2001

W9-DDD-241

2001

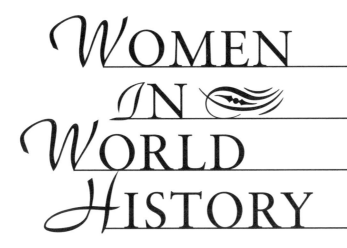

WOMEN IN WORLD HISTORY

A Biographical Encyclopedia

WOMEN IN WORLD HISTORY

A Biographical Encyclopedia

VOLUME
13
R-Schr

Anne Commire, Editor
Deborah Klezmer, Associate Editor

YORKIN PUBLICATIONS

GALE GROUP

THOMSON LEARNING

Detroit • New York • San Diego • San Francisco
Boston • New Haven, Conn. • Waterville, Maine
London • Munich

Yorkin Publications

Anne Commire, *Editor*
Deborah Klezmer, *Associate Editor*
Barbara Morgan, *Assistant Editor*

Eileen O'Pasek, Gail Schermer, Patricia Coombs, James Fox,
Catherine Cappelli, Karen Rikkers, *Editorial Assistants*
Karen Walker, *Assistant for Genealogical Charts*

Special acknowledgment is due to Peg Yorkin who made this project possible.

Thanks also to Karin and John Haag, Bob Schermer, and to
the Gale Group staff, in particular Dedria Bryfonski, Linda Hubbard, John Schmittroth, Cynthia Baldwin,
Tracey Rowens, Randy Bassett, Christine O'Bryan, Rebecca Parks, and especially Sharon Malinowski.

The Gale Group

Sharon Malinowski, *Senior Editor*
Rebecca Parks, *Editor*
Laura Brandau, *Assistant Editor*
Linda S. Hubbard, *Managing Editor*

Margaret A. Chamberlain, *Permissions Specialist*
Mary K. Grimes, *Image Cataloger*

Mary Beth Trimper, *Production Director*
Evi Seoud, *Assistant Production Manager*

Cynthia Baldwin, *Product Design Manager*
Tracey Rowens, *Cover and Page Designer*
Michael Logusz, *Graphic Artist*

Barbara Yarrow, *Graphic Services Manager*
Randy Bassett, *Image Database Supervisor*
Dan Newell, *Imaging Specialist*
Christine O'Bryan, *Graphics Desktop Publisher*
Dan Bono, *Technical Support*

Library of Congress Catalog Card Number 99-24692
A CIP record is available from the British Library

ISBN 0-7876-6436-7
Printed in the United States of America.

Library of Congress Cataloging-in-Publication Data

Women in world history : a biographical encyclopedia / Anne Commire, editor, Deborah Klezmer, associate editor.
    p. cm.
Includes bibliographical references and index.
ISBN 0-7876-3736-X (set). — ISBN 0-7876-4069-7 (v. 10). —
ISBN 0-7876-4070-0 (v. 11) — ISBN 0-7876-4071-9 (v. 12) — ISBN 0-7876-6436-7 (v. 13) — ISBN 0-7876-4073-5 (v. 14)
    1. Women—History Encyclopedias.2. Women—Biography Encyclopedias.
I. Commire, Anne. II. Klezmer, Deborah.
    HQ1115.W6 1999   99-24692
    920.72'03—DC21

10 9 8 7 6 5 4 3 2 1

Rabbani, Ruhiyyih (1910–2000)

Preeminent member of the Bahai faith. Name variations: Mary Sutherland Maxwell. Born Mary Sutherland Maxwell in New York in 1910; died in Haifa, Israel, on January 19, 2000; only child of William Sutherland (an architect) and May (Bolles) Maxwell; married Shoghi Effendi Rabbani, the last official leader of the Bahai faith (died 1957); no children.

Following the death of her husband Shoghi Effendi Rabbani (known as Shoghi Effendi), the last official leader of the Bahai faith, Ruhiyyih Rabbani (born Mary Sutherland Maxwell) became the preeminent member of the governing legislature of the Bahais, who number more than 5 million and believe in the spiritual unity of all mankind. Because of her link with Bahai's spiritual roots, Rabbani was accorded particular respect within the religious community. "She was totally venerated by millions of people," said Dr. Firuz Kazemzadeh, a Bahai and former Russian professor at Yale, following Rabbani's death in January 2000. "There grew up over the years an adoration for her, unlike anybody else in the Bahai community."

The Bahai religion was founded in Iran in 1863, by Mirza Hoseyn, known as Bahaullah (Glory to God). Some of the first Western Bahais included *Phoebe Hearst, mother of William Randolph Hearst, and Rabbani's grandmother who in 1898 was among the first Americans to make a pilgrimage to Haifa, the center of the Bahai faith. Rabbani's own parents, William and

May Maxwell, were also prominent Bahais and visited Haifa several times, taking their young daughter with them. On one such family visit, Shoghi Effendi asked for Mary's hand in marriage. The proposal surprised her family; although the two had known one another from childhood, there had been no dating between them and a betrothal had not been arranged. "The impression one gets is that he sort of knew her and decided that it was time that he should get married," said Frank Lewis, a professor of Middle Eastern Studies at Yale and also a Bahai.

Rabbani, who had no children, worked closely with her husband, serving as his secretary and performing research for his theological writings. Following his death, she was chosen to serve as one of the nine Hands of the Cause, the body which ran the religion until a permanent council (Universal House of Justice), of which she was also a member, was established in 1963. In her position, Rabbani worked to promote the Bahai faith around the world and was always available to meet with pilgrims to Haifa, where she made her home. "People treated her recollections and interpretations of doctrine with a special degree of reverence," said Lewis. Rabbani wrote a biography about her husband, *The Priceless Pearl*, and also authored a small volume of poetry which reflected the loneliness she endured after her husband's death. "She grieved inside, but you wouldn't have known about it unless you read those poems," said Kazemzadeh. "She was a very strong person."

SOURCES:
"Obituaries," in *The New York Times*. January 23, 2000.

Rabi'a (c. 714–801)

Eighth-century mystic and saint of Islam who was known for her asceticism, miracles, and focus on God as love. Name variations: Rabia; Rabi'a the Mystic; Rabiah of Basra; Rabiah al-Adawiyah or Adawiyya; Rabi'ah, Rabe'a. Pronunciation: ra-be-a. Rabi'a was a renowned holy woman and mystic of Islam. Born Rabi'a al-Adawiya al-Kaisiya in Basra (modern-day Iraq) in 714 or 717 (some sources cite 712); died in 801; daughter of Isma'il; mother's name unknown.

Islam developed in Arabia beginning in 610, and, along with Judaism and Christianity, claims the prophet Abraham as its forefather. The earliest imperative of the fledgling sect was to ensure its own survival and the physical safety of its handful of adherents. By 632, Islam was securely established in Mecca and Medina, and the attention of the new faith turned first to matters of expansion and governance, and then to the task of refining its own ethics and theology. It was not until the 2nd century of Islam (or the 8th century of the common era), that the religion began to articulate and openly embrace its mystical dimension. Rabi'a, a young girl living in Basra, born destitute to a life of seeming obscurity, played a pivotal role in the development of Islamic transcendentalism.

The historical events of Rabi'a's life, recorded principally in *Memoir of the Saints* by Attar, are so overlaid with legend that it is difficult to distinguish fact from fiction. Her biography, therefore, is a pastiche of stories told about her over the centuries by her co-religionists. Rabi'a was born in Basra, the fourth daughter (judging by her name which means "the fourth") of penurious parents. On the day the infant entered the world, her family lacked even the resources to anoint her navel with oil or swaddle her in cloth. Rabi'a's mother asked her husband, Isma'il, to go to the neighbors and request a little oil for the lamp so that the family could care for the child during the night. Isma'il went out, but only pretended to knock on the neighbor's door. He could not bring himself to beg because he had taken a personal vow never to ask for anything from others. Isma'il returned empty handed to his wife saying, "They will not open the door." This story introduces two motifs that continue to be significant in Rabi'a's biography. Many of her miracles involved lamps—a symbol of the illumination she sought and achieved through love. Also, like her father, Rabi'a would eventually be dogmatic about relying for her needs, both physical and spiritual, not on her neighbors, but on God alone.

During that first night of Rabi'a's life, the Prophet Muhammad appeared to Isma'il in a dream, assuring him that his daughter was a queen among women and that her intercession would be desired by 70,000 in the Muslim community. Muhammad instructed Rabi'a's father to go to the governor of Basra and request 400 dinars. The righteous governor recognized that the request had been inspired by the Prophet and gave Rabi'a's family all the gold and silver they needed. When Rabi'a was still a child, however, her parents died, a famine hit the land, and she and her sisters, destitute once more, were separated. Rabi'a turned to begging (and, according to some sources, prostitution) to sustain herself. One day, she was seized in the street and sold into slavery for six dirhams.

Rabi'a's life became almost intolerable. She was put to hard labor, but even more grievous was the fact that because of her duties she was unable to devote her days to an activity which would come to consume her: contemplation of God. Each night, she spent hours in prayer lamenting, "O God if I could I would not rest one hour from serving Thee, but you have set me under the hand of a creature." At one point when the young girl was performing an errand for her master, an ominous stranger (who was not permitted to look upon her unveiled) approached her in the street; she fled, fell, and broke her hand. In despair, Rabi'a cried out, "Lord God, I am a stranger, orphaned of mother and father, a helpless prisoner fallen into captivity, my hand broken. Yet for all this I do not grieve; all I need is Thy good pleasure, to know whether Thou art well-pleased or not." She was reassured by a disembodied voice which promised her she would come to occupy a station that even the angels in Heaven would envy.

It was due to her scrupulous piety that Rabi'a finally obtained release from servitude. She was in the habit of standing in prayer through the nighttime hours. One evening, her master awoke and saw Rabi'a praying; a lantern was suspended over her head which put out a brilliant light irradiating the entire house. The light formed a type of halo called *sakina* or cloud of glory. Frightened by this woman's spiritual power, her master manumitted her.

According to one legend, after her release from bondage Rabi'a became a flute player for a while, but most accounts indicate that the emotionally bruised young woman retired to a life of seclusion and celibacy in the deserts near Basra. After living alone in a hermitage for some time, Rabi'a resolved to fulfill the responsibility incumbent on all faithful Muslims of performing the pilgrimage to Mecca. Upon completing the pilgrimage, Rabi'a returned to Basra where she lived out the rest of her days committed to chastity and the adoration of Allah.

In the late 8th century, Basra was active in the development of Islamic thought. Hasan of Basra (642–728), often called the forefather of Islamic mysticism, was an older contemporary of Rabi'a and, as his name indicates, he lived and taught in Basra. He is best known for ascetic observance of ritual and his thorough distrust of the material world. Hasan's instinctual dread of the immensity and power of God kept him in continual awe of judgment day and often caused him to weep profusely in public. He felt that to laugh or talk lightheartedly was frivolous for those, such as himself, who were truly cognizant of the magnitude of the Creator. In fact, when he first undertook his mystical mission he vowed never to laugh again in this world. Hasan advised his followers to avoid all corrupting influences of the profane, sensual, physical world, and, especially, to eschew contact with women. This admonition to shun women does not seem to have applied, however, to all females; association with Rabi'a was anything but polluting. In fact, according to some sources, Hasan refused to remain at any public gathering at which Rabi'a was not present.

Although the Quran establishes succinct and contrasting roles for men and women, among saints, or the "friends of god," there is no division by gender. The objectives and methods of the Muslim mystic are not dissimilar from those of mystics in numerous other sects: to seek union with the Beloved Divine by renouncing the world, purging the self of selfness, and journeying towards ecstatic illumination. It is because the Muslim mystic (also called a Sufi) seeks to extricate himself from the material—from the flesh—that enlightenment is thought to be equally possible for men and women. Whereas the Muslim woman is largely defined by the body due to her role as bearer and nurturer of children, the female mystic is, in a sense, sexless because her physicality is irrelevant. It is the mind and soul of the mystic that leads her to her goal: union with that Divine Essence which is itself non-material and sexless. In the spiritual life, there is "neither male nor female." The Prophet himself said, "God does not regard your outward forms. . . . Mankind will be raised up according to their intentions." The Muslim theologian Abbas of Tus claimed that on the Day of Resurrection the first person to enter Paradise will be *Mary the Virgin, mother of Jesus, and some thinkers claim that *Fatimah, daughter of Muhammad, was the first *qutb,* or spiritual mother of Sufism.

Mystical thinking was well developed in 8th century Basra, particularly the principle of annihilation of the self and union with God, but Rabi'a furthered and deepened Islamic spiritualism by her development of the doctrine of Pure Love and fellowship with God. That love is suggested in the Quranic verse, "He loves them and they love him" (Sura 5.59). Rabi'a's relationship with God was not intellectual, but it was both gnostic and visceral at the same time, both spiritual and corporeal. She loved God for himself alone and not, like Hasan, out of fear of punishment. One legend of Rabi'a has her walking the streets of Basra, a flaming torch in one hand and a pitcher of water in the other. When asked why, she explained that this symbolic act meant that she would set Paradise on fire and drown Hell "so that these two veils may disappear and nobody

may worship God out of fear of Hell or hope for Paradise, but solely for his own beauty."

Rabi'a expressed her feeling in poems and prayers, and she had long intimate conversations with her Beloved, the Lord. The passion of this woman's commitment is felt in her words, "O Lord, the stars are shining and the eyes of men are closed and kings have shut their doors, and every lover is alone with his beloved, and here am I alone with Thee. . . . Thou art my intimate, and longing for Thee sustains me. . . . I have none beside Thee. . . . Thou art my job, firmly established within me. If Thou art satisfied with me, then O desire of my heart, my happiness has appeared."

> *A* woman who walks in the path of God cannot be called merely woman.
>
> —**Attar**

Rabi'a wanted nothing more than to think of God without ceasing, and she felt remorse when the exigencies of daily life forced her to turn her attention from the divine to the mundane. She lamented the necessity of sleeping, and frequently prayed all night, resting only at dawn, and even then regretfully. Once when the saint had abstained from food and drink for seven days and seven nights, she decided to break her fast with a little water, but she heard the voice of God warning, "Concern for me and the pleasures of the world cannot dwell together in one heart." The fear of losing her Beloved, which this incident provoked, led Rabi'a to cut herself off from any real involvement in the world. One of the most famous stories of this holy woman tells of an exquisitely beautiful spring day when she refused to leave her home because she preferred to remain in a dark house, adoring the creator, rather than to go outside and admire the created order which was pale by comparison. She also eschewed the investigation of theological questions which took her attention away from the pristine and manifest perfection of her Beloved.

Rabi'a's biographers are unambiguous as to the superiority of Rabi'a's form of passionate mystical expression over the labored and mechanical rites of other Sufis. Rabi'a was critical of Sufyan al-Thawri (713–778), an authority on the fine points of Islamic law and praxis, because of his over-confidence in the power of ritual observance and his lack of simple, unmediated devotion. At one point, Ibrahim ibn Adham, Rabi'a's student and a famous Sufi, was on a pilgrimage to worship at the Qa'ba. It took him 14 years to reach Mecca, because five times a day he stopped to perform two prostrations while he prayed. When Ibrahim arrived at Mecca, the sacred Qa'ba was gone. He was appalled and shocked, but reassured by a voice which said, "No harm has befallen your eyes, but the Qa'ba has gone to meet a woman who is approaching this place." That woman was, of course, Rabi'a. When she arrived at Mecca, the Qa'ba returned safely to its place. Ibrahim reproached Rabi'a for disturbing the world order, and she replied, "You traversed [the desert] in ritual prayer (*namaz*) but I with personal supplication (*niyaz*)." In other words, Allah had shown favor to the simple woman whose heart was pure over the highly ritualized devotions of Ibrahim.

The linkage of Rabi'a and Hasan of Basra is meaningful in that underlying their fictive relationship is an implicit judgment on the element of mysticism with which each is associated. One day Rabi'a was walking under Hasan's window, and she felt teardrops fall on her head. When she realized they had come from Hasan she reproved him saying, "O teacher, this weeping is from pride of self," at which he was silenced. Rabi'a's biographer, Attar, records that after a compelling religious discussion of the Truth and the Way, Hasan reflected that compared to Rabi'a, with her simple, sincere faith, he was spiritually bankrupt. Even the deer, gazelle and mountain goat, sensing her oneness with God, were attracted to Rabi'a, but they fled when Hasan approached.

Islamic theology is very insistent on the oneness of God. God is unassociated in his splendor with any other being. For that reason, although Muslims honor Jesus Christ as a great prophet, they do not consider him co-existent with God. By the same token, sainthood as conceived in the Christian scheme is abhorrent to Islam. There are no intermediaries between God and his creation—between God and humanity. Although this principle has undergone some interpretation and variation over time, generally speaking, in Islam the term saint does not imply that a human being has the power to intercede with God. Rather, a saint is a person of special purity and insight. Saints are, however, able to perform miracles, and Rabi'a was credited with many. Or rather, many miracles occurred in her presence. In the Islamic tradition, miracles are always the work of God, not humans. Rabi'a herself rejected the common belief that she was capable of performing miracles and thought that miracles were Satanic temptations to pride and vainglory.

Despite her reluctance, however, Rabi'a's life was suffused with the miraculous. For example, although Rabi'a would not ask God to relieve her poverty, Allah provided food for her table when she had guests or when she was in danger of starvation. When she was on her pilgrimage to Mecca, Rabi'a's camel died (some sources say donkey), but it was miraculously restored to life so that she could finish her journey. Another legend relates that one evening Rabi'a's lantern was broken and dysfunctional, but nonetheless, her abode was illuminated by the light that shone around her person, or, in a similar story, from her fingers. When one of her guests protested that only Moses could set his fingers alight, Rabi'a replied that whoever follows in the footsteps of the prophets can "possess a grain of prophethood." According to al-Munawi, once a thief broke into Rabi'a's cell and tried to steal her veil. When the thief had it in his hands, he was suddenly unable to find the door to leave. He put the veil down and could at once see the door, but when he once more picked up the veil, again the exit was obscured. A voice chided the thief assuring him that Rabi'a was under divine protection. The same author tells of a competition of spiritual powers between Hasan of Basra and Rabi'a. Hasan attempted to keep a prayer mat floating on the surface of the water while he was praying on it, but Rabi'a was able to throw her prayer mat into the air and fly up onto it. Ultimately, however, despite her superior powers, Rabi'a scolded Hasan who had initiated the contest, saying that fish can float and birds fly; "the real work for saints lies beyond both of these."

Rabi'a lived in absolute poverty and practiced a life of extreme denial, so much so that she has been criticized by later Muslim writers because Islam has not traditionally favored radical asceticism, and celibacy has never been an exalted ideal in the Muslim community for men or for women. Although her friends would have willingly satisfied Rabi'a's material needs, she refused aid saying, "I should be ashamed to ask for this world's goods from Him to whom they belong, and how should I seek them from those to whom they do not belong?" Many men wanted to marry her, but she refused, saying she belonged entirely to God. One of her suitors was supposedly Hasan of Basra, although the difference in their ages makes this seem unlikely. Supposedly, when Hasan requested Rabi'a's hand, she insisted that she no longer existed except "in the shadow of [God's] command" so that she was not free to give herself in marriage to a mortal man. She also posed to the holy man a riddle in four parts which dealt with God and judgment day. When Hasan confessed that he could not provide her the answers she sought, Rabi'a responded that with this riddle to solve, she had no time for a husband. So disinterested was she in earthly marriage that she even refused the proposal of the Abbasid Amir of Basra, Muhammad ben Sulayman al-Hashimi, who offered her not only his hand, but an enormous income which would assure her a life of wealth and leisure. She responded to the Amir, "It does not please me . . . that you should distract me from God for a single moment, so farewell."

Although the saint wanted nothing more than to be left in solitude to contemplate her Maker, Rabi'a's reputation for sanctity and miracles attracted disciples to her. Men and women came for prayers or counsel or to listen to her teaching. In fact, many of the most notable Sufis of the next generation (such as Adham of Balkh [d. 770?]) were trained at the feet of this female mystic.

Rabi'a died at the age of about 85 in 801 (one source has her dying as early as 752). By the end of her life, she was frail and often sick, but as she told her friends who tended her in her last illnesses, her most serious malady was separation from God which "all the physicians in the world are powerless to cure." The saint did not fear death, in fact she welcomed it; death would bring her into the presence of the God for whom she had longed her entire life. She always had her shroud, which was made from an animal skin, near her, anticipating the joyful day of death when she would reunite with her Beloved. When she was dying, Rabi'a asked her friends to leave her deathbed to make room for the messengers of God Most High. As they left, they heard the saint making her confession of faith and a voice responding, "O soul at rest, return to thy Lord . . . enter among My servants into My paradise." She was buried at Basra.

After her death, many stories were circulated of Rabi'a's appearances in dreams. A famous legend tells of the holy woman, spirited to the end, and how she escaped the inquisitor angels of the tomb, Mundar and Nakir. She appeared in a dream and informed the dreamer that when Mundar and Nakir tested her with the question, "Who is your Lord?" she replied, "Tell Allah that I, a weak old woman, have never forgotten him, so how could he ask me, 'Who is your Lord?'" In another dream, the saint appeared dressed in fine robes of green silk embroidered with gold. The dreamer asked Rabi'a why she was not wearing the hair-skin shroud and the woolen scarf in which she was buried, and Rabi'a replied that her shroud had been taken from her and carried by the angels to Paradise. From time to time, her admirers sought solace or counsel by visiting her grave. Once visitors to her tomb asked Rabi'a if she had attained the union with God for which she had labored her entire life; they heard a voice respond, "I have."

Although the story of Rabi'a is well known in the Muslim world (so much so that her life provided the plot of an Arab movie), the saint has not received a great deal of attention outside of Islam. Some short stories were written about her in the 14th century, and the 19th-century English author Richard Monckton Milnes wrote a collection of poems titled *The Sayings of Rabi-ah*. Scholarship in the 20th century turned its attention to elucidating the contributions of women around the world and through time, and Rabi'a has benefited from that trend. There are now several works in European languages dedicated to telling this woman's story—a story which transcends the boundaries of one culture.

SOURCES:

Arberry, A.J., trans. *Muslim Saints and Mystics*. London: Routledge & Kegan Paul, 1966.

Bosworth, C.E., *et al.*, eds. *New Encyclopaedia of Islam*. Leiden: E.J. Brill, 1995.

Eliade, Mircea, ed. *Encyclopedia of Religion*. NY: Macmillan, 1987.

Denny, Frederick Mathewson. *An Introduction to Islam*. NY: Macmillan, 1985.

Fernea, Elizabeth Warnock, and Basima Qattan Bezirgan, eds. *Middle Eastern Muslim Women Speak*. Austin, TX: University of Texas Press, 1976.

Smith, Margaret. *Rabi'ah the Mystic, and Her Fellow Saints in Islam*. Cambridge: Cambridge University Press, 1984.

SUGGESTED READING:

Arberry, A.J. *Sufism: An Account of the Mystics of Islam*. NY: Harper Torchbooks, 1970.

Baldick, J. "The Legend of Rabi'a of Basra: Christian Antecedents, Muslim Counterparts," in *Religion*. Vol. 20, 1990, pp. 233–247.

Massignon, Louis. *Essai sur Les Origines du Lexique Technique de la Mystique Musulmane*. Paris: Librairie Philosophique J. Vrin, 1954.

Van Gelder, G.J.H. "Rabia's Poem on the Two Kinds of Love: A Mystification?," in *Verse and the Fair Sex: A Collection of Papers Presented at the 15th Congress of the UEAI 1990*. Edited by F. de Jong. Utrecht, 1993.

Martha Rampton,
Assistant Professor of History, Pacific University,
Forest Grove, Oregon

Rabia of Basra (c. 714–801).

See Rabi'a.

Rabia the Mystic (c. 714–801).

See Rabi'a.

Rabin, Leah (1928–2000)

First lady of Israel (1974–77 and 1992–95). Born Leah Schlossberg on April 8, 1928, in Koenigsberg, Germany (now Kaliningrad, Russia); died of cancer on

November 12, 2000, near Tel Aviv, Israel; father was a textile manufacturer and real-estate investor; attended high school in Tel Aviv; received a teaching degree; married Yitzhak Rabin (1922–1995, prime minister of Israel [1974–77, 1992–95]), on August 23, 1948; children: daughter **Dalia Rabin-Pelossof** *(a lawyer and member of Israeli parliament); son Yuval Rabin.*

First lady of Israel from 1974 to 1977 and again from 1992 to 1995, when her husband Yitzhak Rabin was assassinated, Leah Rabin was warmly admired in the United States and Europe during and after her husband's career, less so in Israel. Strong willed, intelligent, and outspoken, she became an untiring advocate of peace between Israel and the Palestinians after her husband's death, carrying on the cause he had championed, and while she remained a controversial public figure in her country, she had earned the respect of many Israelis by the time of her death from cancer in November 2000.

Leah Rabin was five years old when her father, a well-off textile manufacturer, moved his family from her birthplace of Koenigsberg, Germany (now Kaliningrad, Russia), to Palestine in response to Hitler's ascension to power. Palestine was then under British rule, and Jews comprised somewhat less than 30% of the population. While a high school student in Tel Aviv, Leah met Yitzhak Rabin, who was then a 22-year-old officer in the Palmach, the top force in the underground Jewish militia. After graduating from high school the following year, she attended teachers' college briefly before dropping out to join the Palmach, working on propaganda. (She would later return to college and earn a teaching degree.) The state of Israel was created on May 14, 1948, and in the midst of the ensuing Arab-Israeli war, Leah and Yitzhak were married on August 23, 1948. Yitzhak, who served as brigade commander in that conflict, rose through the hierarchy of the Israeli army in the years that followed, finally becoming chief of staff, while Leah raised their two children. The couple remained close throughout their marriage, partners and confidants in both personal life and politics. After Yitzhak oversaw the strategies that led to Israel winning the Six-Day War (called the June War by Arabs) in 1967, he was named Israel's ambassador to the United States in 1968.

The Rabins were popular hosts in Washington, D.C., where Leah charmed the political establishment. The couple also opened a bank account, the existence of which would come back to haunt them. In 1974, after *Golda Meir* resigned as prime minister in the aftermath of the Yom

Kippur War (called the October War by Arabs), Yitzhak was elected prime minister. Three years later, prior to a general election, the Israeli media made public the fact that the Rabins' U.S. bank account had been kept open, albeit with only a small amount of money, after they returned to Israel (Leah had closed the account on a recent trip to Washington). Since they no longer lived in the U.S., the bank account had been illegal under Israeli law. A scandal erupted, an investigation ensued, and Leah, whom many in the country had come to perceive as arrogant and overly European during her tenure as first lady, stood trial and was fined some $27,000. Yitzhak resigned as prime minister and temporarily withdrew from politics, and his Labor Party lost the election to the opposition Likud Party.

Although her husband remained steadily on her side, Leah was widely blamed for his political downfall, and her name was regularly invoked when he returned to politics some years later and began climbing to the top of the government again. He won reelection as prime minister in 1992, intent upon ending the continual violence between Israel and the Palestinians, and in 1993 Leah accompanied him to Oslo where he signed a historic peace accord with Yasser Arafat (head of the Palestine Liberation Organization and later president of the new Palestinian National Authority). The Oslo accords, while rabidly denounced by ultranationalists on both sides, won Yitzhak Rabin, Arafat, and Shimon Peres, the Israeli foreign minister, the Nobel Peace Prize in 1994. That year Leah also traveled with Yitzhak to Jordan for the signing of a peace treaty with that country, and provoked much indignant comment at home when she lost a piece of jewelry during the signing ceremony and ordered accompanying Israeli army troops to search through the sand for it.

Death threats directed at Yitzhak Rabin became common as the peace process, however slowly and delicately, forged ahead. Both Leah and her husband were heckled in public, and demonstrators held rowdy, emotional rallies against Yitzhak (on occasion calling him a traitor) and the peace process. On November 4, 1995, a religious ultranationalist Jew opposed to peace with the Palestinians assassinated Yitzhak Rabin in Tel Aviv. Leah remained composed during his funeral, crying only once, and received condolences from numerous attending heads of state with stoicism. In the days that followed, however, she gave interviews blasting those Israelis (including Likud head and soon thereafter prime minister Benjamin Netanyahu) whom she perceived as having encouraged with their rhetoric the poisonous divisiveness of the anti-peace process faction, and she remained vocal in support of Israeli-Palestinian peace for the rest of her life.

While Leah Rabin never served in an official government position, in the 1990s she became internationally known for her advocacy of peace, and her opinions on the various twists and turns in the peace process during those years were widely sought and quoted in the world media. (Many nationalists and ultra-religious Jews at home remained markedly less impressed.) In 1997, she published *Rabin: Our Life, His Legacy* (she and her husband had published another memoir, *Wife by His Side*, in 1991). She continued her public activities after being diagnosed with lung cancer in the late 1990s, and only hospitalization prevented her from attending the commemoration of the fifth anniversary of her husband's assassination in early November 2000. She died just over a week later, on November 12, 2000, while Israel was convulsed with the worst Israeli-Palestinian violence it had seen in years. Eulogies poured in from international leaders and politicians, including Arafat, Israeli Prime Minister Ehud Barak, American Secretary of State **Madeleine Albright**, and President Bill Clinton, who noted, "We have lost a dear friend and the Middle East has lost a friend of peace, but the work to which she and Yitzhak dedicated their lives must and will continue." Her coffin lay in state for several days before she was buried beside her husband in Mount Herzl cemetery in Jerusalem.

SOURCES:

Contemporary Authors. Vol. 160. Detroit, MI: Gale Research.

"Leah Rabin," in *The Glasgow Herald* [Scotland]. November 14, 2000.

"Leah Rabin, 72," in *The Day* [New London, CT]. November 13, 2000, p. B4.

"Leah Rabin, Israeli First Lady and Peace Advocate, Dies at 72," in *The New York Times*. November 13, 2000, p. B6.

Newsweek. November 20, 1995, p. 63; November 27, 2000, p. 90.

People Weekly. November 20, 1995.

Jo Anne Meginnes,
freelance writer, Brookfield, Vermont

Rabutin-Chantal, Jeanne Françoise de (1572–1641).

See Chantal, Jeanne de.

Rabutin-Chantal, Marie de (1626–1696).

See Sévigné, Marie de.

Raby, Mary (1777–1855).

See Catchpole, Margaret for sidebar on Mary Reibey.

Rachel (1821–1858)

French tragedian whose talent in the classical French tradition brought her a lifetime post with the Comèdie-Française, during which she was credited with reviving respect in post-revolutionary France for the great dramatists of the ancien règime. *Name variations: Rachel Félix or Felix. Born Elisabeth-Rachel Félix near Aargau, Switzerland, probably in February 1821; died on January 3, 1858, in Le Cannet, France, of tuberculosis; second child of poor Jewish peddlers, Jacques and Thèrese Félix; never married, but her numerous affairs among the European aristocracy produced at least one child.*

A leisurely walk through Paris' famous Père Lachaise Cemetery, that granite and marble index to French social and cultural history, would inevitably present the casual visitor with a bewildering array of familiar names—Balzac, Bizet, Chopin. Drawn by these luminaries, it would be easy to bypass the small tomb of one of their contemporaries, in the form of a petite Greek temple, bearing the single name "Rachel" and standing at the end of the avenue of the same name; nor would it be apparent that they once paid enthusiastic court to the woman they had called *la reine du théâtre*; the woman who had, they said at the time, singlehandedly saved the moribund Comèdie-Française with her electrifying interpretations of the French classics, and who fascinated them even more by an unfettered lifestyle denied to most women of the mid-19th century. She was, in fact, one of the most famous personalities of her time, an international celebrity known on both sides of the Atlantic in an age that had not yet invented the telegraph.

"She was born in the realms of poetry," gushed one of her most ardent supporters in 1840 at the height of her career. There was no need for such metaphorical raptures, for the heights to which Mlle Rachel ascended from a decidedly lowly birth were remarkable enough—a birth so obscure that even the precise date and the name under which she came into the world remain problematical. The date generally given for the event, February 1821, was recalled with imperfect memory many years later by her parents, who had not bothered to officially record the arrival of their second daughter. The fact that it was the same year that the exiled Napoleon had died may have played a part in the parental recollection. Jacques and **Thèrese Félix** had been part of the great Jewish exodus from pogroms and harsh living conditions in Poland and Russia, joining the wave of itinerant peddlers which slowly made its way west, particularly to France, where Napoleon had passed laws designed to integrate Jews into mainstream French culture rather than persecute them. The surname "Félix," in fact, may have been the assigned French transliteration of the family's original Hebrew name, "Baruch." Both names in their respective languages mean "blessed."

Rachel had been born as her parents and an older sister traveled through Switzerland on their way to Lyons, where many Jews found employment in that city's thriving cloth-making industry. The baby girl born at a roadside inn in the canton of Aargau, between Zurich and Basel, may have been named Elisabeth or perhaps Elisabeth-Rachel. (A note written by her to her parents in about 1830 is signed "Elissa," a diminutive for Elisabeth.) When their daughter later became famous, Monsieur and Madame Félix would tell stories of how Rachel, at a tender young age, accompanied her older sister **Sarah Félix** singing and playing the guitar to supplement the meager income the family earned from selling pins, writing paper and other notions from the back of their battered wagon; or how Rachel, at seven years of age, could move passersby to tears with her melancholy rendition of the "Ballad of the Wandering Jew." By 1831, when Rachel was ten and had gained three more sisters, including ◄❧ **Lia Félix**, and a brother, the family had arrived in Paris and settled into the Marais, then a damp, marshy outpost on the eastern edge of the city. A seventh and last child, another daughter, was born as the Félixes joined about 9,000 Jews in Paris at the time, accorded full rights as French citizens under Napoleon's laws.

❧► **Félix, Lia** (b. 1830)

French actress. Name variations: Felix. Born in 1830; third daughter of poor Jewish peddlers, Jacques and Thèrese Félix; pupil of her sister, Rachel (1821–1858).

Lia Félix had hardly been tested as an actress when she was asked to take the lead role in Lamartine's *Toussaint L'Ouverture* at the Porte St. Martin on April 6, 1850. Though the play was not a hit, Félix was favorably received, and several important parts were immediately offered to her. Soon, she came to be recognized as one of the best comedians in Paris. *Rachel took Lia to America with her to play supporting parts. On returning to Paris, Lia appeared at several of the principal theaters, but her health forced her to retire for several years. When she reappeared at the Gaieté in the title role of Jules Barbier's *Jeanne d'Arc*, she had an enormous success.

The first recorded reference to Rachel occurs in the registration records of the school in which she and her older sister were enrolled, where the girls were listed as "Mlles de Sainte-Félix." Little is known of her education, although it is probable Rachel was taught the elements of speech and deportment which were a part of every school-child's curriculum in a society much concerned with the social graces. In later life, Rachel would tell friends that she owed her success to her childhood teachers, especially her vocal coach. This anonymous individual was sufficiently impressed with the young student's dramatic talents to recommend her to an actor friend, one Monsieur Saint-Aulaire, who managed a school for the dramatic arts as well as a theater. Saint-Aulaire was also a member of the prestigious Comédie-Française, the French national theater created by an edict of Louis XIV in 1680 to preserve and present the works of the great classical French playwrights, chief among them being Racine, Corneille, and Molière. Saint-Aulaire's theater, in fact, was called the Théâtre Molière and presented several of the works in the Comédie's repertoire. While Sainte-Aulaire taught his students the highly stylized expressions, gestures, and declamatory acting of the classical stage, he departed from his contemporaries in encouraging his students to graft their own natural sensibilities onto this time-honored stock. He was quickly struck by the depth of emotion in Rachel's acting, particularly in the tragic roles for which she would later become famous.

By 1834, when the great American tragedian Edwin Forrest attended a performance at Saint-Aulaire's theater during a European tour, Rachel was attracting considerable attention. Forrest wrote to friends in America about the "Jewish looking girl" he had seen, a "little bag of bones with the marble face and flaming eyes. If she lives and does not burn out too soon," he predicted, "she will become something wonderful." Also in the audience one night and equally impressed was the treasurer of the Théâtre Française, owned and managed by the Comédie-Française. In October 1836, Rachel was offered a position at the Comédie's own acting school, the Conservatoire, with a yearly stipend of 600 francs. Just 15 years old at the time, Rachel was now virtually assured an eventual position with the permanent company of the Comédie-Française. But her first offer of professional employment came from a private company called the Thèâtre Gymnase. Her father, it was said, negotiated the contract himself and convinced his daughter to leave the Conservatoire before her studies there were completed.

*R*achel

(1821–1858)

So it was that Rachel made her professional début in 1837 in a play written especially for her, *La Vendéene,* set during Napoleon's First Republic of 30 years before. Her portrayal of a peasant girl who undertakes a perilous journey on foot to Paris to plead with the empress *Josephine to spare her condemned father's life brought mixed reviews; while the reaction to her work in her second play for the company, a comedy, was so negative that the Théâtre Gymnase agreed to cancel her contract. Anxious to return to the Conservatoire, Rachel undertook a letter-writing campaign to reclaim her place and won a positive response from the teacher she most respected, Joseph-Isidore Samson. Samson agreed to take her on as a private student and prepare her for the Comédie, of which he, like Sainte-Aulaire, was a member. A year's work with Samson added elegance and sophistication to her technique, so that by February 1838, Samson felt she was ready for the classical stage and arranged for her to sign a year's contract as a *pensionnaire*, or apprentice, with the Comédie.

Rachel took her place in a venerable acting company that was struggling to regain the prestige it had lost at the hands of the French Revolution, during which it was viewed as a relic of the *ancien régime* and an aristocratic anachronism. Renamed the Théâtre de la Nation during the Terror of 1792, it had declined into obsolescence during the Directory in the face of more contemporary plays inspired by the German and English romanticism of the early 1800s. It revived somewhat under Napoleon but lost its momentum with the death of its leading tragedian in 1826. By the 1830s, the king's proud Comédie-Française was playing to half-empty houses while audiences flocked to see that ravishing new art form, opera, being presented at the new Opéra de Paris or to the raffish "boulevard theaters" presenting raucous comedies and social satires by authors like Victor Hugo. Such works would have horrified the old masters of the French stage, whose courtly plays adhered strictly to the Three Unities of the ancient Greeks. Their plots were required to take place within a 24-hour period, their action was limited to one location, and there were no distracting subplots. Any fighting or bloodletting was described in elegant prose rather than shown directly, and every moral position was exhaustively presented in static speeches written in stately alexandrines. But even the Napoleonic nostalgia that had brought the "Citizen King" Louis-Philippe to power eight years before Rachel's debut with the troupe had failed to revive the Comédie-Française.

The company's prospects began to brighten once Rachel stepped onto the stage of the Théâtre Française in June 1838, playing Camille in Corneille's *Horace*. It was, wrote critic Jules Janin, "an unexpected triumph, one of those lucky victories of which a nation like ours can be rightly proud." During the next four months, Rachel played every one of the classic *jeunes princesses*—Hermione in Racine's *Andromaque*, Aménaïde in Voltaire's *Tancrède*, Eriphile in Racine's *Iphegénie in Aulide*, Roxane in Racine's *Bajazet*. Theatergoers flocked to see the new

sensation in such numbers that box-office receipts more than doubled by September, and rose to an unprecedented 6,000 francs a night by October. "Racine and Corneille were living among us once more, as in the great century of Louis XIV," rhapsodized one admirer in remembering that first season, although Rachel's fans were not limited to the theater elite. Bourgeois Paris considered her one of their own after Rachel was presented to Louis-Philippe himself and chose to address him using the common "monsieur" rather than the more respectful "sire." By the end of her second season with the Comédie-Française in 1839, Rachel had been presented with the company's coveted *couronée*, a crown of gilded laurels in which each leaf had been inscribed with the names of her most famous roles. More important, she was given the permanent rank of *socìetaire*, eligible for a seat on the company's governing board.

By the early 1840s, her fame had spread far beyond Paris. After a triumphant tour of the French *états*, Rachel was offered her first appearance outside of France. She was paid 3,500 francs for five performances in May 1841 at Her Majesty's Theater in London and was granted a private audience with the young Queen *Victoria*. "Everybody is now raving about her," wrote Rachel's chief English rival, *Fanny Kemble*. "It is singular that so young a woman should so especially excel in delineations and expressions of this order of emotion," she said, although adding the opinion that Rachel was less successful with more subtle emotional tones.

Since Rachel wrote nothing about her acting that has survived, the reactions of those like Kemble must be relied upon. Many of them dwell on the almost frightening emotional intensity of Rachel's performances. "Her lips tremble, her eyes blaze with maniacal fire, a gesture becomes insanely expressive," wrote one observer of her 1843 portrayal of Racine's *Phédre*, considered the greatest triumph of her career; while Charlotte Brontë, who saw Rachel perform four times in London, thought that "it is scarcely human nature that she shows you; it is something wilder and worse; the feelings and fury of a fiend." Her stage presence was so mesmerizing that even former critics of the old classical theater were drawn to her. Among them were French poet and essayist Théophile Gautier, who thought Rachel had "that supreme gift which makes great tragediennes—authority," and Victor Hugo, who had once ridiculed the staid Comédie-Française but now begged its exciting new star to play his Venetian courtesan in *Angelo*. In 1848, Rachel became the very symbol of France with her stirring recitation of the "Marseillaise" in honor of the creation of the Second Republic under Napoleon III, the nephew of the great Bonaparte.

Rachel's private life was of as much fascination as her acting. Her many affairs with prominent aristocrats were the talk of Paris, even though her acting teacher, Samson, thought there was a "sort of confusion . . . in her small features and closely set eyes." She seemed to hold a particular attraction for relatives and descendants of Napoleon, among them Napoleon III, Prince Napoleon-Joseph-Charles-Paul Bonaparte, whom everyone referred to as "Plon-Plon," and one of Napoleon's illegitimate sons. Gossips claimed that Rachel was so sexually predatory that a special bed was installed in her traveling carriage, allowing her to enjoy the favors of a new consort in every town she visited on tour. There was at least one offspring of these liaisons, a son left in the care of her parents to whom Rachel wrote affectionate letters during her touring. More conversationally minded Parisians jockeyed for invitations to Rachel's famous Thursday afternoon salons at her plush apartments facing the Place Royale (now the Place des Vosges), during which they could study the scratched and battered guitar Rachel claimed she had played as a young girl traveling with her parents. Then there was the collection of daggers Rachel assembled as an inducement for a popular playwright of the day to write for her a version of Judith and Holofernes for the stage, or for when she was playing Racine's murderous Roxane.

Not all of Paris society was amused. "The great tragedienne of our age . . . cannot boast of that which is the patrimony of the humblest and poorest child of the people—an act that proves her identity," sniffed one **Madame de Barrera**, referring to Rachel's lack of a proper birth certificate. Indeed, it was only when her father won a lawsuit against the Comédie-Française, during which he was required to prove that her contract had been signed when she was a minor, that a certificate was finally issued giving the date which has come down to us. Jacques Félix, in fact, took such an active interest in his daughter's career, and the money it produced, that Samson, her acting teacher, was once obliged to throw the man down a flight of stairs and to smash a plaster bust of Rachel to demonstrate how easily her career could be broken. Jacques persisted, lodging a formal complaint when Rachel was forced by the Comédie to tour the provinces with non-company actors, and seeing to it that his son Raphael became Rachel's manager when he himself was too much out of favor.

What Rachel thought of it all can only be guessed. During the disputed tour, she merely wrote back to her mother in regal grammar, "What can I tell you about our triumphs? They continue to be as great as our gifts are."

> *I* am free, and mean to remain free.
> I will have renters, but not owners.
>
> —Rachel

Her triumphs were great enough for word of her to cross the Atlantic. In 1855, Rachel accepted an offer to appear in New York and Boston, much to the dismay of French audiences. Her classical portrayals "speak to the souls of discriminating audiences, not the passions of the masses," huffed the critic Janin; and everyone had heard of the infamous Astor Place riots in New York, in which supporters of the American Edwin Forrest and of the English tragedian William Macready had bloodily clashed when the two men were appearing on separate stages in the city. How, it was asked, could such barbarians appreciate the talents of France's greatest actress? Rachel's manager-brother Raphael thought it prudent to send a carefully prepared biography and press clippings well ahead of his sister's arrival in New York. As she made her transatlantic crossing, New York's elite prepared for their first sight of the woman they anticipated would be a "Jewish sorceress," as the city's press eagerly reported. By the time she left New York for Boston, Rachel wrote serenely back to her mother, "I am making myself commercial; I take and I pile up the dollars." She did not complain about the severe cold she had contracted or the unheated train carrying her northward, but by the time she had completed her Boston engagement, the tuberculosis that had first appeared ten years earlier began to take its toll. (The disease had already claimed the life of her youngest sister the previous year.) On the advice of American doctors, Rachel did not return directly to France but sailed instead for Cuba for a "sun cure." A month in Havana humidity, however, did little to alleviate her condition. Doctors now recommended a spa in Germany known for its healing waters, to be followed by rest in Egypt, where it was thought the drier air would help clear her congested lungs. She seemed to rally somewhat after arriving in Cairo, where Napoleon's legacy of a large French-speaking population made the Egyptian city a kind of Paris in the desert. "Don't think it's so easy to bury people of my race and merit," she wrote defiantly to admirers in Paris, but by late 1857 it became plain that her disease would prove victorious. Rachel calmly put her affairs in order, sending her parents back to France, writing her will, and returning all her love letters to their writers while burning her own correspondence.

She left Egypt for France just after Christmas 1857, making her Mediterranean crossing to Le Cannet, near Nice, in the south of France. It was there that she died, on January 3, 1858, while a *minyan* of Jewish gentlemen from the area chanted at her deathbed. Funeral services were held in Nice, Marseilles, and Lyons as her body made its way back to Paris for final burial. The funeral carriage that carried her to Père Lachaise was attended by 40 guards, in full military uniform, and was followed by the Grand Rabbi of Paris and literary giants such as Prosper Merimée, the elder Alexander Dumas, and the poet Alfred de Musset. It was said that 40,000 came to pay their respects before she was finally laid to rest.

Rachel's influence on the French theater was such that even 40 years after her death, drama critic Françisque Sarcey, who had been barely out of his teens when Rachel strode the boards, clearly remembered her. "Rachel alone could draw receipts in those days," he recalled in the century's last decade. "The nights on which she played, the receipts amounted to ten thousand francs." Sarcey claimed Rachel pocketed the lion's share of those receipts and left many a theater owner in the lurch, but even so, he said, great actresses of the late 19th century owed her their careers. Among them was *Sarah Bernhardt, who remembered meeting Rachel when the great actress paid a visit to the convent school Bernhardt attended as a girl. Even then, Rachel was weakened by tuberculosis. "She . . . had to sit down because she could not get her breath," Bernhardt wrote. "They fetched something to bring her around, and she was so pale, so pale! I was very sorry for her, and Sister Appoline told me that what she did was killing her, for she was an actress."

But Rachel would not have wanted Bernhardt's pity, for she considered the price she paid for her art well worth it. Born to poor Jews in a shabby roadside inn, she had risen to the highest ranks of celebrity and had enjoyed every minute of it. In one of the few surviving photographs of her, she wears one of the elegant classical gowns of her stage wardrobe. A delicate filigreed crown rests on her brow. But she is not striking the tragic pose of one of her heroines. Rather, a mischievous smile is playing on her lips as she gleefully thumbs her nose at us.

SOURCES:

Barrera, Madame. *Memoirs of Rachel.* NY: Harper Brothers, 1858.

Brownstein, Rachel M. *Tragic Muse: Rachel of the Comédie-Française.* NY: Knopf, 1993.

Norman Powers,
writer-producer, Chelsea Lane Productions,
New York, New York

Rachel and Leah

Sisters who were matriarchs of Israel.

Rachel (fl. c. 1500 BCE). Fourth matriarch of Israel. Flourished around 1500 BCE; died in childbirth; grave near Bethlehem is a site of pilgrimage; daughter of Laban; sister of Leah; favorite wife of Jacob and one of the four mothers of the 12 tribes of Israel; children: Joseph and Benjamin.

Leah (fl. c. 1500 BCE). Third matriarch of Israel. Name variations: Lea; Lia. Flourished around 1500 BCE; buried with Jacob in the ancestral cave in Hebron; daughter of Laban; sister of Rachel; first wife of Jacob; children: Reuben, Simeon, Levi, Judah, Issachar, and Zebulun—6 of the 12 tribes of Israel.

According to Genesis, *Sarah and Abraham, prophet and father of three modern religions (Judaism, Christianity, and Islam), had a son named Isaac. When Isaac grew, he married *Rebekah, and the couple conceived twins. When her time came, Rebekah delivered first Esau, then Jacob, who came from the womb clinging to his brother's heel. As the boys matured, Isaac favored Esau and arranged to confer on him his birthright as the eldest son—that being a double portion of the family's possessions and the inheritance of the covenant God made with Abraham. On the day Isaac prepared to bless his first-born, Jacob was able to fool his aged, blind father into thinking he was Esau, and so Jacob succeeded, through fraud, in securing Isaac's blessing and Esau's birthright. In anger, Esau vowed to murder his brother. So, to save her favorite son, Rebekah persuaded her husband to send Jacob off to the land of her brother, Laban, who lived in Paddan-aram (Haran) in Mesopotamia. There, according to Hebrew custom, Jacob would seek a wife among his maternal cousins.

After an arduous journey, Jacob arrived at a well just outside Haran, and there, come to water her father's flocks, was a young shepherdess. The woman was Rachel, daughter of Laban, Jacob's uncle. Jacob was moved to tears by his kinswoman's shapeliness and beauty. After helping with the sheep, he kissed her and determined that she would be his wife. Jacob, having left home empty-handed, had no means by which to pay the bride-price for Rachel, so he agreed to give Laban seven years of service. The seven years passed quickly: "they seemed like a few days, so great was his love for her" (29.20), and at the end of that time the wedding feast was duly celebrated. But Jacob was about to become the victim of a fraud similar to the one he perpetrated on his brother. The comely Rachel had an elder sister named Leah, who was "dull-eyed" and ill-favored. On the night the marriage was to be consummated, Laban veiled Leah and sent her into the bridegroom's darkened tent in place of Rachel, so Jacob laid with Leah, and she became his wife. On discovering the ruse, Jacob demanded to know why he had been hoodwinked, and Laban defended his actions on the grounds that it was the custom of his people that the eldest daughter must marry first. Jacob was determined to have Rachel, so he could do nothing but consent to work another seven years for her hand. At the end of 14 years, when Rachel, too, was his wife, Jacob agreed to go on working for wages in Paddan-aram for seven more years.

Yet the family's problems were not over; conflict arose between the two sisters forced into the awkward position of sharing one husband. God had graced Rachel with a sweetness and beauty, which caused Jacob to treasure her dearly, but her sister Leah, unloved and forgotten, God blessed with progeny. While Rachel remained childless, Leah gave birth to four sons, each time hoping "now my husband will love me" (29.32). In distress at her barrenness, Rachel first reproached Jacob ("Give me children or else I am dead" [30.1]), then finally decided to offer her husband a proxy. She had her maid-servant, *Bilhah, lay with Jacob on the understanding that Bilhah's children would be her own. Through Bilhah, Rachel would "build up a family" (30.3). Bilhah and Jacob had two sons, and Rachel was pleased. She called the second of the two boys Naphtali (struggle), claiming, "With great struggle have I wrestled with my sister, and I have prevailed" (30.8). Leah, who had at this point ceased bearing, hastened to outdo her sister; she also offered her servant to Jacob as a surrogate. Through this girl, *Zilpah, Jacob had two more sons, both to Leah's credit.

This competition between the sisters, to provide their husband with sons, continued. At one point Reuben, Leah's eldest son, brought mandrake plants from the field, and Rachel demanded he give them to her, for mandrakes (in Hebrew *dudaim* or love-givers) were thought to counter infertility. Leah bargained with her son's mandrakes and would only agree to give them to her sister if Rachel would allow her access to Jacob's bed. The deal was struck, and when Jacob returned from the country, Leah informed him, "You are to sleep with me tonight. I have

hired you with my son's mandrakes" (30.16). Leah and Jacob had two more sons and a daughter. God finally took pity on Rachel's "humiliation" and blessed her with a son, who would play a pivotal role in the history of the Hebrews; she named him Joseph.

The time came when Jacob wished to leave the service of Laban and return to the land of Abraham with his two wives, two concubines, eleven sons, one daughter, and manifold flocks, but his father-in-law sought to cheat both Jacob and his two wives. He equivocated about the animals he promised Jacob as wages for his labor and refused his daughters their portion of the bride-price and inheritance, which, by ancestral law, belonged to them. So Rachel, unbeknownst to Jacob, stole from her father the statues of the household gods. The family left Paddan-aram clandestinely, but when Laban heard that Jacob had absconded with his wives and herds, he pursued and overtook them in Gilead, demanding to know why his children had left in stealth and stolen his property. As Jacob was unaware of Rachel's theft, he assured his father-in-law that he had taken only what was his, and that if anyone of his party had stolen from Laban, that person merited death. Rachel hurriedly took the contraband gods from her tent, put them in her camel bags, and sat on them while her father searched in vain, telling him she could not rise because it was her time of the month. Angry words passed between Jacob and Laban, but in the end they agreed that Jacob would return to his homeland on the condition that he treat his wives well and never marry again or return to Laban's territory. The two men erected a stone pillar and ate a sacrificial meal to cement the bargain.

Hark, lamentation is heard in Ramah, and bitter weeping, Rachel weeping for her sons. She refuses to be comforted: they are no more.

—(Jer 31.15)

Once Laban was appeased, Jacob's thoughts turned to home, and he began to plot how to approach his estranged brother, Esau. Soon, upon reentering Edomite country, Jacob learned that Esau was approaching with a force of 400. As what seemed like an opposing army arrived, Jacob divided his family into groups. He placed the servant-girls with their children in front; Leah with her sons were next; but Rachel and Joseph he placed in the back, the most protected position. Despite her inability to increase his wealth in sons, Jacob still loved Rachel most. As it turned out, Jacob's fears were unwarranted; when he and Esau met, the reunion was amicable. Both brothers had prospered and Esau seemed to have forgiven the fact that his brother had stolen his birthright. Jacob and his family rested in the land of Canaan near Shechem.

One day *Dinah, the daughter of Leah, "went out" to visit with the local women, and a Hivite prince named Shechem raped her then claimed to love and want her for his bride. Jacob and his sons were incensed about the insult to Dinah, who had been violated by an uncircumcised man. Hamor, Shechem's father, offered to accept Dinah as his daughter-in-law and suggested to Jacob that his family settle in the area and that the tribes of Jacob and Hamor exchange women as wives, thus forming one kin. Hamor agreed to pay whatever bride-price Jacob might demand for Dinah's hand. The price was heavy—heavier than Hamor knew, for Jacob's sons were plotting against him. They insisted that all the men of Hamor's tribe be circumcised. Hamor and the men of his tribe agreed. All had their foreskins removed, but two days later, while they were still weakened and in great pain, the brothers of Dinah armed themselves, entered the city, killed every male, carried off the women, and plundered the houses in retribution for the rape of their sister.

In fear of retaliation, and on the advice of God, Jacob and his family purged themselves of all foreign gods and fled, which put a strain on Rachel, who was pregnant for the second time. They reached Bethel where God had first appeared to Jacob many years before when he was escaping the wrath of his brother. God again manifested himself, renewed the covenant he had made with Abraham and Isaac, and informed Jacob that he must henceforth be called Israel. The group traveled on toward the Promised Land, and a short distance from Ephrath (Bethlehem) Rachel had a second son whom she named Ben-oni (son of my sorrow), later changed by Jacob to Benjamin (son of my right hand). However, much to Jacob's grief, Rachel died in childbirth. After a lifetime together filled with familial strife and divisive jealousies, Jacob (whose years of life were "few and hard" [47.9]) still treasured her above all else. He buried Rachel by the side of the road to Bethlehem and erected a pillar over the spot so that her name would be remembered. Leah lived on and was buried with Jacob in a cave at Machpelah in Canaan. To the end, although Leah had more of Jacob than Rachel ever did, she never won his love.

Rachel had only two sons with Jacob, but she became the mother figure of the Hebrew na-

tion. From her grave near Bethlehem, centuries after her death, Rachel was uniquely placed to observe the fate of her people. When two tribes of Israel were carried captive into Babylon in 587, they passed the pillar under which Rachel lay buried, and this mother of nations cried out in the wilderness at the misery of her children (Jer. 31.15). And again, Rachel's groans rose from the grave for the Innocents of the tribe of Benjamin massacred by King Herod soon after the birth of Jesus. The *Mater Dolorosa* lamented in pain, echoing the sobs of the mothers of Israel (Mt. 2.18).

Rachel and Leah are remembered quintessentially as mothers. The bearing of children in the kin-based culture reflected in Genesis was a task of great importance. So vital was that function that it became the prime, and often only, method through which women could achieve recognition and validation. As a consequence, when women could not bear, they lost self and societal worth and, like Rachel, had cause to wail "I am dead." (Ironically, having a child killed Rachel.) However, concomitant with their status as mothers, several other important issues relating to the two sisters arise from the narrative (called the Jacob Cycle). Primary among them are (1) Rachel's and Leah's historical (or quasi-historical) position as progenitors of Israel; (2) patriarchy in the Hebrew Bible; (3) the place of Rachel and Leah as characters in world exegetical literature and feminist scholarship; and (4) Rachel's special role as universal mother and theological image of the feminine.

(1) It is unlikely that Rachel and Leah, as portrayed in Genesis, existed historically. The Hebrew Bible is challenging because it represents centuries of accretion, interpolation, and reworking. Questions about the historicity of the events in Genesis are central to a discussion of the text, and the most fruitful approach is to recognize in the Old Testament trace elements of numerous historical periods and myriad levels of meaning conflated, overlapping, juxtaposed, and sometimes standing in stark contradiction. This multiplicity is certainly evident in the stories of the first parents of Israel—cradle of Hebrew history, religion, and Jewish group identity.

Archaeological finds and philological studies have necessitated a thoroughgoing revision of the dating of the events in the Old Testament and their chronological ordering. The material in Genesis comes from traditions which may have begun formation around 1900 BCE but which were committed to writing much later. The earliest author or group of authors of the

Old Testament as we now have it are anonymous, but labeled "J" (for the use of the divine name Jehovah or Yahweh) and "E" (for the use of the Hebrew term *Elohim* for God). Both lived in the 9th century BCE. Much later, sometime between 587 and 400 BCE, another author/s called "P" (Priestly) reworked or added to the writings of "J" and "E." In addition to numerous others who adjusted the texts, around 400 BCE, an editor (or group of editors) known as "R" (Redactor) revised the Old Testament canon in a desire to make one continuous narrative out of a medley of disparate sources. As a result of the fact that the Hebrew Bible was composed and reworked in stages by multiple authors, and because cultural boundaries between Israel and its neighbors were less distinct than once thought, the text consists of ancient Mesopotamian and Canaanite customs, beliefs, and attitudes interspersed with later Hebrew ideologies.

Most Biblical scholars have reached agreement that Genesis, although preserving traces of the historical account of the formation of an-cient Israel's population, is a mythologized narrative which represents a reading back into the earliest legends of institutions which were developed much later. The 12 tribes were not literally the descendants of Jacob's sons, rather, later Hebrew authors composed this simple narrative scheme in order to impose a unity on their own pre-history. There is no consensus on exactly when the 12 tribes formed a common identity. Although some argue that they established a form of political unity after the escape from Egypt, while they wandered in the Sinai desert, most hold that the alliance grew from the unification of independent tribes only after the Israelites conquered Canaan under the leadership of Joshua (c. 1225 BCE). Several of the tribal names come from ancient sites in Canaan, such as the mountains of Naphtali. Over time those who dwelt in these areas assumed the names of the localities. Sigmund Mowinckel posits that Jacob and Israel were originally two distinct persons. Israel was the eponym of a group that moved from the Sinai Peninsula into Canaan and united with indigenous "Habiru" tribes.

This combined people worshiped the single god Yahweh. The polytheistic Jacob tribes were from Northwest Mesopotamia and mixed with "Israel" as both were migrating into Palestine about the same time. Mowinckel holds that all the traditions associated with Rachel and Leah originated with the Mesopotamian contingent of tribes. By contrast, Martin Noth holds that the "Leah tribes" existed as a very early confederation of six Canaanite clans that were joined only later by the two "Rachel tribes," which penetrated Canaan from Mesopotamia, thus increasing the component number of tribes in the confederation to 12. These newcomers brought with them the stories of Jacob, Rachel, and Leah.

"Twelve" is a conventionalized Biblical and Near Eastern figure appearing frequently in Genesis for describing coalitions of peoples. There are 12 tribes of Joktan (10.26–29), Nahor (22.20–24), Ishmael (25.13–16), and Esau (36.10–13). The duodecimal arrangement of the descendants of Israel was artificially maintained even when one tribe disappeared or was split. Twenty different listings of the tribes of Israel appear in the Bible, and only two of them are the same.

We can guess at the early history of the peoples by deconstructing the stories in the Jacob Cycle. The attribution of tribes to Leah and Rachel dates from an early stage of Israelite organization, and tribal historical development and struggles for supremacy are encoded and personified in the tales of the conflict of the two sisters. For instance, the tribe of Judah (from Leah) was antagonistic to the tribe of Benjamin (from Rachel). Further, the attribution of certain tribes to servant-girls may indicate their lower status or late entry into the confederation. At any rate, the legend of the 12 sons of Jacob represents an idealized view of the origins of the people of Israel rather than a historically accurate one. Its purpose was to give Israel a strong identity, and Rachel and Leah are central to every version of the account.

(2) An analysis of the matriarchs of Israel inevitably involves a discussion of patriarchy. The later Biblical authors "P" and "R" were living in a period when the existence of Israel as a nation and Judaism as a religion was threatened. In 722 BCE, the Assyrians destroyed 10 of the 12 tribes, and in 587 the Babylonians conquered the other two tribes of Judah, destroyed most of their sacred and historical writings, and carried the Jews into captivity for 50 years. On their return to Judea from Babylon in 537, in order to rebuild their beleaguered community, members of the endangered society restructured themselves within very tightly controlled limits designed to protect religious traditions and cultural hegemony. The work of "P" and "R" reflect the rigidity of their era, including an inflexible adherence to strict patriarchy and absolute monotheism. Patriarchy is a reference to more than descent patterns; it describes a culture in which the social and ideological repression of women, and the domination of older over younger men, prevail. Some scholars see in Genesis a thoroughgoing and unrelenting imposition of patriarchal values. For them the Bible is androcentric and women are cardboard creations of male narrators' ideas about the other sex. Female characters' only role is to facilitate the stories of fathers, husbands, and sons. Once they have served their purpose, they disappear from the narrative. Their point of view is ignored and their deaths are rarely mentioned.

Other scholars, however, see in Genesis a more complex and less monolithic working out and juxtaposition of various ideas about the role of men and women. Because Genesis was written primarily by "J" in the 9th century BCE, the Jacob Cycle contains vestiges of an early matriarchy. The power of the father in Genesis is not self-evident but is painstakingly constructed and incompletely imposed onto "J's" original material. Jacob is involved in a matrilocal marriage, and his brother Esau is blameworthy because he marries out of the matriline. It is important that the covenant pass through not just the right father, but also the right mother, even if she does not bear the oldest son. Jacob is compelled to obtain the permission of his wives before leaving Paddan-aram. They are willing to leave because their father has denied their rights of lineage by treating them as foreigners. There is a strong sense that the children of Jacob belong to Laban through his daughters, which accounts for his indignation when Jacob flees Paddan-aram with the family. According to one translation, Laban protests, "These daughters are mine, these children are mine, these flocks are mine, everything you see is mine" (Mitchell, 67). Further evidence that the earliest Israelites lived under matriarchal systems can be gleaned from a midrash (Jewish Biblical commentary) which maintains that each of the sons of Jacob, except Joseph, had a female twin whom he married. Some have read this tradition as evidence of cognatic descent patterns (reckoned from both parents). According to the same source, one of the tribes of the Leah federation, that of Dinah, was completely matriarchal. Also, Bilhah and Zilpah were thought to be Laban's daughters by concubines. So all the tribes of Israel were born of the daughters of Laban.

Rachel's theft of her father's teraphim (small idols of gold and silver empowered by the stars to tell the future) is one of the plot elements which best elucidates the tension in the text between conflicting notions of power and lineage. In this story Rachel is not acting under orders from her husband or father, but pursues her own interests. The 1st century CE Jewish historian Josephus claimed that the theft occurred because Rachel wanted to use the idols for bargaining power against Laban if necessary (*Antiquities* 1.19.8). The Genesis Rabba (Jewish Biblical commentary) maintains that Rachel wanted to purge Laban of his idolatry, and another early Jewish source says that she stole the gods so that they would not reveal the fleeing family's whereabouts to Laban. Others have proposed Rachel was simply spiteful, dealing with Laban the way he had dealt with her, or was herself idolatrous in that she was planning to establish an Aramaean-style shrine in her new home. However, non-Biblical Mesopotamian documents (Nuzi tablets) illustrate that perhaps Rachel stole the teraphim because possession of them insured transference of property and/or the hereditary power over the kingroup. In other words, Rachel's was a matriarchal system where leadership of the clan resided in the woman's line, and she wanted the teraphim in order to maintain that authority for her son, Joseph. Some scholars view the inclusion of the plot element in which Rachel bleeds on the teraphim and subsequently dies in Ramah as a device to subvert the matriarchal claims implicit in the story.

Several philologists claim that not only did matriarchal patterns hold in Israel's pre-history, but that the founders of the dynasty were goddesses. Leah translates as "wild cow" and Rachel means "ewe," suggesting vestiges of pagan worship of the female and that the mythological origins of the tribes were at one time traced back to founding goddesses. Throughout Genesis there is a persistent emphasis on the role of Yahweh as life-giver. It is God who opens the wombs of the mothers of Israel. When Rachel cannot conceive, Jacob demands of her, "It is my fault that God closed your womb?" (30:2). Numerous scholars, wondering why so often in Genesis the line of descent of God's chosen people is threatened by sterile wives, have come to the conclusion that it was important for the author/s to establish the generative power of their deity in the face of competition from Canaanite fertility goddesses. Yahweh must be seen as not only the creator of the universe, but also the fountainhead of the mysterious process of female productivity. In the incident of the mandrakes, God's prerogative is threatened. For Rachel to have conceived because of this plant (whose roots resembles the male genitals) would have been a form of sympathetic magic, so one midrash has Rachel giving the mandrakes over to a priest rather than ingesting them, and for this meritorious act of resisting temptation, God rewards her with a child. In this story Rachel's integrity is preserved and so is the omnipotence of God as the well-spring of human life.

(3) Despite their restricted role in the Old Testament narrative, the two sisters have assumed tremendous importance in post-Biblical commentary and, more recently, in feminist scholarship. Although the Bible is sketchy in its characterization of Jacob's wives, subsequent ancient and medieval commentary, particularly by Jewish writers, tends to develop their personas more fully, giving them life and considerably more mettle. Post-Biblical tradition, rather than viewing the sisters as passive (and guiltless) "fields to be ploughed," attributes to them autonomous intentions that do not always align with plans the men in the text have designed for them. Later writers particularly make Leah more concrete, meritorious, and fully human. According to the Babylonian Talmud, Rachel and Leah, like Esau and Jacob, were twins; Leah was the elder, and both sisters were very beautiful. Here the word *rakkôt*, normally translated as "dull-eyed," is read "tender or soft-eyed." Leah only became disfigured through weeping and mourning, to the point that she lost her eyelashes, because she was afraid that she would be forced to marry Esau, whom she had heard was "evil and his trade banditry" (Tanhuma Buber, Gn 152). Despite her ugliness, Jacob would have asked for Leah first, but he hesitated to take the older of his cousins and further defraud Esau of his right as first-born. In medieval mystical exegesis, Leah represents messianic hopes of the fruitful reunion of Israel with God, and Philo (1st century CE Jewish historian) claimed Leah had the virtue of a virgin because she was alienated from men and close to God, she was "out of reach of the passions" (*De Posteritate Caini*, 135). According to a 5th-century CE account, when Jacob discovered he had married the wrong sister, he reproached Leah angrily: "Deceiver, daughter of a deceiver!" But Leah calmly replied, "Is there a teacher without his pupil? I learned from your example. Did you not answer your father when he called Esau?" (Genesis Rabba 70:19). For she had heard Jacob himself explain how he swindled his own brother seven years earlier. Here Leah was complicit in the marriage fraud and unintimidated by her husband's reproof.

Another midrash shows Leah's authoritative traits as she furiously arraigned Rachel who snatched the mandrakes from Reuben. "Give them back at once. . . . [I]s it not enough that you have stolen my husband?" Genesis Rabba finds Leah's bargaining with the mandrakes immodest to the point that it claims her daughter was just like her. Dinah was responsible for her rape because she "went out" and played the floozy, like Leah in the incident of the mandrakes. At the hands of Jewish scholars, the daughters are especially assertive in the face of their greedy father. From the beginning, Rachel advised Jacob not to trust her father, and she warned him that Laban would try to substitute Leah for her. They arranged a series of signals they would exchange on the nuptial night so Jacob would know the woman about to enter his bed was Rachel. But when the wedding night came, Rachel could not find it in herself to allow her less fortunate sister to be shamed, so she showed her the code signals she and Jacob had devised. She lay under the nuptial bed and answered when Jacob spoke so that he would not recognize Leah through her voice. As a reward for this sisterly self-sacrifice, God granted Rachel the privileged position of being mother to Samson, Joshua, and King Saul. Leah repaid Rachel's generosity. After giving birth to six boys, when Leah again conceived, knowing that Jacob was destined to have 12 sons, she prayed for a girl so Rachel would have at least 2 sons. God changed the male fetus to a female and gave Rachel Joseph as a reward for Leah's goodness.

Rachel and Leah have become favored topics for modern feminist Biblical scholars, but evaluations of the sisters differ widely. Some have observed that Old Testament women are given short shrift, that none of the Biblical matriarchs match the human depth and literary complexity of the father figures. Their appearances are designed to bolster the main narrative, which is ultimately about men—male patriarchy and an exclusively male-identified god. **Esther Fuchs** claims that the Genesis authors typically neglect full explanations of motivations behind the female protagonists' decisions, and at crucial points in the narrative the text is opaque regarding women's reactions. For example, the female slaves Bilhah and Zilpah are completely muzzled in the text. Rachel's agony at childbirth is overwritten when Jacob alters her dying words by changing her son's name. Further, mothers often interfere to help sons but not daughters; there are few stories of mother-daughter relationships in the Old Testament. The reader is ignorant as to how Leah responded to the rape of her daughter; in fact, we never hear how Dinah herself felt about her situation. Was the intercourse between her and Shechem really rape?

The author's silence about women's motivations often results in their actions becoming morally troubling. Rachel's theft of her father's teraphim is puzzling because the text does not give enough context for the reader to evaluate it, and the author him/herself neither condemns nor praises the act. Whereas the text provides a full explanation and justification for Jacob's theft of Esau's birthright and his flight from Laban, Rachel's robbery is never made clear so she is never vindicated. Rachel's stealing of the teraphim is tainted with the suspicion of paganism, but in the same scene Jacob's distaste for idolatry is unequivocal because he dismisses the gods as "household objects." The reader remains ambivalent about Rachel who appears deceptive and disloyal. These attitudes echo in medieval commentaries, which interpret Rachel's early death at Ephrath as the unwitting consequence of Jacob's curse on whomever carried off Laban's property.

There is, however, a more positive way to view Rachel's behavior. She may be, in the mind of the Biblical narrator, the female counterpart of Jacob. Like him, Rachel must jockey and scheme to establish her status in the family in which she exists in a state of competitive friction with her sister. Like Jacob, who is favored by his mother and his God, Rachel is younger than her sibling rival, but best loved. Both Jacob and Rachel are forced by circumstances to play the part of "trickster"—a role often assumed by those in positions of powerlessness. Rachel filches her father's teraphim and prevents Laban looking into the camel bags by claiming that she can not rise to kiss him because "the common lot of women" (Gn. 31.35) is upon her. Most have seen this as a reference to menses, some to pregnancy, but in either case she understands the horror Laban has of touching a menstruating or pregnant woman, two conditions considered unclean and polluting in much of the ancient world (see Lev. 15–20). Is she lying to her father? The answer is not clear, but perhaps what is most important is that we see this female protagonist not as mendacious but as resourceful, in much the same light that Jacob is portrayed when he designs stratagems to achieve his ends in the face of Laban's rapacious greed or in obtaining his brother's birthright. Just as Jacob steals the patriline, Rachel steals the matriline.

Much of the ancient and modern commentary on Rachel and Leah has focused on the sisters' relationship. Some have attempted to see beyond the apparent oppression of the two daughters and view Rachel's and Leah's lives as valiant, inventive, and selfless attempts to satisfy the demands of the patriarchal autocracy of their culture and in so doing prove how thoroughly they comprehend God's mandates. According to this reading, the two women recognize that Jacob's romantic preferences and their own jealous competitiveness are standing in the way of God's designs: the building up of his people. Therefore, with one another's help they bear and exercise the maternal prerogative of naming the children who will father the Twelve Tribes of Israel. This story then becomes an analogue of women working together to further communal goals.

Others claim that the primary motives of the women are personal and that there is unremitting conflict between them. Of the 12 sons of Jacob, the names of 8 are related directly to the antagonism between Rachel and Leah. Interestingly, the authorial voice through these chapters is sympathetic to the plight of the sisters. The reader is invited to view the deep hurt produced by the patriarchal system in which Rachel and Leah are trapped. The two sisters are used by a father who cheats them of their inheritance and exploits their husband. The only legitimacy possible to them comes through bearing sons. When Rachel finally delivers her long-desired boy, all she can think of is having more; the name "yosef" means "may the Lord add another son" (30.24). Both sisters secure proxies to get ahead in the race for status. They haggle over who will have access to Jacob's body, fountainhead of the only power these women can attain. The text is not silent about the injustice nor is it indifferent to the two women. Rather it acknowledges the sacrifice of personal happiness required for the building up of the 12 tribes. Leah and Rachel are both active players in the drama of their lives, maneuvering as best they can within the confines of a patriarchal system that the text does not criticize, but implicitly problematizes. The tension in the narrative may be due to multiple authors from different time periods with widely divergent views about patriarchy working with the same inherited material. In short, the author/s portray Rachel and Leah as women unwillingly cast in pivotal roles in a sacred panorama they do not choose; nevertheless, they perform their parts admirably, but as real woman with human foibles.

(4) Even as Jacob preferred Rachel to Leah, Rachel has been the favorite of the two sisters over the centuries in art, literature, and theology. One of the reasons for this is because of the hu-manity of Rachel's love affair with Jacob. Nowhere else in Genesis is the relationship between a man and woman described in such tender and exuberant terms. The spontaneous kiss of Jacob is so imbued with youthful passion that it has been viewed as scandalous by many historical commentators, including the Protestant reformer John Calvin. For Josephus, Rachel embodies the ideal of romantic love. She is the romantic ingenue par excellence, and Jacob is her match. Josephus uses the word "eros" to describe the couple's relationship (*Antiquities* I.288). When Rachel dies, her husband's productive life is over. He sires no more children, and the narrative switches focus from him to his sons. Throughout his life Jacob laments the loss of his beloved and transfers his devotion to her children. According to a medieval midrash, when Reuben complains about Jacob's favoritism, the patriarch responds, "I served Laban for Rachel's sake, not for your mother Leah's. The ploughing and sowing I did in Leah should have been done in Rachel, and Joseph should have been my firstborn" (Graves, 241). Throughout his life he loved Joseph above all and ultimately conferred on him all the privileges due the oldest son. When Jacob was an old man about to die, he lapsed into a sorrowful reverie bemoaning the loss of his beautiful wife and first love (Gn. 48.7). The romance of Rachel and Jacob has inspired important art, especially since the Renaissance, including works by Palma Vecchio, Hendrik Terbrugghen, Hugo Van der Goes, Claude Lorrain, and Marc Chagall. Rembrandt's *Danaë* is about Jacob's unintended marriage to Leah. The romantic relationship has also spawned post-Renaissance literary compositions, including songs, a comic opera, an oratorio, and a ballet. Robert Browning plays on the story of the two sisters in *The Ring and the Book,* and a contemporary novel, *The Red Tent,* by **Anita Diamant** reinterprets the love story for a 21st century audience.

Another reason Rachel has assumed primacy as a mother figure over her sister, despite the fact that Leah had more children, is, paradoxically, Rachel's early barrenness. The motif of the barren woman is not completely negative in the Hebrew Bible. Jewish homilies on Genesis compare the seven days of creation to seven barren women. Female infertility provides a metaphor for the prodigality possible through the intercession of Yahweh. God is able to demonstrate his power and charity through the hopeless Rachel, and for the same reason the barren woman becomes a symbol of Israel during the Babylonian captivity (Is. 49.21, 51.2, 54.1–3). Just as Rachel was without issue but was eventually granted offspring, captive Israel would one day be built up. The plight of the barren matriarchs of Genesis comes to stand for the whole of Israel. The potency of this metaphor explains why Rachel has, from a very early date, been favored over Leah. Despite being the younger sister, Rachel is listed before Leah in the wedding blessing in the Book of *Ruth (4.11). There is also a street named after her in modern Jerusalem called "Mother Rachel Street." Rachel is also favored over Leah in the Christian tradition. She is mentioned in the nuptial mass, and because she had only two children, Rachel, like ❧▶ **Mary of Bethany** (Luke 10.38–42), is a model of the contemplative life. Jesus favored Mary like Jacob did Rachel. Leah, on the other hand, mother of seven children, is like ❧▶ **Martha of Bethany**. She symbolizes the active life of service, one held to be inferior to the life of spiritual meditation. This theme has been developed consistently through the Christian era, including its elaboration by Dante in his *Divine Comedy* (*Purgatory* 27.100–108) and Michelangelo who portrayed Rachel on the tomb of Julius II garbed in the habit of a contemplative nun. Further, Leah with her dull eyes was a Christian metaphor for the synagogue (or the Jewish people) who could not see the truth. Rachel, like the early Christian church, was at first disadvantaged by her barrenness, but came to outdistance her sister and triumph as the mother of all Israel, like the church came to dominate the synagogue.

Finally, Rachel is remembered as the quintessential mother because of the position of her tomb and its mention in Jeremiah 31.15. The tomb of Rachel (called *kever* Rachel) has been over the centuries, and continues to be, a site of pilgrimage, especially on the 14th day of the month of Heshvan—the purported day of her death. Today, pictures of the tomb decorate homes in Israel, and it is replicated on household objects. People, drawing on "the merit of Rachel," take packets of earth from her gravesite to give to exiles or to bury with their loved ones. Childless women measure the tomb with red string, which they attach to their persons hoping God will "open the womb" as he once did for Rachel. But the numinous power of Mother Rachel reaches well beyond her biological function as life-giver.

Jeremiah's lament for the children of Israel held bondage in Babylon (in which Rachel is evoked mourning the fate of her children) is the basis of a long tradition in which she becomes identified with the divine spirit of the Jewish people (the Shechinah). In mystical writings, Rachel is called Mother Zion, and it is at her grave that the

messiah will first appear at the end of time: "And she will rise up/ And kiss him" (Dresner, 205). An elaborate medieval midrash spins a tale of Jeremiah seeking someone to convince the Lord to release his captive people. God will not listen to Moses or any of the patriarchs, but he does respond to Rachel's blandishments by which she reminds him that if she was not envious of Leah on what should have been her own wedding night, how could he be so jealous of foreign gods as to punish his people for worshipping them? God replies, "For thy sake, Rachel, will I restore Israel to their land" (Dresner, 161). In this text, God reveals his female nature through empathy with the mourning mother and Rachel becomes the deliverer of her people. The Lord assures the entombed Rachel weeping in Ramah that her children will return safely: "There shall be a reward for your toil; they shall come back from the land of the enemy" (Jer. 31.16). This verse has attained special prominence as an analogue for God's promise to his people as it is the prophetical reading selected for the second day of the Jewish New Year, Rosh Hashanah, and is incorporated into the evening service. Christians have focused on Rachel crying out in mourning for the children slaughtered by Herod. A liturgical drama, the *Ordo Rachelis,* produced in the 5th century and redacted several times in the Middle Ages, features Mother Rachel bemoaning the fate of the sons of her second son, Benjamin. She is consoled by the promise of the Innocents' resurrection.

Throughout Jewish history, during the Holocaust and the wars Israel fought with its Arab neighbors in the 20th century, the tomb of Rachel has been a symbol and place of solace and miracles. Christians and Muslims, but particularly Jews, have sought out the *kever* Rachel to pray for the deliverance of their people in times of national crisis. During the Yom Kippur War of 1973 when Israel was in peril, Rabbi Hayim Shmulevitch stole to the grave of Rachel late one night and prayed: "O Lord! You said to Rachel: 'Restrain your voice form weeping,' but I say: 'Weep Mama, weep!'" (Dresner, 197). The image of Rachel suffering for humanity has been appropriated by secular culture. Albert Camus (*The Fall*) and Herman Melville (*Moby Dick*) both employ the motif to capture the epitome of maternal empathy. Rachel has become a metaphor for compassion—for motherhood.

Despite their struggles, Rachel and Leah are inexorably paired as matriarchs of Israel. Although Genesis separates beauty and fertility, two aspects of womanhood personified by the rival sisters, the wedding blessing in the Book of Ruth extols both women in one breath, and in

❧▶
Martha and Mary of Bethany.
See Mary Magdalene for sidebar.

so doing implicitly reunites them: "May the Lord make this woman . . . like Rachel and Leah, the two who built up the house of Israel" (Ruth 4.11).

SOURCES:

Bellis, Alice Ogden. *Helpmates, Harlots, Heroes: Women's Stories in the Hebrew Bible.* Louisville, KY: Westminster-John Knox Press, 1994.

Callaway, Mary. *Sing, O Barren One: A Study in Comparative Midrash.* Atlanta, GA: Scholars Press, 1986.

Dresner, Samuel H. *Rachel.* Minneapolis, MN: Fortress Press, 1994.

Graves, Robert, and Raphael Patai. *Hebrew Myths: The Book of Genesis.* NY: Greenwich House, 1983.

Jay, Nancy. "Sacrifice, Descent, and the Patriarchs," in *Vetus Testamentum.* Vol. 38, 1988, pp. 52–70.

Mitchell, Stephen, trans. *Genesis: A New Translation of the Classical Biblical Stories.* NY: HarperCollins, 1996.

Noth, Martin. *The History of Israel.* 2nd ed. NY: Harper & Row, 1960.

SUGGESTED READING:

Alter, Robert. *The Art of Biblical Narrative.* NY: Basic Books, 1981.

Bal, Mieke, ed. *Anti-Covenant: Counter-Reading Women's Lives in the Hebrew Bible.* Decatur, GA: Almond Press, 1989.

Sarna, Nahum M. *Understanding Genesis: The Heritage of Biblical Israel.* NY: Schocken, 1966.

Martha Rampton,
Assistant Professor of History, Pacific University,
Forest Grove, Oregon

Rachilde (1860–1953).

See Vallette, Marguerite.

Radagunda.

See Radegund.

Radcliffe, Ann (1764–1823)

Hugely popular and prolific 18th-century English writer who developed the Gothic novel as a distinctive genre and whose works continued to have a considerable influence on major writers for 20 years after her death. Name variations: her books were always attributed to Ann Radcliffe, never Mrs. Radcliffe, but she was subsequently referred to by her husband and by her literary critics as Mrs. Radcliffe. Pronunciation: RAD-cliff. Born Ann Ward on July 9, 1764, in London, England; died on February 7, 1823, in London; only daughter of William Ward (a haberdasher) and Ann (Oates) Ward; educated probably at home but may possibly have briefly attended the school "for young ladies" run by the writer-sisters Harriet and Sophia Lee in Bath; married William Radcliffe, in 1787; no children.

Lived in London until age eight when her parents moved to Bath; after marriage at St. Michael's Church in Bath (1787), settled in London and began writing novels; visited Holland and Germany with husband (1794); published last novel during her lifetime (1797); spent next 25 years living quietly at home, writing for pleasure and traveling widely in England; in later years, suffered from ill health and traveled less; last novel and extracts from her journals published posthumously.

Selected publications: The Castles of Athlin and Dunbayne: A highland story (T. Hookham, 1789); A Sicilian Romance (2 vols., 1790); The Romance of the Forest: interspersed with some pieces of poetry (3 vols., 1791); The Mysteries of Udolpho: A Romance; interspersed with some pieces of poetry (4 vols., G.G. and J. Robinson, 1792); A Journey made in the Summer of 1794, through Holland and the Western frontier of Germany, with a return down the Rhine, to which are added Observations during a tour to the Lakes of Lancashire, Westmoreland and Cumberland (G.G. and J. Robinson, 1795); The Italian, or The Confessional of the Black Penitents: A Romance (3 vols., T. Cadell Jun. and W. Davies, 1797); "On the Supernatural in Poetry," in New Monthly Magazine (Vol. 16, 1826, pp. 145–152); Gaston de Blondeville; or, The Court of Henry III: Keeping Festival in Ardenne, A Romance and St Alban's Abbey, A Metrical Tale, with some poetical pieces . . . to which is prefixed a Memoir of the Author, with extracts from her Journals (4 vols., Henry Colbourn, 1826).

During the morning of September 3, 1797, a young woman stood on a point immediately below Dover castle looking out over the English Channel. Beside her stood her husband. Having left London two days earlier, they were on a tour of the southeast English counties of Kent and Sussex and enjoying a spell of fine and calm weather. Below them, and to the right, the picturesque town of Dover curved its way along the bay, nestling under the white and green of the sheltering chalk cliffs. As the young woman wrote in her journal later that evening, she and her husband were much struck with the grandeur of the seaview: "the long shades on its surface of soft green, deepening exquisitely into purple." In stark contrast, though, the castle itself, bristling with heavy fortifications, presented a sinister aspect. For the young couple, it was impossible to escape the fact that England was at war with France and Napoleon; below them on the water, could be seen a fleet of merchant mariners sailing down the Channel. They were in convoy formation and heavily protected by ships from the British fleet. In the far distance, the French coast itself was visible, "a white line bounding the blue waters."

The young woman was Ann Radcliffe, a highly prolific and popular writer whose vivid powers of description had already won her critical acclaim and whose latest novel, *The Italian,* was being rapidly snapped up by her adoring public. *The Italian* and her fourth novel, *The Mysteries of Udolpho,* which had appeared three years before, had been prominently heralded in the London press for several weeks, evidence, as **Clara McIntyre** suggests, that the publication of a new book bearing her name was an important event in the literary world. And yet, this young woman, whose books brimmed with detailed descriptions of French and Italian landscapes, is believed to have made only one visit outside England, to Holland and Germany in the summer of 1794. Instead, she took other writers' travel records and let her imagination take wing. The sight of the distant white line of the French coast was the closest she ever came to the dramatic landscapes of Southern Europe that she was able so successfully to evoke.

Radcliffe's novels were the escapist literature of the 1790s, a time of considerable turmoil and uncertainty. The idea of the Gothic "terror" novel was not new. Horace Walpole's *The Castle of Otranto* (1764) already contained many of the elements of this form of fiction: brooding monasteries and remote, half-ruined castles with subterranean passages, winding corridors, mysterious lights, strange noises, and villainous banditti, which form the backdrop for kidnaps, imprisonment, hair-raising escapes and dramatic death-bed resolutions played out by almost stock characters such as innocent and modest young heroines who are never compromised and tend to break into song or poetry at moments of great tension; naive heroes who fall hopelessly in love; sinister, domineering and, usually, aristocratic older men who are prepared to steal from, ravish and ultimately murder their wives, daughters and protégés; and loyal, garrulous servants. Radcliffe's success lay in the way she perfected the genre by her ability to create a sense of excitement and terror in her reader through apparently supernatural happenings and her power to enhance the atmosphere with vivid descriptions of the surrounding scenery—the magnificent peaks of the French Pyrenees, the craggy, desolate Italian Apennines, the architectural glories of Venice. As the titles suggest, her works were also liberally sprinkled with poems. That the reader's credulity was often severely stretched, that the supernatural happenings invariably had a completely rational explanation and that it was always evident that everything would eventually be happily resolved only added to the en-

joyment. To her contemporaries Radcliffe was "The Great Enchantress" who could beguile her readers with the power of her narrative and the romantic beauty of her landscapes.

Despite Radcliffe's huge popularity in the 1790s and during the first half of the 19th century, little is known about her life and personality; it is recorded that when poet ***Christina Rossetti** tried to write a biography some 50 years after Radcliffe's death she was forced to give up the idea because so little information was available. As the *Edinburgh Review* recorded at the time of Radcliffe's death: "The fair authoress kept herself almost as much *incognito* as the Author of *Waverley;* nothing was known of her but her name on the title page. She never appeared in public, nor mingled in private society, but kept herself apart, like the sweet bird that sings its solitary notes, shrouded and unseen." Radcliffe left no letters, diaries, or papers, and her journals are concerned purely with recording her impressions of the world around her and reveal little of her innermost thoughts. The major source for information about her life is the *Annual Biography and Obituary* of 1824, and it is believed that most of the material for this account was supplied by her husband. It must therefore be treated with some caution. However, the only physical description that exists of her comes from this source and is quoted in several works about her. She "was, in her youth, of a figure exquisitely proportioned; while she resembled her father, and his brother and sister, in being low of stature. Her complexion was beautiful, as was her whole countenance, especially her eyes, eyebrows, and mouth."

Ann Radcliffe was born on July 9, 1764, at number 19 Holborn on the fringes of the City of London. Her father William Ward came from Leicestershire and her mother **Ann Oates Ward** from the pleasant Derbyshire town of Chesterfield already noted for its famous church with its crooked, lead-striped steeple. William Ward was a tradesman. He owned a haberdashery shop, a fact which seems to have caused Radcliffe's husband some grief. Her somewhat humble but respectable background was quickly passed over in his account of her life in the *Annual Biography and Obituary:* she was "the daughter of William and Ann Ward, who, though in trade, were nearly the only persons of their two families not living in handsome, or at least easy independence." Much greater play was made of her more illustrious relatives. Her paternal grandmother was a sister of William Cheselden, surgeon to King George II, and renowned throughout Europe for his skill in performing operations to remove gallstones. On her mother's side, there were also connections with the medical profession as her maternal grandmother, **Ann Oates,** was the sister of Dr. Samuel Jebb of Stratford whose son became physician to many eminent people in London and was a favorite with the king who made him a baronet in 1778. On her mother's side, she was also related to Dr. Halifax, the bishop of Gloucester, and more distant ancestors were said to be the De Witt family from Holland who were invited to England during the reign of Charles I to undertake drainage works in the fenlands.

Radcliffe lived in London until the age of eight when her parents left to manage a showroom in Bath which sold the fine pottery, jasper ware, medallions, busts, and plaques produced by Josiah Wedgwood whose decorative wares were widely admired by those of fashionable taste. She was to remain in Bath, although with frequent trips to the capital, until her marriage in 1787. Little is known about Radcliffe's education. It seems that, like the majority of girls of her class and background, she would have been taught at home and given a smattering of skills and knowledge designed to maximize her chances of making a good marriage, the kind of "disorderly" and superficial education so roundly condemned by *Mary Wollstonecraft in her *Vindication of the Rights of Woman* in 1792. The emphasis would have been on accomplishments—needlework, drawing, dancing, singing, piano-playing, perhaps a smattering of European languages. Both McIntyre and Robert Miles are eager to suggest that Radcliffe's education may have been of a more formal nature and that she may have attended the well-regarded school for "young ladies" that writers *Sophia and *Harriet Lee opened in Bath in 1781. This seems unlikely given that she was already 17 when the school opened. However, there is certainly evidence that Radcliffe was acquainted with the Lee sisters, most likely on a social basis, and that the greatest influence they had on her life was through the books they published, particularly Sophia Lee's *The Recess* (1785) which represented an important point in the development of the novel with its blend of what **Aline Grant** terms "history, sentiment, suspense and sensibility," a combination of approaches never attempted before.

And yet Radcliffe's education does seem to have gone beyond mere accomplishments. It was certainly not a masculine, classical education for the account of her life in the *Annual Biography and Obituary* recalls that she "would desire to hear passages repeated from the Latin and Greek classics; requiring, at intervals, the most literal translations that could be given, with all that was possible of their idiom." Yet she was extremely widely read. The allusions in her writings show considerable familiarity with the works of the pre-Romantic English poets and with the plays and poems of Shakespeare. She uses quotations from many different sources as headings to her chapters. There is also evidence that she took much pleasure in music and was knowledgeable about art.

It seems that Radcliffe's wider education owed much to the literary and cultural circle in which some of her more wealthy relatives moved. One of this circle, and a person who had a particularly marked influence on her early development, was Thomas Bentley, a man of many interests, a liberal in politics and religion, an anti-slavery campaigner, and a close friend of the radical Joseph Priestley and a business partner of Josiah Wedgwood. Bentley had been married to Radcliffe's aunt, **Hannah Oates,** and after her death in 1756, another of Radcliffe's aunts agreed to act as his housekeeper. For 16 years, until he remarried in 1772, **Elizabeth Oates** kept house for Bentley and even after his second marriage spent considerable time at his substantial home with its fine gardens in Little Cheyne Row, Chelsea. According to Grant, she was "a kindly, well-disposed, intelligent woman," who frequently invited her niece to spend time with them. Wedgwood's biographer, **Eliza Meteyard,** records that Bentley was a popular man who counted among his friends many prominent people in the literary and scientific world and, although she was still very young at the time, Radcliffe would have been introduced to a stimulating and intellectual group of people which included several forceful women—a friend of Dr. Johnson, Hester Thrale (*Hester Lynch Piozzi), who became a well-known travel writer, historian and critic, the bluestocking *Elizabeth Montagu who produced, among other works, an *Essay on the Writings and Genius of Shakespeare,* and *Anna Letitia Barbauld, classical scholar, editor, poet and essayist.

Bentley died in 1780 when Radcliffe was 16. From then until her marriage seven years later, she appears to have spent most of her time in Bath. It was there that she met William Radcliffe, an Oxford graduate and law student. She was married from her parents' home but, soon after, the couple left Bath to set up house in London where William Radcliffe, who had quickly tired of the law, began a career as a journalist and as part-editor of the *English Chronicle.* He also undertook translations from French.

It was her marriage to William that seems to have established Radcliffe's career as a novelist. As was then the practice of many similar young women, she had already begun to record in her journal vivid accounts of the places and scenery she saw as she traveled between Bath and London. William seems to have been impressed with her literary skill and, when she started to write regularly to fill the long winter evenings while he was away on editorial business or preparing reports on parliamentary debates in the House of Commons, he encouraged her enthusiastically.

Her first novel, *The Castles of Athlin and Dunbayne*, appeared within two years of their marriage. Although not a runaway success, it was sufficiently well received for her publisher to ask for a second. Within a year, she had finished *A Sicilian Romance* and only a year later *The Romance of the Forest*. These first three novels were published anonymously but so successful was *The Romance of the Forest* that when the second edition was issued Radcliffe was happy for her name to appear on the title page. Her fourth novel, *The Mysteries of Udolpho*, published in 1794, set the seal on her reputation, not only in Britain, but also in Europe. By then, she was indisputably the most popular writer of her day.

She was far and away the best-selling English novelist of the 1790s; the most read, the most imitated, and the most translated.

—Robert Miles

That same year, Radcliffe took time off from her novel-writing to accompany her husband on a tour through Holland and Germany to Switzerland. They visited Rotterdam, Delft, and other major towns in Holland and were much impressed with Dutch standards of cleanliness. Germany, however, presented a very different picture. They were soon being accosted by barefooted children who ran out to beg; the land lay uncultivated and signs of recent fighting were much in evidence. As they traveled, they came across bands of wounded soldiers and of wretched French prisoners of war. In many places, they were received with rudeness and sullenness. Nevertheless, their visit to Germany did have some high points, particularly their stay in the beautiful spa town of "Goodesberg" (Bad Godesberg). However, they never made it to Switzerland—the Austrian commander of the garrison at the border post refused to accept that they were English and turned them back. They returned to England and made a tour of the Lake District instead.

Radcliffe may have temporarily abandoned her novel-writing but throughout their journey she made copious notes in her journal and on their return was persuaded to publish an account of their travels. *A Journey Made in the Summer of 1794*, a mainly descriptive work, appeared the following year. Two years later, *The Italian*, arguably the most satisfactory of her novels, was published.

And then, after the appearance of six books in eight years, at the age of 33, Radcliffe suddenly stopped publishing. A slim volume of poems appeared in 1816, but her last novel, *Gaston de Blondeville*, was not published until three years after her death. There has been considerable discussion as to why she should have ceased to write for publication. One suggested explanation is that she was upset by adverse comments about *The Italian*. She certainly seems to have been highly sensitive to criticism. For example, she is reputed to have completely misinterpreted a seemingly innocent remark about her in a letter written by the bluestocking *Elizabeth Carter and to have been extremely upset when *Joanna Baillie's very successful *Plays on the Passions* was wrongly attributed to her by the writer *Anna Seward. However, although some reviewers had compared *The Italian* unfavorably to *The Mysteries of Udolpho*, there was much critical acclaim and her preeminence as a writer of fiction was never questioned. The only really hostile review did not appear until four years later. A more plausible explanation was that her great success was beginning to engender a number of second-rate imitations of her work, the most notorious being Matthew Lewis' *The Monk* (1796), and that she was no longer happy to be associated with this genre of writing. Most likely, though, it was the receipt of a sudden legacy which gave her and her husband greater financial stability and enabled her to give up writing for monetary reward.

Unlike some other women writers of her day, Radcliffe never seemed to have difficulty in reconciling her gender and her success as a writer. Others appear to have been assailed by ambivalent feelings towards the status of women as writers. Although by the 1790s women were more widely accepted as literary figures than 50 years earlier, their works, especially their fictional writings, were frequently treated with indulgence and disparagement by male critics, this despite the fact that it has been estimated that women wrote between two-thirds and three-quarters of the novels published between 1760 and 1790. Equally, although many women argued that women should be allowed greater economic independence, they frequently expressed concern that they should have to demean themselves by writing for money. *Charlotte Smith—who came from a family of landed gentry but was forced to write to support her large family when she finally left her husband after putting up with his profligacy, unfaithfulness, and violence for 27 years—was very bitter because she considered that a woman of her class ought not to be reduced to writing novels for a living. Smith admittedly came from a higher social class than Radcliffe but *Elizabeth Inchbald, the daughter of a poor farmer, also stresses in the preface to her novel *A Simple Story* (1791) that she did not choose to be a writer. She justified her career as a novelist on the grounds that it was financial necessity that had obliged her "to devote a tedious seven years to the unremitting labour of literary productions."

Radcliffe never, as far as is known, made any apology for publishing her novels. However, it is possible that her husband's insistence that she wrote with his blessing and the apparently deliberate policy of keeping her from the public eye may have represented an attempt at legitimation. Certainly in the early days of their marriage Radcliffe's earnings, which were not insignificant, would have made a welcome contribution to the family finances. She is said to have received the handsome sum of £500 for *The Mysteries of Udolpho* and £600 for *The Italian*. (*Jane Austen, admittedly unknown at the time, received only ten guineas for *Northanger Abbey* 20 years later.) Radcliffe's husband seems not to have been a good financial manager and on several occasions ran into debt. In the summer of 1797, Radcliffe received news that her aunt Elizabeth had died, leaving her money, books, and plate. Less than a year later, her father also died and she found herself with a life interest in the rents of a house and land a few miles outside Leicester, his hometown. To this was added considerable property which came to her after the death of her mother in 1800. It is Miles' contention that it was these financial inheritances that "allowed her to quit the embarrassing environs of the romance-writer's Grub Street, where few proper ladies were to be found." It was certainly shortly after her aunt's death that William Radcliffe was able to buy the *English Chronicle* for £1,000. Perhaps, though, Radcliffe merely ceased publishing because her husband was becoming more established in his career and was able to spend more time at home with her.

During the rest of her life Radcliffe continued to write poetry and completed the historical romance *Gaston de Blondeville*, which was published along with some of her poems and extracts from her journals in 1826. *Gaston* was prefaced with a memoir of Radcliffe by the writer Thomas Noon Talfourd, this being the only other authoritative source about her life that appears to exist besides the account in the *Annual Biography and Obituary* of 1824. Talfourd was no doubt briefed by William Radcliffe. Also attached was a statement by the family physician. Radcliffe's failure to publish any further novels, and her quiet, almost secluded, lifestyle in the later years of her life, had attracted considerable comment. Stories circulated that she was suffering from a disoriented state of mind brought on by the excesses of her imagination; that she had been confined in Haddon Hall in Derbyshire (believed, erroneously, to have been the prison of the hapless *Mary Stuart, queen of Scots, who lost her head during the reign of *Elizabeth I); that she had died an early and unhappy death. While such rumors marry fittingly with the substance of Radcliffe's novels, they were untrue. For a number of years, though, Radcliffe did suffer increasingly from attacks of asthma and from recurring chest infections. It is said, for instance, in the memoir appended to *Gaston de Blondeville*, that the Radcliffes, keen theatergoers, always sat in the pit, "partly because her health required warm clothing."

In the autumn of 1822, Radcliffe and her husband visited the resort of Ramsgate in the hopes that the sea air would give her some relief from a painful cough and difficult breathing. Although she gained a brief respite, on January 9, 1823, she began to suffer again and died peacefully in her sleep less than a month later. Her physician's statement records that she remained clear-minded until only a few days before her death. She was buried in London in the cemetery on the Bayswater Road which belongs to St. George's Church, Hanover Square.

Radcliffe's novels remained highly popular until well into the 19th century. Several were dramatized, and editions in French, German, Spanish, and Italian cited in the British Library catalogue are evidence that she was read across Europe. The most successful, such as *The Mysteries of Udolpho*, ran into a number of subsequent editions and all those which were published in her lifetime have been reprinted in recent years. The account of her journey to Holland and Germany and her posthumous novel, *Gaston de Blondeville*, are available in facsimile editions. Care must be taken, though, not to confuse Radcliffe with three other women writers of the period. Wrongly attributed to her in some past editions of her novels has been the feminist polemic *The Female Advocate; or, An Attempt to Recover the Rights of Women from*

Male Usurpation (1799). This was the work of an older woman, *****Mary Ann Radcliffe**. The British Library catalogue also lists works from the same period by **Ann Sophia Radcliffe**. Again, these should not be attributed to Ann Radcliffe.

Radcliffe was writing at the end of a century during which women writers had become increasingly numerous and prolific, and the female reading public had grown rapidly. Of all these women writers, Radcliffe was probably the most widely read. Indeed, E.B. Murray goes as far as to suggest that she enjoyed a popularity which no novelist before her—male or female—had ever experienced. Later well-known writers—Walter Scott, Jane Austen and, subsequently, Charles Dickens and the *****Brontë sisters**—acknowledged their debt to Radcliffe in the many allusions to her works that can be found in their letters and novels. Although Radcliffe may not herself have been their equal, it is impossible to deny the definite and important contribution to the development of the novel that she made and the considerable critical acclaim she received both during her lifetime and after her death.

SOURCES:

Grant, Aline. *Ann Radcliffe: A Biography*. Denver, CO: Alan Swallow, 1951.

McIntyre, Clara. *Ann Radcliffe in Relation to Her Time*. New Haven, CT: Yale University Press, 1920.

Miles, Robert. *Ann Radcliffe: The Great Enchantress*. Manchester: Manchester University Press, 1995.

Murray, E.B. *Ann Radcliffe*. NY: Twayne, 1972.

Talfourd, T.N. "Memoir of the Author" and "Extracts from her Journals" prefaced to Ann Radcliffe's *Gaston de Blondeville, or The Court of Henry III: Keeping Festival in Ardenne, A Romance*. Vol. 1. London: Henry Colbourn, 1826.

SUGGESTED READING:

Frank, F.S. *The First Gothics: A Critical Guide to the English Gothic Novel*. NY: Garland, 1987.

Kelly, G. *English Fiction of the Romantic Period, 1789–1830*. London and NY: Longman, 1989.

Spencer, Jane. *The Rise of the Woman Novelist From Aphra Behn to Jane Austen*. Oxford: Basil Blackwell, 1986.

Stoler, J.A. *Ann Radcliffe: The Novel of Suspense and Terror*. NY: Arno Press, 1980.

Sylvia Dunkley,
Tutor in History at the Department of Adult Continuing Education,
University of Sheffield, England,
with gratitude to Robert Miles of Sheffield Hallam University
for allowing access to a pre-publication copy of his
Ann Radcliffe: The Great Enchantress

Radcliffe, Charlotte Maria

(d. 1755)

Countess of Newburgh. Name variations: Charlotte Maria Radclyffe. Died in 1755; daughter of Charles Livingstone, 2nd earl of Newburgh; married Thomas Clifford (died 1718); married Charles Radcliffe, in 1724.

The granddaughter of Sir James Livingstone, the first earl of Newburgh, Charlotte Maria Radcliffe succeeded her father Charles Livingstone, the second earl of Newburgh, as countess of Newburgh in 1694. Her first husband, Thomas Clifford, died in 1718, after which she rebuffed the matrimonial advances of Charles Radcliffe (later titular earl of Derwentwater). He responded by sneaking into her private room via the chimney and thereby leaving her no choice but to marry him, which she did in 1724.

Jo Anne Meginnes,
freelance writer, Brookfield, Vermont

Radcliffe, Margaret.

See Stanley, Margaret.

Radcliffe, Mary Ann

(c. 1746–after 1810)

Scottish-born writer. Name variations: Mrs. Radcliffe; Mary Anne Radcliffe. Born around 1746 in Scotland; died after 1810; married Joseph Radcliffe, around 1760; children: eight.

Selected writings: The Fate of Velina de Guidova (1790); Radzivil (1790); The Female Advocate; or An Attempt to Recover the Rights of Women from Male Usurpation (1799); Manfrone; or The One-Handed Monk (1809); The Memoirs of Mrs. Mary Ann Radcliffe in Familiar Letters to her Female Friend (1810).

Born in Scotland around 1746, Mary Ann Radcliffe was two years old when the death of her father made her heir to a sizeable fortune. She was raised in her father's Protestant faith, although her mother was Catholic, and at some point moved to England. When she was only 14 she fell in love with and secretly married Joseph Radcliffe, a Catholic in his 30s. Her husband showed a fondness for liquor and bad luck in business, which whittled away her inheritance while she gave birth to eight children over the years. When their marriage finally collapsed, Radcliffe was left to fend for herself and her children. She found such "genteel" (and low paying) work as acting as a governess and as a lady's companion and housekeeper, and later operated a retail shoe store and then a school. By the time she was in her 40s, she had turned to writing and, as "Mrs. Radcliffe," published both *Radzivil* and *The Fate of Velina de Guidova* in 1790.

In the 18th and 19th centuries many women writers published their work using "Mrs." and their married names, and Radcliffe's use of "Mrs. Radcliffe," as well as the Gothic-tinged flavor of her fiction, led to some contemporary confusion between her works and those of *Ann Radcliffe, the enormously popular author of such Gothic extravaganzas as *The Mysteries of Udolpho*. Also in this vein was her brief literary magazine *Radcliffe's New Novelist's Pocket Magazine*, which started and stopped publishing in 1802, and her 1809 novel *Manfrone; or The One-Handed Monk* (published under her full name), which was at first refused by her publisher because of its frank depiction of violence and neurotic sexuality. Its success nonetheless led to a second edition, published in 1819.

Altogether different from her novels, and perhaps of more interest to the modern-day reader, was Radcliffe's *The Female Advocate; or An Attempt to Recover the Rights of Women from Male Usurpation* (1799). With her painful, first-hand knowledge of the precarious existence that women who had only been educated to be wives faced when suddenly forced to earn their own living, she pressed the case for wider employment opportunities for women, and cited the arguments of both *Mary Wollstonecraft and *Hester Chapone. This book later formed part of *The Memoirs of Mrs. Mary Ann Radcliffe in Familiar Letters to her Female Friend* (1810), in which, no doubt drawing on her own experience, she also wrote about the dangers of hasty marriages. There is scant information about Radcliffe's life after the publication of her memoirs, although it is known that she lived in Edinburgh, unwell and supported financially by friends, before her death some time in the early 19th century.

SOURCES:

Shattock, Joanne. *The Oxford Guide to British Women Writers*. Oxford: Oxford University Press, 1993.

Jo Anne Meginnes,
freelance writer, Brookfield, Vermont

Radclyffe-Hall, Marguerite.

See Hall, Radclyffe.

Radegonda or Radegonde.

Variant of Radegund.

Radegonde (d. 1445)

*French princess. Died in 1445; daughter of Charles VII (1403–1461), king of France (r. 1422–1461), and *Marie of Anjou (1404–1463); sister of Louis XI (1423–1483), later king of France (r. 1461–1483).*

Radegund of Poitiers (518–587)

Queen of the Franks and saint. Name variations: Radegond; Radegonde; Radegonda; Radagunda. Born in 518 (some sources cite 519) in Thuringia; died on August 13, 587, at abbey of Sainte Croixe, Poitiers, France; daughter of Berthair, Berthaire, or Berthar, king of Thuringia; married Clothar also known as Lothair I (497–561), king of Soissons and the Franks (r. 558–561), in 534; no children.

Radegund of Poitiers is one of the most famous of medieval saints. She was born a German princess in 518, the daughter of King Berthair of Thuringia. During a battle between the Thuringians and the Franks, her family was killed, and Radegund, only 12 years old, was taken prisoner. She was brought to the Frankish royal court to later become the wife of King Lothair I, who already had four wives (*Guntheuca, *Chunsina, *Ingunde, and *Aregunde) despite his Christian beliefs. Having been raised as a girl of exceptional piety, Radegund was understandably miserable at the court. She was, however, remarkably well educated and could read and converse in Latin. At 18, she was forced to marry Lothair, whom she had grown to despise. He was a cruel, vicious man, and Radegund spent most of her time trying to avoid him.

The biographies written of her tell of Radegund's constant prayer and charitable acts; she even supposedly avoided sleeping with her husband by praying all night beside their bed. After several years, Radegund's intense devotion to God and the fact that she remained childless weakened Lothair's interest in her. She finally found the courage to escape from him when she learned that he had murdered her brother, and feared for her own life. Radegund fled to Noen and found refuge with a bishop who, inspired by the story of this former queen, agreed to consecrate her as a deaconess (a very rare office given to a widowed holy woman who could then act with the authority of a priest).

Around 557, she founded a monastery at Poitiers, which became known as Ste. Croixe and is still standing, but she adamantly refused to become its abbess. Instead, she insisted on performing menial tasks such as cooking and cleaning, which furthered her growing reputation as a holy woman. The monastery became very popular, housing over 200 nuns, and also was known as an important center of learning. Its nuns were highly educated and included several writers; Radegund herself was a poet and corresponded with religious leaders across Europe. The ex-queen also spent her time acting as a peacemaker for various rival political factions in France. She died at Ste. Croixe about age 70.

Two of her close friends wrote biographies of her as a part of their successful campaign to have Radegund canonized; one was her sister nun, **Baudonivia**, and the other was Fortunatus, the wandering poet whom Radegund had patronized. It is from these works that most information about the saint's life is obtained.

SOURCES:

Dunbar, Agnes. *Dictionary of Saintly Women.* Vol. I. London: G. Bell and Sons, 1904.

LaBarge, Margaret. *A Small Sound of the Trumpet: Women in Medieval Life.* Boston, MA: Beacon Press, 1986.

Uglow, Jennifer, ed. *Dictionary of Women's Biography.* NY: Continuum, 1989.

Laura York, M.A. in History,
University of California, Riverside, California

Radner, Gilda (1946–1989)

Popular comic actress and original cast member of NBC's "Saturday Night Live," which, in its early years, transformed television comedy. Pronunciation: RAD-ner. Born on June 28, 1946, in Detroit, Michigan; died of ovarian cancer on May 20, 1989, in Los Angeles, California; daughter of Herman Radner (a prominent Detroit businessman) and Henrietta (Dworkin) Radner; studied drama and education at University of Michigan, 1964–69; married G.E. Smith (a musician), in 1980 (divorced 1982); married Gene Wilder (an actor), on September 18, 1984; no children.

Received Emmy for "Saturday Night Live" (1977–78); received Antoinette Perry (Tony) nomination for Lunch Hour *(1980).*

Television: "Saturday Night Live" (1975–80). Theater: Gilda Radner–Live From New York (1979); Lunch Hour (1980). Film: Gilda Live (1980); Hanky Panky (1982); The Woman in Red (1984). Memoir: It's Always Something (1989).

When NBC's "Saturday Night Live" premiered on October 18, 1975, the generation who had come of age during the Vietnam War and Watergate had not quite learned to make fun of itself. The Not Ready for Prime Time Players, the young renegade group that comprised the original cast, changed all that. Their first show featured an ad with activist-turned-entrepreneur Jerry Rubin selling graffiti wallpaper from the 1960s. The show was hip, relevant, and an instant smash. Suddenly, sitting in front of the television on Saturday night was *the* place to be.

Gilda Radner was one of the reasons. Her eccentric, endearing characters were unlike any her audience had ever seen and at the same time instantly recognizable. Everyone who had ever made a fool of themselves felt a rapport with these characters, and with Gilda.

Radner was born on June 28, 1946, to prosperous Jewish parents who lived in an upper-middle-class suburb of Detroit, Michigan; she had one older brother. Her father Herman Radner had been reared with his ten siblings on Manhattan's Lower East Side, where his father had immigrated from Lithuania. In 1906, when he was 13, his family moved to Detroit. Having dropped out of school in the fifth grade, Herman became a pool hustler until he won enough money to buy a pool hall. In the 1920s, he bought a Canadian brewery, and by the Depression he was so prosperous that he became known as a philanthropist, turning his brewery into a free lunchroom.

In 1937, when Herman was 44, he married **Henrietta Dworkin**, and their son Michael was born in 1941. Gilda, who arrived five years later, once described herself as an "unhappy, fat and mediocre" child. The roots of those feelings seemed to lie in her relationship with her mother, next to whom Gilda felt inadequate. Henrietta had been a beautiful young woman, a legal secretary and frustrated ballet dancer, and had become, according to Gilda and several of her friends, cold and critical.

"If you can decide to be funny, I decided it at age ten," Radner told **Amy Gross** of *Mademoiselle*. "I said to myself, 'You're not going to make it on looks.' . . . I just knew if people said I was fat, I'd laugh and make jokes about it and that would be my world." She was encouraged to be funny by her father and her nanny, the two adults she held most dear. **Elizabeth Clementine Gillies**, Gilda's beloved nanny and mother figure, whom she called Dibby, came to work for the Radners when Gilda was four months old and stayed for eighteen years. A widow with three children, she was warm and totally accepting of Gilda, two things Henrietta Radner was not, and she became not only a close confidant throughout Gilda's entire life, but also an inspiration for much of her most successful comic material.

Her father, who had become the wealthy owner of the Saville, one of Detroit's best hotels, loved show business and the show people who stayed at his hotel. It was Herman who taught Gilda to sing and dance and had her perform for relatives. They loved to go to the theater together, and always sat in the third row of the Riviera for road shows of Broadway productions. According to Gilda, Herman always wanted to be a song-and-dance man: "Some of his spunk must have come out in me, because he used to love to perform. . . . He did magic tricks. He loved to sing, and he could tap dance, and he couldn't carry a

tray of food to the table without tripping to make us kids laugh and make my mother nervous. In the years that I've been performing I feel that some part of my father is back alive in me, back doing what he always wanted to do," she told her friend David Saltman as recorded in his book *Gilda*.

But when Radner was 12, her father was diagnosed with brain cancer which soon made him quite ill. He was never really himself again and died two years later, when she was away at summer camp. Herman Radner's illness and death foreshadowed that of his daughter, and broke her heart.

By her high school years, Radner had made a concerted, successful effort to slim down, and she stayed thin for the rest of her life. Eating and dieting remained an obsession, and she always said that she felt as if she were fat; during the most creative, frenetic "Saturday Night Live" period, she began binge eating and was, for a time, bulimic.

$\mathcal{G}$ilda Radner thought she wasn't beautiful. She was wrong about that.

—Tom Shales

After graduating from the Liggett School in 1964, Radner moved to Ann Arbor to attend the University of Michigan, where she stayed for six years without earning a college degree. Her years in Ann Arbor were fertile, however. College is often a heady experience, and it was perhaps more so in the late 1960s, when the Vietnam War divided the United States, and college students were often at the forefront of social change. Instead of frequenting demonstrations and sit-ins, however, Gilda found herself more at home in the theater. She had comic roles in the University of Michigan and Ann Arbor Civic Theater productions of *The Magic Horn, Lysistrata,* and *Hotel Paradiso,* and leading roles in *The Taming of the Shrew* and *She Stoops to Conquer.*

In 1969, Radner moved to Toronto with a boyfriend, with whom she soon broke up, but she stayed in Canada and took a job at a small, avant-garde theater doing pantomime stories for elementary school children. At 23, she realized that she could actually make a living by being funny (although, as the beneficiary of a trust from her father, she did not need to work at all). After seeing *Hair* and the television series "Monty Python's Flying Circus," says Saltman, she "suddenly understood there could be a whole new direction for clowning and performance comedy, something along the lines of what *National Lampoon* was doing in print." Her first professional role came in 1972, when she was chosen for a Toronto production of *Godspell;* among her cast mates were Paul Shaffer, Martin Short, **Andrea Martin** and others who would go on to become well-known entertainers.

After *Godspell,* Radner joined the Toronto company of Second City, the groundbreaking, Chicago-based comedy revue. It was a tough way to learn, for all acts were improvised, and there were few props. Radner rose to the occasion and began to perfect her comedic characterizations. She was meeting and working with people who were to loom large in her life and career: John Belushi, Bill Murray, Dan Aykroyd and, in the audience, a Canadian producer named Lorne Michaels.

In 1974, after six years in Toronto, Radner moved to New York to work with Belushi on "The National Lampoon Radio Hour." It was a chance for her not only to work with Belushi, whom she considered her mentor and a comedic genius, but also to build on her years in Ann Arbor, where she had done some comic bits on the college radio station. One of her best-known characters, Babwa Wawa, a parody of television journalist *Barbara Walters,* made her first appearance on "Radio Hour." The radio show was followed by *The National Lampoon Show,* a road show that became a hit with college students in Canada and the Northeastern United States. Its producers garnered the courage to open the show in New York, and that run also proved successful. Radner's signature character was Rhoda Tyler Moore, a spoof on the popular television comedy, "The Mary Tyler Moore Show."

Lorne Michaels saw Radner's act again, and she was the first person he asked to join the cast of a new show he was attempting at NBC. She hesitated, having received a much more secure offer to work on a syndicated comedy talk show in Calgary. After polling her friends, as was her habit, Radner decided to risk disaster on a national network rather than safety in syndication. She soon began trying to talk Michaels into signing her favorite performing partners, John Belushi, Dan Aykroyd, and Bill Murray, and she succeeded.

Thus were born the Not Ready for Prime Time Players. In addition to Radner, Belushi, Aykroyd and Murray, the charter members were Chevy Chase, **Jane Curtin, Laraine Newman,** and Garrett Morris. The live, 90-minute comedy show, NBC's "Saturday Night Live," was an immediate hit. At its peak, it attracted an audience estimated at 10 million.

By 1979, after the departures from the show of Chevy Chase and John Belushi, Radner was the first among equals. Her generosity and innocence, as well as her eccentric characters, set her apart. She respected her audience and was loved in return. Her stable of characters had become household names, particularly her group of silly newscasters: in addition to Babwa Wawa, there was Roseanne Roseanadanna, who could elaborate at length on such subjects as nose hair, and Emily Litella, whose hearing problem caused her to expound on "Soviet jewelry" and "violins on television." There was Judy Miller, the self-absorbed Brownie; Lisa Loopner, the high school "nerd"; Rhonda Weiss, the Long Island "Jewish princess"; and they were all a part of Gilda Radner. She was gawky, grinning, often childlike and vulnerable, and she was a star. In 1978, the National Academy of Television Arts and Sciences awarded Radner an Emmy for "outstanding continuing performance by a supporting actress in music or comedy."

The show had an impact on teenagers and young adults far beyond that of any network television show before it. "Saturday Night Live," as Saltman describes it, "was a freewheeling blend of the sacred, the brilliant, and the profane, an international salon of the highest caliber as well as a sex-and-drugs-and-rock-and-roll empire that redefined art, culture, fashion and especially humor." To young Americans, "Saturday Night Live" was the one television program not to be missed. Several of its catch phrases were Gilda's, including "It's always something" and "Never mind."

Radner's exit from "Saturday Night Live" was not particularly pleasant. The success of the Blues Brothers, Belushi and Aykroyd's independent act, had fueled her own ambition, and rightly so; she was every bit as popular as they were. NBC executives, who envisioned her as the Lucy Ricardo of the 1980s, wanted Gilda to have her own show, but she was ambivalent. With Lorne Michaels as her advisor, she decided instead to do a Broadway revue. *Gilda Radner: Live From New York*, which opened in 1979, strained old friendships and was a critical failure. Her talent was unquestioned, but many reviewers found the material too slight. The show closed after four weeks, and the accompanying album and film (called *Gilda Live*) both bombed.

"Saturday Night Live" launched its sixth season in the fall of 1980 with a completely new cast, a new executive producer, and terrible reviews. The show was never as funny and fresh again. Radner, however, had found a measure of personal and professional happiness. She married G.E. Smith, leader of the *Gilda Live* band (and later the band leader on "Saturday Night Live"). She appeared on Broadway once more, with Sam Waterson in *Lunch Hour*. This time, reviews were good.

Radner also began to take film roles. She played the president's daughter in *First Family* in 1980, followed by two films with Gene Wilder, *Hanky Panky* (1982) and *The Woman in Red* (1984). Radner said later that she never felt at home in front of the movie camera; indeed, the most significant result of these roles was a personal one. As she recounted in her memoir, *It's Always Something*: "I had been a fan of Gene Wilder's for many years, but the first time I saw him, my heart fluttered—I was hooked. It felt like my life went from black and white to Technicolor." Six months later, she divorced Smith

and in 1984 a wildly happy Radner married Wilder in the south of France. The next year, the newlyweds filmed *Haunted Honeymoon* in London. But there were problems: Gilda had two miscarriages and spells of fatigue. In 1986, after months of increasingly poor health, she was diagnosed with ovarian cancer.

The next two-and-a-half years were a roller coaster of hospitals and treatments, sickness and health. She brightened up gatherings at the Wellness Community, a cancer-support group in Santa Monica, California, where she delighted in making other people laugh. In 1991, the Santa Monica Wellness Community started a similar group in New York; they called it Gilda's Club. Today, it is an international organization with ten clubs in the United States, one in Canada, one in England, with plans for many more. In March 1988, after an eight-year absence from television, Radner appeared on the "Garry Shandling Show" and told cancer jokes.

Gilda Radner died of ovarian cancer on May 20, 1989, at age 42. That night, hosting the final show of the 14th season of "Saturday Night Live," comedian Steve Martin showed a clip of Gilda romping through a spoof of romantic musicals with him. Afterward, he said, "When I look at this tape, I can't help but think how great she was, and how young I looked. Gilda, we miss you."

SOURCES:

Andrews, Deborah, ed. *The Annual Obituary 1989*. Chicago, IL: St. James Press, 1989.

Moritz, Charles, ed. *Current Biography Yearbook 1980*. NY: H.W. Wilson, 1980.

Radner, Gilda. *It's Always Something*. NY: Simon & Schuster, 1989.

Saltman, David. *Gilda: An Intimate Portrait*. Chicago, IL: Contemporary Books, 1992.

Shales, Tom. *Legends: Remembering America's Greatest Stars*. NY: Random House, 1989.

Smith, Chris. "Comedy isn't Funny," in *New York*. Vol. 28, no. 11. March 13, 1995, p. 31.

SUGGESTED READING:

Zweibel, Alan. *Bunny, Bunny: Gilda Radner: A Sort of Love Story*. NY: Villard Books, 1994.

Elizabeth L. Bland,
reporter, *Time* magazine

Radvanyi, Netty (1900–1983).

See Seghers, Anna.

Radziwell, Barbara (1520–1551).

See Sforza, Bona for sidebar.

Rafael, Sylvia (1938–1985)

Israeli intelligence agent. Name variations: also seen as Raphael. Born in 1938, possibly in South Africa; killed by the PLO in Cyprus in 1985.

At the Munich Olympics in 1972, the Arab terrorist group Black September killed 11 Israeli athletes, 9 of them after a day as hostages. The attack had been planned by Ali Hassan Salameh, a member of the Palestine Liberation Organization (PLO), who was also believed responsible for a number of hijackings and murders. The following year, Mossad, Israel's counter-espionage agency, sent a group of its agents to kill Salameh in Lillehammer, Norway, where he was believed to be hiding. One of these agents was Sylvia Rafael. Rafael and her colleagues mistakenly identified a Moroccan waiter, Ahmed Bouchikhi, as Salameh, and shot him dead in the street in front of his pregnant wife. Some nine agents successfully fled the country, but five were caught, including Rafael, who was carrying a Canadian passport identifying her as Patricia Roxburger. Amid swirling rumors that Norwegian police or members of Norwegian intelligence had assisted the agents, all were tried for the murder and convicted. Rafael, defended by Anneaus Schjodt, one of Norway's top lawyers, received the modest sentence of 5½ years in prison, and served only 22 months before being pardoned and released (as were the other agents). She then married Schjodt.

Described as "chic, attractive," and an "efficient spy," Rafael was greeted warmly upon returning to Israel, and continued to work for Mossad. After several other unsuccessful attempts, Mossad killed Salameh with a car bomb in Beirut in 1979. Six years later, the PLO killed Rafael and two other agents in Cyprus. In 1996, while continuing to deny responsibility, Israel paid an unknown sum of money to Bouchikhi's family as compensation for his murder. After a two-year investigation, in 2000 a government commission determined that Norway had not been involved in the attempted assassination.

SOURCES:
Deacon, Richard. *Spyclopaedia*. London: Futura, 1989.
"Norway solves riddle of Mossad killing," in *The Guardian*. March 2, 2000.

Jo Anne Meginnes,
freelance writer, Brookfield, Vermont

Raftor, Kitty (1711–1785).

See Clive, Kitty.

Ragnetrude (fl. 630)

Queen of Austrasia and the Franks. Name variations: *Rainetrude. Flourished around 630; married Dagobert I (c. 606–639), king of Austrasia (r. 623–628), king of the Franks (r. 629–639); children: Sigibert III (630–656), king of Austrasia (r. 634–656).*

Ragnhild

Queen of the Isles. Married Olva the Red, king of the Isles; married Somerled, 1st lord of Argyll; children: Dugall, king of the Isles and founder of the clan Dougall; Reginald or Ranald, king of the Isles; Angus, king of the Isles.

Ragnhild (fl. 1100s)

Danish royal. Married Hagen Sunnevason (son of Erik Egode, king of Denmark); children: Erik Lam or Lamb, king of Denmark (r. 1137–1146).

Rahab (fl. 1100 BCE)

Biblical woman who harbored Hebrew spies sent by Joshua and helped them escape. Name variations: Rahab comes from Rehabiah (meaning wide or broad). Pronunciation: RAY-hab. Flourished around 1100 BCE; married Salmon, a prince of the tribe of Judah; children: Boaz (who married Ruth).

Referred to in the Bible as a harlot, Rahab lived in a house attached to the city wall of Jericho, where she manufactured and dyed linen. Although raised in a pagan culture of Canaan, she came to believe in the Lord as the one true God. When Joshua was camped in the Jordan valley opposite Jericho, he sent two spies to "scout the city." The spies returned five days later, reporting that they had encountered great danger, but were saved by Rahab, who hid them in stalks of flax on her roof, then helped them escape by rope through a window in the house. When the Israelites later captured Jericho, they spared Rahab and her entire family, who were incorporated into the Jewish people.

Rahab later became the wife of Salmon, a prince of the tribe of Judah. Their son Boaz married *Ruth, who became the mother of Obed, the grandmother of Jesse, and the great-grandmother of David. Thus, Rahab was part of the lineage of King David and an ancestor of Jesus Christ. For her declaration of faith, Rahab was cited in the Epistle to the Hebrews as one of the great heroes of the faith.

Rahel.

Variant of Rachel.

Rahel (1771–1833).

See Varnhagen, Rahel.

Rahn, Muriel (1911–1961)

African-American singer and actress. Born Muriel Ellen Rahn in Boston, Massachusetts, in 1911; died of cancer in New York City on August 8, 1961; daughter of Willie and Bessie Rahn; attended Tuskegee Institute and Atlanta University; awarded degree from the Music Conservatory of the University of Nebraska, at Lincoln; attended Teachers College, Columbia University; studied voice at the Juilliard School of Music, New York; married Charles Rountree, in 1932 (divorced); married Richard Campbell, in 1934.

African-American singer Muriel Rahn began performing while in college and launched her professional career in New York in 1929, with *Eva Jessye's Jubilee Singers. She soon was cast in the Broadway musicals *Blackbirds of 1929* and *Hot Chocolates* (1929–30). Rahn spent 1933 in Paris, singing at the fashionable Chez La DuBarry, before returning to Broadway in 1934 in *Come of Age*, starring *Judith Anderson. Rahn appeared as Carmen, her most important Broadway role, in the Billy Rose production of *Carmen Jones*, which enjoyed a run of 231 performances. She then embarked on an extensive concert tour throughout the United States.

Rahn distinguished herself as the only black member of the opera division of New York City's National Orchestral Association, singing in a number of productions, including Mozart's *Abduction from the Seraglio* and Puccini's *Suor Angelica* and *Gianni Schicchi*. In 1948, she performed the title role in Verdi's *Aïda* with the Salmaggi Opera, and in 1954 played the lead in Richard Strauss' modern opera *Salome*. A review in *Ebony* (January 1955) praised her voice and her acting skill. "The audience cheered Miss Rahn for a versatile exhibition of first-rate singing of a difficult score, believable acting of a complex role and a spirited interpretation of a bizarre dance." Rahn also appeared in two American operas by Harry Freeman: *The Martyr* (1947) and *The Barrier*, which premiered at Columbia University in January 1950. In the latter, her portrayal of the leading character, Cora Lewis, received a glowing review from *The New York Times'* music critic Howard Taubman, who called her "the core of the piece—its fire and artistic conscience." *The Barrier* opened on Broadway in November 1950 and was Rahn's last Broadway appearance.

As an African-American performer, Rahn struggled against exploitation and segregation, although she consistently fulfilled her contract obligations. When Billy Rose failed in his promise to raise her salary in accordance with the success of *Carmen Jones*, she denounced him in an article in *The Chicago Defender*. She also protested segregated seating at the Ford Theater in Baltimore, Maryland, when *The Barrier* was playing on tour; Rahn agreed to perform but picketed the theater while not on stage.

SOURCES:

Smith, Jessie Carney, ed. *Notable Black American Women.* Detroit, MI: Gale Research, 1992.

Barbara Morgan,
Melrose, Massachusetts

Rahon, Alice (1904–1987)

French Surrealist painter and poet. Name variations: Alice Paalen; Alice Phillipot. Born Alice Marie Yvonne Phillipot in 1904 in Doubs, France; died in 1987 in San Angel, Mexico; mother's maiden name was Rahon; married Wolfgang Paalen (an Austrian Surrealist painter), in 1934 (divorced 1947); married Edward Fitzgerald (an American decorator), in 1950 (divorced 1960); no children.

An important member of the Surrealist art movement, Alice Rahon was born Alice Marie Yvonne Phillipot in 1904 to a wealthy family in

Alice Rahon

Doubs, eastern France. Raised in Paris, where she received an excellent education, she composed poetry and was drawn to the emerging Surrealist subculture of Paris of the late 1920s. This movement of intellectuals and artists who rejected the materialism and inequality of 20th-century Western society and sought a higher spiritual meaning in life was predominantly male. (Other noted female Surrealists include *Eileen Agar, *Frida Kahlo, *Meret Oppenheim, and ◄❦ Ithell Colquhoun.) "As a movement it may not question the nature of patriarchy but it at least recognizes its existence," note Grimes, Collins, and Baddeley in *Five Women Painters*. "The fact that desire and sexuality play a pre-eminent role in much surrealist work, forces an understanding of the presupposed gender of both artist and audience, a recognition frequently subsumed in less overtly masculine art."

In 1934, Rahon married Wolfgang Paalen, an Austrian Surrealist painter whom she had met in Paris in 1931. The following year, they became part of the Surrealist movement founded in Paris by André Breton. Under her married name Alice Paalen, Rahon published poetry strongly influenced by imagery of the eastern French countryside of her youth and her travels with Paalen in Spain. In 1936, her first book of poems, *On the Same Ground*, was published by the Surrealists. Another collection, *Hourglass Lying Down*, was illustrated by Pablo Picasso and appeared later that year. Rahon was involved in a brief love affair with Picasso which ended in 1936; she then left Paris with another Surrealist artist, Valentine Penrose, and traveled to India.

Fleeing from the threat of war in Europe in 1939, Rahon and Paalen along with the photographer **Eva Sulzer** traveled to the Pacific Northwest of Alaska, Canada, and the western United States. Rahon's exposure to Native American tribes of the region and their arts and culture would later influence her work. Rahon and Paalen then emigrated to Mexico, settling there in 1940. There they organized the 1940 International Surrealist Exhibition in Mexico City. A third book of Rahon's poetry, *Animal Black*, was published in 1941. She then turned her energies to contributing poetry and articles to the Surrealist journal *Dyn*, which she and Paalen published between 1942 and 1945. Near the end of the war Paalen temporarily renounced Surrealism, though Rahon would remain a strong proponent of its principles of liberty and higher consciousness throughout her life. In 1947, the couple divorced and Paalen returned to Paris, where he committed suicide in 1959.

Colquhoun, Ithell. See Agar, Eileen for sidebar.

Rahon remained in Mexico, settling in the Mexico City suburb of San Angel. There she became a full-time painter and assumed her mother's maiden name of Rahon as her professional name. Around 1950, she married the American decorator Edward Fitzgerald, but they divorced in 1960. Rahon adopted Mexico and its culture to a large degree, using its landscape and symbolism as inspiration for her colorful, abstract, and vibrant paintings, which were exhibited widely in Mexico, the United States, and in Europe until the late 1960s.

Rahon stopped painting in the late 1970s; her last work, *A Giant Called Solitude*, is a brooding testament to the isolation and emotional depression she experienced in her last years, after outliving most of her family and friends. She died in San Angel in 1987, at age 83.

SOURCES:

Caws, Mary Ann, Rudolf E. Kuenzli and Gwen Raaberg, eds. *Surrealism and Women.* Cambridge, MA: MIT Press, 1991.

Chadwick, Whitney. *Women Artists and the Surrealist Movement.* Boston, MA: Little, Brown, 1985.

Gaze, Delia, ed. *Dictionary of Women Artists.* Chicago, IL: Fitzroy Dearborn, 1997.

Grimes, Teresa, Judith Collins, and Oriana Baddeley. *Five Women Painters.* London: Lennard, 1989.

Rosemont, Penelope, ed. *Surrealist Women: An International Anthology.* Austin, TX: University of Texas Press, 1998.

Laura York, M.A. in History, University of California, Riverside, California

Raiby, Mary (1777–1855).

See Catchpole, Margaret for sidebar on Reiby, Mary.

Raiche, Bessica (c. 1874–1932)

First American woman to fly solo. Born around 1874 in Beloit, Wisconsin; died in Balboa, California, on April 10, 1932; married.

Bessica Raiche became the first American woman to fly solo in September 1910, in an airplane she and her husband had made out of wire, silk, and bamboo. (*Blanche Scott had briefly flown solo earlier that month, but she had not been intending to do so, and the flight was judged "accidental" by the Aero Club of America.) Born around 1874 in Beloit, Wisconsin, Raiche was living on Long Island in New York at the time of her first solo flight. After her skirt became tangled in the controls of the plane during her fifth flight, she began wearing riding breeches while flying, further enhancing the reputation for eccentricity she had gained as a result of flying, shooting, and wearing bloomers. Raiche went on to make as many as 25 flights in a single week, and with her husband formed the French-American Aeroplane Company, using piano wire to construct the lightest possible planes. She was awarded a gold medal, inscribed to "the first woman aviator of America," from the Aeronautical Society. After her health forced her to retire from flying, Raiche and her husband moved to California. She became a physician and pursued interests in painting, languages, and music before her death on April 10, 1932.

SOURCES:

Read, Phyllis J., and Bernard L. Witlieb. *The Book of Women's Firsts.* NY: Random House, 1992.

Jo Anne Meginnes, freelance writer, Brookfield, Vermont

Raicho Hiratsuka (1886–1971).

See Hiratsuka Raicho.

Raikh, Zinaida (1894–1939)

Russian actress whose murder in 1939 remains one of the mysteries of the Stalin era. Born in Russia in 1894; murdered in Moscow in July 1939; daughter of Nikolai Andreevich Raikh and Anna Ivanovna Viktorova; married Sergei Esenin (the poet); married Vsevolod Meyerhold (the theater director); children: (first marriage) **Tatiana Esenin**; *Konstantin "Kostia" Esenin.*

Both of Russian actress Zinaida Raikh's husbands were major figures within the hothouse world of Soviet culture. Born in 1894, the daughter of a German-born railway worker and an impoverished gentlewoman, Raikh was working as a secretary for the Socialist Revolutionary newspaper *Delo Naroda* when she met her first husband, the brilliant but unstable poet Sergei Esenin. After having two children, she and Esenin separated. According to her son Konstantin (Kostia), Esenin was infuriated by Raikh's infidelities. Soon after the end of her first marriage, Raikh met and married the highly creative theater director Vsevolod Meyerhold, and became one of his leading actresses. Infatuated with his wife, Meyerhold was driven to despair by the fact that Raikh was almost always surrounded by male admirers. The couple's four-room apartment (a rarity in overcrowded Moscow) on Briusovskii Pereulok became an international salon. Among the guests were members of the foreign press, German theater personalities like Erwin Piscator, and Russian intellectuals of the highest caliber, including Anton Chekhov's widow *Olga Knipper-Chekova,* Constantin Stanislavski, and Vladimir

Mayakovsky. Politicians who frequented Raikh's salon included Leon Trotsky and Nikolai Bukharin, both of whom would later die at the hands of Joseph Stalin. More ominous was the presence of high GPU (secret police) officials, such as the dreaded Genrikh Yagoda. Some observers suspected that Raikh worked for the GPU, serving as a decoy to attract important foreign visitors who might have vital intelligence data.

In January 1938, Meyerhold's theater, known throughout the world for its original, brilliant productions, was "liquidated." It appeared at the time that Meyerhold himself would soon be arrested, but he was thrown a lifeline by his artistic antipode Constantin Stanislavski, who invited him to become artistic director of his Opera Theater. But Stanislavski died, and by June 1939 Meyerhold had been arrested and taken to Moscow's infamous Lubianka prison. At this time, Raikh fiercely resisted four police officers who came to search their apartment. Among the papers removed was an 11-page draft of an old letter to Stalin by Raikh complaining about how

Zinaida Raikh

poorly her husband was being treated despite his many theatrical innovations.

Several weeks later, on the night of July 14, 1939, two men entered her apartment about 1 AM by climbing up to the rear balcony. In a violent struggle, Raikh was stabbed repeatedly. Awakened by her screams, the Meyerholds' elderly housemaid tried to help but was beaten unconscious without catching sight of the intruders, one of whom escaped via the balcony while the other ran down the stairs, leaving traces of Raikh's blood on the wool carpet. The caretaker caught sight of two figures jumping into a large black car waiting at the corner of Gorky Street. On discovering Raikh, he called an ambulance, but she died before reaching the hospital. Her eyes had been gouged out, and there were 42 stab wounds in her body.

Although Zinaida Raikh had been one of the most famous actresses in the Soviet Union, the press carried no announcements of her death. Her burial on July 18, 1939, at the Vagankovo cemetery was attended only by a handful of mourners, including her immediate family. It was obvious that word from the highest quarters had warned people to stay away. The actor Moskvin, who was also a deputy to the Supreme Soviet, told Raikh's father: "The public refuses to bury your daughter." Raikh was buried in the black velvet gown of the character Camille, which she had worn in the last performance at the Meyerhold Theater before it was closed forever on January 7, 1938.

SOURCES:
Bezelianskii, Iurii. *Vera, Nadezhda, Liubov'—: Zhenskie Portrety.* Moscow: OAO Izd-vo "Raduga," 1998.
Braun, Edward. "Meyerhold: The Final Act," in *NTQ: New Theatre Quarterly.* Vol. 9, no. 33. February 1993, pp. 3–15.
———. *Meyerhold: A Revolution in the Theatre.* 2nd ed. Iowa City, IA: University of Iowa Press, 1995.
Conquest, Robert. *The Great Terror: Stalin's Purge of the Thirties.* Rev. ed. Harmondsworth, Middlesex, England: Penguin, 1971.
Fisher, Lynn Visson. "Introduction to Zinaida Raikh Letter to Andrei Bely," in *Russian Literature Triquarterly.* No. 13, 1975, pp. 567–569.
Kafanova, Liudmila. "Meierkhol'd i Raikh," in *Novyi Zhurnal/ The New Review.* No. 186, 1992, pp. 336–356.
MacDonald, Ian. *The New Shostakovich.* Boston, MA: Northeastern University Press, 1990.
McVay, Gordon. "Meierkhol'd's Last Production: Two Letters from Zinaida Raikh to Nikolai Ostrovskii," in *The Slavonic and East European Review.* Vol. 68, no. 3. July 1990, pp. 502–506.
Robinson, Harlow. *Sergei Prokofiev: A Biography.* NY: Paragon House, 1988.
Shentalinsky, Vitaly. *Arrested Voices: Resurrecting the Disappeared Writers of the Soviet Regime.* Translated by John Crowfoot. NY: Martin Kessler Books-The Free Press, 1996.
Vronskaya, Jeanne and Vladimir Chuguev. *A Biographical Dictionary of the Soviet Union 1917–1988.* Munich: K.G. Saur, 1989.

John Haag,
Associate Professor of History,
University of Georgia, Athens, Georgia

Raimond, C.E. (1862–1952).

See Robins, Elizabeth.

Raine, Kathleen (1908—)

English romantic poet who has also produced major works of criticism on William Blake, Samuel Taylor Coleridge, and W.B. Yeats. Born in Ilford, a suburb of London, on June 14, 1908; daughter of George Raine (a schoolteacher and Methodist preacher) and Jessie (Wilkie) Raine; educated at Girton College, Cambridge University, 1926–29; married Hugh Sykes Davies (divorced); married Charles Madge (divorced); children: (second marriage) one daughter; one son.

Received scholarship to study science at Cambridge (1926); published first poems (1929); settled in Penrith, Northumberland (1939); returned to wartime London, published first volume of poems (1943); converted to Catholicism (c. 1944); began relationship with Gavin Maxwell (1952); held post as Research Fellow, Girton College, Cambridge University (1955–61); was Andrew Mellon Lecturer, National Gallery of Art, Washington, D.C. (1962); death of Gavin Maxwell (1969); won W.H. Smith Award (1972); received honorary degree from University of Leicester (1974); founded literary journal Temenos (1980); received Queen's Gold Medal for Poetry (1993).

Selected works—prose: Blake and Tradition *(1968);* Farewell Happy Fields: Memories of Childhood *(1973);* The Land Unknown *(1975);* The Lion's Mouth: Concluding Chapters of Autobiography *(1977);* Blake and the New Age *(1979);* India Seen from Afar *(1991).*

Selected works—poetry: Stone and Flower *(1943);* The Pythoness, and Other Poems *(1949);* The Hollow Hill and Other Poems *(1965);* Six Dreams and Other Poems *(1968);* Living with Mystery, Poems 1987–1991 *(1992).*

Kathleen Raine, who celebrated her 92nd birthday in June 2000, is the author of more than a dozen volumes of poetry, as well as numerous critical studies of such literary figures as William Blake, Samuel Taylor Coleridge, and W.B. Yeats. In addition, she has achieved a reputation as a translator of Honoré de Balzac. Raine has recorded her life's experiences in a multivolume biography, and served as well as editor of the magazine *Temenos*. She stands, in her own words, as a proudly traditionalist poet in her concern for "enduring values" and "the culture of the spiritual view of man." In her devotion to traditional Christianity she has stated that she feels more at home in France, where "it still lingers on," than in her native England. "I think the most dangerous of all illusions is to suppose that the material world completely accounts for all reality and all human experience," she said. Her interests have also come to include India's religious traditions.

Kathleen Raine was born on June 14, 1908, in Ilford, an East London suburb, the daughter and only child of George Raine and **Jessie Wilkie Raine**, both schoolteachers in London. Her father was also a Methodist preacher. The youngster's early childhood in this lower middle-class family was marked by World War I and her evacuation from London. She later claimed to remember the day on which Britain entered the war as a sunny time at the beach, while on holiday with her family. As a small child, she saw the German Zeppelins flying overhead on their way to drop bombs. She took refuge from the war for several years by staying with an aunt in Northumberland near the border with Scotland. In later years, she looked to that area in northern England as her real home, especially in light of her dislike for the cramped and dingy portion of London where her family lived. She later described Ilford as a place where "full consciousness would perhaps make life unendurable."

Raine has repeatedly stated her affinity for Scotland, where her maternal grandmother had been born. She admired that country from which "my mother's people" had come and the Scottish tradition passed down in "song, speech, and heroic story." It was her mother from whom Raine "inherited my love of wandering the moors," and she felt "the poet in me is my mother's daughter." A very different legacy came from her father, a teacher of Latin and English literature, who had risen from a family of poor coal miners in Durham. George Raine "stood for progress, education, and the future," and mingled his Methodist religion with an enthusiasm for socialism and pacifism. In later years, his daughter remembered the sermons he delivered as a "local preacher" praising the League of Nations. It was, however, "a family to which poetry mattered very much," as Raine later told an interviewer, noting that her mother "wrote down my first poems before I could hold a pencil." Living in "an environment of poetry," she found her literary interests deepened by her formal education at Ilford County High School and the tutoring she received from

Kathleen Raine

her father in Latin. A platonic love affair with one of her father's former students centered on their mutual interest in poetry.

George Raine hoped his daughter would follow him in becoming an English teacher and a devotee of his religious beliefs and his socialism, but Kathleen rebelled against such a future. Distressed by the drabness of life in a London suburb, she was inspired by a botany teacher, whom she admired, to study science. She later wrote that, in her youth, she found science "an escape into beauty." After attending a local secondary school, she won a scholarship to Girton College, a women's institution that was part of Cambridge University. There, starting in 1926, she studied natural sciences and received her M.A. degree in 1929. For the young girl from a cramped lower middle-class background, "living as a student at Girton was one of the few perfectly happy times of my life." Part of her joy at college came from her new awareness of her own physical beauty; years later, she learned "that a little Society was formed to watch for me to pass."

Raine enjoyed her formal studies in science, noting how she "contemplated in awe and delight the Book of Nature." But she also began to write poetry at Cambridge, publishing her early works in an undergraduate magazine, *Experiment*. She later recalled her distaste for the "agnosticism, atheism, nihilism" she found in the intellectual environment at the great university and the contempt she encountered toward poets like Shakespeare and Milton whom she revered. She spent one year officially studying psychology but in fact was on "a general course of English and French literature, ancient and modern, undertaken by myself with advice from my friends."

At the close of her college years, Raine found herself with no clear plans for the future. A self-described "neurotic bohemian," she soon entered a loveless marriage with a companion from her literary circle, Hugh Sykes Davies. Raine described the marriage as merely "an alliance against society made by two young people whose only bond was a rejection of all those old values . . . from which we were both in revolt." Davies, who went on to become a professor at Cambridge, offered her the excuse to stay in the university locale. As she expected, however, the marriage soon broke down. She then married Charles Madge, from Cambridge. In the politically heated atmosphere of the time all three—Madge, Davies, and Raine herself—were attracted to Communism. Raine later wrote that she, like the Marxists to whom Madge introduced her, felt that "the current of history which flows in one direction only, flowed the way that they were going."

> *The function of the arts is surely to awaken in people self-knowledge, knowledge of the scope and scale of their own humanity which they may not have been aware of.*
>
> —Kathleen Raine

Madge, an aspiring poet like his wife, went on to become a prominent sociologist. He was a pioneer in the study of public opinion and helped found Mass-Observation, an organization intended to keep a running picture of the views of the British population for the purposes of market research. Raine's marriage to Madge collapsed when she fell in love with still another individual from her circle at Cambridge, whom she has referred to only as "Alistair." Their tie was brought to an end by the outbreak of World War II and Alistair's immediate departure for military service.

Before her marriage to Madge ended, the couple had two children. In her autobiography,

Raine made only elliptical references to the details of her two marriages. She was, however, far more kindly disposed toward Madge than toward Davies, stating that having "hurt a man so fine by marrying him for inadequate, indeed for deeply neurotic, reasons, lies heavily on my conscience." The latter years of the 1930s also saw Raine publishing numerous individual poems in British literary magazines.

Upon the outbreak of the war, at the invitation of friends from her second marriage, Raine and her two children settled near Penrith in Northumberland. Thus, Raine returned to a world of northern England she had cherished since childhood. She later recalled her sense of reconnection to her roots as she had become liberated "from Cambridge, from marriage, from Mass-Observation and Marxism, from Ilford." There, in what she described as a "pleasant sanctuary," she survived on a small allowance from Charles Madge, by taking in boarders, and on the money she could earn reviewing books. In an action about which she wrote remorseful passages in her autobiography, she left her two children with a friend in Northumberland and returned to London, convinced of her need to pursue life as a poet. In the British capital, she found work in a wartime government agency, and published her first book of poetry, *Stone and Flower*, in 1943. It was illustrated by her friend *Barbara Hepworth*. After a period of tormented indecision, Raine converted briefly to Roman Catholicism, probably in 1944.

In the postwar years, Raine remained in London eking out a living by reviewing books, teaching part-time, and doing translations. She soon published a second volume of poems, *Living in Time*. Much of Raine's poetry drew upon her scientific background and featured a precise description of the physical world. Nonetheless, her poetic style reflected her interest in classical philosophy and drew heavily upon the traditions of English Romanticism. Some critics see her emphasis on lyricism as a link to earlier English writers, including William Blake and Edmund Spenser, and Raine has shown little interest in most of the work produced by contemporary poets. Throughout much of her writing, Raine expressed her discomfort with "the bankrupt situation of materialist society." "Poetry at its greatest," she insisted in an interview in 1977, "is the language of the human soul, though which the spirit speaks." One critic described Raine's own achievement by noting that "the most immediately appealing feature of her work, evident in even the earliest of her poems, is its sheer lyric loveliness." By the close of the

1940s, Raine's poetry increasingly reflected her interest in Jungian psychology.

In the years following World War II, Raine also developed into a critic of note. Concentrating on the works of William Blake, she published an initial study of his writing in 1951 and returned to Cambridge as a research fellow at Girton College to pursue this interest between 1955 and 1961. She was invited to give the Mellon Lectures in 1962 on Blake, and her study of his work, *Blake and Tradition*, which appeared in 1968, is her most important volume of criticism and an extensive examination of his symbolic language and its roots in Platonic philosophy. Students of her work have remarked upon her obvious affection for Blake's ideas on the need for humans to preserve their powers of connecting with their deepest emotions. She also found that Blake's writing employed "a traditional language . . . and was not to be understood in terms of a personal system, as many had previously thought, invented by himself." One of her main tasks in studying the poet was "to discover where Blake had made his links with tradition."

Raine has often expressed her deep concern about the breakdown of traditional culture. She sees this as a tragedy that could end the ability to employ common literary allusions. "[T]he poet is working upon a shared background of language and literature and religion and history, which one has to play on like an instrument," writes Raine. Thus, if such "connotations, resonances are lost to a society as a whole, then poetry of real quality becomes impossible."

A central force in Raine's life was her unhappy relationship with the travel writer and naturalist Gavin Maxwell. Maxwell would later become famous as the author of *A Ring of Bright Water*, an account of the landscape and wild life of the sea coast. Raine first met him in the early 1950s, when her publisher and friend arranged for this impoverished artist and poet to paint her portrait. Born into a wealthy family, Maxwell had recently lost his inheritance in a shark fishery scheme. She soon discovered that he too had roots in Northumberland and Scotland. "Gavin was native of my paradise," she wrote about his links with northern England, where his grandfather was the duke of Northumberland. "Gavin belonged to my own people in the country lost before I was born," she noted about his Scottish ancestry. His homosexuality precluded a romantic relationship, but she encouraged him to abandon painting and to return to his career as a writer. He in turn offered her the use of his home near the western coast of Scotland.

Raine dedicated her *Collected Poems*, published in 1956, to Maxwell. But her emotional demands on him, perhaps compounded by the differences in their social backgrounds, led to a widening rift. She suffered a severe psychological blow in 1962 when she learned that Maxwell had decided to marry **Lavinia Jean**, a woman from his own elevated social circle whom he had known for years.

Maxwell's death from cancer in 1969 caused a deep crisis in Raine's life. She now completed her autobiography, noting that "nothing more can, in this life, ever be added" to her thoughts about her experiences. Between 1972 and 1977, Raine presented her readers with this story of her life in three separate volumes: *Farewell Happy Fields*, *The Lands Unknown*, and *The Lion's Mouth*. All three were subsequently collected and published under the single title of *Autobiographies* in 1992.

Raine seemed to take pains to avoid a clear presentation of the facts of her life. Instead, she wrote a rambling, often opaque treatment of her recollections starting with her childhood in Ilford and Northumberland, and continuing down to the early 1970s. Ironically, as a poet who had avoided introspection and personal confessions, Raine now seemed most concerned to present a detailed, even tortured account of her thoughts and feelings. In a deeply hostile review of the three collected works in 1992, Ray Monk in the *Times Literary Supplement* chastised Raine for filling her account of her life with "transcendental twaddle."

In 1980, Raine turned her literary efforts in a new direction in founding the literary periodical *Temenos*. The journal's title, meaning "the shrine" in Greek, reflected its purpose, since Raine sought to found a journal that would celebrate the traditional literary values she saw in danger of distinction. The credo declared: "it is the purpose of *Temenos* to reaffirm the traditional function of the arts as vehicles of the human spirit, awakening and illuminating regions of consciousness of which our materialist culture is increasingly unaware." Her work on *Temenos* and her stature as defender of traditional cultural values brought her the friendship of a like-minded figure of national prominence, Great Britain's Prince Charles. He provided her with a suite of rooms in which to work at his Institute of Architecture.

In 1984, Raine was considered to be a prominent candidate for the post of poet laureate of Great Britain. Although she was not chosen, many critics continued to honor her as the traditionalist grande dame of English verse and used her work as a benchmark by which to measure both the style and the achievement of a younger generation of English poets. In the early 1990s, she occupied an ongoing and important role in the English literary scene. In 1991, she published an account of her travels in India over the previous decade, and in 1992 she presented the public with a new volume of poetry, *Living with Mystery, Poems 1987–1991*. Likewise in 1992, Raine appeared on English radio to lecture on the bicentennial celebration of Percy Bysshe Shelley's birth. Her talk on Shelley's connection to Indian mysticism reflected Raine's interest in spiritual writings from the Asian subcontinent.

In February 1993, Raine obtained a new token of her country's esteem. At the age of 84, she was received at Buckingham Palace by Queen *Elizabeth II and awarded the Queen's Gold Medal for Poetry for 1993. But this happy event was soon followed by an outburst of controversy. In March, in a long newspaper interview in *The Guardian*, she held forth on a variety of topics, such as her continuing dislike for her childhood home in Ilford and her guilt for not being present in her children's early lives. Calling Ilford "a world of people who watch television and never exchange feelings or love with their neighbors . . . prisoners, spiritual prisoners" brought an angry response in letters to the editor.

Despite the passage of years, Kathleen Raine has continued to publish. In 1997, for example, she showed her continuing interest in India's religious heritage by contributing an article to the London *Times* on *The Ten Principal Upanishads*. Here she reiterated her despair at growing up in "a spiritually illiterate civilization" and rejoiced in having discovered this work from India, which speaks "to the deeps of the mind."

SOURCES:

Bloom, Harold, ed. *Twentieth-Century British Literature*. Vol. 4. NY: Chelsea House, 1987.

Duncan, Erika. *Unless Soul Claps Its Hands: Portraits and Passages*. NY: Shocken Books, 1984.

Hamilton, Ian, ed. *The Oxford Companion to Twentieth-century Poetry in English*. Oxford: Oxford University Press, 1994.

Schlueter, Paul, and June Schlueter, eds. *An Encyclopedia of British Women Writers*. Rev. and expanded. NY: Garland, 1988.

Shattock, Joanne. *The Oxford Guide to British Women Writers*. Oxford: Oxford University Press, 1993.

Stanford, Donald E., ed. *Dictionary of Literary Biography*, Vol. 20, *British Poets, 1914–1945*. Detroit, MI: Gale Research, 1983.

SUGGESTED READING:

Grubb, Frederick. *A Vision of Reality: A Study of Liberalism in Twentieth-Century Verse*. London: Chatto and Windus, 1965.

Mills, Ralph J., Jr. *Kathleen Raine: A Critical Essay*. Grand Rapids, MI: William B. Eerdmans, 1967.

Rani, Meena. *The Poetry of Kathleen Raine: A Pursuit of Patterns*. New Delhi: Wisdom Publications, 1989.

Neil M. Heyman,
Professor of History, San Diego State University,
San Diego, California

Rainer, Luise (1910—)

Austrian actress. Born on January 12, 1910 (some sources cite 1909), in Vienna, Austria; married Clifford Odets (a playwright), in 1937 (divorced 1940); married Robert Knittel (a publisher), in 1953 (died 1989); no children.

Selected filmography: (in Austria and Germany) Ja der Himmel uber Wien *(1930),* Sehnsucht 202 *(1932),* Heute kommt's drauf an *(1933); (in U.S.)* Escapade *(1935),* The Great Ziegfeld *(1936),* The Good Earth *(1937),* The Emperor's Candlesticks *(1937),* Big City *(1937),* The Toy Wife *(1938),* The Great Waltz *(1938),* Dramatic School *(1938),* Hostages *(1943),* The Best of Everything *(1983),* The Gambler *(1997).*

Arriving in Hollywood from Austria in 1935 and heralded as the new *Greta Garbo, Luise Rainer immediately distinguished herself by winning back-to-back Academy Awards as Best Actress for her work in *The Great Ziegfeld* (1936) and *The Good Earth* (1937). Over the next several years, however, Rainer fell victim to the studio star system, and by 1939 her career was pretty much over. Years later, the actress reflected on her brief years in Hollywood. "They owned me completely," she said of the studio. "I was a tool in a big mechanical factory."

Rainer made her stage debut in Austria at age 16 and was a student of the world-renowned German actor-director Max Reinhardt. After establishing herself on the stage and in films in Austria and Germany, she was discovered by an American talent scout and brought to Hollywood. Her American film debut in *Escapade* (1935), with William Powell, was unremarkable, although studio head Louis B. Mayer felt she had great potential as a romantic star. He cast her with Powell again in *The Great Ziegfeld* (1936), as the impresario's temperamental first wife *Anna Held. Rainer's most memorable scene, which is believed to have cinched the Oscar for her, comes at the end of the movie, when she fights back tears as she phones Ziegfeld to congratulate him on his second marriage to actress *Billie Burke. Ironically, this scene was almost cut; Mayer thought the film was too long. In addition to winning the Academy Award that year, Rainer also took home the New York Critics' Best Actress Award.

Irving Thalberg, the head of production at MGM, went over Mayer's head to cast Rainer as the saintly peasant wife O-Lan in the highly respected screen version of *Pearl S. Buck*'s bestseller *The Good Earth* (1937). The film was overwhelmingly praised by the critics, although not all of them agreed that Rainer's performance was of Oscar quality. While James Agate called it "an exquisite rendering of what my clever Austrian actress imagines a Chinese peasant woman to be like," others were less diplomatic. "Can it be that the Academy has been dazzled by her stage fame," wrote Max Breen, "or is there really something in her two very limited performances, not perhaps apparent to ordinary mortals, which has transcended anything done in those two years by the great Garbo herself?"

While at the height of what would be fleeting fame, Rainer married playwright Clifford Odets, whom she had met and dated while she was making *The Good Earth*. Reportedly, the bridegroom spent his wedding night working on a screenplay, setting the tone for the tumultuous years that followed. "He screamed at me and then didn't talk for a week. It was very, very difficult," Rainer said about the relationship, "but Odets was a very special and immensely gifted human being, and I loved him." Odets was more guarded about his feelings. "Luise Rainer was one of the several persons in my life who prepared me for life," he wrote in his journal. "Our brief time together was necessary for both of us."

Although Rainer hoped to develop her skill as an actress, Louis B. Mayer never gave her the opportunity. Following *The Good Earth,* he cast her in five forgettable films, including *The Emperor's Candlesticks* (1937), again with Powell, *The Big City* (1937), with Spencer Tracy, and *The Toy Wife* (1938), with Melvyn Douglas. In 1938, following *Dramatic School,* and amid rumors of impending retirement, Rainer took a leave of absence to patch up her failing marriage. During that time, the studio dropped her contract.

After her divorce from Odets in 1940, Rainer made a less-than-memorable Broadway debut in *A Kiss for Cinderella,* followed by a tour in *Joan of Lorraine* by Maxwell Anderson. In 1943,

*Luise
Rainer*

Paramount signed her for *Hostages*, with William Bendix, but the film did not trigger a hoped-for comeback. In 1951, Rainer married English publisher Robert Knittel and settled in London, abandoning her career ambitions. Aside from a few television roles, she did not reemerge on screen until 1983, when she appeared in *The Best of Everything*. Her featured role as a flamboyant Russian dowager in *The Gambler* (1997), for which the 89-year-old Rainer came out of retirement, sparked renewed interest in the actress, who was quick to point out to reporters that she looked much younger in person than in her film makeup. A review of the film in *The New York Times* described Rainer as having "the magnetic presence of an ancient grande dame with an elfin sense of mischief." The actress took umbrage with the word "ancient."

At the time, Rainer revealed that she was working on her memoirs ("Unfinished Symphony") and was also considering a movie based on a novel. "It's a book about saving Venice and saving beauty, about not making materialism the quintessence of existence," she said. "You know, some very beautiful things get lost and forgotten, just as I got lost."

SOURCES:

Gussow, Mel. "Revenge of a Studio Pawn: A Comeback, After 55 Years," in *The New York Times*. July 17, 1999.

Katz, Ephraim. *The Film Encyclopedia*. NY: HarperCollins, 1994.

Lamparski, Richard. *Whatever Became of . . . ?* NY: Crown, 1967.

Shipman, David. *The Great Movie Stars: The Golden Years*. Boston, MA: Little, Brown, 1989.

Barbara Morgan,
Melrose, Massachusetts

Rainer, Yvonne (1934—)

American filmmaker, dancer and choreographer. Born in San Francisco, California, in 1934; studied dance with Martha Graham and Merce Cunningham.

Selected filmography: (shorts) Volleyball/Foot Film *(1967)*, Hand Movie *(1968)*, Rhode Island Red *(1968)*, Trio Film *(1968)*, Line *(1969); (feature lengths)* Lives of Performers *(1972)*, Film About a Woman Who . . . *(1974)*, Kristina Talking Pictures *(1976)*, Journeys from Berlin/1971 *(1980)*, The Man Who Envied Women *(1985)*, Privilege *(1990)*, Murder and Murder *(1996)*.

Yvonne Rainer moved from her hometown of San Francisco to New York City in 1957, intending to study acting, but quickly became more interested in modern dance. She studied dance under *Martha Graham and Merce Cunningham, and in 1962 co-founded the Judson Dance Theater. Focusing on natural movement, Rainer invented the minimalist style of modern dance, resolutely unartificial and unemotional, which **Jessica Wolff** notes "departed radically from the dramatic, emotive forms of both its classical and modern dance precursors." She soon gained a name as a daring choreographer and dancer. Her works often incorporated modern or popular music, and by the mid-1960s she also began using slides, recorded and live voices, short films and narrative within her pieces, creating what have been likened to performance "collages." Her first films in the late 1960s were actually shorts created to accompany dances.

Rainer made her first feature-length production, *Lives of Performers*, in 1972, followed by *Film about a Woman Who . . .* (1974), in which the question implicit in the ellipsis is not answered during the movie. The collage techniques of her shorts are carried over into these longer films, which also often employ disjointed soundtracks. According to Wolff, she "interweaves the real and the fictional, the personal and the political, the concrete and the abstract" in her films, and uses a deliberately distancing, Brechtian style to encourage the audience to examine and engage intellectually with what they are watching. While the issues, often feminist, political, or emotional, in her films frequently can be provocative, they are presented without emotion. Later films include *Journeys from Berlin/1971* (1980), an international co-production made while she was a visiting artist in Berlin that won the 1980 Los Angeles Film Critics' first prize for independent film, *The Man Who Envied Women* (1985), and *Privilege* (1990). Rainer has taught at a number of universities and institutes. She received the American Film Institute's *Maya Deren Award in 1988, and in 1990 she was awarded a MacArthur Foundation "genius" grant.

SOURCES:

Acker, Ally. *Reel Women*. NY: Continuum, 1991.

Katz, Ephraim. *The Film Encyclopedia*. 3rd ed. NY: HarperCollins, 1998.

Lyon, Christopher, ed. *The International Directory of Films and Filmmakers*. Vol. 2: *Directors/Filmmakers*. Chicago, IL: St. James Press, 1984.

Uglow, Jennifer S., ed. and comp. *The International Dictionary of Women's Biography*. NY: Continuum, 1989.

SUGGESTED READING:

Rainer, Yvonne. *The Films of Yvonne Rainer*. Indiana University Press, 1989 (screenplays).

———. *Work 1961–73*. Nova Scotia College of Art and Design, 1974 (illustrated dance notes).

Jo Anne Meginnes,
freelance writer, Brookfield, Vermont

Rainetrude.

Variant of Ragnetrude.

Rainey, Barbara Allen (1948–1982)

First woman to become a U.S. Navy pilot. Born on August 20, 1948, in Bethesda, Maryland; died in a plane crash near Evergreen, Alabama, on July 13, 1982; father was an officer in the Navy; Whittier College, Whittier, California, B.A.; married John C. Rainey (a Navy pilot); children: two daughters.

The daughter of a Navy officer, Barbara Allen Rainey was born at Bethesda Naval Hospital in Maryland in 1948, and grew up in Long Beach, California, where she was active in sports and graduated from Lakewood High School. After attending Long Beach City College, she graduated with a B.A. from Whittier College in Whittier, California, and joined the Naval Reserves as an officer late in 1970. She then applied to the U.S. Naval Flight Training School, and after being admitted completed her flight training in one year. In February 1974, Rainey received her "wings of gold," becoming the first female pilot in the history of the U.S. Navy. She served with the Pacific Fleet Squadron in California, and married a fellow Navy pilot. Rainey left active duty in November 1977, prior to the birth of her first child. She remained in the Naval Reserves, and became qualified to fly a C-118 (DC-6) while pregnant with her second child. Recalled to active duty as a flight instructor in 1981, Rainey was assigned to the air station at Whiting Field in Milton, Florida. She was training another pilot in touch-and-go landings at Middleton Field in Alabama on July 13, 1982, when her plane crashed. She was 34. Rainey was buried with full military honors at Arlington National Cemetery, where her gravestone commemorates her as the "first woman Naval aviator."

Jo Anne Meginnes,
freelance writer, Brookfield, Vermont

Rainey, Gertrude (1886–1939).

See Rainey, Ma.

Rainey, Ma (1886–1939)

African-American blues singer known as the "Mother of the Blues." Name variations: Gertrude Rainey; Madame Rainey. Born Gertrude Malissa Nix Pridgett on April 26, 1886, in Columbus, Georgia; died of heart disease on December 22, 1939, in Rome, Georgia; one of three children of Thomas and Ella Pridgett; married William "Pa" Rainey, in 1904; children: (adopted) son, Danny.

At age 14, made her first stage appearance in a locally produced musical revue in Columbus, Georgia (1900); began touring soon after with traveling tent shows and vaudeville acts; introduced blues numbers into her act (1902); adopted the professional name Ma Rainey after marrying William "Pa" Rainey (1904), with whom she performed a comedy-and-dance routine throughout the South; signed to a recording contract (1923), releasing over 90 blues numbers over the next five years and greatly influencing blues singers who would become better known than herself, such as Bessie Smith and Ethel Waters; watched her career decline during the Depression, leading to her retirement from show business (1935).

After a long, hot day in the parched oil fields of East Texas in the 1930s, workers might seek diversion in one of the traveling carnivals that occasionally passed through the bleak shanty towns scattered among the clanking rigs. After wandering through the tents with bearded ladies, strongmen, and elastic contortionists, some musical entertainment might be found—a collection of tired vaudeville routines and second-rate dance numbers. Few in the begrimed audience would know that the remarkable-looking woman who closed the show, the one in the shabby sequined dress who sang of fickle lovers and lonesome nights with a bottle, had once traveled the Southern vaudeville circuit in style, with her own road show, and that black audiences had come from miles around to hear her; or that the blues and jazz singers they heard on the radio—the ones playing big Northern theaters, making films and touring Europe—owed their success to the woman the barker outside the tent had called "the Black Nightingale."

Ma Rainey would be honored by later generations as the "Mother of the Blues," but no such musical form existed by that name when Gertrude Pridgett was born in Columbus, Georgia, in 1886, one of three children of Thomas and **Ella Pridgett**. The family was not a theatrical one, although it was said that a Pridgett grandmother had taken to the stage just after Emancipation. No doubt Gertrude's parents credited this errant ancestor with their daughter's fascination with the traveling minstrel shows that came through Columbus most summers. These shows, presented by black performers for black audiences, were, ironically, copies of an entertainment form created by whites for white audiences as early as the 1840s. The original minstrel shows were performed by whites in blackface and claimed to accurately represent the songs and dances of African-American slaves in some mythical, halcyon South. After the Civil War, black-originated minstrel shows began touring the South, playing to poor sharecropping families under tents set up in the fields; by Gertrude's time, these "tent shows" had become a standard entertainment form for increasingly mobile black audiences, and were adapted for the stages of urban, Northern theaters. Several permanent companies were touring well-established circuits by the late 19th century, and Gertrude would have delighted in the offerings of Richard and Pringle's Georgia Minstrels, Hicks and Sawyer's Minstrels, the King And Bush Wide-Mouth Minstrels, and Pete Werle's Cotton Blossom Show.

By the time she was 14, Gertrude herself was on the stage in a locally produced revue, "A Bunch of Blackberries," at Columbus' Springer Opera House. Two years later, in 1902, Gertrude joined a tent show and took to the road; and by 1904, she had met William "Pa" Rainey, a song-and-dance man with the Rabbit Foot Minstrels. The two were married in February of that year and developed a song-and-dance routine for the Rabbit Foot show.

"The Foots" was one of the most famous minstrel shows of the time, having been organized by an entrepreneur in Mississippi named F.W. Wolcott. The show toured throughout the South, as far north as Virginia, from late spring through early winter, traveling by railroad and performing under an 80'x110' tent. The stage consisted of wooden boards laid on sawhorses, the footlights were kerosene lanterns, and the acts included comedians, jugglers, novelty acts, and "jungle scenes." At first, Ma and Pa Rainey were part of what was called the "After Show," presented after the main acts had appeared; later, they were moved onto the main bill. They performed with a band made up of drums, violin, bass, and trumpet; sometimes Ma would present a solo act, singing and dancing with a jug band as "Madame Gertrude Rainey"; and as early as 1902, even before she met Pa Rainey, she was singing the blues.

$\mathcal{S}$he jes' catch hold of us, somekindaway.

—Sterling Brown

Ma Rainey once claimed that she had "discovered" the blues when a young girl in a Missouri town in which she was appearing in 1902 came to her with a sad, poignant song about a lover who had disappeared. Ma said she learned the song by heart, began using it as part of her act's encore, and claimed she had spontaneously coined the term "blues" when someone asked her what kind of song it was. Although Ma

Rainey was certainly one of the earliest black performers to standardize the blues for mass consumption, she was merely popularizing a musical form that had been developing for more than half a century. Originally recited unaccompanied as improvised chants based on the work songs, laments, and ballads of plantation-bound slaves, the form had begun to coalesce in the 1890s around a 12-bar structure, with three lines to each stanza, and was usually sung to guitar accompaniment. The term "blues" is thought to derive from the descriptive "blue devils," a term which African-Americans had used since the early 19th century to denote depression or despondency. By the time Rainey's Missouri visitor sang about her lost lover, the blues were already becoming well established, and even Ma later admitted that she heard similar songs in other places on the circuit.

As the blues grew in popularity, so did Ma Rainey's fame, for her voice seemed perfectly suited to the style which people came to call "down home blues." Her voice was not powerful and was sometimes described as harsh, but it was ideally suited to the simple, direct lyrics of the blues, each three-line stanza consisting of two identical first lines and a third line that rhymed with the first. Enthusiastic audiences agreed that no one could put across a blues song like Ma Rainey, and by 1914, when Ma and Pa Rainey joined Tolliver's Circus and Musical Extravaganza, they billed themselves as "Rainey and Rainey, Assassinators of the Blues."

During these World War I years, it is probable that Rainey met, and shared a stage with, the woman on whom she would have the most influence, *Bessie Smith. The two very likely first encountered one another when both were traveling with the Moses Stokes show in 1912, although the cherished story of the Raineys kidnapping a young Bessie from her home and forcing her onto the stage is a false one. While Smith and Rainey shared a liking for stage costuming that included spangled and sequined dresses and heavy necklaces made out of gold coins, and for a style that included much moaning, eye-rolling, and sashaying, they were very different temperamentally. Unlike Smith, known for her hard drinking and sharp, sometimes violent temper, Rainey generally got on with everyone. "I never heard cursin' or nothin' like that," trumpet player Clyde Bernhardt once told biographer **Sandra Lieb**. "Ma Rainey acted more like a religious person, that's the way she appear to you when you'd be talkin' to her. She had a lovely disposition, you know, and personality." Nonetheless,

Ma Rainey

Rainey's comedic patter between songs was often vulgar and sexually frank, to the great delight of her audiences, especially since even Ma would readily admit that she was not an attractive woman. Another musician of her period, Jack Dupree, minced no words in once saying, "she was a really ugly woman. But when she opened her mouth—that was it. You forgot everything. She knew how to sing those blues, and she got right into your heart." During these early years of Ma's career, she and Pa Rainey adopted a son, Danny, who joined their act as "the world's greatest juvenile stepper." But it was Ma people wanted to see, and her act soon became permanently solo. Sometime before the end of the decade, she and Pa Rainey separated; and by 1920, Pa Rainey had died.

As World War I came to an end, the blues were taking the country by storm, especially after the release of the first known blues recording, by a black artist named *Mamie Smith, a Northerner from Ohio. The record sold thousands of copies, and companies sprang up practically overnight to exploit the new phenomenon of "race records." But while Bessie and other blues singers like *Lucille Hegamin, *Ida Cox, and *Sippie Wallace were quickly signed to recording contracts, Ma Rainey had to wait until 1923 before a talent scout for a Wisconsin company called Paramount Records signed her. Part of the reason for Ma's late entry into the recording business was that her older, Southern style of "Classic Blues" was already being eclipsed by a smoother, more sophisticated form developed in Northern urban centers. Another reason was that Ma Rainey, who continued to tour rural areas of the Deep South well into the 1920s, never had a Northern white promoter (as Bessie had in writer Carl Van Vechten), and never developed the wealthier, urban following that launched the careers of such women as *Ethel Waters and *Alberta Hunter. Additionally, Paramount was chronically on the verge of bankruptcy throughout the 1920s and was unable to take advantage of technical advances in studio recording. Rainey was singing into an old-fashioned horn and recording on a wax cylinder long after everyone else was using microphones and metal master discs, making her records noticeably inferior to those of her peers.

Nevertheless, Ma Rainey's first release for Paramount—"Moonshine Blues," recorded in Chicago in 1923—and the nearly 100 more blues numbers she would record over the next five years, expanded her audience beyond the Southern minstrel circuit to larger cities and more opulent settings. Paramount launched an aggressive advertising campaign for her first record, under the headline "Discovered at Last! Ma Rainey, Mother of the Blues!" Later promotions included a Mystery Record contest in which the winner got $14, a free phonograph, and a "souvenir record" with Ma's picture on the label. "The Mother of the Blues doesn't want you to ever forget her," the promotional copy ran, "that's how much she loves her friends!" Also in Paramount's grab bag of slogans and monikers was Rainey's title as "The Gold Necked Woman of the Blues" (referring to her prominent gold necklaces) and "The Paramount Wildcat." Said *Mary Lou

Williams, "Ma was loaded with diamonds, in her ears, round her neck, in a tiara on her head. Both hands were full of rocks, too: her hair was wild and she had gold teeth! What a sight!"

Between 1923 and 1928, Ma Rainey recorded such blues classics as "See See Rider," "Cell Bound Blues," "I Ain't Got Nobody," "Bo-Weevil Blues," "Jelly Bean Blues" and, with Louis Armstrong, "Counting the Blues," in addition to performing them live before packed houses in Chicago, Detroit, Pittsburgh, Philadelphia, Newark, and New York, where she recorded with Fletcher Henderson's band. But she never turned her back on the audience that loved her best, the admirers who crowded into rural opera houses and tents during the cotton season and eagerly looked for the big bus emblazoned with Ma Rainey's name in which she and her company toured. By the mid-1920s, Rainey was a leading star of the so-called "Toby tours," playing black theaters throughout the South run by the Theatre Owners' Booking Association (TOBA). By now, she was touring with her own band, variously called The Harmony Boys, The Jazz Hounds, or the Jazz Wildcats, and would open her show by emerging from a giant Victrola, moaning and shimmying her way into "Moonshine Blues." Her son Danny traveled with her and did a comedy routine with Ma in which he danced and sang to "Mama You Done Put That Thing on Me." "This lad has a good and bright future in front of him as a comedian," reported the *Chicago Defender* after Ma had opened in that city in 1928. "Ma Rainey and the entire company . . . with each and every member doing a Charleston, closes the show. The house shakes with laughter when The Madam displays her Charleston dancing."

Rainey rarely performed before white audiences, but she did appear more frequently than might be thought in Northern cities. She recorded and appeared on at least two occasions in New York, including Harlem's Lincoln Theater, leading to the confusion known as "the mystery of the two Ma Raineys." Since it was generally believed Ma never appeared north of Virginia, a woman who *did* appear in Harlem as "Ma Rainey No. 2" in the 1940s, some years after Rainey's death, led to endless speculation and gossip that Ma was still alive. This second Ma Rainey was, in fact, **Lillie Mae Glover**, a Memphis blues singer who might have appeared with Ma in the 1920s and who recorded for Sun Records in the 1950s as "Big Memphis Ma Rainey." She was still appearing in Memphis night clubs as late as 1981 using that name.

The year 1928 was Ma Rainey's most successful, with 20 titles recorded for Paramount, a lengthy tour of the Midwest and the South with her Paramount Flappers, and the release of a wildly popular song in February called "Ma Rainey's Black Bottom," a bawdy number based on a decade-old dance of that name. Audiences howled with laughter when Ma shimmied her way on stage to sing:

Now I'm gon' to show y'all my black bottom,
They stay to see that dance.

The dance became so famous that even white artists performed it, although in a much sanitized version; and playwright August Wilson used the phenomenon as the basis for his notable play of the same name, first presented in 1984.

Despite these successes, show business was undergoing a rapid change. Just as the old minstrel shows had given way to vaudeville after the First World War, vaudeville was losing its audience to the new media of radio and film by the late 1920s. TOBA's worst box-office year was 1927; theaters which once played to full houses were now closing, and more sophisticated audiences were flocking to dance halls to hear jazz and a new form which combined jazz, blues, and popular music into something called "swing." Even though 1928 was Ma Rainey's best year in terms of popularity, seven members of her show left because they had not been paid, and during the spring tour, Ma was forced to disband the company and join someone else's in order to keep working. The final blow came with the Depression, which hit Rainey's core audience—rural blacks— the hardest. The TOBA circuit expired in the early 1930s; Paramount Records, which released 100 "race records" in 1930, issued less than a dozen in 1931, none at all the following year, and went bankrupt not long after. "The blues ran out," pianist Thomas A. Dorsey, who played with Rainey's touring show, once observed. "I don't know what happened to the blues, they seemed to drop it all at once, it just went *down*."

Ma Rainey recorded her last number for Paramount, "Big Feelin' Blues," in December 1928, and by 1930 had to earn her living by appearing with traveling carnivals and what was left of the old tent-show circuit. Gone was the bus in which she had once toured, and for which she had paid $13,000 in cash; it was replaced with a car chassis that some friends made into a house trailer. She cooked her own meals on a small camp stove and improvised her costumes from bits and pieces of the dresses she had worn in her glory days. While Bessie Smith, Ethel Waters, Alberta Hunter and other contemporaries who had made the transition to swing, bebop,

radio, and films remained in the limelight, Ma Rainey faded into obscurity.

In 1935, after the deaths of both her mother and sister, Rainey retired from show business and settled in her hometown of Columbus, Georgia, joining the congregation at Friendship Baptist Church, where her brother was a deacon. More of an entrepreneur than she is generally given credit for, Rainey had saved enough money from her stage days to buy two theaters in nearby Rome, Georgia—the Lyric and the Airdrome—which she managed until her death from heart disease on December 22, 1939; she had outlived Bessie Smith by two years (Bessie having been fatally injured in a car crash in 1937). Ma Rainey's death certificate lists her occupation as "housekeeper."

Most of Rainey's Paramount recordings remained on a shelf for the next 25 years, impossible to remaster because of their poor quality. But starting in the 1950s, when technology had become sufficiently advanced, many of the old recordings began appearing on the Riverside, Milestone, and Biograph labels; and a revived interest in the blues during the 1970s focused renewed attention on the woman who had prepared the ground under sweltering tents in the fields of the Deep South. "Ma Rainey was a tremendous figure," Southern poet Sterling Brown has said. "She had [the audience] in the palm of her hand. Bessie was the greater blues singer, but Ma really *knew* these people. She was a person of the folk." Without Ma Rainey, the blues would never have made the transition from a segregated African-American folk tradition to a distinct American musical form, from which sprung jazz, swing, bebop, and rock.

Ma Rainey may have wanted to leave some such message for future generations when she sang "Last Minute Blues" in 1932, as her career was in decline. "If anybody asks you who wrote this lonesome song," the lyrics went, "tell 'em you don't know the writer, but Ma Rainey put it on."

SOURCES:

Feather, Leonard. *The New Encyclopedia of Jazz*. 2nd ed. NY: Horizon Press, 1960.

Lieb, Sandra. *Mother of the Blues: A Study of Ma Rainey*. Amherst, MA: University of Massachusetts Press, 1981.

Stewart-Baxter, Derrick. *Ma Rainey and the Classic Blues Singers*. NY: Stein and Day, 1970.

SUGGESTED READING:

*Davis, Angela Y. *Blues Legacies and Black Feminism: Gertrude "Ma" Rainey, Bessie Smith, and *Billie Holiday*. NY: Pantheon, 1998.

RELATED MEDIA:

Ma Rainey's Black Bottom (play with music in two acts) by August Wilson, first opened at the Cort Theater on October 11, 1984, starring **Theresa Merritt** and Charles S. Dutton, directed by Lloyd Richards.

Norman Powers,
writer-producer, Chelsea Lane Productions,
New York, New York

Rainier, Priaulx (1903–1986)

South African-born composer. Born on February 3, 1903, at Howick, Natal, South Africa; died in Besse-en-Chandesse (Auvergne), France, on October 10, 1986; third of four daughters of Ellen (Howard) Rainier and William Gregory Rainier of English-Huguenot descent; studied at the South African College of Music Cape Zaon, and at the Royal Academy of Music in London with Rowsby Woof; studied for a short time with Nadia Boulanger in 1937.

Appointed professor at the Royal Academy of Music (1942), teaching composition there until 1961; elected a Fellow of the Royal Academy (1952); received many commissions from the British Broadcasting Corporation (BBC); awarded an honorary doctorate of music from the University of Cape Town (1982); was the first woman initiated into the Liveryman of the Worshipful Company of Musicians, a guild which dates back to 1500 (1983).

Priaulx Rainier was born in 1903 in a remote area near Zululand, and as a child walked six miles across the vast plain of South Africa to take violin lessons. While she walked, she listened to the sounds of the birds, wild animals, and the wind across the great open spaces. At home, she heard a repertoire of classical music played on the family's grand piano. These early sounds, as well as her innate talent, provided the background for works she would later compose.

In 1920, Rainier won an Overseas Scholarship to the Royal Academy of Music and from that point forward would reside in London. Sir Arnold Bax encouraged her to compose, and in 1937, before the outbreak of World War II, she studied with *****Nadia Boulanger** in Paris. The great French teacher instructed her student to write the first things that came into her head every morning. "You are so jammed with ideas that it becomes a problem and you must sift and sort them," said Boulanger. "All your ideas are of value and you must learn to release them."

Rainier's String Quartet was first performed by the Gertler Quartet in London in 1939, and was later recorded by the illustrious Amadeus Quartet. During the war, this work drew a great deal of attention at the National Gallery Concerts sponsored by *****Myra Hess**. Rainier's Sonata for Viola and Piano was also premiered at the

concerts. The composer Benjamin Britten and his partner Peter Pears often encouraged Rainier to compose new works. In the 1960s, the BBC commissioned her compositions which were then broadcast, as well as six Retrospective Concerts of some of her chamber music in 1973. She was a member of the faculty of the Royal Academy of Music and received an honorary doctorate from the University of Cape Town in 1982. A concert solely devoted to her works was given in London's Wigmore Hall in 1983.

SOURCES:
Cohen, Aaron I. *International Encyclopedia of Women Composers.* 2 vols. NY: Books & Music (USA), 1987.
Gilder, Eric. *The Dictionary of Composers and their Music.* NY: Wings Books, 1985.

John Haag,
Athens, Georgia

Raisa, Rosa (1893–1963)

*Polish-born soprano. Born Rose Burchstein on May 30, 1893, in Bialystock, Poland; died on September 28, 1963, in Los Angeles, California; married Giacomo Rimini (1887–1952, a baritone); studied with *Eva Tetrazzini and Barbara Marchisio.*

Debuted as Leonora in Oberto in Parma (1913); debuted at the Chicago Opera (1913), Covent Garden (1914), Teatro alla Scala (1916); primarily associated with the Chicago Opera (1913–37).

Rosa Raisa was closely associated with the city of Chicago where she performed and was greatly admired for many years. Since the Chicago Opera toured the country every year for three months, she appeared throughout America. Chicago was then a world-class music center, so her importance in that city is significant. In addition, she performed for several seasons in Mexico, South America, and Europe. Her European career was capped by three seasons with Toscanini at the Teatro alla Scala, where she performed in world-premiere performances of *Turandot* and Boito's *Nerone*. Raisa's voice was voluminous and brilliant; she was a true dramatic soprano. Hers was a wide-ranging, physically powerful voice, though weak in the middle range as recordings confirm. Raisa made five groups of recordings from 1917 to 1933, a period in which capturing the full range and power of a voice like hers was difficult. Most of these recordings are not remarkable, but a few demonstrate her great ability. Rosa Raisa is remembered for her work with *****Claudia Muzio**; the two shared nine seasons together in Chicago.

John Haag,
Athens, Georgia

Ralston, Esther (1902–1994)

American actress. Name variations: The American Venus. Born Esther Ralston in Bar Harbor, Maine, on September 17, 1902; died in Ventura, California, in February 1994; daughter of vaudevillians, billed as "The Ralston Family"; married George Webb (a director-actor), in 1925 (divorced 1933); married Will Morgan (a singer), in 1934 (divorced 1938); married Ted Lloyd (a journalist), in 1939 (divorced 1954).

Filmography: Phantom Fortunes (1916); Huckleberry Finn (1920); Crossing Trails (1921); Pals of the West (1922); Remembrance (1922); Oliver Twist (1922); Railroaded (1923); Blinky (1923); The Wild Party (1923, not *Dorothy Arzner's talkie film); Pure Grit (1923); The Marriage Circle (1925); Peter Pan (1925); Goose Hangs High (1925); The Little French Girl (1925); Beggar on Horseback (1925); The Lucky Devil (1925); The Trouble with Wives (1925); The Best People (1925); A Kiss for Cinderella (1925); Woman-handled (1925); The American Venus (1926); The Blind Goddess (1926); The Quarterback (1926); Old Ironsides (1926); Dorothy Arzner's Fashions for Women (1927); Children of Divorce (1927); Arzner's Ten Modern Commandments (1927); Figures Don't Lie (1927); The Spotlight (1927); Love and Learn (1928); Something Always Happens (1928); Half a Bride (1928); The Sawdust Paradise (1928); The Case of Lena Smith (1931); Betrayal (1931); The Wheel of Life (1931); The Mighty (1929); Lonely Wives (1931); The Prodigal (1931); Rome Express (1932); After the Ball (1933); Black Beauty (1933); To the Last Man (1933); Sadie McKee (1934); Romance in the Rain (1934); The Marines Are Coming (1934); Strange Wives (1935); Mr. Dynamite (1935); Ladies Crave Excitement (1935); Hollywood Boulevard (1936); Reunion (1936); As Good as Married (1937); Shadows of the Orient (1937); Letter of Introduction (1938); Tin Pan Alley (1940); San Francisco Docks (1941).

At age two, Esther Ralston joined her parents on stage for her debut in vaudeville with "The Ralston Family." She was billed as Baby Esther, "America's Youngest Juliet." At 14, Ralston made her screen debut in a Hoot Gibson western, while her first sizeable role was in the Lon Chaney production of *Oliver Twist* (1922). Playing the wholesome blonde heroine, Ralston became a highly paid silent-screen star. She appeared as Mrs. Darling in the silent version of *Peter Pan* (1925) and shared the lead with *Clara Bow in *Children of Divorce* (1927). Her first talkie was with Richard Dix in *The Wheel of Life* (1931). The tide turned for the success-

ful Ralston in 1933, when she signed with MGM during the reign of Louis B. Mayer. Mayer deemed Ralston uncooperative and lent her out to other studios for a long line of inferior scripts. Her only important film of this period was *Sadie McKee* (1934), starring *Joan Crawford. In 1936, Ralston was in *Reunion* with the *Dionne Quintuplets. Following three more forgettable films, she took on her last important role in the movie *Tin Pan Alley*, starring *Alice Faye, in which Ralston portrayed the vaudevillian *Nora Bayes.

In 1941, Ralston retired from films to raise her children and play the title role on "Woman of Courage," a radio soap opera (1941–42). Later, she worked at B. Altman's department store in Manhasset, Long Island (1956–61), then took a running part on "Our Five Daughters" for NBC-TV (1961–62). For a number of years, Ralston held an executive position with the Kerr Talent Agency and with an electric company in upstate New York. Her autobiography *Some Day We'll Laugh* was published in 1985.

Ramabai, Pandita (1858–1922)

Indian scholar and reformer who drew international attention to the plight of Hindu widows and whose school offered shelter and education to thousands of these young women. Name variations: Ramabai Medhavi; Saraswati or Sarasvati. Born Ramabai Dongre on April 23, 1858, in Mysore State, India; died at her school for Hindu widows, the Mukti Sadan, in Kedgaon, Bombay Presidency, India, on April 5, 1922; daughter of Anant Sastri Dongre and Lakshmibai (both Sanskrit scholars); educated by parents in Sanskrit and Hindu sacred texts; attended Cheltenham Ladies College in England, 1884–86; married Bipin Beharidas Medhavi (a lawyer), in 1880 (died 1882); children: Manoramabai (b. 1881).

When six months old, family adopted a peripatetic lifestyle, traveling to Hindu holy places and earning money by reciting sacred Sanskrit texts; after deaths of father, mother and sister, Ramabai and her brother continued their travels, arriving in Calcutta (1878), where her remarkable learning brought fame and entrée to educated Calcutta society; brother died and Ramabai married one of his friends, a low-caste but educated lawyer (1880); widowed (1882) and, with young daughter, moved to Poona; founded Arya Mahila Samaj (Indian Ladies' Organization), a reform organization working for the improvement of women's condition; traveled to England (1883); baptized a Christian (September 29, 1883); attended Cheltenham Ladies College (1884–86); lectured and studied in the U.S. (1886–89); published The High-Caste Hindu Woman *(1887), which led to the founding of the Ramabai Association to fund education for high-caste child-widows; returned to Bombay (1889) and opened Sarada Sadan, an institution for the education of widows; school moved to Poona (1890); during famine in Central India, saved hundreds of starving girls and young women (1896); after outbreak of plague in Poona, moved school to Kedgaon on the outskirts of the city; her institution, now called the Mukti Mission, expanded to include a "rescue home" for "fallen women" and an orphanage, in addition to the school; during famine (1900), took in more starving girls, including those of lower castes; awarded Kaiser-i-Hind Medal (1919).*

In 1882, two young widows met in Poona, India. The elder of these, herself only 24, was Pandita Ramabai, already well known in educated Indian circles for her scholarly achievements in the recitation and study of Sanskrit and Hindu sacred texts. The younger, although she had been a widow for seven years, was still only 12 years of age. Married at the age of five, as was the custom among certain high-caste Hindus, she had been widowed shortly thereafter. Her husband's family blamed her for the boy's death and turned her out onto the streets, where she scavenged for food. Ramabai took the child-widow into her own home and, realizing that many other young girls, widowed before they had truly become wives, suffered a similar fate, resolved to publicize their plight and to ameliorate the situation.

Ramabai's devotion to improving the status of women in Indian society was, perhaps, rooted in her family history. Her father Anant Sastri Dongre was a noted Sanskrit scholar. At the age of 44, he had married Ramabai's mother **Lakshmibai (Dongre)**, who was then a mere girl of nine. At the time of their marriage, Lakshmibai, like most Indian women, was illiterate and untutored. Anant Sastri was determined, however, that his young wife should be educated in Sanskrit writing, despite Hinduism's prohibition against education of women and lower castes in Sanskrit and certain sacred texts. Facing the censure of the religious elders in their village, Anant Sastri and his wife sought refuge in the Sangamula Forest where, far from curious onlookers, they engaged in their studies and their religious devotions. Although Lakshmibai proved an apt pupil, she was obliged to study late at night or early in the morning since, in addition to her scholarly and religious duties, she was responsible for all the normal housewifely tasks. However-

er, Lakshmibai found time to instruct her youngest child, Ramabai, in Sanskrit and the sacred texts. The goal of her education, Ramabai later recalled, was not simply the memorization of thousands of verses of Hindu scripture nor the explication of difficult Sanskrit grammatical rules. Rather, Ramabai was taught so that, "I might be able to carry on my own education with very little aid from others."

When Ramabai was about six months old, her father lost all his money and the secluded life in the forest came to an abrupt end. Ramabai, her parents, and her older sister and brother started out on a pilgrimage to Hindu holy places that was to last 16 years. The family supported themselves as *Puranikas* (readers of the Puranas, the Hindu scriptures) and received donations from pilgrims at the sacred sites. Ramabai herself knew over 18,000 verses of the Puranas by heart. Eventually, however, the aging Anant Sastri's eyesight failed, and he was no longer able to direct his wife and children in the reading of the Puranas. As Pandita Ramabai later recalled, neither she nor any of her relatives was suited to any secular employment since their training had been exclusively religious. The family determined to rely on the gods for their support, but their prayers went unanswered and their savings were slowly eaten away.

In 1876, the family's financial problems were compounded by a devastating famine that swept through South India where they were then living. Ramabai's father, mother, and sister died of starvation within a few weeks of each other. Ramabai and her older brother continued their peregrinations to various holy sites, keeping caste rules and studying sacred literature but "our faith in our religion had grown cold." After traveling over 4,000 miles on foot, the siblings arrived in Calcutta in 1878. The pair soon came to the attention of learned Brahmins within the city. It was here that Ramabai acquired the honorific *pandita* (learned one) and also received the title of *Saraswati* (the divine embodiment of language, literary expression and learning) from an assembly of Hindu pandits. Ramabai was an instant sensation, notable not just for her vast learning but also because of the fact that she was 20 years old and still unmarried. Among Brahmins, the caste to which Ramabai and her family belonged, it was common for girls to marry at a very young age. Ramabai's father, however, had refused to betroth his daughter, focusing instead on her education and religious training.

Despite the acclaim for her great knowledge of sacred texts, Ramabai's Hindu faith was quickly eroding. As she read more widely, including texts traditionally forbidden to women, Ramabai was struck by many inherent inconsistencies in Hindu religious teaching. She also became more aware of the subordinate position of women in the Hindu hierarchy: "I was waking up to my own hopeless condition as a woman, and it was becoming clearer and clearer to me that I had no place anywhere, as far as religious consolation was concerned."

In 1880, shortly after her brother's death, Ramabai made a clear break with Hinduism through her marriage to Bipin Beharidas Medhavi. Although her husband had been a close friend of her brother and was, in addition, a well-educated lawyer, he was not a Brahmin. By marrying out of her caste, Ramabai cut herself off from orthodox Hinduism. Ramabai and her husband wedded in a civil ceremony, she later recalled, for "neither of us believed in Hinduism or Christianity." After less than two years of marriage, however, her husband died of cholera, and Ramabai was left a widow with a young daughter, **Manoramabai**.

Although Ramabai spoke several vernacular Indian languages in addition to classical Sanskrit, she had not yet learned English which was, because of the British imperial presence in India, the *lingua franca* of the educated classes. After being widowed, Ramabai resided briefly in Madras but soon departed for Poona to pursue her English studies, where she found that her fame had preceded her. She was a highly controversial figure. In India, although many people still considered themselves orthodox Hindus, others were agitating for reform in their religion, including more education and greater freedoms for women. Orthodox Hindus often censured Ramabai for her iconoclastic behavior and refused to socialize with her. However, Ramabai was hailed by the reformers. They supported her in founding the Arya Mahila Samaj, or Indian Ladies Organization, whose aims were, according to one of Ramabai's friends, to "work for the deliverance of women from the evil practices," such as child marriage and lack of education, and "to work for the removal of the present deplorable condition of women in respect of religion, morality, etc., and for their uplift."

It was in Poona, too, that Ramabai met the child-widow whose plight inspired her to take up her life's work. She later wrote, "As I looked on that little figure my vague thoughts about doing something for my sisters in similar conditions began to take shape [and] I began to place a plan for starting a Home for Hindu widows

before my countrymen and to ask for their help." Despite Ramabai's eloquence and celebrity, however, she could not muster sufficient support among the Hindu reformers of Poona to institute her plan. She determined that she could best rectify the situation of Indian widows if she secured medical training for herself. In 1883, therefore, Ramabai, accompanied by her young daughter, departed for England.

In Poona, Ramabai had studied not only English, but also the tenets of Christianity. Through her instructor, she had been introduced to a member of the Sisters of St. Mary the Virgin, an Anglican order of nuns and, upon her arrival in England, stayed at their convent in Wantage. After several months at Wantage, however, during which time she received secular and spiritual instruction, Ramabai felt compelled to leave. Believing that she could never become a Christian, Ramabai refused to impose on the sisters' hospitality only to disappoint their hopes for her conversion. However, in September 1883, Ramabai returned to Wantage, her doubts

Pandita Ramabai

about Christianity apparently dispelled through her correspondence with another Indian convert, and was baptized on September 29. In 1884, Ramabai left Wantage to continue her studies at Cheltenham Ladies College, under the principal and founder, *Dorothea Beale. Ramabai had financed her voyage to England through the publication of a book in Marathi, *Morals for Women*, and she supported herself at Cheltenham by tutoring in Sanskrit.

In 1886, Ramabai traveled to America at the instigation of a relative, **Anandibai Joshi**, who was about to graduate from the Woman's Medical College of Pennsylvania. (Joshi was the first Indian woman to receive a doctor of medicine degree, but she died shortly after her return to India from America.) Ramabai's sojourn in the United States extended far beyond the intended few weeks' visit. She lectured throughout the country on the condition of Indian women and also studied educational methods. In 1887, she published *The High-Caste Hindu Woman*, a book describing the hardships suffered by child-widows in India. It was an immediate success in the United States. The book and Ramabai's lectures inspired the creation of the "Ramabai Association," whose members pledged to support for ten years a school to be founded by Ramabai for the education of high-caste widows.

Thousands upon thousands of young widows and innocent children are suffering untold misery and dying helpless every year throughout this land, but not a philosopher nor a Mahatma has come out boldly to champion their cause and to help them.

—Pandita Ramabai

In 1889, therefore, Ramabai returned to India and established the Sharada Sadan (House of Learning) in Bombay. The school moved to Poona in 1890. Although Ramabai was now a professed Christian, she and her school received support from Hindu reformers in Bombay and Poona. Indeed, Ramabai had promised her American supporters who were funding the school that no proselytizing would occur. Nonetheless, Ramabai welcomed her young pupils to sit in on her private Christian devotions. In 1894, however, when one of Ramabai's Hindu widows asked to be baptized a Christian, the religious practices at the Sharada Sadan came under attack. Guardians of many of the students withdrew their wards from the institution. Several members of the advisory committee, in tendering their resignations to the Ram-

abai Association in the United States, wrote that the Pandita's "active missionary tendencies" represented "a departure from the original understanding [which] cannot fail, in our opinion, to shake the stability of the Institution and alienate public sympathy from this work." Although reduced in size, Ramabai's school survived this crisis and, abandoning its earlier policy of religious neutrality, adopted an openly Christian stance.

Ramabai's shift away from a policy of religious non-interference at her school undoubtedly resulted from the growth of her own religious feelings. Although she had been baptized in 1883, she was still not fully committed to Christianity. In the U.S., with its many Christian sects, Ramabai had been troubled by the apparent lack of unity among the Christian community. However, in 1891, she underwent an emotional religious conversion. She later wrote that after much reading of the Bible and of a book by an evangelical Anglican cleric, and through attendance at Christian evangelical "camp meetings," she realized that her religious feelings were too intellectual. Then came her spiritual awakening: "[M]y mental eyes were opened, and I who was sitting in darkness saw Great Light, and I felt sure that to me, who but a few moments ago sat in the region and shadow of death, Light *had* sprung up." Thus, Ramabai came to believe that it was her duty as a Christian to spread her religion among her pupils, with the result that, over the years, many of her charges converted to Christianity.

In 1896, a terrible famine swept through central India, killing hundreds of thousands and reducing many others to starvation. Perhaps remembering her own family's sufferings in an earlier famine, or perhaps, as some of her critics charged, taking advantage of a disaster to attract new students for her school after the crisis of earlier years, Ramabai visited the famine-stricken region. "Groups of famished people were sitting around," she wrote, in describing a government-run relief site, "and some were lying in heaps, or sitting or lying on ashes on the bare ground. Some had rags to cover their bodies, and some had none. Many were ill, too weak to move about." In her two visits to the famine area, Ramabai brought back 600 starving girls, of whom 300 stayed in her institution and 300 were sent to other relief organizations. It proved impossible to house the new residents in the facilities in Poona. In addition, plague was sweeping through the city and such a large concentration of people would only exacerbate the spread of the disease. Ramabai decided that it was time to seek a new location for her institution.

Several years earlier, she had purchased a large tract of land in Kedgaon, outside Poona, anticipating the day when her institution must become self-supporting after funding from America ceased. To this site, Ramabai brought her new arrivals. She rechristened her institution "Mukti Sadan" or House of Salvation. The earliest residents built much of the facility themselves, even digging wells to ensure an adequate water supply. Ramabai's new facility offered not only education for girls and young women, but also provided a haven for the orphaned and the friendless. On a more pragmatic level, the residents at Mukti received training in skills such as needlework, printing, carpentry, and masonry. The new institution expanded, eventually providing facilities for over 1,900 residents.

Ramabai was by now almost completely deaf after years of failing hearing. Her responsibilities at Mukti were mainly administrative—although this was no small responsibility in an institution chronically short of cash and reliant on prayer and God's grace to provide for every unforeseen contingency. Volunteers, mostly women from Britain and the United States, carried out most of the day-to-day instruction at Mukti. Some of these women staffed the newly added Kripa Sadan, or Rescue Home, which housed Indian girls who had been working as prostitutes. Ramabai's daughter, Manoramabai, returned from schooling in Britain and America to assist her mother in running the institution and in 1913 herself established a school for high-caste girls about 200 miles from Mukti. Manoramabai was expected to take Ramabai's place as the guiding spirit of Mukti, but she would die unexpectedly in 1921, a short time before her mother's death.

In 1900 another famine racked India, this one centered in the province of Gujarat. Rather than traveling to the famine area herself, Ramabai sent a delegation of 20 of her residents, including a number who had taken refuge at Mukti during the earlier famine. These representatives brought over 1,300 women and children to Mukti. Abandoning her original plan to provide assistance only to girls and women of the higher castes, Ramabai decided to offer succor to female famine victims from all castes and social groups. With this arrival of new residents, the institution expanded to include homes for orphaned boys and girls. Throughout the years, Mukti continued to provide a refuge for famine victims.

Ramabai also continued to work for the spread of Christianity among her charges. Indeed, after the 1900 famine, with the influx of many new residents, Ramabai was concerned that Christian residents, now in the minority, were "in danger of being submerged beneath a tidal wave of grossness and superstition." By December 1901, however, 1,200 of the new inmates at Mukti had converted to Christianity. In 1903, Manoramabai and another instructor at Mukti traveled to Australia to investigate a religious revival in that country. Perhaps inspired by the Australian example, Ramabai formed a "prayer circle" in 1905 that "met together each morning and prayed for the true conversion of all the Indian Christians, including ourselves, and for a special outpouring of the Holy Spirit on all Christians of every land."

The results of these prayers was a "Great Revival" at Mukti, whose aim and consequence, according to one of Ramabai's early biographers, was "the abandonment of evil practices, and the experience of joy in the divine love and the divine forgiveness." Many of the young women at Mukti experienced a burning sensation, thought to signal the descent of the holy spirit into the heart. There were also instances of spontaneous simultaneous prayer and speaking in tongues. Some of the Mukti residents involved in this revival became "Bible women," actively proselytizing for Christianity among their fellow Indians.

Ramabai had long been concerned that the Bible was not accessible to ordinary Indians, most of whom did not, of course, read English. She believed that the translations of the Bible in Marathi (an Indian language spoken in the vicinity of Poona) were misleading because they used Sanskrit words, thus suggesting some correspondence between Hinduism and Christianity. To remedy this situation, Ramabai undertook her own translation of the Bible, using simple everyday Marathi. She worked at this project for nearly 20 years, finishing the task shortly before her death.

In 1919, Pandita Ramabai received the Kaiser-i-Hind medal from the British government in recognition of her work for the women of India. By this time, she was too weak to travel outside of Mukti to receive her honor. Ramabai died on April 5, 1922, but her assistants continued the work at Mukti after her death.

SOURCES:

Dyer, Helen S. *Pandita Ramabai*. London: Pickering and Inglis, n.d.

Fuller, Mary. *The Triumph of an Indian Widow*. NY: Christian Alliance, 1928.

Macnicol, Nicol. *Pandita Ramabai*. Calcutta: Association Press, 1930.

SUGGESTED READING:

Forbes, Geraldine. "Women and Modernity: The Issue of Child Marriage in India," in *Women's Studies International Quarterly*. Vol. 2, 1979, pp. 407–419.

Ramusack, Barbara N. "Women's Organizations and Social Change: The Age-of-Marriage Issue in India," in *Women and World Change*. Edited by Naomi Black and Ann Baker Cotrell. Beverly Hills, CA: Sage, 1981, pp. 198–216.

Mary A. Procida,
Visiting Assistant Professor of History,
Temple University, Philadelphia, Pennsylvania

Rama Rau, Santha (1923—)

Indian travel writer and novelist. Name variations: Santha Rama Rau Wattles. Born Vasanthi Rama Rau on January 24, 1923, in Madras, India; daughter of Benegal Rama Rau (a diplomat) and Dhanvanthi (Handoo) Rama Rau (a social worker and women's rights advocate); educated at St. Paul's Girls' School in London; Wellesley College, B.A., 1944; married Faubion Bowers, in 1951 (divorced); married Gurdon W. Wattles, in 1970; children: (first marriage) Jai Peter.

First book, Home to India, *named a Harper Book Find (1945); won the Mademoiselle Award (1947); received National Association of Independent Schools Award for* My Russian Journey *and adapted E.M. Forster's* A Passage to India *for the stage (1960).*

Selected writings: Home to India *(1945);* East of Home *(1950);* This Is India *(1953);* Remember the House *(novel, 1956);* View to the Southeast *(1957);* My Russian Journey *(1959); stage version of E.M. Forster's* A Passage to India *(1960);* Gifts of Passage *(1961);* The Cooking of India *(1970);* The Adventuress *(novel, 1971); (with Gayatri Devi)* A Princess Remembers: The Memoirs of the Maharani of Jaipur *(1976).*

Santha Rama Rau was born in India in 1923, the daughter of Sir Benegal Rama Rau, a diplomat, and **Dhanvanthi Rama Rau**, a social worker and advocate for improved education and rights for Indian women. Both her parents were of Brahman families. From age six to sixteen she lived in England, where her father was stationed for a time, receiving her education at St. Paul's Girls' School in London and visiting her family in various countries over her vacations. She was with them in South Africa when World War II broke out in 1939, preventing her from returning to England; instead, she traveled with her mother and sisters back to India. Rama Rau explored the country extensively during the next two years, acquainting herself with her heritage, and also began writing magazine pieces. (Among those who gave her encouragement to write was *Sarojini Naidu, a poet who was the first woman to become president of the Indian

National Congress.) Rama Rau then went to the United States to attend Wellesley College, working as a writer for the Office of War Information during her school breaks and graduating with honors in 1944.

Rama Rau's first book, *Home to India*, was published the following year. Based on the experiences she had had during her two-year tour of the country, the book was named a Harper Book Find. She returned to India that same year, writing for several magazines and serving as an editor on the magazine *Trend*. After India gained independence in 1947, her father was named the country's first ambassador to Japan, and she traveled with him to Tokyo to serve as his hostess. She enjoyed the country and the people she met there, but found diplomatic life dull. Rama Rau taught English at a Japanese girls' school and became interested in traditional Japanese theater. This interest led to her meeting her future husband, Faubion Bowers, an American who was serving as censor of the theater under occupation. In 1948, she and Bowers, along with an American woman journalist and an Englishman, traveled through China, Indochina, Indonesia and Siam (now Thailand). This trip as well as her life in Japan is chronicled in *East of Home* (1950).

Rama Rau and Bowers continued their travels after they were married in October 1951. (They would later have one son.) These journeys became the basis for further books, including *This Is India* (1954), *View to the Southeast* (1957) and *My Russian Journey* (1959), which were praised for their liveliness and vivid portrayals of each country's people. Her first novel, *Remember the House*, an examination of the upper class in Bombay, was published in 1956; her second novel, *The Adventuress*, followed in 1971. Rama Rau wrote a stage version of E.M. Forster's *A Passage to India* that was produced in London in 1960 and on Broadway the following year, and continued to publish travel writing in various newspapers and magazines, including *The New York Times, Holiday* and *Horizon*. Following a divorce from Bowers, she married Gurdon W. Wattles in 1970. In 1976, with *Gayatri Devi (b. 1919), she co-authored *A Princess Remembers: The Memoirs of the Maharani of Jaipur*.

SOURCES:

Buck, Claire, ed. *The Bloomsbury Guide to Women's Literature*. NY: Prentice Hall, 1992.

Contemporary Authors, New Revision Series, Vol. 1. Detroit, MI: Gale Research.

Moritz, Charles, ed. *Current Biography 1956*. NY: H.W. Wilson, 1956.

Jo Anne Meginnes,
freelance writer, Brookfield, Vermont

Ramavo (1792–1861).

See Ranavalona I.

Rambaut, Mary Lucinda Bonney

(1816–1900).

See Bonney, Mary Lucinda.

Ramberg, Cyvia Myriam (1888–1982).

See Rambert, Marie.

Rambert, Marie (1888–1982)

Polish dancer and teacher, especially remembered for her ability to recognize and develop brilliant choreographers, whose Ballet Rambert was a significant influence on British ballet. Name variations: Cyvia Rambam; Cesia Rambam; Miriam Ramberg; Miriam Rambert; Dame Marie Rambert. Born Cyvia Ramberg (or Rambam) on February 20, 1888, in Warsaw, Poland; died on June 12, 1982, in London, England; third daughter of a Warsaw bookseller who was registered as Ramberg, although his father's surname was Rambam; attended gymnasia in Warsaw until 1904; one-year course at Sorbonne, 1906 (Certificat d'Etudes Françaises); attended Jacques Dalcroze Institute, 1910; married Ashley Dukes (a playwright), on March 7, 1918; children: Angela Dukes; Helen (Lulu) Dukes.

Saw Isadora Duncan dance in Warsaw (1904); moved to Paris (1906); attended Jacques Dalcroze Institute (1910); joined Ballets Russes to work with Diaghilev and Nijinsky (1912); went to London (1914); gave first public performance (1917); opened a dancing school (1920); launched Frederick Ashton as a choreographer (1926); Ballet Club opened (1931); Ballet Rambert officially formed (1934); Australian tour (1947); named CBE (1953); toured China (1957); awarded Chevalier de la Legion d'Honneur (1957); made first American tour (1959); named DBE (1962); published autobiography (1972).

Marie Rambert, whom *Agnes de Mille once compared to *Ninette de Valois in her influence on the world of dance, was born Cyvia Ramberg in 1888 into a large family living near the center of Warsaw, the capital city of Poland (her father was registered as Ramberg, although his father's surname was Rambam). As a child called Cesia, she was so lively that her nurse nicknamed her "Quicksilver." Rambert was also mischievous; one of her earliest memories was of herself, while very young, teasing her grandmother by alternately demanding and refusing a small new potato swimming in butter on a spoon.

Rambert's mother and father were middle-class intellectuals who introduced their children to literature and drama, although not to the visual arts. They were kind but undemonstrative parents. The Rambergs always employed a number of servants (when she grew older, she would deplore the thoughtless treatment they had received), and Rambert received more overt affection from these servants than from her parents. When she was a young woman living in Paris with her aunt and uncle, she would also consider them more affectionate than her mother and father. As children, Rambert and her siblings spent holidays in the country, where she enjoyed riding on top of peasants' haycarts and dancing to the music of fiddles at open-air fêtes lit by Chinese lanterns and enlivened by fireworks. She always felt a need to be active, and another of her nicknames was "Squirrel," because of her fondness for climbing trees.

Poland was then under the oppressive domination of Russia. Rambert recalled being taken out onto the balcony of her family's apartment to view the nighttime celebrations for the coronation of Tsar Nicholas II of Russia, in November 1894. She was educated at a gymnasia in Warsaw, a state school staffed by Russian civil servants where the lessons—even the Polish lessons—were conducted in Russian. School discipline was severe; pupils were expected to sit completely still in class, which was conducted by a teacher and overseen by a *Klassnaya Dama* who sat at a little table and made notes on each child's behavior and diligence. In charge of these women was a governess who secretly listened at classroom doors to make sure no rules were infringed upon, and whom the students nicknamed *Catherine the Great and *Madame Pompadour. At lunch time, which was also exercise time, the children ate their sandwiches while walking up and down a long corridor, pausing to curtsy to the head governess each time they passed her. Rambert enjoyed her lessons, particularly French, Russian, Polish, and literature, and was good at them without having to work hard. She found it easy to memorize long passages in any language she understood, a gift that she would carry with her into old age. Her favorite lesson, however, was dancing, which included ballet and the complicated ballroom dances of the time. Rambert showed such promise that the school's dancing teacher, Waslaw Slowacki, who came from the Warsaw Opera where Enrico Cecchetti was ballet master, asked the governess to allow her to have extra lessons. His request was refused, as dancing was considered nothing more than a necessary middle-class accomplishment.

Although Rambert was a good scholar, she was so high spirited that her conduct often let her down. She recalled several acts of devilment in her autobiography, *Quicksilver*, and it is perhaps not surprising that when she left school at 16 her academic marks were excellent, but her conduct marks were very poor. That same year, in 1904, Rambert first saw *Isadora Duncan dance. The experience would have a profound effect on her future, although it did not then fire her with enthusiasm. She had seen her first ballet as a child, but did not prefer it over the plays, concerts, and operas she also enjoyed while growing up. (She also loved going to balls, relishing one particular occasion when her partner, an army officer, clicked his heels and said, "With your eyes, Mademoiselle, I could light my cigarette.") She was nonetheless offered the opportunity to travel to St. Petersburg as Duncan's companion, but her political involvement intervened.

*M*ovement, perpetual movement was my element.

—Marie Rambert

Rambert had first become caught up with the political unrest that was sweeping Poland while she was still at school. With friends, she visited a 16-year-old working girl who had been hospitalized after being severely wounded during a demonstration. When the girl died, Rambert accompanied the bereaved mother to arrange the funeral, which was paid for by funds she and her fellow students had secretly collected. As she was the same size and build as the dead girl, Rambert was measured for the coffin and the burial clothes. She also helped deliver illegal propaganda leaflets, and joined a social studies group that met at a different member's home each week. One evening while the group was meeting at Rambert's home, the apartment was raided by the police, who searched for subversive literature, apparently without success. Another day, following a demonstration, Rambert came across the badly mutilated bodies of three workers. Such experiences fanned her enthusiasm for revolution and the overthrow of the tsarist regime, and on May 1, 1905, she took part in a massive political demonstration in Warsaw. When the demonstrators were attacked by mounted Cossacks, Rambert narrowly escaped being injured by a sabre. Her parents, who did not share her revolutionary zeal, determined to get her away from danger. Rather than accompanying Isadora Duncan to Russia, Rambert was sent to live with her maternal aunt and uncle in Paris.

Both her aunt and her uncle, a Frenchman named Marc Pierrot, were doctors working in a poor district of Paris where they were much loved. While Rambert was ostensibly in Paris to study medicine, she instead took the one-year course at the Sorbonne for the Certificat d'Etudes Françaises and threw herself into the social whirl of student life. During the day, she attended lectures, visited museums and art galleries, and took up cycling (a daring activity); in the evening, she went to theaters, cabarets, cafés and balls. At one of the latter, she met Isadora Duncan's brother Raymond Duncan, and was befriended by him and his wife. With their help, she began to make a name for herself as a dancer, and for a long time she always danced in the short tunic they had given her.

Rambert returned to Warsaw when she heard that Isadora Duncan was to dance there again. After the performance, she forced her way into the dancer's dressing room and was summarily ejected. Undeterred, she went the next day to see her at her hotel. Rambert particularly admired Duncan's spontaneity, her innovative choice of music, and her ability to project her feelings to the audience. Before returning to Paris, Rambert spent several months with a friend in the south of France, working on dance routines and training with an acrobatics teacher in Cannes. She also spent some time practicing her dancing with other friends in Normandy. Finally back in Paris, she began to make a reasonable living by charging 100 francs to dance at private soirées. To improve her status as a dancer, she also began to take proper ballet lessons from **Madame Rat** at the Paris Opera, and was bitterly disappointed when appendicitis prevented her from dancing at the opening of the annual exhibition of new paintings at the Salon d'Automne.

In 1910, Rambert went to the Jacques Dalcroze Institute in Geneva for what she thought would be a ten-day summer holiday course. Émile-Jacques Dalcroze had invented what was known as the "gymnastique rhythmique" movement as a way to study rhythm, and many influential musicians attended his school. While she was no musician, Rambert proved so proficient that she remained there for over two years, initially as a student, and then as a teacher. In later years, she would credit Dalcroze with teaching her how to work hard. The institute had moved to Hellerau by November 1912, when Sergei Diaghilev, director of the famous Ballets Russes, and his principal male dancer, Vaslav Nijinsky, paid a visit. They were so impressed with Rambert that Diaghilev engaged her as a member of his company. She was specifically charged with helping the dancers learn their roles in the new ballet being choreographed by Nijinsky, *Le Sacré du Printemps*, a task made difficult because the music by Stravinsky had virtually no melody.

Marie
Rambert

Rambert remained with the Ballets Russes for two years. She was taught by the brilliant ballet master Enrico Cecchetti, and on occasion danced with the company. She also became close friends with Nijinsky, realizing she was in love with him only when he announced his engagement to Romola de Pulski (*Romola Nijinska), also a friend of hers, while the company was traveling by boat to a South American tour in 1913. Diaghilev, too, had been in love with Nijinsky, and he terminated both Nijinsky's and Rambert's contracts after the company's return to Paris. (She continued to have intermittent contact with Diaghilev until his death in 1929.) Rambert again began supporting herself by dancing in private houses, but left Paris for London after the outbreak of World War I in September 1914.

She had been known as Miriam Ramberg in Paris and now took the name Marie Rambert. Those first years in London, she taught the technique of movement at the London School of Eurythmics and studied ballet with *Serafima Astafieva. At the Garrick Theater on February 25, 1917, she gave her first performance of La Pomme d'Or, a ballet created for her by Vera Donnet. The following August, Rambert met her future husband, Ashley Dukes, a playwright who was serving as a captain in the army. In true wartime style, they were married on March 7, 1918, after seven months of letter-writing and only four days of actually seeing each other face to face. Rambert continued to live with friends until Dukes was demobilized. They then rented a first-floor apartment in Campden Hill Gardens, where their two daughters would be born. Eventually, they took over the entire house.

Rambert opened her own dancing school in 1920, and found her life's work. She was an excellent teacher of dance, but her true forté lay in discovering and encouraging choreographers. She believed she achieved this by being so unyielding in her insistence on classical correctness that dancers with creative flair rebelled against the rigidity and so developed their own individual styles. Her earliest success was Frederick Ashton, whose ballet A Tragedy of Fashion was first produced at the Lyric Theater in Hammersmith on June 15, 1926.

Her husband, meanwhile, had had great success in 1925 with his play The Man with a Load of Mischief, and they had begun working towards acquiring a theater of their own. In 1927, with plans to establish both dance studios and a theater, they bought the freehold of a large church hall in Notting Hill Gate. The school boasted a small professional company by 1930 (*Tamara Karsavina was a guest artist that season), and the Ballet Club was opened on February 15, 1931. Membership was select, and performances were given on Sunday nights in Dukes' and Rambert's new theater, which in 1933 was named the Mercury Theater. In the years leading up to World War II, Rambert's school and the Ballet Club flourished, and many famous dancers and choreographers spent time working there. In 1934, in readiness for a four-week season at the Duke of York's Theater in London, the company adopted the name Ballet Rambert. Two of the performances in this season were attended by the duke and duchess of York (later King George VI and Queen *Elizabeth Bowes-Lyon), and Rambert was presented to them in the Royal Box.

During the war years, the company entertained the troops and helped to keep up morale by giving programs in the provinces and at the Arts Theater in London. In 1943, Ballet Rambert received its first public funding, with a grant from the newly formed Council for the Encouragement of Music and the Arts (later renamed the Arts Council). After the war, the company toured Germany for two months, dancing in the garrison theaters of the occupying army. Ballet Rambert set off in August 1947 for a six-month tour of Australia and New Zealand that in reality lasted a year and a half. While in New Zealand, Rambert was introduced to *Helen Keller, whom she later described as "the greatest woman I have ever met." Although the tour itself was a great success, Rambert returned to England with little money. Some dancers had left the company while overseas, and others decamped after their arrival back home. Sets and costumes were in poor condition, and only one booking awaited them.

The Arts Council came to the rescue with a grant of £500, and Rambert set about rebuilding Ballet Rambert. The company toured extensively in Europe over the next few years, during which time Rambert appointed as associate director David Ellis, who was married to her elder daughter Angela Dukes. In 1957, the company was invited to China, where Rambert was met by a former pupil who had returned there to teach in 1939 and had progressed to become director of the National School of Ballet. Rambert was impressed by the work she saw at the school and not a little envious of its resources. When Ballet Rambert performed Giselle, they were puzzled at the lack of applause after the first act until informed of the Chinese custom of never applauding when there was a corpse on stage. Two years later, Ballet Rambert visited the United States for the first time, achieving their greatest success there with Two Brothers, choreographed by Norman Morrice. When Ellis resigned as associate director several years later, Morrice took over the position. By that time, it was proving too costly to support a corps de ballet, and so the company became a group of soloists, enabling them to concentrate more fully on new works while still presenting some of their original repertoire.

Rambert's contribution to British ballet had first been acknowledged in 1953, when she was made a Commander of the British Empire. France awarded her the Chevalier de la Légion d'Honneur in 1957, and in 1962, she was made a Dame of the British Empire. (She also appeared that year on "This is Your Life," a British television program which featured famous celebrities.) Two years later, she received a doctorate from the University of Sussex. Although she relied increasingly on co- and associate directors, Marie Rambert continued to be involved with Ballet Rambert until her death in 1982. In 1987, reflecting its wide range of dance forms, Ballet Rambert was renamed the Rambert Dance Company. Christopher Bruce, recognized as the last choreographer to have actually trained with Rambert, has been its artistic director since April 1994. Rambert Dance Company continues to enjoy an international reputation, and on October 12, 1998, opened the newly rebuilt Sadler's Wells Theater in London with Bruce's *Four Scenes*, a ballet commissioned for the occasion.

SOURCES:

Crisp, Clement, Anya Sainsbury, and Peter Williams, eds. *Ballet Rambert: 50 Years On and On.* London: Scolar Press, 1976.

Rambert, Marie. *Quicksilver: The Autobiography of Marie Rambert.* London: Macmillan, 1972.

COLLECTIONS:

The Rambert Archive in London, England.

Barbara Evans,
Research Associate in Women's Studies,
University College Northampton, England

Rambouillet, Catherine de Vivonne, Marquise de (1588–1665).

See Salonnières.

Rambova, Natacha (1897–1966)

American dancer, playwright, actress, costume and set designer, spiritualist, couturier, and Egyptologist. Name variations: Natasha Rambova; Natacha Valentino. Born Winifred Kimball Shaughnessy on January 27, 1897, in Salt Lake City, Utah; died on June 5, 1966, in Los Angeles, California; daughter of Michael Shaughnessy (a federal marshal) and his second wife Winifred (Kimball) Shaughnessy, later Winifred de Wolfe, later Winifred Hudnut; attended Leatherhead Court, an exclusive boarding school outside of London, England; married Rudolph Valentino (the actor), on May 13, 1922 (divorced January 1926); married Alvaro de Urzáiz (a Spanish tour guide), on August 6, 1934 (divorced 1939); no children.

Natacha Rambova is remembered primarily as the second wife of screen actor Rudolph Valentino, to whom she was married from 1922 until shortly before his untimely death in August 1926. Along with *June Mathis, the screenwriter and Metro-Goldwyn-Mayer executive who gave the Valentino his first starring role, Rambova is credited with transforming the actor into Hollywood's first great screen idol. "Their story was Pygmalion and Galatea in reverse," writes Michael Morris in his biography *Madam Valentino*, "the only time in Hollywood history that a woman fashioned a male star to an image of her imagination and shared that image with millions." Rambova was also the creator of her own exotic persona and reinvented herself many times through the years, whenever interest and opportunity beckoned. Her life beyond Valentino included considerable accomplishments as a costume and set designer, an actress, a fashion designer, a spiritualist, and a scholar of symbolism and ancient Egyptian religions.

Although the name she chose for herself was befitting of a Russian princess, Natacha Rambova was solidly American. Born in 1897 in Salt Lake City, Utah, she was christened Winifred Kimball Shaughnessy but nicknamed "Wink," so as not to be confused with her mother **Winifred Kimball**, a member of one of Utah's most prominent Mormon families. Rambova's father Michael, a Civil War hero and retired federal marshal, made a fortune in mining but lost much of it gambling. Twenty-seven years Winifred's senior, he had been married previously and had had seven children with his first wife. Michael took little interest in his second marriage or in his tiny daughter, preferring to sit and relive his glory days with his drinking buddies. Winifred made up for his absence by doting on her daughter and giving her every luxury. The Shaughnessys divorced in 1900, at which time Rambova was sent to live with her mother's sister **Teresa Werner**, while Winifred pursued a career in the emerging field of interior design. After establishing herself as a decorator, Winifred met and married Edgar de Wolfe, brother of the flamboyant *Elsie de Wolfe who is considered America's first interior designer. Rambova's father, from whom she inherited her ambition, tenacity, and temper, died in 1910, without seeing his daughter again.

Winifred's marriage into the de Wolfe family gave her a solid foothold in her chosen profession. Winning her sister-in-law Elsie's approval, she took over her West Coast business and made millions decorating upscale hotels and private homes. Winifred sent her young daughter to Leatherhead Court, an exclusive boarding school outside London, where she was educated in the arts and humanities. Rambova felt acutely alone in the foreign surroundings but compensated by becoming a voracious reader. "My interest in mythology and legend began as a child," she later recalled, "as I never read any other kind of book." Her obsession with Greek and Roman mythology, as well as Nordic legends, would surface later in her scenic and costume designs.

At 17, with her schooling behind her, Rambova sought independence. Drawn to the ballet from childhood (her idol was *Anna Pavlova), she set out for New York to study with Russian dancer Theodore Kosloff, although at 5'8" she was hardly suited for classical dance. She promptly adopted the name Natacha Rambova and began a passionate affair with Kosloff, with whom she toured both as a dancer and as a costume and set designer for his Imperial Russian Ballet. When Kosloff was drafted for the Cecil B. De Mille film *The Woman God Forgot* (1917), Rambova went along as a designer. Her work was commended in *The Moving Picture World* for the "accuracy of the exteriors, interiors, costumes, and accessories," although *Agnes de Mille, Cecil's niece, contended that the designs were not quite as accurate as the review led readers to believe. "In one scene, *Geraldine Farrar wore a headdress decorated with Bird of Paradise feathers," wrote Agnes, "which they later found out never existed in Mexico at that time."

With the Russian Revolution, Kosloff's finances dried up, and his ballet troupe disbanded. He continued to work sporadically for Cecil De Mille, to whom he would also submit Rambova's designs for scenery and costumes, passing them off as his own. Rambova soon tired of the arrangement, and of Kosloff's philandering, and began designing costumes for *Alla Nazimova, whom she had met when the actress became a student of Kosloff's. Rambova's final break with Kosloff, however, almost cost her her life. While she was attempting to move out of the house they shared, he burst in the door and began shooting wildly at her with a hunting rifle, seriously wounding her in the leg and ending her dancing career. But Rambova never pressed charges against her former lover and later claimed that a jealous ballerina had caused her to give up dancing.

Since Nazimova had almost complete control over all aspects of her projects, she hired Rambova to work on the scenic and costume elements for a series of her films, including *Aphrodite* (which was never completed), *Camille* (1921), *A Doll's House* (1922), and *Salome*

(1923). The women worked so well together that rumors began to circulate that they were lovers. Rambova first met Rudolph Valentino ("Rudy") when he was chosen to play Armand in *Camille*. The handsome Italian immigrant had arrived in the United States in 1913 and had worked as a gardener, waiter, and dancer before finding employment in silent pictures. When cast in *Camille*, he had just completed his first major role in *The Four Horsemen of the Apocalypse* (1921), which had not yet been released. Although Valentino was immediately attracted to Rambova, he was somewhat thwarted by her intimidating manner. "She had been a ballerina and would never let you forget it," said **Patsy Ruth Miller**, who played Nichette in the film. "I was a girl from the midwest, and she had a patronizing attitude toward me. I was not aware that Rudy and Natacha were becoming romantically involved. In fact he used to make jokes about her, saying 'There goes Pavlova!' whenever she passed by." Miller also found Rambova's designs for the film heavy-handed. "She leaned rather heavily on the bizarre, both in decor and personal appearance," she said. "Having been a ballerina, she wore her hair parted in the center and pulled back into the typical ballerina knot. She wore flat shoes, walked with her toes pointed out, and went in heavily for floaty draperies and long beady necklaces. I never saw her dance, but I'm sure it was 'interpretive.'"

Rambova and Valentino began appearing together as a couple at a costume ball in December 1920, although Valentino was still married to his first wife, actress **Jean Acker**, who had locked him out of the bedroom on their wedding night and left him soon after. Valentino moved into Rambova's bungalow, and together they purchased several exotic pets, including a lion cub named Zela. Rambova later recalled that their early years together were their happiest. "We were both poor, still unknown to the world in general, and glorying in our freedom. They were days of laughter, days of dreams, and of ambitious planning for the future." Later, the couple purchased an eight-room house in the Whitley Heights section of Hollywood, which they renovated as their financial situation allowed.

The lovers married in Mexico in May 1922, but their honeymoon was halted when Valentino was arrested on charges of bigamy for having wed Rambova before his divorce from Acker was final. The case generated a firestorm of publicity, making it necessary for Rambova to flee to New York and barricade herself in a hotel. The matter went to court, although the charges were

Natacha
Rambova

subsequently dropped. The entire wedding party testified that the first marriage had not been consummated, and Rudy publicly apologized for the miscalculations concerning his divorce. Shortly after the trial, he hit a snag in negotiations with his studio, resulting in his suspension.

In order to infuse their dwindling coffers during the hiatus, the couple embarked on a 17-week, 40-city dance tour, performing a program of mostly Argentine tangos with an additional Spanish-style folk dance they choreographed themselves. "It was a wonderful thing to see these two exotic and graceful creatures dance," said George Ullman, the couple's business manager. "They always appeared to be dancing for and with each other, for the sole joy of being in each other's company." The couple drew enormous crowds—mostly women—wherever they appeared, their popularity fueled by their recent notoriety. They were "officially married" during a stop in Indiana on March 14, 1923. The following summer, they honeymooned in Europe, where they were greeted like superstars.

From the beginning of her relationship with Valentino, Rambova exercised almost complete control over his career, designing his costumes, handling his publicity, negotiating his fees with the studio, even advising him about how he should make on-screen love to his leading ladies. Later, as his popularity grew, Rambova was forced more and more to shield her creation from the studio moguls who sought to take control from her. In protecting her interests and brokering the best deals for the star, Rambova locked heads with many movie executives in Hollywood, including Adolph Zukor. "She was the stronger personality of the two," he said, "or else her power secured domination over his. It was our custom to give stars a good deal of contractual leeway in their material. Natacha began to insert herself into the smallest details and he backed her in everything." Jesse Lasky echoed Zukor, maintaining that Rambova was at constant odds with the studio and would not arbitrate. "She commanded," he said. "When she insisted on his doing perfumed parts like Booth Tarkington's *Monsieur Beaucaire*, in powdered wigs and silk stockings, we had to take him on her terms to have him at all. She designed his costumes herself, and, to give her due credit, they were magnificent. But we hadn't bargained for a dilettante foil for Rambova costumes."

Although the Valentino craze was without precedent, his appeal was for the most part limited to females. "His posturing, decorative image was focused to seduce the women in the audience, and this made their husbands and boyfriends uncomfortable and envious," writes Morris. "Valentino was a woman's sex object," he adds, "he was a woman's actor, and women were his most loyal fans." Ephraim Katz agrees that Valentino appealed almost exclusively to women: "Male audiences found his acting ludicrous, his manner foppish and his screen character effeminate." Katz blamed Rambova for the downward slide in Valentino's career after 1924, citing her contribution to his increasingly effeminate screen image. His off-camera image was also suspect. Rumors concerning the actor's sex-ual orientation surfaced early in his career and haunted him until his death. In 1926, an anonymous editorial headlined "Pink Powder Puff" appeared in the *Chicago Tribune*, accusing the actor of feminizing American males. "When will we be rid of all these effeminate youths," the writer queried, "pomaded, powdered, bejeweled and bedizened, in the image of Rudy—that painted pansy?" Valentino immediately published a letter in a rival Chicago paper, challenging the anonymous editorial writer to a boxing match, but no one came forth. He would later participate in a one-round exhibition bout with Frank O'Neil, a sportswriter for the *New York Evening Journal*.

Rambova's domination over her husband also extended into their intimate life. Although Valentino longed for a family, Rambova resisted, convinced that motherhood would destroy her career. Although their relationship was seriously undermined by the issue of children, it endured until Valentino signed a three-year contract with United Artists in 1924 which explicitly excluded his wife from participating in his films. It may or may not have been his way of forcing his hand, but whatever the case, Rambova felt betrayed and shut out. She sought to save face by producing her own movie, *What Price Beauty?*, a comic satire she wrote on the indignities women suffer in their quest to be beautiful. The film starred *Nita Naldi*, and included an appearance by a young actress named *Myrna Loy*. The picture, which went three times over budget, was well received in previews but not released until 1928. Lou Mahoney, the Valentinos' handyman and confidant, blamed the studio bosses. "No help came from anyone, no thoughts of trying to get this picture properly released. . . . Their whole thought was that if the picture was a success, Mrs. Valentino would be a success. She would then start producing under the Rudolph Valentino Production Company."

In August 1925, Rambova separated from Valentino and took up residence in the couple's New York apartment, telling reporters that she was on a "marital holiday." When pressed about the separation, she grew defensive. "He knew what I was when I married him," she told one publication. "Homes and babies are all very nice, but you can't have them and a career as well. I intended, and intend, to have a career and Valentino knew it. If he wants a housewife, he'll have to look again." In New York, Rambova sought support through her marital crisis from her mother Winifred, who was now married to her fourth husband, the cosmetics magnate Richard Hudnut, who had legally adopted

Rambova. Winifred had recently become a convert to the teachings of *Helena Blavatsky, the founder of the Theosophical Society, and quickly drew her daughter into the controversial philosophy. Mother and daughter went so far as to employ a medium to conduct seances several evenings a week.

During her separation, Rambova also starred in the film *When Love Grows Cold*, which had a storyline remarkably similar to the unfolding Valentino saga. Upon its release in 1926, it was advertised as "a powerful heart stirring story of a woman's supreme devotion and sacrifice for a man who paid the penalty of 'forgetting' when success came to him." The film's advertisers further capitalized on the Valentino estrangement by billing Rambova as Mrs. Rudolph Valentino, which infuriated her. Swearing she was finished with Hollywood, she turned to the stage, taking the role of a Russian woman in the Broadway production of *The Purple Vial*, for which she received promising reviews. "Natacha Rambova was surprisingly adequate as the girl outwitting the fiendish general," wrote *Variety*. She "has demonstrated sparks of an emotional actress that may ride further in either vaudeville or legit."

While Rambova was in New York, Valentino was seen with actresses *Vilma Banky and *Mae Murray, and had an affair with *Pola Negri, although he continued to wear the platinum slave bracelet Rambova had given him in happier times. Morris claims that the actor continued to hold out hope for a reconciliation with Rambova and was devastated when she obtained a Paris divorce in January 1926. The actor died the following August of a perforated ulcer, which Morris attributes to his broken heart. Rambova, who was in France when she was first informed of Valentino's illness, was deeply concerned, having lost much of her anger and resentment in the months since the divorce. She was grief-stricken at the news of his death, and took to her room for three days, even refusing to eat. Having become deeply involved in spiritualism, she did not attend Valentino's funeral, but sought instead to contact his spirit by employing a medium and holding daily seances. Upon her return to New York the following November, she told the press that she had indeed received messages from Valentino, many of which she later disclosed in the book *Rudy: An Intimate Portrait of Rudolph Valentino by His Wife Natacha Rambova*. For some time, she continued to pursue her psychic interests, joining the Bamberger circle, a group that met every weekend to conduct seances and study theosophy.

In 1927, Rambova embarked on several theatrical, literary, and fashion enterprises. In Boston, she appeared in the mystery thriller *The Triple Cross*, although her performance did not live up to the expectations elicited by her earlier Broadway appearance. She also began writing a play, "All That Glitters," an indictment of Hollywood and her marriage to Valentino. The finished work contained so many uncomplimentary depictions of powerful celebrities that it was considered too controversial to produce. In the summer of 1927, following her appearance in the comedy-drama *Creoles*, she gave up acting and opened an exclusive dress-designing studio on West 55th Street in New York City, where she also had an apartment. Her clothing line echoed her own taste for the exotic and stressed individualized design. "All women should not wear knee length skirts, even if that is the prevailing fashion; clothes that are becoming to the tall, languid type, would not do at all for a short girl of the staccato type, who has to have sharp clothes to express her personality."

Although the clothing enterprise was successful, particularly among actresses and celebrities, Rambova abandoned her business to marry Alvaro de Urzáiz, a Spanish tour guide she met on a trip to Greece. After a whirlwind romance, the couple wed in a civil ceremony in France and settled on the island of Mallorca, where they went into business buying and renovating old houses for tourists. At the request of Alvaro's family, the pair married a second time in a religious ceremony on August 6, 1934, which was covered by the worldwide press. "Don Alvaro bears a striking resemblance to Valentino," wrote one reporter, "having the same Latin type of good looks that characterized the popular film star." The couple's peaceful life on the island was shattered by the Spanish Civil War, which both alarmed and fascinated Rambova. When she denounced the Nationalists for their treatment of former leftist sympathizers, however, she became a political liability and was forced to escape Mallorca on a coal freighter headed for France. Alvaro stayed behind to serve the Nationalist forces, thus placing the dual strain of physical and political separation on the marriage.

In 1936, shortly after arriving in France, Rambova suffered a heart attack which marked the onset of health problems that would plague her for the next 30 years. Adding to her physical woes was the emotional breakup of her marriage to Alvaro, who ultimately left her for another woman. Refusing to be defeated, however, Rambova began a new quest for a meaningful life, becoming a student of symbolism and comparative religion. She now embraced the philosophy of George Gurdjieff, whose teachings were steeped in Asian wisdom and practice. Returning to America in October 1939 and settling near her mother in New York, she joined with James H. Smith to co-author a number of articles on mental and physical exercises for *Harper's Bazaar* and *Town and Country*. The two would later collaborate on the book *Technique for Living*. Rambova also pursued a new interest in astrology, defending the discipline in a number of essays for *American Astrology* magazine.

Through her friend **Maud Van Cortlandt Oakes**, Rambova became acquainted with Paul and **Mary Mellon**, who had awarded Oakes a Bollingen Foundation grant to finance her study of the sand painting of New Mexico's Navajos. Mary Mellon had originally formed the foundation to publish the work of Carl Jung, naming it "Bollingen" in tribute to Jung's castlelike refuge on Lake Zurich. In the summer of 1945, Rambova traveled with Oakes to Guatemala to assist her in studying the pre-Columbian background of the indigenous people living there. Although Rambova put her health at risk to make the trip, it fulfilled her longtime dream to connect with lost or vanishing civilizations. Upon her return to New York, she applied for her own grant "to create an archive of comparative universal symbolism." Writes Morris: "She proposed to collect from museums and private collections sketches and photographs of rare books and manuscripts containing archetypal symbolism." To bring her rediscovery of the past to light, Rambova planned to publish a book, tentatively titled "The Myth Pattern of Ancient Symbolism."

Receiving her first grant in 1946, Rambova sailed for Egypt to analyze symbolic material in antique scarabs. On that trip, she met Alexandre Piankoff, a Russian academician who had fled his country's turmoil in 1917 to pursue Egyptological studies. He introduced her to his French translation of the "Book of Caverns" found in the tomb of Ramses VI. Rambova was so fascinated by it that she abandoned her study of scarabs and returned to New York, where she convinced the Bollingen Foundation to finance a two-year expedition to explore Ramses' tomb and the vaults of the nine pyramids at Sakkara, and to record the religious inscriptions found within the structures. The expedition, which began in 1947, was directed by Piankoff, and included photographer L. Fred Husson, artist Mark Hasselriis, and Egyptologist **Elizabeth Thomas**, who served as an assistant to Piankoff. Rambova was "aristocratic, learned," and "cosmopolitan," said Husson. "The achievements of

the ancient Egyptians appeared to be a constant amazement to her, and she was always searching for clues to explain how and why this was so." He also found her a tough taskmaster. "Natacha demanded the best. She worked hard herself and she expected no less from others." By the end of the expedition, the group had recorded the religious testimony of three separate periods of Egyptian history, data which served as the basis of a series of Bollingen publications called "Egyptian Religious Texts and Representations," which were prepared and translated by Piankoff and edited by Rambova.

Rambova returned to New York in 1951 and taught classes in symbolism, mythology, and comparative religion in her apartment. Hasselriis returned around the same time and continued to work with her for the next 14 years, producing drawings of ancient Egyptian inscriptions and art objects for her archives and publications. Rambova attracted many celebrities to her classes, including artist and scholar **Mai-mai Sze**, costume designer *****Irene Sharaff**, painter **Buffie Johnson**, writer and photographer *****Dorothy Norman**, Indian art expert *****Stella Kramrisch**, and screenwriter ⬧ **Mercedes de Acosta**. Rambova was later displeased to be mentioned in de Acosta's autobiography *Here Lies the Heart* (1960), which transparently referred to de Acosta's intimate relationships with women. Though many of her women friends were gay, Rambova disavowed any sexual intimacies with women.

Beginning in 1953, health problems dominated Rambova's life. Most debilitating of her illnesses was scleroderma, a degenerative disease in which the esophagus and internal organs become fibrous and hard, restricting swallowing and digestion. Despite lack of sleep and weight loss from not eating, she worked tirelessly on the Bollingen Series. In 1954, the first volume, *The Tomb of Ramesses VI*, was published, followed a year later by the second volume, *The Shrines of Tut-Ankh-Amon*. In 1955, Rambova made a last trip to Egypt, stopping in Paris to research in the Louvre for the third volume in the series, *Mythological Papyri*, published in 1957. During this time, Rambova also began donating some of her Egyptian artifacts to the Utah Museum of Fine Arts, to which her mother had been an earlier benefactor. Rambova continued to endow the museum throughout the 1950s, describing in letters to the director how the pieces should be exhibited.

While at work on the Bollingen Series, Rambova was also attempting to complete her volume on symbolism. As her disease progressed, she worked exclusively on her own manuscript

de Acosta, Mercedes. See Garbo, Greta for sidebar.

while Piankoff took over the Bollingen publications. When she felt ready, she sent a draft of her work to Carl Jung for his opinion. Jung handed it over to one of his pupils who found Rambova's hypothesis flawed and suggested further work. Jung's rejection caused the Bollingen Foundation to delay their decision to publish the material, which devastated Rambova. She continued to rewrite in an effort to perfect it, but by this time she was in a race against death. "My health is bad and I have not much more time or strength left, and what I have I wish to use to finish at least this work," she wrote to a friend in August 1958.

Eventually Rambova left New York and took up residence in the Connecticut country house she had purchased with part of her inheritance. She made a last trip to New York in September 1965, to meet with lawyers concerning her will. On September 29, after apparently going berserk in a hotel elevator, she was admitted to Lenox Hill Hospital, where she was diagnosed with paranoid psychosis arising from malnutrition. Her doctors administered shock treatment, which Hasselriis attempted to have halted, knowing that Rambova would have objected to it on moral grounds. He was informed, however, that because he was not a blood relative, he could do nothing to stop the treatment.

Rambova left the hospital in November, under the care of her cousin **Ann Wollen** and Ann's mother **Katherine Peterson**, who took her back to California. There Rambova entered Methodist Hospital in Arcadia, where she remained until January, when she was moved to Las Encinas Hospital in Pasadena. She spent her last months hooked up to feeding tubes, which she described as "purgatory." On June 5, 1966, Natacha Rambova died of a massive heart attack. At her instruction, no embalming took place and no services were held. She was cremated and her ashes were scattered in the northern forest of Arizona, the state in which she experienced the same cosmic mystery she had felt in Egypt.

Rambova left her unfinished manuscript, containing over 1,000 pages of text and numerous photographs and illustrations, to the Brooklyn Museum. Her remaining Egyptian artifacts were given to the Utah Museum of Fine Art, and her Far Eastern collection was donated to the Philadelphia Museum. The remainder of her estate was divided among relatives, friends, and students.

Rambova's place in history is confined for the most part to her relatively short relationship with Valentino, although she deserves broader consideration. It has been suggested that her lack of focus kept her from leaving an indelible mark of her own. "Aunt Winifred always said that Natacha's talents stretched in too many directions," said Ann Wollen; "she strove to be the best in too many fields, and suffered as a consequence."

SOURCES:

Garraty, John A., and Mark C. Carnes. *American National Biography.* Vol. 27. NY: Oxford University Press, 1999.

Katz, Ephraim. *The Film Encyclopedia.* NY: Harper-Collins, 1994.

Morris, Michael. *Madam Valentino: The Many Lives of Natacha Rambova.* NY: Abbeville, 1991.

Barbara Morgan,
Melrose, Massachusetts

Ramée, Louise de la (1839–1908)

Popular English novelist. Name variations: Louise de la Ramee; (pseudonym) Ouida. Born Marie Louise Ramé on January 1, 1839, at Bury St. Edmunds, Suffolk, England; died on January 25, 1908, in Viareggio, Italy; daughter of Louis Ramé (a French instructor) and Susan (Sutton) Ramé; educated in local schools.

Selected writings: Held in Bondage *(1863);* Chandos *(1866);* Under Two Flags *(1867);* Folle-Farine *(1871);* A Dog of Flanders and Other Tales *(1872);* Pascarel *(1873);* Two Little Wooden Shoes *(1874);* In a Winter City *(1876);* Moths *(1880);* Bimbi: Stories for Children *(1882);* Princess Naxaprine *(1884);* Views and Opinions *(1895);* Critical Studies *(1900).*

Louise de la Ramée was born on January 1, 1839, in Bury St. Edmunds, Suffolk, England, the daughter of **Susan Sutton Ramé**, an Englishwoman, and Louis Ramé, a French instructor. A precocious child, she received her early education in local schools and for a time lived with her family in Paris. Following her father's disappearance, Louise and her mother returned to England. There she met Harrison Ainsworth, the editor and owner of *Bentley's Miscellany*, in which her first story was published in 1859. Ainsworth also published her first full-length novel, *Granville de Vigne*, in another of his journals, the *New Monthly Magazine*. *Granville de Vigne* was subsequently published in three volumes under the title *Held in Bondage* (1863) and attributed to "Ouida." She would continue to use this pseudonym, which came from a childish mispronunciation of Louise, for subsequent books, and soon began using it in her personal life as well. (She also glamorized her last name from "Ramé" to "de la Ramée.") *Held in Bondage*, like later novels including *Chandos* (1866) and the hugely popular *Under Two Flags* (1867), depicts with a heavy dose of unreality the lives and loves of the privileged social classes in exotic surroundings, or, as one critic has more kindly put it, "the gallant adventures of dashing and fashionable heroes and heroines." The tale of a French Legionnaire torn between two women, *Under Two Flags* sold millions of copies and with the advent of the movie industry in the 20th century was filmed three times; the last version, made in 1936, starred Ronald Colman, *Claudette Colbert, and *Rosalind Russell.

Ramée published 45 novels, becoming quite wealthy, and frequently parodied, in the process.

Blessed with a sure sense of her own importance (she has been called an egomaniac) and a convenient forgetfulness of her own middle-class background, she lived lavishly, in the presumed style of the upper class about which she wrote, and in *Moths* (1880) condemned its infiltration by lower-class poseurs. Having visited Italy frequently, in 1874 she moved to Florence, where she continued her extravagant lifestyle and frequently quarrelled with friends and her publishers. It is said that she received her guests in her villa standing upon a large white bearskin rug, wearing expensive clothes, and surrounded by

Louise de
La Ramée

her beloved dogs. Her novels during this period include *Folle-Farine* (1871, called "a triumph of modern English fiction" by Edward Bulwer-Lytton), *Two Little Wooden Shoes* (1874) and *Signa* (1875); the popular children's tearjerker *A Dog of Flanders and Other Tales* was published in 1872. *Bimbi: Stories for Children* (1882) also proved quite popular. However, after she moved to Lucca, Italy, in 1894, her work began to fall out of favor, as the three-volume novel typical of the Victorian age began to give way to the single-volume novel. She abandoned fiction and wrote for the *Fortnightly Review, Nineteenth Century*, and *North American Review* both on literature and on causes dear to her heart, which included the campaign against women's suffrage, support for the Boers in South Africa, and the anti-vivisection campaign. Some of these essays were collected in *Views and Opinions* (1895) and *Critical Studies* (1900).

A close acquaintance described Ramée as "intensely cynical," and went on: "She despised humanity and attributed sordid and unworthy motives to innocent actions, and scoffed at virtue, domestic life, and fidelity." Because of her extravagant lifestyle and the sale of her copyrights—common with many women writers of the time—Ramée lived in near poverty in her later years. She received a civil-list pension in 1906 through the intervention of friends, and subsisted on this until her death from pneumonia in Viareggio, Italy, on January 25, 1908. She was buried in the English cemetery at Bagni di Lucca in Italy.

SOURCES:

Buck, Claire, ed. *The Bloomsbury Guide to Women's Literature*. NY: Prentice Hall, 1992.

Drabble, Margaret, ed. *The Oxford Companion to English Literature*. 5th ed. NY: Oxford University Press, 1985.

Kunitz, Stanley J., and Howard Haycraft, eds. *British Authors of the Nineteenth Century*. NY: H.W. Wilson, 1936.

Shattock, Joanne. *The Oxford Guide to British Women Writers*. NY: Oxford University Press, 1993.

Jo Anne Meginnes,
freelance writer, Brookfield, Vermont

Ramirez, Sara Estela (1881–1910)

Mexican poet, teacher, journalist, political activist and feminist who helped lay the political groundwork for the Mexican Revolution of 1910. Name variations: Sarita Ramirez. Pronunciation: Rah-MIR-es. Born Sara Estela Ramirez in 1881 in the Mexican state of Coahuila; died in Laredo, Texas, on August 21, 1910; parents undocumented; attended school in Monterrey, Nuevo Leon, and graduated from Teach-

ers' College, ateneo Fuentes, at Saltillo, Coahuila; never married; no children.

At age 17, moved to Laredo, Texas, and began publishing poems, essays, and literary articles in local newspapers, La Crónica *and* El Demócrata Fronterizo, *and was hired to teach Mexican children at the Seminary of Laredo (1898); joined Partido Liberal Mexicano (PLM), the party working for the overthrow of the Mexican dictator (1901); founded the radical daily newspaper* La Corregidora *(1904); was a journalist for* Vésper, *and prominent member of Regeneracion y Concordia and Club Redención; acted in play* Noema *in Laredo, Texas; founded the literary periodical* Aurora *in Laredo (1910).*

In 1876, Porfirio Díaz ascended to the presidency of Mexico, beginning a dictatorship that would last for 34 years. Díaz favored the wealthy minority, and amidst the extreme sociopolitical oppression that marked his rule, the economic gap between rich and poor became so great, according to **Evangelina Enriquez** in *La Chicana*, that "it is estimated that by 1910, half of Mexico was in the hands of 3,000 families and the real wages of a worker were about one quarter of what they had been in 1800." Out of these conditions arose the Partido Liberal Mexican (the Mexican Liberal Party, or PLM), a group of revolutionaries whose main goal was to awaken the people of Mexico to the idea of political change and to organize communities to act against the Díaz regime. One of the group's early members was Sara Estela Ramirez. Through her poetry, journalism, and political activities, she helped to sow the seeds of the Mexican Revolution of 1910, which would erupt only three months after her early death. Deeply aware of the difficulties faced by Mexican women, Ramirez also helped to establish a firm basis for the emergence of the contemporary Chicana feminist movement, and thus is considered one of the founders of Mexican feminism. While Mexican women had been involved in the struggle for national liberation in the 19th century, it was only around the turn of the 20th century that the liberation of women themselves emerged as an issue complementary to, but separate from, the liberation from oppression of all Mexicans.

Ramirez, known among her close friends as "Sarita," was born in the Mexican state of Coahuila in 1881, only five years after Díaz came to power. Little is known about her early life, except that she was the eldest of two daughters and that she was still quite young when her mother died. Thereafter, she shouldered the responsibilities of caring for her younger sister

María and for her father, who was frequently ill. At age 17, she moved to Laredo, Texas, where her poetry and essays soon began to appear in the local Spanish-language newspapers *La Crónica* and *El Demócrata Fronterizo*. That same year, she accepted a position teaching Spanish to Texas-Mexican children at the Seminary of Laredo. With a teacher's salary that approximated the paltry daily wages of a household servant, she got by on little money, studied English, and observed the miserable living conditions of her students and their families. A caring and articulate teacher, Ramirez soon began to realize the importance of the struggle for freedom to her students' futures, and to voice her concerns about the unjust political situation in Mexico, declaring that the effort to bring about change "begins within the walls of the school."

[O]ur souls like diamonds give out light.

—Sara Estela Ramirez

"The first powerful 20th-century anarchist organization developed around the Liberal Party led by the Flores Magón brothers," writes John Hart. "In the years 1901–10, Flores Magón and the Liberal Party posed the only serious challenge to the Díaz regime and they became a symbol of that resistance." Ramirez was 20 when she joined the PLM in 1901, and soon became involved in developing the party's platform. According to **Shirlene Ann Soto**, by 1906 "provisions for the protection of women and children, including the granting of rights and privileges, to illegitimate children" were included in the platform. The addressing of such "women's" issues is thought to show the influence of teachers like Ramirez. Other early issues included efforts to guarantee improved working conditions and job safety for Mexico's workers. The PLM's activities had not gone unnoticed by the Díaz regime, and all members, both men and women, faced the confiscation of their printing presses, imprisonment, exile, and even assassination.

Among the party's core of women leaders, Ramirez served as one of two contact persons authorized to receive funds for a group of Magónistas in exile. In February 1904, a group of these exiles, including Ricardo Flores Magón, met in Laredo at Ramirez's home, which became the local PLM headquarters. As one of Magón's principal contacts in Texas, Ramirez traveled frequently to and from Mexico, despite the danger involved and much pressure from her family to withdraw from the struggle.

The PLM's most prolific letter writer, Ramirez corresponded with Ricardo Flores Magón from 1901 to 1906. Her letters show her concern for the unity of the group, as she urged members to transcend personal differences in service of the common vision. Unlike Magón, who perceived the working class as frequently unwilling to commit to change, Ramirez had faith that the people would understand and make themselves heard. In September 1903, she wrote:

> We need to educate the people and awaken their energy. Our race is a race of heroes, a worthy race, and it will know how to make itself respected. Let us struggle faithfully for the triumph is ours. We are passing through a crisis that we should undergo with calm, in order to begin again the grandiose task of regeneration.

Magón supported Ramirez's literary efforts, negotiating the sale and publication of a volume of her poetry which he later counted among his favorite books. While Ramirez was an active leader in the PLM, her most striking contribution to the fight for freedom was through her writings, which span the period from her arrival in Laredo in 1898 until her death. In 1904, she founded *La Corregidora* (The Magistrate's Wife), a radical paper which she edited until 1910. The paper was named in honor of *Josefa Ortíz de Dominquez, one of the heroes of the 1810 Mexican War for Independence; this was also, according to Ramirez biographer **Inés Hernandez Tovar**, "one of the few times that women heroines were honored in such a way." Printed and distributed daily out of Mexico City, San Antonio and Laredo, *La Corregidora* called for organized resistance against the Díaz regime through mutualism. In a published speech delivered to the Society of Workers of Laredo, Ramirez described mutualism as the underlying principle which should govern social relations, stressing basic principles of solidarity, cooperation, and goodwill.

Ramirez also wrote for the radical paper *Vésper*, founded by *Juana B. Guitérrez de Mendoza, which had a weekly circulation of 8,000. She established close friendships with Mendoza, **Elisa Acuna y Rossetti** and *Dolores Jimenez y Muro, all of whom established periodicals that addressed important sociopolitical questions of the times and are, like Ramirez, considered founders of Mexican feminism and intellectual precursors of the Mexican Revolution. Ramirez was a prominent member of two groups they founded, the feminist organization *Regeneracion y Concordia*, formed to combat the Díaz dictatorship, and *Club Redención*, an arm of the PLM that challenged the Roman Catholic Church's encouragement of the training of women exclusively for roles as good wives and mothers. *Redención* also evaluated issues related to the role of the church in controlling education and the political participation of clerics.

In 1910, Ramirez founded the literary journal *Aurora*, which became an outlet for her writings as a revolutionary poet and humanist. The journal was named in honor of the daughter of her cousins Jose E. García and **Margarita P. de García**. Attesting to the esteem Ramirez attained from her audience during her lifetime, *Aurora* was glowingly received by *La Crónica*, which praised its "beautiful and select literature, . . . dispersing brilliant light on the foreheads of its readers." The paper went on to note, "We find this teacher, Miss Ramirez, struggling always against adversity, every day more resolved and more firm in her position, sustaining the virtue and the merit of her beautiful productions."

Ramirez never married, and some of her poetry evokes a yearning for a spiritual and emotional complement, and the sorrow of unrequited love. In "The Blank Page," she writes, "That page was for you or for no one; You did not write? . . . let no one touch it," reflecting a lover's rejection and her continuing love. Her *Black Diamonds For Yuly (on her day)* was dedicated to a young orphaned woman with whom Ramirez felt a connection through their common forms of suffering. She does not hide the truth about how difficult Yuly's life will be, but offers the young woman the consolation "that our souls, like diamonds give out light." For Ramirez, faith that good would come from misery was always a strong theme.

As teacher and friend to young Yuly and her students, Ramirez reaffirmed her conviction that their circumstances were the central issues of the revolutionary struggle. They were the inspiration for her to continue the fight against injustice, which she did until her death in 1910 from unknown causes, at the early age of 29. Three months later, the Mexican Revolution for which she had worked began, heralding the demise of the Díaz regime and decades of turmoil that would end, finally, in a nascent democracy. Ramirez's legacy of works, part of the poetic tradition that had long existed within the Mexican-American community, has earned her a reputation as a precursor of both the revolution and of Chicana feminism. In her last published poem, entitled "Rise Up!," and dedicated "to women," Ramirez wrote, "Only action is life; to feel that one lives is the most beautiful sensation."

SOURCES:

Hart, John M. *Anarchism and the Mexican Working Class, 1860–1931.* Austin, TX: University of Texas Press, 1978.

Mirandé, Alfredo, and Evangelina Enriquez. *La Chicana: The Mexican American Woman.* Chicago, IL: University of Chicago Press, 1979.

Mora, Magdalena, and Adelaida R. del Castillo, eds. "Sara Estela Ramirez: Una Rosa Roja en el Movimiento," in *Mexican Women in the United States: Struggles Past and Present.* Los Angeles, CA: UCLA Chicano Studies Research Center, 1980.

Sanchez, Rita. "Chicana Writer: Breaking Out of the Silence," in *La Cosecha: Literatura y la Mujer Chicana.* Edited by Linda Armas (special issue of *De Colores: Journal of Emerging Raza Philosophies,* Vol. 3, no. 3, 1977, pp. 31–37).

Soto, Shirlene A. *The Mexican Woman: A Study of Her Participation in the Revolution, 1910–1940.* University of New Mexico dissertation, 1977. Ann Arbor, Michigan: University Microfilm International, 1980.

Tovar, Inés Hernandez. *Sara Estela Ramirez: The Early Twentieth Century Texas-Mexican Poet.* Houston, TX: Houston University Press, 1984.

SUGGESTED READING:

"Sara Estela Ramirez: A Note on Research in Progress," in *HEMBRA: Hermanas en Movimiento Brotando Raíces de Aztlan.* Austin, TX: Center for Mexican American Studies, University of Texas, 1976.

Zamora, Emilio, Jr. "Chicano Socialist Labor Activity in Texas, 1900–1920," in *Aztlan: International Journal of Chicano Studies Research.* Vol. 6, no. 2. Summer 1975, pp. 221–236.

Rocío Evans,
Chicana feminist writer, Cambridge, Massachusetts

Ramolino, Letizia (1750–1836).

See Bonaparte, Letizia.

Ramoma (1829–1883).

See Ranavalona II.

Ramphele, Mamphela (1947—)

South African doctor, anthropologist, educator, and activist. Born on December 28, 1947, near Pietersburg, South Africa; parents were rural schoolteachers; entered medical school in 1968 and qualified in medicine at the University of Natal in 1972; Ph.D. in social anthropology, University of Cape Town, 1991; BCom. degree in administration, University of South Africa; married and divorced; children: sons Hlumelo and Malusi.

Born to rural schoolteachers in the northern Transvaal, South Africa, in 1947, Mamphela Ramphele determined to become a doctor while growing up under apartheid. In 1968, she entered medical school at the University of Natal, where she became one of the group of political activists associated with Mapetla Mohapi and Steven Biko, who was also a medical student, and joined Biko's Black Consciousness Movement. As well as colleagues, they also became lovers. She qualified in medicine in 1972, and three years later founded the Zanempilo Health Clinic at King William's Town through the auspices of the Black Community Programmes. In 1977, she was arrested and, without a trial, banned to a far corner of the Transvaal, where she continued to work as a doctor. Soon thereafter, she discovered that she was pregnant with Biko's child, and learned that Biko and Mohapi had died under suspicious circumstances while in police custody—Biko supposedly committed suicide by jumping out a window. Ramphele gave birth to her first son, Hlumelo (she would later have a second son, Malusi), and, overcoming her grief, eventually went on to found another health clinic, the Ithuseng Community Health Program, while still in detention at Trichardsdal. She later wrote about Biko and their relationship in her autobiography *Mamphela Ramphele—A Life* (published in the U.S. as *Across Boundaries: The Journey of a South African Woman Leader*), and her frank discussion of the romance (Biko was married, and commands enormous respect for his part in the struggle against apartheid) caused no small amount of controversy and talk in South Africa.

Her banning order was lifted in 1983, and three years later Ramphele became a research fellow at the University of Cape Town. She earned a doctorate in social anthropology there in 1991 (her dissertation was published two years later as *A Bed Called Home: Life in the Migrant Labour Hostels of Cape Town*), and that same year was named a deputy vice-chancellor of the university. She became vice-chancellor in 1996, the first black woman to be appointed to such a post in South Africa; President Nelson Mandela, a friend, gave the speech at her installation ceremony. One of her initial acts was to institute a strong sexual harassment policy. During her tenure, she provided stable leadership and strove to elevate the school into a "World-Class African University," which she described as a pledge both to students and to Africa: "We owe this to the students of today and tomorrow, who deserve a qualification that measures up to the best available anywhere. And we owe it to a country and to a continent that can potentially offer so much—socially, culturally, politically and economically—to human understanding and progress in the new millennium."

In 2000, Ramphele left the University of Cape Town to become the second woman managing director at the World Bank, where as managing director of human development she oversees activities in health, education, and social protection. She dismissed criticism about joining the powerful organization, which has been frequently vilified by many who see its actions in poor and developing countries as brutally heavy-handed, by citing her lifelong commitment to equality and empowerment. Widely respected and no stranger to controversy herself, she is the recipient of numerous awards and honorary degrees.

SOURCES AND SUGGESTED READING:

Monday Paper (University of Cape Town). May 8–15, 2000.

Ramphele, Mamphela. *Across Boundaries: The Journey of a South African Woman Leader*. Foreword by Johnetta B. Cole. Feminist Press, 1997.

Uglow, Jennifer, ed. and comp. *The International Dictionary of Women's Biography*. NY: Continuum, 1989.

"World Bank Appoints New Managing Director." World Bank Group news release, September 24, 1999.

Jo Anne Meginnes,
freelance writer, Brookfield, Vermont

Ramsay, Martha Laurens

(1759–1811)

American diarist. Born on November 3, 1759, in Charleston, South Carolina; died on June 10, 1811, in Charleston; daughter of Henry Laurens (a plantation owner, patriot, and later president of the Continental Congress) and Eleanor (Ball) Laurens; well educated but no record of formal schooling; married David Ramsay (a physician and member of the Continental Congress), on January 23, 1787; children: Eleanor (b. 1787); Martha (b. 1789); Frances (b. 1790); Katharine (b. 1792); Sabine Elliot (b. 1794); David (b. 1795); Jane Montgomery (b. 1796); James (b. 1797); a second Jane Montgomery (b. 1799); Nathaniel (b. 1801); William (b. 1802).

Martha Laurens Ramsay, born in Charleston, South Carolina, on November 3, 1759, was the eighth of thirteen children of **Eleanor Ball Laurens**, the daughter of a planter, and Henry Laurens, who would accumulate a large fortune by 1762 through the rice and slave trades and use this money to buy plantations, at one time owning some 20,000 acres. During a bout of smallpox as a baby, Martha was thought dead and laid out for burial, at which point she revived. An extremely bright child, she was able to read at age three and soon learned French, English grammar, geography, arithmetic and some geometry, although there is no record of any formal schooling. While he did not discourage her studies, her father reminded her that "housewifery" was the most important part of a girl's education. Her mother died in 1770 (eight of her children had predeceased her; one who did not, John Laurens, would go on to become George Washington's confidential secretary), and soon thereafter, around the age of twelve, Martha began taking a serious interest in religion.

She was brought up after her mother's death mainly by an aunt and uncle, James and **Mary Laurens**. Martha lived with them for 11 years, first in Charleston, then in England (1775–78), and then at Vigan in southern France, spending much of the time nursing her uncle. She was an avid reader, interested mainly in education and religion; after she received money from her uncle's will, she spent it on Bibles which she distributed to the locals in Vigan and also set up a school, paying the cost of the teacher's salary. In 1782, her father Henry, who had spent the intervening years as president of the Continental Congress (1777–78), a diplomat, and then a prisoner of war in the Tower of London, joined her in France. In obedience to his wishes, she gave up plans to marry a French suitor, and instead spent most of 1783 and 1784 nursing Henry, who had just participated in the negotiations leading to the Treaty of Paris that ended the Revolutionary War, and who was ill with gout. In 1784, he returned to Charleston, and a year later Martha followed.

At home again, she met her father's physician, David Ramsay, a former member of the Continental Congress who was 10 years her senior and had been married twice before. They were married on January 23, 1787, and over the next 16 years she gave birth to 11 children, 8 of whom survived childhood. In 1791, Ramsay also began keeping a diary, the entries in which are concerned primarily with her inner religious life and family life. She was deeply concerned about and oversaw the moral and secular education of her children, teaching them to read the Bible and later learning Latin and Greek herself in order to instruct her sons in these languages. She provided her daughters with an education equal to what was then obtained in boarding schools. Ramsay believed that her primary duty was to the men in her life, many of whom were involved in public service. She also saw to the training of young slaves.

Ramsay's commitment to religion was of great importance to her. She was raised in the Anglican Church, and eventually became and remained a member of the Congregational Church, but it is interesting to note that for most of her life she did not belong to any one denomination. She knew a number of English evangelicals, including *Selina Hastings, the countess of Huntington, and embraced some of their views, but believed with her husband, as he later put it in her *Memoirs*: "The experimental part of religion has generally a greater influence than its theory." Ramsay died in Charleston on June 10, 1811, at the age of 51. The following year, her husband published her diary as *Memoirs of the Life of Martha Laurens Ramsay*. The *Memoirs* became quite popular, and she was seen as the essence of a proper woman, devoted to her religion and her family, well educated but not spoiled from it, and content with her subordinate place as a woman. The diary was written as a record of religious life interspersed with family life, however, not as a record of her personal feelings and thoughts, and so her innermost thoughts on those issues can never be known. It remains a valuable depiction of one woman's religious life in the early years of the newly established United States.

SOURCES:

Buck, Claire, ed. *The Bloomsbury Guide to Women's Literature*. NY: Prentice Hall, 1992.

James, Edward T., ed. *Notable American Women, 1607–1950*. Cambridge, MA: The Belknap Press of Harvard University, 1971.

Jo Anne Meginnes, freelance writer, Brookfield, Vermont

Ramsay, Patricia (1886–1974)

*English princess and granddaughter of Queen Victoria. Name variations: Lady Patricia Ramsay; Patricia Saxe-Coburg. Born Victoria Patricia Helena Elizabeth on March 17, 1886, at Buckingham Palace, London, England; died on January 12, 1974, in Windlesham, Surrey, England; daughter of *Louise Margaret of Prussia (1860–1917) and Arthur, duke of Connaught (son of Queen *Victoria); married Alexander Ramsay, on February 27, 1919; children: Alexander Ramsay (b. 1919).*

As the daughter of *Louise Margaret of Prussia** and Arthur, duke of Connaught and son of Queen *Victoria**, Patricia Ramsay was born a princess in 1886 but endured an unhappy childhood. Her father's military posts frequently took him abroad, and before she was 25 she had traveled with him to India, Ireland, and the Mediterranean. In 1911, he was named governor-general of Canada, and it was Ramsay rather than her mother who moved with him to Canada to serve as his hostess. She proved so popular with Canadians that "Princess Patricia's Canadian Light Infantry" was named in her honor, and she was made the colonel-in-chief of the regiment. Her father's term as governor-general ended in 1916, and three years later she married Alexander Maule Ramsay and became Lady Ramsay. The couple had one son. A painter who chose not to submit her work for consideration at the Royal Academy, Ramsay lived away from the public eye after her marriage, and died in 1974.

Ramsey, Alice Huyler (1886–1983)

First woman to drive across the United States. Born in Hackensack, New Jersey, on November 11, 1886; died in Covina, California, on September 10, 1983; graduated from Vassar College, 1907; married John Rathbone Ramsey (a lawyer); children: at least one son and one daughter, Alice Ramsey Bruns.

Born in Hackensack, New Jersey, Alice Huyler Ramsey graduated from Vassar College in 1907 and soon married and had her first child, a boy. She was president of the Women's Motoring Club of New Jersey when the Maxwell-Briscoe Company, makers of automobiles, offered to sponsor her and provide a car if she would drive across the country. Ramsey was game, and on June 6, 1909, she set off from New York City in a Maxwell touring car, beginning a 3,800-mile cross-country trip from New York City to San Francisco. She was accompanied in the open car by three passengers, **Margaret Atwood, Hermione Johns** and **Nettie R. Powell**. None of them knew how to drive, so Ramsey handled all of it alone. With advance publicity provided by an editor at the *Boston Herald*, her journey was closely watched both nationally and in the small towns she drove through. Despite rain (they spent 12 days in Iowa, unable to drive because of muddy roads), a mishap involving their front tires and a prairie dog hole, mountains and bad roads, Ramsey and her friends completed the trip in 41 days, reaching San Francisco on August 8, 1909. They had gone through 11 sets of cloth tires. At that time, only about two dozen automobiles had completed coast-to-coast runs, and Ramsey was the first woman even to attempt such a feat.

Alice Ramsey continued driving for the rest of her life, and eventually made nearly 30 more cross-country trips by car. In her later years, she lived in Covina, California; at the age of 90, still driving, she had never had an accident. She died in Covina on September 10, 1983. In October 2000, Ramsey became the first woman inducted into the Automotive Hall of Fame.

SOURCES:

Holmstrom, David. "On the Road with Alice," in *American History*. August 1994.

Read, Phyllis J., and Bernard L. Witlieb. *The Book of Women's Firsts*. NY: Random House, 1992.

"Woman driver makes history then—and now," in *St. Petersburg Times* [Florida]. October 20, 2000.

Jo Anne Meginnes,
freelance writer, Brookfield, Vermont

Ramsey, Elizabeth M. (1906–1993)

American physician and placentologist. Name variations: Elizabeth M. Klagsbrunn; Mrs. Hans A. Klagsbrunn. Born in New York City on February 17, 1906; died in Washington, D.C., on July 2, 1993; daughter of Charles Cyrus Ramsey and Grace (Keys) Ramsey; graduated from Bishop's School, La Jolla, California; Mills College, B.A., 1928; Yale Medical School, M.D., 1932; Medical College of Pennsylvania, D.Sc., 1965; also studied in Hamburg, Germany; married Hans Alexander Klagsbrunn (a lawyer), on January 27, 1934.

Graduated from Yale Medical School as one of two women in her class (1932); while conducting a routine autopsy, discovered and then extensively studied a 14-day-old embryo (1930s); Society for Gynecologic Investigation named her distinguished scientist of the year (1987).

Elizabeth M. Ramsey was born in 1906 in New York City but grew up in California, where she graduated from Mills College in 1928. She went on to study in Hamburg, Germany, and at Yale Medical School, where she was one of two women to graduate in the class of 1932. A few years after that she married Hans Klagsbrunn, a lawyer with whom she would later run a pig and dairy farm in Virginia.

Ramsey worked as a pathologist at Yale Medical School in the 1930s, and while autopsying a woman one day she, along with several colleagues, found a 14-day-old embryo. "It was the most interesting professional thing in my life," she later said, for the embryo, which became known as the "Yale Embryo," was at the time the youngest ever seen. Her discovery led her to extensively study the anatomy of human embryos and to publish her findings. She continued her research by studying monkeys to understand the circulatory system of their embryos and placentas. With Martin Donner of the radiology department at Johns Hopkins, she later used radioactive dyes and X-rays to conclude that the human embryo and placenta have a similar circulation system.

Ramsey was the author of over 100 scientific articles as well as two books, *The Placenta of Laboratory Animals and Man* (1975) and, with Donner, *Placental Vasculature and Circulation* (1982). She spent 36 years working in the Carnegie Institute's embryology department at Johns Hopkins University, where she also taught and lectured. In addition to serving on the Dean's Council of the Yale Medical School, she guest-lectured at Georgetown and George Washington universities, and served on the boards of the National Cathedral Choral Society and the National Symphony Orchestra.

Ramsey was the recipient of the distinguished service award of the American College of Obstetricians and Gynecologists, which also elected her to its hall of fame. She served as a vice president of the American Association of Anatomists, and the Society of Gynecologic Investigation named her its distinguished scientist for 1987. She died of a stroke in 1993 in Washington, D.C., less than two weeks after her husband's death.

SOURCES:

The Day [New London, CT]. July 4, 1993.

Jo Anne Meginnes,
freelance writer, Brookfield, Vermont

Ramsland, Sarah Katherine

(1882–1964)

Canadian legislator who was the first woman elected to the Saskatchewan Legislative Assembly. Name variations: Sarah Katherine McEwen; Sarah Katherine McEwen Ramsland. Born on July 19, 1882, in Buffalo Lake, Minnesota; died on April 4, 1964, in Prince Albert, Saskatchewan, Canada; married in 1906 (husband died, 1918); children: three.

Sarah Katherine Ramsland, born in 1882 in Buffalo Lake, Minnesota, was a teacher in the Minnesota public schools until she married and moved to Saskatchewan, Canada, in 1906. Members of both her and her husband's families had served in the state legislature in Minnesota. In 1917, eleven years after the family relocated to Saskatchewan, Ramsland's husband was elected to the Saskatchewan legislature as a member of the Liberal Party. He died the following year.

Now a single mother of three children, Ramsland gained the Liberal Party's nomination for Pelly riding (district) and won the by-election in 1919, earning the distinction of being the first woman elected to the Saskatchewan Legislative Assembly. She was reelected in the provincial election in 1921. Ramsland stressed the need for rural high schools and libraries. Later, her proposal that men and women be entitled to file for divorce on identical grounds won the overwhelming support of her fellow legislators.

Ramsland left the legislature in 1925, after which she was in charge of the traveling library service of the Saskatchewan Provincial Library and assumed leadership roles in the Women's Canadian Club and the Business and Professional Women's Club. A member of the Eastern Star and the Red Cross, she died in 1964.

Howard Gofstein,
freelance writer, Oak Park, Michigan

Ranavalona I (1792–1861)

Monarch of Madagascar, persecutor of Malagasy Christians, and opponent of European imperialism. Name variations: Ramavo. Pronunciation: rah-nah-VAH-loo-nah. Born Ramavo in Madagascar in 1792; died in Madagascar in 1861; member of the Hova royal family; married King Radama, year unknown; children: Rakoto.

Assumed power upon the death of her husband (1828); met French invasion (1829); began persecution of Malagasy Christians (1836); deprived Europeans of trading privileges (1845); had all Europeans expelled from Madagascar (1857).

Ranavalona I is alternately characterized as a bloodthirsty despot or an anti-imperialist heroine, although the truth of her reign probably lies somewhere in between. Little is known of her life before she ascended the throne at age 36 as the wife and cousin of King Radama I of Madagascar. Ranavalona could neither read nor write, but she proved herself to be a formidable political strategist and a ruler of iron will.

A member of the Hova royal family, she was named Ramavo at the time of her birth in Madagascar in 1792. She was still known as Ramavo when her husband Radama I, an exceptionally able administrator and warrior, modernized the Malagasy (people native to Madagascar) army according to the European model and extended his kingdom at the expense of the other tribes of the island. Perhaps of more lasting significance was his friendly attitude towards Europeans generally. While he hoped to enlist their help in subduing the island, he was also both curious and tolerant of their culture. Although he was not a Christian, he enthusiastically welcomed Protestant missionaries, who opened churches and schools and introduced the printing press, and he was even persuaded to abolish slavery, despite the objections of some of the king's most prominent and powerful subjects. Radama also surrounded himself with European advisors. Unity and material progress, innovation and the readiness to avoid isolationism, and a strong belief in education were the primary characteristics of his reign.

Having produced no heirs, Ramavo was excluded from the succession by Radama. Instead, he chose his nephew Rakotobe as heir. But Ramavo was patient, gathering around her a constituency of counselors and military men. On July 27, 1828, after a prolonged illness, the king—in a fit of delirium brought about either by malaria, blackwater fever and/or the excessive consumption of rum—took his own life. Six days later, Ramavo put all the king's closest relatives to death in a coup d'etat. These included the heir to the throne, the king's cousins and brothers, and the queen mother. Because it was against the law to spill royal blood, each member of the royal family was either strangled or starved to death.

Wearing a massive crown lined with red velvet and sporting seven golden spear points topped with a gold bird (the royal Malagasy emblem), Ramavo ascended the throne, taking the royal name of Ranavalona. The new queen revealed the tenor of her future administration when, two days before the funeral of her husband, she firmly issued a revised code of laws, based upon the legal traditions of the Hova tribe. Her rule would mark the ascendancy of a mixed Hova tribal plutocracy—composed of military men, traders and nobles. For the most part, they were conservative and discontented with the growing European influence in Madagascar.

[Ranavalona I] was one of the proudest and most cruel women on the face of the earth.

—Ida Pfeiffer

King Radama was laid to rest in a coffin made of the melted-down silver of Spanish piasters, French francs, and Mexican dollars. In the royal tomb, he was surrounded by his military uniforms, his weapons, and by the portraits of his European contemporaries, Frederick the Great of Prussia, Napoleon Bonaparte, and George IV of Britain.

To become the female ruler of Madagascar presented few difficulties for Ranavalona, as the Malagasy had long been a matrilineal society. However, increasing European influence during the previous two reigns had led the royal family to adopt a patrilineal succession. To definitively secure her position, Ranavalona therefore declared herself to be a member of the male sex. Obviously, this made the issue of remarriage tricky. It was decided that while the new queen could not remarry, she might have lovers, and that any offspring she had would be declared a child of the dead king. This conformed comfortably with the notions of the islanders, who believed that the spirit of the deceased king still watched over them, and that his spirit returned to the queen's bedchamber at night.

Ranavalona quickly began to implement policies which contrasted profoundly with those of her husband. In November, she refused to grant an interview to the British ambassador and repudiated the Anglo-Malagasy treaty of friendship signed by King Radama. Of infinitely greater significance, however, was her reinstatement of slavery as a social and economic institution of Madagascar.

The queen did retain one significant pillar of her husband's rule. She attempted to emulate his conquests, seeking to expand her kingdom at the expense of the Sakalava tribe. Ultimately, her policy failed, for her aggression drove the Sakalavas to seek French protection. In August 1829, when a punitive French force landed on Madagascar, Ranavalona sent an army of 14,000 conscripts to meet them, but they were defeated. The episode illustrated the military and political vulnerability of Madagascar. Though the French occupied the two small islands of Nossi-Be and Ste. Marie, the defeat strengthened Queen Ranavalona's resolve to oppose any further European interference in the affairs of Madagascar.

On September 23, 1829, the queen gave birth to a son and heir Rakoto, who was to be her only child. His father, one of her generals, was assassinated a year later by Rainiharo, who rose to fill the political vacuum left by his predecessor and became the queen's lover. Rainiharo managed the island's foreign policy with a practiced hand, sending delegates to both London and Paris in an attempt to forestall foreign intervention.

Much of royal policy was decided by using divination-boards known as *sikidy*. Upon these boards, beans were thrown and a mathematical combination divined, which guided important decisions. Apart from intrigue and mysticism, however, chance also played an important part in the early reign of the queen. On a stormy day in November 1831, a shipwrecked castaway named Jean Laborde washed up upon the shores of Madagascar. This young French adventurer had been hunting for sunken treasure off the coast of Mozambique when his ship ran into foul weather. Seeking shelter off the southeast coast of Madagascar, Laborde's ship was caught in a cyclone and sunk.

By royal decree, all castaways were automatically the property of the crown. Although the ruling was designed to discourage European exploration of Madagascar, it meant that men like Laborde were usually received at court. Thus, he was led to the palace of Antan, one of the biggest wooden structures in the world. From its towering steepled roof to the ground, it measured 120 feet, and in the intervening space, balconies and galleries faced in every direction. All told, approximately 15,000 slaves had died in the construction of the building. As well, it was customary to bring a gift for the queen. The present had to be in pairs. Two Mexican dollars, for example, was the gift that Laborde supplied to Ranavalona, who was always formally addressed as "great glory" or "great lake supplying all water."

Upon the recommendation of another French resident, Laborde signed a contract with the government to manufacture rifles and cannons. Thus, a local industrial revolution was started, which would later see 10,000 islanders employed in the manufacture of everything from cloth to soap, rum, sugar and many other staples and luxuries. Laborde and the queen enjoyed a tolerable working relationship for many years, and he was to have a happy influence upon young Prince Rakoto.

There was one innovation, however, that Ranavalona forbade: no roads were to be built, as they might aid an invading European army. The only exception was when the queen herself traveled, in which case an army of slaves built the road in front of her. At night, they erected an entire town for the queen and her court; it was then abandoned in the morning.

In the seventh year of her reign, Queen Ranavalona, aged 43, was stricken by illness, and it was feared that she might die. Once recovered, she attributed her cure to the devotion she had exhibited during her infirmity towards her ancestors. These ancestors, or fetishes (objects regarded as the embodiment of potent spirits), were enshrined in a traditionally decorated, steep-roofed cabin. Neither a person on horseback, nor a European, nor a hog were allowed to enter the grounds or cabins. All fetishes were guarded by their personal sorcerers. The fetish to which Ranavalona attributed her recovery was Majakatsiroa, the "Peerless Sovereign." He took the physical form of a small sack, a sachet, and another small bag carried by a well-known sorcerer. This fetish was also the talisman carried by the monarch into battle.

Attributing her recovery to traditional Malagasy spirituality only reinforced Ranavalona's prejudice towards the Christian missionaries of the island. On February 26, 1835, she enjoined all missionaries to respect the cultural traditions of the nation and to cease baptizing its subjects.

Ranavalona I

(1792–1861)

When this proved ineffective, Ranavalona banned the practice of Christian worship altogether. All missionaries were expelled from Madagascar on June 18, 1835, and all mission schools were closed.

What had begun as an effort to safeguard the culture of Madagascar quickly dissolved, however, into a seemingly endless round of persecutions against the island's Christian converts and the queen's political enemies. On August 14, 1836, Ranavalona ordered the first execution of a Christian convert, a woman of 37 named **Rasalama**. She was speared to death, and her body hurled from a cliff, where the dogs and the carrion picked the corpse clean. Many converts, even of the highest rank, were enslaved, burned at the stake, boiled alive, dismembered, starved to death, flayed alive, or thrown from the rocks upon which the capital stood.

With a new tribal legal system in place, all of Ranavalona's subjects were liable to trial by ordeal, often being forced to ingest poison. Many were simply put to death. Paranoia seems to have gripped the court, as a reign of terror spread across the land. Facilitated by the prodigious secret service which the queen maintained, such terror did not lift until her death. It has been suggested that Ranavalona was responsible for the deaths of fully one half of the island's inhabitants.

In 1845, all Europeans were deprived of their trading privileges in the interior of the country and were informed that forced labor would be required of them. Those who disagreed with this arrangement were asked to leave the island within a fortnight. Not surprisingly, many did.

The queen was famous for the exotic galas she held at the palace every two or three months, usually on the anniversary of her birth, accession, marriage and so on. They took place in the great courtyard in front of the palace, and the elite of Malagasy society attended. They ate beef rice, in honor of the queen, and consumed vast quantities of rum. Such occasions always produced a fantastic display of fashion, with men dressed in Arab, Turkish, Spanish, and French costumes, and women wearing sarongs, saris, and European evening gowns. Native dancers entertained the crowd and the royal family, and as the night wore on the behavior of the guests grew more outrageous.

As the years passed, Ranavalona began to distinguish less and less between her personal fancies and her public duties. She became increasingly disinterested in the administration of the realm, mismanaging the economy and allowing her ministers great latitude. By the early 1850s Prince Rakoto had grown into a young, educated, intelligent man. Largely as a result of his relationship with Laborde, he was sympathetic to European ideas and culture. In January 1854, the prince dispatched a secret letter to Napoleon III, asking the French emperor to send a military expedition to Madagascar in order to depose his mother's advisors. Nothing came of the prince's treacherous communiqué, as the French were preoccupied with events in the Crimea, Mexico and elsewhere.

Luckily for him, Prince Rakoto was one of the few people that the queen did not mistrust. It was not until 1857 that the plot was discovered, and Ranavalona reacted by expelling all Europeans from Madagascar and confiscating their possessions, including the factories of Jean Laborde. The prince's actions were attributed to those of an inexperienced young man, led astray by bad advice. From this period until her death, the queen ruled with an iron fist. The slightest hints of opposition or dissent were crushed ruthlessly.

Four years later, in 1861, Ranavalona died. Her reign, which had lasted for 33 years, had engendered a period of terror and religious persecution on a grand scale, given the size of Madagascar. But Ranavalona's reign also marked a period of cultural renewal. Although several other plots were fomented to depose and assassinate her, she managed to foil them all—a testimony to her political acumen, absolute power, and extensive network of spies. With her death, the era of expansionary conquests ended, and no Malagasy monarch was to ever successfully subdue the entire island. After her death, Ranavalona I was generally referred to as "Ranavalona the cruel."

SOURCES:

Ellis, William. *Three Visits to Madagascar during the Years 1853–1854–1856.* London: John Murray, 1858.

Molet, Louis. *Le Bain Royal a Madagascar.* Tananarive, 1956.

Pfeiffer, Ida. *The Last Travels.* London: Routledge, 1861.

Stratton, Arthur. *The Great Red Island.* NY: Scribner, 1964.

SUGGESTED READING:

Croft-Cook, Rupert. *The Blood-Red Island.* London: Staples Press, 1953.

Hugh Stewart, M.A.,
Guelph, Ontario, Canada

Ranavalona II (1829–1883)

Queen of Madagascar. Pronunciation: rah-nah-VAH-loo-nah. Name variations: Ranavalomanjaka; Ramoma. Born in 1829 in Madagascar; died on July 13, 1883, in Tananarive, Madagascar; daughter of Prince Ramasindrazana of Madagascar; married Radama II, king of Madagascar (died 1863); married Rainilaiarivony, prime minister of Madagascar, in 1869; no children.

The future Queen Ranavalona II was born in 1829 into the royal family of the Imerina, rulers of the largest kingdom on the African island of Madagascar. Called Princess Ramoma, she became the first wife of King Radama II, her cousin, but when he married **Rasoherina**, she was relegated to the status of second wife. Radama II was assassinated in 1863, and Rasoherina was chosen to succeed him. When Rasoherina died in 1868, Ramoma was chosen as the new queen and took the name Ranavalona II. Her election to the throne was allegedly to honor the dynasty's founder's wish that women should rule the Imerina. However, historians believe it was arranged by the prime minister, Rainilaiarivony, who wanted to rule himself with a queen to act as figurehead. He consolidated his power in 1869 with his marriage to Ranavalona II. Nevertheless, Ranavalona was to have a significant impact on Madagascar's history.

Her primary influence was on the religion of the Malagasy people. British and French missionaries had been working on the island for decades, but her reign of 15 years began the Christian period of the Madagascar monarchy and implemented Protestant Christianity as the state religion. Ranavalona II was raised and educated as a Christian, taught by Malagasy pastors converted by the London Missionary Society. Her coronation in 1868 used Christian language and symbols, rejecting the traditional gods of the Imerina. In 1869, she and her husband were baptized in a public ceremony, which was followed by the conversion of most of her subjects.

In 1873 and 1881, Ranavalona and her husband issued new legal codes, which borrowed heavily from European liberal political ideology while preserving royal authority. They also centralized the island's administration and tried to strengthen the military.

In foreign policy, the queen and prime minister followed an "open-door" strategy towards European missionaries and traders, and exiled the traditionalist, anti-European faction at court. Britain and France were particularly eager to dominate the cattle, rice, coffee, sugar, and gold trades of Madagascar, and were threatening the stability of the monarchy. The struggle to maintain the island's independence from the colonial European powers had already erupted once into war by the time of Ranavalona's accession.

During the late 1870s, the threat of annexation by the French became more immediate, despite several treaties recognizing her as ruler of all the Malagasy people of Madagascar. In 1882, she sent an embassy to Europe and the United States to arrange treaties with Germany, France, Italy, America, and Britain, but because of France's increasing domination of the island, the other states were not willing to negotiate with her representatives. Another treaty with the French was signed in 1883, but, soon after, the French government made an ultimatum to the queen demanding that she accept the establishment of a French protectorate over the island, allow the sale of land to French nationals, and pay an indemnity for losses to the French army during the struggle for control of Madagascar. Ranavalona rejected these demands, and in June 1883 the French-Malagasy war broke out, the queen urging her subjects to fight for independence. However, she survived only one month into the war. The queen, about 54 years old, died in her capital city of Tananarive on July 13, 1883.

SOURCES:

Brown, Mervyn. *Madagascar Rediscovered: A History from Early Times to Independence*. Hamden, CT: Archon, 1979.

Mutibwa, Phares. *The Malagasy and the Europeans: Madagascar's Foreign Relations, 1861–1895*. London: Longman, 1974.

Laura York, M.A. in History, University of California, Riverside, California

Ranavalona III (1861–1917)

Last queen of Madagascar. Pronunciation: rah-nah-VAH-loo-nah. Name variations: Razafindrahety. Born in 1861 in Madagascar; died in 1917 in Algiers; daughter of Princess Raketaka of Madagascar; married Rainilaiarivony, prime minister of Madagascar, in 1883; no children.

A princess of Madagascar's ruling family of Imerina, Razafindrahety was the last monarch of the great island, and would witness its annexation as a colony of France. She was chosen by the nobility of the Malagasy people of Madagascar to succeed Queen *Ranavalona II in July 1883, and took the name Ranavalona III. A favorite grandniece of the old queen, Razafindrahety was recently widowed after a brief marriage when she was elected queen. She had been educated in Protestant schools by the London Missionary Society in the capital of Tananarive. Her election was supported by Rainilaiarivony, the prime minister and widowed husband of the late queen, who sought her election in order to continue his own unofficial reign. Ranavalona III and the prime minister married in August 1883.

On her accession, the new queen faced the crisis of an ongoing war with the French, who wanted to establish Madagascar as a colony in order to control its rich natural resources and strategic geographical location off the East African coast. The first French-Malagasy war had broken out in June 1883, and the crown would devote most of its resources to a losing military effort over the next decade. In December 1885, the occupation and destruction of the island's chief ports and cities led Ranavalona to sign a treaty with the French, ending the war and agreeing to a French protectorate. However, the French continued their demands for more control over Madagascar's land and trade, and the second French-Malagasy war followed in 1894–95.

Throughout the early 1890s, Ranavalona III and her husband faced a serious decline in royal authority, as Prime Minister Rainilaiarivony aged and the French military position strengthened. There was a continued armed struggle for possession of land on the island between the Malagasy people and French troops and traders. As traditional authority in the capital of Tananarive was eroded, crime, civil strife, and a breakdown of the island economy followed. Other European nations recognized the legitimacy of the French protectorate and ceased direct diplomatic relations with the Madagascar government, which left it with few potential allies in its struggle to maintain independence. The queen did have some support from the British army, which helped hold off the final conquest of the island. However, in September 1895 the queen was forced to surrender Tananarive to French troops. A few days later, Prime Minister Rainilaiarivony was ousted from office and exiled to Algiers. Queen Ranavalona was retained as a figurehead ruler by the French government, which hoped to use her influence to stave off further rebellion. She made speeches urging her subjects to lay down their arms and accept French rule in the interest of peace, but to little effect.

In early 1896, the French faced renewed opposition with the outbreak of the Revolt of the Menalamba, a nationalist insurrection against all foreign influence and control in Madagascar fought in Ranavalona's name. The threat to French troops and trade caused by the Revolt of the Menalamba was the pretext the French used to formally annex Madagascar in August 1896. A governor-general was installed and a few months later the monarchy and the post of prime minister were formally abolished. In February 1897, Ranavalona III was exiled to Réunion to prevent her from becoming a focus for uprisings among her former subjects. Two years later, she was removed to Algiers where she lived in relative comfort, but under French control, until her death in 1917. In 1939, her ashes were returned to Tana-

narive and interred in the royal tomb. This event generated resurgent nationalist sentiment among the Malagasy, although they would not win back their independence from France until 1960.

SOURCES:
Brown, Mervyn. *Madagascar Rediscovered: A History from Early Times to Independence.* Hamden, CT: Archon, 1979.
Mutibwa, Phares. *The Malagasy and the Europeans: Madagascar's Foreign Relations, 1861–1895.* London: Longman, 1974.

Laura York, M.A. in History,
University of California, Riverside, California

Rand, Ayn (1905–1982)

Pro-capitalist, anti-religious novelist and philosopher, and founder of philosophical "Objectivism." Name variations: Alissa Rosenbaum (1905–1926); Ayn Rand (1926–1929 and in professional life throughout); Ayn O'Connor (1929–1982). Pronunciation: Ayn rhymes with pine. Born Alissa Rosenbaum in St. Petersburg, Russia, on February 2, 1905; died in New York on March 6, 1982; daughter of Fronz Rosenbaum (a chemist) and Anna Rosenbaum; attended schools in Russia; University of Petrograd, B.A. in history, graduated with highest honors, 1924; married Charles Francis "Frank" O'Connor (an actor and painter), on April 15, 1929; no children.

Immigrated to America (1926); became naturalized citizen (1931); was a movie extra and screenwriter in Hollywood, then wardrobe chief for RKO pictures (1926–32); was a screenwriter, playwright, and novelist (1932–44); was a freelance writer and Objectivist leader (1950–82).

Selected writings: We, the Living *(Macmillan, 1936);* Anthem *(Cassell, 1938, revised, 1946);* The Fountainhead *(Bobbs-Merrill, 1943);* Atlas Shrugged *(Random House, 1957);* For the New Intellectual: The Philosophy of Ayn Rand *(Random House, 1961);* The Virtue of Selfishness: A New Concept of Egoism *(New American Library, 1964);* Capitalism: The Unknown Ideal *(New American Library, 1966);* The Romantic Manifesto: A Philosophy of Literature *(World, 1969);* Philosophy: Who Needs It? *(Bobbs-Merrill, 1971);* The New Left: The Anti-Industrial Revolution *(New American Library, 1982);* The Ayn Rand Lexicon: Objectivism from A to Z *(New American Library, 1984). Co-editor and contributor to* The Objectivist Newsletter *(1962–65) and its successor* The Objectivist *(1966–71); writer and publisher of* The Ayn Rand Letter *(1971–76). Columnist for the* Los Angeles Times.

Ayn Rand's claim to fame rests on her huge didactic novels *The Fountainhead* (1943) and

Atlas Shrugged (1957) which developed a cult following among pro-capitalist students in the 1950s and 1960s. Earnest, quirky, and dogmatic, Rand thought of herself as the height of rationality, but her personality and her writings proved just the opposite. A Russian émigré and one of the most outspoken anti-Communists of the 20th century, she glorified capitalism, hated all forms of socialism, and thought of selfishness as a positive virtue.

Alissa Rosenbaum (her original name) was born in St. Petersburg in 1905, the year of the first, unsuccessful, Russian Revolution. Her family were secular Jews and her father ran a prosperous chemist's business. As a girl, she read voraciously and began writing stories which emphasized heroism, self-mastery, and unconquerable determination, to all of which themes she would return as a mature writer. Her family was on a visit to Britain in 1914 when the First World War began and had a difficult journey back to Russia. When she was 12, the Bolshevik Revolution broke out in Russia. Her father's business was seized by the new Soviet state, and the family, impoverished, fled to the Crimea. After three years of Civil War, they returned to their home city, now renamed Petrograd, in 1921. Rand entered the university at the age of 16 and graduated in history before her 20th birthday. She worked for awhile as a guide at state museums, meanwhile learning all she could about America, whose movies and skyscrapers she found intoxicating.

An invitation from relatives who had emigrated to America before the revolution delighted her. It enabled her to get a passport and leave Russia, to which she swore she would never return. After a cursory visit to her relatives, she hurried on to Hollywood, where she hoped to get a part in a film or else become a screenwriter, and changed her name to Ayn Rand. Being physically short and dark, and having a thick foreign accent, she was unlikely to be singled out for starring roles in the Hollywood of the 1920s. But Rand had an iron will. She soon learned to speak and write English effectively and played in several films as an extra, while bombarding the studio chiefs with scenarios and scripts. They were baffled at the unrealistic settings she proposed and the degree of heroic integrity her characters displayed, but were impressed by her productivity. Within six months, she had landed a job with Cecil B. De Mille as a screenwriter's assistant.

Rand met, and soon married, Frank O'Connor, who was another movie extra, bit-part player, and painter. In subsequent years, she at-

tributed to him many of the heroic qualities she created in her fictional heroes even though, according to their friends, he was a mild, unambitious man with little of his wife's drive or determination. The marriage enabled her to become naturalized as a U.S. citizen in 1931. De Mille's studio went out of business in 1928, but she was able to secure a job with the wardrobe department of RKO Pictures and rose to become head of the department by 1932. Hollywood suffered far less than most American industries during the Great Depression—the movies' escapism attracted the anxious and the unemployed—and Rand rose with the boom that accompanied the new "talkies." She regarded her work behind the scenes as no more than a deplorable necessity, however, and was jubilant in 1932 when for the first time she sold a screenplay, "Red Pawn," to Universal Pictures. It was a tale of heroic self-sacrifice by a woman, oddly enough for one who claimed to despise altruism and selflessness. Rand then had the vexation of seeing the studio change its mind: "Red Pawn" never appeared on the silver screen.

Her first real breakthrough came with a play which was variously entitled *Night of January 16, Penthouse Legend,* and *Woman on Trial,* which ran first in Hollywood and then for seven months on Broadway in New York. It was a courtroom drama, arranged so that at the beginning of each performance members of the cast chose 12 members of the audience to be jurors. They heard the evidence and had to decide whether to convict or acquit the female lead of murdering her lover, whose death could also be seen as a suicide. Rand wrote two endings so that the play would wind up in a way appropriate to whichever verdict the jury chose. She was indignant at how often audience-juries found her heroine guilty when Rand's own intention had been to establish the opposite. Autocratic with her work, she also disliked alterations made for the New York stage and was careful in later productions to have final say on matters relating to the script.

Her later plays were less successful, but after 1935 Rand began to concentrate on novels. Her first, *We, the Living* (1936), was another story of the self-sacrificing Russian woman, giving herself sexually to one man in order to help another whom she truly loves. As one of her biographers, James T. Baker, remarks: "This seems to be the only type of self-sacrifice she ever approved." Critics found the novel pathetically didactic and regretted that Rand's moralizing about individualism and against Communism so often impeded the flow of what was, in itself, a gripping adventure story. The decade of the 1930s witnessed the high point of American intellectuals' enthusiasm for collectivism and socialism, and made an uncongenial environment for Rand's ideals. Sales were slow at first but increased as word of Rand spread among the pro-capitalist minority. Even so the book was not reprinted after the first run of 3,000 had sold out, and it remained almost unobtainable until reissued in 1960 in the wake of her second blockbuster, *Atlas Shrugged*.

In the mid-1930s, Rand set to work on her first magnum opus, *The Fountainhead*, the story of an uncompromising architect, Howard Roark. Roark's trials and tribulations are largely caused by the philistine majority who do not share his pure vision, and by mealy-mouthed bureaucrats and collectivists who lack his singleness of purpose. In the end, through sheer force of will and integrity, the granite-like Roark is able to have his own way and build the monumental skyscrapers of which he has always dreamed. Along the way, he tames the petulant female lead, Dominique Francon, with some rough bedroom antics. Dominique, like most of Rand's female characters, takes a masochistic pleasure in being crushed into submission to the will of a lordly man in what are virtually rape scenes.

Rand, in preparing the novel, worked without pay for a New York architectural company and studied the business assiduously for the sake of making her work as authentic as possible. Many of its pages read convincingly as an account of the building business between the wars, especially when Rand has relaxed her grip on the ideological reins for a moment. She broke off from writing this big book to campaign for Wendell Willkie, the Republican presidential candidate in 1940. She had become a fierce opponent of Franklin Roosevelt's New Deal and the big, pseudo-socialist government which, in her opinion, Roosevelt was creating. After Willkie's defeat, which she attributed to his concessions to the left, Rand got back to work. Her manuscript won the enthusiastic admiration of Archibald Ogden, an editor at Bobbs-Merrill, who read an early fragment of *The Fountainhead* in 1941. His employers were cool at first, but Ogden and Rand together convinced them that it was a sound project. Rand then wrote the last half of the book at high speed in 1942 and it appeared on schedule in May of the next year. Like *We, the Living*, it got poor reviews but gathered a strong following of enthusiasts who spread the news by word of mouth. It had sold 100,000 copies by the end of the Second World War, two years later, and Rand was able to sell the movie rights for $50,000 without losing control over the film script.

She returned to Hollywood and spent the late 1940s there, at the Hal Wallis studio, writing screenplays for six months of every year and working on her own fiction for the other six. She was now highly paid, acquiring expensive tastes, and finding the intellectual climate more congenial than it had been in the 1930s. A wholehearted McCarthyite, she was glad to see America in general, and Hollywood in particular, undertaking an anti-Communist "red-hunt" and was a cooperative witness before the House Committee on un-American Activities and at the trial of the "Hollywood Ten." Despite her passionate anti-Communism, however, she agreed with Marxists that religion was a form of mass deception. Her militant atheism made her unacceptable to leading conservative intellectuals such as William F. Buckley, Jr., even though he shared her pro-capitalist outlook.

Rand supervised Warner Bros.' filming of *The Fountainhead* (1949), starring Gary Cooper as Howard Roark and *Patricia Neal as Dominique Francon. By then, sales of the book were approaching the one-million mark, and although the movie was not an overwhelming box-office success it introduced her work to a wider audience than ever before. She was hard at work on an even more ambitious novel, which finally saw the light of day in 1957 as *Atlas Shrugged*. In it, she imagined what would happen if America's entrepreneurial capitalists decided to go on strike. In her view, the nation would collapse without their ingenuity, dedication, and hard work. The plot describes how, one by one, the industrialists disappear under mysterious circumstances, often in Colorado. Ordinary citizens, left behind in a foundering society, sometimes hear the cryptic question, "Who is John Galt?," and learn that ships carrying foreign aid supplies abroad are being blown up on the high seas by a pirate named Ragnar Danneskjold. The novel's climax is the revelation that Galt is none other than the heroic capitalist mastermind who has led the secession, and that Danneskjold is one of his faithful lieutenants, who understands that foreign aid does far more harm than good. In a radio speech which takes up nearly 100 of the book's 800 pages, Galt broadcasts his philosophy to a mesmerized national audience and dictates the terms on which he will return with the other entrepreneurs to revitalize America. This windy, hectoring speech, which brings the novel's action to an unwelcome standstill, is a full statement of Rand's own philosophy, and she had enough

Ayn
Rand

clout by then to force her editors, who wanted it cut drastically, to leave it almost intact. As in *The Fountainhead*, the subplot witnesses the forceful sexual taming by John Galt, the manliest of men, of a proud woman, Dagny Taggart, who is herself the dynamic head of a railroad corporation.

While she was writing *Atlas Shrugged*, Rand met a Canadian psychology student, another secularized Jew who had undergone a name change, from Nathan Blumenthal to Nathaniel Branden. They became ardent friends and, apparently, lovers, even though Branden was just then wooing and wedding another woman, **Barbara Weidman (Branden)**. Returning from Hollywood to New York where Branden was studying for a doctoral degree in psychology, Rand encouraged him to develop a lecture series based on her novels. In 1958, he abandoned psychotherapy and founded the Nathaniel Branden Institute (NBI), where Rand enthusiasts could hear his lectures and attend question-and-answer sessions with the author herself. "She radiates intelligence" wrote one student, adding later that "this short, dumpy, ugly old woman with a dense Russian accent was intellectually exciting, but personally unimpressive." Rand wrote no more fiction after *Atlas Shrugged*, turning instead to treatises. Among her philosophical works, published in the last 20 years of her long life, were *For the New Intellectual* (1961), *The Virtue of Selfishness* (1964), and *Capitalism: The Unknown Ideal* (1966).

There was no one more radical than she in championing the autonomy and supremacy of the individual through the rhetoric of her novels. Philosophically she was a wild and freaky anarchist, an iconoclast, a radical individualist. She created fictional heroes who challenged the authority of Corporate America, who fought the conformity of the American nation-state . . . and brought it down with a resounding crash.

—Jerome Tuccille

The NBI, preaching the Randian philosophy of "Objectivism" in the heady atmosphere of the 1960s, soon developed an eager following of students in search of strong emotional commitments. They accepted from Rand that cigarette-smoking was life affirming, some "true believers" even imitated her taste in brooches and badges in the shape of dollar signs, and shared her craze for black billowing capes, tango dancing, and other seemingly eccentric rather than "objective" tastes. One such convert, Jerome Tuccille, later wrote a humorous memoir about it, in which he noted: "Objectivism can be a wonderfully appealing religion substitute for disaffiliated Jews and Catholics from the middle class who turn to it with a mania formerly reserved for their ancestral religion." It was even more exacting than orthodox religion, he added: "To be in disagreement with the ideas of Ayn Rand was to be, by definition, irrational and immoral. There was no allowable deviation." Rand was sufficiently respected to get lecture invitations at major universities, including Harvard, Columbia, and Johns Hopkins, and won the admiration of several men and women who went on to play prominent roles in national affairs, notably Alan Greenspan, who served as an economic advisor to presidents Ford and Reagan and became chair of the Federal Reserve Board in 1987. But an air of crankishness also attached to Rand, and she was often listed as one of America's colorful but zany counter-culture theorists, especially after the appearance of a long *Playboy* interview in 1964. Theorists of radical libertarianism, such as the economist Murray Rothbard, treated her with more suspicion than enthusiasm.

Success, recognition, and the prosperity of the Branden Institute appear to have gone to Rand's head, and in 1968 the Objectivists split, with Branden, her right-hand man, being expelled amid rumors of sexual misconduct, exploitation of Rand's fiction and philosophy, and clashing egos. According to Barbara Branden, who wrote a graphic biography of the leader, *The Passion of Ayn Rand*, the schism was due to Nathaniel Branden's declaration to Rand that he refused to have sex with her anymore, and her discovery that he had taken another lover. Whatever the rights and wrongs of the episode, which had all the markings of a feud in a fundamentalist church or a Marxist sect, Branden stormed out, leaving Leonard Peikoff, another stalwart supporter, as the chief official exponent of Rand's views. Objectivism lost many of its supporters in the calmer air of the 1970s, but the *Ayn Rand Letter* kept the faithful up to date with her thoughts and activities until the end of 1975, when severe illness forced her to abandon it. She died in New York in 1982, at the age of 77.

SOURCES AND SUGGESTED READING:

Baker, James T. *Ayn Rand*. Boston, MA: Twayne, 1987.

Branden, Barbara. *The Passion of Ayn Rand*. Garden City, NY: Doubleday, 1986.

Harriman, David, ed. *Journals of Ayn Rand*. NY: Dutton, 1997.

Merrill, Ronald E. *The Ideas of Ayn Rand*. La Salle, IL: Open Court, 1991.

Rand, Ayn. *Atlas Shrugged*. NY: Random House, 1957.

———. *For the New Intellectual*. NY: Random House, 1961.

———. *The Fountainhead*. NY: Bobbs-Merrill, 1943.

Tuccille, Jerome. *It Usually Begins With Ayn Rand: A Libertarian Odyssey*. NY: Stein and Day, 1971.

Uhl, Douglas Den, and Douglas Rasmussen. *The Philosophic Thought of Ayn Rand*. Urbana, IL: University of Illinois Press, 1984.

RELATED MEDIA:

The Fountainhead, adaptation by Ayn Rand from her novel, starring Gary Cooper and Patricia Neal, Warner Bros., 1949.

The Passion of Ayn Rand, starring **Helen Mirren, Julie Delpy,** Eric Stoltz, and Peter Fonda, produced by Showtime, 1998.

Patrick Allitt,
Professor of History,
Emory University, Atlanta, Georgia

Rand, Ellen (1875–1941)

American portrait painter. Name variations: Bay Rand. Born Ellen Gertrude Emmet on March 4, 1875, in San Francisco, California; died on December 18, 1941, in New York City; daughter of Christopher Temple Emmet (a lawyer) and Ellen James (Temple) Emmet; educated by tutors and studied art under Dennis Bunker, at the Art Students League, 1889–93, and with sculptor Frederick MacMonnies; married William Blanchard Rand (a gentleman farmer and legislator), on May 6, 1911; children: Christopher Temple Emmet (b. 1912); William Blanchard, Jr. (b. 1913); John Alsop (b. 1914).

Ellen Rand, who was known as "Bay" to her famous cousin Henry James and the rest of her family, was born on March 4, 1875, in San Francisco, California. Her father Christopher Temple Emmet had joined the gold rush in 1849, and though he held a medical degree he subsequently became a lawyer. Her mother **Ellen James Temple Emmet** was related to the celebrated James family (William, Henry and *Alice James), and several of Ellen's relatives were painters, including her first cousins **Rosina Emmet Sherwood** and **Lydia Field Emmet**. Rand grew up in San Francisco and San Rafael, California, moving to the New York City area after her father's death around 1884, and from an early age showed marked skill at drawing and sketching. She was educated by tutors, but art was always her primary interest. She studied under Dennis Bunker in Boston and with William Merritt Chase from 1889 to 1893 at the Art Students League in New York City; by the end of that period, she was already contributing fashion sketches to *Vogue* magazine. While traveling abroad with her family when she was 21, she met famous portrait painter John Singer Sargent in London and sculptor Frederick MacMonnies in Paris. She remained in Paris as a painting student of MacMonnies' for three years. In 1900, Rand returned to New York City and set up a studio in Washington Square South, where *Cecilia Beaux was an upstairs neighbor. At a time when solo shows were unusual, Rand had one in 1902 at the Durand-Ruel Galleries on Fifth Avenue. In 1906, she had a one-woman exhibition of 90 paintings at Copley Hall in Boston, where the only previous solo shows had been dedicated to Sargent, Monet and Whistler.

In 1911, at the age of 36, Ellen married William Blanchard Rand, a state legislator and farmer who lived in Salisbury, Connecticut. The couple had three sons over the next three years,

and she divided her time between the farm, where the family spent summers hunting and horseback riding, and New York City, where she lived with the children the remainder of the year and worked on commissioned portraits. Although most of her work was done for a wealthy clientele, including public officials, heads of industry, society women and admired intellectuals, she was more than simply a society portraitist. The Metropolitan Museum of Art in New York holds her portraits of Augustus Saint-Gaudens and Benjamin Altman, and those she painted of Elihu Root and Franklin Delano Roosevelt have become their official portraits. Her artwork brought much recognition, and she won many awards, including a gold medal at the 1915 Panama-Pacific Exposition and the Beck Gold Medal from the Pennsylvania Academy of the Fine Arts in 1922. She was also elected an Associate of the National Academy of Design in 1926 and an Academician in 1934.

Rand's family finances were devastated by the stock-market crash in 1929, and thereafter she devoted herself to seeing her sons through college by doing as many commissions as possible. Her fees rose to the level of $5,000 per painting, and during the Depression years she painted up to 12 to 15 portraits a year, allowing her to earn what was then a prodigious income. It required an equally prodigious amount of work, however, and Rand died of a heart attack on December 18, 1941. She was buried at the Protestant Cemetery in Salisbury, Connecticut.

SOURCES:

James, Edward T., ed. *Notable American Women, 1607–1950*. Cambridge, MA: The Belknap Press of Harvard University, 1971.
Rubinstein, Charlotte Streifer. *American Women Artists*. Boston, MA: G.K. Hall, 1982.

Jo Anne Meginnes,
freelance writer, Brookfield, Vermont

Rand, Gertrude (1886–1970)

American researcher in the field of physiological optics. Name variations: Marie Gertrude Rand; Gertrude Ferree. Born Marie Gertrude Rand in Brooklyn, New York, on October 29, 1886; died in Stony Brook, Long Island, New York, on June 30, 1970; daughter of Lyman Fiske Rand (president of a manufacturing company) and Mary Catherine (Moench) Rand; graduated from Girls High School in Brooklyn in 1904; Cornell University, A.B., 1908; Bryn Mawr, A.M., Ph.D., 1911; post-doctoral fellow (1911–12) and Sarah Berliner Research Fellow (1912–13), Bryn Mawr; married Clarence Ferree, on December 28, 1918 (died 1942).

Became the first woman fellow of the Illuminating Engineering Society of North America (1952); was the first woman to win the Edgar D. Tillyer Medal of the Optical Society of America (1959); received gold medal from Illuminating Engineering Society of North America (1963).

Gertrude Rand was born into a large family on October 29, 1886, in Brooklyn, New York. She graduated from Girls High School in Brooklyn in 1904 and continued her extensive education at Cornell University in Ithaca, New York, where she received an A.B. degree in experimental psychology in 1908. Going on to Bryn Mawr College in Bryn Mawr, Pennsylvania, she earned both an A.M. and a Ph.D. in psychology in 1911. She remained at Bryn Mawr, first as a postdoctoral fellow, then as a Sarah Berliner Research Fellow, and from 1913 to 1927 as an associate in experimental psychology. In 1918, she married Clarence Ferree, a professor at the college who had overseen her doctoral dissertation. They collaborated professionally, researching the effects of illumination on color perception. Other research they conducted eventually led to the development of the Ferree-Rand perimeter, a tool for diagnosing vision problems which maps the perceptual abilities of the retina.

In 1928, Rand and Ferree moved to the Wilmer Ophthalmological Institute of the Johns Hopkins University School of Medicine. Rand taught there as an associate professor of research ophthalmology and then of physiological optics, and in 1935 became associate director of the Research Laboratory of Physiological Optics in Baltimore. She and her husband also consulted with industries and government agencies. Together they developed glare-control lighting for public places, most prominently the Holland Tunnel in New York City and the Johns Hopkins University Hospital. They also developed visual health and acuity standards for airplane pilots and ship lookouts during World War II, and patented a number of lighting instruments and devices.

After Ferree died in 1942, Rand moved to New York City, where she worked as a research associate at the Knapp Foundation of the Columbia University College of Physicians and Surgeons. There she concentrated her efforts on the detection and measurement of color blindness. In 1952, she was elected a fellow of the Illuminating Engineering Society, making her the first woman so honored. During the 1950s, she was part of a team that developed special plates, called Hardy-Rand-Rittler plates, for use in testing color vision. Rather than simply verifying defective color vision, these plates allowed ophthalmologists and psychologists to pinpoint the type and severity of defect in an individual's color vision.

Rand retired in 1957. Two years later, she became the first woman to win the Edgar D. Tillyer Medal from the Optical Society of America for outstanding research in vision, and in 1963 she was awarded a gold medal from the Illuminating Engineering Society. She died in Stony Brook, Long Island, on June 30, 1970, at the age of 83.

SOURCES:
Read, Phyllis J., and Bernard L. Witlieb. *The Book of Women's Firsts.* NY: Random House, 1992.
Sicherman, Barbara, and Carol Hurd Green, eds. *Notable American Women: The Modern Period.* Cambridge, MA: The Belknap Press of Harvard University, 1980.

Jo Anne Meginnes,
freelance writer, Brookfield, Vermont

Rand, Marie Gertrude (1886–1970).

See Rand, Gertrude.

Rand, Mary (1940—)

British athlete. Name variations: Mary Toomey. Born Mary Rand on February 10, 1940, in Wells, Somerset, England; married Bill Toomey (an American decathlon champion); children: Alison Toomey.

Broke the British national record in the pentathlon with 4,046 points (1957); won the silver medal (1958) and the gold medal (1966), both in the long jump in the Commonwealth Games; won the bronze medal in the long jump in the European championships (1962); shared the world record in the 4x100 relay (1963); won the Olympic gold medal in the long jump, the silver in the pentathlon, and a team bronze in the 400-meter relay (1964).

When asked what she would prefer, an Olympic gold medal or a world record, Mary Rand said she favored the record because she wanted to be the best in the world, "just for a moment." Fortunately, her gold medal and her world record happened simultaneously, in the 1964 Tokyo Olympics. Rand won Britain's first gold medal in women's track and field when she placed first in the long jump with a world record of 22'2¼", six inches higher than *Irena Szewinska of Poland. Rand also took a silver in the pentathlon behind the Soviet Union's Irina Press. Though Rand scored more points than Press in three of the five events, Press' shot put totaled 384 points.

Rand, whose specialties were the long jump, the hurdles, and the pentathlon, felt she came alive on a wet track in Russia long ago in 1959; she was there as second-string hurdler behind her teammate **Carol Quinton**. When Quinton fell after the first or second hurdle, 19-year-old Rand knew instinctively she had to carry the torch. "I'd been in Carol's shadow without being aware of it," said Rand. "When Carol fell, I felt I had to win. And I did. . . . I've never forgotten it."

Rand, Sally (1904–1979)

American dancer and burlesque star. Born Helen Gould Beck on January 2, 1904, in Elkton, Hickory County, Missouri; died on August 31, 1979, in Glendora, California; married and divorced several times; children: one son.

Selected filmography: *The Texas Bearcat (1925); The Road to Yesterday (1925); Bachelor Brides (1926); Gigolo (1926); Man Bait (1926); The Night of Love (1927); Getting Gertie's Garter (1927); The King of Kings (1927); His Dog (1927); Galloping Fury (1927); Heroes in Blue (1927); Crashing Through (1928); A Girl in Every Port (1928); Black Feather (1928); Gold Widows (1928); Bolero (1934).*

The story is told that famous exotic dancer Sally Rand came up with her notorious fan dance during the Depression, when she had so little money to purchase costumes that she improvised a routine using only a couple of ostrich-feather fans. The shapely blonde performer later professed that the difference between mediocrity and stardom was simply "merchandising."

Born in 1904 in Hickory County, Missouri, the daughter of a postal worker, Sally Rand left home at age 13 and took a job in a nightclub in Kansas City. During her early years, she performed in clubs, with carnivals, and even with the Ringling Brothers Circus, before making her way to Hollywood. Changing her name from Helen Gould Beck to Sally Rand, she appeared in a number of silent movies during the 1920s, notably Cecil B. De Mille's classic *King of Kings* (1927), but she was forced out with the advent of sound. After initially performing her fan dance in a speakeasy in Chicago, Rand made her way to the Chicago World's Fair (Century of Progress, 1933–34), riding a white horse from downtown to the fairgrounds à la Lady *Godiva. The publicity stunt earned her a concession on the main midway, and although she was arrested on several occasions during her visit, she was later credited with making the fair a financial success.

After Chicago, Rand organized a dance troupe and toured the United States. She ap-

peared at the San Diego World's Fair in 1936 and at the San Francisco Exposition in 1939, then found steady employment as the headliner at various burlesque houses and clubs across the country. Over the years, her act remained pretty much the same. To the strains of Debussy's *Clair de Lune*, she danced her way across the stage, clad only in two fans, which she cleverly manipulated in such a way that the audiences only caught brief glimpses of her anatomy. "No one knew if she was really naked," writes John J. DuPont in an article on the dancer for *American Heritage* (April 1992), "and her appeal lay largely in the eternal hope that by chance or design she would drop one of her fans." DuPont also points out that Rand's questionable profession made her the subject of numerous off-color stories and jokes. "She became something of a byword for the 1930s definition of *naughty*," he writes.

Rand continued to perform for 40 years, and in 1965 replaced **Ann Corio** as the emcee for the Broadway revue *This Was Burlesque*. Her personal life included several marriages and one son. By the 1960s, the dancer had made several million dollars, which she wisely invested in real estate, including a ranch on which she lived with her mother and son. At the time, she said that al-

Sally Rand

though she no longer needed the money, she still looked forward to work because of the travel and the people she met. Rand died in 1979.

SOURCES:

DuPont, John J. "Bottle Blonde," in *American Heritage*. April 1992, pp. 26–27.
Lamparski, Richard. *Whatever Became of . . . ?* NY: Crown, 1967.
McHenry, Robert, ed. *Famous American Women*. NY: Dover, 1983.

Barbara Morgan,
Melrose, Massachusetts

Randall, Claire (1919—)

First woman secretary of the National Council of the Churches of Christ. Born in Dallas, Texas, on October 15, 1919; Scarritt College for Christian Workers, Nashville, Tennessee, B.A., 1950.

Born in 1919, Claire Randall graduated from Scarritt College for Christian Workers in Nashville, Tennessee, in 1950. She later served as director of the Christian World Mission and, from 1962 to 1973, as program director and associate director of Church Women United. In 1974, she became secretary of the National Council of the Churches of Christ (an organization of 30 Protestant and Eastern Orthodox denominations), making her the first woman in America to hold such a high-ranking religious post. As secretary, she worked toward ecumenism and better ties between the council and the Roman Catholic Church. She also served on the National Commission on International Women's Year from 1975 to 1977, and on the Martin Luther King, Jr., Federal Holiday Commission in 1985. In 1988, she was named national president of Church Women United, a post which she held until her retirement in 1992.

Randall received a number of honorary degrees and awards, including D.D. degrees from Yale University and Berkeley Seminary in Berkeley, California, in 1974, and an L.H.D. degree from Austin College in Sherman, Texas, in 1982. She received the Heritage Society's Woman of the Year in Reli-

Martha Jefferson Randolph

gion Award in 1977, and in 1984 was awarded the Order of St. Vladimir by the Russian Orthodox Church.

SOURCES:

Read, Phyllis J., and Bernard L. Witlieb. *The Book of Women's Firsts.* NY: Random House, 1992.

Jo Anne Meginnes,
freelance writer, Brookfield, Vermont

Randolph, Agnes (1312–1369).

See Dunbar, Agnes.

Randolph, Martha Jefferson (1775–1836)

*American hostess and close companion of her father Thomas Jefferson. Name variations: Patsy Randolph. Born at Monticello, Albemarle County, Virginia, on September 27, 1775; died on October 10, 1836, and was buried in the graveyard at Monticello; eldest daughter of Thomas Jefferson (president of the United States, 1801–09) and Martha (Wayles) Jefferson (1748–1782); married her cousin Thomas Mann Randolph, Jr. (a congressional representative and governor of Virginia), on February 23, 1790; children: twelve, including **Anne Carey Randolph** (b. 1791); Thomas Jefferson Randolph (b. 1792); Ellen (1794– 1795); **Ellen Wayles Randolph Coolidge** (b. 1796, who married Joseph Coolidge, Jr.); **Cornelia Jefferson Randolph** (b. 1799); **Virginia Jefferson Randolph** (b. 1801); **Mary Jefferson Randolph** (b. 1803); James Madison Randolph (b. 1806); Benjamin Franklin Randolph (b. 1808); Meriwether Lewis Randolph (b. 1810); **Septimia Anne Randolph** (b. 1814); George Wythe Randolph (b. 1818).*

Martha Jefferson Randolph was born at Monticello in 1775, the eldest daughter of Thomas Jefferson, future president of the United States, and *Martha Jefferson, a half-niece of *Sally Hemings. A tall redhead with freckles, Martha, known as Patsy, not only resembled her father, but was apparently the most devoted to him of all the six Jefferson children. Only seven when her mother died, she accompanied her father to Philadelphia, where he attended the Continental Congress, and then sojourned with him on a five-year diplomatic mission to Paris, beginning in 1784. Thomas took a great interest in Martha's education, sending her to a series of small private schools in Philadelphia, and to the exclusive Abbaye Royale de Panthémont in Paris, where she studied a traditional feminine curriculum emphasizing the arts. While at school, Martha spent weekends with her father at the Hôtel de Longeac, and during their long separations, she corresponded with him regularly. "His letters from that period now seem excessively didactic and moralistic," writes Dumas Malone in *Notable American Women*, "but she took admonitions with good grace and was in all respects a dutiful daughter. The bond between them grew stronger with the passing years."

On February 23, 1790, only a few weeks following the Jeffersons' return to Virginia, Martha married her cousin Thomas Mann Randolph in a ceremony at Monticello. Young Thomas, who went on to serve as a U.S. congressional representative and the governor of Virginia, was alienated from his own father and became increasingly dependent on his father-in-law, who helped him acquire Edgehill, an estate a few miles from Monticello. Over the course of her marriage, Martha gave birth to 12 children, one of whom did not survive infancy. Although Martha and the children spent a good deal of time with Jefferson when he was at Monticello, she visited her father only twice during his presidency (1801–09): once around 1802 with her sister ❧➤ **Maria Jefferson Eppes**, and a second time between 1805–06, during which she gave birth to her eighth child.

Martha's husband Thomas was said to be of superior intelligence, but he was erratic and a poor manager of money. The family's financial situation continued to deteriorate throughout the marriage, and Thomas Jefferson assumed responsibility for the education of his grandchildren. One of them, his namesake Thomas Jefferson Randolph (b. 1792), took over the management of Jefferson's financial affairs during the last decade of his life. After her father left the White House in 1809, Martha spent most of her time with him at Monticello.

Following Thomas Jefferson's death in 1826 and the death of her husband in 1828, Martha's financial situation grew more acute. Eventually, she was awarded $10,000 from the legislature of South Carolina, which was the only thing that saved her from impoverishment. She lived out her last years with her daughters in Boston and Washington, D.C., and with her son Thomas Jefferson Randolph, who had taken over possession of Edgehill some years earlier. She died of apoplexy on October 10, 1836, and was buried in the graveyard at Monticello.

SOURCES:

James, Edward T., ed. *Notable American Women*. Cambridge, MA: The Belknap Press of Harvard University Press, 1974.

Paletta, Lu Ann. *The World Almanac of First Ladies*. NY: World Almanac, 1990.

Barbara Morgan,
Melrose, Massachusetts

Randolph, Patsy (1775–1836).

See Randolph, Martha Jefferson.

Randolph, Virginia (1874–1958)

African-American educator and social worker. Name variations: Virginia E. Randolph. Born Virginia Estelle Randolph in Richmond, Virginia, on June 6, 1874 (some sources erroneously cite 1870); died on March 16, 1958; daughter of former slaves Nelson and Sarah Elizabeth Randolph; educated at the Bacon School and the City Normal School in Richmond, Virginia; never married; no children.

The Virginia Randolph Education Centers and the Virginia Randolph Museum in Glen Allen, Virginia, stand as testimony to a remarkably dedicated and innovative educator and social worker who spent nearly 60 years trying to improve the lives of both African-American children and their parents in poverty-stricken Henrico County, Virginia. She was a pioneer of vocational education whose teaching methods were widely adopted, both in America and internationally. Randolph was born in 1874 in Richmond, Virginia, in the early years of Reconstruction, one of four children of Nelson and **Sarah Elizabeth Randolph**, who were both former slaves. After her father died in her early childhood, her mother struggled to provide an income for the family. Even while Sarah Randolph worked by day as a housekeeper and by night sewing and washing and ironing clothes, she found time to teach her daughter sewing, knitting, and crocheting. Virginia would later use these practical skills as educational methods in schools. Despite her family's poverty and the fact that she began working at age eight, Virginia managed to receive an education, attending the Bacon and the City Normal schools in Richmond.

Randolph began teaching school at age 16, in Goochland County. In 1892, she was transferred to the Mountain Road School in Henrico County. Segregated education was the norm (it would become state law three years later), and in those years the state of Virginia spent only a little over $1 per pupil per year in black schools, compared to $3 and change per pupil in white schools. The one-room Mountain Road School and its surroundings were in extremely poor condition when Randolph first arrived, but through determination and innovation she improved the grounds and the building. She organized a Willing Workers Club to raise money and supplies for the school (and sometimes solicited cast-off materials from white schools), a Patrons' Improvement

❧
Eppes, Maria Jefferson. See Jefferson, Martha for sidebar.

League, a Sunday School, a Patrons' Day intended to involve parents in their children's education, and a Better Homes campaign to improve the lives and homes of the poverty-stricken families of her students. Randolph stressed not only academics but practical skills including sewing, weaving, woodworking and gardening. This emphasis on vocational training and "learning by doing" was not always appreciated by parents, who once tried to have her removed, but she was resolute in promoting both industrial and academic training. She initiated the first Arbor Day celebration in the state in 1908, when she and her students planted 12 sycamore trees (named for the 12 disciples of Jesus) outside the school; a number of the original trees still stand, and have been named "Notable Trees" of Virginia.

Randolph's innovations had not gone unnoticed by Jackson Davis, superintendent of schools for Henrico County. "Here was a teacher," he once said, "who thought of her work in terms of the welfare of a whole community, and of the school as an agency to help people to live better, to do their work with more skill and intelligence, and to do it in the spirit of neighborliness." Also in 1908, he received funding to name her the first "Jeanes Teacher," charged with spreading her educational methods through black schools in the state. Funded by a $1 million donation from wealthy Quaker philanthropist *Anna Thomas Jeanes, a foundation called the Negro Rural School Fund had been organized the previous year to provide educational assistance to poor black schools. Randolph's methods of improving both education and community became the model for all other Jeanes Teachers, who trained teachers throughout counties and states. The program was employed throughout every state in the South and was later used overseas as well, becoming enormously successful in improving vocational education and community life; while the Fund merged with several other similar programs in the late 1930s to become the Southern Education Foundation, Jeanes Teachers continued to assist black schoolchildren and their communities through 1968. (It should be pointed out that the Negro Rural School Fund's original board of trustees, which included Booker T. Washington, George Foster Peabody, and Hollis S. Frissell, deliberately emphasized industrial education as a means of circumventing white suspicion that educating blacks would lead to the horrifying precedent of their entering traditionally white-dominated professions.)

As a Jeanes Teacher, Randolph oversaw 23 rural schools, visiting them regularly to plan improvements and teaching methods. She also or-ganized community programs tailored to the needs of individual communities. Her detailed "Henrico Plan," a record of the changes instituted in these schools, became a blueprint for school systems throughout the South. The Virginia Randolph Training School, the first high school for black students in Henrico County, was built in 1915, beside the Mountain Road School. As its fame grew over the years, Randolph often took into her home students who lived too far away to commute, and later raised funds to build dormitories. After a fire in 1929, the school was rebuilt and named the Virginia Randolph High School, with an enrollment of over 200 students.

Randolph continued working through the 1940s, and died in 1958. The Virginia Randolph High School is now known as the Virginia Randolph Education Centers, the campus of which includes both Randolph's gravesite and a museum dedicated to her life and achievements. In 1976, the museum was designated a National Historic Landmark and a Virginia Historic Landmark. Randolph was inducted into the Virginia Women's Hall of Fame in 1993.

SOURCES AND SUGGESTED READING:

Bowie, Walter Russell. *Women of Light*. NY: Harper & Row, 1963.

Hine, Darlene Clark, ed. *Black Women in America*. Brooklyn, NY: Carlson, 1993.

Jones, Lance G.E. *The Jeanes Teacher in the United States, 1908–1933*. Chapel Hill, NC: University of North Carolina Press, 1937.

Smith, Jessie Carney, ed. *Notable Black American Women*. Detroit, MI: Gale Research, 1992.

COLLECTIONS:

The Virginia Randolph Museum in Glen Allen, Virginia, includes personal memorabilia and photographs of Randolph.

Jo Anne Meginnes,
freelance writer, Brookfield, Vermont

Rangoni, Alda.

See Este, Alda d'.

Rani of Gondwana.

See Durgawati (d. 1564).

Rani of Gurrah.

See Durgawati (d. 1564).

Rani of Jaipur.

See Gayatra Devi (b. 1919).

Rani of Jhansi.

See Lakshmibai (c. 1835–1858).

Rankin, Annabelle (1908–1986)

Australian politician and diplomat who achieved a number of firsts: first woman whip in the British Com-

monwealth; first Australian woman to hold a federal ministerial portfolio; and first Australian woman to hold ambassadorial rank. Born Annabelle Jane Mary Rankin in Brisbane, Queensland, Australia, on July 28, 1908; died on August 30, 1986; daughter of Annabelle (Davidson) Rankin and Colin Dunlop Wilson Rankin (a cane grower and member of the Queensland Legislative Assembly); attended state schools at Childers and Howard and the Glennie Memorial School, Toowoomba, Queensland; never married.

Created a Dame of the British Empire (1957).

Although she was by no means an advocate of women's liberation in the abstract, indeed often speaking out in favor of the primacy of "the homemaker and the mother," by making a personal choice not to marry so as to devote her full energies to a successful career in politics, Annabelle Rankin was able to achieve a number of important victories for all Australian women. Australian attitudes toward women in public life are, like those of many other nations, a complex mixture of conservative and progressive tendencies. The country was founded as a penal colony in the last decades of the 18th century, and as late as the 1830s most of Australia's European women were either convicts or former convicts. The first six free women settlers arrived in 1793, with only 576 having settled there by 1831. Given the fact that 85% of the convicts, and most of the free settlers too, were male, Australia's population in its early years was heavily male. The 1828 European-born population of 54,700 was only about one-quarter female, and even by 1841, with the total white population at 206,700, only about a third of it was female. The shortage of women served to raise their level of marriage, so that in 1851 77% of New South Wales women over 20 were married. The comparable situation in Great Britain was only 57%. By 1861, the imbalance had changed to 42% of the total population being female, and as the frontier disappeared proportion between the sexes became more balanced, the number of males in 1901 being about 110 to every 100 females.

With the passage of time, Australian women began to achieve a growing number of legal rights. Following the British law of 1870, all of the separate colonies comprising the Australian continent passed laws recognizing a married woman's right to own property separately from her husband, starting with Victoria in 1870, and ending with Queensland and Western Australia in 1890 and 1892, respectively. In public affairs, breakthroughs began in 1894, when South Australia granted its European women the right to vote (Aboriginal women—and men—did not receive the franchise on a national basis until 1962). In 1908, Victoria became the last Australian state to give women the right to vote. Women's right to sit in a legislature was a different matter, with South Australia being the first to grant it in 1895, and Victoria the last, in 1923. Because the vast majority of women tended to vote the same way as their husbands or families, the women's vote had little impact on the political landscape, although there were some exceptions, particularly the defeat of two referendums on conscription during World War I, which many observers attributed to the "women's vote." At least through the 1960s, Australian women on balance tended to vote more for the conservative than for liberal political parties.

Although Australia had been the first country in the world to give women both the right to vote and the right to stand for Parliament with the passage of the 1902 Commonwealth Franchise Act, it would be an astonishing 41 more years before a woman was elected to the nation's federal Parliament. Why? As in most countries before World War II, it was simply not customary or acceptable for women to work outside the home. Those who did so were single women who gave up their jobs when they married, or women forced by financial hardship to provide for their families. Political life before the early 1940s reflected these social realities, and generally women who ran as candidates did so as independents or on the tickets of minor parties. None of the major Australian political parties endorsed a woman candidate for the Senate before World War II. In the states, there were a few exceptions. In Western Australia, which had granted women the right to vote in 1899 and the right to sit in its legislature only in 1920, *Edith Cowan was elected in 1921. In 1929, Irene Longman became a member of the Queensland Parliament. In a 1953 radio interview, Longman noted: "We talk loudly and proudly of our democracy, but there is no true democracy where only one sex is directly represented in the Government of the country."

World War II radically transformed Australia, not only threatening it with a potential Japanese invasion, but also bringing about an acceleration of social and political changes begun decades earlier. In 1943, two women were elected to the federal Parliament: *Enid Lyons of Tasmania (United Australia Party) was elected to the House of Representatives, and Dorothy Tangney of Western Australia (Australian Labor Party) won a Senate seat. Another sign of progress for women took place in 1947, when **Florence Cardell-Oliver** became a cabinet minister in the Western Australia state Parliament.

In 1946, Liberal Party member Annabelle Rankin was elected to the Senate representing Queensland. During her long tenure, which lasted until 1971, Rankin was concerned with a wide range of issues, particularly those connected with housing, health, and communications. Her participation in parliamentary committees included the Senate Standing Committee on Regulations and Ordinances. Born in Brisbane, Australia, on July 28, 1908, Annabelle Rankin was the daughter of **Annabelle Davidson Rankin** and Colin Dunlop Wilson Rankin, a cane grower and member of the Queensland Legislative Assembly. She was educated at state schools at Childers and Howard and the Glennie Memorial School in Toowoomba, Queensland. After she traveled overseas during 1936–37, she worked as a clerk in Brisbane upon her return to Australia. When World War II began, she started her public career and served as YWCA assistant commissioner in charge of welfare work for women's services. After her discharge, she became the state organizer for the Junior Red Cross in 1946. That same year she was elected to the Senate as a Liberal-Country Party representative.

From 1947 to 1949, Rankin served as Opposition Whip in the Senate—the first woman to hold such a position in the British Commonwealth. She was also elected vice president of the Queensland Liberal Party in 1949. In 1951, with a change in government favoring her party, Rankin advanced to the office of Government Whip, a post she would hold until 1966. Her service in Parliament showed her to be sensitive to the needs of women as well as the aged and the young. In recognition of her services to Australia, Rankin was created a Dame of the British Empire (DBE) in 1957. Even more important for not only Rankin but the progress of Australian women was her appointment in January 1966 as Minister of Housing in the administration of Harold Holt; she served in that post until March 1971. "I think the women's vote shows itself on anything that affects general living," said Rankin in July 1969. "After all everything that happens in Parliament affects women in some way or other. I always say 'legislation goes into your home.'" After retiring from the Senate in 1971, Rankin was appointed High Commissioner (ambassador) to New Zealand, thus becoming the first Australian woman named to a top-level diplomatic post. She retired from this position in 1974. In the 1984 redistribution of federal seats, one of the new Queensland seats was renamed Rankin in honor of her many services to her nation.

Dame Annabelle Rankin remained an influential figure until her death on August 30, 1986. That same year, **Joan Child** of the Australian Labor Party became the first woman to be Speaker of the House of Representatives. In 1996, another barrier fell when **Margaret Reid** became the first woman to be elected president of the Australian Senate. In September 1999, there were 22 women out of a total number of 76 members of the Australian Senate.

SOURCES:

Browne, Waveney. *A Woman of Distinction: The Honourable Dame Annabelle Rankin D.B.E.* Brisbane: Boolarong, 1981.

Crystal, David, ed. *The Cambridge Biographical Dictionary.* 2nd ed. Cambridge, UK: Cambridge University Press, 1998.

Docherty, J.C. *Historical Dictionary of Australia.* 2nd ed. Lanham, MD: Scarecrow Press, 1999.

Hidden Women: Locating Information on Significant Australian Women. Carlton, Victoria: Melbourne College of Advanced Education, 1986.

Sawer, Marian, and Marian Simms. *A Woman's Place: Women and Politics in Australia.* 2nd ed. St. Leonards, NSW: Allen & Unwin, 1993.

John Haag,
Associate Professor of History,
University of Georgia, Athens, Georgia

Rankin, Jeannette (1880–1973)

American suffragist and pacifist who was the first woman to be elected to the U.S. House of Representatives. Born Jeannette Pickering on June 11, 1880, at Grant Creek Ranch, near Missoula, Montana Territory; died in Carmel, California, on May 18, 1973, of a heart attack; daughter of Olive Pickering Rankin (a schoolteacher and homemaker) and John Rankin (a rancher and building contractor); University of Montana, B.Sc. in biology, 1902; enrolled in New York School of Philanthropy, 1908; also attended University of Washington; never married; no children.

Joined state of Washington's campaign for women's suffrage (1910); spoke before Montana state legislature on behalf of woman suffrage (1911); became field secretary for National American Woman Suffrage Association (1913); ran a successful campaign for U.S. House of Representatives (1916); voted against declaration of war (1917); appointed delegate to Second International Congress of Women (1919); became field secretary, National Consumers' League (1920); became field secretary, Women's International League for Peace and Freedom (1925); founded Georgia Peace Society (1928); elected to second term in the U.S. House of Representatives (1940); voted once

more against U.S. involvement in a world war (1941);
Jeannette Rankin Brigade organized (1967).

On December 7, 1941, the Japanese bombed Pearl Harbor, an event that caused the Congress of the United States to vote for a declaration of war for the second time in less than 25 years. The debate over the declaration of war was brief, lasting only 40 minutes. The only person to vote against U.S. involvement was Jeannette Pickering Rankin, representative from Montana. But Jeannette Rankin was traveling a road she had traveled before. In 1917, when Congress had debated American entry into World War I, she had voted against that as well. In both cases, her position cost her a seat in Congress. Rankin spent a lifetime speaking her mind, even if her opinions were unpopular, and accepting the consequences.

Jeannette Rankin was a child of the American frontier. She was born to **Olive Pickering Rankin** and John Rankin on June 11, 1880, almost a decade before Montana was admitted to statehood. Despite her birth in a remote Western community, her early years showed no sign of deprivation. She was the oldest of seven; six lived to adulthood. As the child of relatively well-to-do parents, she spent her summers on the family's cattle ranch, and the winters in their home in Missoula. It was one of the finest homes in Missoula, the first to be equipped with hot- and cold-running water, central heating, and a bathtub.

It was the ranch, however, that most interested Rankin. There, she was allowed to exercise a great deal of ingenuity and initiative, traits that her father hoped to encourage. Jeannette was the leader among the children in the family, as well as their caretaker. She also pitched in around the ranch, occasionally acting as veterinarian when none was available. She was known to have stitched a horse's wounded shoulder and amputated the foot of a badly injured dog. On a more traditional note, she also used her time as a child to become an expert seamstress, an occupation she would briefly rely upon as an adult.

Education was not Rankin's first love. As a child, she tended to find school boring, and far less useful than time spent on the family's ranch. She did not do well in school, and often felt inferior to her classmates. Nevertheless, she enrolled at the University of Montana. Her undergraduate education evidently did not form the inspiration for her later accomplishments. She earned a B.Sc. in biology, writing her senior essay about snails. Nurses' training seemed to be a possibility after graduation, but her father encouraged her to look elsewhere for her life's work.

There was little to suggest that Rankin's career would be in public life. She taught briefly in country schools near her parents' ranch, and also worked as an apprentice seamstress. In 1908, evidently unsatisfied with this course, she left Montana to attend the New York School of Philanthropy, where she studied social work, one of the few occupations considered acceptable for young, educated, middle-class women. This led to a brief stint as a social worker in Montana which also proved unsatisfying. Again, Rankin returned to school, departing for the University of Washington.

It was there that Rankin became involved with the cause of women's suffrage. As a student, she joined the women of the state of Washington in their successful campaign for equal voting rights. Rankin claimed to support women's suffrage because of her childhood in the West. The Western environment made harsh demands on its settlers, both male and female, and because they shared these responsibilities equally, Rankin believed women should have equal rights. Her devotion to the cause took her back to Montana, where she spoke to the state legislature in favor of equal suffrage on February 2, 1911, the first woman ever to address that state's legislature. She had discovered her calling—politics.

In her new career as suffragist and political organizer, she visited 15 different states, lobbying for women's rights. She spent 1913 and 1914 as the field secretary for the National American Woman Suffrage Association (NAWSA). Her work for women's suffrage also introduced her to the cause of pacifism. One of her mentors in the women's suffrage movement was **Minnie J. Reynolds**, who argued that peace and suffrage were intimately related issues.

Although Rankin was deeply involved in the suffrage movement, as well as in progressive politics, she never formed the close associations with other female reformers that many other Progressive women enjoyed. She greatly admired women such as *Jane Addams, but she was not a part of the group of women reformers clustered around Addams and Hull House. Her brief relationship with NAWSA ended with a break between Rankin and *Carrie Chapman Catt, the association's leader. Catt was not the pacifist Rankin was, and Rankin's position on World War I guaranteed a split between the two women. Catt believed that Rankin's position on World War I cost the organization support, rather than aiding their cause. Despite beginning her political career in the women's movement, Rankin was not so much identified with feminism as with pacifism.

In 1916, she decided to run for the U.S. House of Representatives, under the campaign slogan "Let the People Know." Rankin ran as a Republican with a Progressive agenda, advocating women's suffrage and protection of children, as well as reform of the election process. Her first opportunity to express her views on war presented itself almost immediately. On April 6, 1917, President Woodrow Wilson asked Congress to vote in favor of a declaration of war against Germany. Rankin was one of 57 representatives to vote against the declaration. In a later justification of her action, she wrote to her constituents that her vote reflected their letters and telegrams which ran 16 to 1 against involvement in the war. In the House of Representatives, she denounced the war as "stupid and futile."

During the rest of her term, Rankin supported a number of progressive causes, such as protective labor laws and women's suffrage. Her stay in Congress, however, would be short lived. She did not receive the Republican nomination in 1918, and was unable to gain support from a third party. She also found that she had lost support from the Montanans who had sent her to Washington in the first place, largely as a result of her vote against the war.

Peace is a woman's job.

—Jeannette Rankin

In the years following World War I, Rankin increasingly devoted her energies to the cause of pacifism. She pursued her interests not from Montana, but from her new home base in Georgia. Although she maintained her Montana citizenship, her real home was not far from Atlanta, a one-room house, with no electricity, running water, or telephone, on 64 acres of land. She made a conscious decision to live in spartan surroundings and teach peace to the local community. Her efforts included clubs for boys and girls, an adult study club, and finally, organization of the Georgia Peace Society in 1928. Her work on behalf of the pacifist cause evidently did not sit well with many Georgians. She was publicly denounced as a communist, a charge she vehemently denied. Indeed, her public record indicated that, if anything, she was generally opposed to communism.

The Georgia Peace Society was coming to the end of its life just as the Second World War was beginning. Rankin strenuously opposed President Franklin Roosevelt's attempts to aid Great Britain in the years before the American declaration of war, often going to Washington, D.C., to testify before Congress. She opposed the arms build-up prior to the war, Lend Lease, the Atlantic Charter, and the prewar draft. She was optimistic that war could be avoided. Because of her devotion to the cause of peace, she entered the political fray again, running as a pacifist Republican, and was elected to a second term in 1940. As an alternative to preparations for war, she proposed that the United States construct a defensive line around itself and its possessions. She also called for a vote by the American people to determine whether the nation should go to war. She often commented that "people never make war; it is always governments." These became moot issues with the Japanese bombing of Pearl Harbor on December 7, 1941.

Although Rankin had been one of 57 representatives to vote against World War I, she was the only representative or senator to vote against World War II. Again, she justified her position to her constituents. She claimed that her vote was based upon pledges she had "made to the mothers and fathers of Montana." She said that she wanted more evidence before casting her vote, and could not, in good faith, vote to take the United States into yet another war. Throughout the remainder of her term, she claimed that the war was the product of British imperialists who had encouraged the president to take provocative actions against the Japanese.

Once again, Rankin's career in Congress was cut short by her vote on the war. When the people of Montana did not return her to Congress, she continued her criticism of Roosevelt and his policies from the sidelines. She hoped that the women of America would come together to vote Roosevelt out of office in 1944, but they let her down. She began looking for new heroes and new causes, and found one in India. Between 1949 and 1971, she visited India seven times. There she researched Indian pacifism, and particularly the techniques of Mohandas Gandhi. She also traveled in Africa, Indonesia, South America, Ireland, Russia, Turkey, Mexico, and Czechoslovakia.

Her voting patterns in these years were curious, reflecting her desire to try to find the candidate most likely to keep the peace. She liked President Dwight Eisenhower, even though he was a military man. He ended the Korean War and seemed to be trying to keep the U.S. out of further conflicts. She was suspicious of John F. Kennedy, and so voted for Richard Nixon in 1960. In 1964, she chose Barry Goldwater, because of Lyndon Johnson's escalation of American involvement in the war in Vietnam. She voted again for Nixon in 1968, but he did not end the Vietnam conflict quickly enough. By 1972, she was supporting George McGovern.

Jeannette Rankin

Rankin remained out of the limelight, so much so that many people were surprised to find that she was still alive when in the 1960s she again became involved in politics. Her reason to reenter the national fray was the war in Vietnam. In 1961, she watched in dismay as President Kennedy sent advisors to Vietnam. President Johnson's further military involvement led her to begin to speak out against American actions. A 1967 speech, made before the group Atlantans for Peace, was picked up by the Associated Press. Her speech notified the country that she was indeed alive and well, and still a pacifist. In her address, she argued that if 10,000 American women put their minds to it, they could end the war in Vietnam.

Her call was heard and heeded by a pacifist group, Women's Strike for Peace. In 1968, they marched on Washington to protest the war. They named their contingent the Jeannette Rankin Brigade, and Rankin herself marched at the front of the procession. Between 5,000 to 10,000 women marched to the Capitol, and Rankin was among 16 women who were allowed to enter the building and present a petition to Congress to end the war. They also demanded that Congress use its power to reform American society. Rankin would continue her activities throughout the remaining years of her life, leading marches and supporting the activities of peace groups. Though she contemplated a third term in Congress, so that she might have the opportunity to vote against yet another war, Rankin was slowing down. In 1972, she moved to a nursing home, where she died in her sleep on May 18, 1973, just short of her 93rd birthday. To the very end, she had continued to fight for the cause she held most dear, peace.

Judy Rankin

SOURCES:

Alonso, Harriet Hyman. "Jeannette Rankin and the Women's Peace Union," in *Montana: The Magazine of Western History*. Vol. 39, no. 2. Spring 1989, p. 3449.

Josephson, Hannah. *Jeannette Rankin, First Lady in Congress: A Biography*. NY: Bobbs-Merrill, 1974.

Wilson, Joan Hoff. "'Peace is a Woman's Job': Jeannette Rankin and American Foreign Policy: The Origins of Her Pacifism," in *Montana: The Magazine of Western History*. Vol. 30, no. 1. January 1980, p. 2841.

———. "'Peace is a Woman's Job:' Jeannette Rankin American Foreign Policy: Her Lifework as a Pacifist," in *Montana: The Magazine of Western History*. Vol. 30, no. 2. April 1980, p. 3857.

SUGGESTED READING:

Block, Judy R. *The First Woman in Congress: Jeannette Rankin*. Morristown, NJ: Silver Burdett, 1978.

Hardaway, Roger D. "Jeannette Rankin: The Early Years," in *North Dakota Quarterly*. Vol. 48. Winter 1980, p. 6268.

Harris, Ted. *Jeannette Rankin: Suffragist, First Woman in Congress, and Pacifist*. NY: Arno Press, 1982.

White, Florence. *First Woman in Congress: Jeannette Rankin*. NY: Messner, 1980.

COLLECTIONS:

Jeannette Rankin Papers, Schlesinger Library, Radcliffe College, Cambridge, Massachusetts; oral history "Activist for World Peace, Women's Rights, and Democratic Government" at the Bancroft Library, University of California, Berkeley; letters to the National Council for the Prevention of War from 1929 to 1939 in Swarthmore College Peace Collection, Swarthmore, Pennsylvania.

Pamela Riney-Kehrberg,
Associate Professor of History,
Illinois State University, Normal, Illinois

Rankin, Judy (1945—)

American golfer. Name variations: Judy Torluemke. Born Judith Torluemke in St. Louis, Missouri, on February 18, 1945; daughter of Paul Torluemke; married Yippy Rankin, in 1967; children: a son.

Was three-time winner of the Vare trophy, also held 26 LPGA victories; won the Corpus Christi Open (1968); won four LPGA events (1973); won the Colgate-*Dinah Shore Open (1976); named Player of the Year (1976, 1977); won the Bent Tree Classic (1976); won the Colgate European Open (1974, 1977); won the Colgate Hong Kong Open and five other tournaments (1976); won the Peter Jackson Classic and five other tournaments (1977).

Born in St. Louis, Missouri, in 1945, Judy Rankin was only six when she began taking golf lessons from her father. At age eight, she won her first title; at age fourteen, she was the youngest player to win the Missouri Amateur, winning it a second time in 1961, two years later. Rankin was the low amateur in the U.S. Women's Open in 1960 at age 15. Two years

later, she turned pro, winning three tournaments in her third year on tour. Although she fought a back injury, Rankin won 26 LPGA victories and the Vare trophy in 1973, 1976, and 1977. She was also named Player of the Year in 1976 and 1977 and became the first woman player to win more than $100,000 in a season. In her last great season, 1977, Rankin led the LPGA Tour in earnings ($122,890) for the second straight season and tied in victories, with five. In 28 events that year, Rankin finished in the top 10 an incredible 25 times. Back problems, however, continued to plague her.

Karin Loewen Haag,
Athens, Georgia

Ransome-Kuti, Funmilayo

(1900–1978)

Nigerian teacher and feminist who led her country-women in protest against the British colonial government (1943–49) and was a political force of international stature (1950s). Name variations: Olufunmilayo Ransome-Kuti; the Lioness of Lisabi-land. Born Frances Abigail Olufunmilayo Thomas in Abeokuta, Nigeria, on October 25, 1900; died in Abeokuta on April 12, 1978; daughter of Daniel Olumoyewa Thomas (a farmer and trader) and Phyllis Moyeni Dese (a dressmaker); attended St. John's Primary School and Abeokuta Grammar School; studied in Great Britain, 1919–22; married Reverend Israel Oludotun Ransome-Kuti, in 1925; children: Dolupo; Olikoye; Fela Anikulapo-Kuti (a singer and musician, known as the king of Afrobeat who died from AIDS in 1997); Beko.

As a teacher of literacy classes, became concerned with issues surrounding the status of women (1930–40s); led thousands in a protest against a special flat tax on women imposed by the British, leading to the resignation of the government and institutional reforms (1947–48); as a member of the Abeokuta Provincial Conference, worked on a new constitution (1948–51); ran unsuccessfully for the House of Assembly in the Egba Division (1951); made second run for a legislative seat (1959); elected a world vice-president of the Women's International Democratic Federation (1952); awarded the Order of Niger for her contributions to the nation (1965); received an honorary doctorate of laws from the University of Ibadan (1968).

When the young Nigerian woman faced racial prejudice while studying in Great Britain around 1920, she took a step that would be appreciated by many youths of African origin. Frances Abigail Olufunmilayo Thomas dropped her Christian name of Frances in favor of Funmilayo, identifying herself proudly with her African origins. In later years, for her continued courage and tenacity, she would become known as the Lioness of Lisabiland.

Funmilayo Ransome-Kuti's family had been entangled with European influences long before her birth. Early in the 19th century, her paternal great-grandparents had been captured by Portuguese slave dealers and transported in a slave cargo before the ship was intercepted by the British and they were repatriated in Sierra Leone. Her grandfather, Ebenezer Shobowale Thomas, grew up to be an Anglican catechist. His son, Daniel Olumoyewa Thomas, became a farmer who traded in palm oil, and married a dressmaker, **Phyllis Moyeni Dese**, in 1894. Both were Christians and prominent members of the Yoruba tribe. Funmilayo Ransome-Kuti, christened Frances Abigail Olufunmilayo Thomas, was their first daughter, born in Abeokuta, Nigeria, on October 25, 1900. A second daughter, **Harriet**, was born in 1903. Ransome-Kuti's parents were educated, and they had high aspirations for their children. The sisters attended St. John's Primary School in Abeokuta, where Ransome-Kuti was a pupil from 1906 to 1913. In 1914, she was one of the first girls to attend the secondary Abeokuta Grammar School, founded in 1908. After graduating in 1919, she went to Great Britain, where she studied music, education, domestic science, and French.

Ransome-Kuti returned to Nigeria in 1922, and taught at Abeokuta Grammar School. In 1925, she married Israel Oludotun Ransome-Kuti, an Anglican minister whom she had met while they were both at grammar school. Also a nationalist, he would be one of the founders of the Nigerian Union of Teachers in 1932, and eight years later would encourage the formation of the Nigerian Union of Students, which subsequently grew increasingly political; he was also largely responsible for the establishment of the University of Ibadan. The couple first resided in the town of Ijebu-Ode, near Abeokuta, where their daughter **Dolupo Ransome-Kuti** was born, followed a year later by their son Olikoye. Sons Fela and Beko would be born in 1938 and 1940, respectively. All the children would attend Abeokuta Grammar School, study in Great Britain, and grow up to contribute actively to the future of their country: Dolupo would become a nurse, Okiloye a doctor and Nigeria's minister of health, Fela an immensely popular musician who challenged the government, and Beko a medical practitioner. The Ransome-Kutis took an egalitarian approach to marriage and family life. Wife and husband were on an equal footing, and their daughter and three sons all shared household chores; equality was a way of life, not merely an ideology.

Initially drawn into a public role because of her husband's position, Ransome-Kuti soon demonstrated her own outstanding qualities of leadership. She had begun literacy classes for adult women in Ijebu-Ode before the couple's return to Abeokuta in 1931. In Abeokuta, she founded a nursery school, and in 1942 she organized the Abeokuta Ladies' Club, which was mostly concerned with charitable work. Ransome-Kuti was again holding literacy classes for women in 1944, when a student requested that newspapers be included in their reading material. As she taught this woman to read newspapers, Ransome-Kuti discovered how many articles asserted the inferior status of women, and began to see a correlation between British colonialism and Nigerian women's loss of rank.

In traditional Nigerian society, women had enjoyed high social status. Expected to support themselves economically, they did so largely through farming and trade, and the country's market women were famous for their astute business practices. They created extensive networks with European trading partners, sold vegetables, palm oil, cloth, and a variety of other goods throughout the country and beyond, such as *Okwei of Osomari, and became quite wealthy. Women's economic significance was reflected in Nigeria's "dual-sex" form of government, in which women essentially ruled over women and men ruled over men. This political system had been taken for granted before British colonial rule, which brought in a male-dominated system of government, law and custom that resulted in a serious loss of position for Nigerian women. Under British rule, the nominal head of government was the *alake*, a traditional Nigerian ruler whose powers had been delineated and greatly increased through the Sole Native Authority system, introduced by the British to facilitate administrative duties and the collection of taxes.

In Ransome-Kuti's literacy classes, the imposition of foreign taxation, as well as the loss of status felt by the market women, soon became an issue of contention. They also began to complain to her about the exorbitant taxes imposed by the British. The situation was made worse as World War II continued and the market women were coerced into selling food to Nigerian soldiers at very low prices. The market women resentfully began to identify new and foreign abuses of power under Alake Ademola, who was not fol-

lowing traditional Nigerian customs, especially in his dealings with women. Supported by the Abeokuta Ladies' Club and the Nigerian Union of Teachers (founded by her husband), Ransome-Kuti helped the market women draw up petitions and swear out complaints against the officials of the alake. Soon they began adding demands to their complaints, for if women were to be taxed, they reasoned, they should receive benefits in return. Ransome-Kuti presented resolutions demanding improved sanitation, medical care, literacy classes, and playgrounds for children.

In 1946, Ransome-Kuti renamed her group the Abeokuta Women's Union (AWU), redefining its activities as essentially political rather than social. The organization now had a threefold political purpose: 1) to unite Nigerian women; 2) to promote women's economic, social, and political rights; and 3) to cooperate with all organizations in fighting for the independence of the Nigerian people. The Abeokuta Women's Union quickly grew to 20,000 members. In the early stages of protest, Ransome-Kuti and the AWU members wrote many letters and petitions. While not declaring an outright rejection of British colonialism, the group did reject the male paternalism inherent in the system. It wanted abolition of the female flat tax rate, the removal of Ademola as alake, the abolition of the Sole Native Authority System, and reform of the administrative system to include the participation of women. When these approaches proved unsuccessful, the AWU prepared for a more dramatic step.

On November 29, 1947, thousands of women marched on the palace of the alake. Just before reaching their destination, Ransome-Kuti commanded all the women to close their eyes, so that anyone who was afraid could leave without shame. None left. The women occupied the palace grounds, where they remained for 24 hours, and beginning on December 8 the vigil was repeated for 48 hours, while the women's markets remain closed. As part of the demonstrations, they carried out mock traditional sacrifices, sang abusive songs, and held a "funeral" for Ademola.

Following the December rally, the Majeobaji Society, a secret men's political group that had been formed in 1947, threw its support behind the women, demanding that the tax against men be raised and the tax against women abolished. The alake refused. On February 12, 1948, Ransome-Kuti was ordered to appear in court for her part in the demonstrations. The tough stance she took there won her widespread admiration. She got into a physical fight with the district officer, and, although she had an idiomatic command of English, chose to speak only in Yoruba and insisted that all replies made to her in English be translated into Yoruba.

The women's political impact was clearly being felt by April 28, 1948, when they made another march, this one lasting five hours, through the streets of Abeokuta. Shaken by this demonstration, the alake suspended taxation, set up a committee to examine tax policy, and agreed to admit women to his advisory council. On July 4, 1948, the Ogboni chiefs, once the alake's strongest supporters, demanded that the Sole Native Authority system be dismantled as it was "not in accordance with native law and custom." They then boycotted meetings of the Egba Council to show their displeasure. The entire town was in a state of unrest on July 7–8, when the women held further mass demonstrations. On July 26, after violence broke out during a demonstration by a group of young men, the alake fled. Women demonstrated again for the next two days. The following January, Alake Ademola abdicated, the flat rate tax on women was abolished, and the Sole Native Authority system ceased to exist.

Ransome-Kuti continued her activist role throughout the 1950s. She became the only woman among the 28 members of the Abeokuta Provincial Conference, which worked on a new constitution from 1948 to 1951. She was a candidate for the House of Assembly in the Egba Division in 1951, but was defeated; full free franchise for Nigerian women would not be granted until 1959, so very few women could vote at that time. Ransome-Kuti served as a member of the Egba Council, however, and was a leader of the National Council of Nigeria and Cameroons (NCNC), a militant political party. By 1952, her influence was felt in the international sphere, when she was made world vice-president of the Women's International Democratic Federation. In this role, she visited a number of countries, including the People's Republic of China. After her husband, who had always supported her work, died of cancer in 1955, she was determined to carry on. Despite the fact that her Christian and democratic principles were well known, the British and Nigerian governments labeled her a communist sympathizer, and in 1957, the government of Nigeria refused to renew her passport until public outcry led it to relent. The following year, her alleged communist connections caused the United States to deny her a visa to attend an International Women's Organization conference, a tactic frequently used at the time against radical feminists.

In 1959, Ransome-Kuti ran again for the House of Representatives. Infighting with the NCNC led her to found her own party, the Commoners' People's Party, but this second bid for election was also unsuccessful. Afterward she became involved in a prolonged campaign against a special water rate that had been imposed on women. After refusing to pay the tax, she and several women were arrested, and then, after further protest, rearrested; her resistance continued until 1960, when the tax was finally abolished. Ransome-Kuti became an advisor to President Kwame Nkrumah of Ghana, and used her leadership position in Nigeria and the international community to speak out against injustice. After the Sharpeville massacre in South Africa, she denounced the murders and offered her support to the outlawed African National Congress. She was also a frequent visitor to Britain, where she lectured on the deterioration of the status of Nigerian women under colonial rule.

May I never let womanhood down.

—Funmilayo Ransome-Kuti

In 1966, the armed forces took over the Nigerian government, and all party politics were proscribed. Ransome-Kuti, who had been awarded the Order of Niger the previous year for her contributions to the country, spoke eloquently against the demise of Nigerian democracy. Her son Fela Anikulapo-Kuti, who by the time of his death in 1997 would be Nigeria's most influential and outspoken musician, joined her in condemning the military regime. In 1968, the University of Ibadan conferred upon her an honorary doctorate of laws. She was also awarded the Lenin Peace Prize by the Soviet Union for her work on behalf of the people of Africa. The clever satirical songs Fela wrote and performed about the regime, however, led to physical attacks on a number of occasions. Ransome-Kuti was staying at her son's house in February 1977 when some 1,000 soldiers arrived to confront him. In the ensuing fray, during which the house was destroyed, soldiers threw Ransome-Kuti from a second-story window. The fall brought on a stroke from which she never fully recovered. She died the following year, on April 12, 1978. A later government inquiry into her death closed by placing the blame on an "unknown soldier." Her son Fela wrote a song, titled "Unknown Soldier," which went: "Dem start magic, dem bring hat, dem bring rabbit, dem bring egg, dem bring smoke," and "then they say: unknown soldier." Funmilayo Ransome-Kuti's funeral on May 5 was attended by thousands who remembered all she had done for women and for

Nigeria, and market women closed their stalls as a mark of respect for the Lioness of Lisabiland.

SOURCES:

Callaway, Helen. *Gender, Culture, and Empire. European Women in Colonial Nigeria.* Urbana, IL: University of Illinois Press, 1987.

Coleman, J.S. *Nigeria: Background to Nationalism.* Berkeley, CA: University of California Press, 1971.

"Fighter for the Rights of Women," in *West Africa.* No. 3171. April 24, 1978, p. 785.

Hatch, John Charles. *Nigeria. A History.* London: Secker and Warburg, 1971.

Johnson-Odim, Cheryl. "On Behalf of Women and the Nation: Funmilayo Ransome-Kuti and the Struggles for Nigerian Independence and Women's Equality," in *Expanding the Boundaries of Women's History: Essays on Women in the Third World.* Cheryl Johnson-Odim and Margaret Strobel, eds. Bloomington, IN: Indiana University Press, 1992, pp. 144–157.

Mba, Nina E. "Olufunmilayo Ransome-Kuti," in *Nigerian Women in Historical Perspective.* Edited by Bolanle Awe. Lagos, Nigeria: Sankore, 1992, pp. 133–148.

Mba, Nina Emma. *Nigerian Women Mobilized: Women's Political Activity in Southern Nigeria, 1900–1965.* Berkeley, CA: Institute of International Studies, 1982.

The New York Times. September 16, 2000.

Okonjo, Kamene. "Nigerian Women's Participation in National Politics: Legitimacy and Stability in an Era of Transition," in *Working Paper #221.* East Lansing, MI: Women and International Development Program, Michigan State University, July 1991.

Karin Loewen Haag,
freelance writer, Athens, Georgia

Raphael, Sylvia (1938–1985).

See Rafael, Sylvia.

Rapoport, Lydia (1923–1971)

Austrian-born American social-work educator who was the first UN inter-regional adviser on family welfare and family planning. Name variations: Lydia Rappoport. Born in Vienna, Austria, on March 8, 1923; died in New York City on September 6, 1971; daughter of Eugenia (Margulies) Rappoport and Samuel Rappoport (a businessman and later a translator); attended public schools; Hunter College, B.A., 1943; Smith College School for Social Work, M.S.W., 1944; received certificate in child therapy from the Chicago Institute for Psychoanalysis; studied at the London School of Economics; studied at the Harvard School of Public Health (1959–60).

The younger of two children born to **Eugenia Margulies Rappoport** and Samuel Rappoport in Vienna, Austria, Lydia Rapoport (who later changed the spelling of her last name) moved with most of her family to the United States in 1932, where her father, who had studied law in Vienna and worked in the grain-trading business, had immigrated in 1928. He worked as a translator in New York City, where the family settled and Lydia attended public schools. After graduating from high school, she went on to earn a bachelor's degree in 1943 as a Phi Beta Kappa sociology major at Hunter College. She then enrolled in an accelerated graduate course at Smith College School for Social Work, and was only 21 when she received a master's degree in 1944. Moving to Chicago, she studied for a certificate in child therapy from the Chicago Institute for Psychoanalysis and worked in several jobs in the field of child guidance. Rapoport made a specialty of diagnosing and treating children with emotional problems while a counselor at the Institute for Juvenile Research, as an intake supervisor at the University of Chicago's Child Guidance Clinic, and then as a supervisor at the Jewish Children's Bureau and the Michael Reese Hospital.

Having won a Fulbright fellowship, Rapoport went to study at the London School of Economics in 1952. While in England, she became friends with Dame *Eileen Younghusband, an influential scholar of social work and educator, and Richard Titmuss, one of the creators of England's National Health Service. Rapoport returned to the United States in 1954, settling in California to be near her brother and his family, and supervised students from the School of Social Welfare at the University of California, Berkeley, who worked at the California State Mental Hygiene Clinic. The following year, she became an assistant professor at the School of Social Welfare, teaching social casework. She studied with Erich Lindemann at the Harvard School of Public Health during 1959–60, and in 1963 was a visiting professor at the Baerwald School of Social Work of the Hebrew University in Jerusalem. There she helped to establish standards for undergraduate curricula in social-work programs, and, although being Jewish had never played a large part in her identity, she was deeply impressed with the people and country.

After her return to Berkeley, Rapoport was named a full professor in 1969. During summer breaks, she also taught at her alma mater, Smith College, and at the University of Chicago School of Social Service Administration. The founder of the Community Mental Health Program at Berkeley, an advanced program for graduate social workers, Rapoport specialized in consultation, supervision, and crisis theory, and it was in these areas that she did her major research and writing. Her most important contribution was her articulation of a theoretical framework for "crisis-oriented brief treatment," which she helped to create as a social-casework specialty. She also helped to define the distinct functions of consultation and supervision within social work, and to establish rules for both supervisors and students.

In January 1971, Rapoport became the first United Nations inter-regional adviser on family welfare and family planning, and moved to New York City. Half a year later, while gearing up to begin a study on social workers' potential usefulness in assisting family planning programs in Israel, she underwent emergency intestinal surgery in New York. She died of acute bacterial endocarditis less than two months later, on September 6, 1971. In tribute, friends set up the Lydia Rapoport Distinguished Visiting Professorship, supported by the Lydia Rapoport Endowment Fund, at Smith College School for Social Work.

SOURCES:

Sicherman, Barbara, and Carol Hurd Green, eds. *Notable American Women: The Modern Period.* Cambridge, MA: The Belknap Press of Harvard University, 1980.

Jo Anne Meginnes,
freelance writer, Brookfield, Vermont

Rask, Gertrud (fl. 1721)

Missionary to the Inuit of Greenland. Flourished around 1721; married Hans Egede, known as the "Apostle of Greenland."

The wife of Hans Egede, a Danish missionary known as the "Apostle of Greenland," Gertrud Rask sailed with her husband to Greenland, where they landed in July 1721, and where Egede later established the colony of Godthåb (now the capital, also called Nuuk). Taking up residence among the Inuit population, the couple embarked on a mission to convert the Greenlanders to Christianity. In the process, they befriended and assisted the Inuits, overcoming the language barrier and the unfamiliar living conditions. Rask died in Greenland, although the date is unknown, and her husband subsequently fell ill and returned to Copenhagen around 1736. Historians later credited the couple with opening a new chapter in the history of Greenland.

Raskin, Judith (1928–1984)

American soprano. Born on June 21, 1928, in New York City; died on December 21, 1984; daughter of Harry A. Raskin and Lillian (Mendelson) Raskin; attended Smith College, B.A., 1949, M.A. (hon), 1963; studied with Anna Hamlin in New York; married Raymond Raskin (a physician), on July 11, 1948; children: two.

Debuted in Central City, Colorado (1956); made television debut as Susanna in Mozart's Le nozze di Fi-garo *with the NBC Opera (1957); made New York City Opera debut in* Cosi Fan Tutte *(1959); made Metropolitan Opera debut (1962); sang at the Met (1962–72); made debut at Glyndebourne (1963); taught at the Manhattan School of Music and the Mannes College of Music.*

Judith Raskin was the rare American singer who did not establish her reputation in Europe before appearing on the American stage. She was born in New York City in 1928; her father was a music teacher at a Bronx high school and her mother taught in an elementary school. As a child, Raskin studied piano and violin, but her vocal studies did not begin until her piano teacher heard her sing. In college, she studied with **Anna Hamlin**. After her marriage in 1948, Raskin devoted herself to family for almost ten years and then successfully auditioned for a role as Susanna in the NBC Opera production of *Le nozze di Figaro*. Success led her in 1962 to a debut at the Metropolitan Opera, where she sang until 1972. Raskin's vocal purity often led to comparisons with *****Elisabeth Schumann**. Despite a late beginning, she established herself as an international star. Ill health, however, forced an early retirement from the stage. Judith Raskin then taught for a number of years at the Manhattan School of Music and the Mannes College of Music before her death in 1984.

John Haag,
Athens, Georgia

Raskova, Marina (1912–1943).

See joint entry under Grizodubova, Valentina.

Ratebzad, Anahita (1931—)

Afghan physician and political leader. Born in 1931 in Guldara, Kabul province, Afghanistan; received M.D., 1963.

Afghanistan was described by Elphinstone Mountstuart, British envoy to the court of Shah Shuja (1808–09), as "a poor, cold, strong, and remote country, [with] a turbulent people." Unfortunately for the populace of Afghanistan, particularly its women, this is still true. When the fundamentalist Taliban movement took over most of the country in the mid-1990s, it closed all schools for girls and women. The modest gains made by Afghan women in the 20th century were thus destroyed during its final decade. Anahita Ratebzad symbolizes this ill-fated attempt to secure human rights. Born in 1931, she was educated in Kabul, at the Chicago School of

Nursing, and finally at Kabul University where she was awarded an M.D. degree in 1963, becoming the first woman physician in the history of Afghanistan. In 1965, Ratebzad was one of three successful female candidates for the Afghan Parliament, and in the same year she founded the Democratic Women's Organization, a branch of the Marxist-inspired People's Democratic Party of Afghanistan (PDPA).

In the pro-Soviet government that ruled Afghanistan in the early 1980s, Ratebzad was the highest-ranking woman member within the PDPA. For a brief period, she was Minister of Social Affairs and Tourism, but was purged when another faction took power. Under the regime of Babrak Karmal, she served as Minister of Education in 1980–81 and was elected to the ruling PDPA Politburo. She also was caretaker of the Ministries of Information and Culture, Higher and Vocational Education, and Public Health. But in 1981 she relinquished these posts, which very likely were barely functioning in a nation embroiled in war, and became a member of the Revolutionary Council's Presidium, a position she held from 1981 through 1988. After 1990, Ratebzad withdrew from public life, and all traces of her have vanished from the public record. With the withdrawal of Soviet support in the late 1980s, the PDPA collapsed, even changing its name in June 1990 to Hizb-i Watan (Fatherland Party). Not only was Marxist doctrine abandoned by the PDPA, but earlier reforms, some proclaiming the legal equality of women, were dropped. The triumph of the extreme fundamentalist Taliban movement in the 1990s heralds the demise of all emancipatory processes for the women of Afghanistan.

SOURCES:

Adamec, Ludwig W. *Historical Dictionary of Afghanistan.* 2nd ed. Lanham, MD: Scarecrow, 1997.

Afghanistan: The Legacy of Human Suffering in a Forgotten War. NY: Amnesty International, 1999.

Ellis, Deborah. *Women of the Afghan War.* Westport, CT: Praeger, 2000.

Iacopino, Vincent. *The Taliban's War on Women: A Health and Human Rights Crisis in Afghanistan.* Boston, MA: Physicians for Human Rights, 1998.

Rahimi, Fahima. *Women in Afghanistan.* Liestal: Stiftung Bibliotheca Afghanica, 1986.

Rahimi, Wali M. *Status of Women: Afghanistan.* Bangkok: UNESCO Principal Regional Office for Asia and the Pacific, 1991.

Women in Afghanistan: Pawns in Men's Power Struggles. NY: Amnesty International, 1999.

RELATED MEDIA:

Burstyn, Linda, and **Marlo Thomas**. "Shroud of Silence: Gender Apartheid in Afghanistan" (video), Los Angeles, CA: Feminist Majority Foundation, 1998.

John Haag,
Associate Professor of History,
University of Georgia, Athens, Georgia

Rathbone, Eleanor (1872–1946)

British feminist, social reformer, and member of Parliament. Born in Liverpool, England, in 1872; died in 1946; daughter of William Rathbone (a social reformer and Liberal MP); cousin of *Rosalind Paget (1855–1948); educated at Kensington High School and Somerville College, Oxford; never married; no children.

Born in Liverpool, England, in 1872, Eleanor Rathbone was prominent in the British feminist movement between World War I and World War II. She inherited a family legacy of social reform and political involvement that was passed down to her by three generations of philanthropists and reformers: her great-grandfather William Rathbone (1757–1809), a merchant who played a prominent role in philanthropic enterprise in Liverpool; her grandfather, also named William (1787–1868), a philanthropist and educator who served one year as Liverpool's mayor; and her father, the third William (1819–1902), a philanthropist, social reformer, and Liberal Party MP whose views greatly influenced those of his daughter.

Rathbone's world broadened considerably when she left Liverpool in 1893 to attend Somerville College at Oxford. After completing work there, she considered focusing on philosophy but chose instead to embrace social work, noting that the contemplation of abstract ideas lost its pleasure in a world "with all its wrongs shouting in one's ears." She soon became deeply involved in the Edwardian suffrage campaign, and joined the "non-militant" National Union of Women's Suffrage Societies (NUWSS). By 1900, her suffragist work in Lancashire had led her to a seat in the union's executive committee. She remained active in the NUWSS until 1919, when in the wake of women's enfranchisement it was transformed into the National Union of Societies for Equal Citizenship (NUSEC), of which she became president. In 1912, she published ideas on family allowances that she had first elaborated eight years before, and she remained active in local government and social questions in Liverpool, forming the Liverpool Women Citizens' Association in 1913 to educate women in public affairs and later sitting on the Liverpool city council until 1935.

Perhaps the most spirited issue in which she was involved during the 1920s was the heated debate between the "old" and "new" feminists. "New" feminists, for whom Rathbone was a vocal advocate, favored discriminatory welfare reforms designed to gain equality for women in their roles as mothers. They insisted that women had distinctive legislative needs separate from those of men, and promoted family allowances to reward women who had families (and who were, in general, financially dependent entirely on their husbands). This would also, Rathbone thought, lessen what she called the "Turk complex," or the pride engendered in some men by the fact that their families were utterly dependent on them. To further these and other feminist aims, in 1922 she ran as an Independent for a parliamentary seat in East Toxteth; the area was highly conservative, however, and she won only 40% of the vote. In 1929, again as an Independent, she won a seat representing the two-member Combined English Universities, which she would hold for the rest of her life.

Throughout the 1930s, Rathbone pressed the case that women were lumped together with men in the national insurance system only when it suited men; unemployment benefits, of which women claimed less than men, were pooled, while health benefits, of which women claimed more, were not. She also argued for a fairer na-

tional insurance policy for married women who held paying jobs. She was not, however, a supporter of legislation enforcing equal pay for women, which she believed would, if passed without concomitant family allowances, be merely a pretext for getting women out of the work force. (That she was correct in this supposition can be seen by the views of some supporters of equal pay, including Oswald Mosley's Union of British Fascists, which hoped that it would return women to their "proper sphere" of the home.) Rathbone's case for family allowances, which she had articulated before 1914, was strengthened by the example of separation allowances during the First World War. The family allowance committee formed in 1917 gained impetus from her 1924 work *Disinherited Family*, a milestone in social reform that one critic considered "perhaps the most important feminist text" since John Stuart Mill's *Subjection of Women*. The Inheritance (Family Provision) Act was enacted in 1938; two years later, she published *The Case for Family Allowances*. Rathbone was also a proponent of birth control (although like most feminists she waited to gain

Eleanor Rathbone

the vote before speaking out on the matter), as she believed the poor could improve their lives if they had fewer children. One of only three women MPs to endorse birth control between the world wars, she contributed financially to the predecessor of the Family Planning Association in the early 1930s, and believed government health clinics should provide birth-control information. (At least some of this advocacy, however, was spurred by fears that birth rates in the working class, which exceeded those of the middle class, eventually would lead to increased power for the working class.)

Rathbone was wealthy, but, as with the rest of her family, her affluence did not necessarily influence her politics. In 1930, for example, she advocated higher taxation of inherited wealth, noting that inheritance itself provided an unfair edge to only a small percentage of the population. Indeed, she seemed somewhat indifferent to her own money; she never traveled first class, and took only working vacations. Rathbone was so focused on her work that there was little time for much else; she had no interest in clothes, frequently forgot to eat, and had a habit of being unable to recall where she had put things. She has been described as squeamish about anything smacking of sex, including naked children, and her sole relaxation was smoking cigarettes. Her companion since the 1920s, **Elizabeth Macadam**, took care of the household with the assistance of a housekeeper. While she was often warm with her close friends, Rathbone also had scant patience with human foibles, and like a number of great lovers of humanity she had high expectations of those actual humans with whom she had contact, and frequently little tolerance for their failings.

Rathbone gave more attention to foreign policy than did many feminists at the time. In the 1920s, she was a strong proponent of rights for Indian women and an end to the traditional practices (such as suttee and the proscription against the remarriage of widows) that oppressed them, and in the early 1930s she spoke out against female circumcision in the British colonies in Africa. Also in the early 1930s, she became a staunch Zionist after a visit to Palestine. The rise of Hitler and reports of his atrocities worried her deeply, as did the prospect of war, and in 1937 she published *War Can Be Averted*, in which she argued against a conflict with Germany. When that appeared inevitable, however, Rathbone shifted gears to throw her full support towards the defeat of Hitler and fascism. Consumed with this aim, she commented that she did not want to die without seeing the outcome of the war. Her wish was granted; she died in 1946, a year after hostilities ended with the Allied victory.

SOURCES:

Harrison, Brian. *Prudent Revolutionaries: Portraits of British Feminists between the Wars*. Oxford: Clarendon Press, 1987.

SUGGESTED READING:

Alberti, Johanna. *Eleanor Rathbone*. London: Sage, 1996.
Stocks, Mary D. *Eleanor Rathbone: "A Biography."* Victor Gollancz, 1949.

Jacqueline Mitchell,
freelance writer, Detroit, Michigan

Rathbone, Hannah Mary

(1798–1878)

British novelist. Born near Wellington in Shropshire, England, on July 5, 1798; died in Liverpool, England, on March 26, 1878; married Richard Rathbone, in 1817; children: six.

Born on July 5, 1798, near Wellington in Shropshire, England, Hannah Mary Rathbone was 19 when she married her half-cousin, Richard Rathbone, with whom she had six children. She was apparently "delicate" in health, but nevertheless wrote and painted and drew.

Rathbone introduced the autobiographic type of historical novel with her 1844 *Diary of Lady Willoughby*, which purported to be a journal written during the civil war that erupted under King Charles I (r. 1625–49). The story proved quite popular, and the book itself was published as a physical replica of a 17th-century volume. Because the *Diary* was published anonymously, some believed it had been written by Robert Southey; Rathbone became instantly famous when the third edition was published with her name. A second volume, bringing Lady Willoughby's journal up to the Restoration, was published in 1847, and the volumes were released together the following year.

In addition to the *Diary of Lady Willoughby*, Rathbone published a volume of poetry and two anthologies of other poets' work, and edited for publication the letters of her grandfather, the Quaker philanthropist Richard Reynolds. She also supplied illustrations for a book on birds. Rathbone died in Liverpool at the age of 79 on March 26, 1878.

SOURCES:

The Concise Dictionary of National Biography. Oxford: Oxford University Press, 1992.
Kunitz, Stanley J., and Howard Haycraft, eds. *British Authors of the Nineteenth Century*. NY: H.W. Wilson, 1936.

Jacqueline Mitchell,
freelance writer, Detroit, Michigan

Rathbone, Josephine Adams

(1864–1941)

American librarian and educator. Born in Jamestown, New York, on September 10, 1864; died in Augusta, Georgia, on May 17, 1941; daughter of Joshua Henry Rathbone (a physician) and Elizabeth Bacon Adams; attended Wellesley College and the University of Michigan; New York State Library School, Albany, New York, B.L.S., 1893; never married; no children.

Josephine Adams Rathbone was born in Jamestown, New York, in 1864. She attended Wellesley College and the University of Michigan before enrolling in America's first library school, the New York State Library School at Albany, New York, which had been founded by Melvil Dewey (of Dewey Decimal System fame). She worked as an assistant librarian of the Diocesan Lending Library at the All Saints Cathedral in Albany during the course of the two-year program, and graduated in 1893.

Rathbone's career officially began when she joined the staff of the Pratt Institute Free Library in Brooklyn, New York—the first free public library in the New York City area—as an assistant cataloguer. She also taught in the Institute's library school, which had opened in 1890 to train Free Library workers. In 1895, it was converted into a general library school under the directorship of *Mary Wright Plummer, who was also the director of the library itself. Rathbone was chosen as the assistant in charge under Plummer, and in 1904, when Plummer relinquished her library post to devote her energies to the school, Rathbone became chief instructor. She patterned the Pratt Institute's curriculum after that of her alma mater, although with a greater emphasis on service in small- or medium-sized public libraries. Described as "brisk and executive-like," she was not overly friendly with her students, but she was passionate about the things she taught. As quoted in the *American Library Association Bulletin* in May 1932, she believed that the key to good librarianship was "to know books and to understand the book needs of people," and to facilitate a "vital relationship" between readers and books.

Pratt Institute was among the best library schools in America by 1911, when Plummer left to join the New York Public Library School. Rather than promoting Rathbone to the top position in the school, however, Pratt officials recombined the directorship of the school and the Free Library, and awarded this title to Edward F. Stevens (who had no experience running a li-

brary school). He enjoyed the prestige of a grander title than Rathbone's (which was "vice-director"), even though she was the primary administrator, and their contacts were tense. Nonetheless, her reputation was widely known. In addition to her contributions to library periodicals, she was a member of the American Library Institute, served as secretary of the New York State Library Club Association (1908), and served the New York Library Club as secretary (1895–97, 1909–10) and as president (1918–19). She was invaluable to the American Library Association, in particular during its work providing books for armed forces personnel in World War I, and served as a member of its council (1912–29) and as president (1931–32).

Rathbone never married or had children, but greatly enjoyed reading and the theater, as well as taking canoe trips, climbing mountains, planting trees and traveling. She retired from the Pratt library school in 1938 and moved to her mother's hometown of Augusta, Georgia, where she lived with a cousin. She became a member of the Philomathic Club and the Colonial Dames of America, and learned how to drive her newly purchased automobile. Rathbone died in Augusta of coronary thrombosis at the age of 76 on May 17, 1941.

SOURCES:

American Library Association Bulletin. May 1932.

James, Edward T., ed. *Notable American Women, 1607–1950.* Cambridge, MA: The Belknap Press of Harvard University Press, 1971.

Jacqueline Mitchell,
freelance writer, Detroit, Michigan

Rathbun, Mary Jane (1860–1943)

American marine zoologist. Born in Buffalo, New York, on June 11, 1860; died in Washington, D.C., on April 4, 1943; daughter of Charles Howland Rathbun (a stonemason) and Jane (Furey) Rathbun; graduated from high school in Buffalo, 1878; George Washington University, Ph.D., 1917; never married; no children.

A self-taught zoologist whose formal education ended with her high school graduation, Mary Jane Rathbun was born in Buffalo, New York, in 1860. She was only a year old when her mother died, and she was thereafter cared for by an elderly nurse. Her father Charles Rathbun had inherited the firm of Whitmore, Rathbun & Company, which owned and operated several large, productive stone quarries. An early curiosity about fossils they found in these quarries would help decide the course of both Rathbun's life and that of her older brother Richard. While

Richard worked as an assistant to Spencer Baird, head of the U.S. Fish Commission, from 1873 (and from 1880 also as curator of marine invertebrates at the National Museum in Washington, D.C.), Mary Jane Rathbun developed an interest in his work. In 1881, she began to spend her summers with him at the Marine Biological Station at Woods Hole, Massachusetts, assisting him as he catalogued specimens.

Rathbun was fascinated by the mysteries of the sea, and pursued her cataloguing tasks with zeal. Her devotion caught the attention of Baird, who in 1884 hired her to work in the fish commission full-time. She was assigned to the National Museum, where she helped to organize, catalogue, and preserve the museum's collections. Two years later, she was transferred from the commission staff to the museum staff, as a clerk and copyist in the department of marine invertebrates, where she would work for the next 53 years. While her brother Richard was curator and head of the department, his responsibilities with the fish commission left him little time for this job. In 1889, he noted in a report to the museum's board of regents that Rathbun was responsible for "not only the care and preservation of the collections, but also, for the most part, the general supervision of the department." Meanwhile she was educating herself in marine biology and zoology. She began to publish in 1891, and over the course of her career would publish some 158 scientific papers. Named assistant curator in 1907, she resigned from this position in 1914, so that her salary could be used to hire an assistant. This move allowed her to remain in the division as an honorary associate in zoology, with more time for research. Her research focused on classifying and describing contemporary and fossil decapod crustaceans (shrimps, crabs and their near relatives), and both her published articles and the exhaustive notes she kept at the museum were consulted for years. In 1917, with a study on marine crabs, she earned a Ph.D. from George Washington University. (She had been granted an honorary master's degree from the University of Pittsburgh the previous year.)

Described as petite and plain-featured, Rathbun, who never married, was known for her kindness and her extensive grasp of her specialty. During World War I, she worked in the Washington chapter of the Red Cross and sent care packages to the foreign scientists with whom she had corresponded and their families. She died at her Washington home in 1943, after having suffered a fractured hip. Among the bequests in her will was $10,000 to the Smithsonian Institution, to be used to study crustacea in memory of her brother.

SOURCES:

Ogilvie, Marilyn Bailey. *Women in Science: Antiquity through the Nineteenth Century.* Cambridge, MA: MIT Press, 1986.

Sicherman, Barbara, and Carol Hurd Green, eds. *Notable American Women: The Modern Period.* Cambridge, MA: The Belknap Press of Harvard University, 1980.

Jacqueline Mitchell,
freelance writer, Detroit, Michigan

Rathgeber, Lisa (1961—)

American bowler. Born in Hillsboro, Illinois, on May 19, 1961.

Named Rookie of the Year (1980); led the tour in match play winning percentage, average, and competition points (1983).

In her first years of competition bowling, Lisa Rathgeber showed significant potential but was often runner-up. Then she was named Rookie of the Year in 1980. Three years later, in 1983, Rathgeber went from promise to first place. On her 22nd birthday, she won the Robby's Midwest Classic, her initial title. The following week, she won the Greater Milwaukee Open, becoming the first bowler in five years to take back-to-back titles. At the end of the season, she led the tour in match play with a .6351 winning percentage, points averaged per game with 208.50, and 9,070 competition points. That year, she was named Woman Bowler of the Year by the Bowling Writers Association of America and the Lind Shoe Player of the Year. Rathgeber won the Roto Grip Classic in 1984.

Karin Loewen Haag,
Athens, Georgia

Ratia, Armi (1912–1979)

Finnish entrepreneur who was the co-founder and managing director of the Marimekko fashion firm, which drew worldwide attention to Finnish design in the 1960s. Born in Karelia, Finland, in 1912; died in 1979; graduated from the Art Industry Central School, 1935; married Viljo Ratia (separated 1969); children: Ristomatti Ratia.

Born in Karelia, Finland, in 1912, Armi Ratia graduated from the Art Industry Central School in 1935. She then opened a weaving firm, and also studied for a time in Tübingen, Germany, with a textile manufacturer. The Soviet occupation of Karelia in 1944 forced Ratia to join the four million refugees fleeing the area, and she settled with her husband Viljo Ratia in Helsinki. Viljo purchased an oilcloth factory, and the couple worked together for the next two years.

In 1951, the Ratias founded the clothing firm Marimekko, intending to build on the recovering fashion industry after the devastation of World War II. Indeed, Marimekko's first collection attracted the war-weary eyes of Europeans with its bright colors. Much of the credit for its success went to the young designer that Armi, as managing director, had hired, **Maija Isola,** who drew on abstract art to create unusual, non-figurative designs. Armi's past experience in advertising gave her a knack for marketing which greatly increased the influence of the fledgling firm.

Despite its early success, Marimekko did not experience ready financial stability. Armi Ratia ran the company according to her ideals of individualism and risk-taking, with little concern for the financial side of the business. In fact, Marimekko existed for four years before clothing production moved out of individual workers' homes to an actual shop. Early clothing models were friends or employees or ordinary people, rather than the ultra-glamorous models fashionable in Paris. Mirroring her minimalist approach to production, Ratia intended Marimekko's designs to reflect purity and simplicity, and in 1953 she hired a woman designer, **Vuokko Eskolin-Nurmesniemi,** to foster this style, the first time a full-time designer had been employed in the clothing industry in Finland. Most of the designers the company hired were women, and while in the early years none had formal design training, the freshness of their ideas had launched the company into the export business by the end of the decade.

In 1960, first lady and fashion trend-setter *Jacqueline Kennedy purchased seven of the company's dresses, thereby making the style a sensation in America. Ratia's genius for marketing—her oft-quoted motto was "design as lifestyle"—led to clothing designs that both reflected and influenced the fashion of the 1960s, with unfussy cuts, brilliant colors, and oversized patterns that meshed well with the pop art that was everywhere. The association between the intellectual-cultural community and Marimekko in the minds of consumers (some called the clothes "a cultural phenomenon") resulted in a boom of production shops to export the products. Throughout this success, Ratia maintained the family atmosphere of the company, and even drew up serious plans to create a community, Marikylä, where all employees and their families would live together, although this never came to fruition due to a lack of money.

In 1968, Marimekko had some 450 employees. That year Ratia was awarded the American Nieman Marcus Award as well as the Order of the Rose, Finland's highest honor. The following year, she and her husband separated, and she stepped down as the company's managing director. However, she returned to the position in 1971, and continued to rework the design line to fit emerging cultural trends, including unisex fashions which proved very popular in the 1970s. With the demise of the "Swinging '60s," Ratia focused on more conservative, practical clothes to match the increasingly busy lifestyles of consumers. She retired from Marimekko in 1976, and died three years later. The company experienced a downturn after her death, so closely was its identity linked to Ratia's personal vision. It nonetheless remained in business under the control of her heirs, and in 1985 was bought by a large business concern, which invested much money but saw it operate at a loss. Bought in 1991 by **Kirsti Paakkanen,** Marimekko now operates in the black, with three factories, numerous retail stores in Finland, extensive licensing and exporting deals in Scandinavia, Europe, and the United States, and a reputation for high-quality clothing and accessories for all ages.

SOURCES:
Pile, John. *Dictionary of 20th-Century Design.* NY: Facts on File, 1990.
Uglow, Jennifer, ed. and comp. *The International Dictionary of Women's Biography.* NY: Continuum, 1982.

Jacqueline Mitchell,
freelance writer, Detroit, Michigan

Rattazzi, Countess (b. 1922).

See Agnelli, Susanna.

Rattazzi, Madame (1831–1902).

See Rute, Mme de.

Rau, Santha Rama (b. 1923).

See Rama Rau, Santha.

Raubal, Geli (c. 1908–1931)

Niece of Adolf Hitler. Born around 1908; died of a gunshot wound in Munich, Germany, on September 18, 1931; daughter of Angela Raubal (half-sister of Adolf Hitler).

On September 18, 1931, Geli Raubal, the daughter of **Angela Raubal** and the 23-year-old niece of Adolf Hitler, was found dead in her bedroom. She had died from a gunshot wound in her chest at the Munich apartment she shared with her uncle. Officially, the death was declared a suicide because the room had been locked from inside, but rumors circulated at the time that Raubal was involved in a passionate affair with Hitler, that he had forced her to model for his pornographic drawings and engage in sado-masochistic sex. There was further speculation that Raubal was pregnant, and that Hitler either murdered her during one of their violent arguments or, fearing a scandal, had the young woman executed. In a 1998 "speculative psychobiography" of Hitler titled *Hitler & Geli*, author Ronald Hayman uncovers discrepancies in the extant documents and testimonies surrounding the case, and theorizes that Hitler did indeed cover up the truth about Raubal's death, then pressured the authorities to pronounce it a suicide. Hayman further suggests that Hitler's affair with his young niece was symptomatic of his contempt for women and of a personality scarred by his abusive father and subservient mother. Hitler later declared that Geli Raubal was the only woman he had ever loved.

SUGGESTED READING:

Hansen, Ron. *Hitler's Niece* (novel). HarperCollins, 1999.

Hayman, Ronald. *Hitler & Geli*. Bloomsbury, 1998.

Raucourt, Mlle (1756–1815)

French actress. Born Françoise Marie Antoinette Saucerotte in Nancy, France, on March 3, 1756; died on January 15, 1815; buried at Père Lachaise; daughter of an actor.

Mlle Raucourt, whose real name was Françoise Saucerotte, was the daughter of a provincial actor who took her to Spain, where she began appearing in dramatic parts at age 12. By 1770, she was back in France at Rouen, and her success as Euphémie in Belloy's *Gaston et Bayard* led to a stint at the Comédie Française, where in 1772 she made her debut as *Dido. Raucourt played all the classical tragedy parts to crowded houses, until her extravagance and personal scandals ended her popularity.

In 1776, she suddenly disappeared from France. Her next three years were spent in the capitals of northern Europe, though some of that time was spent in jail for debt. Wherever she went, scandal seemed to follow. Under protection of the French queen *Marie Antoinette, Raucourt reappeared at the Théatre Français in 1779 and was again triumphant, reprising her former roles which included Phèdre and Cleopatra. At the outbreak of the French Revolution, she was imprisoned for six months with other royalist members of the Comédie Française, and she did not reappear upon the stage of the Comédie until the close of 1793, and then only for a short time. Along with a dozen of the best actors in the company, she founded a rival company, but a summons from the Directory brought her back to the Comédie in 1797. Napoleon gave her a pension, and in 1806 she was commissioned to organize and direct a company to tour Italy, where, especially in Milan, she was enthusiastically received. Raucourt returned to Paris a few months before her death on January 15, 1815. But scandal followed her to her grave. When the clergy of her parish at Saint-Roch refused to accept her body for burial, the crowd of mourners broke down the church doors and were only restrained from further violence with the arrival of an almoner hastily sent by Louis XVIII. She is buried at Père Lachaise.

Ravenscroft, Gladys (1888–1960)

English golfer. Name variations: Mrs. Temple Dobell. Born in Rock Ferry, England, in 1888; died in Wirral, England, in 1960; married Temple Dobell.

Golfer Gladys Ravenscroft won the 1912 British Women's Amateur. When she placed first at the 1913 USGA Women's Amateur, she was the third non-American woman to win the championship. Ravenscroft beat two other Brits to take the prize that year: **Muriel Dodd**, the reigning British champion, and *Marion Hollins, whom she toppled in the final round.

Ravensdale, Baroness (1896–1966).

See Curzon, Mary for sidebar on Irene Curzon.

Raverat, Gwen (1885–1957)

British wood engraver and book illustrator. Name variations: Gwen Reverat. Born Gwendolen Mary Darwin in Cambridge, England, in 1885; died in 1957; daughter of Sir George Howard Darwin (1845–1912, a scientist and professor) and Maud Du Puy (1861–1947, an American); granddaughter of Charles Darwin (1809–1882); studied at Slade School, 1908–11; married Jacques Pierre Raverat (a mathematician who became a painter), in 1911 (died 1925); children: two daughters.

Gwen Raverat was born in 1885, the daughter of **Maud Du Puy**, an American of Huguenot descent, and George Howard Darwin, the second son of Charles Darwin. An eminent scientist in his own right, George was a fellow of Trinity College and elected Plumian Professor of Astronomy in 1883. He married Maud the following year in Erie, Pennsylvania, and they settled into an old refurbished mill house in Cambridge, England, which they called Newnham Grange. Gwen was the first of their four children, and spent her formative years in the small and exclusive society centered at the college. As befitted relatives of the developer of the theory of evolution, her parents encouraged her to think for herself. She detailed the world in which she grew up in her 1952 bestselling memoir, *Period Piece: A Cambridge Childhood.*

Raverat began her training in drawing as early as age nine, and studied painting at the Slade School from 1908 to 1911. In 1911, she married Jacques Pierre Raverat, a mathematician who became a painter. Their two daughters were born in Britain, and the family then lived in France until 1925, when Jacques died, after which Gwen returned to Cambridge. While she painted, designed for the theater, and also did illustration (including drawings for *Spring Morning*, a volume of poetry by **Frances Cornford**, in 1915), she is most known for her wood engravings. Raverat taught herself the art, a rare feat, and was a founding member of the Society of Wood Engravers. Among the enormously successful works which featured her engravings was the *Cambridge Book of Poetry for Children* (1932). Raverat also designed the sets for Ralph Vaughan Williams' ballet *Job*, which remained in use for 20 years. From 1928 to 1939, she wrote art criticism for the periodical *Time and Tide*, and worked for naval intelligence during World War II. She also translated Perrault's fairy tales, which were published posthumously. She died in 1957.

SOURCES:

Grimes, Teresa, Judith Collins, and Oriana Baddeley. *Five Women Painters.* Lennard, 1989.

Raverat, Gwen. *Period Piece: A Cambridge Childhood.* Faber, 1952.

Jacqueline Mitchell,
freelance writer, Detroit, Michigan

Raveskaya, Maria (1805–1863).

See Volkonskaya, Maria.

Rawlings, Marjorie Kinnan

(1896–1953)

American writer, best known for Florida-based works, especially for the transcendental essays in Cross Creek *and the realistic novel* The Yearling, *winner of the Pulitzer Prize in 1939. Name variations: Marjorie Kinnan; (pseudonym) Lady Alicia Thwaite. Pronuncia-tion: KIN-nan. Born Marjorie Kinnan on August 8, 1896, in Washington, D.C.; died on December 14, 1953, of a cerebral hemorrhage; daughter of Arthur Frank Kinnan (an employee of the U.S. Patent Office) and Ida May (Traphagen) Kinnan; graduated from Western High School, Washington, D.C., in 1914; graduated from the University of Wisconsin, 1918, as an English major; married Charles Rawlings (a journalist), in 1919 (divorced 1933); married Norton Baskin (a hotel manager), in 1941; no children.*

Published first story at age 13 in the Washington Post *(1909); was editor of high school newspaper; father died (1913); moved with her mother and brother to Madison, Wisconsin (1914); contributed to Wisconsin Literary Magazine; worked for YWCA in New York City (1918); was a feature reporter for the Louisville, Kentucky,* Courier-Journal *(1920–21); was a reporter for Rochester, New York,* Journal-American *(1922); wrote daily feature column, "Songs of a Housewife" (1926–28), for the Rochester* Times-Union; *moved to Cross Creek, Florida (1928); published "Cracker Chidlings" in* Scribner's Magazine *(1931); received Pulitzer Prize for* The Yearling *(1939); lost five-year invasion of privacy suit brought against her (1948).*

Novels and collections of stories/essays: South Moon Under *(1933);* Golden Apples *(1935);* The Yearling *(1938);* When the Whippoorwill *(1940);* Cross Creek *(1942);* Cross Creek Cookery *(1942);* The Sojourner *(1953);* The Secret River *(posthumous, 1955); numerous short stories in the* Saturday Evening Post, The New Yorker, *and* Scribner's Magazine, *collected in* Short Stories of Marjorie Kinnan Rawlings *(1994), edited by Rodger L. Tarr.*

Marjorie Kinnan Rawlings, although primarily a writer of literature for adults, is best remembered for *The Yearling* (1938). As she envisioned it, the novel would appeal to both adults and children. Her expectations came true: *The Yearling* won the Pulitzer Prize in 1939 and soon became a children's classic. Rawlings was for a decade considered the protégé of esteemed Scribner's editor Maxwell Perkins, who also was the editor of F. Scott Fitzgerald, Ernest Hemingway, and Thomas Wolfe. Nevertheless, by 1950, she had become lost to critics who considered her "only" a children's writer—and a female one at that. Her literary merit has been devalued until recently, when a surge of interest in her works has promoted a reappraisal, positioning her as a champion of nature and its caretakers.

Rawlings always considered herself a raconteur. As a child, she would gather neighborhood children around her and keep them enthralled with stories of adventure and daring. Her penchant for storytelling was nurtured by her family: she would escape from housework if she could say she was writing. Her first attempts at fiction and poetry were good enough to be published in the Washington *Post*, to which she was a frequent contributor from 1910 to 1914. Her father Arthur Kinnan, too, provided ample stimulus for her writings, for every summer the family camped out on some rural property he owned in Maryland, paving the way for his only daughter's intense love of nature. Loving and gentle, Arthur was one of the prototypes for Penny Baxter, the inestimable father of *The Yearling.* His death, when Rawlings was 17, was an emotional blow from which she never fully recovered.

> [T]he earth may be borrowed but not bought. It may be used, but not owned.
>
> —Marjorie Kinnan Rawlings

Rawlings then moved with her mother **Ida Traphagen Kinnan** and younger brother to Madison, Wisconsin, where she attended the university. As an English major, Rawlings contributed several witty stories, reviews, and poems to the *Wisconsin Literary Magazine.* She also garnered good notices as an actress in college productions (one of her fellow thespians was Fredric March). While at Madison, Marjorie met her future husband Charles Rawlings. After graduation in 1918, she moved to New York City, trying unsuccessfully to establish herself with a magazine, and he volunteered for the army and was stationed nearby. Marjorie worked for the YWCA and published in magazines sporadically. Despite her mother's protests, Marjorie married Charles in May 1919. Unable to support themselves in New York after the war, they moved to Louisville, Kentucky, where she began work as a feature reporter at the Louisville *Courier-Journal* in 1920. Here, Rawlings wrote a series of articles entitled "Live Women in Live Louisville" that revealed her feminist bent and her ability to dramatize everyday events.

By early 1922, frustrated with his floundering writing career, Charles accepted a job as salesman with his father's shoe company, and the two moved to Rochester, New York. Marjorie again worked as a journalist, this time as a feature writer for the Rochester *Journal-American* and *Times-Union.* She gave her satiric talents full play by writing for the short-lived *Five O'Clock* magazine in 1924, under the pseudonym of Lady Alicia Thwaite. In May 1926, Marjorie began the unusually grueling schedule of writing a poem a day, five days a week, for the soon-to-be syndicated "Songs of a Housewife." The rhymes do not, however, bear the mark of hurriedness or boredom; they are a daily invitation to look upon motherhood and domesticity with a fresh eye, arguing that being a housewife brought beauty and satisfaction, not just frustration and drudgery.

In 1928, the Rawlingses decided to move again, this time to northcentral Florida to the Cross Creek area, to become owners of an orange grove and pursue their careers as free-lance writers. Finally, Marjorie had her big break, when *Scribner's Magazine* accepted "Cracker Chidlings," vignettes of local Floridians, in 1931. "Jacob's Ladder" and "A Plumb Clare Conscience" followed in quick succession. All three stories were based on her observations of neighbors in Cross Creek, as she brought their world of scratch farming, moonshining, and neighborliness to a new height, seeing them as rare and noble survivors. Her "Gal Young Un," a psychological drama of an older woman married to a ne'er-do-well who brings home his latest fling, a "gal young un," was published in *Harper's Monthly,* and was subsequently awarded the O. Henry Memorial Prize for the Best Short Story of 1932.

Having become the protégé of Scribner's editor Maxwell Perkins, Rawlings was encouraged to write a novel, and Scribner's published her first, *South Moon Under,* in 1933. Rawlings did extensive research for the book, actually living with the Fiddia family, on whom the main characters were based. Like so many of her novels, the story rests on betrayal; Cleve turns in his cousin Lant for moonshining, but Cleve is punished for this duplicity. *South Moon Under* was praised for its description of the Florida environment and its people, whose customs and way of life Rawlings was trying to preserve.

Marjorie's growing success rankled Charles, whose career was still floundering. To no surprise, they divorced late in 1933. After his departure from the Cross Creek orange grove, Rawlings was on her own and relied on the close friendships she had developed with her neighbors for advice and extra help to maintain any crop she hoped to keep. These friends were especially profiled in her semi-autobiographical collection of essays, *Cross Creek,* though it was not completed for publication until 1942.

Golden Apples, Rawlings' next novel, was published in 1935. An experiment in point of view and dialogue, the story was well accepted

Marjorie
Kinnan
Rawlings

for a short time; if uneven in tone, it is still interesting for its perspectives. *Golden Apples* tells the story of the Englishman Tordell, wrongly disinherited from his family's estate, who is forced to manage a Florida orange grove. He takes advantage of the resident brother and sister, Luke and Allie Brinley, even seducing the sister, who dies in childbirth, before he finally realizes his place in the environment: "A man was a puny thing . . . ; transitory and unimportant. When he blended himself with whatever was greater than he, he found peace."

The Yearling, published in 1938, is considered Rawlings' most accomplished novel. It is the story of Jody Baxter, his father Penny, and his mother Ory. The focus is on Jody's maturation, as he learns to take on adult responsibilities. Penny is bitten by a rattlesnake and kills a doe, using her liver to draw out the snake venom. When his father almost dies, Jody begins to feel the pressures of taking care of the family. Nevertheless, Penny allows Jody to adopt the doe's baby fawn, but the fawn is wild and, as it grows, begins to destroy the family's crops, their only means of survival. Barely enduring the stealing of their stock by a vengeful bear, and a destructive hurricane that decimates the land and the animals that could have been hunted for food, the family cannot afford Jody's deer to tip the balance. Jody is forced to shoot his pet. However, this act does not completely push him into manhood, for he flees for three days, running away from his father whom Jody feels has betrayed him. Alone, Jody grows desperately hungry and almost dies; finally he realizes his family would starve if the deer had been allowed to live. He returns home to his mother and now invalid father, ready to take over the running of the farm. "He did not believe he should ever again love anything, man or woman or his own child, as he had loved the yearling. He would be lonely all his life. But a man took it for his share and went on."

The Yearling is memorable for its affectionate portrayal of Penny Baxter, the loving father, wise environmentalist, and respected storyteller. His virtues and values are passed on to his son, although Jody cannot be as idealistic as his father was. His mother's hard practicality, confirmed by the loss of his pet, has made a deep impression on Jody. These characters are vividly described, but the drama is more their conflict with nature. Both creator and destroyer, nature is what drives us and sustains us. Penny's ability to live in harmony with the workings of nature is a primary theme of the novel.

The immediate success of *The Yearling* established Rawlings as the eccentric darling of the media, a position she both milked and mocked. Intrepid reporters who could find their way to Cross Creek might be treated to alligator steak or creamed crab, according to Rawlings' mood. By this time, Rawlings had become an excellent cook, and she drew on supplies indigenous to central Florida—along with her prize Jersey cow's cream. Her penchant for good liquor also was well known, so her frequent visitors ate and drank to their contentment. Among her many guests were Robert Frost and *Zora Neale Hurston. Because of her literary connections, especially with Maxwell Perkins, she was also friends with Fitzgerald, Hemingway, James Still, *Margaret Mitchell, and other writers.

When the Whippoorwill, a collection of Rawlings' previously printed magazine stories, was published in 1940. Included were her award-winning "Gal Young Un" and her other successful first short stories, "Jacob's Ladder," "A Plumb Clare Conscience," and "Alligators." Also included were three stories—"Benny and the Bird Dogs," "Varmints," and "Cocks Must Crow"—which featured the sharp-tongued, "heavy-eating" Quincey Dover and her diminutive husband. Quincey tells these stories in her own Cracker dialect with a winning sense of humor.

With the publication of *Cross Creek* in 1942, Rawlings reached her literary apex. Her stories were as popular with American soldiers abroad as with readers at home. The semi-autobiographical essays in this book are imbued with a definite Wordsworthian view of nature. Humans are stewards of the earth, temporary caretakers, but nature keeps on living, century after century. The stories focus on the changing Floridian seasons, and on her friends Moe, Geechee, Snow, Martha, and Dessie, all long-time residents of the Cross Creek area. The essays are unusual due to their peaceful tellings of the natural environment, but also because Rawlings used real names to describe actual incidents. One person whose name appeared in the book took exception to Rawlings' description. **Zelma Cason**, once a good friend, was offended by Rawlings putting in print her already public use of profanity and by being portrayed as "an ageless spinster resembling an angry and efficient canary." Cason sued Rawlings for libel, and then for invasion of privacy. The suit was unfortunate, for much of Rawlings' time was taken up with this five-year petty legal affair (she was also taking time to respond to the many letters GI's were writing to her from the war). In the end, she was ordered to pay Cason $1.00 in damages, plus court costs. As a result, Rawlings did not have another novel published until the year of her death, in 1953.

The same year that *Cross Creek* was published, 1942, Rawlings published a sort of supplement, *Cross Creek Cookery*. Not an ordinary cookbook, this relates anecdotes and histories concerning the recipes, gathered from her own mother's larder and from friends in Cross Creek. Recipes include "Ruth Becker's Creole Oyster Soup," "Mother's Egg Croquettes," and "Okra a la Cross Creek." The publication of a cookbook was for Rawlings not an oddity but a natural occurrence. She often compared writing to cooking: both were creative acts, and she loved doing both. The theme of food—planting, harvesting, cooking, preserving, eating—was present in every one of her novels, especially in *The Yearling*. The Baxters' menus are described in detail, and the very reason for the climactic action is that the food supply is being destroyed by Jody's pet deer. In 1941, Rawlings had married Norton Baskin, a hotel manager and well-known storyteller. Although Baskin emotionally supported Rawlings' career as a writer, she sensed that being his wife would interfere with her habit of isolation which she considered crucial to her writing. So while she did maintain an apartment with him in St. Augustine, she also kept her house at Cross Creek, to which she returned often to write. Rawlings also bought a house in Van Hornsville, New York, which served as a summer home for her for several years, and a beach house at Crescent Beach, Florida.

During her last few years, Rawlings continued to publish magazine stories, the most no-

table of which is "Mountain Prelude," published in the *Saturday Evening Post* in 1947. Actually a novella, this tells the story of a concert pianist who loses both her husband and her son to plane accidents. She retreats to the mountains of North Carolina to recover, where she meets a boy her son's age who comes to work for her, which forces her to see beyond her grief.

In 1953, Rawlings' last novel, *The Sojourner*, was published by Scribner's. It was the first of her novels to be set in the north. Rawlings drew from memories of her grandparents' farm in Michigan, and so there are apple orchards and snow sleighs and bountiful tables. The protagonist, Ase Linden, resembles Penny Baxter in his spirituality and generosity. His mother favors her other son and wills the farm to him, though he leaves. Ase then is steward of the large farm, never owning it outright. In the end, Ase dies of a heart attack on an airplane, after having traveled to reconcile with his brother. He dies peacefully, not alerting his fellow passengers. His sojourn was ended: "He had been a guest in a mansion and he was not ungrateful." Although

From the movie Cross Creek, starring Mary Steenburgen as Rawlings.

not set in Florida, *The Sojourner* presents the same themes as in the earlier works—the betrayal that life brings, but more important the Wordsworthian stewardship towards the earth, and both an abiding love and respect for nature.

Marjorie Kinnan Rawlings died on December 14, 1953, at Crescent Beach, Florida. She left a legacy of works that live on, keeping vital the ideals of preserving the environment and people's cultures, be it Michigan farmers' or Florida Crackers'. Rawlings saw herself as an anthropologist, an observer dedicated to preserving the records of the daily life of a people and a place destined, because of increasing real estate development, to extinction. In this, she was successful.

SOURCES:

Bellman, Samuel I. *Marjorie Kinnan Rawlings*. NY: Twayne, 1974.

Bigelow, Gordon. *Frontier Eden: The Literary Career of Marjorie Kinnan Rawlings*. Gainesville, FL: University of Florida Press, 1966.

———, and Gloria F. Monti, eds. *Selected Letters of Marjorie Kinnan Rawlings*. Gainesville, FL: University of Florida Press, 1983.

Silverthorne, Elizabeth. *Marjorie Kinnan Rawlings; Sojourner at Cross Creek*. Woodstock, NY: The Overlook Press, 1988.

Tarr, Rodger L., ed. *Marjorie Kinnan Rawlings: A Descriptive Bibliography*.

———. *Max and Marjorie: The Correspondence Between Maxwell E. Perkins and Marjorie Kinnan Rawlings*. Gainesville, FL: University of Florida Press, 1999.

———. *Short Stories of Marjorie Kinnan Rawlings*. Gainesville, FL: University of Florida Press, 1994.

Tarr, Rodger L., and Carol Anita Tarr. Introduction. *Cross Creek* by Marjorie Kinnan Rawlings. 50th Anniversary ed. Jacksonville, FL: South Moon Books, 1992.

SUGGESTED READING:

Acton, Patricia Nassif. *Invasion of Privacy: The Cross Creek Trial of Marjorie Kinnan Rawlings*. Gainesville. FL: University of Florida Press, 1988.

The Marjorie Kinnan Rawlings Journal of Florida Literature (a periodical which includes major articles on Rawlings, edited by Rodger L. Tarr, 1988—).

RELATED MEDIA:

Cross Creek (127 min. film), starring **Mary Steenburgen** and Rip Torn, screenplay by **Dalene Young**, Universal, 1983.

The Yearling (129 min. film), starring Gregory Peck, ***Jane Wyman**, and Claude Jarman, Jr., directed by Clarence Brown, MGM, 1946.

Carol Anita Tarr,
Assistant Professor of English,
Illinois State University, Normal, Illinois

Rawls, Betsy (1928—)

American golfer. Born Elizabeth Earle Rawls in Spartanburg, South Carolina, on May 4, 1928; graduated from the University of Texas.

Won the Vare trophy; was the first woman to serve on the Rules Committee for the U.S. Men's Open; won four U.S. Open titles (1951, 1953, 1957, 1960); won her namesake tournament Betsy Rawls Open (1956); won ten tournaments, including Mount Prospect Women's Open, (1959); all told, won 55 LPGA tournaments.

In the golfing world, Betsy Rawls was known as the "circuit judge" because of her comprehensive knowledge of the rules of golf. She was born in Spartanburg, South Carolina, in 1928, and graduated Phi Beta Kappa from the University of Texas with a degree in math and physics. Rawls did not begin playing golf until she was 17, which is considered rather late. In 1949 and 1950, she won the Texas Amateur championship. In 1951, 1953, 1957 and 1960, she won the U.S. Women's Open championship, and was the LPGA champion in 1959 and 1969. Only ***Kathy Whitworth** and ***Mickey Wright** won more tournaments than Rawls, who had 55 tournament titles.

Betsy
Rawls

But 1959 was the year of Rawls. The soft-spoken golfer won ten titles, nearly 40% of the LPGA's 26-event schedule, setting new standards in women's golf in victories, money winnings, and scoring. She also won the coveted Vare Trophy, awarded to the woman with the lowest cumulative score for the season, with a record-scoring average of 74.03, and became the second player to win the *Patty Berg Award. Rawls was elected to the LPGA Hall of Fame in 1960 and won her last victory at Tucson in 1972. Twice president of the LPGA, she was the first woman to serve on the Rules Committee of the U.S. Men's Open. When she retired in 1975, Rawls was named LPGA first tournament director. In 1981, she began a long reign as executive director of McDonald's championship. She was inducted into the World Golf Hall of Fame in 1987.

Karin Loewen Haag,
Athens, Georgia

Rawls, Elizabeth (b. 1928).

See Rawls, Betsy.

Ray, Charlotte E. (1850–1911)

First African-American woman lawyer in the United States who was also the first woman admitted to the bar in the District of Columbia and the third woman in the country admitted to the practice of law. Born in New York City on January 13, 1850; died in Long Island, New York, on January 4, 1911; daughter of Charles Bennett Ray (a Congregational minister and abolitionist) and Charlotte Augusta Burroughs Ray; sister of H. Cordelia Ray (c. 1849–1916); attended the Institution for the Education of Colored Youth, Washington, D.C.; graduated from Howard University Law School, 1872; married a man with the surname Fraim after 1886.

Born in New York City on January 13, 1850, Charlotte Ray was one of seven children. Her mother **Charlotte Burroughs Ray** was originally from Savannah, Georgia, and her father Charles Bennett Ray was a minister and a well-known abolitionist of African, Indian, and European descent. Charlotte no doubt inherited much of her tenacity and courage from her father, who was not only the editor of the *Colored American* and a prominent religious leader, but also a conductor on the Underground Railroad, helping slaves escape. He ensured that all his children, including Charlotte and her sister *H. Cordelia Ray**, were well educated. Charlotte completed her course work at the Institution for the Education of Colored Youth (which had been founded by *Myrtilla Miner**) in Washington, D.C., in

1869, and became a teacher in the Normal and Preparatory Department at Howard University.

Ray had ambitions for a law career, but knew it would be difficult to gain entry into Howard's law school because she was a woman. When applying, she submitted her name as C.E. Ray to maneuver past gender prejudice, and was accepted. Her highly successful academic career included induction into Phi Beta Kappa. Mention was made of her in the school's 1870 annual report, as "a colored woman who read us a thesis on corporations, not copied from the books but from her brain, a clear incisive analysis of one of the most delicate legal questions." The astonishment that ensued was also duly noted.

Corporation law interested Ray particularly during her studies, and she was acknowledged to have a profound grasp of its complexities. She graduated from law school in 1872, and on April 23 became both the first African-American woman lawyer in America and the first woman admitted to the bar in the District of Columbia. When she opened a law office in Washington, she was only the third woman in the country to do so. (The following year, the Illinois Supreme Court would uphold the denial of a law license to *Myra Bradwell** because of her gender.) Ray had had several black male classmates in law school, and they went on to distinguished careers despite the racial prejudice in the country. Sadly for Ray, who was by all accounts an excellent lawyer, the double whammy of her race and her gender kept potential clients at bay. She was unable to sustain her practice and was forced to close her office.

Ray remained active in the cause to further opportunities for blacks and women. She attended the National Women's Suffrage Association convention in New York in 1876, and in the years after 1895 became an active member of the National Association of Colored Women. She had moved back to New York City by 1879, and, rather than practicing corporation law, she worked as a teacher in the Brooklyn public school system, where her two older sisters were also employed. There is scant information about her later life, although it is known that she was married sometime after 1886 to a man whose last name was Fraim. She died of acute bronchitis in 1911, at the age of 60. The annual award of the Greater Washington Area Chapter (GWAC) of the Women Lawyers Division of the American Bar Association is named the GWAC Charlotte W. Ray Annual Award in her honor.

SOURCES:
Igus, Toyomi, ed. *Great Women in the Struggle*. Just Us Books, 1991.

James, Edward T., ed. *Notable American Women, 1607–1950*. Cambridge, MA: The Belknap Press of Harvard University Press, 1971.

McHenry, Robert, ed. *Famous American Women*. NY: Dover, 1980.

Smith, Jessie Carney, ed. *Notable Black American Women*. Detroit, MI: Gale Research, 1992.

Weatherford, Doris. *American Women's History*. NY: Prentice Hall, 1994.

Jacqueline Mitchell,
freelance writer, Detroit, Michigan

Ray, Cordelia (c. 1849–1916).

See Ray, H. Cordelia.

Ray, Dixy Lee (1914–1994)

American scientist who was head of the Atomic Energy Commission and later governor of Washington. Born Margaret Ray in Tacoma, Washington, on September 3, 1914; died on Fox Island, Washington, on January 2, 1994; graduated from Mills College with a degree in zoology, 1937, M.A., 1938; Stanford University, Ph.D., 1945; never married; no children.

Dixy Lee Ray was born on September 3, 1914, in Tacoma, Washington. Although she was christened "Margaret" and given the nickname "Dick" (short for "that little Dickens"), Ray chose her own name, "Dixy Lee," as a homage to her favorite region and Civil War general. At the age of 12, her independent, can-do attitude began to emerge when she climbed Mount Rainier and thus became the youngest girl to scale Washington's highest mountain. She attended Mills College in California on a full scholarship, studying zoology while also working various jobs on campus, including waiting tables, managing the school theater, and cleaning laboratories, to earn money for living expenses. After completing her undergraduate work in 1937, she earned a master's degree the following year.

After teaching in public schools in Oakland, California, in 1942 Ray entered Stanford University. Three years later, having earned a Ph.D. in biology, she became an instructor in zoology at the University of Washington, where she would remain for 25 years. Ray became an assistant professor in 1947, and an associate professor ten years later. She often traveled internationally to conduct her research, which focused primarily on certain marine crustaceans, especially *Limnoria*, and organisms that attack submerged wood and damage piers, boats, drydocks and wharves. She published a number of papers in various journals, and in 1959 edited *Marine Boring and Fouling Organisms*. The year prior to that, she had produced "Animals of the Seashore," a 15-part series of half-hour television shows about various marine animals that was aimed at a general audience. The meticulously executed series proved popular and was lauded by Ray's fellow scientists, and went on to become something of a staple in schools and on educational television. As noted in *Famous American Women*, Ray was a "leading advocate of ecological research as a prerequisite to understanding the dangers inherent in the unregulated growth of such technologies as chemical manufacturing, energy production, and waste disposal." Long before the rise of the environmental movement, Ray was vocal about the contamination of oceans by radioactive materials and dangerous pesticides. "The balance of nature, of living things, is rapidly being altered," she warned. "And we must stop the destruction of species that comes about when we change the environment by our technological advances without knowing the consequences of our interference with nature."

Ray's experience from 1960 to 1962 as a special consultant in biological oceanography to the National Science Foundation led to her appointment as the director of the newly established Pacific Science Center in Seattle, Washington, in 1963. With her guidance, the center achieved national prominence for its work in encouraging a better understanding of science by the general public. After serving as a member of the President's Task Force on Oceanography in 1969, Ray was nominated for a seat on the Atomic Energy Commission by President Richard M. Nixon in 1972. She resigned from the University of Washington and the Science Center after her appointment to the government was confirmed by the Senate. She was the first woman to undertake a full term on the commission. A year later, she became chair of the commission, a post that brought her arguably more power than that held by any other woman in the federal government. (She continued to live in a motor home, as she had since her arrival in D.C., bemusing much of the political establishment.) Ray worked to improve opportunities for minority job applicants in the field, and championed broader research into the safety of nuclear reactors. Many environmentalists criticized her blunt defense of the nuclear industry and she, in turn, opposed environmental alarmists. After the Atomic Energy Commission was reorganized in 1974, she became assistant secretary for oceans and international environmental scientific affairs at the Department of State.

Ray resigned from this job in 1975 in order to campaign as the Democratic candidate for the governorship of her home state. Despite the burgeoning women's movement, not many women ran for statewide office at that time (only *Ella Grasso of Connecticut had been elected without benefit of a husband who had been governor), and Ray, an "apolitical college professor," was considered a long shot at winning, particularly in a Republican-dominated state. Nonetheless, she was elected by a healthy margin. In 1977, at age 62, she was sworn in as the state's first woman governor.

Ray courted controversy from the very beginning of her four years in office, when she fired almost everyone in the administration who had worked for the previous governor, Dan Evans. Her response to the public clamor was: "No one owns a job. From now on, we'll send them a Kleenex at the time they're fired." Her term rarely went smoothly after that, and her battles with reporters became a hallmark of her administration. Some observers cited her unwillingness to compromise as the primary reason behind her defeat in the Democratic primary to Jim McDermott while seeking re-election. Never one to be idle, she picked up where she had left off in her research and writing, co-authoring the books *Trashing the Planet* (1990) and *Environmental Overkill* (1993) with journalist and longtime friend Lou Guzzo. Ray remained opinion-

ated to the end despite suffering from a severe bronchial condition in the last months of her life, offering public commentary on nuclear issues only days before she died at her home on Fox Island on January 2, 1994, at the age of 79.

SOURCES:

Current Biography. Vol. 55, no. 3. March 1994.
"Dixy Lee Ray," in *The Day* [New London, CT]. January 3, 1994, p. B4.
McHenry, Robert, ed. *Famous American Women*. NY: Dover, 1980.
Poole, Lynn and Gray. *Scientists Who Work Outdoors*. NY: Dodd, Mead, 1963.
Weatherford, Doris. *American Women's History*. NY: Prentice Hall, 1994.

Jacqueline Mitchell,
freelance writer, Detroit, Michigan

Ray, H. Cordelia (c. 1849–1916)

African-American poet and scholar. Name variations: Henrietta Cordelia Ray; Cordelia Ray. Born Henrietta Cordelia Ray in New York City around 1849; died in 1916; daughter of Charles B. Ray (a Congregational minister and abolitionist) and Charlotte Augusta (Burroughs) Ray; sister of Charlotte E. Ray (1850–1911); University of the City of New York, master of pedagogy degree, 1891; attended Sauveneur School of Languages; never married; no children.

Selected writings: Sonnets (1893) and Poems (1910).

Henrietta Cordelia Ray—later known more commonly as Cordelia Ray—was born in New York City around 1849, the second daughter of Charles Ray and **Charlotte Burroughs Ray**. Her family's ancestors were reputedly among the first New England Africans, who had intermarried with Native Americans and the English of Massachusetts. In addition to his duties as a Congregational minister, Charles Ray was involved with the Underground Railroad (the family's home served as a way station for escaped slaves) and was editor of the abolitionist newspaper *Colored American*. He made certain that his children were well educated—all received college degrees—including his three daughters, who went on to distinguished careers. Cordelia's older sister **Florence Ray** became a teacher, and her younger sister *Charlotte E. Ray became the first African-American woman attorney in the country. Cordelia attended the University of the City of New York, graduating in 1891; she also studied French, Greek, Latin, and German at the Sauveneur School of Languages.

Initially taken with her sister Florence's profession, Cordelia started her career as a teacher in the girls' department at Colored Grammar School Number One, but the job quickly palled. Relatively unhindered by financial need, she decided instead to become a writer, concentrating her energies on poetry, although she did continue to teach individual students and small groups privately. She and her sister Florence, who had become an invalid, lived together in Woodside, Long Island. Together they produced a 79-page biography of their father's life and work, *Sketches of Life of Rev. Charles E. Ray*, in 1887.

Poetry was Cordelia's true love, and she published many of her poems in the journal of the African Methodist Episcopal Church, the *AME Review*. At the unveiling ceremony for the Freedman's Monument in Washington, D.C., on April 14, 1876, her 81-line poem "Lincoln" was read; Frederick Douglass gave the keynote address. In 1893, she published a collection of her poetry entitled *Sonnets*; a second volume, *Poems*, appeared in 1910. Her work was typical of the late 19th century: passionless ruminations on the broad themes of platonic love, morality, Christian faith, and nature. Ray wrote mainly philosophical poems, verses lamenting disappointed love, and tributes to those (like her father) who fought for freedom. Only in the latter was there the remotest indication of racial consciousness or a political agenda. She enjoyed a sheltered life, relatively free from the virulent racism endured by so many other African-Americans in the post-Reconstruction era, and her poetry was a reflection of this experience. That she, with a father who had worked for the Underground Railroad, must have known of the suffering of most black Americans has caused modern-day critics to view her with some contempt. Added to the criticism aimed at her subject matter (or lack thereof) has been criticism of her technically excellent but stiff style, which was common at the time but now seems stilted and awkward. While she was not hugely popular in her own day, she was, nonetheless, a published poet in a time of severely restricted opportunities for African-Americans and for women. Ray's works are included in the prestigious scholarly series *Collected Black Women's Poetry*, published in 1988, some 72 years after her death.

SOURCES:

Smith, Jessie Carney, ed. *Notable Black American Women*. Detroit, MI: Gale Research, 1992.

Jacqueline Mitchell,
freelance writer, Detroit, Michigan

Ray, Martha (d. 1779)

Mistress of the earl of Sandwich. Murdered outside the Covent Garden Theatre, London, England, in 1779; mistress of John Montagu (1718–1792), 4th earl of Sandwich (1st Lord of the Admiralty); never married; no children.

The daughter of a London stay-maker, Martha Ray was a talented singer. At age 18, she became the mistress of John Montagu, 4th earl of Sandwich and 1st Lord of the Admiralty, and reportedly had some input into his naval appointments. Montagu was known for employing vast patronage in exchange for bribes and political sway. Ray also became the obsession of James Hackman, a lieutenant in the army and later incumbent of Wiveton, Norfolk. In 1779, when she spurned Hackman's marriage proposal, he was so bereft that he shot her dead as she left the Covent Garden Theatre.

Raye, Martha (1916–1994)

American comedian, actress, and singer. Born Margaret Theresa Yvonne Reed on August 27, 1916, in Butte, Montana; died on October 19, 1994, in Los Angeles, California; one of three children (two girls and a boy) of Pete Reed and Maybelle (Hooper) Reed (both vaudeville performers); attended public schools in Montana and Roman Catholic schools in Chicago, Illinois; attended the Professional Children's School, New York City; married Hamilton (Buddy) Westmore (a Hollywood make-up artist), on May 30, 1937 (divorced 1937); married David Rose (an orchestra leader), on October 8, 1938 (divorced 1941); married Neal Lang (a hotel manager), on June 25, 1941 (divorced 1944); married Nick Condos (a dancer and her personal manager), in March 1944 (divorced 1953); married Edward Begley (a dancer), on April 21, 1954 (divorced 1956); married Robert O'Shea (her bodyguard), on November 7, 1958 (divorced 1962); married Mark Harris (an ex-hairdresser), on September 25, 1991; children: (fourth marriage) **Melodye Raye Condos**.

Selected filmography: Rhythm on the Range *(1936);* Hideaway Girl *(1936);* The Big Broadcast of 1937 *(1936);* College Holiday *(1936);* Waikiki Wedding *(1937);* Mountain Music *(1937);* Artists and Models *(1937);* Double or Nothing *(1937);* The Big Broadcast of 1938 *(1938);* Give Me a Sailor *(1938);* College Swing *(1938);* Tropic Holiday *(1938);* Never Say Die *(1939);* $1000 a Touchdown *(1939);* The Farmer's Daughter *(1940);* The Boys From Syracuse *(1940);* Navy Blues *(1941);* Keep 'Em Flying *(1941);* Hellzapoppin *(1941);* Four Jills in a Jeep *(1944);* Pin Up Girl *(1944);* Monsieur Verdoux *(1947);* Jumbo *(1962);* The Phynx *(1970);* The Concorde—Airport '79 *(1979).*

Known for her booming voice, elastic mouth, and raucous humor, Martha Raye was a veteran of the vaudeville and nightclub circuits by the time she was 19, then went on to conquer Broadway, films, and television. Perhaps the most profound aspect of her career, however, was her tireless work for the USO, entertaining American troops during World War II, the Korean War, and the Vietnam War. In 1969, she was awarded the Jean Hersholt Humanitarian Award for her five trips to Vietnam, during which she not only entertained, but also visited the sick and wounded in field hospitals. In 1993, she received the Presidential Medal of Freedom from President Bill Clinton, who cited her "great courage, kindness and patriotism." While her career flourished, Raye's personal life was a disaster, strewn with failed marriages, periodic breakdowns, and several suicide attempts. "I thought success in show business was the answer to everything," she once said. "It isn't. I don't know what is."

Raye was born Margaret Reed, and known as Maggie, in 1916 in Butte, Montana, the daughter of itinerant vaudeville performers. She joined the family song-and-dance act at the age of three, and as a teenager struck out on her own, playing burlesque houses, musical revues, and nightclubs. As a result, her education was catch-as-catch-can, never taking precedence over her performing schedule. Her early career included stints with the Benny Davis Revue, the Ben Blue Company, and the Will Morrissey Company. She made her Broadway debut in 1934, in Lew Brown's musical comedy *Calling All Stars*, which ran for only 36 performances. The following year, while performing at the Trocadero nightclub in Los Angeles, she caught the attention of film director Norman Taurog, who signed her for the lead opposite Bing Crosby in *Rhythm on the Range* (1936). Her show-stopping rendition of "Mr. Paganini" rocketed the 20-year-old to movie stardom. Raye subsequently made over 30 films, most notable among them *Monsieur Verdoux* (1947), a black comedy in which she played Annabella Bonheur, the indestructible mate of a Parisian wife-killer played by Charlie Chaplin. "Miss Raye makes altogether the best foil for the

Martha Raye

actor's miming," wrote Howard Barnes in his review of the film for the New York *Herald Tribune* (April 13, 1947). "In her rough and tumble scenes with the star something of the gaiety of the early Chaplin masterpieces is recaptured." Because of her association with Chaplin, who at the time was under investigation for alleged Communist activities, Raye was unofficially blacklisted by the film community; it was 1962 before she made her next movie.

During the height of her film career, Raye also co-starred with Al Jolson in the 1940 stage revue *Hold On to Your Hats*. She subsequently appeared on Jolson's radio show for two years, and also made guest appearances with Eddie Cantor, Bob Hope, and other leading radio personalities. When Hollywood dismissed her, she turned to the new medium of television, making numerous guest appearances, as well as hosting her own show on NBC during the 1953–54 season. During the 1950s, she also returned occasionally to the nightclub circuit, and for several years starred at her own establishment, The Five O'Clock Club, in Miami. Raye made her film comeback in the 1962 MGM circus musical *Jumbo*, adding spark to an otherwise lackluster screen version of the original 1936 stage show produced by Billy Rose. In reviewing the film for the New York *Herald Tribune* (December 7, 1962), Paul V. Beckley noted that Raye "can breathe life into [her lines] as only fine clowns can, making the grimace add golden weight to the words."

During the late 1960s, Raye suffered a career slump which she blamed on her USO trips to Vietnam. She remained, however, a staunch defender of the American war effort. "It seems to me a lot of this anti-war stuff is aimed at the wrong target," she said in a 1971 interview, "at our boys over there." The troops returned her affection and respect many times over. "Thousands of Vietnam Veterans and I love and would die for her," said Edmond Orr, of McCool, Mississippi. "She proved in Vietnam that she would do the same for us."

In private life, Raye was nothing like her onstage persona, as Hollywood columnist ◄❧ **Louella Parsons** observed in 1963. "Like many great entertainers who thrive on audience reaction, Martha is 'on' at the drop of a cue," she wrote in a column. "At a party she will sing and clown her heart out for hours. She's boisterous, hilarious, loud. But get her alone and you'll find a soft-spoken, serious, thoughtful woman who talks with honesty and simplicity." As other friends of the actress noted, Raye was frequently lonely and

blue. "Few people actually know me, or take me seriously," she once lamented. Of her many marriages, most of which lasted less than three years, the most enduring was her relationship with Nick Condos, to whom she was married from 1944 to 1953, and with whom she had her only child Melodye. When they divorced, Condos stayed on as her manager, and years later moved back into her home with her. After his death in 1988, Raye never changed the kitchen calendar from the month he died.

During her final years, Raye was plagued by ill health; she had a stroke in 1990, and two years later suffered circulatory problems which forced doctors to amputate her left leg below the knee. In 1991, at age 75, she married ex-hairdresser Mark Harris, who was nearly half her age. "He makes me feel young and womanly," she said about the relationship which raised some eyebrows. "I'm really in love this time." Martha Raye died on October 19, 1994, in Los Angeles. As had been her wish, she was buried among "her troops," veterans of World War II, Korea, and Vietnam, at Fort Bragg, North Carolina.

SOURCES:

Fortin, Noonie. *Memories of Maggie*. San Antonio, TX: Langmarc, 1995.

Graham, Judith, ed. *Current Biography 1995*. NY: H.W. Wilson, 1995.

Katz, Ephraim. *The Film Encyclopedia*. NY: Harper-Collins, 1994.

"Mighty Mouth," in *People Weekly*. October 31, 1994.

Moritz, Charles, ed. *Current Biography 1963*. NY: H.W. Wilson, 1963.

Thomas, Bob. Obituary in *The Day* [New London, CT]. October 20, 1994.

SUGGESTED READING:

Pitrone, Jean Maddern. *Take It from the Big Mouth: The Life of Martha Raye*. The University Press of Kentucky, 1999.

Barbara Morgan,
Melrose, Massachusetts

Raymond, Eleanor (1887–1989)

American architect. Born in Cambridge, Massachusetts, in 1887; died in 1989; graduated from Wellesley College, 1909; master's degree in architecture from the Cambridge School of Architecture and Landscape Architecture, 1919; never married; longtime companion of Ethel Power (an architectural journalist and writer).

A residential architect in the Boston area for over half a century, Eleanor Raymond designed and built her first house in 1919. Her interest was drawn to architecture by a landscaping course she took at Wellesley College, and was further piqued after her 1909 graduation when

Parsons, Louella. *See joint entry on Hopper, Hedda and Louella Parsons.*

she was much taken with buildings she saw while traveling in Europe. She later described herself at that time, in the words of **Doris Cole**, as "an independent young woman, with a preference for individual creative work rather than supervision of others, a growing interest in gardens and buildings, and little desire for marriage and family."

After returning to Boston from Europe, Raymond started out by studying with landscaper Fletcher Steele. Most of his other students were proper young Boston women uninterested in careers, however, and she found these classes unchallenging. Instead, she began working for free in Steele's office, learning by observing, and the experience spurred her to enroll in 1917 in the small Cambridge School of Architecture and Landscape Architecture for women. Landscape architecture was strongly linked to horticulture in the early 20th century, and since she was no horticulturist, she turned more to architecture. Nonetheless, landscape remained a focal point throughout her career, for she gave careful consideration to environment and to meshing her buildings with their surroundings. Raymond graduated with a master's degree in architecture in 1919, and that year both opened an office with Henry Atherton Frost and received her first commission.

While her training had been in the Beaux-Arts style of architecture, which made heavy use of such decorative elements as columns and cornices, Raymond was intrigued by the plain style of old American houses, and she became known for the graceful simplicity of her designs. In 1928, she ended her partnership with Frost and opened a solo office in Boston. Raymond worked exclusively on homes, a professional choice dictated both by the limited commercial contracts available to female architects at the time and her own delight in the possibilities afforded by residential design. Her entire philosophy on historic and contemporary architecture is outlined in her book *Early Domestic Architecture of Pennsylvania* (1931, reprinted 1973), a detailed study of the style of early American architecture and what she called its "unstudied directness in fitting form to function." This was an apt description of her own work, although she also experimented with materials; among her buildings were a Plywood House (1940) and a Masonite House (1944), both created for Boston sculptor **Amelia Peabody** (1890–1984). In 1948, Raymond designed and built a Sun House in Dover, Massachusetts, for Peabody. Created in conjunction with chemist and solar engineer *Maria Telkes, who designed its solar heating system, the Sun House was the first solar-pow-

ered house to be built for occupation in America. (It is still lived in today.)

Raymond worked principally in Massachusetts, and a number of her clients were women whom she knew in Boston and Cambridge, many of them involved in the arts. She lived for some 50 years with architectural journalist and writer **Ethel Power** (who was also an editor of *House Beautiful*), and Power's diary, which she kept for nearly 40 years, contains much information on their lives as well as on Raymond's day-to-day work and design principles. Important among these was her belief that the home should accommodate the client, and so her style evolved to keep pace with the changes that occurred over the decades in the ways Americans lived. Raymond was elected a Fellow of the American Institute of Architects in 1961, and she continued working through the 1970s, utilizing new technologies and building materials but always focusing not on those elements but on the "three fields" of a home, meaning the exterior, the interior, and the landscape. In the words of one client, she was "an architect who combine[d] a respect for tradition with a disrespect for its limitations." She died in 1989.

SOURCES:

Cole, Doris. "Eleanor Raymond," in *Women in American Architecture: A Historic and Contemporary Perspective*. Edited by Susan Torre. NY: Whitney Library of Design, 1977.

COLLECTIONS:

The Eleanor Raymond Collection, which includes documentation of nearly 300 architectural projects, personal papers and photographs, memorabilia, and Ethel Power's diary (1930–68), is in the Special Collections at the Frances Loeb Library of Harvard University.

Jacqueline Mitchell,
freelance writer, Detroit, Michigan

Razafindrahety (1861–1917).

See Ranavalona III.

Razia (1211–1240)

First queen of India, who defied the norms of the time to reign as sovereign, and whose courage, intelligence and pragmatism remain unparalleled in medieval Indian history. Name variations: Razia Sultana or Sultana Razia; Raziya or Raziyya Sultana; Raziyyatuddin or Raziyat-ud-din; Razia Iltutmish (or Altamsh). Pronunciation: Ra-ZEE-ya. Born Raziyat-ud-din ("Devoted to the Faith") in 1211 in Delhi, India; died in 1240 outside of Delhi; daughter of Emperor Shams-ud-din Iltutmish; mother's name unknown; had private tutors for reading and writing; military training; married Altuniya, in 1240; no children.

While investigating the history of India during the 13th century, historians have rarely attributed any advancement or transformation of the nation to the reign of the only queen of India, Razia Sultana. They have emphasized the establishment of Muslim rule in India, the Delhi Sultanate, while singing accolades to various monarchs and their legacies. Sacrificed to traditional history of this era are the endeavors of a queen whose rule was cut short because she was a progressive and lenient monarch and, above all, a woman. Despite her best efforts to redefine the prevailing notions of gender roles and royalty, in the end, she was a victim of the conventionalities of the era.

Razia's short reign of three and a half years has often been relegated, at best, to a cursory discussion, but there is something remarkable about the mettle of the young woman who became queen in a Muslim society. She was a queen who discarded the *purdah* system, who threw off the veil, who rode out in combat dressed like any other soldier, who was committed to enhancing the power and benevolence of the kingdom her father had established. The only queen ever to be crowned at the Delhi court in India, Razia is buried in the recesses of history for the simple reason that she was a woman, a mere blip in the continuum of the reigns of the men who came before and after her.

The spread of Islam had crucial repercussions for the East and for the world. India felt its impact in the 11th century when Muslim rulers of the Persian and Turkish empires began to raid its northwestern provinces. By the 12th century, the Muslims had established a dynasty and a throne at Delhi in North India. They then proceeded to expand and assimilate the empire. The period first dynasty until the advent of the Mughals in the 15th century is designated as the era of the Delhi Sultanate, when several dynasties fought for, and some gained control of, the Delhi throne. The first king to establish an empire which was relatively stable was Razia's father Iltutmish of the Mamluk dynasty. He had established a stable empire not solely by usurping power but also by politic and circumspect rule. Iltutmish's judicious court was Razia's classroom, where she closely observed the working of a monarchy, and its attendant triumphs and travails. Her reign is testimony to lessons learned well.

From an early age, Razia displayed an interest in governmental affairs. She was an outstanding student of administration and diplomacy, and an able military cadet. Her capabilities were obvious to her father. Her first experience with governing the kingdom was when Iltutmish went on the Gwalior expedition, leaving her in charge of affairs of state. Razia outshone the best of his aides and was far more effective than any of her effete brothers. Entrusted with imperial power, she wielded it judiciously. Upon his return in 1228, Iltutmish named his 17-year-old daughter to be his successor. Clearly, Razia had demonstrated that she had the necessary courage, alertness, and requisite training to be a consummate monarch. When the astonished and angry ministers remonstrated against this idea, the king responded: "My sons are given over to the follies of youth; you will find there is no one better able to rule this country than my daughter." Iltutmish prepared for his daughter's succession by adding her name to a series of silver *tankah* (a form of currency). After his death, however, Razia was to bear the burden of her gender until she was finally defeated by the patriarchal order of the day; an arrangement that was upheld and utilized by the nobles of the court.

Following the death of Iltutmish, a colorless rake named Rukn-ud-din Firoz took advantage of the nobles' discomfiture with a queen-regnant (Iltutmish had appointed one of Razia's brothers as her successor). Assisted by his scheming and ambitious mother **Shah Turkan**, Firoz captured the throne. But Shah Turkan's cruelty and Firoz's ineffectiveness as a ruler managed to alienate their most vocal supporters. The Delhi Sultanate quickly fell into chaos and disrepair, a fact that dismayed the populace and nobles alike. Playing a skilled game of imperial chess, Razia took advantage of Firoz's temporary absence from the capital and beat the duo at their own game. Clad in red, as was customary for the aggrieved, she appeared before a congregation of Muslims at their Friday prayers and roused them against Shah Turkan's machinations. Her rhetorical entreaties revived Iltutmish's memory and incited the crowd to support his choice for succession; they proclaimed her queen. Confident in her abilities, she promised an effective and fair government, stating that if she "did not prove her abilities and if she did not prove better than men, her head was to be struck off." The promise astutely circumvented any arguments that might associate her gender with her inability as a monarch. While the people and the army officers put their weight behind her, the earlier objectors had new reason for opposition—judging Razia's coup an entirely unacceptable method of ascending the throne. To thwart them, Razia sowed dissensions among the nobles, ensuring a period of ineffective opposition and thus giving her the opportunity to strengthen her position as the first woman monarch of the Delhi Sultanate.

The sultana's first regal act was to organize the government. The governing structure that she set in place would continue to be the system of choice not only for the Sultanate but, with some changes, for early Mughal rule in India. In 13th-century India, the monarch's firmness was the only justification for her/his existence. Razia appropriated considerable authority from provincial chiefs and firmly established the monarch's position as the locus of all power; she placed her staunchest supporters in the most influential positions of governors and ministers; and she carefully planned to break the monopoly of power held by the Turkish nobles. Discarding her female attire, she rode out in public; she also held open court, thus making herself accessible to the nobility and populace alike. Later opponents deemed this same determination, coming from a woman, as scandalous. But Razia did what any monarch would do: she emphasized the vitality and vigor of her rule. She was openly challenging the monopolization of authority by the military aristocracy. In the first two years of her reign, every revolt by a Turkish noble was suppressed quickly and effectively. Razia herself rode out at the head of the imperial army in order to quell any such opposition and open revolt, and swiftly managed to coerce the rebel leaders. While this tactic was initially effective, it later became apparent that the nobles' submission concealed a latent opposition which would soon surface and bring her rule to an end.

Razia's commitment to consolidation of the Sultanate was evident in her superior military expeditions and diplomacy. The furthest corners of the empire were brought under her authority. She led armies against rebelling Hindu princes, who attempted several times to regain control of their territory from the Muslim rulers. There is only one recorded instance in which Razia delegated military maneuvers to a general; otherwise, she was always at the helm of her forces. Her most ingenious diplomatic move was to make peace with the marauding hordes of the Mongols. By 1238, the Mongols had reached the contiguous territories of the Sultanate. When the king of those territories approached Razia for assistance against the Mongols, she refused to ally with him, displaying a prudent disinclination to court Mongol hostility. Her position was tenuous enough within her borders; she did not need pressures from without. The Mongols, apparently pleased with her decision, respected her borders and never attacked her territories. Tacit-

ly, Razia had convened a non-aggression pact with the Mongols, one that ceased to exist once she was deposed.

One of the more remarkable aspects of Razia's reign was her commitment to progressive reform policies. In order to execute such policies, a monarch needs good advisors and sound counsel. Once Razia had fortified her position by quelling the Turkish nobles, she selected for office those who had displayed commitment to, and support for, the empire. She placed competent and exceptional men in such important posts as commander-in-chief of the army, Lord Chamberlain, Lord of the Stables, and Lord of the Nobles. Now Razia was ready to reconstruct the empire. She declared a policy of religious tolerance towards the Hindus and ordered that the *jaziya* (a tax placed by Muslim rulers on "infidel" subjects) be discontinued; clearly, with this move her rule won much support from the Hindu populace. She often visited various parts of Delhi and surrounding villages to ascertain the condition of her people. Perceiving any grievances, she ordered immediate redress. Razia consciously established a new order under which every subject-citizen, regardless of creed or race, had the same opportunities—distinctions and disparities were removed. Penal code provisions were applicable to all without discrimination. Crimes were punished on the basis of evidence; trial by ordeal was abolished. Interprovincial exchange burgeoned; international trade increased. To encourage trade, Razia centralized authority and developed a uniform system of currency, transport, and communication. To safeguard her empire and territories, the sultana developed a strong, standing army that was recruited, trained, and administered from a central location. In a few short months, the young monarch had consolidated and reconstructed her domain.

[Razia] was a great monarch: wise, just, generous, a benefactor of her realm, a dispenser of equity, the protector of her people, and leader of her armies; she had all kingly qualities, except sex, and this exception made all her virtues of no effect in the eyes of men.

—Minhaj-us-Siraj

Razia's aptitude was not limited to governmental excellence alone, however, for her humanism and intellectual curiosity led to a renaissance of art, literature and philosophy. The presence of a dazzling galaxy of savants and their pursuits gave a fresh aspect to a traditional and military-bound 13th-century monarchy. Razia was dedicated to the cause of education. Her father had established the Nasiri College, which had begun to languish during the Shah Turkan days. Razia revived it. Scholars were brought to the college from far and near; literary instruction as well as military training received new impetus. In order for the fruits of education to reach a wider proportion of people, Razia also established several schools and employed important literary figures as teachers there. Libraries were established and made available to the public. Literary scholars received her court's patronage, as did musicians and painters. Razia's aesthetic inclinations led to a flowering of arts, music, and painting. A much-acclaimed painting of the period shows Razia dressed in military garb with no veil sitting astride her favorite horse. Her advocacy of music as a viable form of art received severe criticism from the *ulema* (Islamic theologians). Her response to such criticism was to point towards the *sufi* (Islamic mysticism) movement that looked upon music as a means of realization attained through ecstasy. On a more temporal level, Razia's endorsement of music allowed for the survival of indigenous Hindu music, which would have declined under the *ulema*'s authority. Under Razia's patronage, compositions of ancient Greek philosophers were translated into Persian and Arabic; the Persian intellectual renaissance was brought to India where Umar Khayyam, Saadi, and Firdausi were read and discoursed; Hindu treatises on science, philosophy, and literature were given special recognition and taught in schools and colleges. Razia's reign was dynamic, energetic, and vital—infectious enough to permeate the entire society. The people viewed her rule as one of great toleration and advancement. But she was still a woman, a fact that continued to beleaguer the nobles.

While Razia's subjects benefited, her centralized authority irked the Turkish nobles. With their supremacy severely curtailed, they were unwilling to remain under the control of the revered woman monarch. They did what they knew best: they revolted, instigating a coup to depose Razia. The irony is that the sultana, deeply involved in governing, did not sense the undercurrents until they became apparent. She was most disturbed about the revolt of the governor of Bhatinda, Altuniya. He was not only one of the more supportive nobles of the empire but also a young man who had proclaimed his undying love for her. Razia personally led her forces against Altuniya but was defeated and then imprisoned. In the meantime, the Turkish

nobles had taken control of the throne in Delhi and placed Balban as their king. Razia, whose pride could not countenance this affront, produced a scheme that would assist her in regaining her throne: she proposed to Altuniya that they marry and then as king and queen of the empire return to Delhi to reclaim what was rightfully theirs. Altuniya agreed, and the couple combined their forces, along with some Hindu troops who joined her in gratitude, to march on Delhi. But that day, October 13, 1240, the imperial armies outnumbered them in strategy and manpower; soon, Razia and her consort found themselves outflanked, outmaneuvered, and thoroughly beaten. She continued to fight until an arrow pierced her left breast, instantly killing her. It was a tragic end to a remarkable career.

Razia was a phenomenal leader with foresight and a catholicity of outlook unmatched in any ruler of the Sultanate. She had a breadth of vision, a liberalism that was unconventional, and an unshakable belief in justice for all subjects. By sheer will, she created a more liberal and humane foundation for the Sultanate. Her courage and imagination did not allow her to admit defeat or bow to the narrow, sectarian beliefs of her times. She did not consider herself disadvantaged as a woman, though she was confronted and killed for that reason. Razia was the first and only queen of India; the woman responsible for elevating the consolidation and reconstruction of India to a high level of decency and morality. In the words of Minhaj-us-Siraj:

> Weep not for her! Her memory is the shrine
> Of pleasant thoughts, soft as the scent of flowers,
> Calm as on windless eve the sun's decline,
> Sweet as the song of birds among the bowers,
> Rich as rain with its hues of light
> Pure as the moonshine of an autumn night,
> Weep not for her!

SOURCES:

Habibullah, A.B.M. *The Foundation of Muslim Rule in India: A History of the Establishment and Progress of the Turkish Sultanate of Delhi, 1206–1290 A.D.* Allahabad, India: Central Book Depot, 1961.

Jackson, A.V. Williams, ed. *Medieval India from the Mohammadean Conquest to the Reign of Akbar the Great.* Volume III. London: Grolier Society, 1903.

Majumdar, R.C., ed. *The History and Culture of the Indian People.* Volume V. Bombay: Bharatiya Vidya Bhavan, 1957.

Zakaria, Rafiq. *Razia: Queen of India.* Bombay: India Printing Works, 1966.

Jyoti Grewal, Assistant Professor of History, Luther College, Decorah, Iowa

Read, Deborah (1707–1774).

See Bache, Sarah for sidebar.

Read, Mary and Anne Bonney

Eighteenth-century pirates.

Bonney, Anne (1700–?). Name variations: Ann Bonny. Born in 1700 in County Cork, Ireland; date of death unknown; daughter of William Cormac and an unknown servant; married James Bonney, in 1718; children: unknown.

Family emigrated to South Carolina; stabbed servant (1713); emigrated to New Providence (1719); met "Calico Jack" Rackham and stole ship (1719); captured Dutch merchantship (1719); met Mary Read (1719); captured by Royal Navy (1720); "Calico Jack" Rackham hung (1720); sentenced to death (1720); disappeared (1721).

Read, Mary (1680–1721). Pronunciation: Reed. Born in 1680 in England; died in Jamaica on April 28, 1721; parents' names unknown; married (husband died c. 1712–13); children: none.

Moved to London (1684); grandmother died (1693); joined Royal Navy (1694); joined British army; fought in War of the Spanish Succession (somewhere between 1702–12); Treaty of Utrecht (1713); signed on as a crew member aboard a Dutch merchantship; captured by pirates and met Anne Bonney (1719); captured by Royal Navy (1720); sentenced to death (1720); died of natural causes (1721).

On a still night in the fall of 1720, a Royal Navy sloop, commanded by Jonathan Barnet, slipped alongside a lone ship riding at anchor off the north coast of Jamaica and demanded identification. The answer came back that she was commanded by "Calico Jack" Rackham. Since Rackham was an infamous pirate, there was a brief exchange of cannon fire before sailors of the Royal Navy swarmed aboard. The skirmish which ensued was bloody and brief. The crew of the pirate ship was drunk and put up only a token resistance before fleeing below decks. Two of the crew, however, stood their ground, fighting furiously with pistols, cutlasses and boarding axes, killing and wounding several Royal Navy sailors. One of these pirates fired a shot into the hold, where the rest of the crew was hiding, and screamed at them to come up and fight like men. Without help, however, the pair was soon overpowered. But their stubborn resistance greatly impressed their captors.

As Jonathan Barnet towed the pirate ship into the harbor, the news of Calico Jack's capture quickly spread throughout Port Royal. Barnet was praised for his bravery by the governor, Woodes Rogers, and received a reward of £200.

But Barnet's triumph was overshadowed by the sensational revelation that the dueling pair of pirates, who had staged such a furious last stand, were not, in fact, men, but women—Anne Bonney and Mary Read. Daniel Defoe, who did much to popularize their story, wrote: "Some may be tempted to think the whole story no better than a novel or romance; but . . . it is supported by many thousand witnesses."

Anne Bonney was the illegitimate daughter of an unknown servant and William Cormac, an Irish attorney. The liaison which resulted in Anne's conception took place while Cormac's wife was in the country for her health. Suspecting her husband of infidelity upon her return, Mrs. Cormac secretly took the place of the servant in bed. "The husband came to bed, and that night played the vigorous lover," according to Defoe, "but one thing spoiled the diversion on the wife's side, which was, the reflection that it was not designed for her."

The Cormacs soon separated, and a few months later the servant gave birth to Anne. To conceal the child's identity, she was dressed as a boy, and Cormac claimed that Anne was the son of a relative. When the charade was discovered and Cormac defied popular convention by setting up housekeeping with his mistress, his clients began to desert him. Sensing the futility of his predicament, Cormac immigrated with his young family to Charleston, South Carolina. Once established in the colonies, he became a prosperous plantation owner and a prominent member of the community.

Anne grew up to be a headstrong and volatile young woman, whose fiery temper often got her into trouble. Local gossip had it that she had stabbed a servant with a table knife when she was only 13. When her mother died, Anne took over the responsibilities of housekeeper, but her father's wealth made her an attractive catch on the Charleston marriage market. She rejected all suitors, however, and on one occasion apparently beat up an ardent young man who tried to seduce or, more probably, rape her.

Like it did for many people of the age, the romance and the adventure of the sea fired Anne's imagination, and she began to frequent the waterfront, disguised as a man. Her father, confident that she would outgrow this eccentricity, humored her and made plans for her marriage. But these were upset when Anne eloped with a young sailor named James Bonney, whom she had met in a dockside tavern. Infuriated by his daughter's disobedience, William Cormac disinherited the newlyweds. For a time, the couple tried to scratch out a living on the Charleston docks. When this proved to be impossible, they set sail for the Bahamas, determined to seek their fortune on the island of New Providence. When James found a job as a paid informant for the governor, reporting on the movements of pirate vessels, Anne did not approve of her husband's occupation and the marriage ran into difficulty.

It was on the island of New Providence that the pirate Calico Jack Rackham first met Anne. In 1719, Governor Rogers had announced an amnesty for all pirates, and Calico Jack Rackham had turned himself in. Soon after, he and Anne fell in love. Since divorce by sale was still being practiced by the British lower classes, Rackham offered to buy Anne from her husband. But James, who detested Rackham, denounced the lovers to the governor, and Rogers threatened to strip and flog Anne publicly if she did not return to her husband. Anne ignored his threats.

With pitch and tar her hands were hard

Though once like velvet soft,

She weighed the anchor, heaved the lead

And boldly went aloft.

—Anon.

To further complicate matters, Rackham was now virtually penniless, having spent most of his money living beyond his means. So Anne plotted with him to seize a sloop riding at anchor in the harbor. The ship—owned by John Haman, a wealthy merchant and privateer who lived on a nearby island—was reputed to be the fastest vessel in the Caribbean.

On a dark and rainy night, Anne Bonney, wearing male clothing, accompanied Rackham and his confederates upon their raid. Once aboard, Bonney, armed with a broadsword and pistols, surprised the night watch and held them at gun point. Rackham and his companions raised the anchor and took the wheel. As they sailed past a fort and a man-of-war at the entrance to the harbor, they managed to outwit the sailors who hailed them, claiming that their anchor chain had broken. Once outside, they raised the mainsail and a loud cheer rose from the crew as they made for the open sea.

Raiding ships between Cuba and Jamaica, the crew prospered. Allegedly, they had no idea of Anne's gender, even when she was put ashore to deliver and abandon a child. Bonney proved an able seafarer and a fierce swordswoman. It seems improbable, however, that she was able to keep her gender a complete secret, given the proximity of life aboard an 18th-century sailing ship.

Like Anne, Mary Read had a troubled childhood. Her mother married a sailor, but he abandoned her while she was pregnant. With a small son and another child on the way, the young mother found herself faced with the prospect of supporting a family. She moved from London to the countryside, hoping to find employment. It was there that Mary was born in 1680. They remained in the country for four years, until financial necessity forced them back to London.

Read's brother died prematurely, and since no one in London knew of Mary's existence, her mother dressed her up in boy's clothing and passed her off as her dead son. The scheme worked well, and Mary's grandmother gave the family an allowance of a crown a week. When Read was 13, however, her grandmother died, and she was forced to earn her own living. She was apprenticed as a footboy to a wealthy French woman, but she craved excitement and ran away to sea, signing on as a cabin boy aboard a British man-of-war. Later she joined the army, serving as an infantryman and dragoon in Flanders during the War of the Spanish Succession. Her bravery earned her the esteem of her fellow soldiers and the admiration of her officers, from whom she won several commendations. No one seems to have suspected Mary Read's gender.

She soon fell in love, however, with a handsome young soldier in her regiment. Although Read managed to conceal her feelings, she began to neglect her military duties. These signs might have passed unnoticed, if not for Read's new habit of accompanying her companion without permission, whenever he was sent on a dangerous mission. She found it increasingly difficult to suppress her feelings. At length, writes Defoe, "as they lay together in the same tent, and were constantly together, she found a way of letting him discover her sex, without appearing that it was done with design."

When the campaign in Flanders concluded (c. 1711–12), Read donned female clothing and married her former comrade-in-arms, much to the delight and amusement of her fellow soldiers. The officers of the regiment took up a collection, which helped the young couple to open a tavern near Breda, in Holland. Named "The Three Horseshoes," the tavern was a popular haunt for officers and soldiers of her old regiment. Initially business prospered, but misfortune soon overtook Read. Her husband died prematurely, and the Peace of Utrecht (1713) deprived the tavern of its clientele.

Hoping to make a fresh start, Mary once again donned male attire and rejoined the army, but she found peacetime soldiering dull and soon deserted. Her love of adventure then led her to enlist on a Dutch merchantship bound for the West Indies. When the vessel was attacked at sea and plundered by pirates, the delicately handsome young English sailor was invited to join the pirates. Mary Read promptly agreed—thus becoming the second, albeit unknown, female crew member. The Dutch ship had been commandeered by Calico Jack and his sidekick Anne Bonney.

The new pirate took Anne Bonney's fancy. Disappointment may have turned to laughter, however, when Bonney discovered that the object of her desire was another woman—Mary Read. Rackham noticed the growing intimacy between Anne and the young Englishman. Jealous, he threatened to cut the latter's throat, forcing Anne to reveal the secret of Read's identity. Rackham never divulged the secret and benefited greatly from Mary Read's presence on board. Together, Bonney and Read made a formidable team. They demonstrated unfailing daring and prowess, thus accounting for much of Rackham's fame and success. As Defoe noted, none among the crew "were more resolute or ready to board or undertake anything that was hazardous."

The crew plundered a number of English ships out of Jamaica and pressed many of their crew members into service. One of these, who won Mary Read's heart, became her messmate and companion, a relationship that followed much the same pattern as her experience in Flanders. "When she found he had a friendship for her, as a man," wrote Defoe, "she suffered the discovery to be made, by carelessly showing her breasts, which were very white." The couple fell in love, and Read later declared before a Jamaican court that they had been married in "the eyes of God." She looked upon her marriage as being as valid as any sanctified by the church.

Then one day the young seafarer quarrelled with a shipmate, who challenged him to a duel. In accordance with the ship's articles, the two opponents were to be set ashore to fight to the death. Read was filled with dread for the safety of her lover. Being a skilled and experienced swordswoman, she insisted on taking his place. At the appointed time, she and the pirate were set ashore and the duel began. Both opponents fired their pistols, missing each other. Then they drew their cutlasses. Read's less agile opponent began to tire. Summoning up his last reserves of strength, he lunged at her and overbalanced. Read almost severed his head with the stroke of her cutlass, and her opponent crumpled slowly to the ground. At her trial, Read acknowledged the veracity of the story, but refused to name her "husband" for fear of implicating him.

Clearly Captain Barnet of the Royal Navy respected the raw courage of the two heavily shackled pirates who stood before the court in November 1720. Their gender, however, still remained a closely guarded secret. Then, Anne Bonney and Mary Read were sentenced by the court to hang, along with Rackham and the rest of his crew. When the judge made a routine inquiry as to whether any of the condemned had anything further to say, the courtroom was astounded by the reply: "Milord, we plead our bellies," answered Bonney and Read. By law, the court could not take the life of an unborn child by hanging the mother. The courtroom erupted in laughter, which soon turned to shocked incredulity when a doctor examined the two prisoners and declared that they were indeed both women and both pregnant.

Rackham was allowed to visit Anne Bonney on the morning of his execution. The reunion was short and acrimonious. Anne, still outraged by his conduct during their capture, muttered, "If he had fought like a man, he need not have been hanged like a dog." This was poor consolation for Rackham, who was hanged later in the afternoon on Rackham's cay, the spot that still bears his name.

Bonney and Read were given separate trials. The evidence against them was damning and included the testimony of **Dorothy Thomas**, one of their victims. Thomas testified that the two

From the play Mary Read, *by James Bridie and Claud Gurney, 1934, starring Flora Robson.*

WOMEN IN WORLD HISTORY

women had berated their follow pirates for not killing her, in order to prevent her from becoming a future witness. Captain Thomas Dillon, the master of a ship captured by Rackham and his crew, testified that the two women were "very profligate, cursing and swearing much, and very ready and willing to do anything on aboard." Neither Bonney nor Read refuted the accusations, and they were sentenced to be hanged after their babies had been born.

They both cheated the hangman, however. Bonney delivered her child and disappeared, probably with the assistance of her father, who wielded considerable influence among the island's planters. Read was not so fortunate. She died in prison, just before she was to deliver her child. Read might have earned a pardon from the court, had it not been for one comment. She was asked by the judge how she could live as a pirate, with the constant threat of prison and the noose hanging over her head. According to Defoe, "as to hanging, she thought it no great hardship, for, were it not for that, every cowardly fellow would turn pirate, and so infest the seas, that men of courage must starve."

The geography of Anne Bonney's and Mary Read's odyssey echoed the imperial hot-spots of contemporary Europe: Ireland, Flanders, Carolina and the Caribbean. They fled the law and the ever-expanding British empire, seeking refuge in the anti-colonial Caribbean pirate fraternity. But they also sought to flee the sexual stereotypes of an era. The changing conditions of 18th-century Europe increasingly disrupted hierarchical power, and made it easier for women to escape the strictures of their gender by donning male clothing. This phenomenon was undoubtedly more common than some historians have suggested, and the fact that only a handful of women were ever caught, is a testament to their ingenuity. In the eyes of the law, European women were perpetually under the control of a male figure—father, husband, brother, uncle, or son. The case of Anne Bonney and Mary Read demonstrates that it was possible to break this cycle and to share in the higher income, higher status world of male society, albeit a lawless one.

SOURCES:

Defoe, Daniel. *A General History of the Pyrates*. London: T. Warner, 1724.

Lucie-Smith, Edward. *Outcasts of the Sea*. London: Paddington, 1978.

McWilliams, Karen. *Pirates*. NY: F. Watts, 1989.

Tryals of Captain Rackham and other Pyrates. London. Pamphlet, 1721.

SUGGESTED READING:

Rankin, Hugh F. *The Golden Age of Piracy*. NY: Holt, Rinehart and Winston, 1969.

RELATED MEDIA:

Gooch, Steven. *The Women Pirates Ann Bonny and Mary Read* (play). London: Pluto, 1978.

Mary Read (play) by James Bridie and Claud Gurney, starring *Flora Robson, premiered in 1934.

Hugh A. Stewart, M.A.,
University of Guelph, Ontario, Canada

Reading, Stella (1894–1971).

See Isaacs, Stella.

Reagan, Nancy (1921—)

American actress and first lady (1981–89). Born Anne Frances Robbins on July 6, 1921, in New York City; daughter of Kenneth Robbins (an insurance salesman) and Edith (Luckett) Robbins Davis (an actress); attended Sidwell Friends School, Washington, D.C.; graduated from Girls' Latin School, Chicago, Illinois; Smith College, B.A., 1943; married Ronald Wilson Reagan (an actor and later president of the U.S.), on March 4, 1952; children: Patricia Anne Reagan, known as Patti (b. 1952); Ronald Prescott Reagan (b. 1958); (stepchildren) Maureen Reagan; Michael Reagan.

Selected filmography: The Doctor and the Girl (1949); East Side, West Side (1950); Shadow on the Wall (1950); The Next Voice You Hear (1950); Night Into Morning (1951); It's a Big Country (1952); Shadow in the Sky (1952); Talk About a Star (1952); Donovan's Brain (1953); Hellcats of the Navy (1957); Crash Landing (1958).

"In many ways, I think I served as a lightning rod," first lady Nancy Reagan wrote in her memoir *My Turn* (1989), referring to the fact that she enjoyed none of the adoration afforded her charismatic husband. "Something about me, or the image people had of me, just seemed to rub them the wrong way." Indeed, during her eight years in the White House, Reagan generated a constant stream of criticism and controversy ranging from trivial to sobering. At first, it was her clothes, her friends, and her plans to re-decorate the White House that came under fire. Later, she was accused of usurping her husband's power, of literally taking control of the actions and appointments of the executive branch. In addition to image problems, Nancy Reagan endured a series of shattering events while she was in the White House, including an assassination attempt on her husband, the deaths of both her parents, and her own and her husband's bouts with cancer. But while she calls her years as first lady the most difficult of her life, she also views them as the most rewarding. "In 1988, during the space of a single week, I stood in the Kremlin with the Gorbachevs, had tea in Buckingham Palace with Queen *Elizabeth [II], visited with [*Margaret] Thatcher at 10 Downing Street, and stopped off a Disney World in Florida with some of my favorite people on earth, the Foster Grandparents," she recalls. Through the difficult times, she says, she had the constant love and support of her husband. Now, a decade out of the White House, Nancy Reagan is losing her husband to Alzheimer's disease, a turn of events made all the sadder in light of the couple's fierce devotion to each other.

Born Anne Frances Robbins in New York, on July 6, 1921, and immediately dubbed Nancy by her mother, Reagan was the only child of Kenneth Robbins, an insurance salesman, and Edith Luckett Robbins (later Edith Davis), a moderately successful actress. Her parents divorced when Nancy was a baby, and she was entrusted to the care of Edith's sister Virginia Galbraith in Bethesda, Maryland, while her mother continued to pursue her acting career. When Nancy was eight, Edith married Dr. Loyal Davis, a prominent Chicago neurosurgeon who taught at the medical school of Northwestern University. The doctor, who had a young son by a previous marriage, took Nancy in, but did not formally adopt her until some years later. Davis, by all accounts, was a brilliant but formidable man who demanded perfection from his students, his colleagues, and his children. "To please Loyal Davis, Nancy emulated him, adopting his compulsion for neatness, his obsession with clothes, his mania for discipline," writes Reagan's unofficial biographer Kitty Kelley, who also portrays Davis as a racist and anti-Semite. Reagan expresses only admiration for Davis. "I was so proud of him," she writes. "Here was this wonderful, handsome, accomplished man—and he was my father!"

While she was still living with her aunt, Reagan was sent to Sidwell Friends, a private Quaker school in Washington, D.C. In Chicago, she attended Girls' Latin, where she was only an average student but twice class president and acted in most of the plays. After high school, she attended Smith College, graduating in 1943 with majors in English and drama. Having long since decided to be an actress, and though she appeared in several plays at college, she obtained most of her early stage experience apprenticing at various New York summer theaters. She landed her first professional acting job through her mother's old friend *ZaSu Pitts, who arranged for her to play a minor role (three lines) in *Ramshackle Inn*, which was on a pre-Broadway tour.

Her first and only Broadway role was as the flower maiden in *Lute Song,* a musical about the Far East, starring Yul Brynner and *Mary Martin. Said Reagan: "Mary Martin and my mother were old friends." In 1949, she was recommended for a screen test at MGM, at which time her family connections were once again called into play. This time, her mother's friend Spencer Tracy saw to it that the test was held under the best possible conditions and was directed by George Cukor, then one of the top directors in Hollywood. As a result, Reagan was offered a seven-year contract with the studio, which she signed in 1949. By most accounts, she was not star material. "You have to have something wonderful to become a star, and Nancy didn't have that wonderful something," said producer Pandro Berman. Reagan's first starring role was as the very pregnant wife of James Whitmore in *The Next Voice You Hear* (1950), but it failed to bring her much attention. She made 11 inconsequential films during the 1950s, including *Night into Morning* (1951), her personal favorite, and *Hellcats of the Navy* (1957), in which she co-starred with her husband. Later on, she was fairly dismissive of her acting résumé. "I never was really a career girl," she told Wanda McDaniel of the Los Angeles *Herald Examiner* in 1980. "I majored in drama at Smith and I became an actress because I didn't want to go back to Chicago and lead the life of a post-debutante. I wanted to do something until I found the man I wanted to marry." In her quest, Nancy dated MGM executive Benny Thau and a number of handsome young Hollywood actors, including Clark Gable, Robert Walker, and, of course, Ronald Reagan.

"My life didn't really begin until I met Ronnie," Reagan writes in her memoir. They met at a Hollywood dinner party, but their first date was arranged. As president of the Screen Actors Guild, Ronald invited Nancy to dinner at the suggestion of director Mervyn LeRoy, to advise her about getting her name removed from a list of Communist sympathizers that had appeared in one of the Hollywood newspapers. Reagan knew right away that he was the man she wanted to marry, but he was not at all so sure about her. "He had been burned in his first marriage, and the pain went deep," she says, referring to Ronald's first marriage to actress *Jane Wyman, with whom he had a daughter Maureen Reagan and an adopted son Michael. It was an on-and-off courtship, and there were rumors at the time that Ronald was still hoping to reunite with Wyman. It wasn't until March 4, 1952, two years after they first met, that the couple finally

Nancy
Reagan

married in a small, private ceremony in Los Angeles, engaging their close friends William and **Ardis Holden** as best man and matron of honor. Following a honeymoon in Arizona, they settled into a house in the Palisades, a half-hour from the Reagan ranch in the Santa Ynez Mountains.

Seven-and-a-half months after the wedding, Nancy gave birth to the couple's first child, **Patti Reagan**, on October 22, 1952. ("Go ahead and count," she quips in her book.) The Reagans' second child, Ronald Prescott Reagan, was born in 1958.

By her own admission, Nancy was more successful as a wife than as a mother. Since Maureen and Michael stayed with their mother after their parents divorced, Reagan faced the usual problems that go with a blended family. She got along well with Maureen before she and Ronald married, but after the relationship deteriorated, mostly from lack of contact. Nancy and Maureen would not reconcile and become friends until the White House years. Ronald's second child Michael was three when his parents divorced, and he was particularly sensitive about being adopted. He spent his early childhood at a boarding school in Los Angeles, and at 14 moved in with the Reagans because he was having trouble living with his mother. Michael was rebellious as a teen and was sent away to school in Arizona. As an adult, his closer ties were with members of his biological family, with whom he was reunited.

Reagan's own daughter, Patti, was independent and rebellious from infancy, and Nancy calls their relationship one of the most disappointing aspects of her life. As a teen, Patti was also sent to boarding school in Arizona, then briefly attended college, dropping out to marry a guitarist in a rock group. After that marriage ended, Patti moved home and briefly reunited with Nancy, but their improved relationship was short lived. After a second marriage, she was rarely seen by her parents. Her condemnation of her family in her 1986 "autobiographical novel" *Home Front* assured a continued estrangement.

Compared to Patti, Ronald, Jr. ("Skipper"), was a docile child, and as such became Nancy's favorite. After his own brief rebellious period, he went on to a career as a dancer with the Joffrey Ballet. Although Ronald, Jr., has always shunned politics, he remained close to his mother. But like the rest of the Reagan children, he has expressed the belief that his parents were so devoted to each other that there was little affection left for their children.

Ronald Reagan's own acting career declined after 1952; since the couple had enormous expenses, Nancy went back to work shortly after Patti was born, appearing in films and television until 1962. In 1954, Ronald signed a contract to host the weekly television series "General Electric Theater" and to travel the country representing General Electric at its plants and conventions, which spurred his interest in politics. Although his decision to run for governor of California in 1966 was a family affair, Nancy was initially ambivalent about campaigning. Particularly terrified of speechmaking, she even-

tually agreed to hold less formal question-and-answer sessions, a format she stuck with throughout subsequent campaigns.

Ronald won the gubernatorial election in a landslide over Pat Brown, and the couple moved to the governor's mansion in Sacramento. They lived there only four months before Reagan declared it a firetrap unsuitable for the children and insisted they move. In April 1967, they relocated to an English-style country house in the suburbs, paying the $1,250 monthly rent themselves. (Friends later purchased the house, but still charged the governor the same rent.)

As first lady of California, Reagan became active in the Foster Grandparents Program, which linked senior citizens with physically and developmentally challenged children. She also served the POW-MIA cause during the Vietnam War and made regular visits to veterans' hospitals. Despite her good deeds, however, Reagan already had her serious detractors. Dubbed "Queen Nancy" by some Californians for refusing to live in the governor's mansion, she was further chastised when she called for donations of furniture from old estates to help decorate the rented house. The press also criticized her association with a wealthy clique of women later dubbed "The Group." They included **Betsy Bloomingdale**, ***Bonita Granville**, **Mary Jane Wick**, **Lee Annenberg**, and **Jane Dar**, all of whom remained her good friends throughout her White House years. Reagan struck a particularly sour note with younger women caught up in the feminist movement of the 1960s. Some faulted her for giving up her career, while others found her insincere. ("The gaze," Reagan's adoring acknowledgment of her husband, became a particular source of ridicule.) **Joan Didion**, who visited Reagan in Sacramento, turned out a scathing article called "Pretty Nancy" for the *Saturday Evening Post*, in which she described Reagan's smile as "a study in frozen insincerity," and portrayed her as "playing out some middle-class American woman's daydream, circa 1948."

It was generally assumed that Reagan had talked her husband into his first run for president in 1976 against Gerald Ford, but she claims that after eight years in Sacramento, she was anxious to return to Los Angeles and a normal life. Once Ronald decided to run, however, she threw herself wholeheartedly into the campaign, which turned out to be an elaborate dress rehearsal. Reagan lost his bid in the primaries, although he built a solid base of support that carried over four years later when he ran for president against Jimmy Carter. This time the exhausting campaign resulted in a landslide victory, and in 1981 the Reagans were on their way to the White House.

Criticism of the new first lady began almost immediately with the "Million Dollar Inaugural," so called because of the hordes of wealthy people and celebrities who descended on the nation's capital. That air of glamour and formality would dominate the Reagan years, giving the impression, writes **LuAnn Paletta**, "that only the socially elite mattered." Early on, there was also a flap over Reagan's plans to redecorate the White House. At the root of the controversy was the fact that the Reagans chose to raise private funds for the project rather than accept the $50,000 government allotment given to each new president for renovations and upkeep. The press made much of the large donations made by many of the Reagans' wealthy friends, and the renovations were often contrasted with rising unemployment and homelessness. **Judy Mann** wrote in the *Washington Post*: "Nancy Reagan has used the position, her position, to improve quality of life for those in the White House." Friends also donated over $200,000 to purchase new china, which became another symbol of Reagan's supposed extravagance. (The china remained in the White House after the Reagans left.)

On March 30, 1981, 70 days into her tenure as first lady, Nancy Reagan was returning from a luncheon when she was informed that the president's party had been involved in a shooting at the Washington Hilton, where the president had delivered a speech to the Building Trades Council of the AFL-CIO. Initially, she was told that the president had not been shot but was at the hospital. Confused, she rushed to the hospital to discover that her husband had indeed been shot and was seriously injured, as was his press secretary Jim Brady, who would spend the rest of his life in a wheelchair. (At first, the president thought he had suffered a broken rib when he was shoved into his car by a Secret Service man. It was not known that he had actually been hit by a bullet from would-be assassin John Hinckley's gun until he collapsed while walking into the emergency room.) Later, after he had surgery to remove the bullet lodged near his heart, Reagan would learn that her husband had come very close to death. The first lady remained by the president's bedside until he was allowed to return to the White House. In her autobiography, she admits that the psychological effects of the shooting were deep and lasted throughout the eight years she spent as first lady, causing her to fear for her husband's life every time he left her side. "I was so shaken by the events of that spring that it took me a couple of years just to say the word, 'shooting,'" she wrote. "For a long time I simply referred to it as 'March 30,' or, even more obliquely, as 'the thing that happened to Ronnie.' For me, the entire episode was quite literally, unspeakable."

It was in this vulnerable period immediately following the assassination attempt that Reagan became involved with San Francisco astrologer **Joan Quigley**, who had formerly volunteered advice on the president's campaign and who now disclosed that she had known March 30 was a dangerous day for the president and that he should have stayed at home. (In *Dutch*, his biography of the president, Edmund Morris suggests that Reagan's interest in astrology went back much further, and that she was consulting **Jeane Dixon** when Ronald was the governor of California.) Filled with guilt at the thought that she might have prevented the attack, Reagan contacted Quigley, who was helpful and comforting. Subsequently, she began to contact her regularly, paying for the astrologer's services through a friend in California. "Joan's recommendations had nothing to do with policy or politics—ever," Reagan states unequivocally in her biography. "Her advice was confined to timing—to Ronnie's schedule, and to what days were good or bad, especially with regard to his out-of-town trips." Reagan's secret was safe until 1988, when departed Chief of Staff Donald Regan published his memoir *For the Record*, revealing that the first lady had relied on astrology. The disclosure humiliated both Reagan and the president.

To counteract Reagan's bad publicity during 1981, the White House staff, together with a group of public-relations specialists, devised the first lady's drug-abuse program, "Just Say No," which capitalized on a subject already of interest to her. It remained her cause for the next seven years, during which she traveled to 64 U.S. cities and 8 foreign countries to visit drug rehabilitation centers and to promote the Just Say No clubs, of which there were over 3,000 by 1988. The drug program would continue after Reagan left the White House, funded for a time under the Nancy Reagan Foundation. She also remained a sponsor of the Foster Grandparents Program and in 1982 published the book *To Love a Child*, which chronicles 12 relationships between foster grandparents and grandchildren who participated in the program.

Nothing boosted Nancy Reagan's ratings with the Washington press corps more, however, than her 1982 appearance at the Press Club Gridiron Dinner. Mid-point in the festivities, she appeared unannounced on stage dressed as a bag lady and singing a parody of "Second Hand Rose," a song called "Second Hand Clothes." The performance culminated with the smashing of a plate which resembled the infamous red china, and elicited a standing ovation. "No one thought that Mrs. Reagan had any slapstick, any self-mockery in her," said Hedrick Smith of *The New York Times*. Virginia governor Charles Robb remarked: "It was one of the most astute moves I've seen in a long time."

The most troubling aspect of Nancy Reagan's tenure as first lady was the growing perception that she had too much power, that she not only had the president's ear, but was directing policy decisions. "Did I ever give Ronnie advice? You bet I did," Reagan says. "I'm the one who knows him best, and I was the only person in the White House who had absolutely no agenda on her own—except helping him." Some have suggested that Reagan became more protective of her husband in an effort to hide the fact that he was slipping mentally, but whatever her motives the result had a devastating effect on morale among the White House staff. Reagan was associated with numerous firings and forced resignations from 1982 onwards, when she ousted her chief of staff Peter McCoy. Some of the most notable victims of her influence were Secretary of State Alexander Haig (1982), Secretary of the Interior James Watt (1983), CIA director William Casey (1987), and Chief of Staff Donald Regan (1987), but there were many others. According to Kitty Kelley, it was not until the Regan resignation that the public began to suspect that the first lady's leverage reached beyond that of a devoted, concerned wife to that of a policymaker.

In the summer of 1985, when the president was operated on for colon cancer, there were those who believed that the first lady was actually running the country. In her defense, Reagan's good friend George Will wrote: "[T]he first lady is a doctor's daughter who, if the 25th Amendment provided for transferring power to First Ladies, could have proven in just eight hours how formidable a person in a size four dress can be. In George Bush's eight hours as acting president, the deficit increased $200 million. Nancy never would have allowed that."

In October 1987, Reagan was diagnosed with breast cancer. Her decision to have a mastectomy instead of a lumpectomy followed by radiation sparked yet another controversy. Doctors around the country criticized her choice of treatment, and the director of the Breast Cancer Advisory Center was quoted in *The New York Times* as saying that

the decision "set us back ten years." Nancy resented the statement, believing that a mastectomy was the sensible thing for her to do and the best way to get it all over with. "I couldn't possibly lead the kind of life I lead and keep the schedule that I do having radiation or chemotherapy," she said. "There'd be no way. Maybe if I'd been twenty years old, hadn't been married, hadn't had children, I would feel completely different. But for me it was right." Reagan was still recovering from surgery when her mother died.

The Reagan administration suffered its most difficult period beginning in 1986, following the disclosure that the United States had sold arms to Iran in order to assist the Contras, the U.S.-backed rebels in Nicaragua. The revelation brought censure from the American public and from both political parties. "We've paid ransom, in effect, to the kidnappers of our hostages," said former President Jimmy Carter. As the matter was investigated, the threat of impeachment arose and the president's ratings tumbled. It was at this time that Reagan was instrumental in the firing of Donald Regan, a matter over which she received some of harshest criticism. Journalist William Safire of *The New York Times* referred to Reagan's "extraordinary vindictiveness," calling her "the power-hungry First Lady."

After the Reagans left the White House to George and *Barbara Bush, they retired to California and private life. Reagan immediately set to work on her memoir, a means by which she could have her say and move on. The Reagans enjoyed only a few good years before the former president was diagnosed with Alzheimer's disease in 1994. Since then, Nancy Reagan has taken on the role of caregiver. "She's providing the rope out there and pulling him through," says Robert Higdon, former head of the Ronald Reagan Presidential Foundation. "Beyond everything, she will always make sure he is taken care of." In 2000, the former first lady carried out an abbreviated tour promoting a book of her love letters from the president. She also remains active in a few causes, including Alzheimer's research and her anti-drug campaign. Most of her time, however, is devoted to the enormous task of overseeing her husband's final days. "She's alone a lot of the time," says a friend. "And she is very lonely."

SOURCES:
Fields-Meyer, Thomas. "To Love and Honor," in *People Weekly*. December 15, 1997.

Katz, Ephraim. *The Film Encyclopedia*. NY: Harper-Collins, 1994.

Kelley, Kitty. *Nancy Reagan: The Unauthorized Biography*. NY: Simon & Schuster, 1991.

Leighton, Frances Spatz. *The Search for the Real Nancy Reagan*. NY: Macmillan, 1987.

Moritz, Charles, ed. *Current Biography 1982*. NY: H.W. Wilson, 1982.

Morris, Edmund. *Dutch: A Memoir of Ronald Reagan*. NY: Random House, 1999.

Paletta, LuAnn. *The World Almanac of First Ladies*. World Almanac, 1990.

Reagan, Nancy, with William Novak. *My Turn: The Memoirs of Nancy Reagan*. NY: Random House, 1989.

Warrick, Pamela. "Nancy's New Role," in the *Los Angeles Times*. August 3, 1997.

SELECTED READING:

Davis, Patti. *Home Front* (novel). NY: Crown, 1986.

Deaver, Michael K., with Mickey Herskowitz. *Behind the Scenes*. NY: William Morrow, 1987.

Reagan, Maureen. *First Father, First Daughter: A Memoir*. Boston, MA: Little, Brown, 1989.

Reagan, Michael, with Joe Hyams. *On the Outside Looking In*. NY: Zebra Books, 1988.

Reagan, Nancy. *I Love You, Ronnie: The Letters of Ronald Reagan to Nancy Reagan*. NY: Random House, 2000.

Reagan, Ronald. *Speaking My Mind*. NY: Simon and Schuster, 1989.

Regan, Donald T. *For the Record: From Wall Street to Washington*. NY: Harcourt Brace Jovanovich, 1988.

Wallace, Chris. *First Lady: A Portrait of Nancy Reagan*. NY: St. Martin's Press, 1986.

Barbara Morgan,
Melrose, Massachusetts

Réage, Pauline (1907–1998).

See Aury, Dominique.

Ream, Vinnie (1847–1914)

American sculptor, known as "the girl who sculpted Lincoln," who was the first female sculptor commissioned by the U.S. government. Name variations: Vinnie Ream Hoxie. Born Vinnie Ream on September 25, 1847, in Madison, Territory of Wisconsin; died in Washington, D.C., on November 21, 1914, of uremic poisoning; buried in Arlington National Cemetery; daughter of Robert Lee Ream (a surveyor, recorder of deeds, and employee of the U.S. Treasury, who died November 21, 1885) and Lavinia (McDonald) Ream (died April 17, 1893); attended public schools and Christian College Academy, Columbia, Missouri, 1857–58; studied sculpture privately with Clark Mills in Washington, D.C., 1863; studied art abroad, 1869–71; married Lieutenant Richard Leveridge Hoxie of the Army Engineers (later brigidier general U.S. Army), on May 28, 1878; children: one son, Richard Ream Hoxie (b. 1883).

Spent childhood in Wisconsin, Missouri and Arkansas; during Civil War (1861–65), moved with family to Washington, D.C.; at age 15, became a postal clerk-copyist and church vocalist (1862); allowed to sketch President Abraham Lincoln at the White House; after his assassination (April 14, 1865), won a Congressional competition for the Lincoln statue for the Capitol—the first woman to sculpt for the U.S. government (August 30, 1866); became embroiled in the impeachment of Andrew Johnson; signed a $20,000 contract for bronze statue of Admiral Farragut (January 28, 1875); after marrying into a wealthy family, gave up sculpting, except as a hobby, to become a Washington society hostess; after a lapse of 18 years, returned to professional sculpting (1906); while working on a statue of Civil War governor Samuel Jordan Kirkwood, was stricken ill at her summer home in Iowa City; returned by private train to Washington for treatment, where she died.

Selected sculptures: Bust of Lincoln (*Cornell University, 1865*); Thaddeus Stevens (*1865*); The Morning Glory (*1865*); Sappho, Typifying the Muse of Poetry (*replica on her grave, 1865–70*); Lincoln (*Rotunda, U.S. Capitol, Washington, D.C., 1865–69*); Ideal Bust (*1868*); Franz Liszt (*1869*); Giacomo Cardinal Antonelli (*1870*); Gustave Doré (*1870*); Albert Pike (*1872*); Chief Justice Morrison R. Waite (*1877*); Admiral Farragut (*Farragut Square, Washington, D.C., 1873–80*); Miriam (*shown 1876 Exposition*); America (*1866–68*); The West (*1866–68*); The Spirit of Carnaval (*shown 1876 Exposition*); Governor Samuel Kirkwood (*1906*) and Sequoyah (*1914, both in Statuary Hall, U.S. Capitol, Washington, D.C.*).

"Both President Lincoln and the Artist were of humble origin; both were born and brought up in the West, and, both, under God, are architects of their own fortune," said Senator Lyman Trumbull in January 1871, as he addressed the distinguished crowd in the Rotunda of the U.S. Capitol. He then unveiled Vinnie Ream's statue of Abraham Lincoln, shown holding a copy of the Emancipation Proclamation. Four and a half years earlier, in the Senate debate over awarding the then 17-year-old girl this $10,000 commission, Massachusetts Senator Charles Sumner had been convinced she couldn't do it, while Jacob Howard of Vermont predicted, "Having in view her sex, I shall expect a complete failure in the execution of this work. I would as soon think of a lady writing the Iliad of Homer; I should as soon think of placing her at the head of an army . . . for the conduct of a great campaign." Despite the naysayers and the fact that she had never before executed a statue in marble, Ream succeeded in creating a better likeness of the martyred Lincoln than any of her competitors. Immediately, newspapers throughout the country published stories about her and "the

Lincoln," forever transforming the image of this tiny, coquettish woman with long black curls into "the girl who sculpted Lincoln" and "the wonder girl from the West." Her colorful background, talent and pioneering spirit, her lobbying ability in Washington, as well as the political controversies surrounding her career, created such a mythical figure that it is hard to distinguish fact from fiction.

Vinnie Ream was a child of the frontier. She was born in 1847 in a log cabin in what would later become Madison, Wisconsin, where the Ream family resided among the Winnebago Indians. Because she was musically talented and had a lovely singing voice as a child, her father Robert Ream, a surveyor and mapmaker for the territory, bought her a guitar from a traveling salesman. After brief instruction, she taught herself and family friends how to play the instrument. She also learned piano without instruction and composed songs. While her mother **Lavinia Ream** initially expected her to become a musician, Vinnie could also draw expertly and paint. By the time she and her older sister **Mary Ream** attended Christian College Academy in Missouri (1857–58), ten-year-old Vinnie wanted to become a sculptor, though she had no idea how that might be accomplished. She knew her family was not wealthy enough to send her to Europe, which was how the famous American sculptors had learned. Still, Vinnie was recognized as the best artist at the academy, and received encouragement from an important visitor, Major James S. Rollins, who later became a U.S. congressional representative. Ream's winning personality also made her a favorite of the academy president who, recognizing her gift, gave her a clipping from the works of Robert Hall that inspired her in later life. Wrote Hall: "No man can ever become eminent in anything, unless he work at it with an earnestness bordering on enthusiasm."

After leaving the academy, the Ream girls joined their parents, who had moved to Fort Smith, Arkansas, across the Arkansas River from Indian Territory (now Oklahoma) which was then inhabited by the five Indian "Nations," who had moved there from the Southeast in the 1820s. Even while living in Missouri, Vinnie had composed songs about Indian lore, which were later published; however, at Fort Smith, the 13-year-old created enduring friendships with two notable, educated Cherokees. The first was John Rollin Ridge (1827–1867), a journalist who wrote the poem "I Love Thee" for which Ream wrote the music before it was published in English and Cherokee in 1880. The other was

Ridge's cousin, Elias Cornelius Boudinot (1835–1890), who later became an Arkansas lawyer, chair of the Democratic state central committee, and would in 1871 name a new Oklahoma settlement "Vinita," after his dear "little Vin." Moreover, after the Civil War, Ream's brother Bob would marry **Anna Guy**, a Choctaw and sister of Governor William Guy of the Chickasaw Nation. Thus, the Reams were Westerners with strong ties with Native Americans before they moved East.

In 1862, when Vinnie was 15, the Ream family moved once again, this time from the Arkansas frontier to Washington, D.C. Because Robert Ream's health was failing, he worked only part-time as an army mapmaker. The cost of living was high in the bustling Union capital during the Civil War. Lavinia Ream took in boarders to supplement the family income, while Vinnie and her sister also ambitiously went to work. (To the family's dismay, their brother Bob ran away to join the Confederate forces, as did their friend Boudinot.) Vinnie became a postal clerk at a salary of $50 a month, and took a second paid position as the first female vocalist in a Washington church, at $300 a year. In her spare time, she was taught the harp by Catholic nuns, which contributed to her angelic public image. Senator Edmund G. Ross of Kansas, an old family friend, boarded with the Reams at their rented house on Capitol Hill within view of the unfinished dome of the Capitol.

Vinnie loved to roam the marble Capitol building, examining the statuary. One day, she met Congressman James S. Rollins, who had admired her drawings at Christian College. Finding Ream knowledgeable about governmental sculpture, and knowing of her desire to become a sculptor, Rollins introduced her to his friend Clark Mills (1810–1883), the foremost sculptor in America, whose studio was in the basement of the Capitol. Mills took the teenager seriously and gave her a lump of clay to test her aptitude for modeling. The result, a bust of a Native American, pleased Mills enough to agree to take Ream on as a part-time apprentice after she turned 16.

While she divided her working hours between the post office and studying with Mills, Ream became obsessed with the idea of modeling a portrait bust of President Abraham Lincoln, of whom she had had fleeting glances several times since she had arrived in Washington. Ream, who was 17 by then, appealed to her friend Rollins to help her arrange to sketch the president while he worked at his desk in the executive mansion. According to her diary, she was

Vinnie Ream

allowed to have half-hour sittings with Lincoln for five months: "I was a mere slip of a child, weighing less than ninety pounds and the contrast between the rawboned man and me was indeed great." In her drawings and clay bust, she depicted Lincoln as she remembered him: "a man of unfathomable sorrow." On Good Friday, 1865, Ream had her regular session with Lincoln; the clay bust she was making of him was almost finished. That evening, when Lincoln was shot at Ford's Theater by John Wilkes Booth, Ream became the last person to have sculpted him from life. When Lincoln died the following day, Vice President Andrew Johnson became president of the United States.

While Lincoln was alive, he was more than just the commander-in-chief of the Union; he also was a controversial political figure who represented Western, partisan interests against New England manufacturing interests; but dead, he was an American martyr. Congress rallied to preserve his memory and responded with a competition for the creation of a life-size marble statue for the Rotunda under the new dome of the Capitol. Although Congress had never awarded an art commission to a woman, Vinnie Ream and *Harriet Hosmer, a Massachusetts sculptor, both applied; but Ream used her numerous political connections in Washington to lobby successfully for the $10,000 commission. A press controversy erupted in which Ream was ridiculed for that lobbying by *Jane Grey Swisshelm, the most powerful woman columnist and a friend of Hosmer, and for using her pretty face to win the commission over more experienced artists. But journalists came to her rescue. Horace Greeley, editor of the New York *Tribune*, commissioned "Little Vin," as he called her, to sculpt a bust of himself. One writer decided Ream resembled the French Romantic novelist *Germaine de Staël, another compared her to *Rosa Bonheur, despite the fact that Bonheur dressed in knickerbocker suits while Ream preferred to sculpt in a long skirt, smock, large apron and old school shoes with rubber toes.

She had a mind of many colours. And there was the very devil of a rush and Forward! March! about her, always in a hurry.

—Georg Brandes

While she worked on the Lincoln model, Ream's studio in the basement of the old part of the Capitol became a Washington tourist attraction. The Louisville *Courier* reported: "She darts in and out of the studios . . . illuminating them like a stray sunbeam, and looking like one of her own beautiful statues into which some modern Pygmalion has breathed the breath of life." Her pet doves flew around the studio and perched on her shoulders while she worked. Gentlemen visited the studio, bringing bouquets of flowers and proposals of marriage. Even Brigham Young, the polygamous Mormon leader, was said to have wanted her to become one of his wives. Women's rights advocate *Elizabeth Cady Stanton also visited Ream's studio with her "Plan to Move on the Works of Man, the Monster"; perhaps not

Opposite page Abraham Lincoln, 1870, by Vinnie Ream, U.S. Capitol Art Collection.

surprisingly, Ream refused to endorse it, because she believed some women reacted with jealousy while some men helped her advance.

But a political crisis threatened to interrupt Ream's work on the model—the impeachment of Andrew Johnson. Because she knew so many congressional representatives and senators, to the point of serving them tea in her studio, certain radical politicians tried to intimidate her into lobbying for impeachment. In the end, the proceedings failed by only one vote—that of Senator Ross, who remained loyal to Johnson. Ross was still boarding with the Reams. For awhile, the angry losers had Ream's studio closed in retaliation, but her many friends in Congress rescued her.

Once the clay and plaster models of "the Lincoln" were completed and approved by Congress in 1869, she received a $5,000 partial payment. So in June 1869, Vinnie Ream, her parents and a cage with the two white doves, with the plaster model safely in the hold of the ship, crossed the Atlantic to France on their way to Italy, where the marble statue would actually be made. Ream studied with Léon J.F. Bonnât in Paris and Luigi Majoli in Rome. She traveled to Carrara to select the block of finest marble, before the professional stonecutter proceeded to cut the statue using thousands of measuring points taken from her plaster model, leaving only (as was customary) one-eighth of an inch of surface for the artist to finish off herself. Ream dazzled the Europeans and members of the American art colonies, receiving many more marriage proposals. She sculpted Gustave Doré, made friends with Danish poet Georg Brandes, and was painted by George Healy in Italian peasant costume. Before the Ream family returned to Washington, the marble Lincoln statue was previewed in Rome and London and highly acclaimed. Finally, they arrived back home, and, much to Vinnie's relief, Congress approved the completed statue and disbursed her second $5,000, which covered her European expenses for a year and a half. The official unveiling of her statue of a sorrowful-looking, downcast Lincoln, wearing a suit covered by a judicial cape and holding the Emancipation Proclamation, was one of the two highlights of her career.

In 1875, Ream won a second government contract—for a colossal bronze statue of Admiral David Farragut. This time, however, she was selected by a congressionally appointed committee, which included the admiral's widow **Virginia L. Farragut**, to receive the contract, because Congress could not agree upon who should get the $20,000 commission. The statue was designed to be placed in the center of Farragut Square in the heart of Washington, and was cast from the propeller of his Civil War flagship, the U.S.S. *Hartford*.

Ever since she had won fame and fortune for the Lincoln statue, Ream was at the center of Washington social life in her new home on Pennsylvania Avenue. She kept busy by sculpting portrait busts and medallions of several famous generals. Her friendship with Boudinot and other Cherokee friends continued, while she added explorer Albert Pike and General George Custer to her coterie. Before the Farragut model was completed, Virginia Farragut introduced Ream to handsome First Lieutenant Richard Leveridge Hoxie, of the Engineer Corps of the U.S. Army, who would retire as a general in 1908. When Ream married Hoxie, in an elaborate Washington ceremony on May 28, 1878, Boudinot refused to attend; many years later, he reputedly whispered her name as he died.

Once Vinnie Ream (now Mrs. Richard Hoxie) finished the Farragut contract, her husband felt the same as did most wealthy men of that era: he did not want his wife working for money. Consequently, sculpting turned into more of a hobby than a livelihood for Ream. She became an outstanding Washington hostess, known for entertaining their many friends by playing her harp and for doing volunteer work with art for the blind. Her "perfect marriage" was marred when her only son Richie, who was born in 1883, became an invalid after he was accidentally shot in the head while he and another child were playing with guns. Later in life, her own vitality was hindered by a chronic kidney ailment. Despite the fact that her husband wished to provide Ream's financial support, he nevertheless wanted to make her happy. As she aged and found it more difficult to climb ladders while sculpting, he used his engineering skill to design for her private studio a special chair on a hoist to lift her within easy reach of her work.

To escape the Washington summers, the Hoxies traveled to the Hoxie family homestead in Iowa City, which Richard had renamed "Vinita" for her. Because of their Iowa connections, in 1906 she was commissioned by the State of Iowa to sculpt a statue of Governor Samuel Kirkwood, as a gift to the U.S. Capitol, for Statuary Hall. The statue was completed in 1913.

Her final noteworthy commission, and the third eventually to stand in Statuary Hall, was requested by the State of Oklahoma—a statue of Sequoyah, the chief who had developed the Cherokee alphabet. Unfortunately, Ream could

not complete the statue before she was overtaken by illness, though she arranged to have well-known sculptor Georg Zolnay complete it according to her design. At the unveiling ceremony, which would occur in 1917, after her death, Senator Robert L. Owen of Oklahoma noted Ream's lifelong friendships with Oklahomans and love for the Cherokee people, in addition to her "magnificent ability as a sculptor of the first rank."

In the early fall of 1914, when Ream fell seriously ill, collapsing in the yard of their summer home in Iowa City, her husband chartered a train to send her back to Washington for treatment. She died of uremic poisoning on November 14, 1914, at age 67, and was buried in Arlington National Cemetery dressed in her white wedding gown and holding her bridal fan.

Vinnie Ream's career paralleled the rise of Western interests on the American political scene. As a teenaged artist, she pioneered in the undeveloped field of American sculpture, in which she did creditable work and progressed with experience. Her musical and artistic talent, combined with good looks, social grace and industriousness, made her one of the most admired women of her time; yet she always retained a certain homespun quality. In a Canadian speech in June 1909, she reflected on her success:

> I am a sculptor, and my life has been a happy one—so happy that I have feared always that I was "eating my white bread" and that some terrible storm was surely to break over me, for it seemed as if Heaven could not give me so much. My work has never been labor, but an ecstatic delight to my soul. I have worked in my studio not envying kings in their splendor; my mind to me was my kingdom, and my work more than diamonds and rubies.

SOURCES:

Brandes, Georg. *Reminiscences of My Childhood and Youth.* London: William Heinemann, 1906.

Campbell, O.B. *The Story of Vinnie Ream.* Vinita, OK: Eastern Trails Historical Society.

Fairman, Charles Edwin. *Art and Artists of the Capital of the United States of America.* Washington, DC: Government Printing Office, 1927.

Hall, Gordon Langley. *Vinnie Ream: The Story of the Girl Who Sculpted Lincoln.* NY: Holt, Rinehart and Winston, 1963.

Hoxie, Richard Leveridge. *Vinnie Ream; Printed for private distribution only and to preserve a few souvenirs of artistic life from 1865 to 1878.* Washington, DC, 1915.

James, Edward T., ed. *Notable American Women, 1607–1950.* Cambridge, MA: The Belknap Press of Harvard University Press, 1971.

Prioli, Carmine A. "'Wonder Girl from the West': Vinnie Ream and the Congressional Statue of Abraham Lincoln," in *Journal of American Culture.* Vol. 12, no. 4. Winter 1989, pp. 1–20.

Stathis, Stephen W., and Lee Roderick. "Mallet, Chisel, and Curls," in *American Heritage.* Vol. 27, no. 2. February 1976, pp. 45–47, 94–96.

Tufts, Eleanor. *American Women Artists, 1830–1930.* Washington, DC: National Museum of Women in the Arts, 1987.

SUGGESTED READING:

Becker, Carolyn Berry. "Vinnie Ream Portrait of a Young Sculptor," in *The Feminist Art Journal.* Vol. 5, no. 3, 1976, pp. 29–31.

Gerdts, William H. *The White Marmorean Flock.* Poughkeepsie, NY: Vassar College Art Gallery, 1972.

Griffin, Maude E. "Vinnie Ream, Portrait of a Sculptor," in *Missouri Historical Review.* Vol. 56, no. 3. April 1962, pp. 230–243.

Heller, Nancy. *Women Artists.* NY: Abbeville, 1987.

Hubbard, Freeman H. *Vinnie Ream and Mr. Lincoln.* NY: McGraw-Hill, 1949.

Lemp, Joan A. "Vinnie Ream and Abraham Lincoln," in *Women's Art Journal.* Vol. 6, no. 2. Fall 1985–Winter 1986, pp. 24–29.

Lomask, Milton. *Andrew Johnson: President on Trial.* NY: Farrar, Straus & Cudahy, 1960.

Sandburg, Carl. *Abraham Lincoln: The War Years.* NY: Harcourt, Brace, 1939.

Thorp, Margaret Farrand. *The Literary Sculptors.* Durham, NC: Duke University Press, 1965.

COLLECTIONS:

Christian College, Columbia, Missouri, owns various items pertaining to Vinnie Ream, as well as her painting of *Martha Washington.

Hoxie Family Papers (12 manuscript boxes and one large portfolio), Library of Congress, Washington, D.C. (these contain her diaries, scrapbooks, photographs of her sculpture and newspaper clippings).

Ten folders of poems, clippings, etc., concerning alumna Ream have been deposited in the Western Historical Manuscripts Collection, University of Missouri Library.

June K. Burton,
freelance writer and Associate Professor Emeritus,
University of Akron, Akron, Ohio

Rebay, Hilla (1890–1967)

German-born artist and director of New York's Guggenheim Museum. Name variations: Baroness Hilla Rebay von Ehrenweisen. Born Hildegard Anna Augusta Elisabeth Rebay on May 31, 1890, in Strasbourg, Alsace, Bavaria; died on September 27, 1967, in Green Farms, Connecticut; daughter of Baron Franz Joseph Rebay (a career army officer) and Antonie von Eicken Rebay; studied at the Dusseldorf Academy and in Paris and Munich.

Exhibited with avant-garde groups like the Secession (Munich), the Salon des Indépendents (Paris), the November Gruppe (Berlin), and the Krater (1914–20); exhibited in Berlin at Herwarth Walden's gallery, Der Sterm (1917); exhibited at the Worcester Museum (1927); exhibited at French and Company (1962).

Though little known outside the New York art community, German-American artist Hilla Rebay was instrumental in establishing a base for non-objective art. Born in Bavaria in 1890, Rebay was a successful painter before arriving in the United States in 1927. She was soon commissioned to render a portrait of the scion of the Swiss-American mining dynasty Solomon R. Guggenheim, who, with his wife *Irene Guggenheim, was an avid collector of old-master art. Rebay convinced the Guggenheims to take a look at the modern-art movement in Germany.

Under her tutelage, the Guggenheims' collection of avant-garde art became so vast that Rebay convinced them to share their private collection with the public. As a result, she was the moving spirit behind the Solomon Guggenheim Museum, which opened in a rented gallery on 54th Street in New York. In 1948, Frank Lloyd Wright was commissioned to design the Guggenheim Museum that now resides on Fifth Avenue between 88th St. and 89th. Over the years, Rebay introduced modern artists like Piet Mondrian, Theo van Doesburg, Georges Vantongerloo, Laszló Moholy-Nagy, Klee, Chagall, and Kandinsky to American audiences. Her collection also contained the works of Henri Matisse, Georges Seurat, Henri Rousseau, Pablo Picasso, and Fernand Léger. Though considered autocratic, Rebay mentored many young artists, contributing money for their supplies and exhibiting their work in shows dedicated to up-and-coming talent; along with many others, she supported *Perle Fine, Jackson Pollock, and Rudolf Bauer for several years. Rebay retired as director of the museum in 1951.

SUGGESTED READING:

Lukach, Joan M. *Hilla Rebay: In Search of the Spirit of Art.* Brazillier, 1983.

Rebecca.

Variant of Rebekah.

Rebekah (fl. around 18th c. BCE)

Jewish matriarch. Name variations: Rebecca; Rebecah. Born in Mesopotamia; buried in Hebron; daughter of Bethuel, Abraham's nephew; married Isaac, son of Abraham; children: two sons, Esau and Jacob.

Rebekah was born and raised in Mesopotamia around the 18th century BCE. Her father was Bethuel, a nephew of the Jewish patriarch Abraham, and she had at least one brother, Laban (the father of *Rachel and Leah). Beyond that, much of her life is a mystery until her

chance meeting with Abraham's servant at the well outside her city. Abraham's family dwelled in the land of Canaan, but he wanted his 40-year-old son Isaac to marry someone from his homeland in Mesopotamia, so he sent his servant to bring home a wife for Isaac. Accompanied by ten camels loaded with bridal gifts of gold, silver, and fine clothing, the servant stopped at a well outside the city of Nahor. There, he asked God for a sign of the future bride: that the chosen one would be she who not only agreed to give him a drink but also volunteered to water his camels.

According to the Bible, Rebekah, who was "very fair to look upon" (Gen. 24:16), approached the well with a pitcher on her shoulder to draw water. When the servant asked for a drink, she readily assented and offered to water his camels as well, thereby fulfilling the sign that she was the one. When she had finished watering the camels, the servant offered her a nose ring and two gold bracelets, and asked to stay with her family. At the house of Rebekah's father, the servant outlined his mission as well as God's revelation to him that Rebekah was the chosen bride. The match seemed particularly fortuitous given the fact that not only was Rebekah from Abraham's homeland, but she was also the powerful patriarch's great-niece. Her relatives agreed to the marriage, and Rebekah left with the servant the following day.

Upon their arrival in Canaan, Isaac and Rebekah were married. During a famine in the region, the couple temporarily moved to Philistine territory in Western Canaan, perhaps no more than 20 miles from the Mediterranean Sea. Rebekah's beauty was such that Isaac worried someone might kill him in order to marry her. To prevent this possibility, he lied about his relationship to her, telling people that he was her brother. The same situation had occurred years earlier with Isaac's parents, Abraham and *Sarah, when they had moved to the region. As had been the case with his father, the deception came to light. The Philistine king, Abimelech, discovered their true relationship, but protected the couple from harm by ordering that no one should molest them on pain of death. They stayed in that land for some time, until Isaac's ever-increasing wealth posed a threat to the Philistines, and they forced him to move to the Valley of Gerar.

Though Isaac loved Rebekah very much, her infertility for 20 years prevented them from having children. This was a very grave situation, meaning as it did not only that Isaac had no heir to his vast wealth, but that God's promise to Abraham that he would establish a nation

Rebekah at the well.

through his family line could not be fulfilled. However, after 60-year-old Isaac pleaded with God for a child, his prayer was answered. Apparently experiencing a difficult pregnancy, Rebekah consulted an oracle which told her: "Two nations are in your womb, two peoples going their own way from birth. One will be stronger than the other; the elder will be servant to the younger" (Gen. 25:23). She delivered twin boys Esau and Jacob; Esau, the firstborn, was reddish and hairy, and Jacob was born clutching at his brother's heel. The rivalry between the boys increased with the favoritism shown by their parents. Isaac favored Esau, who loved hunting and outdoor life, while Rebekah favored Jacob, who was quiet and shrewd, much like she herself. In Isaac's old age, Rebekah successfully plotted to fool her blind husband into giving his blessing to Jacob instead of Esau, as he had intended. In Biblical times, this ceremony conveyed clan leadership, and could not be revoked. To save Jacob from Esau's revenge after this ruse, Rebekah convinced Isaac to send Jacob north to look for a wife from within the circle of her own family.

There is no record that Rebekah ever saw her son again, as he did not return to Canaan until after her death. She was buried in a tomb in the Cave at Machpelah, where Abraham and Sarah also were buried.

SOURCES:

Hinnells, John R., ed. *Who's Who of World Religions.* NY: Simon & Schuster, 1992.

Who's Who in the Bible. Pleasantville, NY: Reader's Digest, 1994.

Woman: Her Position, Influence, and Achievement Throughout the Civilized World. Springfield, MA: King-Richardson, 1900.

Jacqueline Mitchell,
freelance writer, Detroit, Michigan

Reber, Sue Novarra (b. 1955).

See Novarra-Reber, Sue.

Récamier, Juliette (1777–1849)

Parisian woman, one of the most beautiful of her day, who attracted the devotion of many of the leading politicians, writers, and social leaders in Europe and whose salons were among the most popular with Parisian society. Name variations: Madame Récamier or Madame Recamier; Jeanne Françoise Julie Adelaïde Récamier; de Récamier. Born Jeanne Françoise Julie Adelaïde Bernard in Lyons, France, on December 4, 1777; died in Paris, France, on May 11, 1849; daughter of Jean Bernard (a notary of Lyons and later collector of customs in Paris) and Juliette Matton Bernard; married Jacques Rose Récamier (a wealthy banker), on April 24, 1793; no children.

Presided over one of the wealthiest and most popular salons in Paris (1795–1806); lived in exile in Europe (1806–07, 1811–14); returned to Paris and continued to attract the cream of Parisian society to her gatherings (1814–49).

Jeanne Françoise Julie Adelaïde Bernard was born in 1777 into the turbulent world of France. Within 12 years of her birth, the tension of the Bourbon monarchy had erupted into the French Revolution. Over the course of her life, France would be rocked by the Reign of Terror and the rise and fall of Napoleon, only to find itself back under the government of the Bourbon monarchs in 1815. This was a period of intellectual and literary flowering, but it was also a time of shifting political loyalties and uncertainty.

"Juliette," as she preferred to be called, was largely sheltered from the upheavals of the day. Her father Jean Bernard was a notary in Lyons until, in 1784, he was appointed collector of customs in Paris. Leaving Juliette in the care of her mother's sister in Ville-franche, the Bernards moved to Paris, where they remained on the fringes of Parisian society. After several months at Ville-franche, Juliette was moved to live with another of her mother's sisters, a nun at the convent of La Déserte in Lyons. She later recalled her life there "like a vague, sweet dream, with its clouds of incense, its innumerable ceremonies, its processions in the gardens, its chants, and its flowers," and credited this early influence for her later religious faith: "I have been able to retain my religious belief, though coming in contact with persons of such various and contradictory opinions. I have listened to them, understood them, admitted them, as far as they were admissible; but I have never allowed doubt to enter my heart."

When Juliette regretfully left the convent to live with her parents in 1791, her mother **Juliette Matton Bernard** decided to introduce her to the wonders of Parisian society. Although Juliette learned to take great pains with her dress and her toilette, and even learned to play a little on the harp and the piano, she never undertook any academic studies. Her parents entertained regularly, and one of their most constant visitors was an old family friend, Jacques Récamier, a wealthy Lyonese banker. Récamier was described as a handsome man with fair hair and blue eyes and a kindly, optimistic nature. In 1793, he asked Juliette's parents for her hand in marriage. Juliette was 15; Récamier was 42. Despite the difference in their ages, Juliette agreed to the match, and on April 14, 1793, the two were wed in a small civil ceremony, which was celebrated quietly since it occurred at the height of the Reign of Terror.

> [T]his young woman forms a remarkable study, for, at an age when girls dream only of reigning over a heart . . . she was thinking how to dominate men, salons, and society itself.
>
> —Joseph Turquan

Monsieur and Madame Récamier seem to have developed a harmonious, if distant, relationship. Contemporaries as well as later biographers commented upon Jacques' paternal concern for his young wife, and Madame Récamier even admitted to her niece in later years that she had been Jacques' wife in name only. In fact, speculation abounded that Jacques was actually Juliette's father, and that she was the product of an earlier liaison with Juliette's mother in Lyons. Jacques set Juliette up in a well-furnished château but spent most of his nights in a small apartment in Paris closer to his business.

Soon after Juliette's marriage, the Reign of Terror burned itself out, and Parisian society began to reappear. Madame Récamier's beauty drew the attention of the Parisian crowds, and her combination of wealth and good looks gave her a certain level of celebrity uncommon for someone without an aristocratic background. Contemporaries waxed eloquent over her white, glistening shoulders and perfect complexion. Her brown hair and eyes set off a countenance of neat, regular features in her round face. She was noted for her elegant figure, especially for her well-proportioned neck, shoulders and arms. As her celebrity grew, she found herself surrounded by the best of Parisian society. On one occasion, she agreed to take on the responsibility of handing around a purse to collect charitable contributions for the Church of St. Roch. On the day of the collection, the church was so full that people stood on chairs, pillars and altar pieces just to catch a glimpse of the famous beauty. The collection was an immense success, bringing in the unheard-of sum of 20,000 francs.

Monsieur Récamier encouraged his young wife to entertain, realizing that her growing celebrity was good for business, and Juliette enjoyed holding salons and parties. Her entertainments were enormously successful: men of the highest rank and the most celebrated wit competed with each other to honor Récamier, and she became "the inaccessible goal of the ambition of a hundred Don Juans." Most of the highest-ranking members of the French aristocracy had emigrated from France during the Terror, and many of them had returned to find financial ruin. They could not dream of opening salons of their own, and so were willing to bestow the honor of their presence upon the salons of the nouveau-riche. Although she was no wit herself, Madame Récamier was able to attract some of the most distinguished minds of her time to her salons. She was widely praised for her tact, which allowed her to bring together men of contrary ideas or competing political factions in apparent harmony under her roof. Since many of her fêtes kept her up until dawn, she came into the habit of sleeping until four in the afternoon, at which time she rose, took her bath and dressed. If any visitor presented himself before the five o'clock hour, her porter would turn him away, noting "Madame's day has not commenced."

In 1798, Jacques Récamier became convinced that their house was too small, and he bought a house in the Rue de Mont Blanc that had belonged to Jacques Necker and ◀❦ **Suzanne Necker**. It was during this transaction that Madame met and established a lasting friendship with the Neckers' daughter, Madame ***Germaine de Staël**. Monsieur Récamier gave Juliette *carte blanche* to decorate the house without regard to cost, and the luxury and elegance of the furnishings generated a great amount of interest and comment.

Madame de Staël, whose pre-Revolutionary salons had made her one of the most distinguished intellectuals of Paris, took an immediate liking to Madame Récamier. They quickly became close friends and confidantes. Juliette could not equal Madame de Staël in wit or learning, but her charming and sympathetic nature made her popular among the most learned members of Parisian society.

Madame Récamier's reign at the top of Parisian society was not destined to last for long, however. The rampant speculation that accompanied Napoleon Bonaparte's rise to power began to take its toll on her husband's business interests. Napoleon is said to have become much

enamored of Juliette, but when he offered her a position in the household of his sister *Carolina Bonaparte**, she turned him down. Perhaps in response to this unaccustomed rebuff, when Monsieur Récamier's bank suffered a series of reverses a few months later, Napoleon refused a state loan to keep the bank afloat, and Jacques was forced to declare bankruptcy in October 1806.

To their credit, many of Juliette's friends were sympathetic to her plight. Several of the best Parisian families had been reduced to relative penury in the wake of the French Revolution and Napoleon's meteoric rise. The Récamiers left Paris for the provinces, where Juliette was able to "hide from the fashionable world, so often dazzled by her brilliant fêtes, that she was no longer financially able to open her doors," writes one of her biographers. "This saved her from the bitterness of seeing her house put up for sale, and in the meanwhile of living miserably on a single floor." To Juliette's great relief, Madame de Staël, who had been banished by Napoleon in 1803 because her political views were spoken a little too freely, offered her an invitation to join her at her house in Coppet, on the Swiss side of Lake Leman.

While living at Coppet, Juliette met Prince Augustus of Prussia, the heir to the Prussian throne. Augustus was so entranced with Juliette's beauty that he asked her to marry him, although Juliette was already married, and her status as a Frenchwoman, a commoner, and a Catholic made her quite unsuitable as a candidate for the Prussian throne. Madame Récamier was so excited by the offer that she wrote to her husband of 14 years at once, asking for a divorce on the grounds that their marriage had only been a civil one and had never been solemnized by the Church. Unbelievably, Monsieur Récamier wrote back giving his consent to the divorce, but warning Juliette that the king of Prussia was unlikely to approve of the match and that Augustus' reputation in Europe had earned him the nickname "Prince Don Juan." In 1807, Augustus returned to Prussia, and Madame Récamier returned to Paris. They kept up a correspondence for several months, but finally gave up on their scheme. Augustus contented himself with a painting Madame Récamier sent him of herself by the artist François Gérard.

Because of her continuing connection to Madame de Staël, in 1811 Napoleon banished Madame Récamier from Paris, forcing her to live outside a 100-mile radius of the city. For the next several years, until Napoleon was defeated and sent to Elba in 1814, she flitted through the

❦▶
*Necker,
Suzanne. See
Staël, Germaine
de for sidebar.*

provinces, living in a succession of hotels. In 1813, Juliette, accompanied by her seven-year-old niece, whom she had adopted, went to Rome. While she was there, the sculptor Canova made two busts of the great beauty; when Madame Récamier found them to be less flattering than she desired, however, Canova angrily gave them new titles and sold them.

During his wife's exile, Monsieur Récamier had slowly rebuilt his fortune, and Juliette was able to return in 1814 to reclaim her place as queen of Parisian society. Her popularity was not diminished by her prior absence from the social scene, and, at 37, she still had the ability to inspire passion in the hearts of the most successful and famous men of her time. Benjamin Constant, the famous writer and diplomat, became one of her most ardent admirers, and is said to have written some of his most stinging indictments of Napoleon as a result of her influence.

Madame Récamier's contemporaries and her later biographers, some of whom have depicted her as a cold-hearted flirt, have been hard pressed to explain her ability to attract the most distinguished men of her time as admirers. Poorly educated and lacking in political ambition, what did Juliette have to offer her illustrious friends, especially after her husband's fortune failed and her own beauty was dimmed by encroaching age? Biographers have depicted her life story as "the little thread which binds many other stories together." She certainly lived her life for her friends, and perhaps, as one biographer noted, "having no children, Madame Récamier consoled herself by having academicians." She has been much praised for her ability to convert her most ardent lovers into lasting friends. Notes another biographer: "She did not extinguish the passions she inspired. Rather she tempered them." In the absence of a family relationship with husband and children, Madame Récamier "found her pleasure and consolation, one might say her vocation" in friendship. Many of her friends, including Madame de Staël, referred to her often as "benevolent" and "angelic."

Madame de Staël returned to Paris soon after Madame Récamier, but by then she was very ill. Juliette kept constant vigil at her side

Juliette
Récamier

and was stricken with grief when Madame de Staël died. While tending to her dear friend, however, Juliette met the man who would become her most important admirer and closest friend, François Auguste de Chateaubriand. Despite his enormous success as an author, Chateaubriand was melancholy and dissatisfied. Cheered by Juliette's presence, he later claimed that his friendship with Madame Récamier "was . . . a relief to his spirits." He quickly became a permanent fixture in her social circle, and, although he was already married, he did not attempt to hide his devotion to Juliette.

In 1819, Jacques Récamier suffered another reversal of his fortunes, and Madame Récamier separated from him, taking a small apartment in the Convent of L'Abbaye-aux-Bois, where she remained for the rest of her life. Although her rooms there were almost as modest as the nuns' cells, she continued to entertain the cream of Parisian society at numerous receptions. Chateaubriand was a frequent attraction featured at her gatherings, as were Benjamin Constant, the poet Ballanche, and members of the most august houses of France and the rest of Europe. She surrounded herself with literary and political figures as well as leaders of fashion. She had the honor of seeing her friends rise in the political firmament. In 1821, her longtime friend Matthieu de Montmorency became minister for foreign affairs. Soon afterward, Chateaubriand was appointed ambassador to London. In his absences, he wrote to her often of his impatience to be back by her side.

As Juliette entered into middle age, she continued to gather new admirers around her and, what is more, successfully kept the friends of her youth close to her side. Her old admirers became even more devoted to her throughout the passing years. Chateaubriand was dismissed from his political office abruptly in 1825, and, although he served as ambassador to Rome from 1828 to 1829, he never reached the political heights of which he dreamed. He remained Juliette's faithful admirer and daily visitor, however, except when political necessity dictated that he travel. Over the course of the next decade, Madame Récamier began losing many of her friends and family to death. Matthieu de Montmorency died in 1825, and her father died shortly thereafter. In 1830, at age 80, Jacques Récamier succumbed to an inflammation of the chest. Although many biographers note that her grief at her husband's passing was notably absent, other contemporaries claimed that she felt "that she had lost her father a second time."

In that same year, France suffered through yet another revolution, which served to end the political ambitions of many of her friends. Her faithful admirer Chateaubriand gave up his political aspirations and dedicated himself to his writing. But her rooms at the Abbaye-aux-Bois still remained a favorite gathering spot for the literary élite of Paris. Her continuing popularity is evidenced by a soirée she hosted in 1840 to raise money to help flood victims in Lyons. Although the price of the tickets was set at 20 francs, members of Parisian society were known to have bid as much as 100 francs to secure them. All in all, from her overflowing rooms in the Abbaye-aux-Bois, Madame Récamier was able to raise no less than 4,390 francs for her cause.

Into her old age, Madame Récamier was still considered the "Queen of Society." When in 1845, at age 68, she lost her vision to cataracts, she continued to receive visitors in her rooms regularly. In the mornings, she would awaken and have the newspapers read aloud to her, or perhaps go for a drive. Each day at 2:30 in the afternoon, Chateaubriand, despite the fact that he was nearing 80 and in failing health, came to see her, and after an hour's *tête-à-tête* with him, Juliette would receive other visitors for the rest of the afternoon.

Madame de Chateaubriand died in 1847, and within a few months, Chateaubriand asked Madame Récamier to marry him. Pleading their advanced years, she politely refused him and proclaimed her desire to continue their relationship as it had been before. When, in the following year, his health declined further, she attended his bedside until he breathed his last in July 1848.

Separated from all of her closest friends by death, Juliette did not linger much longer. A cholera outbreak in 1849 claimed her among its victims, and she succumbed to the disease on May 11, 1849. By the time of her death, Madame Récamier was esteemed as a relic of a bygone age. As France edged closer to democracy, the aristocracy would become increasingly politically marginalized. To many of them who mourned Juliette's passing, she represented the last of the great leaders of pre-Revolutionary salon culture.

SOURCES:

Brooks, Geraldine. *Dames and Daughters of the French Court.* Freeport, NY: Books for Libraries (reprint 1968).

Hall, Evelyn Beatrice. *The Women of the Salons and Other French Portraits.* Freeport, NY: Books for Libraries (reprint 1969).

Luyster, Isaphene M. *Memoirs and Correspondence of Madame Recamier.* Boston, MA: Knight and Millet, 1867.

Terhune, Albert Payson. *Wonder Women in History.* London: Cassell, 1918.

Turquan, Joseph. *A Great Coquette: Madame Recamier and Her Salon*. NY: Brentano's, 1913.

Wharton, Grace and Philip. *The Queens of Society*. NY: Harper, 1860.

SUGGESTED READING:

Delecluze, Etienne-Jean. *Two Lovers In Rome*. Garden City, NY: Doubleday, 1958.

Levaillant, Maurice. *The Passionate Exiles: Madame de Stael and Madame Recamier*. NY: Farrar, Straus and Cudahy, 1958.

Kimberly Estep Spangler,
Assistant Professor of History and Chair,
Division of Religion and Humanities,
Friends University, Wichita, Kansas

Red Bird (1876–1938).

See Bonnin, Gertrude.

Redburga (fl. 825)

*Queen of Wessex, Kent, and the English. Said to be a sister of the king of the Franks, possibly Louis I the Pious, which would make her a daughter of Charlemagne; married Egbert also known as Egbert III (c. 775–839), king of Wessex, Kent, and the English (r. 802–839), before 825; children: *Edith (d. 871); Æthelwulf or Ethelwulf (b. around 800), king of Wessex and England (r. 839–858); Ethelstan, king of Kent (d. around 851). Redburga's husband Egbert had a long and glorious reign.*

Red Duchess, The (1883–1963).

See Elizabeth von Habsburg.

Reddy, Helen (1942—)

Australian-born singer and actress whose song "I Am Woman" became the anthem of the 1970s feminist movement. Born in Melbourne, Australia, in 1942; married second husband Jeff Wald (divorced 1982); married Milton Ruth, in 1983 (divorced 1996); children: (first marriage) daughter Traci; (second marriage) son Jordan.

Helen Reddy's song "I Am Woman," with the lyrics "I am woman, hear me roar, in numbers too big to ignore," became the anthem of the American feminist movement of the 1970s, and its title a cultural catchphrase so resonant it remains instantly recognizable and still powerful enough, over 30 years later, to evoke ridicule by no small number of people. Reddy herself remained indelibly linked with the song in the public mind, even as she continued to produce hit songs in the 1970s and then became an actress and a nightclub and concert singer.

Reddy was born in Australia in 1942 into a family of performers, making her professional debut on her parents' radio show at age two, when her parents held her up to the microphone. After her dreams of becoming a dancer had to be shelved due to a kidney operation, she decided to become a singer. The rock 'n' roll boom occurring in America in the 1950s did not reach isolated Australia, and Reddy's favorite music was jazz. Only in 1958, when her parents returned from a trip to the U.S. bringing her a gift of the top singles—all 40 of them—did she hear the new genre of music. Chief among the performers on her acquisitions were Chuck Berry and Ray Charles, and Reddy was intrigued. By the 1960s, she had moved on to pop, which she considered "a nice middle ground" between jazz and rock. Now in her early 20s, she had a twice-weekly radio show on the Australian Broadcasting Commission, "Helen Reddy Sings." Despite her success, she longed for more.

In 1966, Reddy entered and won a "Bandstand International" singing contest, the adver-

Helen
Reddy

tised first prize of which was a trip to New York and a recording contract with Mercury Records. In an early hint of trouble, she had to badger company officials for four months to receive her plane ticket. Finally, ticket in hand, she sold her furniture, bought another ticket for her three-year-old daughter (she had been married and divorced), and left Australia with no intention of returning. The promise of a record deal proved to be a sham, as she found when she met with Mercury Records. "I said," Reddy later recalled, "'What's happening about the record deal?' And he said, 'Oh, well, the prize was for an audition, and they sent us a tape, and you sing very nicely, dear, but we were really hoping for a male group; do give us a call before you go back to Australia, and have a nice time while you're here.'" Undaunted, Reddy stayed in New York without a green card, making occasional careful trips to Canada to sing for low pay, and scraped together a living for herself and her daughter while waiting for her big break.

During this precarious financial time, Reddy met Jeff Wald, an agent at the William Morris Agency (his clients included comedian George Carlin and singer Tiny Tim) who would become her husband and manager. They moved to Chicago, where Reddy found work in a theater revue. In 1968, they moved to Los Angeles, but even there, in one of the top music centers in the country, her career remained stalled.

Reddy got her break in 1970 when she landed a spot on "The Tonight Show," which opened doors to a one-single contract with Capitol Records. Under pressure to produce a hit, Reddy chose a song she liked for the A-side of the single, and without much enthusiasm agreed to record "I Don't Know How to Love Him," a song sung by the character of *Mary Magdalene in the rock opera *Jesus Christ Superstar* that had already been recorded by several artists, for the B-side. ("They said to me if it's on the B-side, it doesn't matter. No one listens to the B-side.") When the tapes from the recording session were played, however, all agreed that the B-side song should be on the A-side, and upon its release in 1971, "I Don't Know How to Love Him" went to #13 on the charts. This was enough to secure her a contract for a full album, and that same year Reddy recorded two of them, *I Don't Know How to Love Him* and *Helen Reddy*. However, none of the singles from the albums made the Top 40 chart.

Prior to recording the albums, Reddy had become involved in the growing feminist movement. "When the women's movement, as we called it, first started to happen, it was like I'd come home," she once said. "At long last, there were other people who felt the way I did, that women should be valued." She wanted to include a song about the feminist movement on her first album, but in casting around found nothing that fit the bill. "I finally realized that I was going to have to write the song myself because it simply didn't exist. And that was the genesis of 'I Am Woman.' It was my statement as a feminist." She co-wrote the song (with only two verses) with Ray Burton, and included it on the *I Don't Know How to Love Him* album. "I Am Woman," like the other songs on the album, languished without radio play for over a year, until makers of a feminist documentary, *Stand Up and Be Counted*, requested permission to include the song in their film. Seizing the opportunity, Capitol Records agreed and decided to release the song as a single. Reddy wrote a third verse to make it fit the single format and recorded the song again. Radio stations were not quick to embrace the song, but individual women were. To circumvent the lack of airplay, Reddy sang "I Am Woman" on 19 television variety shows. Women started calling radio stations to request the song, and soon it hit #1 on the charts. That same week, Reddy's second child, son Jordan, was born.

Critical reaction to the song was harsh, perhaps all the more so because "issue" songs of the era were typically rough performances by folk or rock musicians, not lushly orchestrated songs by pop singers. One of the (mostly male) critics called Reddy "a purveyor of all that is silly in the women's lib movement." She nonetheless won a Grammy award for Best Contemporary Female Pop Vocal Performance for "I Am Woman," and caused even more controversy when in her acceptance speech she thanked God "because She makes everything possible." Angry letters poured in. Defending herself in an interview, Reddy said, "I knew any feminist would understand what I was saying; it seemed like the only thing I could say that summed it up." While attacked as a blasphemous feminist by some, she was also criticized for not being enough of a feminist by those who saw her popularity as an obstacle to her political correctness. Despite all the brouhaha, in 1975 the United Nations declared "I Am Woman" the theme song of its International Year of the Woman.

Reddy, meanwhile, was on a roll. Between 1972 and 1976, she released seven albums that made the Top 20, and had two more #1 hits, the narrative songs "Delta Dawn" (about a pitiable insane woman) and "Angie Baby" (about a powerful insane woman). In addition, "Leave Me Alone (Ruby Red Dress)," "You and Me

Against the World," and "Ain't No Way to Treat a Lady" made the Top 10. In 1973, Reddy hosted the premier show of the television rock music variety program "The Midnight Special," and became its regular host in 1975.

As her music dropped off the charts in the later 1970s, Reddy began acting, and made her film debut in 1977, in the Walt Disney feature *Pete's Dragon*. She also began performing cabaret-style concerts in nightclubs, and was one of the first to include songs by Simon and Garfunkel in an act intended for non-rock 'n' roll audiences. She has made numerous television specials and had guest spots on various television series. Reddy has also appeared frequently on stage, in revivals of *Call Me Madame* and *Anything Goes*, among others, as well as starring roles in both the West End and Broadway productions of *Shirley Valentine* and *Blood Brothers*. While she no longer records, she continues to give live concerts, on occasion backed by symphony orchestras or jazz groups. Reddy lives in California, where she served as the state commissioner of parks and recreation for three years.

SOURCES:

The Boston Globe. March 21, 1997, pp. C3–C4.

Gaar, Gillian G. *She's A Rebel: The History of Women in Rock & Roll.* Seal Press, 1992.

People Weekly. June 17, 1996, p. 59.

Roxon, Lilian. *Rock Encyclopedia.* NY: Workman, 1969.

Jacqueline Mitchell,
freelance writer, Detroit, Michigan

Redpath, Anne (1895–1965)

Scottish painter. Born in Galashiels, Selkirkshire, Scotland, on March 29, 1895; died in 1965; daughter of Thomas Brown Redpath (a designer of tweed) and Agnes Frier (Milne) Redpath; graduated from Edinburgh College of Art, 1918; earned teaching certificate from Moray House, 1918; married James Beattie Michie (an architect), on September 20, 1920; children: sons Alastair Milne, Lindsay, David.

Anne Redpath made a name for herself as a painter in many parts of Europe, including Scotland, France, and England. Her paintings and watercolors, belonging to no defined school of art, either traditional or modern, were praised for their "clarity and freshness" and sense of cheerful beauty, and her use of color was judged remarkable. Considered among her best works were her interiors of European churches and townscapes, although she was also particularly noted for her still-lifes and paintings of flowers.

Born in Galashiels, Scotland, on March 29, 1895, Redpath was encouraged to paint at a very early age, as her mother **Agnes Redpath** often made paintbrushes out of her own hair for her four children. While Redpath spent her childhood painting flowers not from nature but from her imagination, it was not until a class at Hawich High School with John Gray, later president of the Royal Scottish Society of Water Colour Painters, that she received formal art instruction. While her mother was supportive of her interest in art, her father Thomas Brown Redpath worried that she would not be able to support herself, and urged her to prepare for a back-up career as a teacher. Obeying his wishes, after graduating from high school in 1913 she studied both at Moray House, for a teaching degree, and at the Edinburgh College of Art. There she earned several prizes, and won a small stipend to study in London.

She graduated from both schools in 1918, and the following year was awarded a postgraduate scholarship for further study at the College of Art. This, in turn, led to a scholarship that enabled her to travel through Europe for a year, seeing art in France, Italy, and Belgium. After her return to Scotland, she married architect James Beattie Michie. They spent the next 15 years living in France, where she gave birth to three sons. Busy with family life, Redpath rarely painted during this time. She nonetheless had two exhibitions of her work, at Saint Omer, in the north of France, and later on the Riviera, at Saint Raphaël. Upon the family's return to Scotland in 1934, when her children were a bit older, she returned to painting. While she painted a series of Scottish landscapes, her works during these years were primarily domestic interiors and still-lifes. She also painted war posters during World War II.

Redpath traveled again in Europe in 1949, and afterwards began painting European landscapes, with a greater use of color. In 1951, she was elected to full membership in the Royal Scottish Academy, the first woman so honored. Her first solo exhibition in London was held the following year; particularly noted by critics were her flower paintings. Redpath frequently lectured in Scotland on art, and made a number of radio broadcasts examining modern painters. She received the Order of the British Empire and an honorary LL.D. from the University of Edinburgh in 1955, and also suffered a coronary thrombosis that forced her to curtail her public life but did not stop her from painting. In 1959, she lost the use of her right arm. She eventually regained control over it, but by that time she had taught herself how to paint using her left arm.

A member of the Society of Scottish Artists from 1943, and of the Royal Society of British

Artists from 1946, Redpath served as president of the Scottish Society of Women Artists from 1944 to 1947, and sat on the board of management of the Edinburgh College of Art for six years. Her paintings are held in public collections in various cities, including Sydney, Australia, and Vancouver, Canada, and in private collections in France, and have been displayed in the British Embassy in Bonn, Germany. She died in 1965.

SOURCES:

Candee, Marjorie Dent, ed. *Current Biography Yearbook 1957.* NY: H.W. Wilson, 1957.
The Concise Dictionary of National Biography. Oxford: Oxford University Press, 1992.

Jacqueline Mitchell,
freelance writer, Detroit, Michigan

Red Sonia or Sonja (1907–2000).

See Kuczinski, Ruth.

Redvers, Isabella de (1237–1293).

See Isabella de Redvers.

Louise
Goff
Reece

Reece, Louise Goff (1898–1970)

American congressional representative (May 16, 1961–January 3, 1963). Name variations: Mrs. Carroll Reece. Born Louise Goff in Milwaukee, Wisconsin, on November 6, 1898; died in Johnson City, Tennessee, on May 14, 1970; daughter of Guy Despard Goff (U.S. senator from West Virginia) and Louise (Van Nortwick) Goff; educated in private schools in Milwaukee and at Miss Spence's School in New York City; married B. Carroll Reece (a 12-term congressional representative from Tennessee), on October 30, 1923 (died 1961); children: Louise Goff Reece (who married George W. Marthens II).

Louise Goff Reece was born on November 6, 1898, in Milwaukee, Wisconsin, and was educated at private schools in Milwaukee and Miss Spence's School in New York City. After marrying Carroll Reece, a Republican member of the U.S. House of Representatives from Tennessee, she involved herself with various business activities and campaigned with her husband during his tenure in Congress. When he died in 1961, in the midst of his 12th term in office, she was endorsed by the First District Republican Committee as a candidate for his House seat. Reece won the nomination from the district convention and defeated Democrat William Faw in the special election of May 16, 1961.

While she had not planned to enter politics, it had not been unknown territory even prior to her marriage, for her father Guy Goff had been a U.S. senator representing West Virginia, and her grandfather Nathan Goff had been a senator and representative from the same state. Reece took the oath of office on May 23, 1961. She served on the Public Works Committee, and in that capacity joined with other Republican committee members to warn of the increased federal spending and bureaucracy they predicted would be caused by the Public Works Acceleration and Coordination Act, which they opposed. Representing the interests of the glass industry in her district, she also urged President John F. Kennedy to restore tariff rates on certain glass products. She initiated a special order in honor of the 45th anniversary of the 19th Amendment, which guaranteed women the right to vote. The final vote for ratification, she noted, had been cast by Tennessee.

Reece declined the opportunity to seek a full term in the 1962 elections, saying the district would be better served by a younger representative. After leaving Congress in January 1963, she returned to Tennessee and to her business activities; she was a member of the board of two banks in Tennessee, and also owned and managed Goff Properties in Clarksburg, West Virginia. Reece remained active in the Republican Party on the state and local level, and died in Johnson City, Tennessee, on May 14, 1970.

SOURCES:
Office of the Historian. *Women in Congress, 1917–1990*. Commission on the Bicentenary of the U.S. House of Representatives, 1991.

Jacqueline Mitchell,
freelance writer, Detroit, Michigan

Reed, Alma (1889–1966)

American journalist. Name variations: (pseudonym) Mrs. Goodfellow. Born Alma Marie Sullivan in San Francisco, California, on June 17, 1889 (she claimed 1894); died on November 20, 1966, in Mexico City, Mexico; daughter of Eugene J. Sullivan and Adelaide Frances (Murphy) Sullivan; married Samuel Payne Reed, on August 8, 1915 (divorced around 1916); no children.

Alma Reed, who was born Alma Marie Sullivan in 1889 in San Francisco, the oldest of ten children of Irish immigrants, decided at an early age that she did not want to live her life in the traditional role of wife and mother. Instead, she shocked her family by becoming a reporter at the *San Francisco Call*, where, because she was a woman, she was assigned to write about tales of woe under the name "Mrs. Goodfellow." Reed nonetheless succeeded in using her articles to challenge public thinking on such critical issues as capital punishment. Her influence was such that when she campaigned to prevent the state execution of Mexican prisoner Simon Ruiz, she succeeded in the face of racial prejudice and conservative opinion on the death penalty. The 17-year-old Ruiz was the first beneficiary of a law that made it illegal to hang prisoners who were under 18 years of age, and Reed became something of a celebrity. The *San Francisco Bulletin* lured her away from the *Call* with the promise of more money and her own column with her picture on it—the only staff writer to receive such recognition at the time.

Reed's role in saving Ruiz opened up the opportunity for her to go to Mexico, when President Alvaro Obregon invited her as his personal guest. Her travels there introduced her to famed muralist José Clemente Orozco, who showed her the wonders of his country and fostered her growing affection for it. When *The New York Times* offered her a job, she took it with the stipulation that she be assigned stories in Mexico. In 1923, while covering an archaeological team from the Carnegie Institute that was surveying the Mayan ruins in Mexico's Yucatán, Reed reported on the thefts from the ruins of irreplaceable artifacts which were subsequently smuggled to Boston's Peabody Museum. Working on this story sparked her own passion for archaeology, which would later take her to the excavation of Carthage in North Africa and the exploration of Cozumel, the Mayan equivalent of Jerusalem. Other famous expeditions included her search for the mythological River Styx and an attempt to locate the fabled lost continent of Atlantis. For this search, she set a record for deep-sea diving when she plunged 500 feet below the surface. *The New York Times* would later call her "the only archaeological reporter in the world."

Reed had briefly married Samuel Payne Reed in 1915, but the couple divorced a year later when it became apparent that he was having an affair. During her first assignment in Mexico, Reed met and fell in love with Felipe Carrillo Puerto, governor of Yucatán, who has been called "the Abraham Lincoln of Mexico" for his efforts to liberate the Indian slaves and improve the quality of life in Yucatán. Although Felipe was married at the time, he created a law legalizing divorce so he could leave his wife for Reed. Political unrest in Mexico, however, resulted in his assassination shortly before their planned marriage in 1924. His death affected Reed deeply, and she never had another relationship that equaled the intensity and commitment of their love affair.

Alma
Reed

In 1928, Reed set up a dazzling salon in Greenwich Village where American and foreign intellectuals and artists gathered, often to discuss world peace. One of these was her old friend from Mexico, José Orozco, now an impoverished artist living in New York City. Orozco was in need of a benefactor to champion his work. Reed stepped in, and the following year they set up a gallery to show his murals and the work of other Mexican and American artists. However, the gallery foundered, and Reed was forced to return to journalism in order to pay the bills. She worked as an art editor for the *Mobile Press Register* of Mobile, Alabama, and also promoted cultural events in a weekly radio program.

In 1950, Reed returned to Mexico to work at the English-language *Mexico City News*. In 1961, she was the recipient of the Royal Order of Benefactions, a high order of Greece, and the Aztec Eagle, the highest decoration the Mexican government can bestow on a foreigner. The latter commemorated her nearly 40 years of writing about Mexican culture. In 1966, she published *Ancient Past of Mexico*, and embarked on a book tour.

Reed died unexpectedly in Mexico City on November 20, 1966, in the midst of a routine operation to remove an intestinal obstruction. Suspicious and grieving friends demanded an autopsy, and the "obstruction" turned out to be an occlusion caused by advanced cancer of the colon. Her body was cremated, and three days later a memorial service was held. Because Reed was a heroine in Mexico, celebrated as "La Peregrina" (the Pilgrim) in a well-known folk song, long-held customs were overlooked so her ashes could be laid to rest beside Felipe Carrillo Puerto. The first full-length biography of Reed, *Passionate Pilgrim: The Extraordinary Life of Alma Reed*, was published by **Antoinette May** in 1993.

SOURCES:

Belles Lettres. Fall 1993, p. 40.
Library Journal. April 1, 1993, p. 100.
May, Antoinette. *Passionate Pilgrim: The Extraordinary Life of Alma Reed*. NY: Paragon House, 1993.
Publishers Weekly. February 22, 1993.

Jacqueline Mitchell,
freelance writer, Detroit, Michigan

Reed, Belle (1848–1889).

See Starr, Belle.

Reed, Donna (1921–1986)

American actress who was best known for her television series, "The Donna Reed Show," and her performance in It's a Wonderful Life. *Name variations:* Donna Adams; Donna Asmus. Born Donna Belle Mullenger on January 27, 1921, in Denison, Iowa; died on January 14, 1986, in Beverly Hills, California; daughter of William R. Mullenger and Hazel Mullenger; attended Los Angeles City College, 1938–40; married William Tuttle (a make-up artist), on January 30, 1943 (divorced 1944); married producer Anthony I. Owen, known as Tony Owen, on June 15, 1945 (divorced 1971); married Grover Asmus (a retired army officer), in 1974; children: Penny Jane, Anthony R., Timothy G., and Mary Anne.

Selected filmography: The Get-Away *(1941)*; The Shadow of the Thin Man *(1941)*; Babes on Broadway *(1942)*; The Bugle Sounds *(1942)*; The Courtship of Andy Hardy *(1942)*; Mokey *(1942)*; Calling Dr. Gillespie *(1942)*; Apache Trail *(1942)*; Eyes in the Night *(1942)*; The Human Comedy *(1943)*; Dr. Gillespie's Criminal Case *(1943)*; Thousands Cheer *(1943)*; The Man From Down Under *(1943)*; See Here, Private Hargrove *(1944)*; Mrs. Parkington *(1944)*; The Picture of Dorian Gray *(1945)*; Gentle Annie *(1945)*; They Were Expendable *(1945)*; Faithful in My Fashion *(1946)*; It's a Wonderful Life *(1946)*; Green Dolphin Street *(1947)*; Beyond Glory *(1948)*; Chicago Deadline *(1949)*; Saturday's Hero *(1951)*; Scandal Sheet *(1952)*; Hangman's Knot *(1952)*; Trouble Along the Way *(1953)*; Raiders of the Seven Seas *(1953)*; From Here to Eternity *(1953)*; The Caddy *(1953)*; Gun Fury *(1953)*; Three Hours to Kill *(1954)*; The Last Time I Saw Paris *(1954)*; They Rode West *(1954)*; The Far Horizons *(1955)*; Ransom! *(1956)*; The Benny Goodman Story *(1956)*; Backlash *(1956)*; Beyond Mombasa *(UK, 1956)*; The Whole Truth *(1958)*; Pepe *(1960)*; Yellow-Headed Summer *(unreleased, 1974)*.

An Iowa farm girl and high school beauty queen, Donna Reed began acting at Los Angeles City College, where she was also voted Campus Queen. She signed a contract with MGM in 1941, and made a series of films under the name of Donna Adams before graduating to starring roles in the mid-1940s. In 1946, Reed portrayed Mary Hatch to Jimmy Stewart's George Bailey in the perennial Christmas favorite *It's a Wonderful Life*, a role that personified the sweet, good-hearted screen image she could never shake. In 1953, after a move to Columbia Pictures, where her second husband Tony Owen was an assistant to Harry Cohn, Reed was cast as a prostitute in *From Here to Eternity*. Although she won an Academy Award for Best Supporting Actress for her performance, it did little to change her image, and she soon was back to her good-girl roles.

When her film career slowed during the 1950s, Reed and her producer-husband developed "The Donna Reed Show," in which she portrayed yet another idealized wife and mother. Although the show had a successful run of eight years (1958–66) and made her a millionaire, Reed later spoke with contempt about the two-dimensional, stereotypical character she played and of the male mentality that dominated television programming.

With United States involvement in the Vietnam War, Reed, a staunch Republican and the mother of two sons of draftable age, became deeply involved in the antiwar effort. She did not resume her career until 1984, when she replaced *Barbara Bel Geddes in the role of Ellie on the popular evening soap opera "Dallas." When Bel Geddes returned in 1985, Reed sued the show's producers for breach of contract. Shortly after receiving a $1 million settlement, she died from pancreatic cancer. She left her Oscar statuette to her hometown of Denison, Iowa, where the Donna Reed Foundation for the Performing Arts was established in her memory.

SOURCES:

Katz, Ephraim. *The Film Encyclopedia.* NY: Harper-Collins, 1994.

Lamparski, Richard. *Whatever Became of . . . ?* 5th series. NY: Crown, 1974.

SUGGESTED READING:

Fultz, Jay. *In Search of Donna Reed.* University of Iowa, 1998.

Barbara Morgan,
Melrose, Massachusetts

Reed, Dorothy (1874–1964).

See Mendenhall, Dorothy Reed.

Reed, Elizabeth Armstrong (1874–1911).

See Reed, Myrtle.

Reed, Esther De Berdt (1746–1780)

Co-founder of the first relief organization during the American Revolution. Born Esther De Berdt on October 22, 1746, in London, England; died of dysentery on September 18, 1780, in Philadelphia, Pennsylvania; daughter of Dennys De Berdt and Martha (Symons) De Berdt; married Joseph Reed (a lawyer), on May 31, 1770; chil-

From the movie It's a Wonderful Life, starring James Stewart and Donna Reed.

$\mathcal{E}$sther
$\mathcal{D}$e
$\mathcal{B}$erdt
$\mathcal{R}$eed

dren: Martha, Joseph, Esther, Theodosia (d. 1778), Dennis De Berdt, George Washington.

Moved to America (1771); was hostess to many delegates to the First Continental Congress (1774); published the broadside The Sentiments of an American Woman *(1780); co-founded the Philadelphia Ladies Association and led a fund-raising campaign to support the Continental Army (1780).*

Born in London, England, in 1746, Esther De Berdt was exposed to Americans and their interests early in life. Her father Dennys De Berdt, an agent for the colonies of Delaware and Massachusetts who helped win the revocation of the Stamp Act, often hosted Americans in his London and country homes. In 1763, one of these visitors, New Jersey lawyer Joseph Reed, met and fell in love with the dainty but lively Esther. After enduring Dennys' objections and Joseph's five-year stay back in America, Esther and Joseph were married in 1770. Dennys De Berdt's death less than two months before their wedding had put the De Berdt family under financial strain. As a result, Esther and Joseph decided not to settle in England, as they had planned, but moved to Philadelphia instead.

As American resistance to England intensified and her husband Joseph became a leading patriot, Esther Reed swiftly and wholeheartedly supported the American cause. In 1774, she hosted delegates to the First Continental Congress, among them George Washington, John Adams, and Samuel Adams, and another delegate enthusiastically referred to her as a staunch "Daughter of Liberty." In 1775, with three children of her own, she wrote to her brother, "if these great affairs must be brought to a crisis and decided, it had better be in our time than in our children's." When the American Revolution erupted, she saw those words realized, and though Joseph was often away serving as Washington's aide, Esther had three more children. One of them died of smallpox in infancy, and the family had to flee Philadelphia three times due to the war.

In 1780, as Esther herself was recovering from smallpox, she founded and industriously led a women's campaign to raise money for Washington's Continental Army. On June 10, 1780, she wrote a broadside, *The Sentiments of an American Woman*, in which she discussed how American women wanted to do more than sit at home and wish the best for the soldiers. Women were determined, she declared, to be "really useful," like "those heroines of antiquity, who have rendered their sex illustrious." Knowing that some men might disapprove of such female enterprise, Reed cleverly hinted that any criticism of such efforts would be "unpatriotic." Her words were so compelling that three days after the broadside appeared, 36 women met to plan ways to implement its ideas. The Philadelphia Ladies Association was formed and set to work.

The association speedily collected about $7,500 in precious-metal coin. Reed wished to give money directly to soldiers, but Washington said the Army, unable to supply uniforms, needed shirts instead. Reed's association produced over 2,000 linen shirts and delivered them by the end of 1780. Sadly, Reed did not live to see the work of the Philadelphia Ladies Association, or the American Revolution, completed. In September 1780, she died suddenly at only 33 of acute dysentery. The work of her innovative association, which demonstrated that women could play an effective role in civic actions, was carried on by *Sarah Bache, the daughter of Benjamin Franklin.

SOURCES:

James, Edward T., ed. *Notable American Women, 1607–1950*. Cambridge, MA: The Belknap Press of Harvard University Press, 1971.

Norton, Mary Beth. "The Philadelphia Ladies Association," in *American Heritage*. April–May, 1980, pp. 102–103.

Read, Phyllis J., and Bernard L. Witlieb. *The Book of Women's Firsts*. NY: Random House, 1992.

Weatherford, Doris. *American Women's History*. NY: Prentice Hall, 1994.

Jacquie Maurice,
freelance writer, Calgary, Alberta, Canada

Reed, Mary (1854–1943)

American Methodist missionary. Born Mary Reed on December 4, 1854, in Lowell, Ohio; died on April 8, 1943, in Chandag, India; daughter of Wesley W. Reed and Sarah Ann (Henderson) Reed; graduated from Ohio Central Normal School in Worthington, 1878.

Taught school (1879–84); joined the Cincinnati branch of the Methodist Women's Foreign Missionary Society and sailed to India (1884); returned to the United States due to ill health (1890); went back to India after being diagnosed with leprosy (1891); appointed superintendent of a leper asylum near Pithoragarh (1892); awarded the Kaisar-i-Hind Medal by the government of India (1917); supervised the asylum and local schools (1892–1938); honored by the American Mission to Lepers (1941).

Born into a deeply religious Ohio family in 1854, by age 16 Mary Reed was very active in her local Methodist church. She taught for five years at a district school before deciding to become a missionary at about age 30. In 1884, she joined the Cincinnati branch of the Methodist Women's Foreign Missionary Society and headed to India.

In January 1885, Reed was assigned a post among Hindu women in Cawnpore, but poor health forced her to delay taking the position. While convalescing at Pithoragarh in the foothills of the Himalayas, she studied Hindustani and observed missionary work at a leper colony in the nearby area of Chandag. After her assignment at Cawnpore, Reed became headmistress of a girls' school in Gonda, but fell ill again in 1890 and had to return to the United States for treatment. Her suspicions that she had contracted leprosy were confirmed by a New York doctor. Interpreting her condition as a call to minister to the lepers she had met, she kept the news from her family and friends and in 1891 returned to Pithoragarh.

Early in 1892, Reed was appointed superintendent of the leper asylum at Chandag, which had been established by the interdenominational British Mission to Lepers in India and the East. Reed lobbied effectively to improve the conditions at the asylum; under her administration, its original huts and stables were replaced by cottages, a chapel, a water-supply system, a school, a small hospital, a dispensary, and even 48 more acres of land. While dealing with all the legal, financial, and supervisory demands of running the asylum, she also cared for patients personally and taught reading and religious classes. For seven years, she also pursued her Methodist missionary work by supervising six village schools and three Sunday schools which lay within a five-mile radius of the asylum.

By 1896, despite her refusal of any medical treatment, Reed's leprosy was all but gone, which amazed her very few outside visitors. In all, she did not leave Chandag for 52 years except for five times—two religious gatherings, a trip to Palestine and to the dentist, and one last visit to the United States. When her leprosy flared again in 1932, treatments were available to control it, but by the time she retired in 1938 she was almost completely blind. Her loss of sight contributed to a fatal accident in 1943.

During her life Reed was much admired for her dedicated service: she received the Kaisar-i-Hind Medal from the government of India in 1917, and was honored by the American Mission to Lepers (later renamed the American Leprosy Missions, Inc.) in 1941. Six years after her death, the Mary Reed Memorial Hospital was built by the American Mission to Lepers.

SOURCES:

James, Edward T., ed. *Notable American Women, 1607–1950.* Cambridge, MA: The Belknap Press of Harvard University Press, 1971.

McHenry, Robert, ed. *Famous American Women.* NY: Dover, 1980.

Jacquie Maurice,
freelance writer, Calgary, Alberta, Canada

Reed, Myrtle (1874–1911)

American novelist. Name variations: Myrtle Reed McCullough; (pseudonyms) Katherine LaFarge Norton, Olive Green. Born Myrtle Reed on September 27, 1874, in Norwood Park, Illinois; died of a sedative overdose on August 17, 1911, in Chicago, Illinois; daughter of Hiram Von Reed and Elizabeth (Armstrong) Reed; graduated from high school, 1893; married James Sydney McCullough (a businessman), on October 22, 1906.

Published first story in juvenile periodical at age ten; published first novel, Love Letters of a Musician *(1899); continued to write highly popular works (1899–1911); committed suicide at age 36 (1911).*

Selected writings: Love Letters of a Musician *(1899);* The Spinster Book *(1901);* Lavender and Old Lace *(1902);* What to Have for Breakfast *(cookbook, 1905);* Weaver of Dreams *(published posthumously, 1911).*

Born on September 27, 1874, into a distinguished family in a Chicago suburb, Myrtle Reed was encouraged from an early age to become an author. Her father Hiram Von Reed was a preacher who established Chicago's first literary periodical, the *Lakeside Monthly*, edited another magazine, and gave religious lectures. Her mother **Elizabeth Armstrong Reed**, a fervent Christian and self-taught scholar whose books on comparative religion and Asian literature earned her membership in English academic societies, also served as president of the Illinois Woman's Press Association for four terms.

At age ten, Myrtle Reed saw her first story appear in a children's periodical, the *Acorn*, and in high school she edited and contributed verse and short stories to the school paper, the *Voice*. During that time, she began corresponding with a young man in Toronto, Canada, James Sydney McCullough, who was also editor of his school's paper. A less serious scholar than her mother, she considered herself a student of philosophy, and was an emotional teenager. A breakdown in high school kept her from attending college, and she wrote idealistic romantic fiction and poetry in energetic spurts of creativity.

Reed graduated from high school in 1893 and began contributing poetry, sketches, and short stories to a handful of periodicals. Essentially unknown at the time, these pieces would later be published in such magazines as *Harper's Bazaar*. After suffering a brutal rejection by a major Chicago publisher, her first novel, *Love Letters of a Musician*, was published in 1899 by George H. Putnam and was so popular that it was in its 15th printing by 1904. In 1901, she published a selection of essays on romantic love and courtship, *The Spinster Book*, and in 1902 published *Lavender and Old Lace*—an immensely successful novel which has been called "[an elaborate] daydream translated into print." Reed churned out five more novels that were embraced by readers for their "sweet and tender sentiment" and often came in lavender covers embellished with ornate art-nouveau patterns.

James Sydney McCullough had moved to Chicago during this period to be near Reed, and her work began showing the influence of his presence. The standard of vulnerable femininity she had rendered in *The Spinster Book* was replaced by a more homey ideal woman. In 1905, under the pen name Olive Green, she published the cookbook *What to Have For Breakfast*, then nine more such books, as well as many articles on domestic subjects under the name Katherine La-Farge Norton. After a nearly 15-year courtship,

Reed and McCullough were married in October 1906, as McCullough settled into a real-estate business.

Reed's tendency to cling to her romantic fantasies of the model husband, wife, and home soon took their toll, however. She set out to re-mold McCullough into her dream husband in often exasperating ways, and in response he took to drinking and staying away on business trips. As her reality failed to match her utopian ideals time and again, Reed's disillusionment and depression began to echo in the tone of her books. She began using the sedative Veronal, and shortly after finishing her brooding novel *A Weaver of Dreams*, she ended her life with an overdose on August 17, 1911. *The Chicago Tribune* appropriately entitled an article on her death "Dies in Bondage to Her Own Fancy."

SOURCES:

James, Edward T., ed. *Notable American Women, 1607–1950*. Cambridge, MA: The Belknap Press of Harvard University Press, 1971.

McHenry, Robert, ed. *Famous American Women*. NY: Dover, 1980.

Jacquie Maurice,
freelance writer, Calgary, Alberta, Canada

Reed, Rowena (1900–1988)

American sculptor and design educator. Name variations: Rowena Kostellow. Born on July 6, 1900; died in September 1988 in New York City; graduated from the University of Missouri in Kansas City; studied sculpture at the Kansas City Art Institute; studied with sculptor Alexander Archipenko, and with Josef Hoffmann; attended the Carnegie Institute of Technology; married Alexander Kostellow.

While studying journalism at the University of Missouri in Kansas City, Rowena Reed developed an interest in art. After graduation, she pursued the study of sculpture at the Kansas City Art Institute and there met teaching assistant Alexander Kostellow, whom she would later marry. She studied under sculptor Alexander Archipenko and with Josef Hoffmann, then went on to the Carnegie Institute of Technology in Pittsburgh, Pennsylvania (later renamed Carnegie-Mellon University), where Kostellow was creating the first American industrial design curriculum.

In 1938, Reed joined Kostellow at the Pratt Institute in Brooklyn, New York, and in 1962 she became industrial design chair there. She retired from that position in 1966, but continued teaching until 1987. An important influence on her students and Pratt's industrial design curriculum, Reed strongly emphasized the artistic and aesthetic components of design. Continuing always to work as a sculptor, she believed that in the teaching of design, function was important, but engineering principles should never eclipse artistic value.

Jacquie Maurice,
freelance writer, Calgary, Alberta, Canada

Reel, Chi Cheng (1944—)

Taiwanese-American track-and-field star. Name variations: Chi Cheng; Mrs. Vincent Reel. Born on March 15, 1944, in Isinchu, Taiwan; married Vince Reel (a track coach).

Broke world records at 100 yards, 100 meters, 220 yards, and 200 meters; named Woman Athlete of the Year (1970); became a coach at Redlands University in Redlands, California.

Chi Cheng Reel was born in Isinchu, Taiwan, in 1944. Her interest in competitive racing began there, in junior high school. Always fast in the children's games that were played in nearby rice paddies and in provincial races, she showed great skill as a sprinter. Vince Reel, an American track-and-field coach, discovered Chi Cheng's talent at the 1962 Asian Games in Taiwan, after she had begun to train in earnest. He convinced her to come to the United States to train with him. In 1964, she made the Olympic team representing Taiwan. That summer in the Tokyo Olympics, while running dead even against the Russian star **Galina Bystrova**, Chi Cheng hit a hurdle and broke her thigh. The injury prevented her further competition and ended that year's hopes for the Taiwanese.

Chi Cheng had surgery on her knee in 1967 and endured pulled muscles in both legs in 1968, but she continued her training. At the 1968 Olympics in Mexico City, she placed third in the hurdles and seventh at 100 meters. By 1970, her legs had healed and her speed had become increasingly apparent. That year, she set world records at 100 yards, 100 meters, 220 yards, and 200 meters, and clocked 10.0 seconds at Portland, Oregon, on June 13, 1970, for the first "even time" 100 yards. She broke or equaled seven world records and lost only one race. Then in December 1970, a knee injury coupled with a snapping hip removed her from competition.

Chi Cheng was named Women Athlete of the Year in 1970, but her pain made even walking difficult. Returning to Taiwan for surgery, she spent 52 days in the hospital. When she returned to America, her running days were over; she first had to learn to walk. Once recovered, Chi Cheng became a track-and-field coach at Redlands University in Redlands, California, with her former coach Vince Reel, now her husband.

Karin L. Haag,
freelance writer, Athens, Georgia

Reel, Mrs. Vincent (b. 1944).

See Reel, Chi Cheng.

Reese, Lizette Woodworth
(1856–1935)

American poet. Born Lizette Woodworth Reese on January 9, 1856, in Huntingdon (later Waverly), Maryland; died on December 17, 1935, in Baltimore, Maryland; daughter of David Reese and Louise Sophia (Gabler) Reese; graduated from high school, 1873.

Taught at various Baltimore schools (1873–1921); published first poem, "The Deserted House" (1874); awarded an honorary Doctor of Letters degree from Goucher College (1931).

Selected works: A Branch of May *(1887);* A Quiet Road *(1896);* "Tears" *(sonnet, 1899);* A Wayside Lute *(1909);* Spicewood *(1920);* Wild Cherry *(1923);* Little Henrietta *(1927);* A Victorian Village *(1929).*

In 1856, Lizette Reese and her twin sister were born in a village two miles from Baltimore, known then as Huntingdon and later as Waverly. Her father David Reese, somewhat of a drifter, served on the Confederate side in the Civil War and was later a prisoner of war. Lizette was schooled mostly in Baltimore public schools and lived her entire life a few miles from the cottage where she was born. The memory of her early rural surroundings stayed with her as an adult and perpetually colored her verse, even as she watched the city of Baltimore gradually swallow up her quiet village.

As a schoolgirl, Reese loved to tell fanciful stories and make up rhymes, and though busy teaching positions later left her almost no free time, the writing of prose and poetry remained lifelong passions. Reese began teaching in Baltimore schools at age 17 and did not retire until 1921. In 1874, at 18, she published her first poem, "The Deserted House," which was inspired by a walk to school. From then until the year she died, she continued to write and publish, although the demands of her teaching career made the process slow and sporadic.

After her first volume, *A Branch of May* (1887), Reese published nine more volumes of poetry. In 1890, three of her poems appeared in Edmund Clarence Stedman's *Anthology*, and in November 1899 her most famous sonnet "Tears" first appeared in *Scribner's Magazine*. During her 14-year retirement, she published more poetry and was active in community projects. Her writings only slowly gained recognition outside of Baltimore, but she was well respected by local citizens and fellow poets. Her 75th birthday was officiated by H.L. Mencken, a longtime supporter, who praised her "poetic integrity." In 1931, Goucher College gave her an honorary Doctor of Letters degree, she was elected to Phi Beta Kappa by the College of William and Mary, and she won the Mary P.L. Keats Memorial Prize.

Both Reese's subject matter and form were traditional, and she believed that poetry should deal in universal human experience. Her communication of these universal experiences is intense and very individual, often with a "nostalgic sadness" and with nature and her own bucolic childhood home as the backdrop. Her work was painstakingly crafted, and, as *Harriet Monroe wrote, "delicately frail and fine, springing from a shy and isolated soul; an expression of wistfulness, of the ache of smothered emotion." Reese died just before her 80th birthday and on her stone are her own words:

> The long day sped,
> A roof, a bed;
> No years,
> No tears.

SOURCES:
James, Edward T., ed. *Notable American Women, 1607–1950.* Cambridge, MA: The Belknap Press of Harvard University Press, 1971.

Kunitz, Stanley J., and Howard Haycraft, eds. *Twentieth Century Authors.* NY: H.W. Wilson, 1942.

McHenry, Robert, ed. *Famous American Women.* NY: Dover, 1980.

Jacquie Maurice,
freelance writer, Calgary, Alberta, Canada

Reeve, Clara (1729–1807)

English novelist and poet. Born in 1729 at Ipswich, England; died on December 3, 1807, at Ipswich; daughter of William Reeve (a Suffolk cleric) and Hannah Smithies.

Selected works: Original Poems on Several Occasions *(1769);* The Old English Baron *(also known as* The Champion of Virtue: A Gothic Story, *1777);* The Two Mentors *(1780);* The Progress of Romance *(1785);* The School for Widows *(1791);* Plans of Education *(1792);* Memoirs of Sir Roger de Clarendon *(1793);* Destination; or Memoirs of a Private Family *(1799).*

Clara Reeve was born in 1729 at Ipswich in England, the eldest of eight children. Her maternal grandfather was King George I's goldsmith and jeweler, and her father William Reeve, from whom she said she "learned all she knew," was a rector and curate. At an early age, under her father's guidance, she began reading such weighty material as parliamentary debates, Rapin's *History of England*, Cato's *Letters*, Plutarch, and Greek and Roman history.

Reeve experienced early disappointment in 1769 with her first published work, *Original Poems on Several Occasions*. In 1772, she translated the 1621 Latin novel *Argenis* under the title *The Phoenix*, before achieving great success with her Gothic novel *The Champion of Virtue: A Gothic Story* in 1777. In the second and subsequent editions, the title of the novel was changed to the better-known *The Old English Baron*, and the book was later translated into French and German. Her *Progress of Romance* (1785) was a critical examination of the history of romance and fiction, presented as a dialogue in which the characters analyze such topics as female writers. Reeve published several other novels before she died at Ipswich in December 1807.

SOURCES:

Buck, Claire, ed. *The Bloomsbury Guide to Women's Literature*. NY: Prentice Hall, 1992.

Shattock, Joanne. *The Oxford Guide to British Women Writers*. NY: Oxford University Press, 1993.

Jacquie Maurice,
freelance writer, Calgary, Alberta, Canada

Reeve, Ella (1862–1951).

See Bloor, Ella Reeve.

Reeves, Helen Buckingham (1853–1920).

See Mathers, Helen.

Reeves, Martha (1941—)

American Motown singer who formed the girl-group Martha and the Vandellas. Born on July 18, 1941, in Eufala, Alabama; daughter of Elijah Reeves, Jr., and Ruby Reeves; graduated from Northeastern High in Detroit, Michigan, in 1959; married "Wiley," in 1967 (divorced); married Willie Dee (divorced); children: Eric Jermel Graham (b. November 10, 1970).

Formed girl-group Martha and the Vandellas (1962); recorded first Top Ten pop single (1963); recorded last Top Forty pop single (1967); released last album as Martha Reeves and the Vandellas (1972); awarded the *Dinah Washington Award from Detroit's Ballentine Belles; won *Dionne Warwick's Soul Award; won Heroes and Legends Award; received Pioneer Award with the Vandellas (1993).

Selected singles: "Heat Wave" (1963); "Quicksand" (1964); "Dancing in the Street" (1964); "Nowhere to Run" (1965); "Jimmy Mack" (1966); "Honey Chile" (1967).

Martha Reeves was born in 1941 in Eufala, Alabama, the daughter of Elijah Reeves, Jr., and **Ruby Reeves**, both musicians. Part of the "great exodus" of African-Americans out of the American South, the Reeves family migrated from Alabama to Detroit in 1942. There, Reeves' singing won her a church talent contest at age three—an event, she later recalled, which got her "hooked on pleasing a crowd" with her voice. By the third grade, she was often selected to sing solos in music class. As a schoolgirl, she dreamed of attaining stardom, inspired by other working-class Detroiters who had made it big.

After graduating from high school in 1959, Reeves spent the next year or so working at a host of low-paying jobs and singing on the side whenever she could. Only 19, she used borrowed identification cards to get into nightclubs, singing on open "showcase" nights and hoping for a break. In the summer of 1960, she joined **Rosalind Ashford, Annette Beard**, and **Gloria Williams** in their girl-group, the Del-Phis, and they competed in Detroit talent contests alongside other groups who also later became famous Motown acts. Reeves did solo performances as well, and after one such show in 1961 got her big break when she was asked by a Motown Records scout to audition for them. She arrived at their offices the next morning, and after learning no auditions were held on that day of the week, found herself answering phones all day and thus landed a job as secretary of the A&R department.

Her secretary's wages were soon supplemented with earnings from singing backup or hand-clapping on other acts' records. By 1962, after filling in for ***Mary Wells** in one recording session, Reeves signed a contract, along with two of the Del-Phis (Beard and Ashford), and became lead singer of Martha and the Vandellas. Later that year Motown creator Berry Gordy sent them, along with other young Detroit acts including ***The Supremes**, Marvin Gaye, The Temptations, and Stevie Wonder, out on a successful tour. Though the group endured some bigotry on the road, their new sound soon began to transcend racial boundaries. In 1963, Martha and the Vandellas became the first group to get an encore on Dick Clark's *American Bandstand*, and that summer they had their first Top Ten hit with "Heat Wave." By 1965, they had churned out other popular hits, such as "Dancing in the

Street" and "Nowhere to Run." In 1965 and 1966, they toured successfully in England, appearing on television shows, including one hosted by Reeves' good friend *Dusty Springfield.

While not performing, Reeves, like all Motown performers, was tutored in modeling, choreography, music theory, and even etiquette. She later said that this was like attending a university. However, behind the success and new poise, Reeves' personal life was often tumultuous. After a few early romantic relationships which ended disastrously, in 1967 she impetuously married a man named Wiley in Las Vegas after a peculiar, sporadic nine-month affair. The marriage ended shortly in divorce. After a brief liaison with a man named Gerald, a rocky relationship marked by drugs and violence, Reeves gave birth to a son in November 1970. In the early 1970s, Reeves' second marriage, to Willie Dee, also quickly dissolved. Violence, misfortune and abuse of prescription and non-prescription drugs continued to plague Reeves off and on until around 1980.

The year 1967 marked the Vandellas' last Top Ten hit for Motown, "Honey Chile." By 1968, Reeves' friendship with **Betty Kelly**, who had joined the Vandellas four years earlier, became strained almost to the point of assault, and Betty was replaced by Reeves' sister **Lois Reeves**. More disrupting personnel changes followed. After a 1968 incident in which Reeves refused to finish recording a song with lyrics she disliked, her relationship with Berry Gordy and Motown began to deteriorate. She acquired a reputation for being difficult to work with. Gordy began attending Reeves' shows on occasion with another of Motown's stars, **Diana Ross**, and criticizing Reeves afterward. Suspicious of Motown's accounting practices, Reeves was reputedly the first star to question them, which further damaged her bond with the company. "I think I was the first person at Motown to ask where the money was going," said Reeves. "Did I find out? Honey, I found my way out the door." By the end of the 1960s, Gordy was pouring more effort into the Supremes than into the Vandellas, and by the early 1970s Reeves' more hard-edged

Diana Ross. See *Supremes, The.*

Martha Reeves (right) and the Vandellas.

soul sound had been virtually cast aside. Gordy concentrated his energies on what he felt was Motown's best bet for moving into movies and television, the pretty Diana Ross with her "little-girl coo."

Martha Reeves and the Vandellas released their last album in 1972. Reeves then went solo, touring and producing several rather fruitless albums with various labels throughout the mid-1970s. Living fast in Los Angeles by then, she balked at the disco trend through the late 1970s, but finally recorded a disco album, *Gotta Keep Moving*, in 1980. By 1983, she had moved back to Detroit, and happily participated in a Motown retrospective television special. The resulting Motown resurgence of the 1980s revived her career, and Reeves toured and recorded again successfully on the "oldies" circuit. By 1991, Reeves, by then a grandmother, was recording for film soundtracks and still performing her old hits. One of the last few Motown "survivors," Reeves received a Pioneer Award in 1993. In the mid-1990s, having plowed through decades of career highs and lows, violent lovers, financial troubles, and bouts with drug abuse, Martha Reeves was still in love with her craft and eager to share it with others.

SOURCES:

Gaar, Gillian G. *She's a Rebel: The History of Women in Rock & Roll.* Seattle, WA: Seal Press, 1992.

Reeves, Martha, and Mark Bego. *Dancing in the Street: Confessions of a Motown Diva.* NY: Hyperion, 1994.

Jacquie Maurice,
freelance writer, Calgary, Alberta, Canada

Regina (d. around 251 CE)

Saint. Martyred in Alesia around 251 CE.

Regina was a Christian martyr who chose to die rather than break a vow of virginity and marry outside her faith. Supposedly born to noble, but heathen, parents, she was baptized by her wet nurse and subsequently disowned by her parents for her conversion. Olybrius, prefect of Gaul, encountered the 15-year-old Regina while she was tending sheep, and desired to make her his wife. When she refused to marry him or deny her faith, Olybrius had Regina imprisoned and tortured. She was whipped and burned with heated iron plates and pincers, but still held firm to her faith and her vow of virginity. To stop her ceaseless prayers, her tormenters finally cut her throat. Her feast day is September 7.

Ruth Savitz,
freelance writer, Philadelphia, Pennsylvania

Regina

Mistress of Charlemagne. Associated with Charles I also known as Charlemagne (742–814), king of the Franks (r. 768–814): children: (with Charlemagne) Drogo (b. 801), bishop of Metz; Hugh (b. 802), abbott of St. Quentin.

Regina, Elis (1945–1982)

Popular Brazilian vocalist. Born Elis Regina Carvalho Costa on March 17, 1945, in Porto Alegre, Brazil; died of a cocaine and alcohol overdose on January 19, 1982, in São Paulo, Brazil; married Ronaldo Boscoli (a composer and producer), in 1967 (divorced six years later); married César Camargo Mariano (a pianist, divorced eight years later); children: (first marriage) João Marcelo; (second marriage) Pedro and Maria Rita.

Sang on-air on the children's radio show "Clube do Guri" and won the show prize at age 12; signed first professional contract at age 13 with Radio Gaucha;

Elis Regina

recorded first album (1961); won Queen of the Disco Club award (1961); awarded Best Singer of The Year (1962); won first prize at her first big music festival (1965); ranked as highest-paid singer in Brazil (1966).

Selected albums: Dois Na Bossa, *with Jair Rodrigues (1965);* Elis Regina & Toots Thielemans *(1969);* Elis Regina in London *(1969); . . . Em Plena Verão (1970);* Elis & Tom, *with Antonio Carlos Jobim (1974);* Elis, Essa Mulher *(1979);* Elis Regina—Montreux Jazz Festival *(recorded 1979, released 1982);* Elis Regina—Personalidade *(1989, posthumous).*

Elis Regina was born the eldest child of a rather poor family in Porto Alegre, Brazil, in 1945. Her mother, a housewife, was Portuguese, and her father, who was seldom steadily employed, was Brazilian. Elis listened to Argentinean radio stations in her family home, and could sing in both Spanish and Portuguese at a very young age. A bright girl, by the time she started grade school she was already reading, writing and counting. At age seven, she attempted to sing on a local children's radio show, "Clube do Guri," but froze at the microphone. At nine, she was shining at her piano lessons, but her family could not afford a piano, so she pursued singing instead.

At age 12, Regina returned to "Clube do Guri" and this time not only overcame her stage fright, but won the prize and the audience. Although still hounded by stage fright—even into her adult life—she sang on the show almost weekly for the following two years, and soon signed her first radio contract with Radio Gaucha. Before reaching age 14, she was a local celebrity and making a better income than her father. At 15, she went to Rio de Janeiro to record her first album, and then two more, and although she intended to return home in between each recording she eventually decided to remain in Rio de Janeiro with her father, who was in search of work there. Her first album came out in 1961, and by 1962 the fiery, driven young woman had two awards on her resumé: Queen of the Disco Club and Best Singer of the Year.

Determined to make a name for herself in Rio's competitive music business, Regina used a fake birth certificate so she could sing in nightclubs, and soon snared a television contract. She was rocketing to fame by age 20, interpreting classic bossa nova tunes in her own passionate style for appreciative São Paulo and Rio audiences. Sometimes she daringly introduced unknown songs by young new composers, or became combative with interviewers and composers. Her brash attitude was seen as irreverent; it made her some enemies and cost her some commercial backing, but it was also a source of her popularity. At a popular music festival in 1965, she sang a controversial song that had almost been censored by the military government in power at the time. Finishing the song with arms outstretched, smiling, and with tears in her eyes, Elis Regina thus began her lifelong career as Brazil's reigning diva. By 1966, at only 21, she was the country's highest-paid vocalist.

Regina's personal life was as intense as her performances on stage. A meticulous organizer and demanding perfectionist, she was also temperamental and insecure about her lack of education. She faced a dilemma with her family, guilty about their economic need, but wanting to be free to build her career. As a result, relations with them were always problematic. She called her friendships "eternal" but would sometimes privately disparage her friends. She admitted her mistrust of others and said she doubted "everything" except her stage. Her first marriage, at age 22, to composer-producer Ronaldo Boscoli was stormy for its entire six-year duration. After their divorce, she held a bitter grudge against him, even making it hard for him to see their son. Her second marriage, to pianist César Camargo Mariano, with whom she was working on an album, was happier and more serene, but also ended in divorce after eight years and two children.

From the mid-1960s until the day she died, Regina was one of Brazil's best-loved and well-known performers, and enjoyed a career marked by few slumps. Some critics have said that with her stage presence and ear for language she could have become one of the world's greatest singers if she had wanted to. Her successes at music festivals of the mid-1960s were followed by a highly popular three-year collaboration with singer Jair Rodrigues. As the 1960s ended, she toured Europe, and recorded in Sweden with Toots Thielemans and in London with Peter Knight. In 1974, she recorded the celebrated album *Elis & Tom* in Los Angeles with Brazilian pop-music virtuoso Antonio Carlos Jobim. From the mid-1970s through 1981, her dance, music, and mime stage shows, *Falso Brilhante*, *Essa Mulher*, *Saudade do Brasil* and *Trem Azul* were huge triumphs.

About the time her second marriage was ending, Regina secretly began using cocaine. By December 1981, she had fallen in love with her lawyer Samuel MacDowell. They planned to marry the following year, but in January 1982 she was found dead in her bedroom, having accidentally overdosed on a mix of Cinzano and cocaine. Brazilians suddenly lost their legendary queen of popular music, the petite enchantress with a giant voice to whom they had given the fitting nicknames Furaçao (hurricane) and Pimentinha (little pepper).

Jacquie Maurice,
freelance writer, Calgary, Alberta, Canada

Regina of Ostrevant

*Saint. Name variations: Saint Regina. Married Albert, count of Ostrevant; children: daughter St. **Renfroie**. Her feast day is July 1.*

Regintrud

*Duchess of Bavaria. Daughter of Dagobert II, Merovingian king of Austrasia (r. 674–678), and possibly *Matilda (fl. 680s); married Theodo II, duke of Bavaria (died 716); children: Lantpert of Haimhram, bishop of Haimhram; **Oda of Bavaria** (fl. 680); Theodebert, duke of Bavaria; Grimoald (d. 725), duke of Bavaria; Theodebald, duke of Bavaria; Tassilo II of Bavaria.*

Regitze.

Variant of Richeza.

Regnier, Jeanne-Marie (1914–1944).

See Khan, Noor Inayat.

Rehan, Ada (1857–1916)

Irish-American actress who was famed for her work in Shakespearean comedies. Born Ada Crehan on April 22, 1857 (some sources cite 1860), in Limerick, Ireland; died of cancer on January 8, 1916, in New York City; daughter of Thomas Crehan and Harriett (Ryan) Crehan.

Ada Rehan, whose real name was Crehan, was born in Limerick, Ireland, on April 22, 1857, and, with her parents, immigrated to the United States in 1865, when she was eight. The family settled in Brooklyn, New York. Her two older sisters, **Hattie** and Kate (known professionally as **Kate O'Neil** and married to playwright Oliver Doud Byron), were drawn into the theatrical profession, and Ada shortly followed suit. At age 14, she premiered on a Newark, New Jersey, stage with a minor role in her brother-in-law's play *Across the Continent*. Her sister Kate later secured a place for Ada in ***Louisa Lane Drew**'s Philadelphia theatrical company. Her debut with the company was so successful that although she had been listed as "Ada C.

Rehan" because of a printing error, she was advised to keep it as her stage name. She stayed with the Drew company for two seasons before moving on to apprentice at Macaulay's Theater in Louisville and stock companies in Albany and Baltimore. In Albany, she is said to have played some 90 characters, among them Ophelia to Booth's Hamlet and Lady Anne to McCullough's Richard III. In 1875, she debuted in New York at Wood's Museum in *Thoroughbred*, which was produced by her sister and brother-in-law.

In 1879, the lovely young Rehan began a 20-year professional and personal association with the leading American theatrical producer, Augustin Daly. Shortly after he opened Daly's Theater in New York that year, Rehan played Fanny Adrianse in his production of *Divorce*, and became his leading lady. Under Daly's tutelage, Rehan's gift for delivering effervescent renditions of charming comedic characters blossomed. Daly was almost tyrannical in the management of his troupe, but the result was a skilled and synchronized team which was the recipe for his success.

Ada Rehan

In his *Vagrant Memories*, the veteran dramatic critic William Winter wrote:

> Daly rendered many, various, and important services to the theater of his time, but his recognition and development of the genius of Ada Rehan was the most valuable of them all. In her the stage was illumined and graced by an actress who not only preserved, but bettered, the brilliant traditions of *Peg Woffington and *Dora Jordan. Her rich beauty, her imposing stature, her Celtic sparkle of mischievous piquancy, her deep feeling, her round, full, clear, caressing voice, her supple freedom of movement, the expressive play of her features, and the delightful vivacity of her action—who that ever appreciated could ever forget them?

The heart of the polished Daly ensemble was the acclaimed group known as the "Big Four": John Drew, *Anne Gilbert, James Lewis, and Rehan. By the time Rehan drew accolades after her London debut in 1884 she was already famous. Her subsequent performances in Paris and other major European cities were just as radiant.

Rehan played more than 200 parts in 26 years, but her best work surfaced in Shakespearean comedies, 17th- and 18th-century "Old Comedies," and American adaptations of German farces. Her Lady Teazle in *The School for Scandal* was extremely successful, but her most legendary role was that of Katherine in *The Taming of the Shrew*, which she first played in 1887 in New York City; her characterizations of Rosalind in *As You Like It* and Viola in *Twelfth Night* were also favorites. She brought Maid Marian to life in Alfred, Lord Tennyson's *The Foresters* at a New York opening in 1892; Tennyson had awarded the play to Daly largely due to Rehan's aptitude for Shakespearean comedy. By 1894, she had partnered with Daly in his new London theater (where she had laid the cornerstone in 1891) and was starring there in a lengthy, triumphant run of *Twelfth Night*. In 1896, she took part in an American tour, but by that time was returning often to England.

Rehan never married, and her enthusiasm for acting died with Daly when her longtime ally passed away in Paris in 1899. Daly had skillfully crafted and managed Ada Rehan the celebrity, and he and Rehan had been extremely close. After his death, she became "indifferent" and "miserable" and retired from the stage for a year. A comeback attempt failed dreadfully, due in part to Rehan's own apathy but also because of the changes taking place in popular theater. Audiences at the beginning of the 20th century were finding outdated and dull the once-fashionable comedic style which was Rehan's specialty. In 1905, she gave a final performance in New York City at the testimonial to *Helena Modjeska; she then spent her days between New York and England until her death in 1916. Opinions on Rehan's talent sometimes varied, but her beauty, charm, humor, and vivacity were commonly appreciated. Although he regarded her acting abilities as dubious, George Bernard Shaw said he found her "irresistible." Her bust, along with *Ellen Terry's, is at the entrance to the Shakespeare Memorial Theater at Stratford-on-Avon.

SOURCES:
James, Edward T., ed. *Notable American Women, 1607–1950*. Cambridge, MA: The Belknap Press of Harvard University Press, 1971.

McHenry, Robert, ed. *Famous American Women*. NY: Dover, 1980.

Winter, William. *Ada Rehan: A Study*. 1898.

Jacquie Maurice,
freelance writer, Calgary, Alberta, Canada

Rehn, Elisabeth (1935—)

Finnish administrator and politician. Born on April 16, 1935, in Helsinki, Finland; B.Sc. (Economics), Helsinki, 1957; D.Sc. (Economics), Helsinki, 1994; D.Sc. (Politics), Turku, 1998; married Ove Rehn, in 1955; children: Veronica, Joakiam, Charlotta, and Johan.

Elisabeth Rehn, who was born in Helsinki in 1935, worked as an office manager for Renecta Ltd. (1960–79) and Rehn Trading Ltd. (1978–79). She also taught vocational guidance and was a member of the Kauniainen City Council from 1973 to 1979. In 1979, as a member of the Swedish People's Party (SFP), she was elected to the Finnish Parliament. She would remain there until 1995. Rehn served as leader of the SFP parliamentary group from 1987 until 1990, when in June of that year she was appointed defense minister. With that appointment, Rehn became the first woman in Europe to hold a defense portfolio, and the second woman in the world to do so. As well, in Finland's presidential election of January–February 1994, Rehn came in second. She was a member of the European Parliament from 1995 to 1996, and spent four years working in the Balkans: first as Special Rapporteur for Human Rights in Bosnia-Herzegovina, the Republic of Croatia, and the Federal Republic of Yugoslavia; and then as UN undersecretary general, Special Representative of the Secretary-General in Bosnia-Herzegovina, from January 16, 1998 to July 15, 1999.

Jacquie Maurice,
freelance writer, Calgary, Alberta, Canada

Rehor, Grete (1910–1987)

Austrian politician and trade union official who was the first woman to hold a Cabinet post in her nation's history (Minister of Social Administration, 1966–70). Born Grete Daurer in Vienna, Austria, on June 30, 1910; died in Vienna on January 28, 1987; father killed in World War I; had two sisters; married Karl Rehor; children: daughter, Marielies Rehor.

In October 1965, Austrian politics underwent a sea change when the 20-year coalition of the conservative People's Party (ÖVP) and Socialists (SPÖ) dissolved. In the March 1966 national elections, the ÖVP won an absolute electoral majority, and on April 19, 1966, Joseph Klaus of the ÖVP announced the formation of a single-party government. Among the most important aspects of these changes was the fact that for the first time in Austrian history, a ministerial portfolio—that of Social Administration—had been awarded to a woman, Grete Rehor. Rehor was born in Vienna in 1910 into a conservative Roman Catholic family. Her father was a state official, her mother a registered nurse. As was the case with countless other families during World War I, the great conflict brought them tragedy. Rehor's father was declared missing in action in 1918. From this point on, economic necessity played an important role in young Grete's life. By age 14, she was working to help with the family budget and pay for her school tuition. Even before she was out of her teens, Rehor had lost her mother and had to abandon any thoughts of higher education. By 1925, she was working in a textile factory. Soon after starting full-time work, Rehor became active in the Christian (i.e., non-Socialist) trade union movement, working without pay. In 1933, she advanced to the post of general secretary of the central organization of Christian textile workers.

The years 1933–34 were crucial in the history of modern Austria, witnessing the end of parliamentary democracy and the creation of an ultra-conservative, authoritarian Corporative State that attempted to create a new "Christian" social order which was neither capitalist nor Communist. Grete's concerns during these years were centered on the needs of her fellow textile workers, but were also personal. In 1935, she married Karl Rehor, a fellow Catholic who also believed that the working class, previously loyal to the Marxist Social Democratic Party, could be won over to conservative political ideals if their social and economic concerns were addressed fairly. In 1938, Grete gave birth to the couple's only child, a daughter named **Marielies Rehor.**

The Rehors were not among those Austrians cheering Adolf Hitler when he proclaimed *Anschluss* (union) between Austria and Germany in March 1938. The new Nazi rulers arrested and briefly imprisoned Karl, and he lost his job. In 1940, he was drafted into the German Wehrmacht. He was declared missing on the Russian front three years later, probably having been killed during the battle of Stalingrad. Despite the risks involved, Grete joined a conservative resistance circle, becoming a member of the "hard core" of anti-Nazi Catholic trade unionists within the Austrian resistance movement. Fortunately, she was never arrested, and survived to see Austria liberated from Nazi German rule in the spring of 1945.

After 1945, Rehor resumed her work as a leading Catholic trade unionist, and in November 1949 began serving as an ÖVP member of the Austrian National Assembly. A conscientious member of her party, she would be reelected several times and serve until her retirement in 1970. In April 1966, Federal Chancellor Joseph Klaus appointed Rehor to the ministerial post of Social Administration. In a bureaucratic welfare state like Austria, this was one of the more important portfolios, and some doubted that a woman—even an experienced trade unionist like Rehor—could do the job. The Viennese mass-circulation newspaper *Der Kurier* speculated, "What will happen when a ministerial meeting drags on too long, will [Rehor] then only be thinking of whether or not her kitchen pots are boiling over?" As it turned out, Rehor's tenure as Minister of Social Administration was full of accomplishments, including her creation in 1966 of a new division for women's issues within the ministry. Although philosophically a conservative who believed that, ideally, society ought to be able to find ways to get women back into the home to be with their children, she was also a realist and pragmatist fully aware that such ideas did not reflect reality for many families. The social welfare net remained strong in Austria during her administration, in some ways becoming even more comprehensive than it had ever been. Rehor retired from her ministerial responsibilities in 1970, withdrawing from politics at the same time. She died in Vienna on January 28, 1987, a respected pioneer for women in Austrian political life.

SOURCES:

Steininger, Barbara. "Grete Rehor," in Herbert Dachs, Peter Gerlich, and Wolfgang C. Müller, eds., *Die Politiker: Karrieren und Wirken bedeutender Repräsentanten der Zweiten Republik*. Vienna: Manzsche Verlags- und Universitätsbuchhandlung, 1995, pp. 479–485.

John Haag,
Associate Professor of History,
University of Georgia, Athens, Georgia

Reibey, Mary (1777–1855).

See Catchpole, Margaret for sidebar.

Reich, Lilly (1885–1947)

German designer and architect who collaborated with the renowned Mies van der Rohe and was a significant creative force in her own right. Born in Berlin, Germany, on June 16, 1885; died in Berlin on December 11, 1947.

Began career as a designer of textiles and women's apparel; directed exhibitions of the influential Deutscher Werkbund, becoming the first woman member of its board of directors; extensively influenced the work of Mies van der Rohe (1920s–1930s), playing a crucial role in designing furniture (the Barcelona Chair) and the interiors of the German pavilion at the Barcelona Exposition (1929); has begun to emerge from his shadow.

Born in Berlin in 1885, Lilly Reich received additional inspiration for her already abundant talents in 1908, when she studied with Joseph Hoffmann in Vienna. There, at his famous Wiener Werkstätte, a group of artists and artisans believed that even in modern times a fusion of beauty and appropriate design could be achieved in fabrics, jewelry, and furniture. Upon her return to Berlin, her career flourished as she moved from being a designer of textiles and women's apparel, one of the few fields then open to women, into other areas of design. In 1912, she became a member of the Deutscher Werkbund (DW), an organization emphasizing the uniquely German aspects of design but clearly influenced by such foreign precursors as the Arts and Crafts movement in England and Austria's Wiener Werkstätte. Even before joining the DW, Reich had been commissioned to design the interior finishing and furnishing of a Youth Center in Charlottenburg. In 1914, she not only helped to organize a DW exhibition in Cologne but was also one of the designers of the section titled "Haus der Frau" (House of Woman). By 1915, her professional reputation was such that she supervised a DW fashion show in Berlin.

At the start of World War I, Reich converted her designer atelier into a dressmaker's shop, which it would remain for the duration of the conflict. By 1920, she had resumed her prewar interests, working as the artistic director of the fashion craft exhibition held in Berlin in February of that year. In October, Reich became the first woman to be elected a member of the DW board of directors, an unprecedented achievement for the time in view of the lingering prejudice that women's capacities in the arts were constitutionally less than those of men.

In 1924, Reich first met the already famous architect Ludwig Mies van der Rohe (1886–1969). Within a short time, they had become both professional collaborators and constant companions, a relationship that would end only when he emigrated to the United States in 1938. A consummate professional like Mies, Reich worked from the beginning of their collaboration in the subordinate role that had been the norm for women in the pre-1914 world of her youth, letting him provide the overall concepts of a project while she worked to fill in the details and refinements.

Once the Mies-Reich collaboration began in earnest around the year 1925, critics began to write with ever more enthusiasm about the quality of his exhibitions. It appears to have been more than a coincidence that Mies' successes in exhibition designs can be dated to the years that he and Reich were artistic and personal partners. These successes included the pathbreaking German pavilion at the 1929 Barcelona Exposition. Reich's input into the design of tubular-steel furniture, for which Mies has traditionally been given credit, was significant if not indeed crucial. Ludwig Glaeser, curator of an exhibition of Mies' furniture given at New York's Museum of Modern Art, has shown that important refinements to the famous tubular-steel side chair are attributable to Reich. She continually explored the visual as well as the tactile play of contrasts between textured surfaces and polished metal. Several scholars have noted that Mies did not fully develop any contemporary furniture in a successful manner either before or after his collaboration with Reich. Such landmarks in the history of modern design as the "Barcelona Chair" and the furniture for the Tugendhat house in Brünn/Brno, Czechoslovakia, should be reinterpreted in light of the fact that Reich's artistic contribution to these and other major works of Mies van der Rohe was a significant one.

In 1932, Reich followed Mies to Dessau, where he had become director of the world-famous design school, the Bauhaus. She accepted an appointment as the director of the Bauhaus' weaving studio and workshop of interior design, but this was a time in German history when elegant and original designs were overshadowed by violence in the streets and the imminent seizure of power by Adolf Hitler's Nazi movement. Not being Jewish and having generally avoided involvement in radical politics, neither Reich nor

Mies believed themselves to be threatened by the Nazis, and when Hitler established his dictatorship over the German Reich in 1933, both decided to remain, at least for the time being. Reich participated in the DW meeting that voted unanimously to conform to the new "German path" of the National Socialist regime, based on purging the nation of "Jewish-Bolshevik," "degenerate," and other allegedly alien cultural influences. Over the next few years, both she and Mies were able to co-exist with the Nazis by concentrating on refining architectural and furniture concepts dating back to the heyday of the Weimar Republic of the 1920s.

By 1937, however, Nazi pressure to conform to an increasingly narrow concept of acceptable norms of design had increased significantly for both Reich and Mies van der Rohe. Although they had been commissioned to participate in a Reich Exposition of the German Textile and Garment Industry, scheduled for Berlin in March and April 1937, only a few weeks before the opening their commissions were revoked. On the other hand, Reich was permitted to participate in the German textile industry exhibit at the Paris Exposition that ran from May 24 through November 26, 1937. Realizing that the situation was deteriorating, Mies visited the United States in 1937 to investigate his opportunities for continuing his career there. In 1938, he relocated permanently in Chicago, becoming director of the architectural department of the Armour Institute (renamed the Illinois Institute of Technology in 1940). In September 1939, with World War II already underway, Reich visited Mies in the United States, but although she made clear her desire to stay, he did little to persuade her to remain. The two would never meet again.

Reich managed to return to Berlin, maintaining a correspondence with Mies that was as much about managing his business affairs in Germany as it was personal. Even as bombs rained down on Berlin, Reich continued to design furniture, including a built-in cabinet for a record player and the furnishings for a corporate conference room. But normal life became increasingly difficult to maintain, and in 1943 Reich's studio on Berlin's Genthiner Strasse was destroyed in an air raid. To escape the deadly bombardments, she moved to the town of Zittau, then, with Berlin in ruins, she returned to the destroyed German capital. As early as June 1945, Reich participated in meetings of architects and designers making plans for a revival of the Deutscher Werkbund in post-Nazi Germany. She began working as an architect, and was commissioned by Hans Scharoun to remodel houses. In August 1945, she wrote to her lawyer: "I have to get back to work, if only so as to exist financially. Our family has become very, very poor, but I do hope that my profession will give me the chance of finding satisfactory employment." This opportunity never presented itself to Reich, whose health collapsed. After a long illness, she died in Berlin on December 11, 1947.

SOURCES:

Da Costa Meyer, E. "Cruel Metonymies: Lilly Reich's Designs for the 1937 World's Fair," in *New German Critique*. No. 76. Winter 1999, pp. 161–189.

Dietsch, Deborah K. "Lilly Reich in Her Own Right at MoMa," in *Architecture*. Vol. 85, no. 3. March 1996, p. 35.

Filler, Martin. "Late-Blooming Lilly," in *House Beautiful*. Vol. 138, no. 3. March 1996, pp. 90, 92.

Hochman, Elaine S. *Architects of Fortune: Mies van der Rohe and the Third Reich*. NY: Weidenfeld & Nicolson, 1989.

Lotz, Wilhelm. "Die Halle II auf der Bauausstellung," in *Zeitschrift für gestaltende Arbeit*. Vol. 6, no. 7. July 15, 1931, pp. 241–249.

McQuaid, Matilda. *Lilly Reich: Designer and Architect*. NY: Museum of Modern Art-Harry N. Abrams, 1996.

Ourousssoff, N. "Lilly Reich," in *Artforum*. Vol. 35, no. 1. September 1996, pp. 113–114.

Pile, John F. *Dictionary of 20th-Century Design*. Reprint ed. NY: Da Capo Press, 1994.

"Die Wohnung unserer Zeit," in *Zeitschrift für gestaltende Arbeit*. Vol. 6, no. 7. July 15, 1931, pp. 249–270.

John Haag,
Associate Professor of History,
University of Georgia, Athens, Georgia

Reichard, Gladys (1893–1955)

American anthropologist. Born Gladys Amanda Reichard on July 17, 1893, in Bangor, Pennsylvania; died of a stroke on July 25, 1955, in Flagstaff, Arizona; daughter of Dr. Noah W. Reichard and Minerva Ann (Jordan) Reichard; graduated from Swarthmore College near Philadelphia, Pennsylvania, 1919; studied under Franz Boas; Columbia University, A.M., 1920, Ph.D., 1925; never married; no children.

*Taught in country and elementary schools (1909–15); earned ***Lucretia Mott*** fellowship for graduate study upon graduation from Swarthmore College (1919); moved to New York to study anthropology under Franz Boas at Columbia University (1919); assisted Boas in classes at Barnard College (1920–21); taught at Barnard College (1923–55); first visited Navajo reservation (1923); studied on a Guggenheim fellowship in Hamburg, Germany (1926–27); became assistant professor (1928); spent four summers living with a Navajo family (1930 on); awarded A. Cressy Morrison Prize in Natural Science by the New York Academy of Sciences (1932); ran the*

*successful Navajo reservation Hogan School (1934);
became professor of anthropology (1951).*

Selected writings: Social Life of the Navajo Indians *(1928);* Melanesian Design *(1933);* Spider Woman *(1934);* Navajo Shepherd and Weaver *(1936);* Dezba, Woman of the Desert *(1939);* Navajo Religion: A Study of Symbolism *(1950);* Navajo Grammar *(1951).*

Born in 1893 into an intellectual Quaker family in Bangor, Pennsylvania, Gladys Reichard was the younger of two daughters. Her mother **Minerva Reichard** died when Gladys was still young, and her father Noah Reichard, a respected physician, later remarried. After graduating from high school, Reichard worked as a teacher for a few years, and in 1919 graduated from Swarthmore College with honors and a fellowship for graduate work. Having acquired an interest in anthropology at Swarthmore, she moved to New York to attend Columbia University and study under the renowned anthropologist Franz Boas.

The reserved Reichard was intensely loyal to Boas on both a personal and an academic level, and he became a father figure to her. She lived in his family home for a year while doing her graduate work, and he helped her find grants, jobs, and publishers. Originally oriented toward studying the "evolution of culture," under Boas' influence Reichard turned her academic focus to linguistics. She earned her degree in 1920, assisted Boas in his instruction at Barnard College, then taught at New York's Robert Louis Stevenson School. After doing some field work with the Native American Wiyot tribe in California in the early 1920s, Reichard went back to teach at Barnard in 1923 and earned her Ph.D. from Columbia in 1925. She taught at Barnard for the rest of her life, achieving the rank of professor of anthropology in 1951.

Reichard first became acquainted with the Navajo people in 1923, through her friend Pliny Earle Goddard, curator of ethnology for the American Museum of Natural History. In 1924, she spent six weeks on the Navajo reservation studying genealogy with Goddard; the work done there formed the basis of her 1928 book on Navajo social life. Not content to simply observe and quickly construct abstract theories, Reichard reflected in her own work Boas' fastidiousness with data, as well as Goddard's ambition to understand and describe a culture as experienced by individuals.

After a few years in Germany studying on a fellowship, Reichard moved on to Idaho to analyze Coeur d'Alene grammar for the *Handbook of American Indian Languages*. When Goddard died suddenly in 1928, however, Reichard returned to the study of the Navajo, editing Goddard's unpublished work and spending summers on the reservation in Arizona. She learned the Navajo language and their rug-weaving techniques. Her innovative book on Navajo weaving, *Spider Woman* (1934), related from the perspective of the weaver, was followed by a more technical exploration of the subject, *Navajo Shepherd and Weaver* (1936), and a fictional work, *Dezba, Woman of the Desert* (1939). In 1934, she ran a federally sponsored school which successfully undertook, for the first time, to teach Navajo speakers to write their native language.

Reichard gathered 20 years of research into *Navajo Religion: A Study of Symbolism* (1950) and *Navajo Grammar* (1951). At the time, however, her work failed to achieve the fame that was enjoyed by fellow Franz Boas students ***Ruth Benedict** and ***Margaret Mead**. In 1955, as Reichard spent yet another summer in her beloved Arizona—where she was planning to retire—she suffered two strokes about one week apart and died in Flagstaff. After her death, her work slowly gained more credit for its quality and sophistication.

SOURCES:

Sicherman, Barbara, and Carol Hurd Green, eds. *Notable American Women: The Modern Period*. Cambridge, MA: The Belknap Press of Harvard University, 1980.

Jacquie Maurice,
freelance writer, Calgary, Alberta, Canada

Reichardt, Louise (1779–1826)

German composer. Born on April 11, 1779, in Paris, France; died on November 17, 1826, in Hamburg, Germany; daughter of Johann Friedrich Reichardt (a composer at the court of Frederick II the Great) and Juliane Benda (a singer, pianist, and composer); studied with her father and with Johann Friedrich Clasing.

Organized and conducted several women's choruses (1817); mainly composed songs; prepared singers for Hamburg's musical festival (1818) but was not allowed to conduct as that was considered inappropriate for a woman.

Louise Reichardt was born in 1779 in Paris, France, the daughter of Johann Friedrich Reichardt, a composer at the court of Frederick II the Great, and **Juliane Benda**, a singer, pianist, and composer. By the time she was 11, four of Louise's songs appeared in an anthology of her father's compositions. In 1808, she began teaching. A year later, Reichardt struck out on her own to seek her fortune in Hamburg, where she supported herself as a teacher, choral conductor, and composer. She adopted the Romantic artistic model. Unlike earlier generations, Reichardt was determined not to depend on royal patronage for her income but rather upon a wider public audience. Most of her songs, written from 1809 until her death in 1826, were popular with the middle-class society which dominated Hamburg; her melodies were memorable and her piano accompaniments simple. Because of its melodic lyricism, Reichardt's music has been compared with that of Franz Schubert. Reichardt was engaged to poet Friedrich Eschen, who suddenly died before their wedding. A second engagement to the painter Franz Gareis was also terminated by death. She was very involved with preparing the Hamburg chorus for public concerts. As a woman, however, she was never allowed to conduct in public. Despite these gender restrictions, Reichardt strongly influenced musical life in Hamburg through her composing, teaching, and behind-the-scenes conducting.

John Haag,
Athens, Georgia

Reiche, Maria (1903–1998)

German mathematician and guardian of Peru's Nazca Lines petroglyphs. Born on May 15, 1903, in Dresden, Germany; died of cancer on June 8, 1998, in Lima, Peru; graduated from a local university in Dresden, 1928; studied with Long Island University scholar Paul Kosok.

Left Germany for Peru (1932); first visited Nazca lines with mentor Kosok (1941); began scientific work in Nazca desert, living most of the time in a small hut there (1946); awarded Peruvian government's highest honor, the Order of the Sun (1993); became Peruvian citizen (1994).

In 1932, Maria Reiche left her native Germany with a mathematics degree and the ability to speak five languages, to become a tutor in Peru. While working as a translator in Lima a few years later, Reiche met Paul Kosok, an American scholar who had come to Peru to investigate recently discovered enormous shallow lines etched into the Peruvian desert floor about 250 miles south of Lima. In 1941, Reiche's life changed when Kosok took her to see the ancient lines near the small town of Nazca. That year, at sunset on June 22, Kosok was standing near one of the long straight lines when he noticed that its direction led straight into the setting sun. He surmised that the line was meant to denote the winter solstice. When six months later Reiche observed another line pointing toward the summer solstice mark, they theorized that the lines might be a celestial calendar more than 1,000 years old.

In 1946, the solitary and feisty Reiche, completely captivated by the mysterious lines, began living in the desert for weeks on end while she cleaned and studied them. When Kosok mapped a convoluted line and found it to be the image of a bird, Reiche's fascination intensified. In 1948, Kosok left Peru. Reiche took over his work and shortly thereafter discovered and mapped 18 more animal images. She spent the next 50 years dwelling in a small house near the puzzling drawings, measuring, charting, studying and protecting them. She theorized and wrote about their significance to the ancient Nazcans, who had scraped the images—which can only be recognized from the air—into the timeless plain. Calling the designs "a very fragile manuscript," Reiche paid guards with her own money to patrol them.

Although residents of Nazca initially thought Reiche was "crazy," in time they appreciated her for bringing needed tourist revenue into their town. After the modern discovery of the lines, and Reiche's work, the huge, fragile images became Peru's second biggest tourist attraction, after Machu Picchu. Over the five decades of her labor, Peruvians came to honor Maria Reiche as a national treasure. They commemorated her birthday every year, and in 1993 presented her with their highest national award, the Order of the Sun. "The Lady of the Lines," as she was known, who became a Peruvian citizen in 1994, tirelessly fought all manner of threats to the lines, largely alone. Even in her elderly years she chased away trespassers in her wheelchair. In 1995, UNESCO designated the Nazca Lines a world heritage site. Yet after Reiche's death in 1998 at age 95, Peruvians still wondered who would carry on her dedication to preserving them and unraveling their secrets.

SOURCES:

Thomas, Robert McG., Jr. "Maria Reiche, 95, Keeper of an Ancient Peruvian Puzzle, Dies," in *The New York Times*. June 15, 1998, p. A21.

Jacquie Maurice,
freelance writer, Calgary, Alberta, Canada

Reid, Beryl (1918–1996)

British character actress. Born on June 17, 1918 (some sources cite 1920), in Hereford, England; died on October 13, 1996, in Slough, England.

Selected filmography: The Bells of St. Trinian's (1954); Two Way Street (1960); The Dock Brief (Trial and Error, 1962); Inspector Clouseau (1968); The

Killing of Sister George *(US, 1968)*; Star! *(US, 1968)*; The Assassination Bureau *(1969)*; Entertaining Mr. Sloane *(1970)*; The Beast in the Cellar *(1971)*; Dr. Phibes Rises Again *(1972)*; The Death Wheelers *(1973)*; Joseph Andrews *(1977)*; Carry on Emannuelle *(1978)*.

A versatile British character actress who was equally adept at comedy and drama, Beryl Reid began her career as a music-hall performer, then graduated to stage and screen. She won wide acclaim in America for her Broadway portrayal of the caustic lesbian radio soap-opera star in *The Killing of Sister George* (1966), a role she reprised in the 1968 film. Reid died in 1996, having developed pneumonia after a knee operation.

Reid, Beth Heiden (b. 1959).

See Heiden, Beth.

Reid, Charlotte Thompson

(1913—)

U.S. Republican congressional representative (1963–71). Name variations: Mrs. Frank R. Reid; (stage name) Annette King. Born Charlotte Leota Thompson on September 27, 1913, in Kankakee, Illinois; daughter of Edward Charles Thompson and Ethel (Stith) Thompson; attended Illinois College in Jacksonville, 1930–32; studied voice privately, 1933–40; married Frank R. Reid, Jr. (an attorney), on January 1, 1938 (died August 1962); children: Patricia Reid (who married George Lindner); Frank R. Reid III; Edward Thompson Reid; Susan Reid.

A native of Kankakee, Illinois, Charlotte Thompson Reid graduated from East Aurora High School in 1930. She spent two years at Illinois College in Jacksonville before deciding to devote herself to the pursuit of a professional singing career. In 1936, she began singing on the radio under the name Annette King, on NBC's Chicago-based *Don McNeill's Breakfast Club*. In 1938, she married Aurora lawyer Frank Reid and soon became active in local politics, although her political career did not begin in earnest until 1962. That year, while he was campaigning for a Republican seat in the U.S. House of Representatives, Frank died. County Republicans chose Charlotte to pick up his candidacy, and she defeated the Democratic nominee.

In Congress from 1963 until 1971, Reid served on the Committee on Interior and Insular Affairs, the Committee on Public Works, and the Committee on Standards of Official Conduct. She championed agricultural price supports on behalf of her district, and supported the creation of a privately funded National Cultural Center in Washington, D.C. She introduced a constitutional amendment to allow public school students to engage in noncompulsory prayer, and opposed many of President Lyndon Johnson's social programs. Reid supported improvements to auto safety standards, a measure to outlaw certain types of rifle sales, a "Truth In Lending Law," and the proposed Equal Rights Amendment. During the Vietnam War, she was a determined advocate of the military policies of Johnson and Nixon.

In 1971, Reid resigned from the House to serve a five-year term on the Federal Communications Commission, following her nomination by President Nixon and confirmation by the Senate. From 1983 to 1985, she served on the President's Task Force on International Private Enterprise, and was a member of the Hoover Institution's Board of Overseers in 1984.

SOURCES:

Office of the Historian. *Women in Congress, 1917–1990.* Commission on the Bicentenary of the U.S. House of Representatives, 1991.

Jacquie Maurice, freelance writer, Calgary, Alberta, Canada

Charlotte Thompson Reid

Reid, Christian (1846–1920).

See Tiernan, Frances Fisher.

Reid, Clarice D. (1931—)

African-American physician and researcher. Born in Birmingham, Alabama, in 1931; graduated from the University of Cincinnati Medical School, 1959.

Born in Birmingham, Alabama, in 1931, Clarice Reid developed an early concern for the health issues of minorities. The only African-American student in her medical school, Reid studied family medicine and pediatrics, areas which familiarized her with diseases affecting children and families. She graduated from the University of Cincinnati Medical School in Ohio in 1959, and became Cincinnati's first African-American with a private practice in pediatrics.

Reid's interest in sickle-cell anemia, a painful and debilitating blood disease which primarily afflicts people of African descent, took her to Washington, D.C.'s Howard University. There, as deputy director of the Sickle Cell Program of the Health Service Administration, Reid promoted awareness of the disease, instructed health professionals in the care of sickle-cell patients, and developed a national program to reduce the disease's death rate. Reid's work contributed greatly to improvements in sickle-cell sufferers' quality of life and life spans. Reid received the U.S. Public Health Service's highest honor, the Superior Service Award.

SOURCES:

Igus, Toyomi, ed. *Great Women in the Struggle.* Just Us Books, 1991.

Jacquie Maurice,
freelance writer, Calgary, Alberta, Canada

Reid, Dorothy Davenport

(1895–1977)

American actress, producer, director, and screenwriter. Name variations: Dorothy Davenport; Mrs. Wallace Reid. Born in 1895 in Boston, Massachusetts; died in 1977; daughter of Harry Davenport (an actor) and Alice Davenport (a silent-screen comedian); married Wallace Reid (an actor), in 1913 (died 1923); no children.

Selected filmography: (as actress) Her Indian Hero *(1909),* The Best Man Wins *(1911),* Almost a Suicide *(1912),* His Only Son *(1912),* Our Lady of the Pearls *(1913),* The Lightning Bolt *(1913),* The Cracksman's Reformation *(1913),* A Hopi Legend *(1913),* The Fires of Fate *(1913),* Retribution *(1913),* The Intruder *(1914),* The Countess Betty's Mine *(1914),* The Accomplished Mrs. Thompson *(1914),* The Way of a Woman *(1914),* The Voice of the Viola *(1914),* A Gypsy Romance *(1914),* The Siren *(1914),* Fruit of Evil *(1915),* The Unknown *(1915),* The Adventurer *(1915),* The Explorer *(1915),* The Way of the World *(1916),* The Unattainable *(1916),* Black Friday *(1916),* The Girl and the Crisis *(1917),* Treason *(1917),* The Squaw Man's Son *(1917),* The Fighting Chance *(1920),* Every Woman's Problem *(1921),* The Test *(1922),* The Masked Avenger *(1922),* The Satin Woman *(1927),* Hellship Bronson *(1928),* Man Hunt *(1933); (as producer)* Human Wreckage *(also act., 1923),* Broken Laws *(also act., 1924),* The Red Kimono *(also act., 1926),* The Earth Woman *(1926),* The Dude Wrangler *(1930),* Honeymoon Limited *(1935),* Women Must Dress *(also co-sc., 1935),* Paradise Isle *(1937),* A Bride for Henry *(1937),* Rose of the Rio Grande *(1938),* Terror in the City *(1966); (as director)* Linda *(also exec. prod., 1929),* Sucker Money *(1933),* Road to Ruin *(also co-sc., 1934),* Woman Condemned *(also co-sc., 1934); (as screenwriter)* Prison Break *(1938),* The Haunted House *(1940),* Redhead *(1941),* Curley *(1947),* Who Killed Doc Robbin? *(1948),* Impact *(1949),* Rhubarb *(1951),* Footsteps in the Fog *(1953).*

The daughter of character actor Harry Davenport and silent-screen star **Alice Davenport**, Dorothy Reid began her own acting career at Biograph in 1909 and became one of their most bankable talents. She starred in numerous silent films, often with her husband, superstar Wallace Reid, whom she married in 1913. As the result of treatment from injuries he suffered in a train accident, Wallace became dependent on morphine and alcohol and died from his addiction in 1923, at the age of 32. Following his death, Reid produced and starred in *Human Wreckage* (1923), a biographical and agonizing account of Wallace's demise which also served as a warning about the dangers of drugs. Reid traveled around the country promoting the film, drawing crowds that were probably as eager to see the movie star as they were to hear the message. Her reception in St. Louis, described by Gerald Perry, was fairly typical:

> Five hundred banners announced her appearance. The health department contributed ambulances and wagons for Mrs. Reid's parade. The Mayor proclaimed Anti-Narcotics week and greeted her at the train station with two brass bands. The parade included twenty-five carloads of disabled veterans from the American Legion Hospital and eighty taxicabs with signs on their spare tires advertising the moviehouse showing of *Human Wreckage.*

After 1923, Reid turned her attention to producing, directing, and screenwriting, forming her own production company in 1925 to produce *The Red Kimono* (1926), which also employed two women writers: *Adela Rogers St. Johns, who wrote the original story, and *Dorothy Arzner, who created the screenplay. Although Reid also directed many of her own movies, she did not take screen credit until *Linda* (1929). In 1934, she directed two feature films, *The Road to Ruin* for True Life Photoplays and *The Woman Condemned* for Marcy Pictures, both moralistic in theme. *The Road to Ruin* "is a frank presentation of the pitfalls of youth," said *Film Daily*, "and it whitewashes none of the characters. The results of their folly, ignorance, and carelessness are pointed graphically for the moral."

Although for years Reid seemed to negotiate quite well through the male-dominated movie business, she appears to have suffered a crisis of confidence in the late 1940s, when she pretty much gave up producing and directing for writing. (She did return to produce *Terror in the City* in 1966.) "Men resent women in top executive positions in films as in any field of endeavor," she said in 1952.

In addition to her work in films, Reid established the Wallace Reid Foundation Sanitarium, a drug-addiction center "for the care of unfortunate addicts." Her love for her husband endured long after his death, and she never remarried. All of her energy was channeled into her work, much of it paving the way for a new wave of women filmmakers.

SOURCES:

Acker, Ally. *Reel Women*. NY: Continuum, 1991.

Katz, Ephraim. *The Film Encyclopedia*. NY: HarperCollins, 1994.

Barbara Morgan,
Melrose, Massachusetts

Reid, Elisabeth Mills (1858–1931).

See Reid, Helen Rogers for sidebar.

Reid, Helen Rogers (1882–1970)

American publisher who, for many years, was the dominant figure of one of the ten best newspapers of the world. Name variations: Mrs. Ogden Mills Reid. Born Helen Miles Rogers on November 23, 1882, in Appleton, Wisconsin; died at her home in New York City on July 27, 1970; daughter of Benjamin Talbot Rogers (a hotel operator) and Sarah Louise (Johnson) Rogers; attended Grafton Hall, Fond du Lac, Wisconsin; Barnard College, A.B., 1903; married Ogden

Mills Reid (editor of the New York Herald Tribune*), on March 14, 1911; children: Whitelaw Reid (a newspaper executive); Elisabeth Reid (1916–1924); Ogden Rogers Reid (a newspaper executive).*

As advertising director, joined staff of New York Tribune *(1918), which became* New York Herald Tribune *(1924); served as vice president (1922–47); chosen president (1947–52); designated board chair (1953–68).*

Even before World War I, it had become obvious that the *New York Tribune* was in trouble. By 1900 "the old lady of Park Row"—as it was called—had ceased earning a profit; by 1912, it was a million dollars in debt. From 1872 to 1912, the *Tribune* had been owned by millionaire Whitelaw Reid, but Reid was so involved with major diplomatic activity in Paris and London that he had starved his own paper. When Whitelaw died in 1912, the paper became the property of his widow ✒➤ **Elisabeth Mills Reid**. A year later, their son Ogden Mills Reid assumed the editorship. Ogden tried to recover the *Tribune*'s status by certain innovations: livelier news coverage, larger headlines, a more attractive typeset, bylines for enterprising reporters, a Sunday comic section, and a galaxy of first-rate journalists, including sportswriter Grantland Rice, humorist Robert Benchley, and columnists Franklin Pierce Adams and Heywood Broun. The *Tribune*, however, still remained in the red.

In 1920, a marked change had occurred. Gross revenues had increased two-and-a-half fold. Eight years later, the paper had turned a profit. In large measure, the *Tribune*'s good fortune was due to a small, fragile-looking woman who, until the age of 36, had no real contact with the newspaper world. In the fall of 1918, Ogden entreated his wife, "The *Tribune* needs you; Come on down to the office, and work the paper's success out with me." Writes the newspaper's most thorough historian, Richard Kluger, "She stayed thirty-seven years, and, for better or worse, became its driving spirit."

Helen Reid started out as an advertising solicitor, not even holding an office in the *Tribune* building. Within two months, however, she became director of the entire advertising department. Her first target was New York's department stores, where her obvious social connections gave her direct access to the owners of Wanamaker's, Macy's, and Gimbel's. Journeying to Detroit, she met personally with automobile manufacturers, followed by a trip to Chicago to confer face-to-face with leading meat packers. Eventually, major advertisers would be invited to lunch in the paper's private dining room, where they would find themselves flattered by mixing with actors, authors, and invariably some of the paper's advertising executives. Driving herself as hard as the lowliest solicitor, she would ask her staff: "What miracles today?"

In 1922, the advertising director was made a vice-president, in which capacity she, more than any other single individual, turned the paper into the second-best daily in the United States, one that in many areas even outdid its arch-rival, *The New York Times*. By 1944, people were saying of Helen Rogers Reid what Disraeli said of Queen *Victoria: "She's not a woman; she's an institution."

On November 22, 1882, Helen Reid was born in Appleton, Wisconsin. Her father Benjamin Talbot Rogers was a failed hotel operator who died when she was three. Her mother **Louise Johnson Rogers** had given birth to 11 children, some of whom still had to be raised. Nonetheless Helen, the last child in the family, had a happy youth. She attended public school in Appleton until the age of ten, when she was sent to Grafton Hall, an Episcopal school for girls in Fond du Lac. One of her older brothers was the headmaster, and Helen, a scholarship student, earned her keep by tutoring.

In 1899, Helen enrolled in Barnard College, where she was an active student, managing plays, singing in the chorus, turning a profit for the yearbook, and volunteering at New York City's Henry Street Settlement. Again compelled to provide her own tuition, she tutored, helped staff the bursar's office, and served as assistant housekeeper in a dormitory. Originally aiming to be a Latin teacher, she found herself enchanted by zoology. Later, writing for the Barnard alumni magazine, she would tell of courses where "the love life of an earthworm became beautiful and exciting" and "the nervous system of the dogfish integrated the history of the world into a rational pattern."

Graduating from Barnard in 1903, Helen Rogers became social secretary to Elisabeth Mills Reid, daughter of California financier Darius Ogden Mills and wife of *Tribune* publisher Whitelaw Reid. Rogers proved herself tactful, adept, and above all extremely competent, making herself indispensable to Elisabeth in both America and Britain, where from 1905 until his death in 1912, Whitelaw was ambassador to the Court of St. James. According to legend, Helen memorized the entire *Social Register* in New York and mastered *Burke's Peerage and Landed Gentry* in London.

❧▶ **Reid, Elisabeth Mills** (1858–1931)

American philanthropist. Born in New York City on January 6, 1858; died while staying at her daughter's villa in Cap Ferrat, Nice, France, on April 29, 1931; daughter of Darius Ogden Mills (a California financier) and Jane Templeton (Cunningham) Mills (daughter of a prominent shipowner and shipbuilder); her brother Ogden Mills was the father of Ogden L. Mills, secretary of the treasury; educated by governesses, at Mlle Vallette's School in Paris, and at the Anna C. Brackett School in New York; married Whitelaw Reid (editor and chief owner of the New York Tribune *and minister to France, 1889–92), on April 26, 1881 (died 1912); children: Ogden Mills Reid (b. 1882, a publisher); Jean Reid (who married Sir John Hubert Ward, equerry to England's Queen *Alexandra of Denmark).*

During the Spanish-American War, Elisabeth Mills Reid was the acting head of the nursing division of the American Red Cross; she was also chair of the American Red Cross in London during World War II. As a philanthropist, she helped establish Dr. Trudeau's T.B. sanitarium and the D.O. Mills training school for nurses, both at Saranac Lake, New York.

Although briefly engaged in 1910 to a budding lawyer, with whom she was not really in love, Helen gained the attention of the Reids' only son, Ogden Mills Reid. A Yale graduate, Ogden was serving his apprenticeship on the *Tribune* staff, beginning as a reporter, then working on the copy, city, rewrite, and night desks. Although he had some innovative ideas for revitalizing the paper, his first love was sports, yachting among them. Helen found the handsome, easygoing Ogden at times charming, at times irresponsible, but eventually succumbed to his marriage proposals. At first, both of Ogden's parents frowned upon the union, doing so on the grounds that Helen came from far more modest means. Elisabeth, however, eventually saw the orderly, responsible Helen as Ogden's ideal mate. When, in March 1911, the couple was married, the senior Reids arrived in Appleton in their own railroad car.

For their first seven years of marriage, Reid was the ideal society wife. She served as a gracious hostess; mastered such sports as swimming, tennis, and yachting; and—during World War I—converted the Reid mansion in Purchase, New York, into a working farm producing dairy products. She started to raise two children: Whitelaw ("Whitey"), born in 1913, and Elisabeth ("Betty"), born in 1916.

In 1917, Reid took on a major civil responsibility, serving as state treasurer for New York's women's suffrage campaign. Because suffragists had written off the Empire State as hopeless, organization lagged and money was tight. Taking advantage of her social ties, Reid held small intimate luncheons for Manhattan matrons, after which she passed the fountain pen. She personally raised more than $500,000, later saying, "Winning the battle in New York in 1917 was winning the battle nationally two years later."

Joining the advertising staff of the *Tribune* in 1918, then becoming vice president in 1922, Helen increasingly became involved in the management side of the paper. In 1924, she was the prime impulse in resisting the takeover bid of Frank Munsey, whose reputation was that of a ruthless buccaneer. With the aid of her mother-in-law, Helen reversed the scenario, helping to arrange the *Tribune*'s purchase of Munsey's *New York Herald* for $5 million. Munsey's *Paris Herald,* not yet reaching the distinction it later attained, was tossed into the deal. The new product, the *New York Herald Tribune,* was fundamentally an enlarged version of the Reids' old paper, with new additions including a radio magazine, some comics, and extensive weather information. New Yorkers would informally use the old name, the *Tribune,* or the more informal *Trib.* Now possessing a respectable circulation and an expanded news coverage, the new *Herald Tribune* was on its way to becoming a truly great newspaper. Moreover, by 1928, it was in the black by over $1 million.

When, in December 1924, her daughter Elisabeth died of typhoid, Helen blamed herself bitterly. For awhile, she even kept Betty's deathmask by her bedside. In June 1925, the 42-year-old Reid gave birth to another son, Ogden Rogers ("Brownie"), and was soon back at work. As one staffer put it, "She believed in the paper the way a religious person believes in God."

*D*ozens of her sex—notably in the entertainment field—are better known to the public at large than Helen Reid is, but few wield such power.

—Mona Gardner

Formally, the *Herald Tribune* was under Ogden's direction. Helen was careful never to intrude on his editorial domain. Indeed, she never wrote a story. When the couple differed, his views usually predominated in editorials, and the paper never adopted Helen's enthusiasm for prohibition. Writes historian Kluger, "As queen, she was closest to the monarch, but she was not sovereign and took pains not to pretend otherwise." Yet, behind the scenes, Reid was already

emerging as the dominant figure. The more she became involved in the paper's management, the more Ogden—always something of a playboy—drank. To this day, no one knows whether he resented her ever-expanding role. By 1925, Ogden had become an alcoholic, and in 1937 he was temporarily hospitalized. Helen often had to cover for him, making excuses for his frequent absences and doing all she could to see that he did not endanger himself. Downgrading feature articles that give her first prominence, she continually referred to him as the real boss of the *Herald Tribune,* calling him "the most independent-minded man I ever met." By the time of World War II, however, there was little pretense that Ogden was running the paper.

Although Ogden always remained titular head, with Helen calling herself his "first mate," the press was quick to discern who was really in charge. In October 1934, a *Time* cover story was titled "Herald Tribune's Lady." In May 1944, the *Saturday Evening Post* ran a two-part series, "Queen Helen." The subheading read: "Hostess to the famous, mistress of an old fortune, a high-powered sales executive with sandpaper persistence, Mrs. Ogden Reid is one of America's remarkable women." A year and a half later, *Time* carried another account, "The *Trib*'s Mrs. Reid"; it referred to her as the "tiny, self-assured vice president."

Under Reid's quiet leadership, the paper achieved genuine distinction. "The Herald Tribune was The Paper," writes journalist David Shaw, "a newspaper that became A Legend, a newspaper with the most illustrious alumni this side of Harvard University or the New York Yankees, a newspaper that became the most celebrated burial ground this side of Westminster Abbey." Though only sixth in circulation among Manhattan's nine dailies, the *Herald Tribune* was superior to most in the caliber of its writing, the comprehensiveness of its coverage, the quality of typography, and the artfulness of its make-up. It won the Ayer Cup for typography and design more than any other paper. Certain departments, notably music and dance, exceeded those of *The New York Times.* Its city coverage was the sprightliest in town, its editorial page a masterpiece. Indeed, newspapering had become a kind of art form.

By the 1940s, the *Herald Tribune* possessed some of the greatest drawing cards in journalism. In 1931, again recruiting the assistance of her mother-in-law, Helen hired Walter Lippmann, the most respected political columnist in America. America's most noted foreign correspondent, *Dorothy Thompson, joined the paper in 1936, though she was fired early in 1941 after having endorsed a third term for Franklin Roosevelt. Despite the strident partisanship and ultra-nationalism of the Reid family, Helen serialized the first serious biography of Woodrow Wilson and the memoirs of Wilson's alter ego, Colonel E.M. House.

Women were not neglected, either as readers or writers. It was with an eye on female subscribers that Reid pushed circulation in the middle-class suburbs of Westchester, western Long Island, and northern New Jersey. Women's pages, fashion coverage, society news, tips in gardening, a plethora of wedding announcements—all gave the *Herald Tribune* a special appeal to suburban women. She expanded the paper's Home Institute, a widely known demonstration kitchen that tested recipes and household products. By 1944, suburban circulation exceeded that of *The New York Times*.

Furthermore, by the mid-1940s, the *Herald Tribune* had more women staff members than any other American daily. On the local staff alone, 13 out of 60 reporters were women, as were half a dozen executives. Some women staffers were particularly talented: **Eugenia Sheppard** (fashion), *Dorothy Dunbar Bromley (social issues), *Clementine Paddleford (food). *Irita Van Doren created a distinguished book section. In 1952, *Tribune* journalist *Marguerite Higgins, known for her coverage of the Korean War, became the most famous war correspondent in the world.

In 1930, with the assistance of *Marie Mattingly Meloney ("Missie"), Helen launched the annual Forum of Current Events. Each October audiences packed the Waldorf-Astoria to attend a three-day marathon of speeches and panels by national and often world leaders. Soon dubbed the Herald Tribune Forum, it became covered by all four radio networks. Another one of her projects, the Herald Tribune Fresh Air Fund, raised funds to send needy children to summer camps.

All this time, Reid was becoming a renowned hostess. Her dinner parties, always given in regal fashion, were famous. She would toss out the question of the moment, then go around the table for comments. Some guests would actually rise and address her as if they were speaking in a public meeting.

In some ways, however, Reid's leadership had its drawbacks. She tended to view the *Herald Tribune* as a business more than as a disseminator of news. In 1927, for example, she ordered a fea-

Helen Rogers Reid

ture writer to put advertising pressure on a fashion house, an act that could jeopardize the paper's editorial integrity. In November 1937, a month after Helen was awarded the Comendador Order of Honor and Merit from the Cuban Red Cross, the paper published a special 40-page Sunday supplement under the banner, "Cuba Today: Land of Peace and Progress." The headline of the lead story read, "Colonel Batista's Life Dedicated to Relieving Cubans from Oppression." As the material was not identified as an advertisement, Helen met with much criticism.

Problems existed in other areas. Salaries were never competitive. Reid would not promote gifted Jewish staffers, causing some of the most talented to gravitate to the more hospitable *Times*. Acting in the belief that *Herald Tribune* readers were people of means, she set higher advertising rates than did the *Times*, hence losing irretrievable advertising and circulation.

Like Ogden, and like Whitelaw before him, Helen was a staunch Republican, though one more liberal than her husband or her father-in-law. Just as Colonel Robert R. McCormick, publisher of the *Chicago Tribune*, represented the party's midwestern isolationist wing, Reid epitomized the Grand Old Party's eastern internationalists. The writer *Clare Boothe Luce went so far as to say that "New York Republicanism was Helen Reid." In 1920, she traveled to Marion, Ohio, there to tell President-elect Warren G. Harding that *Tribune* backing depended on the quality of his appointments. In 1940, her paper played a crucial role in the presidential nomination of Wendell L. Willkie, and in 1952 the *Herald Tribune* showed equal prominence in the nomination of Dwight D. Eisenhower.

An ardent interventionist before Pearl Harbor, during World War II Reid endorsed the compulsory drafting of women. "I am glad to see women in industry," she said. "Their families will be better for it. I want to see fathers back in the home, a more equal division of work and sharing of domestic responsibility."

When, in 1947, Ogden died of cancer, Reid became president of the Herald Tribune corporation and in 1953 chair of the board. Only in 1968, when the Reids sold the paper, would she relinquish controlling stock ownership. As Kluger notes, the *Herald Tribune* "became legally and officially what it had long been in fact—a matriarchy." True, Helen appointed Whitelaw president in 1953, but he found himself occupying essentially a ceremonial role, having to check all matters with his mother. Reid in turn found Whitey inept and in 1955 replaced him with the 29-year-old Brownie. Only an insider—indeed only a Reid, she felt, was able to run the paper.

Things now, however, were different. Perhaps because of age, perhaps because of bad advisers and intimidated sons, perhaps even because of a blind self-confidence, she had lost her magic touch. If Reid had presided over the paper's resuscitation, she also ruled over its demise. By 1951, the *New York Herald Tribune* was more of a holding operation than a healthy business, as seen by its unbalanced books. Moreover, it was sinking further into debt each year.

Retrenchment was the watchword. Unlike the *Times*, the *Tribune* invested little in its plant. Instead of engaging in serious restructuring, it simply slashed expenses. In an effort to cut expenses, it made foolish personnel reductions. Badly needed working capital was used to pay long-standing loans, a matter that should have been resolved years earlier. Outside money was spurned, for Reid feared that it would lead to loss of control. Although the paper could not survive without healthy injections of new capital—and talent as well—outsiders refused to touch the enterprise, fearing that the Reids lacked the competitiveness to make the enterprise work.

Occasionally Reid's judgment was sound, as in 1948, when she fostered the serialization of Eisenhower's World War II memoirs. Yet too often she was badly out of touch. Always more at home with New York socialites, intellectuals, and national policymakers than with the average subway rider, she lost contact with the bulk of the city's population. In addition, she resented employees who left the paper over salary matters, expecting absolute fealty under all working conditions. She became absorbed in trivia, answering the most routine letters personally and becoming far too preoccupied with the Herald Tribune Forum. Most important of all, Reid placed far too much confidence in her business manager, William Robinson, an axe-man whom she made executive vice president, then publisher (a title the paper had never used before). Only in 1953, when losses reached $700,000 a year, did Robinson resign.

Finally, in 1958, Reid sold the *Herald Tribune* to financier John Hay Whitney, at which point she retired from the board of directors. Whitney too was unable to rescue the failing property. In May 1967, now named the *World Journal Tribune* (having merged with several rivals), the depleted remnant of the old *Trib* finally expired.

Even in her old age, Helen Reid was formidable. In its obituary, *The New York Times* noted:

> There was little in Mrs. Reid's appearance to suggest the influence she wielded, nor the force of her character. She stood only an inch over 5 feet; and she looked as fragile as a piece of expensive china. Her hair, at first brown, then gray, and later white, was a fine soft fuzz that curled close to her head. Her large green eyes, however, were alert and probing. According to advertising salesmen who dealt with her, they could be quite unnerving.

She spent her last years quietly on the Reid family estate in Purchase, New York, and at her New York apartment. On July 27, 1970, Helen Reid died in New York City.

SOURCES:

Gardner, Mona. "Queen Helen," in John E. Drewry, *More Post Biographies: Articles of Enduring Interest about Famous Journalists and Journals and Other Subjects Journalistic*. Athens, GA: University of Georgia, 1947, pp. 289–314.

Kluger, Richard. *The Paper: The Life and Death of the New York Herald Tribune*. NY: Knopf, 1986.

COLLECTIONS:

Reid's papers are in the Library of Congress, although some letters remain in the family's possession.

Justus D. Doenecke,
Professor of History, New College of the
University of South Florida,
Sarasota, Florida

Reid, Mrs. Ogden Mills (1882–1970).

See Reid, Helen.

Reid, Rose Marie (1906–1978)

Swimsuit designer and businesswoman whose innovative styling put her at the top of the swimwear industry. Born Rose Marie Yancey on September 12, 1906, in Cardston, Alberta, Canada; died on December 19, 1978, in Provo, Utah; daughter of Marie Hyde Yancey (a designer and seamstress) and William Elvie Yancey (a Church of Latter-day Saints bishop and grocer); married Garreth Rhynhart (divorced summer 1935); married Jack C. Reid (a swimming pool manager and instructor), on November 30, 1935 (divorced April 10, 1946); children: (second marriage) Bruce (b. January 19, 1937); Sharon Reid Alden (b. October 2, 1938); Carole Reid Burr (b. July 18, 1940).

Relocated with family to Weiser, Idaho (1916); after graduation from high school, worked in family grocery and beauty businesses; after marriage, designed a swim suit that led to orders from a Vancouver department store and launched Holiday Togs, Ltd.; total involvement, creative and managerial, led to company's name change to Rose Marie Reid; business sales topped $1 million a year for the first time (1946); entered into partnership with Jack Kessler and relocated in California (1947–49); Rose Marie Reid became the leading fashion house and manufacturer of the swimsuit industry (1950s); named one of the top ten women in America by the Los Angeles Times *(1955); co-winner of the American Sportswear Design Award for the "Sporting Look of the Year" sponsored by* Sports Illustrated *(1958); company sales reached $18.4 million, almost 10% of women's bathing suit sales in the nation (1960); refusing to design bikinis, left the company (1960); sold the rights to her name (1964); shifted to the design and manufacture of synthetic-fiber wigs for women; moved to Provo, Utah, to be with her family; continued civic service involvement, especially as a speaker at university and business meetings, and remained active in the Mormon Church.*

Rose Marie Reid learned sewing and design at her mother's knee. The scraps of material left over from **Marie Yancey**'s work as a seamstress became outfits for the little girl's dolls, right down to their umbrellas. By the time Reid was a teenager, she had absorbed the intricacies of cutting patterns, sewing, constructing and fitting, as well as Marie's axiom: "What makes a designer is when one cannot stand anything as it is. . . . You can always see something that you can do to make it lovelier, more unique, or a fit better."

By then, Reid was reconstructing and restyling clothes for herself and her friends.

Born in 1906, the middle child of seven, Rose Marie Yancey was named after her mother and a great aunt, **Rose Hyde**. The family lived in Cardston, Alberta, Canada, a border community of homesteaders living the hardscrabble existence of short growing seasons, frigid winters, and hostile winds sweeping unhindered for hundreds of miles across the prairie. But the land was made beautiful by wild geese, mountain grouse, deer, elk, and waving fields of grass and grain. There was not a fence for 2,000 miles.

Reid's father Elvie Yancey supplemented the farm's income with carpentry while Marie sewed. The children grew up earning money by doing odd jobs around town. Reid, who wore her hair in golden curls, was a bright student who loved to read. At age eight, considered the age of accountability, she was baptized into the Mormon Church.

Rose Marie was ten in 1916, when the Yanceys moved to Weiser, Idaho, to another farm. The children earned money as fruit packers for other farmers, or worked their own fields, where their father would divert them from the effort with math games and spelling contests. Later, handling the details of business, Reid recalled the exacting use of memory she developed from this quizzing. In the evenings, the children practiced penmanship while listening to their father, a bishop of the Mormon Church, read the scriptures. Marie taught her children to sing trios and duets, while Aunt Rose accompanied them on the piano.

After ten years of toiling on the Weiser farm, Elvie went into the grocery business, and the family at last found success in their combined efforts. The farm years had meanwhile taught Marie another business lesson. In a letter to her sister, she wrote: "If there is a loss to be taken, take it quickly, and go on to other operations that can be profitable." In 1925, the Weiser newspaper reported the purchase by the Yancey family of a combined millinery and ready-to-wear store, offering a "new hemstitching service" and a beauty parlor. Reid went to Boise to learn the beauty salon trade, then alternated with her sister **Marion Heilner** in traveling to the small town of Baker City, Oregon, where the family opened up a second beauty salon business. All these enterprises were wiped out during the Depression by the failure of the local bank.

In the summer of 1935, Rose Marie was living in Vancouver, British Columbia, when her marriage to Garreth Rhynhart, an artist-friend of her brother's, ended in divorce. That November, she married Jack C. Reid, a swimming instructor and manager of a pool. When Jack wanted something to replace the woolly trunks that sagged loosely after only a few minutes in the water, Rose Marie selected non-absorbing fabric of closely-woven duck cloth, and put lacing in the sides for a snugger fit. Swimmers at the pool started to ask where they could get such suits for themselves, and Jack was the first to see the opportunity. With two sample suits, one for men and one for women, created by Rose Marie, they approached the local department store of a national chain. When the buyers gave them an order for ten dozen men's suits and six dozen women's, Reid's Holiday Togs, Ltd., was born.

Reid created six styles of bathing suits and arranged with 16 seamstresses, new owners of Singer sewing machines, to fill the order. After a gross profit of $10,000 in its first year, Holiday Togs moved into a rented factory, where 32 machines turned out Reid's next designs. She would eventually style more than 100 suits per season. By November 1938, a Vancouver newspaper was reporting the return of Rose Marie Reid from a business trip to Baltimore, Maryland: "With the United States tucked in her pocket . . . the Reid 'Skintite' will be seen in the future at all America's smartest beaches." Reid was quoted as saying that 3,000 suits had been shipped to Australia the previous week. But duties levied by U.S. Customs made Reid's suits twice as expensive as comparable lines in the States, causing the entrepreneur to begin thinking about establishing an American manufacturing base.

Preferring to design on live models, Reid put an emphasis on an improved fit, a concept previously unknown in the swimwear field. As she introduced tummy-tuck panels, stay-down legs, and inside brassieres, women's swimsuits became a hot fashion item for the first time. In 1937, the name of her suits appeared on swimmers in the British Empire Games in Australia. Operating on the assumption that "a woman should feel as lovely in a swimsuit as she does in an evening gown," Reid experimented with new fabrics and diversified the market, designing "mother-and-daughter" suits as well as for men and boys, covering all ages. She designed for the bodies of all women, and was the first to provide suits according to women's dress sizes. Her sales jumped from $30,000 to $300,000 in one year.

Bruce, the first of the Reid children, was born in 1937, as the business was just getting under way. Admitted to the hospital, Reid was still cutting out fabric on her hospital bed while preparing for delivery. Her daughters Sharon and Carole were born in 1938 and 1940, respectively. To help with the raising of the children, Marie Yancey, now widowed, came to live with the family. In a new, competitive business, Reid often worked 16 hour days, but kept close to her children by involving them in her work. When she brought the infant Sharon with her on business to New York, newspapers announced that she was the youngest child to ever fly across the country. When Reid designed children's swimwear, her own children modeled them for local Canadian businesses. The year totem poles were appliquéd to one style of Reid's suits, Carole was delegated to cut them out. When the children were older and worked as hired employees, Reid held them to high performance standards, so they would not be seen as taking advantage of family ties.

With both her employees and her outside buyers, Reid's own enthusiasm for her work was contagious. Charismatic in her business contacts, she developed marketing techniques that buyers and trade representatives knew would be profitable, and they gave her suits top priority. Experimenting with new fabrics and trims, she introduced the use of gabardine and cotton, and applied sequins in ways the public immediately found appealing. She also developed a rapport with bankers, which helped the company's expansion. Her total immersion in the business justified the shift in the company's name from Holiday Togs to Rose Marie Reid, which was emblazoned across on the wall of the Vancouver factory. In 1944, with World War II still under way, employment in the company was up to 190, and Rose Marie Reid designs were in more than 500 Canadian retail stores; by 1946, the company controlled more than 50% of the Canadian swimsuit business, and annual sales had grown from $32,000 in 1938 to $834,000 that year; in 1947, they reached $1 million.

In 1946, Rose Marie and Jack were divorced. By the following year, she was intent on transferring the business to the United States. In search of an American business partner, she approached Jack Kessler, a clothing salesman, and his wife **Nina Kessler**, in Seattle, Washington. In both Canada and the U.S., however, World War II had been over less than two years; the manufacturing sectors were retooling for peacetime and beset by shortages. With both machinery and materials of the kind Reid needed in short supply, Kessler followed the advice of his financial advisor, who assumed it would be impossible for Reid to succeed, by setting standards for their equal financial partnership that required the designer to acquire all the sewing machines, fabric, and employees to set up the company.

Reid put in an order with the Singer company for the sewing machines she needed. With her name on a waiting list, she turned up at the Singer factory in Winnipeg and announced that she was there to pick up her purchase. When the distributor was not encouraging, Reid replied that she knew the machines were there and she would wait. Within hours, an order of machines arrived at the factory—the exact number to fill Reid's order, returned by a company that had been forced to close. Because she was there, the distributor agreed to turn them over to her. Said Nina Kessler: "[Reid] was the most organized, unorganized person I knew . . . and she was absolutely fearless. . . . She did what had to be done immediately no matter what anybody thought." Anticipating how the suits would be received, Nina prophesied, "We won't be able to make them fast enough."

The first American manufacturing plant was set up in downtown Los Angeles (the leisure-wear capital of the country), 30 miles from the airport, giving access to easy shipping. On an early buying trip to New York, Reid was in the office of a fabric company executive when she noticed a roll of gold metal thread on his desk. Asking for a piece, she took it back to her hotel room, where she tested it by dipping it in salt water. When she saw that it did not tarnish, she bought 20 yards of the thread in silver and 20 yards in gold, located a weaver and swore him to secrecy. Days later, the thread had been turned into shiny metallic gold and silver fabric, the first of its kind, and Reid set off with the yardage for Los Angeles to begin fitting it onto a model for her new swimsuit line. On September 20, 1946, before 300 national buyers and the press in Los Angeles, Rose Marie Reid, Inc., of California, made its company debut with three showings. At the finale of each show, the metallic gold suit was unveiled, at the unheard-of price of $90.

The show was a sensation. Buyers flocked to the company with their orders for the gold suit—so many that the limits of available cloth forced Reid to turn down three out of four. Trade magazines focused on the gold suit; it was featured by *Apparel Week* and newspapers throughout the country. Overnight, the Rose Marie Reid brand was famous. The company had opened in the U.S. hoping to achieve sales of more than $500,000 in its first year; thanks to the metallic gold suit, that goal was far exceeded. Manufacturers were soon copying Reid's

suits, said one of her major rivals, and those who didn't "went out of business."

Reid bought an estate in the suburb of Brentwood complete with swimming pool, riding stables and garden. She brought the children down from Vancouver, along with Marie and her Aunt Florence, and treated some of her new neighbors to personally designed and fitted swimsuits. She also welcomed use of the house by clubs and civic groups, and for fund-raising events, wedding receptions and activities of the Mormon Church. One day, when Reid was having lunch in the Brentwood village with her accountant, they overheard town officials discussing their lack of funds for repaving the village's roads. Reid promptly volunteered to donate the money. She was dubbed the "village financial angel" by the local newspaper and made honorary mayor. Popular as a speaker, Reid also addressed civic and service clubs, as well as university business schools. She spoke about leadership, the future of women in business, and the necessity of hard work for business success; she herself had been following an exhausting schedule for years.

According to Reid, "nothing is so brutally frank as the bare essentials of a bathing suit." She concentrated on construction and fit, and her early "skintite" suit, with its inch of fabric around the back and up over the shoulder that snapped into place, was revolutionary in holding the suit snugly through any activity on the beach. "Imagineering" was the name she gave to her shaping of suits to accommodate women of all ages and figures. Dividing the female torso into six areas, she created camouflaging devices to minimize imperfections in each, including a "bodice bra," vertical stripes, tummy-control panels, brief skirts and shirrings.

In her designs, Reid continued to experiment, bringing bengaline, satin brocade and velvets into the swimwear field. She used a new synthetic material, plastylon, which combined the characteristics of plastic and nylon for a tidy fit. She employed fashionable and innovative braids and appliqués as trim. One famous style involved a red lobster on a white suit; another had a fish decorated with small sparkling mirrors; and Carole's totem poles were a big hit in Canada. Special fabrics were used such as whites with thin gold metallic stripes, white-and-gold diamond-patterned mattelasse, and stripes of silver and candy pink that suggested a ball gown. She employed a fabric patented as Zelan, a colorfast and lightweight cotton or satin that was body-fitting, unstretchable, and cut to hold its shape. In 1951, *Esquire* featured a Rose Marie Reid design that employed 24-carat gold plating on black-lace fabric, sold exclusively at Lord & Taylor in New York City as the "suit of the year." *Life*'s choice that year as the most outstanding and revolutionary suit was the "Hourglass," with its squeezed-in waist and accented hips made more alluring in a satin-latex fabric. When Lord & Taylor featured Rose Marie Reid suits as "Jewels of the Sea" in its Fifth Avenue windows, its competitor, Saks Fifth Avenue, called the company to order "1,000 of whatever you have and 500 more for Palm Beach" to be sent "at once." By 1952, two plants, one in Montreal and one in Los Angeles, were turning out 1,000 Rose Marie Reid suits a day, and sales had soared to $5 million.

As late as January 1949, the fashion editor of the *Vancouver Daily Province* still referred to Reid as "Vancouver's famous swimsuit maker." For several years, after purchasing her former husband's portion of the company, Reid ran the U.S. and Canadian operations concurrently. As she coped with the company's growing pains in California, however, it eventually proved too much to carry on the designing responsibilities for the Canadian branch as well. On October 20, 1952, the Canadian firm announced the closing of its doors, while Reid's fashions in the U.S. proceeded apace.

The spinoff of the "Hourglass" was the "doubloon" shape, featuring colorfast elasticized taffeta and bengaline. In 1954, Reid created "bloomer bottoms," a suit featuring delicate embroidery that accented the bustline; a widening of the suit just under the arms created an optical illusion, narrowing the waist, while pockets widened the hips. Maintaining her belief in the shaping of her suits to enhance a woman's body as the means to business mastery, she continued to design for "modesty and a little mystery." Throughout the 1950s, she essentially held off the invasion of the European bikini—with its minimum of material and no figure control at all—into the American market. In the late 1950s, her designs triggered another leap in sales with the introduction of bathing-suit knits. Reid was the leader in her field for almost two full decades.

In 1955, Reid was named one the top ten women in America by the *Los Angeles Times*. In June 1958, in featuring the Rose Marie Reid look, the *Dallas Times-Herald* suggested that it had become a catalyst in expanding the role of a woman's swimwear, so that "instead of a single suit, she has a wardrobe, and each suit is part of a costume." The previous month, on May 28,

1958, Reid had been co-winner, along with designer *Bonnie Cashin*, of the Sportswear Design Award sponsored by *Sports Illustrated* for "Sporting Look of the Year."

In the 1950s, the Rose Marie Reid factory in Los Angeles produced 5,000 bathing suits a day, with overtime on occasion doubling that number to meet orders during peak season. After Reid began adding small collections of new swimsuit styles in late summer and at Christmas time, when stores formerly had been sold out of swimwear, the practice became industrywide. Meeting the demands of marketing her suits in 45 countries, Reid continued to refuse to design bikinis, offended by their skimpiness on grounds of both modesty and aesthetics. As the pressure intensified for her to adapt her to these styles, she reassessed her position, and decided instead to get out of the swimwear business. She had received all the recognition her field could bring and was now an extremely rich woman. In 1960, Reid retired from the swimsuit industry and turned to the design and manufacture of synthetic wigs, with a new corporation called the Reid-Meredith Company. Her swimsuit company, unable to maintain its competitive edge, closed its plant within two years. In 1964, she sold the right to the trademark name of Rose Marie Reid to the Jonathan Logan Company, and it is still associated internationally with swimwear.

As a pacesetter in the world of fashion, Reid believed youth gave her credibility, and she worked to maintain an energetic appearance. She also hated for anyone to know her true age. She once wrote to her sister Marion Heilner to say that if Marion did not also start fibbing about her age, Rose Marie was going to become her younger rather than her older sister. Refusing to admit she was older than 32, she smudged her birth date on her driver's license and passport. On December 19, 1978, Reid died at the home of her daughter in Provo, Utah. A hybrid rose, dawn-pink in color, was named for Rose Marie Reid. There is no birth date on her gravestone.

SOURCES:

Alden, Sharon Reid. Two interviews by William G. Hartley, Provo, Utah, 1973 (typescript, Oral History Program Archives, Historical Department of The Church of Jesus Christ of Latter-day Saints, Salt Lake City, Utah).

Burr, Carol Reid, and Roger Petersen. *Rose Marie Reid: An Extraordinary Life Story.* American Fork, UT: Covenant, 1995.

"Introducing Workers to Product," in *Business Week.* November 20, 1954.

Jackson, Kenneth T., ed. *Dictionary of American Biography.* Scribner, 1995.

Lencck, Lena, and Gideon Bosker. *Making Waves,* 1989.

Lothrop, Gloria Ricci. "A Trio of Mermaids—Their Impact upon the Southern California Sportswear Industry," in *Journal of the West*. January 1966.

Obituaries in *The New York Times* and *Los Angeles Times* (both December 22, 1978) and *Deseret News* (December 21, 1978).

Reid, Rose Marie. Interview by William G. Hartley, Provo, Utah, 1973 (typescript, Oral History Program Archives, Historical Department of the Church of Jesus Christ of Latter-day Saints, Salt Lake City, Utah).

Sports Illustrated. June 9, 1958.

"Styling Buoys Swim Suit Maker," in *The New York Times*. October 8, 1960.

"Swimsuits Around the Calendar," in *Fortune*. February 1956.

"Well Suited by the West," in *Sports Illustrated*. November 28, 1955.

Harriet Horne Arrington,
freelance biographer, Salt Lake City, Utah

Reid, Mrs. Whitelaw (1858–1931).

See Reid, Helen Rogers for sidebar on Elisabeth Mills Reid.

Reign of Women (1520–1683)

A 150-year period in the Ottoman Empire when women close to the reigning sultans—mothers, wives, daughters and consorts—exercised exceptional power, often determining domestic policy, negotiating with foreign governments, and acting in the role of regent, as well as leaving architectural monuments to their success.

In the long history of the Ottoman Empire, lasting into the early decades of the 20th century, a relatively brief period is known as the Reign of Women, during which the empire reached its cultural, political and territorial apogee. The significance of the term is a subject of some dispute, since many historians describe the extraordinary political influence held by women during this period as a sign of "decline." In the East as well as the West, women are more commonly blamed for their mistakes than praised for their accomplishments in the political realm, and terms like "ruthless" or "devious" are applied to their eradication of rivals or punishment of foes, while the same behavior in men is termed "decisive" and "authoritative." What is unquestionable, in examining the Reign of Women, which lasted from approximately 1520 to 1683, is the degree of power exercised by women in determining foreign and domestic policy and influencing succession to the Ottoman throne, as well as indulging, in the manner of their male counterparts, in the erection of a few lasting monuments to themselves.

The Ottoman Empire began with the conquest of the city of Constantinople by Mohammed II the Conqueror in 1453. His victory ended the Byzantine Empire which had existed as a Christian kingdom for a millennium after the fall of Rome. At its peak, during the reign of Suleiman the Magnificent, Ottoman territories bridged the continents of Europe, Asia, and Africa; its armies occupied Greece, Albania, Serbia, Bosnia, Croatia, part of Hungary, Moldavia, and some of the area around the Black Sea, as well as parts of modern Iran, Iraq, Palestine, Jordan and Egypt. Under Ottoman rule, the standard of living was much higher generally than in Europe, and urban life was much more pervasive. Silks, spices, baths, libraries, monuments and other accoutrements of civilization were common to its cities. The ancient Greek and Roman manuscripts that would later spark the European Renaissance were then being carefully preserved in the libraries of the Middle East and Islamic Spain, making the empire's scholars the preservers and purveyors of what was then understood of classical science, mathematics, medicine, literature, and art.

The role of women in the upper echelons of this culture has been largely underestimated, partly because of a misunderstanding of its social structure. European women have always been more highly visible in public life, while in the Muslim world, seclusion has been the ideal. In wealthy homes at least, women lived in harems, segregated from men, and when they went into the public, they appeared veiled. In the West, it has therefore often been assumed that women's influence did not extend beyond the family into the political and economic life of their country, when, in fact, nothing could be further from the truth.

To understand about harem life, what is important is to recognize the economics underlying the institution. Since only the wealthy could afford to cloister women and to procure the castrated men known as eunuchs to guard them, the segregation of women was a sign of affluence that only the rich could afford. Among the Muslim poor, women still lived in one-room houses with their male family members and worked alongside them in shops or fields, or at their cottage industries. Among the wealthy, men were also separated from society in some ways. Young males seeking to rise in government service entered the "imperial harem" or the "honored harem" for their training, and when wealthy men were seen in public, they were usually surrounded by a retinue that limited their contact with the general populace. Princes or heirs to the throne often lived separate from the women's harem, in a guarded part of the palace known as the "cage," which could restrict their activities more severely than those of the women.

Contrary to popular perceptions, the imperial harem was not simply a bordello filled with women who lived to fulfill the sultan's every demand. Harems have even been compared with nunneries, since many who lived there remained celibate, never called upon to fulfill any conjugal duties. In addition to housing a sultan's wives or concubines, the harem would be home to his mother, sisters, and children as well as any unmarried or divorced family members. It was a woman's world, ruled by the sultan's mother and, in the event of her death, by his wife or chief consort. Its residents oversaw the large number of servants who maintained it, trained new women when they first entered there, and educated the children born and raised there, including the future sultan.

To some degree, the imperial harem contributed to the ascendancy of women. Segregation gave them their own administrative structure, allowing them to rule themselves. Ruling sultans were far less fearful of their wives, mothers, and daughters than they were of brothers and sons. Many women of the harem became trusted advisors, then came to exercise power in their own right.

> The rise to power of the imperial harem is one of the most dramatic developments in . . . the Ottoman Empire. From almost the beginning of the reign of Süleyman the Magnificent . . . high-ranking women of the Ottoman dynasty enjoyed a degree of political power and public prominence greater than ever before or after.
>
> —Leslie P. Peirce

The practice of polygamy inherent in harem life also contributed to female ascendancy, in that it created a unique bond between mothers and children. While the father in a polygamous household was responsible for all his wives and children, the mothers worked and schemed to secure the best future for their own children. Since a woman could rule only through her son, she had to ensure that he reached adulthood in order for her to gain power. The struggle for survival and success was thus a common bond between mothers and sons, and not usually broken by marriage or succession to the throne. When a sultan came to power, his mother became the second-most powerful person in the empire. During the Reign of Women, she was sometimes

the most powerful. The downside of this aspect of harem life was the frequency of fratricide, removing brothers or half-brothers seen as potential rivals for the throne.

The harem life also allowed some women to achieve power by growing enormously rich. Under Islamic law, women received a dowry, and specified shares in the property of deceased relatives were set aside for the female members of the household. Islamic women were thus guaranteed economic independence that was often greater than many Western women enjoyed. As property owners and litigants in property, they might attain status equal to or greater than some men. Since the sultan held the territory of the empire as his personal domain, royal women benefited from the notion that all members of the dynasty were entitled to a share of the family wealth. One sultana, for example, was assigned the income from 23 villages in the province of Egriboz. In addition to agricultural holdings, it was not unusual for these women to own real estate and business establishments in urban areas. Personal wealth was also acquired in the form of jewels and luxury items received as gifts from the sultan and ambassadors of foreign countries. The mother of one sultan was reported to have 20 chests of gold coins at the time of her death, in addition to agrarian lands and urban properties. Such wealth might be used to pay and supply armies, influence government officials, build monuments, or engender popular support.

Apart from the effects of harem life they held in common, the sultanas who ruled during this 150-year period shared a number of traits. Most were foreign-born captives who entered the imperial harem as young slaves. The Ottoman Empire was a multinational entity, quite accepting of outsiders, and slavery was considered a temporary condition to be overcome; and overcome they did. Most of these women had forceful personalities, engendering great loyalty in their husbands, sons, and daughters, and most were willing to be ruthless to keep their power. They were intelligent survivors.

Many historians begin the Reign of Women with *Roxelana (c. 1504–1558), also known as Hurrem or the laughing one. (*See also separate entry on Roxelana.*) The wife of Suleiman the Magnificent, ruler of the Ottoman Empire from 1520 to 1566, Roxelana was probably the daughter of a Ukrainian priest. Captured as a child and sold into slavery, she perhaps came to the royal harem as a gift to Suleiman. After winning his favor, she eventually became his wife, the first woman actually married to a sultan in more than 200 years. She gave birth to five sons and a daughter, ✤▶ **Mihrimah**, who also became powerful. At a time when a fire partially destroyed the harem in the Old Palace, women and children had long lived completely separate from the rest of the household. Roxelana took advantage of the event to move into the sultan's residence, in the Grand Seraglio, a dramatic break with tradition.

The reign of Suleiman was marked by conquest, and his armies were kept busy occupying much of the Mideast and even parts of Europe. In 1521, he captured Belgrade and occupied part of Hungary; in 1526, his troops killed King Louis II of Hungary in the battle of Mohács; in 1527, his troops sacked Rome; in 1529, they invaded Austria and almost took Vienna. There were also frequent battles with Venice and the coastal towns of Italy. All this time that Suleiman was in the field, Roxelana was his chief advisor and surrogate ruler. She learned to write Turkish so she could report events in the capital as well as advise him, and Suleiman trusted her as he trusted no one else to carry out his orders. At one point, Roxelana had Ibrahim, her husband's vizier, executed for disloyalty, and married her daughter Mihrimah to Rüstem, a vizier of her own choosing. Mother, daughter, and son-in-law eventually conspired in the assassination of Mustafa, the crown prince and eldest son of Suleiman by another woman, so that Selim II, Roxelana's son, could inherit the throne.

From time immemorial, monuments have attested to an individual's prominence and resources. In the Ottoman Empire, the buildings ordered constructed by women and dedicated to them were generally religious in nature—mosques, schools, and mausoleums—although a smaller number of bridges, caravansaries or inns, bazaars, and hospitals were built at their command. Mosques, in particular, were associated with female patrons. In the Ottoman period, 953 mosques were built in Istanbul alone, and 61 of these were built by or for women. Of the 448 buildings designed or renovated by the well-known architect Sinan, 39 were constructed for women. Tomb towers were also major undertakings, requiring substantial resources and labor that indicated the resources a builder could muster; following the downfall of the Byzantines, these structures were also a political statement, indicating the dominance of Islam over Christianity.

In Istanbul, Roxelana oversaw the building of the Haseki complex. Though it was not on an imperial scale because its mosque had a single minaret (royal mosques have two minarets), the

✤▶ Mihrimah (1522–1575)

Princess of the Ottoman Empire. Name variations: Mirhrimah. Born in Constantinople in 1522; died in Constantinople in 1575; only daughter of *Roxelana (c. 1504–1558) and Suleiman or Suleyman the Magnificent (c. 1494–1566), sultan of the Ottoman Empire (r. 1520–1566); married Rüstem, chosen by her mother as her father's vizier; children: Aysha Humashah.

Along with her mother and husband, Mihrimah formed a powerful coalition which influenced domestic and foreign politics. She was the most powerful royal princess of the Ottoman Empire, especially after the death of her mother in 1558, when she became Suleiman's closest advisor.

surrounding complex made it a grand architectural venture. In the mid-1550s, a splendid bath was built in her honor—located on the imperial axis formed by the royal palace, the famous Hagia Sophia, and the premier imperial mosque—with chambers for both women and men, built to serve the staff and worshippers at the mosque. Similar, though smaller, complexes bearing Roxelana's name were also built in Jerusalem, Mecca and Medina. Caravansaries and bridges were other monuments to her power and munificence. When Roxelana died in 1558, the bereaved Suleiman buried her in his mosque, and constructed another mosque, school, and hospital in Istanbul in her memory. The number of these structures as well as their ornate character testify to the power Roxelana exercised in her lifetime.

Royal princesses, like mothers and consorts, could sometimes enjoy physical proximity to the sultan and be members of his palace's inner circle. Under the sultans, it became customary for royal princesses to be married to top-ranking diplomats and grand viziers. If their spouses died or were executed for some wrongdoing, they might be married to a new candidate, resulting in a series of husbands. It was not uncommon for a princess to be pivotal in the redistribution of royal power through divorce and remarriage. Like their mothers, they were considered more trustworthy than a sultan's sons or brothers, which further enhanced their power. Mihrimah (1522–1575) was the only daughter of Suleiman the Magnificent and Roxelana, and the most powerful royal princess of the Ottoman Empire. She is said to have been responsible for the decision of the Ottoman government to seize the island of Malta, paying out of her own fortune to outfit 400 ships.

In 1558, after the death of Roxelana, Mihrimah took her mother's place as her father's closest advisor. Her central role followed the custom of keeping male heirs far from the throne; sultans fearful of coups often plied their sons with alcohol, drugs, and women, a poor preparation for their future leadership. Selim II, Mihrimah's brother and heir to the throne, was known throughout his life as "Selim the Sot." Mihrimah, in contrast, maintained her influence through many reigns, and when she died in 1575 her nephew Murad III had her buried next to her father, Suleiman, an honor not granted even to Roxelana.

One of the Ottoman Empire's wealthiest women, Mihrimah also built monuments which endure to this day. From her dowry and inheritance, she amassed a huge fortune which she used in the construction of buildings and the endowment of charitable foundations. Most of the monuments built by these powerful sultanas had a philanthropic purpose, which were religious, educational, or charitable in nature. Many were located in poor or outlying areas, and some were built especially to aid women. For example, Roxelana's Haseki mosque complex was built near the Women's Market, far from the center of the city or any other mosque. Mosques often included soup kitchens, primary schools, and hospitals, serving as viable community centers as well as religious institutions. The sultanas' concern for the welfare of women is further reflected in the many charities they endowed to help orphans, prostitutes, and other unfortunate women.

Two major mosques were constructed to bear Mihrimah's name, as well as bathhouses and medreses (colleges). Designed by Sinan, the renowned architect of the day, both mosques have two minarets, signifying Mihrimah's royal status. The second of these, the Edirnekapi mosque, has been called one of the most revolutionary buildings of Ottoman architecture, a fitting tribute to a remarkable woman.

In societal terms, these royal women set a standard of behavior for the empire, especially in the concern they demonstrated toward their less-advantaged sisters and their occasional intervention in women's interests. ❧➤ **Sah** Sultana, for instance, an aunt of Mihrimah and the sister of Suleiman, was married to Lutfi Pasha, a grand vizier. According to accounts of the period, Sah protested against her husband's inhumane treatment of a prostitute when he had the woman's genitals mutilated. When Lutfi asserted that he would continue to punish prostitutes in this way, his wife lost her temper, and he beat her. Sah Sultana then divorced him, ending not only the marriage, but Lutfi's career, since Suleiman dismissed his former brother-in-law from further government service.

❧➤ **Nurbanu** Sultana (1525–1583) was another important link in this chain of powerful women. Said to be the illegitimate daughter of two noble Venetian families, she was captured as a slave in 1537, and quickly followed in Roxelana's footsteps by marrying Roxelana's son Selim II (r. 1566–1574). In the imperial harem, Nurbanu became Selim's favorite consort. She gave birth to his first child, a daughter (name unknown), then gave birth to two other daughters (names unknown) and a son, Murad III. Like her powerful mother-in-law, Nurbanu learned to use the intricacies of the Ottoman court to her advantage. Since Selim II was a weak ruler, Nurbanu quickly filled the power vacuum, deciding domestic policies and affairs of state, and is said to have worked particularly to ensure special trading rights for Venice, her native land.

When Nurbanu's son, Murad III (r. 1574–1595), came to the throne, her power became more formalized. Murad created the title *valide* sultan, or mother of the sultan, expressly for her, and during his reign he publicly acknowledged his mother as the second-most powerful person in the empire, following his announcement with a grand public procession. Nurbanu sat regularly on Murad's council of state and concerned herself with all questions of government. In 1577, she also initiated the most ambitious monument built during the Reign of Women: a complex called the New Mosque of the Valide Sultan, built on the shore of Istanbul's famous Golden Horn. The project, not completed until after her death, endures as a testament to her ambitions. When Nurbanu died, a weeping Murad accompanied his mother's coffin on foot, an unprecedented display of affection. He buried her next to his father, Selim II.

❧➤ **Safiye** (d. 1603) was chief concubine during the reign of Murad III. Originally of Venetian origin, she was a daughter of the governor of Corfu. Murad had 20 sons and 27 daughters with a number of women, but Safiye remained his favorite consort. Although she resented his other concubines, she procured beautiful slaves for her husband to maintain her own influence, and in later years she became his sole companion as well as his main political advisor. After her son Mohammed III (r. 1595–1603) ascended the throne, her power increased. In 1590, Giovanni Moro wrote of her, "with the authority she enjoys as mother of the prince, she intervenes on occasion in affairs of state, although she is much respected in this, and is listened to by

His Majesty, who considers her sensible and wise." When the sultan was away on military campaigns, she exercised the full power of regent, and she was particularly determined to look after the interests of her native Venice. During one of the frequent altercations between Constantinople and Venice, it is said that she prevented an Ottoman attack on St. Mark's, and she is credited with obtaining favorable trading rights for Venetian merchants. She corresponded on diplomatic matters with *Catherine de Medici and Queen *Elizabeth I, but she was unpopular with the army and did not long survive her son's death in 1603.

&▶ Kösem (1589–1651) exercised power the longest during the Reign of Women. Greek-born, she was the third wife of Ahmed I (r. 1603–1617), the mother of a large number of Ahmed's children, and eventually his only sexual partner. Christoforo Valier said of her in 1616, "She can do what she wishes with the King and possesses his heart absolutely, nor is anything ever denied to her." Two of her sons became sultans: Murad IV (r. 1623–1640) and Ibrahim I (r. 1640–1648). Her daughters **Ayse**, **Fatma**, **Hanzade**, and perhaps **Gevherhan**, and their husbands, played a role in her acquisition of power by supporting Kösem in her extensive political dealings. The need for Kösem as a stabilizing force was especially important, since both Murad and Ibrahim were unstable, deranged, and often cruel men. To consolidate her power, she allied herself with a faction of Janissaries, the fierce Ottoman troops, bribing them with precious metals she had melted and distributed from the palace treasury. She maneuvered every change of grand vizier and accession to the throne. After Ibrahim was deposed in 1648, Kösem continued as regent for her grandson

&▶ **Sah** (fl. 1500s)

*Ottoman princess. Name variations: Sah Sultana. Born around 1490; daughter of Selim I the Grim, Ottoman sultan (r. 1512–1520) and *Hafsa (d. 1534); sister of Suleiman or Suleyman the Magnificent, Ottoman sultan (r. 1520–1566), and *Hatice; aunt of *Mihrimah (1522–1575); married Lutfi Pasha (a grand vizier).*

&▶ **Nurbanu** (1525–1583)

Ottoman valide sultana. Name variations: Nurbanu Sultan; Nurubanu Sultana. Born Cecelia Venier-Baffo in Venice in 1525; died in Constantinople in 1583; illegitimate daughter of two Venetian noble families; married Selim II the Drunkard (also known as Selim the Sot), sultan of the Ottoman Empire (r. 1566–1574); children: three daughters (names unknown), and Murad III (1546–1595), Ottoman sultan (r. 1574–1595).

Nurbanu, born Cecelia Venier-Baffo, was captured as a slave in 1537. She entered the imperial harem and eventually married Selim II, son of Suleiman the Magnificent and *Roxelana. She became valide sultan (mother of the sultan), the most powerful woman in the empire, when her son Murad III ascended the throne in 1574. Murad unhesitatingly accepted her advice, making Nurbanu the empire's true ruler until her death in 1583.

&▶ **Safiye** (d. 1603)

Ottoman sultana. Name variations: sometimes referred to as Baffa Sultana. Probably born in Venice with the maiden name of Baffa, though birth date unknown; assassinated in Constantinople in 1603; favorite consort of Murad III (1546–1595), Ottoman sultan (r. 1574–1595); children: Mohammed III (1566–1603, also seen as Mahomet, Mehmed, Mehemmed, Mehmet, Mohammed, and Muhammed), Ottoman sultan (r. 1595–1603).

Safiye, sometimes referred to as Baffa, entered the imperial harem as a young girl after being captured as a slave. She was the favorite consort of Murad III and the mother of Mehmed III. She personally corresponded with *Elizabeth I of England and pledged assistance to the English in affairs of state and trade; she also acted as regent during the rule of Mehmed III, starting in 1595.

&▶ **Kösem** (1589–1651)

*Ottoman sultana. Name variations: Kosem Sultan or Sultana; Koesem; Kösem Mahpeyker. Probably born in Greece in 1589; assassinated in Constantinople in 1651; third wife of Ahmed I, Ottoman sultan (r. 1603–1617); children: daughters **Ayse**, **Fatma**, **Hanzade**, and perhaps **Gevherhan**; sons Murad IV (1609–1640), Ottoman sultan (r. 1623–1640), and Ibrahim, Ottoman sultan (r. 1640–1648); grandson: Mohammed IV (1641–1691, also seen as Mahomet, Mehmet, Mehmed, Mehemmed, Mohammed, and Muhammed), Ottoman sultan (r. 1648–1687).*

Kösem became valide sultan when her son Murad IV ascended the throne in 1623; she remained valide sultan when her second son Ibrahim became sultan in 1640. Kösem continued her political role under the reign of her grandson Mehmed IV (r. 1648–1687) until she was strangled by *Hadice **Turhan** Sultan, consort of Ibrahim.

Mohammed IV, under the title of Buyuk Valide (Grandmother). Her power finally ended in 1651, when she was strangled on the orders of her daughter-in-law **Hadice Turhan**.

The most powerful and wealthy of the valide sultanas, Kösem oversaw the construction of the most modest mosque. It was built in the first year of Ibrahim's reign, when none of the concubines of this sole male member of the dynasty had become pregnant. At this point, the extinction of the Ottoman dynasty seemed a real possibility, which may explain why this complex is so unassuming. But Kösem also built a large *han*, or Ottoman office building, which includes shops, offices, and storage space for artisans, tradespeople, and traveling merchants, at the center of the city. Known as the Valide Han, it is the grandest of its kind in the capital.

Hadice Turhan (1627–1683) was the last of the powerful sultanas. She began her ascent to power during the reign of Ibrahim (r. 1640–1648), by managing to attract his attention and giving birth to his first son, Mohammed IV (r. 1648–1687). Unstable and corrupt, Ibrahim spent many hours watching naked girls dive for pearls and rubies that he tossed into a large marble pool while his mother Kösem ruled the empire. He is said to have torn the young prince from Hadice's arms and thrown him into a pool to drown, but the child survived. Hadice's mother-in-law, Kösem, had by this time been de facto ruler of the empire for many decades and was Hadice Turhan's chief rival. When Ibrahim died and Mohammed IV ascended to the throne, Hadice Turhan should have become valide sultan, but Kösem continued to hold onto her rule. After waiting for three years, Hadice Turhan fi-

❧ Hadice Turhan (1627–1683)

Sultana. Name variations: Turhana Sultana; Turkan Sultan. Probably born in Russia in 1627; died in Constantinople in 1683; consort of Ibrahim, Ottoman sultan (r. 1640–1648); children: Mohammed IV (1641–1691, also seen as Mahomet, Mehemmed, Mehmed, Mehmet, Mohammed, and Muhammed), Ottoman sultan (r. 1648–1687).

Hadice Turhan, probably born in Russia in 1627, was the consort of the Ottoman sultan Ibrahim and the mother of Sultan Mohammed IV. After *Kösem refused to relinquish the reins of power as valide sultan when Mohammed IV ascended to the throne, Hadice Turhan had her assassinated in 1651 and ruled in the name of her son until her death in 1683, which ended the Reign of Women.

nally had the old woman strangled and assumed her place as the second-most powerful person in the Ottoman Empire. Far more interested in hunting than in governing, Mohammed IV left ruling to his mother, and the empire flourished under her administration, largely through her selection of some of the ablest viziers of the period. In 1683, her death was noted with the words: "the great pillar of the state has passed away."

It is not surprising that Hadice Turhan decided to complete the New Mosque of the Valide Sultan, begun earlier by Nurbanu. This was the first mosque built by a woman to join the ranks of the imperial mosques, equal in the religious hierarchy to the famous Hagia Sophia. Hadice Turhan's New Valide Mosque featured a large and imposing matriarchal tomb, comparable to the patriarchal tomb Suleiman had built for his mosque. Inside it, her catafalque occupies the most prominent position, with her son, Mohammed IV, buried at her feet and four sultans—Mustafa II, Ahmed III, Mahmud I, and Osman III—buried below him. Attached to the main tomb is a structure known as The Tomb of the Ladies which is filled with palace women, and many princes and princesses are buried in the gardens. More people are said to be buried in and around this tomb than is the case with any other in Istanbul except Suleiman's. The endowment for its maintenance specified that 157 individuals be employed as caretakers.

The complex surrounding the tomb includes the mosque, mausoleums, fountains, bathhouses, and the famous Egyptian bazaar, an L-shaped market made up of 86 shops and six gates. The mosque, like Nurbanu's, included a library. Nurbanu's library was the first established by a woman in Istanbul and held her private collection, which included 16 superb Qur'ans. Turhan's personal interest in the libraries is on record in an imperial command, issued in 1662, for books to be transferred from the palace treasury to the New Valide Mosque and two smaller mosques. Mosque libraries, endowed to support large staffs of calligraphers, artists, bookbinders, and other artisans, were centers of learning for the religious staff and visiting religious students.

Lasting barely more than 150 years, the Reign of Women is a fascinating and complex period of history, when the Ottoman Empire covered the most sophisticated areas of the world. The young slave girls, who learned their way through the intricacies of harem life and survived its intrigues, became some of the most powerful women of their time. Given the opportunity to rule, they held their positions with varying degrees of success, sometimes wisely, sometimes ferociously, and sometimes extremely well.

SOURCES:

Atil, Esin. *The Age of Sultan Süleyman the Magnificent.* NY: Harry N. Abrams, 1988.

Bates, Ulku U. "Women as Patrons of Architecture in History," in *Women in the Muslim World.* Edited by Lois Beck and Nikki Keddie. Cambridge, MA: Harvard University Press, 1978, pp. 245–260.

Bridge, Antony. *Suleiman the Magnificent: Scourge of Heaven.* NY: Franklin Watts, 1983.

Croutier, Alev Lytel. *Harem: The World Behind the Veil.* NY: Abbeville, 1989.

Helly, Dorothy O., and Susan M. Reverby. *Gendered Domains: Rethinking Public and Private in Women's History.* Ithaca, NY: Cornell University Press, 1992.

Inalcik, Halil. *The Ottoman Empire: The Classical Age 1300–1600.* Translated by Norman Itzkowitz and Colin Imber. London: Weidenfeld & Nicolson, 1973.

Kinross, John Patrick Douglas Balfour (Lord Kinross). *The Ottoman Centuries: The Rise and Fall of the Turkish Empire.* NY: William Morrow, 1977.

Lamb, Harold. *Suleiman the Magnificent: Sultan of the East.* NY: Bantam, 1951.

Marcus, Julie. "History, Anthropology and Gender: Turkish Women Past and Present," in *Gender and History.* Vol. 4, no. 2. Summer 1992, pp. 148–174.

Peirce, Leslie P. *The Imperial Harem. Women and Sovereignty in the Ottoman Empire.* NY: Oxford University Press, 1993.

"Roksoliana," in *Encyclopedia of Ukraine.* Vol. 4. Edited by Danylo Husar Struck. Toronto: University of Toronto Press, 1993, pp. 394–395.

Severy, Merle. "The World of Süleyman the Magnificent," in *National Geographic.* Vol. 172, no. 5. November 1987, pp. 552–601.

Karin Loewen Haag, writer, Athens, Georgia

Reignolds, Catherine Mary

(1836–1911)

English-born American actress, dramatic reader, and teacher. Name variations: Kate Reignolds; Kate Winslow. Born Catherine Mary Reignolds on May 16, 1836, near London, England; died of sunstroke on July 11, 1911, in Concord, Massachusetts; daughter of Robert Gregory Taylor Reignolds and Emma (Absolon) Reignolds; married Henry Farren (an actor), in December 1857 (died January 8, 1860); married Alfred Erving Winslow (a merchant), on June 28, 1861; children: Charles-Edward Amory Winslow (b. February 4, 1877).

Catherine Mary Reignolds, or Kate as she was better known, was born in 1836 in England, the eldest of three girls. After her father Robert Reignolds died, her mother **Emma Reignolds** took an acting job in Chicago in 1850, and brought her daughters to the United States. As Emma made her Chicago debut in *Cinderella*, her 14-year-old daughter Kate appeared on the same stage in a small role, her first ever. Kate's mother, as well as her two sisters, **Georgie** and **Jane Reignolds,** continued to pursue acting careers, but Kate was the one who was destined to make a name for herself.

In 1855, after little success in Chicago, Reignolds convinced Edwin Forrest to give her a part in a play at the Broadway Theater in New York. Her performance was impressive enough to bring her more work, and in 1857 she joined Ben De Bar's Opera House company in St. Louis, Missouri, where she associated with some of the most prominent stars of the day, including *Charlotte Cushman. In December of that year, she married another actor in the company, Henry Farren, who died only two years later. In 1860, she played Anne Chute in *The Colleen Bawn* in *Agnes Robertson's final appearance at New York's Winter Garden, and later that year became leading lady of the stock company of the Boston Museum, where she was quite popular.

In 1861, Reignolds married a successful and pedigreed young Boston commission merchant, Alfred Erving Winslow. After 1865, she traveled abroad as a celebrated actress, appearing in London's Princess Theatre in 1868 and then in other major English venues, but Boston would be her home for the rest of her life. A stage accident in England forced her to return to the United States, but after her recovery she resumed touring in America as head of her own company. When her son Charles-Edward Amory Winslow was born in 1877, she quit the public life of the theater, and some years later began giving dramatic readings. William Carson maintains that in choosing this career path, Reignolds (now Mrs. Winslow) was likely emulating *Fanny Kemble.

In 1887, under her married name, Reignolds published a book of memoirs, *Yesterdays with Actors*, and in 1895 published *Readings from the Old English Dramatists*. During the 1890s, she gave private elocution and acting lessons to promising young women; acclaimed actress *Josephine Hull** was one of her most successful students. Reignolds died at age 75 at her summer home in Massachusetts, and was remembered as a gifted, respected and versatile actress who held a prominent place in American theater for over 20 years.

SOURCES:

James, Edward T., ed. *Notable American Women, 1607–1950.* Cambridge, MA: The Belknap Press of Harvard University Press, 1971.

Jacquie Maurice, freelance writer, Calgary, Alberta, Canada

Reik, Haviva (1914–1944)

Jewish resistance fighter. Name variations: Havivah. Born Haviva Emma Reik in Slovakia (now Czechoslovakia) in 1914; executed by the German military during World War II in 1944.

A native of Slovakia (now Czechoslovakia), Haviva Reik emigrated to Palestine in the late 1930s and joined the kibbutz Ma'anit. In 1944, during the Nazi occupation of Slovakia, she and three other volunteers parachuted into their former homeland to assist the Jewish resistance and to spy for the Allied forces. Reik was eventually captured by the German military and executed. In present-day Israel, she is regarded as a national hero; both the kibbutz Lehavot Haviva and the Givat Havivah research center bear her name in tribute.

Reinhard, Anna (1487–c. 1538).

> *See Zwingli, Anna Reinhard.*

Reinhardt, Aurelia Henry
(1877–1948)

American educator, college president, and first female moderator of the American Unitarian Association. Born Aurelia Isabel Henry on April 1, 1877, in San Francisco, California; died on January 28, 1948, in Palo Alto, California; daughter of William Warner Henry and Mollie (Merritt) Henry; graduated from the University of California at Berkeley in June 1898; Yale, Ph.D., 1905; married Dr. George Frederick Reinhardt (founder and director of the University Health Service in Berkeley), on December 4, 1909 (died June 1914); children: George Frederick (b. 1911); Paul Henry (b. 1913).

Born in 1877 in California to parents of New England heritage, Aurelia Henry Reinhardt was the second of six children. She attended the "Boys' High School" in San Francisco for two years before her family moved south to booming San Jacinto in 1890. Aurelia's mother **Mollie Henry**, however, disliked the local schools and "culture" there and soon sent her two eldest daughters back to San Francisco. By 1885, her mother had opened a boardinghouse in Berkeley, and, with her sisters, Aurelia worked there cleaning and serving meals while she attended the University of California.

In 1898, even before she had officially received her bachelor's degree, Reinhardt landed a position at the University of Idaho teaching and coaching dramatics. She taught there for three years before beginning her English graduate studies at Yale in 1901. An energetic woman with a forceful personal presence, she thought of becoming a professional actress but eventually decided in favor of a career in education. At Yale, she enjoyed the study of classical, medieval, and modern languages; her first published work was an English translation of Dante's *De Monarchia*. After receiving her Ph.D. from Yale in 1905, Reinhardt studied abroad on a fellowship for a year, primarily at Oxford and in Italy, before returning to teach in Idaho for three years. While working in Idaho, she made plans to marry but her mother thwarted them, and Aurelia returned to Berkeley in 1908.

At the end of 1909, she married the prominent physician George Reinhardt, an old family friend eight years her senior. They had two sons, George Frederick and Paul Henry, and when her husband died suddenly in 1914 the young widow immediately returned to teaching to support her children. She lectured in English at the University of California extension from 1914 to 1916 before accepting a position as president of Mills College in Oakland, California. Reinhardt's dynamic 27-year administration transformed Mills from an unstable establishment into an important, internationally known institution. Although her leadership was sometimes seen as erratically personal and even dictatorial, she won the admiration of her colleagues and the loyalty of her students.

Aside from her duties on campus, Reinhardt was remarkably active in many community and civic affairs. She gave countless speeches, served as president of Oakland's City Planning Commission in 1919, was national president of the American Association of University Women from 1923 to 1927, and was department of education chair for the General Federation of Women's Clubs from 1928 to 1930. She served on several national councils and boards and was active in many other organizations, including the Daughters of the American Revolution and the Dante Society. A lifelong Unitarian despite her mother's Quaker faith, she became the American Unitarian Association's first female moderator in 1940. Intensely interested in politics, Reinhardt was a Republican elector for California in 1928 and strongly opposed Franklin D. Roosevelt's New Deal economic program. She continued to publish scholarly books and articles, and spent her free time collecting books and studying the flora and fauna of the environs around Mills College.

A serious educator who left a lasting impression on those who knew her, Reinhardt believed that the "amazing objective triumphs of science" of her time did not provide all the answers to her students' questions about life. On campuses everywhere, she observed, "interest in philosophy and religion is on the increase." Meeting foreign students and teachers on her journeys to Europe and elsewhere reinforced her belief that democracy was rooted in and interdependent with religion. After her retirement from Mills College, Reinhardt traveled extensively. In the late 1940s, while visiting her son Fred, who later became an ambassador to Italy, she developed a heart condition and returned to the United States. She died in the home of her son Paul, a physician, on January 28, 1948.

SOURCES:

Current Biography 1941. NY: H.W. Wilson, 1941.

James, Edward T., ed. *Notable American Women, 1607–1950.* Cambridge, MA: The Belknap Press of Harvard University Press, 1971.

McHenry, Robert, ed. *Famous American Women.* NY: Dover, 1980.

Read, Phyllis J., and Bernard L. Witlieb. *The Book of Women's Firsts.* NY: Random House, 1992.

COLLECTIONS:

Mills College holds an extensive collection of Reinhardt's papers, including correspondence, manuscripts, and public addresses.

Jacquie Maurice,
freelance writer, Calgary, Alberta, Canada

Reinhild (fl. 8th c.)

Flemish nun and artist. Flourished in the 8th century in Maasryck, Flanders.

Reinhild, one of many medieval nuns who expressed themselves artistically, lived at the convent of Maasryck in modern-day Flanders, in the region north of France then called the Low Countries. In the 8th century, Catholic convents were still relatively independent places of scholarship; Reinhild was extremely well educated at Maasryck. She became famous for her learning and for her artistic abilities, primarily as a painter but also for her beautiful cloth designs. She was also reported to be highly skilled in copying and illuminating manuscripts.

Laura York,
Riverside, California

Reinig, Christa (1926—)

German feminist writer. Born in Berlin, Germany, in 1926; studied four years at Humboldt University.

Published one of her first poetry collections, Der Abend—der Morgen *(Evening—Morning, 1951);* *published prize-winning radio play,* Aquarium *(1968); published feminist novel,* Die Entmannung *(Emasculation or Castration, 1976).*

Christa Reinig was born in Berlin, Germany, in 1926. Although trained as a florist, she was employed as a factory worker during World War II and aided in the reconstruction of Berlin at the war's conclusion. She entered Humboldt University and, after four years of study in art history and archaeology, accepted a position as curator at the Märkisches Museum in 1957. She remained there until 1964, when she moved from East Germany to West Germany and began to devote most of her time to writing.

Reinig's first works were poems, originally published in East German journals, which were later collected in several volumes. Among these are *Der Abend—der Morgen* (Evening—Morning, 1951); *Die Steine von Finisterre* (The Stones of Finisterre, 1960); and *Die Schwalbe von Olevano* (The Swallow from Olevano, 1969). She also wrote for children, including a book of verse, *Hantipanti* (1972), and a story, *Der Hund mit dem Schlüssel* (The Dog with the Key, 1976). Reinig wrote several radio plays, among them the award-winning *Aquarium* (1968). *Die himmlische und die irdische Geometrie* (Heavenly and Earthly Geometry, 1975), an autobiographical novel, was followed by other novels, such as *Die Entmannung* (Emasculation or Castration, 1976). Additional works include *Orion trat aus dem Haus* (Orion Has Left the House, 1969); *Die Ballade vom blutigen Bomme* (The Ballad of Bloody Bomme, 1972); *Mädchen ohne Uniform* (Girl Without Uniform, 1981); *Feuergefährlich: Gedichte und Erzählungen für Frauen und Männer* (Inflammatory: Poems and Stories for Men and Women, 1982); and *Idleness is the Root of All Love* (poems, published in English in 1991). Much of Reinig's work espoused a radical feminism that condemned the plundering nature of a male-driven society in both the East and West. Her satire and use of the grotesque have incited comparisons to the writings of Mark Twain and Jonathan Swift, respectively.

SOURCES:

Buck, Claire, ed. *The Bloomsbury Guide to Women's Literature.* NY: Prentice Hall, 1992.

Columbia Dictionary of Modern European Literature. 2nd ed. NY: Columbia University Press, 1980.

Kari Bethel,
freelance writer, Columbia, Missouri

Reiniger, Lotte (1899–1981)

Talented German film animator who produced pioneering works in the early 1920s and continued with a productive career for the next 50 years. Pronunciation: LOTT-uh RYE-niger. Born in Berlin, Germany, on June 2, 1899; died in Dettenhausen, West Germany, on June 19, 1981; daughter of Karl Reiniger (a banker) and Eleonore Reiniger; studied with Max Reinhardt, Berlin, 1916–17; studied with Paul Wegener at the Berlin Institut für Kulturforschung, 1918–19; married Carl Koch (an art historian and fellow filmmaker), in 1921 (died December 1, 1963).

Began career as animator (1918); completed first full-length animated film (1926); left Germany for England (1935 or 1936); worked on films in Italy (1939–45); returned to Berlin (1944 or 1945); settled in England (1949); received first prize, Venice Film Festival (1955); received Deutsche Film Prize, Berlin Film Festival (1972); produced final silhouette films in Canada (1974–78); settled in Dettenhausen, West Germany, made the subject of special program and symposium, American Film Festival (1980); honored by Museum of Modern Art, New York (1986).

Selected films: The Adventures of Prince Achmed *(1926);* Dr. Doolittle and His Animals *(1927–28);* Carmen *(1933);* Papageno *(1935);* Snow White and Rose Red *(1955);* Jack and the Beanstalk *(1955);* Thumbelina *(1955);* Aucassin and Nicolette *(1974);* The Rose and the Ring *(1979).*

Lotte Reiniger had the distinction of creating the first full-length animated film. In the years between 1923 and 1926, employing handcut silhouettes and a stand she herself had designed, she thereby anticipated the work that Walt Disney's studio would do a decade later. In both silent films and those of the sound era, her work became known as models of the animator's art. In a tribute to Reiniger at the American Film Festival in 1980, the year before her death, fellow silhouette artist **Diana Bryant** remarked on her ability to "create an illusion even with the gesture of one finger." The resulting movement in a Reiniger film "is so superb that after the first few seconds you forget you are looking at flat paper."

The art of animation, in which Reiniger distinguished herself, preceded the invention of film. Attempts to give drawings the appearance of motion have been traced back to the repetitive images of athletes on ancient Egyptian murals. To create this same effect, the Greeks painted multiple images of a single individual on their vases. In the first half of the 19th century, Belgium's Joseph Plateau and England's William G. Horner invented machines that permitted the viewer to see an apparently moving picture. These machines employed such devices as revolving wheels on which pictures had been placed; the customer watched the changing image through a viewing slot or on a mirror. In 1891, using carbon lights, mirrors, and a revolving drum with hand-colored pictures, France's Emile Reynaud took the process a crucial step further. He projected a moving image on a screen to create a 15-minute show for his Parisian audiences. A musical accompaniment added a further dimension.

The invention of the motion-picture camera and projector made possible the animated films that played so large a role in the popular culture of the 20th century. Cinema became the medium in which Reiniger and other great animators of the modern era have worked. With the camera and the projector, a series of changing images could now be photographed frame by frame, then replayed rapidly before an audience to create the illusion of motion. These images could come from a number of different sources. Artists could make a series of drawings, abstract or realistic, to create a cartoon. Puppets, whose poses could be subtly adjusted from one frame to another, provided an additional means to produce the same effect. Silhouette animation, the art that Reiniger was to lift to its greatest heights, used flat cut-out figures, made up of joined parts that could be moved at will. These were photographed with each pose slightly different from the preceding one.

The growing enthusiasm for animation is reflected in French poet Guillaume Apollinaire's 1914 prediction that it was "the thing of the future." He was referring to the germinal work done by French painter Léopold Survage whose set of almost 200 abstract watercolors, designed to be viewed one after the other, was a crucial step toward filmed animation. "I will animate my painting," Survage declared in 1914. "I will give it movement. . . . I am creating a new visual art in time, that of colored rhythm and rhythmic color."

In these same prewar years, an obscure Englishman, C. Armstrong, apparently preceded Reiniger's techniques for creating an animated film. Armstrong moved flat models with joined parts slightly, photographing each new pose and linking the frames to produce the illusion of motion. Meanwhile, Ladislas Starevitch, a former scientist from Eastern Europe, made complex wooden models of insects and animals with separable, movable body parts. Manipulating these, he produced films based on puppet animation.

Lotte Reiniger was born in Berlin on June 2, 1899, the only child of Karl Reiniger, a bank official, and **Eleonore Reiniger**. Little has been recorded about her early life and family back-

Lotte Reiniger

ground, but some sources note that even as a child she put on shadow shows, including plays from Shakespeare. In these childhood productions, the future animator already displayed her gifts in cutting elegant and graceful silhouettes with nothing more than a pair of scissors and her own sense of a correct pattern. She recalled in 1936 how she found herself cutting silhouettes "almost as soon as I could manage to hold a pair of scissors." Her family apparently encouraged her artistic interests. Attending a lecture by film pioneer Paul Wegener in 1915, she took to heart his message about the possibilities of that medium.

Reiniger was educated at Max Reinhardt's theater school in Berlin. Despite her fondness for acting, she found herself most comfortable in the world of silhouettes and shadow theater. Her debut in producing filmed silhouettes came in 1916; these were handcut figures designed as titles for a film by Wegener, *The Pied Piper of Hamelin*. Wegener had discovered her while she was cutting silhouettes behind the stage in Reinhardt's theater. She performed another task for Wegener, finding a way to move wooden rats and guinea pigs for a sequence in the film; Wegener had tried and failed to capture this part of the story using real animals. Her first silhouette film, *The Ornament of the Loving Heart*, a brief piece completed in 1919, began her extensive career in creating works in this genre.

Wegener introduced Reiniger to a circle of young artists who had formed a studio to produce animated works, one of whom was Carl Koch, Reiniger's future husband. Reiniger and her colleagues became important innovators in the technique of animation, creating their own tools such as a special animation stand with different planes upon which to place silhouettes of various sizes, allowing them to film complex scenes with different figures in the foreground and background. "Animation was in its infancy," wrote Reiniger. "The whole field was virgin soil and we had all the joys of explorers in an unknown country."

The Adventures of Prince Achmed, which Reiniger finished in 1926 after three years of devoted labor, is considered by most film historians to be the first full-length animated film. Described by **Cecile Starr** as "a tale of sorcery and splendor, a kidnapped princess, a magic horse, and friendly and monstrous creatures," the film was financed by a German banker, Louis Hagen, who had been impressed by Reiniger's early work. As Reiniger recalled in 1970, Hagen's plan for a full-length picture in silhouettes at first raised a wave of skepticism in her and in the filmmakers whom she consulted. "Animated films were supposed to make people roar with laughter, and nobody had dared to entertain an audience with them for more than ten minutes."

Undaunted by the task and unencumbered by close ties to the existing film industry, Reiniger decided to accept the assignment. Other leading figures in experimental movie making, who likewise felt themselves outside the ranks of established filmmakers, accepted her invitation to join in the project. These included Koch, whom she

had married in 1921, and such luminaries as Walter Ruttmann and Berthold Bartosch. Notes film historian **Ally Acker**, this talented crew drew on "a compendium of experimental techniques." Bartosch, for example, was a former architect who had produced animated educational films in both Vienna and Berlin since 1918. Ruttmann, after four years of service in World War I, had given up a painting career to enter the field of animation, and in 1921 he had taken the novel step of screening an abstract animated film for a general audience. Their combined ability to create realistic backgrounds augmented Reiniger's talent for producing lifelike figures.

The film was made in a garage studio at Hagen's home in the Berlin suburb of Potsdam. Decades later, Reiniger still remembered the low roof in the attic studio and the need to place the glass plate for the silhouettes close to the floor in order to situate the camera above it. To move her figures, she had to kneel on the seat of an old automobile. *Prince Achmed* was filmed on five reels and ran for more than an hour. It required more than 250,000 photographs to produce its effects, each second of film containing 24 separate shots.

Reiniger had to study the actual movement of people and animals in order to produce seemingly natural movement on the part of her artificial creations. She cut out her figures freehand, making smaller and larger versions of the same figure for use in close-ups or more distant shots. Backgrounds were produced by using layers of tissue paper. Her cutouts were made from black cardboard and thin lead. Each arm and leg was a separate piece joined to the body by wire hinges. Reiniger produced the emotional effects she sought by moving the cutouts slightly with her fingers. By placing a strong light below the glass animation table, she made the black cutout figures highly visible while the same light made wire hinges disappear. A wire attachment in the camera moved the film one frame at a time, as Reiniger delicately altered the position of her figures.

Reiniger's skill in this art became renowned. One of the key scenes in *Prince Achmed* exemplifies the complex results of her efforts. In it two characters, the good witch and the sorcerer, are battling for a magic lamp. As the fight proceeds, the two figures change into different animals, and their struggle conclude with each throwing flames at the other. In later years, one of her young collaborators, animator Pat Martin, described how "the beauty of the outcome" disguised the tedious, skilled labor that went into the finished product. "For each tiny sequence," only a few seconds long, required "sitting in the dark, moving each little figure a fraction of an inch at a time before shooting."

The film's plot came from *The Arabian Nights*, and, like the Disney films that appeared a decade later, it was designed for children. *Prince Achmed*, described by **Gwendolyn Foster** as "one of the most innovative early animation films in history," brought together Reiniger's mastery of silhouette animation and the techniques of Asian shadow plays. Shadow plays in countries like India, China, and Thailand were traditionally used to tell a story by means of movable figures made of non-transparent material whose images were projected on a screen. They had first appeared in Europe in the 17th century.

With the help of Berthold Bartosch, Reiniger injected images of waves to accompany a sea journey in the plot. She added depth to much of the film by making separate negatives of figures she and her collaborators had created, then combining them to compose a single image. For example, Bartosch's ability to pierce a piece of cardboard, to move it gradually for a series of photographs, and then to superimpose one shot over another, created what Eric Walter White described as "a sky of stars moving slowly . . . in different directions and at different speeds." Ruttmann helped produce his effects by using materials such as sand and soap, and he also employed mirrors to add other effects to his designs. Weeks of tedious preparation were needed for many of the more complicated portions of the film.

Despite its imaginative and stunning effects, some critics at the time found the 1926 film too long for an animated piece, but others called it "almost faultless," an achievement filled with "spirit and grace." *Snow White and the Seven Dwarfs*, Walt Disney's first full-length animation feature, would not be released for another 11 years, in 1937.

Reiniger largely abandoned such lengthy films after completing *Prince Achmed*. In the late 1920s, now committed to making shorter animated works, she created three *Dr. Doolittle* films. The second Doolittle film contained one of Reiniger's most famous sequences: the forming of the monkey bridge. As Eric White, a longtime student of her work, writes, this portion of the film, with its complex acrobatics, shows how "Lotte Reiniger articulates her figures with such perfect justice and reasonable fantasy that the illusion is never broken."

She had mixed success, however, in maintaining the circle of talented animators who had worked with her between 1923 and 1926. Bartosch was a key collaborator in the *Dr. Doolittle* films, producing the illusion of a snowstorm and, as in *Prince Achmed*, a seascape. His partnership with Reiniger lasted for nearly a decade. On the other hand, Ruttmann, also Reiniger's key collaborator, gave up animation and turned to documentary filmmaking. Reiniger's attempt in 1929 at a live-action, full-length production, *Running after Luck*, failed, but she was able to salvage a two-reel animated segment of the film that could stand alone.

> She is an artist and her work would be as good if instead of working with film she had been a painter or a musician.
> —Jean Renoir

The advent of sound in films gave Reiniger new challenges for her skills. She now created a number of works featuring a musical background. Mozart's *The Magic Flute* was the musical centerpiece for Reiniger's *Papageno*, with the visual images designed to accompany the operatic score. Similarly, *Carmen* was an animated play composed to match the tunes of Bizet's opera. Despite the difficulty of pairing her images to a great work of music, Reiniger claimed to be inspired by the challenge. *Papageno* offered audiences a series of particularly striking images as Reiniger's figures went through apparently miraculous transformations. One such metamorphosis saw eggs hatched to produce human babies. Another showed birds transformed into dancing girls.

Reiniger and Koch moved to England in the mid-1930s and remained there for several years. A notable success for Reiniger, tapping the work she had done on *Prince Achmed* more than a decade before, was the shadow-play portion of French director Jean Renoir's 1938 film *La Marseillaise*. She also completed numerous children's films in Britain. Material on Reiniger and Koch during the war years is scanty, but they evidently returned to the Continent and spent most of World War II in Italy. Some sources suggest that Reiniger returned to Germany in 1944; others state that she went back to her homeland only after the conflict had come to a close.

In 1949, Reiniger settled in Britain, where she spent most of the next three decades making films for the BBC. The development of television gave Reiniger, who often worked in collaboration with her husband, a new outlet in which to display her abilities. She finished more than a dozen animated films based on myths and fairy tales, including *Aladdin, The Grasshopper and the Ant,* and *Thumbelina.* Widowed in 1963, she gave up her career in filmmaking for a prolonged period of time.

After 11 years devoted to theatrical productions, Reiniger received an invitation in 1974 to make films for the National Film Board of Canada. A notable work that she created for them was *Aucassin and Nicolette,* finished in 1974. With her health deteriorating, she returned to West Germany in 1980 and spent the remaining months of her life in the small village of Dettenhausen, south of Stuttgart, where she died on June 19, 1981.

Reiniger is notable for the sheer duration of her career. It extended from 1918 to a final production in 1980. But she has received her highest tributes for the artistic mastery that she achieved and applied during these decades. Working with nail scissors, black paper, and thin sheets of metal, Lotte Reiniger multiplied two-dimensional silhouettes on a set of flat glass screens into a complex and wondrous film world. Throughout her career, she was able to apply her artistic delicacy to produce a magical flexibility in her characters. Writes Jean Renoir: "Artistically, I have to see her as a visual expression of Mozart's music."

SOURCES:

Acker, Ally. *Reel Women: Pioneers of the Cinema 1896 to the Present.* NY: Continuum, 1991.

The Annual Obituary, 1981. Edited by Janet Pudell. NY: St. Martin's Press, 1981.

Foster, Gwendolyn Audrey. *Women Film Directors: An International Bio-critical Dictionary.* Westport, CT: Greenwood Press, 1995.

Katz, Ephraim. *The Film Encyclopedia.* 2nd ed. NY: HarperCollins, 1994.

Russett, Robert, and Cecile Starr. *Experimental Animation: An Illustrated Anthology.* NY: Van Nostrand Reinhold, 1976.

White, Eric Walter. *Walking Shadows: An Essay on Lotte Reiniger's Silhouette Films.* London: Hogarth Press, 1931.

SUGGESTED READING:

Halas, John. *Masters of Animation.* Topsfield, MA: Salem House, 1987.

Reiniger, Lotte. *Shadow Theatres and Shadow Films.* London: B.T. Batsford, 1970.

White, Eric Walter. *The Little Chimney Sweep (after the Silhouette Film by Lotte Reiniger).* Bristol, Eng.: White and White, 1936.

Neil M. Heyman,
Professor of History, San Diego State University,
San Diego, California

Reischauer, Haru (c. 1915–1998)

Japanese-born American journalist. Name variations: Haru Matsukata. Born Haru Matsukata in Japan around 1915; died in La Jolla, California, on September 23, 1998; granddaughter of Prince Masayoshi Matsukata, former prime minister of Japan; attended the American School in Japan; graduated from Principia College, Illinois, 1937; married Edwin O. Reischauer (a scholar and diplomat), in 1956; children: (stepchildren) Robert, Ann, and Joan.

Cited as second most popular woman in Japan by Christian Science Monitor *(1962); published* Samurai and Silk: A Japanese and American Heritage *(1986); became honorary chair of Harvard's policy advisory committee of the U.S.-Japan relations program (1990).*

Haru Reischauer was born Haru Matsukata in Japan around 1915, to a father who was a Yale graduate and son of Prince Masayoshi Matsukata, prime minister of Japan in the late 19th century, and an American-born mother whose father Rioichiro Arai had moved to the U.S. in the 1870s to begin the direct trading of Japanese silk there. Haru was cared for by English governesses in her childhood before attending the American School in Japan. She later enrolled in Principia College in Illinois, spending her summers with her maternal grandparents at their home in Connecticut before her graduation in 1937.

Haru was working as a journalist in Tokyo in 1956, when she met Edwin O. Reischauer, a widely respected scholar of Japanese history and politics and a faculty member at Harvard who had recently been widowed. They were married that year, and made their home in Belmont, Massachusetts, raising Edwin's three young children from his first marriage to **Adrienne Reischauer**, who died in 1955. Edwin continued teaching at Harvard and Haru reported on Japan for the *Saturday Evening Post* and the *Christian Science Monitor.* In 1961, Edwin was named ambassador to Japan by President John F. Kennedy, whom he had taught at Harvard. With deep personal knowledge of the country and the language, the Reischauers were popular with both the government and the populace in Japan. According to *The Boston Globe,* Haru saw her diplomatic role of ambassador's wife as "associating with Japanese women, bridging the gap between the countries, and talking with the wives of American servicemen who were stationed in Japan." She also actively participated in as many as 14 women's groups at one time. Her term as ambassador's wife was so successful that in 1962 the *Christian Science Monitor* named her the second most popular woman in Japan (the most popular was Crown Princess *Michiko).

Edwin Reischauer resigned as ambassador in 1966, and the couple returned to their careers in

Massachusetts. He consulted for the government on Japan and rose higher in academia, in 1973 establishing Harvard's Japan Institute, of which he was appointed director the following year; the institute was later renamed the Edwin O. Reischauer Institute of Japanese Studies. Haru published a well-regarded memoir, *Samurai and Silk: A Japanese and American Heritage*, in 1986. She moved with her husband to California in 1990, where he died that September. Haru Reischauer served as the honorary chair of the policy advisory committee on U.S.-Japan relations at Harvard from 1990, and as the honorary chair of the Center for East Asian Studies at Johns Hopkins University's School of Advanced International Studies from 1993. She held both positions until her death at the age of 83, on September 23, 1998, in La Jolla, California.

SOURCES:

The Day [New London, CT]. October 2, 1998.

Deptula, Nancy Monteith and Michael M. Hess. *The Edwin O. Reischauer Institute for Japanese Studies: A Twenty-Year Chronicle.* Cambridge, MA: Reischauer Institute, Harvard University, 1996.

Kari Bethel,
freelance writer, Columbia, Missouri

Reisenberg, Clara (1910–1998).

See Rockmore, Clara.

Reisenberg, Nadia (1904–1983)

Lithuanian-American pianist who had a long career teaching at the Mannes College of Music, the Juilliard School, Queens College, and the Rubin Academy in Jerusalem. Born Nina Reisenberg in Vilna (now Vilnius), Russian Lithuania, on July 14, 1904; died in New York City on June 10, 1983; sister of Clara Rockmore (1910–1998); children: Robert Sherman (a pianist).

Nadia Reisenberg was born Vilna (now Vilnius), Russian Lithuania, in 1904. She studied with Leonid Nicolaiev (1878–1942), who also taught Dmitri Shostakovich and *Maria Yudina, at the St. Petersburg Conservatory. In 1922, she immigrated with her family, including her sister *Clara Rockmore, to New York as a refugee from Soviet Russia. At her New York debut at the Aeolian Hall in 1924, Reisenberg played Paderewski's *Polish Fantasy* with the composer himself in the audience. Her talent attracted not only Paderewski but noted piano virtuosos like Josef Hofmann and the leading conductors of the day. She was a musicianly pianist who recorded several neglected works, including Tchaikovsky's Piano Sonata and Paderewski's *Polish Fantasy*. Her son, Robert

Sherman, was a gifted pianist who sometimes played duos with his mother in concert but eventually left performing behind to become executive producer of New York's classical music radio station WQXR. Reisenberg had a long career as a teacher at the Mannes College of Music, the Juilliard School, Queens College of the City University of New York, and the Rubin Academy in Jerusalem. Her distinguished students included Richard Goode and the conductor Myung-Whun Chung. She died in New York City on June 10, 1983. There is an extensive Nadia Reisenberg collection at the International Piano Archives at the University of Maryland. In September 1989, her former students and admirers paid tribute to her memory in New York in a program entitled "Nadia Reisenberg—A Joyful Remembrance."

SOURCES:

Dubal, David. *The Art of the Piano.* NY: Summit Books, 1989.

"Music," in *The New Yorker.* Vol. 65, no. 33. October 2, 1989, p. 24.

Schonberg, Harold C. *The Great Pianists.* Rev. ed. NY: Simon & Schuster, 1987.

John Haag,
Athens, Georgia

Reisner, Larissa (1895–1926)

Russian poet, journalist, revolutionary, and diplomat of the pre-Stalinist Soviet Union who symbolized the heroic idealism of the early Bolsheviks. Pronunciation: La-RISS-a RICE-ner. Born Larissa Mikhailovna Reisner near Vilnius, Lithuania, on May 1, 1895; died of typhus on February 9, 1926, in Moscow; daughter of Mikhail Andreevich Reisner (an aristocrat, lawyer, and socialist of German descent) and Ekaterina Alexandrovna Khitrova (an aristocrat with socialist leanings); attended St. Petersburg University; married Fyodor Raskolnikov, in 1918 (divorced 1924); children: one adopted son.

Fled with family to Germany at age eight because of father's political activities (1903); returned to Russia to live in St. Petersburg (1907); following overthrow of Tsar Nicholas II, became involved in the government under the Bolsheviks (1917); married Raskolnikov (1918); during Civil War, ran espionage operation with Raskolnikov, commanding members of the Russian navy; wrote of her exploits in Letters from the Front; *traveled with Raskolnikov as representatives of the Soviet Republic to Afghanistan, where they carried out diplomatic negotiations (1921); returned to Moscow (1923); went to Germany, became involved with the Polish Communist Karl Radek, and wrote journalistic accounts of life in the Weimar Republic (1923), later compiled as* Hamburg at the Barricades; *returned to Russia, and wrote about mining conditions in the Urals (1924).*

Selected works: Letters from the Front *(1920);* Hamburg at the Barricades and Other Writings on Weimar Germany *(London: Pluto Press, 1977).*

Along the deep Volga River that flows south and east across Russia toward the Caspian Sea, sailors aboard one of the ships in the Volga Flotilla stood at uneasy attention. They were undergoing formal inspection by their new commander, who moved along the line with a beautiful woman at his side. The year was 1918, Tsar Nicholas II had been overthrown, and the Bolsheviks were struggling to keep control against the White Russian forces that had moved their ships along the rivers of the vast Russian steppes, laying waste to towns and villages. Among this crew, there were men more ready to fight to the death for the Bolshevik cause than to have a woman on board, for a common sailors' superstition held that a woman brought bad luck to a ship.

Larissa Reisner

For some time after the newly arrived Deputy Commissar for Naval Affairs, Fyodor Raskolnikov, took charge of naval operations, the worst fears of the sailors seemed to be confirmed. Things continued to go badly for the Soviets. Raskolnikov's wife, Larissa Reisner, was offically there only as a journalist, but when the time came that documents needed to be delivered to other Red forces across rough, dangerous terrain, she became a dedicated volunteer. She took charge of the reconnaissance operations and trained some of the sailors in horseback riding and spying on the White Russians. Over the course of two years, her group became expert riders and scouts, dedicated to the tough-minded disciplinarian who led them on her horse named Beauty, a woman who became a legend and a symbol of hope for the fledgling Soviet Union.

Larissa Reisner was born near Vilnius, Lithuania, on May 1, 1895, the daughter of a wealthy and cultured family of landowners of German descent. Her father Mikhail Andreevich had studied law at St. Petersburg University, and by the time he had completed his doctoral thesis in constitutional law he was a declared Marxist. Her mother **Ekaterina Alexandrovna Khitrova** belonged to one of the oldest and noblest families of the region of West Galicia, but had also been swept up in the socialist movement, defying her parents to attend the meetings where she first met and fell in love with Mikhail Andreevich. In January 1899, Larissa's only brother Igor was born.

Reisner's parents, like many members of the Russian intelligentsia and aristocracy of the time, freely discussed their revolutionary leanings. Guests would be invited to gather around a table laden with food, holding saucers of silver under their tea glasses as they spoke of their deep faith in socialism. The earliest high-ranking opposition to autocratic rule had been a revolt against Tsar Nicholas I in December 1825. The failed coup was carried out by a group of army officers, largely from the nobility, who were known as the Decembrists. Their suffering while in Siberian exile (along with their wives, including *Maria Volkonskaya) would inspire later generations of revolutionaries, including the radical group led by *Sonia Perovskaya which assassinated Tsar Alexander II in 1881.

In Reisner's early years, Russia was an imperial empire rotting from within, but the final collapse would not come until the years of World War I. Meanwhile, the turmoil stirred by its slow demise moved her parents farther to the political left, and also forced them out of their previously sheltered existence. Larissa was two years old when the family moved to Tomsk, where her father had been posted as a professor of law at the first university in Asiatic Russia. Tomsk was a dumping ground for political exiles, and therefore a center of political ferment, in both the university and the local factories. When peasants rioted, estates were looted, officials were assassinated, and campuses were convulsed, people like Professor Reisner, who joined the newly formed Socialist Revolutionary Party, were held accountable. He was expelled from the university in 1903, when Larissa was eight, and the family fled to Germany. With all connections to their families severed, her parents settled into a shabby apartment in Berlin, without the servants or beautiful surroundings enjoyed in the past. Sometimes even food was scarce. Larissa went to school in the working-class district of Zehlendorf, for which she would retain a lasting affection, and was soon fluent in idiomatic German.

Russia's first modern revolution, known as Bloody Sunday, occurred in 1905, when hundreds of workers in St. Petersburg were fired on and killed by government troops for attempting to petition the tsar for a constitution. Reisner's father joined the Bolsheviks, the radical arm of the Social Democratic Party, and the only group showing leadership at the time. By 1907, he was back in Russia as an assistant professor of law at St. Petersburg University. The family rented a modest flat at 25 Bolshaya Zelenina and resumed their lives as members of the cultured elite, enjoying the opera, theater, and ballet, and taking holidays on the Black Sea. Larissa and Igor took riding, skating, and skiing lessons.

After receiving a gold medal for her final school examination at age 17, Reisner longed to attend university. Although women in Russia were officially banned from higher education, attitudes were changing, and through her parents' contacts she eventually became one of the first women to gain admittance to St. Petersburg University. When the tall, elegant young woman entered the lecture halls wearing a well-cut gray English suit with white blouse and man's tie, she made a striking impression, evoking whistles and catcalls. Reisner's frequently noted beauty may have enhanced the confidence she often projected, especially among men of authority. Vsevolod Rozhdestvensky, a poet who later became well known, often led these boisterous, demeaning demonstrations. One day she strode up to him, gave him a mocking smile, stretched out her hand and asked about his poems. The two became close friends. According to one poet's description of her:

When she walked along the street, she seemed to bear her beauty like a torch, and even the coarsest objects gained from her presence a new tenderness and gentleness. . . . Not one man passed her without observing her—and according to the author's own statistical observation, every third would stand rooted to the spot watching her as we passed into the crowd.

In the face of male arrogance, Reisner was also capable of a little mockery. At the end of a sociology lecture salted with incomprehensible jargon, when the pompous young professor sought "the opinion of Larissa Mikhailovna," she replied that the lecture had "shone with rare scholarship" but "omitted to mention the work of Stoll and Schmidt on demographic complexes." Taken aback, the professor countered that he was familiar with this work but found it of little value, much to the amusement of those in the classroom who recognized "Stoll & Schmidt" as the name of well-known pharmaceutical manufacturers.

In depths of legend, heroine, you'll walk,

Along that path your steps will not fade.

—Boris Pasternak, "In Memory of Reisner"

Reisner regarded herself as a poet and writer, and spent a good deal of time discussing literature with a wide circle of friends at the Stray Dog Café, the fashionable meeting place for St. Petersburg's bohemian elite. In 1913, she saw the publication of her long poem, *Atlantida*, and articles on the heroines of Shakespeare. She also became chief editor of *Rudin*, a literary magazine that published the works of newcomers as well as established poets like Boris Sadovskoi, Vladimir Zlobin, and Osip Mandelstam. As editor, she also battled with government censors and struggled financially to keep the magazine in print.

Imperial rule came to an end with the overthrow of Tsar Nicholas II in March 1917. Reisner followed many of her contemporaries in joining the Bolshevik Party, and became involved in a literacy program; illiteracy was rampant in Russia, and some 88% of all women were unable to read. Around this time she met Fyodor Raskolnikov, who had lived in exile, endured prison, and sailed as a naval conscript to Japan, Korea, and the island of Kamchatka. For Reisner, Raskolnikov was the model Bolshevik—a fighter and a self-educated man from a poor background, with a passion for literature and proletarian culture. They were married in the summer of 1918.

Russia, meanwhile, continued in turmoil. On July 3, 1917, 20,000 sailors marched in St. Petersburg in favor of the Bolsheviks taking power. When the demonstration failed, many, including Raskolnikov, were arrested. Alexander Kerensky was soon made prime minister, but his government was weak, and in October the Red Guard took to the streets, joined by women, soldiers and sailors. This time the Bolsheviks were carried into power, and treaty negotiations began to end the war Russia had been fighting against Germany along the western front. On March 16, 1918, the Treaty of Brest-Litovsk was signed, but in May, Japanese troops landed at Vladivostok, and Czech troops in Russia revolted. Loyalties now became divided between the Red Bolsheviks and the White Guard, which, financed by France, Britain, and the United States, carried out a wave of uprisings that led to the occupation of vast areas of the former imperial Russia.

Reisner and her husband rallied against the Whites, and Raskolnikov's ties to the navy led to his appointment as Deputy Commissar for Naval Affairs. Czech forces had captured the central Volga town of Samara, but the broad rivers of Russia allowed the Soviet navy to penetrate deep into the country to recapture the lost territory. It was over the next two years that Reisner carried out her dangerous surveillance work, routinely slipping behind enemy lines on foot or horseback, sometimes accompanied by a handful of men she had trained from one of the ships. Caught once behind enemy lines, she was severely beaten before she escaped.

In 1920, the combat ended, and Reisner returned with Raskolnikov to the city of St. Petersburg, now renamed Petrograd, where they settled into rooms in the old Admiralty Building and renewed contacts with family and friends. A writer first and foremost, Reisner plunged back into literary and political life, writing the hugely popular *Letters from the Front*. The book gave full credit to the men who had fought bravely beside her, but also made clear that Russian women could fight as effectively as men.

In March 1921, Reisner and Raskolnikov went sent by the Commissariat of Foreign Affairs on a diplomatic mission to Afghanistan. This remote mountainous country, ruled by a Muslim emir, was still an essentially feudal society, but of enormous strategic importance to the Bolsheviks. In 1919, the new emir Amanullah Khan had declared independence from Britain, which regarded Afghanistan as strategically important for its continued control of its empire in India. When the British bombed the Afghan cities of Kabul and Jalalabad, the Afghanis had turned to Russia for help, and the Bolsheviks thus regarded Afghanistan as critical to their prestige in Central Asia. Raskolnikov arrived in Kabul as the first full ambassador of Soviet Russia, charged, along with Reisner, with the sensitive task of binding Afghanistan closer to Russia.

Reisner's stature was important in creating close ties with the Afghanis. Apart from organizing teas for diplomats' wives, she played tennis with the emir, tended the embassy's goats, spent time riding a beautiful Afghan stallion named Falcon, and learned to speak some Farsi. She loved this isolated land, which she described thus: "By day, spring is merciful—its blue sky is filled with flowering apple trees, old men sing at the edge of fields thick with narcissi, and women standing amongst the velvety winter crops throw back their *chadris* and smile." She learned the ways of the harem, where the country's most influential women lived, attending their banquets and festivities as a regular guest and learning to dance and play the drums. The emir's mother, the Ulya **Hazrat**, developed such an attachment to Reisner that she promised she would not receive the "evil British ladies." As Soviet influence increased, the British felt threatened, and the governments were alternately engaged in intense negotiations and intermittent threats of war.

Living in luxury, Reisner was troubled by the dire poverty and difficult lives of ordinary Afghanis, especially the women. Her marriage was also under great strain. Although there were pleasures in the diplomatic life, she and Fyodor had been happiest together in the tumult of war and revolution. In May 1923, Reisner left Afghanistan and returned to a very different Soviet Union. Bolshevik rule had brought the economy to its knees, shortages were rampant, and strikes were happening everywhere. Desperate to spark the economy, V.I. Lenin had instituted the New Economic Policy (NEP), which allowed some capitalistic enterprise, but the improvements were resented by dyed-in-the-wool Communists. Reisner avoided ideological issues and pursued her literary and party work. Seeing her marriage as over, she asked the Comintern, which supervised Communist activities outside the Soviet Union, to send her to Germany.

In Berlin, Reisner met Karl Radek, secretary of the executive committee of the Comintern, who was internationally known in Marxist circles for his radicalism, brilliant journalism and scandalous life. Although Radek was married and had a child, he and Reisner became romantically involved. She lived in Berlin and Hamburg in the

German working-class districts she had loved as a child, writing columns for Soviet newspapers that were later compiled in the book *Hamburg at the Barricades*. Reisner's style has sometimes been criticized as overly poetic and flowery, but she could also be deadly accurate in her descriptions of the terrible suffering in Germany. The aftermath of World War I was dreadful for ordinary Germans, in part because of the heavy reparations forced on the country by the Allies and in part due to the worldwide Great Depression.

Reisner returned to Russia in January 1924, shortly before the death of Lenin. Her divorce soon became final, but Radek had fallen from favor in the Communist Party and their relationship had begun to deteriorate. Reisner's writings, describing the scope of the Communist revolution on a human scale, were receiving great acclaim, and she had never been more popular. Before long, she traveled to the Ural Mountains, where she wrote about the difficult lives of the miners, reporting bluntly that Communism had not yet wiped out all hunger and suffering. She also adopted a 12-year-old boy whom she had found starving; he became a permanent member of the Reisner family.

Earlier in life, Reisner had contracted malaria, and she was plagued with recurring bouts of the illness. Back in Moscow in the winter of 1926, she fell sick with typhus, probably from drinking unpasteurized milk, and was admitted to the Kremlin Hospital. The typhus receded, but her body had been severely weakened by malaria. She spent her last days barely conscious, and died on February 9, 1926, a few months short of her 31st birthday. Fifty obituary columns marked her passing, and many people came to mourn during the two days her body lay in state at the House of the Press.

In retrospect, Reisner's death coincides with the end of the Bolshevik Revolution. Once Joseph Stalin grasped the reins of power in the Kremlin, Lenin was quickly reduced to a powerless icon in Red Square, and the lofty ideals of the early Bolsheviks were slowly but surely extinguished. The new, efficient bureaucracy and the threat of the secret police made Stalinism the Soviet Union's only creed, and most of the early Bolshevik revolutionaries and independent thinkers—particularly those of aristocratic background—were ultimately exterminated, as were millions of ordinary Russians. Many such people were friends of Larissa Reisner, and had she lived she no doubt would have suffered the same fate. Since the collapse of Communism, it is worthwhile to remember that there were many who fought for the creation of the Soviet Union, Larissa Reisner among them, whose aspirations for humankind were much higher than Stalin's.

SOURCES:

Crankshaw, Edward. *The Shadow of the Winter Palace: Russia's Drift to Revolution, 1825–1917*. NY: Viking, 1976.

Ehrenburg, Ilya. *First Years of the Revolution, 1918–21*. Translated by A. Bostock and Y. Kapp. London: Macgibbon Kee, 1962.

Lerner, Warren. *Karl Radek: The Last Internationalist*. Stanford, CA: Stanford University Press, 1970.

Marcus, Greil. "Behind the Barricades," in *Rolling Stone*. No. 246. August 25, 1977, p. 63.

Porter, Cathy. *Larissa Reisner*. London: Virago Press, 1988.

Reisner, Larissa. *Hamburg at the Barricades and Other Writings on Weimar Germany*. Richard Chappell, ed. London: Pluto Press, 1977.

Sack, A.J. *The Birth of Russian Democracy*. NY: Russian Information Bureau, 1918.

Venturi, Franco. *Roots of Revolution: A History of the Populist and Socialist Movements in Nineteenth Century Russia*. NY: Grosset and Dunlap, 1960.

Karin Loewen Haag,
freelance writer, Athens, Georgia

Reitsch, Hanna (1912–1979)

German flier and test pilot, now recognized as one of the foremost aviators of the 20th century, who was imprisoned as a Nazi sympathizer after World War II, although her name was later cleared. Born Hanna Reitsch on March 29, 1912, in the village of Hirschberg, in German Silesia; died on August 24, 1979, of a heart attack, in Frankfurt, Germany; daughter of Dr. Willy Reitsch (an eye specialist) and Emy Reitsch (a member of the Austrian aristocracy); graduated from high school and briefly attended medical school; never married; no children.

Broke first world record for gliding (1931); gave up medical school for job with Germany's top research establishment for motorless flight; joined Ernst Udet's elite band of military test pilots (1937); promoted to rank of *Flugkapitän*; flew the FW 61, the world's first viable helicopter (1937); first woman to be awarded the Iron Cross on two occasions (1940, 1942); was one of the last to visit Hitler in his bunker (April 1945); imprisoned after World War II as a Nazi sympathizer; name cleared after two years; authored numerous books; sent to India where she became friends with Jawaharlal Nehru, premier of India, and his daughter Indira Gandhi (1959); at request of President Kwame Nkrumah, founded a gliding school in Ghana (1961).

Selected writings: Fliegen mein Leben (*Flying My Life, 1951*); The Sky My Kingdom (*London: Greenhill Books, 1991*).

On April 26, 1945, World War II was near its end. The Soviet Army occupied part of Berlin, and its anti-aircraft weapons were trained on the skies, when a small German plane carrying a German officer and Hanna Reitsch made its approach to the city. After a burst of gunfire, the officer flying the plane, a general in the Luftwaffe, slumped at the controls. As fuel began to pour out of a wing tank, Reitsch, a flier of worldwide renown, took over the controls and soon managed to land the little Fiesler Storch on a deserted stretch of highway amid the ruins of Berlin, not far from the Brandenburg Gate. The general, almost unconscious, was lifted into a German transport, which conveyed him and Reitsch through the Brandenburg Gate, along Unter den Linden and Wilhelmstrasse, and into Voss-Strasse. Their destination was the bunker of Adolf Hitler, and the officer, General Ritter von Greim, was there to be appointed the new head of the Luftwaffe.

Inside the huge underground structure with its many tunnels, the fliers were greeted by Hitler, his mistress *Eva Braun, and Joseph and *Magda Goebbels and their children. The bunker housed many other occupants as well, most of whom recognized that the end was near. In the next two days, Reitsch spoke with Hitler and recognized that his health was shattered, talked with Magda Goebbels, and played with the Goebbels children. When General von Greim was recovered, the two pilots departed. Many they saw during that visit, including Hitler and the Goebbels children, would die, by their own hand or poisoned by others, without leaving the bunker's walls. Reitsch, one of the foremost aviators of the century as well as of her country, thus witnessed the Third Reich in its final death throes, an experience she would never fully escape.

Hanna Reitsch was born on March 29, 1912, in the picturesque town of Hirschberg, in the German region of Silesia. She was the middle of three children, including an older brother Kurt and a younger sister **Heidi**. Her father Dr. Willy Reitsch was an eye specialist, a quiet brooding man who espoused the Prussian concepts of honor and duty; her mother **Emy Reitsch** was the daughter of an Austrian aristocrat. Her parents merged two separate German cultures: Willy Reitsch was a Protestant, representing the stern disciplined North German tradition, and the Catholic Emy represented the long heritage of German-speaking Central Europe. Both were deeply religious and intensely patriotic, and their love of things German transcended all else, encouraging the devotion to duty and the patriotism that were to mark Hanna Reitsch's life.

Hirschberg stood surrounded by snow-capped mountains, with Austria to the south and Russia to the east, its past symbolic of the intricacies of German history. Six centuries earlier, Silesia had been under Polish rule before it came under German and Austrian domination. After World War I, Czechoslovakia had been created to the south and Poland to the east. Shifting political boundaries and the mixed racial heritage made it virtually impossible to determine the population's true culture, but German had long been the dominant language in Central Europe. In the late 19th and early 20th centuries, the rise of nationalism led some groups to insist on speaking their native languages and demanding political independence. The determination to structure government solely on the basis of racial identities would wreak havoc, a process which continues to this day. National and racial identity became especially lethal after Adolf Hitler and his Nazi party determined that "racial purity" should be a central concept in the restructuring of a modern Germany.

As a child Hanna Reitsch was largely unaware of these larger currents swirling around her. Dr. Reitsch was a much-respected member of the Hirschberg community, Emy Reitsch was greatly loved for her charitable works, and the family lived a frugal, peaceful life. One family tradition was to go to bed very early on Saturday night, awaken around 1 AM on Sunday, and take a tram through the valley to the foot of the mountains and begin a three-hour climb, in order to reach the summit just at the break of dawn. There the family held their own religious service, then stayed until lunch. The parents' mixed religious background did not prevent grace from being said before every meal, and God was ever present in the household.

Hanna was a small but self-confident and rambunctious child who loved adventure and recounting what had befallen her. Life for her was never dull, and she adored being the center of attention. Approaching the end of her school career, she extracted a promise from her father that if she did well in her studies he would allow her to take a course at the gliding school in Grunau. Reitsch's parents had their hearts set on their daughter attending medical school, and had no idea how obsessed she was with flying. She obediently gained admittance to medical school with ease, but before her training began, Reitsch spent a year in a Koloschule, which had been established to prepare young ladies for life and work in Germany's colonies. Although Germany no longer had colonies, her parents felt Hanna

Hanna
Reitsch

needed the training she could get there in practical skills such as cooking, cleaning and farm work. Reitsch was happy at the Koloschule and made many lifelong friends. During that year her father kept his promise; he allowed her to take gliding lessons.

After World War I, gliding had developed in Germany as a peculiarly national sport. The Versailles Treaty had banned Germany from establishing an army or an air force, and the gliding schools became a way of circumventing the treaty to train the country's future pilots. Wolf

Hirth was a famous aviator and director of a school, and when Hanna proved to be a natural pilot she became his star pupil and protégé. As a mark of trust, Hirth allowed her to fly a new glider normally reserved for instructors, with permission to stay aloft for as long as she liked. When she landed after a flight of five-and-a-half hours, she had broken a world record for staying airborne in a glider, the first of many records she would topple in her long career.

As a pilot, Reitsch was fearless. Once, while flying near a thunderstorm, she was suddenly sucked upwards, higher and higher, until the earth below was blotted out. Worried at first about crashing against the 5,200-foot Schneekoppe, the highest peak in the Risesengebirge range, she eventually realized that she was well above it. Reitsch was not warmly dressed, and the air grew colder and colder. Then the glider began to be thrown about violently amid a storm of hail and rain. She had reached 9,500 feet, well above normal altitude for gliding, when her glider began to ice and went into a steep dive. The plunge was interrupted by a series of involuntary loops when the young pilot, rain-soaked and freezing, let go of the controls in hopes that the glider would stabilize. She landed finally in front of an inn on a high mountain ridge, at an altitude of 4,500 feet. Hirth learned of her location with relief.

I had only one desire—to fly as a bird flies, unfettered and wholly free.

—Hanna Reitsch

Reitsch enrolled in medical school where she performed well, but her heart was still in the clouds, and her appetite for adventure had merely been whetted. She began to enter and win gliding competitions, paying her way to one in South America by acting as a double in a film called *Rivalen der Luft,* in which the heroine flew a glider. In South America, she met more pilots and, as always, was the only woman. Back in Germany, she was invited to work for the Deutsche Forschungsanstalt für Segelflug (DFS), Germany's top research establishment for motorless flight. Discovering that she could earn money doing what she loved most in life, she abandoned all thoughts of medical school to join the elite group of German glider pilots.

In 1933, the world of flying in Germany underwent a dramatic change once Hitler became chancellor. He appointed Hermann Goering as his air minister, and in 1935 the Luftwaffe officially came into being. Suddenly, after years of amateur competition and testing, pilots like Reitsch occupied a central place in the plans of the Third Reich. Few except Hitler knew that his generals were devising new military concepts which relied heavily on tank and air warfare.

In later years, the term most frequently used to describe Reitsch was "naive," but her political attitudes mirrored those of millions of Germans. After World War I, their country had been plunged into economic chaos and inflation, due in part to the huge reparations the country was forced to pay the Allies. The worldwide onset of the Great Depression had made matters worse for millions, and in Germany many became disillusioned with democracy. When Hitler first came to power, he was elected chiefly as an economic reformer, with a vision for Germany that seemed the way out of chaos; in the beginning, his plans to achieve "racial purity" were played down. In Germany and in much of the world, he was seen as a leader who stabilized a dangerous political situation, and an infinitely better political alternative than the Communists who had overrun the Russian Empire. Reitsch's view of Nazism was shared not only by most Germans at this time, but by most Americans, Britons, and the French as well.

At the testing center in Darmstadt, Reitsch meanwhile gained renown as one of the world's best pilots. Moving easily from gliders to powered flight, she tested all the newest planes, including the Stuka (not an easy plane for someone her size to manage) and the Dornier bomber, which she piloted with ease. In September 1937, she was paid the singular honor of being invited to join Ernst Udet's elite band of military test pilots at Rechlin near Berlin, and was promoted to the rank of Flugkapitän, a high achievement for anyone, male or female. Despite the military nature of her work, Reitsch was never actually a member of the German military. Her unique status was due partly to her immense talent and partly to the fact that she was a good instrument for propaganda. Photographs of the petite blue-eyed blonde appeared everywhere. In 1937, few people had flown the FW 61, the world's first viable helicopter, when Reitsch, as one of the world's best test pilots, was asked to take it up for a trial run.

Germany changed greatly between 1933 and 1938, as the Nazis tightened their grip on the country. German leftists, as well as other dissidents and undesirables, were sent to concentration camps. From 1933 to 1945, an estimated quarter of a million Germans were incarcerated every year in the Third Reich, and many died in prison. Dissent was not tolerated, even among the "racially pure," and anti-Semitism was on the rise. In November 1938, an event known as Kristallnacht, or the Night of the Broken Glass, foreshadowed the Holocaust, when Nazi thugs burned synagogues, destroyed Jewish property, and otherwise brutalized and humiliated Jews. Reitsch, who had Jewish friends, was horrified, and protested to Goebbels, who explained that "things had simply gotten out of hand." Her opposition was noted and disapproved of in many quarters.

Reitsch was an optimist by nature, and flying was her love. Allowing herself to accept Goebbels' version of events, she returned to the clouds. In 1939, with World War II under way, test flights grew more dangerous, as a variety of harebrained inventions were devised for use by the Luftwaffe. She flew huge troop planes, a rocket plane, and planes designed to cut cables. In 1940, after managing a miraculous escape from a crash in a Dornier plane, she became the first woman ever to be awarded Germany's Iron Cross, Second Class, and met Hitler, who showed admiration for her exploits. In October 1942, she crashed again, when the controls jammed in an unpowered Me 163B. This time her recovery took months, and letters, cards, and gifts poured into her hospital room, including some from highly placed Nazis like Heinrich Himmler. She was also awarded a second Iron Cross.

As the war continued, the German Army bogged down, Hitler became more desperate, and so did Nazi schemes. Back in the cockpit, Reitsch carried out whatever tests were devised, no matter how crackbrained. As rumors began to circulate about Jewish extermination camps, Reitsch attempted to get to the source of the stories, and heard from individuals in the highest circles that the stories were Allied propaganda. In light of the widely circulated tales of German cruelty during World War I that later proved to be unfounded, the lie seemed credible, and Reitsch returned to work, her fears lulled.

By late 1944, Germany was surrounded by Allied troops, and the end of the war was in sight. In April 1945, Reitsch agreed to accompany Ritter von Greim, a friend and valued colleague, on the dangerous trip to Hitler's bunker. The appointment of von Greim as head of the Luftwaffe was a ridiculous gesture since the Allies had already annihilated the German air force, and in der Führer's presence Reitsch realized that Hitler was physically ill and mentally unbalanced. During her stay, Hitler gave her a poison capsule in case she might need it. Leaving Berlin proved as difficult as entering, and Reitsch and von Greim were eventually captured by Allied forces. Von Greim later committed suicide.

Imprisoned for 18 months, Reitsch found her short sojourn in the bunker the subject of public attention. No one was certain that Hitler was actually dead, but her account convinced many that he could not have survived. Interrogated many times by the Americans, she gave a consistently straightforward account. Never a Nazi party member, she viewed herself not as a political figure but as someone who had loyally served her country. At the end of her imprisonment, her name was cleared, but her association with the bunker continued to make good copy. The British historian Hugh Trevor-Roper (who was to be deceived himself in the 1980s by the faked "Hitler diaries") gave her account a garbled treatment that implied she'd had an intimate relationship with Hitler, and her two Iron Crosses, as well as her trip to the bunker, seemed to lend credence to his story. Accounts in the media talked of "Hitler's girlfriend," implying an association which never existed.

Germany, meanwhile, was in a shambles. Depressed and disillusioned, Reitsch managed to hold on, even after learning that her parents, sister, and sister's children were all dead, poisoned by her father who feared what the Soviets might do to his family. Only her older brother Kurt remained alive. Reitsch had been especially close to her mother, and eventually found comfort in her loss by converting to Catholicism, her mother's faith. She made friends with a variety of people, including **Yvonne Pagniez**, a former member of the French resistance, and wrote a book, *Fliegen mein Leben* (Flying My Life), published in 1951.

Gradually Reitsch returned to what she loved best—flying—and her renown led to new friendships around the world. In India, she became close with Prime Minister Jawaharlal Nehru and his daughter *Indira Gandhi. In the U.S., she was a friend of Neil Armstrong, and she enjoyed a visit to the White House as the guest of President John F. Kennedy.

In 1961, when she was approaching 50, President Kwame Nkrumah of Ghana asked Reitsch to found a gliding school in his country. Ghanaian glider pilots had few technological skills, but Reitsch threw herself into the venture, planning the school, importing teachers, and training many pilots. She loved the country and its people, and became a good friend of Nkrumah's. Again, however, she had ignored his dictatorial tendencies, and his ouster came as a shock to her, reinforcing the view that her political instincts were always much weaker than her aeronautical skills.

In the 1960s, Reitsch was a true aviation celebrity, recognized as a grand old lady of the air. She was a founding member of the German Association of Women Pilots and of the 99s, an international women pilots' organization established in the U.S. in 1929. She was interviewed for documentaries, wrote several books, and was recognized especially for her expertise in the pioneering aviation of helicopters. Her schedule remained hectic until August 24, 1979, when she died of a heart attack in her Frankfurt apartment. While some obituaries brought up the old accusations, others emphasized the many records she had broken and the frontiers of flight she crossed.

If Hanna Reitsch had a fault, it may have been that she loved flying too much, enough to allow it to obscure everything else. In the clouds, Reitsch left politics behind, always assuming that the world shared her perspective. She was buried in Salzburg, where her grave is a shrine for Austrian and German glider pilots. There are always lighted candles and fresh flowers by the rugged headstone that bears her name. Reitsch did not fly for political kingdoms whose objectives she never grasped; her kingdom was the air, where the fearless fly free.

SOURCES:

Cook, Joan. "Hanna Reitsch, 67; A Top German Pilot," in *The New York Times.* August 31, 1979, p. B5.

"Final Flight," in *Flying.* Vol. 105, no. 6. December 1979, p. 19.

Fritzsche, Peter. *A Nation of Fliers: German Aviation and the Popular Imagination.* Cambridge, MA: Harvard University Press, 1992.

Habel, Walter, ed. *Wer ist wer? The German Who's Who.* Lübeck: Schmidt Römhild, 1979, p. 957.

Hayman, LeRoy. *Aces, Heroes and Daredevils of the Air.* NY: Julian Messner, 1981.

Lomax, Judy. *Hanna Reitsch: Flying for the Fatherland.* London: John Murray, 1988.

Piszkiewicz, Dennis. *From Nazi Test Pilot to Hitler's Bunker: The Fantastic Flights of Hanna Reitsch.* NY: Praeger, 1997.

Reitsch, Hanna. *The Sky My Kingdom.* Translated by Lawrence Wilson. London: Greenhill Books, 1991.

Shears, David. "Iron Cross Heroine Reitsch Dies," in *Daily Telegraph* [London]. August 30, 1979, p. 15.

Taylor, James and Warren Shaw. *The Third Reich Almanac.* NY: World Almanac, 1987.

Wistrich, Robert S. *Who's Who in Nazi Germany.* NY: Macmillan, 1982.

John Haag,
Associate Professor of History,
University of Georgia, Athens, Georgia

Gabrielle Réjane

Réjane, Gabrielle (1857–1920)

French actress. Name variations: Gabrielle Rejane; Gabrielle Charlotte Reju. Born Gabrielle-Charlotte Réju in Paris, France, in 1857 (some sources cite 1856); died in 1920; studied at the Conservatoire, Paris; married M. Porel (a theater director), in 1902 (divorced 1905); children: a daughter, G. Réjane.

The daughter of an actor, Gabrielle Réjane was born in Paris in 1857 and studied acting under Regnier at the Conservatoire, where she won second prize for comedy in 1874. She made her first stage appearance in 1875, at the Théâtre du Vaudeville, after which her reputation as a player of light comedy grew steadily. Her first great success was in Henri Meilhac's *Ma camarade* (1883), and she soon became known as an emotional actress of rare gifts as well, notably in *Divorçons, Sapho, La Dame aux Camélias, Germinie Lacerteux, Ma cousine, Amoureuse, Lysistrata,* and even Ibsen's *A Doll's House.*

Réjane played in theaters throughout Paris, and made her London debut in 1894. The following year, she visited New York, appearing in the title role of Victorien Sardou's *Madame Sans-Gêne,* believed to be her most notable part, although she was called "provoking and irresistible" as Clotilde in Henri Becque's *La Parisienne* and was famed for her performances in *Zaza* and *La Passerelle*. In her day, she was compared favorably to *Eleonora Duse and *Sarah Bernhardt, but most of the comedies in which she was the toast of Paris are now forgotten, along with their authors. From 1892 to 1905, the actress was married to M. Porel, the director of a vaudeville theater. She opened her own theater, the Théâtre Réjane, in Paris in 1906, and continued acting until the year of her death, when she appeared in Henri Bataille's *La Vierge Folle*.

Réjane was known for her French vivacity and animated expression, which made her unrivalled in the parts she had made her own. In every critique of Réjane there is a pointed reference to her wonderful fluency and flexibility of style, her prolific inventions, her natural transitions of mood, and her refined tastes. Sarcey called her "the very essence of the Parisienne."

Rejcka.
Variant of Ryksa.

Reju, Gabrielle (1857–1920).
See Réjane, Gabrielle.

Remond, Sarah Parker (1826–1894)

African-American anti-slavery advocate. Born in Salem, Massachusetts, on June 6, 1826; died in Rome, Italy, on December 13, 1894; daughter of John Remond and Nancy (Lenox) Remond; educated at Bedford College for Ladies in London; studied medicine at the Santa Maria Nuova Hospital in Florence, Italy, 1866–68; married Lazzaro Pinto, in April 1877.

First lectured against slavery (1842), at age 16; appointed as an antislavery agent for the American Anti-Slavery Society (1856); lectured against slavery extensively in Great Britain (late 1850s).

Sarah Parker Remond was born in Salem, Massachusetts, on June 6, 1826. Her father John Remond was a well-known member of the community, an immigrant from the West Indies whose business ventures included trading in food, wines, and spices, as well as wigmaking, hairdressing, and catering. He gained U.S. citizenship in 1811 and became a lifetime member of the Massachusetts Anti-Slavery Society in the 1830s. Her mother **Nancy Lenox Remond** had been a cakemaker before her marriage, and was an active member of the Salem Female Anti-Slavery Society after its founding in 1832. Remond had five sisters and two brothers.

Remond's educational experience as a child was marred by racial prejudice. She attended Salem public schools until 1835, when she attempted to enroll in high school and was refused entrance because of her color. (The previous year Salem had instituted a separate school for "African" children in response to public pressure to revoke integration at the public girls' school.) The Remonds relocated to Newport, Rhode Island, and enrolled their children in a private school for black Americans. The family returned to Salem in 1841, where Remond continued her education informally by reading newspapers and books borrowed from family friends. She was also heavily influenced by the many abolitionist leaders who came to the Remond home for discussion and fellowship, including William Wells Brown and William Lloyd Garrison.

Remond's brother Charles Lenox Remond, her elder by 16 years, became a well-known anti-slavery lecturer in both the United States and Great Britain in the early 1840s. Remond was 16 when she made her first public-speaking appearance, alongside Charles, in Groton, Massachusetts, in July 1842. Over the next ten years, she learned the techniques of political organizing and continued to improve her education and speaking ability at every opportunity. She first came to prominence among abolitionists in May 1853, when she and two friends refused to sit in the segregated section of the Howard Athenaeum in Boston, where they were attending a performance of a Mozart opera. As she was being roughly ejected from the hall by a police officer, she fell down a flight of stairs. She sued the officer and was awarded $500 in a civil suit, thereby setting an important legal precedent and upholding the principle of desegregation at the theater.

In 1856, at age 30, Remond became an agent of the American Anti-Slavery Society. For the next two years, she lectured widely with her brother in New York State and the eastern half of the United States. During her travels, she encountered many inconveniences brought on by discrimination against blacks and women. Often she had to arrange accommodations with private families because she could not find a hotel that would offer her a room. She came into contact with many other anti-slavery leaders and feminists on her lecture circuit, including *Susan B. Anthony and *Abby Kelley. In May 1858, she appeared on the platform of the annual Women's Rights Convention in New York City.

Looking for more freedom and for opportunities to further her education, which she considered deficient, Remond left the U.S. for Great

Britain. She would spend nearly the whole of the rest of her life abroad. She disembarked in Liverpool in January 1859, and with the support of abolitionist Samuel J. May began an extensive lecture tour. While the last vestiges of slavery in the British Empire had been abolished in 1838, many large manufacturers in Britain were dependent upon cotton imported from the Southern states in the U.S., and thus upon slavery. Remond was the first black woman many Britons had seen, and this often drew very large audiences. If curiosity brought people to her lectures, her dignified and intelligent manner moved many to support her cause. She reduced some listeners to tears as she described the inhumanity and horrors of slavery. In London, Remond also met William and *Ellen Craft, escaped slaves who had fled to England after the U.S. passed the Fugitive Slave Act in 1850.

In November 1859, Remond was involved in another highly publicized case of discrimination when Benjamin Moran, the American legation secretary in London, denied her request for a visa to travel to France on the grounds that because she was a person of color, she did not have rights as a U.S. citizen. In December, the London *Morning Star* picked up the story and ran a scathing article criticizing the United States, which was followed by an account of the incident by Remond. In February 1860, the decision to deny her a visa was upheld by the State Department. With help from some influential British friends, she eventually made her trip nonetheless.

Remond had returned to formal education in October 1859, by enrolling in the Bedford College for Ladies (later part of the University of London). During her two years of study, she continued to lecture during breaks and boarded with the college's founder, abolitionist **Elisabeth Jesser Reid**. Remond stayed in Great Britain throughout the Civil War, working to influence British public opinion to support the Union cause. When slavery was finally legally abolished, she turned her attention to the needs of the many newly freed slaves. Through her involvement with the London Emancipation Society and the Freedmen's Aid Association, she helped raise funds to support former slaves and their families.

After the end of the Civil War, Remond returned briefly to the United States to work with her brother Charles and with Frederick Douglass in the American Equal Rights Association, which sought universal suffrage. In 1866, she moved to Florence, Italy, where she studied medicine for two years at the Santa Maria Nuova Hospital. (It is believed she may have met *Eliz-abeth Blackwell** while studying at Bedford.) Her later life is not well documented, and no records have been found to prove that she enrolled in or completed medical school, although she appears to have worked as a physician. What accounts exist of her life after she left London are gleaned from reports by others, such as reformer **Elizabeth Buffum Chace**, abolitionist Parker Pillsbury, and Douglass, all of whom noted visits with her in their writings. Remond married an Italian, Lazzaro Pinto, on April 25, 1877. She died on December 13, 1894, at age 74, and was buried in the Protestant Cemetery in Rome.

SOURCES:

James, Edward T., ed. *Notable American Women, 1607–1950.* Cambridge, MA: The Belknap Press of Harvard University Press, 1971.

Smith, Jessie Carney, ed. *Notable Black American Women.* Detroit, MI: Gale Research, 1992.

Weatherford, Doris. *American Women's History.* NY: Prentice Hall, 1994.

Kari Bethel,
freelance writer, Columbia, Missouri

Rémusat, Claire, comtesse de
(1780–1821)

French writer and countess. Name variations: Claire de Rémusat or Claire de Remusat; countess of Remusat. Pronunciation: Ray-MU-zah. Born Clair Élisabeth Gravier de Vergennes in 1780; died in 1821; married Comte de Rémusat (a court chamberlain); children: François Marie Charles de Rémusat, known as Charles, comte de Rémusat (1797–1875, a politician and writer).

A noted beauty in the court of Napoleon, Claire, comtesse de Rémusat, was a lady-in-waiting and intimate friend of Empress *Josephine. She was married to Comte de Rémusat, court chamberlain, and her position made her thoroughly acquainted with the intimate life of the Napoleonic reign. Though she wrote an essay on the "Education of Women" which was honored by the Academy, her important work was her *Mémoirs*, published by her grandson long after her death in 1879. They are particularly valuable for the light they throw on the court of the First Empire.

Rémy, Caroline (1855–1929).
See Séverine.

Renard, Rosita (1894–1949)

Chilean pianist. Born in Santiago, Chile, in 1894; died in Santiago on May 24, 1949.

Rosita Renard was born in Santiago, Chile, in 1894. As a young girl, she studied in Berlin with Martin Krause (1853–1918), a renowned teacher whose students included her fellow Chilean Claudio Arrau and the Swiss virtuoso Edwin Fischer. With the onset of World War I, Renard went to New York, where she made her American debut in 1917, and was immediately hailed as one of the greatest living pianists and a worthy successor to *Teresa Carreño, who had died that year.

After the war, Renard went back to Germany, then returned to Chile where she played an important role in reorganizing the Santiago Conservatory. Little was heard from her in the music centers of the world, while she concentrating on her teaching, until the mid-1940s, when the distinguished German conductor Erich Kleiber, a refugee from Nazism, was in Chile and needed a soloist for a performance of a Mozart concerto. Kleiber was overwhelmed when he heard Renard play, and they gave a number of concerts together. He urged Renard to revive her international career, and her Carnegie Hall recital, which took place on January 19, 1949, received praise from the often harsh New York critics. Fortunately the recital was recorded (*Rosita Renard at Carnegie Hall: January 19, 1949*, VAI), and it includes stunning performances of works by Bach, Chopin, Mendelssohn and Ravel. According to one historian of great pianism, she had "a patrician musical mind, a marvelous set of fingers, [and] a singing tone." Renard, who was one of the finest exponents of the late-Romantic style of piano playing, died of encephalitis soon after her New York triumph, in her home city of Santiago, on May 24, 1949.

SOURCES:
Dubal, David. *The Art of the Piano.* NY: Summit Books, 1989.
Schonberg, Harold C. *The Great Pianists.* Rev. ed. NY: Simon & Schuster, 1987.

John Haag,
Athens, Georgia

Renata.

Variant of Renée.

Renaud, Madeleine (1903–1994)

French actress. Born in Paris, France, on February 21, 1903; died in Neuilly, a suburb of Paris, on September 23, 1994; educated at the Conservatoire of Dramatic Art in Paris; married Charles Grandval; married Jean-Louis Barrault (an actor and director), in 1940.

Selected filmography: Vent Debout *(1922);* La Terre qui meurt *(1926);* Jean de la Lune *(1931);* La Belle Marinière *(1932);* La Couturière de Lunéville *(1932);* Mistigri *(1932);* La Maternelle *(1933);* Maria Chapdelaine *(The Naked Heart, 1934);* Hélène *(1936);* L'Etrange M. Victor *(1938);* Remorques *(1941);* Lumiére d'Été *(1943);* Le Ciel est à Vous *(The Woman Who Dared, 1944);* Le Plaisir *(1952);* Le Dialogue des Carmélites *(1960);* The Longest Day *(1962);* Le Diable par la Queue *(The Devil by the Tail, 1969);* L'Humeur vagabonde *(1971);* La Mandarine *(1972);* Des Journeés entières dans les Arbres *(1976);* La Lumière du Lac *(1988).*

Born in Paris in 1903, highly respected French actress Madeleine Renaud was a child when she decided she wanted to act, after being praised by an actor for her recital of a poem at a party. Her mother acquiesced on condition that she study at Paris' Conservatoire of Dramatic Art, which she did on scholarship. In 1923, Renaud became a member of the venerable Comédie Française, beginning a professional relationship that would endure for the next 26 years. She made her stage debut that same year as Agnes in Molière's *L'École des Femmes*. Performing in productions by Molière, Marivaux, and Musset, she acted with the company in Paris and on tour throughout Europe, receiving many favorable reviews from the critics.

While she had a few small roles in films in the 1920s, Renaud made her genuine film debut in 1931, in *Jean de la Lune*. Over the course of the next year she was seen on screen in *La Belle Marinière*, *La Couturière de Lunéville*, and *Mistigri* (all 1932), and also appeared as Ophelia in Charles Grandval's stage production of *Hamlet*. Renaud consistently received the approval of reviewers and audiences, for she was equally successful at dramatic roles, to which she brought what was called a restrained and refined style, and at comedic roles that required a robust and energetic kind of acting.

In 1934, Renaud made the film *Maria Chapdelaine*, for which she received the Grand Prize of the French Cinema, and over the next year she appeared at the Comédie Française in *Le Chandelier* and *Les Fausses Confidences*. She met her future husband and business partner, Jean-Louis Barrault, in 1936 when she starred opposite him in *Hélène*, the film adaptation of a *Vicki Baum novel. (Among his other achievements, Barrault would go on to co-star with *Arletty in Marcel Carné's 1945 masterpiece *Les Enfants du Paradis*.) Jean Grémillon cast Renaud in several of his films over the next years, including *L'Etrange M. Victor* (1938), *Remorques* (1940), *Lumiére d'Été* (1942), and *Le Ciel est à Vous* (1943).

Renaud, who had previously been married to Charles Grandval, married Barrault in 1940, and he joined her at the Comédie Française as a producer, director, and actor. Over the next six years, in addition to her other roles there, Renaud starred in her husband's productions of François Mauriac's *Les Mal Aimés* and Paul Claudel's *Le Soulier de Satin*. The husband and wife team also appeared together in Salacrou's *Les Fiancés du Havre*.

In 1946, Renaud and Barrault left the Comédie Française to form the Madeleine Renaud-Jean-Louis Barrault Company, taking over management of the Marigny Theater. A repertory troupe unsubsidized by the government (unlike the Comédie), the company quickly gained a reputation for showcasing both classics by Molière and Shakespeare as well as adaptations and/or premieres of works by modern writers, including Kafka, Camus, Beckett, Genet, Ionesco, and Anouilh. In addition to staging performances at the Marigny, the Renaud-Barrault Company toured Europe, South America, the United States and Canada, often sponsored by the French government to promote and advance international relations. For its debut in New York City at the Ziegfeld Theater on November 12, 1952, the company performed Marivaux's *Les Fausses Confidences* and Prévert's *Baptiste*. These productions, along with an adaptation of Kafka's *The Trial*, earned the company extensive praise in the New York press; by the end of opening week, over 5,000 people had been turned back from the packed theater. Renaud remained professionally active throughout her life, performing in the film *La Lumière du Lac* in 1988, at age 85. She died on September 23, 1994, in the Paris suburb of Neuilly.

SOURCES:
Candee, Marjorie Dent, ed. *Current Biography 1953.* NY: H.W. Wilson, 1953.
Current Biography, 1994. NY: H.W. Wilson, 1994.
Katz, Ephraim. *The Film Encyclopedia.* 3rd ed. NY: HarperCollins, 1998.

Kari Bethel,
freelance writer, Columbia, Missouri

Renault, Mary (1905–1983)

Bestselling British author whose historical novels, set in ancient Greece, made her the first writer to acquire a worldwide reading audience for novels dealing predominantly with homosexual characters. Name variations: Mary Challans; (pseudonym) Mary Martin.

Pronunciation: Rehn-OHLT. Born Mary Challans on September 4, 1905, in London, England; died on December 13, 1983, at Cape Town, South Africa; daughter of Dr. Frank Challans (a physician) and Mary Clementine Newsome Baxter Challans; attended Levick family school; Clifton Girls School in Bristol; St. Hugh's College, Oxford; and Radliffe infirmary, Oxford; never married; lived with Julie Mullard (a nurse), for approximately 50 years; no children.

Worked as a nurse (1938–45); published first novel, Purposes of Love (1939); won the annual Metro-Goldwyn-Mayer prize for the best novel of the year for her book Return to Night (1947); moved to South Africa (1948); published The Last of the Wine, the first of a series of novels set in ancient Greece (1956); became active in the Women's Defence of the Constitution League (1956); elected a Fellow of the Royal Society of Literature (1959); helped reorganize the PEN Clubs in South Africa (1961); named an honorary fellow of St. Hugh's College (1982).

Selected works: The Charioteer (1953); The Last of the Wine (1956); The King Must Die (1958); The Bull from the Sea (1962); The Mask of Apollo (1966); The Persian Boy (1972); Funeral Games (1981).

Although "Mary Renault" wrote novels which gathered a worldwide audience, she was a bit of a mystery to her reading public. To some readers, "Mary Renault" was a popular historical novelist whose vivid writings about ancient Greece drew both an international following and the admiration of classical scholars. To others, she was an icon of Gay Liberation, a writer who used historical fiction to restore homosexuals to their deserved place in history. Few guessed, however, that "Mary Renault" was a quiet and somewhat retiring former nurse who spent much of her life in near isolation in South Africa; who disliked the term "gay"; and whose name was a nom de plume, originally adopted because of legal prosecutions of homosexuals in her native Britain.

The daughter of Frank Challans, an English physician, and **Mary Baxter Challans**, Renault was born in London in 1905, christened Eileen Mary Challans, and nicknamed "Molly." She grew to adulthood feeling emotionally neglected by both her father and her mother. Mary Challans preferred Renault's younger sister, **Frances Joyce Challans**, while Frank made it clear that he would have preferred sons.

The relationship between her father and mother was acrimonious. Renault recalled frequently hearing them argue behind closed doors, although they would fall to silence when she entered the room. Divorce was not an option, since it would have driven away Dr. Challans' patients and threatened the family with economic hard times. To escape what he perceived as his wife's nagging, Frank frequently withdrew to the privacy of his study, ignoring his wife and daughters for long periods. Renault was allowed to enter her father's study to look at his books, but he gave her little help with them.

When Frank was sent to serve in India during World War I, Renault and her sister were given some attention by a family friend, another physician, who also frequently took them to children's shows and other events. They were allowed to play with his children, often at games of "Cowboys and Indians." Renault, drawing on what she had seen in her father's books, preferred to play "Middle Ages" games involving chivalry and knights. Her mother, disapproving, frequently urged her to act more "feminine."

Other than reading books in her father's library, Renault's early education consisted of a school run by a local family, the Levicks. Lessons in etiquette and social graces were combined with academic subjects, such as elementary French. Renault liked the school, and in 1916 she was recognized as its best student.

During World War I, when Frank was out of the country, the Challans family moved out of their home and lived for a time with Mary Challans' sister, Aunt Bertha, and her husband. When German Zeppelin aircraft began to bomb London, Renault and her sister were sent to live in the countryside for several months.

Renault's father was slow to return home at the end of World War I. When he did, he showed little concern for his daughters' education, preferring instead to spend his time rebuilding his diminished medical practice. Aunt Bertha, who took a special interest in the girls' welfare, insisted that they be sent to a secondary school. In 1919, Renault was sent to Clifton Girls School, a boarding school, near Bristol. She was 15—much older than the other students—and had few friends. Ironically, while she did well in history and English courses, she flunked a Greek language course.

Frank Challans thought it was unnecessary for his daughters to attend college, since he believed that unmarried daughters should stay at home. Even Mary Challans tried to talk Renault out of attending college, saying that female students were "unfeminine." Frank offered Renault an allowance of £20 a year, an amount so small that it would have forced her to continue to live in her parents' home. Only Aunt Bertha offered to help: she loaned Renault sufficient money for her college expenses.

When Renault was admitted to the all-women's St. Hugh's College at Oxford in 1928—with plans to become a schoolteacher—neither of her parents were in the least impressed that she had gained admission to a branch of the prestigious university. St. Hugh's had gained membership in Oxford only five years before, and its women students were not allowed to participate in many activities. Reflecting on her days at Oxford, Renault later commented that "Oxford made me," but added that she would have preferred to have been a man, because "men have more fun." St. Hugh's also gave Renault a new appreciation of ancient Greek culture and history. In a Greek language class, she had the opportunity to study Plato. Renault also enjoyed making frequent visits to the Ashmolean museum to view its casts of objects found during excavations at Knossos, Crete. The Cretan Bull-Jumper was her particular favorite.

She was also deeply impressed with J.R.R. Tolkien, who is best known as the author of a popular trilogy about a mythical past entitled *Lord of the Rings* (1954–55). At Oxford, he was

Mary Renault

one of the professors most sympathetic to women students. Tolkien's rejection of "modernism" and experimentation in fiction left a deep impression on Renault, and his influence would later be reflected in her decision to forge a career as a historical novelist.

When Renault graduated in 1928, she received a class III degree in English literature, an acceptable result, since she had no intention of entering academic life. After graduation, she revisited her parents occasionally, but she also worked at a series of odd jobs—such as civil service clerk and chocolate factory worker—in order to support herself and be able to live apart from them. One visit "home" proved fortuitous: when she told her father that she had been suffering from a sore throat, rashes, and aching joints, he quickly diagnosed her illness as rheumatic fever. For much of 1931 and 1932, she was confined to bed, recovering from what could have been a very serious illness.

Renault later expressed regret that she was never able to reconcile with her father, who underwent an operation for throat cancer in 1940 and was unable to speak for the last months of his life. She made no such expression of regret regarding her mother; in fact, in her novels, mothers are often portrayed in unsympathetic terms.

After graduating from college, Renault began to write short pieces and published occasional poems in magazines under the name of Mary Martin. She also reviewed books for the *Oxford Times* and was allowed to supplement her income by selling the review copies she was given. While walking in the Oxford area in 1933, Renault decided, almost on the spur of the moment, to visit nearby Radcliffe infirmary. She applied for a nursing job, thinking that the hospital experience would provide material for her writings, and was hired. In 1936, after taking additional training, she qualified as a nurse. Although much of her work was in the infirmary's brain surgery ward, she was able to find enough spare time at work to write parts of her novels.

At the infirmary, she met **Julie Mullard**, a fellow nurse who would become her lifelong companion until Renault's death in 1983. For their remaining years of residence in Britain, they would work as nurses in a variety of colleges and private schools, except during World War II, when they worked in the Emergency Medical Corps in Britain. Large parts of Renault's novels were written during spare moments at work.

Renault's first book, *Purposes of Love* (1939), which appeared under the title *Promises of Love* in the United States, was set in a hospital, as were many of her early "contemporary" novels. Rather than publishing under her real name, she chose, beginning with her first novel, to borrow the last name of a character she had admired in another writer's novel. "Mary Renault" wanted to have her new last name pronounced as "rehn-OHLT"; she was not, she joked, a French car. Like most of her novels, *Purposes of Love* was not a "conventional" love story, but a heterosexual love story of some steaminess—her fellow nurses denied to reporters that such things happened in hospitals. In a plot twist toward the end of the novel, however, the female protagonist falls in love with another woman. Homosexuality was a common theme, usually more implicit than explicit, in all of her "contemporary" novels of the 1930s and 1940s. All featured a lead character with a sexually ambiguous name (such as Laurie, Kit, Jan, or Hilary), leaving many readers to wonder if another story lurked beneath the surface.

While lesbianism was in "vogue" in some British literary circles in the years between World War I and World War II—as typified by such books as *Virginia Woolf*'s *Mrs. Dalloway* and *Elizabeth Bowen*'s *The Hotel*—novels describing homosexuality were also subject to prosecution under British law. The sexual ambiguity of Renault's early novels was accompanied by frequent references to ancient Greece. In *Purposes of Love* the references included allusions to Plato's views on controlling desire. Numerous references to Greek antiquity appear in both *Kind are Her Answers* (1940) and *The Friendly Young Ladies* (1944), published as *The Middle Mist* in the United States; in both, quotations from classical Greek writers are sometimes casually dropped into ordinary conversations.

Return to Night (1947), which won the $150,000 MGM Prize for the best novel of the year in 1949 in the United States, was based on ancient Greek theories of birth and rebirth. The main male character, Julian Fleming, is portrayed as the son of a psychologically dominating mother. He is pictured as an unassertive man who lacks self-confidence and wrestles heroically with his own inner conflicts. When he attempts suicide, he is rescued by his female lover, Dr. Hilary Mansell, who is more than ten years older but who subordinates her career to his. Lying on his bed, he is compared to "the flower of Sparta brought back from Thermopylae on a shield." Although the novel impressed the contest's judges, MGM never made it into a motion picture. In the words of one of Renault's biographers, Bernard Dick: "In 1947 a combination of adultery, pseudohomosexuality, bigamy, and literate dialogue would have overwhelmed even Metro-Goldwyn-Mayer." The same fate befell *The King Must Die* (1958), which was purchased for film rights by 20th Century-Fox but never produced as a motion picture.

In 1948, Renault and Mullard moved to South Africa, motivated partly by a better climate and partly by South Africa's lower tax rates—an important factor now that Renault had become a writer of international reputation and earning power. They formed a construction company with two male friends and lived in one of the homes produced by the firm. After many years of rented apartments or nurses' accommodations, it was a welcome change.

The presence of a prominent gay community in South Africa proved to be another advantage of their adopted country, although Renault felt little kinship with the Gay Liberation movement that emerged later. She was suspicious of mass movements; she saw sexuality as an individual matter and worried that movements might threaten the ability of people to move, as they chose, along the full spectrum of sexuality. She also disliked the use of the word "gay," which she regarded as a vulgarization of the French word *gai*.

Nevertheless, she and Mullard found they could not remain silent as the Nationalist government of South Africa moved to impose new laws in support of its policy of apartheid, which made "coloreds" in South Africa into second-class citizens. The new laws also included strict censorship. In response, Renault joined with other writers in 1959 in a project to revive the nearly moribund PEN International chapters in the country. She was also a cofounder of the Women's Defence of the Constitution League, known as the Black Sash, which picketed Cabinet members and stood outside government buildings to protest oppressive laws enacted as part of apartheid. As well, Renault and Mullard demonstrated against government proposals to place legal restrictions on homosexuality. In a letter to a friend, Renault made a rare reference to her own sexuality, writing that "we weren't too delighted (by the proposed restrictions)."

South Africa remained Renault's home for the rest of her life; she became one of the country's most famous writers, showing no desire or inclination to return to her native country. When she had left Britain, the country still had the free and relatively tolerant atmosphere of wartime Britain; but by the late 1940s and the 1950s, there were renewed prosecutions of homosexu-

als. Those same years saw the emergence of McCarthyism in the United States, when "perverts" were assumed to be security risks. When Renault and Mullard took a vacation in Greece in 1961, her publisher assumed that she would visit London as part of the trip and made arrangements accordingly. Despite her publisher's pleas, she flatly refused to travel beyond Greece.

With her novel *North Face* (1948), Renault stopped featuring (ostensibly) heterosexual lead characters. *The Charioteer* (1953), the last of Renault's six "contemporary" novels, included a frank discussion of homosexuality and became a transitional book to the eight historical novels which would follow. *The Charioteer* traced the life of its male lead character, Laurie Odell, from childhood to the awakening of homosexual instincts in his adult years. The title of the novel was derived from Plato's teaching that the soul is a charioteer, pulled by two horses, one trying to reach heaven and the other bound for earth. That image became a metaphor for Odell's inner conflicts, in which he feels himself torn between his Platonic relationship with one male friend and his tumultuous affair with another male. In the words of one writer, Renault wanted her readers to see the characters in many of her novels as "Hellenic souls imprisoned in modern bodies."

*M*ary Renault is one of the major novelists of our time. Her insights are phenomenal, her readings of the fine print of psychological history extremely acute, her rendering of truth as she sees it forthright, courageous, informative, and stirring.

—Richard Weston

The novel also attacked homophobia: when Odell reveals his homosexuality to a heterosexual male friend, the friend becomes distant and uncommunicative. When Odell is a hospital patient and sees a boy fall out of his bed, he hesitates to pick the boy up and place him back in bed, for fear that others will see his act as affection for the boy. The novel's plot also included the firing of a schoolteacher, a man whom Odell admired, for having an affair with one of his younger male students.

Although *The Charioteer* would become a bestseller and make Renault the first author to gather a worldwide reading audience for novels in which the main characters were often homosexual, the novel also caused a split between Renault and her American publisher, William Morrow. While her British publisher, Longmans, did not hesitate to publish the novel, Morrow, stunned by its explicit homosexuality, rejected it.

Ironically, this situation worked to Renault's advantage. When she switched her U.S. publication rights to Pantheon, she discovered that the German expatriates who had founded Pantheon, Kurt and *Helen Wolff, held a high opinion of her work. In publicity for her novels, they emphasized the literary and historical merits of her writings, in contrast to the tendency of Longmans to present her books as adventure stories. One result was that her literary reputation was noticeably higher in the United States than in Britain.

By the middle of the 20th century, a reading audience had been created for Renault's historical novels about ancient Greece. Popular interest had been stimulated by the appearance of such books as Robert Graves' *The Greek Myths* and Sir James Frazer's *The Golden Bough*, as well as by continuing archaeological discoveries. The founder of psychiatry, Sigmund Freud, had also used Greek myths to describe psychological conditions.

Although she dealt mostly with the classical and Hellenistic periods of Greek history, two of her novels—*The King Must Die* (1958) and *The Bull from the Sea* (1962)—were set in pre-Hellenic Minoan civilization, at a time when matriarchy was not uncommon and cults to female fertility flourished. For her first novel set in ancient Greece (*The Last of the Wine*, 1956), Renault devoted two years to general research work, examining archaeological records and historical studies, as well as reading books on sculpture and poetry. She had learned to read Greek, but in preparing for her novels, she often used books in which Latin and Greek texts were interleaved with English translations. In some cases, the inspiration was the actual archaeological finds: *The King Must Die* (1958) was conceived while she wandered among the ruins at Knossos. The thoroughness of her preparation was demonstrated when she complained to Pantheon that the American paperback edition of *The King Must Die* featured a cover illustration depicting classical Greece; the novel, she reminded the publisher, was set in the Mycenaean civilization of earlier Greek history.

Many of these historical novels were written in the first person, as if they were autobiographies, a marked improvement from Renault's early "contemporary" novels, where readers were sometimes confused because the point of view shifted from person to person. *The Last of the Wine* was written as the autobiography of an Athenian named Alexias and gave a first-person account of events in Athens leading up to the execution of Socrates.

The Mask of Apollo (1966) was an epic attempt to portray tragedy on three levels—cultural, philosophical, and political. Its presentation of Athenian society and government drew parallels between the decline of the theater in ancient Greece and the decline of Athens. The myth of Theseus became the basis for two novels set in Minoan Crete, *The King Must Die* (which features a struggle over a matriarchal system that required that the king be sacrificed each year and the queen pick a new co-ruler) and *The Bull from the Sea*.

In 1964, Renault departed from the trend set by her earlier historical novels and wrote a nonfiction book for children, *The Lion in the Gateway: The Heroic Battles of the Greeks and Persians at Marathon, Salamis, and Thermopylae*. She followed that with books about Alexander III the Great, including the novel which gained bestseller status more quickly than any of her other writings, the novel *The Persian Boy* (1972). The story of Alexander the Great's love for a eunuch, it is narrated by the eunuch. Her last novel, *Funeral Games* (1981), described the violent struggles in Greece following the death of Alexander the Great.

Renault was in the midst of writing a long-planned novel about the Middle Ages when she was diagnosed, in the summer of 1983, with lung cancer. Mullard kept the diagnosis from her until almost the end. When she died in December 1983, Renault had gained a reputation as a novelist who not only had been able to recreate the past but had tried to restore an "invisible minority" to its rightful place in history.

While reviewers of her books were divided on the question of their literary merits, she thought her most significant achievements lay elsewhere. She was proud that she had been able to produce historically accurate and carefully researched novels, but she was also proud of her ability to use the past to illuminate contemporary problems. For Renault, ancient Greece was a mirror of the 20th century. To her, the ancient Greeks still "made sense"; she was struck by "how constant human political and social development seems." Why, she wondered, did so many of her readers not see the parallels between ancient Greece and their own times—the wars, the dictators, the violence, and the threats to individual freedom?

SOURCES:

Dick, Bernard F. *The Hellenism of Mary Renault*. Carbondale, IL: Southern Illinois Press, 1972.

Sweetman, David. *Mary Renault: A Biography*. NY: Harcourt Brace, 1993.

Wolfe, Peter. *Mary Renault*. NY: Twayne, 1969.

SUGGESTED READING:

Adams, Stephen. *The Homosexual as Hero in Contemporary Fiction*. London: Vision, 1980.

Bremmer, Jan. *Interpretation of Greek Mythology*. London: Croom Helm, 1987.

Burns, Landon C. *Men are Only Men: The Novels of Mary Renault*. Minneapolis, MN: Critique, 1963.

Graves, Robert. *The Greek Myths*. Baltimore, MD: Penguin, 1955.

Heilbrun, Carolyn G. *Reinventing Womanhood*. London: Gollancz, 1979.

COLLECTIONS:

Some of the correspondence of Renault is housed in the Special Collections division of Mugar Memorial Library at Boston University. Materials originally held by her British publisher, Longmans, are housed in the Archives and Manuscripts Division of the Reading University Library, United Kingdom. Unpublished radio scripts are in the Humanities Reference Room of Love Memorial Library, University of Nebraska, Lincoln, Nebraska.

Niles Holt,
Professor of History, Illinois State University,
Normal, Illinois

Renée de Bourbon (fl. 1477)

Abbess of Fontevrault. Name variations: Renee of Bourbon. Flourished in 1477 in France.

Renée de Bourbon was abbess of Fontevrault, in central France, and spent most of her life trying to rid France's monasteries of corruption. With single-minded determination, the noble-born Renée traveled from one religious foundation to another, preaching, writing letters, and even resorting to armed conflict when the corruption she faced was too severe for mere words. She put much effort into improving her own convent-monastery at Fontevrault, trying to return wayward monks and nuns under her rule to the way of God. Her harsh discipline included the use of oaths of loyalty and even threats of punishment.

Laura York,
Riverside, California

Renée of France (1510–1575)

Duchess of Ferrara. Name variations: Renata of France; Renee of France; Renée of Ferrara; Renée, duchess of Ferraro; Renee, duchess of Italy; (Ital.) Renata di Francia. Born at Blois on October 25, 1510; died in 1575; second daughter of Louis XII, king of France (r. 1498–1515), and Anne of Brittany (1477–1514); sister of Claude de France (1499–1524); married Hercules II also known as Ercole II

(1508–1559, future duke of Ferrara and son of Lucrezia Borgia), in 1528; children: Alfonso II (1533–1597), 5th duke of Ferrara and Modena; Cardinal Luigi d'Este (1538–1586); ❧ Anne of Ferrara (1531–1607, who married Francis of Lorraine, 2nd duke of Guise); *Lucrezia d'Este (1535–1598, duchess of Urbino, who married Francesco Maria II della Rovere); *Eleonora d'Este (1537–1581).

Renée of France was born in 1510, the second daughter of Louis XII, king of France, and *Anne of Brittany. After being betrothed successively to Gaston de Foix, Charles of Austria (the future emperor Charles V), his brother Ferdinand, Henry VIII of England, and the elector Joachim II of Brandenburg, 18-year-old Renée was married with great pomp to Ercole II d'Este, son of the duke of Ferrara and *Lucrezia Borgia; Ercole succeeded his father six years later.

Renée's court became a rendezvous for men and women of letters; her closest friends were *Vittoria Colonna and *Margaret of Angoulême, queen of Navarre (related by marriage to Renée's sister *Claude de France). It was also a refuge for the persecuted French Calvinists. Renée had been raised by her governess Mme de Souboise and an Englishwoman, who had taught her the scriptures from the Wycliffe Bible. Thus, she received Clément Marot and John Calvin at her court, and finally embraced the reformed religion. Her husband, who viewed these proceedings with disfavor, had Calvin arrested for heresy, but Renée secretly backed an armed group who freed Calvin. Ercole then banished her friends, took her children from her, and threw her into prison. When Renée recanted and attended mass, she was released.

After her husband's death in 1559, Renée went back to France and turned her duchy of Montargis, 60 miles southeast of Paris, into a center for Protestantism. "She aided, succoured, and fed as many as she could," noted Saint-Beuve. During the wars of religion, she was harassed several times by Catholic troops, and in 1562 her château was besieged by her son-in-law Francis of Lorraine, 2nd duke of Guise, who referred to her castle as "a nest of Huguenots." Renée died at Montargis and was buried in the castle's chapel, where she and her fellow Protestants had worshipped for 16 years.

SUGGESTED READING:

Fontana, B. *Renata di Francia*. Rome, 1889.

Rodocanachi, E. *Renée de France*. Paris, 1896.

Renée of Montpensier (fl. 1500s).

See Mary of Guise for sidebar.

◀❧
Anne of Ferrara.
*See Morata,
Fulvia Olympia
for sidebar.*

Renger, Annemarie (1919—)

German politician, leader of the Social Democratic Party, who was elected the first woman Speaker of the West German Bundestag in December 1972. Name variations: Annemarie Renger-Loncarevic. Born Annemarie Wildung in Leipzig on October 7, 1919; daughter of Fritz Wildung and Martha (Scholz) Wildung; had four brothers and one sister; married Emil Renger; married Aleksandar Loncarevic; children: (first marriage) Rolf Renger.

A war widow, began working for Social Democratic leader Kurt Schumacher (1945), thus starting an improbable career that brought her to the heights of political life in the German Federal Republic, culminating in her election as Speaker of the Bundestag (December 1972); retired (December 1990).

Born in Leipzig in 1919, the sixth and last child of working-class parents, Annemarie Renger grew up in a Social Democratic environment, her father Fritz Wildung being one of the founders of the German socialist workers' sports movement (a street has been named in his honor in Berlin's Wilmersdorf district). After her family moved to Berlin in 1924, Renger attended a lyceum in the German capital. Expelled from school because of her father's "un-German" Marxist politics, Annemarie was accepted as a trainee in a publishing firm, and then worked as a stenotypist. In 1938, she married Emil Renger, an advertising manager. That same year, she gave birth to their son, Rolf. World War II shattered Renger's life. In summer 1944, her husband was killed fighting near Chartres, France, and three of her four brothers lost their lives on battlefields as German soldiers.

As an impoverished war widow with a young child, she began looking for a suitable job only weeks after war's end. By chance, in May 1945 she read printed excerpts of a speech by Kurt Schumacher, the leader of the Social Democratic Party (SPD). Schumacher, a man of courage and will, had been severely wounded in World War II and had survived the entire 12 years of the Third Reich in a series of concentration camps. Despite her family background, Renger had had little interest in politics. But, moved by his idealism, she wrote and asked him if she might be able to work for him. Amazingly, she soon found herself in Schumacher's presence as a job interviewee.

Renger began working as Schumacher's personal assistant in mid-October 1945. Soon, their relationship turned from professional to personal. Until his death in August 1952, Schumacher

would depend on Renger as a trusted adviser, friend, and companion. In 1953, she successfully ran as a Social Democratic candidate for a seat representing Schleswig-Holstein in the Bundestag (West Germany's parliament). She would retain her parliamentary seat without interruption until 1990. With the passage of time, Renger's responsibilities within the Social Democratic Party grew significantly, so that from 1961 through 1973 she was a member of the SPD Parteivorstand (managing committee), serving as well from 1970 through 1973 as a member of the SPD Parteipräsidium (party council). During the same period, from 1969 until 1972, she was one of the four members of the SPD parliamentary office responsible for the financial, personnel, and organizational affairs of the party within the Bundestag. As the SPD's Bundestag floor manager, Renger was known for her detailed knowledge of parliamentary routine. Despite her hectic schedule during these years, Renger somehow found time to play tennis and drive around Bonn in her sporty Mercedes coupe.

After the SPD won the German Federal Republic's national elections in November 1972, the party leadership nominated Renger for president of the Bundestag. On December 13, she was elected, the first woman to hold that high office. In her post-election address, she indicated her hope that in the future her election would not be regarded as a unique event that would never be repeated: "I am convinced that the women in this chamber have no desire to be regarded as exceptions, or treated differently in any way." Within a short time, Renger had become by any criterion the best-known West German woman in public office. In 1976, she relinquished the Bundestag presidency to run unsuccessfully for the presidency of the Federal Republic, losing to Karl Carstens, the candidate of the Christian Democratic Party. She then became the Bundestag's vice-president, a post she retained until the first national elections of newly unified Germany were held in December 1990. At this juncture, Renger retired from politics.

Among her many activities, Renger was chair of the Bundestag delegates working for better German-Israeli relations and chaired the German Helsinki Human Rights Committee; she was also a leading personality of the German Council for the European Movement, serving as its president for many years. As probably the most respected senior woman in the Social Democratic Party, Renger was honored when she was selected to head the Arbeiter-Samariter-Bund (Workers' Samaritan League). Near to her heart is the Kurt-Schumacher-Gesellschaft (Kurt

Schumacher Society), of which she has been president since 1985.

SOURCES:

Enssle, Manfred J. "Five Theses on German Everyday Life after World War II," in *Central European History.* Vol. 26, no. 1, 1993, pp. 1–19.

"Frau Präsidentin: Annemarie Renger-Loncarevic," in *The New York Times Biographical Edition.* December 1971, p. 2245.

Huber, Antje. *Verdient die Nachtigall Lob, wenn sie singt?: Die Sozialdemokratinnen.* Stuttgart: Seewald, 1984.

Latka-Jöhring, Sigrid. *Frauen in Bonn: Zwanzig Porträts aus der Bundeshauptstadt.* Bonn: J. Latka, 1988.

Merseburger, Peter. *Der schwierige Deutsche, Kurt Schumacher: Eine Biographie.* 2nd ed. Stuttgart: Deutsche Verlags-Anstalt, 1995.

Renger, Annemarie. "Am Ende der Tausend Jahre," in Heinz Friedrich, ed., *Mein Kopfgeld: Die Währungsreform—Rückblicke nach vier Jahrzehnten.* Munich: DTV-Deutscher Taschenbuch, 1988, pp. 79–93.

———. *Ein politisches Leben: Erinnerungen.* Stuttgart: Deutsche Verlags-Anstalt, 1993.

———. *Fasziniert von Politik: Beiträge zur Zeit.* Stuttgart: Seewald, 1981.

Roedl, Franz. "Annemarie Renger—the First German Woman Speaker," in *Central Europe Journal.* Vol. 21, no. 3–4. March–April 1973, pp. 72–74.

John Haag,
Associate Professor of History,
University of Georgia, Athens, Georgia

Renie.

Variant of Renée.

Reno, Janet (1938—)

American lawyer who was the first woman appointed attorney general of the United States. Born in Miami, Florida, on July 21, 1938; eldest of four children of Henry Reno (a police reporter) and Jane (Wood) Reno (an investigative reporter); Cornell University, A.B. in chemistry, 1960; law degree from Harvard University Law School, 1963; never married; no children.

One of 16 women in class of 500 at Harvard Law School; became first woman to head county prosecutor's office in Florida (1978); became first woman appointed attorney general of the United States (1993) and served through two administrations and much controversy (1993–2001); inducted into the Women's Hall of Fame at Seneca Falls, New York (autumn 2000).

Janet Reno, the first woman to be appointed attorney general of the United States, was born in Miami, Florida, on July 21, 1938, the eldest child of two idealistic, strong-minded, and highly individualistic parents. Her father Henry Reno was a Danish-born naturalized American who worked as a police reporter for *The Miami Herald* for 43 years until his death in 1967. Her mother **Jane Wood Reno**, with whom she was very close, worked as an investigative reporter for the *Miami News*. In the 1950s, Jane Reno testified before a U.S. Senate committee about her experience posing as a mother attempting to sell her baby on the black market. In addition, she wrestled alligators, read poetry, was named an honorary princess by the Miccosukee Indians, and built the family home by herself, from the ground up, with help from Henry in the evenings. With such examples before her, Janet Reno made her own mark as a pioneer in law enforcement, gaining both admirers and detractors during an often volatile tenure as the nation's "top cop" in the Clinton administration.

Reno grew up in Dade County, Florida, and attended public school there. After graduating from Cornell University in 1960 with a degree in chemistry, she entered Harvard Law School, where she was one of only 16 women in a class of 500. During her law school years, a prominent Miami law firm denied her a summer internship, stating bluntly that it was rejecting her because she was a woman. That same law firm would eagerly offer her a partnership 14 years later, but in the early 1960s the law profession was dominated by men.

After graduation in 1963, Reno moved back home to Miami to begin her law career with the firm of Brigham and Brigham, where she worked until 1967. She then went on to a junior partnership in her own law firm, Lewis and Reno, until 1971, when she received a political appointment as staff director of the Judiciary Committee of the Florida House of Representatives. During her year-long service there, she helped to draft a constitutional revision allowing a reorganization of the state court system. She ran for a seat in the state legislature the following year, but was defeated. Her disappointment was somewhat mitigated when she learned that Abraham Lincoln, whom she held in great respect, had also lost his first election. Instead of serving in the House, she spent 1973 as a counsel for the state senate's Criminal Justice Committee for the Revision of Florida's Criminal Code.

Reno's next job was in the state attorney general's office of the 11th Judicial Circuit of Florida, the office that presides over Dade County and the Greater Miami area, the largest district in Florida. Unsure of what to do with Reno, Seymour Gelber, administrative assistant to the Dade County state attorney Richard Gerstein, gave her what he considered the make-work job of organizing a juvenile division within the prosecutor's office. Reno demonstrated her commitment, energy, and efficiency by putting together a juvenile court in two months, much to the surprise of her colleagues. In 1976, she returned to private practice with a Miami law firm. Two years later, when Gerstein stepped down from office, he recommended to Governor Reubin Askew that Reno be named his successor until the next election. With her appointment, Reno became the first woman to head a county prosecutor's office in Florida. She was elected to the position in the next election in 1978, receiving 74% of the vote. Despite being a Democrat in a heavily Republican county, she won reelection in the following four elections.

As the largest prosecutor's office in Florida, and the one in which the city of Miami was located, the Dade County office had jurisdiction over the most problems in the state. When Reno took over the office, the county was facing increases in drug trafficking and illegal immigration as well as rising racial tension. Although she became widely respected for her tough fair-mindedness and approachability, her tenure as chief prosecutor was seldom smooth. In her first term of office, in 1980, she was faced with severe criticism and unjust charges of racial bigotry from her mishandling of a case from the previous year, in which four white police officers had beaten Arthur McDuffie, an African-American insurance salesman who was unarmed and handcuffed, to death. Although the officers' guilt seemed clear, they were acquitted by an all-white jury, leading to rioting in the black Liberty City section of Miami that caused the loss of 18 lives and $200 million worth of property damage. Reno took the blame for losing an open-and-shut case, and her critics included not only the African-American community but also the U.S. attorney general, Benjamin R. Civiletti, and Florida governor, Bob Graham. The charges that affected Reno most deeply, however, were those of racism, and she spent the following months repairing the rift between herself and the African-American community. She attended African-American civic and social functions while also increasing the hiring of blacks and Latinos, and focused her energy on issues important to minorities. Her hard work paid off when some of her severest critics became, over time, some of her staunchest supporters and allies.

Through all the ups and downs of trying to maintain racial justice, Reno worked assiduously to improve the welfare of children. She reformed the juvenile justice system, aggressively prosecuting child-abuse cases and pursuing delinquent fathers for child support. These efforts earned her the respect of both women's rights groups and the black community, and even won her mention in a rap song. She also established an innovative drug court in which non-violent offenders without records were not automatically sent to jail, but were instead assigned to counseling, giving them responsibility, accountability, and skills, and reintegrating them into their communities.

The primary criticism leveled at Reno was that she failed to go after political corruption and drug trafficking with sufficient zeal. Law enforcement critics cited her willingness to plea bargain and statistics of low jail time imposed on offenders. Admirers countered this argument by noting that the federal authorities, to which she ceded a number of complex cases, had better resources for prosecution than the state.

After Bill Clinton became president of the United States in 1992, Reno was approached by his associates about becoming attorney general. At the time, her mother was seriously ill with lung cancer, and it was understood that Reno, who continued to live with and care for her mother, would not leave Florida or take on added responsibility while her mother needed her. Jane Reno died on December 21, 1992, and on February 11, 1993, Clinton formally nominated Reno for the position of attorney general, which she accepted.

Before Reno's nomination, two other women had been proposed for the position. Both **Zoë Baird** and Judge **Kimba M. Wood** had withdrawn themselves from nomination after reports of their personal employment of illegal immigrants had provoked much outcry and criticism. In his nomination of Reno, Clinton praised her "unquestioned integrity." "She's demonstrated throughout her career a commitment to principles that I want to see enshrined at the Justice Department," he said. "No one is above the law." (He would find his words confirmed a number of times over the following years, as Reno approved various investigations by independent counsels into his alleged illegal conduct.) During her confirmation hearing, she held her own with self-confidence and a clear grasp of the issues faced by law enforcement and the Justice Department, although she made clear to the committee her personal objections to the death penalty. She was confirmed unanimously by the Senate, and on March 12, 1993, was sworn in as the first woman to serve as U.S. attorney general. After her swearing-in, Reno told reporters that she intended to ensure that

Janet
Reno

women seeking abortions would be protected from physical harassment by anti-abortion groups, making it a felony to obstruct business at abortion clinics. The Freedom of Access to Clinic Entrances (FACE) Act was passed the following year, providing criminal and civil sanc-tions for obstruction of, or interference with, a woman's access to abortion.

As attorney general, Reno stood firm in her belief that prison is not necessarily the best re-sponse to criminal acts, strongly supported the strict principles of due process and protection of the innocent, advocated for reformation and community reintegration of youthful offenders, and demonstrated concern about the elimination of sexual and racial discrimination and about protection of the environment. She also had charge of a number of extremely high-profile cases. In April 1993, not even two months after she became attorney general, she had to make one of the most difficult decisions of her career, regarding the situation at the Branch Davidian Compound outside of Waco, Texas. In February, four agents from the Bureau of Alcohol, Tobacco, and Firearms had been killed and another twenty wounded while attempting to serve a search warrant for weapons violations on David Koresh, leader of the Branch Davidians, a survivalist religious cult that included men, women and children. Koresh had barricaded himself and his well-armed followers inside the complex, threatening all who approached, and a 51-day standoff ensued. On April 19, Reno, convinced that the children inside the complex were being physically abused, sanctioned the Federal Bureau of Investigation to attack the compound with tear gas in order to force those inside to surrender and come out. The attack went badly awry, however, and the compound was set ablaze. (Controversy and conspiracy theories would linger about whether the fire had been set by Koresh himself or by incendiary devices used by the FBI.) In the ensuing inferno, some 86 people, including 17 children, were killed. Reno, clearly struggling with the horror, held a news conference shortly thereafter in which she took full responsibility, but not blame, for the tragedy. Her honesty and visible anguish were refreshing to an audience used to political finger-pointing and public-relations spins, and brought her much personal support and acclaim from the public. Nonetheless, the Waco incident cast a long shadow over Reno's years as attorney general, and the deaths of the cultists—particularly of the children—would remain a potent slur for her opponents.

Reno often chose to act strictly as called for by the law, rather than as called for by public or political opinion. For example, she declined to arrest Sheik Omar Abdel-Rahman—linked to a plot to blow up the World Trade Center—before weighing all the evidence. Despite intense political pressure, she ordered him detained only after he attempted to flee the country. She supported **Lani Guinier**, nominated to head the Department of Justice's Civil Rights Division, even after the Clinton administration withdrew the nomination in the face of Republican attacks. Reno also appointed an independent counsel to investigate President Clinton for wrongdoing in an old real-estate transaction, even though she owed him her job. She continued to refer various, though not all, investigations of possible impropriety to independent counsels (finally seven in all), including the investigation of the president's relationship with White House intern **Monica Lewinsky** that eventually led to his impeachment trial.

Reno presided over several other difficult cases, including the bombing of the Alfred P. Murrah Federal Building in Oklahoma City, Oklahoma, in 1995. The bombing, which occurred on the second anniversary of the Waco fire, killed 169 people. Her personal opposition to the death penalty did not prevent federal prosecutors from seeking, and receiving, the death penalty for bomber Timothy McVeigh. Other terrorist bombings followed, both in the U.S. and overseas. In 1996, Reno was diagnosed with Parkinson's disease, and continued working at the same pace while beginning to receive treatment for her illness. She was among those in the Justice Department and the FBI who came under fire for the protracted and eventually all but dropped investigation of nuclear scientist Wen Lee Ho's alleged theft of national security secrets. No doubt the most visible case in the latter part of her tenure, however, was that of Elián González, the 6-year-old Cuban boy who was found floating on an inner tube in the ocean off Miami in late November 1999.

The rescue of Elián by local Cuban-American fishermen began a lengthy, extraordinarily emotional saga that for months made front-page news around the world. He was one of only three survivors from a boat that had capsized while its occupants were fleeing Cuba; eleven more on the boat, including his mother, had drowned. The boy's extended family in Miami promptly claimed him, as did his father in Cuba. The custody battle that ensued involved the U.S. and Cuban governments, the U.S. court system, and much savvy use of the court of public opinion by both Elián's Cuban-American relatives and their supporters and by Fidel Castro. Huge daily rallies were held in Miami by the Cuban-American community to show support for keeping the boy in the United States, and politicians and pundits tripped over themselves in trying to uphold both the sanctity of the family (which dictated that he should be returned to his father in Cuba) and the sanctity of the fight against Communism (which demanded that he not be forced to grow up in Cuba). Reno focused on the legal issues: American custody and immigration laws. Negotiations between Reno, INS

Commissioner **Doris Meissner**, and the Miami relatives dragged on. Tensions were high in the Cuban-American community in Miami, exacerbated by the city's mayor who, because of comments made, seemed to flout obedience to federal law. On April 22, 2000, federal agents staged a pre-dawn raid on the house of Elián's Miami relatives to reunite him with his father. Videotapes of the raid, in which the screaming child was yanked by an agent from the arms of a supporter while surrounded by agents armed with automatic weapons, were replayed endlessly on television and brought Reno a firestorm of criticism, particularly from the Cuban-American community and Republicans in Washington. "[T]ime had run out," she said in response. "I did until the final moments try to reach a voluntary solution." She later noted that she had "tried my level best to make sure we avoided this situation. . . . I'm satisfied with the result."

Reno dealt with the political fallout from the Elián González case with the sure confidence that the decision made had been the correct one under the law. While she was frequently criticized for foot-dragging during her tenure, supporters noted that this apparent indecision resulted from meticulous study of issues and a deliberate refusal to sacrifice the law to expediency (a policy perhaps reinforced by the early experience of Waco). She survived with equanimity repeated calls for her resignation from political opponents over the years, and gained a great deal of respect from the public for her integrity and independence from both political parties. Reno served until the end of the Clinton administration in January 2001, the longest term for any attorney general since 1829. "It's been a great adventure," she said of her years in Washington. "Now I'm going to go home and sit on my front porch." Shortly after she moved back home to Florida, a group of Cuban-Americans still angry about Elián held a protest outside her house. It was, she told reporters, "a great example of the First Amendment at work."

SOURCES:

Axelrod, Alan, *et al. Cops, Crooks, and Criminologists*. Facts on File, 1996.

Encyclopedia of World Biography. 2nd ed. Detroit, MI: Gale Research, 1998.

Graham, Judith, ed. *Current Biography Yearbook 1993*. NY: H.W. Wilson, 1993.

Martin, Jean, ed. *Who's Who of Women in the Twentieth Century*. Crescent Books, 1995.

The Miami Herald. April 23, 2000; April 25, 2000; February 6, 2001.

The New York Times. January 20, 2001, p. A10; January 21, 2001, p. 19.

Malinda Mayer,
writer and editor, Falmouth, Massachusetts

Rentoul, Annie Isobel (c. 1855–1928).

See Outhwaite, Ida for sidebar.

Rentoul, Annie Rattray (1882–1978).

See Outhwaite, Ida for sidebar.

Repplier, Agnes (1855–1950)

American essayist. Pronunciation: Rep-LEER. Born in Philadelphia, Pennsylvania, on April 1, 1855; died in Philadelphia on December 15, 1950; daughter of John George Repplier and Agnes (Mathias) Repplier; educated at Eden Hall, Sacred Heart Convent in Torresdale, near Philadelphia, and Agnes Irwin's private school in Philadelphia; never married; no children.

First published short stories and sketches (1871); received first national attention for a short story appearing in Catholic World *(1881); traveled and lectured extensively, primarily in Europe (from 1890s); published last essay (1940).*

Selected writings—essay collections: Books and Men *(1888),* Points of View *(1891),* Essays in Miniature *(1892),* Essays in Idleness *(1893),* In the Dozy Hours and Other Papers *(1894),* Varia *(1897),* Philadelphia: The Place and the People *(1898),* The Fireside Sphinx *(1901),* Compromises *(1904),* A Happy Half-Century and Other Essays *(1908),* The Cat *(1912),* Americans and Others *(1912),* Counter-Currents *(1916),* Points of Friction *(1920),* Under Dispute *(1924),* Time and Tendencies *(1931),* To Think of Tea! *(1932),* In Pursuit of Laughter *(1936),* Eight Decades: Essays and Episodes *(1937); (biographies)* J. William White, M.D. *(1919),* Père Marquette *(1929),* Mère Marie of the Ursulines *(1931),* Junípero Serra *(1933),* Agnes Irwin *(1934); (autobiography)* In Our Convent Days *(1905).*

Agnes Repplier was born in Philadelphia in 1855, the daughter of **Agnes Mathias Repplier** and John George Repplier. Her father, who had been a widower when he married Agnes Mathias, was a financially successful retailer of coal for a mining business he owned with his brothers. Although Repplier often implied she was of French descent, both her parents were German.

Repplier received her early education at home from her mother, a woman of strong character with high expectations for her four children. Repplier disliked the formal lessons and the material she was required to learn. However, her incredible memory for verse and stories allowed her to recite much of what was read to her by her mother, and as a result, she did not learn to read for herself until she was almost ten years old. She then read with voracious interest, particularly the poetry of Tennyson and Byron.

In 1867, Repplier began her tumultuous years of formal education when she entered Eden Hall, a girls' school associated with the Sacred Heart Convent in Torresdale, Pennsylvania, outside of Philadelphia. She often rebelled against the strict rules, and in her second year was expelled for insubordination. Her parents then sent her to a new private school in Philadelphia run by *Agnes Irwin, who later became the first dean of Radcliffe College. Within 18 months, Repplier was expelled again, reportedly for refusing to read a book she considered "stupid." Her school years were not without rewards, however, for she became friends with Elizabeth Robins (*Elizabeth Pennell), later a noted writer and art critic, at Eden Hall, and Agnes Irwin, who encouraged Repplier to pursue her writing, became her lifelong mentor and friend.

Repplier's father suffered financial losses in 1871, and she was required by necessity to help supplement the family's income. She began submitting stories to the Philadelphia *Sunday Times* and the *Young Catholic*. Over the next ten years, she continued to publish sporadically in these and other periodicals, and received nationwide notice in 1881 for a short story that appeared in *Catholic World*. In 1884, after she published

several more of her stories, *Catholic World's* founder and editor Father Isaac Hecker, who considered Repplier's plots uninspired, urged her to begin writing essays rather than short stories. Accepting the advice, she turned to writing essays, a form she would never abandon.

In 1886, the *Atlantic Monthly* published her essay "Children, Past and Present," a witty look at the ways in which various famous people had been kept in line during childhood. After that, her work appeared often in the *Atlantic Monthly*. Repplier's topics covered a wide range, including events in everyday life, and incidents from history and literature. Her essays were defined by her refined style, laced with a lightly ironical wit that enthralled her readers (writer *Mary Ellen Chase once called her "the dean of American essayists"). Repplier began her career during a time when essays were highly popular, and soon she was consistently publishing collections of her essays. The first of these, *Books and Men*, appeared in 1888, and she published 17 more collections over the next five decades.

Encouraged by Irwin, Repplier delivered her first lecture in 1890. After that, she spent much of her leisure time traveling and lecturing, making numerous trips to Europe. She also wrote five biographies, two of which, *J. William White, M.D.* (1919) and *Agnes Irwin* (1934), were personal tributes to people important in her life (White had successfully treated her for cancer at the turn of the century). The other three biographies were of figures important in the history of the Roman Catholic Church: *Père Marquette* (1929), *Mère Marie of the Ursulines* (1931), concerning *Marie de l'Incarnation (1599–1672), French educator and founder of the Ursuline Order in New France (Canada), and *Junípero Serra* (1933). Her only autobiographical works were *In Our Convent Days* (1905) and the collection *Eight Decades: Essays and Episodes* (1937), both of which deal with her experiences at Eden Hall.

Repplier, who never married, preferred the conversation and companionship of men to women, and through her travels and correspondences gained the friendship of such well-known men as Oliver Wendell Holmes, Henry James, Theodore Roosevelt, and Walt Whitman. Among the awards bestowed upon her were honorary degrees from the University of Pennsylvania (1902), Temple (1919), Yale (1925), Columbia (1927), Marquette (1929), and Princeton (1935), and the Laetare Medal from Notre Dame (1911). Repplier became one of the first women members of the National Institute of Arts and Letters

Agnes Repplier

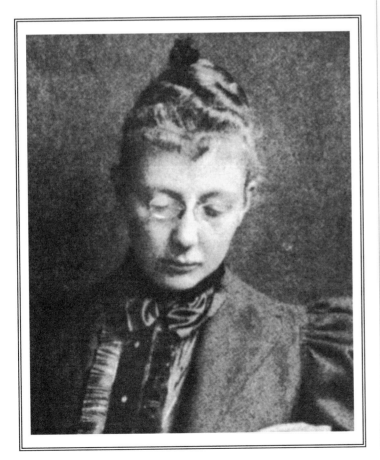

in 1926 (*Julia Ward Howe had been elected in 1907), and two years later she was elected to membership in the American Philosophical Society. In 1935, she received the National Institute of Arts and Letters' gold medal.

When she was not traveling, Repplier lived for many years with her cats in an old red brick house in downtown Philadelphia. She published her last essay in 1940 in the *Atlantic Monthly*, just months before turning 85 years old. She died ten years later, at age 94, and was buried in the family vault at the Church of St. John the Evangelist.

SOURCES:

Edgerly, Lois Stiles, ed. *Give Her This Day.* Gardiner, ME: Tilbury House, 1990.

James, Edward T., ed. *Notable American Women, 1607–1950.* Cambridge, MA: The Belknap Press of Harvard University, 1971.

Kunitz, Stanley J., and Howard Haycraft, eds. *Twentieth Century Authors.* NY: H.W. Wilson, 1942.

McHenry, Robert. *Famous American Women.* NY: Dover, 1980.

Kari Bethel,
freelance writer, Columbia, Missouri

Resnik, Judith (1949–1986).

See Astronauts: Women in Space.

Resnik, Regina (1922—)

American soprano, mezzo-soprano, and stage director. Born on August 30, 1922, in the Bronx, New York; daughter of Sam Resnik (a leather manufacturer) and Ruth (Seidler) Resnik, both immigrated from the Ukraine; Hunter College, B.A., 1942; studied with Rosalie Miller and Giuseppe Danise; married Harry W. Davis (an attorney), on July 16, 1946; children: Michael Philip Davis (b. 1952).

Made concert debut at the Brooklyn Academy of Music (1942); made operatic debut at the New Opera Company (1942), Metropolitan (1944), Bayreuth (1953), Covent Garden (1957); became an opera producer (1971).

Regina Resnik made her operatic debut inadvertently, when the singer for whom she was understudying as Lady Macbeth was suddenly taken ill before the opera's final performance at the New Opera Company in 1942. She won good reviews and a guest appearance with the Opera Nacional in Mexico City, where she performed the following year. Her debut at the Metropolitan Opera in 1944 was similarly unintended; she had been scheduled to sing Santuzza in *Cavalleria Rusticana* on a Saturday night, sever-

al days after the company performed *Il Trovatore*. Early in the week, the soprano who was to sing Leonora in *Il Trovatore* came down with laryngitis, and Resnik, with only 24 hours' notice and one rehearsal, found herself debuting as Leonora. Reviews were positive for both her voice and her courage, and the following year she sang the lead role of Leonore in *Fidelio*, in the Met's first English-language version of that Beethoven opera. Over the next years, she sang such roles as Tosca, Aïda, Butterfly, Donna Anna, and Donna Elvira. She also sang in the American premiers of Benjamin Britten's *Rape of Lucretia* (as the Chorus, 1947) and *Peter Grimes* (1948). Her voice was a shining instrument which coped easily with top notes. She sang at the Wagner festival in Bayreuth for the first time in 1953, as Sieglinde in *Die Walküre*. In 1955, she switched from soprano to mezzo-soprano roles, for which she has been especially remembered. Among these were Marina in *Boris Godunoff*, Amneris in *Aïda*, Ortrud in *Lohengrin*, Giulietta in *Tales of Hoffmann*, and Lucretia in *Rape of Lucretia*. Resnik was a dramatic performer, and this ability combined with her powerful voice made her interpretations memorable. (In 1945, she noted, "I'm not interested in straight singing parts. To me opera is theater, using a singing voice instead of a speaking voice, not just standing around like a singing cow.") Records preserve only some of her work, and some recordings are less than ideal as a demonstration of her artistry. Bernstein's superb recording of *Falstaff* probably best demonstrates her abilities. After Resnik retired from opera, she appeared in a number of concerts as well as musicals. She also achieved considerable success as a director of opera, with productions of *Carmen* in Hamburg, *Elektra* in Venice, and *Falstaff* in Warsaw.

Respighi, Elsa (1894–1996)

Italian composer, organist, pianist, singer, and writer who became a proponent of her husband's music and produced many of his operas after his death. Born Olivieri Sangiacomo in Rome, Italy, on March 24, 1894; died at age 101 in April or May 1996; married Ottorino Respighi (1879–1936), the composer.

Elsa Respighi, born in Rome in 1894, studied piano with Clotide Poce and Giovanni Sgambati and then attended the Accademia de Santa Cecilia, where she graduated in Gregorian chant. While there, she studied advanced harmony and counterpoint under Remigio Renzi and fugue and composition under Ottorino Respighi whom she later married. The couple toured throughout the world and Elsa often sang their compositions. Respighi devoted the latter part of her life to her husband's music. She completed the orchestration of his opera *Lucrezia* and produced *Belfagor, Fiamma, Campana Sommersa,* and *Maria Egiziaca.* Ottorino's music has continued to grow in stature, in no small part due to Elsa's efforts. In 1969, she founded the *Respighi Fondo* in Venice which was dedicated to the propagation of musical culture. Elsa Respighi wrote two operas, *Alcesti* (1941) and *Samurai* (1945), composed four orchestral works as well as a ballet and many vocal works, and also wrote the text for two ballets by her husband as well as his biography.

John Haag,
Athens, Georgia

Restell, Madame (1812–1878).

See Lohman, Ann Trow.

Restituta, Sister (1894–1943)

Austrian nun and nurse who was found guilty by the Nazi People's Court in Vienna on charges of "preparation for high treason." Name variations: Helene Kafka. Born Helene Kafka on May 1, 1894, in Husowitz near Brünn, Moravia (now Brno, Czech Republic); executed in Vienna, Austria, on March 30, 1943.

Born Helene Kafka on May 1, 1894, in Husowitz near Brünn, Moravia (modern-day Brno, Czech Republic), Sister Restituta was a devout Roman Catholic nun and respected nurse who held definite, if unsophisticated, political views. Strong-willed, she worked for years as an operating-room nurse at Vienna's Mödling Hospital. She was critical of the Nazi regime in Austria from its inception. Her opposition to National Socialism's idolatry of the state and glorification of war and racism took tangible form in the last months of 1941, when she refused to remove crucifixes from the patients' wards. She then wrote two pamphlets disparaging the war and Hitler's regime and placed them in the pockets of her patients, all of whom were wounded soldiers. One pamphlet, "German Catholic Youth," referred to an incident in which a unit of Hitler Youths disrupted a Catholic youth meeting in Freiburg im Breisgau; the Catholics were critical of the corruption of young people through Hitler Youth indoctrination. Much of the essay concentrated on itemizing and exposing the anti-Christian essence of the regime. The other pamphlet was a poem, "Soldiers' Song," which condemned the Nazis as an alien horde of "Prussians" who had poisoned the moral character of occupied Austria, had stripped it of its food, gold and art treasures, and whose movement had succeeded in unleashing a bloody war and "poisoned the world with their hatred, turning every other nation into an enemy." It concluded optimistically, by urging soldiers to take up only arms "to fight for a free Fatherland, against the brown slave Reich, for a happy Austria!"

Sister Restituta was denounced to the Nazi authorities by Dr. Stöhr, chief physician of the Mödling Hospital, and as a consequence was arrested on February 18, 1942. Few doubted the outcome of her trial before Vienna's People's Court. The judgment against her, read on October 29, 1942, found her guilty of "treasonous assistance to the foe" and "preparation for high treason," and the sentence was death. She was executed by decapitation in Vienna on March 30, 1943. The prison chaplain, Monsignor Köck, noted in his diary that prior to her death Sister Restituta renewed her nun's vows, that her exemplary demeanor while on death row enabled her to bring several of her fellow prisoners back to the Catholic Church, and that she faced her death with composure, devoutly accepting of the will of God.

SOURCES:
Dokumentationsarchiv des österreichischen Widerstandes, Vienna, file 2695.

Institut für Wissenschaft und Kunst, Vienna, "Biografisches Lexikon der österreichischen Frau."

Luza, Radomir V. *The Resistance in Austria, 1938–1945.* Minneapolis, MN: University of Minnesota Press, 1984.

Rudolf, Karl. *Aufbau im Widerstand: Ein Seelsorgebericht aus Österreich 1938–1945.* Salzburg: Otto Müller Verlag, 1947.

Widerstand und Verfolgung in Wien 1934–1945: Eine Dokumentation. 2nd ed. 3 vols. Vienna: Österreichischer Bundesverlag, 1984.

John Haag,
Associate Professor of History,
University of Georgia, Athens, Georgia

Rethberg, Elisabeth (1894–1976)

German soprano. Name variations: Lisabeth Sättler or Sattler. Born Elisabeth Sättler on September 22, 1894, in Schwarzenberg, Saxony, Germany; died on June 6, 1976, in Yorktown Heights, New York; studied piano and voice with Otto Watrin at the Dresden Conservatory; became an American citizen in 1939; married George Cehanovsky (a baritone), in 1957.

Made her debut in Johann Strauss' Der Zigeunerbaron (1911); appeared as Agatha in Der Freischütz at the Dresden Hofoper (1915); made her debut at Salzburg and Metropolitan Opera (1922), Covent

Garden (1925); created the title role in Strauss' Ægyptische Helena (The Egyptian Helen); made an honorary member of the State Theaters of Saxony (1930); performed at the Met (1922–42) in 30 roles.

Elisabeth Rethberg was born in 1894 into a musical family in Schwarzenberg, Saxony, Germany, and was playing the piano by age four. At seven, she sang the entire *Winterreise* cycle of Schubert. Her training with Otto Watrin emphasized breath control above all else. Having mastered this technique, she undertook no further study. In 1915, Rethberg became a member of the Royal Opera in Dresden. She came to the Metropolitan Opera House in New York City in 1922, in the title role of *Aïda*. For 20 years, from 1922 until 1942, Rethberg starred at the Met, performing Aïda 51 times. In 1926 and 1927, she also sang with the Ravinia Park Opera in Chicago. As well, Rethberg often appeared on radio throughout the 1930s and 1940s.

Toscanini is said to have compared Elisabeth Rethberg's voice to a Stradivarius, calling her one of the world's great sopranos. In 1929, the New York Society of Singers claimed that Rethberg had the world's "most perfect voice." Recordings from 1924 to 1935 document a large compass, even scale, absolute consistency of tone, and effortless production. Opera buffs once spoke of the "Destinn tone" (referring to *Emmy Destinn); during Rethberg's career they spoke of the "Rethberg quality." Rethberg, who learned over 100 roles, was an intelligent, tasteful singer who worked to produce what composers had intended. But her decline was somewhat abrupt, and by 1942 her tone had become forced. Performances recorded during the final years of her career certify that her once great voice was no more.

John Haag,
Athens, Georgia

Retton, Mary Lou (1968—)

American gymnast who, with Korbut and Comaneci, helped change the approach of the sport from ballet to athleticism. Born on January 24, 1968, in Fairmont, West Virginia; daughter of Lois Jean Retton and Ronnie Retton; attended the University of Texas; married Shannon Kelley (a financial analyst), on December 29, 1990; children: three daughters, Shayla Rae Kelley (b. April 12, 1995); McKenna Lane Kelley (b. 1997); Skyla Brae Kelley (b. August 9, 2000).

First woman in the world to complete a variation of the Tsukahara vault; first American woman to win an individual Olympic medal in gymnastics, at Los Angeles (1984); first official female spokesperson for Wheaties.

Born in Fairmont, West Virginia, in 1968, Mary Lou Retton began her gymnastics career on the dance floor, taking ballet, tap, jazz, and acrobatics at age four. When she was seven and enrolled in a gymnastics class at West Virginia University, her mother and coaches soon recognized Retton was destined for great things. She began training at Pete Longdon's Aerial-Port Gymnastics with coach Gary Rafaloski and particularly liked working on gymnastics apparatus, noting, "I just got up and it felt natural." At eight, Retton won the beginner's title at a statewide meet. Four years later, she entered the 1980 Class II nationals, competing against older, more experienced gymnasts and winning the vault event. In 1981, she was made a member of the U.S. junior national team. For the next two years, Retton traveled around the world, winning events in China, Japan, Canada, and South Africa.

Retton was competing in Las Vegas in 1982 when she met the world-famous gymnastics coach Bela Karolyi. She began taking her high school classes by correspondence while training at his U.S. Gymnastics Center in Houston. Karolyi added power to Retton's performance and increased the difficulty of her vaults. After two weeks with her new coach, Retton scored her first perfect ten on the vault. Just a few months later, at the McDonald's American Cup, she won the all-around title, the vault, and the floor exercise, and tied for first place on the uneven parallel bars. In 1983, she became the first woman in the world to complete a variation of the Tsukahara vault—a layout 1½-back somersault with a double twist. Although a stress fracture in her left wrist forced Retton to skip the 1983 World championships, by December of that year she had won the Chunichi Cup in Japan. She successfully defended her American Cup shortly thereafter.

Gymnastics training is always strenuous, but Retton's schedule became even more so as she prepared for the 1984 Olympics in Los Angeles. Spending eight to ten hours a day training, she was chosen as one of eight members on the American women's team. Not long before the games, she tore cartilage in her right knee and had to have arthroscopic surgery; only two days later, she was back on the bars. Retton won five Olympic medals, the most won by any athlete at the 1984 Games; she captured the Olympic gold for the all-around title over her chief competitor, Rumania's **Ecaterina Szabo**, as well as a silver in the vault, and bronze medals in floor exercise, uneven bars, and the team competition.

With the advent of *Olga Korbut, Americans had begun a love affair with female gym-

nasts, but now they had a star of their own. Retton's photo was everywhere, and her light-hearted personality endeared her to fans. She was named 1984 Female Athlete of the Year by the Associated Press, Sportswoman of the Year by *Sports Illustrated*, and became the youngest athlete inducted into the U.S. Olympic Hall of Fame. She also broke the Wheaties endorsement barrier, becoming the first woman athlete ever featured on its cereal box and the first official woman spokesperson for the product.

In 1985, Retton successfully defended her American Cup all-around title. To date, she is the only person to win this title three times. After studying communications at the University of Texas, Retton began serving as a television commentator. An actress as well, she has appeared in several major motion pictures and numerous television shows. She has also been successful as a motivational speaker and newspaper columnist.

In 1994, the U.S. Olympic Committee established the annual Mary Lou Retton Award for athletic excellence, and in February 1995, First Lady **Hillary Rodham Clinton** presented Retton with the **Flo Hyman** Award in recognition of her spirit, dignity, and commitment to excellence. Mary Lou Retton brought a new dynamic to American gymnastics. Olga Korbut and *Nadia Comaneci had changed gymnastics from a graceful ballet exercise to a sport requiring strength, power, and daring, and Retton built on those changes. Thousands of young American girls signed up for gymnastics after her appearance at the 1984 Olympics.

SOURCES:

Retton, Mary Lou, and Bela Karolyi. *Mary Lou: Creating an Olympic Champion.* NY: McGraw-Hill, 1986.

Silverstein, Herman. *Mary Lou Retton and the New Gymnasts.* NY: Franklin Watts, 1985.

Washington, Rosemary G. *Mary Lou Retton, Power Gymnast.* Minneapolis, MN: Lerner, 1985.

Woolum, Janet. *Outstanding Women Athletes: Who They Are and How They Influenced Sports in America.* Phoenix, AZ: Oryx Press, 1992.

Karin L. Haag, freelance writer, Athens, Georgia

Reuss, Eleanor (1860–1917).

See Eleanora of Reuss.

Reuss, princess of.

See Hermine of Reuss (1887–1947).
See Ida of Schaumburg-Lippe (1852–1891).

Reuter, Gabriele (1859–1941)

German novelist. Born in Alexandria, Egypt, on February 8, 1859; died in Weimar, Germany, on November 16, 1941; elder of two children and only daughter of Karl Reuter (a businessman) and Johanne (Behmer) Reuter; some schooling in Wolfenbüttel and Neuhaldensleben, Germany; never married; no children.

Began writing after father's death (1872); published first novel Glück und Geld *(Happiness and Money, 1888); published* Aus guter Familie *(From a Good Family), her most successful novel (1895); published autobiography* Vom Kinde zum Menschen *(From the Child to the Person, 1922).*

Gabriele Reuter wrote about the lives of ordinary, middle-class German women at the turn of the 20th century. Her books describe the psychological bondage imposed on women by the expectations of society and the resulting frustration and anguish of their lives. Although her most famous work, *Aus guter Familie: Leidensgeschichte eines Mädchens* (From a Good Family: The Suffering of a Young Woman), inspired extensive commentary and public debate about women's education and their role in modern society, she denied any social agenda, despite her sympathy with the women's rights movement.

Born on February 8, 1859, Reuter had an exotic childhood in Egypt where her father Karl Reuter was part of a trade delegation to the German embassy. Her mother **Johanne Behmer Reuter** feared that Gabriele would be ill-equipped for proper German society if she continued to live in Egypt, so in 1872 she moved her children to Wolfenbüttel so they could attend appropriate schools. They had not been long in Germany when Gabriele's father died suddenly, leaving the family without income and Gabriele without the means to a formal education.

Reuter, then 13 years old, determined that she must support her family. She had thought of going on the stage, but her father had made her promise that she would do no such thing. Her mother's family included many literary and intellectual women, among them Gabriele's great-grandmother **Philippine Gatterer**, one of the greatest intellects of the German Enlightenment, and **Caroline Engelhard**, a popular novelist of her time. With her family background in mind, Johanne suggested to Gabriele that she enter a writing contest. Although she did not win, an aunt encouraged her to continue to write, and she began submitting small pieces, many of them about Egypt, to the newspapers. One of her cousins, editor of the conservative newspaper *Kreuzzeitung*, helped her get published, but Reuter was not satisfied with her work and stopped writing. She spent the next few years doing household chores and caring for her ailing mother. In 1879, the two of them moved to Weimar, and Reuter—living in what was considered the intellectual center of Germany—began her informal education.

While there, Reuter associated regularly with an aunt and uncle and their friends. Her uncle introduced her to the ideas of Friedrich Nietzsche and to the modern paintings of Arnold Böcklin, whose work shocked the middle-class public, while her aunt provided the perfect example of a devoted, selfless, unfulfilled, and frustrated wife and mother. Reuter began working on a novel about Egypt, encouraged by her aunt who helped her to tighten and simplify her style. The period between 1887 and 1891 seemed to Reuter the turning point for her artistic and personal life. She began to seek out critics and teachers at writers' conferences, for help and encouragement. The critic Karl Frenzel told her to write from her intimate knowledge about life in Germany rather than about Egypt, where she would always be a foreigner, and anarchist John Henry Mackay, with whom she became great friends despite the enormous differences in their worldviews, urged her to escape from her family in Weimar and live her own life. She also began to read such modern writers and thinkers as Charles Darwin, Ernst Haeckel, Arthur Schopenhauer, Emile Zola, Gustave Flaubert, and Guy de Maupassant.

In an epiphany, Reuter understood one day that her mission was to delineate the silent sufferings of girls and women trapped by the society they lived in. Although naturalism, with its grim, detailed descriptions of the lives of the working class, was much in vogue, she recognized that she knew little of the working class and thus had no right to write about them. Middle-class life, on the other hand, was something she understood all too well. She deliberately chose to stay away from the more common dramatic and passionate depictions of middle-class women (exemplified by Flaubert's *Madame Bovary* and Tolstoy's *Anna Karenina*). Her theme became the silent tragedy of daily life, and the focus of her energy was the work that would be *Aus guter Familie*. It was many years before she finished it because her priority was caring for her ill mother. In the meantime, frequent trips to Berlin brought her into the circle of naturalist writers, among them her future publisher Samuel Fischer, and it was to these writers that she first showed her book. Their misinterpretations of her themes horrified her, and she nearly destroyed the novel before deciding that she had presented the truth as she saw it. *Aus guter Familie*, published in 1895, proved to be a phenomenal success, going into 5 editions by 1897 and 18 editions by 1908.

Also in 1895, Reuter moved with her mother to Munich. There she met intelligent, well-spoken feminists whose concerns echoed her own. While she considered working actively in the fight for women's rights, she finally concluded that she would be better employed in dedicating herself to her writing, which was popular with the same middle-class, educated women whom feminists sought to gain as supporters. Nonethe-

less, she remained an advocate of the German women's movement throughout her life. In 1899, she settled with her mother in Berlin, and over the following 20 years wrote almost a book each year. Among these were *Der Lebenskünstler* (The Artist of Life, 1897); *Frau Bürgelin und ihre Söhne* (Mrs. Bürgelin and Her Sons, 1899), much admired by Thomas Mann; *Ellen von der Weiden* (1900), which proved popular enough to merit 65 editions; *Frauenseelen* (Women's Souls, 1902); *Liselotte von Reckling* (1904), also much praised by Thomas Mann; and *Das Tränenhaus* (The House of Tears, 1909), a devastating picture of a maternity house for unmarried, pregnant women scorned by society. Reuter also wrote topical essays, including *Die Probleme der Ehe* (The Problems of Marriage, 1907) and *Liebe und Stimmrecht* (Love and Suffrage, 1914). Her identification with the women's movement can also be seen in the biographies she wrote of contemporary novelist *Marie Ebner-Eschenbach (1904) and of the great 19th-century writer *Annette von Droste-Hülshoff (1905). In 1904, Mann called Reuter "the most sovereign woman living in Germany today."

Reuter published her autobiography, *Vom Kinde zum Menschen* (From the Child to the Person), in 1922. The following year inflation wiped out her life savings, and she lived in a precarious financial state thereafter. She published only a children's book and a fictionalized family history during the grim years of the 1930s. The rise of Hitler at the end of her life was in sad contrast to her ideal of the fulfillment of the individual. She died in Weimar in 1941.

SOURCES:

Buck, Claire, ed. *The Bloomsbury Guide to Women's Literature*. NY: Prentice Hall, 1992.

Garland, Mary. *The Oxford Companion to German Literature*. 3rd ed. Oxford: Oxford University Press, 1997.

Goodman, Katherine R. "Gabriele Reuter" in *Dictionary of Literary Biography*, Vol. 66: *German Fiction Writers, 1885–1913*. Edited by James Hardin. Detroit, MI: Gale Research, 1988.

Malinda Mayer,
writer and editor, Falmouth, Massachusetts

Reventlow, Anne Sophie

(1693–1743)

Queen of Norway and Denmark. Name variations: Anna Sophie von Reventlow; Anna Sofie von Reventlow. Born on April 16, 1693; died on January 7, 1743, in Klausholm; became third wife of Frederick IV, king of Norway and Denmark (r. 1699–1730), on April 4, 1721; children: Christiane Amalie (1723–1724); Frederick Christian (b. 1726); Charles (b. 1728).

Revere, Anne (1903–1990)

American actress who won an Academy Award for her role in National Velvet *but was blacklisted during the McCarthy era. Born on June 25, 1903, in New York City; died of pneumonia on December 18, 1990, in Locust Valley, New York; attended Wellesley College; married Samuel Roser (a stage director), in 1935.*

Selected theater: made Broadway debut in The Great Barrington *(1931); appeared in* Lady With a Lamp *(1931),* Wild Waves *(1932),* Double Door *(1933),* The Children's Hour *(1934),* As You Like It *(1937),* The Three Sisters *(1939),* Cue for Passion *(1958),* Jolly's Progress *(1959), and* Toys in the Attic *(1960).*

Selected filmography: Double Door *(1934);* One Crowded Night *(1940);* The Howards of Virginia *(1940);* The Devil Commands *(1941);* Men of Boys Town *(1941);* The Flame of New Orleans *(1941);* Remember the Day *(1941);* Meet the Stewarts *(1942);* The Falcon Takes Over *(1942);* Are Husbands Necessary? *(1942);* The Gay Sisters *(1942);* Star Spangled Rhythm *(1942);* The Meanest Man in the World *(1943);* Shantytown *(1943);* Old Acquaintance *(1943);* The Song of Bernadette *(1943);* Standing Room Only *(1944);* Rainbow Island *(1944);* National Velvet *(1945);* The Keys of the Kingdom *(1945);* Sunday Dinner for a Soldier *(1945);* The Thin Man Goes Home *(1945);* Don Juan Quilligan *(1945);* Fallen Angel *(1945);* Dragonwyck *(1946);* The Shocking Miss Pilgrim *(1947);* Carnival in Costa Rica *(1947);* Forever Amber *(1947);* Secret Beyond the Door *(1948);* Scudda-Hoo! Scudda-Hay! *(1948);* Deep Waters *(1948);* You're My Everything *(1949);* The Great Missouri Raid *(1951);* A Place in the Sun *(1951);* Tell Me That You Love Me, Junie Moon *(1970);* Macho Callahan *(1970);* Birch Interval *(1976).*

A highly touted character actress and a Tony and Oscar winner, Anne Revere was born in 1903 in New York City and attended Wellesley College. She studied acting at the American Laboratory Theater and worked in stock and repertory before making her Broadway debut in 1931 in *The Great Barrington*. In 1933, she appeared in *Double Door*, then went to Hollywood to reprise her role in the film version a year later. Returning to New York, she was cast as Martha Dobie in *Lillian Hellman's first play, *The Children's Hour* (1934), a controversial drama which brought the subject of lesbianism to the stage for the first time. The play was explosive and ran for 691 performances. Deemed too sensational for the Pulitzer Prize, it won the newly created New York Drama Critics' Circle Award.

In 1940, Revere returned to Hollywood for a more prolonged stay and over the next decade played a series of memorable characters. She won an Academy Award for Best Supporting Actress for her role as *Elizabeth Taylor's mother in *National Velvet* (1945) and was nominated for her supporting roles in *The Song of Bernadette* (1943), based on the story of *Bernadette of Lourdes, and *Gentleman's Agreement* (1947), the film adaptation of *Laura Z. Hobson's novel. Revere also turned in a solid performance in *A Place in the Sun* (1951), playing the mother of Montgomery Clift.

Revere's career came to a crashing halt in 1951, during the McCarthy era, when she was blacklisted by the industry for pleading the Fifth Amendment before the House Un-American Activities Committee. Revere did not work for years. For a time, she and her husband Samuel Roser ran an acting school in Los Angeles; then, in the late 1950s, they moved back East, where Revere returned to the stage and appeared on television. In 1960, she won a Tony for her performance in another Hellman play, *Toys in the Attic*. During the late 1960s, Revere had a running part on the ABC-television soap opera "A Time for Us," but she did not have another substantial screen role until *Birch Interval* in 1976. Anne Revere died, age 87, in 1990.

SOURCES:

Katz, Ephraim. *The Film Encyclopedia.* NY: HarperCollins, 1994.

Lamparski, Richard. *Whatever Became of . . . ?* 1st and 2nd series. NY: Crown, 1967.

Barbara Morgan,
Melrose, Massachusetts

Reville, Alma (1900–1982)

English screenwriter and screen editor. Name variations: Alma Hitchcock. Born in England in 1900; died in 1982; married Alfred Hitchcock (the director), in December 1926; children: Patricia Hitchcock O'Connell (b. 1928, an actress who appeared in Strangers on a Train*).*

Selected filmography: The Ring *(1927);* Juno and the Paycock *(1930);* Murder *(1930);* The Skin Game *(1931);* Rich and Strange *(1932);* Waltzes from Vienna *(1933);* The Passing of the Third Floor Bank *(1935);* The 39 Steps *(1935);* Secret Agent *(1936);* Sabotage *(1936);* Young and Innocent *(*The Girl Was Young, *1937);* The Lady Vanishes *(1938);* Jamaica Inn *(1939);* Suspicion *(US, 1941);* Shadow of a Doubt *(US, 1943);* It's in the Bag *(US, 1948);* The Paradine Case *(US, 1948);* Stage Fright *(1950).*

British-born Alma Reville broke into films in the early 1920s, working as an editor's assistant. She was the "script girl" for Alfred Hitchcock on two of his very early directing projects: *The Pleasure Garden* (1925), and *The Lodger* (1926), which turned out to be his first commercial success. She married the director in 1926 and subsequently edited many of his films. She also collaborated as a screenwriter with him, earning story credits on 16 of Hitchcock's films, and collaborated with other directors as well. Some film historians believe that the characters of Gay Keane in Hitchcock's *The Paradine Case* (1948), Alma Ketter in *I Confess* (1953), and the wife of Detective Oxford in *Frenzy* (1972) are based on Alma Reville. When Hitchcock received the Lifetime Achievement Award from the American Film Institute in 1979, he dedicated it to Reville, noting that without her, "I probably would have ended up at this banquet as one of the slower moving waiters." She died three years later. In 1997, the Alma and Alfred Hitchcock Chair at the University of Southern California was endowed by their daughter **Patricia Hitchcock** O'Connell.

Rexach, Sylvia (1922–1961)

Puerto Rican composer who wrote such songs as "Y Entonces" and "Ola y Arena" that helped elevate Latin American music. Born in Santurce, Puerto Rico, on January 20, 1922; died in Santurce on October 20, 1961; children: Sharon.

Born in Santurce, Puerto Rico, in 1922, Sylvia Rexach played both the piano and the guitar, though she was not formally trained. Her first composition, "Idilio" ("Idyll"), was recorded by the Rafael Muñoz orchestra and sold well. Rexach worked to lend dignity to pop music with such songs as "Y Entonces" ("And Then"), "Alma Adrentro" ("Deep in the Soul"), "Quisiera Ser" ("I Wish to Be"), and "Anochecer" ("Dusk"). "Ola y Arena" ("Surf and Sand") became popular after her death.

Rexach was a founding member and secretary general of the Puerto Rican Society of Writers, Composers, and Musical Editors. A theater in San Juan is named after her. She is credited in *Puerto Rican Women* as having "a poetic imagination and a deep philosophical vein," and with exhibiting courage, humor, and optimism while facing impoverishment and cancer. Rexach died on October 20, 1961, in Santurce.

SOURCES:

Votaw, Carmen Delgado. *Puerto Rican Women.* Washington, DC: National Conference of Puerto Rican Women, 1995.

Kari Bethel,
freelance writer, Columbia, Missouri

Rey, Margret (1906–1996)

German-born American author, with her husband, of the "Curious George" children's book series. Name variations: Margret Elizabeth Rey. Born Margret Elizabeth Waldstein in Hamburg, Germany, on May 16, 1906; died of a heart attack in Cambridge, Massachusetts, on December 21, 1996; daughter of Felix Waldstein (a member of the German Parliament) and Gertrude (Rosenfeld) Waldstein; attended the Bauhaus in Dessau, 1927; Dusseldorf Academy of Art, 1928–29; University of Munich, 1930–31; married H(ans) A(ugusto) Rey (1898–1977, a writer and illustrator), in 1935; no children.

Selected writings: Pretzel *(1944, illustrated by H.A. Rey);* Spotty *(1945);* Pretzel and the Puppies *(1946);* Billy's Picture *(1948).*

Selected writings with H.A. Rey: Raffy and the Nine Monkeys *(1939);* Curious George *(1941);* Elizabite: The Adventures of a Carnivorous Plant *(1942);* Curious George Takes a Job *(1947);* Curious George

Rides a Bike *(1952)*; Curious George Gets a Medal *(1957)*; Curious George Flies a Kite *(1958)*; Curious George Learns the Alphabet *(1963)*; Curious George Goes to the Hospital *(1966)*; Whiteblack the Penguin Sees the World *(2000)*.

Co-editor with Allan J. Shalleck, based on "Curious George" film series: Curious George and the Dump Truck *(1984)*; Curious George and the Pizza *(1985)*; Curious George Goes to a Costume Party *(1986)*; Curious George Goes Fishing *(1987)*; Curious George at the Beach *(1988)*; Curious George and the Dinosaur *(1989)*; Curious George Goes to a Toy Store *(1990)*.

Margret Rey was born on May 16, 1906, in Hamburg, Germany, the daughter of **Gertrude Rosenfeld Waldstein** and Felix Waldstein, a member of the German Parliament. In 1927, she attended the famous Bauhaus in Dessau and spent the following two years studying at the Dusseldorf Academy of Art. Her first job was as a reporter and copywriter in Berlin, Germany. A talented artist and photographer, she held several exhibits of her watercolor paintings in Berlin. In the early 1930s, she moved first to London, England, and later to Rio de Janeiro, where she took jobs as a reporter and a copywriter. In Rio, she also met up again with Hans Augusto Rey, with whom she had been acquainted for a time in Hamburg. A struggling artist, H.A. Rey was then making a living selling bathtubs. Together, they started Brazil's first advertising agency, and in 1935 they were married. In 1936, they moved to Paris.

At the urging of an editor at Gallimard, a French publishing company, Rey worked with Hans to create a story from some humorous drawings he had done for a Paris periodical. The result was *Raffy and the Nine Monkeys* (1939), also published three years later as *Cecily G. and the Nine Monkeys*. The book is the story of a lonely giraffe, Cecily G., who shares her home with a family of monkeys. Rey focused on writing the story, and her husband contributed the illustrations. Their ability to make the absurd seem possible, combined with easy humor and attention to details, earned the couple praise. They also found the formula for their most successful series in Curious George, one member of the book's monkey family, and they were soon writing a story that concentrated on him.

In June 1940, the Reys fled France on bicycles, just hours before the Nazis invaded Paris. Dressed in warm coats and taking nothing but their manuscripts, including the original *Curious George*, they began pedaling south on a rainy predawn morning. They arrived at the French-Spanish border, where they sold their bicycles to customs officials, then boarded a train for Lisbon. The Reys stayed briefly in Rio de Janeiro, then in October 1940 they had their first view of New York harbor; they would remain in America for the rest of their lives. (Margret became a naturalized citizen in 1946.)

The couple took up residence in Greenwich Village and immediately began searching for a publisher for *Curious George*. Within a week, Houghton Mifflin accepted the story for publication. The book, which was destined to become a children's classic, is light and cheerful. In the opening line, the impish monkey is introduced thus: "He lived with his friend, the man with the yellow hat. He was a good little monkey, but he was always curious." George's naive, childlike inquisitiveness forever brings him into situations of innocent mischief from which his friend with the yellow hat saves him, without reproach.

Six years later, in 1947, Rey wrote another Curious George story, again with her husband illustrating, entitled *Curious George Takes a Job*. In all, the Reys published seven books in their "Curious George" series; the last, *Curious George Goes to the Hospital*, earned the Children's Book Award from the Child Study Association of America in 1966. Although only H.A. Rey's name appeared on the first books, each story was a collaboration of ideas, with Margret Rey writing the text and H.A. Rey drawing the illustrations. Rey, who was barely five feet tall, would often act the part of Curious George for her husband, who then made his drawings from her exaggerated poses. Rey was strong-willed, and the couple often debated the plot of the story. (They rarely argued about other things; H.A. Rey once attributed the success of their relationship to the following: "Years ago, we decided that I make all the big decisions and she makes the small decisions. So far in our marriage, there haven't been any big decisions.") In all, the "Curious George" series sold more than 20 million copies worldwide, in 12 different languages. *Pretzel* (1944), the tale of an extremely long dachshund, and *Spotty* (1945), about a brown-and-white rabbit who feels unwanted by his pink-and-white siblings, were works done solely by Rey with her husband contributing the drawings. Appearing toward the end of World War II, the stories advocate tolerance and acceptance.

In 1963, after 20 years in Greenwich Village, the Reys moved to Cambridge, Massachusetts, spending many of their summers at their cottage in Waterville, New Hampshire. Rey ceased writing children's books after her husband's death in 1977. However, with Allan Shalleck she edited over 30 new Curious George stories based on an animated film series. (A stage musical was also based on the Reys' books.) She was involved as well in the marketing of Curious George merchandise, a successful business endeavor that made her a millionaire. Having no children, Rey claimed Curious George as her only offspring, and noted that her ongoing involvement with the creation after H.A. Rey's death made her feel connected to her beloved husband.

Rey taught creative writing at Brandeis University from 1978 to 1984. In 1989, she joined the board of directors of Phillips Brooks House at Harvard University in Cambridge, Massachusetts, and two years later she became the founder and trustee of the Curious George Foundation. In 1996, she donated $1 million each to Beth Israel Hospital in Boston, Massachusetts, and to the Boston Public Library. A lifelong animal lover who with her husband kept pets as varied as turtles, snakes, monkeys and dogs, Rey was also a member of the World Wildlife Fund, the Audubon Society, and the Defenders of Wildlife. She died from complications following a heart attack in Cambridge, Massachusetts, on December 21, 1996.

SOURCES:

Commire, Anne, ed. *Something About the Author.* Vols. 26, 86, and 93. Detroit, MI: Gale Research.
"Margret Rey, 90," in *The Day* [New London, CT]. December 23, 1996, p. B3.
People Weekly. July 29, 1996, p. 28.
Publishers Weekly. January 27, 1997, p. 33.
Time. January 13, 1997, p. 25.

Kari Bethel,
freelance writer, Columbia, Missouri

Reyes, Deborah Elizabeth (b. 1952).

See Meyer, Debbie.

Reynolds, Belle (fl. 1860s)

American Civil War nurse and diarist. Born in Shelburne Falls, Massachusetts; married William Reynolds from Peoria, Illinois, in 1861.

Began traveling with her husband, a lieutenant in the Union Army who was serving in the 17th Infantry of Illinois (August 1861); survived battles and nursed wounded Union soldiers; awarded the commission of major by the governor of Illinois for her bravery and work during the Battle of Shiloh (April 1862); with husband, left the army (1864).

Belle Reynolds, a native of Shelburne Falls, Massachusetts, had been married to William

Reynolds only a few months when the Civil War broke out. William enlisted and became a lieutenant in the Union Army. When his regiment, the 17th Infantry of Illinois, was deployed to southern Missouri in August 1861, Reynolds became determined to follow her husband into battle. She boarded a boat for Cairo, Illinois, on August 10, and joined him the next day at Bird's Point, Missouri. She recorded her experiences over the next three years in her journal.

Of her first experience of camp life, Reynolds wrote: "How could I stay in such a cheerless place. . . . [I]t all seemed too much to endure; but I resolved to make the trial." Having retained the colonel's permission to accompany her husband, she traveled with the regiment by all means available to her, including in the Army wagon, in an ambulance, on a mule, and sometimes on foot, marching with the soldiers and carrying a musket. The regiment traveled often throughout southern Missouri, but seldom encountered danger. Reynolds' journal during this time is filled with descriptions of the beautiful landscape and life in the wilderness.

After spending the winter months in Cape Girardeau, Missouri, the regiment took orders from General Ulysses S. Grant to set out for Tennessee. Reynolds encamped near Pittsburg Landing, with her husband's company. She described the area as "a most romantic spot—high bluffs and deep ravines, little brooks carelessly creeping through the ferns, then rushing down over a rocky precipice, and bounding along to join the river." In contrast to this bucolic scene, she also recorded one of the most complete accounts of what became known as the Battle of Shiloh, in which over 10,000 soldiers on each side were killed in just two days. Union troops were still camped at Pittsburg Landing when the Confederate Army attacked before breakfast on Sunday morning, April 6, 1862. After quickly bidding her husband goodbye as he left for battle, Reynolds herself had to flee with nothing but her bonnet and a basket as Confederate troops descended on the camp. When she reached the safety of the river, she nursed the hundreds of wounded soldiers being treated on boats. The Union forces were being driven towards the river and impending defeat, and Reynolds described a scene of terror, confusion, and carnage. When hope was almost lost, Union gunboats and reinforcements appeared, and the Union Army under Grant won the first great battle of the Civil War.

Reynolds' accounts of the scene are sharp and terrifying. She wrote of her horrifying experiences as she nursed the wounded and dying

Belle Reynolds

soldiers, and described the pain and anguish of the operating room: "These scenes come up before me now with all the vividness of reality. Sometimes I hope it is only a fever-dream, but too well I know it was no dream; for, one by one, they would take from different parts of the hospital a poor fellow, lay him out on those bloody boards, and administer chloroform; but before insensibility, the operation would begin, and in the midst of shrieks, curses, and wild laughs, the surgeon would wield over his wretched victim the glittering knife and saw; and soon the severed and ghastly limb, white as snow and spattered with blood, would fall upon the floor—one more added to the terrible pile." Reynolds' strong will is depicted in her recording of an encounter with doctors who did not desire help from Reynolds and two other women wishing to attend to the wounded. "On one [boat] the surgeon objected to our coming on board, as he 'wanted no women around.' But nothing daunted, we went in search of any who might belong to our regiment."

After the battle, Reynolds was reunited with her husband; his horse had been shot out from beneath him, but he had remained unharmed. Upon his urging, Reynolds boarded a boat heading to a more secure location. Since she was one of the few eyewitnesses to the battle aboard the steamer, she was entreated by the boat's occupants to describe the scene. Governor Yates of Illinois was on board and at that very time drew up a commission, giving Reynolds the rank of major. "I received it, not so much as an honor which I really deserved," she wrote, "but simply as an acknowledgment of merit for having done what I could."

After once again joining her husband, Reynolds moved throughout Tennessee with the regiment, from Jackson to Bolivar to Corinth. In early 1863, her husband was reassigned to Major-General McClernand as aide-de-camp, and in March 1863, Reynolds joined her husband near Vicksburg, Tennessee. After the Union forces overtook Vicksburg, Reynolds' camp life turned more peaceful. Her husband was released from service in the spring of 1864, and Reynolds fades from history with their return to civilian life one year before the end of the Civil War.

SOURCES:

Griffin, Lynne, and Kelly McCann. *The Book of Women: 300 Notable Women History Passed By.* Holbrook, MA: Bob Adams, 1992.

Moore, Frank. *Women of the War; Their Heroism and Self-Sacrifice.* Hartford, CT: S.S. Scranton, 1866.

Kari Bethel,
freelance writer, Columbia, Missouri

Reynolds, Malvina (1900–1978)

Prolific lyricist, musician, and muse of American folk and protest music. Born Malvina Milder on August 23, 1900, in San Francisco, California; died on March 17, 1978, in Berkeley, California; eldest of three children of David Milder and Lizzie (Shenson) Milder; sister of Eleanor Milder Lawrence (b. 1910); University of California at Berkeley, B.A. in English language and literature, 1925, M.A., 1927, Ph.D., 1939; married Ben Goodman (marriage and divorce dates uncertain); married Bud Reynolds (a musician and labor organizer), in 1935 (died 1971); children: **Nancy Reynolds Schimmel** *(b. 1935).*

Inheriting her parents' socialist philosophy and conscience, became a member of the Communist Party (1930s); began to record her thoughts and observations on social justice, world peace, and women's rights in poetry and song; started to perform her music publicly (1940s); was blacklisted for her Communist sympathies because of appearance before the House Un-American Activities Committee (early 1950s); was "discovered" by the socially conscious folk music world (early 1960s); wrote scores of songs, some of them classics which became major hits for well-known

folk artists (mid-1970s); produced several collections of children's songs, as well as establishing her own music publishing company and recording company.

One summer night in 1947, folksinger Pete Seeger found himself talking to a middle-aged, white-haired woman who had approached him after a concert near San Francisco, California. The woman wanted his advice on becoming a singer and songwriter, two professions in which Seeger himself, then only 28, was rapidly advancing. "I usually make a practice of not discouraging people," Seeger remembered nearly 50 years later, "but . . . I think I had in the back of my mind a feeling, 'Gosh, she's pretty old to want to get started as a musician.' I had a lot to learn." Seeger had no idea that, in time, Malvina Reynolds would write for him and others some of the most passionate and popular activist folk music of the coming years.

Born Malvina Milder in San Francisco on August 23, 1900, Reynolds had been raised in a household with a strong sense of social responsibility coupled with a lively respect for the arts. Both her parents, David and **Lizzie Shenson Milder**, were active socialists who exposed their eldest daughter early on to music, poetry, and dance. (A brother, Samuel, was born in 1902 and a sister, **Eleanor Milder Lawrence**, in 1910.) It was David Milder's habit to wake up his household in the morning by playing classical music at high volume on the family phonograph; and one of Malvina's fondest childhood memories was of being taken to the theater by an aunt when she was six years old. "I used to watch the curtain go up and the lights go out, and I was just fascinated," she remembered. She provided her own sort of entertainment to neighborhood children by telling stories with great dramatic flair. She was equally fascinated by music, studying piano and violin during her public school years.

Reynolds' lifelong social activism became evident before she had graduated from Lowell High School, which refused her petition to allow girls to leave the school grounds during lunch—a privilege Malvina pointed out had long been granted to boys. It was not to be her last confrontation with school authorities. As the end of her senior year approached, Reynolds learned she would not be awarded a diploma because of her parents' opposition to World War I, a conflict the Milders considered a deadly exercise in imperialist politics. But she had been such a superlative student that, with the help of several teachers, she was accepted by the University of

Malvina
Reynolds

California at Berkeley without a diploma. The confidence shown in her abilities proved to be well founded. Reynolds made Phi Beta Kappa during her undergraduate years, receiving her B.A. in English language and literature in 1925, her M.A. in 1927, and her Ph.D. in 1939.

Reynolds observed the poverty and suffering of the Depression as a social worker and through the eyes of schoolchildren to whom she taught English. She began to record her impressions in poetry and in song, finding inspiration in the work of two musicians who, like her, gave voice through their music to the frustrations and fears of the downtrodden. Woody Guthrie and Earl Robinson spent the Depression years criss-crossing the country singing "the people's music," using their talents to call attention to the depredations of the country's worst economic crisis in more than a century. Recalling through their music the populist traditions that had unit-ed American workers for generations, they and others like them became a rallying point for the rising labor movement of the times, in which Malvina became increasingly involved after her marriage to Bud Reynolds.

Malvina and Bud had first met at a Socialist meeting in San Francisco when Malvina was in her teens and Bud, originally from Michigan, was in his twenties. Although Malvina had put her college education ahead of Bud's eventual proposal of marriage, the two resumed their re-lationship in the early 1930s soon after both had become members of the American Communist Party. (Malvina's earlier, brief marriage to Ben Goodman had ended in divorce.) Bud was a vig-orous labor organizer and had been instrumen-tal in establishing what would become the Unit-ed Automobile Workers in Detroit. In the manner of all loyal Communists of the time, Malvina and Bud observed a so-called "red wed-ding" in 1934, inviting their friends to a party at which they merely announced they were man and wife. Both were atheists and did not consid-er church or state approval of their union neces-sary, although the marriage was eventually recorded legally after the birth of a daughter, Nancy, in February 1935.

ℒove is something, if you give it away,
you end up having more.
—Malvina Reynolds, from "Magic Penny"

While Bud continued to contribute his orga-nizational skills to the party, music became in-creasingly important to Malvina as a means of expressing her own socialist impulses. "After Woody, I think I was one of the first who was primarily interested in writing songs based on labor and the folk tradition, songs with a social content," she once noted. "I write topical songs because I feel as though they are necessary." By the 1940s, while she worked on an assembly line and in her father's tailor shop, Malvina was per-forming her work in public as part of "The Peo-ple's Songs," a series of fundraising concerts of-fering "songs of labor and the American people" backed by the labor movement and its then-ally, the Communist Party. The proceeds of these concerts were used partly to fund union activi-ties and partly to support a kind of folk music clearinghouse which distributed sheet music of new folk songs. By 1950, "People's Songs" had evolved into the folk-music magazine *Sing Out!*, in which many of Reynolds' songs would be published over the next 25 years. Its inaugural issue featured that anthem of the folk tradition, co-written by Pete Seeger and Lee Hays, "If I Had a Hammer."

But as the nation's post-war anti-Commu-nism began to take hold, the labor movement along with its artistic supporters came under in-creasing government scrutiny by Joseph Mc-Carthy's House Un-American Activities Com-mittee. Along with Seeger and many other Communist sympathizers, Malvina and Bud were blacklisted, although both had resigned from the party in 1947 after taking exception to its rigid bureaucracy that allowed no room for creative experiment. Bud was banned from union activities of any kind and Malvina found it difficult to arrange concert appearances or sell her music. Seeger himself, after refusing to testi-fy before the HUAC, spent the next 17 years in professional limbo. "There was no worse name you could call a person than a Communist," Seeger remembers of those days, "and Woody and I and a lot of other people had sung for Communists and radicals and were proud of it. They were the hardest working people."

Bud found work in house repair and remod-eling, joining Malvina as a California represen-tative for *The National Guardian*, a socialist newspaper. All the while, Reynolds never gave up writing music, sometimes relying on news items and public events for her inspiration. A typical example, from the early 1960s, grew from a *New York Times* article about the tiny nation of Andorra, nestled in the Pyrenees, and its non-existent defense budget:

> They spent four dollars and ninety cents
> On armaments and their defense.
> Did you ever hear of such confidence?

Other songs written during this period include several that have since become folk and pop standards, such as "Magic Penny," "Pied Piper," "Don't Talk to Me of Love," and "We Hate to See Them Go." "She refused to be discouraged," Seeger says, recalling how Reynolds would often call to sing a new song over the telephone to him or, indeed, to anyone whom she thought might help her get it published. "She would not be put down, even though some people called her pushy." The number of new compositions mounted to such a degree that Seeger once joked

Malvina wrote a new song every morning before breakfast.

The turning point in Reynolds' career came in 1957, when Harry Belafonte recorded a song he had co-written with her, "Turn Around," a poignant ballad sung by a parent marveling at the growth of a child. By now, the protest movement that had gone underground during the McCarthy years was emerging stronger than ever, rolling into the 1960s on the voices of such folk groups as the Kingston Trio, the Backporch Majority, and The Weavers (composed of Seeger, Hays, Fred Hillerman, and *Ronnie Gilbert). Many of Reynolds' songs were among their most popular numbers, although Malvina never felt comfortable with the "folk music" designation and probably would have agreed with performer Big Bill Broonzy's opinion, "I guess all songs is folk songs. I never heard no horse sing 'em."

Pete Seeger was rescued from obscurity on the wings of Reynolds' "Little Boxes," a sly swipe at the conformist ethic that so dominated the late 1950s and early 1960s. The inspiration came to her on the way to sing at a meeting of the Friends Committee on Legislation in La Honda, California. Passing through Daly City and driving past the rows of cookie-cutter development houses lining the hills alongside the highway, Malvina had her song about "little boxes on the hillside . . . made out of ticky-tacky" ready by the time she stepped on stage a few hours later, observing:

> And the people in the houses all went to the university,
> Where they were put in boxes, and they came out all the same.
> And there's doctors, and lawyers, and business executives,
> And they're all made out of ticky-tacky,
> And they all look just the same.

Commercial folk acts like the Kingston Trio and the Limeliters gracefully declined to record the song before Seeger did, realizing that Malvina's talent would help him recover his professional fortunes. "'Little Boxes' was actually [Pete Seeger's] first hit single after the long years of the boycott," Malvina later recalled, "and I

Malvina Reynolds

was glad to be the one that helped to break him through that situation. There were many big name people . . . [who] had such respect for Peter that they wanted him to have that song." "Little Boxes" did for Seeger what "Turn Around" had done for Malvina, catapulting him into the public eye and re-establishing his role as a leading figure in the folk music and protest movements. Not long after Seeger released "Little Boxes," he was offered his first network television appearance in 17 years (on "The Smothers Brothers Show") and returned triumphantly to a major concert stage with a sold-out appearance at Carnegie Hall in 1963.

From now on, Malvina's music was rarely absent from the airwaves, record stores or concert tours. "Morningtown Ride" became a number-one hit in Britain in the 1960s; Malvina's environmental protest song "What Have They Done to the Rain?" was recorded by **Joan Baez** in 1962 and again, as a rock number, by The Searchers in 1965, bringing her music to an even wider audience. By the mid-1960s, Malvina was touring the folk music circuit not only in the United States, but in Europe and Japan. She had also become one of the few women at the time adept at the business of writing and recording music, establishing her own music publishing company and record label and releasing six albums for such major labels as Columbia and Folkways as well as her own Cassandra label. She found an entirely new audience when she began publishing her music for children in such collections as *Cheerful Tunes for Lutes and Spoons*, *Tweedles and Foodles for Young Noodles*, and the album *Funnybugs, Giggleworms and Other Good Friends*. It seemed inevitable that Reynolds would make several guest appearances on "Sesame Street" after that revolutionary children's program first appeared on PBS in 1969.

Shortly after Bud Reynolds' death in September 1972, Reynolds was diagnosed with acute pancreatitis. But she refused to let the disease keep her from her usual performance schedule until the afternoon of March 15, 1978, when she fell ill after a photo shoot in Berkeley. Rushed to the hospital, she died during the early morning hours of March 17, 1978.

"What a wonderful person, how I miss her!" Pete Seeger mourned. "I'm only one of millions who have benefitted from her wisdom and stick-to-itiveness. Her life should be an inspiration to many people in many places." At Reynolds' memorial concert, Seeger introduced the song "No Closing Chord," the lyrics of which had been found among Malvina's papers at her death. "Don't play that closing chord for me, baby," she had written:

> I want a wake to wake the dead!
> Some rolling sounds with drums
> And rocking bass,
> And my good comrades dancing
> All around the place.

SOURCES:

The author wishes to thank Nancy Reynolds Schimmel for her help in the preparation of this entry.

Baggelaar, Kristin, and Donald Milton. *Folk Music: More Than a Song*. NY: Thomas Y. Crowell, 1976.

Hitchcock, H. Wiley, and Stanley Sadie. *The New Grove Dictionary of American Music*. Vol. 4. NY: Macmillan, 1986.

Larkin, Colin, ed. *The Guinness Encyclopedia of Popular Music*. Vol. 5. London: Guinness, 1995.

Seeger, Pete. *Where Have All the Flowers Gone?* Edited by Peter Blood. Bethlehem, PA: Sing Out, 1993.

Norman Powers,
writer-producer, Chelsea Lane Productions,
New York, New York

Reynolds, Myra (1853–1936)

American scholar and educator. Born in Troupsburg, New York, on March 18, 1853; died in Los Angeles, California, on August 20, 1936; daughter of Newell Lent Reynolds (a school principal turned minister) and Emily (Knox) Reynolds; graduated from State Normal School, Mansfield, Pennsylvania, 1870; Vassar College, A.B., 1880; University of Chicago, Ph.D., 1895.

Named fellow in English at the University of Chicago (1892); published The Treatment of Nature in English Poetry between Pope and Wordsworth *(1909); became full professor (1911).*

Myra Reynolds was born in 1853 in Troupsburg, Steuben County, New York. Her father Newell Lent Reynolds, a native of Troupsburg, was a school principal who shortly after her birth became a Baptist minister. Her mother **Emily Knox Reynolds** was from nearby Knoxville, Pennsylvania. Reynolds grew up in Tioga County, Pennsylvania, where she developed a love of and appreciation for nature from her father. She completed her early education at Cook Academy, a Baptist school, then moved on to the State Normal School in Mansfield, Pennsylvania, in 1867. After graduating from there in 1870, she disappears from historical view for six years, although it is thought she taught school during that time.

In 1876, at age 23, Reynolds enrolled at Vassar College. She graduated from Vassar with an A.B. degree in 1880 and embarked on a series of jobs in academia: she acted as head of the English department at Wells College in Aurora, New York, from 1880 to 1882; taught at the

Corning (New York) Free Academy from 1882 to 1884; then returned to Vassar as a teacher of English from 1884 to 1892, during which time she took off a year and a half to serve as principal of Woodstock College in Canada. In the fall of 1892, Reynolds began graduate study at the University of Chicago, where she would remain for the rest of her career.

One of Reynolds' initial accomplishments at the university was being named one of the first four fellows in English in 1892. Beginning in 1893, she served as the head of one of the university's earliest women's residence halls, Nancy Foster Hall, a position she held for the next 30 years. In 1894 she became chair of a committee that founded the University of Chicago Settlement, first directed by *Mary Eliza McDowell. In addition to her participation in the growth of the university, Reynolds continued to work on her own career and education. She became an assistant in English in 1894 and earned a Ph.D. the following year. She then moved up within the English department to instructor, then to assistant professor (1897), associate professor (1903), and full professor (1911).

While at the University of Chicago, Reynolds also published several scholarly books. One of the first of these was The Poems of *Anne (Finch), Countess of Winchilsea, published in 1903. Her best-known book, The Treatment of Nature in English Poetry between Pope and Wordsworth, which appeared in 1909, was an extension of her doctoral dissertation. Her last important work, The Learned Lady in England, 1650–1760, an engaging series of personal sketches, was published in 1920.

Reynolds was an influential teacher who was appreciated for her liveliness and positive attitude, as well as her ability to apply her knowledge of and love for art and nature to the study of literature. She retired from the University of Chicago in 1923, at age 70, and spent her retirement years near two of her sisters and their families in Palos Verdes, California. Reynolds died of broncho-pneumonia and uremia in Los Angeles, California, on August 20, 1936, at 83.

SOURCES:

James, Edward T., ed. Notable American Women, 1607–1950. Cambridge, MA: The Belknap Press of Harvard University, 1971.

Kari Bethel, freelance writer, Columbia, Missouri

Rheaume, Manon (1972—)

Canadian professional ice hockey player. Pronunciation: MAY-nohn RAY-ohm. Born in Lac Beauport, Quebec, Canada, on February 24, 1972; married Gerry St. Cyr (a Canadian roller-hockey player); children: one son.

As goaltender, helped Canadian national women's hockey team win gold medal at world championships (1992, 1994); became the first woman to play in the National Hockey League (NHL), as goaltender for the Tampa Bay Lightning (1992); won a silver medal at the Olympics as part of Canada's first women's ice hockey team (1998); retired from Canadian national team (2000) but continued to play professionally in the National Women's Hockey League.

One of the biggest stars of Canadian women's ice hockey and the first woman to play in a National Hockey League game, Manon Rheaume was born in 1972 in Lac Beauport, a suburb of Quebec City in Quebec, Canada. With her two brothers, Martin and Pascal, she was raised in Lac Beauport where their father Pierre managed an outdoor ice rink and coached a boys' hockey team. Rheaume and her brothers were involved in ice skating early on; soon after learning to walk, she learned to skate and by age four was adept at it. As a youngster, Rheaume often watched her brothers play hockey at the rink, and she would join in when they arrived home to play on the makeshift pond her father had made by flooding the backyard. Her other activities, including ballet and skiing, fell by the wayside in favor of her love of hockey. Soon, she was concentrating on goaltending.

Throughout her school years, she played on boys' teams and on youth leagues, and at age 11 became the first girl to play in an International Pee Wee Hockey Tournament. After graduating from high school, Rheaume played on women's hockey teams in Montreal. She also played on Canada's men's Junior B league and, for a short time, on the Junior A level, which is just one step down from the NHL. She recounted to People magazine a Junior A game in which players were trying to scare her with high shots, and she ended up with a three-inch gash above her eyebrow. Regardless of the blood running down her face, Rheaume kept playing: "I didn't want anyone to say I stopped because I was a girl," she said. She was a star on the women's hockey scene, helping the Canadian national women's team win a gold medal at the World championships in Finland in 1992. As goaltender, she gave up only two goals in three games, and was voted Most Valuable Player.

Also in 1992 Rheaume made history when she tended goal in an exhibition game for the

Tampa Bay Lightning, a men's team. It was the first time a woman had played in the NHL, and the first time a woman had seen action in any major professional team sport. After the exhibition game, in which she gave up two goals and made seven saves during the first period, she was given a three-year contract and sent to play for the Atlanta Knights, a minor-league franchise of the Lightning. She noted: "I'm happy to be with Atlanta because I have a good chance to get experience, to learn more. I didn't try to be the first woman to do this, I just want to play." Nonetheless, there were many in the sports world who saw the exposition game and her contract as a cynical publicity stunt (a charge implicitly accepted by the Lightning's general manager, who was quoted as saying he would sign a horse if it could play on skates). *Playboy* magazine offered Rheaume $50,000 to pose nude, which she declined. In December 1992, she played with the Knights in a regular-season game against the Salt Lake Golden Eagles, thus becoming the first woman to play in a regular-season professional hockey game. She later played for a number of other teams, including the Knoxville Cherokees and the Las Vegas Thunder, as well as teams in the Roller Hockey League International.

Rheaume won a second gold medal in the World championships with the Canadian women's hockey team in 1994, and again was voted the team's Most Valuable Player. In 1998, she played with the Canadian women's hockey team at the Nagano Winter Olympics, winning a silver medal. (*See Team USA: Women's Ice Hockey at Nagano.*) Rheaume announced her retirement from the Canadian women's hockey team in 2000, although she continued playing as a forward on a part-time basis with the Montreal Wingstars, part of the highest-level competitive women's hockey league in Canada. Married to a roller-hockey player, she now works as the head of global marketing for women's hockey at a hockey equipment and accessories manufacturer.

SOURCES:
Johnson, Anne Janette. *Great Women in Sports*. Detroit, MI: Visible Ink, 1998.

Kari Bethel,
freelance writer, Columbia, Missouri

Rhind, Ethel (fl. early 20th c.)

Irish artist. Born in Bengal, India; date of death unknown; educated at Londonderry High School; the School of Art, Belfast; and the Dublin Metropolitan School of Art; member of the Guild of Irish Artworkers.

Ethel Rhind was born in Bengal, India, but was educated and worked in Ireland. After she attended Londonderry High School and the School of Art, Belfast, Rhind was awarded a scholarship to study mosaic at the Dublin Metropolitan School of Art in 1902. Six years later, her window in the Old Court Chapel in Strangford, County Down, won first prize at the Royal Dublin Society. Rhind's specialty was creating mosaics from glass set into the plaster of a wall, a technique known as "opus sectile." She used this method in designing the stations of the cross at St. Edna's Church in Spiddal, County Galway. Rhind worked at *Sarah Purser's Dublin workshop, An Túr Gloine (Tower of Glass), and also designed pieces for Grangegorman Church in Dublin and Magheralin Church in County Down. She was a member of the Guild of Irish Artworkers and exhibited her work at the Arts and Crafts Society of Ireland in 1910, 1917, and 1921.

Maria Sheler Edwards,
freelance writer, Ypsilanti, Michigan

Rhoda

Biblical woman. Servant in the house of Mary of Jerusalem.

Rhoda was a servant in the house of *Mary of Jerusalem, the mother of John, also called Mark, possibly one of the writers of the four gospels (Acts 12:12). Mary's residence was the site of the Last Supper and may have also served as the meeting place for the early Christians of Jerusalem. It was also where the disciples gathered to pray for the release of Peter, who had been imprisoned by Herod Antipas. Following Peter's miraculous escape, he was accompanied by an angel to Mary of Jerusalem's door. Rhoda answered his knock, but was so surprised and delighted by his appearance that she ran to tell the others without inviting him in. Peter had to continue knocking until someone finally returned to let him in.

Rhodes, Mary (c. 1782–1853)

American Roman Catholic nun and co-founder of the Sisters of Loretto. Born in or around 1782 in Maryland; died at Loretto, Kentucky, on February 27, 1853; one of seven children (two girls and five boys) of Abraham Rhodes (a planter and slave owner) and Elizabeth Rhodes; educated by the Nuns of the Visitation in Georgetown (now Washington, D.C.); never married; no children.

Moved to Kentucky (1811); with Reverend Charles Nerinckx, founded the Sisters of Loretto (1812); served as mother superior (1812–22).

Mary Rhodes was born in Maryland in or around 1782, one of the last of the seven children of Abraham and **Elizabeth Rhodes**. The Rhodes were Catholic, and Maryland had originally been founded as a haven for Catholics, although they soon lost the upper hand there. Rhodes received her education in Georgetown, Maryland (now Washington, D.C.), from the Nuns of the Visitation. Few details are known about her life before 1811. That year, around age 29, Rhodes went to the Kentucky frontier to visit her brother Bennet, who lived southeast of Bardstown in a community on Hardin's Creek which had been founded by a group of Maryland Catholics in 1786. During her stay, Rhodes found that her brother's children were lacking in secular and religious education and began teaching them. When neighbors asked her to teach their children as well, she consulted with a local missionary priest, Reverend Charles Nerinckx, and the two agreed to open a school for girls. As enrollment at the school increased, Rhodes found assistance from two local women, **Christina Stuart** and **Anne Havern**.

Initially the teachers lived with Rhodes' brother, but the hustle and bustle of his family and friends drove them to an old cabin near the school. Before long, the three women agreed to consecrate their lives, and their educational work, to God. Nerinckx designed a "simple but rigorous rule" for the nascent order and named Rhodes its temporary head. After the rule was approved by Bishop Benedict J. Flaget, on April 25, 1812, Nerinckx formally named their new community Friends of Mary at the Foot of the Cross, and Rhodes and the others took the veil. (The first American order of nuns had been founded only three years earlier, in Maryland, by *Elizabeth Ann Seton.)

The new group, one of the first orders of Roman Catholic nuns on the frontier, soon added three more members. One of these was Rhodes' sister **Ann Rhodes**, who was elected the first mother superior despite being younger than the other members. After her death from consumption only months later, on December 11, 1812, she was replaced by Mary Rhodes, who would serve as mother superior until 1822.

Rhodes and her fellow nuns took their final vows on August 15, 1813. During the ten years that Rhodes acted as mother superior, she established the policies and aims of the community, which was devoted to education. Under her leadership, the campus was expanded and the chapel there became known as "Little Loretto," after the shrine in Loreto, Italy, reputed to be the miraculously transported home of *Mary the Virgin**. The community adopted the name, and ever since has been known as the Sisters of Loretto at the Foot of the Cross. Although its first months had been spent in abject poverty, the order quickly increased its landholdings, and local novices flocked to join to such an extent that at one point the Sisters of Loretto drew the wrath of local families who did not want their daughters withdrawing from the world. Three sister houses had been opened in Kentucky by 1819, and some 30 years later there were branches in Louisiana, Arkansas, and Missouri as well, all devoted to providing Catholic education to children. The original community, which in 1824 had moved some seven miles from its first location, gave its name to the town of Loretto, Kentucky.

Nearly blind in her last years, Rhodes died on February 27, 1853, at the motherhouse of Loretto after 41 years of service as a nun. By the mid-years of the 20th century, there were 70 Loretto communities in the United States.

SOURCES:

James, Edward T., ed. *Notable American Women, 1607–1950*. Cambridge, MA: The Belknap Press of Harvard University, 1971.

Maria Sheler Edwards, freelance writer, Ypsilanti, Michigan

Rhodogune (fl. 2nd c. BCE)

Queen of ancient Parthia. Name variations: Rodogune. Flourished in the 2nd century BCE; daughter of Mithradates I, king of Parthia; sister of Phraates II; married Demetrius II Nicator of Syria.

Rhodogune was the daughter of Mithradates I of Parthia, the king most responsible for the rise of the Parthian Empire, and the wife of Demetrius II Nicator. Mithradates acceded to the throne of Parthia in 171 BCE and began the expansion of Parthian power. By 148 BCE, he had annexed Media (in northwestern Iran) and by 141, Babylonia (in central Iraq)—both at the expense of the Seleucid Empire, the heartland of which lay in western Syria. Mithradates' success in the West came in large part because of dynastic wars which weakened the Seleucid Empire, wars which were rejoined in 146 BCE when the Egyptian king Ptolemy VI forced the divorce of his daughter, *Cleopatra Thea**, from her debauched husband Alexander Balas, so as to replace Balas, both on the throne and in Thea's bed, with Demetrius II Nicator, another Seleucid. In the war which followed, both Balas and Ptolemy VI died, leaving Demetrius in power.

Balas' faction (then led by Diodotus Typhon) rallied around the interests of Antiochus VI, the son of Balas and Thea, to whom Demetrius II Nicator was then married. Through 144 BCE, the armies of Thea's husband fought off those championing her son. However, Demetrius (although he had three children with Thea) failed to meet the expectations of the citizens of Antioch, the Seleucid capital. As a result, the Antiochines drove Demetrius from the city, then offered the Seleucid throne to Antiochus VI, who technically reigned as king until Diodotus executed him in 141 BCE so as to seize the throne for himself.

To recoup his reputation, reverse the Parthian gains in Seleucid lands, and justify a return to the Seleucid throne, in the same year as Antiochus VI's murder, Demetrius began a campaign against Mithradates. Initially, this war went Demetrius' way, but in 140 BCE, he was captured by Mithradates, who first paraded Demetrius as a captive through the contested provinces, and then, seeking political advantage, married him to his daughter Rhodogune. Thereafter Demetrius was treated with respect, for Mithradates hoped that a grateful Demetrius, whom Mithradates intended to place back on the Seleucid throne, would someday respond with pro-Parthian policies. Mithradates further hoped that one day, through Rhodogune, one of his descendants would rule in Antioch.

Coming up with some congenial arrangement in the West had become a priority for Mithradates by 140 BCE, for by that year his policies in the East had fostered the development of threats from that quarter. In addition to his Western wars, throughout his long reign Mithradates also campaigned against the Greek dynasts then ruling in Bactria (modern Afghanistan). His successes there, however, had opened his eastern frontiers to raids from the Sacae, a nomadic nation from the steppes of central Asia once kept in check by the Bactrians. Not wishing to face simultaneous wars on opposing frontiers, Mithradates decided to woo Demetrius. Before any benefit could accrue from the cultivation of Demetrius, however, Mithradates died (peacefully) in 138 BCE. Nonetheless, his successor, Phraates II (the brother of Rhodogune), continued where his father had left off. Trusting that the respect Demetrius had been shown was winning his friendship, Phraates even established his brother-in-law in Hyrcania (northern Iran), where Demetrius apparently possessed large estates, cared for his wife, and knew personal freedom. Certainly, his relationship with Rhodogune seemed to thrive, for with her he is known to have had several children, although their names are unknown. Presumably, as Demetrius fell into the habits of a "family man," Phraates came to trust him more.

Whether or not Demetrius was in fact being won over, events in Antioch undermined the Parthians' hopes for maintaining Demetrius' loyalty. In 138 BCE, Thea, besieged in Antioch by Diodotus, and fearing that Demetrius would never return, while also coming to hate him for his marriage to Rhodogune (and for fathering potential rivals to her children with her), proposed marriage to Demetrius' younger brother, Antiochus VII. Within a year, Antiochus VII married Thea, crushed the faction of Diodotus, and assumed the Seleucid throne himself. In the wake of these events, Demetrius' true loyalties became known as he twice attempted to escape from Parthian lands and his second family. Both times, he was captured and returned to Rhodogune, but it had become clear to all concerned that neither trust, nor emotion, nor responsibility would constrain Demetrius to honor a sense of debt to either Rhodogune or her brother.

By 131 BCE, Antiochus VII had secured the western portion of the Seleucid realm enough for him to worry about the East and his brother. Like his brother before him, Antiochus VII began his eastern war successfully, to the point where he felt secure in demanding the return of Demetrius—supposedly out of piety, but really so as to put him under wraps and remove him as a royal rival. Hoping to stir up trouble between the Seleucid brothers, and by this time understanding Demetrius' character, Phraates released Demetrius. Not long thereafter (in 130 BCE), however, Phraates defeated and killed Antiochus VII in battle, and soon came to rue the premature release of Demetrius. (Nevertheless, perhaps Phraates realized some satisfaction from the fact that among those he captured from Antiochus VII's camp was *Laodice, the daughter of Demetrius and Thea, whom Phraates admired so much that he added her to his harem.) Thereafter, Demetrius left Parthia and Rhodogune for good. Whatever happened to Rhodogune or her children is unknown, but it is likely that they maintained their prominence as the power of Parthia became established. Demetrius' fate, however, is known. Turning westward, he came into immediate conflict with his estranged "wife," Thea. After years of petty strife, at Thea's instigation, Demetrius was murdered by the order of the Seleucid governor of the city of Tyre in 126 BCE.

William S. Greenwalt,
Associate Professor of Classical History,
Santa Clara University, Santa Clara, California

Rhodopis (fl. 6th c. BCE)

Thracian courtesan. Name variations: Rhadopis; Rhodope; (real name) Doricha. Flourished in the 6th century BCE.

In the 6th century BCE, Rhodopis, a Thracian courtesan, was owned by Iadmon from the Greek island of Samos. Iadmon also owned Aesop, the famous fabulist. After profiting from Rhodopis' trade for awhile on Samos, Iadmon relocated her to Naucratis, the Greek emporium tolerated by the Egyptians on one of the arms of the Nile delta so as to facilitate trade with the Greek world. Rhodopis' beauty was legendary. It certainly bedazzled Charaxus of Mytilene (who was the brother of the renowned Greek poet *Sappho); he was so taken by her charms that he purchased her freedom and set her up in her own business. (Not impressed by her brother's infatuation, Sappho wrote a poem which ridiculed his "chivalry.") A free entrepreneur, Rhodopis made a fortune at Naucratis, but not enough to finance the great pyramid at Giza which some of Herodotus' contemporaries (5th century BCE) believed she had erected as a monument to herself. Herodotus, however, knew that the pyramids were much older than Rhodopis. Nevertheless, in order to be remembered, at the end of her career Rhodopis did make a statement of sorts (whether or not she did so with tongue in cheek is not known): she devoted $\frac{1}{10}$th of her net worth to the purchase of as many roasting spits of iron as that sum could buy, and then dedicated them all to Apollo at Delphi where they could be seen for centuries stacked behind the Chian altar. It appears that the local authorities did not quite know what to do with Rhodopis' generosity: being a dedication to the god, however, they could not merely discard her gift.

One anecdote told about Rhodopis concerned one of her sandals, which an eagle is said to have snatched while she was bathing. Having stolen the sandal, the raptor dropped it in the lap of the reigning Egyptian pharaoh Psammetichus, who was so impressed by the quality of its manufacture that he sought out the owner. Once Rhodopis had been discovered, Psammetichus is said to have been so bewitched by her beauty that he married her. Although this was certainly not a historical episode, it is interesting to see in the mythology surrounding Rhodopis an early precursor of the Cinderella tale.

William Greenwalt,
Associate Professor of Classical History,
Santa Clara University, Santa Clara, California

Rhondda, Margaret (1883–1958)

Welsh publisher. Name variations: Lady Margaret Rhondda; Margaret Haig, Viscountess Rhondda; Margaret Haig Thomas; Margaret Mackworth. Born Margaret Haig Thomas in South Wales in 1883; died in 1958; only daughter of David Alfred Thomas (an industrialist) and Sybil (Haig) Thomas; educated privately, then in London and at St. Andrews; spent one year at Somerville College, Oxford; married Humphrey Mackworth, in 1908 (divorced 1923).

Lady Margaret Rhondda was born Margaret Haig Thomas in South Wales in 1883, the only daughter of David Alfred Thomas, an industrialist, and **Sybil Haig Thomas**. Her early years were quite eventful. Joining the protests of the militant suffragists, she was imprisoned and went on a hunger strike. Then, as a business associate of her father's, she was sent to America on the *Lusitania* in 1916. Fortunately, she was rescued from the sinking ship and went on to a viscountcy in 1918. After becoming a successful businesswoman, at one time serving as director of 33 companies, she was granted royal permission to attend the House of Lords.

In 1920, Lady Rhondda founded the weekly *Time and Tide*. For the first six years, it was edited by **Helen Archdale** and closely associated with the feminist organization known as the Six Point Group. When Lady Rhondda became editor (1926–58), the journal's emphasis shifted to politics in general. A leading weekly for nearly 60 years (1920–79), it numbered among its contributors *Winifred Holtby, *Cicely Hamilton, *Stella Benson, *Edith Nesbit, *Rebecca West, ⮞ Viola Meynell, *Katherine Mansfield, *Sylvia Townsend Warner, *Vita Sackville-West, *Dorothy L. Sayers, George Bernard Shaw, G.K. Chesterton, Aldous Huxley, Bertrand Russell, *Storm Jameson, *Gertrude Stein, *Pamela Hansford Johnson, *Rumer Godden, *Kathleen Raine, *Stella Gibbons, *Edith Sitwell, *Stevie Smith, D.H. Lawrence, T.S. Eliot, W.H. Auden, and E.M. Forster. After Lady Rhondda died in 1958, it was learned that she had pumped in £250,000 to subsidize her journal. Though it continued publication for another 20 years, it became a news magazine on the order of America's *Time* and *Newsweek*. Lady Rhondda's memoirs were published as *This Was My World* (1933) and *Notes on the Way* (1937). *The Time and Tide Album* was edited by E.M. Delafield (*Elizabeth Monica Dashwood) in 1932.

SUGGESTED READING:

Eoff, Shirley M. *Viscountess Rhondda: Equalitarian Feminist.* Columbus, OH: Ohio State University Press, 1991.

Meynell, Viola.
See Butler,
Elizabeth
Thompson for
sidebar.

Rhys, Jean (1890–1979)

English novelist and short-story writer. Name variations: Gwen Williams; Ella Williams; Ella or Emma Gray. Born Ella Gwendolen Rees Williams in Roseau, Dominica (West Indies), on August 24, 1890; died in Exeter, England, on May 14, 1979; fourth child of William Rees Williams (a Welsh doctor) and Minna Lockhart (a third-generation Dominican Creole); married Jean Lenglet, in 1919 (divorced 1932); married Leslie Tilden-Smith, in 1934; married Max Hamer, in 1947; children: (first marriage) William Owen (b. December 1919, died three weeks later); Maryvonne Lenglet (b. 1922).

Left Dominica (1907); attended the Perse School, Cambridge, England (1907–08); attended the Academy of Dramatic Art, London (1909); had affair with Lancelot Hugh Smith (1910–12); had affair with Ford Madox Ford (1924); husband Jean Lenglet in prison (1923–24); published four novels (1926–39); convicted of assault (1949); husband Max Hamer in prison (1950–52); Wide Sargasso Sea won W.H. Smith & Son Annual Literary Award (1967); published autobiography Smile Please (1979).

At age 65, Jean Rhys wrote to her daughter **Maryvonne Lenglet**, "[V]ery few people change after well say seven or seventeen. . . . They get *more* this or *more* that and of course look a bit different. But inside they are the same." This, according to Rhys' biographer, **Carole Angier**, applied to Rhys herself who "was stranded in a permanently prescient childhood." Jean Rhys never wanted to grow up, for this meant making decisions and assuming responsibilities such as raising children, getting a job, and handling one's own business affairs. Rhys never did any of these things. She remained, Angier notes, a child plagued by fears, "marooned in a child's imagination, where ordinary adult life is less than half understood."

Rhys "never wanted to be a writer," Angier claims, "all she wanted to be was an ordinary, happy, passive, and protected woman." But Rhys was no ordinary woman, nor was she ever happy. Submissive, dependent, isolated, and alienated from people and places, she led a life that was sad indeed. All of her fictional heroines, and Rhys herself, were "homeless and alone," struggling to survive "in a shifting, uncertain, dangerous world," a world dominated by men who exploited women. Her peripatetic lifestyle and crushing poverty fed her need for security and increased her dependence and vulnerability. She was more proficient at hating than loving, a better writer than a person; she was weak and

self-absorbed. Rhys sought self-knowledge through her writing, and as Angier points out, "she cut everything out of her writing but herself; and in order to write she did the same to her life. She became a near recluse; . . . she never lived an ordinary family life with her daughter. As she grew older she pared more and more away in her writing—her present husbands, her present surroundings." And all of her life she inhabited an inner, private world of her own making, a world of loneliness and isolation, which she viewed "from the perspective of a displaced person."

Rhys was born Ella Gwendolyn Rees Williams in Roseau, Dominica, the West Indies, in 1890, the fourth of five children of **Minna Lockhart Williams** and William Rees Williams. Early in life, Rhys determined that she was different, the only fair member of her family, and that she was ugly. All her life she remembered an encounter with a young man when she was 12 years old; he remarked that she was not pretty. "Oh God, let me be pretty when I grow up. Let me be. Let me be," she wrote later. When she was an old woman, a friend asked Rhys what she would want to be if she were reincarnated: "I would like to be beautiful," she replied.

As a child, Rhys wanted not only to be beautiful, but to be black, to be part of the black culture which was "more alive" and "more a part of [Dominica] than we are." In her novel *Voyage in the Dark* (1934), she says through her heroine Anna, "I always wanted to be black. . . . Being black is warm and gay, being white is cold and sad." In late 19th-century Dominica, white families such as Jean's lived in a world of colonial insularity. Rhys attended a Roman Catholic convent school, but her family discouraged her interest in Catholicism as well as in native culture. Never close to her brothers and sisters, Rhys was largely ignored by her mother, but cherished by her Welsh father who "loved words and books . . . liked odd, eccentric people, and defended them." He taught his reclusive, sensitive young daughter that "if you can't bear something it's all right to run away," and Rhys spent her life running from the fears and misfortunes which haunted her. Dr. Williams was kind, but weak and irresponsible. On the other hand, Rhys' mother represented "strength and protection, but also English superiority, philistinism, and intolerance."

The young Rhys pictured herself as an "outcast," an "alien," in her narrow, confined white world, and she was also aware of "the continued domination of the blacks and the subordinate, reductive role that women had in this culture—the boredom and the feeling of uselessness." Yet she envied the strength and gaiety of the blacks, exemplified by her friend Francine, the model for Francine in *Voyage in the Dark* and for Tia in *Wide Sargasso Sea* (1966). In contrast, Rhys' nurse Meta, "the terror of my life," filled the child's imagination with debilitating fears and demons that tormented the lonely, insecure adult writer: fear of insects, of zombies, of the dark, and of people—"especially people." The child became a woman and "as an artist she matured and grew," writes Angier, "but as a person . . . she [remained] stuck emotionally in childhood." And when she left the West Indies in 1907, at age 16, she carried her demons, and Dominica, with her as she sailed for Southampton, England.

If she thought of herself as an outcast at home, the damp, cold grayness of England only exacerbated her "sense of displacement and cultural rift." Where was the grandeur and elegance of Edwardian England that the West Indian colonials so admired? Everything was "small and mean . . . poor and ugly," and Rhys was miserable. She lived with her strait-laced aunt, **Clarice Rhys Williams**, who enrolled her in Perse High School for Girls. At the rigid, spartan school, Rhys felt clumsy and ignorant, an unsophisticated provincial. After four terms, she asked her father's permission to attend the Royal Academy of Dramatic Art in London to study acting. He agreed, and in 1908, she passed her Oxford and Cambridge Higher Certificate, took the entrance exam for the Academy, and was admitted. However, she quickly became dissatisfied and withdrew, claiming she had learned nothing "except the exact meaning of the word 'snob.'"

When Dr. Williams died in 1909, her mother insisted she return home, but Rhys refused, and, much to her aunt's chagrin, joined the chorus of a musical comedy, "Our Miss Gibbs." The show toured northern England during the winter of 1909; the penetratingly cold climate, the dismal small towns, and poor food and lodgings dispelled any romantic notions she had of life on the stage. The sameness and the tedium of touring were somewhat compensated for by the other chorus girls: attractive and spirited, but often coarse, satirical, and fatalistic, Rhys admired their ability to survive. However, their meager talents and lack of money made them easy prey, and many became prostitutes or, if more fortunate, mistresses. Women, as Jean Rhys wrote in *Voyage in the Dark*, were victims of male exploitation and dominance. She had witnessed their plight and soon would experience a similar fate.

For almost two years, Rhys endured the rigors of itinerant show business. Returning to London, she played in a pantomime of "Cinderella," worked as an artist's model, and posed for advertisements, moving from room to dingy room, clinging to the hope that something wonderful was about to happen. "Real life" turned out to be unhappy, uncertain, and exiguous, but then Rhys fell in love. Her shining knight, her benefactor and lover, was 40-year-old Lancelot Hugh Smith, rich and upper-class, a graduate of Eton and Cambridge, from a respected family of bankers, diplomats, and members of Parliament. Smith was not a handsome Prince Charming, but he was kind, generous, refined, and attentive. The relationship soured, however, probably due to family pressure; Smith's "respectability rejected her," Angier writes, "as she'd been afraid it would." And Rhys "died then, with the end of her first affair—the real death, not the one people know about," as Jean Rhys wrote in *Wide Sargasso Sea* 54 years later. Thomas F. Staley contends that her "bitterness and disillusionment made it impossible for her ever to love with such

openness and excitement again." Her three husbands would inherit the legacy of this love affair. Alone and frightened, Rhys, like the female character she is describing, "knew that she would never belong anywhere; and also that she didn't *want* to belong, not to their world. . . . She knew now what she wanted. She wanted nothing."

But Lancelot had not abandoned his mistress completely; he provided her with a weekly allowance through his solicitors for the next six or seven years. Rhys took the money while hating herself for doing so. "Her habit of reluctant, self-hating dependence had begun," writes Angier, a habit she never had the courage or inclination to break. In 1914, Rhys began to record her feelings and experiences in a notebook which she continued for several years. From her suffering, from the loss of love, the writer Jean Rhys unknowingly emerged. Twenty years later, the first part of her "diary" was the resource for *Voyage in the Dark*. Rhys rarely alluded to the terrible years after the affair ended, but she had learned that life was a battle for survival and if one adheres to the socially acceptable code of morality, "you are trampled to death before you've begun."

There's very little invention in my books. I don't know other people. I have never known other people. I have only ever written about myself.

—Jean Rhys

During World War I, she lived in London in cheap boarding-houses, periodically working again as an artist's model or in the theater, but largely relying on Lancelot's allowance. In 1917, living on Torrington Square in Bloomsbury, she met Jean Lenglet who was half-Dutch, half-French, had fought with the French Foreign Legion in Africa and on the Western Front in Europe, and served as a French secret agent. They were married in Holland in 1919. Rhys vowed never to return to England and was enthusiastic about their move to Paris. In late December 1919, she gave birth to a boy who died of pneumonia three weeks later. Meanwhile, Lenglet had taken a position with the Allied Commission in Vienna where Rhys joined him in the spring of 1920. By the following spring, the Lenglets were able to settle in a fashionable hotel and engage in rather lavish spending. There was money to be made in turbulent postwar Vienna, and Lenglet became involved in several currency exchange schemes. When the Allied Commission moved on to Budapest, Lenglet was accused of having used and lost money appropriated from the Commission and other agencies. He and Rhys, now pregnant, fled Budapest, eventually reaching London via Prague, Warsaw, and Paris. Their daughter, Maryvonne, was born in Brussels in 1922, and by the end of the year the family was back in Paris.

The vagabond life and oppressive poverty fuelled Rhys' insecurity and loneliness. She suggested that Lenglet, who had an interest in journalism, write a few feature articles which she would translate and sell to English-language newspapers. After several unsuccessful attempts to interest editors, Rhys contacted Pearl Adam, wife of the Paris correspondent for *The Times*, whom she had met at a party in London. Asked if she had ever written anything, Rhys showed Adam her diary. Impressed with Jean's style and material, she sent it to Ford Madox Ford, novelist, critic, and editor of the *Transatlantic Review* in Paris. Ford was to be a major influence in Jean Rhys' career; he advised her to read the classical French writers, and provided her with reading lists and copies of contemporary literary magazines containing the best of modern writing. Through Ford, Rhys met other expatriate writers, including Ernest Hemingway and James Joyce. And through Ford, she became a writer and Jean Rhys (she had been known as Ella Williams, then Gwen Williams, then Ella or Emma Gray); she had "found the one thing she could do, and she began to do it." Ford told her to write about what she knew. He read and critiqued her work and acted as a mentor and an anchor in Rhys' inherently disordered life.

In the autumn of 1923, Lenglet was arrested and imprisoned for selling *objects d'art* "of dubious origin." Left with a child and no money, Rhys turned to Ford; her dependence, vulnerability, and passivity dictated her actions. She did not love Ford, but she was desperate, and in the end she lost both Ford and Lenglet who could not forgive her weakness and betrayal: to Rhys, writes Angier, "all that was left was loneliness, fear, drink, and no money, no money." Without a qualm, Rhys again approached Lancelot to provide her with an allowance. **Stella Bowen**, Ford's long-time lover who broke up Rhys' affair with Ford, described Jean as having a gift for writing and being personally attractive, "but on the other side of the balance were bad health, destitution, shattered nerves, an undesirable husband, lack of nationality, and a complete absence of any desire for independence"—a cogent evocation of the present and future life of Jean Rhys. Female vulnerability and male exploitation served as themes throughout Rhys' writings as she examined her own motives and personality through her fictional heroines. She knew by experience, she wrote, that "beneath the passivity and self-destructiveness of women there was a willingness to engage in a desperate struggle for survival, just as beneath the surface ugliness of their lives there was a yearning for beauty, a new dress, an attractive room."

When Lenglet was released from prison, the family settled in Brussels, but the marriage was over. Rhys was, however, able to write several short stories, based on her life with Lenglet, and *The Left Bank* was published by Jonathan Cape in London in 1927. She also completed a draft of *Quartet*, "her most self-centered, vengeful book," notes Angier, and sent it to Cape; they refused to publish it for fear of a libel suit by Ford.

Not to be deterred, Rhys left Lenglet and Maryvonne and went to London to seek a publisher. Here she found a sympathetic editor for *Quartet* (1928) and a new lover. Leslie Tilden-Smith was a literary agent, the Oxford-educated son of an Anglican cleric. Rhys had acquired another caretaker; they lived together, and Jean was free to write while Leslie edited, typed, handled contracts and Rhys' business affairs. He also cooked, cleaned, and did the laundry. But, as Angier notes, Leslie never entered the world Rhys wrote about. She was obsessed with "the loss of love, the loss of hope," and her objective was "to understand her life, and especially her suffering." In *After Leaving Mr. Mackenzie*, the heroine Julia tries "to grapple with nothingness," but never comprehends what it is. Jean/Julia asks, "Why do I suffer?" and she grimly concludes, "*There is no love* . . . there is only 'nothing'—emptiness, and the escape of death." During the 1930s, three of Rhys' major works appeared, *After Leaving Mr. Mackenzie* (1930), *Voyage in the Dark* (1934), and *Good Morning, Midnight* (1939); each received good reviews, but they did not sell well. Rhys was disappointed for "she wrote and rewrote, in an obsessive search for perfection."

Despite her literary production, life with Leslie was not idyllic; financial problems created tensions, and Rhys drank heavily: "her past tormented her," notes Angier, "writing tormented her: she had to drink to write and she had to drink to live." When Leslie's father, who had disapproved of their relationship, died in 1934, they were free to marry. With the money he inherited, Leslie took Rhys on a holiday to her native Dominica in early 1936. At first, she felt "saner and safer" than she had for many years, but Rhys soon became disillusioned as she realized she was considered "one of the old whites," a foreigner, in what now was the blacks' domain. Unwanted, even hated, Rhys "felt more homeless than ever before." Her past had vanished, setting her adrift on a course of further self-destructive behavior. She got drunk, flew into rages, and physically assaulted her husband who did not fight back. In *Good Morning, Midnight*, Rhys examines the fears, the demons that haunted her—"age and ugliness, drunkenness and paranoia"—through her main character, Sasha. Passive and indolent, Sasha is "the stranger, the alien, the old one," or is she "the other—how do I know who the other is? She isn't me." Rhys was beginning to acquire a degree of self-knowledge, but she could not change her ways.

Leslie volunteered for the military when the Second World War began. Rhys joined him at Norfolk, but because of her erratic behavior, Leslie was judged a security risk and was transferred to another base. Eventually, he was posted to London. Rhys had lost touch with Lenglet and Maryvonne during these turbulent times and did not know if they were dead or alive. She later learned that both had worked for the Dutch resistance; Maryvonne spent some time in prison, and Lenglet was in a concentration camp for four years. Agitated, miserable, and on the verge of collapse, Rhys wrote short stories based on her diaries and notebooks filled with invectives directed at people and society and a savage hatred of England, "Rot its mean soul of shit." A few months after the war ended, Leslie died of a heart attack; Rhys recounted this terrible time in a short story, "The Sound of the River." And in a letter to Leslie's daughter from his first marriage, Rhys wrote, "I had all the time the feeling that Leslie had *escaped*—from me, from everyone and was free at last."

Rhys wanted to leave London and to work on her novel which she had titled *Le Revenant* (The Ghost). In a fit of rage, she had burned the first draft that Leslie had typed before the war, but two chapters were later found. Rhys had no money but she would survive, as always. Her rescuer was Leslie's cousin, Max Hamer, a solicitor and executor of Leslie's will. After divorcing his wife, he and Jean married in 1947, the happiest of her marriages, she said. But Max was not the man who could "save" Jean from her paranoia and destructive behavior. Unworldly, sweet-natured, and "full of get rich quick schemes," Max spent most of his time on business in London where they lived. Rhys was depressed, drank heavily, and ate little. And being alone only magnified her fears and released her demons. In spring 1949, Rhys finally exploded, slapped the face of a neighbor man whom she claimed was rude to her, and was brought up on assault charges. She was found guilty. In June 1949, she was remanded into custody and spent five days in the hospital wing of Holloway Prison. Judged sane, she was placed on probation for two years and sent home. Again, Rhys tried to exorcise her pent-up animosities against the nameless, faceless "them" by writing a short story, "Let Them Call It Jazz." Through her black heroine, who was sent to Holloway, Rhys asserts that "if they treat you wrong over and over again the hour strikes when you burst out." Jean was already retreating "further and further into self-absorption, self-pity, and anger," typically blaming others for her own unhappiness. But, as Angier notes, "it wasn't the others, it was herself," and Rhys' acrimony only became more incapacitating as she grew older.

By early 1950, Rhys was a mental and physical wreck, all her books were out of print, and she was forgotten. But trouble seemed to be a permanent part of her existence; Max was arrested in January for illegal financial dealings, tried at the Old Bailey, found guilty, and sentenced to three years in prison at Maidstone. Carole Angier wonders if Max had done it for Jean; poverty frightened her, and she longed for comfort and glamour. Both Lengley and Max ended up in prison, convicted of fraud. Both were "natural gamblers," but, Angier concludes, "the force of Jean's need drove them further than they would have gone without her."

Rhys moved to Maidstone to be near Max. She wrote nothing from 1949 to 1951, when she began a new diary at the Ropemakers' Arms pub in the town. Part of this diary was published in her autobiography, *Smile Please* (1979). From the diary, it is evident that she wanted to live, to do something worthwhile. Angier claims the Ropemakers' diary is not simply a diary but a "drama. . . . it is a trial. . . . *The Trial of Jean Rhys*," who confesses, "I learnt everything too late." Rhys admits that she is guilty of a multitude of sins but there is also good in her—she is a writer: "If I stop writing my life will have been an abject failure. It is that already to other people. But it could be an abject failure to myself. I will not have earned death."

Max was released from prison in 1952, and he and Jean returned to London. Unable to resume his career as a solicitor, Max was also stripped of his Navy pension. From 1953 to 1956, they moved from London to Wales to Cornwall, living on the charity of Rhys' brother Edward and of friends. After years of poverty, obscurity, and debilitating bouts of drinking and depression, Rhys would once again be "rescued"

from penury and literary limbo. In October 1956, the actress **Selma Vaz Dias** placed a notice in the *New Statesman* asking Jean Rhys to contact the British Broadcasting Corporation (BBC). Selma had adapted *Good Morning, Midnight* into a monologue to be broadcast on the radio, but she needed Rhys' permission for the performance. Rhys met with Selma, finalized the arrangements, and the program aired in May 1957. Shortly thereafter, Rhys received a letter from Francis Wyndham, an editor at the publishing house André Deutsch. Wyndham asked if she was still writing, and Rhys promptly replied that she was working on a novel, "Mrs. Rochester," the story of Antoinette Cosway, based on Rochester's mad wife in **Charlotte Brontë*'s *Jane Eyre*. By June, Rhys had sold the option on her novel to Deutsch, promising to finish the book by March 1958, an optimistic estimate, for it was not completed until March 1966. "Mrs. Rochester," retitled *Wide Sargasso Sea*, "turned out to be the most difficult, ambitious, fascinating, elusive book she had ever written." "A demon of a book," Rhys noted.

Jean had originally had the mad Antoinette as sole narrator, but in 1959, she completely revised the book twice; in the final version, Antoinette is the narrator of Part I and Rochester of Part II. To write from a man's point of view was especially difficult for Rhys, but Rochester "is by far the most complex and fully drawn male she has ever accomplished." Rhys' novels and short stories have been compared to those of **Colette* and **Katherine Mansfield*; like them, Rhys was able to create, writes Angier, "an entirely feminine world—a world where the ordering and interpretation are exclusively feminine, and a world where the feminine consciousness is not seen in the reflection of a masculine world." In *Wide Sargasso Sea*, Mrs. Rochester's story is Rhys' story, the story of a West Indian girl who leaves her native land, loves a man who hates her (Lancelot Hugh Smith, in Rhys' case), goes insane, and dies in "a cold, grey" country (England, "the embodiment of hell"). This is considered by many to be Rhys' best, and culminating, novel. The themes are well developed and many—"that the beauty of the world hides cruelty," notes Angier, "that dream reveals reality, that there is no love." In Part II, narrated by Rochester, Rhys acknowledges that men suffer too, that everyone is weak in some way and that through weakness "cruelty and hurt enter the world." But it is Antoinette who is rejected and isolated, finally descending into madness. As was Rhys, Antoinette is rejected by her mother, by the blacks of her homeland, especially Tia

(Francine) who was her childhood friend, and by the West Indian white population who will not accept her and therefore "consign her to the 'outside' forever." "I have only ever written about myself," Rhys once said, and in *Wide Sargasso Sea* she reveals her ability to give structure to memories, feelings, fears, and regrets from her childhood to her old age. The image of steps, or stairs, which she employs here is particularly trenchant, for at the top of the stairs Antoinette's, and Rhys', "own future waits—an old forsaken woman."

While working on *Wide Sargasso Sea*, Rhys had a myriad of problems that at times overrode her desire to finish her novel. From 1957 on, Max was in poor health from a series of strokes. Rhys herself was aging and ill; drinking, "black moods," and anger still dominated her life as she tried to care for her husband. Max had always been an obstacle to Rhys' writing for he had never understood the effort and dedication required to produce a book. Undoubtedly, he resented her shutting him out of her life when she was struggling to write, and struggle she did. The conflict often left Jean with a choice between Max and her work, and unfortunately Max usually won. Rhys had told Leslie Tilden-Smith when he complained about her detachment, "I don't see how you can write without shutting everything else out." Angier further notes that "Jean's core of being a writer, which was a core of loneliness and separation, remained."

Rhys' brother Edward bought the aging couple a bungalow in a small village in Devon called Cheriton Fitzpaine in September 1960. Finally, Rhys had a room of her own, but she worked on her novel only sporadically. However, she was able to complete several short stories which appeared in *Art and Literature*. In 1963, Rhys had a heart attack in London where she had gone to work on the novel; in September, Max entered the hospital. Rhys was alone, an intolerable situation for she could not bear being alone, and when she was "she cracked." There were indications that she had a nervous breakdown again; she was convinced that people in Cheriton Fitzpaine thought she was a witch, they stole from her and attacked her. Max had written to Rhys from the hospital, "You deserve something better than me. I wish you had it." On March 7, 1965, Max Hamer died, leaving Rhys on her own. Her isolation would deepen when she ended her friendship with Selma Vaz Dias over broadcasting rights to Rhys' stories and novels. Rhys had signed a legal agreement to give Selma 50% of all proceeds from movie, stage, television and radio performances of her works, "anywhere in the world," and granted Selma "sole artistic control" over the adaptations. Legal and financial matters always frightened Rhys, and she would sign documents "to stop the panic" that she experienced. Later, Rhys realized what she had done and took legal action to modify the agreement. A mutual friend persuaded Selma to accept a third of any proceeds and to relinquish artistic control. Henceforth, Selma's name was added to Rhys' list of those "who had used her and let her down."

At the age of 76, Rhys had been "rediscovered" by the literary community with the publication of *Wide Sargasso Sea* (1966), for which she won the W.H. Smith and Son Annual Literary Award. She was labeled a "modern classic writer," and her previous works were reissued. She was also recognized by being made a fellow of the Royal Society of Literature.

Rhys was lauded for "her strong originality and her remarkable insight into the feminine psyche," and for her examination of "the panic and emptiness of modern life." But the recognition came too late; Rhys had no one with whom to share her success, and she was too old to enjoy her new celebrity status. In fact, Rhys was becoming more reclusive as she aged. She begrudged interviews, claiming they were untruthful or inaccurate.

In 1975, Rhys, at age 85, began to write her autobiography. But for some reason "she lost faith in the value of her work." Alone and isolated, drunk and angry, she raged against the world, blaming everyone for her unhappiness, except herself. She refused to admit she was responsible for anything that had happened to her, insisting "that people, events, her own fate, swept her along against her will." A creature of stunning contradictions, Rhys both hated and loved her own passivity and paranoia, writes Angier, "because they made her feel a victim, but let her feel innocent."

Jean Rhys had three husbands and at least two lovers, yet her fictional heroines were always isolated beings, as she was in real life. Curiously, she admitted that she preferred the company of men to that of women, but she sympathized with women, women like herself who were lonely and unhappy, the "outcasts" of society. And, as Angier writes, "The truth was that, even with her husbands—even with her daughter, even with her loving friends—she was alone. She was always alone." People, including her husbands and lovers, were a mystery to her for "she knew only herself." In addition, Rhys' view of the world was "tragic and pessimistic. . . .

Her solipsism and her pessimism combined to make her writing exactly what she said it was: a quest for self-knowledge, and nothing to do with anyone else." Writing further isolated Rhys from people and from life, and at times, but not often, she questioned whether it was worth the resultant solitary life.

Rhys hated being old as passionately as she hated being alone, dependent, and poor. Unlike her characters in *After Leaving Mr. Mackenzie* who "have been to the human well and have seen dust instead of their reflections," Rhys' reflection is mirrored in her novels and stories where each heroine is Jean Rhys during various stages of her life. Angier states that Jean thought she had never lived because of her self-imposed, but necessary, isolation from people and places. For Jean Rhys, life was a prison, "the prison of her isolated, unloved self" from which she escaped only through her writing. In an interview in *Paris Review* in 1979, Rhys said "To give life shape—that is what a writer does. That is what is so difficult."

Rhys' health failed rapidly after she broke her hip in March 1979. Several mild strokes ensued; she refused to eat or speak, slowly lost consciousness, and died in the afternoon of May 14, 1979, at the hospital not far from her cottage in Cheriton Fitzpaine.

Jean Rhys' life was an anguished one, for as Angier affectingly writes, "She had been given a supreme gift of knowing how to write; she had not been given the gift of knowing how to live. . . . She didn't want admiration as a writer; she wanted love and acceptance and belonging as a woman. She never found them. . . . Her life was unbearably sad; only her art was triumphant."

SOURCES:
Angier, Carole. *Jean Rhys*. London: Viking, 1985.
O'Connor, Teresa. *Jean Rhys: The West Indian Novels*. NY: New York University Press, 1986.
Staley, Thomas F. *Jean Rhys: A Critical Study*. London: Macmillan, 1979.

SUGGESTED READING:
Angier, Carole. *Jean Rhys: Life and Work*. London: Penguin, 1992.
Howells, Coral Ann. *Jean Rhys*. NY: St. Martin's Press, 1991.
James, Louis. *Jean Rhys*. London: Longman Group, 1978.
LaGallez, Paula. *The Rhys Woman*. London: Macmillan, 1990.
Nebeker, Helen. *Jean Rhys: Woman in Passage*. Montreal: Eden Press, 1981.
Plante, David. *Difficult Women: A Memoir of Three*. NY: Atheneum, 1983.
Wolfe, Peter. *Jean Rhys*. Twayne, 1980.
Wyndham, Francis, and Diana Melly, eds. *Jean Rhys: Letters 1931–1966*. London: André Deutsch, 1984.

COLLECTIONS:
The Jean Rhys Collection is located in the McFarlin Library of the University of Tulsa, Tulsa, Oklahoma.

Jeanne A. Ojala,
Professor of History, University of Utah,
Salt Lake City, Utah

Riabouchinska, Tatiana (1917–2000).
See Toumanova, Tamara for sidebar.

Riario, Caterina Sforza (1462–1509).
See Sforza, Caterina.

Ribeiro, Ingeborg (b. 1957).
See Lorentzen, Ingeborg.

Riberio da Silva, Ana Maria de Jésus (c. 1821–1849).
See Garibaldi, Anita.

Ricard, Marthe (1889–1982)

French spy, reformer, and feminist. Born Marthe Betenfeld in German-occupied eastern France in 1889; died in 1982; married Henri Richer (a grocer, died in World War I); married Thomas Crompton (died); married a man named Ricard.

Served as a spy in World War I; awarded the Cross of the Légion d'Honneur (c. 1918); served in the French resistance in World War II; elected to Paris city government (c. 1945).

Marthe Ricard was born Marthe Betenfeld in eastern France in 1889, while Germany still occupied that region following the Franco-Prussian War. In 1911, at age 22, Ricard qualified to fly as a pilot. After her first husband Henri Richer was killed in the Battle of Verdun during World War I, Ricard served her country as a spy for the French secret service. She has been credited with gaining information about German submarine movements from Baron von Krohn, a German military aide with whom she had formed an intimate relationship. After the war's end she was decorated with the Cross of the Légion d'Honneur in recognition of her services.

Ricard then married Thomas Crompton and moved to his homeland of England. After he died, she returned to France and worked for the resistance during World War II. She was married a third time, to a French man whose last name was Ricard. Soon after the war, she was elected a city councilor in Paris, in which position she fought legalized prostitution, a system she believed exploited women. As a result of her campaign, Parisian brothels were closed in 1945, and similar legislation affecting all of France was enacted a year later. In the early 1970s, however, aware of the continuing exploitation of women working as street prostitutes, Ricard suggested that legalizing some prostitution could offer more protection to those women. She died at the age of 93 in 1982.

SOURCES:

Uglow, Jennifer S., ed. and comp. *The International Dictionary of Women's Biography.* NY: Continuum, 1982.

Maria Sheler Edwards,
freelance writer, Ypsilanti, Michigan

Ricci, Nina (1883–1970)

Italian-born Paris fashion designer. Born Maria Nielli in Turin, Italy, in 1883; died in 1970; family moved to France in 1890; married Louis Ricci; children: Robert.

Nina Ricci was born Maria Nielli in Turin, Italy, in 1883. Her family moved to France in 1890. Having learned the fashion industry as an apprentice dressmaker in Paris, she soon became a head designer. Ricci created her designs by using fabric draped directly on a mannequin, in order to achieve the soft and light look that made her clothes popular. Together with her husband Louis, a successful jeweler, Ricci opened her own store in 1932, at age 49. Their son Robert joined the business and worked as its manager and director. He also added perfumes to the Ricci line, including the highly successful L'Air du Temps. While others have worked as head designers for the firm (Jules-François Crahay, 1954–63, Gérard Pipart, 1963—, and **Myriam Schaefer**, 1993—), Ricci's elegant and feminine styles have remained the trademarks of her label.

Maria Sheler Edwards,
freelance writer, Ypsilanti, Michigan

Riccoboni, Marie-Jeanne
(1713–1792)

French novelist. Name variations: Jeanne Riccoboni. Born Marie-Jeanne Laboras de Mézières in Paris, France, in 1713 (some sources cite 1714); died on December 6, 1792; married Antoine François Riccoboni, in 1734 or 1735 (separated); companion to Marie-Thérèse Biancolleli, from 1753 to 1792.

Selected writings: (fiction) La vie de Marianne *(The Life of Marianne, 1745 [some sources cite 1765]),* Lettres de Mistriss Fanni Butlerd *(Letters from Mistress Fanny Butlerd, 1757),* Histoire de M. lemarquis de Cressy *(The History of the Marquis de Cressy, 1758),* Lettres de Milady Juliette Catesby *(Letters from Juliette Catesby, 1759),* Histoire de Miss Jenny *(The History of Miss Jenny, 1762),* Amelia, 1762; *(nonfiction)* Histoire d'Adélaïd *(The History of Ade-*

laide, 1766), Lettres d'Elisabeth-Sophie de Vallière *(Letters of Elisabeth-Sophie de Vallière, 1772),* Lettres de Milord Rivers *(Letters of Lord Rivers, 1776),* Les Amours de Roger et Gertrude *(Roger and Gertrude in Love, 1780),* Histoire de Christine, reine de suab *(The History of Christine, Queen of Swabia, 1783),* Histoire de deux juenes ami *(The Story of Two Young Friends, 1786),* Ernestine *(1798); (play)* Les Caquets *(The Gossipers, 1761); (correspondence)* Lettres de Mme R. à Diderot *(Letters from Mme R. to Diderot)* in Diderot, Oeuvres *(1798),* Correspondence de Laclos et de Mme R *(The Correspondence of Laclos and Mme R., 1864), and* Mme Riccoboni's Letters to David Hume, David Garrick and Sir Robert Liston 1764–1783 *(1976).*

Marie-Jeanne Riccoboni was born Marie-Jeanne Laboras de Mézières into a bourgeois family in Paris in 1713. In 1734, at age 21, she married Italian actor Antoine François Riccoboni, son of actress **Helena Virginia Riccoboni** and actor-playwright Lodovico Riccoboni. Riccoboni herself tried acting, but met with little success. She soon separated from her husband, and from the age of 40 lived the rest of her life with her companion **Marie-Thérèse Biancolleli**, who was also an actress.

Riccoboni launched her literary career with a continuation of Marivaux's unfinished novel *La vie de Marianne* (The Life of Marianne) in 1745. Her next three novels, *Lettres de Mistriss Fanni Butlerd* (Letters from Mistress Fanny Butlerd, 1757), *Histoire de M. lemarquis de Cressy* (The History of the Marquis de Cressy, 1758), and *Lettres de Milady Juliette Catesby* (Letters from Juliette Catesby, 1759), provided Riccoboni with the means to quit the theater and continue writing. She also collected a small pension from the crown until such practices were abruptly ended with the French Revolution in 1789.

Riccoboni wrote her books in letter form, with romantic themes. Her heroines are typically strong women ensnarled in unresolvable conflicts with men who are their moral inferiors. Her work has been described as clever and written with real pathos, and was admired for its perceptive descriptions of love and friendship. (A later critic, however, noted that "Madame Riccoboni is an especial offender in the use of mechanical aids to impressiveness—italics, dashes, rows of points and the like.") One of her later novels, *Lettres de Milord Rives* (Letters of Lord Rivers, 1776), recounts the relationship between two Frenchwomen who prefer their union to love between men and women. She wrote one play, *Les Caquets* (The Gossipers), in 1761, and her last novel, *Ernestine*, which appeared posthumously in 1798, was considered by some to be her masterpiece. Riccoboni died destitute at the age of 79 on December 6, 1792.

SOURCES:

Buck, Claire, ed. *The Bloomsbury Guide to Women's Literature.* NY: Prentice Hall, 1992.

Harvey, Sir Paul, and J.E. Heseltine, eds. *The Oxford Companion to French Literature.* Oxford: Clarendon Press, 1959.

Maria Sheler Edwards,
freelance writer, Ypsilanti, Michigan

Rice, Alice Hegan (1870–1942)

American novelist known for her popular **Mrs. Wiggs of the Cabbage Patch.** *Name variations: Alice Caldwell Rice. Born Alice Caldwell Hegan in Shelbyville, Kentucky, on January 11, 1870; died in Louisville, Kentucky, on February 10, 1942; only daughter and eldest of two children of Samuel Watson Hegan and Sallie P. (Caldwell) Hegan; attended Miss Hampton's private school in Louisville, Kentucky; honorary Litt.D. degrees from Rollins College, 1928, and the University of Louisville, 1937; married Cale Young Rice (a poet), on December 18, 1902 (died January 24, 1943); no children.*

Selected writing: (fiction) Mrs. Wiggs of the Cabbage Patch *(1901),* Lovey Mary *(1903),* Sandy *(1905),* Captain June *(1907),* Mr. Opp *(1909),* A Romance of Billy-Goat Hill *(1912),* The Honorable Percival *(1914),* Calvary Alley *(1917),* Miss Mink's Soldier and Other Stories *(1918),* Turn About Tales *(co-written with C.Y. Rice, 1920),* Quin *(1921),* Winners and Losers *(co-written with C.Y. Rice, 1925),* The Buffer *(1929),* Mr. Pete and Company *(1933),* The Lark Legacy *(1935),* Passionate Follies *(co-written with C.Y. Rice, 1936),* Our Ernie *(1939); (nonfiction)* On Being "Clinnicked": A Bit of a Talk over the Alley Fence *(1931),* My Pillow Book *(1937),* Happiness Road *(1942); (autobiography)* The Inky Way *(1940).*

Born in 1870, Alice Hegan Rice had a privileged childhood in Kentucky. When her father Samuel Watson Hegan went on frequent business trips, he placed his wife **Sallie P. Hegan** and two young children in the largest hotel in Louisville, the Galt House. Summers and holidays were spent at the country estate of her maternal grandfather, Judge James Caldwell, roaming through the cow pasture, climbing trees, and paddling in the creek. As the imaginative first grandchild, she entertained a host of young aunts and uncles and adoring younger cousins with her stories and finagled them into performing in her plays.

Until the age of ten, Rice was schooled at home, principally by a favorite aunt who had a keen mind and a love of literature. When she was finally sent for formal education, it was to a private girls' school whose teachers were concerned more with imparting social graces than with solid academics. Writing was Rice's strongest subject, and she often wrote other students' compositions for them. When she was 15, she submitted to a newspaper, unsigned, a parody of Ik Marvel's *Reveries of a Bachelor* which she titled *Reveries of an Old Maid.* She was highly pleased when it was published, and even more so when the piece received responses branding her an "acrimonious spinster."

At the age of 16, Rice discovered her social conscience while attending Sunday school at a mission in a poor neighborhood with a friend. When they arrived, the lesson was being disrupted by a gang of boys outside who were dangling a dead cat in the window. Rice offered to address the matter and enticed them with a story on the church steps. She recounted a tale that she had just read titled *Picayune Pete or Nicodemus the Dog Detective* and was such a hit that she was asked to continue through the summer. It was an unusual Sunday school class, filled as it was with the doings of pirates and murderers and gangsters, but it introduced her to the world of the underprivileged and to the poor neighborhood, known as the Cabbage Patch, where the boys lived. Rice combined this newfound awareness of poverty with a character based on a destitute woman who came periodically to her mother's house, asking for food and talking to whomever would listen, and began writing her first novel. With the encouragement of the aspiring young women writers (including *Ellen Churchill Semple and *Annie Fellows Johnston) of the Authors Club of Louisville, of which Rice was a member, *Mrs. Wiggs of the Cabbage Patch* was born.

The story of an indomitably cheery though poverty-stricken widow with five children, *Mrs. Wiggs* was published in 1901 by the first publisher to which Rice sent it, the Century Company in New York City. The most popular of her many works, it was a wildly successful bestseller that was made into a stage play in 1904 and into a film starring *ZaSu Pitts and W.C. Fields in 1934. The book has been translated into French, German, Swedish, Danish, Chinese, Japanese, and Braille, and is still in print. (Of the woman who had inspired Mrs. Wiggs, Rice noted: "Visitors descended upon her in droves. . . . They took palings from her fence and leaves from her trees as souvenirs, and made snapshots of her whenever she showed herself. In vain I offered to move her to a better house in a cleaner neighborhood. She preferred to stay where she was and enjoy the drama of fighting the intruders, sometimes with words, and sometimes, alas, with pails of slop.")

On December 18, 1902, Alice married Cale Young Rice, a poet and playwright. Inseparable for the rest of their lives, the Rices spent much of their time traveling around the world, spending summers in Maine or Florida, and becoming part of the literary scene in London and New York.

Rice's subsequent works drew upon her wish to make people aware of the conditions in which the poor lived, as well as upon her personal experiences during World War I as a hospital volunteer. In the early 20th century, there was an active social reform movement in the United States and Great Britain aimed at improving the working and living conditions of the poor. Through her writings, Rice became a participant in this movement and supported **Louise Marshall**'s efforts to found the Cabbage Patch Settlement House in Louisville in 1910, becoming a member of the board. Her book *Calvary Alley* (1910) was written with the express aim of creating a public outcry over conditions in the urban slums, and she was also a close friend of muckraker extraordinaire *Ida Tarbell. Nonetheless, like her husband, she had no affection for the grimly realistic fiction (exemplified by Sinclair and Steinbeck) of the early decades of the 20th century, and a number of her stories, while not uncommon for their time, now would be considered racially insensitive.

Rice wrote more than 20 books, and, while none of her subsequent works achieved the success of *Mrs. Wiggs*, five others were turned into silent films: *Lovey Mary* (1903), the sequel to *Mrs. Wiggs*, starring *Marguerite Clark (1926); *Sandy* (1905), starring Jack Pickford (1918); *Mr. Opp* (1909), starring Arthur Hough; *A Romance of Billy-Goat Hill* (1912); and *Calvary Alley* (1917), starring **Ann Pennington**.

The onset of the Great Depression badly affected the Rices' finances, and although she suffered from poor health Rice continued writing in those years because she needed the money. She died at her home in Louisville in 1942, age 72, and was buried at Cave Hill Cemetery. Her husband, despondent over losing her, committed suicide less than a year later.

SOURCES:

Commire, Anne, ed. *Something About the Author.* Vol. 63. Detroit, MI: Gale Research.

James, Edward T., ed. *Notable American Women, 1607–1950.* Cambridge, MA: The Belknap Press of Harvard University, 1971.

Kunitz, Stanley J., and Howard Haycraft, eds. *Twentieth Century Authors.* NY: H.W. Wilson, 1942.

Malinda Mayer,
freelance writer, Falmouth, Massachusetts

Rice-Davies, Mandy (b. 1944).

See Keeler, Christine for sidebar.

Rice-Pereira, Irene (1902–1971).

See Pereira, Irene Rice.

Rich, Adrienne (1929—)

One of modern-day America's most distinguished and influential poets and feminist theorists. Born Adrienne Cecile Rich in Baltimore, Maryland, on May 16, 1929; eldest of two daughters of Dr. Arnold Rice Rich (a professor of pathology at Johns Hopkins University's School of Medicine) and Helen Jones Rich (a trained composer and pianist); educated at home, primarily by her mother, until the fourth grade, though her father, who had a fine library, encouraged her to both read and write poetry; attended Roland Park Country School in Baltimore, 1937–47; entered Radcliffe College in Cambridge, in 1947, elected to Phi Beta Kappa, graduated cum laude in 1951; her younger sister Cynthia graduated from Radcliffe five years later; married Alfred Haskell Conrad (an economist at Harvard), in 1953 (committed suicide 1970); lived with Michelle Cliff (1976—); children: David (b. 1955); Paul (b. 1957); Jacob (b. 1959).

Published first volume of verse, A Change of World, in the Yale Younger Poets Series (1951); received the first of many distinguished awards, a Guggenheim fellowship, to study and travel abroad (1951–52); published second volume of poetry, inspired by her travels abroad, The Diamond Cutters (1955); received a second Guggenheim fellowship (1961) and spent the year in the Netherlands with husband and children; published third volume of verse, Snapshots of a Daughter-in-Law (1963); both style and content of work began to change, reflecting her conversion to an increasingly radical feminism; published two subsequent volumes of poetry (1960s), reflecting the social and political turmoil engendered by both the civil-rights movement and the war in Vietnam; moved to New York (1966) where her husband taught at the City College of New York while she taught writing part-time at both Columbia University and CCNY; marriage unraveled after the move to New York and Alfred Conrad committed suicide (1970); while teaching part-time at several colleges and universities and raising her sons alone, continued to write poetry, receiving the National Book Award (1974) for her seventh volume of verse, Diving into the Wreck; *came out as a lesbian in* Twenty-One Love Poems *(1976); published first prose work* Of Woman Born: Motherhood as Experience and Institution *(1976); entered a long-term relationship with the Jamaican-born writer and editor Michelle Cliff (1976); moved to Santa Cruz, California, with Cliff (1984), where both women continue to write about, and in support of, the outsiders and the oppressed.*

Writings: Ariadne: A Play in Three Acts and Poems *(Baltimore: J.H. Furst, 1939);* Not I, But Death, A Play in One Act *(Baltimore: J.H. Furst, 1941);* A Change of World *(New Haven: Yale University Press, 1951);* The Diamond Cutters, and Other Poems *(NY: Harper, 1955);* Snapshots of a Daughter-in-Law: Poems, 1954–1962 *(NY: Harper & Row, 1963; London: Chatto & Windus-Hogarth Press, 1970);* Necessities of Life: Poems, 1962–1965 *(NY: Norton, 1966);* Selected Poems *(London: Chatto & Windus-Hogarth Press, 1967);* Leaflets: Poems, 1965–1968 *(NY: Norton, 1969);* The Will to Change *(NY: Norton, 1971);* Diving into the Wreck: Poems, 1971–1972 *(NY: Norton, 1973);* Poems: Selected and New, 1950–1974 *(NY: Norton, 1975);* Of Woman Born: Motherhood as Experience and Institution *(NY: Norton, 1976);* Twenty-One Love Poems *(Emeryville, CA: Effie's Press, 1976);* The Dream of a Common Language: Poems, 1974–1977 *(NY: Norton, 1978);* On Lies, Secrets, and Silence: Selected Prose, 1966–1978 *(NY: Norton, 1979);* A Wild Patience Has Taken Me This Far: Poems, 1978–1981 *(NY: Norton, 1981);* Sources *(Woodside, CA: Heyeck Press, 1983);* The Fact of a Doorframe: Poems Selected and New, 1950–1984 *(NY: Norton, 1984);* Your Native Land, Your Life *(NY: Norton, 1986);* Blood, Bread, and Poetry: Selected Prose, 1979–1985 *(NY: Norton, 1986);* Time's Power: Poems 1985–1988 *(NY: Norton, 1989);* An Atlas of the Difficult World: Poems 1988–1991 *(NY: Norton, 1991);* Adrienne Rich's Poetry and Prose: Poems, Prose, Reviews, and Criticism *(edited by Barbara Charlesworth Gelpi and Albert Gelpi, NY: Norton, 1993);* Collected Early Poems, 1950–1970 *(NY: Norton, 1993);* What Is Found There: Notebooks on Poetry and Politics *(NY: Norton, 1993);* Dark Fields of the Republic: Poems, 1991–1995 *(NY: Norton, 1995);* Midnight Salvage: Poems, 1995–1998 *(1999); (essays)* Arts of the Possible: Essays and Conversations *(2001).*

One of the most influential American poets of the 20th century, and one of the most remarkable persons of our age, Adrienne Rich continues to read her poetry to audiences that number in the thousands. Both her poetry and her prose works are required reading in many college and university courses in literature, women's studies, feminism and feminist theory. In addition, Rich has been a social and political activist since the early 1960s, championing pacifism, the environment, abortion rights, and equal rights for all—gay or straight, male or female, white, black, brown or Asian, able or disabled. Rich has long sought, in her writings and in her life, alternatives to patriarchal capitalism, which system she believes is not just anti-woman, but anti-human at its core, and destructive of the environment.

Rich is also an educator, lecturer, and editor, and a recipient of numerous awards, prizes and honorary degrees. Over a period of 50 years she has also traveled widely in the United States, in Europe, in Central America and elsewhere. Yet only those who have met Rich face to face or have read her poems written since the late 1970s are aware that she is physically disabled and in constant pain. When barely out of college she developed rheumatoid arthritis and has faced several operations for the crippling disease since the early 1980s. Until the 1980s, Rich spoke of pain only in general terms in her verse, but in *Your Native Land, Your Life: Poems* (1986) she became very specific:

> I feel signified with pain
> from my breastbone through my left shoulder
>   down
> through my elbow into my wrist is a thread of
>   pain.

Rich has also written about another acute pain—the suicide of her husband Dr. Alfred Conrad in October 1970. In *Diving into the Wreck: Poems, 1971–1972* (1973), she wrote of the coming 20th anniversary of their marriage in 1953:

> Next year it would have been twenty years
> and you are wastefully dead.

In *The Washington Post,* **Elizabeth Kastor** (June 8, 1993) described Rich as "a small woman and the hunched back, the cane she leans on, the hands gnarled by rheumatoid arthritis all somehow make her look smaller. . . . She walks without bending her left leg, swinging it along in a slow arc with each pace, and the few steps up to the lectern seem to require an act of physical will."

She was born Adrienne Cecile Rich in Baltimore, Maryland, on May 16, 1929, the eldest of two daughters of Dr. Arnold Rice Rich, a professor of pathology at Johns Hopkins University's School of Medicine, and **Helen Jones Rich**, a trained composer and pianist. Her father, who

Adrienne Rich

treated her like a son, introduced her to the major poets from the 16th to the first half of the 20th century when she was still a child. Rich began writing verse at the age of five. Some of her poems and two plays were published by the time she was twelve. It is not surprising, then, that Rich received early recognition for her verse. Her first volume of poems, *A Change of World* (1951), showed considerable originality though the poems were also influenced by earlier, mostly male, poets such as Donne, Keats, Longfellow, Yeats, and such contemporaries as

Thomas, Stevens, Frost, McNeice, and Auden. In elegant, well-crafted and mostly rhymed verse, Rich sought "detachment from the self and its emotions," believing then, as did W.H. Auden, that "without detachment no art is possible." Auden was so impressed with Rich's poetry that he chose *A Change of World* to receive the Yale Younger Poets Award in 1951, the same year she graduated from Radcliffe College.

Rich's aim of universality and self-detachment continued in her second volume of verse, *The Diamond Cutters* (1955). However, by 1963, when her third volume of verse, *Snapshots of a Daughter-in-Law* appeared, Rich had undergone a real "change of world." Having married Alfred H. Conrad, an economist teaching at Harvard, and given birth to three sons—David, Paul, and Jacob (born in 1955, 1957, and 1959), Rich eschewed universality as a "white male voice" and began to write in a woman's voice and about women's lives. Both her own experience as wife and mother, and the revival of feminism, triggered the change and convinced Rich that *with* detachment no art was possible.

I loved the sound, the music of poetry from the very beginning. It seemed a way of finding out about life. Things could be said in poems that could be said in no other way.

—Adrienne Rich

In her earliest poems, Rich paid homage to largely male poets, but as her feminist awareness increased she wrote more and more about women in general, as well as about specific women. Beginning in the 1970s, Rich acknowledged her debt to and admiration for such women poets as *Anne Bradstreet, *Emily Dickinson, H.D. (*Hilda Doolittle), *Muriel Rukeyser, *Sylvia Plath, *Anne Sexton and others. She also dedicated a poem to *Emily Carr, a very fine Canadian artist of the first half of the 20th century little known outside her country. One of Rich's most haunting poems is dedicated to *Ethel Rosenberg who, at the height of the anti-Communist hysteria of the late 1940s and 1950s, was convicted, along with her husband Julius, of conspiracy to commit espionage. Despite a chorus of protest in the United States and abroad, they were electrocuted in mid-1953.

Since the 1960s and continuing to this day, Rich's poetry has also addressed the major issues and problems of the last 50 years: anti-Semitism, racism, sexism, abortion rights, homophobia, violence against women and disastrous wars from Vietnam to the Persian Gulf. In addition, she has long protested our hostility to left-wing revolutionary movements in Cuba, Chile, and Nicaragua. Rich passionately believes that poetry is powerful, that it can change us for the better and lead us to create a world where true equality, love, social and economic justice, and peace will prevail.

Rich laments that only in the United States is poetry viewed as a luxury read by a small elite, rather than as a necessity of life. She notes that everywhere else in the world—Asia, Africa, Europe, the Middle East and Latin America—political poetry is viewed as normal and is honored by non-authoritarian governments and condemned by authoritarian regimes. Poets in other countries are often appointed to diplomatic posts and/or elected to the legislature, something that rarely happens in the United States.

The Clinton administration did seek to honor Rich in 1997, but she refused to accept the National Medal for the Arts because of her disapproval of many of our government's policies here and abroad. Earlier, in 1974, Rich refused to accept the National Book Award unless and until two other nominees, the poet *Audre Lorde and the novelist **Alice Walker**, were also honored. The three accepted the award in the name of all women and donated the cash prize to the Sisterhood of Black Single Mothers.

A woman who has the courage of her convictions, Rich came out as a lesbian in 1976, six years after her husband's suicide and when her youngest son Jacob was 17. She retains close ties with her sons, and in 1987 celebrated her 58th birthday at Jacob's home in Vermont. *The Dream of a Common Language: Poems, 1974–1977* (1978), her 11th volume of verse, included *Twenty-One Love Poems* (1976). In the 12th poem, Rich, recalling an early love, writes:

> We were two lovers of one gender,
> we were two women of one generation.

In an unnumbered piece between the 14th and 15th poems, Rich tells her beloved, "Whatever happens to us, your body will haunt mine—tender, delicate." In the poem "Transcendental Etude" in *The Dream of a Common Language*, dedicated to **Michelle Cliff**, the Jamaican-born naturalized American writer and editor with whom Rich has shared her life for over 20 years, she writes:

> two women, eye to eye
> measuring each other's spirit, each other's limitless desire,
> a whole new poetry beginning here.

Although Rich has written essays about lesbianism, it is in her poetry that she is able to say things about women loving women that, to quote her, "could be said in no other way."

It is also in her poetry that Rich has been able to say things about other aspects of her identity. "Split at the root" is the way she has characterized herself, a once-married lesbian who is "neither Gentile nor Jew, Yankee nor Rebel." Although she was born to a Southern Protestant mother (and therefore not a Jew under Jewish law) and a totally assimilated Jewish father from the North, it was not until the 1980s that she confronted her Jewish heritage and examined the effects of the Holocaust on her own life and writing.

In 1976, Rich's first prose work, *Of Woman Born: Motherhood as Experience and Institution*, appeared. It proved so popular that W.W. Norton, which has published most of Rich's numerous works, issued a tenth anniversary edition in 1986. Relying on her own experience as a mother of three sons and a great deal of research, Rich argued that being a good mother is neither innate nor instinctual, but a quality that is learned only with a great deal of pain, patience and self-discipline.

In 1979, Norton published Rich's first volume of essays, *On Lies, Secrets and Silence: Selected Prose 1966–1978*. The essays pay homage to the pioneer feminists, *Elizabeth Cady Stanton and *Susan B. Anthony, and to a number of women poets as well as the novelists *Charlotte Brontë and *Virginia Woolf. Rich also included four essays on one of her chief concerns for over 40 years, the education of women. In addition, she returned to the subject of motherhood (and motherlessness) in three essays. In one of her two essays on lesbianism, Rich reminded her audience that "we must remember that we have been penalized, vilified, and mocked, not for hating men, but for loving women."

Her two subsequent volumes of essays, *Blood, Bread and Poetry: Selected Prose, 1979–1986* (1986) and *What is Found There: Notebooks on Poetry and Politics* (1993), as the titles suggest, reiterate her lifelong concern with poetry. Her fifth and latest volume of essays, *Arts of the Possible: Essays and Conversations* (2001), also centers on creativity.

Rich has taught at some of the most prestigious colleges and universities from one end of the United States to the other. In the 1960s and 1970s she taught at Swarthmore, Columbia, New York University, the City College of New York, Brandeis and Rutgers. In the early 1980s, she also taught at Cornell. Since moving to Santa Cruz, California, in 1984, she has taught at Scripps College and Stanford University. Her longest stint of teaching has been at San José State University, from 1984 to the present. Rich has also given guest lectures at many colleges and universities and has received at least five honorary doctorates in literature, including ones from Smith College (1979), Harvard University (1990) and Swarthmore College (1992).

Finally, from 1952 to the present Rich has probably received more awards than any other American poet living or dead. She received two Guggenheim fellowships, in 1952 and 1961. She was the recipient of a Bollingen Foundation grant in 1962, a National Endowment for the Arts grant in 1970, the Fund for Human Dignity Award of the National Gay Task Force in 1981, the first Ruth Lilly Poetry Prize of $25,000 in 1986, a MacArthur Foundation fellowship in 1994, the Tanning Prize of the Academy of American Poets in 1996 and the Lannon Foundation's Lifetime Achievement Award in 1999.

Adrienne Rich has written a great deal and a great deal has been written about her, mostly by literary critics. Although Rich's poetry and prose have been deemed too political and too polemical by some critics, female and male, the vast majority of studies of her work, which, including essays and reviews as well as monographs, number over 50, view Rich with the highest regard.

Margaret Atwood, the distinguished Canadian novelist and critic, writes in *Second Words: Selected Prose*: "Adrienne Rich is not just one of America's best feminist poets, or one of America's best woman poets, she is one of America's best poets." Dick Allen, a *Hudson Review* critic, predicts that Rich "will be read and studied for centuries to come." As we enter the new millennium Rich remains a powerful role model for us all, having accomplished so much despite considerable physical and psychic pain.

SOURCES:

Cooper, Jane R., ed. *Reading Adrienne Rich: Reviews and Re-visions, 1951–81*. Ann Arbor, MI: University of Michigan Press, 1984.

Dickie, Margaret. *Stein, Bishop, and Rich: Lyrics of Love, War, and Place*. Chapel Hill, NC: University of North Carolina Press, 1997.

Gelpi, Barbara C., and Albert Gelpi, eds. *Adrienne Rich's Poetry: A Norton Critical Edition*. NY: Norton, 1975.

Keyes, Claire. *The Aesthetics of Power: The Poetry of Adrienne Rich*. Athens, GA: University of Georgia Press, 1986.

Meese, Elizabeth. "Adrienne Rich" in *Dictionary of Literary Biography*, Vol. 67. Detroit, MI: Gale Research, 1988.

SUGGESTED READING:

Rich, Adrienne. *Diving into the Wreck: Poems, 1971–1972*. NY: Norton, 1973.

———. *The Fact of a Doorframe: Poems Selected and New, 1950–1984*. NY: Norton, 1984.

———. *Of Woman Born: Motherhood as Experience and Institution*. NY: Norton, 1977.

———. *On Lies, Secrets, and Silence: Selected Prose, 1966–1978*. NY: Norton, 1979.

———. *Snapshots of a Daughter-in-Law: Poems, 1954–1962*. NY: Harper & Row, 1963.

Anna Macías,
Professor Emerita of History, Ohio Wesleyan University,
Delaware, Ohio

Rich, Elizabeth (fl. 1710).

See Montagu, Lady Mary Wortley for sidebar.

Rich, Louise Dickinson (1903–1991)

American author. Born Louise Dickinson in Huntington, Massachusetts, on June 14, 1903; died in Mattapoisett, Massachusetts, on April 9, 1991; daughter of James Henry Dickinson (a newspaper editor) and Florence Myrtie (Stewart) Dickinson; Massachusetts State Teachers' College, B.Sc., 1924; married Ralph Eugene Rich (a businessman), on August 27, 1934 (died 1945); children: Rufus and Dinah.

Selected writings: We Took to the Woods *(1942);* Happy the Land *(1946);* Start of the Trail: The Story of a Young Maine Guide *(1949);* My Neck of the Woods *(1950);* Trail to the North *(1952);* Only Parent *(1953);* Innocence Under the Elms *(1955);* The Coast of Maine: An Informal History *(1956);* Peninsula *(1958);* Mindy *(1959);* The First Book of the Early Settlers *(1959);* The First Book of New World Explorers *(1960);* The First Book of the Vikings *(1962);* The Natural World of Louise Dickinson Rich *(1962);* The First Book of China Clippers *(1963);* State O' Maine *(1964);* The First Book of the Fur Trade *(1965);* The First Book of Lumbering *(1967);* The Kennebec River *(1967);* Star Island Boy *(1968);* Three of a Kind *(1970);* The Peninsula *(1971);* King Philip's War, 1675–76 *(1972);* Summer at High Kingdom *(1975).*

Louise Dickinson Rich loved the outdoors, evident from the many books she wrote about natural history and living in the woods. From the time of her marriage to Ralph Rich in 1934 until his death in 1945, the Rich family lived in a camp on the Rapid River in the backwoods of northern Maine. After Ralph died, Rich began writing to support herself and her two children. Her two autobiographical books, the bestselling *We Took to the Woods* (1942) and *My Neck of the Woods* (1950), are accounts of the Richs'

isolated life in the wilderness and of their necessary resourcefulness during such emergencies as the birth of their first child. Among her other works are the young adult novels *Trail to the North* (1952), *Start of the Trail* (1949), and *Summer at High Kingdom* (1975), as well as many history books for children. Rich died of congestive heart failure in 1991.

Malinda Mayer,
freelance writer, Falmouth, Massachusetts

Rich, Mary (1625–1678)

Irish diarist, memoirist, and countess of Warwick. Name variations: Mary Boyle. Born at Youghal near Cork, Ireland, in 1625 (some sources cite 1624); died in Essex, England, in 1678; seventh daughter and thirteenth child of Richard Boyle, 1st earl of Cork; married Charles Rich, 4th earl of Warwick, in 1641 (died 1673); children: one son (died at age 21).

A privileged child of the rich and influential Richard Boyle, 1st earl of Cork, Mary Rich was independent, headstrong, and rebellious. At age 14, much to her father's displeasure, she refused the suitor he had chosen for her because, as she later explained, "living so much at my ease, I was unwilling to change my condition." Her father had recently moved to the Savoy in London and was the center of a bustling social life which his daughter actively participated in and very much enjoyed.

It was in London that she met the "poverty stricken" young Charles Rich, second son of the earl of Warwick, whose impecunious state of £1,300–£1,400 per year placed him far from the hope of ever attaining the hand of the great earl's daughter. Nonetheless, for two years he secretly courted her, and Mary reported him to be "a most diligent gallant to me, applying himself, when there were no other beholders in the room but my sister, to me; but if any other person came in he took no more than ordinary notice of me." When at 16 years of age Mary contracted the measles, Charles was so anxious about her that their relationship was discovered. Mary was sent to the country in disgrace, but not before accepting him as her fiancé. Her father held out for two weeks before finally agreeing to the match and providing her with a dowry, whereupon she insisted on eloping since she was "always a great enemy to a public marriage."

After the nuptials in 1641, Rich had one son on whom she lavished affection. When he fell ill in 1646, she made a vow to God that she would become a "new creature" if her son recovered.

He did, and Rich, who had always held out against Puritanism because she enjoyed society so much, became a convert in the middle of the English Civil War between the Puritans and the Royalists. Her home in Essex was soon a refuge and hiding place for Puritan ministers and bishops who had escaped from London, and she helped to hide armaments from the Royalist soldiers during the siege of Colchester. When her son died of smallpox at the age of 21, she relied strongly on her faith to see her through the ordeal.

Rich's husband Charles, who was a member of Parliament during the war, became the 4th earl of Warwick when his brother died in 1659, thus making Mary Rich, countess of Warwick. When Charles died in 1673, he left to her the whole of his estate for her lifetime. She used her fortune to help those in need and was renowned for both her devotion and her charity.

Rich began a religious diary in 1666, and maintained it through the rest of her life. She began to write her autobiography in 1672, but died in 1678 without completing it, although some of her devotional writings were published in 1686. Her diaries are preserved in the British Museum.

SOURCES:

Buck, Claire, ed. *Bloomsbury Guide to Women's Literature.* NY: Prentice Hall, 1992.

The Concise Dictionary of National Biography. Oxford: Oxford University Press, 1992.

Dick, Oliver Lawson, ed. *Aubrey's Brief Lives.* Ann Arbor, MI: University of Michigan Press, 1957.

Malinda Mayer,
freelance writer, Falmouth, Massachusetts

Rich, Penelope (c. 1562–1607)

English noblewoman who inspired Philip Sidney's **Astrophel and Stella.** *Name variations: Lady Penelope Rich; Penelope Blount; Penelope Devereux; Stella. Born Penelope Devereux around 1562 (some sources cite 1560); died on July 7, 1607, in Westminster, London, England; daughter of Walter Devereux, 1st earl of Essex, and Lettice Knollys (c. 1541–1634, a cousin of Elizabeth I); married Robert Rich, 3rd Baron Rich, later earl of Warwick, in 1581 (divorced 1605); married Charles Blount, 8th Lord Mountjoy, earl of Devonshire, in 1605 (died 1606); children: (first marriage) six, including Robert Rich (1587–1658), 2nd earl of Warwick, and Henry Rich (1590–1649, beheaded), earl of Holland; (second marriage) five, including eldest son Mountjoy Blount (c. 1597–1665), Baron Mountjoy and earl of Newport.*

A great-grandniece of **Anne Boleyn* and the inspiration for one of the most famous sonnet sequences in English literature, Penelope Rich inherited her fiery temperament and famous beauty from her mother **Lettice Knollys*, who was a cousin of Queen **Elizabeth I*. Lettice frequently irritated England's most famous monarch to distraction, and as she grew up Penelope did the same. On one occasion when Elizabeth was visiting Penelope's father Walter Devereux, 1st earl of Essex, Penelope so irritated the queen that Elizabeth banished the girl to her room. Later in life, Penelope would correspond under an assumed name with nobles in Scotland who were plotting against Elizabeth. When her brother Robert Devereux, earl of Essex, was in disfavor at court, Penelope wrote Elizabeth a sarcastic letter that provoked the queen to have Penelope confined to her house.

When she was 14, Penelope Rich caught the eye of the celebrated poet and soldier Sir Philip Sidney. At one point, Penelope's father suggested a marriage between Sidney and his daughter, and there is some speculation that they may have been engaged. But Devereux died in 1576, and Penelope and her siblings became the wards of Henry Hastings, earl of Huntingdon, who was a strict Puritan. He betrothed Penelope to Robert Rich, 3rd Baron Rich. She resisted vigorously, but despite her complaints was married to Robert Rich in 1581. After her marriage, she paid somewhat more attention than she had previously bothered to Sidney, who wrote one of the greatest sonnet sequences of the English language, *Astrophel and Stella*, about her. Published in 1591, five years after Sidney's death from a wound sustained at the battle of Zutphen, the 108 sonnets of the sequence were hugely popular, reinvigorating the sonnet form, and are believed to have influenced Shakespeare. The sonnets detail an unhappy, apparently unconsummated love (Stella refuses Astrophel, and he kisses her only once, while she is asleep), and the exact relationship between Penelope and Sidney after her marriage is unclear. On the other hand, it is quite clear that her marriage was not happy, although she gave birth to six children with Robert.

Penelope's assertiveness was to prove lethal to her younger brother Robert Devereux, the second earl of Essex. Though a favorite of Queen Elizabeth in his early years, Robert was high-strung and quick to anger, even in the presence of the queen. His political service to Elizabeth was marked by many successes and failures and, as a result of one of his later failures, he was tried for contempt and disobedience in June 1600. He lost his lands and was confined to his house. He soon regained his liberty, but continued to play politics badly. Goaded on by Penelope, who was no friend to the queen, Robert and some followers attempted a rebellion to force Elizabeth to fire some of his political enemies from her advisory council. The insurrection failed miserably, and Robert surrendered. He was imprisoned, condemned to death, and beheaded on February 25, 1601.

Her brother's execution did not dampen Rich's rebelliousness, but she did not risk her neck in open antagonism of the queen. (Her son Henry Rich would later be beheaded for his part in the civil war during the reign of Charles I.) Penelope remained popular at court, taking part in masques by Samuel Daniel and Ben Jonson presented there. As well, poets Henry Constable and John Davies also addressed sonnets to her, and several poets dedicated their works in her honor. However, her married life became a scandal. Before she had ever married Robert Rich, Penelope had been in love with Charles Blount, 8th Lord Mountjoy, to whom she had secretly promised herself in marriage. Around 1595, while still married, she began an open relationship with Blount, who was another favorite of the queen's. They had five children, whose paternity he acknowledged, and Rich legally was separated from her husband in 1601. In November 1605, she was formally granted a divorce from Robert Rich; one condition of the divorce decree was that neither party would ever marry again. Penelope would have nothing of it, and a little over a month later, on December 26, 1605, she married Blount. In doing so, she openly broke church law, and her children with Blount were declared illegitimate. Both she and Blount were banished from the queen's court, where they had held high standing. Blount died less than six months later, and Penelope died within a year of his death. John Ford's 1633 tragedy *The Broken Heart*, while set in Sparta, is alleged to have been inspired by Penelope Rich's life.

SOURCES:
The Concise Dictionary of National Biography. Oxford: Oxford University Press, 1992.

Drabble, Margaret, ed. *The Oxford Companion to English Literature*. 5th ed. Oxford: Oxford University Press, 1985.

Patrick Moore,
Associate Professor of English,
University of Arkansas at Little Rock

Richardis.

Variant of Richilde.

Richardis von Stade (d. 1152).

See Stade, Richardis von.

Richards, Ann Willis (1933—)

Governor of Texas. Name variations: Ann Willis; Ann Richards. Born Dorothy Ann Willis in Lakeview, Texas, on September 1, 1933; daughter of Robert Cecil Willis (a pharmaceutical salesman) and Iona (Warren) Willis (a dressmaker); educated at Waco High School; Baylor University, B.A., 1954; University of Texas, Austin, teaching certificate, 1955; married David Read Richards (a lawyer), in 1953 (divorced 1984); children: Cecile, Dan, Clark, and Ellen.

Served as county commissioner, Travis County, Texas (1976–82); served as state treasurer of Texas (1982–90); gave keynote speech at the Democratic National Convention (1988); served as governor of Texas (1990–94).

Only the second woman in Texas history to be governor of the state, Ann Willis Richards won election in 1990 with a combination of intelligence, organizational skills, compassion, humor, and down-home political savvy. She was born in 1933 in Lakeview, Texas, the daughter of Robert Cecil Willis, a pharmaceutical salesman, and **Iona Warren Willis**, a dressmaker. Richards noticed at an early age that her parents worked constantly, and she inherited their energy, which was to serve her well. She was active on the debate team in high school and represented her school at the Texas Girls State, which taught students about the workings of state government.

After marrying David Richards in 1953, and graduating from Baylor University a year later, Richards moved with her husband to Dallas, Texas, where he became an attorney and she taught junior high school. She stopped teaching when she had her first child, and over the next years volunteered in political campaigns for Democratic politicians while raising her four children. In the early 1960s, David worked as a staff lawyer for the Civil Rights Commission in Washington, D.C., where Richards frequently watched sessions of the Senate from the visitors' gallery and met a number of important Democrats. She continued her political activities after their return to Texas in 1962, and by the late 1960s, Richards had developed a reputation as a fine campaign manager, especially for female candidates. In 1974, she managed the campaign of **Wilhelmina Delco**, who became the first black woman ever elected to the Texas House of Representatives.

In 1975, a group of local Democrats suggested to David Richards that he run for Travis county commissioner, a seat held by a Democrat. Instead, after David and Richards decided that she would be the better candidate, Richards announced her candidacy. With backing from many liberal and women's political groups, she campaigned relentlessly throughout the Democratic primary and won the nomination with nearly three times as many votes as the incumbent. She continued campaigning widely, using a savvy mix of newspaper and television coverage, and won the general election with 63% of the vote. The campaign gained her not only the post of county commissioner, but much favorable publicity throughout the state. Richards used the visibility of the post to push for issues she believed in, including ratification of the Equal Rights Amendment.

Richards developed a drinking problem over the years, which came to a head late in September 1980, when several of her friends and children staged an "intervention." She spent four weeks in October 1980 at St. Mary's Alcohol Treatment Unit in Minneapolis, Minnesota. After successfully completing the program, she returned to work, but her marriage began to fail, and she and her husband separated. (They would divorce in 1984.)

After four successful years as a county commissioner, in 1981 Richards decided to run for the state treasurer's office. One of her competitors for the Democratic Party nomination was Warren G. Harding, but his campaign self-destructed after he was indicted on two counts of official misconduct. Her other opponent, Lane Denton, exposed Richards' bout with alcoholism (a disease which was still not much talked about at the time), but lost his chance to score points with suspicious voters when he also falsely claimed that she still drank and that she beat her children. Richards capitalized on Denton's mistakes to win the Democratic primary, and campaigned with much support from the Texas Women's Political Caucus to easily win election against her Republican opponent. In her election-night speech she noted, "Many young women thought there were things a woman couldn't do. Tonight we showed statewide politics is open to them." She had just become the first woman in 50 years to hold state office in Texas.

Richards was a highly successful state treasurer. Until her tenure, no treasurer had ever put Texas state funds in interest-bearing accounts before paying them out for state expenditures. Her shrewd financial management helped the state earn an unexpected $141 million during one fiscal year. In addition, she was beginning to receive increasing nationwide attention, and in 1984 she was invited to second the nomina-

tion of Walter Mondale at the Democratic National Convention. In 1986, she was reelected as treasurer.

Richards' political career got a huge boost when she gave the keynote address at the 1988 Democratic National Convention. George Bush, the Republican nominee for the presidency of the United States, had adopted Texas as his home, and Richards was therefore the perfect Democrat to criticize him and his candidacy. Her brilliant speech brought the house down when she listed Bush's failures and then added, "Poor George, he can't help it—he was born with a silver foot in his mouth." After Bush won the election, he referred to Richards only as "that woman."

Her success as state treasurer and her triumph at the 1988 Democratic National Convention convinced Richards to run for governor of Texas. (Only one woman, *Miriam A. Ferguson, had ever been elected governor of Texas, and she had been swept into the office 50 years prior by

Ann Willis Richards

voters who knew they were actually electing her husband, impeached ex-governor Jim Ferguson.) Once again Richards faced a nasty primary election, with much comment from her opponent and the press about her alcoholism. Rumors of drug use surfaced as well, briefly damaging her standing in the polls before her opponent was himself smeared with revelations about alleged use of illegal drugs. Richards won the nomination. During the summer and fall of 1990, she faced Clayton Williams, the Republican nominee. The gubernatorial campaign was hard-fought, closely watched even nationwide, and hugely expensive for the time: the candidates' combined spending was estimated at over $46.7 million. (When Richards received contributions from San Francisco, some Republicans "smeared" her by claiming she was a lesbian out to advance gays in politics.) Plugging education as her main issue, Richards received much support from women and minorities, and her strong defense of the right to choose gained her the votes of many Republican women. Williams, meanwhile, made repeated and very public verbal gaffes, several of them particularly offensive to women, that called his judgment into question. On November 6, 1990, in what the press labeled "the biggest upset in Texas political history," Richards won the election with 50% percent of the vote to Williams' 47%.

Richards' term as governor had mixed results. As one of the few women governors in the country, and as a famously blunt-spoken politician who advanced women's causes and women in political life, she was widely praised for appointing many women and minorities to important positions in state government. She created reforms in insurance laws and state ethics, appointing *Barbara Jordan as her counselor on ethics, and established the Texas state lottery to generate additional revenues. In 1992, she chaired the Democratic National Convention. However, some of her appointees failed her, her office staff grew enormously in size and cost, much to critics' vociferous dismay, and many voters complained that she spent too much time publicizing herself on the national political stage. In 1994, when she ran for reelection against Republican nominee George W. Bush, the son of the former president and himself later president, she was defeated. The following year Richards joined the Austin branch of a white-shoe Washington law firm, where she works as a lobbyist for a number of large corporations.

SOURCES:

Crawford, Ann Fears, and Crystal Sasse Ragsdale. *Women in Texas.* Austin, TX: State House Press, 1992.

Shropshire, Mike, and Frank Schaefer. *The Thorny Rose of Texas: An Intimate Portrait of Governor Ann Richards.* Birch Lane, 1994.

Weatherford, Doris. *American Women's History.* NY: Prentice Hall, 1992.

Patrick Moore,
Associate Professor of English,
University of Arkansas at Little Rock

Richards, Audrey Isabel

(1899–1984)

English social anthropologist. Born in London, England, on July 8, 1899; died on June 29, 1984; daughter of Sir Henry Erle Richards (a diplomat and law professor) and Isabel (Butler) Richards; Newnham College, Cambridge University, M.S., 1922; London School of Economics and Political Science, Ph.D., 1929.

Awards and honors: awarded the Wellcome Medal for applied anthropology and the Rivers Memorial Medal for field work; named commander of the Order of the British Empire (1955); president of the Royal Anthropological Institute (1960–62); president of the African Studies Association (1963–66); named fellow of the British Academy (1967).

Selected writings: Hunger and Work in a Savage Tribe *(1932);* Land, Labour and Diet in Northern Rhodesia *(1939);* Bemba Marriage and Present Economic Conditions *(1940);* Chisungu: A Girl's Initiation Ceremony among the Bemba of Northern Rhodesia *(1956);* The Changing Structure of a Ganda Village: Kizozi, 1892–1952 *(1966);* The Multicultural States of East Africa *(1969);* Some Elmdon Families *(co-written with Jean Robin, 1974).*

Born in England in 1899, Audrey Isabel Richards spent her childhood in India (which was then a British colony), where her father served on the British Viceroy's Council. She returned to England in 1911, when her father became a law professor at Oxford University, and attended boarding school. Richards then studied natural sciences at Newnham College of Cambridge University from 1919 to 1922. Afterwards, she worked in Germany for the Ambulance Unit Family Welfare Settlement, and was a secretary in the labor department of the League of Nations from 1924 to 1928.

In 1926, Richards enrolled as a graduate student in anthropology at the London School of Economics, where she was a student of Bronislaw Malinowski, the founder of the functional school of anthropology. (Functional anthropologists believe that human institutions can be best understood if they are studied within the context of the entire culture surrounding those institutions.) Influenced by Malinowski's teachings, Richards became a functionalist herself; her doctoral thesis, for which she was awarded a Ph.D. in 1929, was subtitled "A Functional Study of Nutrition among the Southern Bantu." The thesis was published in 1932 as *Hunger and Work in a Savage Tribe.*

Between 1930 and 1934, Richards spent two and a half years in Africa studying the Bemba tribe in Zambia (formerly Northern Rhodesia), while also lecturing in social anthropology at the London School of Economics. As an anthropologist, she was careful not to be too tidy in her categorizations of human social behaviors. She was not afraid of the loose ends, or unexplained data, that remain after an anthropologist's analysis, for she was aware that any analytical framework had its limits, especially if she were studying a social group that was undergoing rapid change.

Richards published a number of books over the course of her career, and lectured in social anthropology at the University of Witwatersrand in Johannesburg, South Africa, from 1938 to 1940. During World War II, she worked on the staff of the British Colonial Office in London. After the war, she taught social anthropology at the University of London until 1950. Richards spent the next six years as director of the East African Institute of Social Research at Makerere University College in Kampala, Uganda, where she supervised numerous Institute fellows and associates conducting dozens of surveys and studies. She held a number of important teaching and administrative positions in social anthropology between 1956 and her retirement in 1967.

Richards worked hard to be an attentive hostess to the many friends who visited her. She was also a generous friend. After her mentor Bronislaw Malinowski's wife **Elsie Masson** died in 1935, Richards became the guardian of their three daughters for a time, and stayed in touch with them for many years. She also had a fine sense of humor and was not averse to telling stories on herself. Once, while studying a village in Essex, England, as she sat "in what I hoped was the conventional pose of poker-face and blank psycho-analytical, shock-proof visage," she wrote, she "was startled by an informant in an area where religious factions were political factions and political feeling ran high. My visitor suddenly shouted, 'You! You say you are not a Protestant, not a Catholic and not a Muslim. There isn't such a person!' and he stumped off."

The recipient of numerous awards and honors, including the Wellcome Medal, the OBE,

and a term as president of the Royal Anthropological Institute, Richards died on June 29, 1984, little more than a week before her 85th birthday.

SOURCES:

The Concise Dictionary of National Biography. Oxford: Oxford University Press, 1992.
Contemporary Authors. Vols. 21–24, 1st revision. Detroit, MI: Gale Research, 1977.
Contemporary Authors. New Revision Series, vol. 27. Detroit, MI: Gale Research, 1989.
Proceedings of the British Academy: 1992 Lectures and Memoirs. Oxford University Press.

Patrick Moore,
Associate Professor of English,
University of Arkansas at Little Rock

Richards, Beah (1926–2000)

African-American actress, poet, and playwright. Born Beah Richardson in Vicksburg, Mississippi, on July 12, 1926 (one source cites 1920); died of emphysema in Vicksburg on September 14, 2000; daughter of Wesley Richardson (a Baptist minister) and Beulah Richardson (a seamstress); attended Dillard University in New Orleans; married artist Hugh Harrell (divorced).

Selected filmography: Take a Giant Step *(1960);* The Miracle Worker *(1962);* Gone Are the Days! *(1963);* Guess Who's Coming to Dinner *(1967);* In the Heat of the Night *(1967);* Hurry Sundown *(1967);* The Great White Hope *(1970);* Mahogany *(1975);* Inside Out *(1987);* Drugstore Cowboy *(1989);* Homer and Eddie *(1989);* Beloved *(1998).*

Beah Richards, whose career on stage and in movies and television stretched over half a century, was born in Vicksburg, Mississippi, in 1926. She knew from an early age that she was going to be an actor, although there were no theaters in Vicksburg, and certainly not for her; she later recalled how, growing up in the segregated South long before the civil-rights movement, she was stoned and jeered at by white children on her way to school.

Richards left Mississippi to attend Dillard University in New Orleans, and then moved to San Diego, California, where she studied dance and acting. She made her professional debut there at the Old Globe Theater in 1948. Two years later, she moved to New York City, where like many other struggling actors she found stage work irregularly. To supplement her income, she taught in a charm school. One of her first major New York roles was in 1954, as the grandmother in the Off-Broadway revival of *Take a Giant Step* (six years later, despite being still in her 30s, she would play the same role in the film version). In 1958, with a number of others, including Godfrey Cambridge, Richards co-founded the Harlem Community Theater. The following year she was cast as the understudy for the part of Lena Younger in the Broadway premiere of *Lorraine Hansberry's *Raisin in the Sun*. Richards landed her first on-stage role on Broadway in 1959, in *The Miracle Worker*, based on the story of *Helen Keller and ◄ Anne Sullivan Macy. Two years later, she was back on Broadway in the hit satire *Purlie Victorious*, written by Ossie Davis and also starring Davis and *Ruby Dee. All three would reprise their roles in the 1963 film version of the play, *Gone Are the Days!*

Her breakthrough role came in the 1965 Broadway play *The Amen Corner*, by James Baldwin. Richards starred in the central role of Sister Margaret Alexander, a woman who has dazzled her Harlem congregation for many years with her charisma and aggressive piety. But when her estranged husband, a good-for-nothing musician, comes home to die, she has to confront her false piety, and she risks losing her congregation and her son, whom she has tried to keep on the straight and narrow. Although the play closed in New York after only 12 weeks (she then went with it to Los Angeles), Richards won rave reviews. She received the *Theatre World* Award and the New York Drama Critics Circle Award for her performance, and topped the Drama Critics Poll of the trade magazine *Variety*. She worked steadily in theater, movies, and television for the rest of her life.

Richards also wrote poetry and plays, including an exploration of segregation, *All's Well That Ends*; in 1971, her play *One Is a Crowd*, which she had written 20 years earlier, received excellent reviews in Los Angeles. A collection of poems, *A Black Woman Speaks*, was published in 1974, including the long title poem which she often performed on stage as a one-woman show. The following year she won an Emmy award for her performance of *A Black Woman Speaks* on television. Richards frequently directed television shows and plays as well, often in California, where she made her home for many years, and taught courses at the University of Southern California. In her writing and her public-speaking engagements, she was a voice against racism and against the employment of African-American actors in unflattering, stereotypical roles. During one conference on stereotyping African-Americans in film, she pointed out that any actor, regardless of personal fame, could change social stereotypes simply by refusing to perform such roles. She herself rejected many such demeaning roles, but worked steadily nonetheless.

Throughout her career, Richards was often cast as a mother or grandmother, invariably dignified and wise, including her role as Sidney Poitier's mother in *Guess Who's Coming to Dinner* (1967), for which she received an Academy Award nomination, as James Earl Jones' mother in *The Great White Hope* (1970), and in numerous guest spots on television series. She was inducted into the Black Filmmakers Hall of Fame in 1974, and won another Emmy in the late 1980s for a guest role on the series "Frank's Place." She made her final appearance on film in 1998, as Baby Suggs in the screen version of *Toni Morrison's novel *Beloved*, opposite *Oprah Winfrey. Richards suffered from emphysema in her last years, but continued working, and won another Emmy award for a guest appearance on the television drama "The Practice" in September 2000. She died that same month in Vicksburg, where she had returned earlier in the year.

SOURCES:

The Day [New London, CT]. September 16, 2000.

❧▶

Macy, Anne Sullivan. See Keller, Helen for sidebar.

From the movie Hurry Sundown, *starring Beah Richards.*

Katz, Ephraim. *The Film Encyclopedia*. 3rd ed. NY: HarperCollins, 1998.

The New York Times. September 16, 2000, p. A13.

Smith, Jessie Carney, ed. *Notable Black American Women*. Detroit, MI: Gale Research, 1992.

Patrick Moore,
Associate Professor of English,
University of Arkansas at Little Rock

Richards, Cornelia Wells Walter

(1813–1898).

See Walter, Cornelia Wells.

Richards, Dorothy Pilley (1893–1986).

See Pilley, Dorothy.

Richards, Ellen Swallow

(1842–1911)

American chemist, founder of the American domestic-science movement, food-reform advocate, and early environmentalist who was the first woman student and faculty member at MIT. Name variations: Ellen Swallow; Ellen Henrietta Richards. Born Ellen Henrietta Swallow in Dunstable, Massachusetts, on December 3, 1842; died of heart disease at her Boston home on March 30, 1911; only child of Mary (Taylor) Swallow and Peter Swallow (a farmer); graduated from Vassar, 1870; awarded science degree from Massachusetts Institute of Technology (MIT), 1873; married Robert Hallowell Richards, in 1875; no children.

Was the first woman to obtain a science degree from MIT (1873); began women's classes in Women's Laboratory, MIT (1876); published The Chemistry of Cooking and Cleaning *(1882); was an instructor in sanitary chemistry, MIT (1884–1911); created the New England Kitchen (1890); organized and was elected first president of the American Home Economics Association (1908); published* Euthenics *(1910).*

Many middle-class American women in the late 19th century complained that they had no adequate goals in their lives. Strongly encouraged by social convention to marry and bear children, to find fulfillment in their homes, they said it was not enough. Some found the remedy in social reform and settlement house work, helping their less fortunate neighbors and gaining a sense of vocation. Others joined the Women's Christian Temperance Union, and a daring minority agitated for votes for women. Ellen Richards, founder of the American domestic-science movement and a public-health crusader, took a path which was both progressive and conservative. Her aim was not so much to take women out into the wider world but to bring one aspect of that world, science, into every home.

She was born Ellen Henrietta Swallow in Dunstable, Massachusetts, on December 3, 1842, the only child of **Mary Taylor Swallow** and Peter Swallow, both farmers. She grew up frail but soon developed a strong will and a range of intellectual interests. Educated at home for the first 16 years by parents who served as her schoolteachers, Richards also learned the domestic arts from her mother, including baking and embroidery. The family became shopkeepers, and Ellen showed a good head for business and organization. In 1864, aged 22, she became a local schoolteacher, then moved to Worcester, Massachusetts, to enjoy several years as an independent breadwinner. Several men courted her but she resisted their advances, after discovering that many married women suffered miserable, constricted lives. She wrote to a cousin that she had no wish to marry or bear children. Recalled to her parents because of her mother's illness, Richards endured two years of sickness and depression but shook herself out of it when she learned of the new Vassar College for women, recently founded in upstate New York. She resolved to enroll there and used her savings in beginning a more formal education. When her funds were exhausted, she tutored less gifted women and paid her way through college, making a favorable impression on her professors.

Graduating from Vassar in 1870 with a distinguished record, especially in the sciences, Richards then applied for graduate study in chemistry at the Massachusetts Institute of Technology (MIT). She was admitted as a "special student," becoming the first woman to study there, and was excused from payment of fees. Richards tried to reassure her professors that she was no feminist radical by volunteering to sew buttons for the men, sweep the laboratory floors, and in other ways make symbolic gestures of submission to male power. "Prof. A. accords me his sanction when I sew up his papers or tie up a sore finger, etc.," she wrote of her ingratiating efforts. "Last night Prof. B. found me useful to mend his suspenders, which had come to grief, much to the amusement of young Mr. C. I try to keep all sorts of such things as needles, thread, pins, scissors, etc. around. . . . They are getting to come to me for anything they want and they almost always find it."

In 1873, Richards became the first women science graduate of MIT; she then persuaded the institute to let her use some vacant campus buildings to set up a laboratory for a Women's Education Association class in chemistry, which she taught, unpaid. The women in her classes learned "Household chemistry," studying the chemical makeup of domestic food products and learning how to trace unwanted additives in foods. In those days, before the passage of any Pure Food and Drug laws (the first came in 1906), this was a worthwhile and necessary job—adulterated foods and milk were a common hazard of American city life. Richards emphasized not only the added safety but also the dignity of being a domestic scientist: "The woman who boils potatoes year after year, with no thought of how or why, is a drudge, but the cook who can compute the calories of heat which a potato of given weight will yield is no drudge." She was also at work as assistant to MIT's Professor William Nichols who had been commissioned to survey the purity of the state's water supply. He too found her an excellent helper and a fine scientist—together they drew up the world's first diagrammatic map of an area's naturally occurring chlorine content in water.

Richards . . . ran her own home as if it were an extension of the Women's Laboratory, and conducted regular tests on the products and technologies introduced into her housekeeping. She called her house . . . the 'Center for Right Living' and hoped it would exemplify the way in which the highest scientific standards could enhance daily life if they were applied to eating, sleeping, breathing, house construction, house-cleaning, and home decoration.

—Laura Shapiro

Richards contributed more than $1,000 each year to the Women's Laboratory, until MIT finally agreed to admit women as ordinary students in 1884. Despite her pioneering in the field, she was not an advocate for equal educational opportunity for women. She feared that if large numbers of women were admitted most would fail their courses, and provide ammunition to men who opposed any women's higher education. Her policy, pursued after 1891 in the Association of Collegiate Alumnae (later the American Association of University Women), which she helped found, was to educate small numbers of women to a high intellectual standard rather than large numbers to a lower standard. One of her teachers and admirers at MIT was a professor of geology and mining, Robert Hallowell Richards. She translated articles from German periodicals for him and did several experiments with a care and confidence which im-

pressed him, and for a time seemed intent on a career in mineralogy. Her thesis was a study of the element Vanadium; on the strength of it, Vassar gave her an honorary M.A. She continued to write papers on minerals, became the only female member of the 4,000-member American Institute of Mining and Mineralogical Engineers in 1879, and wrote a textbook, *First Lessons in Minerals*, in 1882.

In 1875, Ellen Swallow married Robert Richards, and they moved to the suburb of Jamaica Plain, four miles from MIT. In the first years of their marriage, they traveled widely, gathering geological specimens. They honeymooned in the mines of Nova Scotia, and later crossed most of Europe, the Americas, even the North Pole, on behalf of their work. They then renovated their home, modifying the water and sewage system, redesigning the windows, heating, and air flow, and trying to turn it into the ideal safe, hygienic home, which their hundreds of visitors could use as a model for their own. The couple appears to have been ideally suited to one another—each helped the other's career as far as possible.

Nearby at the "Center for Right Living," a laboratory, some of her women students tested food products for adulterative elements. They discovered, for example, that a product sold as "cinnamon" was often a blend of sawdust, mustard, and starch. Ellen Richards (she always used her married name) became, in effect, an early consumer advocate, gaining influential legislators' support, warning other women against inferior products in magazine articles, and pressuring fraudulent manufacturers and wholesalers to reform their ways. She lectured widely on her discoveries across the nation and began to gain a respectable reputation throughout the states. After teaching at MIT unpaid for 12 years, she was finally given a paid faculty position there in 1886, as instructor in "Sanitary Chemistry," but was never awarded the coveted Ph.D. degree. (Smith College gave her an honorary doctorate in 1910.) In a Boston speech of 1892, she introduced the principle of ecology into America. Coined by Ernst Haeckel, a German evolutionary biologist, it meant the study of human interactions with the environment, and nicely fitted Richards' own interdisciplinary work in nutrition, sanitation, mineralogy, and chemistry.

Unlike the radical suffragists of her era, Richards still believed that a woman's place was in the home, but in her eyes a housewife should be a domestic "scientist," albeit a scientist who still knew how to provide a soothing shelter for

Ellen Swallow Richards

her husband and children. She argued for extensive study in the domestic arts, so that women could recover the lost knowledge which their foresisters had possessed (such as spinning, weaving, soap and candlemaking) before industrialization and urbanization presented packaged alternatives to the traditional methods. Among the new types of knowledge all women ought to acquire, she said, were plumbing, construction, an understanding of infections and bacteria, principles of nutrition, and nursing. They should learn to be good cooks, even if they could afford servants, and should know how to make everything in their houses hygienically clean. To develop this kind of outlook, education would have to "awaken a spirit of investigation in our girls as it is often awakened in our boys" and would have to show girls that "science has a very close relation to everyday life."

She became an active member of the Society to Encourage Study at Home, which had been founded in 1873 and was, in effect, the first correspondence-course university for women. Her task was to design and supervise its science curriculum, which soon became its second most popular offering (after history). Richards lived in an era when new machines were a source of acute excitement for Americans, but characteristically she believed women should not merely use them but learn exactly how they worked. Her teaching, while theoretically sound, had strong vocational and practical goals, too. Correspondence with students brought her into contact with many discouraged women. She wrote them encouraging letters and sent them copies of her book *Health*, a compendium of scientific and common-sense ideas for self-preservation.

Her principles were presented more systematically in another book, *Chemistry of Cooking and Cleaning* (1882), which also investigated the chemistry of digestion. Against some domestic scientists and nutritionists who favored an almost puritanical severity in diet and forgot about details like flavor, the level-headed Richards reminded women that food still had to taste good, or else its consumers would never feel inclined to eat it. But she added that too many spices were bad for the digestive system, "like the too frequent and violent application of the whip to a willing steed." Another of her publications, *The Dietary Computer*, tabulated the nutrition of different foods against the cost, enabling poor housewives to get the most food quality for their pennies; in the following years, she wrote a succession of these economy-minded booklets, *The Cost of Living* (1899), *The Cost of Food* (1901), *The Cost of Shelter* (1905), and *The Cost of Cleanness* (1908).

Richards, like many of her New England contemporaries, had every confidence in herself and in the essential superiority of her ways—she was a strong believer in the supremacy of white Anglo-Saxons and some of her rhetoric has, by our standards, an uncomfortable racist edge. She won the support and the financial backing of *Pauline Agassiz Shaw and Edward Atkinson, two Boston philanthropists, who funded a large survey of the eating habits of Boston's working people and the dangers of heavy alcohol consumption. Atkinson had risen from humble origins in the textile trade. As an abolitionist, he had funded John Brown's raid on Harper's Ferry in 1859, and was now himself a food-reform enthusiast. He wrote *The Science of Nutrition* (1896) and invented the handy "Aladdin Oven," a kind of portable kerosene stove which Richards and her friends used in their food experiments. He was also an advocate of healthy homemade "sterile bread," made in his own kneading machine and devoid of the pernicious whitening agents used by commercial bakers.

Together with a domestic science reformer who had studied the issue in Europe, **Mary Hinman Abel**, Richards and Atkinson created the New England Kitchen in 1890, a center designed to transform Boston workers' diets for the better by giving them wholesome grains, vegetables, and fruits in place of fatty meat, beer, and cheap sweets. Whatever the nutritional merits of its food, however, the New England Kitchen never won much enthusiasm from the local people. Middle-class food faddists came to eat there but workers stayed away. Some of the food went to captive audiences (schoolchildren and prisoners), and the creators ate a little of it, but it was never a commercial success. It did, however, enhance the prestige of scientific food advocates among reformers, and Richards found herself increasingly in demand as a nutrition advisor at public institutions, schools, asylums, and hospitals. *Jane Addams sent some of her Hull House volunteers from Chicago to study with Richards in Boston.

Ellen Richards declined to participate in establishing a women's exhibit at the Chicago World's Fair in 1893, because she believed that women had already achieved equality with men and that a separate exhibit was inappropriate. To her, feminism had an old-fashioned air to it and by the 1890s, she said, "Women have now more rights and duties than they are fitted to perform." But she was present at the fair, supervising an ad hoc version of the New England Kitchen where she cooked her ideal foods and distributed literature on scientific housekeeping. In general, Richards did not hold women in high esteem. It seemed to her that they were too slow to adopt better methods and new ideas. As the historian **Laura Shapiro** shows, "she harangued her sex relentlessly. In her view women had to wake up, face new ideas, accept the help that science and technology offered, and give up the irrationality that characterized femininity. 'Women . . . have feared the thunder and ignored the microbe. They have the habit of shrieking at the sight of a toad. . . . Women cannot see why water will not run uphill. . . . They need the influence of the scientific spirit.'"

Richards was certainly an exceptional woman in her range of interests and her level of scientific skills. With her friend Atkinson, she also did pioneer work in the reduction of fire hazards in textile mills, by studying the propensity of lubricants to break down and catch fire, and trying to perfect fire-resistant oils. Later, she built on her ecological ideas, recognizing the interdependence of people, animals, and the natural world, appealing for more attention to water purity, and, as usual, writing extensively on the issue. Her book *Air, Water, Food* (1900) outlined the nature of these interdependent elements, and she followed up in 1904 with *The*

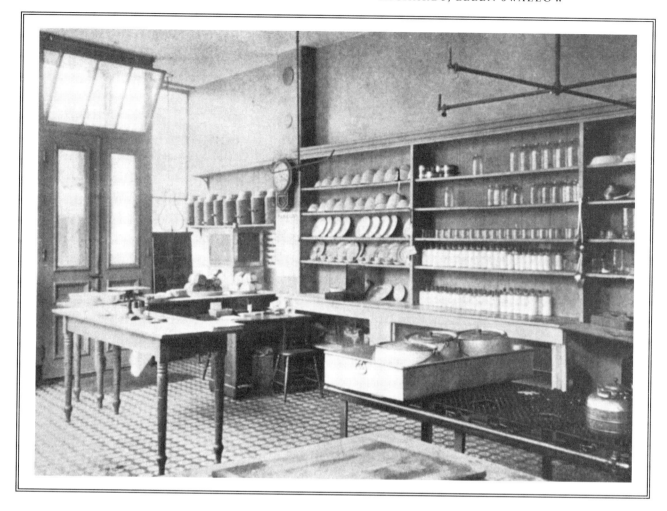

The New England Kitchen, Pleasant Street, Boston.

Art of Right Living, which sounds a familiar environmental note:

> We seem to have assimilated so deeply the idea that man is lord of all the earth that . . . we do not grasp the thought that man must be lord of himself, also, if he is not to succumb to nature's rule in the end. . . . We react to our environment, therefore we must act upon it to make it satisfactory.

But her views on ecology, as on domestic affairs, were practically oriented—she was certainly no "deep ecologist." In *Euthenics: The Science of Controllable Environment* (1910), she made the argument for environmental improvement in terms of its profitability, and showed the vast saving in human capital which could be realized by improved air and water conditions. She outlined a virtual utopia in which citizens' environmental safety committees played a large public role in close cooperation with private industry, schools, and government.

Richards was a regular participant in domestic-science summer conferences, held at Lake Placid, New York, from 1899. In 1908, at the tenth annual meeting, the participants decided to constitute themselves the American Home Economics Association, and they chose Richards as their first president. She tried to prevent it from becoming a women's organization and welcomed the participation of state university departments of dairying, agriculture, and nutrition. Overwork forced her to resign after two years, now aged 68, but she continued to work at an unending round of commitments which included membership of over 200 advisory panels. Ellen Richards died exhausted after a series of heart attacks in March 1911. Her husband lived on in their exemplary home until his death in 1944 at the age of 100, a living testimony to the invigorating regimen, clean air, and good diet his wife had pioneered.

SOURCES:

Clarke, Robert. *Ellen Swallow: The Woman Who Founded Ecology.* Chicago, IL: Follett, 1973.

Hunt, Caroline. *The Life of Ellen H. Richards.* Boston, MA: Whitcomb & Barrows, 1912.

Richards, Ellen. *The Chemistry of Cooking and Cleaning: A Manual for Housekeepers.* Boston, MA: Estes & Lauriat, 1882.

RICHARDS, ELLEN SWALLOW

Shapiro, Laura. *Perfection Salad: Women and Cooking at the Turn of the Century.* NY: Farrar, Straus and Giroux, 1986.

Yost, Edna. *American Women of Science.* Philadelphia, PA: Frederick A. Stokes, 1943.

Patrick Allitt,
Professor of History, Emory University,
Atlanta, Georgia

Richards, Laura E. (1850–1943)

American novelist, poet, and short-story writer. Born Laura Elizabeth Howe in Boston, Massachusetts, on February 27, 1850; died on January 14, 1943; daughter of Samuel Gridley Howe (Boston reformer and educator who founded the Perkins Institute for the Blind) and Julia (Ward) Howe (1819–1910); sister of Maud Howe Elliott (1854–1948); tutored at home by private teachers, later attended local schools; married Henry Richards (an architect and illustrator), on June 17, 1871; children: Alice Maude Richards; Rosalind Richards; Henry Howe Richards; Julia Ward Richards; Maud Richards (died in childhood, 1885); John Richards; Laura Elizabeth Richards.

Laura E. Richards

Laura E. Richards, daughter of Samuel Gridley Howe and *Julia Ward Howe, was born in

1850 and grew up in a house called "Green Peace" in South Boston. Next door was the Perkins Institute for the Blind where she and her siblings played and made friends with the students and their teachers. Richards was named for her father's first pupil, *Laura Bridgman. "As a child I did not think of the wonder of her, any more than of that of sunrise, or a tree, or any other miracle," wrote Richards. "She was Laura; she was blind, deaf and dumb; Papa had brought her out of prison." Before long, Richards was reading *Elizabeth Barrett Browning's *Rhyme of the Duchess May* to an aging blind employee of the institute's workshop.

Richards adored Green Peace, describing it from the day she began to write, she claimed, "first in *Five Mice in a Mouse-trap*, again in *When I Was Your Age.*" The family spent their summers in Lawton's Valley, a few miles from Newport, Rhode Island. At age ten, Richards started writing, and she would publish 80 books in her lifetime. By the time she wrote *Captain January* in 1889, she had already penned many juveniles. "I think this story went to every reputable publisher, or to all that I knew about, in this country, and to several in England. No one would have it." Finally published in 1891, *Captain January* sold three million copies. It was first filmed in 1924, starring *Baby Peggy; the second version, starring *Shirley Temple (Black), was filmed by 20th Century-Fox in 1936.

In 1876, Richards moved with her husband Henry Richards to his boyhood town of Gardiner, Maine, where she lived until her death. There, for 30 or more summers, the couple ran Camp Merryweather, a camp for boys. Richards also helped establish the town's high school, library, office of the district nurse, and befriended a shy neighbor, later known as the poet Edwin Arlington Robinson. Her writer friends included *Sarah Orne Jewett and *Margaret Deland.

Along with the Pulitzer Prize-winning book on her mother, *Julia Ward Howe, 1819–1910* (1916), which she wrote with her sister *Maud Howe Elliott, Richards wrote biographies on *Elizabeth Fry (1916), *Abigail Adams (1917), *Joan of Arc (1919), Laura Bridgman (1928), and on her father Samuel Gridley Howe (1935). Like her mother, Richards remained productive well into her advanced years. Her autobiography *Stepping Westward* was written when she was 81; she died at the age of 93.

SOURCES AND SUGGESTED READING:

Commire, Anne. *Yesterday's Authors of Books for Children.* Vol. I. Detroit, MI: Gale Research, 1977.

266 *WOMEN IN WORLD HISTORY*

Richards, Laura E. *Stepping Westward* (autobiography), 1931.

Richards, Linda (1841–1930)

American nurse and educator. Born Melinda Ann Judson Richards on July 27, 1841, in Potsdam, New York; died on April 16, 1930, in Boston, Massachusetts; youngest daughter of Sanford Richards and Betsy (Sinclair) Richards; graduated from the New England Hospital for Women and Children nursing school, 1873; never married; no children.

Became America's first nursing school graduate (1873); served as first president of the American Society of Superintendents of Training Schools (1894); served as head of the Philadelphia Visiting Nurses Society.

Melinda Ann Judson Richards, called Linda, was born in 1841 in Potsdam, New York, and named after missionary ***Ann Hasseltine Judson** because her father hoped she would grow up to become a missionary. The family, which included Linda's three older sisters, lived briefly in Watertown, Wisconsin, before the death of Sanford Richards when Linda was only four years old. Her mother **Betsy Sinclair Richards** then moved the family to Vermont, where the girls were raised in Derby and Lyndon. Richards received much of her education at an academy in Barton, Vermont. She was 13 years old, and had recently joined the Baptist Church, when her mother died. She then went to live with a physician by the name of Masta, earning her keep in his home by serving as a "born nurse." (Born nurses in those days were women who visited and helped the sick and bedridden.)

Richards took her first paying job during the Civil War, at the Union Straw Works in Foxboro, Massachusetts. She remained at the Straw Works for seven years before quitting in 1870 to work at Boston City Hospital. At the time, there were no nursing schools at which professional nurses could receive formal training, and they performed the most menial chores in hospitals; nursing was considered a job appropriate only for those unable to find better work, and nurses themselves were usually uneducated and often slovenly or heavy drinkers. It had been Richards' desire to work as an assistant nurse, but what she found at Boston City Hospital came as a sad surprise, and she left within three months. Two years later, Dr. ***Susan Dimock** became resident physician and administrator of the New England Hospital for Women and Children, and the hospital set up a training school for nurses. Richards promptly enrolled as a student, and one year later, in 1873, became the first of five women to graduate from the first nursing school in U.S. history.

After graduating, Richards spent one year as night supervisor of the first American training school modeled after ***Florence Nightingale**'s nursing principles, the Bellevue Training School in New York City. She then moved back to Boston to work at the Boston Training School (later the Massachusetts General Hospital School of Nursing). Despite the innovations of nurses' training schools, only a few of these programs came into existence, and they were plagued by ambivalence among hospital medical staffs who were skeptical of the importance of trained nurses. Richards' work at the Boston Training School and other institutions was significant in that she established a sense of credibility among the schools with which she was associated. It was through her persistent example that superintendents of training schools served simultaneously as superintendents of nurses in their hospital environments. Richards was subsequently named supervisor of the nursing staff at the Boston Training School, a position she held until her resignation in 1877. That year, she traveled to England to observe the training schools set up by Florence Nightingale and to consult personally with Nightingale herself. Upon her return to the United States, she set about creating a training school for nurses at Boston City Hospital that both would follow Nightingale's precepts and be deeply connected with the hospital itself. She met with success, and the school opened in 1878. As had been her practice in the past, she served as matron of the hospital and as superintendent of the school.

Richards, who was in poor health, took one leave of absence during her tenure at Boston City Hospital before resigning in 1885. She then volunteered at the American Board of Commissioners for Foreign Missions, which sent her to Japan in 1886. There she established the first Japanese nursing school, at Doshisha Hospital in Kyoto. Richards supervised the school and evangelized for five years before returning to the United States in 1891, again because of poor health.

In 1892, Richards founded a school at Methodist Episcopal Hospital in Philadelphia. Between 1893 and her retirement in 1911, she headed the nurses' training schools at New England Hospital for Women and Children, at Taunton Insane Hospital in Massachusetts, and at the Michigan Insane Asylum in Kalamazoo. She also worked at Brooklyn Homeopathic Hospital, Hartford Hospital, and the University of

Pennsylvania Hospital in Philadelphia, and established a training school at Worcester Hospital for the Insane. In 1894, she became the first president of the American Society of Superintendents of Training Schools, and she was a member of the committee that established the predecessor of the nursing education division at Columbia University's Teachers College. After her retirement, Richards lived in rural Lowell, Massachusetts, and privately published her memoir, *Reminiscences of Linda Richards*. She was rendered an invalid after suffering a cerebral hemorrhage in 1925, and died in a Boston hospital on April 16, 1930. The Linda Richards Award, given in recognition of an unprecedented contribution to the field of nursing, was instituted by the National League for Nursing in 1962.

SOURCES:
Edgerly, Lois Stiles, ed. *Give Her This Day*. Gardiner, ME: Tilbury House, 1990.

James, Edward T., ed. *Notable American Women, 1607–1950*. Cambridge, MA: The Belknap Press of Harvard University, 1971.

McHenry, Robert, ed. *Famous American Women*. NY: Dover, 1980.

Gloria Cooksey,
freelance writer, Sacramento, California

Richards, Shelah (1903–1985)

Irish actress, manager and producer. Born Sheila Geraldine Richards in Dublin, Ireland, on May 23, 1903; died at Ballybrack, County Dublin, Ireland, on January 19, 1985; daughter of John William Richards and Adelaide Roper Richards; educated at Alexandra College, Dublin, and at finishing school in Paris; married Denis Johnston, on December 28, 1928 (divorced 1945); children: Jennifer Johnston (b. 1930, a novelist); Michael Johnston.

Born in 1903, Shelah Richards came from a Dublin legal family with no involvement in the theater, although in her own generation she and her cousin *Geraldine Fitzgerald became two of the most prominent Irish actresses of their time. Richards described her mother **Adelaide Roper Richards** as "a wonderful woman who was a vegetarian and for a time had been a suffragette who had even chained herself to the railings in St. Stephen's Green until my father said that he could not run a respectable practice if she did these things."

Richards' interest in the arts developed early. Her godmother was the artist **Beatrice Elvery** (Lady Glenavy) whose salons she attended with her parents when still a child. When she was 16, Richards met W.B. Yeats, and he was reported to have inquired, "Who is the girl with a head like a lion?" She started acting with the Dublin Drama League, and at 12 hours' notice was asked to replace **Eileen Crowe** in the role of Mary Boyle in Sean O'Casey's *Juno and the Paycock* at the Abbey Theatre. According to family lore, the first her father knew of her acting career was when friends congratulated him on her Abbey success. In 1926, Richards created the role of Nora Clitheroe in O'Casey's next production, *The Plough and the Stars*. She was also the first actress to tackle the lead in Yeats' *The Player Queen* since *Maire O'Neill. "Everyone said how glorious Molly O'Neill had been," said Richards, "and that intimidated me a bit. I was very young." She played other leading roles at the Abbey and traveled to New York with the company.

Richards married the playwright Denis Johnston in 1928. In 1938, she left the Abbey to appear on Broadway in *Molly Keane's *Spring Meeting* which starred *Gladys Cooper and A.E. Mathews. When war broke out the following year, Richards was advised to stay in America, but her two children Michael and Jennifer were in Dublin and she returned. During the war years, Richards ran her own company with Nigel Heseltine at the Olympia Theatre in Dublin; they scored particular successes with Paul Vincent Carroll's *The Strings are False* and Sean O'Casey's *Red Roses for Me*. Her daughter, the novelist **Jennifer Johnston**, used to creep into the theater to watch her mother rehearse. "My mother was of course the epitome of the career woman. She did marvelous things on stage, but then my mother was a very extraordinary person. She wasn't like other people's mothers. . . . You just had to be so different to cope with the sort of life she was leading." By the end of the war, however, Richards' marriage to Denis Johnston was over.

Richards took over the Abbey School of Acting and employed such designers as Louis le Brocquy. In the 1950s, she produced J.M. Synge's *The Playboy of the Western World* in Edinburgh, London and Dublin with *Siobhan McKenna, who was a close friend. She directed the same play in Toronto's Library Theatre in 1965. For many years, she was also a drama adjudicator in Irish amateur drama competitions.

The Irish television service, RTE, was launched at the end of 1961, and at the age of nearly 60 Richards became one of the first producers and one of the few women to work for the new station. She had the distinction of directing the first Irish play during RTE's opening week and of being nominated for a Best Actress award in another RTE production, "Trial at Lisieux."

Although she specialized in drama, Richards produced a wide range of other programs, including documentaries, religious telecasts, and soap operas. Of the latter, she produced the first two important soaps ever screened by RTE, *Tolka Row* (written by ***Maura Laverty**) and *The Riordans*. Of her drama productions for RTE, the most notable were Denis Johnston's *The Moon on the Yellow River*, Shaw's *Arms and the Man* and Synge's *Riders to the Sea*, with Siobhan McKenna. One of her colleagues recalled her ability to coax quality performances from her actors, who respected her directorial qualities. Another felt that "she managed, with her marvelous expertise and experience to bridge the gap between theater and broadcasting, to translate the theatrical experience into a completely different medium."

In the early days of RTE Richards attracted the attention of a government watchdog who was scrutinizing the staff for any signs of left-wing radicalism. Richards was, he reported, a "non-Catholic" who had shown a lack of respect towards one priest who was being interviewed for a program. He suggested that she be replaced by a more Catholic producer. She wasn't. She retired from RTE in the early 1970s, and later made a number of recorded interviews in which she recalled the highlights of her career and the personalities she had known. On her 80th birthday in 1983, a special party was held at the Abbey and the song "Nora," which Jack Clitheroe sings to Nora in *The Plough and the Stars*, was sung to her. She was by that time the last surviving member of the original 1926 cast. The song was sung again in 1985, at her funeral in St. Anne's Church in central Dublin, where she had been married.

SOURCES:

Irish Times. Dublin. January 21–23, 1985.

Quinn, John, ed. "Jennifer Johnston" in *A Portrait of the Artist as a Young Girl*. London: Methuen, 1986.

Deirdre McMahon,
lecturer in history at Mary Immaculate College,
University of Limerick, Limerick, Ireland

Richardson, Dorothy (1873–1957)

English writer associated with the development of modern psychological fiction who wrote Pilgrimage, *a work of autobiographical fiction consisting of 13 novels, or "chapter-volumes," published between 1915 and 1938. Name variations: Dorothy M. Richardson; Mrs. Alan Odle. Born Dorothy Miller Richardson on May 17, 1873, in Abington, Berkshire, England; died on June 17, 1957, at a nursing home at Beckenham in Kent; third child of Charles Richardson (a successful merchant of wine and provisions turned "gentleman") and Mary Miller (Taylor) Richardson; educated at home and in various private schools, including Southwest London College; married Alan Odle (an artist), in 1917 (died 1948).*

Raised with three sisters in the comparative luxury afforded by her father's upward social mobility; educated by a governess and in private schools until reversals in the family fortunes resulted in her acceptance of a teaching position in Germany (1891); returned to England after six months to teach at a private school; after father's bankruptcy (1893), took a position as governess in London's West End; began a career as a dental assistant-receptionist-secretary in London (1896–1908); also began an association with H.G. Wells that developed into a brief affair and remained a longterm friendship; at his suggestion, began to write essays and reviews for journals; supplemented meager income by translating; published first book, The Quakers Past and Present, *and an anthology,* Gleanings from the Works of George Fox *(1914); published* Pointed Roofs, *her first novel and the beginning of the extended work that would become* Pilgrimage *(1915); continued writing individual novels or "chapter-volumes" in ongoing series, along with other writing and translations (1916–38), culminating in the publication of* Pilgrimage *in four volumes (1938); began a 13th part of* Pilgrimage *entitled* March Moonlight *(1944).*

Major writings: Pilgrimage *(four volumes, 1938); (individual "chapter-volumes")* Pointed Roofs *(1915),* Backwater *(1916),* Honeycomb *(1917),* The Tunnel *and* Interim *(1919),* Deadlock *(1921),* Revolving Lights *(1923),* The Trap *(1925),* Oberland *(1927),* Dawn's Left Hand *(1931),* Clear Horizon *(1935).* Dimple Hill, *not published separately, was included in the 1938 four-volume "omnibus" edition of* Pilgrimage; March Moonlight, *unfinished and previously unpublished, was included in the 1967 reissue of* Pilgrimage.

Dorothy Richardson devoted her creative life to a single project: a work of fictionalized autobiography that would capture with truth, completeness, and reality the life story of her heroine Miriam Henderson. Miriam's narrative, like Dorothy Richardson's, is the record of her quest to understand her unique and unfolding identity and her relationship to the people, circumstances, and events of the world she inhabits. Richardson pursued this project, begun in 1912 when she was 39, with a singular consistency of purpose until incapacitated by the illnesses that led to her death in 1957. The result, a novel in 13 parts entitled *Pilgrimage*, embodies the inevitable difficulties of such an undertaking.

Wells, Catherine (d. 1927)

English author. Name variations: Amy Catherine Robbins. Born Amy Catherine Robbins; died in 1927; married H.G. Wells (English novelist, sociological writer, and historian), in 1895; children: George Philip Wells (b. 1901); Frank Wells (b. 1903).

Catherine Wells was 20 years old when she enrolled in a biology laboratory being taught by H.G. Wells at University Tutorial College in London in 1892. Just a year later, at the end of 1893, Wells left his first wife **Isabel Mary Wells** and eloped with Catherine, whom he always called Jane. The two lived together without benefit of clergy (being evicted several times by landlords outraged by their immoral behavior) until Wells was divorced, and married in 1895. H.G. Wells was notoriously promiscuous with both long- and short-term partners, a fact of life which Catherine apparently accepted with equanimity, although sources also state that they ceased physical intimacy after the birth of their second son in 1903. Among his lovers during their marriage were *Dorothy Richardson, *Margaret Sanger, and *Rebecca West, with whom he fathered one of his several out-of-wedlock children in 1914. When journalist **Hedwig Verena Gatternigg** attempted suicide in Catherine and H.G.'s home after arguing with him, Catherine took her to the hospital. The couple remained emotionally close throughout their marriage, although some have noted H.G.'s tendency, in his personal writings, to objectify her as the standard Victorian "angel of the home" (oddly enough, given the circumstances of their early years together). He once wrote of his wife, "She stuck to me so sturdily that in the end I stuck to myself. I do not know what I should have been without her." Catherine Wells died of cancer in 1927, after having suffered for some time. A year later, H.G. published her stories and poems in *The Book of Catherine Wells.*

SOURCES:
Steffen-Fluhr, Nancy. "Paper Tiger: Women and H.G. Wells," in *Science Fiction Studies*. No. 37, vol. 12, part 3. November 1985.

In its attempt to be a truthful and complete representation of the consciousness of its main character's developing interior life, the work lacks the resolution and closure traditionally associated with the novel form. While adhering strictly to Richardson's conception of experience and reality as essentially subjective and timeless, the novel nonetheless provides a detailed and objective historical record of the time, locales, intellectual and cultural milieus, and pervasive moods that characterize the external world through which Miriam Henderson journeys in her quest for an intense personal vision that will finally be transcendent. As a novel consciously informed by an aesthetic of truth to inner experience, it exposes the often problematic and unsatisfying qualities of fiction that attempts to erase the boundaries between life and art. Perhaps most important, the very consistency with which Richardson maintains her technique in representing the perspective of the single, subjective consciousness of Miriam over a period of some 23 years unfortunately demonstrates how an initially revolutionary technique can become conventional before exhausting its chosen subject matter in a 2,000 page, four-volume novel. Such difficulties account to some extent for the history of Dorothy Richardson's critical reputation as a novelist. Originally praised for her innovation in rendering interior states of mind and feeling, she later lost critical esteem as her technique was surpassed by the virtuosity of James Joyce and *Virginia Woolf. More recently, *Pilgrimage* has been revalued for its significance as a historical and cultural document.

The subject matter of Richardson's novel is essentially autobiographical. Miriam Henderson's life clearly reflects the life of Richardson, whose inner world seemed to expand and deepen as external circumstances narrowed her choices and increased her material difficulties. The third of four daughters of Charles Richardson and **Mary Taylor Richardson**, Dorothy Miller Richardson disappointed her father by not being born the male heir he had hoped for. Charles had inherited a successful family business from his father Thomas, a grocer and wine merchant in Abington near Oxford. Within a year of her birth, Thomas Richardson died and Charles inherited £8,000, which enabled him to advance his social status by selling out the business and establishing himself as a member of the newly prosperous middle class. Using his income and leisure to pursue his interests in the arts and sciences, he scrupulously avoided further social contact with those involved in "trade" and was for a while able to provide his family with a comfortable home cared for by a staff of servants, private schooling, frequent vacations to the sea, and time to pursue personal interests.

As a child, Dorothy was early impressed by the intensity of her responses to the natural world, both in the garden of her home at Abington and at the seashore at Dawlish where the family spent holidays. During a financial setback in 1881, the Richardsons moved to Worthing on the Channel coast for reasons of economy and for Mary Richardson's health. Dorothy remembered this time of her childhood as unsettling and vaguely unhappy. When her father recovered financially in 1883 and moved the family to Putney, a fashionable suburb outside London, she recalled their new, luxurious home as a "continuous enchantment." She and her younger sister **Jessie Richardson** were taught at home by a governess for two years before enrolling in 1885 in Miss Sandell's "ladies school" (later Southwest London College), where Dorothy studied languages, mathematics, literature, science, logic, and psychology, and had the opportunity to develop her interest in music. The Richardson daughters were educated like most middle-class Victorian women who would never have to make their way independently in the world. Their mother, like many Victorian wives of her class, suffered frequent periods of depression during which she complained of the "uselessness" of her life.

Charles Richardson, in his role as *paterfamilias*, probably lived beyond his means and certainly speculated unwisely, for the family fortunes again began a downward turn in 1888, this time a decline from which they would not recover. Within two years, his daughters, who had enjoyed the social, cultural, and educational privileges that came with their father's elevated class standing, were forced to seek employment. At 17, Dorothy applied for a position as a pupil-teacher in Germany and left home early in 1891, accompanied by her father, to assume her duties as an English teacher in the province of Hanover.

This separation from her old life marked the beginning of Richardson's personal pilgrimage and became the impetus and subject matter for her life's work. Her experiences in Germany are recalled in *Pointed Roofs*, published in 1915, through the persona of Miriam Henderson, who begins her life's journey with a new Saratoga trunk, the emblem of the accumulated memories, feelings, and experiences she carries with her into an uncertain future.

The 14-year gap between Dorothy Richardson's experiences as a young woman first encountering the world as an independent agent and the retelling of those experiences through Miriam in the first "chapter-volume," as Richardson preferred to call the parts of her extended novel, marked a time of unsettling transition for England as well as for Richardson. With the end of the Victorian era, England witnessed the passing of its national stability, prosperity, and preeminence and faced its future with diminishing certainty, resources, confidence, and power. Richardson, returning to England after her six-month sojourn in Germany, faced the prospect of her father's impending bankruptcy by teaching first at a private school in Finsbury Park—a period recorded in her second chapter-volume, *Backwater*—then as a governess in London's West End—the basis of the third chapter-volume, *Honeycomb*. Late in 1895, she left her position to care for her mother, whose depression intensified as the family suffered increased financial strain and disintegration. Mary Richardson's suicide by slashing her throat with a kitchen knife while under Dorothy's care in 1895 marked for Richardson a final, violent severance from an almost idyllic past, a past that persisted nonetheless at the level of memory in a consciousness she perceived increasingly as moving fluidly between past and present time.

Thus the perspective Richardson brought to her first novel of a young woman's crossing a threshold toward independence and self-awareness had been shaped by the wrenching changes in her personal life and the history of her country and culture, as well as by an urgent desire to discover a source of meaning and value that would transcend loss and change. For this reason, her work has come to be appreciated in recent years as a record of a woman's perspective on English culture in the first part of the 20th century as well as for its innovative use of the "stream of consciousness," a term first used by William James but first applied by ***May Sinclair** to a literary work, in her review of Richardson's *Pointed Roofs*.

> [Dorothy Richardson] is one of the rare novelists who believe that the novel is so much alive that it actually grows.
>
> —Virginia Woolf

Two significant changes in 1896 established new directions for Richardson's life. The first was leaving behind the confinement and conventionality of female roles associated with semi-genteel employment as a teacher or governess to enter the modern world of work as a "new woman" of the turn of the century by becoming a dental assistant and secretary. She found a room of her own in an attic on the edge of Bloomsbury, where her growing sense of solitary independence would thrive despite the cramped material conditions she was to endure for many years. Her expanding spirit found more than ample social contact as she took London for a companion during this stage of her pilgrimage, attending lectures, sermons, and speeches, exploring new religious and philosophical ideas, and discovering groups devoted to personal and social renewal for the new century through socialism, anarchism, free love, feminism, vegetarianism, and a range of other reformist issues. The experiences of these years are recorded in *The Tunnel*, published in 1919.

The second important event of this period was her meeting with writer H.G. Wells, through a friendship reestablished with Amy Catherine Robbins (◀❦ **Catherine Wells**), a schoolmate of her former Putney years who was now married to Wells. From this association, Richardson expanded her acquaintance among literary and political groups and, inspired by new ideas and encouraged by Wells, began to consider the possibility of writing herself. She published her first article, "The Russian and His Book," in October 1902 in *Outlook*, which she described as an "obscure . . . anarchist monthly." She turned to freelance journalism and translation to supplement her barely livable income and to provide a break from the routine of her job, which she found increasingly stultifying. Her friendship with Wells and Amy deepened as she visited them in Kent, and they met her on frequent trips to London. Her relationship with Wells is represented in *Pilgrimage* through Miriam's relationship to Hypo G. Wilson, first in *The Tunnel* (1919), then in greater detail in *Revolving Lights* (1923) and *Dawn's Left Hand* (1931). Richardson never denied the parallel of the explicitly intimate relationship depicted between Miriam Henderson and Hypo G. Wilson to her affair with Wells, which began in 1905. In fact, late in her life she told an interviewer her novel was "distinctly autobiographical. Hypo was Wells, Miriam in part myself."

The years from 1904 to 1912 proved to be stressful for Richardson as she continued to shape the unique consciousness that would become the subject of her work. As she met new friends, engaged new political and philosophical ideas, adopted new sexual views, and discovered her ability as a writer, the tensions of personal relationships and a changing lifestyle took their toll. Her friendship with Benjamin Grad, a Russian-Jewish immigrant whom she had known since her early days in London, became troubled when she could neither agree to marry him nor let him go. The fatigue and oppression of her work at the dentistry office were not relieved by a holiday in Switzerland, financed by her concerned employer in 1904. In 1905, she moved from her attic to share a room in Woburn Walk, across the street from a room occupied by W.B. Yeats, with a woman she had met at a women's club she had recently joined. In the same year, she began her brief sexual relationship with Wells, whose energy and vitality attracted her as much as his aggressive assertion of intellectual and personal dominance put her off. Later in the year, a young drama student and militant suffragist named **Veronica Leslie-Jones**, a resident at the women's club, became passionately infatuated with Dorothy, who was first flattered by her charm and affection but soon threatened by Leslie-Jones' need to absorb her cherished privacy through her possessive, demanding love. At the same time, Richardson had begun reviewing books regularly for her friend Charles Daniel's newly launched monthly, *Crank: An Unconventional Magazine*. After two years at Woburn Walk, she moved back to Endsleigh Street, where Veronica was living. As Richardson came to realize the impossibility of continuing her relationship with Wells, she discovered that she was pregnant. In the late spring or early summer of 1907, she had a miscarriage. By August, months of emotional turmoil moved toward resolution when Benjamin Grad and Veronica, at Dorothy's suggestion and to her relief, became engaged and Dorothy had disentangled herself from the liaison with Wells. She took a leave from the dental office to recover physically and emotionally in Sussex. Her initiation as an independent woman into the modern world represented by her ten years in London was complete.

◀❦

See sidebar on the previous page

Dorothy Richardson

In Sussex, Richardson discovered a new dimension of herself as a writer. Although she continued to write reviews for Daniel's magazine, she also felt a need to speak of her own perception and experience. After returning briefly to London for Veronica and Benjamin's wedding, she left to spend the winter in Switzerland, where she wrote the first of a series of articles (she called them "middles") to be published by the *Saturday Review*. These pieces, falling somewhere between descriptive sketches and personal narratives, foreshadow the autobiographical fiction of *Pilgrimage*.

Upon her return to England in the spring of 1908, Richardson fell ill with influenza and stayed with her sister. During her recuperation, she resigned from the dental office and went to live with a family of Quakers on their farm in Sussex. For the next three years, she lived quietly, reading, writing, picking strawberries, traveling to the market with the farm's produce, and finding serenity and spiritual renewal in the rhythms of nature and the simple, reverent life of the Quakers. During this time, she was exploring her interior life—the memories, feelings, and thoughts that would shape the book she needed to write.

In 1912, she went with novelist J.D. Beresford and his wife **Evelyn Roskams Beresford** to spend the spring in Cornwall and stayed on alone through the fall and winter, living on ten shillings a week. She returned to London early in 1913 with the manuscript of *Pointed Roofs* and took a room in St. John's Wood, then an artists' quarter. After showing her manuscript to Beresford and making some revisions, she sent it to a publisher. When it was rejected, she put it in a trunk and turned to several different kinds of writing. She wrote articles on dentistry for the *Dental Record*, sketches for the *Saturday Review*, and reviews for *Plain Talk*; she also translated works on nutrition and healthful living from French and German, began writing a book, *The Quakers Past and Present*, and collected materials for an anthology, *Gleanings from the Works of George Fox*, both of which were published in 1914. At age 40, she was determined to make her way as a writer.

In 1915, Richardson moved into an attic room at Queen's Terrace, St. John's Wood. In September, through the efforts of Beresford, *Pointed Roofs* was published by Duckworth, and Richardson promptly began work on *Backwater*, the second chapter-volume of *Pilgrimage*, based on her experience as a teacher at Finsbury Park after her return from Germany. At her new lodgings she met another tenant, Alan Odle, a very tall, very thin young artist whose pale face, pointed ears, long, graceful hands with pointed nails, and tattered but elegant black velvet coat gave him an almost otherworldly appearance. His black-and-white drawings of highly decorated, hectic crowd scenes filled with grotesque figures—often part human and part animal—shocked and then fascinated her. They reflected a sardonic, irreverent, often scatological view of human nature reminiscent of Hogarth and a satiric style similar to Aubrey Beardsley's. Odle looked more than eccentric, even among the artists and bohemians who frequented the famous Café Royal, where he spent most of his nights, coming back to his lodgings in the early morning hours. He took to having the breakfast provided for lodgers in the common room in the basement, where he ate in silence across the table from Richardson. In time, they began to talk, and Richardson was impressed by his intelligence, his politeness that verged on formality, and his wide reading, which included *Pointed Roofs*. Odle took little notice of his material conditions or his health, devoting himself entirely to his art. He lived on an allowance from his father and occasional fees he earned as an artist and illustrator, primarily for a magazine called *The Gypsy*, which caused a small stir by announcing in its initial issue, published in the midst of the Great War, that Art "was of more importance than the fate of nations." Moved to solicitude by his pale looks, a disturbing cough, and his seeming indifference to worldly concerns, Richardson encouraged him to be more attentive to his diet and health. Their friendship continued on a fairly formal basis. During the summer of 1916, while she was in the country working on *Honeycomb*, the third volume of *Pilgrimage*, Alan wrote to tell her of his conscription into the army and his reexamination by army doctors, who diagnosed him as consumptive, with perhaps six months to a year to live if he remained in London. Although a specialist Odle later consulted did not find lesions in either lung, the doctor was not confident about the state of Alan's health and recommended rest and good food, preferably in the country, a recommendation Alan felt he had not the means to follow. Richardson returned to London in July with her completed revisions of *Honeycomb*, and a month later, on August 29, married Alan Odle. She was 44 and he was 29, although she gave her age as 37. Apparently, Alan never knew her age through all the years of their marriage, although one suspects that it made not a bit of difference to him.

Shortly after their marriage, they established a pattern they would follow with little deviation for the next 20 years, until it was disrupted by the outbreak of World War II. The routine took them away from London's dampness to live frugally from fall through winter in the generally mild and bracing climate of Cornwall, where she wrote and he sketched on a daily schedule that included regular meals and walks along the cliffs; then during a short spring holiday in a rented Cornwall cottage with domestic help, they rested from work and housekeeping before returning for the summer to Alan's two rooms in Queen's Terrace, which were let out during the winter months. In London, they rode the buses, visited galleries, went to plays and films, and visited and entertained friends for tea in their rooms. In the ten years following their marriage, Richardson published six volumes of *Pilgrimage*, several short stories, reviews, poems, and essays. Her work received favorable critical notice in the context of the development of the psychological novel, and her narrative method of using Miriam Henderson's single central consciousness to capture and convey the subjective nature of time and reality linked her with Proust and Joyce, and later with Virginia Woolf, as a writer who was forging new directions for modern fiction. *Interim*, the fifth chapter-volume of *Pilgrimage*, was published in installments in the *Little Review* from June 1919 to January 1920, along with Joyce's *Ulysses*. Richardson was pleased and amused to share in Joyce's notoriety when the January issue was seized by the New York Post Office as obscene. She had established a small but loyal group of admiring readers and enjoyed a modest fame in literary circles, but was never a popular or commercial success. Alan Odle's recognition as an artist was similarly limited. He had a solo show of his drawings in London in 1919, published his illustrated *Candide* in 1922, and was part of a four-person exhibition of book illustrators in 1925.

Their routine was broken in 1924 when Dorothy and Alan spent the winter in Switzerland and ten days in Paris in the spring before returning to England. Between 1917 and 1927, Richardson had published seven chapter-volumes of *Pilgrimage*: *Honeycomb, The Tunnel, Interim, Deadlock, Revolving Lights, The Trap*, and *Oberland*, taking Miriam Henderson through experiences that closely paralleled her own from 1895 to 1904 and bringing her extended novel to nine volumes. Her first real "block" in writing *Pilgrimage* occurred in 1928 when she reached back to recreate the difficult and painful times she experienced in 1905 and 1906. *Dawn's Left Hand*, the volume that recounts her illness, fatigue, and near breakdown of this time, was not published until 1931. Exhausted and drained by her recreation of these painful memories, and under economic pressures, Richardson turned from her novel to undertake five book-length translations in the next three years. By the end of 1934, the strain of her work left her seriously ill. After her recovery in 1935, another chapter-volume, *Clear Horizon*, appeared. Under the assumption the work was now complete, J.M. Dent issued an "omnibus" edition of *Pilgrimage* in four volumes in 1938, including the previously unpublished *Dimple Hill*. Both Dent and Richardson hoped this edition would create a new audience that might not have read all of the individual volumes as they had come out since 1915 or had not been able to appreciate the work as a whole. They also hoped to restore flagging critical enthusiasm for Richardson's work. The edition did not meet their expectations, partly because the outbreak of World War II established a new national preoccupation and partly because Richardson's technique and subject matter no longer had the novelty and freshness of appeal they had had in 1915. The world had changed once more.

In 1939, Dorothy Richardson and Alan Odle spent their last summer in London. Amidst the chaos of the mobilization of troops and the relocation of women and children, they had a difficult time making travel arrangements to Cornwall, where they spent the duration of the war. As they became accepted as full-time residents of Cornwall, their routine now included sharing fears of invasion with neighbors, listening to war reports and Churchill's speeches on their wireless, and serving coffee and tea in their cottage to soldiers stationed in the village. Alan continued to work on illustrations for an edition of Rabelais; Dorothy continued writing. Between 1939 and 1946, she published a review of *Finnegans Wake*, three short stories, and three sections of *March Moonlight*, the final, unfinished chapter-volume of *Pilgrimage*. After Alan Odle died suddenly of apparent heart failure on February 14, 1948, she lived alone in Cornwall at Hillside, the cottage they had made their home since 1945. In 1952, illness and debility made living alone any longer impossible, and her sister-in-law, **Rose Odle**, arranged for her to live at the nearby Dunrovan Hotel until 1954, when she was moved to a nursing home in Kent where she died on June 17, 1957.

SOURCES:

Blake, Caesar R. *Dorothy Richardson*. Ann Arbor, MI: University of Michigan Press, 1960.

Fromm, Gloria G. *Dorothy Richardson: A Biography*. Athens, GA: University of Georgia Press, 1994.

———. *Windows on Modernism: Selected Letters of Dorothy Richardson*. Athens, GA: University of Georgia Press, 1995.

Glikin, Gloria. "Dorothy M. Richardson: The Personal 'Pilgrimage,'" in *PMLA*. Vol. 78. December 1963, pp. 586–600.

Staley, Thomas F. *Dorothy Richardson*. Twayne's English Author Series. Boston: G.K. Hall, 1976.

Woolf, Virginia. Review of Dorothy Richardson's *The Tunnel*, in *Times Literary Supplement*. February 13, 1919.

SUGGESTED READING:

Richardson, Dorothy. *Pilgrimage*. 4 vols. NY: Knopf, 1967.

Patricia B. Heaman, Ph.D.,
Professor of English, Wilkes University,
Wilkes-Barre, Pennsylvania

Richardson, Dot (1961—)

American Olympic softball player and orthopedic surgeon. Born Dorothy Richardson on September 22, 1961; daughter of Ken Richardson (an Air Force mechanic) and Joyce Richardson; graduated from the University of California, Los Angeles; University of Louisville, M.D.; Adelphi University, master's degree in exercise and physical health.

Named the NCAA (National Collegiate Athletic Association) player of the decade (1989); member of the U.S. Olympic gold medal-winning softball team (1996, 2000).

Born in 1961, Florida native Dorothy "Dot" Richardson was the fourth of five children of Ken and Joyce Richardson. She grew up in various locations around the United States and abroad while her father was employed as a mechanic for the U.S. Air Force. As a child, Richardson was well coordinated and very quick, a natural athlete who loved sports. She played with the Little League in her home state of Florida, but moved up to an adult women's team, the Union Park Jets, by age ten. At 13, Richardson joined the Orlando Rebels to become the youngest member of a women's softball team in a major fast-pitch league. She joined the U.S. women's national team in 1979, while still in high school. Between 1986 and 1996, the women's national team won three World championships, achieving a record of 110 wins and a single loss. The team also won gold medals at the Pan American Games in 1979, 1987, 1995, and 1999.

In 1980, Richardson enrolled at Western Illinois University, where she displayed a record-setting batting average of .480 in college women's competition. The following year, she transferred to the University of California at Los Angeles (UCLA), where she continued her undergraduate curriculum in premedical studies and qualified three times as an all-American in women's softball. In 1983, she was a co-winner with *Jackie Joyner-Kersee of the UCLA All University Athlete Award.

After graduating from UCLA, Richardson entered the University of Louisville Medical School, where she specialized in orthopedic surgery. In order to train and compete with the 1996 U.S. Olympic team for the debut of the women's fast-pitch softball competition, Richardson, who was in residency at the University of Southern California Medical Center in Los Angeles, requested and was granted a one-year leave of absence from her medical duties. Playing with her on the U.S. national team at the Olympics in Atlanta, Georgia, were teammates *Lisa Fernandez, Michele Smith, Michele Granger, Kim Maher, and Sheila Cornell. Richardson, who played in the decisive game of the softball competition despite suffering a ruptured disc, hit the winning home run to score a 3–1 victory over the Chinese national team, winning a gold medal for the United States.

After the Olympics, Richardson signed a deal to endorse a line of sports equipment and returned to medicine. In 1997, she published her autobiography, *Living the Dream*, with sports journalist Don Yaeger. That same year, she received the *Babe Didrikson Zaharais Award for female athlete of the year. Now an orthopedic surgeon in Los Angeles as well as one of the best softball players in the game, Richardson was inducted into the Florida Hall of Fame in 1999. At the 2000 Olympics in Sydney, she and her teammates on the U.S. women's softball team beat Australia 1–0 in the bronze medal game and went on to beat Japan 2–1, again winning the gold medal.

SOURCES:

People Weekly. June 24, 1996, pp. 81–82; August 19, 1996, p. 47; August 25, 1997, p. 35.
Publishers Weekly. December 30, 1996, p. 18.
Time. April 29, 1996, p. 34.

Gloria Cooksey,
freelance writer, Sacramento, California

Richardson, Ethel Florence Lindesay (1870–1946).

See Richardson, Henry Handel.

Richardson, Gloria (1922—)

African-American civil-rights activist. Name variations: Gloria St. Clair Hayes Richardson; Gloria Richardson Dandridge. Born Gloria St. Clair Hayes on May 6, 1922, in Baltimore, Maryland; daughter of John Edwards Hayes and Mabel Pauline (St. Clair) Hayes; granddaughter of Herbert Maynadier St. Clair;

graduated from Howard University, 1942; married and divorced; married Frank Dandridge, in mid-1960s; children: (first marriage) one daughter, Donna.

Gloria Richardson stood at the forefront of the Cambridge Movement, which began in 1961 in Cambridge, Maryland, and peaked in 1963, in the wake of martial law, rioting, and federal intervention. Richardson, who was born in Baltimore on May 6, 1922, moved with her parents John Edwards Hayes and **Mabel St. Clair Hayes** to Cambridge when she was six years old. She graduated from Frederick Douglass High School (now Maces Lane High School) before entering Howard University, from which she graduated in 1942. Richardson's grandfather Herbert Maynadier St. Clair, who sat on the Cambridge City Council from 1912 until 1946, was only the second African-American to hold such a position in Cambridge, a city that historically was a large slave-trading site. Yet even before the Civil War, the town's population included hundreds of freed African-American citizens. Although the

free African-American population was enfranchised to vote as early as 1800, their interests and their causes remained totally unrealized because of racial bigotry. Richardson was aware that despite her grandfather's prominence in the city government, the St. Clair family, along with the rest of the African-American population, was treated as second-class citizenry because of segregationist policies held over from the days of slavery. Richardson blamed bigotry and segregation for many misfortunes suffered by her family and her African-American peers, including discrimination in education and job opportunities, ill health, and inadequate housing.

Richardson affiliated herself with the Cambridge Non-violent Action Committee (CNAC), and in June 1962 she assumed the position of co-chair of that group. During that same year, CNAC, with the help of the Northern Student Movement, initiated a program called Project Eastern Shore. The Eastern Shore activists initially made a push for more widespread African-American voter registration and then undertook an effort to oust the incumbent state senator, Frederick C. Malkus, and other segregationists who blocked the passage of statutes that would outlaw the practice of maintaining separate public facilities for African-Americans.

By the spring of 1963, the segregationist policies of Cambridge had worsened, and a series of demonstrations ensued under the organization and leadership of CNAC. Protests and demonstrations resulted in the arrests of 80 protesters during the month of March and 62 more on a single day in May, including Richardson, her mother, and her daughter. The extraordinary number of arrests in March alone resulted in the formation of a Committee on Interracial Understanding (CIU) to negotiate with the presiding judge on behalf of all of the protesters. The judge agreed to consider specific demands of Richardson's contingency with regard to desegregation, decent housing, police brutality, and other issues.

The arrested African-Americans were released, and the public demonstrations continued. To Richardson's credit, the protests proceeded peacefully. Despite the tension, the need for outside intervention never arose until May 31, when Richardson herself lost patience over the arrest of 15-year-old **Dinez White** (she had been kneeling in prayer and protest), who was subsequently refused reasonable bail. Richardson appealed to the federal government in Washington, D.C., specifically to Attorney General Robert F. Kennedy, for assistance with a mount-

Gloria Richardson

ing list of civil-right violations on the part of the Cambridge authorities. By June 10, when Dinez White and a 15-year-old boy were sentenced to open-ended terms in reform school, Cambridge erupted in wide-scale violence including shootings and arson. Bombs were discovered, and more African-Americans were arrested. Within three days, the minority districts of Cambridge were sealed off with roadblocks imposed by Maryland state troopers. The majority white population took to the streets in counter-protest, and state officials imposed martial law and called out the National Guard on June 14. With the minority protesters confined within certain areas of the city, Richardson attempted to recruit outside demonstrators from other communities, but her plan failed because the outsiders were rerouted by law enforcement and ushered away from the city. The confrontation escalated until July 10, when the National Guard troops pulled out of Cambridge. At that point, pandemonium broke loose. Two African-American citizens were beaten brutally, and the National Guard returned that same day. This time, the troops imposed even tighter curfews. Rioting and shooting were rampant. The troops resorted to throwing tear gas at the protesters. By evening, the situation had deteriorated significantly. Richardson was arrested a third time on July 15.

The demonstration ceased temporarily on July 16, when the city formed a biracial commission to negotiate an end to the protests. But on July 17, President John F. Kennedy publicly admonished the protesters for resorting to violence. Richardson took exception to the president's comments and sent a letter to Kennedy. In fear of a resurgence of violence, the Maryland Bar Association agreed to intervene but failed to bring the parties to the negotiation table. Richardson issued an ultimatum that the moratorium would end unless good-faith negotiations began by July 18 at 7 PM. A committee convened in Washington, and on July 23, President Kennedy, Mayor Calvin Mowbray of Cambridge, and Gloria Richardson signed the Treaty of Cambridge, against Richardson's personal predilection. Richardson later broke ranks with the National Association for the Advancement of Colored People (NAACP) branch of Cambridge over specific details of the treaty.

The Cambridge Movement spearheaded by Gloria Richardson is recognized historically as the first grassroots civil-rights movement to erupt beyond the Deep South. Unlike predecessor movements, this social rebellion addressed specific issues, conditions, and policies, rather than vague complaints about civil rights.

Richardson, who later moved to New York City and worked for the Department for the Aging there, is recognized for her crucial role in integrating the city of Cambridge.

SOURCES:

Brock, Annette K. "Gloria Richardson and the Cambridge Movement" in *Women in the Civil Rights Movement*. Edited by Vicki L. Crawford, *et al.* Bloomington, IN: Indiana University Press, 1993.

Smith, Jessie Carney, ed. *Notable Black American Women*. Detroit, MI: Gale Research, 1992.

COLLECTIONS:

The Ralph J. Bunche Oral History Collection at Howard University, Washington, D.C., includes a 1967 interview with Gloria Richardson.

Gloria Cooksey,
freelance writer, Sacramento, California

Richardson, Henrietta (1870–1946).

See Richardson, Henry Handel.

Richardson, Henry Handel

(1870–1946)

Australian author, best known for her trilogy The Fortunes of Richard Mahony *(1915–1929), who did not achieve fame until she was almost 60. Name variations: Henrietta Richardson; Ethel Florence Lindesay Richardson. Born Ethel Florence Lindesay Richardson near Melbourne, Australia, on January 3, 1870; died at home near Hastings, England, on March 30, 1946; eldest child of Walter Lindesay Richardson (a medical doctor) and Mary Bailey Richardson; educated at home until 1883; attended the Ladies Presbyterian College in Melbourne, 1883–88, and continued her study of the piano at the Music Conservatorium in Leipzig, Germany, 1889–92; married John G. Robertson (chair of German and Scandinavian literature at the University of London), on December 20, 1895; no children.*

Gave up a musical career (1892) after becoming engaged to John G. Robertson; lived in Strasbourg, France (1897–1903), where her husband taught German literature and where she translated two works by Scandinavian authors and began writing her first novel, Maurice Guest; *lived in London, where her husband served as chair of German and Scandinavian literature at the University of London while she, working under the pen name of Henry Handel Richardson, completed* Maurice Guest, The Getting of Wisdom *and* The Fortunes of Richard Mahony *(1903–33); with the publication of* Ultima Thule *(1929), the third and final volume in the Mahony series, finally won universal praise in the English-speaking world; awarded the Australian Literature Society's Gold Medal (1930); nominated for the Nobel Prize*

(1932); following husband's death, moved to "Green Ridges" in Sussex (1934), where she continued to write until her death 12 years later.

Selected writings: Richardson wrote slowly, completing only six novels (the last was The Young Cosima, *1939) over a period of 41 years;* The Getting of Wisdom *and the trilogy* The Fortunes of Richard Mahony *are regarded as her finest work.*

Ethel Florence Lindesay Richardson, who adopted the pen name Henry Handel Richardson, was born in 1870 near Melbourne, Australia, and set four of her six novels in her native land. However, because she lived abroad for 58 of her 76 years and was steeped in European literature, she is widely regarded as an expatriate writer. Both her parents were immigrants; her father Dr. Walter Lindesay Richardson was born in Ireland while her mother **Mary Bailey Richardson**, the daughter of a solicitor, was born in England. Her parents maintained strong ties with their respective families and in 1874, when Ethel was only four and her sister Lillian barely two, the prosperous family sailed for England. The children were left with their English relatives while Walter and Mary Richardson took the traditional grand tour of the European Continent.

I love every moment at my desk. How else could I have kept on writing all these years, getting nothing for it but starvation fees and obscurity.

—Henry Handel Richardson

On the Richardson family's return to Melbourne in 1875, they discovered that their investments had been wiped out. To make matters worse, Walter, who apparently had contracted syphilis in the gold fields during the early 1850s, gradually lost his mind and spent his last year in an insane asylum, dying at home in August 1879. Home in 1879 was the village of Koroit, in the remote western region of Victoria, where Mary Richardson supported her children by serving as the village's postmistress.

The terrible reversal of fortune, the constant quarrels over money, and the bleakness of life in Koroit haunted Ethel Richardson for the rest of her life. Worst of all, she could never forget that she felt only relief when her father died. It was no doubt to exorcise the ghosts of the past that, between 1910 and 1929, Richardson wrote a trilogy of novels, *The Fortunes of Richard Mahony*, largely inspired by her father's fortunes and misfortunes in Australia and abroad.

Richardson's life dramatically changed in 1883, when she entered the Ladies Presbyterian College, a prestigious preparatory school in Melbourne. Thanks to her mother's wise administration of what was left of the family's fortune, Ethel was able to graduate from the college in 1887. By the time she arrived at the college, Richardson was an accomplished storyteller, a voracious reader and a promising young pianist. Mary, who had great ambitions for both Ethel and Lillian, must have been immensely pleased when Richardson won the Senior Pianoforte Scholarship in 1886, followed by First Class Honors in Senior English and History in 1887. Encouraged by the school's headmistress and Ethel's music teachers, Mary Richardson used the proceeds from the sale of her home to finance a year abroad. In 1889, she enrolled her daughters at the Music Conservatorium in Leipzig, Germany, where Ethel studied piano while Lillian studied the violin.

What was to have been a year's residence and study abroad turned into a permanent departure from Australia for Mary Richardson and her daughters. They lived in Leipzig for more than four years, years that Richardson remembered as among the happiest of her life. There she met John G. Robertson, a Scot who was completing his doctorate in German literature at Leipzig's university, and by 1892 the couple became engaged. That year Richardson informed her mother and her dismayed music teachers at the Conservatorium that she was giving up her studies because of her engagement to Robertson. Unlike Richardson's puzzled teachers, Mary understood that Ethel was abandoning a career as a concert pianist because of her terror of being stared at.

Ethel's marriage to John Robertson in Dublin, Ireland, on December 20, 1895, "must have been the greatest single stroke of luck that ever befell Richardson," according to the biographer and critic **Dorothy Green**. A prolific scholar and highly engaged teacher, Robertson encouraged his wife to immerse herself in contemporary French, German, Russian, and Scandinavian literature and to become first a translator and then a writer of fiction. The couple moved to Strasbourg in the fall of 1897, where Robertson was appointed lecturer and then professor of German literature at the university there. Within a month of their removal to Strasbourg, Mary Richardson died in Munich, where she was living with her daughter Lillian. Her mother's death in November 1897 at the age of 57 devastated Richardson, increasing greatly her dependence on her husband for emotional, moral and financial support.

Also, Ethel and her sister Lillian, who married an optometrist, Dr. Otto Neustatter of Munich, in 1899, remained very close, especially when both settled in England.

Encouraged by Robertson, in the months after their marriage Richardson translated into English the Danish writer J.P. Jacobsen's tragic novel *Niels Lyhne*, and the Norwegian writer B. Bjornson's popular short novel, *The Fisher Lass*. By 1897, Richardson began her first novel, *Maurice Guest*, about a failed musician whose obsessive love for a faithless woman drives him to suicide. Heavily influenced by *Niels Lyhne* and by

the novels of Flaubert, Dostoevsky, and Tolstoy, Richardson took ten years to complete the lengthy *Maurice Guest*, which was published in London by Heinemann in 1908.

Maurice Guest was praised by some critics, such as Frank Harris, John Masefield, and Carl Van Vechten, but was judged to be morbid, depressing, dull and verbose by many others. Undaunted, Ethel, who had by now adopted the pen name of Henry Handel Richardson, went on to write a largely autobiographical novel about her years at the Ladies Presbyterian College, *The Getting of Wisdom*, which Heinemann published

Henry
Handel
Richardson

in 1910. Many years later, the novel was praised as one of the most penetrating studies ever written about the mind of an adolescent girl, but in 1910 a number of English and especially Australian critics judged that Richardson maligned the Ladies Presbyterian College. They were disturbed by the novel's frank treatment of the obsessive love of Richardson's protagonist Laura for a fellow student, Evelyn. Laura was Richardson, of course, and Evelyn, as Richardson revealed in her unfinished memoir, *Myself When Young*, was **Constance Bulteel**. The two women remained friends for life and corresponded with each other until Bulteel's death in 1942.

Both *Maurice Guest* and *The Getting of Wisdom* were written in England, where Robertson accepted an appointment as professor of German and Scandinavian literature at the University of London in 1903. Except for a two-month visit to Australia in 1912, Richardson was to spend the remainder of her life, from 1903 to 1946, in England. At the University of London, Professor Robertson gained fame as a brilliant teacher and prolific scholar while his wife, who apparently was not interested in having children, spent each morning for over 40 years writing at her desk. A shy, reclusive woman, Richardson really did love every moment at her desk, and once asserted that "to write is to live."

By 1912 and after Richardson had returned from a two-month visit to Australia, she embarked on what was to be her major preoccupation for the next 17 years: writing a fictionalized account of her father's life. In 1917, Heinemann published her third novel, *Australia Felix*, the first volume in the Richard Mahony trilogy, which concerned her father's success as a gold miner and as a physician in Australia. Only a few critics noticed the novel, and it soon went out of print. As undaunted as ever, and urged on by her husband and a small circle of friends, Richardson went on to write the sequel, *The Way Home*, about her family's sojourn abroad in the mid-1870s. The novel ended with the family's dispirited departure for Australia after discovering that Richard Mahony's investments had failed. In both *Australia Felix* and *The Way Home*, Richardson depicted her father as an outsider, who never seemed to feel at home in England, or Australia, or anywhere else. Richardson also felt like an outsider most of her life. In *Myself When Young*, she stated that her husband "always maintained that, in my imaginary portrait of Richard Mahony I had drawn no other than my own."

When *The Way Home* appeared in 1925, it was largely ignored and barely sold 1,000 copies. Yet Richardson persevered and within three years completed the final volume of the trilogy, *Ultima Thule*, which concerned her father's last years and tragic death. When Heinemann informed Richardson that they could not bear the costs of publishing *Ultima Thule* because of heavy losses from *The Way Home*, Robertson came forward and paid the publishing expenses. To the immense surprise of Richardson and her circle, *Ultima Thule* was widely praised as Australia's greatest novel. The critic Gerald Gould wrote in *The London Observer* that the novel "is a masterpiece, worthy to rank with the greatest and saddest masterpieces of our day." Within months after its appearance in January 1929, Heinemann was able to reimburse Robertson, publishing five additional impressions in six months. In the United States, *Ultima Thule*, which was published by Norton, was so popular that it was taken up by the Book-of-the-Month Club and sold 80,000 copies in the first month alone. In addition, Richardson's first four novels were soon brought back into print in the United States and England. Finally, in 1930 she was awarded the Australian Gold Medal for Literature and in 1932 was nominated for the Nobel Prize.

But Richardson's happiness at achieving fame and fortune after many years of "starvation fees and obscurity" was short-lived. In 1933, her husband died after a brief illness. Her friend, secretary and travel companion, **Olga Roncoroni**, later recalled that Richardson was inconsolable. "In him I lose husband, father, brother rolled in one," she wrote. "He was everything to me."

Tired and ill, in 1934 Richardson sold the house in London she had shared with her husband for nearly 30 years and, with her ever-faithful friend Roncoroni, retired to "Green Ridges," a house by the sea near Hastings in Sussex. There Richardson took up writing again, completing her sixth and last novel, *The Young Cosima*, in 1939. Like her first novel, *Maurice Guest*, it was set in the musical world of late 19th-century Germany, and like all her novels was concerned primarily with character and human relationships. However, unlike Richardson's first five novels, *The Young Cosima* was about historic figures: *Cosima Wagner, the daughter of Franz Liszt, her first husband, the musician Hans Von Bulow, and her second husband, the composer Richard Wagner. The novel did not sell well, for it appeared at the wrong time, on the eve of World War II. In addition, it concerned the wrong people, for both Cosima and Richard Wagner, Hitler's idol, were rabidly anti-Semitic.

There is evidence, especially in her autobiographical novel *The Getting of Wisdom*, that Richardson harbored anti-Semitic sentiments long before she wrote *The Young Cosima*. Unfortunately, Richardson was not alone in this, as Henry James and T.S. Eliot, to name but two, were also anti-Semitic. When critics praise Richardson's lack of prejudice and open-mindedness, they ignore her attitude towards Jews and instead focus on her "dispassionate acceptance" of another despised minority: homosexuals. The theme of homosexuality appears in *Maurice Guest*, *The Getting of Wisdom*, *The Young Cosima*, and in some of Richardson's short stories. In her unfinished autobiography, *Myself When Young*, Richardson confessed that her love for Constance Bulteel at the Ladies Presbyterian College in Australia "stirred me to my depths, rousing feelings I hadn't known I possessed. The attraction that this girl had for me was so strong that few others have surpassed it."

In the last seven years of her life, from 1939 to 1946, Richardson, despite increasing illness, continued to write. She began but never completed a novel, *Nick and Sanny*, about London low life, worked on her memoirs, and wrote short stories. In 1996, it was discovered that Richardson, who never abandoned the piano and practiced every day, wrote over 50 songs in her last years.

Even before Richardson's death in 1946, she fell into obscurity once again, and was dismissed by many Australians, including her fellow novelist *Miles Franklin, as unauthentic and unrepresentative of Australian literature. But beginning in the 1970s and continuing into the late 1990s, Richardson has been rediscovered by Australian writers, critics, and filmmakers. The consensus now is that her novels are among the most important yet produced by an Australian writer.

SOURCES:

Elliott, William D. *Henry Handel Richardson*. Boston, MA: Twayne, 1975.

Green, Dorothy. *Ulysses Bound: Henry Handel Richardson and Her Fiction*. Canberra: Australian National University Press, 1973.

*Palmer, Nettie. *Henry Handel Richardson: A Study*. London and Sydney: Angus & Robertson, 1950.

From the movie The Getting of Wisdom, starring Susannah Fowle.

Purdie, Edna and Olga M. Roncoroni, eds. *Henry Handel Richardson: Some Personal Impressions.* London and Sydney: Angus & Robertson, 1957.

Triebel, Louis. *Henry Handel Richardson: Australian Novelist and Lover of Wisdom.* Hobart, Tasmania: Cat & Fiddle Press, 1976.

SUGGESTED READING:

Lever, Susan, and Catherine Pratt, eds. *Henry Handel Richardson: The Getting of Wisdom, Stories, Selected Prose and Correspondence.* St. Lucia, Queensland: University of Queensland Press, 1997.

Richardson, Henry Handel. *The Fortunes of Richard Mahony.* 3 vols. London and Sydney: Penguin, 1971.

———. *Myself When Young.* NY: W.W. Norton, 1948.

RELATED MEDIA:

The Getting of Wisdom (100 min. Australian film), starring **Susannah Fowle**, screenplay by **Eleanor Witcombe** and **Moya Iceton**, directed by Bruce Beresford, produced by Southern Cross, 1977.

Anna Macías,
Professor Emerita of History,
Ohio Wesleyan University, Delaware, Ohio

Richardson, Katy (1864–1927)

English mountaineer. Born Kathleen Richardson in 1864; died in 1927; lived and climbed with French mountaineer Mary Paillon at Oullins, near Lyons, France.

Made 6 first ascents and 14 first ascents by a woman; climbed the Aiguille de Bionnassay and traversed the Eastern Ridge to the Dôme du Goûter (1888).

Between 1882 and 1893, Katy Richardson made over 100 major ascents, including the first traverse of the East Ridge and Ice Ridge to the Dôme du Goûter. The last few years of her climbing career, she shared the rope with her companion **Mary Paillon.**

Richensia of Nordheim (1095–1141)

Holy Roman empress. Name variations: Richenza of Northeim. Born in 1095; died on June 10, 1141; daughter of Henry the Fat, duke of Saxony, and *Gertrude of Meissen (d. 1117); married Lothair II (b. 1075), Holy Roman emperor (r. 1125–1137), around 1100; children: *Gertrude of Saxony (1115–1143).

Richesa of Lorraine (d. 1067)

Queen of Poland. Name variations: Rycheza; Richeza of Palatine, countess Palatine. Born around 1000 in Lorraine, France; died on March 31, 1067 (some sources cite 1063); daughter of Ezzo, count Palatine, and *Matilda of Saxony (978–1025); niece of Otto III; married Mieszko II (990–1034), king of Poland (r. 1025–1034), around 1013; children: *Richesa of

Poland (fl. 1030–1040); *Gertrude of Poland (d. 1107); Casimir I the Restorer (1015–1058), king of Poland (r. 1038–1058).

Richesa of Poland (fl. 1030–1040)

Queen of Hungary. Name variations: Richeza or Rycheza. Flourished between 1030 and 1040; daughter of Mieszko II (990–1034), king of Poland (r. 1025–1034) and *Richesa of Lorraine (d. 1067); married Bela I, king of Hungary (r. 1060–1063); children: St. Ladislas I (1040–1095), king of Hungary (r. 1077–1095); Geza I, king of Hungary (r. 1074–1077); *Helen of Hungary (who married Zwoinimir, king of Croatia); *Sophie of Hungary (d. 1095); Lanka of Hungary (who married Rstislav, prince of Tmutarakan).

Richey, Helen (1910–1947)

American aviator. Born in 1910 in Pennsylvania; died in 1947.

Was the first woman to fly airmail transport (December 31, 1934); was the first woman to become a licensed instructor (1940); was a flight instructor with rank of major, U.S. Army; discharged (1944); established world record for continuous flight: 9 days, 21 hours, 42 minutes (1933); established world record for Class C plane speed of 55 minutes across 100 kilometers at Langley Field in Virginia (1936); held world altitude record for a midget plane–18,448 feet (1936).

Aviator Helen Richey was born in 1910, just seven years after the initial airplane flight at Kitty Hawk, North Carolina. Richey, of McKeesport, Pennsylvania, was the first woman in America to qualify for a pilot's license, and in August 1933 she completed 1,000 solo hours to qualify for a license as an air transport pilot. On December 30, 1933, Richey broke the world record for continuous flight (with refueling) in her plane, *The Outdoor Girl.*

Richey secured employment as a pilot for Central Airlines and on December 31, 1934, made aviation history as the first woman to fly airmail transport. In 1940, she was the first woman to be licensed as an instructor by the Civil Aeronautics Authority. During World War II, Richey joined the Aviation Transport Auxiliary, which assigned her to transport bombs between the munitions factories and the air bases. Later, as a flight instructor for the U.S. Army, she achieved the rank of major.

Although she never crashed a plane, and despite her accomplishment and bravery, Richey's career grew stagnant. Some suggested that this was because of her lack of physical strength, which made it difficult for her to control heavy trimotor planes, especially under adverse weather conditions. Others, including the lost aviator *Amelia Earhart, suggested that the pilots' union, among others, discriminated against Richey because of her gender.

SOURCES:
Read, Phyllis J., and Bernard L. Witlieb. *The Book of Women's Firsts*. NY: Random House, 1992.

Gloria Cooksey,
freelance writer, Sacramento, California

Richeza.
Variant of Ryksa.

Richeza Eriksdottir (fl. 1200s)
*Scandinavian princess. Name variations: Regitze. Flourished in the 1200s; daughter of *Agnes of Brandenburg (d. 1304) and Erik V Klipping or Clipping, king of Denmark (r. 1259–1286); married Niels of Werle also known as Nicholas II von Werle; children: Sophie (who married Gerhard).*

Richier, Germaine (1904–1959)
French sculptor. Born in 1904 in Grans, Bouches-de-Rhîne, near Arles, France; died in 1959 in Juan-Les-Pins; attended Montpelier École des Beaux Arts, 1922–25; married Otto Baenninger (a sculptor), in 1929.

Sculpted The Toad (1942); *won the sculpture prize at Sâo Paolo Biennale (1951).*

Germaine Richier was born near Arles, France, in 1904, and raised on a farm. Her talent grew spontaneously, even in the absence of nurturing by her father who was biased against women artists. Despite her father's opinion, Richier studied at the Montpelier École des Beaux Arts in 1922. She later studied with Auguste Rodin's student, Emile-Antoine Bourdelle, between 1925 and 1929. By 1930, Richier was noted for her bronze busts and other figures, and in 1934 held her first solo show at the Galerie Max Kaganovitch in Paris. During World War II, Richier took refuge in Switzerland, but even in that neutral environment she developed emotional scars from the war. In contrast to her earlier works that demonstrated the classical influence of Charles Despiau, Richier's later figures were given to symbolism, free-form, and somber attitudes, with disturbing images of death and powerful, distorted figures. Her *Don Quichotte de la Forêt* (Walker Art Center, Minneapolis) is characteristic of her surrealistic work. In 1968, a

"Hommage Germaine Richier" was held at the Musée Rodin, in Paris. Other retrospectives followed in London (1973), and in Paris (1992).

Gloria Cooksey,
freelance writer, Sacramento, California

Richilda.
See Richilde.

Richilde (d. 894)
Saint, queen of France, and Holy Roman empress. Name variations: Richardis or Richilda, princesse d'Ecosse; Saint Richardis or Saint Richilda. Died in 894; daughter of Erchingen (a powerful lord of the Nordgrau); married Charles III the Fat (839–888), king of Germany (r. 876–887), king of France (r. 884–887), and known as Charles II, Holy Roman emperor (r. 881–887), in 877.

As chronicled in Englebert's *Lives of the Saints*, Richilde was caught up in the events of the 9th century: the ineptness of her husband Charles III the Fat, who was eventually deposed at the Diet of Tribur, and the downfall of the Carolingian empire. A short time before her husband's death on January 13, 888, Richilde was accused of adultery. Claiming that the marriage had not been consummated and that she remained a virgin, she retired to the abbey of Andlau and died there. In 1049, Pope Leo IX venerated her remains. Her feast day is September 18.

Richilde (1034–1086)
Countess of Hainault and Flanders. Name variations: Richildis, Richilda; countess of Namur. Born about 1034 in Hainault (Belgium); died on March 15, 1086, in Flanders; daughter of Renier or Rainier V, count of Hainault; married Herman, count of Hainault; married Baldwin VI the Peaceable, count of Flanders (r. 1067–1070), in 1055; married William FitzOsbern, 1st earl of Hereford; children: (second marriage) Arnulf III the Unlucky (1055–1071), count of Flanders; Baldwin II (b. 1056), count of Hainault; Gilbert de Gant.

Richilde was the daughter of Rainier V, the ruler of Hainault, an important medieval province of northwestern Europe. As his only surviving child, Richilde inherited the county on his death. Her first husband, Herman, from the Flemish ruling family, became count of Hainault at the time of their marriage. After Herman's death, Richilde married his relative Baldwin VI, the reigning count of Flanders, around 1055.

The counties of Flanders and Hainault were temporarily united under their joint rule, and the couple had three sons.

In 1070, Baldwin VI was killed in battle against his brother, Robert the Frisian, who disputed Baldwin's right to rule Flanders. Though Richilde became regent of Flanders for her eldest son Arnulf III, she ruled for only a few months. In 1071, Robert the Frisian, who claimed that Richilde had no right to rule and that she was exploiting her subjects with heavy taxation, attempted to seize control of Flanders with the support of Holy Roman Emperor Henry IV. Richilde successfully appealed to the emperor's enemy, King Philip I of France, for aid in protecting her son's inheritance, and war ensued. In February 1071, Richilde led her own troops to meet Robert the Frisian's army at the battle of Ravenshoven, near Cassel in Prussia. Her army was defeated, she was taken prisoner, and her son Arnulf was killed. Philip I gave up Richilde's cause after this disastrous battle, and Robert was invested as count of Flanders.

Richilde was released from prison some time later and allowed to return to her county of Hainault. She married a third time and continued to rule jointly with her son Baldwin II of Hainault until her death in 1086, about age 52.

SOURCES:
Echols, Anne, and Marty Williams. *The Annotated Index of Medieval Women.* NY: Marcus Wiener, 1992.
Nicholas, David. *Medieval Flanders.* London: Longman, 1992.

Laura York, M.A. in History,
University of California, Riverside, California

Richilde (d. 1100)

Saint. Name variations: Blessed Richilde. Died in 1100.

Richilde lived as a recluse with the Benedictines at Hohenwart (Bavaria). Her feast day is August 23.

Richilde (fl. 1300s)

Danish royal. Name variations: Richardis. Flourished in the 1300s; married Valdemar also known was Waldemar III (1314–1364), king of Denmark (r. 1326–1330, deposed), duke of Schleswig (acceded 1325); children: Henry; Valdemar or Waldemar.

Richilde of Autun (d. around 910)

*Queen of France. Name variations: Richild; Richilda; Richildis. Died around 910 in France; daughter of Count Beuves (Biwin or Buwin) and Richilde of Lotharingia; became second wife of Charles I the Bald, king of France (r. 840–877), known also as Charles II, Holy Roman emperor (r. 875–877), in 870; children: *Rothild (c. 871–c. 928); Charles (b. 876); stepchildren: *Judith Martel and Louis II the Stammerer (846–879), king of France (r. 877–879).*

Richilde of Autun, who came from a noble Frankish family, was the mistress of Charles I the Bald, king of the Franks, for several years before they married in 870, one year after the death of his first wife *Ermentrude. Richilde was crowned queen in a special ceremony and went on to become a crucial member of Charles' administration. She ruled as an equal authority with her husband, in the established tradition of Frankish queens. Besides direct involvement in legislation, judicial decisions, and political negotiations, Richilde was an important patron of artists during the "Carolingian renaissance," a period during Charles' rule characterized by high intellectual achievement in the arts and sciences. When Charles died in 877, he left the government in Richilde's control. She first attempted to use her influence to have her brother crowned, but eventually she yielded to public pressure and allowed her stepson to succeed to the throne as Louis II the Stammerer.

SOURCES:
Anderson, Bonnie S., and Judith P. Zinsser. *A History of Their Own.* Vol. I. NY: Harper & Row, 1988.

Laura York,
Riverside, California

Richiza (fl. 1251)

*Queen of Norway. Name variations: Richiza Birgersdottir. Flourished around 1251; daughter of Birger of Bjälbo, regent of Sweden, and *Ingeborg (d. 1254); married Haakon the Younger (1232–1257), king of Norway (r. 1240–1257), in 1251; married Henry I, prince of Werle, in 1262; children: (first marriage) Sverker Magnus.*

Richizza of Denmark (d. 1220)

*Queen of Sweden. Name variations: Rikisa of Denmark; Rikisa Valdimarsdottir or Waldimarsdottir. Died on May 8, 1220; daughter of *Sophie of Russia (c. 1140–1198) and Waldemar or Valdemar I the Great (b. 1131), king of Denmark (r. 1157–1182); sister of *Ingeborg (c. 1176–1237/38), queen of France; sister of Canute VI (1163–1202), king of Denmark (r. 1182–1202), and Waldemar II the Victorious (1170–1241), king of Denmark (r. 1202–1241); mar-*

ried Eric X, king of Sweden (r. 1208–1216), in 1210; children: *Ingeborg (d. 1254); Erik XI (b. 1216), king of Sweden (r. 1222–1250); Helen (who married Knut Johnsson); Margaret, also known as Marta (who married Niels Sixtenson).

Richizza of Poland (1116–1185)

Polish princess. Name variations: Richza; Ryksa. Born on April 12, 1116, in Poland; died on June 16, 1185; daughter of Boleslaus III (b. 1084), king of Poland, and *Salomea (d. 1144); married Magnus, in 1129; married Sverker also known as Swerker I the Elder, king of Sweden (r. 1133–1156); married Vladimir, Prince of Novgorod; children: (first marriage) Knud or Canute III, king of Denmark (r. 1146–1157); Neils; (second marriage) Boleslaw; Sune Sverkersson (b. around 1132); (third marriage) *Sophie of Russia (c. 1140–1198).

Richman, Julia (1855–1912)

American educator and children's rights activist. Born in New York City on October 12, 1855; died in Paris, France, on June 24, 1912; daughter of Moses Richman (a painter and glazier) and Theresa (Melis) Richman; graduated from New York Normal College, 1872; graduate work in the school of pedagogy at New York University, 1897–98; never married; no children.

Julia Richman, born to Jewish parents in New York City in 1855, was ten years old when she entered the New York city public school system that later would be the focus of much of her life's work. In 1870, she enrolled in a two-year course at the New York Normal College (later Hunter College of the City University of New York), and after her graduation returned to the public school system as a teacher despite her father's protests. She was named vice-principal of the school at which she taught ten years later, and in 1884 was named principal of the girls' department at P.S. 77.

Over the course of the 19 years Richman spent as principal at P.S. 77, she was also deeply involved with Jewish educational concerns. She served as the first president of the Young Women's Hebrew Association from 1886 to 1890, was a member of the Jewish Chautauqua Society's educational council from 1889 to 1898, and served as chair of the committee on religious school work for the Council of Jewish Women from 1895 to 1899. She was active in the Educational Alliance, which promoted the assimilation of Jewish immigrants, from its founding in 1889, particularly in the classes run by the alliance that helped to prepare immigrant children for their entrance into the public schools. A member of its board of directors beginning in 1893, Richman used her position within the public school system to help foster the alliance's goals.

Richman was promoted to a district superintendent of city schools in 1903, and chose to work in a district on the city's Lower East Side, which at the time was a crowded, poor neighborhood inhabited primarily by Jewish immigrants. She also moved to the Lower East Side, a far cry from the genteel uptown environs in which she had previously lived. Richman saw her mission as assisting the education of and adjustment to America not only of the 23,000 schoolchildren in the district but of their families and neighbors as well. She did this with typical determination and forcefulness (one of her neighborhood campaigns spurred some locals to start a petition requesting removal of "this self-constituted censor of our morality"), but always with her focus firmly on the welfare and development of schoolchildren. She co-wrote a series of six textbooks on arithmetic, cajoled the school board into setting up classes for developmentally disabled and physically challenged children, instituted separate schools for children with delinquency and truancy problems, set up eye examinations in the schools, and started a program of school lunches for qualified children. Understanding the economic world in which most of her pupils lived, she also made available a job counselor for those who were forced to quit school in order to work. From 1906, her home became the "Teachers House," where principals and teachers in her district met with each other and with three social workers to formulate improvements in the schools.

Richman retired as school superintendent in 1912, leaving behind her a vastly improved school environment on the Lower East Side. Having lectured on education and written articles published in such journals as *Forum, Educational Review,* and *Outlook,* she planned to concentrate on her community work and on writing and public speaking. She traveled to Europe that summer, but became ill in Paris and died there after an appendectomy, at the age of 56. Julia Richman High School in New York City was named in her honor.

SOURCES:

James, Edward T., ed. *Notable American Women, 1607–1950.* Cambridge, MA: The Belknap Press of Harvard University, 1971.

Read, Phyllis J. and Bernard L. Witlieb. *The Book of Women's Firsts.* NY: Random House, 1992.

Gretchen Monette,
freelance writer, Ferndale, Michigan

Richmond, countess of.

See Beaufort, Margaret (1443–1509).

Richmond, duchess of.

See Alice (1201–1221).
See Fitzroy, Mary (c. 1519–1557).
See Villiers, Frances (c. 1633–1677).
See Stuart, Frances Teresa (1647–1702).

Richmond, Mary E. (1861–1928)

American founder of professional social work who pioneered the casework methodology and helped to establish training programs for social workers. Born Mary Ellen Richmond on August 5, 1861, in Belleville, Illinois; died on September 12, 1928, in New York City; daughter of Henry Richmond (a carriage blacksmith) and Lavinia (Harris) Richmond; never married; no children.

Served as assistant treasurer, Baltimore Charity Organization Society (BCOS, 1889); volunteered as a friendly visitor; promoted to general secretary of BCOS (1891); moved to Philadelphia to become general secretary of the Society for Organizing Charity; named director of the Charity Organization Department of the Russell Sage Foundation in New York City (1909); led Charity Organization Institute, a summer training program for social workers (1910–22); awarded honorary degree from Smith College (1921).

Selected writings: Friendly Visiting Among the Poor *(1899);* The Good Neighbor in the Modern City *(1907);* Social Diagnosis *(1917);* What is Social Case Work *(1922);* Child Marriages *(1925);* Marriage and the State *(published posthumously, 1929);* The Long View *(published posthumously, 1930).*

In the last decades of the 19th century, Mary E. Richmond was among a generation of American women whose search for socially meaningful and intellectually rewarding work yielded few options. Richmond would go on to become the founder of social work, in essence creating a new profession. In doing so, she dramatically improved the level of assistance provided to the troubled and poor. Richmond also elevated the status of women's work by transforming what had been only a volunteer activity for women into a legitimate, remunerative career recognized for its societal value.

She was born on August 5, 1861, in Belleville, Illinois, to which her father Henry Richmond, a blacksmith, had moved the family in order to reap high wages by producing gun carriages during the Civil War. The family soon returned to Baltimore, their original home, where Mary spent her youth. She was the only one of four children to survive childhood. Her mother **Lavinia Harris Richmond** died of tuberculosis when Mary was three. Although her father remarried, she had little to do with his new family, and when she was seven he too died of tuberculosis. Now the charge of her maternal grandmother and two aunts, Mary went to live with them in the inexpensive Baltimore boarding house which was run by her grandmother. While not always lucrative, the boarding house did provide an intellectually eclectic atmosphere for Mary. Her grandmother and one of her aunts frequently advocated what at the time were deemed "radical" causes, and as a result Mary heard lively discussions about antivivisection, woman's suffrage, racial issues, and spiritualism. The boarding house was also the site of séances. At age ten, Richmond would later recall, she was able to discern the fakery involved in these events and was amazed that some of the adult participants could not.

Rather than attend school in her early years, Richmond was taught at home by her grandmother. A precocious child and early reader, she was nine when Dickens died and is said to have wept inconsolably upon hearing the news. She wrote to an aunt: "[L]ast Saturday I heard of Dickens' death but it was good news when I heard that his book was in the hands of the Editor, so I expect to read it." Richmond began to attend grammar school at age 11 and at 13 entered Baltimore's Eastern Female High School, a demanding institution which provided a rigorous course of training. In 1878, at age 16, she graduated as one of the youngest members of her class.

Upon graduation, Richmond relocated to New York City. There she and an aunt lived together in a small, inexpensive one-room apartment, and they worked together for a publishing house which produced works on such controversial topics as agnosticism. As a general clerical worker, Richmond worked 12-hour days. At night, she pursued a course of self-education, teaching herself shorthand. Her occasional attendance at Cooper Union lectures and at Henry Ward Beecher's church in Brooklyn seems to have provided the only bright spots in a bleak existence. When her aunt returned to Baltimore due to illness, Richmond remained alone in a strange city, where her isolation, boredom with her job, and extremely low wages made for what she would later regard as the hardest time of her life. She nonetheless persisted in her work for two years before being forced to return to Baltimore in 1880 to recuperate from a case of malaria.

After her illness, Richmond found employment as a bookkeeper at a Baltimore stationers. She remained there from 1881 until 1888, when she went to work as a bookkeeper and office assistant at a Baltimore hotel. During these years, she joined the Unitarian Church and found companionship with other members of the congregation. Fellow church members introduced her to music, which would become a lifelong love. Through the church, she led a class on Shakespeare for young congregants and for young working-class women. Richmond also became active in a literary club.

Perhaps as a result of this increased intellectual and social activity, she began to look for more rewarding employment. For a late 19th-century American woman, finding socially acceptable, mentally stimulating work was a challenge. Although teaching was considered an acceptable profession for a woman, Richmond lacked the educational qualifications and political influence to secure a teaching post. In late 1888 or early 1889, she responded to an advertisement for an assistant treasurer position with the Baltimore Charity Organization Society (BCOS). She had no training or experience with philanthropic work, and the job paid the same salary as her current bookkeeping position, yet it must have seemed to offer greater rewards, for when it was tendered to Richmond, after some deliberation and arguments with her aunt, she accepted.

Before Richmond assumed her new position, friends from the church helped her to finance a week-long trip to Boston so that she could observe the work of the Associated Charities there and gain some idea of the nature of her new undertaking. This trip exposed her to independent women who through their work for the charitable organization were beginning to create the foundations of social work. The system of charity organizations of which Richmond was to become a part was a relatively new development in the history of charitable giving, and based on a concept imported from England. Charitable groups were widespread in large cities in the United States, but their efficiency was brought into question in the late 19th century. After the depression of 1873 left many citizens unemployed and impoverished, various philanthropic groups had responded to this need. It was feared, however, that the lack of coordination between the charities would allow wealthy donors to be exploited.

Charity organization societies arose to systematize efforts between charities, insure that only the "worthy poor" received assistance, and guarantee that charities did not duplicate each others' efforts and give to the same individuals repeatedly. Not only did these goals require that organizations work together, but they also required that charities come to know the individual circumstances of the needy more intimately. "Friendly visitors"—volunteers affiliated with a charitable society—were recruited to visit with and investigate the lives of the impoverished. They were given the responsibility of determining whether or not individuals were among the "worthy poor" and, if so, what type of assistance would be most useful. Charity organizations reasoned that only careful, efficient, and informed assistance would truly help the needy.

While these organizations were trying to better society and help the poor, their approach was often extremely judgmental. Frequently the poor were personally blamed for their economic situation, despite the fact that their lives were often ruled by economic forces outside their control. Strong distrust of the economically disadvantaged was also evident in the organizations' approach as they constantly searched to uncover swindlers who were out to take advantage of philanthropists' generosity. Meanwhile, friendly visitors were often bitterly resented by those they were trying to help, for some visitors rather than being "friendly" were patronizing, nosy, and intrusive. Modern-day scholars find both much to laud and much to question in the 19th-century charity organization. While Richmond began her career by following the established norms of these organizations, she was to be in large part responsible for their transformation.

Upon joining the BCOS, she embraced the goals and assumptions of the society. Her official duties were fund raising for, and promotion of, the organization. Soon she volunteered to be a friendly visitor in her spare time. In her second annual assistant treasurer report, she discussed some of the work she had done with one family:

> As a volunteer visitor in one of our districts, I persuaded an acquaintance to spend about $50 on a family for which I was visitor. . . . He has the . . . satisfaction of knowing that he has removed a family to a cheaper and cleaner home, saving them $5.00 a month in rent, has stopped their begging, raised one of their number from a bed of sickness, and sent three of the children to school.

Richmond's work for the BCOS was impressive, and in 1891 she was appointed general secretary, a position of far greater leadership. The appointment was testimony to her unusual capabilities, for in the past the job had been filled by older men with advanced degrees in political economy.

Realizing that friendly visitors needed broader, more standardized training, Richmond offered informal classes to volunteers working with the BCOS, for whom she also put together a manual. She began to believe that paid agents, rather than volunteer "visitors," were most effective in helping the poor. This was an important step towards the development of social work as a profession. Another step was taken in 1897 at a conference in Toronto, when she called for the establishment of a training school for friendly visitors, or, as she began to refer to them, caseworkers. During this time, Richmond started to reconceptualize the role of the visitor. She began to believe that rather than making the detection of fraud and the determination of "worthiness" one of their prime functions, caseworkers should have as their focus the investigation of needy individuals' conditions in order to better help them. And, in order to investigate effectively, caseworkers needed training. This need was met the following year (1898) when the New York Charity Organization Society began to offer a Summer School in Applied Philanthropy. The following year, Richmond was teaching a course there. Also in 1899, her first book, *Friendly Visiting Among the Poor*, which described effective techniques for friendly visitors, was published and well received.

In 1900, noting that the BCOS seemed to be on stable financial and administrative footing, Richmond accepted an offer to become general secretary of Philadelphia's Charity Organization Society. In a city where the charity system was disorganized and uncoordinated, she worked successfully to centralize the administration of charitable efforts, while also continuing to do casework in addition to her administrative tasks.

This work did not absorb all of Richmond's time, and she involved herself in state and municipal reform politics. She worked to pass wife-desertion and non-support bills as well as state laws regulating child labor, to establish a juvenile court, and to investigate housing conditions. While concerned with passing some legislation to better society, Richmond, unlike many Progressive reformers of the time, believed that one-on-one work with individuals and families was the most important and effective means by which to help people. By interacting with those in need, caseworkers would become familiar with larger problems facing society and could work to better conditions. Meanwhile, caseworkers would be enriched by their personal contact with people from other social and economic classes.

In Philadelphia, Richmond continued to teach and write. She was a frequent teacher at the Summer School of Applied Philanthropy, and when this institution began offering classes year round, she taught during the winter as well. (This institute became the New York School of Social Work and in 1940 became affiliated with Columbia University.) In 1906, she taught a course at the University of Pennsylvania. Thereafter, the Pennsylvania School of Social and Health Work was established, and many of her biographers claim the founding of this institution was an indirect result of Richmond's 1906 course. She also began to offer advice to other cities and their charity organizations. At first, informative materials were exchanged on a monthly basis between different cities. Then in 1905 this exchange was made formal with the establishment of the Field Department of Charities magazine. Richmond served as the editor of this new department, a position which increased her fame and made her a national figure in the developing field of social work. Her second book, *The Good Neighbor in the Modern City*, appeared in 1907 and was well received, particularly by the charity and social-work community.

In 1909, Richmond left Philadelphia for a position with New York's influential Russell Sage Foundation, founded in 1907 by *Margaret Olivia Sage*, where her position was director of the Charity Organization Department. During her years in New York, Richmond's teaching and writings were profoundly influenced by the growing interest in social work and the increase in numbers of social workers. Such developments necessitated the organization of the growing body of knowledge about social problems and their treatments. Her efforts during the 1910s and 1920s to organize and provide knowledge were central to the professionalization of the field. During these years, Richmond produced a methodology and offered a set of standards for social workers.

While at Russell Sage, Richmond began to collect caseworker reports and other background information for a book she had contemplated writing years before in Baltimore. To the case reports and records sent to her by 57 different agencies she added information gained from a study of law and psychology. The resulting work, entitled *Social Diagnosis*, was published in 1917 and is considered her finest work. As a guide for workers on the best way to investigate the circumstances of the people they were trying to help, *Social Diagnosis* detailed how and where to find different types of information as well as how to use this information to help clients. Richmond outlined her goals for the work in the opening chapter of the book:

> When a human being, whatever his economic status, develops some marked form of social difficulty and social need, what do we have to know about him and about his difficulty . . . before we can arrive at a way of meeting his need? . . . The primary purpose of the writer, in attempting an examination of the initial process of social case work, is to make some advance toward a professional standard.

Richmond also worked to set standards for caseworkers through education. From 1910 to 1922, she held the Charity Organization Institute, summer programs for caseworkers and their supervisors. In addition, she taught at a number of schools of social work during these years. In 1920, she became a charter member of the American Association of Social Workers, and in 1921 Smith College recognized her efforts to establish social work on a firm foundation by awarding Richmond an honorary Master of Arts degree, for "establishing the scientific basis of a new profession."

In an effort to popularize the key concepts and goals of the social-work profession and introduce them to a larger lay audience, in 1922 she wrote *What is Social Case Work?* In this volume, Richmond reaffirmed her belief that social casework, when well practiced, was of profound benefit not only to the client but also to the caseworker; ideally, both should grow as a result of their relationship.

Throughout her life, Richmond was repeatedly bothered by a bronchial condition. Beginning in 1918, her health began to decline, and she gradually reduced her activities. After 1922, she no longer held the summer institute, and she began to spend less time at the Russell Sage Foundation and more time working out of her home near Columbia University.

The issue of most concern to her between 1922 and the time of her death in 1928 was marriage laws. Richmond believed that many family problems originated in unstable marriages. Thus she urged the state to take a more active role in administration of marital laws, led a campaign to make states require physical examinations prior to issuing marriage licenses, and advocated raising the minimum age for marriages. As a result of her interest in this subject, she co-authored two books on the topic: *Child Marriages* (1925) and *Marriage and the State* (published posthumously, in 1929).

Early in 1928, Richmond was diagnosed with inoperable cancer. Throughout that year, she continued to work on the proofs of *Marriage and the State*. On September 12, 1928, she died at home in New York. Her many writings and students continued to perpetuate her ideals long after her death. Indeed, modern social work, while it has evolved since Richmond's time, still bears the mark and many of the values of its founder.

SOURCES:

James, Edward T., ed. *Notable American Women, 1607–1950*. Vol III. Cambridge, MA: Belknap Press, 1971.

Lubove, Roy. *The Professional Altruist: The Emergence of Social Work as a Career, 1880–1930*. Cambridge, MA: Harvard University Press, 1965.

Pumphrey, Muriel. "Mary E. Richmond—The Practitioner," in *Social Casework*. Vol XLII, no. 8. October 1961, pp. 375–385.

Rich, Margaret E. "Mary E. Richmond: Social Worker, 1861–1928," in *Social Casework*. Vol XXXIII, no. 9. November 1952, pp. 363–370.

Richmond, Mary. *The Long View: Papers and Addresses*. Edited with biographical notes by Joanna C. Colcord. NY: Russell Sage Foundation, 1930.

Woodroofe, Kathleen. *From Charity to Social Work—In England and the United States*. London: Routledge & Kegan Paul, 1968.

SUGGESTED READING:

McCormick, Mary J. "A Legacy of Values," in *Social Casework*. Vol XLII, no. 8. October 1961, pp. 404–409.

Pumphrey, Muriel W. "The 'First Step'—Mary Richmond's Earliest Professional Reading, 1889–91," in *Social Service Review*. Vol XXXI, no. 2. June 1957, pp. 145–163.

———. "Mary Richmond's Process of Conceptualization," in *Social Casework*. Vol XXXVIII, no. 8. October 1957, pp. 399–406.

COLLECTIONS:

Personal scrapbooks, correspondence, and interviews with friends and colleagues are located in the Mary E. Richmond Archives, Library of the Columbia University School of Social Work in New York City.

Susan J. Matt,
Cornell University, Ithaca, New York

Richsa.

Variant of Ryksa.

Richter, Elise (1865–1943)

Austrian Romance language scholar. Born on March 2, 1865; died in Theresienstadt concentration camp in 1943.

In 1907, Elise Richter became the first woman to hold a faculty position in an Austrian university. She became an associate professor at the University of Vienna in 1921, and in 1922 founded the Verband der akademischen Frauen Österreichs, which she headed until 1930. Richter died in Theresienstadt concentration camp in 1943.

SOURCES:

Andraschko, Elisabeth. "Elise Richter—eine Skizze ihres Lebens," in Waltraud Heindl and Marina Tichy, eds., *"Durch Erkenntnis zu Freiheit und Glück . . ."*: *Frauen an der Universität Wien (ab 1897)*. Vienna: WUV-Universitätsverlag, 1990, pp. 221–231.

John Haag,
Athens, Georgia

Richter, Gisela (1882–1972)

English-born American archaeologist. Born Gisela Marie Augusta Richter in London, England, on August 15, 1882; died in Rome, Italy, on December 24, 1972; daughter of Jean Paul Richter (an art historian) and Luise Marie (Schwaab) Richter; received bachelor's degree from Girton College, Cambridge, 1905; studied at the British School of Archaeology, 1904–05; Trinity College, Dublin, Litt.D., 1913; Cambridge University, A.M., 1933, Litt.D.; never married; no children.

Archaeologist Gisela Richter was born in England in 1882, into a cultured family with a strong appreciation for art, literature, and classical beauty. Her father Jean Paul Richter was a well-known art historian with a special interest in Italian painting, and her mother **Luise Marie Schwaab Richter** both wrote and painted; her older sister **Irma Richter**, with whom she had a close relationship throughout their lives, would grow up to become a painter. The Richters lived in Florence, Italy, for the first ten years of Gisela's life, after which they moved to London, where she continued her education at Maida Vale High School. When she became a bit older, she and Irma often took trips to the museums of Rome and attended lectures on ancient art. By the time she was in her teens, Richter had become, in her own words, "enamoured of Greek and Roman art and decided to become an archaeologist."

Richter attended Girton College, Cambridge, where she found that she already knew much of what was being taught in the undergraduate archaeology classes but greatly enjoyed her courses in history and classical languages. During her last year at college, in 1904–05, she attended the British School of Archaeology in Athens, Greece, where she was the only woman in her class and was not permitted to live on campus. She received her bachelor's degree in 1905 for a thesis on Attic vases. A few months later, Richter traveled to the United States with American archaeologist *Harriet Boyd Hawes, and took a temporary job helping to organize an exhibit on Greek vases at the Metropolitan Museum of Art in New York City. This temporary post soon turned into a lifelong position; she would remain at the Metropolitan Museum until her retirement in 1948.

Named assistant curator of classical art in 1910, Richter was elevated to curator 15 years later. The museum's collections of Greek, Roman, and Etruscan art were being steadily augmented during these years into world-class collections, and Richter was soon an acknowledged expert in all facets of archaic art aside from architecture. (She was awarded several graduate degrees on the basis of her writings.) Richter spent three months of each summer traveling in Europe, visiting with family and colleagues. In 1928, she was named the museum's purchasing agent; among the most important of her acquisitions for the museum was an early Greek marble statue of a young man, almost undamaged and at first suspected by some of being counterfeit. Richter published a number of highly regarded studies, including *The Craft of Athenian Pottery* (1923), *Sculpture and Sculptors of the Greeks* (1929), *Kouroi* (1942), and the popular *Handbook of Greek Art* (1959). She also wrote several publications for the Metropolitan Museum, among them *Red-Figured Athenian Vases* (1936), *Handbook of the Greek Collection* (1953), and *Catalogue of the Engraved Gems, Greek, Etruscan, and Roman* (1956).

After her retirement, Richter, who became an American citizen in 1917, moved with her sister to Rome in 1952. There she continued to research and write on archaic art, and to provide assistance and the benefit of her experience to younger researchers. She was granted a number of honorary degrees in recognition of her contributions to archaeology, and in 1968 received the gold medal of the Archaeological Institute of America. Richter published *My Memoirs, Recollections of an Archaeologist's Life*, in 1972, and died in her sleep that December. She was buried beside her sister, who had predeceased her, in the Protestant Cemetery in Rome.

SOURCES:

Sicherman, Barbara, and Carol Hurd Green, eds. *Notable American Women: The Modern Period*. Cambridge, MA: The Belknap Press of Harvard University, 1980.

Gretchen Monette,
freelance writer, Ferndale, Michigan

Richter, Marga (1926—)

American composer. Born in Reedsburg, Wisconsin, on October 21, 1926; daughter of Paul Richter and Inez (Chandler) Richter (a soprano); studied piano at the Juilliard School of Music under *Rosalyn Tureck and composition with William Bergsma and Vincent Persichetti; married Alan Skelly (a professor of philosophy), in 1953; children: Michael and Maureen.

Marga Richter's paternal grandfather would not permit his children to study music. As a result, her father Paul Richter was devoted to music and married **Inez Chandler Richter**, a soprano. Their daughter Marga was born in 1926. On Saturday afternoons, if the Metropolitan Opera featured Wagner on its radio broadcasts, Paul Richter locked the front doors, allowing no one access or egress until the performance was over. Marga began studying piano at age three and composition at twelve. From the beginning, she used the 12-tone scale, though at the time she had heard very little contemporary music. Richter continued her studies at the Juilliard School of Music, where she majored in composition. She was one of the youngest composers to have her compositions programmed on the Composers Forum series in New York.

Richter married Alan Skelly in 1953 and after their two children were born devoted herself more to home and family than to composition. "I'm glad, I think, that I didn't have commissions coming in and deadlines to meet while the kids were growing up," she said. Once her children were grown, however, she returned to composition, and the interval seemed to have borne creative fruit. In 1968, she began to compose *Landscapes of the Mind I*, and produced six other major works in a ten-year period. She also received endowments, including a grant from the *Martha Baird Rockefeller* Foundation, the Tucson Symphony, and the National Endowment for the Arts, as well as a dozen stipends from the New York State Council on the Arts. Many American orchestras included her compositions in their programs. **Jessye Norman** included Richter's songs in recitals, and her compositions were increasingly performed internationally.

SOURCES:
Block, Adrienne Fried, and Carol Neuls-Bates, comps. and eds. *Women in American Music: A Bibliography of Music and Literature*. Westport, CT: Greenwood Press, 1979.

Cohen, Aaron I. *International Encyclopedia of Women Composers*. 2 vols. NY: Books & Music (USA), 1987.

COLLECTIONS:
Tapes and interviews held at the Graduate Center of the City University of New York, Project for the Oral History of Music in America.

John Haag,
Athens, Georgia

Richter, Ulrike (1959—)

East German swimmer. Born on June 17, 1959.

Won Olympic gold medals in the 100-meter backstroke, 200-meter backstroke, and the 4x100-meter medley relay in Montreal (1976); held the world record for 100-meter backstroke at 1:01.51 (1976); held the world record for the 4x100-meter relay at 4:07.95 (1976); won the World championship in the 100-meter backstroke (1973, 1975).

East Germany walked away with most of the women's gold medals in swimming in the Montreal Olympics of 1976. Ulrike Richter won the gold in the 100-meter backstroke, beating teammate **Birgit Treiber** and setting an Olympic record of 1:1.83. She also took the gold in the 200-meter backstroke, once again ahead of Treiber, setting another Olympic record of 2:13.43. With teammates **Hannelore Anke**, ⚑▶ **Andrea Pollack**, and *****Kornelia Ender**, Richter then won a team gold medal in the 4x100-meter medley relay.

Richthofen, Else von.

See von Richthofen, Else.

Richthofen, Frieda von (1879–1956).

See Lawrence, Frieda.

Ricker, Marilla (1840–1920)

American lawyer and suffragist. Name variations: Marilla Young Ricker. Born Marilla Marks Young in New Durham, New Hampshire, on March 18, 1840; died on November 12, 1920 in Dover, New Hampshire; daughter of Jonathan Young and Hannah (Stevens) Young; attended Colby Academy in New London, New Hampshire; married John Ricker (a farmer), on May 19, 1863 (died 1868); no children.

Was the first woman to have a vote officially acknowledged, although not counted (1871); was the first woman appointed U.S. commissioner in the District of Columbia (1891); dubbed the "Prisoner's Friend" by area newspapers because of her legal work on behalf of prisoners (1890s).

At a time when women were expected to remain at home to care for their families, Marilla Ricker sought the right to vote for women, and she spent her life pursuing legal rights and political equality for the underprivileged. Her parents, Jonathan and **Hannah Young**, raised their four children to be freethinkers, without the gender prejudices of the day. Born in New Durham, New Hampshire, on March 18, 1840, Marilla

◀⚑
Pollack, Andrea.
See Caulkins,
Tracy for sidebar.

was the oldest daughter and began her education early. While her mother taught her to read, her father encouraged her education in politics and philosophy. Bright and energetic, she became a teacher at the age of 16 and had completed a year's worth of training at the Colby Academy in New London, New Hampshire, when the Civil War broke out. Ricker sought to join the Union forces as a nurse, but her lack of nursing experience forced a return to teaching.

On May 19, 1863, Marilla married John Ricker, a wealthy farmer 33 years her senior. John, a progressive thinker like her father, believed in equality, a characteristic that no doubt appealed to her. He died, however, five years later. In 1872, as a well-off widow, Ricker began a four-year sojourn abroad, where she became fluent in various languages. She spent much of this time absorbing the ideas of social reformers such as Charles Bradlaugh, editor of the *National Reformer*, and *Annie Besant*, advocates of self-determination, political equality and birth control.

By the time she returned to America, Ricker had decided to pursue a legal career, determined to focus her attention and energy on helping the oppressed. Although she settled in Washington, D.C., Ricker spent her summers in New Hampshire, and protested conditions in the New Hampshire state prison to the governor of that state in 1879. She also set in motion legislation to grant prisoners the right to send sealed letters to the governor without the interference of prison wardens. Ricker was likewise successful in her 1890 petition to the State Supreme Court to grant women the right to practice law in New Hampshire, although there is no evidence that she herself took advantage of this opportunity.

On May 12, 1882, Ricker passed the District of Columbia bar. Her initial appearance in court was as an assistant counsel in the Star Route mail fraud case of 1882. Her law practice occupied her energies that first year and kept her schedule full, as she was appointed notary public in the District of Columbia by President Chester A. Arthur. In this role, she took further steps toward helping the underprivileged by allowing prisoners to make depositions before her when they did not have the money to pay other city notaries. Within two years, Ricker was appointed U.S. commissioner by the District's Supreme Court judges, becoming the first woman in the District of Columbia to secure such a position.

Acting in this quasi-judicial role furthered her experience and on May 11, 1891, Ricker was admitted to the bar of the Supreme Court of the United States. She never lost sight of her goal of assisting the oppressed, and she played a pivotal role in ending the District of Columbia's "poor convict's law," which allowed indigent criminals to be held indefinitely if they were unable to pay their fines. For this and other efforts to help prisoners and prostitutes, Ricker earned the nickname "Prisoner's Friend" in the area newspapers. While she concentrated on criminal law during the first years of her practice, she went on to focus on banking and financial legislation and then, from the turn of the 20th century, on reforming labor laws.

Ricker is also known for being the first woman in a non-western state (some of which enfranchised women in the late 19th century) to have a vote officially acknowledged, although it was not counted. In 1870, she demanded the right to vote, claiming that, because she was a taxpayer, the 14th Amendment to the Constitution guaranteed her the right. She voted the following year, and while that ballot was not counted, she continued to protest and demand her rightful place in the voting booth every year thereafter when she paid her taxes.

Ricker was a lifetime member of the National American Woman Suffrage Association (NAWSA) and of the National Legislative League, and continued to assist the cause of suffrage as a delegate to various conventions representing the New Hampshire Woman Suffrage Association. Although a staunch Republican, she supported her friend *Belva Lockwood*'s candidacy for president of the United States by heading the New Hampshire ticket of electors for the Equal Rights party during Lockwood's run in 1884. For the most part, however, Ricker maintained her ties with the Republican Party, campaigning in 1888 and 1892 for Republican candidates.

Never moving far from her political goals, Ricker lobbied President William McKinley for an appointment as minister to Colombia in the hopes of opening diplomatic opportunities for women. Although she had extensive support in this effort, she was denied the post. Undeterred, she announced her candidacy for governor of New Hampshire in 1910. Her filing fee for this position was refused on the grounds that since she could not vote, she could not run.

Ricker spent the last years of her life publishing essays, including the collections *I Don't Know, Do You?* (1916) and *I Am Not Afraid, Are You?* (1917), which attacked the clergy and labeled religious reverence "mental suicide." Among her most respected works is *Four Gospels* (1911), which compared the lives and works of Thomas Paine and Robert Ingersoll with those of John Calvin and Jonathan Edwards. Ricker, who was informal and had a lively sense of humor, enjoyed expounding upon her favorite subjects, producing a number of pamphlets and articles, and contributing to the *Dover Tribune* and *Truthseeker* magazine. She lived her final two years in Dover, New Hampshire, in the home of John W. Hogan, editor and publisher of the *Dover Tribune*. Ricker died of a stroke at age 80; her ashes were spread around a favorite tree on the family farm where she had been born.

SOURCES:

James, Edward T., ed. *Notable American Women, 1607–1950*. Cambridge, MA: The Belknap Press of Harvard University Press, 1971.

Read, Phyllis J., and Bernard L. Witlieb. *The Book of Women's Firsts*. NY: Random House, 1992.

Judith C. Reveal,
freelance writer, Greensboro, Maryland

Rickert, Edith (1871–1938)

American educator and writer. Born Martha Edith Rickert in Dover, Ohio, on July 11, 1871; died in Chicago, Illinois, on May 23, 1938; daughter of Francis Rickert and Josephine (Newburg) Rickert; Vassar College, A.B., 1891; University of Chicago, Ph.D., 1899.

Selected writings: (novels) Out of Cypress Swamp *(1902),* The Reaper *(1904),* Folly *(1906),* The Golden Hawk *(1907),* The Beggar in the Heart *(1909),* Severn Woods *(1930); (poetry collection)* American Lyrics *(ed. with Jessie Paton, 1912); (scholarly works)* The Writing of English *(with John M. Manly, 1919),* Contemporary British Literature *(with Manly, 1921),* Contemporary American Literature *(with Manly, 1922),* New Methods for the Study of Literature *(1927),* The Text of the Canterbury Tales, Studied on the Basis of All Known Manuscripts *(with Manly, 8 vols., 1940); (children's story collections)* The Bojabi Tree *(1923),* The Blacksmith and the Blackbirds *(1928),* The Greedy Goroo *(1929).*

Edith Rickert was born on July 11, 1871, in Dover, Ohio, the oldest of four daughters of Francis and **Josephine Rickert**. Raised in La Grange, Illinois, she attended public school in Chicago and went on to Vassar where her interest in creative writing blossomed. While at Vassar, she won recognition for the best short story written by an American undergraduate. She graduated in 1891.

By 1894, Rickert had begun work on her graduate degree at the University of Chicago, studying English literature and philology. Dur-

ing the next two years, she supported herself by teaching in high schools in the Chicago area and then went to Europe for a year of study. Upon her return to the States, she went back to Vassar, where she taught English while working on her dissertation on the Middle English romance *Emaré*. She earned her Ph.D. from the University of Chicago in 1899, and continued teaching at Vassar for another year.

In 1900, Rickert left Vassar and America for England, where she remained for a satisfying and productive nine years. While researching and editing medieval texts, she published five novels: *Out of Cypress Swamp* (1902), *The Reaper* (1904), *Folly* (1906), *The Golden Hawk* (1907), and *The Beggar in the Heart* (1909). In addition, she published over 50 short stories and produced numerous translations of medieval literature.

Forced by economic need, Rickert returned in 1909 to America, where she found editorial work with D.C. Heath & Co. and the *Ladies' Home Journal*. However, she never strayed far from her educational background and also wrote and edited textbooks. In 1912, she collaborated with **Jessie Paton** on the collection *American Lyrics*.

When World War I broke out, Rickert aided the war effort in the employ of the War Department's codes and ciphers division. Here she worked for the first time with John M. Manly, a medieval scholar with the University of Chicago. After the war, Rickert and Manly collaborated on *The Writing of English* (1919), *Contemporary British Literature* (1921), and *Contemporary American Literature* (1922). Many credit their accomplishments in this area as being largely responsible for bringing an air of respectability to and acceptance of the study of contemporary literature in the academic world. In 1924, she accepted an associate professorship at the University of Chicago, and in 1930 she became a full professor there.

Writing in all forms remained an integral part of Rickert's life. In an attempt to establish and define acceptable guidelines for the analysis of writing style, she wrote *New Methods for the Study of Literature* (1927). A ponderous tome, it was used at the University of Chicago on dissertation works, but seldom cited outside of this environment. While her scholarly activities were at the forefront of her work, during these years at the university she also produced three volumes of children's tales, *The Bojabi Tree* (1923), *The Blacksmith and the Blackbirds* (1928) and *The Greedy Goroo* (1929), as well as her last novel, *Severn Woods* (1930).

For all her prolific writing, Rickert is best remembered for her scholarly work, in particular her research on Chaucer. She and Manly embarked in 1930 on this, their most ambitious project. Spending time between England and America, they began preparing *The Text of the Canterbury Tales, Studied on the Basis of All Known Manuscripts* (1940). The stress of producing such a mammoth work took its toll on Rickert's health. She was seriously ill by 1935, and on May 23, 1938, she died of a coronary thrombosis. Edith Rickert was cremated and her ashes were buried at Oak Woods Cemetery in Chicago. Her work with Manly on Chaucer, in eight volumes, was published two years after her death.

SOURCES:

James, Edward T., ed. *Notable American Women, 1607–1950.* Cambridge, MA: The Belknap Press of Harvard University, 1971.

McHenry, Robert, ed. *Famous American Women.* NY: Dover, 1980.

Judith C. Reveal,
freelance writer, Greensboro, Maryland

Riddell, Charlotte (1832–1906)

Irish-born British novelist and short-story writer. Pronunciation: Riddle. *Name variations: (pseudonyms) Mrs. J.H. Riddell; F.G. Trafford; R.V. Sparling; Rainey Hawthorne. Born Charlotte Eliza Cowan in Carrickfergus, County Antrim, Ireland, on September 30, 1832; died in London, England, on September 24, 1906; daughter of James Cowan (a high sheriff) and Ellen (Kilshaw) Cowan; married Joseph Hadley Riddell, in 1857 (died 1880); no children.*

Selected writings: Zuriel's Grandchild *(1856);* The Ruling Passion *(1857);* The Moors and the Fens *(1858);* City and Suburb *(1861);* George Geith of Fen Court *(1864);* Home, Sweet Home *(1873);* Above Suspicion *(1876);* Weird Stories *(1882);* Berna Boyle *(1882);* A Struggle for Fame *(1883);* Mitre Court *(1885);* Miss Gascoyne *(1887);* The Nun's Curse *(1888);* Idle Tales *(1888);* The Head of the Firm *(1892);* The Banshee's Warning *(1894).*

Known in Victorian England as the "Novelist of the City" for her books about the financial and business worlds, and best known to modern readers as an exemplar of the Victorian-era ghost story, Charlotte Riddell was born Charlotte Cowan in a small town in County Antrim, Ireland, in 1832. Her father James Cowan served as the county's high sheriff, and Riddell grew up in quite comfortable circumstances, receiving a suitable education and reportedly writing a full novel by the age of 15. Her father's death when she was around 21 reduced her and her mother **Ellen Kilshaw Cowan** to straitened circumstances. Within a few years they decided to move to London, for Riddell hoped to earn her living as a writer, one of the few semi-respectable professions open to women at the time. They arrived in London in the mid-1850s, and found life there hard and money short.

Riddell's first two novels were long thought to have been lost, but finally were identified as *Zuriel's Grandchild* (1856), under the pseudonym R.V. Sparling, and *The Ruling Passion* (1857), under the pseudonym Rainey Hawthorne. It seems likely she earned little money from them, and her mother died of cancer around 1857. Shortly thereafter, Riddell was married to a civil engineer, Joseph Hadley Riddell, whose poor head for business meant that she ended up supporting them both with her writing, and keeping to a punishing schedule to pay off the debts he incurred. Her third novel, *The Moors and the Fens* (1858), under the pseudonym F.G. Trafford, finally brought some success, and she continued to publish under this pseudonym until 1866.

Despite its personal drawbacks, Riddell's marriage was important to her writing, for it was through Joseph that she gained many details of life in "the City," as the financial heart of London is known. She put this information to use in many of her most popular novels, including *City and Suburb* (1861), *Mitre Court* (1885) and *The Head of the Firm* (1892). It also formed the background for her breakthrough, and most successful, novel, published in 1864. *George Geith of Fen Court*, the story of a cleric who leaves his wife, his congregation, and the religious life to become an accountant in the City, went through several editions, and was adapted into a play that was popular on the stage through the 1880s.

Riddell's work found a ready audience for nearly a quarter of a century after the publication of *George Geith*. She began publishing as Mrs. J.H. Riddell in 1866, and over the course of her career wrote some 46 novels (some anonymous ones may have yet to be discovered). Considered among the best of these which do not focus on the financial world are *Home, Sweet Home* (1873), *Miss Gascoyne* (1887), and *The Nun's Curse* (1888). *A Struggle for Fame* (1883) was said to have been autobiographical, focusing on her own struggle to become a successful writer; *Berna Boyle* (1882) was one of her rare novels set in her native Ireland; and *Above Suspicion* (1876) was a "sensation" novel (at one time, Riddell was almost as popular as

*Mary Elizabeth Braddon, author of *Lady Audley's Secret*, the sensation novel par excellence). She also edited *Home Magazine* and *Anna Maria Hall's *St. James's Magazine* for several years in the 1860s, and contributed regularly to periodicals and Christmas annuals.

Riddell published a number of short stories, and it is for her ghost stories that she is now primarily remembered and read. (She also wrote four novels with supernatural themes, *Fairy Water* [1873], *The Uninhabited House* [1874], *The Haunted River* [1877], and *The Disappearance of Mr. Jeremiah Redworth* [1878], but these have rarely been republished and currently are all but unavailable.) She published ghost stories in the popular Christmas annuals, and released three collections: *Weird Stories* (1884), *Idle Tales* (1888), and *The Banshee's Warning* (1894). Riddell is considered one of the best of the Victorian ghost story writers; some have placed her just below J.S. LeFanu, the acknowledged master of this crowded genre. A number of her stories, including "The Old House in Vauxhall Walk," "Nut Bush Farm," "Diarmid Chittock's Story," "Walnut-Tree House," "Hertford O'Donnell's Warning," and "Forewarned, Forearmed," are now classics, held as standards of the genre and frequently anthologized.

Riddell's husband died in 1880, leaving substantial debts which she paid off with her writing. This became increasingly difficult as her work fell out of fashion beginning in the 1890s, and she grew steadily poorer and began to suffer from ill health. Her poverty was somewhat alleviated after 1901, when she became the first writer to receive a pension from the Society of Authors, but her last years were not spent in comfort. She died of cancer in London in 1906.

SOURCES:

Bleiler, E.F. "Introduction," in *The Collected Ghost Stories of Mrs. J.H. Riddell*. NY: Dover, 1977.

The Concise Dictionary of National Biography. Oxford: Oxford University Press, 1992.

Newmann, Kate, comp. and ed. *Dictionary of Ulster Biography*. The Institute for Irish Studies, Queen's University of Belfast, 1993.

Shattock, Joanne. *The Oxford Guide to British Women Writers*. Oxford: Oxford University Press, 1993.

Judith C. Reveal,
freelance writer, Greensboro, Maryland

Riddles, Libby (b. 1956).

See Butcher, Susan for sidebar.

Ride, Sally (b. 1951).

See Astronauts: Women in Space.

Ridge, Lola (1873–1941)

Irish-born American poet. Name variations: Rosa Delores Ridge. Born Rose Emily Ridge on December 12, 1873 (some sources cite 1883), in Dublin, Ireland; died in Brooklyn, New York, on May 19, 1941; daughter of Joseph Henry Ridge and Emma (Reilly) Ridge; attended Trinity College; studied art under Julian Ashton at the Academie Julienne; married David Lawson, on October 22, 1919; no children.

Selected writings: The Ghetto *(1918);* Sun-Up and Other Poems *(1920);* Red Flag and Other Poems *(1927);* Firehead *(1929);* Dance of Fire *(1935).*

Lola Ridge led an eclectic life from her birth in Ireland in 1873 (some sources follow her lead and put it in 1883) until her death in Brooklyn in 1941. Christened Rose Emily, she preferred to be called Rosa Delores but wrote as Lola Ridge. While still a child she moved with her mother to New Zealand and later to Sydney, Australia. She attended Trinity College in Australia and later studied art under Julian Ashton at the Academie Julienne. Although she initially directed herself toward a career as an artist, she soon changed course and became a poet.

In the spring of 1907, after her mother's death, Ridge immigrated to America. Settling in New York, she supported herself through a variety of professions ranging from factory worker to illustrator to model and author. Ridge soon found her way to Greenwich Village, and focused her energy on writing poetry. In 1908, she published in San Francisco's *Overland Monthly* and also contributed to *Mother Earth*, published by *Emma Goldman. It was in 1918, however, that she received critical acclaim, when her poem "The Ghetto" appeared in the *New Republic*. Although she herself was not Jewish, Ridge drew on her own immigrant status to identify with the plight of Jewish immigrants in America. "The Ghetto" was the title poem of her first volume of poetry released that same year. Praise came quickly from such established poets as Stephen Vincent Benét, Horace Gregory and *Marya Zaturenska.

Ridge's poetic subjects tended toward the far left of the political spectrum, and she dedicated herself and her work to radical causes. This leaning comes through in *Sun-Up and Other Poems* (1920) and *Red Flag and Other Poems* (1927), in which she offered encomiums to left-leaning heroes as varied as the Roman slave Spartacus and the triumphant Bolsheviks. After the First World War, she revived the magazine *Others*, while also serving as an editor of

Broom and contributing to *The Left* and *New Masses*. Although much of her work appeared in these radical magazines, she also published in traditional magazines such as *Harriet Monroe's *Poetry* and the *Saturday Review of Literature*.

Ridge was among those leftist poets and writers, including *Dorothy Parker, *Edna St. Vincent Millay*, and John Dos Passos, who conducted demonstrations on behalf of Nicola Sacco and Bartolomeo Vanzetti, the Italian anarchists sentenced to death (many believed framed) in 1921 for murder in the course of a robbery. After Sacco and Vanzetti were executed in 1927, Ridge wrote *Firehead* (1929), in which she used the subject of the crucifixion of Jesus to allude to the martyrdom of the pair. Her most successful poem, "Three Men Die," from her last volume, *Dance of Fire* (1935), likewise linked the deaths of the two men to Christ's crucifixion.

Ridge was married on October 22, 1919, to David Lawson. She spent a great deal of her adult life in fragile health, and contracted pulmonary tuberculosis in 1929. Praised by **Hildegarde Flanner** for her "tense and vigorous poetic thinking," Ridge was recognized on a number of occasions for her artistic and skillfully written work. She won *Poetry* magazine's Guarantor's Prize (1923), the Shelly Memorial Award in two consecutive years (1934 and 1935), and a Guggenheim fellowship (1935). She died at her home in Brooklyn on May 19, 1941. That same year, Samuel A. DeWitt established the Lola Ridge Memorial Award, which was presented in her memory until 1950.

SOURCES:

James, Edward T., ed. *Notable American Women, 1607–1950*. Cambridge, MA: The Belknap Press of Harvard University, 1971.

Kunitz, Stanley J., and Howard Haycraft, eds. *Twentieth Century Authors*. NY: H.W. Wilson, 1942.

Judith C. Reveal,
freelance writer, Greensboro, Maryland

Ridgway, Rozanne Lejeanne

(1935—)

American diplomat and ambassador. Name variations: Roz Ridgway. Born on August 22, 1935, in St. Paul, Minnesota; daughter of H. Clay Ridgway and Ethel Rozanne (Cote) Ridgway; Hamline University in Minnesota, B.A., 1957; married Theodore (Ted) Deming (an officer in the Coast Guard), in 1983.

Became the first woman to actively participate in a presidential summit, at the Geneva conference between President Ronald Reagan and Soviet Premier Mikhail Gorbachev (November 1985).

After graduating from Hamline University in Minnesota, 21-year-old Rozanne Ridgway entered the Foreign Service in 1957, at a time when women were neither wanted nor welcomed there. Her first assignments took her to Manila and Palermo where she gained experience in personnel and visa issues, but did not move her career forward with any speed. Her mentor George Vest encouraged her to maintain her standards and work hard, a recommendation she took to heart. By 1967, she landed a position as a class 4 political officer in Oslo, Norway, working for Ambassador *Margaret Tibbetts*. Later, with Tibbetts' encouragement, she accepted a position as desk officer for Ecuador.

During her tenure as desk officer, Ridgway became embroiled in the fishery war, when Ecuador seized 51 American fishing vessels. Washington canceled its aid program as well as foreign military assistance before Ecuador removed the military from power. While still in Ecuador, Ridgway moved to deputy director in the Latin American policy office, where she continued working with fisheries. She considered this a vital learning time, when she honed her writing and analytical skills. While attached to the delegation charged with negotiating tuna agreements with Chile, Ecuador and Peru, Ridgway was christened "Tuna Roz." Upon the completion of this assignment, Ron Spiers, ambassador to the Bahamas, offered her a position in the Bahamas.

Ridgway, who did not accept all assignments presented to her, had the knack of being able to turn down a position without causing animosity. In one situation, an undersecretary offered Ridgway the temporary position of special assistant in access and fisheries affairs. Someone was needed to fill in while a replacement was sought. Ridgway refused the temporary position but suggested herself for the permanent deputy assistant secretary post and got the job. Within a year, her team had rewritten postwar international fisheries laws as they applied to the United States as well as negotiated bilateral fishing treaties with 14 nations. This accomplishment earned her a second informal title, "Lobster Lady of the Bahamas."

Though Ridgway was then offered the post of ambassador at the embassy in Trinidad-Tobago, she had tired of living and working on islands. Instead, she asked for the ambassadorship to Finland, and her request was granted. She saw her mission in Finland as one of facilitating Finnish-American dialogue, which during the Cold War was sometimes strained by Finland's determinedly neutral status. Her diplomacy and tact easily won over Finnish society.

In 1980, Ridgway returned to the United States to work as a counselor in the State Department, one of the most disappointing years in her career. She soon realized that she was there only to fulfill gender diversity requirements. Stuck in a dead-end job with few duties, she was relegated to virtual obscurity until a fisheries problem with the Canadians arose. As Secretary of State Al Haig was preparing for President Ronald Reagan's 1981 Canadian summit in Ottawa, he was told by the Canadian foreign minister that the summit would be a disaster if a commercial fishing conflict over scallops off of George's Island were not resolved. Ridgway was called upon to fix the conflict. Shuttling between Ottawa, Washington and New England, she eventually put forth a solution which was unanimously passed in the Senate.

Ridgway's name was proposed for several positions, but nothing surfaced until she was offered the ambassador's post in East Germany. She agreed, even though she married Captain Theodore Deming, an officer in the Coast Guard, before leaving the States. After the wedding, she headed for East Germany, and Deming remained at his assignment in Alaska.

In February 1985, Secretary George Schultz suggested that Ridgway consider becoming assistant secretary for European and Canadian Affairs. The nomination appeared to be going smoothly until Senator Jesse Helms of North Carolina suggested that her loyalty to the Reagan administration was questionable given her earlier service to Democratic President Jimmy Carter. There was considerable wrangling by Helms over situations that had occurred during Ridgway's post in East Germany, and it took the efforts of Senators Charles Mathias, Ted Kennedy, John Kerry, Claiborne Pell and Joe Biden to finally win the vote. Although her relationship with her new boss, George Schultz, had its rocky moments, they grew to respect one another. Ridgway's experience in this capacity led to her becoming the first woman to actively participate in a presidential summit, when she took part in the November 1985 Geneva conference between President Ronald Reagan and Soviet Premier Mikhail Gorbachev.

Given her experience, many thought Ridgway would achieve the personal rank of career ambassador. The number of positions, however, is based on the percentage of career ministers and by the time a position opened, it went to George Vest. On May 22, 1989, Ridgway re-

ceived the Diplomatic Award from the American Academy for Diplomacy. She retired a month later. At her retirement ceremony, she received the Distinguished Honor Award, her department's highest recognition, and the Wilbur J. Carr Award, given to a career officer for special achievements as an assistant secretary. On Foreign Service Day in 1992, Ridgway received the Director General's Cup, during a ceremony in which she was described as a "brilliant negotiator, a diplomat of uncommon skill and a superior strategist." By 1995, she had become president of the Atlantic Council.

SOURCES:

Morin, Ann Miller. *Her Excellency: An Oral History of American Women Ambassadors.* NY: Twayne, 1995.

Judith C. Reveal,
freelance writer, Greensboro, Maryland

Riding, Laura (1901–1991)

Important American poet and contributor to literary modernism who stressed the unique ability of poetry to penetrate a reality beyond that of the senses. Name variations: *Laura Reichenthal; Laura Riding Gottschalk; Laura Riding Jackson.* Born on January 16, 1901, in New York City; died on September 2, 1991, of heart failure, in Sebastien, Florida; daughter of Nathan Reichenthal (a garment worker and labor activist) and Sarah (Sadie) Edersheim Reichenthal (a garment worker); attended Brooklyn Girls' High School, 1914–18; attended Cornell University, 1918–21; married Louis R. Gottschalk, in 1920 (divorced 1925); married Schuyler Jackson, on June 20, 1941 (died 1968).

Moved with husband to Urbana, Illinois (1921); moved with husband to Louisville, Kentucky, and submitted first work to Fugitive *(1923); won Nashville Poetry Prize (1924); joined Robert and Nancy Graves in England, published first book of poetry (1926); assumed the name "Laura Riding" (1927); founded Seizin Press with Graves (1928); attempted suicide, moved to Spanish island of Mallorca (1929); left Spain for Brittany (1938); Schuyler Jackson reviewed her poems for* Time *magazine (1938); ended relationship with Robert Graves, settled in Pennsylvania (1939); abandoned writing poetry, settled in Florida (1941); participated in BBC broadcast explaining her long literary silence (1962); awarded Bollingen Prize for poetry (1991).*

Selected works: (poetry) The Close Chaplet *(1926),* Love as Love, Death as Death *(1928),* Collected Poems *(1938),* Selected Poems: In Five Sets *(1970); (prose)* A Survey of Modernist Poetry *(with Robert Graves, 1927),* The Telling *(with Schuyler Jackson,*

1972), Rational Meaning: A New Foundation for the Definition of Words (1997).

Laura Riding was a major American poet of the first half of the 20th century. Seen as a prodigy when her work first appeared in the 1920s, she later abandoned writing for an extended period of time starting in the late 1930s. She was also an important literary critic, who played a crucial role in promoting the work of *Gertrude Stein. As an editor and critic, she had a particularly strong influence on the English poet and novelist Robert Graves, with whom she also maintained a close personal relationship for 13 years. Riding's poetry, which was distinguished by its verbal precision and the absence of devices like metaphor, attracted only a small reading audience. Notes **Joyce Wexler**, her career contained a "tragic irony" since "as her pursuit of truth became purer, her audience shrank." Riding's verses featured such themes as death and the denunciation of physical sexuality. Her turbulent life was marked by a suicide attempt and by fre-

quent occasions when she changed her name as a symbol of her efforts to reshape her identity.

The future poet was born to immigrant Jewish parents in New York City on January 16, 1901. Her father Nathan Reichenthal had grown up in the Polish province of Galicia and arrived in the United States 17 years before Laura's birth. He worked as a tailor in the sweatshop conditions of the New York garment industry, became a widower after a brief marriage to an immigrant from Hungary, and then married the woman who became Laura's mother, **Sarah Edersheim Reichenthal**, whom her family called Sadie. Sadie, who had been born in the United States of German-Jewish immigrant parents, was a psychologically troubled woman whose life had also been shaped by the harsh conditions she experienced while working in the garment industry.

Nathan tried unsuccessfully to start his own clothing business, but, by his own, perhaps dramatized, account of his life, became an important figure in the New York labor movement and in labor journalism. His various business efforts made the family a highly mobile one, and Riding attended a number of schools in the East and Midwest during her childhood years. As a devotee of American socialism, Nathan encouraged Laura to consider a career as a political activist, a plan she wholeheartedly rejected by her teenage years. Her ambition to become a poet led to a bitter quarrel with her father at the age of 15. This family outburst, along with the young girl's troubled relationship with her bitter and domineering mother, prompted Riding's decision to move in with her half-sister, **Isabel Reichenthal**. A secretary in a publishing firm who soon married one of the editors, Isabel herself published poetry and encouraged Laura's literary aspirations.

The stay with Isabel provided a rare interlude of stability for Riding. So too did her four years at Girls' High School in Brooklyn, where she began to distinguish herself academically. A scholarship, one of three that she won, allowed the young girl, still only 17, to enroll at Cornell University in the fall of 1918. In her second year there she fell in love with her young history instructor, Louis Gottschalk. Two years after beginning her higher education, she dropped her academic program and left college when she and Louis were married on November 2, 1920. Riding then followed her new husband to several junior academic positions, starting at the University of Illinois in 1921. The couple moved to Kentucky two years later when Louis took up a

Laura Riding

position at the University of Louisville. She made several unsuccessful attempts to complete her undergraduate degree at the two institutions where her husband taught. Deeply dissatisfied with the role of faculty wife in an isolated Midwestern town, she threw herself into literary activity, writing both novels and poetry.

As the wife of a young academic in the South, Riding entered the annual poetry contest put on by the Fugitive Group of Nashville, Tennessee, in 1923. The Fugitives were a group of teachers and students at Vanderbilt University including such future literary luminaries as John Crowe Ransom and Allan Tate. They were laying the foundation for the New Criticism movement of the following decades. The first poem she ever published, entitled "Dimensions," appeared in the group's magazine *The Fugitive* in the August–September issue of 1923. Riding shared the Fugitives' view that new forms of poetry free of traditional rhetorical devices must be created. Four more of her works were published in the same journal the following February.

After this breakthrough in her writing career, Riding entered a period of personal crisis. Her marriage was in difficulty, in large part due to her husband's lack of sympathy with her literary ambitions. All of her future relationships were with men who shared her devotion to poetry. When at the close of 1924 she visited the Fugitives in Nashville, she began a brief love affair with Tate. The cause of the relationship's collapse points to a fundamental theme in Riding's life: her intense personality and her arrogant propensity to dominate any group in which she found herself. Around this time, she was hospitalized, probably for a nervous breakdown. After her release, she separated from Gottschalk, and the two eventually divorced in 1925. That same year, the aspiring poet returned to New York and settled in Greenwich Village for several months. A love affair followed with fellow poet Hart. But by the close of 1925, she was so disillusioned with the poets' circles she had discovered in New York—perhaps due to their lack of serious purpose—that she accepted an invitation to cross the Atlantic.

The invitation came from the young but well-known English poet Robert Graves. Graves had been an admirer of Riding for some time, praising her by name in an essay, "Contemporary Techniques of Poetry," he had published in July 1925. A correspondence between the two developed during the remainder of the year. By mid-winter, Graves wanted her to join him, his wife, artist **Nancy Nicholson** (1900–1977), and their four

children for a stay of several months in Egypt where he was to teach at a university. She would supposedly be a good companion for Nancy and a useful collaborator for Robert in completing a book he was writing on modern poetry.

In England, where she arrived in January 1926, Riding met Robert and his family and almost immediately left with them for Egypt. According to one of Graves' biographers, the English poet "had found someone of great intelligence and originality, who listened with interest to his ideas, and whose head teemed with ideas of her own." Riding herself remembered that there had been an immediate attraction between them. Once settled in Egypt, Robert, Nancy, and Laura established what some authors describe as an intimate three-way relationship. Many acquaintances, however, thought that the sexual relationship between Graves and Riding began only when the group returned to England the following year. Riding's close association with Graves began with their common literary interests and, from the early days of their acquaintance, they were enthusiastic literary collaborators.

In 1927, after returning to England, then taking a trip alone to Vienna, Graves and Riding settled down together in an apartment in the London neighborhood of Hammersmith. There they completed an influential study of modern verse entitled *A Survey of Modernist Poetry* (1927). Later in their lives, each insisted on claiming the lion's share of the originality that had gone into the book. Nonetheless, writes Richard Graves, there is "little doubt that hers was usually the controlling intelligence at work." Riding's contribution to the work included a sharp criticism of many modern poets. She castigated those who were immersing themselves in such eccentricities as the poetry of China. And she was equally harsh in condemning poets who drew too much inspiration from the classics. According to Riding's biographer **Deborah Baker**, the book showed that the American poet "was ready to imagine a new poetry." Although the new poetry Riding and Graves lauded had unfamiliar forms, they insisted that the poem's form had to develop out of the theme it presented. Richard Graves sees the book as a defense of the type of modernist poetry Riding herself was writing. With its emphasis on judging a poem solely on the basis of its internal verbal relations and its call for close textual analysis, this work made a fundamental contribution to the development of the New Criticism movement. A symbol of the young American's growing sense of self-confidence and independence came in another one of her name changes. She had gone to England referring to herself as "Laura Riding Gottschalk." Now, she became simply "Laura Riding."

As a successful and prominent author, Robert Graves was able to advance Riding's career. He arranged for her work to appear in print, insisting that he would not deal with his various publishers unless the firms agreed to publish Riding's poetry as well. Unfortunately, the sales of her verse remained at an extremely low level. By contrast, he did well from sales of his popular book on the wartime exploits of Lawrence of Arabia (T.E. Lawrence). Meanwhile, Riding turned much of her formidable energy to writing literary criticism. With Graves' money in hand, the two of them also began their own publishing venture, the Seizin Press. Riding's second volume of poetry, *Love as Love, Love as Death*, was the initial book to appear under the new imprint.

Perhaps all along truth had been Laura Riding's pursuer rather than the imagined quarry.

—Deborah Baker

Baker finds hints of Riding's mental anguish in the poet's work of the late 1920s and notes that even in "her earliest unpublished poems, Riding's poetry could be viewed as intensely suicidal." The poem "In Nineteen Twenty-Seven," for example, gives hints of the suicide attempt that marked Riding's life only two years later. By the spring of 1927, her personal life was complicated by her relationship to the Anglo-Irish poet Geoffrey Phipps. Phipps subsequently declared that he no longer wanted to be on intimate terms with Riding, and this apparently destroyed her remaining mental equilibrium. Throwing herself from a window in her apartment in the Hammersmith neighborhood of London on April 27, 1929, Riding suffered severe but not fatal injuries. These included a broken spine and broken pelvis. The initial diagnosis mistakenly added a fractured skull and, equally mistaken, concluded that Riding would not survive her injuries. A subsequent assessment of her condition suggested she would be permanently crippled. Eventually, the forecast was improved to indicate a complete recovery in time.

In November 1929, Riding and Graves settled in the small town of Deya on the Spanish Mediterranean island of Mallorca. The possibility that Riding might be prosecuted for her attempt to kill herself had not materialized, but the two still felt the need to escape the scandal. Gertrude Stein, who was both Laura's friend and her poetic protégé, had recommended the island as a getaway.

As Baker has put it, instead of being devastated by the experience she had just undergone, "in the months following her suicide attempt, Riding appeared to gain in vitality . . . entering a period of intense and remarkable creativity." She composed a long poem, "Laura and Francisca," which described her decision to live in Mallorca and her affection for a local village child. Signs of concern for her personal appearance, including a new interest in the elegant Spanish clothing and jewelry to be found on the island, matched her creative energies. In the six years they spent on the island, the couple was bolstered by the financial success of Graves' memoir of his service in World War I, *Good-bye to All That*, and a historical novel, *I, Claudius*. Through the 1930s, Riding busied herself with a variety of writing and editing projects. These ranged from editing Graves' work to writing novels both singly and in collaboration with others.

The complex relationship between Riding and Graves now came to include her renunciation of sexual relations. She had first discussed her dissatisfaction with physical sex in an essay published in 1928. In 1933, she was even more decisive on the subject. In a brief autobiographical entry for *Authors Today and Yesterday*, she now stated directly, "I think that bodies have had their day," and claimed that the basic tie between men and women should be "between the male mind and the female mind." For Baker, this public renunciation of sex was an initial step in "the heated search for truth." That same year Graves described Riding's confident and overbearing personality to one of his friends: "She is a great natural fact like fire or trees or snow and either one appreciates her or one doesn't."

Riding's strong personality and her authoritative views on the nature of literature and poetry led to her intellectual domination over a series of visitors to her household in Mallorca. This literary circle in Deya included a number of young English and American poets who had sent her samples of their work and, following intense correspondence, decided to join her on the Spanish island. For a time the rising British intellectual and mathematician Jacob Bronowski fell under her spell, but he, like many others, broke away following a bitter quarrel.

The outbreak of the Spanish Civil War in July 1936 quickly involved Mallorca. The island where Riding and Graves had their home became a military stronghold for the Nationalist rebels led by General Francisco Franco. At the urging of the local British consul, the two hastily abandoned their home and were evacuated on a battleship to France by the Royal Navy. They returned to England vainly hoping that the Civil War would end soon and permit them to reestablish a home in Mallorca.

The darkening political scene in Europe not only ruled out a return to Mallorca, it also pushed Riding into a rare political excursion. She began a campaign of letter writing that came to include letters to 400 key figures in European and American political and intellectual circles. Each letter asked what could be done by intelligent individuals hoping to "live a peaceful, civilized existence" in an increasingly politicized European environment. Riding had hopes that such direct and personal contact with influential leaders might somehow avert the war that now loomed over the Continent. She took 65 of the responses, added her own extensive commentaries, and published the collection in a volume entitled *The World and Ourselves*. The book also included Riding's plan for a new organization for society, one that would create what Baker calls "a woman-centered system of government." Meanwhile, Riding's poems of the final years of the 1930s pointed toward her impending abandonment of poetry itself. She spoke enthusiastically of the need to abandon all imagery and literary device and, writes Baker, "to speak without guile, wit, or decoration."

All hopes of returning to Spain vanished by the start of 1939 as the Civil War continued, and in April Riding and Graves sailed for New York. That summer, they settled on a farm in New Hope, Pennsylvania, as the guests of **Kit Jackson** and Schuyler Jackson, a literary critic who had lauded Riding's poems in a recent review in *Time* magazine and with whom she had corresponded. Soon, a romantic liaison developed between Laura and Schuyler. Kit, who had a mental breakdown and tried to strangle her young daughter **Griselda Ohannessian** (later publisher of New Directions), filed for divorce. (**Miranda Seymour**, Graves' official biographer, wrote a controversial novel about the incident, *The Summer of '39*. As well, versions of this story appear in one Riding biography, three Graves biographies, and a memoir by T.S. Matthews, part of their inner circle and later editor of *Time*.) On June 20, 1941, Schuyler and Laura married; she now took her last name change, becoming Laura Riding Jackson.

Pressed for funds, the Jacksons settled in Wabasso, Florida, a small town on the Atlantic coast, where they hoped to earn their living farming two small grapefruit groves. The two busied themselves with one of Riding's longstanding projects, a dictionary of the English language that would indicate the precise meaning of words. She believed that only a poet had sufficient command of English to permit the realization of such an effort, which she entitled *The Dictionary of Rational Meaning*. The project dragged on for years.

Around the time of her marriage to Jackson, Riding formally abandoned her work as a poet. An acquaintance recalls seeing her burning a mass of papers at the farm in New Hope shortly before she and Jackson were wed. Baker believes that these were Riding's poems, and that she did well to abandon poetry at a time when "her poetry had become increasingly didactic" and she herself was lacking in "the emotional reserves required to endure the demands of her art." **Barbara Adams** sees Riding's decision as more ambiguous, noting that it was not clear "whether she deliberately gave up writing poetry, or whether she gradually lost the creative urge."

In their remote new home, which lacked even a telephone and electricity, the newly married couple worked the land in the face of numerous climatic and financial crises. They also collaborated on their massive linguistic study, *Rational Meaning*, devoted to "knowledge of the meaning of words." Notes Joyce Wexler, since they regarded "poetry as a dead end, together they sought truth via linguistic study."

After decades of illnesses that doctors could never successfully diagnose, Schuyler Jackson died on July 4, 1968. Now alone in the world, Riding completed *Rational Meaning*. Portions of it appeared in various journals starting in the 1970s. She gradually returned to literary circles, establishing written contact with a number of poets and teachers of literature, and she received a Guggenheim grant to support her while she wrote her memoirs. In 1970, she permitted the publication of *Selected Poems: In Five Sets*, a group of works from *Collected Poems*, which she had originally published in 1938. In her book *The Telling*, which appeared in 1972, Riding discussed her need to turn away from poetry and to pursue the study of words as the route to an understanding of truth.

A new interest in Riding's poetry developed among English and American critics starting in the 1970s, and she engaged in lengthy, often contentious correspondence with the writers in order to correct what she saw as inaccuracies or attacks on her ideas. In one case she attempted to rewrite a scholarly dissertation on her work; in another, she first authorized a biography, then broke with the author after the latter had put ten years into the effort.

Laura Riding died of heart failure on September 2, 1991, in Sebastien, Florida. Her modest funeral was attended by only 30 mourners and held in the small and primitive bungalow where she had lived for nearly 50 years. Shortly before her death, the writer, who had abandoned the creation of verse decades before, received Yale University's Bollingen Prize for poetry. The extended study of language upon which she and her late husband had labored for so long, *Rational Meaning*, finally appeared in its entirety in 1997.

SOURCES:

Adams, Barbara. *The Enemy Self: Poetry and Criticism of Laura Riding*. Ann Arbor, MI: UMI Research Press, 1990.

Baker, Deborah. *In Extremis: The Life of Laura Riding*. NY: Grove Press, 1993.

Quartermain, Peter, ed. *American Poets, 1880–1945*. 2nd series. Detroit, MI: Gale Research, 1986.

Seymour, Miranda. *Robert Graves: Life on the Edge*. NY: Henry Holt, 1995.

———. *The Summer of '39* (novel). NY: W.W. Norton, 1999.

Vendler, Helen. "The White Goddess," in *The New York Review of Books*. November 18, 1993, pp. 12–18.

Wexler, Joyce Piell. *Laura Riding's Pursuit of Truth*. Athens, OH: Ohio University Press, 1979.

SUGGESTED READING:

Canary, Robert H. *Robert Graves*. Boston: Twayne, 1980.

Fromm, Harold. "Myths and Mishegaas: Robert Graves and Laura Riding," in *The Hudson Review*. Vol. 44, no. 2. Summer 1991, pp. 189–202.

Graves, Richard Perceval. *Robert Graves: The Years with Laura, 1926–1940*. London: Weidenfeld and Nicolson, 1990.

Neil M. Heyman,
Professor of History, San Diego State University,
San Diego, California

Ridler, Anne (1912—)

English poet and dramatist. Born Anne Bradby in Rugby, Warwickshire, England, on July 30, 1912; daughter of Henry Christopher Bradby and Violet (Milford) Bradby; attended Downe House School in Berkshire; graduated from King's College in London with a degree in journalism, 1932; married Vivian Ridler, in 1938; children: four.

Selected writings: (poetry) Poems *(1939),* The Nine Bright Shiners *(1943),* The Golden Bird *(1951),* A Matter of Life and Death *(1959),* Dies Natalis *(1980),* Ten Poems *(with E.J. Scovell, 1984),* New and Selected Poems *(1988); (verse dramas)* Cain *(1943),* Henry Bly *(1947),* The Trial of Thomas Cranmer *(1956).*

Born Anne Bradby in Rugby, Warwickshire, England, in 1912, Anne Ridler started her life in the academic world of her father, who was a housemaster of Rugby School. Her early education at Downe House School in Berkshire was complemented by six months in Florence and Rome. In 1932, she graduated from King's College in London with a degree in journalism. From 1935 to 1940, Ridler worked as a secretary to T.S. Eliot at Faber & Faber. In 1938, she married Vivian Ridler, later a printer at the University of Oxford.

In 1939, Ridler published *Poems*, her first collection. "It was Eliot who first made me despairing of becoming a poet," she wrote; "Auden . . . who first made me think I saw how to become one." The threads of domesticity and religion weave their way through her works, as she contemplates the various levels of love. *The Nine Bright Shiners* (1943) reflects her anticipation at facing motherhood; *The Golden Bird* (1951), focuses on the pain and anxiety of separation, and *A Matter of Life and Death* (1959) highlights the sadness of children growing to adulthood.

Ridler also wrote plays, translated opera libretti, and edited the works of Charles Williams, James Thomson, Walter de la Mare, Thomas Traherne, George Darley, and William Austin. Her dramatic style is often compared to that of T.S. Eliot. Among her plays are *Cain* (1943), *Henry Bly* (1947), and *The Trial of Thomas Cranmer* (1956). Ridler's later poetry collections include *Dies Natalis* (1980) and *New and Selected Poems* (1988), and she collaborated with E.J. Scovell in 1984 on *Ten Poems*.

SOURCES:

Buck, Claire, ed. *The Bloomsbury Guide to Women's Literature*. NY: Prentice Hall, 1992.

Shattock, Joanne. *The Oxford Guide to British Women Writers*. Oxford: Oxford University Press, 1993.

Judith C. Reveal,
freelance writer, Greensboro, Maryland

Rie, Lucie (1902–1995)

Austrian-born British potter. Born in Austria in 1902; died in 1995.

Born in Austria in 1902, Lucie Rie fled Nazism in 1938 to continue her work in freedom and went on to become both internationally acclaimed and the most famous potter in the United Kingdom. A 1982 BBC film by Sir David Attenborough documented her life and work. At the time of her death, Attenborough noted: "She was a small, quiet lady who would always dress in white, normally a trouser suit. She had an astonishing authority and would be able to prick pretension in a way that would leave you gasping."

SOURCES:

"Dame Lucie Rie," in *The Times* [London]. April 3, 1995, p. 19.

Horsnell, Michael. "Lucie Rie, inspiration to potters, dies at 93," in *The Times* [London]. April 3, 1995, p. 3.

Riefenstahl, Leni (1902—)

One of the most innovative, influential film directors of the 20th century, who made Triumph of the Will *for the Nazi Party and* Olympia *for the IOC, both considered classics, and whose work for the Nazis virtually blocked her from directing after World War II. Pronunciation: LANE-ee REEF-in-shtall. Born Helene Berta Amalie Riefenstahl in Berlin, Germany, on August 22, 1902; daughter of Alfred Riefenstahl (an owner of a plumbing business) and Berta (Scherlach) Riefenstahl; attended Realgymnasium and Kunstakademie in Berlin; began studying classical ballet in 1919; married Peter Jacob, in 1944 (divorced 1946); no children.*

Discovered during dance recital by impresario Max Reinhardt (1923); injured a knee, ending her dance career (1924); made first film appearance, in Der Heilige Berg *(The Holy Mountain, 1926); after the founding of her own film company, directed* Das Blaue Licht *(The Blue Light, 1932),* Sieg des Glaubens *(Victory of Faith, 1933),* Triumph des Willens *(Triumph of the Will, 1935),* Olympia *(1938),* Tiefland *(Lowland, 1944); appointed "film expert" to Germany's National Socialist Party by Adolf Hitler (1933); received the Staatspreis (1935); won the gold Venice Biennale medal (1936); won the Grand Prix of the Exposition Internationale des Art et des Techniques for* Triumph of the Will *(1937); briefly held prisoner after World War II for supposed pro-Nazi activities but released and her name cleared; received a gold medal from the International Olympic Committee for* Olympia *(1948); a Hollywood panel of judges named* Olympia *one of the ten finest motion pictures of all time (1955); traveled extensively in Africa and produced book* The Last of the Nuba *(1973); continued into her 90s to work in photography and film.*

In the darkened movie theater, Nazi banners flood the screen, and thousands of men holding torches march past in the night. Searchlights sweep the sky, stopping to train on the flags and on an enormous statue of an eagle overlooking a high podium. Slowly the river of flags pours past tens of thousands of spectators, coming closer and closer until nothing can be seen but the flags, moving forward as if they have a life of their own. One figure finally emerges. As he stands at attention on the vast podium the camera focuses in, until the viewer is looking at Adolf Hitler, bathed in the glow of the searchlights.

This sequence and many like it were filmed by Leni Riefenstahl, the only female film director hired by the German Third Reich. Anyone who doubts the power of Hitler's propaganda has only to watch her classic film *Triumph of the Will*. Acknowledging the tremendous magnetism of her work, Riefenstahl would not allow it to be screened in modern Germany. Yet she has spent most of her long life denying that it was created with any evil intent. All of her films, she has maintained, were simply art, nothing more. So powerful are her images, however, that the debate about her work continues.

Leni Riefenstahl was born into a middle-class Berlin family on August 22, 1902. Her mother **Berta Scherlach Riefenstahl** was born in what would become Poland. Her father Alfred Riefenstahl was the owner of a plumbing engineering firm. Leni was educated at a Realgymna-

Leni Riefenstahl

sium and at the Kunstakademie in Berlin, and began taking dancing lessons in 1919. Studying classical ballet with **Eduardova** and **Jutta Klammt** and modern dance with *****Mary Wigman**, she wanted to pursue a dancing or acting career, but was adamantly opposed in this by her father, who exercised strict control over his oldest daughter, rarely allowing her to leave home unattended until she was 21.

In 1923, Alfred Riefenstahl agreed to finance a solo dance recital on the condition that Leni would give up dancing if the performance proved unsuccessful. Contrary to his expectations, her debut that year brought her to the attention of Max Reinhardt, the famous impresario, who engaged her for his Deutsches Theater in Berlin. Later she toured under Reinhardt's sponsorship, performing modern dances of her own creation in Zurich, Prague, and other European cities. In 1924, her dancing career was abruptly ended when she cracked her knee-cap.

Leni Riefenstahl was as resolute as she was beautiful. Her father's frequent beatings and abuse of her mother made her determined to live as an independent woman. After her knee injury thwarted her dancing career, she saw the movie *Mountain of Destiny* and decided to become a film actress. She contacted the director, Dr. Arnold Fanck, and impressed him so greatly that he hired her as the only woman in his crew. In 1926, Fanck created a role especially for her in his *Der Heilige Berg* (The Holy Mountain, 1926), about a young dancer turned mountain climber. This was followed by the comedy *Der Grosse Sprung* (The Big Leap, 1927). In 1929, she appeared in *Das Schicksal von der Habsburg* (The Fate of the Habsburgs) and *Die Weisse Hölle von Piz Palü* (The White Hell of Piz Palü). Her first sound film, *Stürme über dem Montblanc* (Storms over Mont Blanc), came out in 1930, followed by the skiing comedy *Der Weisse Rausch* (White Frenzy) in 1931.

From the beginning of her career, Riefenstahl was interested in film production and quickly demonstrated her technical and directing abilities. Fanck taught her how to edit film, and when the French found *White Frenzy* too long, she successfully cut it down. In 1931, she founded her own film company, Leni Riefenstahl Studio Films, to produce her next movie, *The Blue Light*. She recruited Bela Balazs, the distinguished Hungarian writer, to help her with the screenplay. To shoot night scenes during daylight, she pushed the Agfa film company to develop a new film stock. She decided to direct the film, as it was cheaper than hiring someone else, and also played the starring

role of Junta, the mountain girl who scales heights alone. By now, Riefenstahl was one of Germany's most popular actresses.

Although she preferred to direct, she agreed to star in *S.O.S. Eisberg* (S.O.S. Iceberg, 1932–33), a German-American co-production directed by Fanck. The shoot proved eventful. Cracking ice floes threatened the lives of cast members and starving Eskimo dogs ate anything on the set made of fur or leather. The polar bears from the Berlin Zoo were uncooperative, and chronic cystitis and ingrown toenails added to Riefenstahl's list of woes, but she prevailed.

Filmmaking was in its infancy when Leni Riefenstahl began her work as a director. Many techniques now taken for granted had yet to be invented. For example, telephoto lenses did not produce usable footage at night in an unlit crowd, so ways around filming such scenes had to be devised. In order to obtain the best low-angle shots, Riefenstahl had a trench dug in which to place the camera. For elevated shots, she used a fire-truck ladder or rooftop. Sometimes small elevators were placed on flagpoles to shoot wide panoramas. Camera equipment of the period was also extremely heavy and cumbersome, so that moving a camera to achieve a shot could be a huge task in itself. Grueling effort was required to produce effects which are today considered commonplace. Riefenstahl's use of the camera to such excellent effect called for technical improvements in equipment that have made her influence on film production an enduring legacy.

Leni Riefenstahl's involvement in acting and directing began during a tumultuous period of German history. After World War I, a defeated Germany plunged into economic chaos, partly because of the enormous reparations exacted by the Allies. Inflation first wiped out savings and capital, then the worldwide Great Depression made matters worse. While an influx of refugees from Eastern Europe seemed to unbalance the country, the arts flowered in these chaotic conditions. Novels, plays, films, music, and art all took new and exciting directions. The creators of this cultural renaissance were Germans and Jewish refugees from Eastern Europe, an extremely fertile collaboration. Some were leftists, or communists, and in their minds capitalistic Europe had failed, bringing war and deprivation to millions. Intrigued by the new social experiments being attempted in the Soviet Union, they identified with the champions of equal rights for women and workers.

In addition to economic and social chaos, new technologies also challenged the status quo.

Motion pictures, radio, phonographs, and air travel were changing the old world forever. Inundated by social change, a poor economy, and the forces of technology, Germany grew more and more unstable. As economic and political conditions worsened throughout the 1920s, one political party gained increasing power. The National Socialists, led by Adolf Hitler, blamed leftists, communists, and Jews for social unrest and economic instability. The Nazis rejected modern art and modern music. Jazz, for example, was anathema to them. Their prescription for Germany was a return to the traditional social order

in which Germans controlled their own fate. Cultural ferment must cease.

Although Hitler and his followers rejected modernity in the arts, they eagerly embraced new technologies. Hitler often criss-crossed the country by plane, one of the first leaders to do so. He also understood the power of radio and films. It was this combination of fascist ideology with new technology which proved to be so lethal.

In 1933, Hitler became chancellor of Germany. Already, in 1932, he had approached Riefenstahl asking her to make films about him

Leni
Riefenstahl

and his movement once he attained power. He believed films would play an important role his regime. In 1933, Riefenstahl made a film of the National Socialist Party congress in Nuremberg entitled *Sieg des Glaubens* (Victory of Faith). The film was withdrawn after Ernst Roehm and other leaders of the Storm Troopers were purged in 1934, and no prints are in existence. Desiring a second film about the 1934 Nuremberg Nazi Party congress, Hitler approached Riefenstahl once more. She was reluctant, not because of politics but because she wanted full artistic control. Joseph Goebbels, Hitler's propaganda minister, was extremely powerful, and like many Nazis he felt that a woman's place was in the home, not the studio. Riefenstahl accepted Hitler's offer only on the condition that she would have direct access to him and that she would exercise complete control over the project. Her decision to work for Hitler was not unusual. In the early 1930s many in Germany, and indeed throughout the world, viewed Hitler in a positive light. During the Great Depression, his economic objectives seemed commendable. Furthermore, National Socialism seemed a much preferable alternative to Bolshevism. At the time, Riefenstahl's attitudes toward Hitler mirrored those of millions of Germans, Europeans, and Americans who badly miscalculated the German leader's intentions.

If her statements are sincere, she has never grasped, and still does not grasp, the fact that she, by dedicating her life to art, has given expression to a gruesome regime and contributed to its glorification.

—American intelligence report on Leni Riefenstahl, May 30, 1945

By 1934, the Nazis had perfected the staging of large political gatherings. It is estimated that 777,000 people participated in the Nuremberg Rally that September. Riefenstahl demanded and got a crew of 120 to film this enormous event, and 30 cameras, equipped with the latest wide-angle and telescopic lenses, were procured. No expense was spared. Trenches were dug for those low-angle shots, and special camera towers were constructed. *Triumph of the Will* begins with Hitler's plane descending from the clouds on the medieval city. Scenes of joyous Germans dressed in traditional folk costumes, an aerial view of the beautiful medieval buildings, and columns of marching Storm Troopers are only a few of the powerful scenes in this two-hour movie. Riefenstahl was also innovative with the use of sound, combining the dramatic effects of Wagnerian opera with snatches from speeches. *Triumph of the Will* still rivets the viewer, even today.

Regardless of the political implications of this movie, the Berlin premiere of *Triumph of the Will* on March 29, 1935, is considered a landmark in motion-picture history. Riefenstahl's innovative techniques changed the art of filmmaking. The movie received Germany's Staatspreis in 1935, the Venice Biennale gold medal in 1936, and the Grand Prix of the Exposition Internationale des Arts et des Techniques in Paris in 1937.

After making a short film, *Tag der Freiheit* (Day of Freedom), about the Wehrmacht in 1935, Riefenstahl began a film about the 1936 Olympics, held in Germany. Her goal was to emphasize the excitement of competition and the beauty of the human body. Officially authorized by the International Olympic Committee (IOC), the film was produced by her own company and financed by the government. Despite criticism about her Nazi sympathies, critics have found little evidence that Riefenstahl infused the film with Nazi propaganda. In fact, a major highlight of the film involves the record-breaking feats of Jesse Owens, a black American athlete. Certainly no believer in "racial purity" would feature such a defeat of "Aryan" contenders. In 1948, the International Olympic Committee belatedly awarded Riefenstahl a gold medal for *Olympia*. In 1955, it was named one of the ten finest motion pictures of all time by a jury of prominent Hollywood filmmakers.

In 1940, with World War II under way, Riefenstahl began work on the movie *Tiefland* (Lowland). For some time, she had been having great difficulties with the Nazi propaganda machine, particularly with Propaganda Minister Goebbels, her nemesis. Goebbels was notorious for his numerous liaisons, especially with film stars. As Leni Riefenstahl was a film star, he considered her fair game, but she rejected his advances. When he tried to control her work, Riefenstahl went directly to Hitler. Her defiance eventually affected her film work; as well, as the war continued, fewer and fewer resources were available for making motion pictures. After 1943 and the defeat at Stalingrad, it became increasingly apparent that the Third Reich would last much less than a thousand years.

At the end of the war, Riefenstahl was briefly held prisoner by both the Americans and the French, who were certain that her role in the National Socialist Party must have been prominent. In fact she had never joined the party, and it became apparent that an overwhelming desire to make movies, not a fanatical devotion to Nazism, accounted for the works she had produced. She was blacklisted nonetheless, and, although her name had been cleared in court, her equipment and films were confiscated and not returned to her until 1954.

In 1956, Riefenstahl visited Africa with the thought of making a film. She became intrigued with the Mesakin Nuba, an isolated tribe in the Nuba Mountains in Korodfam province of southern Sudan. Six years later, in 1962, she was the first white woman to receive permission from the Sudanese government to visit the Nuba. Once there, she learned the Nuban language and customs and took motion pictures as well as still photos of the tribe. These prints were sold to magazines such as *Life, Der Stern*, and *L'Europeo* and were published in book form as *The Last of the Nuba* in 1973. In 1972, she was commissioned by the London *Sunday Times* to photograph the Olympic Games in Munich. Other assignments have included a series on Mick Jagger, the rock star. In her 90s, Riefenstahl decided to film underwater. Since she was in extremely good physical condition, she lied about her age, passing for 72, learned to scuba dive, and took several underwater photographs. In March 2000, at age 97, Riefenstahl suffered minor injuries, including a few broken ribs, when a helicopter in which she was riding to revisit the Nuba tribe crashed in the Sudan.

Leni Riefenstahl's association with the Third Reich cost her a great deal, and the debate about her motives has never ended. Some compare her with Charlie Chaplin, who was forced out of American films because of his leftist sympathies. Others believe that *Triumph of the Will* could never have been made "by anyone not fanatically at one with the events depicted." Many are appalled by the fanaticism portrayed in the Nuremberg rallies. In her defense, Riefenstahl points out that the participants had no idea that they were being photographed, as telephoto lenses were used. She simply documented the emotions felt by the crowd. In our own era, there is still uncertainty about the role played by film or taped events in shaping public consciousness. In technological terms, cameras are not a new invention, but clearly their impact on human behavior is still not fully understood.

Since it is not possible to determine Riefenstahl's motivation, one is left with her legacy, which remains enduring. Technologically, she made contributions which continue to influence motion pictures. Her creative directing and filming techniques, as well as her innovative use of soundtracks, are proof of her genius. By any assessment, Leni Riefenstahl is one of the most important filmmakers of the 20th century. As for

Triumph of the Will, this film depicts not only a Nazi rally but a beautiful centuries-old medieval city which is no more. Near the end of the war, Nuremberg was obliterated by Allied bombs.

More important, Riefenstahl's movie documents a destructively powerful political movement. There are some who deny the evils of the Third Reich, even going so far as to claim that the Holocaust was a fabrication. *Triumph of the Will* leaves no doubt about what happened in Germany. The leap from the fervor of Nuremberg to the horrors of Auschwitz is a short one. Riefenstahl's gift to the world is the documentation of a horrific episode in human history. Its viewing should be required for future generations so that they, too, will understand the meaning of the words, "Never again."

SOURCES:

"American Intelligence Report on Leni Riefenstahl—May 30th, 1945," in *Film Culture*. No. 77. Fall 1992, pp. 34–38.

Bawden, Liz-Anne. *The Oxford Companion to Film*. London: Oxford University Press, 1976.

Berg-Pan, Renata. *Leni Riefenstahl*. Boston: Twayne, 1980.

Canby, Vincent. "Leni Riefenstahl, In a Long Close-up," in *The New York Times*. October 14, 1993, pp. B1, B4.

Deutschmann, Linda. *Triumph of the Will: The Image of the Third Reich*. Wakefield, NH: Longwood Academic, 1991.

Gunton, Sharon R., ed. "Leni Riefenstahl," in *Contemporary Literary Criticism*. Vol. 16. Detroit, MI: Gale Research, 1981, pp. 519–527.

Heck-Rabi, Louise. "Leni Riefenstahl," in *International Dictionary of Films and Filmmakers*, Vol. 2: *Directors*. Edited by Nicholas Thomas. Chicago, IL: St. James Press, 1991, pp. 694–698.

Hinton, David B. *The Films of Leni Riefenstahl*. London: The Scarecrow Press, 1978.

Hitchens, Gordon. "Interview with a Legend," in *Film Comment*. Vol. 3, no. 1. Winter 1965, pp. 4–31.

Infield, Glenn B. *Leni Riefenstahl: The Fallen Film Goddess*. NY: Thomas Y. Crowell, 1976.

Leffland, Ella. "The Life but not the Times," in *Los Angeles Times*. September 26, 1993, p. 13.

Riefenstahl, Leni. *Leni Riefenstahl: A Memoir*. NY: St. Martin's Press, 1993.

Simon, John. "The Führer's Movie Maker," in *The New York Times Book Review*. September 26, 1993, pp. 1, 26–29.

Taylor, John Russell. "Leni Riefenstahl," in *Cinema: A Critical Dictionary*. Vol. II. Edited by Richard Roud. NY: Viking, 1980, pp. 866–871.

Welch, David. *Propaganda and the German Cinema, 1933–1945*. Oxford: Clarendon Press, 1983.

RELATED MEDIA:

The Wonderful, Horrible Life of Leni Riefenstahl (181 min. documentary), directed by Ray Müller, Kino Video, 1995.

John Haag,
Associate Professor of History,
University of Georgia, Atlanta, Georgia

Riepp, Mother Benedicta

(1825–1862)

*Founder of the first Benedictine convent in America.
Name variations: Mother Benedicta. Born Maria
Sybilla Riepp on June 28, 1825, in Waal in the Bavarian province of Swabia; died on March 15, 1862, in St.
Cloud, Minnesota; oldest of three children of Johann
Riepp (a glassblower) and Katharina (Mayr) Riepp.*

Mother Benedicta Riepp was born Maria
Sybilla Riepp on June 28, 1825, in Waal in the
Bavarian province of Swabia. At age 19, she entered the Benedictine Convent of Saint Walburga
in Eichstätt, where she took her final vows in
1849. She then became a teacher and mistress of
novices at the convent. In 1852, at the request of
Abbot Boniface Wimmer, monk of Metten
Abbey in Bavaria, Riepp sailed for America with
two companions to establish the first Benedictine convent there. They settled in the German
colony of St. Marys, Elk County, Pennsylvania,
the site of an existing Benedictine monastery,
and established St. Joseph's Convent and School,
of which Mother Benedicta became superior.

In the course of 15 years, nine independent
convents were established from the original community, but not without hardships. Enduring jurisdictional disputes with Abbot Wimmer and the
motherhouse, in 1859 Riepp returned to Europe
in order to secure independence for the American
convents. Although she was successful in separating from the motherhouse, the American convents
were placed under the authority of their respective
diocesan bishops. Wimmer also had Riepp removed as superior of St. Joseph's. Returning to
America, she spent her last years at convents in
Erie, Pennsylvania, and St. Cloud, Minnesota, and
died in St. Cloud on March 15, 1862. By 1964,
over 30 independent convents traced their origin
to the first convent in St. Marys.

SOURCES:

James, Edward T., ed. *Notable American Women,
1607–1950.* Cambridge, MA: The Belknap Press of
Harvard University, 1971.
McHenry, Robert, ed. *Famous American Women.* NY:
Dover, 1980.

Barbara Morgan,
Melrose, Massachusetts

Rigby, Cathy (1952—)

*American gymnast. Born on December 12, 1952, in
Long Beach, California; daughter of Anita Rigby and
Paul Rigby (an aeronautical engineer); married Tommy
Mason, in January 1973; married Tom McCoy (a producer); children: Bucky, Ryan, Theresa, and Kaitlin.*

*Earned highest U.S. scores in gymnastics at Summer Olympics in Mexico City (1968); was the first
American woman to win a medal (silver for balance
beam) in international gymnastics competition, at
World championships (1970); placed first in all-around at the World Cup gymnastics championships
(1971); holds 12 international medals, 8 of them gold;
studied acting and singing for ten years; made her theatrical debut as Dorothy in* The Wizard of Oz *(1981);
named one of America's Most Influential Women in
Sports by ABC-TV's "Wide World of Sports" (1987);
named Mother of the Year (1992); with husband, became executive producer of the McCoy-Rigby Series
at the La Mirada Theater for the Performing Arts in
La Mirada, California (1994); began touring the
country and returned to Broadway with* Peter Pan
(1998), earning a Tony nomination for her performance; toured with Annie Get Your Gun *(1999).*

Cathy Rigby came into the world two
months premature and weighing less than four
pounds, but she was destined to leave her mark.
With weak lungs that were repeatedly attacked
by infection, she spent her first five years in and
out of hospitals. But Cathy's mother **Anita
Rigby**, who used crutches as a result of polio,
was an inspiration to her five children, and
Cathy was soon rollerskating and riding a bike.
Enrolled in a trampoline class, she mastered the
backflip the first night. In 1963, the 11-year-old
joined the Southern California Acrobatic Team,
organized by Bud Marquette. Soon she was determined to become a world-class competitor. In
1967, Rigby placed second in her age group at
her first national meet in Chicago. A year later,
she was a member of the U.S. Olympic gymnastics team and headed for Mexico City. Placing
seventh in the balance beam and 16th in all-around scoring, Rigby had the best finish ever
achieved by an American gymnast.

Once home, Rigby was determined to do
even better in the 1972 Games, spending hours
working on innovative jumps, flips and turns. In
1970, with scores of 9.9 and 9.8, she won a silver
medal on the balance beam at the World championship games in Lyubliana, Yugoslavia, becoming the first American woman to win a medal in
international competition. A year later, she won
a gold medal at the Miami World Cup Gymnastics championships, scoring 38.35 out of a possible 40 points and capturing the women's events.

But Rigby's little girl image was beginning to
chafe. She was now 19, secretly dating Tommy
Mason, trying to maintain her weight of 93
pounds, and tired of pigtails. "I would like to let

my hair grow," she complained, "but Bud wouldn't let me. . . . He doesn't want me to grow up." Years later, she would reveal that she had also been battling anorexia and bulimia for 12 years and had gone into cardiac arrest twice because of it. When *Christy Henrich, a 22-year-old American gymnast, died of multiple organ failure after her weight plummeted to 47 pounds in 1994, Rigby burst into tears at the news. "I felt frustrated and angry," she said. "The sport is fertile ground for anorexia." *Nadia Comaneci has admitted succumbing to the same eating disorder.

Finding it difficult to concentrate, Rigby paid for lapses with injuries. She was at the top of women's gymnastics in America when she fell and fractured her toe at the U.S. Olympic trials in May 1972. Then, while she was struggling through the floor exercise the following day, the broken toe caused her to injure her ankle, tearing ligaments on a difficult flip combination. Although Rigby had to withdraw from the competition, she was made a member of the Olympic team.

Though few realized it at the time, the 1972 Olympic Games in Munich were a turning point for American gymnasts. *Olga Korbut was the star of the Games and Americans were enthralled. The U.S. women's team finished fourth in team competition. This dramatic improvement of the U.S. team, led by Rigby who placed seventh on the balance beam and tenth overall, went almost unnoticed by the press and public who were riveted by Korbut's every leap and vault. Rigby retired from gymnastics in 1973 and opened two gymnastic clubs in Anaheim and Mission Viejo, California. She also went on to a career on the stage, having studied acting and voice for ten years. She has starred in *The Wizard of Oz*, *Paint Your Wagon*, *Meet Me in St. Louis*, and *Annie Get Your Gun*, and was nominated for a Tony award for her performance in *Peter Pan*. She and her second husband Tim McCoy are executive producers of the McCoy-Rigby Series at the La Mirada Theater for the Performing Arts in La Mirada, California.

SOURCES:

Hollander, Phyllis. *100 Greatest Women in Sports*. NY: Grosset & Dunlap, 1976.

Jacobs, Linda. *Cathy Rigby: On the Beam*. St. Paul, MN: EMC, 1975.

Sabine, Francene. *Women Who Win*. NY: Random House, 1975.

Woolum, Janet. *Outstanding Women Athletes: Who They Are and How They Influenced Sports in America*. Phoenix, AZ: Oryx, 1992.

RELATED MEDIA:

Faces of Recovery, an award-winning video on eating disorders, produced by McCoy-Rigby Entertainment.

Karin L. Haag,
freelance writer, Athens, Georgia

Cathy
Rigby

Rigby, Elizabeth (1809–1893).

See Eastlake, Elizabeth.

Riggin, Aileen (1906—)

American Olympic diver and swimmer. Name variations: Aileen Riggin Soule. Born Aileen Riggin in Newport, Rhode Island, on May 2, 1906; married Dwight D. Young (a doctor injured in World War II), in 1924 (died); married Howard Soule.

Won the Olympic gold medal in women's springboard diving in Antwerp (1920); won the Olympic bronze in 100-meter backstroke and silver in springboard in Paris (1924).

A few days after her 14th birthday, in the 1920 Olympic Games held at Antwerp, Belgium, Aileen Riggin won the first women's springboard title, setting a 32-year pattern for the U.S. springboard diving team. She would hold the record as the youngest to win a gold medal in springboard until 13-year-old *Marjorie Gestring of the U.S.

Aileen Riggin
(left)

won the competition in 1936. In 1924 in the Paris Olympics, Riggin became the only competitor to win both swimming and diving medals by coming in third in the 100-meter backstroke and second in the springboard. **Sybil Bauer** of the U.S. took the gold in the backstroke, while teammate ***Elizabeth Becker-Pinkston** won the springboard gold medal.

In 1984, when an Olympic official telephoned 78-year-old Riggin at her home in Hawaii to invite her to the Los Angeles Games, he politely inquired if she could still walk. Well, yes, she said, in fact she was still swimming. In 1991, Riggin set six world records in freestyle and backstroke sprints in the World Masters for those in her age group: swimmers who were 85 to 89 years old.

Riggs, Betty (1899–1975).
See Brent, Evelyn.

Riguntha (fl. 580s)
Frankish princess. Flourished in the 580s; daughter of *Fredegund (c. 547–597) and Chilperic I, king of Soissons (r. 561–584), king of the Franks (r. 561–584); betrothed to the Visigothic prince Reccared.

Rikisa.
Variant of Richizza.

Riley, Corinne Boyd (1893–1979)
American U.S. congressional representative. Born Corinne Boyd on July 4, 1893, in Piedmont, Greenville County, South Carolina; died on April 12, 1979, in Sumter, South Carolina; graduated from Converse College, Spartanburg, South Carolina, 1915; married John Jacob Riley (1895–1962, a U.S. congressional representative).

Taught in secondary schools in South Carolina (1915–37); served as field representative, South Carolina State Text Book Commission (1938–42); was associated with Civilian Personnel Office, Shaw Air Force Base, Sumter, South Carolina (1942–44); elected as a Democrat to the 87th Congress, by special election (1962).

Corinne Riley was born Corinne Boyd in Piedmont, Greenville County, South Carolina, in 1893. She attended public schools and graduated from Converse College in Spartanburg, South Carolina, in 1915. Riley then became a teacher, enjoying a career in South Carolina's secondary schools until 1937. A field representative for the South Carolina State Text Book Commission until not long after the United States entered World War II, Riley spent most of the war working with the Civilian Personnel Office at Shaw Air Force Base in Sumter, South Carolina.

Riley married a fellow South Carolinian, John Jacob Riley, a World War I veteran who served in the House of Representatives from 1945 to 1949 and again from 1951. After her husband's death on New Year's Day, 1962, Riley was urged by both the Democratic and Republican committees from South Carolina to run for the remainder of his term representing the Second Congressional District. Riley was reluctant at first, but agreed to run before the end of January, defeating **Martha T. Fitzgerald**—an 11-term member of the South Carolina House of Representatives—in the primary. She was elected unopposed as a Democrat to the 87th Congress by a special election, promising to pursue her husband's conservative agenda.

Assigned a seat on the Committee on Science and Astronautics, Riley introduced a bill authorizing the General Services Administration to transfer surplus property to the Aiken Historical Society in South Carolina, for use as a historical monument. Aiming to benefit an educational television station in her district, Riley also used her short time in Congress to support legislation requiring both ultra- and high-frequency channels on all television sets. Riley served from April 1962 until January 1963, and did not seek reelection to the 88th Congress. After her public service ended, Riley continued to reside in Sumter, South Carolina, where she died in 1979.

SOURCES:

Office of the Historian. *Women In Congress, 1917–1990.* Commission on the Bicentenary of the U.S. House of Representatives, 1991.

Paula Morris, D.Phil.,
Brooklyn, New York

Riley, Dawn (1964—)

American sailor who became the first woman to captain and manage a boat in the America's Cup. Born in 1964 in Michigan; graduated from Michigan State University.

Sailed with first all-women's Whitbread Round the World Race team (1989); became first woman invited to try out for an America's Cup team (1991); won first place in Santa Maria Cup, Baltimore, Maryland, and Women's Cup, Portofino, Italy (1992); was team captain of the first all-women's crew in the America's Cup (1995); set a record in the 153-mile Newport-to-New-York Race (1997); named Rolex Yachtswoman of the Year (1999); became first woman to manage and captain an America's Cup team (2000).

Born in Michigan in 1964, Dawn Riley grew up with saltwater in her veins and an education in sailing that stretched back three generations. Her great-grandfather was a sail-maker who passed on his knowledge of sailing to his daughter, Riley's grandmother. She in turn passed the love of sailing to her son Chuck, who continued the tradition with his daughter Dawn. At 13, Dawn had the opportunity of a lifetime when her family took a year and sailed their 36-foot wooden boat down the Eastern Seaboard to Grenada.

After high school, Riley entered Michigan State University as an advertising major, but stayed with her first love as she captained the women's sailing team for the school. Unable to obtain work in advertising after her graduation, she moved to Florida and took work as the only female crew member on a Frers 45. Although she faced stiff competition and sometimes unkind remarks from her male counterparts, she did not let the comments take her away from the job she signed on for, and that year the boat won its class in competition.

In 1989, Riley was part of an all-female Whitbread Round the World team organized

by British sailor **Tracy Edwards**. Edwards' boat, *Maiden*, completed the difficult nine-month ordeal, sailing 32,000 miles and capturing second place. In 1991, Bill Koch invited Riley to try out for his *America³* team in the America's Cup race; she became the first woman invited to try out with an otherwise all-male America's Cup team. Along with the opportunity to display her skills in a race of this magnitude, Riley suddenly found other women looking to her to set the standards for them to follow. Through this experience she continued to build her reputation as a sailor, and in 1993 she was asked to take over the skipper position in an all-woman crew that had already begun the Whitbread Round the World Race. The race seemed cursed with a sometimes incompetent crew, financial woes, and a boat that suffered structural difficulties midway. She completed the race, but counted it as one of her most exhausting experiences.

Home for a short time, Riley faced a challenging and ultimately disappointing race when Koch asked her to lead an all-female crew in the 1995 America's Cup. This was the first all-female crew in the history of the race, which began in 1851, and Riley and her crew

Corinne Boyd Riley

trained for months with single-minded determination on their *America³* yacht. (*See America³.*) Although they had to switch to a different yacht, *Mighty Mary*, in the midst of the semifinals, and tactician **Jennifer Isler** was replaced by a male tactician with greater experience (a move Riley heartily endorsed in hopes of winning), their boat was fast and the crew was highly competitive. In the semifinals, Riley and her crew handily beat their closest competitor, Dennis Conner, only to find as they pulled into the dock that the San Diego Yacht Club had ordered a rematch. Faced with television cameras, Riley swore a blue streak instead of crying. The rematch generated much controversy and discussion that was only heightened when Conner's boat *Stars & Stripes* went on to lose the America's Cup to a New Zealand boat. Nonetheless, Riley's participation in the race and her handling of the boat and the team had changed the face of competitive sailing forever. In the three years after the boat's first sailing, there were 25–30% more women on boats than ever before.

Riley maintained her competitive edge by honing her skills at every opportunity. In June 1997, she and her crew set a new record in the 153-mile Newport-to-New-York Race, finishing in 13 hours and 39 minutes. However, Riley had her sights set on even bigger goals: designing and captaining her own skipper, *America True*, for the year 2000 America's Cup. Racing in the America's Cup is enormously expensive; boats are built and owned by syndicates, and with *America True* Riley became the first woman head (or CEO, as they are called) of an America's Cup syndicate. Beyond the challenge of managing over 100 employees and volunteers, Riley successfully took on the role of publicist to find corporate sponsors for the $24 million she needed. For once, her gender worked to her advantage, as companies were eager to fund women sailors. She was aided in the building of her boat by Koch, who allowed her access to the research he used in the building of *Mighty Mary*. Riley herself took no notice of gender in putting together a crack sailing team, concerned only with finding the best individual for each job. In

Dawn Riley

February 2000, she became the first woman to captain and manage a boat in the America's Cup. *America True* performed well in the first legs of the race in New Zealand, but opted not to continue when faced with particularly bad weather in a harbor notorious for its tricky winds. New Zealand's *Black Magic* again captured the Cup; shortly thereafter, Riley announced her intentions of racing *America True* in the next America's Cup. "If you can dream it," she says, "you can do it."

SOURCES AND SUGGESTED READING:

Newsday. February 22, 1998, p. C33.

Riley, Dawn, with Cynthia Flanagan Goss. *Taking the Helm.* Boston, MA: Little, Brown, 1995.

"Sailor of the Century," in *Condé Nast Sports for Women.* December 1997.

Judith C. Reveal,
freelance writer, Greensboro, Maryland

Riley, Mary Velasquez (1908–1987)

First female Apache tribal council leader. Born in 1908; died in 1987.

Born in 1908, Mary Velasquez Riley was raised in Arizona on the White Mountain Apache Reservation, and in 1958 became the first woman elected to the tribal council. She remained in a leadership role for the next 20 years, promoting economic development and independence. Her concern for the destiny of her tribe spurred her to lobby Congress for support of the tribe's efforts to maintain its self-respect and heritage. As a result, the Apaches developed the Sunrise Ski Resort and the Fort Apache Timber Company. Both enterprises were wholly owned and operated by the tribe, and because of Riley's shrewd sense of business management both also became multimillion-dollar entities. The tribe acknowledged her tremendous contribution by naming the Mary V. Riley Tribal Educational Center in Whiteriver, Arizona, in her honor. She died in 1987.

Judith C. Reveal,
freelance writer, Greensboro, Maryland

Rimini, Francesca da (d. 1285?).

See Francesca da Rimini.

Rimskaya-Korsakova, Yulia (1878–1942).

See Veysberg, Yuliya Lazarevna.

Rina.

Variant of Catherine or Katherine.

Rincón de Gautier, Felisa (1897–1994).

See Gautier, Felisa Rincón de.

Rind, Clementina (c. 1740–1774)

American newspaper publisher and editor. Born around 1740, possibly in Maryland; died in 1774 in Williamsburg, Virginia; married William Rind (a printer), between 1758 and 1765 (died 1773); children: four sons and one daughter.

The exact date and location of Clementina Rind's birth remain unclear, but there is no mystery about her impact on the role of women in publishing in colonial America. Sometime between 1758 and 1765, she married printer William Rind, who worked on the *Maryland Gazette.* When the paper's partners protested the Stamp Act of 1765 by suspending publication of the *Gazette*, William was encouraged by a group of liberals to move his family to Williamsburg, Virginia, and there publish a "free paper."

On May 16, 1766, the *Virginia Gazette* was in business, and its motto "Open to ALL PARTIES, but Influenced by NONE" was taken seriously by both publisher and readers. When

Mary Velasquez Riley

William died in August 1773, Clementina assumed the role of editor and publisher, managing the press from the back of her brick house on behalf of her five small children. The extended family and staff included John Pinkney, a relative, apprentice Isaac Collins, and a slave called Dick.

Rind maintained the integrity of the newspaper, carefully following the design set forth by her husband. The news covered both national and international events as well as shipping news. Rind supplemented, as needed, with excerpts from her readers' correspondence, including essays, articles and poems. Many of her female readers were responsible for the submissions which Rind printed, resulting in a strong female point of view reflected in the paper. The *Virginia Gazette* was both erudite and eclectic in its subject matter, and through her articles and editorials Rind showed an interest in news on the scientific and educational fronts. She was especially interested in educational issues that related to the College of William and Mary.

The paper was so successful that Rind was able to expand it and, within six months of assuming responsibility as editor, was able to purchase "an elegant set of types from London." The House of Burgesses quickly appointed her public printer and continued to support her with public business, much to the dismay of her competitors.

In August 1774, both her health and her business suffered. Though payments due to her went unpaid, she remained confident that this was a short-term situation which would change to her advantage. Within a month, however, she died. Rind had managed the paper only from August 1773 until September 25, 1774, but she had made an impression on the people of Williamsburg and was missed by her many patrons, who prepared poetic eulogies in her memory. She is believed to have been buried next to her husband at Bruton Parish Church. Rind left no will, and her children were cared for by John Pinkney and the society of Freemasons, of which William Rind had been a member.

SOURCES:

James, Edward T., ed. *Notable American Women, 1607–1950.* Cambridge, MA: The Belknap Press of Harvard University Press, 1971.

Judith C. Reveal,
freelance writer, Greensboro, Maryland

Rinehart, Mary Roberts

(1876–1958)

American novelist and war correspondent. Born Mary Roberts on August 12, 1876, in Pittsburgh, Pennsylvania; died on September 22, 1958, in Brooklyn, New York; daughter of Thomas Beveridge Roberts (a sewing machine salesman) and Cornelia (Grilleland) Roberts; graduated from Pittsburgh Training School for Nurses, 1896; married Stanley M. Rinehart (a surgeon), in April 1896 (died 1932); children: Stanley, Jr.; Alan; Frederick.

Was the first American correspondent to report from the front lines during World War I (1915); was the first reporter to interview England's Queen Mary of Teck (1915).

Selected writings: The Circular Staircase (1908); The Man in Lower Ten (1909); When a Man Marries (1909); The Window at the White Cat (1910); The Amazing Adventures of Letitia Carberry (1911); The Case of Jennie Brice (1913); The After House (1914); Kings, Queens and Pawns (1915); Tish (1916); Bab: A Sub-Deb (1917); The Amazing Interlude (1918); Dangerous Days (1919); A Poor Wise Man (1920); Sight Unseen and the Confession (1921); The Red Lamp (1925); Tish Plays the Game (1926); Lost Ecstasy (1927); This Strange Adventure (1929); The Door (1930); My Story (autobiography, 1931); Miss Pinkerton (1932); The Album (1933); The Doctor (1936); Tish Marches On (1937); The Wall (1938); The Great Mistake (1940); Haunted Lady (1942); The Yellow Room (1945); Episode of the Wandering Knife (1950); The Swimming Pool (1952); The Frightened Wife and Other Murder Stories (1953).

Born Mary Roberts on August 12, 1876, in Pittsburgh, Pennsylvania, Mary Roberts Rinehart was the older of two daughters of **Cornelia Grilleland Roberts** and Thomas Beveridge Roberts. Although her childhood was not overtly unhappy, Mary grew up with the specter of poverty and a vengeful God, the latter caused by her parents' religious conviction which focused on the Old Testament. This childhood sense of danger at her doorstep would later color the mystery novels for which she became famous. Genuine tragedy struck the household when Thomas committed suicide in 1895.

Rinehart graduated from the Pittsburgh Training School for Nurses the following year, and married Stanley M. Rinehart, a young surgeon, in April 1896. The Rineharts immediately started a family, and she was the mother of three boys by the time she was 25. In 1903, the family experienced a crisis that would ultimately change Rinehart's life. A stock-market crash left them $12,000 in debt, and Rinehart took the reins to change their fortunes. She submitted a short story to *Munsey's Magazine* and received

$34 in payment. Encouraged by this success, she sold 45 more short stories in the course of one year, earning $1,800.

Rinehart's first full-length novel, *The Circular Staircase*, was published in 1908. A fu-

sion of the detective story with the humorous novel, this book was the prototype of nearly all the mysteries she would later write. While it was not an instant success, it received a warm critical reception, and kept selling; eventually, *The Circular Staircase* became an all-time bestseller, with sales topping 800,000 by the mid-1950s. Her second novel, *The Man in Lower Ten*, was published the following year to rapid success. It became the first detective novel by an American writer to make the bestseller list, and for years thereafter, so the story goes, railroad passengers avoided sleeping in the "lower 10" berth. Rinehart's disparate fans included Herbert Hoover, Theodore Roosevelt, and *Gertrude Stein.

Rinehart cast a long shadow over the development of 20th-century detective fiction, both in character types and in matters of plot. Her stories are generally told by lively, intelligent, unmarried women in their middle years whose intuitive hunches mesh well with the more systematic work of an official detective. One of her most enduringly popular creations, Letitia Carberry—a middle-aged amateur detective otherwise known as Tish—is a prime example of a Rinehart heroine. Often considered a more daring version of *Agatha Christie's Miss Marple, she first made her literary appearance as part of a series of short stories published in the *Saturday Evening Post* (later collected in the 1911 volume *The Amazing Adventures of Letitia Carberry*). So delighted were the *Post's* editors with Rinehart's work that they personally solicited more Tish stories from her. Another distinguishing characteristic of Rinehart's mysteries is her deviation from the typical "one-murder" story, in which the entire novel is constructed around the solving of a single crime. Instead, the murderers in her books kill a number of victims, some of whom are known to the narrator, throughout the course of the story, and often try to kill the narrator herself.

Critics of Rinehart's mysteries point to her devotion to the "Had I But Known" device (of which she was the prime exemplar), typified in a phrase such as "Four lives might have been spared if I had only remembered." Rinehart also received criticism for relying extensively on improbable coincidences, for prolonging the narrative by withholding information, and for the inclusion of romantic subplots that had little to do with the action, but she was praised for her tightly constructed mysteries, brisk pacing, and comic relief. In addition, one of her novels actually solved a crime: *The After House* (1914), which she based on the true story of several murders that had been committed on a yacht at sea, caused that case to be reopened, an innocent man to be released after nearly 20 years in prison, and the real murderer (the one she had fingered in her novel) to be arrested and convicted.

While she is remembered primarily for her mysteries, Rinehart also wrote numerous romance novels, and these constituted eight of her eleven bestsellers. Most of these stuck closely to society's mores; her women narrators, usually married, fell in love with another man but in the end resigned themselves to their marriages. Male narrators, more often than not, were rescuing the objects of their affections from bad engagements. Rinehart also wrote several plays with Avery Hopwood, including *Seven Days* (1909) and *The Bat* (1920), a dramatization of *The Circular Staircase*. A story about the eerie experiences of a woman mystery writer and her maid in a rented mansion, *The Bat* proved highly successful; it was filmed in 1915, 1927, and 1930, made for television starring *ZaSu Pitts in 1953, and again adapted as a movie in 1959, starring *Agnes Moorehead and Vincent Price.

In addition to her fiction writing, Rinehart achieved no small amount of fame during World War I as the first American correspondent to report from the front lines. Although most newspaper editors at this time refused to sign women as war correspondents, Rinehart's success allowed her to demand, and receive, a considerable amount of leeway from her editors at the *Saturday Evening Post*. They recognized that they needed her stories to fuel sales, and she made it clear that she did not intend to let what then seemed the single biggest event of the century go by unattended. The *Post* therefore established her as an official foreign correspondent, with credentials, an expense account, and letters of introduction.

Rinehart found her nursing experience beneficial in her reports on the war. When the British authorities refused to allow correspondents access to the front, Rinehart approached the Belgian Red Cross and convinced them that, with her nursing background, she could aptly describe to her American readers the Belgian soldiers' plight. She was three weeks at the front before any other correspondents were allowed to make the journey. Her work at the front lines gave her insight and opportunities that other reporters missed. Though Rinehart was the first to write of the use of poison gas by the Germans, the *Post*, obedient to America's neutral status, refused to print the story; another reporter's news of poison gas was soon published in a New York newspaper. On her return to London, she was granted an exclusive interview with England's Queen *Mary of Teck, who expressed special concern for the nursing of the many wounded soldiers, and another with Winston Churchill, who tried to limit his conversations with reporters. Rinehart then went home to America, but she was determined to return to Europe as a nurse should the United States become involved. Ironically, when America finally entered the war, the War Department refused Rinehart permission to travel. She found a way around this problem by reporting on conditions at local training camps. Secretary of War Newton D. Baker was so impressed with her accounts that in 1918 he sent her to France to advise the War Department as to what the troops at the front required. Rinehart was one of the few women allowed to cover the disarmament conference. To her dismay, she was excluded from all male circles and found no outlet where she could compare notes. This experience resulted in her participation in several suffragist movements in Chicago and Pittsburgh. She drew upon many of her experiences during this time to write several books, most notably *Kings, Queens and Pawns* (1915), *Bab: A Sub-Deb* (1917), *The Amazing Interlude* (1918), and *Dangerous Days* (1919). Her heroines in these books always fulfilled what she saw as the task of women during war: service.

Tragedy dogged Rinehart throughout her life. Her husband died in 1932; in 1947, her cook attempted to kill her; and in 1948, her home in Bar Harbor, Maine, was destroyed by fire. Her mother's death after being scalded by boiling water, and Rinehart's own troubles with ill health and accidents, cemented her understanding of the uncertainty of life. She underwent surgery for breast cancer and shared that experience with her readers in "I Had Cancer," an article published in *Ladies' Home Journal* in July 1947. As with her other life experiences, Rinehart used these misfortunes as fodder for her writing and had published her autobiography, *My Story*, in 1931.

Throughout her writing life, Rinehart produced over 60 books—many for the publishing house Farrar & Rinehart, which was established by her sons. By some accounts she was on the bestseller list more often and for a longer time than any other American author. Among the awards she received were an honorary doctorate from George Washington University in 1923, and the Mystery Writers of America Special Award in 1953. Rinehart died in her sleep in New York on September 22, 1958. At the time, her books had sold over 10 million copies.

SOURCES:

Contemporary Authors. Vols. 108, 166. Detroit, MI: Gale Research, 1983, 1999.

Edwards, Julia. *Women of the World: The Great Foreign Correspondents*. Boston, MA: Houghton Mifflin, 1988.

Kunitz, Stanley J., and Howard Haycraft, eds. *Twentieth Century Authors*. NY: H.W. Wilson, 1942.

McHenry, Robert, ed. *Famous American Women*. NY: Dover, 1980.

Publishers Weekly. March 21, 1994, p. 59.

Read, Phyllis J., and Bernard L. Witlieb. *The Book of Women's Firsts*. NY: Random House, 1992.

Sicherman, Barbara, and Carol Hurd Green, eds. *Notable American Women: The Modern Period*. Cambridge, MA: The Belknap Press of Harvard University, 1980.

Twentieth-Century Literary Criticism. Vol. 52. Detroit, MI: Gale Research, 1994.

SUGGESTED READING:

MacLeod, Charlotte. *Had She But Known: A Biography of Mary Roberts Rinehart*. NY: Mysterious Press, 1994.

Judith C. Reveal,
freelance writer, Greensboro, Maryland

Ringart (fl. 822–825)

Queen of Aquitaine. Flourished from 822 to 825; daughter of Theutbert, count of Madrie; married Pepin I (797–838), king of Aquitaine (r. 814–838), in 822; children: Pepin II (b. 823), king of Aquitaine; Charles (b. around 825), archbishop of Mainz.

Rinser, Luise (1911—)

German novelist, short-story writer, diarist and essayist. Born in 1911; daughter of devout Catholics; studied psychology and became a teacher.

Luise Rinser's largely autobiographical writings mirror the tragedy of Germany in the 20th century. Her first book, *Die gläsernen Ringe* (The Glass Rings, 1940), concerns a woman growing up under National Socialism. Though a great success in 1941, the second edition was banned. Arrested by the Nazis in October 1944 on charges of high treason and disruption of the military, Rinser survived only because the documentary evidence against her was burned in an air raid, but she spent the last months of World War II in prison. After the war, she became one of the best-known German writers of the postwar period, publishing such works as *Gefängnis-Tagebuch* (Prison Diary, 1946), *Hochebene* (High Plateau, 1948), *Die Stärkeren* (Those Who Are Stronger, 1948), and the highly acclaimed *Jan Lobel aus Warschau* (Jan Lobel from Warsaw) and *Mite des Lebens* (Middle of Life, 1950). She published her autobiography, *Wolf umarmen* (Embracing the Wolf), in 1981.

SUGGESTED READING:

Frederiksen, Elke. "Luise Rinser's Autobiographical Prose: Political Engagement and Feminist Awareness," in *Faith of a (Woman) Writer*. Westport, CT: Greenwood Press, 1988, pp. 165–171.

Hinze, Diana Orendi. "The Case of Luise Rinser: A Past That Will Not Die," in Elaine Martin, ed. *Gender, Patriarchy, and Fascism in the Third Reich: The Response of Women Writers*. Detroit, MI: Wayne State University Press, 1993, pp. 143–168.

John Haag,
Athens, Georgia

Rinshi (fl. 900s)

Japanese royal. Flourished in the 900s; married Fujiwara no Michinaga (966–1028, head of the famous Fujiwara family during their period of greatest power and influence), in 987; children: daughters *Shoshi (fl. 990–1010), Kenshi, Ishi, and Kishi, and son Yorimichi (who became emperor).

In 987, Fujiwara no Michinaga took Rinshi, the daughter of a high-ranking court official, as his principal wife, and their union proved particularly fruitful. In addition to sons, Rinshi had several daughters, whom Michinaga was able to make good use of in improving his own position. As was the custom of the times, Michinaga eventually took a secondary wife or consort, a woman by the name of **Meishi**. Meishi had three children, daughter **Kanshi** and sons Yorimune and Yoshinobu.

Riperton, Minnie (1947–1979)

African-American singer. Name variations: (pseudonym) Andrea Davis; Minnie Riperton Rudolph. Born in Chicago, Illinois, on November 8, 1947 (some sources cite 1948); died on July 12, 1979, in Los Angeles, California; married Richard (Dicky) Rudolph (a musician and producer); children: Marc; Maya.

Had #1 hit with "Loving You" (1974); received an award for courage and public service from President Jimmy Carter (1977); became first African-American woman named national educational chair of the American Cancer Society (1978).

Selected albums: Come to My Garden *(1970);* Perfect Angel *(1974);* Adventures in Paradise *(1975);* Stay in Love *(1977);* Minnie *(1979);* Love Lives Forever *(1980).*

Gifted with a five-octave voice, Minnie Riperton was born in Chicago on November 8, 1947, and began studying voice, opera, and ballet at age ten. Only four years later, she joined an all-girl group called the Gems, and started working at Chicago's Chess Records as a receptionist. During this time, she lent her voice as a backup singer for such famous artists as **Etta James** and Johnny Nash. In the mid-1960s, Riperton became the lead singer of a soul group, the Rotary Connection, which released a number of albums and opened for such acts as Jefferson Airplane, Sly and the Family Stone, ***Janis Joplin**, and the Rolling Stones. She also recorded as a solo artist under the name Andrea Davis. She released her first album under her own name, *Come to My Garden*, in 1970. By the following year, however, having grown weary of the music business, she temporarily retired.

Riperton returned to music by touring as a backup singer for artists including **Roberta Flack** and Quincy Jones, and in 1973 signed with Epic Records. She found fame with the release of her album *Perfect Angel*, produced by legendary singer and musician Stevie Wonder, the following year. The album became an instant smash, propelled by the international hit single "Loving You," which reached the top of the charts in both America and England. Co-written by Riperton and her husband Dicky Rudolph, the song made full use of her amazing vocal range. She often used her voice instrumentally, creating a sound that fused pop, soul, and jazz. (In the 1990s, "Loving You" would be used in television commercials for Burger King.)

Riperton released two more albums for Epic, *Adventures in Paradise* (1975), which reached the Top 20, and *Stay in Love* (1977). However, her career slowed significantly when she was diagnosed with breast cancer and had a mastectomy at age 29. Riperton did not hide her fight with cancer, which at the time was still often considered an improper subject for discussion, but toured the talk-show circuit and candidly told other women about her surgery and treatment. In 1977, President Jimmy Carter presented her with an award for her bravery and dedication to public awareness of breast cancer. The following year, the American Cancer Society named her its national educational chair—the first African-American woman ever chosen for this position.

Despite her illness, Riperton continued making music. She signed with Capitol Records and in April 1979 released the album *Minnie*, which included the hit singles "Memory Lane" and "Lovers and Friends." Only a few months later, on July 12, 1979, Riperton lost her battle with cancer. In 1980, Capitol posthumously released her last album, *Love Lives Forever*. Still much admired by a select audience, Riperton is also credited with influencing the next generation of women singers (such as **Whitney Houston** and **Mariah Carey**) who use their wide-ranging voices instrumentally.

SOURCES:

Bane, Michael. *Who's Who in Rock.* NY: Everest House, 1981.

Clarke, Donald, ed. *The Penguin Encyclopedia of Popular Music.* NY: Viking, 1989.

Hardy, Phil, and Dave Laing. *Encyclopedia of Rock.* NY: Schirmer Books, 1988.

Hine, Darlene Clark, ed. *Black Women in America: An Historical Encyclopedia.* Brooklyn, NY: Carlson, 1993.

The New York Times Biographical Service. July 1979, p. 980.

Nite, Norm N. *Rock On.* Vol. 2. NY: Thomas Y. Crowell, 1978.

People Weekly. June 17, 1996.

Ann M. Schwalboski,
teacher and writing specialist,
University of Wisconsin-Baraboo/Sauk County

Ripley, Martha Rogers (1843–1912)

American physician and suffragist. Born Martha George Rogers in Lowell, Vermont, on November 30, 1843; died on April 18, 1912, in Minneapolis, Minnesota; daughter of Francis Rogers and Esther Ann (George) Rogers; attended Lansing High School; graduated from Boston University Medical School, 1883; married William Warren Ripley, on June 25, 1867; children: Abigail Louise; Clara Esther; Edna May.

Elected president of the Minnesota Woman Suffrage Association (mid-1880s); founded the Maternity Hospital, a home for unwed mothers, in Minneapolis, Minnesota (1887).

In 1939, a memorial plaque was placed in the Minnesota State Capitol's rotunda to honor "a champion of righteousness and justice," Martha Rogers Ripley. Born Martha George Rogers in Lowell, Vermont, in 1843, she moved with her parents to Iowa where the family—which eventually included four younger siblings—farmed and helped escaped slaves. Martha attended Lansing High School, but never graduated. Although she was employed as a teacher, she wanted to work in the field of medicine. Too young to be accepted for service as a nurse during the Civil War, she instead contributed to the war effort by raising money for the U.S. Sanitary Commission.

In June 1867, Ripley married William Warren Ripley, a rancher originally from Massachusetts, and shortly thereafter they moved to Middleton, Massachusetts, where William operated a saw mill. After the birth of her three daughters, Ripley became a police matron, but an epidemic of illnesses that swept through the area prompted her to act on her medical aspirations. In 1883, she earned an M.D. from Boston University Medical

School (from which one of her sisters had also graduated). This degree proved pivotal to her family's economic survival when a mill accident left her husband severely injured, and he was unable to work. The Ripleys moved close to relatives in Minneapolis, Minnesota, where Martha supported the family by opening a medical practice. Her husband drove the buggy for her when she made house calls at night. As a specialist in obstetrics and children's diseases, Ripley fought to decrease the infant mortality rate. The crowning achievement of her successful practice was her establishment of the Maternity Hospital. Always demonstrating an advanced social consciousness in her work, Ripley initially established the hospital as a home for three unwed mothers in 1886. It quickly became evident that larger facilities were needed, and the permanent facility opened a year later. The hospital provided medical as well as social care for women regardless of economic need or marital status, and included indigent infants in its humanitarian mission. Ripley's prominent place in society was augmented by her position as professor of children's diseases at the Homeopathic Medical College, and her lecture tours in medical schools in nearby states.

Beyond acting as an advocate for women's health, Ripley was a dedicated activist in the cause for women's rights. She had joined women's suffrage groups at both the state and regional levels back in Massachusetts in 1875, working with *Lucy Stone and her husband Henry B. Blackwell (brother of *Elizabeth Blackwell), and after the family's move to Minneapolis she quickly won election as president of the Minnesota Woman Suffrage Association. She pushed for female representation on the city school board and demanded reforms within the schools, which she criticized for placing too heavy a burden on students. Ripley also joined in the effort to change the legal age of consent from 10 years to 18. Concerned about the impact of urban growth on public health, she promoted the incineration of garbage, pure water, better quarantine facilities, playgrounds, and the cremation of the dead.

Ripley's work came to an end when she died of a heart condition on April 18, 1912, after an illness brought on by exposure to harsh weather. Her body was cremated and her ashes added to the cornerstone of a Maternity Hospital building erected in her honor.

SOURCES:

James, Edward T., ed. *Notable American Women, 1607–1950.* Cambridge, MA: The Belknap Press of Harvard University, 1971.

Ann M. Schwalboski,
teacher and writing specialist,
University of Wisconsin-Baraboo/Sauk County

Ripley, Sarah Alden (1793–1867)

American scholar and teacher. Name variations: Sarah Alden Bradford Ripley. Born Sarah Alden Bradford in Boston, Massachusetts, on July 31, 1793; died in Concord, Massachusetts, on July 26, 1867; daughter of Gamaliel Bradford III (a prison warden and reformer) and Elizabeth (Hickling) Bradford; married Samuel Ripley (a minister), on October 6, 1818 (died 1847); children: Elizabeth; Mary Emerson; Christopher Gore; Phebe Bliss; Ezra; Ann Dunkin; Sophia Bradford; one who died young.

Born in 1793 in Boston, Massachusetts, Sarah Alden Ripley was one of nine children of Gamaliel Bradford III and **Elizabeth Hickling Bradford**. She began her education during visits to her grandfather's home in Duxbury, Massachusetts, where she studied with Dr. John Allyn, a minister who did not share the common belief that only boys should be educated. In Boston, she continued her studies in Greek and Latin with the help of a man named Cummings; her father, a progressive warden at Charlestown State Prison and a descendant of *Priscilla Alden, taught her French and Italian. Her mother, poor in health, often left the care of the other children to Sarah, although she still found time to read Sophocles, Theocritus, Tacitus and Seneca.

In 1809, at age 16, Ripley met *Mary Moody Emerson, aunt of poet Ralph Waldo Emerson. Mary Emerson tried to mold the girl's intelligence by pressuring Ripley to accept Calvinism. Though Ripley rejected Calvinism and its harsh strictures, she did meet the Reverend Samuel Ripley, Mary Emerson's half-brother, and agreed to marry him in accordance with her father's wishes. In 1818, Sarah moved into Samuel's home in Waltham, Massachusetts, where he served as the minister of the First Parish Church and owned a small boarding school for boys. This began Ripley's career as a teacher of Latin and Greek and housemother not only to the boys at the school, but to her own seven surviving children as well. Despite her increased responsibilities, Ripley continued to read and study many subjects including theology, philosophy, chemistry and botany. Ralph Waldo Emerson, her friend and nephew by marriage, later noted that "her delight in books was not tainted by any wish to shine, or any appetite for praise or influence." Harvard University President Edward Everett said that Ripley could have been a professor of any subject, and she was known as a Greek scholar of national prominence.

In 1846, Ripley and her husband retired to Concord, Massachusetts, where he died a year later. To ease her grief, she continued reading Greek, including Homer's tragedies. At 70, she decided to read *Don Quixote*, so she taught herself Spanish. Ripley died of a stroke on July 26, 1867. Her portrait hangs in the "Old Manse" in Concord, Massachusetts.

SOURCES:

Edgerly, Lois Stiles, ed. *Give Her This Day: A Daybook of Women's Words.* Gardiner, ME: Tilbury House, 1990.

James, Edward T., ed. *Notable American Women, 1607–1950.* Cambridge, MA: The Belknap Press of Harvard University Press, 1971.

Ann M. Schwalboski,
teacher and writing specialist,
University of Wisconsin-Baraboo/Sauk County

Ripley, Sophia (1803–1861).

See Fuller, Margaret for sidebar.

Rippin, Jane Deeter (1882–1953)

American social worker who founded the first women offenders' detention home and was named national director of the Girl Scouts. Born Jane Parker Deeter in Harrisburg, Pennsylvania, on May 30, 1882; died in Tarrytown, New York, on June 2, 1953; daughter of Sarah Emely (Mather) Deeter and Jasper Newton Deeter; Irving College, B.S., 1902, A.M., 1914; married James Yardley Rippin (an architect and contractor), on October 13, 1913.

As an advocate for women and children, Jane Deeter Rippin played an important role in developing court systems geared to women and in organizing programs aimed at steering them away from delinquency. She was born Jane Parker Deeter in 1882 in Harrisburg, Pennsylvania. By example, the five Deeter children discovered early on that women could be as independent as men; fed up with housework, their mother **Sarah Deeter** hired servants and earned money to pay them by giving private voice lessons. At the same time, Jasper Deeter sent only his sons to private school, while Jane and her sisters attended the local public schools. Rippin's oldest sister, **Ruth**, raised geese in order to earn enough money to send Jane to Irving College in Mechanicsburg, Pennsylvania. She earned a bachelor of science degree in 1902 and began work as assistant to the principal of Mechanicsburg High School.

Six years later, Rippin switched careers and took a position as assistant superintendent of Meadowbrook's Children's Village, a Pennsylvania foster home and orphanage. In 1910, she became a caseworker in Philadelphia for the Society for the Prevention of Cruelty to Children and the next year founded the Coop, a cooperative boardinghouse, with five other women. A forerunner of modern cooperative living, the Coop soon allowed men to join as auxiliary members; one of the first male members was James Yardley Rippin, an architect and contractor whom Jane married on October 13, 1913.

The Rippins' marriage was a solid example of the principles of equality at work. When Rippin earned her A.M. degree from Irving College a year after the wedding and received an appointment as Philadelphia's chief probation officer, James fully supported her acceptance of such an important position. Her father, on the other hand, felt that her $5,000 annual salary was more than a woman was worth, and disowned her when she disobeyed his order to turn down the job. (Two years later, she nonetheless took him into her home to care for him as he was dying.) Rippin supervised probation work for five courts: domestic relations, women's court for sex offenders, petty criminal court for unmarried mothers, and the courts for juveniles and miscreants. Her innovation of psychological and social testing as well as the designation of an advocate social worker for each defendant contributed to the expansion of her staff from 3 to 365. Rippin continued fighting for social reform and, in 1917, opened the first detention home for female offenders. Unlike a traditional prison, the home offered testing and treatment, a court and an employment agency. Rippin believed that education was the key to rehabilitation. She also attempted to establish a center for alcoholic women (this was blocked by local authorities) and provided family courts with nurseries.

The same year the detention home opened, the War Department's Commission on Training Camp Activities asked Rippin to head up efforts to supervise women around southwest military bases in conjunction with the enforcement of liquor and prostitution laws. She not only enforced these laws, but also formed and directed centers which provided women with alternatives to crime. Her success was such that she became director of the commission's section on women and girls in 1918. Rippin and her staff worked with more than 38,000 "delinquent" women and raised more than half a million dollars in the course of her tenure as director.

A study on delinquency sponsored by Rippin had a two-fold effect: it later facilitated the establishment of the United Service Organization (USO), in 1941, and it awakened Rippin's interest in the importance of organizations specifically geared towards girls. As a means of keeping young girls out of trouble, she became closely associated with the Girl Scouts of America (GSA) with her appointment as national director in 1919. In the course of her 11-year service in one of the top spots in the GSA, she transformed the Scouts, which had been incorporated in 1915 by *Juliette Gordon Low, into a well-run, up-to-date organization with a membership of over 250,000. She assisted in the development of the international World Association of Girl Guides and Girl Scouts, and established a continuing tradition—the annual cookie sale. Rippin's failing health dictated the end of her tenure in 1930, although she would remain an active member of the GSA's National Advisory Council until close to her death.

In 1931, she began another career as a journalist and director of research for women's news for The Westchester County Publishers. However, a stroke partially paralyzed her five years later, and necessitated a long period of rehabilitation. Day by day she fought her way back to health by relearning words and sentence structure. She did at last overcome the paralysis and returned to her journalism career until a final stroke rendered her unconscious on March 13, 1953. She never regained awareness and died nearly three months later at her home in Tarrytown, New York.

SOURCES:

Sicherman, Barbara, and Carol Hurd Green, eds. *Notable American Women: The Modern Period.* Cambridge, MA: The Belknap Press of Harvard University, 1980.

Ann M. Schwalboski,
teacher and writing specialist,
University of Wisconsin-Baraboo/Sauk County

Riquetti, Gabrielle-Marie-Antoinette de, Comtesse de Martel de Janville.

See Martel de Janville, Comtesse de (1850–1932).

Ristori, Adelaide (1822–1906)

Italian actress. Born Adelaide Ristori in Cividale del Friuli on January 30, 1822 (some sources cite 1821); died on October 9, 1906, in Rome, Italy; daughter of strolling players; married Giuliano Capranica del Grillo (an Italian marquis), in 1847 (died 1861); children: one son, Georgio Capranica del Grillo, a marquis.

One of the leading actresses of the European theater, Adelaide Ristori took to the stage at age four while her parents were members of a touring theatrical company. At 14, she enjoyed her first success in the title role in Silvio Pellico's tragedy *Francesca da Rimini*, and was only 18 when, for the first time, she played *Mary Stuart in an Italian version of Johann Schiller's play. It would become one of her most famous roles.

As a member of the Sardinian company and the Ducal company at Parma, Ristori played the lead in Carlo Goldoni's *La Locandiera*, Augustin Scribe's *Adrienne Lecouvreur*, Vittorio Alfieri's *Antigone*, and Shakespeare's *Romeo and Juliet*. Following a short retirement after her marriage to Giuliano Capranica del Grillo at age 25, Ristori returned to the stage and appeared regularly in Turin and the provinces.

It was not until 1855 that she paid her first professional visit to Paris. Though initially received coolly, she took the city by storm in the title role of Alfieri's *Myrrha*. The appearance of a rival to the great French actress *Rachel set off a furious partisanship, and Paris was divided into two camps. Gallery theatergoers fought over the merits of their respective favorites. Though the two famous women never actually met, Rachel seems to have known that Ristori harbored no ill will toward her. In 1856, a tour in other countries was followed by another visit to Paris, when Ristori appeared in Giuseppe Montanelli's Italian translation of Gabriel Legouvé's *Medea*. She repeated this success in London.

In 1857, Ristori visited Madrid, playing in Spanish to enthusiastic audiences, and in 1866 she paid the first of four visits to the United States, where she won acclaim, particularly in Paolo Giacometti's *Elizabeth*, an Italian study of the English queen. After her final performance of *Maria Stuart* in New York in 1885, she retired from professional life. She died on October 9, 1906, in Rome.

Adelaide Ristori

Adelaide Ristori's *Ricordi e studi artistici (Studies and Memoirs*, 1888) tells of a fascinating career and is particularly valuable for the chapters devoted to the psychological makeup of the characters of Mary Stuart, *Elizabeth I, Myrrha, Phèdra and Lady Macbeth (*Gruoch). In her interpretation of these roles, Ristori combined instinct with intelligence.

SUGGESTED READING:

Daily Telegraph. London, October 10, 1906.
*Field, Kate. *Adelaide Ristori: A Biography*. New York, 1867.
Kingston, E. Peron. *Adelaide Ristori: A Sketch of her Life*, 1856.

Rita.

Variant of Margaret.

Rita of Cascia (1381–1457)

Italian patron saint of parenthood and the impossible. Name variations: Margarita of Cascia; Rita La Abogada de Imposibles. Born in Roccabornena (also seen as Roccaparena), Umbria, Italy, in 1381 (some sources cite 1377 or 1386); died of tuberculosis on May 22, 1457 (some sources cite 1447) at the Augustinian convent at Cascia; married a noble at age 12; children: two sons.

Born in 1381, Rita of Cascia was exceptionally pious during her youth and intent on joining the Augustinian convent in Cascia. Her parents insisted she wed, however, and when she was 12 they arranged her marriage to a young noble. Rita endured physical and emotional abuse from her ill-tempered husband. He was also unfaithful. For the next 18 years, she remained patient and forgiving, continuously praying for him, as well as for their two sons who were increasingly influenced by their father's cruelty. Rita felt that her prayers were answered when her husband realized the consequences of his behavior and ceased his abuse. Her joy was short-lived, because he was soon stabbed to death by an assassin. While her sons craved retaliation, Rita did not want them to avenge their father's death. Rather, she prayed for the death of her sons. Again, she felt that her prayers were answered when they both took ill. Rita then attempted to comfort them, convincing them that forgiveness would ease their minds. In the end, her sons died pardoning their father's assassin.

After their deaths, Rita returned to Cascia to join the Augustinian convent, but was denied entry because she was no longer a virgin. She persevered, however, and in 1413, after her third application, the rules for entry were relaxed and she was accepted. As a member of the convent, Rita worked tirelessly to aid the ill and to convert negligent Christians. In 1441, reacting to a sermon regarding the thorns of St. James della Marca, Rita experienced extreme pain in her forehead, and an open wound appeared, possibly from a thorn. The wound became so unsightly that Rita was secluded from her convent sisters for nine years. In 1450, healed, she traveled with her convent sisters to Rome for the year of the jubilee. The wound returned, however, and Rita was again secluded from others until her death on May 22, 1457. She was canonized on May 24, 1900.

Due to the belief that St. Rita of Cascia has provided so many miraculous responses to her devotees, she has been referred to as the "saint of the impossible." Traditionally, she has been appealed by those suffering from spousal abuses, infertility, difficult marriages, and desperate or insurmountable causes. Her feast day is May 22.

Ann M. Schwalboski,
freelance writer, University of Wisconsin,
Baraboo/Sauk County

Ritchie, Anna Cora Mowatt

(1819–1870).

See Mowatt, Anna Cora.

Ritchie, Anne Isabella (1837–1919)

British novelist and essayist. Name variations: Anne Thackeray; Lady Ritchie; Anna Isabella Ritchie; Lady Anne Thackeray Ritchie; Mrs. Richmond Ritchie. Born Anne Isabella Thackeray in 1837 in England; died in February 1919 on the Isle of Wight; eldest daughter of William Makepeace Thackeray (1811–1863, the novelist) and Isabella Gethin Shawe; aunt of Virginia Woolf; educated privately; married her cousin Richmond Thackeray Willoughby Ritchie, also seen as Sir Richard Ritchie, in 1877; children: two.

Selected writings: (fiction) The Story of Elizabeth (1863), The Village on the Green (1867), Old Kensington (1873), Miss Angel (1875), Mrs. Dymond (1885); (essay collections) Toilers and Spinners (1874), A Book of Sybils (1883); Blackstick Papers (1908), From the Porch (1913); (biographies) Madame de Sévigné (1881), Records of Tennyson, Ruskin and Browning (1892), Alfred Tennyson and His Friends (1893); contributed material to Dictionary of National Biography.

The elder daughter of **Isabella Gethin Shawe** and eminent novelist William Makepeace Thackeray, Anne Isabella Ritchie was born in 1837 and grew up surrounded by many of the leading literary figures of the Victorian era, several of whom became the subjects of biographical studies she wrote later in life. Anne and her sister spent their early years in Paris with their grandparents because their mother had been hospitalized with mental illness, but they re-

turned to London in 1847. There, the girls associated with the children of Charles Dickens and met several celebrated writers. Anne helped her father by copying out his manuscripts, and she began publishing her own work in *Cornhill Magazine*. After her father's death in 1863, Anne expanded her literary contacts to include the poets Tennyson, Robert and *Elizabeth Barrett Browning, and Swinburne; novelists *Charlotte Brontë and George Eliot (*Mary Anne Evans); and critic John Ruskin. As the aunt of *Virginia Woolf, whom she influenced, Anne was also linked to the first generation of modern writers. Lady Ritchie's first novel *The Story of Elizabeth* (1863) was based upon her childhood in Paris. She became known for novels with domestic settings and themes, in particular *The Village on the Green* (1867) and *Old Kensington* (1873). The inspiration for her fourth novel *Miss Angel* (1875) was the life of 18th-century painter *Angelica Kauffmann, and her fifth novel *Mrs. Dymond* (1885), often considered one of her best, was set during the Franco-Prussian War (1870–71).

In 1877, at age 40, Anne married Richmond Ritchie, her second cousin. Though he was 17 years younger than she, the marriage was said to be a success, and the couple had one son and one daughter. Richmond, who worked in the Indian civil service, was knighted in 1907, which bestowed upon Anne the title Lady Ritchie. After her marriage, she shifted her attention from fiction to essays and biographies, which, written in a "graceful and lucid style," are considered her best works. Her nonfiction titles include *Toilers and Spinners* (1874), which exposed the difficulties of unmarried, unemployed women, and *A Book of Sibyls* (1883), a collection of essays about women writers. Lady Ritchie also wrote *Madame de Sévigné* (1881), a biography of the 17th-century letter writer *Marie de Sévigné, *Records of Tennyson, Ruskin and Browning* (1892) and *Alfred Tennyson and His Friends* (1893), and the essay collections *Blackstick Papers* (1908) and *From the Porch* (1913). She contributed essays to the *Dictionary of National Biography* and wrote introductions to the biographical editions of her father's works (1898–99). In 1903, Ritchie was elected a fellow of the Royal Society of Literature, and she served as president of the English Association from 1912 to 1913. Ritchie was the model for the character of Mrs. Hilbery in Virginia Woolf's *Night and Day*.

SOURCES:

Buck, Claire, ed. *The Bloomsbury Guide to Women's Literature*. NY: Prentice Hall, 1992.

The Concise Dictionary of National Biography. Oxford: Oxford University Press, 1992.

Drabble, Margaret, ed. *The Oxford Guide to English Literature.* 5th ed. Oxford: Oxford University Press, 1985.

Kunitz, Stanley J., and Howard Haycraft, eds. *British Authors of the Nineteenth Century.* NY: H.W. Wilson, 1936.

Shattock, Joanne. *The Oxford Guide to British Women Writers.* Oxford: Oxford University Press, 1993.

Elizabeth Shostak,
freelance writer, Cambridge, Massachusetts

Ritchie, Jean (1922—)

American folk singer and folklorist. Born in Viper, Kentucky, on December 8, 1922; daughter of Balis W. Ritchie (a former schoolteacher and farmer) and Abigail (Hall) Ritchie; attended Cumberland College in Williamsburg, Kentucky; University of Kentucky in Lexington, A.B., 1946; married George Pickow (a photographer), on September 29, 1950; children: Jonathan Balis; Peter Ritchie Pickow.

Received Fulbright grant (1952) to study folk music of the British Isles; sang at first annual Newport Folk Festival (July 1959).

Selected recordings: Children's Songs and Games from the Southern Mountains *(1957);* Folk Concert in Town Hall, New York *(1959);* British Traditional Ballads in the Southern Mountains, Volumes 1 and 2 *(1960);* Precious Memories *(1962);* High Hills and Mountains *(1979);* None But One *(1981).*

Selected writings: The Swapping Song Book *(1952);* A Garland of Mountain Song *(1953); (memoir)* Singing Family of the Cumberlands *(1955);* From Fair to Fair: Folk Songs of the British Isles *(1966).*

Born in 1922 into a musical family whose ancestors had been among the first to settle in the Cumberland Mountain region of Appalachia in the 1700s, Jean Ritchie grew up hearing and singing the traditional songs that her family had passed along for generations. She made her life's work the preservation of this musical heritage, which the Library of Congress had catalogued in the 1930s.

Ritchie was the youngest of 14 children born to Balis W. Ritchie, a former teacher who had turned to farming after losing his hearing, and **Abigail Hall Ritchie**. Though the family was poor and the children worked hard at farm chores, they enjoyed a happy home life and often amused themselves by singing and sharing songs with neighbors.

Balis Ritchie valued learning and helped most of his children receive a solid education.

Jean attended Cumberland College in Williamsburg, Kentucky, worked briefly as a teacher during World War II, and later transferred to the University of Kentucky in Lexington. There she majored in social work and also received some formal musical training. After graduating Phi Beta Kappa in 1946, she worked briefly as a teacher in Kentucky before moving to New York City to take a job as a music counselor at the Henry Street Settlement. In New York, Ritchie began to sing and play the dulcimer for friends, and she met folklorist Alan Lomax, who helped arrange singing appearances for her. He once called her "one of the finest pure mountain singers ever discovered." Within a few years, Ritchie gave up social work to fully devote her energies to her music.

In 1950, Ritchie married photographer George Pickow. She made her first solo public appearance that same year at the Greenwich Mews Playhouse and began doing regular radio performances. In 1952, she received a Fulbright grant to travel with Pickow throughout England, Scotland, and Ireland to trace the origins of Appalachian folk songs. While in England, she appeared at the Royal Albert Hall and sang on BBC radio. Ritchie returned to the United States in 1953, where she worked on several book projects. Oxford University Press had published her first book, *The Swapping Song Book*, in 1952. Oxford also published her portrait of her family, *Singing Family of the Cumberlands* (1955), which received highly favorable reviews. In 1959, Ritchie sang to great acclaim at the first annual Newport (Rhode Island) Folk Festival, of which she was one of the original directors. Ritchie has commented that one of her primary reasons for studying and promoting folk music was the fact that, by the 1940s, radio broadcasts of other types of songs had begun to threaten Appalachian native music. By popularizing traditional songs, she saw herself as preserving an important part of America's cultural heritage. Ritchie has represented the United States at international folklore conferences and served on the first folklore panel of the National Endowment for the Arts. Her work was central in inspiring the American folk music renaissance of the 1960s.

Though Ritchie cut back on her performance schedule while her two sons, Jonathan and Peter, were young, she maintained her interests in folk music and culture and continued recording and performing. Her two-volume album *British Traditional Ballads in the Southern Mountains*, based on her Fulbright research, was issued in 1960. She also released an album of dulcimer instruction, *The Ap-palachian Dulcimer* (1964), as well as *High Hills and Mountains* (1979), and *None But One* (1981), which received the *Rolling Stone* Critics Award as best folk album of the year. Though most of the songs Ritchie has recorded are traditional ballads, she has also written original material; among the best known are "The L&N Don't Stop Here Anymore," "Black Waters," and "Blue Diamond Mine." She has recorded and performed with a number of notable folk musicians, including Doc Watson, Happy Traum, Kenny Hall, Frank Hicks, *Odetta, Sonny Terry, and Brownie McGhee, and has been joined on her later albums by her sons who play banjo, dulcimer, guitar, pennywhistle, dobro, autoharp, bass, and recorder. Ritchie's performance of "Amazing Grace" can be seen in the PBS home video of that name.

SOURCES:

ASCAP Biographical Dictionary. 4th ed. NY: R.R. Bowker, 1980.

Carlin, Richard. *The Big Book of Country Music.* NY: Penguin, 1995.

Hitchcock, H. Wiley and Stanley Sadie. *The New Grove Dictionary of American Music.* London: Macmillan, 1986.

LaBlanc, Michael L., ed. *Contemporary Musicians.* Detroit, MI: Gale Research, 1991.

McHenry, Robert, ed. *Famous American Women.* NY: Dover, 1980.

Morehead, Philip D. with Anne MacNeil. *The New International Dictionary of Music.* Meridian, 1991.

Moritz, Charles, ed. *Current Biography Yearbook 1959.* NY: H.W. Wilson, 1959.

Elizabeth Shostak,
freelance writer, Cambridge, Massachusetts

Ritchie, Mrs. Richmond.

See Ritchie, Anne Isabella (1837–1919).

Rittenhouse, Jessie Belle

(1869–1948)

American poet and critic. Born Jessie Bell Rittenhouse in Mount Morris, New York, on December 8, 1869; died in Detroit, Michigan, on September 28, 1948; daughter of John E. Rittenhouse (a farmer) and Mary J. (MacArthur) Rittenhouse; graduated from Genesee Wesleyan Seminary, Lima, New York, 1890; married Clinton Scollard (a poet and professor), in 1924 (died 1932); no children.

Selected writings: The Younger American Poets *(1904);* The Door of Dreams *(1918);* The Lifted Cup *(1921);* The Secret Bird *(1930);* My House of Life *(memoir, 1934);* Moving Tide: New and Selected Lyrics *(1939).*

Best known for such works as *The Younger American Poets* (1904) and *The Little Book of Modern American Verse* (1913), Jessie Belle Rittenhouse did much to advance the cause of modern American poetry in the early 20th century. She was born in Mount Morris, New York, in 1869, the daughter of John E. Rittenhouse, a farmer, and **Mary J. Rittenhouse**. Jessie's paternal ancestor, William Rittenhouse, came to Philadelphia in 1688 from Germany, and one of his descendants, David Rittenhouse, became an eminent scientist and inventor. Her maternal ancestors had immigrated to upstate New York from Scotland in 1800.

The fifth of seven children, Jessie attended the village school in Conesus, New York, and later studied at the Nunda Academy. She went on to the Genesee Wesleyan Seminary in Lima, New York, where she was noted for her abilities in literature and languages. After graduating in 1890, she returned to her family and worked briefly as a teacher. Soon, however, Rittenhouse embarked on a career in journalism, contributing feature articles to local newspapers. While she was researching a story in 1894, a cousin of the young poet and professor Clinton Scollard gave her a book of Scollard's poems. Rittenhouse, who admired the collection, offered to review it for the *Buffalo Express*. Pleased, Scollard's publisher began regularly sending Rittenhouse new poetry titles that she reviewed to increasing notice and which introduced her to a broad range of new work in poetry.

In 1899, Rittenhouse decided to concentrate exclusively on literary criticism. She moved to Boston, a city that was then a literary center, where she made the acquaintance of *Louise Chandler Moulton, who presided over a salon of poets seeking to break with outdated Victorian and Romantic influences and develop more original poetic work. Rittenhouse focused her attention on several new poets and published *The Younger American Poets* to admiring reviews in 1904. The book, considered a groundbreaking study, was widely read and discussed. The next year, she moved to New York City, where she reviewed regularly for *The New York Times Review of Books* over the next decade. She also co-founded the Poetry Society of America in 1910, serving for ten years as the organization's first secretary. In 1913, Rittenhouse published *The Little Book of Modern American Verse*, an anthology that sold over 1,000 copies and was instrumental in creating a receptive audience for new poetry. She followed this work with *The Little Book of American Poets* (1915), *The Second Book of Modern Verse* (1919), *The Little*

Book of Modern British Verse (1924), and *The Third Book of Modern Verse* (1927), all of which were both commercially successful and influential. During these years, she lectured widely throughout the country. A close friend of poet *Sara Teasdale, Rittenhouse also published several volumes of her own poems, including *The Door of Dreams* (1918), *The Lifted Cup* (1921), *The Secret Bird* (1930), and *Moving Tide: New and Selected Lyrics* (1939), which was awarded a gold medal from the National Poetry Center.

In 1924, Rittenhouse married Clinton Scollard, whose work she had first promoted 30 years earlier; this was his second marriage. The couple divided their time between Kent, Connecticut, and Winter Park, Florida, where Rittenhouse lectured on modern poetry at Rollins College. With Scollard, she co-edited *The Bird-Lover's Anthology* (1930) and *Patrician Rhymes* (1932), and, after his death in 1932, she edited Scollard's selected work in *The Singing Heart* (1934). Rittenhouse also wrote a memoir, *My House of Life* (1932). She received a medal for distinguished service from the Poetry Society of America in 1930, and died in Detroit, Michigan, on September 28, 1948.

SOURCES:

James, Edward T., ed. *Notable American Women, 1607–1950.* Cambridge, MA: The Belknap Press of Harvard University, 1971.

Kunitz, Stanley J., and Howard Haycraft, eds. *Twentieth Century Authors.* NY: H.W. Wilson, 1942.

McHenry, Robert, ed. *Famous American Women.* NY: Dover, 1980.

Elizabeth Shostak,
freelance writer, Cambridge, Massachusetts

Ritter, Louise (b. 1958).

See Balas, Iolanda for sidebar.

Ritter, Thelma (1905–1969)

American actress. Born in Brooklyn, New York, on February 14, 1905; died on February 5, 1969; graduated from the Manual Training High School, Brooklyn, and the American Academy of Dramatic Arts; married Joseph Moran (an actor), on April 21, 1927; children; Joseph; Monica Ann.

Selected filmography: Miracle on 34th Street *(1947);* A Letter to Three Wives *(1949);* All About Eve *(1950);* The Mating Season *(1951);* The Model and the Marriage Broker *(1951);* With a Song in My Heart *(1952);* Pickup on South Street *(1953);* Rear Window *(1954);* The Proud and the Profane *(1956);* Pillow Talk *(1959);* The Misfits *(1961);* Birdman of Alcatraz *(1962);* Move Over, Darling *(1963);* The Incident *(1967);* What's So Bad About Feeling Good? *(1968).*

One of the few character actresses ever to receive star billing, Thelma Ritter was equally at home on stage, screen, and television. She was the winner of an Emmy and a Tony, and had been nominated for six Academy Awards. "Show business is my life, that's all," the wry-faced actress once remarked.

Born in Brooklyn, New York, in 1905, Ritter took to the stage at an early age, perhaps influenced by her father who was a distinguished singer. Throughout high school, she did bit parts in stock and worked summers in a candy store and as a switchboard operator to pay her tuition at the American Academy of Dramatic Arts. During the 1920s, she joined the Poli Theater's stock company in Elizabeth, New Jersey; although she gained valuable experience playing a wide variety of roles, her career failed to ignite. Following her marriage to fellow actor Joseph Moran in April 1927, she settled into suburban domesticity, but it was no substitute for show business. "I missed it, and I wanted to get back into it somewhere," she said later. In 1944, she began making the rounds in radio, and within a year she was featured on such programs as "The Theater Guild of the Air," "Mr. District Attorney," "Big Town," and "The Aldrich Family." In 1946, through a high-school friend who happened to be married to the film's director, she landed a walk-on part in *Miracle on 34th Street*, as the harried housewife who scolds Santa Claus for promising her son too many Christmas toys. After viewing the rushes, Darryl Zanuck was so impressed with Ritter's performance that he padded the role significantly.

Small but juicy parts in several subsequent films, including *A Letter to Three Wives* (1949), led Ritter to her breakthrough role as the wise-cracking maid in *All About Eve* (1950), which Bosley Crowther called "screamingly funny" and which earned the actress her first Academy Award nomination. A year later, she was nominated once for *The Mating Game* (1951), this time for her performance as a well-meaning mother-in-law. "Miss Ritter's invincible sincerity as well as her dry and dour comicality invest the proceedings not only with authentic gaiety but with a kind of human dignity rarely encountered in such films," wrote the critic for *The Christian Science Monitor*. Ritter received subsequent nominations for her supporting roles in *With a Song in My Heart* (1952), *Pickup on South Street* (1953), *Pillow Talk* (1959), and *Birdman of Alcatraz* (1962).

In 1955, Ritter made her television debut in Paddy Chayevsky's *The Catered Affair*, in a role he wrote specifically with her in mind. For her portrayal of the Bronx housewife who invests all of her hopes and dreams in an elaborate wedding for her daughter, Ritter won an Emmy Award. Two years later, she took Broadway by storm, winning accolades and a Tony Award for her portrayal of the alcoholic waterfront harpy Marthy in the musical *New Girl In Town*, based on Eugene O'Neill's *Anna Christie*. Critic Tom Donnelly, of the New York *World-Telegram and Sun*, hailed Ritter as "a small, bedraggled tigress, burning brightly and hilariously through the night."

When not acting, Ritter was active in civic and philanthropic work, particularly with the Girl Scouts and the American Cancer Society. She was also an avid reader, plowing through a book a day, and rereading her favorite author Charles Dickens on a yearly basis. "Off stage she is a gracious and witty woman who can punch out off-beat, sophisticated lines with the skill of a Noel Coward," wrote Fern Marja, who interviewed Ritter for the New York *Post Magazine* (September 16, 1957). The actress, who was the mother of two children, made her last film in 1968 and died the following year, at age 64.

SOURCES:

Candee, Marjorie Dent, ed. *Current Biography 1957*. NY: H.W. Wilson, 1957.

Katz, Ephriam. *The Film Encyclopedia*. NY: Harper-Collins, 1994.

Moritz, Charles, ed. *Current Biography 1974*. NY: H.W. Wilson, 1974.

Barbara Morgan,
Melrose, Massachusetts

Riva, Maria (b. 1924).

See Dietrich, Marlene for sidebar.

Rivé-King, Julie (1854–1937)

American musician and composer who became the first great American woman pianist. Name variations: Julie Rive-King. Born on October 30, 1854, in Cincinnati, Ohio; died on July 24, 1937, in Indianapolis, Indiana; daughter of Leon Rivé (a painter) and Caroline (Staub) Rivé; studied piano in the United States with Henry Andres, William Mason, and Sebastian Bach Mills, and abroad with Carl Reinecke, Adolf J.M. Blassmann, Wilhelm Albert Rischpieter, and Franz Liszt; married Frank H. King (a businessman who became her manager), in 1878 (died 1900); no children.

American pianist and composer Julie Rivé-King was born in Cincinnati, Ohio, the daughter

of Leon Rivé, a painter, and **Caroline Staub Rivé**, French immigrants who moved to Cincinnati in 1854, the year of her birth. Her musical talent emerged at age five, at which time she began studying with her mother, a musician and alumna of the Paris Conservatory. Julie made her first public appearance at the age of eight at one of her mother's concerts, and around that time began formal instruction under Henry Andres. She later studied in New York with William Mason and Sebastian Bach Mills and in Leipzig with Carl Reinecke (1872), and briefly took lessons from Franz Liszt. In 1874, she made her European debut at the Euterpe Musical Association of Leipzig, performing Beethoven's Third Concerto and Liszt's Second Hungarian Rhapsody. For her American debut on April 24, 1875, with the New York Philharmonic Society, she played Liszt's Concerto in E flat and Schumann's "Faschingsschwank aus Wien." A year later, she married Frank H. King, an executive of the Decker Company, the manufacturer of the pianos on which she frequently performed. King had previously managed her concerts, and he would continue to do so until his death in 1900.

By 1936, when she gave up performing, Rivé-King had become the first great American

Julie
Rivé-King

woman pianist. She had given over 4,000 concerts and recitals in the United States and Canada, 500 of which were with orchestras, and had appeared with Theodore Thomas' Chicago orchestra more than 200 times. At the height of her career, she was praised by W.S.B. Mathews, a Chicago pianist and editor of *Music*, as having established "a new standard of concert playing" in the United States. Her extensive repertoire of 500 compositions included both classical and Romantic works, which she performed with equal skill, and her inclusion of American composers made her one of the most influential musicians in the country. She also frequently played her own compositions, including *Polonaise héroïque*, *On Blooming Meadow*, *Bubbling Spring*, and Impromptu in A Flat.

Little is known of Rivé-King's private life, although she was said to have possessed an unassuming personality and to have made lasting friendships both within music circles and beyond. Following her retirement, she gave class lessons at the Bush Conservatory of Music and its successor, the Chicago Conservatory, continuing to teach until shortly before her death in 1937, at age 82.

SOURCES:
Coolidge, Arlan R. "Rivé-King, Julie," in *New Grove Dictionary of American Music*. Vol. 4, p. 50.

Dubal, David. *The Art of the Piano*. NY: Summit Books, 1989.

James, Edward T., ed. *Notable American Women, 1607–1950*. Cambridge, MA: The Belknap Press of Harvard University Press, 1971.

McHenry, Robert, ed. *Famous American Women*. NY: Dover, 1980.

Schonberg, Harold C. *The Great Pianists*. Rev. ed. NY: Simon & Schuster, 1987.

Barbara Morgan,
Melrose, Massachusetts

Rivera, Frida (1907–1954).

See Kahlo, Frida.

Rivera, Pilar Primo de (1913–1991).

See Primo de Rivera, Pilar.

Rivers, Pearl (1849–1896).

See Nicholson, Eliza Jane.

Rives, Amélie (1863–1945)

American author. Name variations: Amelie Louise Rives; Amélie Rives Troubetzkoy; Princess Troubetzkoy. Born Amélie Louise Rives in Richmond, Virginia, on August 23, 1863; died in Charlottesville, Virginia, on June 15, 1945; daughter of Alfred Landon Rives (a civil engineer) and Sarah (MacMurdo) Rives; *educated privately; married John Armstrong Chanler (a lawyer), on June 14, 1888 (divorced 1895); married Prince Pierre Troubetzkoy (a Russian portrait painter), on February 18, 1896; no children.*

Published first story in the Atlantic Monthly *(1886); established literary reputation with the novel* The Quick or the Dead? *(1888); active in movements promoting Southern writing; best-known works include the novels* Shadows of Flames *(1915) and* Firedamp *(1930); also wrote several plays and championed educational reform and women's suffrage.*

Born into a socially distinguished Southern family in Richmond, Virginia, during the Civil War, Amélie Rives was raised in a privileged and genteel environment that nurtured her love of literature. Among her ancestors were such well-known Revolutionary War figures as Colonel William Cabell and Dr. Thomas Walker, as well as her grandfather William Cabell Rives, who served on a diplomatic mission to France before the Civil War and completed a three-volume biography of James Madison. From her grandmother, too, Amélie inherited a literary legacy, for **Judith Page Walker Rives** published several books. Amélie grew up on the family estate at Castle Hill, near Cobham in Albemarle County, Virginia. When she was seven, her father, formerly acting chief of engineers for the Confederacy, took a position as head civil engineer of the Mobile and Birmingham Railroad, and the family moved to Mobile, Alabama. Amélie continued to spend summers at Castle Hill, which she always thought of as her home.

Educated privately, Rives developed an intense love of literature. From her early years, she enjoyed writing stories; she later recalled, "When my grandmother disapproved and quietly took the paper from me, I began to write on the wide hems of my starched white petticoats!" She also became skilled at horseback riding, though she refused to participate in the upper-class ritual of foxhunting, which she considered cruel. A beautiful and charming young woman, Rives made her social debut in Newport, Rhode Island. Yet she was more interested in artistic endeavors than in high society. She had published her first short story, "A Brother to Dragons," anonymously in the *Atlantic Monthly* in 1886, after which more stories and poems appeared in other magazines. Her literary reputation was made with the 1888 publication of her first novel, *The Quick or the Dead?*, which was severely criticized for its frank treatment of a young widow's passionate affair but became a bestseller.

In 1888, Rives married socialite lawyer John Armstrong Chanler of New York, a great-grandson of millionaire John Jacob Astor. The couple lived in Virginia and England, where Rives soon became associated with "The Souls," a group led by *Margot Tennant Asquith, Arthur Balfour, and George, Lord Curzon. At the same time, Rives separated from her husband, divorcing him in 1895. The following year, she married acclaimed portrait painter Prince Pierre Troubetzkoy, son of a Russian noble and an American mother; this second marriage proved much happier than her first. Rives traveled extensively with her husband, and mingled in artistic and social circles. In 1898, a serious illness threatened her reputation and her marriage. Prescribed massive doses of morphine while suffering from a severe case of rheumatic fever, Rives became addicted to the drug—a fact that became publicized and created a scandal. Withdrawing to Castle Hill, Rives struggled to overcome her addition and, by 1902, was again in good health. She drew on this difficult experience in her 1915 novel *Shadows of Flames*, one of the first realistic presentations in American literature of the experience of drug addiction.

Rives continued writing successfully for the next 25 years, producing novels, stories, and poems, as well as several plays, some of which had Broadway productions, and some of which, like *Herod and Mariamne*, were written in verse. Her works have been associated with the Southern literary renaissance, in which Rives' friend *Ellen Glasgow was prominent, but many literary historians consider Rives to have followed more European and cosmopolitan models. Critics point out that Rives remains notable as one of the first American writers to have been influenced by new theories of psychology and mental illness, as seen in such novels as *Shadows of Flames* and *Firedamp* (1930). When asked to judge her own literary accomplishments, she named *Augustine the Man*, a drama in blank verse published in England, as her favorite. In addition to her literary work, Rives was intensely interested in movements for education reform and women's suffrage.

After Prince Troubetzkoy's death in 1936, Rives withdrew to Castle Hill, where she mourned her husband and lived quietly for her remaining years. She was distressed to learn in 1941 that this marriage had stripped her of her American citizenship, which she took steps to regain, considering American democracy to be "a religion, a great faith." She died of heart disease in 1945 at a nursing home in Charlottesville, Virginia.

SOURCES:

Edgerly, Lois Stiles, ed. *Give Her This Day*. Gardiner, ME: Tilbury House, 1990.

James, Edward T., ed. *Notable American Women, 1607–1950*. Cambridge, MA: The Belknap Press of Harvard University, 1971.

Kunitz, Stanley J., and Howard Haycraft, eds. *Twentieth Century Authors*. NY: H.W. Wilson, 1942.

Elizabeth Shostak, freelance writer, Cambridge, Massachusetts

Amélie Rives

Rizpah

Biblical woman. Daughter of Aiah; concubine of King Saul; children: (with Saul) sons, Armoni and Mephibosheth.

The daughter of Aiah, Rizpah became one of the concubines of King Saul, with whom she had two sons, Armoni and Mephibosheth. Following Saul's death, Rizpah became intimate with Abner, the commander-in-chief of Saul's army. This so infuriated Ishbosheth, one of Saul's sons with another woman, that he accused Abner of immorality and disloyalty. Enraged, Abner transferred his allegiance from Saul to David.

Rizpah is also notable for her maternal devotion. During the early years of David's reign at Jerusalem, Rizpah's sons, along with Saul's five other sons, were killed by hanging as retribution for Saul's wrongdoing. Rizpah kept vigil over her children's suspended bodies for five months, protecting them from wild beasts and birds of prey. When David heard of this, he had the bodies taken down and buried.

Rizzotti, Jennifer (1974—)

American basketball player and coach. Born in New Fairfield, Connecticut, on May 15, 1974; attended University of Connecticut; married.

Led University of Connecticut women's basketball team to NCAA championship (1995); named First Team All-America by Kodak, Associated Press (AP) and United Press International (1995–96); named AP Player of the Year (1995–96); named outstanding woman college athlete (1997); was the top pick of the New England Blizzard in the American Basketball League (ABL); was twice named to the

ABL all-star team; joined the Houston Comets of the WNBA after the ABL folded; began coaching at the University of Hartford, becoming the youngest women's basketball coach in Division I (1999).

Basketball player Jennifer Rizzotti helped pave the way for women athletes in the United States to enjoy lucrative and respectable professional careers. A native of New Fairfield, Connecticut, Rizzotti excelled in basketball as a high school student, despite the fact that she was not particularly tall. During her college years at the University of Connecticut, the 5'6" point guard was central to the success of the women's team, the Huskies. She played 135 games during four seasons, and set school records in assists (637) and steals (340). She also became the only athlete at the school to ever exceed 1,000 points (1,540) and 500 assists (637). Rizzotti helped lead the team to the NCAA championship in 1995, with a perfect 35–0 season. In 1996, she played on the R. William Jones Cup Team in Taiwan. Rizzotti was also named First Team All-America by Kodak, Associated Press (AP) and United Press International (UPI) for the 1995–96 season, and was chosen as AP Player of the Year in 1996. During her senior year, in which she maintained a GPA of 3.456, Rizzotti won the Honda-Broderick Cup as the nation's outstanding woman college athlete.

After her successful college career, Rizzotti joined the New England Blizzard, a newly formed women's team in the American Basketball League (ABL). She served as a passionate advocate for women's sports, emphasizing the sense of pride and accomplishment that athletics can offer to young women and men, in addition to making a solid contribution to her team. When the ABL dissolved in 1999 because of financial difficulties, Rizzotti joined the championship Houston Comets team in the Women's National Basketball Association (WNBA). Although eclipsed by the stellar play of high-profile teammates *Cynthia Cooper and *Sheryl Swoopes, Rizzotti was a valuable asset in the Comets' run for a third-straight WNBA championship.

Elizabeth Shostak,
freelance writer, Cambridge, Massachusetts

Robards, Rachel (1767–1828).

See Jackson, Rachel Donelson.

Robb, Isabel Hampton (1860–1910)

Canadian-born nursing educator. Name variations: *Isabel Adams Hampton. Born Isabel Adams Hampton in Welland, Ontario, Canada, in 1860; died in Cleveland, Ohio, on April 15, 1910; daughter of Samuel James Hampton and Sarah Mary (Lay) Hampton; earned teaching certificate from Collegiate Institute in St. Catherines, Ontario; graduated from Bellevue Hospital Training School for Nurses in New York City, 1883; married Hunter Robb (a physician and professor of gynecology), in 1894; children: Hampton; Philip Hunter.*

Born Isabel Adams Hampton in 1860 in Welland, Ontario, Canada, Isabel Hampton Robb grew up in an efficient, Spartan household with her parents and six siblings. She earned a teaching certificate from Collegiate Institute in St. Catherines, Ontario, but her aspirations were in nursing. She completed courses at New York City's innovative Bellevue Hospital Training School for Nurses, which followed *Florence Nightingale's model for nursing education, in 1883, and began her nursing career in Rome, Italy, caring for ill English and American tourists.

In 1886, Robb started work at the Illinois Training School for Nurses at Cook County Hospital in Chicago, as superintendent of nurses. In an effort to improve the educational standards of nursing schools, she proposed the first graded course of study for nurses in the country. In 1889, her leadership qualities caused her to be chosen as superintendent of nurses and principal of the nurses' training school at the newly opened Johns Hopkins Hospital in Baltimore. She endeavored to raise the standards of the nursing program by working to expand the two-year curriculum to three years, establish an eight-hour workday, and enlarge the school's budget. Although these goals were met only after her tenure as superintendent, Robb was instrumental in pushing the school to new levels of excellence. Not content to be an agent of change locally, she desired to see a common standard set for nursing programs across the country. To this end, she became a founding member of the American Society of Superintendents of Training Schools for Nurses of the United States and Canada (after 1912, the National League of Nursing Education), established under her leadership.

Isabel's 1894 marriage to Dr. Hunter Robb, an associate in gynecology at Johns Hopkins, brought an end to her work with that specific hospital, but did not stop her activity in nursing organizations at the national level. From her home base in Cleveland, Ohio, where her husband worked as professor of gynecology at Western Reserve University, Robb played a central role in the founding of the Nurses' Associated Alumnae of the United States and Canada (after 1911, the American Nurses' Association, the name by which it is still known). She presided as its first president from 1897 to 1901 and endeavored to set legal standards of nursing that would encompass all states. In a joint venture with *Mary Adelaide Nutting, her successor at Johns Hopkins, she set in motion the development of a course in hospital economics at Teachers College of Columbia University. Her career also included the writing of two textbooks, *Nursing: Its Principles and Practice* (1893) and *Nursing Ethics* (1900), and her election to the presidency of the Society of Superintendents in 1908. Her life and work ended unexpectedly when she was crushed to death between two streetcars on April 15, 1910.

SOURCES:

James, Edward T., ed. *Notable American Women, 1607–1950*. Cambridge, MA: The Belknap Press of Harvard University Press, 1971.

Read, Phyllis J., and Bernard L. Witlieb. *The Book of Women's Firsts*. NY: Random House, 1992.

Brenda Kubiac,
freelance writer, Chesterfield, Michigan

Robb, Lynda Bird (b. 1944).

See Johnson, Lynda Bird.

Robe, Shirley Pettis (b. 1924).

See Pettis, Shirley Neil.

Roberts, Caroline Alice (1848–1920).

See Elgar, Alice.

Roberts, Dorothea Klumpke (1861–1942).

See Klumpke, Dorothea.

Roberts, Eirlys (1911—)

English consumer activist. Born in London, England, in 1911; daughter of a doctor; attended Clapham High School in London; earned a Classics degree from Girton College, Cambridge; married John Cullen, in 1941.

Born the daughter of a London doctor in 1911, Eirlys Roberts made her mark on European society by campaigning for consumer reform. She began her career as a sub-editor for the Amalgamated Press, and moved into military and political intelligence in the mid-1940s. After taking part in a United Nations Mission to Albania from 1945 to 1947, she settled into a job in the Information Division of the Treasury.

Roberts founded the Consumers' Association in 1957, heading up the research and editor-ial division, and creating the pioneer publication *Which?* in 1961. Through *Which?*, Roberts advocated greater safety and efficiency standards for products as well as public accountability. The accessible style of the journal and the detailed product reports she included made it a success, with a circulation of seven million. In addition to her efforts in these arenas, she served as part-time director of the Bureau of European Consumer Organizations, based in Brussels (1973–78); chair of the Research Institute for Consumer Affairs; and chair of the Environment and Consumer Protection sub-committee of the European Economic Community. For her service, she was awarded the Order of the British Empire (OBE) in 1971 and was made Dame Commander of the British Empire (DBE) six years later.

Brenda Kubiac,
freelance writer, Chesterfield, Michigan

Roberts, Elizabeth Madox
(1881–1941)

American novelist and poet. Born in Perryville, Kentucky, on October 30, 1881; died in Orlando, Florida, on March 13, 1941; daughter of Simpson Roberts and Mary Elizabeth (Brent) Roberts; graduated from high school in Covington, Kentucky, 1900; attended the State College (later the University) of Kentucky; University of Chicago, Ph.B., 1921; never married; no children.

Selected writings: (poetry) In the Great Steep's Garden *(1915),* Under the Tree *(1922); (novels)* The Time of Man *(1926),* My Heart and My Flesh *(1927),* Jingling in the Wind *(1928),* The Great Meadow *(1930),* A Buried Treasure *(1931),* He Sent Forth a Raven *(1935),* Black is My Truelove's Hair *(1938); (short-story collections)* The Haunted Mirror *(1932),* Not by Strange Gods *(1941).*

Elizabeth Madox Roberts was born on October 30, 1881, and grew up in Springfield, Kentucky. Her education began early while listening to her father narrate Greek and Roman myths, as well as stories from Kentucky history. She graduated from high school in Covington, Kentucky, and for a time attended the State College of Kentucky (later the University of Kentucky), but left without graduating due either to problems with her health or her finances. She then taught school in her hometown and nearby villages for ten years. Roberts' teaching experiences in the rural areas of Kentucky expanded her knowledge of country speech and folk ballads, a valuable asset in her later writings.

In 1910, a visit with relatives in the mountains of Colorado inspired Roberts to write seven poems, which were published with photographs of mountain flowers in the book *In the Great Steep's Garden* (1915). A mutual acquaintance at the University of Kentucky put her in touch with University of Chicago professor Robert Morss Lovett, who persuaded her to attend the University of Chicago. Roberts earned a philosophy degree there in 1921 and graduated Phi Beta Kappa. That same year, she won the Fiske Prize from the University of Chicago for poems later published in *Under the Tree* (1922).

After graduation, Roberts returned to Kentucky and focused primarily on writing novels. However, she did not wholly abandon poetry, infusing her fiction with vivid symbolism and a narrative style much like that of her contemporary *Virginia Woolf, whose free-floating prose abandoned realism in order to better convey the interior life of the characters. Using her familiarity with the state and people of Kentucky, Roberts closely linked her writing to them. Kentucky women pioneers are the focus of some of her most prominent novels. Their search for self necessitates a struggle against nature and fate that reflects Roberts' early education in mythology.

*E*lizabeth
*M*adox
*R*oberts

Her first novel, *The Time of Man* (1926), reworked *The Odyssey* into the epic story of a pioneer woman's life, and was translated into several languages. Her more somber second novel, *My Heart and My Flesh* (1927), made use of the scandals and people of her hometown of Springfield to explore the theme of rebirth which would appear in other novels. Her 1928 novel *Jingling in the Wind* expressed Roberts' opinion on the follies of society through a combination of satire, comedy and fantasy. She returned to the historical novel genre for her fourth book *The Great Meadow* (1930). The heroine in the story is Diony Hall, a strong, imaginative woman who is the archetypal protagonist of Roberts' writing. Some critics claim that this story about a pioneer woman's settling in middle Kentucky is one of the greatest American historical novels.

Roberts was also a gifted short-story writer, as demonstrated in the volumes *The Haunted Mirror* (1932) and *Not by Strange Gods* (1941). She won the O. Henry short story award in 1930. Her poetry continued to receive recognition as well, winning the John Reed Memorial Prize of Poetry in 1928 and the Poetry Society of South Carolina's prize in 1931.

In the mid-1930s, Roberts' health problems worsened, and she was diagnosed with Hodgkin's disease in 1936. To alleviate her suffering, she began to spend her winters in Florida. Despite her illness, Roberts continued to write. Her last novel, *Black Is My Truelove's Hair* (1938), managed to reflect the serenity of her earlier writings even though she was aware that her death was near. Roberts died in Orlando, Florida, of anemia, at age 55, and was buried in Springfield, Kentucky.

SOURCES:
Buck, Claire, ed. *The Bloomsbury Guide to Women's Literature.* NY: Prentice Hall, 1992.
James, Edward T., ed. *Notable American Women, 1607–1950.* Cambridge, MA: The Belknap Press of Harvard University, 1971.
Kunitz, Stanley J., and Howard Haycraft, eds. *Twentieth Century Authors.* NY: H.W. Wilson, 1942.
McHenry, Robert, ed. *Famous American Women.* NY: Dover, 1980.

Brenda Kubic,
freelance writer, Chesterfield, Michigan

Roberts, Kate (1891–1985)

Welsh nationalist, writer, publisher and journalist. Born in North Wales in 1891; died in 1985; attended the University College of North Wales, Bangor; married Morris T. Williams, in 1928.

Kate Roberts was born in 1891 and brought up near Caernarfon, in the slate-quarrying area

of North Wales, where her father was a quarry-
man and her mother looked after their small
holding. She studied at the University College of
North Wales, Bangor, and began her career as a
teacher of Welsh in South Wales during the Depression. She married Morris T. Williams in
1928, and together they bought the publishing
firm of Gwasg Gee in Denbigh and its Welsh-
language paper, *Y Faner* (The Banner). Many of
her articles were written for this publication.

Roberts felt that her creative writing was inspired by tragedy and loss: the sufferings caused
by World War I, by quarrying accidents, and by
the austerity of working-class life as endured by
women in domestic settings. Her wish to trans-
mute her observations into action caused her to
join the Welsh Nationalist Party (Plaid Cymru),
whose aim is self-government for Wales, and to
write for its newspaper *Y Ddraig Goch* (The Red
Dragon). There was a break of 12 years in
Roberts' writing, which she resumed after the
death of her husband in 1946 and then continued until she was in her 90s. Her short stories
are reminiscent of those of Chekhov and Maupassant, her books for children sharply observed
and without sentimentality. Roberts was honored by the University of Wales, the Honourable
Society of Cymmrodorion, and the Welsh Arts
Council. On her death she left half of her estate
to Plaid Cymru.

SOURCES:

Berresford-Ellis, Peter. *Celtic Women*. London: Constable, 1995.

Evans, Gwynfor. *Welsh Nation Builders*. Llandyssul:
Gomer, 1988.

Elizabeth Rokkan,
translator, formerly Associate Professor,
Department of English, University of Bergen, Norway

Roberts, Margaret (b. 1925).

See Thatcher, Margaret.

Roberts, Marguerite (1905–1989)

*American screenwriter. Name variations: Maggie
Roberts; Marguerite Sanford. Born in Clarks, Nebraska, on November 26, 1905; died of atherosclerosis on
February 17, 1989, in Santa Barbara, California; attended Colorado State Teaching College; married
twice, second time to John Sanford (a writer).*

*Filmography: Jimmy and Sally (1933); Sailor's
Luck (1933); Peck's Bad Boy (1934); College Scandal
(1935); Florida Special (1936); Forgotten Faces
(1936); Hollywood Boulevard (1936); Rose Bowl
(1936); Turn of the Moon (1937); Wild Moon (1937);
Meet the Girls (1938); Escape (1940); Honky Tonk
(1941); Ziegfeld Girl (1941); Somewhere I'll Find You*

*(1942); Dragonseed (1944); Desire Me (1947); If the
Winter Comes (1947); The Sea of Grass (1947); Am-
bush (1949); The Bribe (1949); Soldiers Three (1951);
Diamond Head (1962); Rampage (1963); Lorett's
Many Faces (1965); Five Card Stud (1968); True Grit
(1969); Norwood (1970); Red Sky at Morning
(1971); Shoot Out (1971).*

A screenwriter for Fox and MGM during
the 1930s and 1940s, Marguerite Roberts was
one of a handful of women of the time who
made her reputation creating "men's films."
Clark Gable, for whom she wrote several box-
office hits, including *Honky Tonk* (1941) and
Somewhere I'll Find You (1942), once said that
she "writes men with more balls than any other
guy on this lot." Roberts was accused of being a
Communist during the dark era of the House
Un-American Activities Committee; she was
blacklisted and did not work for over a decade.
She reemerged in the 1960s, however, to write
her most celebrated screenplay, *True Grit*
(1969), a western based on a novel by Charles
Portis, which John Wayne called the best script
he had ever read.

It is hardly surprising that Roberts was
drawn to the western. Born in Nebraska, she
was raised in Colorado, and was astride a horse
almost as soon as she could walk. Her grandfather, who came to Colorado by covered wagon,
was a sheriff, and her father was a town marshal. "He never carried a gun," Roberts said
about her father, "but all the bad men were
afraid of him. He was short and stocky, but
some people said he was the strongest man in
Colorado and nothing scared him." Roberts recalled that her family was poor and her mother
took in laundry to earn extra money. It became
her ambition to find a good job so her mother
could lead an easier life. Roberts attended Colorado State Teaching College to prepare for a
teaching career, but she got sidetracked when
she married a traveling jewelry merchant who
took her on the road with him. The marriage endured only as far as California, where Roberts
decided to settle.

Following a stint as a reporter and as an unsuccessful writer of crime fiction, Roberts developed an interest in screenwriting. In 1927, she
took a job at Fox as secretary to the studio head
Winfield Sheehan. She later apprenticed in the
script department, working with chief script editor Al Lewis. Once on her own, she experimented with several different genres, writing the
screenplay for *Peck's Bad Boy* (1934), a vehicle
for Jackie Cooper, as well as *Hollywood Boule-*

vard (1936), a melodrama exploiting the more tawdry aspects of the film business. Moving to MGM, where she created *Honky Tonk* (1941), a western adventure starring Clark Gable and *Lana Turner, Roberts found a comfortable niche. Gable liked her style so much that he asked her to work on his next film, *Somewhere I'll Find You* (1942), the story of two war correspondents. Roberts went on to become one of MGM's most respected and highly paid screenwriters, earning enough money to send some home to her mother, and to support her second husband John Sanford, who was pursuing his own writing career.

While at MGM, Roberts did not write exclusively for male stars, although she preferred writing male characters. "At Metro it was very difficult to write for women since [the studio] had such old-fashioned ideas," she said. "There were two kinds of women—whores and angels—and they didn't make for interesting people." Roberts ran into particular difficulty when she was working on the rewrites for *Sea of Grass* (1947), a western in which *Katharine Hepburn played the wife of a cattle tycoon (Spencer Tracy) who places his work before family. Roberts wanted to have the Hepburn character threaten to leave, but director Elia Kazan would not hear of it. "Kazan's politics were very liberal at the time, but he was a chauvinist, and politics, for him, didn't enter into that."

Roberts' own politics would prove to be a force in her career. During the late 1930s, she and Sanford had joined the Communist Party, more in hopes of establishing social reform than inciting revolution, writes **Lizzie Francke** in *Script Girls*. Her political views surfaced in *Escape* (1940), an adaptation of the novel by **Ethel Vance** which centers on an American's rescue of his mother from a Nazi concentration camp just before World War II. Called "far and away the most dramatic and hair-raising picture yet made on the sinister subject of persecution in a totalitarian land" by critic Bosley Crowther, the film was one of 25 investigated by the Senate Subcommittee on War Propaganda. In this case, Francke explains, the Producers' Association, representing management and the Screen Writers Guild (of which Roberts was a militant member), was successful in warding off indictment. But Roberts was not so lucky in September 1951, when she, along with many others in the Hollywood community, was called before the House Un-American Activities Committee. At the time, MGM was so fearful of losing her that they encouraged her to name a few names in order to vindicate herself, but Roberts stood

firm, pleading the Fifth Amendment and refusing to cooperate. As a result, her contract with the studio was terminated and her name was dropped from the credits of *Ivanhoe*, the film she was working on at the time.

After her return to work in the '60s, Roberts wrote the screenplays for such films as *Diamond Head* (1962), *Rampage* (1963), *Five Card Stud* (1968), and the memorable *True Grit* (1969), which won an Academy Award for John Wayne. Roberts ended her career with yet another western, *Shoot Out* (1971), an adaptation of Will James' novel *The Lone Cowboy*, starring Gregory Peck. She died in 1989.

SOURCES AND SUGGESTED READING:

Francke, Lizzie. *Script Girls*. London, England: British Film Institute, 1994.

Halliwell, Leslie. *Halliwell's Film Guide*. 4th ed. NY: Scribner, 1983.

Sanford, John. *Maggie: A Love Story*. Barricade, 1993.

Barbara Morgan, Melrose, Massachusetts

Roberts, Rachel (1927–1980)

Welsh actress who won the British Film Academy's Best Actress award for Saturday Night and Sunday Morning. *Born on September 20, 1927, in Llanelly, Wales; died on November 26, 1980, in Los Angeles, California; youngest of two daughters of Richard Roberts (a minister) and Rachel Ann (Jones) Roberts; attended Swansea High School; graduated from the University of Wales; attended the Royal Academy of Dramatic Art; married Alan Dobie (an actor), in 1955 (divorced 1961); married Rex Harrison (an actor), in March 21, 1962 (divorced 1971); no children.*

Selected filmography in UK, unless otherwise indicated: Valley of Song (Men Are Children Twice, *1953);* The Weak and the Wicked *(1954);* The Good Companions *(1957);* Our Man in Havana *(1959);* Saturday Night and Sunday Morning *(1960);* This Sporting Life *(1963);* La Puce à l'Oreille (A Flea in Her Ear, *Fr.-US, 1968);* The Reckoning *(1969);* Doctors' Wives *(US, 1971);* The Wild Rovers *(US, 1971);* The Belstone Fox *(Free Spirit, 1973);* O Lucky Man! *(1973);* Alpha Beta *(1973);* Murder on the Orient Express *(1974);* Picnic at Hanging Rock *(Austral., 1976);* Foul Play *(US, 1978);* Yanks *(1979);* When a Stranger Calls *(US, 1979);* Charlie Chan and the Curse of the Dragon Queen *(US, 1981).*

Rachel Roberts died by her own hand on November 26, 1980, at age 53. At the time of her death, the talented but troubled actress had all but destroyed her acting career with alcohol and drugs and a desperate obsession with her second husband, Rex Harrison, to whom she was married from 1962 to 1971. "I've never ever got over my halcyon days with him and however much I try, I can't," Roberts wrote shortly before her death. Those close to her were initially stunned at her suicide, unaware of the depths of her despair until the discovery of her journal not long after her death. The diary, which she kept during the last 18 months of her life, chronicles the suicidal depression that ultimately engulfed her.

Rachel Roberts (dubbed Ray at an early age) was born in 1927 in the small Welsh town of Llanelly, although the family moved to the more sophisticated city of Swansea when she was seven. Her father, a Baptist minister, was gentle and loving, but it was her strict and overprotective mother who dominated her upbringing. A shy child with an inferiority complex, she began to change gradually in her teens, when she discovered her talent for recitation and play acting. In high school, she became the star of the school plays and something of a trend-setter, although she still suffered dark periods of self-doubt.

Roberts blossomed during her years at the University of Wales, a rural college on the sea coast, where she took advantage of every acting opportunity available to her. "I knew then she had great things in her," said a friend, referring to her performance in *Juno and the Paycock*. "She had a wonderful face for portraying suffering. There are very few actresses who can show suffering in all three dimensions—with body, expression and feeling." Roberts' next stop was the Royal Academy of Dramatic Art, where she wilted a bit under the strict program of study. Wanting more opportunities to act rather than study, she left before completing the course and joined a repertory company in Swansea. After a year, she moved on to Stratford-upon-Avon, but left after a season without having distinguished herself. She worked for a time at the Irving Theatre Club in London, then went to West Germany to entertain the British troops in a revue called *Intimacy at 8:30*. Returning home, she spent another season at Stratford, where she met actor Alan Dobie, whom she married in 1955.

Following her marriage, Roberts continued to pursue her acting career which consisted mostly of minor stage and film roles. Her breakthrough part was that of the blowsy, unfaithful wife in the "New Wave" British film *Saturday Night and Sunday Morning* (1960), for which she won the British Film Academy's Best Actress award. She went on to play a similar type in *This Sporting Life* (1963), with Richard Harris, earn-

ing a nomination for an Academy Award as Best Supporting Actress. In the interim between the films, Roberts divorced Alan Dobie to become the fourth wife of Rex Harrison, whom she had met in 1960, when she played opposite him in the Chekhov play *Platonov* at the Royal Court. (Harrison had been married previously to **Marjorie Thomas**, *****Lilli Palmer** and *****Kay Kendall**.)

Marriage to Harrison seriously stalled Roberts' career. "I'm not ambitious any more," she admitted following the nuptials. "I don't want to be a great success, to be a star, to have an acting career and be a public figure for fifty-two weeks of the year." When Harrison was selected to play Professor Higgins in the film version of *My Fair Lady* (1964), the couple relocated to Hollywood, where Roberts felt like an outsider. Pretty much confined to the house because she did not drive, Roberts started drinking, and the marriage began to suffer the first signs of stress.

The couple returned to Europe in 1964, and Roberts found work in *Maggie May*, Lionel Bart's updated lay version of the story of Christ and *****Mary Magdalene**, but her drinking forced her to leave the production mid-run. She resumed her role as a dutiful housewife to Harrison, but with an undercurrent of resentment that fractured the relationship. She had film roles in *A Flea in Her Ear* (1968), opposite her husband, and in *The Reckoning* (1969), at which time she admitted to a reporter that allowing her career to lapse had been a mistake. "I did really make a superhuman effort to give up the desire to act. To just completely forget about it. But I could not. It's in your blood and that's that."

Following her divorce from Harrison, who had left her for actress **Elizabeth Harris**, Roberts returned to Los Angeles, but her obsession with her failed marriage hindered her ability to move forward. "I got drunk. I got lower and lower, though still coasting along on the strength of old memories. . . . I wasn't facing life realistically. I was running from it in a mad, 'exciting' disguise." Work seemed to be the one thing that could bring Roberts back into focus. She landed a role in the American production of *The Effect of Gamma Rays on Man-in-the-Moon Marigolds*, staged at the Huntington Hartford Theater, and then in 1972 returned to London's Royal Court in *Alpha Beta*, the chronicle of a destructive middle-class family, with Albert Finney, who had been her co-star in *Saturday Night and Sunday Morning*. Her role as the mistreated and mistreating wife won her the *Evening Standard* Best Actress award, but the character, whose emotional troubles were close to her own, proved a burden to her. While awaiting the play's transfer to the West End after its initial run, Roberts appeared on a talk-show drunk and out of control. She was subsequently hospitalized to dry out.

In 1973, the actress starred in two plays, *The Visit* and *Chemin de Fer*, staged "back to back" by the New Phoenix Company and directed respectively by Harold Prince and Stephen Porter. The roles—Clara Zachanassian in the first, and Francine in the second—demanded a transition from drama to farce, which Roberts carried off with aplomb, receiving a Tony nomination for each of the characterizations, the first "double" in the history of the award. But she was still battling her emotional problems with alcohol and pills. Prince recalled her as "tremendously disciplined" on stage and was surprised by what he saw and heard about her offstage behavior. He recalled receiving a phone call from his colleague, director John Dexter, who had been in Sardi's one evening after a performance of *The Visit*. "Suddenly, out of the corner of his eye, he saw something moving. He looked round. What he witnessed was Rachel crawling towards him *over the tops* of the intervening tables, and when she got near enough to him she hissed, 'That Hal Prince is the coldest son of a bitch I've ever seen in my life.'"

Through the remainder of the 1970s, Roberts continued to drink in excess, but somehow managed to pull herself together enough to maintain a low-level career. In 1976, after roles in the films *Murder on the Orient Express* (1974) and *Picnic at Hanging Rock* (1976), and a tour in the British play *Habeas Corpus*, Roberts was contracted to play the feisty but lovable housekeeper, Mrs. McClelland, on the television sit-com "The Tony Randall Show." During the run of the show, Roberts outwardly appeared to be under control, although she was slipping emotionally and still drinking. Randall later said that he never saw her "other" side. "If anyone had told me she was wild and ungovernable and hooked on alcohol, I simply wouldn't have been able to reconcile that with the woman who played in the show with me for two years." In her journal, Roberts had nothing but disdain

From the movie This Sporting Life, *starring* Richard Harris *and* Rachel Roberts.

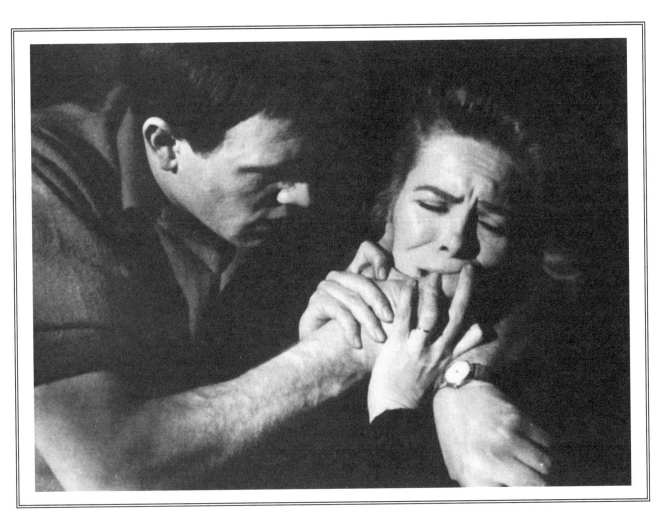

for her role on the Randall show, calling it the "most hateful and humiliating job, degrading and upsetting."

After the series was canceled, Roberts appeared in the British TV film "The Old Crowd" and made several features, including *Yanks* (1979), the John Schlesinger film about wartime England. Around this time, she began going to the Los Angeles Public Library to write her journals, an activity that seemed to calm her inner chaos. In March 1979, however, after returning from a South Seas holiday with her current lover Darren Ramirez, she began what she described as "this spiral of suicidal depression." She still attempted to work, appearing in a summer-stock production of *The Sorrows of Gin* and a short-lived pre-Broadway tour of *Once a Catholic*, but now she was having trouble remembering lines and was often out of control. "Her condition was very noticeable," recalled Ramirez, following the close of *Once a Catholic*. "She would be crying all the time and unable to get herself out of bed. She had begun receiving Lithium treatment to help calm her and keep her spirits up." Roberts also began attending AA meetings and working with a psychiatrist.

While in this precarious state, Roberts decided she wanted to teach and somehow obtained a position as a lecturer in the drama department of Yale University. At the time, playwright Athol Fugard was also at Yale to stage a production of his new play *A Lesson from Aloes*, and it was the hope of Lloyd Richards, then dean of the Yale Drama School, that Roberts would play the leading female role in the work, opposite James Earl Jones. Roberts reluctantly agreed to the part, although her character Gladys was also in the throes of an emotional breakdown. "In addition to Gladys's history of mental instability the fictional character and the real-life woman had something else in common which Fugard was certainly not privy to at that time," writes Alexander Walker, who edited Roberts' journals. "Gladys has been keeping personal journals which, before the play opened, had been seized in a security raid and used as evidence against her husband's political associates. This, it was suggested, had triggered her mental breakdown."

Fugard gradually became aware of Roberts' drinking, her obsession with Harrison, and her fear of performing in his play. Rehearsals were agony and her teaching also began to suffer. Eventually, she was forced to leave the play and Yale. In her journal, Roberts wrote that she was relieved about the play and did not want to act

again: "I want to live. I hate acting and everything connected with it. . . . I really only want to talk and drink and eat. Perhaps Rex will help me do all these things and then I can feel protected in the bargain."

Ironically, Roberts' last feature film role was the comic Mrs. Dangers in the 1980 detective parody *Charlie Chan and the Curse of the Dragon Queen*. She called it "an agitated, lonely ordeal." Soon afterwards, she began a series of hospital stays in England and the United States, but her depression remained untouched by any of the treatments she received. She ended her life by ingesting an overdose of barbiturates after having telephoned both Harrison and Ramirez to say goodbye. The last entry in her journal served as her farewell message:

> I can't control it any more and I've been trying with all my failing strength. I'm paralyzed. I can't do anything and there seems to be no help anywhere. What has happened to me? Is it that my dependence over the years on alcohol has so severely debilitated me that now, without it, I just cannot function at all? Or is it that my nervous system from birth has always been so very frail that life for me is too much to cope with? That I was the hopelessly dependent little girl who found everything too hard to handle, so that my intelligence and talent have been overcome now that I'm in my fifties and I can't understand it? Day after day and night after night, I'm in this shaking fear. What am I so terribly frightened of?
> Life itself, I think.

SOURCES:
Katz, Ephraim. *The Film Encyclopedia*. NY: Harper-Collins, 1994.

Walker, Alexander, ed. *No Bells on Sunday: The Rachel Roberts Journals* (with a documentary biography by Alexander Walker). NY: Harper & Row, 1984.

Barbara Morgan,
Melrose, Massachusetts

Roberts, Sally (1884–1955).

See Martin, Sara.

Robertson, Agnes (1833–1916)

Scottish actress. Name variations: Agnes Kelly Robertson. Born in Edinburgh, Scotland, on December 25, 1833; died in London, England, on November 6, 1916; daughter of Thomas Robertson; married Dionysius Lardner (Dion) Boucicault, also known as Dion Boucicault the Elder (1822–1890, an actor and dramatist), in 1853 (divorced 1889); children: Dion William; Eva (or Eve) Boucicault; Darley George ("Dot") Boucicault, later known as Dion Boucicault *the Younger (1859–1929, an actor, manager and stage director who married actress *Irene Vanbrugh); Patrice Boucicault; Nina Boucicault (1867–1950, an actress); Aubrey Boucicault (an actor and writer).*

Born on December 25, 1833, in Edinburgh, Scotland, Agnes Robertson was said to have begun her acting career at age ten, with an appearance at the Theatre Royal in Aberdeen. Little is known about her early years, although some reports say she may have acted with *Fanny Kemble and William Charles Macready. In 1850, at age 16, Robertson appeared on stage at the Princess' Theatre in London, and may have come under the guardianship of the theater's manager Charles Kean at this time. During her three-year association with the Princess' Theatre, she appeared in several plays, including *The Vampire* and *The Prima Donna* by prolific Irish playwright Dion Boucicault the Elder. A romance developed between Robertson and Boucicault, and when she left for America in August 1853, he followed her a few weeks later. Though no date is known, it is generally assumed that they married shortly before, or shortly after, their move to the United States.

Robertson's first North American appearance was in Montreal, Canada, in September, followed by her New York debut at Burton's Theater on October 22, 1853, playing multiple roles in *The Young Actress*, a musical farce adapted by Boucicault. She quickly became one of the most popular actresses in America. Her petite beauty and the sweetness she conveyed through characters like Jessie, the Scottish servant maid in *Jessie Brown, or The Relief of Lucknow* (1858), and Eily O'Connor in the enduringly popular *The Colleen Bawn* (1860), earned her the nickname "the fairy star." Boucicault wrote most of the plays in which she appeared, and he tailored her characters to complement her unique charm, particularly as a sweet and simple peasant girl, and occasionally showcasing her voice in ballads. Robertson also starred in successful productions of *Dot and Smike* (1859), *The Octoroon* (1859), and *Jeanie Dreams* (also called *The Heart of Midlothian*, 1860). In 1860, Robertson returned with Boucicault to England, where she was known as "the Pocket Venus" by theater audiences. Her 12-year stay in England included roles in Boucicault's *Arrah-na-Pogue* (1865) and *The Long Strike* (1866). In 1872, she returned to America for a year-long revival of some of her most popular roles.

The following two decades proved to be personally tumultuous for Robertson as she en-

Boucicault, Nina. See Adams, Maude for sidebar.

dured Boucicault's repeated infidelities. The two were often apart, with Robertson acting principally in London and Boucicault residing in the United States. She went so far as to initiate divorce proceedings, but halted the process in 1883. The final straw, however, occurred in 1885, when Boucicault departed for an Australian tour with two of their children and **Louise Thorndyke**, one of his longtime acting partners. In Australia, Boucicault married Thorndyke, claiming he had never legally married Robertson. Robertson sued for divorce, which was granted along with court costs on June 21, 1888; it became final six months later. Boucicault died the following year.

Robertson's final appearance occurred at the Princess' Theatre in 1896. She died in London on November 6, 1916. Her legacy to the theater lived on in three of her six children: Aubrey became an actor and writer; Dion Boucicault the Younger enjoyed a successful career as an actor, manager and stage director, creating roles in several of A.A. Milne's plays; and **Nina Boucicault** had a distinguished acting career both in movies and on stage, where she originated the role of Peter Pan for J.M. Barrie.

SOURCES:

James, Edward T., ed. *Notable American Women, 1607–1950.* Cambridge, MA: The Belknap Press of Harvard University, 1971.

Brenda Kubiac,
freelance writer, Chesterfield, Michigan

Robertson, Alice Mary (1854–1931)

American educator and politician who was the first woman to preside over the U.S. House of Representatives (1921). Born Mary Alice Robertson at Tullahassee Mission, Indian Territory (now Tullahassee, Oklahoma), on January 2, 1854; died in Muskogee, Oklahoma, on July 1, 1931; daughter of William Schenck Robertson and Ann Eliza (Worcester) Robertson (both missionary teachers); received early education at home; attended Elmira College in New York, 1871–73; never married; children: adopted daughter, Suzanne Barnett.

Born on January 2, 1854, Alice Mary Robertson grew up at the Tullahassee Mission in what was then Indian Territory (now Oklahoma). Her father William Schenck Robertson had journeyed to the remote territory five years before Alice's birth to take control of the newly formed Tullahassee boarding school, a joint venture between the Creek Indian government and the Presbyterian mission board. Both he and her mother **Ann Worcester Robertson** were missionary teachers. Alice's maternal grandfather was the famous Congregational minister Samuel A. Worcester, who had served as a missionary to the Cherokees. Robertson spent her early life at the mission, before attending Elmira College in New York from 1871 to 1873. However, she cut her education short so that a younger sister could also have a college education.

Robertson continued her association with Native Americans into adulthood when she took a position as a clerk in the Office of Indian Affairs in Washington, D.C. She resigned in 1879 and returned to Tullahassee to teach at the mission school. When a fire destroyed the school, she became secretary to Captain Richard H. Pratt, superintendent of the Carlisle Indian School in Pennsylvania. Two years later, she again returned to Tullahassee to assist her mother in raising funds to build a new school, proving adept at the task. In 1885, Robertson was given the responsibility of running a Presbyterian mission girls' boarding school at Muskogee. Her efforts paved the way for the boarding school's expansion in 1894 into a coeducational college. Known as Henry Kendall College, the fledgling college also benefited from Robertson's teaching of English, history, and civics. (It would later be moved to Tulsa and renamed the University of Tulsa.)

When the federal government took control of Indian education in 1897, Robertson decided to pursue the position of federal supervisor of Creek schools. Her determination prevailed, and she resigned from Henry Kendall College in 1899, to begin the following year what became the exhausting work of federal supervisor. The constant reports and school site visits kept her busy, as did her appointment and certification of teachers. At her suggestion, President Theodore Roosevelt, a personal friend, appointed Robertson postmistress of Muskogee in 1905. She held that position until 1913, when the Wilson administration took over.

Robertson retired that year and settled into farming just outside of Muskogee, where she lived with her adopted Native American daughter, **Suzanne Barnett**. Together they bred dairy cattle and grew vegetables. Robertson also established a successful cafeteria in Muskogee that served hungry troops when military trains rolled through town during World War I. Robertson's delivery of coffee and refreshments to the soldiers was so greatly appreciated that she became known in training camps as "Miss Alice." Her cafeteria soon expanded its services to become the Muskogee Red Cross service and a model for other Red Cross stations to follow.

Even though Robertson herself had opposed women's suffrage, she was persuaded to run for Congress on a Republican ticket after the ratification of the 19th amendment in 1920. (The only woman previously elected to Congress was *Jeannette Rankin, who served from 1916 to 1919 after Montana granted women the right to vote.) Robertson based her campaign on the principles of Christianity and patriotism, and beat incumbent William W. Hastings. Her victory in predominantly Democratic Oklahoma came at a time when Republican landslide victories occurred nationwide. She was the only woman member of Congress and garnered much public attention as a result, although her career was fairly unremarkable. She was assigned to the House Committee on Indian Affairs, the Committee on Expenditures in the Interior Department, and (somewhat less appropriately) the Committee on Woman Suffrage. On June 20, 1921, she became the first woman to preside over a session of the House of Representatives, when she announced the vote for the funding of a U.S. delegation to Peru for the

*Alice
Mary
Robertson*

centennial celebration of Peru's independence. As a conservative, she opposed U.S. entry into the League of Nations and toed the Republican Party line on most issues, with the noted exception of her opposition to the Sheppard-Towner Act of 1921, which provided federal aid to state maternal and child health-care programs. She argued that the act was an intrusion on personal rights by the government, but her opposition angered her female constituents, including the Daughters of the American Revolution. Robertson was also an opponent of such women's political groups as the League of Women Voters and the National Women's Party. In addition to alienating women's groups, Robertson made veterans unhappy by voting against the Soldiers' Bonus Bill, although she voted to increase financial support for Army and Navy nurses. Having severely weakened her support base, she lost the 1922 election to Hastings. She also failed to win an appointment to the Bureau of Indian Affairs in the Harding administration.

Following her defeat, Robertson returned to Oklahoma and served briefly as a welfare worker at the Veterans Hospital in Muskogee. She ended her diverse career as the Washington correspondent for the *Muskogee News* and as an employee of the Oklahoma Historical Society. Robertson died of cancer of the jaw in 1931 and was buried at Greenhill Cemetery in Muskogee, Oklahoma.

SOURCES:
James, Edward T., ed. *Notable American Women, 1607–1950.* Cambridge, MA: The Belknap Press of Harvard University Press, 1971.

McHenry, Robert, ed. *Famous American Women.* NY: Dover, 1980.

Office of the Historian. *Women In Congress, 1917–1990.* Commission on the Bicentenary of the U.S. House of Representatives, 1991.

Read, Phyllis J., and Bernard L. Witlieb. *The Book of Women's Firsts.* NY: Random House, 1992.

Brenda Kubiac,
freelance writer, Chesterfield, Michigan

Robertson, Brenda May (1929—)

First woman elected to the New Brunswick Legislative Assembly. Born on May 23, 1929, near Sussex, New Brunswick, Canada; Mount Allison University, B.Sc. (Home Econ.), 1950; married Wilmont Waldon Robertson; children: three.

Born on May 23, 1929, in Sussex, New Brunswick, Canada, Brenda May Robertson was active in political circles prior to her election to the New Brunswick Legislative Assembly. She served as president of the New Brunswick

Women's Progressive Conservative Association as well as president of the New Brunswick Association of Home Economists. Her activism resulted in her election as a Progressive Conservative to the New Brunswick Legislative Assembly on October 23, 1967, making her the first woman member of the assembly. She worked tirelessly to reduce unemployment and improve social programs, health care and conditions for underprivileged children as youth minister (1970–74), minister of social welfare (1971–72), minister of social services (1972–74), minister of health (1976, 1978–82), and minister for social program reform (1982–84).

Robertson's efforts on behalf of her New Brunswick constituents were recognized when she was appointed to the Canadian Senate on December 21, 1984. As a senator, she continued to devote herself to social reform. Her committee memberships included the Standing Committee on External Affairs, chair of the Fisheries Committee, and deputy chair of the Standing Committees on Social Affairs, and Science and Technology.

Robertson and **Solange Chaput-Rolland** cowrote *Chère Sénateur* (Dear Senator), a 1992 behind-the-scenes look at the operation of the Senate which includes the authors' personal perspectives as women senators. As of the late 1990s, Robertson continued to serve in the Senate.

Howard Gofstein,
freelance writer, Oak Park, Michigan

Robertson, Carole (d. 1963).

See Davis, Angela for sidebar.

Robertson, E. Arnot (1903–1961)

British novelist and film critic. Name variations: Eileen Arnot Robertson; Eileen Arbuthnot Robertson; Mrs. Henry Ernest Turner. Born Eileen Arbuthnot Robertson in Holmwood, Surrey, England, in 1903; committed suicide in London, England, on September 21, 1961; daughter of G.A. Robertson (a doctor); educated at Sherbourne Girls' School, and in Switzerland and Paris; married Henry Turner (general secretary of the Empire Press Union), in 1927; children: one son.

Selected writings: Cullum *(1928);* Three Came Unarmed *(1928);* Four Frightened People *(1931);* Ordinary Families *(1933);* Thames Portrait *(1937);* Summer's Lease *(1940);* The Signpost *(1943);* Devices and Desires *(1954);* Justice of the Heart *(1958);* Strangers on my Roof *(posthumously released, 1964).*

Born Eileen Arbuthnot Robertson in Surrey, England, in 1903, E. Arnot Robertson grew up under the shadow of disappointment, because she did not excel in the sports or music that were most valued by her family. To compensate, she started writing, choosing exotic locations as settings for her novels. She was a world traveler—beginning with her attendance at schools in Switzerland and Paris in addition to her unhappy education at Sherbourne Girls' School—but she chose to locate her stories in places unfamiliar to her, such as Singapore, Malaya, Greece, Zanzibar and Hong Kong. Her first novel, *Cullum* (1928), was the story of an affair between a girl and a womanizing writer. *Three Came Unarmed*, the story of three children raised in Borneo and transplanted in England, appeared the same year.

However, it was not until 1931 that Robertson gained wide recognition, with her novel *Four Frightened People*, which flipped the plot of *Three Came Unarmed* by focusing on four English characters in a jungle. Her 1933 bestseller, *Ordinary Families*, portrayed a middle-class household who shared her own real-life family's passion for sailing. It was adapted as a film by Cecil B. De Mille in 1934. Robertson's subsequent novels, *Thames Portrait* (1937), *Summer's Lease* (1940), *The Signpost* (1943), *Devices and Desires* (1954), *Justice of the Heart* (1958) and *Strangers on my Roof* (1964), were never as notable as her early writings.

Following World War II, Robertson began working as a film critic, and made the news with a libel suit against MGM after the movie studio banned her from screenings because of her hostile reviews. Although she won the first round of the lawsuit, the House of Lords overturned the ruling. In the spring of 1961, Robertson's husband of more than 30 years drowned in a boating accident; five months later, she committed suicide.

SOURCES:

Shattock, Joanne. *The Oxford Guide to British Women Writers*. Oxford: Oxford University Press, 1993.

Brenda Kubiac,
freelance writer, Chesterfield, Michigan

Robertson, Florence (1870–1946).

See Richardson, Henry Handel.

Robertson, Kelly McCormick (b. 1960).

See McCormick, Kelly.

Robertson, Madge (1849–1935).

See Kendal, Madge.

Robertson, Margaret Brunton (1849–1935).

See Kendal, Madge.

Robertson, Marjorie (1904–1986).

See Neagle, Anna.

Robertson, Mrs. Wybrow (1847–1884).

See Litton, Marie.

Robeson, Eslanda Goode

(1896–1965)

African-American activist and wife of Paul Robeson.
Name variations: Eslanda Cardoza Goode Robeson; Essie Goode; Essie Robeson. Born Eslanda Cardoza Goode in Washington, D.C., in 1896; died of cancer at Beth Israel Hospital in New York City on December 13, 1965; daughter of John Goode (a former slave and a clerk in the War Department) and Eslanda (Cardoza) Goode; attended public schools in New York City; attended University of Illinois, 1912–14; Columbia University, B.S., 1920; studied anthropology at London University, 1935–37; studied at the London School of Economics, 1938; enrolled in doctoral course at Hartford Seminary, c. 1939; married Paul Robeson (the activist and actor), on August 17, 1921; children: son Paul (Pauli) Robeson, Jr. (b. 1927).

Born Eslanda Cardoza Goode in Washington, D.C., in 1896, "Essie," as she was known by her intimates, was the wife of the dynamic performer and activist Paul Robeson. Although not as well known as her famous husband, Eslanda Robeson by no means hid in his shadow. Through her writings and actions, she advocated racial equality and withstood considerable political and social pressure in the course of her long activist career.

Eslanda came from a distinguished lineage. Her mother **Eslanda Cardoza Goode** was a descendent of the prominent Sephardic Jewish Cardozo (name spellings vary) family of Charleston, South Carolina, and her mother's father Francis Lewis Cardozo had been secretary of state and secretary of the treasury of South Carolina during Reconstruction. Once called "the most highly educated Negro in America," he was also principal of one of the first secondary schools for blacks in Charleston, South Carolina. Eslanda's father died from an alcohol-related illness when she was six years old. Her mother then moved to New York City with Eslanda and her two brothers to avoid Washington's segregated schools. Eslanda Cardoza Goode served as a role model for her daughter by studying osteopathy and beauty culture, eventually opening a successful practice that catered to such members of the New York elite as **Kate Davis Pulitzer** (Mrs. Joseph Pulitzer) and **Edith Kingdon Gould** (Mrs. George J. Gould). The Harlem environment in which she grew up also profoundly impacted the girl, arriving as she did at the start of the Harlem Renaissance.

In 1912, Eslanda left to study at the State University of Illinois, but returned two years later to complete her undergraduate education at Columbia University. Through close friendships with John Reed and other activists, she developed left-wing political views and a deep commitment to social change. She graduated from Columbia with a degree in chemistry in 1920, and began work as an analytical chemist and technician in the surgery and pathology department at Columbia Presbyterian Medical Center—probably the first black woman to do so. While there, she met her future husband, Paul Robeson, who had come to the hospital for treatment after a football accident. Already a well-known figure by this time, he had moved to Harlem in 1919 after graduating Phi Beta Kappa from Rutgers University and was pursuing a law degree at Columbia. The pair married on August 17, 1921.

It was Eslanda who suggested the change of career that would also change the scope of their lives; she convinced Paul to take the lead in a YMCA production of *Simon the Cyrenian*, his first role in what would be a long and distinguished career in the theater. Audiences were thrilled by his depiction of the black African who carried Christ's cross, and offers to play other roles quickly poured in from prominent theater groups. Although quality roles were few and far between for a black man in the 1920s, Paul Robeson refused to act in any play which depicted blacks as savages or stereotypes.

Having determined that there was no real future for a black man in the legal profession, despite an offer to join a prestigious white law firm, Paul accepted an offer to act in London. Eslanda resigned her position at the hospital in 1925 in order to accompany him. Soon Paul was the toast of two continents and was regularly performing in both the United States and Europe. He showcased his powerful baritone voice on a European concert tour in 1926, and Eslanda decided to give up chemistry altogether to become his full-time manager. She also gave birth to their only son, Paul, Jr., in 1927, although she left him in her mother's care for most of his childhood so she could be free to manage her husband's career.

Eslanda released her first book, a revealing biography of Paul Robeson, in 1930. *Paul Robeson, Negro* reflected her admiration for her hus-

band and highlighted her part in directing his career, but it also did not hide the couple's marital troubles. She was frank about the possibility of her husband's engaging in extramarital affairs, which apparently contributed to their separation from 1930 to 1933. They eventually were able to renew their partnership, both professionally and personally.

Despite their tremendous success, the Robesons continued to be victimized by bigotry and segregation in the United States. They found the more racially tolerant atmosphere of Europe refreshing, particularly in England where the British aristocracy lionized the pair. At a British Labour Party luncheon at the House of Commons in 1928, the Robesons found themselves intensely sympathetic to Labour's views on social equality, a leftist affiliation they would stretch even further when they traveled in the Soviet Union for a year in 1935. They were impressed by the ethnic tolerance among the Soviets, and their outspoken support of certain Communist ideas would later result in tremendous hardship. Eslanda and Paul also traveled to Spain during the Civil War to support the antifascists.

In the midst of her busy schedule, Eslanda decided to act on her growing interest in Africa and embark on a study of anthropology. She studied anthropology for two years at London University, and followed this with a year at the London School of Economics. Although frustrated by the underlying prejudices of her colleagues, Eslanda determined to follow through with her degree, and journeyed to Africa with her young son in 1936 to complete her field work. This trip, and what she learned by examining the myriad economic, cultural, and political realities of Africa, influenced her deeply. Her desire for racial equality took on a Pan-African slant as she recognized the importance of racial pride and unity for the defeat of racism as an ideology.

Eslanda returned with her husband to the United States in 1939 and began her doctoral studies at the Hartford Seminary in Connecticut. However, she was not content to remain in the academic world. She and Paul joined with other influential blacks to found the Council on African Affairs in 1941. This council worked to inform American public opinion on current events in Africa, with a view to rallying black and progressive-minded public circles of the United States to the support of the African peoples in their struggle for independence. Eslanda was one of the most outspoken and articulate members of this organization and was often blunt in her criticism of western colonial powers.

The mid-1940s brought significant accolades to the Robesons as Eslanda's book *African Journey* appeared in 1945 and Paul received the Spingarn Medal that same year. While a scholarly work, *African Journey* was not so much analytical as it was descriptive of the living habits and cultural customs of different tribes, complete with photographs taken by Eslanda. Both provocative and enlightening, it was a landmark work in the sense that it was the first by an American to show the need for reform among the colonial powers. This theme of colonialism became a focal point of Eslanda's later writings; she strongly believed that the end of World War II hearkened a new era of freedom from European colonizers for emerging nations in Asia and Africa.

While Paul went to Europe to entertain victorious Allied troops, Eslanda went as a delegate to the San Francisco Conference, the founding convention of the United Nations. Representing the Council on African Affairs, she hoped to influence the fledgling United Nations to act as a mediator between European colonial powers and their colonies. As the Cold War deepened during these postwar years, Eslanda expressed strong opinions about what she saw as a wayward American foreign policy, arguing that by demonizing Communism, the American government wanted to avoid economic and social problems rooted in racism and colonialism. She hoped to influence the political system from the inside by contributing to the establishment of the Progressive Party. She worked on Henry A. Wallace's presidential campaign, and ran as a Progressive candidate in her own right for secretary of the state of Connecticut in 1948. Two years later, she made a bid for Connecticut's at-large congressional seat. In 1949, she teamed up with Nobel Prize-winning author *Pearl S. Buck to write *An American Argument*. Set up as a dialogue between the two women, Eslanda argued that the United States failed to be a complete democracy, particularly in its treatment of its black citizens. She believed that, while legislation was essential in securing equal rights for African-Americans, a united black protest was needed to spur the process along.

The powerful political stands of the Robesons did not escape the notice of the U.S. government. The House Un-American Activities Committee called up both Robesons to question them about their Communist affiliations and beliefs at a time of national hysteria over the possible Communist threat to the American way of life. Although the committee failed to find anything incriminating in their testimonies, the U.S. government nonetheless revoked their passports,

effectively ending Paul's career as a concert singer. (His reputation in America had already been damaged by an anti-Communist riot at a concert site where he had been scheduled to perform.) The Robesons' income dropped catastrophically, from more than $100,000 a year to $2,000. They were forced to sell their estate in Connecticut in order to live. Foreign governments and cultural groups, both Communist and otherwise, were loud in their condemnation of the persecution, but Washington remained unwilling to reissue their passports. Eslanda refused to be silenced; despite her own troubles, she continued to speak out against injustice wherever she saw it. She followed news of the burgeoning civil-rights movement with avidity, and took part in the Prayer Pilgrimage to Washington, D.C., organized by Martin Luther King, Jr., in 1957.

After nearly ten years, the situation finally began to turn around for the Robesons. In 1958, Paul received an invitation to sing at Carnegie Hall; it was his first concert there in almost a decade. That same year, they finally were issued passports, and promptly traveled to Great Britain and then on to the Soviet Union. However, the years had taken their toll on both Eslanda and Paul. In 1959, they were hospitalized for fatigue and other complaints. In 1963, they traveled to East Germany, where Eslanda spoke to a crowd of more than 20,000, and the East German government awarded her the Peace Medal and the *Clara Zetkin Medal in honor of her work for world peace. Still suffering from poor health and fatigue, they then returned to the United States.

While she remained bluntly critical of inequality, colonialism, and imperialism, Eslanda Robeson's health continued to decline. She died of cancer at Beth Israel Hospital in New York City on December 13, 1965. Her husband Paul Robeson followed her in death in 1976.

SOURCES:

Sicherman, Barbara, and Carol Hurd Green, eds. *Notable American Women: The Modern Period*. Cambridge, MA: The Belknap Press of Harvard University, 1980.

Smith, Jessie Carney, ed. *Notable Black American Women*. Detroit, MI: Gale Research, 1992.

Weatherford, Doris. *American Women's History*. NY: Prentice Hall, 1994.

Brenda Kubiac,
freelance writer, Chesterfield, Michigan

Robespierre, Charlotte (1760–1840)

French author. Name variations: Marie-Marguerite-Charlotte Robespierre; Charlotte de Robespierre; Charlotte Carrault. Born Charlotte Robespierre on February 5, 1760, in Arras, France; died on August 1,

1840, in Paris; daughter of François Robespierre and Jacqueline-Marguerite (Carrault, also seen as Carraut) Robespierre; sister of Maximilien Robespierre (1758–1794, lawyer and diplomat who served on the Committee of Public Safety during the Reign of Terror in the French Revolution); never married; no children.

Charlotte Robespierre is best known for the memoirs she composed on her famous brother Maximilien Robespierre, perhaps the central figure of the French Revolution, and on her own experiences during the Revolution. She was born in southern France in 1760, the daughter of a successful lawyer of Artois. The sudden death of her mother in childbirth in 1764 led to the breakdown of the family; her father became despondent and in 1766 abandoned his children to relatives and moved to Munich, where he died in 1777. The children—Maximilien, the oldest, was only six—were separated, and Charlotte and her younger sister **Henriette Robespierre** were adopted by their aunts.

In 1768, the girls were sent to a convent for poor girls in Tournai to be educated. Henriette died at the convent in her teens, and in 1777 Charlotte returned to Arras. When Maximilien began his law practice there in 1782, Charlotte came to live in his quiet and austere home, keeping house for him and, later, for their younger brother Augustin. During this time, Charlotte became engaged to her brother's friend, the professor and later revolutionary Joseph Fouché, but although the engagement lasted for years, the marriage never transpired.

By 1789, Maximilien's flourishing career had led, with Charlotte's enthusiastic support, to his election to the national Estates-General. Through most of his career, Charlotte was a devoted follower of her brother's increasingly radical ideas of liberty and democracy. She even became involved to a degree in the political life of Arras, always as Maximilien's supporter. The chaos and violence of the early years of the Revolution kept Charlotte and Augustin away from Paris, but their correspondence with Maximilien, who had quickly emerged as one of the Revolution's key leaders, kept them informed of events in Paris.

After Augustin was elected to the National Convention in 1792, he and Charlotte finally joined Maximilien in Paris, where they set up a household together. As the sister of the de facto ruler of France, Charlotte was a witness to the politics of the innermost circle of the Jacobin leadership. In 1793, she even accompanied Augustin on one of his political missions to the Midi region of France. However, the Robespierre home was far from harmonious. Charlotte's open jealousy of Maximilien's friends led him to return to his old boarding house in 1793, just as her disapproval of Augustin's many love affairs led him to move in with friends for a time. Her sibling relationships had deteriorated completely by the spring of 1794, when both brothers began to suspect Charlotte of opposing the Revolution and the new Republic they were leading. Despite the patriotic stance toward the Revolution taken in her memoirs, Charlotte was, like many of the French, divided in her feelings about the Revolution. She loved her brothers deeply and had always supported their patriotism and the principle of liberty, but at the same time she apparently opposed on moral grounds the widespread violence and bloodshed for which Maximilien was responsible. Her brothers also suspected Charlotte's complicity in the anti-Robespierre intrigues cropping up in their inner Jacobin party circle, although there is no evidence that she was involved in any of the conspiracies against him.

In May 1794, Maximilien arranged to have Charlotte sent back to Arras. Fearing for her safety, Charlotte fled from her escort and returned to Paris, where she made an unsuccessful attempt to reconcile with her brothers. This alienation probably worked to save Charlotte's life after the Revolution's leadership turned against Maximilien's tyranny in the summer of 1794. He and Augustin were arrested as traitors to the Republic on the Ninth of Thermidor (July 26) and executed two days later. Suspected of similar crimes, Charlotte herself was arrested on July 30. She fully expected to be executed, but she was released in a general pardon after 15 days.

Although Charlotte survived for another 36 years, little is known of her after 1794. Never marrying, she remained in Paris for the rest of her life, living under her mother's family name of Carrault. None of her relatives survived the Revolution. In 1803, she applied for and was granted an annual stipend from the government of Napoleon Bonaparte, from accounts administered by her former fiancé, Fouché, who was a minister of the interior. The pension continued under King Louis XVIII's reign.

In 1828, she composed her will, leaving her few possessions to the daughter of a friend. In this document, Charlotte also protested vigorously against the accusations, made in 1818 by former Robespierrists, that her pension from the king was a reward for secretly opposing Maximilien during the Revolution. She staunchly asserted her complete loyalty to her brothers and to the former Republic.

It was probably lingering distress caused by these accusations that led Charlotte, with the aid of another former Revolutionary, Albert Laponneraye, to compose her memoirs. The book is less her own memoirs than her recollections and opinions about Maximilien, describing in glowing terms his childhood, character, and career, and ending with her release from prison following the execution of her brothers. Clearly Charlotte intended her book to rehabilitate her dead brother's memory from accusations of tyranny and to clear her own honor by proving that she had always been a loyal sister to him. Published in 1837, the book came to be relied upon by historians as the only evidence for Maximilien Robespierre's formative years. Charlotte Robespierre died three years after she completed her book, at age 80, and was buried in Paris.

SOURCES:

Fleischmann, Hector. *Charlotte Robespierre et Ses Mémoires*. Paris: Albin Michel, 1910.

Matrat, Jean. *Robespierre; or the Tyranny of the Majority*. Trans. by Alan Kendall. NY: Scribner, 1971.

Laura York, M.A. in History, University of California, Riverside, California

Charlotte Robespierre

Robilant, Daisy di (fl. 1922–1933).

See Di Robilant, Daisy.

Robin, Mado (1918–1960)

French soprano. Born in Yseures-sur-Creuse near Tours, France, on December 29, 1918; died in Paris, France, on December 10, 1960; studied with Giuseppe Podestà.

Born in Yseures-sur-Creuse, near Tours, France, on December 29, 1918, Mado Robin began her singing career as a concert artist before moving on to the opera stage. She was well known in French regional theaters as well as in Brussels and Monte Carlo. In 1945, she sang Gilda from *Rigoletto* and Queen of the Night at the Paris Opéra. In 1953, she sang Constanze from Mozart's *Die Entführung*. Robin also sang at the Opéra-Comique and appeared in Brussels, Liège, and San Francisco. She was best known for her roles of Lakmé and Lucia, although some felt her extreme facility for coloratura, as well as her very high range, were displayed to their greatest advantage in such roles as Stravinsky's *The Nightingale*.

John Haag,
Athens, Georgia

Robine, Marie (d. 1399).

See Women Prophets and Visionaries in France at the End of the Middle Ages.

Robins, Elizabeth (1855–1936).

See Pennell, Elizabeth Robins.

Robins, Elizabeth (1862–1952)

American actress, novelist, playwright and author of nonfiction who made her home in Britain, became a suffragist, and promoted women's causes. Name variations: Claire, Clara or C.E. Raimond; Mrs. George Parks; Bessie; Lisa. Pronunciation: RAY-mond. Born Elizabeth Robins on August 6, 1862, in Louisville, Kentucky; died in Brighton, Sussex, England, on May 8, 1952; daughter of Charles Ephraim Robins (a banker and metallurgist) and Hannah Maria Crow; attended Putnam Female Seminary, Zanesville, Ohio; married George Richmond Parks, on January 12, 1885 (committed suicide in 1887); no children.

Left home for the New York stage in her teens, toured in various companies, and worked for the Boston Museum Company where she met her actor husband; following his death (1887), toured with Barrett and Booth; visited Norway (1888) and settled in England; popularized Ibsen on the British stage, play-

ing the first Hedda Gabler in English (1891) and creating the role of Hilde in The Master Builder (1893); managed, produced and wrote plays and co-founded The New Century Theatre; retired from the stage (1902); published first of 14 novels pseudonymously (under name C.E. Raimond, 1894), also wrote plays, several volumes of short stories and nonfiction; wrote bestselling Klondike tale The Magnetic North (1904) after a trip to Alaska to visit brother Raymond; launched suffrage drama in Britain with her play Votes for Women! (1907); sat on the Executive Committee of the suffragist Women's Social and Political Union (1907 to 1912); helped convert Dr. Octavia Wilberforce's Sussex house into a women's convalescent home (1920s).

Major theatrical roles—in repertory and on tour in America (1881–88): The Count of Monte Cristo; A Celebrated Case; Forgiven; Julius Caesar; The Merchant of Venice.

Major theatrical roles—in London, England (1888–1902): Pauline in Her Own Witness (1889); Liza in The Sixth Commandment (1890); Mrs. Linden in A Doll's House (1891); title role in Hedda Gabler (1891); Constance in The Trumpet Call; Claire de Cintré in The American (1891); Hilde Wangel in The Master Builder (1893); Rebecca West in Rosmersholm (1893); Princess Zicka in Diplomacy (1893); Asta in Little Eyolf (1896); Ella in John Gabriel Borkman (1896–97); title role in Mariana (1897); Lucrezia in Paolo and Franchesca (1902); Alice (final role) in Eleanor (1902).

Novels and collected short stories (under the name C.E. Raimond) George Mandeville's Husband (1894), The New Moon (1895), Below the Salt (1896), The Open Question: A Tale of Two Temperaments (1898); *(under name Elizabeth Robins)* The Magnetic North (1904), A Dark Lantern (1905), The Convert (1907), Under the Southern Cross (1907), Come and Find Me! (1908), The Florentine Frame (1909), Where Are You Going To . . . ? (1913, published in America as My Little Sister), Camilla (1918), The Messenger (1919), The Mills of the Gods and Other Stories (1920), Time Is Whispering (1923), The Secret That Was Kept (1926).

Plays: (Anonymous) Alan's Wife (co-authored with Florence Bell, 1893); Elizabeth Robins, Votes for Women! (1907).

Nonfiction: Way Stations (1913); Prudence and Peter (co-authored with Octavia Wilberforce, 1928); Ibsen & the Actress (1928); Theatre and Friendship: Some Henry James Letters (1932); Both Sides of the Curtain (1940); Raymond and I (1956); also Anonymous, Ancilla's Share (1924).

Elizabeth
Robins

Hailed as England's first great intellectual actress, Elizabeth Robins was neither English nor formally trained for the stage. Seven years' schooling at the Putnam Female Seminary in Zanesville, Ohio, was the sum total of her formal education. Yet in the early 1890s, this highly intelligent, sensitive American woman made an enormous impact on the London stage, bringing Henrik Ibsen's new drama to life and in the process shocking and delighting theatergoers and critics.

She had been born in Louisville, Kentucky, in the summer of 1862, during the Civil War, the eldest daughter of Charles Ephraim Robins and **Hannah Maria Crow**; her parents had seen more prosperous times and their marriage was not to last. She had two sisters, three brothers and a half-brother (who died in his teens). The birth of Raymond, the youngest child, precipitated their mother's mental decline and in the mid-1880s she entered an asylum. Robins' father had abandoned the sedentary life of a banker for mining engineering and as a teenager Robins spent some months living with him in a mining camp in Colorado. Although she had lived on Staten Island, New York, as a child, her formative years were spent at her paternal grandmother's home in Zanesville. Her grandmother became her touchstone, closer to her than both parents and a thinly disguised portrait of this stern, yet loving, old woman appears in Robins' most autobiographical novel *The Open Question*.

Still in her teens and with no family history or encouragement of acting, Robins took herself to New York in search of fame. From her first small part in 1881, she was blessed with a combination of luck and talent, aided (and hindered) by her good looks and helped by the chance discovery of a wealthy distant relative. Initially calling herself Claire Raimond, she toured with several companies including that of James O'Neill (father of Eugene). She spent several years at the renowned Boston Museum Company where she met and married a histrionic young actor, George Parks. They had no children. Prone to depression and jealous of her minor successes in relation to his, he drowned himself in the Charles River after two and a half years. Distraught—she never remarried—Robins threw herself into Shakespearean parts, traveling around the United States on an exhausting tour with the veteran actors Barrett and Booth.

In the summer of 1888, she came to Europe for the first time, accompanying **Sara Bull**, widow of the Norwegian violinist Ole Bull, to the family's idyllic island off the west coast of Norway. Stopping in London en route home, she was captivated by the London stage and the possibility of acting there. Encouraged to stay by Oscar Wilde and several actor-managers, she kept postponing her passage and finally made England her home for the rest of her life. Although in her mid-20s and a highly experienced actress, she was forced to start again from the bottom in her search for work and fame. These depressing early years in London are recollected in a volume of her memoirs published in 1940 called *Both Sides of the Curtain*.

Yet her timing was fortuitous. Ibsen's great prose dramas were beginning to reach Britain, and after seeing a performance of *A Doll's House* on the London stage, Robins was captivated. It was she who now proceeded to make Ibsen a household name in Britain. She raised the money for and produced (with another American actress, **Marion Lea**) the first *Hedda Gabler* in English in the spring of 1891. Robins played the part of Hedda to much critical acclaim though she felt her best part to be the one she created in Britain, that of Hilde Wangel in *The Master Builder* in 1893. She organized a successful subscription season for a number of Ibsen's plays and worked closely with her friend and lover, Ibsen's translator William Archer. Together, they founded in 1897 the New Century Theatre. Robins was dedicated to obtaining decent parts for women, breaking the stranglehold and abuse of the actor-manager system, and introducing stimulating European drama to the English stage. She maintained that "no dramatist has ever meant so much to the women of the stage as Henrik Ibsen."

Robins continued acting until 1902, but in 1900 she had made a lengthy visit to her brother Raymond in Alaska. This intrepid journey at the time of the gold rush resulted in typhoid fever which hastened her retirement from the stage (though it is interesting to note that this also coincided with the end of Ibsen's great dramatic contributions). Alaska also provided something more positive: material for journalism and novels, most notably a bestseller about the Klondike entitled *The Magnetic North* (1904), for which she was compared to Daniel Defoe.

Ever conscious of the need to help pay for her mother's medical bills and to meet the costs of a younger brother's medical training as well as making her own ends meet, Robins had long been only too aware of the precariousness of the stage as an extended livelihood for a woman. She had, therefore, for some years seen writing as an alternative means of earning money and had been writing stories and articles since the late 1880s. Her early stories and novels were pseudonymous.

Her first novel, the satirical *George Mandeville's Husband*, was published in 1894 under the name of C.E. Raimond. Her identity was revealed after the publication of her American epic *The Open Question* (1898). She also co-wrote (anonymously), with her close friend **Florence Bell** (Lady Bell), a play about infanticide called *Alan's Wife*, based on a Swedish short story and set in northern England. Robins also played the main part of Jean Creyke on the London stage.

Between the early 1890s and 1926, she had 14 novels published, many of them addressing critical yet risqué social issues such as divorce, abortion, and prostitution. She wrote numerous short stories for journals in Britain and the United States (two collections of these were also published in book form). Her suffrage novel *The Convert* (1907) was reprinted in America and Britain in the 1980s. It grew out of her successful play *Votes for Women!* which was performed at the Royal Court Theatre London, inaugurating suffrage drama. Robins became a committed suffragist, sat on the committee of the militant Women's Social and Political Union from 1907 to 1912, and was first president of the Women Writers' Suffrage League. She replaced *Emmeline Pankhurst** on a Scottish speaking tour when the suffragist leader was in prison. Yet although she was persuaded to speak frequently for the cause and was a very powerful, persuasive performer, Robins detested public speaking and preferred to convert by the written word. She published a number of pamphlets on suffrage and a collection of her suffrage speeches and writings, *Way Stations*, was released in 1913.

Feminism remained one of the main defining forces of Robins' life. During the First World War, she worked for a time as a librarian in a London military hospital entirely staffed by women. When peace came, she wrote frequently in the press on equal rights issues and was a founder member of the board of the influential weekly feminist paper *Time and Tide* and a member of the Six Point Group. She was especially interested in the plight of women doctors and spent her later years with a pioneer woman doctor, *Octavia Wilberforce**. In the late 1920s, they converted Wilberforce's 15th-century Sussex house into a rest home for women recuperating from illness or stress. In 1924, Robins published anonymously a weighty work entitled *Ancilla's Share*. Subtitled *An Indictment of Sex Antagonism*, it was also a paean to peace. Two years later, she wrote her final novel.

Elizabeth Robins' address book and diary (which she kept for most of her long life) read like a *Who's Who*. Her close friends ranged from the poet John Masefield to the politician Sir Edward Grey, the actress Dame *Sybil Thorndike** and writer *Virginia Woolf**. A volume of her correspondence with her compatriot Henry James was published in 1932 as *Theatre and Friendship*. She took the leading role in his play *The American* on the London stage. Her favorite brother Raymond, a well-known human rights activist in the States, married ❧ **Margaret Dreier Robins**, president of the American Women's Trade Union League. Elizabeth Robins was a part owner of their Florida home and frequently visited America.

Robins, Margaret Dreier. See Dreier Sisters.

> One of the most notable events in the history of the modern stage, [Elizabeth Robins' performance in *Hedda Gabler*] marks an epoch and clinches an influence.
> —*The Sunday Times*, 1891

She retained her American citizenship throughout her life and spent World War II back in the United States. A number of her novels are set there while one, *Camilla* (1918), reflects the author's own transatlantic life by being set in both America and Britain. Robins made her final visit to her home country (flying the Atlantic in place of her old long sea voyages) at the age of 88. She died in Brighton on the south coast of England on May 8, 1952, in her 90th year.

SOURCES:

Elizabeth Robins' diaries and correspondence in her Papers at the Fales Library, New York University Library.

SUGGESTED READING:

Gates, Joanne E. *Elizabeth Robins: Actress, Novelist, Feminist*. Tuscaloosa, AL: University of Alabama Press, 1994.

John, Angela V. *Elizabeth Robins: Staging a New Life*. New York and London: Routledge, 1995.

Marcus, Jane. "Art and Anger," in *Feminist Studies*. Vol. 4, 1978, p. 69–98.

Stowell, Sheila. *A Stage of Their Own: Feminist Playwrights of the Suffrage Era*. Manchester: Manchester University Press, 1992.

Thomas, Sue. "Elizabeth Robins," in *Victorian Fiction Research Guide*. No. 22. University of Queensland, Australia, 1994.

COLLECTIONS:

Correspondence and Octavia Wilberforce's unpublished autobiography, The Fawcett Library, London Guildhall University, England.

Correspondence in the Harry Ransom Humanities Research Center, University of Texas at Austin.

Elizabeth Robins Papers, Fales Library, New York University Library.

Angela V. John,
Professor of History, University of Greenwich,
London, United Kingdom

Robins, Margaret Dreier (1868–1945).

See Dreier Sisters.

Robins, Mrs. Raymond (1868–1945).

See Dreier Sisters for Robins, Margaret Dreier.

Robinson, Agnes Mary F. (1856–1944).

See Duclaux, Agnes Mary F.

Robinson, Anastasia (c. 1692–1755)

English opera singer. Name variations: Countess of Peterborough. Born in Italy around 1692; died in Southampton, England, in April 1755; daughter of Thomas Robinson (a portrait painter); studied under Dr. Croft, Sandoni, and Baroness Lindelheim; married Charles Mordaunt, 3rd earl of Peterborough, around 1722 (died 1735).

Born in Italy near the end of the 17th century, Anastasia Robinson studied singing in London under Dr. Croft, Sandoni, and **Baroness Lindelheim**. She made her operatic debut in London in the pasticcio *Creso* in 1714 and went on to sing the soprano roles of Almirena in *Rinaldo* and Oriana in *Amadigi*, and in A. Scarlatti's *Pirro e Demetrio*. Because of illness, she began to sing as a contralto in 1719, including such roles as Matilda in *Ottone*, Teodata in *Flavio*, and Cornelia in *Giulio Cesare*. She also sang in operas by Porta and Bononcini. Robinson was known more for the charming expressiveness of her presentation than for her technical virtuosity. She remained on the London stage until 1724, two years after she secretly married Charles Mordaunt, 3rd earl of Peterborough. It was said that he did not publicly acknowledge her until just before he died on his yacht off Lisbon on November 21, 1735. Upon retiring, she maintained a musical salon highlighting the works of Greene, Bononcini, and Tosi, among others. She died in Southampton, England, in 1755.

Brenda Kubiac,
freelance writer, Chesterfield, Michigan

Robinson, Anna Johnstone (1913–1992).

See Johnstone, Anna Hill.

Robinson, Betty (1911–1997)

American Olympic track athlete. Name variations: Elizabeth Robinson; Betty Robinson Schwartz. Born in Riverdale, Illinois, on August 23, 1911; died in Colorado on May 17, 1997; married Richard S. Schwartz (an upholsterer), in 1939; children: Richard and Jane.

Became first woman to win an Olympic gold medal in track and field in the Amsterdam Games, and also won silver in relay (1928); won second gold medal as member of relay team in the Berlin Olympics (1936).

Not only was Betty Robinson the first woman to win a gold medal for track and field in the Olympics, she also made a miraculous comeback eight years later when she won a second gold medal after recovering from a debilitating accident. Born in Riverdale, Illinois, on August 23, 1911, Robinson was just 16 years old when an assistant track coach at her high school saw her sprint for a train in 1928 and could not believe his eyes. The following day, he timed her as she ran in the school corridor, and encouraged her to enter a meet. ("Till then," she later noted, "I didn't even know there were women's races.") On the day of the meet three weeks later, she had to stop by the local sporting goods store to purchase a pair of spiked shoes. Unbeknownst to her, Robinson was competing with women from the Illinois Athletic Club. When she came in second to **Helen Filkey**, the club's outstanding runner, Robinson was asked to join.

The young runner started practicing, taking the train to Harvey High School, 25 miles away, three times a week. The Olympic tryouts were the first event Robinson ran for the club. Not only did she win, but she broke a world record and went on to the final Olympic tryouts in New Jersey. In Newark, Robinson finished second to **Elta Cartwright** from California in the 100 meters. Only four months after she took up the sport, 17-year-old Robinson was on her way to the 1928 Olympics in Amsterdam, where women's track and field would be part of the Games for the first time.

In those days, track and field was not sophisticated: runners dug holes for each of their feet before the start, training was lax, equipment was poor, racing diets and opportunities for support were almost nonexistent. Despite this, most modern women are running only a second faster than Robinson and some of her competitors; the 100-meter world record she broke in those first tryouts in 1928 was with a time of 12.0 seconds, compared with the great *Florence Griffith Joyner*'s world record of 10.49 in 1988.

During the ocean crossing, Robinson and her teammates worked out on a linoleum track laid out on the deck of the ship. In Amsterdam, the 16-year-old unknown was not favored, but in her trial heat of the 100-meter race she finished second, and in her semi-final heat she finished first, becoming the only American to go into the finals. The first women's track-and-field event held in the 1928 Olympics was the 100-meter dash; Canadians *Fanny Rosenfeld and **Ethel Smith** were highly favored. With three false starts in the finals and two runners disqualified, the inexperienced Robinson became increasingly jittery. But when the gun went off, Robinson and Rosenfeld ran side by side in an extremely close race. Only when friends jumped the railing and came onto the field did Robinson realize she had won the gold, with a time of 12.2 seconds. "When the flag went up [to declare the winner] after the race," she later recalled, "I started cry-

ing like a baby." The finish was so close that two judges disagreed and Canada protested. Even so, Fanny Rosenfeld was awarded the silver and Ethel Smith the bronze. Robinson's gold in track and field was the first of many that American women would win in the decades to come. Later in the Games, Rosenfeld and her Canadian teammates won the gold in the 4x100-meter relay, but the American team came in second, giving Robinson a silver medal to add to her gold.

As a memento of her historic win, thenpresident of the American Olympic Committee

Betty
Robinson

Douglas MacArthur gave Robinson a gold charm shaped like the world. When she returned home, she was greeted by ticker-tape parades in New York City and Chicago and presented with a diamond watch from her fans and a silver cup from her high school.

Three years later, tragedy appeared to end her promising career when she was seriously injured in a plane crash. Both she and the cousin with whom she was flying survived the crash, but Robinson was in the hospital for nearly three months, two of them in a coma, suffering from severe head injuries, a broken arm, and a broken leg. Her leg was stabilized with a silver rod and pin and encased in a cast from her hip to her heel. After she spent another four months in a wheelchair and on crutches, the injured leg was one-half inch shorter than the other. Robinson remained out of competition for three and a half years.

When she began to run again in 1936, she could not bend her knee enough for a crouching start and had to start instead from a standing position. Even so, she was the fifth of six women, including **Harriet Bland**, **Annette Rogers**, and *****Helen Stephens**, to make the Olympic relay team in Berlin. While Hitler sat comfortably in his box seat, assured that the German relay women could not lose, he watched horrified as Germany's **Marie Dollinger** and a teammate dropped the baton on the last pass. The Americans, anchored by Robinson and the 1936 100-meter winner Helen Stephens, won the gold medal on the 4x100-meter relay by eight yards.

At the end of her running career, Robinson had held records in the 50, 60, 70, and 100 yards. She was inducted into the National Track and Field Hall of Fame, the United States Track and Field Hall of Fame, and the Helms Hall of Fame. After her retirement from competition, she continued her interest in the sport by becoming a coach, timer, and public speaker. Many years later, she said, "I still can't believe the attention I get for something I did so long ago." After suffering from cancer and Alzheimer's disease, Robinson died in 1997 at the age of 87.

SOURCES:

Carlson, Lewis B., and John J. Fogarty. *Tales of Gold.* Chicago, IL: Contemporary Press, 1987.

Grace and Glory: A Century of Women in the Olympics. Washington, DC: Multi-Media Partners, 1996.

Greenspan, Bud. *100 Greatest Moments in Olympic History.* Los Angeles, CA: GPG, 1995.

The New York Times. May 21, 1997.

Malinda Mayer,
writer and editor, Falmouth, Massachusetts

Robinson, Elizabeth (1911–1997).

See Robinson, Betty.

Robinson, Harriet Hanson
(1825–1911)

American mill girl and suffragist. Born Harriet Jane Hanson in Boston, Massachusetts, on February 8, 1825; died in Malden, Massachusetts, on December 22, 1911; daughter of William Hanson (a carpenter) and Harriet (Browne) Hanson; married William Stevens Robinson (a newspaper editor and abolitionist), in 1848 (died 1876); children: Harriette Lucy Robinson (later Harriette R. Shattuck); Elizabeth Osborne Robinson; William Elbridge Robinson (died of typhoid at age five); Edward Warrington Robinson.

Harriet Robinson was born on February 8, 1825, in Boston, Massachusetts, the only daughter of four children of William Hanson, a carpenter, and **Harriet Browne Hanson**. Harriet's parents were descended from English colonists to New England, and her maternal grandfather, Seth Ingersoll Browne, had fought in the Revolutionary War. When William Hanson died in 1831, financial difficulties forced the family to move to the mill town of Lowell. There they survived by taking in boarders, with the children earning extra money in local jobs.

At age ten, Harriet began working in the mill as a bobbin doffer. A year later, she led the other young workers in a protest with older workers over a wage cut, a hint of her life of activism to come. Unlike work in horrific conditions experienced by many child laborers at other factories, work in the Lowell mills was relatively relaxed in that era, with time for play and reading. Through the early 1840s, mill owners even provided time for schooling and church, of which Harriet took advantage until age 15.

Although she was not a frequent contributor to the *Lowell Offering*, the famous monthly literary magazine of the Lowell mill girls, Harriet met her future husband through a poem she submitted to the magazine. William Stevens Robinson, an editor with the *Lowell Courier*, noticed the poem and fell in love with the poet. The two married on November 30, 1848, and Harriet became her husband's editorial assistant. Finances were a constant struggle as William went from one journalistic assignment to another in the aid of abolition, and Harriet soon followed him in his convictions. Their home was a hotbed of abolitionist talk, and William fueled discussions with his militant column published under the pen name "Warrington." During the three years in the mid-1850s that they lived in Concord, Massachusetts, Harriet came into contact with such famous New Englanders as Henry David Thoreau and Ralph Waldo Emerson.

At the start of the Civil War, the family was living in Malden, Massachusetts, where Harriet sewed mittens for Boston contractors and her husband won election as clerk of the state house of representatives in 1862, significantly easing the family's financial strain. After the war, their concerns shifted from abolition to women's suffrage, and their oldest daughter, Harriette Lucy Robinson (later **Harriette R. Shattuck**), joined their crusade. Following William's death in 1876, Robinson and her daughter continued their activist work.

The suffragist movement in Massachusetts suffered from factional divisions, and by the early 1880s, Robinson had switched allegiance from *Lucy Stone and the majority of New England suffragists to rival *Susan B. Anthony's National Woman Suffrage Association (NWSA). Robinson and her daughter organized a chapter of the NWSA in Massachusetts. They spoke before a special Senate committee in Washington in 1882, promoted Benjamin F. Butler for governor of Massachusetts in an unsuccessful effort to encourage his support for the cause during 1882–83, and valiantly petitioned Congress for removal of their political disabilities in 1889. Robinson would not see the fruit of her efforts, for women would not gain the right to vote until 1920, nine years after her death.

Robinson was an active member of various women's clubs, including the New England Women's Club, which she founded with *Julia Ward Howe in 1868. She also served on the first board of directors of the General Federation of Women's Clubs early in the 1890s. She wrote a number of books as well, including *Massachusetts in the Woman Suffrage Movement* (1881), *"Warrington" Pen Portraits* (1877), a biography of her husband, and *Loom and Spindle* (1898), a memoir of her time in the Lowell mills. The latter two volumes are considered important historical depictions of their time. Other works include *Captain Mary Miller* (1887), a novel, and *The New Pandora* (1889), a verse play. Robinson died at her home in Malden on December 22, 1911, of complications from a bacterial infection, and was buried in Sleepy Hollow Cemetery at Concord. Her papers are held at the Schlesinger Library at Radcliffe College.

SOURCES:

James, Edward T., ed. *Notable American Women, 1607–1950.* Cambridge, MA: The Belknap Press of Harvard University, 1971.

Brenda Kubiac,
freelance writer, Chesterfield, Michigan

Robinson, Jane Bancroft

(1847–1932)

American Methodist deaconess leader. Name variations: Jane Marie Bancroft; Jane Marie Bancroft Robinson. Born Jane Marie Bancroft in West Stockbridge, Massachusetts, on December 24, 1847; died in Pasadena, California, on May 29, 1932; daughter of George C. Bancroft (a Methodist minister) and Caroline J. Orton; graduated from Emma Willard's seminary, 1871; graduated from New York State Normal School in Albany, 1872; Syracuse University, Ph.B., 1877, Ph.M., 1880, Ph.D., 1884; attended the University of Zurich, 1886–87; married George Orville Robinson (a lawyer), in 1891 (died 1915); children: four stepchildren.

Born on December 24, 1847, in West Stockbridge, Massachusetts, Jane Bancroft Robinson was the only surviving child of George C. Bancroft, a Methodist minister, and his second wife **Caroline J. Orton**. Jane had two half-siblings from her father's first marriage, one of whom, **Henrietta Ash Bancroft**, became closely associated with the deaconess work to which Jane later devoted her life. George Bancroft's service to small parishes in New York and New England never lasted more than two years at a time, so the family moved frequently throughout Jane's childhood. Her mother was an intelligent and well-read woman, despite having little formal education, and she inspired Jane in her own studies.

Robinson began her impressive academic career at *Emma Willard's seminary in Troy, New York. She graduated in 1871, then graduated from the New York State Normal School in Albany the following year. She earned the first of her three degrees from Syracuse University, a Ph.B., in 1877, adding to that a Ph.M. in 1880 and a Ph.D. in 1884. (She would be elected to Phi Beta Kappa in 1907, and receive two honorary doctorates, from Syracuse University in 1919 and from the University of Southern California in 1929.) Robinson's doctoral thesis, *A Study of the Parliament of Paris and Other Parliaments of France*, was published in 1884. While working towards her Syracuse degrees, she became dean of the Woman's College and professor of French language and literature at

Northwestern University in Evanston, Illinois. During the course of her eight-year association with the college, she founded the Western Association of Collegiate Alumnae, an early model of the American Association of University Women.

In the mid-1880s, Robinson was the first recipient of the history fellowship of newly formed Bryn Mawr College, which opened up further avenues of study to her. In the course of two years' traveling in Europe with her parents, she attended the University of Zurich and audited a history *conférence* at the University of Paris. While there, she became the first woman to be admitted to the École Pratique des Hautes Études.

The most important aspect of Robinson's time in Europe had nothing to do with academics, however. A study she conducted of European Protestant laywomen organized in social service—otherwise known as deaconesses—sparked a desire in her to see a similar movement among American Methodist women. Both American Lutherans and Episcopalians had small beginnings in this area, but the Methodist General Conference did not formally recognize the need to organize deaconesses until 1888. (*Lucy Meyer had nonetheless opened the first American deaconess home in Chicago in 1887.) Robinson released her findings upon her return to the United States in the report *Deaconesses in Europe and Their Lessons for America* (1889), and took control of the newly formed Deaconess Bureau. Formed as an offshoot of the Methodist Woman's Home Missionary Society, the bureau organized laywomen into groups of charity workers supported by the church. They were provided with room and board in lieu of salary, and were intended, in their mission statement, to "minister to the poor, visit the sick, pray with the dying, care for the orphan, . . . [and] devote themselves in a general way to such forms of Christian labor as may be suited to their abilities." Robinson spent the next 20 years with this as her main focal point. She declined a professorship of history at Ohio Wesleyan University in order to travel, lecture, and write in support of deaconess work. By the end of the century, she had charge of 32 deaconess homes, schools and hospitals.

The rapid growth of the movement and the scores of independent deaconess homes made it difficult to maintain order and control. Robinson fought to bring deaconess work under the centralized control of the Woman's Home Missionary Society in the hope that it would facilitate the placement of deaconesses. A General Deaconess Board was established in 1908, but its largely advisory role failed to fulfill her hopes for greater order. (Deaconess work finally fell under the supervision of a single bureau seven years after Robinson's death.)

In 1891, she married George Orville Robinson, a Detroit lawyer and widower, in Cincinnati, Ohio, and became a mother to his four children from his first marriage. George was an active Methodist layman and founder of the Michigan *Christian Advocate* who aided his wife's work by giving generously to the construction of deaconess institutions. A longtime vice-president of the Woman's Home Missionary Society, Robinson became president in 1908, serving in that position until 1913. Three years after George's death in 1915, she began living with her half-sister Henrietta in a sizeable home on 11 acres in Pasadena, California. In 1897, Henrietta had resigned her position as professor of English at Albion College to take on the role of field secretary of the Deaconess Bureau, later becoming general superintendent of deaconess work.

Jane Robinson's dedication included her own generous contributions of more than $10,000 to the California Institute of Technology in Pasadena, California, and the donation of her home and land for the construction of retirement homes for deaconesses and ministers. Robinson suffered a stroke in March 1932 while traveling and was hospitalized in Albuquerque, New Mexico. She died two months later, on May 29, 1932, in Pasadena.

SOURCES:

James, Edward T., ed. *Notable American Women, 1607–1950.* Cambridge, MA: The Belknap Press of Harvard University, 1971.

Brenda Kubiac,
freelance writer, Chesterfield, Michigan

Robinson, Jo Ann (1911–1992)

African-American who was a chief participant in the historic Montgomery Bus Boycott (1955–56) that led to the desegregation of the bus system in Montgomery, Alabama, and sparked the civil-rights movement nationwide. Name variations: Jo Ann Gibson Robinson. Born Jo Ann Gibson on April 17, 1911, near Culloden, Georgia; died on August 29, 1992, in Los Angeles, California; graduated with a teaching degree from Fort Valley State College; Atlanta University, M.A. in English; married briefly to Wilbur Robinson; children: one who died in infancy.

Born on April 17, 1911, near Culloden, Georgia, in the segregated South, Jo Ann Robinson was the youngest of 12 children. She was educated in the segregated public schools of Macon and earned her teaching degree at Fort Valley State College. Robinson worked as a public school teacher in Macon for five years before moving to Atlanta, where she earned a master's degree in English from Atlanta University. She next spent a year teaching at Mary Allen College in Crockett, Texas, after which she took a position as a professor of English at Alabama State College in Montgomery in 1949.

Social unrest over segregationist policies was just beginning to ferment that year, and Robinson quickly became involved with two African-American groups that proved pivotal in the civil-rights struggles, the Dexter Avenue Baptist Church and the Women's Political Council (WPC), founded in 1946 by another professor at Alabama State, **Mary Fair Burks**. The WPC was comprised of professional women who worked in the areas of delinquency and voter registration to improve the status of African-Americans in the city. Robinson assumed the presidency of the organization in the 1950s.

Six years before *Rosa Parks made history by refusing to give up her bus seat to a white rider, Robinson suffered abuse at the hands of a white bus driver, who yelled at her and threatened her for sitting in the front of a bus in December 1949. She and other middle-class black friends who had suffered similar indignities petitioned Montgomery officials to end the harassment, to no avail. The seed of what would become the historic Montgomery Bus Boycott of 1955–56 was planted at that time. Robinson and her associates in the WPC began to look for an individual around whom they could build a bus boycott to force the desegregation of the Montgomery bus system. In May 1954, as the impact of the Supreme Court's recent decision in *Brown* v. *Board of Education* began sinking in across the nation, Robinson, as president of the WPC, sent a letter to the mayor of Montgomery noting that a bus boycott was an option if treatment of African-Americans in the transit system did not improve. Believing that the person who would serve as a rallying point for the African-American community must be of impeccable character, Robinson rejected the cases of two African-American women who had previously challenged seating on buses.

Robinson and other activists discovered their heroine in December 1955, when a Montgomery seamstress named Rosa Parks was arrested after refusing to give up her seat towards the front of a city bus. Jo Ann Robinson quietly went to Alabama State College in the middle of the night to run

Jo Ann Robinson

off thousands of fliers on the college's mimeograph machine, advocating a boycott that was originally intended to last only one day. As more African-American church and civic leaders took up the cause, the Montgomery Improvement Association (MIA) came into existence to organize the effort, with Martin Luther King, Jr., and Ralph Abernathy taking lead roles. Robinson served on the executive board of the MIA and edited its newsletter. Although she kept a low profile in the boycott in order to avoid trouble with Alabama State College, Robinson was at the heart of activities throughout the 381-day protest. The U.S. Supreme Court ruled that segregated seating was unconstitutional on November 13, 1956. On December 20, the court's order was served on Montgomery officials, and the boycott ended.

The protest precipitated Robinson's departure from Alabama State College, along with that of 11 other activists. She taught for one year at Grambling College in Grambling, Louisiana, then moved to Los Angeles, where she worked as an English teacher in the public school system until her retirement in 1976. She stayed involved in women's community groups until her health declined seriously shortly after the publication of her memoir, *The Montgomery Bus Boycott and the Women Who Started It*, in 1987. The Southern Association for Women Historians honored Robinson with a publication prize in 1989, but she was too ill to accept the award in person. She died in 1992.

SOURCES:

Crawford, Vicki, Jacqueline Anne Rouse and Barbara Woods, eds. *Women in the Civil Rights Movement:*

Trailblazers and Torchbearers, 1941–1965. Bloomington, IN: Indiana University Press, 1993.

Griffin, Lynne, and Kelly McCann. *The Book of Women: 300 Notable Women History Passed By.* Holbrook, MA: Bob Adams, 1992.

Hine, Darlene Clark, ed. *Black Women in America: An Historical Encyclopedia.* Brooklyn, NY: Carlson, 1993.

"I'm not going to ride the bus," in *U.S. News & World Report.* December 11, 1995, pp. 52, 54.

SUGGESTED READING:

Robinson, Jo Ann Gibson. *The Montgomery Bus Boycott and the Women Who Started It: The Memoir of Jo Ann Gibson Robinson.* Knoxville, TN: University of Tennessee Press, 1987.

RELATED MEDIA:

"Boycott," starring Jeffrey Wright, Terrence Howard, **CCH Pounder** as Jo Ann Robinson, and Carmen Ejogo as *Coretta Scott King, directed by Clark Johnson, first aired on HBO on February 24, 2001.

Jane E. Spear,
freelance writer and editor, Canton, Ohio

Robinson, Joan Violet (1903–1983)

British post-Keynesian economist who developed the theory of imperfect competition and linked neoclassical economic theory to that of Karl Marx. Born Joan Violet Maurice on October 31, 1903, in Camberley, England; died on August 5, 1983, in Cambridge, England; daughter of Helen (Marsh) Maurice and Major-General Sir Frederick Maurice; attended St. Paul's Girls' School and Girton College, Cambridge University; married E.A.G. Robinson (an economist), in 1926; children: two daughters.

Awards: honorary fellow at Girton College, Newnham College, and King's College, all Cambridge.

Father retired from the British Army (1918); admitted to Cambridge University (October 1922); passed the Economics Tripos, Cambridge (1925); taught in India (1926–28); returned to Cambridge (1928); appointed junior assistant lecturer (1931); appointed full lecturer (1937); appointed reader (1949); husband retired (1965); appointed full professor (1965); became chair of the Economics Faculty (1965); retired from Cambridge University (September 30, 1971); suffered a stroke (February 1983).

Selected writings: The Economics of Imperfect Competition *(London: Macmillan, 1933);* Essays in the Theory of Employment *(London: Macmillan, 1937);* Introduction to the Theory of Employment *(London: Macmillan, 1937);* An Essay on Marxian Economics *(London: Macmillan, 1942);* The Rate of Interest and Other Essays *(London: Macmillan, 1952);* The Accumulation of Capital *(London: Macmillan, 1956);* Exercises in Economic Analysis *(London: Macmillan, 1960);* Essays in the Theory of Economic Growth *(London: Macmillan, 1962);* Eco-

nomic Philosophy *(London: C.A. Watts, 1962);* Economics—an Awkward Corner *(London: Allen & Unwin, 1966);* Freedom and Necessity *(London: Allen & Unwin, 1970);* The Cultural Revolution in China *(London: Penguin, 1970);* Economic Heresies: Some Old-fashioned Questions in Economic Theory *(London: Macmillan, 1971);* An Introduction to Modern Economics *(NY: McGraw-Hill, 1973);* Contributions to Modern Economics *(Oxford: Basil Blackwell, 1978);* Collected Economic Papers *(Oxford: Basil Blackwell, 1979);* Aspects of Development and Underdevelopment *(Cambridge: Cambridge University Press, 1979);* Further Contributions to Modern Economics *(Oxford: Basil Blackwell, 1980).*

The daughter of **Helen Marsh Maurice** and Major-General Sir Frederick Maurice, Joan Violet Robinson was born in Camberley, Surrey, on October 31, 1903. When she was 15, her father resigned from the British Army due to public scandal, having accused Prime Minister Lloyd George of deliberately misleading Parliament about the strength of British forces on the Western Front towards the end of World War I. His open letter, published in several London newspapers, rocked the government, and led to Sir Frederick's resignation. The action echoed the behavior of her great-grandfather, Frederick Denison Maurice, a Christian Socialist who forfeited the chair of theology at King's College, London, after his disavowal of eternal damnation. Joan Robinson came to share similar character traits. She was self-assured and unconventional, stubborn and principled.

Following her matriculation at St. Paul's Girls' School, Robinson gained admission to Cambridge University in October 1922, studying economics at Girton College. The works of Alfred Marshall and Arthur C. Pigou greatly influenced her early thinking. While Marshall retired from Cambridge in 1924, his writings, which assumed either perfect competition or monopoly in the economy, remained tremendously influential. In later life, Robinson was to reassess his views:

> The profit motive contains no mechanism to ensure that technical progress will take digestible forms.... Modern capitalism is well adapted to produce fabulous technical successes but not to provide the basis for the noble life accessible to all that Marshall dreamed of.

When Robinson was an undergraduate, Pigou, Marshall's student, was still teaching at the university. John Maynard Keynes also taught there, dividing his time between Cambridge University and London University. At the time, Keynes' lectures focused primarily on orthodox monetary theory and policies. The environment at Cambridge was steeped in a deep conservatism.

In 1925, Robinson graduated with second class honors. The following year, she married economist Austin Robinson, who was six years her senior and taught at Corpus Christi College, Cambridge. Soon after the wedding, the couple moved to India. There, Austin served as tutor to the Maharajah of Gwalior, while Joan taught at the local school. Upon their return to England in 1928, Robinson's husband was offered a position as a lecturer in economics at Cambridge University.

Returning to Cambridge, Robinson undertook the supervision of undergraduate students, as well as research into economic theory. Keynes had become the editor of the *Economic Journal*, and Piero Sraffa, who led the attack against Marshallian economics, had joined the faculty. Keynes attracted many scholars of like mind to Cambridge, including Frank Ramsay, Ludwig Wittgenstein, and Richard Kahn. Robinson and Kahn developed a professional partnership which was to last for the rest of their lives. A spirit of liberalism and innovation permeated the institution.

In 1931, Joan Robinson was appointed junior assistant lecturer. Economists at Cambridge were increasingly conscious of the problems surrounding the meaning of the theory of value, in light of perfect competition. The rethinking of value theory was to advance a stage because of an essay that Charles Gifford had written to Austin Robinson in 1931. Wrote Austin:

> He used a concept, I think derived from something that Yntema had written, that I subsequently suggested naming "marginal revenue." It so happened that Richard Kahn was lunching with us that day. I passed on to Joan and him the idea that Charles Gifford had produced, and they started playing with it. Gradually the game became more serious. It became substantially easier to tackle a number of problems. And out of this grew Joan's first book.

Her *Economics of Imperfect Competition* appeared in 1933.

Up to this point, there had been little analysis of market forces which did not assume either perfect competition or pure monopoly. Joan Robinson demonstrated great analytical skill, particularly when dealing with the problem of the classification of market forces. She attacked Marshall's theory of perfect competition, which was defined as a situation in which the products of one company could be substituted for those of another. Monopoly characterized a situation in which there were no substitutes for the products of a company. Piero Sraffa suggested that each company should be treated as a separate monopoly, and economic sectors should be treated as oligopolies. As a result, Robinson argued that goods were often partial substitutes for one another. Her theory analyzed price and output in the two marketplaces. She concluded that monopolistic corporations restricted output in order to maintain high prices, thus resulting in poor performance at the manufacturing level. Such companies also engaged in cartel behavior, wrote Robinson:

> So long as all adhere to the same set of conventions each can enjoy his share of the market, and each can imagine that he is acting according to strict rules of competition, though in fact the group as a whole, by unconscious collusion, are imposing a mild degree of monopoly upon the market.

The Economics of Imperfect Competition won international recognition. Perfect competition assumed that government regulation of the economy should be confined to the regulation of aggregate effective demand, and that the allocation of a nation's resources should be left to the free market. Competition, however, Robinson argued, did not effectively allocate available resources, given the socio-political agenda of a society. Neither could competition regulate aggregate demand. *Imperfect Competition* taught an entire generation of economists the geometrics of price theory. Writes **Dorothy Lampen Thomson:**

> Robinson's pioneer work on imperfect competition did provide a major breakthrough in theoretical economics by revitalizing price theory, stimulating research into various aspects of microeconomic behaviour, and causing analysis of market behaviour once again to become relevant to the real economy—a world populated by oligopolies.

During the early 1930s, Keynes was in the process of completing his revolutionary work *The General Theory of Employment, Interest and Money*, which was published in 1936. Robinson became increasingly influenced by his views. Along with Kahn, Sraffa, Sir Roy Harrod and James Meade, Robinson became part of what later was known as the "Cambridge Circus." The Circus played a vital role in critiquing and editing the drafts of Keynes' book.

His research focused on the profound social implications of employment, and appealed to Robinson's evolving social consciousness as Britain suffered through the ravages of the Great Depression. Keynes' thesis stressed that equality of savings and investment was maintained by variations in the level of income and the level of unemployment, not merely by adjustments to the rate of interest as neoclassical economists had suggested.

In Robinson's view, Keynes' work constituted a fundamental change in economic theory, challenging all previous doctrine. As a result, she published *Essays on the Theory of Employment* and *Introduction to the Theory of Employment* in 1937. Both works clarified the Keynesian analysis of investment, savings, unemployment, interest rates, and price. Robinson became one of the leading popularizers of Keynes' work. She argued that interest rates did not remunerate the financial sacrifice of savings. She also elucidated the role of disguised unemployment and generalized the Marshall/Lerner theory of international trade.

By the end of the decade, Robinson began to delve into Marxist economic theory. She described her Marxist writings as an attempt to "separate the wheat of science from the chaff of ideology." Robinson sought to reinstate Marx as a preeminent economic analyst, while shedding much of the political baggage associated with his writings. She emphasized the historical, social, and institutional structures which affected distribution, and juxtaposed these with the conventional analysis of resource allocation and equilibrium. While she was sympathetic to Marxian analysis, her decoupling of his economic and political philosophies fostered antagonism among doctrinaire Marxists. Wrote Robinson years later:

> For a discussion of the problems nowadays found to be interesting—growth and stagnation, technical progress and the demand for labour, the balance of sectors in an expanding economy—Marxian theory provides a starting point where academic teaching was totally blank. . . . Marx, as a scientist, proclaimed this grand program, and made an impressive start upon it. But it got very little further. A school of thought flourishes when the followers continuously revise and sift the ideas of the founder, test his hypotheses, correct his errors, reconcile contradictions in his conclusions, and adapt his method to deal with fresh matter. It takes a great genius to set a new subject going; the disciples must admire, even reverence, the master, but they should not defer to him. On the contrary, they must be his closest critics.

During the postwar era, Robinson's work *The Accumulation of Capital* (1956) sought nothing less than a reconstruction of economic theory. This book is widely accepted as an example of Robinson at her intellectual best. The title echoes those chosen by both Adam Smith and *Rosa Luxemburg. Robinson recast the definitions of capital accumulation, labor supply, tech-

nical innovation, and natural resources in Keynesian terms, and in light of her own analysis of writings by Marshall, Marx, Luxemburg, and others. Robinson's focus on the process of capital accumulation in the building of a capitalist economy attacked the traditional concept of the production function and elicited angry responses from conventional economists. As Warren J. Samuels noted:

> She has generally and pointedly challenged the complacency of conventional economists more concerned with analytical and professional respectability and career and less with the exigent problems of distribution, poverty, and injustice and oppression resident, for example, in class use of government.

Robinson's later research moved towards a dynamization of Keynesian economics, which gradually evolved into a post-Keynesian theory of economic growth. The contributions made by Robinson, however, were not purely in the realm of economics. She also sought to deal with larger philosophical issues. In *Economic Philosophy* (1962), she argued that an economy should have a moral underpinning. "Some standard of morality is necessary for every social animal," she wrote. "Any economic system requires a set of rules, an ideology to justify them, and a conscience in the individual which makes him strive to carry them out."

In 1965, Joan Robinson was promoted to full professor and took over the chair of economics. During the 1960s, she sparked the so-called "Cambridge Controversies" over the neoclassical theory of capital and the associated principle of marginal productivity. The debate was an acrimonious one, which pitted Cambridge University against Harvard.

Robinson, who retired from the chair of economics on September 30, 1971, continued to lecture occasionally at Cambridge and maintained a rigorous schedule of lectures at various international institutions. Throughout her career, she traveled extensively, giving public lectures and seminars around the world. Hundreds of students in Asia, Africa, Europe, South and North America were exposed to her ideas first-hand. Robinson was extremely popular with her students. She inspired great admiration among some colleagues, and distrust among her conservative political foes in the academic community.

During the late 1970s, King's College, where John Maynard Keynes had taught, finally agreed to drop its longstanding objection to the admission of female students. This move was welcomed wholeheartedly by Robinson, who

Joan
Violet
Robinson

became the college's first female honorary fellow. In February 1983, Joan Robinson suffered a stroke. She died six months later.

Robinson's works influenced an entire generation of economists. Her *Economics of Imper-* *fect Competition* propelled microeconomics into the mainstream. *Introduction to the Theory of Employment* was one of the most widely read prewar popularizations of Keynesian economics. Her 1942 work, *An Essay on Marxian Economics*, framed Karl Marx as a forerunner of

Keynes, and remains one of the most important works on the subject. In 1956, *The Accumulation of Capital* marked a departure in Robinson's development as an economic theoretician, by attempting to dynamize Keynes and propose a new analysis of long-term capital growth. Her writings demonstrated that not all economists wrote poorly. As John Eatwell pointed out, "Her books and articles are often outstanding examples of English prose."

The economics of Joan Robinson were characterized by two fundamental assumptions. Firstly, that any economic theory must take into account specific social factors. Thus, any analysis must address issues such as the ownership of the means of production, control of the process of production, and the superstructure of social control. Secondly, any serious economic analysis must accept the unique nature of historical time. Economic theory cannot exist in a vacuum. Both prerequisites were antithetical to neoclassical economics. Wrote Eatwell:

> Joan Robinson's unique contribution to economics lies not only in her recognition of the full significance of the Keynesian revolution, and its relationship to Marxian theory, but also in the manner in which, on these bases, she has forged new theoretical tools to tackle a remarkable variety of economic problems. Moreover, beneath the sophistication of her theoretical writings lies a clarity version, exemplified by the way she dissects and simplifies the most complex of problems. It is this combination of originality, sophistication and the ability to identify the crucial elements in complex phenomena, which gives her writings such vitality. Her work has always been, and continues to be, a formidable challenge to orthodoxy of all kinds.

Robinson was the only woman of her generation to achieve prominence in the field of economic theory. This says as much about the difficulty of economic theory, as it does about the involvement of women in higher education. In 1971, *The New York Times* conducted a study which classified 101 social science contributions, in 62 major fields of endeavor. Joan Robinson was the only woman named in the survey.

Joan Robinson thrived on scholarly interaction and debate. Thus, one finds traces of Alfred Marshall, A.C. Pigou, John Maynard Keynes, Piero Sraffa, Michal Kalecki, Richard Kahn, and Karl Marx in her writings. She possessed a strong ability to synthesize and incorporate the ideas of others into her own research. This ability made her one of the leading unorthodox economists of the 20th century. Her approach to economics is best summed up by the words of Pietro

Pomponazzi, the Italian Renaissance philosopher: "It is better to be a heretic if one wishes to find the truth."

SOURCES:

Blaug, Mark, ed. *Joan Robinson (1903–1983) and George Shackle (1903–1992).* Aldershot: Edward Elgar, 1992.

Feiwel, George R. *Joan Robinson and Modern Economic Theory.* NY: New York University Press, 1989.

Loasky, Brian J. *The Mind and Method of the Economist.* Aldershot: Edward Elgar, 1989.

Screpanti, Ernesto, and Stefano Zamagni. *An Outline of the History of Economic Thought.* Trans. by David Field. Oxford: Clarendon Press, 1993.

Skouras, Thanos. "The Economics of Joan Robinson," in *Twelve Contemporary Economists.* Ed. by J.R. Shackleton and Garth Locksley. NY: John Wiley and Sons, 1981.

Spiegel, Henry William. *The Growth of Economic Thought.* Durham, NC: Duke University Press, 1983.

Thomson, Dorothy Lampen. *Adam Smith's Daughters.* NY: Exposition Press, 1973.

SUGGESTED READING:

Harcourt, Geoffrey C. "Harcourt on Robinson," in *Contemporary Economists in Perspective.* Ed. by William Brief and Kenneth G. Elzinga. Greenwich, CT: Jai Press, 1984.

Hugh A. Stewart, M.A.,
Guelph, Ontario, Canada.

Robinson, Julia B. (1919–1985)

American mathematician. Name variations: Julia Bowman Robinson. Born Julia Bowman on December 8, 1919, in St. Louis, Missouri; died on July 30, 1985, in Oakland, California; daughter of Ralph Bowers Bowman and Helen Hall Bowman; studied with a private tutor at age ten, following a year of quarantine after bout with scarlet fever; attended San Diego State College; University of California at Berkeley, Ph.D., 1948; married Raphael Robinson (an assistant professor of mathematics), in December 1941; no children.

Demonstrated that there is no automatic method of deciding which equations have integer solutions (1961); first woman mathematician elected to the National Academy of Science (1976); became first woman president of the American Mathematical Society (1982).

Born in 1919 in St. Louis, Missouri, Julia B. Robinson contracted scarlet fever at the age of nine. Her year-long study with a private tutor following her quarantine and bouts with rheumatic fever awakened an intense interest in mathematics that stayed with her when she returned to the classroom in ninth grade. She graduated from high school at age 16 with honors in mathematics and science and received the Bausch-Lomb medal for excellence in science.

Robinson's mother **Helen Hall Bowman** had died two years after giving birth to her, and following her father Ralph Bowman's second marriage the family moved to San Diego, where Julia enrolled at nearby San Diego State College. There she majored in mathematics and prepared to become a teacher, which was the only certain career path for mathematicians at the time. The onset of the Great Depression in the 1930s had accelerated the loss of her father's savings, leading to his depression and suicide at the beginning of Robinson's sophomore year in college. With financial help from her aunt and sister, Robinson transferred to the University of California at Berkeley for her senior year. There she encountered a stimulating environment with mathematicians like herself. She also met and married an assistant professor at the school, Raphael Robinson. Due to a rule that prohibited members of the same family from working in the same department, Julia Robinson gave up her teaching assistantship in the mathematics department. However, the rule did not prevent her from working with Jerzy Neyman in the Berkeley Statistical Laboratory on classified military projects during World War II. Around this time, Robinson suffered two miscarriages, probably related to her childhood illnesses, and she experienced a serious depression.

Robinson continued her Ph.D. studies under the well-known Polish logician Alfred Tarski. Her dissertation, *Definability and Decision Problems in Arithmetic*, proved the algorithmic unsolvability of the theory of the rational number field. In 1948, Robinson set out to work on David Hilbert's Tenth Problem; she would pursue this mathematical conundrum for most of her career. With the help of mathematicians Martin Davis and Hilary Putnam, who had sent her their work on a theorem, Robinson discovered a solution to the Tenth Problem, which was presented in 1961. Robinson's foundational work paved the way for Yuri Matijasevic to prove nine years later that no general method for determining solvability exists. Robinson also worked at the RAND corporation, the famous think-tank, theorizing about the zero-sum game, and on a problem in hydrodynamics for the Office of Naval Research.

In 1976, Robinson became the first woman mathematician elected to the National Academy of Sciences. Appointed full professor at Berkeley that same year, she carried only a quarter of the usual teaching load due to failing health, which also caused her to step down as president of the Association of Presidents of Scientific Societies. She became the first woman officer of the American Mathematical Society in 1978, and four years later was named its first woman president. The MacArthur Foundation awarded Robinson a fellowship prize of $60,000 for five years. She found the attention "gratifying but embarrassing," and further noted, "Rather than being remembered as the first woman this or that, I would prefer to be remembered as a mathematician should, simply for the theorems I have proved and the problems I have solved." In 1985, the year after Robinson discovered she had leukemia, she was elected to the American Academy of Arts and Sciences. She died on July 30, 1985.

SOURCES AND SUGGESTED READING:

Dunham, William. *The Mathematical Universe*. NY: John Wiley & Sons, 1994.

Feferman, Solomon, ed. *The Collected Works of Julia Robinson*. Providence, RI: American Mathematical Society, 1996.

McMurray, Emily J., ed. *Notable Twentieth-Century Scientists*. Detroit, MI: Gale Research, 1995.

Read, Phyllis J., and Bernard L. Witleib. *The Book of Women's Firsts*. NY: Random House, 1992.

Zilboorg, Caroline, ed. *Women's Firsts*. Detroit, MI: Gale Research, 1997.

Jane E. Spear,
freelance writer and editor, Canton, Ohio

Robinson, Kathleen (1901–1983)

Australian theatrical producer. Born in 1901 in Melbourne, Australia; died on December 28, 1983; daughter of Mary Louise (McKay) Robinson and Matthew John McWilliams Robinson; attended Frensham School in Mittagong, Australia; studied in London at the Royal Academy of Dramatic Art; studied production in London.

Kathleen Robinson was born in 1901 in Melbourne, Australia, the only child of Matthew McWilliams Robinson and **Mary McKay Robinson**, the niece of millionaire pastoralist Sir Samuel McCaughey. Kathleen's love of theater began after seeing an elaborate production of *Ben Hur* with her mother. She was further encouraged to participate in theatrical productions at the Frensham School in Mittagong. In April 1923, Robinson appeared in a production of *The Scarlet Pimpernel* while living in Sydney. Although it was only a benefit performance for the Ryde Homes for Incurables, she received critical acclaim.

Robinson moved to London with her parents and studied at the Royal Academy of Dramatic Art. She eventually joined an Australian tour with Lewis Casson and Dame *Sybil Thorndike and played minor roles in *St. Joan*, *Madame Plays Nap*, and *Macbeth*. After her father's death in 1929, Robinson and her mother moved back to London, where she studied theatrical production. From 1932 until 1935, she ran the Westminster Theatre with Osmond Daltry. Her production of *Arms and the Man*, with rehearsals attended by the playwright George Bernard Shaw, traveled throughout Europe.

On her return to Sydney in 1940, Robinson took a lease on the Minerva Theater at Kings Cross with co-director Alex Coppel, and formed Whitehall Productions. Intending to create a company of native Australians, she established an academy for dramatic art in 1944 and offered training to veterans of World War II. Peter Finch was one of several well-known Australian actors who got their start at the Minerva.

Robinson's determination and financial support kept the theater alive for ten years, but Whitehall could not operate at a loss indefinitely. MGM bought the Minerva Theater in 1948 to use as a cinema. Although Robinson initially won a case to prevent Whitehall's eviction from the theater, poor health resulting from a combi-

nation of low blood pressure and a debilitating fall in early 1950 forced her surrender of the Minerva. She died on December 28, 1983.

SOURCES:

Radi, Heather, ed. *200 Australian Women*. NSW, Australia: Women's Redress Press, 1988.

Jane E. Spear,
freelance writer and editor, Canton, Ohio

Robinson, Mary (1758–1800)

English actress, author, and mistress of King George IV of England. Name variations: Perdita Robinson; Mrs. Robinson; (pseudonym) Anne Frances Randall. Born Mary Darby of Irish descent in Bristol, England, on November 27, 1758; died in Windsor Park, Berkshire, on December 26, 1800; daughter of a whaling captain named Darby; mother's maiden name was Seys; married Thomas Robinson (a clerk in London), in 1774; children: Mary Elizabeth Robinson (b. around 1775); another daughter who died in infancy.

Born in 1758, Mary Robinson was the daughter of an Irish whaling-ship captain who abandoned his family to set up a factory in Labrador. In 1774, she married Thomas Robinson, a clerk in London, where her stunning beauty brought her to the attention of London society. Thomas was arrested for debt the following year, and Mary shared his imprisonment with their young daughter. Gifted as a child, she had been encouraged to write verses and completed the collection *Poems* while in King's Bench prison. It was published in two volumes in 1775.

Following her release, David Garrick, who earlier had been struck by her looks, offered Mary an engagement at Drury Lane. She made a successful debut as Juliet in 1776, and continued to act at Drury Lane for several years. On December 3, 1779, Robinson opened in the role of Perdita in Garrick's version of *The Winter's Tale*. Her beauty so captivated the 18-year-old George, prince of Wales (later King George IV), that he began a correspondence with her, signing his letters "Florizel." Robinson rejected her suitor, and his promise of £21,000 when he turned 21, until she arrived home earlier than usual to find her husband in bed with one of their maids. For about two years, Robinson was mistress to the prince; then he deserted her, dishonoring his bond for £21,000 (though she agreed to return his love letters for £5,000 down, £500 per annum). Owing to the hostility of public opinion because of the affair, she feared a return to the stage. Instead she had relationships with several well-known men, including Colonel Banastre

$\mathcal{M}$ary
$\mathcal{R}$obinson
(1758–1800)

Tarleton, later a member of Parliament from Liverpool (with whom she was involved until 1798), and turned to writing.

Robinson published several collections of poetry, among them *Sight: The Cavern of Woe and Solitude* (1793) and *The Sicilian Lover: A Tragedy* (1796), and was a member of the Della Cruscan poets' circle, along with *Hester Lynch Piozzi and *Hannah Cowley. She also published a number of novels, including *Vancenza* (1792), *The Widow* (1794), *Hubert de Sevrac* (1796), *Walsingham* (1796), and *The Natural Daughter* (1799), which the public bought eagerly because of the scandal attached to her name. Robinson counted among her friends *Mary Wollstonecraft and William Godwin, and in 1799, under the pseudonym Anne Frances Randall, published a book about marriage called *A Letter to the Women of England on the Injustice of Mental Subordination*. Partially paralyzed as the result of an earlier miscarriage, and suffering from ill health in her later years, Robinson died in 1800, at age 42, without finishing her memoirs. These were edited by her daughter Mary Elizabeth Robinson and published the following year. There are numerous portraits of Robinson from her years as an actress, including those by Joshua Reynolds, Thomas Gainsborough, John Hoppner, Richard Cosway, and George Romney.

SUGGESTED READING:

Robinson, Mary. *Memoirs of Mrs. Robinson.* 4 vols., Richard Phillips, 1801 (new edition, edited and with an introduction by Martin J. Levy, published as *Perdita: The Memoirs of Mary Robinson*, Dufour, 1995).

Robinson, Mary (d. 1837)

Famed English beauty known as the Buttermere Beauty. Name variations: Mary of Buttermere; Maid of Buttermere; the Buttermere Beauty. Died in 1837; married to infamous forger and imposter John Hatfield under false pretenses, in 1802; married Richard Harrison; four children.

Mary Robinson, also known as the Buttermere Beauty, achieved such fame for her looks that Samuel Taylor Coleridge, William and *Dorothy Wordsworth, and Charles and *Mary Lamb all found her to be the most beautiful woman in England at the beginning of the 19th century. In 1802, she married John Hatfield, a notorious bigamist and forger who had already deserted at least two wives in addition to serving time in debtors' prison. Hatfield won Robinson's heart by pretending to be a man named Alexander Augustus Hope, but the following year his deception came out in a trial that capti-

vated all of England. He was convicted of forgery and hanged in Carlisle.

The legend of Mary Robinson inspired poets to write verses extolling her virtue and grieving over her marriage to the scoundrel Hatfield. Coleridge and the Wordsworths recorded notes of the trial and circumstances in their journals. Later on, Robinson married Richard Harrison of Caldbeck, a town with a population of over 1,000 in the Northern Fells. They had four children. Robinson slipped into a quiet and genteel life, but her story remained famous even after her death in 1837.

SOURCES:

Bragg, Melvyn. *The Maid of Buttermere.* NY: Putnam, 1987.
The Concise Dictionary of National Biography. Oxford: Oxford University Press, 1992.

Jane Spear,
freelance writer and editor, Canton, Ohio

Robinson, Mary (1944—)

Human-rights lawyer and feminist who helped to advance the legal rights of Irish women and who was elected the first woman president of Ireland. Name variations: Mary Bourke. Born Marie Terese Winifred Bourke on May 21, 1944, in Ballina, County Mayo, Ireland; only daughter and third child of Aubrey de Vere Bourke and Tess O'Donnell Bourke (both doctors); attended Miss Ruddy's School, Ballina, 1948–54, Convent of the Sacred Heart, Mount Anville, Dublin, 1954–61, finishing school in Paris, 1961–62; Law School, Trinity College Dublin, B.L., 1968; Harvard Law School, LL.M., 1969; married Nicholas Robinson, on December 12, 1970; children: Tessa (b. 1972); William (b. 1974); Aubrey (b. 1981).

Awards: Member of the Royal Irish Academy; Hon. Bencher, King's Inns, Dublin, and Middle Temple, London; honorary Professor of Law, Manchester University; honorary fellow, Trinity College, Dublin; honorary member, New York Bar Association; honorary doctorates of law from National University of Ireland and universities of Brown, Cambridge, Montpellier, Liverpool, St. Andrews, Melbourne, Columbia, Poznan, Toronto, Fordham, Queen's Belfast, Rennes, Coventry (1990–97); European Media Prize (1991); Special Humanitarian CARE Award (1993); International Human Rights Award (1993).

Elected to the Irish Senate (1969) and remained there until 1989; was Reid Professor of Constitutional and Criminal Law at Trinity College (1969–75); lecturer in European Community Law (1975–90); introduced in senate first bill to legalize sale of contraceptives (1971); joined Irish Labour Party (1976); stood unsuccessfully for the Dail (1977, 1981); was a member of Dublin City Council (1979–83); introduced first bill to provide for divorce (1980); was a member of the New Ireland Forum (1983–84); was a member of Advisory Commission of Inter-Rights (1984–90); resigned from the Labour Party (1985); was a member of International Commission of Jurists (1987–90); founder and director of Irish Centre for European Law (1989); was a member of Euro Avocats (1989–90); announced candidacy for president of Ireland (April 1990); elected president (November 7, 1990); decided not to seek re-election (March 12, 1997); appointed UN High Commissioner for Human Rights (June 1997).

At first glance, there is little in Mary Robinson's background to explain her career as a socialist, radical human-rights lawyer. Both her parents were doctors, and the strong legal tradition in her father's family had its connections with the British imperial civil service. Her uncle, Paget Bourke, was knighted by Queen *Elizabeth II in 1957. She was born Marie Terese Winifred Bourke on May 21, 1944, in Ballina, County Mayo, the only daughter in a family of five. According to **Olivia O'Leary** and **Helen Burke**, Robinson often had to contend against the wishes and ambitions of her mother **Tess O'Donnell Bourke**. "She was the earth mother, the centre of everything," said Robinson. "She was very, very warm, dominant. She had very strong views on things, which could lead to clashes." Robinson also felt that she could at times be quite "snobbish" which only reinforced her daughter's commitment to equality. Said one of her brothers: Mary "wasn't a clothes horse, wasn't interested in make-up, wasn't interested in the finer things some girls are interested in and which my mother wanted to lavish on her only daughter." However, there were other clues to Mary Robinson's subsequent career in her family background. One of her great-uncles had been involved in the secret revolutionary organization the Irish Republican Brotherhood of the 1860s and 1870s. But of more immediate influence was learning from her father Aubrey Bourke's medical practice the harsh effects of rural poverty and emigration in Ballina and the surrounding countryside. Mayo was one of the poorest parts of Ireland and was particularly affected by emigration. Robinson's interest in the law was spurred by her grandfather H.C. Bourke, a prominent lawyer in Ballina to whom she was close. He was, she recalled, "a great fighter in court. . . . He would always come up with further arguments."

The Bourkes were comfortably well-off. They lived in an imposing house in the center of the town and employed a nanny and servants. Mary attended a small private school run by Miss **Claire Ruddy** and then went to convent boarding school at Mount Anville in Dublin. She was so impressed by the nuns' commitment to the principles of social justice that she briefly considered becoming a nun. Her academic performance at Mount Anville was creditable, and her mother encouraged her to study law at university. First, however, Mary spent a formative year at finishing school in Paris in 1961–62. She saw films which would never have reached Ireland, she visited art galleries, and she read widely, "everything from Kafka to Camus. . . . I was a compulsive reader. Being in an intellectual environment was so nice, so different." In Paris, she learned how to question things, especially the role of the Catholic Church which in Ireland could be authoritarian and oppressive. She also became aware of gender differences in Paris. After her return to Ballina, she spent a year at home working for her entrance to Trinity College, Dublin, where she had decided to study law. The changes brought about by her year in France resulted in communication problems with her parents, but she nonetheless remained on good terms with them.

The Trinity Law School serviced Irish professional legal bodies and also the British Colonial Service (as members of her own family had done). Though the school was not known for its liberalism, the winds of change which were blowing through Irish society in the early 1960s were beginning to make themselves felt at Trinity. Robinson's intellectual commitment stood out from the majority of undergraduates who enjoyed a more social existence. One of her acquaintances, Nicholas Robinson, took a more light-hearted view of his legal studies and was also a talented cartoonist. In her second year, Mary won a prestigious scholarship which gave her a measure of financial independence. She attended college debating societies but was greatly irked by the fact that two of the most prominent societies, the Historical and the Philosophical, excluded women. She became auditor of the Law Society and editor of the student law review, *Justice.* The subject of her inaugural paper for the Law Society was a prescient one in terms of her career: "Law, Morality and the need to separate Church and State." She was advised by a number of people not to deliver it.

Robinson graduated with a first-class degree in law in 1967, then won a scholarship to Harvard Law School. Harvard was a formative

Mary
Robinson
(1944—)

experience. "I had a law degree, but I hadn't really been encouraged to think," she said. "I benefited from a kind of Harvard arrogance. You have the right to question. The fact that you're young doesn't stop you from having thoughts and developing them." The people she met at

Harvard "were much more prepared to accept responsibility, to seek and want involvement. . . . Everything was up for examination." She arrived in the middle of nationwide demonstrations on Vietnam and civil rights which led to debates within Harvard on the teaching of law and the lack of equal participation. Lecturers included such distinguished lawyers as Abram Chayes, Alan Dershowitz, Archibald Cox and Paul Freund. Bourke also attended economics lectures by John Kenneth Galbraith. She earned her first-class master's degree in 1968 and returned to Ireland, where she became a part-time law tutor at Trinity and an apprentice barrister on the Irish western circuit.

The more we are ready to branch out and fulfill ourselves in the life of the country, the more doors will open in the face of quiet ability.

—Mary Robinson

In summer 1969, Robinson decided to stand for the senate, the upper house of the Irish Parliament, as one of the candidates for the three Trinity College senate seats. The Trinity electorate was aging, male, conservative and Protestant; Robinson was young, female, liberal and Catholic. Although she confounded expectations by winning a seat, there were factors working in her favor: she was appointed to the five-year Reid Professorship in Law at Trinity which strengthened her academic credentials; the troubles in Northern Ireland had erupted and were prompting a reassessment of the nature of Irish society; and the Irish women's movement was just getting underway. One of her most active supporters was Nicholas Robinson, whom she married in December 1970. Though her parents did not attend the wedding, this was not, as has been reported, because he was Protestant; there was, in fact, a long tradition of mixed marriages within the Bourke family. Rather, her parents were unimpressed by his dilettante attitude toward the law and his interest in art and cartoons. Their daughter was also aware that "over-love and possessiveness was a large part of it." The rift was soon healed.

After her senate election, Robinson told an interviewer that the best way for a woman to overcome prejudice was "not to emphasize that you are a woman but to show that you can do a job efficiently and well." But women's issues soon dominated her political and legal career. She was particularly critical of the constitutional ban on divorce and the criminal laws against contraceptives. In 1971, she was one of the co-sponsors of a senate bill to change the contraception laws. The first legislative attempt of its kind, the bill aroused a storm of controversy. Robinson and the other co-sponsors were denounced from the pulpits of Catholic churches throughout Ireland, and her parents walked out of their own local church in Ballina after one

such castigation. The bill was refused a first reading, but when a second bill was introduced in November 1973 it passed the first stage and instigated the first ever parliamentary debate on the subject. By this time, however, the legal position had changed completely when the Supreme Court overturned the 1935 law banning the sale and import of contraceptives as a violation of marital privacy. Robinson acted for the appellant, **Mary McGee**.

The landmark McGee case proved to Robinson and other lawyers that the law could be used as a major instrument of reform. She was also aware, after Ireland joined the European Community in 1973, that recourse could be had at the European Court of Justice and the European Court of Human Rights. Robinson stressed this point to the Irish Women's Liberation Movement (IWLM) when it sought her advice, although she herself had considerable reservations about the stridency and some of the publicity-seeking activities of the IWLM. She reinforced her belief in the law over the next 17 years, during which she acted in a series of landmark cases: the abolition of all-male, ratepaying juries in 1976; the 1979 Airey case on the right to free legal aid in civil cases (of which Robinson was particularly proud); the 1980 Murphy case on equal tax treatment for married couples; the McDonald case, also in 1980, ensuring proper provision of local authority accommodation for families of Travelers who were being evicted; and three key judgements in 1988—the Hyland case on equal provision of social welfare payments to married people, the Norris case on gay rights, and the Telecom Eireann case in which Robinson represented women workers demanding equal pay for equal work. In 1989, she was defense counsel in the *SPUC* v. *Grogan* case on the provision of abortion information. Despite these legal and legislative achievements, Robinson was never entirely comfortable in either the senate or the Law Library (where most barristers were based). Both institutions were male-dominated, with a "boys at the bar" culture that changed very slowly.

In 1976, Robinson joined the Labour Party, but this was also to prove an uncomfortable relationship. The party was largely based in the trade-union movement and among the rank and file there was a distrust of middle-class intellectuals like Robinson. There were also personality problems. Robinson's inherent shyness, which she struggled for years to overcome, often made her seem cold, distant and aloof. In the 1977 general election, she decided to stand for the lower house of the Irish Parliament, the Dail, and was selected as one of the four Labour candidates for the Dublin constituency of Rathmines West. However, the campaign was dogged by divisions within the Labour Party at the local and national level, and she lost by 400 votes. She stood again as a Labour candidate in the 1981 election, this time for the largely working-class constituency of Dublin West. She lost more comprehensively this time: Travelers were unpopular in the constituency and her involvement in the McDonald Travelers judgment the previous year worked against her. Some women voters also disapproved of the fact that she had just had a baby (her third child Aubrey), who accompanied her for part of the election campaign. However, Robinson continued to be re-elected to the senate. In 1984, she had high hopes that she would be nominated as attorney general to the coalition government in which Labour was a partner, but the job went to someone else, to her bitter disappointment. This increased her disenchantment with the party and its leader, Dick Spring. At the end of 1985, she resigned from the Labour Party because of her disagreement with the new Anglo-Irish agreement on Northern Ireland, which she felt had ignored the views of the Northern Ireland unionists.

Robinson had also made her views clear during the two referendum campaigns on abortion and divorce which convulsed the country between 1983 and 1986. She predicted that the insertion of a pro-life clause in the Irish constitution in 1983 would lead to pregnant women being pursued in the courts, a prediction borne out in the notorious "X" and "C" cases in the 1990s. In 1986, Robinson was unimpressed by the government's ill-prepared and apathetic handling of the referendum proposing an end to the ban on divorce, which was defeated. (The referendum would eventually be passed on November 25, 1995.) In 1989, after 20 years, Robinson decided not to seek re-election to the senate. Rather, she and her husband intended to build up the Irish Centre for European Law at Trinity. Then, in February 1990, they received a visit from a senior Labour party member, John Rogers, who had been appointed attorney general over Robinson in 1984.

Rogers wanted Robinson to consider standing as the Labour candidate in the Irish presidential election. The Irish president, who is the head of state, is elected every seven years by popular vote, but there had been no presidential election since 1974. The Labour leader, Dick Spring, was determined that in 1990 there would be no agreed candidate and that an election should be held. After discussion with other party members as to the kind of candidate they wanted, Robinson's name quickly emerged. She was extremely surprised by the proposal but, at her husband's urging, considered it seriously. In April, they met Spring and other Labour leaders, and she agreed to accept the Labour nomination but only if she could remain independent. She did not wish to rejoin the Labour Party and told Spring that she would be more valuable as a candidate if she maintained her autonomy. Spring reluctantly agreed; he later conceded that her instincts on this were correct. Robinson quickly gathered around her a trusted campaign team of whom the most important was **Bride Rosney**, her closest friend and confidante since the 1970s. Journalist Eoghan Harris, an unofficial member of her team because of his controversial, polemical reputation, played a key role in the early stages of the campaign. Harris emphasized the need for Robinson to build a broad platform of support outside her core Labour/liberal constituency and the need to tackle media preconceptions and criticisms of her head on. These points became the basis of the Robinson campaign strategy. With the help of her advisers, Robinson also changed her appearance, sporting an elegant new wardrobe and a new hairstyle.

The campaign was launched on May 1, 1990. Although she was the first woman ever to stand as a candidate for the Irish presidency, Robinson received comparatively little press coverage concerning her nomination and the initial stages of her campaign. However, she began campaigning months before any of the other candidates, who waited until autumn, and by then she had a head start. She did months of solid canvassing in the villages and towns of rural Ireland and paid particular attention to local press and radio. The aim was to reassure conservative rural voters that she was not a dangerous radical. Much more reluctantly, Robinson also agreed to expose her family to the public gaze in a feature for the celebrity magazine *Hello*, the first time this had been done in an Irish election although it has since become standard practice. Many political observers believed that Robinson's shyness and reserve would make canvassing particularly difficult for her. This was true in the early stages of her campaign but the warmth of the welcome she received eased her stiffness considerably. It was also true that once she sensed she could win, she was determined to change her personal style if this ensured victory. Tensions developed between her campaign team and the Labour Party election team but they were kept under control. Once the other candidates entered the field that October, the campaign became more intense, and Robinson began to make mistakes, notably when she gave a floundering explanation about her support for gay rights and access to condoms. In the end these mistakes did not matter, particularly when her chief rival, the Fianna Fail candidate Brian Lenihan, was forced to resign from the government because of a political scandal. The week before the election, a member of Lenihan's campaign team made a pointed personal attack on Robinson and her family in a radio interview which provoked widespread criticism and a backlash. Robinson won the election on November 7 by 86,557 votes and won 25 out of a total of 41 constituencies, including every one of the Dublin constituencies. In her acceptance speech, she paid tribute to the women of Ireland who "instead of rocking the cradle, rocked the system."

At her inauguration on December 3, 1990, guests from women's organizations, from social welfare organizations, and from Northern Ireland were particularly prominent, which set the tone for her presidency. Her first months did not go smoothly, however. The president's residence, Áras an Uachtaráin (generally known as the Áras), was an 18th-century house badly in need of refurbishment. The reorganization of the staff also created ill will. But these were minor irritations compared to Robinson's strained relations with the prime minister, Charles Haughey. Haughey's style was strongly presidential and apart from his annoyance at the defeat of his candidate, Brian Lenihan, he was aware that Robinson's election had changed the presidency irrevocably. For much of its history since 1938, the presidency had been the preserve of retired politicians, all men. The president's powers were limited but important, particularly (1) discretion in refusing a dissolution of the Dail; (2) the appointment of a council of state to advise the president; and (3) referral of a bill to the Supreme Court for a decision on its constitutionality. The president could not leave the country without the government's permission, but the government also had to keep the president "generally informed" about its policies. Robinson found that invitations to her for various events would be withdrawn or else would be forwarded to her from Haughey's department with the words "not appropriate for the president" written on them. She was refused permission to travel to England to give the prestigious Dimbleby Lectures on BBC television. In summer 1991, Haughey arrived at the Áras with legal opinions from a senior lawyer as to her powers and functions under the constitution but since constitutional law was Robinson's own bailiwick, she easily saw through this challenge. Haughey left

office in January 1992, and Robinson's relations with her three subsequent prime ministers, Albert Reynolds, John Bruton, and Bertie Aherne, were for the most part excellent.

Robinson fulfilled her election promise to welcome groups to the Áras from all walks of life, from every sector of the community, in both parts of Ireland. Most of her entertainment budget, which was increased by the government, went on tea and cakes for the thousands of visitors each year representing Travelers, the homeless, the physically and mentally handicapped, the unemployed, community groups, women's groups, gay and lesbian groups, among others. She also paid six visits to Mountjoy Prison in Dublin. But she had a keen instinct for the importance of the formal and ceremonial side of her office and felt she had to bring a sense of the office to the people she visited and who visited her in order to show that she valued their work. "It was a President they wanted, not a community worker," she once observed.

Robinson was anxious to further Anglo-Irish relations and to help improve relations between Northern Ireland and the Republic of Ireland. She considered it an anomaly that while Irish government ministers met their British counterparts on an almost daily basis, there had been no formal meeting between the respective heads of state, the British monarch and the Irish president, since Irish independence in 1921. In the three years after her election Robinson had informal meetings with individual members of the British royal family. In May 1993, she became the first Irish president to meet a British monarch, Queen Elizabeth II, at Buckingham Palace, and in 1996 she paid the first formal state visit to Britain as a guest of the queen. These moves were widely welcomed, but her attempts to establish better relations with Northern Ireland proved more difficult. Robinson's presidency coincided with the beginning of the long process to try to secure agreement between the two divided communities in Northern Ireland, nationalist and unionist, after over 20 years of bitter sectarian strife which had cost thousands of lives. Her sympathy for the unionists after the 1985 Anglo-Irish Agreement had led to her departure from the Labour Party, but unionist friendliness towards her evaporated rapidly in June 1993 when Robinson accepted an invitation to west Belfast to meet community representatives. West Belfast was one of the core areas of IRA support and in meeting community representatives she was bound to meet members of the IRA's political wing, Sinn Fein. The British government was furious and asked the Irish prime minister, Albert Reynolds, to stop her. Although the Irish foreign minister, Dick Spring, had reservations about Robinson's Belfast visit, Reynolds regarded it as a key step in his moves to bring the IRA and Sinn Fein toward a cease-fire. Robinson shook hands with the Sinn Fein leader, Gerry Adams, an action which provoked a vitriolic reaction from sections of the British and Irish press. Neither then nor subsequently did Robinson express any regret for her gesture. Adams stated later that her visit marked the first breach in the isolation of his community.

Robinson traveled more widely than any of her predecessors. When visiting Britain, America, Canada, South America, Australia and New Zealand, she was anxious to meet the people of the far-flung Irish diaspora. She had mentioned the diaspora in her inaugural speech in 1990 and "Cherishing the Diaspora" was the subject of her first presidential address to both houses of the Irish Parliament in February 1995. Although the address received a lukewarm response in Ireland, it was more enthusiastically received by emigrant communities abroad. One of the most potent images of Robinson's presidency was the light she kept burning in one of the windows of the Áras as a symbol of the diaspora. But she was also taking an increasing interest in other areas. In October 1992, despite concerns about her security, she visited Somalia which was devastated by famine and civil war. In 1994, she was the first head of state to go to Rwanda after the horrendous genocide there. In both countries, she was critical of the United Nations' response and said so in a number of speeches at the UN. The main lesson she had learned was that political crises could not be solved by short-term responses alone, and that aid agencies needed to be more aware of the political aspects of situations like Somalia and Rwanda. She was also the first head of state to visit the International Criminal Tribunal for the Former Yugoslavia.

Her active interest in the UN prompted speculation that she would like a UN post, and she was mentioned as a possible secretary-general. This raised the question of whether she would seek a second term as president. Her family believed she had achieved all she could in the post, and she herself considered that she could not remain a fresh voice for another seven years. On March 12, 1997, Robinson announced that she would not seek another term but expressed her interest in seeking the UN post of High Commissioner for Human Rights. With the support of the Irish government, she was appointed to that post. Her last engagement as president was on September 12, 1997. Later that day, she flew to Geneva to take up her new position. The morale of her new staff was at rock bottom and her office was facing immense challenges in countries like Rwanda and Algeria. But they were challenges Robinson was determined to meet.

SOURCES:

Finlay, Fergus. *Mary Robinson: A President with a Purpose.* Dublin: O'Brien Press, 1990.

Horgan, John. *Mary Robinson: An Independent Voice.* Dublin: O'Brien Press, 1997.

Irish Times. Dublin, March 13, 1997.

O'Leary, Olivia, and Helen Burke. *Mary Robinson: An Authorised Biography.* London: Hodder & Stoughton, 1998.

O'Reilly, Emily. *Candidate: The Truth behind the Presidential Campaign.* Dublin: Attic Press, 1991.

O'Sullivan, Michael. *Mary Robinson: The Life and Times of an Irish Liberal.* Dublin: Blackwater Press, 1993.

Siggins, Lorna. *Mary Robinson: The Woman Who Took Power in the Park.* Edinburgh: Mainstream, 1997.

RELATED MEDIA:

"President—Mary Robinson 1990–1997," television documentary by Radio Telifis Eireann (RTE), broadcast on October 8, 1997.

Deirdre McMahon,
lecturer in history at Mary Immaculate College,
University of Limerick, Limerick, Ireland

Robinson, Mary F. (1856–1944).

See Duclaux, Agnes.

Robinson, Mrs. Perdita (1758–1800).

See Robinson, Mary.

Robinson, Ruby Doris Smith
(1942–1967)

Civil-rights activist, founding member of the Atlanta Student Movement and the Student Non-Violent Coordinating Committee, and outstanding organizer who urged those in the movement for racial justice not only to work for goals which would benefit poor- and middle-class African-Americans but to risk their lives in the process. Name variations: Rubye. Born Ruby Doris Smith in Atlanta, Georgia, on April 25, 1942; died of cancer in Atlanta on October 9, 1967; second of seven children of J.T. Smith and Alice Smith (who operated a beauty parlor and a used-furniture business out of their Atlanta home); attended Price Hill High School; graduated and made her debut in 1958; entered Spelman College of Atlanta University in 1959; received B.A. in physical education, 1964; married Clifford Robinson, in 1963; children: Kenneth Toure Robinson (b. 1965).

Joined Atlanta Student Movement and Atlanta Committee on Appeal for Human Rights (1960); attended founding meeting of SNCC (1960), elected to executive committee (1962), executive secretary (1966).

Ruby Doris Smith Robinson quickly achieved legendary status within the ranks of the Student Non-Violent Coordinating Committee (SNCC). Her bold defiance of segregationist policies, her "100% shit detector," and her unique ability to merge the passion of a field activist with the careful attention to detail of an effective administrator, made her, in James Forman's words, "one of the true revolutionaries of the civil rights movement."

There is no written record of her short life, but her accomplishments as an organizer can be most fully documented in the daring projects she was instrumental in implementing for SNCC—especially the jail-no bail campaigns, the Freedom Rides of 1961, the Freedom Summer program of 1964, and the voter registration campaigns of 1965 and 1966—and her individual passionate acts for racial justice. For example, Julian Bond and Robinson were part of a SNCC delegation determined to visit Africa in 1964 when they learned that their plane had been overbooked. As Bond later recalled, Robinson remained determined to leave on schedule, rejected the airline's requests to take a later flight and stormed onto the jetway, where she conducted a one woman sit-in until the group was allowed to follow their original schedule.

Yet Ruby Doris Smith Robinson was not raised to be confrontational. Born April 25, 1942, Ruby Doris was the second child of J.T. Smith and **Alice Smith**, who used their 794 Frazier Street home in Atlanta to provide a comfortable middle-class life for their seven offspring. While the children played and studied in the main part of the Smith home, their parents ran a successful small business out of an addition to the house. African-American businesses and clientele and segregated schools formed the backdrop of Robinson's early world. She attended Price High School where she accompanied the school marching band as a majorette. Following local custom, she made her debut in black Atlanta society in 1958. And, like most middle-class African-American women in Atlanta, the following year she enrolled in Spelman College, the women's college of Atlanta University which had a reputation for merging finishing-school skills with academic preparation. Her first year in college passed uneventfully.

In 1960, inspired by the sit-in at the Greensboro, North Carolina, Woolworth's, Robinson joined the Atlanta Committee on Appeal for Human Rights and attended the April 1960 meeting, called by students and *Ella Baker to discuss ways to marshal student protest, which gave birth

to SNCC. When SNCC established its field office in Atlanta, Robinson quickly devoted most of her time to the young organization. Consequently, when SNCC activists debated what action to take when students were arrested in January 1961 for trying to desegregate a Rock Hill, South Carolina, lunch counter, Robinson had proved her commitment to the organization and therefore was in a position to have her voice heard in debate. She suggested that SNCC encourage its members to refuse bail and thereby fill the jails, and, in early February, she went to Rock Hill to practice her own suggestion. She then served a 30-day jail term, marking the first time that a civil-rights activist refused bail and served a full sentence. In May, she joined the Freedom Rides organized by SNCC and again endured beatings and served her full sentence. Yet many activists believe that her greatest contribution to the Rides was yet to come. Once the violence escalated, Robinson worked the phones across the nation to recruit students to replace those riders who were arrested; thus, she not only kept the program going but also pressured the Kennedy administration into action. She finished the year in McComb, Mississippi, helping SNCC coordinate its voter-registration drive. By April 1962, her leadership in SNCC was so well known that she was elected one of three at-large members to the SNCC Executive Committee, ultimately becoming James Forman's special assistant. The following year, she joined SNCC full time.

Robinson spent her time at SNCC trying to make the movement stay attuned to realistic change rather than to lofty, unimplementable ideals. By the spring of 1964, she decided that civil rights was a dead issue since integration had little relevance to those poorer African-Americans concerned "with the basic necessities of life." She argued that "a new strategy" was needed, especially one "with new and creative tactics" that would clearly show "how our work is affecting basic changes in the power structure." Furthermore, she believed that SNCC's decentralized structure and uncoordinated approach to the media undermined its effectiveness. Rather than respond to every issue racism provoked, she argued that SNCC "needed to define its ideology, establish specific goals, and explain in very definite terms how it will project itself in the mass media." Consequently, when students at Fisk University appealed to SNCC for aid in organizing their protests, she responded by traveling with Cordell Reagon to Nashville to help coordinate their efforts.

In the midst of this intense political commitment, she also found time to make a commitment of a more personal nature. After a short, very private courtship, Ruby Doris Smith married Clifford Robinson, a quite, private man who was not involved in SNCC activities. In 1965, she gave birth to their son, Kenneth Toure Robinson.

By 1966, Robinson's leadership skills would be challenged in a different way. Many members had become dissatisfied with the sitting leadership. James Forman had served as executive secretary since 1961 and John Lewis had served as chair since 1963. Forman announced that he did not want to seek reelection, but Lewis remained willing to dedicate his time and energy to SNCC. Many SNCC activists thought Lewis too mainstream and resented the time he spent working with the White House Conference on Civil Rights and his very public fund-raising tours. Stokeley Carmichael, whose stature in SNCC increased with his success in urging African-American Alabamians to support the Black Panther Party on election day, appealed to those frustrated with Lewis. Yet Lewis still won the election and Robinson was chosen to replace Forman as executive secretary. The vote was contested illegally, and another ballot initiated. Although this time Carmichael, with support of white staffers, easily defeated Lewis, Robinson's support remained firm and she became the first and only woman to lead SNCC.

Her tenure as executive secretary would be short-lived, because a rare cancer would kill her within a year. Nevertheless, her contributions to SNCC during this period were notable because she could maintain the delicate balance between black nationalism and integration and between feminism and the historic prejudice against African-American men. Repeatedly, she urged staffers and volunteers alike to demonstrate a commitment to work "rather than sit around talking about white people." When **Mary King** and **Casey Hayden** submitted their famous manifesto "The Position of Women in SNCC," Robinson supported them and even accompanied them on an earlier sit-in in Forman's office. Yet despite her awareness of sexism, throughout her six-year commitment to SNCC, Robinson's priority remained the prejudice that oppressed African-Americans.

When she assumed the leadership of SNCC, the organization was in financial chaos and its energies were drained by a myriad of projects promised by activists and volunteers who were given free rein by its decentralized structure. Once she became executive secretary, Robinson had an immediate impact on SNCC. Media releases became more coordinated, projects were

evaluated, and monies better budgeted. This leadership led many activists within SNCC to believe that she could revive the floundering organization. However, within a few months, cancer destroyed her energy. She died on October 9, 1967, in Atlanta, age 27.

SOURCES:

Carson, Claiborne. *In Struggle: SNCC and the Black Awakening of the 1960s.* Cambridge, MA: Harvard University Press, 1981.

Fleming, Cynthia Griggs. "Black Women Activists and the Student Nonviolent Coordinating Committee: The Case of Ruby Doris Smith Robinson," in *The Journal of Women's History.* Vol. 4, no. 3. Winter 1993, pp. 64–82.

Giddings, Paula. *When and Where I Enter: The Impact of Black Women on Race and Sex in America.* NY: Morrow, 1984.

King, Mary. *Freedom Song.* NY: Morrow, 1987.

SUGGESTED READING:

Fleming, Cynthia Griggs. *Soon We Will Not Cry: The Liberation of Ruby Doris Smith Robinson.* Rowman & Littlefield, 1998.

Garland, Phil. "Builders of a New South," in *Ebony.* Vol. 21. August 1966.

Washington, Cynthia. "We Started from Different Ends of the Spectrum," in *Southern Exposure.* Vol. 5. Winter 1977.

Allida M. Black,
Visiting Assistant Professor of History and American Studies,
Penn State University, Harrisburg

Robison, Mary (1858–1942).

See Robson, May.

Robison, Paula (1941—)

American flutist. Born Paula Judith Robison in Nashville, Tennessee, on June 8, 1941; married Scott Nickrenz (a violist); studied flute with Julius Baker at the Juilliard School of Music and with Marcel Moyse.

Took first prize in the Munich Competition (1964); was the first American to win first prize for flute in the Geneva International Competition (1966); with husband, served as artistic co-director of the Spoleto Festival of Two Worlds in Italy and Charleston, South Carolina (1977) and the Spoleto-Melbourne, Australia Festival of Three Worlds (1986).

Paula Robison established her career as a flutist by performing the works of new composers and often commissioning pieces to be written for her from the likes of Leon Kirchner, Oliver Knussen, Toru Takemitsu, and Alberto Ginastera. Along with her husband Scott Nickrenz, she has been active with the Spoleto Festival, an international event which has taken place on three continents. Here, too, Robison has encouraged new works to be performed. A highly skilled musician, she was the first American flutist to win the Geneva International Competition. She has performed as a soloist with leading orchestras throughout the world as well as with chamber groups. In 1978, Robison joined the faculty of the Juilliard School of Music.

John Haag,
Athens, Georgia

Robsart, Amy (c. 1532–1560)

English noblewoman who died under mysterious circumstances. Name variations: Lady Amy Dudley; Lady Amye Dudley. Born Amye Robsart around 1532 (some sources cite 1535) in Norfolk, England; died on September 8, 1560, at Cumnor Hall, North Berkshire, England; daughter of Sir John Robsart; married Robert Dudley (c. 1532–1588), earl of Leicester (r. 1563–1588), on June 4, 1550; no children.

The life and death of Amy Robsart has been the subject of fiction by many writers, including Sir Walter Scott. She was born around 1532 into the minor English nobility of Norfolk, her father's only legitimate child. Growing up in the northern English countryside, Robsart was not well educated and probably could not write. Nevertheless, her beauty and her large inheritance from her father brought her a marriage into one of England's most prominent families, the Dudleys, hereditary dukes of Northumberland. In June 1550, about age 15, Amy married Robert Dudley, whom she had met only briefly. His father John Dudley was the duke of Northumberland. The wedding took place at the royal palace of Sheen, with the young King Edward VI as host. At first, the marriage was a success, and the couple lived happily enough on Amy's inherited estates in Syderstone, Norfolk. But Dudley began to spend more time at court as he gained the king's favor, visiting his wife less and less often.

When Edward VI died in 1553, Dudley and his family supported the claims of the Protestant Lady *Jane Grey over those of Edward's Catholic half-sister *Mary (I). After Mary came to the throne, Robert Dudley and his brothers were imprisoned as traitors in the Tower of London for over a year; their father was executed. Amy, Lady Dudley, was allowed to visit Dudley occasionally, but even after he was released in October 1554 they still spent little time together.

When *Elizabeth I succeeded Mary in 1558, Robert Dudley quickly rose to a position of prominence at court. Although she gave him some minor offices but few real responsibilities, Elizabeth clearly favored Dudley over her many courtiers, and they were constantly together. Coupled with Elizabeth's refusal to marry any of her suitors, her obvious fondness for Dudley led to widespread rumors of a love affair. Soon it was being said that Dudley had ordered the poisoning of his wife so he himself could marry Elizabeth, and that Elizabeth refused to marry anyone but Dudley.

Robsart was aware of the rumors, despite her distance from the intrigues and gossip of the London court. Throughout the years Robert was serving at court, Amy rarely appeared there herself. Instead, she moved frequently between the Dudley and Robsart rural estates and homes in London, seeing her husband only every few months. Lady Dudley managed their estates and finances, even down to details such as the selling of wool produced on the Syderstone lands. She also led an active social life, and enjoyed riding, hunting, and boating. However, she suffered from very poor health, possibly from breast cancer. Her ill health only encouraged the rumors of a plot by her husband and the queen to poison her. Stories were also set about to the effect that she was suffering from cancer and would soon die. Quadra, the Spanish ambassador, reported to the king of Spain that the queen had repeated this rumor to him.

In 1560, at her husband's bidding, Robsart set up residence at Cumnor Hall, a house near Oxford rented by his agent Anthony Forster or Forrester, a member of Parliament for Abingdon. On September 8, Lady Dudley's servants, returning from the Abingdon Fair, found her dead at the foot of the staircase at Cumnor Hall. Queen Elizabeth had Robert Dudley confined as soon as word reached London. Amy's sudden death understandably caused a major scandal. Many suspected that Dudley and Elizabeth had ordered her death; others believed that she died naturally but that Dudley had been waiting for news of her death to pursue marriage with the queen. A coroner's jury, which Robert Dudley did his best to pack and influence, concluded that she died from an accidental fall down the stairs. There were no witnesses, but her maid reported that Amy had been depressed and had often prayed for an end to her desperation. Whether this desperation was caused by her cancer or her bad marriage is unclear. However, the statement led to a widespread conjecture of suicide, caused by Dudley's neglect of his wife.

No evidence ever surfaced linking Dudley or Elizabeth to Robsart's death, except a vaguely worded diplomatic letter suggesting that the queen had spoken of Amy's death a day before it happened. Yet the decision the queen and Dud-

Amy
Robsart

ley made to cut short the inquiry into her death caused further suspicion. Of course Dudley and Elizabeth did not marry, nor is it likely that the queen ever seriously considered him as a possible husband. But when news of Amy's death reached the foreign courts, the queen's enemies eagerly tried to use the accusation of a murder plot against her to alienate her allies and justify claims that she was unfit to govern England.

Lady Dudley was buried after an elaborate funeral at Worcester College, Oxford. Lord Dudley was created earl of Leicester in 1563 and eventually married *Lettice Knollys (c. 1541–1634).

SOURCES:

Jenkins, Elizabeth. *Elizabeth and Leicester*. NY: Coward-McCann, 1961.

Richardson, Aubrey. *The Lover of Queen Elizabeth: Being the Life and Character of Robert Dudley, Earl of Leicester, 1533–1588*. NY: Appleton, 1908.

Laura York,
Riverside, California

Robson, Eleanor (1879–1979).

See Belmont, Eleanor Robson.

Robson, Flora (1902–1984)

British actress who was nominated for an Academy Award for her performance in **Saratoga Trunk.** *Name variations: Dame Flora Robson. Born on March 28, 1902, in South Shields, County Durham, England; died in July 1984; graduated from Palmer's Green High School; bronze medal graduate of the Royal Academy of Dramatic Art; never married; no children.*

Selected theater: made stage debut as the ghost of Queen Margaret in Will Shakespeare *(Shaftesbury Theatre, November 1921); performed in repertory with Ben Greet's Pastoral Players (1922–23); performed in repertory with J.B. Fagan's company at the Oxford Playhouse (1923–24); appeared as Annie in* Fata Morgana *(Ambassadors' Theatre, September 1924), the stepdaughter in* Six Characters in Search of an Author *(Cambridge Festival Theatre, around 1929), Abbie Putman in* Desire Under the Elms *(Gate Theatre, 1931), Mary Paterson in* The Anatomist *(Westminster Theatre, 1931), Olwen Peel in* Dangerous Corner *(Lyric Theatre, May 1932), Eva in* For Services Rendered *(Globe Theatre, November 1932), Varya in* The Cherry Orchard, *Queen Katharine in* Henry VIII, *Isabella in* Measure for Measure, *Gwendolen in* The Importance of Being Earnest, *Mrs. Foresight in* Love for Love, *Ceres in* The Tempest *and Lady Macbeth in* Macbeth *(all with Old Vic-Sadler's Wells, 1933–34); appeared in title role in* Mary Read *(His Majesty's Theatre, November 1934), title role in* Mary Tudor *(Playhouse Theatre, December 1935), as Anna Christopherson in* Anna Christie *(Westminster Theatre, April 1937); made New York debut as Ellen Creed in* Ladies in Retirement *(Henry Miller Theater, New York, March 1940); appeared as the Duchess of Marlborough in* Anne of England *(St. James Theater, New York, October 1941); toured as Elizabeth in* Elizabeth the Queen *(1942); appeared as Thérèse Raquin in* Guilty *(Lyric, Hammersmith Theatre, London, April 1944); toured provinces in title role in* Ethel

Fry *and as Agnes Isit in* A Man About the House *(1945); appeared as Margaret Hayden in* A Message for Margaret *(Westminster Theatre, August 1946), Lady Macbeth in* Macbeth *(National Theater, New York, March 1948), Lady Cicely Waynflete in* Captain Brassbound's Conversion *(Theatre Royal, Windsor, March 1948), the mother in* Black Chiffon *(Westminster Theatre, May 1949, and 48th St. Theater, New York, 1950), Paulina in* The Winter's Tale *(Phoenix Theater, June 1951), the governess in* The Innocents *(Her Majesty's Theatre, 1952), Mrs. Alving in* Ghosts *(Old Vic, November 1958, and Prince's Theatre, April 1959), Miss Tina in* The Aspern Papers *(Queen's Theatre, August 1959), Gunhild Borkman in* John Gabriel Borkman *(Duchess Theatre, December 1963), Miss Prism in revival of* The Importance of Being Earnest *(Haymarket, February 1968), the mother in* Ring Round the Moon *(Haymarket, October 1968), Agatha Payne in* The Old Ladies *(Westminster, November 1969).*

Selected filmography in UK, unless otherwise noted: A Gentleman of Paris *(1931);* Dance Pretty Lady *(1931);* One Precious Year *(1933);* Catherine the Great *(1934);* Fire Over England *(1937);* Farewell Again *(Troopship, 1937);* I Claudius *(unfinished, 1937);* Wuthering Heights *(US, 1939);* Poison Pen *(1939);* The Lion Has Wings *(1939);* We Are Not Alone *(US, 1939);* Invisible Stripes *(US, 1939);* The Sea Hawk *(US, 1940);* Bahama Passage *(US, 1943);* 2,000 Women *(1944);* Great Day *(1945);* Caesar and Cleopatra *(1945);* Saratoga Trunk *(US, 1946);* The Years Between *(1946);* Black Narcissus *(1947);* Frieda *(1947);* Holiday Camp *(1947);* Good Time Girl *(1948);* Saraband for Dead Lovers *(Saraband, 1948);* The Tall Headlines *(The Frightened Bride, 1952);* Malta Story *(1953);* Giulietta e Romeo *(Romeo and Juliet, It.-UK, 1954);* High Tide at Noon *(1957);* No Time for Tears *(1957);* The Gypsy and the Gentleman *(1958);* Innocent Sinners *(1958);* 55 Days at Peking *(US, 1963);* Murder at the Gallop *(1963);* Guns at Batasi *(1964);* Young Cassidy *(UK-US, 1965);* Those Magnificent Men in Their Flying Machines *(1965);* Seven Women *(US, 1966);* The Shuttered Room *(1967);* Eye of the Devil *(1967);* Cry in the Wind *(Gr.-UK, 1967);* Fragment of Fear *(1970);* The Beast in the Cellar *(1971);* La Grande Scrofa nera *(It., 1972);* Alice's Adventures in Wonderland *(1972);* Dominique *(1978);* Clash of the Titans *(1981).*

Born on March 28, 1902, Flora Robson was just six years old when her father, a marine engineer, entered her in a recitation competition near their home in South Shields, England. Following

Flora's performance of "Little Orphan Annie," which already displayed the beautiful musical voice for which she would become known, he stood and proudly pronounced his daughter "our next *Ellen Terry." With her father's encouragement, Flora continued to enter and win contests in and around London, where the family moved when she was still quite small. At 17, after graduating from Palmer's Green High School, she entered the Royal Academy of Dramatic Art. It was there that she realized she was not as pretty as the other girls and that her plainness might seriously undermine her career in the theater. Although she graduated from the academy with a bronze medal, she was totally lacking in self-confidence. Even after she became a successful actress, she never lost her fear or her desire to be beautiful.

Fresh out of drama school, Robson somehow managed to land a one-line role as the ghost of Queen Margaret in a Cambridge production of *Will Shakespeare*, which ran for 62 performances and gave her a chance to rub shoulders with more experienced actors. From there, she joined Ben Greet's Pastoral Players to gain more experience in Shakespeare. After a year, she moved on to J.B. Fagan's repertory company at Oxford Playhouse, where she expanded her skills, prompting, understudying, and playing an occasional small part, including the unwanted woman in *The Return of the Prodigal*, her best role thus far. At the end of her second season, however, her contract was not renewed, leaving Robson once again unsure of her future. Unable to find immediate work, she returned home, taking a job as a personnel-public relations officer at the Shredded Wheat Company at Welwyn Garden City, where she also directed the amateur theater group. She stayed there four years, almost abandoning her dreams of a professional theater career.

It was Tyrone Guthrie who got the young actress back on track. The director, whom Robson had first met at the Oxford Playhouse, was in Welwyn Garden City to judge an amateur drama festival when he looked up Robson and encouraged her to join him at the Cambridge Festival Theatre, where he was going to direct.

From Ladies in Retirement, *starring Flora Robson.*

She took him up on the suggestion and spent 18 months in Cambridge, playing leads one week and maids the next in a wide repertory of plays. She won the respect of her colleagues and for the first time gained some well-deserved outside recognition, boosting her self-esteem.

Director Peter Godfrey gave Robson her next opportunity, casting her as Abbie in Eugene O'Neill's *Desire Under the Elms*. Six months later, she played Mary Paterson, a drunken Scots harlot, in *The Anatomist*, her breakthrough role. "Here is an actress," wrote St. John Ervine, one of the most influential critics of the day. "If you are not moved by this girl's performance, then you are immovable and have no right to be on this earth. Hell is your place."

Having finally established herself, Robson moved on to more steady employment, including roles in *Othello*, *Dangerous Corner*, and *For Services Rendered*. In 1933, she was invited to join the Old Vic-Sadler's Wells company headed by Charles Laughton. She spent a season with the company, appearing in six productions directed by her mentor Tyrone Guthrie. Her roles included Varya in *The Cherry Orchard*, Katherine in *Henry VIII*, Isabella in *Measure for Measure*, and Gwendolen in *The Importance of Being Earnest*, which provided Robson a welcome opportunity to play comedy. In 1934, she appeared in the title role of *Mary Read*, a play by James Bride that was commissioned by Alexander Korda, who at the time also signed her to her first film contract. He dropped her four years later because he thought she was suitable only for playing queens. Robson, however, continued throughout her career to portray memorable characters in numerous British films and some Hollywood productions, including the classic screen version of *Emily Brontë's Wuthering Heights* (1939) and an adaptation of *Edna Ferber's Saratoga Trunk* (1946), for which Robson was nominated for an Academy Award for Best Supporting Actress.

In 1940, Robson made her New York stage debut at the Henry Miller Theater in the role of Ellen Creed in *Ladies in Retirement*. She stayed in the United States for several years, playing in *Anne of England* and touring summer theaters as *Elizabeth I* in *Elizabeth the Queen*. The actress made a return visit to New York in September 1948 to play Lady Macbeth (*Gruoch*) opposite Michael Redgrave.

Robson was particularly masterful in highly charged roles, as was evident in her 1944 portrayal of Thérèse Raquin in *Guilty*, a stage adaptation of the Zola novel. "This was emotional acting of rare power," reported critic **Audrey Williamson**, "in which face, voice and gesture mirrored the sickening agony and fear of a character not strong enough to face the consequences of murder. Obliged to play against her physical type, she nevertheless painted a nervously vital portrait of the sensuous and passion-fevered Thérèse." Robson was also memorable as a disturbed mother who turns shoplifter in *Black Chiffon* in 1949. "Miss Robson is magnificent in this part," wrote T.C. Worsley. "Is there any other actress playing today who can suggest so much feeling with so little fuss? . . . So real is her behaviour, so totally convincing the illusion she creates, that we hardly notice during the play the improbabilities or the skirtings which the play tails off into." Harold Hobson also praised the actress for her restraint. "Flora Robson is true and unexaggerated, as she always is in the presentation of emotional distress," he wrote.

Robson seemed only to improve with age, winning the *Evening Standard* Award as Best Actress in 1960 for her performance in *The Aspern Papers*. "Flora Robson, as Miss Tina, gives a performance that must surely rank as the greatest in her career," proclaimed Peter Roberts. "Watch her, for instance, in the second act when she appears in an unfamiliar best dress with an unfamiliar coiffure. She is in a state of agitated expectancy yet has spoken no line that hints of a new dress, coiffure, or, indeed, of agitation. But she conveys all these things, and much more, in a few seconds." In 1969, when Robson appeared as Agatha Payne in *The Old Ladies*, her last West End appearance, age still had not dulled her cutting edge. "Flora Robson played the villainous Mrs. Payne with a gleeful sense of black humour," wrote Hugh Leonard. "Self-preservation was the keynote, whether Dame Flora was popping a slice of cake into her reticule or negotiating the stairs with the concentration of a bomb-disposal expert."

The actress, who never married, lived alone with her dog in an old house in Brighton that was filled with prints and treasures her father brought home from his visits to Japan. Her social life included visits to concerts and the theater, as well as numerous social obligations connected with her status as a Dame Commander of the British Empire (conferred in 1960). She had many close friends and admirers among her colleagues, although her closest confidant was apparently a 5-year-old boy named Lee, her next-door neighbor. "Lee has his own television stool in Flora's sitting room and a little coffee-table of his own on which he places his tipple-limejuice, which is kept with the grown-ups' alcoholic drinks in the sideboard," wrote Eric Johns, detailing Robson's great affection and respect for children. "He is made thoroughly at home and never fussed over like a child. Flora has taught him to write and to speak grammatically, so he is streets ahead of the other boys in his class at school."

Although she left the stage in 1969, Robson came out of retirement in 1974 to narrate *Peter and the Wolf* at the Brighton Festival. She continued to make films as late as 1981, when she appeared as one of three eyeless witches in *Clash of the Titans*. Robson died in 1984.

SOURCES:

Hartnoll, Phyllis, and Peter Found. *The Concise Oxford Companion to the Theatre.* Oxford: Oxford University Press, 1993.

Johns, Eric. *Dames of the Theatre.* New Rochelle, NY: Arlington House, 1974.

Morley, Sheridan. *The Great Stage Stars.* Australia: Angus & Robertson, 1986.

Shipman, David. *The Great Movie Stars: The Golden Years.* Boston, MA: Little, Brown, 1995.

Barbara Morgan,
Melrose, Massachusetts

Robson, May (1858–1942)

Australian-born actress. Name variations: Mary Robison. Born Mary Jeannette Robison on April 19, 1858, in Wagga Wagga, New South Wales, Australia; died on October 20, 1942, in Los Angeles, California; one of four children of Henry Robison (a retired sea captain) and Julia Robison; attended convent schools in England, Brussels, and Paris; married Charles Livingston Gore (a rancher), in 1874 (died 1884); married Augustus Homer Brown (a police surgeon), on May 29, 1889 (died 1920); children: (first marriage) three.

Selected filmography: The Trial of the Lonesome Pine *(1914);* How Molly Malone Made Good *(1915);* A Night Out *(1916);* The Prodigal Wife *(1918);* A Broadway Saint *(1919);* The Lost Battalion *(1919);* Paradise *(1926);* The King of Kings *(1927);* The Rejuvenation of Aunt Mary *(1927);* The Angel of Broadway *(1927);* A Harp in Hawk *(1927);* Chicago *(1927);* The Blue Danube *(1928);* Mother's Millions *(1931);* Letty Lynton *(1932);* Red-Headed Woman *(1932);* Strange Interlude *(1932);* Little Orphan Annie *(1932);* The White Sister *(1933);* Reunion in Vienna *(1933);* Dinner at Eight *(1933);* Lady for a Day *(1933);* Dancing Lady *(1933);* Alice in Wonderland *(1933);* You Can't Buy Everything *(1934);* Straight Is the Way *(1934);* Lady by Choice *(1934);* Grand Old Girl *(1935);* Vanessa *(1935);* Her Love Story *(1935);* Reckless *(1935);* Anna Karenina *(1935);* Wife vs. Secretary *(1936);* Rainbow on the River *(1936);* A Star Is Born *(1937);* The Adventures of Tom Sawyer *(1938);* Bring-

ing Up Baby *(1938);* The Texans *(1938);* Four Daughters *(1938);* They Made Me a Criminal *(1939);* Daughters Courageous *(1939);* Nurse *Edith Cavell *(1939);* Four Wives *(1939);* Granny Get Your Gun *(1940);* Irene *(1940);* Four Mothers *(1941);* Playmates *(1941);* Joan of Paris *(1942).*

Described as the "grand old lady" of stage and screen, May Robson stumbled into acting out of necessity and became one of America's most enduring and beloved character actresses. Robson's career, spanning 60 years, encompassed the gas-lit theaters of New York's Bowery as well as the modern Technicolor cameras of the Hollywood studio.

Robson was born Mary Jeannette Robison in 1858 in New South Wales, Australia, where her father Henry, a sea captain, had retired for his health. Following his death, her mother **Julia Robison** took her four young children to London, where Robson attended Sacred Heart Convent. She later spent time at convent schools in Brussels and Paris, before abandoning her education at the age of 16 to elope with Charles Livingston Gore, who was just two years her senior. After several years in Fort Worth, Texas, the couple moved to New York, where Gore died in 1884, leaving Robson a widow with three small children to support. Over the next few years, Robson earned a paltry living by painting china and menus for Tiffany's and by teaching painting to children. Two of her own children, a girl and a boy, died during this period, one of diphtheria and the other of scarlet fever.

Robson was passing a theatrical agency when, on a whim, she decided to audition for a role in the melodrama *Hoop of Gold*. She was cast as both the ingenue and the cockney servant, Tilly. It was the latter role which gained the most attention when Robson made her debut at the Brooklyn Grand Opera House on September 17, 1883. From that time on, she made an effort to develop her talent for more eccentric parts, disguising her face behind layers of greasepaint to take on the often grotesque

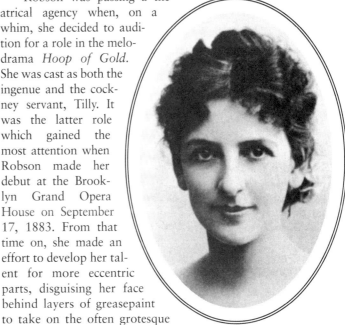

May Robson

appearance of the stock comic characters. "I can't act unless I'm a fright," she once admitted. "If I appear as May Robson unmolested, I'm so self-conscious that I'm a dead failure."

Robson performed with a number of different theater companies during her early career, including the A.M. Palmer Company at the Madison Square Theater, Daniel Frohman's company at the Lyceum, and Charles Frohman's at the Empire. Not long after her second marriage to Augustus Homer Brown, a New York police surgeon, in 1889, Robson began acting under her own management. Over the next several years, she was able to obtain a greater variety of roles, notably in *Dorothy Vernon of Haddon Hall* (1904), in which she played Queen *Elizabeth I, her first serious role, and *Cousin Billy* (1905), in which she appeared undisguised for the first time in 18 years. She received particular acclaim for her roles in *The Mountain Climber* (1906) and *The Rejuvenation of Aunt Mary* (1907), her first starring role and one she would reprise on tour for a decade. In 1911, Robson tried her hand at writing, thinking she could create her own starring vehicle. Her first effort, *The Three Lights* (later changed to *A Night Out*), written in collaboration with Charles T. Dazey, failed in production. She never put pen to paper again.

As early as 1914, Robson began appearing in silent films for Vitagraph and other companies, but it was not until the death of her second husband, in 1920, that she began to break her ties to New York and concentrate more on her movie career. Already into her 60s when she moved to Hollywood in 1927, she made the film version of *The Rejuvenation of Aunt Mary* that year, then went on to play a series of character roles that endeared her to movie audiences throughout the 1930s and early 1940s. Usually cast as the domineering society matron or the crusty old sidekick, she is best remembered for her remarkable portrayal of the Damon Runyon character Apple Annie in Frank Capra's *Lady for a Day* (1933), for which she was nominated for an Academy Award as Best Actress. Also notable were her performances in *Dinner at Eight* (1933) and *Bringing Up Baby* (1938). Robson also won the love and respect of her Hollywood colleagues, who affectionately called her "Muzzey" and marveled at her dedication and stamina. She continued to work until shortly before her death, even though cataracts in both eyes rendered her nearly blind. The actress died shortly after completing *Joan of Paris* (1942), at age 84.

SOURCES:

Block, Maxine, ed. *Current Biography 1942*. NY: H.W. Wilson, 1942.

James, Edward T., ed. *Notable American Women, 1607–1950*. Cambridge, MA: The Belknap Press of Harvard University Press, 1971.

Katz, Ephraim. *The Film Encyclopedia*. NY: Harper-Collins, 1994.

McHenry, Robert, ed. *Famous American Women*. NY: Dover, 1983.

Barbara Morgan,
Melrose, Massachusetts

Rocha, Alicia de la (b. 1923).

See Larrocha, Alicia de.

Roche, Baroness de la (1886–1919).

See Quimby, Harriet for sidebar on Elise-Raymonde Deroche.

Roche, Josephine (1886–1976)

American labor leader and U.S. Treasury official. Born Josephine Aspinwall Roche in Neligh, Nebraska, on December 2, 1886; died in Bethesda, Maryland, on July 13, 1976; daughter of John J. Roche (a mine owner) and Ella (Aspinwall) Roche; Vassar College, B.A., 1908; Columbia University, M.S.W., 1910; married Edward Hale Bierstadt (a broadcast writer), on July 2, 1920 (divorced 1922); no children.

Became first woman police officer in Denver, Colorado (1912); operated the Rocky Mountain Fuel Company, the second largest coal mining company in Colorado (1927–39); first woman to serve as Assistant Secretary of the Treasury of the United States, under President Franklin Roosevelt (1934–37); named one of ten outstanding women in the United States (1936); organized and ran the United Mine Workers' welfare and retirement fund (1947–71).

Josephine Roche was born in Neligh, Nebraska, on December 2, 1886, a child of privilege as the daughter of millionaire mine operator John J. Roche. When she was 12, her father denied her request to visit the mines on account of the danger involved, prompting her to ask, "Then why is it safe enough for the miners?" This early sympathy eventually developed into an unyielding commitment to the improvement of labor conditions that affected change far beyond her father's Rocky Mountain Fuel Company. Although as a wealthy society woman she easily could have ignored the problems of labor, she chose to identify with downtrodden workers from the early years of the labor movement.

Roche developed her activist beliefs while at Vassar College, graduating in 1908 with an ardent desire to improve the welfare of children and fight crime. For a year following her graduation, she worked as a probation officer in Denver, Colorado, where her family had moved in 1906. She left that job to pursue a master's degree in social work at Columbia University in New York. Social reformer, labor advocate and later U.S. Secretary of Labor *Frances Perkins also spent that year at Columbia, and the two became good friends, sharing similar ideas on social reform and public welfare issues. Roche worked for the New York Probation Society while finishing her degree (granted in 1910), and afterwards probed further into social and industrial investigations for Columbia and the Russell Sage Foundation, founded by *Margaret Olivia Sage.

When she returned to Denver in 1912, Roche became Denver's first woman police officer, and was said to be more successful in controlling crime than the city's best male officers. When interoffice conflicts forced her out of the job, she became the executive secretary of the Colorado Progressive Society. Roche devoted herself to this endeavor until 1915, when she took an assignment in Europe during World War I as a special agent for the Belgian Relief Commission. Her brief return to Denver as director of the Girls' Department in the city's juvenile court was interrupted by her appointment by President Woodrow Wilson to serve on the Committee on Public Information and as director of the Foreign Language Information Service when the United States entered the war in 1918. Roche was responsible for coordinating editors of foreign-language newspapers in the government's efforts to disseminate information about U.S. activities to foreign populations. She remained in that post until 1923, when she became the director of the editorial division of the U.S. Children's Bureau in Washington. In 1925, she returned to Denver as referee of Denver's juvenile court.

When Roche's father died in 1927, she inherited his shares in the Rocky Mountain Fuel Company, the second largest coal mining company in Colorado at the time. She quickly proved that her ownership in the company did not affect her loyalty to her ideals; she justified a strike at the company before the State Industrial Commission by citing intolerable working conditions. Indeed, Roche had inherited stock in a company rife with abuse of its workers. The company frequently cheated miners out of their full wages through the use of illegal scales for weighing the coal, and poor working conditions hampered miners' productivity in addition to contributing to numerous accidents and diseases. Her father had employed Pinkerton agents as moles to keep tabs on those miners who had dared discuss organizing, and a recent riot spurred by workers who belonged to the International Workers of the World (IWW or "Wobblies") had resulted in the deaths of six miners. The Industrial Commission's investigation of the riot ended with the recommendation that the miners be allowed to unionize, a recommendation with which Roche fully agreed. Other stockholders took exception to her efforts on behalf of the miners, and received an even greater shock when she proposed that the United Mine Workers of America be invited to unionize the Rocky Mountain workers. Roche took the shareholders up on their threats to sell their stocks, and quickly acquired a majority interest. Her first order of business was to appoint union-friendly officers in the company. She herself became vice-president; the new counsel was Edward P. Costigan, attorney for the United Mine Workers; and the director and manager was John P. Lawson, a former president of the Colorado State Federation of Labor whose unjust sentence of life imprisonment in connection with the infamous Ludlow massacre of miners and their families had been overturned by the Supreme Court. Roche followed that move by announcing that the company was ready to sign a union contract with the workers as soon as they organized. The 1928 contract was one of the first industrial union agreements west of the Mississippi.

Assuming the presidency of the company in 1929, Roche initiated sweeping changes. Rocky Mountain Fuel offered the highest wages of any company in Colorado, at $7 a day, and vastly improved working conditions in the mines. Workers responded to Roche's changes with greater productivity on an average of three tons more coal per day than other mining companies in the state. Roche also backed out of agreements with other contractors designed to eliminate competition by dividing the markets among themselves, earning the ire of her competitors. In retaliation, other mining companies initiated a pricing war, drastically reducing their prices by cutting their workers' pay. Rocky Mountain employees came to Roche's aid by lending the company half their wages until the pricing war ended. By 1932, Roche had come out on top. Rocky Mountain Fuel had doubled its share of coal in the state, and workers put in more days of work per year than did those at any other company. Although Roche had to slash the daily wage to $5.25 in order to stay competitive during the Depression, she still was able to offer $0.25 more than other companies.

Roche's leadership in the mining industry also gave her a leadership role in the formation of the National Bituminous Coal Code, and she worked actively as a member of the Bituminous Coal Authority. In 1934, publicly prodded by a number of newspaper editors, she entered politics, running for governor of Colorado with the campaign slogan "Roosevelt, Roche and Recovery." Her political platform backed Roosevelt's New Deal and called for a change in the state income tax. She had the support of liberals across the state and the country, and swept the vote in cities, but lost the election largely because of gender prejudice among conservatives in rural areas of the state.

Despite her defeat, Roche returned to Washington in 1934, when President Roosevelt appointed her the first woman to serve as the Assistant Secretary of the Treasury. Taking the helm of the U.S. Public Health Service (which was then part of the Treasury), she successfully coordinated the government's various health services and initiated studies of chronic disease and rural sanitation. As part of her job, she acted as the Secretary of the Treasury's representative to the President's Cabinet Commission on Economic Security, lending a hand to that commission's establishment of the National Social Security Act. Her other appointments included chair of the executive committee of the National Youth Administration and chair of the interdepartmental committee to coordinate the health and welfare activities of the U.S. government.

In 1937, Roche resigned her treasury position in order to fill a leadership gap in Rocky Mountain Fuel, which was experiencing a downturn in the competition with natural gas fields and oil. She was unable to secure financial help from the company's bondholders, and her failure to create a compromise after two years led her to step down as head of the company in 1939. That same year she became president of the National Consumers' League, and continued her political work in the area of health.

In 1947, labor leader John L. Lewis recruited Roche as the first director of the United Mine Workers' welfare and retirement fund. During her 24-year administration of the fund, $2.5 billion was collected, with $1.2 billion paid out in pensions and another $900 million spent on medical care for miners and their families. The American Public Health Association cited the fund as a model health services program and awarded it the Albert Lasker Award in 1956. *American Women* named Roche one of the ten outstanding women in the United States in 1936, and in 1941 the Federation of Women's Clubs cited her as one of the women making great strides in the first half of the 20th century. She

retired from the UMW welfare and retirement fund in 1971, when she was in her mid-80s, and died in Bethesda, Maryland, in July 1976.

SOURCES:

Bernikow, Louise. *The American Women's Almanac*. NY: Berkley, 1997.

Bird, Caroline. *Enterprising Women*. NY: New American Library, 1976.

Block, Maxine, ed. *Current Biography 1941*. NY: H.W. Wilson, 1941.

The New York Times Biographical Service. July 1976, p. 1059.

Jane E. Spear,
freelance writer and editor, Canton, Ohio

Roche, Mazo de la (1879–1961).

See de la Roche, Mazo.

Roche, Regina Maria (c. 1764–1845)

Irish novelist. Name variations: Regina Maria Dalton. Born Regina Maria Dalton in Wexford County, Ireland, around 1764; died in Waterford, Ireland, on May 17, 1845; daughter of Captain Blundel Dalton; married Ambrose Roche, in 1793 or 1794 (died 1829).

Selected writings: The Vicar of Lansdowne (1789); The Maid of the Hamlet (1793); The Children of the Abbey (1796); Clermont (1798); The Nocturnal Visit (1800); The Discarded Son; or, The Haunt of the Banditti (1807); The Houses of Osma and Almeria; or, The Convent of St. Ildefonso (1810); The Monastery of St. Colomb (1812); Trecothiek Bower (1813); London Tales (1814); The Munster Cottage Boy (1819); The Bridal of Dunamore and Lost and Won: Two Tales (1823); The Tradition of the Castle; or, Scenes in the Emerald Isle (1824); The Castle Chapel (1825); Contrast (1828); The Nun's Picture (1834).

An early appreciation of literature turned into a full-time passion for Regina Maria Roche, a Dubliner who published 16 novels. Two of these—*The Vicar of Lansdowne* and *The Maid of the Hamlet*—were published under her maiden name of Dalton, before she married Ambrose Roche in 1793 or 1794. It was her third novel, *The Children of the Abbey*, that brought Roche to fame. Ten editions of that novel, plus a mention in ***Jane Austen**'s *Emma*, established her as a popular writer (*Children of the Abbey* rivaled the success of ***Ann Radcliffe**'s *Mysteries of Udolpho*). Roche would continue to write in *Abbey*'s vein—described as both Gothic and realist—for the remainder of her career. Her novel *Clermont* received another Austen mention: it was described as "horrid" in *Northanger Abbey*. Roche published 11 titles after 1800, and *Chil-*

dren of the Abbey remained in print as late as 1882. She died at her home in Waterford, an Irish seaport, at age 81.

SOURCES:

The Concise Dictionary of National Biography. Vol. III. Oxford: Oxford University Press, 1992.

Kunitz, Stanley J., ed. *British Authors of the Nineteenth Century.* NY: H.W. Wilson, 1936.

Shattock, Joanne. *The Oxford Guide to British Women Writers.* Oxford: Oxford University Press, 1993.

Stephen Tschirhart,
freelance writer, Birmingham, Michigan

Rochefort, Christiane (1917–1998)

French feminist writer of novels and nonfiction who harshly condemned the abuse of women in what she considered a brutalized, patriarchal society. Pronunciation: Christie-AHN Roch-FOR. *Born on July 17, 1917, in a working-class district of Paris; died on April 24, 1998, at Le Pradet, France; studied for several years at the Sorbonne; married for four years.*

Returned to Paris after spending several childhood years in the province of Limousin (1922); became successful author with the publication of her first book (1958); won Roman Populiste award (1961); film version of Le Repos du guerrier *appeared (1962); fired as press attaché at Cannes Film Festival (1968); participated in Mouvement de Libération des Femmes (MLF) demonstration at the Tomb of the Unknown Soldier (1970); participated in MLF campaign publicizing prominent women who had undergone abortions (1971); joined pro-abortion group Choisir (1972); won the Prix Mèdici for* La Porte du Fond *(1988).*

Select works—fiction: Le Repos du guerrier *(Warrior's Rest, 1958);* Les Petits enfants du siècle *(Children of the Century, 1961);* Les Stances à Sophie *(Cats Don't Care for Money, 1963);* Une Rose pour Morrisson *(A Rose for Morrisson, 1966);* Printemps au parking *(Blossom on the Tarmac, 1969);* Archaos ou le jardin étincelant *(Archaos or the Glittering Garden, 1972);* Encore heureux qu'on va ver l'été *(Luckily Summer Will Come Soon, 1975);* Quand tu vas chez les femmes *(Now It's Time for the Girls, 1982);* La Porte du Fond *(Rear Exit, 1988);* Conversations sans paroles *(Conversations without Words, 1997).*

Selected works—nonfiction: Les Enfants d'abord *(Children First, 1976);* Le Monde est comme deux chevaux *(The World Is Like Two Horses, 1984).*

A leading feminist author, Christiane Rochefort wrote over a dozen books, including both novels and nonfiction. Her works, which incorporate large doses of black humor, presented a scathing picture of women's constricted life and subordination in modern French society. A key theme of much of her writing was the way in which a woman's loving impulses were likely to be manipulated and betrayed. Rochefort's feminist writing has been described by **Diana Holmes**, a leading scholar of her work, as "closer to that of Anglo-American feminist novelists than to that of her French contemporaries." Holmes points in particular to **Marilyn French** and **Fay Weldon** as the English-language authors whom Rochefort most resembles.

Working mainly within the conventional forms of the novel, Rochefort was able nonetheless to present a number of radical messages. Her interest in sexuality, as well as her consistent frankness in discussing relations between men and women, often brought accusations that her writing was pornographic. She was especially vocal in expressing her concern for children's rights. Her most successful and influential book was *La Porte du Fond* (Rear Exit). Published in 1988, it raised in memorable fashion the dilemma of a young girl who is abused for seven years by her father.

Rochefort found a special target in the shallowness and oppression of a consumer society, and she stressed the harmful role of such desired possessions as automobiles and television sets. Some of her novels were set in an imaginary past or future, devices which she used in order to explore the injustices of present-day society. Others took place explicitly within contemporary French life where she found the world of new housing projects to be harsh and intolerable. "I sadly realize the oppressive power of modern urbanism," she wrote. Nonetheless, while the author's earlier works pointed out society's problems, in her later writing she offered what **Lucille Frackman Becker** called "alternative societies, utopias conceived from the feminist point of view."

Rochefort's heroines were faced with the situation familiar to women of marrying a man whom they love and from whom they expect a satisfying life. But she made it clear how such expectations were doomed to be disappointed in a society that devalued women and refused to endorse their wishes and ideas. Her bitter and ironic tone often reached the reader through a narration presented by the main female character in the story.

Rochefort was never forthcoming about her background, but at her publisher's insistence she provided some information about her life. The writer was born in the 14th arrondissement, a working-class district of Paris, on July 17, 1917, studied a variety of subjects for a time at the Sorbonne, and dabbled in "painting, drawing, sculpting, making music." She also wrote for her own pleasure. To support this life of artistic exploration, she took a number of office jobs, worked as a newspaper correspondent, and wrote film criticism. For a time, she held the post of press attaché for the Cannes Film Festival. Her apparent unruliness in that post led to her dismissal in 1968.

Her writing career began late with the publication of her first novel when she was 41 years old. The first three of Rochefort's novels appeared between 1958 and 1963. Each was identifiably set in the France of the era, and each reflected the concerns of the female narrator. Rochefort was particularly interested in examining how the desires of her heroines collided with society's limited offering of roles for women, and her militant stance was a precursor of French feminist writing which soon began to appear in large quantities. In the view of Holmes, "All her writing is fuelled by a spirit of militant opposition to the dominant values of her society and by the belief that writing has a political function." Rochefort claimed that she wrote with anger against an unjust world. It was a world that she saw as dominated by a male elite and characterized by smoothly running institutions based upon the principles of technological progress and economic growth. In such a world, women's needs and desires were guided or suppressed in the interest of the male elite. Holmes suggests that Rochefort's work tried to challenge this unjust arrangement "by implying an alternative femininity that would be subversive rather than supportive of the patriarchal order."

Anger is one of the constants in my work—it has to be, simply because there are numerous reasons to be angry.

—Christiane Rochefort

When *Le Repos du guerrier* (*Warrior's Rest*) appeared in 1958, it was a spectacular commercial success that reached the bestseller list and was translated into 20 languages. Here Rochefort presented a less self-aware heroine than those who appeared in her later works, but she began to make clear her view that a woman's sexual appetites exposed her to a range of exploitation. The heroine, Geneviève Le Theil, is only partially conscious of the way in which society manipulates her. Infatuated by the sexual pleasure she gets from her alcoholic lover, she supports him, even as he abuses her and uses her money to sink even deeper into his addiction. Her life takes another unfortunate turn when

she is hospitalized for tuberculosis. Rochefort closes her story with Geneviève married to the same ne'er-do-well. She is about to bear his child, and he is trying to use medical help to cope with his addiction. Thus, at the novel's close, the heroine is still tied to a dominant, but visibly flawed male companion. The book was made into a film in 1962 by Roger Vadim starring **Brigitte Bardot**.

Her second novel, *Les Petits Enfants du siècle* (*Children of the Century*), won her critical acclaim, and for it she received the Roman Populiste prize. The book directed its satire at the government policies that encouraged French women to have large numbers of children. Narrated by a young woman from one of these large families, the book condemned the era's social conformity and state intrusion into private life. In Rochefort's view, woman's subordinate role was bolstered by the temptations of a consumer economy. Since the most ready way to increase the family income was to have another child and to draw the resulting state benefits, the urge for possessions plunged women ever deeper into domestic busywork and unwise pregnancies. The book's young protagonist remarks bitterly that she was born only "because of family welfare payments and a legal holiday." Writes Holmes, "it is a related cluster of policies and attitudes that are the objects of the novel's angry derision." In Becker's words, women are degraded by the French system of promoting family life which offers financial rewards for having children and "has transformed the institution of marriage into a legalized form of prostitution."

At the close of the book, Rochefort deliberately shocks the reader by altering the attitude of the heroine. The woman, who throughout the story had irreverently cried out against the cult of motherhood with which she was surrounded, ends up pregnant and ready to marry her baby's father. He is a television installer who will provide well for her. The two of them were looking for an apartment in one of the country's new working-class housing developments, and the woman was reassured when she realized that she would be able to get a maternity grant from the government.

In her third work, the satire *Les Stances à Sophie* (*Cats Don't Care for Money*), Rochefort placed her story in a more elevated middle-class family in the France of the 1960s. Nonetheless, the process of bringing a woman into conformity with the needs of a patriarchal state remained a key theme for Rochefort. Céline, the heroine of the novel, is married to Philippe, a rising young executive in the booming French economy of the time. Earlier on she had pursued a hedonistic lifestyle, and Philippe is shown in a constant effort to circumscribe his wife's expression of her personality by defining what proper behavior should be for a woman. Céline is forced into the role of a child-like creature whose ideas cannot be taken seriously. Her husband's directions for her conduct instruct Céline to "be pretty and silent." In both *Les Petits Enfants du siècle* and *Les Stances à Sophie*, writes Holmes, "the acquisition of a gendered identity is seen as a process of repression and coercion."

At the close of *Les Stances à Sophie*, however, the heroine demonstrates her independence from her husband and his tangle of restrictions on her behavior by deliberately using vulgar French expletives. She "reclaims the right to a verbal vulgarity that is itself a rejection of codes of feminine propriety," notes Holmes. She also finds a close friendship with another woman that develops into a sexual relationship. Thus, unlike the heroines in her first two novels, Céline escapes the rigid framework of the male-dominated marriage into which she has fallen. According to Becker, this work drew on Rochefort's life for material. She too was married to an affluent Frenchman for several years, and she too moved from heterosexual into homosexual relationships.

In 1966, Rochefort turned to a more unconventional style in her dystopian novel *Une Rose pour Morrisson* (A Rose for Morrisson). It presented a picture of the future in the same way that Aldous Huxley and George Orwell had done. Some critics saw this society as a highly colored version of the French state with its pronatalist policies. The dictatorial regime Rochefort pictured was particularly concerned to subordinate young women to an oppressive, male-dominated social order. However, unlike male authors such as Huxley and Orwell, Rochefort filled her novel with successful rebels against that regime. The novel ended with the onset of a rebellion like the actual eruption of French workers' and students' discontent in the spring of 1968.

Rochefort's writing took a different direction in her fifth novel, *Printemps au parking*

From the movie Love on a Pillow, *starring Brigitte Bardot and Robert Hossein, adapted from Christiane Rochefort's* Le Repos du guerrier.

(Blossom on the Tarmac). The author now created a male hero, a 17-year-old student. He leaves home, wanders around Paris, and comes under the influence of a young Parisian intellectual who points him toward revolutionary activism. Alone among Rochefort's novels, *Printemps au parking* ends with two lovers happily linked together, although they are the male partners of a homosexual relationship.

Six years after *Une Rose pour Morrisson*, Rochefort's sixth novel *Archaos* presented a utopian alternative for society. Here a repressive kingdom resembling a state out of medieval Europe was transformed into a feminist utopia, a land of sexual freedom and human liberation. It was a world of supernatural abundance in which the hens produced dozens of eggs each day. Its society was so attractive that enemy spies and soldiers who manage to penetrate it were too charmed to return home. As **Frances Bartkowski** put it in her study of feminist utopian writing, Rochefort presented an "androgynous arcadia of polymorphous perversity" and placed it in "a nostalgic arcadian past."

Rochefort matched her literary criticism of man-oriented French society with an active political role. She was an early member of the French movement for women's liberation, Mouvement de Libération des Femmes (MLF), despite the fact that most members belonged to a much younger generation. Rochefort participated in an important public event sponsored by the MLF. On August 26, 1970, she joined a group of women at France's Tomb of the Unknown Soldier where they displayed a banner to remind the onlookers that half of France's population consisted of—presumably undervalued—women.

The following year Rochefort joined more than 300 other women, including *Simone de Beauvoir** and **Catherine Deneuve**, in declaring that they had obtained abortions. Rochefort and her fellow campaigners intended to challenge the laws forbidding abortion and also to increase access to contraception for French women. In 1972, Rochefort joined the pro-choice group Choisir (Choice).

Rochefort's growing emphasis on the problems of feminism led her to a bitterly humorous contribution to the French language. She took the masculine noun *écrivain*, meaning writer, and adopted the feminine noun *écrivisse*, meaning "crayfish," as its feminine equivalent. This verbal invention, writes Holmes, "was characteristic of Christiane Rochefort's humour and linguistic optimism."

In addition to her novels, Rochefort used nonfiction to present her criticism of modern society. In *Les Enfants d'abord* (*Children First*), which appeared in 1976, she took up the issue of children's rights. With typically heated statements, Rochefort declared that children were an oppressed minority and parent-child relations hopelessly corrupt. The family, which she continued to see as one of the worst features of a patriarchal society, silenced children in the home. Meanwhile, the school system brainwashed them to fit society's purposes

Rochefort's concern for children and the harm they suffered in contact with their parents took a new turn in the late 1980s. She now entered the heated debate over the sexual abuse of children within the family. In *La Porte du Fond*, she spoke out on the question of responsibility for such repulsive actions: did that responsibility reside solely in the adult, or did the child share in the culpability?

The book was written from the standpoint of the victim, recalling from her present-day adult perspective childhood events 20 years in the past. The father's viewpoint was conspicuous by its absence. Instead, in the child's mind, the reader discovered how the father manipulated the girl and, for a period of seven years, forced her to accept his intrusions on her body. In the view of critic **Margaret-Anne Hutton**, Rochefort was directing much of her ire at the entire structure of a patrimonial society with a special jab at traditional Freudian theory. Sigmund Freud had come to assert that his patients' memories of childhood sexual assaults were nothing more than fantasies. He stated as well that female children developed incestuous wishes toward their fathers as a normal part of their sexual development.

Rochefort dedicated the book to Jeffrey Masson, author of *The Assault on Truth*. In that book, he had defended the sexual abuse memories of children as genuine. Masson and others condemned Freud for cowardice in refusing to face the possibility that many adult males were, in fact, sexual predators toward their own daughters. She also broadened her attack to include Christian beliefs, whose commandment seems to require a child to honor her father in all circumstances. And she struck as well at the patriarchal nuclear family, in which the father enjoys the powers of a military dictator. Writes Hutton, "In an age when the legal rights of children are coming under increasing scrutiny, Rochefort has produced a powerful and timely text." Despite the emotional nature of the material, Rochefort told the story in a sober and measured fashion that drew wide-ranging critical praise. Her success was marked most clearly when she received the prestigious Prix Mèdici in 1988 for the book.

Rochefort remained active as a writer and involved citizen to her death, appearing frequently on French television to offer her views on literature. She published a final brief novel, *Conversations sans paroles* (Conversations without Words), in 1997. That same year, she also presented her public with *Adieu, Andromède*, a collection of aphorisms, prose poems, and other miscellaneous writing. In a last surge of political activity, she took on the right-wing political party Front National and opposed its efforts to censor books. Rochefort died at the age of 80 on April 24, 1998, at her home in Le Pradet near the Mediterranean port of Toulon.

Diana Holmes has characterized Rochefort's vision as "a Romantic one, with overtones of Rousseauism." Rochefort saw the human condition as one "which in its natural state can achieve the most cosmic of harmonies, but which is deformed and shrunken by societies whose whole culture radiates from principles of power and of materialism." In the view of Lucille Frackman Becker, Rochefort "carries on the tradition of those who refuse to accept the world as it is . . . who seek to establish a free and equitable society."

SOURCES:

Atack, Margaret, and Phil Powrie, eds. *Contemporary French Fiction by Women: Feminist Perspectives.* Manchester, Eng.: Manchester University Press, 1990.

Bartkowski, Frances. *Feminist Utopias.* Lincoln, NB: University of Nebraska Press, 1989.

Becker, Lucille Frackman. *Twentieth-Century French Women Novelists.* Boston, MA: Twayne, 1989.

Bridgford, Jeff, ed. *France, Image and Identity.* Newcastle, Eng.: Newcastle Polytechnic, 1987.

Crosland, Margaret. *Women of Iron and Velvet and the Books They Wrote in France.* London: Constable, 1976.

Holmes, Diana. *French Women's Writing, 1848–1994.* Atlantic Highlands, NJ: Athlone, 1996.

Hutton, Margaret-Anne. "Assuming Responsibility: Christiane Rochefort's Exploration of Child Sexual Abuse in *La Porte du Fond*," in *The Modern Language Review.* Vol. 90, no. 2. April 1995, pp. 333–344.

Kessler-Harris, Alice, and William McBrien. *Faith of a (Woman) Writer.* NY: Greenwood Press, 1988.

Sartori, Eva Martin, and Dorothy Wynne Zimmerman, eds. *French Women Writers: A Bio-Bibliographical Source Book.* Westport, CT: Greenwood Press, 1991.

SUGGESTED READING:

Green, Mary Jean, Lynn Higgins, and Marianne Hirsh. "Rochefort and Godard: Two or Three Things about Prostitution," in *The French Review.* Vol. 52. February 1979, pp. 440–448.

Jardine, Alice A., and Anne M. Menke, eds. *Shifting Scenes: Interviews on Women, Writing, and Politics*

in Post-68 France. NY: Columbia University Press, 1991.

Penrod, Lynn Kettler. "Consuming Women Consumed: Images of Consumer Society in Simone de Beauvoir's *Les Belles Images* and Christiane Rochefort's *Les Stances à Sophie*," in *Simone de Beauvoir Studies.* Vol. 4, 1987, pp. 1959–1975.

RELATED MEDIA:

Love on a Pillow (French-Italian film, 102 min.), titled *Le Repos du Guerrier* in France, starring Brigitte Bardot and Robert Hossein, directed by Roger Vadim, 1963.

Neil M. Heyman,
Professor of History, San Diego State University,
San Diego, California

Rochefoucauld, Edmée de la
(1895–1991).

See La Rochefoucauld, Edmée, Duchesse de.

Rochester, countess of.

See Hyde, Jane (d. 1725).

Rockefeller, Abby Aldrich
(1874–1948)

American philanthropist. Born Abby Greene Aldrich on October 26, 1874, in Providence, Rhode Island; died on April 5, 1948, in New York; one of the eight children, five sons and three daughters, of Nelson Wilmarth Aldrich (a businessman turned politician) and Abby Pearce (Chapman) Aldrich; tutored at home; attended Miss Abbott's School for Young Ladies, Providence, Rhode Island, in 1893; became first wife of John D. Rockefeller, Jr. (b. 1874), on October 9, 1901; children: **Abby Rockefeller** *(b. 1903); John Davison Rockefeller III (1906–1978); Nelson Aldrich Rockefeller (b. 1908); Laurance Spelman Rockefeller (b. 1910); Winthrop Rockefeller (1912–1973); David Rockefeller (b. 1915). John D. Rockefeller, Jr., also married* ***Martha Baird Rockefeller.**

The daughter of **Abby Chapman Aldrich** and a powerful U.S. senator from Rhode Island, Nelson Wilmarth Aldrich, Abby Aldrich Rockefeller was born in 1874 and grew up in homes in Providence and Washington, D.C. She was strongly influenced by both her father's wealth and his passion for art and books. Well educated at home by a Quaker tutor and later at Miss Abbott's School in Providence, she developed into an intelligent, compassionate, and charming young woman, whose outgoing personality and sense of adventure drew people to her like a magnet. Following her coming-out party in 1893, Abby immersed herself in volunteer work in Providence and read widely in her father's library. She also accompanied the senator on several trips abroad and frequently filled in for her mother as his hostess at official Washington events.

As a young debutante, Abby entertained a legion of eligible suitors, among them John D. Rockefeller, Jr., the only son of the founder of the Standard Oil Trust, who was a student at Brown University. The product of a Puritanical upbringing, John was a stiff, serious-minded young man, and hardly seemed a match for the bright, gregarious Abby. However, she obviously saw beyond his shyness and lack of social skills. "She treated me as if I had all the *savoir-faire* in the world and her confidence did me a lot of good," he later told his biographer. After a seven-year courtship, the couple married on October 9, 1901, at the Aldrich summer home on Warwick Neck, Rhode Island. Following a honeymoon at Pocantico Hills near Tarrytown-on-the-Hudson, the home of the elder Rockefellers, they lived a short time with John's family in New York City before moving into a rented house nearby. (Ten years later, they built a larger home on the same block.)

Abby Aldrich Rockefeller with grandchildren.

"Perhaps, indeed, no two partners in marriage could have been less innately similar than they," wrote biographer *Mary Ellen Chase of the Rockefeller union. For Abby, this meant a period of adjustment, both to her husband's reclusive personality and to the public hostility toward the Standard Oil monopoly overseen by her father-in-law. During her first 15 years of marriage, Abby's life largely revolved around the couple's six children, a daughter and five sons. She tended to the children's religious and cultural education, protected them from publicity, and helped to soften the blows of their father's stern discipline. She also instilled in them her deeply felt conviction that with wealth came responsibility.

Abby's influence on the public and private life of her husband was also considerable. She introduced him to the world of art and served as an unofficial consultant when he built Rockefeller Center and restored Colonial Williamsburg. In 1914, during a miners' strike against the managers of the Colorado Fuel and Iron Company, the company's hired enforcers caused the deaths of some 18 to 20 miners and members of their

families, including 2 women and 11 children, in what became known as the Ludlow massacre. The public outcry that ensued was directed against John and his father (both major absentee stockholders in the company). Abby worked closely with labor expert and future Canadian prime minister William Lyon MacKenzie King to help rebuild and expand labor relations.

"John D. Rockefeller, Jr., esteemed his wife for her sharp, intuitive judgment and her original insights and depended on her for emotional comfort and validation," writes **Bernice Kert**. "He quite literally wanted her nearby whenever possible and was relaxed only in her presence. Abby met such needs unreservedly, whatever the price, and it can safely be stated that such a relationship brought her passion, satisfaction, and stress in equal measure."

Public hostility toward the Rockefellers dissipated somewhat after the dissolution of the Standard Oil Trust and the oil industry's contribution to the Allied victory during World War I. As a result, Abby felt free to enter into a period of public service. Having served on the board of the Providence YWCA as a debutante, she reestablished her bonds with the organization as a member of the national board of the YWCA in New York, for which she served as vice president and as chair of many of its committees. As head of the National Housing Committee, she was instrumental in the building of the Grace Dodge Hotel in Washington, D.C., for professional and business women. She also devoted her time and attention to International House, a meeting place in New York for foreign students which was built with money donated by her husband.

Perhaps the public project nearest to Abby's heart was the Bayway Community Center, which grew out of her concern for the immigrant employees of the Standard Oil Company. In 1920, she had a model worker's house erected in Elizabeth, New Jersey, on a plot of land on which the Standard Oil Company (New Jersey) had constructed some 50 small houses for its employees. Originally, it was to serve as a model for possible future homes, but when Abby realized that the community desperately needed a meeting place, she turned the model home into a Community Cottage, with rotating activities. Cooking classes, a young mother's club, and a baby clinic quickly attracted the women of the neighborhood. "I held twenty-five naked, squirming babies today in our new baby clinic at Bayway," Rockefeller wrote her daughter in 1921, "some of whom took the occasion to drench me. Most of them were fat, rosy, and cheerful, but once in a while they all began to howl at once. I had a wonderful time." In 1926, when the cottage needed more space for its functions, Abby and the Standard Oil Company together built a Community House adjoining it, which held a clubroom and a gymnasium. In 1939, it was expanded again with another addition, in which was housed eight bowling alleys for the men of Bayway. By 1947, realizing how important the center was to its employees, the Standard Oil Company took over the expense of maintaining the buildings, which serviced nearly 97,000 people in that year alone. Abby, however, remained close to the center until her death, attending club functions, decorating various rooms, and even bringing art works from her own collection to the center so that her friends there could enjoy them. "It was never what she did for us, though that was very much," said one of Bayway's immigrant residents after Abby's death. "It was not even what she taught us, though she taught us many new and good things. There was something inside her that got quick inside us and made us cry and laugh at once. What was inside her somehow knew the things that were inside us."

In the late 1920s, Abby developed an all-absorbing interest in modern art, a passion not shared by her husband, who held firmly to the Renaissance and 19th-century masters (as well as Chinese porcelains and medieval tapestries, of which he had an outstanding collection). In deference to John, Abby made most of her modern art purchases with "Aldrich money" and hid them on the 7th floor of the 54th Street mansion, in a children's playroom she had converted to a gallery. In 1929, at the suggestion of her friend *Edith Halpert, Rockefeller also began collecting American "primitives," or folk-art, eventually amassing a collection of about 400 objects (now preserved in one of the restored houses at Williamsburg, Virginia).

Although she was not the sole founder of the Museum of Modern Art, as has sometimes been stated, Rockefeller was certainly the spark which set things in motion and the persistent force behind the museum's survival. ✥➤ **Lillie Bliss** and *Mary Sullivan joined with Abby in founding the museum in 1929, convincing A. Conger Goodyear, then president of the Albright Gallery of Buffalo and a modern-art enthusiast, to serve as its first president. The museum was initially housed in rented quarters at 730 Fifth Avenue and opened its doors on November 7, 1929, with an exhibition of 19th-century French painters. Abby's involvement in the early years

✥➤ *See sidebar on the following page*

Bliss, Lillie (1864–1931)

American philanthropist and co-founder of the New York Museum of Modern Art. Born Lillie Plummer Bliss in Boston, Massachusetts, on April 11, 1864; died in New York City on March 13, 1931; younger of two daughters and second of four children of Cornelius Newton Bliss (a textile commission merchant and secretary of the interior under President McKinley) and Elizabeth Mary (Plummer) Bliss; privately educated; never married; no children.

Born in 1864 in Boston, Massachusetts, Lillie Bliss moved to New York City with her family in 1866, when her father, a textile merchant, became president of Bliss, Fabyan & Company. He also served variously as head of the Protective Tariff League and treasurer of the Republican National Committee, and from 1897 to 1899 was secretary of the interior under President William McKinley. Lillie frequently served as her father's hostess on official occasions, filling in for her mother who suffered from ill health.

Bliss began to support New York's cultural activities as early as 1907, backing the Kneisel Quartet and serving on the advisory committee of the Juilliard Foundation. That same year, she purchased a painting by Arthur B. Davies, an American artist who shared her enthusiasm for contemporary European art and from whom she learned a great deal about Post-Impressionism. She may have provided financial backing for the epochal Armory Show of 1913, of which Davies was a major organizer, although her preference for anonymity makes it difficult to know for certain. At the Armory Show, Bliss purchased two Renoirs, a Degas, and two Redons, initiating a collection of modern French art that would become one of the finest in the United States. In subsequent years, she acquired paintings by Gauguin, Cézanne, Seurat, Matisse, Modigliani, and Picasso, as well as by Davies, whose work she continued to collect until her death. At her family's insistence, Bliss kept her collection hidden away in the attic, although her mother did allow a few Cézannes to be hung in the house proper. Bliss, however, did find a coterie with whom she could openly share her aesthetic judg-

ments, among them stage performers Walter Hampden, *Ruth Draper, and *Ethel Barrymore, and musical personalities Richard Aldrich and Charles M. Loeffler.

Like *Abby Aldrich Rockefeller, Bliss had hopes of establishing a permanent collection of modern art within the city, and in 1929 the two women, along with *Mary Sullivan, another friend sympathetic to their cause, had lunch with A. Conger Goodyear, the president of the Albright Gallery of Buffalo and also a modern-art enthusiast. At the meeting, the Museum of Modern Art was launched, with Goodyear agreeing to chair the organizational committee.

Unfortunately, Lillie Bliss died of cancer in 1931, not long after the museum had sponsored its first major exhibition. Although in the final months of her life she had switched her patronage from art to charity, she did make provisions in her will to ensure that the Museum of Modern Art would have a permanent place in the city. Along with generous bequests to the New York Hospital, the Broadway Tabernacle, and other benevolent organizations, Bliss left the museum a collection of 150 artworks with the caveat that the enterprise be established on a "firm financial basis" within three years. Following her death, her brother Cornelius Bliss, executor of her estate, determined that an endowment of $1 million would be necessary to secure the bequest, but because of the Depression, he instead accepted $600,000, the final amount the museum managed to raise within the allotted time.

Bliss, like Rockefeller, both encouraged and supported freedom of expression in the art world, and through her efforts established the modern-art movement in the United States and guaranteed it continuance. In her "From a Letter to a National Academician," which was published after her death as part of a catalogue of her collection, Bliss admonished older artists for their intolerance of innovation, which she called "a state of mind incomprehensible" to someone who enjoyed finding the new practitioners of music, painting, and literature.

SOURCES:

James, Edward T., ed. *Notable American Women, 1607–1950.* Cambridge, MA: The Belknap Press of Harvard University Press, 1971.

of the museum included gifts of paintings, drawings, and sculptures from her own collection, as well as contributions of money and land from her and her husband, who eventually succumbed to his wife's enthusiasm if not her aesthetics. In 1932, the museum moved into a private Rockefeller-owned house on West 53rd Street, and in 1939, into its own newly erected glass, marble, and steel edifice, also on Rockefeller land.

Throughout the rest of her life, Abby took a profound interest in the museum's collection and in the works of living American artists, whom she supported by purchasing their work and by offering them personal encouragement. Her interest in art, however, went beyond her individual preferences, as Bernice Kert points out. She believed that art belonged to the people, and that all art, even the most extreme, deserved to be seen. "To me art is one of the great resources of my life," she wrote to her son Nelson Rockefeller. "I feel that it enriches the spiritual life and makes one more sane and sympathetic, more observant and understanding." True to her convictions, by 1940 Abby had given most of her private collection to the museum, including works by Americans Walt Kuhn, Peter Blume, Charles Sheeler, and Preston Dickinson, and Europeans Pablo Picasso, Amedeo Modigliani, and Henri Matisse, among others. The 1,600 etchings, lithographs, and woodcuts that comprised her print collection made the museum the greatest repository of 20th-century prints in the world.

In her last years, Rockefeller was slowed somewhat by a pesky heart, which began to drain some of her extraordinary energy. She reluctantly gave in to periods of rest, spending the winters of 1947 and 1948 in Arizona, where she fell in love with the deserts and mountains, as well as the constant sunshine. "Now I can understand better why there were ancient sunworshippers," she wrote. "I'm almost one myself." In early April, back in New York, she spent two days at a family reunion she had planned at Pocantico, the large house and grounds of which were overrun with spring flowers and with her beloved grandchildren. Returning to New York City on April 4, Rockefeller called her sister Lucy in New York before retiring, telling her that she had just had the most beautiful time of all her 74 years. She died early the next morning, on April 5, 1948.

Following her death, Abby Rockefeller was remembered for her spirit and generosity, particularly by the art community, which had benefited so greatly from her largesse. Henri Matisse designed a stained-glass window for the Union Church of Pocantico as a memorial to her, and the Museum of Modern Art opened the Abby Aldrich Rockefeller Print Room, in recognition of her interest in prints and serving as a remembrance of all she had contributed to the museum as a whole. Alfred Barr, who served as the museum's first director, wrote to Abby's son Nelson that her interest in modern art was a lesson in courage. "Not only is modern art artistically radical but it is often assumed to be radical morally and politically and sometimes indeed it is. But these factors which might have given pause to a more circumspect or conventional spirit did not deter your mother."

SOURCES:
Chase, Mary Ellen. *Abby Aldrich Rockefeller.* NY: Macmillan, 1950.
Garraty, John A., and Mark C. Carnes. *American National Biography.* Vol. 18. NY: Oxford University Press, 1999.
*Saarinin, Aline B. *The Proud Possessors.* NY: Random House, 1958.
SUGGESTED READING:
Kert, Bernice. *Abby Aldrich Rockefeller: The Woman in the Family.* NY: Random, 1993.
Stasz, Clarice. *The Rockefeller Women: Dynasty of Piety, Privacy, and Service.* St. Martin's, 1995.
COLLECTIONS:
Abby Rockefeller's correspondence, diaries, and other papers are held at the Rockefeller Archive Center, Pocantico Hills, North Tarrytown, New York.

Barbara Morgan, Melrose, Massachusetts

Rockefeller, Blanchette Hooker
(1909–1992)

American philanthropist. Born Blanchette Ferry Hooker on October 2, 1909, in New York City; died at age 83 in Briarcliff Manor, New York, on December 2, 1992; daughter of Elon Huntington Hooker and Blanche (Ferry) Hooker; married John D. Rockefeller III (1906–1978), on November 11, 1932; children: Sandra Ferry Rockefeller (b. 1935); John (Jay) Davison Rockefeller IV (b. 1937); Hope Aldrich Rockefeller (b. 1938); Alida Davison Rockefeller (b. 1949).

Blanchette Rockefeller was born in 1909 as the heir to the fortune generated by her father, Elon Huntington Hooker, through his Hooker Chemical Company. Described as "lively" and "outgoing," she never relinquished the socially prominent role she received first as a member of the Hooker family and later as the wife of millionaire heir John D. Rockefeller III. Blanchette participated in her husband's business career while raising their four children; her only son, Jay Rockefeller, later became the governor and Democratic senator of West Virginia. She increased her influence on New York's cultural scene when she became president of the Museum of Modern Art, which had been founded by her mother-in-law *Abby Aldrich Rockefeller. Renowned for her varied roles in philanthropy, art, and politics, Rockefeller died at her home in New York from Alzheimer's disease complicated by pneumonia on December 2, 1992.

SOURCES:
"Blanchette Rockefeller: Art museum president, mother of U.S. senator," in *The Day* [New London, CT]. December 2, 1992.
"Milestones," in *Time.* December 14, 1992.
SUGGESTED READING:
Stasz, Clarice. *The Rockefeller Women: Dynasty of Piety, Privacy, and Service.* St. Martin's, 1995.

Stephen Tschirhart, freelance writer, Birmingham, Michigan

Rockefeller, Cettie (1839–1915).
See Rockefeller, Laura Spelman.

Rockefeller, Edith (1872–1932).

See McCormick, Edith Rockefeller.

Rockefeller, Happy (b. 1926).

See Rockefeller, Margaretta "Happy."

Rockefeller, Laura Spelman

(1839–1915)

Affluent American and wife of John D. Rockefeller. Name variations: Cettie Spelman Rockefeller. Born Laura Celestia Spelman in 1839; died in 1915; married John D. Rockefeller (1839–1937, founder of Standard Oil and philanthropist), on September 8, 1864; children: Elizabeth or **Bessie Rockefeller** *(1866–1906);* **Alice Rockefeller** *(1869–1870);* **Alta Rockefeller** *(1871–1962);* ***Edith Rockefeller McCormick** *(1872–1932); John D. Rockefeller, Jr. (1874–1960).*

When her children were young, Laura Spelman Rockefeller, the wife of one of the richest men in America, once noted to a neighbor, "I am so glad my son has told me what he wants for Christmas, so now it can be denied him." Laura and John D. Rockefeller raised their children with stern discipline and few luxuries; although they lived in a mansion and had a grand country estate, the younger ones wore their older siblings' hand-me-downs, and all the children earned their allowances by doing chores. Laura and John had met in high school, and were devoted to each other throughout their marriage. Although Laura loved music and literature and her husband did not, both were religious and serious-minded, somewhat uncomfortable with the temptations offered by the enormous wealth John had acquired, and they believed strongly that life was for duty, not enjoyment. Indifferent to the social whirl to which her position entitled her, Laura suffered from tuberculosis for a number of years, and spent the last six years of her life in a wheelchair. She died in 1915. Among the some $530 million which her husband gave away in his lifetime was a donation to Atlanta's Spelman College, founded by *Sophia B. Packard, which in return was named in honor of Laura's parents. At his request, he was buried beside her after his death in 1937.

SUGGESTED READING:
Stasz, Clarice. *The Rockefeller Women: Dynasty of Piety, Privacy, and Service.* St. Martin's, 1995.

Rockefeller, Margaret (1915–1996)

American conservationist. Name variations: Peggy Rockefeller; Peggy McGrath. Born Margaret Mc-Grath in 1915; died in New York on March 26, 1996; married David Rockefeller (b. 1915, son of ***Abby Aldrich Rockefeller**); children: David Rockefeller, Jr. (b. 1941);* **Abby Aldrich Rockefeller** *(b. 1943);* **Neva Goodwin Rockefeller** *(b. 1944);* **Margaret Dulany Rockefeller** *(b. 1947); Richard Gilder Rockefeller (b. 1949);* **Eileen McGrath Rockefeller** *(b. 1952).*

Her love of farming, animals and agriculture was the hallmark of her career as a conservationist, but Margaret Rockefeller, known as Peggy, was equally at ease with the state dinners and other urban accoutrements of her husband's professional career as the chair of the Chase Manhattan Bank. Both Margaret and David Rockefeller were highly regarded philanthropists; Margaret was not only a founding board member of American Farmland Trust—a national land-preservation group—but the sole founding member of the Maine Coast Heritage Trust. Established in 1970, the Trust held more than 66,000 acres in Maine by the mid-1990s. Rockefeller was also a trustee of the New York Philharmonic Orchestra and served on the board of the New York Botanical Garden. She died of complications from heart surgery in New York on March 26, 1996.

SOURCES:
"Margaret Rockefeller: Conservationist; at 80," in *Boston Globe.* March 27, 1996.

SUGGESTED READING:
Stasz, Clarice. *The Rockefeller Women: Dynasty of Piety, Privacy, and Service.* St. Martin's, 1995.

Stephen Tschirhart,
freelance writer, Birmingham, Michigan

Rockefeller, Margaretta "Happy"

(b. 1926)

American socialite. Name variations: Marguerite. Born Margaretta Fitler Murphy in 1926; married Dr. James Murphy (divorced 1963); married Nelson Aldrich Rockefeller (1908–1979, governor of New York and vice-president of U.S.), in May 1963; children: (first marriage) four; (second marriage) Nelson Aldrich, Jr. (b. 1964); Mark Fitler Rockefeller (b. 1967). Nelson's first wife was Mary Todhunter Rockefeller.

In May 1963, Nelson Aldrich Rockefeller, who was in his second term as governor of New York and was considered a frontrunner for the Republican presidential nomination, married Margaretta "Happy" Murphy. She had been divorced five weeks previously, and as a condition of her divorce gave up custody of her four young children. Nelson Rockefeller's standings in the polls took a nosedive; there had been little public mention of his own divorce from *Mary Todhunter Rockefeller the previous year, but his re-marriage caused a furor. The ensuing Republican primary campaign, which pitted Nelson Rockefeller against Barry Goldwater, was hard-fought and nasty, and it is generally believed that public reaction to Nelson's marriage to Happy, and the skillful fanning of such emotions by hard-line Republicans, lost Nelson the nomination and delivered control of the Republican Party from the "Eastern liberals" to the deeply conservative faction that controls it to this day. After Goldwater was nominated at the national convention in 1964, Nelson Rockefeller was booed during his concession speech. Goldwater then took the podium to deliver his (in)famous acceptance speech, in which he told the crowd, "I would remind you that extremism in the defense of liberty is no vice . . . [and] moderation in pursuit of justice is no virtue."

Happy and Nelson's first son had been born just a month earlier. They had a second son in 1967, and Happy served as first lady of New York while Nelson was reelected governor in 1966 and 1970. He ran for and lost the Republican presidential nomination again in 1968, against Richard Nixon, and chose not to run for a fifth term as governor in 1973. The following year, Happy was diagnosed with breast cancer. She underwent a radical mastectomy, and used her position as a public figure to advocate for early breast-cancer detection. Later that year, Nixon resigned from the presidency in the aftermath of the Watergate scandal, and Gerald Ford, as the new president, named Nelson Rockefeller vice-president. He and Happy lived in Washington for the remainder of Ford's term, which ended in January 1977. Happy Rockefeller continued to live in New York City after Nelson's death from a heart attack in 1979, and in 1991–92 served as an alternate representative to the UN General Assembly.

Rockefeller, Martha Baird

(1895–1971)

*American philanthropist and pianist. Born Martha Baird Allen in 1895; died in 1971; became second wife of John D. Rockefeller, Jr. (1874–1960). John D. Rockefeller, Jr., was first married to *Abby Aldrich Rockefeller (1874–1948).*

Born in 1895, Martha Baird Rockefeller studied piano with Artur Schnabel, and performed in recitals and as a solo pianist before re-tiring in 1931. Twenty years later, she married John D. Rockefeller, Jr., scion of the wealthy Rockefeller family, and after his death in 1960 inherited a considerable amount of money. She used this inheritance to set up the Martha Baird Rockefeller Fund, which distributed study grants to numerous young musicians, many of whom later became prominent. The fund was discontinued in 1982, 11 years after her death.

Rockefeller, Mary Todhunter

(1907–1999)

American socialite. Born Mary Todhunter Clark in 1907; died on April 21, 1999, in New York City; married Nelson Aldrich Rockefeller (1908–1979, governor of New York and vice-president of U.S.), on June 23, 1930 (divorced 1962); children: Rodman Clark Rockefeller (b. 1932); Ann Clark (b. 1934); Steven Clark Rockefeller (b. 1936); (twins) Michael Clark Rockefeller (1938–1961) and Mary Clark Rockefeller (b. 1938). Nelson Rockefeller married Margaretta "Happy" Rockefeller in 1963.

A longtime advocate of nurses' education, Mary Todhunter Rockefeller served as first lady of New York State during the first gubernatorial term of her husband Nelson Aldrich Rockefeller. They were married for over 30 years, before divorcing in 1962 as a consequence of his affair with *Margaretta "Happy" Rockefeller, whom he married the next year. Shortly after Mary and Nelson separated in 1961, their youngest son Michael disappeared while traveling in Papua New Guinea; despite extensive land and sea searches with assistance from the Australian and Dutch militaries, he was never found. (There has been much speculation that he was killed by local headhunters.) Mary Rockefeller served on the National Advisory Health Council and the Defense Advisory Committee on Women in the Services during the 1950s, and on the board of the National League of Nursing for many years. She was honored for "27 years of outstanding achievement on behalf of the nursing profession and the health care of the American people" by the New York County of Registered Nurses in 1959, received a distinguished service award from the National League of Nursing in 1971, and was granted an honorary degree from Hunter College in recognition of her volunteer efforts in 1980.

SOURCES:
The Boston Globe (obituary). April 23, 1999, p. B11.

Rockefeller, Peggy (1915–1996).

See Rockefeller, Margaret.

Rockford Peaches (1940–1954)

Championship women's baseball team.

For 12 years, played in the All-American Girls Baseball League (AAGBL, 1940–1954); won four AAGBL pennants (1945, 1948, 1949, and 1950).

In 1992, the glory days of the Rockford Peaches and the All-American Girls Baseball League (AAGBL) was revisited in the **Penny Marshall** film *A League of Their Own*, starring **Geena Davis**, **Madonna**, **Rosie O'Donnell**, and Tom Hanks as the burned-out baseball player who goads the Rockford, Illinois, team to several League pennants. Though it may have hedged a bit on accuracy, the movie brought back to life, however briefly, one of the great eras in American sports.

The Rockford Peaches

The Rockford Peaches were part of the AAGBL from its inception in 1943, and won four League championships in 12 years, all of them under the management of Bill Allington (played by Hanks), one of the more colorful characters in baseball. The team was at the bottom of the League standings in 1944, when Allington took over management duties. Having spent 20 years playing baseball in the minors, he had been coaching women's baseball since 1939 and had contributed some top players to the AAGBL. A no-nonsense manager who groomed his players in the basics of baseball, he turned the team around in a few short months. In September 1944, 3,133 fans braved unseasonably cold weather at Beyer Stadium (dubbed the "Peach Orchard" by sports writers) to watch Rockford hurler **Carolyn Morris** pitch a 9–0 no-hitter against the visiting Blue Sox. Fans were so excited that they thrust $1, $5, and even $10 bills at the players for particularly savvy plays, while the women in turn handed out autographed photos to the fans.

Allington demanded complete dedication from his players, who included stars like *Dorothy Kamenshek** and *Rose Gacioch**. Although he drilled his players mercilessly and frequently was bitingly sarcastic, he also looked after them like a mother hen. When **Dorothy Wiltse** was playing for the Minneapolis

Millerettes and Allington was with the Peaches, she fell in the dugout and broke her coccyx bone, although she was unaware of the injury at the time. Allington noticed that something was wrong when she took the mound to pitch, and he saw to it that she was taken to a hospital. Gacioch recalls that when she began slowing down in right field, Allington turned her into a pitcher, benefiting the team, but also prolonging her career. "There's not so much ground to cover when you pitch," he told her.

The Rockford team hit their zenith in 1945, with a roster that included **Jo Lenard, Kay Rohrer, Dottie Green, Betty Carveth, Helen Filarski**, Dottie Kamenshek, **Irene Kotowicz, Alva Jo Fisher, Millie Deegan, Olive Little, Dottie Ferguson, Jean Cione**, Carolyn Morris, Rose Gacioch, and **Snookie Harrell**. They won their first League championship that year and were rewarded with a swelling fan base. The newspapers reported their games on the front page of the sports section, along with articles on major-league games. The Peaches won a second and third championship in 1948 and in 1949, although by that time attendance had already begun to decline.

In 1950, the Rockford Peaches went after their fourth championship, minus a few of their star players. (Rohrer left to play softball, Little retired to start a family, and Lenard, Deegan, and Cione had been traded.) Even fewer fans were in attendance, although those who showed were as enthusiastic as ever, jeering at the buses bringing rivals into town, and raising money to help out injured catcher **Ruth Richard**, who was confined to a leg cast for several months.

In 1951 and 1952, the Peaches lost the series championships to the South Bend Blue Sox. At the end of the '52 season, Allington left the team to manage elsewhere, possibly due to a salary dispute. Under new manager Johnny Rawlings, the team continued its decline. By June 1954, during the AAGBL's last year, they had slipped to last place in the league, which was down to only five teams. Often, less than 100 fans were on hand to watch the team play. "It was the same all around the Midwest," writes **Barbara Gregorich**, "as people turned to new recreational opportunities, bought new cars and drove them on newly constructed expressways to bigger cities, or sat home and watched television. . . . The All-American Girls Baseball League died while people were looking the other way."

SOURCES:

Gregorich, Barbara. *Women at Play: The Story of Women in Baseball*. NY: Harcourt Brace, 1993.

RELATED MEDIA:

A League of Their Own (127 min. film), starring Geena Davis, Madonna, Tom Hanks, Rosie O'Donnell, directed by Penny Marshall, 1992.

Barbara Morgan,
Melrose, Massachusetts

Rockmore, Clara (1910–1998)

Lithuanian musician who was recognized as the master of the theremin, an electronic musical instrument. Name variations: Clara Reisenberg. Born Clara Reisenberg in Vilna (now Vilnius), Lithuania, in 1910; died in New York on May 12, 1998; sister of *Nadia Reisenberg (1904–1983).

Born in Lithuania in 1910, Clara Rockmore was admitted to the St. Petersburg Conservatory as a violinist at age five, the youngest musician to enroll at the time. Her musical career took an unexpected turn, however, when she took up the theremin, an electronic musical instrument invented in 1919 by Russian physicist Leon Theremin. The theremin, played by waving hands between two antennae to alter musical pitch and volume, has been compared to a wordless soprano voice or an enchanted cello and enjoyed early attention in science-fiction movies. Rockmore was the recognized master of the instrument; according to one source, she was as adept with the theremin as musical legend Jimi Hendrix was with the electric guitar. Rockmore appeared in the film *Theremin: An Electronic Odyssey* in 1994, and again in a 1998 video documentary, *Clara Rockmore, the Greatest Theremin Virtuosa*. She died in Manhattan on May 12, 1998, approximately one month after that documentary's release.

SOURCES AND SUGGESTED READING:

"Clara Rockmore, 88: Virtuosa on unusual instrument," in *The Day* [New London, CT]. May 12, 1998.

Darreg, Ivor, and Bart Hopkin. "Still Nothing Else Like It: The Theremin," in *Experimental Musical Instruments*. Vol. 8, no. 3. March 1993.

"This Musician Also Could Play The Air Guitar," in *Wall Street Journal*. March 25, 1998.

Stephen Tschirhart,
freelance writer, Birmingham, Michigan

Rodd, Kylie Tennant (1912–1988).

See Tennant, Kylie.

Rodgers, Elizabeth Flynn (1847–1939)

Irish-born American labor leader and chief executive officer of the Women's Catholic Order of Foresters. Born Elizabeth Flynn in Woodford, Ireland, on Au-

gust 25, 1847; died of a cerebral hemorrhage in Wauwatosa, Wisconsin, on August 27, 1939; daughter of Robert Flynn and Bridget (Campbell) Flynn; married George Rodgers (an iron worker, died 1920); children: ten.

First woman to become a Master Workman with the Knights of Labor (1886).

Though she was born in 1847 in Ireland, Elizabeth Flynn immigrated with her family to London, Ontario, early in her life. She was educated there, and at some point married George Rodgers and started a family. They moved to Chicago, Illinois, where George's job as an iron molder led him to active involvement in the labor movement around 1876. He joined the Knights of Labor, one of the largest and most powerful of the early labor groups and one which accepted all workers. Rodgers also joined the Knights of Labor, reputedly the first woman in Chicago to do so, and became head of an all-woman local assembly in September 1881. She served in a variety of roles within the organization before being appointed Master Workman (president) of her district—including all the Knights of Labor assemblies in Chicago and its suburbs except for the stockyard area—following the death of the incumbent in 1886. At that point, the organization claimed over 700,000 members nationwide. Later that year, Rodgers was nominated for the post of general treasurer at the Knights' national convention. Attending with her husband and infant son (who gained a fair share of publicity), she cited her ten young children in declining the post. However, 1886 also had seen the deaths of seven police officers during the infamous Haymarket Riot in May, and the repercussions of the riot, for which seven rioters were sentenced to death and four hanged, severely impacted public acceptance of the labor movement. The Knights of Labor's enrollment and power declined sharply, and Rodgers left the labor movement around 1887 for a role as a partner in a printing firm. With 12 others, she formed the fraternal life insurance agency Women's Catholic Order of Foresters. The former Knights of Labor Master Workman served as High Chief Ranger (chief executive officer) of this organization until 1908. Rodgers died of a cerebral hemorrhage at age 92, in the home of a daughter in Wauwatosa, Wisconsin, in 1931.

SOURCES:

James, Edward T., ed. *Notable American Women, 1607–1950*. Cambridge, MA: The Belknap Press of Harvard University, 1971.

Read, Phyllis J., and Bernard L. Witlieb. *The Book of Women's Firsts*. NY: Random House, 1992.

Stephen Tschirhart,
freelance writer, Birmingham, Michigan

Rodiani, Onorata (d. 1452)

Italian artist and military leader. Name variations: Honorata Rodiana. Died in 1452 in Cremona; never married; no children.

An Italian woman from the emergent bourgeois class, Onorata Rodiani was trained as a professional painter and began a successful career in that field, as did a surprising number of women from late medieval cities. However, Rodiani was forced to give up her painting when she murdered a man in self-defense; while working on commission at the palace of Gabrino Fondolo, she had been attacked by one of Fondolo's courtiers and stabbed him to death. Frightened for her life, she fled her home and eventually joined a troop of mercenary soldiers. She received a pardon from the city authorities, and returned to Cremona. It is reported that she died in battle leading a troop of soldiers in the defense of Cremona from its Venetian enemies.

Laura York,
Riverside, California

Rodnina, Irina (1949—)

Soviet ice skater. Born in the USSR on September 12, 1949; married Alexsandr Zaitsev or Zaitzev (her pairs partner), in 1975; children: at least one son.

Won ten World and ten European titles, as well as three Olympic gold medals in pairs competitions (1969–80): with Alexei Ulanov, won four World championship titles (1969–72) and the gold medal at the Sapporo Olympics (1972); with Alexsandr Zaitsev, won six World championships in pairs (1973–78) and the Olympic gold medal (1976, 1980).

Irina Rodnina inherited the mantle of *Ludmila Protopopov, one half of the dominant Soviet pairs team known as the Protopopovs. Between 1969 and 1972, Rodnina skated successfully with Alexei Ulanov, winning four consecutive World championship titles. But at the 1972 Olympics at Sapporo, Japan, when they won the gold medal, their partnership was coming to an end, and everyone knew it. Ulanov had fallen in love with another Russian skater, **Ludmila Smirnova**, who with her partner Andrei Suraikin had won the silver medal in the same event. A dejected Rodnina stood on top of the podium, Ulanov by her side, Smirnova to her right, while the band struck up the Soviet national anthem. Then, she went home and looked for another partner, and all of Russia helped.

After a nationwide search, Alexsandr Zaitsev was chosen in 1973. Though Zaitsev was three years younger than she, the couple jelled immediately and won the European Paris Competition in Zagreb, Yugoslavia, in 1974, with the highest number of maximum six marks awarded for one performance in an international championship. The highly emotional Rodnina was the dominant skater, performing technically difficult routines. Zaitsev was reserved and intellectual. But they meshed, noted *Time*, "like the gears in a Swiss watch." In 1975, they married; a year later, in the 1976 Olympics at Innsbruck, they won the gold medal.

Coming into the 1980 Olympics at Lake Placid, America's **Tai Babilonia** and Randy Gardner were expected to be tough competitors, because they had upset the Soviets in the 1979 World championships. They had not, however, competed against Rodnina and Zaitsev, who at that time had been in temporary retirement awaiting the birth of their son. But at Lake Placid Gardner pulled a groin muscle and fell four times while warming up for the short program, and he and Babilonia were forced to withdraw. Rodnina and Zaitsev took to the ice to win their second Olympic gold medal. With ten Worlds and three Olympic medals, Rodnina had tied the record of major championship titles in ice skating set by *Sonja Henie. Rodnina retired in 1980 and became a highly successful coach of pair skaters.

SOURCES:

Time. February 2, 1976, pg 65.

Rodogune.

Variant of Rhodogune.

Rodoreda, Mercè (1909–1983)

Spanish author. Name variations: Merce Rodoreda. Born in Barcelona, Spain, on October 10, 1909 (some sources cite 1908); died in 1983; married and separated; children: one.

Born in Barcelona on October 10, 1909, Mercè Rodoreda was only allowed to attend school until age nine and often lamented her lack of formal education. As a teenager, she married her mother's brother, with whom she had a child. After separating from her husband, she began writing, using Catalan rather than Spanish. Rodoreda finished five novels (she later disowned four of them, retaining only the Crexells prize-winning *Aloma* [1938]) and a number of short stories in the mid-1930s. The Spanish Civil War interrupted her writing and her life. A supporter of the socialists and the Republic, she fled to France when Francisco Franco and the National-

ists triumphed in 1939. In exile, she became the mistress and housekeeper of Joan Armand Obiols, another Catalan writer. When Obiols, who was married, refused to break with his wife, Rodoreda felt used and betrayed by her own love for him.

When the Second World War ended, Rodoreda took up her writing again. She found little pleasure during a visit to Franco-controlled Barcelona and decided to live in exile, first in Paris and later in Geneva. A collection of short stories, *Vint-i-dos contes*, won the Victor Català prize in 1957. In 1962, she published *La plaça del Diamant* (*The Time of the Doves*), her most celebrated work and a masterpiece of Iberian literature. As with her other writings, it portrayed the failure of human relations, especially between the sexes, in some ways a reflection of her own experiences. Her later publications include another collection of short stories *La meva Cristina i altres contes* (1984), and the novels *Jardí vora el mar* (1967), *Mirall trencat* (1974), and *Quanta, quanta guerra* (1980). At her death in 1983, she left several drafts of another major novel, *La Mort e la Primavera*.

SOURCES:

Arnau, Carme. *Mercè Rodoreda*. Barcelona: Edicions 62, 1992.

Irina Rodnina and Alexei Ulanov.

Pope, Randolph D. "Mercè Rodoreda's Subtle Greatness," in *Women Writers of Contemporary Spain: Exiles in the Homeland*. Ed. by Joan L. Brown. University of Delaware Press, 1991, pp. 116–135.

Kendall W. Brown,
Professor of History,
Brigham Young University, Provo, Utah

Rodrigues, Amalia (1921–1999)

Portuguese fado singer known as "the soul of the nation" whose career spanned more than 50 years and made her Portugal's best-loved performer. Born Amalia Rodrigues in the slums of Lisbon in 1921 (she was never sure of the exact day; her grandmother told her it was in the cherry season, early summer); died on October 6, 1999; daughter of a trumpet player who died young and a mother who sold fruit in the street market; attended school until age 12; married Francisco Cruz (divorced in less than a year); married Cesar Seabra (an engineer), in 1961.

A petite woman dressed in black walked the narrow streets near the center of Lisbon, browsing through the items displayed by vendors in their stalls. Her appearance was ordinary, but as she passed by, older women were occasionally seen to cross themselves and make a reverential bow. The woman they paid tribute to was Amalia Rodrigues, the fado singer revered throughout Portugal. Known for her long career in nightclubs and on radio and television, she has been compared with France's *Edith Piaf and America's *Billie Holiday, but Rodrigues, for the Portuguese, was not simply a great singer; she was a cultural icon, the embodiment of the soul of the people.

Portugal is a small country with a complex culture that bears traces of the many migrations it has seen over the past 2,000 years. Phoenicians, Greeks, Celts, Romans, Suevi, Visigoths, Muslims (both Arab and Berber), Jews, Italians, Flemings, Burgundian French, black Africans, and Asians have all left their imprint within its borders. It is one of Europe's oldest nation states, and, except for a brief period under Spanish rule, has been a sovereign state since 1140. Its maritime culture began through fishing, but knowledge of the sea eventually led the Portuguese to foreign invasions and the establishment of myriad colonies. For a time, the country was the third largest colonial empire in the world. It remained relatively prosperous through the 18th century, but then fell on harder times. In 1908, King Charles I and his heir Luís were murdered by anarchist Republicans, bringing down the Portuguese monarchy. Chaos followed the assassina-

tions: over the next 16 years, 45 governments were formed and dissolved. Political instability severely affected the country's economic life, and the poor, such as the Rodrigues family, were particularly hard hit. The military took over the government in 1926, and four years later António de Oliveir Salazar, a professor of economics from Coimbra University, became prime minister and established a dictatorship which would last for 40 years. Politically and culturally conservative, Salazar wielded enormous influence at every level, including the arts.

This, then, was the world into which Amalia Rodrigues was born in 1921, and the background for fado, the musical genre with which she is so closely identified. The term derives from *fatum*, the Latin word for fate, and means a traditional urban song performed by either a woman or a man (singers of either sex are called *fadistas*), although women singers have long dominated the art. Some scholars trace the genre through Brazilian and African roots back to Muslim, Moorish, and North African elements mixed in with the Hispanic. It also has connections to the bitter 18th-century ballads composed by Portuguese convicts on their way into exile and forced labor in Portugal's African colonies, which were picked up and brought back to Lisbon by Portuguese sailors. The music is essentially urban, and strongly associated with Lisbon's slums; it was part of the city's popular culture by the 18th century. The first great fadista was **Maria Severa**, a Gypsy (Roma) prostitute whose singing became popular in the 1830s. For 26 years, Severa devoted her life to love, bullfights, wine, and fado, and the black shawl usually worn onstage by women fadistas is considered a tribute to her memory. The essential element conveyed in a fado song is *saudade*, a word that all but defies translation into English. Although its origin is obscure, some suggest that the word derives from the Latin *solitate*, from which the English "solitary" is also derived. Others identify it with the Arabic word *saudawi*, which refers to someone stricken with melancholy and a longing to be alone. Saudade is a common term in colloquial Portuguese, suggesting both a kind of nostalgia and yearning as well as a sweet remembrance of persons and things from the past. Said Rodrigues, "I have so much sadness in me. . . . I am a pessimist, a nihilist. Everything that fado demands in a singer I have in me."

Rodrigues was born in a working-class district of Lisbon, the daughter of a trumpet player who died young and a mother too poor to raise her. She was sent to stay with her grandmother, who earned her living by doing embroidery, and

at age 12 quit school to go to work. She was employed for a time as a dressmaker's apprentice, but she hated the tedious sewing inside the cramped shop, and escaped by selling fruit with mother in the market. Rodrigues enjoyed being out in the open air of the streets, and legend has it that she first sang in public at the market, while she sold her oranges. Her brothers, however, disliked the attention she drew, and forced her to take another job in a cannery. She missed singing in the streets, and of the cannery job later said, "I wanted to kill myself every day."

Meanwhile, she began performing at various festivals in her district, particularly the one known as the "March of Lisbon," and always found people ready to listen. When Rodrigues was 18, a neighbor introduced her to a guitarist who played at the Retiro da Severa, one of the best fado clubs in Lisbon. Impressed by her voice, the guitarist arranged an audition for her at the club. Her talent was quickly recognized, and she was soon performing at the Retiro da Severa. "Five months later," she later said, "I already had top billing in a theater. I didn't have to struggle—it was very easy."

Rodrigues' sudden ascent to fame and fortune in the 1940s opened new worlds for the poor girl from the slums. Night after night she appeared throughout Lisbon in various casas de fado, the café/taverns where families and people of all ages came to hear their favorite music. Onstage, Rodrigues wore a long, full black gown which covered everything but her hands, without jewelry save for a diamond pendant on occasion. Accompanied by two to four musicians on the viola, guitar, and the portuguesa (a long-necked lute dating from the Renaissance), she sang songs about love, jealousy, and the sadness of parting while the crowd sat motionless through every wailing note.

I am a pessimist, a nihilist. Everything that fado demands in a singer I have in me.

—Amalia Rodrigues

Long after success made Rodrigues the family breadwinner, her life continued to be dominated by her brothers. When she fell in love with Francisco Cruz, a guitarist, her brothers objected and refused to approve the match. They finally gave her their permission to marry him, after which she divorced Cruz within a year. She also expanded her performances into larger theaters, and began to star in movies. Salazar called her "the soul of Portugal." Juan, count of Barcelona and father of the future King Juan Carlos I of Spain, once came onstage during a performance to kiss her hand. Rodrigues could afford the best accompanists and was booked into the country's best theaters, and Portuguese poets vied to write lyrics for her to sing; the country was at her feet.

Outside Portugal, Rodrigues' first triumph was at the Olympia in Paris in 1953, followed by successful engagements at La Vie en Rose and Mocambo in the United States. In 1966, she appeared at Lincoln Center in New York City with the New York Philharmonic, under the direction of Andre Kostelanetz. Recordings also made her singing widely known in Portuguese-speaking communities overseas, helping to establish her reputation worldwide. As Rodrigues noted, "Families used to go to the casa de fado every day to listen. It wasn't a restaurant, a cafe or a night club. You had a drink and listened. . . . Now there are no more casas de fado, but the fado is [everywhere] . . . even on television." Even when the advent of new media caused many of the old taverns to fall on bad times, fado remained the "national song, the expression of the people," and Amalia Rodrigues was its soul.

In 1961, after remaining single for 20 years, Rodrigues married for a second time, to Cesar Seabra, an engineer. They lived for a time in Brazil, where Rodrigues had many fans, before returning to Lisbon because she felt that her people wanted her home again. The couple bought an 18th-century home where Rodrigues, by now a wealthy woman, delighted in tending the garden. She was always loyal to her extended family, spending her money freely and never forgetting those who had shared her poverty-stricken youth. Portugal's most highly paid performer, she continued to appear onstage, albeit somewhat more infrequently than in earlier years, and any performance she gave was a guaranteed sellout.

Although she was never a political partisan, Rodrigues did find her life affected by Portuguese politics. At the beginning of the Salazar regime, fado music was highly criticized, but the reputation of the form was gradually rehabilitated as an expression of traditional Portuguese culture. In that phase, it was natural for Salazar to identify with Rodrigues and heap praise on her, angering some of her fans who opposed the dictator and the attention given her from the highest echelons of government. Ignoring her critics, Rodriguez said, "The Portuguese are jealous lovers. They say that I drink, that I am a spy, that I work for the secret police, that I sing only for ministers." And she continued to sing. After Salazar's death in 1970 and the military coup four years later that finally ended the country's dictatorship, both Rodrigues and fado came under new criticism. Some accused her of having profited from her favored position during Salazar's regime, a charge she hotly denied, claiming "I always sang fado without thinking of politics." Fado itself came under fire for being reactionary and fatalistic, and there were those who felt that the country would benefit both culturally and emotionally if the genre were banished in favor of the more international rhythms of rock and jazz. Pop fado emerged, adding drums and clarinet to traditional guitar accompaniment, and performers like **Maria da Fé** sang to a more positive jazz beat, while **Tereza Tarouca** revived the classical aristocratic fado sung by fidalgos (those of noble birth), which was lighter and less urban. For a while, the new sounds seemed to put fado under the threat of extinction.

But the music of Amalia Rodrigues spoke as eloquently to Portugal's younger generation as it had to their parents, and fado refused to die. Her recording of "Grandola Vila Morena" swept the country at the end of the dictatorship, demonstrating that she was a true democrat, and the socialist government gave her the Order of Santiago, the nation's highest honor. Perhaps it was the singer's poor background that helped her to understand the people of her country better than anyone. "Five centuries ago, many Portuguese sailors roamed the world's seas," she said. "This is how the fado began. They were far from home and their loved ones, facing unknown worlds; they lived under difficult conditions and truly suffered, submitting to the uncertainties of fate. For us, the Portuguese, the fado is a kind of atavism." For decades, Portuguese continued to fall silent to listen when Amalia Rodrigues, the soul of her country, sang fado. When she died on October 6, 1999, the government declared a three-day period of national mourning, and all political activity in the country's general election campaign was suspended.

SOURCES:

"Amalia Rodrigues," in *The Economist*. October 16, 1999, p. 93.

"Fado in Manhattan," in *Time*. Vol 60, no. 13. September 29, 1952, p. 65.

"Folk Singers: The Joys of Suffering," in *Time*. Vol. 87, no. 25. June 24, 1966, p. 62.

"Folksingers: You Ain't Been Blue," in *Time*. Vol. 83, no. 6. February 7, 1964, pp. 68–69.

"High Priestess of Fado Singing Returns Nostalgically to Lisbon," in *The New York Times*. August 29, 1964, p. 8.

Mervin, Sabrina, and Carol Prunhuber, eds. *Women Around the World and Through the Ages*. Atomium, 1990, pp. 192–193.

Pareles, Jon. "Fado by Amalia Rodrigues," in *The New York Times*. November 6, 1990, p. C14.

"Queen of Sorrows," in *Newsweek*. Vol. 73, no. 6. February 10, 1969, pp. 76–77.

Sheperd, Richard F. "She Sings the Sad Fado," in *The New York Times*. June 12, 1966, sec. 2, p. 16D.

Wheeler, Douglas L. *Historical Dictionary of Portugal*. London: Scarecrow Press, 1993.

Karin Loewen Haag,
freelance writer, Athens, Georgia

Rodríguez, Ana (1938—)

Anti-Castro Cuban political activist and author.

Name variations: Ana Rodriguez. Born in Cuba on April 17, 1938; daughter of Filiberto Rodríguez and Juana Hernandez Rodríguez; attended University of Havana and the Cetec University.

Confined in Cuba as a political prisoner (1961–79); emigrated to United States (1980); wrote Diary of a Survivor, *inspired by her 19-year prison term, to bring attention to the human-rights abuses occurring in Cuban women's prisons (1995).*

Ana Rodríguez was born in 1938 and grew up in a middle-class family near Havana, Cuba, during the reign of dictator Fulgencio Batista. While attending high school and the University of Havana, she was involved in the anti-Batista movement and was initially a supporter of revolutionary Fidel Castro, despite reservations about his Communist connections. Following Castro's 1959 takeover of the Cuban government, Rodríguez's disillusionment with Communist rule led to her participation in the pro-democratic Cuban underground. Her activities included distributing anti-Castro propaganda and assisting in smuggling Cuban government documents to the American embassy.

Arrested in 1961 and convicted of engaging in anti-revolutionary activities, she was sentenced to 30 years in prison, to be followed by

Ana Rodríguez

30 years of house arrest. Her moving story of life as a political prisoner in Cuba is recounted in her autobiography, *Diary of a Survivor: Nineteen Years in a Cuban Women's Prison*. The account chronicles the prolonged physical and mental abuse which was inflicted upon Rodríguez and her fellow political prisoners. Throughout the ordeal, Rodríguez maintained her dignity and self-respect while refusing to submit to political "re-education" programs.

Rodríguez was released from prison in 1979 as a result of negotiations between the Cuban and U.S. governments. Shortly thereafter, she and her family were granted exit visas and emigrated to Miami, where Rodríguez resumed medical studies she had begun 20 years earlier in Cuba.

SOURCES:

Rodríguez, Ana, and Glenn Garvin. *Diary of a Survivor: Nineteen Years in a Cuban Women's Prison*. NY: St. Martin's, 1995.

Linda S. Walton,
freelance writer, Grosse Pointe Shores, Michigan

Rodríguez, Evangelina (1879–1947)

Dominican Republic family planning advocate, educator, social reformer, and her nation's first woman physician, who risked her life on countless occasions opposing the Trujillo dictatorship. Name variations: Evangelina Rodriquez; Andrea Evangelina Rodríguez Perozo. Born out of wedlock as Andrea Evangelina Rodríguez Perozo in Higuey, Dominican Republic, in 1879; died in San Pedro de Macoris, Dominican Republic, on January 11, 1947; University of the Dominican Republic, medical degree, 1909; attended University of Paris, graduating in 1925; never married; children: one adopted daughter, Selisete.

Became the first Dominican woman physician (1909); studied in France (1921–25); after returning home, worked to improve the lives of the poor, particularly women.

Evangelina Rodríguez began her life in extremely unpromising circumstances in 1879 in Higuey, Dominican Republic; she was born female, out of wedlock, and of part-African descent. As an infant, she was first abandoned by her mother; then her father abandoned her, passing her back to her mother. Evangelina's grandmother provided her with shelter and some emotional support, but life was hard for the young girl, who along with her grandmother earned a precarious living by selling *gofio*, a sweet made from ground corn and sugar, on the streets of their town. Although her impoverished and illiterate father, who worked in the sugar cane indus-

try, would occasionally visit her, Evangelina never was able to discover anything about her mother, who disappeared from her life without a trace.

Rodríguez grew up in San Pedro de Macoris, which at that time was the most important city in the Dominican Republic. Although officially abolished, de facto slavery still existed, and a highly segregated society based on skin color and racial identity determined virtually all aspects of life. To resist these discriminations, Afro-Dominicans practiced solidarity, and a number of organizations enabled them to survive as a community. A black ladies' social club embracing all classes showed interest in Evangelina, who from her earliest years gave evidence of being both intelligent and ambitious. By selling *gofio*, Rodríguez was able to buy supplies for primary school, where tuition was free. Secondary school, however, represented a major hurdle, but good fortune intervened. A private secondary school for girls had recently opened its doors. Though its high tuition made it impossible for Rodríguez, the school's headmistress, **Anacaona Moscoso**, found her a job teaching adult literacy classes at a local night school, thus enabling her both to subsist and pay tuition.

After completing her secondary schooling, Rodríguez continued her work as a teacher. Then in October 1903, she began to study medicine at the University of the Dominican Republic. She received her medical degree in 1909, the first woman in the Dominican Republic to achieve this. Since there were sufficient doctors already practicing in San Pedro de Macoris, Rodríguez chose to begin her career in the small town of Ramon Santana. Here, confronted with poverty and social injustice, she treated poor patients free of charge or for the few centavos they could spare. Rodríguez also handed out great quantities of medicine for free, realizing that her patients simply could not afford them. For over a decade, she treated the poor, saving little money with which to make possible her professional dream, of embarking on more advanced studies in the specialized areas of gynecology and pediatrics.

During her years in Ramon Santana, Rodríguez became more politically aware as she witnessed the exploitation of peasants and sugar-cane workers, both by the local white elite caste and by U.S. corporations which took over the most valuable land in the area. In later years, she would also clash with the one individual who in her eyes embodied all the evils besetting her destitute nation, the dictator Rafael Trujillo.

In 1921, having finally saved sufficient funds, Rodríguez sailed for France, where she studied gynecology, obstetrics, and pediatrics at the University of Paris, graduating in 1925. Once back in the Dominican Republic, she worked even more effectively with her indigent patients, treating their illnesses, delivering their babies, and offering medical counsel. Increasingly aware of the social roots of many illnesses, she also moved into the area of social work. An alarmingly high incidence of sexually transmitted illnesses convinced her that prevention was almost always a more desirable strategy than cure. She began to visit local prostitutes where they worked, giving them advice and free medical treatment. As a result, Rodríguez found herself at the storm center of criticism and opposition by local conservative elements, especially the Roman Catholic clergy who condemned the "immoral and sinful" nature of her philosophy of medicine, in particular her advocacy of birth control and family planning. Her response to administering to prostitutes was uncompromising: "Yes, I go there; they are not bad women, they are just poor women who cannot find other work."

By the 1930s, when the Trujillo dictatorship was establishing an iron grip on the Dominican Republic, Rodríguez was using her hours away from her medical practice to actively participate in a small but vigorous women's movement. Advocating women's suffrage and broad social and economic reforms, Dominican feminists published a journal, *Femina*, to which Rodríguez contributed articles. She also published poetry in local journals and newspapers, and even wrote a novel entitled *Selisete*, named after her adopted daughter. By the late 1930s, Rodríguez had become an outspoken opponent of the Trujillo dictatorship—something that endangered her life and cost her many friendships and potential allies in her medical mission to assist the poor. Her political consciousness, already significantly raised during her years of study in France, was further sharpened by contacts with Republican refugees from the Spanish Civil War, who brought to the Dominican Republic radical notions of social change, including plans for peasant emancipation based on agrarian reform and an agrarian bank system.

Then tragedy struck. Rodríguez began to show signs of mental illness, probably paranoid schizophrenia. Eventually, she neglected herself physically and became ever more defiant of those who had long chosen to ostracize her for her radical views. Mocked for being an "ugly black woman," she retaliated by flaunting her Afro-Dominican heritage, no longer straightening her hair but braiding it in Afro style. She now chose to dress in the fashion of poor black

women, and wore men's shoes instead of the high heels favored by the upper classes of the island. As Rodríguez's illness progressed, her adopted daughter's father arrived to take her into his own home. "I get poison pen letters under my door," she said. "Even in the street when I pass by, people throw insults at me." Although the torments did not seem to break her spirit, in private she confessed to a friend that the taunts did hurt deeply, "For them I'm either kept by a man or not interested in men." Like so many Dominican women, Rodríguez had been scarred by a *machismo* culture profoundly destructive of the essential humanity of half of the nation's population.

In 1946, a massive strike of sugar-cane workers in the eastern part of the Dominican Republic seriously threatened the stability of the Trujillo dictatorship. Trujillo's response was typically brutal. He sent some of his most notorious enforcers to San Pedro and La Romana, where pro-strike was strongest. Several strike leaders were arrested and hanged in public, with their bodies left suspended for days to serve as a deterrent to any further labor militancy. Because of her well-known opposition to Trujillo, the regime sent out agents to find the mentally im-

Dominican Republic stamp honoring Evangelina Rodríguez, issued 1985.

paired but still defiant Rodríguez, whom it called a "Communist instigator of a workers' rebellion." The order was given that she be found dead or alive. Eventually she was found, on one of the long treks she often made on foot between the towns of Pedro Sanchez and Miches. Taken to San Pedro, she was mercilessly interrogated, finally being released on a deserted track near Hato Mayor. For a woman already suffering from mental illness, malnutrition, and exhaustion, this would be a mortal blow. On January 11, 1947, Rodríguez died in San Pedro de Macoris, much mourned by thousands of her poor patients who had remained loyal to her even as she wasted away in both mind and body. The Dominican Republic honored Evangelina Rodríguez by depicting her on a commemorative postage stamp issued on September 26, 1985.

SOURCES:

"Evangelina Rodriguez 1879–1947," in *People* [London]. Vol. 19, no. 1, 1992, p. 21.

Huston, Perdita. *Motherhood by Choice: Pioneers in Women's Health and Family Planning.* NY: The Feminist Press, 1992.

Zaglul, Antonio. *Despreciada en la Vida y Olvidada en la Muerte: Biografía de Evangelina Rodríguez, la Primera Médica Dominicana.* Santo Domingo: Editora Taller, 1980.

John Haag,
Associate Professor of History,
University of Georgia, Athens, Georgia

Rodríguez de Tió, Lola

(1843–1924)

Puerto Rican writer and political activist. Name variations: Lola Rodriguez de Tio. Born in San Germán, Puerto Rico, on September 14, 1843; died in Havana, Cuba, on November 10, 1924; daughter of Sebastián Rodríguez de Astudillo (dean of judiciary in Puerto Rico) and Carmen Ponce de León; married Bonocio Tió Segarra (a publicist and poet), in 1863; children: Patria (b. 1865) and Mercedes (1870–1873).

Selected writings: Mis Cantares *(My Songs, 1876);* Claros y Nieblas *(Fair Weather and Fog, 1885);* Mi Libro de Cuba *(My Book on Cuba, 1893);* Claros de Sol *(Sunshine).*

Revered in both Cuba and Puerto Rico, Lola Rodríguez de Tió used her talents as a writer and poet to promote Puerto Rican liberty and democracy at a time of Spanish dominance. She was born into the island's ruling class on September 14, 1843, the daughter of Sebastián Rodríguez de Astudillo, dean of the Magistracy of Puerto Rico, and **Carmen Ponce de León**, who counted among her ancestors Ponce de León, the explorer and first governor of the colony. Rodríguez de Tió was a bright child, and her instruction in religious schools and from private tutors was guided by her mother, an educated, well-read woman. It was rare for women to be educated in Puerto Rico; most women, especially poor women, were illiterate. It was rarer still for a woman to be an intellectual, but Rodríguez de Tió, who had shown early promise as a poet, was supported and encouraged by poet **Ursula Cardona de Quinones**. Her understanding of the disparity of opportunity for women made Rodríguez de Tió one of Latin America's most influential early feminists.

At age 20, she married Bonocio Tió Segarra, a respected and influential journalist and poet. Partners in life and politics, the couple were a thorn in the side of the government. The colony of Puerto Rico had been long abused, suffering corruption and brutality under Spain's colonial governors. Puerto Rico's visionary patriot Eugenio María de Hostos, who would spend much of his life in exile, was an important influence on Rodríguez de Tió. His eloquent writings inspired many others to call for independence from Spain. Rodríguez de Tió's home in Mayaguez became a salon where the leading intellectuals, including Hostos, discussed politics and called for revolution. Forthright in her opposition, she boldly challenged the government.

The work for which Rodríguez de Tió is best known, and which caused her to be deported, was "La Borinqueña." In 1868, she composed a fiery lyric for a traditional melody, then read it aloud at a literary gathering at her home to immediate acclaim. "Awake, Borinqueños, for they've given the signal!," it begins. "Awake from your sleep, for it's time to fight!" "La Borinqueña" became Puerto Rico's national anthem, although Rodríguez de Tió's lyrics were later replaced with the more sentimental lyrics of Manuel Fernandez Juncos. When the Lares Uprising of 1868 brought about a repressive response from the government, Rodríguez de Tió and her husband, given hours to leave the island, went into exile in Caracas, Venezuela. They grew closer to Hostos who was already living there, and Rodríguez de Tió was a matron of honor at his wedding in 1878.

The family was finally allowed to return to Puerto Rico in 1885, but once again Rodríguez de Tió's writings drew the wrath of the government. "Nochebuena," a tribute to political prisoners, was published in 1887, the "terrible year" of the "Componte." In 1889, Rodríguez de Tió and her family were exiled to Cuba. She would devote the rest of her life to achieving independence for both her homeland and Cuba, but would never again live in Puerto Rico.

Their political activity for Cuban independence caused Rodríguez de Tió and her husband to be expelled from Havana in 1892. They joined a group of Cuban exiles in New York City, where Rodríguez de Tió met Cuban patriot and poet José Martí, who regarded her as an equal in poetry and in politics. This period in her life was one of intense political activity—the group of political exiles created the Cuban Revolutionary Party in 1895. When Martí was killed in Cuba later that year, the exiles carried on their efforts through political clubs. Rodríguez de Tió was elected president of "Ruis Rivera" in 1896, and secretary of another club, "Caridad," in 1897. She and her family returned to Cuba in 1899 after the Spanish-American War, and she worked for the rest of her life for social justice and the betterment of the condition of women in Cuba.

Rodríguez de Tió became a member of the Cuban Academy of Arts and Letters in 1910, and was named Patron of the Galician Beneficent Society in 1911. She remained active in politics, and served as inspector general of the private schools in Havana and in the Ministry of Education. Lola Rodríguez de Tió is a national hero in Puerto Rico, and while her worth as a poet is a matter of dispute among literary critics, her place in Puerto Rican letters is not. Although her Romantic style is considered derivative by some, her verses are well known and have been widely influential. Rubén Darío, considered Spanish America's greatest modern poet, called Rodríguez de Tió "the Daughter of the Isles." Chief among her works are *Mis Cantares* (My Songs, 1876), *Claros y Nieblas* (Fair Weather and Fog, 1885), *Mi Libro de Cuba* (My Book on Cuba, 1893), and *Claros de Sol* (Sunshine). She died in Havana on November 10, 1924, at age 81.

SOURCES:

Notable Hispanic American Women. Book 2. Detroit, MI: Gale Research, 1998.

Votaw, Carmen Delgado. *Puerto Rican Women*. Washington, DC: National Conference of Puerto Rican Women, 1995.

Linda S. Walton,
freelance writer, Grosse Pointe Shores, Michigan

Roebling, Emily (1844–1903)

American woman who supervised the building of the Brooklyn Bridge. Name variations: Emily Warren Roebling; Mrs. Washington Roebling. Born Emily Warren in 1844 in Cold Spring, New York; died in Trenton, New Jersey, and buried in Cold Spring, New York, in 1903; *daughter of Phebe (Lickley) Warren and Sylvanus Warren; married Washington Roebling (a chief engineer), on January 18, 1865, in Cold Spring, New York; children: John A. Roebling II (b. 1867).*

Met Washington Roebling (1864); New York Bridge Company established and John Roebling hired as chief engineer (1867); John Roebling died (July 6, 1869); Washington Roebling became chief engineer of the Brooklyn Bridge project (1869); illness of Washington Roebling (1872); Emily took crash course in engineering (1872); began to act as unofficial chief engineer for Brooklyn Bridge (1872); New York State Legislature took over Brooklyn Bridge project (1875); Tay Bridge disaster (December 1879); Emily escorted Ferdinand de Lesseps on his visit to New York (February 1880); crossed Brooklyn Bridge for the first time (spring 1880); Trustees of Brooklyn Bridge attempted to dismiss Washington Roebling (1882); defended her husband before the American Society of Civil Engineers (1882); Brooklyn Bridge opened (May 24, 1883); moved to Trenton, New Jersey (1884).

Emily Roebling

On May 24, 1883, the Brooklyn Bridge was opened in a ceremony presided over by the president of the United States. It was a day of national celebration. Almost every state in the union sent a representative, and thousands of spectators crammed into specially built bleachers to witness the proceedings. Businesses in Brooklyn and New York were closed. The bridge, which had taken 13 years to build at the cost of $21 million and 20 lives, was the longest span in the world, and represented an engineering feat of monumental proportions.

For 11 of those 13 years, the construction of the Brooklyn Bridge had been supervised by Emily Roebling, wife of chief engineer Washington Roebling. Washington had inherited the project from his father John, who died of tetanus after an accident in the spring of 1869 while surveying the site. In 1872, Washington Roebling in turn became ill, and supervision of the project fell to his wife.

Born in Cold Spring, New York, in 1844, Emily Warren came from a prominent county family. Her father Sylvanus Warren was a local businessman and friend of Washington Irving, the author of *Rip Van Winkle* and *The Legend of Sleepy Hollow*. Engineering ran in the Warren family. Emily's brother, G.K. Warren, was a general in the Union Army, had taught mathematics at the West Point Military Academy, and was passionately interested in military engineering. Notes David McCullough, "It seems his influence had much to do with her . . . subsequent interest in science, and botany in particular." During the latter part of the Civil War, G.K. Warren was a member of the commission assigned to examine the construction of the Union Pacific Railway and was charged with surveying the Gettysburg battlefield.

By and by it was common gossip that hers was the real mind behind the great work and that this most monumental engineering triumph of the age was actually the doing of a woman.

—David McCullough

Emily Roebling's early life seems to have been a conventional one. Her future husband had been a colonel in the Union Army, and G.K. Warren's aide de camp. The couple married on January 18, 1865, after a six-week whirlwind romance. Writing to his sister **Elvira Roebling**, Washington described his new wife:

> She is dark brown eyed, slightly pug-nosed, lovely mouth and teeth, . . . and a most entertaining talker, which is a mighty good thing you know, I myself being so stupid. She is a little above medium size and has a most lovely complexion.

After the war, Washington returned to work for his father's engineering firm. He and Emily moved to the city of Brooklyn and purchased a lovely house overlooking the harbor. Brooklyn had grown into the third largest city in the United States, surpassing both Chicago and Boston in size. The only way to cross the East River to Manhattan, however, was by ferry. In winter, crossings were often suspended due to ice.

In 1867, John Roebling was hired as chief engineer by the New York Bridge Company. The company proposed to build a bridge which would link Brooklyn and Manhattan. There could be no piers or drawbridges, said a contemporary commentator, the bridge had to take "one grand flying leap from shore to shore." The plan called for a 5,989-foot suspension bridge, strung across the East River by steel cables which were to be anchored by two monumental towers. John

Roebling characterized the Brooklyn Bridge as a part of "the great flow of civilization from East towards the West." The bridge was not without its detractors, however. A representative of the Standard Oil Company argued that it would divert trade to Philadelphia. Landlords were furious when both New York and Brooklyn expropriated their properties to make way for the project. Others, such as harbor pilots and sea captains, claimed the bridge would be a hazard to navigation. Several lawsuits resulted, all of which failed to halt construction.

By the time Washington Roebling became chief engineer of the project at the age of 32, the foundations of the towers were under construction. Two pneumatic caissons, like diving bells, were employed. They were made without bottoms, half the size of a city block, and compressed air was pumped into them to keep water out as workers labored inside them, excavating a portion of the floor of the East River. The men entered the caissons' atmosphere through air locks. As the workers dug, the caissons sank farther down into the river bed.

Some of the workers began to suffer from a mysterious disease. Men dropped dead on the spot. Others complained of terrible pains in their joints and of paralysis. When doctors finally diagnosed their affliction as the bends, it was too late to help. Caused by too-rapid decompression, nitrogen bubbles were released into their bloodstreams with crippling results. Washington Roebling soon fell victim to the condition. Unable to move and virtually blind, he became a bedridden invalid. The only person he was able to communicate with was his wife Emily. His condition remained a closely guarded secret.

Without any formal training, Emily Roebling undertook a crash course in variable calculus and engineering. In the beginning, she functioned as a vital link between her husband and the workers in the field. As Edward Ellis noted, "She served as an extension of his brain, and functioned as field marshall on the construction site." As time went on, however, Emily undertook ever-increasing responsibilities and was soon treated by many as the chief engineer of the project. She often inspected the bridge personally, and also attended social functions on her husband's behalf.

Emily Roebling was responsible for all of her husband's correspondence with bridge officials. It seems probable that she did more than merely transcribe his orders. As McCullough points out: "By and by it was common gossip that hers was the real mind behind the great work and that this most monumental engineering triumph of the age was actually the doing of a woman." The trustees of the project grumbled over her increasing involvement, and newspapers often commented on it. One newspaper article described her as having a "scientific bent of mind."

The master mechanic of the bridge, E.F. Farrington, was the first to cross the Brooklyn Bridge, in August 1876, riding a chair slung between the two towers. Farrington also gave a popular series of lectures to packed audiences. A reporter for the *New York Star* wrote, "It is whispered among the knowing ones over the river that

Mr. F's manuscript is in the handwriting of a lady, whose style and calligraphy are already familiar in the office of the Brooklyn Bridge." Although there is no proof of this assertion, many people at the time believed it to be true.

Controversy between members of the Board of Trustees was frequent, and Emily often mediated disputes in order to safeguard her husband's health. When furious board members stormed into the house one day, she tactfully cautioned them not to upset her husband before they went in to see him. Washington described her role as "invaluable." "I had a strong tower

Brooklyn Bridge

to lean upon," he said, "my wife, a woman of infinite tact and wisest counsel."

When construction officials or contractors called at the Brooklyn Heights house, Emily Roebling always exhibited a perfect command of the technical details of the project. Many contractors began to correspond with her personally. Over the years, she dealt with various scandals connected with the bridge and its suppliers. When a furor erupted in 1879 concerning the honesty of the Edge Moor Iron Company, company representatives wrote to Emily and assured her of their good intentions. No mention of her husband was made.

At various times, construction of the bridge was delayed due to lack of funds. By 1875, however, the New York State Legislature took over the project. The city of Brooklyn paid for and owned two-thirds of the bridge, while New York City footed one-third of the cost and owned a corresponding share. Thus, until its completion, the project was well funded.

But the Tay Bridge disaster of December 1879 renewed public skepticism about the bridge's safety. One of the largest and most celebrated bridges in the world, the Tay Bridge in Scotland collapsed during a gale. A train which was crossing it at the time dropped 90 feet into frigid waters, killing all 70 passengers. A board of inquiry blamed the engineer, Sir Thomas Bouch, for a poor design that did not accurately anticipate wind loads. On New Year's Day, the banner headline in the *New York Herald* read: "Will The Tay Disaster Be Repeated Between New York and Brooklyn?"

Emily Roebling appreciated the delicate calculations which had gone into the design of the Brooklyn Bridge. As she watched the spans progress from the window of her home, she no doubt worried whether the Tay Bridge disaster might be repeated. After all, the East River was a stormy one and, like the Firth of Tay, it was located near the sea. Nonetheless, she remained confident of the designs of her father-in-law and her husband.

The French diplomat Ferdinand de Lesseps arrived in New York in late February 1880. After inspection of the bridge in the company of Emily, he told reporters that he was greatly impressed. Later in the week, when he announced to the American Society of Civil Engineers that he was planning to construct a canal across Panama, Roebling was among the women present.

In the same month, the annual dinner of the alumni of the famous Rensselaer Polytechnic In-

stitute took place. Several of the assistant engineers from the Brooklyn Bridge project were invited, and the main speaker of the evening described the bridge and its construction. As much was said about the role of Emily as that of her husband. The assistant engineers in particular idolized her. In his after-dinner remarks, an engineer proposed a special toast:

> Gentleman, I know that the name of a woman should not be lightly spoken in public, but I believe you will acquit me any lack of delicacy or of reverence when I utter half articulated upon my lips, the name Mrs. Washington Roebling.

From the window of his home, Washington watched the bridge rise, year by year, brick by brick. Emily remarked later that he had not spent that much time at the window. One glance of his "practiced eye" told him if things were progressing properly. Although his eyesight improved over the years, Washington's world still remained somewhat blurry.

In the spring of 1880, when the steel-beamed floor was put into place, Emily drove to the construction site, where she met the members of the Board of Trustees. It was a crucial moment, as the bridge now spanned the East River. The group set out across wooden planks that had been erected on the steel floor. Leading the way was Emily Roebling, accompanied by the mayor of Brooklyn, William Howell. Seagulls screeched overhead, while ships steamed quietly past below. The wind tugged at the hats of guests. It was the first crossing of the Brooklyn Bridge on a roadway. When the impressed group arrived in New York, a bottle of champagne was uncorked and the assembled guests drank to Emily's health.

In 1882, when a dispute erupted among the Board of Trustees over the cost of the project, an attempt was made to unseat Washington Roebling as chief engineer. One of the few members to defend him was Seth Low. Afterwards, Emily wrote to Low from Newport:

> I take the liberty of writing to express my heartfelt gratitude for your generous defense of Mr. Roebling at the last meeting of the Board of Trustees. Your words were a most agreeable surprise to us as we had understood you were working in full sympathy with the Mayors of the two cities and the Comptroller of New York. . . . Can you see me at your office some morning[?]

In the same year, she addressed the American Society of Civil Engineers, the first woman ever to do so. The confidence she displayed and her intimate knowledge of the details of the project greatly impressed those present. Her address in Washington's defense renewed their faith in her husband as the chief engineer.

Because Washington Roebling was too ill to attend, the Roeblings watched the opening festivities of the Brooklyn Bridge from the vantage point of their Brooklyn Heights home. After the ceremony, Emily entertained President Chester Arthur, who had once been the customs collector of New York harbor. Other dignitaries included Grover Cleveland, then governor of New York, and Franklin Edson, mayor of New York City. Washington Roebling made a brief appearance, then returned to his room.

Fighting ignorance, corruption, and the elements, all three Roeblings had built the Brooklyn Bridge. A French traveler, Paul Bourget, recorded his impressions of the colossal span:

> You see great ships passing beneath it and this indisputable evidence of its height confuses the mind. But walk over it, feel the quivering of the monstrous trellis of iron and steel interwoven for the length of sixteen hundred feet at a height of one hundred and thirty feet above the water; see the trains that pass over it in both directions, and the stream of boats passing beneath your very body, while carriages come and go, and foot passengers hasten along, an eager crowd, and you will own that these people have a right to plume themselves on their audacity, on the go-ahead which has never flinched.

After the completion of the bridge, the Roeblings moved to Trenton, New Jersey. Since his health remained fragile, Washington never undertook another engineering project. Neither did his wife, which is perhaps indicative of her attitude towards the experience. Emily died at the age of 47, in 1903, and she was buried in her home town of Cold Spring. Washington lived to be 84.

A conventional woman by the standards of the day, Emily Roebling supervised the building of the Brooklyn Bridge only when her husband proved incapable of doing so. While a sense of loyalty certainly motivated her, the Roebling family also faced financial disaster had she not shouldered the burden. Throughout the building of the Brooklyn Bridge, she remained her husband's faithful confidant and companion, safeguarding his health and privacy. She played the role of emissary, diplomat, secretary, purchasing agent, spokesperson, and engineer. Without her efforts the Brooklyn Bridge might never have been completed, and the United States would have been bereft of its first monumental architectural achievement.

SOURCES:

Fiske, Stephen. *Off-Hand Portraits of Prominent New Yorkers.* NY: Lockwood & Son, 1884.

Jackson, Donald C. *Great American Bridges and Dams.* Washington: The Preservation Press, 1988.

Hopkins, H.J. *A Span of Bridges.* London: David & Charles, 1970.

McCullough, David. *The Great Bridge.* NY: Simon and Schuster, 1972.

Steinmann, David B., and Sara Ruth Watson. *Bridges and Their Builders.* NY: Dover, 1957.

Woleher, Curt. "The Bridging of America: The Roebling Saga," in *American Heritage.* April 1991.

SUGGESTED READING:

Schuyler, Hamilton. *The Roeblings: A Century of Engineers, Bridge Builders and Industrialists.* Princeton, NJ: Princeton University Press, 1931.

Hugh A. Stewart, M.A.,
Guelph, Ontario, Canada

Roebling, Mary G. (1906–1994)

American banker and first female governor of the New York Stock Exchange. Born Mary Gindhart in West Collingswood, New Jersey, on July 29, 1906; died in Trenton, New Jersey, on October 25, 1994; daughter of Isaac Gindhart, Jr. (a telephone company employee) and Mary W. (Simon) Gindhart (a music teacher); graduated from Moorestown High School;

Mary G. Roebling

*attended finance classes at the University of Pennsylvania; attended banking and finance courses at New York University; married Arthur Herbert (died); married Siegfried Roebling (a banking and steel-cable magnate who was the grandson of Washington and *Emily Roebling, died 1936); children: (first marriage) Elizabeth Herbert (Mrs. E.H. Dutch); (second marriage) Paul Roebling.*

Became first woman to head a major bank when she became president of the Trenton Trust Company (1937); became first woman to hold a policy-making position on any major stock exchange (1958).

Mary Roebling's early years as a young mother and widow gave no indication that she would become a trailblazer for women in America's financial industry. The daughter of Isaac D. Gindhart, Jr., a telephone company employee, and **Mary W. Gindhart**, a music teacher, Roebling grew up and completed high school in Moorestown, New Jersey. While still a teen, she married Arthur Herbert, and three years later found herself a widow with a baby daughter. Out of necessity she became a secretary at a Philadelphia brokerage firm, while taking finance classes at the University of Pennsylvania at night. She left her employment to marry successful industrialist Siegfried Roebling, only to find herself widowed again, with another infant, in 1936.

Upon her husband's death, Roebling inherited a controlling interest in the Trenton Trust Company, an institution reeling from the effects of the Great Depression. Although she had no financial need to work, she was determined to restore the financial health of the bank. Roebling became president in 1937 and chair of the board of directors in 1941. Her lack of experience in the banking industry prompted her to attend classes in finance at New York University over a six-year period, but much of Roebling's success stemmed from her ability to promote her bank with women customers. Her strategies included holding financial teas to encourage wealthy women to establish trust funds with Trenton Trust. Known for her personal style (she was voted the "best-dressed banking woman" in 1958), Roebling promoted her bank in the same way by hiring professional window dressers to give Trenton Trust a new look. The small touches, such as her sponsorship of art shows, the bank's distribution of thousands of living shamrocks on St. Patrick's Day, and the displaying of her customers' merchandise at the bank, made a large difference. Her success in attracting women customers resulted in a 20-year increase in assets, from $17 million in 1937 to $90 million by 1960. In the process of making her bank wealthy, Roebling acquired a fortune of her own; she was considered one of America's ten richest women by 1957, with personal assets estimated at between $125 million and $200 million. She was driven in a silver Rolls-Royce, wore couture clothing and hung Picassos in her bathrooms, and while traveling once was robbed of the $375,000 worth of jewelry and furs she had with her in her hotel suite.

Because of her success and stature as the first woman to head a major American bank, Roebling was elected the first woman governor of the American Stock Exchange in 1958. She served as one of the three public members on that board until 1962, and was responsible for bringing the public's perspective to board deliberations. In her rapid rise through the ranks of business, Roebling did not forget to create professional opportunities for other women. She hired only women tellers at Trenton Trust's main branch and founded the American Women's Council, of which she was a director. She was also a vocal advocate for a female vice-president of the United States.

Roebling herself never served in elected office, but maintained a strong presence in government, business and community affairs. Her administration of Trenton Trust resulted in leadership positions with other companies, including Wings, Inc., the Fleron Supply Company, the Colonial Operating Company, the Standard Fire Insurance Company, and the Walker-Gordon Laboratory Company. She also served as an emeritus member of the advisory committee on women in the services for the U.S. Defense Department, as well as a vice-president of the National Defense Transportation Association. On the international front, Roebling was a delegate to the Atlantic Congress of NATO, and a trustee of the U.S. Council of the International Chamber of Commerce.

Trenton Trust was acquired by National State Bank in Elizabeth, New Jersey, in 1972, and Roebling served until 1984 as chair of the merged banks, which had assets of $1.2 billion. In 1978, she was involved in organizing the Women's Bank N.A. of Denver, the first federally chartered bank organized by women. Roebling died at her home in Trenton, New Jersey, in 1994.

SOURCES:

Graham, Judith, ed. *Current Biography*. Vol. 56, no. 1. January 1995.

Moritz, Charles, ed. *Current Biography Yearbook 1960*. NY: H.W. Wilson, 1960.

Time. November 7, 1994, p. 23.

Linda S. Walton,
freelance writer, Grosse Pointe Shores, Michigan

Roebling, Mrs. Washington

(1844–1903).

See Roebling, Emily.

Rogatis, Teresa de (1893–1979)

Italian composer, guitarist, pianist, and lecturer. Name variations: married name was Feninger. Born in Naples, Italy, on October 15, 1893; died in Naples on January 8, 1979; married; children: Mario Feninger (a pianist).

Born in Naples in 1893, Teresa de Rogatis was a child prodigy who gave her first recital at age seven. She studied piano, composition, counterpoint, harmony, conducting, and voice at the Conservatorio San Pietro at Majella in Naples. While in Egypt on a concert tour, she married and settled in Cairo. In the late 1950s, Rogatis helped found the National Conservatory of Egypt, where she also taught piano and guitar. She returned to Italy in 1963 and continued to teach and compose. Of over 60 works written by her, half were for piano. Her son Mario Feninger, who was also a concert pianist, founded the Teresa de Rogatis Foundation to publish and distribute his mother's compositions.

John Haag,
Athens, Georgia

Rogers, Adela (1894–1988).

See St. Johns, Adela Rogers.

Rogers, Clara Kathleen (1844–1931)

English-born composer, singer and teacher. Name variations: Clara Doria. Born Clara Kathleen Barnett in Cheltenham, England, on January 14, 1844; died in Boston, Massachusetts, on March 8, 1931; daughter of John Barnett (a composer); married Henry Munroe Rogers (a Boston attorney), in 1878.

Born in Cheltenham, England, in 1844, Clara Kathleen Rogers showed an early interest in composition. She became, at age 12, the youngest student ever accepted by the Leipzig Conservatory, where she studied singing and piano, but not composition, since this area was at the time closed to women. After graduating from Leipzig in 1860 with honors, Rogers continued her studies with Hans von Bülow and others in Berlin, and began a singing career. She made her debut under the name Clara Doria in Milan, and enjoyed a successful career in Italy and England. In 1871, she made her New York debut, but her performing career ended seven

years later with her marriage to Henry Munroe Rogers, a Boston attorney. She then concentrated on composing, although she occasionally appeared as a performer to play her own works and was appointed a professor at the New England Conservatory of Music in 1902. Most of her compositions were songs that used choice texts, and she set them effectively within the then-reigning tradition of German Romanticism; many of these works remain eminently singable and a number of them deserve to be revived. She also composed violin and cello Sonatas and, in her student years, crafted a String Quartet. Rogers wrote several books on the art of singing as well as a three-volume autobiography.

John Haag,
Athens, Georgia

Rogers, Dale Evans (1912–2001)

American actress, singer and author who as Dale Evans teamed with Roy Rogers to star in numerous Westerns for Republic Studios. Name variations: Dale Evans; Frances Fox. Born Frances Octavia Smith in Uvalde, Texas, on October 31, 1912; died in Apple Valley, California, on February 7, 2001; daughter of Walter Hillman and Bettie Sue (Wood) Smith; attended high school in Osceola, Arkansas; married Thomas Frederick Fox, in 1928 (divorced 1930); married Dale Butts (divorced); married Roy Rogers (an actor and singer), in 1947 (died 1998); children: (first marriage) Tom Fox, Jr. (b. 1929); (third marriage) Robin (1950–1952); Sandy (adopted); Dodie (adopted); Debbie (adopted); stepchildren: Cheryl, Linda, and Dusty.

Selected films—as Dale Evans: Orchestra Wives (1942); Girl Trouble (1942); Swing Your Partner (1943); The West Side Kid (1943); In Old Oklahoma (1943); The Cowboy and the Senorita (1944); Song of Nevada (1944); The Yellow Rose of Texas (1944); Don't Fence Me In (1945); Hitchhike to Happiness (1945); Utah (1945); Sunset in El Dorado (1945); Heldorado (1946); My Pal Trigger (1946); Under Nevada Skies (1946); Song of Arizona (1946); Apache Rose (1947); Bells of San Angelo (1947); Slippy McGee (1948); The Golden Stallion (1949); Twilight in the Sierras (1950); Pals of the Golden West (1951).

Selected albums: (with Roy Rogers) The Bible Tells Me So, A Child's Introduction to the West, Christmas is Always, The Good Life, Hymns of Faith, In the Sweet By and By, Jesus Loves Me, Many Happy Trails, 16 Great Songs of the West, Sweet Hour of Prayer; (solo) Country Dale, Dale Evans Sings, Faith, Hope and Charity, Favorite Gospel Songs, Heart of the Country, It's Real, Reflections of Life, Sweeter as the Years Go By, Totally Free, Western Favorites.

Selected writings: Angel Unaware *(1953)*; My Spiritual Diary *(1955)*; Christmas is Always *(1958)*; Dearest Debbie *(1965)*; Salute to Sandy *(1965)*; Time Out Ladies! *(1966)*; The Woman at the Well *(1970)*; Where He Leads *(1974)*; Let Freedom Ring *(1975)*; Grandparents Can *(1983)*.

As a young teenage mother doing secretarial work at an insurance company, Dale Evans Rogers could not have envisioned that she would become one of the most popular Western film heroines of her generation. Born Frances Octavia Smith in 1912, she moved with her family from Uvalde, Texas, to Osceola, Arkansas, where she attended high school. Rogers was still a teenager when she met and married Tom Fox. Shortly after the birth of their son in 1929, Fox deserted his young bride, and Rogers made ends meet by working as a stenographer at an insurance company.

Rogers' placement with the company proved to be fortuitous. When her employers discovered she could sing, they found her work as a vocalist on a company-sponsored radio station. Her voice won her increasingly high-profile positions on radio programs in Memphis, Louisville, and Dallas, until she finally wound up a star on the Chicago airwaves. At the suggestion of a program director in Louisville, she took the name Dale Evans. She also met and married Dale Butts, a pianist and songwriter, during this time. They collaborated on a number of songs, including the widely popular "Will You Marry Me, Mr. Laramie?" Their personal collaboration was not as successful as their professional one, however, and the two divorced.

That hit song brought Rogers to the attention of a Hollywood scout, who suggested she try out for a part in Paramount's *Holiday Inn* in 1942. The movie stalled briefly in production (it was then made without her), so Rogers decided to sign a year-long contract with Twentieth Century-Fox. While waiting for a movie role, she maintained an active career by recording albums, entertaining U.S. military forces, and continuing her radio engagements with some of America's top programs.

Although she had two small roles in musicals, Rogers' contract with Twentieth Century-Fox expired without a major film debut. She next signed on with Republic, the studio that would produce nearly all of her films. Her break came in 1944, when she was offered the second female lead in *The Cowboy and the Senorita* starring another Republic actor, Roy Rogers. Audiences so delighted in the pairing of Roy and Dale that the two

made another 19 formula Westerns in the next three years. He became known as the "King of the Cowboys" and she earned the moniker "Queen of the West." The wholesome couple became familiar figures in over 30 Western-themed movies, including *Sunset in El Dorado* (1945), *Utah* (1945), *My Pal Trigger* (1946), *Under Nevada Skies* (1946), *Song of Arizona* (1946), *Bells of San Angelo* (1947), *The Golden Stallion* (1949), *Bells of Coronado* (1950), and *Pals of the Golden West* (1951). Much of Dale's success was driven by her gutsy heroines—characters of independence and brains who stood apart from the traditional Hollywood portrayal of helpless women in need of saving. Of her role as Toni Ames in *Don't Fence Me In* (1945), she noted, "I like to be active in a role, and hate namby-pamby heroines. Toni was a pleasant departure from the usual Western role, in which the girl just stands around while men do violent and admirable things." Her appearance in *Motion Picture Herald*'s poll as one of the top moneymakers of 1947—the first woman to do so—verified her stardom.

The Roy Rogers-Dale Evans pairing was successful off-screen as well. After Roy's wife **Arlene Rogers** died in 1946, Roy and Dale married the following year. In 1948, they collaborated on radio to create "The Roy Rogers Show," then moved the show to the new medium of television in 1951, producing the weekly series of half-hour Western films until 1957. The show proved to be hugely successful, earning some of the highest ratings for an action program at the time. Roy and Dale, along with Roy's Palomino stallion Trigger ("the smartest horse in the movies") and Dale's horse Buttermilk, became American icons; the show's enduring theme song, "Happy Trails to You," was one of Dale's compositions. At the height of their popularity there were some 2,000 fan clubs worldwide devoted to Dale and Roy, and their lucrative merchandising deals allowed innumerable American girls and boys to dress like their heroes in fringed clothing and holster belts. In addition to their own program, the pair guest-starred on numerous other television programs throughout the 1950s and made a brief comeback as television stars with an hour-long variety program, "The Roy Rogers and Dale Evans Show," in 1962. They also took their Western act on the road, making appearances on the rodeo circuit in colorful costumes. Dale was the only woman to receive star billing at Madison Square Garden when she appeared there in 1952 as part of the World Championship Rodeo.

Like his wife, Roy was a talented singer, and the two recorded both solo albums and collaborative efforts in music careers which spanned

Dale
Evans
Rogers

five deced. Dale record-
ed several albums for children and highlighted her distinct
brand of Western tunes. Her albums included some of her own compositions such as
"Aha, San Antone," which sold in excess of
200,000 copies. Roy and Dale Rogers debuted
the first of their Christian albums with the 1950
release *Hymns of Faith*. Both were committed
Christians, and their faith had a large impact on
their professional lives. They worked closely
with evangelist Billy Graham in his crusades, as
well as with theologian Norman Vincent Peale.
Many of their recordings are gospel-oriented
and much of their later television work was done
for Christian broadcasting. Dale also wrote the
well-known children's
song "The Bible Tells Me
So" ("Jesus loves me, this I know,
for the Bible tells me so").

Dale's faith was particularly evident in her
writings, several of which were inspired by personal tragedies. She wrote *Angel Unaware* about
her and Roy's first child, Robin, who was born
developmentally disabled and died shortly before her second birthday. It was a bestseller in
1953, and Dale donated the royalties to the National Association for Retarded Children. The
profits from her second book, *My Spiritual
Diary* (1955), also went to support the treatment of mental retardation, and enjoyed equal

popularity. When her nine-year-old adopted daughter Debbie died in a church bus accident in 1964, Dale penned a touching remembrance to her, published as *Dear Debbie*. The following year, another adopted child, Sandy, died of alcohol poisoning in Germany, and Dale wrote the tribute *Salute to Sandy*. Dale's autobiography, *The Woman at the Well* (1970), was another publishing success, selling over 275,000 hardcover copies. She had published 25 inspirational works by 1988, including *Time Out Ladies!* (1966), *Where He Leads* (1974), *Let Freedom Ring* (1975), and *Grandparents Can* (1983).

Roy and Dale Rogers showed no signs of slowing down even into their 70s. In 1985, they returned to television with the show "Happy Trails Theater," which featured the pair discussing their past films with guest stars. Dale had a chance to shine on her own as host of "The Dale Evans Show," which appeared the same year on the Trinity Christian broadcasting station. Still singing, she maintained an active concert and speaking schedule into the 1990s. Roy Rogers died in 1998. Dale Evans Rogers died at age 88, at her home in Apple Valley, California, in February 2001. The Roy Rogers and Dale Evans Museum, in Victorville, California, celebrates the memory of the sanitized, singing West presented in their films, and includes among its exhibits the original, now stuffed, Trigger and Buttermilk.

SOURCES:

Dent, Marjorie Candee, ed. *Current Biography Yearbook 1956*. NY: H.W. Wilson, 1956.

Katz, Ephraim. *The Film Encyclopedia*. 3rd ed. HarperCollins, 1998.

The New York Times. February 8, 2001, p. A28.

Parish, James Robert, and Michael R. Pitts. *Hollywood Songsters*. NY: Garland, 1991.

Linda S. Walton,
freelance writer, Grosse Pointe Shores, Michigan

Rogers, Deborah Read (1707–1774).

See Bache, Sarah for sidebar on Deborah Read.

Rogers, Edith Nourse (1881–1960)

U.S. congressional representative (1925–60) who served the longest span of any woman and gained a national reputation advancing the cause of the American veteran. Born Edith Francis Nourse on March 19, 1881, in Saco, Maine; died on September 10, 1960, in Boston, Massachusetts; daughter of Franklin D. Nourse (a mill manufacturer) and Edith Frances (Riversmith) Nourse; attended Rogers Hall, Lowell, Massachusetts, and Madame Julien's, Neuilly, France;

married John Jacob Rogers (a lawyer and U.S. congressional representative), in 1907.

When, in 1925, the 5th Congressional District of Massachusetts elected a vivacious, slightly plump woman in her mid-40s as its congressional representative, many lawmakers predicted that her legislative career would be brief indeed. At the time, she was only the sixth woman ever to have even been elected to the House of Representatives; none of her female predecessors had yet made a major mark there. Indeed, she herself planned to stay in the House of Representatives only a few years. Who would have thought that Edith Nourse Rogers would remain some 35 years, thereby establishing a record for the longest span of service ever held by a woman? And who would have thought that Rogers, who was never in the limelight, would become extremely influential behind the scenes, playing the leading role in the creation of both the Women's Army Corps, commonly known as the WACs, and the GI Bill of Rights?

On March 19, 1881, Edith Frances Nourse was born in Saco, Maine, a mill and shipping town about 15 miles south of Portland. A descendant of 17th-century Puritans, she could trace her ancestors to *Priscilla Alden, the subject of Henry Wadsworth Longfellow's poem "The Courtship of Miles Standish," and to **Rebecca Nurse** (or Nourse), hanged as a witch in Salem in 1692. Franklin Nourse, her Harvard-educated father, managed a large textile mill that inadvertently served as her private playground. Her mother **Edith Riversmith Nourse** engaged in volunteer work among the town's poor.

When Edith was 14, the Nourse family moved to Lowell, Massachusetts, long a textile town and located 25 miles from downtown Boston. There Franklin became mill agent for the city's second largest cotton firm. No longer educated by a private tutor, young Edith attended Lowell's Rogers Hall, a small private girls' school, from which she graduated in 1899. She completed her education at Madame Julien's, a finishing school in Neuilly, near Paris, France. Upon returning home, she lived a life typical of many upper-class young women, participating in Lowell's social, welfare, and Episcopal church activities while attending luncheon and theater parties in Boston.

In the fall of 1907, Edith Nourse married John Jacob Rogers, a graduate of Harvard University and its law school. Practicing law in Lowell with his brother-in-law, John Rogers ran for Congress in 1911 as a regular Republican. Defeating candidates from the Progressive (Bull Moose), De-

Nurse, Rebecca.
See Witchcraft Trials in Salem Village.

mocratic, and Socialist parties, he began a string of six straight victories. Upon arriving in Washington, D.C., Edith Nourse Rogers first lived the life of a socialite, in the process showing a flair for entertaining that she never lost.

Edith Rogers' life changed both markedly and permanently when she went to Europe in 1917. She accompanied her husband, who was part of a delegation of the House Foreign Affairs Committee involved in a "secret" unofficial mission to Britain. With the United States a full-scale belligerent in World War I, Edith threw herself into war work, taking the first step in what would be a veritable career of aiding American service personnel. As a member of a Red Cross party, she accompanied her husband to battle zones, in the process becoming so familiar with base and field hospitals that she left Europe as something of a national expert. As part of the Women's Overseas Service League, she held the status of inspector. One could find her at the early morning shift at the YMCA Eagle Hut in London or, wearing her Red Cross garb, caring for wounded doughboys in France. Upon returning home in early 1918, she became Washington's first "Gray Lady," a term used for dedicated war volunteers sporting gray uniforms. While John served briefly in the field artillery, Edith worked at Washington's Walter Reed military hospital, where she became known as the soldiers' "angel of mercy" and where she remained until 1922. Even after the armistice, she and her husband went back to Europe, there to visit hospitals and ambulance stations in England and France.

Still a member of Congress, John Rogers became a charter member of the American Legion; Edith Rogers joined its auxiliary. In 1922, President Warren G. Harding named Edith his personal representative in charge of assistance for disabled veterans, an appointment renewed by presidents Calvin Coolidge and Herbert Hoover. Her salary: $1.00 per year. Her task: inspecting veterans' hospitals. Crisscrossing the nation, often by plane, she visited every military hospital in the nation, often popping up unexpectedly. When the patients expressed any complaints, she took them personally to the White House. A number of reforms resulted. By now she was recognized as a national authority on such matters.

Edith Rogers' first foray into national politics began rather innocuously. In 1924, she served as a presidential elector for her husband's district. As secretary of all the electors, she was the first woman ever to deliver the official tally to the president of the Senate. That year her husband, who had reached the peak of his career, came

down with Hodgkin's disease, dying in March 1925. With the backing of ex-military personnel, business leaders, and party stalwarts, Edith Nourse Rogers, the name she henceforth always used, ran for her husband's seat. That June, she won the Republican primary in an exceedingly low turnout, but receiving over 80% of the votes cast. Later that month, she won the special election, defeating former Democratic governor Eugene N. Foss by well over a two-to-one ratio.

In this 1925 race, and in 18 succeeding ones, Edith Nourse Rogers had one clear advantage: the 5th Congressional District was solidly Republican. At the same time, it was an extremely diverse region, including the industrial city of Lowell and such historical villages as Lexington and Concord. Suburbs impinged upon both farm and factory, and old-stock Yankees intermingled with foreign-born laborers.

> *For years, [Edith] Rogers has been the conscience of the Veterans' Administration, and God knows that bureaucratic behemoth needs one.*
>
> —Robert S. Allen and William V. Shannon

Even during the New Deal, Rogers remained popular in Middlesex County, her political base. From the early 1940s on, she never had to confront a primary contest. In three campaigns, she met with no Democratic opponent. When the national Democratic Party won landslide victories, she still could receive 60% of her district's vote. By 1938, she was the only Republican woman in the House. She was not afraid to oppose New Deal legislation, so much so that in the early 1940s the liberal *New Republic* gave her a 90% negative rating on domestic policy.

As always the cause of ex-military personnel was her top priority. No veteran's problem was too trivial to demand her full attention and in this sense her constituency was always a national one. Within five years after entering Congress, she was able to secure a $15 million appropriation to build a nationwide network of veterans' hospitals. She guided the bill through the House over the opposition of the committee's chair.

When, however, the controversial bonus issue arose in 1932, she backed President Hoover in opposing the bill. World War I veterans were demanding an advance payment of $2.4 billion, a sum that would have hopelessly strained a federal budget already unbalanced and produced rampant inflation. On June 15, the House passed the bill 209 to 176, but the Senate balked. The issue was a highly emotional one, as veterans (called the Bonus Army) camping on the outskirts of Washington were forcibly removed by federal troops.

In 1933, Rogers was one of the first in Congress to speak against Hitler's treatment of the Jews, writing an article in the black journal *Crisis* that July. In a bipartisan effort to aid victims of Nazi terror, in February 1939 she and Senator Robert F. Wagner (Dem.-N.Y.) introduced identical bills to permit, over a single two-year period, 20,000 refugee children from Germany to enter the United States. This proposal marked the first major attempt to liberalize the immigration act of 1924. It originated in the efforts of the Non-Sectarian Committee for German Refugee Children, an effort launched in 1938 by Dr. **Marion Kenworthy**, director of the Department of Mental Hygiene of the New York School of Social Work. The committee was backed by leading social workers, jurists, labor leaders, educators, and clergy and was headed by Clarence E. Pickett, executive secretary of the American Friends Service Committee. Although the bill provided that the refugees needed sponsors, so as not to become a public charge, patriotic and veterans groups, including Rogers' frequent backer, the American Legion, opposed the law. Nativism, anti-Semitism, and economic insecurity were obvious factors in its defeat. Foes saw the children's bill as a first step in opening the nation's door, resulting in a veritable flood of refugees. The State Department also opposed the measure, arguing that any move to change immigration laws would result in more restrictions, not less. President Franklin Roosevelt felt himself in no position to back legislation that would inevitably lead to controversy. He had recently faced major defeats in his efforts to "purge" his party of anti-New Deal Democrats. Furthermore, the Republicans had made significant gains in the elections of 1938. Once war broke out in 1939, making emigration from Nazi-occupied areas even more difficult, the question became moot. The bill never reached the floors of Congress.

Such sympathy for refugees did not prevent Rogers from frequently voicing isolationist sentiments. In 1936, she declared that "our own troubles are so numerous and so difficult that we have neither the time or inclination to meddle in the affairs of others." Never again, she continued, would the United States "pull the chestnuts out of the fire for some other nation." In the fall of 1939, she opposed Roosevelt's proposal of cash-and-carry, whereby belligerents, primarily the Allies, could receive arms provided they avoid taking out loans and transported the goods themselves. In March 1941, she voted against the lend-lease act, asking, "Would not this bill tie our destiny to that of the European war leaders whose actions we are unable to control practically for all time . . . ?" Once the Western powers fought to mutual exhaustion, she warned, the Soviets would attempt to communize the world. Rogers, however, was not a rigid isolationist. Before World War II, she favored the fortification of Guam. In 1940, she voted for the selective service act and a year later she supported extending the service terms of the draftees. In the fall of 1941, she backed FDR's request for arming American merchant ships and permitting them to enter belligerent ports, a measure that passed Congress less than a month before Japan attacked Pearl Harbor.

During World War II, Rogers' knowledge of the armed forces—and her political clout—was invaluable both to the military and to the Roosevelt administration. On May 28, 1941, she first introduced a bill to create a Women's Auxiliary Army Corps. She modeled her proposal upon the British Auxiliary Territory Service, which she had observed firsthand during World War I. The bill provided that WAACs (or WACs, for in 1943 the "Auxiliary" was dropped) wear an Army uniform, receive pay on a scale similar to that of the regular Army, and live in barracks under Army discipline.

In Congress, Rogers' proposal led to a spirited floor fight. What would happen, asked critics, when young females were officially employed at the rough, all-male domain of army camps? Besides, who would do the nation's washing and mending? In 1942, it took pressure from George C. Marshall himself to secure passage of the bill. As chief of staff, Marshall realized that in America's women there existed a large pool of already trained personnel, already more competent in the desk jobs for which male personnel would have yet to be schooled. In time, Congress authorized the Navy WAVES (Women Accepted for Voluntary Emergency Service), the Army Air Corps WASPS (Women's Auxiliary Service Pilots), the Coast Guard SPARS (from the service's Latin motto *Semper Paratus*), and the Marine Corps Women's Reserve. In all, some 350,000 women donned uniforms.

As in World War I, Rogers inspected hospitals overseas. In the course of a visit to Italy, she was subject to German fire. By now, she had became so popular with troops that a small group of soldiers in the South Pacific adopted the middle-aged congresswoman as their company's pinup girl.

In 1944, Congress passed the GI Bill of Rights. As Rogers was crucial to its crafting,

President Roosevelt appropriately presented her with the signature pen. Spearheaded by the American Legion and passed unanimously by Congress, the GI Bill offered veterans aid in purchasing housing, loans to start businesses, and monthly stipends to help meet education costs. A veteran could have up to $500 a year for college tuition and books and at least $50 for living expenses. By 1956, when the programs ended, close to 8 million veterans, about 50% of those who had served, had received benefits: 2.2 million attended colleges, 3.5 enrolled in technical schools, and 700,000 received agricultural instruction.

Little wonder that when the war ended in the summer of 1945, Rogers was preeminent in veterans' matters. In 1947, when the Republicans took over Congress, she became chair of the House Veterans' Affairs Committee. She later sponsored the Korean Veterans Benefits bill, a permanent Nurse Corps in the Veterans Administration, and legislation to support the development of prosthetic appliances and automobiles for amputees. Wrote the political columnists Robert S. Allen and William V. Shannon, "Servicemen, whether they fought at San Juan Hill, Château-Thierry, Guadalcanal, or in the Bulge, know she is one

Edith
Nourse
Rogers

politician who can be depended on." She was seen, quite correctly, as the GIs' representative, a powerful voice on behalf of those individuals invariably frustrated with the inefficiency that accompanies huge bureaucracies, particularly one whose growth was as astronomical as the VA. Over half of the 1,242 bills she introduced during her career dealt with military matters.

Until the early 1950s, Rogers strongly supported the bipartisan foreign policy articulated by Senator Arthur H. Vandenberg (Rep.-Mich.). She backed the United Nations, Truman's 1947 bill aiding Greece and Turkey, and the European Recovery Program, popularly known as the Marshall Plan. In 1950–51, during what was called the Great Debate over America's global role, she opposed such party leaders as Herbert Hoover and Senator Robert A. Taft (Rep.-Ohio) by endorsing the sending of American forces to Europe. In 1952, she supported Universal Military Training.

By the mid-'50s, however, a more strident form of nationalism surfaced. Rogers not only supported the House Committee on Un-American Activities; she also backed the investigations of Senator Joseph McCarthy (Rep.-Wis.), even contributing to a memorial volume upon his death. In 1953, she called upon the U.S. to withdraw its support from the UN. In fact, if member nations admitted Communist China, the U.S. should expel the organization from American soil. A year later, however, when Vice President Richard Nixon suggested sending U.S. troops to Indochina, Rogers contended that the area was a singularly bad place in which to fight a war.

Rogers' intense activity on behalf of the veteran never caused her to neglect her constituency. She secured lucrative "pork barrel" projects for her district, including funds for improvement and flood control for the Merrimack River Basin. She was credited with having brought to Massachusetts more than $1 billion worth of civil and military manufacturing contracts. She was so adamant on behalf of her area's textile industry that author **Hope Chamberlin** writes, "It seemed to some of her colleagues that she extolled the versatile virtues of cotton morning, noon, and night. On occasion she even forsook her modish ensembles for cotton dresses and urged all congressmen to wear cotton suits." She fought high textile tariffs and was a particularly strong opponent of Secretary of State Cordell Hull's reciprocal trade treaties.

At one point Rogers attacked a trade treaty with Czechoslovakia. Her district contained the heart of the nation's shoe industry, which feared Czech competition. When a Czech shoe manu-facturer sought to establish schools in the U.S., she presented proof that such schools were in reality factories, where the "student" wage could "wreck the higher-paid, unionized domestic shoe industry." When she received a letter warning her to "keep your mouth shut or else," she was provided with police protection.

In 1949, a 67-year-old Rogers faced the threat of scandal. The wife of one of her longtime staff members, naval Captain Harold A. Latta Lawrence, named her as correspondent in a contested divorce case, alleging a "close and intimate relationship" for 20 years. The congresswoman and the captain vehemently denied the charge. Rogers emerged unscathed, for several months later a district court judge ordered all reference to her removed from the record. Lawrence remained as her aide, continuing to manage her political campaigns, becoming coexecutor of her estate, and even inheriting her house in Saco.

Politically, the 1950s saw Rogers as solidly entrenched as ever. When, late in the decade, the Democratically controlled Massachusetts legislature sought to "carve up" her district, House majority leader John W. McCormick, himself from South Boston, prevented the move. At the same time, she was declining both physically and mentally. In 1955, her attendance in the House started dropping, and she was giving signs that she felt "persecuted" by the House Republican leadership. By 1960, she was only supporting her party on one-third of all roll-calls. Yet, when she died of a heart attack on September 10, 1960, Rogers was preparing for her 19th election campaign. She had entered Boston's Massachusetts General Hospital under the assumed name of Edith White so as to avoid jeopardizing her chances in the forthcoming race. The *Boston Globe* commented simply, "Whoever is chosen to succeed her, it will probably be a long time before the position she occupied will, in the larger sense, be filled."

SOURCES:

Chamberlain, Hope. *A Minority of Members: Women in the U.S. Congress*. Praeger, 1973.

Schuck, Victoria. "Edith Nourse Rogers," in Barbara Sicherman and Carol Hurd Green, eds., *Notable American Women: The Modern Period*. Cambridge, MA: Belknap Press of Harvard University Press, 1980, pp. 587–589.

SUGGESTED READING:

Wyman, David S. *Paper Walls: America and the Refugee Crisis, 1938–1941*. University of Massachusetts Press, 1968.

COLLECTIONS:

The Edith Nourse Rogers Papers are in the Schlesinger Library, Radcliffe College, Cambridge, Massachusetts.

Justus D. Doenecke,
Professor of History,
New College of the University of South Florida

Rogers, Ginger (1911–1995)

American film star, dancer and actress who through verve, grace and hard work captured the public's imagination, particularly when she danced with Fred Astaire. Born Virginia Katherine McMath in Independence, Missouri, on July 16, 1911; died on April 25, 1995, at her home in Rancho Mirage, California; daughter of Lela Owens McMath (a secretary) and William Eddins McMath (an electrical engineer), who separated before her birth; attended public schools in Kansas City, Missouri, and Fort Worth, Texas; married Edward Jackson Culpepper, on March 29, 1929, in New Orleans (divorced July 1931); married Lew Ayres (an actor), on November 14, 1934 (divorced 1940); married John Calving Briggs II, on January 16, 1943 (divorced 1948); married Jacques Bergerac (an actor), on February 7, 1953 (divorced 1957); married G. William Marshall (a producer), on March 16, 1961 (divorced March 1967); no children.

Awards: Texas State Charleston Champion (November 1925); Academy Award for Best Actress (1940) for her performance in Kitty Foyle; *granted Lifetime Achievement at Kennedy Center Honors (1992).*

Made Broadway musical debut in Top Speed *(December 25, 1929); made film debut in* Young Man of Manhattan *(1930); made final film* Harlow *(1965); published* Ginger: My Story *(1991).*

Filmography: Young Man of Manhattan *(1930);* Queen High *(1930);* The Sap from Syracuse *(1930);* Follow the Leader *(1930);* Honor Among Lovers *(1931);* The Tip Off *(1931);* Suicide Fleet *(1931);* Carnival Boat *(1932);* The Tenderfoot *(1932);* The Thirteenth Guest *(1932);* Hat Check Girl *(1932);* You Said a Mouthful *(1932);* 42nd Street *(1933);* Broadway Bad *(1933);* Gold Diggers of 1933 *(1933);* Professional Sweetheart *(1933);* A Shriek in the Night *(1933);* Don't Bet on Love *(1933);* Sitting Pretty *(1933);* Flying Down to Rio *(1933);* Chance at Heaven *(1933);* Rafter Romance *(1934);* Finishing School *(1934);* Twenty Million Sweethearts *(1934);* Change of Heart *(1934);* Upper World *(1934);* The Gay Divorcee *(1934);* Romance in Manhattan *(1934);* Roberta *(1935);* Star of Midnight *(1935);* Top Hat *(1935);* In Person *(1935);* Follow the Fleet *(1936);* Swing Time *(1936);* Shall We Dance *(1937);* Stage Door *(1937);* Having a Wonderful Time *(1938);* Vivacious Lady *(1938);* Carefree *(1938); (as dancer-actress* *Irene Castle*)* The Story of Vernon and Irene Castle *(1939);* Bachelor Mother *(1939);* Fifth Avenue Girl *(1939);* Primrose Path *(1940);* Lucky Partners *(1940);* Kitty Foyle *(1940);* Tom Dick and Harry *(1941);* Roxie Hart *(1942);* Tales of Manhattan *(1942);* The Major and the Minor *(1942);* Once Upon a Honeymoon *(1942);* Tender Comrade *(1943);* Lady in the Dark *(1944);* I'll Be Seeing You *(1944);* Weekend at the Waldorf *(1945);* Heartbeat *(1946); (as* *Dolly Madison*)* Magnificent Doll *(1946);* It Had to Be You *(1947);* The Barkleys of Broadway *(1949);* Perfect Strangers *(1950);* Storm Warning *(1950);* The Groom Wore Spurs *(1951);* We're Not Married *(1952);* Monkey Business *(1952);* Dreamboat *(1952);* Forever Female *(1953);* Black Widow *(1954);* Beautiful Stranger *(U.K.,* Twist of Fate, *1954);* Tight Spot *(1955);* The First Traveling Saleslady *(1956);* Teenage Rebel *(1956);* Oh Men! Oh Women! *(1957);* The Confession *(*Seven Different Ways *or* Quick Let's Get Married, *shot in 1964, released in 1971); (as* *Jean Harlow's *mother)* Harlow *(1965).*

Ginger Rogers is indelibly linked with her dancing partner Fred Astaire, but her true partner in life, as she was always the first to say, was her mother **Lela Rogers**. "My mother went though hell, fire, and damnation to take care of me," she said tartly when she was 80, "and my mom was falsely accused of being a bitch." Rogers, in her heyday a lithe blonde of 5'5" and 105 pounds, clearly had the talent and drive necessary, but her mother, who tried unsuccessfully to make a career for herself as a screenwriter, set her daughter on the path to stardom.

Her parents separated before she was born as Virginia McMath in Independence, Missouri, in 1911, and, during the ensuing custody battle, her father William McMath kidnapped her. The court deemed this "reckless behavior" and awarded her to her mother Lela and curtailed his visiting rights. Rogers would see little of him before his death when she was 11. She spent her early years in Kansas City with her maternal grandparents and a family of aunts and cousins, one of whom gave her the nickname Ginger. Her mother pursued work as a screenwriter in Hollywood and, after she landed a job with Fox in New York, she sent for her daughter, who was then five. The child was offered a film contract, but Lela declined, saying she was too young and that working conditions for child actors were too harsh. While Lela worked, Ginger stayed alone in the apartment playing with her toys until she was enrolled in public school. Mother and daughter lived together for a year until Lela joined the Marines in 1918 and helped edit the Corps' newspaper, *The Leatherneck*. In 1920, Lela married a wounded veteran, John Rogers, and although he never adopted his stepdaughter, Ginger assumed his last name. The new family moved to Fort Worth, where one of Ginger's playmates was ***Mary Martin**. They had an informal club called The Cooper Street Gang. When they grew from climbing trees to performing, Lela wrote a play called "The Death of St. Denis" for them, cast Ginger in the lead, and made her a black satin dress trimmed in red.

John Rogers became a successful insurance broker, but he was plagued by lung problems as a result of being gassed during World War I. When doctors said his condition was hopeless and he was on the brink of death, the family turned to a Christian Science practitioner who seemed to effect a miraculous cure.

Sure he was [a great dancer], but don't forget that Ginger Rogers did everything he *did . . . backwards and in high heels.*

—Bob Thaves

Meanwhile, Lela took a job reviewing plays and films for the *Fort Worth Record*. Each afternoon after school, Ginger met her mother at the local theater, where she came to know the performers. The vaudevillian Eddie Foy, Jr., taught her the Charleston, and when one of his siblings was too ill to perform their act, he asked Ginger to fill in. Soon afterward, on November 9, 1915, wearing a homemade dress encrusted with rhinestones, she won the state Charleston championship in Dallas, and embarked on a five-week tour on the Interstate Time, a Southwest theater chain. Rogers dropped plans to be a schoolteacher, and her professional life began with her mother acting as manager.

Lela hired a girl and a boy to appear with Rogers in a group called "Ginger and The Redheads," and, at the age of 14, Ginger went on tour, carrying a large doll so that she would look young enough to qualify for children's rail fares. Lela was determined her daughter would succeed and wrote an act filled with childish patter and gags. In Memphis, when she learned that the manager planned to fire Ginger ("Nuts. She's terrible. Cancel her out."), Lela raced backstage, grabbed her daughter, and hurried her in full makeup to a nearby Chinese restaurant. The two remained there until her afternoon show, which was filled with school kids who loved Ginger's act and saved her job. Against Lela's better judgment, the theater chain booked Ginger in New York, the most demanding venue in the country. Though *Variety*'s reviewer quickly panned her with "This kid with the baby talk is no good in New York," Lela put the criticism to constructive use. She cut the baby talk, rewrote the act, and had Ginger drop her singing voice five tones, all the while using spare minutes at her

Opposite page

Ginger

Rogers

portable sewing machine where she sewed new costumes for her daughter.

They moved on to a more prestigious vaudeville circuit. While Rogers was appearing in Dallas, she was thrilled when Jack Culpepper, a singer and old boyfriend of one of her aunts, came backstage to see her. She had had a crush on him for years, and a few weeks later, to her mother's fury, she married him. "I had been part of the adult entertainment world for years, but still had not reached a personal maturity. I really had never been alone with a man. Harboring thoughts of Jack all those years on the road, I had convinced myself I was in love with him," Rogers wrote in her autobiography. The marriage quickly foundered, as did that of her mother's. Soon they both were divorced and in New York pursuing Ginger's career on Broadway. She made her musical debut in *Top Speed* in December 1929, a few weeks after the stock-market crash. Critic Brooks Atkinson described her as "an impudent young thing . . . who carries youth and humor to the point where they are completely charming." By day, Rogers made films for Paramount on Long Island. In her first, *Young Man of Manhattan* (1930), she played a wisecracking flapper and spoke a *Mae West*-type line, "Cigarette me, Boy," that caught the audience's imagination.

Rogers was chosen as the ingenue star of the George Gershwin musical *Girl Crazy*, which opened on Broadway on October 14, 1930, and she earned $1,000 per week during its 45-week run. During rehearsals, its writers called in a dancer named Fred Astaire to improve the choreography. Rogers was required to do eight shows a week on Broadway, and in her spare time she made films and occasionally appeared at the Blue Angel. Her schedule allowed her only five hours' sleep, but she managed to make time for one date with Astaire. The two went dancing at the Casino in Central Park to the music of Eddy Duchin. Before a romance could develop, Rogers was offered a contract with RKO and left for the West Coast in June 1931.

To Lela's outrage, the studio bleached Ginger's chestnut hair to blonde. Rogers liked the new color, thinking it softened her features and improved her looks, but waited two days before telling her mother she wanted to keep her hair that way. Lela was mostly annoyed that she had not been consulted, and finally admitted that she was beginning to like it herself. The best of the 14 films Rogers made over the next two years were *42nd Street* (1933), which set the mold for the genre of backstage romance and featured her as "Anytime Annie," a social climbing chorus girl, and *Gold Diggers of 1933*, in which she sang "We're in the Money" in a costume studded with coins. Her real breakthrough came in *Flying Down to Rio*, also in 1933. Astaire, who had recently arrived in Hollywood, had been hired by RKO for a part in the film. When he needed a partner for a brief dancing number, he asked, "Where is Ginger Rogers? Isn't she on this lot?" Studio heads had loaned her to Paramount and quickly recalled her. Producers were unsure whether full-length dances would appeal to movie audiences, but the Rogers-Astaire number, "The Carioca," was so successful that the picture was re-shot to incorporate her into the story. The two appeared as secondary characters to the stars, *Dolores Del Rio and Gene Raymond, but they were launched on a remarkable dancing partnership. In her autobiography, Rogers noted with some slight wistfulness that, at the time, Astaire had recently married, and she was on the brink of marrying actor Lew Ayres, so whatever romantic possibilities there might have been for them were never realized.

Rogers was loaned out to make films for Fox and Warner Bros. before she and Astaire were teamed again in *Roberta* (1935), with music by Jerome Kern, which starred *Irene Dunne and Randolph Scott, and introduced a model named *Lucille Ball. Despite her work on other lots, Rogers practiced with Astaire eight hours a day for six weeks before filming each number. When she was called away for non-musical films, their choreographer Hermes Pan stood in for Rogers as Astaire twirled him around the sound stage; Pan then taught her the routines when she returned to RKO. The Rogers-Astaire numbers in *Roberta*—"I Won't Dance" and "Smoke Gets in Your Eyes"—became classics.

Other Rogers-Astaire RKO films followed: *The Gay Divorcee* (released in 1934, before *Roberta*), Irving Berlin's *Top Hat* (which many regard as their best collaboration, 1935), *Follow the Fleet* (1936), *Swing Time* (her personal favorite, 1936), *Shall We Dance* (1937), and *Carefree* (1938). She spent Sundays and holidays rehearsing, many nights recording her songs, and some nights after midnight standing through fittings. Her marriage to Lew Ayres, who was the favorite of her five husbands, foundered under their separate schedules. In 1938, after her marriage ended, she bought a ranch on the Rogue River near Medford, Oregon, and also built a house on the highest point overlooking Beverly Hills. It included a tennis court, projection room, and, as she was a teetotaler, a soda foun-

tain, for which she became famous. She gave popular and well-publicized parties where, because she followed Christian Science, no liquor was served. Despite the sobriety, the atmosphere led her guests to attempt amazing feats. The night she rented out the Rollerdome in Culver City, Humphrey Bogart strapped on skates and jumped three chairs in succession before attempting a cartwheel. He ended up sliding 15 feet on his trouser pants, to the delight of a photographer for *Life*.

Rogers' competitive spirit was clear in all she did. She was regarded as one of the best amateur athletes in Hollywood. As she regularly beat men at tennis, ping pong, and bowling, friends nicknamed her "Champ." She also took pride at being a fair Sunday painter, which she said was her only true relaxation from performing.

Meanwhile, studio executives kept Lela busy by putting her in charge of a workshop for young contract players, including *Betty Grable and Lucille Ball. Ball, who ended up owning RKO as well as becoming America's top television star, said that Rogers and her mother had done more to promote her career than had anyone else in her early years. At one point, the two were said to have kept RKO from firing Ball after she accidentally pelted *Katharine Hepburn with a cup of coffee.

Her fame as Fred Astaire's gossamer partner was not enough to satisfy Ginger Rogers. She was determined to show that she had the talent to be a successful dramatic actress. Though she was RKO's top star, she begged for the role of Queen *Elizabeth I opposite Hepburn in *Mary, Queen of Scots*. To convince director John Ford that she could do it, she tested for the role in full costume under an assumed name. Her stunt was reported in the press, but studio executives decided the embittered Elizabeth would not suit her image.

The 1937 film *Stage Door* was, by her own description, a milestone in her career, because it afforded her her first real opportunity to show her acting ability. Rogers starred opposite Hepburn, her rival as the most important star at RKO. Hepburn had just appeared in a series of movies that flopped, and executives hoped that *Stage Door*, a story about aspiring actresses in a New York boarding house, would revive her career. The film was also a showcase for starlets such as Ball, *Eve Arden, and *Andrea Leeds, who shared top billing with Hepburn and Rogers. Director Gregory LaCava, who adapted it from the *Edna Ferber-George S. Kaufman stage play, based much of the dialogue on the actresses' personalities—Hepburn's patrician aloof-

ness and Rogers' careless accessibility. Although Andrea Leeds won an Oscar for Best Supporting Actress, Rogers treasured her favorable reviews, particularly one from *The New Republic*: "This is the first chance she has had to be something more than a camera object and stand forth in her own right, pert and charming and just plain nice, her personality flexible in the actor's expression." Rogers noted in her autobiography: "I just loved having the word *actor* applied to me."

Although she was a top moneymaker at RKO, Rogers found that the studio undervalued her, a point that became particularly clear when Mark Sandrich, who directed the earliest Rogers-Astaire films, advised her to take dancing, singing, and acting lessons. Rogers accepted the fact that she earned less than Astaire, but she also learned that the weekly salaries of the character actors Edward Everett Horton and Victor Moore were double her own. In her autobiography, she claimed that agents and studio heads consistently disparaged the contributions of actresses, but through persistence and the help of the studio head Pandro Berman, Rogers managed to increase her salary to $3,000 per week in the middle of 1939, and to have the sympathetic George Stevens replace Sandrich. Because Astaire developed their routines with their choreographer Hermes Pan, he was regarded as the stronger partner. Rogers felt that she received insufficient credit for her own suggestions, such as doing their number "Let's Call the Whole Thing Off" in *Shall We Dance* (1937) on roller skates and the idea of leaping "over the tables" in a sequence in *Carefree* (1938). **Anna Kisselgoff**, chief dance critic of *The New York Times*, wrote: "Ginger Rogers was a better dancer than most people gave her credit for. She may have swooned and dipped into many a romantic swoon, but her footwork was as precise as Astaire's."

Astaire allowed that Rogers was the only one of his dancing partners (who later included *Judy Garland and *Lucille Bremer) who never cried in rehearsals. **Arlene Croce** wrote in 1972 that "Ginger Rogers danced with love, with pride in the beauty of an illusion and with one of the most elegant dancer's bodies imaginable. . . . She avoided any suggestion of toil or inadequacy." In his strip "Frank and Ernest," cartoonist Bob Thaves summed up her achievement in a line that many borrowed. He drew a cartoon showing a bedraggled woman and two men standing in front of a poster advertising a "Fred Astaire Film Festival." "Sure he was great," gripes the woman to the men, "but don't forget that Ginger Rogers did everything *he* did . . . backwards and in high heels."

Rogers' most important films of the war years were *Bachelor Mother* (1939), a role she accepted over her better judgment, and *Kitty Foyle* (1940), for which she won that year's Academy Award for Best Actress. "This is the greatest night of my life," she said in her acceptance speech. "I want to thank the one person who has stood by me faithfully: my mother."

In the 1942 *Roxie Hart* for Twentieth Century-Fox, based on the play *Chicago*, Rogers played an ambitious, wisecracking dancer who confesses to a murder committed by her husband so that she will make headlines. Years later, it became a cult film and was turned into the Broadway show *Chicago* starring *Gwen Verdon.

With earnings of $292,150, Rogers was the highest paid Hollywood star in 1945 and the eighth highest salary-earner in the United States. Meanwhile, her mother Lela became a founding member of the Motion Picture Alliance for the Preservation of American Ideas to Combat Communist Infiltration of Hollywood. Ginger herself had been concerned with dialogue that had a "Communist turn" in her 1943 film *Tender Comrade*. She objected to speaking the line "Share and share alike," and so the producer

Ginger Rogers and Fred Astaire.

gave such speeches to other actors. Lela appeared at hearings of the House Un-American Activities Committee (HUAC) in 1947, which was the start of the Communist witch hunts. The writer and the director of *Tender Comrade*, Dalton Trumbo and Edward Dmytryk, were both blacklisted as a result of HUAC investigations.

Ginger Rogers turned 40 in July 1951. Partly because of her age, and partly because of the rise of television, her film career inevitably began to wind down. She again proved herself to be a stalwart trooper and returned to Broadway in *Love and Let Love*, on October 19, 1951. The run lasted a month. On a vacation to France, she met Jacques Bergerac, a 25-year-old lawyer from Biarritz. She married him and made him her costar in the 1954 film *Twist of Fate* (released as *Beautiful Stranger* in the United Kingdom), although their marriage ended in divorce in 1957. She was also married to William Marshall, a producer, from 1961 to 1967.

In the 1960s and 1970s, Rogers toured with *Annie Get Your Gun*, *Hello Dolly*, *Mame*, *Coco*, and *Forty Carats*, among others. As Peter B. Flint noted in her obituary in *The New York Times*, reviewers attributed her enduring career to a dualistic personality; she could be both tough and vulnerable, ingenuous and calculating, and she had a talent for mimicry and affectation. An ardent Republican and Christian Scientist to the end, Ginger Rogers died on April 25, 1995, at her home in Rancho Mirage, California.

SOURCES:

Author's interview with Ginger Rogers. February 25, 1992.

Current Biography. April 1967. NY: H.W. Wilson, 1967.

The New York Times (obituary). April 26, 1995.

Rogers, Ginger. *Ginger: My Story*. NY: HarperCollins, 1991.

Time. April 10, 1939.

RELATED MEDIA:

Hollywood: The Golden Years. BBC Television Productions in Association with RKO Pictures, 1987.

Kathleen Brady,
author of *Lucille: The Life of Lucille Ball* (Hyperion) and
Ida Tarbell: Portrait of A Muckraker (University of Pittsburgh Press)

Rogers, Grace Rainey (1867–1943)

American art collector and philanthropist who donated large sums of money and art to the Cleveland Museum of Art, the Metropolitan Museum of Art, and the Museum of Modern Art. Born in Cleveland, Ohio, on June 28, 1867; died in Greenwich, Connecticut, on May 9, 1943; one of four children of William J. Rainey (a businessman who made a fortune in the coke industry) and Eleanor B. (Mitchell) Rainey; educated at Mrs. Mittleburger's School in Cleveland; married Henry Welsh Rogers (a New York businessman), on September 28, 1907 (divorced 1918); no children.

Grace Rainey Rogers was one of the 20th century's greatest patrons of the arts. The daughter of wealthy Cleveland businessman William J. Rainey, she developed an early interest in art due to the influence of her mother **Eleanor B. Mitchell Rainey**, an art collector and philanthropist in her own right. Rogers received her education at Cleveland's Mrs. Mittleburger's School, and her frequent trips to Europe in the course of her youth served to launch what would be an extensive private art collection, starting with 18th-century French paintings as well as Persian art.

Divorced in 1918 and childless, Rogers spent much of her later life supporting various art museums. She was a fellow of the Metropolitan Museum of Art and an original trustee of the Museum of Modern Art, both located in New York City. She also supported the Cleveland Museum of Art, as a member of the advisory council as well as through one of her most noteworthy gifts, the Rousseau de la Rottière Room. Its sumptuous contents had been designed for the comptroller general of finance during the reign of Louis XV, and had occupied a room in her New York appartment prior to her donation of it to the museum in 1942. Other significant philanthropic contributions included the Paul J. Rainey Memorial Gates for the Bronx Zoo, which she commissioned in 1934 in memory of her brother Paul J. Rainey, an explorer and wildlife motion-picture photographer who had died in 1923. The Audubon Society received his Louisiana animal farm, renamed the Paul J. Rainey Wildlife Sanctuary, as a gift from Rogers. She also took interest in and gave generously to the Society for the Prevention of Cruelty to Animals, the Children's Aid Society, and *Dorothy Eustis' The Seeing Eye, an organization committed to providing seeing-eye dogs to the blind.

Some of Rogers' most significant donations occurred after her death at age 75 in 1943. Her bequest of $696,000 to the Museum of Modern Art made possible the construction of an art center for amateurs—named the Grace Rainey Rogers Memorial Annex—in 1951, and the Metropolitan Museum built the Grace Rainey Rogers Auditorium in 1954 with the $731,000 she left it in her will. The Cleveland Museum received a smaller, although still significant, amount totaling $235,000. Rogers also willed $200,000 to the Eleanor B. Rainey Memorial Institute, founded by her mother.

SOURCES:

James, Edward T., ed. *Notable American Women, 1607–1950*. Cambridge, MA: The Belknap Press of Harvard University, 1971.

Linda S. Walton,
freelance writer, Grosse Pointe Shores, Michigan

Rogers, Harriet B. (1834–1919)

American educator of the deaf. Born Harriet Burbank Rogers in North Billerica, Massachusetts, on April 12, 1834; died in North Billerica, Massachusetts, on December 12, 1919; fourth of five daughters of Calvin Rogers (a farmer) and Ann (Faulkner) Rogers (the daughter of a woolen manufacturer); attended local schools; graduated from Massachusetts State Normal School in West Newton in 1851; never married; no children.

Began private instruction of a young deaf girl (1863); opened her own school for deaf children (June 1866); appointed director of Clarke Institution for Deaf Mutes (1867); resigned due to ill health (1886).

Harriet B. Rogers was the first American woman to teach deaf children solely through the use of the German oral method of speaking and lip reading. Rogers started her career in teaching after graduating from the Massachusetts State Normal School in 1851. She taught for a time in country schools and for several years at the Westford (Massachusetts) Academy. Rogers' eldest sister, **Elisa Ann Rogers**, was also a teacher, and had taught *Laura Bridgman, the first successfully educated deaf and blind child in the United States. It was through Elisa Ann that Rogers was asked to take on **Fanny Cushing**, a young deaf girl, as a private student in 1863. Though she was unsure of her qualifications for the task, Rogers decided that it was the path her life was meant to take. The Cushings wanted their daughter to learn how to speak even though the predominant method for teaching the deaf in the United States at the time was through manual alphabet or sign language. One of Rogers' friends gave her a newspaper article about a German school where the deaf were taught to speak by physically feeling breath patterns and vocal vibrations on the teacher's chest and throat, and then attempting to reproduce the same physical effects themselves. Rogers was able to use this method with Cushing and was quite successful.

In 1865, Rogers met Gardiner Greene Hubbard, a lawyer, businessman, and member of the Massachusetts State Board of Education. Hubbard's young daughter **Mabel Hubbard** (later Mrs. Alexander Graham Bell) had become deaf, and he experienced dismay in 1863 at his inability to provide her with a teacher to help her learn to speak. He and his wife had managed to teach their daughter to speak and read lips somewhat before she completely lost her ability to hear. In 1864, Hubbard had tried unsuccessfully to charter a school for the deaf based on speech and lip reading. After meeting Rogers, he encouraged her to solicit more students and open her own school, which she did with five students in Chelmsford, Massachusetts, in June 1866. Hubbard did not give up on chartering a school, and was finally able to obtain financial support for the school's endowment from John Clarke of Northampton, Massachusetts. On June 1, 1867, a charter was granted for the Clarke Institution for Deaf Mutes (later Clarke School for the Deaf), and Rogers was named the school's director. This was the first school in the United States to teach the deaf exclusively through speech and lip reading.

The Clarke School was considered exceedingly experimental, because the prevailing belief at the time was that manual alphabet and sign language were the only practical forms of communication for the deaf. At first, it was primarily female teachers who embraced the new oral method. They often felt that it was their mission to see the method succeed against staunch opposition from teachers of sign language, who were mostly men and who looked upon the oral method with disdain and labeled its proponents as "visionary enthusiasts." A competition of sorts ensued between the two methods. Rogers and her dedicated group of teachers were on the forefront of the "oralists." In 1871–72, Rogers spent a year in Europe where she studied German schools using oral principles to teach the deaf. While the German method was intended for the partially deaf and those who had lost their hearing after the age of four, Rogers proved it could be effective for many children who were born deaf. Over time, the number of oral schools increased, and traditional schools began to implement a method that taught and employed speech in the classroom while students continued to use sign language outside of the classroom. Another sign that the oral method was gaining approval occurred when the American Instructors of the Deaf, at its 1886 convention, encouraged all efforts to instruct deaf students on how to speak and read lips. In 1890, the American Association to Promote the Teaching of Speech to the Deaf was formed.

Rogers remained director of the Clarke School, with assistance from *Caroline A. Yale beginning in 1873. By 1884, Rogers took a leave of absence and went to Colorado in an effort to alleviate bronchial problems, but her failing health forced her to resign as director in 1886. She lived out the rest of her days in North Billerica, where she spent some of her time supervising a local kindergarten. A lifelong Unitarian, Rogers died of chronic bronchitis and emphysema in 1919, at the age of 85.

SOURCES:

James, Edward T., ed. *Notable American Women, 1605–1950*. Cambridge, MA: The Belknap Press of Harvard University, 1971.

McHenry, Robert, ed. *Famous American Women*. NY: Dover, 1980.

Read, Phyllis J., and Bernard L. Witlieb. *The Book of Women's Firsts*. NY: Random House, 1992.

Susan J. Walton,
freelance writer, Berea, Ohio

Rogers, Mother Mary Joseph

(1882–1955)

American who founded the Maryknoll Sisters of St. Dominic. Name variations: Mary Josephine Rogers; Mollie Rogers. Born Mary Josephine Rogers on October 27, 1882, in Roxbury, Massachusetts; died on October 9, 1955, in New York City; daughter of Abraham Rogers and Mary Josephine (Plummer) Rogers; attended public school in Jamaica Plain, Massachusetts; graduated from West Roxbury High School; Smith College, B.A., 1905; Boston Normal School, teacher's certificate, 1909.

Returned to Smith to work and organize a mission-study class for Catholic undergraduates (1906); resigned from Smith and went to Boston to help Reverend James Anthony Walsh propagate the Catholic faith (1908); received a teacher's certificate (1909) and taught in Boston for next three years, while helping Walsh with mission magazine; moved to Maryknoll Seminary to assist Walsh and became intent on forming a women's religious community (1912); first group of Maryknoll nuns took vows (1921); elected superior general of order (1925); established first contemplative branch of community of religious women (1933); after years of service, declined reelection as superior general (1947).

Mary Josephine Rogers was born in 1882 in Roxbury, Massachusetts, one of eight children of Abraham and **Mary Plummer Rogers**. Growing up in a middle-class family, she attended public schools in Jamaica Plain and West Roxbury, Massachusetts, then earned her B.A. at Smith College in June 1905. While there, she became interested in a group of young Protestant women who were being sent off to foreign missions. It was this experience that, years later, led Rogers to found the Maryknoll Sisters of St. Dominic, a missionary congregation.

When Rogers returned to Smith in 1906 to teach, she was also asked to promote some kind of religious group for Catholic students. She responded by forming a small Catholic mission club which eventually became the Smith Newman Club. Seeking advice for the club, she contacted Father James Anthony Walsh in Boston. His warm welcome and helpful suggestions led her to resign her position at Smith in 1908, and she went to Boston and volunteered to help him with his mission magazine, *The Field Afar*. Rogers also enrolled in Boston Normal School, received her teaching certificate in 1909, and taught for three years while continuing her work with Walsh. In 1912, Walsh opened Maryknoll Seminary near Ossining, New York, to prepare American priests for service in mission areas. Assisting the priests at Maryknoll were six young women, including Rogers, who served as secretaries and became known as the Teresians. Although the women aspired to the religious life, their role was generally perceived as one of supporting the Maryknoll men. Their desire to form a religious community continued to develop, however, and in 1914, after a difficult search, they enlisted members of the Sisters Servants of the Immaculate Heart of Mary to come from Pennsylvania to provide training. After two years, Walsh, Rogers and the other sisters decided on a simpler, more flexible order, and the women became part of the Dominican family. The group finally received approval as a religious congregation from Rome in 1920, after a period of instruction with the Sinsinawa Dominicans. From the beginning, Maryknoll women worked among the Japanese in California and Seattle, and in 1921, six sisters ventured to China. In 1925, the order met and elected Mary Josephine Rogers, now Mother Mary Joseph, as superior. She served as the congregation's leader until 1946, at which time, knowing Rome would not allow her to continue in her post because of her lengthy tenure, she declined renomination.

The priests and sisters of Maryknoll continued to cooperate closely and exchange ideas freely. Mother Mary Joseph provided bold leadership to the order, emphasizing duty of service and the need for professional preparation. While concerned with the preservation of the faith and worship of God, she felt that service to God could be seen in service to fellow humans, an unusual viewpoint at that time. Under her guidance, Maryknoll sisters who were in training were never "tried" on their spiritual progress; she believed that their responses to later challenges would provide proof enough.

Mother Mary Joseph also believed strongly in the power of prayer and meditation, and in 1933 she established a contemplative branch of the order, where cloistered sisters offered their lives in prayer and penance for the work of missions worldwide. Cloisters were also later established in New Mexico, the Sudan, and Guatemala (1980s), and in Thailand (1991). Maryknoll sisters were expected to be fully qualified for their work. Most sisters were involved in some form of social service and received professional preparation. Initially serving mostly in the Far East, Maryknoll sisters diversified over the years and extended their reach around the world, working in Africa, Micronesia, the Mid-East, and Latin America. Mother Mary Joseph remained an important and constructive influence in the order she had founded until her death from peritonitis in New York City on October 9, 1955.

SOURCES:

James, Edward T., ed. *Notable American Women, 1605–1950.* Cambridge, MA: The Belknap Press of Harvard University, 1971.

Jo Anne Meginnes,
freelance writer, Brookfield, Vermont

Rogers, Wanda.

See Marvelettes.

Rohan, Jacqueline de (c. 1520–1587).

See Rothelin, Jacqueline de Rohan, Marquise de.

Rohan-Montbazon, Marie de

(1600–1679)

Duchesse de Chevreuse and French intriguer at the royal court. Name variations: Marie de Rohan; Marie de Rohan-Montbazon, duchesse de Luynes. Born Marie de Rohan-Montbazon in December 1600; died at Gagny, near Paris, on August 12, 1679; daughter of Hercule de Rohan, duke of Montbazon; married Charles d'Albert, duke of Luynes, in 1617 (died 1621); married Claude de Lorraine, duke of Chevreuse (son of *Catherine of Cleves and Henry I of Lorraine, 3rd duke of Guise), in 1622.

Considered one of the most engaging women of her day, Marie de Rohan-Montbazon was born in 1600, the daughter of Hercule de Rohan, duke of Montbazon. In 1617, she married Charles d'Albert, duke of Luynes, who died four years later. She then married Claude de Lorraine, duke of Chevreuse. Despite numerous affairs, she kept the friendship of both of her husbands in their lifetimes.

The duchess was one of the most formidable women at court and a good friend of *Anne of Austria, queen and wife of Louis XIII, king of France. Wrote Louis Auchincloss in *Richelieu*: She "has assumed the role of charmer in the nineteenth-century fiction where Richelieu plays the villain. Both in fiction and fact she was the very essence of what he was trying to tame in the French nobility. She was everything that Richelieu was not: beautiful, healthy, imaginative, sympathetic, romantic, witty. She cared nothing for crowns or laws but much for individuals and power. She was a brigand with a brigand's code of honor. Yet Richelieu was fascinated by her." Even though Richelieu was aware of her enmity, he tried to win her over. But in what is known as the *Conspiration des Dames*, the duchess was caught, in cahoots with Queen Anne and the ☙➤ **Princesse de Condé**, conspiring to thwart Cardinal Richelieu's royal matchmaking in respect to the king's brother. Richelieu then forced Marie to leave France.

While she was in England, King Charles I became so enamored of her that he stipulated "the rescission of her banishment" as a condition in a treaty with France. On the death of Louis XIII, the duchess returned to France but was coldly received by the queen regent, her former friend Anne of Austria. Having acted in concert with Cardinal de Retz against French cardinal and diplomat Jules Mazarin (a close advisor to Anne), Rohan-Montbazon was sent into exile for a second time.

SOURCES:

Auchincloss, Louis. *Richelieu.* Viking, 1972.

Rohde, Ruth Bryan Owen

(1885–1954)

American speaker, author, U.S. congressional representative, diplomat, and first woman envoy. Name variations: Ruth Bryan Owen; Ruth Bryan Leavitt. Pronunciation: Rohde rhymes with soda. Born Ruth Baird Bryan on October 2, 1885, in Jacksonville, Illinois; died of a heart attack on July 26, 1954, in Copenhagen, Denmark; daughter of **Mary Baird Bryan** (a lawyer) and William Jennings Bryan (a well-known politician); attended elementary school, Lincoln, Nebraska; Monticello Seminary, Godfrey, Illinois (1899–1901); and University of Nebraska (1901–1903); married William Homer Leavitt, on October 3, 1903 (divorced 1909); married Reginald Altham Owen, on May 3, 1910 (died 1927); married Borge Rohde, on July 11, 1936; children: (first marriage) **Ruth "Kitty" Leavitt** (b. 1904), John Baird

◄☙
*Condé,
Princesse de.*

*See Longueville,
Anne for sidebar
on Charlotte of
Montmorency.*

Leavitt (b. 1905); (second marriage) Reginald Bryan Owen, Helen Rudd Owen.

Awards: several honorary degrees and many awards, including the Danish Order of Merit conferred by King Frederick IX (1954); inducted into the Florida Women's Hall of Fame (1992).

Served as Bryan's presidential campaign secretary and manager (1908); was a Chautauqua lecturer (1919–28); served as a nurse in World War I; served as faculty member and on University of Miami board of regents (1925–28); elected U.S. congressional representative from Florida (1928–32); appointed U.S. minister to Denmark (1933–36); named presidential appointee to San Francisco Conference to create the United Nations (1945); named alternate delegate to Fourth United Nations General Assembly (1949–50); served as acting president of the Institute for International Government (1952–53).

Selected writings: The Elements of Public Speaking *(1931);* Leaves from a Greenland Diary *(1935);* Denmark Caravan *(1936);* The Castle in the Silver Wood and Other Scandinavian Fairy Tales *(1939);* Picture Tales From Scandinavia *(1939);* Look Forward, Warrior *(1942);* Caribbean Caravel *(1949).*

Like her father William Jennings Bryan, Ruth Bryan Owen Rohde was a politician, the first woman elected to Congress from the Old South. Like him, she was a spellbinding speaker on the Chautauqua circuit, booked coast to coast at town and city lecture halls. When President Franklin Roosevelt chose her to be the first woman to head an embassy overseas, he received an irate letter from one of Rohde's fans back in her childhood home of Lincoln, Nebraska, berating him for sending her to a foreign country. "We don't feel we are so deeply indebted to any country that we need give them the prize of all American women," she protested. "Heavens knows it's seldom enough we have a taste of the white meat. So why send the choice bit to the Danes?" The president's secretary replied that FDR was sorry to hear of the woman's disappointment, but was "very glad indeed that Mrs. Owen [accepted] this very important post." So off Rohde went in May 1933, with three of her four children and three grandchildren, to another rendezvous with history.

Rohde had been making history nearly all her life. It was a family tradition. Her grandfather, Silas Bryan, had been an Illinois state senator and circuit court judge. Her father, who had moved the family to Nebraska to improve his political prospects, was elected to Congress at the age of 30 when Ruth was just five years old. He often took his daughter with him to the Capitol, carrying her on his shoulder.

In 1896, William Jennings Bryan was nominated as the Democratic candidate for president following his electrifying "Cross of Gold" speech. While Republican William McKinley conducted a sedate "front porch" campaign, Bryan took his family on an 18,000 mile cross-country speaking tour, and the 11-year-old Ruth was delegated to help answer fan mail. He ran again in 1900, but he was defeated both times, and Ruth learned to accept criticism and political rejection philosophically.

After two years at the University of Nebraska, and a stint at *Jane Addams' Hull House where she developed a concern for children that would mark her entire career, Rohde left school to marry an artist nearly twice her age on the day after her 18th birthday. The couple had two children: Ruth, called Kitty (b. 1904), and John (b. 1905). Shortly thereafter, they separated. Ruth managed her father's third and final unsuccessful run for the presidency in 1908. The following year, she and her husband divorced. Rohde, as the sole support of her children, began her lifelong vocation as a lecturer, substituting for her father on the Chautauqua circuit. In 1910, she married Reginald Owen, an Englishman she had met in Europe, and spent two happy years with him in Jamaica, where their son Reginald Bryan was born.

At the outbreak of World War I, her husband was sent to the Middle East, while Ruth worked in London with Mrs. Herbert Hoover (*Lou Henry Hoover) in the American Women's War Relief Fund Association. Just before civilian travel was halted, Rohde took her baby to Egypt, enrolling in a nursing course in order to work with the British Volunteer Aid Detachment in Cairo war hospitals. Her husband, who became one of her patients when he developed kidney disease, remained an invalid for the rest of his life. As a result of her wartime experiences, Ruth became a tireless advocate for peace.

The Owens moved to Florida, where the warm weather was expected to benefit Reginald; Ruth's parents had also settled there. Once again Rohde's income was needed to support her family, and she resumed her Chautauqua lectures just eight months after the birth of her fourth child, **Helen Rudd Owen**. She often felt torn between her family and work responsibilities, as when her lecture schedule prevented her from attending her older daughter's wedding.

Ruth
Bryan
Owen
Rohde

After her father's death in 1925, Rohde continued the tradition of public service, running for Congress in 1926, although the political climate was not friendly to women; just six years earlier, Florida had failed to ratify the 19th Amendment granting women the right to vote.

Despite losing the race, and the death of her husband in 1927, Rohde ran again in 1928, covering the Fourth Congressional District, over 500 miles long, in a green Ford coupe, making as many as seven speeches a day. After her election, her defeated opponent challenged her right to hold office. American law at the time of her marriage had deprived women who married foreigners of their citizenship. In 1925, the Cable Act had restored her nationality, but her opponent claimed that she had therefore been a citizen less than the constitutionally required seven-year minimum. Rohde argued her own case before the House of Representatives. She was not only admitted, but the prestigious Committee on Foreign Affairs increased their membership by one to include her. She was re-elected in 1930, and worked all four years for economic development in the state as well as for feminist goals like a Cabinet-level Department of Home and Child. In 1932, she was defeated on the issue of prohibition, which she had always supported, although she herself was not a total abstainer.

The first "Madame Minister" . . . has proved two things: first, that a woman diplomat can serve her country as ably and acceptably as a man, and second, that she has several hurdles to cross before she enjoys equal status.

—*The New York Times*, September 1, 1936

Women fared well in Franklin D. Roosevelt's administration, with *Frances Perkins in the Cabinet and *Nellie Tayloe Ross as director of the U.S. Mint. Rohde was named minister to Denmark, the highest ranking office (at that time the U.S. did not have an ambassador) and the first woman head of mission. She served in Copenhagen a little over three years, winning recognition for her trade negotiations and her efforts to interpret the two cultures to each other. She also studied the Danish social programs, models for those being initiated back in the United States. Because of currency fluctuations, Rohde's salary was effectively cut by 40%, so she spent her summers once again on the lecture circuit. Sometimes she spoke about the New Deal's accomplishments, and James Farley, FDR's campaign manager, urged her to take part in the 1936 campaign.

When Ruth returned to the States in July 1936, it was with the surprising news that she intended to marry Captain Borge Rohde of the Danish King's Life Guards. The wedding was held in the Roosevelts' church in Hyde Park, and the president and the first lady *Eleanor Roosevelt hosted the wedding reception. By her marriage, Ruth Rohde became a Danish citizen, and her dual nationality, as well as her heavy speaking schedule, prompted calls for her to resign from her post. She agreed, apparently without

bitterness, despite the fact that men married to foreign nationals were never called upon to make the same sacrifice. Soon after the start of her campaign trip in a car with a trailer, she injured her leg in an accident, and had to spend over a month in the hospital. She gamely made a nationwide speech from her bed.

During the war, Rohde wrote a book calling for a "union of nations," and in 1945 was named to the Public Liaison Division of the State Department to participate in the San Francisco Conference leading to the organization of the United Nations. In 1949, Harry Truman appointed her U.S. Alternate Representative to the Fourth Session of the U.N. General Assembly, where she served until the following year. She founded the Institute for International Government to support the United Nations in 1952, and acted as president for one year.

By 1954, after more than 50 years of demanding public service, Rohde was ready to retire. She and her husband set off on a world cruise, and in early July stopped in Denmark, where Ruth received the Danish Medal of Merit from King Frederick IX. A few days after the ceremony at the Royal Palace, Ruth suffered a heart attack. Shortly after leaving the hospital several weeks later, she suffered a second and fatal heart attack on July 26. Her ashes were buried in the Ordrup Cemetery outside of Copenhagen.

SOURCES:

Chamberlin, Hope. *A Minority of Members: Women in the U.S. Congress*. NY: Praeger, 1973.

Vickers, Sarah P. "The Life of Ruth Bryan Owen: Florida's first congresswoman and America's first woman diplomat" (unpublished dissertation), 1992.

Kristie Miller, author of *Ruth Hanna McCormick: A Life in Politics, 1880–1944* (University of New Mexico Press, 1992)

Röhl, Ulrike (1934–1972).

See Meinhof, Ulrike.

Rohlfs, Anna Katharine Green (1846–1935).

See Green, Anna Katharine.

Rokeya, Begum (1880–1932).

See Hossain, Rokeya Sakhawat.

Roland, Betty (1903–1996)

Australian dramatist and writer. Name variations: Elizabeth Maclean. Born Elizabeth Maclean in Kaniva, Victoria, Australia, on July 22, 1903; died in 1996; daughter of Roland Maclean (a physician) and Matilda (Blayney) Maclean; attended Church of England girls' grammar school in Melbourne, Australia; mar-

ried Ellis H. Davies, in 1923 (divorced 1934); married Guido Baracchi (a journalist), in the 1930s (died 1975); children: (first marriage) Peter Ellis Davies; (second marriage) Gilda Baracchi.

Selected writings: (plays) The Touch of Silk (produced 1928, published 1942), Morning (produced 1932, published 1937), Granite Peak (televised 1952); (children's books) The Forbidden Bridge (1961), Jamie's Discovery (1963), Jamie's Summer Visitor (1964), The Bush Bandits (1966), Jamie's Other Grandmother (1970); (travelogue) Sydney in Colour and Black and White (1965); (memoirs) Lesbos, the Pagan Island (1963), Caviar for Breakfast (1979); (novels) The Other Side of Sunset (1972), No Ordinary Man (1974), Beyond Capricorn (1976).

Betty Roland was born Elizabeth Maclean in the town of Kaniva in 1903, and spent her early years in the Australian bush. She took the surname "Roland"—her father's given name—in 1951. Her formal education ended relatively early, as she dropped out of school at the age of 16 and started her writing career as a journalist for *Table Talk* and the *Sun News-Pictorial*. Roland demonstrated a talent for drama with her first full-length play, *The Touch of Silk*, produced by the Melbourne Repertory Theatre in 1928. The production was a significant accomplishment for the young writer, given the fact that theaters rarely staged Australian drama at the time. Her next play, *Morning*, was produced in 1932, and was subsequently published in a 1937 anthology.

After Roland's ten-year marriage to Ellis Davies ended in the early 1930s, she became involved with Guido Baracchi, a journalist and well-known Australian Communist. In 1933, they eloped to Russia, where she worked as a journalist for 15 months and developed her own Communist beliefs. Her return to Australia in 1935 and subsequent membership in the Communist Party caused Roland to write a series of political sketches, many of them performed as street theater. Her only full-length political play, *Are You Ready, Comrade?*, won the Western Australian Drama Competition in 1938.

By 1939, Roland's disillusionment with Communism prompted her to abandon political theater for radio plays, at which she proved adept. Her best-known radio presentation, "Daddy Was Asleep," aired in 1945, and her three-act play *Granite Peak* was successful enough to be televised in England in 1952. She spent a number of these years outside of Australia, traveling and living in England and other

countries, but returned permanently to Australia in 1971. There, one of her radio programs, the serial "A Woman Scorned," found new life on television in 1983, as the basis for the popular series "Return to Eden." Roland wrote several books for children as well as three novels, *The Other Side of Sunset* (1972), *No Ordinary Man* (1974) and *Beyond Capricorn* (1976). *Caviar for Breakfast* (1979), a memoir, concerns her experiences in Russia during the 1930s.

SOURCES:

Buck, Claire, ed. *The Bloomsbury Guide to Women's Literature*. NY: Prentice Hall, 1992.

Contemporary Authors. Vol. 103. Detroit, MI: Gale Research, 1982.

Wilde, William H., Joy Hooten, and Barry Andrews. *The Oxford Companion to Australian Literature*. Melbourne, Australia: Oxford University Press, 1985.

Susan J. Walton,
freelance writer, Berea, Ohio

Roland, Eudora (1781–1858).

See Roland, Madame for sidebar.

Roland, Madame (1754–1793)

French intellectual who was among the first women to have a marked impact as a journalistic correspondent. Name variations: Marie-Jeanne Roland de la Platière; Manon Roland; Manon Phlipon. Pronunciation: RO-lun. Born Marie-Jeanne Phlipon on March 17, 1754; guillotined on November 9, 1793; only child of Pierre-Gatien Phlipon (d. 1788), a master engraver aided by his wife, Marie-Marguerite (Bimont) Phlipon (d. 1775); provided with tutors; spent one year at a convent school; and had time to peruse books at leisure; learned English and Italian as well as her native French; married Jean-Marie Roland de la Platière, in 1780; children: one daughter, Marie-Thérèse-Eudora (Madame Champagneux, 1781–1858).

Focused on her education and constant reading until the death of her mother (1758–75); helped to manage her father's shop, wrote an essay on the education of girls and met her husband (1775–80); served as her husband's editor, researcher, and coauthor (1780–89); observed and wrote

Madame Roland

about the French Revolution that would claim her life (1789–93).

Born on March 17, 1754, to Pierre-Gatien Phlipon and **Marie-Marguerite Phlipon**, the future Madame Roland was named Marie-Jeanne Phlipon but would be known as Manon to her friends and relatives. Her father was a skilled Parisian engraver who employed a number of apprentices and sold intricately detailed snuffboxes, frames, and watchcases to wealthy members of the French royal court. Like most wives of master artisans at the time, Manon's mother divided her time between household duties and helping her husband in the shop. Both parents had no personal interest in intellectual pursuits, but when their daughter demonstrated an aptitude for such things, they encouraged it.

Manon Phlipon was taught to read when she was not quite four, and she took to books with a passion. The Phlipons provided their daughter with a succession of tutors. Though Gatien was not a member of France's elite, he sold his wares to the elite, and there may have been the hope that a young woman of learning and refinement might attract a husband above her station. The complexities of 18th-century France were such that not a few members of the elite dabbled in intellectual activities. In these circles, having a brilliant wife was interpreted as an asset to a socially and politically active man. An only child, Manon was being prepared for this role, which also included training in singing, viola, and guitar, so that she might better entertain.

Under the influence of her mother's devout Catholicism, much of Roland's initial endeavors in learning was of a religious bent. At seven, she astounded her parish priest with her knowledge of theological detail as she prepared for her first communion. At nine, however, she ran across a French translation of Plutarch's *Lives*, and her interest in earthly progress was born. In her *Memoirs*, Madame Roland reminisced that this introduction to Plutarch made her a believer in the republican form of government through the historic examples of ancient Athenians and Roman republicans therein portrayed.

Before Roland fully embraced a secular intellectual world, she made one last attempt to immerse herself in religion. At age 11, she begged her parents to allow her to enter a convent for the salvation of her soul. Distraught, but still trying to be supportive of their daughter, the Phlipons agreed on the condition that she try convent life as a student-boarder for one year before making a final decision. On May 7, 1765, she entered Paris' Convent of the Ladies of the Congregation. She was so advanced that the nuns quickly placed her in the older girls' classes, where she made two lifelong friends: 18-year-old **Henriette Cannet** and her 14-year-old sister **Sophie Cannet**. Both were daughters of a fairly comfortable provincial family of lesser nobles from Amiens.

In 1766, Roland decided to leave the convent and began to exhibit doubts where Christian dogma and her society's mores were concerned. These doubts first came to be revealed in a lifelong correspondence which she initiated with the Cannet sisters. Ironically, she said that she first became aware of the onslaughts that could be leveled against Catholic religious dogma by reading Catholic attacks on Protestants. By noting that different Christian sects held different dogmatic interpretations, she began to question the absolute validity of any dogmatic interpretation.

During this same period, Grandmother Phlipon, her father's elderly mother, decided to take Manon to visit **Madame de Boismorel**, a wealthy noblewoman whose children she had helped to raise as a servant. Roland was shocked when the noblewoman had Grandmother Phlipon sit on a low stool while Madame de Boismorel and her lap dog sat on a sofa. Manon was developing an aversion to the traditions of a French society built on rank, privilege and limited opportunities. By 14, she would be prepared to become a follower of the Enlightenment movement and its thinkers called *philosophes*.

The 18th-century Enlightenment aspired to apply the methods of the 17th century's Scientific Revolution to human social interaction. If Galileo and Newton had discovered physical laws for nature by using reason and sensory experience, the intellectuals of the Enlightenment movement hoped to spread knowledge of science, and to combat superstition and decadence by applying reason and experience in order to promote human social, political, and economic progress. Above all else, they believed that this would be made possible by means of free expression and individualism. Officially banned and censored in France, works of the Enlightenment were nonetheless sold in the backrooms of printers' shops. Some members of the aristocratic elite actually embraced a smattering of Enlightenment doctrines, but the royal government and organized religion insisted on drawing a line beyond which discussion would go no further.

By 14, Roland resorted to circulating libraries to read works of the Enlightenment like the *Encyclopedia* edited by Denis Diderot. Not only was this encyclopedia highly critical of miracles, magic and religious dogma; it was also highly laudatory where the practical, profitable, and beneficial activities of artisans were concerned, defining the exact methods of making everything from cloth to gunpowder. To understand technological progress better, Roland taught herself algebra, geometry, physics, and natural history. Order, for her as for the *philosophes*, meant the regular, scientific laws of nature devoid of all special miracles. However, unlike many of her favorite authors, she continued to attend church throughout her life, since she saw organized religion as a means of promoting morality and order among the mass of ordinary people who could not arrive at principles of decorum through reason alone. She also felt that the Christian religion provided ordinary French citizens with comfort as they groaned under 18th-century burdens of underemployment, price inflation, rural landlessness, and increased taxation.

In June 1775, Roland's mother died suddenly. The 21-year-old scholar was now called upon to take over management of the household while her father's fortunes were declining through poor investments and an overzealous dedication to lotteries. Helping in her father's shop, she entertained many elite customers with her wit and intellect, and she used her leisure time to continue her own studies.

In 1776, Roland began an in-depth and extensive reading of the theoretical works and fiction of Jean-Jacques Rousseau. Unlike other *philosophes*, Rousseau emphasized that civilization and the arts had actually hurt humanity by distorting and diverting natural instincts which provided for human survival in the wild. Despite a sexism which made Rousseau denigrate women to a second-class status, Roland found much in his thinking that was attractive. His works helped her to develop a non-Biblical religious sensibility founded on a nearly mystical veneration of Nature and of "Nature's God." Rather than believing the teachings of any single, nonverifiable book, one was to feel the divine presence in the beauty and order of Nature, which transcended the follies of human civilization. Rousseau also confirmed Roland's conclusion that social ranks based on birth were human contrivances to order society. Though hierarchy might not completely disappear, ranking might be based on talent and intellect rather than parentage. This vision appealed to a young woman who had been offended by her grandmother's being treated like a child in the presence of nobility. To Sophie Cannet, she wrote

that Rousseau lifted a veil from her tired eyes so that she was finally able to see the "magnificent scene of the universe." Sophie, however, failed to support Roland in this pursuit. After all, she was of the provincial nobility, and here was an author denouncing all rank based on birth and ascribed status. Still, the heartfelt friendship survived all this, just as Roland was able to remain friends with **Sister Saint-Agatha**, a nun she had met while at the convent school. Differences of opinion in the realm of ideas were not enough to destroy the human relationships which Manon built on kindness and common experience.

> *Burning to profit from [revolutionary] circumstances, [the ambitious] succeed soon enough, using flattery to mislead the people and to turn them against their true defenders, in order to render themselves powerful and respected.*
>
> —**Madame Roland**

The year 1776 was a busy one for Madame Roland, and she anonymously entered one of the numerous literary competitions sponsored by the intellectual discussion groups of the day. The Academy of Besançon sponsored an essay contest in which the question was whether the education of women could make men better citizens. In her entry, Roland argued that women should be educated, but that reform must be general and not rely solely on the improvement of one sex through the influence of the other. Girls and boys both were to be educated. For whatever reason, the Academy decided not to name a winner that year, though Roland's anonymous entry was one that received high praise from the jury. She also met her future husband in 1776. A 42-year-old inspector of manufactures in Amiens, Picardy, Jean-Marie Roland de la Platière was one of the royal bureaucrats with Enlightenment sympathies who frequented her father's shop. He was her senior by some 20 years, but in him she found a kindred spirit who valued her intellect. The longtime bachelor appeared to have his doubts, but the marriage contract was finally signed in January 1780.

By 1781, the Rolands were settled in Amiens, the provincial capital of Picardy. Madame Roland spent much of the year facilitating the publication of her husband's *Letters from Italy*, and she soon became his secretary, editor, researcher, and even coauthor. Jean-Marie was in the process of preparing a number of monographs on several manufacturing processes, and Roland quickly familiarized herself with both technical details and theoretical arguments in favor of free trade and deregulation of craft production. She became integral to the completion of Jean-Marie's *Dictionary of Manufactures, Arts, and Trades*, which appeared successively in 1784, 1785, and 1790 as part of the publisher Panckoucke's revised edition of Diderot's *Encyclopedia*. Despite the complete nature of the partnership, however, it was Jean-Marie who received public acclaim as the sole author of these works.

On October 4, 1781, Roland gave birth to daughter Eudora (◄ **Madame Champagneux**). Against doctor's orders and the social customs of her class, she decided to breast-feed her daughter herself, rather than sending her out to a wet-nurse. In this, she was following the teachings of Rousseau who saw nursing as central to the development of human bonds. As with other aspects of her life, Roland read all she could about nursing in medical dictionaries and Diderot's *Encyclopedia*. A reliable maid named **Marguerite Fleury** was found to aid her with childcare and housekeeping, thus providing Madame Roland with time for intellectual and business activities.

In 1784, Jean-Marie decided to apply for an official patent of nobility, which would improve his social standing, and Madame Roland went to Paris in pursuit of the title. On March 18, she left Amiens with Fleury, who was quickly becoming her confidante as well as maid. In her letters to Jean-Marie, Roland revealed how difficult it was to gain the patent, and that she had chosen instead to make an application, on his behalf, to the general inspectorship of Lyons—a position with far more prestige and responsibility than that of Amiens. Jean-Marie gave his support when he was apprised of this endeavor, and he was soon to learn that Manon gained the post for him within three days of the application. She also negotiated an excellent salary and retirement benefits. From 1784 to 1789, the Rolands lived a routine life in Lyons and nearby Villefranche-sur-Saône. Manon started to educate her daughter, but she found, to her disappointment, that Eudora was far more interested in playing than in reading. Then, in 1789, Madame

Roland was catapulted into the public arena by the French Revolution.

Since May, elected representatives to France's Estates General had been struggling with King Louis XVI over matters of tax reform. As the representatives of France's commoners began to challenge absolute royal power in legislative matters, Louis XVI assembled troops to threaten them. On July 14, 1789, a Parisian crowd stormed the fortress of the Bastille in search of armaments to protect their representatives from the king. Under this pressure, Louis agreed to become a constitutional monarch. In Lyons, Madame Roland began to take an active interest in the changes around her—changes which promised to reform the society of privileged birth she had always detested. She began a career as the Lyons correspondent for a revolutionary newspaper, *Patriote français*, which was published in Paris by Jean-Pierre Brissot de Warwille, a lawyer who had met the Rolands in the spring of 1787. Between 1789 and 1790, Madame Roland wrote Brissot, who then extracted long excerpts from her letters for anonymous publication in his paper. Her unpaid correspondence included accounts of public demonstrations in support of the revolution, but she also reported that the nobles of Lyons and the provinces were more opposed to the loss of their privileges than many among the Parisian elites. She wrote that in small cities, "pride and vanity create more distance between the professions than there ever was in Paris between a bourgeois and a titled aristocrat." Hatreds were intense, and she worried that ignorant commoners, without the guidance of established traditions and religion, would soon drift into anarchy, blindly attacking any and all scapegoats to compensate for the difficulties which they faced in their lives.

On February 1, 1791, Madame Roland's husband was appointed by the municipal government of Lyons to go to Paris and negotiate a loan to revitalize commerce and manufacturing in Lyons. He successfully completed his mission by August 1791. Coming to the attention of the leading elected officials who then held sway in the government, he was named minister of the interior by France's newly elected Legislative Assembly at the end of March 1792. His experience with internal commerce and trade issues seemed to make him an ideal choice. The only problem was that the members of the Assembly were then separating into opposing factions who imagined different futures for the new France. Madame Roland's husband, like their family friend Brissot, soon identified with the Girondins, who favored limited, decentralized

☙► **Champagneux, Madame** (1781–1858)

Daughter of Madame Roland. Name variations: Eudora Roland. Born Marie-Thérèse-Eudora de la Platière on October 4, 1781; died in 1858; daughter of ***Madame Roland** (1754–1793, a journalist) and Jean-Marie Roland de la Platière.*

government. Their chief opponents were the Jacobins, headed by Maximilien Robespierre—a group which favored centralization and active government intervention on behalf of the poor. The new ministers, like Jean-Marie Roland, demonstrated marked Girondin tendencies. They spent hours with a king who was intent on deflecting them from consequential issues, and this willingness to compromise with Louis XVI eventually stigmatized the Girondins.

Ever the working observer, Madame Roland quickly became one of the many spectators in the gallery of the Assembly. There she made note of the events and personalities of the revolution in great detail, and her idealistic vision of a revolution free of selfish ends was quickly shattered. She wrote of her increasing awareness that many of the people's representatives were far more interested in promoting their own careers than in promoting the common welfare. She did note that the Jacobin leader Robespierre seemed incorruptible and dedicated to Rousseauian goals above all else. At the time, she did not know that Robespierre and she would become bitter enemies, and

that she would later write that he was the puppet of the Parisian mobs and their demagogues.

Since 1791, the Rolands' Parisian abode had served as a gathering place for those with Girondin sympathies. Brissot and his colleagues gathered in what would be known as the Salon of Madame Roland, where political theories and policies were discussed at the end of legislative sessions. Such salons, hosted by famous women of the day, were typical of the Enlightenment, and they aided immensely in the exchange of information and ideas. Unlike other women who hosted such salons, however, Madame Roland sat quietly throughout the meetings, serving the men and doing her needlework. In her writings, she admits to having bitten her tongue at times, but, with the instincts of a reporter, she quietly observed, eventually recording what she witnessed in her *Memoirs*.

The rifts between Girondins and Jacobins grew all the while, and when King Louis XVI tried to flee the country in order to join a counter-revolution abroad, the Jacobins saw

Mme Roland in the prison of Ste. Pélagie.

their opportunity to seize power. After the king's execution in January 1793, they used gutter language to stir crowds in their speeches and newspaper essays. The Girondins responded in *La Sentinelle*, a newspaper financially underwritten by Jean-Marie at the behest of Manon. However, with no immediate solutions to the economic difficulties faced by the urban multitudes, the Girondins, who had compromised with the "traitor king," quickly became the scapegoats of Jacobin rhetoric. As early as December 7, 1792, Madame Roland had been called before the legislature which was now known as the National Convention. She was actually charged with having been a moving force behind the royalist conspiracy, but she so eloquently defended herself that the Convention rose in a standing ovation after her presentation.

On January 22, 1793, the day after Louis XVI's execution, Jean-Marie Roland resigned his post as minister of the interior. Among other things, he saw the execution of the king as excessive, and, in a surviving document, he wrote that he resigned since there was no longer any man in the Convention who would oppose the Jacobins. However, the public turmoil merely added to domestic troubles then being experienced by the Rolands. Manon had recently told Jean-Marie that she had fallen in love with a young Girondin legislator named François Léonard Buzot, who was making his mark by combating the Jacobins. However, she also told her husband that she admired him for his intellect and could not leave him at a time when he needed her support, even though the revolutionary government had introduced legal divorce into France. By stating that she had to be honest and tell him the painful truth, Roland perhaps was emulating the call to veracity found in the novels of Rousseau and others. A man approaching 60, Jean-Marie chose this time of disappointment to announce his official retirement from public life.

Completely in control of the government by the end of May, the Jacobins decided to arrest Jean-Marie and other Girondin partisans. Learning of these plans, Madame Roland determined to appear before the National Convention yet again. She immediately preceded to the Convention, but was kept waiting at the door. Manon hurried back to her husband at that point, and he then decided to make his escape from Paris. While Madame Roland approved of this decision, she decided to remain behind and persevere in trying to gain access to the Convention. The two parted, never to see each other again. Around midnight, soldiers arrived at the Rolands' apartment, and Madame Roland was arrested as part of the "Girondin conspiracy against the republic." She now awaited her trial in custody, writing the *Memoirs* which have been the source of much information regarding her life. Composed in prison, her *Memoirs* have, in fact, become her major contribution to French letters. They contain numerous sketches of some of the leading figures of the French Revolution, including Robespierre and Brissot.

While she was incarcerated, Madame Roland was permitted reading material and visits from the maid Fleury, who was allowed to purchase articles of comfort for her mistress. Still, conditions were crowded, and, though physical torture was not employed, verbal abuse was practiced consistently. Beyond prison walls, Jacobin newspapers published innumerable articles, inventing nonexistent orgies at which Madame Roland had officiated. This highly visible woman was now being attacked falsely in such a way as to maximize sentiment against her.

On October 24, the trial of the Girondins began in earnest. Madame Roland admitted in writing that she contemplated suicide, but she would not do it in order to speak on behalf of her friends. In fact, to the bitter end, testimony to her dedication as a friend persisted. Sister Saint-Agatha, despite the religious differences which existed between them, came to visit her former charge on a number of occasions. Roland kept in touch with the Cannet sisters, and Henriette, now a widow, actually came to prison and offered to take Manon's place so that she could escape in disguise. Of course, Madame Roland refused to allow this sacrifice, which would have cost Henriette her own life.

On November 8, Madame Roland went to trial. When she took the stand, she started a prepared speech in defense of the Girondins and of Jean-Marie's service as minister of the interior. The judges intervened, saying it was not permitted to sing the praises of known traitors. She then appealed to the assembled spectators, but the Jacobin press had done its job, and the crowd denounced her as a traitor to the republic. The judges' decision was a foregone conclusion. Madame Roland was condemned to death as one of the participants in a conspiracy against the "indivisibility of the Republic, and the liberty and safety of the French people." She was allowed no appeal, and on November 9, 1793, she was guillotined. Her last words were, "O Liberty, what crimes are committed in thy name!" Word of his wife's execution reached Jean-Marie Roland the very next day. That night, he committed suicide. Her lover Buzot, who was incoherent upon learning of her death on November 15, took his own life in June of the following year.

In her *Memoirs*, Madame Roland wrote observations and character sketches which continue to be used by historians of the French Revolution. In short, she has become the historian's correspondent at the scene. Through her writings, she warns future generations that ambitious individuals will constantly seek ways to sway poorly educated and desperate throngs. On a more personal level, she still allowed herself to soar while discussing the ideals of Rousseau and other Enlightenment thinkers, even though she had seen many of those hopes and goals shattered by harsh reality.

SOURCES:

Clemenceau-Jacquemaire, Madeleine. *The Life of Madame Roland*. Translated by Laurence Vail. London: Longmans, Green, 1930.

Doyle, William. *The Oxford History of the French Revolution*. Oxford: Clarendon Press, 1989.

Furet, François, and Mona Ozouf, eds. *A Critical Dictionary of the French Revolution*. Translated by Arthur Goldhammer. Cambridge, MA: The Belknap Press of Harvard University Press, 1989.

May, Gita. *Madame Roland and the Age of Revolution*. NY: Columbia University Press, 1970.

Roland, Marie-Jeanne. *Mémoires de Madame Roland*. Edited by Paul de Roux. Paris: Mercure de France, 1986.

Abel A. Alves,
Assistant Professor of History,
Ball State University, Muncie, Indiana,
and author of *Brutality and Benevolence: Human Ethology, Culture, and the Birth of Mexico* (Greenwood Press, 1996)

Roland, Pauline (1805–1852)

French socialist journalist and activist whose agitated, tragic life reflected typical features of the Romantic movement. Pronunciation: paw-LEEN ro-LAH. Born Marie-Désirée-Pauline Roland on June 6, 1805, at Falaise (Calvados); died at Lyons of pneumonia and exhaustion on December 16, 1852, and was buried there; daughter of Joseph-Jouachine Roland (d. 1806, a postmaster) and Françoise-Marie-Adélaide Lesne (d. 1833); educated at a boarding school and tutored by Desprèz (1827–31); never married; children: (with Adolphe Guéroult) son, Jean-François Roland (b. 1835); (with Jean-François Aicard) Maria (1837–1839); Moïse (1839–c. 1852); Irma (c. 1841–1923).

Went to Paris to join Enfantin's Saint-Simonians (1832); liaison with Jean-François Aicard (1834–47); published histories of France and England (1835, 1838, 1844); wrote for Saint-Simonian gazettes (mid-1830s); wrote for Pierre Leroux's journals (1841–48); lived at Leroux's commune at Boussac (1847–48); founded a teachers' association and, with Jeanne Deroin, a union of associations (1849); arrested, tried, *and imprisoned (1850–51); arrested and deported to Algeria (1852).*

Writings: Histoire de France abrégé pour l'enseignement des deux sexes, depuis les temps les plus reculés jusqu'à nos jours (Paris: Lecomte & Pougen, 1835); Histoire d'Angleterre, depuis les temps les plus reculés jusqu'à nos jours (2 vols., Paris: Desessart, 1838); Précis d'Histoire d'Angleterre, d'Écosse et d'Irlande, ou Histoire du Royaume-Uni, depuis les temps les plus reculés jusqu'à nos jours (Paris: Didot, 1844); (with G. Lefrançais and Perot) Aux Instituteurs: l'Association des Instituteurs, Institutrices et Professeurs socialistes (Paris: Imprimerie Schneider, 1849); idem., Association fraternelle des Instituteurs, Institutrices et Professeurs socialistes: programme d'éducation (Paris: au siège de l'Association, 1849).

When Pauline Roland, aged 27, set off on November 17, 1832, from her native town of Falaise (Calvados) in Normandy, she was not, like most provincials then and now, seeking her fortune. Rather, as a convert, she was anticipating spiritual

Pauline Roland

fulfillment among the devotees of a new secular religion, Saint-Simonianism. Unfortunately for her hopes, this cult, founded by Louis-Claude de Rouvroy, Comte de Saint-Simon (1760–1825), and then headed by Barthélémy-Prosper Enfantin (1796–1864), was in decline as a result of Enfantin's trial (July 1832) and imprisonment (December 15, 1832–August 1, 1833) for public immorality. Upon his release, he and most of his leading disciples went off to Egypt for three years to await the Female Messiah, who would confirm Enfantin's teachings. The movement never recovered from the Egyptian episode. Enfantin, an engineer by training, became a railway promoter who helped form the Paris-Lyons-Marseille (PLM), France's largest system. Roland knew the Saint-Simonians were in difficulty when she set out, but she would have had no suspicion that the cult was doomed, for she was a true believer and remained so long after most followers had given up.

Pauline and her younger sister **Irma Roland** (1806–1839) were the children of Joseph Roland, postmaster of Falaise, and **Françoise Lesne Roland**. When Joseph died in 1806, Françoise obtained his job. (After 1848 women would be forbidden to hold such posts.) Françoise provided Pauline and Irma a good education at a local boarding school, but Pauline left at age 11½ due to illness, Irma later. Because girls were not admitted to the high school (*collège*), Françoise finally secured them a tutor named Desprèz, an instructor at the school who was married and seven years Pauline's senior. Desprèz was virtually the sole local Saint-Simonian, a subscriber to *Le Globe*, the sect's paper, and friend of Michel Chevalier, a leading Saint-Simonian and later a notable economist and government adviser. Roland had been extremely pious in her childhood but had given up Catholicism. Under the tutelage of Desprèz, she became enthralled by Saint-Simonianism—and by Desprèz, a pale, thin, romantic-looking man trapped in an unhappy marriage. They shared a passionate platonic love from 1827 to 1831.

Saint-Simonianism, a product of the Enlightenment, was a socialist religion ("utopian," according to Marx) emphasizing technology and work. Humans should conquer nature, not each other. Useful work is what is truly fulfilling, and it should be employed to end the suffering of "the most numerous and poorest class." It would free workers but also women, for men and women are equal. Roland found this sexual equality one of Saint-Simonianism's strongest attractions; as she wrote, "I feel myself almost equal to the best [of men] and much superior to the ordinary."

It was Enfantin, Saint-Simon's successor, who developed Saint-Simonianism into a full-blown cult, with a rigid hierarchical organization, rituals, and costumes. Until November 1831, he and Saint-Armand Bazard were co-high priests, but at that point Bazard broke away because of Enfantin's increasingly strange theories on sex and women. Saint-Simonianism preached the liberation of both mind and body. With Enfantin, the religion became more emotional and sensual. He advocated free love, rehabilitating the flesh by satisfying the natural sex drive. He was probably sincere; certainly he was the leading beneficiary of this doctrine. Enfantin was, indeed, an amazing specimen: brilliant, physically magnificent, and (in Chevalier's words) "one of the great magnetizers who exist or have ever existed." Men and women alike gravitated to him, the latter notably so when he decided that the final confirmation of the doctrine would come from the Female Messiah, a kind of perfect woman who would soon appear. Not a few women hoped they would prove to be the predestined One. It seems likely that Pauline Roland harbored some such hope for a time.

She had not rushed into Saint-Simonianism and certainly had serious doubts about Enfantin's sexual ideas, which seemed to her to be a thinly disguised condoning of adultery. Yet, his version of Saint-Simonianism chimed with her extreme sensibility. At Desprèz's urging, she began a long, passionate correspondence, overflowing with questions, confidences, and romantic agonizings, with **Aglaé Saint-Hilaire**, a woman painter charged by Enfantin with indoctrinating female converts. In 1831, Pauline's mother forbade her and Irma to have any more contact with Desprèz, but the three vowed to keep the faith even to martyrdom. (When Desprèz kissed Pauline's hand at their parting, it was their first physical contact.) Pauline finally accepted Enfantin's sex doctrine. In a May 13, 1832, letter to Aglaé she said she now believed Enfantin's was the voice of God. She then vowed to refrain from destroying Desprèz's marriage; in her mind, this sacrifice legitimized her later sexual conduct. From early childhood, she had identified sacrifice with virtue, a theme that would remain powerful throughout her life.

When Françoise told her daughters in 1832 that she could no longer support them, Pauline gladly fled Falaise for Paris to join the disciples of the soon-to-be imprisoned Enfantin. She found poorly paying places as a teacher of geography, history, French, English, and Italian in private schools. The little money she had, from the sale of her diamonds, she gave to Aglaé to help Enfantin. On the eve of his imprisonment, she finally met him in person, but he was cool, probably having been put on his guard by the jealous Aglaé, who was tiring of Roland's effusions and suspecting she was aspiring to be recognized as the predestined One. To Aglaé, Pauline in fact had once candidly admitted to "a bit of a romantic tinge in ideas and too much exaltation." When Enfantin was released in August 1833, Roland begged to spend some time with him, but she received no reply. Meanwhile, Roland's relationship with Aglaé having faded (it would end in September 1835), Enfantin had made Charles Lambert, a mining engineer, her father-confessor. She entered a platonic love affair with him and badly wanted to accompany him and Enfantin to Egypt. Unable to go, she continued to correspond with him.

Lambert left her in charge of the spiritual welfare of a group of young men, including Adolphe Guéroult, a brilliant young journalist at *Le Globe* and *Le Temps*. After very serious thought, she decided to put into practice Saint-Simon's doctrine of saving both spirit and flesh by flesh and spirit. She had vowed she would never marry unless society changed the imbalance between the sexes, and she now steeled herself to raise as their sole parent any children she might bear, accepting no obligatory support from any father. A virgin in her 29th year, she concluded that sexuality could be used as a means of indoctrinating converts. She thus embarked on "carnal moralization," becoming a kind of holy prostitute in order to convert and save the men in her circle. Her literal application of Enfantin's most radical ideas made her perhaps unique among his followers; certainly it scandalized many. Fundamental to Pauline Roland throughout her life, however, was making her acts conform to her ideals.

Described as "tall" (at 5'3"), with a broad brow, oval face, chestnut hair, brown eyes, and a somewhat large nose and mouth, Roland possessed charm and even beauty. She found she enjoyed sex: "Glory to God, it was good," she wrote. Although she probably gave herself to many, she fell in love with Guéroult, who, she wrote, had never been loved by a woman and whose wounded heart only a woman could cure. "I was his mother in love," she wrote to Lambert. Wrote Guéroult: "We loved each other without promises, without any vows. It was love in all its freedom and at the same time full of confidence and loyalty." Enfantin's "ideas were strongly at work here." Roland soon put his faith to the test. She became pregnant and then, on June 20, 1834, had sex with Jean-François

Aicard while Guéroult was out of town. She immediately informed him, and on his return a long conversation ensued. He showed himself "noble and religious," as she put it; they remained friends but no longer lovers. When she gave birth to a son on January 13, 1835, she named him after Aicard; the son learned that Guéroult was his father only after her death.

Roland began a liaison with Aicard that would last until 1847. He had come to Paris from Toulon in 1830 to study law and had fallen in with Saint-Simonianism, from which, however, he became estranged in 1832 because of Enfantin's sexual theories. He was a voluble, hot-blooded southerner, handsome, athletic, proud, and easily offended. Pauline met him when he was disillusioned and despairing. He took pity on her poverty, while she wanted only to be loved and to "save" him and make him happy again. Roland would have three children with Aicard: Maria (1837–1839), Moïse (1839–c. 1852), and Irma (c. 1841–1923). In addition, of course, she raised Jean-François, and in the latter 1840s she took in **Aline-Marie Chazal**, daughter of the deceased social reformer *Flora Tristan* (1803–1844) and later mother of the painter Paul Gauguin. Roland took sole responsibility for her children, asserting that "woman alone is the family."

> *P*auline Roland, this generous fanatic who had the illusions of a child and the character of a hero! This crazy woman, this martyr, this saint.
>
> —George Sand

She and Aicard lived off the money from his meager legal work and their writings for struggling left-wing publications. Through Aicard, she met Pierre Leroux (1797–1871), a dissident Saint-Simonian working out his own version of socialism. Leroux gradually replaced Enfantin as Roland's "father," although she never became as mystically attached to him as to Enfantin. While pregnant with her first child, she began writing (up to 14 hours a day) for Leroux's *Encyclopédie nouvelle*, intended to be the successor to the great 18th-century work. The pay was poor, and the project died in 1841. She also produced a textbook short history of France (1835). In 1838, she published a similar history of England; a revised version for adults, an original historical comparison of England, Scotland, and Wales, appeared in 1844. Notably, she stressed social and cultural matters at the expense of traditional political and military affairs.

Roland also contributed occasional articles and reviews to periodicals. Since items often appeared anonymously or under pseudonyms or first names, it is impossible to establish a firm bibliography. She probably wrote for *La Femme libre* (c. 1832) and certainly its successor, the first French feminist review (and written only by women), *Suzanne Voilquin*'s *La Femme nouvelle/La Tribune des femmes*, followed in its turn by *Le Journal des femmes*—all short-lived Saint-Simonian gazettes of the mid-1830s. She also wrote for Leroux's *Revue encyclopédique* and for *Le Temps*, thanks to Guéroult, as well as *Eugénie Niboyet*'s *Conseiller des femmes* (Lyons). In the 1840s, she contributed to Leroux's and *George Sand*'s *Revue indépendant* (from 1841), Leroux's *La Revue sociale* (from 1845) and the weekly *L'Éclaireur de l'Indre* (from 1843); in 1847, Leroux named her, Luc Desages, and Grégoire Champseix joint directors of *L'Éclaireur*. Her subjects were exceptionally varied: history and geography; biographical essays on English figures; women's concerns, especially labor conditions; peasant life and issues—and so forth.

Roland and Aicard's liaison was predictably stormy, with episodes worthy of Balzac, their contemporary. Briefly, they lived in Paris until around 1838, when Aicard returned to Toulon for two years to deal with his parents' affairs. There he fell in love with a Saint-Simonian friend's ravishing 17-year-old bride, Victoire, who reciprocated. Aicard then, amazingly, persuaded his friend to treat Victoire henceforth only as a sister or daughter. But one day Aicard discovered them violating the "contract" and told Roland everything. She choked down her hurt while sticking by her Saint-Simonian tenets. At his request, she moved to Toulon to fortify him against further temptation. In 1839, Pauline's sister died as did her daughter Maria (deeply distressing events for her), and she gave birth to Moïse. With Aicard, she moved back to Paris, where Irma was born around 1841. But Aicard, a weak man, still loved Victoire. In 1845, when he had to go to Toulon again, he discovered she felt likewise. Roland refused to accept the renewal of what she acidly called "a petty love affair [*amourette*] without import and without dignity." In April 1847, abandoned in Paris, in debt, and desperately wanting to keep her brilliant eldest son in boarding school, she begged Aicard for 17,500 of the 35,000 francs she had loaned him from her sister's bequest and her own earnings over 12 years. Having spent it, he sent her 2,000 from his father's account—a Balzackian ending to this sad tale.

Roland still held to Saint-Simonianism even though by the latter 1830s the cult itself had dis-

solved. But she had learned that free love was not for her and now conceded that marriage had much to recommend it.

Pierre Leroux came to her rescue. In late 1847, she joined his socialist community at Boussac (Creuse), where he had her found a school. His socialism became hers. He had excised the authoritarian, elitist, and cultic features of Saint-Simonianism while retaining its emphasis on a moral transformation of humanity, mystical exaltation, pacifism, female equality, and rejection of all exploitation of man by man. Boussac, founded in 1844, was slowly failing, but the year at the commune, where everyone received the same wage and all profits were put into agriculture, was the happiest of Roland's life. She began applying educational ideas she later spelled out in her teachers' association.

The Revolution of 1848, begun in February with the overthrow of Louis-Philippe (r. 1830–1848) and the proclamation of the Second Republic (1848–52), ultimately ended the Boussac experiment. Contrary to many accounts, Roland did not go to Paris until December 1848, after Boussac had failed, and did not participate in the women's club scene; in 1852, she wrote she had "too much intelligence and seriousness for that." She was not inactive, however. She drew notice when she tried to vote in the municipal elections of February 27 and lodged an official protest (denied in April) when she was refused. She probably contributed an article to Niboyet and *Jeanne Deroin*'s *La Voix des femmes* (The Women's Voice), and at *L'Éclaireur* she supported Leroux's candidacy for the National Assembly, arguing that workers and peasants, not the rich, should be chosen. Leroux won a by-election on June 8; *L'Éclaireur* folded, however, after the June Days insurrection.

From Boussac, Roland sent three open letters to Leroux, published in *Le Peuple* (The People, November 27, December 11 and 18), setting forth her socialist credo. While individual rights must be respected, humans can act usefully only in association. Private capital should disappear, with the state alone owning the instruments of production. Individual property should be permitted only to meet the ordinary needs of life; there should be neither rich nor poor. An elected council should direct all operations of production, distribution, and consumption by communities, with women enjoying full rights to vote and hold office. In a striking departure from her previous views, she endorsed marriage, which should be a union between legal equals based on love and faithfulness; divorce, while allowed, should result in the children being given to others to raise.

As Boussac shut down, she considered taking to the road (à la Flora Tristan) to proclaim "the new religion," but she finally decided to go to Paris. There Roland soon became involved in the associationist movement—workers' cooperatives—and journalism. She worked at *L'Opinion des femmes* (run by Deroin and **Désirée Gay**), which treated women's issues, and as an anonymous editor at *La Tribune des Peuples*, which promoted the liberation of subject nationalities, e.g., the Poles and Italians. Later, between January 1850 and January 1851, Roland published four fine articles in *La République* examining workers' cooperatives.

On February 6, 1849, she answered a call from a teacher, Perot, to meet to start a teachers' association. In April, internal debates led Deroin, Roland, and seven others to withdraw from this and form an association of socialist teachers. At length, on September 30, Roland, Perot, and Gustave Lefrançais, as a provisional executive committee of the Association of Schoolmasters, Schoolmistresses, and Professors, launched a general appeal to teachers.

A co-author, Roland heavily influenced the ambitious program contained in the appeal. It was a typical '48ist scheme, at once sensible and naive. Its core concept was the education of all individuals—male and female—to their full potential. (To Roland, equal education would by itself solve the problems of poverty and the inequality between husbands and wives.) Individual aptitude alone, not family background, should govern placement and progress. By age 18, all should be capable to some degree in "the three" modes of knowledge—manual, scientific, and artistic. The scheme proposed six three-year stages, each with age-specific goals. The most radical idea was the compulsory enrollment of children from birth to three in nurseries and from three to six in daycare facilities staffed by professionals. Roland wanted women free to work: maternity is "a duty of the woman, a sacred duty, even rigorous; but at no time should it be considered her only duty." If a woman did not wish to leave her child, she would be trained to join the staff.

Meanwhile, Deroin, an ex-Saint-Simonian with whom Roland worked in complete harmony, asked her to be a (symbolic) candidate in the May 13–14 elections to the national Legislative Assembly. Mistrustful of politics, Roland declined, and Deroin herself ran instead. Acting on a plan first envisaged by Flora Tristan, Deroin went on to found an umbrella organization of the cooperatives, the Union of Fraternal Associations of Workers. Roland, representing the teachers, joined the Executive Committee and took charge of administration. After a preliminary convention (August 23), delegates from 104 associations formally established the Union (October 5). It promoted an ambitious project to unite production and consumption among the associations so that individuals could be self-sufficient and not have to resort to public markets. The plan's leitmotif was not equal pay per se but the assurance of fair distribution to all according to their needs.

Predictably, the conservative government took a dim view of socialist organizations, despite the teachers' and Union's efforts to stay strictly within the law. Police pressure mounted from March 1850. On May 29, they arrested 38 men and 9 women (including Deroin) at a general assembly. Roland was arrested shortly afterward during searches of dwellings. They were charged with plotting to overthrow the government. Roland's indictment described her as an unwed mother, a communist socialist, and "an enemy of marriage." The Associations Affair trial, held before packed galleries on November 12–14, silenced the women's movement in France for the next 20 years. Roland, Deroin, and **Louise Nadaud** received six months in prison (much lighter sentences than the men's); when their appeals failed, they were incarcerated from January 2 to July 2, 1851, at Saint-Lazare, under the fairly liberal rules of political confinement.

Roland read Plato and the New Testament while in prison, and, said Deroin, worked among the thieves and prostitutes "with a noble persistence" to restore their self-respect. She moved toward a religious socialism: "The democratic and social Republic is what Jesus of Nazareth called the Kingdom of God." She continued to write even though she found her contacts drying up. On April 25, the *Feuille du Peuple* (The People's Page) printed her article "Does a Woman Have a Right to Liberty?"; and *La Liberté de Pensée* (The Freedom of Thought) published in its 43rd and 45th issues long articles on ideals and morality, the first one dedicated to her eldest son. She (with Deroin) also appealed to American feminists for solidarity; in reply, the Second National Women's Rights Convention named *Lucretia Mott to correspond with the French movement.

Upon her release, Roland was destitute. She had received word in prison that an uncle had left her 12,000 francs, which she dreamed of using to pay her debts and help the teachers' association to found a socialist commune. But the bequest became tied up in the courts. Friends had cared for her children while she was imprisoned; she could not support them now by herself. To keep them and herself alive and rescue her failing teachers' association, she begged money from (mostly poor) friends—Lambert turned her down—and imagined publishing ventures, e.g., almanacs and cheap editions of the classics. She could have fled to Belgium or (like Deroin and Leroux) to England, but she stayed fast: "I await my fate," she wrote on January 16, 1852. "Whatever happens, I shall suffer it in conformity with my principles."

She did not have long to wait. After Louis-Napoleon Bonaparte (the future Napoleon III) seized power on December 2, 1851, resistance flickered and a crackdown followed. Roland, contrary to legend, did not participate in the uprising. She did bravely visit prisoners and intercede for them. The authorities, who thought she had fled, finally woke up and arrested her on February 6, 1852, for insurrection, belonging to secret organizations, and posting placards calling for resistance. She appeared before the judge on February 10. To his questions, she defiantly replied, "Actively, I took no part in the insurrection, but in my heart I took an active part." She was sentenced on March 24 to deportation to Algeria for life, for having participated in charity lotteries for prisoners' families (false), for belonging to women's clubs (false), and for being a notorious socialist propagandist, which she was. As she remarked, she was really condemned for her opinions, friends, and participating in the 1848 revolution.

Algerian exile had three categories: 1) imprisonment, 2) confinement to a town and forbidden self-employment, and 3) the same but allowed self-employment. Roland received "Algeria minus" (2). Because her son Moïse was too ill to accompany Roland, friends cared for him until he died soon after she left. They also supported Jean-François and Irma at schools. Throughout her remaining ordeal, the separation from her children tormented her, especially when she felt duty-bound to refuse to appeal or accept any conditional release. While waiting at Saint-Lazare to be transported, she wrote (April 15) in bitterness and idealistic fervor (and in faithfulness to Leroux's doctrine of poverty) that she hoped they would always be poor because rising in this world can only come at the expense of others.

She left for Algeria on June 23 with 10 women and 210 men, sailing from Le Havre to Mers-el-Kabir. After being held at grim Fort Saint-Grégoire near Oran, she was sent by boat on July 10–11 with 13 women to the Convent of the Good Shepherd at El-Bier, near Algiers, a facility mostly for prostitutes and ruled by a strict Bavarian baroness. Many of the women converted or requested pardon, but not Roland. The baroness recommended she be sent to Sétif. Roland took ship to Bougie on July 28 and from there rode to Sétif by mule for several days across the Kabylie in a blazing heat. At Sétif, she worked in a small hotel as a laundress and cook for two francs a day plus the government's one-franc subsidy—not enough to send anything to her children.

Meanwhile, George Sand, the poet Béranger, and others tried in vain to get her released. By autumn, however, the government, concerned about public reaction to the deaths of female deportees, offered to release them if they would repent and swear allegiance. Many women accepted these terms, but Roland still held firm. The government's anxiety grew when Jean-François won first place in a national Latin examination. Fearing he would interrupt the prize ceremony with a political appeal, it increased the pressure on Roland, transferring her to the kasbah (native quarter) at Bône and even threatening her with the "dry guillotine" in Cayenne (Devil's Island). Anguished, she refused all conditions. Exasperated, the government in late October remitted her sentence.

The return of the now-famous exile became an agony. She arrived at Philippeville exhausted and took ship for Marseille. Clad only in a thin robe and canvas shoes, she endured a storm-ridden six-day passage, lying on deck, chilled to the bone and desperately seasick. In late November, she left Marseille for Paris and her children, but at Lyons she halted, sick and utterly worn. Jean-François sped to her bedside, but he arrived too late for her to recognize him. She died at 10 PM on December 16, 1852. Enfantin, who had just settled in Lyons as a railway official, dryly noted in his diary, "Death of Pauline Roland." Police agents watched her burial closely. It is not known if he was one of the five brave souls who showed up.

Both Jean-François and Irma eventually became professors, she in England. To Aicard's credit, he watched over them, and after his death Victoire did the same.

Pauline Roland became an icon of the Left in Europe. Victor Hugo, France's greatest Romantic writer, enshrined her with a poem in *Les Châtiments* (The Punishments), his savage indictment of the regime of "Napoléon le Petit." She indeed typified the Romantic age (c. 1780–1850) in its passion for both individual liberty and human solidarity. She took liberty to the farthest reaches when she called for women to bear children outside the bonds of the male-dominated institution of marriage. Yet at the same time she affirmed a total responsibility for the children and for all those who are, in Saint-Simon's phrase, society's "most numerous and poorest."

Gentle, strong, compassionate, and fearless, Roland was no publicity-seeker and humbly admitted her faults. She was self-sacrificing to the verge of masochism, could be preachy, and lacked intellectual originality. She was also a naïf, and for that she paid a terrible price. From Saint-Lazare in 1851, she confessed to Lefrançais that "setting out twenty years ago under the influence of this false theory that the mother alone is the family, having recognized its error, I see myself condemned to live this life in all its rigor." She modified her ideas, it is true. But, as **Edith Thomas** observed, few persons in any age have demonstrated such a thirst to make one's life conform to one's highest thoughts and words. It was a thirst which brought her, fittingly, to a romantic end: a victory wrapped in tragedy.

SOURCES:

Adler, Laure. *l'Aube du féminisme: les premieres journalistes (1830–1850)*. Paris: Payot, 1979.

Bidelman, Patrick Kay. *Pariahs Stand Up! The Founding of the Liberal Feminist Movement in France, 1858–1889*. Westport, CT: Greenwood Press, 1982.

Decaux, Alain. *Histoire des françaises*. Vol. 2: *La Révolte*. Paris: Perrin, 1972.

Dictionnaire biographique du mouvement ouvrier français. Dir. Jean Maitron. Paris: Éditions Ouvrières, 1969—.

Elwitt, Sanford. "Leroux, Pierre," in *Historical Dictionary of France from the 1815 Restoration to the Second Empire*. 2 vols. Ed. by Edgar Leon Newman. Westport, CT: Greenwood Press, 1987.

Groult, Benoîte. *Pauline Roland, ou comment la liberté vint aux femmes*. Paris: Robert Laffont, 1991.

Michaud, Stéphane. "Deux approches du changement social: Flora Tristan et Pauline Roland au miroir de leur correspondance," in *Flora Tristan, George Sand, Pauline Roland: Les Femmes et l'invention d'une nouvelle morale, 1830–1848*. Paris: Éditions Créaphis, 1994.

Moses, Claire Goldberg. *French Feminism in the Nineteenth Century*. Albany, NY: State University of New York Press, 1984.

Thibert, Marguerite. "Une Apôtre socialiste de 1848: Pauline Roland," in *La Révolution de 1848*. Vol. 22, 1925–26, pp. 478–502, 524–540.

Thomas, Edith. *Pauline Roland: Socialisme et féminisme au XIXᵉ siècle*. Paris: Marcel Rivière, 1956 (contains a bibliography of Roland's journalism and correspondence).

SUGGESTED READING:

Agulhon, Maurice. *The Republican Experiment, 1848 to 1852*. Cambridge: Cambridge University Press, 1983.

Carlick, Robert B. *The Proffered Crown: Saint-Simonianism and the Doctrine of Hope*. Baltimore, MD: Johns Hopkins University Press, 1987.

Emerit, Marcel. *Pauline Roland et les déportées d'Afrique*. Paris: Empire Français, 1948.

Goldstein, Leslie F. "Early Feminist Themes in French Utopian Socialism: The Saint-Simonians and Fourier," in *Journal of the History of Ideas*. Vol. 43, 1982, pp. 91–108.

Lefrançais, Gustave. *Souvenirs d'un révolutionnaire*. Brussels: Bibliothèque des Temps Nouveaux [1902].

Manuel, Frank. *The New World of Henri Saint-Simon*. Notre Dame, IN: University of Notre Dame Press, 1963.

Moses, Claire B. "Saint-Simonian Men/ Saint-Simonian Women: The Transformation of Feminist Thought in 1830s France," in *Journal of Modern History*. Vol. 54, 1982, pp. 240–267.

Perlberg, Marilyn Ann. "Men and Women in Saint-Simonianism: The Union of Politics and Morals." University of Iowa dissertation, 1993.

Price, Roger. *The French Second Republic: A Social History*. Ithaca, NY: Cornell University Press, 1972.

Rabine, Leslie Wahl. *Feminism, Socialism, and French Romanticism*. Bloomington, IN: Indiana University Press, 1993.

Roland, Pauline, Arthur Ranc, and Gaspard-Léonce Rouffet. *Bagnes d'Afrique: Trois Transports au Algérie après le coup d'État du 2 décembre 1851*. Ed. by Fernand Rude. Paris: Maspero, 1981.

Weil, Kan. "Spectacular Bodies: Women and the Discourse of the Saint-Simonians," in *Nineteenth Century Contexts*. Vol. 16, 1992, pp. 33–45.

COLLECTIONS:

Amsterdam: International Institute of Social History.

Paris: Archives de la Ministère de la Guerre; Bibliothèque de l'Arsenal; Bibliothèque historique de la ville de Paris, Fonds Enfantin.

David S. Newhall,
Pottinger Distinguished Professor of History
Emeritus, Centre College,
and author of *Clemenceau: A Life at War* (1991)

Roland de la Platiere, Marie-Jeanne Phlipon (1754–1793).

See Roland, Madame.

Roland Holst, Henriëtte (1869–1952)

Dutch Socialist militant, poet, and essayist, held in high regard for her contributions to her country's modern literature, whose anti-Nazi stance was vital to the morale of the Dutch resistance movement during World War II. Name variations: Henriette Roland Holst; Henriëtte Roland Holst-van der Schalk or Henriëtte Roland Holst van der Schalk. Born Henriëtte Goverdina Anna van der Schalk on December 24, 1869, in Noordwijk, the Netherlands; died on November 21, 1952, in Amsterdam; daughter of a wealthy family of the Dutch bourgeoisie; married Richard Nicolaüs Roland Holst (an artist and writer), in 1896; no children.

Published first volume of poetry (1895); with husband, joined Dutch Social Democratic Labor

Party (1897); published Capital and Labor in the Nineteenth Century *(1902); withdrew from politics (1912); returned to politics in opposition to World War I (1914); was a founding member of the Dutch Communist Party (1918); disillusioned with the Soviet system on visit to Russia (1921); quit the Dutch Communist Party (1927); became the voice of the Dutch resistance movement through her poetry (1940–45).*

Born in the North Sea resort town of Noordwijk in 1869, Henriëtte Roland Holst came from a highly respected family, wealthy members of the Dutch bourgeoisie, and grew up in her family's large and beautifully furnished mansion. She was a critically acclaimed poet by age 26, having published sonnets in the leading literary journal *De Nieuwe Gids* and, in 1895, seeing the publication of her first volume of poetry, *Sonnets and Poems Written in Terzinas*. Much of her early verse was in the Romantic tradition of Percy Bysshe Shelley, whom she also resembled in her support for the downtrodden and her advocacy of social revolution. Other formative influences were English social critic William Morris and leading Dutch poet Albert Verwey, as well as the ideas espoused by Dante and Spinoza.

In 1896, she married Richard Nicolaüs Roland Holst, a talented artist who would teach for many years at the Royal Academy of Graphic Arts, serving as its director from 1926 to 1934. The couple settled in Bloemendaal, not far from Amsterdam, whose artistic and political circles they began to frequent. In Amsterdam as in other cities, intellectual battles raged about the contemporary struggle between capital and labor. While Henriëtte had long been concerned about the condition of the poor, she had little or no knowledge of politics at this time. As she wrote in her autobiography more than 50 years later, it was her husband who introduced her to the complexities of political theory and practice. The year after their marriage, in April 1897, they joined the Dutch Social Democratic Labor Party. Thus abandoning the privileged class to which she had been born, and influenced by Herman Gorter, a gifted poet of the period, Roland Holst focused on her quest for a more just society. As one of her Dutch biographers, K.F. Proost, wrote in 1937, "She was driven by her vision and indignation, and for more than 40 years with her enormous energy and interest she devoted herself orally and in writing to propaganda for a socialist society."

Well versed in Marxist theory, in 1902 Roland Holst published an impressively researched historical study, *Capital and Labor in the Nineteenth Century*. Despite her intellectual grasp of Socialist ideology, it was primarily her strong sense of humanitarian duty that drew her to the workers' movement, and this was eloquently expressed in her 1903 volume *The New Birth*. By this time she was doing editorial work for the Socialist theoretical journal *De Nieuwe Tijd* and was editing the party's newspaper, *De Tribune*. Her socialist bent can also be seen in her books of this period, among them the poetry collection *Upward Roads* (1907), *The Rebels* (1910), a lyric verse drama celebrating the failed Russian revolution of 1905, and *Thomas More* (1912), a drama exploring the conflict between the individual and society. Later dramatic works included *Michael* (1916), *Children of this Time* (1931), and *The Mother* (1932).

Within a few years of joining the Social Democratic Labor Party, Roland Holst had aligned herself with its "Tribunist" faction, a militant circle that took its name from the newspaper and held the reformist party leadership responsible for all but abandoning Marxist fundamentals. The Tribunists were mostly intellectuals of middle- and upper-middle-class background whose vision of Socialism was highly idealistic and, in the final analysis, probably unrealistic. By 1909, Roland Holst had become disillusioned with the compromises inherent in party politics and joined a militant splinter group calling itself the Left Social Democratic Labor Party. During this period, her friendship with *Rosa Luxemburg, the German Social Democratic leader and radical agitator, brought her into contact with the most revolutionary tendencies of pre-1914 continental European socialism, and also tested her acceptance of Marxist doctrine. Radical politics and splinter-group activities failed to fulfill her idealistic notions of what society should become, however, and in 1912 she decided to withdraw entirely from the Socialist movement.

The break was painful for her. In her 1912 book *The Woman in the Woods*, Roland Holst described the feelings of anguish, bitterness and emptiness that overwhelmed her as she isolated herself from the cause she still felt strongly drawn to. Comparing herself to the poet Dante, Roland Holst felt lost in a forest, but without a guide to lead her from the wilderness. Forced to rely on her own intuition and judgment in the making of difficult decisions, she reflected her sense of powerlessness and pain in the following lines from *The Woman in the Woods*:

> She remained alone amidst
> them who fought, full of burning pain,
> longing for a god, to pray to him
> to be also a man in her heart.

Her political withdrawal ended with the start of World War I in 1914. In the bloodbath that engulfed Europe, Roland Holst, like other proponents of Marxist theory, saw an extraordinary opportunity: If workers throughout the world were to unite with members of their class rather than with their own nationalist governments, such a people's movement could end once and for all the root causes of war and human suffering. And the Netherlands, as one of Europe's few remaining neutral states, was an ideal place for breeding this new spirit of proletarian internationalism. In 1915, Roland Holst became head of the small and short-lived but vocal Netherlands Revolutionary Socialist League, a group attempting to fuse the ideals of socialism and pacifism. That same year she traveled to Switzerland to attend the Zimmerwald conference, where participants first heard the impassioned call of Vladimir Lenin to "turn the imperialist war into a proletarian world revolution."

Inspired by the Russian revolutionary, and energized by such an ambitious agenda, Roland Holst worked to engage the Dutch working class in creating the foundations for a truly radical movement. She edited and wrote for *Die Vorbote*, the review published by the Zimmerwald left group of internationalist Socialists, which included the radical communists Karl Radek and Anton Pannekoek. In her articles for the journal, she stated her belief that the international working-class movement would soon recover from its temporary infatuation with nationalism exhibited by the war.

In November 1917, Roland Holst enthusiastically greeted the revolution in Russia led by Lenin; the following year, she became a founding member of the Dutch Communist Party, which aimed to create a workers' state based on social justice and true freedom. When the Comintern, the Leninist organization dedicated to bringing about a world revolution, opened its Amsterdam bureau in November 1919, she became a member of its first executive committee. She was also a leading participant in the Communist conference held in Amsterdam the following February. Soon thereafter, she went to Strasbourg to advocate the Leninist revolution at an important French Socialist congress.

In 1921, Roland Holst went to Soviet Russia as an honored guest and important speaker at the Third Congress of the Comintern. Soon after this trip, however, she privately began to voice her misgivings about what she had witnessed there. She deplored the lack of freedom she had found within the Communist Party and

the revolution's high cost to ordinary people; she also believed that the Soviet Union appeared to be evolving rapidly into a brutal bureaucratic dictatorship distorted by ceaseless warfare against enemies of the state. In this, she became one of the first to perceive the brutal excesses that would characterize the Soviet Union under Joseph Stalin. The hope she had expressed in 1918, that the revolutionary forces of the day could somehow achieve social justice with minimal use of violence, was now beginning to seem a bit naive. Her book *Sunken Borders*, predicting that "the gentle forces will win in the end," contained clear signs that this militant Socialist and revolutionary was experiencing a growing sense of spirituality very much at odds with the leadership in the Soviet Union:

> God grows in us: in you in me in all
> the more we prepare ourselves with courage
> for the battle for the sake of the conscious life of
>   mankind
> and for the penetrating gratification of Love.

In her 1923 book *Between Two Worlds*, Roland Holst rejected the Russian Revolution, terming it "a dreadful disease, a life-and-death crisis in the body of society." By November 1927, the tenth anniversary of the Bolshevik revolution, she resigned from the Dutch Communist Party, abandoning the Soviet Russian model of revolutionary social transformation and the emerging evils of Stalinism. Sympathizing with the breakaway position of Leon Trotsky, she made clear that her commitment to social justice remained undimmed, and that year she founded a splinter group, the Independent Communist Party.

Man's sorrow often will not let me sleep.
—Henriëtte Roland Holst

Decades earlier, in her Marxist phase, Roland Holst had been intrigued by the pacifist ideas of the Russian writer and social visionary Count Leo Tolstoy. At that time she had rejected nonviolence as a viable option for the disadvantaged and oppressed Dutch workers; before 1914, she had believed that anti-militarism in the form of isolated and individual acts of noncompliance or disobedience was a useless tactic. She even held that the proletariat should demand arms in preparation for the day when power would be theirs in a workers' republic. After 1927, however, having discovered the flaws of dogmatic Marxism, she became increasingly convinced that the use of violence could only debase and pervert the ideals of any just cause. Influenced by the Dutch pacifist theologian Bartolomeus de Ligt, Roland Holst became convinced that Socialism and Christianity need not oppose each other.

In 1928, she read a total of 22 works by and about Tolstoy. One result of this intensive study was the article "Tolstoi, the Great Wrestler for Truth," published in *Liberation,* the journal of the minuscule League of Religious Anarcho-Communists. In this article, while granting that Karl Marx was "a scientific genius," Roland Holst argued that Tolstoy, the poetical genius, had also offered profound insights into the nature of modern society, particularly moral ideals that orthodox Socialists had never taken seriously. Asserting that a meaningful new agenda for the Socialist movement must address moral issues, she acknowledged Marx as a major force in Socialist ideology, but proposed that his ideas needed to be humanized and tempered by Tolstoy's ideals.

She was also attracted to the ideas and personality of Mohandas K. Gandhi, India's saintly "Mahatma" and an advocate of political independence achieved through non-violent means. Gandhi's ideas are explored in several of her books published during this period, particularly the verse collections *Between Two Worlds* (1923) and *Between Time and Eternity* (1934). Unlike the Russian Revolution, the Indian independence movement never appeared to lose sight of the necessity of keeping ends and means morally connected, and in the 1930s, Roland Holst devoted considerable energies to Gandhi's cause. She established a Dutch Society of the Friends of India, raising funds and spreading the message of Gandhian nonviolence through its bulletin, *Friends of India,* and spoke about the movement throughout Europe. Throughout the 1930s, she continued to rank Tolstoy and Gandhi as two of the greatest "Heroes of the Spirit" ignored by a morally exhausted Western civilization. In 1935, she praised the great Russian writer in *Friends of India*: "A God-searcher of immense dimensions, a searcher of truth, that was the real essence of Tolstoi, that he was both in his immortal literary work, and in his apostolical activities." Her sensitive biography of Gandhi would be published in 1947, the year India achieved political independence.

Approaching 70 by the 1930s, Henriëtte Roland Holst was a venerated literary figure and the subject of a biography, but she was largely inactive in politics throughout that decade, which also saw the death of her husband in 1938. In May 1940, however, the German invasion of her country instantly reignited her inherent passion for justice. She joined several resistance circles, and during the five brutal years of

Nazi occupation she wrote poems and essays expressing her feelings about the evils of Fascism. Printed by the press of the Dutch underground, these works were passed from hand to hand, and sometimes memorized by the resistance members who were risking their lives daily as they hid Jews and smuggled weapons to be used in the fight against Nazi occupying forces.

After the liberation of the Netherlands in May 1945, Roland Holst was universally acclaimed as one of the pillars of strength who enabled the Dutch people to survive the bloody foreign occupation. The following year, her powerful resistance poems were collected and published as *From the Very Depths*. By then in her late 70s, she remained active in public as well as literary life. For some time after the liberation she contributed articles to *The Flame,* the journal of the small but vocal anti-Stalinist faction of Netherlands Trotskyites.

In 1949, Roland Holst published her autobiography, *The Fire Burned On,* and on the occasion of her 80th birthday was awarded an honorary doctorate from the University of Amsterdam. She had spent her entire life in one of the world's smallest and most densely populated nations, and her life there was reflected in a line of one of her best-known poems: "Holland, you give no space but to the mind." Rich in honors, friends, and years, Henriëtte Roland Holst died in Amsterdam on November 21, 1952. Recent scholarly interest in her life and achievements tends to confirm the evaluation at the time of her death of several leading Dutch newspapers, which described her as the greatest woman produced by the Netherlands in a century.

SOURCES:

Baker, Gary Lee. "Henriëtte Roland Holst-van der Schalk and the Hunchback of Theology: Reconciling the Unreconcilable," in *Canadian Journal of Netherlandic Studies*. Vol. 14, no. 2. Fall 1993, pp. 8–13.

Brouwer, Piet. "Le Thomas More de Henriëtte Roland Holst," in *Moreana: Bulletin Thomas More.* Vol. 25, no. 97. March 1988, pp. 9–20.

Gorman, Robert, ed. *Biographical Dictionary of Marxism.* Westport, CT: Greenwood Press, 1986.

Josephson, Harold, ed. *Biographical Dictionary of Modern Peace Leaders.* Westport, CT: Greenwood Press, 1985.

Lazitch, Branko, and Milorad M. Drachkovitch. *Biographical Dictionary of the Comintern.* New rev. ed. Stanford, CA: Hoover Institution Press, 1986.

Meijer, Reinder P. *Literature of the Low Countries: A Short History of Dutch Literature in The Netherlands and Belgium.* Assen: Van Gorcum, 1971.

"Mme. Roland Holst Dies at Age of 82," in *The New York Times.* November 23, 1952, p. 88.

Prins, Johanna C. "Henriëtte Roland Holst van der Schalk (1869–1952)," in *Canadian Journal of Netherlandic Studies.* Vol. 11, no. 2. Fall 1990, pp. 43–45.

Roland Holst, Henriëtte. *Het vuur brandde voort: Levensherinneringen*. Amsterdam: V.h. Van Ditmar, 1949.

Simons, Wim J. *Henriëtte Roland Holst*. Utrecht: Desclée De Brouwer, 1969.

Weevers, Theodoor. *Poetry of the Netherlands in its European Context 1170–1930*. London: University of London, the Athlone Press, 1960.

Zweers, A.F. "Leo Tolstoj's Role in Henriëtte Roland Holst's Quest for Brotherhood and Love," in *Canadian Review of Comparative Literature*. Vol. 7, no. 1. Winter 1980, pp. 1–21.

John Haag,
Associate Professor of History, University of Georgia,
Athens, Georgia

Roldán, Luisa (1656–1704)

Spanish sculptor of the 17th century. Name variations: Luisa Roldan; La Roldana; Luisa de los Arcos. Born Luisa Ignacia Roldán in Sevilla, Spain, in 1656; died in Madrid in 1704; daughter of Pedro Roldán (a sculptor) and Teresa de Mena y Villavicencio; sister of **Maria Roldán**, *who also helped their father produce sculpture; married Luis de los Arcos (a sculptor), in 1671; children: two.*

A native of Sevilla, Spain, Luisa Roldán was born in 1656, the daughter of Pedro Roldán, a sculptor of some renown, and **Teresa de Mena y Villavicencio**. Luisa was piously educated by her mother. Roldán, who had learned her father's craft, married another sculptor, Luis de los Arcos, in 1671, and they sculpted together in their own studio. One of their most important commissions involved works for the cathedral in Cádiz. Roldán's skill surpassed that of her father, as indicated by an oft-repeated anecdote. He was commissioned to produce a statue of St. Ferdinand for the cathedral in Sevilla, but it failed to please the patrons. She made some modifications in her father's work, to the delight of the cathedral chapter, which thought it was an entirely new statue.

As Luisa Roldán's fame spread, she attracted the attention of Cristóbal Ontañón. In 1692, Ontañón brought Luisa and her husband to Madrid and presented them at the court of Charles II, king of Spain. A commission for a statue of St. Michael for the monastery at El Escorial soon followed. Impressed by her works, the crown appointed her sculptor to the court on June 21, 1695, with an annual stipend of 100 ducats, retroactive to her arrival in Madrid. Roldán produced a number of religious pieces and achieved particular renown for small polychrome clay (terra-cotta) grouped figures for Nativity scenes, a technique virtually unknown before this time. Her most important pieces include *The Death of Saint *Mary Magdalene, The Annunciation*, and *The Mystical Marriage of St. Catherine*. Roldán died in Madrid in 1704.

SOURCES:

García Olloqui, María Victoria. *"La Roldana": escultora de cámara*. Sevilla: Diputación Provincial de Sevilla, 1977.

Kendall W. Brown,
Professor of History,
Brigham Young University, Provo, Utah

Rolfe, Lady Rebecca (c. 1596–1617).

See Pocahontas.

Rollins, Charlemae Hill
(1897–1979)

African-American librarian and author. Born in Yazoo City, Mississippi, on June 20, 1897; died on February 3, 1979; daughter of Allen G. Hill (a farmer) and Birdie (Tucker) Hill (a teacher); attended elementary school, founded by her parents, and black secondary schools in St. Louis, Missouri, and Holly Springs, Mississippi; graduated from high school at Western University in Quindoro, Kansas; attended one year at Howard University in Washington, D.C.; attended library school at Columbia College, Chicago, Illinois, 1932; attended graduate library school at the University of Chicago, 1934–36; married Joseph Walter Rollins, on April 8, 1918; children: Joseph Walter Rollins, Jr. (b. 1920).

As head of the children's department at the George Cleveland Hall branch of the Chicago Public Library, sought to increase the visibility of African-Americans in books for children; after retirement, made her own contribution through her publications Christmas Gif', an Anthology of Christmas Poems, Songs, and Stories Written by and about Negroes *(1963),* They Showed the Way *(1964),* Famous American Negro Poets for Children *(1965),* Famous Negro Entertainers of Stage and Screen *(1967), and* Black Troubadour, Langston Hughes *(1971).*

A distinguished librarian and authority on black literature, Charlemae Hill Rollins was born in Yazoo City, Mississippi, on June 20, 1897. Her family later moved to the town of Beggs in Indian Territory (now the state of Oklahoma), where the Hills, finding no school available for black children, founded their own. Rollins credited her grandmother, a former slave, with instilling in her a passion for books. She finished elementary school when she was 13 and then attended black secondary schools in St. Louis, Missouri, and Holly Springs, Mississippi. In 1916, she graduated from high school at Western University in Quindoro, Kansas, a segregated boarding school. After passing the required teaching exam, Rollins taught in Beggs for a short time before attending Howard University in Washington, D.C., for a year. She then returned to Oklahoma and married Joseph Walter Rollins on April 8, 1918. During World War I, her husband served in the U.S. Army in France while Rollins remained in Oklahoma. Upon his return in 1919, the couple moved to Chicago. Their son Joseph Walter Rollins, Jr., was born the following year.

Attracted to the library profession because of her love for books and her background in teaching, Rollins was hired by the Chicago Public Library in 1927 and assigned to the Harding Square Branch Library as a children's librarian. She realized she needed to enhance her education, and attended the library school at Columbia College in Chicago during the summer of 1932 with funds provided by the library. She then went on to attend the graduate library school at the University of Chicago from 1934 to 1936. With the opening of the George Cleveland Hall Branch Library in the early 1930s, Rollins was named the head of the children's department, a position she would hold for the rest of her career. Named after a prominent black surgeon who was on the library's board of directors, the branch library was the first to be built in a black neighborhood in Chicago, and soon became a center for cultural, educational and recreational activities for the community.

Rollins proved to be a warm and approachable librarian who offered inspiration and worthwhile instruction on the world of literature to children, parents and educators. One of the young patrons whom Rollins was able to encourage was *Gwendolyn Brooks, who would grow up to become a Pulitzer Prize-winning poet. During the Depression, Langston Hughes was a frequent visitor to the library and discussed his poetry with patrons there. Rollins was disturbed, however, by the lack of children's books relating to the African-American experience. She submitted a research paper to one of her instructors at the University of Chicago on the topic. The paper was later published as the pamphlet "The Negro in Children's Books." Rollins continued her research of the situation and the National Council of Teachers of English published her work, *We Build Together, a Reader's Guide to Negro Life and Literature for Elementary and High School Use*, in 1941, with revised editions in 1948 and 1967. Rollins was considered an expert in this specialized field and was inundated with requests from publishers to review manuscripts as well as invita-

tions to lecture, write and teach at various colleges and universities. Her course on children's literature became a required subject for education majors at Roosevelt University in Chicago. She was also committed to involvement in professional organizations and was active in state and national library associations. She chaired the Elementary Section of the Illinois unit of the Catholic Library Association in 1953–54 and the Children's Section of the Illinois Library Association in 1954–55. After serving as vice-president and president-elect of the Children's Services Division of the American Library Association (ALA) in 1956, the following year she became the first African-American president of the division. She also served on the editorial advisory board of *World Book Encyclopedia* and *The American Educator*.

After her retirement in 1963, Rollins focused her energy on writing. She wrote the biographical works *They Showed the Way* (1964), *Famous American Negro Poets for Children* (1965), *Famous Negro Entertainers of Stage and Screen* (1967), and *Black Troubadour, Langston Hughes* (1971), which was awarded the *Coretta Scott King** Award from the New Jersey Library and Medal Association. She also wrote *Christmas Gif', an Anthology of Christmas Poems, Songs and Stories Written by and about Negroes* (1963).

Rollins received many honors for her achievements, including the Library Letter Award from the American Library Association (1953), the Grolier Foundation Award (1955), three Negro Centennial Awards (1963), and the Woman's National Book Association's *Constance Lindsay Skinner** Award (1970). She was elected to honorary life membership of the American Library Association in 1972. In 1974, she was awarded a doctorate of humane letters from Columbia College in Chicago. The Chicago Library paid tribute by dedicating a room to her at the Carter G. Woodson Regional Library in 1977. Rollins died on February 3, 1979, at the age of 81. On October 21, 1989, by proclamation of Mayor Richard M. Daley, the children's area of the George Cleveland Hall Branch Library was named the Charlemae Hill Rollins Children's Room.

SOURCES:

Smith, Jessie Carney, ed. *Notable Black American Women*. Detroit, MI: Gale Research, 1992.

Susan J. Walton,
freelance writer, Berea, Ohio

Romance, Viviane (b. 1912)

French actress. Born Pauline Ronacher Ortmanns (also seen as Ortmans) on July 4, 1909, in Roubaix, France.

Selected filmography: Il est chamant *(1931);* Ciboulette *(1933);* Lilliom *(1934);* Les Yeux noirs *(*Dark Eyes, *1935);* La Bandera *(1935);* La Belle Equipe *(*They Were Five, *1936);* L'Ange du Foyer *(1937);* Mademoiselle Docteur *(*Street of Shadows, *1937);* Naples au baiser de feu *(*The Kiss of Fire, *1937);* Le Puritain *(1938);* Prison de femmes *(*Marked Girls, *1938);* L'Etrange Monsieur Victor *(1938);* Le Joueur *(1938);* La Maison du Maltais *(*Sirocco, *1938);* Gibraltar *(*It Happened in Gibraltar, *1938);* L'Esclave blanche *(*The Pasha's Wives, *1939);* La Tradition de Minuit *(1939);* Angelica *(1940);* La Vénus aveugle *(1941);* Une Femme dans la Nuit *(1941);* Cartacalha *(1942);* Feu Sacré *(1942);* Carmen *(1943);* La Boite aux Rêves *(1945);* Panique *(*Panic, *1946);* L'Affaire du Collier de la Reine *(*The Queen's Necklace, *1946);* La Colère des Dieux *(1947);* La Carrefour des Passions *(1947);* Maya *(also prod., 1950);* Passion *(also prod., 1951);* Au Coeur de la Casbah *(1952);* La Chair et le Diable *(*Flesh and Desire, *also prod., 1953);* Gueule d'Ange *(*Pleasures and Vices, *1955);* L'affaire des poisons *(1955);* Pitié pour les vamps *(also prod., 1956);* Mélodie en sous-sol *(*Any Number Can Win, *1963);* Nada *(1973).*

Winner of the Miss Paris title in 1930, French actress Viviane Romance (born Pauline Ortmanns) entered films as an extra and within a year was earning star billing. She appeared in such films as Fritz Lang's *Lilliom* (1934), Abel Gance's *Vénus aveugle* (1941), and Julien Duvivier's *Panique* (1946). In addition to acting, Romance produced several movies during the 1950s, including *Maya* (1950), *Passion* (1950), *Le Chair et le Diable* (*Flesh and Desire*, 1953), and *Pitié pour les vamps* (1956). The actress appeared in her last film, Claude Chabrol's *Nada*, in 1973.

Romano, Francesca (fl. 1321)

Licensed surgeon of Calabria, Italy. Name variations: Francesca Romana. Flourished in 1321 in Calabria; married Matteo de Romano.

Francesca Romano, one of the few medieval women allowed to study medicine at a university, was from the Italian bourgeoisie, and received permission to enter the medical school at the University of Salerno to take a degree in surgery. Unlike most women doctors, who used folk knowledge and empirical evidence in healing, Romano studied the theoretical, often nonsensical art of medicine the universities provided male doctors. She had to learn Latin and possibly Greek, and read treatises by such classical authors as Aristo-

tle and Galen on anatomy and physiology and their connections to astrology and other supernatural forces. In 1321, having successfully completed her training (which most likely did not involve any actual contact with patients), Romano was granted a license to practice surgery by Charles, duke of Cambria. Her professional career unfortunately went undocumented.

SOURCES:
Uitz, Erika. *The Legend of Good Women: The Liberation of Women in Medieval Cities.* Wakefield, RI: Moyer Bell, 1988.

Laura York,
Riverside, California

Roman empress.
See Rome, empress of.

Romanov, Alexandra (1825–1844).
See Alexandra Nikolaevna.

Romanov, Anastasia (1901–1918).
See Anastasia.

Romanov, Anna (fl. 1550)

*Russian aristocrat. Name variations: Romanova. Flourished around 1550; daughter of *Eudoxia Jaroslavovna (1534–1581) and Nikita Romanov (1530–1586); married Ivan Troiekurow.*

Romanov, Anna (1632–1692)

*Russian princess. Born Anna Mikhailovna Romanov on July 14, 1632; died on October 26, 1692; daughter of *Eudoxia Streshnev (1608–1645) and Michael (1596–1645), tsar of Russia (r. 1613–1645); married Boris Morozov.*

Romanov, Anna or Anne (1795–1865).
See Anna Pavlovna (1795–1865).

Romanov, Catherine.
See Catherine of Mecklenburg-Schwerin (1692–1733).
See Catherine of Russia (1788–1819).

Romanov, Catherine (1827–1894)

*Duchess of Mecklenburg-Strelitz. Born Catherine Michailovna Romanov on August 28, 1827; died on May 12, 1894; daughter of *Helene of Wurttemberg (1807–1873) and Grand Duke Michael of Russia (1798–1849); married George (1824–1876), duke of Mecklenburg-Strelitz, on February 16, 1851; children: Nickolas (b. 1854); **Helena Marie of Mecklenburg-***

Strelitz (1857–1936); George Alexander (b. 1859); Charles Michael (b. 1863).

Romanov, Catherine (1878–1959).

See Catherine Romanov.

Romanov, Elizabeth (1826–1845)

Grand duchess of Luxemburg. Born Elizabeth Michailovna Romanov on May 26, 1826; died on January 28, 1845; daughter of *Helene of Wurttemberg (1807–1873) and Grand Duke Michael of Russia (1798–1849); married Adolphe, grand duke of Luxemburg, on January 31, 1844.

Romanov, Euphamia (fl. 1550)

Russian aristocrat. Name variations: Romanova. Flourished around 1550; daughter of *Eudoxia Jaroslavovna (1534–1581) and Nikita Romanov (1530–1586); married Ivan Sitzki.

Romanov, Hélène.

See Helena Pavlovna (1784–1803).
See Helena of Russia (1882–1957).

Romanov, Irina (fl. 1601)

Russian aristocrat. Name variations: Romanova. Flourished around 1601; daughter of *Eudoxia Jaroslavovna (1534–1581) and Nikita Romanov (1530–1586); married Ivan Godunov (d. 1610), in 1601.

Romanov, Irina (1627–1679)

Russian princess. Born in 1627; died in 1679; daughter of *Eudoxia Streshnev (1608–1645) and Michael (1596–1645), tsar of Russia (r. 1613–1645).

Romanov, Irina (1895–1970).

See Irina.

Romanov, Marie.

See Maria Nikolaevna (1819–1876).
See Marie Alexandrovna (1853–1920).

Romanov, Martha (fl. 1550)

Russian aristocrat. Name variations: Martha Romanova. Flourished around 1550; daughter of *Eudoxia Jaroslavovna (1534–1581, matriarch of the House of Romanov) and Nikita Romanov (1530–1586, patriarch of the House of Romanov); married Boris Tscherkaski.

Romanov, Martha (1560–1631).

See Martha the Nun.

Romanov, Mary.

See Marie Alexandrovna (1853–1920).
See Marie Pavlovna (1890–1958).

Romanov, Natalya (1674–1716)

Grand duchess of Russia. Name variations: Natalie Alexinov Romanov. Born Natalya Alexinova Romanov on September 4, 1674; died on June 29, 1716; daughter of *Natalya Narishkina (1651–1694) and Alexis I (1629–1676), tsar of Russia (r. 1645–1676); sister of Peter I the Great (1672–1725), tsar of Russia (r. 1682–1725).

Romanov, Olga.

See Olga of Russia (1822–1892).
See Olga Constantinovna (1851–1926).
See Olga Alexandrovna (1882–1960).

Romanov, Sophie (1634–1676)

Russian princess. Born on September 14, 1634; died in 1676; daughter of *Eudoxia Streshnev (1608–1645) and Michael (1596–1645), tsar of Russia (r. 1613–1645).

Romanov, Vera (1854–1912).

See Vera Constantinovna.

Romanov, Xenia (1876–1960).

See Xenia Alexandrovna.

Romanov, Yekaterina Ivanova (1692–1733).

See Catherine of Mecklenburg-Schwerin.

Romanova, Anastasia.

See Anastasia Romanova (d. 1560).
See Anastasia Romanova (1860–1922).

Romanova, Maria (1886–1954).

See Ulanova, Galina for sidebar.

Romanovsky-Krassinsky, Princess (1872–1971).

See Kshesinskaia, Matilda.

Romans, queen of the.

See Matilda of Saxony (c. 892–968).
See Marshall, Isabel (1200–1240).
See Sancha of Provence (c. 1225–1261).
See Falkestein, Beatrice von (c. 1253–1277).

Romanzini, Maria (1769–1838).

See Bland, Maria Theresa.

Romary, Janice-Lee (1927—)

American fencing champion and athletic administrator. Name variations: Janice-Lee York. Born Janice-Lee York in San Mateo, California, on August 6, 1927; daughter of Shelby Loren York and Jeanette Adele (Wollmer) York; University of Southern California, A.B., 1949; married Charles Gerald Romary, on November 26, 1953; children: Lisa, Loren, and Charles.

Won ten national championships (1950, 1951, 1956, 1957, 1960, 1961, 1964, 1965, 1966, 1968); was a member of six Olympic teams (1948, 1952, 1956, 1960, 1964, 1968); was the first woman chosen to carry the American flag during the parade of champions in the Montreal Olympics (1968).

Unlike most sports, fencing allows lifelong competition, as Janice Romary's career demonstrates. From 1948 to 1968, she competed for the United States at six Olympic Games and won ten national championships. It may have been her constancy on the scene that caused the 40-year-old Romary to be selected to be the first woman to carry the American flag at an Olympiad, in Mexico City in 1968. Her long experience no doubt also played a role when she was appointed commissioner of fencing for the Los Angeles Olympic Organizing Committee in 1984. Romary is a member of the Fencing Hall of Fame.

Karin Loewen Haag,
Athens, Georgia

Romashkova, Nina (b. 1929).

See Ponomareva-Romashkova, Nina.

Rombauer, Irma S. (1877–1962)

American author of The Joy of Cooking. *Born Irma von Starkloff in St. Louis, Missouri, on October 30, 1877; died in St. Louis on October 14, 1962; younger of two daughters of Hugo von Starkloff (a physician and surgeon) and Clara (Kuhlman) von Starkloff; educated at boarding schools in Switzerland; briefly attended Washington University; married Edgar Roderick Rombauer (a lawyer), on October 14, 1899 (died February 1930); children: Marion Rombauer Becker (1903–1976, an author); Edgar Rombauer.*

The author of America's classic cookbook, Irma S. Rombauer privately published the first slim edition of *The Joy of Cooking* in 1931. After selling 3,000 copies, she revised and enlarged the volume, adding additional recipes and the step-by-step method which, along with its chatty style, became one of the book's unique features. Another

was its money-back guarantee. Published in 1936 and updated many times since, it is still standard issue in kitchens throughout America, particularly for beginning or uncertain cooks. "I started out with *The Joy of Cooking*," said renowned chef *Julia Child. "It always has sensible ideas that other books don't have. And I always felt that Mrs. Joy was at my elbow helping out."

Of German heritage, Rombauer was born Irma von Starkloff in 1887 in St. Louis, Missouri, the daughter of Hugo von Starkloff, a successful surgeon who had come to the United States from Stuttgart, and **Clara Kuhlman**, who had immigrated from Germany and in 1873 had assisted **Susan Blow** in founding the first public-school kindergarten in the United States. When Rombauer was 12, her father was appointed U.S. consul in Bremen, Germany, affording her the opportunity to see much of the world at a young age. She received most of her education at boarding schools in Lausanne and Geneva, and briefly attended the school of fine arts at Washington University after returning to St. Louis in 1894. "I was brought up to be a 'young lady,'" she later recalled, "heaven save the mark! I played the piano poorly, embroidered and sewed, painted on China, and entertained 'callers.' As a family

Irma Rombauer (left) with Marion Rombauer Becker.

we travelled extensively . . . filled our hours with opera-going, gallery-visiting and letter writing. All utterly delightful and almost useless from a practical standpoint."

It was not until her marriage in 1899 that Rombauer fully realized the gaps in her practical education. Her husband Edgar, a lawyer and an avid camper and camp cook, guided her around the kitchen. Gradually, Rombauer became more interested in food and cooking, trying out new recipes on her family, which grew to include a daughter **Marion Rombauer Becker** and a son Edgar. As she gained confidence, Irma began entertaining more, eventually becoming one of St. Louis' most delightful hostesses and finest cooks. Rombauer was also active outside the home, joining a variety of the city's civic and cultural organizations.

In 1930, Rombauer's husband Edgar, who had suffered from manic depression, committed suicide. Her children, now grown and starting families of their own, persuaded Irma to compile a cookbook of the dishes that had so delighted them while growing up. Eager for diversion, she turned to the task, using as a guide an earlier compilation she had put together for a cooking course she had given at her church. The first *Joy of Cooking*, which Rombauer paid to have published, contained 500 recipes interspersed with the author's casual and witty culinary chat. An example was Rombauer's advice on serving alcohol to guests: "Most cocktails containing liquor are made today with gin and ingenuity. In brief, take an ample supply of the former and use your imagination."

The second expanded edition of the cookbook, published by Bobbs-Merrill in 1936, was hardly a runaway bestseller, but sold well and steadily. In 1943, the publisher revised the book again, incorporating another of Rombauer's books, *Streamlined Cooking*, which she had published with only moderate success in 1939. The new edition of *Joy* flew off the shelves, setting sales records that only *Fannie Farmer's Boston Cooking-School Cook Book* had previously reached. Its enormous success in the competitive cookbook field was due in part to its inclusion of basic information on such things as meal planning, table settings, trussing a bird, and filleting a fish. Another selling point was Rombauer's method of listing the ingredients as the mixing process proceeds.

The book was revised a third time in 1951, when Rombauer's daughter Marion, who had assisted her mother previously, became its co-author. In later years, Rombauer gradually turned over most of the responsibility of the cookbook

to her daughter, although she was always ready to answer a query or to acknowledge (in longhand) a letter from a fan. In 1943, newly married **Trish Hooper** phoned Rombauer in a panic. The inexperienced bride was having five people over for dinner and had bought seven packages of spaghetti to feed them, thinking that she would need that much because it was so thin. When it appeared that the boiled spaghetti might start flowing out the door, she called Rombauer. "She was wonderful," Hooper told *Time* magazine some 54 years later. "She told me to put as much spaghetti as would fit into the largest bowl I owned and then pour sauce over it. What wouldn't fit in the bowl I was to pile around the base of my rosebushes." It was "good mulch," Rombauer said.

Rombauer wrote a third cookbook, *Cookbook for Girls and Boys* (1946), but like *Streamlined Cooking*, it was never as successful as *Joy*, which by 1953 had sold over 1.3 million copies and made Rombauer a rich woman. Despite her wealth, she continued to live a simple life, dividing her time between an apartment in St. Louis and a hideaway home she built on a ten-acre wooded lot in Pevely, Missouri. Rombauer suffered a stroke in 1954, and died of a heart attack in 1962, leaving *The Joy of Cooking* in her daughter's hands.

Marion Rombauer Becker continued to supervise revisions of the cookbook every ten years or so, purging it of dated information and attempting to keep up with modern innovations. Food critic James Beard took exception to at least one revised edition, complaining that Marion had deviated too far from her mother's intent. "[I]t included far too many French and Italian recipes, and robbed the book of some of the delicious Rombauer humor and personality," he wrote. "Irma Rombauer is one of the great women of American cookery and deserves to be known in her original state of joy."

Following Becker's death in 1976, the cookbook's copyright became the property of Ethan Becker (youngest son of Marion and architect John Becker), who became embroiled in a lawsuit with then-publisher MacMillan over profit rights, among other issues. The legal wrangling went on until 1994, when Simon & Schuster, which had purchased MacMillan, ended the impasse. Bringing Ethan on board for another expanded revision of the book, which had not been updated since 1975, Simon & Schuster hoped to boost sales (already doing well at 100,000 per year) by adding contemporary standards of nutrition and allowing for changing lifestyles. Three years in the making, the new *Joy* was launched in November 1997, containing a record 2,500 recipes, most of them extensively revised versions of old stand-bys, like tuna casserole, and new additions, such as Buffalo wings, grilled pizza, dim sum, and tapas. The result, according to *Publishers Weekly*, is a cookbook that "advances that tradition with distinction and some calculated flair."

SOURCES:

Candee, Marjorie Dent. *Current Biography 1953*. NY: H.W. Wilson, 1953.

Gray, Paul. "Ode to Joy," in *Time*. November 10, 1997.

Green, Michelle, and Cindy Dampier. "Relighting the Fire," in *People*. November 17, 1997.

"Letters to the Editor," in *Time*. December 1, 1997.

McHenry, Robert, ed. *Famous American Women*. NY: Dover, 1983.

Sicherman, Barbara, and Carol Hurd Green, eds. *Notable American Women: The Modern Period*. Cambridge, MA: The Belknap Press of Harvard University Press, 1980.

SUGGESTED READING:

Mendelson, Anne. *Stand Facing the Stove: The Story of the Women Who Gave America* The Joy of Cooking. NY: Holt, 1996.

Barbara Morgan,
Melrose, Massachusetts

Rome, empress of.

Rome, Esther (1945–1995)

American writer and advocate for women's health.
Name variations: Esther Seidman. Born Esther Seidman on September 8, 1945, in Norwich, Connecticut; died of breast cancer on June 24, 1995, in Somerville, Massachusetts; graduated from Brandeis University, 1966; Harvard Graduate School of Education, M.A., 1968; married Nathan Rome; children: Judah and Micah.

Was a founder of the Boston Women's Health Book Collective which produced the pioneering Our Bodies, Ourselves *(early 1970s); served as an advocate for a variety of women's health issues, particularly breast cancer, body image, nutrition, and eating disorders; served as a consumer representative for the U.S. Food and Drug Administration committee that investigated the potential hazards of silicone breast implants and ran a support group for women with silicone implant difficulties (early 1990s).*

A leading advocate for women's health who insisted that many fitness issues were cultural and economic as well, Esther Rome graduated cum laude from Brandeis University in 1966. She then went on to earn an M.A. in teaching from the Harvard Graduate School of Education in 1968. While Rome had a love for the field of medicine that dated back to the second grade, as a child she had decided that she could not be a doctor because, at the time, very few women became doctors. She would nonetheless have a dramatic impact on the field of women's health.

In 1969, Rome became involved with the growing feminist movement when she met a small group of women at Emmanuel College through a workshop called "Women and Their Bodies." The workshop turned out to be instrumental in Rome's founding, with several other women, of the Boston Women's Health Book Collective (BWHBC). In 1970, the collective put out its first book, *Women and Their Bodies*, a guide to the physical and psychological aspects of being female. It was printed on newsprint and initially sold for a mere 75 cents, the profits from which went back into the collective. In 1971, they changed the name of the book to *Our Bodies, Ourselves*, and within a few short years more than 350,000 copies of the book had been sold. The women then decided to incorporate as a private operating foundation and signed a book contract with Simon and Schuster. *The New Our Bodies, Ourselves* was also a bestseller when it appeared, and the various editions of the book have been integral to the rapid growth of the women's health movement. By the start of the 21st century, over 4 million copies had been sold, and translations had appeared in some 19 languages, including Russian, Thai, Chinese, Serbian, and Japanese. "Cultural adaptations" of the book have been produced in Egypt and were planned for Francophone Africa, and in 2000 the BWHBC, in collaboration with women's groups from the Americas and the Caribbean, published *Nuestros Cuerpos, Nuestras Vidas*, a Spanish-language version that presents health information in light of Hispanic culture and mores. In 1998, the BWHBC published *Our Bodies, Ourselves for the New Century*.

In addition to Rome's association with the Boston Women's Health Book Collective, she was also well known for her vocal advocacy of women's health issues. She often criticized the way women's health issues were handled both by the medical community and the media. Some of her main targets were body image, cosmetic surgery, nutrition, eating disorders, sexually transmitted diseases, breast implants, breast cancer, and the connection between tampons and toxic shock syndrome. She armed herself with an extensive knowledge of medical studies and made herself readily available to journalists. She was constantly in demand as a valuable resource for women's health stories that were broadcast on national television and printed in newspapers all over the country. Rome also served as a consumer representative on the U.S. Food and Drug Administration committee that investigated the potential hazards of silicone breast implants in the early 1990s; the committee's findings brought about a partial ban on the implants. She also started a support group for women with silicone implant difficulties.

Alice Lee Roosevelt

Rome succumbed to one of the women's health issues she had so vigorously campaigned about, dying from breast cancer on June 24, 1995, at the age of 49. She had continued working with co-author **Jane Hyman** up until her death on her last book, *Sacrificing Our Selves for Love*, which was published in 1996. A practicing Jew who kept a kosher home, Rome was buried at B'nai B'rith Cemetery in Peabody, Massachusetts.

SOURCES:
The Boston Globe. June 26, 1995.

Susan J. Walton,
freelance writer, Berea, Ohio

Romero, Pilar Miro (1940–1997).
See Miró, Pilar.

Romsey, abbess of.
See Ethelflaeda (fl. 900s).
See Ethelflaeda (c. 963–c. 1016).
See Marie of Boulogne (d. 1182).

Rooke, Emma.
See Emma (1836–1885).

Rookh, Lalla (fl. 1600s).
See Lalla Rookh.

Roos, Margaret (b. around 1388).
See Fitzalan, Margaret.

Roos, Margaret (fl. 1420)

English aristocrat. Name variations: Lady Grey of Ruthin. Flourished around 1420; daughter of William Roos, 7th baron Roos, and *Margaret Fitzalan (b. around 1388); married Reginald Grey, 3rd Baron Grey of Ruthin; children: John Grey.*

Roosevelt, Alice (1884–1980).
See Longworth, Alice Roosevelt.

Roosevelt, Alice Lee (1861–1884)

American socialite who was the first wife of Theodore Roosevelt and the mother of Alice Roosevelt Longworth. Name variations: Alice Hathaway Lee; Alice Hathaway Lee Roosevelt; Mrs. Theodore Roosevelt. Born Alice Hathaway Lee on July 29, 1861, in Boston, Massachusetts; died on February 14, 1884, in New York, New York; second daughter of George Cabot Lee (a banker) and Caroline Watts (Haskell) Lee; married Theodore Roosevelt (future president of the U.S.), on October 27, 1880, in Brookline, Massachusetts; children: one daughter, Alice Roosevelt Longworth (1884–1980).

At a party during his junior year at Harvard, young Theodore Roosevelt is said to have pointed to a stunning young woman across the room. "See that girl?," he said. "I'm going to marry her. She won't have me but I am going to have her." Indeed, Alice Hathaway Lee, a Boston debutante, wanted no part of Theodore Roosevelt and turned down his first proposal. His persistence, however, eventually won her over, and the couple married in October 1880. Present at the ceremony was the woman whom everyone had thought Theodore would marry—

his childhood companion, *Edith Kermit Carow (Roosevelt).

It was a happy union, though Alice had to adjust to Teddy's more adventuresome side. During a trip to Switzerland soon after the wedding, he undertook a trek up the Matterhorn, while she nervously awaited his return in a hotel room. The newlyweds settled in New York City, where Theodore entered politics as a precinct worker and, within a short time, was elected to the state assembly. During his second term, Alice was expecting their first child, so she did not join him in Albany. *Alice Roosevelt Longworth was born on February 12, 1884, but her mother became very ill. By the time Theodore returned home, his wife had developed serious kidney complications and was unconscious. She died two days later, age 22, the same day Theodore Roosevelt's mother **Martha Bulloch Roosevelt** died of typhoid fever, one floor away in their 57th Street house. Inconsolable, he wrote of his wife: "When my heart's dearest died, the light went from my life forever." Vacating his assembly seat, Theodore left the baby with his sister **Anna Roosevelt Cowles** and fled to his ranch in North Dakota. He never spoke of his first wife again, and there is no mention of her in his autobiography. In 1886, he quietly married Edith Kermit Carow, who would later become first lady.

SOURCES:

Melick, Arden David. *Wives of the Presidents.* Maplewood, NJ: Hammond, 1977.

Paletta, LuAnn. *The World Almanac of First Ladies.* NY: World Almanac, 1990.

Barbara Morgan,
Melrose, Massachusetts

Roosevelt, Anna Hall (1863–1892)

*American socialite and mother of Eleanor Roosevelt. Name variations: Mrs. Elliott Roosevelt. Born Anna Livingston Ludlow Hall in 1863; died of diphtheria on December 7, 1892; daughter of Valentine G. Hall and Mary Livingston Ludlow Hall; sister of Elizabeth Livingston "Tissie" Hall Mortimer, Edith Livingston Ludlow "Pussie" Hall Morgan, and Maude Hall Waterbury Gray; married Elliott Roosevelt (brother of U.S. president Theodore Roosevelt), on December 2, 1883; children: (Anna) *Eleanor Roosevelt (1884–1962); and sons Elliott Roosevelt, Jr. (1889–1893) and Gracie Hall Roosevelt (b. 1891).*

Roosevelt, Betsey (1908–1998).

See Cushing Sisters for Betsey Cushing Whitney.

Roosevelt, Edith Kermit Carow
(1861–1948)

First lady of the United States from 1901 to 1909. Name variations: Mrs. Theodore Roosevelt; Mrs. Theodore Roosevelt, Sr. Born on August 6, 1861, in Norwich, Connecticut; died on September 30, 1948, in Oyster Bay, New York; eldest daughter of Charles Carow and Gertrude Elizabeth (Tyler) Carow; attended Miss Comstock's Academy in New York; became second wife of Theodore Roosevelt (U.S. president, 1901–09), on December 2, 1886, in London, England: children: Theodore Roosevelt, Jr. (1887–1944), Kermit Roosevelt (1889–1943), and Quentin Roosevelt (1897–1918), all killed while in service to their country; Archie Roosevelt (1894–1979), who served in both world wars; Ethel Carow Roosevelt (1891–1977); (stepdaughter) Alice Roosevelt Longworth (1884–1980).

Edith Kermit Carow was born in Norwich, Connecticut, in 1861 and spent a carefree, privileged childhood in New York's Union Square—not far from her future husband, Theodore Roosevelt. The Carows and the Roosevelts traveled in the same social circle, and their children became neighborhood pals. As youngsters, Theodore and Edith shared a love of outdoor activities and often swam and hiked together at the Roosevelt summer retreat on Long Island. They may have been romantically linked for a time as teenagers, but their paths separated when Theodore entered Harvard University. There he met and fell in love with *Alice Lee (Roosevelt), whom he married in 1880. But Alice died four years later, shortly after giving birth to their daughter, *Alice Roosevelt Longworth. Although Edith attended Theodore's wedding, she did not see or hear from him until he contacted her again in 1885. It was an uneasy reunion. Historians speculate that Theodore harbored some guilt and Edith may have resented second-choice status. They apparently resolved their problems or found a way to live with them, however. Theodore traveled to London, where Edith had moved with her

Edith Kermit Carow Roosevelt

mother, and they quietly married there in December 1886. After a long honeymoon, they returned to New York.

Edith insisted that Theodore's daughter Alice live with them. With the addition of five children of their own, it became a large and lively family. With residences in New York City and Long Island, Edith tended to home and children while Theodore pursued his political career. Within 14 years, he served as president of the New York City Police Board, assistant secretary of the navy, and governor of New York State. He also established himself as a colorful and controversial character, and it was often Edith who provided advice when things got out of hand. He begrudgingly admitted, "Whenever I go against her judgment, I regret it." Concerned about the drain on family finances, Edith opposed Theodore's attempts to win public office, and she did not widely participate in the campaign for the vice presidency in 1900. After the election, she rarely went to Washington, until President William McKinley's assassination elevated her young husband to the presidency in 1901.

The Roosevelts brought renewed energy and vibrancy to the White House. The children, ranging in age from debutante Alice to four-year-old Quentin, had little respect for the dignity of their environment as they raced down halls, slid down banisters, and tried, without much success, to keep tabs on a barnyard assortment of pets. It was not unusual to glimpse a pony en route to the children's rooms via the mansion's elevator. In the midst of this unruly brood, Edith is said to have stood apart, sometimes appearing "detached" from the world around her. She has been characterized as possessing such a remarkable sense of self that neither her large family nor her status as first lady could "shake her certainty that she knew what was appropriate." It was, no doubt, this self-confidence that allowed her to risk making substantial changes in the way the White House was managed.

In an effort to shield her family from what she considered an overzealous and intrusive press, Edith banned reporters from the White House, releasing instead posed portraits of herself and the children. Although very little information accompanied these photographs in various publications, public curiosity appeared to be satisfied. Edith probably would have opted for the additional privacy of a separate presidential residence, but settled instead for extensive renovations of the mansion, creating a distinct division between official and family quarters.

To handle correspondence and to control the information that went out of the White House, Edith hired a social secretary, **Belle Hagner**. She also employed professional caterers to provide food for official dinners, thus saving herself for what she considered more urgent duties. Through weekly meetings with Cabinet wives, Edith set limits on entertainment, kept expenses down, and gained assurance that her parties would never be judged inferior. She may have also used these occasions to set boundaries on behavior. It seems that during one such meeting, she firmly advised a married woman to end her relationship with a foreign diplomat or risk being excluded from Washington's social events.

The first lady presided over an abundance of social occasions, most not lavish, but renowned for their interesting mixes of distinguished men and women from all walks of life. In their first full year in office, the Roosevelts held some 180 events in a six-month period. The press marveled at Edith's stamina. The social highlights of the administration were the debuts of daughters Alice and *Ethel Carow Roosevelt, and the wedding of Alice to U.S. Congressional Representative Nicholas Longworth in 1906.

Edith took care to insure that her own contributions, as well as those of past first ladies, would be remembered. She continued the presidential china collection, begun by *Caroline Harrison, with the addition of her own 120-place setting of English Wedgwood. She also initiated a portrait gallery to memorialize all the presidents' wives. Following her example, subsequent administrations arranged for official portraits of first ladies as well as of presidents to be left behind as a permanent record.

After winning the election of 1904 with an unprecedented popular vote, Theodore had vowed not to run again. He turned over the White House to William Taft in 1909 and embarked on an African adventure, leaving Edith behind for 15 months. They met in Egypt for a subsequent world tour. Following Theodore's death in 1919, Edith set out on her own adventure, which she called "Odyssey of a Grandmother." Traveling extensively, she rejoiced in being free of the shackles of married life, which she felt impeded "those born with the wanderfoot." She later contributed some of her experiences to a travel book written by her children, and also teamed up with her son Kermit to write a book on her ancestors. Throughout her later years, she remained active in the Republican Party and campaigned for Herbert Hoover in 1932. Outliving three of her sons, Edith Roosevelt died at age 87, and was buried next to her husband in Young's Cemetery in Oyster Bay. Her portrait, with daughter Ethel Roosevelt, was painted by *Cecilia Beaux.

SOURCES:

Caroli, Betty Boyd. First Ladies. NY: Oxford University Press, 1987.

McConnell, Jane and Burt. Our First Ladies: From Martha Washington to Lady Bird Johnson. NY: Thomas Y. Crowell, 1964.

Melick, Arden David. Wives of the Presidents. Maplewood, NJ: Hammond, 1977.

Paletta, LuAnn. The World Almanac of First Ladies. NY: World Almanac, 1990.

Barbara Morgan,
Melrose, Massachusetts

Roosevelt, Eleanor (1884–1962)

American reformer, humanitarian, UN diplomat, and the most effective woman ever in American politics who was frequently called "First Lady of the World." Born Anna Eleanor Roosevelt on October 11, 1884, in New York City; died November 7, 1962 in New York City; daughter of Elliott Roosevelt and Anna Ludlow Hall Roosevelt (both socialites); educated at Allenswood, Wimbledon Park, England; married Franklin Delano Roosevelt (1882–1945, governor of New York State as well as U.S. president, 1932– 1945), on March 17, 1905; children: Anna Eleanor Roosevelt Dall Boettiger (b. May 3, 1906); James Roosevelt (b. December 23, 1907, a U.S. congressional representative); Franklin Delano Roosevelt, Jr. (March 1909–November 1909); Elliott Roosevelt (b. September 23, 1910); Franklin Delano Roosevelt, Jr. (b. August 17, 1914, a U.S. congressional representative); John Aspinwall Roosevelt (b. March 13, 1916).

Served as director, national legislation committee, League of Women Voters (1920); was chair, finance committee, women's division, New York State Democratic Committee (1924–28); was co-chair, bureau of women's activities, Democratic National Campaign Committee (1928); was editor, Women's Democratic News (1925–28); began radio program (1934); wrote newspaper column, "My Day" (1935–62); was a delegate to UN General Assembly (1945–53); served as permanent chair of UN Commission on Human Rights (1947–48); served as chair, John F. Kennedy's Commission on the Status of Women (1961).

Selected writings: It's Up to the Women (Frederick A. Stokes, 1933); (ed.) Hunting Big Game in the Eighties (Scribner, 1933); (edited by Rose Young) Why Wars Must Cease (Macmillan, 1935); This is My Story (Harper & Bros., 1937); This Troubled World (H.C. Kinsey, 1938); The Moral Basis of Democracy (Howell,

Saskin, 1940); (with Frances Cooke Macgregor) This Is America (Putnam, 1942); If You Ask Me (Appleton-Century, 1946); This I Remember (Harper & Bros., 1949); (with Helen Ferris) Partners: The United Nations and Youth (Doubleday, 1950); India and the Awakening East (Harper & Bros., 1953); (with William De Witt) UN: Today and Tomorrow (Harpers, 1953); Ladies of Courage (Putnam, 1954); It Seems to Me (W.W. Norton, 1954); On My Own (Harper & Bros., 1958); You Learn by Living (Harper, 1960); The Autobiography of Eleanor Roosevelt (Harper, 1961); (with Helen Ferris) Your Teens and Mine (Doubleday, 1961); Book of Common Sense Etiquette (Macmillan, 1962); Tomorrow is Now (Harper & Row, 1963); Eleanor Roosevelt's Christmas Book (Dodd Mead, 1963); (edited by Maurine Beasley) The White House Press Conferences of Eleanor Roosevelt (Garland, 1983); (edited by Rochelle Chadakoff) Eleanor Roosevelt's My Day; Volume I: Her Acclaimed Columns, 1936–1945 (Pharos, 1989); (edited by David Embridge) Eleanor Roosevelt's My Day; Volume II: The Post-war Years—Her Acclaimed Columns, 1945–1952 (Pharos, 1990); (edited by David Embridge) Eleanor Roosevelt's My Day; Volume III: First Lady of the World: Her Acclaimed Columns, 1953–1962 (Pharos, 1991); (edited by Allida M. Black) What I Hope to Leave Behind: The Essential Essays of Eleanor Roosevelt (Carlson, 1995).

Though it was dusk and the heat in Bombay remained stifling, a thousand Hindus were standing patiently in front of the Taj Mahal hotel. Then a 68-year-old woman, sporting what *Time* magazine called a "grandmotherly, garden club dress," came out of the hotel and entered an open automobile. When she climbed in, she did not sit down. Instead, she faced the applauding crowd, bowed her head, and folded her hands before her in a Hindu posture called *namaskar*. The crowd, surging 15 deep against the police lines, roared with delight, jostling across the hotel lawns and smashing flower pots in the process, chanting "Eleanor Roosevelt *zindbad*!" ("Long live Eleanor Roosevelt"). As the tumult continued, ER (as historians would later call her) straightened and dropped her arms, but the crowd would not let her go. Time and again she would bow her head and fold her arms. Finally she swayed, an aide caught her arms, she sat down unsteadily, and the car drove off. This welcome, given in March 1952, was typical of the reception bestowed upon the woman often called "the first lady of the world."

On October 11, 1884, Anna Eleanor Roosevelt was born in New York City. (She never used the name Anna except in legal matters.)

Her father was Elliott Roosevelt, younger brother of future president Theodore Roosevelt, who was her godfather. Her mother was *Anna Hall Roosevelt, scion of Hudson valley aristocracy, being a descendant of the prominent Livingstone family. As her biographer and close personal friend Joseph Lash notes: "To the extent that there has been a ruling class in the United States she was a member by birth." The oldest of three children, Eleanor was caught between a loving, charming, but dissolute father and a cold, disapproving, highly neurotic mother. Possessing a strong inferiority complex, she later recalled herself as "a solemn child, without beauty. I seemed like a little old woman entirely lacking in the spontaneous joy and mirth of youth." "I never smiled," she added. Her mother, thought by Eleanor to be "one of the most beautiful women I have ever seen," nicknamed her two-year-old daughter "Granny," saying, "She is such a funny child, so old-fashioned." Her father, however, was so supportive that ER once said, "He dominated my life as long as he lived and was the love of my life for many years after he died." Yet, exiled from his home because of alcoholism and philandering, he was legally separated from Eleanor. Because of the family's prominence, personal tragedy became widely publicized. A New York Herald headline once read: "ELLIOTT ROOSEVELT DEMENTED BY EXCESSES. Wrecked by Liquor and Folly, He is Now Confined in an Asylum for the Insane near Paris." Only quarrels within the family and disagreement among physicians kept him from being declared insane.

At age 29, Anna Hall Roosevelt died of diphtheria. Because Anna was so socially prominent, the event was covered in the New York press for days. All Anna's children, eight-year-old Eleanor included, were sent to the Tivoli, New York, where they lived with their grandmother, **Mary Ludlow Hall** (Mrs. Valentine G. Hall). Eleanor's doting father tried to compensate for the loss, writing her frequently and buying her a pony. His visits nonetheless were infrequent. He might leave her outside the door of his club for hours while he became totally inebriated. Living with mistresses and addicted to drugs as well as alcohol, he died of a fall when Eleanor was nine.

Now, more than ever, Eleanor's world was one of seclusion, even if she were surrounded by governesses, tutors, and French and German maids. She was, she later recalled, timid, withdrawn, and frightened of "practically everything"—mice, the dark, other children—as well as of displeasing the adults with whom she lived.

To Theodore's wife, Aunt *Edith Carow Roosevelt, she was indeed "a poor little soul." Living with Grandmother Hall had its drawbacks, for the budding adolescent was forced to keep her pigtails and wear hideous clothing. As it was believed her spine was curved, she was put into a corrective brace for over a year. Grandmother Hall did exhibit kindness as well as discipline, however, encouraging her in piano, language study, and creative writing. Uncles and aunts were also present, though their reaction to her was decidedly mixed. If uncles Eddie and Valentine were chronic alcoholics, "Vallie" shooting bird shot at her from an upstairs window, aunts Tissie, Pussie, and Maude (**Elizabeth "Tissie" Hall Mortimer, Edith "Pussie" Hall Morgan,** and **Maude Hall Waterbury Gray**) introduced her to opera, theater, and the dance.

When Eleanor reached 15, Grandmother Hall sent her to Allenswood, a finishing school for society daughters just outside London. Headmistress **Marie Souvestre**, daughter of a well-known French philosopher and novelist, was an unmarried and high-minded free-thinker and political liberal. All classes were conducted in French. Souvestre took an instant liking to Eleanor, turning her into a privileged assistant and traveling companion during holidays. At Allenswood, this awkward, shy American girl blossomed, becoming an able student in languages and literature and the idol of younger classmates.

Returning to New York at age 17, Eleanor lived with her cousin **Susie Parish** and her husband Henry Parish, Jr., and, under pressure from her grandmother, made her debut at the Assembly Ball. She was no longer an awkward adolescent; she had become tall, slender, and "willowy." But she found debutante life stifling, so she involved herself in settlement work. A leader of the Junior League, she visited slum children and taught dancing, literature, and calisthenics at the Rivington Street Settlement. She also joined the Consumers' League, investigating working conditions in garment factories and department stores. Not only did she see how the poor actually lived; she encountered an entire generation of women reformers. "The feeling that I was useful was perhaps the greatest joy I experienced," she once said.

During Eleanor's coming-out period, she got to know her fifth cousin Franklin D. Roosevelt, then a senior at Harvard. Franklin was handsome as he was charming, and the couple soon fell in love. True, as biographer **Blanche Wiesen Cook** notes, FDR was not the ideal suitor: "He was less serious than many; not as rich as others; was con-

Eleanor
Roosevelt

sidered by some frivolous and frothy, and by others arrogant and deceitful." At the same time, Franklin was attentive in the extreme, making no secret of admiring her intelligence and relying on her advice. Furthermore, so Cook writes, "she perceived he needed her, and in many ways

Franklin resembled Eleanor's romantic image of her father—that debonair man who had been the first to call her Little Nell." Franklin's mother, *Sara Delano Roosevelt, thought the couple too young to marry and insisted that they keep their engagement secret for a year.

Despite Sara's attempts to prevent the union, on March 17, 1905, the 23-year-old Franklin and the 20-year-old Eleanor were married. Uncle Theodore, Franklin's sixth cousin, gave away his niece, stealing the limelight in the process. "Well, Franklin," Theodore quipped, "there's nothing like keeping the name in the family." Press coverage concentrated on Eleanor, not Franklin, for as the direct niece of the incumbent president, she was the Roosevelt who really mattered. FDR biographer Geoffrey Ward notes that Franklin's "love of Eleanor was real, but her closeness to the immediate family of the man he admired most on earth must have been an important part of her dowry."

The newlyweds remained in New York while Franklin studied law at Columbia University. As keeper of the purse strings, Sara totally dominated the couple. Biographer Lash writes of ER, who had been on the verge of forming her own identity: "She totally subordinated herself to her husband and her mother-in-law. Their wills became hers; not what she wanted, but what they wanted, mattered." At first, Eleanor, still starved for affection, welcomed Sara's attention, calling her "Mama" and waiting on her continually. She later recalled with obvious regret that there was always someone "to decide everything for me." The very New York townhouse in which they lived was next to Sara's; the two houses had a common entrance and connecting doors, leading to matching dining and drawing rooms that could be opened for joint entertaining. When Eleanor complained to Franklin that she was living in a house that was "not in any way" hers, one "which did not represent the way I want to live," her husband called her "quite mad" and left the room. Even if Franklin and his mother often differed, ER always felt that their first loyalty was to each other. Only at their summer home at Campobello Island in New Brunswick, Canada, did she feel mistress of her own house.

From 1906 to 1916, ER became mother to six children. In 1909, when one son died of influenza after seven months, she wrongly blamed herself, for she had been unable to breast-feed him. ER later noted, "Franklin's children were more my mother-in-law's children than they were mine." Sara on her part told the children, "I was your real mother. Eleanor merely bore you." Sara's generous gifts to her grandchildren continually undercut Eleanor's efforts to exercise needed parental authority.

In November 1910, with his official residence at Hyde Park, Franklin was elected the Democratic assemblyman from Dutchess County. When FDR briefly became a leader of anti-Tammany forces in Albany, ER found herself an astute firsthand observer of legislative proceedings. Finally away from Sara, Eleanor found her marriage fulfilling for the first time.

President Woodrow Wilson appointed Franklin assistant secretary of the navy in January 1913, and Eleanor successfully assumed the role of Washington hostess. When in April 1917, the United States entered World War I, ER could finally free herself from tedious social duties. Many mornings, she rose at 5:00 AM to coordinate the canteen for soldiers arriving at Washington's Union Station, where as many as ten troop trains pulled in each day. With **Addie Daniels**, wife of Wilson's secretary of the navy and FDR's boss, Eleanor also organized the Navy Red Cross. Even after the Armistice, she fought to improve conditions at St. Elizabeth's Hospital for the mentally ill and daily visited troops in the city's naval hospital.

In September 1918, Franklin returned from an inspection trip to Europe stricken with double pneumonia and influenza, the latter a disease that took a heavy toll as war was coming to an end. While her husband was bedridden, Eleanor discovered love letters written by **Lucy Page Mercer**, her own personal secretary and a person she had trusted implicitly. ER later confided to a friend: "the bottom dropped out of my own particular world, and I faced myself, my surroundings, my world honestly for the first time." Considering herself a failure as a woman, she offered to divorce Franklin. For a variety of reasons—concern for the children, pressure from Sara, FDR's political ambitions, Lucy's feelings of guilt as a Roman Catholic over marrying a divorced man—the union formally remained intact, but any intimacy vanished. Henceforth, Eleanor resolved to design an independent life for herself. Knowledge of the affair only became public in 1968.

Although learning of Franklin's infidelity briefly led the 30-year-old Eleanor to feel abandoned, the world of politics brought the couple back into the limelight. In 1920, FDR received the Democratic nomination for the vice-presidency. His troubleshooter Louis McHenry Howe, whose gnome-like appearance and brash demeanor ER first found repellent, renewed her interest in politics, consulting her on a variety of campaign matters, including drafts of her husband's speeches. As was also true of her husband, she had originally hoped that Herbert Hoover would receive the Democratic presiden-

Eleanor
Roosevelt

tial nomination, saying the Wilson protégé was "the only man I know who has firsthand knowledge of European questions and great organizing ability and understands business not only from the capitalistic point of view but also from the worker's standpoint."

After Franklin lost the vice-presidential race, the Roosevelts returned to New York, where Eleanor became active in the League of Women Voters. At the time of her marriage, she had gone so far as to oppose women's suffrage, thinking it violated the female's traditional role;

now she was coordinating the League legislative program. She became particularly close to attorney **Elizabeth Read** and her lifelong partner, educator and journalist **Esther Lape**, and their Greenwich Village home served her as a sanctuary for many years. When in 1920, ER prepared a monthly report as director of the League's national legislation committee, Read served as her researcher. In 1922, Eleanor joined the Women's Trade Union League, which sought maximum hours and minimum wages for female employees, and occasionally she even picketed a recalcitrant firm. Her opposition to the Equal Rights Amendment was based on her fear that it would destroy the few laws that protected women in the marketplace. Although she briefly backed prohibition, she soon realized the 18th amendment to the Constitution was unenforceable.

She would rather light candles than curse the darkness.

—Adlai Stevenson

Other ER causes included the World Court and publisher Edward Bok's award for international peace. She supported American entry into the League of Nations, though in 1920 she had backed the reservations put forth by Senator Henry Cabot Lodge and wanted assurances that Congress alone retained the power to declare war. In 1931, she claimed that men could not be trusted to work for peace. "Any successful crusade," she told the City Club of New York, "must be conducted by the women of all countries." Because of her peace activities, J. Edgar Hoover, director of the newly created Federal Bureau of Investigation, began a detailed file on her in 1924. "One of the wonders of modern history," according to biographer Cook, it ended up totaling about 4,000 pages.

In the summer of 1921, while sailing at Campobello, Franklin contracted polio, which left his lower limbs useless. Hour by hour, through long nights, Eleanor continually nursed him. Cooperating with Louis Howe, she successfully fought Sara's efforts to relegate him to the life of a country squire. Franklin, she believed, could only find fulfillment by reentering politics.

Mastering public speaking and political organization under Howe's skillful tutelage, ER represented her husband until he could resume normal activity. She first mobilized the women of Dutchess County, then served as financial chair of New York state's Democratic Party. Especially active in Al Smith's 1924 campaign for governor of New York, she fought in vain to have the national party platform endorse such

reforms as equal pay for women workers and a 48-hour work week. From 1925 to 1928, she edited the *Women's Democratic News*, after which she executed her leadership of the monthly surreptitiously.

In 1922, Eleanor Roosevelt had made the acquaintance of two women who, for a decade, were her closest friends: former suffragists **Nancy ("Nan") Cook** and her lifelong partner, **Marion Dickerman**. Dickerman, an educator and social worker, had run unsuccessfully for the New York legislature in 1919. Together with *Caroline O'Day, later congressional representative from New York, and **Elinor Morgenthau**, whose husband became FDR's secretary of the treasury, ER, Cook, and Dickerman dominated the women's division of the state Democratic Party. All during the 1920s, the five toured each county into the state, agitating for a host of reforms—public housing, unemployment insurance, worker's compensation, child labor legislation, the eight-hour day.

With Cook and Dickerman, ER moved in 1926 into Val-Kill, a stone cottage just constructed at Hyde Park. There the three women jointly managed a nonprofit crafts factory that reproduced early American furniture and employed farm laborers jobless in winter. Although they dissolved Val-Kill industries only in 1938, the close friendship was already unraveling by 1932. Eleanor thought that Cook and Dickerman were becoming too susceptible to the charm of her husband Franklin. Furthermore, the two intensely disliked a new woman in ER's life, Associated Press correspondent *Lorena ("Hick") Hickok, who first became close to ER during the 1932 presidential race and who resided in the White House from 1941 to 1945.

In 1926, ER and Dickerman also purchased Todhunter, a private progressive school for girls in New York City. Eleanor only severed ties in 1938. Deliberately modeling herself after Mme Souvestre, she served as vice-principal. Even while Franklin was governor of New York, ER spent three days a week at Todhunter, teaching history, sociology, economics, and government. By this time, FDR's unmarried secretary, **Marguerite ("Missy") LeHand**, was serving as his hostess. At Hyde Park and later at the "Little White House" in Warm Springs, Georgia, ER was treated increasingly as a visitor, albeit an honored one.

Eleanor Roosevelt co-chaired the women's division of the Democratic Party in 1928, putting the bulk of her time on Al Smith's bid for the presidency. Given her other party activities, she occupied the most powerful political positions ever held by a woman. Though Smith lost, FDR was chosen governor of New York in that very election. Eleanor quickly became the "legs and ears" of her husband, accompanying him on inspection trips to homes for the aged, state hospitals, and prisons. By then, she was becoming financially independent of Franklin, never a good businessman. Her writing for *McCall's* and *Redbook* brought her thousands of dollars. On the lighter side, in June 1932 she edited a short-lived magazine entitled *Babies, Just Babies*. During the 1932 campaign that propelled Franklin to the White House, ER again organized the women's division of the Democratic National Committee, working with party activist *Molly Dewson to mobilize thousands of female precinct workers.

Once first lady, Eleanor Roosevelt broke precedent in several significant ways. The earliest involved efforts to publicize her views. She was the first president's wife to hold weekly press conferences, limited to women reporters and often centering on women's issues. On December 30, 1935, she began her newspaper column "My Day," distributed through United Features Syndicate. For its first three years, the column centered on domestic matters, and she was not above describing family scrambled-egg feasts on Sunday evenings. By 1939, however, ER addressed general political topics, ranging from pleas for larger welfare appropriations to attacking the anti-interventionist foreign policy of Herbert Hoover. She would continue the column until September 14, 1962, less than two months before her death. Over the years, she wrote monthly columns for *Women's Home Companion*, *Ladies' Home Journal*, and *McCall's*. Her tone might have been naive and her prose full of clichés but she always communicated warmth, sincerity, and genuine concern. The same could be said about her radio program, begun in 1934 and whose profits went directly to the American Friends Service Committee. By 1939, she was so popular that WNBC dubbed her "The First Lady of Radio." In 1935, she contracted with a lecture agency to engage in two tours per year; here, she drew $1,000 per lecture, stupendous in depression America and some of which remained private income.

From the documentary The Eleanor Roosevelt Story.

Second, ER cracked the tradition that the first lady was primarily the social leader of Washington, whose activities were supposedly limited to receiving foreign diplomats, members of Congress, and top administrators—and their spouses. While she certainly did her share of state entertaining, she was forever on the road, so much so that no one knew where "Eleanor Everywhere" would appear next. The most famous cartoon of the decade showed a grinning coal miner, laboring in the bowels of the earth and crying out in astonishment, "For gosh sakes, here comes Mrs. Roosevelt." It was rumored that Arctic explorer Admiral Richard Byrd always set up two places for dinner at the South Pole "in case Eleanor should drop in." One weary reporter who had been following her slavishly said, "Please make Eleanor tired, just for one day." In 1940, *Life* magazine reported:

> During the last seven years, Mrs. Roosevelt has, at a temperate estimate, traveled 280,000 miles, written one million words, earned and given away over half a million dollars, delivered several hundred lectures, radio speeches and interviews to the press; knitted several dozen tiny garments for Roosevelt babies, cooked hot dogs and poured a second cup of coffee at several dozen picnics and probably not wasted as much time as the average person does in one week. With the unaccountable exception of South Dakota, she has visited every State in the Union, most of them more than once. She has talked, intimately, to more people, and covered, attentively, more American territory than the most garrulous and peripatetic Fuller Brush man.

Third, ER was a most vocal advocate for groups that she believed her husband was overlooking. She found government posts for many women, strongly supported the arts and writers' projects of the Works Progress Administration (WPA), and brought Southern sharecroppers and Northern garment workers to the White House. Hearing about the struggle of Appalachian farmers to reclaim their land, she became a champion of a model subsistence homestead community at Arthurdale, West Virginia. Here, she sought, without significant success, to construct model homes and recruit industry to aid stranded coal miners living on a tributary of the Monongahela River. At times, she would even send a personal check to a letter writer in need. According to New Deal official Will Alexander, whenever she received a missive pleading for aid:

> She looked at the thing and decided whose business it was in the government to find out about it, and sent that letter with her own initials on it and wrote, "Find out about this

letter. You know what it's all about." You'd better do it. She never forgot.

Fourth, few New Dealers did as much to advance the status of African-Americans. Fighting to assure equal access to blacks in New Deal relief programs, Eleanor Roosevelt said, "It is a question of the right to work and the right to work should know no color lines." She sought vigorously but unsuccessfully to obtain Franklin's support for legislation defining lynching as a federal crime. As World War II approached, she strongly argued for eliminating discrimination in the armed forces and in defense employment. At the same time, in June 1940, she urged black labor leader A. Philip Randolph to forego his threat of a mass march on Washington to gain defense jobs, arguing that the protest would backfire. In 1939, she resigned from the Daughters of the American Revolution in protest of the DAR's denying black artist *Marian Anderson permission to perform at Washington's Constitution Hall, an auditorium owned by the organization. Anderson ended up singing to 75,000 people from the Lincoln Memorial, in part through ER's intervention.

Fifth, ER saw herself as a strong protector of America's youth. Above all, she feared that continued depression might make young people susceptible to extremist movements. The National Youth Administration of 1935 was basically her creation. It employed thousands of high school and university students, thereby enabling them to continue their studies. In 1940, ER endorsed a form of compulsory youth service for both sexes. Two years later, she wrote in "My Day," "all of us—men in the service and women at home—should be drafted and told what is the job we are to do. So long as we are left to volunteer we are bound to waste our capacities and to do things which are not necessary." In 1944, she wanted continuation of the draft after World War II ended, recommending a year of military service for all males. In 1953, she came out for universal military training. Such ideas always remained with her. When, for example, the Peace Corps was formed in 1961, she wanted it mandatory for every American youth and to include possible service within the United States.

Between 1936 and 1940, ER ardently supported the American Student Union (ASU) and the American Youth Congress (AYC), both prone to heavy Stalinist influence. She was dismayed, however, when in February 1940 the Communist-dominated AYC booed the president and took a "Yanks-are-not-coming" posture. Soon afterwards, she quietly severed her ties, transferring her energies to the International Students' Service. At that time, she became devoted to the ASU's former executive secretary, Joseph Lash. An idealistic young man of strong reformist bent, Lash had resigned his post in protest against Communist infiltration. Deeply disappointed in the shady business careers and frequent marriages of her sons (eighteen marriages among four sons), ER found in Lash not only ideological compatibility but the "good son" she never had.

In 1939, Gallup polls found Eleanor leading Franklin in popularity 67% to 58%. Yet, as was the case with her husband, ER drew bitter opposition as well as strong support. Her pro-black positions led to accusations that she favored miscegenation. Her support for such groups as the AYC created the charge of being a Soviet "fellow traveler." Her radio, journalistic, and lecture activities brought charges that she was "cashing in" on her role as first lady. Even in a generally favorable cover story published in 1952, *Time* quoted her as having once said, "Though Mr. Stalin is a dictator, his efforts have been to help the people prepare themselves for greater power." Offering a parody of Edgar Allan Poe's "The Raven," one writer found her overbearing in her willingness to bestow advice:

> And this expert ever flitting,
> Never sitting, never quitting,
> Never tending her own knitting,
> Doles her pills of fancied knowledge,
> Wisdom from her bursting store.

In all her reformist efforts, it was Eleanor who uniquely had Franklin's ear. At times acting as if she were assistant president of the United States, ER continually sought to bring the cause of the oppressed to her husband's attention, allowing him in turn to use her activism as a liaison to the left. The president, however, frequently refused to act as she wished. Once he manifested genuine fury when she interrupted his 20-minute cocktail period by bringing him a sheaf of papers. She remained, however, "the conscience of the administration." Concerning the New Deal in general, she said that its measures "helped but did not solve the fundamental problems." In speaking of the general American experience, "We had bought ourselves time to think." Writing later about her relationship with Franklin, she said:

> He might have been happier with a wife who had been completely uncritical. That I was never able to be and he had to find it in some other people. Nevertheless, I think I sometimes acted as a spur, even though the spurring was not always wanted or welcome. I was one of those who served his purposes.

In the wake of World War I, ER found armed conflict absolute folly, going so far as to oppose the sale of toy soldiers and to resolve never again to sell a war bond. In 1929, when she took her sons to Europe, she made sure that they visited the military cemeteries. In 1935, she supported passage of the first neutrality act, though she soon sought a law that would distinguish between aggressor and victim. "The war idea is obsolete," she said. Two years later, she served with Admiral Byrd as co-chair of the No-Foreign-War Crusade, a group opposing increased armament. Like Franklin, Eleanor hoped that the Munich Conference of September 1938 would avoid war.

Already, however, ER's pacifism was yielding to her anti-fascism. In October 1935, she supported sanctions against Italy, then in the process of invading Ethiopia, and during that same year she endorsed her husband's program of naval rearmament. Appalled by the bombings of China and Spain, she wrote a friend early in 1938:

> I have never believed that war settled anything satisfactorily, but I am not entirely sure that some times there are certain situations in the world such as we have in actuality when a country is worse off when it does not go to war for its principles than if it went to war.

Little wonder ER sought the lifting of the arms embargo on Republican Spain and later regretted she did not push Franklin harder. Once World War II broke out, she backed the interventionist policies of her husband. In December 1939, she wrote in her column, "We must now weep for Finland," just invaded by the Soviet Union. By 1940, she was spearheading the effort to open the nation's doors to Europe's refugee children and to Jewish fugitives from Hitler.

Eleanor opposed a third term for Franklin in 1940, finding the temptations of power too great. Yet, once her husband had made up his mind to run again, she acquiesced. When Franklin sought his liberal secretary of agriculture, Henry A. Wallace, as running mate, he had ER address a reluctant Democratic convention over the matter. Without her, many said, Wallace could not have carried the convention.

In September 1941, ER became deputy director of the Office of Civilian Defense (OCD), whose director was Fiorello La Guardia. It was the only official job she ever held during her husband's presidency, and she was far from successful in the post. She had hoped to use the OCD as a major New Deal agency, one serving to alleviate wartime stresses of migration, unemployment, housing, and health. New York's flamboyant mayor, however, was more interested in such mundane matters as fire-fighting equipment. In February 1942, she resigned under congressional fire, saying, "I offered a way to get at the President and in wartime it is not politically wise to attack the President."

If ER was ever compromised, it was over the administration's internment of Japanese-Americans, many of them bona fide United States citizens. Over 100,000 people were ejected from their homes on the West Coast and forced to live in "relocation centers" in Western deserts and Arkansas swampland. In April 1943, at Franklin's request, Eleanor visited the detention camps. That October, in an article for *Collier's* magazine, she claimed that the evacuation was carried out with "remarkable skill and kindness." In press accounts, she stressed their gardening skills and emphasized that their "loyalty" must be assured before they could return home. Never once did she publicly express disapproval. Nonetheless, from the start, she was personally shaken by the internments. When, however, she protested privately to her husband, he rebuffed her icily.

With the onset of World War II, ER took a maternal interest in America's GIs. In one column she disparaged the booster tone of war reporting, such as a dispatch reading, "Only six bombers failed to return." She responded, "That little word 'only,' when it is read by a woman whose son or whose husband was on one of those lost bombers, creates a deep sense of bitterness." During the summer of 1943, in a 23,000-mile trip, she visited field hospitals and front-line installations in Australia and the South Pacific. Commented the hard-bitten Admiral William F. ("Bull") Halsey:

> When I say she inspected those hospitals, I don't mean that she shook hands with the chief medical officer, glanced into a sun parlor, and left. I mean that she went into every ward, stopped at every bed, and spoke to every patient: What was his name? How did he feel? Was there anything he needed? Could she take a message home for him? I marveled at her hardihood, both physical and mental. She walked for miles, and she saw patients who were grievously and gruesomely wounded. But I marveled most at their expressions as she leaned over them. It was a sight I will never forget.

When Franklin died of a cerebral hemorrhage at Warm Springs, Georgia, on April 12, 1945, Eleanor bore the news with discipline and dignity. "The story is over" was all she told one reporter, an understandable comment as she had just discovered that Lucy Mercer, whose last name was now Rutherford, had been with

Franklin when he died. Writes biographer J. William T. Youngs in summarizing their marriage, "No one word seems to describe their complex relationship: neither love, nor hostility, nor admiration, nor annoyance was the all-encompassing ingredient of their life together."

If anything, after Franklin's death, ER increased her public activity. She resumed her radio shows and lecture tours, in time adding a program in a new media called television. She feared that her husband's successor, Harry S. Truman, was a mere political hack; in 1944, she had wanted the Democratic convention to renominate Wallace for the vice-presidency. In 1948, while she was openly supporting Truman's election, her endorsement was belated and unenthusiastic. Privately she referred to him as "a weak and vacillating person [who] made such poor appointments in his Cabinet." She would continually write long letters to the new president, imploring him to maintain the Fair Employment Practices Committee, desegregate housing and education, develop a genuinely internationalist foreign policy, and work towards nuclear disarmament.

Early in December 1945, Truman appointed ER one of the five U.S. delegates to the first United Nations General Assembly in London. As she stood for the remnants of New Deal liberalism and still drew much popularity, the appointment was obviously political. Yet she worked hard enough to win the respect of such prominent Republican delegates as John Foster Dulles and Senator Arthur H. Vandenberg. In April 1946, she began work on the U.N. Human Rights Commission, where as chair she was entrusted with drafting an international bill of rights. Finally on December 10, 1948, the Universal Declaration of Human Rights passed the General Assembly. Unquestionably she had been its driving force. That October, *Time* magazine suspected she was the best-known woman in the world.

When World War II first drew to a close, Eleanor Roosevelt feared the breakup of the wartime alliance. She initially favored sharing atomic secrets with the Soviets and opposed the abrupt severance of lend-lease to that nation. Hence, in March 1946, she opposed Winston Churchill's "Iron Curtain" speech, which called for an Anglo-American military alliance and a showdown with the Soviet Union. Germany, she claimed, should never be permitted again to engage in heavy industry, much less rearm. In 1947, she found the Truman Doctrine and a naval show of force in the eastern Mediterranean too strident. Within a year, however, she was supporting the broad outlines of the U.S. response to the Soviet Union, including the Marshall Plan, the North Atlantic Treaty Organization (NATO), and American entry into the Korean War. More than once, she responded to Soviet charges of American injustice by proposing that each country submit to investigation of its social conditions. Her formula for getting along with the Russians: "Have convictions; Be Friendly; Stick to your beliefs as they stick to theirs; Work as hard as they do."

In 1947, ER refused to support the newly formed Progressive Party, with its platform of accommodation towards the Soviet Union, instead helping to spearhead the Americans for Democratic Action, a group which espoused domestic social reforms and support of Truman's foreign policy. To the end of her life, she remained its honorary chair. At the same time, she strongly opposed the activities of Wisconsin Senator Joseph R. McCarthy, whom she saw as suppressing legitimate dissent by trampling heedlessly on civil liberties. Believing Alger Hiss innocent of treason, she refused to condemn the former State Department official while manifesting a strong dislike for Hiss' major foe, California Congressional Representative Richard Nixon.

By the 1940s, ER was headed towards a confrontation with the Roman Catholic Church. Her support for Republican Spain, sponsorship of the American Youth Congress, protests against censorship, discreet support of birth control, and outspoken opposition to federal aid to parochial schools all created tensions with the Roman Catholic Church. In July 1949, America's most powerful Catholic cleric, Francis Cardinal Spellman, denounced her "record of anti-Catholicism" as "discrimination unworthy of an American mother." She defended herself in a column that ended, "The final judgment, my dear Cardinal Spellman, of the worthiness of all human beings is in the hands of God." At the behest of Pope Pius XII and Democratic Party boss Ed Flynn, the cardinal made his peace, but the episode left its scars.

During the 1950s, Eleanor Roosevelt remained very much in the public eye, even though in 1952 newly elected president Dwight D. Eisenhower failed to reappoint her to the U.N. She immediately became the unofficial ambassador-at-large of the American Association for the United Nations, in which capacity she visited the Middle East, Asia, and Europe. By 1954, ER was finding the atomic bomb an instrument of genuine deterrence. Opposing unilateral nuclear disarmament, she went so far as to call the A-

"IT'S HER."

Bill Mauldin's cartoon appeared on November 11, 1962, four days after the death of Eleanor Roosevelt.

bomb "the one real assurance of peace on earth." Two years later, she defended its use in 1945 as being necessary to end the Pacific war quickly. As Eleanor Roosevelt entered her 70s, she continued her travels—to India, Japan, and twice to the Soviet Union, where she interviewed Nikita Khrushchev.

Throughout the postwar years, ER ardently supported Zionism and the nation-state of Israel. She rejected repatriation for Palestinian refugees, claiming Israel would be foolish to "take people who would be dangerous citizens, antagonistic to them and their ideas." Similarly she opposed arms shipments to Arab states, some of which, she said, were under Soviet control. When in 1956 the Eisenhower administration condemned the joint British-French-Israeli invasion of Egypt, she accused the president of siding with "the Kremlin" and "dictator" Gamal Abdel Nasser.

Always a power in the Democratic Party, from 1952 through 1960 ER strongly supported the bids of the witty and urbane governor of Illinois,

Adlai Stevenson, for the presidency. She initially opposed the presidential candidacy of John F. Kennedy, intensely disliking his father Joseph, finding the young Massachusetts senator evasive on McCarthy, and fearing the political influence of the Roman Catholic Church. During the 1960 campaign, however, she endorsed his election. In 1961, Kennedy appointed her to a Special Session of the U.N. General Assembly and made her chair of his Commission on the Status of Women. Appalled by the Bay of Pigs invasion of that year, she served on the abortive "Tractors for Freedom" Committee, formed in order to negotiate with Fidel Castro over prisoners taken in its wake. She called for the demilitarization of Central Europe, pleaded for a test-ban treaty, and sought to have the budding Vietnam crisis turned over to the U.N.

Around 1947, at age 63, ER had fallen in love with her physician, David Gurewitsch, who was 15 years her junior. Conducting a discreet romance, the couple would travel together. When Gurewitsch married in 1958, Eleanor shared a home on Manhattan's East Side with the couple. On November 7, 1962, age 78, Eleanor Roosevelt died at her home in New York City from a rare bone-marrow form of tuberculosis.

SOURCES:

Black, Allida M. *Casting Her Own Shadow: Eleanor Roosevelt and the Shaping of Postwar Liberalism.* NY: Columbia University Press, 1996.

Cook, Blanche Wiesen. *Eleanor Roosevelt: Volume One, 1884–1933.* NY: Viking, 1992.

Goodwin, Doris Kearns. *No Ordinary Time; Franklin and Eleanor Roosevelt: The Home Front in World War II.* NY: Simon & Schuster, 1994.

Lash, Joseph P. *Eleanor and Franklin: The Story of Their Relationship Based on Eleanor Roosevelt's Private Papers.* NY: W.W. Norton, 1971.

———. *Eleanor: The Years Alone.* NY: W.W. Norton, 1972.

Roosevelt, Eleanor. *On My Own.* NY: Harper, 1958.

———. *This I Remember.* NY: Harper and Bros., 1949.

———. *This is My Story.* NY: Harper and Bros., 1937.

SUGGESTED READING:

Asbell, Bernard, ed. *Mother and Daughter: The Letters of Eleanor and Anna Roosevelt.* NY: Coward, McCann, & Geoghegan, 1982.

Berger, Jason. *A New Deal for the World: Eleanor Roosevelt and American Foreign Policy.* NY: Columbia University Press, 1981.

Cook, Blanche Wiesen. *Eleanor Roosevelt: Volume II, 1933–1938.* NY: Viking, 1999.

Glendon, Mary Ann. *A World Made New: Eleanor Roosevelt and the Universal Declaration of Human Rights.* NY: Random House, 2000.

Hareven, Tamara K. *Eleanor Roosevelt: An American Conscience.* Chicago, IL: Quadrangle, 1968.

Hoff-Wilson, Joan and Marjorie Lightman, eds. *Without Precedent: The Life and Career of Eleanor Roosevelt.* Bloomington, IN: Indiana University Press, 1984.

Lash, Joseph. *Love, Eleanor: Eleanor Roosevelt and Her Friends, 1943–1962.* Garden City, NY: Doubleday, 1982.

———. *A World of Love.* NY: Doubleday, 1982.

Roosevelt, Elliott, and James Brough. *Mother R.: Eleanor Roosevelt's Untold Story.* NY: Putnam, 1977.

———. *An Untold Story: The Roosevelts of Hyde Park.* NY: Putnam, 1973.

Roosevelt, James, with Bill Libby. *My Parents: A Differing View.* Chicago, IL: Playboy Press, 1976.

Streitmatter, Rodger, ed. *Empty Without You: The Intimate Letters of Eleanor Roosevelt and Lorena Hickok.* NY: Free Press, 1998.

Ward, Geoffrey C. *Before the Trumpet: Young Franklin Roosevelt, 1882–1905.* NY: Harper and Row, 1985.

———. *A First-Class Temperament: The Emergence of Franklin Roosevelt.* NY: Harper and Row, 1989.

Youngs, J. William T. *Eleanor Roosevelt: A Personal and Public Life.* Boston, MA: Little, Brown, 1985.

RELATED MEDIA:

"Eleanor and Franklin" (television docudrama), starring **Jane Alexander** (Eleanor), Edward Herrmann (Franklin), **Rosemary Murphy** (Sara Delano), **Mackenzie Phillips** (Eleanor in younger years), script by James Costigan, directed by Daniel Petrie, 1976.

"Eleanor, First Lady of the World" (television docudrama), starring **Jean Stapleton** (Eleanor); **Gail Strickland** (Eleanor's daughter Anna Roosevelt Dall Boettiger), script by Caryl Ledner and **Cynthia Mandelberg**, directed by John Erman, 1982.

"The Eleanor Roosevelt Story" (Oscar-winning documentary film), narrated by Archibald MacLeish, Eric Sevaried, Francis Cole, directed by Richard Kaplan, 1965.

Sunrise at Campobello (play), written by Dore Schary, 1957.

Sunrise at Campobello (film), starring ***Greer Garson** (Eleanor), Ralph Bellamy (Franklin), Hume Cronyn (Louis Howe), **Ann Shoemaker** (Sara Delano), written and produced by Dore Schary, directed by Vincent J. Donehue, 1960.

COLLECTIONS:

The papers of Eleanor Roosevelt are in the Franklin D. Roosevelt Presidential Library, Hyde Park, New York.

Justus D. Doenecke,
New College of the University of South Florida,
Sarasota, Florida

Roosevelt, Mrs. Elliott (1863–1892).

See Roosevelt, Anna Hall.

Roosevelt, Ethel Carow (1891–1977)

*First daughter of the United States. Name variations: Mrs. Richard Derby. Born in 1891; died in 1977; daughter of Theodore Roosevelt (U.S. president, 1901–08) and *Edith Kermit Carow Roosevelt (1861–1948); half-sister of *Alice Roosevelt Longworth (1884–1980); married Richard Derby.*

Roosevelt, Mrs. James (1908–1998).

See Cushing Sisters for Betsey Cushing Whitney.

Roosevelt, Sara Delano (1854–1941)

Mother of Franklin Delano Roosevelt. Born Sara Delano in September 21, 1854; died at her home in Hyde Park, New York, following an acute circulatory collapse, on September 7, 1941; seventh of eleven children of Catherine Lyman Delano *(daughter of a prominent Massachusetts family of jurists and financiers) and Warren Delano (business associate of James Roosevelt); married James Roosevelt of Hyde Park (known as Squire James), in October 1880; children: one son, Franklin Delano Roosevelt (1882–1945), president of the United States (1932–1945). James Roosevelt was first married to* Rebecca Howland Roosevelt *who died in 1876; they had a son, James Roosevelt (Rosy) Roosevelt.*

Roosevelt, Mrs. Theodore.

See Roosevelt, Alice Lee (1861–1884).
See Roosevelt, Edith Kermit Carow (1861–1948).

Roper, Margaret More (1505–1544)

English scholar. Born in 1505; died on December 25, 1544; buried at St. Dunstan's Church, in Canterbury, with her father's head in her arms; eldest daughter of Sir Thomas More (1478–1535, English scholar and statesman who was slain for his opposition to detaching England from the spiritual authority of the Roman Catholic Church) and Jane Colt More (c. 1488–1511); had one brother John More (who married Anne Cresacre *in 1529), and two sisters, Elizabeth More Daunce or Dancy (b. around 1506, who married William Daunce on September 29, 1521, the same day Margaret married), and Cecily More Heron (b. around 1507, who married Giles Heron in 1522); tutored by her father and other scholars; married William Roper, of Wellhall in the Parish of Eltham, in Kent, in 1521; children: five, including* *Mary Roper Basset, *English writer and translator (fl. 1544–1572).*

Works: English translation of Erasmus' A Devout Treatise upon the Paternoster (1523); letters to Thomas More, April 1534–July 1535.

Margaret More Roper was born in 1505, the eldest daughter of Sir Thomas More and *Jane Colt More. Thomas, a famous classical scholar, believed that women should be equally educated with men. Thus, Margaret and her sisters, Elizabeth More Daunce and Cecily More Heron, received the same classical education—in Latin, Greek, logic, philosophy, and religion—that their brother John More did. The children were tutored by other scholars as well as by their father and were much admired for their intellectual capabilities.

Roper stood out the most and, notably, won great praise for her intelligence and modesty from the Dutch scholar Desiderius Erasmus, who was also a family friend; he called her "the flower of all the learned matrons in England." Roper devoted a great deal of time to study, particularly to philosophy, but all that remains of her work are letters to her father and a translation of Erasmus' *A Devout Treatise upon the Paternoster*, published in 1523.

Margaret had five children with her husband, William Roper, after they married in 1521. Though her early life was very happy, she was greatly distressed by the execution of her father, who had refused to take the Oath of Supremacy that recognized Henry VIII as head of the Church of England. Margaret's still extant letters are to Thomas More from the period during which he was held in the Tower of London. He was executed in 1535. Roper saved her father's books and papers; she also rescued his head from a stake on London Bridge after 14 days, preserving it in a leaden box until there was an opportunity for its inclusion in the family vault in St. Dunstan's, Canterbury. For this she was questioned by the King's Council but never prosecuted.

SOURCES:

Buck, Claire, ed. *Bloomsbury Guide to Women's Literature*. NY: Prentice Hall, 1992.
Kersey, Ethel M. *Women Philosophers: a Bio-critical Source Book*. NY: Greenwood Press, 1989.

Catherine Hundleby, M.A. Philosophy, University of Guelph, Guelph, Ontario, Canada

Roper, Mary (fl. 1544–1562).

See Basset, Mary Roper.

Roque, Jacqueline (d. 1986)

Second wife of Pablo Picasso. Name variations: Jacqueline Hutin; Jacqueline Picasso; Madame Z. Died from a self-inflicted gunshot wound on October 19, 1986; married an engineer or civil servant by the name of Hutin (divorced); married Pablo Picasso (1881–1973, the artist), on March 2, 1961; children: (first marriage) one daughter Catherine Hutin. Picasso's first wife was *Olga Khoklova.

Jacqueline Roque became the second wife of artist Pablo Picasso in 1961, when he was 80 and she was 35. By all accounts, she was obsessively devoted to Picasso, although some of his biographers question her motives. "Picasso became the tool through which she could assert her will over the rest of the world," wrote **Arianna Huffington**, "the means through which she could experience a sense of power that, even if her imagination had not been as limited as it was, she would never have imagined possible."

Roque knew Picasso as early as 1953, while he was in the process of ending his eight-year affair with *Françoise Gilot. At the time, she had recently divorced her first husband (a man by the name of Hutin) and was living near Vallarius with her six-year-old daughter **Catherine Hutin**. Roque was employed as a sales clerk at Madura's pottery in Vallarius, where Picasso had a studio and where she apparently posed for several paintings: *Portrait de Jacqueline aux mains croisèes*, which portrays her seated on the ground with her hands clasped around her drawn-up knees, and *Portrait of Madame Z*. Picasso called Roque Madame Z, after her house "Le Ziquet" (the little goat). In both portraits, painted in June 1954, Roque's adoration of the artist is quite apparent, although Picasso was then reluctant to enter into a deep commitment. "I could not possibly go to bed with a woman who had had a child by another man," he told a friend. Roque remained just another of Picasso's numerous female diversions for some time and was treated badly by the artist. Even after they became lovers, he frequently ordered her away, taking her back begrudgingly when she threatened to harm herself. Eventually, Roque's devotion simply wore him down, says Patrick O'Brian in his biography *Picasso* (1976). "[L]assitude, consciousness of age, and a longing for peace in which to work induced Picasso to give in. There may well be other factors of which one knows nothing, but that was the only explanation those who knew him well at the time could give. To them it seemed that he just gave up the struggle."

In 1955, Roque and her daughter moved with Picasso into a large villa in the district of La Californie, outside Cannes. It was there, according to Huffington, that "he and Jacqueline settled into a life of being devoured in the process of devouring each other—she by her smothering possessiveness and he by crushing first her spirit and then her humanity." Roque became Picasso's nursemaid, secretary, and housekeeper, and, symbolic of his dependence upon her, he began to call her "Maman." "And of all the women in his life, Jacqueline looked most like his mother," explains Huffington, "and came to look more and more like her as she grew stockier and sturdier with every year." Even while recovering from stomach surgery in 1957, Roque rose from her sickbed in order to tend to Picasso's needs.

As a result, she suffered from a debilitating fatigue from which she never recovered and which frequently caused her to hobble around like an old woman.

In March 1961, the couple secretly married with only necessary witnesses in attendance. From that time on, they divided their time between two residences: Château de Vauvenargues, in a lonely valley under the Montagne Sainte-Victoire, a house that Roque found sinister and lonely, and Mas Notre-Dame-de-Vie, in Mougins, near Cannes. "Marriage transformed Jacqueline from victim to victor," writes Huffington, "and crossing the line from mistress to wife unleashed the destructiveness that had been nursed in her through six years of being treated as something subhuman." In the years that followed, Roque sought to deepen her own relationship with Picasso by destroying his emotional bonds with others, namely his children with other women. From the time of her marriage, she attempted to separate the artist from his past life, and even went so far as to refer to Picasso's paintings of the period as "their children."

In 1965, Picasso was devastated by the publication of Françoise Gilot's book *Life with Picasso*, in which she recounted her private life, sparing few details of her turbulent relationship with Picasso. A short time later, the artist was hospitalized for prostate surgery, which took a further toll on his spirit. By 1969, however, he was recovered and enjoying another productive period. It was as though he thought he could ward off death by working, a belief that Roque shared. "They were co-conspirators in a tragic game of hide-and-seek," says Huffington, "tacitly determined to smother death with busy business: he busy with work, she busy with him."

Picasso cheated death until April 8, 1973, after which there was a long drawn-out battle to settle his estate. In the end, Roque inherited the largest portion, almost three-tenths of the total, including the two houses. She survived Picasso by 13 years, during which she arranged for a number of exhibits of his work from her large collection. On the night of October 15, 1986, after making final arrangements for an exhibition at the Spanish Museum of Contemporary Art in Madrid to open on October 25, Picasso's 105th birthday, Jacqueline Roque committed suicide, shooting herself in the temple. She was buried next to her husband in the park of the Château de Vauvenargues.

SOURCES:

Daix, Pierre. *Picasso: Life and Art*. Translated by Olivia Emmet. NY: HarperCollins, 1993.

Huffington, Arianna Stassinopoulos. *Picasso: Creator and Destroyer*. NY: Simon and Schuster, 1988.

O'Brian, Patrick. *Picasso*. NY: Putnam, 1976.

Barbara Morgan,
Melrose, Massachusetts

Ros, Amanda (1860–1939)

Irish writer. Name variations: Anna Margaret M'Kittrick; Amanda M'Kittrick Ros; Amanda McKittrick Ros; Amanda Malvina Fitzalan Anna Margaret McLelland Ros; (pseudonym) Monica Moyland. Born Anna Margaret M'Kittrick in Drumaness, County Down, Ireland, on December 8, 1860; died on February 3, 1939; daughter of Edward Amlane M'Kittrick (a school principal); educated at Drumaness School and Marlborough Teacher Training College in Dublin, Ireland; married Andy Ross, in 1887 (died 1917); married Thomas Rodgers (a farmer), in 1922 (died 1933).

Eccentric author of Irene Iddesleigh *(1897),* Delina Delaney *(1898), and* Helen Huddleson *(posthumous, 1969), works which inspired one critic to call her the "worst novelist in the world"; developed a cult following in England; published collections of poetry* Poems of Puncture *(1913) and* Fumes of Formation *(1933); wrote ballads during World War I that were printed in broadsheets under the pseudonym Monica Moyland.*

Amanda Ros was born Anna Margaret M'Kittrick in 1860, although she claimed that her mother had named her Amanda Malvina Fitzalan Ann Margaret McLelland M'Kittrick, after the heroine from her favorite novel, *Regina Maria Roche*'s *Children of the Abbey*. Ros became as famous for this overblown style of eccentricity as for her writing, which was described as "uniquely dreadful" for its artificial plots and florid narratives. Growing up in Drumaness, County Down, Ireland, she attended the school where her father served as principal. She trained at the Marlborough Teacher Training College in Dublin, Ireland, from 1884 to 1886, and then took a post at Millbrook National School in Larne, Ireland.

Ros claimed to have been writing since age four and pegged the creation of her first novel, *Irene Iddesleigh*, sometime before she turned 16. However, it is more likely that she produced the novel within five years of the time she self-published it in 1897, using the money given to her by her husband as a tenth anniversary gift for just such a purpose. It sold well enough to enable Ros to build a house, appropriately named "Iddesleigh," and to publish a second novel, *Delina Delaney*, in 1898. These books serve as prime examples of the shortfalls of Ros' writing style, which relied on powerful coincidences and absurd turns of events to propel her plots about high-bred men hopelessly in love with peasant girls after one glance and characters who die of shock brought on by bad news. She was especially well known for her flowery and alliterative phrasing, to which she often sacrificed meaning in complicated run-on sentences.

Ros used her writing to take revenge on her enemies in bald-faced attacks not even remotely masked as satire. She was particularly brutal in regards to the legal profession, which she felt had cheated her out of her inheritance of a lime kiln in 1908. Characters such as Mickey Monkeyface McBlear and Barney Bloater bore the brunt of her ill-will towards lawyers, which was so virulent that she included a completely extraneous section in her last novel, *Helen Huddleson* (completed by her biographer after her death and published in 1969), for the express purpose of highlighting how evil she thought them to be. She explored her enmity further in her collection of poems entitled *Poems of Puncture* (1913).

Neither did critics of her work escape her notice; those who attacked her writing often found themselves the subjects of derisive poems, as critic Barry Pain was after he criticized *Irene Iddesleigh*. Her anger unsoftened by Pain's death, Ros wrote of him as a "rodent of State" in her poem "The End of 'Pain,'" published in her second poetry collection, *Fumes of Formation* (1933). Much of the collection is devoted to her hatred of critics. Ros made reviewer W.B. Wyndham the subject of a 10,000-word essay, "St. Scandalbags," published posthumously in 1954; and "Donald Dudley: Bastard Critic" starts off what would have been a lengthy collection of sketches about her enemies in the unfinished "Six Months in Hell." Ros referred to critics in general as a "maggoty throng," "claycrabs of corruption," and "hogwashing hooligans."

If Ros were no friend to her critics, she did have a group of admirers at St. John's College in Cambridge, England, who helped elevate her to the level of cult status. Those claiming to admire her included Mark Twain, who kept one of her books in his library of "hogwash literature," and Aldous Huxley, who wrote about her work in the 1923 essay "Euphues Redivivus." Ros herself took her writing very seriously, and also composed ballads during World War I under the pseudonym Monica Moyland. She joined what she termed "the boundless battalion of the breathless" in 1939.

SOURCES:

Drabble, Margaret, ed. *The Oxford Companion to English Literature.* 5th ed. Oxford: Oxford University Press, 1985.

Hogan, Robert, ed. *Dictionary of Irish Literature.* Rev. ed. Westport, CT: Greenwood Press, 1996.

Newmann, Kate, ed. and comp. *Dictionary of Ulster Biography.* The Institute of Irish Studies, The Queen's University of Belfast, 1993.

SUGGESTED READING:

Loudan, Jack. *O Rare Amanda: The Life of Amanda McKittrick Ros,* 1954.

Susan J. Walton,
freelance writer, Berea, Ohio

Rosa (1906–1983)

*Duchess of Wurttemberg. Born on September 22, 1906, in Parsh near Salzburg; died on September 17, 1983, in Friedrichshafen; daughter of *Maria Cristina of Sicily (1877–1947) and Peter Ferdinand (1874–1948), archduke of Austria.*

Rosa, Anella de (1613–1649)

Neapolitan painter. Name variations: Anna di Rosa or Aniella Beltrano. Born in Naples in 1613; possibly murdered in 1649; a pupil of Francesco di Rosa; niece of Massimo Stanzioni; married Agostino Beltrano (a painter).

Both pupils of Massimo Stanzioni, Anella de Rosa and her husband Agostino Beltrano were Neapolitan painters who flourished about the middle of the 17th century. Agostino was a good fresco painter and "more than ordinary in his coloring in oil." The talented and beautiful Anella, who acquired a reputation as a historical artist, painted in the same style and worked with her husband. The pictures attributed to her were highly praised, especially that of the *Birth and Death of the Virgin* in the church of Santa Maria de' Turchini. In 1649, according to a Neapolitan art gossip named De' Dominici, Anella was stabbed to death by her husband in a fit of jealous rivalry, over favoritism shown by their master Stanzioni. The 36-year-old survived her wounds only long enough to pardon him. Agostino then fled to France and wandered as an outcast until 1659, when he returned to Naples and resumed his work. He lived, tormented by remorse, until 1665.

But the entire murder theory is debunked by **Germaine Greer** in *The Obstacle Race.* Greer claims that the true scandal was Anella de Rosa's reverence for her master Stanzioni, causing her to become his "willing collaborator, transferring his sketches to the canvas, often doing nearly all

the painting, leaving to him only the finishing touches to faces and hands" if the "work in question was a private commission." In 1638, an explosion brought down the roof of Santa Maria de' Turchini, destroying Anella de Rosa's only authenticated work—though *The Drunkenness of Noah* in the Calbresi Collection (Rome) and *Isaac Blessing Jacob* in the Majetti Collection have been attributed to her.

SOURCES:

Clement, Clara Erskine. *Painters, Sculptors, Architects, Engravers, and Their Works.* Hurd & Houghton, 1874.

Greer, Germaine. *The Obstacle Race.* NY: Farrar, Straus, 1979.

Rosa, Anna di (1613–1649).

See Rosa, Anella de.

Rosa, Euphrosyne Parepa (1836–1874).

See Parepa-Rosa, Euphrosyne.

Rosa di Viterbo (1235–1252).

See Rose of Viterbo.

Rosamond the Fair (c. 1145–1176).

See Clifford, Rosamund.

Rosana (1226–1310).

See Humilitas of Faenza.

Rosanova, Olga (1886–1918).

See Rozanova, Olga.

Rosa of Lima (1586–1617).

See Rose of Lima.

Rosas, Encarnación de (1795–1838)

*Argentinean first lady and wife of dictator Juan Manuel de Rosas. Name variations: Encarnacion de Rosas; Encarnación Ezcurra de Rosas. Born Encarnación Ezcurra y Arguibel on March 25, 1795; died on October 19, 1838; came from an upper-class Buenos Aires family; married Juan Manuel de Rosas (1793–1877), whose dictatorship was one of the harshest in 19th-century Latin American history, in 1813; children: daughter Manuela; sons Juan Bautista and Juan Manuel. Juan Manuel de Rosas also had five illegitimate offspring with his mistress *María Eugenia Castro (two sons, Joaquín and Adrian, and three daughters, Nicanora, Angela, and Justina).*

Born in Buenos Aires in 1795 to immigrant parents, Encarnación Ezcurra y Arguibel spent a childhood that witnessed the final years of Spanish rule and the rebellion that brought independence to Argentina. In 1813, she fell in love with and married Juan Manuel de Rosas, despite opposition from his mother, who aspired to a more prestigious match. Grazing land was easily obtained on the vast Argentine pampas by those willing to seize it from the Indians who roamed there. Juan Manuel soon acquired a huge ranch and set up a *saladero*, or meat-salting plant, to export beef. Encarnación remained in their home in Buenos Aires, receiving frequent visits from Juan Manuel, who spent much of the year attending to his growing interests in the countryside. In the political turmoil that beset the new nation, Juan Manuel also emerged as a military leader, who opposed liberalism, democracy, and disorder. Encarnación's own forceful personality was much like her husband's, and she shared his political and cultural views.

In 1829, Rosas was elected governor of the Buenos Aires province and granted absolute power. For three years, he ruled as dictator. Encarnación worked to rally support for her husband among the lower classes through extra-official patronage. He left power in 1832, chaos ensued, and he was returned as dictator in 1835, partly through the support of the Sociedad Popular Restaurador. Encarnación distributed gifts and public offices to the Sociedad's leaders, and they in turn harassed her husband's enemies, especially the liberal Unitarios. She also ran his urban household and raised their two surviving children, Juan and Manuela. Following a long illness, Encarnación de Rosas died in 1838.

SOURCES:

Lynch, John. *Argentine Dictator: Juan Manuel de Rosas, 1829–1852.* Oxford: Clarendon Press, 1981.

Kendall W. Brown,
Professor of History,
Brigham Young University, Provo, Utah

Rosay, Françoise (1891–1974)

One of the greatest actresses of the French cinema, whose career spanned more than six decades. Name variations: Francoise Rosay. Born Françoise Bandy de Nalèche in Paris, France, on April 19, 1891; died in Paris on March 28, 1974; graduated from the Conservatoire National de Déclamation, Paris; married Jacques Feyder (a director), in 1917; children: three sons.

Selected filmography: Falstaff *(1913);* Têtes de femmes, femme de têtes *(1916);* Crainquebille *(1923);* Gribiche *(1926);* Les Deux Timides *(1928);* Le Procès de Mary Dugan *(The Trial of Mary Dugan, 1929);* The One Woman Idea *(US, 1929);* Si l'Empereur savait ça! *(English version,* His Glorious Night, *and German version,* Olympia, *1930);* Le Petit Café *(Playboy of Paris, 1930);* *Jenny Lind *(A Lady's Morals, 1931);* The Magnificent Lie *(US, 1931);* La Chance *(1931);* Le Rosier de Madame Husson *(He, 1931);* L'Abbé Con-

stantin *(1933);* Remous *(Whirlpool, 1933);* Le Grand Jeu *(1934);* Pension Mimosas *(1935);* Maternité *(1935);* La Kermesse héroïque *(Carnival in Flanders, also appeared in German-language version,* Die klugen Frauen, *1935);* Jenny *(1936);* Un Carnet de Bal *(1937);* Drôle de drame *(Bizarre Bizarre, 1937);* Paix sur le Rhin *(1938);* Ramuntcho *(1938);* Le Joueur d'Echecs *(The Devil Is an Empress, 1938);* Les Gens du Voyage *(Fahrendes Volk, 1938);* Die Hochzeitstreise *(Ger., 1939);* Elles étaient Douze Femmes *(1940);* Une Femme disparait *(Portrait of a Woman, Switz.-Fr., 1942);* Half-Way House *(UK, 1944);* Johnny Frenchman *(UK, 1945);* Macadam *(Back Streets of Paris, 1946);* Saraband for Dead Lovers *(Saraband, UK, 1948);* Quartet *(UK, 1948);* The Naked Heart *(Maria Chapdelaine, UK-Fr., 1950);* Donne senza Nomme *(Women Without Names, It., 1950);* September Affair *(US, 1951);* The Thirteenth Letter *(US, 1951);* L'Auberge rouge *(The Red Inn, 1951);* Les Sept Péchés capitaux *(The Seven Deadly Sins, 1952);* That Lady *(UK, 1954);* La Reine Margot *(1954);* The Seventh Sin *(US, 1957);* Interlude *(US, 1957);* Me and the Colonel *(US, 1958);* Le Joueur *(1958);* The Sound and the Fury *(US, 1959);* Du Rififi chez les Femmes *(Riff Raff Girls, 1959);* The Full Treatment *(Stop Me Before I Kill!, UK, 1961);* Frau Cheney's Ende *(Ger.-Switz., 1961);* Le Cave se rebiffe *(The Counterfeiters of Paris, 1961);* The Longest Day *(US, 1962);* Up from the Beach *(US, 1965);* La 25e Heure *(The 25th Hour, 1967);* Faut pas prendre les Enfants du Bon Dieu pour des Canards sauvages *(Operation Leontine, 1968);* Un Merveilleux Parfum d'Oseille *(1969);* Der Fussgänger *(The Pedestrian, Ger., 1974).*

Born in Paris in 1891, Françoise Rosay attended school in Versailles and studied acting in Paris at the National Academy of Declamation. She made her stage debut in *Fantaisies Parisiennes* in 1908, then joined a French theatrical troupe that was performing in St. Petersburg, Russia, in 1912. The following year, she made her film debut in *Falstaff.* The highly versatile Rosay also sang as a member of the Paris Opera during the years 1916–18.

In 1916, she appeared in Belgian-born director Jacques Feyder's film *Têtes de femmes, femme de têtes.* Rosay, who married Feyder in July 1917, had a small role in his *Crainquebille* (1923) and appeared as a rich American woman who adopts a working-class boy in his *Gribiche* (1926). In 1928, she accompanied her husband to Hollywood, surfacing the next year in *The One Woman Idea* as well as in several of Feyder's French versions of the new sensation, talkies. In one of these, Ferenc Molnar's *Olympia* (1930), Rosay appeared in both a French and German version. In these and other films, she mastered dramatic skills that would soon make her one of the greatest actresses of the French cinema.

Returned to France, Rosay starred with Fernandel in 1931 in *Le Rosier de Madame Husson* (The Virtuous Isidore). By the mid-1930s, she had become a star and was featured in such films as *Un Carnet de Bal* (1937) and Marcel Carné's *Jenny* (1936). In this, Carné's first full-length film, Rosay played a key role in assuring not only its success but its very existence. She offered the young director her services free of charge, having become aware of Carné's talent while he worked as an assistant to her husband. With dialogue by Jacques Prévert and the outstanding acting of Rosay, *Jenny* enabled Carné to launch his career with a quality product. Also of considerable interest is Rosay's performance in the surrealist film of 1937, *Drôle de drame*.

The most outstanding film from this period of Rosay's career, and likely her best-remembered film role, was that of the leader of the Flemish women who dealt with the problems of survival in a conquered town in the 1935 film *La Kermesse héroïque* (Carnival in Flanders). In a story set in Flanders in 1616, Rosay portrays the Burgomaster's wife who welcomes and flirts with the Spanish commander. This tongue-in-cheek comedy, a lavish reconstruction down to the last detail, is set in the real-life Belgian town of Boom. Some film historians have argued that this sophisticated, cynical film is a pioneer feminist screen comedy.

When France was defeated in the summer of 1940, Rosay and Feyder fled to Switzerland in order to avoid being pressured to work for either the Vichy collaborationist regime or the Germans. After completing a film in Switzerland, Rosay went to England while Feyder remained in Geneva. She worked as a broadcaster for the Free French in London, and by the end of the war was in liberated North Africa. There, she worked as a director of Radio Algiers in charge of cultural broadcasting, a position she held from 1944 through 1947. For her wartime activities, she was later awarded the Legion of Honor.

After her husband's death in 1948, Rosay continued to work in films as well as on stage, although she had initally thought of retirement, believing she could never work again without her husband. "But everywhere," she noted, "the film people are nice and keep me busy. They think of me as being only tragic and strong. But I

can be very, very comic—maybe something like *Marie Dressler.*" In the 25 years between her husband's death and her own, Rosay appeared in an average of one film a year and occasionally performed on stage in Paris and London. From 1956 through 1967, she taught a course in dramatic art in Paris. In 1961, she made her New York stage debut, starring as *Catherine II the Great* in *Once There Was a Russian*. Among the better-known films of the final years of her long career are *The Longest Day* (1962), and her last, Maximilian Schell's *The Pedestrian*, which she filmed in Munich in the summer of 1973 when she was 82 years old. Some motion picture historians have suggested that Françoise Rosay shared with *Arletty the ability to be both world-weary and touching.

SOURCES:

Crisp, Colin. *The Classic French Cinema, 1930–1960.* Bloomington, IN: Indiana University Press, 1993.

Harvey, S. "Bonnes Femmes: Making International Stars in the French Cinema," in *Film Comment.* Vol. 17, no. 6, 1981, pp. 40–47.

Legrand, Catherine, and Robyn Karney, eds. *Chronicle of the Cinema.* London: Dorling Kindersley, 1995.

O'Leary, Liam. "Rosay, Françoise," in Nicholas Thomas and James Vinson, eds., *International Dictionary of Films and Filmmakers.* 2nd ed. Vol. 3. Chicago, IL: St. James Press, 1990–94, pp. 1056–1058.

Vincendeau, Ginette, ed. *Encyclopedia of European Cinema.* NY: Facts on File, 1995.

Williams, Alan Larson. *Republic of Images: A History of French Filmmaking.* Cambridge, MA: Harvard University Press, 1992.

John Haag,
Associate Professor of History,
University of Georgia, Athens, Georgia

Rosé, Alma (1906–1944)

Austrian-Jewish violinist and conductor of the women's orchestra at the Auschwitz-Birkenau concentration camp, portrayed in the book and film **Playing for Time,** *whose efforts saved countless musicians condemned to the camps. Name variations: Alma Rose. Born Alma Maria Rosé in 1906 in Vienna, Austria; died in Auschwitz on April 4, 1944, only a few months before the liberation of the camp in January 1945; daughter of Arnold Rosé (a concertmaster of both the Vienna Philharmonic Orchestra and the Court Opera Orchestra [State Opera Orchestra after 1918]) and Justine Mahler (sister of Gustav Mahler); sister of Alfred Rosé (1902–1975, a noted conductor who escaped to the U.S. and Canada).*

Following in her father's footsteps, studied the violin and was a virtuoso performer by her teens; with her father, recorded *Concerto for Two Violins and Orchestra of Johann Sebastian Bach* (1931); struck out on her own and established a solid career in Austria *and other European nations (mid-1930s); the Nazi annexation of Austria (March 1938) ended her father's career in Vienna, but he continued to perform in Great Britain; did not follow her father into exile but remained in Europe; arrested in the Netherlands and sent to Westerbork (1942); transported to Auschwitz, where she became conductor of that concentration camp's women's orchestra (1943).*

Born in Vienna in 1906 when that imperial metropolis was the political and cultural heart of Central Europe, Alma Rosé could boast of extraordinary musical genealogy. Her mother **Justine Mahler** was highly musical, which was not surprising given the fact that she was the sister of Gustav Mahler (1860–1911), conductor of the Vienna Philharmonic and Court (later State) Opera orchestras and composer of some of the greatest works of late German Romanticism. Her father Arnold Rosé was one of the most highly respected musicians in the German-speaking world. Though her parents had wanted a boy, they did everything possible to see to it that Alma became a musician. At birth, a tiny violin was already in her room. The family de-

Alma Rosé

termined she would become a child prodigy like her father.

Arnold Rosé, born Arnold Josef Rosenblum in Jassy in the Bukovina province of the Austrian empire (today Iasi, Romania), had triumphed over anti-Semitic prejudices through the sheer force of his musical genius. He made an acclaimed debut in 1879 at the famous Gewandhaus concerts in Leipzig and by 1881 had become concertmaster of both the Vienna Philharmonic and Court Opera orchestras—posts he would hold with distinction for 57 years. Arnold Rosé was also a brilliant chamber music performer, founding his own lauded string quartet in 1882. In such a rich musical milieu, young Alma's natural talent quickly flourished, and by her early 20s she began a successful career as a violin virtuoso. A permanent testimonial to her talent is her recording with her father of the Concerto for Two Violins and Orchestra of Johann Sebastian Bach. Transcribed in 1931, this moving rendition appeared in CD format in the early 1990s.

Despite the anti-Semitism which pervaded Viennese public life, the Rosés established satisfying careers for themselves. In the 1930s, it appeared the family name would continue to be prominent in musical circles. Alfred Rosé, Alma's brother, was becoming known as a fine conductor, while her own musical skill and artistic taste captivated audiences both inside and beyond the borders of Austria. The Nazi seizure of power in Germany in 1933 ended these possibilities, however. Restrictions increased as anti-Semitic legislation grew, shattering hopes and dreams.

Most of Alma Rosé's energy went into her work, and like many artists she ignored the swirling turmoil of the 1930s. The family was unprepared when her father was summarily terminated as concertmaster of the Vienna Philharmonic and State Opera orchestras after the Anschluss, the Nazi occupation of Austria in March 1938. Arnold fled to London as a penniless refugee, where, at age 75, he reconstituted his famous string quartet which delighted British music-lovers for another half-decade.

Alma decided to remain in Europe. Whether because of stubbornness or political naivete, she refused to cross the English Channel. In the late 1930s, she went to France, which had a large community of German-speaking refugees in Paris. When the Nazis invaded and occupied France in May 1940, she went to the Netherlands. German conquest and occupation of that neutral country quickly led to restrictions against both native-born Dutch Jews and Jewish refugees like herself. It was difficult for Rosé to understand why she was persecuted. She was little interested in Judaism either as a faith or as a cultural tradition. She lived for music, her one consuming passion.

Life in the Netherlands rapidly deteriorated, and in 1942 the Nazi Final Solution was implemented. Although many Dutch men and women took great risks to save Jews (Yad Vashem in Jerusalem has given more awards for rescue achievements to the Dutch than to the people of any other nation), the country was small, flat, and treeless, with no place to hide. There was also a significant group (80,000) of Dutch Nazis who often assisted German occupation officials in tracking down "the divers"—Jews who had gone into hiding. Of the more than 150,000 Dutch and foreign-born Jews in the country in 1940, only about 20,000 survived the war. Unable to hide, Rosé was arrested in 1942 and sent to Westerbork before being moved to Auschwitz.

The small Polish district town of Oswiecim, 50 kilometers southwest of Cracow, was located in the Austrian half of the Austro-Hungarian Monarchy until 1918, when it became part of independent Poland. Oswiecim was incorporated into Nazi Germany in October 1939 after the defeat and occupation of Poland and given the name Auschwitz. Located near the Sola River, a tributary of the Vistula, Auschwitz was essentially unpleasant and unhealthy, a humid and foggy valley with swampy soil. Evacuation of the local population created an area of 40 square kilometers in which a vast complex of facilities was built to house, exploit, and murder large numbers of Jews, Poles, Soviet prisoners of war, and other groups deemed undesirable by the Nazi regime. According to the SS bureaucracy, these individuals had committed offenses which were "relatively light and definitely correctable." The main camp, known as Auschwitz I, rapidly expanded and accommodated 18,000 prisoners by the end of 1941, which grew to 30,000 by 1943. Construction of Auschwitz II, known as the Birkenau camp, began in October 1941.

Women were first sent to Auschwitz I in late March 1942. At first, the women's camp was relatively small, consisting of 999 German women brought from the Ravensbrück concentration camp and an equal number of Jewish women prisoners from Slovakia. By the summer of 1942, the population of the women's section had swollen to 6,000, and it was decided to transfer the women's section to Birkenau, which by January 1944 held 27,053 female prisoners. These women lived under horrifying conditions and some among their number were constantly being selected for the gas chambers. The first Auschwitz prisoners were Poles who had been engaged in resistance, but by 1942 more and more Jews were brought to the camps.

Upon arriving, Rosé was examined by an SS physician in charge of determining who would be put to work and who sent immediately to the gas chamber. Educated, articulate, and in good health, Rosé was allowed to live. The next years of her brief life would be dominated by music even in the face of death. Her efforts not only would allow Rosé to live but would save the lives of countless other women as well. Music often served a utilitarian purpose. Marches were played when prisoners went to work in the morning and when they returned to their barracks. At the Janowska camp, a "Death Tango" was performed during the *Selektionen* that decided whether newly arrived prisoners would live or die.

Orchestras, bands, choirs and other large musical ensembles were a hallmark of Nazi concentration camps. As early as 1933, a choir of 120 performed at the Lichtenburg camp. In Buchenwald in the late 1930s, the SS commanded that a motley orchestra of guitars, harmonicas, and various brass instruments perform regularly. The influx of many talented Viennese Jewish musicians in 1938 resulted in an expansion of musical activity in several camps. In Buchenwald, cabaret performances, including music and songs, briefly showcased the talents of stars like Hermann Leopoldi before the SS banned such displays of impudence. When war vastly expanded the SS concentration-camp empire, many more orchestras were created. Prisoners often brought instruments with them. These were kept when their owners were gassed so that a broad selection was always available to incoming inmates. At the main Auschwitz camp, a brass band of 120 players, a symphony orchestra of 80, a dance band of 20, and a jazz ensemble of 5 performers entertained. Even camps exclusively created as extermination facilities—Belzec, Maidanek, Sobibor and Treblinka—had orchestras.

The camp commander, *Maria Mandel, immediately recognized Alma Rosé's talents and appreciated her musical heritage. A "great music lover" who spared no effort to improve the cultural life of her camp, particularly its musical environment, Mandel came from a very different world than did her prisoner. Born in the village of Münzkirchen, Upper Austria, in 1912, Mandel was typical of the poor, rural people who often joined the Nazi party. Alma Rosé's affluent family—sophisticated and internationally respected—lived in a world unknown to the commandant from the backward Austrian provinces. Meeting someone of Rosé's caliber likely never would have happened to Mandel had she not been put in charge of a death camp. She appreciated the celebrity status which beckoned in the twisted environment of the concentration camp universe.

Rosé leaped at the opportunity to become part of the concentration-camp orchestra. Music had long been her only escape, even in the outside world. Furthermore, being a member of an orchestra gave a woman prisoner distinct advantages over other prisoners. Mandel's musicians enjoyed a protected status. Their block was kept in better repair than those of the clerical staff or prisoners assigned to the cooking unit, and they were able to rehearse in a building that was kept comfortably warm in wintertime. Although their rations were still inadequate, they received more than ordinary prisoners, and they were relatively well dressed in blue cloth dresses and caps. The orchestra was usually busy, playing at roll call and performing martial tunes for the exhausted women who came marching back to their barracks after a day of forced labor. All official occasions included music. Rosé's elevation to conductor of the orchestra placed her in a grotesque position. She operated in a camp founded to humiliate, dehumanize, exploit, and exterminate its inmates under administrators determined to foster a warped version of "culture" within its walls.

Alma Rosé, a tall, dignified woman with dark hair, had a striking presence. As conductor, she assumed the role of a *Kapo*, which gave her great power over the work and even the lives of her ensemble members. In all Nazi concentration camps, the *Kapo* saw to it that the rules of the camp were meticulously followed. The traditional authoritarian role of orchestra conductor was thus greatly reinforced by the camp culture. Rosé took full advantage of her position, pushing her musicians to the outer limits of skill and endurance. She was motivated by fear and determination, as she knew the orchestra could survive only if its performances pleased its captors. The role of the authoritarian musician came quite naturally to Rosé. Like many German-speaking Jews, she was totally assimilated into German culture and typically assumed that her cultural heritage was superior to that of the Poles, French, and other non-German members of her orchestra. Above all, she was determined to use her knowledge of German culture to survive in an extremely hostile environment.

Many problems faced Rosé. Hers was anything but a conventional orchestra. Composed of ten violins, a flute, reed pipes, two accordions, five mandolins, three guitars, and a percussion section of cymbals and drums, it was an odd mixture of instruments. Recognizing that sound was of utmost importance, Rosé pressed *Fania Fénelon, a Jewish musician from Paris who had never before done such work, to orchestrate music. Despite her family heritage, Rosé was not a conductor. She was a virtuoso violinist who read the score as any player would. Her conducting skill was often rudimentary and left much to be desired. Recognizing her weaknesses, she compensated with hours of practice, driving orchestra members to play 12-to-17 hours a day. This regime took its toll on orchestra members, but gradually the ensemble improved. Often, there was "nightwork," a ghastly time when the orchestra entertained SS men. Each day Rosé's musicians entertained kept them alive—quite literally they were "playing for time."

Alma Rosé was the link between demanding captors and frightened, undernourished musicians. Often, these women could not decide who they hated most—the Nazis or their conductor. Rosé's power over them symbolized their powerlessness in the face of the Nazi system of racial hatred and extermination. Sometimes Rosé seemed inhuman, driving them to the limits of physical endurance. Despite their bitterness, the women often felt great unity while playing. Rosé was transformed, even transfigured, when playing her violin. Fénelon describes her as an "incomparably beautiful" young woman who "gave off an extraordinary sensuality." While playing, "her relaxed mouth softened, half-opened; her eyes misted over; her body trembled. Alma was in the throes of love. We were silent, we listened and forgot. When she stopped and put down her bow, the desire to applaud was irresistible. But it was very, very short, the length of a piece of music. Then, instantly, Alma became inhuman once again."

Rosé was isolated. She told Fenelon that her family had always "thought like Germans. . . . I hardly knew we were Jewish." Rosé never seemed to comprehend the enormity of what had happened her. For example, being tattooed "worried" her somewhat because she refused to accept its purpose. Her survival tool was her music which provided temporary release and escape from the threat of the gas chambers. In this, she proved correct. Despite their fear and suffering, Rosé and her orchestra experienced some transcendingly glorious moments. When she conducted Beethoven's Fifth Symphony, a work whose opening bars were the symbol of Allied victory, the women were transported. Ignoring the unconventional nature of their ensemble, they played "in a state of grace because [on that occasion] the symphony soared, compelling and marvelous."

Each day brought new perils, however. Once when Reichsführer-SS Heinrich Himmler visited the camp, he did not compliment Rosé on her work. This incident caused great fear for the conductor and her orchestra. In their world, criticism could mean death. Rosé cultivated Himmler, hoping to play for German troops.

By the spring of 1944, the war was not going well for the Nazis, and tension increased. More and more trainloads of Jews arrived. Fewer and fewer survived while the crematoriums worked overtime. Though Rosé worked harder than ever to survive, eventually Auschwitz claimed her as yet another victim. She became suddenly ill and died on April 4, 1944. Meningitis and spotted typhus were epidemic in the camp. Poison was also suspected, after an autopsy, and SS doctors declared that to be the cause of her death. One Frau Schmidt, a German camp supervisor, was strongly suspected as the culprit. This may well have been what happened. Operating in the highly charged camp environment, Rosé may have made enemies who felt she had escaped death for far too long.

Rosé's funeral reflected the bizarre nature of Auschwitz. The SS erected a catafalque for her body next to the camp medical room. Covered with a profusion of white flowers, mainly lilies, her face was calm, relaxed and beautiful. Her long hands, crossed on her breast, held a flower. Surrounded by her sobbing musicians, she lay in state while members of the SS filed past the foot of her bed, respectfully removing their hats. Maria Mandel was inconsolable. In a small room of one of Adolf Hitler's worst death camps, Nazi captors and Jewish prisoners mourned the passing of a remarkable woman.

As German armies continued to crumble, more and more prisoners were exterminated, but Alma Rosé's orchestra survived. After Auschwitz was liberated in January 1945, these women began their lives anew. For several decades, this strange chapter in history was all but forgotten, and like so many who died in the Holocaust, Alma Rosé was barely remembered. But the image of this fiercely determined musician forcing her orchestra to "play for time" did not die. Orchestra members realized that her efforts had saved them from the ovens. Alma Rosé's conducting career can only be termed a nightmare, but she always believed that the power of music would triumph over the power of darkness.

Opposite page

*E*rnestine

*R*ose

SOURCES:

Adelsberger, Lucie. *Auschwitz: Ein Tatsachenbericht.* 3rd ed. Berlin: Lettner-Verlag, 1960.

Boult, Adrian Sir. "Rosé and the Vienna Philharmonic," in *Music and Letters.* Vol. 32, no. 3. July 1951, pp. 256–257.

Czech, Danuta. *Auschwitz Chronicle.* NY: Henry Holt, 1990.

Dunin-Wasowicz, Krzysztof. *Resistance in the Nazi Concentration Camps 1933–1945.* Warsaw: PWN—Polish Scientific Publishers, 1982.

Fénelon, Fania. *Playing for Time.* NY: Atheneum, 1977.

Gutman, Yisrael, and Michael Berenbaum, eds. *Anatomy of the Auschwitz Death Camp.* Bloomington, IN: Indiana University Press, 1994.

Hart, Kitty. *Return to Auschwitz: The Remarkable Story of a Girl Who Survived the Holocaust.* NY: Atheneum, 1983.

Hoch, Moshe, Marian Fuchs, Gila Flam, and Eddie Halpern. "Music, the Holocaust," in Israel Gutman, ed., *Encyclopedia of the Holocaust.* Vol. 3. London: Collier Macmillan, 1990, pp. 1022–1026.

Kautsky, Benedikt. *Teufel und Verdammte: Erfahrungen und Erkenntnisse aus sieben Jahren in deutschen Konzentrationslagern.* Zurich: Büchergilde Gutenberg, 1946.

Koller, Gabriele, and Gloria Withalm, eds. *Die Vertreibung des Geistigen aus Österreich: Zur Kulturpolitik des Nationalsozialismus.* 2nd rev. ed. Vienna: Zentralsparkasse und Kommerzialbank, Wien [1986].

Kuhn, Annette, and Valentine Rothe. *Frauen im deutschen Faschismus.* 2nd ed. Düsseldorf: Schwann, 1983, vol. II, pp. 200–204.

Laks, Szymon. *Music of Another World.* Trans. by Chester A. Kisiel. Evanston, IL: Northwestern University Press, 1989.

Langbein, Hermann. *Menschen in Auschwitz.* Vienna: Europa, 1972.

Potter, Tully. "Arnold Rosé: The Last Flowering of Old Vienna," in *The Strad.* Vol. 105, no. 1246. January 1994, pp. 232–233 and 235–236.

"Professor Arnold Rosé," in *The Times* [London]. August 26, 1946, p. 7.

Röder, Werner, and Herbert Strauss, eds. *International Biographical Dictionary of Central European Emigrés 1933–1945.* 4 vols. Munich: K.G. Saur, 1983.

Weinzierl, Erika. "Österreichische Frauen in nationalsozialistischen Konzentrationslagern," in *Dachauer Hefte.* Vol. 3, no. 3. November 1987, pp. 166–204.

SUGGESTED READING:

Newman, Richard, with Karen Kirtley. *Alma Rosé: Vienna to Auschwitz.* Timer-Amadeus, 2000.

John Haag,
Associate Professor of History,
University of Georgia, Athens, Georgia

Rose, Ernestine (1810–1892)

Polish-born reformer who was an early advocate of women's rights and for the abolition of slavery in the United States. Born Ernestine Louise Siismondi Potowski on January 13, 1810, at Piotrków, Russian Poland; died on August 4, 1892, in Brighton, England; only child of Isaac Potowski (a rabbi); mother's

name not recorded; had no formal education; married William Rose, in 1835; no children.

Selected writings and lectures: Speech of Mrs Rose, a Polish Lady, at the Anniversary Paine Celebration, in New York, January 29, Year of Independence, 74th-Christian Era *(1850);* An Address on Woman's Rights Delivered Before the People's Sunday Meeting, in Cochituate Hall, on Sunday Afternoon, October 19, 1851 *(1851);* Review of Horace Mann's Two Lectures Delivered in New York, February 17th and 29th, 1852 *(1852);* "*Speech of Mrs. E. L. Rose at the Woman's Rights Convention, Held in Syracuse, September 1852,*" *in* Woman's Rights Commensurate With Her Capacities and Obligations: A Series of Tracts *(1853);* A Defense of Atheism, Being a Lecture Delivered in Mercantile Hall, Boston, April 10, 1861 *(1881);* Two Addresses Delivered at the Bible Convention, Hartford, Conn., in June 1853 *(1888); various newspaper articles in the* Boston Investigator *(from 1831).*

Ernestine Rose was born on January 13, 1810, in the small Polish village of Piotrków which was then part of the Russian Empire. Her father Isaac Potowski was a prominent local rabbi and a strict adherent of a particularly rigorous and austere interpretation of Judaism. He raised his only child on the basis of a belief that the only proper place for a woman was in the home and that her only function was to obey her male elders. What Ernestine's mother (whose name does not appear in any contemporary record) thought about this situation is not known. It is probable, however, that she acquiesced with her husband's position and did her best to raise her daughter in accordance with traditional Jewish customs and mores.

Not surprisingly, given his beliefs, Isaac saw no purpose in sending Ernestine to school. On the other hand, he did encourage her from an early age to study the Torah and the Talmud, the two principal Jewish religious texts. This was unusual inasmuch as such instruction was normally given only to male children. Moreover, Isaac soon complemented this instruction by hiring a private tutor to teach his daughter Hebrew. Rose would later recall, with some pride, how she would often drive her tutor to frustration by incessant questions about various aspects of her studies. Clearly, she had a sharp and enquiring mind which was further evidenced by her own attempts to teach herself foreign languages (particularly German) so that she could read works of literature in their original form.

Rose continued her religious studies until she was 14 years old. Then, for reasons that re-

main obscure, she rebelled and formally abandoned her Judaic beliefs. Isaac's reaction to this development is unknown, but relations with Ernestine appear to have continued normally for the next two years. It was then that he decided, in accordance with rabbinical custom, to choose a husband for his daughter. When Ernestine was informed, she was outraged and refused to have anything to do with this proposal.

The situation was further complicated when Isaac promised the prospective husband a substantial dowry, money which actually belonged to Ernestine, who had inherited it from her recently deceased mother. According to Jewish custom in Poland at the time, if no good reason could be adduced for breaking a betrothal then the dowry would still revert to the bridegroom. Whether Ernestine liked it or not, Isaac assumed his responsibility to pay the dowry and was determined that she should hand over her legacy.

For her part, Rose realized that her only recourse would be an appeal to secular law. Accordingly, she set out for the town of Kalisz where, remarkably for a 16-year-old, she acted as her own attorney in a successful defense of her rights. Then, in order to demonstrate that she had fought the case as a matter of principle and not for reasons of personal gain, Ernestine voluntarily turned all of her inheritance over to her father.

Shortly after, Isaac married a woman little older than Ernestine. Stepmother and stepdaughter quickly developed a mutual antipathy for one another and, in these increasingly difficult domestic circumstances, Ernestine decided to leave home. She traveled first to Berlin (the capital of the kingdom of Prussia) where she discovered that, as a Polish Jew, she was subject to certain restrictive laws that effectively limited her ability to find employment as well as the length of time she could remain in the country. Rose refused to accept these constraints and decided to appeal to the highest authority. In an act of remarkable audacity, she asked for and received an audience with King Frederick William III. The latter was so impressed by the young woman before him that he granted her a special exemption from these laws.

Ernestine's next problem was to earn a living. Once again, she utilized her sharp intelligence by inventing a process by which some specially treated chemical paper, when burned, dispelled cooking odors. This turned out to be a great commercial success and provided Ernestine with enough money to live comfortably as well as to travel widely throughout Germany. It was in the course of these frequent journeys that she first became aware of the full extent of poverty and misery to which the working class (particularly women and children) was then subject.

In 1829, Rose left Germany and continued her travels in Belgium and Holland. The following year, she visited France and was in Paris to witness the July revolt which overthrew King Charles X. Ernestine was so impressed with the revolutionary movement that, when a parallel uprising broke out in Poland a few weeks later, she made plans to return and take part in the attempts to free her own country. She only got as far as the Polish frontier, however, where the police refused to permit her (and other potential revolutionaries) to travel farther. In any case, it was too late; the Polish uprising had been firmly crushed by government authorities.

Three years later, Rose moved to London, England, where she supported herself through the sale of her chemical paper and by giving lessons in Hebrew and German. There she met several of that country's most famous social reformers, such as *Elizabeth Fry (whose work in alleviating prison conditions was becoming internationally known) and Thomas Paine (the great democratic theorist of the American and French revolutions). The person who made the greatest impact on her, however, was Robert Owen, who was then in his early 60s, and who subsequently referred to Ernestine as his daughter.

Owen's career had been based on the theoretical principle that human character is the direct product of its surrounding environment. Human wickedness is the result of the milieu of poverty and misery in which individuals live, but this can be reversed by providing such improvements as better working conditions, good housing, as well as educational and recreational facilities. Owen had attempted to implement this principle on several occasions—at New Harmony in Indiana in the mid-1820s and, a little earlier and more successfully, at New Lanark in Scotland—but few of his model communities lasted for long. Nevertheless, his basic principle had a significant impact on the emerging trade-union movement in Britain as well as on various other associations for social reform.

When Ernestine met Owen, the latter was principally engaged in traveling throughout Great Britain giving lectures to workers on his theory of social improvement. In 1835, he asked Rose to address one such meeting in London. Despite her yet hesitant command of the English language and thick foreign accent, she proved a considerable success. Later the same year, Ernestine met William Rose, a thoughtful and cultured man who made a modest living as a jeweler and silversmith and who considered himself a follower of Owen. Shortly after, the couple were married in a civil ceremony and, early the following year, emigrated to New York where they established a small business (a combined jewelry and perfumery store).

In the mid-1830s, married women in the state of New York enjoyed few, if any, legal rights. All their property effectively belonged to their husbands who were also permitted to appropriate any wages they earned; they had no standing to sue or be sued in the courts; and they were denied the opportunity to vote. Not all men accepted this situation and, in May 1836, Thomas Hertell introduced a bill into the New York state assembly that contained provisions designed to address these injustices. That legislation was defeated, and it took another 12 years before a greatly amended and much-diluted bill was eventually enacted recognizing a woman's right to keep her own property.

Emancipation from every kind of bondage is my principle.

—Ernestine Rose

Throughout these 12 years, Rose traveled the length and breadth of the state gathering signatures on petitions designed to keep the issue before the legislature. At the same time, she kept an increasingly busy schedule of speaking engagements at which she addressed various issues of social reform, particularly the abolition of slavery. Throughout her life, Rose refused to accept any fee for her public appearances and insisted on paying her own traveling expenses. Fortunately, their business provided sufficient financial means for this while her husband William generously extended his moral support. Despite her youth, religious background and marked foreign accent, Rose quickly became a popular speaker. She was known as the "Queen of the Platform," and one newspaper noted approvingly, after a particularly successful meeting, that "she handled her logic as deftly as a needle."

In July 1848, the first Woman's Rights Convention held in the United States was convened in Seneca Falls, New York, "to discuss the social, civil and religious rights of woman." During the convention, *Elizabeth Cady Stanton, a prominent women's rights activist, moved that the convention support the franchise for women. At that time, this was a radical proposal, and the motion was only passed after a heated and divisive debate among the delegates present. Although Rose did not attend this meeting, she was a featured speaker at the first National Woman's Rights Convention held in Worcester, Massachusetts, two years later, where she was elected to the organization's central executive committee. For the next 19 years, she attended every New York state and national convention on women's rights in her capacity as organizer and speaker. Despite furious attacks in the popular press and their frequent interruption by outraged clerics and drunken mobs, these conventions gradually attracted increasingly larger and more enthusiastic audiences.

Throughout these years, Rose continued to gather and present petitions to the New York state assembly in Albany pressing for extensions of women's rights. Due to her growing reputation, she was granted the rare distinction, on several occasions, of being allowed to address the main assembly, or one of its legislative committees, in person. By 1855, she reached the height of her popularity as a public speaker in towns and cities throughout the United States. In the same year, however, the constant strain finally took a toll on her health. When her doctor advised a change of scene, she traveled to England to visit her old friend Robert Owen. On returning to New York six months later, Rose found that her continued association with Owen made some of the more conservative female reformers uncomfortable; this, in turn, made her position in the women's movement more tenuous.

In 1860, two important events occurred. First, in March, the New York assembly finally passed an act Concerning the Rights and Liabilities of Husband and Wife. This bill granted many of the demands which Rose and her colleagues had been making for the previous 12 years, with the important exception of the right to vote. Unfortunately, the victory was short lived because, two years later, the legislation was amended in a manner distinctly unfavorable to the women's cause. The second major event that year was Abraham Lincoln's election as president of the United States.

Although Rose identified herself with the Democratic Party and Lincoln was a Republican, she strongly supported him for his stance against slavery. She did not believe, however, that the president's position went far enough. Lincoln argued that there should be no further extension of slavery into those territories then seeking to become full states of the union. On the other hand, however, he was willing to tolerate it in those Southern states where it currently existed. The latter position was unacceptable to Rose who believed that slavery was an intrinsic

evil that should be abolished everywhere as quickly as possible. Just as all American women should enjoy the same legal and social rights as their male counterparts, so, similarly, all African-Americans should enjoy the same privileges as other citizens.

Although Rose championed the Northern cause during the Civil War, she was frequently critical of the manner in which Lincoln's administration handled the conflict. Despite this, she served on the policy-making committee of the Women's National Loyal League, an organization created in 1863 with the aim of collecting one million signatures on a petition expressing support and solidarity with the aims of the federal government.

Following the end of the war, the 13th Amendment to the Constitution was proclaimed which formally outlawed slavery throughout the United States. Though Rose and her fellow reformers were pleased, they were disappointed that their own demand for suffrage was rejected at the same time. Their frustration was increased shortly afterwards by the 14th and 15th amendments which were intended to grant (male) African-Americans the right to vote. Both the federal government and the mainstream abolitionist movement rejected the women's demand for suffrage on the grounds that many states would not accept this radical proposal. It was believed that any attempt to include female suffrage in the proposed amendments might result in their complete rejection and hence the continuation of slavery.

This decision left Rose and many other female reformers bitter, especially in light of the support they had previously afforded the abolitionist cause. Their subsequent attempts to come to terms with this situation and formulate a new strategy of reform only served to precipitate a major split in their ranks. In 1869, Rose joined the executive committee of the markedly more radical National Woman's Suffrage Association, while the conservative faction formed the rival American Woman's Suffrage Association (these organizations would not merge again until 1889). Rose took little part in running the new organization. She was now close to 60 years of age and neuralgic and rheumatic pains had left her a semi-invalid.

Later that year, the Roses decided to leave America and retire in Europe. They visited France and Switzerland (where Ernestine attended the Congress of Peace in Lucerne) before settling near London. For the next few years, she continued to speak occasionally on the subject of women's rights but, after a short trip to New York in 1873 to settle her outstanding financial affairs, she retired from public life.

In latter years, Rose's health continued to decline, and she was largely confined to her home. She still read avidly and often sent letters to her old colleagues in the United States, advising them on various issues of concern to the reform movement. In 1882, her husband died. Despite entreaties from friends in America to return, Rose stubbornly refused to leave England. Her last years were spent in increasing poverty in the seaside town of Brighton, not far from London, where she died on August 4, 1892, at the age of 82.

SOURCES:

Barnard, L.E. "Ernestine L. Rose," in *History of Woman Suffrage*. Vol. 1. Edited by Elizabeth Cady Stanton, Susan B. Anthony, and *Matilda Joslyn Gage (reprinted, NY: Arno Press, 1975).

O'Connor, Lillian. *Pioneer Women Orators: Rhetoric in the Ante-Bellum Reform Movement*. NY: Columbia University Press, 1954.

Suhl, Yuri. *Eloquent Crusader*. NY: Julian Messner, 1970.
——. *Ernestine Rose and the Battle for Human Rights*. NY: Greenberg, 1956.

SUGGESTED READING:

Davis, Paulina. *A History of the National Women's Rights Movement from 1850 to 1870*. NY: Journeymen Printers' Co-operative Association, 1871.

Foner, Philip. *History of the Labor Movement in the United States*. NY: International Publishers, 1947.

Irwin, Inez Haynes. *Angels and Amazons: A Hundred Years of American Women*. NY: Doubleday, Doran, 1933.

Kolmerten, Carol A. *The American Life of Ernestine L. Rose*. Syracuse University, 1998.

Dave Baxter,
Department of Philosophy, Wilfrid Laurier University,
Waterloo, Ontario, Canada

Rose, Helen (1904–1985)

American costume designer. Born on February 2, 1904, in Chicago, Illinois; died in Palm Springs, California, in November 1985; daughter of William Bromberg and Ray (Bobbs) Bromberg; attended Chicago Academy of Fine Arts; married Harry Rose, on December 28, 1929; children: one daughter, Judy Rose.

Selected filmography: Hello Frisco Hello (1943); Coney Island (1943); Stormy Weather (1943); Ziegfeld Follies (1945); The Harvey Girls (1946); Till the Clouds

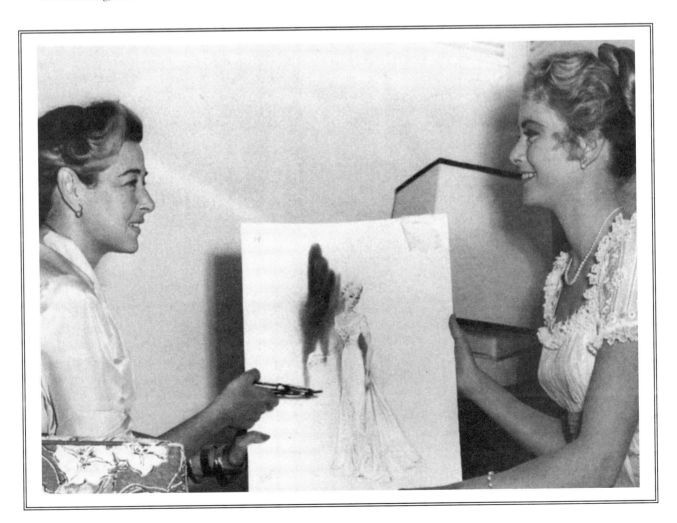

Helen Rose (left) with Grace Kelly.

Roll By *(1947)*; Good News *(1947)*; Homecoming *(1948)*; Act of Violence *(1949)*; Take Me Out to the Ball Game *(1949)*; Father of the Bride *(1950)*; Annie Get Your Gun *(1950)*; Three Little Words *(1950)*; Summer Stock *(1950)*; The Toast of New Orleans *(1950)*; The Great Caruso *(1951)*; The Belle of New York *(1952)*; The Merry Widow *(1952)*; The Bad and the Beautiful *(1952)*; The Story of Three Loves *(1953)*; Dream Wife *(1953)*; Mogambo *(1953)*; Executive Suite *(1954)*; Rhapsody *(1954)*; Rose Marie *(1954)*; The Glass Slipper *(1955)*; I'll Cry Tomorrow *(1955)*; Interrupted Melody *(1955)*; Love Me or Leave Me *(1955)*; The Tender Trap *(1955)*; Bedevilled *(1955)*; High Society *(1956)*; The Power and the Prize *(1956)*; The Opposite Sex *(1956)*; The Swan *(1956)*; Tea and Sympathy *(1956)*; Designing Woman *(1957)*; Silk Stockings *(1957)*; Cat on a Hot Tin Roof *(1958)*; The Gazebo *(1959)*; Butterfield 8 *(1960)*; The Courtship of Eddie's Father *(1963)*; Goodbye Charlie *(1964)*; Mister Buddwing *(1966)*; How Sweet It Is *(1968)*.

One of Hollywood's most renowned costume designers, Helen Rose was born in Chicago in 1904 and studied at the Chicago Institute of Fine Arts. Following a move to Los Angeles in 1929, she designed costumes for nightclubs and for Fanchon and Marco's Ice Follies for many years. Her first film designs were for three Fox musicals: *Hello Frisco Hello*, *Coney Island*, and *Stormy Weather* (all 1943), after which she moved to MGM, where she remained for the next three decades.

During her career, Rose was nominated for ten Academy Awards and won the coveted statue for *The Bad and the Beautiful* (1952) and *I'll Cry Tomorrow* (1955), the story of *Lillian Roth. Although she costumed some of Hollywood's most beautiful leading ladies, including *Elizabeth Taylor, *Lana Turner, and *Grace Kelly, Rose gained more notoriety as the designer of Kelly's wedding dress for her marriage to the prince of Monaco in 1956 than for any of her movie designs. The recognition helped her establish a successful fashion business after her retirement from films in the late 1960s. The designer died in 1985.

SOURCES:

Katz, Ephraim. *The Film Encyclopedia*. NY: HarperCollins, 1994.

Leese, Elizabeth. *Costume Design in the Movies*. NY: Dover, 1991.

Barbara Morgan,
Melrose, Massachusetts

Rose, Margo (1903–1997)

American puppeteer who, with her husband, animated the puppet Howdy Doody. Born Margaret Skewis *in Inway, Iowa, on January 31, 1903; died in Waterford, Connecticut, on September 13, 1997; daughter of Charles Skewis and Myrtle Skewis; graduated from Cornell College, Iowa, in 1924; married Rufus Rose (a puppeteer), in 1930 (died 1975); children: Christopher, James, Rufus.*

Was one of the founders of Puppeteers of America (1937); with husband, made the first full-length film using marionettes, Jerry Pulls the Strings (1938); animated the puppet Howdy Doody for television show (1952); received the President's Award for Artistic Achievement and the Connecticut Commission on the Arts' Excellence in the Arts Award; inducted into the Connecticut Women's Hall of Fame (1997).

Margo Rose, a noted pioneer in American puppetry, always claimed that she could trace her interest in puppetry to the days in her childhood when she and her sister would attach strings to their teddy bears and perform shows. Rose eventually turned this childhood amusement into a lifelong passion and career, earning a vaunted position among premier American puppeteers and distinction as the "grande dame of puppetry in America."

When Rose was a student at Cornell College in Iowa in the early 1920s, she attended a performance by the famous Tony Sarg Marionettes. This show and the encouragement of a college professor inspired her to make her own marionettes and also, upon graduating in 1924, to begin her own show. In 1927, she shortened her name from Margaret to Margo, joined Tony Sarg's troupe, and toured for several years as an actor and puppeteer. Not only did Margo gain valuable experience with the troupe, but she also met her future husband and partner when Rufus Rose joined the Tony Sarg Marionettes in 1928. Margo soon traveled to Italy to study sculpture, and after her return she and Rufus were married in Storm Lake, Iowa, in 1930. The following year, they left Sarg to form the Rufus Rose Marionettes.

While Rufus was more outgoing than his wife (he also later became a leader in the Connecticut General Assembly), Margo, despite her quiet, unassuming manner, was an equal contributor in their creative partnership. Her husband engineered and built puppets from wood, and Margo designed and modeled the puppets' heads, created their costumes, and cared for the puppets when they traveled.

Struggling to subsist during the Great Depression, the Roses found their survival ensured when Tony Sarg asked them to perform at the Chicago World's Fair in 1933. They were able to capitalize on the visibility they garnered at the fair and traveled across the country with their productions, performing two shows each day, six days a week, and frequently traveling daily. By 1938, they had also made the first full-length commercial film using marionettes, *Jerry Pulls the Strings*.

After the U.S. entered World War II and gas shortages became widespread, the Roses stopped traveling with their show and assisted instead in the war effort. While her husband worked at Electric Boat in Groton, Connecticut, Margo Rose volunteered with the American Red Cross. They did not abandon their art altogether, however. In 1943, they built a home in Waterford, Connecticut, which doubled as a studio and theater, and from there they launched the first festival for Puppeteers of America, a group they had helped to establish in 1937.

After the war, Rose resumed her puppetry. In 1952, she and her husband were hired to animate puppets for the "Howdy Doody Show," a commitment they maintained for ten years. In 1965, the couple was also instrumental in establishing the Eugene O'Neill Memorial Theater Center in Waterford, Connecticut, and in 1976 the theater barn there was named in their honor.

Following her husband's death in 1975, Margo began teaching puppetry, energetically sharing her talents with the National Theater Institute at the Eugene O'Neill Memorial Theater Center, the Institute for Professional Puppetry Arts, and the National Puppetry Conference. She also volunteered in the Waterford Public Schools, was a member of the Unitarian Universalist Church in New London, Connecticut, and was active in Literacy Volunteers. She was a recipient of the Connecticut Commission on the Arts' Excellence in the Arts Award and of the President's Award for Artistic Achievement, and she and her husband have been credited with influencing the very direction of American puppetry. Well-known puppeteers including Jim Henson, who developed the Sesame Street characters and the Muppets, and Burr Tillstrom, creator of the popular early television show "Kukla, Fran, and Ollie," acknowledged their debts to the Roses. Margo Rose was inducted into the Connecticut Women's Hall of Fame in May 1997, and died four months later, at age 94.

SOURCES:

The Day [New London, CT]. May 10, 1997, pp. A1, A8; September 15, 1997, pp. A1, A5; September 21, 1997, pp. C7, C9.

Lisa S. Weitzman, freelance writer, Cleveland, Ohio

Rose, Saint.
See *Rose of Viterbo (1235–1252)*.
See *Rose of Lima (1586–1617)*.

Rosenberg, Anna M. (1902–1983)

American public official, businesswoman, and labor relations consultant. Name variations: Anna Marie Rosenberg. Born Anna Maria Lederer in Budapest, Hungary, on June 19, 1902; died in New York City in 1983; second daughter of Albert Lederer (a furniture manufacturer) and Charlotte (Bacskai) Lederer (an author and illustrator of children's books); married Julius Rosenberg (a rug merchant), on October 12, 1919 (died); married Paul Gray Hoffman (administrator of the Marshall Plan, 1948–50), in 1962; children: (first marriage) Thomas Rosenberg.

Awarded the Medal of Freedom (October 20, 1945); became the first woman decorated with the U.S. Medal for Merit (May 28, 1947); received Horatio Alger Award (July 1949); served as assistant secretary of defense (1950–53).

Born in Budapest, Hungary, in 1902, Anna M. Rosenberg immigrated to the United States with her family in 1912. Just two years later, Rosenberg, who even as a teenager was noted for her leadership skills, organized a political club at her high school in New York and helped mediate in a students' strike against compulsory military training. She later acted as head of a delegation that brought a petition to the city's Board of Aldermen, seeking a shorter school day in order to relieve overcrowded classrooms. Inspired by her father's vehement belief that anyone born outside of the United States owed a special obligation to the country, Rosenberg ultimately combined her leadership skills with a strong commitment to public affairs and rose to the upper echelons of the U.S. government.

During the early days of World War I, Rosenberg worked part-time at a base hospital in Manhattan and also sold liberty bonds and thrift stamps on street corners. She briefly interrupted her schooling to marry Julius Rosenberg, a soldier who would later become a rug merchant, on October 12, 1919. After her husband was sent overseas, Rosenberg volunteered to work at the New York Debarkation Hospital. She also became a naturalized U.S. citizen in 1919.

After the war, citizenship in hand, Rosenberg listened to her husband's encouragement and entered politics only a short time after ratification of the 19th Amendment in 1920 had granted women the right to vote. She was elected to the Seventh Assembly District in Manhattan in the early 1920s and immediately began to cultivate key political contacts, among them *Belle Moskowitz, the chief advisor for Governor Al Smith. Rosenberg soon developed a reputation for negotiation and diplomacy, and by 1924 had opened her own office as a public-relations, personnel, and labor consultant. Her renowned success in resolving labor problems caught the attention of many; after Franklin D. Roosevelt became governor of New York in 1929, he frequently consulted with her.

Rosenberg quickly rose in national prominence. In 1934, she accepted her first federal appointment as assistant to Nathan Straus, Jr., then the regional director of the National Recovery Administration (NRA) for the New York area. She succeeded him as regional director after he resigned the following year, although the NRA was soon struck down as unconstitutional by the Supreme Court. From 1936 to 1937, she served as the New York regional director of the Social Security Board. In 1937, she became a member of the New York City Industrial Relations Board and was named chair of the subcommittee on bill of rights and general welfare of the New York State Constitutional Committee. Fiorello La Guardia once said of her, "She knows more about labor relations and human relations than any man in the country."

Rosenberg continued her active involvement in public affairs throughout World War II. Appointed to several posts, she became a director of the Office of Defense and regional director of the Health and Welfare Services (1941–42), consultant to the Retraining and Re-employment Administration (1941–42), and director of Region 2, New York State, of the War Manpower Commission (1942–45), the only woman to hold such a position. Concurrently she held membership in the New York City and State War Councils and in the policy committee of the Office of Coordinator of Inter-American Affairs, and the secretaryship of the President's Combined War Labor Board. Notably, while with the War Manpower Commission, Rosenberg forced the union of the Henry J. Kaiser Pacific Coast plants to accept African-American labor, and she also helped to define the "Buffalo Plan" of labor priorities in industry. Wartime also found her in the European Theater of Operations, sent there as the personal observer of both President Roosevelt and his successor, Harry Truman. For this work, Rosenberg received the Medal of Freedom in October 1945, and in 1947 she became the first woman to receive the Medal for Merit.

Immediately following the end of the war in August 1945, Rosenberg resigned from government duty and returned to her private practice. From then until President Truman, at the special request of Defense Secretary George C. Marshall, named her assistant secretary of defense in November 9, 1950, she accepted only honorary civic and governmental positions. Rosenberg ultimately accepted her new role at the Department of Defense as a patriotic duty. "Feminine and frilly as she is," observed *Eleanor Roosevelt (Rosenberg was known for her dainty hats and gold bangles), "with the Army, Air Force, and Marine Corps and the nation's top industrialists and labor leaders to choose from, [Marshall] wanted her." Rosenberg entered the highest post in the national military establishment ever held by a woman when she was sworn into office on November 15, 1950, charged with coordinating the manpower activities of the Defense Department. Although her confirmation by the Senate was delayed by unfounded rumors that she had attended Communist-front meetings, she was unanimously approved on December 21, 1950.

One of Rosenberg's primary tasks as assistant secretary was to develop the preparedness goals for the Defense Department. Eventually known as the Universal Military Service and Training Bill, this legislation sought to maintain equitable distribution of manpower between the armed forces, farms, and industry, and its chief provision called for the training of 18-year-olds. As well, at Rosenberg's instigation some 50 women were included on an advisory committee that followed the Women's Armed Services Integration Act.

Rosenberg's tenure at the Pentagon was not long, and this may have been due at least in part to the times, which saw both rising anti-Semitism in America and the deepening of the Cold War. (As well, she may have suffered some prejudice because of the closeness of her name to that of *Ethel Rosenberg, whose 1951 sentence of death for spying for the Soviet Union was carried out in 1953.) When Eisenhower assumed the presidency in 1953, Rosenberg left the public sector, returned to New York, and again became president of her consulting firm, Anna M. Rosenberg Associates. In 1961, she was elected to the New York City Board of Education, and the following year she married for a second time, to Paul Gray Hoffman. A collector of French art, Rosenberg remained active in a number of philanthropic organizations and foundations. She lived in New York City until her death in 1983, at the age of 81.

SOURCES:

McHenry, Robert, ed. *Famous American Women.* NY: Dover, 1980.

Rothe, Anna, ed. *Current Biography 1951.* NY: H.W. Wilson, 1951.

Weatherford, Doris. *American Women's History.* NY: Prentice Hall, 1994.

Lisa S. Weitzman,
freelance writer, Cleveland, Ohio

Rosenberg, Ethel (1915–1953)

American activist sentenced to death for espionage who went to the electric chair resolutely proclaiming her innocence. Born Esther Ethel Greenglass on September 28, 1915, in the Lower East Side of New York City; died in the electric chair at Sing Sing Prison, New York, after five jolts of electricity on June 19, 1953; burial site unknown; daughter of Barnet Greenglass (a sewing machine repairer) and Tessie (Fiet) Greenglass; sister of Bernard and David Greenglass; half-sister of Samuel Greenglass; attended local grammar schools, Seward Park High School, 1926–31; attended acting class at Clark House, 1931–33; granted secretarial certificate, Public School 4, 1932; studied modern dance, Henry Street Settlement House, and child development, New School for Social Research, 1944; married Julius Rosenberg, on June 18, 1939; children: two sons, Michael Allen Rosenberg Meeropol (b. March 10, 1943) and Robert Harry Rosenberg Meeropol (b. May 14, 1947).

Employed as shipping clerk, National New York Packing and Shipping Company (1932–35); took voice classes, Schola Cantorum (1935) and Carnegie Hall Studios (1936); attended acting class, Lavanburg Drama Group (1937); hired as stenographer, Bell Textile Company (1936–1940); was a union activist with Ladies Apparel Shipping Clerks Union (1935–38), Workers Alliance of America (1935–38), and Ladies Auxiliary, Federation of Architects, Engineers, Chemists, and Technicians (1936–40); hired as clerk, Census Bureau (1940); served on East Side Defense Council to Defend America and Crush Hitler (1941–43); indicted and imprisoned, after bail was denied, for conspiracy to commit espionage (August 11, 1950); convicted (March 29, 1951); sentenced to death by Judge Irving Kaufman (April 5, 1951); transferred to Sing Sing Prison where she was the only woman in the Condemned Cells; National Committee to Secure Justice in the Rosenberg Case formed (November 1951); appeal denied by U.S. Court of Appeals (February 25, 1952); Supreme Court refused a certiorari (October 13, 1952); Judge Kaufman refused to reduce sentence (January 2, 1953); Eisenhower refused clemency (February 11, 1953); Supreme Court again refused certiorari (May 25, 1953); Judge Kaufman denied motion to hear new evidence (June 8, 1953); Supreme Court refused to grant new trial (July 19, 1953); executed after Eisenhower again refused clemency (June 19, 1953).

At noon on Thursday, April 5, 1951, Ethel Rosenberg stood with her husband Julius Rosenberg in a New York City courtroom, as Judge Irving Kaufman prepared to announce her sentence for conspiracy to commit espionage. Incarcerated since her indictment the previous August, Rosenberg steadfastly denied that she and her husband passed atomic secrets to the Soviets. The state had not presented an air-tight case against her and few expected that she would receive the same sentence as her co-defendants. Only two other women had ever been convicted of treason against the United States: *Iva Toguri ("Tokyo Rose") in 1949, and *Mary E. Surratt, whose trial occurred in the wake of Lincoln's assassination in the final days of the Civil War. While the climate of the 1950s was militaristic, it was one of a cold hostility rather than of armed conflict.

Fully aware of the intense public interest in this case, Judge Kaufman took the time to explain his reasoning before he announced his decision. Staring down from the bench, he told Rosenberg that her crime was "worse than murder." Kaufman then proceeded to lay the groundwork for her sentence:

> The evidence indicated quite clearly that Julius Rosenberg was the prime mover in this conspiracy. However, let no mistake be made about the role which his wife, Ethel Rosenberg, played in this conspiracy. Instead of deterring him from pursuing his ignoble cause, she encouraged and assisted the cause. She was a mature woman. . . . She was a full-fledged partner in this crime . . . [guided by a] love for [the] cause . . . [that] was even greater than [her] love for [her] children.

Kaufman then sentenced her to death by electrocution.

The jury found Rosenberg guilty because her younger brother David Greenglass, who had given her name to the FBI, testified against her in exchange for a lighter sentence. In widely publicized and unsubstantiated testimony which riveted the nation, Greenglass told the FBI that his sister was a Communist, that she avidly encouraged him to help Julius Rosenberg obtain the confidential information he sought, and that she typed the messages her husband supplied to the Soviets. After charges against David were dismissed, the Greenglass family closed ranks, sided with

David, turned their backs on Ethel, and abandoned the two Rosenberg sons, Michael and Robert, to a series of foster homes until they were adopted by Rosenberg's old roommates, Abel and **Anne Meeropol**, in 1957.

Dissension was not new to the Greenglass household. Indeed, even though she was the first of three children, Ethel Rosenberg always felt like an outsider and went to her grave believing that her mother never cared for her. Born in 1915 into an immigrant household constantly striving to keep above the poverty line, Rosenberg lived with her family in a coldwater, windowless, three-room tenement in the Jewish Lower East Side of New York City—a life that Rosenberg often labeled penurious. Her mother **Tessie Greenglass**, embittered by her husband Bernard's inability to meet her economic expectations and housebound after having three children in six years, increasingly made Ethel the target of her discontent.

$\mathcal{T}$he case is not too strong against Mrs. Rosenberg. But for the purpose of acting as a deterrent, I think it is very important that she is convicted, too, and given a stiff sentence.

—Myles Lane, U.S. Attorney

Determined to leave this household as soon as possible, young Ethel threw herself into her school work, finishing grammar school with honors, skipping a year in high school, and, against her mother's vehement protests, acting and singing in school productions. She dreamed of a college education and a career in the theater. Yet the Great Depression forced her to put aside these aspirations and in 1932 she enrolled in a six-month secretarial course offered by Public School 4. That summer, she found work as a shipping clerk with the National New York Shipping and Packing Company.

Throughout the Depression, Rosenberg strove to balance her need for work with her love for the stage. Since she continued to live at home and her father's income continued to drop, her wages went to her mother. The tension between mother and daughter increased as Ethel tried to keep enough of her earnings to pay for voice lessons at Carnegie Hall. Undeterred when Tessie ultimately demanded that all her wages be turned over to the family, Ethel worked the New York City-New Jersey amateur-night circuit to earn the money she needed to continue the lessons.

As working conditions worsened in the National plant, Rosenberg's desire for a career in music became even more fervent. She auditioned for the Schola Cantorum, a professional chorus that performed at Carnegie Hall, and much to her delight became its youngest member. She eagerly accepted the invitation of National coworkers who were loosely affiliated with the Young Communist League's Group Theater to participate in the sing-alongs they often held in supporters' apartments. As word of her talent spread throughout the plant, she began to make new friends and to achieve the recognition her family denied her.

Gradually, she grew confident in her ability to speak for herself off stage. Angry that men made more than she did for the same work, Rosenberg protested, only to have her wages cut for alleged mistakes. Thus, when the Ladies Apparel Shipping Clerks Union began to recruit National workers, Rosenberg not only responded quickly but became one of the union's most stalwart organizers. When the union called a city-wide strike on August 19, demanding better wages and collective bargaining, she not only supported the strike but threw herself into boosting the morale of her fellow strikers. She traveled the city urging workers to support the union jobs, recruited members to walk various picket lines, and served food at the strike soup kitchens.

On Friday, August 30, she joined a contingent of women who successfully prevented National trucks from leaving their warehouses by lying down in the street. As she and her coworkers celebrated their success, they were attacked by a small group of nonunion men swinging lead pipes. Although she escaped unharmed, the attack horrified her, and later she would often tell friends that this attack "started her speaking up against injustice."

Rosenberg returned to National after the strike failed and continued to meet with management to speak out in favor of the union. The first few weeks were tense, but she was confident her job was secure. However, when National executives fired Paul Goldblatt, a leader of the strike whom she admired greatly, Rosenberg protested his dismissal only to find herself dismissed for not having the company's best interests at heart. She appealed to the National Labor Relations Board which, after a five-month delay, found "that Ethel Greenglass was discharged because of her union membership and activities," and ruled that she should be reinstated. By that time, however, she had found a better-paying job as a part-time stenographer with Bell Textile Company. Suddenly, not only did she have more money but she also had more time to pursue her artistic training.

By 1936, work, politics and art were integral parts of Rosenberg's life. She joined Local 65 of the United Wholesale and Retail Union, auditioned for the avant-garde Clark Players, expanded her Carnegie Hall Studio lessons to include voice and piano, and joined the Workers' Alliance, a socialist assembly that would soon join with the Communist-affiliated Unemployed Councils and become known as the Popular Front. While she would never be as involved with the Workers' Alliance as she had been with the leadership of the Shipping Clerks Union, she continued to support strikers by entertaining picketers, union members and Popular Front supporters with romantic songs supporting the Spanish Civil War. Thus, when the International Seaman's Union decided to hold a benefit that December, they immediately asked Rosenberg to perform. She accepted and went to the December gathering alone. She left, however, in the company of an 18-year-old engineering student from City College, Julius Rosenberg.

Quickly, the two young people discovered how much they had in common. A love of the arts, a commitment to Communist politics, and a shared ethnic heritage led to a fiercely passionate courtship. Soon they became inseparable. As her friend from the Clark Players recalled to Rosenberg biographer **Ilene Philipson**, "Every time I went over to Ethel's he was there studying and she was typing his homework." Another remembered that she "was very much involved with Julius to the exclusion of others." When they did get together with friends on weekend nights, politics dominated the discussion.

Engineering never fascinated Julius. Indeed, after the California labor leader Tom Mooney was unjustly convicted, politics occupied all his intellectual zeal. Arguing that everyone knew that City College engineering students were labeled leftists and therefore had a difficult time finding work, Julius wanted to drop out of school and find a less taxing job that would allow him not only to help support his parents but also to devote his life to what he really cared about. Ethel disagreed and convinced him to balance his commitment to politics and school the way she tried to balance her commitment to art and work. Julius acquiesced, but quickly began to spend more time organizing his fellow students than he did studying engineering.

On June 18, 1939, Ethel Greenglass married Julius Rosenberg in a small civil ceremony. Unable to afford their own apartment because Julius was still in college, the Rosenbergs moved in with Marcus and **Stella Pogarsky**, friends

Ethel Rosenberg

from the Young Communist League. Julius began attending campus meetings of the Federation of Architects, Engineers, Chemists and Technicians (FACET), a Communist union of white-collar workers, and Ethel quickly joined its Ladies Auxiliary. While Julius spent Friday nights at FACET meetings, Ethel attended lectures on politics and art sponsored by the Group Theater and the Lavanburg Dramatic Group. Julius made his commitment to Communism official by joining the party on December 12, 1939. There is no record of Ethel's membership. However, the FBI began a file on her in 1940 after one of her fellow tenants told the bureau that Ethel Rosenberg had signed nominating petitions for Communist candidates.

The Rosenbergs' economic fortunes began to change in 1940. She joined the U.S. Census Bureau as a part-time clerk typist, and in the fall of 1941 the U.S. Signal Corps employed Julius as a junior engineer. After a brief scare, when Julius survived a loyalty hearing after the FBI released its information on Ethel and their friends to the Signal Corps, the Rosenbergs relaxed. The couple now had money to move into their own apartment in a new housing project, Knickerbocker Village, and to let Ethel devote her time to volunteer for political activity. Supporting the United States' entry into World War II, she gave all her time to the East Side Conference to Defend America and Crush Hitler (later renamed the East Side Defense Council) and became personal secretary to its head, Carl Marzani.

Soon Rosenberg's priorities changed. She gave birth to her first son Michael in March 1943. Moreover, since the Signal Corps had stationed Julius on temporary assignment in Camden, New Jersey, she had to deal with her newborn son by herself. Her political work subsided, due to a mixture of parenting responsibilities and pressure from her political colleagues to stay home and tend house. Her health deteriorated in 1944 and 1945 when illnesses associated with her childhood bouts with curvature of the spine resurfaced. Furthermore, Michael was a precocious child who constantly demanded all of his mother's attention. Convinced that children should be encouraged rather than disciplined, Rosenberg allowed Michael's tantrums to control the household. Afraid she was failing her son, she sought guidance from a social worker at the Jewish Board of Guardians and enrolled in a child psychology class at the New School of Social Research. The birth of her second son Robert in May 1947 exacerbated these tensions.

Politics took a backseat to childrearing. Her progressive approach to parenting only accentuated the political conflicts she had with her family. In March 1949, her father, the only real ally she had in the Greenglass family, died. With Julius working 14-hour days trying to manage a small machine business, she felt increasingly isolated and began to question her capabilities. Resolute in her politics, she nevertheless remained full of doubt about herself as a mother and a daughter. After months of internal debate, she finally broke with the Communist position on psychiatry and entered psychoanalysis with Dr. Saul Miller.

Relations between the Rosenbergs and the Greenglass family became even more tense after David Greenglass joined in Julius' unsuccessful business ventures. Tessie Greenglass, David's wife **Ruth Greenglass**, and his older half-brother Sam Greenglass all agreed that Julius was a bad financial and political influence on David. Sam continued to offer to pay Julius' way to Russia if he would just leave David alone, and Tessie declared that nothing the Rosenbergs did would ever be rewarding. Ruth believed that her husband David was underpaid and overworked. But David continued to support the Rosenbergs until Julius objected to his leaving the shop early three

afternoons a week to attend night classes. In May 1950, Greenglass offered to sell his share of the business to the Rosenbergs, but money was scarce and he received only a promissory note for half of his initial investment.

Earlier that year, Klaus Fuchs, a German-born scientist, had confessed to British intelligence that he passed atomic information to the Soviets. In May, while the Rosenbergs were completing financial negotiations with David Greenglass, Harry Gold, a Philadelphia chemist, admitted to the FBI that he had been Fuchs' courier and named David Greenglass, who had been assigned to the Los Alamos Atomic Project as a machinist, as his contact. On June 15, Greenglass signed a confession saying that he had passed a "sketch of a high-explosive lens mold" to Gold after Julius Rosenberg had requested that Greenglass give him information Gold could pass on to the Soviets. Ethel Rosenberg was never mentioned. The following day, the FBI questioned Julius Rosenberg and the Rosenbergs retained an attorney. A month later, on the evening of July 17, the FBI searched the Rosenberg apartment and arrested Julius. The next day, Ethel invited the press into her shabby apartment in an attempt to prove to them how absurd she thought the charges against her husband were.

Ethel Rosenberg then took control of Julius' business transactions, strove to calm her high-strung children's anxieties, and worked with her husband's attorney. She became even more isolated. The Greenglass family severed all ties with her. Neighbors shunned her. Her only support came from Julius' parents.

FBI records show that the government had planned from the moment of Julius' arrest to use "any additional information concerning Ethel Rosenberg . . . as a lever against her husband." J. Edgar Hoover agreed, responding to this request enthusiastically. Consequently, Rosenberg was summoned before the grand jury on August 2, 1950. Outwardly composed to the point of stoicism and completely unaware of the charges leveled against her, she followed her attorney's advice and answered most questions asked her by invoking the Fifth Amendment. The jury released her.

The experience scared her. She worried that her children might be left alone and tried to make contingency plans for their welfare. She made an appointment with the Jewish Community Homemakers Service to find a home for her sons should anything happen. The Service was busy and could only meet with her on the afternoon of August 11, the morning of which she was scheduled to reappear before the grand jury.

This time the jury indicted her on broad conspiracy charges, alleging that she had "had a discussion with Julius Rosenberg and others" on November 1, 1944, and "with Julius Rosenberg, David Greenglass, and others" on January 10, 1945. Unable to meet a $100,000 bail, she was detained in the Women's House of Detention in New York for eight months on the charge of conspiracy to commit espionage. She sent her children to live with Tessie Greenglass, only to find that her mother relinquished them to the Hebrew Children's Home in November, where they lived before going to a series of foster homes in 1952.

The chief evidence against her was supplied by her sister-in-law, Ruth Greenglass. The day Julius was arrested, Ruth was interviewed by the FBI. She told the agents that while visiting the Rosenbergs' apartment in November 1944, Julius had asked her to get information from Dave, who was then stationed at Los Alamos, in order to help Soviet-American relations "as far as this atomic information was concerned." Ruth claimed that when she appeared hesitant, Ethel interjected that "she should at least ask her husband . . . if he would furnish this type of information." Although David had not mentioned this in his confession, when confronted with his wife's statement he changed his testimony to match hers.

James McInerney, director of the Criminal Division of the U.S. Justice Department, told the FBI that although Rosenberg was still of great value as a "lever" to use against her husband, there was not enough evidence to convict her. Prosecuting attorney Myles Lane agreed and on February 8 told the Joint Congressional Committee on Atomic Energy that "the case is not too strong against Mrs. Rosenberg. But for the purpose of acting as a deterrent, I think it is very important that she is convicted, too, and given a stiff sentence."

Indeed, no specific charges were made against her until three weeks before her trial and again they came from Ruth Greenglass. Ruth now claimed that Ethel had typed the information that Julius had allegedly passed to the Soviets. Even though there had been no mention of this in David Greenglass' testimony and the FBI had recovered no typed information, the government used this deposition as the linchpin of its case against Ethel Rosenberg. When confronted by the FBI, David Greenglass again supported his wife's recollections.

Ethel Rosenberg's trial began on March 6, 1951, and lasted 23 days. Most expected conviction, but few anticipated a death sentence. J. Edgar Hoover recommended that she be sentenced to 30 years in prison. *The Kaufman Papers* show that even Roy Cohn, who would later join Senator Joseph McCarthy's staff and who supported the death penalty, conceded that "if Mrs. Rosenberg were sentenced to a prison term there was a possibility she would talk." Yet Judge Kaufman had never entertained any sentence other than execution.

Following her sentencing, Rosenberg spent two years in solitary confinement as the only incarcerated woman in Sing Sing prison. She could meet Julius once a week, but a wire-mesh screen separated them. At first, she refused to see her children because she was afraid of the impact visiting their mother in prison might have on them, but after a year, she relented and allowed them to come see her. Even then, however, the visits were infrequent.

The Rosenbergs relied on letters to stay in touch. These documents, which were published as *Death House Letters* in a desperate attempt to raise money to support the Rosenberg sons, reveal a much more passionate Ethel than the public saw during her trial. Here, Rosenberg the wife and mother dominates Rosenberg the activist. Although they show a woman angry that the government subjected Julius and her to prison for actions she vehemently denied doing, the letters also clearly reveal a woman extremely tormented by the separation from her husband and children and who is desperately searching for a home for her sons.

Although their conviction had inspired two years of legal challenges and international protests, the appellate courts refused to hear new evidence and rejected petitions of clemency. President Dwight Eisenhower also denied her petition for clemency. Judge Kaufman set June 15 as the date of execution.

Attorneys for the Rosenbergs appeared before Kaufman on June 8 to argue that newly discovered evidence of Ruth Greenglass' role in the FBI investigation proved perjury and subornation of perjury. Kaufman recessed for 15 minutes only to return to the court, deny their appeal, and read a 30-minute statement he had prepared in advance.

The Court of Appeals affirmed Kaufman's ruling on June 10. On Friday, June 12, Rosenberg attorneys appealed to the Supreme Court to issue a stay of execution so that the defense might file a motion for a new trial, which would include the recently uncovered evidence. The Supreme Court rejected the motion by a 5–4 vote. The following day, while Rosenberg was saying goodbye to her sons, Justice William O. Douglas granted a stay until the court could rule on whether or nor the Atomic Energy Act of 1946 was applicable to the case. Attorney General Herbert Brownell asked the court to stay in session to rule on the question that Douglas had cited in his announcement. On Wednesday, June 19, the court vacated Douglas' stay by a 5–3 vote. Eisenhower again refused clemency, later writing his son John that "in this instance it is the woman who is the strong and recalcitrant character, the man who is the weak one. She has obviously been the leader in everything they did in the spy ring." The Rosenbergs were executed that evening, still proclaiming their innocence.

In 1995, 42 years later, U.S. intelligence agencies declassified a series of telegrams between Moscow and KGB operatives in America during the 1940s that had been intercepted by the forerunner of the National Security Agency. Julius Rosenberg was mentioned by code names a number of times in these documents, primarily as a recruiter of other spies and receiver of classified information. One telegram from 1944 states that "Ethel," the wife of the code-named spy identified by the U.S. as being Julius Rosenberg, "knows about her husband's work." In 1997, a retired KGB officer, Alexander Feklisov, confirmed that he had been the spy handler for Julius Rosenberg, whom he claimed passed him not only information about the lens mold but also an actual radar-controlled proximity fuse, called one of the first "smart" weapons, which Soviet scientists were able to copy through reverse engineering, produce, and use. Feklisov stated that Ethel Rosenberg had been aware of her husband's spying, but had not been a spy herself, had played no part in his network, and "wasn't doing anything for" the Soviets.

SOURCES:

Meeropol, Michael. *The Rosenberg Letters: The Complete Edition of the Prison Correspondence of Julius and Ethel Rosenberg*. NY: Garland, 1994.

—— and Robert. *We Are Your Sons: The Legacy of Ethel and Julius Rosenberg*. Urbana, IL: University of Illinois Press, 1975.

National Committee to Reopen the Rosenberg Case. *The Kaufman Papers* in *Hearings before the Sub-Committee on Criminal Justice of the Committee on the Judiciary, House of Representatives 97th Congress, First and Second Sessions on Federal Criminal Law Revision*, Serial No. 132, *Congressional Record*. December 122, 1982, 2237–2403.

Nizer, Louis. *The Implosion Conspiracy*. Garden City, NY: Doubleday, 1973.

Philipson, Ilene. *Ethel Rosenberg: Beyond the Myths*. NY: Franklin Watts, 1988.

Schneir, Walter, and Miriam Schneir. *Invitation to an Inquest*. NY: Pantheon, 1983.

SUGGESTED READING:

Carmichael, Virginia. *Framing History: The Rosenberg Story and the Cold War*. Minneapolis, MN: University of Minnesota Press, 1993.

Meyerowitz, Joanne. "Beyond the Feminine Mystique: A Reassessment of Postwar Mass Culture, 1946–1958," in *Journal of American History*. Vol. 79, no. 4. March 1993, pp. 1455–1483.

Stern, Sol, and Ronald Radosh. "The Hidden Rosenberg Case," in *New Republic*. June 23, 1979.

RELATED MEDIA:

"The Unquiet Death of Julius and Ethel Rosenberg," a television documentary.

Allida Black, Visiting Assistant Professor of History and American Studies, Penn State University, Harrisburg, Pennsylvania

Rosendahl, Heidemarie (1947—)

West German athlete. Name variations: Heide Rosendahl; Heidemarie Ecker. Born in West Germany on February 14, 1947; daughter of a national discus-thrower.

Won the silver medal in pentathlon in the European championships (1967), won the gold medal (1971); won an Olympic gold medal in the long jump, a team gold in the 4x100-meter relay, and a silver in the pentathlon in Munich (1972).

Heidemarie Rosendahl began her successful sports career at age 19, taking a silver in the pentathlon in the European championships held in Budapest. She was injured in Mexico City in the 1968 Olympics, finishing 8th in the long jump and withdrawing from the pentathlon. At the World University Games in Turin in 1970, Rosendahl broke the world long-jump record with a jump of 22'5¼"; she then went on to win the European pentathlon title in Helsinki the following year.

In the 1972 Olympics in Munich, Rosendahl took a gold medal in the long jump over **Diana Jorgova** of Bulgaria. She also won a silver in the five-event pentathlon; *****Mary Peters** of Great Britain took gold with a world record of 4,801 points. In the 4x100-meter relay, Rosendahl anchored the West German team of **Christiane Krause**, **Ingrid Mickler**, and **Annegret Richter** to win the gold medal in 42.81. In the event, Rosendahl had to stay ahead of East Germany's *****Renate Stecher**, then considered the fastest woman in the world.

Rosenfeld, Fanny (1903–1969)

Canadian track-and-field star and sportswriter. Name variations: Bobbie Rosenfeld. Born in Katrinaslov, Russia, on December 28, 1903; died in December 1969.

Won a gold medal in the 4x100-meter relay and a silver in the 100-meter sprint in the Amsterdam Olympics (1928).

Born in Katrinaslov, Russia, in 1903, Fanny Rosenfeld grew up in Canada, playing softball and hockey with the fellows. In her teens, she bobbed her hair so it would not interfere in sports and from that point forward became known as "Bobbie." Although she had a local reputation as a sprinter, Rosenfeld did not take up track and field until she was 19. In 1922, she moved to Toronto with her family. There, she kept books for a chocolate factory and played softball and ice hockey on the company team. She also began her running career, accumulating Canadian titles and setting national records. In 1925, Rosenfeld tied the world record of 11.0 for the 100-yard dash. At the Ontario Ladies Track and Field championships that same year, she won the discus, 220-yard dash, low hurdles, and long jump, placing second in the 100-yard dash and javelin. Rosenfeld played tennis as well, and won the Toronto Ladies Grass Court Tennis title in 1924. After she qualified for the team, Rosenfeld represented Canada in three events in the 1928 Amsterdam Olympics. She won a gold in the 4x100-meter relay and many fans felt she won the 100 meters against American sprinter *Betty Robinson; even the judges disagreed. When the decision went to Robinson, who had been beaten by Rosenfeld in the semifinal, Canada lodged a protest to no avail. In an era before photo finishes, some races remained in dispute. In any case, Rosenfeld took the silver, and her teammate **Ethel Smith** won the bronze.

Not long after the Olympics, Rosenfeld was laid up with arthritis and spent the next 18 months on crutches. She battled the disabling arthritis for the rest of her life. For over 20 years, starting in 1937, she wrote the column "Feminine Sports Reel" for the *Toronto Globe and Mail*. She joined the promotion department at the *Globe and Mail* in 1957, 12 years before her death.

SOURCES:

Slater, Robert. *Great Jews in Sports*. Middle Village, NY: Jonathan David, 1983.

Wallechinsky, David. *The Complete Book of the Olympics*. NY: Viking, 1988.

Karin Loewen Haag,
Athens, Georgia

Rosenthal, Hedwig Kanner (1882–1959).

See Kanner-Rosenthal, Hedwig.

Rosenthal, Ida Cohen (1886–1973)

Russian-born American manufacturing executive and founder of Maidenform, Inc. Born Ida Kaganovitch in Rakov, Russia, on January 9, 1886 (one source cites 1889); died of pneumonia in New York City on March 29, 1973; eldest of four girls and three boys of Abraham Kaganovitch (a Hebrew scholar) and Sarah (Shapiro) Kaganovitch, who changed the family name to Cohen after immigrating to the United States; married William Rosenthal (a manufacturer and designer), on June 10, 1906 (died 1958); children: Lewis Rosenthal (1907–1930); Beatrice Rosenthal Coleman (b. 1916).

Born in 1886 in Rakov, Russia, near Minsk, Ida Cohen Rosenthal left her family and her homeland at the age of 16 and moved to Warsaw, Poland. There, she worked as a dressmaker while studying mathematics and Russian in the evenings. In 1904, she joined her sister Ethel and immigrated to the United States to escape the threat of the tsarist regime. Her parents joined them and their other children in the United States in 1909, and her father and three brothers eventually organized A. Cohen & Sons of New York City, wholesalers of clocks, silverware, and cut glass.

When Ida first arrived in the United States, she opened her own small seamstress shop in Hoboken, New Jersey. On June 10, 1906, she married William Rosenthal, one of the early ready-to-wear dress manufacturers, and he joined her in the management of the shop. Hoping to capitalize on the growing demand for ready-to-wear clothes, the Rosenthals moved their shop to Washington Heights, New York, in 1918, and, as the company began to prosper, ultimately employed some 20 seamstresses.

In the early 1920s, Ida's friend **Enid Bissett** persuaded her to become a partner in a dress shop in Manhattan. The women realized that customers expected fashions to fit, regardless of their own body shape, and the short, flat flapper dresses popular in the 1920s certainly revealed many body types. Ida tackled the challenge by addressing the issue of shape rather than dress. She began to make a simple two-cup container designed specifically for each customer's breasts, which gave support without crushing the chest, and included them with each dress purchase. Not only did this "gimmick" improve initial sales, but customers also quickly realized that their personal "brassieres" made all outfits fit more neatly, and they eagerly returned to buy more. (Prior to Rosenthal's invention, women for the most part had depended on painfully tight corsets or clothing to support their breasts, although in 1914 *Caresse Crosby had patented a "backless brassiere" made mostly out of two handkerchiefs.)

Ida and her partner soon realized the niche market they had discovered, and in 1923, with an initial investment of $4,500, the two women incorporated the Maiden Form Brassiere Company. (The name would be changed to Maidenform in 1960.) Ida's husband William was a gifted designer and amateur sculptor, and by 1924 he had again joined his wife in business. He focused his talents on the complex puzzle of designing a system for mass-producing brassieres for all sizes and shapes of women, and it was he who established the precursors to the modern A-, B-, C-, and D-cup sizes. Less than 15 years later, the company's gross earnings were over $4.5 million per year; by the mid-1960s, gross earnings had increased to some $40 million.

Not quite five feet tall, Ida Rosenthal was the commanding force in the Maidenform business and held sway by commanding others to sit when addressing her. As she aptly described herself in *Time* in October 1960, "Quality we give them. Delivery we give them. I add personality." She was treasurer and director of sales and advertising while her husband handled design and production, particularly in the company's formative years, and served as company president. When Enid Bissett was forced to retire in the 1940s due to health reasons, the Rosenthals remained the principal managers of the company, and Ida herself assumed the presidency after her husband died in 1958. An observer of the company once remarked in *Fortune* magazine, "Mrs. R. knows everything about the business."

Rosenthal's boundless energy never wavered. She capitalized on the trend in fashion in the 1930s which, unlike the boyish look of the 1920s, emphasized women's figures, and later she ensured that Maidenform received priority in obtaining materials during World War II. In the 1960s, she spent much of her time visiting Maidenform's interests in over 100 countries, and oversaw the company's expansion into sportswear in 1961. In 1963, she visited the Soviet Union as a member of an industrial study exchange team and was excited about the nascent market opportunities she saw there. At 80, she still made at least two overseas business trips each year.

Rosenthal was a director of the Bayonne (New Jersey) Industrial YMCA and of the Bronx Lebanon Medical Center, and was an active member of the Anti-Defamation League. With her husband, she founded Camp Lewis, a Boy Scout camp in New Jersey, established New York University's Judaica and Hebraica Library, and was an important contributor to the establishment of Yeshiva University's Albert Einstein College of Medicine in New York City. After her retirement, Rosenthal's daughter **Beatrice Coleman** took over Maidenform, which over 80 years after its founding remains a large and profitable business. Rosenthal died in New York City in 1973, at age 87.

SOURCES:

Bailey, Brooke. *The Remarkable Lives of 100 Women Healers and Scientists.* Holbrook, MA: Bob Adams, 1994.

Bird, Caroline. *Enterprising Women.* NY: New American Library, 1976.

Sicherman, Barbara, and Carol Hurd Green, eds. *Notable American Women: The Modern Period.* Cambridge, MA: The Belknap Press of Harvard University, 1980.

Lisa S. Weitzman, freelance writer, Cleveland, Ohio

Rosenthal, Jean (1912–1969)

American designer of architectural and theater lighting. Born Eugenie Rosenthal on March 16, 1912, in New York City; died on May 1, 1969, in New York City; only daughter and one of three children of Morris Rosenthal and Pauline (Scharfmann) Rosenthal (both physicians); attended the Ethical Culture School, Bronx, New York; attended Bill Fincke's Manumit School, Pawling, New York; graduated from Friends' Seminary, Manhattan, New York; attended the Neighborhood Playhouse, 1928–30; attended Yale University Drama School, 1931–33; never married; no children.

A pioneer in the craft of lighting design, and the originator of many techniques still in use, Jean Rosenthal is considered by some to have been nothing short of a genius at evoking mood and creating special effects. One of only a handful of women in technical theater during her time, she fought constantly against discrimination, but was eventually accepted and even sought after. Before her untimely death from cancer in 1969, Rosenthal designed over 4,000 theatrical productions, including dance, opera, plays, and musicals, and also consulted on dozens of architectural lighting projects. *Martha Graham, with whom Rosenthal worked for 37 years on various dance projects, once called her a "pure person." "I have never known her to compromise," said Graham. "If she could do it, she would, if not she said no. Hers was the religion of the individual—dedication to as near perfection as possible. She never deviated from that . . . and had discovered the wonder of life. That is not easy."

Rosenthal was born in New York City in 1912, the second child of two busy physicians. (A second boy would later complete the family.) Weighing only five pounds at birth, she thrived on a diet of sour cream and bananas served up by the family's "one in help," a fat Hungarian cook. The Rosenthal children were educated in various progressive schools in and around New York City, and were afforded every opportunity the city had to offer to supplement their formal education with theater, opera, ballet, and museum visits. Because of her unconventional education, however, Rosenthal was turned down by several colleges, and ended up at the Neighborhood Playhouse, where her parents believed she would have the opportunity to "enlarge her horizons." "There I met the people who have had the most lasting and dominant influence on my life and way of thinking," Rosenthal wrote in her book *The Magic of Light.* "Louis Horst, Martha Graham, **Laura Elliott,** ❧▶ **Irene Lewisohn**—and of these Martha Graham was certainly the most important."

Rosenthal soon discovered that she hated performing and dancing, a fact which may have subconsciously precipitated a fall down a flight of stairs in which she injured her back. Sidelined, she drifted backstage, becoming a technical assistant to Graham, who fascinated her. After 18 months, Rosenthal left the playhouse and, probably through her mother, was accepted into the George Pierce Baker Workshop at Yale University. There, she was totally immersed in the theater, studying with those involved in the profession outside the university as well as within it. Of special significance was her lighting course with Stanley McCandless, a taciturn Scotsman who had difficulty communicating, but from whom she nevertheless learned a lot. "If I never did learn anything really practical from him, I did learn an orderliness, a way of organizing it," she wrote. "I have come to know since that if you can organize your ideas in the theater, you have half a chance of putting them over."

Rosenthal left Yale in 1933, during the Depression. Economically secure and living at home, she did some non-paying theater work, then joined the One Act Project, which was part of the WPA Federal Theater Project. It proved to be an extraordinary experience for the 21-year-old, whose variety of responsibilities included working as an assistant to John Houseman, and participating in the historical first performance of Marc Blitzstein's propaganda musical about labor unions, *The Cradle Will Rock* (1937), after which everyone associated with the production was fired. Rosenthal then went to work as the technical director for the Mercury Theater, which was the brainchild of Houseman and Orson Welles. In her down time, she continued to work with Martha Graham and began what would be an 18-year association with Lincoln Kirstein and his Ballet Society. Dance remained one of Rosenthal's favorite forms of theater, and she would later design for the New York City Ballet and the American Ballet Theater, among others. "If I leave anything to posterity," she once said, "it will be, I think, most importantly in the field of dance lighting."

In 1940, while sporadically engaged with Orson Welles and the ballet, Rosenthal, together with **Helen Marcy** and **Eleanor Wise,** two fellow Yale Drama Workshop graduates, opened a small firm called Theater Production Service (TPS), which offered complete design service for shows and for theaters. The business endured for years, although it had difficulty surviving during the war, when supplies became hard to obtain. Although it never made a great deal of money, Rosenthal said it provided her with a "sense of organized professional continuity."

Throughout most of her early career, Rosenthal was associated with lyric rather than commercial theater, and it wasn't until the late 1950s that she began to concentrate on more classic Broadway shows. (In 1957, she designed three musicals, including the very popular *West Side Story*.) Rosenthal always found repertory the most satisfying venue for her work in that it was a continuing effort in which respect and friendship had time to flourish. Commercial theater brought Rosenthal numerous contacts, but usually not friendships. One of the most harrowing factors in all of her collaborative efforts was sex discrimination. The world of technical theater was a dominantly male bastion, and it set up instant barriers. "She had a hard time in the theater," recalled John Houseman. "There was constant and long-term and even violent opposition to her from the electricians because she was a woman, in the beginning a child, and show business is death on women, especially in the technical end." To overcome the rudeness she frequently encountered, Rosenthal developed a tranquil, courteous, but impersonal façade. However, knowledge remained her most useful weapon in the battle for acceptance. "I did know my stuff, and I knew that the technicians knew theirs. I honored, truly, their knowledge and their prerogatives. And gradually they came around—from stagehands to directors—to honor mine."

◀❧

Lewisohn, Irene.
See Lewisohn, Alice and Irene.

Rosenthal had a second career as a consultant, and in that capacity worked mostly on designs for professional and academic theater buildings, although she also consulted on the illumination for the Mauna Kea Beach Hotel, in Hawaii, and the Pan American World Airways Terminal at the John F. Kennedy Airport, in New York. "It is hectic and dangerous to lead the life of a consultant," she once said in a speech, referring to clashes between clients, architects, and vendors. "These forces are all applied to the consultant, and if he or she has humor, judgment, and the ability to sort out the essential aims of each of the people involved, then I think the consultant serves a proper purpose."

Rosenthal, who never married, lived her entire life in a succession of apartments on Manhattan's East Side. Late in her life, she was drawn to nature and established a second home on Martha's Vineyard, where she said the air was the softest and the light the most delicate in the world. She died there of cancer on May 1, 1969, shortly after designing the lighting for Martha Graham's production of *Archaic Hours*, at the New York City Center.

SOURCES:
Rosenthal, Jean, and Lael Wertenbaker. *The Magic of Light*. Boston, MA: Little, Brown, 1972.
Wilmeth, Don B., and Tice L. Miller. *Cambridge Guide to American Theatre*. NY: Cambridge University Press, 1993.

Barbara Morgan,
Melrose, Massachusetts

Rosenwald, Edith (1895–1980).

See Stern, Edith Rosenwald.

Rose of Burford (fl. 15th c.)

Wool merchant of England. Flourished in the late 15th century.

Rose of Burford, an English wool merchant whose early life is obscure, was probably born into a merchant or gentry family. She was well educated—not in the classical fields of literature, music, and Latin, but the areas in which a merchant needed expertise, for example, trading law, mathematics, banking, and export law. Rose became a wholesaler, exporting raw English wool to Calais and selling it to textile manufacturers there. By running her own business, she qualified as a *femme sole* ("woman alone"); in medieval times, this phrase signified a woman who could conduct transactions independently and in her own name, making her an equal with male merchants. Rose retained this status even

when she married another wool merchant, for she kept her business separate.

Her husband was extremely wealthy and worked directly for the king, Edward II, to whom he loaned a large amount of money for England's war against Scotland. Rose, too, appears in royal documents as a merchant to the crown, and also when she requested repayment of her husband's loan after his death. This request began a rather long legal procedure for the widow, who was forced to appear at the royal court five more times to demand the money, which was not forthcoming due to the administration's tight financial situation. Finally, Rose offered the officers of the crown a compromise: that instead of receiving a lump sum equivalent to the loan amount plus interest, she would accept having the loan paid off through reductions of the business taxes she was assessed, to which the royal court agreed. Rose remains a figure in documents of the royal treasury for some years after this settlement.

SOURCES:
Uitz, Erika. *The Legend of Good Women: The Liberation of Women in Medieval Cities*. Wakefield, RI: Moyer Bell, 1988.

Laura York,
Riverside, California

Rose of Lima (1586–1617)

Peruvian mystic and ascetic who was the first person born in the Americas to be canonized by the Roman Catholic Church. Name variations: Rosa de Lima; Rosa de Santa María; Rosa of Lima. Born Isabel Flores de Oliva on April 20 or 30, 1586, in Lima, Peru; died on August 24, 1617, also in Lima; daughter of Gaspar de Flores and María de Oliva; never married; no children.

Confirmed at Quives (1597); took habit as Dominican tertiary (1606); said to have saved Lima from pirates (1615); canonization proceedings begun (1618); beatified (1668); canonized (1671).

A new society, 16th-century Peru grew out of the subjugation of the once-great Inca Empire by the Spanish conquistadors and the equally important subjugation of the conquistadors themselves by agents of the Spanish crown. By 1550, the western coastal and mountainous regions of South America had come under the effective control of the king of Spain's personal representative, the viceroy, whose capital was at Lima. Founded in 1535, this city had a population consisting mostly of native Americans, Africans, and persons of mixed descent, but it was dominated by a tiny Spanish elite, which traced its right to rule to its participation in the conquest and the early civil wars. More important than wealth to this elite's self-identity was its claim to racial purity, its loyalty to the Spanish monarchy, and its devotion to the Roman Catholic Church, the feast days of whose saints marked the passage of the year.

The saints of the Church were among the most important culture heroes of the time. Their lives were a principal theme for artists and writers, and were one of the most common subjects of books to be found in colonists' private libraries. Certainly, the saints were considered fit objects for imitation, and occasionally an individual would appear in society who, to the people around her or him, seemed to demonstrate an exceptional holiness. Such extraordinary virtue might be characterized by contempt for worldly goods, comforts, or pleasures, or by great acts of charity or compassion toward the less fortunate. Another possible sign might be some peculiar trait of behavior or personality that seemed evidence of a unique relationship with God. In this pre-scientific age, stories of supernatural occurrences, such as apparitions, prophecies, or miracles, were readily believed and tended to spread rapidly, contributing as they did so to such an individual's reputation for sanctity. If a person's fame became sufficiently widespread in his or her own time, it might well lead to demonstrations of popular devotion upon his or her death and, ultimately, to calls for canonization, that is, the official recognition of sainthood by the Church.

This process may be observed in the life of the woman who came to be called Rose of Lima, the first person born in the New World to be declared a saint by the Roman Catholic Church. Born in Lima on April 20 or 30, 1586, Rose was one of several children of Gaspar Flores and **María de Oliva**, a Spanish couple resident in the capital. Her parents christened her Isabel, after her maternal grandmother **Isabel de Herrera**, but very early she came to be called Rosa, or Rose, instead. According to a story repeated at the time, the change of name was inspired by Mariana, an Indian maidservant in the Flores household, who, when young Isabel was still a baby, declared that she was so beautiful that she looked like a rose, a European flower only recently imported to Peru. An impetuous person, María de Oliva was so delighted by the servant's observation that she gave immediate instructions that, henceforth, the child should be called by the new name. Only the infant's original namesake refused to cooperate; for years, the old

woman insisted upon addressing her granddaughter as Isabel.

A native of Puerto Rico, Gaspar Flores was considerably older than his wife. He was a soldier who sometime before 1548 had come to Peru, where he saw military action against a rebellious faction of Spaniards led by Gonzalo Pizarro and also in frontier campaigns against unsubdued Indians. Later in life, about the time he decided to marry and start a family, Flores was rewarded for his service with a comfortable assignment as a harquebusier (a soldier armed with a specific style of gun) in the viceregal guard, a largely ceremonial position which did not pay much but which was safe and enabled him to live with his wife, children, and mother-in-law in Lima. Because they were of pure Spanish blood, the Floreses belonged to the city's elite. They lived in a large house in the prestigious downtown section, but they were not wealthy and had to engage in a number of different economic activities to make ends meet. To bring in extra income, María taught children to read and write, while Rose learned to do embroidery and sewing, and she also peddled the fruit and flowers the family grew in their garden.

In the mid-1590s, Gaspar Flores moved his family to the mountain town of Quives, where he had been appointed superintendent of the mines. In 1597, the town was visited by the famous archbishop of Lima, Toribio Alfonso de Mogrovejo (1538–1606), who was making an inspection tour of his archdiocese and offering to administer confirmation to those young people who had achieved the appropriate age. When Rose's family presented her for the sacrament, the respected prelate confirmed her under the religious name Rosa de Santa María, thereby giving the Church's sanction to the change made years before on her mother's whim. Now, even the stubborn grandmother began to call the child Rose. Because both Rose and Toribio de Mogrovejo would ultimately be canonized, devout Catholics have since attributed special significance to the brief encounter between them in the tiny stone church at Quives.

One obstacle to a full understanding of Rose's brief life, and especially of her development as a woman, is the scarcity of documentation. Rose was not an intellectual, although she did have artistic talents. She played musical instruments and enjoyed singing, sometimes making up her own songs, but her poetry was undistinguished and she left no great body of written correspondence. Although Rose is remembered as a gifted mystic, she wrote no books of devotion, and, unlike other religious women of her time, she never penned a spiritual autobiography.

The fact is that most of what we know about Rose comes from statements made in her canonization proceedings by people who had known her in life. For obvious reasons, such testimony tended to concentrate on examples of virtue or special gifts, and, what is more, it tended to resemble closely stories repeated about other saints, suggesting that witnesses may have been guided more by what they thought holy people were supposed to do and say than by what they actually observed. A further complication is that persons who aspired to a virtuous life frequently sought to imitate the behavior of their own favorite saints. For example, several stories told about Rose of Lima are similar to episodes from the career of the Italian mystic *Catherine of Siena (1347–1380), whom she was known to admire and whose life she had read. Did Rose deliberately copy Catherine, or did the people around her merely attribute Catherine's deeds to her? It is unlikely that we shall ever know.

> $\mathcal{D}$ead over three hundred years,
> [Rose of Lima] still lives.
>
> —Frances Parkinson Keyes

Difficulties with the historical record aside, the stories told about Rose of Lima in her own time and afterward portray her as an individual who, even as a young girl, showed a peculiar vocation for prayer and self-denial. By all accounts headstrong, as were her mother and grandmother, Rose preferred solitude and prayer to the company of other children, and, with the help of her brother Hernando Flores, who was devoted to her, she built herself a rustic hermitage in the garden of the Flores home in Lima. It was also at an early age, perhaps so early that she could not fully comprehend its implications, that she made a private vow of perpetual chastity. If Rose had been a lovely baby, she grew into an attractive young woman, but she showed no interest in the many suitors who came to her parents' house, and once, when her brother Hernando teased her by calling attention to her beautiful hair, she took a pair of scissors and cut it off.

We are told that Rose's lack of interest in men was a disappointment to her mother and father, who hoped to see her make an advantageous marriage. Dutifully, she agreed to grow her hair back and wear pretty dresses, but she was not happy doing so. In colonial Peru, if a woman of the elite did not marry, the only honorable al-

ternative state was the religious life, of which one usually thinks in terms of the cloister. In fact, Rose did attempt on two occasions to enter a convent. The first time, she changed her mind because of parental objections; the second time, she did not even consult Gaspar and María, but she backed out at the last minute because of a message she claimed to have received from *Mary the Virgin. Those who are skeptical of supernatural intervention attribute Rose's failure to become a cloistered nun to her unwillingness to defy the will of her mother and father, or to the Flores family's continued dependence on the income from her needlework and flower sales.

For Rose, the solution to her dilemma lay in becoming a *beata*, a woman who had taken religious vows but who lived and worked in the outside world. In 1606, in imitation of her ideal Catherine of Siena, Rose joined the Third Order of the Dominicans, which permitted her to become betrothed to Jesus Christ, while continuing to live at home with her parents and brothers and sisters. A tertiary, as members of third orders were called, was entitled to wear the habit of the parent order, but was not required to do so. In Rose's case, she preferred the white and black Dominican garb to the feminine dresses her mother had insisted upon; it remained her unvarying mode of dress until her death, and in it she became a familiar sight in the streets and churches of Lima.

In an apparent effort to make herself more worthy of her heavenly bridegroom, to whom she did not formally sanctify her spiritual marriage until Palm Sunday, 1617, Rose subjected herself for years to painful acts of self-torture, often with the reluctant assistance of her devoted servant Mariana, who had cared for her as an infant. She regularly flogged herself with a metal chain, and, to permit herself to experience bodily pain as a constant companion, she fastened an iron belt tightly about her waist, placed a lock on it, and threw the key into a well. To emulate the sufferings of Jesus Christ, she had made for herself a pewter crown of thorns. This crown, which she wore every day, dug into her flesh and frequently caused her to bleed, but she hid it from public view under a wreath of roses, because she considered it prideful to call attention to her own struggle for virtue.

Despite Rose's efforts at discretion, word spread of her visions and other mystical experiences, and her excessive acts of mortification. One result of her growing fame was a visit from representatives of the Lima tribunal of the Holy Office of the Inquisition, who came to determine for themselves whether the young woman's unusual behavior was inspired by God or by the devil. Following a lengthy interrogation in front of witnesses, during which Rose replied calmly and modestly to all of their questions, the inquisitors declared their finding that her gifts were of the Holy Spirit. The ecclesiastical authorities took no further notice of Rose, while the people close to her, and those who came to hear of her, became increasingly convinced that a peculiarly holy person walked in their midst.

Aspiring to be touched in some way by the same holiness, citizens of Lima sought Rose's company and favor. Her devotees included persons of wealth and influence, such as the royal accountant Gonzalo de la Maza and his wife **María de Uzátegui**, whose palatial residence became a second home to her. Rose's powerful admirers included also at least one viceroy's wife, the marquise of Montes Claros. If Rose welcomed the friendship and protection offered by the de la Mazas and their two small daughters, we are told that she accepted the attentions of other aristocrats with courtesy but great reluctance. From her point of view, the luxury of life in Lima's ruling households was inconsistent with the ideal of humility in God's service.

Much of Rose's time was spent in good works. Her most important private charity was an infirmary that she established in her parents' home for the treatment of the poor. At first, Rosa's mother María de Oliva was skeptical of this operation which brought some of Lima's most wretched inhabitants to her front door, but, as in so many other things in her relationship with her unusual daughter, she later came to accept it and even attended to the patients herself when Rose was away from the house on other matters. Gradually, Rose built a small following of young women who admired her and wanted to emulate her, and she decided to found a Dominican convent dedicated to Catherine of Siena. According to a story of the time, her mother scoffed at the grandness of the project, as well as at Rose's reported prediction that María herself would one day be a nun in the proposed community, but, after Rose's death, the convent was established, and María de Oliva did end her days cloistered there.

As it had been in her childhood, the garden of the Flores home in Lima remained Rose's favorite place, where she claimed that she "heard the voice of the Lord God . . . in the cool of the day." We are told that, in this peaceful retreat where she still kept the rustic cell Hernando had helped her build years before, Rose conducted conversations not only with God and the saints, but also with the plants and animals. On one occasion, she is said to have told María de Uzátegui, who visited her there and complained of mosquito bites, that the insects always left her alone. "We have an agreement," Rose said, "they do not sting me and I do not kill them."

It was natural that a young woman who was thought to enjoy such harmony with God's creatures should be credited with working miracles as well. One such event is supposed to have occurred in Lima in 1615, when the Dutch pirate Joris van Spilbergen (1568–1620), who had been raiding Spanish settlements along the Pacific coast of South America, attempted to attack the city. According to one of several versions of this story, when Spilbergen's men assaulted a church where women and children had taken refuge, they came face to face at the altar with Rose, who had gone there to invite martyrdom by defending the eucharist from desecration. Cowed by the sight of the young woman in the Dominican habit, her arms outstretched in supplication, the pirates retreated from the scene, returned to their ships, and sailed away.

Although Rose is universally described as a beautiful woman, apparently she was not robust. We are told that she was thin, which should not surprise us because she fasted long and often, and she appears to have been in chronically poor health, perhaps, once again, because of the physical abuse to which she subjected herself. Sometime after the reported encounter with the pirates, her condition began to worsen, and we are told that she accurately foretold the date of her own death. During the final months of her life, Rose went to live in the Lima home of her powerful friends, the de la Mazas, and it was there that death overcame her on August 24, 1617.

By the time she died, Rose's reputation for holiness was well known in Lima and its jurisdiction, and news of her passing inspired massive demonstrations. There was a near riot at her funeral, as faithful followers, hungry for relics, mobbed the bier in a frantic attempt to snatch pieces of her habit and even of her corpse. It was finally necessary for the authorities to cancel the ceremony and proceed with the interment in secrecy. In 1618, only months after Rose's death, officials in Lima opened an inquiry into her life and virtues as a first step toward presenting her cause to the pope as a candidate for canonization. The formal process was a lengthy one, but at home Rose was already a saint by popular acclamation. Her little cell in the garden of her parents' home became a pilgrimage shrine, and her followers venerated her relics as well as an image of her that hung in the Dominican church. In 1624, the Inquisition ordered an end to this unsanctioned cult, but the campaign for official recognition of Rose's sanctity continued. A major milestone occurred in 1668, when Pope Clement IX declared Rose to be "blessed," the stage known as beatification, which authorized the faithful to venerate her within her own diocese. Only three years later, in 1671, Rose finally achieved official acknowledgement of her sainthood when Clement X formally announced her canonization.

SOURCES:

Keyes, Frances Parkinson. *The Rose and the Lily: The Lives and Times of Two South American Saints.* NY: Hawthorn Books, 1961.

Martín, Luis. *Daughters of the Conquistadores: Women of the Viceroyalty of Peru.* Albuquerque, NM: University of New Mexico Press, 1983.

Vargas Ugarte, Rubén, S.J. *Vida de Santa Rosa de Santa María.* 2d ed. Lima: Tipografía Peruana, 1951.

SUGGESTED READING:

Maynard, Sara. *Rose of America: The Story of Saint Rose of Lima.* NY: Sheed & Ward, 1943 (for young readers).

Stephen Webre,
Professor of History, Louisiana Tech University,
Ruston, Louisiana

Rose of Viterbo (1235–1252)

Franciscan preacher and saint. Name variations: Rosa di Viterbo. Born in 1235 in Viterbo, Italy; died in 1252 (some sources cite 1253 or 1261) in Viterbo; never married; no children.

Rose of Viterbo, an Italian holy woman, was born in Italy in 1235. Unlike so many famous medieval holy women, she was not from the ruling classes. She was a peasant who wanted to join a Franciscan convent, but, without a dowry, she could not be accepted. Instead, she joined the informal tertiary order of Franciscans, a group who traveled constantly to preach in the streets. Rose, who never married, became a well-known figure in Viterbo, giving sermons on various sins, urging residents to oppose heretical movements and making political speeches as well. She gained a considerable following of believers who thought her capable of performing miracles, and felt she bore a special message from God. She is an excellent example of the "popular" medieval saint, an unlettered woman whose following was sufficiently large to pressure the Church into naming her a saint.

SOURCES:

Dunbar, Agnes. *Dictionary of Saintly Women.* Vol. I. London: G. Bell, 1904.

Echols, Anne, and Marty Williams. *An Annotated Index of Medieval Women.* NY: Markus Wiener, 1992.

Laura York,
Riverside, California

Rosman, Alice Grant (1887–1961)

Australian novelist. Name variations: (pseudonym) Rosna. Born in Dreamthorpe, Kapunda, South Australia, in 1887; died in 1961; daughter of Alice Mary (Bowyer) Rosman (a poet); attended the Dominican Convent in Cabra, South Australia.

Selected writings: Miss Bryde of England *(1916);* The Tower Wall *(1917);* The Back Seat Driver *(1928);* The Window *(1928);* Visitors to Hugo *(1929);* The Young and Secret *(1930);* Jock the Scot *(1930);* The Sixth Journey *(1931);* Benefits Received *(1932);* Protecting Margot *(1933);* Somebody Must *(1934);* The Sleeping Child *(1935);* Mother of the Bride *(1936);* Unfamiliar Faces *(1938);* William's Room *(1939);* Nine Lives: A Cat of London in Peace and War *(1941).*

Alice Grant Rosman was born in South Australia in 1887, and attended the Dominican Convent in Cabra. She was still a child when she began writing stories, a passion she shared with her mother **Alice Mary Bowyer Rosman**, who published a verse collection entitled *An Enchanted Garden* in 1916. Rosman's first short story was published in the Adelaide *Southern Cross*, and her work appeared in *Aunt Eily's Christmas Annual* in 1902, when she was just 15 years old. Her sketches, stories, and poems were later featured in Australian anthologies, newspapers, and magazines including the *Native Companion*, the *Lone Hand*, and the *Gadfly*, as well as in the Adelaide *Bulletin*, for which she wrote from 1908 to 1911 under the name "Rosna."

In 1911, Rosman traveled with her family to London for the coronation of King George V. She remained in England and joined the literary staff of the *British Australasian* (also referred to as the *British Australian and New Zealander*) and the editorial staff of the *Grand Magazine*. In 1927, however, she relinquished her journalism positions to concentrate on her novel writing.

Rosman quickly earned international acclaim for her novels. *The Window* (1928) sold 100,000 copies. *Visitors to Hugo* (1929), which sensitively combined a psychiatric setting with humor, firmly established her reputation and became the standard by which her subsequent works were judged. Rosman was the author of over 15 novels, the best of which have been described as "domestic romances in comfortable households."

SOURCES:

Kunitz, Stanley J., and Howard Haycraft, eds. *Twentieth Century Authors*. NY: H.W. Wilson, 1942.

Wilde, William H., Joy Hooten, and Barry Andrews. *The Oxford Companion to Australian Literature*. Melbourne, Australia: Oxford University Press, 1985.

Lisa S. Weitzman,
freelance writer, Cleveland, Ohio

Rosna (1887–1961).

See Rosman, Alice Grant.

Ross, Araminta "Minty" (1821–1913).

See Tubman, Harriet.

Ross, Betsy (1752–1836)

Celebrated creator of the first American flag. Name variations: Elizabeth Ross; Elizabeth Ashburn; Elizabeth Claypoole; Elizabeth Griscom Ross Ashburn Claypoole. Born Elizabeth Griscom in Philadelphia, Pennsylvania, on January 1, 1752; died in Philadelphia on January 30, 1836; daughter of Samuel Griscom (a builder) and Rebecca (James) Griscom; married John Ross, on November 4, 1773 (died 1776); married Joseph Ashburn, in June 1777 (died 1782); married John Claypoole, on May 8, 1783 (died 1817); children: (second marriage) Zillah Ashburn (b. 1779), who died young; Eliza Ashburn (b. 1781); (third marriage) Clarissa Sidney Claypoole Wilson (b. 1785); Susan Claypoole (b. 1786); Rachel Claypoole (b. 1789); Jane Claypoole (b. 1792); Harriet Claypoole (b. 1795), who died as an infant.

Betsy Ross, whose name has been as familiar to generations of American schoolchildren as those of *Pocahontas and *Sacajawea, was born in Philadelphia in 1752, into a family that eventually included 17 children. She was the daughter of **Rebecca Griscom** and Samuel Griscom, a builder who allegedly worked on the construction of Independence Hall in Philadelphia. Both were members of the Society of Friends, also known as Quakers, and Betsy probably attended the Quaker school on South Fourth Street. She learned needlework from her mother and was talented enough to receive contracts for military flags throughout her lifetime.

On November 4, 1773, Betsy married John Ross, who had been apprenticed to an upholsterer, and the newlyweds started their own upholstery business. But John was an Episcopalian, not a Quaker, and Betsy was cast out of the Society of Friends; she would later become a member of the Society of Free Quakers or "Fighting Quakers." In January 1776, while on militia duty,

John died in an accidental gunpowder explosion. Ross took over the upholstery business, which would thrive until her retirement at age 75.

In 1777, one month after she married her second husband Joseph Ashburn, Ross provided "ship's colours, etc." (a flag) for Pennsylvania's navy. Along with making flags, Ross supplemented the upholstery business' income by investing in livestock and property, including some 190 acres in Cumberland County. The couple had two children, Zillah (b. 1779), who died young, and **Eliza Ashburn** (b. 1781). But Joseph Ashburn was also a military man, a first mate on the brigantine *Patty*, and their marriage was cut short by the American Revolution. The British captured Ashburn's ship in 1781 and sent him to a British prison, where he died in 1782. A friend of Ashburn's named John Claypoole visited Ross to deliver a last message from her husband. In 1783, less than a year after this meeting, they married. Ross and Claypoole had five daughters: Clarissa Sidney Claypoole (b. 1785), **Susan Claypoole** (b. 1786), **Rachel Claypoole** (b. 1789), **Jane Claypoole** (b. 1792), and Harriet Claypoole (b. 1795), who died as an infant. After John Claypoole died in August 1817, Ross continued living in Philadelphia where she ran the upholstery business until 1827, when she passed it down to a daughter. She died in Philadelphia in January 1836.

Betsy Ross was an active, accomplished woman, the mother of seven children and a successful businesswoman and real-estate investor. She became legendary, however, for her disputable involvement in the creation of the nation's first flag.

George Ross, an uncle of Ross' first husband, was a well-known patriot, a signer of the Declaration of Independence and a friend of George Washington. According to legend, George Ross, George Washington, and Robert Morris visited Betsy Ross in June 1776—or, by some accounts, as late as 1777—as members of a secret committee of the Continental Congress seeking a flag for the nascent nation. Betsy suggested a design to Washington, who then made a pencil sketch of it. Washington originally wanted six-pointed stars, but Ross preferred them five-pointed because they were easier to cut.

No contemporary documents or accounts of these events exist. Because working to further the patriots' cause was considered treason against Britain, these activities were understandably suppressed at the time. Nonetheless, if George Washington secretly commissioned Ross to create a flag, he never recorded her contribution—and he was unusually conscientious about thanking women who helped in the fight for independence, among them ***Phillis Wheatley** and ***Eliza Pinckney**. Furthermore, an account written by Washington on January 4, 1776, stated, "We hoisted the union flag in compliment to the United States." Therefore, Washington already had a flag and most likely would not have asked Ross to create another.

Since many flags were used by different military units during the American Revolution, and considering Ross' occupation and her close rela-

tions to prominent political figures such as her late husband's uncle, it is possible that Ross created at least one of these flags. There are no accounts in the records of the Continental Congress of any committee concerned with the creation of a flag, but on June 14, 1777, the U.S. Congress resolved: "That the flag of the U.S. be thirteen stripes, alternate red and white, that the union be thirteen stars, white in a blue field representing a new constellation." Ross was not mentioned here either (and credit for this design is often given to Francis Hopkinson, a lawyer, writer, and signer of the Declaration of Independence).

Betsy Ross

Ross was first connected publicly with the flag almost 100 years after the American Revolution. In March 1870, at a meeting of the Pennsylvania Historical Society, her grandson William Canby presented a history of the family, including the popularly known tale that his great-aunt had created the flag. He claimed that his Aunt Clarissa had heard it from her mother, Betsy Ross. The story was impossible to check because the participants were no longer alive. *Harper's Monthly* printed the tale in July 1873. Within the next decade, children's American history textbooks presented it as fact, making Ross one of the few women mentioned in history schoolbooks (a state of affairs that would continue throughout most of the 20th century). Ross' Philadelphia home, where she may have fashioned the flag, became a historical monument in 1887. Twelve years later, a painting of the event was displayed at the Columbian Exposition. Clearly her grandson's story struck a chord in American culture that has continued to ring for more than a century.

SOURCES:

James, Edward T., ed. *Notable American Women, 1607–1950.* Cambridge, MA: The Belknap Press of Harvard University, 1971.

Johnson, Thomas H. *The Oxford Companion to American History.* NY: Oxford University Press, 1966.

McHenry, Robert, ed. *Famous American Women.* NY: Dover, 1980.

Read, Phyllis J., and Bernard L. Witlieb. *The Book of Women's Firsts.* NY: Random House, 1992.

Weatherford, Doris. *American Women's History.* NY: Prentice Hall, 1994.

Kelly Winters,
freelance writer, Bayville, New York

Ross, Blanche (c. 1897–1969).

See Rubenstein, Blanche.

Ross, countess of.

See Bruce, Matilda (c. 1285–c. 1326).
See Ross, Euphemia (d. after 1394).
See Leslie, Euphemia (d. after 1424).
See Leslie, Mary (d. 1429).

Ross, Diana (b. 1944).

See Supremes, The.

Ross, Elisabeth Kübler (b. 1926).

See Kübler-Ross, Elisabeth.

Ross, Elizabeth (1883–1953).

See Haynes, Elizabeth Ross.

Ross, Euphemia (d. 1387)

Queen of Scotland. Name variations: Euphemia of Ross; countess of Moray. Died in 1387; daughter of

*Hugh Ross, 4th earl of Ross, and *Matilda Bruce (c. 1285–c. 1326, sister of Robert I the Bruce); married John Randolph, 3rd earl of Moray; became second wife of Robert II Stewart or Stuart (1316–1390), king of Scots (r. 1371–1390), around May 2, 1355; children: David Stewart, earl of Strathearn (c. 1356–c. 1382); Walter Stewart, earl of Atholl and Caithness (c. 1360–1437); *Egidia Stewart (who married William Douglas of Nithsdale in 1387); *Katherine Stewart (who married David Lindsay, 1st earl of Crawford). Robert II's first wife was *Elizabeth Muir.*

SUGGESTED READING:

Sutherland, Elizabeth. *Five Euphemias: Women in Medieval Scotland, 1200–1420.* NY: St. Martin's Press, 1999.

Ross, Euphemia (d. after 1394)

Countess of Ross. Died after September 5, 1394; interred at Fortrose Cathedral, Ross and Cromarty; daughter of William Ross, 3rd earl of Ross, and Mary Og (daughter of Angus Og, lord of the Isles); married Walter de Lesly, earl of Ross (some sources cite Andrew Leslie), around 1361; married Alexander Stewart (c. 1343–1394), 1st earl of Buchan (r. 1382–1394), known as the Wolf of Badenach (some sources cite a 1405 death date), around July 22, 1382; children: (first marriage) Alexander Leslie, 7th earl of Ross; Mary Leslie (d. 1429, who married Donald MacDonald, lord of the Isles).

The daughter of William Ross, 3rd earl of Ross, and **Mary Og**, Euphemia Ross married Walter de Lesly around 1361. Twenty years later, now the countess of Ross, she married Alexander Stewart, 1st earl of Buchan, who was known as the Wolf of Badenach for his excessive cruelty. Alexander had seven children out of wedlock with **Margaret Atheyn**. In 1390, the bishop of Moray ordered Alexander to return to his wife Euphemia. In retaliation, he led a raid on the town of Elgin and burned its cathedral.

Ross, Harriet (1821–1913).

See Tubman, Harriet.

Ross, Ishbel (1895–1975)

Scottish-born American journalist and writer. Name variations: Isabel Rae; Ishbella Rae. Born Ishbella Margaret Ross in Sutherlandshire, Scotland, on December 15, 1895; died on September 21, 1975, in New York City; daughter of David Ross and Grace (McCrone) Ross; educated at the Tain Royal Academy in Ross-Shire, Scotland; married Bruce Rae (a journalist and editor), in 1922; children: Catriona.

Selected writings: Through the Lich-Gate: A Biography of the Little Church Around the Corner *(1931);* Marriage in Gotham *(1933);* Promenade Deck *(novel, 1933);* Ladies of the Press: The Story of Women in Journalism by an Insider *(1936);* Fifty Years a Woman *(novel, 1938);* Isle of Escape *(1942);* Child of Destiny: The Life Story of the First Woman Doctor *(1949);* Margaret Fell: Mother of Quakerism *(1949);* Journey Into Light: The Story of the Education of the Blind *(1951);* Proud Kate: Portrait of an Ambitious Woman *(1953);* Rebel Rose: Life of Rose O'Neal Greenhow, Confederate Spy *(1954);* Angel of the Battlefield: The Life of **Clara Barton (1956);* First Lady of the South: The Life of Mrs. Jefferson Davis *(1958);* The General's Wife: The Life of Mrs. Ulysses S. Grant *(1959);* Silhouette in Diamonds: The Life of Mrs. Potter Palmer *(1960);* *Grace Coolidge *and Her Era: The Story of a President's Wife (1962);* Crusades and Crinoline: The Life and Times of **Ellen Curtis Demorest and William Jennings Demorest (1963);* An American Family: The Tafts, 1678 to 1964 *(1964);* Charmers and Cranks: Twelve Famous American Women Who Defied the Conventions *(1965);* Taste in America: An Illustrated History of the Evolution of Architecture, Furnishings, Fashions, and Customs of the American People *(1967);* Sons of Adam, Daughters of Eve *(1969);* The Expatriates *(1970);* The Uncrowned Queen: The Life of **Lola Montez (1972);* The President's Wife: Mary Todd Lincoln *(1973);* Power with Grace: The Life of Mrs. Woodrow Wilson *(1975).*

Born in Sutherlandshire, Scotland, in 1895, the second of two children, Ishbel Ross knew from an early age that she wanted to be a writer. She was a voracious, catholic reader, and her dreams of becoming a writer were fed by the glimpses she caught of her neighbor Rudyard Kipling, whom she often saw walking with his children. At 20 years of age, after attending Tain Royal Academy in Ross-Shire, Scotland, Ross emigrated to Toronto, Ontario. Though she wanted to be a reporter, she had to take other jobs before anyone would assign her a story. The Canadian Food Board hired her as a publicist, and the library at the *Toronto Daily News* provided her with employment. Finally, suffragist *Emmeline Pankhurst* succumbed to her requests for an interview. Ross proclaimed that she "was never a great suffrage sympathizer" but acknowledged her debt to Pankhurst for providing her with the first step toward a long and successful career of writing about notable women.

In 1919, Ross left Canada for New York City, where she became a general assignment reporter and member of the editorial staff for the *New York Tribune* and later, when it merged with the *New York Herald*, for the *Herald-Tribune*. The number of male reporters fighting overseas in World War I made it easier for women to enter the male-dominated newspaper world. Furthermore, Ross and other women reporters received assignments for front-page stories; on most other papers, these were always given to men. She covered fires, explosions, and prize fights, and interviewed immigrants and college students. Ross was especially interested in aviation, and she often waited all night at airports for the early trans-Atlantic flights to arrive. She interviewed Edward, duke of Windsor (briefly Edward VIII), when he visited the United States, and Charles A. Lindbergh on his triumphant return from the first solo trans-Atlantic flight. She covered sensational crimes, such as the 1926 trial of **Frances Hall** for the murder of her husband Edward Wheeler Hall and **Eleanor Mills*, and the kidnapping and murder of Charles and **Anne Morrow Lindbergh*'s infant son in 1932. Ross attended the presidential inaugurations of Warren G. Harding, Calvin Coolidge, and Herbert Hoover, and reported the death of inventor Thomas Edison.

Ross received a byline only for some of her stories, a situation she brushed off as the result of being a reporter rather than a feature writer, but she was held in high esteem by her colleagues. According to **Barbara Belford** in *Brilliant Bylines*, Stanley Walker, city editor at the *Herald-Tribune*, who often spoke poorly of women journalists in general, said that Ross had "unflustered competence," and referred to her as "the perfect newspaperman"; while reporter Dick West noted, "Her intense blue eyes made you feel that she was sizing you up, coolly and completely. . . . She had a dignity, a self-possession that inspired respect. . . . All her stories had a depth and a texture that no one could match. Her insights brought people and events to life in print."

In 1922, Ross married Bruce Rae, a Scottish-born journalist whom she had met while they were covering a highly publicized divorce case. He worked for *The New York Times*, so the two often had to compete with each other for the same story. Their personal styles, like their writing styles, were very different. Rae was described as a temperamental, sharp-tongued perfectionist, while Ross was quiet and solitary. She emphasized vivid dramatic and visual details, while he focused on mood. They claimed that although their personalities sometimes led to strife at home, they did not discuss the stories they both covered.

Ross and Rae were paid by the column inch for their stories on the Hall-Mills murder case. By the time it ended, they had made enough money to take six months off and embark on a cruise around the world. *Promenade Deck*, Ross' first novel, was inspired by and based on this trip. It became a bestseller and later a movie. In anticipation of the birth of her first—and only—child, Ross quit her job at the *Herald-Tribune*. She continued to write prodigiously, however, focusing on nonfiction books, especially biographies.

One of Ross' best-known books is *Ladies of the Press*, which researchers still rely on for accounts of early women journalists in the United States. Originally published in 1936 and reprinted in 1974, the book remains the only source for quotations, anecdotes, and background information on many reporters. Interestingly, Ross did not include herself in the book, although she was an accomplished journalist and prolific writer. Most of her other books were biographies of famous women, many of them connected to famous men. Among these were **Margaret Fell: Mother of Quakerism* (1949), *Rebel Rose: Life of *Rose O'Neal Greenhow, Confederate Spy* (1954), *First Lady of the South: The Life of Mrs. Jefferson Davis* (1958, about **Varina Howell Davis*), *The General's Wife: The Life of Mrs. Ulysses S. Grant* (1959, about **Julia Grant*), *Silhouette in Diamonds: The Life of Mrs. Potter Palmer* (1960, about **Bertha Honoré Palmer*), and *Power with Grace: The Life of Mrs. Woodrow Wilson* (1975, about **Edith Bolling Wilson*). In many cases, such as in *The President's Wife: *Mary Todd Lincoln* (1973), Ross presented these women as important figures in their own right, not simply as the wives or companions of well-known men. As a result of introducing these women to the general public, she often received invitations to lecture or speak about them on the radio.

Ross' husband died in 1962. She remained healthy and active in her later years, and encouraged younger writers in their careers. She also continued to write, completing 10 books in the 13 years between her husband's death and her own. Her daughter suffered from mental illness, and Ross may have been motivated to write so much because she needed money for Catriona's medical treatment. At age 79, she wrote, "I'm as healthy as a horse, and it will be eighty years I reach next December." A month later, on September 21, 1975, Ross fell from a window of her fourth-story apartment. Although police did not

exclude the possibility of suicide, the cause of her death remains uncertain.

SOURCES:

Belford, Barbara. *Brilliant Bylines*. NY: Columbia University Press, 1986.
Contemporary Authors. Vols. 61–64 and 93–96. Detroit, MI: Gale Research.

Kelly Winters,
freelance writer, Bayville, New York

Ross, Ishobel (1890–1965)

Scottish nurse. Born on the Isle of Skye on February 18, 1890; died in 1965; daughter of James Ross (who is credited with the development of the famous liquor, Drambuie); attended Edinburgh Ladies College; married; children: daughter Jess Dixon.

Born on the Isle of Skye in 1890, Ishobel Ross attended Edinburgh Ladies College and then worked as a teacher at Atholl Crescent School. In 1914, soon after the outbreak of the First World War, Ross attended a lecture by

*Elsie Inglis about the Scottish Women's Hospital Unit. Ross eventually volunteered to accompany Inglis to Serbia, where a hospital unit was being established, arriving in nearby Salonika, Greece, on August 22, 1916. She would remain on the Balkan front until July 1917. Ross kept a diary of her experiences. "The bombardment has begun," she wrote on September 12, 1916:

> The guns started at 5 a.m. this morning and have gone steadily ever since. The noise is quite deafening and seems much nearer than it really is. A Serbian officer told us that we are only 5 miles from the fighting. It is awful to think that every boom means so many lives lost. They say the bombardment will continue for four or five days. Some of us went to the top of the hill tonight and saw the flashes from the guns. What a gorgeous night too, with the moon shining and the hills looking so lovely. The thought of so much killing and chaos so near to all this beauty made me feel very sad.

Ross died in 1965. Her daughter **Jess Dixon** brought the diary to the attention of the Aberdeen University Press; it was published in 1988 as *Little Grey Partridge: First World War Diary of Ishobel Ross Who Served with the Scottish Women's Hospitals in Serbia*.

Ross, Lillian (1926—)

American journalist and writer. Born on June 8, 1926, in Syracuse, New York; daughter of Louis Ross and Edna (Rosenson) Ross; children: Erik Jeremy Ross (adopted).

Selected writings: Picture *(1952);* Portrait of Hemingway *(1961);* Reporting *(1964);* Talk Stories *(1966);* Here But Not Here: A Love Story *(1998).*

Lillian Ross wrote for *The New Yorker* for more than 50 years, beginning in 1945, when she was not yet 20. For most of those years, *The New Yorker* was in its heyday as the most respected and influential magazine in the country, under the editorship of the legendary William Shawn. Ross became well known for her laudatory portraits of movie stars, famous writers, and other celebrity subjects, including John Huston and Ernest Hemingway. To write a piece, Ross first became friends with her subject, eschewing the traditional notion that a journalist should remain impartial. "I don't want to write about people I don't like," she told R.Z. Sheppard of *Time*. "If I like them, I like them with my being, and I'm not going to stop liking them after they have become useful to me." Sheppard noted, "She instinctively understood that the best way to become successful and well known

was to write about the famous." Ross also claimed to have been one of the first writers to use the techniques of fiction in nonfiction articles, a *New Yorker* hallmark also associated with her contemporaries A.J. Liebling and Joseph Mitchell (whom she credited with influencing her style) and with such later writers as Tom Wolfe and **Susan Sontag**.

Ross has written 11 books, but it was her memoir *Here But Not Here: A Love Story* that created the most waves. The book, published in 1998, details the 40 years she spent working and living with William Shawn, who had been fired from *The New Yorker* in 1987, died in 1992, and whose reputation amongst the literati was that of something close to a saint. While their longtime affair had not been the most closely guarded of secrets, the book was controversial because **Cecille Shawn**, his wife of 63 years, was still alive when it was published. "I think it's irrelevant," Ross told R.Z. Sheppard in *Time*, when asked why she would publish a memoir about an affair with a married man whose wife was still alive. "There were no secrets, really, that were divulged. We never went underground, and he talked with her about what was happening with him and with me immediately."

Ross met Shawn in 1952, when she was 25. He was 45 and had been married for 24 years. As **Laura Shapiro** reported in *Newsweek*, "One day in the office the two simply stared at each other, then raced uptown to the Plaza Hotel." Cecille Shawn refused his request for a divorce, so within a few years Shawn was living part of the day in an apartment with Ross ten blocks from the one he lived in the rest of the time with his wife and two sons. In the book, Ross is very candid about her arrangement with Shawn, which Sheppard remarked was "daring even by today's forgiving standards" (although she never explains why he did not simply leave her or leave his wife). Shawn ate his meals with Ross, stopped back at his family's apartment, returned to Ross' place for late-night television, went home to spend the night with his family, and had a private bedside telephone line installed in his room so he could spend time chatting with Ross each night. (His sons were apparently told he was working during all these absences.) After Ross adopted a son in the 1960s, she and Shawn raised him together. Their relationship continued until his death.

Ross quit *The New Yorker* in protest after Shawn was fired, criticizing those writers who did not. A few years after his death, she returned to write for the magazine under new editor **Tina**

Brown, earning accusations of hypocrisy that seemed to bother her no more than did the later criticisms of her memoir.

SOURCES:

Contemporary Authors. Vols. 9–12, 1st rev., vols. 45–48, new rev. Detroit, MI: Gale Research, 1974.
Newsweek. May 4, 1998, p. 71.
The New York Times. May 7, 1998.
Time. June 1, 1998.

Kelly Winters,
freelance writer, Bayville, New York

Ross, Martin (1862–1915).

See Somerville and Ross.

Ross, Mother (1667–1739).

See Cavanagh, Kit.

Ross, Nellie Tayloe (1876–1977)

American politician, director of the U.S. Mint, and first woman governor. Born Nellie Tayloe on November 29, 1876, near St. Joseph, Missouri; died in Washington, D.C., on December 20, 1977; daughter of James Wynns Tayloe (a merchant and farmer) and Elizabeth (Blair) Tayloe; had private tutoring and occasional public schooling in Missouri and Kansas; had two years of training in Omaha, Nebraska as kindergarten teacher; married William Bradford Ross (later governor of Wyoming), on September 11, 1902 (died 1924); children: (twins) George and Ambrose (b. 1903); Alfred (b. 1905, died young); William Bradford II (b. 1912).

Worked for Cheyenne, Wyoming, community activities, including Cheyenne Woman's Club, Boy Scouts and Episcopal Church (1902–22); was wife of governor (1922–24); elected governor of Wyoming (1925–27); served as vice-chair, Democratic National Committee (1928–33); served as director of U.S. Mint (1933–53).

On November 4, 1924, the voters of Wyoming were electing a governor, and many filed in and out of the garage of the Executive Mansion, a regularly designated polling place. They were watched from an upstairs window by Nellie Tayloe Ross, widow of the governor who had suddenly died a month before. Despite her initial reluctance, Nellie Ross had been persuaded to accept the Democratic Party's nomination as his successor at an emergency convention. She thought the people looked "unusually grave and resolute," and she wondered "how many—if any—were casting their ballots for me." She remained alone in her room that night with only a telephone beside her. The phone began to ring,

with reports of a national Republican landslide in which the Democratic presidential nominee received one of the lowest votes on record. Yet Nellie Ross, a Democrat in a Republican-majority state, a woman running for governor just four years after the 19th Amendment provided all American women with the vote, was elected by an ample margin; the more than 43,000 votes she received exceeded those received by any previous candidate in the history of the state and made her the first woman governor in the nation.

Nellie Tayloe's early life gave no promise of the long public career ahead. Born in 1876 near St. Joseph, Missouri, Nellie was a sickly child whose mother died when she was young. She later recalled that her father, a merchant and "gentleman farmer," and three brothers tended to spoil her, and she believed she must have been "weak and inefficient." Her infrequent attendance at public schools had to be supplemented by private tutors, but she studied hard and earned good grades. She graduated from a two-year course in Omaha, Nebraska, to prepare her to teach kindergarten, but her health prevented her from a career as a teacher.

In 1902, she married William Bradford Ross, a young lawyer who had moved to Cheyenne, Wyoming, the year before to begin his practice. The couple had twin sons, George and Ambrose, in 1903. Another son was born in 1905, but died at the age of ten months when, left briefly unattended in his carriage on the lawn, the carriage overturned and he was smothered in the blankets. A fourth son, William Bradford II, was born in 1912. Nellie Ross was not, according to her own account, "militantly or aggressively identified . . . with public affairs." Still, she was involved in the community. In addition to activities in her church and the Boy Scouts, she became a member of the elite Cheyenne Woman's Club. In later years, she deplored its exclusivity—at the time of her election there were only 25 members—but she admitted that its demands on members to prepare and present as many as three lengthy papers every year on the history, literature, art, philosophy and religion of many different countries gave her the sort of training in public speaking that men might have received in county boards, municipal councils, and legislative halls. Her husband discussed many of his cases with her, and listened to her criticisms with respect. In the evenings, since their three active boys made it hard to find "any person brave enough" to care for them at night, the couple entertained themselves by reading aloud to each other, which Ross later credited with strengthening her voice for public speaking. She also thought that the experience of meeting the constant demands of babies transformed her into a useful and self-reliant person. Despite her later accomplishments, she believed that women found greatest happiness and fulfillment in the role of wife and mother.

Although the Democratic Party was in the minority in Wyoming at the turn of the century, William Bradford Ross was elected county attorney in 1904, after winning a well-publicized case against local officials who would not enforce recently enacted laws against gambling. After his return to private life, Nellie hoped he would not be drawn into politics again, and he agreed that holding public office might jeopardize the practice he was building. In 1922, however, the Democrats urged William to run for the governorship, and Nellie did not thwart his ambition. A split in the Republican Party resulted in his victory. In addition to her responsibilities as Wyoming's first lady for official entertaining, Nellie Ross continued to discuss her husband's business with him. They traveled together on official trips, and she helped him write his speeches. On Labor Day, 1924, he asked her to help him compose a short proclamation, after his secretary proved unequal to the task. He thought so

Nellie Tayloe Ross

highly of her assistance that afterwards he joked · about writing a letter of recommendation to attach to his will.

Shortly afterwards, following an operation on September 24, Governor Ross unexpectedly developed septic phlebitis and died on October 2. A special election was called to fill the vacancy for the two remaining years of his four-year term. The State Democratic Committee urged Nellie Ross to run, and nominated her despite her reluctance to do so. Finally she consented and filed. Although concerned that she might not have the physical stamina to do the job, she was eager to see her husband's unfinished work completed, and to find work which would absorb her. She did not doubt her ability to do the job, believing that she understood her husband's program better than anyone else. She also admitted to having been influenced by the rumor that the state might offer her a pension, since she "recoiled" from the idea of an unearned "gratuity."

Nellie Ross did not campaign during the short time which remained, but she released two letters to the public. In one, she promised to do all she could to implement her husband's agenda; in the other, she assured women voters that she would do her utmost to give no one cause to say that women should not hold high executive office. Her opponent Eugene Sullivan was handicapped by ties to the oil industry while public indignation was still raw from the Teapot Dome scandal. Ross believed that many who voted for her wished to pay tribute to her husband by supporting her. Woman suffrage had been granted first in the Wyoming Territory, in 1869; now, over 50 years later, the state of Wyoming elected the first woman governor. She was, it was said, the first governor ever inaugurated in a hat, and stylish hats became her trademark.

Nellie Tayloe Ross became the first woman governor only by a narrow margin; another woman, *Miriam A. "Ma" Ferguson, was elected in Texas on the same day, but inaugurated two weeks after Ross. There was, however, an important difference between them: Ferguson was running for a seat vacated by her husband James who was impeached in 1917 and barred from holding state office. His supporters had elected his wife supposing that she would be merely his proxy. Governor Ross, as a widow, was entirely responsible for her own administration.

Because she had been so familiar with her husband's work, Ross was not particularly daunted by the challenges. When pondering difficult questions in the governor's office with its restful atmosphere of dark rich furniture and soft blue upholstery, she said, "the thought often occurred to me that probably none of those other governors, looking down at me from the walls above, knew at first any more about such matters than I did, and they, like me, just had to investigate and learn."

Nellie Ross faced formidable challenges. The only Democrat in any elective office in the state house, she faced a Republican legislature and a Republican majority on the boards that conducted much of the state's business. Some speculated that she might dismiss all her male employees and pardon all convicted felons. The press, too, was far from friendly; on one occasion, when the road she was traveling to the western border of the state crossed into Idaho for a few miles, a local paper reported that during her absence from the state, the acting governor would be in charge. Not surprisingly, her proposals—for tax relief for farmers and legislation to require county, school board, and state councils to publish budgets before levying taxes—were defeated.

Ross realized that the hostile legislature not only sought to challenge her, they felt confident that because she was a woman, they would prevail. She successfully fought against amendments to a banking reform law that would have curtailed the governor's prerogatives and compromised the effect of the reform. On another occasion, a law creating a new office was held up because the legislature did not approve of the governor's likely choice to fill it. They promised to pass the bill if she would promise not to appoint him. "The governor is not bargaining with the legislature," she replied. The bill passed. She also dismissed a sheriff from office because of violation of the Prohibition laws. Her adherence to principle in these cases would later cost her crucial votes in the next election.

Another political liability was incurred when she vetoed a bill calling for a special election in the event of a Wyoming vacancy in the U.S. Senate, arguing that a special election would be too costly. Wyoming's octogenarian senator, Francis E. Warren, had just been elected to a sixth term. Her political rivals were fearful that he might die, and she would appoint a Catholic advisor during a time when the Ku Klux Klan had influence in Wyoming politics. During the campaign, they contended that a "vote for the woman Governor is a vote for a Democratic Senator." In a predominantly Republican state, it proved a compelling argument.

Almost as trying as partisan rivalry was the intense scrutiny she endured as a "Lady Governor." Motion-picture directors wanted to film her making bread. Character readers analyzed her photographs. Strangers wishing to visit her at home became angry when turned away, even when she was ill.

In her 1926 reelection campaign, Governor Ross ran on her record, forbidding any negative campaigning or use of any paid workers. She made no attempt to appeal to women voters as such, merely challenging her opponents to point to a single act where she had failed because she was a woman. Though no such accusation was made, the Republican nominee, Frank C. Emerson, simply repeated again and again that the governorship was no place for a woman. She lost by less than 1,300 votes in an election in which other Democratic candidates were defeated by far larger margins. Afterwards, observing that the change of a single vote in each precinct would have secured her reelection, Ross believed she should have organized the state's women.

There are no leisure moments in the life of a woman governor, but neither are there any dull ones.

—Nellie Tayloe Ross

Ross took this observation into her next job, when she became vice-chair of the Democratic National Committee in 1928. She seconded the nomination of Alfred E. Smith at the national convention that year, seeing hope for his election in the "great masses of people who have not surrendered utterly to materialism, but who are still jealous for the spiritual welfare of the nation." She campaigned for him throughout the fall, working closely with *Eleanor Roosevelt. Ross insisted that a "dry" like herself could still support the governor of a state which had repealed its Prohibition enforcement laws, and that a Protestant could support a Catholic to reaffirm freedom of conscience.

She continued to organize women voters from a Washington, D.C., office during the next four years, encouraged that the Democratic Party seemed to consider that "women are not voters merely, but co-workers with men." She hoped that women would join parties because of ideological reasons, rather than family tradition. "If universal suffrage is to mean only an increased number of votes . . . directed by masculine opinion," she said, "it will mean only a duplication of votes and not a contribution to the . . . advancement of the country." Through speeches and journal articles, she urged the election of Democrats to Congress in 1930. In 1932, she undertook a nationwide speaking tour on behalf of the Democratic presidential candidate, Franklin Delano Roosevelt.

Pointing out that the Republican administrations throughout the 1920s had appointed few women to important posts, she urged the Democrats to improve on that record, and collaborated with *Molly Dewson, Eleanor Roosevelt and others to help them do so. Franklin Roosevelt appointed Nellie Tayloe Ross director of the Mint, where she supervised the manufacture of all coins and was responsible for the safekeeping of the government's stocks of gold and silver. She took office on May 3, 1933, and served for the next 20 years. "The business of the mint is different from any other business," she discovered. "There is real romance in it."

The Mint's activities had been limited because of the Depression, but as new monetary laws were enacted, her small staff was severely stressed. When business improved during the following year, the demand for coin increased activities, and, by 1940, the Mints were operating 24 hours a day, every day. Staff, working and storage space, and machinery were added, and three new Mint depositories were constructed. In 1940, Ross was appointed to head the Treasury Assay Committee to randomly test coins minted during the previous year. In addition to being the first woman director of the Mint, Ross was the first woman to have her likeness on a Mint medal, and the first to have her name on the cornerstone of a government building.

Although she had resigned her position on the Democratic National Committee to accept her appointment to the Mint, Ross took a temporary leave of absence from her official post to work full-time on the 1936 campaign. She served as an alternate on the platform committee, as did several other New Deal women, and their ideas on child labor, consumer interests, housing, education, civil liberties, and world peace made their way into the platform. In 1940, the Hatch Act, passed the previous year, limited political activity by government workers, much to Ross' chagrin.

Reappointed to another five-year term in 1938, and again in 1943, Ross was faced with new challenges during the war years, which saw an increased demand for coins for vending machines and jukeboxes, as well as for cash-and-carry stores and excise taxes. Spiraling pressure on the coin supply and metal shortages led her to issue the controversial zinc-coated penny. By the time she retired in 1953, she had supervised the coinage of two-thirds of the Mint's production since it was founded in 1792. After leaving office, the woman who had never gone on a public platform before her husband's death continued

to be in demand as a speaker and, in 1969, boasted that she had "lectured in every state in the Union, in many of them repeatedly." At the centennial celebration of Yellowstone Park, Ross, in her 90s, delivered a memorable address.

Although Nellie Tayloe Ross had always given her age as "over twenty-one," she allowed her 100th birthday to be celebrated along with the Bicentennial of the American Revolution. She died in Washington, D.C., the following year. Although she was 48 before she assumed public office, she had demonstrated that women, given the opportunity, could rise to the occasion. "I have never contended that women are *better* fitted than men for political life," she wrote, "but surely there is no basis for belief that they are *less* so."

SOURCES:

Brown, Mabel E., ed. *First Ladies of Wyoming 1869–1990*. The Wyoming Commission for Women, 1990.

Ross, Nellie Tayloe. "The Governor Lady: Nellie Tayloe Ross," in *Good Housekeeping*. August 1927, p. 30; September 1927, p. 36; October 1927, p.72.

Ware, Susan. *Beyond Suffrage: Women in the New Deal*. Cambridge, MA: Harvard University Press, 1981.

SUGGESTED READING:

Roosevelt, Eleanor, and *Lorena Hickok. *Ladies of Courage*. NY: Putnam, 1954.

COLLECTIONS:

Ross papers are at the University of Wyoming in Laramie and additional official records are at the Wyoming State Archives in Cheyenne. Information on her public career can be found at the Franklin D. Roosevelt Library and the Harry S. Truman Library, as well as in the Joseph C. Mahoney papers at the University of Wyoming.

Kristie Miller,
author of *Ruth Hanna McCormick: A Life in Politics 1880–1944*
(University of New Mexico Press, 1992)

Ross, Violet Florence (1862–1915).

See Somerville and Ross.

Rossetti, Christina (1830–1894)

Celebrated Victorian poet who first drew public attention to the Pre-Raphaelite movement. Name variations: (pseudonym) Ellen Alleyne. Born Christina Rossetti in London, England, on December 5, 1830; died of cancer at her residence in London on December 29, 1894; buried at Highgate Cemetery; daughter of Gabriele Rossetti (an Italian refugee and later professor of Italian at King's College, London) and Lavinia Polidori Rossetti; sister of ❧ Maria Francesca Rossetti (1827–1876), Dante Gabriel Rossetti (1828–1882), the famous painter and poet, and William Michael Rossetti (1829–1906), a civil servant and for some time the mainstay of the family; never married; no children.

Enjoyed the same educational advantages as her siblings; at an early age, was encouraged to mix freely with adults—a rarity in Victorian families of the time; remained unmarried, despite two engagements: James Collinson (1848) and Charles Bagot Cayley (1866); suffered from a mysterious malady, exophthalmic bronchocele (1871–73), and remained an invalid the rest of her life.

Poetic works: Goblin Market and other poems *(1862);* The Prince's Progress *(1866);* Sing-Song *(nursery rhymes, 1872);* A Pageant *(1881);* New Poems *(unpublished poems collected by her brother William and printed after her death in 1896).*

Works of religious edification: Speaking likenesses *(1874);* Seek and Find *(1879);* Called to be Saints; Letter and Spirit *(1882);* Time Flies: a Reading Diary *(1885);* The Face of the Deep *(1892);* Verses *(1893).*

Like many female writers and artists in the past, Christina Rossetti suffered from the belief that she was intruding into what was essentially thought of as a male world. This was compounded by the fact that her brilliant, but perhaps cossetted brother, Dante Gabriel Rossetti, was a leading founder of what came to be known as the Pre-Raphaelite brotherhood. This was a circle of young men—Ford Madox Brown, Thomas Woolner, Holman Hunt, and Sir John Everett Millais—resolved to abandon the conventionalities inherited from the 18th century, and to revive the detailed elaboration and mystical interpretation of nature that characterized medieval art. Inevitably, when people thought of *Rossetti,* they thought of Dante Gabriel (though to be fair, he always encouraged his sister's poetic work), and this was to last throughout Christina's lifetime, and for many years thereafter.

Though some critics would disagree with Ford Madox Ford, grandson of Madox Brown, that Christina was "the most valuable poet that the Victorian Age produced" (indeed, when he made this statement in 1911, many readers thought it lunatic), posterity has awarded her her due and has taken some of the more exalted Victorian writers, such as Alfred, Lord Tennyson, Robert Browning, Matthew Arnold, and Algernon Swinburne, down a peg. As the critic C.H. Sisson explains, "The simplicity and directness of her language, the intimate fall of her rhymes, make her immediately accessible in a way that the more oversized figures are not."

Born in London in 1830, Christina Rossetti was the youngest of four children who appeared one after another in the space of four years. Her father Gabriele Rossetti arrived in London as a

Rossetti, Maria Francesca (1827–1876)

English author. Born in 1827; died in 1876; daughter of Gabriele Rossetti (an Italian refugee and later professor of Italian at King's College, London) and **Lavinia Polidori**; *sister of* *Christina Rossetti *(1830–1894), Dante Gabriel Rossetti (1828–1882), and William Michael Rossetti (1829–1906).*

Maria Francesca Rossetti wrote *A Shadow of Dante* (1870). In 1874, age 47, she became an Anglican nun.

refugee from the French-controlled Kingdom of Naples in 1824. He was the son of a blacksmith and locksmith, and had become in turn an official operatic librettist and the custodian of ancient bronzes in the Naples Museum. But he dabbled too much in politics for the likings of the Bourbon kings and hence took refuge in England. As well as becoming professor of Italian at King's College, London, Gabriele also published patriotic verse which was subsequently banned in Italy—thus earning him something of a reputation as a revolutionary. In 1826, he married **Lavinia Polidori**, daughter of Gaetano Polidori, who had at one time been secretary to the poet Alfieri, and had witnessed the fall of the Bastille in 1789 before crossing to England to teach Italian. He too was a writer and established a small printing press in London.

Christina thus grew up in a family circle both literary and intellectual—if not particularly well off. A constant stream of Italian exiles visited her father's house, and, as the children were fluent in the language (Christina was to later write some of her verse in Italian), they were able to take part in political, artistic, and literary conversations with this flashy circle. But Christina did not develop, as one perhaps might have expected, into a sociable and expansive woman. Even when she later mixed intimately with the Pre-Raphaelite brotherhood, she maintained that sense of reserve and isolation that was to characterize so many of her poems. As Ford Madox Ford later wrote, "While her arty brother and his friends were intent on amazing the world," Christina sat "up in the fireless top back bedroom on the corner of the cracked washstand," writing "on the back of old letters."

This sense of isolation can partly be explained by the fact that Christina was profoundly religious by temperament. As a member of a family of ardent Italian patriots, she could hardly become a Catholic (the pope was firmly against any idea of Italian unification). But her devotion assumed a high Anglican character, and she found much congenial occupation in church work and the composition of books of religious edification—particularly in the latter part of her life.

This religious absorption had the unfortunate result of causing an estrangement between herself and a suitor to whom she was deeply attached. James Collinson was a painter with connections with the Pre-Raphaelite brotherhood. In 1850, Dante Gabriele introduced him to his sister, and Christina seems to have fallen in love with him. Collinson, however, had converted from Anglicanism to Catholicism, and Christina refused his proposal of marriage. But when Collinson became an Anglican again, she accepted him. Then, this "right meaning man, of timorous conscience" as William Rossetti described him, once more became a Catholic; this was the last straw as far as Christina was concerned. The renunciation of her lover was a blow from which Christina Rossetti never fully recovered; it accounts for the melancholy and morbid character of much of her poetry. A further suitor appeared in 1866—a scholar called Charles Bagot Cayley. Again, religion interposed to bring the affair to nought. Cayley was an agnostic, an outlook that was anathema to Rossetti.

> *Christina Rossetti seems . . . to be the most valuable poet that the Victorian age produced.*
>
> —Ford Madox Ford

There is no doubt that in her youth Christina was both vivacious and witty, as evidenced by a prose piece she wrote as an adolescent, "Maude, a Story for Girls." Clearly a self-portrait, the narrative occasionally reveals the young Christina. In one scene where Maude writes a melancholy sonnet beginning, "Yes, I too could face death and never shrink," the heroine then "yawned, leaned back in her chair, and wondered how she could fill her time till dinner." Although Christina remained lively and witty in her conversation throughout her life, the experience of her unhappy love affairs undoubtedly accentuated a disposition to self-denial and renunciation, which was to become an ordinary habit of mind. The first four lines of the poem "L.E.L" sum up the adult Rossetti:

> Downstairs I laugh, I sport and jest with all;
> But in my solitary room above
> I turn my face in silence to the wall;
> My heart is breaking for a little love.

And again in "The Prince's Progress," she expresses the agony of hopeless love and chances missed:

> Too late for love, too late for joy,
> Too late, too late!

> You loitered on the road too long,
> You trifled at the gate.

It is interesting to speculate how Christina's life and her work might have changed had she accompanied *Florence Nightingale to the Crimea in 1855, as was at one time proposed. The distressed circumstances of her family, however, caused by the death of her beloved Polidori grandparents in 1853 and the disabling illness which afflicted her father, necessitated her remaining in England. Her outward life was thus to remain quiet and uneventful even by 19th-century standards.

The first recorded verses Rossetti composed, and dictated when she was too young to write, are reputed to have been: "Cecilia never went to school/ Without her Gladiator." The first known written record is a poem written for her mother's birthday when Christina was 12, and printed by her grandfather, Gaetano Polidori, at his private press. A little volume of verse was privately printed in the same manner in 1847. A few years later, when her brother, Dante Gabriel, and his Pre-Raphaelite friends founded a literary journal called *The Germ*, Christina, though only 19, contributed several poems of great beauty, under the pseudonym Ellen Alleyne.

In 1862, her first published volume *Goblin Market and Other Poems* was printed (with a frontispiece in black-and-white by Dante Gabriel). It contains some of her best work, and indeed many critics believe that Christina attained a height which she never reached again. The title poem was the first Pre-Raphaelite writing to catch the imagination of the reading public; thus this quiet, introspective young woman stole a march on her more well-known poetic colleagues (Swinburne's *Atalanta in Calydon* was published in 1865, and Dante Gabriel's *The Blessed Damozel* not until 1870). The poem is highly original in conception, style, and structure. Some critics consider it to be as imaginative as Coleridge's *Ancient Mariner* and comparable only to Shakespeare for the insight shown into "unhuman but spiritual natures." Moreover, "it has," as the critic David Wright says, "a vitality and sensuousness allied to simplicity, clearness, and intellectual coherence, in notable contrast to the lushness of most of the poetry of the period." *Goblin Market* has often passed for a poem for children, a tribute to its immediacy and the dancing lilt of the rhymes:

> Morning and evening
> Maids hear the Goblins cry
> "Come buy our orchard fruits,
> Come buy, come buy."

Christina
Rossetti

But as a fairy tale of temptation and devotion, it contains strong religious and sexual undertones.

Other poems in this first volume also contain great power and beauty. "Up-hill" expresses a world-weariness and religious stoicism which must have been a theme familiar to the reader of 1862. But its simplicity of language was new:

> Does the road wind up-hill all the way?
> Yes, to the very end.
> Will the day's journey take the whole long day?
> From morn to night, my friend.

In "In The Round Tower at Jhansi," Rossetti finds a theme dear to her heart. It is the story of a true incident which took place during the Indian Mutiny (1857–1858), and tells of a young couple preparing to commit suicide rather than be torn to pieces by "The swarming howling wretches below":

> Kiss and kiss: "It is not pain
> Thus to kiss and die.
> One kiss more."—"And yet one again."—
> "Good-bye."—"Goodbye."

Goblin Market and Other Poems was unsurpassed by Rossetti's later volumes of poetry—*The Prince's Progress* (1866) and *A Pageant* (1881)—but like the first volume, both contain lyrical poems of great beauty. In the title poem of *The Prince's Progress*, Dante Gabriel's hand can be seen at work. Christina wrote the last 60 lines of what was to become a 500-line poem in a single day in 1861. Four years later, at her brother's behest, she wrote the long narrative, allegorical lines to precede the original verses. This was a departure from the lyrical style in which Rossetti excelled, and consequently the end result lacks the spontaneity of *Goblin Market* (she did, however, resist her brother's suggestion that she should include a tournament in it, in the best Victorian tradition).

In "Memory" from the 1866 volume, Rossetti writes again about the renunciation of her lovers. Her style is one of controlled passion yet simplicity:

> I shut the door to face the naked truth,
> I stood alone—I faced the truth alone.

and later:

> None know the choice I made; I make it still.
> None know the choice I made and broke my
> heart,
> Breaking mine idol: I have braced my will
> Once, chosen for once my part.

In other poems from these two volumes, particularly when nature and art combine, the result is exquisite. "A Birthday" sees Rossetti in an exalted mood:

> My heart is like a singing bird
> Whose nest is in a watered shoot:
> My heart is like an apple-tree
> Whose boughs are bent with thickest fruit.

"An Apple Gathering" returns to the more melancholy theme of love that never bears fruit, using the plucking of apple blossom as a simile (once plucked, no apples will appear):

> I plucked pink blossoms from mine apple tree
> And wore them all evening in my hair

> Then in due season when I went to see
> I found no apples there.

Rossetti's feelings are conveyed so intensely that even her less important lyrics contain some touch of genius. Her nursery rhymes (*Sing-Song*, 1872), though not comparable to true nursery rhymes handed down through the ages, show a certain deftness:

> Who has seen the wind?
> Neither you nor I:
> But when the trees bow down their heads
> The wind is passing by

As she grew older and her health failed, Rossetti increasingly devoted herself to religious writing. Where poems do appear, as in *Called to be Saints* (1881) and *Time Flies* (1885), they are merely adjuncts to a course of devotional reading. Though almost unreadable to the modern scholar, they were popular in their day, and contain nothing of the sentimental moralism which afflicted so much of Victorian religious writing. Her Christmas carol, "In the bleak mid-winter," is still a favorite among Christian communities throughout the world.

Christina Rossetti died of cancer on December 29, 1894, in Torrington Square, London, after a long illness. In 1896, her unpublished poems, gleaned from many periodicals, were published by her surviving brother William, who included a short introduction of her life. Rossetti's reputation rests on the fact that her verse contributed significantly to the direction in which the poetry of the 20th century was to move. But she will perhaps be best remembered and appreciated for the searing directness, integrity, and lyricism of her poetry.

SOURCES:

Breen, Jennifer. *Victorian Women Poets.* Everyman, 1994.

The Complete poems of Christina Rossetti. Lousiana State University Press, 1979.

Leighton, Angela. *Victorian Women Poets: A Critical Reader.* Blackwell, 1996.

MacBeth, George. *Victorian Verse.* Penguin, 1986.

Marsh, Jan. *Christina Rossetti: Poems and Prose.* Everyman, 1994.

Sisson, C.H. *Christina Rossetti.* Carcanet Press, 1984.

SUGGESTED READING:

Christina Rossetti: The Illustrated Poets. Oxford University Press.

Faxon, Alicia Craig. *Dante Gabriel Rossetti.* Abbeville Press, 1989.

Ricks, Christopher. *The New Oxford Book of Victorian Verse.* Oxford University Press, 1990.

Thomas, Frances. *Christina Rossetti: A Biography.* London, UK: Virago, 1994.

Christopher Gibb,
freelance writer and editor
and Oxford University scholar, London, England

Rossetti, Mrs. Dante Gabriel

(1829–1862).

See Siddal, Elizabeth.

Rossetti, Elizabeth (1829–1862).

See Siddal, Elizabeth.

Rossetti, Maria Francesca (1827–1876).

See Rossetti, Christina for sidebar.

Rossi, Countess de or di.

See Sontag, Henriette (c. 1803–1854).

Rossi, Properzia de (c. 1490–1530)

Italian sculptor. Name variations: Properzia de' Rossi; Properzia di Rossi. Born around 1490 in Bologna, Italy; died in 1530 in Bologna.

Properzia de Rossi, a famous Italian sculptor, lived in Bologna, a city which produced many talented women artists at the end of the Middle Ages. Medieval values and social structures were giving way to a renascence of classical art and a focus on the individual. Properzia was born around 1490, into a wealthy if not noble family, about a year after the return of her father from the galleys, where he had passed 18 years, having been condemned for manslaughter.

She was instructed in drawing and painting by Marc Antonio Raimondi, but showed the most aptitude and love for sculpture and carving. As a young woman, she created works praised widely for their beauty; around 1520, she began accepting public commissions. She first devoted herself to *intaglios* (definition) so minute as to require extraordinary delicacy of handling and enormous patience. She carved a glory of saints on a cherry-stone, upon which 60 heads could be counted, which now reposes in the cabinet of gems at the Uffizi. Other microscopic works executed for Count Camillo Grassi are preserved by his descendants in the Palazzo Manili. Rossi next turned to arabesques, marble ornaments, lions, griffins, vases, eagles, and heads. She modeled the bust of Count Guido Pepoli now in the sacristy of the basilica of St. Petronius. She was employed to assist in finishing the reliefs about the portal which Giacomo della Quercia had left unfinished. She also executed two bas-reliefs now in the St. Petronius sacristy, which represent *Joseph and Potiphar's Wife* and *Solomon receiving the Queen of *Sheba*. Her later works seem to have been influenced by her contact with Il Tribolo.

Properzia benefited from a new cultural emphasis on the education of women, but despite her capabilities, the men she competed with consistently maintained that women artists like Properzia were incapable of invention and of genius, and that public commissions (i.e., highly paid, visible works) should be reserved for those capable of ingenious creations (i.e., male artists). The increasing freedoms and individual fame male artists enjoyed did not extend to their female counterparts, who were judged as much, if not more, for their "deportment" and ladylike behavior as for their paintings, statues, and other works. (It is written that Properzia had a temper like her father's and was twice arraigned in court for displaying it.)

Nevertheless, Properzia continued sculpting. When Pope Clement VII visited Bologna in 1530, he desired to see her, but she had died a few days before, around age 40. Her lover, Antonio Galeazzo Malvasia de' Bottigari, would not marry for many years thereafter. Properzia de Rossi was greatly admired by the people of Bologna, if envied and put down by male artists for overstepping the bounds of femininity by her success.

SOURCES:

Anderson, Bonnie S., and Judith P. Zinsser. *A History of Their Own, vol. I.* NY: Harper & Row, 1988.

Chadwick, Whitney. *Women, Art and Society.* London: Thames & Hudson, 1990.

Clement, Clara Erskine. *Painters, Sculptors, Architects, Engravers, and Their Works.* Hurd & Houghton, 1874.

Laura York, M.A. in History, University of California, Riverside, California

Rossianka (1744–1810).

See Dashkova, Ekaterina.

Rostopchina, Evdokiya

(1811–1858)

Russian poet, author, and host to one of Russia's most active 19th-century literary salons. Name variations: Evdokia or Evdokiia Rostopchina; Countess Rostopchina. Born Evdokiya Petrovna Sushkova in Moscow on December 23, 1811; died on December 3, 1858; her mother died while Evdokiya was still young, and her father, due to his civil service, was frequently absent; married Count Andrei Rostopchin (a conservative aristocrat), in 1833.

Evdokiya Rostopchina was a Russian poet, author, and host to one of Russia's most active 19th-century literary salons. Countess Rostopchina gained renown throughout Russia because of her intellect, her well-respected poetry, and her salon which was visited by all of the major literary personages of the era. Her principal literary legacy is her poetry, and although it has not received ample critical attention since her own day, the poetry possesses considerable merit. By any account, Rostopchina herself remains a significant component of the intellectual and literary history of Russian Romanticism of the 1830s and 1840s.

Evdokiya Petrovna Sushkova was born in Moscow on December 23, 1811, shortly before its evacuation during the war with Napoleon. Her mother died while Evdokiya was still young, and her father, due to his civil service, was frequently absent during her childhood. Consequently, the young Sushkova was raised primarily by her maternal grandparents. According to her brother, her childhood was not particularly happy due to her mother's early death and to her general isolation. However, she clearly found reward in her education. Her family provided her with a governess and the standard domestic education of a young aristocratic girl: lessons in languages, literature, history, geography, and piano. Her passionate interests in languages and literature motivated tireless study and reading, even during her adolescence. She learned French as a natural consequence of being a member of the Russian gentry, and German was included in her education. This passion would continue throughout her life, leading her to independent study of English and Italian. Her love for literature led her to exhaustive reading of the family library, and her own poetic endeavors apparently started at a early age. While still young, she met several established Russian poets, and the assistance of Prince Pyotr Vyazemskii and Baron Anton Delvig led to Sushkova's first major publication, the lyric "Talisman," in 1831.

Sushkova matured into a debutante of Moscovite aristocratic society. In 1833, she married Count Andrei Rostopchin, a conservative aristocrat of high social standing. All contemporary accounts of the marriage indicate that the new Countess Rostopchina (Russian family names add the feminine ending of "a") had little attachment to her husband. Count Rostopchin was considered a "good match" for the well-educated and socially graceful Sushkova. The couple first lived in a Rostopchin country estate and then moved to St. Petersburg in 1836.

Although not necessarily rewarded by her marriage, Rostopchina flourished during the 1830s in terms of social interaction and literary involvement. The congenial Rostopchina developed relationships with all of the literary and artistic luminaries of the age. Aleksander

Pushkin, Mikhail Lermontov, and Nikolai Gogol—the two principal poets and the principal prose writer of Russia in the 1830s—were regular guests and correspondents, and Rostopchina was among the last members of St. Petersburg society to see Pushkin before his death in a duel in 1837. Similarly, Lermontov stayed with Rostopchina during his last visit to St. Petersburg in 1841. The list of her associations encompasses virtually every noted personage of Russian society during the period. Rostopchina's best-remembered activity of the 1830s was her creation of one of the most active literary salons in Russian society. Indeed, she soon acquired such respect and status that appearances in her salon came to be career accomplishments for emerging, aspiring poets and writers. The salon also received virtuoso musicians, including the international celebrity Franz Liszt.

Rostopchina was herself active in literary endeavors, primarily lyric poetry. Among the principal contexts for literary exchange during Russian Romanticism were readings given at salons, such as Rostopchina's own, and the interchange of so-called "album verse" (individuals possessed a personal "album" in which others would write poetic entries). Rostopchina was quite active in both these areas. She also composed verse of a more serious nature and published a number of lyrics in preeminent literary journals. In 1839, she released a book containing two of her more noted prose tales, "Rank and Money" and "The Duel," and her first verse collection was compiled and released in early 1841. She would continue to compose verse for the rest of her life, publishing primarily in journals.

In 1845, the Rostopchin family went abroad and spent two years in Poland, Germany, France, and Evdokiya's beloved Italy. Upon their return to Russia, they went to Moscow, and Rostopchina would spend almost all of her remaining years either in Moscow or in the Rostopchin country estate outside the city. The late 1840s and the 1850s were fruitful years for the tireless author and poet. She quickly reestablished her custom of hosting "literary evenings," and in Moscow, as in St. Petersburg, Rostopchina attracted all of the established and emerging literary personalities of the day. During this period, the countess composed a number of her longer works: the drama in blank verse, "The Woman Recluse," in 1849; the novel in verse *The Poetry and Prose of Life: The Diary of a Young Woman* and several prose novels during the 1850s; and several more society tales. Moreover, her production of lyric verse from this time includes some of her most remembered pieces and two of the more controversial ones: "A Marriage by Force" in 1845, which aroused imperial censure due to its political subtexts concerning the Russian control of Poland, and "To My Critics" in 1856, which responded to assaults by political-ideological literary critics who were gradually assuming editorial control over the journals. Regardless of politically or socially motivated criticism, most rigorous critics, poets, and authors responded warmly to Rostopchina's oeuvre, and especially to her poetry.

Rostopchina's evolving political perspectives bear mention in her biography, for she was a significant and especially paradoxical influence on the view of social issues within the Russian literary community. Nineteenth-century Russian intellectual life, particularly during the 1840s, experienced the debate between what were then known as the "Slavophiles" and the "Westernizers." Most individuals, other than the most ideologically strident advocates, did not pledge slavish adherence to one group or the other, and Rostopchina warmly received both Slavophiles and Westernizers into her salon. As for her own perspectives, she has been regarded both as a Western-leaning figure and as a political and social conservative. She was certainly concerned with a woman's opportunities to participate in the literary community, and conservative criticism, saying that a woman should not (or could not) write poetry, was not an uncommon response to Rostopchina's compositions. Her advocacy of "womanhood" and her vision of "how women should write" (the title of one of her compositions) led her to be called the "Russian *George Sand." The title is, however, somewhat misleading, for Rostopchina's vision of the feminine was far more aesthetic and largely unpolitical. She, like most male poets of her day, saw "the Muse" and "Beauty" as feminine quantities, and as such certain inspirations and observations on beauty were accessible singularly to women. Her most politically charged observation on women concerned a woman's role in the beau monde, and as one who valued her privacy and often wrote of female withdrawal from society, Rostopchina was not favorably disposed to the social edicts which constricted a woman's pursuit of solitude.

If such attitudes bespeak a Western-oriented perspective, other aspects of Rostopchina's life point in quite the opposite direction. The countess was a Russian patriot, albeit a Russian patriot who loved to go abroad. Her social attitudes and her perspectives on the power of artistic beauty were perhaps firmly in tune with the Romantic spirit of the 1830s, but by the rise of the

utilitarian and "democratic" critics in the 1850s, Rostopchina was seen as retrograde and perhaps even reactionary. These critics advocated equality of the sexes according to a pre-Marxist style of socialism and believed that literature, particularly literature dealing with women, should have a primarily political goal of achieving social change. Rostopchina, with her vision of beauty and her idea of the linkage between the feminine and the beautiful, rejected the notion of literature as social force and rejected this view of women. For her love of Russia and her rejection of such utilitarian literature and utilitarian social organization, Rostopchina frequently acquires the label of "conservative" in the 1850s. The label is perhaps appropriate insofar as she clung to her Romantic world view long after the decline of Romanticism. Yet it misleads the modern reader in light of the 20th-century political connotations associated with the word, and Rostopchina never displayed slavish adherence to the imperial Russian government or to conventional, aristocratic reactionary politics.

The last two years of Countess Rostopchina's life marked a period of gradual deterioration of her health and extended physical suffering borne with courage and good spirit. Despite the visibly evident pain, she still received visitors with her renowned warmth and hospitality, and she still worked regularly. Her last visitor of note, the French novelist Alexander Dumas, arrived in the fall of 1858 with a request for her reminiscences on Lermontov, and he observed both her poor health and her good cheer in his own notes on the meeting. Rostopchina fulfilled Dumas' request and added a translation of a Pushkin lyric into French. She accompanied the reminiscences with a poignant note saying that she would likely be dead by the time he received the material. In fact, she was right, and Evdokiya Rostopchina died on December 3, 1858.

Evdokiya Rostopchina contributed to Russian literature with her literary salons, her prose fiction, and her poetry. The significance of the literary salons should not be discounted, for such salons represented the venues of literary and intellectual exchange. Thus, in a manner of speaking, they constituted the geographical site of literary evolution and ferment. Furthermore, as a woman, Rostopchina—like the other significant woman belletrist of the age, *Karolina Pavlova—encountered resistance within the conventional literary society. That is, writing was often seen as an "inappropriate" activity for women of high society. The leading men of Russian literature largely did not share such an opinion, however, and reminiscences of Rostopchina uniformly express respect for the countess and testify to her insight and wit. As a salon host, Rostopchina acquired a reputation as a keen reader and listener, and her opinions exhibited an identifiable impact on the "spirit of the age."

Rostopchina's prose, while widely read during her lifetime, is not the strength of her literary corpus. Her poetically oriented literary mind does not translate well to prose, and these works often suffer from "over-stylized" and "over-written" prose and a cumbersome excess of description. The literary structures, moreover, rely heavily on Romantic conventions. In short, the works reflect the age and do not translate well beyond the Romantic context. Nevertheless, within that context, the prose and particularly the society tales exhibit a keen eye for satire. The most well-remembered tales—"Rank and Money," "The Duel," and "A Happy Woman"—comprise clever exposures of social vanities, empty pursuits, and aristocratic pride.

Rostopchina earned most of her praise for her poetry, and her verse is her primary literary legacy. Unfortunately, although numerous contemporary critics placed her among the premier poets of the late 1830s and the 1840s, her star faded quickly after her death. The socialist and utilitarian critics' condemnation led to the branding of Rostopchina as an aristocratic, salon poet, and this appellation placed her out of favor with the Marxist critics dominating the Soviet period. Nonetheless, Rostopchina composed a number of works esteemed by poets both of her day and of subsequent generations.

Her poetry is not of uniform quality, but certain pieces well deserve the esteem expressed by Pushkin and Lermontov. The stronger pieces emerge from her paradoxical persona, and they reflect a strong, passionate intellect grappling with troubling truths. The weaker pieces suffer from the same shortcomings apparent in her prose, and to the 20th-century reader, such works appear overstated and affected.

The paradoxes about Rostopchina are numerous: she loved her salon and her solitude; she was renowned for her good cheer but was said to have had an unhappy childhood and marriage; she was expressive but restrained. These qualities translate to her poetry, and thus it is characterized by the suggestion of passion without explicit statement, by a call for restraint and feeling, and so on. Perhaps the most interesting paradox lies in the fact that Rostopchina employs the implicitly "confessional" nature of lyric poetry—an illusion of internal reflection in a form intended for public reading—to express her need for privacy. Such is the case of her lyric "How Women Should Write." Here she describes the ideal "poetess" who feels deeply but who alludes to such feeling with restraint:

> Speech not completed with an understanding
>   smile
> Embellished with a warm tear;
> The inner impulse forged by the imagination,
> Decorum would struggle with enthusiasm,
> And wisdom guard every word.
> Yes! A woman's soul must shine in the shadow,
> Like a lamp's light in a marble urn,
> Like the moon at dusk through the cover of
>   storm-clouds;
> And warming life, unbeheld, glimmers.

Rostopchina frequently wrote poetry about poetic composition itself, and she often combined these contemplations of inspiration and creation with her notions of the feminine. This impulse produced a poetic credo whereby women poets, by virtue of being women, had something distinct to offer the literature; they viewed creation differently and indeed created according to different standards. In a poetic epistle to Vasili Zhukovski, a prominent male poet, she writes, "I am a woman! . . . in me thought and inspiration / should be bound together by gentle humility." In this same vein of poetry on poetry, the countess often composed contemplations expressing doubts about her poetic gifts, celebrations of her love of poetry, and reminiscences on her poetic career. More than once she reflected on her childhood spent with numerous poetry readings. By the 1850s, such lyrics assumed a more melancholy tone for she had become a personality out of place with changing literary tastes and standards. In her well-known "To My Critics," she observes:

> I have parted with the new generation,
> My path diverges from it;
> In understanding, spirit and conviction
> I belong to another world.
> I revere and invoke other gods
> And speak in a different tongue;
> I am a stranger to them, amusing, this I know,
> But I am not embarrassed before their judgment.

She continues the metaphor of "revering other gods," and the metaphor recollects the Romantic notion of poetry as divine communion. Yet in the age of socialism, utilitarianism, and pragmatic literature, the divine becomes nothing more than an outmoded convention, and the lyric concludes: "Unwisely, as a solitary priestess, / I stand before an empty altar!"

Countess Rostopchina concluded her 1841 collection of verse with the lyric "The Unfinished Sewing," and the work is based on a metaphor equating a woman sewing with Rostopchina's composition of verse. "The Unfinished Sewing" represents yet another example of poetry on poetry, but in this instance, Rostopchina appears to let us a bit further into her creative world—or at least she suggests that we press deeper beyond her poetic restraint, for beneath the understated exterior lies her "disburdened" soul:

So many sweet and lively memories
Return when I survey them,
So many feelings, meditations,
Were worked into this gaudy cloth,
As I disburdened here my soul!

The hour when woman sews her modest seam
Brings silence, peace, and space for sweet reflection;
Far from the worldly crowd, she's sunk in contemplation;
Enjoys a rest from parties, carriage rides;
Has respite from the world, from visitors, from strife;
Then she may read her soul, may gaze upon herself.
Full work-table to hand, she sits at her round frame,
And stitches rapidly, absorbed in what she sews.

SOURCES:

Kelly, Catriona, ed. *An Anthology of Russian Women's Writing.* Oxford: Oxford University Press, 1994.

Perkins, Pamela, and Albert Cook, eds. *The Burden of Sufferance: Women Poets of Russia.* NY: Garland, 1993.

Rostopchina, Evdokiya. "Rank and Money" (short story), in *Russian and Polish Women's Fiction.* Ed. and trans. by Helena Goscilo. Knoxville, TN: University of Tennessee Press, 1985.

Unfortunately, although several good collections of Rostopchina's literature exist in Russian, she has rarely been translated into English and has not attracted substantial English-language critical commentary. Works cited above appear in translation.

Andrew J. Swensen,
Western Michigan University,
Kalamazoo, Michigan

Roswitha (c. 935–1001).

See Hrotsvitha of Gandersheim.

Roth, Lillian (1910–1980)

American actress-singer whose life was portrayed in the movie I'll Cry Tomorrow. *Born Lillian Rutstein on December 13, 1910, in Boston, Massachusetts; died on May 10, 1980, in New York City; oldest daughter of Arthur Rutstein and Katie (Silverman) Rutstein (later changed to Roth); attended the Professional Children's School, New York City; married David Lyons (died); married William Scott (divorced); married Judge Benjamin Shalleck (divorced); married Eugene Weiner (divorced); married Edward Goldman (divorced); married Mark Harris (divorced); married Thomas Burt McGuire (divorced 1963); no children.*

Broadway plays: The Inner Man *(1917);* Penrod *(1918);* The Betrothed *(1918);* Shavings *(1920);* Artists and Models *(1923);* Padlocks of 1927 *(1927);* Harry Delmar's Revels *(1927);* Earl Carroll's Vanities of 1928 *(1928);* Midnight Frolics *(1929);* Earl Carroll's Vanities of 1931 *(1931);* Earl Carroll's Vanities of 1932 *(1932);* Revels of 1935 *(1934);* I Can Get It for You Wholesale *(1962);* 70 Girls 70 *(1971).*

Selected filmography: Pressing's Crusaders *(1918);* Illusion *(1929);* The Love Parade *(1929);* The Vagabond King *(1930);* Animal Crackers *(1930);* Sea Legs *(1930);* Paramount on Parade *(1930);* Madame Satan *(1930);* Honey *(1930);* Take a Chance *(1933);* Ladies They Talk About *(1933);* Alice, Sweet Alice (Communion, *1977);* Boardwalk (cameo, *1979).*

Actress-singer Lillian Roth is probably remembered more for her fall from grace than for her successful performing career, which included vaudeville, the Broadway stage, and early sound movies. As the result of personal problems and alcohol abuse, the former child star disappeared from the limelight in the 1930s, then made a modest comeback after the publication of her autobiography *I'll Cry Tomorrow* (1954), which was filmed a year later starring *Susan Hayward. Hayward was nominated for an Academy Award for her efforts. Rebuilding a career, however, was difficult for Roth, who was never able to recapture the glory of her early years.

Lillian Roth, who was named for *Lillian Russell, was born in Boston, Massachusetts, in 1910, the oldest of two daughters of Arthur Rutstein and **Katie Silverman Rutstein**, Russian immigrants who would change their name to Roth. When she was six, her mother took her and her sister Ann to Educational Pictures in New York, hoping to find work for them in the movies. Neither child was hired to act, although Lillian was drafted to pose for the company trademark, the statue of a child holding the lamp of knowledge. Katie Roth had better luck at Goldwyn Studios, then located in Fort Lee, New Jersey. There, the girls appeared primarily in bit parts and as extras. Meanwhile, Lillian also found employment on Broadway, making her debut in August 1917 in *The Inner Man*, as the daughter of Wilton Lackaye. Subsequently billed as "Broadway's Youngest Star," she went on to appear in *Penrod* and *The Betrothed* (both 1918), then signed with B.F. Keith to tour in vaudeville with her sister. During this period, Lillian introduced the songs "When the Red, Red Robin Comes Bob Bob Bobbin' Along" and "Ain't She Sweet," both of which went on to become standards.

As Roth approached adulthood, she continued in vaudeville and on Broadway, where she became a popular attraction in *Earl Carroll's Vanities* (1928, 1931, and 1932), and in Ziegfeld's *Midnight Frolics* (1929), among other shows. Her film career was launched with the advent of talkies, when the industry began looking for stage personalities who could sing as well as act. Roth made her movie debut in the musical short *Lillian Roth and Piano Boys* (1929), singing "Ain't She Sweet," then signed a contract with Paramount. Her first feature film was *Illusion* (1929), in which she appeared as herself and offered up a captivating rendition of the song "When the Real Thing Comes Your Way." Her first acting role of note was as Lulu the maid in *The Love Parade* (1929), with *Jeanette MacDonald** and Maurice Chevalier. As James Parish and Michael Pitts point out, most of Roth's film appearances were as a specialty act

rather than as an integrated part of the plot. In the Marx Brothers comedy *Animal Crackers* (1930), for example, in which she played the daughter of a rich hostess who is in love with an artist, the narrative goes on hold while she sings "Why Am I So Romantic?"

By 1930, Roth was beginning to tire of her film assignments and quit Paramount. Later, when offered a contract with Warner Bros., she turned it down, preferring to work in vaudeville. In the summer and fall of 1934, she also starred on her own radio program, "The Lillian Roth Show," on CBS.

It was during the 1930s that Roth's personal life seriously began to undermine her career. After the death of her first husband David Lyons, she started drinking. There followed a string of marriages and divorces throughout the decade, which only caused increasing emotional pain and fueled her alcoholism. While her film and Broadway career gradually slipped away, she was for a time able to pull herself together for occasional work in nightclubs and vaudeville, but by the 1940s, her health was seriously deteriorating, and she was finally convinced by doctors to enter a rehabilitation facility. She emerged in 1946, at which time her friend Milton Berle attempted to get her back to work, but she suffered several setbacks that made it difficult to reestablish her career.

In Alcoholics Anonymous, Roth met Thomas Burt McGuire, whom she married in 1947. McGuire took over managing her career, which began a slow turn-around with several nightclub bookings. Her comeback was further aided by her appearance on the Ralph Edwards television program "This Is Your Life," in 1953. As a result of response to the program, Roth, in collaboration with Mike Connolly and Gerold Frank, wrote her autobiography *I'll Cry Tomorrow*, which sold over a million copies and was eventually translated into 20 languages. The book, combined with the hit movie a year later, ignited renewed interest in Roth and created a slight surge in her career. She made several dramatic appearances on television, played in summer stock, and made two bestselling record albums, *I'll Cry Tomorrow* and *Lillian Roth Sings*. She published a second, less-successful autobiography, *Beyond My Worth*, in 1958, and in 1962 returned to Broadway in the musical *I Can Get It for You Wholesale*, which ran for 301 performances. However, the following year her marriage to McGuire ended, causing her to resume drinking and to lose the momentum she had gained.

In the late 1960s, Roth moved back to New York, where, between sporadic club dates and

*Lillian
Roth*

occasional appearances on the television talk-show circuit, she worked at various menial jobs to make ends meet. She did a final turn on Broadway in 1971, in the unsuccessful Kander and Ebb musical *70 Girls 70*, and had brief roles in the horror film *Alice, Sweet Alice* (1977) and in *Boardwalk* (1979). The singer-actress died in a nursing home on May 10, 1980, following a massive stroke.

SOURCES:

Katz, Ephraim. *The Film Encyclopedia*. NY: Harper-Collins, 1994.

Kinkle, Roger D. *The Complete Encyclopedia of Popular Music and Jazz 1900–1950*. Vol. 3. New Rochelle, NY: Arlington House, 1974.

Lamparski, Richard. *Whatever Became of . . . ?* 3rd series. NY: Crown, 1970.

Parish, James Robert, and Michael R. Pitts. *Hollywood Songsters*. NY: Garland, 1991.

Barbara Morgan,
Melrose, Massachusetts

Rothelin, Jacqueline de Rohan, Marquise de (c. 1520–1587)

French aristocrat jailed for sheltering Huguenots. Born around 1520; died in 1587; daughter of Charles de Rohan and Jeanne de Saint-Séverin; married François of Orleans-Longueville, marquis de Rothelin (died 1548); children: one son.

Jacqueline de Rohan, Marquise de Rothelin, the daughter of Charles de Rohan and **Jeanne de Saint-Séverin**, was born around 1520. Her husband, François of Orleans-Longueville, marquis de Rothelin, died in 1548. While watching out for her son's interests in Neuchâtel, she was brought into contact with religious reformers in Switzerland. Jacqueline, who embraced Protestantism, turned her château at Blandy, in Brie, into a refuge for Huguenots. In 1567, she was imprisoned for harboring Protestants.

Rothenberger, Anneliese (1924—)

German soprano. Born in Mannheim, Germany, on June 19, 1924; daughter of Joseph and Sophie (Haeffner) Rothenberger; studied with Erika Müller at the Mannheim Conservatory; married Gerd W. Dieberitz (a journalist), on July 1, 1954.

Debuted in Koblenz (1943), Hamburg State Opera (1946–56), Salzburg (1954), Metropolitan Opera debut (1960).

Anneliese Rothenberger created the title role in Sutermeister's *Madame Bovary* and Telemachus in Liebermann's *Penelope*. Other forays into modern opera included Hindemith's *Mathis der Maler*, Liebermann's *Die Schule der Frauen*, and Berg's atonal *Lulu*. She was also known as a specialist in Mozart and Strauss. With her career mainly concentrated at the Hamburg and Vienna Staatsoper, Rothenberger made numerous recordings of complete operas and operettas. She was also a skilled actress.

John Haag,
Athens, Georgia

Rothenburger-Luding, Christa (1959—)

East German cyclist and speedskater. Name variations: Christa Luding; Christa Luding-Rothenburger. Born Christa Rothenburger in Weisswasser, German Democratic Republic, on December 4, 1959; married Ernst Luding (a skating coach), in 1988.

Won a gold medal in the 500-meter speedskating race in the Olympic Games in Sarajevo (1984); was the World sprint-skating champion (1984, 1988); became World champion in the 1,000-meter speedskating race (1986); won a silver medal in the 500-meter speedskating race and a gold medal in the 1,000-meter race in the Olympic Games in Calgary (1988); won a silver medal in the 1,000-meter cycling race in the Olympic Games in Seoul (1988); became the first athlete to win medals in both the Summer and Winter Olympic Games in the same year (1988); won a bronze medal in the 500-meter speedskating race in the Winter Olympics in Albertville (1992).

Christa Rothenburger-Luding became known as an "athlete for all seasons," one of those rare people who competes at a world-class level in two different sports, winning impressive victories in both speedskating and bicycling. Her first sport was speedskating; but early in her training, her coach (and later husband) Ernst Luding pressed her to take up cycling during the off-season. Initially, she was not enthusiastic, later saying, "I was convinced that as soon as I tried to ride, I would undoubtedly topple right over," but her misgivings proved false. Since both sports require strength and speed, she took to cycling readily. After the East German Sports Federation finally granted her permission to do so, she began competing in both speedskating and cycling.

The 24-year-old East German athlete made an explosive entry onto the Olympic scene in 1984, when she won the 500-meter speedskating event at the Winter Games in Sarajevo with a time of 41.02 seconds. The 1984 World sprintskating champion became the World champion in the 1,000-meter speedskating event two years later—the same year she upset Estonian **Erika Salumae** at her first international cycling competition to take the gold medal. These victories were a preview to her stellar Olympic showing in 1988 when she skated to a gold medal in the 1,000-meter event at the Winter Olympics in Calgary, Canada. She narrowly missed earning a second gold medal in the 500-meter race when she came in second to American *Bonnie Blair by just two one-hundredths of a second.

The 1988 Summer Olympics in Seoul, Korea, provided Rothenburger-Luding with the unique opportunity to win gold medals in both the Summer and Winter Olympics. Only one other athlete had accomplished the feat: American boxer Eddie Eagan had won a gold medal in bobsledding 12 years after winning the gold in lightweight boxing in 1920. However, Rothenburger-Luding's rival, Salumae, was also competing in the women's cycling 1,000-meter sprint, which was on the Olympic program for the first time that year. After three days of competition, the only two women still in the running for the gold were Salumae, the world champion in 1987, and Rothenburger-Luding, the world champion in 1986, setting up a historic Olympic showdown. In the final heat of the 1,000-meter race, the pair battled to the finish. With just 200 meters to go, Rothenburger-Luding was in the lead, but Salumae edged forward until the two were even, wheel to wheel. Just before the finish line, Salumae pushed ahead and won by only a split second. Rothenburger-Luding was philosophical about the loss. "It was so close," she said. "After the final race I talked with my husband Ernst. We both agreed that the difference was only six inches at the finish." Despite coming in second, at age 28 Rothenburger-Luding became the first athlete ever to win medals at the Winter and Summer Olympics in the same year—an accomplishment that became impossible to equal after the two-year shift of the Winter Games in 1994 permanently split the Summer and Winter Games. She went on to win yet another medal at the 1992 Olympics in Albertville, France, taking the bronze in the 500-meter speedskating event.

SOURCES:
Grace & Glory: A Century of Women in the Olympics. Washington, DC: Multi-media Partners, 1996.
100 Greatest Moments in Olympic History. Los Angeles, CA: GPG, 1995.

Kelly Winters,
freelance writer, Bayville, New York

Rothhammer, Keena (1957—)

American swimmer. Born on February 26, 1957.

Keena Rothhammer won the gold medal in Munich in 1972 for the 800-meter freestyle with a world-record time of 8:53.68. *Shane Gould of Australia came in second and **Novella Calligaris** of Italy placed third. Rothhammer also won a bronze medal in Munich in the 200-meter freestyle.

Rothild (c. 871–c. 928)

*Countess of Maine. Born around 871; died around 928; daughter of *Richilde of Autun (d. around 910) and Charles I the Bald, king of France (r. 840–877), also known as Charles II, Holy Roman emperor (r. 875–877); married Rotger also known as Roger, count of Maine; children: Hugh I, count of Maine.*

Rothilde (fl. 840)

*German princess. Flourished around 840; daughter of Lothair I, Holy Roman emperor (r. 840–855) and *Irmengard (c. 800–851); sister of Louis II (c. 822–875), Holy Roman emperor (r. 855–875), and Lothair II, king of Lorraine (r. 855–869); married Guido of Spoleto; children: Guido of Spoleto, Holy Roman emperor (r. 891–894).*

Rothrude (d. 724).

See Chrotrud.

Rothschild, Baroness Henri de (1874–1926).

See Rothschild, Mathilde de.

Rothschild, Judith (1921–1993)

American painter and philanthropist. Born in 1921 in New York City; died on March 6, 1993, in New York City; daughter of Herbert Rothschild (owner of a furniture manufacturing company); Wellesley College, B.A.; studied with Reginald Marsh of the Art Students League in New York City; attended the Cranbrook Academy of Art in Bloomfield Hills, Michigan; studied with Hans Hofmann and Karl Knaths; studied with Stanley William Hayter at Atelier 17 in New York City; married for 23 years to Anton Myrer (a novelist, divorced).

Born in New York City in 1921, Judith Rothschild began her 55-year painting career as a teenager. She had the opportunity to study with numerous distinguished artists, including Reginald Marsh, Hans Hofmann, Karl Knaths and Stanley William Hayter, and graduated from Wellesley College. During the 1950s and early

1960s, Rothschild moved from her initial abstract, geometric style to landscape and figurative painting. In her later paintings, she synthesized abstract elements with representational forms, often drawing from and alluding to mythology and literature. Her style changed again in the early 1970s, when her visual vocabulary expanded to include a broad emotional and thematic range.

Rothschild's paintings were shown internationally and are in the collections of the Metropolitan Museum of Art, the Guggenheim Museum, the Whitney Museum of American Art, the National Gallery in Washington, D.C., and the Fogg Art Museum in Cambridge, Massachusetts, as well as many other museums and private collections. In the course of her lifetime, she contributed to the art world as founder and president of the American Abstract Artists Association, in addition to serving on the boards of the American Federation of Arts, the MacDowell Colony, the New York Studio School, and the Provincetown Fine Arts Work Center. She was also artist-in-residence at Syracuse University, and a guest artist at the Pratt Institute and the Rhode Island School of Design during the 1970s.

When she died of a stroke in 1993, at age 71, Rothschild left an estate that included her own paintings as well as art by Matisse, Mondrian, Brancusi, Picasso, and Gris. Her will stipulated that this multimillion dollar estate be sold and the proceeds given to galleries and museums for the purchase of works by contemporary American artists.

SOURCES:

The Day [New London, CT]. March 3, 1993.

Heller, Jules, and Nancy G. Heller, eds. *North American Women Artists of the Twentieth Century.* NY: Garland, 1995.

The New York Times Biographical Service. March 1993, p. 345.

The Paintings of Judith Rothschild: An Artist's Search. Metropolitan Museum of Art brochure, 1998.

Kelly Winters,
freelance writer, Bayville, New York

Rothschild, Mathilde de

(1874–1926)

Baroness. Name variations: Baroness or Baronne Henri de Rothschild; Baroness or Baronne de Rothschild. Born Mathilde Weissweiler on May 17, 1874; died on August 12, 1926; married Henri de Rothschild, on May 22, 1895; children: James Nathaniel de Rothschild (b. 1896, who married **Claude Dupont***); Nadine Charlotte de Rothschild (1898–1958, who married Adrien Thierry); Philippe de Rothschild* *(1902–1935, who married* **Elisabeth de Chambure** *[d. 1945] and* **Pauline Fairfax Potter***).*

Baroness Mathilde de Rothschild was known for her charity events in turn-of-the-century Paris. At the time of the baroness' death in 1926, *Janet Flanner named her the "most progressive member" of the conservative House of Rothschild.

Rothschild, Miriam (1908—)

British entomologist and naturalist. Born Miriam Louisa Rothschild on August 5, 1908, in Ashton Wold, England; daughter of Charles Rothschild (a banker and naturalist) and Rozsika von Wertheimstein Rothschild; granddaughter of Nathan Mayer Rothschild, Baron Rothschild (the British financier); niece of Walter Rothschild; educated privately; married George Lane, in 1943 (divorced 1957); children: six.

Despite the virtual absence of any formal education, became a highly regarded scientist and naturalist, specializing in the study of fleas and other insects; made a fellow of the Royal Society (1985); named Commander of the British Empire (CBE); published numerous books on insects and gardens.

Miriam Rothschild was born in 1908 on the sprawling country estate north of London built by her father, banker Charles Rothschild, part of the famous British banking family. Charles was one of two sons of Nathan "Natty" Mayer Rothschild, head of the banking firm of N.M. Rothschild & Sons, who was made a baron by William Gladstone and was the first Jew to sit in the House of Lords. The brilliant financier was so powerful that the popular press considered him to be the real ruler of England, and he groomed his sons, Charles and Walter Rothschild, in the banking business. Although they dutifully played their roles, neither of them took a real interest in the family business; instead, they were passionate about the natural world. Charles was a well-known amateur entomologist who discovered the rat flea *Xenopsylla cheopis*, carrier of the bubonic plague, while on a trip to Egypt. One of Miriam's first forays into the world of entomology was to continue her father's study of fleas, a subject in which she herself would become an expert.

Although she no doubt inherited some of her love of insects from her father, Miriam was actually much closer to her uncle, Walter Rothschild, since her father's illness and eventual suicide when she was 15 prevented a close relationship with him. Walter was an eccentric and a world-famous collector, taxonomist, and naturalist. Using the family's abundant wealth, he financed and participated in an international collecting expedition which resulted in more than 2,000,000 butterfly specimens, 30,000 bird skins, 300,000 beetles, and 144 giant turtles. It was the most extensive private collection of insects in the world, and eventually became part of the British Museum. He was the subject of Miriam's biography *Dear Lord Rothschild* (1983), the title of which was taken from the salutation of the 1917 letter to him from British Foreign Secretary Arthur J. Balfour (now known as the Balfour Declaration), in which the British government promised to support establishment of a Jewish homeland in Palestine.

Miriam herself was breeding ladybugs before she turned five. Despite having no formal education (her family believed it would stifle her creativity), she became a brilliant scientist and naturalist, starting with her studies in marine biology at the University of London's biological station in Naples, Italy, in the late 1920s. In 1932, she moved on to the Marine Biological Station in Plymouth, where the discovery that flatworms had infested some mollusks led her to the study of parasites. Over the following years, she concentrated on parasites, hosts, and other related marine animals, working long hours and amassing many specimens and cultures. This ended in 1939, when the research station in Plymouth, including her laboratory and everything in it, was destroyed by German bombs. She returned to the Rothschild estate, which was being used as a U.S. Air Force field. Over 300 missions flew from the base, and Rothschild made the acquaintance of American pilot and actor Clark Gable during this time; the two often went shooting together. As was revealed much later, she was also engaged in more serious war efforts, as one of many scientists who worked on the Enigma project to break Germany's secret code.

After her marriage to British war hero George Lane in 1943, Rothschild had four children and adopted two more. (She and her husband would remain friends after their 1957 divorce.) Her family responsibilities significantly reduced her free time, but she still managed to engage in a serious study of fleas. She catalogued her father's collection, publishing a five-volume study as a result, and became known as a leading authority on bird fleas. In 1952, she published *Fleas, Flukes & Cuckoos*, a popular study which made her subject understandable to the lay reader. For this she became known as the "Queen of the Fleas." Rothschild was the first to photograph and record the flea's leap, an impressive accomplishment of nature, equivalent to a human being jumping to the top of Rockefeller Center thousands of times without stopping. Her other important research centered on the rabbit flea, which carries a disease fatal to its host.

Rothschild also contributed to research on mites and ticks, the gull-like bird called a skua, and butterflies and moths. With this latter research, she made discoveries about the relationships between insects and plants, in particular how insects use plant poisons as a defense mechanism. She worked on this with Nobel Prize-winner Tadeus Reichstein. She reported how the monarch butterfly defends against birds and spiders by storing poisons from the milkweed plant, to which it has developed immunity. Rothschild completed similar studies with ladybugs, discovering that a single egg can be extremely poisonous even to a much larger creature, and caterpillars, which feed on toxic plant seeds as protection from predators. Another of her experiments was to determine if a bird's fear of hornets was inherited or learned. She placed a magpie raised by hand with no exposure to the insect in a cage with a hornet that had had its stinger removed. She was surprised to discover that the bird instinctively refused to go near the insect.

Later, Rothschild's attention turned to wildflowers, which she raised on her estate. By growing wildflowers as a cash crop, she hoped to reintroduce them as a popular roadside and garden item. In the space of three years she recreated the equivalent of a medieval meadow, with its variety of grasses and flowers common to that time period. Many of her wildflowers require harvesting by hand, making seed expensive, but her work raised public interest in the project.

Rothschild's varied interests made her a scientist and naturalist held in the highest regard. She received numerous awards and honors, among them an honorary degree from Oxford University in 1968 for her contribution to anatomy, chemistry, entomology, pharmacology, neurophysiology and zoology. In 1985, she received the highest honor in British science when she was made a fellow of the Royal Society. She was also named a Commander of the British Empire (CBE). Rothschild has written and co-written numerous scientific papers and books; a number of her later works on gardens are written for the general reader, and have made her one of the most respected modern experts on gardens. "I must say," she told an interviewer for *Smithsonian*, while in her late 70s, "I find everything interesting."

SOURCES:

McCullough, David. "A Rothschild who is known as Queen of the fleas," in *Smithsonian*. June 1985, pp. 139–153.

Notable Twentieth-Century Scientists. 1st ed. Detroit, MI: Gale Research, 1995.

Martha Jones, M.L.S.,
Natick, Massachusetts

Rothwell, Evelyn (1911—)

English oboist. Born in Wallingford, England, on January 24, 1911; studied under Leon Goossens at the Royal College of Music; married Sir John Barbirolli (the conductor), in 1939.

Women were rare in symphony orchestras until the 1930s, and those like Evelyn Rothwell were pioneers. After studying at the Royal College of Music, she joined the Covent Garden Opera touring orchestra (1931). She played with the Scottish Orchestra (1933–36), the Glyndebourne Festival Orchestra (1934–39), and the London Symphony Orchestra (1935–39). When she married the conductor John Barbirolli in 1939, Rothwell began a solo career. Many compositions were dedicated to her by such composers as *Elizabeth Maconchy, Gordon Jacob, Arnold Cooke, Stephen Dodgson, Edmund Rubbra, and Arthur Benjamin. In 1934, she gave the first performance of the rediscovered Mozart Oboe Concerto. Rothwell has written several books on oboe technique and repertoire and was appointed a professor at the Royal Academy of Music, London, in 1971.

John Haag,
Athens, Georgia

Rotrou.

Variant of Chrotrud and Rotrud.

Rotrou of Belgium (d. 724).

See Chrotrud.

Rotrud (800–841)

*French princess. Born in 800; died in 841; daughter of *Ermengarde (c. 778–818) and Louis I the Pious (778–840), king of Aquitaine (r. 781–814), king of France (r. 814–840), and Holy Roman Emperor (r. 814–840).*

Rotrude (c. 778–after 839).

See Irene of Athens for sidebar.

Rouet, Catherine or Katherine (c. 1350–1403).

See Beaufort, Joan (c. 1379–1440) for sidebar on Swynford, Catherine.

Rouet, Philippa (c. 1348–c. 1387)

*French wife of Geoffrey Chaucer. Name variations: Philippa Chaucer; Philippa de Ruet or Philippa de Roet. Born around 1348; died around 1387; daughter of Sir Payne Roelt (a knight from Hainault, France, who arrived in England with the train of Edward III's queen Philippa of Hainault); sister of *Catherine Swynford (c. 1350–1403); married Geoffrey Chaucer (the poet); children: Thomas Chaucer; grandchildren:* ❧ *Alice Chaucer.*

French-born Philippa Rouet probably met Geoffrey Chaucer while at court attending *Philippa of Hainault. The queen may have helped arrange the match.

◆❧
Chaucer, Alice.
See Margaret
of Anjou
(1429–1482) for
sidebar.

Rountree, Martha (1911–1999)

American radio and television producer. Name variations: Martha Presbrey. Born in Gainesville, Florida, on October 23, 1911; died on August 23, 1999, in Washington, D.C.; second oldest of five children; sister of Ann Rountree Forsberg; attended the University of South Carolina; married Albert N. Williams, Jr. (a magazine and radio writer), in 1941 (divorced 1948); married Oliver M. Presbrey (a television producer and advertising executive), on June 18, 1952 (died 1988); children: Martha Presbrey Wiethorn; Mary Presbrey Greene.

A pioneer radio and television producer, Martha Rountree was co-creator of "Meet the Press," the newsmaker series that began as a radio program in 1945, moved to television in 1948, and is currently that medium's longest-running series.

Rountree set her sights on a journalism career at the age of nine. Born in 1911 in Gainesville, Florida, and raised in Columbia, South Carolina, she attended the University of South Carolina, but left college early to become a reporter for the Tampa *Tribune*. In 1938, she moved to New York, where she freelanced for several magazines and wrote advertising copy. A year later, she and her sister **Ann Rountree Forsberg** began Radio House, a production company that produced transcribed programs and singing commercials. One of Rountree's early successes, and radio's first panel show, was "Leave It to the Girls," which began broadcasting in April 1945. The show was comprised of a panel of several well-known celebrities who answered questions—mostly concerning affairs of the heart—sent in by listeners. A single male guest represented the masculine point of view.

Rountree first met her future partner Lawrence E. Spivak when she submitted a story to the *American Mercury*, of which he was then editor. (She later worked as a roving editor for the magazine.) In 1945, she and Spivak joined forces to create "Meet the Press," a first-of-its-kind radio news program on which a panel of journalists interviewed prominent media personalities, eliciting their opinions on controversial issues. In the early years of the show, Rountree served as the moderator, while Spivak was the permanent member of the panel. The program was an instant success; early guests included President Harry S. Truman, Henry A. Wallace, and Senator Robert A. Taft. "I think it is important that the public should hear its elected officers speak out and take their stand in answer to direct questions, without preparation or oratory," Rountree once said, referring to the show's unrehearsed format. "There is nothing so refreshing as unadorned conviction."

"Meet the Press" won the George Foster Peabody Award in 1947, and moved to television in 1948, where it continued to capture awards, including the Radio and Television Arts Sciences Award (1951), the Sylvania Award (1951), and a second George Foster Peabody Award (1952). In 1951, Rountree was personally honored by a citation from the Women for Achievement and selected as the outstanding woman in television by the National Fraternity for Women in Journalism. That same year, she and Spivak produced a second discussion program, "Keep Posted" (later changed to "The Big Issue"), in which two guests on opposing sides of a newsworthy issue were questioned by a panel of notables. They also collaborated with Frank McNaughton and Rountree's husband Oliver Presbrey to produce yet another news program, "Washington Exclusive," which aired in 1953. It presented six senators from both political parties in a debate format.

Rountree lost a coin-toss to Spivak and had to sell her share in "Meet the Press" and "The Big Issue" in the fall of 1953. Spivak would remain its executive producer and moderator for the next 20 years. Since his retirement, the show has been headed by Bill Monroe, Marvin Kalb, Roger Mudd, and Tim Russert. Rountree, who was the only woman to ever moderate the program, moved on to form her own production company with Presbrey and Robert Novak. A clause in her sales contract prevented her from producing any show similar to "Meet the Press" for a period of two years, so the first program created by Rountree Productions, entitled "Press Conference," did not go on the air until mid-1956. *Variety* described the new show as "a no-holds-barred, give-and-take between a roomful of reporters and a top drawer, newsworthy subject." Rountree's role was as "referee or press adviser to the guest of the day." On the first show, U.S. Attorney General Herbert Brownell disclosed the Department of Justice's hitherto unrevealed intention to prosecute General Motors for alleged antitrust violation. His candor drew some protests from magazine and newspaper journalists who objected to a government official "breaking" a story of such national concern on commercial television. "Press Conference," despite critical acclaim, did not have the staying power of "Meet the Press," lasting only until July 1957.

Rountree, a tall, attractive blonde with a soft southern accent, was married in 1941 to writer Albert N. Williams, Jr. They divorced in 1948, and Rountree then married Presbrey. During the height of her career, she made her home in Washington, D.C., where she was acquainted with the city's most prominent diplomats, Cabinet members, and Congressional leaders. "Yielding to Martha's cajolery, they often use her programs for major pronouncements," reported *Life* magazine in June 1952. She also formed Leadership, a nonprofit research foundation,

Martha Rountree

serving as its president until 1988. Once characterized by ✥▶ **Millicent Hearst** as "a diesel engine under a lace handkerchief," Rountree was proud of her blunt, down-to-earth style of reporting. "Freedom of the press is America's first line of defense," she said in a speech to a Chicago women's group. "It is something that must be fought for continuously—not taken for granted." Martha Rountree died in Washington, D.C., in August 1999.

SOURCES:

Brown, Les. *Les Brown's Encyclopedia of Television*. Detroit, MI: Visible Ink Press, 1992.

Candee, Marjorie Dent, ed. *Current Biography 1957*. NY: H.W. Wilson, 1957.

"Martha Rountree, 87, a Creator of 'Meet the Press,'" (obituary) in *The New York Times*. August 25, 1999.

Barbara Morgan,
Melrose, Massachusetts

Rourke, Constance (1885–1941)

Author and scholar of American folklore and culture who sought to recover and revalue American traditions. Pronunciation: Roark. Born Constance Mayfield Rourke on November 14, 1885, in Cleveland, Ohio; died on March 23, 1941, after a fall, in Grand Rapids, Michigan; daughter of Henry Rourke (a designer of hardware specialties) and Elizabeth Constance (Davis) Rourke (a schoolteacher and proponent of the kindergarten movement); Vassar College, B.A., 1907; attended Sorbonne, 1908–09; never married; no children.

After death of father, moved with mother to Grand Rapids, Michigan (c. 1887); graduated from high school (1902); graduated from Vassar College (1907); traveled in Europe (1908–10); served as English instructor at Vassar (1910–15); published first article, "The Rationale of Punctuation" (1915); began writing assignments for various journals (1918); was introduced to Van Wyck Brooks (1920); published first book, Trumpets of Jubilee (1927).

Selected writings: Trumpets of Jubilee (New York, 1927); Troupers of the Gold Coast, or The Rise of Lotta Crabtree (New York, 1928); American Humor: A Study of National Character (New York, 1931); Davy Crockett (New York, 1934); Audubon (New York, 1936); Charles Sheeler: Artist in the American Tradition (New York, 1938); The Roots of American Culture (edited and with a preface by Van Wyck Brooks, New York, 1942). Numerous articles in The Dial, The New Republic, The Freeman, The Saturday Review of Literature, and other journals.

According to Constance Rourke's biographer Samuel Bellman, at the time of her 1902 grad-

uation from high school in Grand Rapids, Michigan, classmates predicted that she would attend the elite women's college, Vassar, captivate young gentlemen, and marry "a well-known man from Harvard." Rourke did, in fact, attend Vassar, following an extra year of study in Grand Rapids with a high-school English teacher, but after college she returned to the home of her mother, where they remained in a close and interdependent relationship until the time of her death. Nevertheless, Rourke maintained an acute independence of intellect that was to lead to a number of outstanding contributions to American culture.

Constance Mayfield Rourke was born in Cleveland, Ohio, on November 14, 1885, the daughter of Henry Rourke, an Irish immigrant who designed lighting and door fixtures, and **Elizabeth Davis Rourke**, who took the name Constance upon reaching adulthood, and was a teacher interested in the progressive educational theories of the day. The couple had met in the early 1880s in St. Louis and traveled around the East and Midwest after they married.

Within a year of Constance's birth, Henry Rourke contracted tuberculosis and went to a sanitarium in Colorado to recuperate. The mountain air did not correct his condition, and he died in 1887 or 1888. His widow and daughter moved to Grand Rapids, in search of a livelihood.

At first, Mrs. Rourke supported her daughter by giving private art lessons to children. Within a few years, she began to teach in the local public schools and worked to establish kindergartens, which were a relatively new innovation at the time. In 1892, she became a school principal, a post she held at various schools until the mid-1920s. Colleagues generally remembered her as authoritarian and temperamental; some even termed her a tyrant.

Throughout their lives together, Constance and her mother nevertheless enjoyed a very close relationship, although other relationships may have suffered as a result. Rourke grew up a loner, with no intimate friends and little involvement in social activities with her peers. **Joan Shelley Rubin** writes that "as a high school student Rourke was reportedly an aloof, bookish, unfashionably dressed girl."

During her four years at Vassar in Poughkeepsie, New York, Rourke found the separation from her mother somewhat difficult, but she did well as a student. She studied English and became involved in a few activities: drama, debate, and, briefly, the college's settlement asso-

✥▶
Hearst, Millicent.
See Davies,
Marion for
sidebar.

ciation. According to Rubin, her courses in English reenforced many of the progressive educational beliefs her mother had espoused. Her professors taught that literature should be democratic, accessible to and useful for everyone in a society. Literature and cultural forms, in fact, should be drawn upon to strengthen and improve social life. The idea that culture could be a means of productive change in society was to undergird Rourke's future work.

Just as had happened in high school, she made few close friends during her college years, but her abilities as a student garnered her respect. Upon graduation from Vassar in 1907, she was awarded the William Borden Fund, which provided her with $1,500 for travel and study in Europe. Rourke returned to Grand Rapids, where she taught for a year, before setting out with her mother for Europe.

It is what the past has to say to the precarious, strange, and tragic present that is significant.

—Constance Rourke

Following her plan to survey European educational methods and literary criticism, Rourke studied at the British Museum and the Sorbonne, and traveled to Italy, Switzerland, Germany, and Austria. By the end of the journey in 1910, she had made up her mind that she wanted to write instead of teach. Nevertheless, she was in need of an income, and she returned to Poughkeepsie that year as a private tutor. Soon she was offered a position at Vassar as an instructor of English, which she accepted, and again, the separation from her mother proved emotionally painful. She planned to return to Grand Rapids, but actually stayed at Vassar until January 1916.

Rourke stopped teaching in 1915, possibly because of her health. Her biographers note variously that she feared the tuberculosis which had killed her father, and that she either suffered from a mild nervous breakdown or heart problems during that year. Her health continued to be a bother until the mid-1920s, when the root of her discomfort was discovered to be a prolapsis of the stomach, and the problem was remedied. In 1916, Rourke was back in Michigan with her mother, but facing financial difficulties. In 1917, she was forced once again to go back to the profession she had hoped to leave.

Now, however, she began to balance her teaching schedule with the writing she had long hoped to do. Her first published article, "The Rationale of Punctuation," had appeared in the *Educational Review* in 1915. Three years later, in 1918, she wrote her first book review for the *New Republic*, then published her first full article (on vaudeville theater) in the same magazine the following year.

In Grand Rapids, Rourke had a number of suitors and rejected several marriage proposals. She became engaged at one point but broke it off, perhaps because she feared a loss of freedom to pursue her own concerns. Her article on vaudeville had marked a transition in her interests, from education to literature and culture, and in 1920 Rourke began to travel to New York City, where she cultivated connections with editors, writers, and critics in search of writing assignments she could fulfill back in Grand Rapids. As Rubin points out, it was this periodic travel away from her mother which allowed her to stay in Grand Rapids with adequate employment and income.

In 1920, Rourke had the good fortune to be introduced to one of the leading figures in New York's circle of critics—Van Wyck Brooks, editor of the *Freeman*. Brooks employed her to write reviews for his journal, but, more important, he ultimately provided her with a new focus and purpose. In his own work, Brooks had offered a series of observations about American culture with which Rourke found that she vehemently disagreed, and it was in opposing his conclusions that she found new subject matter.

Writing in the early years of the 20th century, Brooks and others proposed that America lacked a worthy cultural tradition, particularly compared to that of European countries. According to Brooks, American culture was shallow because Americans were too concerned with their material existences in a capitalist society. Such concerns and such a society bred a lack of imagination and a lack of community and shared beliefs. Like other culture critics of the time, Brooks denied that there was a tradition of cultural and artistic achievement to which contemporary Americans could feel connected. Many critics also doubted the presence in America of any folk traditions out of which grander forms might develop. The picture they painted was of a nation utterly barren of culture. Beginning in the 1920s, the rediscovery of the lost and undervalued cultural life of America became Rourke's mission.

Rourke and Brooks remained on good terms, stimulated by each other's conclusions, and Brooks actually suggested the topic that became Rourke's first book, a group study of five prominent 19th-century individuals: Lyman

Beecher and his son Henry Ward Beecher (both Protestant ministers); Lyman's daughter *Harriet Beecher Stowe, author of *Uncle Tom's Cabin*; newspaper editor and politician Horace Greeley; and circus founder and entrepreneur P.T. Barnum. During the mid-1920s, while turning out numerous well-received reviews, Rourke wrote her group biography, which was published in 1927 under the title *Trumpets of Jubilee*. The book was a study of individuals which sought to uncover more than mere biographical data; Rourke herself claimed that biographies were of interest to her only insofar as they served to illustrate widespread cultural trends. In the words of Kenneth Lynn, a student of Rourke's work, "her aim was to define the American character by evoking and interpreting the popular or folk taste of a bygone era, in this case by studying the lives of five Americans of the mid-19th century who had an enormous popular appeal." For the serialization of the work in *Woman's Home Companion*, a popular magazine, Rourke received $10,000.

In her second book, *Troupers of the Gold Coast, or The Rise of Lotta Crabtree*, published in 1928, Rourke followed a similar approach, focusing this time on the life of a now-forgotten entertainer, *Lotta Crabtree (1847–1924), and theater in San Francisco during the late-19th century.

During the '20s and '30s, Rourke was frequently away from Grand Rapids. While she continued to dislike the separation from her mother, she was welcomed into Eastern literary circles, where she met such well-known authors as Thornton Wilder, William Carlos Williams, and Malcolm Cowley. She also traveled to small towns around the country, spending a great deal of time on research and conducting interviews for her books, which she enjoyed enormously. In *Twentieth Century Authors*, she wrote about her research techniques:

> [M]y work has also included to a large extent what may be called "living research," that is, talking with old timers roundabout the country, particularly in small towns, listening to their autobiographies—plenty of them have the gift!—looking at provincial art, which has its special fascinations, listening to old music. If my work had meant only research in libraries, I don't believe I could have stayed with it, for as far as I can discover I am not a bookish person.

In 1931, Constance Rourke published *American Humor: A Study of the National Character*, considered her finest work and the one for which she is most remembered. Describing the comic images of Yankees, loggers, strolling play-

Constance Rourke

ers, miners, explorers, religious leaders, and boaters which surfaced and resurfaced in American humor and literature, she uncovered the mythic figures which had populated the literary and comic imagination of the nation, and frequently related their stories to the literature of more recognized American authors such as Hawthorne, Melville, and Poe. Underneath comedy, Rourke also found deep feeling, and proposed that American humor has had as its unconscious object the goal of uniting a disparate people. In her closing chapter, she claimed: "If the American character is split and many-sided at least a large and shadowy outline has been drawn by the many ventures in comedy. A consistent native tradition has been formed, spreading over the country."

By attempting to provide evidence of the creative tradition in America which Van Wyck Brooks denied, Rourke hoped to give to creative writers a sense of continuity upon which they could build. The critic, she argued, by tracing and illuminating historical and cultural patterns, was tendering a necessary and important service to the nation's artists by offering them a tradition and a past.

During the 1930s, Rourke published three more books. The first was a biography written for children about Davy Crockett, a logical subject for Rourke because of the significant role Crockett played in the folk traditions and myths of the 19th century. Movie rights to the book were sold, although the film was never produced. In 1936, she produced a biography of naturalist and artist John James Audubon, and in 1938 she finished her sixth and final book, on artist Charles Sheeler, entitled *Charles Sheeler: Artist in the American Tradition*, pursuing her favorite themes.

During the 1930s, while she continued to write articles and reviews for a variety of journals, Rourke broadened the scope of her work as one of the organizers of the National Folk Festival in St. Louis, and in 1934, she became one of the editors of the *Index of American Design*, which was part of the Federal Art Project set up by the U.S. government under the New Deal.

Always concerned about the relationship of cultural forms to the broader society, Rourke became increasingly worried about the threat posed to democratic life by the flowering of fascism in Europe during the 1930s. She became publicly active in antifascist campaigns, making speeches on the need to oppose Germany, first recommending economic sanctions and later supporting military ones. In her piece written for *Twentieth Century Authors* around 1940, she stated her view of the importance of studying American history, which she saw as buried and in need of uncovering, "because we are now pressed to understand and fully use all the forces of democracy."

In 1941, arriving home after attending a meeting of the Grand Rapids chapter of the Committee to Defend America by Aiding the Allies, Rourke slipped on her front porch and injured her back. Her mother was asleep, and Constance did not disturb her, finally managing to get in the house and up to bed. She was hospitalized the next day with a cracked vertebrae and seemed to be recovering well when she collapsed and died from an embolism resulting from her fall. Her mother survived her by only a few years. One last work of Rourke's was published posthumously, salvaged from the manuscript and notes already produced for her next project. The book, entitled *The Roots of American Culture*, was edited and introduced by Van Wyck Brooks who by then had come to agree with Rourke's assessment of American culture.

In his preface, Brooks wrote: "Constance Rourke had assembled proofs of a rich creative life in our past, and she had found indications in it of distinctive native American elements."

SOURCES:

Bellman, Samuel I. *Constance M. Rourke.* Boston, MA: Twayne, 1981.

Kunitz, Stanley J., and Howard Haycraft, eds. *Twentieth Century Authors.* NY: H.W. Wilson, 1942.

Lynn, Kenneth. "Rourke, Constance Mayfield," in *Notable American Women, 1607–1950: A Biographical Dictionary.* Vol. 3. Cambridge, MA: Harvard University Press, 1971.

Rourke, Constance. *American Humor: A Study of the National Character.* NY: Harcourt, Brace, 1931.

———. *The Roots of American Culture.* Edited by Van Wyck Brooks. NY: Harcourt, Brace, 1942.

Rubin, Joan Shelley. *Constance Rourke and American Culture.* Chapel Hill, NC: University of North Carolina Press, 1980.

SUGGESTED READING:

Hyman, Stanley Edgar. *The Armed Vision: A Study in the Methods of Modern Literary Criticism.* NY: Vintage Books, 1955.

Lynn, Kenneth. *Visions of America: Eleven Literary Historical Essays.* Westport, CT: Greenwood Press, 1973.

COLLECTIONS:

Beinecke Rare Book and Manuscript Library, Yale University, Margaret Marshall Manuscripts, uncatalogued.

Susan J. Matt, Ph.D. candidate,
Department of History, Cornell University,
Ithaca, New York

Roussel, Nelly (1878–1922)

Advocate of women's rights, one of France's finest orators of her time, who was a leading proponent of birth control and "integral" feminism. Pronunciation: NELL-ee roo-SELL. Born in Paris, France, on January 5, 1878; died in Paris of tuberculosis on December 18, 1922; educated at elementary school and by herself at home; married Henri Godet (b. 1863), in 1898; children: daughter Mireille Godet and son Marcel Godet (born between 1899 and 1904); another son (b. 1901, died in infancy).

Converted to left-wing causes following marriage to Henri Godet (1898); experienced three exceptionally difficult childbirths (1899–1904); met Paul Robin, the leading advocate of birth control ("neo-Malthusianism," 1900); went on tours lecturing on birth control and women's rights (1901–13); testified at the trial of Hervé and other anti-militarists (1905); brought a lawsuit against L'Autorité but lost (1906–07); opposed the war (1914–18); testified at Hélène Brion's trial for antiwar activities (1918); wrote and spoke against the advocates of large families (neo-natalists) and for women's suffrage (1919–22); started a school to train women speakers (1920).

Writings: Par la révolte *(introduction by Sebastien Faure, privately printed, 1903);* Quelques discours *(privately printed, 1907);* Quelques lances rompus pour nos libertés *(preface by É. Darnaud, Paris: Giard & Brière, 1910);* Pourquoi elles vont à l'Église? Comédie en un acte *(privately printed, 1910);* Paroles de combat et d'espoir *(preface by Madeleine Vernet, Paris: Éditions de l'Avenir social, 1919); (poetry)* Ma Forêt *(Paris: Éditions de l'Avenir social, 1921);* Trois conférences *(preface by Mme O. Laguerre, Paris: Giard, 1930);* Derniers combats, recueil d'articles et de discours *(preface by Han Ryner, Paris: Imprimerie l'Émancipatrice, 1932);* L'Éternelle sacrificé *(translated by Jette Kjaer, edited by Maïté Albistur and Daniel Armogast, Paris: Syros, 1979).*

Journalism: some 200 articles in 46 newspapers and periodicals, e.g., Paris qui passe *(her first article, Oct. 29, 1899),* Le Libertaire *(S. Faure),* La Fronde *(Marguerite Durand),* Le Petit Almanach féministe illustré, L'Action *(Henri Béranger; her most prolific outlet: 60 articles, Jan. 26, 1904–Nov. 21, 1908),* Régénération, Rénouvation, Génération consciente, Le Néo-Malthusien, Le Journal des femmes *(Marie Martin),* La Femme affranchie *(Gabrielle Petit),* L'Équité, La Voix des femmes *(Colette Reynaud; her most frequent outlet after the war),* La Mère éducatrice *(Madeleine Vernet),* La Libre Pensée International *(of Lausanne).*

At age 35, Nelly Roussel's mother (a "sensitive and timorous" woman, according to Nelly's daughter) had married into a monied Parisian professional family. Nelly was born in 1878 and grew up with all the advantages of her station yet seems not to have put great store by them. She was raised as a devout Catholic and educated through the elementary level. But at age 15, her parents ended her schooling, as was customary for girls. By nature friendly and extroverted, she now felt bitterly frustrated, for she was also very bright and studious. To end her education simply because she was a female struck her as a rank injustice.

Roussel had, however, a sympathetic grandfather who had urged her to read widely on her own. He also inspired her with his passion for the theater and encouraged her to become perhaps an actress—a calling thought not altogether respectable in her social milieu. Whether she received any formal training is unclear. That she had a natural talent for acting is undeniable; it contributed greatly to her success as an orator.

At age 20, Nelly met Henri Godet, 35, a struggling sculptor and engraver. Only months later, on June 4, 1898, they married and ever afterward remained a devoted pair. Marriage marked a decisive turning in Roussel's life. She had married for love, not by arrangement as was still common in the bourgeoisie. And her husband soon converted her from Catholicism to freethinking and left-wing, anarchist-flavored politics. Marriage also brought her three traumatic childbirths between 1899 and 1904. A daughter **Mireille Godet** and a son Marcel Godet survived; another son, who nearly cost her her life, died at four months in 1901. As she later testified, her experiences in childbirth were critical in converting her to the cause of birth control—and they occurred at the very time (1900) she had fallen under the spell of birth control's leading advocate in France, Paul Robin (1837–1912).

Robin entered Roussel's life when his son married Godet's sister. At least half-seriously, Roussel called him "the new Christ." He was a teacher who had been driven abroad in 1865 for his socialist opinions—to Brussels, then Geneva, where he mingled with the anarchist Michael Bakunin, and London, where he became a close friend of Karl Marx. Returning to France after the Republican victory in 1879, he was put in charge of the Cempuis orphanage, near Paris, where he introduced coeducation of boys and girls, a radical idea. His activities in promoting birth control—he had joined the cause in London—led, however, to his firing in 1894 and made him something of a celebrity. In 1896, he founded the League of Human Regeneration and launched a campaign through lectures and the League's journal. Robin sought to turn Malthusianism away from conservatism and make family planning the base of a new, free humanity. He viewed it as an alternative to Marx's road to socialism. Overpopulation was not just an economic issue, but one of morals and liberty. Small families among the workers would lead to better health, more education, higher wages, and fewer soldiers to fight capitalism's wars.

Such ideas profoundly influenced Roussel's thinking. To them she added her views on other women's issues. In 1901, she began speaking on behalf of the League to any group or meeting that would sponsor her, notably freethinking, pacifist, and mixed masonic groups, and especially the People's University, a flourishing adult education network begun in 1898 by Georges Delherne. From 1901 to 1913 and after World War I until her death in 1922, Roussel delivered 236 addresses, sometimes to audiences numbering over 2,000, wrote some 200 articles for 46 different publications, and published 6 books.

Her husband handled most of the arrangements, while her mother and an aunt cared for her children during her absences. Especially in the prewar years, Roussel spoke regularly in the provinces, which she found woefully unenlightened about women's concerns. Altogether, down to 1913 she went on tour ten times. In April–June 1905, her busiest stint, she delivered 34 speeches in 15 departments; from 1906 to 1910, she averaged six provincial lectures per year, usually one or two in small locales. At various times, she also spoke abroad, in Belgium, Austria, Hungary, and Switzerland.

As a public speaker, Nelly Roussel made a deep impression on her audiences. She was blessed with strikingly good looks—an oval face with a fine forehead; black, turned-up hair; deep-socketed brown eyes; a slender figure always dressed in black, which set off her luminously white skin. Her voice was in a low register, warm and pure. Described as "magnetic" and "seductive" at the podium, she gave an impression of energy combined with fragility. Her manner was spirited, her gestures vigorous, her hands and face expressive, her pronunciation refined, and her vocabulary impeccable, full of brilliant images. She spoke extemporaneously or from notes, thus preserving a freedom to respond to her audiences. The printed versions of her speeches were derived from stenographic notes, which she carefully reviewed. As a rule, she would end her speech with a reading of "Through Revolt," a theatrical scene she had written which was also sold at the door. She once observed that the most important element in speechmaking is complete command of the subject, followed by organization and apt, well-turned phrasing, the whole capped by a masterful delivery, without which all is lost. She had to a high degree the instincts and skills of a first-class debater. Her speeches are models of trenchant argumentation set forth in vigorous, readily understood language.

Despite her involvement with public issues, Roussel never joined a political party: "I have always been—I am so irremediably—an independent." But her sympathies lay almost entirely with the socialist left. She was no uncritical leftist, however. In the Couriau affair (1913), which concerned the unions' hostility to women workers, she subjected the unions and Marxian socialism to a feminist critique. Moreover, the feminist organizations she joined were moderate and reformist. She was an officer of the Fraternal Union of Women (UFF), member of the executive committee of the largest women's organization, the National Council of French Women

(CNFF), and the Paris representative of Émile Darnaud's mostly provincial Republican Feminist Committee (CRF). She hoped to move them toward more radical positions, especially on birth control and abortion. The reformists, by far the majority in the women's movement, never did feel comfortable with her; her views confined her popularity mainly to the left-wing militants. Her warm personality, however, preserved her from the ostracism suffered by *Madeleine Pelletier, a fellow radical.

Roussel's stance on birth control inevitably got her into a court case, which she lost. In 1906, a right-wing paper, *L'Autorité*, attacked neo-Malthusianism. She sued to force the paper to print her reply. Her letter advocated contraception not just for health reasons, which was legal, but also—without recommending chastity—to avoid the suffering of childbirth or to further a woman's general well-being. On May 22, the judge said the paper was not bound to print a reply which defended practices which are "immoral and anti-social" and which would "arrest the progress" of humanity and be "a cause of weakness and decadence" should the nation adopt them.

To advocate contraception in France in her day was to hoe a very hard row. Likewise with pacifism. As did most feminists, she saw a natural affinity between women and the peace movement. She opposed war and militarism during her whole career. War is a "crime," she said, a "social monster." In 1905, for example, she testified in favor of Gustave Hervé and other antimilitarists at their trial. In December 1914, with the First World War now raging, she confessed she didn't know which was strongest in her—sadness, anger, or disgust—when contemplating "a humanity capable of such a formidable and criminal folly." She expressed pity for the German people and regret that the French delegates left the 1915 meeting at The Hague of the International Alliance for Women's Suffrage after it transformed itself into a congress against war. The calls in France to ban Germany from the rest of humanity appalled her. She had to be careful, however, to avoid prosecution. She spoke at fund-raisers for the National Committee for Medical Dogs (they were used to find the wounded), and in *L'Équité*, from November 1915 until it folded in June 1916, she wrote sentimental columns about women's courage and the need to respect the weak, themes which did not sell well in the year of Verdun, writes Charles Sowerwine. Still, she shunned the mainstream. When the writer-politician Maurice Barrès won some support among women in 1916 for a proposal to grant the vote to war widows, she took her usual hard line: "We do not want to vote by proxy, vote as delegates, as substitutes. We want to vote as free citizens." And when a teacher, *Hélène Brion, was tried in March 1918 for antiwar activities, Roussel was one of only a few (including *Marguerite Durand and *Séverine) who parted with most feminists and appeared as witnesses for her.

After the war, Roussel's radicalism and zeal, if anything, only increased. Applauding the Russian Revolution after the 1919 elections, Roussel called for her compatriots to become "bolshe-viks"—although, even so, she did not join the Communist Party. Intense debates raged around three issues of the highest importance to her: peace, women's suffrage, and birth control. On the peace issue, she became outspoken to the last degree. The war had been plotted by an international band of capitalists—munitions makers, bankers, speculators—and the people had been led to support them by appeals to blind patriotism. The soldiers had not been heroes by going off to war but "cowards" for not opposing it. Moreover, they might not have gone at all if women had not insisted on praising them. Protes-

Nelly
Roussel

tors should have cried not so much "Down with war!" as "Down with the warriors!" Everyone, even front-line nurses, shared guilt for having supported, even indirectly, this mad slaughter.

As for the suffrage and birth-control issues, the campaigns were hot and the outcomes terribly discouraging. The Chamber of Deputies passed a suffrage bill only to see it die in the Senate. (Women would not receive the vote in France until 1944.) Meanwhile, a powerful, noisy, neo-natalist campaign urged having large families ("a social calamity," snapped Roussel, "repopulidolitry") to make up for the terrible battlefield losses and thus help protect the country from a far more populous Germany. It won passage of a law (1920) forbidding the giving of contraceptive information or advising or aiding abortion. To Roussel, these concerns were vital to women. She issued a call (first articulated by **Marie Huot** in 1892) for women to go on strike, a "womb strike" (*grève des ventres*), until their just demands for peace, civil rights, and control of their bodies were met. Her proposal only outraged most of the public, women included.

If you knew, O men, how much happier you will be when women will be happier!

—Nelly Roussel

Roussel continued to contribute articles, usually to *La Voix des femmes* (The Women's Voice). From April 1920 to June 1921, moreover, she spoke 21 times. But she was visibly failing. In 1921, she published a collection of poems, *Ma Forêt* (My Forest), which revealed her anguish and doubts. The sad truth was that near the end of the war she had contracted tuberculosis. Perhaps foreseeing her end, in 1921 she took up **Alice Jouenne**'s project to found a school, "Women's Voice," to train speakers, "a phalanx of militants," as she described them, "active, audacious, well-informed . . . feminist, socialist, pacifist, internationalist."

The disease could not be stayed. Roussel's voice and pen faded from the scene, and on December 18, 1922, in her 45th year, she died. The women's movement in France had lost a powerful advocate at a time when it never needed one more. Not until the latter 1930s did it surge again to serious strength.

Nelly Roussel was most identified with the issue of birth control. Her signal achievement was to incorporate it into feminism generally to form an "integral" feminism, writes **Elinor-Ann Accampo**. Hers was not a popular cause: the CNNF, no less, was a major promoter of the anti-contraception law of 1920.

Roussel viewed the right to control one's own body as the foundation of rights to full citizenship. Nothing enraged her more than the spectacle of all-male legislators chosen only by men laying down laws on childbearing: "Ask us!" At the base of errors and prejudice about contraception she put women's ignorance, the (French) medical establishment's blind conservatism, and, above all, religion, especially the Roman Catholic Church's teachings. Contraception is contrary to "nature?" But "cruel Nature" (a constant in her thought) can be subjected through free choice, the foundation of Science and Progress. How, she asked, can taming the forces of reproduction be "immoral" when the use of vaccines and flood-control is not? The taming, for that matter, is essential for humanity's future: "At no time, in no country, and under no form of social organization will unlimited fecundity be possible."

Roussel was the only prominent feminist to emphasize the pain and risk of childbirth—"a dreadful tragedy that must be lived through to be understood in its unspeakable terror." It is for the woman "and no one else to decide if she is to become a mother. We are dealing with an individual right here, the most imprescriptible and most sacred of all." She roundly denied she was somehow opposed to motherhood as such; it should be, in fact, the most honored and best-recompensed of all social functions. Not motherhood, but poverty, ill-health, and conditions dangerous for childbirth are the enemies. She denied, too, that she advocated contraception so women could live lives of easy pleasure—a red-herring argument. Sexuality, she asserted, is a given in men but also in women, a statement which was still thought rather shocking. Unlike Madeleine Pelletier, another "integral" feminist, Roussel did not foresee or desire a unisex future; maternity marks a basic, unalterable difference between the sexes. Marriage, unfortunately, had become "a worm-eaten fortress," and free unions would be ideal. But she admitted that they were at present too likely to be unstable. As for abortion, it is a woman's right to decide the matter, although she regarded it as an extreme measure; as a rule, it is better to prevent than to cure.

Roussel was no one-issue fanatic. She spoke and wrote on the whole range of questions affecting women. Prominent among these was the suffrage, of course, although she was not one of the feminists who fixated on it; by itself, it was only "a key to unlock the door." Joining the National League for the Women's Vote (LNVF) because she had found the French Union for Women's Suffrage (UFSE) too timid, she became one of its stars (with Pelletier, Durand, Séverine, and *Maria Vérone) and enthusiastically tore into the arguments against female suffrage. The right to vote confers a fundamental mark of human dignity in a democracy. But the Code Napoléon put women in the same legal category as lunatics, criminals, and children. Would women misuse the ballot? "The education of the voter comes with voting." What could women possibly add to bring more "incoherence, injustice, or stupidity to the structure you have built?" To an important thesis among leftists that women were too influenced by the Church, she asked acidly what they (the leftists) had ever done to detach them from religion: "the cabaret is for a man what the church is for a woman: a place of stupefaction and perversion. If you tell me . . . that the dévotes of the church are not ripe for emancipation, I shall reply that the drunks of the cabaret are not any more so!"

In the area of education, "the first chapter of all social issues" (and the subject of her first article, in 1899), she strongly supported coeducation. She blamed parents for trying to make children behave like themselves, miring them in traditional roles. Blaming parents was something new, anticipating *Simone de Beauvoir's analysis. Regarding employment, she asserted that it is solely for women to decide if they are ill-suited to an occupation. Economic independence is a "vital necessity" for women's progress. As did most socialists, she favored eventual collectivization of household tasks, which professionals equipped with the new or soon-to-be-invented machines would do. She won no points among the socialists, however, when she described the parties as masculiniste on women's issues no matter what the party platforms said. Contrary to the Marxists, she maintained that winning the class struggle would not solve all the problems of women, "the proletariat of the proletariat." Simply because they are women, they find all social issues more complicated for them.

Across the whole spectrum of women's issues, Nelly Roussel took positions most of which by the end of the 20th century would seem all but self-evident. Courage was her most salient attribute. For a woman of her time to speak in public meant braving scorn and laughter simply for trying, and all the more so when speaking out on the subjects she chose. Her untimely death sorely wounded the cause of feminism.

SOURCES:

Accampo, Elinor-Ann. "The Rhetoric of Reproduction and the Reconfiguration of Womanhood in the French Birth Control Movement, 1890–1920," in *Journal of Family History.* Vol. 21. July 1996, pp. 351–371.

Albistur, Maïté, and Daniel Armogathe, eds. *Le Grief des femmes.* Vol. 2: *Anthologie des textes féministes du second empire à nos jours.* Paris: Éditions Hier et Demain, 1978.

———. *Histoire du féminisme français, du moyen âge à nos jours.* Vol. 2: *De l'empire napoléonienne à nos jours.* Paris: Éditions des Femmes, 1977.

Bard, Christine. *Les Filles de Marianne: Histoire des féminismes 1914–1940.* Paris: Fayard, 1995.

Cova, Anne. "Féminisme et natalité: Nelly Roussel (1878–1922)," in *History of European Ideas.* Vol. 15, 1992, pp. 663–672.

———. "French Feminism and Maternity Theories and Policies, 1890–1918," in Gisela Bock and Pat Thane, eds., *Maternity and Gender Politics: Women and the Rise of the European Welfare State, 1880s–1950s.* NY: Routledge, 1991.

Hause, Steven, with Anne Kenney. *Women's Suffrage and Social Politics in the French Third Republic.* Princeton, NJ: Princeton University Press, 1984.

Klejman, Laurence, and Florence Rochefort. *L'Égalité en marche: Le Féminisme sous la Troisième République.* Paris: Éditions de la Fondation nationale des sciences politques, 1989.

Offen, Karen. "Roussel, Nelly," in *An Encyclopedia of Continental Women Writers.* Ed. Katherine M. Wilson. NY: Garland, 1991.

Rabaut, Jean. *Histoire des féminismes français.* Paris: Éditions Stock, 1978.

Roberts, Mary Louise. *Civilization Without Sexes: Reconstructing Gender in Postwar France, 1917–1927.* Chicago, IL: University of Chicago Press, 1994.

Ronsin, Francis. *La Grève des ventres: Propagande néo-malthusienne et baisse de la natalité en France, 19e–20e siècles.* Paris: Aubier Montaigne, 1980.

Roussel, Nelly. *Derniers combats: Recueil d'articles et de discours.* Préface de Han Ryner. Paris: L'Émancipatrice, 1932.

———. *L'Éternelle sacrifiée.* Maïté Albistur and Daniel Arbogathe, eds. Jette Kjaer, tr. Paris: Syros, 1979.

Sowerwine, Charles. *Sisters or Citizens? Women and Socialism in France since 1876.* Cambridge: Cambridge University Press, 1982.

Waelti-Walters, Jennifer, and Steven C. Hause, eds. *Feminism in the Belle Epoque: A Historical and Literary Anthology.* Tr. Jette Kjaer, Lydia Willis, and Jennifer Waelti-Walters. Lincoln, NB: University of Nebraska Press, 1994.

SUGGESTED READING:

Agulhon, Maurice. *The French Republic, 1879–1992.* Tr. Antonia Nevill. Oxford: Basil Blackwell. 1993.

Demeulenaere-Douyère, Christianne. *Paul Robin (1837–1912): Un natalist de la liberté et du bonheur.* Paris: Publisud, 1994.

McLaren, Angus. *A History of Contraception from Antiquity to the Present Day.* Oxford: Basil Blackwell, 1990.

———. *Sexuality and Social Order: The Debate over the Fertility of Women and Workers in France, 1770–1920.* NY: Holmes & Meier, 1983.

McMillan, James F. *Housewife or Harlot: The Place of Women in French Society.* NY: St. Martin's Press, 1981.

Smith, Paul. *Feminism in the Third Republic.* Oxford: Clarendon Press, 1996.

Wright, Gordon. *France in Modern Times.* 5th ed. NY: W.W. Norton, 1995.

COLLECTIONS:

Paris: Bibliothèque Historique de la Ville de Paris, Fonds Bouglé, dossier Nelly Roussel; Bibliothèque Marguerite Durand, dossier Nelly Roussel.

David S. Newhall,
Pottinger Distinguished Professor
of History Emeritus, Centre College,
author of *Clemenceau: A Life at War* (1991)

Roux, Maria de (c. 1821–1849).

See Manning, Maria.

Rovere, Giulia della

Duchess of Ferrara. Name variations: Giulia d'Este. Married Alfonso d'Este (1527–1587), duke of Ferrara; children: Alfonsino (1560–1578, who married Marfisa d'Este); Cesare (1562–1628), duke of Ferrara (r. 1597), duke of Modena (r. 1597–1628). Cesare married Virginia de Medici (*Virginia d'Este).

Rovere, Lucrezia della (1535–1598).

See Este, Lucrezia d'.

Rovere, Vittoria della (d. 1694).

See Medici, Vittoria de.

Rowe, Elizabeth Singer

(1674–1737)

English poet and writer. Name variations: Elizabeth Singer. Born Elizabeth Singer on September 11, 1674, in Ilchester, Somerset, England; died of apoplexy in Frome, Somerset, England, on February 20, 1737; daughter of Walter Singer (a Nonconformist minister) and Elizabeth Portnell; probably educated at a religious boarding school; married Thomas Rowe, in 1710 (died 1715).

Selected writings: Poems on Several Occasions: Written by Philomela *(1696);* Friendship in Death *(1728);* Letters Moral and Entertaining *(1729–33);* The History of Joseph *(1736);* Devout Exercises of the Heart *(1737);* Miscellaneous Works *(1739).*

Born in 1674 in Somerset, England, Elizabeth Singer Rowe was the eldest of three daughters. Her father Walter Singer was a Nonconformist minister who had once been imprisoned for his religious beliefs; he met his wife **Elizabeth Portnell** when she visited the prison. Later, Walter became a well-to-do merchant in Frome, in Somerset, England.

Rowe was most likely educated at a local boarding school, where the curriculum, in addition to religious and academic subjects, would have included the usual studies in music and drawing considered indispensable to the educated young woman of the time. She began writing poetry at an early age, and published some poems anonymously in the *Athenian Mercury* (1694–95), edited by John Dunton. In 1696, Dunton published her *Poems on Several Occasions: Written by Philomela.* This volume included reprints of several of her initial poems; other early poems were later reprinted in Dunton's *Athenian Oracle* in 1704. Dunton thought highly of Rowe, calling her "the richest genius of her sex."

Rowe's writing led her to an acquaintance and later friendship with the family of Lord Weymouth, particularly his son Henry Thynne and daughter *Frances Seymour, countess of Hertford, later the duchess of Somerset. Writer Matthew Prior met Rowe at Longford, the Thynnes' residence, and reportedly fell in love with her. Although he did not win her heart, he did use his literary influence to help her publish two Latin translations in Tonson's *Poetic Miscellanies V* in 1704.

In 1709, Rowe met her future husband Thomas Rowe, a classical scholar 13 years her junior who shared her Nonconformist upbringing. They married in 1710, and five years later he died of tuberculosis. Rowe spent the rest of her life in seclusion, devoting herself to charitable work. In 1728, she published her most well-known and popular work, *Friendship in Death in Twenty Letters from the Dead to the Living.* It went through many editions and was also translated into French and German. Rowe followed this with another heavily moralistic tome, *Letters Moral and Entertaining,* which appeared in three parts from 1729 to 1733. In 1736, she published a long poem in eight books, *The History of Joseph,* which was based on the Biblical story.

Elizabeth Rowe died of apoplexy at Frome in February 1737. Before her death, she had requested her friend Isaac Watts to edit a collection of her prayers, and this appeared as *Devout Exercises of the Heart* later that year. The book was popular enough to merit several editions, one of which was published in America in 1792. The compilation *Miscellaneous Works,* edited by her brother-in-law Theophilus Rowe, was published in 1739.

Rowe's work was popular, widely read, influential, and frequently reprinted and translated. She was credited with being the first English poet to combine the qualities of romantic and religious verse. She was aware that as a woman writer, she had few predecessors and would not receive as much support as male writers. In her preface to *Poems on Several Occasions*, Rowe wrote that male writers monopolized the tradition of writing, and fostered the belief that women did not have as much sense or intelligence as they did. She protested these assertions, declaring them "Violations of the liberties of Free-born English women."

SOURCES:

Buck, Claire, ed. *The Bloomsbury Guide to Women's Literature*. NY: Prentice Hall, 1992.

The Concise Dictionary of National Biography. Oxford: Oxford University Press, 1992.

Shattock, Joanne. *The Oxford Guide to British Women Writers*. Oxford: Oxford University Press, 1993.

Kelly Winters,
freelance writer, Bayville, New York

Rowlandson, Mary

(c. 1635–after 1682)

Colonial American whose memoirs of her years in captivity with the Narragansett tribe were published in 1682. Born Mary White Rowlandson around 1635 in Somersetshire, England; died after 1682 in Wethersfield, Connecticut; daughter of John White and Joane West White; married Reverend Joseph Rowlandson, in 1656, in Lancaster, Massachusetts; children: Joseph (b. 1661); Mary (b. 1665); Sarah (1669–1676).

Mary Rowlandson is known for the memoirs she composed after being held captive by Narragansett Indians. She was born in Somersetshire, England, around 1635, but as a child she traveled with her Puritan family to the colony of Massachusetts. About age 21, she married a minister, Joseph Rowlandson of Lancaster, Massachusetts, then had three surviving children. In February 1676, Lancaster was attacked and burned by a party of Narragansett Indians during the Native American uprising against the English colonists known as King Philip's War. Joseph was away at the time. Mary tried to shelter many of Lancaster villagers in her home, but the house was invaded and many of its occupants killed, including Mary's sister and other family members. Rowlandson and her infant Sarah were wounded and taken captive, as were her two older children. Separated from her children, Mary was held captive as a slave for three months, suffering from terrible hunger and cold as well as from bullet wounds. The Narragansett Indians, themselves suffering from the devastation of the war and the harsh winter and constantly on the move in search of food, shared little of their meager food supply with their English captive. Her daughter Sarah died from starvation after a week.

Rowlandson worked for the Indians as a servant and seamstress. As she records in her memoirs, an Indian gave her a Bible seized in a raid which helped sustain her morale and faith during her captivity. A devout Puritan, Rowlandson resisted the urge to try to escape and instead waited patiently for her freedom. After three months, the Indians allowed her to be ransomed by her husband for £20; her two remaining children were eventually freed as well. King Philip's War ended in August, and the Rowlandsons settled in Boston, then in Wethersfield, Connecticut. Joseph Rowlandson died in November 1678.

Rowlandson's vivid memoirs of the captivity were published in 1682 as *The Sovereignty and Goodness of God*; as the title indicates, the book focuses on her religious faith during her captivity. She composed the memoirs as a spiritual lesson for the benefit of her children, in which her trial and deliverance are examples of God's desire that Christians suffer for their faith to prove their worthiness for salvation. At the same time, the book is a fascinating, detailed account of day-to-day life among the Narragansett in a period of great hardship and violence. It became a model for other autobiographies, and is considered a classic colonial American work. The exact year of Rowlandson's death is not known.

SOURCES:

James, Edward T., ed. *Notable American Women, 1607–1950*. Cambridge, MA: The Belknap Press of Harvard University, 1971.

Rowlandson, Mary. *The Captive: The True Story of the Captivity of Mrs. Mary Rowlandson*. Tucson, AZ: American Eagle, 1987.

Laura York, M.A. in History,
University of California, Riverside, California

Rowson, Susanna (1762–1824)

Bestselling English-born novelist, essayist, poet, dramatist, lyricist, actress, and educator. Born Susanna Haswell on or about February 5, 1762, in Portsmouth, England; died in Boston, Massachusetts, on March 2, 1824; daughter of William Haswell (a British naval officer) and Susanna (Musgrave) Haswell (who died shortly after her daughter's birth); educated at home; married William Rowson, in 1786; no children.

Brought to America by her father (1767); returned to England (1778); served as governess until publication of her first novel (1786); continued writing novels and joined a theatrical touring company with husband (1792); joined Philadelphia New Theater Company (1793) and then Federal Street Theater in Boston (1796); retired from stage (1797); established a Young Ladies' Academy in Boston where she served as headmistress until her retirement (1822).

Selected writings: author of the first bestselling novel in American history, Charlotte Temple: A Tale of Truth *(London, 1791, Philadelphia, 1794); also wrote eight other didactic novels, five plays on patriotic themes, two volumes of poetry, and six pedagogical works on geography, history, religion, and spelling.*

In 18th-century European and American society, middle-class women were expected to marry, raise a family, and limit their activities to the domestic sphere. But what if one's parents were suddenly plunged into poverty and/or the man one married was a poor provider, as happened to Susanna Rowson? In such cases, a woman was forced to work, and that is what Rowson did, from her 16th year in 1778 until her retirement in 1822.

A versatile, talented woman of great sense and sensibility, Rowson is a lesson in survival. Her mother **Susanna Musgrave Haswell**, the daughter of a commissioner of customs at Portsmouth, England, died less than ten days after her daughter's birth. A few years later, her father William Haswell, a captain in the British Navy, had to leave his daughter in the care of her nurse and relatives when he was appointed a collector of royal customs in the colony of Massachusetts.

In America, Captain Haswell married **Rachel Woodward**, the daughter of a Hingham merchant, and they settled in a charming house at Hull on the tip of Nantasket Peninsula near Boston. In 1767, Haswell returned to England to fetch his five-year-old daughter and her nurse. The voyage to America almost ended in tragedy, for food supplies ran dangerously low and the ship was almost wrecked as it entered Boston Harbor during a wintry storm. Later, the themes of death in childbirth and shipwrecks were to appear in several of Rowson's novels.

Cavendish, Georgiana. *See Lamb, Caroline for sidebar.*

Susanna Rowson

From 1768 to 1774, Susanna lived an idyllic life in Massachusetts, educated at home and so well read by the age of 12 that the Haswells' summer neighbor, the famous patriot James Otis, referred to her as "my little scholar." However, the American Revolution ended this idyll, and by 1775 Captain Haswell's property was confiscated when he refused to side with the Americans. Susanna and her family endured considerable hardship for the next three years. Finally, in 1778 the Haswells were exchanged for American prisoners in Canada and set sail for England via Halifax.

By the time Rowson returned to England she was 16, her two half-brothers were less than ten years old, and her father and stepmother were ill and penniless. In all probability, Susanna served as a governess for the next eight years. She also sold lyrics to music publishers and, hoping to supplement her meager income, in 1786 she published her first novel, *Victoria*. Rowson found a patron who could guarantee her subscribers, and she dedicated her novel to ◀ **Georgiana Cavendish** (1757–1806), duchess of Devonshire, an intelligent and learned patron of the arts who also wrote poems and novels. Struggling to support herself and her family (which now included a third half-brother), and past her 24th year, Susanna put aside her misgivings and later that year (1786) married William Rowson. An acquaintance of her father's, William was a handsome and affable man, a fine trumpeter, and a horseman of the guard. In addition, he was part owner of what Susanna's father believed to be a thriving hardware business.

Susanna's misgivings about William were soon confirmed; he was a poor provider with a drinking problem. As a result, after her marriage Rowson continued to write and publish novels, most of them about women like herself who, against terrible odds, sought to earn a living while maintaining their virtue. However, at that time few novelists could make a living from their writings. For example, her classic novel of seduction and betrayal, *Charlotte Temple: A Tale of Truth* (1791), brought her instant fame, but very little money.

To make matters worse, by 1792 William's hardware business collapsed and dire need drove Susanna, William, and his younger sister **Charlotte Rowson** to seek employment in English provincial theaters. Each of them had some talent as musicians, singers and dancers, but they earned less than a bare subsistence on the stage. In 1793, the three eagerly accepted a contract with the New Theater in Philadelphia. That year,

Susanna embarked on her third and last voyage across the Atlantic.

When the Philadelphia company went bankrupt in 1796, the Rowsons joined the newly opened Federal Theater in Boston. Within a year, however, that theater also closed and Susanna, Charlotte, and William were forced to abandon the stage. Between 1793 and 1797, Susanna had acted 129 different parts in 126 different productions. In addition, she had written at least five musical plays on patriotic themes, such as *Slaves in Algiers* (1793), that were published and performed in Philadelphia and Boston.

Aware that schools for well-off young women aged 11 to 16 were the rage in the young Republic, in November 1797, and helped by a wealthy patron, Rowson decided to establish a Young Ladies' Academy in Boston. The school, which was moved several times in the Boston area, was a success and for over 20 years was to provide the financial stability that previously had eluded Susanna. Though largely self-educated herself, Rowson was an experienced governess whose novels and other writings were didactic in purpose. She offered her students a thorough education that included arithmetic, geography, geometry, grammar, history, reading, religion and writing. For an extra fee, the older students could also take classes in dancing, French, embroidery, needlework, music, and painting.

Rowson was an innovative and imaginative "preceptress" who offered classes in piano, a new instrument that was just appearing in wealthy American homes. In addition, she was highly aware of the importance of sea power in history; in her textbooks on history and geography and even spelling, she taught her students about navigation in history. She was also a pioneer in women's studies. In three of her six textbooks, she included considerable material on women, especially learned women who were models of bravery, intelligence and intellectual accomplishment. Her feminist intent was clear—to prove that women are the intellectual equals of men. In Rowson's texts and in her teaching she also wanted her students to associate ideas and to think for themselves so that they could continue their education on their own, as she had done.

Susanna made a deep impression on her students. One of them, **Eliza Southgate Bowne**, described her as "an amiable lady, so mild, so good, no one can help loving her; she treats all her scholars with . . . tenderness. . . . No woman was ever better calculated to govern a school than Mrs. Rowson." Another student, **Mary Batchelder**, near death in 1869, wrote of Susanna: "dear, generous, kind hearted woman. Lord grant that we may meet in heaven." Endowed with many gifts, and goaded on by a lifelong need to earn a living, Susanna Rowson led an eventful and productive life in an exciting time of revolutionary change in America and Europe.

SOURCES:

Birdsall, Richard D. "Susanna Haswell Rowson," in *Notable American Women: 1607–1950*. Vol. III. Cambridge, MA: Harvard University Press, 1971, pp. 202–204.

Dexter, Elizabeth Anthony. *Career Women of America, 1776–1840*. Boston, MA: Houghton Mifflin, 1950.

Nason, Elias. *Memoir of Mrs. Susanna Rowson*. Albany, NY: Joel Munsell, 1876.

Rowson, Susanna Haswell. *Charlotte Temple: A Tale of Truth*. NY: Oxford University Press, 1987.

SUGGESTED READING:

Parker, Patricia L. *Susanna Rowson*. Boston, MA: Twayne, 1986.

Weil, Dorothy. *In Defense of Women: Susanna Rowson (1762–1824)*. University Park, PA: Pennsylvania University Press, 1976.

Anna Macías,
Professor Emerita of History,
Ohio Wesleyan University, Delaware, Ohio

Roxana.

Variant of Roxane.

Roxana (fl. 350 BCE)

Macedonian noblewoman. One of seven wives of *Philip II, king of Macedonia (r. 359–336 BCE). Philip's other wives were* **Audata**, *****Olympias**, **Meda**, *****Nicesipolis**, *****Philinna**, *and* **Cleopatra of Macedon**.

Roxane (c. 345–310 BCE)

Bactrian warrior-princess. Name variations: Roxana; Roxané. Born around 345; murdered in 310 BCE (some sources cite 311); daughter of Oxyartes, a Bactrian noble; married Alexander III the Great (356–323 BCE), king of Macedonia (r. 336–323 BCE), in 327 BCE; children: Alexander IV, king of Macedonia.

Probably in October 331, after his great victory over the Persian king Darius III at the battle of Gaugamela, Alexander III the Great, king of Macedonia, proclaimed himself "King of Asia" (not a Persian title). Yet, the war against Darius was not over, for the twice-beaten Persian king fled farther east to try to mobilize an effective defense against the Macedonian. In July 330, however, a group of generals led by Bessus, the satrap (governor) of Bactria and Sogdiana (parts of modern Pakistan, Afghanistan, Turkmenistan, Uzbekistan, and Tajikistan), lost faith in Darius, murdered him, and proclaimed Bessus king of Persia in Darius' stead. Alexander's official position vis-a-vis Darius shifted after the latter's execution: once an adversary, in death Darius became Alexander's honored predecessor, and his murder and the elevation of Bessus became acts of usurpation. Alexander announced his intention—since he had "rightly" won Darius' throne through honorable combat, not murder—to avenge Darius' murder and punish Bessus' treachery in the traditional Persian manner.

Bessus retired to his satrapies and prepared for Alexander's coming. In late 330, after consolidating his power in modern-day Iran, Alexander followed him, but by a somewhat more circuitous route. During the winter of 330–29 BCE, he crossed the Hindu Kush from the southwest by way of the region of Kabul, and attacked the valley of the Oxus River (Bactria proper) from the south during the spring and summer of 329. At first, Alexander's audacity and strategic insight carried the day. Bessus was captured, physically mutilated—the customary Persian punishment for regicides—and put to death. Next, Alexander moved north into the flood plain of the Jaxartes River (Sogdiana), on which he founded a city as a start to a general regional reorganization. It then became obvious to the locals that Alexander was going to attempt to regulate this frontier, which abutted the vastness of central Asia, more closely than the Persians had. Such a plan implied a degree of centralization which the Persians had never imposed, and it also threatened to wreak havoc with the local economy which depended to a significant extent upon the trade route which traversed Asia all the way to China. This realization sparked a widely popular and hard-fought guerilla war (from autumn 329 through spring 327), confronting Alexander with the most difficult fighting he had faced in Asia.

The geographical and human obstacles Alexander encountered in Bactria and Sogdiana were so daunting that he came to realize that he would never secure the region by physical force alone. He therefore turned to tact and diplomacy in an attempt to win over the trust of influential local leaders. One of the most important of these was Oxyartes, who had supported Bessus and who was a participant in the uprising against Alexander. The sources are not in agreement about the timing of the capture of Oxyartes' family, but it is most likely that Alexander apprehended Oxyartes' wife and daughters in 328, and that he flaunted their good treatment so as to entice Oxyartes to surrender, which the latter did in the spring of 327. Soon thereafter, Alexander

completely won over Oxyartes by marrying Oxyartes' daughter Roxane. Some of our sources report that Alexander fell in love with Roxane at first sight, and indeed, she apparently was beautiful. At the heart of this marriage, however, was high politics, for Oxyartes (and, through him, his formerly hostile nation) was being offered an intimate alliance with the most powerful man of his time. Moreover, this was Alexander's first marriage and thus his request for Roxane constituted a very special compliment to all associated with her—a fact neither missed nor appreciated by the many within the Macedonian aristocracy who would have killed to have been so honored. It should be noted that when Alexander married Roxane, he had already been king for almost a decade, he had no viable heir, and he had put himself in harm's way many times. Responsible monarchs took care of their succession. Whether Alexander's prolonged bachelorhood was a matter of irresponsibility, a matter of sexual preference, a matter of politics (that is, he had not previously selected a bride so as not to anger all of those whose daughters had *not* been selected), or some combination of all three, his marriage to Roxane is a testament to the military resistance offered by her people. This latter point becomes especially poignant when it is realized that Alexander's "orientalization" (his occasional adoption of Asian dress and etiquette, and increasingly his readiness to employ Asian manpower to fill military and political posts) was already a growing problem for his Macedonians.

Alexander rewarded Oxyartes first by making him an advisor and then by naming him as the satrap of Paropamisus, the strategic region in the Hindu Kush (around Kabul) which dominated the passes between Bactria and ancient India. Oxyartes would continue to serve in that capacity until the wars which arose after Alexander's death. Roxane accompanied her husband to India where, probably in 326, she delivered a child which died soon after its birth. Little else is known about Roxane during Alexander's lifetime except that her status was threatened when Alexander married (324) two additional wives (*Statira III and *Parysatis II), who were both products of the Achaemenid royal house. When Alexander died near Babylon in June 323, Roxane was again pregnant. It was probably more to protect the interests of her unborn child than simple jealousy which induced Roxane to connive with the Macedonian general, Perdiccas, to secretly murder both Statira and Parysatis soon after Alexander was dead.

When Roxane gave birth to a son, Alexander IV, in September 323, he immediately came to share in the kingship with his mentally incapacitated uncle Philip III, under Perdiccas' regency. Joint kingship was unprecedented in Macedon, as (probably) was the installation of a non-Argead regent. The political ambiguities of the situation, coupled with the rivalries and ambitions current among Alexander's top generals, virtually assured the outbreak of civil war among the most powerful Macedonians. As such, Perdiccas jealously maintained possession of Roxane and the kings in the hope that he could consolidate his control over military rivals, in part by issuing edicts in the kings' names. This ploy failed to convince most of his peers, however, who considered Perdiccas' regency to be more the product of good luck than of merit: although there were older and more respected Macedonians alive when Alexander died, none of these were at Babylon when Alexander passed, a fact which gave Perdiccas a jump on his rivals. Civil war erupted when Perdiccas' authority was challenged, initially by Antigonus and Ptolemy. Both of these generals appealed to Antipater (the most senior and respected Macedonian then living), whom Alexander had left in charge in Europe when he invaded Asia, and Antipater joined the anti-Perdiccan coalition. In the struggle which followed, after an unsuccessful invasion of Egypt (where Ptolemy was encamped), Perdiccas was murdered by some of his own officers (321). Thereafter, Roxane and the kings (with *Eurydice [c. 337–317 BCE] in tow, since she was then the wife of Philip III) fell under the authority of Antipater, who brought them all to Macedonia, where they remained in security until the old general died in 319.

Just before he died, Antipater appointed Polyperchon, one of his adjutants, as the next regent. Why Antipater did not name his own son, Cassander, to the post has caused some debate, but undoubtedly the old Argead loyalist read the situation correctly: that is, if an Argead were ever to again rule in his own name—and that meant Roxane's son, who would not be old enough to rule for well over a decade—then a regency acceptable to all powerful Macedonians would have to be established. Perdiccas' biggest problem had been that he had neither the age nor the experience to convince his peers that it should be he and *no other* who should control the kings. Just as Perdiccas did not possess the reputation to be accepted by his peers, neither did Cassander, who had not even served under Alexander during the conquest of Persia, a fact which mattered greatly to those who had been with Alexander. (Antipater did not face the same criticism since he had long served the Argead house, since Alexander had trusted the homeland to him while the king was away, and since Antipater had fought during Alexander's lifetime, albeit in Europe, not Asia.) Antipater did miscalculate, however: although Polyperchon made a first-rate second in command, he lacked the talent to dominate at the next level.

Cassander, who felt betrayed by his father, rebelled against Polyperchon's regency. Others, who were jealous of Polyperchon's new status, followed suit. As Cassander made his move, he was approached by Eurydice (as the would-be power behind Philip III) to become her champion, so that she could end the joint kingship in favor of her husband. This development brought *Olympias, the mother of Alexander the Great and grandmother of Alexander IV, into the fray, and the kingdom became factionalized behind the two kings. Roxane was unable to establish herself in Olympias' place because she was not intimate with individual Macedonian power-brokers and their ways, and because the Macedonians generally still resented her foreignness. Olympias (aided by her cousin Aecides, the king of Epirus) made common cause with Polyperchon to save the life of her grandson, and took decisive action. In 317, both Philip III and Eurydice fell into Olympias' hands, and both were summarily executed.

During this time, the young Alexander was betrothed to **Deidameia**, the daughter of Aecides, a match which, had the marriage occurred, would have been another in a series which linked the political destinies of Macedon and Epirus. It was Olympias, not Roxane, who arranged this betrothal. The union never materialized, however, because Cassander took Pydna, a Macedonian seaport, had Olympias put to death, and seized Roxane and Alexander IV (316). Whether or not Cassander at that time began to map out the course which would elevate him to kingship (beginning in 306, he and several others all claimed that status), he did inaugurate a series of acts (including his marriage to the Argead princess *Thessalonike, whom he captured along with Roxane and her son) which paved the way for his eventual assumption of the throne.

Of course, the existence of Alexander IV was a problem for Cassander and any other Macedonian with royal ambitions, because the memories of the young king's father and grandfather Philip II were revered among the general Macedonian population. Not wanting to provoke outrage through the mishandling of Alexander IV or Roxane, Cassander put both under whatever "protective" custody the fortified citadel in Amphipolis (under the command of a trusted supporter named Glaukias) could provide. Although Cassander claimed to act in Alexander's interests, he did deprive the young king of his pages and other royal perquisites. There Roxane and Alexander remained, probably knowing most of the comforts of life, until after a treaty was signed by Cassander, Ptolemy and Antigonus, one of the provisions of which was that each of them would retain their current authority until Alexander reached maturity. This treaty was a death sentence, because when Alexander reached puberty (310–09), many Macedonians began to question openly why Cassander had not yet begun the process of educating the prince in a manner befitting a future king. Both Roxane and Alexander were then murdered, although their deaths were kept secret for a time. Eventually the fact of their deaths was announced, but Cassander refused to admit that there had been anything sinister about their ends. Alexander seems to have been interred in one of the rich tombs recently excavated in the burial grounds of the Argead house, located at ancient Aegae. Where Roxane was laid to rest is unknown, but it certainly was far from her home. Perhaps Cassander's execution of Roxane was a kind of blessing, for once she left the security of her mountainous homeland, Roxane became little more than a pawn, tolerated only because she had given birth to the great Alexander's only legitimate heir.

William Greenwalt,
Associate Professor of Classical History,
Santa Clara University, Santa Clara, California

Roxelana (c. 1504–1558)

Captured slave who became wife and consort of the sultan Suleiman, reinstated marriage among the Ottoman rulers, influenced her husband's foreign and domestic policies, consolidated her power by wiping out rivals, and initiated a period of Ottoman history known as the "reign of women." Name variations: Hurrem or Khurrem (Joyful or The Laughing One); Hurrem Sultana; Roxalana, Roxalena, Rossa, Roksoliana. Pronunciation: ROCKS-uh-LAN-ah. Born (probably) Aleksandra Lisowska around 1504 in the town of Rogatin, near Lvov; died on April 15, 1558, in Constantinople; daughter (probably) of a Ruthenian priest; mother unknown; married Suleiman or Suleyman the Magnificent, Ottoman sultan (r. 1520–1566), in 1530; children—five: sons Mehmed; Selim II, Ottoman sultan (r. 1566–1574); Beyazit or Beyazid or Bayezid (d. 1561), Jehangir; and daughter Mihrimah (1522–1575).

Remained Suleiman's domestic and foreign advisor and closest confidante, while eliminating his eldest son, Mustafa, as heir to the throne, and paving the way for the ultimate succession of her own son, Selim.

Toward the middle of the 16th century, European trade representatives witnessed signs of an extraordinary event in Constantinople, the capital of the Ottoman Empire. The sultan Suleiman I the Magnificent had ruled there since 1520, the leader of troops that dominated Turkey, the Balkans, and parts of Hungary and the Middle East, and occasionally posed a threat to Europe by laying siege as they once did to the city of Vienna. But Suleiman's empire was also a powerful trading partner with the West, and held riches beyond anything imaginable in Europe. In his land, the wealthy and powerful wore expensive silks, bathed in warm, scented baths, ate food seasoned with exotic spices, and read manuscripts inherited from the collapsed Roman Empire. In 1530, England's Sir George Young, reporting back to his government by diplomatic pouch, made close observations of daily life, and also wrote about a period in which the city's houses were festooned with garlands, streets were illuminated, and a succession of tournaments, feasts, and processions featured "wild beasts, and giraffes with necks so long they as it were touched the sky," all events marking the marriage of the sultan to his longtime consort, Roxelana, the mother of several of his children, and the woman to whom he had been faithful for many years.

The lavish celebration of royal marriages was common to Europe as well as to the East, but the remarkable political implication underlying this event was the fact that in the past two centuries no powerful Turkish sultan had married, preferring to produce heirs through temporary liaisons with slaves and concubines. The marriage of Suleiman to Roxelana was a radical break with this tradition, signifying the powerful influence of an extraordinary woman.

The origins of Roxelana are obscure. According to Polish tradition, she was Aleksandra Lisowska, the daughter of a Ruthenian priest, born in 1504, in the town of Rogatin, near Lvov, in the western Ukraine, which was then part of Poland; her name may derive from a term meaning "Ruthenian maiden." During this period, Tartar tribes from the East made frequent raids into the Ukraine to obtain booty and slaves. One such captive was a girl of fair complexion with reddish-blonde hair, making her a valuable prize and a worthy gift for the sultan.

Despite the trauma of abduction to a foreign land far from all she knew and loved, Roxelana became known in the harem for her merry ways. She was sometimes punished for refusing to follow the harem rules, but when she was beaten she never cried; because of her happy nature, she was called Hurrem, meaning "joyful."

The harem in which Roxelana was installed was a social institution with a long history in the Middle East, where polygamy had been a traditional practice long before the region became Muslim. The nomadic, pre-Islamic, Turkic tribes frequently engaged in warfare, and Turkic women often fought side-by-side with the men and otherwise enjoyed considerable equality; Turkic culture prized girls, and mediatory prayers often requested the birth of a female. Change in customs regarding women was probably due more to Persian influence than to conversion to Islam. Persia had been influential in the region since Greek and Roman times, and its patriarchal social system was considered superior to Turkic nomadism. As Turkish rulers came to dominate the former Byzantine Empire, one of the Persian customs they adopted was the rigid segregation of women, a social convention that actually overcame religious teaching to bring the harems into existence. Islam, meanwhile, actually improved women's status, as it guaranteed them greater property rights than those enjoyed by their European counterparts; and it limited to four the number of wives a man could marry. The Koran itself did not sanction harems or the veiling of women.

The word *harem* referred both to a portion of a house set aside for women and children, and to a man's wife or wives. Large houses and palaces were divided into the harem and the *selamlik* (men's section). The seclusion of women became connected with economic standing, as only the wealthy could afford to segregate women. Poor peasant women lived in cramped one-room houses, working alongside their men to sustain daily life. While poor women were veiled in public, their freedom of movement was relatively unrestricted. All women, rich or poor, gained little protection from the institution of marriage. A husband had the right to divorce his wife whenever he wished, merely by informing her orally or in writing, "I divorce thee." Divorce, however, was extremely uncommon. Sexual purity, an important factor in marriage, was also a driving force behind the creation of harems. Since the honor of husbands and family rested on the purity of women, strict measures were taken to ensure limited contact with the opposite sex. When women left the harem, they were veiled, taking their seclusion with them.

The harem was guarded by eunuchs who protected the women and acted as go-betweens with the outside world. Eunuchs were male slaves who had been captured while young and castrated in order to serve in this unique function. (Castration was also practiced in Europe; for centuries, thousands of young boys were castrated in order to retain lovely soprano voices into adulthood and to perform in choirs and operas.) In royal palaces, a harem might consist of hundreds or even thousands of women, children, and eunuchs. Ornate furniture, luxurious baths, expensive clothing, rich food, and female servants were provided for the inhabitants. Normal activities consisted of supervising the housework, looking after the children or embroidering. Although women could visit some female neighbors or go to Turkish baths, they rarely left the harem.

By the 14th century, a number of factors had led to the decline of marriage among Ottoman rulers. One factor may have been the fear that if a sultan were defeated in war, his wife would be carried off as a trophy. Another factor was economic: since the groom traditionally gave his new wife a dowry which was then her property, one or more wives for an Ottoman sultan could cause a draining of the coffers. It must also be noted that as the Ottomans enjoyed greater and greater military success, it became increasingly customary for beautiful captives to be added to the harem without the status of a wife. Whatever the reasons, by the reign of Suleiman the Magnificent, all women in the royal harem were concubines rather than wives.

It is not known when Roxelana came to Suleiman's harem. She may have been presented to him as a gift when he became sultan in September 1520. As a slave, she would have entered the complicated hierarchy of the harem with lowly status. A woman's fortunes were tied to those of her son, and therefore the highest-ranking female in the kingdom was the sultan's mother, known as *haseki sultan* (princess favorite); beneath her was the *bas haseki sultan* (chief), mother of the sultan's eldest son. Next were the women promoted to *ikbal* or *hasodalik* (fortunate) once they had been invited to share the sultan's bed. Beneath them were the *gözde* (in favor), or women who might eventually share the sultan's bed. The *gedikliler* (privileged ones) and the *sagirdeler* (novices) formed the two lowest ranks, to which Roxelana initially belonged.

Roxelana was slight and limber, but apart from her reddish hair was no particular beauty; her joyous, fearless nature was what made her stand out. She liked to adorn herself with bright ornaments and wear unusual costumes, and on his visits to the harem, Suleiman began to talk with her because of his interest in the lands to the North. On the day he left his scarf on her shoulder as a sign that he wished to sleep with her, she was immediately raised to a *gözde*.

> [S]uch love does [Suleiman] bear her . . . that they say she has bewitched him.
>
> —Luigi Bassano

In 1521, when Roxelana gave birth to Suleiman's son, named Mehmed, she became the third most powerful woman in the harem. Rivalry was inevitable in such a system, and *Gülabahar Sultana, the mother of Mustafa, the sultan's eldest son, began to display her anger at the favors shown Roxelana. But when Gülabahar attacked and insulted Roxelana, tearing her hair, scratching her face, and saying, "Traitor, sold meat, you want to compete with me?," she miscalculated the resourcefulness of her opponent. When Suleiman next summoned Roxelana, she refused to come, sending the excuse that since she was "sold meat," with a scratched face and torn-out hair, she was unworthy to be in the sultan's presence. It was an act that could have cost her her life.

Impressed by Roxelana's fearlessness and more intrigued than ever, Suleiman sent for Gülabahar and asked if the story were true. Gülabahar replied not only that it was, but that Roxelana had gotten what she deserved. Shortly thereafter, Suleiman made his son Mustafa governor of Mansia, a province far from the seat of power; this change required Gülabahar to accompany him.

Before long, Suleiman began marrying off many of his concubines and slaves and became faithful to Roxelana. Between 1521 and 1524, she gave birth to three more sons and continued to consolidate her power. She also understood Suleiman better than did anyone else, and became much more than just a bedroom companion. The sultan was a poet, and Roxelana also had poetry in her blood. Because her written Turkish was poor, she worked to master the language, and many letters and poems to the sultan followed. She had spies who kept her informed of what was happening throughout the empire, and as her hold over the sultan increased, so did her conviction that slavery and concubinage were not for her. She was determined to become his legal wife, and this she achieved, according to the report of the festivities in 1530.

In 1534, with the death of Suleiman's mother *Hafsa Hatun, Roxelana's duties increased as she became the sultan's political confidante. When he was away at war, which was often, her letters to him were filled with important information about events in the palace and capital. She was one of the few people he trusted completely, and he knew that her spies would inform her of any plots against him. Jealously guarding her proximity to her husband, she identified new rivals, in particular the sultan's inseparable friend and companion Ibrahim. Married to the sultan's sister *Hatice Sultana, he held considerable power as grand vizier, until Roxelana began to undermine his position. During a military campaign Ibrahim played into her hands when he signed a document using the title of sultan. Striking swiftly, Roxelana exposed this arrogance, and Suleiman ordered the execution of his friend on March 15, 1536.

When a fire partially destroyed the harem in the sultan's old palace, Roxelana took the opportunity to make another break with tradition by moving into the sultan's residence in the grand seraglio, Topkapi; until that time, women and children had lived away from the sultan, in completely separate facilities. In new quarters located directly behind the throne room, she was closer than ever to the seat of the sultan's power. When Suleiman wanted to build his wife a new palace and return to the traditional lifestyle, Roxelana distracted him by encouraging the construction of the *Süleymaniye*. With the mosque of Suleiman the Magnificent, the harem gradually became part of the grand seraglio, and Roxelana never lived separately from her husband again.

Extending her influence beyond internal politics to foreign affairs, Roxelana served as Suleiman's chief diplomatic contact with Europe and assumed a powerful role as the sultan's voice in diplomatic relations. Her correspondence with Sigismund I, king of Poland, helped to maintain peace with Poland, and in 1548, she began an ongoing exchange of letters with the new king, Sigismund II, writing that she would be glad to petition Suleiman on his behalf and convey any messages to the sultan. After Suleiman's troops conquered Baghdad, she wrote to **Sutanim**, the sister of the Safavid monarch Sha Tahmasp, that the conquest had been aimed not at "destroying the lands of the Muslims" but at "repairing the houses of religion and adorning the lands of God's law."

In the Ottoman Empire, polygamy meant that there was often more than one rival for succession to the throne. This competition often was resolved through assassination; at the time of his

La piu bella e piu fauorita donna
del gran Turcho dita la Rofsa

In Venetia per Mattio Pagan in Fr
zaria ten per infegna la Fed.

Roxelana

own succession, Suleiman had been the only male who lived to follow the rule of his father. Inevitably, Roxelana became engrossed in the issue of succession, since Suleiman's firstborn, Mustafa, blocked the path to the throne for her own sons. Because Mustafa was handsome and popular with both the army and the people, the sultan's consort waited until this popularity played into her hands.

Meanwhile, as her sons reached the age when they were traditionally given provinces to govern, she defied custom yet again, by remaining in Constantinople with her husband instead of accompanying a son to his new post. Since heirs were always a focal point for potential coups, she also began to work on Suleiman's fears of being overthrown. The sultan became increasingly paranoid about the intentions of Mustafa. Informed of a forged letter to the shah of Persia, supposedly written by Mustafa, about a plan to dethrone him, Suleiman had his son killed, and the succession of Roxelana's own son was thus insured.

Roxelana was not popular among the Ottoman people; she had broken too many conventions, and many considered her responsible for Mustafa's death. Some said openly that his assassination was the result of "the plotting of women and the deceit of the dishonest son-in-law." That son-in-law was Rustem, the husband

Mihrimah. *See Reign of Women.*

of her daughter ◄❧ **Mihrimah**, who through Roxelana's intrigues had risen to the powerful position of grand vizier. It was a violation of the tradition against allowing relatives of the sultan to hold important political positions, which Suleiman had allowed because Mihrimah was his great favorite. Thus, in the eyes of many, Roxelana and Rustem became viewed as an evil duo on the political landscape, thwarting the efforts of a good sultan.

Roxelana died in 1558, after a long illness. Suleiman had her buried in his new mosque, and ordered another mosque built in her name, along with a school and a hospital, near the women's market. After her death, two of Roxelana's sons, Selim and Beyazit, fought over the succession. Beyazit had been his mother's favorite, but he intrigued with the shah of Persia, and the sultan had him assassinated. Suleiman survived his wife by only a few years, until 1566, and was succeeded by Selim (II), who proved to be a weak ruler. By then, the real power of the throne was in the hands of Mihrimah and **Aysha**

Humashah, daughter and granddaughter of Roxelana, continuing what came to be known as "the reign of women." This era, begun when Roxelana moved into the grand seraglio, was to last through the next 150 years of Ottoman history. (See also *Reign of Women.*)

Many historians who have criticized Roxelana and the "reign of women" praise Suleiman for the triumphs of the Ottoman Empire and blame Roxelana for its failings. In fact, Roxelana was like Suleiman in using her power for both good and evil, and leaving a record of successes as well as failures. Whether viewed as a positive or negative force in history, she unquestionably was not a negligible one.

SOURCES:

Atil, Esin. *The Age of Sultan Süleyman the Magnificent.* NY: Harry N. Abrams, 1988.
———. *Turkish Art.* NY: Harry N. Abrams, 1980.
Bridge, Antony. *Suleiman the Magnificent: Scourge of Heaven.* NY: Franklin Watts, 1983.
Croutier, Alev Lytel. *Harem: The World Behind the Veil.* NY: Abbeville Press, 1989.
Inalcik, Halil. *The Ottoman Empire: The Classical Age 1300–1600.* Trans. by Norman Itzkowitz and Colin Imber. London: Weidenfeld & Nicolson, 1973.
Kinross, John Patrick Douglas Balfour (Lord Kinross). *The Ottoman Centuries: The Rise and Fall of the Turkish Empire.* NY: William Morrow, 1977.
Lamb, Harold. *Suleiman the Magnificent: Sultan of the East.* NY: Bantam, 1951.
Peirce, Leslie P. *The Imperial Harem: Women and Sovereignty in the Ottoman Empire.* NY: Oxford University Press, 1993.
"Roksoliana," in *Encyclopedia of Ukraine.* Vol. 4. Edited by Danylo Husar Struck. Toronto: University of Toronto Press, 1993, pp. 394–395.

Karin Loewen Haag,
freelance writer, Athens, Georgia

Gabrielle Roy

Roy, Gabrielle (1909–1983)

French-Canadian writer. Born on March 22, 1909, in St. Boniface, Manitoba; died of heart failure on July 13, 1983; youngest of 11 children of Léon Roy and Mélina Roy; sister of Bernadette "Dédette" Roy; attended Winnipeg Normal Institute; married Marcel Carbotte (a physician), in 1945.

Selected works: Bonheur d'occasion (1945, published in English as The Tin Flute, 1947); La Petite Poule d'Eau (1950, published in English as Where Nests the Water Hen, 1951); Rue Deschambault (1955, published in English as Street of Riches, 1956); La Montagne Secrète (1961, published in English as The Secret Mountain, 1962); Ces Enfants de ma vie (1977, published in English as Children of My Heart); (autobiography) La Détresse et l'enchantment (1984, published in English as Enchantment and Sorrow, 1987); Letters to Bernadette (1990).

Born the youngest of 11 children in St. Boniface, Manitoba, in 1909, Gabrielle Roy was four years old when her father lost his longtime job and the family, never well-to-do, faced dire financial straits. The effects of poverty would later play a large role in Roy's writings. Gabrielle, who was close to her mother **Mélina Roy**, helped as best she could by studying hard enough to win cash prizes for her schoolwork; the money she was awarded was sufficient to pay for most of her freshman year at college. After graduating from the Winnipeg Normal Institute, she spent seven years as a teacher, much of it in her hometown of St. Boniface.

In 1937, much to her mother's dismay, Roy gave up her secure teaching job in the midst of the Depression and traveled to Europe. There she published for the first time, with several articles appearing in a French magazine. Imminent war forced her return to Canada in 1939. Settling in Montreal, she supported herself by working as a freelance journalist and began writing what would become her first novel, *Bonheur d'occasion* (1945). The first close examination of postwar life in Montreal, it was a realistic study of the defeated derelicts of a modern, industrialized city, and marked the beginning of a new era in French-Canadian literature. In 1947, *Bonheur d'occasion* won the French Prix Fémina, and an English translation published that year, *The Tin Flute*, received Canada's Governor-General's Award.

Roy's next novel, *La Petite Poule d'Eau* (1950, published in English as *Where Nests the Water Hen*, 1951), was written partly in France, where she lived for three years in the late 1940s with her new husband. It was followed by *Rue Deschambault* (1955); the English translation of that novel, *Street of Riches*, also won the Governor-General's Award, in 1957, as did her final novel, *Ces enfants de ma vie* (*Children of My Heart*), in 1978. A private woman who preferred to keep public appearances to a minimum, Roy maintained a longtime correspondence with her sister **Bernadette Roy**, a nun, before Bernadette's death in 1970. These letters were published in English in 1990 as *Letters to Bernadette*. Roy's autobiography, *La Détresse et l'enchantment* (published in English as *Enchantment and Sorrow*), appeared in 1984, one year after her death from heart failure.

SOURCES AND SUGGESTED READING:

Roy, Gabrielle. *Enchantment and Sorrow: The Autobiography of Gabrielle Roy.* Trans. by Patricia Claxton. Toronto: Lester & Orpen Dennys, c. 1987.

———. *Letters to Bernadette.* Trans. by Patricia Claxton. Toronto: Lester & Orpen Dennys, c. 1990.

Royall, Anne (1769–1854)

Colonial writer who is considered one of the first women journalists in America. Name variations: Anne Newport Royall. Born Anne Newport on June 11, 1769, near Baltimore, Maryland; died on October 1, 1854, in Washington, D.C.; daughter of William Newport (a farmer) and Mary Newport; married William Royall (a farmer who had served in the American Revolution), in 1797 (died 1813); no children.

Selected writings: Sketches of History, Life and Manners in the United States *(1826);* The Tennessean *(novel, 1827);* The Black Book; or, A Continuation of Travels in the United States *(3 vols., 1828–29);* Mrs. Royall's Pennsylvania *(2 vols., 1829);* Mrs. Royall's Southern Tour *(3 vols., 1830–31);* Letters from Alabama *(1830).*

Anne Royall was born Anne Newport on June 11, 1769, near Baltimore, Maryland, the older of two daughters of **Mary Newport** and William Newport, a small farmer who was still loyal to the king of England. The loss of his land and the hostility of his neighbors towards his political stance prompted him to move his family to the western Pennsylvania frontier. By 1775, the Newports bought land near Hannastown in Westmoreland County. Anne learned to read from her father, and later attended a one-room log schoolhouse nearby.

William Newport died about 1775, most likely in a skirmish with Native Americans. Anne's mother Mary Newport married a man named Butler, and after his death she moved her family down the Shenandoah Valley to Virginia, hoping for help from family friends or relatives. When Anne was 16, they moved to Sweet Springs in Monroe County (now part of West Virginia). Mary became a servant to Captain William Royall, a wealthy farmer who was a personal friend of George Washington and had served in the American Revolution. Captain Royall had one of the largest libraries in Virginia, was a Freemason, and was an avid admirer of Voltaire and Thomas Paine. Known as an eccentric to his neighbors, he set his slaves free and refused to fence in his cattle. Royall took Anne as his protégé, let her read anything in his library, and taught her his theories about life and society. They were married in 1797.

After her husband's death in 1813, Anne Royall left what she called the "cold, dreary, hard-frozen hills" of western Virginia and moved to Alabama with three servants and her inheritance. She lived well until 1823, when some of her husband's relatives managed to void his will by accusing her of adultery. Destitute, and with her reputation in tatters, she went to Washington to ask for the widow's pension due her since Captain Royall had been a veteran; these negotiations would drag on into her old age.

In order to make a living, Royall began traveling throughout the country and writing accounts of her trips. Despite her previous complaints about life in Virginia, she seemed unbothered by hard travel on foot, by stagecoach and by steamer. Throughout the 1820s, alone and with almost no money, she visited nearly every important town in the United States, taking notes in shorthand. She produced five books in ten volumes about her travels, which are still considered important sources of information about America in that era: *Sketches of History, Life and Manners in the United States* (1826); *The Black Book; or, A Continuation of Travels in the United States* (three vols., 1828–29); *Mrs. Royall's Pennsylvania* (two vols., 1829); *Mrs. Royall's Southern Tour* (three vols., 1830–31); and *Letters from Alabama* (1830). She also wrote a novel, *The Tennessean* (1827), and a play, *The Cabinet*; these latter two, unlike her travel books, were not well regarded.

The style of her travel books reveals Royall's opinionated and at times vitriolic temperament. In her straightforward, readable, if sometimes disjointed prose, she heaped praise or criticism on the people and places she visited, naming names and unconcerned about offending public opinion. Her irascible temper got her in trouble on at least two occasions. In 1829, after she called a pillar of the community "a damned old bald-headed son of a bitch" (in public, twice), she was taken to court and charged with being a "common scold"—a charge unused since Puritan times that had been dug from dusty law books solely to punish her. She was convicted, much to her humiliation (and to the delight of her detractors, no doubt), but the court declined to sentence a 60-year-old woman to the prescribed punishment of ducking in a pond; instead, she was fined ten dollars, which her lawyer paid. In another instance, during a fight about Freemasonry, which she wholeheartedly supported, she suffered a broken leg after being thrown down a flight of stairs.

However, Royall's tenacity and uncompromising principles led to her establishment as one of America's first female journalists when, on December 3, 1831, she began publishing *Paul Pry*, a weekly Washington, D.C., paper featuring gossip and her sharp-tongued comments. Dressed in an ill-fitting child's plaid coat, she prowled the halls of Congress, cajoling people to buy her publications; those who declined frequently found themselves unflatteringly featured in the following week's edition. According to legend, she once caught President John Quincy Adams swimming in the Potomac River, and sat on his clothes until he agreed to let her interview him. This story is probably fanciful, however, for she counted Adams and his wife *Louisa Catherine Adams among her truest friends; Adams, who supported her efforts to receive her widow's pension, once likened her to "a virago errant in enchanted armor."

Paul Pry was published until November 19, 1836, when it was succeeded by *The Huntress*, which Royall edited for nearly 20 years, until July 2, 1854. She promoted her political views and private agendas (such as Sunday mail delivery), and publicized graft and scandal, much to the terror of corrupt politicians. Royall believed anyone in public life was fair game for her attacks. She despised missionaries and ministers, denouncing them as "monsters" who were "glutted with women and money . . . aiming to overturn our government and establish the reign of terror"; she also thought that booksellers who stocked a preponderance of books from England were conspiring against America. While her strong opinions earned her many enemies, she also had admirers in government who respected the sincerity and courage of her views.

In her old age, Royall finally received the pension for which she had been fighting for so long. She chose a lump sum rather than a yearly benefit, and her husband's legal heirs took half of it. After she paid her debts and legal fees, she received ten dollars for her trouble. Seven of these she gave to her loyal friend and printing assistant, **Sally Stack**, leaving her with three dollars. Penniless, she died in Washington, D.C., on October 1, 1854, only three months after shutting down *The Huntress*, and was buried in the Congressional Cemetery.

SOURCES:

James, Edward T., ed. *Notable American Women, 1607–1950*. Cambridge, MA: The Belknap Press of Harvard University, 1971.

McHenry, Robert, ed. *Famous American Women*. NY: Dover, 1980.

Read, Phyllis J., and Bernard L. Witlieb. *The Book of Women's Firsts*. NY: Random House, 1992.

Woodward, Helen Beal. *The Bold Women*. NY: Farrar, Straus and Young, 1953.

Kelly Winters,
freelance writer, Bayville, New York

Royce, Sarah (1819–1891)

American pioneer and writer. Name variations: Sarah Eleanor Bayliss Royce. Born Sarah Eleanor Bayliss in Stratford-on-Avon, England, on March 2, 1819; died in

San Jose, California, in 1891; daughter of Benjamin Bayliss (a businessman) and Mary T. Bayliss; educated at the Albion Female Seminary in Rochester, New York; married Josiah Royce, in 1847 (died 1889); children: Mary Royce; Hattie Royce; Ruth Royce; Josiah Royce.

Wrote A Frontier Lady: Recollections of the Gold Rush and Early California *(1932), an autobiographical account of her family's westward trek to California during the gold rush.*

Sarah Royce was born in Stratford-on-Avon, England, in 1819, shortly before her family moved to America. They settled in Rochester, New York, where her father began a merchandising business and Sarah later attended the Albion Female Seminary. In 1847, she married Josiah Royce, a fellow English immigrant who had moved to Canada with his family. A restless individual always moving in search of a better life for his family, he was well suited to the pioneering times in which he lived.

In 1848, Royce and her husband headed west with their infant daughter, **Mary**, with California as their destination. It took them until April 1849 to reach Iowa, by which time the full frenzy of the gold rush had swept the country, and thousands upon thousands were traveling to California. Royce is known for her vivid account of the journey, which she wrote over 30 years after the trip. Based on the diary she kept off and on during the trek, *A Frontier Lady: Recollections of the Gold Rush and Early California* (1932) was intended to be read by her son Josiah, who was writing a history of pioneer times in California.

On the trip, the Royces endured the hardships common to all migrants to California. They began the trip in a large wagon train with others seeking gold, but were left behind when they rested on Sundays in observance of the Sabbath. By early October, they were still in the desert west of the Great Salt Lake, and a missed fork in the trail led them to waste their precious reserves of food, water, and energy. Sarah walked to lighten the weight on the exhausted oxen that were pulling their wagon, and they took the straw out of their mattresses to feed the animals; all along the trail, they found piles of things that other pioneers had abandoned in order to ease their loads. The Royces were soon forced to do the same.

Lost and suffering, Royce, who was a fervent member of the Disciples of Christ, turned to her faith. "I had known what it was to *believe* in God, and to pray that He would never leave us," she wrote of this time in the desert. "He came so near

that I no longer simply *believed* in Him, but *knew* his presence." This mystical knowledge remained with her long after the trek was completed.

The Royces managed to reach the Carson River, and in the middle of October set off for the Sierra Nevada mountains. They would not have survived this decision had a government relief expedition not found them and helped them across before snow closed the mountain passes they traveled through. To Royce, this was yet another example of God's guidance and protection. At the Continental Divide, she wrote, "Through what toils and dangers we had come to reach that point; and as I stood looking my farewell [to the east], a strong desire seized me to mark the spot in some way, and record at least one word of grateful acknowledgment. Yes, I would make a little heap of stones." However, as there were no stones to be found, and no sticks or trees either, she left no sign of their passing.

When they reached California, Royce's husband tried to make a living in several different mining jobs. The couple now had three more children, **Hattie**, **Ruth**, and Josiah, and the family lived in the settlement of Grass Valley. They owned very little and led a very simple life, but Royce had acquired several books, including a Bible, a volume of Milton, several histories, a book of children's stories she had found in an abandoned wagon, and an encyclopedia. She taught school in her home to make up for the lack of a local school. She also held religious services in her home whenever a cleric was available.

After 12 years in Grass Valley, the family moved to San Francisco, where the children could attend better schools. The younger Josiah returned East to attend Harvard in 1882; he eventually became a philosophy professor. The elder Josiah, Royce's husband, died in 1889. After his death, Royce went back East for a year, but then returned to San Jose, California, where she lived with her daughter Ruth. In 1891, at age 72, she was knocked against the wall in a post office and died from "nervous shock."

SOURCES:

Edgerly, Lois Stiles, ed. *Give Her This Day: A Daybook of Women's Words.* Gardiner, ME: Tilbury House, 1990.

James, Edward T., ed. *Notable American Women, 1607–1950.* Cambridge, MA: The Belknap Press of Harvard University, 1971.

Kelly Winters,
freelance writer, Bayville, New York

Royde-Smith, Naomi Gwladys
(1875–1964).

See Macaulay, Rose for sidebar.

Royden, A. Maude (1876–1956)

English preacher. Name variations: Agnes Maude Royden. Born in 1876; died on July 30, 1956; daughter of Sir Thomas Royden, 1st baronet of Frankby Hall; educated at Cheltenham Ladies' College and Lady Margaret Hall, Oxford; received a Doctor of Divinity from Glasgow University, 1931; married George W.H. Shaw.

Was the first woman to become a pastor of the Church of England (late 1910s), although she was never officially ordained; became Britain's first female Doctor of Divinity (1931).

A. Maude Royden was born in 1876, the youngest daughter (among so many children that she once noted "We never got to know each other") of Sir Thomas Royden, 1st baronet of Frankby Hall in Birkenhead, England. She was educated at Cheltenham Ladies' College and Lady Margaret Hall in Oxford. Royden then became a social worker and, starting in 1900, worked at Victoria Women's Settlement in Liverpool and in the rural parish of Luffenham for three years. She was active in the women's suffrage movement, and lectured on suffrage for six years. As a member of the National Union of Women's Suffrage Societies, she served as editor of the organization's journal, *Common Cause.*

The First World War caused Royden to broaden her concern for the ethical and religious aspects of the women's movement to include any individual in need. Determining that the Church of England was the best vehicle for her humanitarian efforts, she became a licensed lay reader of the church. She proved so effective that the bishop of London granted her a special license to preach, making her the first female pastor in the Church of England. Although she was never officially ordained, Royden made the most of this opportunity by taking leadership roles in the churches she served. From 1917 to 1920, she was assistant preacher at City Temple in London.

In 1920, Royden and Dr. Percy Dearmer founded a nondenominational church called the Fellowship Services. During her 16-year association with this church, she became the first female Doctor of Divinity, with a degree awarded by Glasgow University in 1931, and also received an honorary LL.D. from Liverpool University in 1935. Royden hoped to elevate her parishioners with religious optimism in the midst of trying times, and worked to enact social change by organizing the "International Peace Army" with a professed aim of ending the Sino-Japanese War in the early 1930s. She continued her efforts to create a better world when World War II hit Europe, maintaining that the war "is forcing us from smug, middle-class, complacent Christianity into something dangerous and hard—the responsibility of loving our enemies."

Royden traveled widely, preaching in the United States, Australia, New Zealand, India, and China on such topics as "What Sort of a World Would You Want?" and "The World Crisis and Religion." She also wrote a number of inspirational books, among them *The House and the Church* (1922), *The Church and Woman* (1924), *Here—and Hereafter* (1933), and the most well known, *A Threefold Cord* (1947), in which she wrote about her marriage to Reverend George W.H. Shaw.

Royden has been described as "a small graying woman with a limp," but despite her unprepossessing appearance, she was a forceful and dynamic speaker. She could "stand before an audience and discuss commonplace topics without the scraping of a chair, the rustling of a paper, or any other sign of restlessness among her listeners." Although she was clearly a scholar, her listeners reported that they were most deeply impressed by "the force of her humanity." She died in 1956.

SOURCES:
Block, Maxine, ed. *Current Biography 1942.* NY: H.W. Wilson, 1942.
Candee, Marjorie Dent, ed. *Current Biography Yearbook 1956.* NY: H.W. Wilson, 1956.
The Concise Dictionary of National Biography. Oxford: Oxford University Press, 1992.

Kelly Winters,
freelance writer, Bayville, New York

Royer, Clémence (1830–1902)

French autodidact, philosopher, scientist, feminist, translator, and social critic whose works were alternately scorned, praised, and ignored. Name variations: Clemence Royer; Clémence-Auguste Royer; Lux. Pronunciation: Clay-MONCE Raw-yeah. Born Clémence-Auguste Royer on April 21, 1830, in Nantes, France; died in Paris, France, on February 5, 1902; daughter of Augustin-René Royer (a commissioned officer in the French army and entrepreneur) and Josephine-Gabrielle Andouard; partner of Pascal Duprat; children: son, René Duprat (b. March 6, 1866).

Translator of Charles Darwin's Origin of Species; *author of 5 books and over 150 articles, reviews, and monographs ranging in subject matter from anthropology to economics to ethics to feminism to politics to various natural and social scientific disciplines. First woman member of the Société d'Anthropologie de Paris; recipient of Legion of Honor award (1900).*

Selected writings: translation of Darwin's Origin of Species, *with extensive introduction and footnotes (1862, 1866, 1870);* Théorie de l'impôt, ou la dîme sociale *(Theory of Taxation, or the Social Tithe, 1862); (novel)* Les Jumeaux d'Hellas *(The Twins of Hellas, 1864);* Origine de l'homme et des sociétés *(Origin of Man and Societies, 1869);* Le Bien et la loi morale: ethique et téléologie *(Goodness and Moral Law: Ethics and Teleology, 1881);* Natura Rerum: la Constitution du monde, dynamique des atomes, nouveaux principes de philosophie naturelle *(The Nature of Things: the Constitution of the World, Energy of Atoms, and New Principles of Natural Philosophy, 1900).*

In a culture in which women are barred from formal education beyond early grades and excluded from professional associations because of their gender, the opportunities for fame and acclamation are rare. This is especially true in the so-called "masculine" fields of science and philosophy. Clémence Royer sought to create her own opportunities in such a culture by educating herself, by finding supportive male colleagues, by gaining publicity with her French translation of Darwin's *Origin of Species*, and by refusing to be silenced. Royer herself reported that the highest praise noted French linguist and critic Ernest Renan could give her was to say, "She was almost a man of genius." For the articulate feminist, this description was hardly a compliment.

Born in 1830 in Nantes, France, Clémence Royer lived a troubled childhood. Shortly after her birth, her father resigned his commission in the army to participate in the royalist insurrection against Charles X and later in a legitimatist rebellion against Louis-Philippe. Her family fled from place to place, settling at last in Lausanne, Switzerland, which provided the locale for some of her earliest memories. In 1835, the family returned to France, where her father was tried for and acquitted of treason. Royer and her parents then went to Paris, where her father tried his hand at business, but succeeded only in losing most of the family fortune.

During this time in Paris, Royer apparently attended a number of primary schools, but received most of her education at home. This education was not structured and seemed to follow her parents' literary bent emphasizing literature, poetry, and theater. When she was ten, her parents decided that she should have a more formal education and enrolled her in a convent school in Le Mans. Here her natural intelligence was immediately recognized, and she finished the first classes in three months, winning all of the prizes.

At this school, she also received her first formalized religious training. During the next two years, her religious confusion, active imagination, and intense mysticism created a mental and emotional response that seems, from her autobiography, to have been a type of nervous breakdown. Finally, in 1843 her parents felt it necessary to remove her from this environment and took her back to Paris. During the next few years, she read and reread the classical authors, enjoyed music, and sewed.

The Revolution of 1848 was an important event in her intellectual, political, and personal development. Intellectually, she adopted as her heroes Lamartine and Michelet. Politically, she abandoned the royalist politics of her upbringing and adopted a rational belief in republicanism. Personally, she began to define herself and her mission in terms of a *Joan of Arc figure who would liberate humanity from the dogmatism, prejudices, errors, and lies that imprisoned humankind and held back its progress. She was unsure how to fulfill this mission, but had to make some pragmatic decisions following the death of her father in 1850. He had squandered the family fortune on business and political failures, and she realized that with the small dowry left, there was little chance that she could marry as she would like. Moreover, her view of marriage, based on the domestic turmoil of her parents' union, was not something that attracted her, so she decided to prepare herself for a career.

Royer began by publishing some poetry in minor periodicals, but when she tried to write prose, became aware of her real lack of education. Thus, at the age of 20, she started to relearn everything. Her re-education commenced with the most elementary rules of grammar and arithmetic. In two years, she passed three examinations without a failure, the last one being with honors. Both her autobiography and the biographical sources are unclear at this point as to where this education took place and who gave the exams, but **Geneviève Fraisse** suggests that they were probably the *brevet élémentaire*, the *brevet supérieur*, and the exams of the *Hôtel de Ville*. In her autobiography, Royer mentioned two courses that strongly influenced her during this time: Michelet's work on Roman history, which she viewed as a negation of all Christian history and which revealed to her a sense of historical criticism, and the course on physics given at the Conservatoire des Arts et Métiers by Alexandre-Edmond Becquerel, which was for her a negation of all miracles.

Hence between 1850 and 1853, she worked, in the words of her autobiography, "to acquire the only diplomas then accessible to women." These diplomas assured her of a career, and in 1854 she went to Great Britain to teach French and piano in a girls' boarding school at Haverfordwest, Pembrokeshire, Wales. While there, she studied English language and literature and continued to reexamine and revise her religious views, now with the added data that came from her exposure to Protestant sectarianism.

She returned to France in 1855 and spent the summer at a school in an old château in Touraine, where she replaced one of the teachers who was on vacation. Utilizing the school library, she continued her self-education. As a result of this reading, and discussions with the school's priest, she rejected traditional Christianity and its domination of culture and learning. Bitter that she had been betrayed by what she viewed as false teachings that had misled her reason, she came to the conclusion that the mission she had sensed in 1848 was now clear to her. She was to discover Truth and communicate it to all who had been likewise deceived.

> *All that I know I have stolen by sheer force, and I had to forget everything that I had been taught in order to learn for myself.*
>
> —Clémence Royer

In the summer of 1856, Royer returned to Lausanne, where she had experienced safety as a toddler and where she believed she would have the safety to learn and to follow Reason where it led. Using the library in Lausanne, she read voraciously and broadly for four years. But she was not just acquiring knowledge. In 1858, she wrote a piece for a contest that contained the primitive form of her atomic theory that would be found in her last book, *Natura rerum*. She also gave a lecture on logic organized by the famous Swedish novelist *Fredrika Bremer. When this lecture met with great success, Royer decided to offer the following year a complete course, comprised of 40 lessons, on the Philosophy of Nature and History. Only the first lesson of the series was printed, but it contains the initial expressions of Royer's "equal but different" form of feminism and of the need for women to be actively engaged in the scientific enterprise. She affirmed that as long as science remained exclusively in the hands of men, it would never penetrate either the family or society. This "equal but different" form of feminism would be a focal point in several of Royer's works, and she would put it into practice through her own involvement with the feminist movement in France during the final decades of her life.

In 1860, she submitted a manuscript (*Théorie de l'impôt, ou la Dîme sociale*) to a contest sponsored by the State Council of the canton of Vaud to settle the question of tax reform. Pierre Joseph Proudhon, one of the principal French socialists who had earlier denied that women had any intellectual capacities, also submitted a manuscript. When the prize was announced, Royer and Proudhon shared the honor, a situation that the press found ironic and newsworthy. As a result, Royer's work was publicized through Europe, and she began publishing in the *Journal des Économistes*, while continuing to contribute to the *Nouvelle Économiste*, a journal published by Pascal Duprat.

Duprat had brought his family to Lausanne just shortly before Royer arrived there. His supportive responses to Royer's work encouraged her, but gradually their relationship became more than that of intellectual comrades. Duprat left his family and the debts incurred by his wife in 1860, and began meeting Royer at various places throughout Europe during his travels. Finally, in 1865, Royer and Duprat decided to form a companionate marriage. Their son René was born the following year.

During this period of awakening emotions, Royer continued to be extremely productive intellectually. In fact, it was in 1862 that she published the first French translation of Darwin's *Origin of Species*. It is ironic that Royer, a woman who cherished her independence, should be known to most scholars primarily in her subordinate role as Darwin's French translator. Moreover, many scholars of this period have long accused Royer of distorting Darwin's text to serve her own philosophical and scientific purposes. More recently, some scholars have shown Royer to have been more faithful to the text and more critically astute than had been believed.

Royer translated two more editions of *Origin of Species* (1866 and 1870), but in the last (3rd) French edition, argued passionately against Darwin's theory of pangenesis, causing Darwin to withdraw permission for Royer to continue with the translations. She did not see this action, however, as a setback. By this time, she had published at least 24 articles, reviews, and monographs on a variety of topics, the aforementioned treatise on tax reform, a two-volume novel (*Les Jumeaux d'Hellas*), and a major book applying Darwinian theory to the evolution of humans and human society (*Origine de l'homme et des sociétés*). Especially with this latter book, she believed that she had intellectually moved beyond Darwin. The book was published just three months before the outbreak of the Franco-Prussian war in 1870, however, and by the time things had settled down in France, Darwin had published *The Descent of Man*. According to her autobiography, many people believed that her book was the translation of Darwin's, "probably in accordance with the public's prejudice that the translator of a first work never does anything more than translations."

There were a growing number of intellectuals, however, especially among liberal republicans in the anthropological community, who recognized Royer's contributions, and after some debate, she was elected in 1870 as the first woman member of the Société d'Anthropologie. Though this was an honor, her position within the organization was that of a second-class citizen, for she was not allowed to serve on committees, become an officer, or gain professionally—or economically—as a result of her membership. It did, however, provide her a venue for promulgating her views and for debating issues about which she felt passionately. Increasingly she used this forum to disseminate her feminist and scientific beliefs concerning women and their roles in society. She argued for increased education and economic freedom for women, a position that many of her colleagues were willing to support. However, some of her proposals were too extreme for them, especially after the election of the new conservative monarchist government in 1873. One of those extreme proposals was a change in the legal relationship established in the Napoleonic Code between husband and wife. In that Code, wives had no legal rights. Royer contended that marriage should involve a contract in which both partners had equal rights and obligations, including the opportunity for women to initiate divorce proceedings. She also advocated changes in attitudes and behaviors surrounding sexuality and childbirth, including the right of motherhood outside of marriage. In developing these arguments she directly challenged the Roman Catholic Church and indirectly all forms of Christianity.

Her comments, expressed in a paper entitled "*Sur la natalité*," read before the Société in 1874 and scheduled for publication in the organization's journal the following year, were suppressed by the leaders of the Société in deference to other professional colleagues, to the clerical leaders in the country, and to the new governmental leaders. In 1877, the Paris police denied her request to speak on a related topic in a lecture series organized by her friend **Céline Renooz Muro**, a Belgian writer. **Joy Harvey**, who has studied Royer extensively, argues that

Clémence Royer

this denial explains why Royer did not participate in the first Congress on the Rights of Women held in Paris in 1878.

During the decade preceding this Congress, the French feminist movement had developed a new vigor and had begun to lobby for changes in laws and attitudes. Royer had been espousing feminist causes since her days in Lausanne, and she became involved in the International Congresses for the Rights of Women sometime in the early 1880s. Although ill, she chaired the history session of this group in 1889 as one of its honorary presidents. She gradually became more active in the women's movement by joining a mixed Masonic lodge (1893) and by writing for the feminist newspaper *La Fronde* when it was formed in 1897.

Royer's participation in the feminist movement and her sensitivity to the plight of women were grounded in the philosophical system she had developed over 40 years of study and reflection. They were undoubtedly increased, moreover, by her own troubles following the death of Duprat in 1885. She had no rights to Duprat's estate, and no source of income other than public lectures and her own writings, which she had difficulty getting published and more difficulty getting sold. She petitioned the government for a pension, and for four years received a small grant. Finally, around 1890, Royer, feeling forsaken, accepted "free" room and board in the Maison Galignani, a home of "indigent men and women of letters," where she lived until her death.

Poverty and opposition did not, however, halt her productivity. Between 1890 and 1900, she published over 20 articles and a book in which she developed her grand theory of nature (*Natura rerum*). Moreover, regardless of her feelings of abandonment, a number of her friends were still seeking to honor her. In 1897, over 250 celebrated intellectuals, including two political leaders—Georges Clémenceau and Anatole France—the celebrated chemist Marcellin Berthelot, and the writer Emile Zola, attended a banquet organized by the Bleus de Bretagne, a republican organization of Brittany, to honor the life and work of this celebrated Breton. In 1900, *La Fronde* carried a four-part review of her last book, *Natura rerum*, which predicted that some day Royer would receive the glory that was due her. That glory came when, on August 16, 1900, the Minister of Public Instruction named Royer a Chevalier of the Legion of Honor because of her services as a "*femme de lettres, écrivain scientifique*" (woman of letters and scientific writer). She received her certificate and cross on November 12, and her friends organized a second banquet as a tribute to her on November 16, to celebrate what they considered a long overdue honor.

Royer's health continued to decline during the year following this second banquet. Asthma had taken its toll, and she began to cough up blood. She also suffered from an intestinal problem, and some of her friends believed she had a kidney disease. Unable to complete her weekly assignment for *La Fronde* early in 1902, Royer sent word that she needed some rest. When her friend **Mary Léopold Lacour** noticed on February 5 that the weekly article was absent, she went to see her, only to find her in a coma. Help was summoned, Royer was given oxygen to help her breathe, and she gradually regained consciousness. She made it known to Lacour that she did not want a priest called. Lacour left for supper, and when she returned, Royer had died. She was buried on February 10, 1902, in the cemetery of Neuilly. A number of friends and colleagues attended her burial, speaking of her powerful mind and her impish and sparkling good nature.

Following her death, many of her writings were lost, but for a while she was not forgotten. In 1913, the International Freethought Society undertook a subscription drive to raise funds to honor Royer. The project was to place a marble plaque on the house in Praz-Parey, near Lausanne, where Royer had stayed while re-educating herself. This was accomplished in September 1913. In 1930, two events honored the centenary of Royer's birth: one on May 4, which was an all-day affair including a visit to her grave, dinner, and lectures; and one on June 12, which was an evening of lectures by scientific and literary personalities. These activities attest to the impact of Royer's life and thought within some groups a full quarter century after her death. She continued, however, to be marginalized by both the academic community and the feminist movement. Interest in her and her work later reemerged, as historiographical methods evolved in the history of science to include an understanding of socio-cultural influences and as women's studies became more scholarly and less hagiographic. Today Clémence Royer is recognized as an exceptional woman who rose above the limitations imposed by 19th-century French culture. Her contributions to the natural and social sciences were sometimes brilliantly insightful and sometimes remarkably naive and erroneous. In these ways, she paralleled the intellectual path of many men of whom the same could be said, but she did it without the possibility of formal learning and without the support of the professional academic community. As she said near the end of her life, what she accomplished was a result of "sheer force" and against many obstacles, but that accomplishment fulfilled an important role in the French intellectual community and within the French feminist movement.

SOURCES:

Fraisse, Geneviève. *Clémence Royer: Philosophe et femme de sciences*. Paris: Éditions de la Découverte, 1985.

Harvey, Joy. *"Almost a Man of Genius:" Clémence Royer, Feminism, and Nineteenth-Century Science*. New Brunswick, NJ: Rutgers University Press, 1996.

Miles, Sara. *Evolution and Natural Law in the Synthetic Science of Clémence Royer*. Ph.D. dissertation that includes the transcription of Royer's handwritten autobiography, an English translation of her *Introduction to Philosophy for Women*, and her prefaces to the 1st and 3rd French editions of *L'Origine des espèces*. University of Chicago, 1988.

SUGGESTED READING:

Harvey, Joy. "'Strangers to Each Other': Male and Female Relationships in the Life and Work of Clémence Royer, 1830–1902," in *Uneasy Careers and Intimate Lives: Women in Science 1789–1979*. Edited by Pnina G. Abir-Am and Dorinda Outram. New Brunswick, NJ: Rutgers University Press, 1987, pp. 147–171.

Miles, Sara. "Clémence Royet et *De l'origine des espèces: Traductrice ou traîtresse?*" in *Revue de Synthèse*. 4th series. 1989, pp. 61–83.

Moses, Claire Goldberg. *French Feminism in the Nineteenth Century*. Albany, NY: State University of New York Press, 1984.

COLLECTIONS:

Correspondence, papers, and dossier are located at both the Bibliothèque Marguerite Durand, Paris, and the French National Archives, Paris.

Sara Joan Miles, Ph.D.,
Vice President for Institutional Effectiveness
and Professor of History and Biology,
Eastern College, St. Davids, Pennsylvania

Rozanova, Olga (1886–1918)

Prominent Russian avant-garde painter who devoted her final years to developing a form of art appropriate to the society created by the Bolshevik Revolution of 1917. Name variations: Rosanova. Pronunciation: Roe-ZAHN-ova. Born Olga Vladimirovna Rozanova at Malenki, Vladimir Province, in 1886; died of diphtheria in Moscow on November 8, 1918; daughter of Vladimir Rozanov; attended Bolshakov School and Stroganov Institute, Moscow, 1904–10, Zvantseva School of Art, St. Petersburg, 1912–13; married Alexei Kruchenykh (a poet), in 1916.

Moved to Moscow to study art (1904); exhibited works in St. Petersburg with Union of Youth (1910); moved from Moscow to St. Petersburg (1911); began to illustrate her future husband's books (1912); wrote major manifesto on her artistic principles (1913); exhibited paintings at "Free Futurist Exhibition" in Rome (1914); exhibited first non-objective painting (1915); helped organize Supremus group, adopted Suprematism, used collage technique for Universal War (1916); joined IZO and Proletkult (1918); posthumous exhibition of her work in Moscow (1919).

Major works: The Poet (Tretyakov Gallery, Moscow, 1912); Factory and Bridge (NY, 1912); Dissonance, Man in the Street (Hutton Gallery, NY, 1913); Nonobjective Composition (State Russian Museum, St. Petersburg, 1914); Workbox (Tretyakov Gallery, Moscow, 1915); Non-Objective Composition (Collages from Universal War, Tretiakov Gallery, Moscow, 1916); Green Stripe (Tretyakov Gallery, Moscow, 1917).

Olga Rozanova was a leading Russian painter in the first two decades of the 20th century. Like many of her contemporaries such as *Liubov Popova, she absorbed the changing impulses of the larger world of European art, for example working in both Cubist and Futurist styles between 1913 and 1916. By those years, she had followed other leading Russian artists to the opinion that art had to go far beyond the mere representation of visible objects. In the view of a number of critics, though she never traveled outside her own country, Rozanova brought original personal elements to the various genres in which she created her art.

Rozanova did particularly memorable work as the illustrator for books produced during the war by her husband, the Futurist poet Alexei Kruchenykh, whom she married in 1916. With the outbreak of revolution in 1917, she threw herself enthusiastically into the heated political environment. During the short time left to her before she died of diphtheria in 1918, the young painter and illustrator worked actively in the new artists' groups that developed under the aegis of Russia's Bolshevik government.

Russia in the early 20th century, the country in which Rozanova grew to adulthood and took her place in the artistic world, contained a troubled society on the brink of vast changes. Ruled by an inept monarch, Nicholas II, the political system was divorced from the needs of Russia's population with its masses of impoverished peasants. Its growing percentage of factory workers, themselves peasants recently transplanted from the villages of the country, lived in urban squalor. Shaken by defeat in the Russo-Japanese War of 1904–05, the old order in Russia was directly threatened by several varieties of committed revolutionaries. Those who saw the peasantry as the engine of revolution, the Populists, had been disrupting Russian life—even employing assassination of government leaders to do so—since the 1870s. The revolutionary threat was augmented in the 1890s by the emergence of a Marxist revolutionary movement. With such daring and talented leaders as V.I. Lenin and Leon Trotsky, the extreme Bolshevik faction of Marxists succeeded in coming to power in November 1917.

The art world was a lively part of this turbulent society. It welcomed the entry of women painters like Popova, *Alexandra Exter, and *Natalia Goncharova. Both traditional Russian folk art and the latest developments to arrive from Paris, the Continent's capital of the arts, stimulated the minds and paint brushes of Russia's artists. Rozanova was an important component within this section of Russian life.

At a time when Russian artists had a plethora of influences from which to choose, Rozanova managed to tap many of the new currents. In the view of some critics, she followed the path set down by her colleagues, but others find that she maintained a high degree of individuality. A basic view of her work came in 1962 from **Camilla Gray**, who found Rozanova's role on the Russian avant-garde scene "not that of an innovator, but . . . [that] of a talented follower." Such a view of Rozanova's limited role as an innovator may be overstated. More recently, she has been ranked more highly. For example, when Vasily Rakitin, a noted art historian, introduced her work to an exhibition of Russian avant-garde artists in Cologne in 1979, he characterized Rozanova vividly. For him, she was "artistically independent to the point of audacity," a painter who "absorbed everything and depended virtually on nobody."

Olga Rozanova was born in 1886 in the small town of Malenki in Vladimir Province northeast of Moscow. Details about her early life are scanty, but she is known to have moved to Moscow to study art around 1904, pursuing her studies there until 1910. She began in a private studio, the Bolshakov Art School, then entered the Stroganov School of Applied Art. In 1911, she moved to St. Petersburg, Russia's capital city. There she plunged into the world of avant-garde art. She also continued her education at St. Petersburg's Zvantseva Art School in 1912 and 1913.

She loved to contravene herself, and enter heart and soul into the new. It was only her premature death that finally stopped Rozanova's forward march.

—Vasily Rakitin

Rozanova took a key step in her career when she joined the Union of Youth in St. Petersburg. This was an important group of young artists, all of them enthusiastically committed to breaking with the conventions of the past. Through her membership, Rozanova came into contact with the most active artists in Russia. These included Goncharova and David Burliuk. In the words of M.N. Yablonskaya, the stimulation provided by the Union of Youth led Rozanova to conclude that she would not pursue a course of study abroad. Thus, both before and during her brief period as a leading artist, she distinguished herself from other major figures in her country's art world by the fact that she never left Russia.

The Union of Youth became far more than a round table for avant-garde painters. It soon had sections for dramatists and musicians, and, in 1913, the "Gilea" group of avant-garde poets joined as well. One of these poets, Kruchenykh, played a growing role in Rozanova's life, first as an artistic collaborator, then as her husband.

Along with many of her contemporaries, Rozanova absorbed the ideas of Cubism and, especially, Futurism. Cubism arrived in Russia from France and featured the effort to view objects, such as faces, simultaneously from a number of different angles. Futurism, on the other hand, originated in Italy and was characterized by an interest in showing the dynamism of modern life, featuring representations of objects in motion. Both reached Russia shortly before the outbreak of war in 1914. The young Rozanova, still only in her 20s, was a poet as well as a painter, and she helped promote Futurism with her writing as well as her work in the visual arts.

In her fundamental statement of her artistic principles, "The Bases of the New Creation and the Reasons Why It is Misunderstood," published in 1913, she eloquently defended the guidelines of the avant-garde. "Only modern art," she wrote, "has advocated the full and serious importance of such principles as pictorial dynamism, volume and equilibrium." To the conservatives of the art world, she declared boldly, "Messrs arts critics and veterans of the old art are being true to themselves in their fatal fear of what is beautiful and continually renewing itself." Thus, the artist must proceed confidently to explore the new. "The future of art," she insisted, "will be assured only when the thirst for eternal renewal in the artist's soul becomes inexhaustible." Rozanova did not confine her defense of modern art to the written page. As a speaker as well as an artist, she took a leading role in the Union of Youth's efforts to defend free artistic expression in public debate.

In the opinion of **Margaret Betz**, the basic shift from representational art to one "which virtually obliterated all references to the phenomenal world" began in Russia in 1912 and 1913 in the production of prints. Similar developments in painting ensued. According to Betz, Rozanova not only participated in this move of Russian modernists toward abstraction, but "left perhaps the clearest line of development" of the change in her lithographs of March 1913, published in the Union of Youth magazine. The same 1913 issue brought her essay "The Bases of the New Creation" before the public.

The prints, notably three containing remnants of landscape painting, show how Rozanova's eye was searching for a deeper reality. Great sweeping curves combined with a rearrangement of real objects—putting a utility pole above a bridge, for example—to move away from representation. In these and in similar works produced in late 1913 and early 1914, Rozanova may have set a basis for Kasimir Malevich, generally considered the father of Russian abstract art, to move forward into the complete abstraction of the form he called "Suprematism." Ironically, as Betz puts it, Rozanova apparently hesitated after establishing herself as a pioneer in the move to abstraction; she then followed her mentor Malevich when he was the first to muster the courage for the ultimate step away from representational art.

In the wartime years, travel outside Russia was impossible, but the artistic scene within the country continued to be lively. For example, regular gatherings took place in the apartment of Lev Bruni in St. Petersburg (renamed Petrograd at the start of the war); Rozanova and other leading artists traveled between Moscow and Petrograd to keep their colleagues linked to artistic developments in Russia's two great urban centers. She participated in several of the avant-garde exhibitions of the time, including the Tramway V exhibition in Petrograd in March 1915 and The Store exhibit in Moscow in March 1916. For the 0.10 exhibit in Petrograd in January 1916, she produced a number of abstract sculptures. These have since disappeared, although several of her sketches for them have survived.

Before Malevich and Rozanova both moved on to abstract art, he was her mentor as she developed her style in Cubism and Futurism. Malevich had been profoundly influenced by leading French Cubists such as Pablo Picasso and Georges Braque in 1913 and 1914. His use of a collage effect, in which objects like photographs and newspaper clippings appear to overlap one another to give depth to a painting's surface, was a technique typical of Cubism. Rozanova employed it in works like *Workbox* and *Hairdresser's*, both completed in 1915.

There was, however, no clear break between the periods in which Rozanova worked in Cubism and Futurism. As one of her colleagues put it, "Rozanova does not take the essence from these tendencies, but only their means of expression." An important Futurist work by Rozanova entitled *Geography* was painted in 1914–15. It showed the interior of a machine, a typical Futurist device. It also followed the Futurist technique of inserting letters of the alphabet and parts of words into the painting. In this case, Rozanova used letters of both the Western and the Cyrillic alphabets to suggest the words "France," "Amerique," "Paris," and "England." Her Futurist work *Composition of Shining Objects*, presented at the 1915 "Exhibition of Leftist Trends" in Petrograd, was a more abstract example of her ongoing exploration of this style.

In her continuing investigation of different artistic possibilities, Rozanova turned to abstract painting. Her principal mentor remained Male-

Writing Desk *by Olga Rozanova, 1914.*

vich, and she took her place as a key member of his Suprematist group. According to Yablonskaya, it was in the years 1915 and 1916 that Rozanova followed Malevich into complete abstraction, "a mystical, non-objective style of painting which he named 'Suprematism.'" Her stature within Malevich's Suprematist coterie can be seen in her role as Malevich's executive secretary for his stillborn journal *Supremus*. Her work on *Supremus*, even though the journal did not come to actual publication, led her into the area of applied art. In preparing the section of *Supremus* devoted to these issues, she designed embroidery and textiles. These new ventures were to become important following the Bolshevik Revolution of November 1917, when Rozanova and other leading artists redirected their skills to serve the practical needs of Russia's masses.

But her originality, even in the realm of abstract painting, shone through in her emphatic use of color. A notable example of this was her 1917 painting *Green Stripe*, in which a single, multihued green stripe runs vertically down the center of a painting against a cream-colored background. Her love for color and her desire to incorporate it into both her Cubist and Suprematist work has been emphasized by such art critics as **Larissa Zhadova**. Even in her collages, according to Zhadova, Rozanova placed "combinations of pink to lilac or pink to red ranges with blues, sometimes accompanied by striking chords of yellows and greens."

In cooperation with Alexei Kruchenykh, Rozanova served as illustrator for several books of Futurist poetry from 1913 to 1916. Just as her painting in these years encompassed both Futurism and Cubism, so too did her style of illustrating Kruchenykh's works. Her work on the 1913 book *A Forestly Rapid*, for example, employed the techniques of Futurism, but by 1915, when she did the illustrations for *Transrational Book*, Cubism became the dominant genre. In 1916, in illustrating Kruchenykh's *Universal War*, Rozanova moved on to Suprematism and employed abstract forms. In this effort, she used actual collages to accompany the 12 poems that made up her husband's book. This remarkable artistic product had to be turned out by hand, one copy at a time. Against a background of paper colored dark blue, Rozanova placed her collages consisting of fabric and semi-transparent paper. As usual, she added an intensely personal note, in this case varying the Suprematist style. In one of the prints, consisting of geometrical shapes placed in a dynamic relationship with one another, she placed silhouettes of both a man and an airplane, thereby bringing earthly shapes into the austere abstraction of Suprematism.

Rozanova later recalled the feelings that accompanied her work on *Universal War*, suggesting that her future political radicalism had its origins in her reaction to the bloody conflict in which Russia was engaged. "The war did its business with us," she wrote, and "changing the world to a new speed, it gave a malignant background to our lives, against which everything seemed tragic or insignificant."

The turbulent Russia that followed the Bolshevik Revolution of November 1917 saw many young artists rally to the new, radical regime. "Believing that art belonged to the proletariat and should reflect the essential elements of industrial and urban life," according to **Whitney Chadwick**, Rozanova stood in the center of such circles. In 1918, the new government created a Department of Fine Arts (IZO) as part of the Commissariat for Public Education. Artists like Rozanova, who were sympathetic to the aims of the revolution, gathered in this organization. With the financial help of the government, IZO set up dozens of art museums throughout the country.

Rozanova also participated in the "Higher Technical-Artist Studios," known by their Russian abbreviation as *Vkhutemas*. These were training institutions for the country's future artists. Shortly before her death, she founded and led the Industrial Art Section of IZO. Despite the chaotic conditions, as the revolution developed into the Civil War that raged over much of the country, she traveled extensively to build up a system of industrial art centers where the principles of the revolution could be applied in fields such as textiles and woodworking. Her journeys took her hundreds of miles outside Moscow to remote locales such as Bogorodsk and Ivanovo-Voznesensk.

A further sign of Rozanova's commitment to the revolution was her membership in Proletkult. Intended to create a proletarian culture appropriate for a society that had brought the workers and their representatives to power, the organization drew the support of sympathetic artists like Rozanova. A fundamental view of Proletkult was that the art of a proletarian society like Soviet Russia could be produced only by the proletariat, i.e., the factory workers. This meant that Rozanova accepted the view that much of the artistic heritage of the past had to be discarded.

Russia's population in the years following the upheaval of 1917 was decimated by epidemic diseases, and Rozanova was an early victim of this national tragedy. The young artist was taken ill with diphtheria, showing the first signs of infection while decorating a plane at an airfield near Moscow. She was helping to prepare a celebration marking the first anniversary of the Bolshevik revolution. Carried away unconscious, she never recovered. The young artist and supporter of the revolution died on November 8, 1918.

Rozanova's career was thus cut tragically short while she was only 32. She was honored by a commemorative exhibition of her works set up only a few weeks later in early 1919. The collection of 250 paintings showed her sweeping evolution as an artist, containing some of her early paintings done in the Impressionist manner and extending down to recent abstract works reflecting the Suprematist movement. Such a display of her work vividly illustrated the philosophy she had summarized in 1913: "There is nothing worse in this world than the unchanging face of an artist."

SOURCES:

Betz, Margaret. "Graphics of the Russian Vanguard," in *Artnews*. Vol. 75, no. 3. March 1976, pp. 52–54.

Bowlt, John E., ed. and trans. *Russian Art of the Avant-Garde: Theory and Criticism*. Rev. and enl. ed. Thames & Hudson, 1988.

Chadwick, Whitney. *Women, Art, and Society*. London: Thames & Hudson, 1990.

Gray, Camilla. *The Great Experiment: Russian Art, 1863–1922.* NY: Harry N. Abrams, 1962.

Harris, Anne Sutherland, and Linda Nochlin. *Women Artists: 1550–1950.* NY: Alfred A. Knopf, 1976.

Lodder, Christina. *Russian Constructivism.* New Haven, CT: Yale University Press, 1983.

Rudenstine, Angelica Zander. *Russian Avant-Garde Art: The George Costakis Collection.* NY: Harry N. Abrams, 1981.

Yablonskaya, M.N. *Women Artists of Russia's New Age.* Edited by Anthony Parton. London: Thames & Hudson, 1990.

Zhadova, Larissa A. *Malevich: Suprematism and Revolution in Russian Art, 1910–1913.* NY: Thames & Hudson, 1982.

SUGGESTED READING:

Andrews, Richard, and Milena Kalinovska, eds. *Russian Constructivism, 1914–1932: Art into Life.* NY: Rizzoli, 1990.

Slatkin, Wendy. *Women Artists in History: From Antiquity to the 20th Century.* Englewood Cliffs, NJ: Prentice-Hall, 1985.

Neil M. Heyman,
Professor of History, San Diego State University,
San Diego, California

Rozengolts-Levina, Eva (1898–1975)

Russian artist. Name variations: Eva Levina-Rozengolts; Eva Rozengolts. Born Eva Rozengolts in Vitebsk, Russia, in 1898; died in Moscow in 1975; daughter of Klara Frumkin Rozengolts; educated at the Alekseev High School in Vitebsk; entered the School of Dentistry at Tomsk University; studied with sculptor Anna Golubkina; studied with painter Robert Falk; married a man named Levine; children: Elena Levina (b. around 1928).

Eva Rozengolts-Levina was born in 1898 and grew up in a large, gregarious family in Vitebsk, Russia. Her mother **Klara Frumkin Rozengolts** was deeply interested in art, and studied drawing and painting at the People's Art College under "World of Art" painter Mstislav Dobuzhinsky and artist **Vera Ermolaeva**. Eva, like her mother, was passionate about art, but her father wanted her to have a more stable profession. In accordance with his wishes, she became a hospital nurse, and later studied at the School of Dentistry at Tomsk University. In 1919, she traveled to Moscow, where she met such artists as the sculptor Stepan Erzya.

The Russian Revolution interrupted all her pursuits, and Rozengolts-Levina nursed dying Red Army soldiers on the front during a typhus epidemic. Her family did not escape tragedy during this time; three of her five brothers were killed in the war. In 1920, she returned to Moscow, hoping to pursue her dream of becoming an artist. She began as a student of sculptor *Anna Golubkina, but their partnership did not last long. Golubkina thought her insufficiently serious, and their relationship was stiff and awkward. Despite Golubkina's poor opinion of her, Rozengolts-Levina idolized her teacher, and their work together eventually led her to meet the painter Robert Falk.

In October 1921, Rozengolts-Levina became Falk's student, and switched from sculpting to painting. She found the change of mediums intensely rewarding, as the immediacy of the canvas appealed more to her than did the slow development of sculpting. She also proved to be gifted with colors and blossomed under the guidance of Falk. So important was he to her development as an artist that it was reported that she finished a painting and dedicated it to his memory on October 1 for many years of her life. He thought just as highly of her talent; he once told his students that he thought of Rozengolts-Levina as the only legitimate reason for his career as a teacher. Falk's mark as a teacher is particularly evident in Rozengolts-Levina's early work, in which she endeavored to incorporate his lyrical humanitarianism in her depictions of everyday people. His technique can also be seen in her layering of full brush strokes and her use of large-scale canvases. In 1925, Rozengolts-Levina completed her training and received permission from Soviet authorities to travel abroad. One of her brothers was working in London as a member of the Soviet Trade Delegation, and in 1926 she traveled there and visited the Tate Gallery.

In the 1930s, Rozengolts-Levina began working on smaller canvases, and increased the power of her imagery. She used pastels as her medium, and her images evoked spiritual suffering and travail. During this period, she became more socially active and aware; she was concerned that workers were rarely exposed to art, and, in line with Stalinist dictates, wanted to use her art to help build a new socialist society. As Rozengolts-Levina became more introspective throughout this decade, she worked more on cityscapes, such as *Chimneys*, which evokes tension and fear with a depiction of large smokestacks over a nighttime town beneath a glowing sky. In *Moscow River at Twilight*, the river is a threatening current in an apocalyptic scene.

It is for her later work, however, that Rozengolts-Levina is now best known. In 1949, the secret police took her from her home with only the clothes on her back, and she was exiled to Siberia. Her crime was being Jewish and the half-sister of Arkady Rozengolts, who had been executed during one of the great Stalinist purges eleven years previously. For six years she performed heavy manual labor at a timber works on the Enisei River in the harsh Krasnoyarsk region, suffering in frigid temperatures and sleeping on rented floor space in the homes of peasants. Her mother and her daughter **Elena Levina**, a geologist then in her 20s, were allowed to send her the art supplies she requested, and Rozengolts-Levina kept two sketchbooks during her exile. On infrequent occasions she was also able to supplement her tiny wages with commercial art such as lampshades and fans. She was allowed to join her last remaining brother in his exile in Kazakhstan in 1955, two years after Stalin's death. The following year, after seven years of exile, she received permission from government officials to return to Moscow, where she was granted a small apartment and a small pension.

Rozengolts-Levina spent the rest of her life distilling into art her sufferings in Siberia and the suffering she had seen all around her. Working at a table in her Moscow apartment, she created 227 drawings in seven series, all small enough to fit on the table. The early series, *Trees* (1956–60), *Marshes* (1960–61), *Sky* (1960–63), and *People: Plastic Compositions* (1965–68), stark and heavily worked evocations of a bleak, devastated world, are done in ink. In the later series, *Landscapes* (1968–70), *People: Plastic Compositions* (1970–74), and *Sky* (1970–74), some of which concern the same scenes as in earlier series, Rozengolts-Levina used pastels, creating a lighter, less agonized feeling that implies she has made her peace with her memories.

While a number of younger artists and critics knew Rozengolts-Levina in her later years and greatly admired her work, the political climate in the Soviet Union at the time was such that displaying it openly was out of the question, although some of the drawings were quietly purchased by the State Pushkin Museum of Fine Arts. She died in 1975, at age 77, without having seen a public exhibition of her later art. Elena Levina remained a champion of her mother's work, and in the late 1970s dared to give a one-night exhibit of her drawings in Moscow, which was attended by some 300 equally daring people. Word of mouth about Rozengolts-Levina's work continued to grow, and in 1996, after the collapse of the Soviet Union, the first exhibit devoted to her art opened at the State Tretiakov Gallery. In 1999, **Joan Afferica**, an American history professor who had met Elena Levina and first seen Rozengolts-Levina's work at her home in the 1980s, succeeded in bringing an exhibit of 56 of the Siberian drawings to America. Eva Rozen-

golts-Levina's "Life and Work," curated by Afferica, opened at the National Museum of Women in the Arts in Washington, D.C., in June 1999. Rozengolts-Levina's international reputation has continued to grow apace with interest in her work, to the satisfaction of her daughter, who noted during the American exhibit: "What matters to me most is that it will go into the history of art." The poet Evgeny Vinokurov once said of Rozengolts-Levina that "her drawings are severe and, in the main, dark in tone and in their lighting. Yet one of her favorite words was 'joy.' She would not sit down to work until she experienced the joy—although it might be a bitter kind of joy—which was necessary for her creativity. This was the stimulus and the source of her work."

SOURCES:

"Stunning Chronicle of Suffering and Renewal by Russian Artist Eva Levina-Rozengolts on view at the National Museum of Women in the Arts June 17–September 26, 1999," National Museum of Women in the Arts press release, June 1999.

The Washington Times. July 31, 1999, p. D3.

Women Artists of Russia's New Age. NY: Rizzoli, 1990.

Kelly Winters,
freelance writer, Bayville, New York

Rubashov, Rachel (1888–1975).

See Katznelson-Shazar, Rachel.

Rubens, Alma (1897–1931)

American actress. Name variations: billed as Alma Reuben or Reubens during early career. Born Alma Smith in San Francisco, California, in 1897; died in 1931; married Franklyn Farnum (an actor), in 1918 (divorced); married Daniel Carson Goodman (a director, producer, author and physician), in 1923 (divorced 1925); married Ricardo Cortez (an actor), in 1926.

Selected filmography: The Half-Breed *(1916);* Reggie Mixes In *(1916);* Intolerance *(1916);* Truthful Tulliver *(1917);* The Americano *(1917);* The Firefly of Tough Luck *(1917);* I Love You *(1918);* The Answer *(1918);* The Love Brokers *(1918);* Madame Sphinx *(1918);* The Painted Lily *(1918);* The Ghost Flower *(1918);* Restless Souls *(1919);* Diane of the Green Van *(1919);* Humoresque *(1920);* Thoughtless Women *(1920);* The World and His Wife *(1920);* Find the Woman *(1922);* The Valley of Silent Men *(1922);* Enemies of Women *(1923);* Under the Red Robe *(1923);* Gerald Cranston's Lady *(1924);* Is Love Everything? *(1924);* The Rejected Woman *(1924);* Cytherea *(1924);* Week End Husbands *(1924);* The Price She Paid *(1924);* The Dancers *(1925);* East Lynne *(1925);* She Wolves *(1925);* The Winding Stair *(1925);* A Woman's Faith *(1925);* Fine Clothes *(1925);* The Gilded Butterfly *(1926)*; Siberia *(1926)*; Marriage License? *(1926)*; The Heart of Salome *(1927)*; The Masks of the Devil *(1928)*; Show Boat *(1929)*; She Goes to War *(1929)*.

A stunning blonde star of over 40 silent pictures, Alma Rubens died in 1931, age 34, from complications arising from an addiction to heroin. The actress, who had a musical-comedy background, made her first film in 1916 and became a screen regular soon after. She appeared in such well-known films as *Intolerance* (1916), *Humoresque* (1920), and an adaptation of *Edna Ferber*'s *Show Boat* (1929), in which she played Julie, a character whose life was as tortured as her own.

Actress *Eleanor Boardman, who worked on Rubens' last picture, *She Goes to War* (1929), was aware that something was terribly wrong with Rubens, but unaware of the cause. During the shoot, Rubens would steal clothing from the dressing rooms of other actresses and disappear suddenly from the set. Her tumultuous personal life had included three marriages, the first of which, to actor Franklyn Farnum, lasted about three months. She was later married to Daniel Carson Goodman, a director-producer, and to Ricardo Cortez, an actor-director who had been groomed by Paramount as a possible heir to Rudolph Valentino.

SOURCES:

Drew, William M. *Speaking of Silents*. NY: Vestal Press, 1989.

Katz, Ephraim. *The Film Encyclopedia*. NY: Harper-Collins, 1994.

Rubenstein, Blanche (c. 1897–1969)

American who ran the famed Ritz Hotel in Paris with her husband and assisted the French Resistance during the Nazi occupation. Name variations: acted briefly as Blanche Ross; Blanche Rubenstein Auzello. Born in Manhattan, New York, around 1897; killed in Paris, France, on May 29, 1969; youngest of seven children (five girls and two boys) of Isaac Rubenstein and Sara Rubenstein; married Claude Auzello (a hotel manager), around 1924; no children.

The beautiful and spirited daughter of German-Jewish émigrés who had come to New York as newlyweds, Blanche Rubenstein decided early in life that she wanted to have a career rather than follow the path of her four sisters into matrimony. Her brother Sylvester, a film salesman, arranged an introduction for her at the Pathé movie studio, where she had roles in a few silents and also met and befriended actress

*Pearl White, star of the popular series *The Perils of Pauline* (1914). In 1923, White accompanied Rubenstein to Paris, where White hoped to jump-start her career, and where Rubenstein was to rendezvous with Egyptian Prince J'Ali Ledene, then her paramour. At their Paris hotel, however, Rubenstein caught the eye of Claude Auzello, the assistant manager. Auzello, a war hero, had trained as a lawyer, but opted for the hotel business after his discharge from the military. Eventually, Rubenstein gave up her prince and her film career to marry Auzello and take up permanent residence in Paris. The marriage was tumultuous almost from the beginning, primarily because of Auzello's desire to keep a mistress. Rubenstein finally came to accept her husband's dalliance, evening the score by occasionally reuniting with her prince.

While Auzello was negotiating to build a hotel of his own, he received an opportunity he could not refuse, that of assistant manager of Paris' premier hotel, the Ritz. Rubenstein did everything in her power to help her husband in his important new position, even changing her religion because of the Ritz's prejudice against Jews. Throughout the 1920s and 1930s, Rubenstein assisted her husband in the hotel, which hosted such luminaries as Ernest Hemingway, F. Scott Fitzgerald, J. P. Morgan, and Cole Porter. "The hotel was an incredible place," she later recalled, "the men stood out, sharp, brilliant, the women were beautiful, and everybody was rich." Rubenstein's own beauty and charm perfectly complemented her husband's managerial skills. She was particularly savvy at listening to the gossip among the clientele, which enabled her to anticipate their special needs. She also fostered personal relationships with the staff, who were more inclined to respond to a friend than an employer. With much credit due to his wife, Claude was promoted to manager of the hotel in the mid-1930s.

In the summer of 1939, with war inevitable, Claude worried about his wife's Jewish heritage and urged her to return home for the duration, but she stubbornly refused. Following the Nazi occupation of Paris, when the Ritz was taken over by German soldiers, Claude became involved with the French Resistance, relaying to them information he learned from the Nazi officers residing within earshot. Rubenstein, through her friendship with **Lily Kharmayeff**, a member of the French underground, also became involved as a messenger for the Resistance; she was caught and imprisoned several times. During her second incarceration, Blanche was shipped by truck to Fresnes, which was known to be the first stop en route to German labor camps. Charged with harboring enemies of Germany, aiding fugitives, and engaging in acts of terrorism, she was kept in isolation and questioned incessantly. After a month, the interrogations stopped, but Rubenstein heard shootings in the courtyard, and tortured yells through the corridors, causing her to believe she probably would be killed within a short time. What she did not know was that American troops had arrived in Paris, and the Germans were preparing to evacuate. When she was again questioned, she was told that if she named her friend Lily a whore and a Jew, she would be freed. Instead of betraying Kharmayeff, however, she blurted: "I am a Jew, not Lily. I was born on the east side in New York, the Jewish section. My name is Rubenstein. My parents came from Germany." The truth, coupled with her near-delirium from lack of food, led the interrogator to believe she was mad; thus, when her captors left the camp by truck, they left her behind. Rubenstein, realizing she was free, began trudging up the road toward the city.

Blanche was reunited with Claude, and together they witnessed the liberation of Paris, but the glory days of the Ritz were over. For the next 20 years, Rubenstein clung to the hope of recapturing the past, appearing each afternoon in the bar, wearing the latest fashion and keeping watch for her old friends to reappear. "It was her nature to believe she would soon get back everything the war years took away," said Claude. "It was not mine to be so optimistic."

During the 1960s, Rubenstein began suffering fainting spells and was forced to curtail her activities. Claude fell out of favor with the hotel owner, and slipped into a suicidal depression that went unchecked by those closest to him. On the night of May 29, 1969, he shot his wife with a German revolver he had found in the hotel following the liberation. He then turned the revolver on himself.

SOURCES:
Marx, Samuel. *Queen of the Ritz*. Indianapolis, IN: Bobbs-Merrill, 1978.

Barbara Morgan,
Melrose, Massachusetts

Rubenstein, Ida (1875–1961).

See Brooks, Romaine for sidebar.

Rubin, Barbara Jo (1949—)

American jockey. Born in Highland, Illinois, on November 21, 1949.

Was the first female jockey to defeat male riders in a major race in Florida (1969); won many races and

became a media star for four years before injury forced her retirement.

"I have seen the greatest jockeys in the country since 1913 and not one has a better style," wrote Willie Ratner in the *Newark Evening News*. Barbara Jo Rubin "'sits' a horse like Don Meade and that's saying a lot. Her back is absolutely horizontal. Straight as a ruler and she holds her head high. . . . She also has a pair of shoe strings for reins." Rubin's love of horses began with the movie *National Velvet*, starring *Elizabeth Taylor. In addition to riding and collecting show ribbons as a child, she enjoyed playing baseball and football, was a good calf roper, and even rode bulls until her mother threatened to take away her horse unless she stopped. Despite a six-month bout in the hospital with polio when she was six, Rubin was a natural athlete.

While growing up in Miami, Rubin found her way to the Tropical Park racetrack, where she became an exercise girl at three dollars per horse. "She was an exceptional rider," said one owner. "The tough horses would run away from the boys in the morning workouts. After Barbara Jo got on the tough ones, there were no problems. I think she talks to horses."

In the late 1960s, when *Kathy Kusner applied to the Maryland Racing Commission to become a jockey and then won a court case allowing her onto the track, many women followed. Rubin was among the first, applying to the senior steward at Tropical Park on January 14, 1969. Not long after, she was granted her license and 11 male jockeys boycotted a race in which she was scheduled to ride. Fined $100, they were threatened with greater fines if they refused to ride with women. Then it got ugly. Someone threw a rock through Rubin's dressing-room window. Rumors were followed by innuendo. Some resorted to slander, maintaining that Rubin had been given her license only because of an affair with an influential track official. The male jockeys took a stand, declaring they would not ride horses for any owner who allowed Rubin to ride. One owner, Brian Webb, called their bluff and ended the open rebellion, though the jockeys' wives remained critical, claiming a woman on the track endangered their husbands' lives.

Rubin proceeded to prove herself. She won a race at Nassau's Hobby Horse Hall track in the Bahamas. On February 22, 1969, while riding Cohesian, she became the first woman jockey to win in the United States, prevailing by a neck at Charles Town, West Virginia. She was also the first woman to win a major race. By March 14, she had won seven races and was ready to ride a bay named Bravy Galaxy at Aqueduct. A two-year-old with no track record and odds at 13 to 1, Bravy Galaxy was a speedball with Rubin on his back, and she triumphed before a crowd of over 25,000. After the race, fellow jockeys doused her with a bucket of water, a traditional gesture after an apprentice's first win. By April 4, Rubin had won 11 races.

Women jockeys were media celebrities in the late 1960s and early 1970s. Rubin's visage appeared in countless magazines and newspapers; she appeared on "The Ed Sullivan Show" and "The Today Show." However, she was shy by nature, and her main interest was in racing rather than publicity. She continued to compete, winning 23 out of 98 races in her career. "When I rode," said Rubin, "I was a little crazy. Like, I didn't care about going down or anything. And when we went into the turn, they were all looking up at me wondering, 'When is she going to drop out?' . . . I'd just smile at them. And all of a sudden I looked and they'd all dropped back." But injury is a jockey's greatest threat, and in four years Rubin suffered through three major incidents. In October 1969, a horse flipped over the starting gate at Assinaboa Downs in Canada, crushing both her knees. She recovered and got back in the saddle. In March 1970, her horse went through a fence which resulted in blood clots in her legs and five months on the sidelines. In the summer of 1971, her quarter horse, Junior, reared up and came down backward on top of Rubin, crushing her pelvis. When this last injury resulted in permanent pain, she hung up her racing colors.

SOURCES:
Haney, Lynn. *The Lady Is a Jock*. NY: Dodd, Mead, 1973.

Karin L. Haag,
freelance writer, Athens, Georgia

Rubinstein, Helena (1870–1965)

Polish-born American entrepreneur who founded the Helena Rubinstein cosmetics empire. Born on December 25, 1870, in Cracow, Poland; died on April 1, 1965, in New York City; daughter of Horace Rubinstein (an egg merchant), and Augusta (Silberfeld) Rubinstein; attended the University of Cracow and briefly studied medicine in Switzerland; married Edward Titus (a journalist), in 1908 (divorced 1937 or 1938); married Prince Artchil Gourielli-Tchkonia, in 1938 (died 1956); children: (first marriage) Roy (b. 1909), Horace (b. 1912).

Helena Rubinstein was born on December 25, 1870, in Cracow, Poland, the oldest of eight daughters of Horace Rubinstein and **Augusta Silberfeld Rubinstein**. She attended the University of Cracow and briefly studied medicine in Switzerland, before joining an uncle in Australia while in her early 30s. As the oft-repeated story goes, Rubinstein brought 12 pots of her mother's face cream with her to Australia, and soon her new Australian friends were begging her for some of their own. Taking out a loan, she imported cases of the cream and opened a small beauty shop in Melbourne where she also gave one-on-one instruction on skin care. The praises of her influential clients brought business to the shop, and Rubinstein's unflagging energy further bolstered sales. In this first stage of success, she established an 18-hour work day which she would maintain throughout her life. In her autobiography, *My Life for Beauty*, Rubinstein wrote that she was "confident and relaxed only in business."

By 1908, her sister **Ceska Rubinstein** took over the Australian business while Helena headed for London with $100,000 to begin her cosmetics empire. She studied dermatology with experts in Paris, Vienna, and London, and set up a successful beauty salon in the latter city with her "Creme Valaze," developed by chemist Jacob Lykusky (also seen as Lukusky), as the founding product. In 1908, Rubinstein married Edward Titus, an American journalist. When World War I began, they moved with their two sons from Paris to Greenwich, Connecticut. Rubinstein built salons in San Francisco, Boston, and Philadelphia, in addition to selling her wares in department stores. Now known as "Madame," Rubinstein partnered with actress *Theda Bara in creating the vamp look.

Rubinstein's return to Paris in 1918 also signaled her entrance into the world of art. In addition to amassing a considerable collection of her own (she claimed she was conditioned from her business to buying in bulk), she surrounded herself with artists who sought her patronage, notably Modigliani, Chagall, Braque and Dufy. Her husband likewise immersed himself in artistic endeavors through his founding of the Black Mannequin Press, which published such modern writers as D.H. Lawrence. Rubinstein's accumulation of wealth led Salvador Dali to portray her chained to a rock with ropes of emeralds as a symbol of her slavery to her material possessions. In actuality, she could be very casual with her belongings, once stashing a million dollars' worth of jewelry—including some once worn by *Catherine I of Russia—in a cardboard box under her bed.

Rubinstein's marriage began to fall apart toward the end of the 1920s. Recognizing that the problem lay largely in her inability to scale back her work, she tried to lighten her load by selling her American business. However, when the stock market crashed a year later, she could not resist repurchasing it for a fraction of her selling price. Rubinstein and Titus were divorced in 1937 or 1938, and in 1938 she married Prince Artchil Gourielli-Tchkonia, a Russian prince 20 years her junior. As a tribute to him, she created a cosmetics line for men and named it for him.

Rubinstein based her success on daily beauty routines which she devised but never followed herself, claiming not to have the time. She emphasized concentrated, individual attention and pampering of customers, and was the inventor of the "Day of Beauty" concept at her salons. She was also skilled at inventing attractive, enticing packaging and promotional techniques. Beyond her innovations in the marketing of cosmetics and beauty treatments, Rubinstein also initiated changes in the development of cosmetics themselves. She championed the use of silk in cosmetics and sold the first tinted face powder and foundation. She also developed various medicated creams (her claims for which once got her in trouble with the Food and Drug Administration) and waterproof mascara. As with the head of any successful business, Rubinstein was not without her enemies. She had a longstanding feud with rival *Elizabeth Arden, whose marketing approach was somewhat more deliberately upscale than Rubinstein's. In 1938, Arden hired away Rubinstein's general manager and 11 staff members, but Rubinstein got her revenge by hiring Arden's ex-husband. Arden, too, then married a Russian prince (from whom she was later divorced).

Rubinstein provided jobs to several of her sisters and their children, including niece ✥▶ **Mala Rubinstein**, as well as to her son Roy, and was generous to causes she believed in. She gave large sums to Israel and founded the Helena Rubinstein Pavilion of Contemporary Art in Tel Aviv. In 1953, she founded the Helena Rubinstein Foundation to provide funds to health organizations, medical research, and rehabilitation, noting, "My fortune comes from women and should benefit them and their children to better their quality of life." In addition, she gave funds to the America-Israel Cultural Foundation and provided scholarships to Israeli students.

Rubinstein's husband died in 1956, and her younger son Horace died two years later. She did not slow down, however, remaining active until the end of her life and never retiring from her business. As she grew older, she held business meetings in her bedroom, directing from her elaborate Lucite-framed bed. She published her autobiography, *My Life for Beauty*, in 1964, and died of a stroke in New York City the following year, at the age of 94.

SOURCES:

O'Higgins, Patrick. *Madame: An Intimate Biography of Helena Rubinstein.* NY: Viking, 1971.

Sicherman, Barbara, and Carol Hurd Green, eds. *Notable American Women: The Modern Period.* Cambridge, MA: The Belknap Press of Harvard University, 1980.

Kelly Winters, freelance writer, Bayville, New York

✥▶ **Rubinstein, Mala** (1905–1999)

Polish-born cosmetics executive. Name variations: *Mala Kolin; Mala Rubinstein Silson.* Born Mala Kolin in Cracow, Poland, on December 31, 1905; died in July 1999 at a hospital in Manhattan; niece of Helena Rubinstein (1870–1965); sister of Oscar Kolin (d. 1995, chair of Helena Rubinstein, Inc.); married Victor Silson.

Mala Rubinstein was born Mala Kolin in Cracow, Poland, in 1905. At age 18, she moved to Paris to learn the cosmetics business from her aunt *Helena Rubinstein, and worked at the company from the 1920s to the 1970s until its sale to L'Oréal. As vice president in charge of creative services for Helena Rubinstein, Inc., Mala wrote several books on beauty.

Rubinstein, Mala (1905–1999).

See Rubinstein, Helena for sidebar.

Ruck, Berta (1878–1978)

British novelist and illustrator. Name variations: *Amy Roberta Ruck; Mrs. Oliver Onions.* Born Amy Roberta Ruck in Murree, India, in 1878; died in Aberdovey, Merioneth, Wales, on August 11, 1978; daughter of Arthur Ashley Ruck (a British army officer and later chief constable) and Elizabeth Eleanor D'Arcy; attended the Lambeth School of Art, Slade School of Art, and an art college in Paris; married Oliver Onions (a writer who later changed his name to George Oliver), in 1909; children: two sons.

Selected writings: His Official Fiancée (1914); The Wooing of Rosamond Fayre (1915); The Girls at His Billet (1916); In Another Girl's Shoes (1916); Three of Hearts (1917); Sweethearts Unmet (1919); Disturbing Charm (1919); Bridge of Kisses (1920); Sweet Stranger (1921); Arrant Rover (1921); Subconscious Courtship (1922); The Wrong Mr. Right (1922); Sir or Madam? (1923); Dancing Star (1923); Clouded Pearl (1924); Leap Year Girl (1924); Lucky in Love (1924); The Immortal Girl (1925); Kneel to the Prettiest (1925); Pearl Thief (1926); Her Pirate Partner (1927); The Maid of a Minx (1927); Money for One (1928); The Youngest Venus (1928); One of the Chorus (1929); The Unkissed Bride (1929); Offer of Marriage (1930); Today's Daughter (1930); Missing Girl (1930); Post-War Girl (1930); Wanted on the Voyage (1930); Dance Partner (1931); The Lap of Luxury (1931); It Was Left to Peter (1932); This Year, Next Year, Sometime— (1932); Change for Happiness (1933); Sudden Sweetheart (1933); Eleventh Hour Lover (1933); Understudy (1933); Best Time Ever

(1934); Sunburst (1934); A Story-Teller Tells the Truth (1935); Star in Love (1935); Sunshine Stealers (1935); Half-Past Kissing Time (1936); Spring Comes to Miss Lonelyheart (1936); Love on Second Thoughts (1937); Mock-Honeymoon (1937); Love Comes Again Later (1938); Wedding March (1938); Money Isn't Everything (1939); Romance Royal (1939); Jade Earrings (1941); Spinster's Progress (1942); Footlight Fever (1942); A Smile for the Past (1959); A Trickle of Welsh Blood (1967); Shopping for a Husband (1967); An Asset to Wales (1970); Ancestral Voices (1972).

Berta Ruck was born in 1878 in Murree, India, the oldest of eight children of a British army officer serving there. When she was two years old, her family moved to Wales, where she lived with her paternal grandmother in Merionethshire until 1888. Ruck attended St. Winifred's School in Bangor, and had a brief job as a nanny in Germany. With the aim of becoming a book illustrator, she attended the Lambeth School of Art, and received a scholarship to the Slade School of Art. After studying at another art school in Paris for a year, she started a job illustrating stories in the *Idler* and *Jabberwock*.

Ruck switched to a writing career after becoming convinced she could create stories every bit as good as those she was illustrating. She began contributing to magazines such as *Home Chat* and received encouragement from writer and friend *Edith Nesbit. Ruck married Oliver Onions, a writer known for his ghost and detective stories, in 1909. Three years later, a publisher noticed a story of hers in *Home Chat*, and asked her to make it into a novel. The book *His Official Fiancée* (1914) was instantly successful in Britain as well as in the United States, and set the stage for her long career as a novelist. She was prolific, publishing up to three books a year over the next 50-odd years; her last novel was published in 1967, when she was 89.

Ruck's books were updated romantic fairy tales, often set in Wales, with Cinderella plots featuring worthy but poor or ignored heroines who triumph over travail and finally marry rich, adoring men. She also wrote several autobiographical books, including *A Story-Teller Tells the Truth* (1935), *A Smile for the Past* (1959), *A Trickle of Welsh Blood* (1967), *An Asset to Wales* (1970) and *Ancestral Voices* (1972). She was very popular throughout her long life; in the 1920s, a *Berta Ruck Birthday Book* was published, and she spoke to the troops during World War II. Ruck, who died when she was 100, attributed her longevity to her lifelong passion for swimming outdoors in all sorts of weather; in winter, she often had to first break the ice on the water.

SOURCES:

The Concise Dictionary of National Biography. Oxford: Oxford University Press, 1992.

Kunitz, Stanley J., and Howard Haycraft, eds. *Twentieth Century Authors*. NY: H.W. Wilson, 1942.

Shattock, Joanne. *The Oxford Guide to British Women Writers*. Oxford: Oxford University Press, 1993.

Kelly Winters,
freelance writer, Bayville, New York

Rudkin, Margaret (1897–1967)

American businesswoman who founded Pepperidge Farm Bakeries. Born Margaret Fogarty on September 14, 1897, in New York City; died on June 1, 1967, in New Haven, Connecticut; daughter of Joseph I. Fogarty and Margaret (Healy) Fogarty; educated in public high schools; married Henry Albert Rudkin (a stockbroker), on April 8, 1923 (died 1966); children: Henry, Jr. (b. 1924); William (b. 1926); Mark (b. 1929).

Born on September 14, 1897, Margaret Rudkin grew up in New York City with her parents Joseph and **Margaret Fogarty** and four younger siblings. The family lived in a four-story brownstone in what is now a section of Manhattan known as Tudor City, and young Margaret learned to bake and cook from her Irish grandmother who lived with them. When Margaret was 12, her grandmother died, and the family moved to Flushing, Long Island (now part of Queens). She attended public schools there and graduated as valedictorian of her class.

Aiming for a career in business, Margaret became a bookkeeper at a local bank, the first woman to be hired at that institution. In 1919, she took a job at the brokerage firm of McClure, Jones & Co., where Henry Albert Rudkin was a partner in the firm. Though 12 years older than Margaret, he had the advantage of being an Irish New Yorker, and the two were married on April 8, 1923. The firm did well on Wall Street, and the Rudkins bought 125 acres near Fairfield, Connecticut, built a mansion in the Tudor style, and called it Pepperidge Farm after a much-loved pepperidge tree in the front yard.

The Rudkins were both interested in horses, hunting and polo, and the house originally had a garage for 5 cars and stables for 12 horses. However, the Depression and a bad polo accident that forced Henry's leave of absence from work for six months brought an end to their expensive recreational pursuits. Margaret sold the horses and most of the cars, let the full-time servants go, and began devising ways to make money at home.

Although she had servants to do much of the housework, Rudkin frequently did the cooking herself, using recipes from her collection of old cookbooks. While some sources suggest that she began baking bread in 1937 in order to provide wholesome, additive-free slices for her son Mark, who suffered from asthma, in her official history she wrote only that she began because she was interested in providing "proper food for children." "They say life begins at forty," she said. "Well, that's how old I was when I baked that first loaf." Her original efforts to make stone-ground whole wheat bread turned out "as hard as rock and about one inch high." She continued to experiment, and eventually perfected a recipe. In August 1937, she sold her first batch of loaves to a grocer in Fairfield.

The bread was expensive—more than twice the price of commercial loaves—because it used fresh ingredients such as butter and whole milk. It sold well, however, and demand grew; that fall, she hired several workers and moved the bakery from the kitchen to the garage, where she had more room. She made white loaves with unbleached flour, and soon had a standing order for 24 loaves a day from the prestigious Charles & Company specialty store in New York City. For the first few weeks, Henry Rudkin delivered the bread when he commuted in to Wall Street.

Rudkin received glowing publicity about her bread, an important factor in her success. Articles praising her bread appeared in the *New York Journal and American*, the New York *Herald Tribune*, the *World Telegram*, and *Reader's Digest*. Orders poured in from all over the United States, Canada, and overseas. In 1940, she borrowed $15,000 to move the bakery from the farm to a former auto salesroom and hospital in Norwalk, Connecticut. Within a year, she was producing more than 50,000 loaves a week, mostly white bread although she still made whole wheat bread and added other items. She rewarded Benjamin Sonnenberg, the man who had suggested the *Reader's Digest* article, by giving him a 5% interest in the business; by 1960, this would be worth more than $1 million.

Pepperidge Farm became a major firm during the 1940s and 1950s. Margaret Rudkin oversaw the daily operations of the bakery as president, while Henry Rudkin, who quit his Wall Street job to become chair of the company, handled finances and marketing. In 1947, the company moved production to a new plant in Norwalk. Other plants were opened in Pennsyl-vania in 1949 and Illinois in 1953. Rudkin also bought a frozen pastry line from a New Hampshire firm, as well as cookie recipes from the Delacre bakery in Belgium. In the 1950s, Rudkin, who was described as "slim and sophisticated, with gorgeous red hair, green eyes, and a milk-white skin," began appearing in television commercials for her products, although the company's sales were always driven more by word of mouth than by heavy advertising.

In 1960, the company was making profits of $1.3 million on sales of $32 million. That year, Rudkin sold the business to the Campbell Soup Company in exchange for Campbell stock worth $28 million. She continued to run Pepperidge Farm, and was also a director of Campbell Soup. In 1962, her son William became president of Pepperidge Farm, and she took over her husband's job as chair until he died in May 1966. Five months later, Margaret stepped down as chair of the company. By this time she was very ill with breast cancer, for which she had been treated with surgery ten years earlier. She died in June 1967 in New Haven, Connecticut.

Rudkin's success was due not only to her business acumen, but also to her love of cooking and passionate interest in her products. She treated her employees well, paying them more than other companies paid similar workers; for the company's 20th anniversary in 1957, each of the 1,000 employees gave a dollar to buy her a 15th-century cookbook, *De Honesta Voluptate et Valetudine*, which she used for inspiration when she wrote the bestselling *The Margaret Rudkin Pepperidge Farm Cookbook* in 1963. Before she died, she gave her extensive collection of cookbooks to the Pequot Library in Southport, Connecticut, and donated money to the Yale-New Haven Hospital and other institutions.

SOURCES:
Griffin, Lynne, and Kelly McCann. *The Book of Women: 300 Notable Women History Passed By*. Holbrook, MA: Bob Adams, 1992.
Moritz, Charles, ed. *Current Biography Yearbook 1959*. NY: H.W. Wilson, 1959.
Sicherman, Barbara, and Carol Hurd Green, eds. *Notable American Women: The Modern Period*. Cambridge, MA: The Belknap Press of Harvard University, 1980.

Kelly Winters,
freelance writer, Bayville, New York

Rudolph, Wilma (1940–1994)

African-American sprinter who grew up with doctors debating whether or not she would ever walk unassisted and went on to become a legendary track star as the first American woman to win three gold medals in one Olympics. Name variations: (nick-

name) Skeeter. Born Wilma Glodean Rudolph on June 23, 1940, in St. Bethlehem, Tennessee; died on November 12, 1994, at her home in Brentwood, Tennessee, of brain cancer; daughter of Eddie Rudolph and Blanche Rudolph; Tennessee State University, B.A., 1963; married William Ward, on October 14, 1961 (divorced 1962); married Robert Eldrige, in 1963 (divorced 1976); children: (with Eldrige) Yolanda (b. 1958), Djauna (b. 1964), Robert (b. 1965), and Xurry (b. 1971).

Awards: Associated Press' Athlete of the Year Award (1960, 1961); Helms World Trophy for the North American Continent (1960); Los Angeles Times award (1960); Mademoiselle award (1960); The New York Times selection as one of the ten most outstanding women in U.S. (1960); European Sportswriters' Association award for Most Outstanding Athlete of the Year (1960); Sports Magazine award (1960); National Newspaper Publishers Association's award (1960); Babe Didrickson Zaharias Trophy for Outstanding Female Athlete in U.S. (1960); James E. Sullivan Award as the nation's outstanding amateur athlete (1961); Women's Sports Foundation's America's Greatest Women Athletes' award (1984); National Collegiate Athletic Association's Silver Anniversary Award (even though she competed before the NCAA sponsored women's championships in any sport, 1990); first National Sports Award (presented by President Clinton, 1993); enshrinement in the Black Sports Hall of Fame (1973), National Track and Field Hall of Fame (1974), and U.S. Olympics Hall of Fame (1978); Tennessee State University named an indoor track in her honor (1988), and the U.S. Olympics Committee established the Wilma Rudolph Scholarship Fund after her death (1994).

Became youngest member of U.S. women's track-and-field team (1956); competed in the Olympics and won four medals (1956, 1960); retired (1962), becoming a teacher and speaker.

Records (in high-school basketball and women's Negro league): highest individual point total for one game, 53 (1956); member of first team to score 100 points in a game (1957); highest individual, season point total, 803 in 25 games (1957); member, championship team (1957).

Records (Olympic): bronze medal in 400-meter relay (1956); gold medal in 100 meter, 11.0 (1960); gold medal in 200 meter, 24.0 (1960); gold medal in 400-meter relay, 44.5 (1960); was the first American woman to win three gold medals at one Olympics (1960).

Records (world): 60-yard dash, 6.8 (1961); 70-yard dash, 7.8 (1961); 100 meters, 11.2 (1961); 200 meters, 22.4 (1959); 4x100 relay (anchor), 44.4 (1960).

By the start of the 4x100 relay at the Rome Olympics in 1960, 20-year-old Wilma Rudolph had already won two individual-event gold medals, but her American teammates *Martha Hudson, *Lucinda Williams and *Barbara Jones had been shut out. U.S. women's track coach Ed Temple would later recall that Rudolph's greatest desire was a medal for her fellow runners, all of whom, like Rudolph, attended Tennessee State. After the first three legs of the race, the U.S. team was out front, but the final baton hand-off to Rudolph took two tries and erased their lead. It didn't matter. The 6'1", long-striding sprinter not only made up the difference, but was alone at the finish line. The U.S. women's team won its first Olympic gold medal in the relay, and Wilma Rudolph became the first American woman to win three gold medals in one Olympics.

The sixth of Eddie and **Blanche Rudolph**'s eight children, Wilma Rudolph was born prematurely in 1940 after her mother had a fall; her parents were afraid that their 4.5-pound newborn would not make it through the first night. Eddie had a number of children from a previous marriage, and in her autobiography Rudolph counted herself as number 20 of 22. Several years of sickness ensued. Frail and slender, Rudolph endured a bout of double pneumonia at age four which was followed immediately by scarlet fever; more than once she was expected to die. "All I can remember," she would later write, "is being ill and bedridden."

Soon after her birth, the family moved from St. Bethlehem, Tennessee, to a town four miles down the road—Clarksville: population approximately 11,000 and located 43 miles from Nashville. Her mother, a devout church-going Baptist, worked as a domestic, and her father, who was less religious but a strict disciplinarian, was a porter and handyman. Aided by the love and support of her family, and the encouragement of the town's black doctor, Wilma learned to fight against her illnesses. She would later recall a turning point which occurred while she was lying in bed suffering through yet another fever: a conscious decision to stop succumbing to the aches and the urge to drift away. "I think I started acquiring a competitive spirit right then and there," she wrote, "a spirit that would make me successful in sports later on. I was mad, and I was going to beat these illnesses no matter what." Rudolph's competitive will to win would one day be publicly tested in the ultimate arena of amateur athletics. But first she needed to summon the will to walk.

In addition to her other illnesses, a mild form of polio resulted in a crooked and partially paralyzed left leg, with the foot turned inward. As doctors debated whether or not she would ever walk, Rudolph began six years of physical therapy. Two African-American doctors at Meharry Medical College in Nashville fitted her leg with a corrective metal brace, then prescribed regular massage and heat treatments. Once a week for several years, on her mother's day off, Blanche and Wilma rode together in the back of the bus to Nashville. In between trips, her mother and siblings massaged her leg several times a day. "With all the love and care my family gave me," she wrote, "I couldn't help but get better."

Indeed, with treatment she made progress, at first walking by hopping on one leg and then working hard to conceal her brace-aided limp. In private, she would sneak out of the brace, check for signs of improvement, and little by little attempt to use the bad leg. After five years of therapy, she shocked her parents and doctors by walking unassisted. At age 9½, she took the brace off in public, and by the time she was 12 the device went back to Nashville. Once not expected to walk, Rudolph was playing basketball in her bare feet. She was finally free and determined to fit in. Recalling playmates who did not want her on their team, she wrote: "All of my young life I would say to myself, 'One day I'm going to be somebody very special.'"

Racial inequality, however, was more difficult to overcome. During Rudolph's youth, the law of the land and the guiding tenet of racial relations was "separate but equal," but, especially in the South, blacks were not equal. For instance, white bankers denied credit to blacks, and in Clarksville—which was 75% white and segregated—the town's largest employer, a tire company, first banned black employees and later offered them only the poorest jobs. Two of Rudolph's brothers who served in black units during World War II had to ride in the back of the bus and drink from separate water fountains on their way home. When Rudolph and her mother arrived in Nashville for her treatments, it did not matter if they were hungry; the bus-depot restaurant did not serve blacks. One of the first dates carved into **Maya Lin**'s civil-rights memorial in Montgomery, Alabama, is December 1, 1955. On that day, Wilma Rudolph was already 15 years old when *Rosa Parks refused to give up her bus seat, initiating the Montgomery bus boycott and the civil-rights movement. But in the late '40s and early '50s, caught between the pincers of poverty and racism, her parents and teachers saw little choice but to quietly accept the world as it was. Rudolph heeded their message to stay out of trouble while chan-

neling her rage, vowing "to never serve coffee to white ladies in bed on Saturday mornings." The all-black schools Rudolph would attend skirted the issues, promoting black heroes but avoiding the subject of bigotry. Although the winds of change were gathering, they were a long way from Clarksville.

By the time Rudolph was a junior at Burt High School, she had become, of all things, a basketball star. High-school coach Clinton Gray nicknamed her "Skeeter" because she was "little, fast and always in the way, like a mosquito." Gray made Rudolph pay her dues, keeping her on the bench during her freshman year. Despite continuing hurdles, like the social pressures to avoid sport and exercise (many thought such activities unwomanly), Rudolph kept practicing with anyone she could. She finally starred as a sophomore, in one game scoring a record 53 points.

Gray also coached Burt's rag-tag track team, which was mostly an excuse to keep the girls in shape for basketball during the off-season. When he drove them to meets in his nine-passenger DeSoto wagon, his wife packed the meals because they could not get served at whites-only restaurants. To everyone's surprise, including her own, Rudolph excelled on the track. One season she ran 20 different races and won them all. Her confidence developed and her personality blossomed. As Burt High's fastest runner, she was buoyant and cocky when she stepped up to the starting line in Tuskegee, Alabama, at her first major meet away from home, but she failed to lead the way over a single finish line. Better-trained competitors with less raw talent used technique and strategy to beat her in the first few races. She came home with her pride shattered and, demoralized, eventually just gave up.

But the defeat gnawed at her. She sulked and drifted, until at her lowest point she found her familiar resolve. Rudolph decided to stop relying on natural ability, to train hard daily, to be honest with herself, and to never again give up. Ultimately, she would look back on her ability to learn from failure, and her decision to run again after the crushing defeat in Tuskegee, as a major turning point and lifelong guiding lesson.

Rudolph's first love was still basketball, and it was thanks to her playing that she was spotted by Edward Temple. A part-time women's basketball referee, Temple traveled the state scouting and recruiting prospects for his day job as coach of Tennessee State University's women's track team. His legendary team of Tigerbelles—tigers on the track, Southern belles off—eventually produced 40 female Olympians and 14 American medals during his 44 years as a coach. Temple invited Rudolph, still a high-school sophomore, to attend a summer camp for track. The youngest member there, she improved dramatically under Temple's demanding training and tutelage. She also met a second guiding influence, two-time Olympian *Mae Faggs—the senior member and matriarch of the Tigerbelles—who generously encouraged and assisted Rudolph.

> If you can pick yourself up after a crushing defeat, and go on to win again, you are going to be a champion.
>
> —Wilma Rudolph

Jackie Robinson, the first black ballplayer to play in the major leagues, was also an inspiration. Rudolph met him when he attended a meet in Philadelphia with a Brooklyn Dodgers teammate, and Robinson took the time to talk to a few of the competitors. He encouraged her to keep running. "For the first time in my life," she later noted, "I had a black person I could look up to as a real hero." Role models in her sport, particularly women, were scarce. Black women had broken the barrier, with *Alice Coachman winning a gold medal in 1948 in the long jump, but there was no television coverage and women received little press. The women's results for the AAU Nationals in Seattle and the U.S. Olympic Trials, which Rudolph was to attend, would not be published in the papers.

Before her team arrived in Seattle, she had a good deal to learn. In deference to the senior members of the team, she had been holding back. Mae worked to convince her to go all-out, to run to beat everyone, so as to ultimately help the team by running as an individual. Rudolph proved to be a good student. At the 100-meter finals, she tied Faggs in a dead-heat finish, insuring the two of them a slot on the Olympic team. After Greyhound buses to Nashville, Coach Gray's DeSoto, and Coach Temple's caravans, the 16-year-old, 89-pound Rudolph boarded a plane to Los Angeles, then went on to Hawaii and the Fiji Islands before finally arriving in Melbourne, Australia, for the 1956 Olympic games.

In Australia, far away from her coach and family, she suffered an early blow: elimination in the semifinals of the 200-meter heats. Nevertheless, the Melbourne Games were a learning experience. At the opening ceremonies, Rudolph had met *Betty Cuthbert, Australia's best runner, who went on to become the star of the games. Watching Cuthbert claim three gold medals helped lift Rudolph out of her 200-meter elimination blues. Encouraged to refocus, she went all-out during the 4x100 relay. She ran in the third position on a team that included Mae Faggs and helped the U.S. win a bronze medal.

The Melbourne games previewed a coming sea change in track and field, an approaching era of domination by the U.S. women's track and field team. The '56 team planted the seeds for a remarkable series of upcoming accomplishments, especially by black women. *Mildred McDaniel won a gold medal in the high jump, *Willye White performed in the first of a record five Olympics for the U.S. team, and Wilma Rudolph made her Olympic debut. As well, four African-Americans teamed up to run in the relay finals for the first time. With a bronze medal hanging around her neck and the Burt High School Band belting out the national anthem, Rudolph came home the hero of Clarksville to finish her junior year.

Back in school, she excelled in basketball, averaging 35 points a game on the state championship team, and in track. Her romance with Robert Eldrige, a friend since the second grade who became the star of the football and track teams, turned serious. During a routine physical, Rudolph discovered that she was four months' pregnant, and her father forbade future contact with Robert. The unwed Rudolph was seven months' pregnant when she walked up to accept her high-school diploma. Her daughter Yolanda was born in July 1958.

After the pregnancy, Rudolph's weight rose to 129 pounds. To the new mother and the people around her it looked as if her career might end as quickly as it started. Although she had fallen from grace in Clarksville, Rudolph had both a strong record of fighting against the odds and the support of Coach Temple and her family. With sports scholarships not available to women (until 1968), she started college by joining a work-aid program to cover tuition and board, while her older sister Yvonne cared for the infant Yolanda. Rudolph converted her extra weight to muscle, trained hard, and ran well at Tennessee State. At the Nationals in Corpus Christi, she posted a 22.9 in the 200 meters. Rudolph had her first world record and a return ticket for the summer Olympics.

She arrived in Italy during 1960 to find the heat and humidity of Rome exactly like that of her Tennessee training grounds. The coach of the U.S. women's team that year was Ed Temple, and no one knew her better. Motivated by the memory of defeat, Rudolph was ready, and the world was, literally, watching: the Olympics were being televised for the first time. Eurovision transmitted live to 21 European countries.

In the U.S., CBS paid $660,000 for the rights to fly film from Rome. In the stands, there were more than four times as many fans as the entire population of Clarksville watching Rudolph each day when she entered the 100,000-seat-capacity Stadio Olympico. The Italians called her the Black Gazelle, because of her long legs and graceful style. Fans would chant, "Vil-ma Vil-ma," each time she ran.

On the final day of practice, Rudolph ran through sprinklers in a practice field to cool off and stepped in a hole which twisted her ankle. The swelling and discoloration looked disas-trous, but she was lucky to have a full day to re-cuperate—with the ankle taped, iced and elevat-ed—before the preliminaries for her first event, the 100 meter. It would be five days before she would have to truly test the ankle, in the turns on the 200-meter course and in the 4x100 relay.

No one knew it at the time, but the winner of all three events was pretty much predeter-mined when Rudolph stepped out of bed the fol-lowing morning and her ankle, though hurting, held fast under her full weight. Eight years after shipping her leg brace back to the Nashville hos-pital, Rudolph won all there was to win in Rome.

Wilma
Rudolph

Thriving on the energy in the arena, she prepared methodically for her first event. Unfazed by the pressure, she sometimes slept on the trainer's table between heats. After tying the world record of 11.3 in the semifinals, she took the 100-meter gold medal in 11.0 seconds, finishing nearly six meters ahead of the second-place runner, **Dorothy Hyman** of Great Britain. Next she won the 200-meter sprint in 24.0, after running an Olympic record of 23.2 in her opening heat. Finally, after setting a world record of 44.4 in the semifinals, Ed Temple's Tigerbelles won the 4x100-meter relay with a time of 44.5—despite the poor baton pass. Rudolph's six-foot stature, confidence, and story of endurance made her larger than life. The world was fascinated by her grace on the track, astonished by her success, and enthralled by her elegance. A sparkling personality and broad smile further endeared her to fans. She and Cassius Clay—the boxing gold-medal winner in Rome who later changed his name to Muhammad Ali—became fast friends. Together, smiling and confident, they stood as bright young symbols of a changing America.

But while Rudolph won three medals and fame, her victories brought no fortune. The 1960 Olympics were part of a now bygone, strictly amateur, era. Endorsement contracts, training stipends, and appearance fees did not exist. Rudolph and her teammates gave Americans, especially black Americans, hope and inspiration while helping to pave the way for a professional circuit. Female athletes would eventually earn million-dollar contracts for wearing a particular brand of shoes, but pioneers like Rudolph received no direct monetary reward, and had little opportunity to financially exploit their sudden fame.

Rudolph was a superstar, nevertheless, and her life changed dramatically. Immediately after the Olympics, Temple took the team on a tour of London, Athens, Amsterdam, Cologne, Frankfurt, and Berlin. Pope John XXIII granted the team an audience. While Temple watched over the whole team, Rudolph traveled without a manager or an agent. But she had an innate ability to respond to her fans through all the banquets, parades, and appearances, and never tired of signing autographs. When she finally returned home to Clarksville, to a parade, a carnival, and a dinner held in her honor, she used her power to influence change by threatening to boycott the parade unless it was desegregated. By standing tall, she brought the town together in celebration.

Rudolph returned to college, earned a bachelor's degree in education, and continued to run.

The first child in her family to graduate from college, she was also the first woman invited to several prestigious men's track and field meets, including the Melrose Games, the New York Athletic Club Meets, and the L.A. Times Games. After a meet in Washington, D.C., she met with President John F. Kennedy. In 1960, she married William Ward, but they divorced the following year; the marriage is not discussed in her autobiography. She retired from the track in 1962: "Because I couldn't top what I did. . . . I'll be remembered for when I was at my best." In 1963, she traveled on two final goodwill tours and came back to Clarksville to marry her childhood friend and the father of her first child, Robert Eldrige. Rudolph took a job teaching second grade while coaching high-school basketball and track in Tennessee, for $400 a month. But after running in stadiums throughout the world, she could not settle down back home, where she was making little money and felt stagnated as a teacher. With little call in the South for her services, she accepted a position as a director of a community center in Indianapolis for $600 a month. Still somewhat unfulfilled in Indiana, she moved on to work for the Jobs Corps in Poland Springs, Maine. A year later, in 1967, at the request of Vice President Hubert Humphrey, she went to work for Operation Champ, the athletic outreach program, in Detroit. Rudolph also taught at a Detroit high school which was located in what would be the center of the worst Detroit rioting in 1968. At the time, the civil-rights movement was in full swing and racial tensions soared in America. Rioting broke out in the ghettos of Newark, Los Angeles, Detroit and other American cities. Rudolph left Detroit in 1968 on the day that civil-rights leader Dr. Martin Luther King, Jr., was assassinated. In the bus station in Nashville, as she waited with her family to transfer to Clarksville, her children were spat on by a white man who was later arrested by the police.

This proved to be a difficult time for Rudolph, who had tired of serving as a figurehead and having her celebrity exploited for little gain. Some of her jobs were mundane and often unproductive. There was financial stress, and at one point she had tax problems. After having a total of four children together, she and her husband divorced in 1976. The greatest female athlete of her time watched from the sidelines as her world records fell. She sold some of her medals. Cassius Clay, partly in sympathy for the black power movement and in protest of the Vietnam War, had thrown his gold medal into a river.

The difficult years, however, did not diminish Rudolph's spirit. She spent the rest of her life working officially and unofficially as a teacher and role model, and at times holding simultaneous positions, for the next 25 years. She served as a movie-studio representative; a network radio co-host; an administrative analyst for UCLA; an executive for a Nashville bank, a Nashville hospital and an Indianapolis baking company; a representative for Minute Maid orange juice; a coach at Depauw University in Greencastle, Indiana; and president of the Wilma Rudolph Foundation, a nonprofit organization devoted to teaching youngsters that they could overcome obstacles, just as she had. Finally, she formed her own company, based in Indiana, and became a full-time motivational speaker. Here, she was at her best and most enjoyed working with children.

Despite her retirement from the sport, Rudolph never totally left the track. Temple talked to her once a month, and she often came back to help with his young runners. Olympic greats—such as *Evelyn Ashford and *Jackie Joyner-Kersee—describe Rudolph as an idol, as someone who was always willing to listen and provide encouragement. Knowing what it had been like to be alone as a teenager in Melbourne and to have been too poor to bring anyone in her family to Rome, she helped start a trust fund for families of athletes going to Seoul in 1984.

On November 12, 1994, Wilma Rudolph died of brain cancer at her home in Brentwood, Tennessee. At her funeral, the Olympic flag draped her casket. An estimated 4,000 mourners paid their respects. They spoke of her accomplishments on the track, her abiding commitment to the Olympic movement, and her work with children. Her success on the track changed the sport and helped change the country. Rudolph joins Jesse Owens and other sports legends whenever stories are told about Olympic pioneers, the civil-rights movement, and profiles in courage. "Whenever I was down," wrote *Florence Griffith Joyner, "I thought how dedicated Wilma was to overcome the obstacles. That motivated me to push harder. . . . She not only taught me how to sprint but how to go the distance in life." Said Benita Fitzgerald-Brown, 1984 Olympic champion in the hurdles, "She showed it was OK for a woman to be powerful and black and beautiful."

SOURCES:

Biracree, Tom. *American Woman of Achievement: Wilma Rudolph*. NY: Chelsea House, 1988.

Guttman, Allen. *The Olympics: A History of the Modern Games*. Chicago, IL: University of Illinois Press, 1984.

Jacobs, Linda. *Wilma Rudolph: Run for Glory*. St. Paul, MN: EMC, 1975.

Joyner, Florence. "Florence Joyner Pays Tribute to the late Wilma Rudolph," in *Jet Magazine*. December 2, 1994, p. 51.

Litsky, Frank. "Wilma Rudolph, Star of 1960 Olympics, Dies at 54," in *The New York Times*. November 13, 1994, p. 53.

Mallon, Bill, and Ian Buchanan. *Quest for Gold: Encyclopedia of American Olympians*. NY: Leisure Press, 1984.

Moritz, Charles. *Current Biography*. NY: H.W. Wilson, 1961.

Page, James A. *Black Olympian Medalists*. Boulder, CO: Libraries Unlimited, 1991.

Rhoden, William C. "The End of a Winding Road," in *The New York Times*. November 19, 1994, Sports Section, p. 33.

Rudolph, Wilma. *Wilma: The Story of Wilma Rudolph*. NY: Signet, 1977.

Smith, Jessie Carney. *Notable Black American Women*. Detroit, MI: Gale Research, 1992.

U.S. Bureau of the Census. Sixteenth Census of U.S.: 1940. Vol. 2, Part 6. Washington, DC: U.S. Department of Commerce, 1942.

———. U.S. Census of the Population: 1960. Vol. 1, Part 44, Tennessee. Washington, DC: U.S. Department of Commerce, 1963.

Wolfe, Alexander, and Richard Obrien. "Fast Train From Clarksville," in *Sports Illustrated*. November 28, 1994, p. 13.

PERSONAL INTERVIEWS:

Charlene (Clifton) Rudolph of Brentwood, Tennessee, and Edward Temple of Nashville, Tennessee.

RELATED MEDIA:

"Wilma: The Story of Wilma Rudolph" (98 min. television movie), starring Cicely Tyson and Shirley Jo Finney as Wilma, directed by Bud Greenspan, NBC, 1977.

Jesse T. Raiford,
President of Raiford Communications, Inc.,
New York, New York

Ruffin, Josephine St. Pierre

(1842–1924)

African-American civic leader and reformer. Born Josephine St. Pierre in Boston, Massachusetts, on August 31, 1842; died in Boston on March 13, 1924; daughter of John St. Pierre (a clothing dealer) and Elizabeth (Menhenick) St. Pierre; educated at the Bowdoin School; married George Lewis Ruffin (a lawyer, legislator and judge), in 1858 (died 1886); children: Hubert St. Pierre Ruffin; Florida Yates Ridley; Stanley Ruffin; George Lewis Ruffin; Robert Ruffin (died in infancy).

Josephine St. Pierre Ruffin was born in Boston, Massachusetts, in 1842, the youngest of six children of John and **Elizabeth St. Pierre**. Her mother came from Cornwall, England; her father, of African, French, and Indian descent, sold new and used clothing and was the founder of the Zion Church in Boston. Josephine attended public schools in Charleston and Salem, and later went to a private school in New York to avoid Boston's segregated school system. In 1855, after the system changed, she returned to Boston and attended the Bowdoin School.

In 1858, 16-year-old Josephine married 21-year-old free black George Lewis Ruffin, with whom she soon sailed to the less racist environs of Liverpool, England. Six months later, however, they returned, and George began working as a barber. They aided the Union Army during the Civil War by recruiting soldiers for the black regiments and serving in the Home Guard. Their work on behalf of the African-American population continued after the war, when Josephine organized the Kansas Relief Association to collect money and clothing for Southern blacks who had migrated to Kansas. George graduated from law school in 1869, and later built his own law practice, served as a state legislator and city council member, and became the first black municipal judge in Boston before his death in 1886. Josephine was a prominent community leader in her own right as an organizer, journalist, club woman, and volunteer. She was the editor of a black newspaper, the weekly *Boston Courant*, and was a member of the New England Women's Press Association.

Expanding her interests beyond the black community, Ruffin served on the executive board of the Massachusetts Moral Education Association, and was a volunteer visitor for Associated Charities for 11 years. She worked for women's suffrage and associated with reformers such as *Julia Ward Howe, *Lucy Stone, and *Ednah Dow Cheney. She was also a member of several white women's organizations, including the New England Women's Club and the Massachusetts State Federation of Women's Clubs, for which she was a member of the executive board.

In February 1893, Ruffin founded the Woman's Era Club with her daughter, **Florida Ridley**, and *Maria Louise Baldwin, the principal of a local high school. Intended to further the goals of African-American women and all African-Americans, the club, which was open to women of any race, provided scholarships to good students, and initiated many reforms and racial advancements. Ruffin and her daughter also founded the *Woman's Era*, the club's monthly illustrated magazine that was the first periodical owned, published and managed by black women in the United States.

Ruffin's focus on activist organizations for women provided the inspiration for a national organization of black women; its first national conference was held in Boston at Berkeley Hall

in July 1895, under her direction. Ruffin believed that it was in black women's interest to "teach an ignorant and suspicious world that our aims and interests are identical with those of all good aspiring women." Showing that they were dignified and concerned with working toward a better world, black women could break through negative stereotypes.

When the conference led to the founding of the National Federation of Afro-American Women (NFAAW), Ruffin successfully campaigned to have *Margaret Murray Washington, wife of Booker T. Washington, as president. In 1896, the NFAAW merged with the Colored Women's League, led by **Helen C. Cook**, to form the National Association of Colored Women (NACW), a single strong organization that would further the clubs' mutual objectives of improvement and social reform. Its first president was *Mary Church Terrell, and Ruffin, one of seven vice-presidents, remained editor of the *Woman's Era*, which became the official journal of the nascent organization, until 1900. The magazine was effective in publicizing and promoting the organization's goals, among them suffrage, education, culture, patriotism, and child welfare.

Ruffin became involved in a controversy with the General Federation of Women's Clubs (GFWC), which, despite having many members supportive of reform, sought to exclude black women. The GFWC had invited the Woman's Era Club to join, but did not realize it was an organization of black women until Ruffin attended the GFWC's biennial convention in Milwaukee, Wisconsin. She was there representing the Woman's Era Club and the New England Women's Press Association. The GFWC president **Rebecca Lowe** returned the Woman's Era Club dues and asked the club to return its certificate of membership. Ruffin was told that she could not enter the convention as a member of the black Woman's Era Club, but would be allowed to attend as a member of the white New England Women's Press Association.

Ruffin refused to accept these racist conditions. Her stand for civil rights received publicity throughout the nation, and most newspapers supported her. Some state delegations protested and several Massachusetts clubs withdrew from the GFWC, but the organization retained its whites-only policy for several decades. The incident spurred many black women's clubs to develop their own goals and organize various reforms to assist their communities.

Ruffin remained active in civic and charitable work throughout her life. She was one of the 56 charter members of the NAACP, and was a member of many black and white civic organizations. She fully believed that the future would be better for black women. Ruffin worked to further the cause until only weeks before her death from nephritis on March 13, 1924, in her Boston home. Many prominent people, both black and white, attended her funeral, and many organizations mourned her loss.

SOURCES:

Smith, Jessie Carney, ed. *Notable Black American Women*. Detroit, MI: Gale Research, 1992.

Kelly Winters,
freelance writer, Bayville, New York

Ruggiero, Angela (b. 1980).

See Team USA: Women's Ice Hockey at Nagano.

Ruilly, Macette de.

See French "Witches" (14–16th centuries).

Rukeyser, Muriel (1913–1980)

American poet, student of contemporary affairs, and political activist. Pronunciation: ROO-kaiser. Born in New York City on December 15, 1913; died on February 12, 1980, in New York City; daughter of Lawrence B. Rukeyser (an engineer and businessman) and Myra Lyons Rukeyser; attended Ethical Culture Center and Fieldston School, 1921–30, Vassar College, 1930–32, Columbia University, 1931–32; married Glynn Collins (a painter), in 1945 (annulled 1945); children: William Laurie Rukeyser (b. 1947).

Arrested while attending Scottsboro trial in Alabama (1933); won Yale Series of Younger Poets competition (1935); visited West Virginia, witnessed early stage of Spanish Civil War (1936); held post in Office of War Information (1943); moved to California (1945); returned to New York (1954); taught at Sarah Lawrence (1954–67); suffered first stroke (1966, some sources indicate 1964 or 1968); made trip to Hanoi (1972); named president of PEN, and journeyed to South Korea (1975); won Copernicus Prize of American Academy of Arts and Letters and suffered second stroke (1977).

Major works: (poetry) Theory of Flight (1935), U.S. 1 (1938), A Turning Wind (1939), Wake Island (1942), The Green Wave (1948), Body of Waking (1958), Breaking Open: New Poems (1973), The Gates (1976); (prose) Willard Gibbs (1942), The Life of Poetry (1949), One Life (1957), The Orgy (1966), The Traces of Thomas Hariot (1971); (translation) Selected Poems of Octavio Paz (1963).

Muriel Rukeyser was a significant and often controversial American poet and prose writer in the middle decades of the 20th century. In addition to her poetic output, she also produced three biographies, a novel, and essays, as well as translating the work of poets from a number of other languages into English. Although born to an affluent American Jewish family, she turned much of her attention to political and social injustices in the United States and abroad. An activist as well as a writer, Rukeyser found herself jailed on several occasions.

Many critics have evaluated Rukeyser's work largely in terms of its political elements, and, in fact, her political concerns were in evidence throughout her writing career. Others such as fellow poet Kenneth Rexroth have taken a larger view of her literary achievement. They point out that Rukeyser also delved deeply into aspects of her own personality. Notes **Virginia Terris**, most critics have focused so exclusively on "themes of social protest" in her work that they have missed the fact "that her greatest creative strengths have manifested themselves in her poems of intimate human relationships and myth-making." For example, Rukeyser produced a body of verse that explored such issues as her experiences as a woman, and some critics interpret a number of her poems as the attempt of a lesbian or bisexual to confront her hidden identity.

Rukeyser's last years coincided with the rise of modern feminism in the United States, and her relationship to those interested in defining, and perhaps changing, women's social roles has been an important issue for scholars seeking to interpret her life and work. She was not among those in the 1970s and 1980s who criticized men and their behavior and the traditional social roles which women had been forced to accept. Thus, she has been interpreted by some feminists as something less than a committed member of their ranks. Nonetheless, a fellow poet, ***Anne Sexton**, greeted her as "Muriel, mother of everyone," and novelist **Erica Jong** has called her the "mother of us all." **Louise Bernikow**, in a tribute to Rukeyser shortly before the poet's death, castigated earlier critics for playing down "the female-centeredness of her work."

Rukeyser's personality showed few signs of the tragic melancholy many readers associate with modern poetry. On the contrary, she expressed her optimism about personal and social transformation and was openly critical of poets like ***Sylvia Plath** and T.S. Eliot who seemed oppressed by their experiences. Her omnivorous hunger for experiencing as many aspects of the world around her as possible, ranging from aviation to various unpopular political causes, has led some students of her work to compare her to the 19th-century American poet Walt Whitman.

Despite her early success when she won the Yale Prize for Younger Poets in 1935, Rukeyser's reputation fell short of consistent, official acclaim during her lifetime. The optimism she displayed as well as the clear political message in much of her work put her out of step with her most honored contemporaries, and she was sometimes the target of bitter and personalized attacks. In 1953, for example, one scholarly student of Rukeyser's work, M.L. Rosenthal, wrote critically of the poet's lack of irony, her tendency to include areas of her personal life in her verse, and also of her "unaccountable optimism." Notes **Louise Kertesz**, "A woman Whitman, a woman whose work recalls the boldness and scope of Whitman's, was offensive to critics of the forties and fifties." More recently, critics like **Suzanne Gardiner** have accented the value in Rukeyser's approach, praising her role in "a poetic tradition that insists on including within its scope the workings of power and history." It is a tradition that "does not accept the given world as it is, injustices intact, but insists on transformation."

She saw poets as gifted leaders with a mission to encourage all human beings to realize their greatest human potential . . . and she prodded them—and herself—to do it.

—Alberta Turner

Rukeyser was born in New York City on December 15, 1913, the daughter of Lawrence Rukeyser, an engineer by training who was a partner in a construction firm, and **Myra Lyons Rukeyser**, who claimed to be the direct descendant of a famous Jewish sage of the 1st century, Rabbi Akiba. As the child of an affluent Jewish family in New York's Upper West Side, Rukeyser received a stellar education at such renowned institutions as the Ethical Culture Center and the Fieldston School. Even as a teenager, she expressed an interest in both writing and political concerns. As she recorded in a poem about her childhood, Rukeyser noted that she answered her father's query about her ambitions by stating she wanted to be someone like *Joan of Arc. Also in later years, she recalled how her parents hoped she would become "a bridge-playing, golf-playing woman," and a doctor's wife.

Rukeyser's early years were disrupted by both family and public difficulties. Like many young people in the 1920s, she became fascinated and troubled by the Sacco-Vanzetti murder trial in which two Italian immigrants were convicted by an apparently biased court in Massachusetts. Her father and especially her mother were disturbed by her rejection of their world of wealth and privilege. Then, in an ironic turn, the Rukeyser family's circumstances changed with a series of financial difficulties. This brought Muriel's schooling to an abrupt halt after she had spent two years at Vassar and Columbia, and she ended her formal education after her sophomore year. The family fortunes were eventually restored, but friction between the young woman and her parents apparently continued. Some sources indicate that Muriel and her sister were eventually disinherited by their father.

Rukeyser drifted into left-wing journalism and covered the trial of the "Scottsboro Boys" in 1933. Nine African-American youths, ranging in age from 13 to 21, were convicted of raping two white girls, **Victoria Price** and *Ruby Bates, and sentenced to be executed in Alabama. The trial led to Rukeyser's arrest by the local police for the crime of talking to black reporters and carrying in her suitcase a set of posters publicizing a conference for black students at Columbia. While in jail, she fell ill with typhoid. In 1936, she went on to work as an investigative reporter in West Virginia, studying the effects of lung disease on the local miners. As Rukeyser discovered in 1978 when she obtained a copy of her FBI file, such activities had put her and her family under government surveillance since the early 1930s.

Rukeyser had begun writing poetry as a high school student, and she had even managed to have some early poems published in a particularly prestigious outlet, *Harriet Monroe's *Poetry: A Magazine of Verse*. Despite her financial difficulties and work as a journalist, she continued to put her spare hours into writing poetry in the early 1930s. With the aid of poet Stephen Vincent Benet, she refined her most recent work and submitted it successfully to the Younger Poets competition held by Yale University Press. The resulting published volume began with poems about her childhood and adolescence; it then went on to consider the wonders of technology such as aviation that had now become commonplace. She herself had learned to fly in the early 1930s. *Theory of Flight* concluded with Rukeyser's concern for the trial of the "Scottsboro Boys."

The overall message of *Theory of Flight* was an optimistic assertion of human ability. Individuals could overcome their personal fear, whether it be of learning to fly or of protesting social injustice. Writes Kertesz: "The technological achievement of flight is here urged as a symbol

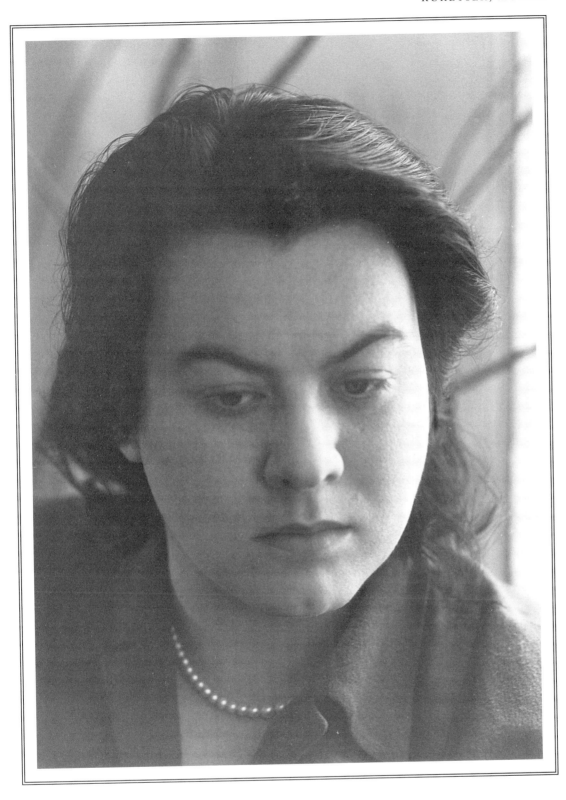

Muriel
Rukeyser

of what can be accomplished in human relationships, private and public." At the time some critics like **Eunice Clark** in *Common Sense* responded with notably enthusiastic praise to her expression of contemporary concerns. She declared that Rukeyser's poetry "is the kind that makes people act a little more valiantly when they have understood it" and cited her "deep positive humanity."

Some students of her work point out that Rukeyser's poetic technique was fully formed by the time *Theory of Flight* appeared in 1935, giving her an initial burst of public recognition. Here as in her later work, Rukeyser employed long sentences in a free-verse style. She addressed the reader directly, and she used space in a deliberately provocative fashion. For example, she placed extra spaces between lines and separated punctuation marks from the sentences they were designed to regulate. The influence of Walt Whitman was evident in the style she adopted although her call for revolution differed from Whitman's celebration of the American reality that existed at his time.

Traveling in Europe in 1936, Rukeyser went to Spain to cover a series of athletic contests sponsored by a workers' organization. It was intended to stand in contrast to the official Olympics being held at the time in Nazi Germany. She soon found herself in the midst of the Spanish Civil War, and she wished to remain in the country in order to aid the Loyalist side. But her lack of useful skills made it clear to Rukeyser that she had to be evacuated with other foreigners. She left behind a German lover, Otto Boch, who was later killed fighting for the Loyalists.

Upon her return to the United States, the young poet moved to California to help put out an anti-Fascist magazine, *Decision*, headed by Klaus Mann, son of the distinguished German novelist Thomas Mann. That same year Rukeyser published *U.S. 1*, in which she presents a documentary in poetic form on the suffering from silica poisoning of the miners in Gaule Bridge, West Virginia, whom she had visited in 1936.

An interesting view of Rukeyser's early work has been presented by Kenneth Rexroth. He denies any propagandistic element, noting that Rukeyser's first writing "was overtly social in its concerns, but it was far removed in style from the approved utterances of the Left." Nor did Rukeyser, in his view, share the political activist's desire to agitate and to call others to action. Her poems were instead expressions "of responsibility, of abiding moral concern."

For a time, Rukeyser's poetry continued to receive recognition in the form of prizes and grants. In 1941, she received a prize from the National Institute of Arts and Letters for "Soul and Body of John Brown," her latest poem. Two years later, she obtained additional support for her work through a Guggenheim foundation grant. But the latest trends in American poetry, centered on the New Criticism movement, turned away from political and social concerns and rejected the possibility of human progress. New Criticism called for a poetry of irony and ambiguity, far dif-

ferent from the work Rukeyser insisted on doing. Notes Kertesz, Rukeyser's writing "in the forties and fifties flaunted standards then in vogue" and her stubbornness in clinging to her own standards in poetry "left her wide open to the attacks of the literary establishment."

During World War II, Rukeyser not only held a government post, working in the poster division of the Office of War Information in 1943, but turned her poetic talents to wartime subjects. She spoke out against the anti-Semitism of the time, declaring: "To be a Jew in the twentieth century" was to be offered "the gift of torment." In the poem "Wake Island," she lauded the heroism of the American fighting man. At the close of the war, however, she became a vocal critic of the use of atomic bombs against the Japanese cities of Hiroshima and Nagasaki. The wartime years also saw her produce an significant work of prose, a pioneering biography of the important 19th-century scientist Willard Gibbs. Her style offended some specialists in the field. One reviewer declared that it "borders on the cryptic," and another castigated Rukeyser for her "fragmentary sentences and round-robin chapters." More positive comments praised her daring in undertaking such a challenging work and her effort to picture the scientific mind at work and its lessons for inquiring minds in other fields.

Like many literary figures who took part in the Office of War Information, Rukeyser left disillusioned when she became convinced that it was presenting the public with propaganda rather than real information. She then lived in California for a number of years, teaching for a time at the California Labor School. These years also brought her a brief marriage, which she had annulled in short order.

In her postwar years, a new element came into Rukeyser's life as well as into her poetry when she gave birth to a child in 1947. Her personal life had been complicated by a love affair with a married man. When she discovered she was pregnant, Rukeyser rejected the possibility of an abortion and chose to raise her son as a single mother. Students of her life have failed to unearth much about the circumstances of her pregnancy. Nonetheless, becoming pregnant and giving birth drew her poetry emphatically toward an examination of her female identity. Her "Nine Poems for the Unborn Child" traced the experience of moving through pregnancy to the point when she could directly address her newborn child.

Rukeyser raised her son, returning to New York to continue her part-time work as a college teacher at Sarah Lawrence. Her duties as a parent somewhat limited her literary output in the 1950s, but when she returned to active publishing—with *Body of Wakening* in 1958—her experiences in giving birth continued as a major part of her literary vocabulary. The year before she had again turned to a biography, *One Life*, the story of Wendell Willkie. Written in an imaginative, poem-like fashion, *One Life* features a fictional German child whose experiences are used to highlight the very different ones Willkie faced.

Sometime in the mid-1960s, Rukeyser suffered a stroke, and, by the close of the decade, the poet was in failing health. She gave up her teaching position at Sarah Lawrence in 1967. Her physical difficulties—she was at times partially paralyzed and suffered a speech impediment—became a topic she explored in her poetry. Despite her illness, Rukeyser became active in the anti-Vietnam War movement. In 1972, she went to Washington to protest against the Asian conflict. Placing herself on the floor of the U.S. Senate led to her arrest and a short stint in jail. Her son William (sometimes known as Laurie) likewise protested the war, going to Canada rather than accept a call from his draft board.

The United States was only one location in which Rukeyser made political statements in the form of flamboyant actions. In 1975, she was elected the leader of PEN, the international organization of authors, and, in that capacity, she went to South Korea to protest the imprisonment of poet Kim Chi-Ha. Kim had been condemned to death for his political poetry, and it is possible that Rukeyser's protest—she stood a vigil in front of the Westgate Prison near Seoul where he was confined—helped to save his life. Moreover, many of her poems continued to move along political lines with open praise for young activists. In her last collection, *The Gates*, published in 1976, she directly complimented those who protested the Vietnam War in Washington demonstrations, and she went on to describe her experiences in South Korea. But this collection contained as well an eloquent description of her recovery from her stroke.

Despite her illnesses, Rukeyser was as productive in her final decade as in her early years. She presented the public with three volumes of poetry—*The Speed of Darkness* (1968), *Breaking Open* (1973), and *The Gates* (1976)—as well as her novel *The Traces of Thomas Hariot* (1971). Terris has written that the first two of these works are notable for Rukeyser's love poems and the exploration of her own emotions they present. Nonetheless, some reviewers continued to emphasize and to castigate the political element in her work. Thomas Stumpf in *Carolina Quarterly* criticized *Breaking Open*, with its references to the war in Vietnam and racial oppression in the United States, as poetry that "like rolled oats, is unappetizing but good for you.... Poetry that is fatally in love with exhortations."

In 1977, Rukeyser was honored by the American Academy of Arts and Letters with the Copernicus Award for "her lifetime achievement as a poet and her contribution to poetry as a culture force." The citation also lauded her commitment to "ideas of freedom" and her actions, including her poetry, in defense of such freedom.

Muriel Rukeyser died in New York City on February 12, 1980. Her complete collected works had appeared in print the year before. Nevertheless, for many students of her work she remains an unjustly neglected writer. Writes *Adrienne Rich: "How do we reach her? Most of her work is out of print.... Included in a major current anthology, her poems are preceded by patronizing and ignorant commentary." In an earlier evaluation of Rukeyser's writing, Terris took a more optimistic position. She expected an eventual revival of interest in Rukeyser. Precisely because "so many explorations [into Rukeyser's writing] remain to be undertaken," she wrote, "is the surest way I know to say Rukeyser is a *significant* poet of our century, one whose place is assured."

SOURCES:

Bernikow, Louise. "Muriel at 65: Still Ahead of Her Time," in *Ms.* January 1979, pp. 14–18.

Davidson, Cathy N., and Linda Wagner-Martin, eds. *The Oxford Companion to Women's Writing in the United States*. NY: Oxford University Press, 1995.

Gardiner, Suzanne. "'A World That Will Hold All the People': On Muriel Rukeyser," in *The Kenyon Review*. Vol. 14. Summer 1992, pp. 88–105.

Gilbert, Sandra M., and Susan Gubar, eds. *The Norton Anthology of Literature by Women: The Tradition in English*. NY: W.W. Norton, 1985.

Gould, Jean. *Modern American Women Poets*. NY: Dodd, Mead, 1984.

Kertesz, Louise. *The Poetic Vision of Muriel Rukeyser*. Baton Rouge, LA: Louisiana State University, 1980.

Myers, Jack, and David Wojahn, eds. *A Profile of Twentieth-Century American Poetry*. Carbondale, IL: Southern Illinois University Press, 1991.

Quartermain, Peter, ed. *American Poets, 1880–1945*. 2nd Series. Detroit, MI: Gale Research, 1986.

Rexroth, Kenneth. *American Poetry in the Twentieth Century*. NY: Herder and Herder, 1971.

Rich, Adrienne. "Beginners," in *The Kenyon Review*. Vol. 15. Summer 1993, pp. 12–19.

Terris, Virginia A. "Muriel Rukeyser: A Retrospective," in *American Poetry Review*. Vol. 3. May–June, 1974, pp. 10–15.

Neil M. Heyman,
Professor of History, San Diego State University,
San Diego, California

Rumania, queen of.

See Elizabeth of Wied (1843–1916).
See Marie of Rumania (1875–1938).

Rumford, countess of.

See Lavoisier, Marie (1758–1836).

Rumsey, Mary Harriman

(1881–1934)

American social welfare leader. Name variations: *Mary Harriman. Born Mary Harriman on November 17, 1881, in New York City; died on December 18, 1934, in Washington, D.C.; daughter of Edward Henry Harriman (a financier and railroad magnate) and Mary Williamson (Averell) Harriman; sister of W. Averell Harriman (ambassador to the Soviet Union and governor of New York); educated at the Brearley School in New York; graduated from Barnard College, 1905; married Charles Cary Rumsey (a sculptor), on May 26, 1910 (died 1922); children: Charles Cary, Jr. (b. 1911); Mary Averell Harriman (b. 1913); Bronson Harriman (b. 1917).*

Born on November 17, 1881, in New York City, Mary Harriman Rumsey was the first of Edward Henry Harriman and **Mary Williamson Averell Harriman**'s six children. Her father was a financier and young Mary grew up in comfortable wealth, which greatly increased at the turn of the 20th century when her father gained control of the Union Pacific and Southern Pacific railroad systems. The family, in addition to being wealthy, was close, and Rumsey's parents were keenly interested in the education and training in the Episcopal faith of all their children.

Rumsey spent most of her childhood in New York City, with frequent vacations to the family's various estates and ranches across the nation. Her entire family enjoyed the outdoors and even joined a scientific expedition to Alaska organized by Edward Harriman in 1899. Rumsey was especially close to her father, and discussed his railroad expansion plans with him; after he took control of Union Pacific, he took Mary and her sister **Cornelia Harriman** on an inspection tour of the Union Pacific railway system.

Despite her wealthy upbringing, Rumsey was keenly aware that others were not so fortunate. In 1901, she founded the Junior League for the Promotion of Settlement Movements. It was later renamed the Junior League of New York, and from this organization developed the Junior League movement which remains active in cities across the country to this day. The purpose of the Junior League was to encourage wealthy, influential girls and women to devote more time, energy, and resources to the community. Her parents encouraged her in this endeavor, and likewise promoted her entrance into Barnard College, which awakened her interest in sociology and the burgeoning new "science" of eugenics, which was then still quite respectable. Six years after her graduation in 1905, she became a lifelong trustee of the school.

Edward Harriman died in 1909, after which Rumsey became involved in managing Arden, the family estate and dairy farm in New York. She also advised her mother on charitable activities, although the exuberant daughter often conflicted with her more formal mother. Mary married Charles Cary Rumsey, a sculptor hired to decorate Arden House, on May 26, 1910. They settled at Sands Point, Long Island, where their home life combined their interests in horses, polo and art. They also owned a farm near Middleburg, Virginia, where Rumsey applied her longstanding interest in eugenics to cattle breeding, and her interest in community service to creating the Eastern Livestock Cooperative Marketing Association. During World War I, Rumsey became involved in the Community Councils that were organized as part of a plan for national defense.

After her husband died in an automobile accident in 1922, Rumsey devoted more time to social causes. She was named a trustee of the United Hospital Fund of New York in 1925, and played a leading role in the Women's Auxiliary of that institution. Going against her family's Republican tradition, she, with her brother Averell Harriman, supported the presidential candidacy of New York Governor Al Smith in 1928, and after the stock-market crash of 1929, helped neighborhoods deal with the financial aftermath.

Rumsey's enduring friendship with *Eleanor Roosevelt and her support of New Deal policies led President Franklin D. Roosevelt to appoint her chair of the Consumers' Advisory Board of the National Recovery Administration (NRA) in 1933. Although the board was unpopular with business and labor interests (as was the entire NRA, which was soon declared unconstitutional), Rumsey kept its agenda on track in the fight against price mark-ups and price discrimination against cooperatives. She played an integral role in protecting consumers' interests during the NRA's establishment of its industrial fair practices code. She also worked to create county consumer-protection councils that would support the efforts of the board. During this time, she shared a house in Washington with Secretary of

Labor *Frances Perkins, who was a close personal friend.

During a fox hunt on her Virginia farm in November 1934, Rumsey suffered several broken bones in a fall from her horse. Pneumonia set in as she recovered from the fall, and she died just a month later, on December 18, in Washington Emergency Hospital. After her funeral at St. Thomas' Episcopal Church in Washington, D.C., she was buried next to her parents in the village graveyard in Arden.

SOURCES:

James, Edward T., ed. *Notable American Women: 1607–1950.* Cambridge, MA: The Belknap Press of Harvard University, 1971.

McHenry, Robert, ed. *Famous American Women.* NY: Dover, 1980.

Kelly Winters,
freelance writer, Bayville, New York

Runcie, Constance Faunt Le Roy

(1836–1911)

American composer and pianist whose music was enormously popular in the 19th century. Born Constance Faunt Le Roy in Indianapolis, Indiana, on January 15, 1836; died in St. Joseph, Missouri, on May 17, 1911; daughter of Robert Henry Faunt Le Roy (an astronomer) and Jane Dale (Owen) Faunt Le Roy; married James Runcie (an Episcopal cleric); children: two sons and two daughters.

Both of Constance Runcie's parents were amateur musicians: her father was an astronomer who also composed and her mother, who was a daughter of the British social reformer Robert Owen, played the piano and harp. Constance was born in Indianapolis in 1836 and spent her childhood in New Harmony, Indiana. In 1852, she began a five-year training period in piano and composition in Stuttgart, Germany. When she returned with her family, they settled again in New Harmony. There she met and married James Runcie in 1861, and founded the first organized women's club in the United States with a constitution and by-laws. She also began to compose songs, a symphony, and chamber music. Runcie may have been the first American woman to compose a symphony, but unfortunately it was never published and the manuscript remains lost. Her songs and chamber music, which have also vanished, were very likely the first such works by an American woman. Although her music was enormously popular in its day, it was seldom played after her death. Runcie's autobiography, *Divinely Led*, was published in New York in 1895.

SOURCES:

Mathews, William S.B. *A Hundred Years of Music in America.* NY: AMS, 1971.

Willard, Frances, and Mary A. Livermore. *A Woman of the Century.* Buffalo: 1893.

John Haag,
Athens, Georgia

Rundle, Elizabeth (1828–1896).

See Charles, Elizabeth.

Rupilia Faustina (fl. 90 CE)

*Roman noblewoman. Flourished around 90 CE; married M. Annius Verus; children: *Faustina I (c. 90–141 CE); M. Annius Verus; M. Annius Libo.*

Russell, Ada Dwyer.

See Lowell, Amy for sidebar.

Russell, Alys Smith (1866–1951).

See Berenson, Mary for sidebar.

Russell, Anna (1911—)

English-born Canadian contralto and comedian. Name variations: Claudia Anna Russell-Brown. Born in 1911 in London; daughter of Claude Russell-Brown and Beatrice Russell-Brown; twice married and divorced; no children.

Anna Russell turned a failing opera career into international fame as a musical satirist. Born in London in 1911 into a prosperous family, Russell early showed signs of musical talent and received a thorough education in classical music in schools in Suffolk, Brussels, and Paris. She then spent five years studying cello, composition, and piano in addition to voice at the Royal College of Music in London. She was often in trouble at school for failing to take her studies seriously and for the comical songs she would write and perform for other students. She then started as a contralto on the concert circuit in Britain, with only moderate success. She was convinced, as she wrote in her memoir, that she had a "tin voice" not suited for the rigors of opera singing. Nevertheless she went on to perform in a Canadian troop show during World War II.

It was as a performer in the Toronto Symphony Orchestra in 1935 that Russell first rendered humorous material professionally, at the conductor's suggestion. Audience response was so positive that she gradually switched from traditional performances to her own comic compositions. She debuted in a recital at New York's Town Hall to great success. Her career took off and she was soon performing her own material in concerts, often solo, across Canada, Europe, the United States, and Japan. By the mid-1950s, Russell was giving over 200 performances a year, including numerous television appearances.

In the late 1950s, Russell joined the New York City Center Opera Company as the Witch in *Hansel and Gretel*, and reprised the role in the movie version of the opera and on stage with the San Francisco Cosmopolitan Opera Company. She also starred in a musical version of *The Importance of Being Earnest* in 1957; in that year as well, Russell became a naturalized citizen of the United States, where she was living while not on tour abroad. Her compositions satirized the excesses of classical music and operatic styles, but also poked fun at the Broadway musical and folk music genres. Her most famous routines were her analysis of Wagner's "Ring of the Nibelung" cycle and "How To Write Your Own Gilbert and Sullivan Opera." These and other routines were recorded on three albums by Columbia, released in 1953 and 1972. She also released a satirical book, *The Power of Being a Positive Stinker*, in 1955.

Annie Russell

Her career was at its height between the late 1950s and the mid-1960s, but she was still in demand in the mid-1970s. Russell then lived and worked in Australia for about nine years, returning to the United States in 1983. In 1985, at age 74, she gave a televised farewell performance in Baltimore, also released as an album. Her autobiography was published in the same year. Russell then retired to Unionville, Ontario.

SOURCES:

Russell, Anna. *I'm Not Making This Up, You Know*. NY: Continuum, 1985.

RELATED MEDIA:

The First Farewell Concert (85 min. video), Video Artists International (recorded live at the Baltimore Museum of Art, the program includes her analysis of Wagner's Ring Cycle, a Gilbert and Sullivan operetta, and her folk tune "Jolly Old Sigmund Freud").

Laura York, M.A. in History, University of California, Riverside, California

Russell, Annie (1864–1936)

American actress. Born on January 12, 1864, in Liverpool, England; died of myocarditis on January 16, 1936, in Winter Park, Florida; daughter of Joseph Russell (a civil engineer) and Jane (Mount) Russell; married Eugene Wiley Presbrey (a stage manager), on November 2, 1884 (divorced 1897); married Oswald Yorke (an English actor), on March 27, 1904 (died 1931).

Born in Liverpool, England, in 1864, Annie Russell was five years old when she immigrated with her family to Canada, where her father Joseph Russell soon died. Russell went on the stage at age eight to help support her mother **Jane Mount Russell** and two younger siblings, making her first professional appearance in a production of *Miss Moulton* at the Montreal Academy of Music in 1872. Six years later, she joined a Gilbert and Sullivan company and made her first New York appearance in *H.M.S. Pinafore* at the Lyceum Theater in May 1879. The following year, she toured South America and the West Indies with a repertory company, playing a variety of roles from young boys to elderly women. She then returned to New York, and the Madison Square Theater, where she made herself look older with the help of an elaborate hairdo and a long dress in order to win the title role in the stage version of *Frances Hodgson Burnett*'s *Esmeralda*, which ran for 350 performances and then toured for a year. The wholesome role made her a star, and she toured for two years in the equally wholesome *Hazel Kirke*, before joining A.M. Palmer's company in Madison Square. She married Eugene Wiley Presbrey, a stage manager for the A.M. Palmer Company, on November 2, 1884.

Russell appeared in several plays throughout the 1880s, including *Broken Hearts* (1885), *Engaged* (1886), *Elaine* (1887), and *Captain Swift* (1888), but problems with her abusive husband aggravated her poor health. Friends raised $3,000 in a benefit performance for her, and she used the money to flee her husband (they would be divorced in 1897). She then spent two years in Italy, recovering.

Russell returned to the New York stage in 1894, in *The New Woman*. The following year, she became the leading woman in Nat Goodwin's company, and in 1896 appeared in *Sue*, by Bret Harte and T.E. Pemberton. *Sue* moved to London in 1898, where it was a hit. In the next several years, Russell appeared in *A Royal Family*, *Miss Hobbs*, *Catherine*, *The Girl and the Judge*, and *The Younger Mrs. Parling*, all wholesome roles she later dismissed as "Anniegenues." On March 27, 1904, she married English actor Oswald Yorke, and in London in November 1905, she starred in the premier production of George Bernard Shaw's *Major Barbara*, which the playwright directed. She returned to New York in 1906, where for one season she gave an unusual and highly regarded performance as Puck in *A Midsummer Night's Dream*.

Russell believed that theater should promote education and morality, and would not appear in plays she considered low or profane; because of this, she never performed in some of the greatest plays of her time. (She particularly disliked Ibsen's work.) Although she was one of the most highly paid female actors—earning $500 a week—Russell complained, perhaps accurately, that audiences wanted only to be amused, not to watch "splendid plays" or to be morally uplifted. She believed that if high-minded women supported the theater, the dignity of the American stage could be protected.

By 1912, Russell had saved enough money and found enough supporters to form the Annie Russell Old English Comedy Company, which during the sole year of its existence produced well-received revivals of *She Stoops to Conquer*, *Much Ado About Nothing*, and *The Rivals*. During World War I, she worked with the Salvation Army and the Red Cross, and assisted French war orphans, all to the detriment of her health. In 1918, after a tiring two years touring in *The Thirteenth Chair*, she retired from performance. Some years later, her longtime friend *Mary Louise Curtis Zimbalist donated funds to build a theater in her honor at Rollins College in Winter Park, Florida. Russell, who became a professor of theater arts at the college, came out

of retirement to perform in Browning's *In a Balcony* at the inauguration of the Annie Russell Theater in 1932, and also performed there the following year in *The Thirteenth Chair*. She continued teaching at Rollins until her death on January 16, 1936.

SOURCES:

James, Edward T., ed. *Notable American Women, 1607–1950*. Cambridge, MA: The Belknap Press of Harvard University, 1971.

McHenry, Robert, ed. *Famous American Women*. NY: Dover, 1980.

Kelly Winters,
freelance writer, Bayville, New York

Russell, Annie (1868–1947).

See Maunder, Annie Russell.

Russell, Mrs. Bertrand.

See Berenson, Mary for sidebar on Russell, Alys Smith (1866–1951).

See Russell, Dora (1884–1986).

Russell, Dora (1894–1986)

English feminist, educator, writer and peace activist whose accomplishments have often overshadowed by the fact of her marriage to Bertrand Russell. Name variations: Dora Black; Countess Russell; Mrs. Bertrand Russell. Born Dora Winifred Black in London, England, on April 3, 1894; died in Porthcurno, Cornwall, England, on May 31, 1986; daughter of Frederick William Black (later Sir Frederick Black, a civil servant) and Sarah Isabella Davisson; won a graduate fellowship from Girton College, Cambridge, 1918; studied French Enlightenment in London and Paris; married Bertrand Arthur William Russell, later 3rd earl Russell, on September 27, 1921 (divorced 1935); married Patrick Grace, in 1940 (died 1948); children: (first marriage) John (b. 1921) and Kate (b. 1923); (with Griffin Barry) Harriet (b. 1930) and Roderick (1932–1983).

Won a scholarship to Cambridge University (1912); traveled with father to U.S. (1917) and was awarded the MBE for her contribution to the war effort; traveled alone to Russia at height of the post-revolutionary civil war and accompanied Bertrand Russell to China (1920); published three important books, Hypatia, The Right to be Happy *and* In Defense of Children *(1925–32); founded and ran a primary school based on advanced educational concepts (1927–43); worked for women's rights, nuclear disarmament and international understanding as an active member of the Six Points Group, the Married Women's Association, the Women's International Democratic Federation and other groups; organized and led the Women's Caravan of Peace (1958); published* The Religion of the Machine Age, *a summation of her views on industrialization, first drafted in the 1920s (1983); completed the third volume of her autobiography,* The Tamarisk Tree, *at age 91 (1985).*

Selected writings: Hypatia or Woman and Knowledge *(NY: E.P. Dutton, 1925);* The Tamarisk Tree: My Quest For Liberty and Love *(London: Virago, 1977);* The Tamarisk Tree 2: My School and the Years of the War *(London: Virago, 1980);* The Dora Russell Reader: 57 Years of Writing and Journalism, 1925–1982 *(foreword by Dale Spender, London: Pandora Press, 1983);* The Tamarisk Tree 3: Challenge to the Cold War *(London: Virago, 1985).*

Dora Black Russell, the former Countess Russell, was 64 when she loaded ten like-minded souls into her weathered, old bus on May 26, 1958, and set out from London on the three-month odyssey which she had named the Women's Caravan of Peace. With tents, cooking facilities, food and little money, Russell's fiery zeal and her unquenchable spirit of adventure propelled the group through Western and Eastern Europe and the Soviet Union, spreading the message of international peace and disarmament. During the entire journey, she later wrote in her autobiography, "there had not been one day when we were not speaking, meeting people or travelling; we were never more than three nights in one place, at times driving all night to keep appointments."

Dora Black was born into a middle-class English family in 1894 and grew up during a turbulent period which saw "women's emancipation, changing sex relations, the expansion of industrialism, revolution and the rising of the working class." In all these developments, Russell later recorded, "my personal life and thought were involved." One of four children, she had a happy childhood, and she describes her parents as devoted and faithful, although she remembers her mother's embarrassment when she felt she might have been overspending her housekeeping budget and had to account to her father. In that unequal power relationship were, perhaps, the roots of Dora's later espousal of feminism. Fortunately, Frederick Black believed that his daughters should be as well educated as his son.

By age 16, Dora had passed most of the examinations necessary for admission to university. Hoping to obtain a scholarship in modern languages at Girton College, Cambridge, she was sent to Germany for a year to study the language intensively. Russell was clearly an able student; she recalled that after her time away, "I could speak German well enough to be taken for a native, and I spoke English for a time with a German accent." Upon her return, Dora's father tutored her in Latin and Greek, essential for university admission at that time, and she found herself inspired by the Greek tale of Medea, the woman driven mad enough to kill her own children by the contempt and ingratitude of her lover. This drama about an ancient "sex war" was to provide inspiration for Russell's first book, *Hypatia*, written some 13 years later. It was also to lure her towards the theater; she was sure that she wanted to write for the stage and longed to become an actress.

Russell won her scholarship easily and in 1912 began her studies in modern history and literature as well as languages at Cambridge. One of the first university colleges for women, Girton College was "like a large girls' boarding school." Separation of the sexes was enforced with almost military rigor; chaperons had to accompany the young ladies whenever they met with young men. "Looking back," Russell wrote in her autobiography, "I have wondered how women ever managed to free themselves from their corsets, frills and furbelows and the iron straightjacket imposed on them by religion, morality and social sanctions."

The first volume of Russell's three-volume autobiography, collectively titled *The Tamarisk Tree*, is subtitled "My Quest for Liberty and Love." That quest was to begin with two discoveries she made at Cambridge: the Heretics Society and Bertrand Russell. While some of the young women at Girton became extremely religious and spent their free time on retreats and in the chapel, Dora and a few other independent-minded women obtained permission to leave the college and went off to the Heretics, a society which called upon its members "to reject authority in matters of religion and belief, and to accept only conviction by reasonable argument." The chief organizer of the society was C.K. Ogden, a multitalented and mercurial eccentric who was to become a close friend and to have a significant influence in Dora's life.

Bertrand Russell, one of the greatest intellects of the 20th century, was in his mid-40s and already a well-known philosopher and mathematician in 1916 when Dora was invited to join her friend, mathematician ***Dorothy Wrinch**, on a walking tour with Bertrand and another mathematician. Now 22, Dora had obtained a first-class degree and was studying French literature in London while pondering her future. She admired Bertrand's outspoken condemnation of the

Dora
Russell

war and was appalled to find that the group was not allowed to walk near the coast since the authorities feared that he might signal to the enemy.

In 1917, Dora accompanied her father on a voyage to the United States. Frederick Black had been instructed by the Admiralty to obtain American oil for the British war effort, and, given the danger of submarine attack, he could not ask his regular staff to assist him. For her contribution to the war effort, Dora was subsequently awarded the MBE. On her return to

London, she was among the spectators who attended the court session at which Bertrand was sentenced to six months' imprisonment for his antiwar writings. Dora also learned that Girton had awarded her a three-year research fellowship. The fellowship came with a room at the college and an income of £3 per week, enough to establish her long-sought financial independence. To augment her cherished "sense of liberty," she also purchased a season train ticket to London, so that she could travel there to continue her research and visit her friends whenever she wished.

On her return to Cambridge, Russell wrote for Ogden's *Cambridge Magazine*, became secretary of the Heretics Society, and delivered her own paper on 18th-century Christianity to the group. Looking back in old age, she marveled at her "scholarship of those days." She delighted in the intellectual atmosphere and seemed to have found her life's vocation as a university teacher, although still not without casting longing glances towards the world of the theater. But Russell's plans for her future were soon to be completely transformed.

Knowing that she traveled frequently between Cambridge and London, in June 1919 Wrinch asked Dora to bring a small folding table from the university which Bertrand needed for his London flat. To thank her, he invited her to tea, and, in what was probably her first conversation alone with him, she expressed her strong disapproval of conventional marriage, her belief in free love, and her conviction that children were entirely the concern of their mother. "Well, whoever I have children with it won't be you," remarked Bertrand. "I felt tempted to answer, 'Nobody asked you, Sir,'" said Dora, "but refrained." Bertrand was still married to his first wife, ◀❖ **Alys Smith Russell**, although the two had been separated for some years.

After this inauspicious beginning, Dora was somewhat surprised to receive Bertrand's invitation to join him and a group of friends on a reading holiday the following month. Making it clear that he had more than a holiday in mind, Bertrand asked if she would marry him if he obtained a divorce. Dora assured him that she had no wish to marry him or anyone else; indeed, she had convinced Girton College that some time in France was essential for the furtherance of her research, and she was planning to leave England at the end of the summer.

The idyllic holiday convinced Dora that her approach to life and her values were in tune with those of Bertrand and also made it evident "that

❖▶
Russell, Alys Smith. *See Berenson, Mary for sidebar.*

he did not know how to look after himself and . . . needed some woman sturdy enough to take care of him." Bertrand's reassurance that he would not expect her, as his wife, to "grace the head of his table" was her first inkling that he might, one day, succeed his childless brother Frank to an earldom. But while titles meant nothing to Dora, she was, despite herself, falling in love and, in an era where most women still had to make the painful choice between marriage and a career, her vision of independence was fading. In her autobiography, Russell graphically described her dilemma:

> I doubt if he ever realized just what he was asking of the person I then was. He was twenty years ahead of me in age and achievement. . . . I was a young woman of deeply-cherished modern views, just arrived at independence and now desirous of spreading her wings; afraid of the entanglements, suspicious of the wiles of men who were forever scheming to drag women back into the legal, domestic and sexual bondage from which feminist pioneers were attempting to escape and deliver their sisters.

She knew that Bertrand had only just ended one affair and there were rumors that he had had another but "knowing what I might be capable of feeling for him, I could never love lightly. Thus I might become absorbed, swallowed up entirely in his life and never able to become what I aspired to in my own person." She left for Paris in October 1919, but her letters to Ogden, the only person in whom she confided, clearly indicate that the struggle with herself was far from over: "I AM young, and the kind of slavery he wants me to accept is what he, at my age, would have emphatically denounced. . . . I do want to try and do what is best for his work and him without destroying myself."

Bertrand joined Dora in Paris in the spring of 1920, and the two traveled together to Spain for a holiday. Knowing that he wanted a child, she made no attempt to prevent conception, yet she was still unwilling to relinquish either her university fellowship or her dreams of an acting career. In a letter to Ogden, she confessed: "I am afraid of the consequences if I cut myself free of him, both to him and to me, and yet he won't take less than everything from me." Independent woman that she was, and fervently wished to continue to be, Russell loved children and felt that, if she had a child, she could "bear country life and a domestic tyrant."

However, it was not tranquil country life which lay in Dora's immediate future; Bertrand invited her to accompany him to Russia. The Russian Revolution had broken out in 1917, and the country was still in turmoil, with the White and Red armies engaged in a bitter Civil War. At the last moment Bertrand was offered a place with a visiting delegation of Labour politicians; Dora, sympathetic to the Bolsheviks and now eager to see the revolution for herself, decided to go alone. She undertook a difficult and tortuous journey to get into the country. Living conditions, even for foreigners, were harsh, and she was frequently in some danger during her visit, but she relished the experience. Her time in Russia culminated in hearing Lenin speak at the Third International Congress in Moscow on the day before her departure; she left reluctantly and only because of Bertrand's urgent summons. Returning to England on August 4, 1920, she learned that Bertrand had been invited to China, was leaving almost immediately, and wanted her to go with him.

Russia had made a deep and lasting impact upon Dora: "I had had the good fortune to be one person, uncommitted, not bound to any political allegiance, who had been able to get into Russia at this moment in history." She had seen "a vision of the making of a future civilization" and she saw herself, "with my unpolitical fresh eyes and the background of my studies," as "the only person in England who could interpret the true essence of what was happening in the Soviet Union." She therefore saw it as her mission to "contribute something to the making of peace between East and West."

Dora's main contribution to spreading the word about Russia emerged as a chapter in Bertrand's own book, written while they were in Paris that August, on the way to China. The two were treated as celebrities by the Chinese; Bertrand had been invited to teach, but Dora was also given the opportunity to speak to large, appreciative audiences and to write. She wrote to Ogden that they lived in "disgraceful luxury"; the ready availability of servants made it possible for the couple to work and to explore one another's personalities. Looking back, Dora described the time in China as "the happiest months of my whole life."

In March 1921, while they were still in China, Bertrand became seriously ill with pneumonia, and Dora nursed him back from the brink of death. By then, she was fully aware of the depth of her affection: "I loved Bertie with adoration and almost worship. He was lover, father-figure, teacher, a companion never at a loss for a witty rejoinder." She also became aware, once the crisis was over, that she was pregnant. As Bertie was still weak, they decided to return to England, where the news that Bertrand's divorce was now final reached them. He pressed Dora to marry him. She insisted that she would live with him and have his children without the despised legal sanction, but was finally persuaded that she could be denying her unborn child the possibility of an earldom if she resisted. The marriage took place that summer, and John, their first child, was born on November 16, 1921.

The family spent the next six years in London, a time "packed so full of social and political life that I now wonder how we had time and energy for it all," she said. Bertrand had decided to support his family by writing, and Dora started work on a book to be called *The Religion of the Machine Age*. She was bitterly disappointed to find that neither her husband nor Ogden, now an influential book editor, understood its basic thesis on the evils of mechanization in modern society. Daunted, she put the book aside, and it was not to be published for more than 60 years. In 1922, the pair were back at Cambridge, reading papers for the Heretics Society; the following year, Dora worked with Bertrand on their shared book, *The Prospects of Industrial Civilization*. By this time, she had become deeply involved in the fight to give women access to reliable birth control.

> Though at no time a professional politician, I have never been able to escape its clutches. . . . Many times I have tried to get myself free . . . to pursue other less demanding and harrowing occupations, but there was always some human problem, need, injustice, from which in conscience, one could not turn aside.
>
> —Dora Russell

The repressive attitude towards birth control which existed in England during the 1920s was clearly demonstrated in the fight to distribute a pamphlet by *Marie Stopes. In 1923, Stopes, having established Britain's first birth-control clinic and written the pioneering work *Married Love*, prepared a cheap and simple pamphlet on contraception, containing essential explanatory diagrams. When the pamphlets were seized by the police and condemned as obscene, Dora led the court appeal against the police action. She did not win the case, nor had she expected to, but the following year, with a Labour government in power, the pamphlet was published once again. This time, however, it appeared without the controversial diagrams. While Dora found her political home within the Labour Party for most of her life, it sometimes failed to act as boldly in the defense of principle as she would have wished.

Russell campaigned actively for the Labour Party in the December 1923 election, with her second child, **Kate**, delaying her arrival obligingly until December 29. In the summer of 1924, Dora ran for Parliament as a Labour Party candidate. "I knew," she wrote, "that there was no chance of winning, but I could carry on my crusade for social justice and the rights of women." She helped establish the Workers' Birth Control Group to function within the Labour Party for reform of the law regarding contraception: Dora had come to realize that women would never be "truly free and equal with men until we had liberated mothers."

Having abandoned, for the time being, her work on industrialism, partly because her arguments had not been understood but also because she feared that her ideas would be attributed to her husband, Dora had turned once again, in the hectic year before Kate's birth, "to my old and chief ambition, the theater, in which no question of rivalry between us could arise." During the winter of 1922–23, she worked as an understudy in various London theaters. Learning she was pregnant at the end of the theater season, in the spring of 1923, Dora regretfully realized that she was facing the end of her theatrical ambitions. Ogden had been trying to persuade Dora to sign a book contract and stop dissipating her energies, and she now began to consider the offer seriously; "all my life," she later wrote, "I have tried to do too many different things. I wonder if this is not a perpetual dilemma for women."

Russell took up the cause of women in general and mothers in particular in her first book, *Hypatia or Woman and Knowledge*, published in 1925 and dedicated to her daughter. Its bold, combative tone is immediately established in the book's preface:

> *Hypatia* was a University lecturer denounced by Church dignitaries and torn to pieces by Christians. Such will be the fate of this book: therefore it bears her name. What I have written here I will not change for similar episcopal denunciations.

In part a history of feminism and wholly a polemic, *Hypatia* proclaims that the "sex war" for women's equality still rages and that women must be made equal members of society, unhampered by marriage or maternity. Marriage, the author asserts, is:

> a barrier for most of us to free public activity; a life-long contract only to be broken in disgrace and public disgust; aunts, uncles, social duties that exasperate and are totally unnecessary; the common view that henceforth husband and wife are one and indivisible, and the wife for ever to be burdened with her husband's duties and affairs.

For mothers, overcoming the stigma associated with sex and access to birth control was essential; sex, she argued, was as much an instinctive need for women as it was for men and "the prevention of conception brings them no loss of poise, health or happiness." Working women in particular must be able to control their fertility: "We want better reasons for having children than not knowing how to prevent them." Nor should women with children be shut out of public life; once her children are in suitable schools, she should be free to do the work for which she is best fitted. "In this way her opinion would count, and her attitude to life help to permeate the community, which is otherwise left to be guided by the outlook of the single woman and the male."

More broadly, *Hypatia* was a plea for toleration and equality; "Grant each man and woman the right to seek his or her own solution without fear of public censure. . . . The wrong lies in rules that are barriers between human beings who would otherwise reach a fuller and more intense understanding of one another." The book's appeal was so strong and so universal that a representative of the Spanish periodical *El Sol* went to England in 1926 to meet the author and offer her a contract to write a regular column for the newspaper. Russell wrote the column for five years, examining such topics as morality, rationalism, education, marriage and motherhood from a feminist perspective.

Hypatia ended with a call for reform of men's education which trained them to accept a dualist philosophy, elevating the mind and diminishing or despising the importance of the body. "If we are to make peace between man and woman . . . it is essential that men should make a more determined attempt to understand what feminists are seeking." It was to education that Dora now turned her attention. In 1927, she published *The Right to be Happy*, her book on the proper nurturing of the human spirit, and in the autumn of that year she put her ideas into practice with the opening of Beacon Hill School. With their older child now five, it seemed to Dora and Bertie that their ideas about child-rearing might be of benefit to others, and they established the school for children up to the age of 12 in a house they had purchased from Bertie's brother.

For the next 15 years, Dora's main task was the running of the school. She put into practice ideas which were then considered radical, developing an environment where there was no competitiveness, no physical punishment, where the children were included in the decision-making process and where Western ideas about conventional religion, the duality of mind and body, and the value of industrialism were steadfastly avoided. For the first four years, Bertrand advised and supported her, but, from the beginning, the bulk of the responsibility was hers. Even so, Dora continued to pursue a variety of other interests. In 1928, she gave a series of lectures in the United States based on her recent book and it was there that she met Griffin Barry, a freelance journalist with Communist sympathies. They began an affair and, with Bertrand's approval, visited Russia together in 1929. Later that year, Dora found herself pregnant with Barry's child.

Having assured one another that theirs was not a conventional marriage and that it had been undertaken only to legitimize their children, Dora and Bertrand had both had affairs after their marriage. Bertrand knew that she wanted more children and dissuaded her from any consideration of abortion once he learned the news. "You won't find me tiresome about it," he assured her. However, by the time Dora and the new baby joined Bertrand at their summer house in Cornwall in July, he told her that he had fallen in love with **Margery Spence (Russell)**, the woman who was later to become his third wife.

In 1931, Dora became a countess when Bertrand inherited the earldom on his brother's death. The following year, when she was away giving birth to her second child by Griffin Barry, Bertrand left the school and effectively ended the 11-year marriage. Dora, still very much in love with her husband, felt hurt and abandoned:

> I had married him at his urgent request to legitimize our son, on the understanding that this marriage was not to be regarded in the orthodox legal sense. I did not lay claim to object to his infidelities, nor to forgive him for them; I did not hold that they required forgiveness. The possessive tone of "my wife," "my husband," did not exist in my vocabulary.

The next three years were consumed by the tortuous and difficult process of obtaining a divorce; Bertie wished to marry Spence and legitimize any children they might have. The end result was that "Bertie got everything he wanted and I nothing except a modest allowance which would come to an end on his death." There were acrimonious disputes about the future of the children. Predictably, Dora's next book, *In Defense of Children*, which appeared in 1932, concerned itself with issues of the rights of children, for "children, like women and the proletariat, are an oppressed class."

Griffin Barry returned to the U.S., and Dora struggled on alone at the school. In 1933, she hired Paul Gillard as a secretary and gradually fell in love with him. In November 1933, he was found dead in mysterious circumstances. Pat Grace, a friend of Paul's, took his place at the school which Dora had been forced to move from Beacon Hill after the divorce became final. Grace, whom Dora was to marry in 1940, was a working-class fascist, very unlike her aristocratic first husband, and yet, Dora observed, he shared with Bertrand "a certain impishness, contempt for pomp, a lack of respect for authority, a sense of purpose in life allied with delight in its adventure—these were all qualities that I admired."

The steady, reliable Pat labored with Dora at the school, which experienced its most successful period in the two years before the Second World War broke out in 1939. In 1940, the school building was requisitioned by the War Office, and it was forced to move once more, this time to Dora's house in Cornwall. Because of staff shortages, she was now "teacher, matron and cook." On the brink of complete exhaustion, Dora finally closed the school in 1943 and began working for the Ministry of Information in London. She found her work congenial; since the Soviet Union was now an important ally in the war against Hitler, Russell was assigned to work on *The British Ally*, a newspaper which the British government was publishing in Moscow. The paper, and Dora's job, lasted until 1950.

Living in London allowed Russell to reestablish her links with feminist groups, including the Six Points Group and the Married Women's Association. Also, once her government work ended and she felt able to speak and act freely once again, she resumed her work for birth control, nuclear disarmament, and international peace through such groups as the Women's International Democratic Federation and the Women's International League for Peace and Freedom. Residing in London also allowed Dora to provide a home for whichever of her children happened to be there but she blamed its polluted air, at least in part, for the early death of Pat, her "comrade in arms," in 1948.

The early 1950s saw Dora once again in the Soviet Union, at the Vienna Peace Congress, and at the Commission on the Status of Women in the United States. In 1958, inspired by the Aldermaston Peace March, she planned and led the Women's Caravan of Peace. However, her work for humanity continued against a backdrop of family troubles and tragedies. Her eldest son John began to experience bouts of severe depression following the failure of his marriage. Dora vigorously opposed Bertrand's efforts to have him confined to a mental hospital, and she gradually assumed the full burden of caring for him for the rest of his life. Her younger son Roddy, who resisted military service in the Korean War and opted instead to work in a coal mine, was involved in an accident which shattered his spine and left him in a wheelchair until he died at the age of 50. But neither Roddy's death nor the suicide of her granddaughter **Lucy Russell**, who burned herself to death to protest the Vietnam War, diminished in any way Dora's unshakable faith in humanity. Indeed, she saw in their sacrifices "the only hope of human survival."

Retirement to her beloved house in Cornwall, "a source of renewal and a refuge from despair," saw Dora Russell continuing to write and continuing to care passionately about humanity until her death at the age of 92. Her devotion to feminism and world peace continued undiminished, as did her opposition to the corrupting influence of industrialization. Her study of *The Religion of the Machine Age*, which she had been discouraged from completing in the 1920s, was finally published in 1983. She completed the third volume of her autobiography in 1985, the year before her death, and it reveals a voice that was as distinctive and fearless in her ninth decade as it had been 60 years earlier in her first book. The final volume ends with a plea for a new philosophy of life which would reconcile the peoples of the earth with one another and allow us to respect the world in which we live. Wrote Russell:

> We do not want our world to perish. But in our quest for knowledge, century by century, we have placed all our trust in a cold, impartial intellect which only brings us nearer to destruction. We have heeded no wisdom offering guidance. Only by learning to love one another can our world be saved. Only love can conquer all.

SOURCES:

Russell, Dora. *The Dora Russell Reader: 57 Years of Writing and Journalism, 1925–1982*. Foreword by Dale Spender. London: Pandora, 1983.

———. *Hypatia or Woman and Knowledge*. NY: Dutton, 1925.

———. *The Tamarisk Tree: My Quest For Liberty and Love*. London: Virago, 1977.

———. *The Tamarisk Tree 2: My School and the Years of the War*. London: Virago, 1980.

———. *The Tamarisk Tree 3: Challenge to the Cold War*. London: Virago, 1985.

Spender, Dale. *There's Always Been a Women's Movement This Century*. London: Pandora, 1983.

(Dr.) Kathleen Garay,
Assistant Professor of History and Women's Studies,
McMaster University, Hamilton, Canada

Russell, Dorothy Stuart
(1895–1983)

English pathologist. Born in 1895; died in 1983; educated at Perse High School for Girls in Cambridge; graduated from Girton College in Cambridge, 1918; London Hospital Medical College, M.B., B.S., 1923, M.D., 1930.

Born in 1895, Dorothy Stuart Russell became a well-known pathologist and professor of pathology. She began her academic career at Perse High School for Girls in Cambridge, England, and graduated with first-class honors from Girton College in 1918. Her time at the London Hospital Medical College, from which she received M.B. and B.S. degrees in 1923 and an M.D. in 1930, helped launch her accomplishments in research in the field of pathology. Russell wrote well-regarded treatises on various aspects of pathology, including "A Classification of Bright's Disease" (1929) and "Observations on the Pathology of Hydrocephalus" (1940, republished 1967). She worked at the Nuffield Department of Surgery in Oxford from 1940 until 1944. While serving as the director of the Bernhard Baron Institute of Pathology from 1946 until 1960, she also taught morbid anatomy. Russell's *Pathology of Tumours of the Nervous System*, co-written with L.J. Rubinstein, was published in 1959. In addition to being the first female member of the Medical Research Society, she was an honorary fellow and member of several distinguished academic and professional societies related to medicine and pathology, including the Royal Society of Medicine and the Royal College of Pathology. She died in 1983.

SOURCES:

The Concise Dictionary of National Biography. Oxford: Oxford University Press, 1992.

Kelly Winters,
freelance writer, Bayville, New York

Russell, Elizabeth (1540–1609)

English writer. Name variations: Lady Elizabeth Russell; Lady Elizabeth Cooke; Lady Elizabeth Hoby. Born Elizabeth Cooke in 1540 in Essex, England; died in 1609; daughter of Sir Anthony Cooke and Anne Fitzwilliam Cooke; sister of Anne Cooke Bacon (1528–1610) and Mildred Cooke Cecil; married Sir Thomas Hoby, in 1558 (died 1566); married John, Lord Russell, in 1574 (died 1584); children: (first marriage) Elizabeth Hoby (died young), Anne Hoby (died young), Edward Hoby, Thomas Hoby; (second marriage) Francis Russell (died young), Elizabeth Russell (died young), and Anne Russell, Lady Herbert.

The poet and translator Elizabeth Russell was one of four daughters of **Anne Fitzwilliam Cooke** and Anthony Cooke, tutor to the young English king Edward VI. Like many Renaissance intellectuals, the Protestant Anthony Cooke provided his daughters with an exceptional humanist education in languages and literature; their home was referred to as the "female university." In 1553 the family went into exile in Germany when the Catholic *Mary I succeeded as queen of England, returning after Mary's death in 1558.

At age 18, Elizabeth married Thomas Hoby, the English ambassador to Paris. Hoby was, like his wife, both a scholar and a Calvinist reformer of the emerging Anglican Church. The couple had four children. As part of her continued studies of theology and classical languages, Russell translated a Latin treatise by Bishop John Ponet on the sacrament of the Eucharist. When Hoby died in 1566, Elizabeth composed touching elegies in Latin for his monument at Bisham Abbey in Berkshire. In 1570, she wrote epitaphs to honor the memory of her two young daughters who died a week apart at ages seven and nine.

In 1572, Russell worked with her two sisters, *Anne Cooke Bacon** and **Mildred Cooke Cecil**, to write dedicatory prefaces in Greek verse for a treatise on scientific knowledge which was presented to Queen *Elizabeth I. Two years later, she married John, Lord Russell, heir to the earl of Bedford, with whom she had three children, though two were to die young. When John died in 1584, Elizabeth composed a cycle of Greek and Latin verses in his memory which adorn the tomb she had erected for him in Westminster Abbey. As do all her known verses, the Russell elegies demonstrate the centrality of her Calvinist beliefs in the primacy of faith and predestination.

As the widow of a wealthy aristocrat Russell became actively involved in the management of her children's inheritance. She also used her close family connections at the royal court (her sister Mildred was the mother of Robert Cecil, the queen's secretary of state) to seek help with financial and property disputes.

In 1605, Russell finally published her translation of Ponet's treatise on the Eucharist, completed decades before, as *A Way of Reconciliation of a good and learned man, touching the Truth, Nature, and Substance of the Body and Blood of Christ in the Sacrament*. She had not thought it politically wise to publish sooner, given Ponet's radical theology; the work was dedicated to her only surviving daughter, **Anne, Lady Herbert.**

Russell commissioned her own monument to be built at Bisham Abbey and gave detailed instructions for its decoration and epitaphs. She died in 1609, at age 69.

SOURCES:

Schleiner, Louise. *Tudor and Stuart Women Writers.* Bloomington, IN: Indiana University Press, 1994.

Schlueter, Paul, and June Schlueter, eds. *Encyclopedia of British Women Writers.* New Brunswick, NJ: Rutgers University Press, 1998.

Laura York, M.A. in History, University of California, Riverside, California

Russell, Elizabeth Mary, Countess

(1866–1941).

See Arnim, Elizabeth von.

Russell, Gail (1924–1961)

American actress. Born on September 21, 1924, in Chicago, Illinois; died on August 27, 1961, in Los Angeles, California; second child of George Russell (an auto bond salesman) and Gladys (Barnet) Russell; attended Santa Monica High School, Santa Monica, California; married Guy Madison (an actor), on August 31, 1949 (divorced 1954); no children.

Selected filmography: Henry Aldrich Gets Glamour *(1943);* Lady in the Dark *(1944);* The Uninvited *(1944);* Our Hearts Were Young and Gay *(1944);* Salty O'Rourke *(1945);* The Unseen *(1945);* Duffy's Tavern *(1945);* Our Hearts Were Growing Up *(1946);* The Bachelor's Daughters *(1946);* Calcutta *(1947);* Angel and the Badman *(1947);* Variety Girl *(1947);* Night Has a Thousand Eyes *(1948);* Moonrise *(1948);* Wake of the Red Witch *(1948);* Song of India *(1949);* El Paso *(1949);* The Great Dan Patch *(1949);* Captain China *(1949);* The Lawless *(1950);* Air Cadet *(1951);* Seven Men From Now *(1956);* The Tattered Dress *(1957);* No Place to Land *(1958);* The Silent Call *(1961).*

Gail Russell didn't long to be a movie star. A shy, introverted child who spent most of her time in her room and fled from guests, she dreamed of a career in art. When she turned into a stunning teenager, however, and caught the eye of a Paramount executive, her mother wangled a screen test. "Mother dragged me there," Russell said later. Without any training or visible talent, Russell was terrified, but her dark hair, blue eyes, and even features photographed beautifully and the studio saw great potential in her.

Paramount first cast Russell in the role of a high-school vamp in *Henry Aldrich Gets Glamour* (1943), which required little more than standing around looking pretty. During the shooting of her second film, *Lady in the Dark* (1944), she suffered a debilitating attack of stage fright, the first of many. "I would stand on the set with the director, actors and technicians surrounding me," she recalled later, "and I would panic. I could not remember a line or often even move." While her co-star *Ginger Rogers cajoled her through her fears, Russell later turned to alcohol to numb the terror.

In *The Uninvited* (1944), Russell played Stella Meredith, a young woman at the mercy of a ghost bent on destroying her. The film, a smash hit (as was its theme song "Stella by Starlight"), catapulted Russell to stardom. She also scored a success portraying *Cornelia Otis Skinner in *Our Hearts Were Young and Gay* (1944), an autobiographical account of Skinner's travel to Europe with her friend **Emily Kimbrough** (played by *Diana Lynn). Russell reprised the role in the sequel *Our Hearts Were Growing Up* in 1946. Also notable was *Night Has a Thousand Eyes* (1948), co-starring Edward G. Robinson, made during the mid-point of Russell's career, at which

Jane Russell

time Hollywood was beginning to sense that she was in trouble. But the actress received her best reviews for the sleeper *The Lawless* (1950), in which she played a Mexican-American newspaper reporter who helps to free a young Mexican man wrongly accused of rape.

In 1949, Russell had married actor Guy Madison, although it was rumored that she was then involved romantically with John Wayne, her co-star in *The Angel and the Badman* (1947) and *Wake of the Red Witch* (1948). The marriage was a tumultuous union that ultimately ended in divorce in 1954. In the meantime, Russell's drinking increased, and by 1952 her movie career was at a standstill. In 1953, she was cited as correspondent in the divorce case brought by **Esperanza Wayne** against her husband John, an accusation which exacerbated the actress' alcoholism. Later that year, after a number of drunk-driving arrests, she entered a sanitarium in Seattle for treatment.

In 1955, following her divorce, Russell returned to the screen in *Seven Men from Now*, produced by John Wayne. She appeared in several subsequent films, the last of which, *The Silent Call*, was filmed early in 1961. In August of that year, after her neighbors had not seen her for several days, the actress was found dead in her apartment in Los Angeles, where she had lived for some time under the name of Mrs. Robert Moseley, Guy Madison's actual name. The cause of death was reported as acute and chronic alcoholism. "There was always a sense of pressure, no time to think or relax," Russell once said about her life as a movie star. "I just wanted to be alone to take stock, and it wasn't possible. Film work was just too demanding."

SOURCES:

Katz, Ephraim. *The Film Encyclopedia*. NY: HarperCollins, 1994.

Roberts, Barrie. "Gail Russell: Dark Star," in *Classic Images*. October 1992, pp. 24–28.

Barbara Morgan,
Melrose, Massachusetts

Russell, Lady Hamilton (1875–1938).

See Scott, Margaret.

Russell, Jane (1921—)

American actress. Born Ernestine Jane Geraldine Russell on June 21, 1921, in Bemidji, Minnesota; married Bob Waterfield (a football player and coach), in 1943 (divorced 1968); married Roger Barrett (an actor), in 1968 (died); married a third time; children: adopted three children with first husband.

Selected filmography: The Outlaw *(1943);* Young Widow *(1946);* The Paleface *(1948);* His Kind of Woman *(1951);* Double Dynamite *(1951);* The Las Vegas Story *(1952);* Macao *(1952);* Montana Belle *(1952);* Son of Paleface *(1952);* Gentlemen Prefer Blondes *(1953);* The French Line *(1954);* Underwater! *(1955);* Foxfire *(1955);* The Tall Men *(1955);* Gentlemen Marry Brunettes *(1955);* Hot Blood *(1956);* The Revolt of Mamie Stover *(1956);* The Fuzzy Pink Nightgown *(1957);* Fate Is the Hunter *(1964);* Johnny Reno *(1966);* Waco *(1966);* The Born Losers *(1967);* Darker Than Amber *(1971).*

A tall, voluptuous brunette, Jane Russell spent most of her acting career attempting to overcome her initial image as a sex symbol. Discovered in 1941 by producer-director Howard Hughes, who was conducting a nationwide search for a sensual leading lady for his movie *The Outlaw*, Russell met all his requirements. The film, tame by modern-day standards, caused a furor among the censors when it was previewed in 1941 and as a result was not released until 1943. "The publicity campaign took even longer than the production of the movie," recalled Russell, whose sultry pose in a haystack would never be forgotten. "I spent nearly two years doing publicity photos while Howard fought with the Hays Office [Hollywood's censorial board] over censorship. They wouldn't allow the film to be released without certain cuts in suggestive scenes. In the meantime, since I was under a seven-year contract to Hughes, he sent me out every day to get my picture taken. It would be hard for people to forget me." Indeed, the sexpot image settled like a shroud over Russell, who was once introduced by Bob Hope as "the two and only Miss Russell."

The daughter of a former actress, Russell was already well trained in her craft when Hughes decided to make her a star, having studied acting at Max Reinhardt's Theatrical Workshop and with *Maria Ouspenskaya. Following *The Outlaw*, she made a number of films she would just as soon forget, although by then she was trapped by her contract. "I loathed making *Young Widow*," she said, referring to her second film in 1946. "We had three directors at various times on the picture. It was like plowing through mud." Russell's best film role was opposite *Marilyn Monroe in an adaptation of *Anita Loos' *Gentlemen Prefer Blondes* (1953), in which the two (as showgirl and ditsy blonde), romp through Paris looking for rich husbands. Russell later appeared in nightclubs and on television and in 1971 replaced **Elaine Stritch** in the Broadway musical *Company*.

For 25 years, Russell was married to her high school sweetheart, football player and later coach Bob Waterfield. In her autobiography, *My Path and Detours* (1985), she calls the marriage "a mixture of happiness and brutality." The couple adopted three children before divorcing in 1968, after which Russell married actor Roger Barrett, who died just months after the wedding. The actress later wed a real estate agent and settled in Sedona, Arizona. Through the years, she has remained active as a volunteer with WAIF, an adoption agency that places children from other countries with American parents.

SOURCES:

Blowen, Michael. "Just One of the Fellas," in *Boston Globe.* October 17, 1985.

Katz, Ephraim. *The Film Encyclopedia.* NY: HarperCollins, 1994.

Barbara Morgan,
Melrose, Massachusetts

Russell, Jane Anne (1911–1967)

American biochemist and endocrinologist who was recognized as the world authority on carbohydrate metabolism during the 1940s and 1950s. Name variations: Jane A. Russell; Jane Russell Wilhelmi. Born on February 9, 1911, in Los Angeles County (now Watts), California; died of breast cancer on March 12, 1967, in Atlanta, Georgia; daughter of Josiah Howard Russell (a rancher and deputy sheriff) and Mary Ann (Phillips) Russell; graduated from the Polytechnic High School in Long Beach, California, 1928; University of California at Berkeley, B.S., 1932; Institute of Experimental Biology, Ph.D., 1937; married Alfred Ellis Wilhelmi (a scientist and professor), on August 26, 1940.

The career of biochemist Jane Anne Russell demonstrates both the level of achievement reached and the difficulties faced by women in scientific research in the 1940s and 1950s. Although Russell worked in her chosen field for over three decades, eventually produced over 70 publications, received numerous prestigious awards, and had substantial influence in shaping science policy, she did not receive formal recognition and a promotion to full professor until 1965, when she was terminally ill.

Russell was born on February 9, 1911, in California, the last of the five children of Josiah Howard Russell and **Mary Ann Phillips Russell.** The family was poor; her father built a homestead near Los Angeles, earning a living as a rancher and deputy sheriff. Russell was an excellent student, especially talented in mathematics. She graduated second in her class from Polytechnic High School in Long Beach, California, after two years of study, and entered the University of California at Berkeley at age 17. By the time she graduated Phi Beta Kappa four years later, she was first in her class and had earned the University Gold Medal, a Stewart Scholarship, and the Kraft prize.

Russell continued her studies with graduate work at Berkeley, financing her education by working as a technician for Edward S. Sundstroem, the chair of the department. In 1934, she received the California Fellowship in Biochemistry and, the following year, the Rosenberg Fellowship. As a Ph.D. candidate, she worked in the Institute of Experimental Biology, researching the role of pituitary hormones in carbohydrate metabolism. Before even receiving her doctorate in 1937, she had published six papers on this topic and had several others under preparation. She collaborated with Carl and *Gerty T. Cori, who would share the Nobel Prize in medicine in 1947, on carbohydrate research at Washington University in St. Louis. Russell's recognized genius was in her design of comparatively uncomplicated experiments that uncovered important information for the resolution of unanswered questions.

By the time she began work as a National Research Council fellow at Yale University in 1938, Russell was considered an international expert in the field of carbohydrate metabolism. Her research had shown that during times of carbohydrate deprivation, an unknown agent maintained levels of tissue carbohydrate, including blood glucose (she later identified this unknown factor as growth hormone). This research brought attention to the existence of balancing factors in carbohydrate metabolism, and provided grounding for later studies of body growth, maintenance and breakdown.

During her time at Yale, Russell continued her work on the hormonal regulation of carbohydrate metabolism. She collaborated with Alfred Ellis Wilhelmi, whom she would marry in 1940 and who worked with the growth hormone which Russell later showed to be the regulator of the activity of pituitary extracts. Fellowships supported her work before she became an instructor in 1941. Her nine years in this position earned her numerous prestigious scientific distinctions usually granted only to full professors, such as the Ciba Award in 1946. Despite these accomplishments and the fact that she was a world-renowned authority in her field, Russell was never formally recognized by Yale through academic promotions. This glaring omission later became cited as an example of discrimination against women in academia.

In 1950, Russell moved with Wilhelmi to Emory University in Atlanta, Georgia, where she became an assistant professor and he was named professor and chair of the department of biochemistry. She continued to earn recognition for her research at Emory by expanding her focus to include nitrogen metabolism; as a result of her studies in this area, she postulated that the growth hormone was essential for the prevention of the breakdown of structural proteins—a theory later proved correct. She was considered an excellent teacher as well, known for the clarity of her lectures and her enthusiasm for helping students.

Russell's move to Atlanta corresponded with the beginning of her four-year involvement with the National Institutes of Health study section on metabolism and endocrinology. She later became a member of the National Research Council Committee for the Evaluation of Post-Doctoral Fellowships and a member of the highly regarded National Science Board. In 1958, she joined the editorial board of the American Physiological Society. She was named Atlanta's Woman of the Year in Professions in 1961, the same year that she and Wilhelmi shared the Upjohn Award of the Endocrine Society. She finally had been promoted to associate professor at Emory in 1953, but still did not earn promotion to full professor until 1965, three years into her battle with breast cancer. She died in Atlanta in 1967. In 1976, Emory University instituted the annual Jane Russell Wilhelmi Memorial Lecture in her honor.

SOURCES:

Bailey, Brooke. *The Remarkable Lives of 100 Women Healers and Scientists.* Holbrook, MA: Bob Adams, 1994.

Sicherman, Barbara, and Carol Hurd Green, eds. *Notable American Women: The Modern Period.* Cambridge, MA: The Belknap Press of Harvard University, 1980.

Kelly Winters,
freelance writer, Bayville, New York

Russell, Katherine (1829–1898).

See Russell, Mother Mary Baptist.

Russell, Lady (1636–1723).

See Russell, Rachel.

Russell, Lillian (1861–1922)

Comic opera singer, actress, and political activist who was widely hailed as the embodiment of Ameri-

can Beauty. Name variations: Nellie; Diamond Lil. Born Helen Louise Leonard on December 4, 1861, in Clinton, Iowa; died on June 6, 1922, at her home in Pittsburgh from "complications" (some sources report her death as the result of a fall that did not, at the time, seem serious); daughter of Charles Egbert Leonard (a newspaper and book publisher) and Cynthia Leonard (a political activist and women's rights advocate); attended private schools in Chicago: Convent of the Sacred Heart grammar school and Park Institute, a finishing school; studied voice privately with Leopold Damrosch, a well-known Brooklyn voice coach; married Harry Braham (an orchestra conductor), in 1880 (divorced); married Edward Solomon (a musician), in 1883 (divorced); married John Haley (an actor), in 1894 (divorced); married Alexander Pollock Moore (a newspaper publisher), in 1912; children: (first marriage) son who died in infancy; (second marriage) Dorothy Solomon.

Family moved to Chicago, Illinois (c. 1863–65); moved to New York City with her mother to study for an opera career (1878); made first stage appearance as a chorus girl in H.M.S. Pinafore (1879); made professional debut at Tony Pastor's, billed as "The English Ballad singer" (1880); first comic opera "The Pie Rats of Penn Yann" (a parody of The Pirates of Penzance) was a hit at Tony Pastor's (1881); sang in genuine Gilbert and Sullivan productions, such as Patience and The Sorcerer, as well as other musicals; lived and worked in England (1883–85); returned to New York to play at the Casino where she enjoyed some of her greatest successes, including Princess Nicotine and An American Beauty; was at the peak of her singing career (1890s); shifted from comic opera to burlesque, working with the famous comedy team of Weber and Fields (1899); endured voice problems (1906), making a shift from singing to acting a necessity; joined Weber and Fields again in production of Hokey-Pokey (1912); appeared in her only film, Wildfire, with Lionel Barrymore (1914); during last few years, concentrated on political and personal concerns, campaigning actively for Theodore Roosevelt (1912) and Warren G. Harding (1920), and wrote a column for two Chicago papers; sold war bonds during World War I; though not a union officer, helped negotiate a settlement for the first Actors Equity strike (1919); worked for women's suffrage and appointed to investigate immigration problems.

Because she was known for both her good nature and her beauty, comic-opera singer Lillian Russell was often sought out for important "firsts." In May 1890, she took part in the first long-distance telephone call by singing a song from Offenbach's *The Grand Duchess* into the funnel of a New York telephone. By a miracle of science, the president and other dignitaries heard her lovely voice in Washington, D.C. A short time later, Thomas A. Edison asked Russell to sing, this time for one of his first voice recordings. She was then asked to test the now-famous acoustics of the nearly completed Carnegie Hall, but when asked to sing the "Star-Spangled Banner" neither she nor any of the other wealthy elite in the room knew the words. A German immigrant painter came down off a scaffold and wrote the lyrics on his brown paper lunch sack so she could continue with the test. Russell ruefully admitted that she went home and memorized the song so she would never again be caught in that embarrassing situation. Ironically, in her later years, she would campaign to severely limit immigration in a nativist attempt to keep America "American" and not have it culturally influenced by immigrants. Her unflinching willingness to share her failings with the American public, paired with her belief that some people were more fit than others to be "Americans," illustrates the complex nature of the woman who was known simply as "Lil" and also as the "American Beauty."

On December 4, 1861, Lillian Russell was born Helen Louise Leonard, but the family just called her Nellie. The youngest of five daughters, Russell enjoyed a close relationship with both her mother **Cynthia Leonard**, a prominent and outspoken women's rights activist and suffragist, and her father Charles E. Leonard, a quiet newspaper and book publisher. While Russell was expected to mind her manners and obey her parents, she was also encouraged to think independently. Cynthia was a radical political activist who enjoyed the close friendship of such women as suffragist *Susan B. Anthony. Charles, from whom Russell got her easy-going nature, published the works of the "great agnostic" Robert Ingersoll at a time when few publishers would dare to bring on the public's wrath by doing so.

Charles Leonard dubbed his daughter "airy, fairy Nellie," a nickname that stayed with her throughout her life, although it later changed to "airy, fairy Lillian" to match her stage name. Cynthia Leonard tried to instill in her daughters a respect for their own ability, truth, and God. The last two concepts were a bit vague, however, for five-year-old Nellie. When told that God would hear her if she lied, Russell replied indignantly, "I don't think He can amount to much if He's snooping around trying to catch little girls in lies." As an adult, she avoided lying. She also kept others from snooping by being charmingly frank about what she wanted to share and simply omitting the things that she did not wish to discuss. For her entire life, she remained "airy fairy," or somewhat unearthly, to those who loved her.

Russell attended school at the Convent of the Sacred Heart, where at age ten she made her stage debut as a child captured by Gypsies (Roma). She danced, played a tambourine, and had a few spoken lines. The mother superior warned Cynthia that her daughter was talented: "Dangerously talented; she will require careful watching." While Russell's mother did not take the caution to heart, it was well known to the family that Nellie intended to become a great actress. During the next few years, Nellie decided instead that she would become an opera singer. Her clear soprano voice led her family to believe her dream was possible. After she left "finishing school" (the Park Institute on the west side of Chicago), her mother took her, along with one of her sisters, to New York so that Russell could train for an opera career with Professor Leopold Damrosch. The relocation effectively separated Russell's mother and father. Few clues exist as to why the move became a permanent one.

While studying for the opera, Russell played a chorus girl in the operetta *H.M.S. Pinafore* in order to become familiar with the "essentials of the stage." This was supposed to be a short stint to boost her stage confidence, but, without her mother's knowledge, Nellie accepted an offer from Tony Pastor to sing for $75 a week at his theater. Pastor billed her as "Lillian Russell, the English Ballad Singer," to keep her mother in the dark. So, while Cynthia attended her evening meetings on women's rights, Russell would sneak out to the theater. For awhile, she kept her secret, until her mother went to Tony Pastor's theater one night and saw her daughter on the stage. While Cynthia had hoped Nellie would make her career in opera, she did not strenuously object to the career shift. Nellie, who thought that her new name sounded musical, would be Lillian Russell for the rest of her life.

In 1880, Russell married Harry Braham, a much-older orchestra conductor, but career conflicts and the tragic death of their infant son ended the union. Her career, however, was a success, and her salary rose accordingly. Various theater managers tried, with increasingly better offers, to lure her into signing a contract. Russell wrote in her autobiography that in 1883, "I began to think it was fun to sign contracts promiscuously." Indeed, she signed five contracts with five different managers for the same

season. Her response to the legal tangle that ensued was to elope to England with a musician, Edward Solomon. While there, she performed in a number of musical revues, had a daughter **Dorothy Solomon**, and, for a short time, lived in near poverty. She returned to the stage, and her career was in full force by the time she traveled back to the United States. Shortly after, Edward Solomon, who unbeknownst to Russell had one wife too many, was arrested for bigamy. Russell was shocked. Though she announced an annulment of the marriage to the press in 1886, she was very much in love with her husband and did not actually file until 1893.

At the peak of her popularity, Lillian Russell symbolized American femininity. She was tall and blonde, with a fair complexion and the ample, hour-glass curves that late 19th-century Americans loved. Her physical characteristics appealed to those who based nationalistic identity on Yankee tradition. From the 1870s on, the American public seemed intent on finding an embodiment of American beauty. Charles Darwin's *Origin of Species: The Preservation of Favored Races in the Struggle for Existence* was often used to "prove" that certain ethnic groups were physically and mentally superior to others. This line of thinking led many Americans to believe that North Americans from Anglo-Saxon stock were in the process of evolving into a superior type. They thought that English-speaking Anglo-Saxons would soon control the world, and so were interested in finding men and women who illustrated this superiority and "proved" the theory. While American women from many ethnic backgrounds were beautiful, the popular press dubbed Lillian Russell the "American Beauty"; she personified what was then considered the ultimate expression of American womanhood.

Russell had not sought this type of approval, but because of her enormous popularity, she could affect public opinion on many topics. She was able, for example, to support women's suffrage and women's rights while reassuring the public that having the vote would not make a woman less feminine. If Lillian Russell could advocate women's suffrage and still retain her femininity, so could others. As a child, she had charmed everyone with her manners and beauty but physically fought with the neighborhood boys who suggested that girls were not equal to them. As an adult, she continued to charm and also continued to fight for gender equality.

In 1890, Russell met and befriended "Diamond Jim" (James Buchanan) Brady, a business-

Lillian
Russell

man who had worked his way up from poverty to become one of the richest men in America. Always platonic, this friendship would continue for the rest of her life. Brady, who was known for his enormous appetite and his public display of wealth, showered Russell with so many diamonds that the press dubbed her "Diamond Lil." They would regularly meet for late suppers after her evening performance, often with an interesting array of companions. Although Brady consumed course after course, Russell often matched his consumption. Particularly fond of corn on the cob, they fascinated fellow diners during the Chicago World's Fair with the huge pile of corn cobs that accumulated nightly at their table. Although public taste ran to full-figured women, this sort of hobby tended to over-pad Russell's already well-cushioned curves. She retained her celebrated beauty by turning to diet and exercise.

*W*hat has Life meant to me? Just a waiting game for something better. Doing as much good as possible, finding as much pleasure as possible, being as just and generous in thought and deed as possible.

—Lillian Russell

Russell manifested an interesting combination of abandon and discipline. While she accumulated extravagant clothes and belongings, lived a lavish lifestyle, and matched Brady corn cob for corn cob, she also routinely worked hard to maintain her voice and beauty, and never stinted on her political beliefs. She seldom drank more than half a glass of champagne because it was bad for her voice. In court, she demanded that she never be made to wear revealing tights on stage, supposedly to keep warm in drafty theaters and therefore protect her voice, but perhaps also because of the caloric results of those late night suppers. Exercise and sports for women rapidly gained popularity at the end of the 19th century, but the press often compared athletic women unfavorably with preferred passive femininity. Russell, who had an iron-clad will when it came to exercise, became a vocal proponent of active lifestyles for women.

As soon as the safety bike was mass-produced in the 1890s, allowing women to ride a bicycle without becoming tangled up in their skirts, Lillian Russell hit the streets with flying pedals. In many circles, a woman riding a bicycle was still considered shocking, but Russell's popularity helped make the bicycle acceptable for women. Brady gifted Russell with a gold-plated bicycle with her initials formed from diamonds

and emeralds on the handlebars. She reported she made use of the machine "every morning, rain or shine," often riding with her good friend and fellow actress *Marie Dressler. She also took the bicycle with her whenever she toured, even in Europe. Frequently asked about her beauty secrets, Russell gave interviews that praised exercise as a beauty necessity. While exhibiting manners and refinement, she reminded the American public that women were strong, vigorous, and capable of action.

While the 1890s brought much critical acclaim and wealth to Russell, it was also a period of personal disappointment. In 1894, she wed for the third time, but the marriage was a disaster from the start. Her new husband, John Haley, had met and courted her only to advance his own acting career. By all accounts, Haley was unwilling, or unable, to consummate the marriage, and their relationship swiftly deteriorated into hostility. For awhile, they continued to work together, but friends and then the press became increasingly aware of their marital difficulties. After five months, the couple separated for good. When Haley aired petty complaints about Russell, the press responded by ridiculing her three failed marriages. Parodying the title of her successful role, "The Queen of Brilliants," they called her the "The Queen of Divorces." Though the public clucked over her private life, they flocked to hear her clear soprano voice soar effortlessly to high C. She was at the peak of her popularity. Women and men alike adored her.

In the 19th century, the theater was not a diversion for "nice" women, particularly those in the middle to upper class. Comic opera, at which Lillian Russell excelled, bridged the gap between serious opera and other theatrical entertainments, raising their level of respectability. At the turn of the century, Russell helped make another form of entertainment acceptable to both sexes of all classes. In 1899, she joined the popular vaudeville comic team of Weber and Fields. Vaudeville was on its way to expanding its audience.

Russell often remarked that she continued to study throughout her career, first with her voice, and later with her acting. In 1906, her flawless voice began to show signs of wear. Although she was warned that she was overusing it (serious opera performers sang fewer high C notes in order to protect their throats), Russell had continued to delight her audiences night after night with difficult music. Her voice now needed serious rest. In a risky career move, Russell took on her first non-singing role in a play, and, although her next few plays received mixed reviews, the American public seemed as enthralled with her speaking performances as they had been with her singing performances. In 1912, she rejoined Weber and Fields, who had recently reunited after a bitter feud, and they enjoyed renewed commercial success.

The year 1912 saw increased political activism from Russell. She stumped vigorously for Theodore Roosevelt's unsuccessful presidential campaign, during which she stressed such reforms as the eight-hour work day. The year also brought happiness when she married Alexander Pollock Moore, a newspaper publisher and prominent progressive Republican. Russell and Moore enjoyed both marital contentment and a shared commitment to political activism. She continued her stand on women's suffrage with renewed activism, walking behind *Inez M. Boissevain in the 1913 Washington, D.C., suffrage parade which resulted in street rioting when the police refused to protect the 8,000 women marchers. Russell publicly addressed the unfairness of a democratic nation that would not allow some of its citizens the ballot, pointing out that she paid a great deal of taxes and had zero "representation" to show for it.

During an interview with journalist and author *Djuna Barnes in 1915, Russell requested that Barnes "begin the interview with the name of Lillian Russell but end it with the name of such as was Cynthia Leonard." Russell seems to have based her career on the same sentiment. She began as Lillian Russell, the singer, and was cherished for her voice and beauty. She ended her career, however, with her concern over public issues and with the activities that were important to both her parents. Following her father's interest in the written word, Russell began her own newspaper column. Though she wrote for the *Chicago Daily Tribune* and the *Chicago Herald*, her commentary was read nationally through syndication. The publishers wanted her to give beauty tips. When Russell stressed that beauty came from within, not from the way people looked to others, her editor wired, "Write less about soul and more about pimples."

With America's entry into World War I, Russell volunteered time and money to sell war bonds. Addressing thousands, she held rallies for recruitment, urging young men to come forward and enlist; many followed her call. When some of those same young men came back from the war wounded, they joined her on stage to sell more war bonds. In recognition of her work, Russell was appointed an honorary sergeant of the U.S. Marine Corps and wore her new uniform to public events and photo calls. Like many other women, Russell tied her patriotic efforts to women's suffrage. If it were appropriate for women to take on patriotic roles, then it was appropriate for them to vote.

In 1920, Russell campaigned for Warren G. Harding, and following his election he appointed her a commissioner for the study of immigration. Coming at a time when mass immigration to the States had increased urban crowding and other problems, her 1922 report suggested stopping immigration for five years, then, if immigration were resumed, to severely limit it. In order to lessen foreign influence on American life, the report proposed that immigrants live in the United States for 21 years before they were allowed to become citizens. "Our melting pot is overcrowded," wrote Russell, and she warned that unless something was done, "there will no longer be an America for the Americans." Social Darwinists, including many prominent Americans, felt that unless Anglo-Saxon traditions as well as genes remained dominant in the U.S., the country would no longer be "American."

In preparation for the report on immigration, Russell traveled to Europe to see firsthand the postwar conditions that made so many Europeans eager to come to America. On the return trip, she fell onboard ship. Although she admitted she was injured, she did not consider the fall important, and it is doubtful she received much medical attention. Shortly thereafter, back at home in Pittsburgh, she became ill. Lillian Russell died on June 6, 1922. It was reported that she died of "a complication of diseases." There is no evidence to pinpoint what that might mean, though most accounts assume the fall caused internal injuries that led to her death. At President Harding's order, she was buried with full military honors.

SOURCES:

Auster, Albert. *Actresses and Suffragists: Women in the American Theater, 1890–1920*. NY: Praeger, 1984.

Banner, Lois. *American Beauty*. NY: Alfred A. Knopf, 1983.

McArthur, Benjamin. *Actors and American Culture, 1880–1920*. Philadelphia, PA: Temple University Press, 1984.

Morell, Parker. *Lillian Russell: The Era of Plush*. NY: Random House, 1940.

Russell, Lillian. "Lillian Russell's Reminiscences," in *Cosmopolitan*. February–September 1922.

SUGGESTED READING:

Burke, John. *Duet In Diamonds: The Flamboyant Saga of Lillian Russell and Diamond Jim Brady in America's Gilded Age*. NY: Putnam, 1972.

COLLECTIONS:

Harvard Theater Collection, Harvard University (clippings); papers from 1878 to 1886, University of

Rochester Library, New York (letters); Robinson Locke Dramatic Collection, New York Public Library Performing Arts Research Center at Lincoln Center (scrapbooks).

JoAnne Thomas,
Instructor of History and Women's Studies,
Western Michigan University, Kalamazoo, Michigan

Russell, Lucy (c. 1581–1627)

*English patron of poets. Name variations: Lucy, Countess of Bedford; Lucy Harington. Born around 1581; died in 1627; daughter of John Harington, 1st Baron Harington of Exton, and **Anne Harington**; married Edward Russell, 3rd earl of Bedford, in 1594.*

Born around 1581, Lucy Russell was a patron of some of the foremost English poets of her day. Ben Jonson and John Donne praised her in their work. Jonson wrote three of his epigrams—the 76th, 84th, and 94th—for her, in which he called her his muse, thanked her for her financial gifts, and delighted in her friendship. In the 94th epigram, he refers to her as "Lucy, you brightness of our sphere, who are / Life of the muses' day, their morning star." Donne also wrote several poems addressed to her, including an elegy after her death. Some

critics, particularly in the following centuries, implied that these writers' financial dependence on Russell sparked their unflagging admiration far more than did the actual quality of her character, but this seems at least much exaggerated if not completely spurious. Donne's poem "To the Countess of Bedford," which discusses how virtue is usually tinged with some sort of vice and vice with some bit of virtue, seems explicitly to deny any who would malign her name, stating that while his poem "do / Stand on two truths, neither is true to you." Her generosity, at any rate, is unquestionable. She received a large inheritance from her father John Harington, 1st Baron Harington of Exton, and spent most of it financing writers; in addition to Jonson and Donne, she helped support poet Michael Drayton, poet and playwright Samuel Daniel, and poet, playwright and translator George Chapman. Although Russell is known primarily for her financial support of various literary figures, she apparently wrote verse herself, as evidenced by allusions to her work in the writing of others. None of her writings survive, however.

SOURCES:

The Concise Dictionary of National Biography. Oxford: Oxford University Press, 1992.
Lodge, Edmund. *Portraits of Illustrious Personages of Great Britain.* Vol. 3. London: William Smith, n.d.

Kelly Winters,
freelance writer, Bayville, New York

Russell, Margery (d. around 1380)

English merchant. Died around 1380 in Coventry, England.

Margery Russell, an English merchant, traded internationally in a variety of goods and, though married to another merchant, ran her business as a *femme sole*, or "woman alone," from the town of Coventry. She was well educated in those areas in which a businesswoman needed special knowledge, including arithmetic and trading law. She used her knowledge to great advantage, successfully pursuing in court those whom she felt had taken advantage of her. She even went to the royal court for redress when one of her ships was attacked and plundered by Spanish pirates. With a sense of justice perhaps odd to modern observers, the court granted Russell permission to compensate her loss through seizure of Spanish cargo in nearby ports. Spanish traders lodged a complaint against her soon afterwards for taking goods valued at more than she had lost. After this, Russell disappears from the court records.

Lucy Russell

SOURCES:

Echols, Anne, and Marty Williams. *An Annotated Index of Medieval Women*. NY: Markus Wiener, 1992.

Laura York,
Riverside, California

Russell, Mary Annette, Countess

(1866–1941).

See Arnim, Elizabeth von.

Russell, Mother Mary Baptist

(1829–1898)

Irish-born Roman Catholic nun who founded St. Mary's Hospital, the first Catholic hospital on America's West Coast. Name variations: Katherine Russell; Sister Mary Baptist; Mary Baptist Russell. Born in Newry, County Down, Ireland, on April 18, 1829; died in San Francisco, California, on August 6, 1898; daughter of Arthur Russell (a sea captain and brewer) and Margaret (Hamill) Russell; educated by a governess and in private schools; never married; no children.

Established the House of Mercy, a shelter for unemployed women (1855); founded St. Mary's Hospital, the first Catholic hospital on the West Coast (1857); established the Magdalen Asylum for reformed prostitutes (1861).

Mother Mary Baptist Russell was born Katherine Russell into a large and comfortably wealthy family in Ireland on April 18, 1829. Her parents, Arthur and **Margaret Hamill Russell**, made sure that their children practiced their Catholic beliefs, and lived out their own faith by ministering to the starving men and women of their town. During the Great Famine in Ireland, Margaret Russell managed the relief efforts for those people who were most destitute. Inspired by her mother's charity, Katherine, with two of her sisters, entered the Sisters of Mercy convent in Kinsale in 1848. The following year, Katherine cared for the victims of a cholera outbreak. She received her habit the same year, and became a full-fledged sister in 1851, taking the name Sister Mary Baptist.

In 1854, Russell answered a call for help in San Francisco to care for victims of another cholera outbreak. Her order, the Sisters of Mercy, had recently established a branch there, and the archbishop appointed Russell its mother superior. She left Kinsale with eight other nuns and novices, and embarked on the work that would shape the rest of her life. In the course of the next five years, Russell not only worked with the poor and sick, but also established institutions which allowed her to continue this work on a broader, more far-reaching basis. While she initially ran a hospital for San Francisco and the surrounding county under contract from the city, after two years questions arose about the separation of church and state, and she ended the arrangement in 1857. That year Russell founded St. Mary's Hospital, the first Catholic hospital on the West Coast, where nuns from the Sisters of Mercy nursed countless poor and sick people.

In addition to nursing, Russell also involved the Sisters of Mercy in the education of the poor and the protection of unemployed women. In 1855, the Sisters of Mercy, under her direction, established a night school for adults and a shelter for unemployed women called the House of Mercy. In 1861, Russell also created the Magdalen Asylum (named in reference to ***Mary Magdalene**), a shelter for young women trying to escape from prostitution which housed nearly 200 women over the next eight years. She visited death-row inmates at San Quentin, as well as inmates at local and county jails. She established a home for the aging and infirm, and provided, among other things, daily hot meals for the poor of San Francisco during particularly hard times. She also established Catholic schools for children in Sacramento and San Francisco.

In order to maintain the broad scope of her charity work, Russell had to ensure funding for her programs and homes. In this endeavor, too, she worked diligently. She organized a society for Catholic lay women in 1859, and encouraged its members to contribute to the causes of the Sisters of Mercy. When Russell died in 1898 at the age of 69, she left behind a powerful legacy of charitable work and devotion to others; a local newspaper recognized her as the "best-known charitable worker on the Pacific Coast." Because of her generosity, her managerial skills, and her diligence in pursuing funding, she guaranteed that the work to which she had dedicated her life would continue long after her death. Her brother Matthew Russell published *The Life of Mother Mary Baptist Russell, Sister of Mercy*, in 1901.

SOURCES:

Edgerly, Lois Stiles, ed. *Give Her This Day: A Daybook of Women's Words*. Gardiner, ME: Tilbury House, 1990.

James, Edward T., ed. *Notable American Women, 1607–1950*. Cambridge, MA: The Belknap Press of Harvard University, 1971.

Newmann, Kate, comp. *Dictionary of Ulster Biography*. The Institute of Irish Studies, the Queen's University of Belfast, 1993.

Andrea Bewick,
freelance writer, Santa Rosa, California

Russell, Rachel (1636–1723)

English aristocrat. Name variations: Rachel Wriothesley; Rachel Vaughan; Lady Russell. Born in September 1636 (some sources cite 1637) in Hampshire, England; died on September 29, 1723, in Southampton; daughter of Thomas Wriothesley (1607–1667), 5th earl of Southampton (r. 1624–1667), and Rachel Massuy de Ruvigny also seen as Rachel de Massue (b. 1603); married Francis Vaughan, Lord Vaughan, in October 1654 (died 1667); married William Russell, Lord Russell, in August 1669 (beheaded 1683); children: (first marriage) two who died young; (second marriage) **Rachel Russell** (1674–1725, who married William Cavendish, 2nd duke of Devonshire), **Catherine Russell** (1676–1711, who married John Manners, 2nd duke of Rutland), Wriothesley Russell (b. 1680), duke of Bedford.

The life of Rachel Russell is preserved in hundreds of her letters and in the numerous treatises she composed. She was one of four surviving children of Thomas Wriothesley, 5th earl of Southampton, and his aristocratic French wife **Rachel de Massue**. The years of Rachel's childhood on her father's country estate in Hampshire correspond to the period of the English Civil War of the 1640s and early 1650s. Rachel

Rachel Russell

grew up without close attachment to either of her parents; her mother died in childbirth when Rachel was three, and her father was absent from his children for months at a time, serving as a moderate Royalist leader in the House of Lords in London. As a result, Rachel formed extremely close lifelong relationships with her sisters, **Elizabeth** and **Magdalene Wriothesley**. The Wriothesley children were raised in the Anglican Church, but their religious upbringing was strongly influenced by Puritan piety as well. However, piety would not play much of a role in Rachel's personal life until many years later.

In 1654, Thomas Wriothesley arranged a marriage for Rachel, then aged 16, with Francis Vaughan, son of the earl of Carbery, also 16. It was an unhappy marriage from the beginning. She had two children who each survived only a few days. In her later autobiographical writings, Rachel passes over the years of this youthful first marriage with little comment. She makes no direct mention of her husband, who died of the plague in March 1667.

Widowed and childless at age 30, Rachel returned to her family estates, where her father died only two months after her husband. With no surviving sons, Thomas left his vast fortune and estates to be divided among his daughters. Along with a large income, Rachel inherited Southampton House, her father's favorite country estate. She divided her time between Southampton and her home in London, where she eventually met and fell in love with William Russell, a wealthy but not noble member of Parliament.

Rachel married William in August 1669. The couple had similar personalities—genial, warmhearted, intelligent, with a deep interest in politics—and shared Anglican religious beliefs tolerant of dissenters. Rachel's many letters to and about her husband show that they were passionately in love throughout their marriage. She had three children, all of whom lived to adulthood, to whom she and William were loving and affectionate parents. With William's encouragement Rachel became involved in current affairs and in the management of the Wriothesley and Russell estates. Religious devotion also began to play a more important role in her life at this time.

The couple shared reform-minded Whig politics as well. They both feared King Charles II would re-establish Catholicism and create an absolutist state, but William was drawn to more extreme reformist policies than was his more moderate wife. As William rose in political importance to become leader of the House of Commons, Rachel played an increasingly important role as his unofficial advisor. She used her social connections and family members highly placed in Parliament and the royal court to gather information on William's political opponents, reporting to her husband on political events and gossip when he was away from London. This intrigue became more dangerous after William emerged as the head of parliamentary opposition to King Charles II. Despite Rachel's many warnings, after 1681 William became involved in conspiracies to dethrone the king.

In 1683, William was arrested and tried for treason. Rachel and their children were allowed to visit him in the Tower of London, where he and Rachel devised plans for his defense. She did everything in her power before and during the trial to get him released, including appealing to the king, procuring the best lawyers, and petitioning every highly placed official she could. She even appeared at the trial herself, although it was extremely unusual for a woman to be allowed into a courtroom. Despite her best efforts, William was convicted for his plots with the French against the king, and, although Rachel made personal appeals to Charles to pardon him, William was executed as a traitor on July 21.

Rachel's correspondence from the months following the execution reveal how deeply she mourned. To her husband's supporters, she became a political symbol, the grieving widow of a patriotic martyr. Rachel contributed to this image, struggling with the administration to get William's final speech published, and continuing to support those who wanted to reform the government. They finally succeeded in 1688, when James II was deposed in the Glorious Revolution by the Protestant William of Orange. One of William's first acts as king was agreeing to Rachel's petition to have her husband's conviction overturned posthumously and to reverse the attainder that had denied the Russells their legal and property rights.

This restored the Russell family honor and legal rights, and, combined with the friendship of the king, it also restored Rachel's social status among the aristocracy. She now could expand her previous role as a mother into that of the widowed matriarch of an important family. She used this new status to the political and financial benefit of herself and her children—expanding and managing her properties in London and Hampshire, negotiating marriages for her children, and conducting business ventures. She also used her status at the royal court to influence royal and church appointments for the benefit of her extended family.

Lady Russell's health and eyesight began to fail around 1702, when she was 65, but she continued her many business affairs and maintained an active social life well into her 70s. She then retired to her estate at Southampton House, where she died at age 85 in 1723.

SOURCES:
Schwoerer, Lois G. *Lady Rachel Russell*. Baltimore, MD: Johns Hopkins University Press, 1988.
Russell, John. *The life of William, Lord Russell; with some account of the times in which he lived*. London: Longman, 1820.

Laura York, M.A. in History, University of California, Riverside, California

Russell, Rosalind (1908–1976)

American actress, famed for her performances in **Auntie Mame** *and* **Gypsy***. Born on June 4, 1908, in Waterbury, Connecticut; died of cancer on November 28, 1976, in Los Angeles, California; one of seven children of Clara Russell and James Russell (a trial lawyer); had a Catholic school education before graduating from New York's American Academy of Dramatic Arts in the mid-1920s; married Frederick Brisson (a producer); children: one son, Lance.*

Won several parts on the stage before making film debut in *Evelyn Prentice* (1934); enjoyed great success in a string of comedies (1940s) in which she often played bright, witty career women; appeared in her most famous role as Auntie Mame both on Broadway (1956) and in the film adaptation (1958); nominated four times for an Oscar, was given a specially created award for the charity work which marked much of her later life (1972).

Films: Evelyn Prentice (1934); The President Vanishes (1934); Forsaking All Others (1934); The Night Is Young (1935); West Point of the Air (1935); The Casino Murder Case (1935); Reckless (1935); China Seas (1935); Rendezvous (1935); It Had to Happen (1936); Under Two Flags (1936); Trouble for Two (1936); Craig's Wife (1936); Night Must Fall (1937); Live Love and Learn (1937); Man-Proof (1938); Four's a Crowd (1938); The Citadel (1938); Fast and Loose (1939); The Women (1939); His Girl Friday (1940); Hired Wife (1940); No Time for Comedy (1940); This Thing Called Love (1941); They Met in Bombay (1941); The Feminine Touch (1941); Design for Scandal (1941); Take a Letter Darling (1942); My Sister Eileen (1942); Flight for Freedom (1943); What a Woman (1943); Roughly Speaking (1945); She Wouldn't Say Yes (1945); Sister Kenny (1946); The Guilt of Janet Ames (1947); Mourning Becomes Electra (1947); The Velvet Touch (1948); Tell It to the Judge (1949); A Woman of Distinction (1950); Never

Wave at a Wac *(1953)*; The Girl Rush *(1955)*; Picnic *(1956)*; Auntie Mame *(1958)*; A Majority of One *(1962)*; Five Finger Exercise *(1962)*; Gypsy *(1962)*; The Trouble with Angels *(1966)*; Oh Dad, Poor Dad, Mama's Hung You in the Closet and I'm Feeling So Sad *(1967)*; Rosie *(1967)*; Where Angels Go, Trouble Follows *(1968)*; Mrs. Pollifax—Spy *(1971)*.

No one could ever have accused Rosalind Russell of being timid. "It's important to make news," she once said, a statement she put diligently into practice during her 40 years on the stage and in movies. She played bright, brassy career women at a time when most American women were relegated to kitchens or charity bazaars; she sang the lead in musicals with a voice that even she compared to "a crow with a sore throat"; and she fearlessly took on roles ranging from nuns to murderers to the mother of a stripper. Her versatility so impressed theater critic Brooks Atkinson that he once suggested that she run for president. "She can dance and sing better than any president we have had," he observed. "She is also better looking and has a more infectious sense of humor."

Her energy and intensity might have been born from the competition that came from having three brothers and three sisters. Russell was the middle-born of the Irish-Catholic brood raised by James and **Clara Russell** in Waterbury, Connecticut. Her father had put himself through Yale Law School by playing semi-professional baseball and had gone on to become a successful trial lawyer by the time Rosalind was born on June 4, 1908. She had been named for, of all things, a steamship—the S.S. *Rosalind*, on which her parents had taken a cruise to Nova Scotia just before her birth. The energetic performances that marked her adult career were already much in evidence during her childhood as the roughneck of the family. Before she was 16, she had broken a leg jumping out of a hayloft and fractured a wrist in a leap off a wall, not to mention snapping a collarbone in a fall during a race and breaking an arm falling off a horse. Despite these adolescent catastrophes, she grew into a statuesque, 5'7" young woman much admired for her luxurious black hair, and successfully completed ten years of parochial school education, graduating in 1924.

Her schooling continued despite her father's early death in 1927, for James Russell left a comfortable estate and instructions that his children would receive no income from it until three years after completing their college education. Accordingly, Rosalind attended Marymount

College in Tarrytown, New York, where she was drawn to the conviviality of the school's drama club and first took to the stage in several of its productions. Such was her attraction for the theater that she was allowed to leave Marymount in her sophomore year and transfer to the American Academy of Dramatic Arts in Manhattan, her mother being of the opinion that her daughter's addiction would quickly run the course. Besides, Rosalind promised that her interest in drama extended only to teaching it, certainly a respectable means for a young woman to make her way in the world. But before graduating from the Academy in 1929, Russell had appeared in several more student productions and had gotten herself noticed by two producers scouting talent for their summer theater upstate, in Lake Saranac. She was offered $150 a week for the coming season. Russell's devotion to the stage only intensified during the rigorous schedule of summer stock, in which she often played two different roles each week. "We rehearsed all morning, played golf all afternoon, and stayed up all night," she said fondly of those weeks under the summer stars. "We lived on youth, energy and no sleep. It was a wonderful summer."

After an autumn in Boston with a British repertory company, Russell made her Broadway debut early in 1930 in a revue called *The Garrick Gaieties*, staged by the Theater Guild, in which she sang and did sketches. After a tour with the show, she was back on Broadway in April 1931 for the comedy *Company's Coming*, although the show closed after only eight performances, and she took to the road again for the next three years with an assortment of stock companies. By 1934, Russell had learned to troupe with the best of them. She knew how to master a role quickly and instinctively, how to get a character across to the audience with a minimum of fuss and self-analysis, and how to take on a challenge with impeccable self-confidence. It all came in handy when a talent scout for Universal saw a performance in Newark, New Jersey, and offered her a screen test. She would test, Russell replied, only in Los Angeles; only if she were paid $100 for each test; and only if any forthcoming contract guaranteed her $300 a week. Universal fussed and complained, but Russell not only received $900 for her nine Hollywood tests but was offered a seven-year contract with a guarantee of, not $300, but $400 a week.

Further surprises were in store for her new employers. Upon learning that MGM might offer her a test for its upcoming production of the J.M. Barrie play *What Every Woman*

Knows, Russell arranged a meeting with Universal head Carl Laemmle, Jr. She arrived wearing an unflattering dress, heavy, caked makeup, and a sorrowful expression. After hearing her complaints that she was unhappy in Hollywood and wanted to return to New York, Laemmle agreed to cancel her contract with no penalties. His reaction on learning a few days later that Russell had signed with MGM is not recorded. Although she was not offered a part in the Barrie film, Russell made her screen debut in 1934's *Evelyn Prentice*, a weepy melodrama starring **Myrna Loy* and William Powell, the studio's most popular screen couple.

Between 1934 and 1936, Russell made nine films for MGM and three more on loanout, usually playing the woman who loses her man to the leading lady. Since her characters were often fashionable, sophisticated society women, she referred to these early years in Hollywood as her "Lady Mary" period. A short-lived attempt at playing mantrapper roles followed, in films like *China Seas* and *Reckless*, with little success ("Rosalind Russell exhibits an excess of dental charm" was one of the kinder reviews); while a starring role in *The Casino Murder* was the result of the studio's decision to use her as a threat in its ongoing battle with Myrna Loy's demands for higher salaries. Russell was paired with Paul Lukas in the film as a second-string Nick and Nora Charles, and, while Loy might have gotten the message, *The Casino Murder* fizzled at the box office. A second attempt was more successful—1935's *Rendezvous*, in which the studio cast her opposite Powell, Loy's usual screen partner in the successful "Thin Man" series. Russell received her first screen success as the girl who enlists Powell to help uncover a Washington spy ring. "Miss Russell gets her first leading assignment . . . and ripens into full flower," enthused *Variety*, while Richard Watts in *The New York Times* thought that "Miss Russell is one of the most interesting and beautiful of the cinema's new lady sophisticates [and is] one of the film's greatest pleasures."

Despite the respectful reviews that greeted her next few pictures, MGM was reluctant to cast her in the part that became Russell's breakthrough role, as the deliciously malicious Sylvia Fowler in the studio's 1939 production of *The Women*, based on **Clare Booth Luce*'s scathing satire of New York society women. Rosalind's battle to win the role included five screen tests for director George Cukor, who flatly told her she wasn't right for it, and a personal appeal to Irving Thalberg, MGM's head of production. "Some of my best friends think I'm funny," she told him, in hind-

sight an understatement from the woman who would in just a few years become the favorite comedian of millions of moviegoers. Russell threw herself into the role with her usual gusto, her on-screen fistfight with **Paulette Goddard* resulting in not a few actual cuts and bruises. Nor did she flinch off-screen in the face of a more formidable opponent, **Norma Shearer*, Thalberg's wife and the film's nominal star, when it was announced that Shearer's contract forbade any other woman from sharing top billing. Russell's answer was a three-day "sick leave," forcing the film to shut down until Shearer relented. The picture was a great success. "*The Women* brought me acceptance as a comedienne," Rosalind later said, and "also brought me my husband."

The husband in question was Danish-born theatrical agent Frederick Brisson, who had seen her in *The Women* during a transatlantic crossing. Brisson arrived in Hollywood as Russell was shooting *His Girl Friday*, in which she played the fast-talking, sharp-witted newspaper reporter Hildy Johnson. Brisson's friendship with

Rosalind Russell

the film's director, Howard Hawks, failed to produce a date; and while Rosalind's co-star, Cary Grant, sympathetically arranged a dinner date, it was nearly a year before Rosalind finally accepted Brisson. Grant served as best man at their wedding on October 25, 1941. Brisson became a well-known Hollywood agent during the next decade and earned the moniker "the Wizard of Ros" for his expert handling of his wife's career, including her decision not to renew her contract with MGM in 1942 and to work instead on a freelance basis. By then, she had appeared in four films in less than two years, all comedies, two of which, *Hired Wife* and *No Time for Comedy*, were released at the same time. "If Rosalind Russell doesn't capture all the votes for best screen comedienne this year," *The New York Times* observed in 1941, "it certainly won't be her fault."

With her "Lady Mary" phase now behind her, Russell became known for playing intelligent, business-minded women comfortably at ease among more perplexed male executives. There was, for example, the secretary in *Hired Wife* who agrees to marry her boss so his company can be transferred to her to avoid a lawsuit; the insurance company executive in *This Thing Called Love* whose statistical analysis of successful marriages induces her to delay consummating her own for three months to ensure its survival; and the judge in *Design for Scandal* who manages to save a trial lawyer from professional ruin. In her first picture after leaving MGM, 1942's *Take a Letter, Darling*, she had been promoted to the level of boss, playing an advertising executive with a male secretary and easily inhabiting a luxurious suite with a view of the Empire State Building and a huge desk peppered with telephones. "A woman in business faces many problems that men don't," she says in the picture. "Among those problems are *men*."

> *Acting is standing up naked and turning around very slowly.*
> —Rosalind Russell

But it was an uncharacteristic role that same year as a wide-eyed girl from Ohio that brought Russell her first Academy Award nomination. *My Sister Eileen*, based on a series of short stories by *Ruth McKenney* published in *The New Yorker*, observed the efforts of Rosalind's Ruth Sherwood and **Janet Blair**'s Eileen to make it big in New York after arriving in Greenwich Village from a small Midwest town. Russell would maintain a close association with the role, playing Ruth again in a broadcast version on Lux Radio Theater, and in a musical version called

Wonderful Town on Broadway and on television. It was the first indication that Rosalind could handle roles outside of the social satires for which she had become known, although it didn't seem much of a change to her. "It's fine to have talent, but talent is the last of it," she said. "In an acting career, as in any acting performance, you've got to have vitality. The secret of successful acting is identical with a woman's beauty secret: joy in living."

With America's entry into World War II, Rosalind added bond rallies, fundraising appearances and charity work to her already full schedule, starring in two pictures during 1943 and, amazingly, giving birth to a son, Lance, in May of that year. Finally, she later told *Time* magazine, "I just got up one morning and fell in a heap." Her collapse was diagnosed as nervous exhaustion. Months of rest at home were ordered, and rumors began circulating that Russell would retire. "The collapse slowed me up long enough to realize that after a wonderful career, you either retire or go on to something you've never undertaken before," she said later. Typically, it was the latter course that she chose.

Roughly Speaking, the first film released after her collapse, was an attempt to combine her comedic talents with serious material—in this case, the true story of a wealthy woman who loses everything to a gigolo of a husband but triumphs in the end. Her next two choices were even more surprising. *Sister Kenny* was based on the story of *Elizabeth Kenny, an Australian nurse who developed one of the first treatments for infantile paralysis. Although the film performed badly at the box office, critics were impressed with her dramatic abilities and Rosalind received her second Academy Award nomination. Then came 1947's *Mourning Becomes Electra*, in which she starred as the murderous Lavinia with Raymond Massey and Michael Redgrave in the film adaptation of Eugene O'Neill's tortured story of family hatreds and betrayals. The film was an even worse failure than *Sister Kenny*, and Rosalind later claimed she had done the picture only as a favor to the director, Dudley Nichols, with whom she had worked on several of her earlier movies. "I didn't particularly enjoy making the O'Neill film. It never fitted into the medium," she said. Audiences agreed. "When people stay away from it, as they are likely to do," critic Bosley Crowther accurately predicted, "it will not be because it is an 'adult picture,' but because it is just plain bad."

Smarting from such critical bruising, Russell returned to comedy roles in two films produced by her husband's film company and began to consider returning to the stage, from which she had been absent for ten years. She embarked with uncharacteristic caution on this new endeavor, touring during 1951 and 1952 in a production of John van Druten's *Bell, Book and Candle* to good reviews before taking on a full-blown Broadway role. "What makes you walk away is fear," she later wrote, "and you've got to conquer fear to live with yourself." Her triumphant return to Broadway in 1953's *Wonderful Town*, based on *My Sister Eileen*, completely obliterated whatever fears she might have had. The show, with a score by Leonard Bernstein and lyrics by *Betty Comden and Adolph Green, arrived at the Winter Garden in February after tryouts in Boston, New Haven, and Philadelphia. Russell hurt her back in New Haven when a chorus boy dropped her during a dance number; went on with the flu and a 103-degree temperature in Boston; and learned an entirely new opening number and a completely rewritten second act before the show premiered in Philadelphia. Her musical re-creation of Ruth Sherwood

(with **Edie Adams** as Eileen) won her the New York Critics' Circle Award and a Tony during her 15 months with the show, during which she never missed a performance until leaving in 1954 because of a film commitment. The film was Joshua Logan's 1955 production of William Inge's *Picnic*, in which Russell turned in a touching performance as the lonely Rosemary, the spinster schoolteacher who is desperate to marry a man she's been dating for years. "I was very flattered that Josh Logan would see me as an old maid schoolteacher in Kansas," she once recalled. "I had been playing those Park Avenue dames for so many years."

While shooting *Picnic*, Russell received the galley proofs of a book written by Patrick Dennis, a memoir about growing up with a charmingly eccentric aunt. "You are my Auntie Mame for stage and screen," he said in the note attached to the proofs. Russell took the compliment to heart. She opened on Broadway in *Auntie Mame* in October 1956 to such rapturous reviews that the show, the most expensive pro-

From the movie Gypsy, *starring Rosalind Russell.*

duced on Broadway that year, made its investors over a million dollars during its 17-month run. Russell successfully transferred the role to film in 1958 to earn her fourth Academy Award nomination. She announced a temporary retirement after the picture was completed, although she did not divulge that the reason for her absence was breast cancer. Nor did anyone but her family know of the two mastectomies she underwent, in 1960 and in 1965, before she was given a clean bill of health.

She was sufficiently recovered from the first operation to start work on a string of three pictures in 1961, all based on stage plays and all released in 1962. She played a Jewish mother who falls in love with a Japanese businessman in *A Majority of One*, a troubled housewife who falls in love with a younger man in the family drama *Five Finger Exercise*, and the aggressively ambitious Mama Rose in *Gypsy*. While the first two films did mediocre business and she was taken to task by the critics for her work in *Five Finger Exercise*, *Gypsy* captured the hearts of both audiences and reviewers. The film was based on stripper *Gypsy Rose Lee's memoirs of her early years in burlesque under her mother's tutelage, and adapted from the successful Broadway musical which had starred *Ethel Merman as Mama Rose; Russell told reporters that she approached it not as a musical but as a great story with music. "People come to a musical to hear good music, but if I'm in it, they know they're going to hear damn *little* music. But they can hope for a good story," she said. That's exactly what audiences got. "Hold yer hats and hallelujah!," bubbled *Time* in its review of the film. "The old girl rips, roars, romps, rampages and rollicks through this raucous musical."

But *Gypsy* would prove to be Russell's last triumph, on stage or screen. Her film work during the late 1960s was more interesting for its variety than for its quality. She played a Mother Superior at a girls' school in Disney's 1966 *The Trouble with Angels* and in the 1968 sequel; an eccentric widow in Arthur Kopit's black comedy *Oh Dad, Poor Dad, Mama's Hung You in the Closet and I'm Feeling So Sad*; and a madcap millionaire mother committed to an asylum by her greedy daughters in *Rosie*. In 1969, she was felled by rheumatoid arthritis and again had to stop working. The side effects from the steroids used to treat the disease were troublesome, and she later regretted her public announcement of her condition, claiming it made the studios nervous about hiring her. "Loss of health is the worst thing that can happen to anybody," she said. The disease had become so crippling by the early 1970s that she was able to work in only one film, 1971's *Mrs. Pollifax—Spy*, produced by her husband with a screenplay she had adapted herself from **Dorothy Gilmore**'s novel. She used the pseudonym C.A. McKnight, her mother's maiden name, just as she had 15 years earlier for a film called *The Unguarded Moment*, written for *Esther Williams in 1956. *Mrs. Pollifax* was her last screen appearance.

She turned to fundraising activities for charities and appearances for the National Council of the Arts with such vigor that, in 1972, she was awarded the American Academy's Jean Hersholt Award for Humanitarian Service, and attended a sold-out "Tribute to Rosalind Russell" at New York's Town Hall in 1974. Asked during the proceedings what she considered her greatest achievement, Russell promptly retorted "Being alive." The response was more than quick-witted repartee. Although her struggles with arthritis had long been public knowledge and Russell openly discussed her condition in her autobiography, only her family knew that her cancer had returned. "One disease to a book is enough," she told her husband. Weakened by a broken hip that required surgery early in 1976, she died peacefully at home on November 28.

Her husband saw to it that the autobiography she had been writing during the last two years of her life was published posthumously, in 1977. Russell had drawn its title from her most famous role. "Life's a banquet," Auntie Mame tells her adoring nephew, "and most poor suckers are starving." In shaping and guiding her own career, Rosalind Russell had seen to it that her plate was always full, and her guests always well fed.

SOURCES:
Russell, Rosalind, with Chris Chase. *Life Is a Banquet.* NY: Random House, 1977.
Yanni, Nicholas. *Rosalind Russell.* NY: Pyramid, 1975.

Norman Powers,
writer-producer, Chelsea Lane Productions,
New York, New York

Russell, Sarah (1915–1988).

See Laski, Marghanita.

Russia, empress of.

See Vassiltschikov, Anna.
See Sophia of Byzantium (1448–1503).
See Anastasia Romanova (d. 1560).
See Maria of Circassia (d. 1569).
See Sobakin, Marta (d. 1571).
See Godunova, Irene (d. 1603).
See Maria Skuratova (d. 1605).
See Mniszek, Marina (c. 1588–1614).

See Dolgorukova, Marie (d. 1625).

See Sophia Alekseyevna for sidebar on Maria Miloslavskaia (1626–1669).

See Narishkina, Natalya (1651–1694).

See Grushevski, Agraphia (1662–1681).

See Marpha (1664–1716).

See Saltykova, Praskovya (1664–1723).

See Eudoxia Lopukhina (1669–1731).

See Catherine I of Russia (1684–1727).

See Anna Ivanovna (1693–1740).

See Elizabeth Petrovna (1709–1762).

See Catherine II the Great (1729–1796).

See Sophia Dorothea of Wurttemberg (1759–1828).

See Elizabeth of Baden (1779–1826).

See Marie of Hesse-Darmstadt (1824–1880).

See Marie Feodorovna (1847–1928).

See Alexandra Feodorovna (1872–1918).

Russia, grand duchess of.

See Anna Pavlovna (1795–1865).

See Helene of Wurttemberg (1807–1873).

See Olga of Russia (1822–1892).

See Marie Alexandrovna (1853–1920).

See Maria of Mecklenburg-Schwerin (1854–1920).

See Ella (1864–1918).

See Helena of Russia (1882–1957).

See Olga Alexandrovna (1882–1960).

See Karadjordjevic, Helen (1884–1962).

See Alexandra Feodorovna for sidebar on Olga (1895–1918).

See Alexandra Feodorovna for sidebar on Tatiana (1897–1918).

See Anastasia (1901–1918).

Russudan, Rusudan, or Rusudani.

See Tamara for sidebar.

Rute, Mme de (1831–1902)

French novelist. Name variations: Marie-Laetitia-Studolmine Wyse; Mme de Solms; Comtesse Rattazzi. Born in County Cork, Ireland, in 1831; died in 1902; daughter of Sir Thomas Wyse and Laetitia Bonaparte (daughter of Lucien Bonaparte); married three times.

Selected writings: Bicheville (1865); Les Mariages de la Créole (1866).

Mme de Rute was born Marie-Laetitia-Studolmine Wyse in County Cork, Ireland, into a family whose fortunes were largely determined by political intrigue. Her father Sir Thomas Wyse was an English noble. Her mother **Laetitia Bonaparte** was the daughter of Lucien Bonaparte and his second wife *****Alexandrine Jouberthon Bona-** **parte**. Lucien's relationship with Alexandrine was not condoned by his older brother, Emperor Napoleon I (who had attempted to bribe Lucien into divorcing her), and so their ten children and their children's children, including Laetitia and her daughter, were never recognized as Bonapartes by the French ruling family.

After her first marriage, Mme de Rute, then known as Mme de Solms, lived in France until forced to leave by Napoleon III's disapproval in 1853. She later returned to France, where her novel *Bicheville* (1865), which was set in Florence, was published. However, she was forced to leave the country again in 1865, after her subsequent novel, *Les Mariages de la Créole* (published the following year in Brussels), was refused publication.

SOURCES:
Harvey, Sir Paul, and J.E. Heseltine, comp. and eds. *The Oxford Companion to French Literature.* Oxford: Oxford University Press, 1959.

Andrea Bewick,
freelance writer, Santa Rosa, California

Ruth (fl. 1100 BCE)

Moabite widow of the Old Testament, model of unwavering devotion, who moved with Naomi, her mother-in-law, to Judah where she met and married Boaz and became the great-grandmother of King David. Flourished around 1100 BCE; born in Moab; possibly the daughter of King Eglon of Moab; married Mahlon (son of Naomi and Elimelech); married Boaz; children: (second marriage) son Obed (grandfather of King David).

According to the Book of Ruth, during the time of the Judges a famine ravished the land of Judah, and Elimelech, an Israelite of Bethlehem, **Naomi**, his wife, and two sons, sought their livelihood in neighboring Moab. While in Moab, Elimelech died, and ten years later his sons followed him to the grave. Now Naomi was left alone with her two daughters-in-law, Moabite women whom her sons had married while in exile. Destitute, Naomi decided to return to her homeland in Judah where the famine which drove her family out had subsided. She urged her sons' wives to return to their mothers' homes and seek new marriages with Moabite men. Despite their tears and pleas, Naomi insisted, explaining that she was too old to bear more sons who might become husbands to the two widowed women. One daughter, *Orpah, reluctantly heeded her mother-in-law's entreaty and, kissing Naomi, returned home. But the other daughter, Ruth, steadfastly refused to leave, in-

See sidebar on the following page

❧▶ Naomi (fl. 1100 BCE)

Biblical woman. Name variations: Noemi. Born in Bethlehem, in Judah; married Elimelech; mother-in-law of Ruth; children: Mahlon (who married Ruth); Chilion (who married Orpah).

Said to be an outstanding beauty, Naomi made her home in Bethlehem with her husband Elimelech and her sons Mahlon and Chilion, until the great famine forced the family to migrate to Moab, east of the Dead Sea. Over the next ten years, Naomi lost both her husband and her sons, after which she made plans to return to her homeland. Although she told her daughters-in-law, *Ruth and *Orpah, to return with their families in Moab and find new husbands, Ruth, Mahlon's widow, insisted on accompanying her mother-in-law, saying, "Wherever you go, I will go" (Ruth 1:16). The women reached Bethlehem at harvest time, and Ruth went to work gleaning in the fields. There she met Boaz, a wealthy kinsman of Naomi's late husband. Having no claim to Elimelech's estate, but hoping to keep it in the family, Naomi encouraged Ruth to seek the favor of Boaz. Ruth and Boaz eventually married and had a son Obed, who was the grandfather of King David.

sisting that wherever Naomi went she would go, where Naomi found shelter, so would she. Naomi's people would be Ruth's people and Naomi's God, Ruth's God. Where Naomi died, so would Ruth. The two arrived empty-handed in Bethlehem, and when the women of the town asked, "Could this be Naomi?," the widow insisted that she now be called "Mara," which means "bitter," because of her misfortune. She did not realize that, through God's ineffable agency, redemption stood right beside her in the person of Ruth, her foreign, widowed, and childless daughter-in-law.

It was the beginning of the barley harvest, and Ruth agreed to go to the fields to glean the grain the reapers left behind; this was, by law, a privilege of the poor (Lv 19.9–10; Dt 24.19–22). She happened onto the land of a particular farmer named Boaz, meaning "in him is strength," who was a wealthy kinsman of Naomi's husband. Ruth waited for hours to meet the proprietor and seek special permission to glean his fields and collect grain from among the sheaves. Boaz not only confirmed Ruth's right to glean, but told her to stay close to his servant girls, drink from his workers' jars, and share the midday meal with his reapers. This way the men in the field would not bother her. He even instructed his reapers to intentionally abandon, in Ruth's path, grain that had already been reaped. Boaz had heard of the Moabite's

kindness to Naomi and sought to reward it, even though Ruth was a foreigner and from a tribe unfriendly to Judah. She thanked her benefactor who, she claimed, had treated her as one of his own "maidservants." At the day's end, Ruth returned to her mother-in-law with her abundant gleanings. When she told her about Boaz, Naomi praised God for his goodness, for she knew that Boaz was in a position to act as her *gō'ēl* (redeemer) because of his relationship to her husband. A *gō'ēl* was a relative who had particular obligations within the kin-group, one of which was to purchase a relative's land if that land had to be sold out of economic need; this way property was maintained within a clan (Lv 25.25, 47–55). Naomi began to devise a plan.

Ruth continued to glean in Boaz's fields through the barley harvest and into the wheat harvest. At the end of the season, Naomi revealed her daring scheme to her daughter-in-law. Ruth was to bathe, perfume herself, dress in her finest clothes, and go stealthily to the threshing-floor where Boaz would be spending the night near the piles of newly winnowed grain. She was to keep herself concealed until Boaz was fulsome from eating and drinking; when he lay down to sleep, Ruth was to "uncover his feet." Naomi concluded her instructions with the enigmatic: "He will tell you what next to do." Ruth followed her mother-in-law's instructions. Around midnight (in the Bible, the time of reckoning), she sidled up to Boaz, lifted his blanket, and lay beside him. He awoke startled and asked who was there. Ruth revealed her identity, "I am your handmaid." She urged Boaz to spread his robe over her—thus becoming her protector—and also to act as *gō'ēl* to Naomi, that is, to buy her land. Boaz was pleased by both requests; he was no longer young, and he praised Ruth for placing duty before vanity. Instead of seeking a young, more attractive mate, Ruth had considered Naomi's welfare, for only by marriage within Naomi's clan could Ruth be the instrument of her mother-in-law's security. However, Boaz informed Ruth of an obstacle to her second request; there was another man in town who was a closer relative to Naomi's husband than he, and that man had first rights as redeemer. Boaz assured his would-be bride that he would see what he could do. The two spent the night together on the threshing floor, and in the morning Boaz filled Ruth's shawl with six measures of barley and helped her slip away unnoticed.

That day Boaz went to the town gate, the venue for legal translations in ancient Judah, and found Naomi's kinsman (not named in the text) who had legal rights with regard to the property of Naomi. Before ten elders Boaz asked the kinsman if he wished to buy Naomi's land, which presumably she could not work herself, to keep it from leaving the clan. When the kinsman replied, "I shall redeem it," Boaz informed the witnesses that he himself would "acquire" Ruth and that their first son would be pledged to Ruth's dead husband, Mahlon, "in order to perpetuate the memory of the deceased upon his estate." In other words, the property in question would be inherited by the child of Ruth and Boaz (acting as proxy for Mahlon). This changed the circumstances; the kinsman withdrew his offer to buy the land so the property fell to Boaz. To seal the bargain, a sandal was exchanged between the two men, according to the legal customs of Israel.

All in Bethlehem were pleased by the turn of events. The townswomen praised the once-alien Ruth, and compared her to the most esteemed matriarchs of Israel: *Rachel, ❦➤ Leah, and Tamar. The couple had a son, Obed, who would carry on the line of Elimelech and Naomi and become the grandfather of the great King David. Naomi was no longer "bitter." The women of Bethlehem professed, "Blessed be the Lord who, on this very day, did not deny you a redeemer."

The Book of Ruth is one of only two canonical Biblical texts named after a woman. Its length (four chapters); simple, symmetrical structure; and modest narrative style belie the ideological and literary complexity of this masterful tale. Scholarly research on *Ruth* has centered on the date of its composition, the role of divine intervention, the genre or literary mode of the story, social and legal features, and, most recently, on feminist issues. (When the word *Ruth* is italicized in this entry it refers to the Biblical book rather than to Ruth, the character.)

Ruth was accepted into the canon in the mid-2nd century BCE. In the Jewish tradition, the book belongs to the third division of the Hebrew Bible known as the Writings, and it is among a smaller collection of *Megilloth* (five scrolls) which, since the early Middle Ages, have been recited at major festivals, *Ruth* being read at Shavu'ot, the Feast of Weeks (or Pentecost), which marks the harvest festival of the first-fruits in mid-April. This is most likely because the story starts during the barley harvest and ends with the wheat harvest. In most Hebrew Bibles, *Ruth* follows Proverbs which ends with a poem in praise of a "worthy woman." The placement of the Book of Ruth is controversial because of the uncertainty of the date of its composition. The first line of *Ruth* reveals that the

events occurred "Long ago, in the time of the judges" (c. 1350–1050 BCE), but it is not at all clear whether this assignation is literal or fictive. Also, although the last six verses of the book place the events three generations before the life of King David (c. 970), many scholars argue that the genealogy of David was tacked on after the tale was composed and so provides no sure information about the book's composition.

The date of *Ruth* is important because the historical context of its production could provide insight to the author's message. Scholars tend to divide into two broad groups as to the date of the book: those who believe it to have been written before the Jews were carried into exile in Babylon (587 BCE), and those who argue that the book is post-exilic, written after the Jews returned from Babylon (537 BCE), likely in the 5th or 4th century BCE. Most of the arguments for the date of *Ruth* are based on three factors: linguistic clues, legal customs, and external evidence. *Ruth* contains some Aramaic words, and Aramaic began to supplant Hebrew only after the Babylonian exile, but this evidence is not conclusive because well before the Babylonian period, Hebrew included a few Aramaic loan-words and phrases.

Those hoping to date *Ruth* based on legal traditions note that the laws of property transaction and marriage described in the story do not square with Israelite practices as laid out in Deuteronomy (25.5–10), written in the 7th and 8th centuries BCE. For instance, there has been some confusion over the trading of the shoe ceremony at the gate when Boaz redeems Naomi's property. More important, the custom of levirate marriage (the arrangement whereby the brother of a deceased man marries the man's widow and raises children in the name of the deceased) is broadened or misinterpreted in *Ruth*. Modern scholars are by no means agreed on whether levirate marriage plays a role in the story at all. Many translations of the scene at the city gate have Boaz telling the next-of-kin that if he acts as *gō'ēl* and buys Naomi's land he must also marry Ruth to perpetuate Mahlon's line. But neither the kinsman at the gate nor Boaz are brother-in-law to Ruth, so neither is obliged to marry her under the obligations of levirate marriage. In whatever way the puzzling scene at the gate is interpreted, the legal evidence in *Ruth* is no more conclusive than linguistics in dating the book. *Ruth* could have been written before the marriage laws articulated in Deuteronomy were set, i.e. before the 8th century. Or, as those who claim the book is post-exilic argue, the imprecision about marriage and property laws may

Leah. See joint entry under Rachel and Leah.

mean the book was written when the legal customs it describes were archaic, had undergone development, or were no longer understood or enforced. After all, the author prefaces the sandal ceremony with, "This was formerly done in Israel," which presupposes the readers' unfamiliarity with the ancient procedure. But some writers counter that *Ruth* was intentionally placed in an ambiguous, distant past to give it a hoary, mythic quality. Another possibility is that the story of *Ruth* experienced a long period of development and transmission (either oral or written) and was finally recorded in its present form after the exile; this could account for the inconsistencies and snippets of law, language, and custom from various periods of Israelite history.

*W*here you go, I will go, and where you stay, I will stay. Your people shall be my people, and your God my God. Where you die, I will die, and there will I be buried. . . . Nothing but death shall divide us.

—Ruth to Naomi (1.16–17)

A third criteria for dating has to do with Israel's relationship to Moab. The Book of Ruth is audacious in its celebration of a Moabite heroine. Not only is Ruth a woman of great merit comparable to Israel's matriarchs, Leah and Rachel, but she is the ancestor of King David. This is startling because Moab and Israel were traditional enemies. Moabites refused to feed the Israelites when they were starving, and Moab was the home of Balak, who summoned Balaam to curse Israel (Nm 22–24). The Moabites battled with Saul (1 Sm 14.47), and Moabite women corrupted Hebrew men (Nm 25). Deuteronomy 23.2–6 says no Moabite "shall enter the assembly of the Lord even to the tenth generation." On a moralistic level, the Moabites were thought to be polluted as the race came about as a result of Lot's incest with his unnamed eldest daughter (Gn 19.30–38), and both Ezra (9–10) and Nehemiah (13.23–29) forbid marriage between Israelites and Moabites. It has been suggested that *Ruth* must have been written during a period when relations between Moab and Israel were tranquil: late 5th to mid-4th century BCE. By the same reasoning, some date the book to the much earlier monarchical period (c. 1000), when many neighboring peoples were incorporated into the political kingdom of Israel without rancor.

Controversies over dating and interpretation are closely related in an important issue concerning Ruth's marginality: she is a woman, without a male protector, childless, and foreign.

Much is made of her foreignness; it is mentioned several times. When Boaz first sees Ruth in his fields, he asks, "To whom does she belong?" The response summarizes her status: "This woman is an unmarried Moabitess." In the Middle Ages, rabbinic commentators (Jewish religious leaders) were uncomfortable enough with the ethnicity of Ruth that they tendered various proposals to bring the story into line with Biblical proscriptions; hence, some Rabbis said that it was only Moabite men whom the Book of Deuteronomy forbade becoming Jews. Others claimed that Elimelech did not allow Mahlon and Chilion to marry Moabite women; they did so after their father died, and this violation of deuteronomic law was the cause of their deaths. Also, Elimelech himself was punished with death for escaping to Moab during famine.

How and why, then, was a poor, childless Moabite woman raised to the status of Israel's national heroines? One possibility is that the Book of Ruth was written partially as a protest against Israelite exclusiveness or xenophobia. When the Persians defeated the Babylonians in 537 BCE, they allowed the Jews held captive in Babylon to return to their homeland. These returning refugees faced the challenge of reintegrating themselves into the population which had remained in Judah and of reorganizing society under Persian overlordship. In this atmosphere of uncertainty, attitudes rigidified as to who was a "legitimate Jew" and who a foreigner. Both Ezra and Nehemiah categorically exclude from legitimacy the progeny of mixed marriages between Moabites and Israelites. For some, the Book of Ruth, despite its serene, nonpolemical tone and idyllic surroundings, is a critique against this kind of particularism. Another explanation for elevating Ruth, of such objectionable heritage, to a position of honor is that it was well known that King David had a strain of Moabite blood; therefore, it behooved the Rabbis to come to terms with this "fact" and to bolster Ruth's fitness as progenitor to Israel's greatest king by presenting the Moabite ancestress in the best possible light. They attempted to underplay Ruth's foreignness by focusing on her conversion or comparing her with Abraham—both were foreigners, chosen by God to leave their homelands and become forbearers of illustrious individuals. Though not implied in the text, she was said by the Rabbis to be lovely like a girl of 14, modest (she gleaned sitting down, not bending over), and the daughter of King Eglon of Moab. Ruth became, at the hands of medieval commentators (both Jewish and Christian), the ideal of female beauty and comportment.

But was she such a model of perfect womanhood? Some feminist commentators agree with the opinion of the Rabbis but evaluate the merit of her character differently. They view Ruth as a poor role model, arguing she is too submissive and obedient. For this group of scholars, the premise of the Book of Ruth is that the protagonist willingly and uncritically submits to the "degrading" custom of levirate marriage which ensures the patrilineage of a dead male, and, in this case, fills a gap in the patriarchal hierarchy leading up to King David. Most feminist scholarship, however, tends to see Ruth in a more "favorable" light as courageous, inventive, pro-active, and even subtly subversive. For them *Ruth* is a story of two female protagonists, fiercely loyal to each other, struggling to survive in and transform their patriarchal world.

It is the women in *Ruth* who play the dominant, active, and morally commendable roles. Jack Sasson, in his folkloric analysis, has determined that Ruth plays the part of "hero" which is traditionally filled by a male. She actively pursues her goals, overcomes adversity, and brings her quest to a successful conclusion. While in Moab she refuses to leave her mother-in-law, despite being pressed to do so three times. Ruth makes sure she meets Boaz face to face on her first day of gleaning; she will not glean without his permission, although that permission is not necessary. On the threshing floor, she exceeds the instructions given her by Naomi and, through creative improvisation, initiates the chain of events that not only provides her a husband, but assures her mother-in-law an heir and the ownership of her property. Boaz, the prominent male in the story, is always a secondary character and largely a foil for Ruth. His sluggishness highlights her virtues to good advantage (the Jewish Midrash portrays him as 80 years old and has him die after only one day of marriage). Although the author does not censure Boaz for dereliction of duty in not recognizing his clan responsibility, he is passive and dependent on the imaginative manipulation of the women. "He has patriarchal power, but he does not have narrative power. He has authority within the story but not control over it" (Trible 176). He sleeps while Ruth acts.

In opposition to the view of some feminists that *Ruth* deconstructs the gender boundaries of the rigid male-dominated culture in which the character finds herself, it can as easily be said that Ruth, above all characters in the book, is the most prescient and solicitous of the needs of the patriarchy. She becomes the agent for mending broken bonds and assuring the permanence

of God's ordained social order. For this reason, Ruth is paralleled to ❧➤ **Tamar** (Gn 38), a woman who also understood the necessity of continuation of the male line. Tamar was the wife of Er, son of Judah. When Tamar's husband died, she married his brother, Onan, according to the demands of levirate marriage. Onan also died, and Tamar was returned to her "father's house." She was distraught because the imperative of fostering sons in the name of her deceased husband weighed heavy on her. Tamar dressed herself as a prostitute and, veiled, seduced her father-in-law, Judah. When she became pregnant, he voiced the judgment of the Jewish tradition in his praise: "She has been more just than I." She recognized her duty to family.

Ruth is also compared to Leah and Rachel, the two wives of Jacob, who resourcefully satisfied the demands of the patriarchal laws of their culture and in so doing proved how thoroughly they comprehended God's mandates. Jacob loved the beautiful Rachel, who appeared to be barren, and shunned the less alluring but fertile Leah. The two women recognized that Jacob's trivial preferences and their own jealous competitiveness were standing in the way of God's designs: the building up of his people. Therefore, with one another's help they both had children, who fathered the Twelve Tribes of Israel (Gn 30.1–25). Just as these two women working together built God's elect nation, another pair of women collaborated to restore it. (Naomi and Ruth sometimes even are conflated in the text. For instance, when Ruth has Obed the townswomen say, "Naomi has a son.") Lot was the son of Abraham, who, well before the time of Ruth, separated from his father's people on the Plain of Jordan (Gn 13.7–13). Lot was the father of Moab, who was born of Lot's eldest daughter. She seduced her father by "trickery" in order that his line might not die out (Gn 19.30–38). Lot was forefather to Ruth the Moabite, and Boaz was the descendent of Abraham. Therefore, in Obed, Ruth's son, the ancient rift was mended for the blood of Lot and Abraham mixed in his veins. Further, through a harmonious collaboration, or as the text says, by "clinging together," Ruth and Naomi become

❧➤ **Tamar** (fl. 1100 BCE)
Biblical woman. Flourished around 1100 BCE; married Er (son of Judah, died); married his brother Onan (son of Judah, died); children: (with Judah) twin sons, Perez and Zerah.

the ancestral mothers of the king who united and led the Twelve Tribes of Israel. The women featured in *Ruth* (Rachel, Leah, Tamar, Naomi, and Ruth), each in her own way, weave together the torn fabric of family and thereby restore and redeem the Lord's people.

Both historical commentators and modern scholars have noted that the women extolled in *Ruth* employ sexual stratagems to achieve their ends. (Even the male protagonist, Boaz, is associated with dubious carnal activity; he is the son of the prostitute *Rahab [Mt 1:5; Heb 11.31].) The vignette of Ruth and Boaz at the threshing floor has attracted attention because of the sexual tension caused by its ambiguity. Those who see Ruth as a model of virtue—ancestor of both David and Jesus (Mt 1.5–16)—are anxious to interpret the scene exactly as written: Ruth uncovers Boaz's feet and lies by them. In so doing she follows her mother-in-law's instructions and makes herself a symbol of great humility. But a careful philological investigation reveals that the metaphoric language may be meant to describe the couple's betrothal and its consummation. One scholar, referring to Naomi's instructions to Ruth, interprets the Hebrew *gillit margelotaw* (which is usually translated "uncover his feet") as "take your clothes off at the place by his feet." "Foot" (*regel*) is a common Biblical euphemism for penis. When Boaz awakens startled and asks who is there, Ruth responds, "Ruth, your *āmāh*," which means "marriageable woman." She implores Boaz to "spread [his] cloak over [his] maidservant," asking that Boaz take her as his woman. The word for cloak is *kānāp*, which also means "wing," and the phrase Ruth uses is a Biblical metaphor for betrothal (Ezekiel 16.8). After the discussion the two "lie down." Whether they sleep the night away or consummate their secret betrothal is left provocatively ambiguous. Ephrem the Syrian (d. 373 CE), a Christian theologian, felt no confusion about the activities of Ruth and Boaz that night, nor did he question the virtue of their motives. In his *Hymns of Nativity* Ephrem wrote, "The throbbing coal went up and fell down in Boaz's bed. She saw the high priest who was hidden in his loins: fire for his incense. She ran and was a heifer for Boaz. She would bring forth [Christ], the fatted calf" (15). The comparison the men at the gate make between Ruth and Tamar reinforces the likelihood that Ruth and Boaz had intercourse that night on the threshing floor. In both cases, the woman, adorned and anointed, takes the initiative to the same worthy end. The grain Boaz gives Ruth in the morning, which is possibly a betrothal gift, is meant also

for Naomi who came back from Moab "empty." Now she will have both grain and children. When Ruth returns home, Naomi asks her the strange question, "Who are you?," which some have read as, "Whose wife are you?" Naomi is asking her daughter-in-law whether the betrothal has been accomplished. Ruth relates "all that the man had done to her."

Traditionally, Jewish scholarship has attributed the authorship of *Ruth* to the prophet Samuel (Babylonian Talmud, *Baba Bathra* 14b), the same man who purportedly wrote Judges, but that seems unlikely because Samuel died before David became king. Recently, convincing arguments have been proffered that *Ruth* was authored by a woman, possibly an old wise-woman, which may account for the book's empathy with Naomi. One scholar identifies the writer as *Tamar (fl. 1000 BCE), daughter of King David. However, attaining proof that the person who actually committed the story to writing was a woman is less promising (perhaps less interesting) than the studies that investigate the way that *Ruth* reflects a woman's culture, voice, and textual authority. Authorial activity and literacy need not be equated. There is a decided absence of androcentrism in the story; women—their concerns and perspectives—comprise the substance of the narrative. For instance, while in Moab Naomi tells Orpah and Ruth to return to their mothers' houses, not the more common "father's house."

Another hint that *Ruth* may be authored (if not actually committed to writing) by a woman/women is the role of the Bethlehemite female "chorus" which provides the communal voice. Although the townswomen do not have the legislative or judicial power that the men exercise at the city gate, they have authority and the capacity to assess and articulate group values. It is they who pronounce for the reader the final judgment on the events of the narrative, interpreting the impact of the elders' legal decisions and harmonizing them with the women's world around which the narrative revolves. Although the climax of the story and the point at which all of its elements are integrated is the birth of a son, the women of Bethlehem pronounce Ruth worth more even than the "fullness" of seven sons.

There are many issues in *Ruth* upon which consensus has not been reached, but scholars tend to agree on the import of the book's theology. In *Ruth*, God's universal causality and lordship are ever-present, though hidden—expressed not through miracles, revelations, or displays of power, but within the lives of common people of unpretentious, even unsavory, backgrounds. The ancient historian Flavius Josephus (d. around 100 CE) wrote, "God . . . advanced David [to dignity and splendor], though he were born of such mean parents" (*Antiquities* V.ix.4). God is an invisible character in the story, but he does direct human action and finally answers all prayers. In the barley fields, when Ruth asks Boaz why he is taking notice of her when she is a foreigner, the term she uses is *nochria* which means "someone who is seen." She is seen because she is strange. She describes herself from Boaz's perspective because she knows that she is dependent on his gaze, just as she is dependent on God's gaze or grace. In this sense Ruth epitomizes the position of all humans with respect to God.

A second theological function of the book is to celebrate particular virtues, such as faithfulness (both human and divine) and *hesed*, meaning "just charity," or "duty willingly performed." The setting of the story is likely the period of the Judges because those were dark days; the Israelites were disregarding their covenant, and moral leadership was lacking. "In those days Israel had no king, and everyone did as he saw fit" (Jgs 21.25). By contrast, Ruth puts duty first, and, through her offspring, Israel is supplied the leadership it lacks. For many Israelites, the most important word of the book was the last one: David.

The genre of *Ruth* is debatable. It has been called an idyll, a simple pastoral story with no evil characters, comedy, historical novel, subversive parable, folk tale, short story, old Canaanite oral poem, and nursery tale. It is well suited to public performance; no other book in the Hebrew Bible has a higher ratio of dialogue to narrative text. Like ancient story-telling, only two characters engage in conversation at a time. The text is skillfully constructed with a classical literary configuration employing careful patterning based on numerology, chiasmi, assonance, punning, and play on names. Stylistic factors have been employed in efforts to date the book. The delicate psychological portrayal of characters similar to court histories of David, the gracious manners, and even specific phrases resemble the patriarchal narratives in Genesis, Samuel, and Kings.

Some scholars view *Ruth* as, at base, folk mythology artificially freighted by redactors and commentators with political and theological overtones. Many have looked for parallels to the story's heroines in the literatures of neighboring cultures. Ruth has been compared with near eastern "deceptive goddesses" associated with motifs of sexual exchange, drunkenness, and feasting. Sasson suggests that Boaz was frightened of Ruth when he was awakened on the threshing floor because he thought she might be the female demon Lilith. The text calls Naomi both "the pleasant one" and "the bitter one," a pair of appellations known as an epithet of Anat, a Canaanite goddess. Some writers also have seen a connection to the Greek myth of Demeter: Naomi and Ruth are the two sides of womanhood—youth and age—like Demeter and Persephone, and the story is set during the harvest. Naomi has been compared to the Egyptian Isis, a widow who seeks an heir for her deceased husband. *Ruth* may be connected to fertility myths of Canaanite origin: Bethlehem means "house of bread" and clan territory around Bethlehem is Ephratha meaning "fertility." The famine mentioned at the beginning of *Ruth* may originally have been the result, not the cause, of Naomi's departure.

The compelling story of Ruth has inspired surprisingly little great art and literature. The most famous medieval artistic treatment is from the 12th century *Admont Bible* which treats the subjects of Ruth gleaning and the couple's marriage. Nicolas Poussin's (d. 1665) portrayal of *Summer* shows Ruth among the gleaners, and Rembrandt van Rijn's (d. 1669) *The Jewish Bride* is likely a representation of the nuptials of Boaz and Ruth. The widows' return to Judah is commemorated in the Dutch painter Willem Drost's (d. 1680) *Ruth and Naomi*. William Blake (d. 1827) produced a watercolor of Naomi, Ruth, and Orpah in Moab, and Jean François Millet (d. 1875) portrays Boaz instructing Ruth to lunch with his reapers in *Harvesters Resting*.

Both Jewish and Christian commentaries on *Ruth* were produced in the Middle Ages, and in the modern period a few plays and poems in Spanish, French, German, and English have been based on the tale. John Keats' "Ode to a Nightingale" (1819) mentions Ruth: "Perhaps the self-same song that found a path/ Through the sad heart of Ruth when, sick for home,/ she stood in tears amid the alien corn," and one of the most moving poems in Victor Hugo's *La légende des siècles* (1859), "Booz endormi," explores the elderly Boaz's mysterious experience of love. Two contemporary novels by American authors have appeared since World War II: *Ruth* (1949) by Irving Fineman, and *The Song of Ruth: A Love Story from the Old Testament* (1954) by Frank G. Slaughter.

Most modern discussion about *Ruth* focuses on its date and author and how that author understood and reflected his or her own culture.

However, a story as rich as *Ruth* is not limited to the function it had in its original place and time. In any milieu Ruth is a woman to be revered for her devotion and admired for her spirit. Although she is cooperative and selfless, we need not see Ruth as subservient because she supports community values; quite apart from subverting a narrow patriarchy, she appropriates and humanizes it.

SOURCES:

Bellis, Alice Ogden. *Helpmates, Harlots, and Heroes: Women's Stories in the Hebrew Bible.* Louisville, KY: Westminster Press, 1994.

Brenner, Athalya, ed. *A Feminist Companion to Ruth.* Sheffield: Sheffield Academic Press, 1993.

Campbell, Edward F. *Ruth.* 2nd ed. The Anchor Bible, vol. 7. Garden City, NY: Doubleday, 1975.

Fewell, D.N., and D.M. Gunn. *Compromising Redemption: Relating Characters in the Book of Ruth.* Louisville, KY: Westminster Press, 1990.

Knight, Douglas A., and Gene M. Tucker, eds. *The Hebrew Bible and Its Modern Interpreters.* Philadelphia, PA: Fortress Press, 1985.

Larkin, Katrina J.A. *Ruth and Esther.* Sheffield: Sheffield Academic Press, 1996.

Meyers, Carol. *Discovering Eve: Ancient Israelite Women in Context.* NY: Oxford University Press, 1988.

Sasson, Jack M. *Ruth: A New Translation with a Philological Commentary and a Formalist-Folklorist Interpretation.* 2nd ed. The Biblical Seminar. Sheffield: JSOT Press, 1989.

Trible, Phyllis. *God and the Rhetoric of Sexuality.* Philadelphia, PA: Fortress Press, 1978.

Wolde, Ellen van. *Ruth and Naomi.* Translated by John Bowden. Macon, GA: Smyth and Helwys, 1998.

SUGGESTED READING:

Brenner, Athalya, and Fokkelien van Dijk-Hemmes. *On Gendering Texts: Female and Male Voices in the Hebrew Bible.* Leiden: Brill, 1993.

Gow, M.D. *The Book of Ruth: Its Structure, Theme and Purpose.* Leicester: Apollos, 1994.

Gray, John. *Joshua, Judges, and Ruth.* Grand Rapids, MI: Eerdmans, 1986.

Hals, Ronald M. *The Theology of the Book of Ruth.* Philadelphia, PA: Fortress, 1969.

Hubbard, R.L. *The Book of Ruth.* Grand Rapids, MI: Eerdmans, 1991.

Jöuon, Paul. *Ruth: commentaire philologique et exégétique.* 2nd ed. Biblical Institute Press. Rome, 1986.

LaCocque, André. *The Feminine Unconventional: Four Subversive Figures in Israel's Tradition.* Minneapolis, MN: Fortress Press, 1990.

Myers, Jacob M. *The Linguistic and Literary Form of the Book of Ruth.* Leiden: Brill, 1955.

Zakovitch, Y. *Ruth: A Commentary.* Jerusalem: Magnes, 1990 (for Jewish reading of Ruth).

Martha Rampton,
Assistant Professor of History, Pacific University,
Forest Grove, Oregon

Ruth-Rolland, J.M. (1937–1995)

Central African official. Name variations: Jeanne-Marie Ruth-Rolland. Born in 1937; died in Paris, France, on June 4, 1995.

Trained as a teacher, Jeanne-Marie Ruth-Rolland became the director of social services in the army of the Central African Republic. She was also an adviser to the prime minister on women's issues and a campaigner on behalf of the homeless children of the republic's capital, Bangui. But her candor was anathema to the republic's military ruler, General Andre Kolingba, and she was imprisoned for five years (1986–91). Upon her release, she joined the Cabinet as its minister of social affairs in 1992–93. She died in a hospital in Paris of unreported causes at age 58.

Rutherford, Margaret (1892–1972)

English actress who rose to stardom in middle age and created an ensemble of eccentrics for film and stage, including Agatha Christie's Miss Marple. Born Margaret Taylor Rutherford on May 11, 1892, at 15 Dornton Road, Balham, England; died on May 22, 1972, at Chalfont St. Peter, England; daughter of William Rutherford Benn and Florence (Nicholson) Benn; married (James Buckley) Stringer Davis (an actor), on March 26, 1945; children: adopted four children, including writer **Dawn Langley Hall Simmons** *(d. September 18, 2000, who before her sex-correction operation in 1968 was known as Gordon Langley Hall).*

Filmography: Dusty Ermine *(Hideout in the Alps, 1936);* Talk of the Devil *(1936);* Beauty and the Barge *(1937);* Catch as Catch Can *(1937);* Quiet Wedding *(1940);* The Yellow Canary *(1943);* The Demi-Paradise *(Adventure for Two, 1943);* English Without Tears *(1944);* Her Man Gilbey *(1944);* Blithe Spirit *(1945);* Meet Me at Dawn *(1946);* While the Sun Shines *(1947);* Miranda *(1948);* Passport to Pimlico *(1949);* The Happiest Days of Your Life *(1950);* Her Favorite Husband *(The Taming of Dorothy, 1950); (cameo)* The Magic Box *(1951);* Curtain Up *(1952);* Castle in the Air *(1952);* Miss Robin Hood *(1952); (as Miss Prism)* The Importance of Being Earnest *(1952);* Innocents in Paris *(1953);* Trouble in Store *(1953);* The Runaway Bus *(1954);* Mad About Men *(1954);* Aunt Clara *(1954);* An Alligator Named Daisy *(1955);* The Smallest Show on Earth *(1957);* Just My Luck *(1957);* I'm All Right Jack *(1959);* On the Double *(1961);* Murder She Said *(1961);* The VIPS *(1963);* Murder at the Gallop *(1963);* The Mouse on the Moon *(1963);* Murder Ahoy *(1964);* Murder Most Foul *(1964); (cameo)* The Alphabet Murders *(1966);* Chimes at Midnight *(1966);* A Countess from Hong Kong *(1967); (voice)* The Wacky World of Mother Goose *(1967);* Arabella *(1968).*

Margaret Rutherford was 13 when she learned that her father, whom she had been told had died in India nursing the sick when she was a baby, had not died at all. Instead, he was living in Broadmoor, an asylum for the criminally insane. Throughout her life, she kept the news secret, fearful of exposure that would end her career and fearful for her own sanity.

Soon after her parents married in 1882, her father William Rutherford Benn, having manifested symptoms of manic-depression, had entered the Bethnal House Asylum in East London. William was known to talk to himself and quote from the Bible. His father, the Reverend Julius Benn, a dedicated evangelist who worked with the poor, was concerned for his son and arranged to have him stay at a home in Matlock to live with a "Godly and properly Christian couple" for a period of rest. Margaret's mother **Florence Benn**, too young to cope, heartily agreed. Thus, it was the Reverend Benn who accompanied his son to Matlock and stayed the night with him before returning home. The next morning, Reverend Benn was dead. The *Derbyshire Times* (March 7, 1883) reported that when the master of the cottage in Matlock entered the guest room, he found William Rutherford Benn standing "silent and erect in front of him in his night dress, his throat, beard, hands, night dress, legs and feet, dripping with blood, and without uttering a sound he dramatically pointed to the bed." He had smashed his father's skull in with a Staffordshire chamberpot, then unsuccessfully tried to take his own life by slitting his throat with a small pocket knife.

William's brother John came to his aid at the inquest, exhorting the judge to allow evidence as to William's state of mind, but the judge would have none of it and pronounced him guilty. When William, however, confused the chief constable with Pontius Pilate, he was remanded to Broadmoor. Seven years later, William was released and turned over to the care of his brother. Because of all the publicity, William legally dropped his surname and went by his mother's maiden name, Rutherford. Meanwhile, Florence had remained true, writing him daily, and the couple reunited. Now known as Mr. and Mrs. Rutherford, they moved into a home in Balham. There, on May 11, 1892, Margaret Taylor Rutherford was born.

Five years later, the family moved to India, where William, a poet at heart, worked as a silk merchant. Like his father, William also spent long hours working with the poor and nursing victims of cholera. When Florence became preg-

nant once again, William offered to send her back to England but she refused. It was now Florence, nearing term, who was manifesting restless and disturbed behavior. William wired for her sister Bessie to come help. But before Bessie could arrive, an Indian servant found Florence hanging from a tree. She had killed herself. The ordeal sent William over the edge once more. In October 1902, he was admitted to the Northumberland House Asylum. Over a year later, when he showed signs of homicidal tendencies, he was removed to Broadmoor where he remained until he died in 1921, age 66.

The unmarried Aunt Bessie, who lived in Wimbledon, became Rutherford's mother. After consulting the rest of the extended family, Bessie told Margaret her father had died. "I was allowed my own dream world," recalled Rutherford, "which my adoptive mother punctuated with her discipline. For instance, my back was weak, so every day I was made to lie motionless on the floor while she read to me in French. Later in my career I have been many times complimented on my carriage, ability to wear period clothes, and my meticulous French accent. This is all due to those morning sessions on the floor with Aunt Bessie."

Rutherford, known to family as Peggy, grew up lonely, her loneliness lessened only by occasional visits from a favorite cousin; the two wrote plays together. By age eight, Margaret knew she wanted to be an actress. Another cousin, however, was so against theater that Margaret had to "write a part for her where she was confined to a dark dreary cupboard for most of the performance."

At 13, the news of her father's existence sent Rutherford into "a fit of deep depression with long periods of silence broken occasionally by crying." Bessie, despite the significant drain to her finances, wanted her cherished daughter to experience a change of scene and learn something of the real world. Shortly after, in 1906, Rutherford was sent to Raven's Croft School, then located in Upper Warlingham, Surrey.

When Peggy Rutherford informed the headmistress that she intended to be a professional actress, she was immediately steered to the piano, a more respectable artistic endeavor for a lady. Unlike actresses, pianists did not form liaisons with the prince of Wales. Rutherford, who enjoyed the school, stayed an extra year because she loved taking care of the "little ones." "I have always had this motherly instinct," she once said, "and people find it easy to share their problems with me." Returning to Wimbledon to live with her adoptive mother while giving piano lessons, Rutherford became a familiar figure, biking to the homes of her students. But she still longed to be an actress. When Aunt Bessie dug down and found a little more money for acting lessons, Rutherford began studying with an old Shakespearean actor named Acton Bond and joined her local drama society. She spent some time during World War I reciting poetry to convalescing soldiers.

But after the war, Bessie endured a series of strokes and needed Margaret's care. "With her usual sense of order," wrote Rutherford's biographer and adopted daughter **Dawn Langley Simmons**, Bessie "calmly announced one morning to a tearful Margaret, 'It is quite unfair to you. I am taking much too long to die.' Moments later she was gone." The year was 1925 and Rutherford was now 33. With her small inheritance as well as money from the sale of the Wimbledon house, she rented a bedsitter (one-room apartment) in London, next door to Holloway Prison, and engaged a 60-year-old maid, **Elizabeth Orphin**, because Margaret was "bad with a sewing needle"; the two would remain good friends until Elizabeth's death years later.

With the help of acquaintances, Margaret managed to scare up an audition with the intimidating *Lilian Baylis, who ran the Old Vic. Though Baylis seemed less than impressed, she accepted Rutherford as a trainee actress for the 1925 September–May season. Unfortunately, it turned out to be only one season of nine roles; then Baylis let her go. For the next two years, Rutherford was once again biking to piano students. She joined the Wimbledon Amateur Theatrical Society and quickly learned two things: she had a knack for making people laugh and she thrived on it. She was finally engaged as an understudy for **Mabel Terry-Lewis** in *A Hundred Years Old* at the Lyric in Hammersmith. When Terry-Lewis took ill, Rutherford went on for 15 weeks. In 1929, she worked a season in repertory at the Grand in Fulham; 29 parts gave her ample experience. Between jobs, Margaret began to experience deep depression, a pattern that would continue the rest of her life; she was terrified that she might go mad.

While appearing in Ben Travers' comedy hit *Thark* at the Oxford Playhouse, Rutherford met Stringer Davis, an actor seven years her junior. Their courtship would last 15 years. Invited to join **Esmé Church**'s company at Croydon's Greyhound Theater, she suggested Davis sign with the theater as well. There, she played opposite Donald Wolfit as Mrs. Solness in *The Master Builder*. Though an impressed Wolfit claimed that she was the best Solness he had ever worked with and had the makings of a great tragic actress, Rutherford, despite her efforts, was acquiring a substantial reputation as a character actress and beginning to be typecast. "The parts I had been given had begun to show signs of the eccentricity that I later developed into my own special technique," she said.

In 1933, a small part at the Lyric in *Wild Justice* grew during rehearsals and the play was transferred to the West End. Following that, she reprised *The Master Builder* with Wolfit at the Embassy Theater, Swiss Cottage, and then went into rehearsal for *Jane Cowl's *Hervey House*, which starred *Gertrude Lawrence and *Fay Compton. Though the play had a short run, Rutherford's reviews were glowing. After that, she was featured in Robert Morley's *Short Story*, directed by Tyrone Guthrie. She was also handed her first film, *Dusty Ermine*, in another role which was expanded as the filming progressed. Margaret Rutherford was now working steadily.

In 1938, while playing the part of Aunt Bijou Furze in *The Spring Meeting*, a play by *Molly Keane and John Perry (written under the joint name M.J. Farrell), the character actress attained stardom. Her reputation now secure, she was offered the part of Miss Prism in the milestone production of Oscar Wilde's *The Importance of Being Earnest*, with John Gielgud directing and *Edith Evans as Lady Bracknell. (In 1947, Rutherford would replace Evans as Lady Bracknell for the North American tour; she remained, however, Miss Prism for the film version.) *Earnest* opened for eight charity performances at the Globe in January 1939 and was revived for a short run at Golders Green Hippodrome.

When World War II intervened, Stringer joined the military and along with most of the British army was rescued from the beach at Dunkirk. But Rutherford, who was living with her close friend and stand-in **Grace Bridges**, had a career that was sizzling. She agreed to play the menacing Mrs. Danvers to *Celia Johnson's Mrs. de Winter in *Daphne du Maurier's *Rebecca*. The play opened in April 1940 and only closed because a bomb shuttered the theater that September. Rutherford followed that with the role of Madame Arcati, the ditzy medium in Noel Coward's *Blithe Spirit*, though she warned Coward that she had great respect for mediums and would play Arcati straight. Of Madame Arcati, the critic for the *Tatler* wrote: "Miss Rutherford is not one of your pale anaemic dabblers in the psychic but a thoroughly hearty, bi-

Margaret
Rutherford

cycling *bon viveuse*, breathing deeply and skipping about with a triumph when she brings off a coup. To see her Madame Arcati get up from an armchair is a lesson in eccentric observation." *Blithe Spirit* ran for 1,997 performances. Despite the fact that Rutherford loathed long runs, she stayed with the show for over a year. (The play would be filmed in 1945 with David Lean directing.) From Prism to Danvers to Arcati, Rutherford had put her stamp on three magnificent roles in a row. Another favorite part of hers would be that of Lady Wishfort in William Congreve's *The Way of the World*, again directed by Gielgud at the Lyric in Hammersmith.

Near war's end, on March 26, 1945, Rutherford married Stringer Davis. "Ours was one of those romances that took a long time to bloom," she said. "For many years he had his mother, whom he loved dearly, to consider and I had my career. It was the war separation that changed everything. [He] suddenly realized that there is nothing worse in life than loneliness and that perhaps after all he might be husband material. It took him all that time to find himself in that respect, if you see." Since her career had eclipsed his, Rutherford generally had written in her contracts that Stringer be given a small role. In the 1950s, the couple lived on the second floor of Old Hall in Highgate, ex-home of Francis Bacon. *Rumer Godden and her husband lived on the main floor and the couples became friends. Mr. and Mrs. Stringer Davis would eventually settle at Elm Close, Gerrards Cross, outside London.

Rutherford, still concerned about her mental health, suffered when not working. In 1956, she had an extended bout with depression. "My nerves aren't the best," she told Howard Thompson of *The New York Times*. "I've had two breakdowns. Work can be a cure, but psychiatry saved me." In a BBC interview, she told Alex McIntosh: "One only has a breakdown when one feels that the whole of one's object for living has gone. One has lost one's roots, one has lost one's bearings; that, I think, is almost the deepest sadness that can be imagined in the world today and it is for that, that I have the most compassion, for people who are in that state, I think because I have been in that state myself." She called it her "melancholia." A bad patch required rest in a nursing home, or a guesthouse near the sea. For that reason, Rutherford took in orphans, many people who had lost their way. Among these were writer Gordon Langley Hall, then a 19-year-old who had been born with a swollen clitoris, been deemed a boy, and had lived with the unattended abnormality until she underwent a sex-correction operation in 1968, became Dawn Langley Hall, got married and became Dawn Langley Simmons, and had a child.

In 1962, Rutherford received an OBE (Officer of the Order of the British Empire) from Queen *Elizabeth II. Shortly thereafter, she was offered the role of Miss Marple, *Agatha Christie's stellar woman sleuth, in *Murder, She Said* for MGM. In order to take the part, Rutherford had to break a long-held rule. Because of her father, she had refused to do any role having to do with crime. But Rutherford was told that Marple was involved with solving puzzles, not crime; besides, Stringer had been offered the role of the village librarian. When she finally accepted, everyone was happy except Agatha Christie, who deplored the casting until she met Rutherford on the set and they became boon companions. Rutherford would go on to make three more "Miss Marple" movies.

Next came the role of the duchess of Brighton in the movie *The VIPs* with *Elizabeth Taylor and Richard Burton. At first, Rutherford turned down the job, but the writers were willing to listen to her criticism and came up with a duchess who had "both substance and integrity," noted Rutherford. That same part won her an Academy Award for Best Supporting Actress in 1963.

Another prolonged depression arrived in June 1965 and she had to bow out of a production of the *Solid Gold Cadillac* in London. Rutherford was also having trouble with her memory. As Mrs. Malaprop in the 1966 production of *The Rivals* at the Haymarket, she sometimes had to create her own malapropisms because she wasn't always sure of the lines. Even so, that same year Orson Welles requested her presence in his movie *Chimes at Midnight*. But, hired for a cameo in another movie, her problem grew worse, and her small scene had to be shot over so many times that she was replaced. "On that terrible day," wrote Eric Johns, "she was discovered hunched on a chair in the hall of her own home, sobbing her heart out as she repeated over and over again, 'I've been sacked!'" Essentially, it was the end of her career.

In 1967, with her inclusion in the queen's New Year's Honors List, she became Dame Margaret Rutherford. That November, while filming *Arabella*, an Italian movie in Rome, the 75-year-old Rutherford fell in her hotel room and broke her hip. Though the Italian doctor begged her to stay with her hip in plaster for a month, she returned to London. From then on, she walked with two canes.

Margaret Rutherford had always been much too generous with her money and barely one step ahead of the English tax collector. Now, with no income, she was forced to sell her beloved Elm Close, and she and Stringer moved to a small bungalow at Chalfont St. Peter. She died there on May 22, 1972. Stringer followed 14 months later, on August 7, 1973. Margaret Rutherford, brilliant at comedy, once said to a friend, "I never play for laughs."

SOURCES:
Johns, Eric. *Dames of the Theater.* New Rochelle, NY: Arlington House, 1974.

Simmons, Dawn Langley. *Margaret Rutherford: A Blithe Spirit.* NY: McGraw-Hill, 1983.

Rutherford, Mildred (1851–1928)

American educator and Confederate apologist. Name variations: Miss Millie. Born Mildred Lewis Rutherford in Athens, Georgia, on July 16, 1851; died in Athens on August 15, 1928; daughter of Williams R. Rutherford and Laura Battaille Rootes (Cobb) Rutherford (sister of Thomas Reade Rootes Cobb who established the Lucy Cobb Institute for Girls); graduated from the Lucy Cobb Institute for Girls; never married; no children.

Mildred Lewis Rutherford was born in 1851 into a prominent, large and wealthy family in Athens, Georgia, a decade before the Civil War would devastate her home state. Her parents had strong ties to the South; both were from well-known families who had settled in Virginia before the American Revolution, later moving to Georgia. Rutherford inherited her commitment to education from her father and an uncle, who were prominent figures in Georgia's schools. Her father Williams R. Rutherford, a professor of mathematics at the University of Georgia, also ran a boys' school in Athens, while her mother **Laura Cobb Rutherford**'s brother Thomas established the Lucy Cobb Institute for Girls (named after his daughter) in 1858.

The Southern Confederacy was another Rutherford family passion. During the Civil War, two of Rutherford's uncles served as generals in the Confederate Army. Rutherford worked with her mother and sisters on behalf of the Soldiers' Aid Society, providing food and bandages for Confederate soldiers. These strong ties to family, tradition, and the South shaped her childhood and adulthood. After the Confederacy lost the Civil War, she spent the rest of her life working to promote the values that she believed the Old South embodied.

Rutherford graduated from the Lucy Cobb Institute in 1868, ten years after its founding and three years after the end of the Civil War. She spent several years teaching in public schools in Atlanta before returning to the Institute as principal in 1880. She would remain there for the next 46 years, working to educate young women in the traditions and manners of the antebellum South. Known to her students as "Miss Millie," she wrote the textbooks for her literature class-es, including *English Authors* (1890), *American Authors* (1984), *French Authors* (1906), and *The South in Literature and History* (1907), placing greater emphasis on the morality of writers than on the artistic merit of their work. Rutherford believed that some Southern writers had not received their proper place in the pantheon of American literature and advocated for their greater visibility at the national level (she felt that Joel Chandler Harris, author of the "Uncle Remus" stories, was the neglected equal of Walt Whitman and William Dean Howells). The lack of objective, critical content in her textbooks limited their usefulness to later generations, except in cases where she provided biographical data on more obscure writers.

Rutherford also worked on behalf of Southern and states' rights. She was very active in the Daughters of the Confederacy, serving as historian and honorary president, and helping to establish several new chapters. She was considered particularly effective as a lecturer, sometimes appearing in mid-19th-century costume to add atmosphere to her defense of the South in lecture halls throughout the country. In a series of pamphlets printed in the mid-1920s, she accused Northern historians of distorting the motives of the South during the Civil War, and insisted that the war was precipitated by the North more with the aim of destroying the economic base of the South by ending slavery than with the aim of ending slavery itself. She also took stands against women's suffrage, child labor laws, and national prohibition, arguing that they violated states' rights.

Mildred Rutherford was a member of the Young Women's Christian Association, serving for some 15 years on its national board; she also took charge of the Athens City Mission Board, and became head of an industrial home for girls which her sister Bessie had founded. However, her fight on behalf of the vanished South in which she had grown up was her life's work. She was ill with Bright's disease and arteriosclerosis in her later years, before contracting hypostatic pneumonia and dying on August 15, 1928, in Athens. Three years after her death, the Lucy Cobb Institute closed its doors as well.

SOURCES:
James, Edward T., ed. *Notable American Women, 1607–1950.* Cambridge, MA: The Belknap Press of Harvard University, 1971.

Andrea Bewick,
freelance writer, Santa Rosa, California

Ruth the Gleaner (fl. 1100 BCE).

See Ruth.

Ruthven, Jocelyn Otway (1909–1989).

See Otway-Ruthven, Jocelyn.

Rutkiewicz, Wanda (1943—)

Polish mountaineer. Born in Lithuania on February 4, 1943; acquired a Master of Science in computer science; married in 1970 (divorced 1973); married Helmut Scharfetter, in 1982 (divorced 1984).

Made the first all-women's ascent of the North Face of Matterhorn (1978); was the first European woman and first Pole to climb Mount Everest (1978); made the first all-female ascent of Nanga Parbat, without oxygen or high altitude porters; ascended K-2 (1986).

Wanda Rutkiewicz was born in 1943 in Lithuania, but her family moved to Wrockaw, Poland, when she was four. At school, she was a talented athlete, excelling in high jump, volleyball, shot-put, and javelin, but it was not until her first rock climb at 18 in southwest Poland

Wanda Rutkiewicz

that she heard the "explosion" which would set her course. From then on, she climbed every weekend, traveling three hours and walking one hour to get to the rocks, and sleeping in caves in the forest below.

In 1964, Rutkiewicz attended a rescue course in the Austrian Alps. The next few years brought success and failure. Two of her climbs were with **Halina Krüger-Syrokomska**; they ascended the East Face of the Grépon and the Trollryggen East Pillar in Norway. Rutkiewicz's first big mountain expedition, however, was in 1970, a combined Polish-Russian ascent of Peak Lenin (23,406 ft.) in the Russian High Pamirs. It was not a happy experience. In contrast, she regarded the next expedition as the best of her life. In 1972, Rutkiewicz, along with **Alison Chadwick-Onyszkiewicz** (one of Britain's most accomplished climbers), her husband Janusz Onyszkiewicz, and seven others, climbed Noshaq (24,580 ft.), the second-highest summit in the Hindu-Kush. Rutkiewicz and Chadwick became close friends.

With **Danuta Wach** and **Stefania Egierszdorff**, Rutkiewicz made the second ascent of the North Pillar of the Eiger in the Western Alps in 1973. On her next expedition to the High Pamirs, sponsored by the Soviet Mountaineering Federation, Rutkiewicz fell ill from oedema and had to be helicoptered to Base Camp. At the time, she had no idea how fortunate she was. Fifteen mountaineers would die on that venture.

The year 1975 saw her leading the Polish Women's Karakorum Expedition up Gasherbrum II (26,362 ft.) and Gasherbrum III (26,090 ft.) between the Indian subcontinent and central Asia. On that undertaking, Chadwick-Onyszkiewicz made it to the top of GIII, the highest peak first climbed by a woman. Wanda was close behind.

In 1978, after a life-threatening bout of meningitis the preceding year, Wanda, along with **Anna Czerwinska, Krystyna Palmowska,** and **Irena Kesa**, attempted the first women's winter ascent of the North Face of the Matterhorn. Though they reached the summit, bad weather and Kesa's severe frostbite forced a helicopter rescue.

That October, Rutkiewicz became the first Pole and the first European woman to climb Mount Everest. But she was the only woman in the Franco-German expedition and faced not only the bitter cold but open resentment and anger. "Perhaps in Germany," said Wanda, "they do not have many independent women climbers who are leading and deciding for themselves." On leaving Base Camp, she learned that Alison Chadwick-Onyszkiewicz and **Vera Watson** had fallen to their deaths while attempting a first ascent of the center summit on Annapurna I.

Rutkiewicz preferred all-women expeditions: "If men and women are members of the same expedition, a man either consciously or subconsciously will take over the leadership in the mountains, or a woman consciously or subconsciously will give the leadership to the better one and will concentrate only on the problem of 'whether *she* will climb to the top.'" There is nothing wrong with this until a woman subverts her independent abilities. "Therefore it is necessary to test one's abilities and to learn to be independent in the mountains, not only to learn how to climb."

In 1981, while preparing for K-2 (the second-highest mountain in the world at 28,250 ft.), Rutkiewicz fell 650 ft. and broke her leg; four operations followed. Terrible weather, as well as the sudden death of Halina Krüger-Syrokomska, would force a retreat of the first all-women's K-2 expedition in 1982. Though Wanda could not climb, she had been at the Base Camp, leading the expedition. "At 1:30 p.m. Halina reported by radio to Base Camp," said Wanda. "She was in normal spirits and gave a colourful and funny report of the climb. . . . Anna [Czerwinska] and Halina were lying in their tent after eating and were talking lazily. Suddenly, without warning, in the middle of their conversation Halina became unconscious and died within a few minutes." Halina's body was brought back to Base Camp and buried at the foot of K-2. In the spring of 1984, with a healed leg, Rutkiewicz made another attempt, only to be defeated by bad weather once more.

For Wanda, there was to be one more fateful attempt. In the summer of 1986, as a member of a small French expedition that consisted of Maurice and **Liliane Barrard** and Michel Parentier, they reached Base Camp on May 22 and were the first expedition on the mountain to attempt Abruzzi Ridge. On June 23, Rutkiewicz reached the summit, a summit she felt was "much more beautiful and more difficult than Mount Everest." But her euphoria was short lived. On the descent, Liliane and Maurice Barrard were lost in a snowstorm. That summer, 11 others would die attempting to ascend K-2, including Britain's **Julie Tullis**.

SOURCES:

Birkett, Bill, and Bill Peascod. *Women Climbing: 200 Years of Achievement.* London: A. & C. Black, 1989.

Rutledge, Ann (1813–1835)

Abraham Lincoln's legendary love. Born Ann Mayes Rutledge in Kentucky on January 7, 1813; died of typhoid in Illinois on August 25, 1835; daughter of James Rutledge (a mill-owner and tavernkeeper) and Mary Ann (Miller) Rutledge; never married; no children.

Described by her fiancé John McNamar as "a gentle Amiable Maiden without any of the airs of your city Belles but winsome and Comly withal a blond in complection with golden hair, cherry red Lips & a bonny Blue Eye," Ann Rutledge was the famed beloved of Abraham Lincoln. She was born in Kentucky in 1813, and as a child traveled with her family to Illinois, where her father James Rutledge, along with a man named John M. Cameron, set up a sawmill that soon became the locus of a town they named New Salem. James and **Mary Ann Rutledge** would have ten children in all, of whom Ann was the third-born. She reputedly was the only girl educated at the local school run by Mentor Graham, and a grammar book with her signature on the cover is now in the Library of Congress. As the town prospered, James Rutledge opened a tavern which also offered accommodations to travelers, and it was there that the future president boarded when he arrived in New Salem in 1831. Though Ann was engaged to John McNamar, a friend of Lincoln's, legend has it that her romance with Lincoln marked Lincoln's life forever.

In 1833, McNamar, a young merchant, traveled back to New York to take care of his parents. Before leaving, he bought a farm for Rutledge, and her family moved there with her to await his return. McNamar's absence lengthened with the complications of his father's death and his own long illness. During this time, although he was no longer boarding with her family, Lincoln allegedly fell in love with Ann Rutledge. She died of typhoid (or "milk fever" or "brain fever") in 1835, before McNamar's return. Lincoln's extreme grief over Rutledge's death (some reportedly feared for his sanity) gave rise, after his own death, to the widespread theory that she had been his one true love. In their book *Mentor Graham: The Man Who Taught Lincoln* (1944), Kunigunde Duncan and D.F. Nickols quote the ex-schoolmaster Graham as saying of Rutledge that she was "Beautiful and ingenious—amiable—kind—exceptionally good scholar in all the common branches including grammar. She was beloved of everybody and she loved everybody. Lincoln and she were engaged—Lincoln told me so—told me he felt like committing suicide after her death but I [told] him of God's higher purpose. He told me he thought so too—somehow—couldn't tell how."

The story of this lost love gained wide currency through William Herndon, Lincoln's one-time law partner, who soon after the president's assassination began researching his life with plans to write a biography. As most mid-to-late-20th-century accounts have it, Herndon, who had a high opinion of his intuitive powers, believed he could read other people's minds, and constructed the story on the basis of vague reminiscences given by those who had lived in New Salem 30 years before. He added his own imaginative inventions, such as a fictional wedding day disrupted by Lincoln's decision not to marry Rutledge, flavored them with his dislike of Lincoln's wife, *Mary Todd Lincoln, suggesting that their marriage was hollow and portraying Mary Todd as a harridan (a characterization perpetuated by many Lincoln biographers), and spun the whole story for the first time during a public lecture in November 1866. Grief over the president's assassination was still raw, and the romance of the tale could not help but attract believers, although Mary Todd Lincoln stoutly refused to countenance it as anything but untrue. *Herndon's Lincoln*, published by Herndon and a co-writer in 1889, reiterated the story of Lincoln's supposed tragic love, and this was included in most of the plethora of books about the president subsequently written. The young Ann Rutledge, beloved of one of the most revered Americans and cut down in her prime, became a figure of American romance. Herndon refused to offer his evidence for inspection, however, and it was not until 1942, after his research materials had been acquired by the Library of Congress, that historians were able to assess the evidence for the love story. What little they found led them to conclude that it was, in fact, only a story.

In more recent years, however, some historians have begun to declare that there was an actual romance, and perhaps an implied engagement, between Rutledge and Lincoln during the years that McNamar was away from New Salem. More recent interpretations of the relationship between Rutledge and Lincoln can be found in John Evangelist Walsh's *The Shadows Rise: Abraham Lincoln and the Ann Rutledge Legend* (1993) as well as two of historian Douglas L. Wilson's books on Lincoln, *Lincoln Before Washington: New Perspectives on the Illinois Years* (1997) and *Honor's Voice: The Transformation of Abraham Lincoln* (1998), all published by the University of Illinois Press. In 1890, Ann Rutledge's remains were moved from the Concord burying ground outside New Salem,

which Lincoln had often visited after her death, and transferred to the cemetery in the nearby town of Petersburg, Illinois. Her tombstone there, erected in 1921, bears the epitaph composed for her by Edgar Lee Masters in his *Spoon River Anthology*, which includes the words:

> I am Ann Rutledge who sleep beneath these weeds,
> Beloved in life of Abraham Lincoln,
> Wedded to him, not through union
> But through separation. Bloom forever, O Republic,
> From the dust of my bosom!

SOURCES:

The Day [New London, CT]. February 22, 1998, p. H2.

Duncan, Kunigunde and D.F. Nickols. *Mentor Graham: The Man Who Taught Lincoln*. Chicago, IL: University of Chicago Press, 1944.

James, Edward T., ed. *Notable American Women, 1607–1950*. Cambridge, MA: The Belknap Press of Harvard University, 1971.

Wilson, Douglas L., and Rodney O. Davis, eds. *Herndon's Informants: Letters, Interviews, and Statements About Abraham Lincoln*. Urbana, IL: University of Illinois Press, 1997.

Andrea Bewick,
freelance writer, Santa Rosa, California

Ruysch, Rachel (1664–1750)

Dutch painter of flowers and still-lifes. Born in Amsterdam, Holland, in 1664; died in Amsterdam in 1750; daughter of Anthony Frederick Ruysch (a professor of anatomy and botany) and Maria (Post) Ruysch; apprenticed to Willem van Aelst; married Juriaen Pool (a portrait painter), in 1693; children: ten.

Considered a major international artist in her lifetime as well as after her death, Dutch painter Rachel Ruysch created detailed and exquisitely colored flower arrangements, often with outdoor settings and including small mammals, reptiles, and insects. The genre, a specialty much in vogue among women in Holland and elsewhere during the 17th century, was often dismissed as "womanish," but Ruysch seems to have achieved a profundity in her paintings that could not be ignored. Today, her work fetches a high price among collectors.

Ruysch was born in Amsterdam in 1664, to distinguished parents. Her father Anthony Frederick Ruysch was a professor of anatomy and botany, as well as an amateur artist, and her mother **Maria Post Ruysch** was the daughter of the architect Pieter Post. Ruysch's artistic talent emerged early, and at age 15 she became the student of the sophisticated flower and still-life painter Willem van Aelst. Two of her earliest dated works, a flower painting, and a study of insects and a this-tle plant in a landscape (1685), reveal a remark-able technical skill in one so young. Adopting van Aelst's asymmetrical, spiraling compositions, she developed them to perfection. "Her taste in choos-ing and balancing blooms, colours, light and backgrounds was perfect," writes **Germaine Greer** in *The Obstacle Race*, "the finish of her painting soft, clear and flawless."

In 1693, Ruysch wed portrait painter Juri-aen Pool, and throughout 50 years of marriage produced ten children while also keeping her ca-reer afloat. In 1701, she and her husband be-came members of The Hague guild, and, from 1708 to 1716, she was court painter to the Elec-tor Palatine, Johann Wilhelm von Pfalz; her fam-ily lived for some time at his court in Düsseldorf. In 1716, the Pool household settled back in Am-sterdam, where the artist remained active until three year before her death in 1750. Two of her late flower paintings, dated 1747, are also marked with her age, 83, under the signature.

Ann Sutherland Harris and **Linda Nochlin**, in *Women Artists: 1550–1950*, cite one of Ruysch's simpler flower paintings, *Still Life with Flowers and Plums* (1703), as one of the best ex-amples of her compositional skills and ability to suggest movement, "as if a gentle breeze were ruf-fling the whole arrangement." The authors also point out that in the artist's more elaborate flower pieces, those including insects—particularly bee-tles, butterflies, grasshoppers, and dragonflies—she often depicted groups of specimens seldom ever seen together in the same season, indicating an idealized representation. "She is in effect fol-lowing the doctrine that it was the artist's duty to select from nature and to portray perfectly what nature could only render imperfectly." Ruysch sometimes introduced new flora and fauna from Dutch trading voyages into her works, as well as unusual varieties of flowers, fruits, and insects.

According to Harris and Nochlin, Ruysch's lifetime output of about 200 paintings is substan-tial compared to earlier women artists, but it is not so impressive when compared to her male Dutch contemporaries, who often turned out upwards of 800 works in a lifetime. Still, given her domestic responsibilities, Ruysch was obviously a women of great discipline and vitality. Her younger sister **Anna Elisabeth Ruysch** (c. 1680–1741), also painted, but little is known about her.

SOURCES:
Greer, Germaine. *The Obstacle Race*. NY: Farrar, Straus & Giroux, 1979.
Harris, Ann Sutherland, and Linda Nochlin. *Women Artists: 1550–1950*. L.A. County Museum of Art: Knopf, 1976.
Sterling, Susan Fisher. *Women Artists*. NY: Abbeville Press, 1995.

Barbara Morgan,
Melrose, Massachusetts

Ryan, Anne (1889–1954)

American artist. Born on July 20, 1889, in Hoboken, New Jersey; died on April 18, 1954, in Morristown, New Jersey; only daughter and oldest of four children of John Ryan (a banker) and Elizabeth (Soran) Ryan; graduated from the Academy of St. Elizabeth's Con-vent, in Convent Station, New Jersey; attended St. Eliz-abeth's College; married William J. McFadden (a lawyer), in 1911 (separated 1923); children: (twins) William and Elizabeth McFadden; Thomas McFadden.

Finding her metier at the age of 50, Anne Ryan enjoyed a short but intense art career, first painting and then creating the abstract collages of paper and fabric for which she became known. Hilton Kramer found unusual intimacy in Ryan's small creations, noting that her work has "the air of a private communication, of something confided with affection and delicacy."

Anne Ryan was born in Hoboken, New Jer-sey, in 1889, the only daughter and eldest of four children of John Ryan and **Elizabeth Soran Ryan**, wealthy Irish-Catholics. Both parents died when she was still a child, and she and her brothers were raised by their grandmother. After completing preparatory school at the Academy of St. Elizabeth's Convent, Ryan briefly attended St. Elizabeth's College, leaving in 1911 to marry William J. McFadden, then a young law student. The couple had three children: twins, William and Elizabeth (1912), and Thomas (1919).

The marriage did not endure, failing in part because of Ryan's desire to move beyond a life of domesticity. Following a legal separation in 1923, Ryan resumed her maiden name and moved to New York City's Greenwich Village, where she wrote poetry (*Lost Hills* was pub-lished in 1925) and worked on a novel. From 1931 to 1933, she lived on the island of Major-ca, writing poetry, stories, and articles, some of which were published in *The Literary Digest* and *Commonweal*. During the summer of 1932, she visited Paris with her older children.

Returning to Greenwich Village in 1933, Ryan moved in with her younger son and con-tinued to write; for a brief time, she also ran a restaurant to make ends meet. At age 50, per-haps inspired by the vibrant, young artistic com-munity around her (friends included Hans Hof-mann and Tony Smith), she discovered painting and had her first solo exhibition of oil paintings in 1941. That same year, she joined British surrealist Stanley Hayter's Atelier 17 to study printmaking. There, influenced by Hayter's abstract work, she produced a number of woodblock prints and engravings.

The turning point in Ryan's artistic career was her exposure to an exhibit of collages by the German master Kurt Schwitters at the Rose Fried Gallery in 1948. Inspired, Ryan began to experiment in the new medium, at first using "found objects," such as postage stamps, ticket stubs, candy wrappers, and fragments of pictures to create her collages. Soon, she became more individualistic in her selection of materials, choosing textiles with distinctive weaves and textures, and a variety of fine papers, including some specially handmade by Douglas Howell. Many of these materials she allowed to age or "ripen" in order to produce a "faded or worn quality." The resulting works have been described variously as "lyrical" and "otherworldly." **Charlotte Streifer Rubinstein** writes: "Their calm spiritual quality stems from her early contact with the Catholic mystics and her familiarity with the poetry of Rainier Maria Rilke and Gerard Manley Hopkins, among others." Poet John Ashbery compared Ryan's compositions to the work of Charles Ives, John Cage, and *Marianne Moore, noting that her art goes "beyond 'mysteries of construction' . . . into mysteries of being which, it turns out, have their own laws of construction." The first public showing of Ryan's collages was at the Betty Parson's Gallery in 1950. The following year, her work was included in the exhibition "Abstract Painting and Sculpture in America" at the Museum of Modern Art.

Ryan spent her last years living with her daughter **Elizabeth McFadden** in Greenwich Village. After suffering a stroke in 1954, she moved in with her son in Morristown, New Jersey, where she died on April 18, just shy of her 65th birthday. In 1974, a major exhibition, "Anne Ryan Collages," was held at the Brooklyn Museum, sparking renewed interest and appreciation in the artist.

SOURCES:

Bailey, Brooke. *The Remarkable Lives of 100 Women Artists*. Holbrook, MA: Bob Adams, 1994.
Rubinstein, Charlotte Streifer. *American Women Artists*. Boston, MA: G.K. Hall, 1982.
Sicherman, Barbara, and Carol Hurd Green, eds. *Notable American Women: The Modern Period*. Cambridge, MA: The Belknap Press of Harvard University Press, 1980.

COLLECTIONS:

Anne Ryan's papers are located at the Archives of American Art, Washington, D.C.

Barbara Morgan,
Melrose, Massachusetts

Ryan, Catherine O'Connell (1865–1936).

See Inventors.

Ryan, Elizabeth (1892–1979)

American tennis player. Name variations: Bunny Ryan. Born in Los Angeles, California, in 1892; died of a stroke while at Wimbledon, England, in July 1979; daughter of a British immigrant to America; never married.

Won the Russian championship (1914); won 19 doubles titles and 7 mixed-doubles titles at Wimbledon; won 4 mixed-doubles titles in France and 2 in the United States.

Though she played in two Wimbledon singles finals, Elizabeth "Bunny" Ryan was known as the best player of her era who never won a major singles title. Born into a wealthy household in Los Angeles, she learned to play tennis with her elder sister **Alice Ryan**. In 1904, the 12-year-old Ryan moved with her mother to England where she would continue to live for most of her life.

Until her death in 1979, Ryan held the record for the greatest number of Wimbledon wins, most of them in doubles while partnering some of the best players in tennis, including *Suzanne Lenglen. Between 1912 and 1934, she won an incredible 659 titles. Dubbed "Miss Chop and Drop," Ryan was a strong volleyer with a malevolent chopped forehand and a lethal drop shot; ground strokes were not her strong suit.

In 1979, *Billie Jean King was looking for her 20th Wimbledon doubles title and a chance to break the long-held Ryan record of 19. But when King and *Martina Navratilova took the match from **Betty Stove** and **Wendy Turnbull** in three sets, King had no interest in rejoicing, because she "could not stop thinking of Elizabeth." After suffering a stroke the day before at the All England Club, Wimbledon, the 88-year-old Ryan had died en route to the hospital.

Rycheza.

Variant of Richesa.

Ryder, Sue (1923–2000)

British social worker and philanthropist. Name variations: Baroness Ryder of Warsaw; Lady Ryder. Born Margaret Susan Ryder in England in 1923; died in Bury St. Edmunds, England, on November 2, 2000; married a naval officer (killed in World War II); mar-

ried Leonard Cheshire (a social worker, war hero, and holder of the Victorian Cross), in 1959 (died 1992); children: (second marriage) Jeremy Cheshire; Elizabeth Cheshire.

Sue Ryder devoted her entire life to the care of others. She was born in England in 1923 into a prosperous farming family, and spent her early childhood living on the outskirts of Leeds, near some of the city's worst slums. The children she saw on the streets during the Depression provided her with her first lesson in the misery of poverty. During the 1930s, the Ryder farm also fell on hard times; the family moved to a summer cottage in Thurlow, Suffolk.

With the outbreak of war in 1939, Ryder left school and volunteered for the FANYs (First Aid Nursing Yeomanry). After training, she was assigned to the Special Operations Executive (SOE), a unit involved in organizing sabotage and supporting resistance movements in occupied countries. Attached to the Polish section, "The Bods," as they were called, Ryder endured extreme danger and hardships and lost many of her compatriots on various missions. It was a highly motivated group, however, and further inspired Ryder to devote her life to the relief of human suffering. She later served in North Africa and Italy, and at war's end performed relief work in France and Poland. She became so enamored of the Polish nation that she would take the name Warsaw as part of her title when she was elevated to the House of Lords as a life peer in 1979.

In 1953, using a small inheritance and borrowed money, Ryder established the first Sue Ryder Home in Suffolk, England, a refuge for concentration camp survivors as well as the mentally and physically ill. In 1959, she went into partnership and married Leonard Cheshire, a British war hero and founder of the Cheshire Homes for the disabled. (At 18, Ryder had married a young naval officer, but he had been killed in the war just a few weeks after the wedding.) Through the Sue Ryder Foundation, she would found 24 Sue Ryder Houses in Britain and 80 other centers in 20 nations, including Eastern Europe and India. She also set up 500 Sue Ryder charity shops, where she was known to purchase her own clothes. The homes serve patients with cancer, the physically handicapped, the elderly, the mentally ill, and those suffering from Huntington's disease. Some of the facilities also offer home visits, bereavement counseling, and respite care. In 1979, the queen mother, *Elizabeth Bowes-Lyon, inaugurated the Sue Ryder Foundation Museum in Cavendish. "It is intended," said Ryder, "to show the misery in the world and the needs which exist more vividly than the written word could do. It is not dedicated to me." Ryder was the author of two autobiographies: *And the Morrow Is Theirs* and *Child of My Love*.

SOURCES:

"Baroness Ryder, 77, Charity Organizer, Dies," in *The New York Times*. November 7, 2000.
This England. Spring 1987, p. 74; Spring 1998, p. 79.

Barbara Morgan,
Melrose, Massachusetts

Rye, Maria Susan (1829–1903)

English social reformer and feminist. Born in London, England, in 1829; died in 1903 in Hempstead, England; educated at home.

Born in London in 1829, Maria Susan Rye was the first of nine children of a liberal, bookish lawyer. She received her education at home, and as a teenager began working with the poor of her community through her local church; this impulse to fight on behalf of the disadvantaged would shape her life. Her first and primary interest lay in securing basic rights for women. In the mid-19th century, married women in England could not own property, and under the law any property inherited by a married woman from her relatives immediately passed into the hands of her husband. In 1856, Rye became secretary of a committee supporting the Married Women's Property Bill, designed to rectify this injustice. Beyond the property issue, she was also concerned about the lack of employment opportunities for middle-class women, and was a member of the Society for Promoting the Employment of Women. In 1859, she opened a law stationers' business with the express intent of hiring middle-class women to work for her.

So many women applied for positions in this business and other projects that Rye was affiliated with, such as the Telegraph School, founded by Isa Craig (*Isa Knox), and the Victoria Press, founded by *Emily Faithfull, that she began promoting the idea of emigration to countries with greater opportunities. For middle-class women who could not find work, the idea of emigrating offered a certain degree of hope. In 1861, Rye helped establish the Female Middle Class Emigration Society, which for nearly a decade helped educated women pursue opportunities in Canada, Australia, and New Zealand.

During the course of her journeys to some of these countries, Rye became aware of the plight of poor children there, many of whom were orphaned on the journey from England because of the terrible conditions on board ship. In 1868, Rye established homes for impoverished children in both London and Canada. Numerous youngsters from the London home were sent to the one in Canada, which cared for them after their long journey and helped them make the transition to their new land by assisting in the procurement of jobs and more permanent housing. (This sending out of the country of "gutter" children, not all of whom were orphans, while praised by some, caused others to denounce her as a destroyer of poor families and a manipulative entrepreneur.) Rye was also influential in the creation of the Church of England Waifs and Strays Society in 1891, with which she remained closely involved during the remainder of her life. Before her death in 1903, she claimed responsibility for sending some 4,000 destitute English children on to new lives in Canada.

SOURCES:

The Concise Dictionary of National Biography. Oxford: Oxford University Press, 1992.

Uglow, Jennifer, ed. and comp. The International Dictionary of Women's Biography. NY: Continuum, 1982.

Andrea Bewick,
freelance writer, Santa Rosa, California

*Leonie
Rysanek*

Rygier-Nalkowska, Zofia (1884–1954).

See Nalkowska, Zofia.

Ryksa (1116–1185).

See Richizza of Poland.

Ryksa (fl. 1288)

Queen of Poland. Name variations: Richeza, Richizza, or Rycheza; Richiza Valdemarsdottir. Flourished around 1288; daughter of Waldemar or Valdemar I (b. 1243), king of Sweden (r. 1250–1275), and *Sophie of Denmark (d. 1286); married Przemysl II (1257–1296), duke of Cracow (r. 1290–1291), king of Poland (r. 1290–1296), in 1285; children: *Ryksa of Poland (1288–1335, who married Vaclav, king of Bohemia and Poland, r. 1300–1305).

Ryksa of Poland (d. 1185)

Queen of Castile and Leon. Name variations: Richeza of Poland. Died on June 16, 1185 (some sources cite 1166); daughter of Wladyslaw also known as Ladislas II the Exile (1105–1159), king of Hungary (r. 1162); became second wife of Alphonso VII, king of Castile and Leon (r. 1126–1157), in July 1152 or 1153; children: Fernando (b. 1154); *Sancha of Castile and Leon (1164–1208). Alphonso VII was also married to *Berengaria of Provence.

Ryksa of Poland (1288–1335)

Queen of Bohemia, Hungary, and Poland. Name variations: Richeza or Rycheza; Richsa; Rejcka; Ryksa Elizabeth; Elisabeth or Elizabeth-Ryksa; Elizabeth of Poland. Born in 1288 (some sources cite 1286); died on October 19, 1335, in Koniggratz; daughter of Przemysl II (1257–1296), king of Poland (r. 1290–1296) and *Ryksa (fl. 1288); second wife of Vaclav or Waclaw or Wraclaw II also known as Wenceslas II (1271–1305), king of Bohemia (r. 1278–1305), and Poland (r. 1300–1305); second wife of Rudolph or Rudolf III (1281–1307), king of Bohemia and Poland (r. 1306–1307). Wenceslas II's first wife was *Judith (1271–1297); his third was *Elizabeth of Poland (fl. 1298–1305).

Rysanek, Leonie (1926–1998)

Austrian soprano. Born on November 14, 1926, in Vienna, Austria; died of bone cancer on March 7, 1998, in Austria; studied with Alfred Jerger, Rudolf Grossman, and Clothide Radony von Ottean at the Vienna Conservatory; married E.L. Gaussmann (a musicologist).

Made debut in Innsbruck (1949); sang in the first postwar Bayreuth Festival (1951); debuted at Covent Garden (1953), Vienna State Opera (1954); made American debut in San Francisco (1956); debuted at Metropolitan Opera (1959); celebrated her 25th anniversary at a Metropolitan Opera Gala (1984); gave last performance at the Met (1996).

Leonie Rysanek found fame at age 24 when she appeared as Sieglinde in Wagner's *Die Walkuere* at the first postwar Bayreuth festival. Over the next 40-odd years she would appear on major international opera stages over 2,100 times, in the process gaining an ardent following and a reputation as a consummate singer as well as a passionate actress. Unlike some singers whose voices deteriorate with the years, hers actually grew stronger, and she made many recordings which document her evolution as a singer and artist. Rysanek appeared widely throughout Europe, including performances in Vienna, Milan, Hamburg, Berlin, Paris, and Munich, but found her home on the stage of the Metropolitan Opera House in New York City in 1959, while performing as Verdi's Lady Macbeth. She sang at the Met to great success for the next 25 years, performing 20 roles in a total of 298 performances. At one of these, a performance of Wagner's *The Flying Dutchman*, the audience was so enthralled by her portrayal of Senta that applause lasted throughout the intermission, ending only when the conductor lifted the baton to begin Act 3. In 1984, Rysanek was honored by a Gala celebrating a quarter of a century on the stage of the great house; in January 1996, as she gave her final performance there (at age 70), she received a 20-minute standing ovation. An honorary member of the Vienna State Opera, Rysanek was fêted in her homeland of Austria as well, where she was one of the country's most well-known women. She remained active until only a few months before her death from bone cancer in March 1998.

SOURCES:

The Day [New London, CT]. March 9, 1998.
The New York Daily News. March 9, 1998.
Time. March 23, 1998, p. 39.

John Haag,
Athens, Georgia

temptation, the joys of parenthood, and the evils of government corruption.

Although Siti binti Saad has been dead since 1950, her voice still booms out of transistor radios and tape decks in Africa, India, and parts of the Arab world. Usually the words are sung in Swahili, but sometimes the language is Arabic or Hindustani. The island of Zanzibar is now part of the modern republic of Tanzania, but throughout that region, her music still speaks to the present.

Siti binti Saad was probably born in 1880, although the exact date is not known. Her birthplace was the village of Kisuani, six miles from the port of Zanzibar Town, and she was known first as Mtumwa binti Saad, a name which she later changed. Formal schooling for girls was not introduced on the island until the 1920s, and like many of her contemporaries, Siti never learned to read, but she had a restless intelligence, a quick memory, and a gift for mimicry that were to stand her in good stead. She loved to sing, at home and while working in the fields. She learned the pottery-making traditional among local Fumba women, and began to move from village to village to sell her wares. In 1910, when she was about 30, she moved to Mtoni. The following year, after a musician named Musa Bulushi promised to teach her how to follow string music, she left village life behind and moved to the port town of Zanzibar.

In Siti binti Saad's day, many African men and women were abandoning the traditional life of the village for the greater opportunities offered by the city. Women who left were frequently ones who had been abandoned by their husbands or otherwise stranded economically, without family or home. Arriving in the urban centers with few job skills, they risked being driven into prostitution out of the sheer need to eat and survive. When Siti arrived in Zanzibar Town, singing was not even known as a profession open to women along the East African coast. Fortunately, the combination of changing conditions, a powerful voice, and an energetic talent soon worked together in her favor.

In the city, Siti began to learn singing and Arabic from another musician, Mhusin Ali. According to one contemporary, she "possessed a wonderfully retentive mind and her power of grasping things and mastering them was unimaginable." Simply by mimicking what she had just heard, she learned the techniques of singing in Arabic or Hindustani with perfect intonation, and joined a group of four men—Subeti Ambari, Buda Swedi, Mwalimu Shaaban,

Saad, Siti binti (c. 1880–1950)

African singer and recording star from the island of Zanzibar whose recordings in Swahili, Arabic, and Hindustani continue to be heard in many parts of Africa, India, and the Arab-speaking world. Name variations: Siti bint Saad. Born Mtumwa binti Saad in Kisuani, near Zanzibar Town, probably in 1880; died in 1950; remained illiterate throughout her life, but took singing lessons in Zanzibar Town beginning in 1911.

Just off the East African coast at the edge of the Indian Ocean lies the island of Zanzibar, a trading center that for many centuries has served as the funneling point, like the neck of an hourglass, for the surrounding Arab, African and India cultures. Monsoon winds filled the triangular sails of Arab dhows, blowing the open-decked boats toward the island's ports. They came bearing cargoes of dried fruits, Indian fabrics and spices to trade for the ivory, gold, and other wares of Africa, then waited for the shift in prevailing winds to blow them back across the ocean. In the 1920s, one dhow drawn up at Zanzibar Town was the yacht-like vessel of Abdul-Wahab, a wealthy captain from the Persian Gulf who owned a fleet of trading ships. When his luxurious private ship reached the port, the popular club singer Siti binti Saad would be invited aboard with her orchestra to perform on the carpeted decks, in front of hangings of silk. In that setting reminiscent of the Arabian nights, she would raise her powerful voice in well-known songs about love, hate, and Mbaruku. At first, her musical engagements were a failure, until she found a way to differentiate her presentation from those of other performers, by acting out her songs. She also had a huge voice. As her reputation began to grow, it was said that she could be heard miles away, especially at night. If hooligans disrupted her performance, she could quell the disturbance without the use of a microphone. Singing at weddings, parties, and public functions, Siti combined her booming voice and acting skills to slowly build a reputation. She was a new, unique kind of performer, going against the traditional view of East African women as shy and dependent in public.

In Zanzibar, there was a well-established tradition of musical clubs, with performances in Arabic, dating back to 1900. Songs in Swahili were generally restricted to all-day picnics where the songs constituted the main entertainment, or festivals of Swahili song and dance, where Siti frequently performed. Swahili originated as the language of Zanzibar's Bantu people; the term comes from the Arabic word *sahil*, meaning coast. Over the thousands of years of coastal trade, many Arabic, Indian, Persian, English and Portuguese words were injected into it as it became the preferred language of commerce throughout the large oceanic region and along African continental paths of Arab trade. Ultimately the convergence of Arab, African, and Indian cultures, as well as of the Muslim religion, that occurred through this trade, made Swahili the *lingua franca* over large portions of the African continent, and independent of all borders.

In the 1920s, Siti binti Saad began to widen her reputation as a Taarab singer, performing in Swahili. Other women—**Bib Jokha, Bibi Mwana Iddi Hasan, Binti Issa** and **Bi Mkubwa Saidi**—all became famous as female Taarab singers, but she was the first true professional in the field, singing to large audiences and eventually making recordings. Like other aspects of life on the island of Zanzibar, the Taarab musical form is East African in origin with an oriental character. The term itself may mean pleasure or something pleasant, or it may derive from the word "Arab." In 1870, Sultan Barghash invited musicians from Egypt to play at his court, and was so taken with the music they called "Taarab" that he sent Muhammed Ibrahim to Egypt to learn how to perform it. A Taarab orchestra was founded at the sultan's palace, and African and Arabic elements began to blend over time. By the 1920s, it had evolved into a new form of popular music when an orchestra of African perform-

ers appeared singing Taarab songs in Swahili. In Zanzibar Town, as customers flocked to the "Changani clubs" like Silver Day and Golden Night to hear the Swahili Taarab songs, both Siti and the clubs grew famous.

It was during this period that Siti performed nightly on the dhow of Abdul-Wahab. In 1928, her local fame led to the signing of her first recording contract with Abdulkarim Hakim Khan, an agent for His Master's Voice, a recording company located in Bombay, India. *Um Kalthum, the famous Egyptian singer, was already making records in Arabic, and Indian recordings were popular as well. Now Khan saw the potential of a huge new market for songs in Swahili. East Africans would not only buy the recordings, he reasoned, but the machines to play them, and Khan was also in the business of selling gramophones.

With the contract signed, Siti and her Taarab group made a concert tour of India. Hearing the local music, the singer soon recognized the potential of the subcontinent as a market for her recordings, and learned to mimic songs sung in Hindustani. Back in Zanzibar, the recording stampede was soon on, with His Mas-

Siti binti Saad

ter's Voice setting up a local recording studio, and another agent, Gokaldas S. Rughani, seeking her out to record for America's Columbia Records. Singing in Arabic for Arabs, in Hindustani for Indians, and in Swahili for everyone, Siti became one of the first modern popular singing stars, tapping into a huge audience which was ostensibly separated by culture but actually bound together by a common language, religion, and strong economic ties. As radios and records reached an ever-widening audience, coffee shops and cafés throughout the region were flooded with the sound of Siti's voice.

Performance tours eventually took Siti binti Saad to Tanganyika, Kenya, and Uganda as well as India. Singing her Taarab songs, so rich in imagery, she also widened public recognition of the polyglot trading language of Swahili as a language of international cultural stature.

Siti binti Saad died in 1950, at age 70. "When you play on the flute at Zanzibar," goes an old Arab proverb, "all Africa as far as the lakes dances." Like a Zanzibar flute, Siti was heard throughout Africa, much of the Arab world, and India. Fully understanding her own gifts, she wrote in one of her songs:

Beauty and comely countenance
do not matter
Nor grandeur
That despises tradition
A big loss it is
To lack intelligence.

SOURCES:

Kurz, Laura S. *Historical Dictionary of Tanzania.* London: Scarecrow, 1978.

Lodhi, Abdulaziz Y., Anette and Gunnar Rydström. *A Small Book on Zanzibar.* Stockholm: Författares Bokmaskin, 1979.

Maw, Joan, and David Parkin, eds. *Swahili Language and Society.* Vienna: Beiträge zur Afrikanistik, 1984.

Oliver, Roland, ed. *The Cambridge History of Africa.* Cambridge: Cambridge University Press.

Osaki, Lilian Temu. "Siti Binti Saad: Herald of Women's Liberation," in *SAGE: A Scholarly Journal on Black Women.* Vol. 7, no. 1. Summer 1990, pp. 49–54.

Robinson, Pearl T. "Women in Rural Africa: The Political and Policy Imperatives," in *SAGE: A Scholarly Journal on Black Women.* Vol. 7, no. 1. Summer 1990, pp. 2–3.

Suleiman, A.A. "The Swahili Singing Star Siti Bint Saad and the Tarab Tradition in Zanzibar," in *The Journal of East African Swahili Committee.* Vol. 39, no. 1–2, 1969, pp. 87–90.

Zawari, Sharifa M. *Say It in Swahili.* NY: Dover, 1972.

Karin Loewen Haag,
freelance writer, Athens, Georgia

Saadawi, Nawal el (b. 1931).

See El Saadawi, Nawal.

Saarinen, Aline (1914–1972)

American art critic and television commentator. Name variations: Aline B. Louchheim; Mrs. Eero Saarinen. Born Aline Milton Bernstein in New York City on March 25, 1914; died in New York City on July 13, 1972; only daughter and middle of three children of Allen M. Bernstein (owner of an investment and industrial counseling firm) and Irma (Lewyn) Bernstein; graduated from the Fieldston School, New York City, 1931; Vassar College, A.B., 1935; Institute of Fine Arts, New York University, A.M., 1941; married Joseph H. Louchheim (a public welfare administrator), on June 17, 1935 (divorced 1951); married Eero Saarinen (1910–1961, an architect), on December 26, 1953 (died September 1961); daughter-in-law of *Loja Saarinen (1879–1968); aunt of *Pipsan Saarinen Swanson (1905–1979); children: (first marriage) Donald Louchheim (b. 1937), Harry Louchheim (b. 1939); (second marriage) Charles Eames Saarinen (b. 1954).

Aline Saarinen was born Aline Milton Bernstein in New York City in 1914, the only daughter and middle of three children of Allen M. Bernstein, owner of an investment and industrial counseling firm, and **Irma Lewyn Bernstein.** Raised in what her father termed a "high brow" family, Saarinen was encouraged in cultural and artistic pursuits from an early age, and later recalled her girlhood dream as wanting to be "intelluptuous." At nine, she made her first trip to Europe, where her older brother Charles Bernstein guided her through French chateaux and Gothic cathedrals, sparking her interest in art and architecture. Later, at Vassar College, she was further influenced by the art courses she took with John McAndrew and **Agnes Ringe.** Elected to Phi Beta Kappa in her junior year, and the recipient of a Vassar College fellowship, she also served as an art critic for the *Vassar Miscellany News* and in her senior year was editor of the yearbook, *Vassarion.* Immediately upon graduating in 1935, Aline married Joseph Louchheim, a public welfare administrator. In the fall of that year, she enrolled at the Institute of Fine Arts, New York University, to study the history of architecture. By the time she received her A.M. degree in 1941, she was the mother of two boys, Donald (b. 1937) and Harry (b. 1939). During World War II, while her husband served in the Navy, Aline put her career plans on hold to work as executive secretary of the Allegheny County Rationing Board in Pittsburgh and as a nurse's aide for the Red Cross in Washington, D.C.

In 1944, with her family reunited in New York City, Saarinen launched her career as an assistant at *Art News* magazine. After two years of covering gallery and museum exhibits, she became managing editor and began writing under her own byline. In 1946, in celebration of the 75th anniversary of the Metropolitan Museum of Art, the magazine sponsored the book *5,000 Years of Art*, which contained photographs and reproductions of artworks from 3000 BCE to 1946, along with Saarinen's commentary. *The New York Times* praised the work as outstanding and in December 1947 hired her as an associate art editor and art critic. In addition to producing articles on a wide variety of art-related subjects for the *Times*, she also wrote for the *Atlantic Monthly, House Beautiful*, and other magazines.

Aline and Joseph were divorced in 1951, and in 1953 she married renowned Finnish architect Eero Saarinen; they had met two years earlier when she interviewed him for an article. The couple relocated to Bloomfield Hills, Michigan, where Eero's firm was headquartered, and where Saarinen gave birth to a son Eames in December 1954. Having by this time been promoted to associate art critic at the *Times*, she continued to work for the paper while handling public relations for her husband's firm. With the aid of a Guggenheim fellowship awarded in 1957, she also produced another book, *The Proud Possessor* (1958), a biographical study of major art collectors.

Following her husband's sudden death in 1961, Saarinen carried out his plans to move the firm to New Haven, Connecticut, and also saw to it that the ten buildings being developed by Eero were completed. In 1962, she published the biography *Eero Saarinen on His Work*.

In 1962, Aline was asked to appear on television to discuss Rembrandt's *Aristotle Contemplating the Bust of Homer*, which the Metropolitan Museum of Art had recently purchased at great expense. Her performance was so engaging and down-to-earth ("highbrow without being highblown," said one reviewer) that it led to further guest appearances and finally to a third career as an art critic. In 1963, she became art and architecture editor for the "Sunday Show" on NBC and art critic for the daily "Today" show. A year later, in October 1964, she broadened her purview, becoming the third woman correspondent for NBC News (following *Pauline Frederick and *Nancy Dickerson), as well as the moderator of "For Women Only," an informative television panel program that focused on women's issues. In 1971, Saarinen was named chief of the NBC Paris News Bureau, the first woman ever appointed to head a foreign television division. Happily committed to her work, she only complained of the dreadful pace, remarking, "You almost have to be a widow to do it."

Throughout her career, Saarinen received numerous awards, including the International Award for Best Foreign Criticism at the Venice Biennale (1951), the American Federation of Arts Award for best newspaper criticism (1953), and two honorary degrees. The only woman member of the U.S. Fine Arts Commission in Washington, she was offered the post of ambassador to Finland in 1964, but turned it down. She died of a brain tumor in July 1972 in New York City.

SOURCES:

Candee, Marjorie Dent, ed. *Current Biography 1956.* NY: H.W. Wilson, 1956.

Read, Phyllis J., and Bernard L. Witlieb. *The Book of Women's Firsts.* NY: Random House, 1992.

Sicherman, Barbara, and Carol Hurd Green, eds. *Notable American Women: The Modern Period.* Cambridge, MA: The Belknap Press of Harvard University, 1980.

COLLECTIONS:

Aline Saarinen's papers are located at the Archives of American Art, Washington, D.C.

Barbara Morgan,
Melrose, Massachusetts

Saarinen, Mrs. Eero (1914–1972).

See Saarinen, Aline.

Saarinen, Eva Louise (1905–1979).

See Swanson, Pipsan Saarinen.

Saarinen, Loja (1879–1968)

*Finnish-born weaver and textile designer. Name variations: Loja Gesellius; Loja Gesellius Saarinen; Louise Gesellius; Louise Saarinen. Born Louise Gesellius on March 15, 1879, in Finland; died in April 1968; sister of architect Herman Gesellius; studied art in Finland and Paris; married (Gottlieb) Eliel Saarinen (1873–1950, an architect), on March 6, 1903; mother-in-law of *Aline Saarinen (1914–1972); children: Eero Saarinen (1910–1961, an architect); Eva Lisa Saarinen Swanson (1905–1979), a designer known as Pipsan Saarinen Swanson.*

Loja Saarinen was born Louise Gesellius on March 15, 1879, in Finland. A significant influence on the design aspects of modern textile production, she studied art in Finland and Paris before marrying noted Finnish architect Eliel Saarinen, who was at the time in partnership with her brother Herman Gesellius. The Saarinens immigrated to the United States in 1923, and settled near Ann Arbor, Michigan, where

Eliel took a teaching position at the University of Michigan. He later was commissioned to design several art schools at Cranbrook, in Bloomfield Hills, Michigan, one of which, Cranbrook Academy of Art, he also headed for many years. Loja also joined the creative community at Cranbrook, becoming director of the weaving shops in 1930, and serving as department head until her retirement in 1942. From 1928 on, Loja also headed her own textile studio.

Her carpet and textile designs, many of which were developed for her husband's buildings, were widely exhibited and won numerous awards. Her style combined Modernist design with traditional Scandinavian weaving and Art Deco techniques of the 1920s and 1930s. In addition to practicing her craft, Saarinen also taught many of the distinguished textile designers and weavers who have perpetuated her style and technique. Her designer daughter *Pipsan Saarinen Swanson also taught at Cranbrook.

SOURCES:

Block, Maxine, ed. *Current Biography 1942*. NY: H.W. Wilson, 1942.

Pile, John. *Dictionary of 20th-Century Design*. NY: Roundtable Press, 1990.

Saarinen, Louise (1879–1968).

See Saarinen, Loja.

Saarinen, Pipsan (1905–1979).

See Swanson, Pipsan Saarinen.

Saba, queen of (fl. 10th c. BCE).

See Sheba, Queen of.

Sabatini, Gabriela (1970—)

Argentinean tennis player. Name variations: Gaby Sabatini. Born in Buenos Aires, Argentina, on May 16, 1970; daughter of Osvaldo Sabatini (an automotive executive) and Beatriz Sabatini.

Began playing tennis at age six; moved to Florida at age 12 to continue training; dropped out of school at 14 in order to devote herself to professional tennis; joined the professional tour, became the youngest semifinalist in the history of the French Open, and was named Rookie of the Year (1985); won a silver medal at the Olympic Games in Seoul, South Korea (1988); ranked number three in the world (1989, 1991, 1992); won the U.S. Open (1990); won the Australian Open (1995); retired (1996).

Born into affluence in Buenos Aires, Argentina, on May 16, 1970, Gabriela Sabatini was learning how to swing a tennis racket and place a serve by age six. Her early display of talent and drive was nurtured by her parents, Osvaldo and **Beatriz Sabatini**. Osvaldo, an automotive executive, enrolled her in private tennis lessons by the time she was seven.

When she was ten, Sabatini was ranked first in her nation's twelve-and-under division. Shortly thereafter, she moved to Florida to continue her tennis training. In 1985, she joined the professional tour and quickly accelerated to the top of the rankings. In that same year, she became the youngest person ever to reach the semifinals of the French Open, attaining a 17th-place ranking in the world, and was named Rookie of the Year by *Tennis* magazine.

Despite—or because of—her success, several of her advisers worried that Sabatini was trying to accomplish too much too soon. Dick Dell, a sports agent who signed her just after she turned 14, acknowledged his concerns to *Sports Illustrated*'s Bruce Newman (May 2, 1988): "I am for anything that would give her an outlet outside tennis. Instead of being in school every day with girls her own age, she was thrown into an adult world." Sabatini did not take correspondence courses or continue her schooling after moving to the United States. In addition, she did not speak English during her first three years in Florida, and her natural shyness often was interpreted as aloofness. However, she could not be dissuaded from her rigorous schedule of training and touring, playing 20 out of 27 weeks on four continents her rookie year.

Over the next several years, Sabatini continued to progress in the sport until she was ranked 5th in the world in 1988. This final leap into the top ranks occurred, in part, because she changed coaches and playing styles. In 1987, Sabatini hired Angel Gimenez, a former Davis Cup player from Spain, to improve her conditioning and stamina. Her new training included running up to an hour each day and increasing her practice time on court in order to offset her problem of tiring too easily during matches. That year, she beat *Martina Navratilova in both the Italian Open in May and the Virginia Slims championship in October, although she was unable to make it past the semifinals in the French Open or the quarterfinals in the U.S. Open and Wimbledon. In 1988, her hard work paid off. *Steffi Graf, the German tennis player who had long been Sabatini's rival, had won all of their 11 matches. At the 1988 Virginia Slims tournament in Boca Raton, Florida, Sabatini upset Graf by winning their final match in two sets. Several weeks later, she beat Graf in another tournament, proving that the powerful teenager had

Gabriela
Sabatini

been replaced by an experienced professional whose endurance and variety of strokes had taken her to the top.

Despite setbacks in 1988—Sabatini lost both the U.S. Open and the Summer Olympics finals to Graf—she earned $1 million and won the silver medal at the Summer Olympics. She continued strongly in 1989, winning tournaments and more money, but was unable to capture the major titles. Fans and foes alike began to wonder if the Argentinean tennis player could ever be ranked #1.

With her failure at the 1990 French Open, Sabatini decided to switch coaches again. This time she hired Carlos Kirmayr, a former top-ranked Brazilian. She stopped working with weights—which had added bulk when she needed speed—and began seeing a sports psychologist. Kirmayr diagnosed Sabatini as overthinking her game, and urged her to pursue other interests, such as photography, French, and sightseeing. She also ended her longstanding doubles partnership with Graf that had won them the women's doubles championship at Wimbledon in 1988.

The change was a large factor in her outstanding victory in the U.S. Open in 1990 against Graf; she beat Graf again at the Virginia Slims championship later that year, although she ultimately lost the tournament to **Monica Seles** in a historic five-set final that lasted nearly four hours. While Sabatini continued to beat Graf into 1991, she found a new rival in Seles, who defeated her again in the finals of the Lipton International Players championship in Key Biscayne, Florida, in 1991. The pair traded wins throughout the year, with Sabatini ranked just behind Seles. By April 1991, Sabatini's career earnings reached $4 million, the 5th-highest total on the women's tour. (Like other tennis players, Sabatini endorsed various products; she was the first woman athlete to sign a multimillion-dollar contract with Pepsi and the first to have a perfume named after her.) But the year ended on a shaky note for Sabatini, as she lost to Graf at Wimbledon, to **Jennifer Capriati** at the U.S. Open, and to Seles at the Virginia Slims championship.

The year 1992 proved more promising, as Sabatini rallied from her defeat at the Australian Open to win five tournaments in the first five months. However, she was bothered by tendinitis and had several disappointing losses that year, including dropping Wimbledon to Graf and the U.S. Open to *Mary Joe Fernandez. Sabatini would not win another major tournament until 1995, when she took the Australian Open. During these years, Sabatini suffered from injuries and motivation problems. Though she was committed to the game, she had a difficult time keeping up with some of the younger players on the tour. In 1996, after another long year of injuries and tough competition, Sabatini retired from the sport at the age of 26. While still playing exhibition matches, she concentrated more on her endorsement deals, and by 2001 was marketing some seven internationally popular perfumes.

SOURCES:

The Day [New London, CT]. October 23, 1996, pp. D1, D5.

Dictionary of Hispanic Biography. Detroit, MI: Gale Research, 1996.

Graham, Judith, ed. *Current Biography 1992*. NY: H.W. Wilson, 1992.

Johnson, Anne Janette. *Great Women in Sports*. Detroit, MI: Visible Ink, 1998.

Moritz, Charles, ed. *Current Biography*. NY: H.W. Wilson, 1992.

Andrea Bewick,
freelance writer, Santa Rosa, California

Sabba.

See Sambethe.

Sabbe (fl. 10th c. BCE).

See Sheba, Queen of.

Sabin, Ellen (1850–1949)

American educator and administrator. Born Ellen Clara Sabin in Sun Prairie, Wisconsin, on November 29, 1850; died in Madison, Wisconsin, on February 2, 1949; daughter of Samuel Sabin (a farmer) and Adelia Sabin; educated at the local school; attended the University of Wisconsin, 1886–89; never married; no children.

Became the first woman principal and the first woman superintendent of schools in Portland, Oregon.

Born into a farm family in Wisconsin in 1850, Ellen Sabin, called Ella by her intimates, was the oldest of eleven children. Her father had made his fortune in California during the gold rush that began in 1849, and then returned to Wisconsin to settle down. Sabin grew up on a 300-acre farm and attended school at the local schoolhouse, where she quickly excelled. When she was 15, she entered the University of Wisconsin and also began teaching in her hometown of Sun Prairie. Her development of a system of visual aids in the teaching of geography was one of her earliest innovations in the field of teaching. She then moved from third- and fourth-grade classes in Sun Prairie to a seventh-grade class in Madison, winning appointment as principal of the Fourth Ward School within months of arriving there.

In 1872, Sabin's father again sought adventures in the West and moved the family to Eugene, Oregon. Sabin quickly resumed her work, establishing her own one-room schoolhouse as competition to the rundown schoolhouse in Eugene. She gained a great deal of attention for a paper she presented at the State Teachers' Institute in Salem, Oregon, and, at age 22, was nominated for state superintendent of schools. Although she turned down the offer, she did take a teaching post at the Old North School of Portland. As it had in Wisconsin, her performance there merited her ascending to the position of principal a year later, the first woman so appointed in Portland.

While principal, Sabin continued her innovative approach to teaching. Rather than using corporal punishment as discipline, she met with students and their families, often traveling through dangerous neighborhoods to visit them at home. She encouraged her students' skills by establishing a tutoring program whereby more able pupils helped those who were struggling. Though she insisted on a mastery of traditional subjects, she also recognized the need for practical training. Sabin helped the boys get jobs by speaking with overseers at businesses and factories. She spent 1886 in Europe, receiving training in educational procedures, and upon her return to Portland in 1887 became superintendent of Portland's schools. No other large U.S. city had a woman in such a position.

During these years, Sabin's reputation increased, and in 1891 she signed on as president of Downer College for Women in Wisconsin. Although the job paid only half what she had received in Portland, she looked forward to the freedom to develop the institution, unfettered by committees or school boards. Quickly realizing that the school's backwater location put it at a disadvantage, in 1895 she began to orchestrate its merger with the poorly led Milwaukee College for Women. She became president of the new institution, Milwaukee-Downer College, upon the merger's completion in 1897. During her tenure, Milwaukee-Downer College expanded greatly, gaining full recognition from the college accreditation board, tripling its endowment, and expanding to a 43-acre campus. Once again, Sabin emphasized traditional learning and practical skills, and the school offered bachelor's degrees as well as diplomas in nursing and home economics.

The recipient of honorary doctorates from Grinnell College and Benoit College and a member of several educational associations, Sabin retired in 1921. In 1945, she was honored by the Wisconsin branch of the American Association of University Women, which named its national graduate fellowship after her. Ellen Sabin died in Madison, Wisconsin, on February 2, 1949, age 98. Milwaukee-Downer College would remain in operation until 1964, when it merged with Lawrence University in Appleton, Wisconsin.

SOURCES:

James, Edward T., ed. *Notable American Women, 1607–1950.* Cambridge, MA: The Belknap Press of Harvard University, 1971.

Andrea Bewick,
freelance writer, Santa Rosa, California

Sabin, Florence (1871–1953)

American physician and medical researcher who made substantial contributions to the fields of histology, immunology, and public health and fought for women's rights within and outside her profession.

Pronunciation: SAY-bin. Born Florence Rena Sabin on November 9, 1871, in Central City, Colorado; died on October 3, 1953, in Denver; daughter of George Kimball Sabin (a mining engineer) and Serena (Miner) Sabin; graduated from Vermont Academy, 1889; Smith College, B.S., 1893; Johns Hopkins School of Medicine, M.D., 1900; never married; no children.

Awards: Baltimore Association for the Advancement of University Education for Women fellowship (1901); Naples Table Association Prize (1903); numerous honorary degrees, including a Doctorate of Science from Smith College (1910); appointed first woman full member of the Rockefeller Institute for Medical Research (1925); elected first woman member of the National Academy of Sciences (1925); Annual Achievement Award, Pictorial Review (1929); National Achievement Award, Chi Omega Sorority (1932); M. Carey Thomas Prize, Bryn Mawr College (1935); Trudeau Medal, National Tuberculosis Association (1945); *Jane Addams Medal for distinguished service by an American woman (1947); Medal for Achievement, University of Colorado (1947); American Woman's Association Medal for eminent achievement (1948); Lasker Award, American Public Health Association (1951); Distinguished Service Award, University of Colorado (1953); *Elizabeth Blackwell Citation of the New York Infirmary (1953).

Was instructor in zoology, Smith College (1895–96); interned at Johns Hopkins Hospital (1900–01); was a fellow under Franklin Paine Mall, Department of Anatomy, Johns Hopkins School of Medicine (1901–02); as instructor, Department of Anatomy, was the first woman on the Johns Hopkins medical faculty (1902–05); was an associate professor (1905–17); was the first woman promoted to full professorship at Johns Hopkins School of Medicine, becoming a professor of histology in the Department of Anatomy (1917–25); was the first woman president of the American Association of Anatomists (1924–26); was a member of the Research Committee of the National Tuberculosis Committee (1926); was a member of the Rockefeller Institute for Medical Research (1925–38); served on advisory board, John Simon Guggenheim Memorial Foundation (1939–47); served on the board of directors and was vice-president for three years of the Children's Hospital, Denver (1942–46); served as chair, Sabin Committee, Governor of Colorado Post-War Planning Committee

(1944); was manager, Denver Department of Health and Welfare (1947–51); served as president, Western Branch of the American Public Health Association (1948); served as chair, Board of Health and Hospitals, Denver (1951). Book-length publications: Atlas of the Medulla and Midbrain *(Friedenwald Co., 1901);* Franklin Paine Mall: The Story of a Mind *(Johns Hopkins Press, 1934).*

During the late 19th century, women found it difficult to obtain a high-quality medical education. Many medical schools refused to admit them entirely, believing that women lacked the intellectual capacity, scientific objectivity, and physical stamina necessary to practice medicine. Although there were several all-female medical colleges in the United States, the quality of education available at these institutions, and at most medical schools in the country for that matter, paled in comparison to what was available at the renowned medical colleges of Europe.

In the early 1890s, a group of physicians and scientists affiliated with the Johns Hopkins University began plans for a medical school that would equal and perhaps even surpass the great European institutions of medical education. This grandiose scheme required a large amount of money, however, and in 1890 the trustees of Johns Hopkins began a fund drive to raise capital for the new institution. Soon after, a group of women headed by *M. Carey Thomas, dean and future president of Bryn Mawr College, and ◄ Mary E. Garrett, heiress to the Baltimore and Ohio Railroad fortune, founded the Baltimore Women's Committee to help gather money for the project. Garrett offered to contribute $60,000 to the university, provided (1) baccalaureate degrees were required for admission, which was unusual at the time; and (2) women were admitted and educated on the same (as opposed to equal but separate) basis as men.

Although the trustees agreed that the requirements for admission would raise the standards and status of the medical college, they were vehemently opposed to Garrett's request to admit women. Like many male physicians and scientists of the period, the trustees believed that the presence of women in medicine degraded the status of the profession as a whole, and that women as a class were incapable of being good physicians and medical scientists. They therefore felt that admitting women would defeat the purpose of creating a prestigious, high-quality institution of medical education. It was only when the fund-raising campaign faltered in 1893, and Garrett raised her contribution to $300,000,

that the trustees grudgingly agreed to accept Garrett's conditions. Among the early graduates of this outstanding new medical school was Florence Sabin, who would become the preeminent woman scientist of her generation.

Born in 1871 in a humble frame house in Central City, a mining town near Denver, Colorado, Sabin had little inkling of her future accomplishments and fame as a scientist. Her early life was primitive despite her father's income as a mining engineer: the family home was poorly constructed and had no plumbing, electricity, or heat. Her childhood was also disrupted by a series of deaths within her immediate family, the most unsettling of which was the loss of her mother on Florence's seventh birthday. Florence and her older sister, **Mary Sabin**, were then shuttled between relatives and boarding schools in Denver, Chicago, and Vermont.

According to Mary, Florence's bent toward medicine was foreshadowed in her early days in Central City, when, in May 1874, a devastating fire destroyed much of the town center. Florence's father George Sabin had gone to help fight the fire and returned with singed whiskers and a blackened hand and face. Watching her younger sister tenderly clean her father's wounds, Mary predicted that Florence would someday enter the healing profession. There were also physicians in Sabin's family tree; her grandfather had been a country doctor in Vermont, and her father had studied medicine for a few years before deciding mining was more profitable. As well, the loss of her mother at such a young age may have influenced her eventual career choice.

At Smith College, where she received her undergraduate education, Sabin's interest in medicine was nurtured by Dr. **Grace Preston**, who was the college physician and an instructor in physical education and hygiene. Preston warned Sabin that becoming a physician would be difficult: "Being a woman doctor is pioneering even now," she told Florence, but added that "you have pioneer blood in you," referring to Sabin's roots on the Western frontier. Preston told her about the work of the Baltimore Women's Committee to open Johns Hopkins Medical School to women, and encouraged the young woman to try to gain admittance to the first medical school class. Preston inspired Sabin, and she agreed that her "pioneer spirit" gave her the backbone to fight for her and other women's right to study medicine.

Unfortunately, her father's health was failing and his business had fallen on hard times, and

Garrett, Mary E.
See Thomas, M.
Carey for sidebar.

Florence was forced to find the funds for medical school on her own. To raise money, she taught mathematics for several years at Wolfe Hall in Denver, which she had attended while she was a young girl, and then spent a year teaching zoology at Smith College. Finally, in 1896, Sabin had earned enough to afford the expensive tuition at Johns Hopkins Medical School.

Sabin's attendance at Johns Hopkins was fortunate, because the employment situation for women in medicine was extremely bleak during her lifetime. Women who overcame discrimination in admissions policies and managed to receive a medical diploma nonetheless had difficulty finding jobs in the field and were excluded from internships and residencies at most hospitals in the United States. The high-quality education available at Hopkins compared to other medical schools at the time, and the connections she made with prominent male scientists at that institution, undoubtedly gave Sabin an edge when it came to finding employment. While at Hopkins, she came under the influence of Franklin P. Mall, a professor of anatomy and perhaps the leading scientist at Johns Hopkins, who would have a marked influence on her education and future career. As a student under Mall's direction, Sabin worked on developing a three-dimensional model of the brainstem of newborn infants and made a major contribution to the understanding of the structure of the human brain. Published in 1901 as *An Atlas of the Medulla and Midbrain*, the model became a popular anatomical text of the day. In addition to her substantial accomplishments in medical research, Sabin was also an outstanding medical student and graduated third in her class in 1900.

Yet even Sabin's stellar credentials were not enough to assure her the same recognition and rewards as male scientists. After graduation, she encountered some resistance to her request for an internship at the Johns Hopkins Hospital. There were only 12 openings available to the graduating class, 4 of which were highly prized positions with Dr. William Osler in internal medicine. Since the top student in Sabin's class was too unhealthy to pursue an internship and the second student chose surgery, there should have been no obstacles to Sabin's appointment as an intern in internal medicine. The male faculty were somewhat reluctant to appoint women to these positions, however, partly because they believed male students were more deserving. In addition, these positions were considered unsuitable for women because they entailed contact with male patients in the "colored" wards of the hospital. Although the faculty eventually relented and allowed Sabin and another woman classmate to become internal medicine interns, many of their male classmates protested that these female students had "robbed" them of their rightful positions. The hospital superintendent shared a similar mistrust of women physicians, and even accused Sabin and the other female intern of having "abnormal sex interests" because of their willingness to work in a black male ward.

Although the Hopkins trustees resigned themselves to the presence of women as medical students and interns, they continued to bar women from faculty positions, regardless of their qualifications. Fortunately, Sabin's work had caught the attention of the same group of Baltimore women who had been responsible for opening the medical school to female students. After gaining Mall's approval, the Baltimore Women's Committee set up a fellowship for Sabin in the Department of Anatomy under Mall's supervision. During her tenure as a fellow, Sabin began research on the development and structure of the lymphatic system, work that would occupy her for a number of years. When her fellowship expired in 1902, Mall kept her on as an assistant instructor in the Department of Anatomy, which made her the first woman on the Johns Hopkins faculty. Despite this recognition from her mentor and her educational qualifications, her male colleagues continued to call her "Miss," rather than "Doctor," Sabin.

Rather than publicly protest this unequal treatment by her male colleagues, Sabin quietly dedicated herself to her research and teaching, with the hope that if she worked hard and avoided controversy, she would eventually receive the praise she deserved. Between 1902 and 1925, she focused on studying the origins of blood cells and the lymphatic system. One of her most significant accomplishments in this area was her demonstration that the lymphatic system arises from buds on the blood vessels, disproving an older theory that the lymphatics arose from the tissue spaces and then grew toward the blood vessels.

At first, acknowledgment of Sabin's scientific accomplishments came largely from other women. For example, in 1903 one of her papers on the lymphatic system was awarded a $1,000 prize from the Naples Table Association, an organization dedicated to promoting scientific research by women. In 1910, Smith College awarded her an honorary Doctorate of Science in recognition of her outstanding scientific accomplishments. She received numerous other awards from women's organizations throughout her life, including the Annual Achievement Award from *Pictorial Review* in 1929, the National Achievement Award from Chi Omega Sorority in 1932, and the M. Carey Thomas Prize in 1935.

Sabin also gradually won some measure of respect from male scientists, although it was half-hearted at times. In 1917, she was promoted to full professor in the Department of Anatomy at Hopkins, the first woman to attain this goal. However, her male colleagues never fully accepted her as an equal, as is demonstrated by their failure to appoint her as chair of the department following Mall's death in 1917. Instead, Sabin endured the humiliation of watching one of her own students, whom many of her friends considered her inferior in experience and talent, promoted above her to chair. Although Sabin was disappointed, she made no formal complaints about this episode to the Johns Hopkins administration.

While she never outwardly protested unfair treatment from men, Sabin did support some feminist causes. Throughout her career, she maintained close contact with the members of the Baltimore Women's Committee, who, in addition to supporting Sabin and other women's scientific careers, fought diligently for women's suffrage and other feminist issues. Sabin herself wrote countless letters to Maryland legislators, marched in suffrage parades, and worked tirelessly to convince her male colleagues of the importance of the suffrage issue. In 1909, she happily pointed out that all the full professors at the medical school, with the interesting exception of the professor of obstetrics, supported women's suffrage.

Sabin was aware that other women scientists tended to be underrecognized, and she worked quietly behind the scenes to improve some conditions for female colleagues. For example, when she was notified that she had been selected for an award from a particular organization, she would frequently turn the award down and suggest that one of her younger, less recognized colleagues should be honored instead. Similarly, when she served on the advisory board of the Guggenheim Memorial Foundation, she ensured that women received equal consideration for these awards. She warned younger women scientists that professional success would not come easily, despite the efforts of herself and other established female scientists to improve the situation for women in science. Indeed, she advised female students considering scientific careers to "be prepared to work hard for work's sake, without thought of what it may bring them in the way of personal acclaim and emolument."

By adhering to her own standards of hard work and humility, Sabin achieved a level of scientific renown that no woman had before. In 1924, she was elected the first female president of the American Association of Anatomists. The following year, she was elected to the National Academy of Sciences, the first woman ever to receive such a highly coveted position. Also in 1925, she left the Johns Hopkins Medical School to accept a position as a member of the Rockefeller Institute for Medical Research, again the first woman to be so honored. At the Rockefeller Institute, she spent 13 years working on various projects on the immune system, including a groundbreaking study on the immune response to tuberculosis. Her work at the Institute won her widespread acclaim from female and male scientists alike.

After leaving the Rockefeller Institute in 1938, Sabin retired to her home state of Colorado to spend more time with her sister Mary, who by this time was her only surviving relative. Sabin sustained an active intellectual life even in retirement, and maintained close contact with her friends and former colleagues in Baltimore and New York. She did not remain in retirement long, for in 1944 she accepted a request from Governor John Vivant of Colorado to serve on his Post-War Planning Committee and assist in the state's health needs. Sabin soon discovered that Colorado's public-health system was riddled with political corruption and bureaucratic inefficiency, and she essentially began a one-woman campaign for reforms. With the same zeal she had devoted to the suffrage campaign, Sabin collected information on the state's health institutions, and lobbied legislators and officials to support and more adequately finance public-health programs. Her hard work resulted in the passage of a series of public-health bills, commonly referred to as the "Sabin laws," which significantly improved the amount of funding allotted to various regulatory agencies. These laws also substantially improved the health and welfare of the citizens of Colorado, particularly those who suffered from tuberculosis. Within two years after passage of the Sabin laws, the death rate from tuberculosis in the state was cut in half. Despite her advanced age, Sabin continued to work on behalf of public and environmental health issues in Colorado throughout the late 1940s and early 1950s. In 1947, her achievements in public health were recognized by her election as president of both the Western Branch of the American Public Health Association and the Denver Board of Public Health, as well as her unanimous appointment as honorary fellow of the American Public Health Association.

It was only when her sister became increasingly ill during 1951 that Sabin finally withdrew from all professional activities. Eventually, the strain of caring for her invalid sister wore Florence down, and her own health gradually declined throughout 1953. That October, Sabin died of a heart attack, just a few days shy of her 82nd birthday. In her obituary in the Denver *Post*, she was called the "First Lady of American

Science," a tribute demonstrated by the numerous awards and honorary degrees she received throughout her life and the buildings named for her at the University of Colorado School of Medicine and at Smith College. In 1956, recognition of her life's accomplishments culminated in the installation of a bronze statue in the National Statuary Hall in Washington, D.C., in honor of "Florence Sabin, Teacher-Scientist-Citizen."

SOURCES:

Andriole, Vincent T. "Florence Rena Sabin—Teacher, Scientist, Citizen," in *Journal of the History of Medicine and Allied Sciences*. Vol. 14. July 1959, pp. 320–350.

Bluemel, Elinor. *Florence Sabin: Colorado Woman of the Century*. Boulder, CO: University of Colorado Press, 1959.

Brieger, Gert H. "Florence Rena Sabin," in *Notable American Women: The Modern Period*. Eds. Barbara Sicherman and Carol Hurd Green. Cambridge, MA: Harvard University Press, 1980.

Kubie, Lawrence S. "Florence Rena Sabin," in *Perspectives in Biology and Medicine*. Vol. 4. Spring 1961, pp. 306–315.

McMaster, Philip D. and Michael Heidelberger. "Florence Rena Sabin," in *Biographical Memoirs of the National Academy of Sciences*. Vol. 34, 1960, pp. 271–319.

Phelan, Mary K. *Probing the Unknown: The Story of Dr. Florence Sabin*. NY: Thomas Y. Crowell, 1969.

SUGGESTED READING:

Glazer, Penina Migdal, and Miriam Slater. *Unequal Colleagues: The Entrance of Women into the Professions, 1890–1940*. New Brunswick, NJ: Rutgers University Press, 1987.

Morantz-Sanchez, Regina Markell. *Sympathy and Science: Women Physicians in American Medicine*. NY: Oxford University Press, 1985.

Rossiter, Margaret W. *Women Scientists in America: Struggles and Strategies to 1940*. Baltimore, MD: Johns Hopkins University Press, 1982.

COLLECTIONS:

Florence Sabin Papers, Sophia Smith Collection, Smith College, Northampton, Massachusetts.

Florence Sabin Papers, American Philosophical Society, Philadelphia, Pennsylvania.

Heather Munro Prescott,
Associate Professor of History,
Central Connecticut State University,
New Britain, Connecticut

Sabin, Pauline Morton (1887–1955)

American political reformer. Name variations: Pauline Smith; Mrs. Charles H. Sabin. Born Pauline Morton in Chicago, Illinois, on April 23, 1887; died of bronchopneumonia on December 27, 1955, in Washington, D.C.; younger of two daughters of Paul Morton (a railroad executive and later president of the Equitable Life Assurance Society whose brother founded Morton Salt) and Charlotte (Goodridge) Morton; granddaughter of J. Sterling Morton (U.S. secretary of agriculture); educated in private schools and abroad; married James Hopkins Smith, Jr., on February 2, 1907 (divorced); married Charles Hamilton Sabin (president of Guaranty Trust Company of New York), on December 28, 1916 (died 1933); married Dwight F. Davis (former U.S. secretary of war, governor-general of the Philippines, and donor of the Davis Cup tennis trophy), on May 9, 1936; children: (first marriage) Paul Morton Smith (1908–1956); James Hopkins Smith (b. 1909), who became assistant secretary for the navy.

Pauline Morton Sabin was considered the "mother" of prohibition reform in America. In 1929, after observing nine years of lawlessness, bootlegging and gangster rule, she threw herself into the fight to repeal the 18th Amendment to the Constitution. Though a lifelong Republican, Sabin put principles above party and in 1932 supported Franklin D. Roosevelt for the presidency, because he came out for repeal. Sabin had been a member of the Republican Committee of Suffolk County, New York (1919); a member of the Republican State Executive Committee of New York (1920); president of the Women's National Republican Club (1921); delegate to the Republican National Convention (1924); and a member of the Republican National Committee. She resigned from the committee in 1929 to organize the Women's Organization for National Prohibition Reform, of which she was made national chair. After winning her fight against prohibition in 1933, Sabin pushed just as energetically for political reforms in New York City.

Sabina (88–136 CE)

Roman empress who was the wife of Hadrian. Name variations: Vibia Sabina. Born in 88 CE; daughter of Matidia I (d. 119 CE) and L. Vibius Sabinus; married Hadrian, Roman emperor (r. 117–138 CE).

Sabina was born in 88 CE, the daughter of L. Vibius Sabinus and *Matidia I, the maternal granddaughter of G. Salonius Matidius Patruinus and *Ulpia Marciana, and the grandniece of Ulpia's brother M. Ulpius Traianus (Trajan). When Sabina was ten years old, Trajan became emperor of Rome. Thus, she was in a powerful position when she came to be of marriageable age. Sabina had a younger sister, *Matidia II, named after their mother as Sabina bore the feminine version of their father's name. Although Sabina's family was both Roman and aristocratic, it also had provincial ties, for long before her birth it had been among the first to settle in Italica, a Roman colony in Spain.

Sabina's importance was connected with the successful career of her granduncle Trajan, whose brilliant military service caused Emperor Domitian to elevate him to the uppermost echelon of the Roman political elite before that unpopular emperor was assassinated in late 96. Although he was somewhat sullied by his close association with Diocletian, Trajan's competency and extensive connections led Domitian's childless successor, Nerva, to adopt him in 97. As a result, when Nerva died a few months later (98), the empire fell into Trajan's lap. Thus unexpectedly elevated to supreme authority, Trajan had a need to consolidate his rule, and a common way to do so in ancient Rome was to judiciously exploit political marriage.

Trajan and his wife *Plotina, however, were childless. As a result, soon after their young grandniece Sabina reached puberty, she was married (in 100) to P. Aelius Hadrianus (Hadrian, b. 76 CE), a distant relative: Hadrian's great-grandfather was the grandfather of Trajan and Ulpia Marciana. Whatever else this marriage did, it purposely rejected a close connection between the family of Trajan (and Hadrian) and any other within the Senatorial nobility. As such, Trajan both avoided angering all of the other Senatorial families who might interpret Sabina's marriage as a snub and avoided entangling alliances with another clan which surely would have thought itself at least the social equal of Trajan's family.

Despite the political rationale behind this union and Plotina's enthusiasm for the match, Trajan is said to have had reservations about Hadrian as Sabina's husband, although the nature of these reservations is nowhere explained. Trajan's hesitancy over Sabina's marriage is all the more puzzling because, even before his elevation to imperial status, Hadrian had been established as Trajan's military and political protégé. Perhaps it was not the match itself, but the youth of Sabina at the time of its consummation which concerned Trajan. Another possible source of Trajan's concern might have been his knowledge of Hadrian's sexual orientation. One thing seems certain: although the union would not be happy, it is hardly likely that Trajan could have predicted Sabina's and Hadrian's personality clash, since Sabina was little more than a child when she wed. Hadrian also seems to have been cool to the match, but accepted it as necessary for his continued advancement. Regardless of the reservations involved, when this marriage was celebrated a new age was dawning, and

Sabina became an important link between the two men who would determine the shape which that future would take.

As the reign of Trajan unfolded productively, it became apparent that the woman in Hadrian's life was not to be Sabina, but Plotina, who was so enthusiastic a promoter of Hadrian's interests that some suspected her of being in love with him. If so, however, hers was more the affection of a mother than that of a lover. Being without a son of her own, Plotina lavished her maternal affections upon the next best thing. Nevertheless, she pampered Hadrian in a way as to intrude into the relationship between Hadrian and Sabina. This alone did not undermine their marriage, for at least two other factors stunted the development of much emotional and physical intimacy between Hadrian and Sabina. First, to whatever degree Hadrian might have been susceptible to feminine beauty (at least one source claims that he occasionally seduced the wives of important associates), he clearly harbored primarily homosexual inclinations. The most obvious evidence

Sabina

for this involved Hadrian's favorite, Antinoos, a handsome youth whom Hadrian kept close by his side even when traveling. On one such expedition, to Egypt in 130, Antinoos met a mysterious death by drowning in the Nile. Hadrian's grief as a result of this loss was so excessive that he founded a city (Antinoopolis) at the site, named a star after him, and dedicated statues to his memory in religious sanctuaries throughout the empire. Contemporary tongues wagged about the emperor's devotion.

The second factor which precluded the development of intimacy between Sabina and Hadrian was Sabina herself. Undoubtedly pampered as a child, accustomed to being the center of much attention, and excited by the prospects of her politically significant marriage, she was, it is probable, quickly disillusioned by Hadrian's private aloofness, and her marginal (if publicly proper) role in his life. As a result, the sting—not of rejection, but of indifference—bred anger in Sabina, and then hatred. She was known to throw tantrums and to be ill-tempered in Hadrian's presence, and she even made it a source of some pride to have it known that the reason Hadrian remained childless was that she refused to have sex with him.

When Trajan died in 117 in Asia Minor (after having been engaged in a war of conquest for the complete control of Mesopotamia), Plotina delayed an announcement of the death until she had assured Hadrian's uncontested accession. This was necessary because, although Hadrian had emerged as the obvious successor of Trajan by that time, the emperor had never formally adopted him as his legal heir. Why Trajan had not done so before 117 is a matter of conjecture, as is whether he actually lived long enough to adopt Hadrian. Plotina, who was with her husband when a stroke (some thought poison might have been involved) laid him low, claimed that Trajan had adopted Hadrian on his deathbed. However, the fact that the publication of this adoption came in letters which *she*, not Trajan, wrote and sent to Rome has allowed many, then as well as now, to question what really happened after Trajan fell ill. Regardless, Hadrian replaced Trajan, and quickly consolidated his hold on the throne. Plotina helped him do so and stood staunchly at his side until she herself died around 122, after which Hadrian had her deified.

Thereafter, it would be only Sabina who graced the arm of Hadrian on appropriate public occasions, for although their mutual antipathy held, they remained married. Undoubtedly they did so because the Romans expected their emperors to be married. As well, Sabina was too well placed for Hadrian to abandon, and she provided cover for his homosexual affairs. (By and large, the Romans tended to disdain homosexuals.) Although she loathed Hadrian, Sabina enjoyed being the empress of Rome, with all of its perquisites.

Hadrian's was mostly a peaceful reign, and was characterized by his extensive travels throughout the empire. Sabina accompanied her husband on these state visits to the provinces (including that to Egypt when Antinoos died), so there is ample testimony to the continuation of her public status throughout the Roman world. She was styled as the "Augusta" (after 128) and widely recognized as the "new Hera" (after 129), and her portrait even graced many a contemporary coin. Thus did Hadrian broadcast his "respect" for his spouse. Those close to the palace, however, knew a different story: their private altercations and disdain continued until death did them part. Although Hadrian maintained his distance from Sabina as much as possible, he clearly kept a close eye on her affairs. In 122, while the imperial couple was visiting Britain, two of Sabina's associates—Septicius Clarus (a praetorian praefect) and Seutonius Tranquillus (a director of correspondence and the famous imperial biographer)—were dismissed from public service, supposedly because they were "too informal" in their relationship with Sabina, but really because they were her friends. In the wake of these dismissals, Hadrian announced that he would have divorced Sabina too, if she had been a "private citizen." Thus did he admit how important she was to his possession of the throne.

So did Sabina and Hadrian coexist until her death in 136. With their well-established antipathy widely if not universally known, it comes as no surprise that some blamed Sabina's death on Hadrian, either through poisoning or enforced suicide. Since the two had put up with one another for 36 years, however, there is no compelling reason to believe that Hadrian had a hand in Sabina's demise, although he surely took pleasure in her passing. Regardless, even in death Hadrian maintained an appropriate piety toward her memory by both proclaiming her a goddess and seeing to it that her ashes were placed in his mausoleum. Indeed, there is even a tinge of poetic justice in the fact that the fates of the two would be tied together for all of eternity, since both Hadrian and Sabina shared honorific inscriptions originally situated over the doorway of their common tomb.

William S. Greenwalt,
Associate Professor of Classical History,
Santa Clara University, Santa Clara, California

Sabina (b. 166).

See Faustina II for sidebar on Vibia Aurelia Sabina.

Sabina, Poppaea (d. 47).

See Messalina, Valeria for sidebar.

Sabina, Poppaea (d. 65).

See Agrippina the Younger for sidebar.

Sabine of Bavaria (1492–1564)

Duchess of Wurttemberg. Born on April 23, 1492; died on August 30, 1564; daughter of Albert IV the Wise (1447–1508), duke of Bavaria (r. 1465–1508); married Ulrich VI (1487–155), duke of Wurttemberg (r. 1503–1519, 1534–1550), on March 2, 1511; children: Christof (b. 1515), duke of Wurttemberg.

Sabine of Brandenburg-Ansbach (1529–1575)

*Electress of Brandenburg. Name variations: Sabine von Brandenburg-Ansbach or Anspach. Born on May 12, 1529; died on November 2, 1575; daughter of George of Ansbach (b. 1484) and Hedwig of Munsterberg (d. 1531); became second wife of John George (1525–1598), elector of Brandenburg (r. 1571–1598), on February 12, 1548; children: *Sophie of Brandenburg (1568–1622). John George's first wife was *Sophie of Liegnitz (1525–1546); his third was *Elizabeth of Anhalt (1563–1607).*

Sablé, Madeleine de Souvré, Marquise de (c. 1599–1678)

French writer of letters and maxims. Name variations: Magdeleine, Marquise de Sable, Sablé, or Sabele; Madame de Sablé. Born around 1599; died on January 16, 1678; daughter of Gilles de Souvré, marquis de Courtenvaux (tutor of Louis XIII and marshal of France); married Philippe Emmanuel de Laval, marquis de Sablé, in 1614 (died 1640); children: four.

Following the death of her husband in 1640 which left her in somewhat straitened circumstances, Madame de Sablé took rooms in the Place Royale, Paris, with her friend the **Countess of St. Maur.** There she established a literary salon almost rivaling that of the ❧➤ **Marquise de Rambouillet** in importance. Sablé's salon was frequented by *Marie-Madeleine de La Fayette and Antoine Arnauld, and contributed to the production of the maxims of La Rochefoucauld. In fact, the *Maximes et Pensées diverse* of the Marquise de Sablé were composed before those of La Rochefoucauld, though not published until after her death.

In 1655, she retired, with the Countess of St. Maur, to the Convent of Port Royal des Champs, near Marly. (*See also Port Royal des Champs, Abbesses of.*) When that establishment was closed, the two moved to Auteuil in 1661. In 1669, Madame de Sablé took up her residence in the Port Royal convent in Paris, where she died on January 16, 1678.

Sablière, Marguerite de la (1640–1693).

See La Sablière, Marguerite de.

Sabuco, Oliva de Nantes Barrera (1562–1625)

Spanish philosopher and medical writer. Name variations: Luisa. Born in Alcarez, Spain, in 1562; died in Alcarez in 1625; fifth of eight children of Bachiller Miguel Sabuco and Francisca de Cozar; sister of Alonso Sabuco; married Acacio de Buedo of Alcaraz, in 1580.

Selected works: Nueva filosofía de la naturaleza del hombre, no conocido ni alcanzada de los grandes filosofos antiquis, laquel mejora la vida y salud humana . . . escuta y sacada a luz par Doña Oliva Sabuco de Nantes Barrera, natural de la ciudad de Alcare (1587); Vera medicine y vera filosofia, oculta a lost antiguos, en dos dialogos (1587).

Nueva filosofía de la naturaleza del hombre, the philosophical treatise of Oliva Sabuco, was first published in 1587. Shortly after, Oliva's father Miguel Sabuco gave his oldest son Alonso Sabuco a "letter of power" in which Miguel claimed authorship of the work published under his daughter's name. She had been "named its author only to confer honor on her," he wrote in the letter, and she had no legal or personal interest in it. He then sent Alonso and his wife to Spain in an unsuccessful attempt to have the treatise published there under Miguel's name. But Miguel never paid their expenses for the trip (Oliva's husband Acacio de Buedo eventually did) and eventually retracted the statement of his authorship. When his letter was unearthed by historians at the beginning of the 20th century, authorship again became an issue, but the treatise is once again accepted as Oliva's work.

A second edition of the work was published in 1588 (and one further edition was pirated). But the book was suppressed, and all but two copies, parts of which had been erased, were de-

❧➤

Rambouillet, Marquise de.

See Salonnières for sidebar.

stroyed by the Inquisition. Then in 1622 it was republished in Portugal. The book is considered to have been very influential. Sabuco's philosophy harks back to the classical tradition, and uses the classical dialogue format, to examine the order of nature and humanity. She presaged René Descartes in her concern over the interaction of the soul and the body, placing their nexus in the brain. The treatise is now usually published along with her writing on medicine, *Vera Medicine*, a colloquy originally published in 1587, which includes a philosophical discussion of the human body and emotions, as well as medical advice.

SOURCES:

Dowling, John. "Oliva Sabuco de Nantes Barrera," in Katharina Wilson, ed., *Encyclopedia of Continental Women Writers*. NY: Garland, 1991.

Hurd-Mead, Kate Campbell. *A History of Women in Medicine, from the Earliest Times to the Beginning of the Nineteenth Century*. Haddam, CT: Haddam Press, 1938.

Kersey, Ethel M. *Women Philosophers: a Bio-critical Source Book*. NY: Greenwood, 1989.

Waithe, Mary Ellen, ed. *A History of Women Philosophers*. Boston, MA: Martinus Nijhoff, 1987–95.

Catherine Hundleby, M.A. Philosophy,
University of Guelph, Guelph, Ontario, Canada

Sacagawea (c. 1787–c. 1812 or 1884).

See Sacajawea.

Sacajawea (c. 1787–c. 1812 or 1884)

Native American who served as a guide and interpreter for the historic Lewis and Clark Expedition in 1805–06 as they traveled up the Missouri River and westward to the Pacific Ocean. Name variations: Sacagewea; Sacagawea; Sakajawea; Sakakawea; "Bird Woman" (translated from the language of the Hidatsa, a tribe within the Shoshoni); "Boat Pusher" (translated from Shoshoni); sometimes called Janey in Clark's journal. Pronunciation: Tsi-ki-ka-wi-as in Hidatsa, rendered phonetically in English as Sakakawea, or, in Clark's journal as "Sah-kah-gar-we-a," later amended to "Sacajawea" by expedition member George Shannon (which was accepted as the standard form for the name from 1893). Born into a tribe of Northern Shoshonis, in what is now the Lemhi Valley of Idaho, around 1787; died as early as 1812, in childbirth, or (according to a minister who claimed to have officiated at her burial) as late as April 9, 1884; married Touissant Charbonneau (common-law, without benefit of church or state), a fur trapper and guide; children: Jean Baptiste, nicknamed "Pomp" which is Shoshoni for "first born" (b. February 11 or 12, 1805); Bazil

(adopted, son of her deceased sister); possibly a daughter, Lizette (or Lisette).

Spent 20 months as guide for President Jefferson's expedition to explore the country's new holdings in the West (1805–06), then passed out of history except for a few unreliable references.

The only definitive information known about Sacajawea, whose name has become intrinsically linked with one of the greatest adventures in American history, dates from the 20 months she spent as a guide with the famous Lewis and Clark Expedition, which set out to explore and map the United States' newly acquired Louisiana Territory in 1804–06. A small, resilient Shoshoni woman with a newborn baby on her back, she earned the respect of the explorers she led and may very well have won the heart of expedition leader Captain William Clark. Despite attending to the needs of her young son and being subjected to an aging husband (some reports indicate that he may have acquired her in a gambling game; others that she was sold to him as a slave; and still others that he received her in a trade), Sacajawea remained unfailingly cheerful throughout the journey. With her baby, she was a symbol of the expedition's peaceful (or at least non-warlike) intentions to the Indian tribes they encountered and thus served as the explorers' ambassador of good will as they made their historic journey.

Sacajawea was born into a tribe of Northern Shoshonis somewhere in what was later called the Lemhi Valley in the modern state of Idaho. The date of her birth was around 1787 or 1788, according to the European Christian calendar. Her childhood was interrupted when she was kidnapped by another Shoshoni tribe called the Hidatsa, and it ended when she became the wife of Touissant Charbonneau, a French-Canadian fur trader living among the Hidatsa and Mandan Indians. Her marriage was *à la façon du pays* (after the fashion of the country), a common-law relationship without benefit of church or state ceremony. In the records of Lewis and Clark, Charbonneau was acknowledged as a good interpreter but characterized as brutish, clumsy, prone to panic, and not particularly capable of performing the tasks assigned to him. Other documentary sources which allude to him suggest that he was competent, and his reputation may have suffered largely in comparison to his admirable wife.

The Lewis and Clark Expedition for which Sacajawea would become famed was authorized by President Thomas Jefferson even before he had arranged for the purchase of the vast area of land, known as the Louisiana Territory, west of the Mississippi River, from Napoleon's France. Also called the Louisiana Purchase, this area was defined by the watershed of the Missouri River branch of the Mississippi River (meaning that all the land drained by streams and rivers that flowed into the Missouri River, then into the Mississippi River, was part of the territory).

Headed by two captains, Meriwether Lewis (President Jefferson's private secretary) and William Clark (the younger brother of the famous Revolutionary War general George Rogers Clark), the Lewis and Clark expedition assembled near St. Louis in the fall of 1803 to explore this territory. Their party was made up of 14 soldiers, 9 civilian Kentucky volunteers, 2 French rivermen, a professional hunter, and Clark's personal servant, a black man named York; later, there were to be additions and subtractions from this original group. Jefferson also authorized the expedition to cross over the Continental Divide and the northern Rocky Mountains to reach the Pacific Ocean. All along the way, they were to learn what they could about the minerals, plants, animals and Indian populations occupying the region.

Departing St. Louis in May 1804, the expedition did not reach new territory until November, when they set up winter quarters among the Mandan Indians in the middle of present-day North Dakota. At what was Fort Mandan, the group took on two interpreters and their wives, who were Indian. One of these couples was Charbonneau and Sacajawea. On February 11 or 12, after a difficult labor, Sacajawea gave birth to a son. Although given the European Christian name of Jean Baptiste Charbonneau, the boy was known by his Shoshoni name of "Pomp," meaning "first born." (Some accounts record that it was Clark who gave the infant, for whom he had much affection, the nickname Pomp, because the child was so bouncy.)

On April 7, 1805, when the spring weather allowed the expedition to set out from Fort Mandan, the other interpreter and his wife remained behind, making Sacajawea now the only woman member of the expedition. From the beginning, the young mother endeared herself to the men by identifying edible berries and roots, which she picked industriously without complaint. While such activities were likely unremarkable to Sacajawea, her contributions to life on the expedition impressed the European-American observers, especially Captain Clark. She also mended clothes and moccasins and

nursed the sick and injured, all while caring for her infant son.

Sacajawea first distinguished herself on May 14 when she saved many valuable supplies after a boat capsized. Originally seated in the rear of the boat with Pomp strapped on her back, she held on to the boat as it turned on its side and fished lost items out of the swirling water, including cases of instruments, compasses, books, and clothing. Lewis, who never became as fond of her as Clark, was especially grateful for her rescue of his precious copy of Benjamin Barton's *Elements of Botany*. Her calm effectiveness was especially notable in contrast to the panic displayed by her husband who could not swim. On May 20, in recognition of her feat, a river along their route was named in her honor. (A later journal noted, however, "With less gallantry, the present generation calls it Crooked Creek.")

> *P*icture a slight, active Indian girl, with the black hair and copper skin of most Shoshonis of her time . . . who set out for the Pacific with Lewis and Clark with a baby on her back.
>
> —**Harold P. Howard**

By the summer of 1805, the explorers had arrived in the Shoshoni territory from which Sacajawea had been stolen in her childhood. There she began her service as interpreter and good-will ambassador. In August, she broke her customary stoic calm when enjoying an emotional reunion with her brother Cameahwait, a Shoshoni chief. She learned that of her family only he, another brother (who was absent), and her eldest sister's son Bazil were still alive. Sacajawea immediately adopted Bazil.

That autumn, assisted by maps drawn for them by Chief Cameahwait and by Sacajawea's knowledge of edible vegetation, the expedition traversed the Bitterroot Mountain Range (which separates modern Montana and Idaho), to make the momentous crossing from the Missouri River into the Columbia River basin. In November, with winter closing in, they trudged down the Columbia to the coast. By the first of the year, they arrived exhausted at Fort Clatsop, near the modern city of Portland, Oregon, to spend the rest of the winter. The decision as to where they would winter had been made by vote, with the votes of both Sacajawea and Clark's servant York counted equally with the others.

During the first six months of 1806, the Walla Walla and Nez Perce Indians helped the beleaguered explorers by restoring their food supplies and even healing their wounds. Although these Pacific Northwest Indians were already favorably disposed to the European-American explorers (their disillusionment would come later), the presence of Sacajawea and her baby, who was by now a toddler, no doubt helped to smooth relations.

At the end of June, recrossing the Bitterroot Mountains entailed considerable hardship for the party. By the time they re-entered Montana, Sacajawea again proved of great assistance. In early July, the captains separated their expedition into two groups. Lewis took the northern route to follow the Missouri River as it bends north toward what is now Great Falls. Clark chose the shorter route from the Missouri River's source at Three Forks (the junction of the Jefferson, Madison, and Gallatin Rivers) directly across southern Montana just north of Yellowstone Park. Remaining with Clark, Sacajawea was able to assure him that their southern group was following the right track. On their way down the Yellowstone River, which courses northeastward, they proceeded toward what is now the city of Livingston. Lewis' northern group was not so fortunate, enduring a skirmish with some Blackfoot Indians, but eventually did rejoin Clark's group (August 12) at the mouth of the Yellowstone River where it joins the Missouri River near the Montana-North Dakota boundary.

Sacajawea's journey ended in August 1806 at the Hidatsa-Mandan village, where she and her husband were relieved of their duties (the expedition party would arrive back at St. Louis the following month). For his services, Charbonneau received a voucher for just over $500. Sacajawea received no compensation for her role on the journey, and Clark noted in a letter to her husband (August 20, 1806): "Your woman who accompanied you that long dangerous and fatigueing rout to the Pacific Ocean and back, deserved a greater reward for her attention and Services on that rout than we had in our power to give her at the Mandans." Clark gave the family an opportunity to experience the world of Europeans at the thriving trading post on the banks of the Mississippi. Charbonneau accepted the offer, taking Sacajawea and Pomp (no word about Bazil) into St. Louis. But neither Charbonneau nor Sacajawea were city people, and when he decided to return to the Upper Missouri she went with him, leaving her son in St. Louis (where Pomp's education was supervised by Clark). While there are scattered references to the subsequent lives of the men—Charbonneau, Pomp, and even Bazil—Sacajawea disappears from all reliable European-American documentation.

Several references in Indian oral traditions and European documents, which have been largely discredited, suggest that Sacajawea lived to a ripe old age. In the early years of the 20th century, *Grace Raymond Hebard and Charles A. Eastman pieced together the traditional Shoshoni accounts into the following tale. After 1806, Charbonneau took a new wife, which Sacajawea tolerated. She left him, however, after he whipped her once too often. Sacajawea then wandered for several years before marrying a Comanche (whose language is related to that of the Shoshoni), with whom she had five children. Outliving her husband after he was killed in battle, in the 1860s she was reunited with Pomp, now called Baptiste, and her own people. Subsequently, she was tenderly cared for by her adopted son Bazil, who had suffered a crippling leg wound and was a sub-chief for the famous Chief Washakie. According to one unsubstantiated account, Sacajawea was killed by hostile Indians near what is now Glasgow, Montana, in 1869. The more accepted version is that she lived until April 9, 1884, when she was formally buried by an Episcopal missionary named Reverend John Roberts on the Wind River Reservation in Wyoming. A historical marker on the reservation reads: "Sacajawea, Died April 9, 1884. A Guide with the Lewis and Clark Expedition, 1805–1806. Identified, 1907, by Rev. John Roberts Who Officiated at Her Burial."

It is most likely though that Sacajawea died in childbirth about six years after the expedition at Fort Manuel, in what is now South Dakota, on December 20, 1812. According to an entry in a diary kept by a John Luttig: "This evening the wife of Charbonneau, a Snake squaw, died of putrid fever. She was a good and the best woman in the fort, aged about 25 years. She left a fine infant girl." Given the European ignorance of Indian tribes and widespread difficulties in spelling Sacajawea's name, we should probably conclude that this was her actual death notice. In 1813, after the fort was burned by Indians, Luttig applied to the court to be appointed guardian of the girl, named Lizette, as well as for a boy declared to be about ten years old named Touissant (a name he shared with Sacajawea's husband). When Luttig died in 1815, his name was erased from the court record and replaced by that of "William Clark."

A notebook owned by Clark discovered in 1955 perhaps clinches the argument. On the outside of the book, which Clark apparently used between 1825 and 1828, he listed the names of all who were on the expedition, with

Sacajawea

notations as to what happened to each of them following the journey. He has been proven definitely wrong about only one member who lived to be almost one hundred years old. Beside Sacajawea's name he wrote one word: "Dead." Clark himself died in 1838.

In Clark's journal of the expedition, on April 7, 1805, he wrote out a phonetic spelling of her name, "Sah-kah-gar-we-a," apparently intending that the "g" be pronounced hard, but for the official edition this spelling was amended by George Shannon, a college-educated member of the expedition (and a better speller), who insisted that the name be spelled Sacajawea. Elliott Coues adopted this latter spelling in his massive history of the expedition, published in 1893, and it has since been accepted as standard. In Hidatsa, the language of the tribe who kidnapped the young girl away from her people, the phonetic rendering of her name was "Tsi-ki-ka-wi-as" which became "Sakakawea" in English. The name meant "Bird Woman" in Hidatsa, while the meaning in Shoshoni was "Boat Pusher." European-American biographers have preferred to perpetuate the former, more exalted, translation.

After Sacajawea guided her party through Indian country, up the Missouri River to its headwaters and source, over the Continental Divide to the Pacific Ocean, and then back down the Missouri River to St. Louis, she retreated back into the obscurity from whence she came. In her place emerged an American legend. In addition to Sacajawea Creek, Montana (named for her by Lewis and Clark), many natural sites were named in her honor including the Sacajawea Lakes in Washington (at Longview) and North Dakota (formerly Lake Garrison) as well as the Sacajawea Mountain Peaks in Montana (Bridger Range), Wyoming (Wind River Range), Idaho (Lost River Range), and Oregon (Wallowa Range). The subject of numerous statues, paintings, historic markers, and musical compositions, she also appears on an American gold-colored $1 coin which replaced the *Susan B. Anthony dollar in 2000. In his biography *Sacajawea*, Harold P. Howard concludes his study with the picture of "an Indian girl bearing a baby on her back, gathering berries along a riverbank for a boatload of [European] explorers bound on America's great westward adventure."

SOURCES:

Coues, Elliott. *A History of the Expedition Under the Command of Captains Lewis and Clark.* 3 vols. New York, 1965 (first published in 4 vols., 1893).

Hebard, Grace Raymond. *Sacajawea: Guide of the Lewis and Clark Expedition.* Los Angeles, 1957 (first published in 1932).

Howard, Harold P. *Sacajawea.* OK: University of Oklahoma, 1971.

SUGGESTED READING:

De Voto, Bernard, ed. *The Journals of Lewis and Clark.* Boston, 1963.

Lewis, Meriwether. *The Lewis and Clark Expedition.* Edited by Nicholas Biddle. 3 vols. Philadelphia, 1961 (first published in 1814).

———, and William Clark. *Original Journals of the Lewis and Clark Expedition.* Edited by Reuben Gold Thwaites. 8 vols. New York, 1904.

Moulton, Gary E., ed. *The Journals of the Lewis and Clark Expedition.* University of Nebraska, 1983.

David R. Stevenson,
Associate Professor of History,
University of Nebraska at Kearney, Nebraska

Sacharissa (1617–1684).

See Sidney, Lady Dorothy.

Sacher, Anna (1859–1930)

Austrian hotel proprietor, owner of Vienna's world-famous Hotel Sacher, who was famed for the elegance of her hotel and her colorful personality. Born Anna Maria Fuchs in Vienna, Austria, on January 2, 1859; died in Vienna on February 25, 1930; daughter of Johann Fuchs; married Eduard Sacher (1843–1892, a hotel owner), in 1880; children: Anna Sacher; Fanny Sacher; Eduard Sacher.

Born in 1859 in Vienna's Leopoldstadt district into modest circumstances (her father was a butcher), Anna Maria Fuchs would become world renowned as Anna Sacher, owner of her city's incomparable Hotel Sacher. In 1880, she married Eduard Sacher, one of three sons of Franz Sacher, who was originally a cook in Prince Metternich's kitchen and was able to improve his station by founding a successful wine shop and delicatessen. Eduard too had started out as a cook, but after working in Paris and accumulating some capital, he opened a tavern that introduced into Vienna a remnant of naughty Paris—*Chambre separées*, discreet rooms where wealthy males could dally with young women of light virtue. Having accumulated more capital, in 1873 Eduard inaugurated a new hotel—known as the Hotel Sacher—that guaranteed Vienna's aristocrats and top bourgeoisie not only the best in dining and accommodations but a multitude of *Chambre separées* for their private pleasures.

Eduard died prematurely in 1892, but the establishment named after him was never in danger of faltering. The same high standards of quality were maintained, and even enhanced, by his widow, who quickly became known universally as "Frau Sacher." Attractive as a young woman, Sacher saw her beauty fade as she grew older, but she more than made up for this with her formidable personality. Smoking a cigar, she would often be seen in public accompanied by her pair of toy French dogs. Despite Anna Sacher's eccentricities, few details of her hotel ever escaped her, and its standards never slipped. Assisted by longtime headwaiter Franz Wagner, she ran a tight ship for almost four decades.

One of the hotel's most famous features was its fabled Sachertorte, a chocolate tart deemed incomparable by many a gourmet. The hotel also boasted fine cuisine, superb wines, an excellent location (across the street from the Hofoper, today's State Opera House, and only a few minutes by foot from the Hofburg, the Imperial Palace), and Anna Sacher's reputation for discretion. She never revealed what went on in her hotel's numerous *Chambre separées*, which served as places of assignation for many a Habsburg archduke. For Emperor Franz Joseph I, who pointedly never set foot in the Hotel Sacher, the establishment was an ominous barometer of his realm's (and family's) moral decay, and he regarded it as little better than a high-class bordello. It was in the Hotel Sacher that Franz Joseph's heir and only son, Crown Prince Rudolf, asked his current mistress, **Mizzi Caspar**, if she would be willing to enter into a suicide pact with him. After she responded to his offer with laughter, Rudolf chose to end his life in January 1889 with someone who was willing to die with him, teenager ***Marie Vetsera**.

Anna Sacher chose never to write her memoirs. Even so, a vast number of stories about her have been printed since her death, and they make fascinating reading, even if some are apocryphal. Sacher, whose hotel flourished in the long Indian summer before the Habsburg Empire met its demise at the end of World War I, revealed many noble qualities during that devastating conflict. Wartime food rationing ended the glorious menus and buffets of the pre-1914 age, and many of her regular aristocratic guests no longer came to Vienna, remaining instead on their rural estates where food supplies were relatively plentiful. As the situation worsened, the always generous Sacher fed and provided lodging for poor students. For this, she would receive the Goldene Verdienstkreuz (Golden Achievement Cross), one of the highest honors of the newly created Republic of Austria, which emerged after 1918.

Sacher's last years were not always happy. Postwar Vienna in the 1920s was a metropolis full of starving beggars, desperate bourgeois, and aristocrats too proud to beg. Inflation and class conflict made the new world a much less glamorous place, even if the vast majority in the "good old days" had never been able to enjoy the leisure and elegance of that epoch. Old and in poor health, in April 1929 Sacher withdrew from the management of her beloved hotel, placing it under the administration of trustees. She felt betrayed by her son Eduard, who had forged an alliance with the Hotel Sacher's arch-competitor, Demel's coffee house and pastry shop (owned by Karl and ***Anna Demel**), and wished to keep the establishment from his control after she passed from the scene. Anna Sacher died in Vienna on February 25, 1930. Before she was

Anna Sacher

buried outside the city, in Dornbach, her funeral cortege first moved with great solemnity around her internationally renowned hotel. Respectfully, the many Viennese who were present that day bowed their heads as Frau Sacher passed by for the last time.

SOURCES:

Brown, Catherine. "Recipe for a Proper Viennese Whirl," in *The Herald* [Glasgow]. January 16, 1993, p. 9.

Eybl, Franz M. *Ganz Wien ist ein Beisel: Literarische Eindrücke aus Wiener Hotels & Gaststätten.* Vienna: Döcker, 1998.

Hagen, Ernst. *Hotel Sacher: In deinen Betten schlief Österreich.* Vienna: Paul Zsolnay, 1976.

Johnston, William M. *The Austrian Mind: An Intellectual and Social History.* Berkeley, CA: University of California Press, 1972.

Maier-Bruck, Franz. *Das grosse Sacher Kochbuch: Die österreichische Küche.* Munich: Schuler, 1975.

Matthew, Christopher. *A Different World: Stories of Great Hotels.* NY: Paddington, 1976.

Mazakarini, Leopold Karl. *Das Hotel Sacher zu Wien.* Vienna: Orac, 1976.

"Mme. Sacher," in *The Times* [London]. February 26, 1930, p. 16.

Seeliger, Emil. *Hotel Sacher: Weltgeschichte beim Souper*. Berlin: Schaffer, 1939.

Sherwell, Philip. "Chocolate Soldiers Go into Battle," in *The Sunday Telegraph* [London]. March 14, 1993, p. 23.

"Tafelspitz und Sachertorte," in *Volksblatt-Magazin* [Vienna]. February 12, 1988, pp. 2–3.

Wagner, Renate. *Heimat bist Du grosser Töchter: Österreicherinnen im Laufe der Jahrhunderte*. Vienna: Edition S/Österreichische Staatsdruckerei, 1992.

Watkin, David. *Grand Hotel: The Golden Age of Palace Hotels, An Architectural and Social History*. Secaucus, NJ: Chartwell, 1984.

RELATED MEDIA:

"Hotel Sacher" (film), directed by Erich Engel in 1939, Chicago: International Historic Films, 1985.

"Legendary Hotels of the World. . . . The Imperial Hotels of Vienna," NY: A&E Home Video, 1997.

John Haag,
Associate Professor History,
University of Georgia, Athens, Georgia

Sachiko, Hidari (b. 1930).

See Hidari Sachiko.

Sachs, Nelly (1891–1970)

German-Jewish poet and playwright who was awarded the Nobel Prize for Literature in 1966 for her work commemorating the suffering of Holocaust victims.

Pronunciation: SAX. Born Leonie Sachs on December 10, 1891, in Berlin, Germany; died on May 12, 1970, at St. Görans-Hospital in Stockholm, Sweden; buried next to her parents in the Jewish cemetery in Haga Norra, Stockholm; daughter of William Sachs (a manufacturer) and Margarete (Karger) Sachs; attended Dorotheen-Schule (public school) in Berlin-Moabit, 1897–1900 (had to leave because of poor health); received private lessons until 1903; attended the exclusive Aubert-Schule, a private girls' school in Berlin, 1903–08; never married; no children.

Awards: Poetry award of the Swedish Radio (1958); prize for poetry from the Association of German Industry (1959); Droste Prize for poets (1960); city of Dortmund named her the first winner of the newly established Nelly-Sachs-Prize (1961); Peace Prize of the German Book Sellers Association (1965); named honorary citizen of Berlin (1967).

Grew up in Berlin; poems first published in the Vossische Zeitung *(Berlin, 1929); published poems in* Berliner Tagblatt *(1932); published poems in the Jewish paper* Der Morgen *(1936–38); her father, a wealthy manufacturer, died (1930); endured Nazi Germany's policies against Jews (1933–40); fled with mother to Sweden (1940); published first and only prose book,* Legenden und Erzählungen *(1921); published first volume of poetry with the East Berlin Auf-*bau Verlag (1947); translated Swedish poetry into German and edited anthologies of Swedish poetry (1947, 1958, 1963 and 1965); death of her mother (1950); journeyed to Germany, Zürich, and Paris, and met poet Paul Celan with whom she had corresponded since 1954 (1960); hospitalized, with short interruptions, for paranoia and persecution mania (1960–63); together with S.Y. Agnon, awarded Nobel Prize for Literature (December 10, 1966); dedication and ceremonial opening of a Nelly Sachs room at the Kungliga Library in Stockholm (December 10, 1971).

Selected works: Legenden und Erzählungen *(Legends and Stories, 1921);* In the Habitations of Death *(1947);* Eclipse of the Stars *(1949);* Eli: A Mystery Play of the Sufferings of Israel *(1951);* And No One Knows How to Go On *(1957);* Flight and Metamorphosis *(1959);* Journey into a Dustless Realm *(1961);* Death Still Celebrates Life *(1961);* Glowing Enigmas I–IV *(1963–66);* Die Suchende *(1966).*

Together with the Israeli writer S.Y. Agnon, Nelly Sachs was awarded the 1966 Nobel Prize for Literature, marking the high point of her career. While her poetry was largely ignored in the 1940s and 1950s, it became increasingly popular in the wake of a student movement, and Germany's attempts to come to terms with its National Socialist past. In the 1960s, Sachs, an important German-Jewish voice commemorating the Holocaust, was celebrated as one of the greatest German-language poets, though she lived in Sweden. Stylized by the press into a tragic and solemn cult figure, she received numerous honors and awards. The literary public perceived Sachs as a symbol of a German-Jewish reconciliation and misinterpreted her hopes for Germany's younger generation as a sign that the nation's past could now be laid to rest.

In 1966, before the Jewish World Congress, the Jewish philosopher Gershom Scholem spoke of an immeasurable abyss between Germans and Jews and declared the German-Jewish dialogue a dangerous illusion. By honoring Sachs' work, many Germans believed that the hopelessly divisive relationship between German and Jews could be overcome, that forgiveness could be attained, and that a reconciliation was possible after all. Conveying honors on a Jewish poet provided Germany with the opportunity to display its remorse. In her poetry, Sachs remembers the Jewish suffering without directing words of hatred or thoughts of revenge against the perpetrators. Thus, by honoring Sachs, the German literary public was able to pay tribute to the victims of the Holocaust without being confronted with their own repressed feelings of guilt about the unspeakable atrocities. In 1967, the Swedish writer Olof Lagercrantz called upon German readers to accept Sachs as a fellow German who was forced to leave her native country, and not as a stranger who can suddenly be turned into an honorary citizen.

Sachs' popularity was short-lived. In the past 30 years, her work has not received much attention, either from the reading public or from the literary establishment. Although most of her major works of poetry have been translated into English, at present they are no longer in print. Her biography is representative of thousands of Jews of her generation who were able to escape the horrors of National Socialism in Germany. The experience of persecution and exile, the remembrance of the Holocaust, and the awareness of the dangers of nationalism and anti-Semitism are an integral part of her work. Recognizing that her own fate was shared by many of her generation, Sachs emphasized the symbolic meaning of her work and insisted that her own life was insignificant. The biography she wrote for the Nobel Prize Committee consisted of three sentences: "Nelly Sachs was born on December 10, 1891 in Berlin. On May 16, 1940 she came with her mother to Sweden as a refugee. Lives in Stockholm since 1940 and works as a writer and translator." Sachs carefully guarded her private life; even friends remarked on her tendency to conceal large parts of herself. Therefore, despite the availability of her letters and notes, little is known about her; biographical research has been limited to mostly facts and dates.

Leonie "Nelly" Sachs was born in Berlin in 1891, the only daughter of **Margarete Karger Sachs** and William Sachs, a wealthy inventor and manufacturer. Both parents came from assimilated Jewish families, and the Sachs household was conservative-liberal and non-religious. As was the case with many upper-class Jews, assimilation was a fact of life and membership in the Jewish community was a formality. Sachs grew up in a villa in the area around the Tiergarten in Berlin. Her early childhood was seemingly idyllic and carefree. The Sachs family had servants, and Nelly enjoyed playing in the garden with her pets. Her father, who loved to read and admired the genius of Leonardo da Vinci and Johann Wolfgang von Goethe, was an accomplished musician and a great fan of the music of the Classical and Romantic age. He also had an extensive collection of crystals, rocks, corals, fossils, and books on insects and flowers. Later, rocks and butterflies became central motifs of Sachs' poetry. Her father, a com-

plex and emotionally withdrawn man, died of cancer in 1930, and it was the unconditional love and cheerfulness of her mother that gave her courage in the years of persecution and exile.

Young Nelly perceived dance to be her element, but it was her tragic fate, she said later, that kept her from fulfilling that dream. Thus, she turned to language as a form of expression. From 1897 to 1900, Sachs attended public school but had to withdraw for health reasons. She received private tutoring until 1903, when she began attending the exclusive private Aubert-Schule. Graduating in 1908, she continued her life as an upper-class daughter without training or profession, then began writing poems and painting in watercolors at age 17. Until the Nazis came to power in 1933, Nelly and Margarete Sachs did not have to worry about their standard of living.

In 1921, Sachs published *Legenden und Erzählungen* (*Legends and Stories*), in which she clearly imitated the style of Swedish writer *Selma Lagerlöf, whom she admired. In later years, Sachs distanced herself from this work—and from her poems written before 1942—and refused to have the stories reprinted. Though she sent her book to Lagerlöf and received a thank-you note praising her stories, Sachs' early work lacks both independence of thought and a style of its own.

I wrote in order to be able to survive.

—Nelly Sachs

Sachs did not participate in the spirited intellectual life of Berlin in the 1920s and had no contact with the artistic circles of the time. Apparently she lived her life apart from the coffee-houses and knew little of the Expressionist movement, the theater and cabaret scene, and even other Jewish women poets in Berlin, such as *Else Lasker-Schüler and *Gertrud Kolmar. Sachs did, however, visit several lectures on Romanticism at the University of Berlin and met two of her lifelong friends, **Gudrun Harlan** and **Vera Lachmann**; both would be instrumental in arranging for Sachs' escape from Nazi Germany.

After Hitler's rise to power in 1933, Sachs and her mother endured the German harassment and persecution of Jews. They were no longer allowed to attend cultural events or use the street-cars and public gardens. They were not allowed to keep pets and could not receive stamps to obtain milk, meat, fish, or fruit. Sachs was summoned by the Gestapo, the German security force, to appear for an interrogation. Afterwards, she suffered a complete paralysis of the larynx for five days. Sachs compared her inability to speak to the muteness of a fish, and later the silent suffering of fish became a central motif of her poetry.

In 1939, when the Nazi policy of the destruction of European Jewry moved toward its "final solution," Gudrun Harlan traveled to Sweden in the hope of saving Sachs' life. Harlan had planned a trip earlier that year to try to obtain a Swedish visa for Nelly and Margarete, but she had been hit by a car and had to spend several months in the hospital. After her release, she sold her living-room furniture to finance the train ride to Sweden. On crutches and with no knowledge of Swedish, Harlan made her way to Selma Lagerlöf, who apparently wrote a letter on Sachs' behalf. Harlan was also able to get an audience with Swedish Prince Eugene and convinced him to help Sachs obtain a visa for Sweden. In May 1940, Sachs received an order to keep herself available for transport to a work camp. On the very same day, she received her transit visa for Sweden. When she requested an exit visa from Germany, a Gestapo official advised Sachs to tear up her transport order, exchange her train tickets for airplane tickets, and leave Germany immediately. Thus, with a small suitcase and five Reichsmark each, which was all they were allowed to take, Sachs and her mother arrived in Stockholm on May 16, 1940, a few days before the borders were closed and the ban on emigration was put in force.

After living in a home for refugees in Stockholm, Sachs received a one-room apartment from the Jewish Warburg Foundation, in which she lived for the rest of her life. The first years of exile were extremely difficult, but the love and sense of responsibility for her mother kept Sachs alive. She earned some money through translation and received a permanent visa in 1944. Because of the cramped quarters, writing became difficult. Afraid to disturb her mother's sleep, Sachs did not want to turn on the light at night in the room they shared. Therefore, she composed her poems in her thoughts and wrote them down the next morning. Her breakthrough as a poet came in the winter of 1943–44: "I wrote as if I were in flames," she later remarked. The Holocaust, exile, Jewish mysticism, and Israel as a land of peace and belonging became consistent themes of Sachs' poetry. She contributed to the establishment of a new tradition in literature, Holocaust literature, in which death, dehumanization, the passing of time, the disintegration of reality, the corruption of reason and morality, speechlessness, the violent end to childhood and innocence, and the escape into madness were central themes and motifs.

Death and life under the constant threat of extinction recur throughout *In the Habitations of Death* (1947):

> O the chimneys
> On the ingeniously devised habitations of death
> When Israel's body drifted as smoke

By matching the divergent concepts of habitat and death, Sachs unmasks the duplicity of the concentration camps. The "ingeniously devised habitations" are not places where people live, but where they die, and the smoke that drifts through the chimneys stands in contrast to the smoking chimney of a home associated with warmth and nourishment.

> O the habitations of death,
> Invitingly appointed
> For the host who used to be a guest—

Here, the habitations of death represent a reversal of expectation: death, an occasional guest in the home, is the host and master of the habitations of death. The insidiousness of the invitation and hospitality demonstrates the systematic dissolution of the perception of reality. The victims are confronted with a new reality that defies all previous expectations.

The theme of the murder of children is taken up in the third poem. At the camps, children are robbed of their innocence and the fundamental trust inherent in the mother-child relationship is destroyed. "O the night of the weeping children!" speaks of the terror of the children branded for death. Deprived of their dolls and pets and separated from their mothers, they spend the night alone "in the nests of horror" devoid of love and security.

> Sleep may not enter here.
> Terrible nursemaids
> Have usurped the place of mothers

Instead of love and hope for the future, there is a "wind of dying" in the air which blows over the hair "that no one will comb again."

After the death of her mother in 1950, Sachs experienced an existential crisis. Life had lost its meaning and purpose. She turned to Jewish mysticism for solace and studied the hasidic writing of the Jewish philosopher Martin Buber. The influence of Jewish mysticism upon Sachs' poetry becomes prevalent in the works of the 1950s. The themes of exile, the longing for deliverance, and the loss of language now took on mystical dimension and are seen in the context of the Cabala and the Biblical experience of the exiled

Jews. The cycle of creation and destruction is prevalent in both *And No One Knows How to Go On* and *Flight and Metamorphosis*. No arrival is possible without death, one poem states, as Sachs redefines flight as both a religious experience and an existentialist mode. However, she also expresses a longing for love, deliverance from suffering, and "rest during flight."

In 1960, Sachs returned to Germany for the first time since her escape to Sweden in 1940. To avoid having to spend the night there, she took a hotel in Switzerland and crossed Lake Constance on the day she was to receive the Droste Prize in Meersburg. In Zürich, she met German-Jewish writer Paul Celan, who had grown up in a remote area of Rumania, the Bukovina. Celan, a survivor of a work camp, had lost his parents in the Holocaust and now lived in Paris. He had corresponded with Sachs since 1954, but only met her, together with the Austrian poet *Ingeborg Bachmann, at the hotel in Zürich in 1960. Celan was undergoing an acute crisis caused by a persecution mania, self-doubts, and the rise of anti-Semitism in Germany. The meetings with Sachs in Zürich and Paris, where she visited him after her excursion to Germany, seemed to help him conquer his fears and overcome his crisis, though only temporarily. Sachs and Celan admired each other's works and formed a deep bond of friendship. In *Death Still Celebrates Life*, which she wrote in a mental hospital in 1961, Sachs describes the "Marvel of encounters," which appears to refer to her meeting with Celan, as a conversation of two minds:

> far beyond their bodies
> that mourn like orphans
> down to the tips of their toes
> with abandonment.

Upon her return to Stockholm, Sachs fell into a state of deep depression, paranoia, and persecution mania. In her own words, she lived through a "descent into hell," experiencing hallucinations and obsessive delusions. She felt secretly observed and pursued by spies. "The insufferable happened, and I was unable to put into words what truly stood behind that which brought me to the brink of spiritual and physical destruction," she wrote to Celan in December 1960. With short interruptions, she spent the next three years in a hospital and a convalescent home. Harlan and Celan rushed to her side, but Sachs refused to see Celan out of fear of infecting him with her terrors. *Journey into a Dustless Realm* and *Death Still Celebrates Life*, both written during her illness, testify to Sachs' torment and anguish: "Who calls," the lyrical I asks in the poem under this title and answers, "My own voice!" "Who answers?" it inquires next and replies, "Death!"

In her acceptance speech for the Peace Prize of the German Booksellers' Association in 1965, Sachs spoke of the need to continue the despairing search for peace: "Together let us remember with sorrow the victims and let us go out anew—plagued by fear and doubt—to search again and again for a new opportunity" which may be afar "but nevertheless exists." On De-

cember 10, 1966, her 75th birthday, Sachs received the Nobel Prize for Literature. To her it seemed as if a fairy tale had become reality. At the end of her acceptance speech in Stockholm, she cited the poem "Fleeing" from *Flight and Metamorphosis*: "Fleeing, what a great reception on the way," the poem begins, recalling her flight to safety from Germany to Sweden. The poem ends by giving expression to the feeling of loss which is counterbalanced by the ability to accept change:

> I hold instead of a homeland
> the metamorphoses of the world

Nelly Sachs died on May 12, 1970, the day Paul Celan was buried in Orly near Paris. He had drowned himself in the river Seine around April 20. On December 10, 1971, which would have been her 80th birthday, the Swedish prime minister Olof Palme opened the Nelly Sachs room of the Kungliga Library in Stockholm. The room recreates Sachs' small apartment and contains her furniture and books. Sweden, Sachs' chosen land of exile, honored the German refugee and poet, who suffered from and kept alive the haunting memory of the Holocaust.

SOURCES:

Bahr, Ehrhard. *Nelly Sachs*. Munich: Beck, 1980.
Berendsohn, Walter. *Nelly Sachs*. Darmstadt: Agora, 1974.
Kessler, Michael, and Jürgen Wertheimer. *Nelly Sachs: Neue Interpretationen*. Tübingen: Stauffenburg, 1994.
Nelly Sachs zu Ehren. Frankfurt: Suhrkamp, 1966.
Wiederman, Barbara, ed. *Paul Celan-Nelly Sachs Briefwechsel*. Frankfurt: Suhrkamp, 1994.

SUGGESTED READING:

Sachs, Nelly. *The Seeker and Other Poems*. NY: Farrar, Straus & Giroux, 1970.
———. *O The Chimneys: Selected Poems, including the verse play ELI*. NY: Farrar, Straus & Giroux, 1967.
Wiederman, Barbara, ed. *Paul Celan-Nelly Sachs: Correspondence*. Translated by Christopher Clark. Sheep Meadow, 1995.

Karin Bauer,
Assistant Professor of German Studies,
McGill University, Montreal, Canada

Sackville-West, Vita (1892–1962)

English poet, novelist, short-story writer, biographer, and gardener whose unusual lifestyle was portrayed in her son's book Portrait of a Marriage. *Name variations: Lady Victoria Mary Nicolson. Born Victoria Mary Sackville-West at Knole in Kent, England, on March 9, 1892; died at Sissinghurst Castle, Kent, on June 2, 1962; only child of Lionel Sackville-West, 3rd Lord Sackville, and his cousin Victoria Sackville-West; attended Miss Wolff's School, London; married Harold Nicolson (later Sir), on October 1, 1913 (died at Sissinghurst, May 1, 1968); children: Benedict*

"Ben" Lionel Nicolson (b. August 6, 1914); Nigel Nicolson (b. January 19, 1917).

Bought Long Barn (1915); had an affair with Violet Keppel Trefusis (April 1918–summer 1921); met Virginia Woolf (December 1922); won Hawthornden Prize for The Land *(1927); bought Sissinghurst Castle (1930); with Harold, went on lecture tour of U.S. (1932); won the Heinemann Prize for* The Garden *(1946); awarded Companion of Honor in New Year's Honors List (1947); received Honorary Doctor of Literature, Durham University (1950); knighthood bestowed on Harold Nicolson (1953); Sissinghurst passed to the National Trust (1969).*

Vita Sackville-West, a proud aristocrat, loved women (sexually and emotionally) and her gentle, passive, homosexual husband Harold Nicolson. She was passionate, selfish, eccentric, and complex, the product of exclusive upper-class English society of the early 20th century. Statuesque, sophisticated, well traveled, and well connected, Sackville-West cherished her independence which she was able to maintain in her "open" marriage and her numerous love affairs; all her relationships were conducted on her terms, and she convinced herself that she could love her accommodating husband while being "in love" with her female lovers. A prolific writer, Sackville-West produced 15 books of poetry, 12 novels, 3 collections of short stories, 6 biographies, and 17 works of nonfiction, mostly on gardening and travel. She was a modern woman who hated the modern world, a feminist in attitude and lifestyle who repudiated the feminist label. Vita loved country living, flowers, and dogs; she ignored politics and detested marriage as an institution which devoured a woman's identity.

Vita Sackville-West had two deep and abiding attachments in her life—her beloved husband and Knole, her ancestral home. Queen *Elizabeth I gave Knole to her cousin, Thomas Sackville, and it had remained in the family since the 16th century. Knole constituted a kind of self-contained small town; it allegedly had 365 rooms, 52 staircases, and 7 courtyards. The complex of stone buildings, dating from the 15th century, covers more than six acres, and when Vita was born, the Sackvilles employed about 60 full-time servants. The family could trace its history back to Herbrand de Salkaville who came to England with William the Conqueror in 1066. The second Baron Sackville-West, Vita's grandfather, had sired five illegitimate children, including Vita's mother, **Victoria Sackville-West**, with a Spanish dancer known as **Pepita**. Lacking a legitimate heir, Knole and the noble title would pass to the baron's nephew Lionel Sackville-West, who married his cousin Victoria in the Chapel at Knole in 1890. Thus, Vita inherited her dual nature from her father's solid Kentish stock and her Latin mother. The handsome young couple entertained lavishly; old noble families, the rich and famous, and royalty, including King Edward VII, were frequent guests.

Vita was an unruly child who resented other children intruding into her world at Knole; she treated them so roughly that most of her playmates refused to come to tea or the dance class on the estate. She loved her father more than her mother who had a fierce temper and criticized Vita's untidy habits and "her silences," not wanting to look at the child "because I was so ugly," Sackville-West recalled. Brought up by nurses and governesses, Vita was a secretive, imaginative child. She spoke French by the age of seven and began writing poems, plays, and historical novels when she was twelve. Her parents disapproved of her concentration on writing, fearing she would become eccentric and too intellectually inclined. Vita ignored their admonishment and between 1906 and 1908, she composed three plays and a novel, all in French. Her "fantasy world," which revolved around Knole, her ancestors, and herself, was augmented by a complex family situation. By the time Vita was seven years old, her parents' marriage had changed into a convenient and mutually tolerated *ménage à quatre*—Vita's father and his mistress **Olive Rubens**, her mother and her mother's wealthy admirer Sir John Murray Scott, known as Seery. Infidelity was common among the upper classes who maintained a public image of marital stability, thus avoiding scandal. Indeed, the Sackvilles' "open marriage" made an impression on their daughter who "became too knowing, while remaining childishly innocent." Sackville-West easily accepted the objects of her parents' affection, with whom she lived quite amicably at Knole and during frequent visits to Seery's apartment and villa in Paris or his hunting lodge in Scotland.

As an adolescent, Sackville-West attended Miss Woolff's School in London; the girls at this exclusive establishment were encouraged to be conscious of who they were and what their families represented. Vita considered herself unpopular, "a prig and a pariah," but she did well in her studies and was fiercely competitive. At age 12, she made two friends who would change her life: **Rosamund Grosvenor** and ten-year-old *Violet Keppel (Trefusis)**, whose mother *Alice Keppel** was King Edward VII's mistress. The day she met Violet, Sackville-West wrote a song, "I've got a friend," innocently unaware that their "love" for one another would last a lifetime. Travel on the Continent was an integral part of education for upper-class children, and in 1908, Vita, Violet and their governesses went to Florence, Italy—Vita had learned Italian as well as French. At age 16, she was almost six feet tall, a striking young woman; she attracted the unpleasant attentions of her well-regarded godfather, the Honorable Kenneth Halleyburton Campbell, who tried to rape her several times. She refused to confide in her parents—Campbell was an old family friend—but as she told a companion later, "Perhaps it accounts for much," referring to her negative attitude towards men and sex, and her attraction to women.

In 1909, Sackville-West had her "coming out," which she did not enjoy. When the death of Edward VII curtailed social functions, she happily concluded, "Thus can the tragedies of great Kings be turned to the uses of little people." But she and her father dutifully attended the funeral and later the coronation of King George V. Having made her debut in society, Sackville-West was eligible for marriage, a prospect that had little appeal for her. Despite her lack of interest in men, while in Florence in the spring of 1909, the Marchese Pucci, from an old Florentine family, fell in love with her and followed her back to England. Fortunately, her parents were against Pucci's suit, and he eventually abandoned his courtship. That autumn, Vita, her mother, and Seery went to Russia where they were guests of Count Joseph Potocki on his estate in the Ukraine, which covered 100 square miles. The opulent, princely lifestyle of the family did not impress Sackville-West as much as did the miserable conditions of the peasants who grovelled at Potocki's feet as he lashed at them with a dog-whip. Vita later said she could understand why Russia erupted in revolution in 1917.

Old Lord Sackville, Vita's grandfather, had died in 1908, and her father inherited Knole and the title. However, the old man's illegitimate children laid claim to the estate; in the ensuing court case, Lionel and Victoria won the judgment. Now legally secure in their rights to the property and title, Lord and Lady Sackville returned home to the enthusiastic applause of their servants at Knole. The death of the king and the prolonged court case had interfered with Vita's social commitments, including being introduced to suitable young men. Lord Sackville feared Vita would marry a "soul" (an intellectual), though she was being courted by Viscount Lascelles and the heir to the dukedom of Rutland. But at a dinner party in London in June 1910, Vita met Harold Nicol-

son, an Oxford graduate who worked in the Foreign Office. He was definitely a dreaded "soul," but Lady Sackville liked him, and so did Vita. There was an obstacle, however, of which Harold was not aware—Vita was involved in a liaison with Rosamund Grosvenor. Vita characterized their affair as "almost exclusively physical," but V. Glendinning claims they never "made love" in the technical sense: "They did not think of it." Vita saw no conflict between loving Rosamund and not discouraging Harold who wanted to marry her. "I was very fond of [Rosamund]," Vita recalled later, "but she was quite stupid." Stupid or not, Vita had no intention of abandoning her for a man, however gentle, clever, and accommodating he might be.

Lady Sackville and Vita made frequent trips to Italy and southern France, two of Vita's favorite places. Tea with former French Empress *Eugénie and balls and lavish parties at the great houses of friends kept Vita circulating among possible suitors, several of whom proposed to her. However, she hesitated to commit herself to Harold or any man; she preferred to be with Rosamund, as she explained to Harold in a letter. Harold probably understood her love for Rosamund for he was attracted to young men and was currently infatuated with a Frenchman at his diplomatic post in Constantinople. Vita knew she loved Rosamund, but she would not have been able to give their kind of love a name, just as she was ignorant of "the physical realities of male homosexuality." Years later, she would reproach Harold for not enlightening her on a subject that became a major feature of their married life: "I knew nothing about homosexuality," she wrote. "You should have told me about yourself, and have warned me that the same sort of thing was likely to happen to myself. It would have saved us a lot of trouble and misunderstanding."

Sackville-West shied away from marriage and Harold, for, as she told him, she "had only just begun to live and to make friends." But Harold persisted despite Vita's declared preference for Rosamund and her obvious "distaste for the idea of marriage." Why then did she marry, and why choose Harold instead of one of the aristocratic and landed young men who pursued her? Perhaps because she and Harold were "more than lovers, they were friends." Harold understood Vita's nature and needs, and, most important, her desire to write, to become a recognized poet. (Her first published poem, "A Dancing Elf," appeared in The English Review in 1913.) Vita already knew, too, that "some men seem born to be lovers, others to be husbands; [Harold] belongs to the latter category."

*V*ita
*S*ackville-
*W*est

She was not mistaken, and this unusual couple were married in the chapel at Knole on October 1, 1913. Vita was given a diamond and emerald necklace by her mother and a sculpture from Rodin, one of Lady Sackville's ardent admirers. The newlyweds would have few financial wor-

ries, despite Harold's moderate income; Lady Sackville had inherited the bulk of Seery's vast fortune and was a generous benefactor.

Shortly after the wedding, the couple set out for Constantinople with Vita's maid Emily and

Harold's valet "Wuffy." Harold found great satisfaction in his Foreign Office career, but Vita disliked diplomatic life with its emphasis on protocol and precedence—and in which she was Mrs. Harold Nicolson, subsuming her own individual identity. In June 1914, Vita and Harold were in England awaiting the birth of their son and the imminent outbreak of war. Vita was pleased to learn that the Bodley Head publishing house had taken her book *Poems of West and East*, which would come out in 1917. On August 6, 1914, Benedict Lionel was born at Knole; inexplicably Vita asked her father's longtime paramour, Olive Rubens, to be the godmother, which outraged Lady Sackville. The Nicolsons were living in London that autumn, enjoying an active social life despite the war on the Continent. In March 1915, they purchased their first large country house, Long Barn, in Kent. Here Vita began her lifelong enthusiasm for gardening and wrote the first of her many garden poems. They also purchased a house on Ebury Street in London, but Vita preferred country living, and Long Barn was "home." Sackville-West would eventually acquire a national reputation for her expertise on plants and garden design and regularly contribute articles to journals such as the popular *Country Life.*

The first great sorrow of [Vita's] life was that, by an accident of gender, Knole could never be hers; the second, the realization that she was not a "great" writer.

—Victoria Glendinning

A stillborn son in 1916 was followed by the birth of Nigel the next year. The family considered Long Barn their primary residence where Vita could devote her time to poetry and her garden. Harold, however, did not share Vita's attachment to the land and historic manor houses. He considered entering politics, which Vita despised as much as the diplomatic service. During the war years, she did volunteer work at the local Red Cross, but the war did not prevent the Nicolsons and their society friends from attending grand weekend house parties. At a party in October 1917, Harold was compelled to tell Vita that he suspected he had contracted a venereal disease, and she would have to consult a doctor. This disclosure forced Harold to reveal his active homosexual life; after discussing this revelation, Vita responded "quickly and quietly," and they resumed their "normal" life; but from this time on, marital sex was no longer a part of their relationship. This was a crucial turning point in their lives and would lead to the only real crisis to threaten their marriage.

Sackville-West was gaining recognition as an accomplished poet, and her *Poems of West and East* received favorable reviews. In 1918, she began a novel, *Heritage* (1919), in which she explores her own double heritage through the character Rawdon Westmacott who was of Spanish-Kentish ancestry, as was Vita. This duality is also found in her view of love—"love as passion and as loyal companionship"—which originated in her fiction and ended as a reality. Vita developed an all-consuming passion for her friend Violet Keppel which led into conflict with Harold, her loyal companion. At the time, Harold was immersed in his career and often absent from Long Barn. In April 1918, Violet came to visit, and Vita revealed to her the sexual complexity of her marriage. Violet, in turn, told Vita "how much she loved her and why, and in what ways." As Vita wrote later, she felt she was "beginning life again in a different capacity."

"The adventure had begun," as Glendinning describes it. Vita longed for excitement and adventure, "for places where no one will want me to order lunch, or pay housebooks." And as she explained to Harold, Violet could rescue her from "a sort of intellectual stagnation, a bovine complacency." However, this passionate love affair nearly wrecked her marriage. During their three-year liaison, Vita and Violet spent a great deal of time abroad—Vita always feared scandal—faithfully writing to Harold every day. Periodically, Vita returned to Long Barn to immerse herself in the solitude that was essential to her well-being. She was especially pleased when her first published novel, *Heritage*, received good reviews. And she had already begun writing *Challenge*, a romantic novel featuring herself as Julian and Violet as Eve. In her real-life affair, Vita had taken to wearing men's clothes and appearing in public with Violet, both in London and abroad, disguised as her "husband" and calling herself Julian. Even Violet's marriage to Denys Trefusis in 1919, which was mutually agreed to be platonic only, did not diminish Violet's love for Vita. Nor did the affair affect Harold's commitment to his wife. (Vita never allowed herself to be referred to as "wife.") Harold was a delegate to the Paris Peace Conference in 1919, trying to juggle his demanding duties and his bizarre marital situation: Vita had informed Harold that she intended to "elope" with Violet. "Why do you imagine that there is nothing between eloping with Violet and cooking my dinner?" Harold inquired. When Vita carried out her threat and eloped with Violet in 1920, Harold and Denys "finally rescued them" in a hotel room in Amiens, France. Their escape from their respective spouses was foiled, but Vita never forgot the depth of her affection for her lover. In January 1921, the women once again fled abroad; but Vita was now torn between her love for Harold, her sons, and her passionate attachment to Violet. However, when Vita learned that their escapade threatened to provoke a scandal, she became frightened and gradually drew back from her lover. While the affair was still a fresh memory, Vita wrote a kind of confession of this tangled tragicomic affair which her son Nigel found in a locked box after Vita died and published in his *Portrait of a Marriage*.

When Lady Sackville read the proofs of Vita's novel *Challenge*, she was appalled to recognize Eve as Violet; she admitted she did not understand same-sex attraction, but she tried. She certainly was not ignorant of Vita's proclivities since her daughter confided in her concerning her most personal thoughts and doings. Under pressure from her mother and Violet's parents, Vita withdrew the book and paid the publisher to recover the "rights" to the novel. Beginning with the publication of *The Dragon in Shallow Waters* in 1921, which became a bestseller, Sackville-West entered a productive period. Her short story, "The Heir," centers around the love of a man for a great manor house; surprisingly there are no women in the story. But Vita's interest in poetry was foremost, and she contributed poems to the *Mercury* though "the most interesting and personal pieces of writing" were never published, according to Glendinning. She also worked on a play called "Marriage," "a feminist piece." To be free, Vita wrote in the play, one must be selfish, but women need time to be free, to be alone. And further, a man, she asserts, is never identified on legal documents as a "married man" but a woman is a "married woman" and loses her own name, her separate self. The play was never finished because she "had not solved the problem," at least not at this time. But Vita Sackville-West—the woman, not the writer—would achieve a degree of freedom unknown to most women of her age, would spend, by choice, long periods alone, and would live and publish under her maiden name. Vita's book of poetry *Orchard and Vineyard*, which contained poems about Kent, love poems written during her liaison with Violet, and to her friend, *Dorothy Wellesley, appeared in 1921. Vita was not the only writer in the family; Harold worked on his scholarly, well-written life of Alfred, Lord Tennyson. His work was solid and intellectually appealing, but his books never acquired the wide readership Vita's work attracted. Vita's deep attachment to Knole and her

ancestors is reflected in her history *Knole and the Sackvilles* (1922). When it was completed, she wrote to her cousin Eddy Sackville-West, heir to Knole, that the Sackvilles "*were* a rotten lot, and nearly all stark raving mad. You and I have got a jolly sort of heredity to fight against." Rotten and mad, perhaps, but Vita was proud of her illustrious lineage. In 1923, she edited *The Diary of Lady *Anne Clifford*, a spin-off of the Knole book, and completed *Grey Wethers*, both published that year.

Sackville-West was now an established author, admired and appreciated by some of the leading literary figures of the period, including George Moore, Aldous Huxley, *Edith Sitwell, and the cliquish Bloomsbury group which included Leonard and *Virginia Woolf, Clive Bell, Duncan Grant, and Virginia's sister *Vanessa Bell. Sackville-West continued to publish poetry and articles on a variety of subjects in several reputable periodicals, and her books were well received. In recognition, she was elected to the PEN Club. Domestic affairs were never allowed to interfere with Vita's work; servants, a secretary, and a governess for the boys left her "free and alone" to pursue her writing, gardening, and her love affairs. Harold spent weekdays in London or on the Continent on diplomatic business while Vita lived at Long Barn with brief sojourns into London. She had not yet begun to isolate herself from society in London or the aristocratic country estates of friends. She knew, and liked, Winston Churchill, always at ease among her upper-class peers. Vita had a loving marriage and a great deal of independence; she remained Vita Sackville-West, even to Harold, and without guilt indulged in numerous love affairs with women. Harold, too, had a series of relationships with men who were his "intellectual equals," but he was "never a passionate lover," according to his son Nigel, so the "physical element" of these affairs was secondary and did not interfere with his work. Nigel says that Harold "saw Vita as the companion of a lifetime" although she took no interest in his career; when Harold was appointed to the staff of the League of Nations after World War I, Vita did not even know what the League was. But Vita's liaisons, which at times consumed her entire being, never diminished her love for Harold: "I love you more than myself, more than life, more than the things I love," she wrote to him in 1919. This sentiment remained valid to the end of her life.

On December 14, 1922, Vita met Virginia Woolf for the first time. Woolf was fascinated by Vita's aristocratic demeanor, "no false shyness or modesty. . . . She is . . . hard, handsome, manly; inclined to double chin." If Violet was Vita's great passion, Virginia Woolf's "friendship was the most important fact in Vita's life, except Harold," Nigel asserts. This friendship turned to love and then to physical intimacy. But Harold no longer saw Vita's love affairs, her "muddles" he called them, as a threat to their marriage. They shared a home, their sons, many friends, and their love of travel, which they often did together. Even Vita's affair with Geoffrey Scott, whom she met in Florence, did not alarm Harold. Of this short-lived romance, Nigel writes, Vita "smashed [Scott's] life and finally wrecked his marriage," then ended this "experiment in love because he was a man, because he was an impossible rival to Harold, and because he was replaced by someone. . . a woman, a genius, Virginia Woolf."

When Harold was posted to Teheran, Persia (now Iran), in 1925, Vita did not accompany him. But the following year, she joined him for the coronation of Shah Reza Pahlavi with side trips to India and Iraq where she was invited to tea with the king of Iraq. In Teheran, Vita finished her long poem *The Land*, for which she received accolades from the British literary community. Vita's relations with Virginia began to worry Harold who wanted to avoid any scandal that might affect his career. In truth, Harold was carrying on an affair, though discreetly, with Raymond Mortimer. Vita did not object to this, telling Harold, "I don't mind who you sleep with, so long as I may keep your heart."

Sackville-West loved to travel, especially to France and Italy, but she loved Long Barn more. She returned to England in the spring, content to be alone and to concentrate on her writing and her garden. She wrote to Harold that she intended to be "very eccentric and distinguished, and never see anyone." In September 1926, *The Land* was published and sold well; its 2,500 lines are a celebration of Kent and the "farmer's yearly round." Pleased at the critics' reviews, Sackville-West noted, "I *will* get myself into English literature. Somehow or another." Vita and Harold were elected fellows of the Royal Society of Literature, and Vita gave a lecture to the members in October. In early 1927, before leaving again for Teheran, Vita won the Hawthornden Prize for *The Land*. From her experiences in Persia, she wrote two insightful travel books, *Passenger to Teheran* and *Twelve Days*.

Sackville-West's intention to "never see anyone" did not apply, of course, to Virginia and the several other women with whom she was carrying on concurrent affairs. None of her lovers, except Violet, ever posed a threat to Vita's and Harold's consensual "open marriage." This is obvious from the daily letters they exchanged, even when living together. In her correspondence, Vita makes clear that their marital arrangement would not suit "ordinary people," for only intelligent people, like themselves, could make marriage work, any marriage. And Vita was grateful that their "liaisons" were separate from "the more natural attitude we have towards each other." To Sackville-West, marriage was claustrophobic from which her liaisons provided relief, an outlet for her "restlessness and excess energy." She composed love sonnets for her lovers, many of which Harold judged to be too "b.s." (back-stairs or homosexual) to ever be printed. At least 14 women were romantically involved with Vita for rather lengthy periods of time, but, inexplicably, she failed to realize that the women who loved her were more seriously committed to the affairs than she was. However, Vita never completely severed these emotional ties, and former lovers were prone to exact "emotional alimony" from her.

Despite Sackville-West's propensity for entanglements, she was a prolific writer and a sound business woman, managing her money, lands and tenants. Trees were planted, flower gardens proliferated, and her manor house at Long Barn was refurbished, all at her expense. Harold's salary was his own, and Vita often chided him for not being able to live within his means. Vita also was expected to bring up Benedict and Nigel who, she admitted, interrupted her life. In fact, Vita was never on intimate terms with her sons, and Nigel acknowledges that they were closer to Harold than to their mother.

Virginia Woolf's friendship with Vita culminated in a literary masterpiece, *Orlando*, which revolves around Vita, Knole, and Harold. Spread over three centuries, the story follows Orlando (Vita), a young man in the reign of Queen Elizabeth I who turns into a young woman in the 18th century; thus, the author skillfully incorporates Vita's dual natures into a single portrait. No attempt was made to hide Vita's identity, for three of the eight photographs in the novel are of her. Vita was flattered to be the subject of *Orlando*; she admired Virginia's intelligence and imagination, and appreciated her support: Virginia and Leonard Woolf owned Hogarth Press which published 16 of Vita's works from 1924 to 1933. Other, larger publishing houses tried to convince Sackville-West to change publishers, but she refused. The Woolfs appreciated her loyalty. Lectures to various literary and cultural groups and talks on BBC radio allowed Vita to expound on modern poetry and express her views on "The Modern Woman"; in the latter, she declared that "Women *cannot* combine careers with normal life because they love too much. Men don't." Similar opinions are expressed in her novel *All Passion Spent* (1931). A married man, she wrote, could "enjoy his free, varied and masculine life with no ring on his finger or difference in his name." Vita adamantly defended similar rights for women and condemned "ordinary" marriage. In June 1929, she and Harold discussed the subject on the BBC; Harold claimed that "a man's work was a necessity, and a woman's career a luxury," and asked Vita if she thought "the joys of motherhood" were not adequate compensation, to which she retorted, "No, most emphatically I don't." Nigel Nicolson said his father did not particularly like women, and Vita made no secret that she preferred women to men, but opposing views seem to have had no bearing on their love for one another.

On a visit to Italy with Harold, Vita got the idea for her most commercially successful book, *The Edwardians* (1930), "her own romance of Knole" and a way of life that no longer existed. The book would be popular "for snobbish reasons alone," she told Virginia. Before it was completed, Vita had published a collection of lesbian poems, which Harold told her were not good, and a biography of Andrew Marvell (1929).

Place was always important to Vita; her roots, her Sackville identity were at Knole, but her home was at Long Barn which she had made into a showplace. However, in 1930, the possibility of a poultry farm locating next door forced Vita to consider moving. The moment she laid eyes on Sissinghurst Castle (in Kent), she had to have it. It was "a complex of ruins" on seven acres of "muddy wilderness," with no electricity or water, and not one habitable room. To Vita, it was magnificent, "Sleeping Beauty's Castle." Most important, it had a family connection: in 1554, Thomas Sackville had married the daughter of the owner. In Vita's mind, it was a "family house." A few days after the purchase, Vita planted a lavender bush "as an act of faith." In time, her faith would be rewarded as Sissinghurst became known as one of the most beautiful gardens in England and was opened to the public. Vita indulged her love of nature and enjoyed the solitude of her splendid ruins. Harold did not share her enthusiasm for renovation and isolation. He was beginning to feel old, useless, poor, and depressed. Having left diplomatic service, he tried journalism and in 1935 entered politics and served as a member of Parliament for ten years; he lived in London, coming home only on weekends. Vita, too, suffered from depression periodically, despite her diverse interests and time-consuming love affairs. Something was missing in her life. She refused to be involved in any way in politics, even turning down most invitations to events at Buckingham Palace. To relieve her tension and depression, Vita needed a passionate love affair, "the only thing that lifts life out of a trough," she believed. And though she "loved and moved on to new lovers," writes Glendinning, she "always kept in touch, even friends, with her lovers." But with Vita, no affair was permanent or remained exclusive for long. Only Harold was a constant in her complicated, often turbulent life.

Vita and Harold had more in common than their love for one another; they shared similar attitudes and biases. They were condescending towards the dull-witted, stolid middle-class ("bedints" in Sackville language) and were prejudiced against Jews and "colored" people, according to Nigel. In the 1930s, Harold joined Oswald Mosley's New Party. Vita "loathed" Mosley and his right-wing followers, and Harold disassociated himself from the group when Mosley openly embraced fascism. Vita found satisfaction not in politics but in local cultural events, writing poetry and novels, and acquiring new lovers. The Nicolsons were well known in the United States and were invited to undertake a lecture tour in 1932; they discussed marriage on radio shows, and Vita lectured on novel-writing to groups from New York to California. "Los Angeles is hell," Sackville-West wrote, and "Americans have an unequalled genius for making everything hideous." But she was impressed with the Grand Canyon and other natural marvels and intended to return to America.

The following year, Vita began giving a series of talks on gardening for the BBC which were then printed in the *Listener*. The program was extremely popular and earned Vita a nationwide reputation as an expert gardener. This kind of public exposure was uncharacteristic, for Sackville-West was becoming increasingly reclusive and conservative. At Sissinghurst, Vita's rooms in The Tower were physically separated from Harold's quarters and the boys' residence; Nigel comments that he and Ben entered Vita's sanctuary only about a half dozen times in the 30 years the family resided at Sissinghurst. Living in separate accommodations suited Vita who "had no talent or taste for the commonality of family life." In her Tower, Vita found refuge from the modern world which she hated. She was anti-Republican in the Spanish Civil War, and had no sympathy for King Edward VIII's "dilemma over Mrs. Wallis Simpson" (*Wallis Warfield, duchess of Windsor), that "piece of trash," as Vita fumed. But her interest in Knole and her ancestors never diminished. In reviewing the Knole succession case of 1910, she revived her interest in her Spanish "gypsy" grandmother. The result was *Pepita* (1937), "one of the most personal, humane and lively of all her books," writes Glendinning. Sackville-West was not religious, but her affinity for exceptional females led to books on *Joan of Arc and saints *Thérèse of Lisieux and *Teresa of Avila.

As Europe moved closer to war, Vita withdrew even more among her flowers at Sissinghurst, contributing articles entitled "Country Notes" that regularly appeared in the *New Statesman.* She tried to avoid thinking about an armed conflict, "Otherwise one would go mad—one would become a lunatic in a world of maniacs." In the autumn of 1938, local inhabitants were issued gas masks. Vita and Harold were against appeasing Hitler, but they also did not believe Britain could win a war against Germany. However, Vita continued to make long-term plans for her garden "as an act of faith" in the future, and in May 1939, she opened the garden to benefit charity. When the "wicked folly" of war finally came, she was made an ambulance driver and was involved with the Women's Land Army. Harold was asked to join Churchill's wartime government, working in London. A German invasion of England was expected, and Harold obtained pills for Vita in case suicide became necessary. Sissinghurst lay on the flight path of German bombers, between the Channel ports and London; frequent air battles occurred in the Kent area, and Knole was damaged. In March 1941, Virginia Woolf committed suicide; her last novel, *Between the Acts,* was said to be her "letter of farewell to Vita," as *Orlando* "was her letter of love." Vita's *Grand Canyon,* set in World War II, was rejected by Leonard Woolf's Hogarth Press as "profoundly defeatist" and not appropriate for the times. In the book, the Germans are victorious and many Europeans flee to the United States which eventually signs a treaty with Germany. Published in 1942, it was not a success.

Vita felt all the more alienated from a rapidly changing world as she learned of plans for Britain's postwar welfare state. It was dreadful, she asserted, "The proletariat being encouraged to breed like rabbits . . . as though there weren't too many of them already . . . and everyone being given everything for nothing." Harold, however, supported the proposed changes. Sackville-West thought public funding should go instead to "extended education" and higher teachers' salaries.

The real world was found wanting, but Sissinghurst, Vita's "one magnificent act of creation," largely compensated for what was lacking. Between 1939 and 1958, she published ten works on gardening; *The Garden* won the Heinemann Prize in 1946. In this beautiful long poem, Vita says about flowers: "They cannot break the heart, as friend/ Or love may split our trust for ever." Her weekly gardening articles for the *Observer* made her "more widely known and more eagerly read than anything else she ever wrote."

Sackville-West was among a select number of British subjects to be recognized on the King's New Year's Honors List in 1947. She also undertook lecture tours in North Africa and Spain for the British Council. In 1950, she was awarded an Honorary D. Litt. from Durham University. Three years later, Harold was granted a knighthood, and became Sir Harold Nicolson—Vita, however, refused to be called "m'lady." Advancing age, painful arthritis, and further isolation did not prevent the Nicolsons from traveling and meeting new people. Sissinghurst drew increasing numbers of visitors, one of whom was the queen mother (*Elizabeth Bowes-Lyon) who came to visit the gardens and have lunch: "I shall have to put on a skirt," was Vita's first reaction. Winter cruises with Harold to Indonesia, South America, the Far East, and Africa afforded Vita a respite from writing and gardening. At age 63, she was honored by the Royal Horticultural Society, bought a Jaguar car, and fell in love again; as Glendinning notes, Vita's "great adventure was never over."

On a New Year's cruise in 1962, Vita began hemorrhaging; when she returned to England, she underwent surgery and was diagnosed with cancer. Vita Sackville-West died at Sissinghurst in June; Harold died there from a heart attack four years later. Always to be associated with the name of Vita Sackville-West are Knole and Harold Nicolson, "the only person in whose love I trust." They helped to define her life and to mold her into an independent, memorable woman.

SOURCES:

Glendinning, Victoria. *Vita: The Life of Vita Sackville-West.* Middlesex, Eng.: Penguin, 1983.

Nicholson, Nigel. *Portrait of a Marriage.* NY: Atheneum, 1980.

SUGGESTED READING:

Nicolson, Nigel. *Virginia Woolf: A Penguin Life.* NY: Viking, 2000.

Stevens, Michael. *Vita Sackville-West: A Critical Biography.* London: Michael Joseph, 1973.

Todd, Janet, ed. *Dictionary of British Women Writers.* London: Routledge, 1989.

Troutmann, Joanne. *The Jessamy Brides: The Friendship of Virginia Woolf and Vita Sackville-West.* University Park, PA: Pennsylvania State University Press, 1973.

Watson, Sara Ruth. *Vita Sackville-West*. NY: Twayne, 1973.

CORRESPONDENCE:

Vita Sackville-West's letters, diaries, notebooks, and correspondence are in Sissinghurst Castle, Kent; diaries of Lady Sackville and Vita's early diaries are located in the Lilly Library, Bloomington, Indiana.

Jeanne A. Ojala,
Professor of History,
University of Utah, Salt Lake City, Utah

Sadako (r. 976–1001)

*Empress of Japan. Reigned from 976 to 1001; member of the powerful and influential Fujiwara family and daughter of Fujiwara Michitaka (d. 990); niece of Fujiwara Michinaga (966–1028), a major figure in Japanese history; sister of Shigei Sha. *Sei Shōnagon (c. 965–?), author of the Japanese masterpiece* Makura no sōshi *(The Pillow Book), served as Sadako's lady-in-waiting.*

Sadako (1885–1951)

*Empress of Japan. Name variations: Princess Sadako; Taisho empress. Born in 1885; died on May 17, 1951; daughter of Prince Kujo Michitaka; married Yoshihito Haru-no-miya (Emperor Taisho), emperor of Japan (r. 1912–1926), on May 10, 1900; children—four sons: Prince Michi (b. April 29, 1901, reigned as Emperor Hirohito, r. 1926–1989); Prince Yasuhito Chichibu (June 1902–1953, who married *Chichibu Setsuko); Prince Takamatsu (b. January 1905); Mikasa.*

Empress Sadako was born in 1885, the daughter of Prince Kujo Michitaka and a member of the aristocratic Fujiwara clan that had provided royal brides for centuries. She married Yoshihito Haru-no-miya when he was crown prince of Japan in May 1900. Twelve years later, he would become emperor of Japan.

In 1901, Sadako's first son Prince Michi was born; he would later occupy the Japanese throne for 63 years as Emperor Hirohito. Following long-established custom, after 70 days the infant Michi was taken away from Sadako and entrusted to a foster parent, the 70-year-old vice-admiral Count Kawamura Sumiyoshi. When the count died, the child was returned to the baroque atmosphere of Akasaka Palace, a miniature replica of Versailles that was his parents' official residence. He and his brother Prince Chichibu rarely saw their unaffectionate father and were allowed only weekly visits to Sadako.

Emperor Yoshihito died on Christmas Day, 1926; Sadako lived on in seclusion in her palace in downtown Tokyo as the dowager empress until 1951. She is credited with helping her husband to encourage the inculcation of Western ideas.

Sadat, Jehan (1933—)

Egyptian first lady who, unlike wives of previous Egyptian leaders, played a prominent role in Egyptian politics, particularly in advancing the cause of women's rights. Name variations: Gehan Sadat; Jihan Sadat. Born in 1933 in Roda Island, Egypt; daughter of Safwat Raouf (a physician) and Gladys Charles Cotrell; Cairo University, B.A. in Arabic literature, 1978, M.A., 1980, Ph.D. in literary criticism, 1986; married Anwar Sadat (president of Egypt, 1970–81), in 1949 (assassinated 1981); children: Loubna, Noha, Jihan and Gamal.

Jehan Sadat was born on Roda Island in Egypt in 1933, the third of four children, and grew up in a middle-class household in Cairo. Her father Safwat Raouf, an Egyptian doctor, was a practicing Muslim; her British mother **Gladys Charles Cotrell** was Christian. Jehan's parents met in England while Safwat was at the University of Sheffield studying medicine. Although her mother never converted to Islam or adopted many Arab customs, the Raouf children were raised in the Islamic faith. However, they also ate English breakfasts, had a Christmas tree, and were exposed to many British women, who had much freer lifestyles than did Arabic women. Jehan had a happy childhood. She attended an all-girl government school at the age of 11, and received an excellent education, learning English and classical Arabic, math, science, and many other disciplines.

Following the deaths of two close relatives when she was 13, Jehan turned for solace to the Quran, the holy book of Islam, and became deeply religious. She was also interested in politics and Egyptian nationalism. After World War II, she supported the removal from Egypt of the British, who continued to hold a controlling influence in the country even after the official end of its protectorate status in 1936. Ironically, Jehan's love for her country was in part inspired by her mother's pride in her native Britain, since Jehan desired to emulate her mother's nationalism with her own pride in Egypt.

When Jehan was 15, she accepted an invitation to stay with her aunt in Suez. There she met military hero Anwar Sadat, who was also an ardent nationalist actively fighting for the removal of the British. Twice Jehan's age, Sadat had already experienced a great deal as a soldier.

Along with future Egyptian president Gamal Abdel Nasser, Sadat was one of the leaders of the Free Officers Committee, a secret revolutionary society committed to the liberation of Egypt both from the British and from King Farouk's corrupt regime. Sadat had been imprisoned for collaborating with two German spies in 1942, and again in 1946 after being linked to several attacks on pro-British officials, including the assassination of Finance Minister Amin Osman Pasha. Although Anwar had been acquitted of this crime and released from prison, Jehan's parents were still leery of their romance. Besides the age difference and Anwar's revolutionary activities, he was also an impoverished divorcee with three children. Jehan eventually talked her parents into supporting their marriage, which took place in May 1949.

Having been court-martialed after the incident with the German spies, Sadat had to earn a living as a journalist until influential friends restored his army commission in 1950. As a captain stationed in the Sinai Desert, he remained active in the Free Officers Committee. The growing tension between the British and Egyptians developed in many Egyptian circles into an equal resentment towards Farouk, which finally made possible the long-hoped-for revolution. On July 22, 1952, Sadat joined with Nasser in a bloodless coup which forced Farouk from the country and established Nasser as the new Egyptian leader. In 1958, Egypt was renamed the United Arab Republic to reflect Nasser's pan-Arab policies, and Sadat held several high-level positions within the Nasser government. In the course of the tempestuous tenure of Nasser's presidency, during which Egypt became embroiled in military conflicts with Israel over Israel's occupancy of Arab Palestine, Sadat was one of the few officials to remain in Nasser's favor. His strict adherence to Nasser's political philosophies netted him the vice-presidency in 1969 as well as the nickname "Major Yes-Yes." When Nasser died of a heart attack less than a year later, Anwar Sadat ascended to the presidency and Jehan Sadat joined him in the spotlight.

Although political wives were expected to remain out of sight, Jehan was determined not to follow in the footsteps of her passive predecessors. She was well aware of the subservient condition of Egyptian women, who were often valued less than cows in the villages, and early on began advocating for change. In 1967, she set up a cooperative in the village of Talla so peasant women could obtain a degree of economic independence from their husbands by making and selling crafts. To emphasize education for women, Jehan enrolled in Cairo University to study Arabic literature at the age of 41. She graduated in 1978, and went on to receive her master's degree in 1980. She took her examinations on television, both to set an example as an educated woman and to prove that she did not cheat. In 1979, her influence over her husband resulted in the passage of a set of laws, known as "Jehan's Laws," whereby 30 seats in the Egyptian Parliament were set aside for women, and women were granted the power to divorce their husbands for polygamy or repudiation and retain custody of their children.

Somewhat of a politician in her own right, Jehan presided over the meetings of the Monufiya People's Council, a local legislature of the region in which Anwar had grown up, for several years starting in 1969. She brought many improvements to the area through her efforts to increase the number of day-care facilities and for birth-control measures to help stem Egypt's burgeoning overpopulation. She also held several other high-level positions. During the Suez Canal war of 1974, she chaired the Egyptian Red Crescent (similar to the Red Cross) and the Egyptian Blood Bank Society, and was honorary chair of the Supreme Family Planning Council. She was head of the Egyptian Society for Cancer Patients, the Society For Preservation of Egyptian Antiquities, the Scientific Association for Egyptian Women, and the Society for the Welfare of University and Higher Institute Students, which raised funds to buy books and clothes for students. She also established orphanages and a facility for rehabilitating handicapped veterans.

Although the extent of her influence over Anwar Sadat's policies is not known, Jehan supported her husband in his often controversial policy decisions. With Islamic fundamentalism on the rise in the 1970s, Sadat came under fire for aligning himself with Western powers. He had actively sought friendly relations with the United States by divesting Egypt of Soviet officials and diplomatic ties in the early 1970s. While he had pronounced his loyalty to Nasser's pan-Arab policies on taking the office of the president, Sadat changed the country's name from the United Arab Republic to the Arab Republic of Egypt, indicating the primacy of Egyptian interests over those of other Arab countries. But while these decisions alarmed many Arab fundamentalists, it was Sadat's willingness to negotiate a peace treaty with Israel which truly incensed the extremist element in Egypt. Officially signed in 1979, the peace agreement between Israel and Egypt resulted in Anwar Sadat's and Israeli Prime Minister Menachem Begin's winning the Nobel Peace Prize in 1978, but it also made him numerous enemies. Jehan herself scandalized many with her independence and activism, her Western mannerisms and her willingness to grant personal interviews to Western magazines. (She had, nonetheless, refused to meet with *Leah Rabin in 1975 when both were attending the International Women's Year Conference in Mexico City.) Anwar, however, supported her, inviting her to walk next to him in public rather than the traditional five paces behind, and making sure she was the first person to shake hands with visiting dignitaries.

On October 6, 1981, a spectacular military parade was held in Cairo to commemorate the anniversary of the Yom Kippur surprise attack on Israel. Sadat was attired in full uniform and flanked by bodyguards and Egyptian dignitaries. A small band of assassins who had commandeered one of the many passing military vehicles jumped out and approached the reviewing stand, spraying rifle fire at the president and killing him instantly. Amazingly, Vice President Hosni Mubarak, just a few feet away, was not injured. Jehan Sadat, safe behind the bulletproof glass her husband refused to use, could only watch in horror.

Sadat's funeral was attended by a galaxy of Western leaders, including three former U.S. presidents—Richard Nixon, Gerald Ford and Jimmy Carter—but very few Islamic leaders. The streets of Cairo were deserted, as a curfew had been imposed. The shock and regret expressed in Europe and the United States stood in marked contrast to the response in Arab capitals, which ranged from muted to openly joyful.

After Anwar's assassination, Jehan went into seclusion for a year. When she emerged from her period of mourning, she resumed lecturing and doctoral studies at Cairo University. In 1984, the president of the University of South Carolina—which had given Jehan an honorary doctorate in 1979—asked her to teach at the school. She accepted the invitation, and also took on a lectureship at the American University in Washington, D.C. She left the University of South Carolina in 1986 over a salary dispute and became a visiting professor at Radford University in Virginia, earning her doctorate in literary criticism from Cairo University that year as well. In addition to a heavy lecturing schedule, she became a professor of international studies at the University of Maryland in 1993, and endowed a chair there in the name of her dead husband.

SOURCES:

Commire, Anne, ed. *Historic World Leaders*. Detroit, MI: Gale Research, 1994.

Current Biography 1971. NY: H.W. Wilson, 1971.

Moritz, Charles, ed. *Current Biography Yearbook 1986*. NY: H.W. Wilson, 1986.

Sadat, Jehan. *A Woman of Egypt*. NY: Simon & Schuster, 1987.

Ruth Savitz,
freelance writer, Philadelphia, Pennsylvania

Sadeler, Agnes (fl. 1386)

Rebellious English serf. Name variations: Sadler. Flourished around 1386 in Ramsley (Romley), England.

Little is known about Agnes Sadeler, a rebellious English serf. She is listed in court records of 1386 as being the leader of the villagers of Ramsley when they rose against their feudal lord. Sadeler was accused of gathering the rebels together, and of rallying the villagers when they refused to work for their overlord, demanding that they be freed from their bondage to him. For this, she was declared an outlaw by the courts.

Laura York,
Riverside, California

Sadlier, Mary Anne (1820–1903)

Irish-born author. Name variations: Mary Anne Madden; Mary Ann Sadlier; Mrs. J. Sadlier. Born Mary Anne Madden on December 31, 1820, in Cootehill, County Cavan, Ireland; died on April 5, 1903, in Montreal, Canada; daughter of Francis Madden (a merchant); married James Sadlier (a publisher), in November 1846; children: three daughters, including Anna T. Sadlier (a writer); three sons; one foster son.

Selected writings: The Blakes and the Flanagans (1855); Willie Burke: A Tale of the Irish Orphan in America (c. 1856); Bessy Conway (1862); Catechism of Sacred History and Doctrine (1864); Maureen Dhu (1870); Purgatory: Doctrinal, Historical, and Poetical (1886); De Fromental (1887); (with daughter, Anna T. Sadlier) Stories of the Promises (1895).

Although Mary Anne Sadlier published her first poems in the London periodical *La Belle Assemblée* at age 18, she produced her most serious work after immigrating to North America at age 24. The author of nearly 60 novels, many of which originally appeared in serial form in Catholic newspapers, she explored in her work the cultural and religious dimensions of Irish immigration in the United States, with a distinctively conservative Catholic perspective. Despite her distrust of literature on moral grounds, Sadlier used the novel as a forum for providing young Irish Catholics with models for ways to resist what she felt were the damaging effects of

American liberal Protestantism. She affirmed the values of the traditional Irish patriarchal family and hierarchical society, and argued against American individualism. A strong voice for conservative Catholicism, Sadlier was praised for her treatment of Irish Catholic issues, and won the Laetare Medal from the University of Notre Dame in 1895.

She was born Mary Anne Madden on December 31, 1820, in Cootehill, County Cavan, Ireland. Her father Francis Madden was a successful merchant who raised Mary Anne following the death of her mother while the girl was quite young. He suffered business losses in the 1840s and soon died, after which she sailed for New York City in 1844. In November 1846, she married James Sadlier, co-owner (with his brother, Denis) of a Catholic publishing house. The couple then moved to Montreal, Canada, where James managed a branch of the firm and Mary Anne gave birth to three daughters and three sons. She and her husband also took in a foster son. During her 14 years in Montreal, Sadlier published a collection of short stories, several novels, and contributed to numerous Catholic journals, including the *Boston Pilot*, the *New York Tablet*, *The Literary Garland*, and *The American Celt*. The family returned to New York in 1860, by which time Sadlier had gained a reputation as a Catholic writer for her poetry and fiction in defense of the faith (sometimes produced on request).

In New York City, Sadlier cultivated a wide circle of literary, clerical, and lay acquaintances, hosting weekly receptions at her East Broadway house as well as at her summer home in Far Rockaway. She also supported Catholic charities. Those in her circle included Archbishop Hughes of New York and the Irish statesman and poet Thomas D'Arcy McGee, whose *Poems of D'Arcy McGee* she edited in 1869.

Sadlier wrote out of her concern for Irish youth, constructing such characters as Bessy Conway in her novel of the same name to show the moral dilemmas faced by Irish servant girls. Her other novels, also didactic in nature, addressed conflicts facing young Irish immigrants to America. Despite artistic flaws, her novels were quite popular with their intended audience, and are now considered important depictions of Irish immigrant life of the era. *Willie Burke: A Tale of the Irish Orphan in America* sold 7,000 copies following its publication around 1856. Other significant titles include *The Blakes and the Flanagans* (1855), *The Confederate Chieftains* (1860), *Aunt Honor's Keepsake* (1866), *Confessions of an*

Apostate (1868), and *De Fromental* (1887). After the death in 1869 of her husband, who had often suggested topics for her books, Sadlier focused her writing increasingly on religious and historical themes. Later works included two produced collaboratively, *Catechism of Sacred History and Doctrine* (1864), with *Mother Angela Gillespie, and *Stories of the Promises* (1895), with her daughter **Anna T. Sadlier**, who herself enjoyed a career as a well-known Catholic writer. She also published a translation of Matthieu Orsini's *Life of the Blessed Virgin, Mother of God* (1885) and wrote *Purgatory: Doctrinal, Historical, and Poetical* (1886). Sadlier returned to Montreal in the 1880s to be near her children, and died on April 5, 1903.

SOURCES:

James, Edward T., ed. *Notable American Women, 1607–1950*. Cambridge, MA: The Belknap Press of Harvard University, 1971.

McHenry, Robert, ed. *Famous American Women*. NY: Dover, 1980.

Lolly Ockerstrom,
freelance writer, Washington, D.C.

Sáenz, Manuela (1797–1856)

South American revolutionary and companion to Simón Bolívar, the Liberator of South America, who accompanied him into combat, saved his life on two occasions, fought for his reputation, and guarded his papers until her death. Name variations: Manuela Saenz. Born Manuela Sáenz on December 27, 1797, in Quito, Ecuador; died on November 23, 1856, in Paita, Peru; daughter of Simón Sáenz de Vergara (a well-born Spanish adventurer) and María Joaquina de Aispuro (a wealthy woman in her own right); briefly attended a convent school; married James Thorne (an English merchant), in 1817; no children.

Sent to a convent school, from which she fled with a military officer (1814); fell in love with Simón Bolívar (1822); remained Bolívar's companion in the revolutionary cause until independence from Spain was achieved (1824); was separated from Bolívar at time of his death (1830); lived to see Bolívar reinstated as a hero (1842).

Wakened at midnight by barking dogs, Manuela Sáenz sat up, realizing that someone was moving about in the house. She shook the man next to her, whispered for him to get up, quickly helped him dress, and handed him his sword and pistol. He escaped through the window before she let in the men pounding on the door. They searched the room, demanding to know the whereabouts of her companion, and

Sáenz answered that he was at a council meeting—she had been waiting for him herself. One man struck her in the face, sure that she was lying, then the intruders left by the open window themselves. A short while later that night, Sáenz rejoined her companion in the town plaza. He was Simón Bolívar, the heroic general known as the Liberator of South America, and it was the second time she had saved his life. When they returned home, Bolívar would say to her, "You are the Liberatrice of the Liberator."

Manuela Sáenz was born out of wedlock on December 27, 1797, in Quito, Ecuador. Her father Simón Sáenz de Vergara was a well-born Spanish adventurer and a married man with four children. Her mother **María Joaquina de Aispuro** was a woman of a wealthy and aristocratic family who raised her daughter in affluent circumstances. Of Manuela's birth, Hugo Mocay wrote, "She was born in a magnificent bed covered with velvet lined in satin and adorned with an abundant fringe and a precious gold ornament, with a coverlet in the same style and sheets embroidered in Belgian lace." The child grew up in the home of her maternal grandparents, where her father was a regular visitor and fiercely affectionate toward his daughter. He even tried to persuade his legitimate children to accept her, without success.

After Quito was sacked by rebel factions during one of the region's ongoing civil wars, Manuela and her mother left the city for their Catahuango hacienda, or ranch, where Manuela learned to ride horseback, read the classics, and speak English among playmates and companions who were chiefly black slaves. In the colonial frontier culture of South America, which was dominated by Spain and the Catholic Church, the upper levels of society officially adhered to strict standards of behavior, but women in the New World were actually allowed considerable freedom relative to the times. In this free-wheeling society, Manuela grew up knowing how to smoke, drink and swear, and experienced "the tormented delights of love" during her teenage years; she also became enamored of the revolutionary politics then sweeping the continent, where many people, inspired by the recent revolutions in North America and France, longed for liberation from Spain.

In an effort to tame her adventuresome spirit, Sáenz was sent to a convent at age 17. Unfortunately, the chosen convent was "notorious for its libertine practices," and Manuela soon fled it with a military officer, Fausto de Elhuyar; their passionate affair lasted several weeks before she

was returned to her mother. She had grown into a beautiful woman who loved being the center of attention when, three years later, she was married to an English merchant, James Thorne, who at 40 was twice her age. Thorne doted on his bride, and their lavish wedding celebration lasted three days. The couple set up a luxurious household and Sáenz, whose interest in revolutionary politics had remained strong, became a host for clandestine political meetings. But politics was apparently not enough to keep her occupied, and when she resumed her affair with Fausto, Thorne decided to move his wife from Quito to a hacienda outside Lima, Peru.

Delighted to be living in the "City of the Viceroys," Sáenz quickly became friends with the similarly intelligent, attractive and flirtatious **Rosita Campuzano**, who shared Sáenz's passion for revolutionary politics. Soon both women were holding salons in support of revolutionary action, organizing women into groups to raise money for shipbuilding and uniforms. During this time Campuzano became the lover of General José de San Martín, the military figure known as the Protector of Peru.

> *L*earn to love and do not leave me, not even to go with God Himself.
>
> —Simón Bolívar, in a letter to Sáenz

In April 1822, after the death of her mother, Sáenz was summoned back to Quito to collect her inheritance, but she may also have been sent away from Lima by her husband. Two months later, on June 16, 1822, Simón Bolívar arrived in Quito. At age 39, the man still in the process of liberating what would become the independent countries of Venezuela, Colombia, Ecuador, Panama, Peru and Bolivia was at the height of his influence. He had been born in Caracas, on July 24, 1783, the son of a noble Spanish family. In 1801, he had married **Maria Teresa Toro**, in Spain, and the couple returned to Venezuela in 1803. When his wife died of yellow fever, Bolívar had pledged never to marry again, but to devote his life to freeing Venezuela from Spain. A brilliant general as well as a statesman who understood the implications of democracy, Bolívar became a legend in his own time, leading armies throughout the continent, trekking through uncharted wilderness, and relying on limited resources during most of some 200 bloody battles in which he was eventually engaged.

On the night of June 16, Manuela Sáenz danced with Bolívar at the governor's palace, beginning what was to be a lifelong love affair. The two shared much in common. Both admired the same heroes, thinkers, and writers, and both were veterans in the fight against Spain. Both also had reputations as devotees of eros as well as revolution. If Bolívar was past his prime—due mainly to the rigors of his long campaign and to the symptoms of the tuberculosis that would eventually kill him—the passionate Manuela Sáenz was the physical and intellectual tonic he needed.

Bolívar's military actions kept him constantly on the move, and Sáenz was soon traveling with him. An excellent equestrian, she adopted an outfit of red pants and a black velvet poncho, with her loose curls falling out from under a plumed hat. She also became skilled with a sword and pistol. Although Bolívar remained the ladies' man he had always been, both recognized the uniqueness of their relationship. Sáenz became chief confidante, secretary and advisor to the Liberator, reading to him when he was tired and caring for him when he was sick. She alone was entrusted with his personal records. Bolívar's aide-de-camp, Daniel Florencio O'Leary, eventually proposed that she be made a colonel, and people began to refer to her as "Bolívar's woman."

On December 9, 1824, Spain's power over the New World finally ended at the battle of Ay-

Manuela Sáenz

acucho, Peru. Bolívar returned to Bolivia, named in his honor, where he established schools, distributed land to the Indians, and implemented new irrigation and mining techniques. Unfortunately, his vision of a united South America was soon subsumed by those eager to carve out personal fiefdoms for themselves, and power grabs became the order of the day. Before long a series of civil wars broke out which were to consume political energy on the continent for the next half-century. Even the ambitious friends of Bolívar turned against him, leading to his rescue by Sáenz on two occasions. The first time, in August 1828, she got news that his enemies intended to kill him in Bogotá, Colombia, at a masked ball. Unable to warn him ahead of time, Sáenz arrived at the gathering, unkempt and apparently drunk, making such a scene that Bolívar unknowingly thwarted the murderers' plot by leaving; the second time, she prevented the attempted assassination in his bed.

As the political intrigues worsened, Bolívar's past feats were thrown into disrepute. His military victories were said to have been won by other generals, or else he was portrayed as a bloodthirsty monster, blamed for atrocities committed by both sides. Sáenz found herself attacked as a common prostitute and castigated for her loyalty to the former hero, now viewed as a mere murderer. The South America created by Bolívar had begun to splinter into Venezuela, Colombia, Ecuador, Peru, and Bolivia by January 1830, when Bolívar resigned from the last of his official duties. He was ill and most of his personal fortune had been spent on freeing the various parts of the continent. Refusing both a pension and a gift from his uncle, he sold his fine horses, some furnishings and jewels, and set out with Manuela for the Colombian port of Cartagena, intending to sail for Europe.

The money was soon gone, however, and Bolívar, perhaps realizing that he was near death, sent Sáenz away. Still she remained loyal. When Sáenz returned to Bogotá for the Feast of Corpus Christ on June 9, 1830, she learned she was to be burned in effigy, a display arranged by Bolívar's nemesis, Francisco de Paula Santander. Fearing Sáenz's reaction to the display, the authorities stationed armed guards around the plaza. Sáenz rushed to the plaza brandishing a pistol, intent on destroying the effigy which she viewed as an insult to Bolívar. Her opponents were cowed. On June 23, she wrote to a newspaper:

> If even the withdrawal of this hero from public life has failed to calm your rage and you have chosen me as your target, I can say to you: you can do whatever you want to

me, you can threaten my very existence, cowards that you are, but you cannot make me betray my respect and friendship for General Bolívar and my gratitude to him. Those of you who consider this to be a crime reveal only the pettiness of your own minds, while I demonstrate the constancy of my spirit by vowing that you shall never make me vacillate or fear.

Bolívar died on December 17, 1830; Sáenz lived another 26 years, generally impoverished and persecuted by some who demanded her imprisonment. When pressured to hand over Bolívar's papers, she responded defiantly, "You will neither get papers nor books; I shall deliver them to no one unless you prove to me by law that he is an outlaw." Banished for awhile to Guaduas, she let a poisonous snake bite her in the hope she could join her dead lover; later she was exiled to Jamaica. Finally she settled in the Peruvian coastal town of Paita, where she ran a shop catering to sailors and was sought out by such notable visitors as Giuseppe Garibaldi, Ricardo Palma, and a young whaler named Herman Melville.

At age 50, Manuela dislocated a hip, which left her an invalid until her death a decade later, on November 23, 1856, during a diphtheria epidemic. She was buried in a common grave, and the papers of Bolívar which she had so jealously guarded were burned by townspeople in their attempt to halt the spread of the disease. She had lived long enough, however, to see Bolívar restored to his rightful place in history, following the publication of the memoirs of his aide, O'Leary, 12 years after the general's death. Manuela Sáenz, for a long time relegated to the back pages of history, recently has become more recognized for her contributions during the struggle for independence and for her unfailing loyalty to the Liberator.

SOURCES:

Ballesteros, Mercedes. *Manuela Sáenz, el ultimo Amor de Bolívar*. Madrid: Fundacion Universitaria Española, 1976.

Bushnell, David. *The Liberator, Simón Bolívar: Man and Image*. NY: Alfred A. Knopf, 1970.

Gil-Montero, Martha. "Manuela & Simón," in *Américas*. Vol. 42, no. 2, 1990, pp. 6–15.

Malta, Demetrio Aguilera. *Manuela, La caballeresa del sol: A Novel*. Carbondale, IL: Southern Illinois University Press, 1967.

Masur, Gerhard. *Simón Bolívar*. Rev. ed. Albuquerque, NM: University of New Mexico Press, 1969.

McNerney, Robert F., Jr. *Bolívar and the War of Independence*. Austin, TX: University of Texas Press, 1970.

Nicholson, Irene. "Simón Bolívar," in *The Liberators: A Study of Independence Movements in Spanish America*. NY: Frederick A. Praeger, 1969, pp. 153–263.

Paine, Lauran. *Bolivar the Liberator*. London: Robert Hale, 1970.

von Hagen, Victor W. in collaboration with Christine von Hagen. *The Four Seasons of Manuela: The Love Story of Manuela Sáenz and Simón Bolívar*. NY: Duell, Sloan and Pearce, 1952.

Karin Loewen Haag,
writer, Athens, Georgia

Saewara (fl. 630)

Queen of East Anglia. Flourished around 630; daughter of Saethryth, an abbess; married Anna, king of East Anglia (r. 635–654); children: Saint *Sexburga (d. 699?); *Elthelthrith (630–679); *Withburga; (stepdaughter) *Ethelburga (d. 665). King Anna's second wife was *Hereswitha.

Safford, Mary Jane (1834–1891)

Civil War nurse, physician, and reformer. Name variations: Mary Jane Safford Blake. Born on December 31, 1834, in Hyde Park, Vermont; died on December 8, 1891, in Tarpon Springs, Florida; youngest child of Joseph Safford (a farmer) and Diantha Little Safford; attended schools in Illinois, Vermont, and Montreal, Canada; graduated from New York Medical College for Women, 1869; advanced medical training at the General Hospital of Vienna, medical centers in Germany, and at the University of Breslau; married James Blake, in 1872 (probably divorced 1880); children: (adopted) Margarita Safford; Gladys Safford.

Nicknamed the "Cairo Angel" for her service to wounded Union soldiers in Cairo, Illinois, during the Civil War; credited with being the first woman to perform an ovariotomy (early 1870s); was one of the first women elected to the Boston School Committee (1875).

A descendant of Thomas Safford, who left England in 1630 and became a founder of the Massachusetts Bay Colony, Mary Jane Safford led a distinguished career as a physician and professor of medicine in the 19th century. Her medical career began during the Civil War, when she almost singlehandedly nursed the sick and wounded in Cairo, Illinois, over the objections of officers and surgeons. Resolutely making daily rounds, Safford delivered material aids to patients from a small basket while behind her followed a porter carrying a larger basket of provisions. Together they toured the primitive tent hospitals, braving the mud behind the levee to deliver relief to the sick. Determined to serve the Union despite the limitations imposed upon her gender, Mary Safford, like *Louisa May Alcott and *Clara Barton, entered nursing, the only wartime role socially acceptable for women at that time. The same determination she showed as a volunteer nurse surfaced later in her career, as she undertook medical training and engaged with issues relating to women's medical and social conditions.

Safford was born on December 31, 1834, in Hyde Park, Vermont, the youngest of five children of Joseph Safford and **Diantha Little Safford**. The family moved to Crete, Illinois, when she was three, and her father established a new homestead and farm there. When her mother died in 1849, Mary returned to New England to attend school in Bakersfield, Vermont; after graduating, she studied French for a year near Montreal, Canada, then studied German while living with a German family. Following her return to Illinois, she lived first in Joliet, then in Shawneetown, where she taught in a public school. She resided with an older brother, Alfred Boardman Safford, a successful businessman who helped fund the construction of the school building where she was employed. In 1858, they moved to Cairo, Illinois, where Alfred became a well-to-do banker and public benefactor.

Cairo quickly became an important military supply depot and training center at the start of the Civil War in 1861, because of its strategic position at the juncture of the Mississippi and Ohio rivers. When sickness broke out, spawning a host of tent hospitals, Mary began her self-styled relief mission. She tended to both the physical and psychological needs of patients, providing them with food, handwork, games, and reading and writing materials with funding from Alfred. Working closely with surgeons, she prepared meals for patients based on individual dietary needs. She also met the energetic "Mother" *Mary Ann Bickerdyke, who trained her in nursing techniques. Described as having a "pleasant voice and winning manner," the petite Mary Safford became known among her patients as the "Cairo Angel." She worked tirelessly, five times accompanying wounded men to hospitals in nearby towns on the *City of Memphis*, the Sanitary Commission's transport ship. Following the Battle of Shiloh, she served aboard the *Hazel Dell*, working to the point of collapse.

To regain her health, Safford went on an extended European tour in the summer of 1862, joining the party of an old friend from Joliet, the former governor of Illinois, Joel A. Matteson. Her continued interest in medicine drew her to visit hospitals while she was in Europe, and she became determined to attend medical school. Upon her return to America, she entered Dr. *Clemence S. Lozier's New York Medical College for Women, and graduated in 1869. That summer, she attended a women's suffrage convention in Chicago presided over by her friend *Mary A. Livermore.

During the fall of 1869, Safford returned to Europe to take advanced studies in surgery at the General Hospital of Vienna. She remained in Europe for nearly three years, also studying at medical centers in Germany. At the University of Breslau, she was credited with being the first woman to perform an ovariotomy. In 1872, she opened a private practice in Chicago, where she earned a reputation both as a worthy physician and as an advocate of women's dress reform. The same year, she married James Blake and moved with him to Boston, where she joined the faculty of the newly formed Boston University School of Medicine as professor of women's diseases. Also maintaining a private practice and working on the staff of the Massachusetts Homeopathic Hospital, Safford focused her activities on women's issues, writing on dress, hygiene, and exercise, and striving to improve the conditions of working-class women. In 1875, she became one of the first women elected to the Boston School Committee.

Mary Jane Safford is thought to have divorced in 1880, when she resumed the use of her maiden name. She retired in 1886 because of frail health, and with her two adopted daughters, **Margarita** and **Gladys Safford**, moved to Tarpon Springs, Florida, to join her brother Anson P.K. Safford, the former territorial governor of Arizona. She died in Florida in 1891, only a few weeks before her 57th birthday.

SOURCES:
James, Edward T., ed. *Notable American Women, 1607–1950.* Cambridge, MA: The Belknap Press of Harvard University, 1971.
McHenry, Robert, ed. *Famous American Women.* NY: Dover, 1980.

Lolly Ockerstrom,
freelance writer, Washington, D.C.

Safiye Sultana (d. 1603).
See Reign of Women.

Sagan, Leontine (1889–1974)
Jewish actress and film director who achieved critical acclaim before being forced to flee Nazi Germany for South Africa in 1933 and went on to co-found the National Theatre in Johannesburg. Name variations: *Leontine Fleischer; Leontine Sagan-Fleischer; Leontine Fleischer-Sagan; Leontine Schlesinger.* Pronunciation: *Leon-teen-AH ZAH-gahn. Born Leontine Schlesinger on February 13, 1889, in Budapest, Hun-*

gary; died in Pretoria, South Africa, of cerebral thrombosis on May 20, 1974; daughter of Josef Schlesinger and Emma (Fasal) Schlesinger; attended elementary school in Vienna, Austria, and elementary and secondary school in Johannesburg, South Africa; attended the Acting School of the German Theater (Reinhardt School) in Berlin for the two-year course (1910–12); married Dr. Victor Fleischer (an archivist, dramatist, and novelist); children: not known.

Awards: Lion of San Marco at the Venice Film Festival (1932) for Mädchen in Uniform (variously translated as Maidens in Uniform, Girls in Uniform, and Children in Uniform).

Moved from Vienna to Johannesburg with her parents sometime after 1900; returned to Berlin to attend the Acting School of the German Theater (1910); member of the Cooperative of German Stage Actors (Genossenschaft Deutscher Bühnen-Angehöriger, GDBA, 1912–34), acting in various cities, including Vienna, Frankfurt am Main, and Berlin; directed Mädchen in Uniform (1931), which brought her worldwide acclaim, and her second and only other film Men of Tomorrow (also titled Young Apollo), in the United Kingdom (1932); remained in UK after National Socialist takeover and toured South Africa (1933); produced operettas by Ivor Novello in London, Glasgow, New York, and other cities (1934–39); worked as a stage director in Johannesburg and Capetown, South Africa (1939–42); helped co-found the National Theatre in Johannesburg; produced for the theater and BBC in London after 1943; returned to South Africa (1950s), where she worked as a director and impresario there and in Rhodesia until her death.

Major theater credits: (under direction of Erich Pabst) acted in Onkelchen hat geträumt at the Komödie (Comedy) in Berlin (Aug.–Sept. 1924); (under direction of Carl Sternheim) performed in 1913 at the Komödie (1924); appeared as Der Glaube (Faith) in Jedermann and Liza in Der lebende Leichnam (The Living Corpse) at the National Theater in Basel, Switzerland, during a tour with Max Reinhardt's acting company (1926); directed Freudiges Ereignis (Little Accident) at the Komödie (1929); directed Children in Uniform at the Duchess Theater in London (her first production in England, 1932); subsequently produced Finished Abroad (1933); produced and acted in Children in Uniform and Nine Till Six in South Africa (1933); worked in London (1933–39); directed Richard III for the Oxford University Dramatical Society (1934); played Lady Anne at the Open Air Theatre (June 1934); directed and produced numerous plays, including Murder in Mayfair (1934), Glamorous Night (1935), Two Share a Dwelling (1935), Vicky (1935), O Evening Star (1936), Careless Rapture (1936), The Old Maid (1936), Balalaika (1936), Crest of the Wave (1937), Venus in Silk (1937), Paprika (1938), The Scarlet Pimpernel (1938), and The Dancing Years (1939); returned to South Africa (1939–43); produced Arc de Triomphe (1943), A Night in Venice (1944), and Gay Rosalinda (1945) in London.

Leontine Sagan learned acting from two masters of 20th-century theater, Max Reinhardt and Victor Barnowsky. Although the biographical details of her life remain scant, it is clear that she was far ahead of her time. Her films Mädchen in Uniform (1931) and Men of Tomorrow (1932), which used new photography and sound techniques and handled radical subject matter, established Sagan as one of the great directors in pre-World War II Germany and Britain.

Born in 1889 in Budapest, Hungary, Sagan was old enough to be fully aware of the turn-of-the-century renaissance that took place in Europe prior to the outbreak of the First World War in 1914. In fact, she spent part of her childhood in Vienna, the city that epitomized this cultural revolution, before her family relocated in South Africa in the early 1900s. The family's move was by no means unusual, since many Jewish immigrants left Europe between 1901 and 1914 in order to escape the racism and prejudice prevalent there.

Sagan certainly must have been influenced by the events taking place around her while she was enrolled in primary school in Vienna, and these may well have sparked her interest in the theater when she attended secondary school in South Africa. In 1910, she returned to Europe where she had been accepted at the Acting School of the German Theater in Berlin, founded and directed by Reinhardt. In attempting to develop a "theater for the masses" before World War I, he had become famous, and he consistently sponsored, supported, and encouraged numerous novice actors, actresses, film directors, producers and artists in the 1920s and 1930s.

Following completion of her two-year course of study, Sagan began acting professionally and promptly joined the Cooperative of German Stage Actors (Genossenschaft Deutscher Bühnen-Angehöriger, GDBA) in 1912. It is uncertain when she first began using her stage name "Sagan"; however, she first appears under this name in the 1912 edition of the New Theater Almanac (Neuer Theater Almanach), the official publication of the GDBA.

During 1912 and 1913, Sagan played bit roles in Teplitz, Germany, and other smaller towns, intent on building her reputation as a stage actress. In 1914, she landed her first full-time professional job with a theater company at the Albert Theater in Dresden. In 1915, she was back in Austria at the Neue Wiener Bühne (New Vienna Stage), where she remained only one year before leaving for Frankfurt am Main. Sometime during 1915 or 1916 (the exact date and place are unknown), Sagan married Dr. Victor Fleischer, archivist for the reigning prince of Liechtenstein in Vienna, director of the Frankfurter Verlagsanstalt (Frankfurt Publishing House), and later a freelance dramatist in Berlin. In Frankfurt, Sagan established permanent residence with her husband and was active as an actress, especially in the Neues Theater (New Theater), the Frankfurter Kammerspiele (Frankfurt Chamber Theater), and the Schauspielhaus (Acting House). She had at least three different residences while in Frankfurt, before finally settling in an apartment on the Corneliusstrasse where she lived from 1921 to 1927.

> 𝒯rankfurt's most intelligent actress was [Leontine] Sagan.
>
> —Rudolf Frank

It is difficult to be certain how many acting jobs Sagan actually had at any given time. She was employed full-time at various theaters in Frankfurt am Main, while appearing concurrently in Vienna, Berlin, and very possibly in other large European cities. In 1926, she took part in a tour of Switzerland with Max Reinhardt's theater troupe, performing as "Glaube" (Faith) in *Jedermann* and as Liza in *Der lebende Leichnam* (The Living Corpse), both roles typically associated with *Helene Thimig. That same year, she performed for the first time in Berlin. Sagan appeared at two theaters in Frankfurt am Main in the 1928–29 season, and also in Berlin at the well-known Renaissance Theater and the Englisches Theater Deutscher-Schauspieler e.V. (The English Theater for German Actors), which produced English plays for the interested elite. By 1930, she was working full-time at these two theaters, and living in an apartment in Berlin-Wilmersdorf.

Although Leontine Sagan was well known in theater circles by the middle 1920s, she first achieved worldwide recognition for two films that she directed in the early 1930s. Using her highly developed skills accumulated from nearly 20 years of work in the theater as an actress and director, she became an instant celebrity when her first film *Mädchen in Uniform* (*Girls in Uniform* or *Maidens in Uniform*), starring **Dorothea Wieck** and **Hertha Thiele**, was released in 1931. Based on the play *Gestern und Heute* (*Yesterday and Today*) by *Christa Winsloe, *Mädchen in Uniform* was the first German film to be cooperatively produced. The Deutsche Film Gemeinschaft, comprised of cast members and crew, was formed especially for this purpose, and shares of company stock were distributed in lieu of salaries. This unusual production arrangement alone would have secured *Mädchen in Uniform* a place in film history; because the movie was an artistic achievement as well, it established Sagan as one of the top motion-picture directors in interwar Germany.

Sagan, who worked on the film under the supervision of Carl Froelich, received the Lion of San Marco at the 1932 Venice Film Festival for *Mädchen*, and the movie attained widespread critical acclaim for its fresh filming and sound techniques as well as for its superb handling of a lesbian theme. In fact, *Mädchen in Uniform* is regarded as the first truly radical lesbian film. Its structure is a mixture of montage and narrative sequences. Sagan pioneered the use of superimposition of one character's face over another's to convey the psychological bond between them. This technique is used especially to show the attraction between the teacher Fräulein von Bernburg and her student Manuela von Meinhardis. Sagan also utilized shadows to add depth and emotion. For instance, she used this technique in the lighting and shooting of the school's back staircase to symbolize the girls' confinement. They are not allowed to use the well-lighted front stairs, which are reserved for the teachers and administrative personnel.

The film's frank treatment of lesbianism and Prussian discipline at a German girls' school was also far ahead of other films at this time. The movie, with its anti-fascist, anti-authoritarian, and anti-patriarchal themes, is truly amazing when one considers that it was shot only two years before Adolf Hitler's rise to power. Perhaps it was for this reason that *Mädchen in Uniform* was considered so scandalous upon its original release, a reputation it kept for many years to come.

After her tremendous success, Sagan quickly started work on a new project in Great Britain, the film *Men of Tomorrow*, released in 1932. This was one of the first films produced by the Korda Studios, founded by brothers Alexander, Vincent, and Zoltan Korda, who had immigrated from Hungary in 1932 after having produced numerous successful films in their homeland. All three went on to notable film careers in Britain.

Sagan's influence on theater and filmmaking in the late 1920s and early 1930s was immense. Her novel techniques and original production methods revolutionized German theater, and this expertise was transferred to Britain when she decided to stay there following the National Socialist seizure of power in 1933. That year, despite huge success in London, Paris and Berlin, *Mädchen in Uniform* was banned by National Socialist Cultural Minister Joseph Goebbels for the unhealthy "moral attitude" that it promoted. Under these conditions, it was certainly safer for Sagan to stay in England. Sadly, after the release of *Men of Tomorrow*, which only had slight success, Sagan never again worked as a motion picture director. From then on, she contented herself with stage productions.

Without adequate language skills, it would have been nearly impossible, even for someone as talented as Sagan, to find work in London. Many émigré artists had difficulty finding work in England and America, and as the number of refugees increased after 1938, the situation would become even more dire. But Sagan's childhood and adolescence in South Africa had

Leontine
Sagan

prepared her well for work in the U.K.; she had a superb command of the English language. In 1933, she toured South Africa with the "Capetown Repertoire Society," directing and acting in various productions. Despite the job situation, she was able to find work upon her return to London in 1934. She produced plays for the Oxford University Dramatical Society, notably *Richard III* in 1934, and operettas by Ivor Novello in London, Glasgow, New York, and other cities from 1934 to 1939.

In 1939, Sagan helped found the Austrian exile theater "The Lantern" in London; she is listed on the theater's official letterhead as a sponsor. "The Lantern" became one of the best-known refugee theaters in Britain and actively promoted the British cause in the fight against fascism during World War II. Many of those involved with "The Lantern" also worked for the BBC developing programming for broadcast into occupied Europe. In addition, Sagan was actively involved in the Austrian exile PEN Club as a sponsor and patron of the arts, along with author Stefan Zweig and other notable Austrians. PEN (Poets, Playwrights, Essayists, Editors and Novelists) had been founded in 1921 in London to combat racial hatred and intolerance.

Sagan again returned to South Africa in late 1939 and helped co-found the National Theatre in Johannesburg. Afterwards, she worked as a director at the new theater, toured extensively, and produced throughout South Africa and Rhodesia. She was instrumental in the development of South African theater during the Second World War and was one of the best-known actresses and stage producers in the country. In 1943, she returned to London with her husband Victor Fleischer and began work for the BBC. They remained in London for the duration of the war, and Fleischer died there in 1951. Following the death of her husband, Sagan returned to South Africa where she again took up an active role in the theater of her adopted home. For the next 23 years, until her own death on May 20, 1974, she produced and directed in South Africa. As far as is known, she never remarried, and her death certificate lists her as "widowed."

In 1981, Sagan's film *Mädchen in Uniform* celebrated its London revival, and in recent years there has been more critical attention paid to her work, but to date no biography of Sagan has been published, and there are large gaps in the information available on her.

SOURCES:

Arnsberg, Paul. *Die Geschichte der Frankfurter Juden seit der Französischen Revolution, Bd. III*. Darmstadt: Eduard Roether, 1983, p. 412.

Brüne, Klaus, ed. "Mädchen in Uniform," in *Lexikon des Internationalen Films*. Reinbek bei Hamburg: Rowohlt, 1988, p. 2381.

Deutsches Bühnenjahrbuch. Berlin: Verlag F.U. Günther & Sohn, 1915–35.

Institut für Zeitgeschichte (Institute of Contemporary History), Munich, Germany. "Abridged Death Certificate of Leontine Sagan-Fleischer from the Republic of South Africa, May 14, 1980."

Goble, Alan, ed. *The International Film Index, 1895–1990*. Vol. 2. Munich: Bowker-Saur, 1991, p. 1480.

International Biographical Dictionary of Central European Emigrés 1933–1945. Volume II. Ed. by Herbert A. Strauss and Werner Röder. Munich: K.G. Saur, 1983, p. 1009.

Jüdisches Lexikon. Ein enzyklopädisches Handbuch des jüdischen Wissens in vier Bänden. Bd. II. Berlin: Jüdischer, 1968 (reprint from 1928), p. 679.

Katz, Ephraim. *The International Film Encyclopedia*. London: Macmillan, 1982, p. 1009.

Krusche, Dieter, and Jürgen Labenski. *Reclams Film Führer*. 9. Aufl. Stuttgart: Philipp Reclam jun., 1993, pp. 339–340.

Letter from Mr. Herbert Koch, Registry Archive of the City of Vienna, Austria, March 15, 1996.

Lyon, Christopher, and Susan Doll, eds. "Mädchen in Uniform," in *The International Dictionary of Films and Filmmakers: Volume I*. London: Macmillan, 1987, pp. 273–274.

Uglow, Jennifer S., and Frances Hinton, eds. *The Macmillan Dictionary of Women's Biography*. London: Macmillan, 1982, pp. 407–408.

Die Vertreibung des Geistigen aus Österreich. Zur Kulturpolitik des Nationalsozialismus. Ausstellungskatalog Hrsg. von der Zentralsparkasse und Kommerzialbank, Wien, in Zusammenarbeit mit der Hochschule für Angewandte Kunst in Wien. Jänner–Februar, 1985.

Walk, Joseph. *Kurzbiographien zur Geschichte der Juden, 1918–1945*. Munich: K.G. Saur, 1988, p. 323.

Who Was Who in the Theatre, 1912–1976. Detroit, MI: Gale Research, 1978.

SUGGESTED READING:

Berghaus, Günter, ed. *Theatre and Film in Exile: German Artists in Great Britain, 1933–1945*. Oxford: Berg, 1989.

Pally, Marcia. "Women in Love: Filmmakers who choose Lesbianism as a Subject," in *Film Comment*. Vol. 22. March–April 1986, pp. 35–39.

RELATED MEDIA:

Mädchen in Uniform (98 min.), starring Hertha Thiele (as Manuela von Meinhardis), Dorothea Wieck (as Fräulein von Bernburg), **Emilia Unda** (as the Headmistress), **Ellen Schwanneke** (as Ilse von Westhagen), **Hedwig Schlichter** (as Fräulein von Kosten), and **Gertrud de Lalsky** (as Manuela's aunt), directed by Leontine Sagan, Deutsche Film Gemeinschaft, 1931.

Mädchen in Uniform (95 min. remake of 1931 version), starring *Romy Schneider** (as Manuela von Menhardis), directed by **Geza von Radvanyi**, CCC, 1958.

Men of Tomorrow (also titled *Young Apollo*), starring Robert Donat (as Julian Angell) and *Merle Oberon** (as Ysobel d'Aunay), directed by Leontine Sagan, Korda Studios, 1932.

Gregory Weeks,
University of Graz, Austria

Sage, Juniper.

See Brown, Margaret Wise.
See Hurd, Edith Thacher.

Sage, Kay (1898–1963)

American painter whose works embodied an elegant and refined form of Surrealism. Name variations: Katherine Linn Sage; Katherine Sage Tanguy; K. di San Faustino or Kay di San Faustino; Princess di San Faustino. Born Katherine Linn Sage in Albany, New York, on June 25, 1898; died of a self-inflicted gunshot wound on January 8, 1963, in Woodbury, Connecticut; daughter of Henry Manning Sage (heir to an industrial fortune and a member of the New York Legislature) and Anne Wheeler (Ward) Sage (daughter of an Albany physician); educated at various girls' schools including Brearley and Foxcroft in the United States as well as in Europe, 1908–15; attended Corcoran Art School, 1919–20; attended Italian art schools in Rome and private study with individual artists, 1920–23; married Prince Ranieri di San Faustino, in 1925 (divorced, marriage annulled by Catholic Church, 1935); married Yves Tanguy, in 1940 (died 1955).

Parents divorced (1908); worked as a government censor during World War I (1917–18); had first solo exhibit (1936); moved to Paris (1937); attended International Surrealist Exhibit in Paris and held her first exhibit there (1938); returned to the U.S. to live (1939); had first solo exhibit there (1940); moved to Woodbury, Connecticut (1941); won Watson F. Blair Purchase Prize at Art Institute of Chicago (1945); exhibited work at Catherine Viviano Gallery, New York City (1950); made first postwar trip back to Europe (1953); eyesight began to fail (1958); made first suicide attempt (1959); first full-scale retrospective showing of her work (1960).

Major works: Monolith *(Albany Institute of History and Art, 1937);* Egg on Sill *(Mattatuck Museum, Waterbury, Connecticut, 1939);* Danger, Construction Ahead *(Yale University Art Gallery, 1940);* I Saw Three Cities *(The Art Museum, Princeton University, Princeton, N.J., 1944);* The Unicorns Came Down to the Sea *(Philadelphia Museum of Art, 1948);* This is Another Day *(Sheldon Memorial Art Gallery, University of Nebraska-Lincoln, 1949);* Tomorrow is Never *(Metropolitan Museum of Art, New York, 1955).*

Katherine Linn Sage was an American heiress and socialite who transformed herself into a major figure in the art world of the mid-20th century. Although she enjoyed the benefits of inherited wealth throughout her life, she abandoned the role of social dilettante, as well as her marriage to her first husband, an Italian noble, in 1935 to become a serious artist. Upon moving to Paris, the center of the European art world, in 1937, she took the name Kay Sage and quickly came under the influence of such Surrealist painters as André Breton and her future husband Yves Tanguy.

Despite the unwillingness of most Surrealist painters to take a woman colleague seriously, Sage managed to enter the Surrealist circle and to learn from the leaders of the movement while developing her own unique style. Her close relationship and eventual marriage to Tanguy served for a long period to put her achievements in his shadow. Nonetheless, in the years after 1940 when she had relocated to her home country of the United States, and especially from 1946 onward, she began to produce paintings of striking originality which won her a considerable degree of recognition. Her work is distinguished from that of many of her fellow Surrealists by the lack of living creatures and the absence of any attempt to tell a complex narrative. Instead, she created an eerie world of geometric shapes, draperies, and lattices. Feminist art critics like **Whitney Chadwick**, working in the last several decades, have promoted recognition of Sage as a major artist who was long overshadowed by the males who dominated Surrealism.

Sage made no concessions to critics and buyers who might have been uncomfortable with her grim visions. Many critics such as **Elizabeth Martin** and **Vivian Meyer** have commented on the painter's longtime use of a dark palette, "the haunting air of melancholy and unease which pervades much of her work." For Chadwick, Sage's works were "barren vistas stripped of human habitation." Moreover, she gave no hint of the mind-set that directed her work. Of her own gripping images, Sage noted, "There is no reason why anything should mean more than its own statement." Nonetheless, some viewers found her achievement noteworthy. As critic James Thrall Soby put it, Sage's art "creates its own silence: lovely, serene, and memorable."

Kay Sage was also a talented writer. Fluent in three languages—a result of spending much of her childhood and early adult years in Europe—she could write verse in French and Italian as well as in English. In the final years of her life, she found her work as a painter hindered by her deteriorating eyesight. As a consequence she turned her creative efforts toward poetry.

The Surrealist movement in which Sage claimed a position flourished in Europe during the period between World War I and World War II. Surrealist art reflected the shock that World War I had brought to European life and to the sensibilities of European artists. It sought, for example, to combine unlikely groups of images in order to open the door to the subconscious mind. When World War II made France a dangerous and inhospitable place for such artists, approximately a dozen major Surrealists took refuge in the United States. Many critics contend that the American art world that was just departing from the socialist realism of the 1930s took crucial inspiration from the Surrealist refugees. "It is incontrovertible that not only was there a new mode of painting developing in New York," notes **Martica Sawin**, "it was emerging among those artists who had the greatest amount of contact with the Surrealist emigrés." Sage's earlier relationship with the Surrealist movement in Paris in the late 1930s, and the inspiration she drew from the Surrealist circle, was an early harbinger of this wave of artistic cross-fertilization.

Katherine Linn Sage was born into a family of wealth and privilege on June 25, 1898, in Albany, New York. She was the daughter of Henry Manning Sage and **Anne Ward Sage**. Her father's family had passed on to him a fortune based on lumber and real estate, and, at the time of Katherine's birth, Henry Sage was already a rising Republican member of the New York State Legislature. Henry and Anne Sage had a troubled marriage, with Anne unwilling to devote herself to the duties expected from a socially prominent politician's wife. The two effectively separated when Katherine and her sister were young, and the marriage came to a formal end in 1908. By then Katherine and her mother, sometimes accompanied by Katherine's sister, had begun to spend most of their time traveling in Europe. Rapallo, a seaport and winter resort in Italy, was a favorite residence for the females of the Sage family, and, for Katherine, after visits to her father, returning to Rapallo "seemed like going home."

Sage's adolescence was marked by her unusual family situation, her extensive travel, and the absence of any stability in her education. She attended a handful of private girls' schools in both the United States and Europe between 1908 and 1915. These years gave the young woman both a taste for solitude and, paradoxically, a veneer of social sophistication. One cousin described her as having "the essence of elegance, cosmopolitan glamour and savoir faire." Her talent for languages became evident as her residence in several foreign countries made her completely at home in French and Italian. Among her intimates, she enjoyed showing off her skill in using both the language of the educated and the coarser forms of popular speech. But Sage exhibited other talents as well. Even as a young child, the future artist showed an interest in painting.

The outbreak of World War I in 1914 pushed the Sage women to return to the United States. In 1917 and 1918, Katherine used her linguistic talents to work in the U.S. Government Censorship Office in New York. A shadowy wartime love affair with an older man made her reluctant to accompany her mother back to Europe, and, with the onset of peace, she spent some time at the Corcoran School of Art in Washington, D.C.

In the fall of 1920, Sage returned to Europe, where she spent the next two decades of her life. To her family, Katherine's interest in art still seemed the dilettantish desire of a wealthy young woman with time on her hands, but a testimony to the seriousness of her attraction to painting was evident when she continued her art studies in Italy in the early years of the 1920s. Her paintings from this period showed some talent, but they were conventional pieces such as portraits of young girls. Notes her biographer **Judith Suther**, these works differ in every respect—"subject matter, mood, and technique"—from her mature efforts after 1940. Sage subsequently dismissed the significance not only of her early works but of the teachers who had provided her with the technical tools she would subsequently employ. As she grew older, she contended that she was a self-taught artist.

In Suther's words, Sage spent "the aimless years" of her life from the mid-1920s through the mid-1930s as the wife of an Italian aristocrat, Prince Ranieri di San Faustino. They met in 1923 and were married, first in a civil ceremony on March 30, 1925, then in a religious wedding the following day. Although she continued to paint for a time, her social life as an Italian princess soon pushed her active work as an artist aside. Her husband held a variety of nebulous and undemanding positions mainly arranged for him by Henry Sage, his father-in-law, and other members of his family. The young socialite couple traveled extensively.

The decade of her marriage saw Sage grow increasingly restless with both her aimless existence and her charming but unambitious husband. The death of close relatives—her father in 1933 and her sister the following year—may have focused her discontent and motivated her to make a sharp turn in her life. Another factor may have been her acquaintance with the American poet Ezra Pound. The two met frequently to discuss their shared interest in the arts.

Sage's emergence as a serious and ambitious artist came in December 1936, when she put on display six oil paintings at a Milan art gallery. These works were, in Suther's words, "experimental abstract compositions." Another mark of her new sense of purpose was her decision to move to Paris, the artistic capital of the Continent. The Parisian art world had always intimidated her, but she apparently now felt ready to make an attempt to join it. She had an amicable separation from Ranieri and agreed, so that he could remarry, to let him end their marriage via a papal annulment.

In Paris, Sage's wealth allowed her to set herself up in style in early 1937 in one of the city's most glamorous neighborhoods. One year later, she received a lasting influence on her career as a painter when she attended the International Surrealist Exhibit in the early months of 1938. Although Sage had already encountered Surrealist art during a visit to Paris in 1936, Suther calls the 1938 exhibit "the catalyst that fired her imagination." She now abandoned any ties to traditional painting and plunged feverishly into the new style. In the fall of 1938, she exhibited six of her paintings, of which five drew heavily on Surrealist techniques. At approximately this time Sage first encountered Yves Tanguy, a merchant sailor turned Surrealist painter with whom she quickly fell in love.

Sage's view of herself as a Surrealist painter did not gain her easy entry into Surrealist circles. These were filled with resolutely masculine artists like André Breton who offered no welcome to female colleagues, despite the fact that Breton had been impressed by her exhibition in the fall of 1938. Her financial independence probably combined with her fiery desire to become a serious artist to help her shrug off the half-hostile, half-indifferent response she evoked. Her entry into the world of Surrealist artists was eased somewhat through her romantic link with Tanguy. Nonetheless, some of Tanguy's established friendships, notably the one with André Breton, came under strain as he turned his attention to Sage. In addition, her wealth and her aristocratic bearing and title grated on the nerves of Surrealists who were both poor and openly contemptuous of the gap between Europe's social classes. Although she provided them with money in time of need and helped several to reach the United States after the outbreak of World War II, Sage was viewed with distrust and often open dislike.

Sage progressed swiftly as a painter in the last years of the 1930s. Her contact with the Surrealists between 1937 and 1939 saw her stimulated as never before. As war approached in the summer of 1939, she was silent about her reactions to the growing political crisis. An American citizen, she was free to return to the United States as the conflict started to involve Europe. It was her social status and high-level connections, however, that helped her to bring Tanguy along with her. She left in October 1939, and Tanguy, freed from French military service on medical grounds, followed a month later. Back home, she continued to display a solid indifference to the great political events transpiring except as they affected Surrealist art and her acquaintances among the circle of Surrealist artists.

The time in Paris provided the groundwork for an outburst of creativity that appeared when she was back on American soil. In those earlier years, notes Suther, "she had been painting steadily, preparing the way for the distinctive Surrealist style that emerged in her pictures from the 1940s." Sage participated in a number of shows of Surrealist art, most of them greeted

Kay Sage

without enthusiasm by American art critics unfamiliar with the Surrealist movement. But she was determined to build a personal reputation as a painter. Her first one-woman show in the United States—in which she displayed seventeen paintings done in the past three years—took place in June 1940 at the Matisse Gallery in New York City.

A crucial painting in this initial exhibit was *Danger, Construction*, completed in 1940. It seemed to show a prehistoric landscape combined with rock formations and a group of the "sentinel figures" that would become one of her chief artistic motifs. Critics took due note of her social prominence by referring to her as "princess," but they also perceived the power of her pictures' dream-like quality while noting that she was not as obscure or frightening as her fellow Surrealists. An American surrealist with an accessible style may have had a particular appeal in an artistic venue that had never embraced the movement. The exiled Surrealists newly transplanted to New York, writes Dickran Tashjian, "merely heightened the cultural ambivalence felt by many American artists and writers toward the European avant-garde now in their midst."

With her first marriage severed by both church annulment and civil divorce, Sage formalized her longtime love affair with Yves Tanguy by marrying him in August 1940. In November 1941, the two moved to the small town of Woodbury, Connecticut, and, four years later, decided to make it their permanent home. A traditional artists' colony, Woodbury was removed from the immediate frenzy of New York City's artistic scene. In particular, it distanced her from immediate contact with many of the exiled Surrealists such as André Breton who rewarded her generosity with surliness. With Kay's fortune available to them, she and Yves were able in 1946 to establish themselves in a comfortable home on the northern fringe of Woodbury, using the barn to provide them with a set of studios for their work. Ironically, their house was the former poor farm for 19th-century Woodbury's residents. One of the couple's favorite recreations was holding informal shooting matches for their friends, using the extensive set of guns Tanguy collected at their home.

Sage's painting became even more striking by the mid-1940s, even as critics continued to refer to her primarily as the wife of Yves Tanguy. *I Saw Three Cities*, completed in 1944, featured a particularly dominant "sentinel figure" towering over sail-like vertical slabs. Her use of color employed intense greens and bright reds in marked contrast to the grays, greens, and browns that had been featured in her earlier work. Shadows also came to play an increasingly important role in the imagined world she was busy exploring. It is possible that she deliberately made her figures less and less organic in order to draw a clear line between her work and her husband's. Ironically, Sawin suggests that the sharper focus and brighter colors in Tanguy's own work at this time may have come from his close contact with Kay Sage and "the decisive shapes, sharp edges, and strong light of her paintings."

A breakthrough in the range of acceptance for Sage's work came in 1945 when she won a prize from the Art Institute of Chicago. She now regularly received invitations to participate in national exhibits in locations ranging from the Palace of the Legion of Honor in San Francisco to the Corcoran Gallery of Art in Washington, D.C. A new motif in her work—along with shadows and sentinel figures—was scaffolding and latticework. Since the house at Woodbury was undergoing extensive renovation at this time, the new forms came apparently from the practical side of Sage's life. On the other hand, as Suther notes, they may represent "the inner reconstruction Sage had begun upon leaving Rapallo" in the mid-1930s.

Their small circle of friends remarked on the strong personal differences between Sage and her husband. She struck most of those who met her as a chilly, remote figure who still carried herself with the airs of an American heiress and an Italian princess. Yves Tanguy, on the other hand, was often a drunken buffoon whose party behavior included butting his head against those of his guests in order to see whose was harder. His behavior in public often included openly insulting his wife. In a more discreet way, Sage also engaged in heavy drinking while they lived together in Connecticut. The strains on her personality may have come from the fact that their friends and acquaintances still saw him as the more significant artist.

For some students of her work, Sage reached artistic maturity with her 1950 exhibit at the Catherine Viviano Gallery in New York. By then, the troublesome set of European Surrealists had returned home and thus freed her energies to concentrate on her easel. Her works now showed a new level of refinement and elaboration of earlier themes such as drapery and latticework. Sage's style increasingly focused on perfecting her earlier techniques. She rejected the practice of the European Surrealists in conducting an endless round of casting off old motifs and restlessly seeking new ones.

By the early 1950s, New York critics increasingly lauded Sage's work. Moreover, they did so without the backhanded compliments of earlier years in which they had characterized her work as an accessible and elegant form of Surrealism. In 1952, for example, *The New York Times* did not even mention Surrealism in remarking upon "the dream world that she both creates and renders on canvas with encyclopedic fidelity." Nonetheless, positive judgments of Sage's work were often laced with remarks about its chilly and intellectualized character.

Sage's life took a decisive turn downward in January 1955 when Tanguy suffered a fatal cerebral hemorrhage. His health had been precarious for years, and in 1953 he was found to be suffering from a stomach ulcer and high blood pressure. Kay Sage's efforts to wean him away from hard liquor seemed to have some success, but he apparently never made an effective recovery. Her husband's death sent her into years of despair that cut off her career as a painter. Notes Sawin, she "stayed on in the house she and Tanguy had shared, increasingly lonely, depressed and alcoholic." Her work as a painter continued, but she mainly repeated the motifs she had established in the previous decade and a half. Her works now bore somber titles far different from the playful ones she had favored before, e.g. *For the Wind to Tear*, *The Circle Never Sleeps*, *Tomorrow is Never*.

Sage's talents as a writer had been evident as early as her teenage years. During her first marriage, when it had been difficult for her to paint, she apparently turned most of her creative energy to poetry; none has survived. There is some evidence that she wrote poetry during the late 1930s when she was beginning her career as a Surrealist painter. In the 1940s, she continued to produce a trickle of what Suther calls "laconic rhymes" to reflect her inner feelings. Now, in the aftermath of Tanguy's death, she turned increasingly away from painting, impelled in part by the fact that her eyesight was growing weaker. In 1955, she put together a record of her life in an imaginatively constructed autobiography that she called *China Eggs*. In 1958, in another concession to her eyesight problems, she began producing collages.

By the late 1950s, Sage was in the grip of unmanageable depression. After pondering the possibility of ending her life for several years, she made an unsuccessful suicide attempt with sleeping pills in early 1959. Surgery later that year and again in June 1960 failed to improve her eyesight, and her success in publishing poetry—several volumes appeared written in Sage's fluent French—did not lift her spirits. Even a showing of her paintings at the Viviano Gallery in April 1960—the first complete retrospective of her work—and the uniformly favorable notices it received made no permanent impression on her failing spirits. Perhaps addled by alcohol, she suffered a damaging fall in her home in late 1960. Then on January 8, 1963, in the home in Woodbury, where she had remained after her husband's death, she used a gun to end her life.

SOURCES:

Caws, Mary Ann, *et al.*, eds. *Surrealism and Women*. Cambridge, MA: MIT Press, 1991.

Chadwick, Whitney. *Women, Art, and Society*. London: Thames & Hudson, 1990.

———. *Women Artists and the Surrealist Movement*. London: Thames & Hudson, 1985.

Martin, Elizabeth, and Vivian Meyer. *Female Gazes: Seventy-Five Women Artists*. Toronto: Second Story Press, 1997.

Sawin, Martica. *Surrealism in Exile and the Beginning of the New York School*. Cambridge, MA: MIT Press, 1995.

Sicherman, Barbara, and Carol Hurd Green, eds. *Notable American Women: The Modern Period*. Cambridge, MA: The Belknap Press of Harvard University, 1980.

Suther, Judith D. *A House of Her Own: Kay Sage, Solitary Surrealist*. Lincoln, NE: University of Nebraska Press, 1997.

Tashjian, Dickran. *A Boatload of Madmen: Surrealism and the American Avant-garde, 1920–1950*. NY: Thames & Hudson, 1995.

SUGGESTED READING:

Chadwick, Whitney, and Isabelle de Courtivron, eds. *Significant Others: Creativity and Intimate Partnership*. NY: Thames & Hudson, 1993.

Dunford, Penny. *A Biographical Dictionary of Women Artists in Europe and America since 1850*. NY: Harvester Wheatsheaf, 1990.

Fine, Elsa Honig. *Women and Art: A History of Women Painters and Sculptors from the Renaissance to the 20th Century*. Montclair, NJ: Allanheld and Schram, 1978.

Neil M. Heyman,
Professor of History, San Diego State University,
San Diego, California

Sage, Margaret Olivia (1828–1918)

American philanthropist who was one of the top public benefactors in the early 20th century. Name variations: Margaret Olivia Sage; Olivia Sage; Mrs. Russell Sage. Born Margaret Olivia Slocum in Syracuse, New York, on September 8, 1828; died in New York City on November 4, 1918; daughter of Joseph Slocum (a merchant) and Margaret Pierson (Jermain) Slocum; attended Syracuse public schools; graduated from the Troy Female Seminary, 1847; married Russell B. Sage (a financier), on November 24, 1869 (died 1906); no children.

When Margaret Olivia Sage inherited more than $63 million from her husband's estate upon his death in July 1906, she quickly became one of America's premier philanthropists. Her first project was to establish the Russell Sage Foundation in memory of her husband, who had amassed a fortune in wholesale groceries, the stock market, railroads and money-lending. Begun in 1907 with a $10 million endowment (at the time the largest-ever single gift for the public good) which she later increased by $5.6 million, the Russell Sage Foundation was intended to improve living and social conditions in the United States. Its trustees were granted almost total authority for distributing money, most of which provided support for numerous small organizations and charities. Margaret Sage donated huge numbers of modest sums to hospitals, churches, homes for the elderly, the YWCA and YMCA, Bible tract societies, and the American Seaman's Friend Society. As her philanthropic work progressed, her focus remained on education, religion, and welfare, although she also supported such causes as fresh air funds, humane treatment for animals, milk inspection, the Women's Christian Temperance Union, and the women's suffrage movement.

Sage was born on September 8, 1828, in Syracuse, New York, the daughter of Joseph Slocum and **Margaret Jermain Slocum**. Both her parents came from families whose ancestors had settled in America during colonial times; Joseph Slocum, a well-to-do merchant, traced his lineage to Anthony Slocum, who immigrated from England to Massachusetts in 1630, although she later also claimed that he had been related to Miles Standish. (After her husband's death, she would assert that his ancestors had fought on the side of William the Conqueror.) Known as Olivia in her youth, Sage went to local schools in Syracuse before attending the Troy Female Seminary in Troy, New York. By the time she graduated in 1847, her family faced financial hardship, and she therefore accepted a teaching post at the Chestnut Street Seminary in Philadelphia. Although Sage resigned from teaching after only two years because of ill health, she maintained a lifelong interest in women's education. For the next two decades, she taught infrequently when her health permitted.

At the age of 41, she married Russell B. Sage, a millionaire businessman, former congressional representative, and widower whose first wife had been a close friend of hers at the Troy Female Seminary. Although Russell Sage had acquired millions of dollars from business ventures and the stock market, he was not noted for his generosity. Only at Margaret Sage's urging did he fund the education of 40 Native American children, donate $50,000 to the Woman's Hospital of the State of New York, and provide money for a dormitory at the Troy Female Seminary. The Sages maintained homes in New York City, Long Island, and Sag Harbor; from these locations, Sage acted on her conviction that her gender and her station in life commanded her to work for the benefit of society. Although she felt that a woman's first duty was to her home, she also believed women to be the moral superiors of men, and that as such they had a special responsibility to work for the improvement of social systems. A lifelong Presbyterian, she took a keen interest in home and foreign missions.

Many of Sage's religious and social beliefs reflected upper-class 19th-century American culture, particularly her attitudes toward servants and the poor. She perceived servants as misled and wayward children, and her concern about the "moral filth" of the poor led her to insist on the need for missionary work among them. (She also considered giving money directly to the needy "the very worst thing to do.") At the same time, she gave generously to institutions fostering women's education, and purchased a new campus for her own alma mater in Troy, by then called the *Emma Willard School after its founder, in 1910. Six years later, after consultation with *Eliza Kellas, the school's principal, she used its old buildings to start Russell Sage College for women's vocational education. Other universities and colleges also benefited from Sage's generosity. Harvard University received a dormitory, named Standish Hall at her request, Yale acquired the Pierson-Sage campus (both of these gifts honored her parents' colonial lineages), and Syracuse University received $16 million. For a time, the teachers' college at Syracuse was named the Margaret Slocum Sage Teachers' College. Her patronage extended as well to 13 other leading Eastern men's and women's colleges and to 2 black colleges, Tuskegee Institute and Hampton Institute, each of which received $800,000. She also gave $800,000 to the New York Public Library. Missions, various religious societies and other ministries received some $7.5 million.

Sage also provided financial support for the Children's Aid Society, the Charity Organization Society, the Woman's Hospital and the Presbyterian Hospital, as well as other welfare institutions. Among the cultural institutions she provided with sizable donations were the New York Botanical Gardens, the Metropolitan Museum of Art, the American Museum of Natural History, and the

New York Zoological Society. She purchased 70,000 acres on Marsh Island off the Louisiana coast and presented it to the government as a bird refuge, and also purchased Constitution Island, the former home of ❧➤ **Anna** and **Susan Warner** in the Hudson River, and gave it to the U.S. Military Academy. In all, her charitable financial contributions amounted to about $80 million, placing her in the same league as such better-known philanthropists as Andrew Carnegie, J.P. Morgan, and John D. Rockefeller. Margaret Sage died in New York City on November 4, 1918, at age 90. She continued her philanthropy posthumously with bequests in her will for many of her favorite charities, including the Russell Sage Foundation. Both the foundation and Russell Sage College remain in operation.

SOURCES:

James, Edward T., ed. *Notable American Women, 1607–1950*. Cambridge, MA: The Belknap Press of Harvard University, 1971.

McHenry, Robert, ed. *Famous American Women*. NY: Dover, 1980.

Lolly Ockerstrom,
freelance writer, Washington, D.C.

Sage, Mrs. Russell (1828–1918).

See Sage, Margaret Olivia.

Sager, Ruth (1918–1997)

American geneticist. Born on February 7, 1918, in Chicago, Illinois; died of cancer on March 29, 1997, in Brookline, Massachusetts; graduated from the University of Chicago, 1938; Rutgers University, M.S., 1944; Columbia University, Ph.D., 1948; married Arthur Pardee.

Ruth Sager distinguished herself early in her career with a major discovery in the field of genetics. At a time when few women were represented in the sciences, Sager's investigations into the location of genetic material in cells changed the direction of genetic research. Following her groundbreaking discovery in 1953, she taught and conducted research at some of the most prestigious scientific and medical institutions in the United States.

Sager was born in Chicago in 1918 and graduated from the University of Chicago in 1938. Following the completion of an M.S. in plant physiology in 1944 at Rutgers University, she continued her studies at Columbia, receiving a Ph.D. in genetics in 1948. She served as a Merck Fellow for three years at the National Research Council, and then became an assistant in biochemistry at the Rockefeller Institute for Medical Research (later Rockefeller University). With support from the U.S. Public Health Service and the National Science Foundation, she began her investigations into genetic theory.

Challenging the prevailing notion regarding the location of the genetic material in cells, Sager examined alternative theories that suggested the possibility of a second genetic system governing heredity existing outside the chromosomes. In 1953, while conducting experiments in the cells of the green alga *Chlamydomonas*, she discovered a gene regulating sensitivity to streptomycin outside the chromosomal structure in the cells. Further experimentation revealed three significant factors: many non-chromosomal genes in the plant could be passed on by either the male or the female partner in sexual reproduction; such genes controlled a range of hereditary characteristics; and these genes had the ability to replicate and remain active throughout several generations. Sager's findings pointed to a new paradigm for genetic research.

For the next 20 years, Sager's career led her to research posts at several different institutions, including her alma mater, Columbia University, where she was research associate in zoology from 1955 until she advanced to senior research associate in 1961. Beginning in 1966, she served as professor of biology at Hunter College of the City University of New York. She was appointed a Guggenheim Research Fellow in 1972–73. By 1975, she was on the staff of Boston's Dana-Farber Cancer Institute, an affiliate of Harvard University Medical School, while also serving as professor of cellular genetics at Harvard Medical School. Sager retired from the school as professor emerita in 1988, but continued working at Dana-Farber, eventually becoming chief of cancer genetics there. Her groundbreaking research merited her election to the National Academy of Sciences in 1977. Having devoted herself to research in cancer genetics, Sager herself died of cancer of the bladder at her home in Brookline, Massachusetts, on March 29, 1997.

SOURCES:

McHenry, Robert, ed. *Famous American Women*. NY: Dover, 1980.

"Ruth Sager, 79," in *The Day* [New London, CT]. April 4, 1997.

Lolly Ockerstrom,
freelance writer, Washington, D.C.

Sagittinanda, Turiya (b. 1937).

See Coltrane, Alice.

Sah Sultana (fl. 1500s).

See Reign of Women.

Anna and Susan Warner. *See joint entry under Warner, Susan.*

Saiki, Patricia Fukuda (1930—)

U.S. Republican congressional representative (January 3, 1987–January 3, 1991). Name variations: Patricia Fukuda; Mrs. Stanley Mitsuo Saiki. Born Patricia Fukuda in Hilo, Hawaii, on May 28, 1930; daughter of Kazuo Fukuda and Shizue (Inoue) Fukuda; attended public schools in Hilo; University of Hawaii at Manoa, B.S., 1952; married Stanley Mitsuo Saiki, on June 19, 1954; children: Stanley Mitsuo Saiki; Sandra S. Saiki; Margaret C. Saiki; Stuart K. Saiki; Laura H. Saiki.

Patricia Fukuda Saiki was born in Hilo, Hawaii, in 1930, of Japanese ancestry. After attending public school in Hilo, she went to the University of Hawaii at Manoa, graduating with a B.S. in 1952. She then taught junior and senior high in the public schools before entering politics as a Republican. Serving first as a delegate to the Hawaii State Constitutional Convention in 1968, she was elected to the Hawaii House of Representatives later that year. She remained in the Hawaiian House until 1974, when she was elected to the state senate, where she served from 1974 to 1983. In 1982, Saiki became the Republican nominee for lieutenant governor, and from

Patricia Fukuda Saiki

1983 to 1985 she served as chair of the Republican Party of Hawaii.

By 1986, Saiki was living in Honolulu, which enabled her to run in a special election to fill the vacancy left when Cecil Heftel resigned as representative from Hawaii's First Congressional District in order to run for governor. Although she lost the special election to Neil Abercrombie, she won the Republican primary for the general election which was held on the same day. Saiki then won the general election held in November, defeating Democratic candidate Mufi Hannemann to become the first Republican to represent Hawaii in the U.S. House of Representatives since the islands achieved statehood in 1959. During her two terms in the House, Saiki served on the Committee on Banking, Finance and Urban Affairs, the Select Committee on Aging, and the Committee on Merchant Marine and Fisheries. She was instrumental in helping to secure authorization for additional land for the Kiluea National Wildlife Refuge, and co-sponsored the bill to provide compensation for Japanese-Americans interned during World War II. Saiki left the House after receiving the Republican nomination for the U.S. Senate in 1990, although she lost that election to Democrat Daniel K. Akaka of Honolulu.

Saiki returned to Honolulu upon leaving Congress, but soon became the director of the Small Business Administration under President George Bush. She ran for governor again in 1994, also unsuccessfully, and two years later chaired the special advisory council on small business for Senator Bob Dole's presidential campaign.

SOURCES:

Office of the Historian. *Women In Congress, 1917–1990.* Commission on the Bicentenary of the U.S. House of Representatives, 1991.

Lolly Ockerstrom,
freelance writer, Washington, D.C.

Saimei, Empress (594–661).

See Kōgyoku-Saimei.

Saint, Eva Marie (1924—)

American actress who won an Academy Award for her performance in On the Waterfront. *Born on July 4, 1924, in Newark, New Jersey; younger daughter of John Saint (a businessman) and Eva Saint; Bowling Green State University, Bowling Green, Ohio, B.A., 1946; married Jeffrey Hayden (a producer-director), on October 27, 1951; children: two.*

Selected filmography: On the Waterfront *(1954);* That Certain Feeling *(1956);* A Hatful of Rain *(1957);* Raintree County *(1957);* North by Northwest *(1959);*

Exodus *(1960)*; All Fall Down *(1962)*; 36 Hours *(1964)*; The Sandpiper *(1965)*; The Russians Are Coming, the Russians Are Coming *(1966)*; Grand Prix *(1966)*; The Stalking Moon *(1969)*; Loving *(1970)*; Cancel My Reservation *(1972)*; Nothing in Common *(1986)*.

Eva Marie Saint's "essential characteristic is serenity," noted *Mademoiselle*, following her Oscar-winning movie debut as the convent-reared girl in *On the Waterfront*. Over the course of her career, Saint has also been cited for the sensitivity and compassion she brings to the craft of acting. Reviewing her portrayal of the traveling companion in the Broadway play *A Trip to Bountiful* (1953), for which she received the Drama Critics Award, Walter Kerr observed: "She just nudges the role into existence, working softly, placidly, and with infinite attractiveness."

Saint was born in 1924 in Newark, New Jersey, but grew up in Delmar, New York, near Albany. Originally planning to become a teacher, she attended Bowling Green State University, where she soon discovered that her talents lay elsewhere. After acting in several college plays and spending two summers as a guide at a NBC radio station in New York, Saint graduated in 1946 and left for New York, to launch her career in radio. "With me," she later told Oscar Godbout of *The New York Times*, "there were years of doing small things, soap operas, ads, modeling, then the snowball just seemed to grow." In 1948, certain that she wanted to be an actress, Saint enrolled at the Actors Studio.

From radio, Saint moved gracefully into television, playing dramatic roles on such shows as "Robert Montgomery Presents," "Studio One," and "Philco Playhouse," and winning the 1954 Sylvania award as "the best dramatic actress in television." *The Trip to Bountiful*, which provided Saint with her first major role on Broadway, was actually adapted from the television play in which she also appeared. Saint's Broadway run was followed by the female lead in the film *On the Waterfront*, starring Marlon Brando and directed by the legendary Elia Kazan. Saint's delicate persona added a decidedly romantic note to the otherwise gritty film, which was adapted from the exposé of racketeering on the New York docks by Malcolm Johnson. A.H. Weiler of *The New York Times* found Kazan's choice of Saint inspired. "She is sweet, intelligent, and appealing in the role . . . poignant, tender, and moving." *The Christian Science Monitor* concurred, calling Saint "a compassionate actress who possesses beauty and something much more."

Eva Marie Saint

Saint appeared in a smattering of films throughout the next two decades, although her unique personality and talent made it increasingly difficult for her to find appropriate vehicles. Notable among her later roles was the long-suffering wife in *A Hatful of Rain* (1957) and the cool-headed spy in the Hitchcock comedy-thriller *North by Northwest* (1959). Her last film appearance was in *Nothing in Common* (1986).

SOURCES:
Candee, Marjorie Dent, ed. *Current Biography Yearbook 1955*. NY: H.W. Wilson, 1955.
Scott, Walter. "Personality Parade," in *Boston Sunday Globe Parade*. February 4, 2001.

Barbara Morgan,
Melrose, Massachusetts

St. Albans, duchess of (c. 1777–1837).

See Burdett-Coutts, Angela for sidebar on Mellon, Harriot.

St. Denis, Ruth (1877–1968)

One of the greatest figures in the dance world in the first half of the 20th century and a founder of modern dance. Name variations: Mrs. Edwin Shawn. Born Ruth Dennis on January 20, 1877, in Newark, New

Jersey; died on July 21, 1968; eldest child of Thomas L. Dennis (an inventor) and Ruth Emma (Hull) Dennis (one of the first licensed woman doctors in the U.S.); married Ted Shawn, on August 13, 1914 (separated, 1928).

Began theatrical career (1893); made New York debut (January 1906); went on European tour (1906–09), American tour (1909–10), H.B. Harris coast-to-coast tour (1910–11), southern tour (1914), cross-country concert tour (1914–15); helped found Denishawn (summer 1915); went on Denishawn concert and vaudeville tours (1915–17), vaudeville tours (1918–19); went on cross-country tour (1921), Mayer tours (1922–25), Asian tour (1925–26), Judson tour (1926–27), Ziegfeld Follies tour (1927–28); gave concerts, especially at Lewisohn Stadium (1928–32); closed Denishawn (1931); published Lotus Light, *a book of poetry (1932); appeared as part of* Dance International *at Radio City Music Hall, New York (1937); published autobiography,* An Unfinished Life *(1939); founded School of Natya with La Meri (1940–42); gave last public performance, at Jacob's Pillow (August 1964).*

Ruth St. Denis and *Isadora Duncan, though they never worked together, were the two founders of what is now known as modern dance. In 1890s America, there was no serious dance form of any kind except for the corps de ballet at the Metropolitan Opera and an occasional solo performer visiting from Europe. Yet this was the era when women first began to think seriously of emancipation from traditional women's roles, and both of these dancers, as much by their free-wheeling ways of life as by their art, inspired a generation of young women as perhaps no women had ever done before. Thanks to their efforts and their example, dancing became rampant in America, and barefoot college girls were romping on lawns in tunics, striking poses and forming "Grecian urns." More important, however, they created a new medium of human expression that revolutionized the art of the dance, molding a dance idiom for the 20th century, as Stravinsky did for 20th-century music and Picasso for 20th-century art.

Ruth St. Denis was born Ruth Dennis in Newark, New Jersey, in 1877, the eldest of two children. Her father T.L. Dennis, a Civil War veteran, inventor, and impractical dreamer, eventually drifted into alcoholism. Her mother **Ruth Hull Dennis**, one of the first licensed woman doctors in the United States, was, in the words of the day, "a woman of advanced views." Be-

cause her husband was irresponsible, Ruth Hull Dennis was the sole provider for the family, and it was she who had the greatest influence upon the lives of her daughter and her son "Buzz" (he was never given a proper name), who was born in 1887. A suffragist and free-thinker who campaigned against corsets and long dresses, Ruth Hull Dennis was a possessive woman responsible for driving off all her daughter's suitors until St. Denis was nearly 40.

Ruth grew up on a farm at Pin Oaks, near Newark, where she was able to run and felt the inspiration of nature, and where she received her first religious instruction from her mother who read to her from the Bible at the end of each day. She attended public school, but her regular education was supplemented by lessons at a dance school in Somerville, New Jersey, at night, as well as by the teachings of Delsart on movement taught to her by her mother. Her parents both recognized her talents and encouraged her to develop them. With a flair for acrobatics and mimicry, St. Denis soon decided that she wanted a career in show business. At 16, she went on the stage as a dancer at Worth's Museum in Manhattan. From then on, she worked continuously in cheap music halls, variety shows, and touring road companies, occasionally modeling for a department store and briefly attempting classical ballet.

In 1898, St. Denis had a bit part in a play produced by Austin Daly. After Daly's sudden death, she danced in David Belasco's London production of *Zaza*, starring the famed *Leslie Carter. She then returned to New York and was hired by Belasco, for whom she worked for the next five years. During this period, she attracted numerous suitors, including the famous architect Stanford White (later murdered by Harry K. Thaw) and even Belasco himself. Urged on by her mother, Ruth rejected them all. It was Belasco who nicknamed her "Saint Dennis," because of her resistance to his charms. From this, the stage name Ruth St. Denis was born.

While on tour in 1903 with the Belasco production of *Madame DuBarry*, she saw an Egyptian scene in an ad for Egyptian Deities cigarettes in Buffalo, New York, and in that moment divined her mission in life: the propagation of dance as a universal medium. She began to steep herself in the cultures of the East, eventually coming under the influence of Hindu dance. She then devised several "oriental" dances, setting them to the music from Delibe's opera *Lakmé*. Gathering together a motley company, she succeeded in getting an engagement in New York, where she opened at the Hudson Theater in

Manhattan in January 1906. Using the surname St. Denis for the first time, she performed *Incense, The Cobra* and, finally, *Radha*, her solo interpretation of a classical Indian temple dance (she would dance *The Cobra* as late as 1966, when she was 89). Purity of form or authenticity were not concerns to St. Denis at that moment, nor would they ever be; she was an interpreter and an artist, not an ethnographer.

In physical appearance, St. Denis was tall and lanky, with long arms and legs, and a face that was pretty in her youth. Her dances were characterized by deep backbends, graceful spins, and great extensions of her long limbs.

Though lacking in energy and force, they were nevertheless beautiful because she was a born, instinctive dancer. Her first audience, comprised of some of the cream of New York society (patrons of the arts who were in a position to launch the careers of anyone they admired), was spellbound, and the theater was sold out for each performance. In this way, Ruth St. Denis became a name in the world of dance. She was soon invited to perform at luxurious homes and private clubs by some of the wealthiest patrons of the arts in New York, Boston, Philadelphia, and elsewhere. The money earned allowed her to establish some financial security.

Meanwhile, after her success in New York, St. Denis chose as her manager the promoter Henry B. Harris, who immediately booked her in London. From there, she went to France and then to Germany, where she had her greatest triumph, then on to Prague, Vienna, Düsseldorf, Hamburg, Brussels, Budapest, Nürnberg, Graz, Monte Carlo, Munich, and Breslau. As a rule, she performed in variety theaters or music halls, but in time she also appeared in major theaters and opera houses. Her recitals were always solo performances, and during this period she devised the cycle of Indian dances that were to make her famous. (In performing alone, St. Denis was not unique; Isadora Duncan and ◄✣ **Mata Hari** also gave solo recitals.) Elegant and graceful, St. Denis had great style and early introduced into her dances a rippling effect with the movement of her arms that was totally original.

While in France, she saw and learned from the American dancer *****Loie Fuller**, who pioneered in the use of theatrical lighting and who had mastered the art of performing with fabrics designed to illuminate the movements of her body. St. Denis spent nearly three years in Europe, returning to the United States in 1909, where she immediately embarked on two American tours sponsored by Harris (1909–10, 1910–11). On December 12, 1910, she finally succeeded in staging her first full-length dance, *Egypta*. Harris lost money on this production, as well as on her last tour, and St. Denis was forced to return to vaudeville to enable him to recoup. Harris perished in the sinking of the *Titanic* in April 1912. Without him, St. Denis toured in vaudeville for three years but found it a meager living, and she augmented her income by once again giving private performances for society groups. By now, she had become as interested in Japanese dance as she had been in that of Egypt and India. To this period belong several of her dances on Japanese themes, especially *O-mika*.

There was a furious dance craze in America in the years immediately prior to the First World War, and St. Denis thought that she might do better if, like *****Irene Castle**, she had a partner. In the spring of 1914, she advertised for someone to fill the role. The turning point in both her life and career occurred when she first met her future husband and dance partner, Ted Shawn. Edwin Myers Shawn was born in Kansas City, Missouri, on October 21, 1891, and was raised in Denver, Colorado. He attended the University of Denver where he first saw St. Denis perform on her coast-to-coast tour in March 1911. Originally planning to become a minister, Shawn was so struck by St. Denis that he turned to a career

✣►
Mata Hari.
See Zelle,
Margaretha.

in dance. By 1913, he had begun to make a reputation for himself in Los Angeles with a partner named **Norma Gould**. Together, they introduced the then-fashionable "Tango Teas" to the West Coast, where Shawn produced the first dance film, *Dance of the Ages*, for the Edison Company. He then went on a tour with Gould that took them to New York. There, Shawn taught dance, eventually meeting St. Denis through one of his pupils. When Shawn went to see his idol at her home in New York, they chatted for hours, the first of many such conversations. St. Denis later remarked that this first discourse never really ceased for the rest of their lives.

In the spring of 1914, St. Denis, "assisted by Ted Shawn with **Hilda Beyer**," toured the southeast. Ruth did her Indian and Japanese dances. Shawn did his own solos (*Dagger Dance, Dance Russe, Pipes of Pan*, etc.) and lightened the program by dancing the latest ballroom crazes (Argentine tango, fox trot, maxixe) with Beyer. That summer, St. Denis and Shawn were married in New York. She was 37; he was 23. Years later, referring to her husband in a journal, St. Denis would write: "He is easily the greatest male dancer in the world today." Nijinsky, of course, was no longer dancing; Nureyev was yet to come. While there seems to be no doubt that she was in love with the young, handsome dancer (at least in the beginning), Shawn, although certainly captivated by St. Denis and dazzled by her artistry, was attracted to other men. Ultimately, this soured the marriage, though it was never legally terminated.

Once married, St. Denis and Shawn launched the Ruth St. Denis School of Dancing and the Related Arts, soon called simply Denishawn, which opened in the summer of 1915 in Los Angeles. The school, largely Shawn's brainchild, could not survive on tuitions alone, so the couple closed it in the fall and arranged a concert at the Hudson Theater in New York. The concert was a huge success and led to a strenuous vaudeville engagement that took them across the entire country, giving two performances a day. A Denishawn tour followed in 1916–17, this time consisting of a proper company. St. Denis and Shawn were accompanied by 11 of their students, billed as the "Denishawn Dancers."

Throughout the 16 years of its existence (1915–31), Denishawn would be the most important, most original, and most interesting dance company in America. Above all, it would school some 75 dancers, including such future luminaries as *****Doris Humphrey**, Charles Weidman and the incomparable *****Martha Graham**.

By her own admission, St. Denis was not a very good teacher and never hid the fact that the teaching system at Denishawn was developed largely by Shawn. Since much of what she did was improvised and then simply repeated, there wasn't much technique involved in her dance and thus not that much that she could really teach. Two years or so with her company made one sufficiently a disciple to be able to teach the newcomers, so much so that Doris Humphrey, already a dance instructor before joining Denishawn, was immediately set to teaching, and Martha Graham was given her first classes after only two years with the company. Graham had first seen St. Denis dance in Los Angeles in 1911, an experience that changed her life. She joined the company in 1916, remaining until 1923, when she went on to forge a career that made her arguably the greatest American dancer and choreographer of the 20th century. The tribute to what Martha Graham learned at Denishawn is enshrined in the first five chapters of *Agnes de Mille's biography of her, chapters that are virtually a biography of Ruth St. Denis and Ted Shawn and a capsule history and appreciation of their company. As the fame of Denishawn grew, many stars of stage and screen would come to study there, among them *Ina Claire, *Colleen Moore, Lenore Ulric, *Mabel Normand, *Ruth Chatterton and *Myrna Loy. When the *National Geographic Magazine* printed its first color photograph, it was of Ruth St. Denis and Ted Shawn dancing.

In 1917, during World War I, Shawn entered the army, and St. Denis reorganized the company so as to continue touring in vaudeville without him. It was at this time that the company was joined by Doris Humphrey, who had been teaching at her own school in Oak Park, a suburb of Chicago, but yearned to give up teaching in order to actually dance. After Shawn returned from the war, Denishawn toured for a second year in vaudeville, after which St. Denis again reorganized the company for concert appearances. The new company launched its career with a tour of the Western states, performing several new dances—*Soaring, Valse Caprice*—choreographed both by St. Denis and her dancers and set to music ranging from Bach through Chopin.

At the end of this tour, the Shawns purchased a home in Eagle Rock, a suburb of Los Angeles, where they also rented a suitable building to house their company. Three tours in vaudeville followed under the aegis of Daniel Mayer; they also toured England in 1922. These concert tours lasted for four years and were both theatrical and highly eclectic, including square dances, American Indian dances, and Spanish dances, as well as the usual oriental or pseudo-oriental numbers that the company's audiences had learned to expect. An excellent singer, St. Denis did not hesitate to introduce vocals and even dialogue into her compositions. She created what she called "Rhythmic Choirs" to execute religious dances, which she hoped would later be performed in churches and other houses of worship. The programs were strenuous and the touring exhausting, but St. Denis, with her endless energy, good humor, and enthusiasm, kept the company alert and on its toes.

Denishawn was a large company as dance ensembles go. Besides St. Denis, Ted Shawn, and Louis Horst as musical director, it included some 15 dancers in the company at any one time, and it offered a full season of engagements. Dancers were allowed not only to teach but to choreograph dances for the company which were then performed. Nothing like that was to exist in dance companies in later years. Denishawn provided its dancers with food, shelter, and business management, so that they could devote themselves almost totally to their art, an advantage that no longer existed anywhere in the United States after Denishawn closed.

St. Denis had her dancers attempt virtually every type of dance known, from American Indian to East Indian, from Japanese to Javanese, from Spanish to Russian to Greek. She believed that all dance was the property of all dancers and refused to allow herself to be limited by national considerations. For this reason, she saw no need to develop what might be considered an "American dance." Whether with pseudo-Hindu (*Radha*, 1906), pseudo-Egyptian (*Egypta*, 1910), pseudo-Japanese (*O-mika*, 1913), pseudo-Arab (*Ouled Nail*, 1914) or pseudo-Aztec (*Xochitl*, 1921), St. Denis cloaked the essential inauthenticity of her dances in artistic and religious vision. Shawn was no more interested in authenticity than she; if anything, he was less interested. Staging "good theater" and producing "what worked" was his forte. Inordinately proud of his physique, he flaunted himself in ever skimpier costumes, fought for more solo time, and was adept at staging dances designed to show himself to best advantage. In the end, there were many both inside the company and out who felt that Shawn was St. Denis' evil genius in this regard and that he had abased her art.

In 1925, Denishawn set off on the now-famous tour of the Orient, departing from Seattle for Japan, China, Singapore, Malaya, Rangoon,

India (where the company spent five months), Ceylon, Java, and Cambodia. Everywhere, the couple cooked up publicity stunts to attract audiences, and St. Denis visited temples, palaces and bazaars, gathering inspiration for costumes and bits and pieces of oriental dances for future reference. The tour concluded with a return trip to Japan and then the voyage to San Francisco in December 1926. Denishawn then went on a four-month cross-country tour to New York under the management of Arthur Judson.

In the winter of 1927, the Shawns began a tour with the Ziegfeld Follies, the annual musical extravaganza designed to imitate the Folies Bergère in Paris. With the money thus earned, they were able to purchase a property near Van Cortlandt Park in the Bronx as the home of what was to be called "Greater Denishawn." Strict rules applied there, among them a limit on the number of Jewish students to 10% of the total and a strict supervision of morals. It was these restrictions along with artistic disagreements that led Doris Humphrey to leave the company. Despite their differences, however, Humphrey always spoke well of St. Denis.

By the late 1920s, it became clear to St. Denis (as it had long been to those around her) that Shawn's influence was damaging her artistic career. She had compromised, sold out. In 1928, their marriage, though never legally terminated, came to an end in what was tactfully referred to as an "artistic separation." Much that is negative has been written about Shawn, his ruthlessness, his ambition, the way he used St. Denis to build a career that otherwise would not likely have gotten off the ground. Though he was a homosexual, it is probable that he was genuinely stifling this side of his nature at the time he married St. Denis. On the other hand, there seems little doubt that St. Denis, by her own account a virgin at 37 when she met him, feared physical sexuality, so much so that their marriage may well have been a practical union for both partners. As her marriage turned sour, St. Denis began taking up with young men among her students. In a letter written nearly 30 years before she died and only published after her death, she called herself a "stupid, blind, egotist . . . attracting defenseless boys who need a friend and mother and instead find an impossible lover," and spoke ruefully of the harm that she had done to her husband, blaming him for nothing. In any case, there is no question that Shawn had a major influence on the direction of St. Denis' career and, through Denishawn which was his idea, on the development of modern dance.

Denishawn did not long survive the separation of its founders. Ted Shawn made his first trip to Europe in the spring of 1930, dancing alone in Germany and Switzerland before returning to join St. Denis and the company for its fourth annual appearance at Lewisohn Stadium that summer. The following season, 1930–31, he returned to Europe and then came back to New York for the Lewisohn engagement where, for the last time, he danced with St. Denis. That fall, he toured as "Ted Shawn and His Dancers." Thus, in 1931, the Denishawn Company was dissolved, its dancers going their separate ways. Louis Horst, who was its pianist from 1915 to 1925, went on to become the musical director for Martha Graham as well as a teacher and the founding editor and critic of *Dance Observer*.

After the closing of Denishawn, "the dark years" closed in on St. Denis. No longer young, without funds, her school and company gone and the Great Depression in full swing, she not only found it difficult to secure bookings but suffered the artistic indignity of seeing her life's work suddenly pass out of style, replaced by the harsher dance forms of the 1930s, many of them choreographed and performed by her former pupils. She reformed her rhythmic choir, designing programs for its performances; she developed masques and pageants for church groups. Occasionally, she appeared in what was left of vaudeville and did a little teaching. In 1932, she published a book of poetry and in 1939 completed an autobiography, *An Unfinished Life*.

As St. Denis grew older, her religious impulses grew more pronounced. In her spiritual life, she was eclectic. A Christian Scientist and a believer in reincarnation, she passed through several religious phases and dabbled in Hinduism and Theosophy. "There was a god in her," said Charles Weidman. Wrote de Mille: "If her dances were a sham, they nevertheless evoked great emotions in her audience, and she projected an aura of mysticism and importance." In her later years, St. Denis dreamed of establishing a temple-school for the development of sacred dance, "a place," she said, "which had the motivations of a church with the instrumentation of the stage." Although she was able to attract a number of ministers and priests to her idea, and she did create great religious ballets such as *The White Madonna*, *The Blue Madonna of St. Marks*, and the *Gregorian Chants*, performing them in many major churches, she was never to found a church-theater of her own. Instead, for several years she passed from the realm of the theater into that of academia. In

1938, she was invited to establish the dance department at Adelphi College in Long Island, New York.

The revival of St. Denis' theatrical career began in 1937, when, at nearly 60, she appeared as part of a great two-month-long dance festival at Radio City Music Hall in New York entitled *Dance International*. There she had a triumph performing the "oriental" dances that had made her famous, and there she met the famed ethnic dancer *La Meri, who had invented the very term "ethnic dance." Quickly becoming friends, the two women founded the School of Natya in New York City in 1940. Their partnership was crowned with success, both teaching students and occasionally performing together.

On July 11, 1941, St. Denis was invited to perform her original Hudson Theater program of 1906 at the Jacob's Pillow Dance Festival founded by Ted Shawn, a historic event at which she not only had an artistic triumph but achieved the status of a certified legend. Her *Radha* was filmed on this occasion. St. Denis' career then resumed almost at full throttle with appearances at Carnegie Hall, Adelphi College, Jacob's Pillow and on tour. For several years, she

Ruth
St.
Denis

made her home in an apartment on East 59th St. in New York that had once housed Isadora Duncan, and she often danced at the Duncan Studio on the same street. In 1942, the School of Natya was merged with the Ethnologic Dance Center. When the United States entered the Second World War, St. Denis briefly worked as a riveter in a California war plant and thereafter made Hollywood her home for the rest of her life.

Although St. Denis was concertizing in New York City as late as 1952 (when she was 75), she spent her last years teaching at colleges, traveling about the country giving lectures, and showing films of herself and of her beloved Denishawn. Although no motion pictures are known to exist of Isadora Duncan, Ruth St. Denis was too keen a showwoman to allow her art to go unrecorded. She and Shawn had made their motion picture debut in 1916 (doing a "Babylonian dance" in D.W. Griffith's famed spectacle *Intolerance*) and were filmed several times dancing alone, together, and with the whole of Denishawn. As she grew older, she also tried her hand at acting, most notably giving a creditable performance in *The Madwoman of Chaillot*.

A disorganized person, St. Denis relied on those around her to keep her life in order, and she was never free from assorted lackeys whose services were usually rendered in the hope of getting something more in return. Vibrant, vivacious, witty, irreverent and wonderful company, she never lacked for real friends, however, and she was anything but lonely in her last years. Her home-cum-studio on Cahuenga Boulevard was both school and theater to her and also the seat of the Ruth St. Denis Foundation, which was the business end of her plans for her temple-theater. In time, she had what amounted to a complete reconciliation with Ted Shawn and frequently appeared at Jacob's Pillow until she was deep into her 80s.

While busy with plans at age 91, among them a dancing choir of women past 50 and a television series based on the psalms, Ruth St. Denis died on July 28, 1968, after a short illness. Ted Shawn died in 1972. By all accounts, St. Denis' early dances were colorless and her music banal, but everything she did was imbued with her own presence and character that made whatever she did on stage seem more than it was. Deeply religious, she considered her new dance to be a religious exercise, and, throughout her life, she was able to convey this to her audiences. To see Ruth St. Denis was an experience meant to be more than an entertainment. Her audiences knew this, and she never let them down.

SOURCES:

Cohen, Selma Jean, ed. and comp. *Doris Humphrey: An Artist First*. Middletown, CT: Wesleyan University, 1972.

de Mille, Agnes. *The Life and Work of Martha Graham*. NY: Random House, 1956, 1991.

St. Denis, Ruth. *An Unfinished Life: An Autobiography*. London: George G. Harrap, 1939.

Terry, Walter. *Miss Ruth: The "More Living" Life of Ruth St. Denis*. NY: Dodd, Mead, 1969.

SUGGESTED READING:

Shawn, Ted. *Ruth St. Denis: Pioneer and Prophet*. 2 vols. New York, 1920.

Terry, Walker. *Ted Shawn: Father of American Dance*. NY: Dial, 1976.

COLLECTIONS:

The journals of Ruth St. Denis are on deposit at the library of the University of California, Los Angeles; the Denishawn archives are in the Dance Collection of the Library and Museum of the Performing Arts at Lincoln Center in New York.

Robert H. Hewsen,
Professor of History, Rowan University,
Glassboro, New Jersey

St. George, Katharine (1894–1983)

U.S. congressional representative. Born Katharine Delano Price Collier in Bridgnorth, England, on July 12, 1894; died in Tuxedo Park, New York, on May 2, 1983; second daughter and third of four children of Price Collier (an Iowa-born writer, Unitarian minister and European editor of Forum *magazine) and Katharine Delano (sister of* *Sara Delano Roosevelt, *the mother of Franklin Delano Roosevelt); cousin of President Franklin D. Roosevelt; educated at private schools in England, France, Switzerland, and Germany; married George St. George, in April 1917; children:* **Priscilla St. George.**

Served as U.S. representative from New York (January 3, 1947–January 3, 1965); became executive vice-president and treasurer of the St. George Coal Company (1947); was first woman to become chair of a Republican campaign committee in New York State; her proposed Equal Rights Amendment for women (1959) became law in the form of the Equal Pay Act (1963).

Katharine St. George was born Katharine Delano Price Collier in 1894 in Bridgnorth, England, of American parents. Her distinguished family lineage included Philippe de la Noye, a Huguenot who had journeyed to Plymouth Colony in 1621, and Isaac Allerton, who had served as the pilgrims' business agent. She was also the first cousin of future president Franklin Delano Roosevelt on her mother's side, and pursued a political career at the same time that her more famous relative made his run for office.

When Katharine was two, her father relinquished his job as European editor of *Forum* magazine and returned with the family to the United States. The Colliers settled in Tuxedo Park, New York, famous as the first haven created specifically for millionaires and as the place where the men's dinner jacket came into vogue. Like other fashionable society girls, Katharine received her education in private schools in England, France, Switzerland, and Germany, starting at age 11, then made Tuxedo Park her permanent home base after her father's death in 1913. She married George St. George, a clerk for J.P. Morgan and Company, in April 1917, and became involved in such local civic affairs as the Red Cross and the board of education. Two years after their marriage, George took ownership of a coal brokerage, eventually becoming chair of the board with Katharine acting as executive vice-president and treasurer. She also became an avid dog breeder, raising prize English setters and pointers and becoming the president of the English Setter Club of America.

St. George was also active in the Republican Party, eventually ascending to the presidency of the Tuxedo Park Republican Club as well as the governorship of the Woman's National Republican Club. Despite her high profile in local politics, she took a six-year hiatus after her cousin Franklin's successful Democratic bid for the presidency in 1932. When rumors circulated that Roosevelt would seek a third term in 1940, St. George reentered the political arena with renewed vigor as treasurer of the Orange County Republican Committee. No longer content just to support the candidacies of others, she hoped to win the Republican nomination for a campaign for the State Assembly in the early 1940s. When her bid was rejected, however, she continued to work for other candidates as chair of the county campaign committee, the first woman in New York State to hold such a post. She aligned herself with Governor Thomas E. Dewey in his unsuccessful attempt to unseat her cousin Franklin.

St. George finally had her chance to step into the political spotlight when she campaigned for the U.S. House of Representatives on the Republican ticket. Her campaign platform promised support for veterans—to whom she pledged homes and jobs—farmers, and labor unions. Elected in 1946, St. George listed among her priorities the relaxation of government control over private enterprise and the strengthening of American foreign policy. She had hoped to further these aims through participating on the House Committee on Foreign Affairs, but she was instead appointed to the Committee on Post Office and Civil Service, the Committee on Government Operations, the Committee on Armed Services, and the Rules Committee.

Despite her small physique (5'2" and 110 lbs.), St. George made her political presence felt from the first of her nine terms in Congress. One writer noted, "Mrs. St. George has been active and vocal on occasion, during her first session in Congress, conducting herself with the confidence of long experience in political life." She supported the constituents of her milk- and poultry-producing district by proposing bills which would allow for the use of surplus butter in rations provided to the military, and fought reductions in dairy price supports. She also worked to stabilize the broiler and egg industry through her proposed establishment of market regulations. Women also benefited from St. George's efforts; she presented legislation to include the Women's Army Auxiliary Corps under the provisions of the Veteran's Administration law during her first term and attempted to present before the House a proposed Equal Rights

Katharine St. George

Amendment for women in 1950. Although the Judiciary Committee denied the latter request, she eventually achieved her goal when the Equal Pay Act, guaranteeing equal pay for men and women, became law in 1963.

St. George's committee work extended her influence in several directions. She advocated the delegation of the power to increase postal rates to the Postmaster General in 1953, and throughout the decade pressed for the establishment of a federal safety division in the Labor Department. An ardent capitalist, St. George argued against granting Veteran's Administration gratuities to any member of an organization that advocated the overthrow of the U.S. government. She responded to the Supreme Court's 1963 prohibition of official school prayer by introducing a joint resolution to allow for the overriding of the Court's decisions by a two-thirds majority vote of both Congress and the Senate. She firmly believed that government employees should adhere to a common code of ethics and voted against a measure passed in 1964 that increased the salaries of federal career employees.

St. George's run for a tenth term in 1964 resulted in her defeat by John G. Dow. She returned to civic activities in Tuxedo Park, chairing the Tuxedo Park Republican town committee until 1979. She died on May 2, 1983, and was buried in St. Mary's-in-Tuxedo Church Cemetery.

SOURCES:

Office of the Historian. *Women In Congress, 1917–1990.* Commission on the Bicentenary of the U.S. House of Representatives, 1991.

Rothe, Anna, ed. *Current Biography 1947.* NY: H.W. Wilson, 1947.

B. Kimberly Taylor,
freelance writer, New York, New York

St. James, Lyn (1947—)

American race-car driver. Name variations: Evelyn Cornwall. Born Evelyn Cornwall on March 13, 1947, in Willoughby, Ohio; daughter of Alfred Cornwall and Maxine (Rawson) Cornwall; educated near Cleveland at the Andrews School for Girls; earned a piano-teaching certificate from the St. Louis Institute of Music, 1967; married John Carusso, in 1970 (divorced 1979); married Roger Lessman, in February 1993; children: (stepchild) Lindsay.

First woman to average more than 200 miles per hour on an oval track, at Alabama's Talladega Superspeedway, and first woman to win a solo North American professional road race, at Watkins Glen, New York (both 1985); won the SCCA (Sports Car Club of America) Florida Regional championship (1976 and

1977); won, along with male teammates, the GTO class of the Daytona 24 Hours marathon (1987 and 1990); finished in 11th place in the Indianapolis 500, becoming the second woman to participate in that race, and won Rookie of the Year honors (1992).

Lyn St. James changed her name from Evelyn Cornwall when she decided to race professionally, inspired by the television actress **Susan St. James**. She was born in Willoughby, Ohio, in 1947, the only child of a sheet-metal worker, and attended an all-girls school near Cleveland, where she was committed to learning to play the piano. Her mother felt the piano would give her something to fall back on throughout her life, and would exert a refining influence. St. James' love of cars was derived in part from her mother, who was dependent on them because of an impairment. She viewed cars as a means to attaining mobility and power. While in high school in the 1960s, St. James attended a drag race one night with friends. A male friend challenged her to try racing; she did, and she won. The thrill of the experience stayed with her for years. After earning a piano-teaching certificate from the St. Louis Institute of Music, she took a job as a secretary and taught piano lessons on the side. In 1970, she married fellow race-car enthusiast John Carusso, and the two began competing in local Sports Car Club of America (SCCA) races.

In 1976 and 1977, St. James won the SCCA Florida Regional championship, and in 1978 she advanced to the SCCA runoffs in Atlanta, Georgia, amateur racing's national championship. Her engine blew up, but the experience steeled her resolve to get sponsors, spare cars, and top-notch equipment; she was intent on becoming a professional race-car driver. Shortly thereafter, she changed her name and, in her first season as a professional, won the Top Woman Driver award in the International Motor Sports Association Kelly American Challenge Series. The Ford Motor Company agreed to sponsor St. James in 1981, and she became part of the company's motorsports program, selling Ford products on tours across America and racing under the Ford name.

St. James' fame as a driver increased markedly when she won a professional road race at Watkins Glen in New York in 1985. The victory marked the first time a woman had won a solo professional road race in North America. That same year brought another first as she became the first woman to average more than 200 miles per hour on an oval track, a milestone marked at Alabama's Talladega Superspeedway. She set a second speed record at that track in

1988, and won—along with male teammates—the GTO class of the Daytona 24 Hours marathon in 1987 and 1990.

In 1988, St. James started driving Indy cars, following in the footsteps of driver *Janet Guthrie, who in 1976 was the first woman to qualify for the prestigious Indianapolis 500 race. But unlike Guthrie, St. James was the first woman to compete full-time on the Indy professional circuit. Though she lost Ford as a corporate sponsor in 1991, she found other companies willing to back her, such as J.C. Penney, Agency Rent-A-Car, Goodyear, and Danskin, in 1992. That year, she became the second woman to qualify for the Indianapolis 500, finishing her Indy debut in 11th place. The impressive finish was enough to garner Rookie of the Year honors for the 45-year-old. She qualified again in 1993, but finished 25th in a field of 33 because of engine trouble. She continued to qualify for races throughout the 1990s.

St. James published *Lyn St. James' Car Owner's Manual* in 1984 and also wrote a weekly column for the *Detroit Free Press-Detroit News*, in which she addressed readers' questions about their vehicles. In addition, she served as director of consumer relations for the Car Care Council, a trade group that addressed safety and maintenance concerns on behalf of car and truck owners. She was also active in the Woman's Sports Foundation for many years and served as its president from 1990 to 1993. The year her presidency ended, she started the Lyn St. James Foundation, to help others develop into professional race-car drivers, particularly young women who hoped to break into the male-dominated sport. She also advanced the development of young women in the area of self-esteem through her creation of the Indianapolis Make a Difference campaign in 1994; St. James, who claimed to be drawn to the sport of racing in part because the helmet made her anonymous, hoped to deflect such self-esteem problems in other girls through the campaign's sports and leadership programs.

SOURCES:

Contemporary Newsmakers. Issue 2. Detroit, MI: Gale Research, 1993.

Johnson, Anne Janette. *Great Women in Sports*. Detroit, MI: Visible Ink, 1998.

Oglesby, Carole A., ed. *Encyclopedia of Women and Sport in America*. Oryx, 1998.

B. Kimberly Taylor,
freelance writer, New York, New York

St. Johns, Adela Rogers (1894–1988)

American journalist, author, and educator. Born Adela Nora Rogers in Los Angeles, California, on May 20, 1894; died on August 10, 1988, in Arroyo Grande, California; daughter of Earl Rogers (a prominent trial lawyer) and Harriet (Greene) Rogers; attended Hollywood High School, from which she received an honorary diploma in 1951; married William Ivan St. Johns (a journalist), on December 24, 1914 (divorced 1929); married Richard Hyland (divorced); married Francis Patrick O'Toole (divorced); children: (first marriage) William Ivan St. Johns II; **Elaine St. Johns***; McCullah St. Johns; Richard Rogers St. Johns.*

Worked as a reporter for the San Francisco Examiner *(1913),* Los Angeles Herald *(1914–18),* International News Service *(1925–49),* Chicago American *(1928), and* New York American *(1929); wrote 15 books and 13 screenplays; considered the first woman sportswriter in the U.S.; was the first woman faculty member of the graduate school of journalism at the University of California at Los Angeles (1950–52).*

Adela Rogers St. Johns, born Adela Rogers in Los Angeles, California, in 1894, was the daughter of Earl Rogers and **Harriet Greene Rogers**. An avid reader and writer from childhood on, she published her first story in the *Los Angeles Times* in 1903, at age nine. Her formal schooling ended with her departure from Hollywood High School without a diploma after failing a math course, although the school granted her an honorary diploma in 1951. Her father was a prominent trial lawyer who once defended Clarence Darrow on a jury-tampering charge, and St. Johns spent most of her youth in his law office due to the stormy relationship between her parents. When she was 18, her father introduced her to William Randolph Hearst, who hired her for seven dollars a week to write for the *San Francisco Examiner*. St. Johns continued to work as a reporter for various newspapers between 1913 and 1928, and held the unofficial title of veteran "sob sister" of American journalism. She went on to work for Hearst newspapers for 40 years.

In 1914, at age 20, St. Johns began working at the *Los Angeles Herald* and married *Herald* colleague William I. St. Johns. In 1931, she earned the sobriquet of the world's greatest "girl" reporter with her controversial 16-part exposé on the treatment of the city's indigent for the *Herald*. She covered all beats, encompassing crime, local politics, sports, and society stories, but was noted for her inside scoops on the Hollywood film community. As well, St. Johns wrote profiles for *Photoplay* magazine of many leading film stars, including *Clara Bow, Clark Gable, *Greta Garbo, Rudolph Valentino, and Tom Mix.

During the early 1920s, St. Johns left newspaper reporting to raise her children and turned to writing screenplays and fiction, as well as features for such leading magazines as *Saturday Evening Post, Good Housekeeping, McCall's, Ladies' Home Journal, Cosmopolitan, Redbook, Reader's Digest, Harper's Bazaar.* Her first published short story "The Tramp" was based on her experiences in Hollywood. Many of her stories were published in book form; although critics gave them mixed reviews, they were popular with readers. St. Johns returned to full-time newspaper work in 1925 and filed a wide variety of stories, all of which were marked by her distinctively frank, emotional style. During the Depression, she posed as an unemployed woman to expose how callously the poor were treated by both employment agencies and charitable organizations. In 1935, she covered the trial of Bruno Richard Hauptmann, the accused kidnapper and murderer of Charles and *Anne Morrow Lindbergh's infant son, and moved to Washington to report on national politics in the mid-1930s. At the 1940 Democratic National Convention, she revealed how special effects were used to create the illusion of a spontaneous floor demonstration in support of Franklin D. Roosevelt's renomination, specifically for the benefit of radio listeners. Her coverage of the assassination of Senator Huey Long (1935), the abdication of Edward VIII (1936) and subsequent marriage to Wallis Simpson (*Wallis Warfield, duchess of Windsor), and other major news stories made her one of the best-known reporters of her era. As a sports reporter, she worked with such illustrious colleagues as Ring Lardner, Damon Runyon, and Grantland Rice, while following most of the major sporting events in the United States. She covered the controversial Jack Dempsey-Gene Tunney "long count" fight in 1927, as well as the Kentucky Derby, World Series, Rose Bowl, Olympics, and U.S. Open at Forest Hills. Adela and William St. Johns were divorced in 1929; she married twice more—to Richard Hyland and Francis Patrick O'Toole—but both marriages ended in divorce.

St. Johns conducted the daily radio program "Woman's Viewpoint of the News" for some time, and retired from newspaper work in 1948 in devote her time exclusively to books. She published a biography of her father, *Final Verdict* (1962), and recounted facets of her life and thoughts in *The Honeycomb* (1969) and *Some Are Born Great* (1974). Many of her novels embraced religious themes, the most notable being the 1966 bestseller *Tell No Man.* Numerous films were based on her early novels and short stories, chief among them *Pretty Ladies* (1925), *The Single Standard* (1929), *Scandal* (1929),

Free Soul (1931), *A Woman's Man* (1934), *I Want A Divorce* (1940), and *Government Girl* (1943). St. Johns enjoyed working in Hollywood, though she perceived her screenplays merely as a way to pay bills.

In 1950, she became the first woman faculty member of the graduate school of journalism at the University of California at Los Angeles (UCLA). In 1970, she was awarded a Medal of Freedom by President Richard M. Nixon and emerged from retirement to cover *Patricia Hearst's kidnapping in 1976 for the *San Francisco Examiner.* Adela Rogers St. Johns died in 1988, at age 94.

SOURCES:

Contemporary Authors. Vols. 108 and 126. Detroit, MI: Gale Research.
McHenry, Robert, ed. *Famous American Women.* NY: Dover, 1980.

B. Kimberly Taylor,
freelance writer, New York, New York

St. Léon, Fanny (1817–1909).

See Cerrito, Fanny.

Sainte-Marie, Buffy (1941—)

Cree folk singer, songwriter, and activist, internationally known for her protest songs in the 1960s, who founded organizations to benefit Native Americans.
Name variations: Beverly Sainte-Marie. Born on February 20, 1941, on the Cree Piapot reservation in Craven, Saskatchewan, Canada; adopted daughter of Albert C. Sainte-Marie and Winifred Kendrick Sainte-Marie; graduated from the University of Massachusetts, 1963; married Dewain Kamaikalani Bugbee, in 1967; children: (with actor Sheldon Wolfchild) son Dakota Starblanket Wolfchild (b. 1977).

Selected discography: It's My Way *(March 1964);* Many a Mile *(February 1965);* Little Wheel, Spin and Spin *(April 1966);* Fire and Fleet and Candlelight *(June 1967);* I'm Gonna Be a Country Girl Again *(April 1968);* She Used to Want to Be a Ballerina *(1971);* Moonshot *(1973);* Buffy *(1974);* Sweet America *(1975);* Changing Woman *(1975);* Coincidence and Likely Stories *(1993);* Up Where We Belong *(February 1996).*

Singer and songwriter Buffy Sainte-Marie was born in 1941 on the Cree Piapot reservation in Saskatchewan, Canada. Orphaned in the first months of her life, she was adopted by a Massachusetts couple, Albert C. Sainte-Marie and **Winifred Kendrick Sainte-Marie**, who was part Micmac Indian. Although the family lived in an all-white community, Winifred often spoke to

her daughter, nicknamed "Buffy," about her Indian history.

At age four, Sainte-Marie was creating poems and teaching herself to play the piano. She began to craft her own distinctively poetic songs, after her father presented her with a guitar for her 16th birthday. While an honors student at the University of Massachusetts, she sang in local coffee shops, attracting a following. In 1963, she graduated with a philosophy degree as one of the school's top ten seniors. Not long after, Sainte-Marie moved to New York City where she found a welcoming home in Greenwich Village's folk movement and performed in nightclubs, including the Bitter End, the Gaslight Cafe, and Gerde's Folk City.

Vanguard Records released Sainte-Marie's first album, *It's My Way*, in 1964. Along with antiwar folk singer **Joan Baez**, Sainte-Marie rose to international prominence in the 1960s as a folk singer and songwriter, and she produced a number of gold records. Her unique singing style incorporated the Creek mouthbow and traditional Native "vocables" (characteristic syllables without meaning used in repetition). Her recordings reflected a range of musical styles, including contemporary folk songs, old American folk standards, popular love songs, antiwar ballads, and songs celebrating her Indian heritage. Sainte-Marie also recorded songs protesting the injustices inflicted on Native Americans, such as "My Country 'Tis of Thy People You're Dying" (from the 1966 album *Little Wheel, Spin and Spin*), one of the most searing protest songs of the time. During the height of the turbulent antiwar era, some of Sainte-Marie's releases were banned from radio and television, and her outspoken views on both the Vietnam War and the treatment of Native Americans resulted in an FBI record, most of which "was blacked out with magic marker," she later noted. "I don't know what they ever suspected me of."

Sainte-Marie's antiwar "Universal Soldier" is considered a classic, and her "Now That the Buffalo's Gone" is often listed as the first Indian protest song. Elvis Presley covered her song "Until It's Time for You to Go" from her *Many a Mile* album (1965). Sainte-Marie also appeared on numerous television shows throughout the 1960s and early 1970s, including "The Tonight Show" with Johnny Carson. When she accepted a television contract for an episode of "The Virginian," she insisted that only Native Americans be cast as Indians and assisted with the script, thus contributing to an episode which received high praise for its authenticity. In the 1960s, Sainte-Marie settled in Kauai, Hawaii, where she remained throughout the 1990s.

Co-written with Jack Nitzche, her song "Up Where We Belong" earned an Academy Award as the theme song for the movie *An Officer and a Gentleman*. With proceeds from Joe Cocker and **Jennifer Warnes**' cover of this song, Sainte-Marie supported her work as an activist. In addition to founding the Native North American Women's Association, which sponsored theater, arts and education projects, she created the Nihewan Foundation, a law-school scholarship fund for Native Americans funded by proceeds from her concerts. By 1975, more than 20 Native Americans had completed law school thanks to her foundation.

Sainte-Marie had a son, Dakota Starblanket Wolfchild, in 1977 with actor Sheldon Wolfchild. She joined the cast of "Sesame Street" from 1976 to 1981, and Dakota appeared on the show as well, with mother and son featured in educational episodes about contemporary Native American family life. She performed mainly overseas after 1981, continuing to draw enormous crowds, and became well known as a visual artist working with digital technology. Recorded by more than 100 artists in seven languages, her songs have been performed by music greats including ***Janis Joplin**, **Barbra Streisand**, and **Tracy Chapman**.

SOURCES:

Bataille, Gretchen M. *Native American Women*. NY: Garland, 1993.

"Buffy Sainte-Marie," in *People Weekly*. June 17, 1996.

Malinowski, Sharon, ed. *Notable Native Americans*. Detroit, MI: Gale Research, 1995.

Roxon, Lillian. *Lillian Roxon's Rock Encyclopedia*. NY: Grosset & Dunlap, 1969.

B. Kimberly Taylor,
freelance writer, New York, New York

Saint Mars, Gabrielle de

(1804–1872)

French novelist. Name variations: Gabrielle de Saint-Mars; Vicomtesse de Saint-Mars; Marquise de Poilow or du Poilloüe; (pseudonyms) Marie Michon, Jacques Reynaud, and Countess Dash or Comtesse Dash. Born Gabrielle-Anne Cisterne de Courtiras on August 2, 1804, in Poitiers, France; died on September 11, 1872, in Paris; married E.-J. du Poilloüe de Saint Mars, in 1824 (separated 1834); children: one son.

Gabrielle de Saint Mars was a popular fiction writer for nearly 40 years. Although she claimed an aristocratic heritage, she was born into a middle-class family in 1804 in Poitiers, France; little is known about her upbringing. At age 20, she married E.-J. du Poilloüe de Saint Mars, a cavalry officer and viscount, and moved to Paris. Her husband's noble title allowed Saint Mars to enter the intellectual life of Parisian high society and become fairly well educated. Her marriage failed, however, and she separated from her husband around 1835.

Saint Mars began to write professionally to support herself and her son, finding benefactors among her friends in the Parisian elite. With the aid of her friend and patron, the novelist

Alexander Dumas *père*, Saint Mars became a journalist for the *Revue de Paris* in the late 1830s before she turned to writing novels. She published under several pen names, which was not unusual among women writers of the time; her first and favorite pseudonym, Countess Dash, was chosen because it suited her aristocratic pretensions. In 1839, she published her first novel, *Le jeu de la reine* (*The Queen's Game*). It met with moderate success, and encouraged her to publish new works, mostly formulaic historical romance novels concerning real and fictional nobles, set in pre-Revolutionary France; new works would appear regularly for the next three decades. Her books, appealing to the nostalgia and romanticism of the 19th-century French elite, became quite popular and sold well for many years.

Saint Mars is believed to have ghost-written several of Dumas' shorter fictional works, and is known to have written for his *Mousquetaire* (The Musketeer) in the 1850s, under the name Marie Michon. Theirs was a close personal and literary relationship. Saint Mars had a keen eye for detail and for the idiosyncrasies of her contemporaries, skills she revealed in the literary "portraits" she contributed to *Le Figaro*. In the late 1860s, she composed a six-volume set of memoirs, *Memoires des Autres* (*Memories of Others*), a gossipy and nostalgic look at her life and friendships. Saint Mars died in Paris at age 68 in 1872. Her memoirs were published in 1896.

SOURCES:
Buck, Claire, ed. *The Bloomsbury Guide to Women's Literature.* NY: Prentice Hall, 1992.
Wilson, Katharina, ed. *An Encyclopedia of Continental Women Writers.* NY: Garland, 1991.

Laura York, M.A. in History,
University of California, Riverside, California

St. Martin-Permon, Laurette de (1784–1838).

See Abrantès, Laure d'.

St. Michel, Elizabeth de (1640–1669).

See Pepys, Elizabeth.

Sakajawea or Sakakawea (c. 1787–c. 1812 or 1884).

See Sacajawea.

Sakharov, Elena (b. 1923).

See Bonner, Elena.

Salaberga of Laon (d. around 665)

Sainted abbess of Laon. Born in France; died around 665; married Blandinus Boson, a Frankish noble; chil-dren: at least six, including Anstrude of Laon, an abbess. Her feast day is September 22.

Little is known about the early life of Salaberga of Laon. Born in France in the mid-7th century, she came from the Frankish nobility, and seems to have always felt drawn to a religious life. But Salaberga was unable to fulfill this calling, due to pressure from her parents to lead a more conventional life. Thus she married Blandinus Boson in her teens and gave birth to at least six children, including a daughter, *Anstrude of Laon. After her children had grown and she had been widowed, Salaberga, who did not wish to marry again, was able to live as she had wanted to.

She became an active religious woman, using her own resources to found no less than seven churches. Taking the vows of a nun, she gained a widespread reputation for her piety, generosity, and energetic personality. Salaberga took her responsibilities seriously, and did not want to relinquish control over her churches or convents to any male church officials. She became one of the numerous holy women of the 7th century who had more authority than women were supposed to, taking on the duties of a priest, and managing the spiritual and material lives of more than 300 nuns. Salaberga of Laon was highly respected and after her death her followers pushed successfully for her sainthood. Her daughter Anstrude succeeded her as abbess.

Laura York,
Riverside, California

Salavarrieta, Pola (1795–1817)

Colombian rebel in the fight for independence. Name variations: La Pola; Policarpa Salavarrieta. Born Policarpa Salavarrieta in Guaduas, Colombia, on February 22, 1795; executed in Bogotá, Colombia, on November 14, 1817; daughter of José Joaquin Salavarrieta and Maríana (Rios) Salavarrieta.

Born in 1795 in Guaduas, Colombia, into a respectable Creole family, Pola Salavarrieta and her brothers became revolutionaries during the independence movement; she played a key role in the patriot underground, first in Guaduas and then in Bogotá. Colombia was a viceroyalty of Spain when Salavarrieta trained as a seamstress and used her skills to gain positions in the homes of Spanish royalist women in Bogotá. She passed on the political information which she overheard in these homes to rebels who were trying to overthrow the Spanish.

Colombian two-peso banknote honoring Pola Salavarrieta.

After authorities uncovered her covert activities, she was captured and imprisoned by the Royalists. Accused of espionage and subversion against the Spanish crown and condemned to death, she and seven or eight accomplices were either shot or hanged as republican agents in Bogotá's main plaza on November 14, 1817. As she courageously walked to her death, Salavarrieta (or "La Pola," as she came to be called) shouted a tirade against Spanish oppression and urged her people to avenge her death. Her execution in the public square inspired popular sympathy, and her story became that of a legendary resistance hero. She was one of approximately 50 female agents who were executed before Colombia achieved independence in 1819. Salavarrieta was the first Latin American woman commemorated on a postage stamp, her image appearing on a 1910 independence-centennial issue. She also appears on a 1977 two-peso Colombian banknote.

SOURCES:

Davis, Robert H. *Historical Dictionary of Colombia.* Metuchen, NJ: Scarecrow, 1993.

Mahoney, M.H. *Women in Espionage.* Santa Barbara, CA: ABC-CLIO, 1993.

Tenenbaum, Barbara A., ed. *Encyclopedia of Latin American History and Culture.* Vol. 5. NY: Scribner, 1996.

SUGGESTED READING:

Henderson, James D., and Linda Roddy Henderson. *Ten Notable Women of Latin America.* Chicago, IL: Nelson-Hall, 1978.

Barbara Morgan,
Melrose, Massachusetts

Sale, Madame de (1308–1348).

See Noves, Laure de.

Salem Witchcraft Trials.

See Witchcraft Trials in Salem Village.

Salih, Halide (c. 1884–1964).

See Adivar, Halide Edib.

Salisbury, countess of.

See Mohun, Elizabeth.

See Grandison, Katharine (fl. 1305–1340) in Siege Warfare and Women.

See Montacute, Maud (fl. 1380s).

See Holland, Eleanor (c. 1385–?).

See Margaret of Anjou for sidebar on Alice Chaucer (fl. 1400s).

See Pole, Margaret (1473–1541).

See Howard, Catherine (d. 1672).

Salisbury, duchess of.

See Montacute, Alice (c. 1406–1463).

Sallé, Marie (1707–1756)

French ballerina and choreographer. Name variations: Marie Salle. Born in 1707; died in 1756; daughter of an acrobat and theatrical performer; studied with Françoise Prévost, Jean Balon, and Blondy; lived with Rebecca Wick.

A great deal is known of those on the periphery in the life of Marie Sallé, but not much is known about the great *danseuse* herself. Her adoring fans, however, were quick to fill in the gap. They claimed she was a child prodigy, that she was a virgin who scorned men, that she was an inventor of a new style of dance. Marie Sallé was indeed a prodigy. As a nine-year-old, she

made her center-stage debut on October 18, 1716, at the Lincoln's Inn Fields in London, following the performance of a play. She and her 11-year-old brother danced and delighted the audience; so much so, they were signed for a return engagement.

Marie Sallé was born in 1707 into a large theatrical family who toured the small towns of France; her uncle François Moylin, known as Francisque, was a comedian-tumbler and the manager of their traveling troupe which included Moylin's brother, his sister and her husband (the acrobat Sallé), another sister and her husband (the clown Cochois), and all their children, including Sallé and **Marianne Cochois** (another future ballerina).

The young Marie must have shown potential, because the family arranged for her to become a pupil of *Françoise Prévost, as well as Jean Balon and Blondy. In 1727, age 20, Sallé reluctantly left her dance-partner and beloved brother and made her Opéra de Paris debut. Her greatest success that season was in Prévost's *Les Caractères de la danse*, arranged as a *pas de deux* with Antoine Laval. But Sallé was not happy. She was ill prepared for the backstage intrigues and the press' eagerness to promote a rivalry with fellow *danseuse* *Marie-Anne Cupis de Camargo. Sallé's style was one of grace and expressive mime; Camargo was more technical, more athletic. Poets sang Sallé's praises. Wrote Voltaire: "*Ah! Camargo, que vous êtes brilliante/ Mais que Sallé, grands dieux, est ravissante!*" (Ah! Camargo, you are brilliant/ But Sallé, great gods, is ravishing!) The public was particularly disappointed when Sallé did not become embroiled in scintillating, scandalous escapades. In fact, she spurned a long line of suitors, which led to the virgin motif in all serious speculation.

To further Sallé's misery, the Opéra de Paris eschewed change. Throughout its existence, it had employed the same manner of costumes: male dancers wore masks; women danced in tall wigs, jewels, feathered headdresses, voluminous skirts and panniers. The fact that movement was severely impeded by all this did not come into question. Between engagements, Sallé fled to London to dance with her brother. She was a huge success, and her fame in London reached its height.

On her return to Paris in 1731, she learned of her brother's death, and the following year left the Opéra, taking a year off. In 1733, she was invited to perform at the Comédie-Italienne in a one-act play written by friends, François Riccoboni and Jean-Antoine Romagnesi. Knowing that the Italians would be far more receptive to her ideas and would also allow her a chance to choreograph, she agreed. But the director of the Opéra de Paris was incensed. Because of the long-standing rivalry between the two companies, he made a formal complaint to the king's minister, and Mlle Sallé was politely informed that if she insisted on performing with the Italians she would be imprisoned in the For-l'Evêque. Backing out of the engagement, she once again left for London.

On February 14, 1734, Sallé opened in *Pygmalion* at Covent Garden and made ballet history. She had created her own ballet, let her hair flow freely, had chosen her own costumes—a simple muslin dress and slippers without heels—and had tried to communicate inner feelings rather than settle for technical effect. From that time on, *Pygmalion* has been cited as the forerunner of Jean Georges Noverre's *ballet d'action*, a ballet that told a story. Shortly thereafter, Sallé appeared in another ballet of her own creation, *Bacchus and Ariadne*. Both productions were the rage of London, and Sallé was now an acclaimed dancer, choreographer, and innovator. "It was not by leaps and antics that she touched one's heart," wrote Noverre. Paris took note; newspapers gushed as they told their readers about her revolutionary ideas, her abundant salary, and her would-be lover who had offered her huge sums but was refused because of the ballerina's renowned chastity.

The conclusion of the 1735 season in London did not fare as well. Composer Georg Friedrich Handel had inserted ballet numbers expressly arranged for Sallé into five of his operas. On April 16, when she appeared in his *Alcina* dressed as a boy, she was hissed. Some critics speculated that the heckling did not come from the entire audience but from a rival opera group of Handel's, though there might have been another reason. Rumors had already surfaced in London about Sallé's amorous preferences. Rumors turned into a minor scandal when she returned to France in the company of Mlle **Manon Grognet**, a dancer from the Drury Lane Theatre who was the target of Paris scandalmongers because of her lesbian tendencies. Ex-suitors of Sallé's felt betrayed and foolish; friends abandoned her. Marie Sallé's name was now added to crude verses and scornful lampoons, including those by Voltaire.

Nonetheless, she was rehired by the Opera in August 1735 for her last and longest Paris engagement. The time was auspicious. Camargo had gone into a six-year, self-imposed retirement; as well, there was a new and brilliant composer, Jean-Philippe Rameau, and a new dancing partner, David Dumoulin. Because of her fame, Sallé was allowed to impose some choreography on the season's opener, Rameau's *Les Indes galantes*. Though slow in achieving popularity, it eventually recaptured Sallé's fickle public. But the Opéra's management insisted on retaining their backlist of tired favorites for the rest of a mediocre season. Thus, in June 1739, Sallé turned in her notice. She was 32.

For the next five years, until 1745, she lived quietly in Paris in an apartment on the rue Saint-

Honoré with her friend **Rebecca Wick**. Though Sallé sat for two portrait painters, Jean Fenouil and Maurice La Tour, she was not seen in public. From 1745 to 1747, she danced at Versailles with Dumoulin in 20 ballets, then retired for another five years. In 1752, she participated in four ballets at Fontainebleau. Her relationship with Wick endured throughout. Five years before she died in 1756, Sallé named her "*amiable amie*" as her sole heir.

SOURCES:

Migel, Parmenia. *The Ballerinas: From the Court of Louis XIV to Pavlova.* NY: Macmillan, 1972.

Salminen, Sally (1906–1976)

Finnish author. Born in Vargata on the Åland Islands on April 25, 1906; died in Copenhagen, Denmark, on July 19, 1976; daughter of Erika Norrgaard and Hindrik Salminen; married Johannes Dührkop (a Danish painter), in 1940.

Sally Salminen was born in 1906 and grew up in a family of 12 children on the Åland Islands, an archipelago of 80 inhabited islands in the Gulf of Bothnia, forming part of Finland. She went to school there and afterwards got a job in the general store at Vargata. Always an avid reader, she had dreams of seeing the larger world and becoming a writer. At 18, she therefore moved to Stockholm and later to Linköping. To mitigate her primitive schooling, she took classes in Swedish, mathematics and bookkeeping, which eventually enabled her to progress from salesgirl to cashier and bookkeeper.

In the meantime, an elder brother had emigrated to America, and in March 1930, Salminen and one of her sisters set out for New York. While there, she started *Katrina*, the novel which would bring her world fame. She wrote it in pencil at the end of a day's work as a maid, resting on her knees by her bed or sitting on a park bench, all 600 pages. The book concerned a young bride who arrives on one of the outlying Åland Islands to find that the house her new husband has erected, well appointed in her imagination, is in fact a poor little shack with none of the basic amenities. Friends typed the manuscript which won first prize in a 1936 literary competition sponsored jointly by a Swedish and Finnish publishing company. The prize money enabled Salminen to return to Åland and start a life as a full-time writer. She also resumed her acquaintance with the Danish painter Johannes Dührkop whom she married and later accompanied to Denmark.

Two novels were published in 1939 and 1941, after which Salminen wrote a series about an Åland emigrant: *Lars Laurila* (1943), *New Land* (1945), *Small Worlds* (1949) and *The Star and the Chasm* (1951). Shy and reserved, Salminen nonetheless made contacts with Danish writers, moved about the country, and actively participated in the Danish Resistance movement during World War II. As soon as the borders were reopened, she and her husband initiated the extended travels they would pursue for many years, making lengthy stops in places which would serve as inspiration for both. *Prince Efflam* (1953)—arguably her best novel—is set in Brittany, and a trip to Algeria and Jerusalem inspired two travel books: *Jerusalem* (1970) and *Journeys in Israel* (1971).

Between 1966 and 1974, Salminen wrote four autobiographical works detailing her stays in the United States and Denmark. Her last major work, *On the Ocean* (1963), is set on the island of Fano on the west coast of Denmark. Her stay in that country, her marriage to a Dane, and her travels with him gave her a wider horizon than she would have had staying at the Åland Islands, as she had contemplated doing on her return from America. It made her writing more difficult, however, because she continued to write in Swedish in a Danish-speaking environment which invariably colored her own language and weakened its effect.

Salminen has been called an "immigrant in life," and she spoke of herself as an outsider. The sudden and overwhelming fame which followed the publication of *Katrina* was difficult for her to handle. She felt herself thrust into a new world and confronted by scores of people, all of whom seemed more intelligent and better educated than she. They would ask questions she could not always answer, and even after she had written several other books, they would insist on talking about *Katrina*. At first, Salminen felt flattered, but she grew weary of being "the author of *Katrina*." She wanted to move on but felt herself fettered by her own creation:

> Katrina became a big and hateful monster stomping through the world. I heard her footsteps as she trampled my peace and quiet and I constantly had to eat her up. I had lived off my work with that book for one and a half years, devoured it as a drunken glutton. . . . I had had my fill. I did not want to hear any more about it.

Ironically, *Katrina* refuses to go away. Sixty years after its publication, it keeps appearing in new editions.

Sally Salminen was deeply engaged in social and cultural issues. At her death, a Danish journalist summed up the author's life as a "steady fight for freedom, freedom to learn, to write, to become knowledgeable about people, art and culture." An indefatigable questioner, a defiant, persistent seeker of justice, Salminen would burn with anger and resentment at unprovoked infringements or injustice. However, wrote the journalist, in the presence of love and trust, she would "show her tender heart and quiet wisdom in the steady, clear gaze of her eyes."

SOURCES:

Sallys Saga: En minnesbok om Sally Salminen. Ed. Anna Bondestam. Borgaa: Schildts, 1986.

Inga Wiehl,
Yakima Valley Community College,
Yakima Valley, Washington

Salmon, Lucy Maynard

(1853–1927)

American historian and educator. Born on July 27, 1853, in Fulton, New York; died in Poughkeepsie, New York, on February 14, 1927; daughter of George Salmon and Maria Clara (Maynard) Salmon; University of Michigan, B.A., 1876, A.M., 1883.

Descended from Puritans on both sides of her family, Lucy Maynard Salmon was born in 1853, in the small mill town of Fulton, New York, the only daughter of George Salmon and **Maria Maynard Salmon**. In addition to her older brother, she had three half-brothers from her father's previous marriage. George Salmon was an active Presbyterian who served as director of the Fulton bank and owner of a successful tannery. Prior to her marriage, Maria Salmon served as principal of the Fulton Female Seminary. She died when Lucy was only seven years old. The stepmother whom Lucy acquired the following year was evidently more concerned with her step-daughter's spiritual development than with her health and contentment. After attending schools in Oswego, Lucy became a student at Falley Seminary (formerly the Fulton Female Seminary, now reorganized as a coeducational institution). Shy and depressed, Salmon was sent by her worried parents to stay with relatives in the Midwest.

A cousin encouraged her to apply to the University of Michigan, which she entered in 1872 following a year of high school in Ann Arbor. Under the tutelage of Charles Kendall Adams, Salmon fell in love with history and, after graduating in 1876, spent five years in an Iowa high school, first as assistant principal, then as principal. During 1882, she returned to Ann Arbor for

a year of graduate work in European history as well as English and American constitutional history, earning her A.M. degree. Salmon then taught in Terre Haute, Indiana, at the State Normal School before taking a fellowship at Bryn Mawr College (1886–87) where the subject of her graduate work was American history.

The year-long fellowship ended with Salmon's acceptance of a teaching position at Vassar College as its first history teacher. In 1889, she became a full professor and would remain at Vassar until the end of her career. Salmon proved to be an influential member of the college faculty, not only in the construction of Vassar's fledgling history department, but also in the greater administration of the college. She took particular interest in developing the school's library and campaigned with other faculty members for a less structured curriculum in order to give students the freedom to pursue their own academic interests. Unhappy with the college's conservative outlook, she pressed for more liberal policies that would give greater voice to the faculty. In addition, by conducting her classes as seminars rather than lectures, she focused on the teacher-student relationship while emphasizing an awareness of current events as a backdrop to the study of history. Under her direction, history classes were popular among students, and in time Salmon's department, which she chaired, grew to include six additional professors.

Salmon's own scholarly work reflected broad interests. Her focus on civil and domestic service had already begun taking shape in her master's thesis, *History of the Appointing Power of the President* (1885). In her 1897 work *Domestic Service* (1897), she pioneered the use of statistical methods in the study of the subject, and she disclosed her dislike for the class distinctions evident within Vassar's service system—a disapproval which surfaced again in her *Progress in the Household* (1906). Two books published in 1923 were born out of Salmon's interest in journalism, *The Newspaper and the Historian* and *The Newspaper and Authority*.

Following a two-year sabbatical to Europe starting in 1898, Salmon moved off-campus with Vassar librarian **Adelaide Underhill**. She became active in the Women's City and County Club; and when the American Historical Association was founded in 1884, she joined as a charter member, going on to serve on the executive committee between 1915 and 1919. Instrumental in the founding of the Association of History Teachers of the Middle States and Maryland, Salmon served as the first president of that organization. In addition, she helped to organize the Western Association of Collegiate Alumnae, which merged into the Association of Collegiate Alumnae at the national level.

Salmon was a pacifist and dedicated suffragist at a time when the Vassar administration banned political activity in support of the suffrage movement. At age 70, she successfully avoided compulsory retirement, and a few years later, in 1926, her alumnae friends organized the Lucy Maynard Salmon Fund for Research to provide monies for her to continue working. She died of a stroke in 1927 and was buried in the Poughkeepsie Rural Cemetery. Two of Salmon's works, *Why Is History Rewritten?* (1929) and *Historical Material* (1933), were published posthumously.

SOURCES:

James, Edward T. *Notable American Women, 1607–1950.* Cambridge, MA: The Belknap Press of Harvard University, 1971.

Gloria Cooksey,
freelance writer, Sacramento, California

Salm-Salm, Agnes, Princess

(1840–1912)

American war relief worker. Name variations: Agnes Leclercq; Agnes, princess Salm Salm. Born Agnes Elisabeth Winona Leclercq Joy on December 25, 1840, in Vermont (some sources cite Quebec or Baltimore); died in Karlsruhe, Germany, on December 21, 1912; daughter of William L. Joy and Julia (Willard) Joy; married Felix Constantin Alexander Johann Nepomuk, Prince Salm-Salm (a German mercenary), in Washington, D.C., on August 30, 1862 (died in battle on August 18, 1870); married Charles Heneage, in 1876.

Served as a federal hospital worker during American Civil War; accompanied husband to Mexico (1866); pled for life of Emperor Maximilian (1867); received Grand Cordon of the Order of San Carlos (1867); was a relief worker during Franco-Prussian War (1870); received Prussian Medal of Honor; recommended for the Iron Cross; published Zehn Jahre aus meinem Leben *(Ten Years of My Life, 1875).*

Agnes, Princess Salm-Salm, followed her husband, Prince Felix Salm-Salm, a German soldier of fortune, from one battleground to another, bringing relief to wounded and imprisoned soldiers in the United States, Mexico, and Prussia. Little is known of her early life. She was born on December 25, 1840, in Vermont, though some sources indicate her place of birth as Quebec or Baltimore, and may have been an actress or circus performer. She met her husband in 1862, in Washington, D.C., where she had es-

tablished herself under the name Agnes Leclercq. The prince was at the time a colonel and chief of staff under the command of General Louis Blenker, and three months after their marriage in August of that year, he was put in command of the 8th New York Infantry, possibly due to the efforts of his wife. Inseparable from her husband, Princess Salm-Salm accompanied him wherever he was stationed.

During the American Civil War, Agnes became well known in the camps and federal hospitals where she cared for and comforted the sick and injured. By the end of the war, Felix had achieved the rank of brigadier general by brevet, on April 13, 1865, and later became the military governor of Atlanta. This success was due, in large part, to the popularity and influence of Agnes who was much loved for her cheerfulness and sympathy.

In February 1866, Felix offered his services to Emperor Maximilian of Mexico, and Agnes soon became a trusted member of the court of Maximilian and his empress *Carlota. An archduke of Austria, Maximilian had accepted the throne in the mistaken belief that the people had voted him their king. In truth, his ascension was part of a secret conspiracy between Mexican conservatives (who wanted to overthrow the liberal government of President Benito Juárez) and the ambitious French emperor Napoleon III (who wanted to expand his empire). Maximilian had angered all sides by taking seriously his position as a benevolent monarch, maintaining many of Juárez's reforms, attempting to abolish peonage, refusing to return confiscated land holdings to the Roman Catholic Church, and using his own money to replenish the empty treasury of the Mexican government.

At the end of the American Civil War, the French Army, which had been promised to Maximilian for his support, were forced to withdraw under the terms of the Monroe Doctrine. In March 1867, with the French gone, Juárez and his army entered Mexico City. Prince Salm-Salm was with Maximilian when he was betrayed and captured at Querétaro on May 15, 1867. Agnes rode back and forth between the prison and Liberal headquarters at San Luis Potosi to negotiate terms, find means of delaying the judicial proceedings, and plead with Juárez to release the emperor and her husband. Her efforts became the subject of a well-known painting by Manuel Ocaranza, and Maximilian showed his gratitude by decorating her with the Grand Cordon of the Order of San Carlos. Although many European heads of state petitioned for Maximilian's release, he was executed at Querétaro in June. Felix, however, was set free, thanks to the indefatigable Agnes.

After the death of the emperor, the Salm-Salms returned to Europe where, in recognition of all she had done on behalf of Maximilian, Agnes was rewarded by Archduchess *Sophie of Bavaria, Maximilian's mother, with a miniature portrait of him set in an emerald bracelet. She was also granted a pension by the emperor of Austria, Franz Joseph I. Felix was appointed major of the Queen Augusta regiment of the Prussian guards and, with special permission granted by General von Steinmetz in July 1870, Agnes accompanied him as part of his staff with the army of invasion during the Franco-Prussian War. Prince Salm-Salm was killed leading his battalion in the battle of Gravelotte on August 18, 1879. Both before and after his death, the princess continued to organize hospitals and distribute supplies to the sick and wounded. Generals commanding the soldiers to whom she had ministered recognized her efforts with letters of gratitude. She also received the Prussian Medal of Honor, made of metal from a captured cannon, and a bracelet from Empress *Augusta of Saxe-Weimar. She was recommended for the Iron Cross, but was denied it as this honor was reserved for men.

The remainder of Princess Salm-Salm's life was relatively uneventful. She published an autobiography, *Zehn Jahre aus meinem Leben* (Ten Years of My Life), in 1875, and remarried in 1876, to a member of the British embassy stationed in Berlin. In 1899, she returned to the United States to restore to the survivors flags of the 8th and 68th New York regiments, which her husband had commanded. She was made an honorary member of both the Blenker Veteran Association and the New York chapter of the Daughters of the American Revolution. She returned to the United States again in 1900, this time to solicit funds to equip an ambulance corps for the relief of those wounded in the South African Boer War. She died in Karlsruhe, Germany, on December 21, 1912.

SOURCES:

Johnson, Rossiter, ed. *The Twentieth Century Biographical Dictionary of Notable Americans.* Boston, MA: Biographical Society, 1904.

McHenry, Robert, ed. *Famous American Women.* NY: Dover, 1980.

Malinda Mayer,
writer and editor, Falmouth, Massachusetts

Salome (c. 65 BCE–10 CE)

Influential sister of Herod the Great. Born around 65 BCE; died around 10 CE; daughter of Antipater, a wealthy Idumaean, and Cyprus (c. 90 BCE–?); sister of Herod the Great; married Joseph (executed in 28 BCE); married Costobar (divorced); married Alexas; children: (second marriage) Alexander; Herod; Antipater; Berenice (c. 35 BCE–?); and another unnamed daughter.

Antipater and *Cyprus (an Arabian) had four sons—Phasael, Herod the Great, Joseph, and Pheroras—and a daughter, Salome. A wealthy Idumaean, Antipater backed Hyrcanus over Aristobulus in the 60s BCE, as the Hasmonian house of Judea engaged in internecine rivalries (*See Berenice [c. 35 BCE–?]*). In the process, Antipater came to know well many Romans who, at the time, were expanding their imperium throughout the region, including the military-minded Pompey the Great. Somewhat later (in 48), Antipater advanced the interests of his family by sending troops to the aid of Julius Caesar when the latter was militarily beleaguered in Alexandria. As rewards, Caesar appointed Antipater to the position of procurator and granted him Roman citizenship. Antipater was poisoned in 43 by an Arabic rival named Malichus, but he nevertheless paved the way for the later success of his most famous offspring, Herod the Great.

Herod and his brothers continued the political rise begun by their father, and they also did so in collusion with the extension of Roman power throughout the East. The late 40s and 30s, however, were a period of great turmoil, with Rome experiencing a civil war fought between the Caesarians and the assassins of Julius Caesar, the rise of the Second Triumvirate, and the great showdown between Octavian (later Augustus) and Marc Antony. Nonetheless, in 42 Herod held a Roman governorship in Palestine and in 40 (the same year his older brother, Phasael, died) was appointed Judea's king by the Roman Senate. When the rift between Octavian and Antony grew, Herod backed the latter, both because of his military reputation and because Antony's power base lay in the eastern Mediterranean. In 31, however, Antony fell to the forces of Octavian. Herod was quick to make amends to the new master: in 30 when Octavian was on the island of Rhodes, Herod approached him, offering loyalty and support. As a result of this pilgrimage, Octavian reconfirmed Herod's authority in Judea.

It should be noted that Herod was, in essence, a foreign appointee, a fact which did not endear him to many of his subjects, although the popular Hasmonian dynasty (which had ruled Judea for over a century) was clearly in serious decline. Herod's status within his realm was initially insecure (in fact, he remained politically paranoid throughout his entire life), but he overcame the reservations of many by divorcing his first wife **Doris** (by no means of humble birth, but not of royal status) in 42 in order to marry ❧▶ **Mariamne the Hasmonian** (in 37, although they were betrothed in 42). Mariamne was a stunning beauty from the Hasmonian house. Before his divorce and remarriage, Herod and Doris had a son, also named Antipater, from whom Herod initially distanced himself after his marriage to Mariamne so as to give political precedence to the sons he would have with her. This treatment of Antipater was not only necessary, because Mariamne provided Herod with a valuable link to the deposed dynasty, it was also Herod's wish, for he was besotted by his new wife. Although Herod doted on Mariamne, she did not return his affection in its intensity. There appears to have been two main reasons for her coolness: first, in order to secure his newly won throne, Herod had executed Mariamne's brother Jonathon and grandfather Hyrcanus lest either ignite a movement to restore the Hasmonian house to power; and second, because his family was nowhere near as exalted as hers (notwithstanding the obvious edge in political acumen Herod had over any of the contemporary Hasmonians). Nevertheless, Mariamne and Herod had five children: three sons, one unnamed, who died young, Alexander and Aristobulus I; and two daughters, **Salampsio** and ❧▶ **Cypros**.

Acutely aware of her effect on Herod, and recognizing his political need for her family connections, Mariamne lorded over her husband, his family, and his court, making it clear that she felt superior to all. Although Herod tolerated this behavior, neither his mother Cyprus nor his sister Salome were anywhere near as forgiving of the slights they received by Mariamne's actions and words, and they sought opportunities to turn Herod against his queen. Thus was Herod's court divided into factions, each seeking not only a recognition of superior status, but, even more so, the political influence which came with superior status. An opportunity to undermine Mariamne's authority presented itself before the fall of Antony. (Perhaps) doctoring the evidence, Salome accused Mariamne of having sent a portrait of herself to Antony in Egypt, where he was then established as the consort of *Cleopatra VII. The reason she had done so, alleged Salome, was that Mariamne had hoped to attract Antony's amorous attention. This allegation did two things: first, it incited in Herod suspicions of infidelity; and second, it roused his fear that a jealous Cleopatra VII might avenge herself upon him, his interests, and/or Mariamne herself.

Both to protect Mariamne and to keep an eye on her, Herod placed her under the supervision of Salome's husband Joseph whom Herod regarded as trustworthy. Herod, however, made the mistake of issuing to Joseph a command he meant to keep secret from Mariamne: in the event of a successful Egyptian attempt on Herod's life, Joseph was to kill Mariamne. Joseph understood this order as a manifestation of Herod's love—that he wished to be with his beloved even in the underworld, if the worst came to pass. Whether or not this was the case, the naive Joseph broke his troth with Herod and revealed Herod's instruction to Mariamne, hoping thereby to convince her that Herod's love was true, so that she might respond in kind. Not at all pleased by the information Joseph had revealed, Mariamne is said to have responded to Herod, while he was in the process of proclaiming his devotion, by declaring that he had a funny way of expressing love, insofar as he had made provisions for her execution. Stunned by her retort, Herod proclaimed that Joseph would never have revealed the secret decree unless Joseph himself had been so enamored of Mariamne as to have attempted to seduce her. When the issue became known to Salome, who did not care overmuch for Joseph, she saw her opportunity to attack her nemesis: Salome assured her brother that what he suspected was true—Joseph *had* seduced Mariamne. Grief-stricken, Herod ordered the executions of Mariamne and Joseph (in 29).

This episode embittered Herod's court, for the sons of Mariamne would never forget the murder of their mother, and they never forgave the rest of Herod's family, especially Salome, for their role in Mariamne's downfall. Indeed, the strong emotions unleashed by Mariamne's death were not allowed to settle, for Herod recalled Doris and Antipater in the wake of Mariamne's disgrace and these created their own faction to promote Antipater as Herod's heir. (Herod also married several other times and maintained a polygamous household. Lesser wives and their children compounded the court's factionalization.) Antipater's main problem was this: although he was older than his stepbrothers, the status of his mother was lesser than had been Mariamne's. As a result, any hope of Antipater's becoming Herod's political heir meant that he had to do everything he could to antagonize the bitterness created by Mariamne's execution. This was not very difficult, but with time, Herod began to think seriously about an emotional reconciliation with Mariamne's children. The issue

Mariamne the Hasmonian. See *Berenice (c. 35 BCE–?) for sidebar.*

Cypros. See *Berenice (28 BCE–after 80 CE) for sidebar.*

of who would become Herod's political heir became acute in 17, when Herod retrieved Alexander and Aristobulus from Rome, where they had been deposited for three reasons: to put some geographical distance between them and Herod in the hopes that the memory of Mariamne's murder would fade; to begin their formal education in the Roman manner; and to make valuable political contacts with the imperial elite.

Once Alexander and Aristobulus were back in Jerusalem, Herod began their political rehabilitation in part by planning their marriages in such a way as to be politically advantageous to Herod and his dynasty (c. 15). Herod arranged the marriage of Alexander to a princess from Cappadocia named **Glaphyra**. This union solidified Herod's international standing, and many interpreted it as a prelude to a reevaluation of the succession question. For Aristobulus, Herod had another kind of marriage in mind—the younger living son of Mariamne would begin, Herod hoped, to reconcile the various factions into which his family was split by being married to Salome's daughter, *Berenice (by her second husband, Costobar). Sadly, harmony was not to be so simply resurrected.

Antipater knew these marriages imperiled his prospects. He proceeded to do everything he could to undermine Herod's growing faith in Mariamne's sons without (if he could) appearing to do so in a vindictive way, for Herod had grown somewhat maudlin about his executed wife, and appeared intent upon assuaging his guilt by promoting the interests of her sons. Fortunately for Antipater, he had allies to help him with his campaign. First among these was Salome, who feared the retribution which would certainly result if the sons of her hated rival ever held real power: this fear was hardly allayed by the marriages of Mariamne's sons. A second factor in Antipater's favor was Alexander and Aristobulus themselves, for they were easily goaded into trumpeting their general bitterness and also into exhibiting their genuine disdain for most of Herod's family, since only they and their sisters had a Hasmonian ancestry. Neither were the sons of Mariamne helped by their marriages, for Alexander's wife, Glaphyra (like Mariamne herself), flaunted her noble birth while sneering at the more humble origins of the likes of Salome. Even more undiplomatic, because of her descent, Glaphyra demanded precedence over all of the ladies of Herod's court, including Salome—a dictate which won her few friends.

This was bad enough for Salome, but the marriage of Aristobulus to Berenice was even worse. Although the relationship between Aristobulus and Berenice was often a good one, Aristobulus was never reconciled with Salome, for he (like his brother) never forgot the role that she had played in their mother's death. Thus, when marital troubles arose, Aristobulus would bemoan the fact that his brother had married royalty, while he himself had "only" merited a daughter of Salome. In addition, Aristobulus even once went so far as threaten that when Herod was no more, he and Alexander would put Salome to work weaving in the company of slaves. When talk like this got back to Salome, she reported it to Herod, who was displeased that Mariamne's sons would not let bygones be bygones, although guilt long delayed any punishment.

Anarchy began to reign at Herod's court, with rumors and allegations flying freely. Each member of Herod's family assured the aging king that he or she was his only true friend, whereas everyone else was but a snake waiting to strike. One particularly nasty altercation exploded after Herod gave some of the fabulous clothes once owned by Mariamne to some of the women of his family. When Alexander and Aristobulus learned of this "sacrilege," they are alleged to have threatened (although they later denied it to a furious Herod) that a time would come when the clothes would be recalled and the women caught wearing them attired in haircloth. Such talk, quickly brought to Herod's ears by the likes of Salome, not only belittled the status of the women in Herod's family, it also attacked Herod's royal prerogative. It was suggested that Alexander and Aristobulus, ingrates both, thought of their legitimacy and political prospects as coming from their mother and *not* from Herod. Could a political coup be in the making? As time passed, Herod's paranoia made him think it increasingly likely.

Compounding the complexity of the situation, however, was the fact that Herod did not always think he could trust those who attacked Mariamne's sons. Salome, so often Herod's ally and an especially good source for court gossip, herself came into conflict with her brother in 14. Her other brother, Pheroras, in order to deflect Herod's displeasure from himself, revealed that Salome had fallen in love with one Syllaeus (the son of Obadas, one of Herod's regional enemies), when that Arabian prince visited Jerusalem on a diplomatic mission. Apparently, Syllaeus experienced a similar attraction, although Salome's appeal might have been more political than physical, for she was about 50 at the time. Herod allowed the relationship to develop to the point where Salome divorced Costobar, and wedding plans began to be made. It seems that Herod exploited this affair to undermine the position of Obadas, but the marriage fell through when Syllaeus refused circumcision, one of Herod's conditions without which he would not approve the marriage. This demand was obviously imposed in order to sever Syllaeus' ties to his father and native culture. Salome was devastated by the development, but Herod held firm with the result that he strained his relationship with his sister. Somewhat after this affair (c. 9), some truce between Herod and Salome was in place, for he betrothed her (initially over her objections) to a political friend named Alexas. Salome seems to have had children only with Costobar: these being Alexander, Herod, Antipater, Berenice, and another daughter whose name is unknown.

In 7, an even greater crisis exploded primarily because of Herod's need to maintain close contacts with Rome. Herod traveled to Rome more than once on diplomatic business, but matters at home prevented him from doing so as frequently as he would have liked in order to preserve the intimacy he so wished to maintain with the imperial family. In his stead he therefore often made use of Alexander (who had remained popular in Rome since his school days) and Salome (who was a close friend of Augustus' wife *Livia) as political and personal emissaries. However, in Alexander's case, success in Rome (and Judea) was counter-productive, for, as his diplomatic star rose, Herod, encouraged by Salome and Antipater, increasingly feared that Alexander was not entirely trustworthy. Nor did Alexander's behavior allay Herod's anxiety, for the more important he became, the more ostentatious he acted at court, never noticing the negative impact this had on Herod. Finally, Herod's patience broke, and he formally accused Alexander of treachery on the slimmest of evidence. Herod's fury was made all the more intense when Alexander—trying desperately to shake Herod's renewed faith in the allegations Salome had made against him—accused her of having once forced him to have sex with her. Tried before a Roman judge, Alexander was convicted and executed, as was Aristobulus whom detractors (certainly including Salome) implicated in his brother's "crimes." Aristobulus, too, had tried to ruin Salome before his fall by alleging that she had not severed contact with Syllaeus, and that she was acting as his spy against Herod. If there were any truth in this charge, Herod did not believe it.

For three years thereafter, Antipater reigned as Herod's heir-presumptive. Herod, however, never able to free himself from Mariamne's memory, eventually rued the executions of her sons. As he had once before, Herod attempted to atone for past errors by making restitution to the offspring of those who had suffered as a result of those mistakes. When he openly acknowledged the children of Alexander and Aristobulus at court and began to make plans for their future, Antipater came to realize that his own was by no means secure. Indeed, in 4, just 5 days before disease took Herod, Antipater was executed at his father's command for attempting to appropriate too much authority to himself before the old man was gone. Salome played a role in Antipater's ruin, for she more than any other made sure that Herod knew all about Antipater's behind-the-back politicking.

Perhaps Salome's most positive contribution came in the immediate aftermath of Herod's death at Jericho. Just prior to that passing, Herod had issued a vicious command to Salome, Alexas and the local military garrison. Herod doubted that his subjects would mourn his death; rather, he suspected that the sounds of laughter would sully the dignity of his passing. So he ordered the murder of a large number of Jewish leaders whom he had already rounded up and incarcerated in Jericho's hippodrome. After their slaughter had been effected, Herod reasoned, there would be no rejoicing to stain his demise—for his memory might be hated, but the pain brought on by a massacre would douse all joy. Thinking this excessive, Salome and Alexas disobeyed, telling the guard that Herod had changed his mind. They then saw to it that the hostages were released before the soldiers had second thoughts about executing Herod's order.

Herod had made several wills during his lifetime, but his last split up most of his realm among Archelaus, named king of Judea proper, Antipas, designated tetrarch of Galilee, and Philip, appointed tetrarch of Trachonitis. All of these heirs were Herod's sons by lesser wives. This will was contested, however, primarily by Antipas (with the support of most of his family), who had been named as Herod's sole heir in an earlier will. Thus, when all concerned traveled to Rome to have Herod's bequests ratified by Augustus, a large family contingent, including Salome and her son, Antipater, went along to voice their opinions about the arrangements. Supposedly, Salome was open in her support for the priority of Archelaus, but when depositions were presented she and her son spoke on behalf of Antipas. Augustus carefully considered all of the evidence as well as the general situation in the East and decided to ratify most of Herod's last provisions, with the most important deviation being that Archelaus was named ethnarch, not king, of Judea.

Herod remembered Salome in his will with a generosity which suggests that whatever disagreements the two had ever had, he considered her a loyal supporter at the time of his death. In addition to a substantial amount of cash, Salome also received the revenues, amounting to about 60 talents of silver annually, from three important cities: Jamnia, Azotus and Phasaelis (although the cities fell under the political authority of Archelaus). The latter provision broke with Jewish tradition and suggests just how much Herod's family had accommodated themselves to the more widespread hellenistic culture. In addition to these bequests, Augustus gave Salome a large palace at Ascalon, perhaps as a sop when he decided in favor of Archelaus over Antipas. Salome lived until 10 CE. When she died, Livia inherited all of her property, a fact which demonstrates both the intimacy of their relationship and the distance which separated Salome from her surviving kin.

William Greenwalt,
Associate Professor of Classical History,
Santa Clara University, Santa Clara, California

Salome II (fl. 1st c.)

Biblical saint. Flourished in the 1st century in Galilee; married Zebedee; children: John the Evangelist; James the Greater.

The Galilean Salome, mentioned in the books of Mark and Matthew in the New Testament, was the wife of Zebedee, a prosperous fisherman, and lived on the Sea of Galilee, probably at Capernaum. She was the mother of the apostles John the Evangelist and James the Greater, and was herself a devoted follower of Jesus. Referred to in Matthew only as the mother of the sons of Zebedee, she is recorded there as being ambitious for the prestige of her sons and is said to have asked Jesus to allow them to sit on either side of him in his kingdom. Salome is also recorded in Mark as being a witness, along with *Mary Magdalene and *Mary of Cleophas, the mother of James, to Jesus' crucifixion and the resurrection. Some scholars have identified Salome as the sister of *Mary the Virgin, the mother of Jesus.

Laura York, M.A. in History,
University of California, Riverside, California

Salome III (c. 15 CE–?)

The Jezebel of the New Testament. Flourished around 15 CE; daughter of Herodias and Herod Philip I; granddaughter of Herod the Great; married her father's half-brother Herod Philip II, the Jewish tetrarch

of Batanea, Trachonitis, and Auranitis (died 34 CE); married her cousin Aristobulus IV (son of Herod IV, the full brother of Salome's mother Herodias); children: (second marriage) at least three sons, Herod VI, Agrippa III, and Aristobulus V.

The daughter of Herod Philip I and *Herodias, Salome III was a scion of the Herodian royal house of Biblical fame, and doubly descended from its founder, Herod the Great. Salome III's father was the son of the great Herod and **Mariamne II** (one of his ten attested wives), while Herodias was the daughter of Aristobulus I (Herod the Great's son with another of his wives, *Mariamne the Hasmonian) and *Berenice (the daughter of Herod the Great's sister, *Salome). The endogamous tendency of the Herodian dynasty is as evident in the two known marriages of Salome III as it was in those of her immediate ancestors, for her first husband, her uncle Herod Philip II, the Jewish tetrarch of Batanea, Trachonitis, and Auranitis (a post held only because of Roman approval), was her father's half-brother. Sometime after the death of Herod Philip II in 34 CE, Salome III married her cousin Aristobulus IV, the son of Herod IV (the full brother of Salome's mother Herodias). Salome III's second marriage produced at least three sons: Herod VI, Agrippa III, and Aristobulus V, so we must assume that it was congenial and lasted for some time. However, by the middle third of the 1st century CE the political clout of Salome's family was declining as the Roman Empire was becoming more directly institutionalized in the East, with the result that we know little about Salome's adult life, her marriages, or the fates of her sons.

Regardless, Salome III's lasting fame was earned when she was probably no more than 14 or 15 years of age. At that time, her mother was no longer married to Salome's father. After Salome's birth, Herodias had become intimate with Herod Antipas (then tetrarch of Galilee and of Peraea), the son of Herod the Great and *Malthace, and thus the half-brother of Herodias' husband, Herod Philip I. Herod Antipas was also married at the time, but their mutual attraction caused each to divorce so that they could marry. The affair created a scandal both because of the initial adultery leading to two divorces and because of the blood affinity of the principals. One prominent figure of the time—John the Baptist—was extremely critical of Herod Antipas and Herodias—especially so of the latter for her willingness to be intimate with two sons of her own grandfather. John pronounced the marriage of Herod Antipas and Herodias illicit—a perhaps meaningless condemnation from somebody without influence, but especially dangerous from one whose religious ministry was growing in popularity among the people whom Herod Antipas wanted to rule without trouble. Herodias begged her husband to put an end to John's continuous censure, but this Herod Antipas was for a time loath to do, lest by so acting he arouse the anger of John's followers and thus foment rebellion against his own authority. Herod Antipas' qualms, however, did not save John from imprisonment in the fortress at Machaerus, where he languished for an unknown period of time.

If the accounts of the gospels of Matthew and Mark can be trusted for their historical content in this instance, John sat in prison until a celebration of Herod Antipas' birthday, an event celebrated lavishly with a banquet (one must assume at Machaerus) attended by all of the important public and private figures of Herod's realm. At this feast, Salome III (the honoree's young stepdaughter) performed a dance which was so well received by those assembled as to induce from Herod a promise that Salome could have anything from him which she desired, up to the worth of one-half of his realm. Probably flustered and certainly inexperienced in such public recognition, Salome is reported to have consulted with her mother about what she should request from her stepfather. Young enough to be under her mother's domination still, Salome is said to have returned to Herod Antipas with a request for the head of John the Baptist. Although the accounts continue with the tetrarch's attempt to persuade Salome to accept another token of his appreciation, she is said to have insisted (upon her mother's urging) for the death of John. Fearing a loss of public face before those assembled in his honor, Herod Antipas apparently conceded. In the most gruesome record of the event, Herod not only had John executed but also ordered that his head be presented to Salome on a platter in fulfillment of her request.

William S. Greenwalt,
Associate Professor of Classical History,
Santa Clara University, Santa Clara, California

Salomé, Lou or Louise von (1861–1937).

See Andreas-Salomé, Lou.

Salomea.

Variant of Salome.

Salomea (d. 1144)

Queen of Poland. Name variations: Salome of Berg-Schelklingen. Died on July 27, 1144; daughter of Henry, count of Berg; second wife of Boleslaw III Krzywousty also known as Boleslaus III the Wry-

Salome III with the Head of St. John the Baptist.

mouthed (1085–1138), king of Poland (r. 1102–1138); children: *Richizza of Poland (1116–1185); Boleslaus or Boleslaw IV the Curly (1125–1173), king of Poland (r. 1146–1173); Mieszko III Stary (1126–1202), king of Poland; Henryk (1132–1166); Dobronega Ludgarda; **Judyta** (who married Otto I, margrave of Brandenburg); *Agnes of Poland (b. 1137); Casimir II (1138–1194), king of Poland (r. 1177–1194). Boleslaus III's first wife was *Zbyslawa.

Salomea (1201–c. 1270).

See Salome of Hungary.

Salome Alexandra.

See Alexandra (r. 76–67 BCE).

Salome of Berg-Schelklingen (d. 1144).

See Salomea.

Salome of Hungary (1201–c. 1270)

Saint and queen of Hungary. Name variations: Saint Salomea. Born around 1201; died around 1270;

*daughter of the duke of Cracow; second wife of Bela IV, king of Hungary (r. 1235–1270); children: *Elizabeth of Hungary (who married Henry I, duke of Lower Bavaria); *Anna of Hungary (who married Rastislav, ex-prince of Novgorod); and possibly *Yolanda of Gnesen.*

Salome of Hungary was the second wife of Bela IV, king of Hungary. He was first married to *Maria Lascaris. Upon the death of her husband in 1270, Salome entered the order of the Poor Clares; she died soon after. Her feast day is November 17.

Salomon, Alice (1872–1948)

German reformer who played a key role in the establishment of social work as a profession in her country and was a leader in the new field of social work education. Born in Berlin, Germany, on April 19, 1872; died in New York City on August 29 or 30, 1948; daughter of Albert Salomon and Anna Potocky-Nelken Salomon; had six brothers and sisters, three of whom died in infancy; never married.

Alice Salomon was born in 1872 into a highly assimilated Jewish family in Berlin, her ancestors having settled in the city in the mid-18th century as *Schutzjuden* (protected Jews) under a special dispensation from Prussia's King Frederick II the Great. Salomon enjoyed all the advantages of an upper-bourgeois milieu. Her father Albert, a successful leather merchant, died when she was 13 years old. Alice's mother **Anna Potocky-Nelken Salomon**, who came from a family of bankers, reflected the conservative values of the day by vetoing her daughter's wish to become a teacher. Until Anna's death in 1914, Alice—who alone among her sisters did not marry—lived with her mother. Intellectually frustrated and desiring to contribute to society, in 1893 Salomon became a member of the newly founded Mädchen- und Frauengruppen für soziale Hilfsarbeit (Girls' and Women's Group for Social Assistance), an organization of educated middle-class women whose goal was the creation of a national network of volunteers trained to address the sufferings of the urban poor. Salomon's energy and initiative quickly brought her to the attention of the organization's founders, *Minna Cauer, Jeanette Schwerin, and Professor Gustav Schmoller. After Schwerin's death in July 1899, Salomon became chair of Mädchen- und Frauengruppen. That same year, she established the first full one-year course in social work education in Berlin.

Believing that only a thorough study of the social conditions that underlay poverty would enable society to find the means to alleviate such injustices, starting in the mid-1890s Salomon began to publish articles and books to alert the public to these issues. Over the next half century, she would write 28 books and approximately 250 articles. Although Salomon had not graduated from a gymnasium and had thus not been awarded an Abitur (school-leaving certificate) that qualified her to matriculate at a German university, in 1902 she began auditing courses at the University of Berlin, where women with an Abitur had just been accepted as students. In 1906, her extraordinary academic achievements prompted the Prussian minister of instruction to make a rare exception to the rule prohibiting such students from receiving academic degrees, and in that year she was awarded a doctorate for her dissertation, "The Causes of Unequal Payment for Men's and Women's Work," a problem that remains unresolved.

In 1908, Salomon founded the Soziale Frauenschule (Social Work School for Women) in Berlin-Schöneberg, the first modern and academically grounded interdenominational institution teaching social work skills in Germany. She remained director of this pioneering professional school until 1925. Located in the venerable Pestalozzi-Fröbel Haus, which had been founded decades before by **Henriette Breymann**, a leader of the kindergarten movement, the school would train a large number of Germany's female social workers for more than two decades. Although countless demands were made on Salomon by the school as well as by other educational enterprises, she continued to publish. In her writings, she argued for public acceptance and understanding of, and support for, the emerging profession of social work, which she clearly distinguished from the religiously grounded charitable activities of the past. Modern social work, she argued, was to be defined by its exclusive devotion to increasing the productive and reproductive capacities of welfare recipients for the benefit of society in general.

In 1917, with Germany embroiled in World War I and the services of social workers more in demand than ever, Salomon established the German Conference of Schools of Social Work, a precursor of similar confederations in other countries. Her efforts received a strong vote of confidence from the German state after 1918, when the liberal Weimar Republic granted official certification to her Soziale Frauenschule. In 1925, the year she relinquished her directorship duties in Berlin-Schöneberg, Salomon initiated the creation of and headed the Women's Academy of Germany (Deutsche Akademie für soziale und pädagogische Frauenarbeit), an institution for the promotion of social work research, continuing education, training for institutional leadership, and recruitment for social-work educators.

Above and beyond the immense impact Salomon had on the evolution of the profession of social work in Germany, she was also active in the women's and peace movements. Her close association with *Jane Addams, whom she met at several international conferences, led many of Salomon's contemporaries to refer to her as the "Jane Addams of Germany." Although post-1918 Germany was plagued by the stigma of defeat in war, inflation, and fear of revolution, and was rife with anti-Semitism, Salomon was a loyal German. She had converted to Christianity in 1914, was intensely nationalistic, yet remained proud of her Jewish ancestry, enjoying immense prestige in both Gentile and Jewish circles. Because of her international prestige and a well-deserved reputation for reconciliation and consensus building, Salomon was one of post-1918 Germany's outstanding exemplars of that nation's democratic ideals. Unfortunately, all of these hopeful signs of a new spirit were soon to be shattered in an orgy of violence.

Like most democratic Germans, Salomon was unable to take effective measures against the growing menace of Nazism and anti-Semitism. But as she neared the end of her career in the early 1930s, she was rewarded with many high honors. On the occasion of her 60th birthday in 1932, she was the recipient of many encomiums, the most important of which was an honorary medical degree from the University of Berlin for her accomplishments in social medicine. She also received a silver medal from the Prussian Ministry of State. The path-breaking institution she had founded in 1908 was renamed the Alice Salomon School of Social Work. All of these achievements would come crashing down in ruins after January 30, 1933, when Adolf Hitler was appointed chancellor of Germany.

As a result of the Nazi "civil service reform" law of April 1933, which purged Jews and anti-Nazis from public jobs, Salomon lost her state positions and came under increasing pressure from the Hitler regime to relinquish her other positions. Repeatedly she complied with the Nazis' demand to resign from the presidency of the International Committee of Schools of Social Work, only to be given a vote of confidence by her admiring foreign colleagues when the organization's board of directors unanimously voted

to retain her in the presidential office. By the end of 1933, however, Salomon's pride, the Women's Academy of Germany, had no choice but to announce its "voluntary" dissolution. In 1934, the now Nazi-controlled Prussian Ministry of Instruction decreed that the Alice Salomon School of Social Work would henceforth be known, like all of the other social work academies in the Reich, as a Schule für Volkspflege (Training School for Officials Dedicated to the People's Welfare), and that its curriculum would emphasize the indoctrination of National Socialist tenets—including "racial science"—in the hearts and minds of its student body.

Like many Germans of Jewish ancestry, Salomon decided to remain in Germany despite the ever-increasing humiliations and injustices heaped upon her by the Nazis and their many collaborators. Above all, she felt that she had to remain in order to assist with the orderly departure of her younger social work colleagues, who would be able to continue their careers in their new homes. With the help of the Russell Sage Foun-

Alice
Salomon

dation and a social workers' relief organization called "Hospites," she was urged to leave Germany, if only temporarily, to head a project to compile the first international study of social-work education. In 1937, returning to Berlin after a speaking tour of the United States, Salomon was summoned by the Gestapo, interrogated for hours, and given an ultimatum: to leave Germany within three weeks or be taken to a Konzentrationslager (concentration camp). Besides her Jewish ancestry (the Nazis regarded her as a Vollblutsjüdin ["full-blooded Jewess"] despite her Christian faith), Salomon had long been persona non grata in the Third Reich because of her fame as a champion of women's rights and the rights of the poor and dispossessed. She had also been active in the Bekennende Kirch (Confessing Church—the anti-Nazi wing of the Lutheran denomination) and had an international reputation as a pacifist and internationalist. Finally, she was hated by National Socialist ideologists for writings in which she had been critical of both Social Darwinist principles and the Volkisch emphasis on an irrational biological collectivity grounded on blood and race. One of the key elements in her philosophy of social work was the idea that "the most fundamental law in human relations is the law of interdependence."

Heartbroken at having to leave her native land, Salomon arrived in New York City in 1937. Two years later, in 1939, the Nazi state stripped Salomon of her German citizenship. Her honorary doctoral degree was also annulled. Until she acquired United States citizenship in 1944, she was officially a woman without a country, and technically an enemy alien as well. Even more painful for her was the fact that despite occasional recognition of her achievements, such as public festivities on the occasion of her 70th birthday in 1942, which included a special award for her service to humanity from the International Club of the New York YMCA, she was not able to find significant outlets for the wisdom and insights derived from a long, successful career. Even an invitation from *Eleanor Roosevelt to visit the White House did little to lessen Salomon's despair during the early 1940s. Ruled by criminals, her beloved Germany was now being destroyed in the most violent conflict in history. After the war, she learned that two of her closest relatives had been killed in the Holocaust and that another, brought to despair, had chosen to commit suicide.

Unable to find employment, Salomon spent some of her time with a small circle of friends but much of her energy went into writing her memoirs, entitled "Character is Destiny: An Autobiography." Although she completed it in 1944, and it was written in excellent English, a language she had mastered in her youth, Salomon was unable to find a publisher. The autobiography was not published until 1983, when it appeared in a German translation.

Alice Salomon died alone in her modest Manhattan apartment on either August 29 or 30, 1948. Instead of the many friends and colleagues who would have attended her funeral had the course of history been different, only four or five mourners accompanied her casket to the burial ground in Brooklyn's Evergreen Cemetery. There was no ceremony, and only a simple gravestone with the inscription "Alice Salomon 1872–1948" remains to this day to bear witness to the accomplishments of a remarkable woman.

SOURCES:

Hong, Young-Sun. "The Contradictions of Modernization in the German Welfare State: Gender and the Politics of Welfare Reform in World War I Germany," in *Social History*. Vol. 17, no. 2. May 1992, pp. 251–270.

———. "Gender, Citizenship, and the Welfare State: Social Work and the Politics of Femininity in the Weimar Republic," in *Central European History*. Vol. 30, no. 1, 1997, pp. 1–24.

Koven, Seth, and Sonya Michel. "Womanly Duties: Maternalist Politics and the Origins of Welfare States in France, Germany, Great Britain, and the United States, 1880–1920," in *The American Historical Review*. Vol. 95, no. 4. October 1990, pp. 1076–1108.

Muthesius, Hans, ed. *Alice Salomon, die Begründerin der sozialen Frauenberufs in Deutschland*. Cologne: Carl Heymanns, 1958.

Otto, Hans-Uwe, and Heinz Sünker, eds. *Soziale Arbeit und Faschismus*. Frankfurt am Main: Suhrkamp, 1989.

Pfütze, Hermann. "Arbeit und Glück: Alice Salomons Schriften 1896–1908," in *Merkur: Deutsche Zeitschrift für europäisches Denken*. Vol. 52, no. 12. December 1998, pp. 1170–1174.

Rouette, Susanne. "Mothers and Citizens: Gender and Social Policy in Germany after the First World War," in *Central European History*. Vol. 30, no. 1, 1997, pp. 48–66.

Rupp, Leila J. "Sexuality and Politics in the Early Twentieth Century: The Case of the International Women's Movement," in *Feminist Studies*. Vol. 23, no. 3. Fall 1997, pp. 577–605.

Salomon, Alice. "Character is Destiny: An Autobiography" (unpublished manuscript, Alice Salomon Papers, Memoir Collection, Leo Baeck Institute, NY).

———. *Charakter ist Schicksal: Lebenserinnerungen*. Edited by Rüdeger Baron and Rolf Landwehr, translated by Rolf Landwehr. Weinheim: Beltz, 1983.

Wieler, Joachim. "Destination Social Work: Emigrés in a Woman's Profession," in Sibylle Quack, ed., *Between Sorrow and Strength: Women Refugees of the Nazi Period*. Cambridge, UK: Cambridge University Press, 1995, pp. 265–282.

——. *Er-Innerung eines zerstörten Lebensabends: Alice Salomon während der NS-Zeit (1933–1937) und im Exil (1937–1948)*. Darmstadt: Lingbach, 1987.

——. "Great Teachers: Alice Salomon," in *Journal of Teaching in Social Work*, Vol. 2, no. 2, 1988, pp. 165–171.

——. "A Life Dedicated to Humanity: Alice Salomon under Nazi Rule (1933–37) and in Exile (1937–48)," in *International Social Work*. Vol. 31, 1988, pp. 69–74.

——, and Susanne Zeller, eds. *Emigrierte Sozialarbeit: Portraits vertriebener SozialarbeiterInnen.* Freiburg im Breisgau: Lambertus, 1995.

John Haag,
Associate Professor of History,
University of Georgia, Athens, Georgia

Salomon, Charlotte (1917–1943)

German-Jewish artist whose Life? or Theater?, *a documentation of her life under Nazi rule, is considered to be one of the greatest artistic works of the Holocaust. Name variations: Lotte Nagler. Born Charlotte Salomon on April 16, 1917, in Berlin, Germany; perished in Auschwitz on October 10, 1943; daughter of Albert Salomon (1883–1976, a surgeon who achieved success as a physician and professor at the University of Berlin) and Franziska (Fränze) Grünwald Salomon (who suffered from depressions and committed suicide in 1926); married Alexander Nagler in Nice, on June 17, 1943.*

Admitted to the Art Academy of Berlin as one of that institution's few "non-Aryan" students (1935); expelled from the Academy because she was Jewish (1938); fled to France (early 1939); while in France, created an extraordinary autobiography in art entitled Leben? oder Theater? Ein Singespiel *(Life? or Theater? An Operetta), which was saved from destruction and became recognized as the visual equivalent of the diary of* *Anne Frank.

Charlotte Salomon was born in Berlin on April 16, 1917, the only child in an assimilated middle-class Jewish family. Her father Albert Salomon, a withdrawn, quiet man, had advanced from a modest family in the provinces to become a successful surgeon. After joining the faculty of the University of Berlin in 1921, he was promoted to full professor in 1927. Her mother **Fränze Grünwald Salomon** was the daughter of a prosperous Berlin medical family who prided themselves on their allegiance to German values and culture. When Charlotte was born, German Jews believed they were fully accepted by their Christian neighbors who would always protect them. Over 12,000 Jews died for the Fatherland in World War I, strengthening this belief.

Despite economic stability, Salomon's childhood was unstable for personal and historical reasons. Her aunt, also named Charlotte ("Lottchen"), committed suicide by drowning herself in 1913. (Years before, Charlotte's maternal great-aunt and her husband had also committed suicide.) As well, Germany's defeat in November 1918 led to political turmoil and bloodshed in the streets of Berlin and other cities. Communists unsuccessfully fomented revolution, while embittered war veterans founded the Nazi party. Anti-Semitism grew rapidly, and Jews were accused of treason and war profiteering. But until she was in her teens, Salomon was largely insulated from these corrosive forces. She loved to read and listen to music. After her nanny taught her how to dip a brush and paint, Salomon immersed herself in the world of color and images.

In February 1926, her mother Fränze committed suicide. Nine-year-old Salomon was not told the cause of her mother's death, and only years later did she discover this, as well as other family secrets. Germany's Jews had a high suicide rate, four times that of Catholics and almost twice that of Protestants. Many Jewish families, including Salomon's, were ashamed of this fact, which some regarded as another sign of their otherness and alienation from the larger society.

Despite this tragedy at a young age, Charlotte's childhood remained secure. She grew to love the singer **Paula Lindberg**, who became her stepmother in 1930. A talented mezzo-soprano who specialized in opera and the music of Bach, Lindberg had been born into a rabbi's family in a small German town, and had achieved considerable professional success by the time she married Albert Salomon. Never an outgoing child, Charlotte, or Lotte as her classmates called her, was happiest while alone, reading, dreaming and thinking—just like her father, the distinguished professor. Her peers at the Fürstin-Bismarck Gymnasium on the Sybelstrasse in nearby Charlottenburg would recall that Salomon was a quiet girl with more than a trace of lethargy in her personality. She lacked the self-confidence to be a group leader, and she never talked about or showed her works of art to her classmates. Salomon created an inner life, spending countless hours reading poetry, plays, and novels.

On January 30, 1933, Adolf Hitler was appointed chancellor of Germany and soon established a brutal dictatorship. A new and frightening world began to emerge for Salomon and other German Jews. A national boycott of Jewish businesses took place on April 1, 1933. Anti-Semitic legislation enacted at the same time cost her father his professorship at the University of Berlin; Paula's singing career also ended. At school, Salomon's situation was complicated, for not only were many of her classmates Jewish, but a significant part of the non-Jewish teaching staff and student body resisted Nazi racism. The school's motto, "To Unite You Not in Hatred but in Love," was an ideal many teachers and students believed in. Distressed by what was happening, Salomon voluntarily withdrew from the Fürstin-Bismarck Gymnasium in September 1933. A year later, when Jews were forced to transfer en masse to exclusively Jewish schools, she made no plans to enroll in university classes. She and her parents knew only too well that a Jewish woman with a university diploma had little chance of finding a job in a Nazi-controlled society.

Searching for a vocation, Salomon enrolled in a school of fashion design for Jewish girls, even though her stepmother felt at the time that she had little if any genuine artistic talent. Depressed and at loose ends in the spring of 1934, Salomon took a trip to Rome with her grandparents to celebrate her birthday. The trip transformed Salomon, who was entranced by the warm colors of the Italian culture and the architectural and artistic legacies of many epochs. From this point on, she regarded herself as an artist. Back in Berlin, her lack of interest in fashion design was all too apparent, however, and she was expelled from school. In a moment of uncharacteristic bravado, Salomon attempted to enroll at Berlin's Vereinigte Staatschule für Freie und Angewandte Kunst (Academy of Art), located in an imposing building on the Hardenbergstrasse. Even though she was Jewish, an official permitted her to take the exam, but in the end an "Aryan" candidate was chosen to fill her slot. This experience made Salomon more determined than ever not to abandon art which was the only means to express her emotions in a increasingly hostile world, and she asked her parents to hire a private art tutor. Although skeptical of her gifts, they agreed. Motivated more than ever to learn the basics of draughtsmanship, color, and composition, she finished her private studies in mid-1935 and once again applied for admission to the Art Academy. To her amazement, she was accepted as one of that institution's very few Jewish students, beginning her studies in October 1935.

In the convoluted racial theories which prevailed in Nazi Germany in 1935, individuals of part-Jewish ancestry whose fathers had fought for the Fatherland in World War I could still be admitted on a case-by-case basis. Although she was a "full Jewess," Salomon obviously made a highly favorable impression on the Admissions Committee. She was one of only two candidates of "full-Jewish ancestry" admitted that year. The surviving minutes note that despite her racial background, her artistic abilities were "beyond doubt," and there was "no reason to doubt her German attitude." Although a Nazi student leader objected that the presence of a Jewish female constituted "a danger" to Aryan males, the Admissions Committee argued that no such threat existed because of Fräulein Salomon's "reserved nature."

Salomon began her studies at the Art Academy just as the infamous Nuremberg Laws transforming German Jews into second-class citizens were enacted. Strangely enough, she was able to live a life that remained precariously "normal." Not all of the teachers or students at the Academy were Nazis, and she was generally treated with respect despite her unique status. In 1937, she fell in love with the music teacher and theorist Alfred Wolfsohn (1896–1962), an artist who had been seriously shell-shocked in World War I. As they became intimate, Salomon confided to Wolfsohn her anxieties, including the fear that hers was a life cursed by a family history of mental instability and suicide, which she suspected had led to the deaths of several people near and dear to her, possibly even her own mother. Wolfsohn, old enough to be her father, calmed her fears, encouraging her to work through these concerns by means of her art. In her great work *Life? or Theater?*, Salomon would recollect Wolfsohn's calming effect by presenting him as the character "Amadeus Daberlohn," who counseled her during a period of deep depression, stating, "Instead of taking your own life in such a horrible way, why don't you make use of the same powers to describe your life?"

This calm period was brought to an end with terrifying suddenness during the night of November 9–10, 1938. The Nazi regime, using the death of a Nazi diplomat shot by a distraught Jewish refugee in Paris as a pretext, unleashed a nationwide anti-Jewish reign of terror. In one night, known as *Kristallnacht* (Night of the Broken Glass), scores of Jews were killed; 191 synagogues were burned; and Jewish-owned shops and businesses were destroyed (25 million marks in damages occurred, of which fully 5 million was for broken glass). German Jews lost whatever vestiges of human rights they had retained since 1933. Salomon's father was imprisoned in the notorious Sachsenhausen concentration camp which further underlined the family's peril. Upon his release, the family made plans to leave Germany as quickly as possible.

Charlotte
Salomon

Unlike many desperate German Jews in the late 1930s, the Salomon family had a place of refuge. Charlotte's maternal grandparents, Ludwig and **Marianne Benda Grünwald**, had lived in freedom since 1934. A wealthy German-American friend of theirs, **Ottilie Gobel Moore**

(1902–1972), had settled on the French Riviera in 1928, and while visiting the Grünwalds in Berlin in early 1933, during the first terror-filled days of the Nazi regime, she offered refuge at her villa "l'Ermitage" in Villefranche-sur-Mer. After a brief attempt to settle in Italy in 1934, the

Grünwalds moved to Villefranche, where Moore was committed to caring for a large number of orphans and exiles from Fascist persecution. In January 1939, Charlotte left Germany for France, where she was immediately welcomed by Moore, who offered her the same open-ended hospitality that her grandparents had enjoyed for more than five years. Back in Berlin, Albert and Paula made plans to join the rest of their family. With the help of a non-Jewish Swedish friend, they procured false passports to the Netherlands, where they settled in Amsterdam a few weeks after Charlotte arrived in southern France.

The war raged on, and I sat by the sea and saw deep into the heart of humankind.

—Charlotte Salomon

Salomon quickly settled in with her grandparents, who enjoyed pleasures that were denied the great majority of Jewish refugees. In her first months on France's breathtaking Côte d'Azur, an exuberant Salomon felt personally and artistically liberated. In her own words, she was now "renewed and clear, out of so much suffering and sorrow." Soon, however, dark and ominous forces entered this sunny, untroubled world. In conversations with her grandfather, she received confirmation of what she had long suspected—her mother had committed suicide in a fit of depression.

For the young artist, the forces of anti-Semitism seemed to combine with a genealogy of doom which had taken her mother, her aunt, and her great-grandmother. Wolfsohn had known the secret of her mother's suicide but did not tell her, fearing it might cause self-destruction. Thrown into despair, Salomon suffered a nervous breakdown and tried to jump out a window. Tragically, her grandmother's delicate psychological equilibrium snapped under these trying circumstances in 1940, and she took her own life, adding to the family legacy from which Charlotte Salomon believed she could not escape. She and her grandfather found it impossible to live together, so he moved to Nice while she remained in Villefranche, painting and dreaming.

The horror of learning of her family legacy was soon followed by the German invasion and defeat of France in May and June 1940. The little security remaining in Salomon's life was shattered forever. She and her grandfather were deported to the infamous Gurs detention camp in the Pyrenees. Fortunately, both were released in mid-July 1940 after several weeks' incarceration. They returned to Villefranche, where Salomon poured out her feelings in her art. Aloof and hypersensitive, she did not speak to her grandfather or Moore for days at a time, communicating instead with bright colors on paper.

As violence and insecurity grew, Salomon created a new world through her art. Drawing powerful images to represent her past, whether real or symbolic, she told her story, the essence of her life. In little over a year, from 1941 to 1942, Salomon created a massive sequence of gouache paintings on paper which fused autobiography and documentation of Nazi racism as it impacted on her and those near and dear to her. Entitled *Life? or Theater? (Leben? oder Theater? Ein Singespiel)*, the work consisted of 1,325 paintings. Much more than a diary in pictures, which is what many critics first titled it, the paintings are an autobiographical drama recounting the lives of her lead character "Charlotte Kann" and her family. The work is unique. One critic has argued that it is neither exclusively art nor literature, but "cinema on paper" and thus an important part of the classic period of German film. *Life? or Theater?* has extraordinary power and intensity, in part because of the simple, almost folk-art technique employed by Salomon, who showed little or no objectivity or detachment from what she depicted. Furthermore, she supplied a text for each picture, often speaking to the viewer in the frankest possible terms. For example, one of the gouaches depicted her in gray, showing her grabbing her head with the legend: "Dear God, just let me not go mad." *Life? or Theater?* portrays the end of her beloved stepmother's musical career as a result of Nazi persecution as well as the sudden termination of her father's academic and medical careers. Salomon is depicted becoming alienated from former friends, her school, her native land, language, and family.

The psychological blows Salomon was forced to absorb were almost too much to bear and even then, they did not cease. By 1941, Amsterdam was under German occupation, so she was unable to communicate with her father and stepmother. Despite the kindness of Moore, Salomon was often profoundly depressed. In one of her captions, she observed: "The war raged on, and I sat by the sea and saw deep into the heart of humankind." Only her art was therapy for her emotional burdens. For over a year, she worked as if possessed. Because of the scarcity of paper due to the war, she painted on both sides of sheets to conserve materials, choosing for the final version the side she found most expressive of her ideas.

Despite the emotionally tense and even tragic subject matter of *Life? or Theater?*, parts of the cycle are radiant. Despair and ecstasy mingle as Salomon depicts her life in Berlin pursuing her artistic goals despite Nazi attempts to deny them. Her love for her stepmother, and her relationship with "Amadeus Daberlohn" (Wolfsohn), are touchingly depicted from one picture to the next. The entire work is evocative of post-Romantic German culture in that it mingles death and despair with a lyrical eroticism (Salomon loved music, one of her favorite works being Schubert's "Death and the Maiden," both the *Lied* and the string quartet). In one moving picture, she sings to her grandmother the vocal parts of Beethoven's Ninth Symphony while drawing her face. Much of the work is tagged with musical cues, carefully indicating where popular music of pre-Hitler Germany as well as where compositions by Bach, Mozart, Beethoven, Schubert, Weber, and Bizet should be introduced. Besides her own words, Salomon incorporated quotations from Goethe, Nietzsche, Heine, and Verlaine as well as newspaper headlines and Biblical verse.

While she feverishly attempted to put in permanent form the story of her anguished life, the world around her continued to disintegrate. Although she and her grandfather lived in relatively privileged circumstances for several years because of the kindness of Moore, this situation was to change. In September 1941, when Moore left for the United States with nine refugee children, it was Salomon's last chance to escape the Nazi menace. But the U.S. State Department was unsympathetic to the plight of Jewish refugees, refusing to issue visas, and she doubtless did not want to abandon her aged grandfather or her parents who were still in Amsterdam. Besides, the part of France she lived in was ruled by the collaborationist Vichy French regime, which was anti-Semitic but had many officials who were lax in enforcing its decrees. Even the German occupation of southern France, in November 1942, gave Salomon a ray of hope, for the Côte d'Azur was taken over by Italy, and it quickly became clear that Italian occupation officials would not participate in the deportation of Jewish refugees.

The Nazi death machine ground relentlessly forward, however, coming ever closer. When she completed *Life? or Theater?*, she became concerned about its fate and her own precarious prospects for survival. She entrusted two precious packages to a local physician, telling him, "Keep this safe, it is my whole life." With her great work completed and in safe hands, Salomon's world began to unravel. In February 1943, grandfather Ludwig collapsed on a Nice

street and died. Now alone, she met another Jewish refugee who had benefited from Moore's kindness, Austrian-born Alexander Nagler. Nagler, from a wealthy family, had been pampered in his youth but was now shattered and beaten. He drank too much and seemed incapable of making any realistic plans for the future. Salomon perhaps was drawn to him as much for the emotional security she could provide as for whatever strength he might give her. She married Nagler in Nice on June 17, 1943. Unfortunately, while applying for his marriage license, he had unwisely revealed his true address to the police. By this time, the Côte d'Azur had been occupied by the Germans, and on September 21, 1943, a Gestapo truck arrived at l'Hermitage, arresting Salomon and Nagler. After several weeks' imprisonment at the Drancy camp near Paris, they were "resettled to the east" on October 7, 1943. After a trip of three days and nights, Transport 60 arrived at Auschwitz on October 10. Salomon, five months pregnant, was selected for immediate gassing and was dead before the end of that day.

Charlotte Salomon, Self-Portrait.

Her father Albert and stepmother Paula survived the war, learning about Charlotte's death from her French friends. Moore returned to Villefranche in 1946 and retrieved most of her own possessions as well as Charlotte's paintings. At first, she did not wish to give these to the Salomons, but in 1947 she relented. For a number of years, they remained in Amsterdam unknown to the world. Her work was introduced in 1963 in Germany and the United States when 80 selections from *Life? or Theater?*, labeled a "diary in pictures," appeared in simultaneous publications. This first edition was incomplete and indeed was "edited" in places to the point of bowdlerization because of family sensibilities. (One painting, which depicted her grandfather saying to her, "Oh just do it, kill yourself too, so this yakking of yours can stop!," appeared in print with these words airbrushed out.) In 1981, a virtually complete edition of her work was published, so that the full power of her vision was visible for all to behold. The critic Ad Peterson, who first viewed Salomon's legacy as a "curious document," now spoke of it as a "unique work, with nothing else of its conception and size in art history."

SOURCES:

Costanza, Mary S. *The Living Witness: Art in the Concentration Camps and Ghettos.* NY: The Free Press, 1982.

Eichenbaum, Pola. *Jewish Artists Who Perished in the Holocaust.* Tel-Aviv: Tel-Aviv Museum, 1968 (exhibition catalog).

Felstiner, Mary. "Charlotte Salomon's Inward-turning Testimony," in Geoffrey H. Hartman, ed., *Holocaust Remembrance: The Shapes of Memory.* Oxford, UK: Blackwell, 1994, pp. 104–116, 279–282.

Felstiner, Mary Lowenthal. "Engendering an Autobiography in Art: Charlotte Salomon's 'Life? or Theater?,'" in Susan Gorag Bell and Marilyn Yalom, eds., *Revealing Lives: Autobiography, Biography, and Gender.* Albany, NY: State University of New York Press, 1990, pp. 183–192.

———. *To Paint Her Life: Charlotte Salomon in the Nazi Era.* NY: HarperCollins, 1994.

Griffin, Susan. *A Chorus of Stones: The Private Life of War.* NY: Doubleday, 1992.

Heller, Nadine V. "Cinema on Paper: Charlotte Salomon's Life or Theater?," in *Arts Magazine.* Vol. 64, no. 8. April 1990.

Kaplan, Marion. "Jewish Women in Nazi Germany: Daily Life, Daily Struggles, 1933–1939," in *Feminist Studies.* Vol. 16, no. 3. Fall 1990, pp. 579–606.

Levine, Amy E. "Charlotte Salomon: Psychological Resolution through Art," M.A. thesis, Smith College, 1984.

Rupp, Leila J. "Committing survival," in *Women's Review of Books.* Vol. 12, no. 2. November 1994, pp. 8–9.

Salomon, Charlotte. *Charlotte: A Diary in Pictures.* Comment by Paul Tillich. NY: Harcourt, Brace & World, 1963.

———. *Charlotte: Life or Theater? An Autobiographical Play by Charlotte Salomon.* Trans. by Leila Vennewitz. NY: Viking, 1981.

Stevens, Mark. "Portraits of Pain," in *Newsweek.* Vol. 98, no. 11. September 14, 1981, p. 97.

COLLECTIONS:

Salomon's *Life? or Theater?* is held by the Jewish Historical Museum in Amsterdam, where 60 of her paintings are on permanent display.

RELATED MEDIA:

Charlotte (film), by **Judith Herzberg** and Frans Weisz.

John Haag,
Associate Professor of History,
University of Georgia, Athens, Georgia

Salonina (r. 254–268)

Roman empress. Reigned from 254 to 268; born Cornelia Salonina Chrysogone; married Gallienus (c. 218–268), emperor of Rome (r. 253–268).

Salonina, thought be a cultivated woman, was probably a Greek, possibly from Bithynia. Married to Gallienus, emperor of Rome, she and her husband were friends of Plotinus and other intellectuals. Gallienus also had a concubine named **Pipa**.

Salonnières (fl. 17th and 18th c.)

Women who operated as agents and funding agencies for the most important writers, philosophes, and artists, and who encouraged and supported the founding of the French Academy as well as the writing of the Encyclopedia.

Created in the Marquise de Rambouillet's famous chambre bleue (1618), salons played an important role in the shaping of the French Academy; Lambert opened her salon which was called the "antechamber of the Academy" since she personally selected half of the Academy's members (1710); Tencin put artists, writers, and philosophes on an equal footing with aristocrats at her salon (1729); Geoffrin established a salon which was home to philosophes while a second salon sustained artists; her support over several decades of the writers of the Encyclopedia *was critical to its success; Deffand's rival salon was important for its foreign influence, especially English; Lespinasse included many foreigners as well; salonnières were agents of change and did much to foster modern concepts of equality, democracy, and liberty.*

"Between conversation and civilization, the art of talk and the art of living, there has always been a vital link," writes Peter Quennell in *Affairs of the Mind.* Women played a central role in the development of the salon which has been called the cradle of the French Revolution. Indeed, many of our modern concepts of individual liberty, equality, and democracy were born in this unique French institution. Salons were not receptions. They were groups of carefully selected people who came together to discuss a common topic skillfully directed by a hostess or *salonnière.* Members of salons sought to attain the highest ideals of truth and beauty as well as to emphasize perfection, proportion, and harmony which they believed led to unity and temperance. Freedom, not license, they felt, represented an opportunity to stimulate and enlarge intellectual life.

A salon required two elements—a good hostess and literary lions. Leaders of salons selected participants and directed the flow of conversation. It was commonly said: "Hostesses, like poets, are born, not made." Women in 17th- and 18th-century French salons rose to positions of power and influence because they were agents and granting agencies rather than mere hosts. Their stamp of approval determined what books were read, what plays were attended, and what art was purchased. Salonnières often found funding for their protégés, some of whom they supported entire lifetimes. Their extensive networks were essential to success, and few philosophes, writers, or artists achieved success without their assistance. Their influence was also felt in the creation of cultural institutions like the Academies, the Comédie Française, government pension lists, and the administration of the book trade. The modern world continues to benefit from the influence wielded by this unique group of women.

The ascendancy of French women has several explanations. During the Middle Ages, women were considered supreme; the age of chivalry elevated their status, especially in France. A series of kings' mistresses established a powerful political dynasty which was imitated in the arts. The salonnières' cultural dominance was a counterpart to the political influence already wielded by some women at court. Finally, there was a long tradition of intellectual comradeship between the sexes in France. It is not surprising that given the opportunity, French women gained prominence and a breadth of view not found in other parts of Europe.

The history of the salon begins with ✍▶ **Catherine de Vivonne, Marquise de Rambouillet** (1588–1665), who invited a group of writers, scholars, nobles, and women to regular social gatherings in her *chambre bleue.* Playing a major role in shaping French classical taste, Rambouillet encouraged the original members of the French Academy as they struggled to re-

construct the French language. Boussuet, La Rochefoucauld, *****Marie-Madeleine de La Fayette**, Corneille, *****Marie de Sévigné**, the *****Duchesse de Longueville**, *****Madeleine de Scudéry**, and the *****Duchesse de Montpensier** all met at the Hôtel Rambouillet. Since she proposed so many of the candidates who were selected for membership, Rambouillet's name is inseparably connected with the French Academy, and the tradition of having salonnières select Academy members continued long after her death. Despite the fact that women were excluded from authorship, Mademoiselle de Scudéry and Madame de La Fayette wrote long romances expressing their ideas, dreams, and desires, no doubt influenced by the literary company they kept. La Fayette's much celebrated *Princesse de Clèves* is one of the better-known works by women which emerged from the Rambouillet salon. Many of the women involved in this circle would later found their own salons and become collectively known as the *Précieuses.* These women fundamentally shaped the French Academy.

Salons lost their importance during the reign of Louis XIV when all activity was centralized in the court of the Sun King, then reappeared during the reign of Louis XV. Mme de Lambert's salon was the bridge between 17th-century and 18th-century institutions. A rich widow, ✍▶ **Anne Thérèse de Marguenat de Courcelles, Marquise de Lambert** (1647–1733) had been educated by her stepfather, Bachaumont. When she opened her salon in 1710 in the Palais Mazarin, she insisted upon a high standard of ethics in a time of license. Her salon was characterized as dignified, tranquil, and constructive and was called the "antechamber of the Academy" as she was credited with creating half of the Academy's membership. Lambert was a writer, and although her works, chiefly on education, were ostensibly produced for her children, they were read by a much larger audience. She was also responsible for the substitution of French scientific formulas for Latin ones: Fontenelle facilitated this change in order that Lambert might be able to read his scientific treatises.

The character of the salon alters with the debut of the Marquise de Tencin in 1729. An ex-mistress of Philippe II, duke of Orléans (regent for Louis XV), ✍▶ **Claudine Alexandrine Guérin de Tencin** (1685–1749) was famous for organizing the notorious fêtes at Saint-Cloud. A runaway nun, she was liberal and déclassé, and it seems fitting that her illegitimate son, Jean d'Alembert (1717–1783), was the famous editor of the *Encyclopédie.* Tencin abandoned him to his father, the Chevalier Destouches, who pro-

✍▶

*See sidebar
on the
following page*

✍▶

*See sidebars
on the
following page*

Rambouillet, Catherine de Vivonne, Marquise de (1588–1665)

French salonnière of the first salon who left an indelible mark on the history of French thought, language, and literature. Name variations: Marquise de Rambouillet. Born in Rome in 1588; died in December 1665; daughter of Jean Vivonne, marquis de Pisani, and Julia (or Giulia) Savelli, a Roman woman of noble family; married Charles d'Angennes, marquis of Rambouillet; children: Julie d'Angennes, duchesse de Montausier; Angélique d'Angennes (who was the first wife of the marquis de Grignan).

Known as the founder of preciosity (a manner of thought and exchange which reflected the utmost delicacy of taste), Catherine de Vivonne, marquise de Rambouillet, presided over the first of the salons which were to dominate French intellectual and literary life during the 17th and 18th centuries. "She drew up a new code of behavior, of manners, and of speech," notes one historian, "and she encouraged the intellectual appreciation of beauty, and the study of language and letters." While the ideal of the "cultivated man" which Rambouillet inspired was lauded by many, it was mocked by others, including Molière in his famous *Les Précieuses ridicules.*

She was born in Rome in 1588, the daughter of Jean de Vivonne, marquis of Pisani, and **Julia Savelli**, a Roman of noble birth. At age 12, Catherine was married to Charles d'Angennes, who was to become marquis of Rambouillet. In France, disliking both the coarseness and the intrigue of court life under Henry IV, she conceived of an alternative. There was at the time no precedent for the salon Rambouillet founded in a mansion located near the Louvre. There, at what would be known as the Hôtel Rambouillet, in 1618 she remodeled the structure so as to arrange a suite of large reception rooms for the purpose of gathering intellectuals, nobility, and literary greats for discussion. Rambouillet's salon served as the center of France's social and literary currents for 30 years.

There were likely many reasons for her success. She was not alone in her dislike of the court, and many found her gatherings and the way of life which was developed there a new and welcome avenue of exchange and expression. Her fine tastes have been attributed to her Roman nationality as well as her early training. Although

there is no known portrait of her in existence, she was also reputedly beautiful. Regardless of the qualities which allowed her to preside for so many years over gatherings of France's elite, there is no question as to the enormous extent of her influence. French men of letters owed the advancement of their position to her salon, and, as noted in the 1910 edition of the *Encyclopedia Britannica,* "the almost uniform excellence of the memoirs and letters of 17th-century Frenchmen and Frenchwomen may be traced largely to the development of conversation as a fine art at the Hôtel Rambouillet, and the consequent establishment of a standard of clear and adequate expression." Thanks to Rambouillet's vision, such a standard was engaged in many influential salons that appeared in France and were presided over by women who achieved great importance in French cultural life by following Rambouillet's example.

Among the notable events originating from Rambouillet's salon was a poetry collection on different flowers called the *Guirlande de Julie,* a work composed by the day's most famous poets and addressed to Rambouillet's eldest daughter **Julie d'Angennes** (later duchesse de Montausier). In fact, much of the preciosity which later earned the salon ridicule has been attributed to Julie. By the mid-17th century, Rambouillet's extraordinary influence waned as Louis XIV tolerated no social rivals to his court. She continued to preside over her salon, however, until her death in December 1665.

Lambert, Anne Thérèse de Marguenat de Courcelles, Marquise de (1647–1733)

French salonnière. Name variations: Marquise de Lambert. Born in Paris, France, in 1647; died in 1733; stepdaughter of Bachaumont.

Tencin, Claudine Alexandrine Guérin de (1685–1749)

French writer and society leader. Name variations: Madame de Tencin; Marquise de Tencin. Born in 1685; died in 1749; sister of **Madame de Ferriol**; mistress of Philippe II also known as Philip or Philippe Bourbon-Orleans (1674–1723), 2nd duke of Orléans and regent for Louis XV (1710–1774), king of France (r. 1715–1774); children: illegitimate son, Jean Le Rond d'Alembert (1717–1783), was the famous editor of the Encyclopédie.

vided for his maintenance and education. She was audacious and ambitious, fond of intrigue, highly intelligent, and imaginative, so it was no difficult task to gather the most brilliant minds around her. Whereas Lambert had held separate

salons for nobility and commoners, Tencin included both groups. Influential until her death in 1749, Tencin held the first salon where writers and artists were elevated to the same status as aristocrats: Fontenelle, Marivaux, Montesquieu,

Chesterfield, and Grimm were among those who frequented.

The most famous salonnière, *Marie Thérèse Geoffrin (1699–1777), was a friend and neighbor of Tencin's. Bourgeois rather than aristocratic, Mme Geoffin was the wealthy wife of a glass manufacturer. She began frequenting the Tencin salon before inviting some of its members for Wednesday dinners in 1737. Montesquieu, Voltaire, Diderot, d'Alembert, Lord Shelbourne, Horace Walpole, Grimm, and Bernardin de Saint-Pierre were among her circle. Mme Geoffrin also patronized the arts and began a second salon for artists on Mondays. It was, however, the philosophes who set the tone at Geoffrin's. Her involvement was considerable and she gave large amounts of her fortune to underwrite the *Encyclopédie*. Her reputation was international, and she corresponded with *Catherine II the Great, Empress *Maria Theresa of Austria, and King Stanislaus Augustus of Poland, who was like a son to her. A sober, honest woman, Geoffrin was known for her many acts of kindness to the writers and artists whom she constantly supported as well as for her largesse to the poor. Such was her influence that a common joke of the time went: "I don't know him, but he must have wit, I suppose, since he visits Mme Geoffrin." She was often called the "foster mother of the philosophes."

Mme Geoffrin's most formidable rival was Mme du Deffand. These two remarkable women shared no love for each other although Geoffrin was generally on equitable terms with almost everyone. While Geoffrin is known for her patronage, Marie Anne de Vichy-Chamrond, Marquise du Deffand (1697–1780) is remembered for her voluminous correspondence with Horace Walpole, the Duchesse de Choiseul, and Voltaire. Cultivated and intense, Deffand was dissatisfied by nature. Hers was a stressful life with much inner loneliness and partial failure. Critical of others and of herself, she was her own worst enemy and never at peace. She was born in 1697, the daughter of the Comte de Chamrond. Sent to a convent school in Paris, she declared herself a skeptic though she disapproved of open attacks on the church. She married the Marquis du Deffand, a distant cousin, then became the regent's mistress as well as the mistress of his crony, the Comte de Fargis. Bored with her marriage, she arranged a legal separation from her husband and returned to Paris.

When Mme du Deffand's husband died in 1750, and she regained the part of her dowry that he had retained, she resolved to found a salon. Living in a suite attached to the Convent of St. Joseph, she received guests every day after six. Unlike Geoffrin whose salon was almost all male, Deffand included women. The Maréchale de Luxembourg and the Duchesse de Choiseul were stars at Deffand's, while d'Alembert, Montesquieu, Maupertuis, Beaumarchais, and Lady *Mary Hervey and George Selwyn all frequented the lively and entertaining evenings.

But Deffand began to go blind in her 50s and feared her salon would have to close. In hopes that rest would aid a cure, she decided to visit her birthplace, spending time with her brother, Gaspard de Vichy, and his family. Here she discovered a mystery child, Julie de Lespinasse (1732–1776), who would one day found her own salon. Born in 1732, Julie grew up in the home of a doctor and a midwife, but she was actually the illegitimate daughter of the Comtesse d'Albon whose husband left her after the birth of four children. Subsequently the Comtesse had two other children, a son who became a monk, and her daughter Julie. When the Comtesse died, the 15-year-old Lespinasse turned her annuity of a few hundred francs over to her elder brother; as an orphan, she was penniless from that point forward. Lespinasse was invited to look after the children of Comte Gaspard de Vichy who married one of her half-sisters. Although the Vichy children loved her, the young woman's life was miserable. It seems almost certain that Comte Gaspard had been Comtesse d'Albon's lover and so was, in fact, Julie's father. Wishing to hush up his guilty secret, he took his anger out on the girl. After four miserable years, the young woman had resolved to enter a convent; then Mme du Deffand arrived.

Without realizing Lespinasse was her niece, Deffand took an instant liking to the young girl. Here was someone with whom she could talk, someone who loved the French classics and knew English and Italian. When the girl re-

Deffand, Marie Anne de Vichy-Chamrond, Marquise du (1697–1780)

French patron of fashion and literature. Name variations: *Madame du Deffand; Marquise du Deffand; Marie de Vichy-Chamrond.* Born Marie Anne de Vichy-Chamrond in 1697; died in 1780; daughter of the Comte de Chamrond; sister of Gaspard de Vichy; married the Marquis du Deffand, a distant cousin.

SUGGESTED READING:
Craveri, Benedetta. *Madame Du Deffand & Her World.* Trans. by Teresa Waugh. Godine, 1994.

See sidebar on the following page

Lespinasse, Julie de (1732–1776)

French writer and salonnière whose salon was a meeting place for writers of the Encyclopédie. *Name variations: L'Espinasse. Born Jeanne Julie Éléonore de Lespinasse at Lyons on November 9, 1732; died in Paris on May 23, 1776; born out of wedlock to the Comtesse d'Albon and (probably) Comte Gaspard de Vichy; brought up as the daughter of Claude Lespinasse.*

Julie de Lespinasse was one of two children born out of wedlock to the **Comtesse d'Albon**, whose husband had left her after the births of their first four children. It is likely that Comte Gaspard de Vichy was Julie's father, a fact which was kept secret. She was raised as the daughter of a doctor, Claude Lespinasse, and attended a convent school.

Left penniless following her mother's death, Lespinasse was invited to care for the children of Comte Gaspard de Vichy, who had married Julie's half-sister **Mme de Vichy**. Four years into her engagement as governess, she met *Marie du Deffand who did not realize at the time that Julie was her niece. Employing Lespinasse as her companion, Deffand brought her back to her home in Paris where Lespinasse lived on the floor above. Their alliance, which lasted from 1754 to 1764, grew strained as Lespinasse's popularity with Deffand's salon guests grew. The affections shown toward Lespinasse by philosopher and mathematician Jean d'Alembert (the greatest ornament of Deffand's salon) deepened the estrangement between the two women, and in 1764, following a violent quarrel, Lespinasse founded her own salon in the rue Saint-Dominique.

Although d'Alembert came to share a roof there with Lespinasse, their relationship was free from scandal, allowing him to lead a comfortable existence while she benefited from the influence his presence lent to her salon.

Lespinasse, presiding over the most popular gatherings in Paris, prompted the following laudatory remarks in the *Memoir of Marmontel*: "The circle was formed of persons who were not bound together. She had taken them here and there in society, but so well assorted were they that once there they fell into harmony like the strings of an instrument touched by an able hand. Following out that comparison, I may say that she played the instrument with an art that came of genius." Her salon became the center for the writers of the famous *Encyclopédie*, edited by d'Alembert, and her influence as a respected and beloved woman among great men was widespread.

In her day, even Lespinasse's closest friends were unaware of her amorous obsessions, her legendary passions that would inform her *Lettres* (2 vols., 1809). The Spanish Marquis de Mora was her first attachment, but in 1772 he had to return to Spain because he was dying of consumption. That year, Lespinasse met Comte de Guibert. Her letters to de Guibert, referred to by one historian as "the worthless object of her fatal infatuation," began in 1773 and were ranked by Sainte-Beuve as belonging to the same category of outpourings as those of *Heloise and the Portuguese nun *Mariana Alcoforado. In 1774, Lespinasse wrote to de Guibert: "You know that when I hate you, it is because I love you to a point of passion that unhinges my soul."

Lespinasse's letters reflect the struggle between her feelings for de Mora and her desire for de Guibert. De Guibert's marriage to another and de Mora's death in 1774 on his way back to Paris left her in misery. To calm her nerves, she used opium sedatives, and the deterioration in her health was likely accelerated by both the drug use and her despair. She died on May 23, 1776. Her writings include not only her letters but also two chapters which were meant as a sequel to *Sentimental Journey* by Laurence Sterne.

sponded to the older woman's kindness, Deffand began to envision a life together in Paris with Lespinasse as her paid companion. Her friends suggested the younger woman live in a convent nearby rather than actually living with Deffand, but she would have none of it. Soon Julie de Lespinasse was settled on the floor above her employer and fitted out with new clothes.

Lespinasse adjusted immediately to life in Paris. The daily routine resumed—supper with three or four guests and a larger party each week. There were trips to the opera and the Comédie Française. Since Deffand was an insomniac, the two women often drove around the streets of Paris until 2 AM. For the first time in her young life, Mlle de Lespinasse was treated as an equal. Hénault, La Harpe, the Maréchal de Luxembourg were all enchanted by her, and d'Alembert formed a touching friendship which lasted her lifetime. Lespinasse's charm was a great contrast to Deffand's biting sarcasm. The first trouble came when the older woman refused to allow a young Irish nobleman entry to her home after he fell in love with the charming young woman. Scenes and reconciliations became the order of the day. Estrangement grew when Deffand discovered that her good friend d'Alembert, the greatest ornament of her salon, had transferred his devotion to Lespinasse.

Corneille reading Polyeucte at the Hôtel Rambouillet.

Desiring more of Lespinasse's company, d'Alembert began to arrive early at the "floor above." This informal gathering grew as Turgot, Condorcet, Marmontel, La Harpe and Hénault joined the group. Leaving her bedroom an hour earlier one day, Deffand heard voices upstairs and discovered the existence of a rival salon. In his memoirs, Marmontel describes the ensuing scene as "the most celebrated quarrel in the literary history of eighteenth century France." Making the situation worse, all the guests, old friends of Mme du Deffand, sided with the newcomer, leading to an irreparable breach between the two women. The parting, however, was to prove a blessing for both. Lespinasse spread her wings, while Deffand uncharacteristically relied on her friends in her hour of anguish, thus tasting the depths of enduring friendship for the first time. Within a year, she began a correspondence with Horace Walpole. In this important literary legacy (over 1,000 letters survive), her vibrant spirit emerges triumphant over old age, bitterness, and blindness.

The influence of [these] women in France by the middle of the 18th century had become so powerful that a man could hardly rise without the co-operation of some one of them.

—Helen Clergue

D'Alembert immediately came to his beloved Lespinasse's rescue. Both were illegitimate children of prominent parents and no doubt he understood her situation well. He introduced the young woman to Mme Geoffrin who loved her from the start. She treated her as a daughter and included her as the only woman guest at her Wednesday dinners. With her typical generosity, Geoffrin sold three of Van Loo's paintings from her extensive collection and gave the proceeds to the younger woman who used them to set up her own establishment. Many of Geoffrin's circle also joined this new salon. The two women were great friends, and it was not uncommon for them to call on each other twice a day. Although some refused to attend a salon hosted by "a former companion of Mme du Deffand," most were only too eager to be enrolled as one of her guests. "Madame Geoffrin was feared; Madame du Deffand admired; . . . Julie de Lespinasse loved," said the Marquis de Ségur. Lespinasse gathered a wide variety of guests bound by no common tie. Her salon met daily from five to nine. International visitors were often included and Creutz, the Swedish ambassador, Abbé Galiani, the Neapolitan, and Lord Shelbourne attended when they were in Paris. British aristocrats and intellectuals were lionized in the salons, but particularly in Lespinasse's; she was an Anglophile.

While the salons were cultural institutions of great importance, they also represented a tangled web of human relationships. Adored by many men and women, Lespinasse fell in love with the Spanish Marquis de Mora, 12 years her junior. But de Mora was slowly dying of consumption and had to return to Spain. In 1772, she met Comte de Guibert and was soon again in love. Sainte-Beuve ranks her letters to him, quite justly, with the outpourings of *Heloise,

but the consumptive de Mora was still corresponding with her and the dual passions caused Lespinasse great anxiety. While de Mora wrote her tender letters, she continued her fervent prose to Guibert. During this tumultuous time, de Mora died and Guibert married, a great blow. Throughout d'Alembert remained her staunch and dedicated friend, despite the fact that Lespinasse was so distracted; she lost interest in her salon and her friends. Abetted by opium sedatives to calm her nerves, her health deteriorated, and she became increasingly frail. Lespinasse died leaving small tokens of affections to Mme Geoffrin and d'Alembert.

Salons grew, in part, because of the restrictions life imposed on women in pre-Revolutionary France. It was neither easy nor safe to get about the dirty and uncomfortable streets of Paris. Walks, drives, concerts, lectures, and shopping trips were infrequent. Since they were barred from the outside world, women invited the world to come to them, with amazing results. There were few journals and newspapers to spread new ideas, so the salon—as well as the literary café—became the principal means by which opinion on current events was circulated. Salons also opened new vistas for France. During Louis XIV's reign, the French never looked beyond their borders, confining themselves to their own civilization. It was the 18th-century salon which awoke them to the knowledge that ideas worth attention existed elsewhere.

Salons encouraged platonic friendships and intellectual exchange between women and men. Deffand's friendship with Walpole, d'Alembert's with Lespinasse, and Geoffrin's with Stanislaus Augustus of Poland are examples of the remarkable friendships which were an 18th-century ideal. Salons allowed continuous contact between the sexes. They offered a place where women and men could share common pursuits. This unique institution made substantial contributions to philosophy, literature, and the arts, as well as to the modern view of society. Intellectual liberty, liberty of thought, and liberty of discussion were shared goals. A sense of fraternity and comradeship characterized the best features of the salon. It has been said, "Equality of sex, of mind, and of person was never more conspicuous than in the salon of the eighteenth century."

SOURCES:

Batiffol, Louis, André Hallays, Raul Reboux Nozère, and André Bellessort. *The Great Literary Salons.* London: Thornton Butterworth, 1930.

Clergue, Helen. *The Salon.* NY: Burt Franklin, 1907 (reprint 1971).

Ducros, Louis. *French Society in the Eighteenth Century.* NY: Putnam, 1927.

Glotz, Marguerite, and Madeleine Marie. *Salons du xviiie Siècle*. Paris: Hachette, 1945.

Grand, Serge. *Ces Bonnes Femmes du XVIIIe*. Paris: Pierre Horay, 1985.

Kastner, L.E., and Henry Gibson Atkins. *A Short History of French Literature*. Port Washington, NY: Kennikat Press, 1970.

Lougee, Carolyn C. *Le Paradis des Femmes: Women, Salons, and Social Stratification in Seventeenth-Century France*. Princeton, NJ: Princeton University Press, 1976.

Lough, John. *The* Encyclopédie *in Eighteenth-Century England and Other Studies*. Newcastle upon Tyne: Oriel Press, 1970.

Mason, Amelia Gere. *The Women of the French Salons*. NY: Century, 1891.

Nitze, William A., and E. Preston Dargan. *A History of French Literature*. NY: Henry Holt, 1938.

Quennell, Peter. *Affairs of the Mind: The Salon in Europe and America from the Eighteenth to the 20th Century*. Washington, DC: New Republic Books, 1980.

Roustan, M. *The Pioneers of the French Revolution*. NY: Howard Fertig, 1969.

Tallentyre, S.G. *The Women of the Salons*. NY: Putnam, 1926.

Wade, Ira O. *The Structure and Form of the French Enlightenment*. Vol. I. Princeton, NJ: Princeton University Press, 1977.

Karin Haag,
freelance writer, Athens, Georgia

Salote Topou III (1900–1965)

Queen of Tonga. Name variations: Salote Tupou III; Queen Salote. Born on March 13, 1900; died in 1965; daughter of King George Topou (or Tupou) II; educated at the Diocesan Ladies' College of the Church of England (Auckland) and the University of Sydney; married Sione (John) Fe'iloakitau Kaho (Prince Viliami Tungi or Tugi), in 1917 (died 1941); children: sons Taufa or Tung (b. 1918, later known as King Tafua'ahou Topou IV), and Jione Gu Manumataogo.

Ruled Tonga (1918–65); created an Honorary Dame Commander of the Order of the British Empire (1932), and Honorary Grand Commander of the Order of the British Empire (1945).

When Salote Topou III was born on March 13, 1900, she was the crown princess of the South Pacific kingdom of Tonga, an approximately 250-square-mile region of about 150 coral and volcanic islands. Her family line had governed these islands since the 10th century. In 1845, when Salote's great-great-grandfather had become king of the consolidated State of Tonga, the modern kingdom began. As King George Topou I, he established a constitutional monarchy and reigned until his death at 96 in 1893. Salote's father George Topou II succeeded him, but, due to financial difficulties in the kingdom, in 1900 he ne-

gotiated a treaty with Great Britain whereby Tonga became a British protectorate. Tonga largely maintained its independence as a self-governing region, however. As a tribute to the English monarchs *Charlotte of Mecklenburg-Strelitz and George III, who reigned when the idea of a treaty between Tonga and Great Britain was first entertained, all Tongan monarchs were named after them, with the female monarchs named Salote, Polynesian for Charlotte.

Prior to ascending the throne, Salote Topou III received her education at the Diocesan Ladies' College of the Church of England (Auckland, New Zealand) and at the University of Sydney (Australia). In 1917, her marriage to Sione (John) Fe'iloakitau Kaho, otherwise known as Prince Viliami Tungi, united Tonga's two noblest families. After her father's death, she took the throne on April 12, 1908, and in accordance with Tongan tradition her husband served as Salote's prime minister. They had two surviving sons, the eldest of whom, Prince Taufa Topou, assumed his father's post on the latter's death in 1941.

Queen Salote proved to be an immensely popular ruler both at home and abroad. Her regal physical presence—made more impressive by a height of more than six feet—and gracious

This Tonga postage stamp honoring Salote Topou III was issued in 1920.

demeanor caused *The New York Times* to dub her "Britain's most popular coronation guest." The Tongan people adored her as a benevolent and enlightened monarch, among whose accomplishments was the institution of free and compulsory education. Tongans also enjoyed free medical care as well as a kingdom largely devoid of crime and with ample land and housing. Reported the London *Times*, "Tonga has neither dissensions at home nor enemies abroad and must be one of the happiest countries of the world." Queen Salote's policies brought nearly universal literacy to the islands, which developed a reputation as the most peaceful and harmonious region on earth. (This reputation had been in the makings as early as the 1770s, when English navigator James Cook responded to the hospitality he found on his visits there by naming the region the Friendly Islands.) "There is no question of the high character of Queen Salote," wrote J.C. Furnas of *The New York Times*, she is "universally respected by her people and everybody else in the Pacific."

Queen Salote was a Methodist who served as the head of the Wesleyan Free Church of Tonga and the Tonga Red Cross. In 1932, she was named an Honorary Dame Commander of the Order of the British Empire and in 1945 was elevated to Honorary Grand Commander of the order. Upon her death in 1965, Salote was succeeded by her eldest son who took the throne as King Tafua'ahou Topou IV. Five years later, Tonga regained complete independence from Great Britain.

SOURCES:

Candee, Marjorie Dent, ed. *Current Biography 1953.* NY: H.W. Wilson, 1953.

Jackson, Guida M. *Women Who Ruled.* Santa Barbara, CA: ABC-CLIO, 1990.

Gloria Cooksey,
freelance writer, Sacramento, California

Salov'eva, Poliksena (1867–1924).

See Teffi, N.A. for sidebar.

Salt, Barbara (1904–1975)

American-born British diplomat who in 1962 became the first woman to receive a British ambassadorial appointment. Name variations: Dame Barbara Salt. Born in Oreville, California, on September 30, 1904; died in London, England, on December 28, 1975; daughter of Reginald John Salt and Maud Fanny (Wigram) Salt; had two sisters; educated at Seaford in Sussex; attended universities in Munich and Cologne; never married.

Was first British woman diplomat to be named counsellor (1955), minister (1960), and ambassador (1962); named a Dame Commander of the Order of the British Empire (1963).

Although born in 1904 in California, Barbara Salt was British to the core; she was taken by her parents back to England soon after her birth, where her affluent family settled in Oxford. Her father was a banker; her grandfather was Sir Thomas Salt, chair of Lloyds Bank and a member of Parliament for Stafford. She matriculated at Downs School, Seaford, Sussex, and mastered German in universities in Munich and Cologne. Dame Barbara Salt became a pioneer among women in the world diplomatic corps. From 1933 to 1938, she was employed as a secretary, and it was as a secretary that she began her wartime career in 1940, working for the top-secret Special Operations Executive (SOE) for the British government. Soon, her abilities were recognized, and starting in 1942 she was posted as vice-consul to the SOE office in Tangier, Morocco. Although the details of her work here remain shrouded in mystery, she was engaged in underground anti-Axis propaganda and was promoted to head of the Tangier operations. Salt remained in Tangier until 1946, when she returned to London.

In November 1946, Salt began working at the British Foreign Office, as a temporary first secretary in the United Nations Department. Her appointment in the Foreign Office became permanent in 1949. By this time, she had earned "a sterling reputation" from both her superiors and colleagues because of her "critical and analytical mind, her quickness, her practical common sense, and her mature judgement." After serving briefly in Moscow in 1950 as commercial first secretary of the British embassy, she had to return to London because of poor health. In 1951, she was appointed first secretary at the British embassy in Washington, D.C., being promoted to counsellor *sur place* in 1955. Salt left Washington in 1957 for Tel Aviv, serving there not only as counsellor and consul-general, but also occasionally acting as chargé d'affaires.

She achieved another first when she became the first woman diplomat to be named a minister, as deputy head of the United Kingdom delegation to the 1960 United Nations' disarmament negotiations in Geneva. In 1961, she was transferred to New York as U.K. representative on the Economic and Social Council of the UN. By this time, Salt's health had become precarious. She often suffered from severe migraine headaches but managed to cope.

In April 1962, it was announced that she would be U.K. ambassador to Israel—another historic first for British women. Unfortunately, her health had deteriorated to an alarming degree, and in October of that year she developed thromboses which did not respond to medical treatment. In successive operations, both her legs had to be amputated, and her state of health forced the Foreign Office to cancel her appointment as ambassador to Israel. A brilliant diplomatic career appeared shattered.

Now in a wheelchair, Salt resumed work as soon as she was mobile. The word "indomitable" began to be linked to her name in both press reports and conversations; witnesses commented on her ability to bear pain, disablement, and disappointment. At the time of her retirement in January 1973, she would note, "People keep saying what a tragedy it was that I wasn't able to go to Israel. I don't regard it as such. It's just something you have to live with." Although she was confined to a wheelchair for the rest of her life, Salt's last decade at the Foreign Office was productive. Between 1963 and 1966, she led U.K. delegations in financial negotiations with Israel, Rumania, and the USSR. As a negotiator, she had few equals. Besides being a perfectionist, she could be formidable in her obstinacy and had a superb grasp of details.

When not engaged in delicate negotiations for the Foreign Office, Salt did historical research on the diplomatic history of World War II, but she also served on Civil Service selection boards, and updated a handbook on etiquette for junior diplomats. From 1967 to the end of her career in 1973, she headed the SOE section of the Foreign and Commonwealth Office. Salt always made a strong impression on newly arriving members of the diplomatic service. Elegant in appearance, she was a sparkling and witty speaker, and was able to impart at least some of the wisdom she had gained from her years of service. Among the honors she received were an MBE in 1946, a CBE in 1959, and a DBE in 1963. Dame Barbara Salt died at her home in Montagu Square, London, on December 28, 1975.

SOURCES:

Brimelow, Thomas. "Salt, Dame Barbara" in Lord Blake and C.S. Nicholls, eds. *The Dictionary of National Biography 1971–1980*. Oxford: Oxford University Press, 1986, pp. 755–756.

"Dame Barbara Salt," in *The Times* [London]. January 6, 1976, p. 12.

"Dame Barbara Salt: A Brilliant Diplomatic Career," in *The Times* [London]. December 31, 1975, p. 12.

"Indomitable," in *The Times* [London]. January 11, 1973, p. 16.

Oxbury, Harold. *Great Britons: Twentieth-Century Lives*. Oxford: Oxford University Press, 1985.

John Haag,
Associate Professor History,
University of Georgia, Athens, Georgia

Salter, Susanna Medora

(1860–1961)

First woman mayor in the United States. Name variations: Suzanna Madora Salter. Born on March 1, 1860, in Kansas; died on March 17, 1961, in Norman, Oklahoma.

Susanna Salter was a 27-year-old official of the Women's Christian Temperance Union when she went to the polls to vote in the local elections of Argonia, Kansas (population 500). Once there, she discovered that, according to the ballot, she was a mayoral candidate. Accounts vary as to whether she had been nominated by fellow women's temperance workers or by prankster "Wets," but it is clear that Salter neither campaigned for the post nor, indeed, even knew she had been nominated. On that election day in 1887, the first year in which women were allowed to vote in local elections in the state of Kansas, Salter was elected mayor by a two-thirds majority, making her the first woman in the United States to be elected mayor of any city. She served a one-year term as Argonia mayor for which she received one dollar in wages. Salter died on March 17, 1961, shortly after her 101st birthday.

Gloria Cooksey,
freelance writer, Sacramento, California

Saltykova, Praskovya (1664–1723)

*Russian empress. Name variations: Dowager Empress Praskovya; Praskovia Saltykova; Proscovia or Proskovia Soltykov. Born Praskovya Fedorovna Saltykova on October 21, 1664; died on October 24, 1723; daughter of Feodor Soltykov; married Ivan V Romanov (1666–1696), tsar of Russia (r. 1682–1689), on January 9, 1684; children: Marie (died young); Theodosia (1690–1691); *Catherine of Mecklenburg-Schwerin (1692–1733); *Anna Ivanovna (1693–1740); Proskovia Romanov (1694–1731, who married Ivan Momonov).*

Salviati, Elena (fl. early 1500s)

*Florentine noblewoman. Name variations: Elena Appiani. Flourished in the early 1500s; daughter of *Lucrezia de Medici (b. around 1480) and Jacopo or Giacomo Salviati; sister of *Maria Salviati (1499–1543); married Jacopo V. Appiani.*

Salviati, Lucrezia (b. around 1480).

See Medici, Lucrezia de.

Salviati, Maria (1499–1543)

Florentine noblewoman. Name variations: Maria de Medici. Born Maria de Medici in 1499; died in 1543; daughter of Lucrezia de Medici (b. around 1480) and Jacopo or Giacomo Salviati; sister of *Elena Salviati; married Giovanni (delle Bande Nere) de Medici (1498–1526, son of* *Caterina Sforza), in 1516; children: Cosimo I (1519–1574), ruler of Florence (r. 1537), grand duke of Tuscany (r. 1569–1574, who married* *Eleonora de Medici).*

Born in 1499 into one of the wealthy patrician families of Florence, Maria Salviati was the daughter of Giacomo Salviati and *Lucrezia de Medici (who was the daughter of Florentine ruler Lorenzo "the Magnificent" de Medici). Maria has been praised by biographers as a courageous woman, intelligent, and devoted. She grew up with the boy whom she would eventually marry, Giovanni de Medici, an orphan raised by her parents. Giovanni was one of the few Medici men who earned his living as a mercenary; he came from one of the lesser branches of the wealthy Medici family, and thus did not share in the banking fortune for which the Medici are famous. Maria and Giovanni married in 1516, when she was 17 and he was 18. They had only one child in ten years of marriage: Cosimo I, born in 1519, who in time became ruler of Florence. A military leader and politician of distinction, Maria's son raised the status of the Medici family—who had been ruling Florence without legitimate authority—when he was named the first grand duke of Tuscany by the Holy Roman emperor in 1569.

In an era when ten or more children were the norm for aristocratic families, Maria and Giovanni's one child points to the almost constant separation of husband and wife during their marriage. Giovanni's skills as a soldier led him to higher and higher military ranks, until eventually he was the renowned commander of the pope's army. It was the black armor (*bande nere*, in Italian) that he and his soldiers wore which gave Giovanni the name he is known by, Giovanni "delle Bande Nere." He relied heavily on Maria, despite the fact that she remained in her parents' palace in Florence while he was on campaign. Their copious correspondence is still preserved, and shows the close relationship between the two. In his letters, Giovanni asks Maria for supplies and depends on her to administer their lands. Maria in turn shows herself to be both businesswoman and caring wife in her letters, constantly asking Giovanni to come home from his wars but resigned to taking care of their domestic affairs in his absence. She also offered Giovanni advice on maintaining his professional and political alliances.

When he was wounded in battle in 1525 and the pope withheld pay for his troops, Maria traveled to Rome herself and successfully demanded that he pay Giovanni's soldiers. The next year, at the height of his rise to fame as a military leader, Giovanni died in battle at age 28 and was buried in Mantua. Since he had spent much of his money on his troops, Giovanni left Maria and her young son with little financial security. She spent the next ten years in retirement at the palace of Trebbia outside Florence, devoting herself to raising Cosimo.

It was not just the fact that she was impoverished and widowed that led Maria to retire with her son; she was justifiably afraid for Cosimo's well-being. With Giovanni's death, the seven-year-old boy became one of the few potential heirs to the Medici fortune, since the primary branch had no legitimate male heirs living. This made the boy the possible target of numerous would-be heirs, and so for fear of his life Maria chose to keep him close to her, and away from the political intrigues of Florence. As Cosimo grew and needed her care less, Maria joined the Third Order of St. Dominic and devoted herself to working with the poor and sick of the Tuscan countryside. Their financial needs were taken care of by two benefactors, Filippo Strozzi and the marquis of Mantua.

In 1537, Cosimo, only 17 years old, jumped into Florentine politics on the assassination of the hated Florentine despot Alessandro de Medici by a Medici relative, Lorenzino. Cosimo put himself out to the Florentine patricians as the rightful ruler of the city and received widespread support. An intelligent political strategist, Cosimo soon was able to consolidate his power, which included the execution of his former benefactor, Filippo Strozzi, whom Cosimo feared would raise a faction against him. Maria was shocked and saddened by Cosimo's actions and wrote to him, admonishing him and advising him to back down. Cosimo ignored her requests, and following his coming to power, he saw his mother only rarely. Maria moved from Trebbia to another palace, at Castello. She died and was buried there in 1543. In 1685, her remains and those of her husband were brought to the Medici mausoleum in Florence and reburied together.

SOURCES:

Micheletti, Emma. *The Medici of Florence*. Florence: Scala, 1980.

Young, George F. *The Medici*. 2nd ed. NY: E.P. Dutton, 1911.

Laura York,
Riverside, California

Salvini-Donatelli, Fanny

(c. 1815–1891)

Italian soprano who was the first Violetta. Name variations: Francesca Lucchi. Born around 1815 in Florence; died in June 1891 in Milan.

Fanny Salvini-Donatelli is best remembered as the soprano who created the role of Violetta in the disastrous first performance in March 1853 of the Verdi opera *La Traviata*. Violetta, based on ***Alphonsine Plessis**, is a young woman dying of consumption. When the healthy, very plump Salvini-Donatelli made her appearance on stage, the audience burst into laughter at the thought that she was supposed to have a terminal illness. She had been given the role for her vocal ability, over Verdi's objections that she was miscast. However, her reputation and her voice managed to salvage the opera, and certainly it did not end her career. By the time of *La Traviata*, Salvini-Donatelli was a soprano well known across her native Italy. She debuted in Venice in 1839, and was acclaimed for her flexible and expressive technique. In addition to her performance as Violetta, she sang opera across Italy regularly. In 1842, she went abroad to perform in Vienna, moved on to Paris, and closed her career singing in London in the late 1850s. Salvini-Donatelli retired in 1859 about age 44, but performed again in 1865. She returned to Italy and retired again in Milan, where she died in 1891.

Laura York, M.A. in History,
University of California, Riverside, California

Saman, Mme de (1801–1879).

See Allart, Hortense.

Samaroff, Olga (1882–1948)

Virtuoso concert pianist and advocate for American-born performing artists, who exerted considerable influence on musical life in the U.S. during the first half the 20th century and raised the standards of music education through her students, lectures, and writings. Name variations: Olga Samaroff Stokowski; Olga Stokowski. Born Lucie Mary Olga Agnes Hickenlooper on August 8, 1882, in San Antonio, Texas; died in New York City on May 17, 1948; daughter of Carols Hickenlooper *(a U.S. Army officer) and* Jane Hickenlooper *(an amateur pianist); attended Paris Conservatoire de Musique, graduated with honors, 1898; married Boris Loutzky (a civil engineer), in 1900 (divorced 1904); married Leopold Stokowski (1882–1977, the musical conductor), in 1911 (divorced 1923); children:* Sonya Stokowski.

Married in Berlin (1900); traveled in Germany and Russia, moved to New York City after divorce (1904); made professional concert debut (1904); toured as concert artist in the U.S. and performed extensively in London until second marriage (1911); resumed concert touring (1914); divorced and moved to New York City, accepted a post at the Juilliard School of Music in New York City and at the Philadelphia Conservatory of Music in Philadelphia (1923); after an injury, wrote several books and lectured extensively on music appreciation; died at age 65 (1948).

Selected writings: The Layman's Music Book *(1935, revised as* The Listener's Music Book, *1947);* The Magic World of Music *(1936);* A Music Manual *(1937);* An American Musician's Story *(1939).*

For the child named Lucie Mary Olga Agnes Hickenlooper, preparation for a remarkable career as an international piano soloist began before she was born, with the lives of her mother and grandmother. The daughter of a U.S. Army officer and an amateur pianist, she was born in 1882, in San Antonio, Texas, and received her early musical training from her grandmother, Lucie Palmer Loening Grünewald. Before the American Civil War, **Lucie Palmer** had studied music and received a French education at a New Orleans convent and made her musical debut at age 15, playing a Beethoven piano concerto with the orchestra of the French Opera in New Orleans. After marrying a well-connected German, George Loening, she gave no thought to a professional career, but when in Munich with her husband she frequently played for King Ludwig I of Bavaria. When the Civil War ended, however, she was back in New Orleans, a penniless young widow with two small children to support. Lucie became a piano teacher, and a second marriage took her to Texas, where her daughter from her first marriage, **Jane Hickenlooper**, became the mother of the gifted Olga.

It was the strength of this background that led to Olga's performance, at a very young age, before American composer Edward MacDowell, pianist Vladimir de Pachmann, and William Steinway, head of the famous piano manufacturing firm. All three recommended that the child be taken to Europe for additional training. It was a time when American musicians, no matter how talented or well trained, had great difficulty in developing concert careers in the U.S. without the prestige of European training and press notices. Although there were splendid music schools in the United States, the prejudices against American-trained musicians was so pronounced that developing European credentials were thought to be the only path to a successful career.

At age 12, Olga departed for France, accompanied by her grandmother, and did not see her parents for the next five years. She studied first with composer-pianist Charles Marie Widor at a convent school and took private lessons from François Marmontel, then in his 80s; after a year of preparation, she entered the competition at the Paris Conservatoire de Musique, where she was granted a two-year scholarship, the first ever awarded to an American girl for piano classes. (Most American music students then in Paris were singers.) When Olga began her studies with the eccentric pianist, pedagogue and composer Elie Delaborde, he greeted her at her first lesson with, "Why do you try to play the piano? Americans are not meant to be musicians!" After hearing her perform Schumann's *G Minor Sonata*, however, he decided that with a name like Hickenlooper she must be European after all; eventually he gave her the pet name "Bambola."

Olga's program of study at the Paris Conservatory was rigorous, demanding more than seven hours a day on music and four or five more at academic subjects. In 1898, after graduating with honors, she went with her grandmother to Berlin, another important European musical center, where her studies continued with the Russian pianist and teacher Ernst Jedliczka, who had been a student of the composer Peter Ilyich Tchaikovsky at the Moscow Conservatory. She took lessons from the Australian pianist, author and composer Ernest Hutcheson, who would later become her colleague at the Juilliard Graduate School, and studied organ and composition with Otis Bardwell Boise, an American who later taught at the Peabody Conservatory in Baltimore.

In her memoirs, Samaroff describes the endless succession of debut concerts given by young American musicians in pre-World War I Berlin. The performances, marking the end of student days, were a very expensive means of eliciting press reviews that could be sent to the performer's hometown, and American music magazines solicited advertising for the events at very high fees. In 1900, Olga's grandmother was at work on plans for her Berlin debut when Olga decided instead to marry Boris Loutzky, a Russian civil en-

gineer connected with the Russian Embassy in Berlin. Under pressure from her husband, and also following her own convictions about the role of a wife, Olga stopped performing for three years, but continued to study music and attend occasional concerts while the couple moved in the diplomatic circles of Berlin and St. Petersburg.

According to some accounts, the jealousy of Olga's husband made her life a nightmare. In 1904, she obtained a papal annulment and legal divorce, and returned to the U.S. that September with little money and no alimony. In New York, she approached Henry Wolfsohn, a leading concert manager, who refused to help her prepare for a New York debut because she had neither European press notices nor the resources to return to Europe to achieve them. While she was in Europe, her family had moved from Texas to St. Louis, after losing all their property in the Galveston flood of 1900, so they had no financial support to offer. Jane Hickenlooper came to New York, however, and shared a small room with her daughter at the modest St. Hubert Hotel near Carnegie Hall while trying to persuade Olga to become a music teacher in St. Louis. But Olga, driven by thoughts of the sacrifices her family had already made for her sake, was determined to pursue a concert career. By a stroke of good luck, Wolfson chanced to hear her play at the Steinway showroom, and was impressed enough to agree to arrange a debut concert at Carnegie Hall.

An orchestra had to be hired to accompany Olga, and her mother and grandmother decided to risk all their savings on hiring the New York Symphony Orchestra, to be conducted by Walter Damrosch. Wolfsohn, refusing to represent anyone with the name of Hickenlooper, insisted that Olga change her name. She "combed the family tree" and found the name of a distant Russian relative, Olga Samaroff, which she took as her stage and legal name.

Her New York debut performance was January 18, 1905, the first time Samaroff had ever played with an orchestra. The program included Schumann's *A Minor Concerto*, Liszt's *E-Flat Concerto* and some solo pieces by Chopin; the favorable reviews launched her career, at age 22. Of the risky gamble taken by her mother and grandmother, Samaroff wrote in her memoirs, "I have often wondered how I brought myself to allow them to do it, but the confidence of youth has strength, if not wisdom. I believed in a successful outcome."

Many performance opportunities followed, and through the assistance of a New York patron

Olga
Samaroff

Samaroff played a series of paid engagements. Since Wolfsohn's fees were extremely high, Jane Hickenlooper took over the management of her daughter's budding career. After Samaroff played the Saint-Saëns *C Minor Sonata for Piano and Cello* with the Boston Symphony Quartet, the relatively minor performance received enthusiastic reviews from major critics of the day, and elicited a management contract with the prestigious Charles A. Ellis of Boston, whose clients included the Australian operatic soprano *Nellie Melba, Polish pianist Ignace Jan Paderewski,

Austrian-American violinist Fritz Kreisler, and American soprano *Geraldine Farrar.

If Samaroff advanced relatively easily in her concert career, it was because the trail had been blazed by an earlier generation of American women pianists in the late 19th century. By 1900, women concert players were not considered a novelty in America or in Europe because performers like *Julie Rivé-King, *Amy Cheney Beach, Venezuela-born *Teresa Carreño, *Fanny Bloomfield Zeisler, and *Amy Fay had gained the confidence, respect and admiration of the public as "lady pianists"; in Europe, the ground had been broken by *Clara Schumann and *Sophie Menter in Germany, *Louise Farrenc in France, and *Arabella Goddard in England, among others.

In 1906, Ellis arranged for Samaroff's first solo recital, at London's Steinway Hall. Although the appearance did not prove profitable, Samaroff met some of England's leading personalities of the day, including novelist Thomas Hardy, publisher John Lanes, painter John Singer Sargent, and poet William Watson. By the end of the season, she had been promised an engagement with the London Symphony Orchestra for the following year.

With the superlative European press notices Samaroff had received, Ellis was able to secure some of the highest fees ever paid to a woman pianist, $500–$600 per concert. Samaroff paid Ellis 20% of her fees and was responsible for her own traveling and living expenses, as well as all the costs handled by a press agent for photographs, printing expenses and distribution of leaflets, window cards, and the three-sheet posters then popular. Samaroff gave joint recitals with world-class violinists Fritz Kreisler and Efrem Zimbalist, among others, and performed with every major symphony orchestra in the U.S. and Europe; in 1908, she made records for Welte-Mignon Company in Germany, becoming the first American woman pianist to record.

In 1905, Samaroff met the English-born musician Leopold Stokowski when he was the organist at St. Bartholomew's Church in New York, his first position in the United States. The courtship lasted nearly five years while she continued to perform as many as 80 concerts a season. When they married in 1911, he was conductor of the Cincinnati Orchestra and she ended her stage appearances to devote herself to building Stokowski's career. "I was very much in love, and was quite willing to agree that it was too difficult to combine marriage and a career."

In 1912, Stokowski took the podium for the Philadelphia Orchestra, where he served as sole conductor for 24 years, becoming one of the most charismatic and celebrated maestros of his generation. Samaroff had previously appeared in Philadelphia as a guest soloist with the orchestra's two former directors, Fritz Scheel and Karl Pohlig, and it was widely believed that she handled the negotiations for her husband's contract. She became familiar with the behind-the-scenes politics of American symphony orchestras and tried to be effective as a conductor's wife. In 1914, encouraged by Arthur Judson, the company's manager, she resumed her own career, performing with the Philadelphia Orchestra. Judson also involved her in some of his other projects, but she considered her career as secondary to the duties of her private life as long as the marriage lasted.

During the first few summers of their married life, the Stokowskis spent time in their villa outside Munich, but the outbreak of World War I forced a hurried departure from Germany. The summers of 1916–18 were spent in Seal Harbor, Maine, where they were visited by many famous musician friends. In 1917, Samaroff played the Saint-Saëns *Concerto in G minor* at the Worcester Festival, accompanied by her husband. Several accounts of this performance indicate that she was recovering from some serious illness, generally believed to be a nervous breakdown. In 1920, she played a series of eight concerts, during which she performed all 32 Beethoven piano sonatas, the first American woman pianist to achieve this feat. She was also one of the first women artists to become a member of the Beethoven Association of New York.

In 1921, at age 39, Samaroff gave birth to a daughter, Sonya, in London. That year, she began recording for the Victory Talking Machine Company and from 1921 to 1931 made more than 20 recordings. Always forward-thinking, Samaroff had immediately embraced the new technology of recording and saw its potential in music education. Although many had thought of them as the ideal couple, Samaroff and Stokowski separated in 1923. They continued to maintain a friendship and work together while Samaroff reestablished herself in New York. Meanwhile, record royalties enabled her to buy a house at Seal Harbor, where she spent summers and was aided by a full-time cook, housekeeper, secretary, and an English nurse for the baby.

Always a prolific writer of letters, as well as of plays, poems, essays and fictions that remained unpublished, she began during these years to write about music for *Etude* and other music magazines. She followed the contemporary music scene closely, and was a colleague of the American composer advocate **Claire Reis** in the Town Hall Music Committee and the League of Composers. Samaroff had a reputation for being open-minded, progressive and visionary.

Although the majority of student pianists in music schools were women, who also outnumbered men as teachers, few women gained international influence as performers or teachers. Samaroff became the exception. Without any prior experience, she signed a contract in 1924 to teach piano at the newly established Juilliard Graduate School, then on East 52nd Street in New York City. In 1925, she injured her arm and shoulder in a fall that effectively ended her performing career. Soon after, she was offered the job of music critic for the *New York Evening Post*, replacing British writer and guest music critic Ernest Newman. Samaroff held the post for two seasons, resigning when the paper refused her proposal to expand the department.

In 1928, she was appointed head of the piano department at the Philadelphia Conservatory, and held the post concurrently with her Juilliard position for the next 20 years. That same year, she established the Schubert Memorial, a foundation to help young musicians secure a first performance with a major orchestra, inspired by her own experiences as a young artist. She also set up an annual competition to select a soloist for a performance with the Philadelphia Orchestra in a regular subscription concert.

Samaroff based her teaching on her own hands-on experiences. One of her goals was to make the student independent, both musically and in life. She demanded that students study and analyze a score away from the piano and think of the piano in orchestral terms. She also believed that study and practice were the keys to success in interpretation, and she demanded accuracy and fidelity to the score, insisting that her students "exhaust the printed page."

Samaroff believed that students needed to study music history, theory and literature because "one cannot be musically mature while one is humanly immature." She sent her students to museums, opera, ballets and libraries, encouraging historical research. Often she invited her students to dine in her home with famous personages of the time like conductor Bruno Walter, English pianist Dame *Myra Hess and Russian pianist and conductor Ossip Gabrilowitsch. She invited students to Europe and to stay at her summer home in Maine.

Samaroff often found debut gowns for women students through her society friends, or had a suit tailor-made at her own expense for a male student. During the Depression years of the 1930s, some students lived with her, undertaking housekeeping duties for room and board. Musicales put on in her New York apartment gave young artists an opportunity to perform before audiences of other musicians, famous conductors, patrons of the arts, managers and world-famous personalities. Among the artists supported by her in these ways were Eugene List, who began his studies with her at age 13, African-American *Natalie Hinderas, *Rosalyn Tureck, William Kapell, American composer Vincent Persichetti, and Alexis Weissenberg.

Throughout the 1930s, Samaroff lectured on music appreciation, intent on making "listening more of a real musical activity." In 1935, she wrote *The Layman's Music Book* (with a revised edition published as *The Listener's Music Book*, 1947). She also wrote *The Magic World of Music* (1936) and *A Music Manual* (1937). Samaroff was one of the first to use recordings and other audio-visual aids in her presentations. She was chosen by the State Department to represent the U.S. at the first International Congress of Musical Education in the House of Parliament in Prague, Czechoslovakia, and in 1938 she was the only woman among 21 delegates to Belgium to serve on the Concours Eugène Ysaÿe International Jury.

Samaroff was acutely aware of the prejudices faced by women musicians. In 1937, she wrote an article for the *Music Clubs Magazine*, the publication of the National Federation of Music Clubs, the largest music organization in the U.S., challenging them to work to eliminate these difficulties. In her concert programs she premiered works by women composers, including Americans **Mary Howe** and Amy Cheney Beach, and in her later years she became a role model for other women in the profession, and was often interviewed.

Her autobiography, *An American Musician's Story*, speaks eloquently about many aspects of musical life in the States as well as her own career and personal experiences. She wrote in the conclusion of her book: "As I have observed the profound changes that have taken place in the musical life of my time, it has often seemed to me as though each of us—no matter what the circumstances of our existence may be—sits at a loom fashioned to do its share in the weaving of fate." Olga Samaroff was 65 when she died, in 1948.

SOURCES:

Kline, Donna S. "Olga Samaroff: Teacher Extraordinaire," in *American Music Teacher*. Vol. 38. June–July 1989, pp. 10–15.

Pucciani, Donna. "Olga Samaroff (1882–1948): American Musician and Educator," dissertation, New York University, 1979.

Stokowski, Olga Samaroff. *An American Musician's Story*. NY: W.W. Norton, 1939.

SUGGESTED READING:

Loesser, Arthur. *Men, Women and Pianos: A Social History*. New York, 1954.

Pucciani, Donna. "Olga Samaroff: Pianist and Master Teacher," in *The Piano Quarterly*. Vol. 30, no. 118, 1982, p. 32.

COLLECTIONS:

Correspondence located at the New York Public Library, Music Division at Lincoln Center, and at the Library of Congress, Music Division, in Washington, D.C.

RELATED MEDIA:

Olga Samaroff Performs in 1908 (long-playing record, #665 in "The Welte Legacy of Piano Treasures" series), Recorded Treasures, Hollywood, California, 1963.

Jeannie G. Pool,
freelance writer on music history,
Los Angeles, California

Sambethe

The Jewish Sibyl. Name variations: Sabba; Sambathe. Daughter of Berosos and Erymanthe.

Believed to have been a sibyl (female prophet), Sambethe, the daughter of Berosos and **Erymanthe**, was raised among the Jews of Palestine. Sources are unclear about her ethnicity, for while they place her among the Palestinian Jews, some call her a Babylonian, others an Egyptian, and still others a Persian. The name Sambethe itself, however, is derived from the Jewish word "Sabbath," so that whatever her origin, it appears that she (if, indeed, she was even a historical figure) plied her trade in the general vicinity of Judea. When Sambethe might have lived is unknown. One tradition had her on Noah's ark and perhaps the wife of one of his sons; the first unambiguous reference to her did not come until the 2nd century CE, although it is possible that some contemporaries of Alexander the Great (356–323 BCE) believed that she had foretold of his achievements.

William Greenwalt,
Associate Professor of Classical History,
Santa Clara University, Santa Clara, California

Sammuramat (fl. 8th c. BCE)

Queen of Assyria, either the wife or mother of King Adadnirari III (r. 811–783 BCE), who appears from the legends that have grown up around her to have been one of the most remarkable women of the pre-classical world. Name variations: (Assyrian) Sammuramat; (Greek) Semiramis or Sémiramis, also Semiramide; (Armenian) Shamiram. Pronunciation: sam-mu-RA-mat; semi-RAM-is; Sem-EE-rham-i-day; shah-mi-RAM. Flourished around the 8th century BCE; either the wife or mother of King Adadnirari III (r. 811–783 BCE).

Queen Sammuramat's name has been preserved in an inscription on the back of a statue of the Babylonian god Nabu which was set up in the great temple at Calah by the Assyrian monarch Adadnirari III (r. 811–783 BCE). The inscription reads: "For the life of Adadnirari, king of Assyria, its lord, and for the life of Sammuramat, the lady of the palace and its mistress." And this is all that is known for certain of Sammuramat.

From the description of her as the mistress of the palace, it is clear that she was queen, but whether she came to the throne as the wife of Adadnirari or as his mother has been debated. As his mother, she would have been the widow of Shamshiadad, serving as regent during Adadnirari's minority. Regardless, it seems to be beyond question that she was the historical figure behind the legends of an Assyrian queen known to the Greeks and Romans as Semiramis and to the Armenians as Shamiram. While only generalities may be inferred about Sammuramat from stories of the legendary Semiramis, the latter served as an important player on the pages of ancient accounts which ascribed to her no end of extraordinary accomplishments. The Greek historian of the 2nd century BCE Diodorus of Sicily calls Semiramis "the most renowned woman of whom we have any record."

Our earliest firm date in ancient history is June 15, 763 BCE. On that day, the Assyrian text called the *Eponymous Chronicle* records a total eclipse of the sun from which all the reigns cited in the *Chronicle* can be precisely dated, spanning the years 910–648 BCE. The events described in the *Chronicle* can then be expanded by drawing upon the more ample information provided by the *Assyrian Annals*. From what we can tell from these records, which for the reign of Shamshiadad are rather fragmentary, he was a most warlike ruler who made many campaigns and military expeditions to the west (against the Hittites and Israelis), the northeast (against the Medes, where he became the first Assyrian king to carry his arms to the Caspian Sea), and the south (against the Babylonians). At the time of his son Adadnirari's accession to the throne in 811 BCE, Assyria was the largest state the world had ever known.

Under Adadnirari's vigorous and aggressive rule, Assyria grew even larger and was, moreover, the world's first true empire. Warlike, ferocious and bloodthirsty as they are known to have been, the Assyrians were also the first to perfect the technique of permanent occupation of a conquered country. With their panoply of provinces, governors, and garrison troops, as well as their system of taxation, they may well be said to have originated the very concept of empire, a particular form of government whereby one mighty military power conquered its neighbors and then ruled them on a permanent basis. Such a conquest guaranteed those conquered a modicum of internal peace and prosperity and a certain protection against foreign invasion in return for their continued submission. Not until 1991 did the chain of related empires that began with Assyria—Persian, Median, Alexandrian, Seleucid, Parthian, Roman, Sassanian, Byzantine, Arab, Safavid, Ottoman, Russian and Soviet—come to an end.

The chief source for the legends surrounding the name Semiramis is Ctesias of Cnidus, a Greek doctor who served as court physician to King Artaxerxes II (404–359 BCE) of Persia. While the history of Persia written by Ctesias, known as the *Persica*, did not survive, a great deal of the information it contained was preserved by Diodorus, who incorporated large sections of the *Persica* into his own historical work.

According to the legend passed on by Ctesias and preserved for us by Diodorus, Semiramis was a demi-goddess, the daughter of the Syrian deity Derceto and a handsome mortal youth. The legend relates that the goddess Aphrodite was offended in some way by Derceto and inspired her with love for this mortal, but after bearing the child, Derceto, out of shame and regret, killed her lover and exposed their baby to die. The infant was nurtured by doves, however, which fed her with milk and, when she was old enough to need more nourishing food, cheese stolen from local cowherds. After the cowherds discovered the child, they gave her to Simmas, the keeper of the royal herds of the Assyrian king Ninus. Simmas named her Semiramis, from the Syrian word for "dove." Eventually, Semiramis grew up to be a beautiful girl. One day, she was seen by a royal officer named Onnes, who had been sent to inspect the royal herds. He fell in love with her and secured Simmas' permission to marry her. Two sons were born of this union, Hyapates and Hydaspes, about whom the legend curiously has nothing more to say. Not long afterwards, Onnes was with King Ninus campaigning in Bactriana (Afghanistan). Unable to live without his beautiful wife, he sent for her to join him. We are told that while on the long, hot journey from Syria to Bactriana Semiramis devised the all-enveloping robe worn thereafter by women in the East (the *chador*), both to hide her beauty from the gaze of men and to protect the delicate whiteness of her skin from the sun.

When she arrived in Bactriana, Semiramis observed the siege of a local city. Perceiving that the siege was not going well, and that no one dared attack the acropolis (the fortified high place inside the city) because of its great strength, she also observed that the defenders of the acropolis, secure in its strength, did not hesitate to leave it unguarded from time to time. Semiramis took a number of troops skilled in climbing and seized the fortification, whereupon the city fell. While no explanation is given for her sudden interest in military matters, nor for the origin of her own skill in climbing, without saying so explicitly Diodorus (or Ctesias) seems to indicate that the soldiers, unable to see Semiramis because of her concealing robe, took her to be a man.

King Ninus naturally marveled at the achievement of this woman and quickly became enamored of her. He thus asked Onnes to yield her to him, offering his own daughter Sosane in return. After Onnes' refusal, the king threatened him with blinding if he did not cooperate. So unwilling was Onnes to live without Semiramis, and so fearful was he of the king's rage, that he escaped his dilemma by hanging himself. Ninus then married Semiramis and made her his queen. In time, she had a son, Ninyas. Soon after, the king died and Semiramis, now 20, became ruler in her own right. Nothing is said in the legend about a regency; it is taken for granted that she either had the right to rule in her husband's place or that, owing possibly to her remarkable qualities, no one in a position of authority cared to press the issue.

Semiramis, we are told, began her reign by erecting a great tomb for her late husband some nine stadia (c. 5,460.75 ft.) high and ten stadia (c. 6,067.5 ft.) wide. Eager to achieve great exploits, she then decided to found a great city in Mesopotamia, to be called Babylon. According to the legend, she gathered no less that two-million men to labor on the city which was built on both sides of the River Euphrates, surrounded by walls around 335 feet in height and strengthened by 250 towers. The circumference of these walls (which were built of baked brick [adobe] and sealed with locally available bitumen) came to some 360 stadia (about 40 miles). Outside the wall, the city was protected by a natural defense of impenetrable swamps. Between the wall and the first row of houses within it ran a circumferential roadway.

To link the two halves of the city, Semiramis ordered the construction of a bridge, five stadia (c. 3,033.75 ft.) long, at the narrowest point of the river. The piers of this bridge were set 12 feet apart and it was floored by heavy beams of cypress, cedar and palm logs. An extensive quay was then erected along the river. On either side of the bridge, Semiramis had two lavish palaces constructed, each with its own separate inner and outer circumferential walls. Within the walls of the first palace was built a walled acropolis, and here the queen set up colossal bronze statues of Ninus, herself and the great god of Babylonia, Zeus-Belus (Ba'al). In the center of the city, she erected a great temple to Zeus-Belus, the details of which were lost to Ctesias as the temple was in ruins during his day. He recalled, however, that at the top of the temple there had stood statues of Zeus-Belus and of two Babylonian goddesses to whom he gave the names of the Greek goddesses Hera and Rhea. The walls of these buildings were faced with glazed and painted tiles of the brightest hues, depicting scenes of hunts and battles. Ctesias recalled the great Hanging Gardens of Babylon, one of the Seven Wonders of the World, but admits that these were built later by Nebuchadnezzar II, another king of Babylon, for his Median wife **Amyntis**, who in the flatlands of Mesopotamia missed the mountains of her native land in northwest Iran. Outside the city, at the lowest point in Babylonia, Semiramis is said to have constructed a square reservoir of baked bricks, 300 stadia (c. 182,025 ft.) long on each side and 35 feet deep.

She is also credited with founding other cities along the Tigris and Euphrates rivers, all equipped with emporia, and is said to have set up an obelisk 130 feet long and 25 feet wide and thick which was cut from a single block of stone quarried in Armenia and brought to Babylon. The Greek historian Herodotus adds that Semiramis built numerous dikes in the plain between the Tigris and Euphrates rivers for flood control, and he states that one of the gates of Babylon was named for her.

Diodorus, still drawing upon Ctesias, tells us that after leaving Babylonia Semiramis journeyed to Media to a great mountain called Bagistana. There she laid out a park which was watered by a spring. Moving on in Media, she came to the city of Chauon, where on a high plateau she found a striking rock. Upon the rock, she erected costly buildings and at its foot laid out another park. Semiramis was so enchanted by the scenery and view at Chauon that she spent a long time there. Unwilling to take a lawful husband for fear of losing her royal power to him, she is said to have passed her nights in pleasure with soldiers drawn from her elite guard. Her achievements in the way of constructions did not end there. We are told that she cut a road through the Zercaeus (Zagros) Mountains, built a palace in the Median capital of Ecbatana, and ordered the construction of a long tunnel to bring water to the city from a distant lake. Next, visiting every other province of her realm, Semiramis cut roads through the mountains and made high mounds in the plains to mark the tombs of generals, even building towns on some of these. She next visited Egypt, where, conquering Libya, she is said to have made a journey to the famed oracle at the oasis of Zeus-Ammon in the Libyan desert. There it was prophesied to Semiramis that her son Ninyas would conspire against her, at which time she would disappear, receiving eternal honors. Journeying south to Ethiopia, she toured the country and saw its wonders but shortly gave up the idea of conquering it.

The queen, having put the affairs of Egypt and Ethiopia in order, then journeyed east to the city of Bactra (now Balkh), capital of Bactriana, where, seeking military glory to augment the fame of her building activities, she decided to conquer India. Two years were spent in preparations for waging war on India's ruler King Stabrobates. During this time, Semiramis gathered detailed information regarding the country's wealth in gold, silver, iron, copper and precious stones, and she amassed a gigantic army consisting of 3 million infantry, 200,000 cavalry, 100,000 chariots, and numerous men on camels, as well as 3,000 riverboats that could be dismantled and carried over land. When the invasion was launched, a great war ensued, the course of which is given in great detail by Ctesias. Victorious, Semiramis returned to Babylon where she is said to have died after a reign of 40 years.

According to Diodorus, other historians, such as Athenaeus, laid down far different accounts of Semiramis than Ctesias. In other versions of her story, she came to her power as a courtesan who was beloved by King Ninus because of her great beauty. At first, Semiramis is said to have obtained only a modest position in the palace harem but was later proclaimed a royal wife. She then persuaded the king to give her royal power for five days. Once Semiramis had the scepter and royal robes, she held a great

festival. At a huge banquet given by her during the festival, she convinced the king's miliary commanders and his greatest dignitaries to cooperate in a coup whereby she would seize his throne. On the second day of the festival, Semiramis had the king arrested and thrown into prison, whereupon she proclaimed herself queen and commenced to rule in her own right. While this story may seem a bit more plausible than the one recounted by Ctesias—which made Semiramis the daughter of a goddess—it is actually only another far-fetched tale. The origin of this legend was the memory of a certain Babylonian festival, a

sort of new year's celebration, the most prominent feature of which was the placement of a criminal upon the throne for five days; after that five-day reign, during which the criminal was permitted to issue decrees and use the king's concubines, the criminal was whipped and executed.

Yet another source for stories about Semiramis is the Greek geographer Strabo of Amasia, who died about 20 CE and whose vast *Geography* is a treasure trove of information gathered from innumerable sources otherwise long lost. Strabo confirms the supposed founding of Babylon by Queen Semiramis and of Nineveh, which became the Assyrian capital, by her son Ninus (sic). He tells us that Alexander wished to invade India because he had heard that Semiramis and later Cyrus the Great of Persia had both failed to conquer it. In addition, Strabo records that there were mounds in the Middle East called "mounds of Semiramis"—including those upon which the eastern Anatolian towns of Zela and Tyana were situated—and that canals, walls, roads and bridges were all attributed to her, as well as fortifications equipped with aqueducts, reservoirs, and rock-cut staircases in mountainsides.

On the Armenian side, the late 7th- or early 8th-century Armenian historian Moses of Khoren (Movses Khorenats'i) has much to say about Semiramis, and his account is an excellent example of the growth of her legend in the East. Moses, reluctant to abandon the tales of divinities handed down from the Armenian past, converted pagan deities into heroes of old; thus stories of the goddess Ishtar reached Armenia as the deeds of "Queen Shamiram of Asorestan." In connecting Semiramis with the Armenian town of Van (often called Shamiramakert in Armenian, "built by Semiramis"), Moses became an Armenian witness to the connection between the deeds of Semiramis and the inscriptions on the cliff overlooking the town which had been referred to by Ctesias so long before as "Chauon." The Greek authors—with no "v" in their alphabet in ancient times—even got the name of the town with reasonable accuracy, translating "Van" as "Chauon."

Moses' account of Semiramis is as follows. Voluptuous and lascivious, Semiramis was the wife of the Assyrian monarch King Ninos. She had long heard of the handsomeness of Ara the Fair, who was the son and successor of her husband's vassal King Aram of Armenia. Ara came to the throne, but while her husband was still alive Semiramis was unable to arrange a meeting with him to see his handsomeness for herself. After the death of King Ninos, however, she sent Ara lavish gifts. She commanded him to come to her in Nineveh, giving him the choice of marrying her and becoming her consort or, if he were unwilling to remain in Assyria, simply visiting her and satisfying her lust. Ara, however was devoted to his own queen, Nvart, and refused her repeated offers. Angered, Semiramis marched into Armenia with a large army, hoping thus to impress Ara and bend him to his will. Although she specifically gave orders that he be taken alive if at all possible, Ara was killed in the ensuing battle. The central Armenian plain where he died thereafter bore his name: the Plain of Ayrarat. Semiramis took the body of the fallen

king. With all her magic arts, she tried to bring him back to life by having his corpse licked by the life-giving gods called the Aralez. The gods failed at this attempt. The determined Semiramis—after having Ara's decaying corpse thrown into a ditch and buried—dressed someone else as Ara and had it proclaimed far and wide that the gods had answered her prayers.

Once the war had come to an end, Semiramis found herself unable to leave the beauty of the Armenian countryside and decided to build a royal residence there to escape the summer heat of Assyria. According to Moses, the site chosen for this residence was a high hill overlooking a plain on the shores of a salt lake (Lake Van). After studying the site carefully, Semiramis is said to have assembled 42,000 skilled workers from all over her empire and 6,000 artisans versed in the handling of wood, stone, bronze, and iron. First a great aqueduct was constructed to bring water to the site of the projected city, then the city itself, with its palaces and gardens, was carefully laid out. Most significant in Moses' account is his following description on the cliff overlooking the town of Van in his own time:

> On the side of the rock facing the sun, where today no one can scratch a line with an iron point—so hard is the surface—[she had carved out] various temples, chambers, treasure stores and wide caverns; no one knows how she created such works. And over the entire face of the rock, smoothing it like wax, she inscribed as with a stylus, many texts, the very sight of which would make one marvel.

This description clearly refers to the rock caves and inscriptions that even now, some 12 centuries after Moses, can still be seen on the cliff above the town of Van. These could not have originated, however, with Semiramis. In fact, these inscriptions, while indeed carved in Assyrian cuneiform, are not in the Assyrian language. They are rather in the language of the people of Biainele (or Urartu in Assyrian; Ararat in Hebrew), a local kingdom that flourished in the 9th–6th centuries BCE, and so have nothing to do with any Assyrian queen. By Moses' time, in the late 7th or early 8th century CE, the Persian legends of Semiramis recorded by Ctesias and Diodorus of Sicily centuries before would have become widely known in Armenia. It is interesting to note, however, that the legend attributing Semiramis constructions and inscriptions so far to the north had arisen as early as the time of Ctesias. Moses also goes on to attribute to Semiramis the many other cuneiform inscriptions discovered throughout the Armenian Plateau over the past century or more, and which must have been much more numerous in his time; these too have nothing to do with the Assyrian queen.

Moses goes on to record that while away from Nineveh on her annual summer vacations in Armenia, Semiramis left the government of her empire to the magus Zoroaster, chief of the Medes. Meanwhile, reproached by her sons for her vicious mode of life, she executed them all except Ninyas (Ninuas), the youngest. Moses then notes that Semiramis had a falling out with Zoroaster whom she feared was planning to assume control over her empire. She waged a war against him, which she lost. Fleeing the Mede, Semiramis came to Armenia, where she was killed by the one son she had spared, Ninyas. Moses then concludes his account with a confused recollection of how Semiramis is supposed to have thrown a talisman, apparently made of pearls, into the sea (Lake Van), and he thus explains the Armenian saying: "the pearls of Semiramis into the sea," i.e., "as lost as [?]," or perhaps "as worthless as," "the pearls of Semiramis [cast?] into the sea."

As told by Moses, the story of Ara and Semiramis curiously echoes a tale in Plato's *Republic* which tells of "Er son of Armenios" (Ara, son of Aram in Moses), who, having been slain in battle like Ara, was returned to life after a sojourn in the underworld. This tale parallels the story of the Syrian youth Tammuz the Beautiful. After Tammuz is slain by a boar, the goddess Ishtar (Astarte, i.e. Semiramis) descends into the underworld to bring him back to the realm of the living. Moses' story of Semiramis and Ara goes back to the Sumerians, as the name of the Armenian Aralez referred to by him is derived from the Sumerian Arallu, the land from which none return. In the *Assyrian History* of Ctesias, Ara/Aralez/Arallu turn up as the Assyrian kings Arios and Arialos. These kings are successors of the sun god who was known also as Ninyas the Ninevite, son of Semiramis. The identification of Semiramis with Ishtar accounts for the way in which the legends circulating around the goddess became interwoven with the exploits attributed to the Assyrian queen. Notes **Antonia Fraser:**

> It was this identification with the mysterious and seductive goddesses of the East, such as Astarte (or Ishtar), who first prowled along the edges of the Classical world and then invaded it, which was probably most important in preserving her story. In this manner it was thrillingly carried away from the small patch of historical ground in which it had originally been rooted.

The events described by Moses of Khoren are not the only remnants of the Semiramis story

to be found in Armenia. South of Bitlis a 22-foot-high tunnel carved through a spur of rock that would otherwise block the road through the Bitlis Pass is known as the tunnel of Semiramis, just to cite one example.

It has always been difficult to believe that where there is so much legendary smoke there is not some amount of historical fire. But while it is clear that Sammuramat was the actual person around whom the legends of Semiramis grew, we unfortunately can find nothing in the few facts we know about Sammuramat and the period in which she lived that could give rise to the fantastic exploits credited to Semiramis.

An examination of the nature of kingship in Assyria, which paralleled that of kingship in many other parts of the ancient world, may provide the ultimate source for our understanding of the origins of the legends surrounding Semiramis. The strength of the Assyrian monarchy lay primarily in the well-established monarchical tradition of the Orient which prevented the population, high and low, from imagining any other form of government. The strength of the individual ruler, however, depended only partly on his position within the royal family, and a king could even emerge from outside the main dynasty. The overriding factor in establishing the legitimacy of the monarch was the concept of the divinely appointed king: whoever acquired the throne was ipso facto the chosen representative of Ashur, the chief god of the Assyrian pantheon. The kingship in Assyria, while hereditary in the Sargonid Dynasty, might see the patrilineal succession modified by the decision of the reigning king or tempered by a usurpation which, if successful, endowed the usurper with, again ipso facto, the requisite divine legitimation: Ashur had spoken.

As the king was the viceroy of Ashur, he not only had to rule but also to conduct the sacred cult which made him de facto the High Priest of the state religion. Among his dignities were those of "King of the Four Regions" and "King of the World," both cosmocratic titles that represented the ultimate jurisdiction of the god of whom the king was the representative on earth. While the king himself might not actually own the world, Ashur certainly did, and this rendered the king, ex officio, a cosmocratic ruler by proxy. Although not regarded as a god himself, as was the king of Egypt, Adadnirari was the "light of Ashur" and was expected to possess the twin divine attributes of wisdom and prowess at arms. His education, conducted by tutors, thus would have placed emphasis on military affairs and the handling of weapons (bow and arrow; sword and spear) as well as hunting and falconry; and at least in the case of some Assyrian rulers, the king's education would have involved considerable academic training (Ashur is all-wise, so the king too must be wise).

The king was held to be in his glory under three distinct sets of circumstances: war, wherein he acted in Ashur's capacity as master of the world; the hunt, during which he represented the deity as lord of nature; and the banquet, at which he represented Ashur as the one who bestows all largesse. This oriental concept of kingship was extremely influential. It was passed from the Assyrians to the Persians, and through the vast Persian Empire to countless other peoples of the Middle East, until the coming of Christianity and Islam altered the manner in which kingship was viewed. The real question in regard to the reality behind the legend of Semiramis is whether or not the Assyrians would have countenanced the kingship passing into the hands of a woman. Since Ashur, for example, was a war god, presumably the king must be able to lead his armies into battle. Theoretically, given the nature of ancient warfare, a woman could not do so and this is why no woman was ever allowed to hold the throne of the Roman Empire. Yet the impression one gets from the legends of Semiramis is that the woman behind the legend, likely Sammuramat, did in fact hold the throne and may even have taken part in battles to justify her holding it.

The wonder of a woman leading warriors in battle, going out on the hunt, and undertaking extraordinary building projects normally considered the province of kings, may very well have sparked the legends to begin with. Once the queen held the throne, legends would naturally arise to justify her having been able to do so. Such legends could preserve the notion that women could not rule by asserting that Sammuramat was an exception—she was no ordinary woman. We may assume then that Sammuramat exercised a certain extraordinary authority, hitherto impossible for an Assyrian queen to wield, and that certain military campaigns were launched by her and constructions accomplished by her order that together made her name a byword. In any case, it is beyond question that it soon became customary to attribute any remarkable construction, of which the builder's name had been forgotten, to the by now semi-legendary Assyrian queen.

In addition to being known for her constructions and battles, Semiramis has long been associated with female sensuality and voluptuousness. Fraser notes:

> Her voracious sexual appetites were, like the Queen herself, legendary; the most stalwart soldiers under her command were regularly called into a different kind of service; ungratefully if practically, Semiramis was in the habit of putting her lovers to death immediately after a night of love lest the tale of the Empress' desires should be spread abroad. Even more licentious, as well as unnatural, was the passion that Semiramis was supposed to have nourished for her son Ninyas.

Voltaire's play *Semiramis* (first performed in 1748) dealt with this theme of the love of Semiramis for her son, but placed her feelings in the realm of tragic love, for Voltaire's Semiramis does not know that Arsaces is her son. Other works about Semiramis include the play *Semiramide* by Pietro Metastasio (1698–1782), master of the melodrama, and an opera also entitled *Semiramide* by Gioacchino Rossini (1792–1868) which was based on Voltaire's play and first staged in Venice in 1823. As a vehicle for the American singer *Mary Garden, Rossini's work was performed well into the 20th century, usually staged with grandiose pseudo-oriental sets and bizarre, lavish costuming.

It is interesting that from the data given by Diodorus it is possible to determine the approximate period in which Semiramis is supposed to have reigned according to the Persians from whom Ctesias had his information. Diodorus tells us that the fall of Nineveh (612 BCE) took place 30 reigns after the reign of Semiramis' son Ninyas. Allowing the standard genealogical span of 30 years per generation, this would put Ninyas' death some 900 years before the fall of Nineveh, in 1512 BCE. Moving back another 30 years from the death of Ninyas brings us to 1542 which would mark the death of his mother Semiramis after a reign of 40 years (c. 1582–1542 BCE). But so far as we can reconstruct the chronology for so early a period, at that time there was no kingdom of Assyria.

SOURCES:

Diodorus of Sicily (Diodorus Siculus). *The History*. Loeb Classical Library ed.

Herodotus. *The Histories*. Loeb Classical Library ed.

Fraser, Antonia. *The Warrior Queens*. NY: Alfred A. Knopf, 1989.

Moses Khorenats'i. *History of the Armenians*. Engl. trans. by R.W. Thomson. Cambridge, MA: Harvard University Press, 1978.

Strabo. *Geography*. Loeb Classical Library ed.

SUGGESTED READING:

The Cambridge Ancient History.

Robert H. Hewsen,
Professor of History, Rowan University,
Glassboro, New Jersey

Samoilova, Konkordiya

(1876–1921)

Russian Social Democrat who was a leading Communist organizer of working women. Name variations: Konkordiia Samoilova; K.N. Samoilova-Gromova; (party pseudonyms) Natasha, Vera, and Bol'shevikova; (literary pseudonym) N. Sibirskii. Pronunciation: Sam-OY-lo-va. Born Konkordiya Nikolaevna Gromova in Irkutsk in 1876; died on June 2, 1921, near Astrakhan of cholera; daughter of Nikolai Gromov (a priest); attended gymnasium in Irkutsk, 1884–94, Bestuzhev-Riumin Courses (St. Petersburg), 1896–1901, and Free Russian School of Social Sciences (Paris), 1902–03; married Arkadii Aleksandrovich Samoilov, in 1906; no children.

Was active in the Russian student movement (1897–1901); joined the Russian Social Democratic Labor Party (1903) and became a Bolshevik (1906); was an underground party propagandist (1903–12); was secretary of the editorial board of Pravda *(1912–14) and member of the editorial board of* Rabotnitsa *(1914, 1917); was a party organizer among working women (1917–21); helped organize First Conference of Women Workers (November 1917) and First All-Russian Congress of Working Women (November 1918); head of Zhenotdel operations in Ukraine (1919–20); was a member of the editorial board of* Kommunistka *(1920–21); headed the political department on the agitational steamship* Krasnaia Zvezda *(1920–21). Publications: numerous articles and brochures in Russian on topics relating to working women.*

On February 17, 1913 (o.s.), International Women's Day was celebrated for the first time in tsarist Russia. That day was also the turning point in the revolutionary career of Konkordiya Samoilova. For the past decade, she had been active as an underground propagandist for the Russian Social Democratic Labor Party. Like almost all Marxists, she had argued that the problems of female workers were the same as those of men and that it was separatism to appeal to or organize women in a different fashion than men. Even though the Second International Conference of Socialist Women had called in 1910 for the annual celebration of International Women's Day, Samoilova and her Russian colleagues saw this as a bourgeois feminist ruse of no relevance or interest to the supposedly backward female proletariat in Russia. Nothing was done to mark the day until 1913 when the State Duma or parliament designated February 17 as a holiday. To offset an anticipated feminist observance, Samoilova was told by the Bolsheviks' unenthusiastic Petersburg Committee to organize some kind of counter-demonstration. Under her direction, *Pravda* (Truth) devoted its first three pages to issues of concern to women, and she arranged for a "Scientific Meeting on the Woman Question" at the Kalashnikova Bourse. To mislead the authorities into thinking it was going to be an upper-class, high-brow affair, Samoilova printed five-kopeck tickets which then were distributed free of charge in working districts. Much to the surprise of the party as well as the police, hundreds of working women flocked to the meeting to hear speakers talk about economic and social issues from a female and class perspective. They enthusiastically voiced their approval of speeches which were far more socialistic than "scientific" in tone and content. This response convinced Samoilova that women workers were not as politically backwards as the party had thought, that their special needs had to be addressed, and that efforts should be made to organize them against their oppressors. She was to devote the remaining eight years of her life to this struggle.

Konkordiya Samoilova

Like most prominent women in the Russian Social Democratic movement, Konkordiya Samoilova did not come from a life of poverty and oppression. She was born in the eastern Siberian city of Irkutsk in 1876. Her father Nikolai Gromov was an Orthodox priest who could afford to send her to the local gymnasium for ten years. Like many of her educated contemporaries, both male and female, she realized the need for political change in Russia and explored in her youth the competing theories of the Marxists and the agrarian populists for bringing about reform. For awhile, she considered herself a Tolstoyan interested in educating the peasant masses of Russia. In 1896, after overcoming considerable parental opposition, she and her sister left for St. Petersburg to enroll in the Bestuzhev Courses which offered almost the only form of higher education then open to Russian women. For five years, Samoilova studied philosophy and became involved in the growing student movement. She gave her first public speech in 1897 in protest against the suicide in jail of a fellow female student. Four years later, she was arrested after another student demonstration, jailed for three months for possessing several banned books and a revolver, and expelled from the Bestuzhev Courses. Rather than returning to Irkutsk, she went to Paris where she completed her political education by listening to lectures given by various émigré Marxists at the Free Russian School of Social Sciences. In 1903, she joined the Russian Social Democratic Labor Party and for awhile helped out in the editorial offices of the party's newspaper *Iskra* (The Spark).

In that same year, Samoilova returned to Russia and began nearly a decade of work as an underground propagandist. She moved from city to city organizing propaganda circles in which advanced workers could increase their class consciousness by reading and discussing the classics of Russian and European Marxism. It was dangerous work. On three occasions she was arrested, once on suspicion of participating in the murder of a police agent who had infiltrated one of her circles, and she spent more than two years in tsarist prisons in Tver and St. Petersburg. In 1906, she joined with the Bolshevik wing of the Social Democratic Party and married Arkadii Aleksandrovich Samoilov, a fellow Bolshevik and a lawyer. Six years later, Samoilova was given the job of running the editorial office of the Bolsheviks' new legal newspaper *Pravda* in St. Petersburg. She was soon struck by the volume of letters which the paper received from female workers and by the frustration they revealed when their concerns were not addressed. The enthusiasm and militancy demonstrated several months later on International Women's Day convinced her that the party must devote more attention to organizing these women.

One approach which Samoilova discussed with *Inessa Armand, an émigré Bolshevik with similar concerns, was to publish a special Marxist newspaper aimed specifically at working women. While Armand attempted to get the grudging approval of the male party leaders for the scheme and to raise the necessary money abroad, Samoilova coordinated arrangements for the publication of *Rabotnitsa* (The Woman Worker) in St. Petersburg. On the eve of publication in February 1914, however, she and two other editors were arrested by police seeking to forestall a second observance of International Women's Day. While banished from St. Petersburg, she nevertheless was able to contribute at least three articles to the first Marxist newspaper

devoted to the interests of Russian working women. In 1917, after the overthrow of the tsar, she returned to editing *Rabotnitsa*, and shortly after the Bolsheviks came to power she organized the First Conference of Women Workers in Petrograd (formerly St. Petersburg).

For women like Samoilova, Armand and *Alexandra Kollontai, the culmination of their efforts came in August 1919 when Zhenotdel, or the Women's Section of the Central Committee, was finally established to coordinate party work among Russian women. Samoilova had been instrumental in laying the groundwork for Zhenotdel. She was "a calm, organized, persuasive woman with a talent for compromise," writes **Barbara Clements**, who "possessed enough political realism to curb [Kollontai's] tendency to rush ahead oblivious of party opposition." She showed these talents when she convinced her reluctant male colleagues at the Ninth Party Congress to strengthen Zhenotdel's mandate. "When the chances of putting through some Zhenotdel question . . . were few, we brought up the heavy artillery—Comrade Samoilova," said Kollontai. Samoilova did not, however, consider herself to be a theoretician and much preferred to stay in the background carrying out the decisions of others. She was quite content to help edit Zhenotdel's theoretical journal *Kommunistka* (The Communist Woman) and to coordinate its activities in Ukraine, leaving the leadership of the body to Armand and Kollontai. As a result, she has never been accorded the attention given to her more famous colleagues. In 1920, still depressed over the death of her husband two years earlier, she temporarily returned to an earlier interest when she agreed to serve as a propagandist on the agitational steamship *Krasnaia Zvezda* (Red Star) as it plied the Volga River promoting the cause of the new Soviet state. On a second cruise in 1921 she, like her husband, contracted cholera, died and was buried in Astrakhan at the age of 45. The nearly concurrent loss of its three strong and independent leaders—Samoilova, Armand who had also died of cholera in 1920, and Kollontai who was sent into diplomatic exile in 1922—was a blow from which the embryonic Soviet women's movement never recovered.

SOURCES:

Clements, Barbara Evans. "Samoilova, Konkordiia Nikolaevna," in *Modern Encyclopedia of Russian and Soviet History.* Vol. XXXIII, 1983, pp. 72–73.

Morozova, Vera. "Kompas u kazhdogo svoi," in *Zhenshchiny russkoi revoliutsii* (Women in the Russian Revolution). Moscow, 1982, pp. 101–114.

"Samoilova, Konkordiia Nikolaevna," in *Deiateli SSSR i revoliutsionnogo dvizheniia Rossii* (Personalities of the USSR and the Revolutionary Movement in Russia). Moscow, 1989 [1927], pp. 645–646.

SUGGESTED READING:

Kudelli, P. *K.N. Samoilova-Gromova (Natasha), 1876–1921 gg. (biografiia)*. Leningrad, 1925.

R.C. Elwood,
Professor of History,
Carleton University, Ottawa, Canada

Sampson, Deborah (1760–1827)

Revolutionary War soldier who, disguised as a man, fought in several engagements with the enemy. Name variations: Mrs. Deborah Sampson Gannett; (aliases) Timothy Thayer, Robert Shurtleff, Shurtliff, Shurtlieff, or Shirtliffe, and Ephraim Sampson. Born Deborah Sampson on December 17, 1760, in Plymton, Massachusetts (near Plymouth); died in Sharon, Massachusetts, on April 19, 1827; daughter of Jonathan Sampson (a farmer and sailor) and Deborah (Bradford) Sampson; self-taught and attended local elementary schools; married Benjamin Gannett, on April 7, 1785; children: Mary Gannett; Patience Gannett; Earl Bradford Gannett.

Lived on family farm (1760–66); became an indentured servant (1770–78); unsuccessfully enlisted as a soldier (early 1782); enlisted in the Continental Army (May 20, 1782) as "Robert Shurtleff"; served with army north of New York City and in detachments versus Tories; wounded on head (June 1782) and on thigh (July 1782); went on expedition to Fort Ticonderoga (November 1782); appointed orderly to Gen. John Patterson in Philadelphia (June–September 1783); took ill, gender discovered, and discharged (October 25, 1783); granted pay settlement by Massachusetts (1792); romanticized biography published (1797); joined lecture circuit (1802); granted federal pensions, as a female army veteran (1805 and 1818).

Deborah Sampson symbolizes the patriotic contributions of women during the American Revolution and their rising expectations for greater freedom in domestic and public life. Sampson is the only documented female soldier, masquerading as a man, who served in the ranks of the Continental Army; she is also regarded as the first paid woman lecturer in America.

Large numbers of women participated in the war effort: sewing and mending clothes for the army, raising money, working farms and businesses during the absences of their male relatives, serving as nurses in army hospitals, and even accompanying the army, performing a variety of support duties. Some women, such as the well-known ❧▶ **Margaret Corbin**, ❧▶ **Mary Ludwig Hays McCauley** ("Molly Pitcher"), and **Anna Maria Lane** assisted their husbands at their battle stations. But Deborah Sampson is the only woman who served an enlistment as a soldier, engaging in the same military duties and the rigors of camp, long marches, and even battle as did her male comrades. She was the only woman to receive veteran's pensions for her own military service during the Revolutionary War.

She was born in 1760, in Plymton, Massachusetts, near Plymouth, the eldest of three daughters in a family of five children of Jonathan Sampson, a farmer, and Deborah Bradford Sampson. A high-spirited young woman, Sampson yearned for an easier and more exciting life than the drudgery of farm and household chores. She had a desire to travel. For a poor woman to do so, however, would arouse suspicion that she was a person of ill repute. Not having the resources to act the role of a gentlewoman, why not join the army? Men could, she thought, why not women? Tall for her times (5'8"), muscular, with a wide waist and long nose, though of female voice and countenance, she could well pass for a young soldier if properly attired. Many of the rag-tag infantry of the Continental Army were mere boys.

Sampson boasted a distinguished pedigree. On her mother's side, she was descended from Governor William Bradford of Plymouth colony, and, on her father's, from Miles Standish and *Priscilla Alden, also early Pilgrims. Her father was a heavy drinker and poor provider, and, like many New England farmers, went to sea for part of each year. When Deborah was five, he abandoned the family and soon thereafter died in a shipwreck. Sampson's mother had to send her children to board at other homes. Deborah lived with a pastor's widow for two years, and then resided three years with an elderly relative who died in 1770. In a common practice of the time, Deborah next was taken in as an indentured servant of the Jeremiah Thomas family of Middleboro, Massachusetts. The Thomases were prosperous farmers, and Sampson continued doing farm and household work, becoming an accomplished spinner and seamstress. Thomas allowed her to attend school part-time with his sons and to earn money by having sheep and chickens of her own. Though the indenture ended when Sampson reached her 18th birthday in 1778, she stayed with the Thomas family for several more years. For six months, she was a substitute schoolteacher. In 1780, she was baptized into the First Baptist Church of Middleboro.

In early spring 1782, while staying a few days at the home of Captain Benjamin Leonard,

Margaret Corbin and *Mary Ludwig Hays McCauley*. See entry titled Two Mollies.

Sampson took a suit of clothes belonging to Leonard's son Samuel and, tying her hair in back and taping a cotton strip to compress her breasts, headed to the local recruiting office. She enlisted in the army as Timothy Thayer. Given bounty money, she swaggered boldly to a tavern, and became outrageously inebriated. Her ruse, however, was undone, because an elderly woman, who had been in the same room when Sampson signed her enlistment papers, recognized "Timothy" as Deborah from Sampson's awkward way of holding a quill, having lost most of the use of her forefinger from an accident. Sampson was quickly removed from the army rolls and forced to relinquish that part of the bounty money that she had not spent in the tavern.

She was a remarkable vigilant soldier on her post, and always gained the admiration and applause of her officers.

—*The Independent Gazette*, January 10, 1784

Sampson's erratic behavior raised a few eyebrows in the small New England farming community. Her mother felt that the best way to stay gossip was to quickly find a husband for her daughter. A young man located as a candidate for such a match, however, did not suit Sampson. "I had not [my mother's] eyes to see such perfection in this lump of a man, or that he possessed qualities that would regenerate me," she said, according to her biographer.

> I had no aversion to him at first, and certainly no love, if I have ever understood that noble passion. At any rate, this marry, or not to marry, was decided thus: On a certain parade-day he came to me, with all the *sang froid* of a Frenchman, and the silliness of a baboon, intoxicated, not with love, but with rum. From that moment I set him down a fool, or in a fair way to be one.

Sampson was still determined to join the army but took more care in her disguise than before. She went to Bellingham, and there on May 20, 1782, contacted a recruiting agent, sometimes known as a "speculator," who agreed to sign her up, providing he received part of the bounty money. Sampson enlisted as Robert Shurtleff, the name of her elder brother. Every town divided its male population capable of bearing arms into classes, from whom soldiers for the Continental Army were selected. Sampson represented a class from Uxbridge. According to the policy for Continental enlistments at the time, Sampson signed on for three years or the duration of the war. She was mustered into the service at Worcester by Captain Eliphalet

Thorp on May 23, and assigned to George Webb's infantry company of the Fourth Massachusetts Regiment, commanded by Colonel William Shepard and later by Colonel Henry Jackson. Because she looked too young to shave, other soldiers began calling her "smock face" and "Molly."

The Fourth Massachusetts Regiment was assigned to West Point, and Sampson had no difficulty escaping detection. Again she kept her breasts tightly taped, and she dressed and used the latrines during darkness. Family and friends, disturbed over her disappearance, suspected that she had gone soldiering. When a family friend went to camp searching for her, she successfully avoided him. Sampson wrote her mother that she had found "agreeable work" in "a large but well-regulated family." Members of her church in Middleboro, having for some time despaired of Sampson's waywardness, decided to excommunicate her. The record of the First Baptist Church in Middleboro, September 3, 1782, declares:

> The Church consider'd the case of Deborah Sampson, a member of this Church, who last Spring was accused of dressing in men's clothes, and enlisting as a Soldier in the Army, and altho she was not convicted, yet was strongly suspected of being guilty, and for some time before behaved verry loose and unchristian like, and at last left our parts in a suden maner, and it is not known among us where she is gone, and after considerable discourse, it appeard that as several bretheren had labour'd with her before she went away, without obtaining satisfaction concluded it is the Church's duty to withdraw fellowship untill she returns and makes Christian satisfaction.

Although the war had stalemated after Charles Cornwallis' surrender at Yorktown in October 1781, patrols from George Washington's army, encamped above New York City, which was still held by the British, clashed with enemy units. Bands of Tories and patriots often fought each other on the so-called "Neutral Ground" in Westchester County, located immediately above the city. Sampson and her company were sent to White Plains, and from there sought out enemy detachments along the east side of the Hudson River. In mid-June 1782, Sampson's unit fought with British dragoons and Tories between Tarrytown and Sing Sing. Sampson sustained a sword wound on the left side of her head. Several weeks later, she and 30 other soldiers were ambushed by Tories at East Chester, four miles east of the river. A musket ball pierced her thigh. Sampson feared that the wound was so serious that a doctor would discover her sex. Sent to a hospital of the

French army, six miles away, she was treated by a surgeon, without her gender being discovered. She then was permitted to sleep. "I had slept scarcely an hour, when he again alarmed me," Sampson later recalled. "Approaching me on my mattress of straw, and holding my breeches in his hand, dripping from the wash-tub, 'How came this rent?' said he, putting his finger into it. I replied, 'It was occasioned, I believe, on horseback, by a nail in the saddle or holster.'" As she grew better, the surgeon's "scrutiny diminished," and she rejoined the army before her wound healed. "Had the most hardy soldier been in the condition I was when I left the hospital," she noted, "he would have been excused from military duty." It appears that the bullet was never extracted. Many years later, in 1837, a committee of Congress, hearing a pension claim by her husband as a widower of a war veteran, would state "that the effect of the wound continued through life, and probably hastened her death."

In November 1782, Sampson traveled with her company to Fort Ticonderoga for the purpose of protecting settlers from marauding Indians. She saw some action. The unit, in January 1783, returned to Washington's army, encamped at New Windsor, New York. In June, she was transferred to Philadelphia to serve as an orderly to Major General John Paterson, who, with troops from Washington's army under the command of Major General Robert Howe, had come to the city to quell a mutiny. Soldiers of the Pennsylvania line, demanding back pay before being discharged, had seized the State House where Congress was in session. The legislators quickly fled to Princeton. The mutineers soon dispersed, but Paterson, in charge of court-martials of the leaders of the malcontents, stayed in Philadelphia for several months. While acting as the general's orderly, Sampson came down with "malignant fever" and lay near death. In a hospital ward, Dr. Barnabas Binney attended to her. "Thrusting his hand into my bosom to ascertain if there were motion at the heart," noted Sampson, "he was surprised at finding an inner vest tightly compressing my breasts, the instant removal of which not only ascertained the fact of life, but disclosed the fact that I was a woman!" The startled physician had Sampson brought to his home to recuperate, for the time being agreeing to keep her secret.

Having mended, Sampson joined a party of troops of the Massachusetts 11th Regiment on a land-surveying expedition. The expedition to the Ohio River set out from Baltimore. Once again sick, she had been left at an "Indian camp" and rejoined the troops on their return eastward.

Back in Baltimore, it seems that a young lady of 17 developed a crush on Robert Shurtleff (Deborah), even presenting Sampson with six linen shirts, 25 Spanish dollars, and 5 guineas. Not sure how to react, Sampson encouraged the relationship for awhile, the two going on carriage rides and the like. Finally, on departing Baltimore, Sampson wrote the young lady, signing the letter as "Your Own Sex."

The war had now officially concluded, with the signing of the Peace of Paris on September 3, 1783, and the British prepared to evacuate their last bastion, New York City. In October, Sampson set out for West Point to receive her discharge. While she was traveling in a boat on the Hudson, a squall came up near Elizabeth Town, New Jersey, and a trunk containing clothes and her diary were lost. This was especially unfortunate because if her diary had survived it would have served as corroboration as well as a corrective for her later recollections.

Meanwhile, Dr. Binney had second thoughts about concealing knowledge of Sampson's true sex, and, considering himself duty bound, informed Paterson of his discovery. The general then wrote General Henry Knox, commander of the remnant American army at West Point, revealing that Private Robert Shurtleff was actually Deborah Sampson. All was done with good humor. At West Point, Sampson, dressed in female attire, paraded up and down the ranks of the troops, never recognized by her fellow soldiers. She received an honorable discharge from General Knox on October 23, 1783.

After being discharged, Sampson traveled by ship to New York City and then made her way to Boston. She went to live on a farm owned by her uncle, Zebulon Waters, at Stoughton, Massachusetts. Unable to resist the urge to cross-dress again, she wore men's clothing, passing herself off as Ephraim Sampson, the name of her younger brother. But at last, in spring 1784, she decided to establish permanently her identity as a woman and to wear female attire. Meanwhile, she had become a celebrity of sorts. A New York newspaper, on January 10, 1784, printed a tribute to her as a female hero, which the *Boston Gazette* also carried on February 9, 1784.

Sampson soon attracted a suitor, and on April 7, 1785, married Benjamin Gannett. The couple settled into a two-story farmhouse in Sharon, Massachusetts. They had three children—Mary, Patience, and Earl Bradford. Because of trouble from her war-related thigh wound, Sampson was unable to be of much help in the farm work.

Like so many other New Englanders, the Gannetts had great difficulty in making a livelihood from their small farm. Deborah Sampson had received no pay while in the army. This was not unusual, as most soldiers went unpaid from 1782 to 1783. The Continental currency was worthless. Eventually, states issued veterans "settlement certificates," to be redeemed in the future. Sampson, however, had been given none of these. She evidently had lost her discharge papers. On January 1792, she sent a petition, supported by depositions from persons who attested to her military service, to the Massachusetts legislature. Eight days later, the Massachusetts Assembly granted her the sum of £34, with interest from the date of her discharge in October 1783. The resolution conferring the grant stated that Sampson had "exhibited an extraordinary instance of female heroism by discharging the duties of a faithful, gallant soldier, and at the same time preserving the virtue & chastity of her sex unsuspected and unblemished, & was discharged from the service with a fair & honorable character."

In 1797, Herman Mann of Dedham, Massachusetts, published a biography of Deborah Sampson. Although he interviewed her at length, the book obviously contains much exaggeration and fiction. Both author and subject had regrets over the book's publication, and Mann planned to rewrite it, but died in 1833 before accomplishing this task. His son executed a revision that removed much of the outlandish material, but this work has never been published. In 1866, John A. Vinton published the Mann biography of 1797, along with sharp editorial evaluation of the authenticity of various passages and excerpts from the revised biography.

Herman Mann also prepared a pat speech for Sampson, which she delivered it at the Federal Street Theater in Boston on March 22, 1802, and subsequently at other places in New England and New York until September 9, 1802. She was probably the first woman to go on a paid lecture circuit. The "Address," as it was known, was hardly more than patriotic rhetoric, with no mention of Sampson's specific deeds. As to her own motives, Sampson declared: "Wrought upon at length by an enthusiasm and frenzy that could brook no control, I burst the tyrant bonds which held my sex in awe, and clandestinely, or by stealth, grasped an opportunity, which custom and the world seemed to deny, as a natural privilege."

In 1804, Sampson applied to the U.S. government for a disabled veteran's pension, the only kind of postwar military remuneration awarded at that time. Paul Revere, a neighbor of the Gannetts, wrote to Congressman William Eustis on her behalf:

> I have been induced to inquire her situation & character, since she quitted the Male habit & soldier's uniform: for the more decent apparel of her own sex, & since she had been married and become a mother. Humanity and Justice obliges me to say, that every person with whom I have conversed about Her, & it is not a few, speak of her as a woman of handsome talents, good morals, a dutiful wife, and an affectionate parent. She is now much out of health. She has several children, her husband is a good sort of man, though of small force in business. They have a few acres of poor land, which they cultivate, but they are really poor.
> She has told me that she has no doubt that her ill health is in consequence of her being exposed when she did a soldier's duty & that while in the army she was wounded.

Congress, on March 11, 1805, placed her on the Massachusetts Invalid Pension Roll, providing her a stipend of four dollars a month, retroactive to January 1, 1803. Sampson's stipend was raised to eight dollars a month, under an act of Congress of 1818, which gave pensions to veterans who had served continuously for nine months and who had relinquished state pensions. In her petition to Congress for an increased award, Sampson mentioned that she had been at the battle of Yorktown, in October 1781. Herman Mann, in his biography of Sampson, had also claimed her presence at Yorktown, but offered no specifics or evidence. Unquestionably, Sampson had a faulty memory, as did many old veterans seeking pensions, or she let fantasy dictate reality; her muster certificate, noting her entry into the army and dated May 23, 1782, has survived and is to be found in the Massachusetts Archives, Boston.

On April 19, 1827, Deborah Sampson died at age 66. Several months before her death, when asked the value of her possessions, she replied that all that she had was $20 worth of clothing. She was buried in Rockbridge Cemetery, in Sharon, one wing of which is dedicated as a memorial to Deborah Sampson Gannett.

In 1836, Congress passed an act allowing pensions to widows of deceased Revolutionary War soldiers. Benjamin Gannett took the unprecedented step of applying for a widower's pension. At first, it was deemed that widowers were not covered under the law. The Committee on Revolutionary Pensions, however, decided that the case of Deborah Sampson was a worthy exception. Sampson, as a common soldier, had "fought and bled for human liberty."

[Benjamin Gannett] was honored much by being the husband of such a wife; and as he has proved himself worthy of her, as he has sustained her through a long life of sickness and suffering, and as that sickness and suffering were occasioned by the wounds she received, and the hardships she endured in defence of the country; and as there cannot be a parallel case in all time to come, the Committee do not hesitate to grant relief.

Therefore, Congress, by a special act, gave Gannett a pension of $80 a month in 1837, retroactive to March 4, 1831. He did not live to collect, dying in January 1837 at age 83. Congress then passed another special act, conferring upon the Gannetts' three children, as heirs, the sum of $466.66 to be divided equally among them.

Deborah Sampson's place in history is indeed unique in the history of the Revolutionary War. She was a common soldier among male companions, many of whom were of the roughest sort and riff-raff, yet her gender was undetected. Her experience was more than "theatrical," as one contemporary noted; it verged on the miraculous. But all the more tribute is due her, not only for equalling men in the soldier's life and in combat, but also for having the hardship of maintaining the persona of "Robert Shurtleff." While some anecdotes attributed to Sampson are at least partially fictional and specifics of her military activity are missing, her service is fully documented.

SOURCES:

Davis, Curtis C. "A 'Gallantress' Gets Her Due: The Earliest Published Notice of Deborah Sampson," in *Proceedings of the American Antiquarian Society.* Vol. 91, pt. 2, 1981, pp. 319–323.

Evans, Elizabeth. *Weathering the Storm: Women of the American Revolution.* NY: Scribner, 1975.

Mann, Herman. *The Female Review: Life of Deborah Sampson.* Introduction by John A. Vinton. NY: Arno Press, 1972 (reprint of 1866 edition).

Stickley, Julia W. "The Records of Deborah Sampson Gannett, Woman Soldier of the Revolution," in *Prologue: The Journal of the National Archives.* Vol 4. Winter 1972, pp. 233–241.

SUGGESTED READING:

Doyle, Kathleen. "'Pvt. Robert Shurtleff': An Unusual Revolutionary War Soldier," in *American History Illustrated.* Vol. 23. October 1988, pp. 30–31.

McGovern, Ann. *The Secret Soldier: The Story of Deborah Sampson.* NY: Scholastic, 1975.

Freeman, Lucy, and Alma Halbert Bond. *America's First Woman Warrior.* Paragon House, 1992.

Norwood, William F. *Deborah Sampson, Alias Robert Shirtliff of the Continental Line.* Baltimore, MD: Johns Hopkins Press, 1957.

COLLECTIONS:

Pension file of Deborah Gannett, alias Robert Shurtleff, S32722 (M 804, microfilm roll 1045), National Archives, Washington, D.C.; several documents relating to Deborah Sampson's military service reside in the Massachusetts Archives, Boston.

RELATED MEDIA:

"Deborah Sampson, a Woman in the Revolution" (15 min. video), Phoenix-BFA Films & Video, 1976.

"Women on the Battlefields Molly Pitcher and Deborah Sampson" (15 min. video), Eye Gate Media, 1977.

Harry M. Ward,
Professor of History, University of Richmond, Richmond, Virginia, author of *Colonial America* (Prentice-Hall) and other books on colonial and Revolutionary America

Sampson, Edith S. (1901–1979)

African-American lawyer and judge. Name variations: Edith Spurlock; Edith Clayton. Born Edith Spurlock in Pittsburgh, Pennsylvania, on October 13, 1901; died in October 1979; one of eight children of Louis Spurlock (manager of a cleaning and dying establishment) and Elizabeth (McGruder) Spurlock (a milliner and maker of false hair switches); graduated from Peabody High School in Pittsburgh; attended New York School of Social Work; John Marshall Law School, LL.B., 1925; Loyola University, LL.M., 1927; married Rufus Sampson (a field agent, divorced); married Joseph E. Clayton (an attorney), in 1934 (died 1957); no children.

Was the first woman to receive an LL.M. from Loyola University; was one of the first black women admitted to practice before the U.S. Supreme Court (1934); was the first African-American appointed delegate to the United Nations (1950); was the first black woman elected judge in the United States (1962).

Edith S. Sampson accomplished many firsts in a career path far removed from her poverty-stricken origins. Born on October 13, 1901, in Pittsburgh, Pennsylvania, she grew up in a large family that worked hard to survive. Her father Louis Spurlock managed a shop that cleaned and dyed fabrics, and her mother **Elizabeth McGruder Spurlock** made buckram hat frames and false hair switches. Her parents were frugal by necessity, handing down clothing from child to child and avoiding waste. The children worked as soon as they were able, and Sampson got her first job when she was 14, scaling and boning fish in a fish market. Although the family was poor, their hard work and frugality paid off when they were able to buy a home.

When Sampson graduated from Peabody High School in Pittsburgh, her Sunday school teacher helped her get a position with Associated Charities, and that organization in turn arranged for her to attend the New York School of Social Work. While there, Sampson took a required course in criminology taught by George

W. Kirchwey of the Columbia University School of Law, and received the highest grade in the class. "You are in the wrong field," Kirchwey told her. "You have the earmarks of a lawyer."

Sampson moved to Chicago and worked as a social worker for the Illinois Children's Home and Aid Society, finding placements for orphaned and neglected children in adoptive and foster homes. She again encountered Kirchwey, who was in town to give a speech, and he further encouraged her to enter law school. With his support, she enrolled in the evening program at Chicago's John Marshall Law School in 1922 and became the highest-ranking student of the 95 enrolled in the course on jurisprudence, earning a special commendation from Dean Edward T. Lee.

After receiving her bachelor of laws degree in 1925, Sampson sat for the Illinois bar exam and, despite her shining record, failed it. She attributed her setback to overconfidence and claimed it was the best thing that could have happened to her. Not at all discouraged, she continued her studies at the graduate law school of Loyola University, and in 1927 became the first woman granted an LL.M. from that institution. She passed the bar and was admitted to the practice of law in Illinois the same year.

While in graduate school, Sampson had been appointed probation officer for the Juvenile Court of Cook County, Illinois, thus beginning an 18-year association with that court which she said taught her the practical side of law. She later became a referee for the same court. Her private law practice, which she maintained until 1942, specialized in criminal law and domestic relations. Located on Chicago's South State Street in the middle of black neighborhoods, it became the place where thousands of poor people who otherwise would have been unable to afford representation could come for legal advice. In 1934, Sampson was among the first black women admitted to practice before the U.S. Supreme Court, and in 1947 she was appointed assistant state's attorney of Cook County. She was "a kind of freewheeler," in court, said a friend, "with a completely unorthodox approach to the law." Said Sampson, "I talk from my heart and let the law take care of itself."

Sampson's career took a new turn in 1949 when, as chair of the executive committee of the National Council of Negro Women, she was invited to be one of 26 American civic, cultural, labor, and welfare leaders to participate in an international lecture tour. Using her own money, she traveled throughout the world, participating in public debates about current political ques-

tions and meeting with foreign dignitaries. Sampson was intent on exposing Soviet anti-American propaganda which exploited the condition of blacks in America. Before one audience, she declared that even though American democracy was not yet functioning perfectly, still she "would rather be a Negro in America than a citizen in any other land." Her skill and personality were much admired. Once, while speaking to the League of Pakistani Women, she referred to her efforts to raise $5,000 to cover her travel expenses, and the audience surprised her by collecting the sum and presenting it to her. She accepted the gift and immediately turned it over to the Pakistani league for their social work. When the lecture circuit was made permanent and named the World Town Hall Seminar, Sampson was elected president by the membership. The tour changed her focus. "After visiting and talking with the peoples of other countries," she said, "I knew that I could never make my law practice the primary business of my life; I would have to devote myself to the course of world brotherhood and world peace."

To Sampson's delight, President Harry Truman helped further her goal by appointing her an alternate member of the U.S. delegation to the United Nations in August 1950, substituting for *Eleanor Roosevelt. She was the first African-American appointed as an official U.S. representative. At the UN, Sampson served on the Social, Humanitarian, and Cultural Committee, which covered many areas including land reform, reparation of prisoners, repatriation of Greek children, and radio jamming. Her first appearance was on September 28, 1950, in an appeal to the UN to continue advisory work in social welfare. She was reappointed as alternate delegate again in 1952, and President Dwight D. Eisenhower later made her member-at-large of the U.S. Commission of UNESCO.

Many of Sampson's speeches concerned the status of African-Americans in America. While she admitted to injustices and imperfections in the social structure, she remained adamant in her defense of the United States as a country where the struggle for justice could take place in an atmosphere of hope. She denounced once more the images used by the Soviets in particular to criticize the social plight of American blacks, and hotly defended the U.S. against ideological attack. Her comments met with some criticism from American journalists who thought she overstated the case and made the status of blacks appear more positive than it was, but there were many who approved her stand. In 1961 and 1962, she was appointed to serve on the U.S.

Edith S.
Sampson

Citizens Commission on the North Atlantic Treaty Organization, and in 1964 and 1965, she was a member of the Advisory Committee on Private Enterprise in Foreign Aid.

In 1962, Sampson was elected associate judge of the Municipal Court of Chicago, the first black woman in America to hold a judgeship. Her cases involved domestic relations, and by the late 1960s, as a judge of a branch of the Circuit Court of Cook County, landlord-tenant issues. She was adamantly opposed to evicting tenants, to the dismay of landlords. She was a friend and supporter of Mayor Richard Daley who backed her as a candidate for the court

when William Dawson, a leader in Chicago's black community, opposed her. She also visited Harold Washington, at the time a prosecuting attorney with the mayor's office, to encourage him to work agreeably with the prosecutor's staff.

Toward the end of her life, Sampson received an honorary doctor of laws degree from the John Marshall Law School. Although she had no children, she was much admired by her nieces and nephews, two of whom followed her into the legal profession and became judges. Her strong personality impressed everyone who met her. Said one admirer, "She works like a dynamo, talks like a pneumatic drill, and her warmth penetrates any room she enters." Sampson retired from the bench in 1978 and died the following year at the age of 78.

SOURCES:

Current Biography 1950. NY: H.W. Wilson, 1950.

The New York Times (obituary). October 11, 1979.

Smith, Jessie Carney, ed. *Notable Black American Women.* Detroit, MI: Gale Research, 1992.

Malinda Mayer,
writer and editor, Falmouth, Massachusetts

Sampter, Jessie (1883–1938)

American poet and Zionist activist. Born Jessie Ethel Sampter on March 22, 1883, in New York City; died on November 11, 1938, at Givat Brenner, Palestine; daughter of Rudolph Sampter and Virginia (Kohlberg) Sampter; attended Columbia University, 1902–03; never married; children: (adopted daughter) Tamar.

Selected writings: The Seekers *(1910);* The Coming of Peace *(1919);* The Emek *(1927);* In the Beginning *(1935);* Brand Plucked from the Fire *(1937); (translator)* Far Over the Sea *(1939).*

Poet and Zionist Jessie Sampter belonged to a generation in which many assimilated German-Jewish Americans reconnected with their Jewish roots by helping their impoverished brethren who arrived in America from Eastern Europe after the Russian pogroms of the early 1880s. Sampter did not even know she was Jewish until age eight, yet she would go on to write in her unpublished autobiography "The Speaking Heart": "I have a people, a congregation. It is not in the Church nor in the Synagogue. It is in the streets, in the tenements, in the crowded 'Pale' of Russia and Poland, in the little agricultural settlements in Palestine. . . . It is my people, a chosen people. God has called it, has chosen it for suffering and service."

She was born the second of two daughters in New York City in 1883, into the cultured, well-off family of Rudolph Sampter and **Virginia Kohlberg Sampter**. Both her grandfathers had immigrated from Germany and eventually arrived in New York. Her father was a self-employed attorney and avowed atheist who supported the founding of the Ethical Culture Society by his friend Felix Adler. Not a healthy child, Jessie was educated at home. Her aspirations of becoming a violinist were cut short at age 12 when she contracted poliomyelitis which affected her hands and spine, making a back brace necessary. While she recuperated, Sampter engaged herself in writing articles and poems for the children's magazine *St. Nicholas.* During

1899 and 1900, she made an extended visit to England with her mother and other members of the family to further her education. Upon her return, she spent a year attending Columbia University—her father's alma mater—where she had some study of writing.

By 1909, her sister's marriage, the deaths of her parents, and an unrequited love affair left Sampter bereft of companionship. She applied herself to the formation of study groups among her cousins in order to generate discussion about politics, science, and spiritual matters. These weekly talks inspired her first book, *The Seekers,* which was published in 1910.

Under the influence of Reverend Merle St. Croix Wright, president of the Poetry Society of America, Sampter joined the Unitarian Church. Perhaps an act of even greater influence on Wright's part, however, was his introducing to her the work of the Jewish poet Hyman Segal. Whereas Sampter's earlier attempts to identify spiritually with both orthodox and reformed Jewish synagogues had not met with great success, Segal's poems in the *Book of Pain and Struggle Called the Prophecy of the Fulfillment* (1911), about the Eastern European Jewish immigrant experience, provided her with a spiritual connection to other Jews that until then had eluded her.

Through contact with younger Jewish intellectuals, Sampter learned a modern, social-activist approach to Judaism while developing concern for the hardships faced by Yiddish-speaking Jews of New York's East Side ghetto. At the same time, Sampter was becoming a Zionist. For a time, she resided in a Jewish settlement house, and she became an early leader in the women's Zionist organization Hadassah, which had been founded by *Henrietta Szold, to whom she had been introduced by Segal. To convey the precepts of the Zionist movement to American Jews, Sampter organized a School of Zionism, and her teaching resulted in the publication of two manuals: *Course of Zionism* (1916) and *Guide to Zionism* (1920).

Following her recuperation from a nervous breakdown in 1918, Sampter relocated to Palestine the following year. She would live there until her death, making only three trips back to the States. On her arrival in Jerusalem, she was still too weak to get out of bed and so spent her time making children's toys. As she grew stronger, she went to work among the poverty-stricken Yemenites, and organized night classes for Yemenite working girls. In 1923, Sampter adopted a two-year-old named Tamar who had been orphaned. The following year, she moved to Rehoboth to continue her work with the Yemenites.

As a result of her time in Palestine, Sampter was able to write in both Hebrew and English. In addition to her poetry, prose, biography, Zionist essays, and articles on subjects such as Arab-Jewish relations, she also translated the juvenile poetry of Hayyim Nahman Bialik from the Hebrew to English. Following her travels in Galilee (the center of the kibbutz movement in the 1920s), Sampter's writing was influenced by the communal life she witnessed, as evidenced in her 1927 book of prose poetry *The Emek*. In 1933, she joined the Givat Brenner kibbutz and used her own savings the following year to build a rest home for aging members of the kibbutz. She died there at age 55 on November 11, 1938, after battling both pneumonia and malaria.

SOURCES:

James, Edward, ed. *Notable American Women, 1607–1950*. Cambridge, MA: The Belknap Press of Harvard University, 1971.

SUGGESTED READING:

Badt-Strauss, Bertha. *With Fire: The Life and Work of Jessie Sampter*. NY: The Reconstructionist Press, 1956.

Gloria Cooksey,
freelance writer, Sacramento, California

Sams, Doris (1927—)

American baseball player. Name variations: Sammy. Born on February 2, 1927, in Knoxville, Tennessee.

Doris Sams, a pitcher and outfielder for the Muskegon-Kalamazoo Lassies from 1946 to 1953, was named Player of the Year in 1947 and 1949. She threw a perfect game in 1947, won the batting championship in 1949, and took the home-run title in 1952. Her lifetime batting average was .290.

Samuel, Mrs. Zerelda (c. 1824–1911).

See James, Zerelda.

Samuelson, Joan Benoit (1957—)

American runner and gold-medal winner in the first Olympic marathon for women. Name variations: Joan Benoit. Pronunciation: BAH-noit. Born Joan Benoit on May 16, 1957, in Cape Elizabeth, Maine; daughter of Nancy Benoit and Andre Benoit (a clothing retailer); Bowdoin College, B.A. in history and environmental studies, 1979; married Scott Samuelson, in 1984; children: Abigail (b. 1987); Anders (b. 1990).

Placed first in the Boston Marathon, with a time of 2:35:15 (1979); placed first and set a world record, Boston Marathon, 2:22:43 (1983); placed first, Olympic Marathon Trials, 2:31:04 (1984); won Olympic gold medal and set Olympic record for the women's marathon, 2:24:52 (1984); received Jessie Owens Award (1984); named Women's Sports Foundation Amateur Sportswoman of the Year (1984); set world and American records, Chicago Women's Marathon, 2:21:21 (1985).

In August 1984, Joan Benoit Samuelson arrived in Los Angeles to compete in the first-ever Olympic marathon for women. The International Olympic Committee (IOC) had previously banned women from competing in the event, believing that the long-distance run posed a health hazard to women. The inaugural marathon began early in the morning at the track of Santa Monica City College, while the temperatures remained relatively cool and the smog had yet to reach noxious levels. As the marathon started, the runners remained in a tight group for the first three miles. Samuelson, feeling claustrophobic, broke away from the pack at the four-mile mark. As the miles rolled by, she continued to stretch out her lead. Some of the other runners believed she would fade back after such a quick start, but Samuelson maintained her advantage. At the end of 26 miles, as she emerged from the tunnel into the stadium which led to the final stretch, she could hear the crowd of 77,000 roaring and cheering her on. Weak with emotion, she lowered her head and kept running. As the last 200 meters approached, she waved her cap to the crowd and then broke the finish tape. Winning the gold medal with a time of 2:24:52, Joan Benoit Samuelson finished nearly a minute and a half ahead of her closest competitor. Her accomplishment was all the more remarkable considering the injuries and obstacles she had overcome to achieve it.

Born in Cape Elizabeth, Maine, on May 16, 1957, Joan Benoit was the third of four children, and only daughter, of **Nancy Benoit**, a natural athlete, and Andre Benoit, who had served as a ski trooper during World War II. There were two things the Benoits encouraged in their children from an early age—religion and skiing. The children often attended Sunday Mass in their ski clothes so they could hit the slopes as soon as the service ended. Samuelson's dream of going to the Olympics ended early, when, at age 15, she hit a slalom gate on a ski run and broke her leg. Though it eventually healed, the nerve to ski at a breakneck pace never returned.

The accident was a turning point for Samuelson. Without skiing, she began to focus on both field hockey and track at her high school. In order to rehabilitate her injured leg and prepare herself for competition, she initiated an extended running schedule. What began as an exercise in muscle building became a solitary endeavor that she loved. Her training and natural talent led her to excel as part of the track team.

Samuelson's performance on the high-school running track earned her a scholarship to North Carolina State University. There, her track team finished second overall in the National championships of the Association of Intercollegiate Athletics for Women. In addition, Samuelson was named to the All-America Team. Track and field victories notwithstanding, she was unhappy at North Carolina State and transferred to Bowdoin College in New England where she continued to run and also participated in both swimming and field hockey. Even though most of the running events were too short to showcase her true talent, she was awarded "most valuable player" for track her freshman year. As a junior, she received the award again, this time in recognition of her field-hockey abilities.

During her senior year, Samuelson celebrated her first major victory as a distance runner. The Boston Marathon is one of the most prestigious distance races in the United States. Though it has been run continuously since 1897, women have been allowed to compete only since 1972. The barrier was broken by the one-two punch of ❦▶ **Roberta Gibb** (1966) and ❦▶ **Kathy Switzer** (1967), who registered as K. Switzer and outran marathon officials who tried to confiscate her race number. On a cold, drizzly April day eight years later (1979), Joan Benoit Samuelson lined up to compete in the event. Jumping out early to take the lead, she held it for just over five miles, before dropping back into the pack. At the bottom of the infamous Heartbreak Hill, Samuelson began to pick up speed. By mile 18, she was running alone. While completing the last several miles, she could hear nothing but the deafening clamor of the crowd as it urged her on. She crossed the finish line, taking first place with a time of 2:35:15, setting a new American record and shattering the old course record for women by almost seven minutes.

After winning the marathon, Samuelson was overwhelmed by the public and media attention that followed. There was an invitational dinner at the White House. Newspapers, magazines, and television reporters requested interviews; fans mobbed her. A television agent badgered her to consider a movie deal. The public pressure was so intense that she seriously considered quitting racing.

In the final analysis, Samuelson decided she loved running more than she hated the publicity and, with the hope of qualifying for the 1980 Olympics in the 1,500-meter event, accepted an offer to race and train in New Zealand. Shortly after she arrived, however, the U.S. announced its boycott of the Moscow Olympics. Samuelson returned home, became violently ill, and several days later was diagnosed as having appendicitis. After recovering from an appendectomy, she resumed her training schedule and accepted a job that utilized her running expertise.

Samuelson began work as a consultant for Nike in Exeter, New Hampshire. There, she performed stress tests for shoes and evaluated the effects of oxygen intake utilization on athletes. The job provided a flexible environment, allowing her to train and participate in races. Her first race in 1981 was the New Orleans half-marathon, which she won while setting a new American-best record with a time of 1:13:26. She went on to San Diego and set another half-marathon record of 1:11:16. She then competed in the Boston Marathon and placed third with a time of 2:30:16. This extensive racing schedule took its toll on her body. In December 1981, she was hospitalized again and underwent surgery on both feet. In addition to tendon repairs, the doctor removed bone spurs, scar tissue, and both bursa sacs which had ruptured.

The severity of the surgery altered Samuelson's view on running enormously. It was quite possible she might never race again. "Either my feet wouldn't heal properly and I'd have to stop running or they would be fine and I could do what I liked," she wrote in her autobiography. "Either way, I thought I could cope." By May 1982, it was clear her running career was far from over, and she competed in the 25-kilometer Old Kent River Bank Run. She finished with a time of 1:26:30, taking first and beating the American record by ten seconds. She took second place and achieved a personal best with a time of 32:35 in the ten kilometer L'eggs mini-marathon. For a time, she competed on the European Track circuit and, on her return to the U.S., won the New York ten kilometer race with a time of 33:17. Her greatest triumph, at that point, was undoubtedly the Nike-Oregon Track Club marathon where she finished first with a time of 2:26:11 and set another American record.

By 1983, Samuelson was running over 100 miles a week in preparation for the Boston

✥► Gibb, Roberta (1943—)

American marathon runner. Name variations: Roberta Gibb Bingay; Bobbi Gibb. Born in 1943; graduated from Tufts University and New England School of Law; married to a Tufts University distance runner; children.

In 1984, Joan Benoit Samuelson was honored for winning the first U.S. Olympic Marathon trials. The statue that she tucked under her arm that day was sculpted by Roberta "Bobbi" Gibb, the woman who dared to run the Boston Marathon before it was open to women. Gibb had paved the way for Samuelson, whose early career as an elite runner was very much tied to the Boston race.

Roberta Gibb was born in 1943, grew up in Winchester, Massachusetts, and in 1964 witnessed her first Boston Marathon, which at the time was limited to males. Gibb was so impressed with the race that she fell in love with the idea of running. "I started to train but had no coach, no notion of how to train, no encouragement, no role models," she wrote in her brief autobiography *To Boston With Love*. "So I just kept running farther and farther— curious to see how far I could go and how fast." Gibb felt ready to put her training to the test in 1966, but when she applied to the Boston Athletic Association (BAA) for an official Marathon number, she was turned down on the grounds that women were incapable of covering the 26.2-mile distance. She decided to defy authority and enter the race unofficially. "My outrage turned to humor as I thought how many preconceived prejudices would crumble when I trotted right along for 26 miles," she wrote. Gibb's mother, who thought her daughter had "gone mad," drove her to the starting line in Hopkinton on the morning of the race. Clad in a black bathing suit, her brother's Bermuda shorts, and a blue hooded sweatshirt pulled up to cover her long blonde ponytail, Gibb leapt unnoticed from the bushes at the starting line, joining the 500 official male runners. Growing over-heated as she approached Wellesley, she whipped off her sweatshirt, thus changing the Boston Marathon forever.

Gibb was exhilarated by the response of the Wellesley College women who cheered her on, but after 20 miles, the combination of new shoes, dehydration (she was told water would cause cramps), and the roast beef dinner she had consumed the night before began to take a toll. But she persevered. "I was going to get to that finish line if I had to crawl," she said later. "If I'd dropped out, it probably would have set women's running back 20 years." She finished the race at 125th with an estimated time of 3:21:40, beating 290 male competitors. Still, authorities stood firm on their ban of women from the race.

The following year, Gibb ran again, joined by *Kathy Switzer, a track athlete from Syracuse University who gained official entry by applying as K. Switzer. A few miles into the race, BAA race official Jock Semple jumped off the press bus and tried to remove Switzer, but her boyfriend wrestled him to the ground. Switzer went on to complete the race, coming in an hour behind Gibb, who finished in 3:27:17. In 1968, with women still denied official entry, three women ran with Gibb, who again finished first in the unofficial field. The next year, Gibb did not run, but **Sara Mae Berman** of Cambridge joined the women's field, winning with a time of 3:22:46. She cut her time to 3:05:07 in 1970, and won the field again in 1971. In 1972, BAA officials finally allowed women to enter the Marathon, provided they met the men's qualifying time of 3:30. Eight women met the standard that year, including **Nina Kuscsik**, who became the first sanctioned women's winner, with a time of 3:10:26.

Roberta Gibb, an attorney as well as a sculptor, divides her time between Delmar, California, and Rockport, Massachusetts. She returned to Boston in 1996 to run the 100th Marathon, which also marked the 30th anniversary of her breakthrough run. Interviewed at the time by Associated Press journalist **Carolyn Thompson**, Gibb recalled the headlines from the day after her groundbreaking race. "Hub Bride First Gal to Run Marathon" and "Blonde Wife, 23, Runs Marathon," they read. There were also pictures of her smiling at the finish line and making fudge at home "to show I really was a woman," she said.

SOURCES:
Docherty, Bonnie. "Roberta Gibb paved the way for future generations of women," in *Middlesex News*. April 20, 1997.
Thompson, Carolyn. "Gibb recalls her historic run," in *The Day* [New London, CT]. April 6, 1996.

✥► Switzer, Kathy (1947—)

American runner. Name variations: Kathrine Switzer; Kathy Switzer Miller.

Because of the 100-year "no women allowed" rule in the Boston Marathon, Kathy Switzer registered for the race as K. Switzer in 1967. She arrived at the starting line in a sweatsuit with hat pulled low. During the race, when an official realized she was a woman, he tried to stop her by ripping the racing number off her back. Switzer, and her running partners, fought off the official, and she finished the race. The incident, however, was captured by a photographer and the ensuing publicity tarnished the prestigious marathon. Five years later, in 1972, women were allowed to enter Boston's premiere event. Switzer had helped pave the way. The 33-year old **Nina Kuscsik**, mother of three, was the first winner in the women's division, with a time of 3:08:58, finishing ahead of 800 male runners. In 1974, Switzer won the New York City Marathon with a time of 3:07:29.

SUGGESTED READING:
Switzer, Kathrine. *Running and Walking for Women over 40.* Griffin, 1998.

Marathon. Her training paid off: she finished first with a time of 2:22.43, shaving almost three minutes off the world record. Mobbed by reporters who asked for her secret, she replied: "I run how I feel. When I don't feel good, I find a spot in the pack and hang on. Today I felt great and I went for it." The win was not without controversy, however. During the marathon, another runner who served as a reporter for a local radio station ran beside Samuelson. Some claimed that he called out split times and acted as a pacer. None of the allegations were ever proven and no rule against pacing was passed by marathon officials. Samuelson dismissed the accusations, asserting that the reporter was a nuisance who had trouble keeping pace with her.

In the early days, running was not considered feminine. While training on a country road, I was so embarrassed that when a car came along I would pretend I was picking up returnable bottles.

—Joan Benoit Samuelson

The Boston finish placed Samuelson on the list of favorites to win the 1984 first-ever Olympic women's marathon. She began training for the trials with a determined focus. By mid-March, she felt she was approaching peak condition as an athlete and competitor. On March 17, she began a 20-mile loop run which served as a gauge of her training fitness. As she approached the 17-mile mark, she felt a strange sensation in her knee as "if a spring were unraveling in the joint." By the time she reached home, her knee was stiff and throbbing with pain. Panic-stricken, she went to see the head of the Olympic team physicians. The doctor gave her anti-inflammatory drugs, prescribed rest, and injected her knee with cortisone.

For the next three weeks, Samuelson rested and ran short distances. On the morning of April 10, she took a long run with no pain in her knee. That evening, she had a track workout where she ran three separate miles under five minutes. All appeared well, but as she took her cool-down laps her knee tightened again. The next morning there was no improvement, and she had to abandon her training run and walk home.

On April 12, just one month before the marathon trials, she was given another cortisone shot, but her knee did not respond. Desperate, Samuelson consulted a knee specialist in Oregon. The news was not good. The doctor prescribed five days of complete rest followed by surgery if her knee did not improve.

On April 25, Samuelson underwent arthroscopic surgery. The doctor located and removed an inflamed, fibrous mass called a plica which prevented the joint from functioning properly and caused the pain in her knee. Remaining in the hospital overnight, Samuelson was released with instructions to return in a week. In the meantime, her only allowed exercise was swimming and slow riding on a stationary bicycle. The Olympic Marathon trials were 17 days away.

On April 29, the day before her post-operative examination, she jogged a bit without pain. Though cleared by her doctor to resume running, she was advised to slow down and take it easy. Samuelson had other plans. She began a training schedule that started early in the morning and ended near 11:00 PM. With the help of physical therapy and whirlpool baths, she continued to swim, bike, and run. A few days later, she ran for over an hour without pain. In her determination to compensate for lost time, she ran again that same day and pulled her left hamstring. The injury that had first threatened to keep her out of the Olympic trials now became secondary as she experimented with new forms of therapy to treat the hamstring. One of the newest forms of therapy was minimal electrical neuromuscular stimulation. Samuelson underwent six-to-ten hours of treatment a day until the trials began.

The Olympic Marathon trials were held in Olympia, Washington, on May 12. The course was a flat loop and any woman who had completed a certified marathon with a time under 2:51:16 was eligible to compete. Only the top three finishers, however, would win spots on the Olympic team. As she jogged to the starting line, Samuelson was not sure she could finish, let alone place in the top three. Her knee was tight and the hamstring still hurt even after days of therapy. At the 14th mile of the race, Samuelson took the lead and hung on through pain to cross the finish line first with a time of 2:31:04. She had secured herself a place on the Olympic Marathon team.

So it was that the 5'3" Joan Benoit Samuelson, along with 50 other Olympic hopefuls, lined up at the track of Santa Monica City College one hot summer day in 1984. In the starting pack was Norway's lankier *Grete Waitz, who had been experiencing back spasms the day before. So few tickets were sold for this, the first running of an Olympic women's marathon, that the gates were thrown open to all. Samuelson, with the bill of her painter's cap facing backwards, began, as she said, to follow the "yellow

Opposite page

Joan

Benoit

Samuelson

brick road." Though fearful of "showboating," she moved into the lead and never looked back. It was the modest and unassuming Samuelson who was the first to come running onto the oval of the Los Angeles Coliseum while the crowd roared long and loud. Waitz crossed the finish line 1 minute and 26 seconds later, for a silver medal. Fifty-two years earlier, the Los Angeles Coliseum had cheered when another runner, Juan Carlos Zabala of Argentina, had entered the stadium to win the men's Olympic Marathon of 1932. If he had been running in the same race with Samuelson, Waitz, and those other 1984 pioneer women runners, he would have finished 10th. Samuelson said after the race that she did not want to sound boastful, but "it was a very easy race for me. I was surprised I wasn't challenged at all."

After her Olympic victory, Samuelson enjoyed and later endured the ensuing publicity. Within three days, she had returned quietly to her home in Maine. She hoped to revert to a normal lifestyle but the peace and quiet she longed for never materialized. Her hometown of Freeport celebrated her success with Joan Benoit Day, while Portland held a parade. Maine's Sports Hall of Fame bent its standing rule that members be retired and inducted Samuelson that same year. Aside from being Maine's sweetheart, she found out that the rest of America intended to claim her, and commercial offers from fast food chains and drink companies poured in. Samuelson chose her endorsements carefully. She maintained her contract with Nike and accepted an offer from Poland Spring, a local water company. She told an interviewer from *The New York Times*: "I'm a clean-living person. Nike and Poland Spring are both a natural for me. The others weren't." The marathoner ended 1984 by marrying Scott Samuelson in a church ceremony, with 500 of their friends and family members in attendance.

Samuelson hoped the next year would bring her the peace she so craved and that she could get back to her solo training runs. This was not to happen, however, for she was recognized everywhere she went. Cars would honk as she ran or walked through town. People came to her home seeking autographs or advice. Though Samuelson recognized that the public wanted to share in her victory, it tried her patience, and she again seriously considered giving up running in hopes of regaining her privacy.

During the next three years, she continued to train but stayed off the major marathon circuit and away from the public eye. Her running

was devoted not to placing first or winning prize money but to chasing a faster time. In 1987, while pregnant with her first child, she reentered the Boston Marathon. Despite having trained for the event, she was forced to drop out due to internal bleeding in one of her legs.

In October, she gave birth to her daughter **Abigail** and concentrated on balancing the demands of motherhood and marathon running. Two weeks later, with her daughter packed safely in a carseat by poolside, she resumed lap swimming. Within three weeks, she was running again. Four weeks later, she was running up to 50 miles and by the fifth week she was up to 80 miles.

The next few years saw her return to the marathon circuit but she was plagued by bad luck and injuries. At the New York City Marathon in 1988, she was tripped by a volunteer at a water station and finished third with a time of 2:32:40. In 1989, she finished eighth in the Boston Marathon with a time of 2:37:57. Even so, she continued to train. When her son Anders was born in 1990, Samuelson thought the next year would see her healthy and once again hitting her stride. In March 1991, she competed and placed first in a 15-kilometer race in Cincinnati. After this victory, she again looked toward the Boston Marathon. There she placed fourth with a time of 2:26:54 which delighted her. She continued to race that year but health problems plagued her. While running the New York City Marathon, she suffered an asthma attack and dehydration which contributed to a sixth-place finish.

The ensuing years saw her qualify for the 1992 Olympic Trials but at the last moment she chose not to compete. In October 1998, age 41, she just happened to be in New York, making appearances for Nike, at the time of the city's marathon. Rather than leave for Maine on the intended day, she ran and came in 12th. Samuelson, who races and trains as her health permits, runs because she loves it, and because, as she has said, her life would be incomplete without it. "Winning isn't everything, and it isn't the only thing," she said. "It is one of many things."

SOURCES:

Averbuch, Gloria. *The Woman Runner: Free to be the Complete Athlete*. NY: Simon and Schuster, 1984.

Benoit, Joan, with Sally Baker. *Running Tide*. NY: Alfred A. Knopf, 1987.

Boga, Steven. *Runners and Walkers: Keeping Pace With the World's Best*. Harrisburg, PA: Stackpole, 1993.

Burfoot, Amby. "Cloudy Skies," in *Runner's World*. Vol. 27, no. 2. February 1992, pp. 40–43.

Dowd, Mike. "Samuelson Still Striding 10 Years After," in *Bangor Daily News*. July 1, 1994.

Finn, Robin. "A Runner in Search of Her Own Standard," in *The New York Times*. September 15, 1988.

Janofsky, Michael. "Injury Forces Samuelson to Drop Out of Marathon," in *The New York Times*. November 2, 1990.

———. "Samuelson Poised at Boston Crossroad," in *The New York Times*. April 14, 1991.

Litsky, Frank. "Samuelson Tests Her Resolve," in *The New York Times*. June 3, 1988.

Littlefield, Bill. "Marathon Mom," in *Yankee*. April 1994, p. 98.

Smith, Harold L. "Joan Benoit," in *Great Athletes: The Twentieth Century*. Vol. 2. Pasadena, CA: Salem Press, 1992.

SUGGESTED READING:

Derderian, Tom. *Boston Marathon: The History of the World's Premier Running Event*. Champaign, IL: Human Kinetics, 1994.

RELATED MEDIA:

"Joan Benoit Samuelson—10 Years After" (two-part interview with Samuelson), WVII-Television, Bangor, Maine, 1994.

Gaynol Langs,
independent scholar, Redmond, Washington

Sancha (c. 1178–1229)

First abbess of Lorvano. Born around 1178; died on March 13, 1229, at Lorvano; daughter of *Douce of Aragon (1160–1198) and Sancho I (1154–1211 or 1212), king of Portugal (r. 1185–1211 or 1212).

Sancha de Aybar

Mother of two kings. Mistress of Sancho III the Great (c. 991–1035), king of Navarre (r. 970–1035); children: (with Sancho) Ferdinand or Fernando I, king of Castile and Leon; Ramiro I, king of Aragon (r. 1035–1063).

Sancha of Aragon (d. 1073)

Countess of Urgel. Died in 1073; daughter of *Gilberga (d. 1054) and Ramiro I, king of Aragon (r. 1035–1069); married Pons, count of Toulouse; married Armengol III, count of Urgel; children: *Isabel of Urgel.

Sancha of Aragon (1478–1506).

See Borgia, Lucrezia for sidebar.

Sancha of Castile and Leon (d. 1179).

See Berengaria of Navarre for sidebar.

Sancha of Castile and Leon (1164–1208)

Queen of Aragon. Born on September 21, 1164; died on November 9, 1208, in Sijena; daughter of Alphonso VII, king of Castile and Leon (r. 1126–1157), and his *second wife *Ryksa of Poland (d. 1185); became second wife of Alphonso II (1152–1196), king of Aragon (r. 1162–1196), count of Barcelona (r. 1162–1196), and count of Provence as Alphonso I (r. 1166–1196), on January 18, 1174; children: Alphonso II, count of Provence and Forcalquier (d. 1209); Pedro also known as Peter II the Catholic (1174–1213), king of Aragon (r. 1196–1213); Ramon Berengar, count of Ampurias; Fernando; *Constance of Aragon (d. 1222). Alphonso II's first wife was *Matilda of Portugal (c. 1149–1173).*

Sancha of Leon (1013–1067)

Queen of Leon and Castile. Born in 1013; died on November 7, 1067, in Castile; daughter of Alphonso V, king of Leon, and Elvira Gonzalez of Galicia; married Ferdinand I (c. 1017–1065), king of Castile (r. 1038–1065), around 1032; children: Sancho II (b. around 1037), king of Castile and Leon (r. 1065–1072); Garcia of Galicia (c. 1042–1090), king of Galicia (r. 1065–1090); Alphonso VI (c. 1030–1109), king of Castile and Leon; *Urraca (1033–1101); *Elvira (1038–1101).

Sancha of Leon, who reigned as queen and regent of Castile, was the daughter of Alphonso V, king of Leon, and *Elvira Gonzalez of Galicia. In 1032, Sancha married Ferdinand of Castile, heir to the throne. He succeeded in 1037 (as Ferdinand I), and Sancha thus became queen of Castile; in the meantime, she had inherited the crown of Leon from her father. This united the two kingdoms into Leon-Castile, which became one of the most powerful nations in Western Europe.

Sancha was a popular queen, and one who took her responsibilities seriously. She was involved in the daily administration of the combined kingdoms, and was also an important figure in the *Reconquista* of Spain, the political, religious, and military movement to eliminate Muslim rulers from their strongholds on the Iberian peninsula. Sancha and Ferdinand joined other Catholic leaders in a unified effort to retake Spain, an effort which proved mostly successful from a military standpoint. However, several centuries of Muslim rule had left the peninsula profoundly influenced by Arabic culture, and it retained a large Muslim population even after their governments were dismantled. Sancha was regarded by her subjects as a pious and active woman; when Ferdinand died in 1065, Sancha was chosen as regent of Leon-Castile, a position in which she served well for two years.

SOURCES:
Echols, Anne, and Marty Williams. *An Annotated Index of Medieval Women.* NY: Markus Wiener, 1992.

Laura York,
Riverside, California

Sancha of Provence (c. 1225–1261)

Duchess of Cornwall. Name variations: Sanchia. Born around 1225 in Aachen, North Rhine, Westphalia, Germany; died on November 9, 1261, in Berkhamsted, Hertfordshire, England; buried in Hailes Abbey, Gloucestershire, England; daughter of *Beatrice of Savoy (d. 1268) and Raymond Berengar or Berenger IV (some sources cite V), count of Provence and Forcalquier; sister of *Eleanor of Provence (1222–1291), *Beatrice of Provence (d. 1267), and *Margaret of Provence (1221–1295); married Richard (1209–1272), 1st earl of Cornwall and king of the Romans, on November 23, 1243; children: Richard (died days after birth in 1246); Edmund (1249–1300), 2nd earl of Cornwall; Richard (c. 1252–1296). Richard of Cornwall first married *Isabel Marshall (1200–1240); his third wife was *Beatrice von Falkestein (c. 1253–1277).

Sanchez, Celia (1920–1980)

Cuban revolutionary leader, one of the key personalities in the movement to overthrow Batista, who was a political and personal intimate of Fidel Castro's for two decades. Name variations: Celia Sanchez; Celia Sanchez Mandeley or Manduley; (revolutionary names) Aly and Norma. Born in 1920 in Media Luna, near Manzanillo, Cuba; died in Havana on January 11, 1980; daughter of Dr. Manuel Sanchez Silveira; had four sisters.

Born in 1920 in Manzanillo, Cuba, Celia Sanchez grew up in a large family far removed from the poverty that afflicted most of the nation. Her father, a physician, was patriotic and socially conscious, and he impressed on his five daughters the necessity of striving for a more just world. Working as a company doctor at a sugar mill, he saw firsthand the inequities in a colonial society. When Celia was an adolescent, her father took her up Cuba's highest mountain, Pico Turquino in the Sierra Maestra, to place a bust of revolutionary martyr José Martí, Cuba's George Washington, at the peak. The Sanchez family's political allegiance was to the Ortodoxo (Orthodox) Party, founded in 1947 to bring honest government and social reform to Cuba. In March 1952, however, Fulgencio Batista seized power and rapidly transformed the island republic into a dictatorship based on terror and corruption. Like many liberal Cubans, Celia Sanchez was profoundly opposed to the Batista regime, but like virtually all of them she also felt powerless against the dictatorship, which had almost unlimited power on its side.

On July 26, 1953, Fidel Castro and a small band of militants attempted to spark a national uprising against the dictator by seizing the Moncada barracks in the city of Santiago, capital of Oriente province, the historical cradle of Cuban independence. The attack failed, and many of Castro's colleagues were killed or executed. He, however, survived and was released from prison in an amnesty several years later, going into exile in Mexico. Castro was determined to topple Batista's brutal rule. Sailing from Mexico in a leaky vessel named *Granma*, he and 81 other revolutionaries, including Ernesto "Che" Guevara, went aground on December 2, 1956, south of Niquero near Belic, at Playa de los Colorados. Soon the invaders found themselves being attacked by a much larger unit of Batista's troops. Less than 20 of the original group were able to escape to the nearby Sierra Maestra mountains. Sanchez, who had planned to meet the group on their arrival, had been arrested that morning in nearby Campechuela, and never made it to the beach.

Already at this nascent stage of his eventually successful revolution, Castro had been given important support by Sanchez. She had provided his group with coastal charts and maps of the region, and after the pitiful remnants of Castro's group reached the relative security of the mountains, she provided food and supplies, and established a network of friendly local peasants that enabled the guerrilla band to live off the land.

Shortly after 5 AM, on February 16, 1957, Sanchez and Castro met for the first time in the middle of a pasture, several hundred yards from a friendly peasant's farmhouse. Celia, whose code names were "Aly" and "Norma," had walked all night with a rebel guide to reach the site. Neither of them ever described this first meeting, but the mutual impression must have been formidable, for it marked the birth of an association that would last 23 years, to the day of her death. Joined by fellow rebel leaders Frank Pais and Fidel's brother Raúl, the four talked animatedly until high noon, when for security reasons they decided to move to a nearby canefield where they lunched on delicacies the visitors had brought with them. Castro was fascinated by the dark-haired and attractive Sanchez not only physically, but intellectually. It was clear from the start that she was extremely intelligent and practical, able to argue the fine points of politics and even weapons, of which she had expert knowledge.

Sanchez returned to the rebels' mountain retreat several times, finally joining their growing band permanently before the end of the year. Immediately, she became an indispensable part of Castro's life, taking on the role of personal manager. Unswervingly loyal, she became his shadow, displaying endurance equal to any in the guerrilla band. On patrol, she walked immediately behind Fidel. As his secretary and assistant, she brought order to his life, and she conscientiously saved many of Castro's documents, including messages handwritten before and after battles, preserving them for posterity. Often, her slacks and blouse pockets were stuffed with important papers, for the indefatigable Castro would dictate to her anytime, anywhere.

When Castro appeared to be physically exhausted, Sanchez would insist he rest. Concerned about his physical safety, and convinced that his survival was crucial to the success of their revolution, she took steps to keep him from personally leading attacks on the enemy. No detail of the rebels' daily life appeared to be too insignificant for her to notice. When their prisoners (Batista's soldiers) wrote home, it was Sanchez who arranged that a few pesos be slipped in with the letters; when they ate in a peasant's home, she quietly passed the family a few pesos on their departure.

On January 1, 1959, Castro and his rebel army entered Havana in triumph. Batista had fled only hours before. For the next 21 years, Sanchez would play a key role not only in Castro's private life (perhaps more as a mother figure than as a lover), but also in his new role as Maximum Leader of a revolutionary republic defying the most powerful nation in the world, the United States. With Castro's energies often unfocused because of his abiding dislike of schedules and administrative details, it was Sanchez who brought at least a semblance of direction into his daily life. Officially, as time went by her positions included those of Secretary of both the Presidency and the Council of Ministers, as well as membership in the Central Committee of the Communist Party of Cuba (CPC) and the holding of a seat in the National Assembly. Unofficially, she continued to be the single most important person in Castro's life, serving as his conscience and alter ego. She also wielded much power due to the fact that she functioned as his gatekeeper, controlling access to Cuba's leader. Although in public she followed the official line of "Fidel is always right," privately she was very likely the only person in Cuba who could tell Castro when he was wrong. The only other individual who dared to speak to Castro in such a free and open fashion was Che Guevara, who was killed in Bolivia in 1967.

Sanchez also helped design the extensive Lenin Park complex in suburban Havana, and helped preserve museums and sites of historic interest. Aware that much of the history of the revolution did not exist in conventional written sources, she organized an extensive oral history project to preserve memories of the struggle. To the millions of Cubans who supported the revolution, Sanchez was its human face, particularly when promises were not kept or a grievance or injustice had not been addressed. To many, her warmth and common sense was the genuine article, and on countless occasions she was able to cut through red tape to rectify a problem for an individual, a family, or even a village simply by making a telephone call to the appropriate government agency. The hardening of Cold War tensions and the aging of Cuba's revolution brought with it ominous signs of totalitarian intolerance, but for Sanchez the ideals she had fought for in the Sierra Maestra remained imperishable and unassailable. Her reputation for compassion prompted an old-line Communist to say of her, "If I believed in Christianity I would say that she came as close to sainthood as anyone on earth."

The Castro revolution marked an important chapter in the liberation of Cuba's women. Officially, all discrimination against them was ended, and rhetorically at least, the culture of machismo was declared to be dead and a relic of the past. In reality, of course, considerable inequalities remained. Although much progress was achieved after 1959, the de facto status of Cuban women was still not fully equal to that of men after four decades of revolutionary government. Castro admitted as much when he conceded, "in the corners of our consciousness live on old habits out of the past." Statistics served to underline the situation: although women in the 1980s comprised 36% of the nation's labor force, they comprised only 13% of CPC membership and few of the government's leading officials were women.

Celia Sanchez, a heavy smoker, died of lung cancer in Havana on January 11, 1980. Many Cubans were grief-stricken at her death, none more so than Castro. Some Cubans believed that Castro was suddenly deprived of an essential personal and political "gyroscope." He became withdrawn for a number of months, and observers even claimed to detect a perceptible slowing of the wheels of Cuba's governmental machinery in the period after Sanchez's death. In July 1980, the embattled island's revolutionary leadership suffered the loss of another of its leading women when **Haydée Santamaria** Cuadrado (1927–1980) committed suicide. A veteran of the Sierra Maestra like Sanchez, Santamaria had been a member of the CPC Central Committee since 1965.

Since her death, Celia Sanchez has been virtually canonized by Cuba as the woman who most embodies its revolutionary ideals, with countless hospitals and schools named after her. In January 1985, and again in May 1990, 5 centavo postage stamps were issued in her honor. She was also remembered in 1990 by the minting of 1 peso and 5 peso commemorative coins.

SOURCES:

Alberto, Eliseo. "'La mas hermosa y autoctona flor de la revolucion,'" in *Verde Olivo* [Havana]. Vol. 21, no. 3. January 20, 1980, pp. 4–13.

Bourne, Peter G. *Fidel: A Biography of Fidel Castro*. NY: Dodd, Mead, 1986.

Bunck, Julie Marie. "Women's Rights and the Cuban Revolution," in Irving Louis Horowitz and Jaime Suchlicki, eds., *Cuban Communism*. 9th ed. New Brunswick, NJ: Transaction, 1998, pp. 406–426.

"Celia Sanchez, Aide to Castro," in *The Washington Post*. January 13, 1980, p. D4.

Cuban stamp honoring Celia Sanchez, issued on May 9, 1990.

SANCHEZ, CELIA

"Cuban Leader in Revolution Kills Herself," in *The Times* [London]. July 30, 1980, p. 6.

Directory of Personalities of the Cuban Government, Official Organizations, and Mass Organizations. 2 vols. Washington, DC: Central Intelligence Agency, 1973–74.

Karol, K.S. *Guerrillas in Power: The Course of the Cuban Revolution.* NY: Hill & Wang, 1970.

Llanes, Julio M. *Celia nuestra y de las flores.* Havana: Editorial Gente Nueva, 1985.

Llovio-Menéndez, José Luis. *Insider: My Hidden Life as a Revolutionary in Cuba.* NY: Bantam, 1988.

Lockwood, Lee. *Castro's Cuba, Cuba's Fidel.* Boulder, CO: Westview Press, 1990.

Minà, Gianni. *An Encounter with Fidel: An Interview.* Translated by Mary Todd. Melbourne, Australia: Ocean Press, 1991.

Quirk, Robert E. *Fidel Castro.* NY: W.W. Norton, 1993.

Steffens, Heidi. "Cuba: The Day Women Took over Havana," in *Ms.* Vol. 3, no. 10. April 1975.

Szulc, Tad. *Fidel: A Critical Portrait.* NY: Morrow, 1986.

Thomas, Hugh. *Cuba, or, The Pursuit of Freedom.* NY: Da Capo Press, 1998.

Towers, Roy. "The Reckless Revolutionary," in *The Herald* [Glasgow]. August 13, 1996, p. 11.

Vail, John J. *Fidel Castro.* NY: Chelsea House, 1988.

John Haag,
Associate Professor History,
University of Georgia, Athens, Georgia

Sanchez, Munia Mayor (995–1067).

See Munia Elvira.

Sanchez de Cepeda y Ahumada, Teresa (1515–1582).

See Teresa of Avila.

Sanchia or Sancia.

Variant of Sancha.

Sand, George (1804–1876)

French author of over 100 novels, plays, and essays who gained literary fame during her lifetime and infamy for her unconventional lifestyle. Name variations: Amandine-Lucile-Aurore Dupin; Mme Dudevant. Born Amandine-Aurore-Lucile Dupin in Paris, France, on July 1, 1804; died at Nohant (Berry), France, on June 8, 1876; daughter of Maurice Dupin de Francueil and Antoinette-Sophie-Victoire Delaborde; married Baron Casimir Dudevant, on September 17, 1822 (died March 1871); children: Maurice (b. 1823); (with Stéphane Ajasson de Grandsagne) Solange Sand.

Left Nohant for Paris (January 4, 1831); had affair with Alfred de Musset (summer 1833); filed for legal separation from Dudevant (1836); had affair with Frédéric Chopin (1833–1847); wrote plays, tracts, and open letters supporting social change (1848); published Histoire de ma Vie *(1854–55).*

Aurore Dupin Dudevant, also known as George Sand, was a descendant of a king of Poland on her father's side and of a Parisian bird-seller on her mother's. Her critics vilified her as a loose woman, a political radical, and a "lioness" who devoured her numerous lovers. She further shocked society by dressing as a man and smoking cigars. But to her admirers, including the French literary elite, she was praised for her prodigious production of novels and plays, and as the originator of the genre of rustic, regional literature in France. An independent, free-thinking woman, Sand was an anomaly, even among sophisticated, worldly Parisian society. She was described as a "thinking bosom," and her androgynous lifestyle exhibited her duality—a "man's mind" and a woman's sensitivity and desires.

She was born Amandine-Aurore-Lucile Dupin in Paris, on July 1, 1804, the daughter of Maurice Dupin and **Sophie Delaborde Dupin**. The union of her parents was, in the eyes of her paternal grandmother, an abomination. Her plans to annul the marriage were abandoned, however, when she saw her infant granddaughter, but she persisted in disparaging her "guttersnipe" daughter-in-law Sophie. After Maurice Dupin died in a riding accident in 1808, the elder Mme Dupin won legal custody of Sand. Sophie and Aurore had been living with Mme Dupin at her country estate of Nohant in the Berry region, but friction between the Mesdames Dupin led Sophie to return to Paris. Charming, but uneducated, the young widow led a lifestyle that was deemed "debauched and wanton" by Sand's grandmother-guardian. Proud of her ancestry and social class, the elder Mme Dupin resolved to mold and educate Aurore in the role of the well-born heiress she was.

Maurice Dupin (a direct descendant of Augustus the Strong, king of Poland) was an officer in Napoleon's army when he met Sophie in Italy; she was the mistress of an aging general and mother of an illegitimate daughter, Caroline. Maurice, too, had an illegitimate child, a son Hippolyte Chatiron, age five, who lived at Nohant. Hippolyte and Aurore were educated by their father's tutor, Deschartres, who believed rigorous academic training was essential to both males and females: Latin, Greek, math, history, literature, and science prepared his pupils to function in the secular world. Formal religious instruction was shunned since both Mme Dupin and Deschartres were progressive free-thinkers. Following Rousseau's dictum of educating "the whole child," Aurore played freely with the local peasant children, learned to ride (wearing trousers and boots), and observed nature

through exploration, not dull textbooks. At age 13, Sand was strong-willed and often rebellious, and her grandmother made arrangements for her to attend a convent school in Paris. An excellent student, Aurore embraced religion and declared her intention of becoming a nun. Grand-mother Dupin put an end to such talk and removed her from school in April 1820.

Life at Nohant was pleasant for Aurore. A voracious reader (of everything from Aristotle to Benjamin Franklin) and a skilled rider, she was allowed a great deal of freedom. However, when Mme Dupin died in December 1821, Aurore was again the center of a family dispute between her father's relatives and her mother. Sophie won the custody battle, and Aurore moved to Paris, where she was often bored and restless. On a visit with friends of her father near Paris, Aurore met her future husband.

At age 18, as heiress to Nohant and an investment house in Paris, Sand was not without prospects, despite her mother's lower-class origins. Casimir Dudevant, nine years her senior, was the illegitimate son of Baron Dudevant and heir to his lands and money. Preparing to study law after resigning from the military, Casimir was a stolid and robust young man. Aurore was not averse to him or to the idea of marriage; marriage based on love and mutual respect was the romantic ideal to which Aurore clung all her life but never realized. The marriage contract was signed in August 1822, and less than a month later they were married. Aurore's inheritance was reserved for her, but her husband controlled and managed it, according to the dictates of French law. Aurore would spend much of her life in litigation to overturn her husband's rights to her properties. Her struggle for economic independence provided a recurrent theme in her novels.

> *What a heart of gold she had! What absence of anything petty, mean or insincere! What a brave man she was, and what a good woman!*
>
> —Ivan Turgenev

The young couple settled in Nohant and were actively involved socially and politically in their region of Berry. In June 1823, their son Maurice was born in Paris. Severe depression clouded Sand's joy of motherhood, but this was largely dispelled after a long trip to the Pyrenees with Casimir and several friends. Reciprocal love, the basis of a happy marriage, had not manifested itself according to Aurore's hopes or expectations. Sand took a lover, her childhood friend Stéphane Ajasson de Grandsagne. Less than a year later a daughter, Solange, was born. Throughout her life, Aurore searched for love and sexual fulfillment, and for an outlet for her energy and imagination; as George Sand, she would achieve personal and professional satisfaction and an independence unusual for her time. Aurore Dudevant became a writer, not by accident but by choice.

Two incidents, quite unrelated, changed Aurore's life, and her public identity. In July 1830, she met and fell in love with Jules Sandeau, a 19-year-old from Berry, a student in Paris. A few months later, she found a letter written by Casimir, which was to be opened on his death. The letter detailed his wife's failings, listing his grievances against her. Sand confronted Casimir and announced her intention to live in Paris for part of each year. Casimir agreed to this and to an annual allowance. In January 1831, she left Nohant, and her husband and children. By April, she and Jules Sandeau had published an article in *La Revue de Paris* under the name J. Sand; shortly thereafter, they collaborated on a novel, *Rose et Blanche*, again signed J. Sand. Free from provincial and marital restrictions, Aurore lived openly with Sandeau.

Sand had also written a novel, *Aimée*, for which she needed a publisher. She approached the editor of *Le Figaro* who promptly rejected the work and advised her to make children, not books. However, recognizing a nascent talent, Henri de Latouche suggested that she write articles for his newspaper using the pen-name Jules Sand. A year later (1832), Aurore had two novels, *Indiana* and *Valentine*, published under a nom de plume of her choice: George Sand was born. Favorably reviewed, *Indiana* made her name in the sophisticated, competitive literary circles of Paris. Neither novel was a collaborative effort, for Sand had broken with Sandeau who lacked her discipline and drive and envied her production. Sand commonly wrote 20-to-40 pages each day, working from near midnight to early morning.

Sand's heterodox lifestyle generated as much comment as did her annual publications. In her love affairs, which have been labeled "serial monogamy," Sand was often the pursuer rather than the pursued. When author and critic Prosper Merimée proved to be sexually inadequate, Sand promptly ended their liaison. With none of her lovers was Sand the proverbial "kept woman." Conversely, her lovers were "kept men" who lived with her or in a separate residence, often at her expense. According to **Donna Dickenson**, Sand considered sex natural and that a woman's sex drive was the same as a man's. What was most shocking, however, was Sand's frankness and honesty about sex: she condemned the double standard and defied social convention. Was Sand a feminist and/or a liberated woman? She had open love affairs, achieved economic independence, dressed as a man, and smoked in public. But her view of women's roles did not include participation in public life (the masculine sphere), nor did she support the suffragist goals of the feminists. Sand's life and writings are indicative of this dichotomy.

George Sand's reputation as a writer was assured with the publication of *Lélia* (1833), although it received mixed reviews. Calling attention to the unequal status of women in society, Sand was accused of advocating free love and other morally dangerous ideas. The author and critic Alfred de Musset wrote a favorable review of the book; the same year he (age 22) and Sand became lovers. With an advance on her next novel, the couple left for a holiday in Italy. Relations deteriorated when Sand fell ill and Musset amused himself with other women. His infidelity and unconcern for Sand's welfare hurt her. But when Musset contracted a venereal disease and typhoid fever, Sand nursed him and called in a doctor. Despite her own poor health and caring for Musset, she produced two novels and a series of articles while in Venice. After a lovers' quarrel, Musset returned to Paris. Sand and the doctor became lovers.

On her return to Paris, Sand and Musset reconciled. Her apartment on the quai Malaquais was the scene of an orderly family life—it included Musset and Sand's two children—and a gathering-place for Parisian literati. Women seldom, if ever, attended, which can be explained by Sand's remarks in her *Histoire de ma Vie*: "With very few exceptions I cannot stand women for long. . . . women are usually nervous, anxious creatures. . . . I therefore prefer men to women and I say this without malice." Sand's turbulent affair with Musset lasted only two years (1833–35), but it provided materials for several novels, notably *Elle et Lui* (1858).

Relations with Casimir also caused Sand problems. She and her husband had agreed that Sand would receive control of Nohant in late 1835 and custody of Solange, while Casimir was awarded the investment house in Paris. When Casimir attempted to alter the agreement, Sand was furious and tore up the document. To protect her rights (which were few under French law), she consulted lawyers Gabriel Planet and Michel de Bourges, liberal republican activists from whom Sand became aware of current French socialist thought. When Casimir struck his wife and threatened to shoot her, Sand left Nohant and filed for legal separation (divorce was forbidden in France). She won her case. Separation was granted, Nohant was hers, and she was awarded custody of Solange. Casimir received the investment house and joint custody of Maurice. Still unsatisfied, Casimir appealed the decision. The final judgment in the court at Bourges ended in a vote by the judges of 5 to 5. Public opinion rallied around Sand, and the court found in her favor. She was free.

No doubt her experiences, an unhappy marriage and having to fight for her own properties, affected her ideas on women's inferior status in society. Indeed, Casimir was able to live openly with his housekeeper and their daughter at the Dudevant estate of Guillery in Berry without incurring public censure. Sand and her novels, on the other hand, were declared threats to morality. Despite her miserable marriage and frequent clashes with her husband, Sand never turned the children against their father though they began using Sand as a surname after 1841. George Sand was not interested in Casimir's life at Guillery, except as it affected her children's rights to their father's estate. Losing her investment house to Casimir was not as important to her as retaining her country house in Nohant. Land and local ties meant a good deal to Sand. To the local peasants, she was the respected and generous grande dame of Nohant. However, income from her writing never quite met her financial obligations: Nohant and its staff of servants, her apartments in Paris, and extensive travel consumed much of her re-

George Sand

sources. She also supported various lovers and her children into her old age, paid for her nephew's education, and provided a substantial dowry for her daughter and a poor relative. Sand fed over 40 local peasant families, a gesture that endeared her to her neighbors.

Family and financial problems did not interfere with Sand's prodigious literary output or with her love affairs. She pursued a reluctant Michel de Bourges until he finally succumbed, but their affair was shortlived. Though he failed to convert Sand to his radical socialist views, they shared a common commitment to establishing a republic in France. Brief sexual interludes with an actor and a playwright ended abruptly when Sand met the Polish composer Frédéric Chopin at a friend's salon in Paris. Sand's energy was seemingly inexhaustible; she wrote every day, frequently entertained guests at Nohant (Honoré Balzac, Franz Liszt and his mistress ◀❧ **Marie d'Agoult**, who wrote under the pseudonym Daniel Stern, and Gustave Flaubert, among others), kept a residence in Paris, and engaged in time-consuming sexual exploits. All the while she kept up a semblance of family life for her children. In 1837 alone, Sand had five works published, looked after her sick mother (who died that August), and traveled to Gascony to recover her daughter whom Casimir had kidnapped.

Sand met Chopin in Marie d'Agoult's salon in November 1836. He appeared an unlikely candidate for a love affair. Weak, snobbish, melancholic, and prissy, Chopin presented a sharp contrast to the vigorous, cigar-smoking Sand who needed a challenge to arouse her interest in a man. The timid Pole was such a challenge. Sand courted Chopin with her usual determination. The lovers spent the winter in Majorca with Sand's children. Chopin, suffering from tuberculosis, required constant care, and the primitive conditions on the island exhausted the normally dynamic Sand. She nursed him, revised one novel (*Lélia*), and finished another. From Majorca, the "family" moved on to Marseille and finally settled down at Nohant in mid-1839. Chopin, ever cognizant of social decorum, acted the part of a proper houseguest. Sand was addressed as Mme Dudevant with the formal *vous*. That autumn, the lovers took separate apartments in Paris. Passion had vanished, and Sand's maternal predilections replaced their former bond.

Sand's play *Cosima*, starring **Marie Dorval**, was produced in Paris in 1840. The audience hissed and the reviewers panned it. After seven performances, the play closed, and Sand was hurt, emotionally and financially. But her inter-

est in socialism provided new materials for her work. To bring about social change through her writing became her goal. She and Pierre Leroux founded a socialist newspaper which soon folded; two years later, a similar venture also proved unsuccessful. Socialist themes dominated her novels for a time, but they did not sell well, and Sand's publisher advised her to return to the topics that had made her famous.

Sand's life revolved more and more around Nohant rather than Paris. Writers and artists, family and friends created a lively milieu for her creative energies. Her son Maurice was a rather passive individual; he loved his non-conformist mother but not her Polish lover whom Sand also "mothered." Solange, on the other hand, clashed with Sand and created dissension in the household. A big, stalwart girl, intelligent and musically gifted, she resented her mother's attention and generosity to **Augustine Brault**, a poor female relative. Solange's marriage in 1847 to an uncouth, prodigal sculptor, Auguste Clésinger, was a disaster. When Clésinger struck Sand in anger, she ordered them to leave Nohant. Chopin had sided with Solange, creating a final break with Sand. When he died in 1849, she was unmoved. Years later, she acquired her letters to Chopin and destroyed them. The Sand-Chopin love story has provoked much comment. George Sand as "man-eater," as a devourer of weak, sensitive creatures, entered into legend. It is true that Sand never remained friends with rejected lovers, but she never maligned them either. To her detractors, Sand's blatant display of female sexuality and open defiance of social convention aroused public hostility, even in "enlightened" Paris.

All attention was focused on that city in early 1848. The overthrow of the monarchy and the possibility of creating a republic drew Sand to the capital. As unofficial minister of propaganda, she wrote plays, tracts, and open letters supporting social change, hoping to influence the revolutionary leaders. Her article on revolution was denounced as inflammatory and for causing a serious riot in Paris. Approached by a feminist group to run for a seat in the Assembly, Sand refused, claiming that politics was not a woman's place, and economic independence was essential before women should even be allowed to vote. Marriage and family constituted a woman's sphere. Writing to suffragists, Sand spoke of "your sex," not "our sex." To Sand, men and women possessed different natures, respectively ruled by the head and the heart, by reason and emotion. According to Dickenson, the question then is, how did Sand identify herself? Was she confused about her own identity?

Agoult, Marie d'.
See Wagner, Cosima for sidebar.

Did her androgyny derive from her dislike of women, her preference for men? In her personal journal, Sand assumes the masculine gender in referring to herself, as she did in her professional writings. Indeed, one might conclude that George Sand-Mme Dudevant was her creation of a single entity from the public man-private woman dichotomy she accepted as real.

Disillusioned by the bloody riots and the flaccid republican leadership, Sand left Paris. She was through with politics; however, she traveled to Paris in 1851, to meet with President Napoleon III on behalf of her imprisoned and exiled republican friends. Between 1849 and 1856, many of her plays were staged in Paris, not all successfully. *François le Champi*, written in the Berry dialect with a peasant as hero, was a great hit. Having discarded her socialist themes, Sand saw her work sell well once again. She continued to write novels and plays until her death, often incurring the wrath of Catholic conservatives and the French government. Her fame and talent prompted Sainte-Beuve to nominate Sand for the Prix Gobert, worth 20,000 francs. The 40 men of the Académie Française refused to grant the prize to Sand. Empress *Eugénie (wife of the now Emperor Napoleon III) then offered a comparable sum to Sand who declined the offer. Similarly when an effort was launched to have Sand elected to the Académie, she declined the "honor."

Meanwhile, Sand's personal life continued to revolve around her son Maurice, who married a woman whom Sand loved, and her daughter Solange, who separated from her husband in 1852 and moved near Nohant. Sand also had a new lover, after two brief, banal affairs. Alexandre Manceau was an engraver, 13 years younger than Sand, who remained devoted to her until he died 15 years later. He also served as manager of Nohant, allowing Sand to concentrate on writing and her grandchildren. She was content with Manceau at Nohant, but Maurice, who wanted to assume control of his inheritance and manage his estate, ordered Manceau to leave. Sand chose to leave too. They took a small house near Paris and also rented a studio in the city where she wrote and nursed the tubercular Manceau. When he died, a 61-year-old Sand, alone for the first time, was restless. Success with her plays (*Sarah Bernhardt starred in *The Other*) and her literary friendships determined her residence; she spent the winter months in Paris and summers at Nohant, welcoming visitors such as Flaubert, Ivan Turgenev, and Alexander Dumas *fils*.

In May 1876, while working on the second volume of *Tales of a Grandmother*, Sand suffered from severe gastric distress. Minor surgery and medication were ineffective, and on June 8, George Sand died at Nohant. Two days later, she was buried in the garden of the estate she loved and fought so long to possess. George Sand was one of the foremost Romantic writers of her century, but after she died her reputation as a writer was overshadowed by the infamy of her exploits. Whether she was a liberated woman, a feminist, a socialist, cannot obscure the fact that George Sand earned accolades as one of France's finest Romantic writers.

SOURCES:

Dickenson, Donna. *George Sand: A Brave Man—The Most Womanly Woman*. Oxford: Berg, 1988.

Jordan, Ruth. *George Sand: A Biography*. London: Constable, 1976.

Powell, David A. *George Sand*. Boston, Twayne, 1990.

SUGGESTED READING:

Barry, Joseph. *Infamous Women: The Life of George Sand*. Garden City, NY: Doubleday, 1977.

Cate, Curtis. *George Sand: A Biography*. London: Hamish Hamilton, 1975.

Gerson, Noel B. *George Sand: A Biography of the First Modern Liberated Woman*. London: Robert Hale, 1973.

Jack, Belinda. *A Woman's Life Writ Large*. NY: Knopf, 2000.

Maurois, André. *Lélia: The Life of George Sand*. Trans. by Gerard Hopkins. NY: Penguin, 1977.

Toesca, Maurice. *The Other George Sand*. Trans. by Irene Beeson. London: Dennis Dobson, 1947.

Jeanne A. Ojala,
Professor of History,
University of Utah, Salt Lake City, Utah

Sandel, Cora (1880–1974)

Norwegian author best known for her Alberta trilogy, which was described by the Christian Science Monitor as "one of the most complete portrayals of a woman's life that exist in modern fiction." Name variations: Sara Fabricius; Sara Jönsson. Born Sara Cecilia Margarete Gjørwel Fabricius on December 20, 1880, in Kristiania (now Oslo), Norway; died on April 3, 1974, in Uppsala, Sweden; eldest child and only daughter of Anna Margareta Greger and Jens Schou Fabricius (a naval captain), both from families in which the men traditionally followed professions as government officials; attended public school in Tromsø, North Norway; art training (painting) at Harriet Backer's studio, Kristiania, 1899 and 1905, and in Paris from 1906; married Anders Jönsson (a Swedish sculptor), in 1913 (divorced 1926); children: Erik (b. 1917 in Paris).

Spent two years in Italy with husband (1913–15); spent a period in Brittany where she began to write (1918), otherwise stayed in Paris until 1921; moved to Stockholm, Sweden; had a temporary teaching post in

Tromsø (1922); published short stories under pseudonym; published volume 1 of the trilogy, Alberta and Jacob, *her first novel (1926); divorced (1926), but continued to live in Sweden, except for a brief period in Norway (1936–39); published* Alberta and Freedom *and* Alberta Alone *(1931 and 1939); won first prize in Norwegian short-story competition for novella* Nina *(1939); awarded author's stipend for life by the Norwegian government (1940); published novel* Krane's Café *after the liberation of Norway (1945);* Krane's Café *adapted for the stage (1947), and filmed (1951); moved to Uppsala (1960); exhibited paintings (1972);* Alberta and Freedom *filmed and shown on television (1972).*

Selected short-story collections: En blå sofa *(1927);* Carmen og Maja *(1932);* Mange takk, doktor *(1935);* Dyr jeg har kjent *(1945);* Figurer på mørk bunn *(1949);* Vårt vanskelige liv *(Our Difficult Lives, ed. by Odd Solumsmoen, 1960);* Barnet som elsket veier *(The Child Who Loved Roads, ed. by Steinar Gimnes, 1973).*

Selected novels: Alberte og Jakob *(1926);* Alberte og Friheten *(1931);* Bare Alberte *(1939);* Kranes Konditori *(1945);* Kjøp ikke Dondi *(1958). All Norwegian titles published by Gyldendal, Oslo.*

Selected translations: Alberta and Jacob, Alberta and Freedom, Alberta Alone *(all translated by Elizabeth Rokkan, Peter Owen, London, 1962, 1963, 1965);* Krane's Café *(translated by Elizabeth Rokkan, Peter Owen, London, 1968);* The Leech *(translated by Elizabeth Rokkan, Peter Owen, London, 1960);* Cora Sandel: Selected Short Stories *(translated by Barbara Wilson, Seal Press, Seattle, 1985);* The Silken Thread: Stories and Sketches *(translated by Elizabeth Rokkan, Peter Owen, London, 1986).*

Sara Fabricius was born in 1880 in Kristiania (now Oslo), Norway, 25 years before the establishment of independence from Sweden in 1905. Her mother tongue was Norwegian, she was published in Norway, and she was rewarded with a writer's stipend by the Norwegian government. Yet she lived in other countries for most of her life, and guarded her privacy behind her pseudonym, Cora Sandel. She called this "my mania for anonymity." It should have been sufficient, she thought, for people to read her books. Writes Odd Solumsmoen: "Her detestation of all publicity is identical with her detestation of the superficial, of the sensational, of muddle, of any kind of literary ladies' tea party: in a word, of falsehood." It is significant that she adopted a female pseudonym. To be a 20th-century woman writer, and to write about women in order to champion their cause, became her en-

tire purpose. Her brief autobiography reads: "I was a child in Oslo, a young girl in North Norway, a grown woman in France and Sweden, am growing old during World War II, had a son during the first war, and live in fear that he may be sacrificed during the second."

Sandel's first 12 years were spent in the comfortable circumstances of a large, upper-middle-class family on Oslo's west side. Her father, serving in the navy, came and went, but in 1892 he took a post as a government administrator in Tromsø, a coastal port over half way between the Arctic Circle and the North Cape. The contrast must have been considerable between the Norwegian capital and this isolated outpost, which, at the turn of the century, was linked with the rest of this elongated country only by the regular visits of the coastal steamer, often delayed by storms. The journey took a week from Trondheim; there were two months of winter darkness when the sun never rose above the horizon. But there was no lack of congenial company or of activities such as amateur dramatics, youth clubs, and friendships made at the school for girls at which Sandel was educated. It was her observation of the frustrating and limiting lives imposed on the girls and young women of respectable families (expressed in the first volume of the *Alberta* trilogy) that turned Sandel's ambitions towards a career as an artist. In this she was helped initially by her father, who enabled her to spend some time at the painter *Harriet Backer's studio in Kristiania in 1899 and 1905, and later by an uncle, who assisted her in continuing her training in Paris after the death of her parents. Her need to escape from Norwegian society to the wider world of Europe nevertheless went hand in hand with her parallel loyalty to the language and culture of that society, reflected in the continued, close relationship with her literary friends and her publisher.

After moving to Paris for good in 1906, Sandel concentrated on her painting for the next decade. Her impressions of the Parisian artistic milieu were to find expression in *Alberta and Freedom* 15 years later: café life, the music hall, life classes, the stimulation of other artists, the poverty. "We were frozen and half starved," she said later; and 40 years on she wrote at the beginning of the novel *Krane's Café*, "Poverty is terrible. Of all so-called misfortunes, it's the one that affects you most deeply." Sandel was influenced by artists such as **Oda Krogh**, and by writers such as *Colette, whose *La Vagabonde* she translated into Norwegian and published in 1952. Sandel was also able to continue what proved to be a lifelong friendship, begun at

Cora
Sandel

school in Tromsø, with the pioneer of Norwegian university education for women: *Ellen Gleditsch (1879–1968). She, too, was in Paris, to study with *Marie Curie, and later she became the first woman professor of chemistry at the University of Oslo, as well as president of the Norwegian branch of the International Federation of University Women.

The two years spent in Florence after Sandel married the Swedish sculptor Anders Jönsson were happy ones, but the couple returned to experience a Paris torn by war and suffering material shortages. This period is reflected in some of her short stories. When her art professor, André Lhote, enquired why she was no longer attending his class at Colarossi's, adding that she must not stay away for lack of money, she admitted that she was pregnant. His reply was devastating: "*Alors, c'est fini pour vous.*" (In that case, it's all over for you.) And so it proved where her painting was concerned. Her son Erik was born in 1917. During a stay in Brittany in 1918, she turned to writing; and when the Jönssons moved to Sweden in 1921 her canvases were used to protect her husband's sculptures on the journey. She commented later that ceasing to paint felt like having a leg or an arm amputated. But the notes which were to prove the basis of her trilogy traveled with her in her baggage.

The move to Stockholm was the beginning of the end of Sandel's marriage. In 1922, she left her child and husband to take a post in Tromsø teaching languages. She knew the town; her parents, though now deceased, had never moved south; and it was necessary financially. Her writings tell us that she would have had no wish to be in Oslo where she would have met with the disapproval of her bourgeois relatives. The following year, she returned, however, to Sweden, presumably for the sake of her son, and was not to visit Tromsø again until 1950. She settled outside Stockholm, and in 1926 was divorced from Jönsson. The same year saw the publication in Norway of *Alberta and Jacob*, which established her immediately as an important, though unknown, writer, and aroused the enthusiasm of both critics and public for its depiction of small-town life in North Norway. The initial printing of 9,000 copies was exceptional for such a small population. From now on, having found herself as woman and author, she was known as Cora Sandel.

To tell a little of the truth.

—Cora Sandel

Her independence was, however, again highly precarious where her economy was concerned. She took first prize in a couple of short-story competitions, and her hard work during the '20s and '30s resulted in the publication of several collections of stories in addition to the second and third volumes of the trilogy, a modern *Bildungsroman* in the tradition of Norwegian writer *Camilla Collett's *Amtmandens døttre* (*The District Governor's Daughters*), as well as *Sigrid Undset's *Kristin Lavransdatter* (of which Sandel did not approve). The main theme of Sandel's fiction was that of women trapped by circumstance, often abandoning their hopes or striving for self-fulfillment. Her painter's eye is particularly in evidence in the stories. She is conscious of the effects of light and shadow, and of how her characters play out their scenes in the focus of the light. Her descriptions are built up with the care of a painter giving thought to the form of her images.

In 1940, Sandel attained a certain security through the award of a writer's stipend from the Norwegian government, but the Nazi occupation of Norway cut her off from her homeland for the next five years. During this time, she felt that patriotism demanded that she overcome her shyness and, like other Norwegians in exile in Sweden and the United States, she gave talks defending Norway and challenging the Swedish criticism that their neighbor should have put up a better resistance and not capitulated to the German invasion. She pointed out that such a small country could not buy weapons; there had been,

after all, no question of rearmament, since there had been no involvement in World War I. "We were simply unable to afford cannon and bombers," she said. "We had not given much thought to the matter either. The idea of killing is foreign to a people like ourselves, used to devoting our lives to the daily struggle for existence."

Her stories and reminiscences dating from this period reflect her concern for the wider European situation as well as that of Norway. They include "Berit" ("Blue Anemones," translated by Rokkan), an account of Invasion Day (April 9, 1940) from the viewpoint of a little girl; "Til Lukas," a touching monologue by a Central European refugee writing to her lover who has been arrested by the Nazis (published in an anthology of Norwegian writing in exile, *Utenfor norske grensen* [Outside the Norwegian Frontier], Stockholm, 1943); and an ambitious allegory on Nazi expansion and European foreign affairs in the 1930s and 1940s. She may, in fact, have been one of the few Norwegians living in Sweden who had experienced war at firsthand before 1940 (always excepting those serving in the Norwegian merchant marine during World War I), and this resumption of hostilities was a profound disappointment to her. On Armistice Day 1918, she had written in her diary to her small son: "Peace. You do not understand it and will never understand it, for war will be unthinkable when you are grown up."

Despite these dark events, her humor had not deserted her, as Norwegians were to discover when *Krane's Café* was published in 1945. This was Sandel's tribute to Tromsø, and she admitted that it was her own favorite. The subtitle of the novel is "Interior with figures," and its scenic and dramatic form lent itself to successful adaptation as a play, with an additional act, by the playwright Helge Krog. It was performed for the first time in 1947, made into a film in 1951, and its popularity has been such that it has been staged many times since in Norwegian theaters. A charming collection of anecdotes, *Dyr jeg har kjent* (Animals I have known), subtitled "Stories for young and old," also came out after the Liberation.

Sandel's publisher, Gyldendal, awarded her an annual stipend in 1950 and issued her *Samlede verker* (Collected works) in six volumes two years later, adding a seventh in 1958 after publication of her final novel, *Kjøp ikke Dondi* (*The Leech*). This won second prize in a European literary competition in 1960, when its author was 80 years of age.

Interest in Sandel remained strong in Scandinavia to the end of her long life, the last 14 years of which were spent in semi-retirement in Uppsala. In 1972, when she was 91, 30 of the pictures she had painted in her youth were exhibited in Stockholm; they included landscapes, still-lifes and portraits reminiscent of Cézanne, who was clearly not the "distant ideal" she made him out to be, but a real and visible influence on her work. The same year, she was able to see the television version of *Alberta and Freedom*, a medium scarcely imagined at the time when the novel was written. And in 1973 she was persuaded by Steinar Gimnes to publish stories and reminiscences dating from her early years as a writer, under the title *Barnet som elsket veier* (The Child Who Loved Roads). To her readers' surprise, it included the only poem she is known to have written, "Today the rose has been kissing the orchid," a wry little piece of advice to women revealing the combination of sympathy and irony that is her hallmark as a prose writer. Never, she told them, search for the vanished rose, for nothing is gained by loss. This was written at the age of 92, with the years in Florence in mind, according to her son; but it is interesting to remember that in the early 1970s Norwegian women were involved in the second liberation movement, and Sandel would have been aware of it. Cora Sandel's activities during her last decade were fitting reminders of her lifelong concerns, which continued up to her death in 1974, aged 93.

SOURCES:

Beyer, Edvard, ed. *Norges litteraturhistorie.* Vol. V. Oslo: Cappelen, 1975, pp. 252–265.

Dahl, Willy. *Norges litteratur.* Vols. II and III. Oslo: Aschehoug, 1984.

Essex, Ruth. *Cora Sandel: Seeker of Truth.* NY: Peter Lang, 1995.

Garton, Janet. *Norwegian Women's Writing 1850–1990.* Chapt. 7. London: Athlone Press, 1993.

Lervik, se Hjort. *Menneske og miljø i Cora Sandels diktning.* Oslo: Gyldendal, 1977.

Øverland, Janneken. *Cora Sandel om seg selv.* Oslo: Den norske bokklubben, 1983.

Rokkan, Elizabeth. "Cora Sandel and the Second World War," in *Scandinavica.* Vol. 28, no. 2. November 1989, pp. 155–160.

——. "Cora Sandel's War Story," in *Scandinavica.* Vol. 26, no. 1. May 1987, pp. 5–12.

Solumsmoen, Odd. *Cora Sandel—en dikter i ånd og sannhet.* Oslo: Aschehoug, 1957.

Zuck, Virpi, ed. *Dictionary of Scandinavian Literature.* Chicago, IL: St. James Press, 1990.

RELATED MEDIA:

Alberte og friheten was produced as a television series by Norsk Rikskringkasting, 1972.

Kranes Konditori was dramatized by Helge Krog (1947), and filmed in 1951.

Nina was filmed under the title *Hoysommer,* 1958.

Elizabeth Rokkan,
translator, formerly Associate Professor,
Department of English, University of Bergen, Norway

Sanders, Dorothy Lucie (1903–1987)

Australian writer. Name variations: (pseudonym) Lucy Walker. Born on May 4, 1903 (some sources cite 1907 and 1917), in Boulder Gold Fields, Western Australia; died in 1987; daughter of William Joseph McClemans (a cleric and founder of a grammar school) and Ada Lucy (Walker) McClemans; attended Perth College, University of Western Australia and Claremont Teachers' College, receiving her teaching certificate in 1938; married Colsell Sanders (a professor), on September 5, 1936; children: Jonathan William; (twins) Colin Creeth and Lucyann.

Dorothy Lucie Sanders was born on May 4, 1903, in Boulder Gold Fields, Western Australia, the daughter of **Ada Walker McClemans** and William Joseph McClemans, a cleric and founder of Christ Church Grammar School. Her education consisted of ten years of studies at Perth College and four years as a part-time student at the University of Western Australia. She also received a teacher's certificate in 1938 from the Claremont Teachers' College. On September 5, 1936, she married Colsell Sanders, an emeritus professor and former chair of the Tertiary Education Commission in Western Australia. They had three children.

Sanders is chiefly known for her stories of young women and love. Her novels, several of which are set in Perth, include *Fairies on the Doorstep* (1948), *Waterfall* (1956), *Pepper Tree Bay* (1959), and *Monday in Summer* (1961). Under the pseudonym Lucy Walker, she also wrote *Love in a Cloud* (1960), *The Distant Hills* (1962), *The Man from Outback* (1964), *The River Is Down* (1967), *The Run Away Girl* (1975), and *So Much Love* (1977). She was a contributor of short stories and articles to magazines in Australia and the United Kingdom.

Jo Anne Meginnes,
freelance writer, Brookfield, Vermont

Sanders, Marlene (1931—)

American journalist and television executive. Born on January 10, 1931, in Cleveland, Ohio; daughter of Mac Sanders and Evelyn R. (Menitoff) Sanders; attended Ohio State University, 1948–50; attended the Sorbonne in Paris, 1950; married Jerome Toobin, on May 27, 1958; children: Jeffrey Toobin (a television news correspondent); Mark Toobin.

Television news correspondent and producer Marlene Sanders broke barriers for women in the area of network news throughout her career. She was born in 1931 in Cleveland, Ohio, and attended Ohio State University. Following one year at the Sorbonne in Paris (1950), she set her sights on the theater and was involved with summer-stock and off-Broadway productions before taking a job with a small television station in New York City. Her work with Mike Wallace on his interview show "Night Beat" (1956–58) was followed by a position as assistant director of news and public affairs for New York's radio station WNEW (1962). While there, Sanders wrote her radio documentary "The Battle of the Warsaw Ghetto" for which she received the Writers Guild of America Award in 1964.

The same year, she joined her first major television network, ABC, where she would remain for nearly a decade and a half. During her time there, she became the first woman to anchor a nightly television network newscast (1964), the first woman to report from the Vietnam War (1966), and the first woman vice president of a television network news division (1976). Her promotion to the latter position, as vice president and director of documentaries for ABC, came as a result of her work as a producer of award-winning documentaries, including "Children in Peril" (1972) and "The Right to Die" (1974). Sanders also produced "Woman's Place" (1973), a pioneering documentary which looked at the issue of gender roles. In 1978, Sanders left ABC for CBS to produce the news magazine "CBS Reports." Rejecting a transfer to CBS radio in 1987, she left the network and went to work two years later for New York's public-television station WNET (1989). Her 1989 book *Waiting for Prime Time*, cowritten with **Marcia Rock**, detailed the experiences of female television journalists.

Sanders, a three-time Emmy Award winner, received many honors for her professional achievements over the years, including the Golden Mike Award from *McCall's* magazine in 1964 and the Broadcast Woman of the Year Award from American Women in Radio and Television in 1975. She was a faculty member of New York University as well as of Columbia's Graduate School of Journalism and served as a professional in residence at the Media Studies Center of the Freedom Forum Foundation.

SOURCES:

Read, Phyllis J., and Bernard L. Witlieb. *The Book of Women's Firsts*. NY: Random House, 1992.

Gloria Cooksey,
freelance writer, Sacramento, California

Sanders, Summer (1972—)

American swimmer and gold medalist in the Barcelona Olympics. Born on October 13, 1972; attended Stanford University; married Mark Henderson (an Olympic swimmer), in 1997.

Won eight U.S. National championships; named NCAA Swimmer of the Year (1991 and 1992); won Olympic gold medals for the 200-meter butterfly and the 4x100-meter medley relay, silver medal for the 200-meter individual medley, and bronze medal for the 400-meter individual medley at Barcelona (1992).

Born in October 1972, Summer Sanders showed no interest in the family pool as a toddler, until she leapt in suddenly when her parents weren't looking. At three, she could manage a standard lap; at four, she was beating seven-year-olds; at fifteen, she qualified for the 1988 Olympic trials in the 200- and 400-meter individual medleys and 100- and 200-meter breaststroke. Failure to make the Olympic team did not dampen her elation at what proved to be a strong showing at the trials. Returning to her home in Roseville, California, she set her sights on making the 1992 team.

After graduating from high school, where she was an honors student, Sanders attended Stanford University on an athletic scholarship, majoring in communications. Two years in a row, 1991 and 1992, she received the NCAA Swimmer of the Year title. In March 1992, the 19-year-old Sanders qualified for five events in the upcoming Olympics, including the 200- and 400-meter individual relays and the 100- and 200-meter butterfly. With Olympic competition on the horizon, she relinquished her NCAA eligibility to sign lucrative endorsement contracts.

In Barcelona, the rising swimming star was regarded as a serious contender in all five of her events. Sanders did not disappoint, winning gold in the 200-meter butterfly and the 4x100-meter medley relay, silver in the 200-meter individual medley, and bronze in the 400-meter individual medley. Following her victories, she told *Sports Illustrated*, "I just want to sit down and relax. I want to enjoy the feeling that nobody expects me to do anything great tomorrow." Not since 1984 had a woman swimmer earned four medals during a single Olympiad, and Sanders returned home an American hero.

Her Olympic success brought a host of new opportunities and endorsement offers. In addition to appearing on television as a guest on her favorite soap opera "All My Children" and as a host on MTV, Sanders accepted engagements as a motivational speaker and signed contracts for additional product endorsements. But she never managed to better her times from 1992 and announced that she was ready to retire in December of the following year.

Nearly a year and a half later, when she decided to attempt a comeback to compete in the 1996 Atlanta Games, Sanders faced daunting odds: she had been away from competitive swimming for 17 months. She went into training as a member of the U.S. Swimming Resident National Team. To help her from becoming discouraged at her inability to keep up with the other team members, the coach initially segregated her from the rest of the team by having her swim in her own lane. Performing the most challenging workouts her coach could provide, she increased her speed enough to join the rest of the group by June. Nonetheless, competing against younger swimmers whose training had not been interrupted, Sanders failed to qualify for the 1996 Olympic team.

She was, however, in attendance at the Atlanta Games, serving as a swimming analyst with NBC. She also became part of the story when her steady beau, swimmer Mark Henderson, who had won gold in the 4x100-meter medley relay, proposed to her during the closing ceremonies. (They would marry on July 4, 1997.) Sanders' performance on the network during the Olympics launched her career as a sports commentator. She came on board for Lifetime's coverage of the Women's National Basketball Association (WNBA) during its inaugural season, and beginning in December 1997 covered both the WNBA and the NBA for NBC's "NBA Inside Stuff," of which she became co-host in July of the following year. In 1997, Sanders premiered as the host of a new children's game show, "Figure It Out," on the Nickelodeon Network. Her book *Champions Are Raised, Not Born: How My Parents Made Me a Success* was published in 1999.

SOURCES:

Harris, Beth. "Summer Sanders Fails to Qualify," in *The Day* [New London, CT]. March 13, 1996.

Johnson, Anne Janette. *Great Women in Sports*. Detroit, MI: Visible Ink, 1998.

Starr, Mark. "Ticketless in Atlanta," in *Newsweek*. October 23, 1995.

Gloria Cooksey,
freelance writer, Sacramento, California

Sanders-Brahms, Helma (1940—)

German screenwriter and director. Name variations: Helma Sanders. Born Helma Sanders on November 20, 1940, in Emden, Germany; attended an acting school in Hanover, 1960–62, and Cologne University; never married; children: Anna Sanders.

Selected films: (for TV) Gewalt *(Violence, 1971); (for TV)* Der Angestellte *(The Employee, 1972); (documentary)* Die Maschine *(The Machine, 1973); (for TV)* Die letzten Tage von Gomorrah *(The Last Days of Gomorrah, 1974);* Unter dem Pflaster ist der Strand *(The Sand Under the Pavement, 1975); (for TV)* Shirins Hochzeit *(Shirin's Wedding, 1976);* Deutschland bleiche Mutter *(Germany, Pale Mother, 1980);* Die Berührte *(No Mercy, No Future, 1981);* Flügel und Fesseln *(The Future of Emily, 1984);* Laputa *(1986);* Geteilte Liebe *(Divided Love, 1988);* Apfelbaume *(Apple Trees, 1992); (documentary)* Lumière et compagnie *(Lumière and Company, 1995).*

Helma Sanders-Brahms was born Helma Sanders in Emden along the North Sea in western Germany, on November 20, 1940. Her father was absent during much of her childhood, initially because of World War II and later due to family tension. As a result, her mother, a strong and independent woman, raised Sanders-Brahms almost exclusively on her own. The young girl felt alienated because of her home life, and found escape through her art and cultural pursuits. Even as a child, she harbored an interest in theater and cinema, and decided by the age of ten that she would work in the theater. She read incessantly, went to movies, and wrote her own scripts.

Sanders-Brahms attended an acting school in Hanover, Germany, between 1960 and 1962, and took the advice of teachers who suggested she study direction. During her four years at Cologne University as a drama and literature major, she eschewed the society of other students. "I felt the need to do something different," she said, "to leave the student milieu which was, particularly at that time, divorced from contemporary reality." Instead, she occupied herself in odd jobs as a factory worker, store clerk, and hospital aide in a determined effort to stay closely in touch with real life. "Two or three people died every day in the room where I worked. After a month I couldn't sleep or eat. . . . I was no help to the sick. Too emotional, too sensitive to be effective." After graduating, she taught one year before securing a position at a television station, WDR-3 in Cologne, as an on-air introducer of film classics. Soon, she was producing film shorts and documentaries for WDR, interviewing Italian directors Pasolini, Zeffirelli, and Corbucci, and directing. Her first film for television involved an interview with terrorist *Ulrike Meinhof, one of the leaders of the Baader-Meinhof gang. "The film still exists," says Sanders-Brahms, "but it is very difficult to see it."

Sanders-Brahms considered it both imperative and inevitable that she branch out alone and produce her own work. Her independent nature and unwillingness to compromise her beliefs made it difficult for her to work within the confines of a commercial environment. As such, she joined the New German Cinema movement in constructing her scripts around the political left. The dehumanization brought about by technology and the personal plights of the downtrodden became persistent themes. She created intensely real characters, frequently representative of an imprisoned urban working class.

In 1971, Sanders-Brahms completed her first television film, *Gewalt* (Violence), for WDR. The movie focused on assembly-line workers at a Ford Motor Company plant. *Der Angestellte* (The Employee), made in 1972, was a study of the alienation of a computer programmer, played by Ernst Jacobi, who received the Best Actor award at the San Remo (Italy) film festival for his performance. In 1973, her hour-long documentary *Die Maschine* (The Machine) won the Fipresci prize at Oberhausen.

After 1974, Sanders-Brahms matured quickly into a full-blown artist. She created and produced her own scripts, and earned professional respect and notoriety beyond the borders of her native Germany. Her first international success came with her portrayal of the exploitation of Germany's foreign workers in the film *Shirins Hochzeit* (Shirin's Wedding) in 1976. The late 1970s saw Sanders-Brahms focus more on radical subjectivism than on the political films of a few years before. Like other German women directors of the time, she probed mother-daughter relationships and linked them with Germany's troubled history.

Her development in this direction resulted in one of her most famous works, *Deutschland bleiche Mutter* (Germany, Pale Mother), in 1980. "It is my remembrance," said Sanders-Brahms, "a confrontation with the past." The film, which starred **Eva Mattes** and Ernst Jacobi, also featured Sanders-Brahms' narration and her infant daughter **Anna Sanders**. The narrative follows the psychological deterioration of a woman whose subjugation by her domineering husband manifests itself in facial paralysis. The treatment: removal of all of her teeth, a scene that is both shocking and symbolic. *Deutschland bleiche Mutter* took first prize at three film festivals.

The following year, Sanders-Brahms attempted improvisational film with *Die Berührte*, starring **Elisabeth Stepanek**. That work, which delved into the world of schizophrenia, won the British Film Institute Award under the title *No Mercy, No Future*, in part for its daring approach to a difficult subject. But Sanders-Brahms' personal favorite among her films was *Die letzten Tage von Gomorrah* (The Last Days of Gomorrah, 1974). The piece, a work of science fiction, decries consumer-based culture; in it, a computer factory develops the definitive machine, a television that satiates all human cravings. In the following years, Sanders-Brahms became associated with European art cinema with such films as *Flügel und Fesseln* (The Future of Emily, 1984) and *Laputa* (1986). As her fame evolved, Helma Sanders hyphenated her surname to Sanders-Brahms (composer Johannes Brahms is an ancestor on her mother's side) to clearly distinguish herself from a close contemporary, German director **Helke Sander**.

SOURCES:

Katz, Ephraim. *The Film Encyclopedia*. HarperCollins, 1998.

Unterburger, Amy, ed. *Women Filmmakers & Their Films*. Detroit, MI: St. James Press, 1998.

Vincendeau, Ginette, ed. *Encyclopedia of European Cinema*. NY: Facts on File, 1995.

Wakeman, John, ed. *World Film Directors, Vol. II, 1945–1985*. NY: H.W. Wilson, 1988.

Gloria Cooksey,
freelance writer, Sacramento, California

Sanderson, Sybil (1865–1903)

American soprano. Name variations: debuted under name Ada Palmer. Born Sybil Swift Sanderson on December 7, 1865, in Sacramento, California; died of pneumonia on May 15, 1903, in Paris, France; eldest of four daughters of Margaret Beatty (Ormsby) Sanderson and Silas Woodruff Sanderson (a California state legislator, justice of the state supreme court, and later chief counsel for the Central Pacific and Southern Pacific railroads); educated by governesses and at private schools; studied with Jean-Baptiste Sbriglia and *Mathilde Marchesi *at Paris Conservatory, and with Jules Massenet; married Antonio Terry (a Cuban millionaire), on December 1, 1897 (died December 1898); children: daughter (died in infancy).*

Made debut at The Hague (1888); created the role of Esclarmonde at Opéra-Comique (1889); debuted at Paris Opéra (1894), and Metropolitan Opera (1895).

American-born Sybil Sanderson, whose name is linked with Jules Massenet's operas, is a mystery in the opera world. After Sanderson's debut in *Manon* at The Hague, Massenet considered her the ideal interpreter of the work. Afterwards, he wrote both Esclarmonde and *Thaïs* specifically for Sanderson. She also created

SANDES, FLORA

Saint-Saëns' *Phryné*. It could be that Massenet was infatuated with the beautiful singer, but he also may have been captivated by her ravishing voice and theatrical instinct. Her success in Paris was enormous. She fared less well, however, in her debut at the Met; critics felt her voice was not "of a kind to be associated with serious opera." Earlier appearances at Covent Garden had produced a similar result. It could be that her voice simply did not fill larger houses. Whatever the reason, Sanderson's career withered at the turn of the century. She married in 1897 and gave birth in 1898, but her husband died that same year and her daughter soon after. Her health undermined, Sanderson contracted influenza and died of complications of the disease in 1903, at age 37. She left no recordings.

John Haag,
Athens, Georgia

Sanderson, Tessa (1956—)

British Olympic athlete. Name variations: Theresa Sanderson. Born on March 14, 1956, in St. Elizabeth, Jamaica.

Won the javelin throw at the Commonwealth Games (1978 and 1986); took second place, European championships (1978); set a Commonwealth record of 6,114 points in the heptathlon (1981); came in fourth, World championships, Helsinki, Finland (1983); won gold medal for javelin throw, Los Angeles (1984), setting an Olympic record: 228 feet and 2 inches (69.56 meters).

Tessa Sanderson was born in 1956 in St. Elizabeth, on the island of Jamaica, where she first learned to throw the javelin at age 14. She improved rapidly and gained 30 feet in her throwing distance between 1976 and 1977. By 1980, her distance was within one foot of the world record. Although a clear favorite to medal, Sanderson apparently had an attack of nerves during the Olympic trials and failed to qualify for the Moscow Games that year. It was one of few setbacks in an otherwise stellar career which included first-place wins in the 1978 and 1986 Commonwealth Games, a second-place finish in the European championships in 1978, and a fourth-place position in the World championships in Helsinki in 1983. Although not as well known for her skills in the heptathlon, Sanderson had also set a Commonwealth record in that event with a score of 6,114 points in 1981.

In 1984, four years after failing to compete in Moscow, Sanderson made the most of her second chance at the Los Angeles Olympic Games. She not only qualified, but also set an Olympic record of 69.56 meters for the javelin throw, taking the gold medal. She then settled in Leeds, England, and began work as a sports promotion assistant.

Gloria Cooksey,
freelance writer, Sacramento, California

Sandes, Flora (1876–1956)

English nurse and soldier considered a hero of World War I. Born in Poppleton, outside of York, England, in January 1876; died in Suffolk, England, in November 1956; youngest of eight children; attended finishing school in Switzerland; married Yuri Yudenitch (a Russian colonel), in 1927 (died during World War II); no children.

The only British woman to fight in the trenches during World War I, Flora Sandes was a hero of the Allied Serbian Army and as such was awarded the Kara George Star, the highest Serbian military award (equivalent to the British Victoria Cross). Commissioned as a second lieutenant in June 1919, by a special act of the Serbian Parliament, Sandes also served briefly in World War II, during which she escaped from her Gestapo captors. She later returned to her roots in rural England, where she died in obscurity in 1956.

Sandes, the youngest of the eight children of a vicar, was born in 1876 and grew up near Ipswich in Suffolk, where she prayed nightly that she might miraculously be changed into a boy. As a child, she eschewed dolls and frilly dresses, much preferring to romp in the woods with her brothers. Several years of finishing school in Switzerland during her teenage years did nothing to quell her adventurous spirit. Returning to England, she joined the Ladies Nursing Yeomanry and the St. John Ambulance Brigade, where she received some medical training, although with war on the horizon in 1914, she was turned down for hospital service. Still eager for action, she volunteered with six other Red Cross nurses to travel to the tiny Balkan kingdom of Serbia, to aid the allied army there. After serving for four months without the supplies needed to nurse the wounded, Sandes returned to England to solicit funds and equipment. Upon her return to Serbia, she was stricken in a typhus epidemic, but was among the few to survive.

When Germany and Bulgaria entered the war against the Serbs in 1915, Sandes' medical unit was abandoned and only serving soldiers were allowed to remain with the army. Seeing this as an opportunity, Sandes made a request to join the Serbian Army as a private. Because Serbia and Britain were allies, and Serbian women were allowed to enlist in their country's forces, she was granted her wish. Over the course of the next seven years, during which time she was promoted to sergeant, she endured mountain warfare and front-line battles. In 1916, fighting close to the Bulgarian lines, she was severely wounded by a grenade and sent to Greece, then to North Africa, for surgery. Discharged from the hospital in 1917, Sandes refused a desk job to return to the front line. She served only six months before her injuries forced her to head back to England for further surgery. While convalescing, she formed the Serbian Comforts Fund in London, and published an article on the plight of the Serbs in the *Morning Post*. In 1918, Sandes rejoined the army for the final push to victory. Just before the Armistice, she was stricken with the "Spanish Flu," then killing thousands upon thousands across the globe, from which she also made a miraculous recovery.

After the war, Sandes served in the Serbian Army until 1927, when she was discharged and married Yuri Yudenitch, a former colonel in the

Flora
Sandes

tsar's Imperial Guard who had escaped from Russia after the Bolshevik Revolution in 1917 and joined the Serbs. The couple went to live in Paris, where Sandes took a most unlikely job as wardrobe mistress and chaperon to the **Tiller Girls**, a female dance troupe who appeared at the Folies Bergére in Paris.

During the 1930s, Sandes and her husband returned to England, then drove across Europe and into the former Serbia, now part of the new federation of Yugoslavia. They settled in a country house outside Belgrade, where Sandes gave English lessons and Yuri ran a taxi service. When the Germans invaded Yugoslavia, once again plunging the country into war, Sandes, then in her 60s, was accepted back into the army as a captain. The advance of the Germans was so swift, however, that she and Yuri were captured by the Gestapo. Yuri died in 1941, but Sandes, who escaped, stayed in Belgrade, giving English lessons during the enemy occupation.

Following the liberation in 1945, Sandes returned to England, eventually settling into a cottage near Wickham Market. Memories of her soldiering days would return when least expected. "Sometimes now when playing family bridge for threepence a hundred the memory of those wild nights comes over me, and I am lost in another world," she wrote. "Instead of the powdered nose of my partner I seem to be looking at the grizzled head and unshaven chin of the Commandant, and the scented drawing room suddenly fades away into the stone walls of a tiny hut lighted by a couple of candles stuck into bottles and thick with tobacco smoke, where five or six officers and I sit crowded on bunks or camp stools." In her later years, Sandes was plagued by her war injuries, although a motorized wheelchair allowed her to get around quite well. At age 80, she entered Ipswich hospital, where she died in November 1966.

SOURCES:

"Flora Sandes," in *This England*. Spring 1988, p. 14.

Uglow, Jennifer, ed. *The International Dictionary of Women's Biography*. NY: Continuum, 1982.

SUGGESTED READING:

Burgess, Alan. *The Lovely Sergeant*. Heinemann, 1963.

Sandes, Flora. *The Autobiography of a Woman Soldier*. H.F. & G. Witherby, 1927.

———. *An English Woman Sergeant in the Serbian Army*. Hodder & Stoughton, 1916.

Barbara Morgan,
Melrose, Massachusetts

Sandoz, Mari (1896–1966)

American biographer and historian. Name variations: Mari Macumber. Born Marie Susette Sandoz on May 11, 1896, in Sheridan County, Nebraska; died on March 10, 1966, in New York City; daughter of Jules Ami Sandoz and Mary Elizabeth (Fehr) Sandoz; attended business college for nine months and the University of Nebraska, 1922–31 (non-continuous); married Wray Macumber, in 1914 (divorced 1919).

Selected writings: Old Jules *(1935);* Slogum House *(1937);* Capital City *(1939);* Crazy Horse: The Strange Man of the Oglalas *(1942);* Cheyenne Autumn *(1953);* The Buffalo Hunters *(1954);* Winter Thunder *(1954);* The Horsecatcher *(1957);* Love Song to the Plains *(1961);* The Battle of the Little Bighorn *(1966);* The Story Catcher *(1973).*

Born in 1896, Mari Sandoz was the first of Jules and **Mary Sandoz**'s six children. The family lived near the Niobrara River in the Sand Hills area of northwestern Nebraska. Jules and Mary, his fourth wife, were Swiss immigrants living as homesteaders. He was a trapper, horticulturalist, and locator for new settlers, and he became important in local politics.

As a child, Sandoz learned the skills of trapping and skinning animals along with the domestic chores of cooking and baking. She spoke only German until she was nine. Then she attended the local school, where she learned English. Reading instantly captivated her, especially the work of Joseph Conrad and Thomas Hardy. "By the time I was ten," Sandoz told an interviewer, "I could bake up a 49-pound sack of flour, but would let the bread sour and the baby cry if there was anything to read." When she was nearly 14, she noted, she and her brother "had to dig our cattle out of the snowdrift of a May blizzard, and by night I was snowblind." After a six-week battle with total blindness, Sandoz discovered she "had only one eye left. But it's very useful to me, so it doesn't matter." Regardless of the physical challenge, she attained an eighth-grade education in little over four years.

Sandoz skipped high school, passed the rural teachers' examination, and taught school for five years in two Nebraska counties. She was married briefly to Wray Macumber from 1914 to 1919. Three years after her divorce, she enrolled at the University of Nebraska where she studied intermittently for nine years. She held miscellaneous jobs for support but never graduated.

Sandoz's lack of formal certification never hampered her career, which began at age ten with her first published work in the Omaha *Daily News*. In 1926, one of her many collegiate stories won honorable mention in a *Harper's* magazine contest and, in 1927, her short story,

"The Vine," appeared in *Prairie Schooner*. The death of her father in 1928 set Sandoz to work on her first full-length biography. Despite her dying father's distaste for the writing profession ("You know I consider artists and writers the maggots of society," he once told her), she honored his request that she document the struggles of his life. Her manuscript, *Old Jules*, received curt rejection on first submission, which left Sandoz dejected. She burned much of her other work and swore never to write again, but soon realized that she possessed an innate need to write. She rewrote *Old Jules*, and it won a lucrative nonfiction prize from the Atlantic Monthly Press in 1935. The book received praise for its accuracy and for the wealth of information it contained about the development and settling of the Great Plains.

Sandoz worked for assorted state and local publications in Nebraska between 1927 and 1940. After the release of her second novel, *Capital City* (1939), which was banned in many Nebraska libraries, she left her home state. She taught creative writing at the University of Colorado in 1941, at Indiana University in 1946, and at the University of Wisconsin for almost ten years. In 1943, she made Greenwich Village in New York City her permanent home and immersed herself in exhaustive research and extensive writing.

Sandoz's work revealed a deep involvement with her Western environment, which she perceived as both vigorous and violent. In her first novel, *Slogum House* (1937), set during the pioneer days of Nebraska, she distinguished herself as a controversial author—the book's scheming, grimly ambitious main character, who exploits her children for her own gain, outraged many readers, as did the language Sandoz chose to use. As an "independent liberal," Sandoz projected an uncanny sympathy and commitment for the thought and emotions of Native Americans. Her work was frequently of epic proportion and reflected concepts that were previously non-existent in mainstream literature. Acclaimed for her talent as a researcher, historian, and biographer, she wrote energetically throughout her lifetime and completed more than 20 book-length works.

Of all Sandoz's work, her "Great Plains Series"—or "Trans-Missouri Series"—is considered her great opus. Over the course of nearly 30 years, between 1935 and 1964, she documented a succession of fascinating images of the American West in factual book-length form. The series includes her acclaimed biography of the Oglala

Sioux leader *Crazy Horse*; a detailed retelling of the Cheyenne people's flight from Indian Territory, *Cheyenne Autumn*; and three other historical studies of the Old West. Sandoz, who thoroughly enjoyed the modern media of radio, television, and movies, lived to see *Cheyenne Autumn* produced as a feature film in 1964, directed by John Ford and starring Richard Widmark, **Carroll Baker**, and *Dolores Del Rio. On occasion, she wrote stories for children, including *The Horsecatcher* and *The Story Catcher*.

Sandoz underwent a mastectomy in 1954 and another in 1964. She died of cancer in St. Luke's Hospital in New York City in 1966. According to her wish, her body was returned to the Sand Hills country in Nebraska for burial.

SOURCES:

Commire, Anne, ed. *Something About the Author*. Vol. 5. Detroit, MI: Gale Research.

Contemporary Authors. New Revision Series. Vol. 64. Detroit, MI: Gale Research.

Dictionary of Literary Biography. Vol. 9. Detroit, MI: Gale Research.

Kunitz, Stanley J., and Howard Haycraft, eds. *Twentieth Century Authors*. NY: H.W. Wilson, 1942.

Sicherman, Barbara, and Carol Hurd Green, eds. *Notable American Women: The Modern Period*. Cambridge, MA: The Belknap Press of Harvard University, 1980.

Stine, Jean C., ed. *Contemporary Literary Criticism*. Vol. 28. Detroit, MI: Gale Research.

Gloria Cooksey,
freelance writer, Sacramento, California

Sands, Diana (1934–1973)

African-American actress. Born in 1934; died of cancer on September 21, 1973.

Diana Sands created the role of Beneatha in *Lorraine Hansberry's *Raisin in the Sun* for the Broadway stage and the Hollywood screen. On Broadway, she also appeared in *Blues for Mr. Charlie*, *The Owl and the Pussycat*, *We Bombed in New Haven*, *Gingham Dog*, *Ain't Supposed to Die a Natural Death*, and *Tiger at the Gate*. She received a Theater World Award for her performance in *Tiger, Tiger Burning Bright*. Wrote a friend, **Jane Galvin Lewis**, in *Ms* magazine in December 1973: "Diana said good-bye quietly without many of us who loved her even knowing that she was sick, until almost the end. The only thing one can forget is that she, as a whole person, is gone—all else we'll remember."

Sandwich Islands, princess of.

See Nahienaena (c. 1815–1836).
See Kamamalu, Victoria (1838–1866).
See Kaiulani (1875–1899).

Sandwich Islands, queen of.

See Kamamalu (c. 1803–1824).
See Kinau (c. 1805–1839).
See Kalama (c. 1820–1870).
See Kapiolani (1834–1899).
See Emma (1836–1885).
See Liliuokalani (1838–1917).

Sandwich Islands, queen-regent of.

See Kaahumanu (1777–1832).

Sandys, Diana (1909–1963).

See Churchill, Diana Spencer.

Sanford, Maria Louise (1836–1920)

American educator. Born on December 19, 1836, in Saybrook (now Old Saybrook), Connecticut; died on April 21, 1920, in Washington, D.C.; daughter of Henry Sanford and Mary (Clark) Sanford; attended Meriden Academy; graduated from New Britain Normal School, 1855.

Maria Louise Sanford was born in Saybrook, Connecticut, on December 19, 1836, the third of four children of **Mary Clark Sanford** and Henry Sanford. Following the failure of his shoe store, Henry had moved the family from Georgia to Saybrook prior to Maria's birth. Sanford's education began at age four with her attendance at a country school. In addition, her mother gave her Bible lessons, and told her of the lives of important historical figures; Maria took inspiration from such women as prison reformer *Elizabeth Fry and the founder of Mt. Holyoke Seminary, *Mary Lyon. The debt from Henry Sanford's earlier business failure forced the family's move to Meriden, where he got a job in his brother's factory. Maria supplemented her classes at the Meriden Academy with her own prolific reading and graduated with honors from the New Britain Normal School in 1855.

Sanford began her innovative teaching career in Connecticut towns, earning a reputation as an instructor who cultivated a love of learning in her students as a substitute for the harsh disciplinary tactics common at the time. She was adamant about emphasizing morals in the classroom in addition to secular pursuits, and later lectured on the topic of moral training at teachers' institutes. While devoting herself to her students, she did not neglect her own education, continuing to study history, logic, and the sciences on her own. In the midst of her professional success, Sanford suffered from depression stemming from her father's death in 1859 and the breaking-off of her engagement to a student of theology.

Positions in Parkersville and Unionville, Pennsylvania, in the latter half of the 1860s earned Sanford the love and respect of both communities. So great was her popularity that she narrowly lost an election for superintendent of the school district in Chester County in 1869, even though such a position was unheard of for a woman. Although she was denied the system's superintendency, Sanford still made her influence felt as the principal of a local academy. She introduced new teaching methods to instructors at the four area schools through the establishment of monthly meetings.

In 1869, Sanford accepted the job of English teacher at Swarthmore College; she was promoted to full professor the following year. Her affinity for poetry had its roots in her childhood studies, but during the mid-1870s she also developed an appreciation for art, which she eagerly incorporated into her curriculum. During her innovative art talks, she used slides to illustrate her points. Soon she was devoting three days a week to lecturing, which resulted in criticism from her fellow instructors and a large pay cut in 1878. Her unconsummated love for a married colleague deepened her unhappiness, and she decided to leave Swarthmore in 1879.

In 1880, a meeting with the president of the University of Minnesota resulted in Sanford's appointment there as an assistant professor. Eventually becoming a full professor of rhetoric and elocution, she made an indelible mark on the institution in her nearly 30-year career there. Deliberate and generous, she financed the education of several of her relatives and made herself available to students; she also assisted those in need and provided shelter for the homeless. She was understandably beloved because she refused to erect a barrier between herself and her students, as was then expected.

In the late 1880s, imprudent real-estate investments left Sanford $30,000 in arrears, but, like her father before her, she refused to file for bankruptcy. She was 80 years old before she successfully paid off her entire debt. Her sacrifice necessitated the implementation of a tight budget and unorthodox means of making extra money which sometimes met with the disapproval of her associates, such as her decision to rent art books to students. Her feminist stance also became an area of attack by critics. Despite criticism from the conservative administrators of the university and other members of the school faculty, Sanford garnered sufficient support from students and alumni to see her through the difficult financial times without loss of her position.

Retirement in 1909 did not spell the end of Sanford's public life. She continued to lecture on the topics of art, public affairs, and women's suffrage throughout the country. She also remained active in the Minneapolis Improvement League and the Woman's Welfare League, the former of which she founded in 1892. On the night of April 21, 1920, Sanford died in her sleep in Washington, D.C. She was buried in Mount Vernon Cemetery. Maria Louise Sanford's memory was honored in many ways. The first women's dormitory at the University of Minnesota was named for her, as was a public school in Minneapolis. As well, a statue was erected to her memory in Statuary Hall in the U.S. Capitol Building in Washington, D.C.

SOURCES:

James, Edward T., ed. *Notable American Women, 1607–1950*. Cambridge, MA: The Belknap Press of Harvard University, 1971.

McHenry, Robert, ed. *Famous American Women*. NY: Dover, 1980.

Gloria Cooksey,
freelance writer, Sacramento, California

Sanger, Margaret (1879–1966)

American feminist and flamboyant social activist who led the modern birth-control movement, founded the International Planned Parenthood Federation, and was instrumental in distributing contraception information and opening birth-control clinics around the globe. Born Margaret Louisa Higgins on September 14, 1879, in Corning, New York; died of arteriosclerosis on September 6, 1966, in the Valley House and Convalescent Center in Tucson, Arizona; sixth of eleven children of Michael Hennessey Higgins (a stonemason) and Anne (Purcell) Higgins; attended St. Mary's Catholic School until 8th grade, Claverack College and Hudson River Institute (1896–98), and nurses' training program at the White Plains Hospital (1900–02); married William Sanger, in August 1902 (divorced, after lengthy separation, in October 1921); married James Henry Noah Slee, on September 18, 1922 (died 1943); children: (first marriage) Stuart (b. 1903); Grant (b. 1908), and Margaret "Peggy" (b. 1910).

Attended nurses' training school at the White Plains hospital (1899–1902); married William Sanger and was forced to leave nursing school (1902); lived a conventional life in Hastings-on-Hudson as a wife and mother of three (1902–10); relocated with family to New York City and became involved in Socialist activities, with particular interest in issues of health and sexuality for poor women (1910–14); published The Woman Rebel, indicted for violating obscenity laws,

and fled to Europe where she met Havelock Ellis (1914); returned to U.S. (1915); opened the first birth-control clinic, was arrested, and spent 30 days in prison (1915–16); published The Birth Control Review *(1917–28); published first book,* Woman and the New Race *(1920); incorporated and became president of the American Birth Control League (1921); published second bestseller,* The Pivot of Civilization *(1922); established the Birth Control Clinical Research Bureau (1923); sponsored the World Population Conference in Geneva, Switzerland (1928); organized the National Committee for Federal Legislation for Birth Control (1930–36); with Dr. Hannah Stone, won court battle to license physicians to dispense birth-control information through the mails (1936); traveled to Hawaii, China, and India on behalf of the birth-control movement (1935–36); served as president of the Birth Control International Information Centers, London, England (1930–36); served as vice-president of the Family Planning Organization (1939); was honorary chair of the Planned Parenthood Federation of America (1942); was first president of International Committee on Planned Parenthood (1946); organized the Cheltenham Congress on World Population and World Resources in Relation to the Family (1948), which resulted in the formation of the International Planned Parenthood Federation (IPPF, 1952).*

Awards and honors: received the American Woman's Association Award (1931); the Award of honor of the Town Hall Club, New York City (1936); honorary LL.D. degree from Smith College (1949); the Albert and Mary Lasker Foundation Award from the Planned Parenthood Federation of America (1950); the City of Tucson, Arizona, proclaimed Margaret Sanger Week in March (1965); 3rd class Order of the Precious Crown from Japan (1965); honorary LL.D. degree from the University of Arizona (1966); the Planned Parenthood Federation of America created the Margaret Sanger Award (1966).

In the summer of 1912, while working as a home nurse, Margaret Sanger received a panicked call from Jake Sachs whose wife was dying of blood poisoning after attempting a self-induced abortion. For two weeks, Sanger nursed **Sadie Sachs** back to health in the couple's tenement apartment in the slums of New York's Lower East Side. When Sadie explained to her doctor that she could not afford physically, financially, or emotionally to have more children and asked what she could do to prevent further pregnancies, he patted her on the back and recommended that she persuade Jake to sleep on the roof.

When he left, in tears Sachs begged Sanger to teach her some reliable methods of contraception. Sanger knew there was little information available but promised to do what she could. Busy with her own three children and her work, she forgot about her promise. In October, Sanger received another call from Jake: his wife had attempted another self-induced abortion. Sadie Sachs died ten minutes after Sanger reached their home. By her own recollection, she left the apartment to wander the streets for hours, "thinking, regretting, dreading to stop; fearful of my conscience, dreading to face my own accusing soul." That night she resolved not to "go back again to nurse women's ailing bodies while their miseries were as vast as the stars." Rather than work to lessen the pain of the poor women she served in the crowded homes of New York's tenements, she would make it her mission to bring knowledge of contraception to women of all classes, races, and creeds. In this effort, she went on to lead the modern birth-control movement as an internationally known champion of a woman's right to information about her own body.

Margaret Sanger was born on September 14, 1879, in Corning, New York, the sixth child of Michael and **Anne Purcell Higgins**. Though tubercular and frail from her illness, Anne had five more children after Margaret, while Michael, not a wealthy man, helped deliver them at home. Margaret witnessed these births and with them her mother's weakening condition. All accounts indicate that her parents had a supportive, loving relationship; nonetheless, the coming of children year after year into the Higgins household made an impression on young Margaret about the connections between childbirth, poverty, and women's ill-health.

Michael Higgins was an outspoken freethinker and atheist in a community of devout Catholics. His unpopular political opinions did nothing to help his career as a stonemason, particularly in a community where a stonemason's largest business came from the local Catholic cemeteries. More interested in a good political discussion than in earning money to support his ever-growing family, he had a penchant for supporting radical causes and spending what little funds the family had in lavish gestures. Sanger always maintained that her father left a positive legacy for the Higgins children in terms of his emphasis on independent thinking as well as his encouragement to challenge authority and to leave the world a better place than they found it. But his freewheeling spending and lack of support for the family were not lost on her, nor was the way in which the arrival of each new child overbur-

dened her ailing mother and contributed to her death at 49. Michael, in contrast, lived past 80.

Faced with poverty, the older siblings in the family took jobs to help support the younger ones. Growing up bearing the taunts and harassment of their contemporaries who were taught that the Higginses were "children of the devil," Sanger actively strove to be courageous and to challenge her own fears. To overcome the dread of a certain railroad bridge, for instance, she attempted to traverse it. But she was only halfway across when a train came and was forced to hang from a support between the tracks while the train screamed by overhead. A local farmer helped her back up; she then successfully finished crossing the bridge.

While in 8th grade at a Catholic school, Sanger was ridiculed by a teacher for being tardy and wearing a pair of new, fancy gloves (a present from her sister who worked as a nanny for a wealthy family). The young Sanger marched out of the school, vowing never to return. When she could not be convinced to change her mind, her two oldest sisters, **Mary** and **Nan**, scraped together enough money to send her to Claverack College and Hudson River Institute, a private, preparatory boarding school across the state. Sanger's sisters took care of her tuition while she worked in the school kitchen to pay for her room and board. The years she spent at Claverack (1896–98) were happy. Sanger thrived in the secure atmosphere where she was removed from the daily worries of helping support her struggling family. She performed particularly well at elocution and had a reputation as a leader who encouraged others to challenge the rules of the school. Later she would credit a lecture from the headmaster, after she challenged the school's curfew, with changing her thinking about her own leadership abilities. The headmaster commended her for her charismatic personality but also reminded her that with leadership comes responsibility. Suddenly, the link between developing one's own views on politics and society, and using one's abilities to improve the world (sometimes missing in her father's politics), became clear to Sanger.

Sanger was prevented from finishing her final year at Claverack for lack of funds, and in 1898, age 19, she returned home to help nurse her mother who was in the final stage of tuberculosis. With the harsh reality of her family's poverty, and with her father growing more and more controlling after her mother's death in 1899, Sanger realized that she would have to give up her goal of becoming a doctor. Settling instead on nursing, she entered a training program at the White Plains Hospital. After completing two years there, she began taking summer courses at the Manhattan Eye and Ear Hospital, probably to make up credits she had missed while fighting her own bout with tuberculosis, to prepare for the final year of schooling that would allow her to become a registered nurse. She was 23 when she met William Sanger. Ten years older than Margaret, William was an architect and aspiring artist who whisked her up in a whirlwind of romance and aggressively sought her hand in marriage. The wedding took place in August 1902 and shortly thereafter she wrote to her sister: "I'm very sorry to have the thing occur, but yet I am very, very happy." She was then dismissed from the nursing program at White Plains because married women were not permitted there.

Six months after her marriage, Sanger was pregnant. She was also dealing with a tubercular flare-up and spent the last months of her pregnancy in an Adirondack sanitarium before returning to New York to give birth to a son, Stuart, in 1903. After another stint at the sanitarium to help her regain her health, she returned to the home William was building for them in Hastings-on-Hudson, a town well removed from the pollution and bustle of Manhattan. The couple worked hard on the house, taking pride in a leaded-glass window above the staircase, and were just beginning to move in when the entire dwelling was destroyed by fire due to a faulty furnace. The Sangers rebuilt the home, lived there for eight years, and had two more children, Grant in 1908 and Margaret (Peggy) in 1910. Sanger would later claim that the fire had taught her a valuable lesson about the futility of material things.

During this suburban interlude, Sanger focused on her roles as wife and mother but felt increasingly dissatisfied with her life. Hoping to overcome the onset of some serious rifts in their marriage, the Sangers decided to return to New York City in 1910. From their Manhattan apartment, both Margaret and William involved themselves in the radical labor movement and Socialist politics. She began to work as a home nurse on the city's Lower East Side, meeting Sadie Sachs and watching her die, and encountering many distressing instances of women weakened by childbirth and poverty-induced substandard living conditions. She became involved in the International Workers of the World (IWW) strikes and in 1912 led a group of striking workers' children out of Lawrence, Massachusetts. Her participation in this cause brought her national attention. As the urgency of women's health issues became more clear to her, she was disappointed with the male leadership of the radical political community. Sanger wrote two columns for the socialist newspaper *The Call*—"What Every Mother Should Know" and "What Every Girl Should Know"—which detailed facts of anatomy and of sexually transmitted diseases. "If the unions [are] fighting for better wages and shorter hours," she wrote, "they should be equally concerned with the size of the workingman's family." Influenced by the radical feminist *Emma Goldman (with whom she later would form a rivalry), Sanger began to draw away from the causes of her radical Socialist friends who continued to focus on economic issues. She increasingly regarded "family limitation" as the defining issue of her political activities, and separated herself somewhat from the feminists who were working for suffrage.

Meanwhile, her relationship with William grew more troubled. As his dream of becoming a painter took precedence over supporting the family financially, Sanger was distressed by the seeming similarities between her husband and her father. Her relationships with friends in the labor movement also fueled the breakdown of her marriage. Many of these male friends were anarchists who did not believe in social institutions such as monogamy and marriage, and Sanger now made the sexual freedom of women part of her feminist consciousness as well as part of her own life's practice. In the hopes of rekindling their struggling relationship, in October 1913 the Sangers traveled in France where William studied painting while Margaret investigated the ways in which French women managed to limit their families. Purchasing samples of tampons, suppositories, and douches, Sanger took detailed notes about their uses and was anxious to return to the United States to pass along her knowledge. Likely in recognition that she and William could no longer continue their marriage, Sanger encouraged him to stay in Paris to paint while she returned to New York with the children.

Before going to France, in February 1913 Sanger had come in contact with censorship and the 1873 Comstock Act for an article she wrote about syphilis in *The Call*. Named for its principal supporter Anthony Comstock, the law prevented "obscene materials," including birth-control information, from being distributed through the U.S. mail. Upon her return to New York in 1914, she set out to challenge the notion that information about contraception was obscene. She began to publish a militantly feminist journal, *The*

Margaret
Sanger

Woman Rebel. The radical newsletter, which introduced the now-common term "birth control," published eight issues dealing with such topics as child labor, social hygiene, population growth, and the exploitation of women in industry. Her aim, as cited in the first issue, was "to stimulate women to think for themselves and to build up a conscious fighting character." The post office quickly declared the publication unmailable.

Sanger was indicted on nine counts of violating federal statutes, creating a media firestorm, and faced up to 45 years in prison. Fearing a harsh judgment, she fled the country in October 1914, before going to trial. She left behind 100,000 copies of a pamphlet entitled "Family Limitation," which gave the most detailed instructions on birth control and contraception techniques then available in English. Many of the methods, such as the use of laxatives to induce menstruation, were criticized as ineffective or outdated, but Sanger's pamphlet marked the first effort to bring national attention to the necessity of *all* women having access to available information about birth control.

> *I would* be heard. No matter what it should cost. *I would be heard.*
>
> —Margaret Sanger

While in exile, Sanger toured Europe where she learned that different cultures had different attitudes and methods of family limitation. She spent long hours in the British Museum studying overpopulation. She also traveled to Holland, where she learned about the diaphragm and the Dutch populace's open advocation of birth control as necessary to the quality of life, and to other European countries to discuss with women how they maintained small families. During this year abroad, the 35-year-old Sanger met sexologist Havelock Ellis. Though he was married, they had an affair, then went on to maintain a close friendship. Ellis influenced many of Sanger's permissive ideas about sexuality in general and her feminist consciousness about sexual liberation for women in particular.

Determined to foster a Dutch-style attitude (that birth control was part of a nation's quality of life) to the practice of providing birth-control information in the U.S., Sanger prepared to return home in 1915. In her absence, William Sanger had been imprisoned for distributing a copy of her "Family Limitation" pamphlet, and Sanger had a growing sense of doom. Upon her return, however, she was surprised to see that U.S. public opinion on contraception had taken a more liberal slant; the term "birth control" was in fairly wide use and Anthony Comstock, the author and enforcer of the obscenity laws, was dead.

Because Sanger's direct-action politics were considered lawless, she did not receive the support of the new president of the National Birth Control League, *Mary Ware Dennett. But the unfortunate illness and death of Sanger's young daughter Peggy increased public support for her. Although Sanger was offered a postponement of her trial, the family tragedy had made her even more determined to pursue her cause, and she declined. With hundreds of letters coming to the judge from women who had been helped by Sanger's information, and with support from liberals and feminists in Europe and the U.S., Sanger was determined to strike a victory over the Comstock laws. Seeing how much the tide had turned in favor of open discussion of birth control since Sanger's indictment a year earlier, the prosecutor tried to settle out of court, which Sanger would not do. In February 1916, he dropped all charges against her, and she was free to begin the open, public championing of her cause.

At a dinner in her honor, she said:

> I realize that many . . . cannot sympathize with or countenance the methods I have followed in my attempt to arouse working women . . . . They tell me that *The Woman Rebel* was badly written; that it was crude; that it was emotional and hysterical; that it mixed issues; that it was defiant, and too radical. Well, to all of these indictments I plead guilty.

She did, however, maintain that birth control was not a new or a radical notion, for it had been in existence since Aristotle. It must be made available, she noted, to all women, especially to those of the poor working class.

Sanger had begun to realize the value of broad public support and to understand that the elite liberal constituency could do a great deal for her cause. In 1916, she toured the nation, speaking in Rochester, Detroit, Boston, Milwaukee, St. Louis, Denver, and Los Angeles as well as many smaller towns in between. In all, she gave her lecture 119 times, always to full crowds eagerly awaiting knowledge of contraception. Though meeting opposition from the Catholic Church and some women's clubs, Sanger continued to advocate civil disobedience as a means of achieving greater justice in the availability of birth-control information, but she also continued to court the support of the elite liberal feminists, who were mostly white and upper class. During this time, she was struggling with Dennett, who advocated legislative reform and scorned Sanger's more militant tactics. Oddly, while Dennett advocated the total repeal of the obscenity statutes on free-speech grounds, Sanger was instead happy to promote only reform of the statutes which would allow properly licensed doctors and nurses to be responsible for providing birth-control information to working-class women through organized clinics. Her vision was in part spurred by the Dutch system of socialized public health care that the U.S. would only begin to debate seriously in the last part of the 20th century.

Convinced that it was action, not legislation or speeches, that would bring her goals to fruition, Sanger and her sister **Ethel Byrne** started the first birth-control clinic in the United States. The clinic, located in Brownsville, Brooklyn, opened on October 16, 1916, and some 140 patients waited in line for hours to see the sisters. Nine days later, the clinic was raided and closed down, and Margaret and Ethel were jailed. Ethel promptly went on a hunger strike, asserting that she would "die, if need be, for my sex." The story created a sensation in the New York City press. Supporters crowded the courtroom, but this time public opinion did not sway judicial action. Sanger's open acknowledgement of circulating birth-control information and her unwillingness to promise not to do so again—"I cannot promise to obey a law I do not respect"—earned her a guilty verdict and 30 days in jail.

On appeal, the Sanger decision was upheld, but the appeal nonetheless won a significant victory for the birth-control cause. Although Judge Frederick Crane of the Court of Appeals of the State of New York upheld Section 1145 of the obscenity law that prevented laypersons from distributing birth-control information, the door was opened to an interpretation that doctors and pharmacists might distribute such information not only in the treatment of venereal disease. This victory was an important one in light of Sanger's goal of establishing doctor-run birth-control clinics. Realizing that working-class women were too enmeshed in the struggles of daily life to give energy to her cause and that they had no dispensable income to contribute, Sanger strengthened her courting of elite feminists and began downplaying her more radical past. With the financial help of friends, she founded *The Birth Control Review*, which she would edit and publish until 1928.

In 1919, Sanger was living in a small apartment in New York City, giving most of her income to *The Birth Control Review* and growing fatigued. She still grieved over her daughter's death and struggled to find time to be with her two sons, who were in boarding schools much of the year. Given an advance to write a book, she took her son Grant to California and there wrote *Woman and the New Race*, which was published in 1920. In 1921, with the help of her wealthier friends, she founded the American Birth Control League (which in 1942 would become the Planned Parenthood Federation of America), and served as the organization's first president. After finally receiving the divorce she had demanded from William Sanger (1920), she married millionaire J. Noah Slee in 1922. The

marriage seems to have been one of convenience for Sanger from the beginning, but also one of mutual need. In return for time with Sanger, Slee grudgingly agreed to respect her autonomy and also gave enormous financial support to the birth-control cause. Sanger maintained intimate relations with other men but stayed married to him until his death in 1943.

After a world tour in 1922—in which she organized birth-control clinics in Hawaii, China, and Japan and lectured in England, Scotland and Germany—Sanger returned to the U.S. and began planning for the International Birth Control Conference. In 1923, her newly enhanced financial and social status allowed her to open the Birth Control Clinical Research Bureau in New York City, the first birth-control clinic in the United States to be staffed by doctors. The Birth Control Conference was held in New York City during 1925 and was attended by over 18,000 delegates from more than a dozen nations. Sanger followed this victory by resigning as the president of the American Birth Control League and organizing the World Population Conference in Geneva, Switzerland, in 1927. This conference, which brought together prominent social scientists from all over the globe, resulted in the creation of a small committee focused on international population.

The Geneva conference tapped not only a great deal of Sanger's strength, but also much of Noah Slee's fortune. She returned to the United States to see the Birth Control Clinical Research Bureau raided by police in 1929. The raid and ensuing arrest of eight staff members—resoundingly denounced by the press, the medical profession, and upper-class liberals—provided Sanger's longtime attorney Jonah Goldstein with an opportunity to establish that married women had a right to obtain birth-control information under the law as written, which required that a woman have a medical reason for such information.

In the years between 1930 and 1936, Sanger and others launched a serious effort to write a bill that would establish a woman's right to such information under the auspices of a group entitled the National Committee for Federal Legislation for Birth Control. Though they were unsuccessful in 1931 and again in 1934, their attempts kept birth control at the forefront of public attention. A major victory for the Committee came in 1936 in *United States* v. *One Package*, a case in which Dr. **Hannah Stone**, who ran Sanger's New York Birth Control Bureau, was arrested for receiving a package of contraceptive materials through the mail. The decision in favor of Stone marked the repeal of the last vestiges of the Comstock laws and the beginning of many such decisions, including the American Medical Association's 1937 resolution to accept contraception as a legitimate medical option that needed to be included in medical-school curricula.

By age 56, Sanger had achieved enormous status as the early champion of a cause whose time had come. During the 1930s, she published two autobiographies, *My Fight for Birth Control* (1931) and *Margaret Sanger: An Autobiography* (1938). While these are valuable in what they reveal about how Sanger wanted her life to be viewed, neither accurately portrays her childhood and early radicalism in the labor movement. (Decades later, **Ellen Chesler**'s biographer of Sanger, *Woman of Valor*, would correct many factual errors, some of which Sanger had encouraged.) Sanger traveled extensively, attending such functions as the All-India Women's Conference in 1935 and visiting Hong Kong, Rangoon, and China. While in the U.S. in 1936, she received the Town Hall Club award in the same building which had once locked its doors to one of her meetings.

In 1939, the American Birth Control League and the Birth Control Clinical Research Bureau merged to become the Birth Control Federation of America. In partial retirement after 1939, Sanger witnessed the reaction against birth control and the trend toward "family planning" in this organization. When the Birth Control Federation of America then became the Planned Parenthood Federation of America in 1942, Sanger was elected its honorary chair. In 1946, Sweden's *Elise Ottesen-Jensen convened an international conference in Stockholm that resulted in the founding of the International Committee on Planned Parenthood; Sanger was its first president. In 1948, she sponsored the Cheltenham Congress on World Population and World Resources in Relation to the Family, which resulted in the 1952 formation of the International Planned Parenthood Federation (IPPF), the largest provider of birth-control information in the world.

With many of her dear friends aging and dying—including Havelock Ellis in 1939, Hannah Stone in 1941, and Noah Slee in 1943—Sanger retired to Tucson to spend time with her children and grandchildren but never quit politicking for more advancements in birth-control techniques, including the birth-control pill. She traveled to Japan three times and made a return trip to India in 1959. In the U.S., she continued to receive pressure from Catholics who did not

support birth control or her flamboyant lifestyle. Sanger received many tributes late in life, including honorary LL.D. degrees from Smith College (1949) and the University of Arizona (1966) as well as the highest honor given to women in Japan, the 3rd class Order of the Precious Crown (1965). Other honors include the Margaret Sanger Award created by Planned Parenthood Federation of America for people who demonstrate commitment to the principles of social justice and the Margaret Sanger Medallion for community-level contributions, both created in 1965. Sanger died on September 14, 1966, shortly before her 87th birthday. "When the history of our civilization is written," wrote H.G. Wells, "it will be a biological history and Margaret Sanger will be its heroine."

SOURCES:

Anticaglia, Elizabeth. *12 American Women*. Chicago, IL: Nelson-Hall, 1975.

Baskin, Alex. *Woman Rebel*. NY: SUNY at Stonybrook, 1976.

Chesler, Ellen. *Woman of Valor: Margaret Sanger and the Birth Control Movement in America*. NY: Simon & Schuster, 1992.

Kerber, Linda K., and Jane Sherron De Hart. *Women's America: Refocusing the Past*. 3rd ed. NY: Oxford University Press, 1982.

Lader, Lawrence. *The Margaret Sanger Story, and the Fight for Birth Control*. Westport, CT: Greenwood, 1955.

Muccigrosso, Robert, ed. *Research Guide to American Historical Biography*. Vol. III. Washington, DC: Beacham, 1988.

Sicherman, Barbara, and Carol Hurd Green, eds. *Notable American Women: The Modern Period*. Cambridge, MA: Belknap Press of Harvard University, 1980.

Sweeney, Patricia E. *Biographies of American Women: An Annotated Bibliography*. Santa Barbara, CA: ABC-Clio, 1990.

Tinling, Marion. *Women Remembered: A Guide to Landmarks of Women's History in the United States*. CT: Greenwood, 1986.

SUGGESTED READING:

Gordon, Linda. *Woman's Body: Woman's Right*. NY: Viking, 1976.

Kennedy, David M. *Birth Control in America: The Career of Margaret Sanger*. New Haven, CT: Yale University Press, 1970.

Reed, James. *The Birth Control Movement and American Society: From Private Vice to Public Virtue*. Princeton, NJ: Princeton University Press, 1983.

Sanger, Margaret. *Margaret Sanger: An Autobiography*. NY: W.W. Norton, 1938.

———. *My Fight for Birth Control*. NY: Farrar & Rinehart, 1931.

RELATED MEDIA:

"Choices of the Heart: The Margaret Sanger Story," starring **Dana Delany** as Sanger, first aired on Lifetime network, 1995.

"Woman Rebel," a film about Margaret Sanger, written and directed by Francis Gladstone for "Nova," sponsored by PBS, aired in 1976.

Correspondence and personal papers are housed in over 500 boxes in the Library of Congress collection, which is on microfilm and has a reference guide.

The Margaret Sanger Papers Project, involving Smith College, the Library of Congress, New York University, and the Institute for Research in History, is currently searching out, collecting, and microfilming all available Sanger correspondence and archival materials under the direction of Esther Katz of New York University.

Sophia Smith Collection, Smith College, has papers of the Planned Parenthood Federation of America, and the Margaret Sanger Bureau, and the personal papers of many of her close colleagues.

Sharon L. Barnes, Ph.D. candidate,
University of Toledo, Toledo, Ohio

Sangster, Margaret (1838–1912)

American writer. Name variations: Elizabeth Munson. Born Margaret Elizabeth Munson on February 22, 1838, in New Rochelle, New York; died on June 3, 1912, in South Orange, New Jersey; interred in Cypress Hills Cemetery in Brooklyn; attended Passaic Seminary (a Baptist school) in Paterson, New Jersey, and graduated from Monsieur Paul Abadie in New York, New York; daughter of John Munson and Margaret R. (Chisholm) Munson; grandmother of writer Margaret Elizabeth Sangster (b. 1894); married George Sangster, in October 1858; children: George Munson Sangster (b. 1859).

Selected writings: Hours with Girls *(1881);* Little Knights and Ladies *(1895);* Janet Ward, A Daughter of the Manse *(1902);* Fairest Girlhood *(1906);* An Autobiography: From My Youth Up *(1909);* My Garden of Hearts *(posthumous) (1913).*

Margaret Sangster was born Margaret Elizabeth Munson in 1838 in New Rochelle, New York, the firstborn of two daughters of John and **Margaret Chisholm Munson**, who each had a son from previous marriages. An extremely intelligent child, Sangster could read when she was only four years old. The Munson family, who observed the Presbyterian faith and Calvinist precepts, moved to New York City in 1841, where they remained for five years before settling in Paterson, New Jersey. Sangster was only in her teens when her father died, and an uncle, David Chisholm, stepped in to assist the family.

Sangster received a Baptist education at the Passaic Seminary in New Jersey before graduating from Monsieur Paul Abadie's French and English school in Brooklyn, New York. Even as a young child, Sangster had occupied herself by writing stories and poems. These youthful journals provided a wealth of material that nourished her adult writing career. Her first published work, the short story "Little Janey," led to an extended assignment writing 100 children's stories for a series of illustrations. Margaret pursued her writing career until October 1858, when she married George Sangster, a widower. She willingly accepted the role of mother to his two young daughters, and the couple eventually had a third child, a son named George. George Sangster served in the Union Army during the Civil War, after which the family lived briefly in Norfolk, Virginia, before returning to Brooklyn in 1870.

After the death of her husband in 1871, Sangster wrote to support her family. She contributed to many periodicals, including the *Atlantic Monthly* and *Hearth and Home*, where she secured a permanent position as editor of the children's page in 1873. In time, she became assistant editor of the magazine, a position she used to promote her "mission to girlhood." She offered advice and wrote inspirational and provocative essays for young women on such themes as "The Girl and Her Friends," "The Girl in Business," and "Shall Both Be Wage Earners?" She was one of the popular American poets in the period following the Civil War, and her poems "Elizabeth Aged Nine" and "Are the Children at Home?" were known the country over.

Sangster accepted an editorial position at the *Christian Intelligencer* immediately following the demise of *Hearth and Home* in 1875. She later worked as a literary adviser for Harper & Brothers and as an editor at *Harper's Young People* from 1882 until 1889. She also edited *Harper's Bazaar* for ten years until that magazine ceased publication. At *Harper's*, as at *Hearth and Home*, Sangster's occupation allowed her to share her ideals with the magazine's readership. She even altered the format and limited the fictional content in deference to more service-oriented articles.

Sangster also wrote novels, including *Hours with Girls, Little Knights and Ladies, Good Manners, Radiant Motherhood,* and *My Garden of Hearts,* and signed on as a member of the editorial staff of *Woman's Home Companion*

Margaret Sangster

in 1904. Her magazine articles, though characterized as "preachy," were nonetheless amicable, light, and easy to follow. She made no pretense concerning the literary value of her work, and duly recognized "good writers" such as Charles Dickens and *Jane Austen. Over the years Sangster's political stance evolved to more liberal and feminist beliefs, in part due to her experiences as a wage earner. She died in South Orange, New Jersey, on June 3, 1912.

SOURCES:

James, Edward T., ed. *Notable American Women, 1607–1950.* Cambridge, MA: The Belknap Press of Harvard University, 1971.

McHenry, Robert, ed. *Famous American Women.* NY: Dover, 1980.

Gloria Cooksey,
freelance writer, Sacramento, California

Sankova, Galina (b. 1904)

Russian photojournalist, considered one of the finest to document World War II. Born in 1904 in Russia.

Born in 1904, Galina Sankova became interested in photography in the 1930s, but initially served the Soviet Union as a nurse when World War II began. She gained access to the Russian front after becoming a correspondent for the magazine *Frontovaya Illyustracia* (The Front Illustrated). Sankova endured great peril while documenting the war. Against orders, she stormed into battle in order to accurately record the western front and the Briansk and Don campaigns near Stalingrad. She was present at the 1944 northern offensive at Leningrad and even attended to the injuries of 100 wounded soldiers after a battle.

Sankova, who did not go unscathed, suffered serious injuries in an airplane accident, but she was photographing Russian children in a German concentration camp the following day. Her collection of war photographs—published as *On the Trail of Horror*—made her the preeminent Russian female war photographer, in the distinguished company of **Natasha Bode, Olga Ignatovich, Olga Lander** and **Yelzaveta Mikulina**. Her body of work also includes photographs taken in Siberia. Sankova joined the staff of *Ogonyok* magazine at the war's conclusion.

SOURCES:

Rosenblum, Naomi. *A History of Women Photographers.* NY: Abbeville, 1994.

Ruth Savitz,
freelance writer, Philadelphia, Pennsylvania

Sans-Gêne, Madame (c. 1764–after 1820).

See Lefebvre, Catherine.

Sansom, Odette (1912–1995)

Hero of the French Resistance, known only as Odette, who worked for the British War Department during World War II and, when captured and tortured by the Nazis, refused to divulge classified information.

Name variations: Odette Hallowes; Odette Churchill; (code names) Odette Matayer, Céline, Lise. Born Odette Marie Céline Brailly on April 28, 1912, in France; died in 1995 in England; daughter of Yvonne Brailly and Gaston Brailly (a bank official and soldier); married Roy Sansom, in 1930; married Captain Peter Morland Churchill, in 1947; married Geoffrey Hallowes; children: (first marriage) Françoise (b. 1932); Lily (b. 1934); Marianne (b. 1936).

Joined the Resistance (1942); captured and brought to Fresne Prison in Paris (1943); tortured by the Gestapo (May 26, 1943); transferred to Karlsruhe prison (May 12, 1944); brought to Ravensbrück concentration camp for women in Germany under sentence of death (July 18, 1944); released from Ravensbrück (April 28, 1945); received George Cross from King George VI (November 19, 1946); testified for the prosecution at the War Crimes Court in Hamburg, Germany (December 16, 1946).

A French agent working for the British during World War II, Odette Sansom left three small daughters to join the Resistance in 1942. She was captured six months later and imprisoned in Fresne, the Gestapo prison in Paris. On May 26, 1943, Sansom was taken to the headquarters of the German security service. When she refused to divulge the whereabouts of her spy circuit's wireless operator and another British officer, she not only saved the lives of other agents but enabled them to continue their work for the Resistance.

A specially trained inner core of Nazis, hand-picked by Heinrich Himmler, interrogated her repeatedly. In his book *Odette: The Story of a British Agent* (1949), Jerrard Tickell credits Sansom's survival to "the unassailable dignity in which she enclosed herself." One Nazi interrogator caught her arms and held them behind the back of the chair, wrote Tickell. The other began to unbutton her blouse. "I resent your hands on me or on my clothes," she said. "If you tell me what you want me to do and release one hand I will do it." The interrogator told her to unbutton it. When she did, he pulled back the material and pressed a red-hot poker to her spine. As she fell forward, the interrogator asked, "Where is Arnaud?" Sansom replied, "I have nothing to say."

The torture continued. Still Odette refused to speak. The interrogator calmly told her that his colleague was going to pull out her toenails one by one. In between each "evulsion," he would repeat his questions, telling her she could end "the ceremony" simply by answering the questions. Again, he asked, "Where is Arnaud?" When Sansom would not answer, the man kneeling at her feet fastened pincers around the tip of one of her toenails and pulled. The pain was excruciating. Still, she refused to speak. "Now would you care to tell me Arnaud's address?," the interrogator asked. When Odette again refused, the Nazi systematically tore out each of her toenails, one by one. "How do you feel?," the interrogator asked. "I have nothing to say," Sansom replied.

The interrogator told Odette he was a servant of his führer, Adolf Hitler, and had no regrets for what he did; in fact, he would stop at nothing to get the information he needed. "I am interested to see, monsieur, that you consider it necessary to defend what you have just done," said Sansom. Standing angrily over her, he said, "We Germans have no need to excuse ourselves to subject races. Are you going to answer my questions?" Once more, she refused. Back in her cell, Sansom ripped her prison cloth into strips to bind her feet. She had kept silent, but she knew about the other things the Gestapo did to women and, alone in the darkness of the prison, she feared her strength might not last.

"If I had courage, it was my grandfather's," Sansom told a *London Sunday Times* interviewer in 1990. "Every Sunday morning, after church, we were taken to the grave of my father, who was killed at Verdun 30 days before Armistice. 'It will be your duty,' said my grandfather, 'to do what you can for your country.' I grew up with this sense of duty." Sansom, an elegant, vivacious young Frenchwoman who had been living in England, detested the Nazi system, the police state, and Hitler. Coming from a long line of patriots from the province of Picardy, she rose up against indifference and was outraged when the Nazis took over her nation. She believed that only if England and France survived would freedom and civilization prevail. It was this belief that saw her through her harrowing ordeal.

Odette Marie Céline Brailly was born on April 28, 1912, the first child of Gaston, a bank official in Amiens, and **Yvonne Brailly**. In 1914, her father joined an infantry regiment. Honored for his tenacity and courage at the battle of Verdun, he was later killed as he attempted to save two men missing from his platoon.

Odette was a quiet child. When she was eight, an unidentified disorder caused her to go blind for

two years. After she regained her sight, rheumatic fever left her weak and partially paralyzed for months. While her brother, Louis, went to school at the Lycée, Odette was sent to the Convent of Sainte Thérèse because her mother thought the Normandy air would be beneficial. The nuns considered her volatile, petulant, and stubborn.

At age 14, Sansom moved with her mother to Boulogne, where Odette and her brother ran barefoot over the rocks and cliffs during the holidays. When Louis returned to school, she continued her walks alone and, though she missed him, found an unexpected joy in solitude. Yet, there was an undercurrent of bitterness and turbulence in her. Something about the future seemed to haunt her.

In 1930, Odette met Roy Sansom, an Englishman who was the son of a family friend. A year later, they were married, and their first daughter **Françoise** was born in 1932. They then moved to England where a second daughter **Lily** was born in 1934. Two years later, **Marianne** was born. Four years later, Sansom was following the fall of France in British newspapers, listening to BBC radio reports as refugees choked every road from Paris to Marseilles while Ger-

Odette
Sansom

man troops marched down the Champs-Élysées. Winston Churchill, prime minister of Great Britain, proclaimed his faith that France would be free once more, and Charles de Gaulle, leader of the Free French in London, encouraged his nation to fight back.

Before war broke out in September 1939, Britain had established secret agencies to conduct clandestine operations in Europe. By July 1940, these activities were brought under the control of a central organization, called the Special Operations Executive (SOE), also known as "the Firm" and "the Racket." Each country, including France, had its own section in London. Men and women from the SOE would work within occupied nations, disabling factories, wrecking power houses, and severing lines of communication. Spies were chosen carefully. Selectors, relying on instinct, looked for spirit rather than muscle.

After the British evacuation of Dunkirk, the War Office had made a radio appeal to the public for pictures of the French coast. The purpose of these photos was to determine the exact topography of a particular section. SOE was also monitoring those who brought them in, hoping to find some who were qualified to become agents in France.

By the end of March 1941, the first members of the French Section were in intensive training in Britain. Agents learned how to place explosive matchboxes or fountain pens where they would do the most damage. They learned how to pick locks and pockets, forge signatures, and derail trains. They also learned how to kill silently. Meanwhile, Sansom was feeling powerless. According to the Geneva Convention, women were not allowed to engage in physical combat, but she wanted desperately to fight the Nazis and decided to volunteer for the war effort in any way she could. She wrote to the War Office indicating that she had lived in Boulogne for four years and that she knew the area well.

During her interview, Sansom was puzzled by the questions and by how much the British knew about her. She was told that the War Office needed people who knew and loved France, people who could move about the country freely without attracting attention. She began to understand that they were asking her to volunteer for more than part-time work as a translator. After four months of agonizing indecision over leaving her three children, and still feeling unqualified, she accepted. "Train me," she said. "You will realize I am not what you want."

In July 1942, Sansom began her training at the SOE school, a country house hidden in New Forest, Hampshire. She learned how to fire British guns, how to identify the insignia on German uniforms, how to write, transmit, and receive Morse code, how to handle a canoe, and how to evade answers under SS (Schutzstaffel or "elite guard") interrogation; in short, all the techniques necessary for leading the double life of a spy.

Women were employed by SOE for field work, generally as couriers, and frequently as wireless operators. They were not expected to carry out acts of sabotage or to join in guerilla operations, though there were exceptions. For example, *Violette Szabo fought a rearguard action with German units before being captured near Limoges. Another courier, **Pearl Witherington**, led an underground force of 2,000 young French guerillas, called the Maquis, who specialized in cutting the main Paris-Bordeaux railway. Sansom was trained to serve as a courier and a circuit organizer. This would mean securing an apartment in a specified part of town in France to which the SOE might send other members, either as part of an escape team or to encourage sabotage and action by the French Resistance.

Before spies left England, Scotland Yard detectives scrutinized their clothing. Britain's most prestigious organizations turned out forged papers for them to carry. Agents wore boots and shoes with secret compartments. They hid microdots bearing secret codes on their bodies, or in toothpaste tubes, shoelaces or buttons. Messages were printed on ties, scarves, handkerchiefs, and underwear. A matchstick was made in which the equivalent of nine sheets of paper could be carried and then hidden among the regular matches in the box. Agents memorized codes in verse.

In October 1942, leaving her three daughters at a convent school in Essex, 30-year-old Odette Sansom became a member of the Women's Transport Service, a part of the First Aid Nursing Yeomanry (FANY). Her first mission was to set up a wireless operation at Auxerre. She was to land on the Mediterranean coast and work her way north, where SOE hoped to establish a new circuit. With several other agents, two of them women, Odette sailed from Gibraltar at the end of October aboard a small Polish trading boat. She had already made three unsuccessful attempts to get to France. A week later, they landed on the Riviera in an unoccupied region of France. The following month, after American and British troops landed in French North Africa, the Germans were prompted to enter the unoccupied zone, at which point the Mediterranean coast took on new significance for the SOE.

Captain Peter Morland Churchill (code name "Raoul") was the commanding officer of the Marseilles-Cannes SOE circuit (code name "Spindle"), one of nearly 50 secret organizations run by British agents in occupied France. Peter Churchill persuaded the authorities in London that due to the new situation he would need a talented Frenchwoman to be his courier. Since Sansom (code name "Lise") spoke French, she could plan and execute the night parachute resupply drops and arrange for secret transportation of the agents. Rarely would an assignment be easily completed, nor did agents have the luxury of time. People would cross paths, sometimes in crucial ways, then slip away and never see one another again.

When German counter-intelligence became more of a threat, Churchill moved his circuit of saboteurs and information gatherers to Upper Savoy in February 1943. Odette accompanied him. While on a secret trip to England, he left her in charge. Sansom organized and brought about the largest resupply drops ever made to the Maquis who were hiding in the mountains above the Cote d'Azur in France. But German agents had begun to infiltrate "Spindle" by the time Churchill returned to Annecy on the night of April 14–15, 1943. After he landed by parachute in a remote mountainous area, Churchill and Sansom hid in an inn in St. Jorioz. It was there, the next night, that they were arrested by Italian troops and a German security agent.

En route to the Gestapo prison in Paris, they decided that Sansom would pretend to be Churchill's wife, in order to divert attention from his London mission and the sabotage they had orchestrated in France. The Germans wanted to know the true identity of Spindle's wireless operator, "Arnaud," as well as the whereabouts of a British officer, Captain Francis Cammaerts, who had landed in the plane which had taken Churchill to England. It was at Fresne Prison that they tortured Sansom.

Occasionally, during their imprisonment, Sansom and Churchill managed to meet and talk secretly before he was moved to Germany in February 1944. In June 1943, she was brought before an improvised military court and condemned to death as a British spy. When they told her she was to be executed, listing her many crimes against the Nazi Third Reich, she told them to take their pick of offenses, because they could only kill her once.

Returning to Fresne, Sansom expected to be shot. However, since she had claimed to be the wife of Peter Churchill, and the Germans were not sure of his relationship with Winston Churchill (there was none), they were reluctant to kill her. No underling in occupied Paris was prepared to order the execution of an agent who might, later in the war, be of considerable value to Berlin. Both Churchill and Sansom were therefore retained in Fresne and frequently interrogated for another eight months.

> *I* knew kindness as well as cruelty, understanding as well as brutality.
>
> —Odette Sansom

On May 12, 1944, 25 days before the Allies landed in Normandy, Sansom, along with six other women agents of the SOE, was taken in handcuffs by night train from Fresne to Karlsruhe Prison in Germany. Although they had all parachuted into France and been on similar missions, none of the agents had met. Knowing they were going to die gave them a sense of freedom, and they told each other their real names as well as their code names.

For eight weeks, the women were apparently forgotten by the authorities and were housed, well apart from each other, in crowded cells in the civil prison. Orders arrived from Berlin in July. Three of the women—**Andrée Borrel** ("Denise"), **Vera Leigh** ("Simone"), and **Diana Rowden** ("Juliette")—were taken to the Natzweiler concentration camp in Alsace and summarily executed. Odette's other companions remained at Karlsruhe until September when they were taken to Dachau concentration camp. **Yolande Beekman** ("Yvonne"), **Madeleine Damerment** ("Martine"), and **Eliane Plewman** ("Gaby"), along with *****Noor Inayat Khan**, were executed without trial in Dachau on September 13, 1944. Sansom was the only one officially condemned to die and, ironically, the only one to live.

Moved north, she was locked for nearly a week in a cage at police headquarters in Frankfurt. She was then transported to Halle, where she was again treated brutally. Finally, she was taken to Ravensbrück concentration camp for women. She arrived on July 18, 1944, two days before a now-famous failed plot by members of Hitler's inner circle to assassinate him.

At Ravensbrück, Sansom was put in solitary confinement underground, in an attempt to break her spirit. By October, when her health had just about failed, they moved her to a cell above ground. Roll call (*appel*) in the camps was held outdoors twice a day, no matter the weather—in summer at 5:30 AM, in winter at 4:30 AM. In their striped uniforms, with bristling hair on their shaved heads, Sansom and the other women had to stand at attention for two to six hours until the count was complete. This was hard enough for most prisoners and even worse for those suffering from diarrhea which was epidemic in the camps. Those who stumbled or fell were ordered to the Bunker, a maze of tiny, airless cells. There were beatings, tortures, mutilations and rapes. Women also died from malnourishment, overwork, exposure, lethal injections or obscene experimental surgery. In five years, over 100,000 women died. Though the camp was designed to contain a maximum of 6,000 prisoners, after 1943, there were never fewer than 12,000. Inmates drank ersatz coffee in the morning, watery soup for lunch, and ate bread for dinner while doing heavy labor. Those who managed to live for more than a few weeks or months on this diet had figured out a way to get extra food. They either had a skill the SS valued, a job where they could steal food, or a protector who looked after them.

At any time, there could be a surprise selection for the gas chamber. In desperation, some women would scrape soot with their nails from the prison walls to try to blacken the roots of their gray hair hoping to look younger and be spared death during selection. They would stand on their swollen feet as the Nazis came, smoking and chatting, handing out pink tickets for the crematorium. Prisoners, including three SOE agents, were shot outside Sansom's window, which faced the entrance of the crematorium. In December 1946, giving evidence at a war crimes trial in Hamburg, she would describe how she had seen women being driven screaming and struggling to the crematorium doors.

By the fall of 1944, news filtered back to prisoners that the war had turned against the Germans. As the Russians drew closer, the entire Nazi death operation went into reverse. The Germans began a massive campaign to hide the evidence of their crimes. They scraped out human fat 18 inches thick from crematoria chimneys. They killed anyone they feared might testify. They marched long columns of prisoners out of the camp, by the thousand, past the notorious sign *Arbeit macht frei* (Work makes one free). Some had only rags to cover their feet as they were forced onto the frozen mud. Anyone who fell behind was shot dead.

On April 28, 1945, on her 33rd birthday, Sansom was released from Ravensbrück weighing less than 90 pounds. Still thinking she was going to be executed, she was driven by the Nazi commandant of Ravensbrück, Fritz Sühren, in his Mercedes to the American line. Sühren was hoping to save himself from execution as a war criminal after Germany's defeat. He told the Americans, "This is Frau Churchill," believing that she was related to the prime minister of England. As Odette got out of the car, Sühren stood in the street with her. "And this is Fritz Sühren," she said, "commandant of Ravensbrück concentration camp. Please make him your prisoner." Then she demanded his revolver, put it into her bag, turned and walked into the nearby village. She would keep the pistol as a memento of the war.

Sühren, along with his top-ranking prison staff, was executed following the War Crimes Tribunal at Nuremberg. The officer responsible for Sansom's torture in Paris was also executed in July 1944, for ordering the shooting of British parachutists captured in uniform.

Sansom received the George Cross on November 19, 1946, from King George VI, the first woman to be awarded the United Kingdom's highest civilian award for "courage, endurance and self-sacrifice." Violette Szabo and Noor Inayat Khan were awarded the George Cross posthumously for their bravery. Szabo was shot at Ravensbrück; Khan was brutally interrogated and kept in chains before she was executed at Dachau. On December 16, 1946, Major Stephen Stewart called Odette Sansom as a witness for the prosecution at the War Crimes Court at Hamburg. She wore her FANY uniform and the blue ribbon and silver miniature of the George Cross.

At age 78, in October 1990, Sansom sat with a reporter for the *London Sunday Times*. The journalist summed up the experience:

> Everyone remembers that Odette had her toe-nails torn out by the Gestapo. Some mistakenly say finger-nails: but her torturers stopped short when they realised that even the grotesque pain of the toe-nails could not persuade her to speak (and having been ticked off firmly by Odette myself, for springing a photographer on her, I understand the Gestapo's reluctance to displease her further).

After the war, Odette's marriage to Roy Sansom was dissolved, and she married Peter Churchill. The marriage ended in divorce. Later, she married Geoffrey Hallowes. She lived quietly, carrying on an extensive correspondence. "People in trouble or despair seem to think I am someone of learning to turn to," she explained.

In all, 50 SOE women agents were landed in France during World War II. Fifteen of them were captured by the Nazis. Two of those escaped, and Sansom returned, the lone survivor. In commemoration of those women of the SOE who were executed by the Nazis, there is a plaque at St. Paul's Knightsbridge, dedicated on May 7, 1948. It reads:

> In love and homage to Mrs. Yolande E.M. Beekman, Croix de Guerre, Miss **Danielle Bloch**, Miss Andrée M. Borrel, Miss **Muriel Byck**, Miss Madeleine Damerment, Miss Noor Inayat Khan, Mrs. **Cecily M. Lefort**, Miss Vera E. Leigh, Mrs. Eliane S. Plewman, Croix de Guerre, Miss **Lilian V. Rolfe**, Miss Diana H. Rowden, Mrs. **Yvonne Rudellat**, Mrs. Violette R.E. Szabo, George Cross.

Each Remembrance Day, Sansom placed a cross of flowers there. "That is a permanent link I would not let go of," she said. Odette Sansom died in 1995.

SOURCES:

"British Heroine Honored, Aided French Resistance Despite Gestapo Tortures," in *The New York Times.* August 21, 1946.

Fraser, Antonia, ed. *Heroes and Heroines.* London: Weidenfeld & Nicolson, 1980.

Gleeson, James Joseph. *They Feared No Evil: The Women Agents of Britain's Secret Armies, 1939–45.* London: R. Hale, 1976.

Grove, Valerie. "Life wisdom learnt in the darkness of a torture cell; Odette Hallowes, GC.," in *London Sunday Times.* October 14, 1990.

"The Last Days of Auschwitz, 50 Years Later: Untold Stories From the Death Camp," in *Newsweek.* January 16, 1995, pp. 46–59.

Mahoney, M.H. *Women in Espionage.* Santa Barbara, CA: ABC-CLIO, 1993.

Perles, Alfred, ed. *Great True Spy Adventures.* London: Arco, 1957.

Tickell, Jerrard. *Odette: The Story of a British Agent.* London: Chapman & Hall, 1949.

Stafford, David. *Britain and European Resistance, 1940–45: A survey of the Special Operations Executive with Documents*, 1980.

"Tortured French Woman Decorated by George VI," in *The New York Times.* November 20, 1946.

RELATED MEDIA:

Odette (123 min.), produced in Britain by Lowpert-Dowling-UA, starring *Anna Neagle and Trevor Howard, 1951 (Sansom was technical advisor on the film).

Susan Slosberg, writer, New Rochelle, New York

Santha Rama Rau (b. 1923).

See Rama Rau, Santha.

Sant Jordi, Rosa de (b. 1910).

See Arquimbau, Rosa Maria.

Santolalla, Irene Silva de
(1902–1992)

Peruvian educator and first woman senator in Peru.
Born Irene Silva Linares on May 10, 1902, in Cajamarca, Peru; died on July 30, 1992, in Lima, Peru; daughter of Oscar Silva Burga and Susana Linares de Silva; attended Liceo del Carmen in Cajamarca, Peru; attended Colegio Sagrados Corazones in Lima, Peru; married Fausto Santolalla Bernal, on June 4, 1922; children: **Irene Santolalla Silva**; **Maria Teresa Santolalla Silva**; **Javier Santollalla Silva**; **Nelly Santolalla Silva**.

Founded and was first president of the Peruvian Committee for Collaboration with the United Nations (1949); led movement to enfranchise Peruvian women (1955); was the first woman elected to the Peruvian senate (1956); named "Woman of the Americas" by the Unión de Mujeres Americana (1956); awarded Peru's highest honor, the Order of the Sun (1982).

Irene Silva de Santolalla was born Irene Silva Linares in Cajamarca, Peru, in 1902. Her parents, Oscar Silva Burga and **Susana Linares de Silva**, were well-to-do and respected in the academic circles of northern Peru. Irene, the eldest of 13 siblings, grew to be industrious, energetic, and independent. She attended the Catholic school, Liceo del Carmen, in Cajamarca, and Colegio Sagrados Corazones (Sacred Heart College) in Lima, Peru.

On June 4, 1922, she married engineer Fausto Santolalla Bernal. Unlike many upper-class Peruvian mothers, Santolalla chose to care for her four children herself rather than leave them in the care of servants. She believed that mothers should involve themselves in every aspect of child-rearing in order to raise well-adjusted children, and did not embark on her teaching and writing career until her youngest child was old enough to attend school. At first, Santolalla wrote extensively about early child development and pre-school education. In 1940, she published *Por La Felicidad de Nuestros Hijos* (For Our Children's Happiness).

Although Peruvian women did not receive the right to vote until 1955, Santolalla advocated issues related to women and children in international political circles well before then. She was a regular attendee at major conferences, such as the Lima Congress for the Protection of Children (1943), the First International Congress for the Protection of Children in Rural Areas, held in Montevideo, Uruguay (1945), the first Feminine Spanish-American Congress, held in Madrid (1951), the International Study Congress, held in Oxford (1952), and the World Movement of Mothers, held in Bonn, Germany (1954). Santolalla's international perspective inspired her to organize the first non-governmental committee in the United Nations in 1949.

That same year, she taught family education as a professor at the Catholic University of Peru. In that capacity, she relied heavily on her own writings to develop a curriculum.

Santolalla opened her publicly licensed school, El Instituto de Orientación Matrimonial y Familiar (School of Preparation for Marital and Family Life), in Lima on June 2, 1952. She offered courses in child training, nutrition, interior decorating, and nursing. From an initial enrollment of 8 students, Santolalla's institute grew to 112 students plus a nursery school annex (El Jardín de la Infancia) by June 1955.

Three months later, the Peruvian legislature passed an equal-rights bill for women, after which Santolalla received an appointment from President Manual Odría to organize a women's contingency within the party El Partido Restaurador. She was subsequently elected the first woman senator in Peru, on June 17, 1956. In her six-year career as senator, she continued her crusade on behalf of women and children by authoring a law on family education in 1957. She also helped to found government teacher-training institutes in Peru.

Irene Silva de Santolalla was honored numerous times by a variety of organizations. In 1954, she received a medal from the Ford Foundation for her efforts in disseminating family education. She received the Woman of the Americas award from the Unión de Mujeres Americanas in 1956; in conjunction with that award, a "Day of the Woman of the Americas" was held in her honor on May 5, 1956, including a reception in New York with a salute from the Peruvian ambassador to the United States. She served as the president of Cruzada Pro-Educación de la Futura Madre Peruana and honorary president of the Peruvian National Association of Girl Scouts. In 1982, the Peruvian government honored her with its most prestigious award, the Order of the Sun. Santolalla died on July 30, 1992, in Lima, at age 90.

SOURCES:

Current Biography. NY: H.W. Wilson, 1956.
Current Biography. NY: H.W. Wilson, 1992.
The New York Times (obituary). August 4, 1992.

Gloria Cooksey,
freelance writer, Sacramento, California

Sanuti, Nicolosa (fl. 1453)

Bolognese writer. Flourished around 1453 in Bologna, Italy.

A Bolognese aristocrat, Nicolosa Sanuti was a learned writer who composed several treatises.

She is mostly remembered for an essay she published in response to sumptuary laws enacted in Bologna in 1453. Sanuti, like many wealthy noblewomen, disagreed strongly with male attempts to regulate the dress and jewelry women were allowed to wear. In particular, the Bolognese code specifically denied even aristocratic women the right to wear cloth of silver or gold, but allowed men to do so. The sumptuary code she opposed delineated a careful hierarchy of materials, styles, and colors women of each social class could adorn themselves with; the premise was that women were too concerned with material beauty, which was sinful since it both took women's minds from the spiritual world to come, and, like *Eve, tempted men as well.

Sanuti used her classical education to argue against this popular premise; she created a theory of fashion which spoke of broader issues of women's virtue and of the unfair treatment of women in the law. Her treatise proposed that fashionable clothing and fine jewelry must be considered a reward given to virtuous women, who were denied the financial and political rewards and offices given to virtuous men. Nicolosa felt that fine garments were the only status symbol women were allowed to have, and that if denied such garments, women would be stripped of the signs of their virtue; she supported her arguments with numerous examples from the ancient and contemporary worlds of noble and pious women. Lastly, Sanuti made the somewhat radical statement that women were humanity's only hope of surviving male destructiveness, for women's work and fertility rebuilt families and nations after men's warfare, and brought humanity to a higher moral level. She continued to write for some time, but no other treatise was as widely read as this well-articulated essay.

SOURCES:

Klapisch-Zuber, Christiane, ed. *A History of Women in the West: Silences of the Middle Ages.* Vol. II. Cambridge, MA: Belknap-Harvard, 1992.

Laura York,
Riverside, California

Sapphira (fl. 1st c.)

Woman of the Bible. Flourished in the 1st century CE; *married Ananias.*

According to Luke in the Acts of the Apostles, it was customary for the wealthy in the newly inaugurated Christian movement to liquidate their assets and to cede all of the money thereby raised to the apostles for the upkeep of the whole Christian community. Sapphira and her husband Ananias apparently sold a property in or near Jerusalem to do just this, but instead of turning over all of the profits from the sale, they surrendered only a portion of the total. When the apostle Peter confronted Ananias about his deceit and berated him for attempting to cheat God, it is attested that Ananias dropped dead at his feet. About three hours later, Sapphira (in on the fraud but ignorant of Ananias' fate) also met with Peter who asked her how much money she and her husband had received for their property. After Sapphira maintained the lie, Peter rebuked her, pointed out the men who had just finished burying her husband, and predicted that they would do the same for her. Immediately after Peter uttered his prophecy, Sapphira too dropped dead. She was buried with her husband, with Luke noting the awe inspired within the Christian community by God's power and vengeance.

William Greenwalt,
Associate Professor of Classical History,
Santa Clara University, Santa Clara, California

Sappho (c. 612–c. 557 BCE)

*One of the greatest poets of Lyric Age Greece, who revolutionized Greek literature by writing about her personal thoughts and feelings and by describing her physical surroundings. Name variations: Sapho; Psappho; Psappha. Born around 612 BCE in Eresos, on the island of Lesbos, Greece; died under unknown circumstances around 557 BCE; daughter of Scamandronymus or Scamandrus (probably a noble wine merchant) and Cleïs (probably a noblewoman of Lesbos); had three brothers, Charaxus, Larichus, and Eurygyius; possibly married Cercylas from Andros; children: one daughter, **Cleïs**.*

Moved at approximately six years of age from Eresos to Mytilene, the largest city on Lesbos (c. 606 BCE); founded a school or sorority for young women for the study of music and poetry; banished from Lesbos, possibly for political reasons (c. 598–c. 581 BCE); famous in her own day, honored in busts, statues and coins, and painted on Greek vases with quotes from her verses; after her death, became extremely popular among the Athenians of the 5th century BCE.

Publications: Nine volumes of her poetry were said to have been published during her lifetime or shortly afterward, none of which now exist. Her work is known to modern scholars only in fragments.

To modern scholars, Sappho is a particularly fascinating yet elusive character. She is known to us only through the few fragments of her poetry which have survived the ravages of time and the condemnation of the Medieval Church. Using the pieces of work which have been attributed to her, the sketchy knowledge we have of Greece during the Lyric Age, and the often wildly exaggerated caricatures of Sappho which were written in the later Greek era and during the Roman Empire, scholars have pieced together a shadowy and frustratingly dim approximation of the poet. Over the course of the last 2,000 years, controversy has raged over Sappho's reputed sexual orientation and activities, and that controversy burned ever hotter in the late 20th century in the context of the burgeoning field of gay and lesbian studies. Although we will probably never be able to determine with any accuracy the most intimate details of Sappho's private life, scholars know enough about her to agree that she was one of the world's greatest poetic geniuses.

Sappho was born around 612 BCE in the city of Eresos, on Lesbos, one of the Greek islands in the Aegean Sea. During the Lyric Age of Greece, Lesbos was known for its beautiful women and its sweet wine. Social customs on Lesbos permitted women much more freedom than was allowed in other parts of the known world. Women (at least those who came from the aristocratic class) mixed freely with men in public, were well educated, and often formed literary clubs to cultivate poetry and music. At the time of Sappho's birth, Lesbos was a particularly wealthy island whose citizens had a reputation for luxury. Sappho was born into the aristocracy of that island, and this advantage allowed her to pursue a life of leisure and high culture otherwise uncommon for that day. Historical sources disagree on the name of her father, but the most accurate ones available identify him as Scamandronymus, a noble wine merchant of Eresos. Sappho's mother **Cleïs** was also a member of the aristocratic class. After Sappho's birth, Cleïs would give birth to three sons: Charaxus, Larichus, and Eurygyius.

Sappho was very young when her father died; in one of her poems, she mentions mourning a parent at the untimely age of six. Scamandronymus was possibly a casualty of a ten-year war which broke out in 606 BCE between the cities of Lesbos and Athens over a trading base named Sigeum which had been founded by the Lesbians on the Hellespont. For whatever reason, early in Sappho's life she and her family moved from Eresos to the city of Mytilene, which was the largest on the island. It is possible that Cleïs fled there to live under the protection of members of her extended family; even after the death of Scamandronymus, Cleïs maintained wealth and position in her society which she was able to pass on to her children. In Mytilene, Sappho was well educated. Her poems show that she was very familiar with the works of Homer and Hesiod, and with Greek myths and legends.

No contemporary descriptions of Sappho exist, and later descriptions vary widely. In some, she is depicted as small in stature, with violet-black hair and dark skin. Representations of her on vases and in statuary, however, show her as being of average height and slender form, with the highly stylized facial features which reflect the Greek personifications of female beauty. Some of her ancient detractors referred to her as "ugly," while many of her greatest admirers waxed eloquent upon her beauty. Whether or not she was physically beautiful, it is doubtless that she possessed an irresistible charisma, as witnessed by her great popularity even in her own lifetime.

Sappho began composing poetry perhaps while still in her teens, and she quickly began to attract the admiration of her contemporaries. By the time she was in her 20s, her writings were being circulated, not only on Lesbos, but in other parts of the Greek world and beyond. Her work was revolutionary in several ways. She was one of the first Lyric poets to write from the perspective of individual subjectivity, and thus her work was dramatically different from the heroic epics of Hesiod and Homer. Hesiod had referred to himself as a "conduit of divine inspiration," and had given little information about his personal reaction to the stories which he put into writing. Sappho's work, in contrast to the epics which glorified battles and other public deeds, concentrated upon revealing her private, interior life, her personal reactions to the world around her and to the people she knew. Her poetry is written in a decidedly female voice, another departure from past Greek tradition. For example, her depiction of the legendary Helen differed from Homer's: in Homer's epic, Helen is dragged off to Troy against her will; in Sappho's poem, Helen journeys to Troy "resisting not," leaving behind her noble husband "all for love." In creating her richly imaginative work, Sappho seemed to be conscious that she was opening the door that led to a new means of expression; in several surviving fragments, she expresses confidence that her work will some day bring her immortality.

While still a young woman, Sappho founded a school or sorority for women who were interested in the study of music and poetry. As an aristocratic woman of means, she was able to provide her charges with sumptuous surroundings, good food, and personal slaves to care for their every physical need. Her reputation as a writer brought young women from far-away cities and from the most august of families, pre-sumably to be educated and prepared for their transition into the adult world and marriage.

But Lesbos had been thrown into political upheaval with the ouster of the Penthilidai family, who claimed lineage from Homer's King Agamemnon. In the ensuing struggle for political dominance, a succession of autocrats from the aristocratic families of Lesbos came to power, some of whom allied themselves with the lower classes by promising reforms which would reduce the power of the aristocracy. This upheaval brought about new democratic impulses which prompted frequent rebellions. Possibly within the context of one of these rebellions, a group of young aristocrats, including Sappho, was banished sometime around 598 BCE. She left Lesbos and settled for a time on the island of Sicily, where she continued to write poetry and became something of a celebrity. According to legend, during her sojourn there she married, possibly to a wealthy merchant named Cercylas, and gave birth to a daughter, whom she named Cleïs, after her mother. If indeed Sappho were married, she seems to have been widowed at an early age. There is no mention of her having a husband when she reappeared in her native land sometime around 581 BCE.

Upon her return, Sappho seems to have continued to take young women into her home. As depicted in the remnants of her poetry, she appears to have developed a strong romantic, if not sexual, relationship with some of these women. Many of her poems describe a distant, unattainable object of desire, usually a woman. In the only definitively complete poem of Sappho's which has survived, she prays for help to Aphrodite, the goddess of love:

Richly-throned immortal Aphrodite, daughter of Zeus, weaver of wiles, I pray to you: break not my spirit, Lady, with heartache or anguish;

But hither come, if ever in the past you heard my cry from afar, and marked it, and came, leaving your father's house,

Your golden chariot yoked: sparrows beautiful and swift conveyed you, with rapid wings aflutter, above the dark earth from heaven through the mid-air;

And soon they were come, and you, Fortunate, with a smile on your immortal face, asked what ails me now, and why I am calling now,

And what in my heart's madness I most desire to have: Whom now must I persuade to join your friendship's ranks? Who wrongs you, Sappho?

For if she flees, she shall soon pursue; and if she receives not gifts, yet shall she give; and if she loves not, she shall soon love even against her will.

Sappho

Come to me now also, and deliver me from cruel
anxieties; fulfil all that my heart desires to fulfil, and be yourself my comrade-in-arms.

In other poems, Sappho seems to mourn the loss
of one of her students who was particularly
beloved:

Honestly I wish I were dead. Weeping she left me
With many tears, and said 'Oh what unhappiness
is ours; Sappho, I now, against my will I leave
you.'
And this answer I made to her: 'Go, and fare
well, and remember me; you know how we
cared for you.

If not, yet I would remind you . . . of our past
 happiness.
Many wreaths of violets and roses and . . . you
 put around you at my side,
And many woven garlands, fashioned of flowers,
 . . . round your soft neck,
And . . . with perfume of flowers, fit for a queen,
 you anointed . . .
And on soft beds . . . you would satisfy your
 longing.'

While it is impossible to determine from the content of the poetry alone whether or not Sappho's relationships with these women were sexual, she was living during a time when lines between heterosexual and homosexual love were not so clearly drawn as they are now. While descriptions of sexual relationships between women during this period are rare, descriptions of sexual relationships between young Greek men and boys are quite common. Sappho's work differs from homoerotic writings by men. Many of the poems describing male homosexual (as well as heterosexual) love tend to focus on the idea of conquest of the love object. Sappho's descriptions of romance, however, are exclusively focused on romantic intimacy and sharing between equals.

Sappho's descriptions of romantic longing are deeply personal and lushly descriptive, but her descriptions of nature and her physical surroundings portray the same seductiveness. In another example, she described the night sky: "Oh, evening star, you bring all that the blithe dawn has scattered wide; you bring the sheep; you bring the goats; you bring home the child to its mother." Another favorite of hers was gold, which she described as "a child of Zeus; no moth nor worm devours it; and it overcomes the strongest of mortal hearts." Sappho was especially fond of describing the birds and flowers which could be found in such profusion on Lesbos. She enthusiastically depicts for us "the yearning-voiced messenger of spring, the nightingale," and "the wild-hyacinth which on the mountain-side the shepherd treads underfoot, yet it still blooms purple on the ground." She also writes of her own beloved daughter:

I have a maid, a bonny maid,
As dainty as the golden flowers,
My darling Cleïs. Were I paid
All Lydia, and the lovely bowers
Of Cyprus, 'twould not buy my maid.

Due to her respected position in the Mytilene community, Sappho was given numerous commissions to write hymns for religious festivals. She often referred to herself as the servant of Aphrodite, but in one fragment she describes her frustration at trying to compose a hymn to Adonis while her mind is distracted by desire:

"Be still, my heart!—for me you cannot throw out in rapid hymn-spurting inspiration an Adonis-song which in beauty of style shall please the goddesses; for dishonoring Desire and heart-conquering Aphrodite made you speechless, and brain destroying Peitho from her flagon of gold has poured her sweet nectar upon your wits."

Sappho also wrote a large number of wedding songs. Traditional Greek wedding ceremonies typically lasted several days, with ritual presentation of the couple to each side of the family, music and feasting. In these works, Sappho clearly pays homage to Hera, the goddess of marriage. Many of these are lighthearted teases and optimistic good wishes composed for a choir of maids to sing to the couple on their wedding night. In one example, she writes: "And we maidens spend all the night at this door, singing of the love between you, richly blessed bridegroom, and your bride of the violet-scented breast. And when the dawn is come and you arise and depart, may the great god Hermes direct your feet whither you shall find no more ill-luck than we tonight shall find sleep."

We know that Sappho lived at least well into middle age, for in a few of her fragments she makes reference to her encroaching age: "Ah girls, that I may escape wrinkles!" she writes, and admits in another poem in which she seems to be turning down an offer of marriage that she had no wish to marry a second time since she is past the age of childbearing and cannot bear to live with a younger man: "If my breasts were still capable of giving suck, and my womb were able to bear children, then to another marriage-bed not with trembling feet would I come, but now on my skin age is already causing innumerable lines to go about, and Love hastens not to fly to me with his gift of pain." She advises her suitor: "but if you love me, choose a more youthful companion for your bed, for I cannot endure to be married to a young man. I am too old."

About the death of Sappho nothing is known for certain. An old myth alleged that she threw herself off a cliff after being rejected by a young fisherman named Phaon. Modern scholars have disputed that myth, however, as a later fabrication by Athenian playwrights. After she died, it is believed, her body was cremated, and she was given a hero's burial on Lesbos. At the time, she was considered one of the preeminent poets in all of Greece. Solon, the esteemed leader of Athens, was said to have requested on his deathbed that he be taught Sappho's latest song. Her poetry was copied not only in Greece, but in Egypt (where some of the most important fragments have been discovered), and later in Rome. Nine volumes of her poetry were said to have been collected during her lifetime.

Greek and Roman scholars ranked Sappho's works among the greatest ever created. The Romans were said to have compiled two editions of her poetry, one arranged by subject and the other arranged by meter. She was credited with creating the Mixolydian mode in music, which Plutarch claimed could arouse the passions more than any other. Plato referred to her as the "tenth muse," and Plutarch asserted that her work was "mixed with fire." Aristotle quoted her verses in his *Rhetoric*. Comedians of the Greek Classical Period referred to her work extensively and composed many parodies of her life. Later Greek and Roman poets often adapted, or even copied outright, Sappho's works. Her style was imitated by the Roman poet Horace in his odes.

After the fall of the Roman Empire, Sappho's writings were read and preserved by Byzantine scholars, but they quickly fell out of favor in Western Europe. Medieval clerics perceived her as a dangerous harlot and on several occasions ordered her books to be burned. None of her works survived through the Middle Ages in Europe. The few lines that now exist have been dug out of the sands of Egypt, or, in some cases, were found only as a snippet of a sentence or phrase preserved inside a Greek textbook to illustrate a particular grammatical construction.

When Sappho's works were revived during the Renaissance, many scholars tended to portray her as a woman of bad character, and that legacy has haunted the historical figure of Sappho from that time up to the present. It was only with the arrival of the Romance Movement in the 19th century that efforts were made to rehabilitate her as the great hero of Romanticism. Much of that "rehabilitation" involved explaining away the more seductive and obviously erotic nature of her works by divorcing them from the physical realm. Only in the 20th century have scholars begun to consider what precious little is left of her works at face value. During the last few decades, Sappho has become a hero to feminists and to gay and lesbian scholars. All attempts to reconstruct the poet's sexual life, however, have foundered in the face of the lack of historical evidence.

One factor that has remained constant through the ages is her great popularity. Sappho's writings have been admired in literary circles of every age. Many modern groups, from the strait-laced Victorians to 20th-century feminist scholars, have tried to "own" her, and her biography has often been written to suit a particular agenda. Her poetry is personal, and therefore immediately accessible. She presents a much clearer and more intimate portrait of the ancient Greeks than we can see through any other remnant that remains of that civilization. The passion and feeling exhibited by her work transcend mere sexual expression, and by focusing on the senses, opens our minds to a new appreciation of the world around us.

Sappho's legacy lies in ruined fragments, but as David Robinson noted, "In them we recognize the creator's genius as clearly as in a fragmentary torso of Phidias we see the sculptor's art in every chiselled line." Her works are once again hailed as one of the greatest contributions of Greek culture, and they provide a refreshing alternative to the dominant vision of the ancient world as a logical, masculine, unemotional culture. In Sappho's work we catch a fleeting glimpse of a feminine, emotional and personal world peopled with human beings who, like us, struggle to understand life's beauty, anxiety, excitement and uncertainty.

SOURCES:

Dubois, Page. *Sappho is Burning*. Chicago, IL: University of Chicago Press, 1995.

Elytis, Odysseus. "Preface to Sappho," in *World Literature Today*. Vol. 65, no. 1, 1991, pp. 59–61.

Foley, Helene P. *Reflections on Women in Antiquity*. NY: Gorden and Breach, 1981.

Jenkyns, Richard. *Three Classical Poets: Sappho, Catullus, and Juvenal*. Cambridge, MA: Harvard University Press, 1982.

Lardinois, André. "Lesbian Sappho and Sappho of Lesbos," in Bremmer, Jan, ed. *From Sappho to De Sade: Moments in the History of Sexuality*. London: Routledge, 1989.

Page, Denys. *Sappho and Alcaeus: An Introduction to the Study of Ancient Lesbian Poetry*. Oxford: Clarendon Press, 1955.

Robinson, David M. *Sappho and Her Influence*. NY: Cooper Square, 1963.

Weigall, Arthur. *Sappho of Lesbos: Her Life and Time*. NY: Frederick A. Stokes, 1932.

Kimberly Estep Spangler,
Assistant Professor of History, Chair,
Division of Religion and Humanities,
Friends University, Wichita, Kansas

Sappho of Brabant (1493/94–1575).

See Bijns, Anna.

Sara.

Variant of Sarah.

Sarabhai, Anusyabehn (1885–1972)

Indian labor organizer who founded assorted craft unions that ultimately united into the Textile Labour

Association. Born in 1885; died in 1972; attended London School of Economics.

Anusyabehn Sarabhai was born in Ahmedabad, India, in 1885. Although her family was wealthy, she was orphaned at ten years of age. Two years later, she surrendered unwillingly to an arranged marriage, which she later had annulled. Sarabhai traveled to England in 1911, where she attended the London School of Economics. There she was exposed to the teachings of the Fabian Society, which advocated a slow and non-revolutionary transition to socialism.

When Sarabhai returned to her homeland, she became involved in charitable and philanthropic works. In 1914, she undertook the education of the children of these mill workers, and in 1917 she organized workers into a cohesive group that ultimately called for a labor strike; it was the first labor strike in the history of India. Sarabhai was a colleague of Mohandas Gandhi and supported him in 1918 in his Ahmedabad strike. By 1920, she was instrumental in establishing the Textile Labour Association, a conglomeration of separate unions that she had organized earlier in her career. Throughout her lifetime, Sarabhai assisted with supervision, negotiations, and dispute resolution for the laborers among whom she worked. She died in 1972.

Gloria Cooksey,
freelance writer, Sacramento, California

Saracens, queen of the.

See Mavia (c. 350–c. 430).

Saragossa, Maid of (1786–1857).

See Agostina.

Sarah (fl. 3rd, 2nd, or 1st c. BCE)

Biblical matriarch. Name variations: Sara ("princess"); was originally named Sarai ("mockery"). Flourished in the 3rd, 2nd, or 1st century BCE; married Abram later known as Abraham or Abrahim ("father of a multitude," although his original name appears to have been Abram, "exalted father"); children: Isaac (who married Rebekah).

Sarah's dates cannot be secured, since the historical era of Abraham cannot be established with any certainty. Indeed, suggestions range widely, from the 3rd to the 1st millennium BCE. Originally, Sarah was named Sarai ("mockery"), while Abraham was known as Abram. In the Biblical narrative, Abram and Sarai were man and wife before they began their migration across the Fer-

tile Crescent from the land of Ur, on the Euphrates River, to the Promised Land of Canaan, accompanied by Abram's father Terah and Abram's nephew, Lot. Terah died at Harran, leaving Abram (then 75 years old according to the Bible, making Sarai 65 at the time) to lead the Hebrews on their subsequent journey. Upon coming to Canaan and passing through Shechem, the Lord is said to have given all observable land to Abram and his descendants. However, a famine soon drove the nomadic tribes to Egypt.

Before entering that rich land Abram, knowing that the pharaoh would find Sarai irresistibly beautiful (if somewhat old by modern standards) and fearing his own murder if it became known that she was his wife, convinced Sarai to pretend that she was his sister. Thus fooled into thinking that Sarai was available, the pharaoh is said to have taken her into his harem, in return honoring Sarai's "brother" with gifts of many animals, slaves and precious metals. The Lord, displeased by the pharaoh's appropriation of the woman otherwise assigned, struck his house with plague. When the pharaoh learned that Sarai was Abram's wife, not his sister, he berated Abram for the deception and expelled the Hebrews from Egypt, albeit with all of the gifts he had previously offered.

The historicity of this episode is called into question by the appearance (somewhat later in Genesis) of an alternative version of the story. In this tale, Abram settled in the Negeb between Kadesh and Shur when Abimelech, the king of Gerar, sent for Sarai. In this version Sarai played Abram's half-sister (being of different mothers), and was released only after Abimelech received a dream from the Lord promising death if the king did not return Sarai to Abram at once. Again, Abram and Sarai are said to have been expelled from the vicinity, but not before receiving significant gifts.

Whatever truth may lie in these accounts, upon the Hebrews' return to Canaan the followers of Abram and Lot are said to have split: the former settling near Hebron and the latter in Sodom, in the Jordan River valley. Soon thereafter, it is recorded that Abram saved Lot (who had been captured by enemies of Sodom), whereupon the Lord reiterated his gift of Canaan to Abram and his descendants. These promises were beginning to wear thin with Abram and Sarai, for she had yet to bear her husband any children. Ten years out of Egypt and fearing her own barrenness, Sarai sought legitimate children through an established custom whereby she gave one of her slaves to Abram for child-bearing with the understanding that if the slave gave birth, Sarai would become the acknowledged mother of the child. The slave chosen for this duty was ❧➤ **Hagar**, of Egyptian origin. Abram lay with Hagar and impregnated her—to the joy of Sarai—that is, until Hagar came to make fun of Sarai for her inability to conceive. Put out by Hagar's insolence, Sarai approached Abram for support, but Abram threw the problem back to his wife. As a result and with Abram's tentative support, Sarai began to abuse Hagar, who fled. Thus stood affairs until the Lord intervened, inducing Hagar to return to her service with the promise that her child would be fruitful and produce for her countless descendants. Back with Abram and Sarai (now 86 and 76 respectively), Hagar gave birth to Ishmael, who became (for the time being) Abram's heir.

Thirteen years later, the Lord is said to have appeared again before Abram to renew their covenant with additional promises that his descendants would be numerous, and with additional demands, including the first mention of circumcision. It was at this time that Abram was renamed Abraham and Sarai, Sarah. More to the point for the future, the Lord specifically promised that Sarah would bear a son. At this, the newly renamed Abraham laughed, for he believed that Sarah was well beyond the age of child-bearing. Somewhat later, when Sarah also learned of the Lord's promise, she too laughed, although she is said to have denied doing so when admonished by the Lord. Despite the skepticism of Abraham and Sarah, the Lord brought forth the long-anticipated child, for when Abraham was 100 and Sarah was 90, Isaac ("he laughed") was born. Thus, Abraham had two sons with different mothers, the older with a slave and the younger with his legitimate wife. Nevertheless, this did not long present a problem for precedence, for after Ishmael once ridiculed his younger half-sibling, Sarah approached Abraham and demanded that both Hagar and Ishmael be sent away. Although Abraham initially balked at the prospect, the Lord induced him to act as Sarah demanded, and the pair was driven off, albeit under the Lord's protection.

Thus finally Sarah came to have what she had longed for, a son through whom she could help found a nation. Living to a ripe old age (127, according to scripture), Sarah predeceased Abraham, who purchased the cave/tomb of Machpelah near Hebron (although an alternative tradition places the site near Shechem) from a Hittite named Ephron as her final resting place. There Sarah was eventually joined by Abraham,

❧➤ **Hagar** (fl. 3rd, 2nd, or 1st c. BCE)

Egyptian slave and Biblical woman. Flourished in the 3rd, 2nd, or 1st century BCE; born in Egypt; children: (with Abraham also known as Abrahim) Ishmael.

As related in Genesis, Hagar was the Egyptian slave of *Sarah, who was married to Abraham. Unable to have children, Sarah gave Hagar to her husband, in accordance with accepted custom, so that his line might continue. Upon becoming pregnant, Hagar mocked Sarah for her barrenness. Furious, Sarah took her revenge by treating Hagar so poorly that the pregnant woman ran away. She was stopped by an angel of the Lord, who told her to go back to Sarah. The angel also announced that she would give birth to a son and name him Ishmael, and that through Ishmael her descendants would be "too numerous to be counted." Hagar returned to Sarah and Abraham, and in due course her son Ishmael was born. According to the Bible, the angel's prophecy about her descendants was proved true, for through her son she became the ancestress of all Arabs.

Isaac, *Rebekah, Jacob, and ❧➤ **Leah**—all major figures of early Hebraic history.

William S. Greenwalt,
Associate Professor of Classical History,
Santa Clara University

➤❧
Leah. See joint entry under Rachel and Leah.

Sarah of Görlitz (fl. 1388)

Jewish townswoman of Görlitz. Flourished around 1388 in Görlitz, Germany.

Sarah was a Jewish resident of Görlitz, a medium-sized German town with a fairly large Jewish population. In medieval times, Jews suffered under a variety of discriminatory laws and regulations, many of which were designed to minimize their ability to compete with Christians in business. Under these circumstances, urban Jewish communities could not expect much in the way of social services from the town governments, but had to rely on each other.

Sarah of Görlitz was one such woman who made an important contribution to her community. The only mention of her life is found in town records of 1388, when she, obviously already a wealthy woman, inherited a house from another Jew. Sarah used her money to convert the house into a school for Jewish children (who could not attend Christian schools). She believed in the value of educating both girls and boys, and did her community an important service by her generosity. The school remained in operation for many years.

SOURCES:

Uitz, Erika. *The Legend of Good Women: The Liberation of Women in Medieval Cities.* Wakefield, RI: Moyer Bell, 1988.

Laura York,
Riverside, California

Sarah of St. Gilles (fl. 1326)

Jewish physician of France. Flourished in 1326 in Marseilles; married Abraham, a physician.

Sarah of St. Gilles was a Jewish doctor of Marseilles. Unlike so many medieval women doctors, Sarah seems to have avoided trouble with the local authorities, even though she had a substantial practice and was widely respected for her healing abilities. The records of Marseilles show that in 1326 Sarah was licensed to take on apprentices and that she chose to instruct women in the healing arts. This fact reveals the personal wealth she had amassed, since all apprentices had to be fed, clothed, and housed for up to a year or more at the doctor's expense; in return, Sarah received all the money they earned during their tutelage.

SOURCES:

LaBarge, Margaret. *A Small Sound of the Trumpet: Women in Medieval Life.* Boston, MA: Beacon Press, 1986.

Laura York,
Riverside, California

Sarai (fl. 3rd, 2nd, or 1st c. BCE).

See Sarah.

Sardinia, queen of.

See Henrietta Anne for sidebar on Anne-Marie d'Bourbon-Orleans (1669–1728).

See Marie Clotilde (1759–1802).

See Maria Teresa of Austria (1773–1832).

See Maria Theresa of Tuscany (1801–1855).

See Marie Adelaide of Austria (1822–1855).

Sarfatti, Margherita (1880–1961)

Italian art critic, author, poet, and journalist who helped found the Italian art movement Novecento (Twentieth Century), and for almost two decades was Benito Mussolini's lover and influential adviser. Name variations: Margherita Sarfatti-Grassini; (pseudonyms) Cidie and El Sereno. Pronunciation: Sar-FAHT-tee. Born Margherita Grassini on April 8, 1880, in Venice, Italy; died on October 30, 1961, at her country home near Lake Como; daughter of Amedeo Grassini (a businessman, lawyer, and heir to a large fortune) and Emma (Levi) Grassini; educated at home by her mother and her Swiss governess; at 14, began to be tutored for a number of years by three of the most distinguished and cultured scholars and lecturers in Venice; married Roberto Sarfatti, on May 29, 1898; children: Roberto (1900–1918); Amedeo (b. June 24, 1902); Fiammetta (b. January 1909).

At 15, became a socialist (1895); after her marriage (1898), moved to Milan (1902); began writing for a number of feminist and socialist journals (1901); became art critic for the socialist newspaper Avanti! *(1909); began an intermittent love affair with Mussolini (early 1913); left Socialist Party (October 1915); became cultural editor of Mussolini's newspaper,* The People of Italy *(December 1918), and managing editor of* Hierarchy: A Political Review, *co-founded with Mussolini (January 1922); was instrumental in founding the Novecento (Twentieth Century) art movement (autumn 1922); wrote the first biography of Mussolini, published in English (1925), then in Italian and titled* Dux *(1926); converted to Catholicism (1928); wrote articles for Hearst Press under Mussolini's name (April 1930–1934); toured Brazil and Argentina with Twentieth Century art exhibit (December 1930); ended love affair with Mussolini (late 1931); left positions at* The People of Italy *and* Hierarchy *(1932); made triumphant tour of U.S., culminating with a visit to the White House and the Roosevelts (March–June 1934); fled Italy (November 1938); sailed to Montevideo, Uruguay (October 1939); lived in Montevideo and Buenos Aires (1939–47); returned to Italy (March 1947).*

Selected publications (all in Italian unless otherwise indicated): The Feminist Militia in France *(1915);* The Burning Torch *(1919);* The Living and the Dead *(1919);* Tunisiaca *(Things Tunisian, 1923);* Achille Funi *(1925);* The Life of Benito Mussolini *(in English, 1925, in Italian, titled* Dux, *June 1926);* Il palazzone *(The Large Country House, 1929);* The History of Modern Painting *(1930);* Daniele Ranzoni *(1935);* America: The Search for Happiness *(1937);* Giacomo Girolamo Casanova de Seingalt *(in Spanish, 1943);* Giorgione the Mysterious Painter *(in Spanish, 1944);* Titian or Faith in Life *(in Spanish, 1944);* Mussolini as I Knew Him *(in Spanish, 1945);* Casanova versus Don Giovanni *(1950);* Water Under the Bridge *(1955);* Undervalued Love *(1958).*

Although most famous as the biographer and lover of Benito Mussolini, dictator of Italy from 1922 to 1943, Margherita Sarfatti deserves to be remembered in her own right as one of the most influential Italian art critics and connoisseurs of the 20th century. She was a major figure in Italian cultural life for almost 50 years, and wrote two

800

dozen books and thousands of newspaper articles, mostly on the subject of art. One of Italy's first women art critics, she played a key role in founding the post-World War I Twentieth Century art movement, which proved very influential during the 1920s. In part because of her relationship with Mussolini and in part because of her exceptional intelligence and learning, she became a virtual dictator of the arts during the '20s. Some dubbed her the "uncrowned queen of Italy."

She was born Margherita Grassini on April 8, 1880, in a 15th-century palace located in the Old Jewish Ghetto section of Venice. Her rich and cultured parents were devout Orthodox Jews, but they decided to give her a secular education. Though she never had any formal instruction, she received an exceptional schooling in history, art, and literature from her tutors. Her studies instilled in her an abiding belief in the crucial function that art plays, both in providing moral guidance for society and in demonstrating, to a greater degree than military conquests and political power, the greatness of a country.

When she was 15, a middle-aged professor fell in love with her while she was vacationing. She did not return his love, but she did succumb to his ideas, and converted to socialism. She herself soon fell in love with a brilliant Venetian lawyer, Cesare Sarfatti. Although he was 14 years her senior, she succeeded in convincing him to join the Socialist Party. Her father and mother opposed a marriage, but once Margherita had turned 18 and could no longer be legally prevented from marrying, they decided to accept the inevitable. Two sons, Cesare and Amedeo, and a daughter, **Fiammetta Sarfatti**, were born during the next 11 years.

The Sarfattis' move in October 1902 from beautiful and romantic Venice to modern Milan, the most progressive city in Italy, marked a new period in their lives. Sarfatti became more involved than ever in the political and cultural developments of the time. She joined the group of feminists and Socialists who met at the apartment of the famous ***Anna Kuliscioff**, who along with her husband, the Socialist leader Filippo Turati, helped edit one of the leading Socialist journals. Since Sarfatti had always believed that women were the complete equals of men and should enjoy greater freedom, she became active in feminist journalism and politics. In 1912, she worked closely with Kuliscioff in the founding and publication of *The Defense of Women Workers*, a journal which espoused the cause of Socialist feminism. She also campaigned for sex education in the schools, legalization of divorce, and for a law to make fathers responsible for their illegitimate children.

In 1909, Sarfatti became art critic for the official Socialist Party newspaper *Avanti!* (Forward!). In her articles, she championed such schools of modern art as Post-Impressionism, the Viennese Secession, and Italian Futurism. She believed in bringing art to the masses, but rejected the idea of a social-realist art. As she was making her influence felt in newspaper and journal articles, she also founded an important salon which attracted many artists and writers. Her wealth, discriminating intelligence, and social connections enabled her to build up an important art collection for herself and to influence others in the collection of art.

In 1912, probably during a gathering at Kuliscioff's, Sarfatti met Benito Mussolini, the wild man of the Italian Socialist Party. In many ways, they were social and cultural opposites; Mussolini was the crude son of a small-town blacksmith and Margherita the polished daughter of a wealthy businessman. Nonetheless, Sarfatti and Mussolini immediately became attracted to each other. She was captivated by his energy, his violently aggressive personality, and his reckless bravado; he found fascinating her self-assurance, sophistication, and beauty. Sarfatti's full-figured, blonde looks were precisely the type that Mussolini found irresistible. Unlike many of her feminist or socialist friends, she did not affect a deliberately "unfeminine" or drab proletarian style of dress. Sarfatti loved stylish clothes, expensive perfumes, and fine jewelry, and all this Mussolini found appealing. A close friendship developed and then, in early 1913, they began a love affair. But the relationship was rocky and Mussolini continued to see many other women, including ***Rachele Guidi** who had had daughter ***Edda** (**Ciano**) with him in 1910 and married him around 1916. What kept Sarfatti and Mussolini together was as much their common political and publishing interests as physical attraction. In the autumn of 1913, Sarfatti became one of Mussolini's chief collaborators in producing a new journal, *Utopia: A Biweekly Review of Italian Revolutionary Socialism*. At the same time, Sarfatti worked actively to promote her husband's political career, and in November 1913 he won a seat in Parliament.

World War I transformed both Italy and Sarfatti's relationship with Mussolini. When the rest of Europe went to war in August 1914, Italy remained neutral, and neutrality also became the official policy of the Italian Socialist Party. Mussolini, editor of *Avanti!*, soon became uneasy with this passive approach and in October 1914 broke ranks to denounce German aggression and advocate support for the French, the Belgians, and those Italians still under the domination of Austria Hungary. This led to Mussolini's expulsion from the Socialist Party. Sarfatti and her husband supported Mussolini but hesitated to break openly with the Socialists. In January 1915, she traveled to France to see the war for herself. Her visits to wounded and mutilated soldiers in the hospitals made a deep impression on her. Over the spring and summer of 1915, she wrote an account of her trip to France, *The Female Militia in France*, which described how the women of France were heroically working to save their country from German barbarism. By the fall of 1915, Sarfatti had left the Socialist Party.

> *W*hen I first met her she was the uncrowned queen of Italy. Now she is the crowned pauper of the exiles.
>
> —*Alma Mahler

Swept up in the nationalist fervor, Margherita's young son Roberto joined the army in 1917, but died a few months later, in January 1918, leading *Arditi*, assault troops, against the Austrians. He was barely 17 years old. Roberto's death devastated the Sarfatti family, but brought Margherita and Mussolini closer together. In his newspaper *The People of Italy*, Mussolini glorified young Roberto as a symbol of patriotic heroism; he also provided Sarfatti emotional solace for her loss. Margherita turned away from her Socialist beliefs and embraced a fervent patriotism which alone seemed to justify the sacrifice of her son's life. Like Sarfatti, Mussolini was needier than ever before, isolated from his old allies on the left, but still without supporters on the right or a clear path to the future. Although details about Sarfatti and Mussolini's relationship during the war years are sketchy, sometime over the summer and fall of 1918, their earlier infatuation and friendship deepened into a profound love. According to his sister **Edvige Mussolini**, Benito referred to Margherita as his "Sail," a name conjuring up "images of the sea, of the sky and of adventure."

Sarfatti began to work constantly at *The People of Italy*, assuming considerable responsibility for its editorial and managerial policies, and, in December 1918, became cultural editor for the newspaper. In March 1919, together with Mussolini, she founded *Ardita*, a monthly literary review of *Popolo d'Italia*, and later in the month, attended the founding of the Fascist Movement. In January 1922, Sarfatti became managing editor of the important journal *Gerar-*chia (Hierarchy), which succeeded *Ardita* as a source of cultural criticism and as an unofficial mouthpiece for Mussolini's political views. Although Mussolini was listed as the director, Sarfatti actually ran the journal, hiring its staff, seeking out and choosing its articles, and writing many of them herself. Besides playing a leading role in shaping Fascist cultural policy, Sarfatti loaned the movement large sums. When Mussolini made the difficult decision to stage a coup d'etat and seize power in October 1922, historians Cannistraro and Sullivan suggest that, at a critical point, Sarfatti bolstered him psychologically in following through on his risky plan.

The success of the Fascist March on Rome in pressuring the king to appoint Mussolini prime minister opened the way for Sarfatti to exercise more influence over Italian culture. Mussolini cared little for the visual arts, and allowed Sarfatti to act as his guide. In the chaotic, postwar era, she believed artists should abandon their individual "arbitrary" styles and work toward a "collective synthesis." She wanted a return to the great stylistic traditions of past Italian art, to an art which encouraged devotion to hierarchy, discipline, and order, much like Fascism itself. She came to believe that both classical, Roman art and certain types of Modern art embodied these values and traditions. In 1922, Sarfatti thought she had discovered the desired "collective synthesis" that she had written about earlier in the work of seven of her favorite painters, including Mario Sironi and Achille Funi. She picked up on the suggestion of one of the painters, and widely publicized the group as "the Italian Twentieth Century." In 1923 and again in 1926, she persuaded Mussolini to open exhibitions of her favored group, which came to include such men as Carlo Carrà, Giorgio Morandi, and Gino Severini. In the public's eye, Mussolini's appearances established Novecento (Twentieth Century) as the Fascist artistic movement.

During the 1920s, Sarfatti also served as a member of various governmental committees dealing with cultural matters. In 1924, Mussolini appointed her head of the Italian judging committee for the International Exposition of Decorative Arts in Paris; in addition, she served as vice-president of the exposition itself, and for these services the French government awarded her the medal of the Legion of Honor. While in Paris, she met the famous African-American dancer *Josephine Baker, took an immediate liking to her, and invited Baker to visit her in Italy (which she eventually did).

Sarfatti's cultivation of La Joséphine was but one of many examples of her knack for collecting celebrities. Much of Sarfatti's influence during the '20s was exercised through her brilliant salon, where the famous mixed with young but promising unknowns. After the death of her husband Cesare in 1924, she moved to Rome. Here she proved an ideal salon hostess, a lively and brilliant conversationalist who knew how to draw even the most reclusive guests into the discussion. The list of Italian visitors to Sarfatti's salon included the playwright Pirandello, the inventor Marconi, and the novelist Alberto Moravia. Since her ambition to acquire, or create, celebrities was stronger than any desire for ideological consistency, she supported the careers of many artists and authors who did little to conform to Fascism or in fact opposed the regime. Virtually every distinguished foreign traveler who visited Rome in the late 1920s also called at Margherita's salon. These included French foreign minister Louis Barthou, and the authors André Gide and André Malraux. Sarfatti's close friend, the famous French writer *Colette, often visited her in Rome and at her country home.

Sarfatti exerted great influence over the third Monza International Exhibition of Decorative Arts in 1927. As a member of the organizing committee, she used her experience of the Paris exhibit to transform the way the Monza exhibits were presented. For the first time in Italy, the Monza fair aimed to achieve a collaboration between architects and artists. The entire exhibit became a showcase for modern design. Ever since she had seen Melnikov's Soviet Pavilion and Le Corbusier's work at the Paris Expo, Sarfatti had been won over to the side of modernism, which had its counterpart in Italy in the rationalist architecture of the *Gruppo 7* (Group of Seven). Although Sarfatti's reputation as "dictator of the arts" during the 1920s was exaggerated, it was in large measure due to her that modern art often enjoyed the support of the government. Her efforts therefore helped to raise the artistic quality of Fascist patronage.

More famous than her salon or her influence on art, however, was her role in creating the myth of *Il Duce*, of Mussolini the brilliant, if solitary, leader. In 1924, an Italian literary agent working on behalf of foreign publishing firms approached Sarfatti about writing a biography of Mussolini. Enthusiastic about the project, Mussolini supplied her with various private papers and documents. The first edition of her biography appeared in English in September 1925 as *The Life of Benito Mussolini*, with an introduction by *Il Duce* himself. In the Italian edition, which appeared in June 1926, the title of the book was simply *Dux*, the Latin form of *Duce* or "Leader."

In Sarfatti's biography, Mussolini appears as a man destined for greatness who, by sheer force of will, rose above his poverty-stricken environment. He is a strong, ruthless leader devoid of ordinary human weakness or material self-interest. He is the true heir to the Roman Caesars. In the book, Sarfatti deliberately distorted and omitted aspects of Mussolini's career, such as his support for Fascist hooliganism. The photographs in *Dux* showed Mussolini's wide-ranging talents as party activist, soldier, newspaper writer, world diplomat, sports enthusiast, pilot, and racecar driver. On innumerable occasions in the following decades, the media repeated the photographic images first found in Sarfatti's biography.

Dux was a bestseller at home and abroad. Between 1926 and 1938, 17 editions were published in Italy. The book was translated into 18 languages, and according to some accounts, sold a million copies. It did more than any other book or article to shape the image of Mussolini abroad. It also made Sarfatti a great deal of money.

Already at the end of the '20s, signs began to appear that Sarfatti's personal relationship with Mussolini might be in jeopardy and her position in the Fascist state vulnerable. In response to an

Margherita
Sarfatti

outburst of Mussolini's anti-Semitism, the atheist Margherita converted to Catholicism in 1928. Then in early 1929 Rachele Guidi, Mussolini's legal wife, moved from Milan to Rome. Mussolini wished to project a clearer image of his family as good Catholics, now that the Lateran Accords had led the Vatican to recognize the state of Italy for the first time. He also wanted to keep a closer eye on his daughter Edda who, much to Mussolini's displeasure, had fallen in love with a Jewish lieutenant colonel. Rachele and her children hated Sarfatti and were now in a better position to obstruct her relationship with Mussolini. In January 1930, Sarfatti became the subject of a violent argument between Rachele and Benito, and Mussolini promised to break off their relationship. Moreover, by the summer of 1929, Mussolini had come to feel that his identification with Sarfatti's cherished Twentieth Century movement was an embarrassment, opening him up to unnecessary criticism.

In 1930, Margherita turned 50. No longer the beauty she had once been and prone to various ailments, she also increasingly put on weight even though she tried various dieting drugs to control her appetite. Mussolini hated obesity.

Sarfatti's articles began to appear more and more infrequently in *The People of Italy;* they ended altogether by the end of 1932. In December of that year, she left her position as director of *Hierarchy.* For years, Sarfatti had lived across the street from Mussolini's residence at Villa Torlonia; toward the end of 1931, she moved a number of blocks away. A further sign of estrangement came in early 1932, when Sarfatti waited for hours for an appointment with Mussolini, only to be informed that he would not receive her.

Despite the growing personal distance between them, on occasion *Il Duce* still sought her advice on issues regarding cultural policy. She also continued to ghostwrite articles for Mussolini, as she had done all during the 1920s. The Fascist regime persisted in valuing Sarfatti's knowledge of English and her journalistic skills. She became good friends with many members, especially American members, of the Rome press corps. Indeed, Adrian Lyttelton has judged her "probably the regime's most successful manager of public relations." In April 1930, she signed a four-year contract to write pieces under Mussolini's name (and approved by him) for the Hearst Press. This contract made both her and *Il Duce* a great deal of money.

In 1934, Sarfatti undertook a triumphant tour of the United States. Despite her estrangement from Mussolini, she was received in Washington, D.C., as if she were still the uncrowned queen of Italy. Sarfatti arrived with the warm recommendation of the American ambassador to Rome, who described her as "probably the best-informed woman in Italy" and someone who knew Mussolini's mind intimately. She was invited to tea at the White House where she spent an hour with Franklin D. Roosevelt and a hostile *Eleanor Roosevelt. Her four-month tour, which included Cuba and Mexico as well as the U.S., was filled with a hectic schedule of lectures, interviews, and dinners. In June 1937, she used her experiences as the basis for a book entitled *America: The Search for Happiness.* On her return to Italy, when Sarfatti went to report to *Il Duce* on her meetings with Roosevelt, Hearst, and other prominent Americans, she expected a warm welcome. Instead, Mussolini shouted at her that "America does not count!" since its economic resources were not matched by its military forces, and he brusquely ended their interview.

Disturbed by reports that Sarfatti was gossiping about him, in May 1935 Mussolini ordered Italian newspapers to ignore her completely. Increasingly deprived of political influence, Margherita turned to writing and traveling. In 1930, she published a *History of Modern Painting.* In August–September 1931, she helped organize and gave lectures during an exhibition of Twentieth Century art which toured South America. In 1935, she published a biography of a 19th-century Italian artist, Daniele Ranzoni.

Despite the rocky nature of their relationship, Sarfatti continued to be loyal to Mussolini and Fascism. When Italy invaded Ethiopia, she put to good use her ties with American Ambassador Breckinridge Long, vigorously defending the Italian cause and carrying messages between Mussolini and the American embassy. In the end, Long advised President Roosevelt not to institute an oil embargo against Italy.

Sarfatti's political influence came to an end with Mussolini's proclamation of the Rome-Berlin Axis and his public adoption of anti-Semitic policies. On a personal level, Mussolini began a passionate love affair with the young ✧▶ Clara Petacci and felt less than ever before the need for Margherita's friendship. Sarfatti's last recorded visit with Mussolini was in the spring of 1938. She found him completely changed. Deeply disturbed by Mussolini's growing alliance with Hitler, and especially by the führer's triumphant visit to Rome in May 1938, Sarfatti fled Italy. This was about the same time (November 1938) that the Fascist Grand Council published a whole series of anti-Semitic decrees barring Jews from the professions and government, forbidding them to contract mixed marriages, and prohibiting them from employing non-Jews. Jews were expelled as well from the Fascist Party.

Margherita now began a life of exile, first in Paris and then in Montevideo and Buenos Aires. In return for the safety of her daughter and family in Rome, she kept silent about her relationship with Mussolini and her views on Fascist Italy. In Buenos Aires, she became friends with *Victoria Ocampo, a prominent writer and the editor of *Sud* who hosted the most important cultural salon in the country. Sarfatti now socialized with prominent political and cultural figures, such as the modernist author Jorge Luis Borges. She also published criticism and travel articles, and books on the artists Giorgione and Titian. She finished a book on Casanova. In *Mussolini as I Knew Him*, Sarfatti tried to come to terms with her involvement with *Il Duce* and Fascism. She acknowledged her responsibility for believing in Fascism, and analyzed what she believed were the reasons that had led Mussolini to lose sight of the original goals of the Fascist movement. Margherita had originally thought of publishing *Mussolini as I Knew Him* in the United States, where she would probably have earned a considerable amount of money. But she lost her nerve and instead published the work in 14 installments in the Spanish-language paper *Crítica* during June–July 1945. The series drew little attention.

In March 1947, Sarfatti returned to Italy. Her book *Water Under the Bridge*, published in 1955, was less a memoir of her own life than an account of the people she had known, with the exception of Mussolini, whom she did not mention. She ended her story in 1934. Adventurous and full of curiosity even at 76, in 1956 Sarfatti decided to travel to India, Ceylon, Malaya, Hong Kong, and Japan, even though none of her friends would agree to go with her. She died on October 30, 1961, in her country home, Il Soldo, near Lake Como.

SOURCES:
Cannistraro, Philip. "Sarfatti-Grassini, Margherita," in *Historical Dictionary of Fascist Italy.*
———, and Brian R. Sullivan. *Il Duce's Other Woman: The Untold Story of Margherita Sarfatti, Mussolini's Jewish Mistress and How She Helped Him Come to Power.* NY: William Morrow, 1993.
Lyttelton, Adrian. "Mussolini's Femme Fatale," in *The New York Review of Books.* July 15, 1993, pp. 18–22.

SUGGESTED READING:
Marzorati, Sergio. *Margherita Sarfatti: Saggio biografico.* Como, 1990.

Richard Bach Jensen,
Assistant Professor of History at Louisiana Scholars' College, Northwestern State University, Natchitoches, Louisiana

❧▶ Petacci, Clara (c. 1915–1945)

Italian mistress of Benito Mussolini. Born around 1915; died near Como, Italy, on April 28, 1945.

In 1945, at the close of World War II, the Allied armies had fought their way up the peninsula and threatened to overrun all of northern Italy. In this desperate situation, Benito Mussolini tried to escape into Austria by joining a column of retreating German soldiers. Stopped by communist guerilla fighters near the northern tip of Lake Como, the Germans allowed them to search the convoy and seize Mussolini. On April 28, 1945, these partisans machine-gunned to death the 61-year-old Mussolini and his lover, Clara Petacci, who had insisted on joining him in his final moments.

Sargant, Ethel (1863–1918)

British botanist. Born in 1863 in London, England; died in 1918; daughter of Henry Sargant and Catherine (Beale) Sargant; attended North London Collegiate School and Girton College in Cambridge, 1884.

Was the first woman to serve on the council of the Linnaean Society; served as president of Botanical Section of the British Association meeting (1913); served as president of the Federation of University Women.

Selected writings: A Theory of the Origin of Monocotyledons Founded on the Structure of Their Seedlings; The Evolution of Monocotyledons; and The Reconstruction of a Race of Primitive Angiosperms.

Ethel Sargant was born in London in 1863, the daughter of Henry and **Catherine Beale Sargant**. A student of natural science, Ethel was educated at North London Collegiate School and subsequently graduated from Girton College in Cambridge. From 1892 to 1893, she studied research methodologies at Kew Gardens with D.H. Scott. Sargant spent some time in the observation of working laboratories during a visit to Europe in 1897, including the Bonn laboratory of Adolf Strasburger.

Sargant was a gifted "basic" researcher. She examined specimens for the sole purpose of collecting knowledge, and she had little patience for researchers who embarked on what she considered prejudicial research, performed for the purpose of substantiating preconceived theories. Sargant, who conducted her research experiments largely from her mother's home, eventually moved her residence to Girton Village in Cambridge. She was not renowned for her teaching skills, but was an adept researcher who provided invaluable counsel to students with regard to research methods.

Sargant's principal areas of study included cytology and the morphology of plants. By 1895, she embarked on extensive research into monocotyledons. In the course of her observations and experiments, she studied monocotyledon seedlings, especially to learn how they entrench themselves into the soil. She also studied the vascular systems and phylogenetics associated with those plants. Her writings include *A Theory of the Origin of Monocotyledons Founded on the Structure of Their Seedlings*, *The Evolution of Monocotyledons*, and *The Reconstruction of a Race of Primitive Angiosperms*.

In 1913, Sargant was elected to an honorary fellowship at her alma mater, Girton College, and served as a section president of the meeting of the British Association during that same year. Among other honors, she was accepted as a fellow of the Linnaean Society and distinguished herself as the first woman to serve on the council of that organization. She was also the president of the Federation of University Women. Sargant died in 1918.

SOURCES:
Ogilvie, Marilyn Bailey. *Women in Science*. Boston, MA: Cambridge Press, 1993.

Gloria Cooksey,
freelance writer, Sacramento, California

Saria.

Variant of Sarah.

Sark, dame of.

See Hathaway, Sibyl (1884–1974).

Sarolta (fl. 900s)

Duchess of Hungary. Name variations: Sarolt. Flourished in the late 900s; married Prince Geysa also known as Prince or Duke Geza (r. 970–997); children: St. Stephen I (c. 975–1038), the first king of Hungary; *Sarolta (fl. 1000s); *Judith of Hungary (fl. late 900s); Maria (fl. 995–1025, who married the doge of Venice).

Sarolta, duchess of Hungary, and her husband Duke Geza received baptism late in life from St. Adelbert, the Northumbrian missionary. As a sign of their faith, the couple changed their son's name from Vajk to Stephen and raised him as a Christian. As the Hungarian king Stephen I, he left a remarkable imprint on the history of Europe and the world.

Sarolta (fl. 1000s)

Hungarian princess. Flourished in the 1000s; daughter of Prince Geza (r. 970–997) and Sarolta (fl. 900s); married Samuel Aba, king of Hungary (r. 1041–1044).

Sarraute, Nathalie (1900–1999)

Innovative French writer who helped to devise and popularize the "new novel" or "antinovel" in French literature. Pronunciation: Sa-ROTE. Born Nathalie Cherniak on July 18, 1900 (some sources cite 1902), in Ivanovo-Voznesensk, Russia; died in Chérence, France, in October 1999; daughter of Ilya or Elie Cherniak (a chemist) and Pauline Chatunskaya Cherniak (a writer); attended public school in France, 1905–14, Sorbonne, 1914–20, Oxford University, 1920–21, University of Berlin, 1921–22, University of Paris Law School, 1922–25; married Raymond Sarraute (a lawyer), in July 1923 (died 1984); children: three daughters, Claude Sarraute; Anne Sarraute; Dominique Sarraute.

Left Russia to live part-time in France (1902); parents divorced (1904); began to live permanently with her father in France (1908); started practice of law in France (1925); began to write fiction (1932); published first book, Tropismes (1939); hid from the Germans during occupation of France (1941–43); won International Literary Prize for Les Fruits d'or (1964).

Selected works: (fiction) Tropismes (Tropisms, 1939), Portrait d'un inconnu (Portrait of a Man Unknown, 1948), Martereau (1953), Le Planétarium (The Planetarium, 1959), Les Fruits d'or (The Golden Fruits, 1963), Entre la vie et la mort (Between Life and Death, 1968), Vous les entendez? (Do You Hear Them?, 1972), "disent les imbéciles" ("fools say," 1976), Tu ne t'aimes pas (You Don't Love Yourself, 1989), Ici (Here, 1995); (memoir) Enfance (Childhood, 1983); (essays) L'Ere du soupçon (Age of Suspicion, 1956); (plays) Silence (1964), The Lie (1966), Isma (1970).

Nathalie Sarraute was one of 20th-century France's most distinguished writers. Starting in the 1930s, she became a pioneer in the development of an experimental form of fiction known variously as "the new novel" or "the antinovel." Sarraute claimed to be inspired by the great writers who revolutionized fiction at the start of the 20th century: James Joyce, Marcel Proust, *Virginia Woolf, and Franz Kafka. Starting where they left off, she saw herself "taking up that development again." Eschewing any effort to connect her work to present-day events or political positions, Sarraute, a master of dialogue, concentrated instead on the interior life and thoughts of the human species. In her earliest works, she limited some of the innovations in her style by placing a narrator at the center of plotless stories. In time, even this concession to older forms faded away. Writes **Margaret Crosland**: "Sarraute's work brings the reader not action, drama, or speed, but a prickly, shifting mass of colourless half expressed images indicating a form of communication." In Crosland's view, appreciation of Sarraute's work "depends first of all on one's capacity for enjoying technique in itself."

The French novel, whose development Sarraute influenced significantly, changed in the course of the 20th century, with the assault on old forms intensifying in the years after 1945. French writers increasingly rejected the style of writing personified by Honoré Balzac, which features sharply identified characters, clear plot lines, and a link to a visible line of identifiable events. For Sarraute and likeminded writers, notes Henri Peyre, "World War II, Nazism, the social issues of 1933–39 . . . might just as well have occurred on another planet." Instead, the effort to explore inner reality, notably the psychology of the individual, drew writers away from a literature linked to great public events.

In an interview in 1964, Sarraute expressed her conviction that every true novelist establishes a new form in which to work, but such achievements could never be lasting. "The need to overthrow [today's discoveries] will stimulate new revolts . . . and hence eventually new conventions." She herself had been an active participant in the loosely tied group of "new novelists" since their emergence after World War II. Even in work done in the 1930s, Sarraute anticipated the post-1945 attack on the conventional novel by other writers such as Alain Robbe-Grillet. Her difficult and seemingly eccentric style of writing at first received neither critical nor popular acceptance. Critics began to recognize her talents by the late 1940s, however, and her reputation spread widely in the following decade. Despite the heavy demands she made on her readers, Sarraute found a definite, if not massive, reading public.

Nathalie Sarraute was born in the Russian industrial city of Ivanovo-Voznesensk, near Moscow, on July 18, 1900, the daughter of Elie Cherniak, a chemist, and **Pauline Cherniak**, a writer. Sarraute's parents, both Russian Jews, had met in Geneva, Switzerland, while pursuing an education that was denied to individuals of their religious background in their native coun-

try. The young girl spent her first years moving back and forth between Russia and France, and her father, who had separated from Nathalie's mother and then remarried, settled in Paris in 1908. Fluent in Russian and French as a child, Sarraute learned German as well from the family of her father's second wife. She also became fluent in English at an early age. One student of her work, **Ruth Temple**, considers Sarraute's ability to read authors ranging from Dostoevsky to Joyce in the original as an important influence on her future literary career.

As a child of seven or eight, Nathalie first tried her hand at a novel, but a devastatingly harsh criticism of this first work from a friend of her mother, a professional writer, discouraged her from continuing the effort. Her father, a widely cultured and well-read member of the upper-middle class, engaged his daughter in valuable conversations about great writers. But he also discouraged her from taking up a career along these lines. Nonetheless, the young girl drew stimulus for her literary interests from the Parisian community of exiled Russian intellectuals whom she came to know as she grew up. After graduating from secondary school in Paris, she had three brief periods of study in which she explored a variety of subjects—English, history, sociology—in various institutions of higher education: at the Sorbonne, then at Oxford, and finally at the University of Berlin.

In 1922, Sarraute returned to France to enter the law school at the University of Paris at her father's encouragement. She completed her studies in 1925 and began a career practicing law. While at law school, she had met Raymond Sarraute, a fellow student, and the two were married in July 1923. They had three daughters, and both practiced law. Although Nathalie Sarraute carried out her professional duties with only limited enthusiasm, Raymond Sarraute went on to a distinguished career as an attorney.

In 1932 or 1933, Sarraute gave in to a longstanding urge and began to write fiction, although she would continue to practice law until 1940. Sarraute aimed at a new kind of novel, notes **Germaine Brée**, designed to investigate "a certain unexplored dimension of human psychic reality" as yet untouched in the fiction with which she was familiar. Sarraute later claimed that her legal training helped her work as a creative writer. Giving oral arguments made her think about the nature of spoken language, and the direct writing required in legal briefs helped her escape the complex literary forms that French students normally acquired during their higher education. Her husband strongly encouraged her writing career. Sarraute's work was marked from the start by its innovative and difficult style, and critics were slow to respond in a positive manner. Nor did she quickly find a substantial reading audience.

Her first work, *Tropismes*, which incorporated the writing she had been doing for the last several years, set the pattern for much of what was to follow. Sarraute investigated the relations among human beings as reflected by their imperceptible reactions to one another. Her books were devoid of plot, and often it was difficult to tell which character was speaking. Plunging the reader into uncertainty concerning the events taking place and the individuals describing those events became a hallmark of Sarraute's work.

Tropismes appeared in 1939 after being rejected by two major publishers. She was unable to call the book a novel, describing it instead as "a collection of short texts." It drew its title from the biological phenomenon in which a living organism responds in involuntary fashion to an outside stimulus. The book, which established the basic elements of her writing style for the coming decades, consisted of 19 sketches, ranging in length from one to three pages. When *Tropismes* was republished in 1957, it was expanded to 24 segments. According to Temple, only some of them are truly innovative; others are relatively conventional descriptions of an external reality.

> *I* am concerned only with the inner life which is going on every moment in each of us.
> —Nathalie Sarraute

In each of the innovative pieces of *Tropismes*, however, Sarraute charts the involuntary psychological reaction of an individual to the remarks or actions of another. The common reaction she finds is fear and misunderstanding; the human relations she portrays are unequal ones with one personality under the domination of another. There is little if any action, and it is often difficult, in this germinal work, even to tell who is speaking. Sarraute's aim, then and henceforth in her career, was to immerse her reader in a world in which individuals respond to the often thoughtless and unintended stimuli brought to them by others.

As Sarraute later claimed, she wanted to prevent the reader from seeking the normal guideposts in a written work and to block the reader from identifying the characters whose thoughts were presented and to leave the time and place of events uncertain. Nonetheless, **Gretchen Rous Besser** has found a continuing thread of satire in

Tropismes, with Sarraute taking particular aim at women with "their frivolous concerns and useless occupations." By pouring a degree of gentle ridicule on a largely featureless individual engaging in foibles and habitual behavior, Sarraute, according to Besser, strikes at "all the countless lookalikes who reinforce his mediocrity." This pessimistic book with its stress on the bleakness of human behavior was a commercial failure, and it received only a single review, which appeared in a Belgian journal.

During the years of World War II that followed, the author's Jewish parentage put her life in peril. For two years, Sarraute took refuge in a small country village near Paris, at time pretending to be her daughters' governess, a woman named Nicole Sauvage. When she was betrayed by one of the local residents, she returned to Paris to go into hiding in her home city. Even in this perilous environment, she continued to write.

Between 1948 and 1959, Sarraute finished three books that came somewhat closer than *Tropismes* to the form of a novel. Nonetheless, she continued to focus on the subterranean course of human interactions she had outlined in her first work. There was no attempt to describe her characters' physical features or personalities, no effort to give them names, no discernible plot, no outside events, and no narration. Instead the reader was confronted immediately with the inner thoughts of a character.

Sarraute received an important endorsement of the first of these works, *Portrait d'un inconnu*, from Jean-Paul Sartre. Seeing beyond the apparent clutter of petty events and details that had mystified earlier critics, Sartre lauded her work in a preface to the book when it appeared in 1948. He also promoted it by publishing a chapter in his important journal, *Les Temps modernes*. The book, largely written during the wartime years, concentrated on tropisms within a single personality, an unidentified man who obsessively watches the lives of an elderly father and his daughter. He may be an observant friend of the family, but Sarraute complicates her description of his reactions to them by having him recount events that he did not witness. She also shifts the angle of observation to that of the father. This work, like *Tropismes*, turned out to be a commercial failure. After selling a mere 400 copies, the publisher destroyed the rest of the copies that had been printed. In a preface to a subsequent edition of *Portrait d'un inconnu* in 1957, Sartre used the term "antinovel" to characterize the kind of work Sarraute, now joined by a number of other authors, was doing.

Nathalie
Sarraute

Responding to the indifference with which her earlier work had been received, Sarraute tried to explain her style in a series of essays that she began publishing in 1946. Four of these were gathered into a book, *L'Ere de soupçon*, which appeared in 1956. In the title essay, Sarraute noted that the era of the clearly defined and pictured fictional character was over. Stimulated by James Joyce, Marcel Proust, as well as Sigmund Freud, modern readers did not need or want such guideposts in their novels. Instead, they would welcome works based on inner dialogues with no clear indication of who was speaking or thinking. Sarraute claimed that she was merely trying retrospectively to understand a style of writing she had already developed in intuitive fashion. She also found a valuable ally in the person of Alain Robbe-Grillet. He was not only a writer with similar tastes, but his position as director of an important publishing house, Les Editions de Minuit, gave her a sympathetic outlet for some of her work.

The second of these novels, *Martereau*, still had some conventional elements in it, such as a single narrator and a wisp of a plot. A young man is asked to buy a house for an elderly acquaintance, thereby helping the older man to evade his tax obligations. The narrator is the older man's nephew whose observations and responses to the world form the work's centerpiece.

Sarraute's reputation began its ascent in 1959 with the publication of the third of her postwar works of fiction, *Le Planétarium*. The book was widely and often favorably reviewed, and it has proven to be her most popular work in the eyes of an English audience. One fragmentary element of the plot involves a young man, Alain Guimiez, and his efforts to obtain his aunt's apartment for himself and his wife. Another pertains to a famous author and the younger writers who seek to get to know her. Unlike her first two novels, this book has no main narrator whose interior thoughts provide some kind of centerpiece to the work. As in Sarraute's other works, the most important element is the set of tropisms she presents. These emerge with no indication of the individual mind in which they are to be found. Writes Besser: the reader "is passed like a shuttlecock from one mind to the next, without knowing precisely where [she] is."

In the three novels written from the early 1960s through the start of the following decade, completely unidentified voices dominate the scene. According to Besser, "the result is an undiverted emphasis on the tropisms themselves." In *Les Fruits d'or*, published in 1963, a novel of that same name is at the book's center. Typically, Sarraute gives the reader no idea of the book's contents. Instead, she explores the reactions, i.e., tropisms, the fictitious novel evokes. These include the fear of non-conformity and the sadistic pleasure one personality takes in imposing his standards on someone else. Sarraute appeared anxious to show both the absence of any objective standard for measuring art and consequently the reserve one should exercise toward any critic's opinion. Paradoxically, her book itself won sufficient critical acclaim to receive the International Literary Prize for 1964.

The second of these works, *Entre la vie et la mort*, published in 1968, considers the tropisms in the mind of a writer, including those she/he develops as a result of the tropisms of others. Sarraute's exploration here of the nature of artistic creation received high praise, including novelist *Mary McCarthy's declaration, "one would have said in advance that it was impossible . . . to show how an author composes."

The third, *Vous les entendez?*, which appeared in 1972, considers the world of art from the perspective of the audience, the lover of art to whom the work is presented. A dimly identified father and his children respond to a stone figurine in the family home. The father's affection for the figurine provokes ridicule from his children, and Sarraute works with the consequent tropisms evoked on both sides of the confrontation. Typically for a work by Sarraute, *Vous les entendez?* lacks clearly edged characters. Even the number of children is left uncertain and their reactions merge with those of their father.

In a turn in her writing career, Sarraute began composing radio plays in the early 1960s. The main challenge in such an endeavor lay in using spoken dialogue to convey the subterranean tropisms that she continued to place at the center of her work. French stage director Jean-Louis Barrault succeeded in the difficult task of retaining the main qualities of Sarraute's work while turning several of her radio plays into production for the legitimate theater. By using silences, by focusing on trivial untruths told by one character, by placing a disruptive and provocative figure at the center of a group that must respond to him, Sarraute managed to transfer her literary techniques to the stage.

Sarraute subsequently returned to her emphasis on the novel, producing *"disent les imbéciles"* in 1976. Representing an even greater emphasis than heretofore on abstraction and tropisms, it consists of nothing more than dialogue uttered by several undifferentiated characters who, as Besser notes, "are disembodied voices emitting opinions." The title reflects the book's theme that ideas are important, and that the crude dismissal of an idea as something only "fools say" is the road to calamity. For some critics, this work seemed to mark a somewhat new turn in Sarraute's literary career. She appeared to admit, if only reluctantly, that literature cannot remain mute in the face of social and political concerns.

In 1983, Sarraute produced a book with the provocative title of *Enfance* (Childhood). Apparently a memoir of her childhood between the ages of five and eleven, it was the closest thing to an autobiography this innovative writer had ever produced. But here, too, tropisms dominate the literary scene. Notes Leon Roudiez, "the people mentioned in it are never fleshed out." He claimed that Sarraute composed the book in terms of "the stirring provoked within the child by confrontations with adults." Thus, *Enfance* takes place within the literary framework she had already established.

After a long hiatus, during which her husband died in 1984, Sarraute presented her devotees with an even more abstract work, *Tu ne t'aimes pas*, in 1989. It featured completely anonymous characters, as well as an indistinct narrator (or possibly several narrators). And advancing age did not bring an end to Sarraute's literary productivity. *Ici*, which appeared in 1995, resembled in form her pioneering effort in *Tropismes*, published almost 60 years earlier.

Sarraute's reputation as one of France's most innovative and important writers of the 20th century seems assured. "She cracks open the common place," writes Besser, "and extracts the deeper meaning hidden underneath." In the words of Claude Mauriac, a critic who placed her explicitly at the pinnacle of the literary world, "of all living writers, [she] is the one who has most profoundly and fundamentally renewed our knowledge of mankind."

SOURCES:

Besser, Gretchen Rous. *Nathalie Sarraute*. Boston, MA: Twayne, 1979.

Brée, Germaine. *Women Writers in France: Variations on a Theme*. New Brunswick, NJ: Rutgers University Press, 1973.

Brosman, Catherine Savage, ed. *French Novelists since 1900*. Detroit, MI: Gale Research, 1989.

Crosland, Margaret. *Women of Iron and Velvet and the Books They Wrote in France*. London: Constable, 1976.

Mercier, Vivian. *The New Novel from Queneau to Pinget*. NY: Farrar, Straus and Giroux, 1971.

Peyre, Henri. *French Novelists of Today*. NY: Oxford University Press, 1967.

Roudiez, Leon S. *French Fiction Revisited*. Elwood Park, IL: Dalkey Archive Press, 1991.

Sartori, Eva Martin, and Dorothy Wynne Zimmerman. *French Women Writers: A Bio-Bibliographical Source Book*. NY: Greenwood Press, 1991.

Temple, Ruth Z. *Nathalie Sarraute*. NY: Columbia University Press, 1968.

SUGGESTED READING:

Barbour, Sarah. *Nathalie Sarraute and the Feminist Reader: Identities in Process*. Lewisburg, PA: Bucknell University Press, 1993.

Minoque, Valerie. *Nathalie Sarraute and the War of Words*. Edinburgh, Scotland: Edinburgh University Press, 1981.

Neil M. Heyman,
Professor of History,
San Diego State University, San Diego, California

Sarrazin, Albertine (1937–1967)

French writer whose work was based upon her experiences as a criminal and prison inmate. Pronunciation: Al-bear-TEEN Sarah-ZAN. Name variations: Albertine Damien; Anne-Marie R. Born in Algiers, French North Africa, on September 17, 1937; died of cardiac arrest during surgery on July 10, 1967, in Montpellier, France; married Julien (Jules) Sarrazin (a fellow criminal), on February 7, 1959.

Adopted by a couple in Algiers (1939); moved from Algeria to France, raped by member of her adopted family (1947); incarcerated in reform school (1952); escaped from reform school, rearrested following robbery of a dress store (1953); her adopted family revoked her adoption (1956); escaped from prison, met Julien Sarrazin (1957); freed following several additional terms in prison (1960); injured in automobile accident (1961); new series of crimes and imprisonments (1961–65); her first novels accepted for publication, settled in Montpellier (1965); received Four Jury Prize for La Cavale *(1966); film version of* L'Astragale *appeared (1967).*

Major works: (novels) La Cavale *(The Runaway, 1965),* L'Astragale *(Astragal, 1965),* La Traversière *(The Crossing, 1966); (diaries and other prose works)* Journal de Prison 1959 *(Prison Journal 1959, 1972),* Le Passe-peine, 1949–1967 *(Doing Time, 1949–1967, 1976).*

In her short writing career, Albertine Sarrazin became a noted figure on the French literary scene. Basing her writing, both fiction and nonfiction, upon her eventful and tragic life as a criminal and prison inmate, she received a large measure of popular and critical acclaim in the mid-1960s. Two of Sarrazin's three novels were bestsellers, and her writing received a second surge of critical interest after her death with the rise of feminist concerns as well as renewed interest in prison conditions due to a series of riots in the 1970s. Her voluminous correspondence and her diaries were published posthumously, and her *Journal de Prison 1959* continues to be read widely along with her novels.

Some early critics viewed the quality of her work with some skepticism. Henri Peyre, for example, lauded her "fine sense of comedy" and her "genuine talent as a stylist," but he attributed much of her success to the skill with which her first two books were publicized. In more recent years, **Elissa Gelfand**, the most prominent scholarly student of Sarrazin's writing, has interpreted her work from a different perspective, that of "socio-literary feminist criticism."

Gelfand gives Sarrazin credit for being a significant feminist writer. She sees Sarrazin, in her prison journal but even more so in her novels, as an important example of a woman rejecting the socially imposed identity of a deviant. Instead, Sarrazin insists on her identity "as a writer, not as a criminal." According to Gelfand, Sarrazin, while not a feminist herself, sharply criticizes conventional social standards, thus mirroring a rising feminist consciousness that was rejecting conventional gender and other categories by the 1960s. Other feminist critics such as *Gloria Steinem have been less enthusiastic about Sarrazin, chastising her for a lack of political concerns and for her frequently supercilious descriptions of other women.

Sarrazin's writing is inseparable from her experiences during her brief lifetime. Notes **Margaret Crosland**: "It was the intensity of this restricted life [in prison] which developed her obsessive need to write." Her books described her years in prison, which dominated her world from the early 1950s until 1964 and which constituted nearly one third of her abbreviated lifetime. They dealt as well with the periods she spent immersed in criminal activity. Moreover, some of her writing also examined her thoughts about her role as a writer as she was producing her various works.

*P*erhaps the most rewarding quality in her writing is her irrepressible optimism.

—Margaret Crosland

Sarrazin's writing diverged from the experimental forms prominent in France at the time and featured in the work of such innovative authors as *Nathalie Sarraute and *Marguerite Duras. Instead, her accounts of prison life and criminal activity were traditional narratives. As Gelfand has pointed out, Sarrazin was less interested in the routines of prison life—although she described them in substantial detail—than she was in her personal growth and development within this harsh framework. A number of prominent French women who were imprisoned, starting with Manon Phlipon (*Madame Roland) during the French Revolution, have recorded their experiences. But Sarrazin turned such writing in a new direction by transforming her experiences into fiction. It was, in Gelfand's words, a "sharp turn toward a new literary orientation in prison writing."

Sarrazin's combination of detachment and defiance was also notable. In contradiction of the general public's frequent presumption that confinement in a women's prison means immersion in lesbian relationships, she repeatedly asserted her continuing heterosexual desires. She refused to concede that sexual desire is diminished by being placed behind bars. Instead, she insisted on her continuing attraction to Julien Sarrazin. She rejected the prison custom in which all women were addressed by their maiden names. Even before her marriage to Julien she referred to herself as "La Sarrazine." While her work was repeatedly confiscated or even lost by the individuals in charge of her various places of confinement, she continued to write clandestinely. Even when it came to reflecting on her life as a criminal, Sarrazin insisted on her autonomy. It was not society or even her scarred childhood that pushed her into activities outside the law. "I chose elsewhere, i.e., outside the realm of sanctioned activity," she wrote, "because I have a taste for risk."

The future writer was born in Algiers in French North Africa on September 17, 1937. She was apparently the illegitimate child of a teenage Spanish mother who deposited the baby at the local Welfare Office. It is possible that an Arab was her father. Officials at the Welfare Office gave her the name Albertine Damien. Her subsequent life was shaped in large measure by her adoption, at the age of two, by a French army doctor serving in North Africa and his wife. Various sources identify the elderly couple's family name only by the letter "R." They renamed the child Anne-Marie, and in her obviously autobiographical literary works, Sarrazin used a variant of this new name (Annick or Anick) to designate herself as the narrator.

The adoption was not a happy one. In 1947, after the family returned from Algeria to settle in Aix-en-Provence in southern France, Albertine was sexually assaulted by an adult male relative. Meanwhile, although she proved to be a notably talented student, her relations with her adopted parents deteriorated. Two harsh consequences followed. Her family moved to end their formal relationship with her by annulling the adoption. Meanwhile, in November 1952, her father placed her in a reform school, the Refuge of the Good Shepherd in Marseilles.

Sarrazin escaped in less than a year, using the opportunity offered by a trip outside the school to take her examination to graduate from secondary school. Ironically, before fleeing she took and passed the examination at the exceptionally young age of 16. She made her way to Paris where she reunited with Emilienne, a girl from the school with whom she had established a homosexual relationship. Albertine supported herself by working as a prostitute, but she and Emilienne made an unsuccessful venture into armed robbery. They were quickly arrested, and Sarrazin received a seven-year jail sentence.

The curious combination of a young girl who was a criminal, a gifted student, and a budding literary talent manifested itself during this period. In prison at Fresnes, then in the reformatory at Doullens in Picardy in northeastern France, Sarrazin began to write both poetry and prose. The prose took the form of notes that were later published in her prison journal. Meanwhile, she continued to study for the state examination required for entry into study at the university level. This period also brought her into contact with a new and positive influence. At Doullens, she had regular meetings with Dr. **Christiane Gogois-Myquel**, a psychiatrist who came to appreciate the young woman's literary gifts and encouraged her to go on writing. Sarrazin later dedicated her first book, *La Cavale*, to Gogois-Myquel, whom she referred to cryptically as "my one-sixteenth of a mother."

In April 1957, after four years of incarceration, Sarrazin escaped from the reform school at Doullens. During the breakout, she suffered a broken ankle, but she was saved from recapture by Julien Sarrazin, a truck driver passing by the prison who gave her a lift in his vehicle. This fortuitous meeting led to a relationship that lasted for the remainder of the young woman's life. Julien himself was a veteran criminal, and the two of them now joined their efforts to live as burglars. They were arrested in September 1958, and over the next two years each served a stretch in prison. On February 7, 1959, they were married during an interlude when Julien was temporarily free but Albertine was still confined. She was permitted to leave the prison escorted by guards in order to take part in the wedding ceremony. Both before and after the marriage, Albertine had written lengthy letters to Julien. These constituted an important part of her literary legacy.

A final set of troubles with the law came in the early 1960s. Both Albertine and Julien were arrested in 1961 for burglary, and she served a two-year sentence. Then, in 1964, by which time she was working as a journalist in Alès in southern France, she was taken into custody for petty theft: she had stolen gourmet food and whisky to prepare a coming-home party for her husband. Albertine was now given a prison term—her last—that she completed in August 1965. After her release, she and Julien moved to the remote Cevennes region of central France. Two years later, with her literary career well launched, she and her husband bought a house in the countryside outside the southern city of Montpellier.

The year in which Albertine finished her final prison term (1965) was the same one in which her first two novels, *La Cavale* and *L'Astragale*, appeared. They were published by the firm of Jean-Jacques Pauvert, which Gogois-Myquel had first contacted on Sarrazin's behalf several years before. Both drew upon her experiences of incarceration and the emotions of being released from prison. A third novel, *La Traversière*, appeared a year later.

Sarrazin wrote *La Cavale* secretly in prison in 1961 and 1962; her work on *L'Astragale* was the product of a period of freedom in the spring and summer of 1964. The novels depend largely upon conventional literary techniques, but French critics were immediately impressed by the colorful nature of her personal experiences and the vivid, confident way she had transformed them into fiction. She quickly became an important public personality as her books reached the bestseller list and she was invited to make appearances on television. *La Cavale* was entered in several prize competitions, winning the Prize des Quatres Jurys in Tunisia in the spring of 1966.

Albertine Sarrazin

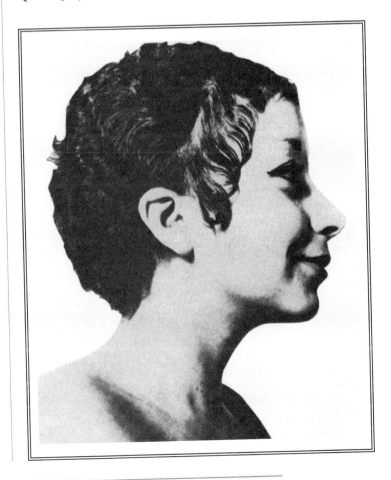

La Cavale takes its narrator through a year and a half of incarceration during the late 1950s in three separate prisons: Amiens, Soissons, and Compiegne. The title comes from the French prison slang word for an escape. The narrator, Annick Damien, is clearly speaking in the author's own voice. She presents a profane, cynical, and knowing view of prison life. From the first page, Annick makes it clear she is a veteran of numerous lock-ups, wise to the ways of such institutions, and always comparing the institution in which she finds herself to the ones she has known in the past. Accepting with equanimity the cast of characters she encounters in prison—fellow inmates and guards—she records in the same measured tone the minor kindnesses and bizarre behaviors she endures. "In the old days, I screamed, I broke things," she says, in the face of a prison that held her securely. Now, however, "I don't scream any more: It is I who watch the prison, I study the old contraption." She manages to detach herself from any close relationship with her fellow prisoners, dealing with them extensively only when it comes to such matters as trading in food and cigarettes. The twin obsessions in her thoughts are the deadening details of the prison routine, living in an all-female society, and her ongoing and imaginative plans for escape.

The only variations to enter the life described in *La Cavale* come with occasional court appearances in which she has a rendezvous with "Zizi," her lover and partner in crime. A notable event in the book comes when she is temporarily released in order to marry him in a nine-minute ceremony at the local mayor's office. The reader is struck by "Annick's" obvious intelligence and storytelling ability, and by the sordid circumstances of confinement into which she has repeatedly allowed her behavior to place her. Writes Sarrazin: "Excessive delicacy is as out of place here as the cultivation of sweet potatoes."

The favorable critical reception *La Cavale* received in France was matched by its popularity with the reading public. In less than a decade, 500,000 copies of the book had been sold in Sarrazin's native country. Elsewhere, the book's reception was less enthusiastic. Critics from the American literary community, like Steinem and John Updike, found the book—almost 500 pages long—to be largely a rambling and self-indulgent exercise.

L'Astragale, although written later, is set in an earlier stage of Sarrazin's life. Less than half as long as *La Cavale*, it describes the young author's escape from prison in 1957 and her first year with her future husband. Its title comes

from the ankle bone that Sarrazin broke jumping from a 30-foot wall in order to get out from behind bars. The first scene places the author at the base of the wall from which she has just plunged, after which she crawls away from the scene of her incarceration. Picked up by the truck driver whom she will later marry, she expresses her joy in unmitigated terms: "A new century begins." After 16 months of freedom, in which she supports herself part of the time by working as a Parisian prostitute, she finds herself once again in the hands of the police and on her way back to prison. The book gave Sarrazin her greatest public acclaim, selling almost a million copies. A film version appeared in 1967.

Both books were translated into English and appeared in the United States within a year. Sarrazin's third novel, *La Traversière*, was likewise autobiographical and dealt mainly with her experiences leading to the publication of *La Cavale*. The only work Sarrazin wrote while living outside a prison environment, the book begins with a bitter and bleak depiction of her adopted family with her overbearing adopted father and his self-effacing wife. It continues with an account of her life after leaving prison, including her droll description of work as a journalist for a provincial newspaper. It appeared in 1966 in French, but it has never been translated into English.

The book is marked by the young author's uncertainty about the possibility of future literary success. It was, in fact, initially rejected by Sarrazin's publisher, and it received a notably harsh response from formerly friendly members of the French literary community. Wrote novelist Hervé Bazin: "Her tool fell from her hands just at the moment when it had become perfectly honed." A critic in the *Times Literary Supplement* (January 1967) expressed discontent in a more muted fashion. Noting Sarrazin's "genuine imaginative talent," the critic asked, "when will she give us a real novel?"

Sarrazin had scarcely any time to relish her literary achievements. Although extensive surgery corrected her broken ankle, she soon experienced a new physical problem in the form of a diseased kidney. On July 10, 1967, during an operation to correct this malady, she died suddenly at the age of 30. Her husband claimed that her death was the result of medical malpractice. He sued and won a substantial settlement which he devoted to the task of publishing all of her remaining writing.

The works that appeared after Sarrazin's death were the products of her first years as a writer. They were diaries and collections of letters, and they drew much of their inspiration from her troubled childhood and her years behind bars. The first was her *Journal de Prison 1959*, which was published in 1972. It was followed four years later by a more extensive collection, *Le Passe-peine, 1949–1967*. The latter work included a description of her precarious life in Paris in 1953 when she survived by working as a prostitute as well as her subsequent incarceration in Fresnes prison.

The brevity of Sarrazin's life and the relatively small body of work she produced is sobering. Nonetheless, notes Gelfand, even though "she did not have the time to mature fully," her work "gives sure form to her inchoate life experience" and it does so with "impressive literary sophistication and originality."

SOURCES:
Brosman, Catharine Savage, ed. *French Novelists since 1960*. Detroit, MI: Gale Research, 1989.

Crosland, Margaret. *Women of Iron and Velvet and the Books They Wrote in France*. London: Constable, 1976.

Gelfand, Elissa D. *Imagination in Confinement: Women's Writing from French Prisons*. Ithaca, NY: Cornell University Press, 1983.

———. "Imprisoned Women: Toward a Socio-Literary Feminist Analysis," in *Yale French Studies*. Vol. 62, 1981, pp. 185–203.

Peyre, Henri. *French Novelists of Today*. NY: Oxford University Press, 1967.

Sarrazin, Albertine. *Astragal*. Translated by Patsy Southgate. NY: Grove Press, 1967.

———. *The Runaway*. Translated by Charles Lam Markmann. NY: Grove Press, 1967.

Sartori, Eva Martin, and Dorothy Wynne Zimmerman, eds. *French Women Writers: A Bio-Bibliographical Source Book*. Westport, CT: Greenwood Press, 1991.

SUGGESTED READING:
Gelfand, Elissa D. "Albertine Sarrazin: A Control Case of Femininity in Form," in *The French Review*. Vol. 51, no. 2. December 1977, pp. 245–251.

———. "Women Prison Authors in France: Twice Criminal," in *Modern Language Studies*. Vol. 11, no. 1, 1980–81, pp. 57–63.

Neil M. Heyman,
Professor of History,
San Diego State University, San Diego, California

Sarre, countess of.

See Marie José of Belgium (b. 1906).

Sartain, Emily (1841–1927)

American mezzotint artist and influential art educator. Born on March 17, 1841, in Philadelphia, Pennsylvania; died on June 17, 1927; daughter of John Sartain (a painter) and Susannah (Longmate) Sartain; studied in Philadelphia at the Pennsylvania Academy of the Fine Arts, 1864–70.

La Piece de Conviction (*also known as* The Reproof) *won a medal at the Centennial Exhibition (1876); employed as art editor of* Our Continent *magazine (1881–83); served as principal of Philadelphia School of Design for Women (1886–1920).*

Emily Sartain was born in 1841 into a family of artists. Her mother **Susannah Sartain** was the descendant of Edward Longmate and John Swaine, both respected English engravers. Emily's father John Sartain was a highly regarded engraver, artist, and publisher who encouraged Emily and three of her brothers in their artistic careers. For six years, she attended the Pennsylvania Academy of Fine Arts, then continued her artistic education in Europe, studying under noted painter Evariste Luminais in Paris and painting copies of famous works in Spain and Italy. In 1878, the Paris Salon accepted two of her paintings, one of which, *La Piece de Conviction* (*The Reproof*), won a medal at the Centennial Exhibition of 1876 in Philadelphia. She was awarded another prize for best picture by a woman at the Pennsylvania Academy of Fine Arts.

Upon her return to the United States, Sartain concentrated on mezzotint engravings. She had learned the technique from her father, and was the only woman to work in the genre. Mezzotints are soft, velvety prints and are made by burning copper or steel plates to produce a very even grain.

Sartain was art editor of *Our Continent* from 1881 to 1883. In 1886, she was encouraged by her friend, the renowned painter Thomas Eakins, to take the position of principal of the Philadelphia School of Design for Women (now the Moore School of Art), the first industrial arts school for women in the United States. Sartain, who strongly believed that commercial artists should be trained as much as fine artists, and that commercial and fine arts should be held to the same standards, used her position to make sweeping changes to the curriculum. She instituted training in the French technique, which concentrates on perspective and on working from live models, and hired Robert Henri and other avant-garde artists as teachers. As an educator, she was instrumental in furthering industrial-design training for women.

Her innovations were soon noted throughout the art world, and Sartain was invited to be a U.S. delegate for several prestigious congresses on commercial art education in Europe. At the World's Columbian Exposition in 1893, she was selected to be a judge of art and chaired the Pennsylvania women's art committee, which decorated the interior of the Pennsylvania Building.

Sartain was also active civically: she was a founder of the New Century Club, president and one of the founders of the women artists' Plastic Club, and president of the Browning Society of Philadelphia. She also founded a summer art school in Virginia. After her retirement in 1920, she spent her summers in Europe and winters in California. Emily Sartain died on June 17, 1927, while visiting relatives in Philadelphia.

SOURCES:

James, Edward T., ed. *Notable American Women, 1607–1950*. Cambridge, MA: The Belknap Press of Harvard University, 1971.

McHenry, Robert, ed. *Famous American Women*. NY: Dover, 1980.

Rubinstein, Charlotte Streifer. *American Women Artists*. Avon, 1982.

Ruth Savitz,
freelance writer, Philadelphia, Pennsylvania

Sarton, May (1912–1995)

Prolific American writer of poetry, fiction, autobiography, and journals who was largely ignored by the literary establishment but always enjoyed an appreciative, loyal, and discerning readership. Born Eléanore Marie Sarton at Wondelgem near Ghent, Belgium, on May 3, 1912; died of breast cancer at York Hospital in York, Maine, on July 16, 1995; only surviving child of George Sarton (famed historian of science) and Eleanor Mabel (Elwes) Sarton (a talented artist and designer); after she and her parents fled Belgium for England in 1914 and settled permanently in Cambridge, Massachusetts, in 1917, attended the notable Shady Hill School, 1917–26, interrupting her studies there to study at the Institute Belge de Culture Française for nine months in 1925; entered the Cambridge High and Latin School in 1926, completing her formal education there in 1929; never married; lived with Judith Matlack, 1945–58; no children.

Joined Eva Le Gallienne's Civic Repertory Theater in New York as an apprentice (1929); founded and directed the Apprentice Theater (1933), later renamed the Associated Actors Theater, Inc., which staged ten European plays as a course at the New School for Social Research in New York and five plays at the Wadsworth Atheneum in Hartford, Connecticut; when company failed (1936), left the theater to devote her life to writing, supporting herself by brief stints of teaching and by yearly lecture tours to colleges and universities throughout U.S.; published first volume of poetry, Encounter in April (1937), followed by first novel, The Single Hound (1938), both of which won high praise in U.S. and Great Britain; completed four novels and five volumes of verse (1939–55) which were also favorably reviewed; after

the 1955 publication of Faithful Are the Wounds (a novel about the suicide of a Harvard University professor), ignored by the literary establishment for years but gained an ever-widening readership with the publication of four autobiographies and seven journals (1959–96); at age 53 and in her tenth novel, Mrs. Stevens Hears the Mermaids Singing (1965), "came out" as a lesbian, which rather than alienating her readers, enhanced her reputation for honesty and courage; old age and illness became major themes in all her writing, winning her yet more devoted readers (1970s–95).

Publications: May Sarton was one of the most productive American writers of the 20th century. Between 1937 and 1955, she wrote and saw published 15 volumes of verse, 19 novels, 11 memoirs and journals, 2 children's books, several plays and other miscellaneous writings. In 1997, W.W. Norton, her publisher for over 30 years, reported that 38 of the over 50 books she wrote were still in print, an indication of the popularity she enjoyed during her lifetime and beyond. An anthology of her best poems, Collected Poems, 1930–1993, was published in 1993. Sarton herself correctly judged that her most enduring novels were Faithful Are the Wounds (1955), Mrs. Stevens Hears the Mermaids Singing (1965), As We Are Now (1973), and A Reckoning (1978). Her memoirs and journals have been unusually popular, especially I Knew A Phoenix (1959), Journal of a Solitude (1973) and The House by the Sea (1977).

The pattern of May Sarton's life—the need to be creative and the need for loving friendships—was established early. The gifted child of gifted parents, Sarton began writing poetry by the age of nine. Her first poems were inspired by **Katherine Taylor**, the director of the innovative Shady Hill School, and by one of its finest teachers, **Anne Longfellow Thorp**, both of whom became "root" or lifelong friends of Sarton. As was the case with many other women poets, going back to *Sappho of ancient Greece, Sarton's muse was always a woman and usually a woman older than herself. In Sarton's poems, mind and heart, work and love, were inextricably entwined.

May Sarton was born Eléanore Marie Sarton at Wondelgem near Ghent, Belgium, on May 3, 1912, the only surviving child of George Sarton and **Mabel Elwes Sarton**, a talented artist and designer. While Sarton looked back on her childhood as a happy one, especially after she was enrolled at Shady Hill School at the age of five, her earliest years were traumatic. After the

German invasion of Belgium in 1914, she and her parents fled to England, taking temporary refuge with her mother's English relatives. A second uprooting came in 1916, when the family set sail for the still-neutral United States. Within a year, the Sartons settled permanently in Cambridge, Massachusetts, where George Sarton, already a highly respected scholar in the new field of the history of science, won a teaching appointment at Harvard University. He was to teach there until his retirement in the 1950s.

George Sarton was totally engrossed in his writing, editing and teaching and that, plus his inconsiderate treatment of Mabel, especially over money matters, alienated May from him until her mother's death in 1950. Sarton adored her mother, for it was Mabel who nourished her talents and her emotional needs, who took care of all the household details, and who worked to help pay for May's expenses at school and at summer camp. Mabel Sarton had a great gift for friendship, and her friends became May's friends as well. Later, women's friendships became a constant theme in all of May Sarton's novels.

In a tribute written in the '70s, Sarton wrote in *A World of Light* that through her mother, "I witnessed extreme awareness of all forms of beauty, and extreme sensitivity to human beings and human relationships. . . . Through my father I understood that a talent is something given, that it opens like a flower, but without exceptional energy, discipline and persistence will never bear fruit." Both parents were "the two people in the world I could feel in total communion about politics, art, religion, all that really matters."

While the Sartons all became American citizens in 1924 and lived in the United States for the rest of their lives, they never lost their European roots, returning to Europe regularly in the 1920s and 1930s and after World War II. In 1925, Sarton interrupted her studies at Shady Hill to attend the Institute Belge de Culture Française in Brussels for nine months. At the Institute, one of her teachers, **Marie Closset**, a poet who wrote under the pen name of Jean Dominique, became Sarton's next muse and a friend for life. Later, Closset became a central figure in Sarton's first novel, *The Single Hound* (1938).

Over a period of 68 years, from 1924 until her last visit to England in 1992, she made at least 25 trips, many by ocean liner, primarily to England, Belgium, and France. During one particularly magical summer, 1936, Sarton met many of England's leading writers and intellectuals, some of whom became root friends. These included the literary critics S.S. Koteliansky and

Basil de Selincourt, the writer *Elizabeth Bowen, and the zoologist Julian Huxley and his wife *Juliette Huxley. *Virginia Woolf, whom Sarton met on several occasions that summer and the next, haunted her for the rest of her days. Years later, Sarton wrote, "My heaven is Bloomsbury."

In 1926, Sarton graduated from Shady Hill School and entered the academically excellent Cambridge High and Latin School. While she was a student there, George Sarton took her to see *Eva Le Gallienne in Ibsen's *Hedda Gabler*. To his chagrin, his daughter fell in love with the theater, and in 1929 Sarton turned down a Vassar College scholarship to accept Le Gallienne's invitation to join her Civic Repertory Theater in New York as an apprentice. While George fumed (but agreed to provide his rebellious and stubborn daughter with a monthly allowance of $100), Mabel Sarton found safe housing for her daughter at the women's McLean Club near the Civic Repertory. During Sarton's four years with Le Gallienne's group, she studied many aspects of the theater, including acting, directing, and

May Sarton

translating and writing plays. Eva Le Gallienne became another of Sarton's lifelong friends, and there were no hard feelings when Sarton formed her own company in 1933, which closed after three years, a victim of the Depression.

Sarton's seven years in the theater were invaluable, for as **Elizabeth Evans** notes in *May Sarton Revisited*, Sarton "took with her excellent dramatic training . . . that has served her well, endowing her with a sense of audience, an awareness of timing, an instinct for character and conflict, an ability to convey emotion, and above all, an awareness of the well modulated speaking voice."

Sarton returned to her first love, writing, and in 1937 her initial volume of poetry, *Encounter in April*, was favorably reviewed. The following year, her first novel, *The Single Hound*, which was set in Europe, received excellent reviews by Orville Prescott in *The New York Times* and Basil de Selincourt in *The London Observer*. Encouraged, Sarton published her second volume of verse, *Inner Landscape*, in 1939. To support herself, she taught creative writing and choral speech at the Stuart School in Boston from 1937 to 1940; later she was to teach courses in writing and literature on temporary appointments at Radcliffe and Wellesley.

During World War II, Sarton satisfied her love of travel, her joy in making new friends, and her need to supplement her modest income by embarking on spring and fall lecture/poetry reading tours at colleges and universities in many regions of the United States. The tours introduced Sarton to succeeding generations of college students and were to become a yearly ritual until ill health forced her to end them in 1987. Although Sarton was not a college graduate (as was also true of two writers she much admired, Virginia Woolf and *Sylvia Townsend Warner), she found early and enduring support for her writings in academia.

In 1945, while vacationing in New Mexico, Sarton met **Judith Matlack**, an unmarried teacher 14 years her senior who taught at Simmons College in Boston. Within weeks, they became close friends, and on their return to Cambridge agreed to live together, a new experience for each of them. George and Mabel Sarton were happy to see their only child settle down at last, and every Sunday until their passing they welcomed their daughter and her gentle and considerate housemate to dinner. Meanwhile, Sarton was delighted to forge strong and lasting bonds with Judith's more numerous family.

Sarton and Matlack settled down to a comfortable routine: while Matlack taught at Simmons, Sarton spent about eight hours at her desk. After Matlack's return at four, they discussed their respective experiences of the day over a drink, and then went for an hour's walk. After a companionable dinner, Matlack graded papers while Sarton resumed work at her desk. Their household was enriched when they adopted a cat they named Tom Jones, who is the subject of one of Sarton's most endearing novellas, *The Fur Person* (1957). Sarton later recalled, in her writings and in interviews, that she spent the happiest years of her life with Matlack. They were certainly very productive years as well, for between 1945 and 1958 Sarton wrote six novels and four volumes of poetry.

In 1958, Sarton's life took a new direction when she decided to buy and restore an old farmhouse in Nelson, New Hampshire, some 85 miles from Cambridge. Many years later in her tribute to Matlack, *Honey in the Hive: Judith Matlack, 1898–1982* (1988), Sarton conceded that her decision to leave Judith was very hard on the latter. However, Sarton never conceded, except indirectly, that she left Matlack because she was in love with another woman. It appears that Matlack, who regretted that she never married, was never able to respond to Sarton's passionate needs. However, after Sarton's departure for New Hampshire they remained close friends until Matlack's death in 1982.

In Nelson, Sarton embarked on a new phase of her literary career, and in 1959 her first memoir, *I Knew a Phoenix*, was published. It was followed by three more memoirs, *Plant Dreaming Deep* (1968), *Journal of a Solitude* (1973), and *A World of Light* (1976). These autobiographical works, and the seven journals Sarton wrote between 1974 and 1994, sold very well and attracted a host of new readers to all of Sarton's writings.

The 15 years in Nelson were especially productive of poetry, and, inspired by one new muse after another, Sarton completed six volumes of verse. She also wrote seven novels, including two of her most highly esteemed works, *Mrs. Stevens Hears the Mermaids Singing* (1965) and *As We Are Now* (1973). The protagonists in both novels are older women, which had always been a constant in Sarton's fiction. What was new was that Mrs. Stevens is a lesbian poet who has come to terms with her sexual identity and is able to help a troubled young man accept his homosexuality. *As We Are Now* is the only novel Sarton ever wrote in which violence occurs, though offstage. The protagonist, Caroline Spencer, ends her life by burning down the nursing home where she and other inhumanely treated residents are confined.

In *Mrs. Stevens Hears the Mermaids Singing*, Sarton is both Mrs. Stevens and the young man struggling with his sexual identity. Despite the fact that Sarton was attracted to older women from her earliest years and appears to have had only one brief affair with a man (Julian Huxley), she was unable to come to terms with her preference for women until she was in her 40s. Like many women of her generation growing into adulthood at a time when lesbianism was viewed with horror, Sarton never came out to her parents, though Mabel Sarton must have been aware that her daughter was, at the very least, woman-centered. And fearful of the label "lesbian writer," Sarton postponed her coming out until she was an established writer. As she explained many times, she considered herself a full human being, a universal writer who wrote for all human beings—young and old, male and female, single or married, gay or straight—rather than a lesbian or woman writer.

With the publication of *Mrs. Stevens*, Sarton gained new readers while losing very few of her admiring fans. Her novel preceded the gay-rights movement by several years and lent the movement considerable support by portraying gays in a convincingly positive light. Sarton came out because she could afford to be honest, whereas lesbians in teaching and other professions who revealed their sexual orientation would very likely face ostracism and lose their jobs as well. Referring to *Mrs. Stevens Hears the Mermaids Singing*, Sarton wrote her good friend Basil de Selincourt, who had been supportive of her work for 30 years, that "now it is done, I doubt if the subject will come up again in any future work." Such was not the case. In Sarton's last two novels, *The Magnificent Spinster* (1985) and *The Education of Harriet Hatfield* (1989), she paid homage to women whose lifelong relationships with other women were accepted and understood by their families and friends.

In 1973, Sarton sold the house in Nelson and moved to a house rented from friends by the sea at York, Maine. Though Sarton dearly loved Nelson and was buried there, she found it too small and too isolated a community for a person past 60. York, on the other hand, was just over the border from Massachusetts and relatively close to Cambridge and Boston's Logan Airport. And York, an upscale summer resort area, had

many more doctors than Nelson, as well as an excellent hospital. The move proved to be a wise and fruitful one in every respect. Sarton had always been an ardent lover of nature, and the sight and sounds of the sea added new imagery and a new dimension to her poetry and prose. During her 20 years at York, Sarton continued her amazing productivity, completing seven volumes of poetry, five novels, two children's books, one memoir and seven journals before her death in 1995.

One reason why Sarton was so productive and more popular than ever during the last two decades of her life was the attention and recognition she received from feminist scholars like **Carolyn Heilbrun** of Columbia University. In 1985, Sarton wrote to a friend that after 1955 she became "old-fashioned, not interesting" to the (mostly male) literary critics. "It was Women's Studies which has brought me back." Beginning in 1972, panels on Sarton's writing were a regular feature at the annual meetings of the Modern Language Association, and courses on her work were offered at a number of colleges and universities. In addition, Sarton was the subject of two studies in the Twayne U.S. Authors Series, **Agnes Sibley**'s *May Sarton* (1972) and Elizabeth Evans' *May Sarton Revisited* (1988). Between 1982 and 1994, four collections of critical essays on her writings appeared, and three anthologies of her writing were also published. And in the 1980s, videos about Sarton or of Sarton reading from her work were also released.

Academia, which had always been supportive of Sarton, showered her with honors in the last decades of her life. She was the recipient of a record 18 honorary degrees, and it was standing-room only wherever Sarton read her poems, gave lectures, or signed copies of her books on college campuses throughout the country. In one of her last poems, "A Fortune," published in *Coming into Eighty*, she recalled that, when she was 34 and out of a job, a reader of tarot cards assured her that, in the end, she would finally achieve money, love, and fame.

> Now I am eighty
> The long game of solitaire
> Has ended
> Exactly as he said
> It must.

However, in addition to fame, love and success, there was also a great deal of illness, pain, and loss in Sarton's last 15 years. In her journal *Recovering* (1980), we learn that Sarton developed breast cancer and underwent a mastectomy in her 68th year. In the later 1980s, she suffered the first of a series of strokes, which, combined with a fibrillating heart, cancer of the lining of her left lung, and irritable bowel syndrome, left Sarton exhausted and depressed. "Everything hurts," she wrote in *Endgame: A Journal of the Seventy-Ninth Year* (1992), and it especially hurt that one by one she had to give up her greatest pleasures: gardening, long walks, traveling, giving lectures and readings, and long visits with friends far and near. The death of many of her older friends added to her anguish and loneliness. A woman of fierce independence, Sarton was forced by illness to accept dependence and rely more and more on help from her friends and those she paid to run errands and care for the house and garden.

Lacking the mental and physical energy to write novels after 1989, Sarton wrote journals, the last of which, *At Eighty-Two: A Journal* (1996), appeared posthumously. They were her lifesavers. Without them, she said, "life would seem empty and without purpose." The principal reason Sarton was able to continue the journals was that she gained a new lease on life after meeting **Susan Sherman** in the mid-1980s. Sherman was an English teacher at the Riverdale School in New York who, before she met Sarton, had spent years reading Sarton's letters and other unpublished writings stored in the Berg Collection of the New York Public Library. After they met, a great and lasting friendship developed between the two women, and they collaborated closely on *May Sarton: Among the Usual Days* (1993), a thematic compilation of excerpts from Sarton's letters and other unpublished writings edited by Sherman.

Sherman was an exemplary and loving friend—driving up to York on weekends, spending her summers with Sarton, and even taking a leave of absence from the Riverdale School one autumn in order to care for the increasingly frail Sarton. Sherman delighted Sarton by always arriving with an armful of flowers and by preparing elegant meals which were accompanied by animated conversation at the dinner table. For Sarton fans, it is comforting to know that her last years were made bearable by Sherman, who also served as a muse for poems that are included in Sarton's *Collected Poems, 1930–1993*. Sarton's very last muse, however, was a "fur person," her beloved cat Pierrot. Her final volume of poetry, *Coming Into Eighty* (1994), was dedicated "to Pierrot, the Muse Mews."

Her friend and literary executor, Carolyn Heilbrun, captured the essence of Sarton's life work when she wrote: "she has written of the old, the sick, the dispossessed, and of the joys and glories of life: flowers, birds, cats, sunrises, and of the endurance of love and the ephemerality and dangers of passion." While the literary establishment has been dismissive of much of her work, Sarton continues to touch the lives of an ever-widening circle of readers because she wrote about the things that really matter.

SOURCES:

Daziel, Bradford Dudley, ed. *Sarton Selected: An Anthology of the Journals, Novels and Poems of May Sarton.* NY: W.W. Norton, 1991.

Evans, Elizabeth. *May Sarton Revisited.* Boston: G.K. Hall, Twayne United States Authors Series, No. 551, 1989.

Hunting, Constance, ed. *May Sarton: Woman and Poet.* Orono, ME: University of Maine, 1982.

Ingersoll, Earl G., ed. *Conversations with May Sarton.* Jackson, MS: University Press of Mississippi, 1991.

Kallet, Marilyn, ed. *A House of Gathering: Poets on May Sarton's Poetry.* Knoxville, TN: University of Tennessee Press, 1993.

Peters, Margot. *May Sarton: A Biography.* NY: Alfred A. Knopf, 1997.

SUGGESTED READING:

Sarton, May. *As We Are Now.* NY: W.W. Norton, 1973.

———. *Collected Poems, 1930–1993.* NY: W.W. Norton, 1993.

———. *The House by the Sea.* NY: W.W. Norton, 1977.

———. *Mrs. Stevens Hears the Mermaids Singing.* NY: W.W. Norton, 1965.

———. *A World of Light: Portraits and Celebrations.* NY: W.W. Norton, 1976.

Anna Macías,
Professor Emerita of History,
Ohio Wesleyan University, Delaware, Ohio

Sartoris, Adelaide Kemble (1814–1879).

See Kemble, Adelaide.

Sas-Adler, Valentine (1898–1942).

See Adler, Valentine.

Sass, Marie Constance (1834–1907)

Belgian soprano. Name variations: Marie Sax. Born in Ghent on January 26, 1834; died in Auteuil near Paris on November 8, 1907; married the baritone Castelmary (divorced 1867).

Marie Constance Sass was born in Ghent in 1834. She was a chansonette-singer in a Paris café, singing under the name Marie Sax, before being discovered and taught by **Mme Ugalde**. Sass made her debut as a soprano at the Théâtre-Lyrique in 1859. She appeared at the Paris Opéra from 1860 to 1871, and in Italy in 1864.

Satchell, Elizabeth (c. 1763–1841).

See Kemble, Elizabeth.

Sati Beg (c. 1300–after 1342)

Il-Khanid queen of Persia. Reigned 1338–1339; born around 1300; died after 1342; niece of Mahmud Ghazan (1295–1304), Il-Khan; daughter of Oljeitu, an Il-Khan; sister of Abu Said; married Choban (a military amir, died); married Arpa Ke'un (died 1336); married Sulaiman; children: (first marriage) daughters Baghdad Khatun and Sorghan Shira.

Sati Beg, a Mongol descended from Genghis Khan, was the niece of Mahmud Ghazan, daughter of Oljeitu, and sister of Abu Said. Her family ruled the much-troubled kingdom of Persia, which was centered in the modern state of Iran, but also included parts of what are now Turkey, Syria, Iraq, Armenia, Azerbaijan, Turkmenistan, Afghanistan and Pakistan. The Mongol control of Persia came as a result of two invasions: Genghis Khan led the earlier and more destructive of these in 1220–21, while Hulegu Khan (Genghis' grandson) followed up with a second expedition in 1256. Initially, Hulegu planned to base himself in Persia as he pursued additional conquests farther west; it was his dream to create a Mongol empire stretching from the Mediterranean Sea to China. This dream, however, never materialized because of the successful resistance offered by the Mamluks, the Muslim masters of Egypt. For over 50 years, the Mongols struggled with the Mamluks (primarily in Syria), a conflict which debilitated Persia. The empire had suffered greatly with the coming of the Mongols, and constant warfare hindered any kind of recovery.

When it became obvious that the tide of Mongol conquest in the west had about run its course, it was decided that the Mongol state should be somewhat decentralized in order to permit the vast empire's localized problems to be faced regionally. The Great Khan ruling in China continued to be recognized as the supreme Mongol authority, but he no longer claimed direct rule over Persia. Instead, the so called Il-Khans came to govern that chaotic region (initially from their capital at Tabriz) as deputies of the Great Khan. These rulers—all the descendants of Genghis and Hulegu Khan—faced a difficult situation because of foreign wars and domestic unrest. Domestically, Persia was afflicted by two major problems. The first of these was religious: the Persia which the Mongols had conquered was Islamic (if torn between the Sunni and Shiite sects), although significant numbers of Buddhists, Christians and Jews lived within its boundaries. The Mongols, however, were initially pagans whose rule was not legitimate in the eyes of the Islamic majority. Hence, there was a crisis concerning the rule of law, with the only real justification for Mongol rule being "might makes right." A second major cause of discontent was taxation, which remained very high under the Mongols in order to pay for the Il-Khanate's many wars.

The greatest of the Il-Khans was Mahmud Ghazan (1295–1304), who began an accommodation with the majority of his subjects by converting to Islam. This helped to consolidate his religious and legal position and went a long way toward justifying Mongol rule to his non-Mongol subjects. Ghazan also did more than any of his Mongol predecessors to put a cap on taxation, to foster economic growth, and to constrain the arrogance of his kingdom's military aristocracy. Ghazan, however, died when he was only 33. He was succeeded by his brother, Khar-Banda, who adopted the throne name of Oljeitu ("Fortunate One"). Oljeitu attempted to further Ghazan's reforms but without as much success. This was due mostly to his primary interests which were more cultural and intellectual than his brother's. In a more peaceful time, Oljeitu may have been a greater king, but as things stood his dedication to the arts allowed others to assert more political and military autonomy than was good for his realm.

Oljeitu was also young (36) when he died in 1316. Unfortunately, his son and heir, Abu Said, was only 12 at the time of his accession. As a result, many chieftains sought personal advantage in rebelling against the new Il-Khan. Fortunately for Abu Said, however, others sought advantage in the defense of his authority. Chief among the latter was the military amir named Choban, a very capable figure with a large family which he put to work in Abu Said's interests. In 1319, Choban helped Abu Said to win a major victory against a rebellious coalition, and he became the Il-Khan's most trusted servant, a position which was publicly ratified by his marriage to Oljeitu's daughter (and Abu Said's sister) Sati Beg. The couple had two daughters, **Baghdad Khatun** and **Sorghan Shira**. Choban was much older than Sati Beg and already had several adult sons.

Thereafter, Choban saw to the entrenchment of his family's influence by the appointment of his sons to powerful positions: in particular, Temur Tash became the viceroy of Rum (Persian Anatolia) and Dimashq Khwaja became the viceroy of Azerbaijan. Despite the extent of Choban's influence, a serious break between him and Abu Said began in 1325. The first cause for this was the growing arrogance and dissolution of Dimashq Khwaja, who had begun to usurp the powers traditionally held by the Il-Khan's vizier. This ambition and the swagger with which it was displayed insulted the now adult Abu Said. A second problem between Abu Said and Choban arose when the Il-Khan became obsessed with Choban and Sati Beg's daughter Baghdad Khatun, who was already married. This did not deter Abu Said, who reportedly invoked an ancient tradition to the effect that the sovereign could claim any woman he wished, regardless of her current marital status. Choban, however, did what he could to douse Abu Said's passion, but his attempt to put some geographical distance between Abu Said and Baghdad Khatun only frustrated the Il-Khan and further inflamed his passion.

In 1326, a threat to Persia's eastern frontier sent Choban into the field on military business. While he was away from court, the arrogance of Dimashq Khwaja so embittered Abu Said that the Il-Khan had Choban's son executed, perhaps on trumped-up charges. Knowing that this was tantamount to declaring war against his powerful amir, Abu Said was ready to free himself of Choban's influence and to begin to rule independently. The struggle between the realm's two most important figures initially split the loyalties of its military class. During his return to the west for a showdown with Abu Said, however, Choban made the mistake of allowing his army to pillage much of the Persian countryside, a blunder which undoubtedly played a role in the desertion of a significant portion of his army on the eve of his would-be confrontation with Abu Said. Thus weakened, Choban retreated to the east, in the hope that he could rally the support he needed to avenge the death of his son. As he prepared for civil war, Choban sent Sati Beg and their child Sorghan Shira back to her brother Abu Said. A second assault against Abu Said never materialized, for Choban was captured by an ally of Abu Said and put to death. Thereafter, Temur Tash fled to Egypt where he was kept as a possible weapon against Persia until the political climate changed, and he, too, was executed. As a demonstration that it was his will which had carried the day, Abu Said married his niece Baghdad Khatun.

With Choban's fall, Abu Said began to rule for himself in earnest, although it was not until 1329 that he reduced the last major domestic threat to his authority. Even then, foreign enemies still existed. In 1335, Abu Said was on his way to deal with a raid led by one Oz Beg, when he was poisoned. Ironically, his murderer was Baghdad Khatun, who was jealous of a younger rival for Abu Said's affections. Heaping irony upon irony, this rival was her niece, Dil-Shad Khatun, the daughter of the same Dimashq Khwaja whom Abu Said had put to death.

Because Abu Said was the last of his direct line, when it came time for the Mongols to select a new Il-Khan they turned to a collateral branch of the ruling family. A majority supported Arpa Ke'un, who attempted to consolidate his control of the throne by marrying Sati Beg. Even with this marriage, however, Arpa Ke'un was unable to win unanimous support for his elevation and his short reign was beset by unrest: in 1336, his governor of Baghdad, Ali Padshah, joined in the disquiet, captured Arpa Ke'un, and had him executed. This murder made Sati Beg twice widowed and unleashed a general civil war which continued into 1338.

In that year, two power-brokers emerged as Persia's most important warlords: Hasan Buzurg (the husband from whom Abu Said had stolen Baghdad Khatun and thus the one-time son-in-law of Choban); and Hasan Kuchak (the son of Temur Tash and thus the grandson of Choban). Each of these rivals sought to be the power behind the throne of some puppet Il-Khan, whose only qualification for the office was that he or she was a descendant of Genghis Khan. Initially, Hasan Buzurg put forward a child named Muhammed as his claimant, but Hasan Kuchak captured and executed him. At the same time, Hasan Kuchak put forward Sati Beg as his choice for Il-Khan, a post she nominally held in 1338–39. The kingdom was too polarized, however, for Sati Beg ever to exert any real authority. To counter Hasan Kuchak's move, Hasan Buzurg next supported one Togha Temur but abandoned him thanks to a ruse devised by Hasan Kuchak. In a letter, Hasan Kuchak proposed the marriage of Sati Beg to Togha Temur, then he let the letter fall into the hands of Hasan Buzurg. Hasan Buzurg's next candidate was Jahan Temur, a move which was popular enough to induce Hasan Kuchak to depose Sati Beg in favor of one Sulaiman, whom Hasan Kuchak then forced Sati Beg to marry.

The two Hasans met in a battle in 1340 to decide the fate of the kingdom. Hasan Kuchak won this engagement, forcing Hasan Buzurg to flee to Baghdad where he jettisoned Jahan Temur and successfully established a new dynasty which severed Iraq, Kurdistan and Azerbaijan from the rest of Persia. As for Hasan Kuchak, he was murdered by his wife shortly after his victory. Sulaiman survived the death of Hasan Kuchak but was deposed, probably in 1342, by Kuchak's brother. Thereafter, Sati Beg and her last husband fall out of the historical record.

William Greenwalt,
Associate Professor of Classical History,
Santa Clara University, Santa Clara, California

Saucerotte, Françoise (1756–1815).

See Raucourt, Mlle.

Saunders, Cicely (1918—)

Founder of the hospice movement for the care of terminal cancer patients and head of St. Christopher's, London, Britain's first modern hospice. Name variations: Cicely Saunders until 1980; Mrs. Cicely Bohusz or Dame Cicely Saunders from 1980. Born in Barnet, north London, England, in 1918; daughter of Gordon Saunders (an estate agent) and Chrissie (Knight) Saunders; attended Roedean School, St. Anne's College, Oxford, and St. Thomas's Hospital, London; married Marian Bohusz-Szyszko (a Polish artist), in 1980; no children.

Worked as a nurse (1939–43); served as an almoner (medical social worker, 1945–51); served as a doctor (1951—); was a research scientist (1957–59); was founder and head of St. Christopher's Hospice (1963—); taught a semester at Yale School of Nursing (1965); was an advocate for compassionate care of the dying, writer, broadcaster, and speechmaker.

Cicely Saunders founded the modern hospice movement, to provide care for dying cancer patients, and established the first British hospice in 1963 (opened 1967). She realized that British doctors and hospitals were dedicated to attempting cures, and that patients who had no prospect of recovery were out of place in their hands. In the 1940s and 1950s, she was ahead of her time in recognizing the close connection between a patient's physical, emotional, and spiritual condition, and drew frequent connections between her medical work and her profound Christian faith. Her hospice, St. Christopher's, and its many imitators throughout the world, are dedicated to care of the whole person at the end of life, rather than taking a narrowly medical view.

Saunders was born in Barnet, north London, in 1918 into an argumentative, ambitious family. She was the oldest of three children and the only daughter. Her father Gordon Saunders was a successful real-estate agent in Barnet. Her mother **Chrissie Saunders**, withdrawn and moody, feuded with him, and the parents separated after 28 stormy years of marriage. Cicely grew up tall and awkward. She was materially privileged and attended Roedean, one of England's elite girls' boarding schools, but hated it, being lonely and shy. In her last years there, however, she began to come out of her isolation and was appointed head of her house. From there she moved, after a year in a "crammer," to St. Anne's College, Oxford, to study philosophy, politics, and economics.

The onset of the Second World War in 1939 decided her to switch to nursing after just one year, despite the opposition of her Oxford tutors. She trained at the *Florence Nightingale school, part of London's St. Thomas's Hospital, but after qualifying with distinction was unable to work as a war nurse because she was not physically strong enough. Saunders had slight curvature of the spine; the hard work made it worse, and led to a slipped disc and other orthopedic difficulties. Returning to Oxford, she finished her degree in 1945 then trained as an "almoner" (medical social worker) so that she could find another way into the helping professions. She already had an undefined sense that she would devote her life to aiding people in pain.

Volunteering to work evenings in St. Luke's hospital for the terminally ill, she learned to appreciate the importance of controlling pain with analgesic drugs, and they became central to her care philosophy thereafter. Further difficulties with her own health, and back surgery that year, made the problem of chronic pain something very close to her own experience.

The summer of 1945 not only saw her graduation; it was also the moment of her parents' emotionally exhausting separation (with her mother making threats of suicide) and of Cicely's own conversion to Christianity. She had had no formal religious upbringing, had declared herself an atheist at school, but now, after years of reading C.S. Lewis and other influential Christian writers, she was converted during a seaside vacation in Cornwall with a group of evangelical friends. Then and later, however, she was able to get along well not only with a wide variety of other Christians (the work of Catholic nuns was influential in her development of hospices) but also with agnostics and atheists, many of whom came to share her sense of mission.

Saunders' formative experience, and one she spoke of often in her subsequent career, was a meeting with David Tesma, a Polish Jew and refugee in England, who was dying of inoperable cancer in 1947. Her two-month contact with Tesma, and her recognition that hospitals offered him no place to die with dignity, resolved Saunders to create such a place. They fell in love and spent as much time as possible together even though he was desperately ill and confined to a hospital bed. Their time together made Saunders realize that the last moments of life can as easily be a time of emotional and personal growth as any other. He bequeathed her £500 in his will to start a hospice for terminal cancer patients and told her, "I will be the window in your home." That money became the nucleus of the funds for St. Christopher's even though 20 years were to pass before it opened. It is striking that when she fell in love again, 12 years later, the man was once again Polish, Antoni Michniewicz, and once again a terminal cancer patient in the last stages of his illness, whose death after a two-month romance brought her to an emotional collapse.

> To talk of accepting death when its approach has become inevitable is not mere resignation on the part of the patient nor defeatism or neglect on the part of the doctor. Certainly they will take no steps to hasten its coming, but for both of them it is the very opposite of doing nothing.
>
> —Cicely Saunders

Friends who sympathized with Saunders' ambition to create a care-center for terminal cancer patients urged her to train as a doctor, so that she could speak with authority in the medical community. Accordingly, she began medical school as a 33-year-old in 1951, back at St. Thomas's Hospital, and graduated in 1957. She also spent as much time as possible at St. Joseph's, a Catholic refuge for the incurably ill. The nuns there made up in enthusiasm and energy what they lacked in formal medical and nursing training, and the place provided a model for the kind of center Saunders would later create. Her advanced views on preventive pain control found a responsive audience among the nuns, and she began to lobby the British medical community for a new approach to medication. In her view, patients would be much happier, more easy to manage, have less sense of helpless dependency, and feel more confident, if they had ready and regular access to the painkillers they needed. Her experiments over a long period of time at St. Joseph's convinced her that this policy did not lead to addiction nor to the need for steadily increasing doses, which was then the orthodox view. She also favored oral over injected drugs, because they too gave the patient less sense of helplessness.

Another novelty in her treatment was her belief that it was best to tell terminal patients that they were in fact dying. Orthodox medical opinion preferred to continue holding out hope. At one point, working at St. Luke's as a visiting doctor, she answered a patient's question "Am I dying?" affirmatively and caused such dismay among the other doctors that she was asked to leave. Central to her philosophy from the 1940s on has been the belief that patients will benefit from preparing for their death rather than hoping vainly to avert it. Saunders realized, of course, and later taught her hospice's staff, that breaking news of this kind was momentous and often harrowing; they studied ways to prepare patients for the news and ways of discerning when they would be ready to learn it.

After years of study, advocacy, lobbying, fund-raising, and teaching, Saunders supervised the creation of a trust, which began work on St. Christopher's Hospice in Sydenham, south London, in 1963 and finished it four years later. Having come from a prosperous family and having been helped out financially by her father at crucial moments in her career, she had the faith that money was always available. She certainly proved to be an extremely talented fund raiser. With tales of her own experiences, and stories of suffering cancer victims, she spoke eloquently to individuals, trusts, and foundations, and was able to attract an influential and wealthy group of donors. A bishop laid the foundation stone and the hospice's first visitor—subsequently its official patron—was Princess *Alexandra of Kent. Like her near contemporary *Mother Teresa, then involved in similar work in Calcutta, Saunders knew just how to blend faith in God's mercy with hard-headed accountancy. Money was essential because she did not want the hospices to be developed or run by the National Health Service (NHS), the nationalized British system of healthcare since 1947. Private funding would offer her more control and more flexibility, but she was careful to work in close collaboration with influential NHS officers, to ensure that they would send and support poor patients, and that lack of funds would be no bar to admission.

Patients at St. Christopher's were treated with palliatives and painkillers sufficient to make the last days of their lives bearable. "With effective pain control," said Saunders, "you are giving the patient space to be themselves. Pain control allows the patient to complete their journey in the search for meaning. You can't tell another person what that meaning is, but you can give them value and help them find their own meaning."

She had also recognized, much earlier than most British doctors, that entire families are involved in the process of death. She therefore created far more liberal visiting hours for patients than conventional British medical facilities, and encouraged children to visit (most hospitals banned them). An on-site day-care center for the doctors' and nurses' own children, and a section for retired employees, added to the hospice's feeling of being a community integrated into daily life rather than shut away from it. Saunders recognized too that bereaved families often needed help when the patient had died, and arranged a "Pilgrims' Club" for them, under the guidance of a prominent psychologist, Dr. Colin Murray Parkes, who joined St. Christopher's staff.

Saunders' influence spread steadily. As longevity increased, terminal care was becoming a pressing issue throughout the developed world. Already renowned for her advocacy and research before St. Christopher's opened, she gave a speech at Yale's School of Nursing in 1963 which led to an invitation to teach there for a semester in 1965. **Florence Wald**, the Yale school's dean, went to work for a year at St. Christopher's soon after it opened. She and *Elisabeth Kübler-Ross, both great admirers of Saunders, were instrumental in spreading the ideals of the hospice movement in the United States, and the first American hospices opened in 1974. They, like English volunteers and supporters, found Saunders a charismatic and sometimes daunting figure, and they repeated the story of an American visitor who asked if she might touch the great founder. "No you can't. I bite," Saunders snapped, adding, "I am not a cult figure." Saunders made a point of working at the hospice into her late 60s, keeping in close touch with the doctors, nurses, and patients, and teaching a rising generation on the basis of her lifetime's experience. By the time she retired from active daily involvement, care for the dying had become an established part of medical practice.

Saunders married late in life. Her brief, sad romances with the two Polish men had drawn her to a study of Polish life and history. One day in December 1963, her eye was caught by a painting in a London gallery exhibition, *Christ Calming the Waters* by the Polish artist Marian Bohusz-Szyszko. She bought it for the chapel of the hospice, on which work had just begun, and wrote the artist a letter of thanks, explaining to him that it would be a source of inspiration to dying cancer patients. He responded by offering her, as a gift, one of his major canvases. They met, and soon fell in love. Though he was married, his wife was still in Poland, behind the Iron Curtain, and they had been separated since 1939. Being a descendant of the haughty Polish Catholic aristocra-

cy and a political refugee, he refused either to be divorced or to accept what might be construed as the charity of a well-to-do English woman. His wife died in 1975, however, by which time he and Saunders had been living together for a decade. Finally, in 1980 he and Saunders married quietly, without alerting any of their friends, families, or admirers. He was already 79 and she 61, but he lived on to the age of 93.

In her 60s, Saunders began to spend more time away from St. Christopher's, visiting hospices around the world, arranging conferences, and still working hard at fund raising. She also lobbied to have the type of terminal care she had pioneered integrated throughout the British medical system rather than confining it solely to hospices. In 1980, she was made a Dame of the British Empire by Queen *Elizabeth II and in 1989 received the Order of Merit, another high honor. She was often asked to speak, broadcast, and write, and published or edited a long series of books and articles on the care of the terminally ill, despite her claim that writing was a terrible struggle for her.

Saunders remained an energetic and controversial figure into her 80s. She was particularly opposed to the voluntary and assisted suicide movement led, in America, by Dr. Jack Kevorkian. "Human nature being what it is," she told a reporter, "euthanasia . . . would not stay voluntary for very long. . . .To legalize the killing of patients is a very dangerous thing to do. You the patient are saying your life is not worth living and I, the doctor, am saying I agree with you." In her view it was much better to palliate the suffering and to counteract the patient's feeling of worthlessness; to her, the last days of life were still an opportunity for personal and spiritual growth. She feared that legalized euthanasia would put intolerable pressure on sick and elderly people to end their own lives prematurely, aware of the liability they might become for their relatives. Of her own impending demise, Saunders told a reporter in 1998: "Everyone else would like to have a stroke on the golf course, but I'd rather have cancer, because it does give us a chance to say thank you, and I'm sorry, and good-bye."

SOURCES:

Downey, Marion. "Founding Light of Hospices Brings Message of Life," in *Sydney Morning Herald*. July 18, 1998.

du Boulay, Shirley. *Cicely Saunders: Founder of the Modern Hospice Movement*. NY: Amaryllis Press, 1984.

Katz, Helena. "A Career of Compassion," in *McGill Reporter*. November 6, 1997.

Saunders, Cicely. *The Management of Terminal Malignant Disease*. London: Edward Arnold, 1984.

————, and Mary Baines. *Living with Dying: The Management of Terminal Disease*. Oxford: Oxford University Press, 1989.

————, and Robert Kastenbaum, eds. *Hospice Care on the International Scene*. NY: Springer, 1997.

COLLECTIONS:

St. Christopher's Hospice, Sydenham, UK; records of the National Health Service, UK.

Patrick Allitt,
Professor of History,
Emory University, Atlanta, Georgia

Saunders, Doris (1921—)

African-American publisher and journalist. Born Doris Evans on August 8, 1921, in Chicago, Illinois; daughter of Alvesta Stewart Evans and Thelma (Rice) Evans; attended Northwestern University, 1938–40; attended Central YMCA College, 1940–41; Roosevelt University, B.A., 1951; Boston University, M.S. and M.A., 1977; attended Vanderbilt University, 1983–84; married Sydney S. Smith (divorced); married Vincent E. Saunders, Jr., on October 28, 1950 (divorced August 1963); children: (second marriage) **Ann Camille Saunders***; Vincent E. Saunders III.*

Established and operated Plus Factor and Information Public Relations (1966); wrote and associate produced "Our People" on WTTW-TV (1968–70).

Doris Saunders was born Doris Evans in 1921 in Chicago, the daughter of Alvesta Stewart Evans and **Thelma Rice Evans**. When her father died during her teenage years, her mother went to work to support the family. From that point on, Saunders and her family lived with her maternal grandparents. While a student at Englewood High School, Saunders developed a mentor-ward relationship with *****Charlemae Hill Rollins**, then the children's librarian at the Hall Branch Library, which had a pronounced affect on young Saunders' future. After high school, she studied at Northwestern University from 1938 until 1940, then transferred to Central YMCA College from 1940 to 1941, at which time she entered an on-the-job training program with the Chicago Public Library system. She remained with that civil service system through 1949, being promoted from junior library assistant to principal reference librarian.

Saunders eventually lost patience with the biased environment at the Chicago Public Library, and on February 1, 1949, accepted a position as librarian for the Johnson Publishing Company, publisher of *Ebony*. She acquired her job, which did not exist prior to her application, on ingenuity. Because of her efforts, the Johnson library would become an important reference library, specializing in contemporary black history during the 20th century. Later, in 1960, she convinced publisher John H. Johnson to create another position for her to oversee an innovative project producing hardcover titles about African-Americans and African-American history. In this capacity, Saunders was responsible for such publications as *Before the Mayflower* by Lerone Bennett, Jr.

In 1966, Saunders founded a public-relations firm, Plus Factor and Information. She contributed articles to the *Chicago Daily Defender* and hosted "The Doris Saunders Show," a lunchtime radio talk show on WBEE in Chicago. She later wrote and associate produced "Our People" for WTTW-TV. At Chicago State University, she served as the director of community relations in 1968, with expanded duties from 1970 to 1972 as acting director of institutional development. Saunders then returned to work for Johnson Publishing, prior to her enrollment in postgraduate studies at Boston University for one year. In 1977, she emerged with a master of science degree in journalism and a master of arts degree in African-American studies. She attended doctoral courses in history at Vanderbilt University from 1983 to 1984. As time permitted, Saunders continued to publish books for Johnson, including one of her own written with **Geraldyn Major**, *Black Society* (1976).

During her years at the Chicago Public Library System, Saunders married and divorced Sydney S. Smith. On October 28, 1950, she married Vincent E. Saunders, Jr., an educator from Chicago. The couple divorced in August 1963, after having two children, Ann Camille and Vincent III. Saunders' professional involvement includes memberships in the National Association of Media Women and the Black Academy of Arts and Letters. She served the Illinois Chapter of the American Civil Liberties Union as a board member, and is a member of the Chicago Leadership Resource Program. Saunders also was a member of the Black Advisory Commission for the 1980 U.S. Census.

SOURCES:

Smith, Jessie Carney, ed. *Notable Black American Women*. Detroit, MI: Gale Research, 1992.

Gloria Cooksey,
freelance writer, Sacramento, California

Saunders, Marshall (1861–1947)

First Canadian author to sell over one million copies of a single book. Born Margaret Marshall Saunders on April 13, 1861, in Milton, Nova Scotia; died on February 15, 1947; daughter of Edward Manning Saun-

ders (a minister) and Maria K. (Freeman) Saunders; never married; no children.

Selected writings: (children) Beautiful Joe: The Autobiography of a Dog *(1893),* Deficient Saints *(1899),* A Tale of Maine *(1899),* Beautiful Joe's Paradise *(1902),* Princess Sukey *(1905),* The Wandering Dog *(1914),* Esther de Warren *(1927); (adult)* The Girl from Vermont *(1910).*

Marshall Saunders was born on April 13, 1861, the eldest child of the Reverend Edward M. Saunders and **Maria Freeman Saunders**, both of whose ancestry in the New World dated back to the Pilgrims' landing at Plymouth Rock. Saunders was born in the house of her maternal grandparents in Milton, a town in the vicinity of Liverpool, Nova Scotia. She lived with her family in the Annapolis Valley in the town of Berwick until 1867, when her father, a Baptist cleric, was reassigned to a church in Halifax, Nova Scotia. When Saunders was 15 years old and ready to attend finishing school, she went to Scotland to study in Edinburgh. She remained abroad for two homesick years, including time spent for enrichment purposes in Orléans, France. When she returned home in 1879, she worked as a schoolteacher. Recognizing her talent, her father encouraged her to write.

Saunders, who was content in her home life, wrote frequently about her surroundings. She was adept at weaving elaborate plots in emulation of those authors whose works her parents most respected—Charles Dickens and Sir Walter Scott. Her earliest works appeared in periodicals when she was 23. Later she began to work on book-length manuscripts with involved, dramatic plots. Her first book *My Spanish Sailor* appeared in 1889. Her second, *Beautiful Joe: The Autobiography of a Dog* (1893), was her most famous, and the only one to remain in print by the end of the 20th century. The story's protagonist-narrator, a dog named Joe, was modeled after an Ontario friend's pet whose ears and tail had been mutilated by its previous owner. The family in the narrative resembled her own, especially Miss Laura, based on Saunders' own sister Laura, who had died at age 17. The book, reissued as *Beautiful Joe: An Autobiography* in 1894, had been written in part as an entry for a Boston-based writing contest, and Saunders had won $200 for the story. She wrote a sequel, *Beautiful Joe's Paradise; or, The Island of Brotherly Love,* in 1902.

Saunders lived in Boston from 1895 to 1898, at which time she relocated to California for two years. Thereafter, she traveled throughout Europe and North America, writing and ob-

serving subjects for her work. She settled in Toronto, Ontario, with one of her younger sisters and a few house pets. Saunders was extremely fond of domestic animals, as was clearly demonstrated by the many animal stories that she wrote. The animals in her writing, notes **Carole Gerson**, "are able to remember, record, and present (with the aid of a human amanuensis) complex information at the intellectual level of a nine-year-old child." Along with encouraging humane treatment of animals, Saunders advocated for the rights of children and often used animals to parallel their vulnerability. In her only work geared to an adult audience, *The Girl from Vermont: The Story of a Vacation School Teacher* (1910), she affirmed her ideas about social justice for the young.

Saunders concluded her writing career in 1927 with her final novel *Esther de Warren: The Story of a Mid-Victorian Maiden,* her personal favorite. Because of poor financial management and harder-to-come-by publishers, she was forced to pursue supplementary income aggressively during the 1920s and 1930s, touring the country with her sister **Grace**, giving slide presentations of "Marshall Saunders and Her Pets" and "Marshall Saunders: Her Life and Literary Adventures." Aging and in failing health, she withdrew increasingly to her residence in Toronto beginning in 1940, assisted for a time by the Canadian Writers' Foundation. She died in relative poverty in February 1947.

Through her work, Saunders attacked such social issues as urbanization and child labor. She successfully attracted international attention to her activist policies in opposition to child exploitation and inhumane treatment of animals. Saunders received an honorary M.A. degree from Acadia University in 1911, and in 1934 she was created a commander of the Order of the British Empire.

SOURCES:
Gerson, Carole. "Margaret Marshall Saunders," in *Dictionary of Literary Biography.* Vol. 92. *Canadian Writers, 1890–1920.* Detroit, MI: Gale Research.
Kunitz, Stanley J., and Howard Haycraft, eds. *Twentieth Century Authors.* NY: H.W. Wilson, 1942.

Gloria Cooksey,
freelance writer, Sacramento, California

Saunderson, Mary (d. 1712).

See Bracegirdle, Anne for sidebar.

Sauvé, Jeanne (1922–1993)

Canadian feminist who was the first woman to be appointed governor-general of Canada. Name varia-

tions: Jeanne Sauvé. Pronunciation: Zhahn So-VAY. Born Jeanne Mathilde Benoît on April 26, 1922, at Prud'homme, Saskatchewan; died on January 26, 1993, in Montreal, Quebec; fifth child of Charles Benoît (a building contractor) and Anna (Vaillant) Benoît; attended Notre Dame du Rosaire Convent, Ottawa, the University of Ottawa, as well as the University of Paris, graduating with a diploma in French civilization, 1952; married Maurice Sauvé, in 1948; children: Jean-François Sauvé (b. 1959).

On October 29, 1984, the new governor-general of Canada was officially sworn into office in an impressive ceremony in the nation's capital, Ottawa. A non-political post, the governor-general is intended to act as the official emissary to Queen *Elizabeth II, representing the interests of all Canadians. What made this particular ceremony unique was the fact that, for the first time in the history of the office, the honor was granted to a woman: Jeanne Sauvé.

She was born on April 26, 1922, in the tiny hamlet of Prud'homme, located about 30 miles north of Saskatoon, Saskatchewan. She was the fifth of seven children of Charles and **Anna Benoît** who had migrated from Quebec ten years previously. Her father was a building contractor who specialized in the construction of small Catholic churches and nunneries. Both parents were native French speakers who strongly believed in the importance and value of Canada's Francophone heritage. These values, however, were difficult to impart in the predominantly Anglophone atmosphere of Saskatchewan where, at that time, there were few French-language schools.

[She was] from the great race of pioneering women who opened the door of Canada's highest institutions to women.

—Pierre Trudeau

Shortly after Jeanne was born, two of her older sisters had been sent east to Ottawa in order to receive their education. The Benoîts, however, were not happy to see their family break up in this manner. Accordingly, in 1925, they abandoned their business in Saskatchewan so that the entire family could be together in the nation's capital.

When Jeanne was six, she began to attend the Notre Dame du Rosaire Convent, a prominent religious school run by the Grey Nuns. For the next 12 years, she consistently impressed her teachers with her keen intelligence (she was always top of her class) and her unselfish willing-

ness to help her fellow students. She took an active part in team sports and games, and developed an excellent command of the English language and a reputation as a self-confident student who could eloquently and forcefully make her point of view understood.

Sauvé would later recall two of the most prominent influences which affected her during this period. First, the surroundings of the convent school instilled in her a sense of religious devoutness which she was to retain for the rest of her life. Second, when she was ten, her father took her on a visit to the House of Commons in the Canadian Parliamentary building. Just outside the chamber stood a bust of *Agnes Macphail, the first woman to be elected to the House. According to Sauvé, her father pointed to the bust and told his daughter that some day she too would become a famous politician.

This mixture of religion and politics proved a powerful attraction. When she was 15, Sauvé joined the Jeunesse Étudiante Catholique (JÉC), one of several Catholic action organizations which then existed in Quebec. Many of these, such as Lionel Groulx's L'Association Catholique de la Jeunesse Canadienne-Français (ACJC), combined a fierce commitment to Quebec nationalism with a very conservative attitude against any form of change to the social structure (particularly the place of women in that structure). The JÉC was distinct, however, in that its members advocated not only the continuance of Quebec within the Canadian federation (albeit with some amelioration in its position), but also certain mild left-wing proposals for enhancing social change and reform.

Sauvé was an active member of the JÉC throughout her remaining years at the convent school. Just prior to her graduation in 1940, she won a scholarship to the University of Ottawa for a Bachelor of Arts degree. She was keen to take up this scholarship, but her father refused to permit it on the grounds that, although generous, it would not be sufficient to cover all her expenses for a full-time education. Deeply disappointed, she eventually managed to make her father agree to a compromise. If she were allowed to take night classes at the university, she would support herself with a regular job during the day. Fortunately, Jeanne soon managed to secure a well-paying position with the federal government as a French-English translator in the Department of National Defense.

Although she greatly enjoyed her university studies, Sauvé became increasingly dissatisfied with the slow pace towards her degree. Accordingly, when two years later, in 1942, she was offered the opportunity to move to Montreal to take up a position as president of the women's section of the JÉC, she willingly agreed. Sauvé's tenure as president proved to be an exciting and invigorating experience. She quickly developed into a first-class public speaker and a highly capable administrator. Moreover, she was introduced to a number of young, dynamic intellectuals, such as Pierre Trudeau, Marc Lalonde, and Gerard Pelletier, who were determined to put into practice their shared views about the place of Quebec in Canada and the need for social re-

form. Finally, she met and fell in love with her future husband, Maurice Sauvé.

In his youth, Maurice had been a strong Quebec nationalist, but his views had modified substantially thanks to his growing awareness that Francophones and Anglophones shared a common interest in a strong, united Canada. He had been the first French-Canadian to be elected president of the National Federation of Canadian University Students and was already a qualified lawyer when he met Jeanne. In 1948, however, he received a scholarship to study at the

Jeanne
Sauvé

London School of Economics in England and, before leaving, he decided to marry. Maurice had clear criteria for a wife; she must be an equal, independent, and willing to pursue her own career. Jeanne fitted these requirements and the subsequent success of their marriage testified to Maurice's insight into her character.

The day after their marriage, the couple set sail for London. For the next two years, Sauvé worked at a series of minor jobs, while her husband worked at his doctoral degree in economics. In 1950, they moved to Paris where both registered at the Sorbonne campus of the University of Paris. While Maurice finished his doctorate, Jeanne managed to complete a diploma course in French civilization and, at the same time, worked part-time in the youth section of the United Nations Educational, Scientific, and Cultural Organization (UNESCO).

The Sauvés returned to Montreal in the summer of 1952 where both found work as union organizers for the Canadian Federation of Labour. Neither was entirely comfortable at this task, and Maurice soon left to take on new responsibilities as a consultant to the Royal Commission on the Economy which convened in Ottawa. Jeanne meanwhile began her own new career as a journalist for the Canadian Broadcasting Corporation (CBC) and its sister French-language network Radio-Canada. Over the next 20 years, she became one of the country's most distinguished public broadcasters, widely regarded as an astute interviewer and insightful commentator on the major political issues of the day. She won many plaudits for the integrity and intelligence which she brought to current affairs programming and for the skill with which she could present difficult and complex issues to the listening public. Sauvé, it is fair to say, set new standards of excellence in broadcasting which have rarely been surpassed to this day.

Her position as a journalist also kept her in regular contact with her old friends Trudeau, Lalonde, and Pelletier who by this time were becoming leading members of the federal Liberal Party. Trudeau would become prime minister of Canada in 1968 and Lalonde would serve as his minister of finance. This political connection was also strengthened by her husband Maurice's decision to enter Parliament. He had originally joined the Liberal Party in 1958 and had won election to the House of Commons four years later. In 1964, he was appointed a Cabinet minister with responsibility for forests and rural development in the government of then prime minister Lester Pearson.

At the end of the 1960s, the great political question in Canada revolved around the position of Quebec in the nation. Trudeau, along with his federal and provincial colleagues, searched vainly for some compromise which would recognize the uniqueness of Francophone Quebec while keeping Canada as a whole united. On the other hand, an increasingly strident nationalist movement began to call for nothing less than the recognition of Quebec as an independent, sovereign country. Matters came to a head in 1970, when a terrorist group—the Front de la Libération du Quebec (FLQ)—launched a series of bombings, kidnappings and murders that eventually led to the government's imposition of the War Measures Act, which effectively curtailed a range of civil and political liberties in Quebec.

Sauvé was deeply concerned with these developments but felt that her position as a public broadcaster did not allow her to fully express her own views on the issues. It was in these circumstances that she decided to abandon journalism and enter politics. As always, Maurice, who had recently lost his own seat in Parliament, encouraged his wife in her decision. Thus, in the general election of 1972, Sauvé was elected as the Liberal Party member for the Quebec riding (district) of Laval des Rapides. She was 50 years of age.

Prime Minister Trudeau immediately invited Sauvé to join the federal Cabinet (she was the first woman from Quebec to be awarded this distinction). Her initial portfolio was as minister of science and technology, where her background training in broadcasting allowed her to make significant contributions, particularly in the area of telecommunications policy. Reelected at the general election in 1974, Sauvé was then assigned to the ministry of the environment before switching to the newly created department of communications a year later.

Following a brief period in 1979 when the Conservative Party held office, the Liberals resumed power in 1980. Trudeau, however, did not want Sauvé back in the Cabinet as he suspected her of covertly supporting one of his opponents in a recent challenge to his leadership. On the other hand, she was too prominent a politician to be simply demoted. He decided instead to appoint Sauvé as (the first woman) speaker of the House of Commons. The holder of this post has a key role to play in the parliamentary system, as he or she regulates all debates and ensures that proper legal and procedural practices are followed in the House.

Sauvé later described her first months in this position as sheer torture. She was slow to learn the names of all 282 members of Parliament and was often too confused to note whether she had accepted equal numbers of questions from the government and opposition sides of the House. Often entangled in points of order and points of privilege, she gave rulings that were angrily rejected by one side or the other. Under her control, debates in the House degenerated into slinging matches and, on more than one occasion, all business had to be abandoned until order could be restored.

Although Sauvé worked hard to learn members' names and memorize the standing orders governing the House's business, she continued to be viewed as a weak speaker. It was not until 1982, when she suggested procedural reforms concerning the way in which parliamentary debates were conducted, that members of Parliament and the media began to show some grudging respect for her efforts. On the other hand, her work in administrating the House met with greater success. She was always an able organizer and set about to cut spending by disposing of many of the perks and privileges which members enjoyed. Sauvé also instituted personnel policies based on merit and a new accounting system for supplies and services. Moreover, she improved security services around the House of Commons and also introduced a daycare center for Commons staff.

When she eventually stepped down from the position in 1984 (following the Liberal Party's defeat in an election), Sauvé was emotionally and physically drained. She began to suffer from a serious respiratory illness, and for a short time her life was believed to be in danger. Her only thoughts were of retiring with her husband to their home in Montreal.

Not surprisingly, when she was first asked by the new Conservative prime minister Brian Mulroney to become governor-general of Canada, Sauvé's instinct was to refuse. On reflection, however, she realized that this position offered her a unique opportunity to promote those principles of Canadian unity that she had argued for throughout her life. For the next six years, Sauvé earned a reputation for the dignity and flair with which she represented the people of Canada at official events at home and abroad.

In 1990, Sauvé stepped down as governor-general and retired to Montreal. She remained active by establishing the Foundation Jeanne Sauvé, a charitable trust which seeks to bring together youth leaders from around the world. Her greatest tragedy, however, was the death of her husband Maurice in 1992. After that her own health rapidly deteriorated. Early in January 1993 she was admitted to hospital in Montreal, where it was discovered that her respiratory condition had given rise to cancer. She died later that month and was honored by the Canadian government with a state funeral.

SOURCES:

Clockie, Hugh. *Canadian Government and Politics.* Toronto: Longmans, 1984.

Jackson, Robert. *Politics in Canada.* Scarborough: Prentice-Hall Canada, 1986.

Woods, Shirley E. *Her Excellency Jeanne Sauvé.* Toronto: Macmillan, 1986.

SUGGESTED READING:

Brooks, Stephen. *Canadian Democracy.* Toronto: McClelland and Stewart, 1993.

COLLECTIONS:

A selection of Jeanne Sauvé's private papers are held in the National Archives of Canada.

Dave Baxter,
Department of Philosophy, Wilfrid Laurier University,
Waterloo, Ontario, Canada

Savage, Augusta (1892–1962)

African-American sculptor and teacher whose work and educational endeavors helped increase opportunities for other black artists. Born Augusta Christine Fells on February 29, 1892 (some sources cite 1900), in Green Cove Springs, Florida; died on March 26, 1962; daughter of Reverend Edward Fells and Cornelia (Murphy) Fells; briefly attended Tallahassee State Normal School (now Florida Agricultural and Mechanical State University); attended Cooper Union Art Program, 1921–24; studied with George Brewster, 1929–30; studied with Félix Beauneteaux, at the Grand Chaumière, France; studied with Charles Despiau, in France; married John T. Moore, in 1907 (died); married James Savage, around 1915 (divorced early 1920s); married Robert L. Poston, in October 1923 (died 1924); children: (first marriage) Irene Connie Moore (b. 1908).

Won the Julius Rosenwald Fellowship (1929 and 1931); was the first African-American member of the National Association of Women Painters and Sculptors (1934); won citations at the Salon d'Automne and the Salon de Printemps at the Grand Palais, Paris; was awarded a medallion at the Colonial Exposition in France.

Selected works: bronze bust of W.E.B. Du Bois, New York Public Library (1922); Lift Every Voice and Sing, *New York World's Fair (1939).*

Destined to be called "one of the nation's most distinguished black artists of the Harlem Renaissance and beyond," Augusta Savage was born in 1892 in Green Cove Springs, Florida, where she worked the red clay, which was native to the area, into a source for her early creativity. "At the mud pie age," she later noted, "I began to make 'things' instead of mud pies." Inspired to share her skills with others even in her youth, she instructed siblings and friends in her sculpting technique. Savage's father, however, was by no means pleased with the works his young daughter produced. A minister who worked as a house painter, he regarded her creations as "graven images" and punished her repeatedly for her efforts. "My father licked me five or six times a week and almost whipped all the art out of me," she said, but she did not let his aggression put an end to her activities; rather, she took care to keep her work hidden from him.

In 1907, while in her mid-teens, she married John T. Moore, with whom she had a daughter, **Irene Connie Moore**, the next year. John died while Irene was still a child. Around the time Augusta married a carpenter and laborer named James Savage, she relocated in 1915 to West Palm Beach, Florida. There, a local pottery factory provided her with clay, and when a statue of *Mary the Virgin was among the pieces she produced, her father began to relent and accept her talents. Local attention also resulted from this work and opened the door for Savage to teach a class in clay modeling to her fellow high-school students for six months. From sculptures of animals, her work evolved to increasingly challenging subjects. Noticed by country-fair superintendent George Currie, she was provided an opportunity to display her work at the country fair, earning $25 in prize money. This sum was increased by local contributions until she was able to support a stint in Jacksonville where she produced busts for wealthy blacks in hopes of generating enough income for formal art training. Although this venture did not prove lucrative, her goal would be achieved after she made her way to New York.

Arriving in Manhattan during 1920 with $4.60 to her name, Savage went to work as an apartment caretaker. A letter of introduction from Currie to the sculptor Solon Borglum made possible her entrance to Cooper Union, where she studied largely with sculptor George Brewster. Cooper Union provided a four-year art program which was tuition free, but, after Savage lost her job three months into her studies, she could not afford living expenses. The school's director provided her with a scholarship so that she could continue, and she took an inexpensive room in Upper Harlem to make ends meet.

Her studies in African art at the 135th Street branch of the New York Public Library brought her to the attention of librarian **Sadie Peterson (Delaney)**. Through Peterson's efforts, Savage received a commission for a portrait of NAACP founder W.E.B. Du Bois for the library. This work, which is still regarded as the finest likeness of Du Bois ever produced, earned her portrait commissions for other black leaders, including of Marcus Garvey, who sat for the sculptor in his Harlem apartment. In addition to the financial support they represented, these commissions earned Savage the black community's recognition.

She became an even more recognizable figure when a summer-school program at France's Palace of Fountainebleau, which was under the auspices of the French government, rejected her application in an overtly racist attempt to exclude Savage because she was black (this was publicly admitted by the selection committee's chair for painting and sculpture). Savage took the matter to the press, and her case was argued by Alfred Martin of the Ethical Culture Society and prominent anthropologist Franz Boas. While the issue was addressed in articles in *The New York Times*—and other leading newspapers, including the *Nation,* lent their voices to the protest—Savage did not gain admittance to the school. However, Hermon MacNeil, a committee member, did not hide his shame of the incident and invited Savage to work with him at College Point, an offer she accepted. "Meanwhile," notes **Jessie Carney Smith**, "Savage became known as a talented troublemaker to be avoided. It has been suggested that the prominent white critics, museum heads, artists, and dealers saw to it that she was excluded from exhibits and galleries."

Neither her experiences with bigotry nor difficulties in her personal life kept Savage from continuing her work. Her third marriage, in October 1923 to journalist and Marcus Garvey associate Robert L. Poston, ended with Poston's death less than six months later (March 1924).

In 1925, Countess **Irene Di Robilant** provided Savage with scholarship funds so that she could study at Rome's Royal Academy of Fine Arts. To raise money for travel expenses, Savage took employment in a laundry. Unable to come up with enough funds to both see to her family matters and make her way to Italy, she was unable to accept Di Robilant's gift. Her luck changed in 1929 when she was awarded the first of two Julius Rosenwald fellowships (the second in 1931). This honor was particularly influenced by what was to become the most popular of Savage's statues, *Gamin,* a portrait of an attractive

Harlem boy. Note Bearden and Henderson, the head she sculpted "caught the vitality, the humanity, the tenderness, and the wisdom of a boy child who has lived in the streets." By the time she won the first Rosenwald fellowship, Onorio Ruotolo, Antonio Salemme, and Hermon MacNeil were among those with whom she had studied, and Savage had developed significant contacts, including the Carnegie Corporation's Frederick P. Keppel who endorsed her fellowship application.

Savage also studied with the sculptor Victor Salvatore who expressed the hope that she would "consider her future work largely in rela-

tion to her own people." This thought was echoed by Rosenwald official George Arthur; while she was studying in Paris during 1930, he offered this advice:

[Avoid becoming] too much imbued with European standards of technique, if they are going to kill the other something which in my opinion some Negro will eventually give to American art, maybe in sculpture, maybe in music, painting or literature. . . . There is just one field in which the Negro has an equal chance with the white man in American life and that field is art. If he follows standards or even the white Americans,

Augusta
Savage

which in turn have copied them from Europe, then the Negro can at best be but a copy of the copy.

While in Paris, Savage had private study with Félix Beauneteaux and Mademoiselle Hadjii at the Grand Chaumière and later with Charles Despiau. Several European galleries showed her work, and she earned citations at the Salon d'Automne and Paris' Salon Printemps at the Grande-Palais, as well as a medallion at the Colonial Exposition. From the Carnegie Corporation, she received another grant which financed her travels in France, Belgium, and Germany.

She returned to New York in 1931, and her work was shown for a second time in a Harmon Foundation exhibit during 1930–31 (her first showing with the foundation had been in 1928). She concentrated on sculptured portraits while working to instruct others in her field. Active in enrolling black artists in the Works Progress Administration's Federal Art Project (FAP), she provided them with studio space at the school she established, Savage Studio of Arts and Crafts. In the 1930s, her students' exhibitions received positive recognition, as did her own work; William Artis, Norman Lewis, and Jacob Lawrence were among those of her students who would receive national attention as artists.

Savage became the first African-American to win election to the National Association of Women Painters and Sculptors (1934). By 1936, she had accepted a position as assistant supervisor of the FAP for New York City. As the Harlem Community Art Center's first director (1937), she worked to develop recreational, artistic, and educational programming. She was also among the main organizers of the Harlem Artists Guild, of which she became the second president.

As one of four women, and the only black woman, commissioned to execute a sculptural work for the 1939–40 New York World's Fair, Savage produced her most famous piece entitled *Lift Every Voice and Sing*. Smith describes the work as a "sixteen-foot harp composed of blacks of various sizes and ages, who lift their voices to sing and form strings, tapered from each head to the base. A mammoth forearm and hand with fingers curved upward, representing the Creator, form the base. In front, the kneeling figure with outstretched arms offers the gift of black music to the world." Unfortunately, funds were not available to have the piece cast in bronze and it was destroyed following the exhibition; photographs of the work remain, however, as testament to Savage's talent. While working on *Lift Every Voice and Sing*, the artist took leave from the Harlem Art Center to complete the project, and she was later disappointed to find that in her absence she had been replaced.

In June 1939, a corporation which Savage headed opened the Salon of Contemporary Negro Art. This was the country's first gallery dedicated to showing and selling art produced by African-Americans. Despite its important work, the gallery had to shut its doors after only a few years because funds were unavailable to keep it running. In the following years, Savage's participation in art promotion and instruction, as well as her own production, declined. After relocating to Saugerties in New York's Catskill Mountains, she is said to have brought in money by raising and selling chickens and eggs. Savage continued sculpting and executed portrait sculptures of tourists. She did return to New York City on occasion to perform repair work on some of her plaster pieces and, as her health failed, eventually moved back there to live with her daughter before dying of cancer in the Bronx on March 26, 1962. Although she died in virtual obscurity, the place in history since secured for Savage as a sculptor and teacher serves to reinforce her motto: "Life is fleeting, Art is eternal."

SOURCES:

Bailey, Brooke. *The Remarkable Lives of 100 Women Artists.* Holbrook, MA: Bob Adams, 1994.

Bearden, Romare, and Harry Henderson. "Augusta Savage," in *Six Black Masters of American Art.* NY: Doubleday, 1972.

Current Biography 1941. NY: H.W. Wilson, 1941.

Rubinstein, Charlotte Streifer. *American Women Artists.* Avon, 1982.

Sicherman, Barbara, and Carol Hurd Green, eds. *Notable American Women: The Modern Period.* Cambridge, MA: The Belknap Press of Harvard University, 1980.

Smith, Jessie Carney, ed. *Notable Black American Women.* Detroit, MI: Gale Research, 1992.

Saville, Helena (1817–1898).

See Faucit, Helena Saville.

Savitch, Jessica (1947–1983)

American reporter and television newscaster who was one of the first female television anchors. Born Jessica Beth Savitch in Wilmington, Delaware, on February 1, 1947; died in New Hope, Pennsylvania, on October 23, 1983; eldest of three daughters of David (Buddy) Savitch (a clothing merchant) and Florence (Spadoni) Savitch (a nurse); graduated from Atlantic City High School, Margate, New Jersey, in 1964; Ithaca College, New York, degree in communications, 1968; married Melvin Korn (an advertising executive), in January 1980 (divorced November 1980); married Donald

Rollie Payne (a gynecologist), on March 21, 1981 (committed suicide August 1981); no children.

One of the first women to break into the male bastion of television news, Jessica Savitch lived her short life intensely focused on her career. She was born in Wilmington, Delaware, in 1947, the eldest of three daughters of David Savitch and **Florence Spadoni Savitch**, and spent her early years in a small town in Pennsylvania. Although she dreamed of becoming a reporter, there were few role models in journalism for girls in the 1950s aside from those women assigned to cover "women's issues," such as homemaking and fashion. When Jessica was 12, David Savitch died of kidney disease at age 33; she never fully recovered. The family moved to Margate, New Jersey, and she switched from a provincial school to the tough, inner-city environment of Atlantic City High School. This was an intimidating experience for Savitch, and she felt lonely and unsettled until, in her sophomore year, she found a niche at radio station WOND in nearby Pleasantville. Soon, she was hanging around the station, reading the news and making announcements. Together with a friend, Savitch created her own show, "Teensville," broadcast on Saturdays; this led to another broadcasting job on Sundays. At age 14, Savitch had become the first regularly scheduled female radio announcer in Atlantic City. She continued at WOND until graduation.

Determined to be a broadcast journalist, despite her family's reservations, Savitch looked for schools that offered degrees in communications and decided on Ithaca College in New York, primarily because it was the cheapest. There, she soon had her first bout with sexism. Denied an on-air position at the college's AM-FM radio station, she protested to the station's male faculty advisor and was told, "There is no place for broads in broadcasting." Her furious appeal to college administrators forced the station to give her the late-night Saturday slot, but the station manager purposely neglected to tell her to shut down the transmitter after her shift, and she was fired after her first night for not doing so.

Frustrated, Savitch began commuting two hours to Rochester, where she found production work, did voice-overs for commercials, and worked as an on-camera model. In 1966, she landed a job with WBBF-AM in Rochester as the weekend disc jockey, the first female Top 40 disc jockey in the area. She was a tremendous success in Rochester, but because of the broadcast range of the station, no one at Ithaca knew of it. She

had no close friends in either place, and at college was generally thought to be a cold, snobbish prima donna. It was during these years that she first began suffering from bulimia and anorexia.

After graduating in 1968, Savitch continued to work part-time for WBBF while looking for a job as a broadcast journalist. Confident that her degree would help, she began sending out her résumé, which was rejected for reasons as varied as her lack of experience—despite that fact that she had been working in broadcasting since the age of 14—to the fear that she was too pretty and would "cause dissension in the news room." Undaunted, she moved to New York City and supported herself by making commercials and modeling while she made the rounds.

In 1969, **Joan Showalter**, personnel director for CBS, hired her as a floating administrative assistant, though she could neither type nor take dictation. Savitch worked for Marvin Friedman, the news director of WCBS radio, an all-news AM station. He thought her background irrelevant since it was not in news, but Charles Osgood and Ed Bradley became mentors, encouraging and teaching her. Although Savitch was starting at the bottom, she never admitted it to her family and friends. Letters always implied that she was already at the top and that her success was assured.

After a year at WCBS, Savitch decided that she was getting nowhere in New York City, so she began seeking work with CBS affiliates in other cities. She received only one offer, from KHOU-TV in Houston, Texas. Because television news had become so persona-driven in the past years, Dick John, manager of the station, was looking for a new personality to embellish the nightly news. He was impressed with her audition tape and, when he met her, with her gumption, for she told him she wanted to be a network anchor by the time she was 30. John hired her as a general assignment reporter in 1971, but Savitch had oversold herself, and initially she was overwhelmed by the work. Cameraman John Shaw took her under his wing, teaching her tricks of the trade and helping her adjust. He also suggested that she pre-record her broadcasts and then play them back through a hidden earphone, repeating what she heard. This became a device that she used for the rest of her career. It allowed her to look directly into the camera while reading the news, a characteristic that was to become her trademark.

For the next two years, Savitch covered every conceivable story, from murder investigations, a skyjacking, and a robbery-in-progress to political scandals, elections, and strikes. She realized early that she was not an investigative journalist, so she covered stories that were already breaking. Savitch never had trouble gathering a story; trouble came from the men with whom she had to work. They saw her as a star and a pretty girl, not as a serious professional. Three months after her arrival in Houston, the news director suggested that Savitch audition for the position of weekend anchor. She pulled her hair back, dressed in an unfussy dark suit, and used her "best male imitation" during the audition. The ploy worked, and she became the first woman television anchor in the South.

While she was in Houston, Savitch also met Ron Kershaw, a reporter from the rival ABC network. Their relationship was probably the closest Savitch had with a man. Both enjoyed the competition of covering the same story, spending their evenings together watching news shows, criticizing them and taking notes. Savitch, however, was more ambitious, working toward the highest position with the greatest possible exposure. Kershaw gave her an engagement and wedding ring, but they never married.

Savitch continued to file up to three stories a day during the week, submitting many of them through the CBS news bureau in Atlanta, Georgia. She competed with other reporters for breaking stories and often tried for an unusual angle. One of her stories about a fire caused by a train derailment gained national exposure when Walter Cronkite broadcast it on the evening news. She was temperamental and egocentric with her colleagues, but the public loved her. On screen, she came across as vivid and dynamic, and she was featured in articles in *TV Guide* and in newspapers. Her popularity helped KHOU capture the #1 slot in the ratings. "She had a real knack for the personal approach, for making herself the center of the story," said a news director. "She understood TV news for what it is—show business. She didn't worry about what journalists with a capital 'J' worry about—she was concerned with putting on a show." Less than a year after she began working in Houston, broadcast executives around the country were trying to woo her.

One admirer was Jim Topping, who had been scouting for talent in local markets. When he became news director of KYW-TV, the NBC affiliate in Philadelphia, he solicited Savitch for samples of her work, and during their interview talked to her about the possibility of becoming an anchor. In November 1972, Savitch signed a five-year contract to be a general assignment re-

porter with KYW. It marked the beginning of the end of her relationship with Kershaw. Although he quit his job in Houston and looked for work in Philadelphia, he was repeatedly turned down because of his relationship with Savitch, and she was too involved in her own career to spend time with him.

Savitch's new job in Philadelphia started out badly. She was viewed as a country bumpkin, and although the hostility she faced was not as open as it had been in Houston, it was still there. She was fortunate to find as a mentor David Neal, the assignment editor whose office was next to Topping's. He saw Savitch's potential and helped her to change her image and acquire a more professional outlook. His advice ranged from makeup and hairstyle to speech lessons and relations with management. Savitch's voice coach, **Lilyan Wilder**, helped her eliminate a lisp.

Kershaw found a job in Baltimore, but Savitch began returning from her visits to him with bruises on her body, wearing sunglasses to cover her face. When she discovered that she was pregnant, she went to New York, without Kershaw, for an abortion. She claimed that she had made the only possible decision, but she was visibly upset for some time afterward.

Four months after beginning her job in Philadelphia, Savitch was chosen to anchor the weekend newscast. Despite her popularity with the public, she was never offered the traditional prerogative of substituting for the weeknight anchors, only one of many actions she interpreted as slights. Tired of the station's attitude toward her during her first year there, Savitch sought and was offered a job with CBS in New York City, but KYW refused to allow her to break her five-year contract. Savitch tried to hold her ground, claiming that she had understood that she could leave if she chose, but the courts ruled against her and upheld the contract. Her response was to stage a one-woman sick-out until the station agreed to raise her salary and help her develop her career. They reached an agreement, but her feelings about KYW were soured forever.

As a way of focusing on a single issue using a single reporter, the station assigned Savitch to do a five-part series on natural childbirth. At first, she was annoyed at being asked to cover "women's news"—a fluff piece—but as she worked on the documentary, she warmed to her subject. The resulting series was a sensation, the first time a live birth had been shown on television, and Savitch received rave reviews. This piece was followed by another series, "Rape . . . the Ultimate Violation," for which she acted as a decoy with an undercover police unit. It won the 1974 Clarion Award from Women in Communications. When shown to legislators in Pennsylvania, New Jersey, and Delaware, it helped the passage of revisions to laws on the treatment of rape victims and the prosecution of rapists. These series and others, on divorce, dieting, and the training of women police officers, were such popular successes that they became a regular feature of the news.

With the success of the documentaries and Savitch's rising popularity (there was even a fan club), she had become too important for periodic reports and weekend news. She was given the job of weeknight co-anchor for "Eyewitness News," with Mort Crim, at 5:30 PM, beginning August 1974, and the ratings immediately soared. Two years later, she became part of a tri-anchor team on the nightly news at 11:00 PM. She also co-hosted "Meetinghouse," a live one-hour weekly prime-time public issue forum. By spring 1975, "Eyewitness News" was holding first place in the ratings. Savitch received both vindication and recognition of her accomplishments when she was invited by Ithaca College to be a visiting professor. She accepted and taught a fall course in 1976, and again in 1978. (She did not, however, meet another goal, that of becoming the first woman anchor on a national network. In 1976, *Barbara Walters began co-anchoring the ABC nightly news.)

However, Savitch's relationships with the station directors, her co-workers, and with Kershaw, continued to disintegrate. When her contract expired in 1977, Savitch received offers from all three major networks. After much thought, many interviews, and consultation with Melvin Korn, an advertising executive whom Savitch found both attentive and stable, she chose NBC as offering the best opportunities, including the possibility of becoming a national anchorwoman. The FCC had prohibited discrimination against women in hiring and promotion in broadcasting in 1971, and NBC had just suffered a humiliating defeat in a sex-discrimination suit brought by its female employees. Savitch, a popular woman broadcaster, came along at a time when the network was trying to change its hiring practices and increase the number of women and African-Americans on-screen. Aware of her own draw and potential, Savitch negotiated a contract that gave her both a good salary and a long list of perks, but caused her to begin her NBC career with the reputation of a spoiled star.

Savitch was attached to the Washington news bureau covering the U.S. Senate (taking over from *Catherine Mackin) and anchored the Sunday edition of the "NBC Nightly News." Two months later, she teamed up with news giants David Brinkley and John Chancellor in a three-way broadcast. Network executives were sufficiently impressed to assign her periodically as a substitute on the weekday "Nightly News"—a position never before held by a woman. She disliked being a reporter again when she had already graduated to anchor status, but NBC insisted. She soon found that she was in over her head, for reporting on the Senate is very different from reporting on fires. At NBC, she was on her own for the first time, without a mentor; she had no local guidance and no one to explain to her how things were done in Washington. In addition, she was constantly ill. As a result, her reports were a disappointment to her bosses, but they had invested so much in her that they kept her going.

Savitch was moved off the Senate beat and onto general assignment. The network still tried to keep up her image, but disappointment was in the

Jessica Savitch

air. In May 1979, she went to Canada to cover an important election which long-time Prime Minister Pierre Trudeau was expected to lose. The assignment was intended to give her exposure, but she knew nothing about Canadian politics. Although she tried to prepare, her report on the "Nightly News" was considered awful, and a subsequent piece was rejected. Her complaints to the president of NBC News did nothing to enhance her reputation, and the producers banned her from reporting for the "Nightly News."

In April 1979, Savitch was assigned to the "Segment Three" unit, putting together documentaries for the "Nightly News." That same month, she asked Korn to marry her. When Kershaw found out, he was so distraught that his friends put him into a private hospital. The wedding was a grand, formal affair at the Plaza Hotel in New York City in January 1980, but afterwards the couple would continue to live in separate apartments. Savitch would also continue to see Kershaw, apparently incapable of breaking up with him. By February 1980, unable to manage both marriage and her career and beset by drug problems, Savitch asked Korn for a divorce. By November, he agreed. Their marriage would last ten months. Meanwhile, between October 1979 and June 1980, Savitch had been a principal reporter for "Prime Time Sunday" (later "Prime Time Saturday"), a weekly news magazine. She had fit her reporting assignments around her hectic schedule of talks, public appearances, interviews, and her wedding, leaving little time for preparation. On return from her honeymoon with Korn, she had discovered she'd been cut back to one Sunday night broadcast.

In the early days of her marriage, Savitch had suffered a miscarriage and felt ill for several months. The gynecologist she consulted, Donald Rollie Payne, recommended minor surgery, and she found herself attracted to his stability, authority, and competence. Soon they were a couple, and he followed her when she went on assignment. By the time her divorce from Korn became final, she was pregnant by Payne and wanted to marry him. Already divorced and a bisexual, Payne was not inclined toward marriage or fatherhood, but apparently felt he had no choice. The nuptials seemed doomed from the beginning. Savitch suffered another miscarriage, and Payne became abusive. She discovered that he was addicted to the amphetamines he had been supplying to her and insisted he get medical help, but on his return from the hospital he was despondent over the loss of his reputation and possibly his career. One night, Savitch returned home to Washington from her weekly broadcast in New York and found Payne hanging by her dog's leash from a pipe in the basement. They had been married five months.

Savitch was back on the job less than a month later. With her contract coming up for renewal, she tried to polish up her credentials and went over the news division's heads, lowering her popularity with her boss considerably. In 1980, she got another chance to boost her career when she was assigned to the highly visible job of podium correspondent for the Republican and Democratic National Conventions. Savitch, however, had not been told what to say or do, and she knew she was ill-prepared and that her performance would be mercilessly scrutinized. She interviewed everyone she could, took key players to lunch, and studied reports on past conventions, but her performance was not a success.

Extremely popular with the public and the press nevertheless, Savitch scored high in popularity polls and was in constant demand on the lecture circuit. She won four Emmy awards during her career, was featured in countless magazines and newspaper articles, and in 1980, she was one of the 12 most popular speakers in the country. With a charismatic presence on camera, Savitch made impressive inroads in a male-dominated field, providing a role model and inspiration where none had been before. However, she was under constant pressure to prove herself, and the strain began to take its toll. She spent her career fighting health problems and abusing amphetamines and cocaine. Her personal relationships with men were tumultuous, unconventional, and unhappy. Her career was her only positive focus, and all her energies were concentrated on it.

By 1982, no longer able to tolerate her ups and downs, the network was losing interest in Savitch. She occasionally substituted for **Jane Pauley** on "Today," and in the fall of 1981, when Tom Brokaw left the program, she co-anchored with Pauley for several weeks. She did news updates and weekend anchoring and occasionally appeared on "Meet the Press." In 1982, she moved to New York City, where she worked on documentaries and served as principal correspondent for A-News Capsules to NBC affiliates. When she was invited to work on "Frontline" for PBS, she went on partial leave from NBC and moved to Boston. Shortly after, her autobiography, *Anchorwoman* (1982), was published. For a time it seemed that "Frontline" might revive her career, but she could no longer sustain the energy that had brought her so far, and she was soon reduced to doing one-minute live bits for NBC.

Concerned about her future, Savitch passed up a new NBC show only to find in 1983 that **Connie Chung** was replacing her as Saturday anchor of "Nightly News." Her problems with drugs were catching up with her; she was frighteningly thin, her skin looked bad, and her nails were bitten to the quick. She checked into a celebrity health spa in an effort to detoxify, but came away as tense and disoriented as when she had gone in. She received a blow in her last contract negotiations when NBC implied, by signing her for only one year rather than three, that it was quietly pushing her out. At the same time, the producers of "Frontline" had decided to decrease her role even further in the coming season. The woman whom *Newsweek* had named "NBC's Golden Girl" had lost her edge. The final blow came in early October 1983, during a 60-second, live spot for "News Digest," when she lost control of herself on the air, slurring her speech in what has been described as a mini-nervous breakdown, with a stricken look on her face. The spot was seen by some 8 to 10 million people.

Twenty days later, a car in which Savitch was riding took a wrong turn in dense fog and went over an embankment into a muddy canal in rural Bucks County, Pennsylvania. Savitch and her companion in the car, *New York Post* executive Martin Fischbein, drowned in shallow water, as did her dog. Her sudden death put to rest all speculation about her career. Despite the downhill rush of her final days, Jessica Savitch was an important part of the changing face of television news and an icon of her time.

SOURCES:

Blair, Gwenda. *Almost Golden: Jessica Savitch and the Selling of Television News.* NY: Simon and Schuster, 1988.

Devine, Elizabeth, ed. *The Annual Obituary 1983.* Detroit, MI: St. James Press, 1984.

"Jessica Savitch of NBC-TV Killed in Car Accident," in *The New York Times Biographical Service.* October 1983.

Lawrence, Sue. "Jessica Savitch (1947–1983)," in *Women in Communication: A Biographical Sourcebook.* Edited by Nancy Signorielli. Westport, CT: Greenwood Press, 1996.

Moritz, Charles, ed. *Current Biography Yearbook 1983.* NY: H.W. Wilson, 1983.

Taft, William H. *Encyclopedia of Twentieth-Century Journalists.* NY: Garland, 1986.

Malinda Mayer, writer and editor, Falmouth, Massachusetts

Savitskaya, Svetlana (b. 1948).

See Astronauts: Women in Space for sidebar.

Savoy, countess of.

See Matilde of Vienne (d. after 1145).

See Clementina of Zahringen (fl. 1150s).
See Margaret of Geneva (fl. late 1100s–early 1200s).

Savoy, duchess of.

See Blanche of Burgundy (1288–1348).
See Mary of Burgundy (d. 1428).
See Louise of Savoy for sidebar on Anne of Lusignan (b. around 1430).
See Yolande of France (1434–1478).
See Margaret of Bourbon (d. 1483).
See Margaret of Austria (1480–1530).
See Beatrice of Portugal (1504–1538).
See Margaret of Savoy (c. 1523–1574).
See Catherine of Spain (1567–1597).
See Christine of France (1606–1663).
See Françoise d'Orleans (fl. 1650).
See Jeanne of Nemours (d. 1724).
See Louisa Christina of Bavaria (fl. 1726).
See Maria Antonia of Spain (1729–1785).
See Louise of Parma (1802–1857).

Savoy, regent of.

See Christine of France (1606–1663).
See Jeanne of Nemours (d. 1724).

Savoy-Carignan, duchess of.

See Este, Catherine d'.
See Maria Christina of Saxony (1779–1851).

Savoy-Carignan, princess of.

See Anna Victoria of Savoy.
See Mancini, Olympia (c. 1639–1708).

Savoy-Piedmont, queen of.

See Maria Theresa of Tuscany (1801–1855).

Saw, Ruth (1901–1983)

English philosopher. Born Ruth Lydia Saw in England on August 1, 1901; died in 1983; daughter of Samuel James Saw and Matilda Louisa (Horner) Saw; sister of Grace Saw (a mathematician); educated at the Country School for Girls in Surrey; Bedford College, University of London, B.A., 1926; Smith College, Ph.D., 1934.

Lecturer in philosophy, Smith College (1927–34); lecturer in philosophy, Bedford College (1939–44); lecturer in philosophy, Birkbeck College (1939–46); reader in philosophy, Birkbeck College (1946–61); member of executive committee of the Aristotelian Society (1946–49), treasurer (1950–62); professor of aesthetics, University of London (1961–64); founder of the British Society of Aesthetics; head of the department of philosophy, Birkbeck College; professor emeritus, Birkbeck College (1964); president of the Aristotelian Society (1965).

Selected works: "An Aspect of Causal Connection," in Proceedings of the Aristotelian Society (New

Series 35, 1934–35); "William of Ockham on Terms, Propositions and Meaning," *in* Proceedings of the Aristotelian Society *(New Series 42, 1941);* "The Grounds of Induction in Professor Whitehead's Philosophy of Nature," *in* Philosophical Studies: Essays in Memory of L. Susan Stebbing *(1948);* The Vindication of Metaphysics: A Study in the Philosophy of Spinoza *(1951);* Leibniz *(1954);* "Dr. Margaret MacDonald," *in* Analysis *(16, 1956);* "Sense and Nonsense in Aesthetics," *in* British Journal of Aesthetics *(1, 1961);* "What is a Work of Art?," *in* Philosophy *(36, 1962);* "Art and the Language of Emotions," *in* Symposium, Proceedings of the Aristotelian Society Supplement *(36, 1962);* "Sense and Reference in Aesthetics," *in* British Journal of Aesthetics *(3, 1963);* "The Logic of the Particular Case," *in* Proceedings of the Aristotelian Society *(New Series 66, 1966);* Aesthetics, an Introduction *(1971).*

Not much is known about the early life of Ruth Saw, except that she was educated at the Country School for Girls in Surrey and her sister **Grace Saw** became a mathematician. After completing her B.A. at Bedford College, University of London, in 1926, she left England for the United States. While working as a lecturer at Smith College from 1927 to 1934, Saw completed her Ph.D. in philosophy. Her interest was in logic and the philosophy of language.

Saw then returned to England and became active in the Aristotelian Society, an organization that fostered intellectual exchange among philosophers. From 1946 to 1949, she served on the Society's executive committee. She also held several positions at University of London's Bedford and Birkbeck colleges, initially as a lecturer. During the 1940s, she was particularly involved with the study of the metaphysical systems, or theories of reality, of Leibniz and Spinoza, and published books on each of these rationalist philosophers.

By the late 1950s, Saw had turned away from metaphysics to aesthetics, the theory of art. She was particularly interested in metaesthetics, the consideration of what would be an adequate aesthetic theory, and she argued that it must be related to a philosophy of language. Her *Aesthetics, an Introduction* (1971) is less a survey of aesthetic theories than it is an exposition of her own views.

From 1950 to 1962, Saw was treasurer of the Aristotelian Society, and from 1961 to 1964 professor of aesthetics at the University of London. During the early '60s, she also founded the British Society of Aesthetics. On her retirement from Birkbeck College in 1964, she received the honor of professor emeritus, and in 1965 she was elected president of the Aristotelian Society (the fifth woman to hold this prestigious position).

SOURCES:

Kersey, Ethel M. *Women Philosophers: a Bio-critical Source Book.* CT: Greenwood Press, 1989.

Waithe, Mary Ellen, ed. *A History of Women Philosophers.* Boston, MA: Martinus Nijhoff, 1987–95.

Catherine Hundleby, M.A. Philosophy, University of Guelph, Guelph, Ontario, Canada

Sawyer, Ruth (1880–1970)

American writer and storyteller. Born on August 5, 1880, in Boston, Massachusetts; died on June 3, 1970; daughter of Francis Milton Sawyer and Ethelinda J. (Smith) Sawyer; attended Miss Brackett's School in New York; attended Packer Collegiate Institute in Brooklyn, 1895–96; Garland Kindergarten Training School, 1900; graduated from Teachers College, Columbia University, B.S. in education, 1904; married Albert C. Durand, on June 4, 1911 (died 1967); children: David Durand (b. 1912); Margaret Durand McCloskey (b. 1916).

Received the John Newbery Medal of the American Library Association (1937), Lewis Carroll Shelf Award (1964), Regina Medal of the Catholic Library Association (1965), *Laura Ingalls Wilder Medal of the American Library Association (1965); received Caldecott Honor Medals for* The Christmas Anna Angel *(1945) and* Journey Cake, Ho! *(1954).*

Selected writings: The Primrose Ring *(1915);* This Way to Christmas *(1916);* Seven Miles to Arden *(1916);* A Child's Yearbook *(1917);* Herself, Himself and Myself *(1917);* Doctor Danny *(1918);* Leerie *(1920);* The Silver Sixpence *(1921);* Gladiola Murphy *(1923);* The Tale of the Enchanted Bunnies *(1923);* Four Ducks on a Pond *(1928);* Folkhouse: The Autobiography of a Home *(1932);* The Luck of the Road *(1934);* Toño Antonio *(1934);* Gallant: The Story of Storm Veblen *(1936);* Picture Tales From Spain *(1936);* Roller Skates *(1936);* The Year of Jubilo *(1940);* The Least One *(1941);* The Long Christmas *(1941);* The Way of the Storyteller *(1942);* The Christmas Anna Angel *(1944);* This is the Christmas: A Serbian Folktale *(1945);* Old Con and Patrick *(1946);* The Little Red Horse *(1950);* Maggie Rose: Her Birthday Christmas *(1952);* Journey Cake, Ho! *(1953);* A Cottage for Betsy *(1954);* The Enchanted Schoolhouse *(1956);* The Year of the Christmas Dragon *(1960);* How to Tell a Story *(1962);* Daddles: The Story of a Plain Hound-Dog *(1964);* Joy to the World: Christmas Legends *(1966);* My Spain: A Storyteller's Year of Collecting *(1967).*

Ruth Sawyer was born in the Back Bay section of Boston in 1880, and had four older brothers. Sawyer's parents, Francis Milton Sawyer and **Ethelinda Smith Sawyer**, were members of the New England gentry. Ethelinda came from Lexington, Massachusetts, and Francis, an importer, boasted colonial ancestry as well. The family relocated to the Upper East Side of New York City in 1881. As a small child, Ruth was cared for by a French governess, and later by a nanny named Johanna; she grew extremely attached to this Irish woman from Donegal who shared a wealth of stories with her young charge. As she became older, Ruth attended Miss Brackett's School in New York.

Sawyer was 14 when her father died in 1894. The family retreated to Maine for a year, and then returned to New York City where Sawyer attended Brooklyn's Packer Collegiate Institute in 1895 and 1896. After graduating from the Garland Kindergarten Training School in Boston in 1900, she worked in Cuba, organizing kindergartens for orphans of the Spanish-American War. That project secured her a scholarship to Teachers College at Columbia University, where she studied folklore and indulged her love of storytelling. Receiving a B.S. in education in 1904, Sawyer secured employment as a professional storyteller with the New York Public Lecture Bureau. In that capacity, she spent two years relating stories to New York's foreign-born population and set up the first storytelling program for children at the New York Public Library. In 1905 and 1907, she made trips to Ireland to research articles for the *New York Sun*. There, she gleaned new material from Irish *sennachies*, the tellers of traditional Irish tales.

While Sawyer was a student at Columbia, she had become acquainted with an opthamologist, Dr. Albert C. Durand. The couple married on June 4, 1911, and moved to Ithaca, New York, where they raised two children, and Sawyer remained devoted to both writing and storytelling. Using her maiden name, as she would for all her works, she published several novels, including *The Primrose Ring* (1915) and *Seven Miles to Arden* (1916). Her children's books included *This Way to Christmas* (1916), *A Child's Yearbook* (1917), and *The Tale of the Enchanted Bunnies* (1923).

Between 1923 and 1933, Sawyer traveled the rural counties of New York, where she shared her stories with the local residents under the auspices of the Cornell University Extension Services. In 1931, she also traveled to Spain to collect folklore and met a Spanish boy who impressed her; on her return home, she wrote *Toño Antonio*, published in 1934. In the process, she befriended *May Massee of Viking Press, who urged Sawyer to write more Spanish stories. She published *Picture Tales from Spain* in 1936 and *My Spain* in 1967.

Sawyer penned one of her most famous works, *Roller Skates*, in 1936. The autobiographical story relates one year in the life of a "freewheeling" young girl who explores New York City on roller skates while her parents are abroad. She embraces life to the fullest, befriending people from a broad spectrum of ethnicities and ages. While championing the spirit of children, Sawyer also injected a degree of realism then rarely seen in children's books when the heroine Lucinda must deal with the deaths (one a murder) of two friends. The book won the Newbery Medal of the American Library Association in 1937, and Lucinda made an appearance in a sequel, *The Year of Jubilo* (1940), later reissued as *Lucinda's Year of Jubilo* (1965).

Ruth Sawyer

Sawyer's stories are characterized by their focus on family relationships. Many of her books are set at Christmastime, including *The Long Christmas* (1941), *Maggie Rose: Her Birthday Christmas* (1952), and *The Year of the Christmas Dragon* (1960).

Sawyer's *The Christmas Anna Angel*, with illustrations by **Kate Seredy**, won the Caldecott Honor for illustrations in 1945. After Sawyer's daughter **Margaret** (**McCloskey**) married the talented, whimsical illustrator Robert Mc-Closkey, mother and son-in-law collaborated on *Journey Cake, Ho!*; it won a Caldecott Medal in 1954. In addition to her many children's stories, Sawyer wrote *The Way of the Storyteller* in 1942 to instruct others in the art of storytelling. The book, which offers samples for storytelling, became a classic guide for teachers, and in 1965 Sawyer made a recording entitled *Ruth Sawyer: Storyteller.*

Sawyer, who was particularly fond of sailing, fishing, and berry-picking, retired with her husband to Gull Rock, in Hancock, Maine, in 1946. They spent their winters in Florida and later moved to Boston, where Sawyer continued her storytelling activities at the Boston Public Library. The couple's final move was to the Hancock House Nursing Home in Lexington, Massachusetts, where Durand died in 1967. Sawyer died of a gastrointestinal hemorrhage on June 3, 1970.

SOURCES:

Contemporary Authors. Vols. 73–76. Detroit, MI: Gale Research, 1978.
Dictionary of Literary Biography. Vol. 22. Detroit, MI: Gale Research, 1983.
Kunitz, Stanley J., and Howard Haycraft, eds. *Twentieth Century Authors.* NY: H.W. Wilson, 1942.
Sicherman, Barbara, and Carol Hurd Green, eds. *Notable American Women: The Modern Period.* Cambridge, MA: The Belknap Press of Harvard University, 1980.

Gloria Cooksey,
freelance writer, Sacramento, California

Sax, Marie (1834–1907).
See Sass, Marie Constance.

Saxe-Altenburg, duchess of.
See Elizabeth of Brunswick-Wolfenbuttel (1593–1650).
See Amelia of Wurttemberg (1799–1848).

Saxe-Coburg and Gotha, duchess of.
See Mary of Wurttemberg (1799–1860).
See Louise of Saxe-Gotha-Altenburg (1800–1831).
See Alexandrina of Baden (1820–1904).

Saxe-Coburg-Saalfeld, duchess of.
See Augusta of Reuss-Ebersdorf (1757–1831).

Saxe-Gotha, duchess of.
See Elizabeth Sophie of Saxe-Altenburg (1619–1680).
See Christine of Baden-Durlach (1645–1705).
See Madeleine of Anhalt-Zerbst (1679–1740).
See Louise Charlotte of Mecklenburg-Schwerin (1779–1801).

Saxe-Hildburghausen, duchess of.
See Louise of Prussia for sidebar on Charlotte (1769–1818).

Saxe-Lauenburg, duchess of.
See Dorothea of Brandenburg (1446–1519).

Saxe-Lüneburg, duchess of.
See Catherine of Brunswick-Wolfenbuttel (1488–1563).

Saxe-Meiningen, duchess of.
See Louise of Hohenlohe-Langenburg (1763–1837).

Saxe-Weimar, duchess of.
See Anna Amalia of Saxe-Weimar (1739–1807).
See Marie Pavlovna (1786–1859).
See Louise of Hesse-Darmstadt (d. 1830).

Saxe-Weimar, grand duchess of.
See Sophia of Nassau (1824–1897).
See Pauline of Saxe-Weimar (1852–1904).

Saxony, countess of.
See Oda (806–913).

Saxony, duchess of.
See Hedwig (d. 903).
See Ulfhild of Denmark (d. before 1070).
See Sophie of Hungary (d. 1095).
See Gertrude of Saxony (1115–1143).
See Matilda of England (1156–1189).
See Helene of Brunswick-Luneburg (d. 1273).
See Cunegunde (d. after 1370).
See Margaret of Saxony (c. 1416–1486).
See Barbara of Poland (1478–1534).
See Amalie of Saxony (1794–1870).
See Alice Maud Mary (1843–1878).
See Adelaide of Saxe-Meiningen (1891–1971).

Saxony, electress of.
See Agnes of Habsburg (c. 1257–1322).
See Margaret of Saxony (c. 1416–1486).
See Agnes of Hesse (1527–1555).
See Anna of Denmark (1532–1585).
See Elizabeth of Wittelsbach (1540–1594).
See Sophie of Brandenburg (1568–1622).
See Hedwig of Denmark (1581–1641).
See Magdalena Sybilla (1587–1659).
See Anna Sophia of Denmark (1647–1717).
See Maria Antonia of Austria (1724–1780).

Saxony, queen of.

See Theresa (1767–1827).
See Amalia of Bavaria (1801–1877).
See Maria of Bavaria (1805–1877).
See Caroline of Saxony (1833–1907).
See Toselli, Louisa (1870–1947).

Say, Lucy Sistare (1801–1885)

American scientific illustrator. Born Lucy Sistare in New London, Connecticut, in 1801; died in Lexington, Massachusetts, in 1885; daughter of Nancy Sistare and Joseph Sistare; married Thomas Say, in 1827 (died 1834).

Born in New London, Connecticut, in 1801, Lucy Sistare Say lived for a time at the New Harmony colony in Indiana, Robert Owen's model cooperative renowned in its time as a center of learning and culture. There, her responsibilities included spinning, knitting, and sewing, and she also involved herself with the free public school and free library at New Harmony—the first such institutions in the United States. In 1827, she married fellow New Harmony member Thomas Say, an entomologist and conchologist. Lucy, who illustrated many of her husband's scientific writings, became noted for her unusually fine drawings of invertebrates, and for other illustrations that she created to accompany his text.

Widowed in 1834, Say left New Harmony and lived with a sister in New York City. Eventually, she brought her late husband's specimen cabinet to the Philadelphia Academy of Natural Sciences. Say, who corresponded with other naturalists, was honored in 1841 as the first woman admitted to the academy.

SOURCES:
Ogilvie, Marilyn Bailey. *Women in Science.* Boston, MA: Cambridge Press, 1993.

Gloria Cooksey,
freelance writer, Sacramento, California

Sayao, Bidu (1902–1999)

Brazilian soprano. Name variations: Bidú Sayão. Pronunciation: Bidoo Sah-YA-oo. Born Balduina de Oliveira Sayao on May 11, 1902, in Niteroi near Rio de Janeiro, Brazil; died from complications of pneumonia after a brief illness on March 12, 1999, in Rockport, Maine; daughter of Pedro de Oliveira (a well-to-do banana planter) and Maria José Costa Sayao; studied with Elena Theodorini, Jean de Reszke, Lucien Muratore, Reynaldo Hahn, and Luigi Ricci; married Walter Mocchi (an impresario), in 1927 (di-

vorced 1934); married Giuseppe Danise (a baritone), in 1947 (died 1963).

Debuted in Rome (1926), at Opéra-Comique in Paris (1926), at Teatro alla Scala (1930), at Metropolitan Opera (1937), at Chicago Opera (1941), at San Francisco Opera (1946); retired (1957).

"It is said that Miss Sayao's success in opera has done more to open the door to careers for other ambitious Brazilian girls of good family than all the women's-rights organizations of her country," noted *Current Biography* in 1942. Were it not for one uncle who had a passion for theater, Bidu Sayao would not have been given a chance to perfect her voice. She began studying with the great Rumanian opera singer **Elena Theodorini** at the age of 14, without her family's knowledge. Her voice had a limited range but Theodorini began to build it with spectacular results. A later teacher, **Emma Carelli**, said: "The voice is limited but sometimes it is the tiny birds who fly the greatest distances and for the longest times!" When her parents were finally told, "they

𝒷idu
𝒮ayao

were only a little less shocked," commented Sayao, "than if they had awakened one morning to discover that I had eloped with a Fiji Islander." It was Theodorini who convinced them that a voice "was something worth cultivating."

In 1925, Sayao made her debut as a concert singer in the Teatro Municipal in Rio de Janeiro, a still-remembered triumph. In 1927, she married her teacher's former husband, Walter Mocchi, who directed the Teatro Municipal in Sao Paulo. At this time, she made Rome her base and began to make extended concert tours and to perform opera in Europe and South America. Sayao met Toscanini in 1936 and was given the part as soloist for Debussy's *La damoiselle élue* at Carnegie Hall, which won great critical acclaim. *Lucrezia Bori had left the Metropolitan, and Sayao was asked to replace her. She remained at the Met for 16 seasons during which she sang 12 roles. Of the 226 performances she made in New York, 38 were broadcast, so recordings of all her Metropolitan roles except Serpina exist. Sayao had a true lyric coloratura with a peculiar sweetness. Although her voice was small, it could always be heard in solo or ensemble from the back of a large hall. When Rudolf Bing became director of the Met in 1950, Sayao's performances were drastically reduced, so she began to concentrate instead on concerts throughout the United States and Canada. In 1958, Sayao retired to the seaside town of Lincolnville, Maine.

SOURCES:

Current Biography. NY: H.W. Wilson, 1942.

"Bidú Sayão, 94, Star Soprano, Dies," in *The New York Times.* March 13, 1999.

John Haag,
Athens, Georgia

Sayers, Dorothy L. (1893–1957)

English translator of Dante's Inferno, *Christian moralist, and detective story writer who created the characters of Lord Peter Wimsey and Harriet Vane. Born Dorothy Leigh Sayers in Oxford, England, on June 13, 1893; died in Witham, Essex, on December 17, 1957; daughter of Reverend Henry Sayers (headmaster of Christ Church Choir School, Oxford) and Helen (Leigh) Sayers; educated at Godolphin School, Salisbury; graduated with first class honors in modern languages from Somerville College, Oxford, 1915; married Oswald Atherton Fleming (a journalist), in 1926 (died 1950); children: (illegitimate) son, John Anthony (b. 1924).*

Began work at Benson's advertising agency, London (1922); published first novel Whose Body? *(1923); gave birth to her son John Anthony in Bournemouth (1924); co-founded the Detection Club (1929); left advertising to become full-time writer-lecturer (1931); published* Gaudy Night *(1935); had first stage success with* Busman's Honeymoon *(1937); had Christian radio play "The Man Born to be King" on BBC (1941); published Dante translation, Cantica I, Hell (1949); published Dante, Cantica II, Purgatory (1955).*

Selected writings: Whose Body? *(1923);* Clouds of Witness *(1926);* Unnatural Death *(1927);* The Unpleasantness at the Bellona Club *(1928);* Strong Poison *(1930);* The Five Red Herrings *(1931);* Murder Must Advertise *(1933);* The Nine Tailors *(1934);* Gaudy Night *(1935);* Busman's Honeymoon *(1937);* (ed.) Great Short Stories of Detection, Mystery and Horror *(1928, 1931, 1934);* (ed.) Tales of Detection *(1936);* (play) The Zeal of Thy House *(1937);* (play) The Devil to Pay *(1939);* (cycle of radio plays) "The Man Born to be King" *(1941–42);* (translation) Dante's *Divine Comedy, the* Inferno *(1949) and* Purgatorio *(1955).*

Dorothy L. Sayers is best remembered for a fine series of detective novels, with suave Lord Peter Wimsey and his beloved Harriet Vane leading the fight against crime. But Sayers was also an outstanding scholar and linguist, one of the first women to be awarded a degree by Oxford University. When mystery writing had freed her of financial anxiety, she turned increasingly to the study of medieval literature and to writing in defense of her ardent Christian faith. She also wrote extensively for the British press, and became a familiar figure on BBC radio during the Second World War, a popular moralist and a gifted lecturer.

Sayers was born in 1893 in Oxford, where her father was head of the choir-school at Christ Church. The family moved to the fen country of Huntingdonshire when he became a parish vicar, and she spent a lonely childhood dedicated to hard study and avid reading. Boarding at the Godolphin School in Salisbury, she had a severe attack of measles which caused most of her hair to fall out. She returned wearing a wig, but suffered a nervous breakdown a few months later. Despite acute health problems, Sayers had a distinguished school career and was back in Oxford in 1912, this time as a student in modern languages. After her first two years, the outbreak of the First World War emptied Oxford of nearly all its male students, many of them never to return. Sayers gained first class honors, the highest possible degree, in her final exams in 1915, but was not able to have the degree formally conferred until 1920, owing to Oxford's slowness to reform its rules on women's education.

In her first years after college, Sayers worked briefly at several different jobs: teaching languages to schoolgirls in Hull, working at Blackwell's, Oxford's publishing and bookselling company, and helping a friend, war veteran Eric Whelpton, to run a private school in Normandy. Though she was in love with Whelpton, he kept their relationship intellectual rather than physical, and, at the end of the year, she returned to England, seeing him rarely thereafter. Sayers was high-spirited, daring, and independent, in some ways an example of the "new woman" of the era. Though she was always politically conservative. she smoked and rode a motorcycle in Oxford and London. She became a devoted fan of detective fiction, reading all the prominent English works in the genre, though many of her literary friends looked down on such works as beneath them. Sayers considered Wilkie Collins' *The Moonstone*, one of the first English mystery novels, a masterpiece. Later essays and introductions to crime story anthologies demonstrated that in addition to becoming a detective story writer herself she was thoroughly acquainted with the whole history and aesthetics of the form.

In 1922, Sayers moved to London as an advertising copywriter where her quick wit and plays on words enabled her to enjoy the work. She lived in a Bloomsbury flat among a humbler group of bohemians than the famous Bloomsbury group, then in its heyday. The work, its amorality, and its perpetual appeal to lust and gluttony, offended her Christian convictions, but she had to admit that she was good at it. She would later put her advertising talent to use in World War II as a propaganda writer.

In 1923, Sayers published her first Peter Wimsey novel, *Whose Body?* It was an immediate success, and from then on she worked steadily for the next 14 years at enlarging the character of Wimsey, giving him a complete family history, and elaborating meticulously researched plots to expand his skills, his character, and his circle of friends. The durable quality of these novels depends partly on Sayers' skill in creating a distinctive atmosphere for each book, usually in a well-drawn area of the English provinces. *The Nine Tailors* (1934), for example, is set in the fen country of her youth. She had a sure gift for regional accents and mores, and made certain that such details as the effects of poisons, the vagaries of the British railway timetable, and the patterns of English church bellringing, were all rendered accurately. It is tempting to see the central figure, Wimsey, as an alter ego for Sayers. He had the money, leisure, and social position she lacked, and moved in a world of erudite wits, exchang-ing just the kind of learned banter of which her advertising colleagues knew nothing. Biographer **Nancy Tischler** writes of the characters:

> Each is an extension of Sayers' own double personality. . . . Sayers was always as middle class as Parker [the policeman] but her tastes were as elitist as Lord Peter's. She lived in small flats, often on back streets, but she loved the lavish country homes of the aristocracy. She might sit alone at a cluttered kitchen table eating orange marmalade out of a tin while she made notes for her books, but she cherished the protocol and respected the cultivated palate of the epicure.

Sayers was skilled in setting up moral ambiguities and tensions in her plots. Wimsey takes a schoolboy's "sporting" pleasure in the hunt for the culprit in each of the mysteries, but when the evidence points unmistakably to the guilty party he loses all relish for the game and regrets having to apprehend and visit retribution on the culprit. Sayers heightened the moral drama in *Five Red Herrings* (1931) by making the victim a horrible character and the murderer a likeable, friendly man whom Wimsey admires.

> There can be few plainer women on earth than Dorothy L. Sayers, and the adjective is an extremely kind one. . . . She was large, raw-boned, and awkward. Just as I have never seen a less attractive woman to look upon, I have never come across one so magnetic to listen to.
>
> —Mary Ellen Chase

In her Bloomsbury period, Sayers had a succession of unsuccessful, usually unrequited, love affairs. In 1923, however, she became pregnant by one of her motorcycling friends but managed to hide the fact from her family and colleagues after he refused to take responsibility for the child. She took a six-months' leave from her job and then moved alone to a private nursing home in Bournemouth to give birth to a boy whom she named John Anthony. She would never say who his father was, and carefully covered her tracks, so that as little as possible could be learned about the entire episode. James Brabazon revealed the facts in his 1981 biography of Sayers. She arranged for John to be raised by a distant relative, **Ivy Shrimpton**, who took in orphans. Sayers paid for his schooling and later "adopted" him informally, though they rarely lived together, and he only found out she was his real mother after World War II, when he applied for a passport and needed a copy of his birth certificate.

In 1926, Sayers married Oswald Fleming, a World War I veteran and minor author, who had written about his war experiences in *How to See the Battlefields* and now worked for the *News of the World* as a motor-racing and crime correspondent. He was the divorced father of two daughters, with whom he was no longer in contact, and seems to have been psychologically damaged by his experiences in the war. Sayers had far more energy than did Fleming, and he became embittered by her greater success, deteriorating into an angry drunkard. As she became more involved in the theater during the 1930s, and then as a lecturer and broadcaster with the BBC, she spent long periods away from their home at Witham, Essex. When he was invited to London parties or dinners with her, he often became drunk and abusive. In true British fashion, however, Sayers never had a harsh word to say about him in public, and if the marriage was a disaster, as seems likely from the remaining evidence, she was certainly not going to admit it. As with the truth about her son, she practiced an extreme reticence about her private life.

In 1929, she and G.K. Chesterton, creator of the detective-priest Father Brown, and like her a spirited defender of Christianity, collaborated in founding the Detection Club, whose members promised to rely on wit and deduction rather than melodrama and coincidence in solving the mysteries they put before their readers. Other members included *Agatha Christie, E.C. Bentley, and Anthony Berkeley. On induction to the club, new members would go through an initiation ritual replete with darkness, torches, a skull on a black pillow, and ceremonial robes, and would have to answer the solemn question: "Do you promise to observe a seemly moderation in the use of Gangs, Conspiracies, Death-Rays, Ghosts, Hypnotism, Trap-Doors, Chinamen, Super-Criminals and Lunatics, and utterly and forever to forswear Mysterious Poisons unknown to Science?" The members financed their club by writing a succession of plays and novels, contributing a chapter each and then passing the work on to the next writer. Sayers contributed to *The Floating Admiral* (1929), *Ask a Policeman* (1933), and *Double Death* (1939), among others.

By 1930, the Peter Wimsey novels had established her reputation, but Sayers felt they had literary weaknesses. She aimed now to write more literary novels of manners, and planned the first of these, *Strong Poison*, as a vehicle for marrying off Wimsey and bringing his career to an end. However, she found Wimsey so popular that she kept the character going. *Strong Poison* was also the novel in which she introduced Har-

riet Vane, an ex-Oxford woman and detective-story writer accused of murdering her former lover. Wimsey falls in love with her and helps exonerate her, but she refuses to marry him when she feels a debt of gratitude which makes her, she believes, unequal to him. Only when she has clearly established her own sense of worth with him, and has revealed Lord Peter's own insecurities, in *Gaudy Night* (1936), does Harriet agree to marry him. *Gaudy Night*, which many Sayers fans regard as her masterpiece, was also an exploration of the need for absolute intellectual integrity, and clearly echoed Sayers' own scholarly interests and moral preoccupations.

In the 1930s, she enlarged her reputation with several successful plays. The first, *Busman's Honeymoon*, was a stage adaptation, written with **Muriel St. Clare Byrne**, of the last Wimsey novel, in which he and Harriet marry and move to a country cottage, interrupting the bliss of newlyweds to solve another murder mystery. It ran for nine months in London's West End. Her next play, *The Zeal of Thy House* (1937), was produced in Canterbury Cathedral as part of the annual Canterbury festival, and took on a more frankly religious subject than any of her earlier works. Set in the Middle Ages, it deals with the rebuilding of a cathedral which has been damaged by fire. The monks have to choose between a profligate man who is a true master-builder, or an upright but less talented architect. They choose the rake, and Sayers argues that this is the right choice: whatever one's personal failings, great works of art speak for themselves and live beyond the fallibility of their creator. In his pride, the builder challenges God himself, but pays the price for his hubris. He falls from his scaffolding and is crippled, learning a new humility and love of God in the face of adversity.

The success of this and other religious plays led to an invitation from the BBC to write a radio play about the life of Christ. Sayers worked hard on the project, but just before its first airing the press learned that it was to be presented in contemporary language, which led to protests from the Protestant Truth Society and the Lord's Day Observance Society, who wanted her to stick with the venerable King James version. Despite their complaints, "The Man Born to be King" was well reviewed and received warmly by a large public. In the late 1940s, her Canterbury play was revived, and she wrote two more religious plays, for Lichfield and Colchester Cathedrals.

Sayers was an outspoken Christian apologist, loyal to the Church of England, but impatient at its sleepiness—too many Anglicans, she said, displayed the "Seven Deadly Virtues"—and at its uneven attitude towards sin. She thought it was too censorious about sex and too negligent about sins which had greater public and social consequences. For example, in one speech, she declared:

> The Church says Covetousness is a deadly sin—but does she really think so? Is she ready to found Welfare Societies to deal with *financial* immorality. . . . Is Dives, like Magdalen, ever refused the sacraments on the grounds that he, like her, is an "open and notorious evil-liver"? Does the Church arrange services with bright congregational singing for Total Abstainers from *Usury*?

Sayers was also dismayed at the way in which social convention and over-familiarity with the Christian story had made it seem dull and tame. In a *Sunday Times* article from 1938, she declared that "The Christian faith is the most exciting drama that ever staggered the imagination of man—and the dogma is the drama." Like Chesterton, her detective-story friend, she found her faith exciting. She became a churchwarden of her parish church, and was a moving figure in

Dorothy L. Sayers

the Society of St. Anne, a discussion group begun in 1942, which brought together Christians and agnostics to discuss religion and ethics, and perform plays (including several of her own). Sayers persuaded such Christian luminaries as T.S. Eliot, C.S. Lewis, Charles Williams, and J.R.R. Tolkien to give speeches there. Like her, they thought of Christianity as joyful and intellectually compelling. In politics and in general outlook a conservative, she belonged in spirit to old Toryism, that branch of English conservatism which predated the industrial revolution. She could therefore speak against the materialism of both capitalism and communism, and on behalf of economic justice, in a way which suggested Christian socialism.

Her last major project, which absorbed much of her interest in the last decade of her life, was a translation of Dante's *Inferno*. She had not tackled it until the war years, when she began reading it during a German air-raid on London, and at once was captivated. Working on it was no simple matter, because she was forced to learn medieval Italian. To make matters worse, her husband resented the project, so that she was only able to work at it when she was away from home or when he was asleep. Her translation aimed to clarify the many obscure references in Dante to scholastic theology, ancient cosmology, courtly love, and Italian history, making the work accessible to the modern reader. Sayers worked to preserve in English Dante's rhyming patterns but accompanied the rhyming version with a prose edition. Widely accepted as superior to all earlier translations, it made Dante a popular subject in Britain for the first time.

Her husband died of a stroke in 1950, following one of his many bursts of uncontrolled bad temper. For the last few years, he had done no work and was regularly drunk in the local pub. She did not mourn for him unduly, but wrote: "I shall miss having him to look after, and there will be no one to curse me and keep me up to the mark." Without his presence, "It seems impossible there should be so many uninterrupted hours in the day." She was still working hard on the third section of her Dante translation, *Paradise*, when she quite suddenly and unexpectedly died of a stroke in 1957. (The translation was completed by **Barbara Reynolds**.) Sayers was mourned as a great British institution, but remembered primarily for her Wimsey novels. In the 1970s and since, she has become the subject of serious analytical study. The Dorothy L. Sayers Society, based in her Witham home, was founded in 1970, and the *Sayers Review*, a journal, in 1976. Attractive to mystery buffs, to

Christians, and to feminists for such essays as "Are Women Human?," she seems likely to enjoy continuing popularity.

SOURCES:
Brabazon, James. *Dorothy L. Sayers: The Life of a Courageous Woman*. London: Victor Gollancz, 1981.
Coomes, David. *Dorothy L. Sayers: A Careless Rage for Life*. Oxford: Lion, 1992.
Durkin, Mary B. *Dorothy L. Sayers*. Boston: Twayne, 1980.
Gaillard, Dawson. *Dorothy L. Sayers*. NY: Frederick Ungar, 1981.
Hannay, Margaret P. *As Her Whimsy Took Her: Critical Essays on the Work of Dorothy L. Sayers*. Kent, Ohio: Kent State University Press, 1979.
Kinney, Catherine. *The Remarkable Case of Dorothy L. Sayers*, 1990.
Reynolds, Barbara. *Dorothy L. Sayers: Her Life and Soul*. St. Martin's, 1993.
———. *The Passionate Intellect: Dorothy L. Sayers' Encounter with Dante*. 1989.
Tischler, Nancy M. *Dorothy L. Sayers: A Pilgrim Soul*. Atlanta, GA: John Knox Press, 1980.

Patrick Allitt,
Professor of History,
Emory University, Atlanta, Georgia

Sayers, Peig (1873–1958)

Irish storyteller. Born Máiréad (Margaret) Sayers in Vicarstown, Dunquin, County Kerry, Ireland in March 1873 (exact date unknown but christened on March 29); died in Dingle, County Kerry, on December 8, 1958; youngest child of Tomás Sayers and Máiréad Ní Bhrosnacháin (Margaret "Peig" Brosnan) Sayers; educated at Dunquin National School; married Pádraig Ó Guithín (Patrick Flint), in February 1892; children: two daughters, four sons.

Swedish folklore scholar Bo Almqvist maintains that it would be hard to find Peig Sayers' match as a storyteller anywhere in the world. According to family tradition, the Sayers family was originally of English origin but by the mid-19th century had become completely gaelicised, dispossessed and poor, ekeing out a living in the remote southwest of Ireland. Her father Tomás Sayers was a renowned storyteller who passed on many of his tales to his youngest child Peig. His own life had been marred by tragedy. He had lived through the Great Famine of the 1840s but after his marriage to **Peig Brosnan** of Castleisland their first nine children had died in infancy. The Sayerses then moved to the townland of Vicarstown, near the village of Dunquin at the westernmost tip of the Dingle Peninsula in County Kerry, in late 1872. Six months later in March 1873 their last child was born. She was always known as Peig, after her mother.

The Dingle Peninsula was an area of outstanding scenic beauty and, by the time of Peig's birth, one of the last bastions of the native Irish language. (These Irish-speaking areas, called the Gaeltacht, were gradually being eroded by the spread of English.) The region was also being eroded by emigration for it was one of the poorest in Ireland and still very much dependent on potatoes as a staple food. America was a magnet for its young people, and there was a long-established process of chain migration whereby emigrant relatives and friends would send the passage money back to other relatives and friends in Ireland. As the youngest child, Peig was cherished by her parents; she was particularly close to her father whom she described as a quiet, sensible man. When she was seven, the family peace was disturbed by her brother Sean's new wife who came to live with them. Her sister-in-law was bad-tempered and took out her anger on Peig and her father. At age 12, Peig was taken out of school and went to work as a servant for the Curran family who were merchants in the nearby town of Dingle.

Sayers was lucky in that she was treated well by her employers. In her autobiography, she writes that after two years with the Currans she became ill and returned to Vicarstown, though she does not describe the illness. She and her best friend, **Cáit Boland**, talked often of emigration, as most of their contemporaries had by now left for America. Then Boland went, promising to send back fare money to Sayers as soon as possible. In the meantime, Peig, expecting the fare within a year, took a job as a farm servant, a notoriously hard form of work. Four years later, Boland wrote Sayers telling her that she had had an accident and would not be able to send the money. This was a major blow. Sayers returned to Vicarstown where her brother arranged a marriage for her with Pádraig Ó Guithín, from Great Blasket Island. The Blaskets, a group of islands some miles off the Dingle Peninsula, were places of great beauty in summer, but in winter they were bleak, desolate, exposed to the Atlantic winds, and often cut off for weeks at a time by the dangerous winter tides. Though arranged, the marriage was happy, and Peig soon made close friends on Great Blasket. She and Pádraig had eleven children, of whom six survived. In summer, the unspoiled, almost archaic way of life of the islands attracted many visitors, including students of the Irish language from Britain and Europe. The Norwegian scholar Carl Marstrander visited the island in 1907 and was deeply impressed with Sayers. Shortly afterwards, Marstrander met the young English scholar, Robin Flower, who was working on Irish manuscripts at the British Museum, and urged him to visit the Blaskets. Flower fell in love with them and their people and visited almost every year for the rest of his life. He became a fluent Irish speaker and was keenly appreciative of Peig Sayers' stories and tales. It was largely through Flower's writings that the academic world was alerted to Sayers' storytelling gifts.

But life on Great Blasket was becoming more difficult. Sayers later described the year 1920 as the worst of her life: her second-youngest child was killed in a cliff accident and by the end of that year two of her other children had emigrated to America. Her husband died in 1921. One by one the rest of her children set out for America in the 1920s. Though her son Micheál left in 1930, he soon returned and earned his living by sheep-rearing and writing poetry. A Dublin teacher, **Máire Ní Chinnéide**, who was a regular visitor to the Blaskets, urged Peig to tell her story to Micheál. He then sent the manuscript pages to Ní Chinnéide in Dublin who edited them for publication. *Peig* was published in 1936. A second volume, *Machnamh Sean-mhná* (An Old Woman's Reflections), also edited by Ní Chinnéide, was published in 1939. The indefatigable Flower urged the head of the Irish Folklore Commission to send a full-time collector to speak to Peig. Thus in 1938, Seosamh Ó Dálaigh (Joseph Daly) arrived; he would spend several years recording 350 ancient legends, ghost stories, folk stories, and religious stories of Peig's on an Ediphone cylinder. Ó Dálaigh recalled that Sayers' forte was the short tale: "from the opening of the narrative one would have no idea where the tale might turn."

By this time the Blaskets were in terminal decline and many islanders left during the Second World War. Peig, her son and her brother-in-law went back to live near Vicarstown on the mainland at the end of 1941. After a bad fall in the late 1940s, her health deteriorated, and she spent the last eight years of her life in the Dingle Hospital. She was remembered by one of the nuns there as "very stately and very dignified." A further volume of autobiography, *Beatha Pheig Sayers*, was published posthumously in 1970.

Sayers' legacy has been complex. For generations of Irish schoolchildren for whom *Peig* was a compulsory set text in the Irish curriculum, her image is negative and, as perceived in the books, her existence seemed to consist of hard work, grief and resignation to the will of God. It was also presented in official circles as the authentic picture of Gaeltacht life, which it certainly was not. These perceptions were helpful neither to the reputation of Sayers herself nor to the language she loved. Scholars have also made the important point that the books were not written by Peig but were reminiscences which she dictated to others; they also observe that the autobiographical genre was not suited to her mode of traditional storytelling. Plans for full publication of her stories (most of which have never been published) are in preparation and should provide the basis for a fairer assessment of her legacy.

SOURCES:

Flower, Robin. *The Western Island.* Oxford: Oxford University Press, 1945. New ed. 1973.

Sayers, Peig. *Peig: The Autobiography of Peig Sayers of the Great Blasket Island.* First published in Irish in 1936 and translated from Irish by Bryan MacMahon. Dublin: Talbot Press, 1973.

———. *An Old Woman's Reflections.* First published in Irish in 1939 and translated from Irish by Seamus Ennis with an introduction by W.R. Rodgers. Oxford: Oxford University Press, 1962.

The Voice of Generations: The Story of Peig Sayers. Radio Telifís Éireann (Dublin) documentary, December 8, 1998.

Deirdre McMahon,
lecturer in history at Mary Immaculate College,
University of Limerick, Limerick, Ireland

Sayre, Zelda (1900–1948).

See Fitzgerald, Zelda.

Saz, Leyla (1850–1936).

See Hanim, Leyla.

Sbislava of Kiev (d. 1110).

See Zbyslawa.

Scala, Beatrice della or Reginna della (1340–1384).

See della Scala, Beatrice.

Scales, Jessie Sleet (fl. 1900)

First African-American public health nurse. Flourished around 1900; born in Stratford, Ontario, Canada; graduated from the Provident Hospital School of Nursing, Chicago, 1895.

Several historians have reached the conclusion that Jessie Sleet Scales was the first black public health nurse active in the United States. A native of southwestern Ontario—which in pre-Civil War times had been a prime terminus for the Underground Railroad—Scales graduated from Chicago's Provident Hospital School of Nursing in 1895, hoping to work in the field of public health. Moving to New York, she was rejected for many jobs simply because of her race, despite the fact that institutionally trained nurs-

es were in short supply at the time. Scales was finally employed in 1900 by the Charity Organization Society to make home visits to black tuberculosis sufferers and convince them to seek medical treatment. Given the post on a two-month trial basis, she did so well that her reports on her work were submitted by her supervisor for publication in the *American Journal of Nursing*, and the editor of the *Journal* remarked on her capabilities and altruism. Scales continued her work with the society for nine years.

SOURCES:

Carnegie, Mary Elizabeth. *The Path We Tread: Blacks in Nursing 1854–1984.* Philadelphia, PA: J.B. Lippincott, 1986.

James M. Manheim,
freelance writer and editor,
Ann Arbor, Michigan

Scarborough, Dorothy (1878–1935)

American novelist and musicologist. Born in Mount Carmel, Texas, on January 27, 1878; died on November 7, 1935; daughter of John B. Scarborough (a lawyer) and Mary Adelaide Scarborough; sister of Martha McDaniel Scarborough and George Moore Scarborough, both writers; received bachelor's and master's degrees from Baylor University in Waco, Texas, 1890s; studied at the University of Chicago; studied at Oxford University in England, 1910–11; Columbia University in New York, Ph.D., 1917; never married.

Selected writings: Fugitive Verses *(1912);* The Supernatural in Modern English Fiction *(1917);* From a Southern Porch *(1919);* In the Land of Cotton *(1923);* On the Trail of Negro Folk-Songs *(1925);* The Wind *(1925);* The Unfair Sex *(1925);* Impatient Griselda *(1927);* Can't Get a Red Bird *(1929);* The Stretch-berry Smile *(1932);* The Story of Cotton *(1933);* A Song Catcher in Southern Mountains *(1937, posthumous).*

Known equally well for a series of realistic novels and for her pioneering investigations of American folk music, Dorothy Scarborough helped to pave the way for the generation of Southern women writers who came to prominence in the middle of the 20th century. Though she wrote and taught in New York for much of her professional life, Scarborough drew upon her Texas origins in her fiction and was perhaps that state's most important contributor to the regionalist style that gained favor between the world wars.

Scarborough was born in the East Texas town of Mount Carmel on January 27, 1878. As a child, she experienced the stark, severe environment of West Texas when her family moved to the town of Sweetwater, hoping the dry climate there would cure her mother's lung disease; West Texas would become the setting for Scarborough's most famous novel, *The Wind*. Her mother's health did improve, and the family moved to Waco, drawn there by Baylor University and the educational opportunities it could provide for the Scarborough children. All three surviving children showed literary talent—Dorothy's sister **Martha McDaniel Scarborough** would write novels, poetry, and a biography of her husband, and her brother George Moore Scarborough became a successful playwright. He moved to Hollywood and, in the 1920s, collaborated with Dorothy on the screenplay for the film version of *The Wind*, which featured silent-screen star *Lillian Gish*.

Scarborough graduated young from Baylor, contributing a piece to the university's literary magazine when she was only 15. She taught English and journalism at Baylor, and made vigorous efforts to further her education, receiving a master's degree from Baylor and taking courses at the University of Chicago. In 1910, Scarborough traveled to England and spent a year at Oxford University, a journey of the body and mind that challenged her and opened up her future career. Returning to her teaching position at Baylor, Scarborough explored her growing interest in folklore with the publication of a group of poems, *Fugitive Verses* (1912), which highlighted black folk songs. Baylor granted her a leave of absence so she could work toward her doctoral degree at Columbia University in New York. Her dissertation on the supernatural in English fiction was completed in 1917 and published by Putnam. With the publication came an offer of a teaching position at Columbia, which Scarborough accepted. While teaching there in the 1920s and 1930s, she found herself much in demand as a commentator and lecturer.

Like many other writers of the 1920s, Scarborough strove in her novels toward a realistic depiction of a single region of the country—in her case, the South and her home state of Texas. *The Wind* (1925) is the story of the devastation wreaked on a cultured woman by the harsh environment of West Texas; the novel's unsentimental depiction of implacable natural forces seized the public's imagination with the aid of Gish's film version. Perhaps inspired by a trilogy of works by novelist Frank Norris that dealt with wheat farming, Scarborough completed three novels that explored the difficult life of Southern sharecropper cotton farmers. *In the Land of Cotton* (1923), *Can't Get a Red Bird* (1929), and *The Stretch-berry Smile* (1932) did not achieve the renown of Norris' books, but, together with *The Wind*, they cemented Scarborough's reputation as an important regional writer and as the voice of a progressive spirit in Southern fiction.

Even before leaving Texas, Scarborough had become interested in the new discipline of folklore, combining her keen observations of the ways and works of the common people around her (vividly on display in her fiction) with the tools of the systematic study of folk cultures. She gravitated especially toward music. *On the Trail of Negro Folk Songs*, published by Harvard University Press in 1925, was still useful to scholars decades later, after many other intensive studies of black folk music had been made. At the time of her death in November 1935, she was at work on another major folk song collection, *A Song Catcher in Southern Mountains*, which was issued posthumously in 1937. The rigors of travel in the mountains may have had deleterious effects on her health.

At Columbia, students of Scarborough's included *Carson McCullers, later famous as an explorer in fiction of Southern culture's bizarre corners. Scarborough put her students in contact with such famous writers as her friends *Edna Ferber and Hamlin Garland, and many of those students rewarded her efforts by maintaining a lifelong correspondence with her. As a writer, Scarborough engaged herself with some of the most important intellectual currents of her time. As a teacher, she encouraged her students to do the same, and her own early career provided an exemplary demonstration of the value of the single-minded pursuit of an advanced education. It enabled her to rise to the top echelon of the American writing profession of her day.

SOURCES:

Crawford, Ann Fears, and Crystal Sasse Ragsdale. *Women in Texas*. Austin, TX: State House Press, 1992.

Kunitz, Stanley J., and Howard Haycraft, eds. *Twentieth Century Authors*. NY: H.W. Wilson, 1942.

James M. Manheim,
freelance writer and editor,
Ann Arbor, Michigan

Scemiophris (fl. 1680–1674 BCE).

See Sobek-neferu.

Scepens, Elizabeth (fl. 1476)

Artist and bookmaker of Belgium. Name variations: Elisabeth Betkin. Flourished around 1476 in Bruges.

Elizabeth Scepens ran a successful art studio in Bruges, Flanders. She studied book production and illustration under the illuminator

William Vrelandt of Bruges, and upon his death took over the large, prolific studio in partnership with Vrelandt's widow. The studio contributed to the production of manuscripts in several ways: with calligraphy, capital decoration, and painted miniatures. Scepens' talent earned her a membership in the Bruges guild of scribes and artists in 1476; the membership was renewed every year until her retirement in 1489.

SOURCES:

Anderson, Bonnie S., and Judith P. Zinsser. *A History of Their Own*, vol. I. NY: Harper & Row, 1988.

Chadwick, Whitney. *Women, Art, and Society*. London: Thames & Hudson, 1990.

Laura York,
Riverside, California

Schacherer-Elek, Ilona (1907–1988).

See Mayer, Helene for sidebar.

Schaffner, Katherine.

See Marvelettes.

Schaft, Hannie (1920–1945)

Member of the Dutch resistance during World War II who protected Jews, gathered vital reconnaissance information, assassinated Germans and Dutch collaborators, and was executed in the last days of the war.

Name variations: Johanna Jannetje Schaft; "Johanna Elderkamp." Born Jannetje Johanna Schaft in Haarlem, the Netherlands, on September 16, 1920; executed on April 17, 1945; daughter of Pieter Schaft (a teacher) and Aafje Talea (Vrijer) Schaft; was a law student in Amsterdam at the time of the German occupation of the Netherlands, in May 1940; never married; no children.

Became an active member of a Communist resistance cell in Haarlem, hiding and assisting Jews who were being rounded up for "resettlement" to the death camps of the East (1941); with Freddie and Truus Oversteegen, carried out assassinations and became known to the German forces as the "red-haired girl" (1942–43); encouraged student solidarity that led to closing down of the Dutch universities (1943); arrested (March 1945) and executed (April 17, 1945), only three weeks before the collapse of Nazi Germany and the liberation of her country.

By the late 1930s, many in the Netherlands felt that they could no longer avoid war. Two decades earlier, during World War I, their country had managed to remain neutral, but with the rise of Nazism in Germany it became clear that this small nation would not be strong enough to defend itself against the aggressive forces gather-

ing to the west. On May 10, 1940, the fears of the 1930s became grim reality when the German Blitzkrieg smashed across the German border into Belgium and the Netherlands. The Dutch queen *Wilhelmina fled to England on May 13, and the next day the German Luftwaffe bombed and destroyed the port city of Rotterdam, killing nearly 1,000 civilians. On May 15, recognizing their situation as hopeless, Dutch military commanders surrendered, as Nazi tanks rolled into the capital city of Amsterdam. That same day, at least 150 Dutch men and women, many of them Jews, committed suicide.

Among the Dutch resolved to resist the Nazi occupiers was a 20-year-old woman named Hannie Schaft, a law student who commuted from her native city of Haarlem to the University of Amsterdam for classes several days a week. Born Jannetje Johanna Schaft in Haarlem on September 16, 1920, she was the daughter of Pieter and **Aafje Vrijer Schaft**. Pieter was a teacher with Social Democratic ideals; Aafje was the daughter of a minister and held equally strong Christian Socialist beliefs. During Hannie's childhood, the most important event had been the death of her 12-year-old sister Annie, in December 1927, of diphtheria. Hannie and her parents were left inconsolable. From that point on, the Schafts were highly protective of their only remaining child, a shy and bookish girl.

Growing up in the 1930s, young Hannie witnessed the conditions of massive unemployment in her country brought on by a worldwide depression, as well as the growing fear of aggression by the Fascist states of Germany and Italy. Many Dutch people, even those who had previously enjoyed a middle-class standard of living like the Schaft family, suffered. By late 1931, 250,000 were out of work, a situation that had worsened in 1934 to 415,000 registered unemployed. In 1932, 400,000 lived below the official poverty line. In the midst of such misery in the Netherlands only radical change seemed to promise relief. Some were drawn to the Fascist ideology of Anton Mussert, whose NSB party received 8% of the vote in the 1935 provincial elections.

Even as a schoolchild Hannie hated Fascism. She was an admirer of the Russian Revolution of 1917 that brought about the Soviet Union, and in one of her class compositions, written in 1936, she noted sarcastically that Mussolini's Italy had "brought civilization" to conquered Ethiopia by using machine guns, bombs and poison gas. During the Spanish Civil War between General Franco's Fascists and the International Brigades who went to Spain to save democracy, she listened eagerly to the radio and read newspaper accounts to keep abreast. Young Schaft's heroes were not movie stars or athletes but enemies of Fascism like Georgi Dimitrov, the defiant Bulgarian revolutionary and courtroom hero of the Reichstag Fire Trial, and Carl von Ossietzky, German anti-Nazi recipient of the Nobel Peace Prize, who was tortured in a German concentration camp and died of this ill-treatment a few days after his release in 1938.

Even more radical than her Socialist parents, Schaft believed that only a profound social revolution could bring an end to economic exploitation, war, and racism. In the fall of 1938, she began her study of law at the University of Amsterdam. Europe was on the brink of war that tragic autumn: the Western allies at the Munich conference, attempting to appease Hitler's appetite for territory, capitulated by giving him strategic sections of Czechoslovakia. In the civil war in Spain, the republic was rapidly succumbing to Franco's militarily superior Fascist forces. At school, Schaft was a student of Professor H.J. Pos, a passionate foe of Fascism and an active member of the Committee of Vigilance, a leading anti-Nazi organization. The young Dutch student had Jewish friends both in Haarlem and in Amsterdam, and concern for them deepened her opposition to Hitler's racist policies.

Following the May 1940 occupation, the Germans initially were not as brutal in Holland as they were in Eastern Europe. By February 1941, however, many Dutch men and women were incensed by the increasing anti-Semitism exhibited by German occupying forces and Dutch collaborators. Amsterdam, which had a large Jewish population, also had the country's largest concentration of Socialists and Communists; it was in Amsterdam, therefore, that Dutch Nazis had wanted to prove their loyalty. At first, the mistreatment of Jews by Dutch storm troopers led to the creation of Jewish Action Groups, working as self-defense units along with non-Jewish groups from working-class neighborhoods to vigorously resist Dutch Nazi provocations. On February 11, a group of Nazis who entered Amsterdam's Jewish quarter met spirited resistance, and one of the Nazis died of his wounds. On February 19, German police became involved, and Jewish defenders sprayed them with acid. Within days, 425 young Jewish men were under arrest as the result of brutal raids, and the population of Amsterdam went on strike in protest of racist policies. The strike, led by defiant Communists, spread quickly to Haarlem and other major Dutch cities, the first significant act of opposition in German-occupied Europe against anti-Semitic policies. For Hannie Schaft, it was also the catalyst drawing her into the fight against Nazi repression.

Late in 1941, she joined the small, Communist-leaning Raad van Verzet (Council of Resistance) cell in Haarlem, one of the many illegal groups organized to resist the Nazi occupation forces and their Dutch collaborators. It was also the most militant. Although not officially a Communist organization, the group was allied to the Communist resistance movement, and all of its members were sympathetic to the political Left. Before Schaft became the third woman in the group, **Truus** and **Freddie Oversteegen**, 17 and 15 respectively, were its only female members. There were also five men.

Hannie's work at first involved assisting Jews who were attempting to escape the tightening dragnet, as the Germans gathered them up to be sent to concentration camps and eventually to extermination facilities farther to the east. Sometimes she hid Jews in her parents' home, where they were given food, encouragement, and false

Hannie Schaft

documents. She also collected funds from sympathetic individuals in Haarlem to support these activities.

With the passage of time, Hannie, Truus, and Freddie began more radical resistance, specializing in the assassination of German Nazi officers and Dutch traitors. The reaction of the Dutch population in Haarlem and elsewhere to these activities was by no means uniformly positive. For one thing, the Germans began taking and shooting a growing number of Dutch hostages in retaliation. There were even objections within the resistance movement, some members of which felt women should not be assassins. Schaft and the Oversteegens strongly disagreed with this viewpoint, and in time the trio became notorious in German and Dutch Nazi circles for their bold effectiveness. Branded as dangerous terrorists, they were the targets of countless hours spent in searching for them, and particularly for the "red-haired girl": Hannie Schaft.

At the end of 1942, when the occupiers authorized 7,000 students to be called up for obligatory labor service in Germany, Schaft joined virtually all her fellow students in defiantly refusing to bow to this measure. The Nazis, attempting to split the student movement by adopting conciliatory tactics, first lowered the number to 3,000; when this still met with opposition, they announced a postponement of the plan with no deadline for a new policy. The crisis deepened again, however, early in 1943. General H.A. Seyffardt and several other leading Dutch collaborators were assassinated. It soon became clear that students had played an important role in these killings, and several hundred young people were arrested and interrogated.

In March 1943, the German Commissioner of the Occupied Netherland Territories, Arthur Seyss-Inquart, enraged by the success of the students, imposed a loyalty oath on students; everyone was required to sign or else relinquish the right to study. Schaft, once considered shy and scholarly, argued forcefully against signing the oath on moral grounds. When 86% of the student body ultimately refused to submit, higher education in the Netherlands was for all practical purposes at an end. Schaft successfully completed her law studies in underground classes, but she was not to live long enough to be awarded her degree.

Earlier, in February 1943, the German defeat at Stalingrad had had a powerful effect on the morale of the Dutch. The Nazis had essentially lost the war, but remained a strong and ruthless foe, determined to hold onto their conquered na-

tions as long as possible. That year, Dutch resistance grew considerably, but the geography of the Netherlands, which lacks both mountains and forests, made it impossible to create the kind of partisan movement that flourished in Yugoslavia and in the Soviet Union. The Dutch functioned as "urban partisans," concentrating on hit-and-run activities and intelligence-gathering operations of value to the Allies. A nationwide Council of Resistance was created, in which Schaft and the Oversteegens played a leading role. The group, which included Communists, Social Democrats, anarchists and liberals, was led by Jan Bonekamp, a factory worker with a clear political vision and an almost total lack of fear.

By this time a prominent figure in the resistance, Schaft worked closely with Bonekamp, who taught her how to use weapons in the woods behind the home of Mari Andriessen, a noted Haarlem sculptor. Schaft soon fell in love with Bonekamp, an unsophisticated, warm-hearted man of the people whose hair was rarely in place. Hannie, in contrast, was an attractive, well-educated, middle-class woman, whose radicalism was based on emotion and education rather than on personal deprivation. To complicate matters, Jan was married and on the Nazi "most wanted" list; he was forced to live in hiding.

Schaft maintained her contacts with the Oversteegens, who had moved to the city of Enschede where they worked as nurses and collected data on a local German military airport. Politically on the left but not a dogmatic Marxist, Schaft studied Karl Marx's Das Kapital but also investigated the great works of Eastern philosophy and the ideals of non-violence espoused by India's Mohandas Gandhi. When not reading philosophy, she and Jan were occupied with attacking strategic facilities. On November 27, 1943, they destroyed the power plant at Velsen. Two days later, in the town of Beverwijk, they carried out the assassination of a notorious collaborator. In January 1944, Schaft was involved in destroying a Haarlem movie theater by arson.

The German authorities became increasingly incensed by their losses. Hitler himself ordered his subordinates in the Netherlands to eliminate the group doing such damage, and, starting in December 1943, an ongoing anti-sabotage policy against the Dutch resistance, known as Aktion Silbertanne ("Silver Fir"), was initiated. If German officials or Dutch collaborators were killed or wounded, Dutch hostages were increasingly shot in retaliation, and German officials began to specialize in anti-resistance cruelties. People like Willy Lages, head of the Aktion, his assistant Emil Rühl, and SS member Maarten Kuijper, a Dutch collaborator, were particularly notorious for their capturing and torturing activities.

In early 1944, Schaft was assigned to prepare a detailed map of German-built fortifications on the Dutch coastline, a difficult and dangerous task which she carried out brilliantly. Access to coastal military zones was highly restricted, but she entered the banned regions with relative impunity. She was poised and confident, spoke excellent German, and was in possession of forged papers identifying her as "Johanna Elderkamp" born in Zurich, Switzerland. Coupling her own observations with information from other resistance members, she was able to provide a complete map, which was sent through resistance channels to London, where it served as the basis for a successful raid by 300 Royal Air Force planes on the German submarine facilities at Ijmuiden on March 26, 1944.

By the spring of 1944, Hannie Schaft and members of her cell were planning new guerrilla activities and maintaining contacts with various groups in the nationwide Council of Resistance network. In April, she and Jan took part in a dramatic guerrilla attack on the Krommenie city hall, where their unit seized documents valuable to the resistance. A few days later, the group carried out an important raid on a chemical facility in Amsterdam. But as the war neared its end, the Haarlem cell's incredible good luck began to run out. During a raid in June 1944, one of its most courageous members, Gerrit Jan van der Veen, was badly wounded and captured by the Nazis, betrayed by a traitor in their midst. On June 12, 1944, less than a week after the Allies had landed on the beaches of Normandy, Gerrit and several others were executed by the Nazis. Bonekamp, Schaft and other surviving members of their cell took an oath to avenge the tragic deaths, and high on their list for elimination was Police Captain Ragut in the town of Zaandam. Ragut was a notorious collaborator, responsible for many deaths in the resistance, whose motives were particularly loathsome as he was not even a Nazi sympathizer; he simply worked for considerable sums of money.

On June 21, 1944, Schaft and Bonekamp cycled to Zaandam, where he managed to shoot Ragut. But as the couple fled the scene, Ragut appeared to be still alive, so Bonekamp returned to finish the job. Meanwhile, Schaft continued to cycle ahead, planning to meet him at a pre-arranged site. Ragut then shot Bonekamp who, severely wounded, staggered to a house for help.

Instead, the inhabitants called the police. Bonekamp lingered on for a number of hours, during which he was recognized by a local collaborator. The anti-resistance expert Rühl arrived, and ordered an injection for Jan to make him talk; Rühl then told the dying man that he was a friend and wanted to take him to his comrades. No longer able to sense the danger, Bonekamp gave Rühl the address of Hannie and her parents just before dying.

A few days later, Nazi police arrived at Schaft's home, arrested her parents, and sent them to German concentration camps. An emotionally distraught Hannie was taken from Haarlem by friends to a safe place and given new identity papers. She told them that she would surrender to the Nazis in exchange for her parents' release. Alarmed at her unbalanced state, the resistance leaders assigned Truus and Freddie Oversteegen to stay with Schaft day and night until she could regain her equilibrium. Slowly, the distraught Schaft got a grip on her emotions, and concluded that her work was more necessary than ever before. She took on a new appearance, with eyeglasses and her hair dyed black. She was no longer the "red-haired girl" the Nazis had been pursuing for so long.

Postage stamp issued on March 22, 1962, by the German Democratic Republic, honoring Hannie Schaft.

After much soul-searching, Schaft and the Oversteegens now concluded that they must avoid involvement in actions that would lead to the loss of innocent lives, Dutch or German, although it might limit some of their actions. Consequently, the trio vehemently opposed plans by the Council to bomb the Universal department store in Amsterdam, arguing that while such raids might weaken German morale, it would inevitably result in the loss of innocent Dutch shoppers and ordinary German soldiers. A plan to kidnap and hold the children of Seyss-Inquart for ransom was also summarily rejected by Schaft, for dropping to the moral level of the enemy. "We are not like the Nazis," she argued, "we of the resistance do not kill children," and neither of these plans were subsequently carried out by the male-led leadership of the council.

In the late summer and early fall of 1944, Schaft gathered information to produce a detailed map of German rocket-launching sites. Southern England was under increasing attacks by Nazi V-1 and V-2 rockets that took lives and were eroding morale, and when her work was completed and forwarded to London, it helped Allied pilots to target the launching facilities. By the autumn of 1944, however, the Dutch citizenry was suffering terribly throughout the lowlands. Food scarcities caused disease and death among infants, the old, and the weak. Schaft and Truus Oversteegen spent almost every day conveying food supplies, literature and weapons from one resistance group to another. The Nazis generally searched women less thoroughly than they did men, so despite a few close calls she was able to function effectively during this time as a courier. But as the war wound down toward the end of 1944, the occupying army became increasingly brutal and arbitrary. One terrible incident involved the village of Putten, which was burned to the ground in retaliation for the resistance killing of a single German officer. Of the 590 men taken from the village to Germany, only about 50 survived the war. In March 1945, when it was clear that the conflict would be over in a matter of days or weeks, a failed attack on Hanns Rauter, Seyss-Inquart's deputy, resulted in the retaliatory execution of more than 250 Dutch prisoners.

In the winter of 1944–45, Schaft's group remained relatively quiet, waiting for the Allies. But the military liberation did not take place, and politics intervened. In London, the Dutch government-in-exile put pressure on the leaders of the resistance to rein in the activities of the leftist and Communist groups operating underground, fearing that they might attempt to seize power when German authority crumbled. Not until early spring 1945 did the Haarlem group resume some of its work, blowing up a train carrying industrial equipment to Germany. On March 15, Schaft and the Oversteegens carried out an assassination attempt against Ko Langendijk, a notorious collaborator, who was wounded but survived. On March 21, Schaft was bicycling to Ijmuiden when she was stopped at a German control point and was unable to get rid of her handbag, which contained copies of the underground Communist paper *De Waarheid*. Worse, she was also discovered to be carrying a pistol. Taken to a prison cell, she maintained her composure through relentless interrogation, but was then sent to Amsterdam and interrogated by Emil Rühl. Recognized as the "red-haired girl," she was warned that without a complete confession, five Dutch girls would be executed, and Hannie broke down and confessed. After the war, Rühl noted that despite the harsh treatment, the longtime resistance fighter behaved with dignity throughout her ordeal.

Had she not been labeled "a dangerous Communist," Schaft might well have lived to see her country's liberation from Fascism. But she did not fall into the category of prisoners that the Germans had informally promised to protect. Because of her dramatic resistance successes and the strong Communist affiliations of her Haarlem group, she was defined as a notorious terrorist. On April 17, 1945, three weeks before the final collapse of Nazi Germany, Aktion leader Lages conveyed the execution order; Schaft was taken from her cell and driven by car to the sand dunes of Overveen. There she was executed by Kuijper, the Dutch SS officer, and hastily buried among the bodies of 421 other Dutch men and women of the resistance for whom the dunes had been an execution ground.

Liberated from their captivity in Germany, Schaft's parents came back to Haarlem hoping to be reunited with their daughter. For awhile there appeared to be hope that she was still alive, but on May 21, the couple received confirmation of her death. Her body was exhumed and on November 27, 1945, in a ceremony attended by Queen Wilhelmina and others of the Dutch royal family, she was honored as part of an impressive funeral in the dunes where she had lost her life seven months earlier. Schaft was reburied along with the 421 other resisters who had given their lives. A modest stone marks her final resting place, noting her name and dates of birth and death as well as the simple phrase, *Zij diende* ("She served").

As the Cold War progressed, Hannie Schaft's reputation suffered. Conservatives labeled her a doctrinaire Communist and cold-blooded terrorist, and standard Dutch reference works omitted mention of her, turning her into a veritable "non-person." In 1952, the police even banned a ceremony in her honor. In Eastern Europe and the Soviet Union, she was harnessed to Cold War propaganda, cited as a Communist resistance heroine although she had never been a member of the party. In March 1962, the German Democratic Republic commemorated her life and work on a postage stamp that was part of a series honoring European anti-Fascist martyrs. By the late 1970s, the Cold War attitudes that had distorted memory of the life and struggles of Hannie Schaft were on the wane, allowing a new generation of scholars to recognize this remarkable young woman, martyred at age 25, for what she truly was, a fighter who helped to save Jews and to liberate her country.

SOURCES:

Haarlems Dagblad (special supplement dedicated to Schaft). May 3, 1975.

Hirschfeld, Gerhard. *Nazi Rule and Dutch Collaboration: The Netherlands under German Occupation 1940–1945.* Translated by Louise Willmot. Oxford: Berg, 1988.

Kock, Erich. *Unterdrückung und Widerstand: 5 Jahre deutscher Besetzung in den Niederlanden 1940–1945.* Dortmund-Brackel: Fritz Brandt-Druck, 1960.

Kooy, G.A. *Het echec van een 'volkse' beweging: Nazificatie en denazificatie in Nederland 1931–1945.* Assen: Van Gorcum, 1964.

Kors, Ton. *Hannie Schaft: Het levensverhaal van een vrouw in verzet tegen de nazi's.* Amsterdam: Van Gennep, 1976.

Krasil'nikov, E.P. "Khanni Skhaft-Geroina dvizheniia soprotivleniia niderlandakh," in *Novaia i Noveishaia Istoriia.* No. 6, 1986, pp. 113–124.

Luykx, P. "Collaboratie," in *Spiegel Historiae.* Vol. 17, no. 7–8, 1982, pp. 382–387.

Menger, Truus. *Toen Nit, Nu Niet, Nooit.* The Hague: Leopold, 1982.

Rijksinstituut voor Oorlogsdocumentatie, Amsterdam, biographical dossiers.

Schwegman, Marjan. "Women in Resistance Organisations in The Netherlands," in Thompson, Paul and Natasha Burchardt, eds. *Our Common History: The Transformation of Europe.* Atlantic Highlands, NJ: Humanities Press, 1982, pp. 297–310.

Strobl, Ingrid. *"Sag nie, du gehst den letzten Weg": Frauen im bewaffneten Widerstand gegen Faschismus und deutsche Besatzung.* Frankfurt am Main: Fischer Taschenbuch, 1989.

Verzetsmuseum, Amsterdam, biographical files.

Vries, Theun de. *Het meisje met het rode haar: Roman uit het verzet 1942–1945.* Amsterdam: Pegasus, 1956.

Warmbrunn, Werner. *The Dutch under German Occupation 1940–1945.* Stanford, CA: Stanford University Press, 1963.

Wildt, Annemarie de, ed. *Je deed wat je doen moest: Vrouwen in verzet.* Amsterdam: 1985.

John Haag,
Associate Professor of History,
University of Georgia, Athens, Georgia

Schalk, Henriëtte van der (1869–1952).

See Roland Holst, Henriëtte.

Schaller, Johanna Klier (b. 1952).

See Klier-Schaller, Johanna.

Scharff-Goldhaber, Gertrude
(b. 1911)

American physicist. Name variations: Gertrude Scharff Goldhaber; Mrs. Maurice Goldhaber. Born Gertrude Scharff in Mannheim, Germany, on July 14, 1911; daughter of Otto Scharff and Nelly (Steinharter) Scharff; attended universities of Freiburg, Zurich, and Berlin; Ph.D., University of Munich, 1935; married Maurice Goldhaber (director of Brookhaven National Laboratory), on May 24, 1939; sister-in-law of **Sulamith Goldhaber** *(d. 1965, also a physicist); children: Alfred Scharff Goldhaber; Michael Henry Goldhaber.*

Born in Mannheim, Germany, in 1911, nuclear physicist Gertrude Scharff-Goldhaber had a long and influential career. Scharff-Goldhaber was a research associate at the Imperial College in London from 1935 to 1939. Following her marriage to Maurice Goldhaber, director of the Brookhaven National Laboratory in Upton, New York, she arrived in the United States in 1939 and became a naturalized citizen in 1944. She was a research physicist at the University of Illinois, Champaign, from 1939 to 1948, an assistant professor from 1948 to 1950, associate physicist at Brookhaven from 1950 to 1958, and senior physicist from 1962 on. At Brookhaven, she was immersed in both theoretical and experimental work, ascertaining the detailed properties of nuclear energy levels and magnetic moments to gain a better grasp of nuclear structure. She served on the Committee on Problems of Women in Physics in 1971.

Scharlieb, Mary Ann (1845–1930)

English physician who was one of the first female judges in England. Name variations: Dame Mary Ann Dacomb Scharlieb. Born Mary Ann Dacomb Bird in 1845; died in 1930; entered Medical School of Madras in India, 1877; London University, M.D., 1888; married W.M. Scharlieb (a lawyer), in 1865.

Dame Mary Ann Scharlieb overcame Victorian prejudice against women in the medical profession and became a noted gynecological surgeon. Scharlieb spent part of her life in India, and was first motivated to seek a medical education from witnessing the dangers that Indian women experienced in childbirth. Dividing her activities between England and India, she amassed a record of accomplishment over a career that lasted a lifetime.

Born Mary Ann Bird in 1845, she married lawyer W.M. Scharlieb before she had reached the age of 20. Scharlieb accompanied her husband to India in 1866. Eleven years later, she qualified for entrance to the Medical School of Madras along with three other women, and studied there for three years, even though the school's superintendent had written disparagingly of the prospect of giving women a medical education. Returning to London, she earned a degree from the Royal Free Hospital in 1882 and was granted an M.D. degree from London University in 1888.

Scharlieb is said to have been a skilled surgeon, but she believed that female doctors should restrict themselves to the fields of midwifery, gynecology, and pediatrics. With the aid of pioneering physician *Elizabeth Garrett Anderson, she established a private practice, and in 1892 obtained the post of chief surgeon at the New Hospital for Women. She served there until 1903. Scharlieb also devoted her professional energies to the medical life of her part-time home of India, for whose cultural traditions she expressed great respect. In the middle 1880s, she played an important role in establishing the Royal Victoria Hospital for Caste and Gosha Women, and worked to form a Women's Medical Service for India during World War I.

Later in life, Scharlieb was richly honored. In 1920, she became one of the first English women named to a judgeship, and in 1926 she received the title of Dame Commander of the Order of the British Empire—the female equivalent of knighthood. She died in 1930.

SUGGESTED READING:

Arnold, David. *Colonizing the Body: State Medicine and Epidemic Disease in Nineteenth-Century India.* Berkeley, CA: University of California Press, 1993.

Blake, Catriona. *The Charge of the Parasols: Women's Entry into the Medical Profession.* London: Women's Press, 1990.

Bonner, Thomas Neville. *To the Ends of the Earth: Women's Search for Education in Medicine.* Cambridge, MA: Harvard University Press, 1992.

James M. Manheim, freelance writer and editor, Ann Arbor, Michigan

Scharrer, Berta (1906–1995)

German-born American neuroscientist who, with her husband, virtually founded the discipline of neuroendocrinology. Born Berta Vogel in Munich, Germany, on December 1, 1906; died in the Bronx, New York City, on July 23, 1995; daughter of Karl Phillip Vogel and Johanna (Greis) Vogel; married Ernst Albert Scharrer (1906–1965, a scientist), in 1934.

In 1937, two German scientists arrived in the United States as refugees from Nazism, "with $4 each and clear consciences." As gentiles, Berta Scharrer and her husband Ernst Scharrer could have remained in Germany; indeed, their careers there might have thrived in view of the fact that the persecution and expulsion of Jewish faculty members had created many desirable openings in Germany's universities and research centers. But the Scharrers' principles could no longer allow them to stomach the increasing inhumanity of the Third Reich. When they arrived in America, they brought with them an already significant amount of scientific knowledge and experience. By 1937, both had made progress in their investigations into a phenomenon they had discovered in the animal kingdom, the ability of some nerve cells to secrete hormonal substances. Working as a team, the Scharrers made major discoveries in this area, which quickly became the new discipline of neuroendocrinology.

Berta Scharrer was born in Munich in 1906, the daughter of a judge. After earning her doctorate in biology in 1930 from the University of Munich, she took a position as research associate in a psychiatric research institute in that city. Berta married fellow biologist Ernst Albert Scharrer in 1934. In 1928, Ernst had discovered what he termed nerve-gland cells in a fish, making the then startling hypothesis that some nerve cells were as much involved in secreting hormonal substances as were cells of the endocrine system. This idea, namely that neurons had a dual function, was revolutionary, indeed heretical. Up to this time, scientific orthodoxy had argued that either cells secreted hormones, in which case they were endocrine cells, or they conducted electrical impulses, making them nerve cells that were part of the nervous system. To carry out their plan of investigating this phenomenon, the Scharrers divided up the animal kingdom between them: Ernst would specialize on vertebrates; Berta would study the invertebrates.

Their research progressed well, particularly after Ernst was named director of the Edinger Institute for Brain Research in Frankfurt am Main. There, as a research associate, Berta made great strides during the next few years, discovering nerve-gland cells in mollusks in 1935, in worms in 1936, and in insects early in 1937. But while their work in the new area of neurosecretion was going well, life in Nazi Germany was becoming unbearable. Even though they were not affected by the regime's racism, the general level of brutality had reached an intolerable level. In 1937, the Scharrers decided to emigrate to the United States, traveling via the Trans-Siberian Railway and the Pacific, and collecting specimens along the way. For the next several years, Ernst held temporary posts at the University of Chicago and New York's Rockefeller Institute.

Berta continued her insect research. At the University of Chicago, she quickly realized that her small laboratory table greatly limited her choice of invertebrate specimens. When a helpful custodian informed her, "We have roaches in the basement, do you want some?," she answered in the affirmative. The Chicago roaches proved to be highly suited for her studies, being small and free for the taking. In 1940, soon after she and her husband arrived in New York City, a further stroke of good fortune took place. In a shipment of South American monkeys to the Rockefeller Institute there were a number of roaches in the bottom of the now-empty crate. These roaches, *Leucophaea maderae*, would become the subjects of Berta Scharrer's research for the next 55 years. She found them preferable to their American cousins because they were larger and slower, and were live-bearers rather than egg-layers.

Although affected by nepotism rules and other forms of discrimination against women scientists in the academic world, Berta ignored these injustices and concentrated on her research. Even though the two did all their work together as a research team, only her husband received a salary and the title of professor, while she remained an unpaid researcher. In 1955, she finally gained long-overdue recognition for her work when both she and her husband were offered joint positions at the newly created Albert Einstein College of Medicine at New York's Yeshiva University. Now a professor, she taught histology (the microscopic structure of tissues), while continuing an ambitious program investigating insect glands. Using the electron microscope, Berta was able to accomplish some of the earliest detailing of the insect nervous system and especially the neurosecretory system. Together with her husband, in 1963 she published *Neuroendocrinology*, which was immediately recognized as a basic textbook in the new discipline.

Ernst died in a swimming accident in Florida in 1965 that almost cost Berta her life. Determined to continue the work both had done for so long, she carried out more research over the next decades. Although she officially retired from Albert Einstein College of Medicine in 1978, she remained an involved scientist. Countless awards and honors came her way over the years, including membership in the U.S. National Academy of Sciences, and receipt of the Kraepelin Medal of the Max Planck Institute in Munich in 1978 and of the U.S. National Medal of Science in 1983.

Scharrer remained active to the end of her long, productive life, in July 1995. At the time, there were many tributes. Wrote Aubrey Gorbman and Howard A. Bern:

> Berta Scharrer was a noble, generous, kind, and humane person. Integrity and modesty were hallmarks of her character and career. She was always approachable and helpful to others. She is missed not only for her qualities as a scientist and teacher, but also for the beauty of her friendships and outlook.

SOURCES:

Florey, Ernst. "The Zoological Station at Naples and the Neuron: Personalities and Encounters in a Unique Institution," in *Biological Bulletin*. Vol. 168, no. 3. June 1985, pp. 137–152.

Gorbman, Aubrey, and Howard A. Bern. "In Memoriam Berta V. Scharrer (1906–1995)," in *General and Comparative Endocrinology*. Vol. 101, no. 1. January 1996, pp. 1–2.

Jones, J. Sydney. "Berta Scharrer 1906–1995," in Kristine M. Krapp, ed. *Notable Twentieth-Century Scientists*. Detroit, MI: Gale Research, 1998, pp. 408–410.

Kass-Simon, G. "Biology Is Destiny," in G. Kass-Simon and Patricia Farnes, eds. *Women of Science: Righting the Record*. Bloomington, IN: Indiana University Press, 1990, pp. 215–267.

Martin, Douglas. "Roach Expert, 88, Bids Goodbye to Her Subjects," in *The New York Times*. February 9, 1995, p. C18.

Oksche, A. "In memoriam Berta Scharrer 1906–1995," in *Cell & Tissue Research*. Vol. 282, no. 1. October 1995, pp. 1–2.

Satir, Birgit H., and Peter Satir. "Berta Vogel Scharrer (1906–1995)," in Louise Grinstein, Carol Biermann and Rose K. Rose, eds. *Women in the Biological Sciences: A Bio-Bibliographic Sourcebook*. Westport, CT: Greenwood Press, 1997, pp. 477–489.

Saxon, Wolfgang. "Berta Scharrer, 88, Research Scientist and Roach Expert," in *The New York Times Biographical Service*. July 1995, p. 1061.

Siebert, Charles. "What the Roaches Told Her," in *The New York Times Magazine*. December 31, 1995, pp. 26–27.

Stay, B. "Berta Vogel Scharrer (December 1, 1906–July 23, 1995)," in *Journal of Insect Physiology*. Vol. 41, no. 12. December 1995, pp. 1017–1018.

Wissig, Steven L. "A Tribute to Berta Scharrer," in *The Anatomical Record*. Vol. 249, no. 1. September 1997, pp. 1–5.

John Haag,
Associate Professor History,
University of Georgia, Athens, Georgia

Scharrer, Irene (1888–1971)

English pianist. Born in London, England, on February 2, 1888; died in London on January 11, 1971; cousin of Myra Hess (1890–1965).

Irene Scharrer was born in London in 1888, studied with Tobias Matthay, and made her successful London debut in 1904. A brilliant but subdued musician, she often played two-piano recitals with her cousin, *Myra Hess. In 1925, Scharrer made her first tour of the United States, performing concertos but also doing excellent work as a recitalist and chamber-music pianist.

John Haag,
Athens, Georgia

Schary, Hope Skillman
(c. 1908–1981)

American executive who founded Skillmill, a textile-manufacturing firm. Name variations: Hope Skillman; Mrs. Saul Schary. Born Hope Skillman in Grand Rapids, Michigan, around 1908; died in New Milford, Connecticut, on May 23, 1981; daughter of Frederic Cameron Skillman and Mary (Christie) Skillman; graduated from Goucher College in Maryland, 1961; married Saul Schary, on December 15, 1934.

Probably the first woman to own a textile-manufacturing company, Hope Skillman Schary was a female chief executive at a time when there were very few women in upper management. After many years as a role model for women hoping to enter the upper echelons of the work force, in later life Schary turned her energies directly to the cause of women's rights, emerging as a leader of longstanding volunteer organizations devoted to the advancement of women.

Born Hope Skillman in Grand Rapids, Michigan, around 1908, Schary was an associate editor at *Parnassus* magazine (1932–33) and *The Fine Arts* (1933–34), both in New York City. As a textile designer, she was an assistant stylist with the Ameritex division of Cohn-Hall-Marx Co. (1934–35), stylist (1935–39), and director (1939–42). She then founded Skillmill, Inc. in 1944. Asked once by an interviewer how she had settled on her chosen career, Schary answered that she needed to become self-sustaining (she was married in 1934 to Saul Schary, an artist) and indicated a more general desire to take advantage of her education, drive, and ambition. Even after its wartime beginnings, Skillmill employed only women for some years. Schary remained the company's chief executive until her retirement in the early 1960s.

Schary then stepped into a leadership position at Fashion Group, Inc., an industry association of 5,000 women, serving as president from 1958 to 1960. Gaining recognition for her work on women's-rights issues, Schary became involved with the National Council of Women of the United States, a volunteer organization with a history stretching back to the late 19th century, and served as its president (1970–72 and 1976–78). At the time of her death in 1981, she held the office of vice president in a similar worldwide organization, the International Council of Women.

James M. Manheim,
freelance writer and editor, Ann Arbor, Michigan

Scheff, Fritzi (1879–1954)

Austro-American soprano. Born in Vienna, Austria, on August 30, 1879; died in New York on April 8, 1954; daughter of a physician and a Wagnerian soprano.

When Fritzi Scheff left the Metropolitan Opera in 1903 after three seasons, it was a decision she would later regret. Born in Vienna, Austria, in 1879, she had trained at the Hoch Conservatory in Frankfurt, debuted in Nuremberg on January 10, 1897, and had sung a variety of operatic roles. But in 1903 she left the Met to appear in *Babette*, an operetta written for her by Victor Herbert. Her greatest triumph was in 1906 in another operetta Herbert wrote especially for her, *Mlle Modiste*. Though Scheff appeared in two other Herbert operettas, she had damaged her career as a classical singer. Soon she was forced to sing in vaudeville, Broadway shows, and in nightclubs in order to survive as a singer. Later she became a star on radio and television. By modern standards, Scheff's decision to become a media star would be considered wise, but she was of the old school and always lamented her choice.

John Haag,
Athens, Georgia

Schekeryk, Melanie (b. 1947)

American folk singer. Name variations: Melanie; Melanie Safka. Born Melanie Safka on February 3, 1947, in Queens, New York; daughter of Fred Safka and Polly Safka; married Peter Schekeryk, on December 31, 1968; children: Leilah (b. 1973); Jeordie (b. 1975); Beau Jarred (b. 1981).

Known to her American and European fans simply as Melanie, Melanie Schekeryk has enjoyed a career as a rock, pop, and folk singer-songwriter for over 30 years. Born in 1947 in New York, she gave her first performance on a radio broadcast at age four. After high school graduation, Melanie went on to study at the American Academy of Dramatic Arts in New York, while performing at night at clubs and coffeehouses. She turned professional in 1967 with a record contract for the Columbia Records label. In 1968, she married music publisher Peter Schekeryk. Melanie performed at the original Woodstock Music and Art Fair in 1969 in Bethel, New York, an appearance which gained her considerable recognition and boosted record sales; her next album, *Candles in the Rain*, sold over a million copies in 1970 and earned her *Billboard*'s award as top female vocalist. Her record label also promoted her work heavily in England and Western Europe, where her records were often in the top ten in sales.

Melanie and her husband started Neighborhood Records in 1971 and released the song which would become her biggest hit, "Brand New Key," a light tune about a pair of roller skates. It sold over 3 million copies and was #1 in the United States. "At the time, it killed me," said Schekeryk, "because it marked me as this cute, ever-so-sunny performer, and I wanted to be deep, dark, and brooding." Her other hit songs include "What Have They Done to My Song, Ma?," "Lay Down," and "Beautiful People." In 1971, Melanie, always politically active and an advocate for a range of social issues, performed for the UN General Assembly and became a spokeswoman for UNICEF, touring to raise money for the fund in 1972. She continued to write and release new albums as well as contribute to political causes throughout the 1970s and 1980s, although she took some time off to care for her three children. Melanie has the distinction of being the first female pop artist to have three albums on *Billboard* charts simultaneously. In 1989, she was honored with an Emmy award for writing "The First Time I Loved Forever" for the television production "Beauty and the Beast: A Distant Shore" for CBS. Now living in Clearwater, Florida, Melanie is perhaps best known in Western Europe, where her blend of rock and folk music styles and her unique, expressive voice have won her many loyal fans. However, she is still popular in the States and continues to write and perform at folk, bluegrass, and pop concerts, with her children serving as backup.

SOURCES:

Larkin, Colin, ed. *The Encyclopedia of Popular Music.* Vol. V. London: Muze UK, 1998.

People Weekly. June 17, 1996, p. 136.

Shaw, Arnold. *Dictionary of American Pop-Rock*. NY: Schirmer Books, 1982.

Melanie

Laura York, M.A. in History, University of California, Riverside, California

Schell, Maria (1926—)

Austrian actress. Name variations: acted as Gritli Schell. Born Maria Margarethe Anna Schell in Vienna, Austria, on January 15, 1926; daughter of Hermann Ferdinand Schell (a Swiss playwright) and Marguerite (de Noé) Schell (an actress); sister of Maximilian Schell (an actor, director, producer, and screenwriter); attended a convent school at Colmar in Alsace; attended business school in Switzerland; attended the School of Theatrical Arts, Zurich; married Horst Hächler (a film director), on April 27, 1957.

Selected filmography: Steibruch *(Switz., 1942);* Der Engel mit der Posaune *(Aus.-Ger., 1948);* Angel With the Trumpet *(UK, 1949);* Die letzte Nacht *(Ger., 1949);* Es Kommt ein Tag *(Ger., 1950);* Dr. Holl *(Angelika, Ger., 1951);* The Magic Box *(UK, 1951);* So Little Time *(UK, 1952);* Tagebuch einer

Verliebten *(Ger., 1953)*; Der träumende Mund *(Dreaming Lips, Ger., 1953)*; The Heart of the Matter *(UK, 1953)*; Die letzte Brücke *(The Last Bridge, Ger.-Yugo., 1955)*; Napoléon *(Fr., 1955)*; Die Ratten *(The Rats, Ger., 1955)*; Gervaise *(Fr., 1956)*; Liebe *(Ger., 1956)*; Rose Bernd *(The Sins of Rose Bernd, Ger., 1957)*; Le Notti bianche *(White Nights, It.-Fr., 1957)*; Une Vie *(End of Desire, Fr.-It., 1958)*; The Brothers Karamazov *(US, 1958)*; Raubfischer in Hellas *(As the Sea Rages, Ger.-Yugo., 1959)*; The Hanging Tree *(US, 1959)*; Cimarron *(US, 1960)*; The Mark *(UK, 1961)*; Ich bin auch nur eine Frau *(Only a Woman, Ger., 1962)*; L'Assassin connaît la Musique *(Fr., 1963)*; Le Diable par la Queue *(The Devil by the Tail, Fr.-It., 1969)*; 99 Mujeres *(99 Women, 1969)*; Night of the Blood Monster *(1971)*; The Odessa File *(UK, 1974)*; Follies Bourgeoises *(Fr., 1976)*; Voyage of the Damned *(UK, 1976)*; So oder so ist das Leben *(also co-prod., Ger., 1976)*; Schöner Gigolo—armer Gigolo *(Just a Gigolo, Ger., 1978)*; Superman *(US, 1978)*; La Passante du Sans-Souci *(La Passante, 1982)*; 1919 *(UK, 1985)*.

Maria Schell

An internationally acclaimed actress who frequently portrayed soulful, downtrodden women, Maria Schell reached the peak of her career in the 1950s, winning the 1954 Cannes Film Festival award as Best Actress for her work in Helmut Kautner's *Die letzte Brücke (The Last Bridge)* and the 1956 Venice Festival prize for René Clement's *Gervaise*. Her much-anticipated American debut, as the sensuous Grushenka in *The Brothers Karamazov* (1958), advanced her career in the United States. During the 1960s, however, Schell's star declined swiftly, largely due to the women's movement and the stronger, less vulnerable female characters written for the screen.

Born in 1926 into a distinguished theatrical family, Schell is the eldest child of Hermann Ferdinand Schell, a Swiss playwright, and **Marguerite de Noé**, a Viennese actress of French and Austrian descent. All three of Schell's younger siblings are also actors, the most famous among them being Maximilian Schell. In 1938, with Hitler's forces on the move, the Schell family left Vienna and settled in Zurich, where Maria attended a convent school. Although she appeared in theatricals as a child, her father insisted that she attend business school before indulging her growing interest in acting.

Schell then took an office job, but her heart was elsewhere. Auditioning for a small role in the Swiss film *Der Steinbruch* in 1942, she was unexpectedly awarded the lead, thus opening the door to an acting career. She subsequently enrolled at the School of Theatrical Arts in Zurich, studying her craft while making a second film and appearing on the Zurich stage. She then did a stint with the State Theater of Bern, further honing her skills in a classical repertory of plays. In 1948, intending to join the Burgtheater, a major German-language repertory company, she was side-tracked by an offer to play the lead in the Austrian film *Der Engel mit der Posaune*. The role led to a seven-year contract with famed film impresario Sir Alexander Korda.

Schell's skills and fluency in several languages led her to starring roles in over 20 European films, including *Die letzte Brücke*, *The Heart of the Matter* (based on Graham Greene's novel), and *Gervaise*, which, in addition to the Cannes award, won the New York Film Critics Award as the Best Foreign Film in 1957 and was nominated for an Academy Award. Between films, Schell continued to perform in the live theater, enjoying the opportunity to develop full characterizations and to do an occasional comic role. In 1957, she married German film director Horst Hächler.

Schell's American debut as Grushenka in *The Brothers Karamazov*, a role coveted by *Marilyn Monroe, was preceded by a *Time* article in which the actress was extolled for her talent, but was also characterized as ambitious and egotistical, charges she denied in a flurry of additional articles. The publicity did much to enhance the success of the film, which also featured Yul Brynner and Lee J. Cobb, who was nominated for an Academy Award in the Best Supporting Actor category. The beautiful German export was immediately cast in two additional Hollywood films, *Hanging Tree* (1959) and *Cimarron* (1961), both westerns. She also starred in three television dramas, including a two-part dramatization of Ernest Hemingway's novel *For Whom the Bell Tolls*.

After 1963, Schell all but retired from films, returning only occasionally for a character role. She acted and served as co-producer of the film *So oder so ist das Leben* (1976). Her last American film was *Superman* (1976) in which she appeared in the much-ballyhooed opening sequence with Marlon Brando, Trevor Howard, and **Susannah York**.

SOURCES:

Katz, Ephraim. *The Film Encyclopedia.* NY: Harper-Collins, 1994.

Moritz, Charles, ed. *Current Biography Yearbook 1961.* NY: H.W. Wilson, 1961.

Barbara Morgan,
Melrose, Massachusetts

Schiaparelli, Elsa (1890–1973)

Influential French couturiere whose designs changed the face of fashion in the two decades prior to World War II. Pronunciation: Skya-pa-RELL-ee. Name variations: Comtesse de Kerlor or Countess de Kerlor. Born Elsa Luisa Maria Schiaparelli on September 10, 1890, in Rome, Italy, to an aristocratic Italian family; died in Paris, France, on November 13, 1973, of complications from a series of strokes; daughter of Celestino Schiaparelli (of ancient Piedmontese lineage) and Maria Luisa Domenitis Schiaparelli (a Neapolitan); educated in private schools in Italy and Switzerland; married Comte William de Wendt de Kerlor (a French theosophist), in 1919 (divorced 1922); children: one daughter, Yvonne "Gogo" de Kerlor (b. 1920).

Defied parents by marrying a French theosophist and moving with him to New York (1919); divorced and moved to Paris (1922); began designing sweaters and casual wear for women; introduced two full collections of casual and formal wear (mid-1930s); was running her own company of several hundred employees and was the most famous purveyor of French haute couture in the world; spent most of World War II in U.S., lecturing and doing volunteer work to raise money for French war victims, though her company continued to operate in France under the supervision of trusted assistants; never regained her prewar popularity but her influence on contemporary fashion is still much in evidence; introduced her last collection (1954).

It was as a mere tourist, a single mother with little money and few prospects, that Elsa Schiaparelli first came to the city with which she would become synonymous. She was on her way from Italy to England that summer of 1913 when train schedules left her in Paris for a ten-day layover. Though she would not return there for nearly ten years, the vibrant artistic energy of the French capital exerted an immediate and powerful effect. She would say years later that "poverty and Paris" were the two greatest influences on her career as the world's most famous *haute couturiere.* "Poverty forced me to work," she said, "and Paris gave me a liking for it, and courage."

Her upbringing had ill prepared her for the task of earning a daily living. Indeed, Elsa Luisa Maria Schiaparelli had been born on September 10, 1890, in an elegant Italian palazzo where Michelangelo and Erasmus had once stayed, and where Queen *Christina of Sweden had lived after abdicating her throne. The Palazzo Corsini housed the Italian Academy of Science's Lincei Library, overseen by Elsa's father, Celestino Schiaparelli, of ancient Piedmontese lineage. The Schiaparellis had been known for centuries for their erudition and intelligence (Elsa's astronomer uncle Giovanni had discovered the "canals" of Mars), so Celestino's choice of the emotionally volatile Neapolitan **Maria Luisa Domenitis** for his wife was one of the few things that managed to ruffle the reserve of his northern relations. The couple's first child, **Beatrice Schiaparelli**, was so strikingly beautiful that Elsa, with her large brown eyes and dark hair, always considered herself a rather plain girl.

With one of the world's most beautiful cities spread around her, and St. Peter's just around the corner, Elsa's childhood did not lack for color or style. All her life, she would remember the swirling scarlet moiré of cardinals' robes, the somber mauve of official church mourning, and the spring explosion of color at Rome's flower market, the Campi dei Fiori. Then, too, there were the costumes and passion of the Italian theater, to which Celestino began taking his younger daughter at an early age to see the great classics of the stage, although he quickly disabused Elsa of her desire to become an actress.

Schiaparellis from time immemorial had abhorred public displays of emotion and firmly believed in the traditional woman's role as homemaker, hostess and child bearer.

But Maria's southern Italian passions ran strong in her younger daughter. When Celestino accepted the chair for Oriental Studies at the University of Rome and moved his family across the Tiber to the via Nazionale, 19-year-old Elsa took over a linen closet in the family's new apartment and spent months pouring out her creative turmoil in a collection of poetry which she published, without her family's knowledge, under the title *Arethusa* in 1911. "I was possessed," Schiaparelli later said of her brief career as an author. "Never since have I experienced such complete pleasure." Her meditations on the nature of love and the human spirit were well-enough received for the volume to be translated into English and German and for one reviewer to note that "Elsa Schiaparelli's poetry is profoundly human and essentially emotional." It was, in fact, the frank passion and emotionalism of the poems that dismayed Elsa's father and led to the quick decision to send her off to a convent in Switzerland while a suitable husband was found for her. Schiaparelli cared for none of the prospects her family presented and instead accepted an offer from an Englishwoman she had met in Florence to take a job in Britain at a progressive school for children. Thus it was that Schiaparelli first saw Paris that summer of 1913.

It's when you can't be extravagant that you become ingenious.

—Elsa Schiaparelli

She arrived during Europe's last burst of creativity before the outbreak of World War I, with Paris the epicenter of the storm of innovation. Elsa's first impression of the city was the relative freedom which allowed French women the same economic opportunities as men, even to own their own businesses, in sharp contrast to her tradition-bound upbringing. Then, too, there was the artistic ferment then seizing Paris—of the Fauvists, with their startling new palettes of scarlets and greens and purples, and the challenging perspectives of the Cubists, shattering the placid landscapes and still-lifes of the previous century. Of even more interest to Schiaparelli during her ten days in the French capital was the activity along the rue de la Paix, the center of a fashion industry that even then laid down the rules for well-dressed women around the world. Fashion was one of the few areas in which the circumscribed lives of aristocratic young ladies could find modest expression, and Schiaparelli herself had been spending much of the allowance which had been assigned to her since the age of 18 on clothing. She was delighted to not only tour the great fashion houses along the rue de la Paix but to accept an invitation to attend a costume ball on her last night in Paris. Elsa managed to throw together a costume consisting of yards of dark blue crepe de chine arranged like a voluminous pair of pajamas (a harbinger of her famous "lounging pajamas" of the 1930s), accented by a brilliant sash of orange silk and a matching turban, all held together by scores of pins which made their presence known as soon as Schiaparelli's first dance partner attempted to put his hands on her.

England could hardly match the excitements of Paris, but Schiaparelli took advantage of the many cultural opportunities London had to offer, the city being only a short train ride from the Kent countryside where her school was located. One evening in late 1913, she attended a lecture on theosophy delivered by a handsome Frenchman of mixed Breton and Polish descent grandly named Comte William de Wendt de Kerlor. In his remarks on spirituality and the underlying unity of spiritual belief, Elsa found many of the same themes she had explored in her own poetry. She gladly accepted an invitation to meet the speaker after his talk, and the very next day, Elsa and de Kerlor were engaged. Ignoring her parents' frantic attempts to block the impending marriage and threats to disinherit their troublesome daughter, the couple wed in a civil ceremony early in 1914. The new Comtesse de Kerlor, blissfully in love if now financially bereft, settled down to a married life interrupted just a few months later, in August 1914, by World War I.

De Kerlor, a pacifist who had long been predicting a spiritual renewal that would save Europe from war, sank into disillusionment and depression. In later life, Schiaparelli rarely spoke of the events of the next four years, although she acknowledged that de Kerlor sought comfort for his distress with other women and that the early glow of the marriage soon dulled. Among de Kerlor's lovers was actress ***Isadora Duncan**, for whom he developed an especially strong passion, which may account for the decision to move with Elsa in 1919 to New York, where Duncan had taken up residence. Schiaparelli was pregnant by the time she and de Kerlor settled into the Hotel Brevoort in Greenwich Village. A daughter the couple named Yvonne was born in 1920, but even the presence of a child failed to save the marriage.

Elsa
Schiaparelli

With help from her mother, Schiaparelli found a small apartment off Sixth Avenue. She earned a living producing translations from Italian for several publishing houses and took whatever other odd jobs she could find. Yvonne, meanwhile, had been diagnosed with infantile paralysis, a disease which would take years and expensive therapy to cure. Despite Schiaparelli's frequent references to the poverty of these years, her daughter cast a different light in her own recollections. "She loved to be dramatic about her financial situation, but . . . her mother sent us money. Mummy got all dressed up every night for her umpteen dinner parties, leaving me with a nanny," Yvonne remembered from a distance of nearly 70 years, still recalling her mother's usual evening farewell of "Well, I must go now!" as she rushed out the door. (Her baby-talk response of "Go, go!" gave Yvonne the nickname, Gogo, for which she would be known for the rest of her life.) Nevertheless, Schiaparelli would always consider these American years to be as crucial to her future as Paris would be. "America has always been more than hospitable and friendly to me," she said many years later, citing the vitality and modernism she found in New York. "[America] made it possible for me to obtain a unique place in the world." During her time in the city, Schiaparelli made friends with other expatriate Europeans who had fled the war, among them Surrealist artists Marcel Duchamp and Salvador Dali, both of whose work would help lend a striking avant-garde air to "the Schiaparelli look."

But Paris beckoned. In June 1922, with her divorce from de Kerlor final, Schiaparelli set sail for France in the company of a wealthy American woman she had befriended who asked for her help in arranging a divorce from her French husband. Not long after arriving in Paris, Schiaparelli designed and constructed a simple evening dress for a cash-strapped friend who had been invited to a formal dinner. It attracted enough attention that the evening's host wondered admiringly who had designed it. The host was Paul Poiret, the leading designer in prewar France, and his interest in her creation inspired Elsa to further experiments. Although she had no experience in the physical process of dress-making, she covered her ignorance well as she produced a few small items for curious friends, often cutting material without a pattern using a pair of kitchen shears. Mistakes were frequently hidden underneath oversized, shawl-like collars she would later formalize as the bolero, or cleverly hidden by a sash. Schiaparelli finally met Poiret, whom she admiringly called the "Leonardo of fashion," at one of the great man's fashion shows and was pleased when he complimented her on her self-designed dress. Encouraged to begin showing some of her sketches to the leading fashion houses of the day, Schiaparelli adapted her mentor's use of color and line to such good effect that she was soon being referred to as "the female Poiret."

But it was with a simple sweater, rather than elegant evening wear, that Schiaparelli launched her assault on the industry. Although sweaters had not been considered a fashion item before the war, their potential became apparent in the early 1920s on the tennis court, where more liberal attitudes had led women to abandon the old, ankle-length cotton skirts and constricting blouses for pleated, knee-length skirts worn with short-sleeved, knitted vests. Elsa's future rival, *Coco Chanel, was among the first to adapt the look into a line for which she coined the phrase "sports wear"; while Jean Patou, who was challenging Poiret's supremacy in male-designed fashion, took Chanel's idea a step further by introducing matched twin-sets of pleated skirt and sweater, creating almost overnight the machine-made sweater industry. Schiaparelli entered the fray during the winter of 1923–24 by producing a simple, hand-knit black-and-white sweater that became immensely popular for its clean lines and Cubist-inspired pattern, so much so that yet another of the wealthy American women who seemed to seek out Elsa offered to provide backing for a modest business. With the money, Schiaparelli purchased a small dress house called Maison Lambal in the Place Vendôme and, in January 1926, introduced her first collection. "The collection, although not large, is carefully conceived and executed," reported Women's Wear Daily. "They are all simple and direct with very fine detail work and pleasing color combinations."

Although Elsa's ambitions for her new company soon outstripped the resources of her first patron, other backers were found for a larger and more elaborate collection introduced in January 1927, which was again cited for its innovative use of color and combinations of fabrics. "Display Number One," as Elsa grandly called the collection, included sweaters made from a newly developed elastic wool blend called kasha, to which she had added crepe de chine skirts with matching scarves and stockings. The designs were drawn from the Futurist art of her Italian adolescence and from the new Art Deco movement. The collection's innovations, revealed to a much wider public when French Vogue published a page of Schiaparelli's designs in its February issue, brought so many new customers to her door that Elsa was obliged to move her showrooms to larger quarters in St. Germain de Prés.

A year later, she convinced her backers to let her rent space on the street which had held such fascination for her more than a decade earlier. She took four small rooms on the attic floor at number 4 rue de la Paix, a space so cramped that clients had to stand on chairs or tables for their fittings after struggling up six flights of creaky wooden stairs. But business was brisk enough for Schiaparelli to proudly mount a plaque at her door, bearing her name in her trademark black-and-white with the slogan "pour le sport," and to take a full-page ad in French *Vogue* for February 1928. There was even press attention in America, where *The New Yorker*'s Paris correspondent ***Janet Flanner** noted: "She is hardly established and is a good bet as a growing influence on the Paris world of sport."

Further innovations followed. There was the line of sweaters in what Schiaparelli called an "Armenian stitch," which had been brought to her attention by an Armenian refugee from Turkey who became Elsa's head seamstress. This new line of sweaters was woven from three yarns of different colors, rather than the usual two. One color was woven in an understitch that formed a kind of lining, shimmering underneath the two top colors and giving the sweater more body. Elsa received her biggest order to date, for 40 copies of the sweater, from Lord & Taylor in New York. She managed to fill the order in two weeks after scouring Paris for six more seamstresses who knew the special stitching technique. By late spring of 1928, the sweaters were selling in New York for $95 each, or nearly $1,000 in modern currency. After the "Armenian Sweater" came a line of "Trompe l'oeil" sweaters, with clever designs of bowties or butterfly wings; and the "Skeleton Sweater," a black sweater with white lines mimicking the bone structure of the chest and giving the alarming appearance of an X-ray. All were hand-knit by Schiaparelli's growing corps of seamstresses and could be accessorized with a collection of carved, tiled or lacquered jewelry Elsa had designed. The "House of Schiap," as her business was now labeled, became so identified with sweaters that Elsa once joked: "My professional life hung on a thread."

Schiaparelli's "Display Number Two" appeared during the summer of 1928, a year and a half after her first collection, and was much more ambitious in scope. It included beach and cruise wear in addition to her new sweater creations; bathing suits were made from the new synthetics, with daring, low backlines and transparent straps to allow for maximum exposure to the sun. There were more traditional knitted tunics for wear with matching jersey shorts, as well as a line of more formal wear, such as a white smock with a pair of appliqued black gloves playfully sewn on the bust and the derriere. Elsa also presented the first in a long line of fragrances, which she simply called "S." It was the world's first unisex fragrance, packaged in an elegant black-and-white box, and was soon followed by her most famous scent, "Shocking." To round out the collection, Schiaparelli included a line of beauty-care products, like patterned sponges and washcloths with sponge linings. Her playfulness with such everyday objects was much remarked upon and brought to mind the Futurists' glorification of the mundane and the skewed humor of the Dadaists. Such observations were not far afield, for Schiaparelli often sought the help of the likes of Dali, Cocteau, or Giacommetti in developing her ideas.

By the time Elsa put her first major collection of formal wear on the Parisian ramps in January 1929, *The Paris Times* was calling her "one of the rare creators," while American *Vogue* thought her triple-length "necklace scarves" in vibrant, Fauvist-inspired colors were "a brilliant invention." Even more popular was the simple knitted tube cap that could be twisted or bunched into whatever shape the wearer wanted. The "Mad Cap" became such a common accessory, especially after film star ***Ina Claire** took to wearing one on screen, that Schiaparelli grew to hate them and threatened to order them off store shelves. But it was her uncanny ability to sense what contemporary women wanted, what Schiaparelli called a "throwaway elegance," that brought such success. "Perhaps more than any other person," *Vogue* said in 1935, "she is responsible for the feeling of spontaneous youth that has crept into everything." Even the economic disasters that followed the stock-market crash of 1929 failed to stop Schiaparelli, whose business was kept afloat by clients in Europe and America so wealthy that the Depression had little effect on them.

Indeed, the 1930s were the golden years for the House of Schiaparelli. Elsa began the decade by buying out her backers and becoming the sole owner of a business that was employing 400 workers by 1932 and which had taken over the entire building on the rue de la Paix. Each year of the decade brought fresh surprises to the ground floor showrooms staffed by well-groomed saleswomen. In 1931 came an elaboration of the culottes Elsa had introduced three years earlier, which she now called the "trouser skirt," quite scandalous among the more conservative elements. ("It should be a penal offence to wear them," sniffed one proper English gentleman.) Then there was Elsa's first formal evening gown, a tight, black crepe de chine sheath with a low back and two sashes which could be tied in the back as a bow or crossed to the front. In a later version, famously worn by ***Marlene Dietrich**, white cocks' feathers sprouted from the shoulders. Later in the 1930s, with rumblings of war coursing through Europe and the grip of the Depression deep and bitter, Schiaparelli produced more severely cut designs bearing such names as "The Skyscraper Silhouette," marked by straight, sharp lines and stiffened and padded shoulders that were so prominent even Elsa referred to them as "trays" or "shelves." There followed the hoop-skirted "Cone Silhouette," then square-cut box capes and box suits, sometimes with a bolero added, along with designs derived from Cossack military uniforms and from men's golfing suits. Schiaparelli proclaimed that her adaptations of men's fashions were her way of solving the inequality of the sexes; she herself never established another long-term relationship with a man after her divorce from de Kerlor. "Some women have achieved a combination of strength and tenderness," she said near the end of her life, "but most of those who have wanted to walk alone have, in the course of the game, lost their happiness." There may not have been tenderness, but Schiaparelli's strength was of formidable proportions. Her employees referred to her reverently, sometimes fearfully, simply as "Madame," and took pains to remain in her good graces. "She wasn't easy, and she always spoke her mind," Gogo said of her mother. "She could be quite scary, even to me. Mummy was a real Italian, fiery and willful."

By mid-decade, there was no doubt that Schiaparelli did, indeed, walk alone. No one could match her brilliant color schemes, developed by spraying the same kind of varnish used for automobile finishes onto white paper until an interesting shade emerged, or her almost architectural styling that viewed the body merely as a framework for line and form. Few others embraced with such enthusiasm the new synthetic materials, including a bizarre glass-like substance called Rhodophane which Schiaparelli fashioned into swim wear and casual attire; and no one else thought to replace the traditional hook-and-eye fastenings of women's clothes with another borrowing from menswear, the zipper, so that even women without maids or patient husbands could slip in and out of their clothes as easily as men. "Why don't you realize that this wonderfully creative woman is expressing our life and times in her little suits and dresses and her unique materials?," *Harper's* challenged its readers in 1937.

By then, Elsa's staff of loyal employees had grown to 600 and was housed in a new, 98-room headquarters at 21 rue de la Paix, while Schiaparelli herself had moved her private quarters to an imposing mansion on the rue de Berri, just off the Champs-Élysée, where the guest lists

at her entertainments included such names as Cunard, Astor, and Vanderbilt. Unlike Coco Chanel, whom Schiaparelli called "that dreary little bourgeoisie," Elsa's upbringing and education brought her acceptance as a social equal from her clients, all of whom regarded her as an artist, not a dressmaker. (Chanel, for her part, often called Schiaparelli "that Italian who's making clothes.") Hollywood's aristocracy adopted her, too, as *Greta Garbo, *Katharine Hepburn and, most notably, *Joan Crawford graced their screen roles with Schiaparelli fashions. Even Elsa's fashion shows became a form of entertainment, known as much for their artistic flair as for their fashions, set against a background of dramatic lighting, specially composed music and fully realized sets. The 1938 show at which she presented her "Circus Collection" sent performers skipping down the aisles, leaping on and off the stage and ramps or climbing in and out of windows; while later that same year, the music chosen for the show introducing her "Commedia dell'arte Collection" included Vivaldi and Scarlatti, as Harlequins and Pulcinellas posed and pirouetted. "Has she not the air of a young demon who tempts women, who leads the mad carnival in a burst of laughter?," Schiaparelli's friend Jean Cocteau wrote of her. "Her establishment . . . is a devil's laboratory. Women who go there fall into a trap, and come out masked, disguised, deformed or reformed, according to Schiaparelli's whim."

Even war failed to stop her momentum, at least at first. The House of Schiaparelli set a five-day sales record in August 1939, just weeks before Hitler invaded Poland. Although the threatened invasion of France emptied Paris and reduced her staff to a mere 150, Schiaparelli managed to introduce on schedule her new collection for 1940. She ironically called it "The Cash and Carry Collection," for its wide, deep pockets were suitable for stuffing with household valuables by women fleeing to the safety of England or America. When the invasion of France finally came in the spring of 1940, Elsa turned her home over to the Quakers for use as a homeless shelter, put her business in the hands of trusted assistants, and left her beloved Paris. She settled first in Biarritz, on the Côte d'Azur, but soon signed a contract for an American lecture tour designed to raise awareness of France's plight in a country which had yet to enter the fighting. The tour began at Lord & Taylor's in New York in September 1940 and lasted until the end of that year. "I am not pessimistic about our future," she told her audiences. "There may be ashes on the fire, but the flames are still there."

The response was generous enough that Schiaparelli was able to return to Paris early in 1941 bearing desperately needed medical supplies as well as money for destitute friends sewn into the lining of her hat. Living in the single room that had been set aside for her in the rue de Berri house, she managed to get another collection designed and introduced for the winter of 1942 before leaving once again for America at the urging of close friends, who feared that Schiaparelli's outspoken criticism of both Hitler and Mussolini before the war would come back to haunt her.

This second sojourn in America lasted until the end of the war. Elsa volunteered for American Relief to France, for which she organized shows of French culture and art to raise money for war victims; and for the American Red Cross, working for a time at Bellevue Hospital as a medical assistant. She had little to do with American fashion houses and, indeed, declined to attend the banquet for the first Coty Awards in 1943—a decision she hotly pointed out to a French cultural delegation to New York which accused her of consorting with the American fashion business at the expense of France. "I have defended the good name of French fashion from the beginning to the end," she protested. "I have always maintained that inspiration can only, and will only, be rooted in Paris." With the war's end and her return to Paris in 1945, she set about designing a new collection while offering the services of her business to the French government for repairing second-hand clothes for those left destitute by the war, and by organizing shows for those still confined to hospitals with war injuries. She did not much publicize the fact that the House of Schiaparelli had actually turned a profit during the war, or that her mansion in the rue de Berri and its treasures had survived intact during the worst years of the Occupation because she had given it for the use of the embassy staff of Brazil, a neutral country during wartime.

But the dominance of Schiaparelli fashions waned as the postwar world threw off whatever remained from before the conflict and made a new start. Although she softened the rigid lines of her earlier collections and brought a new simplicity to her clothes, attention now went to younger designers like Christian Dior, Yves Saint Laurent and Guy Laroche, all of whom had worked for her as stylists. For the first time since opening her business, Schiaparelli started losing money to the New Look, and a hasty attempt to open a mass-market store in New York nearly drove her into bankruptcy. In February 1954, Schiaparelli presented her last formal collection and retired.

The House of Schiaparelli, much reduced in staff but able to stave off financial collapse, remained in operation while Elsa retreated to a house she had purchased in Tunisia. She was not heard from for a month, emerging from her isolation to make promotional appearances during the late 1950s and to keep her name in the public eye by authorizing its use on lines of perfumes and accessories. (Advertisements for "Schiaparelli earrings" could be found in American *Vogue* as late as 1965.) Privately, she lamented the commercialization of fashion, of which she had long accused Chanel. "Young designers . . . can no longer do what they like because of pressures on them to produce lines that sell for a certainty," she wrote. "The daring is gone. No one dreams any more." In the early 1970s, after a series of strokes left her effectively bedridden, Schiaparelli sold the business in the rue de la Paix that had ruled *haute couture* for two decades. Then, on November 13, 1973, the fashion world learned of her passing. Schiaparelli had died peacefully in her sleep, at age 83.

Although she had bemoaned the state of contemporary fashion, her influence is still evident in the bright colors, arresting patterns and unusual materials that she first introduced at a time when the world teetered between two world wars and needed new ways to look at itself. "Madame Schiaparelli trampled down everything that was commonplace," Yves Saint Laurent once said of her. "She slapped Paris. She smacked it. She tortured it. She bewitched it. And it fell madly in love with her."

SOURCES:

Block, Maxine, ed. *Current Biography*. NY: H.W. Wilson, 1940.
Boylan, Nuala. "The Schiaparelli Dynasty," in *Harper's Bazaar*. August 1993.
Schiaparelli, Elsa. *Shocking Life*. NY: Dutton, 1954.
White, Palmer. *Elsa Schiaparelli*. NY: Rizzoli, 1986.

Norman Powers,
writer-producer, Chelsea Lane Productions,
New York, New York

Schiff, Dorothy (1903–1989)

American newspaper publisher who ran the New York Post *for over 30 years. Name variations: Dorothy Hall; Dorothy Backer; Dorothy Thackrey; Dolly Schiff. Born Dorothy Schiff in New York City on March 11, 1903; died in New York City on August 30, 1989; daughter of Mortimer L. Schiff (an investment banker) and Adele A. (Neustadt) Schiff; granddaughter of banker Jacob Schiff; graduated from Brearley School in Manhattan, 1920; attended Bryn Mawr College, 1920–21; married Richard B.W. Hall (a broker), on October 17, 1923 (divorced 1932);*

married George Backer (a publisher), in 1932 (divorced 1943); married Theodore Olin Thackrey (an editor), in July 1943 (divorced 1949); married Rudolf G. Sonneborn (a petroleum executive), in 1953 (separated 1965, divorced); children: (first marriage) Mortimer Ball (b. 1924), Adele Ball (b. 1925); (second marriage) Sarah Ann Backer.

Was the first woman to become a newspaper publisher in New York City; gained control of the New York Post as majority stockholder (1939), and served as director, vice-president, and treasurer (1939–42), and as publisher, president, and owner (1942–76); championed liberal causes and changed the paper to reflect popular tastes; sold paper to Rupert Murdoch (1976).

Dorothy Schiff, the first woman to become a newspaper publisher in New York City, was as much a topic of gossip as the subjects reported in her newspaper, the *New York Post*. A celebrity in her own right, she was friend, acquaintance, and occasionally lover of the influential, powerful, and glamorous personalities of the time, as well as a crusader for social justice and an adamant supporter of President Franklin Roosevelt's New Deal.

She was born in New York City in 1903, the daughter of Mortimer L. Schiff, an investment banker, and **Adele Neustadt Schiff**. Raised in an atmosphere of wealth and privilege, Dorothy was nonetheless neglected by her absent and uninvolved parents and abused by her caretakers. "There was no joy in my growing up," she once said. "None, absolutely none." She married her first husband, Richard Hall, much against her parents' wishes, primarily to escape her unhappy home life. Her marriage, however, brought her no happiness. Like Schiff's parents, Hall was preoccupied with status, money, and power. His concern over his social standing made him wary of her Jewish ancestry, and he saw her as an impediment to his social ambitions. When her parents died in 1931, she became a wealthy woman in her own right and promptly divorced him. She abandoned her conversion to the Episcopal Church and renewed her concern for European Jews.

Schiff married George Backer, a writer and liberal Democrat, in 1932, and found herself in a world of ideas very different from the shallow international set she had known. Backer introduced her to the Algonquin Round Table of writers and to New Deal politics, with its concern for the welfare of the underprivileged and needy. Inspired by her new interest in social service and government reform, Schiff threw herself into a variety of social causes, serving on the boards of various hospitals and child welfare agencies. As a member of the Social Service Committee at Bellevue Hospital for four years, she was introduced to the harsh realities of poverty. She recalled that it was "a sincere attempt to help, but of course it seemed a pretty feeble effort. It seemed to me that what we were doing was putting a little salve on the sore, not curing the disease." She subsequently held board positions for the Henry Street Settlement, Mount Sinai Hospital, and the Women's Trade Union League of New York.

Curious about New Deal politics, Schiff joined the School of Politics of the Women's National Republican Club and studied the unemployment situation from both Democratic and Republican points of view. She concluded that Roosevelt had the best solutions to the problem. After hearing him speak at the 1936 Democratic National Convention, she became such an admirer that she rejected her Republican roots to join the Democratic Party. She was immediately appointed radio chair of the women's division of the Democratic State Committee. She also became close friends with Franklin and *Eleanor Roosevelt. Although there was conjecture that Franklin had once been her lover, she hotly denied it.

In 1937, Schiff became secretary-treasurer of the New York Joint Committee for the Ratification of the Child Labor Amendment. She felt that child labor was "economically stupid, socially unjust, and morally wrong." That same year, Mayor Fiorello La Guardia appointed her a member of the Board of Child Welfare, which provided funds for destitute mothers whose husbands had abandoned them, died, or been disabled. She was chair of two committees for the board, Case Policy and Appeal from Clients and Medical Care. The Board of Child Welfare merged with the Department of Welfare in 1941.

In 1939, Schiff, who had been investing in communications for some time, used her inheritance to buy a controlling interest in the failing *New York Post*, one of three daily evening newspapers in New York City. Founded by Alexander Hamilton in 1801, it was the oldest continuously published newspaper in the nation. Schiff named her husband editor and publisher and herself vice-president and treasurer. In the first two years of her ownership, the paper lost nearly $2 million. Schiff became terrified of bankruptcy, but her ideas would bring success. She wanted the *Post* to have more popular appeal, so she changed it to a tabloid format and added comics, gossip, scandal, glamour, and human interest stories. During the 1940s, contributors of *Post* columns included such notables as Franklin P. Adams, Drew Pearson, Eleanor Roosevelt, *Sylvia Porter, *Elsa Maxwell, and Eric Sevareid. The newspaper became known for crusading liberal causes: it supported trade unions, social welfare legislation, and child labor laws, and called for social justice among the classes.

In 1943, Schiff divorced Backer and married the *Post*'s new editor, Theodore Olin Thackrey. He helped build the paper's circulation and cut its losses, while she became publisher and president, as well as owner. Six years later, she divorced Thackrey and reverted to using her maiden name, although she retained the title of "Mrs." because she thought it more suitable for a grandmother than "Miss."

Admirers of the *Post* consider the years 1948 to 1961, when it was under the editorship of James Wechsler, to be its golden age. Wechsler, with Schiff's direction, made a point of hiring talented reporters and columnists, and Schiff saw to it that there were plenty of features about sex and celebrities. The paper also took on targets that up until then had been immune to criticism, such as the practices of FBI director J. Edgar Hoover, and the uncontrolled anti-Communist persecutions of Senator Joseph McCarthy. From 1951 to 1958, Schiff wrote her own column titled "Publishers Notebook," then "Dear Reader." When she became editor-in-chief in 1962, she stopped writing columns. From 1950 on, there were no longer any financial problems for the *New York Post*. Schiff, however, was never convinced of the financial security of the paper. She constantly complained about her poverty, and kept a tight rein on expenses. She eliminated coverage on matters not directly concerning New York City, and allowed skilled employees to leave for better-paying jobs. She never praised her staff or gave them bonuses because, she claimed, she was not raised that way. Yet, despite her eccentricities, her staff was fond of her and very loyal.

In 1962, a press strike affected the whole of New York City. At first, Schiff joined in the lockout, but a few months before the strike ended, she reopened her plant, complaining that the male publishers had snubbed her during negotiations. Several newspapers went out of business as a result of the strike, but the *Post* survived. By 1967, it was the only remaining evening paper in New York City.

In 1976, Schiff surprised everyone, including her own staff, by selling the *Post* to Australian businessman Rupert Murdoch for $32 million. The negotiations had been kept so secret

that her own paper was scooped on the news. She sold the paper because it was "a terrible headache," she said, although she would stay on as a consultant until 1981. That same year (1976), Schiff cooperated with author Jeffrey Potter in the writing of her biography, *Men, Money, and Magic*. Calling it in later years "that awful book," she revealed intimate details about her childhood and her relationships with many men, both in and out of marriage, and later came to regret much of what she had said. In May 1989, Schiff was diagnosed with cancer, and, characteristically, refused treatment for it. She died in New York City in her apartment on Manhattan's East Side at the age of 86.

Dorothy Schiff

SOURCES:

Current Biography 1945. NY: H.W. Wilson, 1945.

McHenry, Robert, ed. *Famous American Women.* NY: Dover, 1980.

Potter, Jeffrey. *Men, Money, and Magic: The Story of Dorothy Schiff.* NY: Coward, McCann, 1976.

Malinda Mayer,
writer and editor, Falmouth, Massachusetts

Schindler, Emilie (b. 1909)

Czech wife of Oskar Schindler who helped him protect Jewish workers in Zablocie, Poland, from the

Nazi concentration camps. Born Emilie Pelze in 1909 (some sources cite 1907) in Alt-Molstein, Czechoslovakia; daughter of a wealthy farmer; educated in an Austrian convent school; married Oskar Schindler (an industrialist); no children.

Emilie Schindler was 20 years old when she met her future husband, Oskar Schindler, on one of his sales calls in her region of Czechoslovakia. A handsome, fast-talking tractor salesman, Oskar quickly won her heart, and they married six weeks later, much against the wishes of her father. Emilie's new husband was charismatic, but he was also a heavy drinker and lifelong womanizer, which significantly disrupted their marriage.

As the Nazis ascended to power in Germany in the 1930s, Oskar joined the Nazi party and cultivated his political contacts. His influence in the party enabled him to buy a bankrupt enamelware factory in Zablocie, Poland, outside of Cracow. Although war profiteering was his initial motivation for staffing the factory with Jewish workers who would otherwise be taken to the concentration camps, Oskar soon experienced a change of heart. He spent a fortune supplying his Jewish workers with food and bribing Nazi officials to maintain a "hands-off" policy towards his factory. As the war progressed, he even risked his life to ensure that his 1,200-plus workers would remain safely within the protection of his factory.

Oskar's repeated infidelities led to the Schindlers' separation for the first three years of the factory's development—from 1939 to 1942—but Emilie played an equally active role in the saving of the Jews. The Soviet advance necessitated the factory's move from Zablocie to Brinnlitz, Czechoslovakia, in 1944. Incredibly, Oskar convinced the Nazis to allow the workers to move with the factory. There, Emilie hunted down medicine, vitamins and food on the black market to stock the factory's clinic and to increase the Jews' meager rations. One Jew saved by the Schindlers' sacrifices remarked of Emilie, "She kept us alive. She was equal to her husband in everything."

In 1945, the Soviet invasion of Czechoslovakia was inevitable. Although fearful of being captured by Russian troops, the Schindlers waited until the Nazis had left the region, to ensure that the Jewish workers they left behind would not be killed, before fleeing themselves. Saying goodbye to their charges, they dressed in the striped uniforms of the workers and fled toward Switzerland, eventually crossing American lines.

When the war was over, the Schindlers were left penniless since the Soviets had confiscated their property and their personal possessions had been looted. In 1949, a grant from a Jewish relief group helped them emigrate to Argentina where they set up a farm to breed otters. Eight years later in 1957, with the farm mortgaged and failing and their resources at an end, Oskar returned to Germany, ostensibly to seek compensation for their war losses. He never returned and died of a seizure in Frankfurt in 1974. Emilie was forced to sell the farm and live on charity provided by a grateful Jewish community.

Film director and producer Steven Spielberg made a movie about the Schindlers in 1993. Based on the award-winning 1982 book by Thomas Keneally, *Schindler's List* garnered a number of awards and Emilie Schindler—86 years old and in poor health—began to receive attention at her home near Buenos Aires. She found this sudden popularity to be irritating, since her memories of her unfaithful husband were bitter and unhappy. In response to the movie, she published her autobiography, *Where Light and Shadow Meet*, in 1997, in which she presented an iconoclastic view of the man so many viewed as a hero.

SOURCES:

Epstein, Jack. "Savior in the Shadow of Schindler," in *San Francisco Sunday Examiner and Chronicle.* February 20, 1994.

Neill, Michael. "An Angel looks Homeward," in *People Weekly.* Vol. 40. December 13, 1993, pp. 79–80.

Pettit. Jayne. *A Place to Hide: True Stories of Holocaust Rescues.* NY: Scholastic, 1993.

RELATED MEDIA:

Schindler's List (film), starring Liam Neeson as Oskar and **Caroline Goodall** as Emile Schindler, directed by Steven Spielberg, 1993.

Malinda Mayer,
writer and editor, Falmouth, Massachusetts

Schindling, Liselott Linsenhoff
(b. 1927).

See Linsenhoff, Liselott.

Schlafly, Phyllis (1924—).

See Griffiths, Martha Wright for sidebar.

Schlegel, Dorothea von (1764–1839).

See Mendelssohn, Dorothea.

Schlesinger, Leontine (1889–1974).

See Sagan, Leontine.

Schlesinger, Therese (1863–1940)

Austrian Social Democratic leader who was dedicated to the causes of social progress, pacifism, and feminism. Name variations: *Therese Schlesinger-Eckstein.* Born Therese Eckstein in Vienna, Austria, on June 6,

1863; died in Blois/Loire, France, on June 5, 1940; daughter of Albert Eckstein and Amalie (Wehle) Eckstein; married Viktor Schlesinger; children: Dr. Anna Frey (1889–1920).

On November 28, 1905, members of the Habsburg monarchy's conservative elite were both awed and frightened by demonstrations demanding the granting of the ballot to the male working class, who resented being denied this right because of property restrictions. Throughout the nation, which comprised Austria and Hungary, more than one million marched in favor of suffrage. In Vienna alone, a quarter of a million workers wearing red armbands took to the streets. Organized and led by the Social Democratic Party of Austria (Sozialdemokratische Partei Österreichs; SPÖ), their disciplined ranks took four hours to file past the Parliament building on the Ringstrasse. Several years later, an unknown young man from the provinces, Adolf Hitler, watched a similar demonstration in Vienna, later describing how he had observed "with bated breath the gigantic human dragon slowly winding by." Although the anti-Marxist Hitler was convinced that the organized masses had been seduced by their Jewish leaders into becoming "a menacing army," he was clearly impressed by their discipline and the potential power of the organized masses.

How did the SPÖ become a major force in Austrian history, and what role did women play in it? The long and productive life of Therese Schlesinger, one of the most important women in the history of this organization, sheds considerable light on both the successes and the failures of the Austrian Socialist movement. Like most of the leading personalities of European Socialism, she was born into a world of middle-class affluence, in 1863, during Vienna's "golden age" of liberalism. She grew up in a large, loving, and assimilated Jewish family. Therese's father Gustav Eckstein was a successful industrial chemist, inventor and industrialist whose sense of responsibility prompted him to provide significant social benefits for his employees even though in that era of laissez-faire capitalism he was not obligated to do so. Like many members of the liberal bourgeoisie of the day, Gustav was a free thinker in religion and open to new ideas. He was an active member of an influential group of Viennese intellectuals that included the physicist and philosopher Ernst Mach and the social reformer Josef Popper-Lynkeus.

Both Gustav and **Amalie Eckstein** were avid readers of influential new books and enthusias-

tic attenders of Carl Brühl's popular Sunday science lectures on such fresh and controversial topics as Darwinism. Although she was never able to achieve her childhood dream of becoming a teacher, Amalie was widely read, with broad cultural interests, and held strong opinions on various facets of public life that she followed with interest to the end of her life. Blessed with parents who were both intellectually engaged and affluent, Therese and her siblings were immersed from birth in an environment that provided them with material comforts and with mental stimulation.

Gustav's business success enabled Therese to be educated at home by private tutors once she had completed elementary school. Of the eight Eckstein children (six girls, two boys), four of them including Therese would play significant roles in the intellectual and political life of Central Europe. Therese's sister **Emma Eckstein**, who became an outspoken feminist, entered into the history of psychoanalysis as one of the first patients of Sigmund Freud. Therese's brother

Gustav, the youngest, left Vienna for Berlin where he became a noted Social Democratic publicist as one of the editors of the party journal *Die Neue Zeit* (The New Era). Her other brother Friedrich Eckstein was a polymath who because of his family's wealth was able to live the life of a *Privatgelehrter* (private scholar); he studied music theory with the great Anton Bruckner, and included among his friends Sigmund Freud, Hugo von Hofmannsthal, Karl Kraus, and Arthur Schnitzler.

Born too soon, Schlesinger was denied admittance to both secondary and university education, breakthroughs for women that would not take place until the last decade of the 19th century. Society's discrimination only served to strengthen her desire to amass as much knowledge as possible through intensive reading and discussion. She cherished the classic authors of German literature, particularly Friedrich von Schiller, whose idealism and love of freedom made a lasting impression. Schlesinger's sense of social justice inexorably brought her into contact with the rapidly growing Social Democratic movement, which championed the rights of an impoverished industrial working class. She not only began to regularly read *Die Neue Zeit* and the movement's daily *Arbeiter-Zeitung* (Worker's Newspaper) but also mastered the often obscure argumentation that lay at the heart of Karl Marx's massive tome *Das Kapital*. Years later, Schlesinger recalled that while intensively studying the book she often came down with headaches. Many decades later, she would continue to speak to friends of "how much one still needs to read, to understand, and to accomplish." Throughout her life, she would proclaim that her greatest fear was one of "*unwissend zu sterben*" (dying while still ignorant).

Therese Eckstein married Viktor Schlesinger, a bank employee, on June 24, 1888. The happy marriage produced one child, a daughter Anna; it also brought tragedy. At the time of Anna's birth in August 1889, the midwife in attendance infected Therese with erysipelas, a streptococcus infection which made the new mother acutely ill, causing her to be confined to a wheelchair for the next two years. The lifelong aftereffects of the illness included a permanently stiff hip joint and a right leg that shrank significantly. Less than two years after she became ill, in February 1891, Viktor died of tuberculosis. Over the next several years, Schlesinger created a new life for herself. Although self-taught, she had a broad education. This, along with the economic independence that her family's wealth provided, gave her the resources to begin a career dedicated to

helping others. Years later, she described this phase of her life as one of "psychological rescue." Recalling the difficulties she had had to face as a single mother, Schlesinger claimed that her growing involvement in public issues had enabled her to rise above "the poverty of a merely personal circle of interest."

Within a few years, Schlesinger became an active member in Austria's most important women's rights organization, the Allgemeiner Österreichischer Frauenverein (General Austrian Women's Association or AÖF), whose members generally came from comfortable middle-class backgrounds similar to her own. Most of her time as an AÖF member went into journalistic work, writing articles for the newspaper *Die Volksstimme* (The Voice of the People). Generally, Schlesinger's publications were impassioned essays in favor of two of the most important items on the agenda of Austrian feminists, namely women's suffrage and women's admission to all institutions of higher learning. Her first significant non-journalistic activity took place in 1896, when Schlesinger became a member of an investigatory commission under the auspices of the Ethical Society (Ethische Gesellschaft), a reform organization whose ideology was based on a concept of progress free of both religion-based morality and political party allegiances. Comprising 35 members, the commission was charged with gathering detailed information on the life and employment conditions of Vienna's working-class women. One of only five women members of the commission, Schlesinger and her colleagues heard often chilling testimony of economic exploitation and sexual harassment from 300 women. Although the commission's final report was a convincing indictment of the atrocious conditions under which many thousands of women had to work and live, the immediate impact of the study was minimal in a society still dominated by notions of laissez-faire "economic freedom" that perpetuated the problems of the laboring classes. Desiring to bring the details of Viennese working women's misery to as broad a public as possible, Schlesinger traveled to Berlin to present to the First International Women's Congress a report on the degrees of social injustice she and her colleagues had uncovered.

Having become convinced that appeals to middle-class social consciences would never bring about significant improvements in the lives of the working class, in 1897 Schlesinger became a member of the Austrian Social Democratic Party (Sozialdemokratische Partei Österreichs or SPÖ). She was convinced that Socialism, a doctrine in her eyes grounded in values of cooperation, compassion, and rational planning, could bring about a more just society. Schlesinger quickly became known in Social Democratic circles as one of the most dedicated, enthusiastic women in the movement, and she caught the attention of SPÖ founder and leader Victor Adler. In 1901, she was one of the founding members of the Association of Social Democratic Women and Girls (Verein Sozialdemokratischer Frauen und Mädchen), an organization in which she would play a significant role for the next three decades. From the late 1890s, Schlesinger would also be an important member of the women's trade-union movement, which was dominated by the SPÖ, and was active in the secretariat of the bookbinder's union, as well as in the women's section of the large clerical workers' union. At the same time, Schlesinger remained active as an orator and journalist, publishing articles in such SPÖ organs as *Der Kampf* (The Struggle), *Die Unzufriedene* (The Dissatisfied Women), and the always important *Arbeiter-Zeitung*. In 1907, along with her party colleagues *Anna Boschek and *Adelheid Popp, Schlesinger represented the SPÖ at the first International Socialist Women's Conference, held that year in Stuttgart, Germany. In March 1911, she chaired the first SPÖ Women's Conference in Vienna, at which she, Popp, and Adler delivered major addresses.

A convinced pacifist before 1914, Schlesinger often cast a critical eye at the middle-class pacifists led by the redoubtable *Bertha von Suttner. Like a number of other leading Social Democrats in Germany and Austria-Hungary, Schlesinger was shocked and disappointed when the SPÖ leadership gave its support to the Habsburg government when war broke out in August 1914. Almost from the onset, Schlesinger was active in antiwar circles within the left-wing Vienna SPÖ leadership, and was one of the chief organizers of these dissident groups. Along with Friedrich Adler, the physicist son of Victor Adler, Schlesinger was able to create a viable organization of Marxist internationalists opposed to the official "patriotic" line of the party's leaders. A number of prominent women became active in the antiwar group, including **Gabriele Proft, Helene Popper, Isa Strasser, Berta Becker, Marie Bock, Mathilde Eisler**, and **Anna Ströhmer**.

By 1916, Schlesinger was playing a key role in expanding the network of antiwar activists within the Vienna SPÖ. In that same year, she was the founder of an even more activist antiwar circle, the Verein "Karl Marx." Schlesinger su-

pervised the publication of a secret and illegal newsletter for members of the Verein "Karl Marx," which kept them informed of antiwar activities similar to their own that were developing in other warring nations. As Austria-Hungary's people became increasingly weary of the war, the Verein "Karl Marx" increasingly came to the attention of the police, which regarded its antiwar attitudes as subversive if not treasonous. The assassination of the Austrian prime minister, Count Stürgkh, in October 1916 by Schlesinger's close friend Friedrich Adler, brought on harsh government repressive measures. These included suppression of the Verein "Karl Marx," many of whose members were imprisoned. Schlesinger defended Friedrich Adler in public when he was placed on trial for his life in 1917, even though such actions might result in her own imprisonment.

In 1917, she traveled to Stockholm, in neutral Sweden, to represent the antiwar faction of the SPÖ at the third Zimmerwald peace conference of European Social Democratic parties. At this time, she took the radical position that the best way to end the war that was ravaging Europe was to hasten the transformation of the continent's social order. Schlesinger did not approve of the Bolshevik seizure of power in Russia in 1917, and although critical of its leadership, particularly on the issue of the war, remained a loyal member of "her" party, the SPÖ. In 1918, with the collapse of the Habsburg monarchy and the creation of a republican regime in Austria, women finally received the vote. Along with six other women, Schlesinger served in 1919–1920 as a member of Austria's constituent National Assembly (Konstituierende Nationalversammlung). From 1920 through 1923, she served as an SPÖ delegate to the new republican National Assembly, and from 1923 until 1930 was a delegate to the upper house of the Austrian Parliament. A number of important pieces of social legislation in the field of women's education can be attributed to her efforts during this period. Public success was however shadowed by a personal tragedy, the death by suicide in 1920 of Schlesinger's only child, her daughter Anna (Dr. **Anna Frey**).

Throughout the 1920s, Schlesinger spoke for women within the SPÖ. Her prestige allowed her to raise issues that others could only hint at, including the fact that women continued to play a subordinate role within the party. Sometimes frustrated, she could at times leave the problems of Vienna behind when she, along with her old friend Friedrich Adler, worked—not always with success—to recreate the unity of the world Social Democratic movement through the organization of the Socialist International. After 1918, the Socialist International attempted to embody the ideals of democratic socialism in opposition to the Third International, which had its headquarters in Moscow and proclaimed the ideals of proletarian dictatorship along Leninist (later Stalinist) lines. In 1926, Schlesinger helped to formulate the SPÖ position on women's issues for the so-called Linz Program which was published that same year. During these years, she began to prepare for the day when she would no longer be able to carry on her work, the day she would "pass the torch" to the next generation of women Social Democrats. Among Schlesinger's closest friends and collaborators in this group in Vienna was a young woman of talent and stamina, *Käthe Leichter.

The Nazi seizure of power in Germany in 1933, and the piecemeal but inexorable decay of parliamentary democracy in Austria at the same time, would culminate in the bloody suppression of Austrian Social Democracy in February 1934. By this time, Schlesinger was old and sick, so the Austrian dictatorship did not arrest her. She was still alive when Hitler's forces occupied Austria in March 1938, but now, despite her advanced age and physical frailty, she was in great danger, stigmatized by the Nazi regime as "*eine rote Jüdin*" (a Red Jewess). Fortunately, Schlesinger was able to secure an exit permit from the Nazi authorities in 1939, fleeing to France, where she entered a sanatorium-nursing home. On June 5, 1940, she died in the small French town of Blois/Loire, at a time when France had already been militarily defeated by Nazi Germany, and less than two weeks before the swastika would fly over occupied Paris. Fortunately, fate had decided that she would die a natural death instead of being murdered in one of the Third Reich's death camps.

SOURCES:

Anderson, Harriet. *Utopian Feminism: Women's Movements in* fin-de-siècle *Vienna*. New Haven, CT: Yale University Press, 1992.

Bock, Eva. "Therese Schlesinger (1863–1940)," unpublished *Grund- und integrativwissenschaftliche dissertation*, University of Vienna, 1987.

Byer, Doris. "Sexualität—Macht—Wohlfahrt: Zeitgemässe Erinnerungen an das 'Rote Wien,'" in *Zeitgeschichte*. Vol. 14, no. 11–12. August–September 1987, pp. 442–463.

Calkins, Kenneth R. "The Uses of Utopianism: The Millenarian Dream in Central European Social Democracy Before 1914," in *Central European History*. Vol. 15, no. 2. June 1982, pp. 124–148.

Eckstein, Gustav. *Was ist der Sozialismus? Gespräche zur Einführung in den Grundbegriffe des wissenschaftlichen Sozialismus*. Mit einem Vorwort von Karl Kautsky und ein Lebensabriss Gustav Ecksteins

von Therese Schlesinger. Vienna: Verlag der Wiener Volksbuchhandlung, 1931.

Embacher, Helga. "Der Krieg hat die 'göttliche Ordnung' zerstört!," in *Zeitgeschichte*. Vol. 15, no. 9–10. June–July 1988, pp. 347–363.

Glaser, Ernst. *Im Umfeld des Austromarxismus*. Vienna: Europaverlag, 1981.

Gruber, Helmut. *Red Vienna*. NY: Oxford University Press, 1991.

Herrmann, Ursula. "Frauen und Sozialdemokratie 1871 bis 1910," in *Beiträge zur Geschichte der Arbeiterbewegung*. Vol. 41, no. 2. June 1999, pp. 59–71.

Klein-Löw, Stella. "Therese Schlesinger," in Norbert Leser, ed., *Werk und Widerhall*. Vienna: Verlag der Wiener Volksbuchhandlung, 1964, pp. 353–361.

Lewis, Jill. "Schlesinger, Therese," in A. Thomas Lane *et al.*, eds., *Biographical Dictionary of European Labor Leaders*. Vol. 2. Westport, CT: Greenwood Press, 1995, pp. 856–857.

Pleschberger, Werner and Christa Vogt. "Fraueninteressen und SPÖ: Aspekte ihrer Organisationsweise und Ideologie in der Massenpartei," in *Österreichische Zeitschrift für Politikwissenschaft*. Vol. 7, no. 4, 1978, pp. 393–412.

Rabinbach, Anson. *The Crisis of Austrian Socialism: From Red Vienna to Civil War 1927–1934*. Chicago, IL: University of Chicago Press, 1983.

———. "Politics and Pedagogy: The Austrian Social Democratic Youth Movement 1931–32," in *Journal of Contemporary History*. Vol. 13, no. 2, 1978, pp. 337–356.

Riemer, Eleanor S., and John C. Fout, eds. *European Women: A Documentary History, 1789–1945*. NY: Schocken, 1980.

Schlesinger, Therese. *Die Frau im sozialdemokratischen Parteiprogramm*. Vienna: Verlag der Organisation Wien der Sozialdemokratischen Partei, 1928.

———. *Die geistige Arbeiterin und der Sozialismus*. Vienna: H. Heller & Cie., 1919.

———. *Was wollen die Frauen in der Politik?* Vienna: Brand, 1910.

———. *Wie will und wie soll das Proletariat seine Kinder erziehen?* Vienna, 1921, in the pamphlet collection of The Hoover Institution on War, Revolution, and Peace, Stanford University, Stanford, CA: Pam HC 265 Sc.

Steiner, Herbert. "Schlesinger, Therese Eckstein," in Harold Josephson *et al.*, eds. *Biographical Dictionary of Modern Peace Leaders*. Westport, CT: Greenwood Press, 1985, pp. 845–846.

Stimmer, Kurt. *Die Arbeiter von Wien: Ein sozialdemokratischer Stadtführer*. Vienna: Verlag Jugend und Volk, 1988.

Tichy, Marina. "Feminismus und Sozialismus um 1900: Ein empfindliches Gleichgewicht—Zur Biographie von Therese Schlesinger," in Lisa Fischer and Emil Brix, eds., *Die Frauen der Wiener Moderne*. Munich: Verlag für Geschichte und Politik, 1997, pp. 83–100.

———. "'Ich hatte immer Angst, unwissend zu sterben'—Therese Schlesinger: Bürgerin und Sozialistin," in Edith Prost and Brigitte Wiesinger, eds., *"Die Partei hat mich nie enttäuscht . . ." Österreichische Sozialdemokratinnen*. Vienna: Verlag für Gesellschaftskritik, 1989, pp. 135–184.

Wegs, J. Robert. "Working-Class 'Adolescence' in Austria, 1890–1930," in *Journal of Family History*. Vol. 17, no. 4, 1992, pp. 439–450.

John Haag,
Associate Professor of History,
University of Georgia, Athens, Georgia

Schleswig-Holstein, countess of.

See Ulfeldt, Leonora Christina for sidebar on Kristen Munk (1598–1658).

Schleswig-Holstein, duchess of.

See Caroline Matilda for sidebar on Louise Augusta (1771–1843).

Schleswig-Holstein-Sonderburg-Augustenberg, duchess of.

See Adelaide of Hohenlohe-Langenburg (1835–1900).

See Queen Victoria for sidebar on Helena (1846–1923).

See Caroline Matilda of Schleswig-Holstein (1860–1932).

Schleswig-Holstein-Sonderburg-Glucksburg, duchess of.

See Louise of Hesse-Cassel (1789–1867).

See Marie Melita of Hohenlohe-Langenburg (1899–1967).

Schlösinger, Rose (1907–1943)

German anti-Nazi activist and social worker. Name variations: Rose Schloesinger or Schlosinger. Born in Frankfurt am Main, Germany, on October 5, 1907; executed at Berlin's Plötzensee prison on August 5, 1943; married Bodo Schlösinger (a translator at the Foreign Ministry in Berlin), in 1936; children: Marianne Schlösinger.

Born into a working-class Social Democratic family in Frankfurt am Main on October 5, 1907, Rose Schlösinger grew up with ideals that were diametrically opposed to those of the Nazi regime that took over Germany in 1933. Because her mother was a prominent member of the Social Democratic Party, Rose was banned from her career in social work by the Nazis; she eventually found work as an executive secretary in a factory in Chemnitz, Saxony.

In 1936, Rose married Bodo Schlösinger, who worked as a translator at the Foreign Ministry in Berlin. A member of an anti-Nazi circle led by Arvid Harnack since 1932, he shared her feelings that all means should be used to topple Hitler and his henchmen, and the couple worked with underground cells. By 1937, Rose had become active in the underground work of a group of Berlin Communists who cooperated with the Schulze-Boysen-Harnack group (the "Red Orchestra" organization). In time, Nazi intelligence was able to penetrate these groups, and in October 1942 Rose was arrested. She was sentenced to death by the Reich War Tribunal on January 20, 1943. When her husband, who was at the time serving on the eastern front as an interpreter, received word of her sentence, he committed suicide on February 22, 1943, in a Russian farmhouse. Rose Schlösinger was executed by decapitation at Berlin's Plötzensee prison on August 5, 1943.

SOURCES:

Biernat, Karl-Heinz, and Luise Kraushaar. *Die Schulze-Boysen-Harnack Organisation im antifaschistischen Kampf.* Berlin: Dietz, 1970.

Gollwitzer, Helmut, Käthe Kuhn, and Reinhold Schneider, eds. *Dying We Live: The Final Messages and Records of the Resistance.* NY: Pantheon, 1956.

Kraushaar, Luise. *Deutsche Widerstandskämpfer 1933–1945: Biographien und Briefe.* 2 vols. Berlin: Dietz, 1970.

John Haag,
Associate Professor of History,
University of Georgia, Athens, Georgia

Schlossberg, Caroline Kennedy

(1957—)

American lawyer, author, and first daughter. Name variations: Caroline Kennedy. Born Caroline Bouvier Kennedy on November 27, 1957, in New York City; only daughter of John F. Kennedy (1917–1963, president of the United States) and Jacqueline (Bouvier) Kennedy (1929–1994); sister of John F. Kennedy, Jr. (1960–1999); graduated from Concord Academy, near Boston, Massachusetts, in 1975; graduated from Radcliffe College, Boston, in 1960; awarded law degree from Columbia University Law School, 1988; married Edwin Schlossberg (an author and interactive media designer), on June 19, 1986: children: **Rose Schlossberg** *(b. 1988);* **Tatiana Schlossberg** *(b. 1990);* John Schlossberg *(b. 1992).*

"She lives her life reflecting her father's best ideals and her mother's way of honoring those ideals," writes Donald Spoto of Caroline Kennedy Schlossberg, the daughter of President John F. Kennedy and ***Jacqueline Kennedy**, and a member of America's most powerful and prominent political family. While her brother John F. Kennedy, Jr., assumed a more public role, Caroline judiciously protected her anonymity, working quietly behind the scenes on a variety of civic, social, and cultural projects, and choosing carefully each encounter with the media. "She is first and foremost a wife and mother," says Paul Kirk, Jr., chair of the John F. Kennedy Library Foundation and a family friend. "That's a key priority for her. She saw how important it was to her as a child."

Born in New York City in November 1957, Caroline Kennedy was raised out of the public eye by her mother following the assassination of her father in 1963 when she was five. She was educated at the Convent of the Sacred Heart in New York, and the Concord Academy, near Boston. While at Concord, she spent her summers attempting to broaden her horizons. At 15, she lived among the coal miners of East Tennessee for six weeks, photographing and interviewers their families. Other summers, she traveled to Hong Kong and worked for NBC, producing documentaries on Sweden and the Middle East. Following her graduation from Concord, she studied art appreciation in London for a year before entering Radcliffe College, Harvard. She also worked as an intern in her uncle Ted Kennedy's Senate office. After receiving her undergraduate degree in 1980, Caroline went to work for the Film and Television Development Office of the New York Metropolitan Museum of Art. While there, she met her future husband Edwin Schlossberg, a multimedia designer and writer 13 years her senior, whom she married in June 1986 in Cape Cod, Massachusetts, in as "private a wedding as a Kennedy could have," writes **Margaret Carlson**, "registering her Luneville Old Strasbourg china ($50 for a five-piece setting) at Bloomingdale's." Her cousin **Maria Shriver** was her matron of honor, and her brother John began the initial toast: "All my life there has just been the three of us—Mommy, Caroline and I."

In June 1988, Caroline graduated from Columbia University Law School and also gave birth to her first child Rose, named after her grandmother *Rose Fitzgerald Kennedy. The Schlossbergs had a second child Tatiana in 1990 and a third, John, named after Caroline's brother, in 1993. Schlossberg passed the bar exam in 1989, and began researching her first book, *Our Defense: The Bill of Rights in Action*, written with her Columbia schoolmate and friend **Ellen Alderman**. Although she did not exploit her mother's publishing contacts for her book, she had no qualms about using her celebrity status to sell it. "If my name makes more people want to read it, that's fine," she told an interviewer in 1991. A second book with Alderman, *The Right to Privacy*, published in 1995, is a scholarly work. The two authors also posted a lengthy

piece, "Expectation of Privacy," on the Mighty Words Web site. "If we do not protect our privacy it will be taken from us," they wrote. "And if we accept intrusion, we will be conditioned to expect less privacy than we deserve in a free society." Many view Schlossberg's defense of privacy as a personal mission.

In 1989, Caroline, with her mother and brother, founded the Profile in Courage Awards, given annually by a 12-member panel of the Kennedy Library Foundation to a public official who has engaged in an act of political bravery. Caroline, who has been active in the selection process, personally phones the winners and travels to Boston to help present the award at a ceremony at the Kennedy Library. Following Jackie's death in 1994, Caroline also assumed her mother's place in the New York cultural scene, becoming an honorary chair of the American Ballet Theater. In 1997, she took over as president of the Kennedy Library Foundation and also joined the Board of the Citizens Committee for New York City, which supports local volunteer groups.

Most of Schlossberg's energies, however, are focused on her children, and she is very much a hands-on mom. The Schlossbergs divide their time between their primary residence in Manhattan and a weekend house on Long Island. Almost daily, Caroline walks her daughters to the same private school she herself attended, where she and her husband are active in parent-teacher activities. "They come to parent-teacher nights, they come to assemblies when the kids are performing," says a friend. "The kids have been brought up in a solid, not a frivolous, way."

"Caroline had some of the remote, mysterious quality of her mother," wrote Carlson. "When I met her for the first time, I expected to hear that whisper, see a will-o'-the-wisp, but found instead someone with a firm voice, incredibly self-possessed and with a day-to-dayness about her. You could picture that she could make her way in Manhattan, hailing taxis and going to the movies and taking her children for ice cream in Central Park without causing a fuss."

In July 1999, Caroline Kennedy Schlossberg came under the glare of the media once more. Her brother John was killed when the Piper Saratoga he was piloting crashed off the coast of Martha's Vineyard, Massachusetts, also killing his wife **Carolyn Bessette** and her sister **Lauren Bessette**. Caroline was now the sole survivor of Camelot's First Family. "The Kennedy legend is her franchise," says presidential scholar Stephen Hess. "It's her legacy." In the days to follow, in

addition to her immediate family, she relied heavily on the support of her Uncle Ted, the Kennedy patriarch whose own burden over the loss of his nephew was immense. "Without Teddy, I don't think I could have gotten through the past few months," Schlossberg said in her opening remarks at a November 2000 fundraiser for the senator. But most of those close to Caroline believe in her strength and fortitude. "She knows that John would want her to be strong and move on with her life," said Joseph Gargan, Caroline's cousin. "That's always been a Kennedy family message: to pick up and carry on."

SOURCES:

Carlson, Margaret. "And Then There Was One," in *Time*. July 26, 1999.

Leamer, Laurence. *The Kennedy Women: The Saga of an American Family*. NY: Villard, 1994.

Ratnesar, Romesh. "Caroline Kennedy: Champion of Civility," in *Time*. August 2, 1999, pp. 49–50.

Smolowe, Jill. "Moving On," in *People Weekly*. May 29, 2000, pp. 100–105.

SUGGESTED READING:

Andrews, Jay David. *Young Kennedys: The New Generations*. Avon, 1998.

Gibson, Barbara, and Ted Schwartz. *The Kennedys: The Third Generation*. Pinnacle, 1993.

Barbara Morgan,
Melrose, Massachusetts

Schmahl, Jeanne (1846–1916)

French feminist. Pronunciation: jhan shmall. Born Jeanne Elizabeth Archer in Great Britain in 1846; died in 1916; naturalized French citizen through marriage to Henri Schmahl in 1873.

Jeanne Schmahl, who was born in England in 1846 to an English father and French mother, went to Paris to study medicine. She never finished her studies but until 1893 practiced as a midwife, living comfortably in a fine residence at the Parc Montsouris with her husband Henri Schmahl, who supported her activities and served discreetly as her secretary. Jeanne had already joined *Maria Deraismes' Society for the Amelioration of Woman's Condition and the Demand of Her Rights when she was strongly drawn into the movement for women's rights by the sad case of a patient of hers. The woman had been fired after

Caroline Kennedy Schlossberg with her brother John F. Kennedy, Jr.

she protested to her employer about his regularly giving her wages to her husband, an alcoholic who beat her. From 1884, she began to work to change provisions of the Code Napoléon (1804—) which denied women the right to dispose of their own income. She became active, too, in the Protestant women's movement for moral and social reform centered around *Sarah Monod and the Versailles Conferences of the 1890s.

Although she supported Deraismes' causes and helped the suffragist *Hubertine Auclert financially, she concluded that removing the Code Napoléon's restrictions on women—which made them perpetual minors before the law—should take precedence over obtaining the vote. She also concluded that the anticlerical republicanism of Deraismes and Auclert was a hindrance to building a large women's movement in France and achieving concrete gains. Hence, in 1893, she founded L'Avant-courrière (The Advance Messenger), an organization focused on persuading Parliament to enact two specific reforms: the right of women to bear legal witness to public and private acts, and the right of women, including wives, to have full control of their own income. She enlisted women from both conservative and liberal circles as co-founders, including *Anne, Duchesse d'Uzès, *Juliette Adam, *Jane Misme and Monod. Her tactics joined an uncompromising feminism with a strict adherence to moderate methods and conservative personal behavior—a combination which had wide appeal and proved effective. Parliament passed the legal witness act in 1897. The income control bill, however, stalled in the Senate after passing the Chamber of Deputies in 1896. It became the most ardently sought bill for women since the divorce law of 1884. To some extent, Schmahl agreed with the socialist feminists: "Where does one start? With the economic interests of women" (1895). England had had the Married Women's Property Act on the books since 1882, and other countries had been enacting such legislation since the 1850s. The Senate finally relented and passed the "Schmahl Law" in 1907.

Having achieved its goal, L'Avant-courrière dissolved itself as it had stated it would do. In the meantime, however, Schmahl had become convinced that the suffrage question had to be pressed despite its political and social divisiveness in France, where the ruling republicans feared that votes for women would give the Roman Catholic Church and the conservatives enough influence to endanger the Third Republic. In 1902, Schmahl was elected as one of the three French delegates to the 1904 organizational meeting of *Carrie Chapman Catt's International Women's Suffrage Alliance (IWSA). Because of disagreements between Auclert and Catt, however, the French delegation did not participate. Isolated and rudderless, the women's suffrage cause in France struggled until Schmahl, having ended L'Avant-courrière, decided to take matters in hand. Once again she viewed the non-partisan approach as the one most likely to rally the widest support. Her longtime friend Jane Misme supported this tactic and in January 1909 opened her La Française to Schmahl, who wrote a series of powerfully argued essays on the suffrage question. On February 13, 1909, with strong support from the National Council of French Women (CNFF), 300 women, representing all but the most militant suffragists, answered her call to organize a national body, the French Union for Women's Suffrage (UFSF). Schmahl was elected president and Misme secretary-general, and in London in April 1909 the UFSF was accepted as the French branch of the IWSA.

Schmahl's presidency came to an early end as the result of the extraordinary success of the head of the membership and propaganda committee, *Cécile Brunschvicg, in attracting new members. Schmahl saw Brunschvicg, an outspoken republican, as threatening the non-partisan character of the UFSF and Schmahl's intention to keep a line open to the Catholics. At the same time, Schmahl's own growing distemper, exacerbated by her domineering manner, was alienating members and undercutting her ability to lead a large organization with a heterogeneous clientele. In a wrenching meeting in December 1910, Brunschvicg was elected secretary-general and Schmahl resigned the presidency rather than accept "a purely honorary role." Misme supported Brunschvicg, while the Duchesse d'Uzès reluctantly stood by Schmahl, whose last years were spent in a deepening isolation.

Despite her sad end, Jeanne Schmahl had made her mark as one of the most influential feminists of her time. It has been said of her that "few other contemporary feminists could claim so direct an influence on legislative reform." The UFSF, of which she was the founder, grew apace and became the principal French organization advocating women's suffrage. Perhaps most important of all, it was her example of moderation and concentration on practicable achievements which "drew increasing numbers of high-born, reform-minded women into social activism," a major result of which was the union in 1901 of French women's organizations into the CNFF.

SOURCES:

Hause, Steven C., with Anne R. Kenney. *Women's Suffrage and Social Politics in the French Third Republic*. Princeton, NJ: Princeton University Press, 1984.

Historical Dictionary of the Third French Republic 1870–1940. 2 vols. Patrick H. Hutton, ed. Westport, CT: Greenwood Press, 1986.

Klejman, Laurence, and Florence Rochefort. L'Égalité en marche: Le féminisme sous la Troisième République. Paris: Presses de la Fondation nationale des sciences politiques, 1989.

Moses, Claire Goldberg. French Feminism in the Nineteenth Century. Albany, NY: SUNY Press, 1984.

David S. Newhall,
Professor of History Emeritus, Centre College,
author of Clemenceau: A Life at War (Edwin Mellen Press, 1991)

Schmich, Mary Theresa (b. 1954).

See Messick, Dale for sidebar.

Schmidgall, Jenny (b. 1979).

See Team USA: Women's Ice Hockey at Nagano.

Schmirler, Sandra (1963–2000)

Canadian member of Olympic curling team. Name variations: (nickname) Schmirler the Curler. Born on June 11, 1963, in Biggar, Saskatchewan; died on March 2, 2000, in Regina, Saskatchewan; daughter of Art Schmirler and Shirley Schmirler; attended school in Biggar, Saskatchewan, and the University of Regina; married Shannon England (a computer systems analyst); children: Sara and Jenna.

Represented high school in sport of curling; was a member of Caledonian Curling Club; made national debut (1987); played in Canadian Mixed championships (1992); won six Saskatchewan Women's championships with Marcia Gudereit, Joan McCusker and Jan Betker; won Scott Tournament of Hearts (1993); won Canadian and world titles (1993, 1994 and 1997); won first full-medal gold in Olympic curling history at Olympic Games in Nagano, Japan (1998); inducted into Canadian Curling Hall of Fame (1999).

Sandra Schmirler was born in 1963 in Biggar, Saskatchewan, where she and her sisters were introduced to the sport of curling by their parents Art and **Shirley Schmirler**. In 1981, while she was still in high school, Sandra's team won the national high-school championship, launching her athletic career in one of Canada's most popular sports. A gifted sportswoman, Schmirler also excelled at badminton, swimming and volleyball.

After graduating from the University of Regina, Schmirler worked at the South East Leisure Centre in Regina, competing as a member of the Caledonian Curling Club. She made her first appearance on the national scene in 1987, playing third for **Kathy Fahlman**'s Saskatchewan rink at the Scott Tournament of Hearts, followed by the 1992 Canadian Mixed championships, playing third for skip Brian McCusker.

Known as "Schmirler the Curler," she was to become a dominant force in her sport, credited with raising the standard for all other competitors. "When you played her, you were in awe," said two-time Canadian champion **Colleen Jones**. "You knew she was better. You knew she was going to win. It was like playing against [Wayne] Gretzky." Schmirler also helped to change the image of curling, long regarded as a second-class sport.

With team members **Marcia Gudereit, Joan McCusker** and **Jan Betker**, Schmirler assured the dominance of the Caledonian Curling Club in the 1990s. In 1991, her team won their first of six Saskatchewan women's championships. In 1993, the team won the Scott Tournament of Hearts, and then, representing Canada, went on to win their first World championship in Geneva, Switzerland. They also won the World championship in Oberstdorf, Germany (1994) and in Bern, Switzerland (1997).

Schmirler's next challenge was to ensure that her rink became the first to represent Canada in curling as a full-medal sport at the 1997 Olympics. Her rink faced the toughest field ever assembled in Canadian curling history, fighting to qualify for the Winter Olympic Games in Nagano, Japan. In the final trials, just weeks after the birth of her first daughter Sara, Schmirler's team won a 9–6 victory over their Calgary competitors. Competing in Nagano, Schmirler and her rink beat the Danish team 7–5, winning the first full-medal gold in Olympic curling history. Devoted to her family as well as to her sport, Schmirler was tremendously popular in Canada—and particularly in Saskatchewan—receiving a hero's welcome on her return home from the Olympics. Her team was voted the Canadian press team of the year for 1998, and she was inducted into the Canadian Curling Hall of Fame in 1999.

Two months after the birth of her second daughter Jenna, and only four months after her father's death from cancer, Schmirler herself was diagnosed with cancer, and she was admitted to Regina General Hospital to undergo emergency surgery. Canadians rallied to support her and help pay her medical expenses. After a final public appearance at the Canadian Junior Curling championships in Moncton, Schmirler died in March 2000 in Regina, Saskatchewan, at age 36. In a statement issued by Prime Minister Jean Chrétien, she was described as "an exemplary sports ambassador for Canada," because of her athletic talent, "her bright, engaging personality and her incredible zest for life."

SOURCES:

"Sandra Schmirler, 36, Dies," in *The New York Times.* March 4, 2000, p. B7.

Macleans. March 13, 2000, p. 56; March 17, 2000, p. 13.

Paula Morris, D.Phil., Brooklyn, New York

Schneider, Claudine (1947—)

U.S. congressional representative (1981–1990). Born Claudine Cmarada in Clairton, Pennsylvania, on March 25, 1947; attended the University of Barcelona, Spain, and Rosemont College in Pennsylvania; Windham College in Vermont, B.A., 1969; attended University of Rhode Island School of Community Planning; fellow at Harvard University Institute of Politics, 1990s.

Claudine Schneider

A U.S. congressional representative from 1981 to 1990, Claudine Schneider devoted her energies to environmental and scientific issues, sponsoring or co-sponsoring significant pieces of legislation and gaining recognition for her involvement with the effort to slow global climate change and for her familiarity with environmental problems generally. After an unsuccessful Senate run in 1990, Schneider emerged as a prominent educator and consultant.

Born Claudine Cmarada in Clairton, Pennsylvania, in 1947, Schneider studied at the University of Barcelona in Spain and at Rosemont College in Pennsylvania. She received her B.A. from Windham College in Vermont in 1969, and after that attended the University of Rhode Island School of Community Planning. Schneider became interested in environmental problems in the 1970s, serving in a variety of governmental and private administrative positions in which she not only learned about the environment but also gained political contacts and influence. She founded the Rhode Island Committee on Energy in 1973, became executive director of the Conservation Law Foundation in 1974, and was named federal coordinator of the Rhode Island Coastal Management Program in 1978.

A late 1970s stint as producer and host of a public affairs television program in Providence, Rhode Island, helped to place Schneider's face and voice before the public. She drew on this influence to challenge incumbent Democrat Edward Beard for election to one of Rhode Island's seats in the U.S. House of Representatives in November 1978. She lost, but two years later she won a rematch with Beard and took her seat in January 1981 as the first Republican elected to the House from heavily Democratic Rhode Island in more than 40 years.

Schneider served on the Committee on Science, Space, and Technology and on the Committee on Merchant Marine and Fisheries, and in 1983 joined the House's Select Committee on Aging. Like many other Republicans from the New England states, Schneider sometimes took progressive stands at odds with other members of her party, and she carried forward the commitment to the environment that she had developed in the 1970s. Schneider was a key player in the effort to stop construction of a controversial nuclear power project, the Clinch River reactor, and worked to ban ocean dumping of medical waste and industrial byproducts. In 1989, she introduced legislation to establish a national energy policy aimed at the reduction of "greenhouse" gas emissions believed to contribute to global warming. She also worked to improve U.S. relations with the Soviet Union in the waning days of Communist rule there, and her efforts resulted in an unprecedented live satellite television transmission linking members of Congress with the Soviet Union's top legislative body. Schneider was given an Emmy award for the nationally broadcast television programs that followed.

In 1990, Schneider challenged entrenched Rhode Island Democrat Claiborne Pell for election to the U.S. Senate and was defeated. In the 1990s, after profiting from a fellowship at Harvard University's Institute of Politics, Schneider became a member of the faculty of Harvard's prestigious John F. Kennedy School of Government. She was also named chair of the board of Renew America, an environmental problem-solving organization, started an energy efficiency enterprise in Latin America, and lectured and worked as a consultant on such diverse issues as strategic military planning, climate change, alternative health care, and leadership training for women.

SOURCES:
Global Climate Change Digest. April 1989.
Office of the Historian. *Women In Congress, 1917–1990.* Commission on the Bicentenary of the U.S. House of Representatives, 1991.

James M. Manheim,
freelance writer and editor, Ann Arbor, Michigan

Schneider, Hortense (1833–1920)

French operatic soprano. Born in Bordeaux, France, on April 30, 1833; died in Paris, France, on May 6, 1920.

A tailor's daughter, Hortense Schneider was born in Bordeaux, France, in 1833, and undertook vocal studies there. She left home at age 16 and made her operatic debut in the city of Agen in 1853 in *La Favorite*, a work by the composer Inès. Said to be strikingly beautiful, she was noticed by the famous actor Berthelier, who introduced her to Jacques Offenbach, the most significant composer of comic opera in 19th-century France. Schneider quickly became the most famous operetta star in Paris, creating the leading roles in Offenbach's *La Belle Hélène, Barbe-Bleue, La Grande-Duchesse de Gérolstein, La Vie Parisienne,* and *La Périchole*. She also earned the consideration of composer Camille Saint-Saëns for the lead role in his weighty opera *Samson and Delilah*.

From the inception of her Paris career in 1855 until her retirement in 1878, she created leading roles in many productions. An international star, she appeared in London in 1867 and in St. Petersburg in 1872. Schneider was a realist who recognized that fame, youth and beauty were all fleeting, and she received in her dressing-room men who could help her face the future financially secure. Thus, she entertained, among others, the prince of Wales, Tsar Alexan-

der II (who argued with his son Grand Duke Vladimir as to who would see Schneider first), Kaiser Wilhelm I of Prussia, Chancellor Otto von Bismarck, the sultan of Turkey, the khedive of Egypt, and the king of Sweden.

For nearly two decades, she was the undisputed queen of the French musical stage; she was also very likely the most talked-about woman in Paris and the most celebrated *grande horizontale* of the time. Whether she was a great singer is difficult to determine, but she had personality and stage presence to spare. Schneider spent the last decades of her long life attending the theater and dispensing charity. She never ran out of funds, having accumulated a sizable collection of diamonds and rubies when she was young and desirable. In 1918 she vigorously applauded the young *Yvonne Printemps, who was then appearing in *La Revue de Paris*; thus the former queen of the Second Empire passed the torch to the woman who would soon emerge as the musical stage queen of the Third Republic.

SOURCES:
Aronson, Theo. *The King in Love: King Edward VII's Mistresses: Lillie Langtry, Daisy Warwick, Alice Keppel and Others.* NY: Harper & Row, 1988.

Schneider, Magda (1909–1996)

German actress. Born in Augsburg, Bavaria, Germany, on May 17, 1909; died in Schöenau, Germany, on July 30, 1996; married Wolf Albach-Retty (a leading actor of Vienna's Volkstheater); children: Romy Schneider (1938–1982, an actress); Wolf-Dieter Albach-Retty.

Born on May 17, 1909, in Augsburg, Germany, Magda Schneider used her training in singing and dancing to begin her acting career in light opera. In 1931, she entered the film industry with her debut film, *Two in a Car*. One of the most popular prewar German actresses, she made more than 70 films, including *The Story of Vicki* and *Be Mine Tonight*. Her most memorable film performance came in 1933 as the romantic lead in Max Ophüls' *Liebelei*, known in English as *Flirtation*. In the 1950s, Schneider acted in a number of supporting roles with her daughter, the actress *Romy Schneider, first in *When the White Lilacs Bloom Again* and later in the popular "Sissi" films, a series about the Austro-Hungarian royal family. The films were released in the United States in 1962 as *Forever, My Love*.

SOURCES:
"Magda Schneider, German Actress, 87," in *The New York Times.* August 2, 1996, p. B7.

Bonnie Burns, Ph.D.,
Cambridge, Massachusetts

Schneider, Romy (1938–1982)

Austrian actress who became famous in the 1950s through her "Sissi" film series, and whose life, like that of the empress she portrayed, ended tragically. Born Rosemarie Albach-Retty in Vienna, Austria, on September 23, 1938; died in Paris, France, on May 29, 1982; daughter of Wolf Albach-Retty (an actor) and Magda Schneider (1909–1996, an actress); married Harry Meyen-Haubenstock (a German actor and director), in 1966 (divorced 1975); married Daniel Biasini, in 1975 (divorced 1977); children: (first marriage) David Christophe (1967–1981); (second marriage) Sarah Magdalena Biasini (b. 1976).

Romy Schneider was born Rosemarie Albach-Retty in Vienna in 1938, only a few months after the city became part of Nazi Germany's Third Reich. That she would become a famous actress was almost predestined, given the fact that she was born to a famous theatrical couple; her father Wolf Albach-Retty was a leading actor of Vienna's Volkstheater, and her mother *Magda Schneider starred in scores of lavish musical films in Germany. In an earlier generation, paternal grandmother **Rosa Albach-Retty** had been one of the most popular actresses of the Austrian theater. Rosemarie, known to family as Romy from her earliest years, was educated at private schools in Berchtesgaden and Salzburg. Interested in painting, she planned to continue her education at art school, but she was also interested in school plays, not only acting in them but directing as well.

In 1953, when Romy was 14, Berlin director Kurt Ullrich cast her as her famous mother Magda's screen daughter in the sentimental film *Wenn der weisse Flieder wieder blüht* (When the White Lilacs Bloom Again). The movie, although of no artistic weight, was a success, and Romy never again returned to school. Near the end of her life, Schneider noted: "To start in this business very young is all very well. But some day or other you have to pay the price for it, and it can be very heavy." Over the next half-dozen years, she was almost always in front of a camera, making nearly a score of films in Germany. One of these, the 1954 film *Mädchenjahre einer Königin* (released in the United States in 1958 as *The Story of Vickie*), was about the adolescence of Britain's Queen *Victoria. Described by one critic as "a pert *Maria Schell," Schneider became popular with mass audiences. In an attempt to work on a higher artistic level, she starred with *Lilli Palmer in the 1958 remake of the classic *Mädchen in Uniform*.

Schneider became one of the European cinema's most famous actresses because of her portrayal of Empress *Elizabeth of Bavaria (1837–1898) in three films directed by Ernst Marischka: *Sissi* (1955), *Sissi, Die Junge Kaiserin* (1956), and *Sissi, Schicksalsjahre einer Kaiserin* (1957). Known as the "Sissi" films, from Elizabeth's nickname, they were sentimental costume dramas, saccharine and escapist—perfect fare for German and Austrian audiences desirous of forgetting about the horrors of Nazism, World War II, and the privations of the early postwar years. When a lengthy amalgam of the three "Sissi" films was shown in the United States in 1962 under the title *Forever, My Love*, *The New York Times* critic noted that while "visually striking," the film was "brimming with warm wholesomeness and almost overwhelming sweetness," with performances ranging "from feeble to broad and the dubbed, kindergarten dialogue is plain ludicrous." Schneider, a potentially fine actress, was being hopelessly typecast in a "Shirley Tempelhof" role.

The intelligent, ambitious Schneider was aware of the dangers of these films, which had made many critics dismiss her as an actress of little consequence who had become permanently trapped in saccharine teenage roles, and despite lucrative offers she turned down the opportunity to appear in further "Sissi" movies. Seeking to expand her horizons, she went to Paris in 1958 to appear in *Christine*, a remake under a French director of the classic film *Liebelei*, one of her mother's greatest successes several decades earlier. Schneider's leading man in *Christine* was French star Alain Delon, with whom she quickly fell in love. She also fell in love with Paris and life in France, and soon transformed herself from a innocent Austrian ingenue into an elegant Parisian actress. Fluent in French, English, and Italian as well as her native German, Schneider was able to win over French audiences and critics alike, appearing successfully on the Paris stage. In 1961, she played opposite Delon in Luchino Visconti's adaptation of John Ford's Jacobean drama, *'Tis Pity She's a Whore*.

Schneider became an internationally acclaimed film star in 1962, when she appeared in the segment directed by Visconti in the multidirector film *Boccaccio '70*. Her performance, as that of a young wife who allows her husband to pay her for sex in order to save their wobbly marriage, was thought to be one of the best in the entire film. In 1962, she also appeared in a small role in *The Trial*, Orson Welles' version of Franz Kafka's great book, in which Schneider caught the attention of critics as a "disturbingly erotic" maidservant. In Carl Foreman's *The Victors* (1962), she was effectively cast in a small role as a young violinist forced into becoming a prostitute in wartime. In Otto Preminger's 1963 production of *The Cardinal*, Schneider made a powerful impression as an impulsive Viennese student who finds herself hopelessly in love with a young priest. She starred with Jack Lemmon in her first Hollywood film, *Good Neighbor Sam* (1963). Though it was a comedy with a flimsy plot, Schneider once again drew critical praise, while *Variety* welcomed her as "a fascinating newcomer to the Hollywood scene." Schneider's comedic talents were further revealed in Clive Donner's *What's New, Pussycat?* (1965), which starred Peter Sellers.

By the mid-1960s, Schneider's private life became increasingly turbulent as her affair with Delon ended. Professionally, she devoted herself to making films with French directors, including Claude Sautet, with whom she made *Les choses de la vie* (The Things of Life, 1970), *César et Rosalie* (1972), a warm-hearted comedy in which she starred with Yves Montand, and *Une histoire simple* (A Simple Tale, 1978). During the 1970s, she was twice awarded a César, the French equivalent of an Oscar. Other notable film roles included that of the assassin's girlfriend Gita in Joseph Losey's 1972 drama *The Assassination of Trotsky*, and a more mature Empress Elizabeth of Bavaria in Visconti's *Ludwig* (1973). Despite personal problems, Schneider remained professionally active to the end of her tragically short life, appearing in such films as Costa-Gavras' *Claire de femme* (1979) and Bertrand Tavernier's *La mort en direct* (Deathwatch, 1979). Her last film appearance was in Jacques Rouffio's *La passante du Sans-Souci*, released in 1982, the year of her death.

Though her professional life was filled with success, Schneider's personal life was in marked contrast. Once describing herself as "proud, hot-tempered, [and] impatient," she was also intelligent, sensitive, and easily hurt. When she and Delon lived openly together in the early 1960s although unmarried, they were hounded by the media, so much so that Schneider characterized the situation as one in which the press made her "feel like a whore." She was determined not to abandon her career for a conventional marriage, noting: "The cinema was in my skin. I couldn't give it up nor did Alain wish me to. I was not made for the kitchen." She admitted that she was not easy to live with: "I have too many moods. Sometimes I think I am too ambitious."

In 1966, within a year of the end of her affair with Delon, Schneider married German actor and director Harry Meyen-Haubenstock. In 1967, she gave birth to a son, David Christophe. She and her husband divorced in 1975. That same year, she married a photographer, Daniel Biasini, with whom she had a daughter, Sarah Magdalena. Schneider's second marriage ended in divorce in 1977. In 1979, her first husband, who had survived a Nazi concentration camp, committed suicide. Schneider had remained friendly with Meyen-Haubenstock and was disturbed by his death. Her health declined, and she had to undergo surgery for removal of one of her kidneys. In July 1981, Schneider received a blow from which she would never recover. While climbing on a fence at the house of his father's parents, her son David Christophe fell onto an iron railing and was fatally impaled. Her own weakened health and the merciless and unrelenting media coverage of the tragedy only increased the intensity of grief resulting from her son's death.

Schneider was found dead in her Paris apartment on May 29, 1982. Police reports initially suggested that the actress had committed suicide, but the public prosecutor later would announce that she had suffered a cardiac arrest. Schneider was buried in the little village of Boissy-sans-Avoir, west of Paris, where only weeks before her

Romy Schneider

death she had purchased a farm and a cemetery plot. Her five-year-old daughter Sarah Magdalena was placed in the custody of her maternal grandmother Magda Schneider. Magda outlived her daughter by more than a decade, dying in July 1996. Although many filmgoers in Germany and Austria had been critical of Schneider's adoption of France as a second home during her lifetime—regarding her as "a star without a homeland"—after her death they became ever more interested in the details of her short, tragic life. Many books and countless articles have been published about her in Germany, and others have appeared as well in France, Switzerland, Russia, Spain, Japan, and the former Czechoslovakia.

Many writers have attempted to explain Schneider's appeal to film audiences. Director Claude Sautet came close to the mark when he described her as "a mixture of poisonous charm and virtuous purity. She is as elevated as a Mozart allegro but aware of the power of her body and her sensuality. Romy is vivacity itself, an . . . actress who transcends the everyday, who has an ethereal quality which is the preserve of only great stars."

SOURCES:

Gaiter, Dorothy J. "Romy Schneider, the Actress, Dies in Paris Apartment at 43," in *The New York Times Biographical Service*. May 1982, p. 652.

Hermary-Vieille, Catherine. *Romy*. 3rd ed. Düsseldorf: M. von Schröder, 1988.

Jürgs, Michael. *Der Fall Romy Schneider: Eine Biographie*. Munich: Paul List, 1991.

Lowry, Stephen, and Helmut Korte. *Der Filmstar*. Stuttgart: J.B. Metzler, 2000.

"Magda Schneider, German Actress, 87," in *The New York Times*. August 2, 1996, p. B7.

Riess, Curt. *Romy Schneider*. 2nd ed. Rastatt: A. Moewig, 1990.

"Romy Schneider," in *The Annual Obituary 1982*. NY: St. Martin's Press, 1983, pp. 242–244.

"Romy Schneider, Versatile Screen Actress," in *The Times* [London]. May 31, 1982, p. 10.

Segrave, Kerry. *The Continental Actress: European Film Stars of the Postwar Era—Biographies, Criticism, Filmographies, Bibliographies*. Jefferson, NC: McFarland, 1990.

Seydel, Renate, ed. *Ich, Romy: Tagebuch eines Lebens*. 3rd ed. Frankfurt am Main: Ullstein, 1991.

"Schneider, Romy," in *Current Biography 1965*. NY: H.W. Wilson, 1965, pp. 369–370.

Schwarzer, Alice. *Romy Schneider: Mythos und Leben*. Cologne: Kiepenheuer & Witsch, 1998.

Schygulla, Hanna. *Romy Schneider: Portraits 1954–1981*. Munich: Schirmer-Mosel, 1988.

Steinbauer, Marie Louise. *Die andere Romy: Momentaufnahmen*. Munich: Von Schröder, 1999.

Talese, Gay. *The Overreachers*. NY: Harper & Row, 1965.

John Haag,
Associate Professor History,
University of Georgia, Athens, Georgia

Schneider, Vreni (1966—)

Swiss Olympic alpine skier. Born in 1966 in Elm, Switzerland; daughter of shoemaker Kaspar Schneider.

First female alpine skier to win three gold medals and the first to win five medals in the Olympic Winter Games.

Vreni Schneider was born in 1966 in Elm, Switzerland, and grew up in that picturesque town near a ski resort in the Swiss Alps. She began skiing at the age of three and was competing in races by the time she was in the first grade. Schneider advanced rapidly through the ranks of the national team and at the 1988 Olympic Winter Games in Calgary, Canada, won gold medals in both the slalom and the giant slalom events. In a sport generally measured by tenths-of-seconds, Schneider won the giant slalom a full second ahead of any other competitor. She startled audiences by winning the slalom by 1.68 seconds in what was termed "the most brilliant single effort of the Alpine in women's Olympic history."

From 1984 to 1992, Schneider won a staggering 38 World Cup races, far outdistancing any other skier of her generation. In 1989, she had a remarkable year, winning the World Cup and setting a record with 14 wins. At the 1994 Olympic Winter Games in Lillehammer, Norway, Schneider overcame a herniated disc that had hampered her at the 1992 Olympics and the 1993 World championships. Though some predicted she would never place, Schneider earned a silver medal in the combined event, a bronze medal in the giant slalom, and a gold in the slalom. Still competing at the close of the 20th century, Schneider opened a sporting-goods store in her hometown of Elm.

SOURCES:

Johnson, Anne Janette. *Great Women in Sports*. Detroit, MI: Visible Ink, 1998.

Bonnie Burns, Ph.D.,
Cambridge, Massachusetts

Schneiderman, Rose (1882–1972)

President of the Women's Trade Union League who struggled for workers' rights, helping to establish the eight-hour day, minimum-wage regulations, and safer working conditions. Name variations: Rosie. Pronunciation: SHNY-der-men. Born Rachel Schneiderman on April 6, 1882 (some sources cite 1884, but 1882 is documented), in the small village of Saven in Russian Poland; died in New York at the Jewish Home and Hospital for the Aged on August 11, 1972; daughter of Adolph Samuel Schneiderman (a tailor) and Deborah (Rothman) Schneiderman; attended public school to

Selected publications: All for One *(Eriksson, 1967).*

ninth grade; attended nightschool at the Rand School of Social Science; never married; no children.

Family moved to New York (1890); spent a year in a Jewish orphanage; began work at 13; founded first women's branch of the United Cloth Hat and Cap Makers' Union (1903); joined the Women's Trade Union League (WTUL) (1905); served as vice president of New York WTUL (1906); co-ordinated garment workers' strikes (1909–14); was national organizer for the International Ladies Garment Workers' Union (ILGWU) (1915–16); was a speaker and organizer for the National American Woman Suffrage Association (1913, 1915, 1917); served as president of New York WTUL (1918–49); helped found International Congress of Working Women (1919); member of WTUL delegation to Paris Peace Conference (1919); ran for U.S. Senate (1920); organized Bryn Mawr Summer School for Women Workers (1921); served as president of the National League (1926); served in the National Recovery Administration (1933–35); secretary of the New York State Department of Labor (1937–43).

Rose
Schneider-
man

On Saturday, March 25, 1911, more than 500 employees of the Triangle Waist Company were working overtime in New York City's ten-story Asch building when the 4:30 power-off bell rang. Leaving their sewing machines for the washrooms, the workers made their way through the narrow rows past wicker baskets overflowing with finished goods—silks, lawns, laces, and the shirtwaists made famous by artist Charles Dana Gibson. Tomorrow's work, layers of lawn alternating with layers of tissue paper, waited on the cutting tables above bins brimming with rags, and in the midst of such fire hazards employees puffed on their cigarettes, versed in the art of blowing smoke under their coats to help their employers ignore such blatant violations of fire regulations. The Asch building was, after all, fireproof.

The fire began in a rag bin. At 4:35, the eighth-floor bookkeeper sent a message to the ninth floor's main offices: "The place is on fire: Run for your lives." From the street below, onlookers, including James Cooper of the New York *World*, watched the first signs of disaster. "For fully a minute," wrote Cooper, "the spectators seemed in doubt as to whether the smoke meant fire or was simply some unusual smoke that might come from a machine. . . . Within another minute the entire eighth floor was spouting little jets of flame from the windows." As it was Saturday, those on the street assumed that the building was deserted until "suddenly something that looked like a bale of dark dress goods was hurled from an eighth-story window. . . . Another seeming bundle of cloth came hurtling through the same window, but this time a breeze tossed open the cloth and from the crowd of 500 persons came a cry of horror. The breeze disclosed the form of a girl shooting down to instant death."

I came to see that poverty is not ordained by heaven, that we could help ourselves.

—Rose Schneiderman

Many workers jumped; others rushed to blackened stairways, locked doors, rusted-shut windows, and a fire escape that collapsed beneath their weight. By the time firefighters connected their hoses, the entire eighth floor was ablaze. Jumping as many as three together towards the safety nets hastily held out on the street below them, the young women brought the nets down to the pavement or ripped holes straight through them. Continued Cooper:

> A young man helped a girl to the window sill on the ninth floor. Then he held her out deliberately, away from the building, and let her drop. He held out a second girl the same way and let her drop. He held out a third girl who did not resist. They were all as unresisting as if he were helping them into a street car instead of into eternity. He saw that a terrible death awaited them in the flames and his was only a terrible chivalry. . . . Quick as a flash, he was on the window sill himself. His coat fluttered upwards—the air filled his trouser legs as he came down. I could see he wore tan shoes.

Nearly 150 workers, most of them Jewish immigrant women, lost their lives in the Triangle Fire because the building failed to meet required safety standards. On April 5, "the skies wept," reported the *World*, as a group of working men and women marched in procession to mourn the fate of "their fellows who perished in the fire at NO. 23 Washington Place, March 25 last." Among the mourners was a woman named Rose Schneiderman. As a union leader and activist, her resolve was intensified: workers would never again be forced to risk their lives to earn their livings.

Born in Russian Poland's village of Saven in 1882, Schneiderman was one of four children of **Deborah Rothman Schneiderman** and Samuel Schneiderman. Samuel's occupation as a tailor forced Deborah to provide for the family on three rubles a week. "Father was inclined to be satisfied with his lot," Schneiderman later recounted, "as long as he could read books and have friends about him"; he shared this pleasure with his family, reading aloud from such works as *The Arabian Nights*. Teaching his daughter to read and write, he encouraged Schneiderman's dream of becoming a teacher and stressed the importance of a formal education. "Like Mother," she later said, "he was not demonstrative, but he shared his love of books with us, reading to us a great deal and helping me with my lessons. In a way it was natural that I should feel closer to him than to Mother. She had a habit of teasing. . . . She would praise me to others but never to my face. Father, on the other hand, always encouraged me openly." But if Schneiderman was occasionally at odds with her mother, she also admired her strength, recalling: "When Mother made up her mind, things happened." Though Deborah Schneiderman had never attended school, she had taught herself to read the Jewish prayer book in order to recite the prayers at synagogue.

Finding it difficult to earn enough money in Poland, Samuel moved his family to New York City when Rose was eight. He died two years later. Deborah was left with four children (one of them a newborn), no income, and no means of providing for her family. Along with her four-year-old brother Charles, ten-year-old Rose was placed in an orphanage run by the Hebrew Sheltering Guardian Society. She was issued a uniform and her hair was shorn. "To say it was humiliating," she later wrote, "is to put it mildly." The girls were marched in line and slept in an enormous dormitory. Disobedience was discouraged with beatings or by locking the girls in a closet for up to 24 hours. They owned only the trunks which housed their dolls and books. Schneiderman, in fact, did not even own a trunk, as her mother could not afford to fill it.

In just under a year, Deborah Schneiderman arrived to reclaim her daughter, but the return to the Lower East Side proved depressing. "Everything looked so drab and dismal," wrote Rose, "I almost wished I was back in the orphanage." For the next two years, she cared for her younger sister while attending school, completing nine grades in four years' time. Then her mother lost her job.

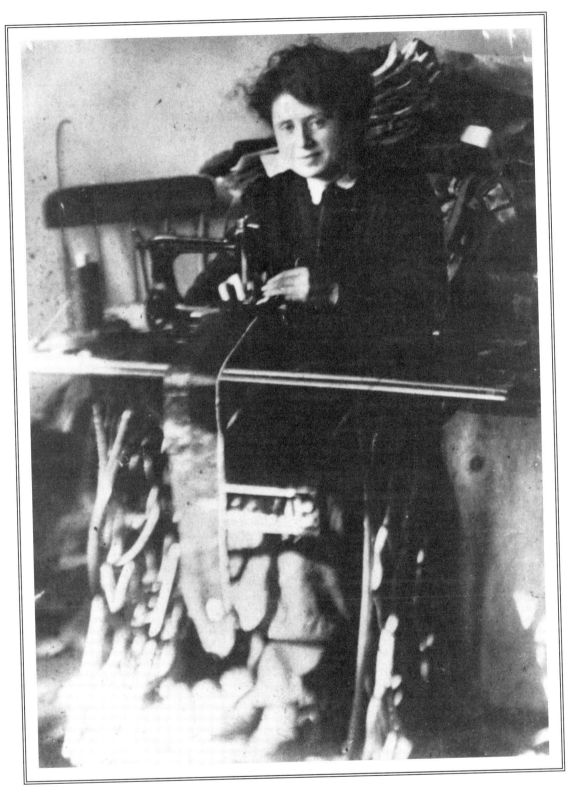

At 13, Rose Schneiderman went to work as a cash girl for Hearn's Department Store, bringing home $2.16 after a 64-hour week. Initially, she tried to continue her formal education through night school but soon found that there were other ways of acquiring knowledge; she read Bible stories in Yiddish to her mother but chose English novels for herself. She also joined the Lady Manchester Club, where she learned parliamentary procedure. Meanwhile, Schneiderman took a position as check girl for another department store and worked the same hours for a nine-cent salary hike. After three years, a neighbor helped her secure a job in a cap factory, despite her mother's disapproval of the less "genteel" post, where she made $6 a week. She soon advanced to sample maker, a position which brought no raise but guaranteed that she would not be laid off during the slack season. During these years, it was she who saw to it that her family was fed, prompting her later reflections of an unhappy childhood marked by a tremendous sense of responsibility.

But when she reached her early 20s, Schneiderman found her life's passion in the labor movement. In 1903, she encountered **Bessie Braut**, a reportedly "radical and progressive" woman who showed Schneiderman that the male workers were at least a little better off because they were organized. Pay advances made by the men were absorbed by the women workers rather than employers; thus, each half-cent increase for the men equaled a half-cent deduction from the women's paychecks. Convinced that the women workers would benefit from their own union, Schneiderman and two coworkers went to the United Cloth Hat and Cap Makers' Union to ask for assistance. They were told to return with 25 signatures. Two days later, they appeared with the signatures, and Local 23—the first women's branch of the Jewish Socialist Hat and Cap Makers' Union—was chartered in January 1903. Schneiderman served as secretary. "To me," she said, "it is the spirit of trade unionism that is most important, the service of fellowship, the feeling that the hurt of one is the concern of all and that the work of the individual benefits all."

The following year, Schneiderman discovered what she later deemed the most important influence in her life: the Women's Trade Union League (WTUL). She recalled that when attending her first meeting, she saw little business transacted, she heard no reports of any kind, and at the meeting's end everyone danced the Virginia Reel. While this did little to subdue her initial reservations about the League, she did encounter *Leonora O'Reilly, a League member who made a marked impression upon her. Schneiderman later made an important connection with ◀⁂ **Margaret Dreier Robins**, another League member, and it was largely due to these friendships that she joined the League in 1905.

O'Reilly, Robins, and ◀⁂ **Mary Dreier** proved strong influences in Schneiderman's life, and she was to work closely with them for many years. Following their examples, she became a more powerful speaker, an "effective, direct, and rather

chic woman." In 1906, she was made vice president of the New York League and by 1909 was a full-time organizer for New York's East Side. Though these new appointments meant she would never finish school, her heart, she said, was in the trade-union movement.

November 1909 heralded the "Uprising of the Twenty Thousand"—one of the largest strikes in the history of the East Side. For three winter months, thousands of immigrant women in the shirtwaist industry protested deplorable working conditions, while Schneiderman served as their coordinator. Prominent society women, such as *Anne Morgan, joined the picket lines. By the strike's end, their union had not been formally recognized, but the women had effected shorter working days, increased pay, and achieved some safety reforms. Still, without a viable trade union, the workers remained without rights and bargaining power.

Eight months after the strike's conclusion, one of the strikers came before the League, urging action, following a fire in Newark, New Jersey, that claimed the lives of 25 working women. The WTUL then demanded an investigation of all factory buildings. Complaints regarding unsafe working conditions ranged from locked doors to barred windows and buildings without fire escapes. A *New York Times* article revealed that 99% of factories checked had serious fire hazards. Despite the overwhelming evidence, no action was taken.

In March 1911, three months after the investigation, the historic Triangle Fire broke out. With 146 dead, the tragedy elicited an outpouring of sympathy from the lower East Side ghetto community. Wrote United Press reporter William Shepherd, "I remembered these girls were the shirtwaist makers. I remembered their great strike of last year in which these same girls had demanded more sanitary conditions and more safety precautions in the shops. These dead bodies were the answer."

History has largely credited Schneiderman with laying the groundwork for the reforms that followed. Six weeks after the fire, during a mass meeting at the Metropolitan Opera House on May 2, 1911, the 29-year-old Schneiderman, with her flowing red hair and biting oratory, delivered a speech that swayed public opinion to the labor movement's side and secured the support of wealthy uptown New Yorkers:

> This is not the first time girls have burned alive in the city. . . . Every year thousands are maimed. The life of men and women is so cheap and property is so sacred. There

⁂▶

Margaret Dreier Robins and *Mary Dreier. See Dreier Sisters.*

are so many of us for one job it matters little if 140-odd are burned to death. . . . But every time the workers come out in the only way they know to protest against conditions which are unbearable, the strong hand of the law is allowed to press down heavily upon us. . . . It is up to the working people to save themselves. The only way they can save themselves is by a strong working-class movement.

Schneiderman addressed rallies throughout the Midwest, advocating not only trade unionism but socialism and suffragism. In 1918, she became president of New York's WTUL—a position she would hold for some 30 years. In the 1920s, she represented the National WTUL at international conferences, ran for U.S. Senate on the Farmer-Labor ticket, and organized the Bryn Mawr Summer School for Working Women. In 1926, she became president of the National League, holding the position until the organization's demise.

When *Eleanor Roosevelt, a woman Schneiderman greatly admired, became a member of the WTUL, the two struck up a close friendship. On frequent visits as a guest at Hyde Park, and through correspondence, Schneiderman educated President Franklin D. Roosevelt in the trade-union movement, eventually becoming one of his trusted advisers. Indeed, FDR liked "Rosie," and as *Frances Perkins pointed out, she "made a good many things clear to Franklin Roosevelt that he would hardly have known in any other way." Schneiderman was the only woman appointed to the Labor Advisory Board of the National Recovery Administration (NRA), and from 1937 to 1943 she served as secretary of the New York State Department of Labor.

At 85, she published her autobiography *All for One*, admitting to a childhood longing to become a teacher. She recalled that one of the proud moments in her life occurred when Eleanor Roosevelt stood up at an AFL-CIO convention and told the audience that Rose Schneiderman had taught her all she knew about trade unionism. A few years after she signed herself into an old-age home, Schneiderman died in New York at the age of 90. By the time of her death, the minimum wage and the eight-hour day had become woven into the fabric of American life.

SOURCES:
Brooks, Tom. "The Terrible Triangle Fire," in *American Heritage*. Vol XIII, no. 5. August 1957, p. 54.

Lagemann, Ellen Condliffe. *A Generation of Women*. Cambridge, MA: Harvard University Press, 1979.

Schneiderman, Rose. *All for One*. NY: P.S. Eriksson, 1967.

SUGGESTED READING:
Papachristou, Judith. *Women Together*. NY: Knopf, 1976.

COLLECTIONS:
Correspondence, papers, and memorabilia located in the Tamiment Library, New York University, and the New York State Labor Library, Department of Labor, New York City.

RELATED MEDIA:
"The Triangle Factory Fire Scandal" (VHS, 2 hrs.), fictionalized account starring **Stephanie Zimbalist, Tovah Feldshue**, and David Dukes, Alan Landsburg Productions, 1979.

Schnell, Betty (1850–1939).
See Hennings, Betty.

Schoff, Hannah Kent (1853–1940)

American welfare worker and reformer. Born Hannah Kent on June 3, 1853, in Upper Darby, Pennsylvania; died in Philadelphia, Pennsylvania, on December 10, 1940; daughter of Thomas Kent and Fanny (Leonard) Kent; attended Longstreth School in Philadelphia; attended the Waltham (Massachusetts) Church School; married Frederic Schoff (an engineer), in 1873 (died c. 1922); children: Wilfred Harvey (b. 1874), Edith Gertrude (b. 1877), Louise (b. 1880), Leonard Hastings (b. 1884), Harold Kent (b. 1886), Eunice Margaret (b. 1890), and Albert Lawrence (b. 1894).

Elected president of the National Congress of Mothers (later the National Congress of Parents and Teachers), a group that lobbied for reform in child labor, marriage laws, and education; lobbied for the passage of legislation in Philadelphia that established a separate juvenile court system; wrote The Wayward Child *(1915) and* Wisdom of the Ages in Bringing Up Children *(1933).*

Born the oldest of five children on June 3, 1853, Hannah Kent Schoff grew up in the Pennsylvania towns of Upper Darby and Clifton Heights. She received her education at the Longstreth School in Philadelphia and the Waltham Church School in Massachusetts before marrying Massachusetts engineer Frederic Schoff in 1873. Schoff spent much of the first 20 years of their marriage raising their seven children. She did not embark on her career in child-welfare reform until the close of the 19th century.

In 1897, Schoff attended the first National Congress of Mothers in Washington, D.C., as a representative of the New Century Club. She rapidly made her influence felt within the Congress and, in 1899, organized the Pennsylvania Congress of Mothers, a state branch of the national organization. Only three years later, she secured promotion to the presidency of the national body and put her powerful administrative abilities to work. Schoff's vision for the National Congress of Mothers included the establishment of parent-teacher organizations within the schools; her success in promoting this agenda was reflected in the group's change of name in 1908 to the National Congress of Mothers and Parent-Teacher Organizations, later the National Congress of Parents and Teachers. In 1910, she was a U.S. delegate to the Third International Congress for Home Education in Brussels. As special collaborator with the U.S. Bureau of Education from 1913 to 1919, Schoff helped establish a federal Home Education Division. She added to her busy schedule by taking on the directorship of the National Kindergarten Association and founding the Philadelphia Alliance for the Care of Babies in 1913.

Schoff was equally devoted to the cause of child-welfare reform, advocating support of child labor legislation, standardized marriage and divorce laws, and federal assistance towards the education of young children through committees within the National Congress. Her 18 years of service to the Congress established its national headquarters in Washington, D.C., and produced 29 more state branches and a membership roll that boasted 190,000. Along with the increased membership, Schoff ensured that the organization had future funding through an endowment fund.

Schoff was every bit as passionate about wayward children in prison as she was about children in school. In 1899, she initiated a movement for reform in the treatment of juvenile offenders after becoming acquainted with the case of an eight-year-old Philadelphia girl arrested and imprisoned for arson. Horrified to learn that the youngster was kept in the same prison as hardened adult criminals, she managed to secure the release of the child into a foster home, where she blossomed. Schoff later conducted a survey and discovered that almost 500 children were incarcerated with adults in Philadelphia's criminal justice system. She formed a committee of the New Century Club that researched the treatment of juvenile offenders across the nation and drew up bills for new legislation. Her ultimate goal was the establishment of separate juvenile courts and detention homes, as well as a probation system for juvenile offenders. In May 1901, the state legislature in Pennsylvania signaled their agreement with her petitions by passing them into law.

Schoff did not interpret this legislative victory as the end of her reform work. Now that her reforms had passed into law, she wanted to make sure that the juvenile court set up in Philadelphia (only the second in the nation) functioned properly. She became president of the Philadelphia Juvenile Court and Probation Association in 1901, serving until 1923, and sat in on nearly every trial that came through the court's doors in an eight-year period. She also took charge in recommending probation officers and raising money for their salaries. Now a recognized expert in this field, she counseled other states in the development of juvenile court systems, and even traveled to Canada as the first woman invited to speak before Parliament.

The year 1909 brought yet another appointment for Schoff when she became chair of the American Committee on the Causes of Crime in Normal Children, under the direction of the U.S. Bureau of Education. She built on her already extensive knowledge of juvenile delinquency through a nationwide survey designed to explore the origins of childhood criminal behavior, and published her findings in *The Wayward Child* in 1915. The book further exposed the need for reform in the legal system as it pertained to children. Schoff also authored a second book, *Wisdom of the Ages in Bringing Up Children*, published in 1933. Her prodigious energy finally tapered off at the close of the 1930s, and she died of a cerebral hemorrhage on December 10, 1940.

SOURCES:

James, Edward T., ed. *Notable American Women, 1607–1950*. Cambridge, MA: The Belknap Press of Harvard University, 1971.

McHenry, Robert, ed. *Famous American Women*. NY: Dover, 1980.

Bonnie Burns, Ph.D.,
Cambridge, Massachusetts

Schofield, Martha (1839–1916)

American educator who devoted most of her life to the advancement of African-American education after the Civil War. Born on February 1, 1839, near Newton, Pennsylvania; died in Aiken, South Carolina, on January 13, 1916; daughter of Oliver Schofield and Mary Jackson Schofield; educated in a private school run by her uncle, John Jackson, in Sharon, Pennsylvania.

Martha Schofield was born on February 1, 1839, into a Pennsylvania family of committed abolitionists who frequently sheltered fugitive slaves escaping to the North prior to the Civil War. The third of five children and one of four daughters, she was raised in a Quaker tradition that promoted equality between and among individuals. In this community, women could hold positions of prominence in local religious meetings, and fugitive slaves were welcomed and aided in their quest for freedom.

After attending a private school in Sharon, Pennsylvania, Schofield went to teach at a Quaker school in Purchase, New York, and later at a school for African-Americans in Philadelphia. In 1865, she volunteered for the Pennsylvania Freedmen's Relief Association and was sent to the Sea Islands of South Carolina. There she established the Garrison School and ran it for a year with another Pennsylvanian, **Mary A. Sharp**. For the next two years, Schofield taught at several island schools, often finding herself engaged in struggles with incompetent or lazy representatives of the Freedmen's Bureau, an agency established in 1865 to aid newly emancipated slaves by providing food and medical supplies, creating schools, and distributing land.

In 1868, Schofield moved to Aiken, South Carolina, in part to improve her health after a bout of tuberculosis. There, she taught at a school that had been established two years previously by the Freedmen's Bureau. In 1870, she donated land for the construction of a new schoolhouse. By the late 1870s, the Freedmen's Bureau had ceased to provide educational funds for black institutions. Schofield took matters into her own hands and raised money to maintain the school in Aiken. In 1886, it incorporated as the Schofield Normal and Industrial School, becoming one of the premier black educational institutions in the South. Founded on the principles of Booker T. Washington, the school offered vocational training in farming, carpentry, blacksmithing, cooking, and sewing, as well as a traditional curriculum. Schofield remained associated with the school for the rest of her life. She died in Aiken at the age of 76.

SOURCES:

James, Edward T., ed. *Notable American Women, 1607–1950*. Cambridge, MA: The Belknap Press of Harvard University, 1971.

Bonnie Burns, Ph.D.,
Cambridge, Massachusetts

Scholastica (c. 480–543)

Catholic saint. Born around 480 in Nursia in Umbria; died in 543 in Monte Cassino; daughter of Europious and Abundantia (according to a 12th-century source); twin sister of St. Benedict of Nursia (c. 480–c. 547).

St. Scholastica was born in Nursia (now called Norcia) in Umbria, part of central Italy, around 480. Scholastica, whose name means "the Well Taught," is known primarily as the twin sister of St. Benedict of Nursia, founder of the monastic tradition in Western Europe. Scholastica devoted her life to pious worship, participated in religious communal life, and founded a convent at Monte Cassino, near her brother's monastery.

At the end of the 5th century, the Roman Empire had virtually collapsed, due in part to economic crises and repeated invasions by Germanic peoples from the North. In the midst of political and social upheaval, Christianity offered a measure of order and discipline in a turbulent world. Scholastica and her brother Benedict, children of a prominent and wealthy family in Nursia, were raised together in a tradition of Christian piety until they reached age 14, at which time Benedict was sent to Rome to be educated in philosophy and law. He was horrified by the worldliness of Rome and left the city for northern Italy, where, after living in self-imposed solitude and poverty for three years, he eventually founded Monte Cassino, the first monastic order in Western Europe. Like Benedict, Scholastica had devoted her life to prayer, discipline, and charity. In the early Middle Ages, women were not allowed to take vows binding them to a religious order until they were 40 years old. In preparation, younger women, if they chose, could establish religious communities where they lived according to strict religious principles. Scholastica participated in such a community until she left for Monte Cassino to be near the brother from whom she had been separated since they were 14. There, she built a convent for herself and her companions and arranged to meet her brother for one day out of the year in a small hut on the mountainside.

In 543, Scholastica and Benedict met for the last time. She and her companions joined Benedict at a traveler's inn on Monte Cassino. As they sat at a table and the hour for them to part approached, Scholastica begged her brother for more time together. Benedict, in his self-discipline, refused on the grounds that he would never pass a night outside the monastery walls. According to Catholic hagiography, Scholastica wept in silence and then paused for a moment, her head bowed and her hands clasped. When she raised her head again, a startling boom of thunder shook the inn, the sky became black, and a wild storm ripped through the night. Benedict, appalled, asked his sister what she had done. Scholastica replied that since Benedict would not grant her wish, she had prayed to God for more time with her brother. God's answer, the raging storm, prevented Benedict from returning to his monastery until the morning. When the storm abated, brother and sister parted for the last time. Scholastica died three days later, and some claim that her soul ascended to heaven in the form of a dove. Benedict buried her body in a grave at the foot of the altar in his church. Four years later, when Benedict died, he was buried in the same grave beside his sister Scholastica.

SOURCES:
Fraser, Mrs. Hugh. *Italian Yesterdays.* Vol. II. NY: Dodd, Mead, 1913.

Bonnie Burns, Ph.D.,
Cambridge, Massachusetts

Scholastica of Champagne

(d. 1219)

*Countess of Macon. Name variations: Scholastica of Champaigne. Died in 1219; daughter of *Marie de Champagne (1145–1198) and Henry I, count of Champagne; married William IV, count of Macon and Vienne.*

Scholl, Sophie (1921–1943)

German student and member of the White Rose resistance movement who was executed with her brother Hans because of their opposition to Hitler's Nazi regime. Born Sophia Scholl on May 9, 1921, in Forchtenberg, Germany; executed with brother Hans on February 22, 1943, at Gestapo headquarters near Munich; daughter of Robert Scholl (mayor of Forchtenberg) and Magdalene (Müller) Scholl (a deaconess in the local church); graduate of the gymnasium and attended University of Munich; never married: no children.

Arrested by the Gestapo because of her brother's activities (1937); finished high school and labor service required by the Third Reich before entering the University of Munich (1942); served as a courier for the White Rose, a small circle of anti-Nazi activists distributing leaflets calling for the overthrow of the Third Reich until arrest at the university on February 18 (1943).

A shower of leaflets rained down on the courtyard of the University of Munich that afternoon in February 1943. More were scattered in the stairways, on window seats and ledges, all denouncing Adolf Hitler and his Nazi regime. As lecture hall doors opened and students and professors poured into the corridors, the young woman and man who had been distributing the forbidden material dashed toward the stairs, but were stopped suddenly by a janitor shouting, "You are under arrest!" With remarkable composure, the pair halted, appearing resigned. In a

short time, the "janitor" had delivered them to the building superintendent, who turned them over to the president of the university, Professor Walther Wüst, who was also an SS-Oberführer in the much-feared German secret police. With all exits barred, the students in the building were ordered to assemble in the courtyard, where they witnessed their fellow students Sophie Scholl and her brother Hans being loaded into a car, headed for the local Gestapo headquarters. Four days later, the two would be executed as traitors to the Third Reich.

The roots of the Scholls' heroism were nurtured in a warm family life. Sophie Scholl was born in Forchtenberg, Germany, on the Kocher River in Baden-Württemberg, on May 9, 1921, three years after her brother Hans. She also had two older sisters, **Inge** and **Elisabeth**, and a younger brother, Werner. Their father Robert Scholl was mayor of Forchtenberg, and their mother **Magdalene Müller Scholl** was a deaconess in the local church. Sophie's parents were well respected in the community as virtuous people with high ideals. Her father was a progressive mayor who worked to bring improvements to his small city, and her mother helped the sick and the poor.

In summer, the Scholl children, especially Sophie, enjoyed swimming in the Kocher. She also loved playing with her dolls. Like her brothers and sisters, Scholl was a good student. She was also gifted as an artist and a writer, producing texts she would illustrate herself. A quiet person who was sometimes withdrawn, she could also be daring, scaling rocks and cliffs that no one else wanted to attempt.

Sophie's parents created a sheltered island for their children in a time when their country endured great unrest. After World War I ended in 1918, Germany had been required to pay reparations for its role in the conflict, and Kaiser Wilhelm II had been forced to abdicate. A democratically elected government had been installed, but a worldwide depression, followed by rampant inflation, had helped to keep Germany unstable. In the 1920s, an Austrian-born veteran named Adolf Hitler formed a new political party which he called National Socialism. Jews and Communists, he said, were responsible for all of Germany's woes. The Nazi Party found sympathizers among many of the country's frustrated, desperate and angry citizens, and the movement gradually gained momentum.

In 1930, Sophie was nine years old when her father was voted out of office. The family moved to Ludwigsburg, and then to Ulm in 1932, where he practiced accounting. A pacifist who had served as a medical orderly in World War I, Robert Scholl now feared the dangerous political currents swirling in Germany. The children, however, remained mostly unaware of the abyss awaiting their generation. Like most German youngsters of the period, they joined the Hitler Youth, perceived at the time as an organization much like the Boy Scouts or Girl Scouts with emphasis on hiking expeditions and camping trips. Everyone could join, except, of course, Jews, leftists, and other "undesirables." The Scholls met the standards of the "racially pure" Germans that Hitler so often spoke about, and although the elder Scholls had reservations about the Hitler Youth, they let their children determine their own activities. They trusted that their example would ultimately be more important than an organization determined to shape the minds of Germany's youth.

While her brother Hans rose quickly in the ranks of the Hitler Youth, Sophie was less carried away with the organization. Angered when two Jewish girls in her class were not allowed to join, she posed the essential question that many Germans in those years neglected to ask: "Why can't Luise, with her fair hair and blue eyes, be a member, while I with my dark hair and dark eyes am a member?" And when Hans and her father argued the issues of Nazi politics, Sophie listened.

In 1936, Adolf Hitler had been in power for three years when Hans attended the Nüremberg rallies, an impressive event of the kind the chancellor used effectively to garner support. For Hans, however, the Nazi political agenda became clear at Nüremberg, and he gradually began to withdraw from the Hitler Youth, becoming involved instead with the German Boys' League of the First of November, known as "d.j.1.11," which had no particular political agenda.

In the meantime, the Nazi regime was moving inexorably toward accomplishing its terrifying goals. At first Hitler's strategy was not directed exclusively toward the Jews, although they were increasingly denied the rights of other citizens. In the early days, the Nazis also targeted fellow Germans, including leftists, Communists, socialists, pacifists, and individuals considered to be "artistically liberal," as well as the mentally defective and Gypsies (Roma), who were exterminated as "racially defective." It is estimated that from 1933 to 1945 approximately a quarter of a million Germans were taken into custody every year, in what proved to be a highly effective means of coercing other Germans into toeing the party line. The dreaded knock on the door was a fear shared by all Germans.

Sophie Scholl

One early morning in November 1937, the Gestapo called at the Scholls' apartment. Magdalene Scholl's response, upon opening the door, was to grab up a basket. "Excuse me gentlemen," she said, "I am in a hurry to get something from the bakery." Leaving the room, she instead went to the apartment's top floor, where she picked up any materials in her two sons' room that she thought might be suspicious, and left on her errand with the materials in her basket. All youth organizations had by this time been banned except for the Hitler Youth, and Sophie, Werner, and Hans were all arrested for Hans' continued activities in the outlawed German Boys' League. Taken into custody, the three were driven from Ulm to Stuttgart, 50 miles in an open truck without warm clothes, on a route that took them through a snowstorm in the windswept mountains. Sophie was released after a day, but Werner was kept for one week and Hans for five weeks. If fellow members of the Hitler Youth had not vouched for him, he might have been sent to a concentration camp.

Following their arrest, Hans and Sophie, then aged 16 and 19, were bound together more closely than ever before. Hans and their sister Inge broke with National Socialism for good, but Sophie, who was often subjected to interrogation by school administrators, officially dropped out later. While such arrests generally accomplished their goal of terrifying the populace, Sophie's self-confidence seemed to be strengthened. She shared the attitude voiced by Hans: "We must bear it in a different spirit from other people. This is a distinction." Coming around to their parents' attitude toward the Hitler regime, brother and sister also felt the support of the elder Scholls who remained an island of moral calm.

Don't we all know, no matter in which times we live, that at a moment's notice God can call us into account?

—Sophie Scholl

On September 1, 1939, Hitler's armies invaded Poland, setting off World War II. As the Germans swept across much of Western Europe and then turned on the Soviet Union, the country began to claim the young for its purposes. Hans was drafted into the army, and Sophie, after receiving her diploma from a German gymnasium (high school), was required to put on a uniform and report to the Krauchenwies labor camp near Sigmaringen on the upper Danube to perform labor service for the Third Reich. Writing, "We live like prisoners," she hoped to complete her service by August 1941, but was instead required to serve another six months in the War Auxiliary Service. Trained as a kindergarten teacher, she then reported to a nursery school in Blumberg, a small town near the Swiss border, where her work proved less onerous.

Hans was sent to the Eastern front, where the Germans' cruelty against the Russians was even greater than their cruelty in Western Europe. Sophie corresponded meanwhile with another young soldier, Fritz Hartnagel, a friend since about age 16; the two had enjoyed hiking and outdoor activities together. Sophie's letters to Fritz, which document her growing determination to resist the Nazis, argue against Fritz's desire to be a good soldier. "I cannot comprehend it," she wrote him, "human beings constantly putting other human beings into mortal danger, over and over again. I will never understand it; I think it is horrible. Do not say it is for the Fatherland."

Hans, more opposed than ever to the evil engulfing Europe, decided to become a medical doctor in the hope of being exempted from combat. On May 9, 1942, Sophie took the train 95 miles from Ulm to join her brother, who had entered the University of Munich. That night they celebrated in his rooms with wine and cake, and she was soon introduced to his friends Alexander Schmorell, Christoph Probst, and Willi Graf, and to a professor, Kurt Huber. All were members of a small, intimate circle who shared an opposition to the Nazis on the grounds of deeply held Christian convictions. The members called themselves the White Rose, a name the origins of which are uncertain, although it may have come from the title of a novel. Committed to action, the youths had secretly acquired mimeograph machines, ink, paper, and other necessities for printing leaflets to carry their message against the Third Reich.

Always under the threat of discovery by the Gestapo, the White Rose began to print and distribute its leaflets through a network of students throughout the country. A courier traveling by train would deposit a bag of materials in a train compartment at the beginning of the trip, sit in another compartment to avoid being caught with the materials, and retrieve them a few minutes before disembarking. Sophie was often such a courier, shuttling between Augsburg, Stuttgart, and Ulm, and White Rose leaflets eventually appeared in Frankfurt, Berlin, Hamburg, Freiburg, Saarbrücken, and even in Salzburg and Vienna; some turned up as far away as Norway, England, and Sweden.

The Gestapo, meanwhile, was growing extremely alarmed, because for the first time in the war, German troops were showing signs of losing. In the fall of 1942, the Red Army showed its mettle, defying Allied predictions that the Soviet Union would fall like ripe fruit. German troops, unprepared for the harsh rigors of a Russian winter, began to bog down, and the Soviet military, guerrillas, and populace fought extremely well, until the two armies became locked in hand-to-hand combat at Stalingrad. After horrifying casualties on both sides, the Soviet armies surrounded and defeated the Nazis, in a turning point of the war.

At the start of 1943, Sophie and Hans returned to Munich after spending Christmas with their family in Ulm. Morale at the university was rapidly deteriorating as students grew tired of being fed into the voracious war machine. When a Nazi leader speaking at a commemorative assembly demanded that the women students "give the Führer a child" rather than hang about the university, some young women rushed for the exits, furious at the insult, and were arrested by the SS. The male students beat up the speaker and held him hostage in exchange for the women. After this incident, more White Rose leaflets appeared and slogans were painted on the walls around Munich, enraging the local Gestapo, which set up a special commission to exterminate the resistance group.

By February, Hans and Sophie Scholl knew that the Gestapo was closing in. With their arrest imminent, they decided to distribute leaflets at the university one more time, provoking their capture on February 18, 1943. Soon after they were taken to Gestapo headquarters, other members of the White Rose were rounded up, until some 80 people had ultimately been captured throughout Germany. A prisoner forced to work at Gestapo headquarters wrote a secret account of the dignity maintained by the sister and brother during the last four days of their lives. A short trial was held, Sophie and Hans were allowed a brief time with their parents for good-byes, and they were executed, along with Christoph Probst, by guillotine in the late afternoon of February 22, 1943. Shortly before the execution, Probst summed up their attitude: "I didn't know dying could be so easy. In a few minutes we meet again in eternity."

Hopes that the White Rose would spark a revolt against the Third Reich proved futile. The University of Munich in fact sponsored large demonstrations against the underground group, and the Gestapo worked relentlessly to annihilate all opposition. The entire Scholl family was sent to prison, except for Werner who was sent back to the Eastern front. Military service there was an almost certain death sentence, as it proved to be in his case.

The Nazis, in an attempt to discredit the White Rose movement, described its members as "typical loners, [who] had transgressed shamelessly against the defensive strength and the spirit of the German nation by smearing house walls with subversive incitements and disseminating fliers fomenting high treason." Their efforts, they said, must be consigned to the flames. The flame which endured, however, was the white, hot flame of truth, which ultimately consumed Adolf Hitler and his minions and reduced the Third Reich to ashes. Sophie Scholl's gift to the world is now ours to tend.

SOURCES:

Die Weisse Rose: Der Widerstand von Studeten gegen Hitler München 1942–43.

Hanser, Richard. *A Noble Treason: The Revolt of the Munich Students Against Hitler.* NY: Putnam, 1979.

Jens, Inge, ed. *At the Heart of the White Rose: Letters and Diaries of Hans and Sophie Scholl.* NY: Harper and Row, 1987.

Postage stamp honoring Sophie Scholl, issued by the Federal Republic of Germany on February 14, 1991.

"The Nazi Student Trial," in *The Nation.* Vol. 156. May 29, 1943, p. 779.

Neuman, Alfred. *Six of Them.* NY: Macmillan, 1946.

Schneider, Michael C. and Winfried Süss. *Keine Volksgenossen: Studentischer Widerstand der Weissen Rose.* Munich: Rektoratkollegium der Ludwig-Maximilians Universität München, 1993 (exhibition catalog).

Scholl, Inge. *Students Against Tyranny: The Resistance of the White Rose, Munich, 1942–1943.* Middletown, CT: Wesleyan University Press, 1970.

Stern, J.P. "The White Rose," in *The Heart of Europe. Essays on Literature and Ideology.* Oxford: Blackwell, 1992.

Vinke, Hermann. *The Short Life of Sophie Scholl.* NY: Harper and Row, 1984.

Wittenstein, George J. "The White Rose: German Youth Resistance to Hitler, 1939–1942," in *Soundings: Collections of the University Library.* Vol. XXII, no. 28, 1991, pp. 61–74.

John Haag,
Associate Professor of History,
University of Georgia, Athens, Georgia

Scholtz-Klink, Gertrud (1902—)

German who became Frauenführerin (female führer) of both the National Socialist Women's Union and of German women in general during the Third Reich, but wielded no power. Born in Adelsheim, Baden,

Germany, on February 9, 1902; married three times; children: eleven.

Joined the Nazi Party (1928); became Frauen-führerin (female führer) of both the National Socialist Women's Union and of German women in general (1934); having escaped punishment (1945), remained convinced that the Third Reich had been beneficial to the German people and particularly to its women.

Married at age 18 to a postal clerk, Gertrud Scholtz-Klink could boast of classic "Aryan" features, including the blonde hair and blue eyes that many Germans in fact do not have. Joining the anti-feminist Nazi Party in 1928 when it was still a small sect on the radical right, Scholtz-Klink had little education and a natural tendency to accept what those (men) in authority told her was right. In 1929, she was appointed Nazi women's leader in the southwestern German state of Baden, which led to a promotion two years later to head the women's group in the state of Hessen. Scholtz-Klink had sound political instincts, always cultivating the male leaders in the Nazi Party, particularly Gauleiter (regional party chief) Robert Wagner. Although she was the head of a large family and a widow (she eventually had eleven children in three marriages), Scholtz-Klink displayed remarkable energy and tenacity when given an assignment. Besides her regional responsibilities, she also became prominent in the early 1930s in the Nazi national organization for women party leaders, the Nationalsozialistisches Frauenschaft (National Socialist Women's Association, or NSF), as well as in the group designed to incorporate the rank and file of Germany's women, the Deutsches Frauenwerk (German Women's Enterprise, or DFW).

The Nazis came to power in 1933, initiating a reign of terror that quickly eliminated their enemies; their private political party became the sole faction within a totalitarian state. The new situation gave Scholtz-Klink an opportunity to greatly expand her power. In 1934, Labor Service chief Konstantin Hierl named her head of the national Women's Labor Service (Frauenarbeitsdienst). That same year, with the support of Erich Hilgenfeldt, director of the Nazi Welfare Association (Volkswohlfahrt), she took charge of both the NSF and the DFW, becoming Reichsfrauenführerin (women's Führer) and thus exercising the same dictatorial power within these organizations as did Adolf Hitler on the national scale (Führerprinzip—the leadership principle). Her youthful energy and obedience to the party hierarchs made her a suitable choice for these posts. By 1939, an estimated six million women were participating in the activities of these two mass organizations.

Because her activities were cut off from the mainstream of Nazi Party activities, Scholtz-Klink enjoyed considerable autonomy within the boundaries of her own bureaucratic organizations. Outside this realm, however, her influence was slight, and Hilgenfeldt reigned supreme. Adolf Hitler often mentioned Scholtz-Klink and her groups in public but did not consult with her. Many German women recognized the essential powerlessness of these organizations and most did not become members. Despite persecution, church-affiliated organizations remained significant places for women to seek moral support during the Nazi years. As a fanatical Nazi, Scholtz-Klink harbored antipathy to Christianity and formally withdrew as a member of the Lutheran church. This move likely only served to embolden some German women not to support her Nazi organizations.

Gertrud Scholtz-Klink's ideals were simple, indeed unsophisticated. She fully accepted her task of bringing German women back to the traditional patriarchal ideals of "*kinder, kirche, küche*" (children, church, kitchen). An effective orator with a rasping voice that somewhat resembled that of Hitler, Scholtz-Klink spoke at countless rallies on the joys of simple domestic chores and child rearing. "The mission of woman," she said, is "to minister in the home and in her profession to the needs of life from the first to the last moment of man's existence." Like those of the male Nazi leaders, her speeches were filled with military images, declaring that "the German woman enthusiastically fights at the Führer's side in his battle for universal recognition of the German race and German culture." Convinced that physical labor would be healthy not only for women but for the future of the German race, she often spoke of how "the German woman must work and work, physically and mentally she must renounce luxury and pleasure." Sometimes her oratory bordered on the absurd, as when she declared during a Nazi rally in 1937 that "even if our weapon is only the wooden spoon, its striking power shall be no less than that of other weapons."

The start of World War II in 1939 opened up great opportunities for all branches of the German state and the Nazi Party, both of which viewed military victories as opening the door for widespread plunder and expansion of power. In the occupied territory of Poland, Scholtz-Klink's NSF organization was active in the transfer of

possessions from Jews and Poles to Volksdeutsche (ethnic Germans). On at least one occasion, Scholtz-Klink personally benefited from these traumatic events. On the eve of the outbreak of war, she sent a special "buyer" to purchase the valuables of the family of **Erna Segal**. For a tiny fraction of their value, Scholtz-Klink acquired the Segals' possessions in a situation very close to extortion because of her power and the desperation of the family to come up with funds to pay a massive "tax" that had recently been levied on Germany's entire Jewish community.

In 1945, Soviet soldiers captured Scholtz-Klink, but she was able to escape, living under an assumed name in the French occupation zone. After she was identified and arrested in 1948, she served 18 months following her conviction by a French military court in November 1948 on a charge of carrying false identification papers. Subsequently included on a Tübingen de-Nazification court's list of "major offenders," Scholtz-Klink benefited from the Cold War which had caused a major change in American policy toward Germany. The West needed Ger-

mans as allies against the Soviet Union, and reminders of the Nazi past were now very much out of place. As a result, Scholtz-Klink was acquitted of war crimes and her sentence of 18 months just happened to coincide with the time she had already served on her earlier conviction. In the early 1950s, she was banned for life from holding any public office in the Federal Republic of Germany. Scholtz-Klink remained utterly unrepentant, publishing in 1978 a collection of speeches and essays entitled *Die Frau im Dritten Reich* (Women in the Third Reich).

SOURCES:

Andrews, Herbert D. "Thirty-Four Gold Medallists: Nazi Women Remember the *Kampfzeit*," in *German History*. Vol. 11, no. 3. October 1993, pp. 293–315.

Cosner, Shaaron, and Victoria Cosner. *Women under the Third Reich: A Biographical Dictionary*. Westport, CT: Greenwood Press, 1998.

Koonz, Claudia. *Mothers in the Fatherland: Women, the Family, and Nazi Politics*. NY: St. Martin's Press, 1987.

Saldern, Adelheid von. "Victims or Perpetrators? Controversies about the Role of Women in the Nazi State," in David F. Crew, ed. *Nazism and German Society, 1933–1945*. London: Routledge, 1994, pp. 141–165.

Gertrud Scholtz-Klink

Scholtz-Klink, Gertrud. *Aufbau des deutschen Frauenar-beitsdienstes.* 2nd ed. Leipzig: Verlag "Der Na-tionale Aufbau," 1934.

———. *Die Frau im Dritten Reich: Eine Dokumentation.* Tübingen: Grabert, 1978.

———. *The Task of the Woman of To-Day: Conference of Women at the Reich Party Rally of Honour, 1936.* Berlin: NSDAP-Deutsches Frauenwerk, 1936.

———. *Verpflichtung und Aufgabe der Frau im national-sozialistischen Staat.* Berlin: Junker und Dünnhaupt, 1936.

"Scholtz-Klink, Gertrud (1902—)," in Dieter K. Buse and Juergen C. Doerr, eds. *Modern Germany: An Ency-clopedia of History, People, and Culture, 1871–1990.* Vol. 2. NY: Garland, 1998, p. 894.

Wistrich, Robert S. *Who's Who in Nazi Germany.* New ed. London: Routledge, 1995.

John Haag,
Associate Professor History,
University of Georgia, Athens, Georgia

Schönbrunn, Gabi.

See Zange, Gabi.

Schöne, Andrea Mitscherlich
(1961—)

East German speedskater. Name variations: *Andrea Schoene or Andrea Schone; Andrea Mitscherlich; An-drea Ehrig. Born Andrea Mitscherlich in East Ger-many in 1961.*

> *Won the world 3,000 meters (1983); won the Olympic silver in the 3,000 (1976); won the Olympic gold medal in the 3,000 (1984).*

In two Olympic tries, speedskater Andrea Schöne could only claim one silver, acquired in Innsbruck in 1976 under her maiden name of Mitscherlich. That year, *Tatiana Averina of the USSR walked home with the gold in the 1,000 and 3,000 meters, with Olympic records in both. At Sarajevo in 1984, Schöne, by then a 23-year-old nurse, finally won the gold medal in the 3,000 me-ters with a time of 4:24.79, beating an Olympic record set by Björg Eva Jensen of Norway in 1980. Schöne's teammate and longtime friend *Karin Kania-Enke came in second for a silver, while teammate *Gabi Schönbrunn (Zange) took the bronze. Schöne also won two silver medals in the 1,000 and the 1,500, both behind Kania-Enke. In 1988 in Calgary, under the name Andrea Ehrig, she took silvers in the 3,000 and 5,000 meters and a bronze in the 1,500 meters.

Schopenhauer, Adele (1797–1849)

German poet and sister of Arthur Schopenhauer. Born Luise Adele Schopenhauer on June 12, 1797, in

Hamburg, Germany; died in 1849 in Bonn, Germany; daughter of Johanna Schopenhauer (1766–1838) and Heinrich Floris Schopenhauer (d. 1805, a merchant); sister of Arthur Schopenhauer (the German philoso-pher); never married; no children.

Adele Schopenhauer, a poet and novelist, was born in 1797 in Hamburg, Germany. After her fa-ther Heinrich Schopenhauer, a merchant in Ham-burg, committed suicide in 1805 when the family business failed, her mother *Johanna Schopen-hauer moved with Adele to Weimar. There, Adele grew up surrounded by the leading writers and artists of Germany who flocked to her mother's biweekly literary salons. Since Johanna turned to writing fiction to support herself and Adele, and her brother Arthur Schopenhauer made his name as a Romantic philosopher, it is not surprising that Adele, well educated, became a writer as well. Among her circle of literary friends were the family of Johann Goethe and the renowned poet *Annette von Droste-Hülshoff. Adele wrote nov-els, including *Anna* (1844) but preferred poetry, and shared with her brother the Romantic sense of the emptiness and superficiality of society. She also had a strong interest in folklore and com-posed children's fairy tales based on popular leg-ends. Adele had a difficult relationship with her brother, who was for a long time estranged from the family, but tried to mediate between him and their mother. After her mother's death, Adele edit-ed many of Johanna Schopenhauer's works. She died in Bonn about age 52.

SOURCES:
Buck, Claire. *The Bloomsbury Guide to Women's Litera-ture.* NY: Prentice Hall, 1992.

Wallace, W. *Life of Arthur Schopenhauer.* St. Clair Shores, MI: Scholarly Press, 1970.

Laura York, M.A. in History,
University of California, Riverside, California

Schopenhauer, Johanna
(1766–1838)

German writer who hosted an influential salon. Name variations: Johanna Henriette Trosiener; Henri-ette Trosiener or Trosina; Madame Schopenhauer. Born Johanna Henriette Trosiener (also seen as Trosi-na) in Danzig, West Prussia, on July 9, 1766; died on April 18, 1838, in Jena, Prussia; daughter of Christian Heinrich Trosiener (a merchant, banker, and senator) and Elisabeth (Lehmann) Trosiener; married Heinrich Floris Schopenhauer (a merchant), on May 16, 1785 (died 1805); children: Arthur Schopenhauer (a philosopher, b. February 22, 1788); Luise Adele Schopenhauer (a poet, b. June 12, 1797)

Selected writings: A Lady Travels: Journeys in England and Scotland from the Diaries of Johanna Schopenhauer.

Now best remembered as the mother of philosopher Arthur Schopenhauer, Johanna Schopenhauer was a novelist and travel writer well known in her time. Her father, a well-to-do Danzig merchant and banker, gave her an excellent education and allowed her to study art. Her intellectual and artistic interests were neglected, however, after her marriage at age 18 to Heinrich Schopenhauer, a 38-year-old merchant of Hamburg. She had two children, Arthur in 1788 and *Adele Schopenhauer in 1797, and devoted herself to their care at their country home outside Danzig. In the early 1800s, most of the Schopenhauer family fortune was lost during a period of rapid inflation and speculation; in consequence, Heinrich committed suicide in 1805. The next year Johanna, after having settled the Schopenhauer finances, moved with her daughter to Weimar, where, at age 40, she began an entirely new life.

Weimar was a cultural center for German literary and artistic figures, and Johanna soon became part of Weimar's social elite. She started a salon where she hosted new and established writers and poets, including Johann Wolfgang von Goethe. Encouraged by her friends, Johanna took up writing herself and also studied painting. In 1810, she published a biography of her friend, the German writer Karl Fernow; she would write and publish for the next two decades, gaining a considerable reputation for herself. Writing across genres, she produced travelogues from her trips abroad, as well as biographies of artists, novellas, story collections, and several full-length novels, the best known being *Gabriele* (1819). Her work became quite popular, and she enjoyed considerable fame across Germany.

Johanna had a close relationship with her daughter, but she was estranged from her son Arthur, later a well-known Romantic philosopher. "The character or will," he once opined, "is inherited from the father; the intellect from the mother." Their strained relationship prior to 1819 is preserved in their often harsh correspondence; Johanna never saw him again after an argument in 1814, during which she apparently threw him down a flight of stairs. In 1819, Arthur broke off all correspondence with his mother following a disagreement over the family finances. In 1828, Johanna moved to Bonn to live with Adele, but when the ruler of Weimar, Karl Friedrich, offered the celebrated author a pension, she accepted and retired to his court at

Jena in 1837. She completed her memoirs before dying at Jena the following year. The memoirs were published in 1924.

SOURCES:

Buck, Claire. *The Bloomsbury Guide to Women's Literature.* NY: Prentice Hall, 1992.

Durant, Will. *The Story of Philosophy.* NY: Washington Square Press, 1961.

Wallace, W. *Life of Arthur Schopenhauer.* St. Clair Shores, MI: Scholarly Press, 1970.

Laura York, M.A. in History,
University of California, Riverside, California

Schratt, Katharina (1855–1940)

Austrian actress who was later companion to Franz Joseph I. Born in 1855 in Baden, Austria; died in 1940; daughter of a middle-class shopkeeper; attended a convent school; studied acting in Vienna; married into the von Kiss family in 1877; children: son Anton (b. 1878).

Katharina Schratt was born in the small town of Baden, Austria, into a solid, middle-class family, in 1855, the daughter of a haberdasher. She first appeared on a stage when she was 11 years old, after persuading the father of a friend to give her a small part in a local production. Her own father was so scandalized that he sent her to a convent school. Once there, the exuberant Katharina did not abandon the theater but instead would drape herself in a bedsheet and perform plays from memory for the other schoolgirls. When the mother superior discovered her antics, she wrote to Schratt's father and requested that he remove his daughter from the school, citing her departure from the usual course of good behavior.

Despite her father's objections to the idea of a woman on the stage, Schratt was soon able to convince him to let her study acting in Vienna. In 1873, she performed for Franz Joseph I for the first time at celebrations for the 25th anniversary of his rule; she was 18 years old and would not begin her liaison with the emperor for another 13 years. In the meantime, she became a popular figure on the stage. As a member of the Stadttheater, she embodied the ideal of young Austrian womanhood, often appearing on floats at carnival time holding a cornucopia, the sign of natural abundance.

In 1877, Schratt left the stage for a time after marrying a Hungarian aristocrat named Kiss whose family had lost their fortune by order of Emperor Franz Joseph during the revolution of 1848. The Kiss family persuaded Schratt to petition the emperor for the return of their lands; she did gain an audience with him, but her petition failed. Eventually, she separated from Kiss, who had mismanaged their money so badly that the authorities at one time seized all of their property, including their clothes. Schratt's son, Anton, born in 1878, was sent to military school.

By 1884, Schratt was a member of the *Burgtheater*, a company supported privately by the emperor, then 53 years old and estranged from his wife *Elizabeth of Bavaria (1837–1898), known as Empress Sissi. The gossip of the period suggests that Franz Joseph had given his wife a venereal disease, a betrayal for which she could never forgive him. After this rupture, he dedicated himself to the management of the empire, while the freedom-loving Elizabeth devoted her time to her charities. At times, however, Elizabeth would have to endure her husband's company, which, as the years wore on, became more and more tedious to her. By 1886, when it became clear that Katharina Schratt had captured the emperor's attention, Empress Elizabeth saw an opportunity to free herself from her husband's

emotional needs and summoned the court actress to a private audience where an agreement was reached between them about Schratt's newest role: companion to the emperor.

Elizabeth requested the court painter, Heinrich von Angeli, to paint a portrait of Schratt as a present to Franz Joseph. Elizabeth also arranged that she and Franz Joseph would pay regular visits to the sittings to view the progress of the work. In this way, she managed the course of the affair between her husband and Schratt, even sending Schratt an emerald ring as a token of her appreciation. The accompanying letter, a clever exercise in double-entendre, thanks Schratt for her sacrifice in sitting for the portrait and expresses the empress' great joy over the cherished gift of a portrait that Schratt's sacrifice had made possible. Throughout the summer of 1886, Franz Joseph continued to meet Schratt, usually accompanied by Empress Elizabeth, who coined the phrase *die Freundin* (woman-friend) to describe Schratt's relationship to the emperor.

By all accounts, this unlikely affair between an autocratic ruler and a burgher's daughter was quite successful. Letters written by Franz Joseph to Schratt indicate his respect and admiration for her. Schratt eased Franz Joseph's loneliness and helped restore a degree of charm and civility to the Hofburg, the royal palace where the emperor spent most of his time. Elizabeth, however, found herself entangled in an odd relationship with Schratt—on the one hand belittling Schratt's attempts to act an aristocratic part, and on the other believing that Schratt embodied a kind of simple good luck that had eluded Elizabeth for most of her life. As the affair continued, Elizabeth began to treat her husband with more affection than she had in years.

Though the last ruler of the Habsburgs found some degree of domestic happiness toward the end of his reign, Austria-Hungary, as his empire was known after 1867, gradually was overshadowed by the Prussian-dominated German Empire. In 1889, Elizabeth and Franz Joseph's only son, Archduke Rudolf, fulfilled a suicide pact with his mistress *Marie Vetsera by shooting her and then himself. In 1898, Elizabeth was assassinated by an Italian anarchist. Finally, in 1914, the emperor's nephew Franz Ferdinand, and Franz Ferdinand's wife *Sophie Chotek, were assassinated by a Serbian nationalist, precipitating the events that led to World War I. Franz Joseph died in 1916 before the end of the war and the final defeat of his empire. Katharina Schratt, the token of good luck to her empress, outlived the Habsburgs and their empire, dying in 1940.

Katharina Schratt

SOURCES:
Haslip, Joan. *The Emperor and the Actress: The Love Story of Emperor Franz Josef and Katharina Schratt.* Dial, 1982.
Kelen, Betty. *The Mistresses: Domestic Scandals of Nineteenth-Century Monarchs.* NY: Barnes & Noble, 1966.

Bonnie Burns, Ph.D.,
Cambridge, Massachusetts

Schreiber, Adele (c. 1872–1957)

Austrian feminist and politician. Name variations: Adele Schreiber-Krieger. Born in Vienna, Austria, around 1872; died in 1957; daughter of a doctor; married a doctor.

Adele Schreiber was born in Vienna around 1872. A rebellious daughter of a doctor, she left Vienna while still young, finding work as a reporter for the *Frankfurter Zeitung* in Berlin. Schreiber threw herself into the cause of women's rights. In addition to helping found the International Women's Suffrage Alliance in 1904 and the German Association for the Rights of Women and Children in 1910, she opened a home for unwed mothers.

Following World War I and the collapse of the monarchy in 1918, German women were granted the right to vote, and Schreiber benefited by winning a seat as a Social Democrat in the first Reichstag. As a member of the constitutional government that ran Germany from 1919 until the rise of Hitler in 1933, she concentrated especially on women's issues, chairing a committee that proposed a bill to make regulated prostitution illegal and serving as president of the German Red Cross. She also retained her journalistic roots by editing women's journals and producing a number of books about mothers and children, among them *Mutterschaft* and *Das Buch von Kinde.*

When Hitler assumed power in 1933, Schreiber went into exile. She lived in Great Britain until 1947, then moved to a town near Zurich, Switzerland. Fluent in five languages, she traveled throughout Europe and the United States, giving lectures and promoting women's causes. In 1956, the year before she died, she coauthored *Journey Towards Freedom,* the history of the International Alliance of Women, for which she had served as vice-president.

Malinda Mayer,
writer and editor, Falmouth, Massachusetts

Schreiber, Lady Charlotte Guest (1812–1895).

See Guest, Lady Charlotte.

Schreiner, Olive (1855–1920)

South African novelist, socialist and feminist who became an important critic of British imperial policy and struggled to reduce the many social restrictions placed on Victorian women. Name variations: Emilie Schreiner; (pseudonym) Ralph Iron. Pronunciation: SHRINE-er. Born Olive Emilie Albertina Schreiner on March 24, 1855, in Wittebergen, South Africa; died in Cape Town, South Africa, on December 10, 1920; daughter of Gottlob Schreiner (a missionary and businessman) and Rebecca (Lyndall) Schreiner; married Samuel Cron Cronwright, on February 24, 1894; children: daughter (died one day after birth on April 30, 1895).

Worked as a governess and began writing novels (1874–1881); published The Story of an African Farm *under pseudonym Ralph Iron (1883); developed her feminism and socialism as member of "Men's and Women's Club" in London; hailed as a feminist pioneer after publication of* Dreams *(1890); became vocal opponent of Cecil Rhodes, British imperial policy, and the Boer War; campaigned for end to racial and gender restrictions on vote in South Africa; defended pacifism and conscientious objectors during World War I; last unfinished work published posthumously (1929).*

Publications: The Story of an African Farm *(1883);* Dreams *(1890);* Dream Life and Real Life *(1893);* The Political Situation *(co-authored by Samuel Cronwright-Schreiner, 1896);* Trooper Peter Halkett of Mashonaland *(1897);* An English South African's View of the Situation *(1899);* Closer Union *(1909);* Women and Labor *(1911); (published posthumously)* Thoughts on South Africa *(1923),* Stories, Dreams and Allegories *(1923),* From Man to Man *(1926), and* Undine *(1929).*

English women of the sprawling British Empire found themselves playing dual and often ambiguous roles. As members of the colonizing race, they benefited from the increased power and opportunities generated by imperialism. As women, however, they were colonized in turn by Victorian gender norms which sharply curtailed their freedom and relegated them to secondary status within colonial and metropolitan society. From beneath these contradictory impulses, a young South African woman named Olive Schreiner emerged as one of the leading and most influential feminists and critics of imperial policy in the 19th and early 20th centuries.

Born in 1855 into an evangelical missionary family stationed in Wittebergen, South Africa, Olive Schreiner was the 9th of **Rebecca Lyndall Schreiner** and Gottlob Schreiner's 12 children.

Christened Olive Emilie Albertina after three dead brothers, Schreiner was known to her family as Emilie for her first 15 years. Her father's preoccupation with mission work left the task of raising and educating the children to Olive's mother. Rebecca Schreiner, faced with life in a series of failing and "uncivilized" mission stations, instilled in her children a stern and unwavering evangelical creed and behavioral code that stressed the importance of duty, proper comportment and the racial superiority of Britons. While all the Schreiner children were taught by their mother at home, Olive's brothers were later sent to school in England in accordance with Victorian beliefs that only men could profit from an extensive education. Olive, on the other hand, was forced to augment her own meager education by reading widely, setting in motion a pattern that she maintained for the rest of her life.

In 1861, under orders from the Wesleyan Missionary Society, Gottlob Schreiner moved the family to Healdtown where he was to run the mission station and its attached vocational school. Four years later, he was dismissed by the mission society in disgrace for breaking its rule prohibiting missionaries from engaging in trade. After nearly three decades as a missionary, Gottlob was forced to try his hand at business in order to make a living. His efforts proved to be a failure, and the family quickly slid into poverty.

In 1867, the three youngest children, including Olive, were sent to live with their older brother, Theo, who had returned to South Africa to take up a position as headmaster and teacher of a small school in Cradock. News about the discovery of diamonds in Griqualand West, an autonomous African state with a growing European population, led to further disruptions in Olive's childhood. When Theo and her younger brother William went to the diamond fields in 1870 in the hopes of raising the family from poverty, Olive was shunted between a series of relatives and family friends. It was in this period that Schreiner finally renounced formal religion and became a freethinker. Despite her mother's teachings, which were enforced by corporal punishment and stinging criticism, Olive began questioning her commitment to religion after the death of a younger sister in 1864. This loss of religious sentiment and the ensuing disapproval from her deeply spiritual family left a hole in her life that was not filled until she read and adopted the philosophies presented in Herbert Spencer's *First Principles*. Spencer and other freethinkers rejected formal religious authority and dogma in favor of science, rational inquiry and speculation. Schreiner's growing commitment to this ideology distanced her from her family and helped foster a lifelong need for independence.

In the midst of this conversion to freethinking ideology, Schreiner suffered the collapse of a whirlwind engagement to Julius Gau, a German businessman whom she had met while traveling between relatives. Eager to put the whole episode behind her, Olive decided in December 1872 to join her brothers and older sister in the diamond fields of Kimberly. Living in a tent city alongside other prospectors, Schreiner had to contend with poor sanitation, disease, lack of food, widespread drunkenness and gambling. Since claims were by no means automatically profitable, the wives and sisters of prospectors supplemented the family income by cooking and cleaning for others. In addition to filling these traditional roles, Schreiner also taught in the local school and began writing short stories in which she started to develop many of the themes and characters that later appeared in her novels.

Barely a year after her arrival, an increasingly sickly Schreiner was forced to leave Kimberly for a sister's home in Fraserburg in search of better health. Life in the tent city of the diamond fields had caused an asthmatic condition which would plague her for the rest of her life. After meeting and befriending Dr. John and **Mary Brown** in Fraserburg, Schreiner decided to pursue a career in medicine. While the Browns encouraged this decision, which would have required study in England or the United States, her family's poverty prevented Olive from enacting her plans.

In an effort to begin contributing to the family income, Schreiner answered an ad in April 1874 for a position as governess, one of the few reputable occupations open to Victorian women of middle-class origins. Since most qualified teachers in South Africa were men who opened their own schools in urban areas, female governesses were in high demand in agricultural communities as a cheap alternative to boarding schools. As single women in strangers' homes, they were, however, subject to a variety of abuses ranging from poor pay to overwork and sexual advances from their employers.

Although her own experiences in a series of governess positions over the next seven years were generally positive, Schreiner was not immune from these problems. Her chief complaints were the inadequate pay and loneliness brought on by isolation in remote farming communities. She was not, however, willing to forego the independence that her work gave her and went so far as to refuse her family's offer of monetary aid. Shortly thereafter, Schreiner explained in a letter to her sister: "I made up my mind when I was quite a little child that as soon as I was able I would support myself for I see no reason why a woman should be dependent on her friends any more than a man should." While this commitment to supporting herself compromised many of her choices later in life, Schreiner's dedication to this principle never wavered.

During the seven years that she worked as a governess, Schreiner completed two novels and began work on a third. Set in South Africa, all three (*The Story of an African Farm*, *Undine* and *From Man to Man*) explored and asserted several different positions on women, freedom, religion and love. In 1880, Schreiner sent the manuscript of *The Story of an African Farm* to the Browns in England and asked them to find her a publisher. Although they were initially unsuccessful, Olive began revising the manuscript and set sail for England in 1881 in the hopes of entering medical school. Shortly after her arrival, Schreiner enrolled in a nurses' training course at the Royal Infirmary in Edinburgh and began studying for the medical school entrance exam. Within a few weeks, ill health forced her to abandon both pursuits and she returned to writing.

In 1882, Schreiner succeeded in finding a publisher for *The Story of an African Farm*, which came out the following year under the pseudonym of Ralph Iron. Her first novel was very well received and Schreiner found herself being introduced into social and literary circles which included such influential figures as Havelock Ellis, *Eleanor Marx-Aveling, Oscar Wilde and H. Rider Haggard. In addition to enabling her to forge close friendships with Marx-Aveling and Ellis, Schreiner's newfound notoriety assured her of an audience and linked her in the public mind with the growing movement for women's emancipation. This link was as much the result of Schreiner's own behavior and independence as it was of the feminist commentary of her main character, Lyndall, who persistently critiqued the social restrictions placed on women by Victorian society.

Shortly after the appearance of her first novel, Schreiner immersed herself in the newly formed "Men and Women's Club," which committed itself to intellectual work aimed at improving the relations between the sexes. As an active member, Schreiner took part in its many discussions on the inadequacy of women's education, the Contagious Diseases Acts (which were designed to curtail the prevalence of venereal disease among prostitutes), and the non-recognition of women's sexuality. She also explored these themes in her extensive correspondence with Havelock Ellis and fellow club-member Karl Pearson. When the club turned its attention to prostitution, Schreiner began researching the problem in detail. After some initial efforts at rescue work, she came to the conclusion that her energies would be better spent on publicizing women's issues through her writing.

As a result of her work, Schreiner developed an intense but short-lived friendship with Pearson. Although biographers speculate that she was in love with him, Schreiner herself consistently denied that they were ever romantically involved. When their friendship collapsed at the end of 1886, Schreiner sank into despair and left England to travel around Europe. While abroad, she began work on an introduction for a new edition of *Mary Wollstonecraft's *A Vindication of the Rights of Woman*. This introduction, never finished, was soon abandoned in favor of a series of allegories, later published as *Dreams*, which explored the constraints placed on women by Victorian society.

Olive Schreiner

On her return to England in 1889, Schreiner, still upset over the loss of her friendship with Pearson, studiously avoided the Club and declined most social invitations. In October, she decided to return to South Africa, after an absence of eight years, in order to concentrate more fully on her work. Prior to her departure, Olive entrusted Ellis with the publication of her allegories on the condition that they be targeted at the rich, whom she felt were most in need of enlightenment. Published in 1890, *Dreams*, with its emphasis on the injustices done to women by Victorian society, appeared as a feminist call to arms.

Shortly after her November 1889 arrival in South Africa, the widespread popularity of *Dreams* led to invitations to appear as a speaker at meetings and social gatherings throughout the British Empire. Anxious to continue her work and plagued by increasingly severe asthma attacks, Schreiner moved to Matjesfontein in search of better health. After settling into her new home, she began grappling with the problems of Victorian colonial society and South African politics in a series of essays which appeared as journal articles in the United States and England between 1891 and 1900. In these essays, collected and published in 1923 as *Thoughts on South Africa*, Schreiner emerged as an opponent of racial and ethnic segregation and as a staunch supporter of the Dutch farmers, called Boers, who had fled British rule after the Napoleonic wars and set up semi-autonomous republics in the Transvaal (also called the Republic of South Africa) and Orange Free State.

Schreiner's involvement in South African politics increased dramatically when her younger brother William, who had returned to South Africa to practice law after attending Cambridge University, became an advisor and, subsequently, attorney-general for the newly formed government of Cecil Rhodes. Rhodes' own rise to political power lay in his control over South Africa's nascent diamond and gold industries. In addition to his control of De Beers Consolidated Mines, however, Rhodes was also given a charter by the British government which empowered his British-South Africa Company to annex and administer new territory as he saw fit. By 1890, Rhodes had used his economic power to forge an alliance with the Afrikaner Bond, a Boer political party dedicated to an autonomous and united South Africa, and to become prime minister of Cape Colony.

Initially impressed by Rhodes' accomplishments, Schreiner quickly became one of his most vocal critics, a position she was to maintain throughout the 1890s. Her actions irreparably damaged her already weakened relationship with her family, since they regarded Olive's critique of Rhodes as an attack on her brother. Despite the pain that this caused her, Schreiner remained firm in her opposition to Rhodes and his official policies, which she attacked in essays and satirical sketches. The basis of these criticisms lay in Schreiner's own anti-capitalist sentiments which had been forged during her years in England. Olive's critique of Rhodes and his government was centered around her belief that governmental policy was set by capitalists with little regard for the needs of the masses. This was subsequently confirmed by Rhodes' efforts to annex the remaining independent African states, impose voting restrictions and a labor tax on the indigenous populations, and inflict corporal punishment on those who hindered South Africa's industrial development.

In the midst of this campaign against government policies, Schreiner met and was courted by her future husband, an ostrich farmer named Samuel Cron Cronwright. After a brief period of indecision in which she worried that marriage would impinge on her independence, she accepted his proposal, and they were married in a civil ceremony in February 1894. At Schreiner's insistence, she retained her own name while he changed his to Samuel Cronwright-Schreiner, thereby making them an anomaly within Victorian society. Within three months, they abandoned Samuel's farm and moved to Kimberly after Olive's asthmatic condition worsened. Shortly thereafter, a pregnant Olive resumed her unsuccessful attempts to complete *From Man to Man*, a task which was to elude her for the rest of her life. Schreiner's grief over the death of her baby a day after its birth in April 1895 was compounded by four subsequent miscarriages. In an effort to alleviate their sadness, both Schreiner and her husband plunged into work and politics.

In August 1895, Samuel delivered a speech on South Africa's political situation to a local Farmer's Association meeting. Although the speech was billed as his own creation, its content and style reveal Olive's extensive input. Published in England the following year as a jointly authored book entitled *The Political Situation*, Samuel's speech argued that capitalists had acquired too much control over South Africa's government and economy. In a much more radical move, Samuel and Olive also called for the expansion of the franchise regardless of race or color and began referring to the so-called "native question" as one of labor, since the issues involved were created by capitalist exploitation.

As the details of the ill-fated 1896 Jameson raid unfolded in the South African press, Schreiner built on the socialist critiques presented in *The Political Situation* and issued a warning that the capitalists' need for unified markets would lead to war between the British and their Boer neighbors. The origins of the raid, part of a plot to complete the British takeover of the Transvaal, were traced back to Rhodes himself and eventually led to the collapse of his government. Rhodes' incurable expansionist impulses were demonstrated later that same year when he used his position as head of the British-South Africa Company to invade and annex the nearby lands of the Matabele and Mashona tribes. Appalled by Rhodes' actions in the newly renamed territory of Rhodesia, Schreiner wrote *Trooper Peter Halkett of Mashonaland*, a scathing attack on capitalist expansion and a warning that its next target would be the Boers rather than the indigenous African peoples.

Convinced that her warnings were falling on deaf ears, Schreiner and her husband went to England in 1897 to visit family and friends. While abroad, she continued her crusade and delivered many speeches warning of the coming war and criticizing British policy in South Africa. These activities and her subsequent speeches on behalf of both the women's movement and conscientious objectors helped to create her image as a brilliant crusader and campaigner. In 1898, Schreiner returned to South Africa in time to see Rhodes defeated at the polls. Although he was replaced as prime minister by her younger brother William, Olive remained convinced that capitalists like Rhodes were attempting to provoke a war with the Boer republics. Her renewed warnings, published in 1899 as *An English South African's View of the Situation*, also went unheeded.

With the outbreak of the Boer War (1899–1902), Schreiner's husband went to England to campaign for an end to the hostilities, while she moved from Johannesburg to Hannover in an effort to relieve her asthma. During the war's initial phase, she wrote very little, preferring instead to devote her time to gathering food and raising money to alleviate local shortages. When she returned to her house in Johannesburg a year after being stranded in Hannover by the imposition of martial law, she found that it had been looted and her manuscripts burned. Schreiner's response was to resume her involvement in politics, this time in direct opposition to her brother's governmental policies which called for the annexation of the Boer republics once they had been defeated. Olive's frequent speeches at conferences opposed to official policy played no small part in the subsequent collapse of her brother's ministry. While the republics were eventually annexed, the 1902 peace treaty, which granted the Boers internal autonomy and allowed them to impose racial restrictions on the franchise, was only a temporary solution to the problem of South African unity.

In the midst of Schreiner's increasing political activity, her husband, who had returned to South Africa in 1900, established a business and entered politics as a member of the Cape Colony Parliament. Although historians speculate that this may have marked the beginning of an estrangement between the couple, they both denied the existence of any marital problems in their correspondence with others. While Samuel busied himself with his parliamentary duties, Olive began campaigning for the nascent South African labor movement, despite her disagreement with its tendency towards racial exclusivity, which she felt unnecessarily hindered the struggle against capitalist exploitation. In addition to her commitment to labor, after the war Schreiner also became heavily involved in the South African women's movement which received a welcome boost from both her notoriety and her ties to suffragists in England.

When negotiations for a new South African constitution were initiated in 1907, she helped form the Women's Enfranchisement League which waged an unsuccessful campaign to secure the vote for women. In tandem with this effort, Olive reconciled with her brother William and joined him in calling for a federated South African republic devoid of racial restrictions on voting rights. They believed that smaller, more loosely controlled states would provide better government and more liberty. Like the campaign to include women in the franchise, these efforts failed and the new constitution instead created the Union of South Africa, a white-controlled, semi-autonomous British Dominion made up of the former Cape Colony, Natal, the Transvaal and the Orange Free State.

Frustrated by the failure of her efforts to secure a decentralized, racially integrated South Africa, Schreiner threw herself even more fully into the women's movement. While continuing her work with suffrage groups and the organization of women's trade unions, she also began to research and write *Women and Labor*. Hailed by many as the bible of the early 20th-century feminist movement, *Women and Labor*, which appeared in 1911, argues that the industrial revolution narrowed and depleted the labor roles available to women until they were reduced to "sex parasites" and childbearing machines. In order for women to regain their rightful place and for society to progress, women had to be allowed to break free of social restrictions and engage in productive labor. Thus, for Schreiner, the women's movement was inextricably linked with the labor movement. Influenced by *Women and Labor*, which met with critical acclaim, feminists throughout the empire revamped their platforms and began pressing for an end to the social restrictions on women's work.

Despite her influence within the feminist community, Schreiner did not always meet with success in this period. In 1913, she resigned as vice-president of the Women's Enfranchisement League as a protest against the League's decision to alter its program in favor of securing a racially based vote for women. Disillusioned and increasingly ill, Schreiner left for Britain in the hopes of getting treatment for her asthma. The outbreak of World War I trapped her in England where she suffered taunts and persecution because of her German name, her pacifism, and her spirited defense of conscientious objectors. During the war, Schreiner called for equal pay for women filling industrial positions formerly occupied by men and began work on "The Dawn of Civilization," a long article published after her death in which she explored and justified pacifism.

Although she had become incapacitated by illness four years earlier, it was not until July 1920 that Samuel ended their long separation and joined her in England. Shocked by her appearance, he canceled a proposed trip to the United States in order to care for his wife. Eager to avoid another damp English winter, Olive set sail for South Africa the following month, leaving her husband to follow after he had tied up their affairs. On arrival at the Cape, Schreiner began raising money for striking African workers and avidly followed press accounts of the civil disobedience campaign organized to protest the issuing of internal passbooks. She was working on these campaigns when she died on December 10, 1920.

Returning after the funeral, Samuel arranged for his wife to be reinterred on the ridge above his old farm at Buffelskop and began writing her biography. Despite her wish that her papers and unfinished manuscripts remain private, over the next decade Samuel produced an edited collection of her letters and oversaw the posthumous publication of several works, the last of which was the semi-autobiographical novel *Undine*

which she had begun as a young governess on the verge of an intellectual awakening.

SOURCES:

Barash, Carol. *An Olive Schreiner Reader.* London: Pandora, 1987.

Berkman, Joyce Avrech. *The Healing Imagination of Olive Schreiner.* Amherst, MA: University of Massachusetts Press, 1989.

———. *Olive Schreiner: Feminism on the Frontier.* Quebec: Eden Press Women's Publications, 1979.

First, Ruth, and Ann Scott. *Olive Schreiner.* NY: Schocken, 1980.

Thurman, Howard. *A Track to the Water's Edge: The Olive Schreiner Reader.* NY: Harper & Row, 1973.

SUGGESTED READING:

Chaudhuri, Nupur, and Margaret Strobel, eds. *Western Women and Imperialism.* Bloomington, IN: Indiana University Press, 1992.

Cronwright-Schreiner, Samuel Cron, ed. *The Letters of Olive Schreiner.* London: Unwin, 1924.

———. *The Life of Olive Schreiner.* London: Unwin, 1924.

Draznin, Yaffa Claire, ed. *My Other Self: The Letters of Olive Schreiner and Havelock Ellis, 1884–1920.* NY: Peter Lang, 1992.

Hobman, D.L. *Olive Schreiner: Her Friends and her Times.* London: Watts, 1955.

Lewis, Jane. *Women in England 1870–1950: Sexual Divisions and Social Change.* Bloomington, IN: Indiana University Press, 1984.

Rive, Richard, ed. *Olive Schreiner Letters.* Oxford: Oxford University Press, 1988.

COLLECTIONS:

Correspondence, papers and manuscripts located in Cradock Library, Cradock, South Africa; South African Library, Special Collections, Cape Town; Humanities Research Center, University of Texas, Austin; the privately owned Fryde Collection, Johannesburg; and the J.W. Jagger Library, University of Cape Town.

Kenneth J. Orosz, Ph.D. candidate in European History, Binghamton University, Binghamton, New York

Schroeder, Louise (1887–1957)

German Social Democratic leader who as deputy mayor of West Berlin was a symbol of defiance against Soviet and Communist pressure during the Berlin blockade of 1948–49, one of the tensest periods of the Cold War. Name variations: Luise Schröder. Born Louise Dorothea Sophie Schroeder in Hamburg-Altona, Germany, on April 2, 1887; died in West Berlin on June 4, 1957; educated in Hamburg; never married.

Appointed acting Oberbürgermeisterin ("lord mayoress," May 8, 1947); stepped down from mayoral post (1951); remained active in politics in West Germany (1950s); City of Berlin began to award an annual Louise Schroeder Medal (1998).

Louise Schroeder was born into a working-class family in the Hamburg suburb of Altona in

1887, and experienced privation from her earliest years. Her father was an unskilled worker whose modest wages from toiling in a brickyard were insufficient to support his large family (eight children, four of whom died in infancy). Her mother had little choice but to supplement the domestic income by working long hours selling vegetables in the neighborhood. Louise's father was a class-conscious proletarian and trade-union member as well as a dedicated Social Democrat, and she sometimes accompanied him to local meetings of the Sozialdemokratische Partei Deutschlands (Social Democratic Party, or SPD). In 1910, when Schroeder became a member of the SPD, she was particularly concerned about the growing danger of a major war in Europe. She was shocked in August 1914 when Europe plunged into World War I, with Germany's participation given the full support of the ostensibly antiwar SPD, whose Reichstag deputies voted unanimously to finance the conflict. Despite this disillusionment, Schroeder remained in the party, becoming chair of its local Altona branch in 1915.

One of the immediate consequences of Germany's defeat and the collapse of its monarchy in 1918 was the achievement of women's suffrage. In January 1919, Schroeder was one of the 41 women elected to the National Assembly that had the task of writing a new, democratic constitution for the German Republic. The nascent state, known as the Weimar Republic, was born in turmoil. As a convinced Social Democrat, Schroeder believed that democracy could only succeed in Germany if it brought social justice and economic stability to the vanquished, embittered nation. She paid attention to the needs of her constituency, which became permanent when her National Assembly seat turned into a Reichstag seat. Her power base in Hamburg-Altona was her position as director of the welfare office in that region. Nationally, Schroeder became an important personality in the SPD when she and *Marie Juchacz founded the Social Democratic Arbeiterwohlfahrt (Workers' Welfare) organization to address the many problems of social distress resulting from the WWI defeat, as well as the resulting inflation and economic instability.

As a Reichstag deputy, Schroeder developed expertise in the area of social-welfare legislation. She was particularly concerned with the problem of venereal disease and prostitution, and proposed legislation that would reform and modernize the nature of state intervention in this area. A skilled bridge-builder and crafter of coalitions, Schroeder worked with some of her political ad-

Postage stamp issued by the West Berlin post office on June 3, 1961, honoring Louise Schroeder.

versaries, including **Christine Teusch** of the Catholic Center Party and **Marie-Elisabeth Lüders** of the middle-class German Democratic Party, to help pass legislation improving state support of mothers and children, even unmarried mothers and children of illegitimate birth.

Schroeder's successful political career ended abruptly in the first months of 1933, when the Nazi Party, having come to power "legally" with Adolf Hitler's appointment as chancellor of Germany on January 30 of that year, quickly initiated a reign of terror and proclaimed a totalitarian state, the Third Reich. In March 1933, Schroeder and other Social Democratic Reichstag deputies voted against the Enabling Act that provided Hitler with the pseudo-legal basis for his dictatorship. Soon after, all Social Democratic elected officials in Germany lost their posts. Many were arrested and taken to concentration camps. Others, like Schroeder, became unemployed and were denied unemployment assistance because of their "un-German" allegiance to the ideals of democratic socialism. Schroeder became an "unperson," and her 1925 guide to social legislation, *Mutter und Säugling in der Gesetzgebung*, relating to women and infants, was placed on the Nazi Index of Prohibited Literature.

Under police surveillance, Schroeder struggled to survive, taking over a small bread shop in her old neighborhood of Hamburg-Altona. Even there, she remained loyal to her Social Democratic ideals, responding pointedly with a "Guten Tag" to any customer who entered her shop with a salutation of "Heil Hitler." After some time, she had to abandon the shop, the target of a boycott by the local Nazis and a business which many former Social Democrats avoided because they feared that the store was under police surveillance.

In 1938, Schroeder moved to Berlin where she found employment as a secretary in a construction firm. Living in the capital of Hitler's Greater German Reich was not only psychologically difficult but physically dangerous, once World War II began in 1939. The target of ever-increasing Allied bombing raids, Berlin would be largely reduced to rubble by the end of the war in 1945. On three separate occasions, Schroeder had her dwelling destroyed in air raids. After one such raid on her district of Friedenau, she had to be rescued from under a pile of rubble. She survived the unrelenting bombings, as well as the bloody battle for Berlin in the spring of 1945, and within days of the end of hostilities embarked confidently on the second stage of her political career. She was 58.

By that summer, Soviet occupation authorities had given permission for the democratic parties of the Weimar period, including the SPD, to be reconstituted. Schroeder was elected to the governing board (*Vorstand*) of the Berlin SPD, and by August 1946 had advanced to the post of vice-chair. At the same time, she served as director of the SPD's recreated social welfare organization, the Arbeiterwohlfahrt. She was also a senior editor (along with Otto Suhr) of the SPD monthly journal, *Das Sozialistische Jahrhundert* (The Socialist Century), a job she held from November 1946 through February 1950. Besides the misery and privation of living in a shattered city, by the end of 1946 Berliners found themselves increasingly at the center of the rapidly emerging east-west conflict that would be known to history as the Cold War. As a four-power occupation zone within the Soviet Occupation Zone (SBZ) of defeated Germany, Berlin took on important symbolism in the struggle between the Soviet Union and the Western nations, led by a triumphant and prosperous United States. Tensions grew markedly after the municipal elections of October 1946, in which the Social Democrats ran strongly, with the Communist-controlled Socialist Unity Party (Sozialistische Einheitspartei Deutschlands, or

SED) winning 26 out of 130 seats in the City Assembly (Magistrat).

By December 1946, the new governing coalition of the city of Berlin was in place, consisting of Felix Ostrowski of the SPD as Oberbürgermeister (lord mayor), and with Ferdinand Friedensburg (Christian Democratic Union, or CDU), Heinrich Acker (SED), and Schroeder (SPD) as his deputies. Most of the other key posts of the municipal government were occupied by non-Communists, which outraged the SED and its Soviet backers. In June 1947, the Berlin City Assembly elected SPD member Ernst Reuter, a strongly anti-Communist Social Democrat who had once been a Communist and had solid anti-Nazi credentials, as the city's Oberbürgermeister. Soviet occupation authorities in Berlin regarded Reuter's election as a provocation, refusing to recognize it and blocking him from assuming the post. Consequently, to keep the city functioning and as a Western response to this Soviet step, the Allied occupation authorities authorized Schroeder to perform his functions as amtierende (acting) Oberbürgermeisterin (lord mayoress), a job she began on a de facto basis on May 8, 1947. To allow her to officially take on this highest position in the municipal government, in June 1948 First Deputy Mayor Ferdinand Friedensburg, recognizing the prestige of both the SPD and Schroeder, whom Berliners had taken to their hearts, stepped aside. That same month, the Berlin Blockade began, with the Soviets closing all land and water routes to the non-Soviet zones in Berlin. In response, the Western allies instituted the famous Berlin Airlift, flying supplies by cargo aircraft to the people in their occupation zones. During these tense months, Schroeder enjoyed the support and respect of the beleaguered city's women, who turned out en masse on July 3, 1948, to protest the Soviet's blockade. Never before had a German woman been entrusted with such a prestigious and important political post, and never before in European history had a city the size of Berlin been governed by a woman.

Supported both by the Allied Kommandatura that controlled the Western sectors of Berlin and the overwhelming majority of Berliners in that part of the city, Schroeder symbolized the determination of non-Communist Berliners not to surrender to Soviet might. Starting on June 23, 1948, and on many occasions after that, she presided cool-headedly over municipal council meetings that were disrupted by Communist demonstrators. As a result of her resolve, Schroeder became the best-known and most-beloved woman in Germany in the late 1940s, a position she continued to enjoy in West Germany throughout the 1950s up to the time of her death. During the blockade of Berlin, which lasted from June 24, 1948 until May 13, 1949, Schroeder resisted Soviet and German Communist pressures on her adopted city. Despite her frail health, she refused to be intimidated either by the Soviets, the SED, or the Allied military authorities. Schroeder also served as a member of the Berlin Municipal Parliament from 1948 through 1950 and continued to live modestly, subleasing a small apartment from a friend at Boelckestrasse 121 in the Tempelhof district. In her leisure hours, she collected and read books. Some Berliners talked of Schroeder only as "Königin Louise," a reference to *Louise of Prussia, the heroic Prussian queen of the Napoleonic epoch. Although Schroeder never married or had children, many affectionately called her the "Mother of Berlin."

Only in December 1948 did Schroeder step back from her post as acting Oberbürgermeisterin of West Berlin, relinquishing duties to Ernst Reuter, who with the informal division of the city was now able to take his elected position. Until 1951, however, she would retain her position as one of West Berlin's deputy mayors. When the blockade finally ended in mid-May 1949, a massive rally of thanksgiving was held at the Schöneberg Rathaus in West Berlin. Reuter, Konrad Adenauer, and other political luminaries made well-received speeches, but one of the high points of the celebration was the appearance on the podium of Louise Schroeder, for whom the crowd of 500,000 West Berliners chanted in unison, "Louise! Louise!"

Because of her courageous stand during the Berlin Blockade and her decades-long defense of democracy and human rights, Schroeder was immensely popular not only in West Berlin but throughout West Germany for the final decade of her life. In 1948–49, she served as president of the German Conference of Cities (Deutscher Städtetag). For a time in 1949, her name was often mentioned as a strong candidate for the post of Bundespräsident (Federal President) of the nascent West German state, the Federal Republic of Germany, although in the end Theodor Heuss was chosen. Schroeder served as a Social Democratic member in the West German Parliament, the Bundestag, from 1949 until her death in 1957. Beginning in 1950, she also represented West Berlin in the Council of Europe. Other honors included being a member of the governing board of the German Red Cross, and, in the final months of her life, she received an hon-

orary doctorate from the University of Cologne and the award of the freedom of the City of West Berlin. She died in West Berlin on June 4, 1957.

Louise Schroeder has been honored by Germany in many ways, including two postage stamps issued by the West Berlin postal authorities. The first of these was a 20 pfennig stamp issued on June 3, 1961, to mark the fourth anniversary of her death, followed by a 50 pfennig stamp released on February 12, 1987, to commemorate the 100th anniversary of her birth. She has also been honored by having a gymnasium named for her in Munich, as well as a street in Berlin, Louise-Schroeder-Platz in the Reinickendorf district. Beginning in 1998, the municipal government of Berlin has awarded a Louise Schroeder Medal to honor individuals whose lives personify Schroeder's lifelong goals of working to bring about a world based on democracy, social justice, freedom, and equality between women and men. The first two recipients of the award were the author **Carola Stern**, in 1998, and the former president of the Berlin Parliament, **Hanna-Renate Laurien**, in 1999.

SOURCES:

Blos, Anna, Adele Schreiber, Louise Schroeder, and Anna Geyer, eds. *Die Frauenfrage im Lichte des Sozialismus.* Dresden: Kaden, 1930.

Dertinger, Antje. "Frauen im Reichstag (IV): Leben für Benachteiligte: Über die parlamentarische Tätigkeit Louise Schroeders," in *Das Parlament.* November 12, 1983, p. 11.

Haydock, Michael D. *City under Siege: The Berlin Blockade and Airlift, 1948–1949.* Washington, DC: Brassey's, 1999.

Herz, Hanns-Peter. "Louise Schroeder," in Claus Hinrich Casdorff, ed., *Demokraten: Profile unserer Republik.* Königstein-Taunus: Athenäum, 1983, pp. 239–246.

Huber, Antje. *Verdient die Nachtigal Lob, wenn sie singt?: Die Sozialdemokratinnen.* Stuttgart: Seewald, 1984.

Koerfer, Marthina. *Louise Schroeder: Eine Frau in den Wirren deutscher Politik.* Berlin: Presse- und Informationsamt des Landes Berlin, 1987.

Löbe, Paul. "Lebensbild einer deutschen Frau," in *Louise Schroder: Ein Frauenleben unserer Zeit.* Berlin-Grünewald: Arani, 1956, pp. 7–21.

Michalski, Bettina. *Louise Schroeders Schwestern: Berliner Sozialdemokratinnen der Nachkriegszeit.* Bonn: Dietz, 1996.

Moeller, Robert G. "Protecting Mothers' Work: From Production to Reproduction in Postwar West Germany," in *Journal of Social History.* Vol. 22, no. 3. Spring 1989, pp. 414–437.

———. "Reconstructing the Family in Reconstruction Germany: Women and Social Policy in the Federal Republic, 1949–1955," in *Feminist Studies.* Vol. 15, no. 1. Spring 1989, pp. 137–169.

Nachlass Paul Hertz, Archiv der Historischen Kommission zu Berlin.

Parrish, Thomas. *Berlin in the Balance, 1945–1949.* Reading, MA: Addison-Wesley, 1998.

Richie, Alexandra. *Faust's Metropolis: A History of Berlin.* NY: Carroll & Graf, 1998.

Schroeder, Louise. *Die Frau und der Sozialismus.* Hamburg: Sozialdemokratische Partei, Landesorganisation Hansestadt Hamburg, 1946.

———. *Mutter und Säugling in der Gesetzgebung.* Berlin: Dietz, 1925.

Schumacher, Martin, *et al.*, eds. *M.d.R.: Die Reichstagsabgeordneten der Weimarer Republik in der Zeit des Nationalsozialismus: Politische Verfolgung, Emigration, und Ausbürgerung, 1933–1945.* Düsseldorf: Droste, 1991.

Tusa, Ann, and John Tusa. *The Berlin Airlift.* NY: Atheneum, 1988.

Wickert, Christl. *Unsere Erwählten.* 2 vols. Göttingen: Sovec, 1986.

Windsor, Phillip. *City on Leave: A History of Berlin, 1945–1962.* London: Chatto & Windus, 1963.

John Haag,
Associate Professor History,
University of Georgia, Athens, Georgia

Schroeder, Patricia (1940—)

U.S. representative, advocate for families and women, who used her position on the House National Security Committee to challenge assumptions about spending priorities. Name variations: Pat Schroeder. Pronunciation: SHROW-der. Born Patricia Scott on July 30, 1940, in Portland, Oregon; daughter of Bernice Lemoin Scott (an elementary schoolteacher) and Lee Combs Scott (a pilot and aviation insurance adjuster); University of Minnesota, B.A. (magna cum laude, Phi Beta Kappa), 1961; Harvard Law School, J.D., 1964; certification from Colorado Bar, 1964; married James W. Schroeder, on August 18, 1962; children: Scott William Schroeder (b. 1966); Jamie Christine Schroeder (b. 1970).

Numerous honorary degrees and awards, including Child Advocacy Award, National Parent-Teacher Association (1990); Distinguished Service to Families Award (1991); Leadership Award, Center for Policy Alternatives (1994); National Women's Hall of Fame (1995).

Family moved from Oregon to Texas, Ohio, and Iowa (1940–58); practiced law and taught law at Denver area schools (1964–72); won 2 primary and 12 general elections (1972–96); served on House National Security Committee (formerly House Armed Services Committee, 1973–96), House Judiciary Committee (1980–96), and House Post Office and Civil Service Committee (1973–94); served as co-chair, Congressional Caucus for Women's Issues (1979–95), deputy whip, Democratic Caucus (1987–96), and chair, House Select Committee on Children, Youth, and Families (1991–93); formed exploratory presiden-

tial campaign committee, raised $1 million in three months (1987); retired undefeated from Congress (1996); became president and chief executive of the Association of American Publishers (1997).

Selected publications: Champion of the Great American Family *(Random House, 1989);* 24 Years of House Work . . . and the Place is Still a Mess *(Andrews McMeel, 1998).*

The young mother who wore her long hair tied back with a velvet ribbon and carried a bag of disposable diapers to her swearing-in as a member of Congress in 1973 was an unlikely candidate for membership on the U.S. House of Representatives Armed Services Committee. Or so thought Congressman Edward Hébert, the elderly and irascible chair who tried to keep her off his committee, and then, when she had doggedly lobbied her way in, tried to keep her in what he imagined was her place. "I hope you're not going to be a skinny *Bella Abzug," was his less-than-cordial greeting. "No," she assured him, "I'm going to be me. I'm going to be Pat Schroeder." The chair and his colleagues soon learned who Pat Schroeder was: a woman who wanted a seat on the committee that controlled nearly 40% of the national budget, to see if money could be saved from military spending and used for other purposes. "When men talk about defense, they always claim to be protecting women and children," she said at the time, "but they never ask the women and children what they think." Unasked, she was about to tell them.

Patricia Scott's parents were strong role models. Her father Lee Scott was a pilot who had been drafted to teach aviation during World War II. After the war, he became an aviation insurance adjuster, and taught Schroeder to fly before she was 16, thus encouraging her to be unconventional. He prized efficient use of time, mowing the grass in his suit because he didn't want to waste time changing clothes. He expected Pat and her older brother Mike to help on projects like rebuilding an airplane or remodeling a house. Schroeder's mother **Bernice Scott** returned to work as an elementary schoolteacher the year Pat entered kindergarten. She never insisted that Pat help in the kitchen but allowed her to choose other chores. As a child, Schroeder suffered from amblyopia or "lazy eye," and for a time had to wear an eye patch. Her father helped her cope with other children's teasing by advising her, "Never frown at your enemies. Smile—it scares the hell out of them." It was a lesson she learned well.

The Scott family moved frequently while Schroeder was growing up: from Portland, Oregon, where she was born in 1940, to Kansas City, Missouri, to North Platte, Nebraska, to Sioux City, Iowa, to Dallas, Texas, to Hamilton, Ohio, and finally to Des Moines, Iowa, where she graduated from high school. The experience helped her learn to make friends. "Starting at three," she remembered, "whenever we moved I had to find kids to play with in the new neighborhood . . . as soon as the moving truck pulled away, I would line up my toys on the sidewalk and sit down next to them. . . . The toys were like flypaper. I made friends almost at once."

Her family believed everyone had a right to a college education but also the responsibility to work for it. Schroeder paid her way by flying out to assess damage at airplane crash sites. She graduated in three years, magna cum laude and Phi Beta Kappa. For awhile, Schroeder had studied Chinese and longed to go to China, but her biggest desire, inspired by her father, had always been to attend law school. His law school dream had been thwarted by the Depression. The Scotts were dubious about her choice of Harvard, where Schroeder was one of only 15 women in a class of 550. On her first day, the man who had been assigned the seat next to hers refused to take his place, remarking that he had never gone to school with a girl and did not plan to start now. He also sneered that she should be ashamed of herself for taking a spot in the class that should have gone to a man. Although Pat found Harvard stuffy and "not very challenging," she did meet one "affable" young man, Jim Schroeder. The two married in 1962. After graduation in 1964, they moved to Denver, where Jim joined a law firm. Pat went into private practice and worked as the field attorney for the National Labor Relations Board until the birth of their son Scott in 1966. Thereafter, she worked part time, teaching law at three local colleges, serving as a hearing officer in the Colorado Department of Personnel, and doing pro-bono work for Rocky Mountain Planned Parenthood. The Schroeders' daughter Jamie was born four years after Scott.

In 1970, Jim ran for the state legislature and Pat worked on his campaign; he was defeated by only 42 votes. Two years later, he joined other Democrats to pick a candidate for Colorado's 1st District in the U.S. House of Representatives. The Republican incumbent, James "Mike" McKevitt, had been a popular district attorney. McKevitt had won in 1970 after a Democratic split following a bitter primary battle, when an anti-Vietnam war challenger had beaten the ten-term Democratic congressman. Worse, redistricting had moved some Democratic neighborhoods into an adjoining suburban district. Most

prospective candidates were reluctant to run against such odds. When someone asked Jim, "What about your wife?," he laughingly dismissed the idea. But at home, the Schroeders realized Pat had good credentials: with labor groups through her work at the NLRB, with education groups through her teaching, and from the growing anti-war movement. Jim urged her to run: "You say you're concerned . . . here's your chance to do something."

Because she was considered a long shot, the Democratic National Committee gave Pat Schroeder no money, and women's groups were also reluctant to support her. She kept her part-time jobs. But her overconfident opponent stayed in Washington until the last month of the campaign, and Schroeder's message on the war, the environment, and child care garnered her 52% of the vote, despite a nationwide landslide for Richard Nixon. Schroeder was one of five women elected to Congress for the first time that year; nine of the eleven female incumbents were reelected. There were no women senators in the 93rd Congress. Congresswoman Bella Abzug (D-NY) called to congratulate Schroeder, but when she learned that the new congresswoman had two children, ages two and six, Abzug flatly stated, "I don't think you can do the job." Schroeder pared down her domestic responsibilities to a minimum, ordering carpeting for their Washington home and even a new car over the phone. Jim gave up his partnership in a Denver law firm and found work with a Washington, D.C., law firm, for awhile as a lobbyist, then at the Department of Agriculture. He began to see more of the children than he had before, a benefit to them all. The children chose to attend public rather than private schools and to use the money saved to accompany their mother on trips. The Schroeders made more time for their family by avoiding the Washington social scene.

Schroeder had been elected on a platform to improve education and clean up the environment, and she believed that money from those programs could be found by cutting the defense budget that stood at nearly $80 billion, 40% of the entire national budget. She managed to win a place on the House Armed Services Committee, over the protests of Hébert, an admitted "male chauvinist" whose reaction to Schroeder, she later recalled, made her first day at Harvard seem like a welcoming party in comparison. He did not consider her worthy to join the committee because she had never been in combat. Schroeder pointed out that neither had most of the male members of his committee. Later described by conservative columnist George Will as a "rhetorical roughneck," Schroeder earned good press coverage for remarks like her complaint that the vision of the committee was "obscured by the shine of military brass." Although the 1974 Military Procurement Authorization bill came out of committee with none of Schroeder's suggestions for change, she filed seven pages of "additional views," criticizing the committee's procedures. She was encouraged when a member who had always previously voted with the chair told her privately that he had come to agree that the committee was little more than a lobby for the Pentagon. "Courage is contagious," said Schroeder. "Maybe next year he'll be willing to [say] it publicly."

Interviewer: "How can you be the mother of two small children and a member of Congress at the same time?"

Schroeder: "Because I have a uterus and a brain and they both work."

Pat Schroeder's first bill, introduced with Senator Walter Mondale, was the Child Abuse and Protection Act to fund local demonstration and counseling programs on child abuse. It tied funds to a state's ability to meet reporting and treatment requirements. As it was her first bill, she learned everything she could about the subject, even attending Mondale's Senate hearings as well as the House Education and Labor Subcommittee hearings. The bill passed overwhelmingly and was signed into law.

Schroeder had begun a career of advocacy for children, women and families. She and other women in Congress began meeting informally soon after her arrival to discuss issues affecting women. In 1977, they formed the Congresswomen's Caucus (later the Congressional Caucus for Women's Issues) to identify the problems women faced and decide what needed to be done. Starting in 1979, Schroeder served as the Democratic co-chair. After 1981, the Caucus introduced into each session of Congress an Economic Equity Act, made up of various bills to help women financially.

Often when Pat Schroeder was interviewed during her first term, she was asked her greatest fear as a freshman in the House. "Losing my housekeeper," she always replied. During her first press conference after the 1972 election, she joined other members of Congress in calling for a bill to remedy the lack of affordable child care. On the House Armed Services Committee, gen-

erals told her privately that inadequate child care for the families of service members was their main personnel problem. Schroeder believed that it was a national responsibility to ensure good care for children, the most valuable national resource. In 1974, she became a member of the House Post Office and Civil Service Committee, and conducted hearings on ways to increase the productivity of the federal work force. She found that parents wanted more control over their schedules, and she introduced a pilot "flextime" program, later made permanent, to allow government workers to choose their own hours. In 1978, she pushed through a Federal Employees Part-Time Career Employment Act which created 10,000 new part-time jobs with pro-rated benefits in the federal government, a boon to working parents. She was an active supporter of Head Start, and enrolled her daughter Jamie in the program.

Soon women from Colorado who were not constituents from Schroeder's district began showing up in her office. "First they see their own Representative, their Congressman," she explained to a *Ms.* Magazine reporter in 1976, "then they come to see me, their Congresswoman." Such visibility was not without its drawbacks. Schroeder admitted that it was sometimes exhausting: "Strangers, men and women, feel free to stop me . . . and tell me everything in their lives that ever went wrong."

In 1977, Schroeder joined 81 colleagues to introduce the Pregnancy Discrimination Act, prompted by a Supreme Court decision which had found General Electric not guilty of discrimination for excluding pregnancy under its disability plan because the condition was "voluntary." Schroeder was indignant to learn that the plan paid for sports injuries, attempted suicides, disabilities incurred during a fight or in the commission of a crime, and vasectomies. The Act became law in 1978. However, a provision to direct employers to reinstate women in their old jobs after childbirth was not included in the final bill. In 1985, Schroeder authored the Family and Medical Leave Act, which required employers with 50 or more employees to provide at least 12 weeks a year of unpaid leave for birth, adoption, or family illness. Unsuccessful during the administrations of Ronald Reagan and George Bush, it was one of the first pieces of legislation signed by President Bill Clinton in 1993.

Often traveling to military bases in the U.S. and overseas, Schroeder became aware of another inequity: women who had foregone careers of their own to accompany their foreign service or

Patricia
Schroeder

military husbands on frequent moves were left without pensions if the marriage ended in divorce. Wives of foreign service officers were particularly shortchanged, as they were expected to contribute to the success of their husbands' careers by entertaining foreign diplomats, as well as by making a family life overseas where problems of health, housing, and education were often overwhelming. In 1977, Schroeder introduced several former spouse bills, for the foreign service, the military, the civil service, and the CIA, each of which had its own retirement program. These bills were enacted into law between 1980 and 1984.

When Ronald Reagan became president in 1981, his budget called for reductions in education, training, social services, health, income security, and justice programs which Schroeder saw as a direct attack on women. Congress established a Select Committee on Children, Youth and Families; Schroeder was a charter member and chair of its Economic Security Task Force. The group took credit for smaller decreases than the administration had requested in programs such as Aid to Families with Dependent Children, food stamps, Medicaid, and public housing. A self-styled fiscally conservative liberal, Schroeder voted against Reagan's 1981 tax cut, because she thought the country could not afford it, and against the 1986 tax-reform bill, because she favored more progressive rates.

Schroeder challenged the belief that most women on welfare had been born into welfare families, claiming that in most states, the majority of women on welfare first experienced poverty following a divorce. The Congressional Caucus for Women's Issues discovered that, even though Congress had enacted a Child Support Enforcement program in 1975, states varied widely in enforcing child-support payments by fathers. The Child Support Enforcement Amendment passed in 1984 and brought some regularity to the collection process, which enabled the federal government to cut expenditures. More important from Schroeder's point of view, the bill signaled that the federal government had a role to play when the economic security of children and families was at stake. She also was concerned with economic equity issues such as tax reform, occupational segregation and affirmative-action programs.

Pat Schroeder continued to work for her goals through the House Armed Services Committee. In 1987, she became deputy whip for arms-control legislation, and authored the nuclear test ban amendment to the 1988 Defense Authorization. When Reagan blamed the budget deficit on "welfare queens," she countered with an accusation that defense contractors who overcharged were the real "welfare queens" of the '80s. At the same time, she worked for other military issues such as improved training and increased pay. She became an early advocate for "burden sharing," calling on America's allies to assume a larger portion of the defense costs in Europe and the Pacific. At that time, the United States was spending $1,115 per citizen on defense, $669 of which went to support NATO,

while France was spending $511 on defense, and Great Britain $488. These countries spent more per capita than the U.S. on health and education, and Schroeder did not think it was coincidental that they had lower rates of infant mortality, teen pregnancy, divorce, and alcohol and drug abuse.

After her first reelection in 1974, Schroeder never had to campaign hard to keep her seat in Congress. She became more partisan in the 1980s, however, campaigning in 1984 against Reagan, whom she characterized as the "Teflon president" because none of the failures of his administration stuck to him. She accused Reagan of investing American tax dollars in the biggest peacetime military budget in history while cutting programs which created better economic conditions for women. In June 1984, she led a march from Capitol Hill to the White House, claiming that "advancing women's rights and defeating Ronald Reagan are synonymous." She was chagrined by his reelection, complaining that the Democrats had "raised the art of losing the presidency to an art form."

In 1987, she was working for a second time as co-chair of fellow Coloradan Gary Hart's presidential campaign, but when Hart was caught in a sex scandal and left the race, Schroeder began to explore the possibility of becoming a candidate herself. She insisted that her candidacy was not merely symbolic: she had a platform and she had served in Congress 15 years, longer than any other candidate that year except Delaware Senator Joe Biden, who withdrew after admitting to plagiarism. But she continued to be seen not as Pat Schroeder but as Everywoman, advancing the struggle of women for a stronger voice in government. She was often asked, "Why are you running as a woman?," to which she would reply: "Do I have an option?" Within three months, she had raised $1 million, but it was only half of what she thought was needed to mount a professional campaign. At a rally of 2,000 supporters in Denver on September 28, she announced she would not be a candidate for president. The crowd, which had been chanting "Run, Pat, Run," groaned loudly, and Schroeder, unprepared for the crowd's powerful reaction, began to cry. Predictably, pundits used the occasion to speculate on women's suitability for high public office. The congresswoman began to keep a file of stories about male politicians and sports figures who cried, to document yet another double standard.

After the U.S. invasion of Panama in 1989, Schroeder introduced legislation to allow women in the army to take part in all military activities, including combat, creating a controversy which intensified during the Gulf War in 1991. Schroeder saw combat restriction as just another job hurdle, pointing out that in modern warfare, women at command headquarters and supply depots were already exposed to fire. The military, she said, was "the last tree house" where women were still being denied education and training. As chair of the House Armed Services subcommittee on research and technology, she led a drive to convert defense technology for use in law enforcement and women's health care.

During the first Clinton administration, starting in 1993, several other acts sponsored by Schroeder were signed into law. In addition to the Family and Medical Leave Act, these included part of an omnibus health bill to include women and minorities in research studies at the National Institutes of Health; an act to give child-care providers access to information on child abusers; an act to garnish the wages of federal retirees in cases of child abuse; and an act to strengthen law enforcement agencies in combatting violent crimes against women. She also voted to increase funding for cancer screening for low-income women, and to further improve child-support collection. She introduced legislation together with **Barbara-Rose Collins** (D-Michigan) to prevent female genital mutilation (also known as female circumcision) from being performed in the United States.

At 55, Schroeder announced her plan to retire at the end of her term in 1996, eager to explore new options while still young enough to do so successfully. She inclined toward a career in education, believing that education was the key to ending poverty. With the flair for coining memorable phrases that had contributed so much to her visibility and success, Schroeder suggested, "Perhaps we should call schools 'stadiums'; they'd get more attention." Iconoclastic to the end, in the spring of 1996 she was the lone dissenter when the House of Representatives voted 404–1 to bestow a Congressional Gold Medal on Reverend Billy Graham.

By the time of her retirement, Patricia Schroeder was the longest-serving woman in Congress, widely respected not only for her tireless efforts on behalf of women and children, but for her shrewd study of arms control and economics. "Unfortunately, the Washington I'm leaving is meaner than it was when I arrived," she wrote, "and that's not good for any of us. . . . They're all about ideology now."

SOURCES:

Barth, Irene. "Congresswoman Pat Schroeder," in *Ms.* June 1976, p. 62.

Chamberlin, Hope. *A Minority of Members: Women in the U.S. Congress.* NY: Praeger, 1973.

Dowd, Maureen. "Women Who Would Be President: Patricia Schroeder: Uncompromising Free Spirit," in *McCall's.* June 1990, p. 66.

Newsweek. November 24, 1975, p. 77; December 18, 1995, p. 38.

Office of the Historian, U.S. House of Representatives. "Patricia S. Schroeder," in *Women in Congress: 1917–1990.* Washington, DC: U.S. Government Printing Office, 1991.

O'Reilly, Jane, and Gloria Jacobs. "Watch Pat Run," in *Ms.* February 1988, p. 44.

People Weekly. September 7, 1987, p. 40.

Reynolds, Barbara. "The Move To Outlaw Female Genital Mutilation," in *Ms.* July–August 1994, p. 92.

Schroeder, Pat, with Andrea Camp and Robyn Lipner. *Champion of the Great American Family: A Personal and Political Book.* NY: Random House, 1989.

Summers, Anne. "Pat Schroeder: Fighting for Military Moms," in *Ms.* May–June 1991, p. 90.

U.S. News and World Report. December 12, 1982.

Viorst, Judith. "Congresswoman Pat Schroeder: The Woman Who Has a Bear By the Tail," in *Redbook.* Vol. 142, no. 1. November 1973, p. 97.

Will, George. *Newsweek.* August 17, 1987, p. 76.

Kristie Miller,
author of *Ruth Hanna McCormick: A Life in Politics 1880–1944*, (University of New Mexico Press, 1992)

Schröder-Devrient, Wilhelmine

(1804–1860)

German soprano. Name variations: Wilhelmine Schroeder-Devrient. Born on December 6, 1804, in Hamburg, Germany; died on January 26, 1860, in Coburg; daughter of Friedrich Schröder (a singer) and Antoinette Sophie (Bürger) Schröder (1781–1868), an actress known as Sophie Schröder; studied with her mother and father in Hamburg; studied with Mozatti in Vienna; married Karl Devrient, in 1823 (divorced or separated 1828); married Herr Van Döring (divorced before 1850); married Baron von Bock, in 1850; children: (first marriage) four.

Made debut as Pamina in Vienna (1821); sang at the Dresden Court Opera (1823–47); toured Europe until her retirement (1856).

Until she was 17, Wilhelmine Schröder-Devrient was trained as an actress by her mother, German actress **Sophie Schröder** (1781–1868), who excelled in tragic roles. At that time, Schröder-Devrient had a remarkable success as Leonore in *Fidelio*. Beethoven, who took note of her acting, offered to write an opera for her. Since the composer was by then completely deaf, her acting had inspired him more than her singing, and dramatic roles would remain her forte. Goethe was also a fan of Schröder-Devrient, as was the composer Wagner.

During her early career, she sang mostly in Vienna, Berlin, Dresden, and Paris, but later she appeared frequently in London. Her private life was stressful and unsettled. Married three times, she was also involved in numerous love affairs. Personal criticism caused Schröder-Devrient untold pain. In Budapest, she once rushed off the stage and collapsed in her dressing room, upset over a fan's comments. Confronting the man, she invited him to send onstage a serene women whose life he admired and have her project passion. "When I have to represent a passion," she told him, "I must possess one, for I can only be carried away by what I feel with great intensity." Her first marriage lasted five years, during which time she had four children. Her second marriage, to a Saxon officer, was brief, but her third marriage proved more stable. Schröder-Devrient was a powerful and passionate singer much admired in her day.

John Haag,
Athens, Georgia

Schroth, Frances (b. 1893).

See Bleibtrey, Ethelda for sidebar.

ACKNOWLEDGMENTS

Photographs and illustrations appearing in *Women in World History, Volume 13,* were received from the following sources:

Courtesy of A/S Gyldendal Norsk Forlag, Oslo, Norway, **p.** 767; Painting *La Tragédie* by Eugène Emmanuel Amaury-Duval, 1855, **p.** 9; © American International Pictures, 1966, **p.** 461; Courtesy of Ann Richards Committee, **p.** 257; © Atlantic Films, 1980, **p.** 281; Photo by Ernest A. Bachrach, **p.** 590; Photo by Cecil Beaton, **p.** 562; Painting by Évariste Carpentier, **p.** 433; Drawing by Alice Danyell, **p.** 66; Painting by Jacques David, **p.** 143; Portrait by Eugene Delacroix, **p.** 763; Courtesy of the *Denver Post*, photo by Jim Richardson, **p.** 915; Painting by Carlo Dolci, **p.** 709; © Daniel Forster, courtesy of America True,

p. 312; Photo by Pearl Freeman, **p.** 241; From a drawing by Elizabeth Moore Hallowell, **p.** 500; Photo by Horst, **p.** 865; Photo by Ward Hutchinson, **p.** 298; © The Imogen Cunningham Trust, 1978, photo by Imogen Cunningham, **p.** 575; © Independent Artists, 1963, **p.** 336; Courtesy of the Embassy of Ireland, Washington, D.C., **p.** 365; Courtesy of the John F. Kennedy Library, **p.** 879; From Captain Charles Johnson's *General History of the Pirates*, 1725, **p.** 125; Photo by Joseph Gray Kitchell, **p.** 327; Courtesy of the Library of Congress, **pp.** 81, 93, 199, 251, 457, 477, 637, 647, 715, 749; Courtesy of the Marjorie Kinnan Rawlings Society, **p.** 109; © Angus McBean, **p.** 617; Photo by Clarence Sinclair Bull for M.G.M., **p.** 41; Courtesy of Sara Joan Miles, **p.** 551; Photos by Nadar, **pp.** 202, 761; Courtesy of the Fales Library, New York University, **p.** 347; © News America Syndicate, 1962, **p.** 465; Painting by C.W. Peale, **p.** 152; Courtesy of the Alice Marshall Collection, Penn State University, Harrisburg, **p.** 135; Courtesy of ProServ, **p.** 633; Courtesy of Cathy Rigby, **p.** 309; © RKO, 1946, **p.** 151; Photo by Jacques Robert, **p.** 809; Courtesy of the Ronald Reagan Library, **p.** 129; Painting by Dante Gabriel Rossetti, **p.** 511; Courtesy of *Running News*, photo by Victor G. Sailer, **p.** 755; Courtesy of Schroder Music Company, photo by Eunice Militante, **p.** 231, photo by Alejandro Stuart, **p.** 233; © Sigma Productions, Inc., 1966, **p.** 260; Painting by Thomas Sully, **p.** 86; Photo by Wolf Suschitsky, **p.** 847; Photo by Asela Torres, **p.** 399; Courtesy of the U.S. Department of Justice, **p.** 215; Courtesy of the U.S. House of Representatives. **pp.** 148, 168, 311, 339, 415, 427, 682, 691, 882; © Universal City Studios, Inc., 1983, **p.** 111; Photo by Jay Te Winburn, **p.** 332; Courtesy of the World Figure Skating Hall of Fame and Museum, **p.** 395.